THE COLLINS
PAPERBACK
GERMAN
DICTIONARY
AMERICAN LANGUAGE EDITION

THE COLLINS PAPERBACK GERMAN DICTIONARY

AMERICAN LANGUAGE EDITION

GERMAN • ENGLISH   ENGLISH • GERMAN

COLLINS
London and Glasgow

First published in this edition 1990

© **William Collins Sons & Co. Ltd. 1990**

ISBN 0 00 433577 5

---

editors/Text
Dagmar Förtsch, Hildegard Pesch,
Lorna Sinclair, Elspeth Anderson

American language consultant/amerikanisches Englisch
Professor Marvin Folsom

editorial staff/Manuskriptbearbeitung
Barbara Christie, Susan Dunsmore, Val McNulty

Printed in Great Britain
Collins Clear-Type Press

INHALT

CONTENTS

Warenzeichen

Note on trademarks

EINLEITUNG

Verständnis der deutschen Sprache

Dieses neue Wörterbuch bietet dem Benutzer einen praktischen, detaillierten Überblick über den modernen Sprachgebrauch, wobei sowohl die Bereiche der Wirtschaft und der Bürautomatisation eingeschlossen sind als auch eine umfassende Auswahl von Abkürzungen, Akronymen und geographischen Bezeichnungen gegeben ist, die man täglich liest. Um das Nachschlagen zu erleichtern, sind auch unregelmäßige Verb- und Substantivformen angegeben, jeweils mit einem Verweis auf den Haupteintrag, wo die Übersetzung gegeben wird.

Ausdrucksfähigkeit im Deutschen

Um die Verständigung und Ausdrucksfähigkeit im Deutschen zu erleichtern, dienen dem Benutzer zahlreiche Angaben, die richtige Übersetzung für den jeweiligen Kontext zu finden; betrachten Sie diese als Hinweisschilder. Die am häufigsten gebrauchten Wörter werden anhand vieler Beispiele für richtige Anwendung ausführlich behandelt.

Ein Begleiter bei der Arbeit

Bei diesem neuen Collins Nachschlagewerk wurde besonderer Nachdruck auf Zuverlässigkeit und Einfachheit gelegt, und es soll Ihnen vor allem im Beruf oder beim Studium nützlich sein. Wir hoffen, daß es Ihnen auf lange Sicht als hilfreiches Arbeitsmittel dient.

INTRODUCTION

Understanding German

This new and thoroughly up-to-date dictionary provides the user with wide-ranging, practical coverage of current usage, including terminology relevant to business and office automation, and a comprehensive selection of abbreviations, acronyms and geographical names commonly found in the press. You will also find, for ease of consultation, irregular forms of German verbs and nouns with a cross-reference to the basic form where a translation is given.

Self-expression in German

To help you express yourself correctly and idiomatically in German, numerous indications – think of them as signposts – guide you to the most appropriate translation for your context. All the most commonly used words are given detailed treatment, with many examples of typical usage.

A working companion

Much care has been taken to make this new Collins dictionary thoroughly reliable, easy to use and relevant to your work and study. We hope it will become a long-serving companion for all your foreign language needs.

ABKÜRZUNGEN

ABBREVIATIONS

Adjektiv	**a**	adjective
Abkürzung	**abk, abbr**	abbreviation
Akkusativ	**akk, acc**	accusative
Adverb	**ad**	adverb
Agrarwirtschaft	**AGR**	agriculture
Anatomie	**ANAT**	anatomy
Architektur	**ARCHIT**	architecture
Artikel	**art**	article
Kunst	**ART**	
Astrologie	**ASTROL**	astrology
Astronomie	**ASTRON**	astronomy
attributiv	**attr**	attributive
Kraftfahrzeugwesen	**AUT**	automobiles
Hilfsverb	**aux**	auxiliary
Luftfahrt	**AVIAT**	aviation
besonders	**bes**	especially
Biologie	**BIOL**	biology
Botanik	**BOT**	botany
britisch	**Brit**	British
Kartenspiel	**CARDS**	
Chemie	**CHEM**	chemistry
Film	**CINE**	cinema
Konjunktion	**cj**	conjunction
umgangssprachlich	**col**	colloquial
Handel	**COMM**	commerce
Komparativ	**comp**	comparative
Computerwesen	**COMPUT**	computers
Kochen und Backen	**COOK**	cooking
zusammengesetztes Wort	**cpd**	compound
Dativ	**dat**	dative
dekliniert	**dekl**	declined
kirchlich	**ECCL**	ecclesiastical
Volkswirtschaft	**ECON**	economics
Eisenbahn	**EISENB**	railroad
Elektrizität	**ELEK, ELEC**	electricity
besonders	**esp**	especially
und so weiter	**etc**	et cetera
etwas	**etw**	something
Euphemismus	**euph**	euphemism
Femininum	**f**	feminine
übertragen	**fig**	figurative
Film	**FILM**	cinema
Finanzwesen	**FIN**	finance
formell	**form**	formal
'phrasal verb', bei dem Partikel und Verb nicht getrennt werden können	**fus**	fused: phrasal verb where the particle cannot be separated from the main verb
gehoben	**geh**	elevated
Genitiv	**gen**	genitive
Geographie	**GEOG**	geography

ABKÜRZUNGEN

ABBREVIATIONS

Geologie	GEOL	geology
Grammatik	GRAM	grammar
Geschichte	HIST	history
scherzhaft	hum	humorous
Imperfekt	imperf	imperfect
unpersönlich	impers	impersonal
unbestimmt	indef	indefinite
untrennbares Verb	insep	inseparable
Interjektion	interj	interjection
interrogativ	interrog	interrogative
unveränderlich	inv	invariable
unregelmäßig	irreg	irregular
jemand	jd	somebody
jemandem	jdm	(to) somebody
jemanden	jdn	somebody
jemandes	jds	somebody's
Rechtswesen	JUR	law
Kartenspiel	KARTEN	cards
Konjunktion	kj	conjunction
Kochen	KOCH	cooking
Komparativ	komp	comparative
Sprachwissenschaft	LING	linguistics
wörtlich	lit	literal
literarisch	liter	literary
Literatur	LITER	literature
Maskulinum	m	masculine
Mathematik	MATH	mathematics
Medizin	MED	medicine
Meteorologie	MET	meteorology
Militärwesen	MIL	military
Bergbau	MIN	mining
Musik	MUS	music
Substantiv	n	noun
nautisch	NAUT	nautical
Nominativ	nom	nominative
Neutrum	nt	neuter
Zahlwort	num	numeral
Objekt	obj	object
oder	od	or
veraltet	old	
sich	o.s.	oneself
Parlament	PARL	parliament
pejorativ	pej	pejorative
Person/persönlich	pers	person/personal
Photographie	PHOT	photography
Physik	PHYS	physics
Plural	pl	plural
Politik	POL	politics
possessiv	poss	possessive
Partizip Perfekt	pp	past participle

ABKÜRZUNGEN

ABBREVIATIONS

Präfix	**präf, pref**	prefix
Präposition	**präp, prep**	preposition
Präsens	**präs, pres**	present
Presse	**PRESS**	
Typographie	**PRINT**	printing
Pronomen	**pron**	pronoun
Psychologie	**PSYCH**	psychology
Imperfekt	**pt**	past tense
Radio	**RAD**	radio
Eisenbahn	**RAIL**	railroad
Relativ-	**rel**	relative
Religion	**REL**	religion
jemand(-en, -em)	**sb**	somebody
Schulwesen	**SCH**	school
Naturwissenschaft	**SCI**	science
schottisch	**Scot**	Scottish
Singular	**sing**	singular
Skisport	**SKI**	skiing
etwas	**sth**	something
Suffix	**suff**	suffix
Superlativ	**superl**	superlative
Technik	**TECH**	technology
Nachrichtentechnik	**TEL**	telecommunications
Theater	**THEAT**	theater
Fernsehen	**TV**	television
Typographie	**TYP**	typography
umgangssprachlich	**umg**	colloquial
Universität	**UNIV**	university
unpersönlich	**unpers**	impersonal
unregelmäßig	**unreg**	irregular
(nord)amerikanisch	**US**	(North) American
gewöhnlich	**usu**	usually
Verb	**v**	verb
intransitives Verb	**vi**	intransitive verb
reflexives Verb	**vr**	reflexive verb
transitives Verb	**vt**	transitive verb
vulgär	**vulg**	vulgar
Zoologie	**ZOOL**	zoology
zusammengesetztes Wort	**zW**	compound
zwischen zwei Sprechern	—	change of speaker
ungefähre Entsprechung	≃	cultural equivalent
eingetragenes Warenzeichen	®	registered trademark

GERMAN NOUN ENDINGS

After many noun entries on the German-English side of the dictionary, you will find two pieces of grammatical information, separated by commas, to help you with the declension of the noun, e.g.: **-, -n** or **-(e)s, -e**.

The first item shows you the genitive singular form, and the second gives the plural form. The hyphen stands for the word itself and the other letters are endings. Sometimes an umlaut is shown over the hyphen, which means an umlaut must be placed on the vowel of the word, e.g.:

dictionary entry	*genitive singular*	*plural*
Mann *m* **(e)s, ¨er**	**Mannes** or **Manns**	**Männer**
Jacht *f* **-, -en**	**Jacht**	**Jachten**

This information is not given when the noun has one of the regular German noun endings below, and you should refer to this table in such cases.

Similarly, genitive and plural endings are not shown when the German entry is a compound consisting of two or more words which are to be found elsewhere in the dictionary, since the compound form takes the endings of the LAST word of which it is formed, e.g.:

for **Nebenstraße**   see **Straße**
for **Schneeball**   see **Ball**

REGULAR GERMAN NOUN ENDINGS

nom		*gen*	*pl*
-ant	*m*	-anten	-anten
-anz	*f*	-anz	-anzen
-ar	*m*	-ar(e)s	-are
-chen	*nt*	-chens	-chen
-ei	*f*	-ei	-eien
-elle	*f*	-elle	-ellen
-ent	*m*	-enten	-enten
-enz	*f*	-enz	-enzen
-ette	*f*	-ette	-etten
-eur	*m*	-eurs	-eure
-euse	*f*	-euse	-eusen
-heit	*f*	-heit	-heiten
-ie	*f*	-ie	-ien
-ik	*f*	-ik	-iken
-in	*f*	-in	-innen
-ine	*f*	-ine	-inen
-ion	*f*	-ion	-ionen
-ist	*m*	-isten	-isten
-ium	*nt*	-iums	-ien
-ius	*m*	-ius	-iusse
-ive	*f*	-ive	-iven
-keit	*f*	-keit	-keiten
-lein	*nt*	-leins	-lein
-ling	*m*	-lings	-linge
-ment	*nt*	-ments	-mente
-mus	*m*	-mus	-men
-schaft	*f*	-schaft	-schaften
-tät	*f*	-tät	-täten
-tor	*m*	-tors	-toren
-ung	*f*	-ung	-ungen
-ur	*f*	-ur	-uren

AUSSPRACHE   PRONUNCIATION

Die Aussprache folgt gewöhnlich in eckigen Klammern nach dem jeweiligen Eintragwort.

In general, we give the pronunciation of each entry in square brackets after the word in question.

Ausnahmen sind:

Exceptions are:

Im deutsch-englischen Teil,
wenn die Aussprache leicht von anderen Einträgen abgeleitet werden kann, die in unmittelbarer Nähe stehen, z.B.:

On the German-English side
Where the pronunciation is easily derivable from related entries in close proximity, e.g.:

fahrend abgeleitet von **fahren**
gefälligst von **gefällig**
Befähigung von **befähigen**

fahrend derived from **fahren**
gefälligst from **gefällig**
Befähigung from **befähigen**

LAUTSCHRIFT   PHONETIC SYMBOLS

alle Vokallaute sind nur ungefähre Entsprechungen

all vowel sounds are approximate only

	à	h*a*t		ō:	*O*per
*a*dd m*a*p	a			ôṅ	Champign*on*
c*a*re *air*	är			œ	sch*ö*n
p*a*lm f*a*ther *o*dd	â	h*a*ben B*ah*n		ōē	*ö*ffnen
	âṅ	*En*semble	*oi*l b*oy*	oi	H*eu*
*a*ce r*a*te	ā	M*e*tall	t*oo*k f*u*ll	ŏŏ	M*u*cke
	ā:	M*e*ter	p*oo*l f*oo*d	ōō	Mus*i*k k*u*lant
	aṅ	Cous*in*		ōō:	K*uh* H*u*t
b*a*t r*u*b	b	*B*all	*ou*t n*ow*	ou	H*au*t
ch*e*ck ca*tch*	ch		p*i*t st*o*p	p	*P*akt
	cḩ	*ich*	r*u*n p*oo*r	r	*R*age
d*o*g r*o*d	d	*d*ann	s*ee* pa*ss*	s	*R*a*ss*e
*e*nd p*e*t	e	h*ä*sslich K*e*tte	s*u*re ru*sh*	sh	*sch*ön
*e*ven tr*ee*	ē	v*i*tal	t*a*lk s*it*	t	*T*al
	ē:	g*ie*ssen	*th*in b*o*th	th	
*a*bove d*a*rk*e*n	ə	B*i*tte	*th*is ba*the*	tḩ	
f*i*t hal*f*	f	*F*aß	*u*p d*o*ne	u	
*g*o lo*g*	g	*G*ast	*ur*n t*er*m	ûr	
*h*ope *h*ate	h	*H*err	*u*se f*ew*	yōō	
*i*t g*i*ve	i	*i*rgend		ü:	k*üh*l
*i*ce wr*i*te	ī	w*ei*t		ü	k*ü*rzlich M*ü*ll
*j*oy le*dg*e	j		v*ai*n e*ve*	v	*w*as
c*oo*l ta*k*e	k	*k*alt	*w*in a*w*ay	w	
	kḩ	ho*ch*	*y*et *y*earn	y	A*dj*ektiv
l*oo*k ru*l*e	l	*L*ast	*z*est mu*s*e	z	Ha*s*e
*m*ove see*m*	m	*M*ast	vi*si*on plea*s*ure	zh	*G*enie
*n*ice ti*n*	n	*N*uß	Betonung	'	stress mark
ri*ng* so*ng*	ng	abdrä*ng*en	zeigt an, daß	·	shows where two
*o*pen s*o*	ō	*O*live M*o*ral	zwei Konsonanten		consonants should
	o	*O*pfer	getrennt auszusprechen		be pronounced
l*aw* d*o*g *o*rder	ô		sind		separately

GERMAN IRREGULAR VERBS

*with 'sein'

infinitive	present indicative (2nd, 3rd sing.)	preterite	past participle
aufschrecken*	schrickst auf, schrickt auf	schrak od schreckte auf	aufgeschreckt
ausbedingen	bedingst aus, bedingt aus	bedang od bedingte aus	ausbedungen
backen	bäckst, bäckt	backte od buk	gebacken
befehlen	befiehlst, befiehlt	befahl	befohlen
beginnen	beginnst, beginnt	begann	begonnen
beißen	beißt, beißt	biß	gebissen
bergen	birgst, birgt	barg	geborgen
bersten*	birst, birst	barst	geborsten
bescheißen*	bescheißt, bescheißt	beschiß	beschissen
bewegen	bewegst, bewegt	bewog	bewogen
biegen	biegst, biegt	bog	gebogen
bieten	bietest, bietet	bot	geboten
binden	bindest, bindet	band	gebunden
bitten	bittest, bittet	bat	gebeten
blasen	bläst, bläst	blies	geblasen
bleiben*	bleibst, bleibt	blieb	geblieben
braten	brätst, brät	briet	gebraten
brechen*	brichst, bricht	brach	gebrochen
brennen	brennst, brennt	brannte	gebrannt
bringen	bringst, bringt	brachte	gebracht
denken	denkst, denkt	dachte	gedacht
dreschen	drisch(e)st, drischt	drasch	gedroschen
dringen*	dringst, dringt	drang	gedrungen
dürfen	darfst, darf	durfte	gedurft
empfehlen	empfiehlst, empfiehlt	empfahl	empfohlen
erbleichen*	erbleichst, erbleicht	erbleichte	erblichen
erlöschen*	erlischst, erlischt	erlosch	erloschen
erschrecken*	erschrickst, erschrickt	erschrak	erschrocken
essen	ißt, ißt	aß	gegessen
fahren*	fährst, fährt	fuhr	gefahren
fallen*	fällst, fällt	fiel	gefallen
fangen	fängst, fängt	fing	gefangen
fechten	fichtst, ficht	focht	gefochten
finden	findest, findet	fand	gefunden
flechten	flichtst, flicht	flocht	geflochten
fliegen*	fliegst, fliegt	flog	geflogen
fliehen*	fliehst, flieht	floh	geflohen
fließen*	fließt, fließt	floß	geflossen
fressen	frißt, frißt	fraß	gefressen
frieren	frierst, friert	fror	gefroren
gären*	gärst, gärt	gor	gegoren
gebären	gebierst, gebiert	gebar	geboren
geben	gibst, gibt	gab	gegeben

infinitive	present indicative (2nd, 3rd sing.)	preterite	past participle
gedeihen*	gedeihst, gedeiht	gedieh	gediehen
gehen*	gehst, geht	ging	gegangen
gelingen*	——, gelingt	gelang	gelungen
gelten	giltst, gilt	galt	gegolten
genesen*	gene(se)st, genest	genas	genesen
genießen	genießt, genießt	genoß	genossen
geraten*	gerätst, gerät	geriet	geraten
geschehen*	——, geschieht	geschah	geschehen
gewinnen	gewinnst, gewinnt	gewann	gewonnen
gießen	gießt, gießt	goß	gegossen
gleichen	gleichst, gleicht	glich	geglichen
gleiten*	gleitest, gleitet	glitt	geglitten
glimmen	glimmst, glimmt	glomm	geglommen
graben	gräbst, gräbt	grub	gegraben
greifen	greifst, greift	griff	gegriffen
haben	hast, hat	hatte	gehabt
halten	hältst, hält	hielt	gehalten
hängen	hängst, hängt	hing	gehangen
hauen	haust, haut	hieb	gehauen
heben	hebst, hebt	hob	gehoben
heißen	heißt, heißt	hieß	geheißen
helfen	hilfst, hilft	half	geholfen
kennen	kennst, kennt	kannte	gekannt
klimmen*	klimmst, klimmt	klomm	geklommen
klingen	klingst, klingt	klang	geklungen
kneifen	kneifst, kneift	kniff	gekniffen
kommen*	kommst, kommt	kam	gekommen
können	kannst, kann	konnte	gekonnt
kriechen*	kriechst, kriecht	kroch	gekrochen
laden	lädst, lädt	lud	geladen
lassen	läßt, läßt	ließ	gelassen
laufen*	läufst, läuft	lief	gelaufen
leiden	leidest, leidet	litt	gelitten
leihen	leihst, leiht	lieh	geliehen
lesen	liest, liest	las	gelesen
liegen*	liegst, liegt	lag	gelegen
lügen	lügst, lügt	log	gelogen
mahlen	mahlst, mahlt	mahlte	gemahlen
meiden	meidest, meidet	mied	gemieden
melken	milkst, milkt	molk	gemolken
messen	mißt, mißt	maß	gemessen
mißlingen*	——, mißlingt	mißlang	mißlungen
mögen	magst, mag	mochte	gemocht
müssen	mußt, muß	mußte	gemußt
nehmen	nimmst, nimmt	nahm	genommen
nennen	nennst, nennt	nannte	genannt
pfeifen	pfeifst, pfeift	pfiff	gepfiffen
preisen	preist, preist	pries	gepriesen
quellen*	quillst, quillt	quoll	gequollen
raten	rätst, rät	riet	geraten
reiben	reibst, reibt	rieb	gerieben
reißen*	reißt, reißt	riß	gerissen
reiten*	reitest, reitet	ritt	geritten
rennen*	rennst, rennt	rannte	gerannt

infinitive	present indicative (2nd, 3rd sing.)	preterite	past participle
riechen	riechst, riecht	roch	gerochen
ringen	ringst, ringt	rang	gerungen
rinnen*	rinnst, rinnt	rann	geronnen
rufen	rufst, ruft	rief	gerufen
salzen	salzt, salzt	salzte	gesalzen
saufen	säufst, säuft	soff	gesoffen
saugen	saugst, saugt	sog	gesogen
schaffen	schaffst, schafft	schuf	geschaffen
schallen	schallst, schallt	scholl	geschollen
scheiden*	scheidest, scheidet	schied	geschieden
scheinen	scheinst, scheint	schien	geschienen
schelten	schiltst, schilt	schalt	gescholten
scheren	scherst, schert	schor	geschoren
schieben	schiebst, schiebt	schob	geschoben
schießen	schießt, schießt	schoß	geschossen
schinden	schindest, schindet	schund	geschunden
schlafen	schläfst, schläft	schlief	geschlafen
schlagen	schlägst, schlägt	schlug	geschlagen
schleichen*	schleichst, schleicht	schlich	geschlichen
schleifen	schleifst, schleift	schliff	geschliffen
schließen	schließt, schließt	schloß	geschlossen
schlingen	schlingst, schlingt	schlang	geschlungen
schmeißen	schmeißt, schmeißt	schmiß	geschmissen
schmelzen*	schmilzt, schmilzt	schmolz	geschmolzen
schneiden	schneidest, schneidet	schnitt	geschnitten
schreiben	schreibst, schreibt	schrieb	geschrieben
schreien	schreist, schreit	schrie	geschrie(e)n
schreiten	schreitest, schreitet	schritt	geschritten
schweigen	schweigst, schweigt	schwieg	geschwiegen
schwellen*	schwillst, schwillt	schwoll	geschwollen
schwimmen*	schwimmst, schwimmt	schwamm	geschwommen
schwinden*	schwindest, schwindet	schwand	geschwunden
schwingen	schwingst, schwingt	schwang	geschwungen
schwören	schwörst, schwört	schwor	geschworen
sehen	siehst, sieht	sah	gesehen
sein*	bist, ist	war	gewesen
senden	sendest, sendet	sandte	gesandt
singen	singst, singt	sang	gesungen
sinken*	sinkst, sinkt	sank	gesunken
sinnen	sinnst, sinnt	sann	gesonnen
sitzen*	sitzt, sitzt	saß	gesessen
sollen	sollst, soll	sollte	gesollt
speien	speist, speit	spie	gespie(e)n
spinnen	spinnst, spinnt	spann	gesponnen
sprechen	sprichst, spricht	sprach	gesprochen
sprießen*	sprießt, sprießt	sproß	gesprossen
springen*	springst, springt	sprang	gesprungen
stechen	stichst, sticht	stach	gestochen
stecken	steckst, steckt	steckte *od* stak	gesteckt
stehen	stehst, steht	stand	gestanden
stehlen	stiehlst, stiehlt	stahl	gestohlen
steigen*	steigst, steigt	stieg	gestiegen
sterben*	stirbst, stirbt	starb	gestorben
stinken	stinkst, stinkt	stank	gestunken

infinitive	present indicative (2nd, 3rd sing.)	preterite	past participle
stoßen	stößt, stößt	stieß	gestoßen
streichen	streichst, streicht	strich	gestrichen
streiten*	streitest, streitet	stritt	gestritten
tragen	trägst, trägt	trug	getragen
treffen	triffst, trifft	traf	getroffen
treiben*	treibst, treibt	trieb	getrieben
treten*	trittst, tritt	trat	getreten
trinken	trinkst, trinkt	trank	getrunken
trügen	trügst, trügt	trog	getrogen
tun	tust, tut	tat	getan
verderben	verdirbst, verdirbt	verdarb	verdorben
verdrießen	verdrießt, verdrießt	verdroß	verdrossen
vergessen	vergißt, vergißt	vergaß	vergessen
verlieren	verlierst, verliert	verlor	verloren
verschleißen	verschleißt, verschleißt	verschliß	verschlissen
wachsen*	wächst, wächst	wuchs	gewachsen
wägen	wägst, wägt	wog	gewogen
waschen	wäschst, wäscht	wusch	gewaschen
weben	webst, webt	webte *od* wob	gewoben
weichen*	weichst, weicht	wich	gewichen
weisen	weist, weist	wies	gewiesen
wenden	wendest, wendet	wandte	gewandt
werben	wirbst, wirbt	warb	geworben
werden*	wirst, wird	wurde	geworden
werfen	wirfst, wirft	warf	geworfen
wiegen	wiegst, wiegt	wog	gewogen
winden	windest, windet	wand	gewunden
wissen	weißt, weiß	wußte	gewußt
wollen	willst, will	wollte	gewollt
wringen	wringst, wringt	wrang	gewrungen
zeihen	zeihst, zeiht	zieh	geziehen
ziehen*	ziehst, zieht	zog	gezogen
zwingen	zwingst, zwingt	zwang	gezwungen

UNREGELMÄSSIGE ENGLISCHE VERBEN

present	pt	pp	present	pt	pp
arise (arising)	arose	arisen	eat	ate	eaten
awake (awaking)	awoke	awaked	fall	fell	fallen
			feed	fed	fed
be (am, is, are, being)	was, were	been	feel	felt	felt
			fight	fought	fought
			find	found	found
bear	bore	born(e)	flee	fled	fled
beat	beat	beaten	fling	flung	flung
become (becoming)	became	become	fly (flies)	flew	flown
			forbid (forbidding)	forbade	forbidden
befall	befell	befallen			
begin (beginning)	began	begun	forecast	forecast	forecast
			forego	forewent	foregone
behold	beheld	beheld	foresee	foresaw	foreseen
bend	bent	bent	foretell	foretold	foretold
beseech	besought	besought	forget (forgetting)	forgot	forgotten
beset (besetting)	beset	beset	forgive (forgiving)	forgave	forgiven
bet (betting)	bet (*also* betted)	bet (*also* betted)	forsake (forsaking)	forsook	forsaken
bid (bidding)	bid (*also* bade)	bid (*also* bidden)	freeze (freezing)	froze	frozen
bind	bound	bound	get (getting)	got	got, (*US*) gotten
bite (biting)	bit	bitten			
bleed	bled	bled	give (giving)	gave	given
blow	blew	blown	go (goes)	went	gone
break	broke	broken	grind	ground	ground
breed	bred	bred	grow	grew	grown
bring	brought	brought	hang	hung (*also* hanged)	hung (*also* hanged)
build	built	built			
burn	burned (*also* burnt)	burned (*also* burnt)	have (has; having)	had	had
burst	burst	burst	hear	heard	heard
buy	bought	bought	hide (hiding)	hid	hidden
can	could	(been able)	hit (hitting)	hit	hit
cast	cast	cast	hold	held	held
catch	caught	caught	hurt	hurt	hurt
choose (choosing)	chose	chosen	keep	kept	kept
			kneel	knelt (*also* kneeled)	knelt (*also* kneeled)
cling	clung	clung			
come (coming)	came	come	know	knew	known
			lay	laid	laid
cost	cost	cost	lead	led	led
creep	crept	crept	lean	leaned (*also* leant)	leaned (*also* leant)
cut (cutting)	cut	cut			
deal	dealt	dealt	leap	leaped (*also* leapt)	leaped (*also* leapt)
dig (digging)	dug	dug			
do (3rd person: he/ she/it/does)	did	done	learn	learned (*also* learnt)	learned (*also* learnt)
draw	drew	drawn	leave (leaving)	left	left
dream	dreamed (*also* dreamt)	dreamed *also* dreamt)	lend	lent	lent
			let (letting)	let	let
drink	drank	drunk	lie (lying)	lay	lain
drive (driving)	drove	driven	light	lighted (*also* lit)	lighted (*also* lit)
dwell	dwelt	dwelt	lose (losing)	lost	lost

present	pt	pp	present	pt	pp
make (making)	made	made	spell	spelled (*also* spelt)	spelled (*also* spelt)
may	might	—	spend	spent	spent
mean	meant	meant	spill	spilled (*also* spilt)	spilled (*also* spilt)
meet	met	met	spin (spinning)	spun	spun
mistake (mistaking)	mistook	mistaken	spit (spitting)	spat	spat
mow	mowed	mowed (*also* mown)	split (splitting)	split	split
must	(had to)	(had to)	spoil	spoiled (*also* spoilt)	spoiled (*also* spoilt)
pay	paid	paid	spread	spread	spread
put (putting)	put	put	spring	sprang	sprung
quit (quitting)	quit (*also* quitted)	quit (*also* quitted)	stand	stood	stood
read	read	read	steal	stole	stolen
rend	rent	rent	stick	stuck	stuck
rid (ridding)	rid	rid	sting	stung	stung
ride (riding)	rode	ridden	stink	stank	stunk
ring	rang	rung	stride (striding)	strode	stridden
rise (rising)	rose	risen	strike (striking)	struck	struck (*also* stricken)
run (running)	ran	run			
saw	sawed	sawn	strive (striving)	strove	striven
say	said	said			
see	saw	seen	swear	swore	sworn
seek	sought	sought	sweep	swept	swept
sell	sold	sold	swell	swelled	swelled (*also* swollen)
send	sent	sent			
set (setting)	set	set	swim (swimming)	swam	swum
shake (shaking)	shook	shaken			
shall	should	—	swing	swung	swung
shear	sheared	sheared (*also* shorn)	take (taking)	took	taken
			teach	taught	taught
shed (shedding)	shed	shed	tear	tore	torn
shine (shining)	shone	shone	tell	told	told
			think	thought	thought
shoot	shot	shot	throw	threw	thrown
show	showed	shown	thrust	thrust	thrust
shrink	shrank	shrunk	tread	trod	trodden
shut (shutting)	shut	shut	wake (waking)	woke (*also* waked)	waked (*also* woken)
sing	sang	sung	waylay	waylaid	waylaid
sink	sank	sunk	wear	wore	worn
sit (sitting)	sat	sat	weave (weaving)	wove (*also* weaved)	woven (*also* weaved)
slay	slew	slain			
sleep	slept	slept	wed (wedding)	wedded	wedded (*also* wed)
slide (sliding)	slid	slid			
sling	slung	slung	weep	wept	wept
slit (slitting)	slit	slit	win (winning)	won	won
smell	smelled (*Brit* smelt)	smelled (*Brit* smelt)	wind	wound	wound
			withdraw	withdrew	withdrawn
sow	sowed	sown (*also* sowed)	withhold	withheld	withheld
			withstand	withstood	withstood
speak	spoke	spoken	wring	wrung	wrung
speed	sped (*also* speeded)	sped (*also* speeded)	write (writing)	wrote	written

ZAHLEN

NUMBERS

ein(s)	1	one
zwei	2	two
drei	3	three
vier	4	four
fünf	5	five
sechs	6	six
sieben	7	seven
acht	8	eight
neun	9	nine
zehn	10	ten
elf	11	eleven
zwölf	12	twelve
dreizehn	13	thirteen
vierzehn	14	fourteen
fünfzehn	15	fifteen
sechzehn	16	sixteen
siebzehn	17	seventeen
achtzehn	18	eighteen
neunzehn	19	nineteen
zwanzig	20	twenty
einundzwanzig	21	twenty-one
zweiundzwanzig	22	twenty-two
dreißig	30	thirty
vierzig	40	forty
fünfzig	50	fifty
sechzig	60	sixty
siebzig	70	seventy
achtzig	80	eighty
neunzig	90	ninety
hundert	100	a hundred
hunderteins	101	a hundred and one
zweihundert	200	two hundred
zweihunderteins	201	two hundred and one
dreihundert	300	three hundred
dreihunderteins	301	three hundred and one
tausend	1000	a thousand
tausend(und)eins	1001	a thousand and one
fünftausend	5000	five thousand
eine Million	1000000	a million

ZAHLEN

NUMBERS

erste(r,s)	1.	first	1st
zweite(r,s)	2.	second	2nd
dritte(r,s)	3.	third	3rd
vierte(r,s)	4.	fourth	4th
fünfte(r,s)	5.	fifth	5th
sechste(r,s)	6.	sixth	6th
siebte(r,s)	7.	seventh	7th
achte(r,s)	8.	eighth	8th
neunte(r,s)	9.	ninth	9th
zehnte(r,s)	10.	tenth	10th
elfte(r,s)	11.	eleventh	11th
zwölfte(r,s)	12.	twelfth	12th
dreizehnte(r,s)	13.	thirteenth	13th
vierzehnte(r,s)	14.	fourteenth	14th
fünfzehnte(r,s)	15.	fifteenth	15th
sechzehnte(r,s)	16.	sixteenth	16th
siebzehnte(r,s)	17.	seventeenth	17th
achtzehnte(r,s)	18.	eighteenth	18th
neunzehnte(r,s)	19.	nineteenth	19th
zwanzigste(r,s)	20.	twentieth	20th
einundzwanzigste(r,s)	21.	twenty-first	21st
dreißigste(r,s)	30.	thirtieth	30th
hundertste(r,s)	100.	hundredth	100th
hunderterste(r,s)	101.	hundred-and-first	101st
tausendste(r,s)	1000.	thousandth	1000th

DEUTSCH-ENGLISCH
GERMAN-ENGLISH

A

A, a [â] *nt* A, a; **das A und O** the be-all and end-all; (*eines Wissensgebietes*) the basics *pl*; **wer A sagt, muß auch B sagen** (*Sprichwort*) in for a penny, in for a pound (*Sprichwort*).

à [â] *präp* (*bes COMM*) at.

a. *abk* = **am.**

A *f abk* (= *Autobahn*) I (*US*), M (*Brit*).

a.A. *abk* (= *auf Anordnung*) by order.

AA *nt abk* (= *Auswärtige(s) Amt*) Dept. of State (*US*), F.O. (*Brit*).

Aal [âl] *m* **-(e)s, -e** eel.

aalen [â'lən] *vr* (*umg*): **sich in der Sonne ~** bask in the sun.

a.a.O. *abk* (= *am angegebenen od angeführten Ort*) loc. cit.

Aas [âs] *nt* **-es, -e** *od* **Äser** carrion; **~geier** *m* vulture.

ab [ap] *präp* +*dat* from ♦ *ad* off; **~ Werk** (*COMM*) ex works; **Kinder ~ 14 Jahren** children from (the age of) 14; **links ~** to the left; **~ und zu** *od* **an** now and then *od* again; **von da ~** from then on; **der Knopf ist ~** the button has come off; **München ~ 12.20 Uhr** (*EISENB*) leaving Munich 12.20; **~ durch die Mitte!** (*umg*) beat it!

abändern [ap'endərn] *vt* alter (*in* +*akk* to); (*Gesetzentwurf*) amend (*in* +*akk* to); (*Strafe, Urteil*) revise (*in* +*akk* to).

Abänderung *f* alteration; amendment; revision.

Abänderungsantrag *m* (*PARL*) proposed amendment.

abarbeiten [ap'árbītən] *vr* slave away.

Abart [ap' árt] *f* (*BIOL*) variety.

abartig *a* abnormal.

Abb. *abk* (= *Abbildung*) ill., illus.

Abbau [ap'bou] *m* **-(e)s** dismantling; (*Verminderung*) reduction (*gen* in); (*Verfall*) decline (*gen* in); (*MIN*) mining; (*über Tage*) quarrying; (*CHEM*) decomposition.

abbauen *vt* dismantle; (*verringern*) reduce; (*MIN*) mine; quarry; (*CHEM*) break down; **Arbeitsplätze ~** make job cuts.

Abbaurechte *pl* mineral rights *pl*.

abbeißen [ap'bīsən] *vt unreg* bite off.

abbekommen [ap'bəkomən] *vt unreg*: **etwas ~** get some (of it); (*beschädigt werden*) get damaged; (*verletzt werden*) get hurt.

abberufen [ap'bərōō:fən] *vt unreg* recall.

Abberufung *f* recall.

abbestellen [ap'bəshtelən] *vt* cancel.

abbezahlen [ap'bətsâlən] *vt* pay off.

abbiegen [ap'bē:gən] *unreg vi* turn off; (*Straße*) bend ♦ *vt* bend; (*verhindern*) ward off.

Abbild [ap'bilt] *nt* portrayal; (*einer Person*) image, likeness; **a~en** [ap'bildən] *vt* portray; **~ung** *f* illustration; (*Schaubild*) diagram.

abbinden [ap'bindən] *vt unreg* (*MED*: *Arm, Bein etc*) apply a tourniquet to.

Abbitte [ap'bitə] *f*: **~ leisten** *od* **tun** make one's apologies (*bei* to).

abblasen [ap'blâzən] *vt unreg* blow off; (*fig umg*) call off.

abblättern [ap'bletərn] *vi* (*Putz, Farbe*) flake (off).

abblenden [ap'blendən] *vti* (*AUT*) dim (*US*), dip (*Brit*).

Abblendlicht [ap'blentlicht] *nt* low beam (*US*), dipped headlights *pl* (*Brit*).

abblitzen [ap'blitsən] *vi* (*umg*): **jdn ~ lassen** send sb packing.

abbrechen [ap'brechən] *vti unreg* break off; (*Gebäude*) pull down; (*Zelt*) take down; (*aufhören*) stop; (*COMPUT*) abort; **sich** (*dat*) **einen ~** (*umg*: *sich sehr anstrengen*) bust a gut.

abbrennen [ap'brenən] *unreg vt* burn off; (*Feuerwerk*) let off ♦ *vi aux sein* burn down; **abgebrannt sein** (*umg*) be broke.

abbringen [ap'bringən] *vt unreg*: **jdn von etw ~** dissuade sb from sth; **jdn vom Weg ~** divert sb; **ich bringe den Verschluß nicht ab** (*umg*) I can't get the top off.

abbröckeln [ap'brœkəln] *vi* crumble off *od* away; (*BÖRSE*: *Preise*) ease.

Abbruch [ap'brōōkh] *m* (*von Verhandlungen etc*) breaking off; (*von Haus*) demolition; (*COMPUT*) abort; **jdm/etw ~ tun** harm sb/sth; **~arbeiten** *pl* demolition work *sing*; **a~reif** *a* only fit for demolition.

abbrühen [ap'brü:ən] *vt* scald.

abbuchen [ap'bōō:khən] *vt* debit; (*durch Dauerauftrag*) pay by standing order (*von* from).

abbürsten [ap'bürstən] *vt* brush off.

abbüßen [ap'bü:sən] *vt* (*Strafe*) serve.

ABC-Staaten [âbātsā:'shtâtən] *pl abk* = Argentinien, Brasilien und Chile.

ABC-Waffen *pl abk* (= *atomare, biologische und chemische Waffen*) ABC weapons (= *atomic, biological and chemical weapons*).

abdampfen [ap'dámpfən] *vi* (*fig umg*: *losgehen/-fahren*) hit the road.

abdanken [ap'dángkən] *vi* resign; (*König*) abdicate.

Abdankung *f* resignation; abdication.
abdecken [àp'dekən] *vt* uncover; (*Tisch*) clear; (*Loch*) cover.
abdichten [àp'diçhtən] *vt* seal; (*NAUT*) caulk.
abdrängen [àp'drengən] *vt* push off.
abdrehen [àp'drā:ən] *vt* (*Gas*) turn off; (*Licht*) switch off; (*Film*) shoot; **jdm den Hals ~** wring sb's neck ♦ *vi* (*Schiff*) change course.
abdriften [àp'driftən] *vi* drift (away).
abdrosseln [àp'drosəln] *vt* throttle; (*AUT*) stall; (*Produktion*) cut back.
Abdruck [àp'dröök] *m* (*Nachdrucken*) reprinting; (*Gedrucktes*) reprint; (*Gips~*, *Wachs~*) impression; (*Finger~*) print; **a~en** *vt* print.
abdrücken [àp'drükən] *vt* make an impression of; (*Waffe*) fire; (*umg: Person*) hug, squeeze; **jdm die Luft ~** squeeze all the breath out of sb ♦ *vr* leave imprints; (*abstoßen*) push o.s. away.
abds. *abk* = **abends.**
abebben [àp'ebən] *vi* ebb away.
Abend [â'bənt] *m* **-s, -e** evening; **gegen ~** towards (the) evening; **den ganzen ~** (**über**) the whole evening; **zu ~ essen** have dinner *od* supper; **a~** *ad* evening; **~anzug** *m* tuxedo; **~brot** *nt*, **~essen** *nt* supper; **a~füllend** *a* taking up the whole evening; **~gymnasium** *nt* night school; **~kasse** *f* (*THEAT*) box office; **~kurs** *m* evening classes *pl*; **~land** *nt* West; **a~lich** *a* evening; **~mahl** *nt* Holy Communion; **~rot** *nt* sunset.
abends *ad* in the evening.
Abendvorstellung *f* evening performance.
Abenteuer [â'bəntoiər] *nt* **-s, -** adventure; (*Liebes~ auch*) affair; **a~lich** *a* adventurous.
Abenteurer *m* **-s, -** adventurer; **~in** *f* adventuress.
aber [â'bər] *kj* but; (*jedoch*) however; **oder ~** or else; **bist du ~ braun!** aren't you brown!; **das ist ~ schön** that's really nice; **nun ist ~ Schluß!** now that's enough! ♦ *ad*: **tausend und ~ tausend** thousands upon thousands; **A~** *nt* but.
Aberglaube [â'bərgloubə] *m* superstition.
abergläubisch [â'bərgloibish] *a* superstitious.
aberkennen [àp'erkenən] *vt unreg*: **jdm etw ~** deprive sb of sth, take sth (away) from sb.
Aberkennung *f* taking away.
aber- *zW*: **~malig** *a* repeated; **~mals** *ad* once again.
Abf. *abk* (= *Abfahrt*) dep.
abfahren [àp'fârən] *unreg vi* leave, depart; **der Zug ist abgefahren** (*lit*) the train has left; (*fig*) we've *od* you've *etc* missed the boat; **der Zug fährt um 8.00 von Bremen ab** the train leaves Bremen at 8 o'clock; **jdn ~ lassen** (*umg: abwiesen*) tell sb to get lost (*umg*) ♦ *vt* take *od* cart away; (*Film*) start; (*FILM, TV: Kamera*) roll; (*Strecke*) drive; (*Reifen*) wear; (*Fahrkarte*) use; **auf jdn ~** (*umg*) really go for sb.

Abfahrt [àp'fârt] *f* departure; (*Autobahn~*) exit; (*SKI*) descent; (*Piste*) run; **Vorsicht bei der ~ des Zuges!** stand back, the train is about to leave!
Abfahrts- *zW*: **~lauf** *m* (*SKI*) descent, run down; **~tag** *m* day of departure; **~zeit** *f* departure time.
Abfall [àp'fál] *m* waste; (*von Speisen etc*) garbage (*US*), rubbish (*Brit*); (*Neigung*) slope; (*Verschlechterung*) decline; **~eimer** *m* garbage can (*US*), rubbish bin (*Brit*).
abfallen *vi unreg* (*lit, fig*) fall *od* drop off; (*POL, vom Glauben*) break away; (*sich neigen*) fall *od* drop away; **wieviel fällt bei dem Geschäft für mich ab?** (*umg*) how much do I get out of the deal?
abfällig [àp'fcliçh] *a* disparaging, deprecatory.
Abfallprodukt *nt* (*lit, fig*) by-product.
abfangen [àp'fángən] *vt unreg* intercept; (*Person*) catch; (*unter Kontrolle bringen*) check; (*Aufprall*) absorb; (*Kunden*) lure away.
Abfangjäger *m* **-s, -** (*MIL*) interceptor.
abfärben [àp'ferbən] *vi* (*lit*) lose its color; (*Wäsche*) run; (*fig*) rub off.
abfassen [àp'fásən] *vt* write, draft.
abfeiern [àp'fiərn] *vt* (*umg*): **Überstunden ~** take time off in lieu of overtime pay.
abfertigen [àp'fertigən] *vt* prepare for dispatch, process; (*an der Grenze*) clear; (*Kundschaft*) attend to; **jdn kurz ~** give sb short shrift.
Abfertigung *f* preparing for dispatch, processing; clearance; (*Bedienung: von Kunden*) service; (: *von Antragstellern*) dealing (*von* with).
abfeuern [àp'foiərn] *vt* fire.
abfinden [àp'findən] *unreg vt* pay off ♦ *vr* come to terms; **sich mit jdm ~/nicht ~** put up with/not get along with sb; **er konnte sich nie damit ~, daß ...** he could never accept the fact that ...
Abfindung *f* (*von Gläubigern*) payment; (*Geld*) sum in settlement.
abflachen [àp'fláhən] *vt* level (off), flatten (out) ♦ *vi* (*fig: sinken*) decline.
abflauen [àp'flouən] *vi* (*Wind, Erregung*) die away, subside; (*Nachfrage, Geschäft*) fall *od* drop off.
abfliegen [àp'flē:gən] *unreg vi* take off ♦ *vt* (*Gebiet*) fly over.
abfließen [àp'flē:sən] *vi unreg* drain away; **ins Ausland ~** (*Geld*) flow out of the country.
Abflug [àp'flōō:k] *m* departure; (*Start*) take-off; **~zeit** *f* departure time.
Abfluß [àp'flōōs] *m* draining away; (*Öffnung*) outlet; **~rohr** *nt* drainpipe; (*von sanitären Anlagen auch*) wastepipe.
abfragen [àp'frágən] *vt* test; (*COMPUT*) call up; **jdn** *od* **jdm etw ~** question sb on sth.
abfrieren [àp'frē:rən] *vi unreg*: **ihm sind die Füße abgefroren** his feet got frostbitten, he got frostbite in his feet.

Abfuhr [áp'foo:r] f -, -en removal; (fig) snub, rebuff; **sich** (dat) **eine ~ holen** meet with a rebuff.

abführen [áp'fü:rən] vt lead away; (Gelder, Steuern) pay ♦ vi (MED) have a laxative effect.

Abführmittel nt laxative, purgative.

Abfüllanlage f bottling plant.

abfüllen [áp'fülən] vt draw off; (in Flaschen) bottle.

Abgabe [áp'gábə] f handing in; (von Ball) pass; (Steuer) tax; (einer Erklärung) giving.

abgaben- zW: **~frei** a tax-free; **~pflichtig** a liable to tax.

Abgabetermin m closing date; (für Dissertation etc) submission date.

Abgang [áp'gáng] m (von Schule) leaving; (THEAT) exit; (MED: Ausscheiden) passing; (: Fehlgeburt) miscarriage; (Abfahrt) departure; (der Post, von Waren) dispatch.

abgängig [áp'gengiĉh] a missing, absent.

Abgangszeugnis nt leaving diploma.

Abgas [áp'gás] nt waste gas; (AUT) exhaust; **a~frei** a: **a~frei verbrennen** burn without producing exhaust; **~katalysator** m **-s, -en** catalytic converter.

ABGB nt abk (Österreich: = Allgemeines Bürgerliches Gesetzbuch) Civil Code in Austria.

abgeben [áp'gä:bən] unreg vt (Gegenstand) hand od give in; (Ball) pass; (Wärme) give off; (Amt) hand over; (Schuß) fire; (Erklärung, Urteil) give; (darstellen) make; „Fahrrad abzugeben" "bicycle for sale"; **jdm etw ~** (überlassen) let sb have sth ♦ vr: **sich mit jdm/etw ~** associate with sb/bother with sth.

abgebrannt [áp'gəbránt] a (umg) broke.

abgebrüht [áp'gəbrü:t] a (umg: skrupellos) hard-boiled, hardened.

abgedroschen [áp'gədroshən] a trite; (Witz) corny.

abgefahren [áp'gəfárən] pp von **abfahren**.

abgefeimt [áp'gəfïmt] a cunning.

abgegeben [áp'gəgä:bən] pp von **abgeben**.

abgegriffen [áp'gəgrifən] a (Buch) welithumbed; (Redensart) trite.

abgehackt [áp'gəhákt] a clipped.

abgehalftert [áp'gəhálftərt] a (fig umg) rundown, dead beat.

abgehangen [áp'gəhángən] a: (gut) ~ (Fleisch) well-hung ♦ pp von **abhängen**.

abgehärtet [áp'gəhertət] a tough, hardy; (fig) hardened.

abgehen [áp'gä:ən] unreg vi go away, leave; (THEAT) exit; (POST) go; (MED) be passed; (sterben) die; (Knopf etc) come off; (abgezogen werden) be taken off; (Straße) branch off; (abweichen): **von einer Forderung ~** give up a demand; **von seiner Meinung ~** change one's opinion; **davon gehen 5% ab** 5% is taken off that; **etw geht jdm ab** (fehlt) sb lacks sth ♦ vt (Strecke) go od

walk along; (MIL: Gelände) patrol.

abgekämpft [áp'gəkempft] a exhausted.

abgekartet [áp'gəkártət] a: **ein ~es Spiel** a put-up job.

abgeklärt [áp'gəkle:rt] a serene, tranquil.

abgelegen [áp'gəlä:gən] a remote.

abgelten [áp'geltən] vt unreg (Ansprüche) satisfy.

abgemacht [áp'gəmáĉht] a fixed; **~!** agreed!

abgemagert [áp'gəmágərt] a (sehr dünn) thin; (ausgemergelt) emaciated.

abgeneigt [áp'gənïkt] a averse (dat to).

abgenutzt [áp'gənōōtst] a worn, shabby; (Reifen) worn; (fig: Klischees) well-worn.

Abgeordnete(r) [áp'gəordnətə(r)] mf dekl wie a elected representative; (von Parlament) Member of Congress (US), Member of Parliament (Brit).

Abgesandte(r) [áp'gəzántə(r)] mf delegate; (POL) envoy.

abgeschieden [áp'gəshē:dən] a (einsam): **~ leben/wohnen** live in seclusion.

abgeschlagen [áp'gəshlágən] a (besiegt) defeated; (erschöpft) exhausted, worn-out.

abgeschlossen [áp'gəshlosən] a attr (Wohnung) self-contained ♦ pp von **abschließen**.

abgeschmackt [áp'gəshmákt] a tasteless; **A~heit** f lack of taste; (Bemerkung) tasteless remark.

abgesehen [áp'gəzä:ən] a: **es auf jdn/etw ~ haben** be after sb/sth; **~ von ...** apart from ...

abgespannt [áp'gəshpánt] a tired out.

abgestanden [áp'gəshtándən] a stale; (Bier auch) flat.

abgestorben [áp'gəshtorbən] a numb; (BIOL, MED) dead.

abgestumpft [áp'gəshtōōmpft] a (gefühllos: Person) insensitive; (Gefühle, Gewissen) dulled.

abgetakelt [áp'gətákəlt] a (fig) decrepit.

abgetan [áp'gətán] a: **damit ist die Sache ~** that settles the matter.

abgetragen [áp'gətrágən] a worn.

abgetrennt [áp'gətrent] a (COMPUT) off-line.

abgewinnen [áp'gəvinən] vt unreg: **jdm Geld ~** win money from sb; **einer Sache etw/Geschmack ~** get sth/pleasure from sth.

abgewogen [áp'gəvō:gən] a (Urteil, Worte) balanced.

abgewöhnen [áp'gəvœnən] vt: **jdm/sich etw ~** cure sb of sth/give sth up.

abgießen [áp'gē:sən] vt unreg (Flüssigkeit) pour off.

Abglanz [áp'glánts] m reflection (auch fig).

abgleiten [áp'glïtən] vi unreg slip, slide.

Abgott [áp'got] m idol.

abgöttisch [áp'gœtish] a: **~ lieben** idolize.

abgrasen [áp'grázən] vt (Feld) graze; (umg: Thema) do to death.

abgrenzen [áp'grentsən] vt (lit, fig) mark off; (Gelände) fence off ♦ vr dis(as)sociate o.s. (gegen from).

Abgrund [áp'grōont] *m* (*lit, fig*) abyss.
abgründig [áp'gründiçh] *a* unfathomable; (*Lächeln*) cryptic.
abgrundtief *a* (*Haß, Verachtung*) profound.
abgucken [áp'gōokən] *vti* copy.
Abguß [áp'gōos] *m* (*KUNST. METALLURGIE*: *Vorgang*) casting; (: *Form*) cast.
abhaben [áp'hábən] *vt unreg* (*umg*: *abbekommen*): **willst du ein Stück ~?** do you want some?
abhacken [áp'hákən] *vt* chop off.
abhaken [áp'hákən] *vt* check off.
abhalten [áp'háltən] *vt unreg* (*Versammlung*) hold; **jdn von etw ~** (*fernhalten*) keep sb away from sth; (*hindern*) keep sb from sth.
abhandeln [áp'hándəln] *vt* (*Thema*) deal with; **jdm die Waren/8 Mark ~** do a deal with sb for the goods/beat sb down 8 marks.
abhanden [áphán'dən] *a*: **~ kommen** get lost.
Abhandlung [áp'hándlōong] *f* treatise, discourse.
Abhang [áp'háng] *m* slope.
abhängen [áp'hengən] *unreg vt* (*Bild*) take down; (*Anhänger*) uncouple; (*Verfolger*) shake off ♦ *vi* (*Fleisch*) hang; **von jdm/etw ~** depend on sb/sth; **das hängt ganz davon ab** it all depends; **er hat abgehängt** (*TEL umg*) he hung up (on me *etc*).
abhängig [áp'hengiçh] *a* dependent (*von* on); **A~keit** *f* dependence (*von* on).
abhärten [áp'hertən] *vtr* toughen (o.s.) up; **sich gegen etw ~** harden o.s. to sth.
abhauen [áp'houən] *unreg vt* cut off; (*Baum*) cut down ♦ *vi* (*umg*) clear off *od* out; **hau ab!** beat it!
abheben [áp'hā:bən] *unreg vt* lift (up); (*Karten*) cut; (*Masche*) slip; (*Geld*) withdraw, take out ♦ *vi* (*Flugzeug*) take off; (*Rakete*) lift off; (*KARTEN*) cut ♦ *vr* stand out (*von* from), contrast (*von* with).
abheften [áp'heftən] *vt* (*Rechnungen etc*) file away; (*Nähen*) tack, baste.
abhelfen [áp'helfən] *vi unreg* (+*dat*) remedy.
abhetzen [áp'hetsən] *vr* wear *od* tire o.s. out.
Abhilfe [áp'hilfə] *f* remedy; **~ schaffen** put things right.
abholen [áp'hō:lən] *vt* (*Gegenstand*) fetch, collect; (*Person*) call for; (*am Bahnhof etc*) pick up, meet.
abholzen [áp'holtsən] *vt* (*Wald*) clear, deforest.
abhorchen [áp'horçhən] *vt* (*MED*) listen to, sound.
abhören [áp'hœrən] *vt* (*Vokabeln*) test; (*Telefongespräch*) tap; (*Tonband etc*) listen to; **abgehört werden** (*umg*) be bugged.
Abhörgerät *nt* bug.
abhungern [áp'hŏŏngərn] *vr*: **sich** (*dat*) **10 Kilo ~** lose 10 kilos by going on a starvation diet.
Abi [á'bē] *nt* **-s, -s** (*SCH umg*) = **Abitur.**
Abitur [ábētōō:r'] *nt* **-s, -e** German school-leaving examination; (**das**) **~ machen** take

one's school-leaving exam.
Abiturient(in *f*) [ábētōōrēent'(in)] *m* candidate for school-leaving certificate.
Abk. *abk* (= *Abkürzung*) abbr.
abkämmen [áp'kemən] *vt* (*Gegend*) comb, scour.
abkanzeln [áp'kántsəln] *vt* (*umg*): **jdn ~** give sb a dressing-down.
abkapseln [áp'kápsəln] *vr* shut *od* cut o.s. off.
abkarten [áp'kártən] *vt* (*umg*): **die Sache war von vornherein abgekartet** the whole thing was a put-up job.
abkaufen [áp'koufən] *vt*: **jdm etw ~** buy sth from sb.
abkehren [áp'kā:rən] *vt* (*Blick*) avert, turn away ♦ *vr* turn away.
abklappern [áp'klápərn] *vt* (*umg*: *Läden, Straße*) scour, comb (*nach* for); (: *Kunden*) call on.
abklären [áp'kle:rən] *vt* (*klarstellen*) clear up, clarify ♦ *vr* (*sich setzen*) clarify.
Abklatsch [áp'klátsh] *m* **-es, -e** (*fig*) (poor) copy.
abklemmen [áp'klemən] *vt* (*Leitung*) clamp.
abklingen [áp'klingən] *vi unreg* die away; (*RAD*) fade out.
abknallen [áp'knálən] *vt* (*umg*) shoot down.
abknöpfen [áp'knœpfən] *vt* unbutton; **jdm etw ~** (*umg*) get sth off sb.
abkochen [áp'koλhən] *vt* boil; (*keimfrei machen*) sterilize (by boiling).
abkommandieren [áp'komándē:rən] *vt* (*MIL*: *zu Einheit*) post; (*zu bestimmtem Dienst*) detail (*zu* for).
abkommen [áp'komən] *vi unreg* get away; (**vom Thema**) **~** get off the subject, digress; **von der Straße/von einem Plan ~** leave the road/give up a plan.
Abkommen *nt* **-s, -** agreement.
abkömmlich [áp'kœmliçh] *a* available, free.
Abkömmling *m* (*Nachkomme*) descendant; (*fig*) adherent.
abkönnen [áp'kœnən] *vt unreg* (*umg*: *mögen*): **das kann ich nicht ab** I can't stand it.
abkratzen [áp'krátsən] *vt* scrape off ♦ *vi* (*umg*) kick the bucket.
abkriegen [áp'krē:gən] *vt* (*umg*) *siehe* **abbekommen.**
abkühlen [áp'kü:lən] *vt* cool down ♦ *vr* (*Mensch*) cool down *od* off; (*Wetter*) get cool; (*Zuneigung*) cool.
Abkunft [áp'kŏŏnft] *f* - origin, birth.
abkürzen [áp'kürtsən] *vt* shorten; (*Wort auch*) abbreviate; **den Weg ~** take a short cut.
Abkürzung *f* abbreviation; short cut.
abladen [áp'lâdən] *vti unreg* unload; (*fig umg*: *Ärger auch*) vent (*bei jdm* on sb).
Ablage [áp'lágə] *f* place to keep/put sth; (*Aktenordnung*) filing; (*für Akten*) tray.
ablagern [áp'lágərn] *vt* deposit ♦ *vr* be deposited ♦ *vi* mature.
Ablagerung *f* (*abgelagerter Stoff*) deposit.
ablassen [áp'lásən] *unreg vt* (*Wasser,*

Dampf) let out *od* off; *(vom Preis)* knock off ◊ *vi:* **von etw** ~ give sth up, abandon sth.

Ablauf *m (Abfluß)* drain; *(von Ereignissen)* course; *(einer Frist, Zeit)* expiration *(US)*, expiry *(Brit)*; **nach** ~ **des Jahres/dieser Zeit** at the end of the year/this time.

ablaufen [áp'loufən] *unreg vi (abfließen)* drain away; *(Ereignisse)* happen; *(Frist, Zeit, Paß)* expire; ~ **lassen** *(abspulen, abspielen: Platte, Tonband)* play; *(Film)* run ◊ *vt (Sohlen)* wear (down *od* out); **sich** *(dat)* **die Beine** *od* **Hacken nach etw** ~ *(umg)* walk one's legs off looking for sth; **jdm den Rang** ~ get the better of sb.

Ableben [áp'lā:bən] *nt (form)* demise *(form)*.

ablegen [áp'lā:gən] *vt* put *od* lay down; *(Kleider)* take off; *(Gewohnheit)* get rid of; *(Prüfung)* take; *(Zeugnis)* give; *(Schriftwechsel)* file (away); *(nicht mehr tragen: Kleidung)* discard, cast off; *(Schwur, Eid)* swear ◊ *vi (Schiff)* cast off.

Ableger *m* **-s, -** layer; *(fig)* branch, offshoot.

ablehnen [áp'lā:nən] *vt* reject; *(mißbilligen)* disapprove of; *(Einladung)* decline, refuse ◊ *vi* decline, refuse.

Ablehnung *f* rejection; refusal; **auf** ~ **stoßen** meet with disapproval.

ableisten [áp'lĭstən] *vt (form: Zeit)* serve.

ableiten [áp'lītən] *vt (Wasser)* divert; *(deduzieren)* deduce; *(Wort)* derive.

Ableitung *f* diversion; deduction; derivation; *(Wort)* derivative.

ablenken [áp'lɛngkən] *vt* turn away, deflect; *(zerstreuen)* distract ◊ *vi* change the subject; **das lenkt ab** *(zerstreut)* it takes your mind off things; *(stört)* it's distracting.

Ablenkung *f* deflection; distraction.

Ablenkungsmanöver *nt* diversionary tactic; *(um vom Thema abzulenken auch)* red herring.

ablesen [áp'lā:zən] *vt unreg* read; **jdm jeden Wunsch von den Augen** ~ anticipate sb's every wish.

ableugnen [áp'loignən] *vt* deny.

ablichten [áp'liȼhtən] *vt* photocopy; *(fotografieren)* photograph.

abliefern [áp'lē:fərn] *vt* deliver; **etw bei jdm/einer Dienststelle** ~ hand sth over to sb/in at an office.

Ablieferung *f* delivery.

abliegen [áp'lē:gən] *vi unreg* be some distance away; *(fig)* be far removed.

ablisten [áp'listən] *vt:* **jdm etw** ~ trick *od* con sb out of sth.

ablösen [áp'lœzən] *vt (abtrennen)* take off, remove; *(in Amt)* take over from; *(Schuld, Hypothek)* pay off, redeem; *(Methode, System)* supersede ◊ *vr (auch einander* ~) take turns; *(Fahrer, Kollegen, Wachen)* relieve each other.

Ablösung *f* removal; relieving.

abluchsen [áp'lŏŏksən] *vt (umg)*: **jdm etw** ~ get *od* wangle sth out of sb.

Abluft *f (TECH)* used air.

ABM *pl abk (= Arbeitsbeschaffungsmaßnahmen) job-creation scheme.*

abmachen [áp'máᴋhən] *vt* take off; *(vereinbaren)* agree; **etw mit sich allein** ~ sort sth out for o.s.

Abmachung *f* agreement.

abmagern [áp'mâgərn] *vi* get thinner, become emaciated.

Abmagerungskur *f* diet; **eine** ~ **machen** go on a diet.

Abmarsch [áp'mársh] *m* departure; **a~bereit** *a* ready to start.

abmarschieren [áp'márshē:rən] *vi* march off.

abmelden [áp'meldən] *vt (Auto)* take off the road; *(Telefon)* have disconnected; *(COMPUT)* log off; **ein Kind von einer Schule** ~ take a child away from a school; **er/sie ist bei mir abgemeldet** *(umg)* I don't want anything to do with him/her; **jdn bei der Polizei** ~ register sb's departure with the police ◊ *vr* give notice of one's departure; *(im Hotel)* check out.

abmessen [áp'mɛsən] *vt unreg* measure.

Abmessung *f* measurement; *(Ausmaß)* dimension.

abmontieren [áp'montē:rən] *vt* take off; *(Maschine)* dismantle.

abmühen [áp'mü:ən] *vr* wear o.s. out.

abnabeln [áp'nâbəln] *vt:* **jdn** ~ *(auch fig)* cut sb's umbilical cord.

abnagen [áp'nâgən] *vt* gnaw off; *(Knochen)* gnaw.

Abnäher [áp'nɛ:ər] *m* **-s, -** dart.

Abnahme [áp'nâmə] *f* **-, -n** removal; *(COMM)* buying; *(Verringerung)* decrease *(gen* in).

abnehmen [áp'nā:mən] *unreg vt* take off, remove; *(Führerschein)* take away; *(Geld)* get *(jdm* out of sb); *(kaufen, auch umg: glauben)* buy *(jdm* from sb); *(Prüfung)* hold; *(Maschen)* decrease; *(Hörer)* lift, pick up; *(begutachten: Gebäude, Auto)* inspect; **kann ich dir etwas** ~**?** *(tragen)* can I take something for you?; **jdm Arbeit** ~ take work off sb's shoulders; **jdm ein Versprechen** ~ make sb promise sth ◊ *vi* decrease; *(schlanker werden)* lose weight.

Abnehmer *m* **-s, -** purchaser, customer; **viele/wenige** ~ **finden** *(COMM)* sell well/badly.

Abneigung [áp'nīgŏŏng] *f* aversion, dislike.

abnorm [ápnorm'] *a* abnormal.

abnötigen [áp'nœtigən] *vt:* **jdm etw/Respekt** ~ force sth from sb/gain sb's respect.

abnutzen [áp'nŏŏtsən] *vt* wear out.

Abnutzung *f* wear (and tear).

Abo [à'bō] *nt* **-s, -s** *(umg)* = **Abonnement**.

Abonnement [àbon(ə)mâ'] *nt* **-s, -s,** *od* **-e** subscription; *(Theater~)* season ticket.

Abonnent(in *f)* [àbonɛ'rən] *m* subscriber.

abonnieren [àbonɛ'rən] *vt* subscribe to.

abordnen [áp'órdnən] *vt* delegate.

Abordnung *f* delegation.

Abort [àbort'] *m* **-(e)s, -e** *(veraltet)* lavatory.

abpacken [áp'pákən] *vt* pack.

abpassen [áp'pásən] *vt* (*Person, Gelegenheit*) wait for; (*in Größe: Stoff etc*) adjust; (*warten auf*) catch; (*jdm auflauern*) waylay; **etw gut** ~ time sth well.

abpausen [áp'pouzən] *vt* make a tracing of.

abpfeifen [áp'pfīfən] *vti unreg* (*SPORT*): (**das Spiel**) ~ blow the whistle (for the end of the game).

Abpfiff [áp'pfif] *m* final whistle.

abplagen [áp'plâgən] *vr* struggle (away).

Abprall [áp'prál] *m* rebound; (*von Kugel*) ricochet.

abprallen *vi* bounce off; ricochet; **an jdm** ~ (*fig*) make no impression on sb.

abputzen [áp'põõtsən] *vt* clean; (*Nase etc*) wipe.

abquälen [áp'kve:lən] *vr* struggle (away).

Abr. *abk* = **Abrechnung; Abreise.**

abrackern [áp'rákərn] *vr* (*umg*) slave away.

abraten [áp'râtən] *vi unreg* advise, warn (*jdm von etw* sb against sth).

abräumen [áp'roimən] *vti* clear up *od* away; (*Tisch*) clear.

abreagieren [áp'räägē:rən] *vt* (*Zorn*) work off (*an* +*dat* on); **seinen Ärger an anderen** ~ take it out on others ♦ *vr* calm down.

abrechnen [áp'reçhnən] *vt* deduct, take off ♦ *vi* (*lit*) settle up; (*fig*) get even; **darf ich** ~? would you like your check now?

Abrechnung *f* settlement; (*Rechnung*) check; (*Aufstellung*) statement (*über* +*akk* for); (*Bilanz*) balancing; (*fig: Rache*) revenge; **in** ~ **stellen** (*form: Abzug*) deduct.

Abrechnungszeitraum *m* accounting period.

Abrede [áp'rā:də] *f*: **etw in** ~ **stellen** deny *od* dispute sth.

abregen [áp'rā:gən] *vr* (*umg*) calm *od* cool down.

abreiben [áp'rībən] *vt unreg* rub off; (*säubern*) wipe; **jdn mit einem Handtuch** ~ towel sb down.

Abreibung *f* (*umg: Prügel*) hiding, thrashing.

Abreise [áp'rīzə] *f* departure.

abreisen *vi* leave, set off.

abreißen [áp'rīsən] *unreg vt* (*Haus*) tear down; (*Blatt*) tear off ♦ *vi*: **den Kontakt** *etc* **nicht** ~ **lassen** stay in touch.

abrichten [áp'riçhtən] *vt* train.

abriegeln [áp'rē:gəln] *vt* (*Tür*) bolt; (*Straße, Gebiet*) seal off.

abringen [áp'ringən] *vt unreg*: **sich** (*dat*) **ein Lächeln** ~ force a smile.

Abriß [áp'ris] *m* **-sses, -sse** (*Übersicht*) outline; (*Abbruch*) demolition.

abrollen [áp'rolən] *vt* (*abwickeln*) unwind ♦ *vi* (*vonstatten gehen: Programm*) run; (: *Veranstaltung*) go off; (: *Ereignisse*) unfold.

Abruf [áp'rõõ:f] *m*: **auf** ~ on call.

abrufen *vt unreg* (*Mensch*) call away; (*COMM: Ware*) request delivery of; (*COMPUT*) recall, retrieve.

abrunden [áp'rõõndən] *vt* round off.

abrüsten [áp'rüstən] *vi* disarm.

Abrüstung *f* disarmament.

abrutschen [áp'rõõtshən] *vi* slip; (*AVIAT*) sideslip.

Abs. *abk* = **Absender**; (= *Absatz*) par., para.

absacken [áp'zákən] *vi* (*sinken*) sink; (*Boden, Gebäude auch*) subside.

Absage [áp'zágə] *f* **-, -n** refusal; (*auf Einladung auch*) negative reply.

absagen *vt* cancel, call off; (*Einladung*) turn down ♦ *vi* withdraw; (*ablehnen*) decline; **jdm** ~ tell sb that one can't come.

absägen [áp'ze:gən] *vt* saw off.

absahnen [áp'zânən] *vt* (*lit*) skim; **das beste für sich** ~ (*fig*) take the cream.

Absatz [áp'záts] *m* **-es, -sätze** (*COMM*) sales *pl*; (*JUR*) section; (*Bodensatz*) deposit; (*neuer Abschnitt*) paragraph; (*Treppen*~) landing; (*Schuh*~) heel; **~flaute** *f* slump in the market; **~förderung** *f* sales promotion; **~gebiet** *nt* (*COMM*) market; sales territory; **~prognose** *f* sales forecast; **~schwierigkeiten** *pl* sales problems *pl*; **~ziffern** *pl* sales figures *pl*.

absaufen [áp'zoufən] *vi unreg* (*umg: ertrinken*) drown; (: *Motor*) flood; (: *Schiff etc*) go down.

absaugen [áp'zougən] *vt* (*Flüssigkeit*) suck out *od* off; (*Teppich, Sofa*) hoover ®, vacuum.

abschaben [áp'shâbən] *vt* scrape off; (*Möhren*) scrape.

abschaffen [áp'sháfən] *vt* abolish, do away with.

Abschaffung *f* abolition.

abschalten [áp'sháltən] *vti* (*lit, umg*) switch off.

abschattieren [áp'shátē:rən] *vt* shade.

abschätzen [áp'shetsən] *vt* estimate; (*Lage*) assess; (*Person*) size up.

abschätzig [áp'shetsiçh] *a* disparaging, derogatory.

Abschaum [áp'shoum] *m* **-(e)s** scum.

Abscheu [áp'shoi] *m* **-(e)s** loathing, repugnance; **a~erregend** *a* repulsive, loathsome; **a~lich** [áp'shoi'liçh] *a* abominable.

abschicken [áp'shikən] *vt* send off.

abschieben [áp'shē:bən] *vt unreg* push away; (*Person*) pack off; (*fig: Verantwortung, Schuld*) shift (*auf* +*akk* onto); (*ausweisen: Ausländer*) deport.

Abschied [áp'shē:t] *m* **-(e)s, -e** parting; (*von Armee*) discharge; ~ **nehmen** say goodbye (*von jdm* to sb), take one's leave (*von jdm* of sb); **seinen** ~ **nehmen** (*MIL*) apply for discharge; **zum** ~ on parting.

Abschieds- *zW*: **~brief** *m* farewell letter; **~feier** *f* farewell party.

abschießen [áp'shē:sən] *vt unreg* (*Flugzeug*) shoot down; (*Geschoß*) fire; (*umg: Minister*) get rid of.

abschirmen [áp'shirmən] *vt* screen; (*schützen auch*) protect ♦ *vr* (*sich isolieren*) cut o.s. off (*gegen* from).

abschlaffen [ảp'shlȧfən] *vi* (*umg*) flag.

abschlagen [ảp'shlȧgən] *vt unreg* (*abhacken*, *COMM*) knock off; (*ablehnen*) refuse; (*MIL*) repel.

abschlägig [ảp'shle:giċḩ] *a* negative; **jdn/etw ~ bescheiden** (*form*) turn sb/sth down.

Abschlagszahlung *f* installment (*US*), interim payment (*Brit*).

abschleifen [ảp'shlīfən] *unreg vt* grind down; (*Rost*) polish off ♦ *vr* wear off.

Abschleppdienst *m* (*AUT*) towing company (*US*), breakdown service (*Brit*).

abschleppen [ảp'shlepən] *vt* (take in) tow.

Abschleppseil *nt* towrope.

abschließen [ảp'shlē:sən] *unreg vt* (*Tür*) lock; (*beenden*) conclude, finish; (*Vertrag*, *Handel*) conclude; (*Versicherung*) take out; (*Wette*) place; **mit abgeschlossenem Studium** with a degree; **mit der Vergangenheit ~ break** with the past ♦ *vr* (*sich isolieren*) cut o.s. off.

abschließend *a* concluding ♦ *ad* in conclusion, finally.

Abschluß [ảp'shlōōs] *m* (*Beendigung*) close, conclusion; (*COMM: Bilanz*) balancing; (*von Vertrag*, *Handel*) conclusion; **zum ~** in conclusion; **~feier** *f* (*SCH*) end-of-term party; **~prüfer** *m* accountant; **~prüfung** *f* (*SCH*) final examination; (*UNIV auch*) finals *pl*; **~rechnung** *f* final account; **~zeugnis** *nt* (*SCH*) leaving diploma.

abschmecken [ảp'shmɛkən] *vt* (*kosten*) taste; (*würzen*) season.

abschmieren [ảp'shmē:rən] *vt* (*AUT*) grease, lubricate.

abschminken [ảp'shmingkən] *vt*: **sich ~** remove one's make-up.

abschmirgeln [ảp'shmirgəln] *vt* sand down.

abschnallen [ảp'shnȧlən] *vr* unfasten one's seat belt ♦ *vi* (*umg*: *nicht mehr folgen können*) give up; (: *fassungslos sein*) be staggered.

abschneiden [ảp'shnīdən] *unreg vt* cut off ♦ *vi* do, come off; **bei etw gut/schlecht ~** (*umg*) to come off well/badly in sth.

Abschnitt [ảp'shnit] *m* section; (*MIL*) sector; (*Kontroll~*) stub; (*MATH*) segment; (*Zeit~*) period.

abschnüren [ảp'shnü:rən] *vt* constrict.

abschöpfen [ảp'shœpfən] *vt* skim off.

abschrauben [ảp'shroubən] *vt* unscrew.

abschrecken [ảp'shrɛkən] *vt* deter, put off; (*mit kaltem Wasser*) plunge into cold water.

abschreckend *a* deterrent; **~es Beispiel** warning; **eine ~e Wirkung haben, ~ wirken** act as a deterrent.

abschreiben [ảp'shrībən] *vt unreg* copy; (*verlorengeben*) write off; (*COMM*) deduct; **er ist bei mir abgeschrieben** I'm finished with him.

Abschreibung *f* (*COMM*) deduction; (*Wertverminderung*) depreciation.

Abschrift [ảp'shrift] *f* copy.

abschuften [ảp'shōōftən] *vr* (*umg*) work o.s. to death.

abschürfen [ảp'shürfən] *vt* graze.

Abschuß [ảp'shōōs] *m* (*eines Geschützes*) firing; (*Herunterschießen*) shooting down; (*Tötung*) shooting.

abschüssig [ảp'shüsiċḩ] *a* steep.

Abschuß- *zW*: **~liste** *f*: **er steht auf der ~liste** (*umg*) his days are numbered; **~rampe** *f* launch(ing) pad.

abschütteln [ảp'shütəln] *vt* shake off.

abschütten [ảp'shütən] *vt* (*Flüssigkeit etc*) pour off.

abschwächen [ảp'shvɛċḩən] *vt* lessen; (*Behauptung*, *Kritik*) tone down ♦ *vr* lessen.

abschweifen [ảp'shvīfən] *vi* wander; (*Redner auch*) digress.

Abschweifung *f* digression.

abschwellen [ảp'shvɛlən] *vi* *unreg* (*Geschwulst*) go down; (*Lärm*) die down.

abschwenken [ảp'shvɛngkən] *vi* turn away.

abschwören [ảp'shvœrən] *vi* *unreg* (+*dat*) renounce.

absehbar [ảp'zā:bȧr] *a* foreseeable; **in ~er Zeit** in the foreseeable future; **das Ende ist ~** the end is in sight.

absehen *unreg vt* (*Ende*, *Folgen*) foresee; **jdm etw ~** (*erlernen*) copy sth from sb ♦ *vi*: **von etw ~** refrain from sth; (*nicht berücksichtigen*) leave sth out of consideration.

abseilen [ảp'zīlən] *vt* lower down on a rope ♦ *vr* (*Bergsteiger*) abseil (down).

abseits [ảp'zīts] *ad* out of the way ♦ *präp* +*gen* away from.

Abseits *nt* (*SPORT*) offside; **im ~ stehen** be offside; **ins ~ geraten** (*fig*) go beyond the pale.

absenden [ảp'zɛndən] *vt unreg* send off, dispatch.

Absender *m* -s, - sender.

Absendung *f* dispatch.

absetzbar [ảp'zɛtsbȧr] *a* (*Beamter*) dismissible; (*Waren*) saleable; (*von Steuer*) deductible.

absetzen [ảp'zɛtsən] *vt* (*niederstellen*, *aussteigen lassen*) put down; (*abnehmen*) take off; (*COMM: verkaufen*) sell; (*von: abziehen*) deduct; (*Theaterstück*) take off; (*entlassen*) dismiss; (*König*) depose; (*streichen*) drop; (*Fußballspiel*, *Termin*) cancel; (*hervorheben*) pick out; **das kann man ~** that is tax-deductible ♦ *vi*: **er trank das Glas aus, ohne abzusetzen** he emptied his glass without pausing for breath ♦ *vr* (*sich entfernen*) clear off; (*sich ablagern*) be deposited.

Absetzung *f* (*FIN: Abzug*) deduction; (*Entlassung*) dismissal; (*von König*) deposing; (*Streichung*) dropping.

absichern [ảp'ziċḩərn] *vtr* make safe; (*schützen*) safeguard.

Absicht [ảp'ziċḩt] *f* intention; **mit ~** on purpose; **a~lich** *a* intentional, deliberate.

absichtslos *a* unintentional.

absinken [ȧp'zingkǝn] vi unreg sink; (*Temperatur, Geschwindigkeit*) decrease.

absitzen [ȧp'zitsǝn] unreg vi dismount ♦ vt (*Strafe*) serve.

absolut [ȧpzōlōō:t'] a absolute.

Absolutheitsanspruch m claim to absolute right.

Absolutismus [ȧpzōlōō:tis'mōōs] m absolutism.

Absolvent(in *f*) m: die ~en eines Lehrgangs the students who have completed a course.

absolvieren [ȧpzolvē:'rǝn] vt (*SCH*) complete.

absonderlich [ȧpzon'dǝrlich̩] a odd, strange.

absondern vt separate; (*ausscheiden*) give off, secrete ♦ vr cut o.s. off.

Absonderung *f* separation; (*MED*) secretion.

absorbieren [ȧpzorbē:'rǝn] vt (*lit, fig*) absorb.

abspalten [ȧp'shpȧltǝn] vt split off.

Abspannung [ȧp'shpȧnōōng] *f* (*Ermüdung*) exhaustion.

absparen [ȧp'shpȧrǝn] vt: sich (*dat*) etw ~ scrimp and save for sth.

abspecken [ȧp'shpekǝn] vt (*umg*) shed ♦ vi lose weight.

abspeisen [ȧp'shpīzǝn] vt (*fig*) put off.

abspenstig [ȧp'shpenstich̩] a: ~ machen lure away (*jdm* from sb).

absperren [ȧp'shperǝn] vt block od close off; (*Tür*) lock.

Absperrung *f* (*Vorgang*) blocking od closing off; (*Sperre*) barricade.

abspielen [ȧp'shpē:lǝn] vt (*Platte, Tonband*) play; (*SPORT: Ball*) pass; **vom Blatt** ~ (*MUS*) sight-read ♦ vr happen.

absplittern [ȧp'shplitǝrn] vti chip off.

Absprache [ȧp'shprȧkh̩ǝ] *f* arrangement; **ohne vorherige** ~ without prior consultation.

absprechen [ȧp'shprech̩ǝn] unreg vt (*vereinbaren*) arrange; **jdm etw** ~ deny sb sth; (*in Abrede stellen: Begabung*) dispute sb's sth ♦ vr: **die beiden hatten sich vorher abgesprochen** they had agreed on what to do/ say *etc* in advance.

abspringen [ȧp'shpringǝn] vi unreg jump down/off; (*Farbe, Lack*) flake off; (*AVIAT*) bale out; (*sich distanzieren*) back out.

Absprung [ȧp'shprōōng] m jump; **den** ~ **schaffen** (*fig*) make the break (*umg*).

abspulen [ȧp'shpōō:lǝn] vt (*Kabel, Garn*) unwind.

abspülen [ȧp'shpü:lǝn] vt rinse; (*Geschirr*) do the dishes.

abstammen [ȧp'shtȧmǝn] vi be descended; (*Wort*) be derived.

Abstammung *f* descent; derivation; **französischer** ~ of French extraction od descent.

Abstand [ȧp'shtȧnt] m distance; (*zeitlich*) interval; **davon** ~ **nehmen, etw zu tun** refrain from doing sth; ~ **halten** (*AUT*) keep one's distance; ~ **von etw gewinnen** (*fig*) distance o.s. from sth; **mit großem** ~ **füh-** ren lead by a wide margin; **mit** ~ **der beste** by far the best.

Abstandssumme *f* compensation.

abstatten [ȧp'shtȧtǝn] vt (*form: Dank*) give; (: *Besuch*) pay.

abstauben [ȧp'shtoubǝn] vti dust; (*umg: stehlen*) pinch; **(den Ball)** ~ (*SPORT*) tuck the ball away.

Abstauber(in *f*) [ȧp'shtoubǝr(in)] m **-s,** - (*umg: Person*) fly-boy, somebody on the make.

abstechen [ȧp'shtech̩ǝn] unreg vt cut; (*Tier*) cut the throat of ♦ vi contrast (*gegen, von* with).

Abstecher m **-s,** - detour.

abstecken [ȧp'shtekǝn] vt (*Fläche*) mark out; (*Saum*) pin.

abstehen [ȧp'shtā:ǝn] vi unreg (*Ohren, Haare*) stick out; (*entfernt sein*) stand away.

Absteige *f* -, **-n** cheap hotel.

absteigen [ȧp'shtīgǝn] vi unreg (*vom Rad etc*) get off, dismount; (*im Hotel*) put up (*in +dat* at); (*SPORT*) be relegated (*in +akk* to); **auf dem absteigenden Ast sein** (*umg*) be going downhill, be on the decline.

abstellen [ȧp'shtelǝn] vt (*niederstellen*) put down; (*entfernt stellen*) pull out; (*hinstellen: Auto*) park; (*ausschalten*) turn od switch off; (*Mißstand, Unsitte*) stop; (*ausrichten*) gear (*auf +akk* to); (*abkommandieren*) order off; **das läßt sich nicht/läßt sich** ~ nothing/something can be done about that.

Abstellgleis nt siding; **jdn aufs** ~ **schieben** (*fig*) cast sb aside.

Abstellraum m storeroom.

abstempeln [ȧp'shtempǝln] vt stamp; (*fig*) brand (*zu, als* as).

absterben [ȧp'shterbǝn] vi unreg die; (*Körperteil*) go numb.

Abstieg [ȧp'shtē:k] m **-(e)s, -e** descent; (*SPORT*) relegation; (*fig*) decline.

abstimmen [ȧp'shtimǝn] vi vote ♦ vt (*Instrument*) tune (*auf +akk* to); (*Interessen*) match (*auf +akk* with); (*Termine, Ziele*) fit in (*auf +akk* with) ♦ vr agree.

Abstimmung *f* vote; (*geheime* ~) ballot.

abstinent [ȧpstēnent'] a (*von Alkohol*) teetotal.

Abstinenz [ȧpstēnents'] *f* teetotalism.

Abstinenzler(in *f*) m **-s,** - teetotaller.

abstoßen [ȧp'shtō:sǝn] vt unreg push off od away; (*anekeln*) repel; (*COMM: Ware, Aktien*) sell off.

abstoßend a repulsive.

abstottern [ȧp'shtotǝrn] vt (*umg*) pay off.

abstrahieren [ȧpstrȧhē:'rǝn] vti abstract.

abstrakt [ȧpstrȧkt'] a abstract ♦ ad abstractly, in the abstract.

Abstraktion [ȧpstrȧktsē̄ō:n'] *f* abstraction.

Abstraktum [ȧpstrȧk'tōōm] nt **-s, Abstrakta** abstract concept; (*GRAM*) abstract noun.

abstrampeln [ȧp'shtrȧmpǝln] vr (*fig umg*)

sweat (away).
abstreifen [ảp'shtrīfən] vt (abtreten: Schuhe, Füße) wipe; (abziehen: Schmuck) take off, slip off.
abstreiten [ảp'shtrītən] vt unreg deny.
Abstrich [ảp'shtriċh] m (Abzug) cut; (MED) smear; ~e machen lower one's sights.
abstufen [ảp'shtoō:fən] vt (Hang) terrace; (Farben) shade; (Gehälter) grade.
abstumpfen [ảp'shtoōmpfən] vt (lit, fig) dull, blunt ♦ vi become dulled.
Absturz [ảp'shtoōrts] m fall; (AVIAT) crash.
abstürzen [ảp'shtürtsən] vi fall; (AVIAT) crash.
absuchen [ảp'zoō:ℏən] vt scour, search.
absurd [ảpzoōrt'] a absurd.
Abszeß [ảpstses'] m -sses, -sse abscess.
Abt [ảpt] m -(e)s, ¨e abbot.
Abt. abk (= Abteilung) dept.
abtasten [ảp'tástən] vt feel, probe; (ELEK) scan; (bei Durchsuchung) frisk (auf +akk for).
abtauen [ảp'touən] vti thaw; (Kühlschrank) defrost.
Abtei [ảptī'] f -, -en abbey.
Abteil [ảptīl'] nt -(e)s, -e compartment.
abteilen [ảp'tīlən] vt divide up; (abtrennen) divide off.
Abteilung f (in Firma, Kaufhaus) department; (MIL) unit; (in Krankenhaus, JUR) section.
Abteilungsleiter(in f) m head of department; (in Kaufhaus) department manager/manageress.
abtelefonieren [ảp'tālāfōnē:rən] vi telephone to say one can't make it.
Äbtissin [epti'sin] f abbess.
abtönen [ảp'tœnən] vt (PHOT) tone down.
abtöten [ảp'tœtən] vt (lit, fig) destroy, kill (off); (Nerv) deaden.
abtragen [ảp'trágən] vt unreg (Hügel, Erde) level down; (Essen) clear away; (Kleider) wear out; (Schulden) pay off.
abträglich [ảp'tre:kliċh] a harmful (dat to).
Abtragung f (GEOL) erosion.
Abtransport m -(e)s, -e transportation; (aus Katastrophengebiet) evacuation.
abtransportieren [ảp'tránsportē:rən] vt take away, remove; transport; evacuate.
abtreiben [ảp'trībən] unreg vt (Boot, Flugzeug) drive off course; (Kind) abort ♦ vi be driven off course; abort.
Abtreibung f abortion.
Abtreibungsversuch m attempted abortion.
abtrennen [ảp'trenən] vt (lostrennen) detach; (entfernen) take off; (abteilen) separate off.
abtreten [ảp'trā:tən] unreg vt wear out; (überlassen) hand over, cede (jdm to sb); (Rechte, Ansprüche) transfer; **sich** (dat) **die Füße ~** wipe one's feet ♦ vi go off; (zurücktreten) step down; **~!** (MIL) dismiss!
Abtritt [ảp'trit] m (Rücktritt) resignation.
abtrocknen [ảp'troknən] vt dry ♦ vi do the drying-up.

abtropfen [ảp'tropfən] vi: **etw ~ lassen** let sth drain.
abtrünnig [ảp'trüniċh] a renegade.
abtun [ảp'toō:n] vt unreg take off; (fig) dismiss; **etw kurz ~** brush sth aside.
aburteilen [ảp'oōrtīlən] vt condemn.
abverlangen [ảp'ferlángən] vt: **jdm etw ~** demand sth from sb.
abwägen [ảp've:gən] vt unreg weigh up.
abwählen [ảp'vc:lən] vt vote out (of office); (SCH: Fach) give up.
abwälzen [ảp'veltsən] vt (Schuld, Verantwortung) shift (auf +akk onto); (Arbeit) unload (auf +akk onto); (Kosten) pass on (auf +akk to).
abwandeln [ảp'vándəln] vt adapt.
abwandern [ảp'vándərn] vi move away.
Abwärme [ảp'vermə] f waste heat.
abwarten [ảp'vártən] vt wait for; **das Gewitter ~** wait till the storm is over ♦ vi wait; **~ und Tee trinken** (umg) wait and see; **eine abwartende Haltung einnehmen** play a waiting game.
abwärts [ảp'verts] ad down; **~gehen** vi unpers (fig): **mit ihm/dem Land geht es ~** he/the country is going downhill.
Abwasch [ảp'vásh] m -(e)s washing-up; **... dann kannst du das auch machen, das ist (dann) ein ~** (umg) ... then you could do that as well and kill two birds with one stone.
abwaschen vt unreg (Schmutz) wash off; (Geschirr) wash (up).
Abwasser [ảp'vásər] nt -s, -wässer sewage; **~kanal** m sewer.
abwechseln [ảp'veksəln] vir alternate; (Personen) take turns.
abwechselnd a alternate.
Abwechslung f change; (Zerstreuung) diversion; **für ~ sorgen** provide entertainment.
abwechslungsreich a varied.
Abweg [ảp'vā:k] m: **auf ~e geraten/führen** go/lead astray.
abwegig [ảp'vā:giċh] a wrong; (Verdacht) groundless.
Abwehr [ảp'vā:r] f - defense (US), defence (Brit); (Schutz) protection; (~dienst) counter-intelligence (service); **auf ~ stoßen** be repulsed; **a~en** vt ward off; (Ball) stop; **abwehrende Geste** dismissive gesture; **~reaktion** f (PSYCH) defense reaction.
abweichen [ảp'vīċhən] vi unreg deviate; (Meinung) differ; **vom rechten Weg ~** (fig) wander off the straight and narrow.
abweichend a deviant; differing.
Abweichler m -s, - (POL) maverick.
Abweichung f (zeitlich, zahlenmäßig) allowance; **zulässige ~** (TECH) tolerance.
abweisen [ảp'vīzən] vt unreg turn away; (Antrag) turn down; **er läßt sich nicht ~** he won't take no for an answer.
abweisend a (Haltung) cold.
abwenden [ảp'vendən] unreg vt avert ♦ vr

turn away.

abwerben [áp'vɛrbən] vt unreg woo away (jdm from sb).

abwerfen [áp'vɛrfən] vt unreg throw off; (Profit) yield; (aus Flugzeug) drop; (Spielkarte) discard.

abwerten [áp'vɛrtən] vt (FIN) devalue.

abwertend a pejorative.

Abwertung f devaluation.

abwesend [áp'vǟ:zənt] a absent; (zerstreut) far away.

Abwesenheit [áp'vǟ:zənhīt] f absence; **durch ~ glänzen** (ironisch) be conspicuous by one's absence.

abwickeln [áp'vikəln] vt unwind; (Geschäft) transact, conclude; (fig: erledigen) deal with.

Abwicklungskosten [áp'viklōōngzkostən] pl transaction costs pl.

abwiegen [áp'vǟ:gən] vt unreg weigh out.

abwimmeln [áp'viməln] vt (umg: Person) get rid of; (: Auftrag) get out of.

abwinken [áp'vingkən] vi wave it/him etc aside; (fig: ablehnen) say no.

abwirtschaften [áp'virtsháftən] vi go downhill.

abwischen [áp'vishən] vt wipe off od away; (putzen) wipe.

abwracken [áp'vrákən] vt (Schiff) break (up); **abgewrackter Mensch** wreck (of a person).

Abwurf [áp'vōōrf] m throwing off; (von Bomben etc) dropping; (von Reiter, SPORT) throw.

abwürgen [áp'vürgən] vt (umg) scotch; (Motor) stall; **etw von vornherein ~** nip sth in the bud.

abzahlen [áp'tsálən] vt pay off.

abzählen [áp'tse:lən] vt count (up); **abgezähltes Fahrgeld** exact fare.

Abzählreim [áp'tse:līm] m counting rhyme (such as "eeny meeny miney mo", for choosing a person).

Abzahlung f repayment; **auf ~ kaufen** buy on the installment plan (US) od on hire purchase (Brit).

abzapfen [áp'tsápfən] vt draw off; **jdm Blut ~** take blood from sb.

abzäunen [áp'tsoinən] vt fence off.

Abzeichen [áp'tsīçhən] nt badge; (Orden) decoration.

abzeichnen [áp'tsīçhnən] vt draw, copy; (unterschreiben) initial ♦ vr stand out; (fig: bevorstehen) loom.

Abziehbild nt transfer.

abziehen [áp'tsē:ən] unreg vt take off; (Tier) skin; (Bett) strip; (Truppen) withdraw; (subtrahieren) take away, subtract; (kopieren) run off; (Schlüssel) take out, remove ♦ vi go away; (Truppen) withdraw; (abdrücken) pull the trigger, fire.

abzielen [áp'tsē:lən] vi be aimed (auf +akk at).

Abzug [áp'tsōō:k] m departure; (von

Truppen) withdrawal; (Kopie) copy; (Subtraktion) subtraction; (Betrag) deduction; (Rauch~) flue; (von Waffen) trigger; (Rabatt) discount; (Korrekturfahne) proof; (PHOT) print; **jdm freien ~ gewähren** give od grant sb a safe conduct.

abzüglich [áp'tsü:kliçh] präp +gen less.

abzweigen [áp'tsvīgən] vi branch off ♦ vt set aside.

Abzweigung f junction.

Accessoires [áksesōārs'] pl accessories pl.

ach [ákh] interj oh; **~ so!** I see!; **mit A~ und Krach** by the skin of one's teeth; **~ was** od **wo, das ist doch nicht so schlimm!** come on now, it's not that bad!

Achse [ák'sə] f -, **-n** axis; (AUT) axle; **auf ~ sein** (umg) be on the move.

Achsel [ák'səl] f -, **-n** shoulder; **~höhle** f armpit; **~zucken** nt shrug (of one's shoulders).

Achsenbruch m (AUT) broken axle.

Achsenkreuz nt coordinate system.

acht [ákht] num eight; **~ Tage** a week; **A~** f -, **-en** eight; (beim Eislaufen etc) figure (of) eight.

Acht f - attention; **hab a~** (MIL) attention!; **sich in a~ nehmen** be careful (vor +dat of), watch out (vor +dat for); **etw außer a~ lassen** disregard sth.

achtbar a worthy.

Achteck nt octagon.

Achtel num eighth; **~note** f eighth note (US), quaver (Brit).

achten vt respect ♦ vi pay attention (auf +akk to); **darauf ~, daß ...** be careful that ...

ächten [eçh'tən] vt outlaw, ban.

achte(r, s) a eighth.

Achter- zW: **~bahn** f roller coaster; **~deck** nt (NAUT) afterdeck.

achtfach a eightfold.

achtgeben vi unreg take care (auf +akk of); (aufmerksam sein) pay attention (auf +akk to).

achtlos a careless; **viele gehen ~ daran vorbei** many people just pass by without noticing.

achtmal ad eight times.

achtsam a attentive.

Achtstundentag m eight-hour day.

Achtung [ákh'tōōng] f attention; (Ehrfurcht) respect ♦ interj look out!; (MIL) attention!; **alle ~!** good for you/him etc!; **~, fertig, los!** ready, set, go!; **„~ Hochspannung!"** "danger, high voltage"; **~ Lebensgefahr/ Stufe!** danger/watch your step!

Achtungserfolg m reasonable success.

achtzehn num eighteen.

achtzig num eighty; **A~er(in f)** m **-s,** - octogenarian.

Achtzigerjahre pl eighties pl.

ächzen [eçh'tsən] vi groan (vor +dat with).

Acker [á'kər] m **-s,** ꞏ field; **~bau** m agriculture; **~bau und Viehzucht** farming.

ackern vti plow (US), plough (Brit); (umg) slog away.
a conto [à kon'tō] ad (COMM) on account.
a. d. abk = **an der** (bei Ortsnamen).
a.D. abk = **außer Dienst.**
A.D. abk (= Anno Domini) A.D.
ad absurdum [àt àpzōōr'dōōm] ad: ~ **führen** (Argument etc) reduce to absurdity.
ADAC m - abk (= Allgemeiner Deutscher Automobil-Club) ≈ AAA (US), AA (Brit).
ad acta [àt àk'tá] ad: **etw** ~ **legen** (fig) consider sth finished; (Frage, Problem) consider sth closed.
Adam [à'dàm] m: **bei** ~ **und Eva anfangen** (umg) start right from scratch od from square one.
adaptieren [àdàptē:'rən] vt adapt.
adäquat [àdekvàt'] a (Belohnung, Übersetzung) adequate; (Stellung, Verhalten) suitable.
addieren [àdē:'rən] vt add (up).
Addis Abeba [à'disà'bābà] nt -, -s Addis Ababa.
Addition [àdētsēō:n'] f addition.
Ade [àdā:'] nt -s, -s, a~ interj bye!
Adel [à'dəl] m -s nobility; ~ **verpflichtet** noblesse oblige.
adelig, adlig a noble.
Adelsstand m nobility; (hoher auch) aristocracy.
Ader [à'dər] f -, -n vein; (fig: Veranlagung) bent.
ADGB m abk (= Allgemeiner Deutscher Gewerkschaftsbund) German trades union federation.
Adhäsionsverschluß [àthezēō:ns'fershlōōs] m adhesive seal.
Adjektiv [àt'yektē:f] nt -s, -e adjective.
Adler [à'dlər] m -s, - eagle.
adlig a = **adelig.**
Admiral [àtmēràl'] m -s, -e admiral.
Admiralität f admiralty.
ADN m abk (= Allgemeiner Deutscher Nachrichtendienst) East German News Agency.
adoptieren [àdoptē:'rən] vt adopt.
Adoption [àdoptsēō:n'] f adoption.
Adoptiv- [àdoptē:f'] zW: ~**eltern** pl adoptive parents pl; ~**kind** nt adopted child.
Adr. abk (= Adresse) add.
Adressant [àdràsànt'] m sender.
Adressat [àdresàt'] m -en, -en addressee.
Adreßbuch nt directory; (privat) address book.
Adresse [àdre'sə] f -, -n (auch COMPUT) address; **an der falschen** ~ **sein** (umg) have gone/come to the wrong person; **absolute** ~ absolute address; **relative** ~ relative address.
adressieren [àdresē:'rən] vt address (an +akk to).
Adressiermaschine f addressing machine.
Adria [à'drēà] f - Adriatic Sea.
Adriatisches Meer [àdrēà'tishəs mā:r] nt

(form) Adriatic Sea.
Advent [àtvent'] m -(e)s, -e Advent.
Adventskranz m Advent wreath.
Adverb [àtverp'] nt adverb.
adverbial [àtvàrbēàl'] a adverbial.
AdW f abk = Akademie der Wissenschaften.
aero- [àārō] präf aero-.
Aerobic [äārō:'bēk] nt -s aerobics sing.
Affäre [àfe:'rə] f -, -n affair; **sich aus der** ~ **ziehen** (umg) get (o.s.) out of it.
Affe [à'fə] m -n, -n monkey; (umg: Kerl) clod.
Affekt m -(e)s, -e: **im** ~ **handeln** act in the heat of the moment.
affektiert [àfektē:rt'] a affected.
Affen- zW: **a~artig** a like a monkey; **mit a~artiger Geschwindigkeit** (umg) like a flash; **a~geil** a (umg) magic, fantastic; ~**hitze** f (umg) incredible heat; ~**liebe** f blind adoration (zu of); ~**schande** f (umg) crying shame; ~**tempo** nt (umg): **in** od **mit einem** ~**tempo** at breakneck speed; ~**theater** nt (umg): **ein** ~**theater aufführen** make a fuss.
affig [à'fiċh] a affected.
Afghane [àfgà'nə] m -n, -n, **Afghanin** f Afghan.
afghanisch a Afghan.
Afghanistan [àfgà'nistàn] nt -s Afghanistan.
Afrika [à'frēkà] nt -s Africa.
Afrikaans [àfrēkàns'] nt - Afrikaans.
Afrikaner(in f) [àfrēkà'nər(in)] m -s, - African.
afrikanisch a African.
afro-amerikanisch [à'frōàmārēkà'nish] a Afro-American.
After [àf'tər] m -s, - anus.
AG f - abk (= Aktiengesellschaft) ≈ corp.; abk = **Amtsgericht.**
Ägäis [ege:'is] f - Aegean (Sea).
ägäisch a: Ä~**es Meer** Aegean Sea.
Agent(in f) [àgent'(in)] m agent.
Agententätigkeit f espionage.
Agentur [àgentōō:r'] f agency; ~**bericht** m (news) agency report.
Aggregat [àgrāgàt'] nt -(e)s, -e aggregate; (TECH) unit; ~**zustand** m (PHYS) state.
Aggression [àgresēō:n'] f aggression.
aggressiv [àgresē:f'] a aggressive.
Aggressivität [àgresēvē:t'] f aggressiveness.
Agitation [àgētàtsēō:n'] f agitation.
Agrar- [àgràr'] zW: ~**politik** f agricultural policy; ~**staat** m agrarian state.
AGV f abk (= Arbeitsgemeinschaft der Verbraucherbände) consumer groups' association.
Ägypten [egüp'tən] nt -s Egypt.
Ägypter(in f) m -s, - Egyptian.
ägyptisch a Egyptian.
aha [àhà'] interj aha!
Aha-Erlebnis nt sudden insight.
ahd. abk (= althochdeutsch) OHG.
Ahn [àn] m -en, -en forebear.

ahnden [ân'dən] *vt* (*geh*: *Freveltat, Verbrechen*) avenge; (*Übertretung, Verstoß*) punish.

ähneln [e:'nəln] *vi* (+*dat*) be like, resemble ♦ *vr* be alike *od* similar.

ahnen [â'nən] *vt* suspect; (*Tod, Gefahr*) have a presentiment of; **nichts Böses** ~ be unsuspecting; **du ahnst es nicht!** you have no idea!; **davon habe ich nichts geahnt** I didn't have the slightest inkling of it.

Ahnenforschung *f* genealogy.

ähnlich [e:n'liĉh] *a* similar (*dat* to); **das sieht ihm (ganz)** ~! (*umg*) that's just like him!, that's him all over!; **Ä~keit** *f* similarity.

Ahnung [â'nōōng] *f* idea, suspicion; (*Vorgefühl*) presentiment.

ahnungslos *a* unsuspecting.

Ahorn [â'horn] *m* **-s, -e** maple.

Ähre [e:'rə] *f* **-, -n** ear.

Aids [ā:dz] *nt* - AIDS.

akad. *abk* = **akademisch**.

Akad. *abk* = **Akademie**.

Akademie [âkâdāmē:'] *f* academy.

Akademiker(in *f*) [âkâdā:'mēkər(in)] *m* **-s,** - university graduate.

akademisch *a* academic.

Akazie [âkâ'tsēə] *f* **-, -n** acacia.

Akk. *abk* = **Akkusativ**.

akklimatisieren [âklēmâtēzē:'rən] *vr* become acclimatized.

Akkord [âkort'] *m* **-(e)s, -e** (*MUS*) chord; **im** ~ **arbeiten** do piecework; ~**arbeit** *f* piecework.

Akkordeon [âkor'dâon] *nt* **-s, -s** accordion.

Akkordlohn *m* piece wages *pl*, piece rate.

Akkreditiv [âkrādētē:f'] *nt* **-s, -e** (*COMM*) letter of credit.

Akku [â'kōō] *m* **-s, -s** (*umg*: *Akkumulator*) accumulator.

akkurat [âkōōrât'] *a* precise; (*sorgfältig auch*) meticulous.

Akkusativ [â'kōōzâtē:f] *m* **-s, -e** accusative (case); ~**objekt** *nt* accusative *od* direct object.

Akne [â'knə] *f* **-, -n** acne.

Akribie [âkrēbē:'] *f* (*geh*) meticulousness.

Akrobat(in *f*) [âkrōbât'(in)] *m* **-en, -en** acrobat.

Akt [âkt] *m* **-(e)s, -e** act; (*KUNST*) nude.

Akte [âk'tə] *f* **-, -n** file; **etw zu den** ~**n legen** (*lit, fig*) file sth away.

Akten- *zW*: ~**deckel** *m* folder; ~**koffer** *m* attaché case; **a~kundig** *a* on the files; ~**notiz** *f* memo(randum); ~**ordner** *m* file; ~**schrank** *m* filing cabinet; ~**tasche** *f* briefcase; ~**zeichen** *nt* reference.

Aktie [âk'tsēə] *f* **-, -n** share; **wie stehen die** ~**n?** (*hum umg*) how are things?

Aktien- *zW*: ~**bank** *f* joint-stock bank; ~**emission** *f* **-, -en** share issue; ~**gesellschaft** *f* joint-stock company; ~**index** *m* **-(es), -e** *od* **-indizes** share index; ~**kapital** *nt* share capital; ~**kurs** *m* share price.

Aktion [âktsēō:n'] *f* campaign; (*Polizei*~, *Such*~) action.

Aktionär(in *f*) [âktsēōne:r'(in)] *m* **-s, -e** shareholder.

Aktionismus [âktsēōnis'mōōs] *m* (*POL*) actionism.

Aktionsradius [âktsēō:nz'râdēōōs] *m* **-, -ien** (*AVIAT, NAUT*) range; (*fig*: *Wirkungsbereich*) scope.

aktiv [âktē:f'] *a* active; (*MIL*) regular; **A~** *nt* **-s** (*GRAM*) active (voice).

Aktiva [âktē:'vá] *pl* assets *pl*.

aktivieren [âktēvē:'rən] *vt* activate; (*fig*: *Arbeit, Kampagne*) step up; (*Mitarbeiter*) get moving.

Aktivität [âktēvēte:t'] *f* activity.

Aktiv- *zW*: ~**posten** *m* (*lit, fig*) asset; ~**saldo** *m* (*COMM*) credit balance.

aktualisieren [âktōōálēzē:'rən] *vt* (*COMPUT*) update.

Aktualität [âktōōálēte:t'] *f* topicality; (*einer Mode*) up-to-dateness.

aktuell [âktōōel'] *a* topical; up-to-date; **eine** ~**e Sendung** (*RAD, TV*) a current affairs program.

Akupunktur [âkōōpōōngktōō:'ər] *f* acupuncture.

Akustik [âkōōs'tik] *f* acoustics *pl*.

akustisch [âkōōs'tēsh] *a*: **ich habe dich rein** ~ **nicht verstanden** I simply didn't catch what you said (properly).

akut [âkōō:t'] *a* acute; (*Frage auch*) pressing, urgent.

AKW *nt abk* = **Atomkraftwerk**.

Akzent [âktsent'] *m* **-(e)s, -e** accent; (*Betonung*) stress; ~**e setzen** (*fig*) bring out *od* emphasize the main points; ~**verschiebung** *f* (*fig*) shift of emphasis.

Akzept *nt* **-(e)s, -e** (*COMM*: *Wechsel*) acceptance.

akzeptieren [âktsäptē:'rən] *vt* accept.

AL *f abk* (= *Alternative Liste*) Alternative Party.

Alarm [álârm'] *m* **-(e)s, -e** alarm; ~ **schlagen** give *od* raise the alarm; ~**anlage** *f* alarm system; **a~bereit** *a* standing by; ~**bereitschaft** *f* stand-by.

alarmieren [álârmē:'rən] *vt* alarm.

Alaska [álás'kâ] *nt* **-s** Alaska.

Albaner(in *f*) [álbâ'nər(in)] *m* **-s, -** Albanian.

Albanien [álbâ'nēən] *nt* **-s** Albania.

albanisch *a* Albanian.

albern [ál'bərn] *a* silly.

Album [ál'bōōm] *nt* **-s, Alben** album.

Aleuten [álôō:'tən] *pl* Aleutian Islands *pl*.

Alg *abk* (*umg*) = **Arbeitslosengeld**.

Alge [ál'gə] *f* **-, -n** alga.

Algebra [ál'gâbrá] *f* - algebra.

Algerien [álgā:'rēən] *nt* **-s** Algeria.

Algerier(in *f*) *m* **-s, -** Algerian.

algerisch [álgā:'rish] *a* Algerian.

Algier [ál'zhē:ər] *nt* **-s** Algiers.

ALGOL [ál'gol] *nt* **-(s)** (*COMPUT*) ALGOL.

Algorithmus [álgörit'mōōs] *m* (*COMPUT*)

algorithm.

Alhi [ál'hi] *abk* (*umg*) = **Arbeitslosenhilfe**.

alias [á'lēás] *ad* alias.

Alibi [á'lēbē] *nt* **-s, -s** alibi.

Alimente [álēmen'tə] *pl* alimony *sing*.

Alkohol [ál'kōhol] *m* **-s, -e** alcohol; **unter ~ stehen** be under the influence (of alcohol *od* drink); **a~frei** *a* non-alcoholic; **~gehalt** *m* proof.

Alkoholiker(in *f*) [álkōhō:'lēkər(in)] *m* **-s, -** alcoholic.

alkoholisch *a* alcoholic.

Alkoholverbot *nt* ban on alcohol.

All [ál] *nt* **-s** universe; (*RAUMFAHRT*) space; (*außerhalb unseres Sternsystems*) outer space.

all- *zW:* **~a'bendlich** *a* every evening; **~bekannt** *a* universally known.

alle *a siehe* **alle(r, s)**.

alledem [á'lədā:m] *pron:* **bei/trotz** *etc* **~** with/in spite of *etc* all that; **zu ~** moreover.

Allee [álā:'] *f* **-, -n** avenue, parkway (*US*).

allein [álīn'] *a, ad* alone; (*ohne Hilfe*) on one's own, by oneself; **von ~** by oneself/itself ♦ *kj* (*geh*) but, only; **nicht ~** (*nicht nur*) not only; **~ schon der Gedanke** the very *od* mere thought ...; the thought alone ...; **~erziehend** *a* single-parent; **A~erziehende(r)** *mf dekl wie a* single parent; **A~gang** *m:* **im A~gang** on one's own; **A~herrscher(in** *f*) *m* autocrat; **A~hersteller(in** *f*) *m* sole manufacturer.

alleinig [álī'niç] *a* sole.

allein- *zW:* **~stehend** *a* single; **A~unterhalter(in** *f*) *m* solo entertainer; **A~vertretung** *f* (*COMM*) sole agency; **A~vertretungsvertrag** *m* (*COMM*) exclusive agency agreement.

allemal [á'ləmâl'] *ad* (*jedesmal*) always; (*ohne weiteres*) with no bother; **ein für ~** once and for all.

allenfalls [á'lənfáls'] *ad* at all events; (*höchstens*) at most.

alle(r, s) [á'lə(r,s)] *a* all; **wir ~** all of us; **~ beide** both of us/you *etc*; **~ vier Jahre** every four years ♦ *ad* (*umg: zu Ende*) finished; **etw ~ machen** finish sth up; (*substantivisch*): **~s Gute** all the best; **vor ~m** above all; **das ist ~s andere als** ... that's anything but ...; **es hat ~s keinen Sinn mehr** nothing makes sense any more; **was habt ihr ~s gemacht?** what did you get up to? ♦ *pron:* **ohne ~n Grund** without any reason, with no reason at all; **trotz ~m** in spite of everything.

allerbeste(r, s) [á'lərbes'tə(r, z)] *a* very best.

allerdings [á'lərdings'] *ad* (*zwar*) admittedly; (*gewiß*) certainly.

allerfrühestens [á'lərfrü:'əstəns] *ad* at the very earliest.

allergisch [áler'gish] *a* allergic; **auf etw** (*akk*) **~ reagieren** be allergic to sth.

Allergie [álārgē:'] *f* allergy.

aller- [á'lər] *zW:* **~hand'** *a inv* (*umg*) all sorts

of; **das ist doch ~hand!** that's a bit much!; **~hand!** (*lobend*) that's wonderful!; **A~hei'ligen** *nt* All Saints' Day; **~höch'ste(r, s)** *a* very highest; **es wird ~höchste Zeit, daß** ... it's really high time that ...; **~höch'stens** *ad* at the very most; **~lei'** *a inv* all sorts of; **~letz'te(r, s)** *a* very last; **der/das ist das ~letzte** (*umg*) he's/it's the absolute end!; **~neu'(e)ste(r, s)** *a* very latest; **~seits'** *ad* on all sides; **prost ~seits!** cheers everyone!

Allerwelts- *in zW* (*Durchschnitts-*) common; (*nichtssagend*) commonplace.

aller- *zW:* **~wenigste(r, s)** *a* very least; **die ~wenigsten Menschen wissen das** very few people know that; **A~werteste(r)** *m dekl wie a* (*hum*) posterior (*hum*).

alles *pron* everything; **~ in allem** all in all; *siehe* **alle(r, s)**.

allesamt *ad* all (of them/us *etc*).

Alleskleber *m* **-s, -** all-purpose adhesive.

Allgäu [ál'goi] *nt part of the alpine region of Bavaria.*

allgegenwärtig *a* omnipresent, ubiquitous.

allgemein [ál'gəmīn] *a* general; **im ~en Interesse** in the common interest; **auf ~en Wunsch** by popular request ♦ *ad:* **es ist ~ üblich** it's the general rule; **A~bildung** *f* general *od* all-round education; **~gültig** *a* generally accepted; **A~heit** *f* (*Menschen*) general public; (*pl: Redensarten*) general remarks *pl;* **~verständlich** *a* generally intelligible.

Allheilmittel [álhīl'mitəl] *nt* cure-all, panacea (*bes fig*).

Alliierte(r) [álēē:r'tə(r)] *mf dekl wie a* ally.

all- *zW:* **~jähr'lich** *a* annual; **~mäch'tig** *a* all-powerful, omnipotent; **~mäh'lich** *ad* gradually; **es wird ~mählich Zeit** (*umg*) it's about time; **A~radantrieb** *m* all-wheel drive; **~seitig** *a* (*allgemein*) general; (*ausnahmslos*) universal; **A~tag** *m* everyday life; **~täg'lich** *a, ad* daily; (*gewöhnlich*) commonplace; **~tags** *ad* on weekdays.

Allüren [álü:'rən] *pl* odd behavior *sing;* (*eines Stars etc*) airs and graces *pl.*

all- *zW:* **~wis'send** *a* omniscient; **~zu** *ad* all too; **~zugern** *ad* (*mögen*) only too much; (*bereitwillig*) only too willingly; **~zuoft** *ad* all too often; **~zuviel** *ad* too much.

Allzweck- [ál'tsvek-] *in zW* all-purpose.

Alm [álm] *f* **-, -en** alpine pasture.

Almosen [ál'mō:zən] *nt* **-s, -** alms *pl.*

Alpen [ál'pən] *pl* Alps *pl;* **~blume** *f* alpine flower; **~veilchen** *nt* cyclamen; **~vorland** *nt* foothills *pl* of the Alps.

Alphabet [álfábā:t'] *nt* **-(e)s, -e** alphabet.

alphabetisch *a* alphabetical.

alphanumerisch [álfánōōmā:'rish] *a* (*COMPUT*) alphanumeric.

Alptraum [álp'troum] *m* nightmare.

als [áls] *kj* (*zeitlich*) when; (*komp*) than; (*Gleichheit*) as; **alles andere ~** anything but; **~ Beweis** as proof; (*bei Vergleichen*):

soviel/soweit ~ **möglich** as much/far as possible; **gerade,** ~ just as; ~ **Kind/ Mädchen** *etc* as a child/girl *etc*; **nichts** ~ nothing but; ~ **ob** as if.

alsbaldig [álsbál'dìçb] *kj*: „**zum** ~**en Verbrauch bestimmt**" "for immediate use only".

also [ál'zō:] *kj* so; *(folglich)* therefore; ~ **wie ich schon sagte** well (then), as I said before; **ich komme** ~ **morgen** so I'll come tomorrow; ~ **gut** *od* **schön!** okay then; ~**, so was!** well really!; **na** ~**!** there you are then!

alt [ált] *a* old; **ich bin nicht mehr der** ~**e** I am not the man I was; **alles beim** ~**en lassen** leave everything as it was; **ich werde heute nicht** ~ **(werden)** *(umg)* I won't last long today/tonight *etc*; ~ **aussehen** *(fig umg)* be in a pickle.

Alt *m* **-s, -e** *(MUS)* alto.

Altar [áltár'] *m* **-(e)s, -äre** altar.

alt- *zW*: **A**~**bauwohnung** *f* old apartment; ~**bekannt** *a* well-known; ~**bewährt** *a* *(Methode etc)* well-tried; *(Tradition etc)* longstanding; **A**~**bier** *nt* *top-fermented German dark beer;* ~**ein'gesessen** *a* old-established; **A**~**ei'sen** *nt* scrap iron.

Altenteil [ál'təntīl] *nt*: **sich aufs** ~ **setzen** *od* **zurückziehen** *(fig)* retire from public life.

Alter [ál'tər] *nt* **-s, -** age; *(hohes)* old age; **er ist in deinem** ~ he's your age; **im** ~ **von** at the age of.

altern [ál'tərn] *vi* grow old, age.

alternativ [áltərnátē:f'] *a*: ~ **wohnen/leben** live an alternative way of life.

Alternativ- *in zW* alternative.

Alternative [áltərnátē:'və] *f* alternative.

Alternativ- *zW*: ~**szene** *f* alternative scene; ~**-Technologie** *f* alternative technology.

alters [ál'tərs] *ad* *(geh)*: **von** *od* **seit** ~ **(her)** from time immemorial.

Alters- *zW*: **a**~**bedingt** *a* related to a particular age; caused by old age; ~**grenze** *f* age limit; ~**heim** *nt* rest home *(US)*, old people's home *(Brit)*; ~**ruhegeld** *nt* retirement benefit; **a**~**schwach** *a* *(Mensch)* old and infirm; *(Auto, Möbel)* decrepit; ~**versorgung** *f* old-age pension.

Altertum [ál'tərtōō:m] *nt* antiquity.

altertümlich *a* *(aus dem Altertum)* ancient; *(veraltet)* antiquated.

alt- *zW*: ~**gedient** *a* long-serving; **A**~**glas** *nt* used glass *(for recycling)*, scrap glass; **A**~**glascontainer** *m* bottle bank; ~**her'gebracht** *a* traditional; **A**~**herrenmannschaft** *f* *(SPORT)* team of players over thirty; ~**klug** *a* precocious; **A**~**linke** *f* *(POL)* long-serving socialists *pl*; **A**~**material** *nt* scrap; ~**modisch** *a* old-fashioned; **A**~**papier** *nt* waste paper; **A**~**stadt** *f* old town.

Altstimme *f* alto.

alt- *zW*: **A**~**warenhändler** *m* second-hand dealer; **A**~**wei'bersommer** *m* Indian summer.

Alu [á'lōō] *abk* = **Arbeitslosenunterstützung**; **Aluminium**.

Alufolie [á'lōōfō:lēə] *f* aluminum foil.

Aluminium [álōōmē:'nēōōm] *nt* **-s** aluminum *(US)*, aluminium *(Brit)*; ~**folie** *f* aluminum *od* aluminium foil.

am [ám] = **an dem**; ~ **Sterben** on the point of dying; ~ **15. März** on March 15th; ~ **letzten Sonntag** last Sunday; ~ **Morgen/Abend** in the morning/evening; ~ **besten/ schönsten** best/most beautiful.

Amalgam [ámálgâm'] *nt* **-s, -e** amalgam.

Amateur [ámátœr'] *m* amateur.

Amazonas [ámátsō:'nás] *m* - Amazon (river).

Ambiente [ámbēen'tə] *nt* - ambience.

Ambition [ámbētsēō:n'] *f*: ~**en auf etw** *(akk)* **haben** have ambitions of getting sth.

Amboß [ám'bos] *m* **-sses, -sse** anvil.

ambulant [ámbōōlánt'] *a* outpatient.

Ameise [â'mīzə] *f* **-, -n** ant.

Ameisenhaufen *m* anthill.

Amerika [ámā:'rēkà] *nt* **-s** America.

Amerikaner(in *f)* [ámárēkâ'nər(in)] *m* **-s, -** American; *(Gebäck)* flat iced cookie or cake.

amerikanisch *a* American.

Ami [á'mē] *m* **-s, -s** *(umg)* Yank; *(Soldat)* GI.

Amme [á'mə] *f* **-, -n** *(veraltet)* foster mother; *(Nährmutter)* wet nurse.

Ammenmärchen [á'mənme:rçḫən] *nt* fairy tale *od* story.

Amok [á'mok] *m*: ~ **laufen** run amok *od* amuck.

Amortisation [ámortēzátsēō:n'] *f* amortization.

amortisieren [ámortēzē:'rən] *vr* pay for itself.

Ampel [ám'pəl] *f* **-, -n** traffic lights *pl*.

amphibisch [ámfē:'bish] *a* amphibious.

Ampulle [ámpōō'lə] *f* **-, -n** *(Behälter)* ampule *(US)*, ampoule *(Brit)*.

amputieren [ámpōōtē:'rən] *vt* amputate.

Amsel [ám'zəl] *f* **-, -n** blackbird.

Amt [ámt] *nt* **-(e)s, -er** office; *(Pflicht)* duty; *(TEL)* exchange; **zum zuständigen** ~ **gehen** go to the relevant authority; **von** ~**s wegen** *(auf behördliche Anordnung hin)* officially.

amtieren [ámtē:'rən] *vi* hold office; *(fungieren)*: **als ...** ~ act as ...

amtierend *a* incumbent.

amtlich *a* official; ~**es Kennzeichen** registration (number), license number.

Amtmann *m*, *pl* **-männer** *od* **-leute**, **Amtmännin** *f* *(VERWALTUNG)* senior civil servant.

Amts- *zW*: ~**arzt** *m* medical officer; **a**~**ärztlich** *a*: **a**~**ärztlich untersucht werden** have an official medical examination; ~**deutsch(e)** *nt* officialese; ~**eid** *m*: **den** ~**eid ablegen** be sworn in, take the oath of office; ~**geheimnis** *nt* *(geheime Sache)* official secret; *(Schweigepflicht)* official secrecy; ~**gericht** *nt* district court; ~**mißbrauch** *m* abuse of one's position;

~**periode** *f* term of office; ~**person** *f* official; ~**richter** *m* district judge; ~**schimmel** *m* (*hum*) officialdom; ~**stunden** *pl* office hours *pl*; ~**träger** *m* office bearer; ~**weg** *m*: **auf dem** ~**weg** through official channels; ~**zeit** *f* period of office.
amüsant [àmüzánt'] *a* amusing.
Amüsement [àmüzǝmáǹ'] *nt* amusement.
amüsieren [àmüzē:'rǝn] *vt* amuse ♦ *vr* enjoy o.s.; **sich über etw** (*akk*) ~ find sth funny; (*unfreundlich*) make fun of sth.
an [àn] *präp* +*dat* (*räumlich*) at; (*auf, bei*) on; (*nahe bei*) near; (*zeitlich*) on; +*akk* (*räumlich*) (on)to; ~ **Ostern** at Easter; ~ **diesem Ort/Tag** at this place/on this day; ~ **und für sich** actually; **jung** ~ **Jahren sein** be young in years; ~ **der ganzen Sache ist nichts** there is nothing in it; ~ **die 5 DM** (*ungefähr*) around 5 marks; ~ **die Arbeit gehen** get down to work; ~ **der Donau/ Autobahn/am Ufer** by *od* on the Danube/ freeway/bank; ~ **der gleichen Stelle** at *od* on the same spot; **jdn** ~ **der Hand nehmen** take sb by the hand; **sie wohnen Tür** ~ **Tür** they live next door to one another; **es** ~ **der Leber** *etc* **haben** (*umg*) have liver *etc* trouble; **ein Gruß/eine Frage** ~ **jdn** greetings/a question to sb ♦ *ad*: **von** ... ~ from ... on; **ohne etwas** ~ with nothing on; **das Licht ist** ~ the light is on.
analog [ànálō:k'] *a* analogous.
Analogie [ànálōgē:'] *f* analogy.
Analogrechner [ànálō:'krecǹnǝr] *m* -**s**, - analog computer.
Analphabet(in *f*) [ànálfàbā:t'(in)] *m* -**en**, -**en** illiterate (person).
Analyse [ànálü:'zǝ] *f* -, -**n** analysis.
analysieren [ànálüzē:'rǝn] *vt* analyze.
Anämie [ànemē:'] *f* -, -**n** anemia (*US*), anaemia (*Brit*).
Ananas [à'nánás] *f* -, - *od* -**se** pineapple.
Anarchie [ànárcěhē:'] *f* anarchy.
Anästhesist(in *f*) [ànestäzist'(in)] *m* -**en**, -**en** anesthesiologist (*US*), anaesthetist (*Brit*).
Anatomie [ànátōmē:'] *f* anatomy.
anbahnen [àn'bánǝn] *vr* open up; (*sich andeuten*) be in the offing; (*Unangenehmes*) be looming ♦ *vt* initiate.
Anbahnung *f* initiation (*von, gen* of).
anbändeln [àn'bendǝln] *vi* (*umg*) flirt.
Anbau [àn'bou] *m* (*AGR*) cultivation; (*Gebäude*) extension.
anbauen *vt* (*AGR*) cultivate; (*Gebäudeteil*) build on.
Anbau- *zW*: ~**gebiet** *nt*: **ein gutes** ~**gebiet für etw** a good area for growing sth; ~**möbel** *pl* unit furniture sing.
anbehalten [àn'bǝhàltǝn] *vt unreg* keep on.
anbei [ànbī'] *ad* enclosed (*form*); ~ **schicken wir Ihnen** ... please find enclosed ...
anbeißen [àn'bīsǝn] *unreg vt* bite into ♦ *vi* (*lit*) bite; (*fig*) swallow the bait; **zum A**~ (*umg*) good enough to eat.
anbelangen [àn'bǝlàngǝn] *vt* concern; **was**

mich anbelangt as far as I am concerned.
anberaumen [àn'bǝroumǝn] *vt* (*form*) fix, arrange.
anbeten [àn'bā:tǝn] *vt* worship.
Anbetracht [àn'bǝtràkǹht] *m*: **in** ~ in view (of +*gen*).
Anbetung *f* worship.
anbiedern [àn'bē:dǝrn] *vr* (*pej*) curry favor (*bei* with).
anbieten [àn'bē:tǝn] *unreg vt* offer ♦ *vr* volunteer; **das bietet sich als Lösung an** that would provide a solution.
anbinden [àn'bindǝn] *unreg vt* tie up ♦ *vi*: **mit jdm** ~ (*umg*) start something with sb.
Anblick [àn'blik] *m* sight.
anblicken *vt* look at.
anbraten [àn'brâtǝn] *vt unreg* (*Fleisch*) brown.
anbrechen [àn'brecǹhǝn] *unreg vt* start; (*Vorräte*) break into ♦ *vi* start; (*Tag*) break; (*Nacht*) fall.
anbrennen [àn'brenǝn] *vi unreg* catch fire; (*KOCH*) burn.
anbringen [àn'bringǝn] *vt unreg* bring; (*Ware*) sell; (*festmachen*) fasten; (*Telefon etc*) install.
Anbruch [àn'brōōkǹh] *m* beginning; ~ **des Tages/der Nacht** dawn/nightfall.
anbrüllen [àn'brülǝn] *vt* roar at.
Andacht [àn'dàkǹht] *f* -, -**en** devotion; (*Versenkung*) rapt interest; (*Gottesdienst*) prayers *pl*; (*Ehrfurcht*) reverence.
andächtig [àn'decǹhtiċh] *a* devout.
andauern [àn'douǝrn] *vi* last, go on.
andauernd *a* continual.
Anden [àn'dǝn] *pl*: **die** ~ the Andes.
Andenken [àn'dengkǝn] *nt* -**s**, - memory; souvenir; (*Erinnerungsstück*) memento, keepsake (*an* +*akk* from).
andere *siehe* **andere(r, s)**.
anderenteils, andererseits *ad* on the other hand.
andere(r, s) [àn'dǝrǝ(r, z)] *a* other; (*verschieden*) different; **am** ~**n Tage** the next day; **ein** ~**s Mal** another time; **kein** ~**r** nobody else; **alles** ~ **als zufrieden** anything but pleased, far from pleased; **von etwas** ~**m sprechen** talk about something else; **unter** ~**m** among other things; **von einem Tag zum** ~**n** overnight; **sie hat einen** ~**n** she has someone else.
andermal *ad*: **ein** ~ some other time.
ändern [en'dǝrn] *vt* alter, change ♦ *vr* change.
andernfalls *ad* otherwise.
andernorts [àn'dǝrnorts'] *ad* elsewhere.
anders *ad* differently (*als* from); **wer** ~? who else?; **niemand** ~ no-one else; **es blieb mir nichts** ~ **übrig, als selbst hinzugehen** I had no alternative but to go myself; **wie nicht** ~ **zu erwarten** as was to be expected; **wie könnte es** ~ **sein?** how could it be otherwise?; **ich kann nicht** ~ (*kann es nicht lassen*) I can't help it; (*muß leider*) I have

no choice; ~ **ausgedrückt** to put it another way; **jemand/irgendwo** ~ somebody/ somewhere else; ~ **aussehen/klingen** look/ sound different.

anders- *zW*: **~artig** *a* different; **A~denkende(r)** *mf dekl wie a* dissident, dissenter.

anderseits [àn'dərzīts'] *ad* on the other hand.

anders- *zW*: **~farbig** *a* of a different color; **~gläubig** *a* of a different faith; **~herum** *ad* the other way round; **~lautend** *a attr (form)*: **~lautende Berichte** reports to the contrary; **~wo** *ad* elsewhere; **~woher** *ad* from elsewhere; **~wohin** *ad* elsewhere.

anderthalb [àn'dərthálp'] *a* one and a half.

Änderung [en'dəröŏng] *f* alteration, change.

Änderungsantrag [en'dərŏŏngsántrâk] *m (PARL)* amendment.

anderweitig [àn'dərvī'tiĉ] *a* other ♦ *ad* otherwise; *(anderswo)* elsewhere.

andeuten [àn'doitən] *vt* indicate; *(Wink geben)* hint at.

Andeutung *f* indication; hint.

andeutungsweise *ad (als Anspielung, Anzeichen)* by way of a hint; *(als flüchtiger Hinweis)* in passing.

andichten [àn'diĉtən] *vt*: **jdm etw** ~ *(umg: Fähigkeiten)* credit sb with sth.

Andrang [àn'dráng] *m* crowd, rush.

andrehen [àn'drā:ən] *vt* turn *od* switch on; **jdm etw** ~ *(umg)* unload sth onto sb.

androhen [àn'drō:ən] *vt*: **jdm etw** ~ threaten sb with sth.

Androhung *f*: **unter** ~ **von Gewalt** with the threat of violence.

anecken [àn'ekən] *vi (umg)*: **(bei jdm/allen)** ~ rub (sb/everyone) up the wrong way.

aneignen [àn'īgnən] *vt*: **sich** *(dat)* **etw** ~ acquire sth; *(widerrechtlich)* appropriate sth; *(sich mit etw vertraut machen)* learn sth.

aneinander [ànínàn'dər] *ad* at/on/to *etc* one another *od* each other; **~fügen** *vt* put together; **~geraten** *vi unreg* clash; **~legen** *vt* put together.

anekeln [àn'ā:kəln] *vt* disgust.

Anemone [ànāmō:'nə] *f* -, **-n** anemone.

anerkannt [àn'erkánt] *a* recognized, acknowledged.

anerkennen [àn'erkenən] *vt unreg* recognize, acknowledge; *(würdigen)* appreciate; **das muß man** ~ *(zugeben)* admittedly, you can't argue with that; *(würdigen)* ... one has to appreciate that.

anerkennend *a* appreciative.

anerkennenswert *a* praiseworthy.

Anerkennung *f* recognition, acknowledgement; appreciation.

anerzogen [àn'ertsō:gən] *a* acquired.

anfachen [àn'fàĥən] *vt (lit)* fan into flame; *(fig)* kindle.

anfahren [àn'fârən] *unreg vt* deliver; *(fahren gegen)* hit; *(Hafen)* put into; *(umg)* bawl out ♦ *vi* drive up; *(losfahren)* drive off.

Anfahrt [àn'fârt] *f (Anfahrtsweg, Anfahrtszeit)* journey; *(Zufahrt)* approach.

Anfall [àn'fál] *m (MED)* attack; **in einem** ~ **von** *(fig)* in a fit of.

anfallen *unreg vt* attack; *(fig)* overcome ♦ *vi (Arbeit)* come up; *(Produkt, Nebenprodukte)* be obtained; *(Zinsen)* accrue; *(sich anhäufen)* accumulate; **die anfallenden Kosten/Reparaturen** the costs/repairs incurred.

anfällig [àn'feliĉ] *a* delicate; ~ **für etw** prone to sth.

Anfang [àn'fáng] *m* **-(e)s, -fänge** beginning, start; **von** ~ **an** right from the beginning; **zu** ~ at the beginning; ~ **Fünfzig** in one's early fifties; ~ **Mai/1978** at the beginning of May/1978.

anfangen [àn'fángən] *vti unreg* begin, start; *(machen)* do; **damit kann ich nichts** ~ *(nützt mir nichts)* that's no good to me; *(verstehe ich nicht)* it doesn't mean a thing to me; **mit dir ist heute (aber) gar nichts anzufangen!** you're no fun at all today!; **bei einer Firma** ~ start working for a firm.

Anfänger(in *f)* [àn'fengər(in)] *m* **-s, -** beginner.

anfänglich [àn'fengliĉ] *a* initial.

anfangs *ad* at first; **wie ich schon** ~ **erwähnte** as I mentioned at the beginning; **A~buchstabe** *m* initial *od* first letter; **A~gehalt** *nt* starting salary; **A~stadium** *nt* initial stages *pl*.

anfassen [àn'fásən] *vt* handle; *(berühren)* touch ♦ *vi* lend a hand ♦ *vr* feel.

anfechtbar [àn'feĉtbâr] *a* contestable.

anfechten [àn'feĉtən] *vt unreg* dispute; *(Meinung, Aussage auch)* challenge; *(Urteil)* appeal against; *(beunruhigen)* trouble.

anfeinden [àn'findən] *vt* treat with hostility.

anfertigen [àn'fertigən] *vt* make.

anfeuchten [àn'foiĉtən] *vt* moisten.

anfeuern [àn'foiərn] *vt (fig)* spur on.

anflehen [àn'flā:ən] *vt* implore.

anfliegen [àn'flē:gən] *unreg vt* fly to ♦ *vi* fly up.

Anflug [àn'flōŏ:k] *m (AVIAT)* approach; *(Spur)* trace.

anfordern [àn'fordərn] *vt* demand; *(COMM)* requisition.

Anforderung *f* demand *(gen* for); *(COMM)* requisition.

Anfrage [àn'frâgə] *f* inquiry; *(PARL)* question.

anfragen [àn'frâgən] *vi* inquire.

anfreunden [àn'froindən] *vr* make friends; **sich mit etw** ~ *(fig)* get to like sth.

anfügen [àn'fü:gən] *vt* add; *(beifügen)* enclose.

anfühlen [àn'fü:lən] *vtr* feel.

anführen [àn'fü:rən] *vt* lead; *(zitieren)* quote; *(umg: betrügen)* lead up the garden path.

Anführer(in *f)* *m* **-s, -** leader.

Anführung *f* leadership; *(Zitat)* quotation.

Anführungsstriche, Anführungszeichen *pl* quotation marks *pl*.

Angabe [àn'gâbə] *f* statement; (*TECH*) specification; (*umg: Prahlerei*) boasting; (*SPORT*) service; **ohne** ~ **von Gründen** without giving any reasons; **~n** *pl* (*Auskunft*) particulars *pl*; **~n zur Person** (*form*) personal details *od* particulars.

angeben [àn'gā:bən] *unreg vt* give; (*anzeigen*) inform on; (*bestimmen*) set ♦ *vi* (*umg*) boast; (*SPORT*) serve.

Angeber(in *f*) *m* **-s, -** (*umg*) show-off.

Angeberei [àngā:bərī'] *f* (*umg*) showing off.

angeblich [àn'gā:pliċḥ] *a* alleged.

angeboren [àn'gəbō:rən] *a* inborn, innate (*jdm* in sb); (*MED, fig*) congenital (*bei* to).

Angebot [àn'gəbō:t] *nt* offer; (*COMM*) supply (*an* +*dat* of); **im** ~ (*umg*) on special offer.

angeboten [àn'gəbō:tən] *pp von* **anbieten**.

Angebotspreis *m* offer price.

angebracht [àn'gəbràḳht] *a* appropriate.

angebrannt [àn'gəbrànt] *a*: **es riecht hier so** ~ there's a smell of burning here; **wie** ~ (*umg*) like mad.

angebrochen [àn'gəbroḳhən] *a* (*Packung, Flasche*) open(ed); **was sollen wir mit dem ~en Abend machen?** (*umg*) what shall we do with the rest of the evening?

angebunden [àn'gəbōōndən] *a*: **kurz** ~ **sein** (*umg*) be abrupt *od* curt.

angefangen *pp von* **anfangen**.

angegeben *pp von* **angeben**.

angegossen [àn'gəgosən] *a*: **wie** ~ **sitzen** fit like a glove.

angegriffen [àn'gəgrifən] *a* exhausted.

angehalten [àn'gəhàltən] *a*: ~ **sein, etw zu tun** be required *od* obliged to do sth ♦ *pp von* **anhalten**.

angehaucht [àn'gəhouḳht] *a*: **links/rechts** ~ **sein** have left-/right-wing tendencies *od* leanings.

angeheiratet [àn'gəhīrātət] *a* related by marriage.

angeheitert [àn'gəhītərt] *a* tipsy.

angehen [àn'gā:ən] *unreg vt* concern; (*angreifen*) attack; (*bitten*) approach (*um* for); **das geht ihn gar nichts an** that's none of his business ♦ *vi* (*Feuer*) light; (*umg: beginnen*) begin; **gegen jdn/etw** ~ (*entgegentreten*) fight sb/sth; **gegen etw** ~ (*Mißstände, Zustände*) take measures against sth.

angehend *a* prospective; **er ist ein ~er Vierziger** he is approaching forty.

angehören [àn'gəhœrən] *vi* belong (*dat* to).

Angehörige(r) *mf dekl wie a* relative.

Angeklagte(r) [àn'gəklâktə(r)] *mf dekl wie a* accused, defendant.

angeknackst [àn'gəknàkst] *a* (*umg: Mensch*) uptight; (: *Selbstbewußtsein*) weakened.

angekommen [àn'gəkomən] *pp von* **ankommen**.

Angel [àng'əl] *f* **-, -n** fishing rod; (*Tür~*) hinge; **die Welt aus den ~n heben** (*fig*) turn the world upside down.

Angelegenheit [àn'gəlā:gənhīt] *f* affair, matter.

angelernt [àn'gəlernt] *a* (*Arbeiter*) semi-skilled.

Angelhaken *m* fish hook.

angeln [àng'əln] *vt* catch ♦ *vi* fish; **A~** *nt* **-s** angling, fishing.

Angel- *zW*: **~punkt** *m* crucial *od* central point; (*Frage*) key *od* central issue; **~rute** *f* fishing rod.

Angelsachse [àng'əlzáksə] *m* **-n, -n, Angelsächsin** *f* Anglo-Saxon.

angelsächsisch [àng'əlzeksish] *a* Anglo-Saxon.

Angelschein *m* fishing license.

angemessen [àn'gəmesən] *a* appropriate, suitable; **eine der Leistung ~e Bezahlung** payment commensurate with the input.

angenehm [àn'gənā:m] *a* pleasant; **~!** (*bei Vorstellung*) pleased to meet you; **das A~e mit dem Nützlichen verbinden** combine business with pleasure.

angenommen [àn'gənomən] *a* assumed; (*Kind*) adopted; **~, wir ...** assuming we ... ♦ *pp von* **annehmen**.

angepaßt [àn'gəpàst] *a* conformist.

angerufen [àn'gərōō:fən] *pp von* **anrufen**.

angesäuselt [àn'gəzoizəlt] *a* tipsy, merry.

angeschlagen [àn'gəshlâgən] *a* (*umg: Mensch, Aussehen, Nerven*) shattered; (: *Gesundheit*) poor.

angeschlossen [àn'gəshlosən] *a* affiliated (*dat* to *od* with), associated (*dat* with).

angeschmiert [àn'gəshmē:rt] *a* (*umg*): **der/die A~e sein** have been had.

angeschrieben [àn'gəshrē:bən] *a* (*umg*): **bei jdm gut/schlecht** ~ **sein** be in sb's good/bad books.

angesehen [àn'gəzā:ən] *a* respected ♦ *pp von* **ansehen**.

Angesicht [àn'gəziċḥt] *nt* **-es, -er** (*geh*) face.

angesichts [àn'gəziċḥts] *präp* +*gen* in view of, considering.

angespannt [àn'gəshpànt] *a* (*Aufmerksamkeit*) close; (*Nerven, Lage*) tense, strained; (*COMM: Markt*) tight, over-stretched; (*Arbeit*) hard.

Angest. *abk* = **Angestellte(r)**.

angestammt [àn'gəshtàmt] *a* (*überkommen*) traditional; (*ererbt: Rechte*) hereditary; (: *Besitz*) inherited.

Angestellte(r) [àn'gəshteltə(r)] *mf dekl wie a* employee; (*Büro~*) white-collar worker.

angestrengt [àn'gəshtrengt] *ad* as hard as one can.

angetan [àn'gətân] *a*: **von jdm/etw** ~ **sein** be impressed by sb/sth; **es jdm** ~ **haben** appeal to sb.

angetrunken [àn'gətrōōngkən] *a* inebriated.

angewiesen [àn'gəvē:zən] *a*: **auf jdn/etw** ~ **sein** be dependent on sb/sth; **auf sich selbst** ~ **sein** be left to one's own devices.

angewöhnen [àn'gəvœnən] *vt*: **jdm/sich etw** ~ get sb/become accustomed to sth.

Angewohnheit [àn'gəvō:nhīt] *f* habit.

angewurzelt [àn'gəvōōrtsəlt] *a*: **wie** ~ **da-**

stehen be rooted to the spot.
angiften [án'giftən] *vt* (*pej umg*) snap at.
angleichen [án'glīċhən] *vtr unreg* adjust (*dat* to).
Angler [áng'lər] *m* **-s,** - angler.
angliedern [án'glē:dərn] *vt* (*Verein, Partei*) affiliate (*an* +*akk* to *od* with); (*Land*) annex.
Anglist(in *f*) [ángglist'(in)] *m* **-en, -en** English specialist, Anglicist; (*Student*) English student; (*Professor etc*) English lecturer/ professor.
Angola [ánggō:'lá] *nt* **-s** Angola.
angolanisch [ánggōlá'nish] *a* Angolan.
angreifen [án'grīfən] *vt unreg* attack; (*anfassen*) touch; (*Arbeit*) tackle; (*beschädigen*) damage.
Angreifer(in *f*) *m* **-s,** - attacker.
angrenzen [án'grentsən] *vi:* **an etw** (*akk*) ~ border on sth, adjoin sth.
Angriff [án'grif] *m* attack; **etw in ~ nehmen** make a start on sth.
Angriffsfläche *f:* **jdm/einer Sache eine ~ bieten** (*lit, fig*) provide sb/sth with a target.
angriffslustig *a* aggressive.
Angst [ángst] *f* **-, -̈e** fear; **~ haben** be afraid *od* scared (*vor* +*dat* of); **~ haben um jdn/ etw** be worried about sb/sth; **jdm ~ einflößen** *od* **einjagen** frighten sb; **nur keine ~!** don't be scared; **a~** *a:* **jdm ist a~** sb is afraid *od* scared; **jdm a~ machen** scare sb; **a~frei** *a* free of fear; **~hase** *m* (*umg*) chicken, scaredy-cat.
ängstigen [eng'stigən] *vt* frighten ♦ *vr* worry (o.s.) (*vor* +*dat*, *um* about).
ängstlich *a* nervous; (*besorgt*) worried; (*schüchtern*) timid; **A~keit** *f* nervousness.
Angstschweiß *m:* **mir brach der ~ aus** I broke out in a cold sweat.
angurten [án'gŏŏrtən] *vtr* = **anschnallen.**
Anh. *abk* (= *Anhang*) app.
anhaben [án'hábən] *vt unreg* have on; **er kann mir nichts ~** he can't hurt me.
anhaften [án'háftən] *vi* (*lit*) stick (*an* +*dat* to); (*fig*) (+*dat*) stick to, stay with.
anhalten [án'háltən] *unreg vt* stop; (*gegen jdn halten*) hold up (*jdm* against sb); **jdn zur Arbeit/Höflichkeit ~** make sb work/be polite ♦ *vi* stop; (*andauern*) persist; (*werben*): **um die Hand eines Mädchens ~** ask for a girl's hand in marriage.
anhaltend *a* persistent.
Anhalter(in *f*) *m* **-s,** - hitch-hiker; **per ~ fahren** hitch-hike.
Anhaltspunkt *m* clue.
anhand [ánhánt'] *präp* +*gen* with.
Anhang [án'háng] *m* appendix; (*Leute*) family; (*Anhängerschaft*) supporters *pl*.
anhängen [án'hengən] *vt unreg* hang up; (*Wagen*) couple up; (*Zusatz*) add (on); (*COMPUT*) append; **sich an jdn ~** attach o.s. to sb; **jdm etw ~** (*umg: nachsagen, anlasten*) blame sb for sth, blame sth on sb; (*: Verdacht, Schuld*) pin sth on sb.

Anhänger *m* **-s,** - supporter; (*AUT*) trailer; (*am Koffer*) tag; (*Schmuck*) pendant; **~schaft** *f* supporters *pl*.
Anhängeschloß *nt* padlock.
anhängig *a* (*JUR*) sub judice; **~ machen** (*Prozeß*) bring.
anhänglich *a* devoted; **A~keit** *f* devotion.
Anhängsel *nt* **-s,** - appendage.
anhauen [án'houən] *vt* (*umg: ansprechen*) accost (*um* for).
anhäufen [án'hoifən] *vt* accumulate, amass ♦ *vr* accrue.
Anhäufung [án'hoifōōng] *f* accumulation.
anheben [án'hā:bən] *vt unreg* lift up; (*Preise*) raise.
anheimelnd [án'hīməlnt] *a* comfortable, cozy (*US*), cosy (*Brit*).
anheimstellen [ánhīm'shtelən] *vt:* **jdm etw ~** leave sth up to sb.
anheizen [án'hītsən] *vt* (*Ofen*) light; (*fig umg: Wirtschaft*) stimulate; (*verschlimmern: Krise*) aggravate.
anheuern [án'hoiərn] *vti* (*NAUT, fig*) sign on *od* up.
Anhieb [án'hē:b] *m:* **auf ~** at the very first go; (*kurz entschlossen*) on the spur of the moment.
anhimmeln [án'himəln] *vt* (*umg*) idolize, worship.
Anhöhe [án'hœə] *f* hill.
anhören [án'hœrən] *vt* listen to; (*anmerken*) hear ♦ *vr* sound.
Anhörung *f* hearing.
Animierdame [ánēmē:r'dámə] *f* nightclub *od* bar hostess.
animieren [ánēmē:'rən] *vt* encourage, urge on.
Anis [ánē:s'] *m* **-es, -e** aniseed.
Ank. *abk* (= *Ankunft*) arr.
ankämpfen [án'kempfən] *vi:* **gegen etw ~** fight (against) sth; (*gegen Wind, Strömung*) battle against sth.
Ankauf [án'kouf] *m:* **~ und Verkauf von ...** we buy and sell ...; **a~en** *vt* purchase, buy.
Anker [áng'kər] *m* **-s,** - anchor; **vor ~ gehen** drop anchor.
ankern *vti* anchor.
Ankerplatz *m* anchorage.
Anklage [án'klágə] *f* accusation; (*JUR*) charge; **gegen jdn ~ erheben** (*JUR*) bring *od* prefer charges against sb; **~bank** *f* dock.
anklagen [án'klágən] *vt* accuse; (*JUR*) charge (*gen* with).
Anklagepunkt *m* charge.
Ankläger(in *f*) [án'kle:gər(in)] *m* **-s,** - accuser.
Anklageschrift *f* indictment.
anklammern [án'klámərn] *vt* clip, staple ♦ *vr:* **sich an etw** (*akk od dat*) ~ cling to sth.
Anklang [án'kláng] *m:* **bei jdm ~ finden** meet with sb's approval.
ankleben [án'klē:bən] *vt:* **Plakate ~ verboten!** post no bills.
Ankleidekabine *f* changing cubicle.

ankleiden [án'klīdən] *vtr* dress.
anklingen [án'klingən] *vi* (*erinnern*) be reminiscent (*an* +*akk* of); (*angeschnitten werden*) be touched (up)on.
anklopfen [án'klopfən] *vi* knock.
anknipsen [án'knipsən] *vt* switch on; (*Schalter*) flick.
anknüpfen [án'knüpfən] *vt* fasten *od* tie on; (*fig*) start ♦ *vi* (*anschließen*) refer (*an* +*akk* to).
Anknüpfungspunkt *m* link.
ankommen [án'komən] *vi unreg* arrive; (*näherkommen*) approach; (*Anklang finden*) go down (*bei* with); **es kommt darauf an** it depends; (*wichtig sein*) that is what matters; **es kommt auf ihn an** it depends on him; **es darauf ~ lassen** let things take their course; **gegen jdn/etw ~** cope with sb/sth; **damit kommst du bei ihm nicht an!** you won't get anywhere with him like that ♦ *vi unpers*: **er ließ es auf einen Streit/einen Versuch ~** he was prepared to argue about it/to give it a try.
ankreiden [án'krīdən] *vt* (*fig*): **jdm etw (dick** *od* **übel)** ~ hold sth against sb.
ankreuzen [án'kroitsən] *vt* mark with a cross.
ankündigen [án'kündigən] *vt* announce.
Ankündigung *f* announcement.
Ankunft [án'koonft] *f* -, **-künfte** arrival.
Ankunftszeit *f* time of arrival.
ankurbeln [án'koorbəln] *vt* (*AUT*) crank; (*fig*) boost.
Anl. *abk* (= *Anlage*) enc(l).
anlachen [án'làkhən] *vt* smile at; **sich** (*dat*) **jdn ~** (*umg*) pick sb up.
Anlage [án'làgə] *f* disposition; (*Begabung*) talent; (*Park*) gardens *pl*; (*Beilage*) enclosure; (*TECH*) plant; (*Einrichtung*: *MIL*, *ELEK*) installation(s); (*Sport~ etc*) facilities *pl*; (*umg*: *Stereo~*) (stereo) system *od* equipment; (*FIN*) investment; (*Entwurf*) layout; **als ~** *od* **in der ~ erhalten Sie ...** please find enclosed ...; **~berater(in** *f*) *m* investment consultant; **~kapital** *nt* fixed capital.
Anlagenabschreibung *f* capital allowance.
Anlagevermögen *nt* capital assets *pl*, fixed assets *pl*.
anlangen [án'làngən] *vi* arrive.
Anlaß [án'làs] *m* -**sses**, -**lässe** cause (*zu* for); (*Ereignis*) occasion; **aus ~** (+*gen*) on the occasion of; **~ zu etw geben** give rise to sth; **beim geringsten/bei jedem ~** for the slightest reason/at every opportunity; **etw zum ~ nehmen** take the opportunity of sth.
anlassen *unreg vt* leave on; (*Motor*) start ♦ *vr* (*umg*) start off.
Anlasser *m* -**s**, - (*AUT*) starter.
anläßlich [án'leslikh] *präp* +*gen* on the occasion of.
anlasten [án'làstən] *vt*: **jdm etw ~** blame sb for sth.
Anlauf [án'louf] *m* run-up; (*fig*: *Versuch*) attempt, try.

anlaufen *unreg vi* begin; (*Film*) be showing; (*SPORT*) run up; (*Fenster*) mist up; (*Metall*) tarnish ♦ *vt* call at; **rot ~** turn *od* go red; **gegen etw ~** run into *od* up against sth; **angelaufen kommen** come running up.
Anlaufzeit *f* (*fig*) time to get going *od* started.
anläuten [án'loitən] *vi* ring.
anlegen [án'lā:gən] *vt* put (*an* +*akk* against/on); (*anziehen*) put on; (*gestalten*) lay out; (*Kartei*, *Akte*) start; (*COMPUT*: *Datei*) create; (*Geld*) invest; (*Gewehr*) aim (*auf* +*akk* at); ♦ *vi* dock; (*NAUT*) berth; **es auf etw** (*akk*) **~** be out for sth/to do sth; **strengere Maßstäbe ~** lay down *od* impose stricter standards (*bei* in); **sich mit jdm ~** (*umg*) quarrel with sb.
Anlegeplatz *m* = **Anlegestelle.**
Anleger(in *f*) *m* -**s**, - (*FIN*) investor.
Anlegestelle *f* landing place.
anlehnen [án'lā:nən] *vt* lean (*an* +*akk* against); (*Tür*) leave ajar ♦ *vr* lean (*an* +*akk* on).
Anlehnung *f* (*Imitation*): **in ~ an jdn/etw** following sb/sth.
Anlehnungsbedürfnis *nt* need of loving care.
anleiern [án'līərn] *vt* (*umg*) get going.
Anleihe [án'līə] *f* -, -**n** (*FIN*) loan; (*Wertpapier*) bond.
anleiten [án'lītən] *vt* instruct.
Anleitung *f* instructions *pl*.
anlernen [án'lernən] *vt* teach, instruct.
anlesen [án'lā:zən] *vt unreg* (*aneignen*): **sich** (*dat*) **etw ~** learn sth by reading.
anliegen [án'lē:gən] *vi unreg* (*Kleidung*) cling.
Anliegen *nt* -**s**, - matter; (*Wunsch*) wish.
anliegend *a* adjacent; (*beigefügt*) enclosed.
Anlieger *m* -**s**, - resident; **~ frei** no thoroughfare – residents only.
anlocken [án'lokən] *vt* attract; (*Tiere auch*) lure.
anlügen [án'lü:gən] *vt unreg* lie to.
Anm. *abk* (= *Anmerkung*) n.
anmachen [án'màkhən] *vt* attach; (*Elektrisches*) put on; (*Salat*) dress; **jdn ~** (*umg*) try and pick sb up.
anmalen [án'màlən] *vt* paint ♦ *vr* (*pej*: *schminken*) paint one's face *od* o.s.
Anmarsch [án'màrsh] *m*: **im ~ sein** be advancing (*auf* +*akk* on); (*hum*) be on the way.
anmaßen [án'màsən] *vt*: **sich** (*dat*) **etw ~** lay claim to sth.
anmaßend *a* arrogant.
Anmaßung *f* presumption.
Anmeldeformular [án'meldəformóolàr] *nt* registration form.
anmelden *vt*. announce; (*geltend machen*: *Recht*, *Ansprüche zu Steuerzwecken*) declare; (*COMPUT*) log on ♦ *vr* (*sich ankündigen*) make an appointment; (*polizeilich, für Kurs etc*) register; **ein Gespräch nach**

Deutschland ~ (*TEL*) place a call to Germany.
Anmeldung *f* announcement; appointment; registration; **nur nach vorheriger** ~ by appointment only.
anmerken [ån'merkən] *vt* observe; (*anstreichen*) mark; **jdm etw** ~ notice sb's sth; **sich** (*dat*) **nichts** ~ **lassen** not give anything away.
Anmerkung *f* note.
Anmut [ån'mo͞o:t] *f* - grace.
anmuten *vt* (*geh*) appear, seem (*jdn* to sb).
anmutig *a* charming.
annähen [ån'ne:ən] *vt* sew on.
annähern [ån'ne:ərn] *vr* get closer.
annähernd *a* approximate; **nicht** ~ **soviel** not nearly as much.
Annäherung *f* approach.
Annäherungsversuch *m* advances *pl*.
Annahme [ån'nâmə] *f* -, **-n** acceptance; (*Vermutung*) assumption; **~stelle** *f* counter; (*für Reparaturen*) reception; **~verweigerung** *f* refusal.
annehmbar [ån'nā:mbâr] *a* acceptable.
annehmen *unreg vt* accept; (*Namen*) take; (*Kind*) adopt; (*vermuten*) suppose, assume; **jdn an Kindes Statt** ~ adopt sb; **angenommen, das ist so** assuming that is so ♦ *vr* take care (*gen* of).
Annehmlichkeit *f* comfort.
annektieren [ånektē:'rən] *vt* annex.
anno [å'nō] *a*: **von** ~ **dazumal** (*umg*) from the year dot.
Annonce [ånōn'sə] *f* -, **-n** advertisement.
annoncieren [ånōnsē:'rən] *vti* advertise.
annullieren [åno͞olē:'rən] *vt* annul.
Anode [ånō:'də] *f* -, **-n** anode.
anöden [ån'œdən] *vt* (*umg*) bore stiff.
anomal [ånōmâl'] *a* (*regelwidrig*) unusual, abnormal; (*nicht normal*) strange, odd.
anonym [ånōnü:m'] *a* anonymous.
Anorak [å'nōråk] *m* **-s, -s** parka.
anordnen [ån'ordnən] *vt* arrange; (*befehlen*) order.
Anordnung *f* arrangement; order; **~en treffen** give orders.
anorganisch [ån'orgânish] *a* (*CHEM*) inorganic.
anpacken [ån'påkən] *vt* grasp; (*fig*) tackle; **mit** ~ lend a hand.
anpassen [ån'påsən] *vt* fit (*jdm* on sb); (*fig*) adapt (*dat* to) ♦ *vr* adapt.
Anpassung *f* fitting; adaptation.
Anpassungsdruck *m* pressure to conform (*to society*).
anpassungsfähig *a* adaptable.
anpeilen [ån'pīlən] *vt* (*mit Radar, Funk etc*) take a bearing on; **etw** ~ (*fig umg*) have one's sights on sth.
Anpfiff [ån'pfif] *m* (*SPORT*) (starting) whistle; (*Spielbeginn*: *Fußball etc*) kick-off; **einen** ~ **bekommen** (*umg*) be bawled out.
anpöbeln [ån'pœbəln] *vt* abuse; (*umg*) pester.
Anprall [ån'prål] *m* impact (*gegen, an +akk* with).
anprangern [ån'prångərn] *vt* denounce.
anpreisen [ån'prīzən] *vt unreg* extol; **sich** ~ sell o.s. (*als etw* as sth).
Anprobe [ån'prō:bə] *f* trying on.
anprobieren [ån'prōbē:rən] *vt* try on.
anpumpen [ån'po͞ompən] *vt* (*umg*) borrow from.
anquatschen [ån'kvåtshən] *vt* (*umg*) speak to; (: *Mädchen*) try to pick up.
Anrainer [ån'rīnər] *m* **-s, -** neighbor (*US*), neighbour (*Brit*).
anranzen [ån'råntsən] *vt* (*umg*): **jdn** ~ tick sb off.
anraten [ån'râtən] *vt unreg* recommend; **auf A~ des Arztes** *etc* on the doctor's *etc* advice *od* recommendation.
anrechnen [ån'rec͟hnən] *vt* charge; (*fig*) count; **jdm etw hoch** ~ value sb's sth greatly.
Anrecht [ån'rec͟ht] *nt* right (*auf +akk* to); **ein** ~ **auf etw haben** be entitled to sth, have a right to sth.
Anrede [ån'rā:də] *f* form of address.
anreden *vt* address; (*belästigen*) accost.
anregen [ån'rā:gən] *vt* stimulate; **angeregte Unterhaltung** lively discussion.
anregend *a* stimulating.
Anregung *f* stimulation; (*Vorschlag*) suggestion.
Anregungsmittel *f* stimulant.
anreichern [ån'rīc͟hərn] *vt* enrich.
Anreise [ån'rīzə] *f* journey there/here.
anreisen *vi* arrive.
anreißen [ån'rīsən] *vt unreg* (*kurz zur Sprache bringen*) touch on.
Anreiz [ån'rīts] *m* incentive.
anrempeln [ån'rempəln] *vt* (*anstoßen*) bump into; (*absichtlich*) jostle.
anrennen [ån'renən] *vi unreg*: **gegen etw** ~ (*gegen Wind etc*) run against sth; (*MIL*) storm sth.
Anrichte [ån'ric͟htə] *f* -, **-n** sideboard.
anrichten *vt* serve up; **Unheil** ~ make mischief; **da hast du aber etwas angerichtet!** (*umg*: *verursacht*) you've started something there all right; (: *angestellt*) you've really made a mess there.
anrüchig [ån'rüc͟hic͟h] *a* dubious.
anrücken [ån'rükən] *vi* approach; (*MIL*) advance.
Anruf [ån'ro͞o:f] *m* call; **~beantworter** *m* (telephone) answering machine, answerphone.
anrufen *vt unreg* call out to; (*bitten*) call on; (*TEL*) phone, call.
anrühren [ån'rü:rən] *vt* touch; (*mischen*) mix.
ans [åns] = **an das**.
Ansage [ån'zâgə] *f* announcement.
ansagen *vt* announce ♦ *vr* say one will come.
Ansager(in *f*) *m* **-s, -** announcer.
ansammeln [ån'zåməln] *vt* collect ♦ *vr* accu-

mulate; (fig: Wut, Druck) build up.
Ansammlung f collection; (Leute) crowd.
ansässig [án'zesiçh] a resident.
Ansatz [án'záts] m start; (Haar~) hairline; (Hals~) base; (Verlängerungsstück) extension; (Veranschlagung) estimate; **die ersten Ansätze zu etw** the beginnings of sth; ~**punkt** m starting point; ~**stück** nt (TECH) attachment.
anschaffen [án'sháfən] vt buy, purchase; **sich** (dat) **Kinder** ~ (umg) have children ♦ vi: ~ **gehen** (umg: durch Prostitution) walk the streets.
Anschaffung f purchase.
anschalten [án'sháltən] vt switch on.
anschauen [án'shouən] vt look at.
anschaulich a illustrative.
Anschauung f (Meinung) view; **aus eigener** ~ from one's own experience.
Anschauungsmaterial nt illustrative material.
Anschein [án'shīn] m appearance; **allem** ~ **nach** to all appearances; **den** ~ **haben** seem, appear.
anscheinend a apparent.
anschieben [án'shē:bən] vt unreg (Fahrzeug) push.
Anschiß [án'shis] m (umg): **einen** ~ **bekommen** get a telling-off/ticking-off.
Anschlag [án'shlák] m notice; (Attentat) attack; (COMM) estimate; (auf Klavier) touch; (Schreibmaschine) character; **einem** ~ **zum Opfer fallen** be assassinated; **ein Gewehr im** ~ **haben** (MIL) have a rifle at the ready; ~**brett** nt bulletin board.
anschlagen [án'shlágən] unreg vt put up; (beschädigen) chip; (Akkord) strike; (Kosten) estimate; **einen anderen Ton** ~ (fig) change one's tune ♦ vi hit (an +akk against); (wirken) have an effect; (Glocke) ring; (Hund) bark.
anschlagfrei a: ~**er Drucker** non-impact printer.
Anschlagzettel m notice.
anschleppen [án'shlepən] vt (umg: unerwünscht mitbringen) bring along.
anschließen [án'shlē:sən] unreg vt connect up; (Sender) link up; (in Steckdose) plug in; (fig: hinzufügen) add ♦ vir: **(sich) an etw** (akk) ~ adjoin sth; (zeitlich) follow sth ♦ vr join (jdm/etw sb/sth); (beipflichten) agree (jdm/etw with sb/sth).
anschließend a adjacent; (zeitlich) subsequent ♦ ad afterwards; ~ **an** (+akk) following.
Anschluß [án'shlōōs] m (ELEK, EISENB, TEL) connection; (weiterer Apparat) extension; (von Wasser etc) supply; (COMPUT) port; **im** ~ **an** (+akk) following; ~ **finden** make friends; ~ **bekommen** get through; **kein** ~ **unter dieser Nummer** number unobtainable; **den** ~ **verpassen** (EISENB etc) miss one's connection; (fig) miss the boat.
anschmiegen [án'shmē:gən] vr: **sich an**

jdn/etw ~ (Kind, Hund) snuggle od nestle up to od against sb/sth.
anschmiegsam [án'shmē:kzâm] a affectionate.
anschmieren [án'shmē:rən] vt smear; (umg) take in.
anschnallen [án'shnálən] vt buckle on ♦ vr fasten one's seat belt.
Anschnallpflicht f: **in Taxis ist jetzt** ~ you now have to wear a seat belt in cabs.
anschnauzen [án'shnoutsən] vt (umg) yell at.
anschneiden [án'shnīdən] vt unreg cut into; (Thema) introduce.
Anschnitt [án'shnit] m first slice.
anschreiben [án'shrībən] vt unreg write (up); (COMM) charge to one's account; (benachrichtigen) write to; **bei jdm gut/ schlecht angeschrieben sein** be well/badly thought of by sb, be in sb's good/bad books.
anschreien [án'shrīən] vt unreg shout at.
Anschrift [án'shrift] f address.
Anschriftenliste f mailing list.
Anschuldigung [án'shōōldigōōng] f accusation.
anschwärzen [án'shvertsən] vt (fig umg): **jdn** ~ blacken sb's name (bei with).
anschwellen [án'shvelən] vi unreg swell (up).
anschwemmen [án'shvemən] vt wash ashore.
anschwindeln [án'shvindəln] vt (umg) lie to.
ansehen [án'zā:ən] vt unreg look at; **jdm etw** ~ see sth (from sb's face); **jdn/etw als etw** ~ look on sb/sth as · sth; ~ **für** consider; **(sich dat) etw** ~ (have a) look at sth; (Fernsehsendung) watch sth; (Film, Stück, Sportveranstaltung) see sth; **etw (mit)** ~ watch sth, see sth happening.
Ansehen nt -s respect; (Ruf) reputation; **ohne** ~ **der Person** (JUR) without respect of person.
ansehnlich [án'zā:nliçh] a fine-looking; (beträchtlich) considerable.
anseilen [án'zīlən] vt: **jdn/sich** ~ rope sb/o.s. up.
ansein [án'zīn] vi unreg (umg) be on.
ansetzen [án'zetsən] vt (anfügen) fix on (an +akk to); (anlegen, an Mund etc) put (an +akk to); (festlegen) fix; (entwickeln) develop; (Fett) put on; (Blätter) grow; (zubereiten) prepare ♦ vi (anfangen) start, begin; (Entwicklung) set in; (dick werden) put on weight ♦ vr (Rost etc) start to develop; **zu etw** ~ prepare to do sth; **jdn/etw auf jdn/etw** ~ set sb/sth on sb/sth.
Ansicht [án'ziçht] f (Anblick) sight; (Meinung) view, opinion; **zur** ~ on approval; **meiner** ~ **nach** in my opinion.
Ansichts- zW: ~**karte** f picture postcard; ~**sache** f matter of opinion.
ansiedeln [án'zē:dəln] vt settle; (Tierart) introduce ♦ vr settle; (Industrie etc) get established.

ansonsten [ánzons'tən] *ad* otherwise.
anspannen [án'shpánən] *vt* harness; (*Muskel*) strain.
Anspannung *f* strain.
Anspiel [án'shpē:l] *nt* (*SPORT*) start.
anspielen *vi* (*SPORT*) start play; **auf etw** (*akk*) ~ refer *od* allude to sth.
Anspielung *f* reference, allusion (*auf +akk* to).
Ansporn [án'shporn] *m* **-(e)s** incentive.
Ansprache [án'shprákhə] *f* (*Rede*) address.
ansprechen [án'shprechən] *unreg vt* speak to; (*bitten, gefallen*) appeal to; (*Eindruck machen auf*) make an impression on; (*Meßgerät auch*) react ♦ *vi* react (*auf +akk* to); **jdn auf etw** (*akk*) **(hin)** ~ ask sb about sth; **etw als etw** ~ regard sth as sth.
ansprechend *a* attractive.
anspringen [án'shpringən] *unreg vi* (*AUT*) start ♦ *vt* (*anfallen*) jump; (*Raubtier*) pounce (up)on; (*Hund*: *hochspringen*) jump up at.
Anspruch [án'shprookh] *m* **-s, -sprüche** (*Recht*) claim (*auf +akk* to); **den Ansprüchen gerecht werden** meet the requirements; **hohe Ansprüche stellen/haben** demand/expect a lot; **jdn/etw in** ~ **nehmen** occupy sb/take up sth.
anspruchs- *zW*: ~**los** *a* undemanding; ~**voll** *a* demanding; (*COMM*) upmarket.
anspucken [án'shpookən] *vt* spit at.
anstacheln [án'shtákhəln] *vt* spur on.
Anstalt [án'shtált] *f* **-, -en** institution; ~**en machen, etw zu tun** prepare to do sth.
Anstand [án'shtánt] *m* decency; (*Manieren*) (good) manners *pl*.
anständig [án'shtendich] *a* decent; (*umg*) proper; (*groß*) considerable; **A~keit** *f* propriety, decency.
anstandshalber [án'shtántshálbər] *ad* out of politeness.
anstandslos *ad* without any ado.
anstarren [án'shtárən] *vt* stare at.
anstatt [ánshtát'] *präp +gen* instead of ♦ *kj*: ~ **etw zu tun** instead of doing sth.
anstauen [án'shtouən] *vr* accumulate; (*Blut in Adern etc*) congest; (*fig auch: Gefühle*) build up.
anstechen [án'shtechən] *vt unreg* prick; (*Faß*) tap.
anstecken [án'shtekən] *vt* pin on; (*Ring*) put *od* slip on; (*MED*) infect; (*Pfeife*) light; (*Haus*) set fire to ♦ *vr*: **ich habe mich bei ihm angesteckt** I caught it from him ♦ *vi* (*fig*) be infectious.
ansteckend *a* infectious.
Ansteckung *f* infection.
anstehen [án'shtā:ən] *vi unreg* line up (*US*), queue (up) (*Brit*); (*Verhandlungspunkt*) be on the agenda.
anstelle [ánshte'lə] *präp +gen* in place of.
anstellen [án'shtelən] *vt* (*einschalten*) turn on; (*Arbeit geben*) employ; (*umg*: *Unfug treiben*) get up to; (: *machen*) do ♦ *vr* line

up (*US*), queue (up) (*Brit*); (*umg*) act; (: *sich zieren*) make a fuss, act up.
Anstellung *f* employment; (*Posten*) post, position; ~ **auf Lebenszeit** tenure.
ansteuern [án'shtoiərn] *vt* make *od* steer *od* head for.
Anstich [án'shtich] *m* (*von Faß*) tapping, broaching.
Anstieg [án'shtē:k] *m* **-(e)s, -e** climb; (*fig: von Preisen etc*) increase (*gen* in).
anstiften [án'shtiftən] *vt* (*Unglück*) cause; **jdn zu etw** ~ put sb up to sth.
Anstifter *m* **-s, -** instigator.
Anstiftung *f* (*von Mensch*) incitement (*zu* to); (*von Tat*) instigation.
anstimmen [án'shtimən] *vt* (*Lied*) strike up (with); (*Geschrei*) set up ♦ *vi* strike up.
Anstoß [án'shtō:s] *m* impetus; (*Ärgernis*) offense (*US*), offence (*Brit*); (*SPORT*) kick-off; **der erste** ~ the initiative; **ein Stein des** ~**es** (*umstrittene Sache*) a bone of contention; ~ **nehmen an** (*+dat*) take offense at.
anstoßen *unreg vt* push; (*mit Fuß*) kick ♦ *vi* knock, bump; (*mit der Zunge*) lisp; (*mit Gläsern*) drink (a toast) (*auf +akk* to); **an etw** (*akk*) ~ (*angrenzen*) adjoin sth.
anstößig [án'shtœsich] *a* offensive, indecent; **A~keit** *f* indecency, offensiveness.
anstrahlen [án'shtrálən] *vt* floodlight; (*strahlend ansehen*) beam at.
anstreben [án'shtrā:bən] *vt* strive for.
anstreichen [án'shtrichən] *vt unreg* paint; **(jdm) etw als Fehler** ~ mark sth wrong.
Anstreicher(in *f*) *m* **-s, -** painter.
anstrengen [án'shtrengən] *vt* strain; (*strapazieren*: *jd*) tire out; (: *Patienten*) fatigue; (*JUR*) bring ♦ *vr* make an effort; **eine Klage** ~ (*JUR*) initiate *od* institute proceedings (*gegen* against).
anstrengend *a* tiring.
Anstrengung *f* effort.
Anstrich [án'shtrich] *m* coat of paint.
Ansturm [án'shtoorm] *m* rush; (*MIL*) attack.
ansuchen [án'shtsoo:khən] *vi*: **um etw** ~ apply for sth; **A~** *nt* **-s, -** request.
Antagonismus [ántágōnis'mōōs] *m* antagonism.
antanzen [án'tántsən] *vi* (*umg*) turn *od* show up.
Antarktis [ántárk'tis] *f* **-** Antarctic.
antarktisch *a* antarctic.
antasten [án'tástən] *vt* touch; (*Recht*) infringe upon; (*Ehre*) question.
Anteil [án'tīl] *m* **-s, -e** share (*an +dat* in); (*Mitgefühl*) sympathy; ~ **nehmen an** (*+dat*) share in; (*sich interessieren*) take an interest in; ~ **an etw** (*dat*) **haben** (*beitragen*) contribute to sth; (*teilnehmen*) take part in sth.
anteilig *a* proportionate, proportional.
anteilmäßig *a* proportional.
Anteilnahme *f* **-** sympathy.
Antenne [ánte'nə] *f* **-, -n** aerial; (*ZOOL*) antenna; **eine/keine** ~ **für etw haben** (*fig*

umg) have a/no feeling for sth.

Anthrazit [ántrátsē:t'] *m* **-s, -e** anthracite.

Anthropologie [ántrōpōlōgē:'] *f* - anthropology.

Anti- [án'tē] *in zW* anti; **~alkoho'liker** *m* teetotaller; **a~autoritär'** *a* anti-authoritarian; **~babypille** [ántēbā:'bēpilə] *f* (contraceptive) pill; **~biotikum** [ántēbēō:'tēkŌŌm] *nt* **-s, -ka** antibiotic; **~held** *m* antihero.

antik [ántē:k'] *a* antique.

Antike *f* **-, -n** (*Zeitalter*) ancient world; (*Kunstgegenstand*) antique.

Antikörper *m* antibody.

Antillen [ánti'lən] *pl* Antilles *pl*.

Antilope [ántēlō:'pə] *f* **-, -n** antelope.

Antipathie [ántēpátē:'] *f* antipathy.

antippen [án'tipən] *vt* tap; (*Pedal, Bremse*) touch; (*fig: Thema*) touch on.

Antiquariat [ántēkvárēāt'] *nt* **-(e)s, -e** second-hand bookstore; **modernes** ~ remainder bookstore/department.

antiquiert [ántēkvē:rt'] *a* (*pej*) antiquated.

Antiquitäten [ántēkvētē:'tən] *pl* antiques *pl*; **~handel** *m* antique business; **~händler(in** *f*) *m* antique dealer.

Antlitz [án'tlits] *nt* **-es, -e** (*liter*) countenance (*liter*), face.

antörnen [án'tœrnən] *vti* = **anturnen.**

Antrag [án'trâk] *m* **-(e)s, -träge** proposal; (*PARL*) motion; (*Gesuch*) application; **einen** ~ **auf etw** (*akk*) **stellen** make an application for sth; (*JUR etc*) file a petition/claim for sth.

Antrags- *zW*: **~formular** *nt* application form; **~gegner(in** *f*) *m* (*JUR*) respondent.

Antragsteller(in *f*) *m* **-s, -** claimant; (*für Kredit etc*) applicant.

antreffen [án'trefən] *vt unreg* meet.

antreiben [án'trībən] *unreg vt* drive on; (*Motor*) drive; (*anschwemmen*) wash up ♦ *vi* be washed up; **jdn zur Eile/Arbeit** ~ urge sb to hurry up/to work.

Antreiber *m* **-s, -** (*pej*) slave-driver (*pej*).

antreten [án'trā:tən] *unreg vt* (*Amt*) take up; (*Erbschaft*) come into; (*Beweis*) offer; (*Reise*) start, begin ♦ *vi* (*MIL*) fall in; (*SPORT*) line up; (*zum Dienst*) report; **gegen jdn** ~ play/fight against sb.

Antrieb [án'trē:p] *m* (*lit, fig*) drive; **aus eigenem** ~ of one's own accord.

Antriebskraft *f* (*TECH*) power.

antrinken [án'tringkən] *vt unreg* (*Flasche, Glas*) start to drink from; **sich** (*dat*) **einen Rausch** ~ get drunk; **angetrunken sein** be tipsy.

Antritt [án'trit] *m* beginning, commencement; (*eines Amts*) taking up.

antun [án'tŌŌ:n] *vt unreg*: **jdm etw** ~ do sth to sb; **sich** (*dat*) **Zwang** ~ force o.s.

anturnen [án'tŌŌrnən] *vt* (*umg: Drogen, Musik*) turn on ♦ *vi* (*umg*) turn you on.

Antwort [án'vort] *f* **-, -en** answer, reply; **um** ~ **wird gebeten** RSVP, please reply by return.

antworten *vi* answer, reply.

anvertrauen [án'fārtrouən] *vt*: **jdm etw** ~ entrust sb with sth; **sich jdm** ~ confide in sb.

anvisieren [án'vēzē:rən] *vt* (*fig*) set one's sights on.

anwachsen [án'váksən] *vi unreg* grow; (*Pflanze*) take root.

Anwalt [án'vàlt] *m* **-(e)s, -wälte, Anwältin** [án'veltin] *f* attorney (*US*), solicitor (*Brit*); lawyer; (*fig*) champion; (*fig: Fürsprecher*) advocate.

Anwalts- *zW*: **~honorar** *nt* retainer, retaining fee; **~kammer** *f* professional association of lawyers; **~kosten** *pl* legal expenses *pl*.

Anwandlung [án'vándlŌŌng] *f* caprice; **eine** ~ **von etw** a fit of sth.

anwärmen [án'vermən] *vt* warm up.

Anwärter(in *f*) [án'vertər(in)] *m* candidate.

anweisen [án'vīzən] *vt unreg* instruct; (*zuteilen*) assign (*jdm etw* sth to sb).

Anweisung *f* instruction; (*COMM*) remittance; (*Post~, Zahlungs~*) money order.

anwendbar [án'ventbâr] *a* practicable, applicable.

anwenden [án'vendən] *vt unreg* use, employ; (*Gesetz, Regel*) apply.

Anwender- *zW*: **~programm** *nt* (*COMPUT*) application program; **~software** *f* application package.

Anwendung *f* use; application.

anwerfen [án'verfən] *vt unreg* (*TECH*) start up.

anwesend [án'vā:zənt] *a* present; **die A~en** those present.

Anwesenheit *f* presence.

Anwesenheitsliste *f* attendance register.

anwidern [án'vē:dərn] *vt* disgust.

Anwohner(in *f*) [án'vō:nər(in)] *m* **-s, -** resident.

Anwuchs [án'vŌŌ:ks] *m* growth.

Anzahl [án'tsâl] *f* number (*an* +*dat* of).

anzahlen *vt* pay on account.

Anzahlung *f* deposit, payment on account.

anzapfen [án'tsàpfən] *vt* tap.

Anzeichen [án'tsìċhən] *nt* sign, indication; **alle** ~ **deuten darauf hin, daß** ... all the signs are that ...

Anzeige [án'tsīgə] *f* **-, -n** (*Zeitungs~*) announcement; (*Werbung*) advertisement; (*COMPUT*) display; (*bei Polizei*) report; ~ **erstatten gegen jdn** report sb to the police).

anzeigen *vt* (*zu erkennen geben*) show; (*bekanntgeben*) announce; (*bei Polizei*) report.

Anzeigenteil *m* advertisements *pl*.

anzeigepflichtig *a* notifiable.

Anzeiger *m* indicator.

anzetteln [án'tsetəln] *vt* (*umg*) instigate.

anziehen [án'tsē:ən] *unreg vt* attract; (*Kleidung*) put on; (*Mensch*) dress; (*Schraube, Seil*) pull tight; (*Knie*) draw up; (*Feuchtigkeit*) absorb ♦ *vr* get dressed.

anziehend *a* attractive.

Anziehung f (*Reiz*) attraction.
Anziehungskraft f power of attraction; (*PHYS*) force of gravitation.
Anzug [án'tsōō:k] m suit; **im ~ sein** be approaching.
anzüglich [án'tsü:kliç̣h] a personal; (*anstößig*) offensive; **A~keit** f offensiveness; (*Bemerkung*) personal remark.
anzünden [án'tsündən] vt light.
Anzünder m lighter.
anzweifeln [án'tsvīfəln] vt doubt.
AOK f - abk = *Allgemeine Ortskrankenkasse.*
APA f abk = *Austria Presse Agentur.*
apart [ápárt'] a distinctive.
Apartheid [ápárt'hīt] f apartheid.
Apartment [ápárt'mənt] nt -s, -s apartment, flat (*Brit*).
Apathie [ápátē:'] f apathy.
apathisch [ápá'tish] a apathetic.
Apenninen [ápenē:'nən] pl Apennines pl.
Apfel [áp'fəl] m -s, = apple; **in den sauren ~ beißen** (*fig umg*) swallow the bitter pill; **etw für einen ~ und ein Ei kaufen** (*umg*) buy sth dirt cheap od for a song; **~mus** nt apple purée od (*als Beilage*) sauce; **~saft** m apple juice.
Apfelsine [ápfəlzē:'nə] f -, -n orange.
Apfel- zW: **~tasche** f apple turnover; **~wein** m cider.
apl. abk = **außerplanmäßig.**
APO, Apo [á'pō] f - abk (= *außerparlamentarische Opposition*) extraparliamentary opposition.
apolitisch [á'pōlē:tish] a non-political, apolitical.
Apostel [ápos'təl] m -s, - apostle.
Apostroph [ápōstrō:f'] m -s, -e apostrophe.
Apotheke [ápōtā:'kə] f -, -n drugstore (*US*), chemist's (shop) (*Brit*).
Apotheker(in f) m -s, - druggist (*US*), chemist (*Brit*).
Appalachen [ápálá'ḳhən] pl Appalachian Mountains pl.
Apparat [ápárát'] m -(e)s, -e piece of apparatus; (*Foto~*) camera; (*Telefon*) telephone; (*RAD, TV*) set; (*Verwaltungs~, Partei~*) machinery, apparatus; **am ~** on the phone; (*als Antwort*) speaking; **am ~ bleiben** hold the line.
Apparatur [ápárátōō:r'] f apparatus.
Appartement [ápárt(ə)mâñ'] nt -s, -s apartment.
Appell [ápel'] m -s, -e (*MIL*) muster, parade; (*fig*) appeal; **zum ~ antreten** line up for roll call.
appellieren [ápelē:'rən] vi appeal (*an +akk* to).
Appetit [ápátē:t'] m -(e)s, -e appetite; **guten ~!** enjoy your meal; **a~lich** a appetizing; **~losigkeit** f lack of appetite.
Applaus [áplous'] m -es, -e applause.
Appretur [áprátōō:r'] f finish; (*Wasserundurchlässigkeit*) waterproofing.
approbiert [áprōbē:rt'] a (*Arzt*) registered,

certified.
Apr. abk (= *April*) Apr.
Aprikose [áprēkō:'zə] f -, -n apricot.
April [ápril'] m -(s), -e April; **jdn in den ~ schicken** make an April fool of sb; **~wetter** nt April showers pl; *siehe* **September.**
apropos [áprōpō:'] ad by the way, that reminds me.
Aquaplaning [ákváplâ'ning] nt -(s) aquaplaning.
Aquarell [ákvárel'] nt -s, -e watercolor (*US*), watercolour (*Brit*).
Aquarium [ákvâ'rēōōm] nt aquarium.
Äquator [ekvâ'tor] m -s equator.
Äquivalent [ekvēválent'] nt -(e)s, -e equivalent.
Ar [âr] nt od m -s, -e (*Maß*) are (100 m²).
AR abk = **Aufsichtsrat.**
Ära [e:'râ] f -, -en era.
Araber(in f) [á'rábər(in)] m -s, - Arab.
Arabien [árá'bēən] nt -s Arabia.
arabisch a Arab; (*Arabien betreffend*) Arabian; (*Sprache*) Arabic; **A~er Golf** Arabian Gulf; **A~es Meer** Arabian Sea; **A~e Wüste** Arabian Desert.
Arbeit [ár'bīt] f -, -en work (*no art*); (*Stelle*) job; (*Erzeugnis*) piece of work; (*wissenschaftliche*) dissertation; (*Klassen~*) test; **Tag der ~** = Labor Day; **sich an die ~ machen, an die ~ gehen** get down to work, start working; **jdm ~ machen** (*Mühe*) put sb to trouble; **das war eine ~** that was a hard job.
arbeiten vi work ♦ vt make ♦ vr: **sich nach oben/an die Spitze ~** (*fig*) work one's way up/to the top.
Arbeiter(in f) m -s, - worker; (*ungelernt*) laborer (*US*), labourer (*Brit*).
Arbeiter- zW: **~familie** f working-class family; **~kind** nt child from a working-class family; **~mitbestimmung** f employee participation; **~schaft** f workers pl, labor force; **~selbstkontrolle** f workers' control; **~-und-Bauern-Staat** m (*DDR*) workers' and peasants' state; **~wohlfahrt** f workers' welfare association.
arbeitet 3. pers sing präs von **arbeiten.**
Arbeit- zW: **~geber** m -s, - employer; **~nehmer** m -s, - employee; **a~sam** a industrious.
Arbeits- in zW labor (*US*), labour (*Brit*); **~amt** nt employment office; **~aufwand** m expenditure of energy; (*INDUSTRIE*) use of labor; **~bedingungen** pl working conditions pl; **~beschaffung** f (*Arbeitsplatzbeschaffung*) job creation; **~erlaubnis** f work permit; **a~fähig** a fit for work, ablebodied; **~gang** m operation; **~gemeinschaft** f study group; **~gericht** nt labor relations board; **~hetze** f work stress; **a~intensiv** a labor-intensive; **~konflikt** m industrial dispute; **~kraft** f workers pl, labor; **a~los** a unemployed, out-of-work; **~losengeld** nt unemployment benefit; **~losenhilfe** f supple-

mentary benefit; ~**losenunterstützung** f unemployment benefit; ~**losenversicherung** f ≈ unemployment compensation (*US*); ~**losigkeit** f unemployment; ~**moral** f attitude to work; (*in Betrieb*) work climate; ~**niederlegung** f walkout; ~**platte** f (*Küche*) work-top *od* surface; ~**platz** *m* place of work; (*Stelle*) job; ~**platzrechner** *m* (*COMPUT*) work station; ~**recht** *nt* labor laws *pl*; **a~scheu** *a* work-shy; ~**tag** *m* work(ing) day; ~**teilung** f division of labor; ~**tier** *nt* (*fig umg*) glutton for work; (*Geistesarbeiter auch*) workaholic; **a~unfähig** *a* unfit for work; ~**unfall** *m* industrial accident; ~**verhältnis** *nt* employee-employer relationship; ~**vermittlung** f (*Amt*) employment office; ~**vertrag** *m* contract of employment; ~**zeit** f working hours *pl*; ~**zeitverkürzung** f reduction in working hours; ~**zimmer** *nt* study.

Archäologe [árçheōlō:'gə] *m* **-n**, **-n**, **Archäologin** f arch(a)eologist.

Arche [ár'çhə] f **-**, **-n**: **die ~ Noah** Noah's Ark.

Architekt(in f) [árçhētekt'(in)] *m* **-en**, **-en** architect.

architektonisch [árçhētektō:'nēsh] *a* architectural.

Architektur [árçhētektōō:r'] f architecture.

Archiv [árçhē:f'] *nt* **-s**, **-e** archive.

ARD f - *abk* (= *Arbeitsgemeinschaft der öffentlich-rechtlichen Rundfunkanstalten der Bundesrepublik Deutschland*) West German broadcasting association.

Arena [árā:'nā] f **-**, **-renen** (*lit, fig*) arena; (*Zirkus~, Stierkampf~*) ring.

arg [árk] *a* bad, awful ♦ *ad* awfully, very; **es zu ~ treiben** go too far.

Argentinien [árgentē:'nēən] *nt* **-s** Argentina, the Argentine.

Argentinier(in f) *m* **-s**, **- Argentine.**

argentinisch [árgentē:'nish] *a* Argentine.

Ärger [er'gər] *m* **-s** (*Wut*) anger; (*Unannehmlichkeit*) trouble; **jdm ~ machen** *od* **bereiten** cause sb a lot of trouble *od* bother; **ä~lich** *a* (*zornig*) angry; (*lästig*) annoying, aggravating.

ärgern *vt* annoy ♦ *vr* get annoyed.

Ärgernis *nt* **-ses**, **-se** annoyance; (*Anstoß*) outrage; **öffentliches ~ erregen** be a public nuisance.

arg- *zW*: ~**listig** *a* cunning, insidious; ~**listige Täuschung** fraud; ~**los** *a* guileless, innocent; **A~losigkeit** f guilelessness, innocence.

Argument [árgōōment'] *nt* argument.

argumentieren [árgōōmentē:'rən] *vi* argue.

Argusauge [ár'gōōsougə] *nt* (*geh*): **mit ~n** eagle-eyed.

Argwohn *m* suspicion.

argwöhnisch *a* suspicious.

Arie [â'rēə] f aria.

Aristokrat(in f) [áristōkrât'(in)] *m* **-en**, **-en** aristocrat.

Aristokratie [áristōkrâtē:'] f aristocracy.

aristokratisch [áristōkrâ'tish] *a* aristocratic.

arithmetisch [áritmā:'tish] *a* arithmetical; ~**es Mittel** arithmetic mean.

Arkaden [árkâ'dən] *fpl* (*Bogengang*) arcade *sing*.

Arktis [árk'tis] f - Arctic.

arktisch *a* arctic.

arm [árm] *a* poor; **~ dran sein** (*umg*) have a hard time of it.

Arm *m* **-(e)s**, **-e** arm; (*Fluß~*) branch; **jdn auf den ~ nehmen** (*fig umg*) pull sb's leg; **jdm unter die ~e greifen** (*fig*) help sb out; **einen langen/den längeren ~ haben** (*fig*) have a lot of/more pull (*umg*) *od* influence.

Armatur [ármâtōō:r'] f (*ELEK*) armature.

Armaturenbrett *nt* instrument panel; (*AUT*) dashboard.

Armband *nt* bracelet; ~**uhr** f (wrist) watch.

Arme(r) *mf dekl wie a* poor man/woman; **die ~n** the poor.'

Armee [ármā:'] f **-**, **-n** army; ~**korps** *nt* army corps.

Ärmel [er'məl] *m* **-s**, **- sleeve; etw aus dem ~ schütteln** (*fig*) produce sth just like that.

Ärmelkanal *m* (English) Channel.

Armenrecht *nt* (*JUR*) legal aid.

Armer *siehe* **Arme(r)**.

Armleuchter *m* (*pej umg*: *Dummkopf*) fool.

ärmlich [erm'liçh] *a* poor; **aus ~en Verhältnissen** from a poor family.

armselig *a* wretched, miserable; (*mitleiderregend*) pathetic, pitiful.

Armut [âr'mōō:t] f - poverty.

Armutszeugnis *nt* (*fig*): **jdm/sich ein ~ ausstellen** show sb's/one's shortcomings.

Aroma [árō:'mâ] *nt* **-s**, **Aromen** aroma.

aromatisch [árōmâ'tish] *a* aromatic.

arrangieren [árânzhē:'rən] *vt* arrange ♦ *vr* come to an arrangement.

Arrest [árest'] *m* **-(e)s**, **-e** detention.

arretieren [árātē:'rən] *vt* (*TECH*) lock (in place).

arrogant [árōgánt'] *a* arrogant.

Arroganz f arrogance.

Arsch [ársh] *m* **-es**, **-̈e** (*umg*) ass (*US!*), arse (*Brit!*); **leck mich am ~!** (*laß mich in Ruhe*) go to hell! (*!*); **am ~ der Welt** (*umg*) at the end of the world; ~**kriecher** *m* (*umg!*) asslicker (*!*); arselicker (*!*); ~**loch** *nt* (*umg!*: *Mensch*) bastard (*!*).

Arsen [árzā:n'] *nt* **-s** arsenic.

Art [árt] f **-**, **-en** (*Weise*) way; (*Sorte*) kind, sort; (*BIOL*) species; **eine ~ (von) Frucht** a kind of fruit; **Häuser aller ~** houses of all kinds; **einzig in seiner ~ sein** be the only one of its kind, be unique; **auf diese ~ und Weise** in this way; **das ist doch keine ~!** that's no way to behave!; **es ist nicht seine ~, das zu tun** it's not like him to do that; **ich mache das auf meine ~** I do that my (own) way; **nach ~ des Hauses** à la maison.

arten *vi*: **nach jdm ~** take after sb; **der Mensch ist so geartet, daß ...** human na-

ture is such that ...
Arterie [ártā:'rēə] *f* artery.
Arterienverkalkung *f* arteriosclerosis.
Artgenosse [árt'gənosə] *m* animal/plant of the same species; (*Mensch*) person of the same type.
Arthritis [ártrē:'tis] *f* -, **-ritiden** arthritis.
artig [ár'tiĊħ] *a* good, well-behaved.
Artikel [ártē:'kəl] *m* **-s**, **-** article.
Artillerie [ártilərē:'] *f* artillery.
Artistik [ártis'tik] *f* - artistry; (*Zirkus-, Varietékunst*) circus/variety performing.
Arznei [ártsnī'] *f* medication, medicine; ~**mittel** *nt* medicine, medicament.
Arzt [ártst] *m* **-es**, **ːe**, **Ärztin** [e:rts'tin] *f* doctor; **praktischer** ~ general practitioner, GP.
Ärztekammer *f* ≈ State Medical Board of Registration (*US*), ≈ General Medical Council (*Brit*).
Arzthelferin *f* doctor's assistant.
ärztlich [e:rts'tliĊħ] *a* medical.
As [ás] *nt* **-ses**, **-se** ace; (*MUS*) A flat.
Asbest [ásbest'] *m* **-(e)s**, **-e** asbestos.
Asche [á'shə] *f* -, **-n** ash.
Aschen- *zW*: ~**bahn** *f* cinder track; ~**becher** *m* ashtray; ~**brödel** *nt*, ~**puttel** *nt* (*LITER, fig*) Cinderella.
Aschermittwoch *m* Ash Wednesday.
Asiat(in *f*) [ázēát'(in)] *m* **-en**, **-en** Asian.
asiatisch *a* Asian, Asiatic.
Asien [á'zēən] *nt* **-s** Asia.
asozial [á'zōtsēál] *a* antisocial; (*Familien*) asocial.
Asoziale(r) *mf dekl wie a* (*pej*) antisocial man/woman *etc*; **Asoziale** *pl* antisocial elements.
Aspekt [áspekt'] *m* **-(e)s**, **-e** aspect.
Asphalt [ásfált'] *m* **-(e)s**, **-e** asphalt.
asphaltieren [ásfáltē:'rən] *vt* asphalt.
Asphaltstraße *f* asphalt road.
aß [ás] *imperf von* **essen**.
Ass. *abk* = **Assessor**.
Assekurant(in *f*) [ásākōōránt'(in)] *m* **-en**, **-en** underwriter.
Assemblersprache [əsem'blərshprâ꣡ħə] *f* (*COMPUT*) assembly language.
Assessor(in *f*) [áse'sor(in)] *m* **-s**, **-en** *graduate civil servant who has completed his/her traineeship*.
Assistent(in *f*) [ásistent'(in)] *m* assistant.
Assistenzarzt [ásisten'tsártst] *m* intern (*US*), houseman (*Brit*).
Assoziation [ásōtsēátsēō:n'] *f* association.
assoziieren [ásōtsēē:'rən] *vt* (*geh*) associate.
Ast [ást] *m* **-(e)s**, **ːe** bough, branch; **sich** (*dat*) **einen** ~ **lachen** (*umg*) double up (with laughter).
AStA [ás'tá] *m* **-(s)**, **-(s)** *abk* (= *Allgemeiner Studentenausschuß*) *students' association*.
Aster [ás'tər] *f* -, **-n** aster.
ästhetisch [estä:'tish] *a* esthetic (*US*), aesthetic (*Brit*).
Asthma [ást'má] *nt* **-s** asthma.

Asthmatiker(in *f*) [ástmá'tēkər(in)] *m* **-s**, **-** asthmatic.
astrein [ás'trīn] *a* (*fig umg*: *moralisch einwandfrei*) straight, on the level; (: *echt*) genuine; (*prima*) fantastic.
Astrologe [ástrōlō:'gə] *m* **-n**, **-n**, **Astrologin** *f* astrologer.
Astrologie [ástrōlōgē:'] *f* astrology.
Astronaut(in *f*) [ástrōnout'(in)] *m* **-en**, **-en** astronaut.
Astronautik *f* astronautics.
Astronom(in *f*) [ástrōnō:m'(in)] *m* **-en**, **-en** astronomer.
Astronomie [ástrōnōmē:'] *f* astronomy.
ASU *abk* = *Arbeitsgemeinschaft Selbständiger Unternehmer*) *association of private traders*; (= *Abgassonderuntersuchung*) exhaust check.
ASW *f abk* (= *außersinnliche Wahrnehmung*) ESP.
Asyl [ázü:l'] *nt* **-s**, **-e** asylum; (*Heim*) home; (*Obdachlosen*~) shelter.
Asylant(in *f*) [ázü:lánt'(in)] *m* **-en**, **-en** person seeking (political) asylum.
Asylrecht *nt* (*POL*) right of (political) asylum.
A.T. *abk* (= *Altes Testament*) O.T.
Atelier [átəlēā:'] *nt* **-s**, **-e** studio.
Atem [â'təm] *m* **-s** breath; **den** ~ **anhalten** hold one's breath; **außer** ~ out of breath; **jdn in** ~ **halten** keep sb in suspense *od* on tenterhooks; **das verschlug mir den** ~ it took my breath away; **einen langen/den längeren** ~ **haben** have a lot of staying power; **a~beraubend** *a* breathtaking; **a~los** *a* breathless; ~**pause** *f* breather; ~**wege** *pl* (*ANAT*) respiratory tract; ~**zug** *m* breath.
Atheismus [átā:is'mŏŏs] *m* atheism.
Atheist(in *f*) *m* atheist; **a~isch** *a* atheistic.
Athen [átā:n'] *nt* **-s** Athens.
Athener(in *f*) *m* **-s**, **-** Athenian.
Äther [e:'tər] *m* **-s**, **-** ether.
Äthiopien [etēō:'pēən] *nt* **-s** Ethiopia.
Äthiopier(in *f*) *m* **-s**, **-** Ethiopian.
Athlet [átlā:t'] *m* **-en**, **-en** athlete.
Athletik *f* athletics *sing*.
Atlantik [átlán'tik] *m* **-s** Atlantic.
atlantisch *a* Atlantic; **der A~e Ozean** the Atlantic Ocean.
Atlas [át'lás] *m* **-** *od* **-ses** , **-se** *od* **Atlan'ten** atlas; ~**gebirge** *nt* Atlas Mountains *pl*.
atmen [ât'mən] *vti* breathe.
Atmosphäre [átmōsfe:'rə] *f* -, **-n** atmosphere.
atmosphärisch *a* atmospheric.
Atmung [ât'mŏŏng] *f* respiration.
Ätna [e:t'ná] *m* **-(s)** Etna.
Atom [átō:m'] *nt* **-s**, **-e** atom; ~**angst** *f* fear of all things nuclear.
atomar [átōmár'] *a* atomic, nuclear; (*Drohung*) nuclear.
Atom- *zW*: ~**bombe** *f* atom bomb; ~**energie** *f* nuclear *od* atomic energy; ~**kern** *m* atomic nucleus; ~**kernforschung** *f* nuclear research; ~**kraftbefürworter(in** *f*) *m* supporter

of nuclear power; **~kraftgegner(in** *f*) *m* opponent of nuclear power; **~kraftwerk** *nt* nuclear power station; **~krieg** *m* nuclear *od* atomic war; **~lobby** *f* nuclear lobby; **~macht** *f* nuclear *od* atomic power; **~meiler** *m* nuclear reactor; **~müll** *m* nuclear waste; **~physik** *f* nuclear physics *sing*; **~pilz** *m* mushroom cloud; **~sperrvertrag** *m* (*POL*) nuclear non-proliferation treaty; **~sprengkopf** *m* nuclear *od* atomic warhead; **~strom** *m* *electricity generated by nuclear power*; **~testgelände** *nt* nuclear testing range; **~versuch** *m* atomic test; **~waffen** *pl* nuclear *od* atomic weapons *pl*; **~wirtschaft** *f* nuclear industry; **~zeitalter** *nt* atomic age.

Attacke [átá'kə] *f* -, **-n** (*Angriff*) attack.

Attentat [átentát'] *nt* **-(e)s, -e** (attempted) assassination (*auf* +*akk* of).

Attentäter(in *f*) [átente:'tər(in)] *m* **-s,** - (would-be) assassin.

Attest [átest'] *nt* **-(e)s, -e** certificate.

attraktiv [átráktē:f'] *a* attractive.

Attrappe [átrá'pə] *f* -, **-n** dummy; **bei ihr ist alles** ~ everything about her is false.

Attribut [átrēbōō:t'] *nt* **-(e)s, -e** (*GRAM*) attribute.

ätzen [e'tsən] *vi* be caustic.

ätzend *a* (*lit: Säure*) corrosive; (*Geruch*) pungent; (*fig umg*) dreadful, horrible.

auch [oukh] *kj* also, too, as well; (*selbst, sogar*) even; (*wirklich*) really; **oder** ~ or; ~ **das ist schön** that's nice too *od* as well; **das habe ich** ~ **nicht gemacht** I didn't do it either; **ich** ~ **nicht** nor I, me neither; ~ **wenn das Wetter schlecht ist** even if the weather is bad; **nicht nur ..., sondern** ~ not only ...but also ...; **ohne** ~ **nur zu fragen** without even asking; **wozu** ~**?** (*emphatisch*) whatever for?; **wer/was** ~ whoever/ whatever; **so sieht es** ~ **aus** it looks like it too; ~ **das noch!** not that as well!

Audienz [oudēents'] *f* -, **-en** (*bei Papst, König etc*) audience.

Audimax [oudēmáks'] *nt* (*UNIV umg*) main lecture hall.

audiovisuell [oudēōvēzōōel'] *a* audiovisual.

Auditorium [oudētō:'rēōōm] *nt* (*Hörsaal*) lecture hall; (*geh: Zuhörerschaft*) audience.

auf [ouf] *präp* +*akk od dat* (*räumlich*) on; (*hinauf*: +*akk*) up; (*in Richtung*: +*akk*) to; (*nach*) after; ~ **der Reise** on the way; ~ **der Post/dem Fest** at the post office/party; ~ **das Land** into the country; ~ **der Straße** on the road; ~ **dem Land/der ganzen Welt** in the country/the whole world; ~ **deutsch** in German; ~ **Lebenszeit** for sb's lifetime; **was hat es damit** ~ **sich?** what does it mean?; ~ **eine Tasse Kaffee/eine Zigarette(nlänge)** for a cup of coffee/a smoke; ~ **meinen Brief hin** because of *od* on account of my letter; **die Nacht (von Montag)** ~ **Dienstag** Monday night; ~ **einen Polizisten kommen 1.000 Bürger** there is one police-

man to every 1,000 citizens; **bis** ~ **ihn** except for him; ~ **einmal** at once ♦ *ad*: ~ **und ab** up and down; ~**, an die Arbeit!** come on, let's get on with it; ~ **und davon** up and away; ~**!** (*los*) come on!; ~ **sein** (*umg: Person*) be up; (*Tür*) be open; **von Kindheit** ~ from childhood onwards; ~ **daß** so that.

aufarbeiten [ouf'árbītən] *vt* (*erledigen: Korrespondenz etc*) catch up on.

aufatmen [ouf'âtmən] *vi* breathe a sigh of relief.

aufbahren [ouf'bârən] *vt* lay out.

Aufbau [ouf'bou] *m* (*Bauen*) building, construction; (*Struktur*) structure; (*aufgebautes Teil*) superstructure.

aufbauen [ouf'bouən] *vt* erect, build (up); (*Existenz*) make; (*gestalten*) construct; (*gründen*) found, base (*auf* +*dat* on) ♦ *vr*: **sich vor jdm** ~ draw o.s. up to one's full height in front of sb.

aufbäumen [ouf'boimən] *vr* rear; (*fig*) revolt, rebel.

aufbauschen [ouf'boushən] *vt* puff out; (*fig*) exaggerate.

aufbegehren [ouf'bəgâ:rən] *vi* (*geh*) rebel.

aufbehalten [ouf'bəhâltən] *vt unreg* keep on.

aufbekommen [ouf'bəkomən] *vt unreg* (*umg: öffnen*) get open; (*: Hausaufgaben*) be given.

aufbereiten [ouf'bərītən] *vt* process; (*Trinkwasser auch*) purify; (*Text etc*) work up.

Aufbereitungsanlage *f* processing plant.

aufbessern [ouf'besərn] *vt* (*Gehalt*) increase.

aufbewahren [ouf'bəvârən] *vt* keep; (*Gepäck*) put in the baggage check.

Aufbewahrung *f* (safe)keeping; (*Gepäck*~) baggage check (*US*), left-luggage office (*Brit*); **jdm etw zur** ~ **geben** give sb sth for safekeeping.

Aufbewahrungsort *m* storage place.

aufbieten [ouf'bē:tən] *vt unreg* (*Kraft*) summon (up); (*Armee, Polizei*) mobilize; (*Brautpaar*) publish the banns of.

Aufbietung *f*: **unter** ~ **aller Kräfte** ... summoning (up) all his/her *etc* strength ...

aufbinden [ouf'bindən] *vt unreg*: **laß dir doch so etwas nicht** ~ (*fig*) don't fall for that.

aufblähen [ouf'ble:ən] *vr* blow out; (*Segel auch*) billow out; (*MED*) become swollen; (*fig pej*) puff o.s. up.

aufblasen [ouf'blâzən] *unreg vt* blow up, inflate ♦ *vr* (*umg*) become big-headed.

aufbleiben [ouf'blībən] *vi unreg* (*Laden*) remain open; (*Person*) stay up.

aufblenden [ouf'blendən] *vt* (*Scheinwerfer*) turn on full beam.

aufblicken [ouf'blikən] *vi* (*lit, fig*) look up (*zu* (*lit*) at, (*fig*) to).

aufblühen [ouf'blü:ən] *vi* blossom; (*fig auch*) flourish.

aufblühend *a* (*COMM*) booming.

aufbocken [ouf'bokən] *vt* (*Auto*) jack up.

aufbrauchen [ouf'brouk͡hən] *vt* use up.
aufbrausen [ouf'brouzən] *vi* (*fig*) flare up.
aufbrausend *a* hot-tempered.
aufbrechen [ouf'brec͡hən] *unreg vt* break open ♦ *vi* burst open; (*gehen*) start, set off.
aufbringen [ouf'bringən] *vt unreg* (*öffnen*) open; (*in Mode*) bring into fashion; (*beschaffen*) procure; (*FIN*) raise; (*ärgern*) irritate; **Verständnis für etw** ~ be able to understand sth.
Aufbruch [ouf'brōōk͡h] *m* departure.
aufbrühen [ouf'brü:ən] *vt* (*Tee*) make.
aufbrummen [ouf'brōōmən] *vt* (*umg*): **jdm die Kosten** ~ land sb with the costs.
aufbürden [ouf'bürdən] *vt* burden (*jdm etw sb with sth*).
aufdecken [ouf'dekən] *vt* uncover; (*Spielkarten*) show.
aufdrängen [ouf'drengən] *vt* force (*jdm on sb*) ♦ *vr* intrude (*jdm on sb*).
aufdrehen [ouf'drā:ən] *vt* (*Wasserhahn etc*) turn on; (*Ventil*) open; (*Schraubverschluß*) unscrew; (*Radio etc*) turn up; (*Haar*) put in rollers.
aufdringlich [ouf'dringlic͡h] *a* pushy; (*Benehmen*) obtrusive; (*Parfüm*) powerful.
aufeinander [oufinān'dər] *ad* (*achten*) after each other; (*schießen*) at each other; (*vertrauen*) each other; **A~folge** *f* succession, series; **~folgen** *vi* follow one another; **~folgend** *a* consecutive; **~legen** *vt* lay on top of one another; **~prallen** *vi* hit one another; (*Truppen, Meinungen*) clash.
Aufenthalt [ouf'enthält] *m* stay; (*Verzögerung*) delay; (*EISENB*: *Halten*) stop; (*Ort*) haunt.
Aufenthalts- *zW*: **~genehmigung** *f* residence permit; **~raum** *m* day room; (*in Betrieb*) recreation room.
auferlegen [ouf'erlā:gən] *vt* impose (*jdm etw sth upon sb*).
auferstehen [ouf'ershtā:ən] *vi untr unreg* rise from the dead.
Auferstehung *f* resurrection.
aufessen [ouf'esən] *vt unreg* eat up.
auffahren [ouf'fârən] *unreg vi* (*Auto*) run, crash (*auf* +*akk* into); (*herankommen*) draw up; (*hochfahren*) jump up; (*wütend werden*) flare up; (*in den Himmel*) ascend ♦ *vt* (*Kanonen, Geschütz*) bring up.
auffahrend *a* hot-tempered.
Auffahrt *f* (*Haus~*) drive; (*Autobahn~*) entrance ramp (*US*), slip road (*Brit*).
Auffahrunfall *m* pile-up.
auffallen [ouf'fálən] *vi unreg* be noticeable; **angenehm/unangenehm** ~ make a good/bad impression; **jdm** ~ (*bemerken*) strike sb.
auffallend *a* striking.
auffällig [ouf'felic͡h] *a* conspicuous, striking.
auffangen [ouf'fángən] *vt unreg* catch; (*Funkspruch*) intercept; (*Preise*) peg; (*abfangen*: *Aufprall etc*) cushion, absorb.
Auffanglager *nt* refugee camp.

auffassen [ouf'fásən] *vt* understand, comprehend; (*auslegen*) see, view.
Auffassung *f* (*Meinung*) opinion; (*Auslegung*) view, conception; (*auch* **Auffassungsgabe**) grasp.
auffindbar [ouf'fintbâr] *a* to be found.
aufflammen [ouf'flámən] *vi* (*lit, fig*: *Feuer, Unruhen etc*) flare up.
auffliegen [ouf'flē:gən] *vi unreg* fly up; (*umg*: *Rauschgiftring etc*) be busted.
auffordern [ouf'fordərn] *vt* challenge; (*befehlen*) call upon, order; (*bitten*) ask.
Aufforderung *f* (*Befehl*) order; (*Einladung*) invitation.
aufforsten [ouf'forstən] *vt* (*Gebiet*) reforest; (*Wald*) restock.
auffrischen [ouf'frishən] *vt* freshen up; (*Kenntnisse*) brush up; (*Erinnerungen*) reawaken ♦ *vi* (*Wind*) freshen.
aufführen [ouf'fü:rən] *vt* (*THEAT*) perform; (*in einem Verzeichnis*) list, specify; **einzeln** ~ itemize ♦ *vr* (*sich benehmen*) behave.
Aufführung *f* (*THEAT*) performance; (*Liste*) specification.
auffüllen [ouf'fülən] *vt* fill up; (*Vorräte*) replenish; (*Öl*) top up.
Aufgabe [ouf'gâbə] *f* -, **-n** task; (*SCH*) exercise; (*Haus~*) homework; (*Verzicht*) giving up; (*von Gepäck*) registration; (*von Post*) mailing; (*von Inserat*) insertion; **sich** (*dat*) **etw zur** ~ **machen** make sth one's job *od* business.
aufgabeln [ouf'gâbəln] *vt* (*fig umg*: *jdn*) pick up; (: *Sache*) get hold of.
Aufgabenbereich *m* area of responsibility.
Aufgang [ouf'gáng] *m* ascent; (*Sonnen~*) rise; (*Treppe*) staircase.
aufgeben [ouf'gā:bən] *unreg vt* (*verzichten auf*) give up; (*Paket*) send, mail; (*Gepäck*) register; (*Bestellung*) give; (*Inserat*) insert; (*Rätsel, Problem*) set ♦ *vi* give up.
aufgeblasen [ouf'gəblâzən] *a* (*fig*) puffed up, self-important.
Aufgebot [ouf'gəbō:t] *nt* supply; (*von Kräften*) utilization; (*Ehe~*) banns *pl.*
aufgedonnert [ouf'gədonərt] *a* (*pej umg*) tarted up.
aufgedreht [ouf'gədrā:t] *a* (*umg*) excited.
aufgedunsen [ouf'gādōōnzən] *a* swollen, puffed up.
aufgegeben [ouf'gəgā:bən] *pp von* **aufgeben**.
aufgehen [ouf'gā:ən] *vi unreg* (*Sonne, Teig*) rise; (*sich öffnen*) open; (*THEAT*: *Vorhang*) go up; (*Knopf, Knoten etc*) come undone; (*klarwerden*) become clear (*jdm to sb*); (*MATH*) come out exactly; (*sich widmen*) be absorbed (*in* +*dat* in); **in Rauch/Flammen** ~ go up in smoke/flames.
aufgeilen [ouf'gīlən] *vtr* (*umg!*) turn on, sexually excite.
aufgeklärt [ouf'gəkle:rt] *a* enlightened; (*sexuell*) knowing the facts of life.
aufgekratzt [ouf'gəkrátst] *a* (*umg*) in high spirits, full of beans.

aufgelaufen [ouf'gəloufən] *a:* ~**e Zinsen** *pl* accrued interest.
Aufgeld *nt* extra charge.
aufgelegt [ouf'gəlä:kt] *a:* **gut/schlecht** ~ **sein** be in a good/bad mood; **zu etw** ~ **sein** be in the mood for sth.
aufgenommen [ouf'gənomən] *pp von* **aufnehmen.**
aufgeregt [ouf'gərä:kt] *a* excited.
aufgeschlossen [ouf'gəshlosən] *a* open, open-minded.
aufgeschmissen [ouf'gəshmisən] *a* (*umg*) in a fix, stuck.
aufgeschrieben [ouf'gəshrē:bən] *pp von* **aufschreiben.**
aufgestanden [ouf'gəshtåndən] *pp von* **aufstehen.**
aufgetakelt [ouf'gətåkəlt] *a* (*fig umg*) all decked out.
aufgeweckt [ouf'gəvekt] *a* bright, intelligent.
aufgießen [ouf'gē:sən] *vt unreg* (*Wasser*) pour over; (*Tee*) infuse.
aufgliedern [ouf'glē:dərn] *vr* (sub)divide, break down (*in* +*akk* into).
aufgreifen [ouf'grīfən] *vt unreg* (*Thema*) take up; (*Verdächtige*) pick up, seize.
aufgrund [oufgrōōnt'] *präp* +*gen* on the basis of; (*wegen*) because of.
Aufgußbeutel [ouf'gōōsboitəl] *m* sachet (containing coffee/herbs *etc*) for brewing; (*Teebeutel*) tea bag.
aufhaben [ouf'håbən] *vt unreg* have on; (*Arbeit*) have to do.
aufhalsen [ouf'hålzən] *vt* (*umg*): **jdm etw** ~ saddle sb with sth.
aufhalten [ouf'håltən] *unreg vt* (*Person*) detain; (*Entwicklung*) check; (*Tür, Hand*) hold open; (*Augen*) keep open; (*abhalten, stören*) hold back, keep back (*bei* from); ♦ *vr* (*wohnen*) live; (*bleiben*) stay; **sich über etw/jdn** ~ go on about sth/sb; **sich mit etw** ~ waste time over sth; **sich bei etw** ~ (*sich befassen*) dwell on sth.
aufhängen [ouf'hengən] *unreg vt* (*Wäsche*) hang up; (*Menschen*) hang ♦ *vr* hang o.s.
Aufhänger *m* -**s,** - (*am Mantel*) hook; (*fig*) peg.
Aufhängung *f* (*TECH*) suspension.
aufheben [ouf'hā:bən] *unreg vt* (*hochheben*) raise, lift; (*Sitzung*) wind up; (*Urteil*) annul; (*Gesetz*) repeal, abolish; (*aufbewahren*) keep; (*ausgleichen*) offset, make up for ♦ *vr* cancel itself out; **viel A**~**(s) machen** make a fuss (*von* about); **bei jdm gut aufgehoben sein** be well looked after at sb's.
aufheitern [ouf'hītərn] *vtr* (*Himmel, Miene*) brighten; (*Mensch*) cheer up.
aufheizen [ouf'hītsən] *vt:* **die Stimmung** ~ stir up feelings.
aufhelfen [ouf'helfən] *vi unreg* (*lit: beim Aufstehen*) help up (*jdm* sb).
aufhellen [ouf'helən] *vtr* clear up; (*Farbe, Haare*) lighten.
aufhetzen [ouf'hetsən] *vt* stir up (*gegen* against).
aufheulen [ouf'hoilən] *vi* howl (*vor* with); (*Sirene*) (start to) wail; (*Motor*) (give a) roar.
aufholen [ouf'hō:lən] *vt* make up ♦ *vi* catch up.
aufhorchen [ouf'horĊHən] *vi* prick up one's ears.
aufhören [ouf'hœrən] *vi* stop; ~, **etw zu tun** stop doing sth.
aufkaufen [ouf'koufən] *vt* buy up.
aufklappen [ouf'klåpən] *vt* open; (*Verdeck*) fold back.
aufklären [ouf'kle:rən] *vt* (*Geheimnis etc*) clear up; (*Person*) enlighten; (*sexuell*) tell the facts of life to; (*MIL*) reconnoiter (*US*), reconnoitre (*Brit*) ♦ *vr* clear up.
Aufklärung *f* (*von Geheimnis*) clearing up; (*Unterrichtung, Zeitalter*) enlightenment; (*sexuell*) sex education; (*MIL, AVIAT*) reconnaissance.
Aufklärungsarbeit *f* educational work.
aufkleben [ouf'klā:bən] *vt* stick on.
Aufkleber *m* -**s,** - sticker.
aufknöpfen [ouf'knœpfən] *vt* unbutton.
aufkochen [ouf'koĊHən] *vt* bring to the boil.
aufkommen [ouf'komən] *vi unreg* (*Wind*) come up; (*Zweifel, Gefühl*) arise; (*Mode*) start; **für jdn/etw** ~ be liable *od* responsible for sb/sth; **für den Schaden** ~ pay for the damage; **endlich kam Stimmung auf** at last things livened up.
aufkreuzen [ouf'kroitsən] *vi* (*umg: erscheinen*) turn *od* show up.
aufkündigen [ouf'kündigən] *vt* (*Vertrag etc*) terminate.
aufladen [ouf'ládən] *unreg vt* load; **jdm/sich etw** ~ (*fig*) saddle sb/o.s. with sth ♦ *vr* (*Batterie etc*) be charged; (*neu* ~) be recharged.
Auflage [ouf'lågə] *f* edition; (*Zeitung*) circulation; (*Bedingung*) condition; **jdm etw zur** ~ **machen** make sth a condition for sb.
Auflage(n)höhe *f* (*von Buch*) number of copies published; (*von Zeitung*) circulation.
auflassen [ouf'låsən] *vt unreg* (*umg: offen*) leave open; (: *aufgesetzt*) leave on; **die Kinder länger** ~ let the children stay up (longer).
auflauern [ouf'louərn] *vi:* **jdm** ~ lie in wait for sb.
Auflauf [ouf'louf] *m* (*KOCH*) pudding; (*Menschen*~) crowd.
auflaufen *vi unreg* (*auf Grund laufen: Schiff*) run aground (*auf* +*akk od dat* on); **jdn** ~ **lassen** (*umg*) drop sb in it.
Auflaufform *f* (*KOCH*) ovenproof dish.
aufleben [ouf'lā:bən] *vi* revive.
auflegen [ouf'lā:gən] *vt* put on; (*Hörer*) put down; (*TYP*) print ♦ *vi* (*TEL*) hang up.
auflehnen [ouf'lā:nən] *vt* lean on ♦ *vr* rebel (*gegen* against).
Auflehnung *f* rebellion.
auflesen [ouf'lā:zən] *vt unreg* pick up.
aufleuchten [ouf'loiĊHtən] *vi* light up.

aufliegen |ouf'lē:gən| *vi unreg* lie on; (*COMM*) be available.

auflisten |ouf'listən| *vr* list ♦ *vt* (*COMPUT*) list.

auflockern |ouf'lokərn| *vt* loosen; (*fig: Eintönigkeit etc*) liven up; (*entspannen, zwangloser machen*) make relaxed; (*Atmosphäre auch*) ease.

auflösen |ouf'lœzən| *vt* dissolve; (*Haare etc*) loosen; (*Mißverständnis*) sort out; (*Konto*) close; (*Haushalt*) break up; (**in Tränen**) **aufgelöst sein** be in tears.

Auflösung *f* dissolving; (*fig*) solution; (*Bildschirm*) resolution.

aufmachen |ouf'mákhən| *vt* open; (*Kleidung*) undo; (*zurechtmachen*) do up ♦ *vr* set out.

Aufmacher *m* (*PRESSE*) lead.

Aufmachung *f* (*Kleidung*) outfit, get-up; (*Gestaltung*) format.

aufmerksam |ouf'merkzàm| *a* attentive; **auf etw** (*akk*) ~ **werden** become aware of sth; (**das ist**) **sehr** ~ **von Ihnen** (*zuvorkommend*) (that's) most kind of you; **jdn auf etw** (*akk*) ~ **machen** point sth out to sb; **A~keit** *f* attention, attentiveness; (*Geschenk*) token (gift).

aufmöbeln |ouf'mœ:bəln| *vt* (*umg: Gegenstand*) do up; (: *beleben*) buck up, pep up.

aufmucken |ouf'moōkən| *vi* (*umg*) protest (*gegen* at, against).

aufmuntern |ouf'moōntərn| *vt* (*ermutigen*) encourage; (*erheitern*) cheer up.

aufmüpfig |ouf'müpfichh| *a* (*umg*) rebellious.

Aufnahme |ouf'námə| *f* -, **-n** reception; (*Beginn*) beginning; (*in Verein etc*) admission; (*in Liste etc*) inclusion; (*Notieren*) taking down; (*PHOT*) shot; (*auf Tonband etc*) recording; **~antrag** *m* application for membership *od* admission; **a~fähig** *a* receptive; **~leiter** *m* (*FILM*) production manager; (*RAD, TV*) producer; **~prüfung** *f* entrance test.

aufnehmen |ouf'ná:mən| *vt unreg* receive; (*hochheben*) pick up; (*beginnen*) take up; (*in Verein etc*) admit; (*in Liste etc*) include; (*fassen*) hold; (*begreifen auch*) grasp; (*beim Stricken: Maschen*) increase, make; (*notieren*) take down; (*photographieren*) photograph; (*auf Tonband, Platte*) record; (*FIN: leihen*) take out; **es mit jdm** ~ **können** be able to compete with sb.

aufnötigen |ouf'nœtigən| *vt*: **jdm etw** ~ force sth on sb.

aufoktroyieren |ouf'oktrōáyē:rən| *vt*: **jdm etw** ~ (*geh*) impose *od* force sth on sb.

aufopfern |ouf'opfərn| *vtr* sacrifice.

aufopfernd *a* selfless.

aufpassen |ouf'pásən| *vi* (*aufmerksam sein*) pay attention; **auf jdn/etw** ~ look after *od* watch sb/sth; **aufgepaßt!** look out!

Aufpasser(in *f*) *m* **-s, -** (*pej: Aufseher, Spitzel*) spy, watchdog; (*Beobachter*) supervisor; (*Wächter*) guard.

aufpflanzen |ouf'pflàntsən| *vr*: **sich vor jdm** ~ **plant** o.s. in front of sb.

aufplatzen |ouf'plátsən| *vi* burst open.

aufplustern |ouf'plōō:stərn| *vr* (*Vogel*) ruffle (up) its feathers; (*Mensch*) puff o.s. up.

aufprägen |ouf'pre:gən| *vt*: **jdm/einer Sache seinen Stempel** ~ (*fig*) leave one's mark on sb/sth.

Aufprall |ouf'prál| *m* **-(e)s, -e** impact.

aufprallen *vi* hit, strike.

Aufpreis |ouf'prīs| *m* extra charge.

aufpumpen |ouf'poōmpən| *vt* pump up.

aufputschen |ouf'poōtshən| *vt* (*aufhetzen*) inflame; (*erregen*) stimulate.

Aufputschmittel *nt* stimulant.

aufraffen |ouf'ráfən| *vr* rouse o.s.

aufräumen |ouf'roimən| *vti* (*Dinge*) clear away; (*Zimmer*) tidy up.

Aufräumungsarbeiten *pl* clearing-up operations *pl*.

aufrecht |ouf'rechht| *a* (*lit, fig*) upright.

aufrechterhalten *vt unreg* maintain.

aufregen |ouf'rā:gən| *vt* excite; (*ärgerlich machen*) irritate, annoy; (*nervös machen*) make nervous; (*beunruhigen*) disturb ♦ *vr* get excited.

aufregend *a* exciting.

Aufregung *f* excitement.

aufreiben |ouf'rībən| *vt unreg* (*Haut*) rub raw; (*erschöpfen*) exhaust; (*MIL: völlig vernichten*) wipe out, annihilate.

aufreibend *a* strenuous.

aufreihen |ouf'rīən| *vt* (*in Linie*) line up; (*Perlen*) string.

aufreißen |ouf'rīsən| *vt unreg* (*Umschlag*) tear open; (*Augen*) open wide; (*Tür*) throw open; (*Straße*) take up; (*umg: Mädchen*) pick up.

Aufreißer *m* **-s, -** (*Person*) smooth operator.

aufreizen |ouf'rītsən| *vt* incite, stir up.

aufreizend *a* exciting, stimulating.

aufrichten |ouf'richhtən| *vt* put up, erect; (*moralisch*) console ♦ *vr* rise; (*moralisch*) take heart (*an* +*dat* from); **sich im Bett** ~ sit up in bed.

aufrichtig |ouf'richhtichh| *a* sincere; honest; **A~keit** *f* sincerity.

aufrollen |ouf'rolən| *vt* (*zusammenrollen*) roll up; (*Kabel*) coil *od* wind up; **einen Fall/ Prozeß wieder** ~ reopen a case/trial.

aufrücken |ouf'rükən| *vi* move up; (*beruflich*) be promoted.

Aufruf |ouf'rōō:f| *m* summons; (*zur Hilfe*) call; (*des Namens*) calling out.

aufrufen *vt unreg* (*auffordern*) call upon (*zu* for); (*Namen*) call out; **einen Schüler** ~ ask a pupil (to answer) a question.

Aufruhr |ouf'rōō:r| *m* **-(e)s, -e** uprising, revolt; **in** ~ **sein** be in uproar.

Aufrührer(in *f*) *m* **-s, -** rabble-rouser.

aufrührerisch |ouf'rü:rərish| *a* rebellious.

aufrunden |ouf'rōōndən| *vt* (*Summe*) round up.

aufrüsten |ouf'rüstən| *vti* arm.

Aufrüstung *f* rearmament.

aufrütteln [ouf'rütəln] *vt* (*lit*, *fig*) shake up.

aufs [oufs] = **auf das.**

aufsagen [ouf'zågən] *vt* (*Gedicht*) recite; (*geh*: *Freundschaft*) put an end to.

aufsammeln [ouf'zåməln] *vt* gather up.

aufsässig [ouf'zesiçh] *a* rebellious.

Aufsatz [ouf'zåts] *m* (*Geschriebenes*) essay; (*Schul~ auch*) composition; (*auf Schrank etc*) top.

aufsaugen [ouf'zougən] *vt unreg* soak up.

aufschauen [ouf'shouən] *vi* look up.

aufscheuchen [ouf'shoiçhən] *vt* scare *od* frighten away.

aufschichten [ouf'shiçhtən] *vt* stack, pile up.

aufschieben [ouf'shē:bən] *vt unreg* push open; (*verzögern*) put off, postpone.

Aufschlag [ouf'shlåk] *m* (*Ärmel~*) cuff; (*Jacken~*) lapel; (*Hosen~*) cuff (*US*), turn-up (*Brit*); (*Aufprall*) impact; (*Preis~*) surcharge; (*TENNIS*) service.

aufschlagen [ouf'shlågən] *unreg vt* (*öffnen*) open; (*verwunden*) cut; (*hochschlagen*) turn up; (*aufbauen: Zelt, Lager*) pitch, erect; (*Wohnsitz*) take up; **schlagt Seite 111 auf** open your books at page 111 ♦ *vi* (*aufprallen*) hit; (*teurer werden*) go up; (*TENNIS*) serve.

aufschließen [ouf'shlē:sən] *unreg vt* open up, unlock ♦ *vi* (*aufrücken*) close up.

Aufschluß [ouf'shlōos] *m* information.

aufschlüsseln [ouf'shlüsəln] *vt* break down (*nach* into); (*klassifizieren*) classify (*nach* according to).

aufschlußreich *a* informative, illuminating.

aufschnappen [ouf'shnåpən] *vt* (*umg*) pick up ♦ *vi* fly open.

aufschneiden [ouf'shnīdən] *unreg vt* (*Geschwür*) cut open; (*Brot*) cut up; (*MED*) lance ♦ *vi* (*umg*) brag.

Aufschneider *m* -s, - boaster, braggart.

Aufschnitt [ouf'shnit] *m* (slices of) cold meat.

aufschnüren [ouf'shnü:rən] *vt* unlace; (*Paket*) untie.

aufschrauben [ouf'shroubən] *vt* (*fest~*) screw on; (*lösen*) unscrew.

aufschrecken [ouf'shrekən] *vt* startle ♦ *vi unreg* start up.

Aufschrei [ouf'shrī] *m* cry; **a~en** *vi unreg* cry out.

aufschreiben [ouf'shrībən] *vt unreg* write down.

Aufschrift [ouf'shrift] *f* (*Inschrift*) inscription; (*Etikett*) label.

Aufschub [ouf'shōō:p] *m* -(e)s, -schübe delay, postponement; **jdm ~ gewähren** grant sb an extension.

aufschürfen [ouf'shürfən] *vt*: **sich** (*dat*) **die Haut/das Knie ~** graze *od* scrape o.s./one's knee.

aufschütten [ouf'shütən] *vt* (*Flüssigkeit*) pour on; (*Kohle*) put on (the fire); (*Damm, Deich*) throw up; **Kaffee ~** make coffee.

aufschwatzen [ouf'shvåtsən] *vt* (*umg*): **jdm**

etw ~ talk sb into (getting/having *etc*) sth.

Aufschwung [ouf'shvōōng] *m* (*Elan*) boost; (*wirtschaftlich*) upturn, boom; (*SPORT*) circle.

aufsehen [ouf'zā:ən] *vi unreg* (*lit*, *fig*) look up (*zu* (*lit*) at, (*fig*) to).

Aufsehen *nt* -s sensation, stir; **a~erregend** *a* sensational.

Aufseher(in *f*) *m* -s, - guard; (*im Betrieb*) supervisor; (*Museums~*) attendant; (*Park~*) keeper.

aufsein [ouf'zīn] *vi unreg* (*umg*) be open; (*Person*) be up.

aufsetzen [ouf'zetsən] *vt* put on; (*Flugzeug*) put down; (*Dokument*) draw up ♦ *vr* sit upright ♦ *vi* (*Flugzeug*) touch down.

Aufsicht [ouf'ziçht] *f* supervision; **die ~ haben** be in charge; **bei einer Prüfung ~ führen** supervise an exam.

Aufsichtsrat *m* board (of directors).

aufsitzen [ouf'zitsən] *vi unreg* (*aufrecht hinsitzen*) sit up; (*aufs Pferd, Motorrad*) mount, get on; (*Schiff*) run aground; **jdn ~ lassen** (*umg*) stand sb up; **jdm ~** (*umg*) be taken in by sb.

aufspalten [ouf'shpåltən] *vt* split.

aufspannen [ouf'shpånən] *vt* (*Netz, Sprungtuch*) stretch *od* spread out; (*Schirm*) put up, open.

aufsparen [ouf'shpårən] *vt* save (up).

aufsperren [ouf'shpərən] *vt* unlock; (*Mund*) open wide; **die Ohren ~** (*umg*) prick up one's ears.

aufspielen [ouf'shpē:lən] *vr* show off; **sich als etw ~** try to come on as sth.

aufspießen [ouf'shpē:sən] *vt* spear.

aufspringen [ouf'shpringən] *vi unreg* jump (*auf +akk* onto); (*hochspringen*) jump up; (*sich öffnen*) spring open; (*Hände, Lippen*) become chapped.

aufspüren [ouf'shpü:rən] *vt* track down, trace.

aufstacheln [ouf'shtåkhəln] *vt* incite.

aufstampfen [ouf'shtåmpfən] *vi*: **mit dem Fuß ~** stamp one's foot.

Aufstand [ouf'shtånt] *m* insurrection, rebellion.

aufständisch [ouf'shtendish] *a* rebellious, mutinous.

aufstauen [ouf'shtouən] *vr* collect; (*fig: Ärger*) be bottled up.

aufstechen [ouf'shteçhən] *vt unreg* prick open, puncture.

aufstecken [ouf'shtekən] *vt* stick on; (*mit Nadeln*) pin up; (*umg*) give up.

aufstehen [ouf'shtā:ən] *vi unreg* get up; (*Tür*) be open; **da mußt du früher** *od* **eher ~!** (*fig umg*) you'll have to do better than that!

aufsteigen [ouf'shtīgən] *vi unreg* (*auf etw*) get onto; (*hochsteigen*) climb; (*Rauch*) rise; **in jdm ~** (*Haß, Verdacht, Erinnerung etc*) well up in sb.

Aufsteiger *m* -s,- (*SPORT*) team promoted to

the top league; **(sozialer)** ~ social climber.

aufstellen [ouf'shtelən] *vt* (*aufrecht stellen*) put up; (*Maschine*) install; (*aufreihen*) line up; (*Kandidaten*) nominate; (*Forderung, Behauptung*) put forward; (*formulieren: Programm etc*) draw up; (*leisten: Rekord*) set up.

Aufstellung *f* (*SPORT*) line-up; (*Liste*) list.

Aufstieg [ouf'shtē:k] *m* **-(e)s, -e** (*auf Berg*) ascent; (*Fortschritt*) rise; (*beruflich, SPORT*) promotion.

Aufstiegschance *f* -, **-n, Aufstiegsmöglichkeit** *f* prospect of promotion.

aufstöbern [ouf'shtœbərn] *vt* (*Wild*) start, flush; (*umg: entdecken*) track down.

aufstocken [ouf'shtokən] *vt* (*Vorräte*) build up.

aufstoßen [ouf'shtō:sən] *unreg vt* push open ♦ *vi* belch.

aufstrebend [ouf'shtrā:bənd] *a* ambitious; (*Land*) up-and-coming.

Aufstrich [ouf'shtrich] *m* spread.

aufstülpen [ouf'shtülpən] *vt* (*Ärmel*) turn up; (*Hut*) put on.

aufstützen [ouf'shtütsən] *vr* lean (*auf +akk* on) ♦ *vt* (*Körperteil*) prop, lean; (*Person*) prop up.

aufsuchen [ouf'zōō:khən] *vt* (*besuchen*) visit; (*konsultieren*) consult.

auftakeln [ouf'tākəln] *vt* (*NAUT*) rig (out) ♦ *vr* (*pej umg*) deck o.s. out.

Auftakt [ouf'tákt] *m* (*MUS*) upbeat; (*fig*) prelude.

auftanken [ouf'tángkən] *vi* get gas (*US*)) *od* petrol (*Brit*) ♦ *vt* refuel.

auftauchen [ouf'toukhən] *vi* appear; (*gefunden werden, kommen*) turn up; (*aus Wasser etc*) emerge; (*U-Boot*) surface; (*Zweifel*) arise.

auftauen [ouf'touən] *vti* thaw; (*fig*) relax.

aufteilen [ouf'tīlən] *vt* divide up; (*Raum*) partition.

Aufteilung *f* division; partition.

auftischen [ouf'tishən] *vt* serve (up); (*fig*) tell.

Auftr. *abk* = **Auftrag.**

Auftrag [ouf'trák] *m* **-(e)s, -träge** order; (*Anweisung*) commission; (*Aufgabe*) mission; **etw in** ~ **geben** order/commission sth (*bei* from); **im** ~ **von** on behalf of; **im** ~ *od* **i.A. J. Burnett** pp J. Burnett.

auftragen [ouf'trágən] *unreg vt* (*Essen*) serve; (*Farbe*) put on; (*Kleidung*) wear out; **jdm etw** ~ tell sb sth ♦ *vi* (*dick machen*) make you/me *etc* look fat; **dick** ~ (*umg*) exaggerate.

Auftraggeber(in *f*) *m* **-s, -** (*COMM*) purchaser, customer.

Auftragsbestätigung *f* confirmation of order.

auftreiben [ouf'trībən] *vt* *unreg* (*umg: beschaffen*) raise.

auftrennen [ouf'trenən] *vt* undo.

auftreten [ouf'trā:tən] *unreg vt* kick open ♦ *vi*

appear; (*mit Füßen*) tread; (*sich verhalten*) behave; (*fig: eintreten*) occur; (*Schwierigkeiten etc*) arise; **als Vermittler** *etc* ~ act as intermediary *etc*; **geschlossen** ~ put up a united front.

Auftreten *nt* **-s** (*Vorkommen*) appearance; (*Benehmen*) behavior (*US*), behaviour (*Brit*).

Auftrieb [ouf'trē:p] *m* (*PHYS*) buoyancy, lift; (*fig*) impetus.

Auftritt [ouf'trit] *m* (*des Schauspielers*) entrance; (*lit, fig: Szene*) scene.

auftrumpfen [ouf'trōōmpfən] *vi* show how good one is, crow.

auftun [ouf'tōō:n] *unreg vt* (*umg*) open ♦ *vr* open up.

auftürmen [ouf'türmən] *vr* (*Gebirge etc*) tower up; (*Schwierigkeiten*) pile *od* mount up.

aufwachen [ouf'vákhən] *vi* wake up.

aufwachsen [ouf'váksən] *vi* *unreg* grow up.

Aufwand [ouf'vánt] *m* **-(e)s** expenditure; (*Kosten auch*) expense; (*Luxus*) show; **bitte, keinen** ~! please don't go out of your way.

Aufwandsentschädigung *f* -, **-en** expense allowance.

aufwärmen [ouf'vermən] *vt* warm up; (*alte Geschichten*) rake up.

aufwarten [ouf'vártən] *vi* (*zu bieten haben*): **mit etw** ~ offer sth.

aufwärts [ouf'verts] *ad* upwards; **A~entwicklung** *f* upward trend.

aufwärtsgehen *vi* *unreg* look up.

aufwecken [ouf'vekən] *vt* wake(n) up.

aufweichen [ouf'vīchən] *vt* soften; (*Brot*) soak.

aufweisen [ouf'vīzən] *vt* *unreg* show.

aufwenden [ouf'vendən] *vt* *unreg* expend; (*Geld*) spend; (*Sorgfalt*) devote.

aufwendig *a* costly.

aufwerfen [ouf'verfən] *unreg vt* (*Fenster etc*) throw open; (*Probleme*) throw up, raise ♦ *vr*: **sich zu etw** ~ make o.s. out to be sth.

aufwerten [ouf'vertən] *vt* (*FIN*) revalue; (*fig*) raise in value.

Aufwertung *f* revaluation.

aufwickeln [ouf'vikəln] *vt* (*aufrollen*) roll up; (*umg: Haar*) put in curlers; (*lösen*) untie.

aufwiegeln [ouf'vē:gəln] *vt* stir up, incite.

aufwiegen [ouf'vē:gən] *vt* *unreg* make up for.

Aufwind [ouf'vint] *m* up-current; **neuen** ~ **bekommen** (*fig*) get new impetus.

aufwirbeln [ouf'virbəln] *vt* whirl up; **Staub** ~ (*fig*) create a stir.

aufwischen [ouf'vishən] *vt* wipe up.

aufwühlen [ouf'vü:lən] *vt* (*lit: Erde, Meer*) churn (up); (*Gefühle*) stir.

aufzählen [ouf'tse:lən] *vt* count out.

aufzeichnen [ouf'tsichnən] *vt* sketch; (*schriftlich*) jot down; (*auf Band*) record.

Aufzeichnung *f* (*schriftlich*) note; (*Tonband~, Film~*) recording.

aufzeigen [ouf'tsigən] *vt* show, demonstrate.

aufziehen [ouf'tsē:ən] *unreg vt* (*hochziehen*) raise, draw up; (*öffnen*) pull open; (:

Reißverschluß) undo; (*Gardinen*) draw (back); (*Uhr*) wind; (*umg*: *necken*) tease; (*großziehen*: *Kinder*) raise, bring up; (*Tiere*) rear; (*umg*: *veranstalten*) set up; (: *Fest*) arrange ♦ *vi* (*Gewitter, Wolken*) gather.

Aufzucht [ouf'tsooχht] *f* (*das Großziehen*) rearing, raising.

Aufzug [ouf'tsoo:k] *m* (*Fahrstuhl*) elevator (*US*), lift (*Brit*); (*Aufmarsch*) procession, parade; (*Kleidung*) get-up; (*THEAT*) act.

aufzwingen [ouf'tsvingən] *vt unreg*: **jdm etw** ~ force sth upon sb.

Aug. *abk* (= *August*) Aug.

Augapfel [ouk'äpfəl] *m* eyeball; (*fig*) apple of one's eye.

Auge [ou'gə] *nt* **-s, -n** eye; (*Fett*~) globule of fat; **unter vier** ~**n** in private; **vor aller** ~**n** in front of everybody, for all to see; **jdn/etw mit anderen** ~**n** (**an**)**sehen** see sb/sth in a different light; **ich habe kein** ~ **zugetan** I didn't sleep a wink; **ein** ~**/beide** ~**n zudrücken** (*umg*) turn a blind eye; **jdn/etw aus den** ~**n verlieren** lose sight of sb/sth; (*fig*) lose touch with sb/sth; **etw ins** ~ **fassen** contemplate sth; **das kann leicht ins** ~ **gehen** (*fig, umg*) it might easily go wrong.

Augenarzt *m* eye specialist, ophthalmologist.

Augenblick *m* moment; **im** ~ at the moment; **im ersten** ~ for a moment; **im** ~**lich** *a* (*sofort*) instantaneous; (*gegenwärtig*) present.

Augen- *zW*: ~**braue** *f* eyebrow; ~**höhe** *f*: **in** ~**höhe** at eye level; ~**merk** *nt* (*Aufmerksamkeit*) attention; ~**schein** *m*: **jdn/etw in** ~**schein nehmen** have a close look at sb/sth; **a**~**scheinlich** *a* obvious; ~**weide** *f* sight for sore eyes; ~**wischerei** *f* (*fig*) eye-wash; ~**zeuge** *m*, ~**zeugin** *f* eye witness.

August [ougoost'] *m* **-(e)s** *od* **-, -e** August *siehe* **September**.

Auktion [ouktsēo:n'] *f* auction.

Auktionator [ouktsēonä'tor] *m* auctioneer.

Aula [ou'lä] *f* **-, Aulen** *od* **-s** assembly hall.

Auma *m* **-** *abk* = *Ausstellungs- Und Messe-Ausschuß Der Deutschen Wirtschaft*.

aus [ous] *präp* +*dat* out of; (*von ... her*) from; (*Material*) made of; ♦ *ad* out; (*beendet*) finished, over; (*ausgezogen*) off; ~ **Erfahrung** from experience; ~ **Spaß** for fun; ~ **ihr wird nie etwas** she'll never get anywhere; ~ **und ein gehen** come and go; (*bei jdm*) visit frequently; **weder** ~ **noch ein wissen** not to know which way to go; **auf etw** (*akk*) ~ **sein** be after sth; **vom Fenster** ~ from the window; **von Rom** ~ from Rome; **von sich** ~ of one's own accord; ~ **und vorbei** over and done with; **ok, von mir** ~ OK, if you like.

Aus *nt* **- : ins** ~ **gehen** go out of bounds.

ausarbeiten [ous'ärbitən] *vt* work out.

ausarten [ous'ärtən] *vi* degenerate; (*Kind*) become overexcited.

ausatmen [ous'ätmən] *vi* breathe out.

ausbaden [ous'bädən] *vt* (*umg*): **etw** ~ **müssen** take the rap for sth.

Ausbau [ous'bou] *m* extension, expansion; removal.

ausbauen *vt* extend, expand; (*herausnehmen*) take out, remove.

ausbaufähig *a* (*fig*) worth developing.

ausbedingen [ous'bədingən] *vt unreg*: **sich** (*dat*) **etw** ~ insist on sth.

ausbeißen [ous'bīsən] *vr unreg*: **sich** (*dat*) **an etw** (*dat*) **die Zähne** ~ (*fig*) have a tough time of it with sth.

ausbessern [ous'besərn] *vt* mend, repair.

Ausbesserungsarbeiten *pl* repair work *sing*.

ausbeulen [ous'boilən] *vt* beat out.

Ausbeute [ous'boitə] *f* yield; (*Gewinn*) profit, gain; (*Fische*) catch.

ausbeuten *vt* exploit; (*MIN*) work.

ausbezahlen [ous'bətsälən] *vt* (*Geld*) pay out.

ausbilden [ous'bildən] *vt* educate; (*Lehrling, Soldat*) instruct, train; (*Fähigkeiten*) develop; (*Geschmack*) cultivate.

Ausbilder(in *f*) *m* **-s, -** instructor; instructress.

Ausbildung *f* education; training, instruction; development; cultivation; **er ist noch in der** ~ he's still a trainee; he hasn't finished his education.

Ausbildungsplatz *m* (*Stelle*) training vacancy.

ausbitten [ous'bitən] *vt unreg*: **sich** (*dat*) **etw** ~ (*geh*: *erbitten*) ask for sth; (*verlangen*) insist on sth.

ausblasen [ous'bläzən] *vt unreg* blow out; (*Ei*) blow.

ausbleiben [ous'blībən] *vi unreg* (*Personen*) stay away, not come; (*Ereignisse*) fail to happen, not happen; **es konnte nicht** ~**, daß** ... it was inevitable that ...

ausblenden [ous'blendən] *vti* (*TV etc*) fade out.

Ausblick [ous'blik] *m* (*lit, fig*) prospect, outlook, view.

ausbomben [ous'bombən] *vt* bomb out.

ausbooten [ous'bō:tən] *vt* (*umg*: *jdn*) kick *od* boot out.

ausbrechen [ous'brechən] *unreg vi* break out; ♦ *vt* break off; **in Tränen/Gelächter** ~ burst into tears/out laughing.

Ausbrecher(in *f*) *m* **-s, -** (*umg*: *Gefangener*) escaped prisoner, escapee.

ausbreiten [ous'brītən] *vt* spread (out); (*Arme*) stretch out ♦ *vr* spread; (*über Thema*) expand, enlarge (*über* +*akk* on).

ausbrennen [ous'brenən] *unreg vt* scorch; (*Wunde*) cauterize ♦ *vi* burn out.

ausbringen [ous'bringən] *vt unreg* (*ein Hoch*) propose.

Ausbruch [ous'brooχh] *m* outbreak; (*von Vulkan*) eruption; (*Gefühls*~) outburst; (*von Gefangenen*) escape.

ausbrüten [ous'brü:tən] *vt* (*lit, fig*) hatch.
Ausbuchtung [ous'bōōkhtōōng] *f* bulge;
(*Küste*) cove.
ausbügeln [ous'bü:gəln] *vt* iron out; (*umg:
Fehler, Verlust*) make good.
ausbuhen [ous'bōō:ən] *vt* boo.
Ausbund [ous'bōōnt] *m*: **ein** ~ **an** *od* **von
Tugend/Sparsamkeit** a paragon of virtue/a
model of thrift.
ausbürgern [ous'bürgərn] *vt*: **jdn** ~ expatriate sb.
ausbürsten [ous'bürstən] *vt* brush out.
Ausdauer [ous'douər] *f* perseverance; stamina.
ausdauernd *a* persevering.
ausdehnen [ous'dā:nən] *vtr* (*räumlich*)
expand; (*Gummi*) stretch; (*Nebel*) extend;
(*zeitlich*) stretch; (*fig: Macht*) extend.
ausdenken [ous'dengkən] *vt unreg* (*zu Ende
denken*) think through; **sich** (*dat*) **etw** ~
think sth up; **das ist nicht auszudenken**
(*unvorstellbar*) it's inconceivable.
ausdiskutieren [ous'diskōōtē:rən] *vt* talk out.
ausdrehen [ous'drā:ən] *vt* turn *od* switch off;
(*Licht auch*) turn out.
Ausdruck [ous'drōōk] *m* **-s**, **-drücke** expression, phrase; (*Kundgabe, Gesichts*~) expression; (*Fach*~ *auch*) term; (*COMPUT*) hard
copy; **mit dem** ~ **des Bedauerns** (*form*)
expressing regret.
ausdrucken *vt* (*Text*) print out.
ausdrücken [ous'drükən] *vt* (*auch vr: formulieren, zeigen*) express; (*Zigarette*) put out;
(*Zitrone*) squeeze.
ausdrücklich *a* express, explicit.
Ausdrucks- *zW*: ~**fähigkeit** *f* expressive-
ness; (*Gewandtheit*) articulateness; **a**~**los** *a*
expressionless, blank; **a**~**voll** *a* expressive;
~**weise** *f* mode of expression.
Ausdünstung [ous'dünstōōng] *f* (*Dampf*) vapor (*US*), vapour (*Brit*); (*Geruch*) smell.
auseinander [ousinàn'dər] *ad* (*getrennt*)
apart; **weit** ~ far apart; ~ **schreiben** write
as separate words; ~**bringen** *vt unreg* separate; ~**fallen** *vi unreg* fall apart; ~**gehen**
vi unreg (*Menschen*) separate; (*Meinungen*)
differ; (*Gegenstand*) fall apart; (*umg: dick
werden*) put on weight; ~**halten** *vt unreg*
tell apart; ~**klaffen** *vi* gape open; (*fig: Meinungen*) be far apart, diverge (wildly);
~**laufen** *vi unreg* (*umg: sich trennen*) break
up; (*Menge*) disperse; ~**leben** *vr* drift
apart; ~**nehmen** *vt unreg* take to pieces,
dismantle; ~**setzen** *vt* (*erklären*) set forth,
explain ♦ *vr* (*sich verständigen*) come to
terms, settle; (*sich befassen*) concern o.s.;
sich mit jdm ~**setzen** talk *od* (*sich streiten*)
argue with sb; **A**~**setzung** *f* argument.
auserkoren [ous'erkō:rən] *a* (*liter*) chosen,
selected.
auserlesen [ous'erlā:zən] *a* select, choice.
ausersehen [ous'erzä:ən] *vt unreg* (*geh*):
dazu ~ **sein, etw zu tun** be chosen to do
sth.

ausfahrbar *a* extendable; (*Antenne,
Fahrgestell*) retractable.
ausfahren [ous'fârən] *unreg vi* drive out;
(*NAUT*) put out (to sea) ♦ *vt* take out;
(*TECH: Fahrwerk*) drive out ♦ *vr* (*ausliefern: Waren*) deliver; **ausgefahrene Wege**
rutted roads.
Ausfahrt *f* (*des Zuges etc*) leaving, departure; (*Autobahn*~, *Garagen*~) exit, way
out; (*Spazierfahrt*) drive, excursion.
Ausfall [ous'fál] *m* loss; (*Nichtstattfinden*)
cancellation; (*das Versagen: TECH, MED*)
failure; (*von Motor*) breakdown; (*Pro-
duktionsstörung*) stoppage; (*MIL*) sortie;
(*Fechten*) lunge; (*radioaktiv*) fallout.
ausfallen [ous'fálən] *vi unreg* (*Zähne, Haare*)
fall *od* come out; (*nicht stattfinden*) be
cancelled; (*wegbleiben*) be omitted;
(*Person*) drop out; (*Lohn*) be stopped;
(*nicht funktionieren*) break down; (*Resultat
haben*) turn out; **wie ist das Spiel ausgefallen?** what was the result of the game?; **die
Schule fällt morgen aus** there's no school
tomorrow.
ausfallend *a* impertinent.
Ausfallstraße *f* arterial road.
Ausfallzeit *f* (*Maschine*) downtime.
ausfegen [ous'fä:gən] *vt* sweep out.
ausfeilen [ous'fīlən] *vt* file out; (*Stil*) polish
up.
ausfertigen [ous'fertigən] *vt* (*form*) draw up;
(*Rechnung*) make out; **doppelt** ~ duplicate.
Ausfertigung *f* (*form*) drawing up; making
out; (*Exemplar*) copy; **in doppelter/
dreifacher** ~ in duplicate/triplicate.
ausfindig [ous'findich] *a*: ~ **machen** discover.
ausfliegen [ous'flē:gən] *vti unreg* fly away;
sie sind ausgeflogen (*umg*) they're out.
ausfließen [ous'flē:sən] *vi unreg*
(*herausfließen*) flow out (*aus* of); (*auslaufen: Öl etc*) leak (*aus* out of); (*Eiter etc*) be
discharged.
ausflippen [ous'flipən] *vi* (*umg*) freak out.
Ausflucht [ous'flōōkht] *f* **-**, **-flüchte** excuse.
Ausflug [ous'flōō:k] *m* excursion, outing.
Ausflügler(in *f*) [ous'flü:klər(in)] *m* **-s**, **-** vacationer (*US*), tripper (*Brit*).
Ausfluß [ous'flōōs] *m* outlet; (*MED*) discharge.
ausfragen [ous'frâgən] *vt* interrogate, question.
ausfransen [ous'frànzən] *vi* fray.
ausfressen [ous'fresən] *vt unreg* eat up;
(*aushöhlen*) corrode; (*umg: anstellen*) be up
to.
Ausfuhr [ous'fōō:r] *f* **-**, **-en** export, exportation ♦ *in zW* export.
ausführbar [ous'fü:rbâr] *a* feasible; (*COMM*)
exportable.
ausführen [ous'fü:rən] *vt* (*verwirklichen*)
carry out; (*Person*) take out; (*Hund*) take
for a walk; (*COMM*) export; (*erklären*) give
details of; **die ausführende Gewalt** (*POL*)

the executive.

Ausfuhrgenehmigung *f* export license.

ausführlich *a* detailed ♦ *ad* in detail; **A~keit** *f* detail.

Ausführung *f* execution, performance; (*von Waren*) design; (*Thema*) exposition; (*Durchführung*) completion; (*Herstellungsart*) version; (*Erklärung*) explanation.

Ausfuhrzoll *m* export duty.

ausfüllen [ous'fülən] *vt* fill up; (*Fragebogen etc*) fill in; (*Beruf*) be fulfilling for; **jdn (ganz)** ~ (*Zeit in Anspruch nehmen*) take (all) sb's time.

Ausg. *abk* (= *Ausgabe*) ed.

Ausgabe [ous'gábə] *f* (*Geld*) expenditure, outlay; (*Aushändigung*) giving out; (*Schalter*) counter; (*Ausführung*) version; (*Buch*) edition; (*Nummer*) issue.

Ausgang [ous'gáng] *m* way out, exit; (*Ende*) end; (*Ausgangspunkt*) starting point; (*Ergebnis*) result; (*Ausgehtag*) free time, time off; **ein Unfall mit tödlichem** ~ a fatal accident; **kein** ~ no exit.

Ausgangs- *zW:* **~basis** *f*, **~punkt** *m* starting point; **~sperre** *f* curfew.

ausgeben [ous'gā:bən] *unreg vt* (*Geld*) spend; (*austeilen*) issue, distribute; (*COMPUT*) output; **ich gebe heute abend einen aus** (*umg*) it's my treat this evening ♦ *vr:* **sich für etw/jdn** ~ pass o.s. off as sth/sb.

ausgebeult [ous'gəboilt] *a* (*Kleidung*) baggy; (*Hut*) battered.

ausgebucht [ous'gəbōo:k̭ht] *a* fully booked.

Ausgeburt [ous'gəbōo:rt] *f* (*pej: der Phantasie etc*) monstrous product *od* invention.

ausgedehnt [ous'gədā:nt] *a* (*breit, groß, fig*: *weitreichend*) extensive; (*Spaziergang*) long; (*zeitlich*) lengthy.

ausgedient [ous'gədē:nt] *a* (*Soldat*) discharged; (*verbraucht*) no longer in use; ~ **haben** have done good service.

ausgefallen [ous'gəfálən] *a* (*ungewöhnlich*) exceptional.

ausgefuchst [ous'gəfōōkst] *a* (*umg*) clever; (*listig*) crafty.

ausgegangen [ous'gəgángən] *pp von* **ausgehen.**

ausgeglichen [ous'gəglik̭hən] *a* (well-)balanced; **A~heit** *f* balance; (*von Mensch*) even-temperedness.

Ausgehan'zug *m* good suit.

ausgehen [ous'gā:ən] *vi unreg* go out; (*zu Ende gehen*) come to an end; (*Benzin*) run out; (*Haare, Zähne*) fall *od* come out; (*Feuer, Ofen, Licht*) go out; (*Strom*) go off; (*Resultat haben*) turn out; (*spazierengehen auch*) go (out) for a walk; (*abgeschickt werden: Post*) be sent off; **mir ging das Benzin aus** I ran out of gas; **auf etw** (*akk*) ~ aim at sth; **von etw** ~ (*wegführen*) lead away from sth; (*herrühren*) come from sth; (*zugrunde legen*) proceed from sth; **wir können davon** ~**, daß** ... we can proceed

from the assumption that ..., we can take as our starting point that ...; **leer** ~ get nothing; **schlecht** ~ turn out badly.

ausgehungert [ous'gəhōōngərt] *a* starved; (*abgezehrt: Mensch etc*) emaciated.

Ausgehverbot *nt* curfew.

ausgeklügelt [ous'gəklü:gəlt] *a* ingenious.

ausgekocht [ous'gəkok̭ht] *a* (*pej umg: durchtrieben*) cunning; (*fig*) out-and-out.

ausgelassen [ous'gəlásən] *a* boisterous, high-spirited; **A~heit** *f* boisterousness, high spirits *pl*, exuberance.

ausgelastet [ous'gəlàstət] *a* fully occupied.

ausgeleiert [ous'gəliərt] *a* (*Gummiband etc*) worn.

ausgelernt [ous'gəlɛrnt] *a* trained, qualified.

ausgemacht [ous'gəmák̭ht] *a* settled; (*umg: Dummkopf etc*) out-and-out, downright; **es gilt als** ~**, daß** ... it is settled that ...; **es war eine** ~**e Sache, daß** ... it was a foregone conclusion that ...

ausgemergelt [ous'gəmergəlt] *a* (*Gesicht*) emaciated, gaunt.

ausgenommen [ous'gənomən] *präp* +*gen od dat, kj* except; **Anwesende sind** ~ present company excepted.

ausgepowert [ous'gəpō:vərt] *a:* ~ **sein** (*umg*) be tired/exhausted.

ausgeprägt [ous'gəprɛ:kt] *a* prominent; (*Eigenschaft*) distinct.

ausgerechnet [ous'gərek̭hnət] *ad* just, precisely; ~ **du/heute** you of all people/today of all days.

ausgereicht [ous'gərik̭ht] *pp von* **ausreichen.**

ausgeschlossen [ous'gəshlosən] *a* (*unmöglich*) impossible, out of the question; **es ist nicht** ~**, daß** ... it cannot be ruled out that ... ♦ *pp von* **ausschließen.**

ausgeschnitten [ous'gəshnitən] *a* (*Kleid*) low-necked.

ausgesehen [ous'gəzā:ən] *pp von* **aussehen.**

ausgesprochen [ous'gəshprok̭hən] *a* (*Faulheit, Lüge etc*) out-and-out; (*unverkennbar*) marked ♦ *ad* decidedly.

ausgestorben [ous'gəshtorbən] *a* (*Tierart*) extinct; (*fig*) deserted.

ausgewogen [ous'gəvō:gən] *a* balanced; (*Maß*) equal.

ausgezeichnet [ous'gətsik̭hnət] *a* excellent.

ausgiebig [ous'gē:bik̭h] *a* (*Gebrauch*) full, good; (*Essen*) generous, lavish; ~ **schlafen** have a good sleep.

ausgießen [ous'gē:sən] *vt unreg* (*aus einem Behälter*) pour out; (*Behälter*) empty; (*weggießen*) pour away.

Ausgleich [ous'glik̭h] *m* **-(e)s, -e** balance; (*Vermittlung*) reconciliation; (*SPORT*) equalization; **zum** ~ (+*gen*) in order to offset; **das ist ein guter** ~ that's very relaxing.

ausgleichen [ous'glik̭hən] *unreg vt* balance (out); reconcile; (*Höhe*) even up ♦ *vi* (*SPORT*) equalize; **ausgleichende Gerechtigkeit** poetic justice.

Ausgleichs- *zW:* **~sport** *m* fitness activity;

~tor *nt* equalizer.
ausgraben [ous'grâbən] *vt unreg* dig up;
(*Leichen*) exhume; (*fig*) unearth.
Ausgrabung *f* excavation; (*Ausgraben auch*)
digging up.
ausgrenzen [ous'grentsən] *vt* shut out, separate.
Ausgrenzung *f* shut-out, separation.
Ausguck [ous'gōōk] *m* look-out.
Ausguß [ous'gōōs] *m* (*Spüle*) sink; (*Abfluß*)
outlet; (*Tülle*) spout.
aushaben [ous'hâbən] *vt unreg* (*umg*: *Kleidung*) have taken off; (*Buch*) have finished.
aushalten [ous'hâltən] *unreg vt* bear, stand;
(*umg*: *Geliebte*) keep ♦ *vi* hold out; **das ist
nicht zum A~** that is unbearable; **sich von
jdm ~ lassen** be kept by sb.
aushandeln [ous'hándəln] *vt* negotiate.
aushändigen [ous'hendigən] *vt*: **jdm etw ~**
hand sth over to sb.
Aushang [ous'hâng] *m* notice.
aushängen [ous'hengən] *unreg vt* (*Meldung*)
put up; (*Fenster*) take off its hinges ♦ *vi* be
displayed ♦ *vr* hang out.
Aushängeschild *nt* (store) sign.
ausharren [ous'hárən] *vi* hold out.
aushäusig [ous'hoiziçh] *a* gallivanting
around, on a spree.
ausheben [ous'hā:bən] *vt unreg* (*Erde*) lift
out; (*Grube*) hollow out; (*Tür*) take off its
hinges; (*Diebesnest*) clear out; (*MIL*) enlist.
aushecken [ous'hekən] *vt* (*umg*) concoct,
think up.
aushelfen [ous'helfən] *vi unreg*: **jdm ~** help
sb out.
Aushilfe [ous'hilfə] *f* help, assistance;
(*Person*) (temporary) worker.
Aushilfs- *zW*: **~kraft** *f* temporary worker;
~lehrer(in *f*) *m* substitute (*US*) *od* supply
(*Brit*) teacher; **a~weise** *ad* temporarily, as
a stopgap.
aushöhlen [ous'hœlən] *vt* hollow out; (*fig*:
untergraben) undermine.
ausholen [ous'hō:lən] *vi* swing one's arm
back; (*zur Ohrfeige*) raise one's hand;
(*beim Gehen*) take long strides; **weit ~**
(*fig*) be expansive; **zum Gegenschlag ~**
(*lit, fig*) prepare for a counter-attack.
aushorchen [ous'horçhən] *vt* sound out,
pump.
aushungern [ous'hōōngərn] *vt* starve out.
auskennen [ous'kenən] *vr unreg* know a lot;
(*an einem Ort*) know one's way about; (*in
Fragen etc*) be knowledgeable; **man kennt
sich bei ihm nie aus** you never know where
you are with him.
auskippen [ous'kipən] *vt* empty.
ausklammern [ous'klámərn] *vt* (*Thema*)
exclude, leave out.
Ausklang [ous'kláng] *m* (*geh*) end.
ausklappbar [ous'klápbár] *a*: **dieser Tisch ist
~** this table can be opened out.
auskleiden [ous'klīdən] *vr* (*geh*) undress ♦ *vt*
(*Wand*) line.

ausklingen [ous'klingən] *vi unreg* (*Ton, Lied*)
die away; (*Fest*) peter out.
ausklinken [ous'klingkən] *vt* (*umg*: *Bomben*)
release ♦ *vr* (*fig*) lose one's head.
ausklopfen [ous'klopfən] *vt* (*Teppich*) beat;
(*Pfeife*) knock out.
auskochen [ous'koḵhən] *vt* boil; (*MED*) sterilize.
auskommen [ous'komən] *vi unreg*: **mit jdm
~** get along with sb; **mit etw ~** get by with
sth; **A~** *nt* **-s**: **sein A~ haben** get by; **mit
ihr ist kein A~** she's impossible to get along
with.
auskosten [ous'kostən] *vt* enjoy to the full.
auskramen [ous'krámən] *vt* (*umg*) dig out,
unearth; (*fig*: *alte Geschichten etc*) bring
up.
auskratzen [ous'krátsən] *vt* (*auch MED*)
scrape out.
auskugeln [ous'kōō:gəln] *vr*: **sich** (*dat*) **den
Arm ~** dislocate one's arm.
auskundschaften [ous'kōōntsháftən] *vt* spy
out; (*Gebiet*) reconnoiter (*US*), reconnoitre
(*Brit*).
Auskunft [ous'kōōnft] *f* **-**, **-künfte** information; (*nähere*) details *pl*, particulars *pl*;
(*Stelle*) information office; (*TEL*) inquiries;
jdm ~ erteilen give sb information.
auskuppeln [ous'kōōpəln] *vi* disengage the
clutch.
auskurieren [ous'kōōrē:rən] *vt* (*umg*) cure;
(*Krankheit auch*) get rid of.
auslachen [ous'láḵhən] *vt* laugh at, mock.
ausladen [ous'lâdən] *unreg vt* unload; (*umg*:
Gäste) cancel an invitation to ♦ *vi* (*Äste*)
spread.
ausladend *a* (*Gebärden, Bewegung*) sweeping.
Auslage [ous'lâgə] *f* store window (display).
Auslagen *pl* outlay, expenditure.
Ausland [ous'lánt] *nt* foreign countries *pl*;
im/ins ~ abroad.
Ausländer(in *f*) [ous'lendər(in)] *m* **-s**, **-**
foreigner.
Ausländerfeindlichkeit *f* hostility to
foreigners, xenophobia.
ausländisch *a* foreign.
Auslands- *zW*: **~aufenthalt** *m* stay abroad;
~gespräch *nt* international call;
~korrespondent(in *f*) *m* foreign correspondent; **~reise** *f* trip abroad;
~schutzbrief *m* international car insurance;
~vertretung *f* agency abroad; (*von Firma*)
foreign branch.
auslassen [ous'lásən] *unreg vt* leave out;
(*Wort etc auch*) omit; (*Fett*) melt; (*Kleidungsstück*) let out; (*Wut, Ärger*) vent (*an
+dat* on) ♦ *vr*: **sich über etw** (*akk*) **~** speak
one's mind about sth.
Auslassung *f* omission.
Auslassungszeichen *nt* apostrophe.
auslasten [ous'lástən] *vt* (*Fahrzeug*) make
full use of; (*Maschine auch*) use to capacity; (*jdn*) occupy fully.

Auslauf [ous'louf] *m* (*für Tiere*) run; (*Ausfluß*) outflow, outlet.

auslaufen *vi unreg* run out; (*Behälter*) leak; (*NAUT*) put out (to sea); (*langsam aufhören*) run down.

Ausläufer [ous'loifər] *m* (*von Gebirge*) spur; (*Pflanze*) runner; (*MET*: *von Hoch*) ridge; (: *von Tief*) trough.

ausleeren [ous'lä:rən] *vt* empty.

auslegen [ous'lä:gən] *vt* (*Waren*) lay out; (*Köder*) put down; (*Geld*) lend; (*bedecken*) cover; (*Text etc*) interpret.

Ausleger *m* **-s, -** (*von Kran etc*) jib, boom.

Auslegung *f* interpretation.

Ausleihe [ous'līə] *f* **-, -n** issuing; (*Stelle*) check out (*US*), issue desk (*Brit*).

ausleihen [ous'līən] *vt unreg* (*verleihen*) lend; **sich** (*dat*) **etw ~** borrow sth.

auslernen [ous'lɛrnən] *vi* (*Lehrling*) finish one's apprenticeship; **man lernt nie aus** (*Sprichwort*) you live and learn.

Auslese [ous'lä:zə] *f* **-, -n** selection; (*Elite*) elite; (*Wein*) choice wine.

auslesen [ous'lä:zən] *vt unreg* select; (*umg*: *zu Ende lesen*) finish.

ausliefern [ous'lē:fərn] *vt* deliver (up), hand over; (*an anderen Staat*) extradite (*an +akk* to); (*COMM*) deliver; **jdm/etw** (*dat*) **ausgeliefert sein** be at the mercy of sb/sth ♦ *vr*: **sich jdm ~** give o.s. up to sb.

Auslieferungsabkommen *nt* extradition treaty.

ausliegen [ous'lē:gən] *vi unreg* (*zur Ansicht*) be displayed; (*Zeitschriften etc*) be available (to the public); (*Liste*) be up.

auslöschen [ous'lœshən] *vt* extinguish; (*fig*) wipe out, obliterate.

auslosen [ous'lō:zən] *vt* draw lots for.

auslösen [ous'lœzən] *vt* (*Explosion, Schuß*) set off; (*hervorrufen*) cause, produce; (*Gefangene*) ransom; (*Pfand*) redeem.

Auslöser *m* **-s, -** trigger; (*PHOT*) release; (*Anlaß*) cause.

ausloten [ous'lō:tən] *vt* (*NAUT*: *Tiefe*) sound; (*fig geh*) plumb.

ausmachen [ous'màkhən] *vt* (*Licht, Radio*) turn off; (*Feuer*) put out; (*entdecken*) make out; (*vereinbaren*) agree; (*beilegen*) settle; (*Anteil darstellen, betragen*) represent; (*bedeuten*) matter; **das macht ihm nichts aus** it doesn't matter to him; **macht es Ihnen etwas aus, wenn ...?** would you mind if ...?

ausmalen [ous'màlən] *vt* paint; (*fig*) describe; **sich** (*dat*) **etw ~** imagine sth.

Ausmaß [ous'màs] *nt* dimension; (*fig auch*) scale.

ausmerzen [ous'mertsən] *vt* eliminate.

ausmessen [ous'mesən] *vt unreg* measure.

ausmisten [ous'mistən] *vt* (*Stall*) muck out; (*fig umg*: *Schrank etc*) tidy out; (: *Zimmer*) clean out.

ausmustern [ous'mōōstərn] *vt* (*Maschine, Fahrzeug etc*) take out of service; (*MIL*: *entlassen*) take out of active duty (*because*

of ill-health or injury).

Ausnahme [ous'nàmə] *f* **-, -n** exception; **eine ~ machen** make an exception; **~erscheinung** *f* exception; **~fall** *m* exceptional case; **~zustand** *m* state of emergency.

ausnahms- *zW*: **~los** *ad* without exception; **~weise** *ad* by way of exception, for once.

ausnehmen [ous'nä:mən] *unreg vt* take out, remove; (*Tier*) gut; (*Nest*) rob; (*umg*: *Geld abnehmen*) clean out; (*ausschließen*) make an exception of ♦ *vr* look, appear.

ausnehmend *a* exceptional.

ausnüchtern [ous'nücchtərn] *vti* sober up.

Ausnüchterungszelle *f* drunk tank (*US*), drying-out cell (*Brit*).

ausnützen [ous'nütsən] *vt* (*Zeit, Gelegenheit*) use, turn to good account; (*Einfluß*) use; (*Mensch, Gutmütigkeit*) exploit.

auspacken [ous'pákən] *vt* unpack ♦ *vi* (*umg*: *alles sagen*) talk.

auspfeifen [ous'pfīfən] *vt unreg* hiss/boo at.

ausplaudern [ous'ploudərn] *vt* (*Geheimnis*) blab.

ausposaunen [ous'pōzounən] *vt* (*umg*) tell the world about.

ausprägen [ous'pre:gən] *vr* (*Begabung, Charaktereigenschaft*) reveal *od* show itself.

auspressen [ous'presən] *vt* (*Saft, Schwamm etc*) squeeze out; (*Zitrone etc*) squeeze.

ausprobieren [ous'prōbē:rən] *vt* try (out).

Auspuff [ous'pōōf] *m* **-(e)s, -e** (*TECH*) exhaust; **~rohr** *nt* exhaust (pipe); **~topf** *m* (*AUT*) muffler (*US*), silencer (*Brit*).

ausquartieren [ous'kvártē:rən] *vt* move out.

ausquetschen [ous'kvetshən] *vt* (*Zitrone etc*) squeeze; (*umg*: *ausfragen*) grill; (: *aus Neugier*) pump.

ausradieren [ous'rádē:rən] *vt* erase, rub out.

ausrangieren [ous'ránzhē:rən] *vt* (*umg*) chuck out; (*Maschine, Auto*) scrap.

ausrauben [ous'roubən] *vt* rob.

ausräumen [ous'roimən] *vt* (*Dinge*) clear away; (*Schrank, Zimmer*) empty; (*Bedenken*) put aside.

ausrechnen [ous'recchnən] *vt* calculate, reckon.

Ausrechnung *f* calculation, reckoning.

Ausrede [ous'rä:də] *f* excuse.

ausreden [ous'rä:dən] *vi* have one's say; **er hat mich nicht mal ~ lassen** he didn't even let me finish (speaking) ♦ *vt*: **jdm etw ~** talk sb out of sth.

ausreichen [ous'rīchən] *vi* suffice, be enough.

ausreichend *a* sufficient, adequate; (*SCH*) adequate.

Ausreise [ous'rīzə] *f* departure; **bei der ~** when leaving the country; **~erlaubnis** *f* exit visa.

ausreisen [ous'rīzən] *vi* leave the country.

ausreißen [ous'rīsən] *unreg vt* tear *od* pull out ♦ *vi* (*Riß bekommen*) tear; (*umg*) make off, scram; **er hat sich** (*dat*) **kein Bein ausgerissen** (*umg*) he didn't exactly strain

himself.
ausrenken [ous'rɛŋkən] *vt* dislocate.
ausrichten [ous'riçtən] *vt* (*Botschaft*) deliver; (*Gruß*) pass on; (*Hochzeit etc*) arrange; (*erreichen*) get anywhere (*bei* with); (*in gerade Linie bringen*) get in a straight line; (*angleichen*) bring into line; (*TYP etc*) justify; **jdm etw ~** take a message for sb; **ich werde es ihm ~** I'll tell him.
ausrotten [ous'rotən] *vt* stamp out, exterminate.
ausrücken [ous'rükən] *vi* (*MIL*) move off; (*Feuerwehr, Polizei*) be called out; (*umg: weglaufen*) run away.
Ausruf [ous'roo:f] *m* (*Schrei*) cry, exclamation; (*Verkünden*) proclamation.
ausrufen *vt unreg* cry out, exclaim; call out; **jdn ~** (*lassen*) (*über Lautsprecher etc*) page sb.
Ausrufezeichen *nt* exclamation mark.
ausruhen [ous'roo:ən] *vtir* rest.
ausrüsten [ous'rüstən] *vt* equip, fit out.
Ausrüstung *f* equipment.
ausrutschen [ous'rootshən] *vi* slip.
Ausrutscher *m* **-s, -** (*umg: lit, fig*) slip.
Aussage [ous'zågə] *f* **-, -n** (*JUR*) statement; **der Angeklagte/Zeuge verweigerte die ~** the accused/witness refused to give evidence.
aussagekräftig *a* expressive, full of expression.
aussagen [ous'zågən] *vt* say, state ♦ *vi* (*JUR*) give evidence.
Aussatz [ous'zåts] *m* **-es** (*MED*) leprosy.
aussaugen [ous'zougən] *vt* (*Saft etc*) suck out; (*Wunde*) suck the poison out of; (*fig: ausbeuten*) drain dry.
ausschalten [ous'shåltən] *vt* switch off; (*fig*) eliminate.
Ausschank [ous'shåŋk] *m* **-(e)s, -schänke** dispensing, giving out; (*COMM*) selling; (*Theke*) bar.
Ausschankerlaubnis *f* license (*US*), licence (*Brit*).
Ausschau [ous'shou] *f:* **~ halten** look out, watch (*nach* for).
ausschauen *vi* look out (*nach* for), be on the look-out.
ausscheiden [ous'shīdən] *unreg vt* (*aussondern*) take out; (*MED*) excrete ♦ *vi* leave (*aus etw* sth); (*aus einem Amt*) retire (*aus* from); (*SPORT*) be eliminated, be knocked out; **er scheidet für den Posten aus** he can't be considered for the job.
Ausscheidung *f* removal; excretion; elimination.
ausschenken [ous'shäŋkən] *vt* pour out; (*COMM*) sell.
ausscheren [ous'shä:rən] *vi* (*Fahrzeug*) leave the line *od* convoy; (*zum Überholen*) pull out.
ausschildern [ous'shildərn] *vt* signpost.
ausschimpfen [ous'shimpfən] *vt* scold, tell off.

ausschlachten [ous'shlåk̇tən] *vt* (*Auto*) cannibalize; (*fig*) make a meal of.
ausschlafen [ous'shlåfən] *unreg vir* sleep late ♦ *vt* sleep off; **ich bin nicht ausgeschlafen** I didn't have *od* get enough sleep.
Ausschlag [ous'shlåk] *m* (*MED*) rash; (*Pendel~*) swing; (*von Nadel*) deflection; **den ~ geben** (*fig*) tip the balance.
ausschlagen [ous'shlågən] *unreg vt* knock out; (*auskleiden*) deck out; (*verweigern*) decline ♦ *vi* (*Pferd*) kick out; (*BOT*) sprout; (*Zeiger*) be deflected.
ausschlaggebend *a* decisive.
ausschließen [ous'shlē:sən] *vt unreg* shut *od* lock out; (*SPORT*) disqualify; (*Fehler, Möglichkeit etc*) rule out; (*fig*) exclude; **ich will mich nicht ~** myself not excepted.
ausschließlich *a, ad* exclusive(ly) ♦ *präp* +*gen* excluding, exclusive of.
ausschlüpfen [ous'shlüpfən] *vi* slip out; (*aus Ei, Puppe*) hatch out.
Ausschluß [ous'shlōōs] *m* exclusion; **unter ~ der Öffentlichkeit stattfinden** be closed to the public.
ausschmücken [ous'shmükən] *vt* decorate; (*fig*) embellish.
ausschneiden [ous'shnīdən] *vt unreg* cut out; (*Büsche*) trim.
Ausschnitt [ous'shnit] *m* (*Teil*) section; (*von Kleid*) neckline; (*Zeitungs~*) clipping (*US*), cutting (*Brit*); (*aus Film etc*) clip, excerpt.
ausschöpfen [ous'shœpfən] *vt* ladle out (*aus* of); (*fig*) exhaust.
ausschreiben [ous'shrībən] *vt unreg* (*ganz schreiben*) write out (in full); (*ausstellen*) write (out); (*Stelle, Wettbewerb etc*) announce, advertise.
Ausschreibung *f* (*Bekanntmachung: von Wahlen*) calling; (: *von Stelle*) advertising.
Ausschreitung [ous'shrītōōng] *f* excess.
Ausschuß [ous'shōōs] *m* committee; board; (*Abfall*) waste, scraps *pl*; (*COMM: auch* ~*ware f*) reject.
ausschütten [ous'shütən] *vt* pour out; (*Eimer*) empty; (*Geld*) pay ♦ *vr* shake (with laughter).
Ausschüttung *f* (*FIN*) distribution.
ausschwärmen [ous'shvermən] *vi* (*Bienen, Menschen*) swarm out; (*MIL*) fan out.
ausschweifend [ous'shvīfənt] *a* (*Leben*) dissipated, debauched; (*Phantasie*) extravagant.
Ausschweifung *f* excess.
ausschweigen [ous'shvīgən] *vr unreg* keep silent.
ausschwitzen [ous'shvitsən] *vt* sweat out.
aussehen [ous'zā:ən] *vi unreg* look; **gut ~** look good/well; **wie sieht's aus?** (*umg: wie steht's?*) how's things?; **das sieht nach nichts aus** that doesn't look anything special; **es sieht nach Regen aus** it looks like rain; **es sieht schlecht aus** things look bad; **A~** *nt* **-s** appearance.
aussein [ous'sīn] *unreg vi* (*umg*) be out; (*zu*

Ende) be over ♦ *vi unpers*: **es ist aus mit ihm** (*umg*) he is finished, he has had it.
außen [ou'sən] *ad* outside; (*nach* ~) outwards; ~ **ist es rot** it's red (on the) outside.
Außen- *zW*: ~**antenne** *f* outside aerial; ~**arbeiten** *pl* work *sing* on the exterior; ~**aufnahme** *f* outdoor shot; ~**bezirk** *m* outlying district; ~**bordmotor** *m* outboard motor.
aussenden [ous'zendən] *vt unreg* send out, emit.
Außen- *zW*: ~**dienst** *m* outside *od* field service; (*von Diplomat*) foreign service; ~**handel** *m* foreign trade; ~**minister** *m* ≈ Secretary of State (*US*), ≈ foreign minister (*Brit*); ~**ministerium** *nt* ≈ State Department (*US*), ≈ Foreign Office (*Brit*); ~**politik** *f* foreign policy; ~**seite** *f* outside; ~**seiter(in** *f*) *m* -**s**, - outsider; ~**spiegel** *m* (*AUT*) outside mirror; ~**stände** *pl* (*bes COMM*) outstanding debts *pl*, arrears *pl*; ~**stehende(r)** *mf dekl wie a* outsider; ~**welt** *f* outside world.
außer [ou'sər] *präp* +*dat* (*räumlich*) out of; (*abgesehen von*) except; ~ **Gefahr sein** be out of danger; ~ **Zweifel** beyond any doubt; ~ **Betrieb** out of order; ~ **sich** (*dat*) **sein/ geraten** be beside o.s.; ~ **Dienst** retired; ~ **Landes** abroad ♦ *kj* (*ausgenommen*) except; ~ **wenn** unless; ~ **daß** except; ~**amtlich** *a* unofficial, private.
außerdem *kj* besides, in addition ♦ *ad* anyway.
außerdienstlich *a* private.
außerehelich *a* extramarital.
äußere(r, s) [oi'sərə(r,z)] *a* outer, external.
Äußere(s) *nt* exterior; (*fig: Aussehen auch*) outward appearance.
außer- *zW*: ~**gewöhnlich** *a* unusual; ~**halb** *präp* +*gen*, *ad* outside; ~**irdisch** *a* extraterrestrial; **A**~**kraftsetzung** *f* repeal.
äußerlich *a, ad* external; **rein** ~ **betrachtet** on the face of it; **A**~**keit** *f* (*fig*) triviality; (*Oberflächlichkeit*) superficiality; (*Formalität*) formality.
äußern *vt* utter, express; (*zeigen*) show ♦ *vr* give one's opinion; (*sich zeigen*) show itself.
außer- *zW*: ~**ordentlich** *a* extraordinary; ~**planmäßig** *a* unscheduled; ~**sinnlich** *a:* ~**sinnliche Wahrnehmung** extrasensory perception.
äußerst [oi'sərst] *ad* extremely, most.
außerstande [ousərshtán'də] *ad* not in a position, unable.
äußerstenfalls *ad* if worst comes to worst.
äußerste(r, s) *a* utmost; (*räumlich*) farthest; (*Termin*) last possible; (*Preis*) highest; **mein** ~**s Angebot** my final offer.
Äußerste(s) *nt:* **bis zum** ~**n gehen** go to extremes.
Äußerung *f* (*Bemerkung*) remark, comment; (*Behauptung*) statement; (*Zeichen*) expression.

aussetzen [ous'zetsən] *vt* (*Kind, Tier*) abandon; (*Boote*) lower; (*Belohnung*) offer; (*Urteil, Verfahren*) postpone; **jdn/sich etw** (*dat*) ~ lay sb/o.s. open to sth; **jdm/etw ausgesetzt sein** be exposed to sb/sth; **was haben Sie daran auszusetzen?** what's your objection to it?; **an jdm/etw etw** ~ find fault with sb/sth ♦ *vi* (*aufhören*) stop; (*Pause machen*) have a break.
Aussicht [ous'zièht] *f* view; (*in Zukunft*) prospect; **in** ~ **sein** be in view; **etw in** ~ **haben** have sth in view; **jdm etw in** ~ **stellen** promise sb sth.
Aussichts- *zW*: **a**~**los** *a* hopeless; ~**punkt** *m* viewpoint; **a**~**reich** *a* promising; ~**turm** *m* observation tower.
Aussiedler(in *f*) [ous'zē:dlər(in)] *m* -**s**, - (*Auswanderer*) emigrant.
aussöhnen [ous'zœnən] *vt* reconcile ♦ *vr* reconcile o.s. (*mit jdm/etw* with sb/to sth); (*einander*) become reconciled.
Aussöhnung *f* reconciliation.
aussondern [ous'zondərn] *vt* separate off, select.
aussorgen [ous'zorgən] *vi:* **ausgesorgt haben** have no more money worries.
aussortieren [ous'zortē:rən] *vt* sort out.
ausspannen [ous'shpánən] *vt* spread *od* stretch out; (*Pferd*) unharness; (*umg: Mädchen*) steal (*jdm* from sb) ♦ *vi* relax.
aussparen [ous'shpárən] *vt* leave open.
aussperren [ous'shperən] *vt* lock out.
Aussperrung *f* (*INDUSTRIE*) lock-out.
ausspielen [ous'shpē:lən] *vt* (*Karte*) lead; (*Geldprämie*) offer as a prize ♦ *vi* (*KARTEN*) lead; **ausgespielt haben** be finished; **jdn gegen jdn** ~ play sb off against sb.
Ausspielung *f* (*im Lotto*) draw.
ausspionieren [ous'shpēönē:rən] *vt* (*Pläne etc*) spy out; (*Person*) spy on.
Aussprache [ous'shprákhə] *f* pronunciation; (*Unterredung*) (frank) discussion.
aussprechen [ous'shpreçhən] *unreg vt* pronounce; (*zu Ende sprechen*) speak; (*äußern*) say, express; **der Regierung das Vertrauen** ~ pass a vote of confidence in the government ♦ *vr* (*sich äußern*) speak (*über* +*akk* about); (*sich anvertrauen*) unburden o.s.; (*diskutieren*) discuss ♦ *vi* (*zu Ende sprechen*) finish speaking.
Ausspruch [ous'shpröökh] *m* remark; (*geflügeltes Wort*) saying.
ausspucken [ous'shpöökən] *vt* spit out ♦ *vi* spit.
ausspülen [ous'shpü:lən] *vt* wash out; (*Mund*) rinse.
ausstaffieren [ous'shtáfē:rən] *vt* equip; (*Zimmer*) furnish.
Ausstand [ous'shtánt] *m* strike; **in den** ~ **treten** go on strike; **seinen** ~ **geben** hold a farewell party.
ausstatten [ous'shtátən] *vt* (*Zimmer etc*) furnish; **jdn mit etw** ~ equip sb with sth.
Ausstattung *f* (*Ausstatten*) provision; (*Klei-*

dung) outfit; (*Aussteuer*) dowry; (*Aufmachung*) make-up; (*Einrichtung*) furnishing.

ausstechen |ous'shtɛchən| *vt unreg* (*Augen, Rasen, Graben*) dig out; (*Kekse*) cut out; (*übertreffen*) outshine.

ausstehen |ous'shtä:ən| *unreg vt* stand, endure ♦ *vi* (*noch nicht dasein*) be outstanding.

aussteigen |ous'shtīgən| *vi unreg* get out, alight; (*aus Gesellschaft*) drop out (*aus* of); **alles ~!** (*von Schaffner*) end of the line!

Aussteiger(in *f*) *m* (*umg*) drop-out.

ausstellen |ous'shtɛlən| *vt* exhibit, display; (*umg: ausschalten*) switch off; (*Rechnung etc*) make out; (*Paß, Zeugnis*) issue.

Aussteller(in *f*) *m* (*auf Messe*) exhibitor; (*von Scheck*) drawer.

Ausstellung *f* exhibition; (*FIN*) drawing up; (*einer Rechnung*) making out; (*eines Passes etc*) issuing.

Ausstellungs- *zW*: **~datum** *nt* date of issue; **~stück** *nt* (*in Ausstellung*) exhibit; (*in Schaufenster etc*) display item.

aussterben |ous'shtɛrbən| *vi unreg* die out; **A~** *nt* extinction.

Aussteuer |ous'shtoiər| *f* dowry.

aussteuern |ous'shtoiərn| *vt* (*Verstärker*) adjust.

Ausstieg |ous'shtē:k| *m* **-(es), -e** (*Ausgang*) exit; **~ aus der Atomenergie** dropping out of using atomic energy.

ausstopfen |ous'shtopfən| *vt* stuff.

ausstoßen |ous'shtō:sən| *vt unreg* (*Luft, Rauch*) give off, emit; (*aus Verein etc*) expel, exclude; (*Auge*) poke out; (*herstellen: Teile, Stückzahl*) turn out, produce.

ausstrahlen |ous'shtrālən| *vti* radiate; (*RAD*) broadcast.

Ausstrahlung *f* radiation; (*fig*) charisma.

ausstrecken |ous'shtrɛkən| *vtr* stretch out.

ausstreichen |ous'shtrīchən| *vt unreg* cross out; (*glätten*) smooth out.

ausstreuen |ous'shtroiən| *vt* scatter; (*fig: Gerücht*) spread.

ausströmen |ous'shtrœmən| *vi* (*Gas*) pour out, escape ♦ *vt* give off; (*fig*) radiate.

aussuchen |ous'zōō:khən| *vt* select, pick out.

Austausch |ous'toush| *m* exchange; **a~bar** *a* exchangeable.

austauschen *vt* exchange, swop.

Austausch- *zW*: **~motor** *m* reconditioned engine; **~student(in** *f*) *m* exchange student.

austeilen |ous'tīlən| *vt* distribute, give out.

Auster |ous'tər| *f* **-, -n** oyster.

austesten |ous'tɛstən| *vt* (*COMPUT*) debug.

austoben |ous'tō:bən| *vr* (*Kind*) run wild; (*Erwachsene*) let off steam; (*sich müde machen*) tire o.s. out.

austragen |ous'trāgən| *vt unreg* (*Post*) deliver; (*Streit etc*) decide; (*Wettkämpfe*) hold; **ein Kind ~** (*nicht abtreiben*) have a child.

Austräger |ous'trɛ:gər| *m* delivery boy; (*Zeitungs~*) newspaper boy.

Austragungsort *m* (*SPORT*) venue.

Australien |oustrå'lēən| *nt* **-s** Australia.

Australier(in *f*) *m* **-s, -** Australian.

australisch *a* Australian.

austreiben |ous'trībən| *vt unreg* drive out, expel; (*Geister*) exorcize; **jdm etw ~** cure sb of sth; (*bes durch Schläge*) knock sth out of sb.

austreten |ous'trä:tən| *unreg vi* (*zur Toilette*) be excused ♦ *vt* (*Feuer*) tread out, trample; (*Schuhe*) wear out; (*Treppe*) wear down; **aus etw ~** leave sth.

austricksen |ous'triksən| *vt* (*umg*: SPORT, *fig*) trick.

austrinken |ous'tringkən| *unreg vt* (*Glas*) drain; (*Getränk*) drink up ♦ *vi* finish one's drink, drink up.

Austritt |ous'trit| *m* emission; (*aus Verein, Partei etc*) withdrawal.

austrocknen |ous'troknən| *vti* dry up.

austüfteln |ous'tüftəln| *vt* (*umg*) work out; (*ersinnen*) think up.

ausüben |ous'ü:bən| *vt* (*Beruf*) practice (*US*), practise (*Brit*), carry out; (*innehaben: Amt*) hold; (*Funktion*) perform; (*Einfluß*) exert; (*Reiz, Wirkung*) exercise, have (*auf jdn* on sb).

Ausübung *f* practice, exercise; **in ~ seines Dienstes/seiner Pflicht** (*form*) in the execution of his duty.

ausufern |ous'ōō:fərn| *vi* (*fig*) get out of hand; (*Konflikt etc*) escalate (*zu* into).

Ausverkauf |ous'ferkouf| *m* sale; (*fig: Verrat*) sell-out.

ausverkaufen *vt* sell out; (*Geschäft*) sell up.

ausverkauft *a* (*Karten, Artikel*) sold out; (*THEAT: Haus*) full.

auswachsen |ous'våksən| *vi unreg*: **das ist (ja) zum A~** (*umg*) it's enough to drive you mad.

Auswahl |ous'vål| *f* selection, choice (*an +dat* of).

auswählen |ous've:lən| *vt* select, choose.

Auswahlmöglichkeit *f* choice.

Auswanderer |ous'vándərər| *m* **-s, -, Auswanderin** *f* emigrant.

auswandern *vi* emigrate.

Auswanderung *f* emigration.

auswärtig |ous'vertich| *a* (*nicht am/vom Ort*) out-of-town; (*ausländisch*) foreign; **das A~e Amt** the State Department (*US*), the Foreign Office (*Brit*).

auswärts |ous'verts| *ad* outside; (*nach außen*) outwards; **~ essen** eat out; **A~spiel** *nt* away game.

auswaschen |ous'váshən| *vt unreg* wash out; (*spülen*) rinse (out).

auswechseln |ous'vɛksəln| *vt* change, substitute.

Ausweg |ous'vä:k| *m* way out; **der letzte ~** the last resort; **a~los** *a* hopeless.

ausweichen |ous'vīchən| *vi unreg*: **jdm/etw ~** (*lit*) move aside *od* make way for sb/sth; (*fig*) sidestep sb/sth; **jdm/einer Begegnung ~** avoid sb/a meeting.

ausweichend *a* evasive.
Ausweichmanöver *nt* evasive action.
ausweinen [ous'vīnən] *vr* have a (good) cry.
Ausweis [ous'vīs] *m* **-es, -e** I.D. card; passport; (*Mitglieds~, Bibliotheks~ etc*) card; **~, bitte** your papers, please.
ausweisen [ous'vīzən] *unreg vt* expel, banish ♦ *vr* prove one's identity.
Ausweis- *zW*: **~karte** *f*, **~papiere** *pl* identification papers *pl*; **~kontrolle** *f* identity check.
Ausweisung *f* expulsion.
ausweiten [ous'vītən] *vt* stretch.
auswendig [ous'vendiçh] *ad* by heart; **~ lernen** learn by heart.
auswerfen [ous'verfən] *vt unreg* (*Anker, Netz*) cast.
auswerten [ous'vertən] *vt* evaluate.
Auswertung *f* evaluation, analysis; (*Nutzung*) utilization.
auswickeln [ous'vikəln] *vt* (*Paket, Bonbon etc*) unwrap.
auswirken [ous'virkən] *vr* have an effect.
Auswirkung *f* effect.
auswischen [ous'vishən] *vt* wipe out; **jdm eins ~** (*umg*) put one over on sb.
Auswuchs [ous'vōō:ks] *m* (out)growth; (*fig*) product; (*Mißstand, Übersteigerung*) excess.
auswuchten [ous'vōōkhtən] *vt* (*AUT*) balance.
auszacken [ous'tsákən] *vt* (*Stoff etc*) pink.
auszahlen [ous'tsálən] *vt* (*Lohn, Summe*) pay out; (*Arbeiter*) pay off; (*Miterbe*) buy out ♦ *vr* (*sich lohnen*) pay.
auszählen [ous'tse:lən] *vt* (*Stimmen*) count; (*Boxen*) count out.
auszeichnen [ous'tsīçhnən] *vt* honor (*US*), honour (*Brit*); (*MIL*) decorate; (*COMM*) price ♦ *vr* distinguish o.s.; **der Wagen zeichnet sich durch ... aus** one of the car's main features is ...
Auszeichnung *f* distinction; (*COMM*) pricing; (*Ehrung*) awarding of decoration; (*Ehre*) honor (*US*), honour (*Brit*); (*Orden*) decoration; **mit ~** with distinction.
ausziehen [ous'tsē:ən] *unreg vt* (*Kleidung*) take off; (*Haare, Zähne, Tisch etc*) pull out; (*nachmalen*) trace ♦ *vr* undress ♦ *vi* (*aufbrechen*) leave; (*aus Wohnung*) move out.
Auszubildende(r) [ous'tsōōbildəndə(r)] *mf* trainee; (*als Handwerker auch*) apprentice.
Auszug [ous'tsōō:k] *m* (*aus Wohnung*) removal; (*aus Buch etc*) extract; (*Konto~*) statement; (*Ausmarsch*) departure.
autark [outárk'] *a* self-sufficient (*auch fig*); (*COMM*) autarkical.
Auto [ou'tō] *nt* **-s, -s** car, automobile (*US*); **mit dem ~ fahren** go by car; **~ fahren** drive; **~bahn** *f* freeway (*US*), motorway (*Brit*); **~bahndreieck** *nt* freeway junction; **~bahnkreuz** *nt* freeway intersection.
Autobiographie [outōbēōgráfē:'] *f* autobiography.
Auto- *zW*: **~fahrer(in** *f*) *m* motorist; driver;

~fahrt *f* drive; **~friedhof** *m* (*umg*) wrecking yard (*US*), car dump (*Brit*).
autogen [outōgā:n'] *a* autogenous; **~es Training** (*PSYCH*) relaxation through self-hypnosis.
Autogramm [outōgràm'] *nt* autograph.
Automat *m* **-en, -es** machine.
Automatik [outōmá'tik] *f* automatic mechanism (*auch fig*); (*Gesamtanlage*) automatic system.
automatisch *a* automatic.
Automatisierung [outōmátēzē:'rōōng] *f* automation.
Automobilausstellung [outōmōbē:l'ousshtelōōng] *f* motor show.
autonom [outōnō:m'] *a* autonomous.
Autonummer *f* license number.
Autopsie [outopsē:'] *f* autopsy, post-mortem.
Autor [ou'tor] *m* **-s, -en, Autorin** [outō:'rin] *f* author, authoress.
Auto- *zW*: **~radio** *nt* car radio; **~reifen** *m* car tire (*US*) *od* tyre (*Brit*); **~rennen** *nt* motor racing.
autoritär [outōrētē:r'] *a* authoritarian.
Autorität *f* authority.
Auto- *zW*: **~unfall** *m* car *od* motor accident; **~verleih** *m*, **~vermietung** *f* car rental.
av. *abk* (= *arbeitsverwendungsfähig*) operable.
AvD *m* - *abk* (= *Automobilclub von Deutschland*) ≈ AAA (*US*), AA (*Brit*).
AVO *f* - *abk* (= *Allgemeine Vergütungsordnung*) general wage regulations.
Avus [ávōōs'] *f* - *abk* = *Automobil-Verkehrs-Und Übungsstrasse.*
Axt [ákst] *f* **-, ̈e** ax (*US*), axe (*Brit*).
AZ, Az. *abk* (= *Aktenzeichen*) ref.
Azoren [àtsō:'rən] *pl* (*GEOG*) Azores *pl*.
Azteke [àtstā:'kə] *m* **-n, -n, Aztekin** *f* Aztec.
Azubi [àtsōō:'bi] *mf* **-s, -s** *abk* (*umg*) = **Auszubildende(r).**

B

B, b [bā:] *nt* B, b; **B-Dur/b-Moll** (the key of) B flat major/minor.
B *f abk* = **Bundesstraße.**
bA *abk* (= *beschränktes Anbaugebiet*) *area of restricted cultivation around nuclear sites.*
Baby [bā:'bē] *nt* **-s, -s** baby; **~ausstattung** *f* layette; **~raum** *m* (*Flughafen etc*) nursing room; **~sitter** [bā:'bēzitər] *m* **-s, -** babysitter; **~speck** *m* (*umg*) baby fat.
Bach [bàkh] *m* **-(e)s, ̈e** stream, brook.
Backblech *nt* baking tray.
Backbord *nt* **-(e)s, -e** (*NAUT*) port.
Backe *f* **-, -n** cheek.

backen [bá'kən] *vti* *unreg* bake; **frisch/knusprig gebackenes Brot** fresh/crusty bread.

Backen- *zW*: ~**bart** *m* sideboards *pl*; ~**zahn** *m* molar.

Bäcker(in *f*) [be'kər(in)] *m* **-s,** - baker.

Bäckerei [bekərī'] *f* bakery; (*Bäckerladen*) baker's (shop).

Bäckerjunge *m* (*Lehrling*) baker's apprentice.

Back- *zW*: ~**fisch** *m* fried fish; (*veraltet*) teenager; ~**form** *f* baking tin; ~**hähnchen** *nt* roast chicken; ~**obst** *nt* dried fruit; ~**ofen** *m* oven; ~**pflaume** *f* prune; ~**pulver** *nt* baking powder; ~**stein** *m* brick.

bäckt [bekt] *3. pers sing von* **backen**.

Bad [bát] *nt* **-(e)s,** ⁻**er** bath; (*Schwimmen*) bathe; (*Ort*) spa.

Bade- [bá'də] *zW*: ~**anstalt** *f* swimming pool; ~**anzug** *m* bathing suit; ~**hose** *f* bathing *od* swimming trunks *pl*; ~**kappe** *f* bathing cap; ~**mantel** *m* bath(ing) robe; ~**meister** *m* swimming pool attendant.

baden [bá'dən] *vi* bathe, have a bath ♦ *vt* bath; **damit kannst du** ~ **gehen** (*fig umg*) you'll get nowhere with that.

Baden-Württemberg [bá'dənvür'təmberk] *nt* Baden-Württemberg.

Bade- *zW*: ~**ort** *m* spa; ~**sachen** *pl* swimming things *pl*; ~**tuch** *nt* bath towel; ~**wanne** *f* bath (tub); ~**zimmer** *nt* bathroom.

baff [báf] *a*: ~ **sein** (*umg*) be flabbergasted.

BAföG, Bafög [bá'fœk] *nt* - *abk* (= *Bundesausbildungsförderungsgesetz*) West German student grants system.

BAG *nt* - *abk* (= *Bundesarbeitsgericht*) West German industrial tribunal.

Bagatelle [bágáte'lə] *f* -, **-n** trifle.

Bagger [bá'gər] *m* **-s,** - excavator; (*NAUT*) dredger.

baggern *vti* excavate; (*NAUT*) dredge.

Baggersee *m* *artificial lake in gravel pit etc.*

Bahamas [báhá'más] *pl*: **die** ~ the Bahamas *pl*.

Bahn [bán] *f* -, **-en** railroad (*US*), railway (*Brit*); (*Weg*) road, way; (*Spur*) lane; (*Renn*~) track; (*ASTRON*) orbit; (*Stoff*~) length; **mit der** ~ by train *od* rail/tram; **frei** ~ (*COMM*) carriage free to station of destination; **jdm/einer Sache die** ~ **frei machen** (*fig*) clear the way for sb/sth; **von der rechten** ~ **abkommen** stray from the straight and narrow; **jdn aus der** ~ **werfen** (*fig*) shatter sb; ~**beamte(r)** *mf* railroad official; **b**~**brechend** *a* pioneering; ~**brecher(in** *f*) *m* **-s,** - pioneer; ~**damm** *m* railroad embankment.

bahnen *vt*: **sich einen Weg** ~ clear a way.

Bahnfahrt *f* railroad journey.

Bahnhof *m* station; **auf dem** ~ at the station; **ich verstehe nur** ~ (*hum umg*) it's all Greek to me.

Bahnhofs- *zW*: ~**halle** *f* station concourse; ~**mission** *f* *charitable organization for helping rail travelers in difficulties*; ~**vorsteher** *m* stationmaster; ~**wirtschaft** *f* station restaurant.

Bahn- *zW*: ~**linie** *f* (railroad) line; **b**~**lagernd** *a* (*COMM*) to be collected from the station; ~**schranke** *f* grade (*US*) *od* level (*Brit*) crossing barrier; ~**steig** *m* platform; ~**steigkarte** *f* platform ticket; ~**strecke** *f* railroad line; ~**übergang** *m* grade (*US*) *od* level (*Brit*) crossing; **beschrankter/unbeschrankter** ~**übergang** crossing with gates/unguarded; ~**wärter** *m* signalman.

Bahre [bá'rə] *f* -, **-n** stretcher.

Baiser [bezā:'] *nt* **-s, -s** meringue.

Baisse [be:'sə] *f* -, **-n** (*Börse*) fall; (*plötzliche*) slump.

Bajonett [báyōnet'] *nt* **-(e)s, -e** bayonet.

Bakelit [bákālē:t'] *nt* ® **-s** Bakelite ®.

Bakterien [báktā:'rēən] *pl* bacteria *pl*.

Balance [báláⁿ'sə] *f* -, **-n** balance, equilibrium.

balancie'ren *vti* balance.

bald [bált] *ad* (*zeitlich*) soon; (*beinahe*) almost; ~ ... ~ ... now ... now ...; ~ **darauf** soon afterwards; **bis** ~! see you soon.

baldig [bál'diᴄʰ] *a* early, speedy.

baldmöglichst *ad* as soon as possible.

Baldrian [bál'drēán] *m* **-s, -e** valerian.

Balearen [báláá'rən] *pl*: **die** ~ the Balearics *pl*.

Balg [bálk] *m* *od* *nt* **-(e)s,** ⁻**er** (*pej umg*: *Kind*) brat.

balgen [bál'gən] *vr* scrap (*um* over).

Balkan [bál'kân] *m*: **der** ~ the Balkans *pl*.

Balken [bál'kən] *m* **-s,** - beam; (*Trag*~) girder; (*Stütz*~) prop.

Balkon [bálkōⁿ'] *m* **-s, -s** *od* **-e** balcony; (*THEAT*) (dress) circle.

Ball [bál] *m* **-(e)s,** ⁻**s** ball; (*Tanz*) dance, ball.

Ballade [bálá'də] *f* -, **-n** ballad.

Ballast [bá'lást] *m* **-(e)s, -e** ballast; (*fig*) weight, burden; ~**stoffe** (*MED*) *pl* roughage *sing*.

ballen [bá'lən] *vt* (*formen*) make into a ball; (*Faust*) clench ♦ *vr* build up; (*Menschen*) gather.

Ballen *m* **-s,** - bale; (*ANAT*) ball.

ballern [bá'lərn] *vi* (*umg*) shoot, fire.

Ballett [bálet'] *nt* **-(e)s, -e** ballet; ~**(t)änzer(in** *f*) *m* ballet dancer.

Ballistik [bális'tik] *f* ballistics *sing*.

Ball- *zW*: ~**junge** *m* ball boy; ~**kleid** *nt* evening dress.

Ballon [bálōⁿ'] *m* **-s, -s** *od* **-e** balloon.

Ballspiel *nt* ball game.

Ballung [bá'lŏōng] *f* concentration; (*von Energie*) build-up.

Ballungs- *zW*: ~**gebiet** *nt* conurbation; ~**zentrum** *nt* center (of population, industry *etc*).

Balsam [bál'zâm] *m* **-s, -e** balsam; (*fig*)

balm.

Balte [bál'tə] *m* **-n, -n, Baltin** *f*: **er ist** ~ he comes from the Baltic.

Baltikum [bál'tēkōōm] *nt* **-s**: **das** ~ the Baltic States *pl*.

baltisch *a* Baltic *attr*.

Balz [bálts] *f* **-, -en** (*Paarungsspiel*) courtship display; (*Paarungszeit*) mating season.

Bambus [bám'bōōs] *m* **-ses, -se** bamboo; ~**rohr** *nt* bamboo cane.

Bammel [bá'məl] *m* **-s** (*umg*): **(einen)** ~ **haben vor jdm/etw** be scared of sb/sth.

banal [bánál'] *a* banal.

Banalität [bánálēte:t'] *f* banality.

Banane [báná'nə] *f* **-, -n** banana; **das ist** ~ (*umg*: *egal*) it's not important.

Bananen- *zW*: ~**schale** *f* banana skin; ~**stecker** *m* jack plug.

Banause [bánou'zə] *m* **-n, -n** philistine.

band [bánt] *imperf von* **binden**.

Band *m* **-(e)s,** ⁻**e** (*Buch*~) volume; **das spricht** ~**e** that speaks volumes ♦ *nt* **-(e)s,** ⁻**er** (*Stoff*~) ribbon, tape; (*Fließ*~) production line; (*Faß*~) hoop; (*Ziel*~, *Ton*~) tape; (*ANAT*) ligament; **etw auf** ~ **aufnehmen** tape sth; **am laufenden** ~ (*umg*) non-stop ♦ *nt* **-(e)s, -e** (*Freundschafts*~ *etc*) bond ♦ [bent] *f* **-, -s** band, group.

Bandage [bándá'zhə] *f* **-, -n** bandage.

bandagie'ren *vt* bandage.

Bandbreite *f* (*von Meinungen etc*) range.

Bande [bán'də] *f* **-, -n** band; (*Straßen*~) gang.

bändigen [ben'digən] *vt* (*Tier*) tame; (*Trieb, Leidenschaft*) control, restrain.

Bandit [bándē:t'] *m* **-en, -en** bandit.

Band- *zW*: ~**maß** *nt* tape measure; ~**säge** *f* band saw; ~**scheibe** *f* (*ANAT*) disc; ~**scheibenschaden** *m* slipped disc; ~**wurm** *m* tapeworm.

bange [bá'ngə] *a* scared; (*besorgt*) anxious; **jdm wird es** ~ sb is becoming scared; **jdm** ~ **machen** scare sb; **B**~**macher** *m* **-s, -** scaremonger.

bangen *vi*: **um jdn/etw** ~ be anxious *od* worried about sb/sth.

Bangladesch [bánggládesh'] *nt* **-s** Bangladesh.

Banjo ['bányō, 'bendzhō] *nt* **-s, -s** banjo.

Bank [bángk] *f* **-,** ⁻**e** (*Sitz*~) bench; (*Sand*~ *etc*) (sand)bank *od* bar; **etw auf die lange** ~ **schieben** (*umg*) put sth off ♦ *f* **-, -en** (*Geld*~) bank; **bei der** ~ at the bank; **die** ~ **sprengen** break the bank; ~**anweisung** *f* banker's order; ~**beamte(r)** *m* bank clerk; ~**einlage** *f* (bank) deposit.

Bankett [bángket'] *nt* **-(e)s, -e** (*Essen*) banquet; (*Straßenrand*) shoulder (*US*), verge (*Brit*).

Bank- *zW*: ~**fach** *nt* (*Schließfach*) safe-deposit box; ~**gebühr** *f* bank charge; ~**geheimnis** *nt* confidentiality in banking.

Bankier [bángkēā:'] *m* **-s, -s** banker.

Bank- *zW*: ~**konto** *m* bank account; ~**leitzahl** *f* bank code number; ~**note** *f*

banknote; ~**raub** *m* bank robbery.

bankrott [bángkrot'] *a* bankrupt; **B**~ *m* **-(e)s, -e** bankruptcy; **B**~ **machen** go bankrupt; **den B**~ **anmelden** *od* **erklären** declare o.s. bankrupt; **B**~**erklärung** *f* (*fig umg*) sellout; declaration of inability.

Banküberfall *m* bank raid.

Bann [bán] *m* **-(e)s, -e** (*HIST*) ban; (*Kirchen*~) excommunication; (*fig*: *Zauber*) spell; **b**~**en** *vt* (*Geister*) exorcize; (*Gefahr*) avert; (*bezaubern*) enchant; (*HIST*) banish.

Banner *nt* **-s, -** banner, flag.

bar [bár] *a* (*unbedeckt*) bare; (*frei von*) lacking (*gen* in); (*offenkundig*) utter, sheer; ~**e(s) Geld** cash; **etw (in)** ~ **bezahlen** pay sth (in) cash; **etw für** ~**e Münze nehmen** (*fig*) take sth at its face value; ~ **aller Hoffnung** (*liter*) devoid of hope, completely without hope.

Bar *f* **-, -s** bar.

Bär [be:r] *m* **-en, -en** bear; **jdm einen** ~**en aufbinden** (*umg*) put (*US*) *od* have (*Brit*) sb on.

Baracke [bárá'kə] *f* **-, -n** hut.

barbarisch [bárbá'rish] *a* barbaric, barbarous.

Barbestand *m* money in hand.

Bärenhunger *m* (*umg*): **einen** ~ **haben** be famished.

bärenstark *a* (*umg*) strapping, strong as an ox; (*umg fig*) terrific.

barfuß *a* barefoot.

barg [bárk] *imperf von* **bergen**.

Bar- *zW*: ~**geld** *nt* cash, ready money; **b**~**geldlos** *a* non-cash; **b**~**geldloser Zahlungsverkehr** non-cash *od* credit transactions *pl*.

barhäuptig *a* bareheaded.

Barhocker *m* bar stool.

Bariton [bá'rēton] *m* baritone.

Barkauf *m* cash purchase.

Barkeeper [bár'kē:pər] *m* **-s, -** barman, bartender.

Barkredit *m* cash loan.

Barmann *m* **-(e)s,** ⁻**er** barman.

barmherzig [bármher'tsiċh] *a* merciful, compassionate; **B**~**keit** *f* mercy, compassion.

Barock [bárok'] *nt od m* baroque.

Barometer [bárōmā:'tər] *nt* **-s, -** barometer; **das** ~ **steht auf Sturm** (*fig*) things look stormy.

Baron [bárō:n'] *m* **-s, -e** baron.

Baronesse [bárōne'sə] *f* **-, -n, Baronessin** *f* baroness.

Barren [bá'rən] *m* **-s, -** parallel bars *pl*; (*Gold*~) ingot.

Barriere [bárēe:'rə] *f* **-, -n** barrier.

Barrikade [bárēkâ'də] *f* **-, -n** barricade.

barsch [bársh] *a* brusque, gruff; **jdn** ~ **anfahren** snap at sb.

Barsch [bársh] *m* **-(e)s, -e** perch.

Bar- *zW*: ~**schaft** *f* ready money; ~**scheck** *m* open check (*US*), uncrossed cheque (*Brit*).

barst [bárst] *imperf von* **bersten.**

Bart [bárt] *m* **-(e)s,** **̈-e** beard; (*Schlüssel~*) bit.

bärtig [bɛːr'tiɕ] *a* bearded.

Barvermögen *nt* liquid assets *pl*.

Barzahlung *f* cash payment.

Basar [bázár'] *m* **-s, -e** bazaar.

Base [bá'zə] *f* **-, -n** (*CHEM*) base; (*Kusine*) cousin.

Basel [bá'zəl] *nt* Basle.

basieren [bázē:'rən] *vt* base ♦ *vi* be based.

Basis [bá'zis] *f* **-, Basen** basis; (*ARCHIT, MIL, MATH*) base; **~ und Überbau** (*POL, SOZIOLOGIE*) foundation and superstructure; **die ~** (*umg*) the grass roots.

basisch [bá'zish] *a* (*CHEM*) alkaline.

Basisgruppe *f* action group.

Baske [bás'kə] *m* **-n, -n, Baskin** *f* Basque.

Basken- *zW:* **~land** *nt* Basque region; **~mütze** *f* beret.

Baß [bás] *m* **Basses, Bässe** bass.

Bassin [básań:'] *nt* **-s, -s** pool.

Bassist [básist'] *m* bass.

Baß- *zW:* **~schlüssel** *m* bass clef; **~stimme** *f* bass voice.

Bast [bást] *m* **-(e)s, -e** raffia.

basta [bás'tá] *interj:* **(und damit) ~!** (and) that's that!

basteln *vt* make ♦ *vi* do handicrafts; **an etw** (*dat*) **~** (*an etw herum~*) tinker with sth.

bat [bât] *imperf von* **bitten.**

BAT *m abk* (= *Bundesangestelltentarif*) West German salary scale for employees.

Bataillon [bátályō:n'] *nt* **-s, -e** battalion.

Batist [bátist'] *m* **-(e)s, -e** batiste.

Batterie [bátərē:'] *f* battery.

Bau [bou] *m* **-(e)s,** *no pl* (*Bauen*) building, construction; (*Aufbau*) structure; (*Körperbau*) frame; (*Baustelle*) building site; *pl* **~e** (*Tierbau*) hole, burrow; (*MIN*) working(s); *pl* **~ten** (*Gebäude*) building; **sich im ~ befinden** be under construction; **~arbeiten** *pl* (*Straßenbau*) roadwork *sing* (*US*), roadworks *pl* (*Brit*); building *od* construction work *sing*; **~arbeiter** *m* building worker.

Bauch [boukh] *m* **-(e)s, Bäuche** belly; (*ANAT auch*) stomach, abdomen; **sich** (*dat*) **(vor Lachen) den ~ halten** (*umg*) split one's sides (laughing); **mit etw auf den ~ fallen** (*umg*) fall on one's face with sth; **~ansatz** *m* beginning of a paunch; **~fell** *nt* peritoneum.

bauchig *a* bulging.

Bauch- *zW:* **~landung** *f:* **eine ~landung machen** (*fig*) experience a failure/flop; **~muskel** *m* abdominal muscle; **~redner** *m* ventriloquist; **~schmerzen** *pl* stomach-ache; **~speicheldrüse** *f* pancreas; **~tanz** *m* belly dance; belly dancing; **~weh** *nt* stomach-ache.

Baud-Rate [boutrá'tə] *f* (*COMPUT*) baud rate.

bauen [bou'ən] *vti* build; (*TECH*) construct; (*umg: verursachen: Unfall*) cause; **auf jdn/ etw ~** depend *od* count upon sb/sth; **da hast du Mist gebaut** (*umg*) you really messed

that up.

Bauer [bou'ər] *m* **-n** *od* **-s, -n** farmer; (*Schach*) pawn ♦ *nt od m* **-s, -**(*Vogel~*) cage.

Bäuerchen [boi'ərɕən] *nt* (*Kindersprache*) burp.

Bäuerin [boi'ərin] *f* farmer; (*Frau des Bauers*) farmer's wife.

bäuerlich *a* rustic.

Bauern- *zW:* **~brot** *nt* black bread; **~fängerei'** *f* deception, confidence trick(s); **~frühstück** *nt* bacon and potato omelet; **~haus** *nt* farmhouse; **~hof** *m* farm(yard); **~schaft** *f* farming community; **~schläue** *f* native cunning, craftiness, shrewdness.

Bau- *zW:* **b~fällig** *a* dilapidated; **~fälligkeit** *f* dilapidation; **~firma** *f* construction firm; **~führer** *m* site foreman; **~gelände** *f* building site; **~genehmigung** *f* building permit; **~gerüst** *nt* scaffolding; **~herr** *m* client (*for whom sth is being built*); **~ingenieur** *m* civil engineer.

Bauj. *abk* = **Baujahr.**

Bau- *zW:* **~jahr** *nt* year of construction; (*von Auto*) year of manufacture; **~kasten** *m* box of bricks; **~klötzchen** *nt* (*building*) block; **~kosten** *pl* construction costs *pl*; **~land** *nt* building land; **~leute** *pl* building workers *pl*; **b~lich** *a* structural; **~löwe** *m* building speculator.

Baum [boum] *m* **-(e)s, Bäume** tree; **heute könnte ich Bäume ausreißen** I feel full of energy today.

baumeln [bou'məln] *vi* dangle.

bäumen [boi'mən] *vr* rear (up).

Baum- *zW:* **~grenze** *f* tree line; **~schule** *f* nursery; **~stamm** *m* tree trunk; **~stumpf** *m* tree stump; **~wolle** *f* cotton.

Bau- *zW:* **~plan** *m* architect's plan; **~platz** *m* building site; **~sachverständige(r)** *mf* building expert; **~satz** *m* construction kit.

Bausch [boush] *m* **-(e)s, Bäusche** (*Watte~*) ball, wad; **in ~ und Bogen** (*fig*) lock, stock, and barrel.

bauschen *vtir* puff out.

bauschig *a* baggy, wide.

Bau- *zW:* **b~sparen** *vi untr* save with a building and loan association; **~sparkasse** *f* building and loan association (*US*), building society (*Brit*); **~stein** *m* building stone, freestone; **~stelle** *f* building site; **~stil** *m* architectural style; **b~technisch** *a* in accordance with building *od* construction methods; **~teil** *nt* prefabricated part (of building); **~unternehmer** *m* contractor, builder; **~weise** *f* (method of) construction; **~werk** *nt* building; **~zaun** *m* hoarding.

b.a.w. *abk* (= *bis auf weiteres*) until further notice.

Bayer(in *f*) [bī'ər(in)] *m* **-n, -n** Bavarian.

bay(e)risch *a* Bavarian.

Bayern *nt* Bavaria.

Bazillus [bátsi'lōs] *m* **-, Bazillen** bacillus.

Bd. *abk* (= *Band*) vol.

BDA *m abk* (= *Bund deutscher Architekten*) association of German architects ♦ *nt abk* (= *Besoldungsdienstalter*) seniority.
Bde. *abk* (= *Bände*) vols.
beabsichtigen [bəáp'ziçhtigən] *vt* intend.
beachten [bəáḳh'tən] *vt* take note of; (*Vorschrift*) obey; (*Vorfahrt*) observe.
beachtenswert *a* noteworthy.
beachtlich *a* considerable.
Beachtung *f* notice, attention, observation; **jdm keine ~ schenken** take no notice of sb.
Beamtenlaufbahn *f*: **die ~ einschlagen** enter the civil service.
Beamtenverhältnis *nt*: **im ~ stehen** be a civil servant.
Beamte(r) [bəám'tə(r)] *m* **-n, -n, Beamtin** *f* official; (*Staats~*) civil servant; (*Bank~ etc*) employee.
beamtet *a* (*form*) appointed on a permanent basis (*by the state*).
beängstigend [bəɛngs'tigənt] *a* alarming.
beanspruchen [bəán'shprōōḳhən] *vt* claim; (*Zeit, Platz*) take up, occupy; (*Mensch*) take up sb's time; **etw stark ~** put sth under a lot of stress.
beanstanden [bəán'shtándən] *vt* complain about, object to; (*Rechnung*) query.
Beanstandung *f* complaint.
beantragen [bəán'trágən] *vt* apply for, ask for.
beantworten [bəánt'vortən] *vt* answer.
Beantwortung *f* reply (*gen* to).
bearbeiten [bəár'bītən] *vt* work; (*Material*) process; (*Thema*) deal with; (*Land*) cultivate; (*CHEM*) treat; (*Buch*) revise; (*umg: beeinflussen wollen*) work on.
Bearbeitung *f* processing; treatment; cultivation; revision; **die ~ meines Antrags hat lange gedauert** it took a long time to deal with my claim.
Bearbeitungsgebühr *f* handling fee.
Beatmung [bəát'mōōng] *f* respiration.
beaufsichtigen [bəouf'ziçhtigən] *vt* supervise.
Beaufsichtigung *f* supervision.
beauftragen [bəouf'trágən] *vt* instruct; **jdn mit etw ~** entrust sb with sth.
Beauftragte(r) *mf dekl wie a* representative.
bebauen [bəbou'ən] *vt* build on; (*AGR*) cultivate.
beben [bā:'bən] *vi* tremble, shake; **B~** *nt* **-s -** earthquake.
bebildern [bəbil'dərn] *vt* illustrate.
Becher [be'çhər] *nt* **-s, -** mug; (*ohne Henkel*) tumbler.
bechern [be'çhərn] *vi* (*umg: trinken*) have a few (drinks).
Becken [be'kən] *nt* **-s, -** basin; (*MUS*) cymbal; (*ANAT*) pelvis.
Bedacht [bədáḳht'] *m*: **mit ~** (*vorsichtig*) prudently, carefully; (*absichtlich*) deliberately.
bedacht *a* thoughtful, careful; **auf etw** (*akk*) **~ sein** be concerned about sth.
bedächtig [bədeçh'tiçh] *a* (*umsichtig*)

thoughtful, reflective; (*langsam*) slow, deliberate.
bedanken [bədáng'kən] *vr* say thank you (*bei jdm* to sb); **ich bedanke mich herzlich** thank you very much.
Bedarf [bədárf'] *m* **-(e)s** need; (*Bedarfsmenge*) requirements; (*COMM*) demand; supply; **alles für den häuslichen ~** all household requirements; **je nach ~** according to demand; **bei ~** if necessary; **~ an etw** (*dat*) **haben** be in need of sth.
Bedarfs- *zW*: **~artikel** *m* requisite; **~deckung** *f* satisfaction of sb's needs; **~fall** *m* case of need; **~haltestelle** *f* flag stop (*US*), request stop (*Brit*).
bedauerlich [bədou'ərliçh] *a* regrettable.
bedauern [bədou'ərn] *vt* be sorry for; (*bemitleiden*) pity; **wir ~, Ihnen mitteilen zu müssen, ...** we regret to have to inform you ...; **B~** *nt* **-s** regret.
bedauernswert *a* (*Zustände*) regrettable; (*Mensch*) pitiable, unfortunate.
bedecken [bəde'kən] *vt* cover.
bedeckt *a* covered; (*Himmel*) overcast.
bedenken [bədeng'kən] *vt unreg* think over, consider; **ich gebe zu ~, daß ...** (*geh*) I would ask you to consider that ...; **B~** *nt* **-s, -** (*Überlegen*) consideration; (*Zweifel*) doubt; (*Skrupel*) scruple; **mir kommen B~** I am having second thoughts.
bedenklich *a* doubtful; (*bedrohlich*) dangerous, risky.
Bedenkzeit *f* time for reflection.
bedeuten [bədoi'tən] *vt* mean; signify; (*wichtig sein*) be of importance; **das bedeutet nichts Gutes** that means trouble.
bedeutend *a* important; (*beträchtlich*) considerable.
bedeutsam *a* significant; (*vielsagend*) meaningful.
Bedeutung *f* meaning; significance; (*Wichtigkeit*) importance.
bedeutungs- *zW*: **~los** *a* insignificant, unimportant; **~voll** *a* momentous, significant.
bedienen [bədē:'nən] *vt* serve; (*Maschine*) work, operate ♦ *vr* (*beim Essen*) help o.s.; (*gebrauchen*) make use (*gen* of); **werden Sie schon bedient?** are you being served?; **damit sind Sie sehr gut bedient** that should serve you very well; **ich bin bedient!** (*umg*) I've had enough.
Bedienung *f* service; (*Kellner etc*) waiter; waitress; (*Zuschlag*) service (charge); (*von Maschinen*) operation.
Bedienungsanleitung *f* operating instructions *pl*.
bedingen [bədi'ngən] *vt* (*voraussetzen*) demand, involve; (*verursachen*) cause, occasion.
bedingt *a* limited; (*Straferlaß*) conditional; (*Reflex*) conditioned; **(nur) ~ gelten** be (only) partially valid; **~ frachtfrei** (*COMM*) C and F.

Bedingung f condition; (*Voraussetzung*) stipulation; **mit** od **unter der ~, daß** ... on condition that ...; **zu günstigen ~en** (*COMM*) on favorable terms.

Bedingungs- zW: **~form** f (*GRAM*) conditional; **b~los** a unconditional.

bedrängen [bədre'ngən] vt pester, harass.

Bedrängnis [bədreng'nis] f (*seelisch*) distress, torment.

Bedrängung f trouble.

bedrohen [bədrō:'ən] vt threaten.

bedrohlich a ominous, threatening.

Bedrohung f threat, menace.

bedrucken [bədrōō'kən] vt print on.

bedrücken [bədrü'kən] vt oppress, trouble.

bedürfen [bədür'fən] vi unreg +gen (*geh*) need, require; **ohne daß es eines Hinweises bedurft hätte,** ... without having to be asked ...

Bedürfnis [bədürf'nis] nt **-ses, -se** need; **~ nach etw haben** need sth; **~anstalt** f (*form*) comfort station (*US*), public convenience (*Brit*); **b~los** a frugal, modest.

bedürftig a in need (*gen* of), poor, needy.

Beefsteak [bē:f'stā:k] nt **-s, -s** steak; **deutsches ~** hamburger.

beehren [bəā:'rən] vt (*geh*) honor (*US*), honour (*Brit*); **wir ~ uns** we have pleasure in.

beeilen [bəī'lən] vr hurry.

beeindrucken [bəīn'drōōkən] vt impress, make an impression on.

beeinflussen [bəīn'flōōsən] vt influence.

Beeinflussung f influence.

beeinträchtigen [bəīn'trechtigən] vt affect adversely; (*Sehvermögen*) impair; (*Freiheit*) infringe upon.

beend(ig)en [bəend'(ig)ən] vt end, finish, terminate.

Beend(ig)ung f end(ing), finish(ing).

beengen [bəe'ngən] vt cramp; (*fig*) hamper, inhibit; **beengende Kleidung** restricting clothing.

beengt a cramped; (*fig*) stifled.

beerben [bəer'bən] vt inherit from.

beerdigen [bəer'digən] vt bury.

Beerdigung f funeral, burial.

Beerdigungsunternehmer m mortician (*US*), undertaker (*Brit*).

Beere [bā:'rə] f **-, -n** berry; (*Trauben~*) grape.

Beerenauslese f wine made from specially selected grapes .

Beet [bā:t] nt **-(e)s, -e** (*Blumen~*) bed.

befähigen [bəfe:'igən] vt enable.

befähigt a (*begabt*) talented; (*fähig*) capable (*für* of).

Befähigung f capability; (*Begabung*) talent, aptitude; **die ~ zum Richteramt** the qualifications to become a judge.

befahl [bəfā:l'] imperf von **befehlen**.

befahrbar a passable; (*NAUT*) navigable; **nicht ~ sein** (*Straße, Weg*) be closed (to traffic).

befahren [bəfā:'rən] vt unreg use, drive over;

(*NAUT*) navigate ♦ a used.

befallen [bəfà'lən] vt unreg come over.

befangen [bəfà'ngən] a (*schüchtern*) shy, self-conscious; (*voreingenommen*) biased; **B~heit** f shyness; bias.

befassen [bəfà'sən] vr concern o.s.

Befehl [bəfā:l'] m **-(e)s, -e** command, order; (*COMPUT*) command; **auf ~ handeln** act under orders; **zu ~, Herr Hauptmann!** (*MIL*) yes, sir!; **den ~ haben** od **führen** be in command (*über* +akk of).

befehlen [bəfā:'lən] unreg vt order; **jdm etw ~** order sb to do sth; **du hast mir gar nichts zu ~** I won't take orders from you ♦ vi give orders.

befehligen vt be in command of.

Befehls- zW: **~empfänger** m subordinate; **~form** f (*GRAM*) imperative; **~haber** m **-s,** - commanding officer; **~notstand** m (*JUR*) obligation to obey orders; **~verweigerung** f insubordination.

befestigen [bəfes'tigən] vt fasten (*an* +dat to); (*stärken*) strengthen; (*MIL*) fortify.

Befestigung f fastening; strengthening; (*MIL*) fortification.

Befestigungsanlage f fortification.

befeuchten [bəfoich'tən] vt damp(en), moisten.

befinden [bəfin'dən] unreg vr be; (*sich fühlen*) feel ♦ vt: **jdn/etw für** od **als etw ~** deem sb/sth to be sth ♦ vi decide (*über* +akk on), adjudicate.

Befinden nt **-s** health, condition; (*Meinung*) view, opinion.

beflecken [bəfle'kən] vt (*lit*) stain; (*fig geh*: *Ruf, Ehre*) besmirch.

befliegen [bəflē:'gən] vt unreg (*Strecke*) fly.

beflügeln [bəflü:'gəln] vt (*geh*) inspire.

befohlen [bəfō:'lən] pp von **befehlen**.

befolgen [bəfol'gən] vt comply with, follow.

befördern [bəfŒr'dərn] vt (*senden*) transport, send; (*beruflich*) promote; **etw mit der Post/per Bahn ~** send sth by mail/by rail.

Beförderung f transport, conveyance; promotion.

Beförderungskosten pl transport costs pl.

befragen [bəfrà'gən] vt question; (*um Stellungnahme bitten*) consult (*über* +akk, *nach* about).

Befragung f poll.

befreien [bəfrī'ən] vt set free; (*erlassen*) exempt.

Befreier(in f) m **-s,** - liberator.

befreit a (*erleichtert*) relieved.

Befreiung f liberation, release; (*Erlassen*) exemption.

Befreiungs- zW: **~bewegung** f liberation movement; **~kampf** m struggle for liberation; **~versuch** m escape attempt.

befremden [bəfrem'dən] vt surprise; (*unangenehm*) disturb; **B~** nt **-s** surprise, astonishment.

befreunden [bəfroin'dən] vr make friends; (*mit Idee etc*) acquaint o.s.

befreundet a friendly; **wir sind schon lange**

(miteinander) ~ we have been friends for a long time.
befriedigen [bəfrē:'digən] *vt* satisfy.
befriedigend *a* satisfactory.
Befriedigung *f* satisfaction, gratification.
befristet [bəfris'tət] *a* limited; *(Arbeitsverhältnis, Anstellung)* temporary.
befruchten [bəfrōōkh'tən] *vt* fertilize; *(fig)* stimulate.
Befruchtung *f*: **künstliche** ~ artificial insemination.
Befugnis [bəfōō:'knis] *f* -, -se authorization, powers *pl*.
befugt *a* authorized, entitled.
befühlen [bəfü:'lən] *vt* feel, touch.
Befund [bəfōōnt'] *m* -(e)s, -e findings *pl*; *(MED)* diagnosis; **ohne** ~ *(MED)* (results) negative.
befürchten [bəfürch'tən] *vt* fear.
Befürchtung *f* fear, apprehension.
befürworten [bəfü:r'vortən] *vt* support, speak in favor of.
Befürworter(in *f*) *m* -s, - supporter, advocate.
Befürwortung *f* support(ing).
begabt [bəgápt'] *a* gifted.
Begabung [bəgâ'bōōng] *f* talent, gift.
begann [bəgán'] *imperf von* **beginnen**.
begatten [bəgá'tən] *vr* mate ♦ *vt* mate *od* pair (with).
begeben [bəgā:'bən] *vr unreg (gehen)* proceed *(zu, nach* to); *(geschehen)* occur; **sich in ärztliche Behandlung** ~ undergo medical treatment; **sich in Gefahr** ~ expose o.s. to danger; **B~heit** *f* occurrence.
begegnen [bəgā:g'nən] *vi* meet *(jdm* sb); *(behandeln)* treat *(jdm* sb); **Blicke** ~ **sich** eyes meet.
Begegnung *f* meeting; *(SPORT auch)* match.
begehen [bəgā:'ən] *vt unreg (Straftat)* commit; *(abschreiten)* cover; *(Straße etc)* use, negotiate; *(geh: Feier)* celebrate.
begehren [bəgā:'rən] *vt* desire.
begehrenswert *a* desirable.
begehrt *a* in demand; *(Junggeselle)* eligible.
begeistern [bəgīs'tərn] *vt* fill with enthusiasm; *(inspirieren)* inspire; **er ist für nichts zu** ~ he's not interested in doing anything ♦ *vr*: **sich für etw** ~ get enthusiastic about sth.
begeistert *a* enthusiastic.
Begeisterung *f* enthusiasm.
Begierde [bəgē:r'də] *f* -, -n desire, passion.
begierig [bəgē:'rich] *a* eager, keen; *(voll Verlangen)* hungry, greedy.
begießen [bəgē:'sən] *vt unreg* water; *(mit Fett: Braten etc)* baste; *(mit Alkohol)* drink to.
Beginn [bəgin'] *m* -(e)s beginning; **zu** ~ at the beginning.
beginnen [bəgin'ən] *vti unreg* start, begin.
beglaubigen [bəglou'bigən] *vt* countersign; *(Abschrift)* authenticate; *(Echtheit, Übersetzung)* certify.

Beglaubigung *f* countersignature.
Beglaubigungsschreiben *nt* credentials *pl*.
begleichen [bəglī'chən] *vt unreg* settle, pay; **mit Ihnen habe ich noch eine Rechnung zu** ~ *(fig)* I've a score to settle with you.
begleiten [bəglī'tən] *vt* accompany; *(MIL)* escort.
Begleiter(in *f*) *m* -s, - companion; *(zum Schutz)* escort; *(MUS)* accompanist.
Begleit- *zW*: **~erscheinung** *f* side-effect; **~musik** *f* accompaniment; **~papiere** *pl* *(COMM)* accompanying documents *pl*; **~schiff** *nt* escort vessel; **~schreiben** *nt* covering letter; **~umstände** *pl* attendant circumstances *pl*.
Begleitung *f* company; *(MIL)* escort; *(MUS)* accompaniment.
beglücken [bəglü'kən] *vt* make happy, delight.
beglückwünschen [bəglük'vünshən] *vt* congratulate *(zu* on).
begnadet [bəgnâ'dət] *a* gifted.
begnadigen [bəgnâ'digən] *vt* pardon.
Begnadigung *f* pardon.
begnügen [bəgnü:'gən] *vr* be satisfied, content o.s.
Begonie [bəgō:'nēə] *f* begonia.
begonnen [bəgo'nən] *pp von* **beginnen**.
begossen [bəgo'sən] *pp von* **begießen** ♦ *a*: **er stand da wie ein** ~**er Pudel** *(umg)* he looked so sheepish.
begraben [bəgrâ'bən] *vt unreg* bury; *(aufgeben: Hoffnung)* abandon; *(beenden: Streit etc)* end; **dort möchte ich nicht** ~ **sein** *(umg)* I wouldn't like to be stuck in that hole.
Begräbnis [bəgre:p'nis] *nt* -ses, -se burial, funeral.
begradigen [bəgrâ'digən] *vt* straighten (out).
begreifen [bəgrī'fən] *vt unreg* understand, comprehend.
begreiflich [bəgrī'flich] *a* understandable; **ich kann mich ihm nicht** ~ **machen** I can't make myself clear to him.
begrenzen [bəgren'tsən] *vt (beschränken)* restrict, limit *(auf +akk* to).
Begrenztheit [bəgrentst'hīt] *f* limitation, restriction; *(fig)* narrowness.
Begriff [bəgrif'] *m* -(e)s, -e concept, idea; **im** ~ **sein, etw zu tun** be about to do sth; **sein Name ist mir ein/kein** ~ his name means something/doesn't mean anything to me; **du machst dir keinen** ~ **(davon)** you've no idea; **für meine** ~**e** in my opinion; **schwer von** ~ *(umg)* slow, dense.
Begriffs- *zW*: **~bestimmung** *f* definition; **b~stutzig** *a* dense, slow.
begrub [bəgrōō:p'] *imperf von* **begraben**.
begründen [bəgrün'dən] *vt (Gründe geben)* justify; **etw näher** ~ give specific reasons for sth.
Begründer(in *f*) *m* -s, - founder.
begründet *a* well-founded, justified; **sachlich** ~ founded on fact.

Begründung *f* justification, reason.
begrüßen [bəgrü:'sən] *vt* greet, welcome.
begrüßenswert *a* welcome.
Begrüßung *f* greeting, welcome.
begünstigen [bəgüns'tigən] *vt* (*Person*) favor (*US*), favour (*Brit*); (*Sache*) further, promote.
Begünstigte(r) *mf dekl wie a* beneficiary.
begutachten [bəgōō:t'áḳhtən] *vt* assess; (*umg: ansehen*) have a look at.
begütert [bəgü:'tərt] *a* wealthy, well-to-do.
begütigend *a* (*Worte etc*) soothing; ~ **auf jdn einreden** calm sb down.
behaart [bəhárt'] *a* hairy.
behäbig [bəhe:'biḳh] *a* (*dick*) portly, stout; (*geruhsam*) comfortable.
behaftet [bəháf'tət] *a*: **mit etw ~ sein** be afflicted by sth.
behagen [bəhá'gən] *vi*: **das behagt ihm nicht** he does not like it; **B~** *nt* **-s** comfort, ease; **mit B~ essen** eat with relish.
behaglich [bəhá'kliḳh] *a* comfortable, cozy (*US*), cosy (*Brit*); **B~keit** *f* comfort, coziness (*US*), cosiness (*Brit*).
behält [bəhelt'] *3. pers sing präs von* **behalten**.
behalten [bəhál'tən] *vt unreg* keep, retain; (*im Gedächtnis*) remember; ~ **Sie (doch) Platz!** please don't get up!
Behälter [bəhel'tər] *m* **-s, -** container, receptacle.
behämmert [bəhe'mərt] *a* (*umg*) screwy, crazy.
behandeln [bəhán'dəln] *vt* treat; (*Thema*) deal with; (*Maschine*) handle; **der behandelnde Arzt** the doctor in attendance.
Behandlung *f* treatment; (*von Maschine*) handling.
behängen [bəhe'ngən] *vt* decorate; (*Wände auch*) hang.
beharren [bəhá'rən] *vi*: **auf etw** (*dat*) ~ stick *od* keep to sth.
beharrlich [bəhár'liḳh] *a* (*ausdauernd*) steadfast, unwavering; (*hartnäckig*) tenacious, dogged; **B~keit** *f* steadfastness; tenacity.
behaupten [bəhoup'tən] *vt* claim, assert, maintain; (*sein Recht*) defend; **von jdm ~, daß ...** say (of sb) that ... ♦ *vr* assert o.s.; **sich auf dem Markt** ~ establish itself on the market.
Behauptung *f* claim, assertion.
Behausung [bəhou'zōōng] *f* dwelling, abode; (*armselig*) hovel.
beheben [bəhā:'bən] *vt unreg* (*beseitigen*) remove; (*Mißstände*) remedy; (*Schaden*) repair; (*Störung*) clear.
beheimatet [bəhī'mátət] *a* domiciled; (*Tier, Pflanze*) with its habitat in.
beheizen [bəhī'tsən] *vt* heat.
Behelf [bəhelf'] *m* **-(e)s, -e** expedient, makeshift; **b~en** *vr unreg*: **sich mit etw b~en** make do with sth.
Behelfs- *zW*: **~ausfahrt** *f* (*Autobahn*) temporary exit; **b~mäßig** *a* improvised,

makeshift; (*vorübergehend*) temporary.
behelligen [bəhe'ligən] *vt* trouble, bother.
Behendigkeit [bəhen'diḳhkīt] *f* agility, quickness.
beherbergen [bəher'bergən] *vt* (*lit, fig*) house.
beherrschen [bəher'shən] *vt* (*Volk*) rule, govern; (*Situation*) control; (*Sprache, Gefühle*) master ♦ *vr* control o.s.
beherrscht *a* controlled; **B~heit** *f* self-control.
Beherrschung *f* rule; control; mastery; **die ~ verlieren** lose one's temper.
beherzigen [bəher'tsigən] *vt* take to heart.
beherzt *a* spirited, brave.
behielt [bəhē:lt'] *imperf von* **behalten**.
behilflich [bəhilf'liḳh] *a* helpful; **jdm ~ sein** help sb (*bei* with).
behindern [bəhin'dərn] *vt* hinder, impede.
Behinderte(r) *mf dekl wie a* disabled person.
Behinderung *f* hindrance; (*Körper~*) handicap.
Behörde [bəhœr'də] *f* **-, -n** authorities *pl*; (*Amtsgebäude*) office(s *pl*).
behördlich [bəhœr'tliḳh] *a* official.
behüten [bəhü:'tən] *vt* guard; **jdn vor etw** (*dat*) ~ preserve sb from sth; **behütet** (*Jugend etc*) sheltered.
behutsam [bəhōō:t'zám] *a* cautious, careful; **man muß es ihr ~ beibringen** it will have to be broken to her gently; **B~keit** *f* caution, carefulness.
bei [bī] *präp* **+dat** (*örtlich*) near, by; (*zeitlich*) at, on; (*während*) during; **beim Friseur** at the hairdresser's; ~ **uns** at our place; ~ **seinen Eltern wohnen** live with one's parents; ~ **einer Firma arbeiten** work for a firm; **ich habe ihm** ~ **der Arbeit geholfen** I helped him with the work; ~ **guter Gesundheit sein** be in good health; ~ **Nacht** at night; ~ **Nebel** in fog; ~ **Regen** if it rains; ~ **offenem Fenster schlafen** sleep with the window open; ~ **Feuer Scheibe einschlagen** in case of fire break glass; **etw** ~ **sich haben** have sth on one; **jdn** ~ **sich haben** have sb with one; **ich habe kein Geld** ~ **mir** I have no money on me; ~ **seinem Talent** with his talent; ~ **Goethe** in Goethe; **beim Militär** in the army; **beim Fahren** while driving.
beibehalten [bī'bəháltən] *vt unreg* keep, retain.
Beibehaltung *f* keeping, retaining.
Beiblatt [bī'blát] *nt* supplement.
beibringen [bī'bringən] *vt unreg* (*Beweis, Zeugen*) bring forward; (*Gründe*) adduce; **jdm etw** ~ (*zufügen*) inflict sth on sb; (*zu verstehen geben*) make sb understand sth; (*lehren*) teach sb sth.
Beichte [bīḳh'tə] *f* **-, -n** confession.
beichten *vt* confess ♦ *vi* go to confession.
Beicht- *zW*: **~geheimnis** *nt* secret of the confessional; **~stuhl** *m* confessional.
beide [bī'də] *pron, a* both; **meine ~n Brüder**

my two brothers, both my brothers; **die ersten** ~**n** the first two; **wir** ~ we two; **einer von** ~**n** one of the two; **alles** ~**s** both (of them); ~**mal** ad both times.

beider- zW: ~**lei** a inv of both; ~**seitig** a mutual, reciprocal; ~**seits** ad mutually ♦ präp +gen on both sides of.

beidhändig [bīt'hendiçh] a ambidextrous.

beidrehen [bī'drā:ən] vi heave to.

beidseitig [bit'zītiçh] a (auf beiden Seiten) on both sides.

beieinander [bīnán'dər] ad together; ~**sein** vi unreg: **gut** ~**sein** (umg: gesundheitlich) be in good shape; (: geistig) be all there.

Beifahrer(in f) [bī'fárər(in)] m -**s**, - passenger; ~**sitz** m passenger seat.

Beifall [bī'fál] m -(e)s applause; (Zustimmung) approval.

beifallheischend [bī'fálhīshənt] a fishing for applause/approval.

beifällig [bī'feliçh] a approving; (Kommentar) favorable (US), favourable (Brit).

Beifilm [bī'film] m supporting film.

beifügen [bī'fü:gən] vt enclose.

Beigabe [bī'gâbə] f addition.

beige [be:'zhə] a beige.

beigeben [bī'gā:bən] unreg vt (zufügen) add; (mitgeben) give ♦ vi (nachgeben) give in (dat to).

Beigeschmack [bī'gáshmák] m aftertaste.

Beihilfe [bī'hilfə] f aid, assistance; (Studien~) grant; (JUR) aiding and abetting; **wegen** ~ **zum Mord** (JUR) because of being an accessory to the murder.

beikommen [bī'komən] vi unreg (+dat) get at; (einem Problem) deal with.

Beil [bīl] nt -(e)s, -e ax (US), axe (Brit), hatchet.

Beilage [bī'lâgə] f (Buch~ etc) supplement; (KOCH) vegetables and potatoes pl.

beiläufig [bī'loifiçh] a casual, incidental ♦ ad casually, by the way.

beilegen [bī'lā:gən] vt (hinzufügen) enclose, add; (beimessen) attribute, ascribe; (Streit) settle.

beileibe [bīlī'bə] ad: ~ **nicht** by no means.

Beileid [bī'līt] nt condolence, sympathy; **herzliches** ~ deepest sympathy.

beiliegend [bī'lē:gənt] a (COMM) enclosed.

beim [bīm] = **bei dem**.

beimessen [bī'mesən] vt unreg attribute, ascribe (dat to).

Bein [bīn] nt -(e)s, -e leg; **jdm ein** ~ **stellen** (lit, fig) trip sb up; **wir sollten uns auf die** ~**e machen** (umg) we ought to be making tracks; **jdm** ~**e machen** (umg: antreiben) make sb get a move on; **die** ~**e in die Hand nehmen** (umg) take to one's heels; **sich** (dat) **die** ~**e in den Bauch stehen** (umg) stand about until one is fit to drop; **etw auf die** ~**e stellen** (fig) get sth off the ground.

beinah(e) [bī'ná(ə)] ad almost, nearly.

Beinbruch m fracture of the leg; **das ist**

kein ~ (fig umg) it could be worse.

beinhalten [bəin'hálten] vt contain.

beipflichten [bī'pfliçhten] vi: **jdm/etw** ~ agree with sb/sth.

Beiprogramm [bī'prōgràm] nt supporting program.

Beirat [bī'rât] m legal adviser; (Körperschaft) advisory council; (Eltern~) parents' council.

beirren [bəi'rən] vt confuse, muddle; **sich nicht** ~ **lassen** not let o.s. be confused.

beisammen [bīzà'mən] ad together; ~**haben** vt unreg: **er hat (sie) nicht alle** ~ (umg) he's not all there; **B**~**sein** nt -**s** get-together.

Beischlaf [bī'shlâf] m (JUR) sexual intercourse.

Beisein [bī'zīn] nt -**s** presence.

beiseite [bīzī'tə] ad to one side, aside; (stehen) on one side, aside; **Spaß** ~! joking apart!; **etw** ~ **legen** (sparen) put sth by; **jdn/etw** ~ **schaffen** put sb/get sth out of the way.

beisetzen [bī'zetsən] vt bury.

Beisetzung f funeral.

Beisitzer(in f) [bī'zitsər(in)] m -**s**, - (JUR) assessor; (bei Prüfung) observer.

Beispiel [bī'shpē:l] nt -(e)s, -e example; **mit gutem** ~ **vorangehen** set a good example; **sich** (dat) **an jdm ein** ~ **nehmen** take sb as an example; **zum** ~ for example; **b**~**haft** a exemplary; **b**~**los** a unprecedented.

beispielsweise ad for instance od example.

beispringen [bī'shpringən] vi unreg: **jdm** ~ come to the aid of sb.

beißen [bī'sən] unreg vti bite; (stechen: Rauch, Säure) burn ♦ vr (Farben) clash.

beißend a biting, caustic; (Geruch) pungent, sharp; (fig auch) sarcastic.

Beißzange [bīs'tsángə] f pliers pl.

Beistand [bī'shtánt] m -(e)s, ⁻e support, help; (JUR) adviser; **jdm** ~ **leisten** give sb assistance/give sb one's support.

beistehen [bī'shtā:ən] vi unreg: **jdm** ~ stand by sb.

Beistelltisch [bī'shteltish] m occasional table.

beisteuern [bī'shtoiərn] vt contribute.

beistimmen [bī'shtimən] vi (+dat) agree with.

Beistrich [bī'shtriçh] m comma.

Beitr. abk = **Beitrag**.

Beitrag [bī'trák] m -(e)s, ⁻e contribution; (Zahlung) fee, subscription; (Versicherungs~) premium; **einen** ~ **zu etw leisten** make a contribution to sth.

beitragen [bī'trágən] vt unreg contribute (zu to); (mithelfen) help (zu with).

Beitrags- zW: **b**~**frei** a non-contributory; **b**~**pflichtig** a contributory; **b**~**pflichtig sein** (Mensch) have to pay contributions; ~**zahlende(r)** mf dekl wie a fee-paying member.

beitreten [bī'trā:tən] vi unreg join (einem Verein a club).

Beitritt [bī'trit] m joining; membership.

Beitrittserklärung f declaration of membership.

Beiwagen [bī'vågən] m (Motorrad~) sidecar; (Straßenbahn~) extra carriage.

beiwohnen [bī'vō:nən] vi (geh): **einer Sache** (dat) ~ attend od be present at something.

Beiwort [bī'vort] nt adjective.

Beize [bī'tsə] f -, -n (Holz~) stain; (KOCH) marinade.

beizeiten [bītsī'tən] ad in time.

bejahen [bəyâ'ən] vt (Frage) say yes to, answer in the affirmative; (gutheißen) agree with.

bejahrt [bəyârt'] a aged, elderly.

bejammern [bəyá'mərn] vt lament, bewail.

bejammernswert a lamentable.

bekakeln [bəkâ'kəln] vt (umg) discuss.

bekam [bəkám'] imperf von **bekommen.**

bekämpfen [bəkem'pfən] vt (Gegner) fight; (Seuche) combat ♦ vr fight.

Bekämpfung f fight od struggle against.

bekannt [bəkánt'] a (well-)known; (nicht fremd) familiar; **mit jdm** ~ **sein** know sb; **jdn mit jdm** ~ **machen** introduce sb to sb; **sich mit etw** ~ **machen** familiarize o.s. with sth; **das ist mir** ~ I know that; **es/sie kommt mir** ~ **vor** it/she seems familiar; **durch etw** ~ **werden** become famous because of sth.

Bekanntenkreis m circle of friends.

Bekannte(r) mf dekl wie a friend, acquaintance.

bekanntermaßen ad as is known.

bekannt- zW: **B~gabe** f announcement; **~geben** vt unreg announce publicly; **B~heitsgrad** m degree of fame; **~lich** ad as is well known, as you know; **~machen** vt announce; **B~machung** f publication; (Anschlag etc) announcement; **B~schaft** f acquaintance.

bekehren [bəkā:'rən] vt convert ♦ vr become converted.

Bekehrung f conversion.

bekennen [bəke'nən] vt unreg confess; (Glauben) profess; **Farbe** ~ (umg) show where one stands ♦ vr: **sich zu jdm/etw** ~ declare one's support for sb/sth.

Bekenntnis [bəkent'nis] nt -ses, -se admission, confession; (Religion) confession, denomination; **ein** ~ **zur Demokratie ablegen** declare one's belief in democracy; **~schule** f denominational school.

beklagen [bəklâ'gən] vt deplore, lament ♦ vr complain.

beklagenswert a lamentable, pathetic; (Mensch) pitiful; (Zustand) deplorable; (Unfall) terrible.

beklatschen [bəklát'shən] vt applaud, clap.

bekleben [bəklā:'bən] vt: **etw mit Bildern** ~ stick pictures onto sth.

bekleckern [bəkle'kərn] vt (umg) stain.

bekleiden [bəklī'dən] vt clothe; (Amt) occupy, fill.

Bekleidung f clothing; (form: eines Amtes)

tenure.

Bekleidungsindustrie f clothing industry, rag trade (umg).

beklemmen [bəkle'mən] vt oppress.

Beklemmung f oppressiveness; (Gefühl der Angst) feeling of apprehension.

beklommen [bəklo'mən] a anxious, uneasy; **B~heit** f anxiety, uneasiness.

bekloppt [bəklopt'] a (umg) crazy.

beknackt [bəknákt'] a (umg) lousy.

beknien [bəknē:'ən] vt (umg: jdn) beg.

bekommen [bəko'mən] unreg vt get, receive; (Kind) have; (Zug) catch, get; **es mit jdm zu tun** ~ get into trouble with sb ♦ vi: **jdm** ~ agree with sb; **wohl bekomm's!** your health!

bekömmlich [bəkœm'liçh] a easily digestible.

beköstigen [bəkœs'tigən] vt cater for.

bekräftigen [bəkref'tigən] vt confirm, corroborate.

Bekräftigung f corroboration.

bekreuzigen [bəkroi'tsigən] vr cross o.s.

bekritteln [bəkri'təln] vt criticize, pick holes in.

bekümmern [bəkü'mərn] vt worry, trouble.

bekunden [bəkōōn'dən] vt (sagen) state; (zeigen) show.

belächeln [bəle'çhəln] vt laugh at.

beladen [bəlâ'dən] vt unreg load.

Belag [bəlâk'] m -(e)s, ̈-e covering, coating; (Brot~) spread; (auf Pizza, Brot) topping; (auf Tortenboden, zwischen Brotscheiben) filling; (Zahn~) tartar; (auf Zunge) fur; (Brems~) lining.

belagern [bəlâ'gərn] vt besiege.

Belagerung f siege.

Belagerungszustand m state of siege.

Belang [bəláng'] m -(e)s importance.

Belange pl interests pl, concerns pl.

belangen vt (JUR) take to court.

belanglos a trivial, unimportant.

Belanglosigkeit f triviality.

belassen [bəlá'sən] vt unreg (in Zustand, Glauben) leave; (in Stellung) retain; **es dabei** ~ leave it at that.

Belastbarkeit f (von Brücke, Aufzug) load-bearing capacity; (von Menschen, Nerven) ability to take stress.

belasten [bəlá'stən] vt (lit) burden; (fig: bedrücken) trouble, worry; (COMM: Konto) debit; (etw mit einer Hypothek) ~ mortgage sth ♦ vr weigh o.s. down; (JUR) incriminate o.s.

belastend a (JUR) incriminating.

belästigen [bəle'stigən] vt annoy, pester.

Belästigung f annoyance, pestering; (körperlich) molesting.

Belastung [bəlá'stōōng] f (lit) load; (fig: Sorge etc) weight; (COMM) charge, debit(ing); (mit Hypothek) mortgage (gen on); (JUR) incriminating evidence.

Belastungs- zW: **~material** nt (JUR) incriminating evidence; **~probe** f capacity test; (fig) test; **~zeuge** m witness for the pros-

ecution.
belaubt [bəloupt'] *a*: **dicht ~ sein** have thick foliage.
belaufen [bəlou'fən] *vr unreg* amount (*auf +akk* to).
belauschen [bəlou'shən] *vt* eavesdrop on.
beleben [bəlā:'bən] *vt* (*anregen*) liven up; (*Konjunktur, jds Hoffnungen*) stimulate.
belebt [bəlā:pt'] *a* (*Straße*) crowded.
Beleg [bəlā:k'] *m* -(e)s, -e (*COMM*) receipt; (*Beweis*) documentary evidence, proof; (*Beispiel*) example.
belegen [bəlā:'gən] *vt* cover; (*Kuchen, Brot*) spread; (*Platz*) reserve, book; (*Kurs, Vorlesung*) register for; (*beweisen*) verify, prove; (*MIL: mit Bomben*) bomb.
Belegschaft *f* personnel, staff.
belegt *a* (*Zunge*) coated; (*Stimme*) hoarse; (*Zimmer*) occupied; **~e Brote** open sandwiches.
belehren [bəlā:'rən] *vt* instruct, teach; **jdn eines Besseren ~** teach sb better; **er ist nicht zu ~** he won't be told.
Belehrung *f* instruction.
beleibt [bəlīpt'] *a* stout, corpulent.
beleidigen [bəlī'digən] *vt* insult; offend.
beleidigt *a* insulted; (*gekränkt*) offended; **die ~e Leberwurst spielen** (*umg*) be in a huff.
Beleidigung *f* insult; (*JUR*) slander; (*schriftlich*) libel.
beleihen [bəlī'ən] *vt unreg* (*COMM*) lend money on.
belemmert [bəle'mərt] *a* (*umg*) sheepish.
belesen [bəlā:'zən] *a* well-read.
beleuchten [bəloich̩'tən] *vt* light, illuminate; (*fig*) throw light on.
Beleuchter(in *f*) *m* -s, - lighting technician.
Beleuchtung *f* lighting, illumination.
beleumdet [bəloim'dət], **beleumundet** [bəloi'mŏŏndət] *a*: **gut/schlecht ~ sein** have a good/bad reputation.
Belgien [bel'gēən] *nt* -s Belgium.
Belgier(in *f*) *m* -s, - Belgian.
belgisch *a* Belgian.
Belgrad [bel'grät] *nt* Belgrade.
belichten [bəlich̩'tən] *vt* expose.
Belichtung *f* exposure.
Belichtungsmesser *m* exposure meter.
belieben *vi unpers* (*geh*): **wie es Ihnen beliebt** as you wish.
Belieben [bəlē:'bən] *nt*: (**ganz) nach ~** (just) as you wish.
beliebig [bəlē:'bich̩] *a* any you like, as you like; **~ viel** as many as you like; **in ~er Reihenfolge** in any order whatever; **ein ~es Thema** any subject you like od want.
beliebt [bəlē:pt'] *a* popular; **sich bei jdm ~ machen** make o.s. popular with sb; **B~heit** *f* popularity.
beliefern [bəlē:'fərn] *vt* supply.
bellen [be'lən] *vi* bark.
Belletristik [belātris'tik] *f* fiction and poetry.
belohnen [bəlō:'nən] *vt* reward.

Belohnung *f* reward.
Belüftung [bəlüf'tŏŏng] *f* ventilation.
belügen [bəlü:'gən] *vt unreg* lie to, deceive.
belustigen [bəlŏŏs'tigən] *vt* amuse.
Belustigung *f* amusement.
bemächtigen [bəmech̩'tigən] *vr*: **sich einer Sache** (*gen*) **~** take possession of sth, seize sth.
bemalen [bəmâ'lən] *vt* paint ♦ *vr* (*pej: schminken*) put on one's war paint (*umg*).
bemängeln [bəme'ngəln] *vt* criticize.
bemannen [bəmá'nən] *vt* man.
Bemannung *f* manning; (*NAUT, AVIAT etc*) crew.
bemänteln [bəmen'təln] *vt* cloak, hide.
bemerkbar *a* perceptible, noticeable; **sich ~ machen** (*Person*) make od get o.s. noticed; (*Unruhe*) become noticeable.
bemerken [bəmer'kən] *vt* (*wahrnehmen*) notice, observe; (*sagen*) say, mention; **nebenbei bemerkt** by the way.
bemerkenswert *a* remarkable, noteworthy.
Bemerkung *f* remark; (*schriftlich auch*) note.
bemitleiden [bəmi'tlīdən] *vt* pity.
bemittelt [bimi'təlt] *a* well-to-do, well-off.
bemühen [bəmü:'ən] *vr* take trouble od pains; **sich um eine Stelle ~** try to get a job.
bemüht *a*: (**darum) ~ sein, etw zu tun** endeavor (*US*) od endeavour (*Brit*) od be at pains to do sth.
Bemühung *f* trouble, pains *pl*, effort.
bemüßigt [bəmü:'sich̩t] *a*: **sich ~ fühlen/ sehen** (*geh*) feel called upon.
bemuttern [bəmŏŏ'tərn] *vt* mother.
benachbart [bənákh'bärt] *a* neighboring (*US*), neighbouring (*Brit*).
benachrichtigen [bənákh'rich̩tigən] *vt* inform.
Benachrichtigung *f* notification.
benachteiligen [bənákh'tīligən] *vt* (put at a) disadvantage, victimize.
benehmen [bənā:'mən] *vr unreg* behave; **B~** *nt* -s behavior (*US*), behaviour (*Brit*); **kein B~ haben** not know how to behave.
beneiden [bənī'dən] *vt* envy.
beneidenswert *a* enviable.
Beneluxländer [bā:'nälŏŏkslendər] *pl*, **-staaten** *pl* Benelux countries *pl*.
benennen [bəne'nən] *vt unreg* name.
Bengel [be'ngəl] *m* -s, - (little) rascal od rogue.
Benimm [bənim'] *m* (*umg*) manners *pl*.
benommen [bəno'mən] *a* dazed.
benoten [bənō:'tən] *vt* mark.
benötigen [bənœ'tigən] *vt* need.
benutzen [bənŏŏ'tsən], **benützen** [bənü'tsən] *vt* use.
Benutzer(in *f*) *m* -s, - user; **b~freundlich** *a* user-friendly.
Benutzung *f* utilization, use; **jdm etw zur ~ überlassen** put sth at sb's disposal.
Benzin [bentsē:n'] *nt* -s, -e (*AUT*) gas(oline)

(*US*), petrol (*Brit*); **~einspritzanlage** *f* (*AUT*) fuel injection system; **~kanister** *m* gas can; **~tank** *m* gas tank; **~uhr** *f* gas gauge.

beobachten [bəō:'baᶄhtən] *vt* observe.

Beobachter(in *f*) *m* **-s,** - observer; (*eines Unfalls*) witness; (*PRESSE, TV*) correspondent.

Beobachtung *f* observation.

beordern [bəor'dərn] *vt*: **jdn zu sich** ~ send for sb.

bepacken [bəpá'kən] *vt* load, pack.

bepflanzen [bəpflân'tsən] *vt* plant.

bequatschen [bəkvát'shən] *vt* (*umg: überreden*) persuade; **etw** ~ talk sth over.

bequem [bəkvā:m'] *a* comfortable; (*Ausrede*) convenient; (*Person*) lazy, indolent.

bequemen [bəkvā:'mən] *vr* condescend (*zu* to).

Bequemlichkeit *f* convenience, comfort; (*Faulheit*) laziness, indolence.

Ber. *abk* = **Bericht; Beruf.**

berät [bəre:t'] *3. pers sing präs von* **beraten.**

beraten [bərâ'tən] *unreg vt* advise; (*besprechen*) discuss, debate ♦ *vr* consult; **gut/ schlecht** ~ **sein** be well/ill advised; **sich** ~ **lassen** get advice.

beratend *a*: **jdm** ~ **zur Seite stehen** act in an advisory capacity to sb.

Berater(in *f*) *m* **-s,** - adviser; **~vertrag** *m* consultancy contract.

beratschlagen [bərât'shlâgən] *vti* deliberate (on), confer (about).

Beratung *f* advice; (*Besprechung*) consultation.

Beratungsstelle *f* advice center.

berauben [bərou'bən] *vt* rob.

berauschen [bərou'shən] *vt* (*lit, fig*) intoxicate.

berauschend *a*: **das war nicht sehr** ~ (*ironisch*) that wasn't very exciting.

berechenbar [bəre'ᶍhənbâr] *a* calculable; (*Verhalten*) predictable.

berechnen [bəreᶍh'nən] *vt* calculate; (*COMM: anrechnen*) charge.

berechnend *a* (*Mensch*) calculating, scheming.

Berechnung *f* calculation; (*COMM*) charge.

berechtigen [bəreᶍh'tigən] *vt* entitle; (*bevollmächtigen*) authorize; (*fig*) justify.

berechtigt [bəreᶍh'tiᶍht] *a* justifiable, justified.

Berechtigung *f* authorization; (*fig*) justification.

bereden [bərā:'dən] *vtr* (*besprechen*) discuss; (*überreden*) persuade.

beredt [bərā:t'] *a* eloquent.

Bereich [bərīᶍh'] *m* **-(e)s, -e** (*Bezirk*) area; (*PHYS*) range; (*Ressort, Gebiet*) sphere; **im** ~ **des Möglichen liegen** be within the bounds of possibility.

bereichern [bərī'ᶍhərn] *vt* enrich ♦ *vr* get rich; **sich auf Kosten anderer** ~ feather one's nest at the expense of other people.

Bereifung [bərī'foong] *f* (set of) tires (*US*) *od* tyres (*Brit*) *pl*; (*Vorgang*) fitting with tires.

bereinigen [bərī'nigən] *vt* settle.

bereisen [bərī'zən] *vt* travel through; (*COMM: Gebiet*) travel, cover.

bereit [bərīt'] *a* ready, prepared; **zu etw** ~ **sein** be ready for sth; **sich** ~ **erklären** declare o.s. willing.

bereiten *vt* prepare, make ready; (*Kummer, Freude*) cause; **einer Sache** (*dat*) **ein Ende** ~ put an end to sth.

bereit- *zW*: **~halten** *vt unreg* keep in readiness; **~legen** *vt* lay out; **~machen** *vtr* prepare, get ready.

bereits *ad* already.

bereit- *zW*: **B~schaft** *f* readiness; (*Polizei*) alert; **in B~schaft sein** be on the alert *od* on stand-by; **B~schaftsarzt** *m* doctor on call; (*im Krankenhaus*) duty doctor; **B~schaftsdienst** *m* emergency service; **~stehen** *vi unreg* (*Person*) be prepared; (*Ding*) be ready; **~stellen** *vt* (*Kisten, Pakete etc*) put ready; (*Geld etc*) make available; (*Truppen, Maschinen*) put at the ready.

Bereitung *f* preparation.

bereitwillig *a* willing, ready; **B~keit** *f* willingness, readiness.

bereuen [bəroi'ən] *vt* regret.

Berg [berk] *m* **-(e)s, -e** mountain; (*kleiner*) hill; **mit etw hinterm** ~ **halten** (*fig*) keep quiet about sth; **über alle** ~**e sein** be miles away; **da stehen einem ja die Haare zu** ~**e** it's enough to make your hair stand on end; **b~ab** *ad* downhill; **b~an, b~auf** *ad* uphill; **~arbeiter** *m* miner; **~bahn** *f* mountain railroad; **~bau** *m* mining.

bergen [ber'gən] *vt unreg* (*retten*) rescue; (*Ladung*) salvage; (*enthalten*) contain.

Berg- *zW*: **~führer** *m* mountain guide; **~gipfel** *m* mountain top, peak, summit.

bergig [ber'giᶍh] *a* mountainous, hilly.

Berg- *zW*: **~kamm** *m* crest, ridge; **~kette** *f* mountain range; **~kristall** *m* rock crystal; **~mann**, *pl*, **~leute** miner; **~not** *f*: **in** **~not sein/geraten** be in/get into difficulties while climbing; **~predigt** *f* (*REL*) Sermon on the Mount; **~rettungsdienst** *m* mountain rescue service; **~rutsch** *m* landslide; **~schuh** *m* walking boot; **~steigen** *nt* mountaineering; **~steiger(in** *f*) *m* **-s,** - mountaineer, climber; **~-und-Tal-Bahn** *f* roller coaster.

Bergung [ber'goong] *f* (*von Menschen*) rescue; (*von Material*) recovery; (*NAUT*) salvage.

Berg- *zW*: **~wacht** *f* mountain rescue service; **~werk** *nt* mine.

Bericht [bəriᶍht'] *m* **-(e)s, -e** report, account; **b~en** *vti* report; **~erstatter** *m* **-s,** - reporter, (newspaper) correspondent; **~erstattung** *f* reporting.

berichtigen [bəriᶍh'tigən] *vt* correct.

Berichtigung *f* correction.

berieseln [bərē:'zəln] *vt* spray with water *etc.*
Berieselung *f* watering; **die dauernde ~ mit Musik** ... *(fig)* the constant stream of music ...
Berieselungsanlage *f* sprinkler (system).
Beringmeer [bā:'ringmā:r] *nt* Bering Sea.
beritten [bəri'tən] *a* mounted.
Berlin [berlē:n'] *nt* **-s** Berlin.
Berliner *a attr* Berlin ♦ *m* **-s**, - *(KOCH)* jelly *(US) od* jam *(Brit)* doughnut.
Berliner(in *f)* *m* **-s**, - Berliner.
berlinerisch *a (umg:* Dialekt) Berlin *attr.*
Bermudas [bermōō:'dàs] *pl:* **auf den ~** in Bermuda.
Bernhardiner [bernhárdē:'nər] *m* **-s**, - Saint Bernard (dog).
Bernstein [bern'shtīn] *m* amber.
bersten [bers'tən] *vi unreg* burst, split.
berüchtigt [bərüċh'tiċht] *a* notorious, infamous.
berücksichtigen [bərük'ziċhtigən] *vt* consider, bear in mind.
Berücksichtigung *f* consideration; **in** *od* **unter ~ der Tatsache, daß** ... in view of the fact that ...
Beruf [bərōō:f'] *m* **-(e)s**, **-e** occupation, profession; *(Gewerbe)* trade; **was sind Sie von ~?** what is your occupation *etc?*, what do you do for a living?; **seinen ~ verfehlt haben** have missed one's vocation.
berufen *unreg vt (in Amt)* appoint *(in +akk* to; *zu* as) ♦ *vr:* **sich auf jdn/etw ~** refer *od* appeal to sb/sth ♦ *a* competent, qualified; *(ausersehen):* **zu etw ~ sein** have a vocation for sth.
beruflich *a* professional; **er ist ~ viel unterwegs** he is away a lot on business.
Berufs- *zW:* **~ausbildung** *f* vocational *od* professional training; **b~bedingt** *a* occupational; **~berater** *m* vocational counselor *(US)*, careers adviser *(Brit)*; **~beratung** *f* vocational guidance; **~bezeichnung** *f* job description; **~erfahrung** *f* (professional) experience; **~feuerwehr** *f* fire department *(US) od* service *(Brit)*; **~geheimnis** *nt* professional secret; **~krankheit** *f* occupational disease; **~kriminalität** *f* professional crime; **~leben** *nt* professional life; **im ~leben stehen** be working *od* in employment; **b~mäßig** *a* professional; **~risiko** *nt* occupational hazard; **~schule** *f* vocational *od* trade school; **~soldat** *m* professional soldier, regular; **~sportler** *m* professional (sportsman); **b~tätig** *a* employed; **~unfall** *m* occupational accident; **~verbot** *nt:* **jdm ~verbot erteilen** ban sb from his/her profession; *(einem Arzt, Anwalt)* strike sb off; **~verkehr** *m* commuter traffic; **~wahl** *f* choice of a job.
Berufung *f* vocation, calling; *(Ernennung)* appointment; *(JUR)* appeal; **~ einlegen** appeal; **unter ~ auf etw** *(akk) (form)* with reference to sth.
Berufungsgericht *nt* appeal court, appellate

court *(US)*.
beruhen [bərōō:'ən] *vi:* **auf etw** *(dat)* **~** be based on sth; **etw auf sich ~ lassen** leave sth at that; **das beruht auf Gegenseitigkeit** the feeling is mutual.
beruhigen [bərōō:'igən] *vt* calm, pacify, soothe ♦ *vr (Mensch)* calm (o.s.) down; *(Situation)* calm down.
Beruhigung *f* reassurance; *(der Nerven)* calming; **zu jds ~** to reassure sb.
Beruhigungs- *zW:* **~mittel** *nt* sedative; **~pille** *f* tranquillizer.
berühmt [bərü:mt'] *a* famous; **das war nicht ~** *(umg)* it was nothing to write home about; **~-berüchtigt** *a* infamous, notorious; **B~heit** *f (Ruf)* fame; *(Mensch)* celebrity.
berühren [bərü:'rən] *vt* touch; *(gefühlsmäßig bewegen)* affect; *(flüchtig erwähnen)* mention, touch on; **von etw peinlich berührt sein** be embarrassed by sth ♦ *vr* meet, touch.
Berührung *f* contact.
Berührungspunkt *m* point of contact.
bes. *abk (= besonders)* esp.
besagen [bəzá'gən] *vt* mean.
besagt *a (form: Tag etc)* in question.
besaiten [bəzī'tən] *vt:* **neu ~** *(Instrument)* restring.
besänftigen [bəzenf'tigən] *vt* soothe, calm.
besänftigend *a* soothing.
Besänftigung *f* soothing, calming.
besaß [bəzàs'] *imperf von* **besitzen**.
besät [bəze:t'] *a* covered; *(mit Blättern etc)* strewn.
Besatz [bəzàts'] *m* **-es**, **⁻e** trimming, edging.
Besatzung *f* garrison; *(NAUT, AVIAT)* crew.
Besatzungs- *zW:* **~macht** *f* occupying power; **~zone** *f* occupied zone.
besaufen [bəzou'fən] *vr unreg (umg)* get drunk *od* stoned.
beschädigen [bəshe:'digən] *vt* damage.
Beschädigung *f* damage; *(Stelle)* damaged spot.
beschaffen [bəshá'fən] *vt* get, acquire ♦ *a* constituted; **so ~ sein wie** ... be the same as ...; **B~heit** *f* constitution, nature; **je nach B~heit der Lage** according to the situation.
Beschaffung *f* acquisition.
beschäftigen [bəshef'tigən] *vt* occupy; *(beruflich)* employ; *(innerlich):* **jdn ~** be on sb's mind ♦ *vr* occupy *od* concern o.s.
beschäftigt *a* busy, occupied; *(angestellt)* employed *(bei* by).
Beschäftigung *f (Beruf)* employment; *(Tätigkeit)* occupation; *(Befassen)* concern; **einer ~ nachgehen** *(form)* be employed.
Beschäftigungs- *zW:* **~programm** *nt* employment scheme; **~therapie** *f* occupational therapy.
beschämen [bəshe:'mən] *vt* put to shame.
beschämend *a* shameful; *(Hilfsbereitschaft)* shaming.
beschämt *a* ashamed.
beschatten [bəshá'tən] *vt* shade;

(Verdächtige) shadow.
beschaulich [bəʃhou'liçh] *a* contemplative; *(Leben, Abend)* quiet, tranquil.
Bescheid [bəʃhīt'] *m* **-(e)s, -e** information; *(Weisung)* directions *pl*; ~ **wissen** be well-informed *(über +akk* about); **ich weiß** ~ I know; **jdm** ~ **geben** *od* **sagen** let sb know; **jdm ordentlich** ~ **sagen** *(umg)* tell sb where to go.
bescheiden [bəʃhī'dən] *unreg vr* content o.s. ♦ *vt:* **etw abschlägig** ~ *(form)* turn sth down ♦ *a* modest; **B~heit** *f* modesty.
bescheinen [bəʃhī'nən] *vt unreg* shine on.
bescheinigen [bəʃhī'nigən] *vt* certify; *(bestätigen)* acknowledge; **hiermit wird bescheinigt, daß** ... this is to certify that ...
Bescheinigung *f* certificate; *(Quittung)* receipt.
bescheißen [bəʃhī'sən] *vt unreg (umg!)* cheat.
beschenken [bəʃheng'kən] *vt* give presents to.
bescheren [bəʃhā:'rən] *vt:* **jdm etw** ~ give sb sth as a present; **jdn** ~ give presents to sb.
Bescherung *f* giving of presents; *(umg)* mess; **da haben wir die** ~! *(umg)* what did I tell you!
bescheuert [bəʃhoi'ərt] *a (umg)* stupid.
beschichten [bəʃhiçh'tən] *vt (TECH)* coat, cover.
beschießen [bəʃhē:'sən] *vt unreg* shoot *od* fire at.
beschildern [bəʃhil'dərn] *vt* signpost.
beschimpfen [bəʃhim'pfən] *vt* abuse.
Beschimpfung *f* abuse, insult.
beschirmen [bəʃhir'mən] *vt (geh:* *beschützen)* shield.
beschiß *imperf von* **bescheißen**.
Beschiß [bəʃhis'] *m* **-sses** *(umg)*: **das ist** ~ that is a cheat.
beschissen *pp von* **bescheißen** ♦ *a (umg!)* bloody awful, lousy.
Beschlag [bəʃhlāk'] *m* **-(e)s, -e** *(Metallband)* fitting; *(auf Fenster)* condensation; *(auf Metall)* tarnish; finish; *(Hufeisen)* horseshoe; **jdn/etw in** ~ **nehmen** *od* **mit** ~ **belegen** monopolize sb/sth.
beschlagen [bəʃhlā'gən] *unreg vt* cover; *(Pferd)* shoe; *(Fenster, Metall)* cover; ~ **sein** be well versed *(in od auf +dat* in) ♦ *vir (Fenster etc)* mist over.
beschlagnahmen *vt* seize, confiscate.
Beschlagnahmung *f* confiscation, sequestration.
beschleunigen [bəʃhloi'nigən] *vt* accelerate, speed up ♦ *vi (AUT)* accelerate.
Beschleunigung *f* acceleration.
beschließen [bəʃhlē:'sən] *vt unreg* decide on; *(beenden)* end, close.
beschlossen [bəʃhlo'sən] *a (entschieden)* decided, agreed; **das ist** ~**e Sache** that's been settled ♦ *pp von* **beschließen**.
Beschluß [bəʃhlōōs'] *m* **-sses, -schlüsse** deci-

sion, conclusion; *(Ende)* close, end; **einen** ~ **fassen** pass a resolution.
beschlußfähig *a:* ~ **sein** have a quorum.
beschmieren [bəʃhmē:'rən] *vt (Wand)* bedaub.
beschmutzen [bəʃhmōō'tsən] *vt* dirty, soil.
beschneiden [bəʃhnī'dən] *vt unreg* cut; prune, trim; *(REL)* circumcise.
beschnuppern [bəʃhnōō'pərn] *vr (Hunde)* sniff each other; *(fig umg)* size each other up.
beschönigen [bəʃhœ'nigən] *vt* gloss over; **beschönigender Ausdruck** euphemism.
beschränken [bəʃhreng'kən] *vt* limit, restrict *(auf +akk* to) ♦ *vr* restrict o.s.
beschrankt [bəʃhrángkt'] *a (Bahnübergang)* with barrier.
beschränkt [bəʃhrengkt'] *a* confined, narrow; *(Mensch)* limited, narrow-minded; *(pej:* *geistig)* dim; **Gesellschaft mit** ~**er Haftung** corporation *(US)*, limited company *(Brit)*; **B~heit** *f* narrowness.
Beschränkung *f* limitation.
beschreiben [bəʃhrī'bən] *vt unreg* describe; *(Papier)* write on.
Beschreibung *f* description.
beschrieb [bəʃhrē:p'] *imperf von* **beschreiben**.
beschrieben [bəʃhrē:'bən] *pp von* **beschreiben**.
beschriften [bəʃhrif'tən] *vt* mark, label.
Beschriftung *f* lettering.
beschuldigen [bəʃhōōl'digən] *vt* accuse.
Beschuldigung *f* accusation.
beschummeln [bəʃhōō'məln] *vti (umg)* cheat.
Beschuß [bəʃhōōs'] *m:* **jdn/etw unter** ~ **nehmen** *(MIL)* (start to) bombard *od* shell sb/sth; *(fig)* attack sb/sth; **unter** ~ **geraten** *(lit, fig)* come into the firing line.
beschützen [bəʃhü'tsən] *vt* protect *(vor +dat* from).
Beschützer(in *f)* *m* **-s, -** protector.
Beschützung *f* protection.
beschwatzen [bəʃhvà'tsən] *vt (umg:* überreden)* talk over.
Beschwerde [bəʃhvā:r'də] *f* **-, -n** complaint; *(Mühe)* hardship; *(pl: Leiden)* pain; *(INDUSTRIE)* grievance; ~ **einlegen** *(form)* lodge a complaint; **b~frei** *a* fit and healthy; ~**frist** *f (JUR)* period of time during which an appeal may be lodged.
beschweren [bəʃhvā:'rən] *vt* weight down; *(fig)* burden ♦ *vr* complain.
beschwerlich *a* tiring, exhausting.
beschwichtigen [bəʃhviçh'tigən] *vt* soothe, pacify.
Beschwichtigung *f* soothing, calming.
Beschwichtigungsgerede *nt* patronizing talk.
beschwindeln [bəʃhvin'dəln] *vt (betrügen)* cheat; *(belügen)* fib to.
beschwingt [bəʃhvingt'] *a* cheery, in high spirits.

beschwipst [bəshvipst'] *a* tipsy.

beschwören [bəshvœ'rən] *vt unreg* (*Aussage*) swear to; (*anflehen*) implore; (*Geister*) conjure up.

beseelen [bəzā:'lən] *vt* inspire.

besehen [bəzā:'ən] *vt unreg* look at; **genau ~** examine closely.

beseitigen [bəzī'tigən] *vt* remove.

Beseitigung *f* removal.

Besen [bā:'zən] *m* **-s**, - broom; (*pej umg*: *Frau*) old bag; **ich fresse einen ~, wenn das stimmt** (*umg*) if that's right, I'll eat my hat; **~stiel** *m* broomstick.

besessen [bəze'sən] *a* possessed; (*von einer Idee etc*) obsessed (*von* with).

besetzen [bəze'tsən] *vt* (*Haus, Land*) occupy; (*Platz*) take, fill; (*Posten*) fill; (*Rolle*) cast; (*mit Edelsteinen*) set.

besetzt *a* full; (*TEL*) engaged, busy; (*Platz*) taken; (*WC*) occupied (*US*), engaged (*Brit*); **B~zeichen** *nt* busy signal (*US*), engaged tone (*Brit*).

Besetzung *f* occupation; (*von Stelle*) filling; (*von Rolle*) casting; (*die Schauspieler*) cast; **zweite ~** (*THEAT*) understudy.

besichtigen [bəzich'tigən] *vt* visit, look at.

Besichtigung *f* visit.

besiedeln *vt*: **dicht/dünn besiedelt** densely/ thinly populated.

Besied(e)lung [bəzē:d'(ə)loong] *f* population.

besiegeln [bəzē:'gəln] *vt* seal.

besiegen [bəzē:'gən] *vt* defeat, overcome.

Besiegte(r) [bəzē:k'tə(r)] *mf dekl wie a* loser.

besinnen [bəzi'nən] *vr unreg* (*nachdenken*) think, reflect; (*erinnern*) remember; **sich anders ~** change one's mind.

besinnlich *a* contemplative.

Besinnung *f* consciousness; **bei/ohne ~ sein** be conscious/unconscious; **zur ~ kommen** recover consciousness; (*fig*) come to one's senses.

besinnungslos *a* unconscious; (*fig*) blind.

Besitz [bəzits'] *m* **-es** possession; (*Eigentum*) property; **~anspruch** *m* claim of ownership; (*JUR*) title; **b~anzeigend** *a* (*GRAM*) possessive.

besitzen *vt unreg* possess, own; (*Eigenschaft*) have.

Besitzer(in *f*) *m* **-s**, - owner, proprietor.

Besitz- *zW*: **~ergreifung** *f*, **~nahme** *f* seizure; **~tum** *nt* (*Grundbesitz*) estate(s *pl*), property; **~urkunde** *f* title deeds *pl*.

besoffen [bəzo'fən] *a* (*umg*) drunk.

besohlen [bəzō:'lən] *vt* sole.

Besoldung [bəzol'doong] *f* salary, pay.

besondere(r, s) [bəzon'dərə(r, s)] *a* special; (*eigen*) particular; (*gesondert*) separate; (*eigentümlich*) peculiar.

Besonderheit *f* peculiarity.

besonders *ad* especially, particularly; (*getrennt*) separately; **das Essen/der Film war nicht ~** the food/film was nothing special *od* nothing to write home about; **wie geht's dir? — nicht ~** how are you? — not too hot.

besonnen [bəzo'nən] *a* sensible, levelheaded; **B~heit** *f* level-headedness.

besorgen [bəzor'gən] *vt* (*beschaffen*) acquire; (*kaufen auch*) purchase; (*erledigen*: *Geschäfte*) deal with; (*sich kümmern um*) take care of; **es jdm ~** (*umg*) sort sb out.

Besorgnis *f* **-**, **-se** anxiety, concern; **b~erregend** *a* alarming, worrying.

besorgt [bəzorkt'] *a* anxious, worried; **B~heit** *f* anxiety, worry.

Besorgung *f* acquisition; (*Kauf*) purchase; (*Einkauf*): **~en machen** do some shopping.

bespannen [bəshpá'nən] *vt* (*mit Saiten, Fäden*) string.

bespielbar *a* (*Rasen etc*) playable.

bespielen [bəshpē:'lən] *vt* record.

bespitzeln [bəshpi'tsəln] *vt* spy on.

besprechen [bəshpre'chən] *unreg vt* discuss; (*Tonband etc*) record, speak onto; (*Buch*) review ♦ *vr* discuss, consult.

Besprechung *f* meeting, discussion; (*von Buch*) review.

bespringen [bəshpri'ngən] *vt unreg* (*Tier*) mount, cover.

bespritzen [bəshpri'tsən] *vt* spray; (*beschmutzen*) spatter.

besser [be'sər] *a* better; **nur ein ~er ... just a** glorified ...; **~e Leute** a better class of people; **~gehen** *vi unreg unpers*: **es geht ihm ~** he feels better.

bessern *vt* make better, improve ♦ *vr* improve; (*Menschen*) reform.

besserstehen *vr unreg* (*umg*) be better off.

Besserung *f* improvement; **auf dem Weg(e) der ~ sein** be getting better, be improving; **gute ~!** get well soon!

Besserwisser(in *f*) *m* **-s**, - know-all.

bestand *imperf von* **bestehen**.

Bestand [bəshtánt'] *m* **-(e)s**, ⁼e (*Fortbestehen*) duration, continuance; (*Kassen~*) amount, balance; (*Vorrat*) stock; **eiserne(r) ~** iron rations *pl*; **~ haben, von ~ sein** last long, endure.

bestanden *a*: **nach ~er Prüfung** after passing the exam ♦ *pp von* **bestehen**.

beständig [bəshten'dich] *a* (*ausdauernd*) constant (*auch fig*); (*Wetter*) settled; (*Stoffe*) resistant; (*Klagen etc*) continual.

Bestands- *zW*: **~aufnahme** *f* stocktaking; **~überwachung** *f* stock control, inventory control.

Bestandteil *m* part, component; (*Zutat*) ingredient; **sich in seine ~e auflösen** fall to pieces.

bestärken [bəshter'kən] *vt*: **jdn in etw** (*dat*) **~** strengthen *od* confirm sb in sth.

bestätigen [bəshte:'tigən] *vt* confirm; (*anerkennen, COMM*) acknowledge; **jdn (im Amt) ~** confirm sb's appointment.

Bestätigung *f* confirmation; acknowledgement.

bestatten [bəshta'tən] *vt* bury.

Bestatter *m* **-s**, - mortician (*US*), undertaker

(*Brit*).
Bestattung *f* funeral.
Bestattungsinstitut *nt* funeral home (*US*), undertaker's (*Brit*).
bestäuben [bəshtoi'bən] *vt* powder, dust; (*Pflanze*) pollinate.
beste *siehe* **beste(r,s)**.
bestechen [bəshte'çhən] *unreg vt* bribe ♦ *vi* (*Eindruck machen*) be impressive (*durch* because of).
bestechend *a* (*Schönheit, Eindruck*) captivating; (*Angebot*) tempting.
bestechlich *a* corruptible; **B~keit** *f* corruptibility.
Bestechung *f* bribery, corruption.
Bestechungs- *zW*: **~gelder** *pl* bribe *sing*; **~versuch** *m* attempted bribery.
Besteck [bəshtɛk'] *nt* -(e)s, -e knife, fork and spoon, cutlery; (*MED*) set of instruments; **~kasten** *m* cutlery canteen, cutlery tray.
bestehen [bəshtä:'ən] *unreg vi* be; exist; (*andauern*) last; **die Schwierigkeit/das Problem besteht darin, daß ...** the difficulty/problem lies in the fact that ..., the difficulty/problem is that ...; **~ auf** (+*dat*) insist on; **~ aus** consist of ♦ *vt* (*Kampf, Probe, Prüfung*) pass; **B~** *nt*: **seit B~ der Firma** ever since the firm came into existence *od* has existed.
bestehenbleiben *vi unreg* last, endure; (*Frage, Hoffnung*) remain.
bestehlen [bəshtä:'lən] *vt unreg* rob.
besteigen [bəshtī'gən] *vt unreg* climb, ascend; (*Pferd*) mount; (*Thron*) ascend.
Bestellbuch *nt* order book.
bestellen [bəshte'lən] *vt* order; (*kommen lassen*) arrange to see; (*nominieren*) name; (*Acker*) cultivate; (*Grüße, Auftrag*) pass on; **wie bestellt und nicht abgeholt** (*hum umg*) like orphan Annie; **er hat nicht viel/nichts zu ~** he doesn't have much/any say here; **ich bin für 10 Uhr bestellt** I have an appointment for *od* at 10 o'clock; **es ist schlecht um ihn bestellt** (*fig*) he is in a bad way.
Bestell- *zW*: **~formular** *nt* purchase order; **~nummer** *f* order number; **~schein** *m* order coupon.
Bestellung *f* (*COMM*) order; (*Bestellen*) ordering; (*Ernennung*) nomination, appointment.
bestenfalls ['bestən'fáls] *ad* at best.
bestens [bes'təns] *ad* very well.
beste(r, s) [bes'tə(r, s)] *a, superl von* **gute(r, s)** best; **sie singt am ~n** she sings best; **so ist es am ~n** it's best that way; **am ~n gehst du gleich** you'd better go at once; **jdn zum ~n haben** pull sb's leg; **etw zum ~n geben** tell a joke/story *etc*; **aufs ~** in the best possible way; **zu jds B~n** for the benefit of sb; **es steht nicht zum ~n** it does not look too promising.
besteuern [bəshtoi'ərn] *vt* tax.
bestialisch [bestêâ'lish] *a* (*umg*) awful,

beastly.
besticken [bəshti'kən] *vt* embroider.
Bestie [bes'tēə] *f* (*lit, fig*) beast.
bestimmen [bəshti'mən] *vti* (*Regeln*) lay down; (*Tag, Ort*) fix; (*beherrschen*) characterize; (*ausersehen*) mean; (*ernennen*) appoint; (*definieren*) define; (*veranlassen*) induce; **du hast hier nicht zu ~** you don't make the decisions here; **er kann über sein Geld allein ~** it is up to him what he does with his money.
bestimmend *a* (*Faktor, Einfluß*) determining, decisive.
bestimmt *a* (*entschlossen*) firm; (*gewiß*) certain, definite; (*Artikel*) definite ♦ *ad* (*gewiß*) definitely, for sure; **suchen Sie etwas B~es?** are you looking for anything in particular?; **B~heit** *f* certainty; **in** *od* **mit aller B~heit** quite categorically.
Bestimmung *f* (*Verordnung*) regulation; (*Festsetzen*) determining; (*Verwendungszweck*) purpose; (*Schicksal*) fate; (*Definition*) definition.
Bestimmungs- *zW*: **b~gemäß** *a* as agreed; **~hafen** *m* (port of) destination; **~ort** *m* destination.
Best- *zW*: **~leistung** *f* best performance; **b~möglich** *a* best possible.
Best.-Nr. *abk* = **Bestellnummer**.
bestrafen [bəshtrâ'fən] *vt* punish.
Bestrafung *f* punishment.
bestrahlen [bəshtrâ'lən] *vt* shine on; (*MED*) treat with X-rays.
Bestrahlung *f* (*MED*) X-ray treatment, radiotherapy.
Bestreben [bəshträ:'bən] *nt* -s, **Bestrebung** [bəshtretä:'bˉoˉong] *f* endeavor (*US*), endeavour (*Brit*), effort.
bestrebt [bəshträ:pt'] *a*: **~ sein, etw zu tun** endeavor (*US*) *od* endeavour (*Brit*) to do sth.
bestreichen [bəshtrī'çhən] *vt unreg* (*Brot*) spread.
bestreiken [bəshtrī'kən] *vt* (*INDUSTRIE*) black; **die Fabrik wird zur Zeit bestreikt** there's a strike on in the factory at the moment.
bestreiten [bəshtrī'tən] *vt unreg* (*abstreiten*) dispute; (*finanzieren*) pay for, finance; **er hat das ganze Gespräch allein bestritten** he did all the talking.
bestreuen [bəshtroi'ən] *vt* sprinkle, dust; (*Straße*) (spread with) grit.
Bestseller [bestse'lər] *m* -s, - best-seller.
bestürmen [bəshtür'mən] *vt* (*mit Fragen, Bitten etc*) overwhelm, swamp.
bestürzen [bəshtür'tsən] *vt* dismay.
bestürzt *a* dismayed.
Bestürzung *f* consternation.
Bestzeit *f* (*bes SPORT*) best time.
Besuch [bəzˉoˉoˑkh'] *m* -(e)s, -e visit; (*Person*) visitor; **einen ~ bei jdm machen** pay sb a visit *od* call; **~ haben** have visitors; **bei jdm auf** *or* **zu ~ sein** be visiting sb.

besuchen vt visit; (SCH etc) attend; **gut besucht** well-attended.
Besucher(in f) m **-s,** - visitor, guest.
Besuchs- zW: **~erlaubnis** f permission to visit; **~zeit** f visiting hours pl.
besudeln [bəzōō:'dəln] vt (Wände) smear; (fig: Namen, Ehre) sully.
betagt [bətâkt'] a aged.
betasten [bətâs'tən] vt touch, feel.
betätigen [bətε:'tigən] vt (bedienen) work, operate ♦ vr involve o.s.; **sich politisch ~** be involved in politics; **sich als etw ~** work as sth.
Betätigung f activity; (beruflich) occupation; (TECH) operation.
betäuben [bətoi'bən] vt stun; (fig: Gewissen) still; (MED) anesthetize (US), anaesthetize (Brit); **ein betäubender Duft** an overpowering smell.
Betäubung f (Narkose): **örtliche ~** local anesthetic (US) od anaesthetic (Brit).
Betäubungsmittel nt anesthetic (US), anaesthetic (Brit).
Bete [bā:'tə] f **-, -n: rote ~** beet (US), beetroot (Brit).
beteiligen [bətī'ligən] vr (an +dat in) take part, participate; (an Geschäft: finanziell) have a share; **sich an den Unkosten ~** contribute to the expenses ♦ vt: **jdn ~** give sb a share od interest (an +dat in).
Beteiligung f participation; (Anteil) share, interest; (Besucherzahl) attendance.
Beteiligungsgesellschaft f associated company.
beten [bā:'tən] vti pray.
beteuern [bətoi'ərn] vt assert; (Unschuld) protest; **jdm etw ~** assure sb of sth.
Beteuerung f assertion; protest(ation); assurance.
Beton [bātôn'] m **-s, -s** concrete.
betonen [bətō:'nən] vt stress.
betonieren [bātōnē:'rən] vt concrete.
Betonmischmaschine f concrete mixer.
betont [bətō:nt'] a (Höflichkeit) emphatic, deliberate; (Kühle, Sachlichkeit) pointed.
Betonung f stress, emphasis.
betören [bətœ'rən] vt beguile.
betr. abk (= betreffend, betreffs) re.
Betr. abk = **Betreff.**
Betracht [bətrâḳht'] m: **in ~ kommen** be concerned od relevant; **nicht in ~ kommen** be out of the question; **etw in ~ ziehen** consider sth; **außer ~ bleiben** not be considered.
betrachten vt look at; (fig auch) consider.
Betrachter(in f) m **-s,** - onlooker.
beträchtlich [bətreḳht'liḳh] a considerable.
Betrachtung f (Ansehen) examination; (Erwägung) consideration; **über etw** (akk) **~en anstellen** reflect on od contemplate sth.
betraf [bətrâf'] imperf von **betreffen.**
Betrag [bətrâk'] m **-(e)s, ²e** amount; **~ erhalten** (COMM) value received; **b~en** [bətra'gən] unreg vt amount to ♦ vr behave.

Betragen nt **-s** behavior (US), behaviour (Brit); (bes im Zeugnis) conduct.
beträgt [bətrε:kt'] 3. pers sing präs von **betragen.**
betrat [bətrât'] imperf von **betreten.**
betrauen [bətrou'ən] vt: **jdn mit etw ~** entrust sb with sth.
betrauern [bətrou'ərn] vt mourn.
beträufeln [bətroi'fəln] vt: **den Fisch mit Zitrone ~** sprinkle lemon juice on the fish.
Betreff m: **Betr: Ihr Schreiben vom ...** re od reference your letter of ...; **~ Bewerbung** re job application.
betreffen [bətre'fən] vt unreg concern, affect; **was mich betrifft** as for me.
betreffend a relevant, in question.
betreffs [bətrefs'] präp +gen concerning, regarding.
betreiben [bətrī'bən] vt unreg (ausüben) practice (US), practise (Brit); (Politik) follow; (Studien) pursue; (vorantreiben) push ahead; (TECH: antreiben) drive; **auf jds B~** (akk) **hin** (form) at sb's instigation.
betreten [bətrā:'tən] vt unreg enter; (Bühne etc) step onto; **"B~ verboten"** "keep off/out" ♦ a embarrassed.
betreuen [bətroi'ən] vt look after.
Betreuung f: **er wurde mit der ~ der Gruppe beauftragt** he was put in charge of the group.
betrieb [bətrē:p'] imperf von **betreiben.**
Betrieb m **-(e)s, -e** (Firma) firm, concern; (Anlage) plant; (Tätigkeit) operation; (Treiben) traffic; **außer ~ sein** be out of order; **in ~ sein** be in operation; **eine Maschine in/außer ~ setzen** start a machine up/stop a machine; **eine Maschine/Fabrik in ~ nehmen** put a machine/factory into operation; **in den Geschäften herrscht großer ~** the shops are very busy; **er hält den ganzen ~ auf** (umg) he's holding everything up.
betrieben [bətrē:'bən] pp von **betreiben.**
Betriebs- zW: **~anleitung** f operating instructions pl; **~ausflug** m firm's outing; **~ausgaben** pl revenue expenditure; **b~eigen** a company attr; **~erlaubnis** f operating permission; **b~fähig** a in working order; **~ferien** pl company vacation sing; **~führung** f management; **~kapital** nt working capital; **~klima** nt (working) atmosphere; **~kosten** pl running costs pl; **~leitung** f management; **~rat** m workers' council; **~rente** f company pension; **b~sicher** a safe, reliable; **~stoff** m fuel; **~störung** f breakdown; **~system** nt (COMPUT) operating system; **~unfall** m industrial accident; **~wirt** m management expert; **~wirtschaft** f economics.
betrifft [bətrift'] 3. pers sing präs von **betreffen.**
betrinken [bətring'kən] vr unreg get drunk.
betritt [bətrit'] 3. pers sing präs von **betreten.**
betroffen [bətro'fən] a (bestürzt) amazed, perplexed; **von etw ~ werden** od **sein** be

affected by sth ♦ *pp von* **betreffen.**
betrüben [bətrü:'bən] *vt* grieve.
betrübt [bətrü:pt'] *a* sorrowful, grieved.
betrug [bətrōō:k'] *imperf von* **betragen.**
Betrug *m* **-(e)s** deception; (*JUR*) fraud.
betrügen [bətrü:'gən] *unreg vt* cheat; (*JUR*)
defraud; (*Ehepartner*) be unfaithful to ♦ *vr*
deceive o.s.
Betrüger(in *f*) *m* **-s,** - cheat, deceiver.
betrügerisch *a* deceitful; (*JUR*) fraudulent;
in ~**er Absicht** with intent to defraud.
betrunken [bətrōōng'kən] *a* drunk.
Bett [bet] *nt* **-(e)s, -en** bed; **im** ~ in bed; **ins**
od **zu** ~ **gehen** go to bed; ~**bezug** *m* duvet
cover; ~**decke** *f* blanket; (*Daunen*~) quilt;
(*Überwurf*) bedspread.
bettelarm [be'təlárm] *a* very poor, destitute.
Bettelei [betəli'] *f* begging.
Bettelmönch *m* mendicant *od* begging
monk.
betteln *vi* beg.
betten *vt* make a bed for.
Bett- *zW*: ~**hupferl** *nt* (*süddeutsch*) bedtime
sweet; **b**~**lägerig** *a* bedridden; ~**laken** *nt*
sheet; ~**lektüre** *f* bedtime reading.
Bettler(in *f*) [be'tlər(in)] *m* **-s,** - beggar.
Bett- *zW*: ~**nässer** *m* **-s,** - bedwetter;
~**schwere** *f* (*umg*): **die nötige** ~**schwere**
haben/bekommen be/get tired enough to
sleep; ~**vorleger** *m* bedside rug; ~**wäsche**
f, ~**zeug** *nt* bedclothes *pl*, bedding.
betucht [bətōō:kht'] *a* (*umg*) well-to-do.
betulich [bətōō:'liċh] *a* (*übertrieben besorgt*)
fussing *attr.*
betupfen [bətōō'pfən] *vt* dab; (*MED*) swab.
Beugehaft [boi'gəháft] *f* (*JUR*) coercive detention.
beugen [boi'gən] *vt* bend; (*GRAM*) inflect ♦
vr (*sich fügen*) bow (*dat* to).
Beule [boi'lə] *f* **-, -n** bump.
beunruhigen [bəōōn'rōō:igən] *vt* disturb,
alarm ♦ *vr* become worried.
Beunruhigung *f* worry, alarm.
beurkunden [bəōō:r'kōōndən] *vt* attest, verify.
beurlauben [bəōō:r'loubən] *vt* grant a vacation to; (*suspendiert sein*) have been relieved of one's duties.
beurteilen [bəōō:r'tīlən] *vt* judge; (*von Buch
etc*) review.
Beurteilung *f* judgement; (*von Buch etc*) review; (*Note*) mark.
Beurteilungsgespräch *nt* appraisal interview.
Beute [boi'tə] *f* **-** booty, loot; (*von Raubtieren
etc*) prey.
Beutel *m* **-s,** - bag; (*Geld*~) purse; (*Ta-
baks*~) pouch.
bevölkern [bəfœl'kərn] *vt* populate.
Bevölkerung *f* population.
Bevölkerungs- *zW*: ~**explosion** *f* population
explosion; ~**schicht** *f* social stratum;
~**statistik** *f* vital statistics *pl.*
bevollmächtigen [bəfol'meċhtigən] *vt*

authorize.
Bevollmächtigte(r) *mf dekl wie a*
authorized agent.
Bevollmächtigung *f* authorization.
bevor [bəfō:r'] *kj* before; ~**munden** *vt untr*
dominate; ~**stehen** *vi unreg* be in store (*dat*
for); ~**stehend** *a* imminent, approaching;
~**zugen** *vt untr* prefer.
bevorzugt [bəfō:r'tsōō:kt] *ad*: **etw** ~ **abfertigen** *etc* give sth priority.
Bevorzugung *f* preference.
bewachen [bəvá'khən] *vt* watch, guard.
bewachsen [bəvák'sən] *a* overgrown (*mit*
with).
Bewachung *f* (*Bewachen*) guarding; (*Leute*)
guard, watch.
bewaffnen [bəváf'nən] *vt* arm.
Bewaffnung *f* (*Vorgang*) arming;
(*Ausrüstung*) armament, arms *pl.*
bewahren [bəvá'rən] *vt* keep; **jdn vor jdm/
etw** ~ save sb from sb/sth; **(Gott) bewahre!**
(*umg*) heaven *od* God forbid!
bewähren [bəve:'rən] *vr* prove o.s.;
(*Maschine*) prove its worth.
bewahrheiten [bəvár'hītən] *vr* come true.
bewährt *a* reliable.
Bewährung *f* (*JUR*) probation; **ein Jahr Gefängnis mit** ~ a suspended sentence of one
year with probation.
Bewährungs- *zW*: ~**frist** *f* (period of) probation; ~**helfer** *m* probation officer; ~**probe** *f*:
etw einer ~**probe** (*dat*) **unterziehen** put sth
to the test.
bewaldet [bəvál'dət] *a* wooded.
bewältigen [bəvel'tigən] *vt* overcome;
(*Arbeit*) finish; (*Portion*) manage; (*Schwierigkeiten*) cope with.
bewandert [bəván'dərt] *a* expert, knowledgeable.
Bewandtnis [bəvánt'nis] *f*: **damit hat es folgende** ~ the fact of the matter is this.
bewarb [bəvárp'] *imperf von* **bewerben.**
bewässern [bəve'sərn] *vt* irrigate.
Bewässerung *f* irrigation.
bewegen [bəvā:'gən] *vtr* move; **der Preis bewegt sich um die 50 Mark** the price is
about 50 marks; **jdn zu etw** ~ induce sb to
(do) sth.
Beweg- [bəvā:k'-] *zW*: ~**grund** *m* motive;
b~**lich** *a* movable, mobile; (*flink*) quick.
bewegt [bəvā:kt'] *a* (*Leben*) eventful; (*Meer*)
rough; (*ergriffen*) touched.
Bewegung *f* movement, motion; (*innere*)
emotion; (*körperlich*) exercise; **sich** (*dat*) ~
machen take exercise.
Bewegungs- *zW*: ~**freiheit** *f* freedom of
movement *od* action; **b**~**los** *a* motionless.
Beweis [bəvīs'] *m* **-es, -e** proof; (*Zeichen*)
sign; ~**aufnahme** *f* (*JUR*) taking *od* hearing
of evidence; **b**~**bar** [bəvīz'-] *a* provable.
beweisen [bəvī'zən] *vt unreg* prove; (*zeigen*) show;
was zu ~ **war** QED.
Beweis- *zW*: ~**führung** *f* reasoning; (*JUR*)
presentation of one's case; ~**kraft** *f* weight,

conclusiveness; **b~kräftig** *a* convincing, conclusive; **~last** *f* (*JUR*) onus, burden of proof; **~mittel** *nt* evidence; **~not** *f* (*JUR*) lack of evidence; **~stück** *nt* exhibit.

bewenden [bəven'dən] *vi*: **etw dabei ~ lassen** leave sth at that.

bewerben [bəver'bən] *vr unreg* apply (*um* for).

Bewerber(in *f*) *m* **-s, -** applicant.

Bewerbung *f* application.

Bewerbungsunterlagen *pl* application documents *pl*.

bewerkstelligen [bəverk'shteligən] *vt* manage, accomplish.

bewerten [bəvä:r'tən] *vt* assess.

bewies [bəvē:s'] *imperf von* **beweisen**.

bewiesen [bəvē:'zən] *pp von* **beweisen**.

bewilligen [bəvi'ligən] *vt* grant, allow.

Bewilligung *f* granting.

bewirbt [bəvirpt'] *3. pers sing präs von* **bewerben**.

bewirken [bəvir'kən] *vt* cause, bring about.

bewirten [bəvir'tən] *vt* entertain.

bewirtschaften [bəvirt'sháftən] *vt* manage.

Bewirtung *f* hospitality; **die ~ so vieler Gäste** catering for so many guests.

bewog [bəvō:k'] *imperf von* **bewegen**.

bewogen [bəvō:'gən] *pp von* **bewegen**.

bewohnbar *a* inhabitable.

bewohnen [bəvō:'nən] *vt* inhabit, live in.

Bewohner(in *f*) *m* **-s, -** inhabitant; (*von Haus*) resident.

bewölkt [bəvœlkt'] *a* cloudy, overcast.

Bewölkung *f* clouds *pl*.

Bewölkungsauflockerung *f* break-up of the cloud.

beworben [bəvor'bən] *pp von* **bewerben**.

Bewunderer(in *f*) *m* **-s, -** admirer.

bewundern [bəvoon'dərn] *vt* admire.

bewundernswert *a* admirable, wonderful.

Bewunderung *f* admiration.

bewußt [bəvoost'] *a* conscious; (*absichtlich*) deliberate; **sich** (*dat*) **einer Sache ~ sein** be aware of sth; **~los** *a* unconscious; **B~losigkeit** *f* unconsciousness; **bis zur B~losigkeit** (*umg*) ad nauseam; **~machen** *vt*: **jdm etw ~machen** make sb conscious of sth; **sich** (*dat*) **etw ~machen** realize sth; **B~sein** *nt* consciousness; **bei B~sein** conscious; **im B~sein, daß** ... in the knowledge that ...

Bewußtseins- *zW*: **~bildung** *f* (*POL*) shaping of political ideas; **b~erweiternd** *a*: **b~erweiternde Drogen** mind-expanding drugs; **~erweiterung** *f* consciousness raising.

bez. *abk* (= *bezüglich*) re.

Bez. *abk* = **Bezirk**.

bezahlen [bətsá'lən] *vt* pay (for); **es macht sich bezahlt** it will pay.

Bezahlung *f* payment; **ohne/gegen** *od* **für ~** without/for payment.

bezaubern [bətsou'bərn] *vt* enchant, charm.

bezeichnen [bətsīch'nən] *vt* (*kennzeichnen*)

mark; (*nennen*) call; (*beschreiben*) describe; (*zeigen*) show, indicate.

bezeichnend *a* characteristic, typical (*für* of).

Bezeichnung *f* (*Zeichen*) mark, sign; (*Beschreibung*) description; (*Ausdruck*) expression, term.

bezeugen [bətsoi'gən] *vt* testify to.

bezichtigen [bətsich'tigən] *vt* accuse (*gen* of).

Bezichtigung *f* accusation.

beziehen [bətsē:'ən] *unreg vt* (*mit Überzug*) cover; (*Bett*) make; (*Haus, Position*) move into; (*Standpunkt*) take up; (*erhalten*) receive; (*Zeitung*) subscribe to, take; **etw auf jdn/etw ~** relate sth to sb/sth ♦ *vr* refer (*auf +akk* to); (*Himmel*) cloud over.

Beziehung *f* (*Verbindung*) connection; (*Zusammenhang*) relation; (*Verhältnis*) relationship; (*Hinsicht*) respect; **diplomatische ~en** diplomatic relations; **seine ~en spielen lassen** pull strings; **in jeder ~** in every respect; **~en haben** (*vorteilhaft*) have connections *od* contacts.

Beziehungskiste *f* (*umg*) dead-end relationship.

beziehungsweise *ad* or; (*genauer gesagt auch*) that is, or rather; (*im anderen Fall*) and ... respectively.

beziffern [bətsi'fərn] *vt* (*angeben*) estimate (*auf +akk, mit* at).

Bezirk [bətsirk'] *m* **-(e)s, -e** district.

bezirzen [bətsir'tsən] *vt* (*umg*) bewitch.

bezogen [bətsō:'gən] *pp von* **beziehen**.

Bezogene(r) [bətsō:'gənə(r)] *mf dekl wie a* (*Scheck etc*) drawee.

Bezug [bətsōō:k'] *m* **-(e)s, -e** (*Hülle*) covering; (*COMM*) ordering; (*Gehalt*) income, salary; (*Beziehung*) relationship (*zu* to); **in b~ auf** (*+akk*) with reference to; **mit** *od* **unter ~ auf** (*+akk*) regarding; (*form*) with reference to; **~ nehmen auf** (*+akk*) refer to.

bezüglich [bətsü:'lich] *präp +gen* concerning, referring to ♦ *a* concerning; (*GRAM*) relative.

Bezugs- *zW*: **~nahme** *f* reference (*auf +akk* to); **~person** *f*: **die wichtigste ~person des Kleinkindes** the person to whom the child relates most closely; **~preis** *m* retail price; **~quelle** *f* source of supply.

bezuschussen [bətsoo:'shoosən] *vt* subsidize.

bezwecken [bətsve'kən] *vt* aim at.

bezweifeln [bətsvi'fəln] *vt* doubt, query.

bezwingen [bətsvi'ngən] *vt unreg* conquer; (*Feind auch*) defeat, overcome.

bezwungen [bətsvoo:'ngən] *pp von* **bezwingen**.

Bf. *abk* = **Bahnhof; Brief**.

BfA *f - abk* (= *Bundesversicherungsanstalt für Angestellte*) *Federal insurance company for employees*.

BFM *nt - abk* (= *Bundesfinanzminister(ium)*) *Federal minister/ministry of finance*.

BfV *nt - abk* (= *Bundesamt für Verfassungsschutz*) *Federal Office for Pro-*

tection of the Constitution.
BG *f abk* (= *Berufsgenossenschaft*) *professional association.*
BGB *nt - abk* = **Bürgerliches Gesetzbuch.**
BGH *m - abk* (= *Bundesgerichtshof*) *Federal Supreme Court.*
BGS *m - abk* = **Bundesgrenzschutz.**
BH *m* **-s, -(s)** (= *Büstenhalter*) bra.
Bhf. *abk* = **Bahnhof.**
BI *f abk* = **Bürgerinitiative.**
bibbern [bi'bərn] *vi* (*umg*: *vor Kälte*) shiver.
Bibel [bē:'bəl] *f* **-, -n** Bible.
bibelfest *a* well versed in the Bible.
Biber [bē:'bər] *m* **-s, -** beaver.
Biberbettuch *nt* flannelette.
Bibliographie [bēblēōgráfē:'] *f* bibliography.
Bibliothek [bēblēōtā:k'] *f* **-, -en** (*auch COMPUT*) library.
Bibliothekar(in *f*) [bēblēōtākár'(in)] *m* **-s, -e** librarian.
biblisch [bē:'blish] *a* biblical.
bidirektional [bēdērektsēōnál'] *a* bidirectional; **~es Drucken** bidirectional printing.
bieder [bē:'dər] *a* upright, worthy; (*pej*) conventional; (*Kleid etc*) plain.
Biedermann *m* **-(e)s, -männer** (*pej geh*) petty bourgeois.
biegbar [bē:k'bâr] *a* flexible.
Biege *f*: **die ~ machen** (*umg*) buzz off, split.
biegen [bē:'gən] *unreg vtr* bend; **sich vor Lachen ~** (*fig*) double up with laughter; **auf B~ oder Brechen** (*umg*) by hook or by crook ♦ *vi* turn.
biegsam [bē:k'zâm] *a* supple.
Biegung *f* bend, curve.
Biene [bē:'nə] *f* **-, -n** bee; (*veraltet umg*: *Mädchen*) chick.
Bienen- *zW*: **~honig** *m* honey; **~korb** *m* beehive; **~stich** *m* (*KOCH*) *cake coated with sugar and almonds filled with custard or cream*; **~wachs** *nt* beeswax.
Bier [bē:r] *nt* **-(e)s, -e** beer; **zwei ~, bitte!** two beers, please; **~brauer** *m* brewer; **~deckel** *m*, **~filz** *m* beer mat; **~krug** *m* beer mug; **~schinken** *m* ham sausage; **~seidel** *nt* beer mug; **~wurst** *f* ham sausage.
Biest [bē:st] *nt* **-es, -er** (*pej umg*: *Mensch*) (little) wretch; (*umg*: *Frau*) bitch (*!*).
biestig *a* beastly.
bieten [bē:'tən] *unreg vt* offer; (*bei Versteigerung*) bid ♦ *vr* (*Gelegenheit*) be open (*dat* to); **sich** (*dat*) **etw ~ lassen** put up with sth.
Bigamie [bēgámē:'] *f* bigamy.
Bikini [bēkē:'nē] *m* **-s, -s** bikini.
Bilanz [bēlánts'] *f* balance; (*fig*) outcome; **eine ~ aufstellen** draw up a balance sheet; **~ ziehen** take stock (*aus* of); **~prüfer** *m* auditor.
bilateral [bē:'látārál] *a* bilateral; **~er Handel** bilateral trade; **~es Abkommen** bilateral agreement.
Bild [bilt] *nt* **-(e)s, -er** (*lit, fig*) picture; photo;

(*Spiegel~*) reflection; (*fig*: *Vorstellung*) image, picture; **ein ~ machen** take a photo od picture; **im ~e sein** be in the picture (*über* +*akk* about); **~auflösung** *f* (*~schirm*) resolution; **~band** *m* illustrated book; **~bericht** *m* pictorial report; **~beschreibung** *f* (*SCH*) description of a picture.
bilden [bil'dən] *vt* form; (*erziehen*) educate; (*ausmachen*) constitute ♦ *vr* arise; (*durch Lesen etc*) improve one's mind; (*erziehen*) educate o.s.
bildend *a*: **die ~e Kunst** art.
Bilder- [bil'dər] *zW*: **~buch** *nt* picture book; **~rahmen** *m* picture frame.
Bild- *zW*: **~fläche** *f* screen; (*fig*) scene; **von der ~fläche verschwinden** (*fig umg*) disappear (from the scene); **b~haft** *a* (*Sprache*) vivid; **~hauer** *m* **-s, -** sculptor; **b~hübsch** *a* lovely, pretty as a picture; **b~lich** *a* figurative; pictorial; **sich** (*dat*) **etw b~lich vorstellen** picture sth in one's mind's eye.
Bildnis [bilt'nis] *nt* (*liter*) portrait.
Bild- *zW*: **~röhre** *f* (*TV*) cathode ray tube; **~schirm** *m* (*TV, COMPUT*) screen; **~schirmgerät** *nt* (*COMPUT*) display unit; **~schirmtext** *m* teletext; **b~schön** *a* lovely; **~sichtgerät** *nt* video display terminal (VDT), visual display unit (VDU).
Bildung [bil'dōong] *f* formation; (*Wissen, Benehmen*) education.
Bildungs- *zW*: **~gang** *m* school (and university/college) career; **~gefälle** *nt* educational incline; **~lücke** *f* gap in one's education; **~politik** *f* educational policy; **~roman** *m* (*LITER*) Bildungsroman, *novel concerned with the intellectual or spiritual development of the main character*; **~weg** *m*: **auf dem zweiten ~weg** through night school/the Open University *etc*; **~wesen** *nt* education system.
Bildweite *f* (*PHOT*) distance.
Bildzuschrift *f* reply enclosing photograph.
Billard [bil'yàrt] *nt* **-s, -e** billiards; **~ball** *m*, **~kugel** *f* billiard ball.
billig [bi'liċh] *a* cheap; (*gerecht*) fair, reasonable; **~e Handelsflagge** flag of convenience; **~es Geld** cheap/easy money.
billigen [bi'ligən] *vt* approve of; **etw stillschweigend ~** condone sth.
billigerweise *ad* (*veraltet*) in all fairness, reasonably.
Billigladen *m* discount store.
Billigung *f* approval.
Billion [bilēō:n'] *f* trillion (*US*), billion (*Brit*).
bimmeln [bi'məln] *vi* tinkle.
Bimsstein [bims'shtīn] *m* pumice stone.
bin [bin] *1. pers sing präs von* **sein.**
binär [bēne:r'] *a* binary; **B~zahl** *f* binary number.
Binde [bin'də] *f* **-, -n** bandage; (*Arm~*) band; (*MED*) sanitary napkin; **sich** (*dat*) **einen hinter die ~ gießen** od **kippen** (*umg*) put a

few drinks away.

Binde- *zW*: **~glied** *nt* connecting link; **~hautentzündung** *f* conjunctivitis; **~mittel** *nt* binder.

binden *vt unreg* bind, tie ♦ *vr* (*sich verpflichten*) commit o.s. (*an* +*akk* to).

bindend *a* binding (*für* on); (*Zusage*) definite.

Binde- *zW*: **~strich** *m* hyphen; **~wort** *nt* conjunction.

Bindfaden *m* string; **es regnet Bindfäden** (*umg*) it's sheeting down.

Bindung *f* bond, tie; (*SKI*) binding.

binnen [bi'nən] *präp* +*dat od gen* within; **B~hafen** *m* inland harbor; **B~handel** *m* internal trade; **B~markt** *m* home market.

Binse [bin'zə] *f* -, **-n** rush, reed; **in die ~n gehen** (*fig umg*: *mißlingen*) go to pot.

Binsenwahrheit *f* truism.

Biographie [bēōgráfē:'] *f* biography.

Biologe [bēōlō:'gə] *m* **-n**, **-n**, **Biologin** *f* biologist.

Biologie [bēōlōgē:'] *f* biology.

biologisch [bēōlō:'gish] *a* biological.

birgt [birkt] *3. pers sing präs von* **bergen**.

Birke [bir'kə] *f* -, **-n** birch.

Birma [bir'má] *nt* **-s** (*veraltet*) Burma.

Birnbaum *m* pear tree.

Birne [bir'nə] *f* -, **-n** pear; (*ELEK*) (light) bulb.

birst [birst] *2./3. pers sing präs von* **bersten**.

bis [bis] *ad, präp* +*akk* (*räumlich*: ~ *zu/an* +*akk*) to, as far as; (*zeitlich*) till, until; (~ *spätestens*) by; **Sie haben ~ Dienstag Zeit** you have until *od* till Tuesday; **~ Dienstag muß es fertig sein** it must be ready by Tuesday; **~ hierher** this far; **~ wann gilt der Fahrplan/ist das fertig?** when is the timetable valid till/will that be finished by?; **~ in die Nacht** into the night; **~ auf weiteres** until further notice; **~ bald!/gleich!** see you later/soon; **~ auf etw** (*akk*) (*einschließlich*) including sth; (*ausgeschlossen*) except sth; **~ zu** up to ♦ *kj* (*mit Zahlen*) to; (*zeitlich*) until, till; **von ... ~ ...** from ... to ...

Bisamratte [bē:'zámrátə] *f* -, **-n** muskrat (beaver).

Bischof [bi'shof] *m* **-s**, **⁻e** bishop.

bischöflich [bi'shœfliç] *a* episcopal.

bisexuell [bēzeksōōel'] *a* bisexual.

bisher [bishä:r'] *ad*, **bisherig** *a* till now, hitherto.

Biskuit [biskvē:t'] *m od nt* **-(e)s**, **-s** *od* **-e** biscuit; **~gebäck** *nt* sponge cake(s); **~teig** *m* sponge mixture.

bislang [bislàng'] *ad* hitherto.

biß [bis] *imperf von* **beißen**.

Biß *m* **-sses**, **-sse** bite.

bißchen [bis'çhən] *a, ad* bit.

Bissen [bi'sən] *m* **-s**, **-** bite, morsel; **sich** (*dat*) **jeden ~ vom** *od* **am Munde absparen** watch every penny one spends.

bissig [bi'siç] *a* (*Hund*) snappy; vicious;

(*Bemerkung*) cutting, biting; „**Vorsicht, ~er Hund**" "beware of the dog".

bist [bist] *2. pers sing präs von* **sein**.

Bistum [bis'tōō:m] *nt* bishopric.

bisweilen [bisvī'lən] *ad* at times, occasionally.

Bit [bit] *nt* **-(s)**, **-(s)** (*COMPUT*) bit.

Bittbrief *m* petition.

Bitte [bi'tə] *f* -, **-n** request; **auf seine ~ hin** at his request; **b~** *interj* please; (*als Antwort auf Dank*) you're welcome; **wie b~?** (I beg your) pardon?; **b~ schön!** it was a pleasure; **b~ schön?** (*in Geschäft*) can I help you?; **na b~!** there you are!

bitten *unreg vt* ask (*um* for); **aber ich bitte dich!** not at all; **ich bitte darum** (*form*) if you wouldn't mind; **ich muß doch (sehr) ~!** well I must say! ♦ *vi* (*einladen*): **ich lasse ~** would you ask him/her to come in now?

bittend *a* pleading, imploring.

bitter [bi'tər] *a* bitter; (*Schokolade*) plain; **etw ~ nötig haben** be in dire need of sth; **~böse** *a* very angry; **~ernst** *a*: **damit ist es mir ~ernst** I am deadly serious *od* in deadly earnest; **B~keit** *f* bitterness; **~lich** *a* bitter ♦ *ad* bitterly.

Bittsteller(in *f***)** *m* **-s**, **-** petitioner.

Biwak [bē:'vák] *nt* **-s**, **-s** *od* **-e** bivouac.

Bj., BJ *abk* = **Baujahr**.

Blabla [blâblâ'] *nt* **-s** (*umg*) waffle.

blähen [ble:'ən] *vtr* swell, blow out ♦ *vi* (*Speisen*) cause flatulence *od* wind.

Blähungen *pl* (*MED*) wind.

blamabel [blámá'bəl] *a* disgraceful.

Blamage [blámá'zhə] *f* -, **-n** disgrace.

blamieren [blámē:'rən] *vr* make a fool of o.s., disgrace o.s. ♦ *vt* let down, disgrace.

blank [blángk] *a* bright; (*unbedeckt*) bare; (*sauber*) clean, polished; (*umg*: *ohne Geld*) broke; (*offensichtlich*) blatant.

blanko [bláng'kō] *ad* blank; **B~scheck** *m* blank check (*US*) *od* cheque (*Brit*); **jdm einen B~scheck ausstellen** (*fig*) have complete trust in sb; **B~vollmacht** *f* carte blanche.

Bläschen [ble:s'çhən] *nt* bubble; (*MED*) small blister.

Blase [blá'zə] *f* -, **-n** bubble; (*MED*) blister; (*ANAT*) bladder.

Blasebalg *m* bellows *pl*.

blasen *vti unreg* blow; **zum Aufbruch ~** (*fig*) say it's time to go.

Blasenentzündung *f* cystitis.

Bläser(in *f***)** [ble:'zər(in)] *m* **-s**, **-** (*MUS*) wind player; **die ~** the wind (section).

blasiert [blázē:rt'] *a* (*pej geh*) blasé.

Blas- *zW*: **~instrument** *nt* wind instrument; **~kapelle** *f* brass band; **~musik** *f* brass band music.

blaß [blás] *a* pale; (*Ausdruck*) weak, insipid; (*fig*: *Ahnung, Vorstellung*) faint, vague; **~ vor Neid werden** go green with envy.

Blässe [ble'sə] *f* - paleness, pallor.

Blatt [blát] *nt* **-(e)s**, **⁻er** leaf; (*Zeitung*) newspaper; (*von Papier*) sheet; (*KARTEN*) hand;

vom ~ **singen/spielen** sight-read; **kein ~
vor den Mund nehmen** not to mince one's
words.
blättern [ble'tərn] *vi*: **in etw** (*dat*) ~ leaf
through sth.
Blätterteig *m* flaky *od* puff pastry.
Blattlaus *f* aphid.
blau [blou] *a* blue; (*umg*) drunk, stoned;
(*KOCH*) boiled; (*Auge*) black; ~**er Fleck**
bruise; **Fahrt ins B~e** mystery tour; **mit
einem ~en Auge davonkommen** (*fig*) get
off lightly; **ein ~er Brief** (*SCH*) *letter informing parents that their child is likely to
have to repeat a year*; **er wird sein ~es
Wunder erleben** (*umg*) he won't know
what's hit him; ~**äugig** *a* blue-eyed;
B~beere *f siehe* **Heidelbeere.**
Blaue *nt*: **das ~ vom Himmel (herunter) lügen** (*umg*) tell a pack of lies.
blau- *zW*: **B~kraut** *nt siehe* **Rotkohl; B~licht**
nt flashing blue light; ~**machen** *vi* (*umg*)
skip work; **B~pause** *f* blueprint; **B~säure** *f*
prussic acid; **B~strumpf** *m* (*fig*) bluestock-
ing.
Blech [blɛҫ] *nt* **-(e)s, -e** tin, sheet metal;
(*Back~*) baking tray; ~ **reden** (*umg*) talk
rubbish *od* nonsense; ~**bläser** *pl* the brass
(section); ~**büchse** *f,* ~**dose** *f* can.
blechen *vti* (*umg*) pay.
Blech- *zW*: ~**schaden** *m* (*AUT*) damage to
bodywork; ~**trommel** *f* tin drum.
blecken [ble'kən] *vt*: **die Zähne** ~ bare *od*
show one's teeth.
Blei [bliⁱ] *nt* **-(e)s, -e** lead.
Bleibe *f* **-, -n** roof over one's head.
bleiben *vi unreg* stay, remain; **bitte, ~ Sie
doch sitzen** please don't get up; **wo bleibst
du so lange?** (*umg*) what's keeping you?;
das bleibt unter uns (*fig*) that's (just)
between ourselves; ~**lassen** *vt unreg* (*aufgeben*) give up; **etw ~lassen** (*unterlassen*)
give sth a miss.
bleich [blaiҫ] *a* faded, pale; ~**en** *vt* bleach;
B~gesicht *nt* (*umg*: *blasser Mensch*) pale-
faced individual.
bleiern *a* leaden.
Blei- *zW*: **b~frei** *a* lead-free; ~**gießen** *nt New
Year's Eve custom of telling fortunes by the
shapes made by molten lead dropped into
cold water*; **b~haltig** *a*: **b~haltig sein** contain lead; ~**stift** *m* pencil; ~**stiftabsatz** *m*
spike heel; ~**stiftspitzer** *m* pencil sharpener; ~**vergiftung** *f* lead poisoning.
Blende [blɛn'də] *f* **-, -n** (*PHOT*) aperture; (:
Einstellungsposition) f- stop.
blenden *vt* blind, dazzle; (*fig*) hoodwink.
blendend *a* (*umg*) grand; ~ **aussehen** look
smashing.
Blender *m* **-s, -** con-man.
Blessur [blɛsōō:r'] *f* **-, -en** bruise.
Blick [blik] *m* **-(e)s, -e** (*kurz*) glance, glimpse;
(*Anschauen*) look, gaze; (*Aussicht*) view;
Liebe auf den ersten ~ love at first sight;
den ~ senken look down; **den bösen ~ ha-**

ben have the evil eye; **einen (guten) ~ für
etw haben** have an eye for sth; **mit einem
~ at a glance.**
blicken *vi* look; **das läßt tief ~** that's very
revealing; **sich ~ lassen** put in an appearance.
Blick- *zW*: ~**fang** *m* eye-catching object;
~**feld** *nt* range of vision (*auch fig*);
~**kontakt** *m* visual contact; ~**punkt** *m*: **im
~punkt der Öffentlichkeit stehen** be in the
public eye.
blieb [bliⁱp] *imperf von* **bleiben.**
blies [bliⁱs] *imperf von* **blasen.**
blind [blint] *a* blind; (*Glas etc*) dull; (*Alarm*)
false; ~**er Passagier** stowaway.
Blinddarm *m* appendix; ~**entzündung** *f*
appendicitis.
Blindekuh [blin'dəkōō:] *f*: ~ **spielen** play
blind man's buff.
Blinden- [blin'dən-] *zW*: ~**hund** *m* guide dog;
~**schrift** *f* braille.
Blind- *zW*: ~**gänger** *m* (*MIL, fig*) dud; ~**heit**
f blindness; **mit ~heit geschlagen sein** (*fig*)
be blind; **b~lings** *ad* blindly; ~**schleiche** *f*
slow worm; **b~schreiben** *vi unreg* touch-
type.
blinken [bling'kən] *vi* twinkle, sparkle;
(*Licht*) flash, signal; (*AUT*) indicate ♦ *vt*
flash, signal.
Blinker *m* **-s, -, Blinklicht** *nt* (*AUT*) indicator.
blinzeln [blin'tsəln] *vi* blink, wink.
Blitz [blits] *m* **-es, -e** (flash of) lightning; **wie
ein ~ aus heiterem Himmel** (*fig*) like a bolt
from the blue; ~**ableiter** *m* lightning rod;
(*fig*) vent *od* safety valve for feelings; **b~en**
vi (*aufleuchten*) glint, shine; **es blitzt** (*MET*)
there's a flash of lightning; ~**gerät** *nt*
(*PHOT*) flash(gun); ~**licht** *nt* flashlight;
b~sauber *a* spick and span; **b~schnell** *a,
ad* as quick as a flash; ~**würfel** *m* (*PHOT*)
flashcube.
Block [blok] *m* **-(e)s, ˝e** (*lit, fig*) block; (*von
Papier*) pad; (*POL: Staaten~*) bloc; (*Fraktion*) faction.
Blockade [blokȧ'də] *f* **-, -n** blockade.
Block- *zW*: ~**buchstabe** *m* block letter *od*
capital; ~**flöte** *f* recorder; **b~frei** *a* (*POL*)
unaligned; ~**haus** *nt,* ~**hütte** *f* log cabin.
blockieren [blokē:'rən] *vt* block ♦ *vi* (*Räder*)
jam.
Block- *zW*: ~**schokolade** *f* cooking chocolate;
~**schrift** *f* block letters *pl*; ~**stunde** *f* two-
hour class.
blöd [blø:t] *a* silly, stupid.
blödeln [blø:'dəln] *vi* (*umg*) fool around.
Blödheit *f* stupidity.
Blödian [blø:'dēȧn] *m* **-(e)s, -e** (*umg*) idiot.
blöd- *zW*: **B~mann** *m* (*umg*) idiot; **B~sinn**
m nonsense; ~**sinnig** *a* silly, idiotic.
blöken [blø:'kən] *vi* (*Schaf*) bleat.
blond [blont] *a* blond; blonde, fair-haired.
Blondine [blondē:'nə] *f* blonde.
bloß [blō:s] *a* (*unbedeckt*) bare; (*nackt*)
naked; (*nur*) mere; **mit ~em Auge** with the

naked eye ♦ *ad* only, merely; **laß das ~!** just don't do that!; **wie kann so etwas ~ geschehen?** how on earth can something like that happen?

Blöße [blœ'sə] *f* -, -n bareness; nakedness; (*fig*) weakness; **sich** (*dat*) **eine ~ geben** (*fig*) lay o.s. open to attack.

bloß- *zW*: **~legen** *vt* expose; **~stellen** *vt* show up.

Blücher [blü'çhər] *m*: **er geht ran wie ~** (*umg*) he doesn't mess around.

blühen [blü:'ən] *vi* (*lit*) bloom, be in bloom; (*fig*) flourish; (*umg*: *bevorstehen*) be in store (*jdm* for sb).

blühend *a*: **wie das ~e Leben aussehen** look the very picture of health.

Blume [bloo:'mə] *f* -, -n flower; (*von Wein*) bouquet; **jdm etw durch die ~ sagen** say sth in a roundabout way to sb.

Blumen- *zW*: **~kasten** *m* window box; **~kohl** *m* cauliflower; **~strauß** *m* bouquet, bunch of flowers; **~topf** *m* flowerpot; **~zwiebel** *f* bulb.

Bluse [bloo:'zə] *f* -, -n blouse.

Blut [bloo:t] *nt* -(e)s (*lit*, *fig*) blood; **(nur) ruhig ~** keep your shirt on (*umg*); **jdn/sich bis aufs ~ bekämpfen** fight sb/fight bitterly; **b~arm** *a* anemic (*US*), anaemic (*Brit*); (*fig*) penniless; **~bahn** *f* bloodstream; **b~befleckt** *a* bloodstained; **~bild** *nt* blood count; **~buche** *f* copper beech; **~druck** *m* blood pressure.

Blüte [blü:'tə] *f* -, -n blossom; (*fig*) prime; **~zeit** *f* flowering period; (*fig*) prime.

Blutegel' *m* leech.

bluten *vi* bleed.

Blütenstaub *m* pollen.

Bluter *m* -s, - (*MED*) hemophiliac (*US*), haemophiliac (*Brit*).

Bluterguß *m* hemorrhage (*US*), haemorrhage (*Brit*); (*auf Haut*) bruise.

Blut- *zW*: **~gerinnsel** *nt* blood clot; **~gruppe** *f* blood group.

blutig *a* bloody; (*umg*: *Anfänger*) absolute; (: *Ernst*) deadly.

Blut- *zW*: **b~jung** *a* very young; **~konserve** *f* unit *od* pint of stored blood; **~körperchen** *nt* blood corpuscle; **~probe** *f* blood test; **b~rünstig** *a* bloodthirsty; **~schande** *f* incest; **~senkung** *f* (*MED*): **eine ~senkung machen** test the sedimentation rate of the blood; **~spender** *m* blood donor; **b~stillend** *a* styptic; **~sturz** *m* hemorrhage (*US*), haemorrhage (*Brit*).

blutsverwandt *a* related by blood.

Blutübertragung *f* blood transfusion.

Blutung *f* bleeding, hemorrhage (*US*), haemorrhage (*Brit*).

Blut- *zW*: **b~unterlaufen** *a* suffused with blood; (*Augen*) bloodshot; **~vergießen** *nt* bloodshed; **~vergiftung** *f* blood poisoning; **~wurst** *f* black pudding; **~zuckerspiegel** *m* blood sugar level.

BLZ *abk* = **Bankleitzahl**.

BND *m* -s - *abk* = **Bundesnachrichtendienst**.

Bö(e) [bœ'(ə)] *f* -, -en squall.

Boccia [bot'shá] *nt* *od* *f* bowls *sing*.

Bock [bok] *m* -(e)s, ¨e buck, ram; (*Gestell*) trestle, support; (*SPORT*) buck; **alter ~** (*umg*) old goat; **den ~ zum Gärtner machen** (*fig*) choose the worst possible person for the job; **einen ~ schießen** (*fig umg*) make a boo-boo; **~ haben, etw zu tun** (*umg*: *Lust*) fancy doing sth.

Bockbier *nt* bock (beer) (*type of strong beer*).

bocken [bo'kən] *vi* (*umg*: *Auto*, *Mensch*) play up.

bocklos *a* (*umg*) apathetic, completely uninterested.

Bocksbeutel *m* wide, rounded (*dumpy*) wine bottle containing Franconian wine.

Bockshorn *nt*: **sich von jdm ins ~ jagen lassen** let sb upset one.

Bocksprung *m* leapfrog; (*SPORT*) vault.

Bockwurst *f* bockwurst (*large frankfurter*).

Boden [bō:'dən] *m* -s, ¨ ground; (*Fuß~*) floor; (*Meeres~*, *Faß~*) bottom; (*Speicher*) attic; **den ~ unter den Füßen verlieren** (*lit*) lose one's footing; (*fig*: *in Diskussion*) get out of one's depth; **ich hätte (vor Scham) im ~ versinken können** (*fig*) I was so ashamed that I wished the ground would swallow me up; **am ~ zerstört sein** (*umg*) be shattered; **etw aus dem ~ stampfen** (*fig*) conjure sth up out of nothing; (*Häuser*) build overnight; (*fig*: *Grundlage*): **auf dem ~ der Tatsachen bleiben** stick to the facts; **zu ~ fallen** fall to the ground; **festen ~ unter den Füßen haben** be on firm ground, be on terra firma; **~kontrolle** *f* (*RAUMFAHRT*) ground control; **b~los** *a* bottomless; (*umg*) incredible; **~personal** *nt* (*AVIAT*) ground personnel *pl*; **~satz** *m* dregs *pl*, sediment; **~schätze** *pl* mineral wealth *sing*.

Bodensee [bō:'dənzā:] *m*: **der ~** Lake Constance.

Bodenturnen *nt* floor exercises *pl*.

bog [bō:k] *imperf von* **biegen**.

Bogen [bō:'gən] *m* -s, - (*Biegung*) curve; (*ARCHIT*) arch; (*Waffe*, *MUS*) bow; (*Papier*) sheet; **den ~ heraushaben** (*umg*) have got the hang of it; **einen großen ~ um jdn/etw machen** (*meiden*) give sb/sth a wide berth; **jdn in hohem ~ hinauswerfen** (*umg*) fling sb out; **~gang** *m* arcade; **~schütze** *m* archer.

Bohle [bō:'lə] *f* -, -n plank.

böhmisch [bœ'mish] *a* Bohemian; **das sind für mich ~e Dörfer** (*umg*) that's all Greek to me.

Bohne [bō:'nə] *f* -, -n bean; **blaue ~** (*umg*) bullet; **nicht die ~** not one little bit.

Bohnen- *zW*: **~kaffee** *m* pure coffee; **~stange** *f* (*fig umg*) beanpole; **~stroh** *nt*: **dumm wie ~stroh** (*umg*) as dumb as they come.

bohnern vt wax, polish.
Bohnerwachs nt floor polish.
bohren [bõː'rən] vt bore ♦ vi (fig: drängen) keep on; (peinigen: Schmerz, Zweifel etc) gnaw; **in der Nase** ~ pick one's nose.
Bohrer m -s, - drill.
Bohr- zW: ~**insel** f oil rig; ~**maschine** f drill; ~**turm** m derrick.
Boiler [boi'lər] m -s, - water heater.
Boje [bõː'yə] f -, -n buoy.
Bolivianer(in f) m -s, - Bolivian.
bolivianisch a Bolivian.
Bolivien [bõlē:'vēən] nt Bolivia.
Bollwerk [bol'verk] nt (lit, fig) bulwark.
Bolschewismus [bolshāvis'mōōs] m - Bolshevism.
Bolzen [bol'tsən] m -s, - bolt.
bombardieren [bombárdē:'rən] vt bombard; (aus der Luft) bomb.
Bombe [bom'bə] f -, -n bomb; **wie eine** ~ **einschlagen** come as a (real) bombshell.
Bomben- zW: ~**angriff** m bombing raid; ~**erfolg** m (umg) huge success; ~**geschäft** nt (umg): **ein** ~**geschäft machen** do a roaring trade; ~**politik** f policy of increasing armament expenditure; **b**~**sicher** a (umg) dead certain.
bombig a (umg) great, super.
Bon [bong] m -s, -s voucher; (Kassenzettel) receipt.
Bonbon [bõṅbõṅ'] nt od m -s, -s candy (US), sweet (Brit).
Bonn [bon] nt Bonn.
Bonze [bon'tsə] m -n, -n big shot (umg).
Bonzenviertel nt (umg) posh quarter (of town).
Boot [bõːt] nt -(e)s, -e boat.
Bord [bort] m -(e)s, -e (AVIAT, NAUT) board; **über** ~ **gehen** go overboard; (fig) go by the board; **an** ~ on board ♦ nt (Brett) shelf.
Bordell [bordel'] nt -s, -e brothel.
Bord- zW: ~**funkanlage** f radio; ~**stein** m curb(stone) (US), kerb(stone) (Brit).
borgen [bor'gən] vt borrow; **jdm etw** ~ lend sb sth.
borniert [bornē:rt'] a narrow-minded.
Börse [bœr'zə] f -, -n stock exchange; (Geld~) purse.
Börsen- zW: ~**makler** m stockbroker; **b**~**notiert** a: **b**~**notierte Firma** listed company; ~**notierung** f quotation (on the stock exchange).
Borste [bors'tə] f -, -n bristle.
Borte [bor'tə] f -, -n edging; (Band) trimming.
bös [bœs] a = **böse**; ~**artig** [bœz'-] a malicious; (MED) malignant.
Böschung [bœ̃'shōōng] f slope; (Ufer~ etc) embankment.
böse a bad, evil; (zornig) angry; **das war nicht** ~ **gemeint** I/he etc didn't mean it nastily.
bos- [bõːs'-] zW: ~**haft** a malicious, spiteful; **B**~**heit** f malice, spite.

Boß [bos] m -sses, -sse (umg) boss.
böswillig [bœs'vilìçh] a malicious.
bot [bõːt] imperf von **bieten**.
Botanik [bõtã'nik] f botany.
botanisch [bõtã'nish] a botanical.
Bote [bõː'tə] m -n, -n, Botin f messenger.
Boten- zW: ~**gang** m errand; ~**junge** m errand boy.
Botschaft f message, news; (POL) embassy; **die Frohe** ~ the Gospel; ~**er** m -s, - ambassador.
Bottich [bo'tiçh] m -(e)s, -e vat, tub.
Bouillon [bōōlyõṅ'] f -, -s consommé.
Boulevard- [bōōləvár'] zW: ~**blatt** nt (umg) tabloid; ~**stück** nt light play/comedy.
Bowle [bõː'lə] f -, -n punch.
Bowlingbahn [bõː'lingbân] f bowling alley.
Box [boks] f (Lautsprecher~) speaker.
boxen vi box.
Boxer m -s, - boxer.
Box- zW: ~**handschuh** m boxing glove; ~**kampf** m boxing match.
boykottieren [boikotē:'rən] vt boycott.
BPA nt abk (= Bundespresse- und Informationsamt) Federal press and information office.
BR abk = Bayerischer Rundfunk.
brach [bràḳh] imperf von **brechen**.
brachial [bràḳhēál'] a: **mit** ~**er Gewalt** by brute force.
brachliegen [bràḳh'lē:gən] vi unreg (lit, fig) lie fallow.
brachte [bràḳh'tə] imperf von **bringen**.
Branche [brãñ'shə] f -, -n line of business.
Branchenverzeichnis nt yellow pages pl.
Brand [brànt] m -(e)s, -e fire; (MED) gangrene.
branden [bràn'dən] vi surge; (Meer) break.
Brand- zW: ~**anschlag** m arson attack; ~**herd** m source of the fire.
brandmarken vt brand; (fig) stigmatize.
brandneu a (umg) brand-new.
Brand- zW: ~**salbe** f ointment for burns; ~**satz** m incendiary device; ~**stifter** m arsonist, fire-raiser; ~**stiftung** f arson.
Brandung f surf.
Brandwunde f burn.
brannte [bràn'tə] imperf von **brennen**.
Branntwein [brànt'vīn] m brandy; ~**steuer** f tax on spirits.
Brasilianer(in f) [bràzēlēã'nər(in)] m -s, - Brazilian.
brasilianisch a Brazilian.
Brasilien [bràzē:'lēən] nt Brazil.
brät [bret] 3. pers sing präs von **braten**.
Bratapfel m baked apple.
braten [brà'tən] vt unreg roast, fry; **B**~ m -s, - roast, joint; **den B**~ **riechen** (umg) smell a rat, suss something.
Brat- zW: ~**hähnchen** nt, ~**hendl** nt (süddeutsch, österreichisch) roast chicken; ~**huhn** nt roast chicken; ~**kartoffeln** pl fried/roast potatoes pl; ~**pfanne** f frying pan; ~**rost** m grill.

Bratsche [brât'shə] *f* -, -n viola.
Brat- *zW:* ~**spieß** *m* spit; ~**wurst** *f* grilled sausage.
Brauch [brouḱh] *m* -(e)s, **Bräuche** custom.
brauchbar *a* usable, serviceable; (*Person*) capable.
brauchen *vt* (*bedürfen*) need; (*müssen*) have to; (*verwenden*) use; **wie lange braucht man, um ...?** how long does it take to ...?
Brauchtum *nt* customs *pl*, traditions *pl*.
Braue [brou'ə] *f* -, -n brow.
brauen [brou'ən] *vt* brew.
Brauerei [brouərī'] *f* brewery.
braun [broun] *a* brown; (*von Sonne auch*) tanned; (*pej*) Nazi.
Bräune [broi'nə] *f* -, -n brownness; (*Sonnen*~) tan.
bräunen *vt* make brown; (*Sonne*) tan.
braungebrannt *a* tanned.
Braunkohle *f* brown coal.
Braunschweig [broun'shvīk] *nt* -s Brunswick.
Brause [brou'zə] *f* -, -n shower bath; (*von Gießkanne*) rose; (*Getränk*) lemonade.
brausen *vi* roar; (*auch vr: duschen*) take a shower.
Brause- *zW:* ~**pulver** *nt* lemonade powder; ~**tablette** *f* lemonade tablet.
Braut [brout] *f* -, **Bräute** bride; (*Verlobte*) fiancée.
Bräutigam [broi'tigâm] *m* -s, -e bridegroom; fiancé.
Braut- *zW:* ~**jungfer** *f* bridesmaid; ~**kleid** *nt* wedding dress; ~**paar** *nt* bride and bridegroom, bridal pair.
brav [brâf] *a* (*artig*) good; (*ehrenhaft*) worthy, honest; (*bieder: Frisur, Kleid*) plain; **sei schön ~!** be a good boy/girl.
BRD *f* - *abk* (= *Bundesrepublik Deutschland*) FRG.
Brechbohne *f* green bean.
Brecheisen *nt* crowbar.
brechen *vti unreg* break; (*Licht*) refract; (*fig: Mensch*) crush; (*speien*) vomit; **die Ehe ~** commit adultery; **mir bricht das Herz** it breaks my heart; **brechend voll sein** be full to bursting.
Brech- *zW:* ~**mittel** *nt:* **er/das ist das reinste ~mittel** (*umg*) he/it makes me feel ill; ~**reiz** *m* nausea.
Brechung *f* (*des Lichts*) refraction.
Brei [brī] *m* -(e)s, -e (*Masse*) pulp; (*KOCH*) gruel; (*Hafer*~) oatmeal (*US*), porridge (*Brit*); (*für Kinder, Kranke*) mash; **um den heißen ~ herumreden** (*umg*) beat about the bush.
breit [brīt] *a* wide, broad; **die ~e Masse** the masses *pl*; ~**beinig** *a* with one's legs apart.
Breite *f* -, -n width; breadth; (*GEOG*) latitude.
breiten *vt:* **etw über etw** (*akk*) ~ spread sth over sth.
Breitengrad *m* degree of latitude.
Breitensport *m* popular sport.
breit- *zW:* ~**gefächert** *a:* **ein ~gefächertes**

Angebot a wide range; ~**machen** *vr* spread o.s. out; ~**schlagen** *vt unreg* (*umg*): **sich ~schlagen lassen** let o.s. be talked round; ~**schult(e)rig** *a* broad-shouldered; ~**treten** *vt unreg* (*umg*) enlarge upon; **B~wandfilm** *m* wide-screen film.
Bremen [brā:'mən] *nt* Bremen.
Bremsbelag *m* brake lining.
Bremse [brem'zə] *f* -, -n brake; (*ZOOL*) horsefly.
bremsen *vi* brake, apply the brakes ♦ *vt* (*Auto*) brake; (*fig*) slow down ♦ *vr:* **ich kann mich ~** (*umg*) not likely!
Brems- *zW:* ~**licht** *nt* brake light; ~**pedal** *nt* brake pedal; ~**schuh** *m* brake shoe; ~**spur** *f* tire (*US*) *od* tyre (*Brit*) marks *pl*; ~**weg** *m* braking distance.
brennbar *a* inflammable; **leicht ~** highly inflammable.
Brennelemente *pl* reactor rods.
brennen [bre'nən] *unreg vi* burn, be on fire; (*Licht, Kerze etc*) burn; **wo brennt's denn?** (*fig umg*) what's the panic? ♦ *vt* (*Holz etc*) burn; (*Ziegel, Ton*) fire; (*Kaffee*) roast; (*Branntwein*) distil(l); **darauf ~, etw zu tun** be dying to do sth.
Brenn- *zW:* ~**material** *nt* fuel; ~**(n)essel** *f* nettle; ~**ofen** *m* kiln; ~**punkt** *m* (*MATH, OPTIK*) focus; ~**spiritus** *m* methylated spirits *pl*; ~**stoff** *m* liquid fuel.
brenzlig [brents'lich] *a* smelling of burning, burnt; (*fig*) precarious.
Bresche [bre'shə] *f* -, -n: **in die ~ springen** (*fig*) step into the breach.
Bretagne [brātán'yə] *f:* **die ~** Brittany.
Bretone [brātō:'nə] *m* -n, -n, **Bretonin** *f* Breton.
Brett [bret] *nt* -(e)s, -er board, plank; (*Bord*) shelf; (*Spiel*~) board; **Schwarze(s) ~** bulletin board; **er hat ein ~ vor dem Kopf** (*umg*) he's really thick.
Bretter *pl* (*SKI*) skis *pl*; (*THEAT*) boards *pl*.
brettern *vt* (*umg*) speed.
Bretterzaun *m* wooden fence.
Brezel [brā:'tsəl] *f* -, -n pretzel.
bricht [bricht] *3. pers sing präs von* **brechen**.
Brief [brē:f] *m* -(e)s, -e letter; ~**beschwerer** *m* -s, - paperweight; ~**bombe** *f* letter bomb; ~**freund(in** *f*) *m* pen pal; ~**kasten** *m* mailbox; ~**kopf** *m* letterhead; **b~lich** *a, ad* by letter; ~**marke** *f* postage stamp; ~**öffner** *m* letter opener; ~**papier** *nt* notepaper, writing paper; ~**qualität** *f* (*COMPUT*) letter quality; ~**tasche** *f* wallet; ~**taube** *f* carrier pigeon; ~**träger** *m* mailman (*US*), postman (*Brit*); ~**umschlag** *m* envelope; ~**wahl** *f* absentee ballot (*US*), postal vote (*Brit*); ~**wechsel** *m* correspondence.
briet [brē:t] *imperf von* **braten**.
Brigade [brēgá'də] *f* -, -n (*MIL*) brigade; (*DDR*) (work) team *od* group.
Brikett [brēket'] *nt* -s, -s briquette.
brillant [brilyánt'] *a* (*fig*) sparkling, brilliant; **B~** *m* -en, -en brilliant, diamond.

Brille [bri'lə] *f* -, **-n** spectacles *pl*; (*Schutz~*) goggles *pl*; (*Toiletten~*) (toilet) seat.

Brillen- *zW*: **~schlange** *f* (*hum*) four-eyes; **~träger(in** *f*)**: er ist ~träger** he wears glasses.

bringen [bri'ngən] *vt unreg* bring; (*mitnehmen, begleiten*) take; (*einbringen*: *Profit*) bring in; (*veröffentlichen*) publish; (*THEAT, FILM*) show; (*RAD, TV*) broadcast; (*in einen Zustand versetzen*) get; (*umg*: *tun können*) manage; **jdn dazu ~, etw zu tun** make sb do sth; **jdn zum Lachen/Weinen ~** make sb laugh/cry; **es weit ~** do very well, get far; **jdn nach Hause ~** take sb home; **jdn um etw ~** make sb lose sth; **jdn auf eine Idee ~** give sb an idea.

brisant [brēzánt'] *a* (*fig*) controversial.

Brisanz [brēzánts'] *f* (*fig*) controversial nature.

Brise [brē:'zə] *f* -, **-n** breeze.

Brite [bri'tə] *m* **-n, -n, Britin** *f* Briton, Britisher (*US*); **die ~n** the British.

britisch [bri'tish] *a* British; **die B~en Inseln** the British Isles.

bröckelig [brœ'kəliçh] *a* crumbly.

Brocken [bro'kən] *m* **-s, -** piece, bit; (*Fels~*) lump of rock; **ein paar ~ Spanisch** a smattering of Spanish; **ein harter ~** (*umg*) a tough nut to crack.

brodeln [brō:'dəln] *vi* bubble.

Brokat [brōkát'] *m* **-(e)s, -e** brocade.

Brombeere [brom'bā:rə] *f* blackberry.

bronchial [bronçhēāl'] *a* bronchial.

Bronchien [bron'çhēən] *pl* bronchial tubes *pl*.

Bronze [brōñ'sə] *f* -, **-n** bronze.

Brosame [brō:'zámə] *f* -, **-n** crumb.

Brosche [bro'shə] *f* -, **-n** brooch.

Broschüre [broshü:'rə] *f* -, **-n** pamphlet.

Brot [brō:t] *nt* **-(e)s, -e** bread; (*~laib*) loaf; **das ist ein hartes ~** (*fig*) that's a hard way to earn one's living.

Brötchen [brœt'çhən] *nt* roll; **kleine ~ backen** (*fig*) set one's sights lower; **~geber** *m* (*hum*) employer, provider (*hum*).

brotlos [brō:'tlō:s] *a* (*Person*) unemployed; (*Arbeit etc*) unprofitable.

Brotzeit *f* (*süddeutsch*: *Pause*) break.

Bruch [brookh] *m* **-(e)s,** ⁼**e** breakage; (*zerbrochene Stelle*) break; (*fig*) split, breach; (*MED*: *Eingeweide~*) rupture, hernia; (*Bein~ etc*) fracture; (*MATH*) fraction; **zu ~ gehen** get broken; **sich einen ~ heben** rupture o.s.; **~bude** *f* (*umg*) shack.

brüchig [brü'çhiçh] *a* brittle, fragile; (*Haus*) dilapidated.

Bruch- *zW*: **~landung** *f* crash landing; **~schaden** *m* breakage; **~stelle** *f* break; (*von Knochen auch*) fracture; **~strich** *m* (*MATH*) line; **~stück** *nt* fragment; **~teil** *m* fraction.

Brücke [brü'kə] *f* -, **-n** bridge; (*Teppich*) rug; (*Turnen*) crab.

Bruder [broo:'dər] *m* **-s,** ⁼ brother; **unter Brüdern** (*umg*) between friends.

Brüder- [brü:'dər] *zW*: **b~lich** *a* brotherly; **~lichkeit** *f* fraternity; **~mord** *m* fratricide; **~schaft** *f* brotherhood, fellowship; **~schaft trinken** fraternize, address each other as "du".

Brühe [brü:'ə] *f* -, **-n** broth, stock; (*pej*) muck.

brühwarm ['brü:'vàrm] *a* (*umg*): **er hat das sofort ~ weitererzählt** he promptly spread it around.

Brühwürfel *m* bouillon cube.

brüllen [brü:'lən] *vi* bellow, roar.

Brummbär *m* grumbler.

brummeln [broo'məln] *vti* mumble.

brummen *vi* (*Bär, Mensch etc*) growl; (*Insekt, Radio*) buzz; (*Motoren*) roar; (*murren*) grumble ♦ *vt* growl; **jdm brummt der Kopf** sb's head is buzzing.

Brummer [broo'mər] *m* **-s, -** (*umg*: *Lastwagen*) big truck-trailer (*US*), juggernaut (*Brit*).

Brummi [broo'mē] *m* (*umg*) = **Brummer**.

brummig *a* (*umg*) grumpy.

Brummschädel *m* (*umg*) thick head.

brünett [brünet'] *a* brunette, dark-haired.

Brunnen [broo'nən] *m* **-s, -** fountain; (*tief*) well; (*natürlich*) spring; **~kresse** *f* watercress.

Brunst [broonst] *f* (*von männlichen Tieren*) rut; (*von weiblichen Tieren*) heat; **~zeit** *f* rutting season.

brüsk [brüsk] *a* abrupt, brusque.

brüskieren [brüskē:'rən] *vt* snub.

Brüssel [brü'səl] *nt* **-s** Brussels.

Brust [broost] *f* -, ⁼**e** breast; (*Männer~*) chest; **einem Kind die ~ geben** nurse (*US*) *od* breastfeed (*Brit*) a baby.

brüsten [brüs'tən] *vr* boast.

Brust- *zW*: **~fellentzündung** *f* pleurisy; **~kasten** *m* chest; **~korb** *m* (*ANAT*) thorax; **~schwimmen** *nt* breast-stroke; **~ton** *m*: **im ~ton der Überzeugung** in a tone of utter conviction.

Brüstung [brüs'tōong] *f* parapet.

Brustwarze *f* nipple.

Brut [broo:t] *f* -, **-en** brood; (*Brüten*) hatching.

brutal [brootāl'] *a* brutal; **B~ität'** *f* brutality.

Brutapparat *m*, **Brutkasten** *m* incubator.

brüten [brü:'tən] *vi* hatch, brood (*auch fig*); **brütende Hitze** oppressive *od* stifling heat.

Brüter *m* **-s, -** (*TECH*): **schneller ~** fast-breeder (reactor).

Brutstätte *f* (*lit, fig*) breeding ground (*gen* for).

brutto [broo'tō] *ad* gross; **B~einkommen** *nt*, **B~gehalt** *nt* gross salary; **B~gewicht** *nt* gross weight; **B~gewinn** *m* gross profit; **B~inlandsprodukt** *nt* gross domestic product; **B~lohn** *m* gross wages *pl*; **B~sozialprodukt** *nt* gross national product.

brutzeln [broo'tsəln] *vi* (*umg*) sizzle away ♦ *vt* fry (up).

BSE *abk* = *Industriegewerkschaft Bau, Stei-*

ne, Erden.
Btx *abk* = **Bildschirmtext.**
Bub [boo:p] *m* **-en, -en** boy, lad.
Bube [boo:'bə] *m* **-n, -n** (*Schurke*) rogue; (*KARTEN*) jack.
Bubikopf *m* bobbed hair.
Buch [boo:kh] *nt* **-(e)s,** ‡**er** book; (*COMM*) account book; **er redet wie ein** ~ (*umg*) he never stops talking; **ein** ~ **mit sieben Siegeln** (*fig*) a closed book; **über etw** (*akk*) ~ **führen** keep a record of sth; **negativ/positiv zu** ~**(e) schlagen** make a significant difference, tip the balance; ~**binder** *m* bookbinder; ~**drucker** *m* printer.
Buche *f* **-, -n** beech tree.
buchen *vt* book; (*Betrag*) enter; **etw als Erfolg** ~ put sth down as a success.
Bücherbrett [bü:'chərbret] *nt* bookshelf.
Bücherei [bü:chərī'] *f* library.
Bücher- *zW*: ~**regal** *nt* bookshelves *pl*, bookcase; ~**schrank** *m* bookcase.
Buchfink [boo:kh'fingk] *m* chaffinch.
Buch- *zW*: ~**führung** *f* book-keeping, accounting; ~**halter(in** *f*) *m* **-s,** - book-keeper; ~**handel** *m* book trade; **im** ~**handel erhältlich** available in bookstores; ~**händler(in** *f*) *m* bookseller; ~**handlung** *f* bookstore; ~**prüfung** *f* audit; ~**rücken** *m* spine.
Büchse [bük'sə] *f* **-, -n** can; (*Holz*~) box; (*Gewehr*) rifle.
Büchsen- *zW*: ~**fleisch** *nt* canned meat; ~**öffner** *m* can opener.
Buchstabe *m* **-ns, -n** letter (of the alphabet).
buchstabieren [boo:khshtábē:'rən] *vt* spell.
buchstäblich [boo:kh'shte:pliçh] *a* literal.
Buchstütze *f* bookend.
Bucht [boo:kht'] *f* **-, -en** bay.
Buchung [boo:'khoong] *f* booking; (*COMM*) entry.
Buchwert *m* book value.
Buckel [boo:'kəl] *m* **-s,** - hump; **er kann mir den** ~ **runterrutschen** (*umg*) he can (go and) take a running jump.
buckeln *vi* (*pej*) bow and scrape.
bücken [bü'kən] *vr* bend; **sich nach etw** ~ bend down *od* stoop to pick sth up.
Bückling [bü'kling] *m* (*Fisch*) kipper; (*Verbeugung*) bow.
buddeln [boo:'dəln] *vti* (*umg*) dig.
Bude [boo:'də] *f* **-, -n** booth, stall; (*umg*) place; **jdm die** ~ **einrennen** (*umg*) pester sb.
Budget [büdzhā:'] *nt* **-s, -s** budget.
Büffel [bü'fəl] *m* **-s,** - buffalo.
büffeln [bü'fəln] *vi* (*umg*) cram ♦ *vt* (*Lernstoff*) bone up on.
Büf(f)ett [büfā:'] *nt* **-s, -s** (*Anrichte*) sideboard; (*Geschirrschrank*) dresser; **kaltes** ~ cold buffet.
Bug [boo:k] *m* **-(e)s, -e** (*NAUT*) bow; (*AVIAT*) nose.
Bügel [bü:'gəl] *m* **-s,** - (*Kleider*~) hanger; (*Steig*~) stirrup; (*Brillen*~) arm; ~**brett** *nt* ironing board; ~**eisen** *nt* iron; ~**falte** *f* crease.

bügeln *vti* iron.
Buhmann [boo:'mán] *m* (*umg*) bogeyman.
Bühne [bü:'nə] *f* **-, -n** stage.
Bühnenbild *nt* set, scenery.
Buhruf [boo:'roo:f] *m* boo.
buk [boo:k] *imperf* (*veraltet*) *von* **backen.**
Bukarest [boo:'kárest] *nt* **-s** Bucharest.
Bulette [boole'tə] *f* meatball.
Bulgare [boolgá'rə] *m* **-n, -n, Bulgarin** *f* Bulgarian.
Bulgarien *nt* **-s** Bulgaria.
bulgarisch *a* Bulgarian.
Bull- [bool'] *zW*: ~**auge** *nt* (*NAUT*) porthole; ~**dogge** *f* bulldog; ~**dozer** [bool'dō:zər] *m* **-s,** - bulldozer.
Bulle *m* **-n, -n** bull; **die** ~**n** (*pej umg*) the fuzz, the cops.
Bullenhitze *f* (*umg*) sweltering heat.
Bummel [boo:'məl] *m* **-s,** - stroll; (*Schaufenster*~) window-shopping.
Bummelant [boo:məlánt'] *m* slowpoke (*US*), slowcoach (*Brit*).
Bummelei [boo:məlī'] *f* wandering; dawdling; skiving.
bummeln *vi* wander, stroll; (*trödeln*) dawdle; (*faulenzen*) loaf around.
Bummel- *zW*: ~**streik** *m* slowdown (*US*), go-slow (*Brit*); ~**zug** *m* slow train.
Bummler(in *f*) [boo:m'lər(in)] *m* **-s,** - (*langsamer Mensch*) slowpoke (*US*), dawdler (*Brit*); (*Faulenzer*) idler, loafer.
bumsen [boo:m'zən] *vi* (*schlagen*) thump; (*prallen, stoßen*) bump, bang; (*umg: koitieren*) have sex.
Bund [boo:nt] *m* **-(e)s,** ‡**e** (*Freundschafts*~ *etc*) bond; (*Organisation*) union; (*POL*) confederacy; (*Hosen*~, *Rock*~) waistband; **den** ~ **fürs Leben schließen** take the marriage vows ♦ *nt* **-(e)s, -e** bunch; (*Stroh*~) bundle.
Bündchen [bünt'çhən] *nt* ribbing; (*Ärmel*~) cuff.
Bündel *nt* **-s,** - bundle, bale.
bündeln *vt* bundle.
Bundes- [boo:n'dəs] *in zW* Federal (*bes* West German); ~**bahn** *f* Federal Railways *pl*; ~**bürger** *m* West German citizen; ~**gerichtshof** *m* Federal Supreme Court; ~**grenzschutz** *m* (*BRD*) Federal Border Guard; ~**hauptstadt** *f* Federal capital; ~**haushalt** *m* (*POL*) National Budget; ~**kanzler** *m* Federal Chancellor; ~**land** *nt* state, Land; ~**liga** *f* (*BRD SPORT*) national league; ~**nachrichtendienst** *m* (*BRD*) Federal Intelligence Service; ~**post** *f*: **die (Deutsche)** ~**post** the (German) Federal Post (Office); ~**präsident** *m* Federal President; ~**rat** *m* upper house of West German Parliament; ~**republik** *f* Federal Republic (of West Germany); ~**staat** *m* Federal state; ~**straße** *f* Federal Highway, ≈ 'A' road.
Bundestag *m* West German Parliament.
Bundestags- *zW*: ~**abgeordnete(r)** *mf*

(BRD) German member of Parliament, member of the Bundestag; **~wahl** *f* (Federal) parliamentary elections *pl*.

Bundes- *zW*: **~verfassungsgericht** *nt* Federal Constitutional Court; **~wehr** *f* West German Armed Forces *pl*.

Bund- *zW*: **~falten** *pl (Hose)* waist pleats; **~hose** *f* knee breeches *pl*.

bündig [bün'diç] *a (kurz)* concise.

Bündnis [bünt'nis] *nt* **-ses, -se** alliance.

Bunker [bŏŏng'kər] *m* **-s,** - bunker; *(Luftschutz~)* air-raid shelter.

bunt [bŏŏnt] *a* colored *(US)*, coloured *(Brit)*; *(gemischt)* mixed; **jdm wird es zu ~** it's getting too much for sb; **B~stift** *m* colored pencil, crayon.

Bürde [bür'də] *f* **-, -n** *(lit, fig)* burden.

Burg [bŏŏrk] *f* **-, -en** castle, fort.

Bürge [bür'gə] *m* **-n, -n, Bürgin** *f* guarantor.

bürgen *vi* vouch; **für jdn ~** *(fig)* vouch for sb; *(FIN)* stand surety for sb.

Bürger(in *f)* *m* **-s,** - citizen; member of the middle class; **~initiative** *f* citizen's initiative; **~krieg** *m* civil war; **b~lich** *a (Rechte)* civil; *(Klasse)* middle-class; *(pej)* bourgeois; **gut b~liche Küche** good home cooking; **b~liches Gesetzbuch** Civil Code; **~meister** *m* mayor; **~recht** *nt* civil rights *pl*; **~schaft** *f* population, citizens *pl*; **~schreck** *m* bogey of the middle classes; **~steig** *m* sidewalk *(US)*, pavement *(Brit)*; **~tum** *nt* citizens *pl*.

Burgfriede(n) *m (fig)* truce.

Bürgin *f siehe* **Bürge.**

Bürgschaft *f* surety; **~ leisten** give security.

Burgund [bŏŏrgŏŏnt'] *nt* **-(s)** Burgundy.

Burgunder *m* **-s,** - *(Wein)* burgundy.

Büro [bürō:'] *nt* **-s, -s** office; **~angestellte(r)** *mf* office worker; **~klammer** *f* paper clip; **~kraft** *f* (office) clerk.

Bürokrat [bürōkrât'] *m* **-en, -en** bureaucrat.

Bürokratie [bürōkrātē:'] *f* bureaucracy.

bürokratisch *a* bureaucratic.

Bürokratis'mus *m* red tape.

Büroschluß *m* office closing time.

Bursch(e) [bŏŏrsh'(ə)] *m* **-en, -en** lad, fellow; *(Diener)* servant.

Burschenschaft *f* student fraternity.

burschikos [bŏŏrshēkō:s'] *a (jungenhaft)* (tom)boyish; *(unbekümmert)* casual.

Bürste [bürs'tə] *f* **-, -n** brush.

bürsten *vt* brush.

Bus [bŏŏs] *m* **-ses, -se** bus.

Busch [bŏŏsh] *m* **-(e)s, ⁺e** bush, shrub; **bei jdm auf den ~ klopfen** *(umg)* sound sb out.

Büschel [bü'shəl] *nt* **-s,** - tuft.

buschig *a* bushy.

Busen [bŏŏ:'zən] *m* **-s,** - bosom; *(Meer)* inlet, bay; **~freund(in** *f)* *m* bosom friend.

Bussard [bŏŏ'sárt] *m* **-s, -e** buzzard.

Buße [bŏŏ:'sə] *f* **-, -n** atonement, penance; *(Geld)* fine.

büßen [bü:'sən] *vti* do penance (for), atone (for).

Buß- *zW*: **~geld** *nt* fine; **~- und Bettag** *m* day of prayer and repentance.

Büste [büs'tə] *f* **-, -n** bust.

Büstenhalter *m* bra.

Büttenrede [bü'tənrä:də] *f* carnival speech.

Butter [bŏŏ'tər] *f* - butter; **alles (ist) in ~** *(umg)* everything is fine *od* hunky-dory; **~berg** *m (umg)* butter mountain; **~blume** *f* buttercup; **~brot** *nt* (piece of) bread and butter; **~brotpapier** *nt* ≈ wax paper; **~cremetorte** *f* cream cake; **~dose** *f* butter dish; **~keks** *m* ≈ morning coffee cookie; **b~weich** *a* soft as butter; *(fig, umg)* soft.

Butzen [bŏŏ'tsən] *m* **-s,** - core.

BV *f abk (= Bundesverfassung)* Federal Constitution.

BVA *nt abk (= Bundesverwaltungsamt)* Federal administration office.

BVG *nt abk (= Betriebsverfassungsgesetz)* ≈ Industrial Relations Act; = **Bundesverfassungsgericht.**

BVM *nt abk (= Bundesverkehrsminister(ium))* ≈ Department of Transport.

BW *f abk* = **Bundeswehr.**

b.w. *abk (= bitte wenden)* p.t.o.

BWM *nt abk (= Bundeswirtschaftsministerium)* Federal ministry of trade and commerce.

BWR *m abk (= Bundeswirtschaftsrat)* Federal economic agency.

Byte [bīt] *nt* **-s, -s** *(COMPUT)* byte.

Bz. *abk* = **Bezirk.**

bzgl. *abk (= bezüglich)* re.

bzw. *abk* = **beziehungsweise.**

C

(siehe auch **K** *und* **Z;** *für* **CH** *siehe auch* **SCH)**

C, c [tsā:] *nt* C, c; **C-Schlüssel** *m* alto *od* C clef.

C *abk (= Celsius)* C.

ca. [ká] *abk (= circa)* approx.

Cabriolet [kábrēōlā:'] *nt* **-s, -s** *(AUT)* convertible.

Café [káfā:'] *nt* **-s, -s** café.

Cafeteria [káfātārē:'á] *f* **-, -s** cafeteria.

Calais [kále:'] *nt* **-':** **die Straße von ~** the Straits of Dover.

campen [kem'pən] *vi* camp.

Camper(in *f)* *m* **-s,** - camper.

Camping [kem'ping] *nt* **-s** camping; **~platz** *m* camp(ing) site.

Caravan [ká'ráván] *m* **-s, -s** caravan.

Carnet [kárne'] *nt* **-s** *(COMM)* international customs pass, carnet.

Cäsium [tse:'ziŏŏm] *nt* cesium *(US)*, caesium *(Brit)*.

cbm *abk (= Kubikmeter)* m³.

ccm *abk* (= *Kubikzentimeter*) cc, cm³.

CDU [tsā:dā:ōō:'] *f* - *abk* (= *Christlich-Demokratische Union* (*Deutschlands*)) Christian Democratic Union.

Cellist(in *f*) [tshelist'(in)] *m* cellist.

Cello [tshe'lō] *nt* **-s**, **-s** *od* **Celli** cello.

Celsius [tsel'zēōōs] *a* Celsius.

Cembalo [tshɛm'bálō] *nt* **-s**, **-s** cembalo, harpsichord.

ces, Ces [tses] *nt* -, - (*MUS*) C flat.

Ceylon [tsī'lon] *nt* **-s** Ceylon.

Chamäleon [kámɛ:'lāon] *nt* **-s**, **-s** chameleon.

Champagner [shámpán'yər] *m* **-s**, - champagne.

Champignon [shám'pinyōn] *m* **-s**, **-s** button mushroom.

Chance [shâṅs'(ə)] *f* -, **-n** chance, opportunity.

Chancengleichheit *f* equality of opportunity.

Chaos [kâ'os] *nt* - chaos.

Chaot(in *f*) [káō:t'(in)] *m* **-en**, **-en** (*POL pej*) anarchist (*pej*).

chaotisch [kàō:'tish] *a* chaotic.

Charakter [káráktər'] *m* **-s**, **-e** [kárák'tā:rə] character; **c~fest** *a* of firm character.

charakterisieren [káráktārēzē:'rən] *vt* characterize.

Charakteristik [káráktāris'tik] *f* characterization.

charakteristisch [káráktāris'tish] *a* characteristic, typical (*für* of).

Charakter- *zW:* **c~los** *a* unprincipled; **~losigkeit** *f* lack of principle; **~schwäche** *f* weakness of character; **~stärke** *f* strength of character; **~zug** *m* characteristic, trait.

charmant [shármánt'] *a* charming.

Charme [shárm] *m* **-s** charm.

Charta [kár'tá] *f* -, **-s** charter.

Charterflug [tshár'tərflōō:k] *m* charter flight.

chartern [tshár'tərn] *vt* charter.

Chassis [shásē:'] *nt* -, - chassis.

Chauffeur [shofœr'] *m* chauffeur.

Chaussee [shōsā:'] *f* -, **-n** (*veraltet*) high road.

Chauvi [shō'vē] *m* **-s**, **-s** (*umg*) male chauvinist pig.

Chauvinismus [shōvēnis'mōōs] *m* chauvinism, jingoism.

Chauvinist [shōvēnist'] *m* chauvinist, jingoist.

checken [tshe'kən] *vt* (*überprüfen*) check; (*umg: verstehen*) get.

Chef(in *f*) [shef(in)] *m* **-s**, **-s** head; (*umg*) boss; **~arzt** *m* head physician; **~etage** *f* executive floor; **~redakteur** *m* editor-in-chief; **~sekretärin** *f* personal assistant/secretary; **~visite** *f* (*MED*) consultant's round.

Chemie [c̣h̬āmē:'] *f* - chemistry; **~faser** *f* man-made fiber (*US*) *od* fibre (*Brit*).

Chemikalie [c̣h̬āmēká'lēə] *f* chemical.

Chemiker(in *f*) [c̣h̬ā:'mēkər(in)] *m* **-s**, - (industrial) chemist.

chemisch [c̣h̬ā:'mish] *a* chemical; **~e Reinigung** dry cleaning.

Chiffre [shi'fər] *f* -, **-n** (*Geheimzeichen*) cipher; (*in Zeitung*) box number.

Chiffriermaschine [shifrē:r'máshē:nə] *f* cipher machine.

Chile [tshē:'lā] *nt* **-s** Chile.

Chilene [tshēlā:'nə] *m* **-n**, **-n**, **Chilenin** *f* Chilean.

chilenisch *a* Chilean.

China [c̣h̬ē:'ná] *nt* **-s** China.

Chinese [c̣h̬ēnā:'zə] *m* **-n**, **-n**, **Chinesin** *f* Chinaman, Chinese; Chinese woman.

chinesisch *a* Chinese.

Chinin [c̣h̬ēnē:n'] *nt* **-s** quinine.

Chip [tship] *m* **-s**, **-s** (*COMPUT*) chip.

Chips *pl* chips *pl* (*US*), crisps *pl* (*Brit*).

Chirurg(in *f*) [c̣h̬ērōōrg'(in)] *m* **-en**, **-en** surgeon.

Chirurgie [c̣h̬ērōōrgē:'] *f* surgery.

chirurgisch [c̣h̬ērōōrgish] *a* surgical; **ein ~er Eingriff** surgery.

Chlor [klō:r] *nt* **-s** chlorine.

Chloroform [klōrōform'] *nt* **-s** chloroform.

chloroformieren [klōrōfōrmē:'rən] *vt* chloroform.

Chlorophyll [klōrōfül'] *nt* **-s** chlorophyll.

Cholera [kō:'lárá] *f* - cholera.

Choleriker(in *f*) [kōlā:'rēkər(in)] *m* **-s**, - hot-tempered person.

cholerisch [kōlā:'rish] *a* choleric.

Cholesterinspiegel [c̣h̬ōlestārē:n'shpē:gəl] *m* cholesterol level.

Chor [kō:r] *m* **-(e)s**, **⁻e** choir; (*Musikstück*, *THEAT*) chorus.

Choral [kōrál'] *m* **-s**, **-äle** chorale.

Choreograph(in *f*) [kōrāōgráf'(in)] *m* **-en**, **-en** choreographer.

Choreographie [kōrāōgráfē:'] *f* choreography.

Chor- *zW:* **~gestühl** *nt* choir stalls *pl*; **~knabe** *m* choirboy.

Chose [shō:'zə] *f* -, **-n** (*umg: Angelegenheit*) thing.

Chr. *abk* = **Christus; Chronik.**

Christ [krist] *m* **-en**, **-en** Christian; **~baum** *m* Christmas tree.

Christen- *zW:* **~heit** *f* Christendom; **~tum** *nt* **-s** Christianity.

Christin *f* Christian.

Christ- *zW:* **~kind** *nt* ≈ Santa Claus; (*Jesus*) baby Jesus; **c~lich** *a* Christian; **c~licher Verein Junger Männer** Young Men's Christian Association.

Christus *m* **Christi** Christ; **Christi Himmelfahrt** Ascension Day.

Chrom [krō:m] *nt* **-s** (*CHEM*) chromium; chrome.

Chromosom [krōmōzō:m'] *nt* **-s**, **-en** (*BIOL*) chromosome.

Chronik [krō:'nik] *f* chronicle.

chronisch *a* chronic.

Chronologie [krōnōlōgē:'] *f* chronology.

chronologisch *a* chronological.

Chrysantheme [krüzántā:'mə] *f* -, **-n** chrysanthemum.

CIA ['sē:ï'ā:] *m* - *abk* (= *Central Intelligence Agency*) CIA.

circa [tsir'kå] *ad* = **zirka**.

cis, Cis [tsis] *nt* -, - (*MUS*) C sharp.

clean [klē:n] *a* (*Drogen umg*) off drugs.

clever [kle'vər] *a* clever; (*gerissen*) crafty.

Cliquenwirtschaft [kli'kɔnvirtsháft] *f* (*pej umg*) cliquish practices *pl*.

Clou [klōō:] *m* **-s, -s** (*von Geschichte*) (whole) point; (*von Show*) highlight, high spot.

Clown [kloun] *m* **-s, -s** clown.

cm *abk* (= *Zentimeter*) cm.

C.M.B. *abk* (= *Caspar, Melchior, Balthasar*) the Magi.

COBOL [kō:'bol] *nt* COBOL.

Cockpit [kok'pit] *nt* **-s, -s** cockpit.

Cola [kō:'lá] *f od nt* -, **-s** Coke ®.

Computer [kompyōō:'tər] *m* **-s,** - computer; **c~gesteuert** *a* computer-controlled; **~steuerung** *f* numerical control; **~technik** *f* computer technology.

Conférencier [kōnfārånsēā:'] *m* **-s, -s** master of ceremonies.

Container [kontā:'nər] *m* **-s,** - container; **~schiff** *nt* container ship.

Contergankind [kontergán'kint] *nt* (*umg*) thalidomide child.

cool [kōō:l] *a* (*umg: gefaßt*) cool.

Cornichon [kornēshōn'] *nt* **-s, -s** gherkin.

Couchgarnitur ['koutshgárnē'tōō:r] *f* three-piece suite.

Couleur [kōōlœr'] *f* **-s, -s** (*geh*) kind, sort.

Coupé [kōōpā:'] *nt* **-s, -s** (*AUT*) coupé, sports version.

Coupon [kōōpōn'] *m* **-s, -s** coupon; voucher; (*Stoff~*) length of cloth.

Courage [kōōrá'zə] *f* - courage.

Cousin [kōōzań:'] *m* **-s, -s** cousin.

Cousine [kōōzē:'nə] *f* -, **-n** cousin.

Creme [kre:m] *f* -, **-s** (*lit, fig*) cream; (*Schuh~*) polish; (*Zahn~*) paste; (*KOCH*) mousse; **c~farben** *a* cream.

Crux [krōōks] *f* - (*Schwierigkeit*) trouble; problem.

CSSR [tshā:eseser'] *abk von Name für* **Tschechoslowakei.**

CSU [tsā:esōō:'] *f* - *abk* (= *Christlich-Soziale Union*) Christian Social Union.

Curriculum [kōōrē:'kōōlōōm] *nt* **-s, -cula** (*geh*) curriculum.

Curry(pulver *nt*) [ká'rē(pōōlfər)] *m od nt* **-s** curry powder.

Currywurst *f* curried sausage.

Cursor [kœr'sər] *m* **-s** (*COMPUT*) cursor.

Cutter(in *f*) [ká'tər(in)] *m* **-s,** - (*FILM*) editor.

CVJM [tsā:fouyotem'] *m* - *abk* (= *Christlicher Verein Junger Männer*) YMCA.

D

D, d [dā:] *nt* D, d.

D. *abk* = **Doktor** (*der evangelischen Theologie*).

da [då] *ad* (*dort*) there; (*hier*) here; (*dann*) then; **was gibt's denn ~ zu lachen/fragen?** what's so funny about that?/what is there to ask?; **~ kann man nichts machen** nothing can be done about it; **~ hast du dein Geld!** (here you are,) there's your money; **es war niemand im Zimmer, ~ habe ich ...** there was nobody in the room, so I ...; **was hast du dir denn ~ gedacht?** what were you thinking of?; **~, wo** where ♦ *kj* as.

d.Ä. *abk* (= *der Ältere*) Sen., sen.

DAAD *m* - *abk* (= *Deutscher Akademischer Austauschdienst*) German Academic Exchange Service.

DAB *m* - *abk* = *Deutscher Athletenbund* ♦ *nt* - *abk* (= *Deutsches Arzneibuch*) pharmacopoeia.

dabehalten *vt unreg* keep.

dabei [dåbï'] *ad* (*räumlich*) close to it; (*noch dazu*) besides; (*zusammen mit*) with them/it *etc*; (*zeitlich*) during this; (*obwohl doch*) but, however; **was ist schon ~?** what of it?; **es ist doch nichts ~, wenn ...** it doesn't matter if ...; **bleiben wir ~** let's leave it at that; **es soll nicht ~ bleiben** this isn't the end of it; **es bleibt ~** that's settled; **das Dumme/Schwierige ~** the stupid/difficult part of it; **er war gerade ~, zu gehen** he was just leaving; **hast du ~ etwas gelernt?** did you learn anything from it?; **~ darf man nicht vergessen, daß ...** it shouldn't be forgotten that ...; **die ~ entstehenden Kosten** the expenses arising from this *od* that; **es kommt doch nichts ~ heraus** nothing will come of it; **ich finde gar nichts ~** I don't see any harm in it; **~sein** *vi unreg* (*anwesend*) be present; (*beteiligt*) be involved; **ich bin ~!** count me in!; **~stehen** *vi unreg* stand around.

Dach [dåxh] *nt* **-(e)s, -̈er** roof; **unter ~ und Fach sein** (*abgeschlossen*) be in the bag (*umg*); (*Vertrag, Geschäft auch*) be signed and sealed; (*in Sicherheit*) be safe; **jdm eins aufs ~ geben** (*umg: ausschimpfen*) give sb a (good) talking to; **~boden** *m* attic, loft; **~decker** *m* **-s,** - slater, tiler; **~fenster** *nt* skylight; (*ausgestellt*) dormer window; **~first** *m* ridge of the roof; **~gepäckträger** *m* (*AUT*) roof rack; **~geschoß** *nt* attic story (*US*) *od* storey (*Brit*); (*oberster Stock*) top floor; **~luke** *f* skylight; **~pappe** *f* roofing felt; **~rinne** *f* gutter.

Dachs [dáks] *m* **-es, -e** badger.

Dachschaden *m* (*umg*): **einen ~ haben** have a screw loose.

dachte [dàḳh'tə] *imperf von* **denken**.

Dach- *zW*: **~verband** *m* umbrella organization; **~ziegel** *m* roof tile.

Dackel [dà'kəl] *m* **-s,** - dachshund.

dadurch [dàdŏŏrčh'] *ad* (*räumlich*) through it; (*durch diesen Umstand*) thereby, in that way; (*deshalb*) because of that, for that reason ♦ *kj*: ~, **daß** because.

dafür [dàfü:r'] *ad* for it; (*anstatt*) instead; (*zum Ausgleich*): **in Mathematik ist er schlecht, ~ kann er gut Fußball spielen** he's very bad at maths but he makes up for it at football; **er kann nichts ~** he can't help it; **er ist bekannt ~** he is well-known for that; **was bekomme ich ~?** what will I get for it?; **~ ist er immer zu haben** he never says no to that; **~ bin ich ja hier** that's what I'm here for; **D~halten** *nt* **-s** (*geh*): **nach meinem D~halten** in my opinion.

DAG *f abk* (= *Deutsche Angestellten-Gewerkschaft*) ≈ *Clerical and Administrative Workers' Union*.

dagegen [dàgà:'gən] *ad* against it; (*im Vergleich damit*) in comparison with it; (*bei Tausch*) for it; **haben Sie was ~, wenn ich rauche** do you mind if I smoke?; **ich habe nichts ~** I don't mind; **ich war ~** I was against it; **sollen wir ins Kino gehen? — ich hätte nichts ~** (*einzuwenden*) shall we go to the cinema? — that's okay by me; **~ kann man nichts tun** one can't do anything about it ♦ *kj* however; **~halten** *vt unreg* (*vergleichen*) compare with it; (*entgegnen*) object to it.

dagewesen [dà'gəvà:zən] *pp von* **dasein**.

daheim [dàhīm'] *ad* at home; **bei uns ~** back home; **D~** *nt* **-s** home.

daher [dàhà:r'] *ad* (*räumlich*) from there; (*Ursache*) from that; **das kommt ~, daß ...** that is because ...; **~ kommt er auch** that's where he comes from too ♦ *kj* (*deshalb*) that's why; **~ die Schwierigkeiten** that's what is causing the difficulties; **~gelaufen** *a*: **jeder ~gelaufene Kerl** any Tom, Dick or Harry; **~reden** *vi* talk away ♦ *vt* say without thinking.

dahin [dàhin'] *ad* (*räumlich*) there; (*zeitlich*) then; (*vergangen*) gone; **ist es noch weit bis ~?** is there still far to go?; **das tendiert ~ es** it is tending towards that; **er bringt es noch ~, daß ich ...** he'll make me ...; **~gegen** *kj* on the other hand; **~gehen** *vi unreg* (*Zeit*) pass; **~gehend** *ad* on this matter; **~gestellt** *ad*: **~gestellt bleiben** remain to be seen; **~gestellt sein lassen** leave sth open *od* undecided; **~schleppen** *vr* (*lit: sich fortbewegen*) drag o.s. along; (*fig: Verhandlungen, Zeit*) drag on; **~schmelzen** *vi* be enthralled.

dahinten [dàhin'tən] *ad* over there.

dahinter [dàhin'tər] *ad* behind it; **~klemmen, ~knien** *vr* (*umg*) put one's back into it; **~kommen** *vi unreg* (*umg*) find out.

dahinvegetieren [dà'hinvàgà'tē:rən] *vi* vegetate.

Dahlie [dà'lēə] *f* -, **-n** dahlia.

DAK *f* - *abk* = *Deutsche Angestellten-Krankenkasse*.

dalassen [dà'làsən] *vt unreg* leave (behind).

dalli [dà'lē] *ad* (*umg*): ~, **~!** on the double!

damalig [dà'màličh] *a* of that time, then.

damals [dà'màls] *ad* at that time, then.

Damaskus [dàmás'kŏŏs] *nt* Damascus.

Damast [dàmást'] *m* **-(e)s, -e** damask.

Dame [dà'mə] *f* -, **-n** lady; (*SCHACH, KARTEN*) queen; (*Spiel*) checkers (*US*), draughts (*Brit*).

Damen- *zW*: **~besuch** *m* lady visitor *od* visitors; **~binde** *f* sanitary napkin; **d~haft** *a* ladylike; **~sattel** *m*: **im ~sattel reiten** ride side-saddle; **~wahl** *f* ladies' choice.

Damespiel *nt* checkers (*US*), draughts (*Brit*).

damit [dàmit'] *ad* with it; (*begründend*) by that; **was meint er ~?** what does he mean by that?; **was soll ich ~?** what am I meant to do with that?; **muß er denn immer wieder ~ ankommen?** must he keep on about it?; **was ist ~?** what about it?; **genug ~!** that's enough; **~ basta!** and that's that; **~ eilt es nicht** there's no hurry ♦ *kj* in order that *od* to.

dämlich [dɛ:m'lič̣h] *a* (*umg*) silly, stupid.

Damm [dàm] *m* **-(e)s, ¨-e** dike (*US*), dyke (*Brit*); (*Stau~*) dam; (*Hafen~*) mole; (*Bahn~, Straßen~*) embankment.

dämmen [de'mən] *vt* (*Wasser*) dam up; (*Schmerzen*) keep back.

dämmerig *a* dim, faint.

Dämmerlicht *nt* twilight; (*abends auch*) dusk; (*Halbdunkel*) half-light.

dämmern [de'mərn] *vi* (*Tag*) dawn; (*Abend*) fall; **es dämmerte ihm, daß ...** (*umg*) it dawned on him that ...

Dämmerung *f* twilight; (*Morgen~*) dawn; (*Abend~*) dusk.

Dämmerzustand *m* (*Halbschlaf*) dozy state; (*Bewußtseinstrübung*) semi-conscious state.

Dämmung *f* insulation.

Dämon [de:'mon] *m* **-s, -en** [demō:'nən] demon.

dämonisch [demō:'nish] *a* demonic.

Dampf [dàmpf] *m* **-(e)s, ¨-e** steam; (*Dunst*) vapor (*US*), vapour (*Brit*); **jdm ~ machen** (*umg*) make sb get a move on; **~ ablassen** (*lit, fig*) let off steam; **d~en** *vi* steam.

dämpfen [dem'pfən] *vt* (*KOCH*) steam; (*bügeln auch*) iron with a damp cloth; (*fig*) dampen, subdue.

Dampfer [dàm'pfər] *m* **-s,** - steamer; **auf dem falschen ~ sein** (*fig*) have got the wrong idea.

Dämpfer *m* -s, - (*MUS*: *bei Klavier*) damper; (*bei Geige, Trompete*) mute; **er hat einen ~ bekommen** (*fig*) it dampened his spirits.

Dampf- *zW*: **~kochtopf** *m* pressure cooker; **~maschine** *f* steam engine; **~schiff** *nt* steamship; **~walze** *f* steamroller.

Damwild [dám'vilt] *nt* fallow deer.

danach [dánáx̣h'] *ad* after that; (*zeitlich auch*) afterwards; (*gemäß*) accordingly; (*laut diesem*) according to which *od* that; **mir war nicht ~** (*umg*) *od* **~ zumute** I didn't feel like it; **er griff schnell ~** he grabbed at it; **~ kann man nicht gehen** you can't go by that; **er sieht ~ aus** he looks it.

Däne [de:'nə] *m* -n, -n Dane, Danish man *od* boy.

daneben [dánä:'bən] *ad* beside it; (*im Vergleich*) in comparison; **~benehmen** *vr unreg* misbehave; **~gehen** *vi unreg* miss; (*Plan*) fail; **~greifen** *vi unreg* miss; (*fig*: *mit Schätzung etc*) be wide of the mark; **~sein** *vi unreg* (*umg*: *verwirrt sein*) be completely confused.

Dänemark [de:'nəmárk] *nt* -s Denmark.

Dänin [de:'nin] *f* Dane, Danish woman *od* girl.

dänisch *a* Danish.

Dank [dángk] *m* -(e)s thanks *pl*; **vielen** *od* **schönen ~** many thanks; **jdm ~ sagen** thank sb; **mit (bestem) ~ zurück!** many thanks for the loan; **d~** *präp* +*dat od gen* thanks to; **d~bar** *a* grateful; (*Aufgabe*) rewarding; (*haltbar*) hard-wearing; **~barkeit** *f* gratitude.

danke *interj* thank you, thanks.

danken *vi* (+*dat*) thank; **nichts zu ~!** don't mention it; **dankend erhalten/ablehnen** receive/decline with thanks.

dankenswert *a* (*Arbeit*) worthwhile; rewarding; (*Bemühung*) kind.

Dank- *zW*: **~gottesdienst** *m* service of thanksgiving; **d~sagen** *vi* express one's thanks; **~schreiben** *nt* letter of thanks.

dann [dán] *ad* then; **~ und wann** now and then; **~ eben nicht** well, in that case (there's no more to be said); **erst ~, wenn ... only when ...; ~ erst recht nicht!** in that case no way (*umg*).

dannen [dá'nən] *ad*: **von ~** (*liter*: *weg*) away.

daran [dárán'] *ad* on it; (*stoßen*) against it; **es liegt ~, daß ...** the cause of it is that ...; **gut/schlecht ~ sein** be well/badly off; **das Beste/Dümmste ~** the best/stupidest thing about it; **ich war nahe ~, zu ...** I was on the point of ...; (*zeitlich*: *danach anschließend*): **im Anschluß ~** following that *od* this; **wir können nichts ~ machen** we can't do anything about it; **es ist nichts ~** (*ist nicht fundiert*) there's nothing in it; (*ist nichts Besonderes*) it's nothing special; **er ist ~ gestorben** he died from *od* of it; **~gehen** *vi unreg* start; **~machen** *vr* (*umg*): **sich ~machen, etw zu tun** set about doing sth; **~setzen** *vt* stake; **er hat alles ~gesetzt,**

von Chicago wegzukommen he has done his utmost to get away from Chicago.

darauf [dáróuf'] *ad* (*räumlich*) on it; (*zielgerichtet*) towards it; (*danach*) afterwards; **es kommt ganz ~ an, ob ...** it depends whether ...; **seine Behauptungen stützen sich ~, daß ...** his claims are based on the supposition that ...; **wie kommst du ~?** what makes you think that?; **die Tage ~** the days following *od* thereafter; **am Tag ~** the next day; **~folgend** *a* (*Tag, Jahr*) next, following; **~hin** [-hin'] *ad* (*im Hinblick ~*) in this respect; (*aus diesem Grund*) as a result; **wir müssen es ~hin prüfen, ob ...** we must test it to see whether ...; **~legen** *vt* lay *od* put on top.

daraus [dárous'] *ad* from it; **was ist ~ geworden?** what became of it?; **~ geht hervor, daß ...** this means that ...

darbieten [dár'be̅:tən] *vt* (*vortragen*: *Lehrstoff*) present ♦ *vr* present itself.

Darbietung *f* performance.

Dardanellen [dárdánε'lən] *pl* Dardanelles *pl*.

darein- *präf siehe* **drein-**.

Daressalam [dáresálám'] *nt* Dar-es-Salaam.

darf [dárf] *1./3. pers sing präs von* **dürfen**.

darin [dárin'] *ad* in (there), in it; **der Unterschied liegt ~, daß ...** the difference is that ...

darlegen [dár'lā:gən] *vt* explain, expound, set forth.

Darlegung *f* explanation.

Darleh(e)n *nt* -s, - loan.

Darm [dárm] *m* -(e)s, ⁻e intestine; (*Wurst~*) skin; **~ausgang** *m* anus; **~grippe** *f* gastric influenza; **~saite** *f* gut string; **~trägheit** *f* under-activity of the intestines.

darstellen [dár'shtelən] *vt* (*abbilden, bedeuten*) represent; (*THEAT*) act; (*beschreiben*) describe ♦ *vr* appear to be.

Darsteller(in *f*) *m* -s, - actor; actress.

darstellerisch *a*: **eine ~e Höchstleistung** a magnificent piece of acting.

Darstellung *f* portrayal, depiction.

darüber [dárü:'bər] *ad* (*räumlich*) over/above it; (*fahren*) over it; (*mehr*) more; (*währenddessen*) meanwhile; (*sprechen, streiten*) about it; **~ hinweg** (*fig*) have got over it; **~ hinaus** over and above that; **~ geht nichts** there's nothing like it; **seine Gedanken ~** his thoughts about *od* on it; **~liegen** *vi unreg* (*fig*) be higher.

darum [dáro̅o̅m'] *ad* (*räumlich*) round it; **~ herum** round about (it); **er bittet ~** he is pleading for it; **es geht ~, daß ...** the thing is that ...; **~ geht es mir/geht es mir nicht** that's my point/that's not the point for me; **er würde viel ~ geben, wenn ...** he would give a lot to ... ♦ *kj* that's why; *siehe auch* **drum**.

darunter [dáro̅o̅n'tər] *ad* (*räumlich*) under it; (*dazwischen*) among them; (*weniger*) less; **ein Stockwerk ~** one floor below (it); **was verstehen Sie ~?** what do you understand by that?; ~ **kann ich mir nichts vorstellen** that doesn't mean anything to me; ~**fallen** *vi unreg* be included; ~**mischen** *vt (Mehl)* mix in ♦ *vr* mingle; ~**setzen** *vt (Unterschrift)* put to it.

das [dás] *pron* that; ~ **heißt** that is; ~ **und** ~ such and such ♦ *art siehe* **der.**

DAS *m - abk = Deutscher Automobilschutz.*

dasein *vi unreg* be there; **ein Arzt, der immer für seine Patienten da ist** a doctor who always has time for his patients.

Dasein [dá'zīn] *nt -s (Leben)* life; *(Anwesenheit)* presence; *(Bestehen)* existence.

Daseins- *zW:* ~**berechtigung** *f* right to exist; ~**kampf** *m* struggle for survival.

daß [dás] *kj* that.

dasselbe [dászel'bə] *art, pron* the same.

dastehen [dá'shtā:ən] *vi unreg* stand there; *(fig)*: **gut/schlecht** ~ be in a good/bad position; **allein** ~ be on one's own.

Dat. *abk =* **Dativ.**

Datei [dátī'] *f (COMPUT)* file; ~**name** *m* file name; ~**verwaltung** *f* file management system; ~**verzeichnis** *nt (COMPUT)* directory.

Daten [dá'tən] *pl (COMPUT)* data; ~**bank** *f* data base; ~**erfassung** *f* data capture; ~**satz** *m* record; ~**schutz** *m* data protection; ~**sichtgerät** *nt* video display terminal (VDT), visual display unit (VDU); ~**träger** *m* data carrier; ~**übertragung** *f* data transmission; ~**verarbeitung** *f* data processing.

Datenverarbeitungsanlage *f* data processing equipment, DP equipment.

datieren [dátē:'rən] *vt* date.

Dativ [dá'tē:f] *m -s, -e* dative; ~**objekt** *nt (GRAM)* indirect object.

dato [dá'tō] *ad:* **bis** ~ *(COMM: umg)* to date.

Dattel [dá'təl] *f -, -n* date.

Datum [dá'tōom] *nt -s,* **Daten** date; *(pl: Angaben)* data *pl;* **das heutige** ~ today's date.

Datumsgrenze *f (GEOG)* (international) date line.

Dauer [dou'ər] *f -, -n* duration; *(gewisse Zeitspanne)* length; *(Bestand, Fortbestehen)* permanence; **es war nur von kurzer** ~ it didn't last long; **auf die** ~ in the long run; *(auf längere Zeit)* indefinitely; ~**auftrag** *m* standing order; **d**~**haft** *a* lasting, durable; ~**haftigkeit** *f* durability; ~**karte** *f* season ticket; ~**lauf** *m* long-distance run.

dauern *vi* last; **es hat sehr lang gedauert, bis er ...** it took him a long time to ...

dauernd *a* constant.

Dauer- *zW:* ~**obst** *nt* fruit suitable for storing; ~**redner** *m (pej)* long-winded speaker; ~**regen** *m* continuous rain; ~**schlaf** *m* prolonged sleep; ~**stellung** *f* permanent position; ~**welle** *f* perm, permanent; ~**wurst** *f* German salami; ~**zustand** *m* permanent condition.

Daumen [dou'mən] *m -s, -* thumb; **jdm die** ~

drücken *od* **halten** keep one's fingers crossed for sb; **über den** ~ **peilen** guess roughly; ~**lutscher** *m* thumb-sucker.

Daune [dou'nə] *f -, -n* down.

Daunendecke *f* down duvet.

DAV *m - abk = Deutscher Alpenverein.*

davon [dáfon'] *ad* of it; *(räumlich)* away; *(weg von)* away from it; *(Grund)* because of it; **das kommt** ~! that's what you get; ~ **abgesehen** apart from that; **wenn wir einmal** ~ **absehen, daß** ... if for once we overlook the fact that ...; ~ **sprechen/wissen** talk/know of *od* about it; **was habe ich** ~? what's the point?; *(mit Passiv):* ~ **betroffen werden** be affected by it *od* them; ~**gehen** *vi unreg* leave, go away; ~**kommen** *vi unreg* escape; ~**lassen** *vt unreg:* **die Finger** ~**lassen** *(umg)* keep one's hands *od* fingers off (it *od* them); ~**laufen** *vi unreg* run away; ~**tragen** *vt unreg* carry off; *(Verletzung)* receive.

davor [dáfō:r'] *ad (räumlich)* in front of it; *(zeitlich)* before (that); ~ **warnen** warn about it.

dazu [dátsōo:'] *ad (legen, stellen)* by it; *(essen, singen)* with it; **und** ~ **noch** and in addition; **ein Beispiel/seine Gedanken** ~ one example for/his thoughts on this; **wie komme ich denn** ~? why should I?; ... **aber ich bin nicht** ~ **gekommen** ... but I didn't get around to it; **das Recht** ~ the right to do it; ~ **bereit sein, etw zu tun** be prepared to do sth; ~ **fähig sein** be capable of it; **sich** ~ **äußern** say sth on it; ~**gehören** *vi* belong to it; **das gehört** ~ *(versteht sich von selbst)* it's all part of it; **es gehört schon einiges** ~, **das zu tun** it takes a lot to do that; ~**gehörig** *a* appropriate; ~**kommen** *vi unreg (Ereignisse)* happen too; *(an einen Ort)* come along; **kommt noch etwas** ~? will there be anything else?; ~**lernen** *vt:* **schon wieder was** ~**gelernt!** you learn something (new) every day!; ~**mal** [dá'tsōomál] *ad* in those days; ~**tun** *vt unreg* add; **er hat es ohne dein D**~**tun geschafft** he managed it without your doing *etc* anything.

dazwischen [dátsvi'shən] *ad* in between; *(räumlich auch)* between (them); *(zusammen mit)* among them; **der Unterschied** ~ the difference between them; ~**funken** *vi (umg: eingreifen)* butt in; ~**kommen** *vi unreg (hineingeraten)* get caught in it; **es ist etwas** ~**gekommen** something cropped up; ~**reden** *vi (unterbrechen)* interrupt; *(sich einmischen)* interfere; ~**treten** *vi unreg* intervene.

DB *f abk = Deutsche Bundesbahn.*

DBB *m abk (= Deutscher Beamtenbund)* German Civil Servants Association.

DBP *f abk = Deutsche Bundespost* ♦ *nt abk = Deutsches Bundespatent.*

DDR *f - abk (= Deutsche Demokratische Republik)* GDR.

Dealer(in *f)* [dē:'lər(in)] *m -s, - (umg)* pusher.

Debatte [dābá'tə] *f* -, -n debate; **das steht hier nicht zur ~** that's not the issue.
Debet [dā:'bet] *nt* -s, -s *(FIN)* debits *pl.*
dechiffrieren [dāshifrē:'rən] *vt* decode; *(Text)* decipher.
Deck [dek] *nt* -(e)s, -s *od* -e deck; **an ~ gehen** go on deck.
Deck- *zW:* **~bett** *nt* feather quilt; **~blatt** *nt* *(Schutzblatt)* cover.
Decke *f* -, -n cover; *(Bett~)* blanket; *(Tisch~)* tablecloth; *(Zimmer~)* ceiling; **unter einer ~ stecken** be hand in glove; **an die ~ gehen** hit the roof; **mir fällt die ~ auf den Kopf** *(fig)* I feel really claustrophobic.
Deckel *m* -s, - lid; **du kriegst gleich eins auf den ~** *(umg)* you're going to catch it.
decken *vt* cover; **mein Bedarf ist gedeckt** I have all I need; *(fig)* I've had enough; **sich an einen gedeckten Tisch setzen** *(fig)* be handed everything on a plate ♦ *vr* coincide ♦ *vi* lay the table.
Deck- *zW:* **~mantel** *m:* **unter dem ~mantel von** under the guise of; **~name** *m* assumed name.
Deckung *f* *(Schützen)* covering; *(Schutz)* cover; *(SPORT)* defense *(US)*, defence *(Brit)*; *(Übereinstimmen)* agreement; **zur ~ seiner Schulden** to meet his debts.
deckungsgleich *a* congruent.
de facto [dā: fák'tō] *ad* de facto.
Defekt [dāfekt'] *m* -(e)s, -e fault, defect; **d~** *a* faulty.
defensiv [dāfensē:f'] *a* defensive.
Defensive *f:* **jdn in die ~ drängen** force sb onto the defensive.
definieren [dāfēnē:'rən] *vt* define.
Definition [dāfēnētsēō:n'] *f* definition.
definitiv [dāfēnētē:f'] *a* definite.
Defizit [dā:'fētsit] *nt* -s, -e deficit.
defizitär [dāfētsēte:r'] *a:* **eine ~e Haushaltspolitik führen** follow an economic policy which can only lead to deficit.
Deflation [dāflátsēō:n'] *f* *(WIRTSCHAFT)* deflation.
deflationär [dāflátsēōne:r'] *a* deflationary.
deftig [def'tiċh] *a* *(Essen)* large; *(Witz)* coarse.
Degen [dā:'gən] *m* -s, - sword.
degenerieren [dāgānārē:'rən] *vi* degenerate.
degradieren [dāgrádē:'rən] *vt* degrade.
dehnbar [dā:n'bâr] *a* elastic; *(fig: Begriff)* loose; **D~keit** *f* elasticity: looseness.
dehnen *vtr* stretch.
Dehnung *f* stretching.
Deich [dīċh] *m* -(e)s, -e dike *(US)*, dyke *(Brit)*.
Deichsel [dīk'səl] *f* -, -n shaft.
deichseln *vt* *(fig: umg)* wangle.
dein [dīn] *pron* *(in Briefen:* **D~)** your; *(adjektivisch):* **herzliche Grüße, D~e** Elke with best wishes, yours *od* *(herzlicher)* love, Elke.
deiner *pron* *(gen of* **du)** of you.
deine(r, s) *poss pron* yours.

deinerseits *ad* on your part.
deinesgleichen *pron* people like you.
deinetwegen [dī'nətvā:'gən], **deinetwillen** [dī'nətvi'lən] *ad* *(für dich)* for your sake; *(wegen dir)* on your account.
deinige *pron:* **der/die/das ~** yours.
dekadent [dākádent'] *a* decadent.
Dekadenz *f* decadence.
Dekan [dākân'] *m* -s, -e dean.
deklassieren [dāklàsē:'rən] *vt* *(SOZIOLOGIE:* *herabsetzen)* downgrade; *(SPORT: übertreffen)* outclass.
Deklination [dāklēnátsēō:n'] *f* declension.
deklinieren [dāklēnē:'rən] *vt* decline.
Dekolleté [dākoltā:'] *nt* -s, -s low neckline.
Dekor [dākō:r'] *m od nt* -s, -s *od* -e decoration.
Dekorateur(in *f)* [dākōrátœr'(in)] *m* interior decorator.
Dekoration [dākōrátsēō:n'] *f* decoration; *(in Laden)* window dressing.
dekorativ [dākōrátē:f'] *a* decorative.
dekorieren [dākōrē:'rən] *vt* decorate; *(Schaufenster)* dress.
Dekostoff [dā:'kōshtof] *m* *(TEXTIL)* furnishing fabric.
Dekret [dākrā:t'] *nt* -(e)s, -e decree.
Delegation [dālāgátsēō:n'] *f* delegation.
delegieren [dālāgē:'rən] *vt* delegate *(an +akk* to).
Delegierte(r) *mf* *dekl wie* *a* delegate.
delikat [dālēkât'] *a* *(zart, heikel)* delicate; *(köstlich)* delicious.
Delikatesse [dālēkàte'sə] *f* -, -n delicacy.
Delikatessengeschäft *nt* delicatessen (shop).
Delikt [dālikt'] *nt* -(e)s, -e *(JUR)* offense *(US)*, offence *(Brit)*.
Delinquent [dālingkvent'] *m* *(geh)* offender.
Delirium [dālē:'rēōōm] *nt:* **im ~ sein** be delirious; *(umg: betrunken)* be paralytic.
Delle [de'lə] *f* -, -n *(umg)* dent.
Delphin [delfē:n'] *m* -s, -e dolphin.
Delphinschwimmen *nt* butterfly (stroke).
Delta [del'tá] *nt* -s, -s delta.
dem [dā(:)m] *art* *(dat von* **der, das)** **wie ~ auch sei** be that as it may.
Demagoge [dāmágō:'gə] *m* -n, -n demagog(ue).
Demarkationslinie [dāmárkátsēō:nz'lē:nēə] *f* demarcation line.
Dementi [dāmen'tē] *nt* -s, -s denial.
dementieren [dāmentē:'rən] *vt* deny.
dem- *zW:* **~entsprechend** *a* appropriate ♦ *ad* correspondingly; *(demnach)* accordingly; **~gemäß, ~nach** *ad* accordingly; **~nächst** *ad* shortly.
Demo [dā:'mō] *f* -s, -s *(umg)* demo.
Demographie [dāmōgráfē:'] *f* demography.
Demokrat(in *f)* [dāmōkrât'(in)] *m* -en, -en democrat.
Demokratie [dāmōkràtē:'] *f* democracy; **~verständnis** *nt* understanding of (the meaning of) democracy.

demokratisch *a* democratic.
demokratisieren [dāmōkrátēzē:'rən] *vt* democratize.
demolieren [dāmōlē:'rən] *vt* demolish.
Demonstrant(in *f*) [dāmonstránt'(in)] *m* demonstrator.
Demonstration [dāmonstrátsēō:n'] *f* demonstration.
demonstrativ [dāmonstrátē:f'] *a* demonstrative; (*Protest*) pointed.
demonstrieren [dāmonstrē:'rən] *vti* demonstrate.
Demontage [dāmontâ'zhə] *f* -, -n (*lit, fig*) dismantling.
demontieren [dāmontē:'rən] *vt* (*lit, fig*) dismantle; (*Räder*) take off.
Demoskopie [dāmōskōpē:'] *f* public opinion research.
Demut [dā:'mōō:t] *f* - humility.
demütig [dā:'mü:tiçh] *a* humble.
demütigen [dā:'mü:tigən] *vt* humiliate.
Demütigung *f* humiliation.
demselben *dat von* **derselbe, dasselbe.**
demzufolge ['dā:mtsōō'folgə] *ad* accordingly.
den [dā(:)n] *art akk von* **der.**
denen [dā:'nən] *pron dat von* **der, die, das.**
Denk- [dengk] *zW:* ~**anstöß** *m:* jdm ~anstöße geben give sb food for thought; ~**art** *f* mentality; **d~bar** *a* conceivable.
denken *unreg vi* think; **wo** ~ **Sie hin!** what an idea!; **ich denke schon** I think so; **an jdn/etw** ~ think of sb/sth; **daran ist gar nicht zu** ~ that's (quite) out of the question; **ich denke nicht daran,** das zu tun there's no way I'm going to do that (*umg*) ♦ *vt:* **für jdn/etw gedacht sein** be intended *od* meant for sb/sth ♦ *vr* (*vorstellen*): **das kann ich mir** ~ I can imagine; (*beabsichtigen*): **sich** (*dat*) **etw bei etw** ~ mean sth by sth.
Denken *nt* **-s** thinking.
Denker(in *f*) *m* **-s,** - thinker; **das Volk der Dichter und** ~ the nation of poets and philosophers.
Denk- *zW:* ~**fähigkeit** *f* intelligence; **d~faul** *a* mentally lazy; ~**fehler** *m* logical error; ~**horizont** *m* mental horizon.
Denkmal *nt* **-s, -er** monument; ~**schutz** *m:* **etw unter** ~**schutz stellen** classify sth as a historical monument.
Denk- *zW:* ~**pause** *f:* **eine** ~**pause einlegen** have a break to think things over; ~**schrift** *f* memorandum; ~**vermögen** *nt* intellectual capacity; **d~würdig** *a* memorable; ~**zettel** *m:* **jdm einen** ~**zettel verpassen** teach sb a lesson.
denn [den] *kj* for; (*konzessiv*): **es sei** ~, **(daß)** unless ♦ *ad* then; (*nach Komparativ*) than.
dennoch [den'nokh] *kj* nevertheless ♦ *ad:* **und** ~, ... and yet ...
denselben *akk von* **derselbe** ♦ *dat von* **dieselben.**
Denunziant(in *f*) [dānōōntsēánt'(in)] *m* informer.

Deospray [dā:'ōshprā:] *nt od m* deodorant spray.
Depesche [dāpe'shə] *f* -, -n dispatch.
Deponent(in *f*) [dāpōnent'(in)] *m* depositor.
Deponie *f* dump, disposal site.
deponieren [dāpōnē:'rən] *vt* (*COMM*) deposit.
deportieren [dāportē:'rən] *vt* deport.
Depot [dāpō:'] *nt* **-s, -s** warehouse; (*Bus*~, *EISENB*) depot; (*Bank*~) safe.
Depp [dep] *m* **-en, -en** (*Dialekt pej*) twit.
Depression [dāpresēō:n'] *f* depression.
depressiv *a* depressive; (*FIN*) depressed.
deprimieren [dāprēmē:'rən] *vt* depress.
der [dā(:)r] *def art* the ♦ *rel pron* that, which; (*jemand*) who ♦ *demon pron* this one; ~ **und** ~ so-and-so; ~**art** *ad* (*Art und Weise*) in such a way; (*Ausmaß: vor a*) so; (: *vor v*) so much; ~**artig** *a* such, this sort of.
derb [derp] *a* sturdy; (*Kost*) solid; (*grob*) coarse; **D~heit** *f* sturdiness; solidity; coarseness.
deren [dā:'rən] *rel pron* (*gen sing von* **die**) whose; (*von Sachen*) of which; (*gen pl von* **der, die, das**) their; whose, of whom.
derentwillen ['dā:rənt'vilən] *ad:* **um** ~ (*rel*) for whose sake; (*von Sachen*) for the sake of which.
dergestalt *ad* (*geh*): ~, **daß** ... in such a way that ...
der- *zW:* ~'**glei'chen** *pron* such; (*substantivisch*): **er tat nichts** ~**gleichen** he did nothing of the kind; **und** ~**gleichen (mehr)** and suchlike; ~'**jenige** *pron* he; she; it; (*rel*) the one (who); that (which); ~'**ma'ßen** *ad* to such an extent, so; ~**sel'be** *art, pron* the same; ~'**weil'(en)** *ad* in the meantime; ~'**zeit'** *a* (*jetzt*) at present, at the moment; ~'**zeit'ig** *a* present, current; (*damalig*) then.
des [des] *art gen von* **der.**
des, Des [des] *nt* - (*MUS*) D flat.
Deserteur [dāzertœr'] *m* deserter.
desertieren [dāzertē:'rən] *vi* desert.
desgl. *abk* = **desgleichen.**
desgleichen ['des'glíchən] *pron* the same.
deshalb ['des'hálp] *ad, kj* therefore, that's why.
Design [dēzīn'] *nt* **-s, -s** design.
designiert [dāzēgnē:rt'] *a attr:* **der** ~**e Vorsitzende/Nachkomme** the chairman designate/prospective successor.
Desinfektion [dāzinfektsēō:n'] *f* disinfection.
Desinfektionsmittel *nt* disinfectant.
desinfizieren [dāzinfētsē:'rən] *vt* disinfect.
Desinteresse [desíntəre'sə] *nt* **-s** lack of interest (*an +dat* in).
desselben *gen von* **derselbe, dasselbe.**
dessen [de'sən] *pron gen von* **der, das;** ~**ungeachtet** *ad* nevertheless, regardless.
Dessert [dese:r'] *nt* **-s, -s** dessert.
Dessin [desaṅ:'] *nt* **-s, -s** (*TEXTIL*) pattern, design.
Destillation [destilàtsēō:n'] *f* distillation.
destillieren [destilē:'rən] *vt* distil(l).
desto [des'tō] *ad* all *od* so much the; ~ **bes-**

ser all the better.

deswegen ['des'vā:gən] *kj* therefore, hence.

Detail [dātī'] *nt* **-s, -s** detail.

detaillieren [dātäyē:'rən] *vt* specify, give details of.

Detektiv [dātektē:f'] *m* **-s, -e** detective; **~roman** *m* detective novel.

Detektor [dātek'tor] *m* (*TECH*) detector.

Detonation [dātōnátsēō:n'] *f* explosion, blast.

Deut *m*: **(um) keinen ~** not one iota *od* jot.

deuten [doi'tən] *vt* interpret; (*Zukunft*) read ♦ *vi* point (*auf +akk* to *od* at).

deutlich *a* clear; (*Unterschied*) distinct; **jdm etw ~ zu verstehen geben** make sth perfectly clear *od* plain to sb; **D~keit** *f* clarity; distinctness.

deutsch [doitsh] *a* German; **~e Schrift** Gothic script; **auf gut ~ (gesagt)** (*fig umg*) in plain English.

Deutsche(r) *mf dekl wie* a: **er ist ~r** he is (a) German.

Deutschland *nt* Germany; **~frage** *f* (*POL*) German question; **~lied** *nt* West German national anthem; **~politik** *f* home *od* domestic policy; (*von fremdem Staat*) policy towards Germany.

deutsch- *zW*: **~sprachig** *a* (*Bevölkerung, Gebiete*) German-speaking; (*Zeitung, Ausgabe*) German-language; (*Literatur*) German; **~stämmig** *a* of German origin.

Deutung *f* interpretation.

Devise [dāvē:'zə] *f* **-, -n** motto, device; **~n** *pl* (*FIN*) foreign currency; foreign exchange.

Devisen- *zW*: **~ausgleich** *m* foreign exchange offset; **~kontrolle** *f* exchange control.

Dez. *abk* (= *Dezember*) Dec.

Dezember [dātsem'bər] *m* **-(s), -** December; *siehe* **September.**

dezent [dātsent'] *a* discreet.

Dezentralisation [dātsentrālēzátsēō:n'] *f* decentralization.

Dezernat [dātsernát'] *nt* **-(e)s, -e** (*VERWALTUNG*) department.

Dezibel [dātsēbel'] *nt* **-s, -** decibel.

dezidiert [dātsēdē:rt'] *a* firm, determined.

dezimal [dātsēmál'] *a* decimal; **D~bruch** *m* decimal (fraction); **D~system** *nt* decimal system.

dezimieren [dātsēmē:'rən] *vt* (*fig*) decimate ♦ *vr* be decimated.

DFB *m abk* (= *Deutscher Fußball-Bund*) ≈ Football Association.

DFG *f abk* (= *Deutsche Forschungsgemeinschaft*) German research council.

DGB *m abk* (= *Deutscher Gewerkschaftsbund*) ≈ TUC.

dgl. *abk* = **dergleichen.**

d.h. *abk* (= *das heißt*) i.e.

Dia [dē:'à] *nt* **-s, -s** *siehe* **Diapositiv.**

Diabetes [dēábā:'tes] *m* **-, -** (*MED*) diabetes.

Diabetiker(in *f*) [dēábā:'tēkər(in)] *m* **-s, -** diabetic.

Diagnose [dēágnō:'zə] *f* **-, -n** diagnosis.

diagnostizieren [dēágnostētsē:'rən] *vti* (*MED, fig*) diagnose.

diagonal [dēágōnál'] *a* diagonal.

Diagonale *f* **-, -n** diagonal.

Diagramm [dēágrám'] *nt* diagram.

Diakonie [dēákōnē:'] *f* (*REL*) social welfare work.

Dialekt [dēálekt'] *m* **-(e)s, -e** dialect; **~ausdruck** *m* dialect expression *od* word; **d~frei** *a* without an accent.

dialektisch *a* dialectal; (*Logik*) dialectical.

Dialog [dēálō:k'] *m* **-(e)s, -e** dialog(ue).

Diamant [dēámánt'] *m* **-en, -en** diamond.

Diapositiv [dēápōzētē:f'] *nt* **-s, -e** (*PHOT*) slide, transparency.

Diät [dēe:t'] *f* - diet; **~en** *pl* (*POL*) allowance; **d~** *ad* (*kochen, essen*) according to a diet; (*leben*) on a special diet.

dich [dich] *pron* (*akk von* **du**) you ♦ *refl pron* yourself.

dicht [dicht] *a* dense; (*Nebel*) thick; (*Gewebe*) close; (*undurchlässig*) (water)tight; (*fig*) concise; (*umg: zu*) shut, closed; **er ist nicht ganz ~** (*umg*) he's nuts; **~ machen** make watertight/airtight; (*Person*) close one's mind ♦ *ad*: **~ an/bei** close to; **~ hintereinander** right behind one another; **~bevölkert** *a* densely *od* heavily populated.

Dichte *f* **-, -n** density; thickness; closeness; (water)tightness; (*fig*) conciseness.

dichten *vt* (*dicht machen*) make watertight; seal; (*NAUT*) caulk ♦ *vti* (*LITER*) compose, write.

Dichter(in *f*) *m* **-s, -** poet; (*Autor*) writer; **d~isch** *a* poetical; **d~ische Freiheit** poetic license.

dicht- *zW*: **~halten** *vi* unreg (*umg*) keep one's mouth shut; **~machen** *vt* (*Geschäft umg*) wind up.

Dichtung *f* (*TECH*) washer; (*AUT*) gasket; (*Gedichte*) poetry; (*Prosa*) (piece of) writing; **~ und Wahrheit** (*fig*) fact and fantasy.

dick [dik] *a* thick; (*fett*) fat; **durch ~ und dünn** through thick and thin; **D~darm** *m* (*ANAT*) colon.

Dicke *f* **-, -n** thickness; fatness.

dick- *zW*: **~fellig** *a* thickskinned; **~flüssig** *a* viscous.

Dickicht *nt* **-s, -e** thicket.

dick- *zW*: **D~kopf** *m* mule; **D~milch** *f* soured milk; **D~schädel** *m* = **Dickkopf.**

die [dē:] *art siehe* **der.**

Dieb(in *f*) [dē:p, dē:'bin] *m* **-(e)s, -e** thief; **haltet den ~!** stop thief!; **d~isch** *a* thieving; (*umg*) immense; **~stahl** *m* theft; **~stahlprämie** *f reward for the apprehension of shoplifters.*

diejenige [dē:'yā:nigə] *pron siehe* **derjenige.**

Diele [dē:'lə] *f* **-, -n** (*Brett*) board; (*Flur*) hall, lobby; (*Eis~*) ice-cream parlor.

dienen [dē:'nən] *vi* serve (*jdm* sb); **womit kann ich Ihnen ~?** what can I do for you?; (*im Geschäft auch*) can I help you?

Diener *m* **-s, -** servant; (*umg: Verbeugung*)

bow; ~**in** f (maid)servant.
dienern vi (fig) bow and scrape (vor +dat to).
Dienerschaft f servants pl.
dienlich a useful, helpful.
Dienst [dē:nst] m **-(e)s, -e** service; (Arbeit, Arbeitszeit) work; ~ **am Kunden** customer service; **jdm zu** ~**en stehen** be at sb's disposal; **außer** ~ retired; ~ **haben** be on duty; **der öffentliche** ~ the civil service.
Dienstag m Tuesday; **am** ~ on Tuesday; ~ **in acht Tagen** od **in einer Woche** a week on Tuesday, Tuesday week; ~ **vor einer Woche** od **acht Tagen** a week (ago) last Tuesday.
dienstags ad on Tuesdays.
Dienst- zW: ~**alter** nt length of service; **d**~**beflissen** a zealous; ~**bote** m servant; ~**boteneingang** m tradesmen's od service entrance; **d**~**eifrig** a zealous; **d**~**frei** a off duty; ~**gebrauch** m (MIL. VERWALTUNG): **nur für den** ~**gebrauch** for official use only; ~**geheimnis** nt professional secret; ~**gespräch** nt business call; ~**grad** m rank; **d**~**habend** a (Arzt, Offizier) on duty; ~**leistung** f service; ~**leistungsgewerbe** nt service industries pl; **d**~**lich** a official; (Angelegenheiten) business; ~**mädchen** nt domestic servant; ~**plan** m duty roster; ~**reise** f business trip; ~**stelle** f office; **d**~**tuend** a on duty; ~**vorschrift** f service regulations pl; ~**wagen** m (von Beamten) official car; ~**weg** m official channels pl; ~**zeit** f office hours pl; (MIL) period of service.
diesbezüglich a (Frage) on this matter.
diese siehe **diese(r, s)**.
dieselbe [dē:zel'bə] pron, art the same.
Dieselöl [dē:'zəlœl] nt diesel oil.
diese(r, s) [dē:'zə(r, s)] pron this (one) ♦ a this; **diese Nacht** tonight.
diesig a drizzly.
dies- zW: ~**jährig** a this year's; ~**mal** ad this time; ~**seits** präp +gen on this side; **D**~**seits** nt - this life.
Dietrich [dē:'triċ̣h] m **-s, -e** picklock.
Diffamierungskampagne [difámē:'rōōngskámpányə] f **-, -n** smear campaign.
differential [difárentsēál'] a differential; **D**~**getriebe** nt differential gear; **D**~**rechnung** f differential calculus.
Differenzbetrag [difərents'bətrâk] m difference, balance.
differenzieren [difárentsē:'rən] vt make differences in.
differenziert a complex.
diffus [difōō:s'] a (Gedanken etc) confused.
Digitalrechner [dēḡətál'reċ̣hnər] m digital computer.
Diktaphon [diktáfō:n'] nt dictaphone ®.
Diktat [diktât'] nt **-(e)s, -e** dictation; (fig: Gebot) dictate; (POL auch) diktat.
Diktator [diktâ'tor] m dictator; ~**isch** [-átō:'rish] a dictatorial.
Diktatur [diktátōō:r'] f dictatorship.

diktieren [diktē:'rən] vt dictate.
Diktion [diktsēō:n'] f style.
Dilemma [dēle'má] nt **-s, -s** od **-ta** dilemma.
Dilettant [dēletánt'] m dilettante, amateur; **d**~**isch** a dilettante.
Dimension [dēmenzēō:n'] f dimension.
DIN f abk (= Deutsche Industrie-Norm) German Industrial Standard.
Ding [ding] nt **-(e)s, -e** thing; object; **das ist ein** ~ **der Unmöglichkeit** that is totally impossible; **guter** ~**e sein** be in good spirits; **so wie die** ~**e liegen, nach Lage der** ~**e** as things are; **es müßte nicht mit rechten** ~**en zugehen, wenn** ... it would be more than a little strange if ...; **ein krummes** ~ **drehen** commit a crime/do something wrong; **d**~**fest** a: **jdn d**~**fest machen** arrest sb; **d**~**lich** a real, concrete.
Dings, Dingsda, Dingsbums nt (umg) what-d'-you-call-it; (Person) what's-his/her-name.
Dinosaurier [dēnōzou'rēər] m dinosaur.
Diözese [dēœtsā:'zə] f **-, -n** diocese.
Diphtherie [diftārē:'] f diphtheria.
Dipl.-Ing. abk = **Diplomingenieur**.
Diplom [dēplō:m'] nt **-(e)s, -e** diploma; (Hochschulabschluß) degree; ~**arbeit** f dissertation.
Diplomat [dēplōmât'] m **-en, -en** diplomat.
Diplomatie [dēplōmátē:'] f diplomacy.
diplomatisch [dēplōmá'tish] a diplomatic.
Diplomingenieur m academically qualified engineer.
dir [dē:r] pron (dat von **du**) (to) you.
direkt [dērekt'] a direct; ~ **fragen** ask outright od straight out; ~**er Speicherzugriff** (COMPUT) direct memory access.
Direktion [dērektsēō:n'] f management; (Büro) manager's office.
Direktmandat nt (POL) direct mandate.
Direktor(in f) m director; principal (von Hochschule).
Direktorium [dērāktō:'rēōōm] nt board of directors.
Direktübertragung f live broadcast.
Direktverkauf m direct selling.
Dirigent(in f) [dērēgent'(in)] m conductor.
dirigieren [dērēḡē:'rən] vt direct; (MUS) conduct.
Dirne [dir'nə] f **-, -n** prostitute.
dis, Dis [dis] nt **-, -** (MUS) D sharp.
Disco [dis'kō] f **-s, -s** disco.
Disharmonie [dishármōnē:'] f (lit, fig) discord.
Diskette [diske'tə] f disk, diskette.
Diskettenlaufwerk nt disk drive.
Diskont [diskont'] m **-s, -e** discount; ~**satz** m rate of discount.
Diskothek [diskōtā:k'] f **-, -en** disco(theque).
diskreditieren [diskrādētē:'rən] vt (geh) discredit.
Diskrepanz [diskrāpánts'] f discrepancy.
diskret [diskrā:t'] a discreet.
Diskretion [diskrātsēō:n'] f discretion; **strengste** ~ **wahren** preserve the strictest con-

fidence.

diskriminieren [diskrēmēnē:'rən] vt discriminate against.

Diskussion [diskōōsēō:n'] f discussion; **zur ~ stehen** be under discussion.

Diskussionsbeitrag m contribution to the discussion.

Diskuswerfen [dis'kōōsverfən] nt throwing the discus.

diskutabel [diskōōtá'bəl] a debatable.

diskutieren [diskōōtē:'rən] vti discuss; **darüber läßt sich ~** that sounds like something we could talk about.

disponieren [dispōnē:'rən] vi (geh: planen) make arrangements.

Disposition [dispōzētsēō:n'] f (geh: Verfügung): **jdm zur** od **zu jds ~ stehen** be at sb's disposal.

disqualifizieren [diskválēfētsē:'rən] vt disqualify.

Dissertation [disertátsēō:n'] f dissertation, doctoral thesis.

Dissident(in f) [disēdent'(in)] m dissident.

Distanz [distánts'] f distance; (fig: Abstand, Entfernung) detachment; (Zurückhaltung) reserve.

distanzieren [distántsē:'rən] vr: **sich von jdm/etw ~** dissociate o.s. from sb/sth.

distanziert a (Verhalten) distant.

Distel [dis'təl] f -, **-n** thistle.

Disziplin [distsēplē:n'] f -, **-en** discipline.

Disziplinarverfahren [distsēplēnár'ferfárən] nt disciplinary proceedings pl.

dito [dē:'tō] ad (COMM, hum) ditto.

Diva [dē:'vá] f -, **-s** star; (FILM) screen goddess.

divers [dēvers'] a various.

Diverses pl sundries pl; „~" "miscellaneous".

Dividende [dēvēden'də] f -, **-n** dividend.

dividieren [dēvēdē:'rən] vt divide (durch by).

d.J. abk (= der Jüngere) Jun., jun.; (= dieses Jahres) of this year.

Djakarta [dzhákár'tá] nt Jakarta.

DJH nt abk (= Deutsche Jugendherberge) ≈ Youth Hostels Association.

DKP f abk (= Deutsche Kommunistische Partei) German Communist Party.

DLRG f abk (= Deutsche Lebens-Rettungs-Gesellschaft) German lifesaving association.

DLV m abk (= Deutscher Leichtathletik-Verband) German track and field association.

d.M. abk (= dieses Monats) inst.

DM f abk (= Deutsche Mark) DM.

D-Mark [dá:'márk] f -, - deutschmark, (West) German mark.

DNS f abk (= Desoxyribo(se)nukleinsäure) DNA.

doch [doᶄh] ad: **das ist nicht wahr! – ~!** that's not true! – yes it is!; **nicht ~!** oh no!; **und ~, ...** and yet ...; **wenn ~** if only; **es war ~ ganz interessant** it was really od actually quite interesting; **er kam ~ noch**

he came after all ♦ kj (aber) but; (trotzdem) all the same.

Docht [doᶄht] m -(e)s, -e wick.

Dock [dok] nt -s, -s od -e dock; **~gebühren** pl dock dues pl.

Dogge [do'gə] f -, **-n** bulldog; **deutsche ~** Great Dane.

Dogma [dog'má] nt -s, **-men** dogma.

dogmatisch [dogmá'tish] a dogmatic.

DOK nt abk (= Deutsches Olympisches Komitee) German Olympic Committee.

Doktor [dok'tor] m -s, **-en** [-tō:'rən] doctor; **den ~ machen** (umg) do a doctorate od Ph.D.

Doktorand(in f) [doktoránt '(-din)] m **-en, -en** Ph.D. student.

Doktor- zW: **~arbeit** f doctoral thesis; **~titel** m doctorate; **~vater** m supervisor.

doktrinär [doktrēne:r'] a doctrinal; (stur) doctrinaire.

Dokument [dōkōōment'] nt -s, -e document.

Dokumentar- [dōkōōmentár'] zW: **~bericht** m documentary; **~film** m documentary (film); **d~isch** a documentary.

dokumentieren [dōkōōmentē:'rən] vt document; (fig: zu erkennen geben) reveal, show.

Dolch [dolᶄh] m -(e)s, -e dagger; **~stoß** m (bes fig) stab.

dolmetschen [dol'metshən] vti interpret.

Dolmetscher(in f) m -s, - interpreter.

Dolomiten [dōlōmē:'tən] pl (GEOG): **die ~** the Dolomites pl.

Dom [dō:m] m -(e)s, -e cathedral.

Domäne [dōme:'nə] f -, **-n** (fig) domain, province.

dominieren [dōmēnē:'rən] vt dominate ♦ vi predominate.

Dominikanische Republik [dōmēnē-'kánishə rāpōō'blē:k] f Dominican Republic.

Dompfaff [dō:m'pfáf] m **-en, -en** bullfinch.

Dompteur [domptœr'] m, **Dompteuse** [domptœ'zə] f (Zirkus) trainer.

Donau [dō:'nou] f: **die ~** the Danube.

Donner [do'nər] m -s, - thunder; **wie vom ~ gerührt** (fig) thunderstruck.

donnern vi unpers thunder ♦ vt (umg) slam, crash.

Donnerschlag m thunderclap.

Donnerstag m Thursday; siehe **Dienstag**.

Donnerwetter nt thunderstorm; (fig) dressing-down ♦ interj good heavens!; (anerkennen) my word!

doof [dō:f] a (umg) daft, stupid.

Dopingkontrolle [do'pingkontrolə] f (SPORT) drug test.

Doppel [do'pəl] nt -s, - duplicate; (SPORT) doubles; **~band** m (von doppeltem Umfang) double-sized volume; (zwei Bände) two volumes pl; **~beschluß** m (NATO) NATO Double Agreement; **~bett** nt double bed; **d~bödig** a (fig) ambiguous; **d~deutig** a ambiguous; **~fenster** nt double glazing; **~gänger(in** f) m -s, - double; **~korn** m type *of schnapps;* ~**punkt** *m* colon; **d**~**seitig** *a* double-sided; *(Lungenentzündung)* double; **d**~**seitige Platte** double-sided disk; **d**~**sinnig** *a* ambiguous; ~**stecker** *m* two-way adaptor; ~**stunde** *f* (*SCH*) double period.

doppelt *a* double; (*COMM: Buchführung*) double-entry; (*Staatsbürgerschaft*) dual ♦ *ad:* **die Karte habe ich** ~ I have two of these cards; ~ **gemoppelt** (*umg*) saying the same thing twice over; **in** ~**er Ausführung** in duplicate.

Doppel- *zW:* ~**verdiener** *pl* two-income family; ~**zentner** *m* 100 kilograms; ~**zimmer** *nt* double room.

Dorf [dorf] *nt* -(e)s, ¨er village; ~**bewohner** *m* villager.

Dorn [dorn] *m* -(e)s, -en (*BOT*) thorn; *pl* -e (*Schnallen*~) tongue, pin; **das ist mir ein** ~ **im Auge** (*fig*) it's a thorn in my flesh.

dornig *a* thorny.

Dornröschen *nt* Sleeping Beauty.

dörren [dœ'rən] *vt* dry.

Dörrobst [dœ'rō:pst] *nt* dried fruit.

Dorsch [dorsh] *m* -(e)s, -e cod.

dort [dort] *ad* there; ~ **drüben** over there; ~**her** *ad* from there; ~**hin** *ad* (to) there; ~**hinaus** *ad:* **frech bis** ~**hinaus** (*umg*) really cheeky.

dortig *a* of that place; in that town.

Dose [dō:'zə] *f* -, -n box; (*Blech*~) tin, can; **in** ~**n** (*Konserven*) canned, tinned (*Brit*).

dösen [dœ'zən] *vi* (*umg*) doze.

Dosen- *zW:* ~**milch** *f* evaporated milk; ~**öffner** *m* can opener.

dosieren [dōzē:'rən] *vt* (*lit, fig*) measure out.

Dosis [dō:'zis] *f* -, **Dosen** dose.

Dotierung [dōtē:'rōong] *f* endowment; (*von Posten*) remuneration.

Dotter [do'tər] *m* -s, - egg yolk.

Double [dōō:'bəl] *nt* -s, -s (*FILM etc*) stand-in.

Doz. *abk* = **Dozent.**

Dozent(in *f*) [dōtsent'(in)] *m* -en, -en professor (*für* of).

dpa *f* - *abk* (= *Deutsche Presse-Agentur*) German Press Agency.

Dr. *abk* = **Doktor.**

Drache [drá'khə] *m* -n, -n (*Tier*) dragon.

Drachen *m* -, - kite; **einen** ~ **steigen lassen** fly a kite; ~**fliegen** *nt* (*SPORT*) hang-gliding.

Dragée [drázhā:'] *nt* -s, -s (*PHARM*) dragee, sugar-coated pill.

Draht [drát] *m* -(e)s, ¨e wire; **auf** ~ **sein** be on the ball; ~**esel** *m* (*hum*) trusty bicycle; ~**gitter** *nt* wire grating; ~**seil** *nt* cable; **Nerven wie** ~**seile** (*umg*) nerves of steel; ~**seilbahn** *f* cable railway; ~**zange** *f* pliers *pl;* ~**zieher(in** *f*) *m* (*fig*) wire-puller.

drall [drál] *a* strapping; (*Frau*) buxom.

Drall *m* (*fig: Hang*) tendency; **einen** ~ **nach links haben** (*AUT*) pull to the left.

Drama [drá'má] *nt* -s, **Dramen** drama.

Dramatiker(in *f*) [drámá'tēkər(in)] *m* -s, -

dramatist.

dramatisch [drámá'tish] *a* dramatic.

Dramaturg(in *f*) [drámátōōrk '(-gin)] *m* -en, -en artistic director; (*TV*) drama producer.

dran [drán] *ad* (*umg*) *siehe* **daran;** (*an der Reihe*): **jetzt bist du** ~ it's your turn now; **früh/spät** ~ **sein** be early/late; **ich weiß nicht, wie ich (bei ihm)** ~ **bin** I don't know where I stand (with him); ~**bleiben** *vi unreg* (*umg*) stay close; (*am Apparat*) hang on.

drang [dráng] *imperf von* **dringen.**

Drang *m* -(e)s, ¨e (*Trieb*) urge, yearning (*nach* for); (*Druck*) pressure.

drängeln [dre'ngəln] *vti* push, jostle.

drängen [dre'ngən] *vt* (*schieben*) push, press; (*antreiben*) urge ♦ *vi* (*eilig sein*) be urgent; (*Zeit*) press; **auf etw** (*akk*) ~ press for sth.

drangsalieren [drángzálē:'rən] *vt* pester, plague.

dran- *zW:* ~**kommen** *vi unreg* (*umg: an die Reihe kommen*) have one's turn; (*SCH: beim Melden*) be called; (*Frage, Aufgabe etc*) come up; ~**nehmen** *vt unreg* (*umg: Schüler*) ask.

drasch [drásh] *imperf von* **dreschen.**

drastisch [drás'tish] *a* drastic.

drauf [drouf] *ad* (*umg*) *siehe* **darauf;** ~ **und dran sein, etw zu tun** be on the point of doing sth; **etw** ~ **haben** (*können*) be able to do sth just like that; (*Kenntnisse*) be well up on sth; **D**~**gänger** *m* -s, - daredevil; ~**gehen** *vi unreg* (*verbraucht werden*) be used up; (*kaputtgehen*) be smashed up; ~**zahlen** *vi* (*fig: Einbußen erleiden*) pay the price.

draußen [drou'sən] *ad* outside, out-of-doors.

Drechsler(in *f*) [dreks'lər(in)] *m* -s, - (wood) turner.

Dreck [drek] *m* -(e)s mud, dirt; ~ **am Stecken haben** (*fig*) have a skeleton in the closet (*US*) *od* cupboard (*Brit*); **das geht ihn einen** ~ **an** (*umg*) that's none of his business.

dreckig *a* dirty, filthy; **es geht mir** ~ (*umg*) I'm in a bad way.

Dreckskerl *m* (*umg!*) dirty swine (!).

Dreh [drā:] *m:* **den** ~ **raushaben** *od* **wegbaben** (*umg*) have got the hang of it.

Dreh- *zW:* ~**achse** *f* axis of rotation; ~**arbeiten** *pl* (*FILM*) shooting; ~**bank** *f* lathe; **d**~**bar** *a* revolving; ~**buch** *nt* (*FILM*) script.

drehen *vti* turn, rotate; (*Zigaretten*) roll; (*Film*) shoot; **ein Ding** ~ (*umg*) play a prank ♦ *vr* turn; (*handeln von*): **sich um etw** ~ be about sth.

Dreher(in *f*) *m* -s, - lathe operator.

Dreh- *zW:* ~**orgel** *f* barrel organ; ~**ort** *m* (*FILM*) location; ~**scheibe** *f* (*EISENB*) turntable; ~**tür** *f* revolving door.

Drehung *f* (*Rotation*) rotation; (*Um*~, *Wendung*) turn.

Dreh- *zW:* ~**wurm** *m* (*umg*): **den** ~**wurm haben/bekommen** be/become dizzy; ~**zahl** *f*

rate of revolution; ~**zahlmesser** *m* tachometer.

drei [drī] *num* three; **aller guten Dinge sind
~!** (*Sprichwort*) all good things come in
threes!; (*nach zwei mißglückten Versuchen*)
third time lucky!; **D~eck** *nt* triangle;
~**eckig** *a* triangular; **D~ecksverhältnis** *nt*
eternal triangle; ~**einhalb** *num* three and a
half; **D~einigkeit** [-ī'nićhkīt] *f*, **D~faltigkeit**
[-fál'tićhkīt] *f* Trinity.
dreierlei *a inv* of three kinds.

drei- *zW:* ~**fach** *a* triple, treble ♦ *ad* three
times; **D~fuß** *m* tripod; (*Schemel*) three-
legged stool; **D~gangschaltung** *f* three-
speed gear; ~'**hun'dert** *num* three hundred;
D~kä'sehoch *m* (*umg*) tiny tot;
D~kö'nigsfest *nt* Epiphany; ~**mal** *ad* three
times, thrice; ~**malig** *a* three times.
dreinblicken [drīn'blikən] *vi:* **traurig** *etc* ~
look sad *etc.*
dreinreden [drīn'rā:dən] *vi:* **jdm** ~
(*dazwischenreden*) interrupt sb; (*sich
einmischen*) interfere with sb.
Dreisprung *m* triple jump.
dreißig [drī'sićh] *num* thirty.
dreist [drīst] *a* bold, audacious.
Dreistigkeit *f* boldness, audacity.
drei- *zW:* ~'**vier'tel** *num* three-quarters;
D~'viertelstun'de *f* three-quarters of an
hour; **D~vier'teltakt** *m:* **im D~vierteltakt** in
three-four time; ~**zehn** *num* thirteen; **jetzt
schlägt's ~zehn!** (*umg*) that's a bit much.
dreschen [dre'shən] *vt unreg* thresh; **Skat** ~
(*umg*) play skat.
dressieren [dresē:'rən] *vt* train.
Dressur [dresōō:r'] *f* training; (*für ~reiten*)
dressage.
driften [drif'tən] *vi* (*NAUT, fig*) drift.
Drillbohrer *m* light drill.
drillen [dri'lən] *vt* (*bohren*) drill, bore; (*MIL*)
drill; (*fig*) train; **auf etw** (*akk*) **gedrillt sein**
(*fig umg*) be practiced at doing sth.
Drilling *m* triplet.
drin [drin] *ad* (*umg*) *siehe* **darin; bis jetzt ist
noch alles** ~ everything is still quite open.
dringen [dri'ngən] *vi unreg* (*Wasser, Licht,
Kälte*) penetrate (*durch* through; *in +akk*
into); **auf etw** (*akk*) ~ insist on sth; **in jdn**
~ (*geh*) entreat sb.
dringend [dring'ənt], **dringlich** [dring'lićh] *a*
urgent; ~ **empfehlen** recommend strongly.
Dringlichkeit *f* urgency.
Dringlichkeitsstufe *f* priority; ~ **1** top
priority.
drinnen [dri'nən] *ad* inside, indoors.
drinstecken [drin'shtekən] *vi* (*umg*): **da
steckt eine Menge Arbeit drin** a lot of work
has gone into it.
drischt [drisht] *3. pers sing präs von*
dreschen.
dritt *ad:* **wir kommen zu** ~ three of us are
coming together.
dritte *siehe* **dritte(r, s).**
Drittel *nt* **-s,** - third.

drittens *ad* thirdly.
dritte(r, s) [dritə(r, s)] *a* third; **D~ Welt**
Third World; **im Beisein D~r** in the presence of a third party.
drittklassig *a* third-rate, third-class.
Dr.jur. *abk* (= *Doktor der Rechts-
wissenschaften*) ≈ L.L.D.
DRK *nt* - *abk* (= *Deutsches Rotes Kreuz*) ≈
R.C.
Dr.med. *abk* (= *Doktor der Medizin*) ≈ M.D.
droben [drō:'bən] *ad* above, up there.
Droge [drō:'gə] *f* -, -n drug.
dröge [drœ'gə] *a* (*norddeutsch*) boring.
Drogen- *zW:* **d~abhängig** *a* addicted to
drugs; ~**händler(in** *f*) *m* peddler, pusher;
d~süchtig *a* addicted to drugs.
Drogerie [drōgərē:'] *f* drugstore (*US*), chem-
ist's shop (*Brit*).
Drogist(in *f*) [drōgist'(in)] *m* druggist (*US*),
chemist (*Brit*).
Drohbrief *m* threatening letter.
drohen [drō:'ən] *vi* threaten (*jdm* sb).
Drohgebärde *f* (*lit, fig*) threatening gesture.
Drohne [drō:'nə] *f* -n drone.
dröhnen [drœ'nən] *vi* (*Motor*) roar; (*Stimme,
Musik*) ring, resound.
Drohung [drō:'ōōng] *f* threat.
drollig [dro'lićh] *a* droll.
Drops [drops] *m od nt* -, - fruit drop.
drosch [drosh] *imperf von* **dreschen.**
Droschke [drosh'kə] *f* -, -n cab.
Droschkenkutscher *m* cabman.
Drossel [dro'səl] *f* -, -n thrush.
drosseln [dro'səln] *vt* (*Motor etc*) throttle;
(*Heizung*) turn down; (*Strom, Tempo, Pro-
duktion etc*) cut down.
Dr.phil. *abk* (= *Doktor der Geisteswissenschaften*) ≈ Ph.D.
Dr.rer.nat. *abk* (= *Doktor der Naturwissenschaften*) ≈ Ph.D.
Dr.rer.pol. *abk* (= *Doktor der Staats-
wissenschaften*) ≈ Ph.D.
Dr.theol. *abk* (= *Doktor der Theologie*) ≈
D.D.
drüben [drü:'bən] *ad* over there, on the other
side; (*umg*: *auf DDR/BRD bezogen*) on the
other side.
drüber [drü:'bər] *ad* (*umg*) = **darüber.**
Druck [drōōk] *m* **-(e)s, -e** (*PHYS, Zwang*)
pressure; (*TYP: Vorgang*) printing; (: *Produkt*) print; (*fig: Belastung*) burden, weight;
~ **machen** put pressure on; ~**buchstabe** *m*
block letter; **in ~buchstaben schreiben**
print.
Drückeberger [drü'kəbergər] *m* **-s,** - shirker,
dodger.
drucken [drōō'kən] *vti* (*TYP, COMPUT*) print.
drücken [drü'kən] *vti* (*Knopf, Hand*) press;
(*zu eng sein*) pinch; (*fig: Preise*) keep
down; (: *belasten*) oppress, weigh down;
jdm etw in die Hand ~ press sth into sb's
hand ♦ *vr:* **sich vor etw** (*dat*) ~ get out of
(doing) sth.
drückend *a* oppressive; (*Last, Steuern*)

heavy; (*Armut*) grinding; (*Wetter, Hitze*) oppressive, close.

Drucker *m* **-s,** - printer.

Drücker *m* **-s,** - button; (*Tür~*) handle; (*Gewehr~*) trigger; **am ~ sein** *od* **sitzen** (*fig umg*) be the key person; **auf den letzten ~** (*fig umg*) at the last minute.

Druckerei [drŏŏkərī'] *f* printing works, press.

Druckerschwärze *f* printer's ink.

Druck- *zW:* **~fahne** *f* galley(-proof); **~fehler** *m* misprint; **~knopf** *m* snap fastener; **~kopf** *m* printhead; **~luft** *f* compressed air; **~mittel** *nt* leverage; **d~reif** *a* ready for printing, passed for press; (*fig*) polished; **~sache** *f* printed matter; **~schrift** *f* printing; (*gedrucktes Werk*) pamphlet.

drum [drŏŏm] *ad* (*umg*) around; **mit allem D~ und Dran** with all the bits and pieces *od* (*Mahlzeit*) trimmings *pl.*

Drumherum *nt* trappings *pl.*

drunten [drŏŏn'tən] *ad* below, down there.

Drüse [drü:'zə] *f* **-, -n** gland.

DSB *m* - *abk* (= *Deutscher Sport-Bund*) German Sports Association.

Dschungel [dzhŏŏ'ngəl] *m* **-s,** - jungle.

DSV *m* - *abk* (= *Deutscher Schriftstellerverband*) German Authors' Association.

dt. *abk* = **deutsch.**

DTB *m abk* (= *Deutscher Turnerbund*) German Gymnasts' Association.

DTC *m* - *abk* = *Deutscher Touring Automobil Club.*

Dtzd. *abk* (= *Dutzend*) doz.

du [dŏŏ:] *pron* (**D~** *in Briefen*) you; **mit jdm per ~ sein** be on familiar terms with sb; **D~** *nt:* **jdm das D~ anbieten** suggest that sb uses "du" *od* the familiar form of address.

dübeln [dü:'bəln] *vti* plug.

Dublin [dà'blin] *nt* Dublin.

ducken [dŏŏ'kən] *vt* (*Kopf, Person*) duck; (*fig*) take down a peg or two ♦ *vr* duck.

Duckmäuser [dŏŏk'moizər] *m* **-s,** - yes-man.

Dudelsack [dŏŏ:'dəlzàk] *m* bagpipes *pl.*

Duell [dŏŏel'] *nt* **-s, -e** duel.

Duett [dŏŏet'] *nt* **-(e)s, -e** duet.

Duft [dŏŏft] *m* **-(e)s,** ⁻e scent, odor (*US*), odour (*Brit*); **d~en** *vi* smell, be fragrant.

duftig *a* (*Stoff, Kleid*) delicate, diaphanous; (*Muster*) fine.

Duftnote *f* (*von Parfüm*) scent.

dulden [dŏŏl'dən] *vti* suffer; (*zulassen*) tolerate.

duldsam *a* tolerant.

dumm [dŏŏm] *a* stupid; **das wird mir zu ~** that's just too much; **der D~e sein** be the loser; **der ~e August** (*umg*) the clown; **du willst mich wohl für ~ verkaufen** you must think I'm stupid; **sich ~ und dämlich reden** (*umg*) talk till one is blue in the face; **so etwas D~es** how stupid, what a nuisance; **~dreist** *a* impudent.

dummerweise *ad* stupidly.

Dumm- *zW:* **~heit** *f* stupidity; (*Tat*) blunder,

stupid mistake; **~kopf** *m* blockhead.

dumpf [dŏŏmpf] *a* (*Ton*) hollow, dull; (*Luft*) close; (*Erinnerung, Schmerz*) vague; **D~heit** *f* hollowness, dullness; closeness; vagueness.

dumpfig *a* musty.

Dumpingpreis [dàm'pingprīs] *m* give-away price.

Düne [dü:'nə] *f* **-, -n** dune.

Dung [dŏŏng] *m* **-(e)s** = **Dünger** .

düngen [dü'ngən] *vt* manure.

Dünger *m* **-s,** - dung, manure; (*künstlich*) fertilizer.

dunkel [dŏŏng'kəl] *a* dark; (*Stimme*) deep; (*Ahnung*) vague; (*rätselhaft*) obscure; (*verdächtig*) dubious, shady; **im ~n tappen** (*fig*) grope in the dark.

Dünkel [düng'kəl] *m* **-s** self-conceit; **d~haft** *a* conceited.

Dunkel- *zW:* **~heit** *f* darkness; (*fig*) obscurity; **bei Einbruch der ~heit** at nightfall; **~kammer** *f* (*PHOT*) dark room.

dunkeln *vi unpers* grow dark.

Dunkelziffer *f* estimated number of unnotified cases.

dünn [dün] *a* thin; **D~darm** *m* small intestine; **~flüssig** *a* watery, thin; **~gesät** *a* scarce; **D~heit** *f* thinness; **~machen** *vr* (*umg*) make o.s. scarce; **D~schiß** *m* (*umg*) the runs.

Dunst [dŏŏnst] *m* **-es,** ⁻e vapor (*US*), vapour (*Brit*); (*Wetter*) haze; **~abzugshaube** *f* extractor hood.

dünsten [düns'tən] *vt* steam.

Dunstglocke *f* haze; (*Smog*) pall of smog.

dunstig [dŏŏns'tiċh] *a* vaporous; (*Wetter*) hazy, misty.

düpieren [düpē:'rən] *vt* dupe.

Duplikat [dŏŏplēkàt'] *nt* **-(e)s, -e** duplicate.

Dur [dŏŏ:r] *nt* **-, -** (*MUS*) major.

durch [dŏŏrċh] *präp* +*akk* through; (*Mittel, Ursache*) by; (*Zeit*) during; **~ die ganze Welt reisen** travel all over the world ♦ *ad* through; (*KOCH umg*): **(gut) ~** well-done; **den Sommer ~** during the summer; **8 Uhr ~ past 8 o'clock; ~ und ~** completely; **das geht mir ~ und ~** that goes right through me; **~arbeiten** *vti* work through ♦ *vr:* **sich durch etw ~ arbeiten** work one's way through sth; **~atmen** *vi* breathe deeply.

durchaus [dŏŏrċhous'] *ad* completely; (*unbedingt*) definitely; **das läßt sich ~ machen** that sounds feasible; **ich bin ~ Ihrer Meinung** I quite *od* absolutely agree with you; (*in verneinten Sätzen*): **~ nicht** (*als Verstärkung*) by no means; (*als Antwort*) not at all.

durch- [dŏŏrċh'] *zW:* **~beißen** *unreg vt* bite through ♦ *vr* (*fig*) battle on; **~blättern** *vt* leaf through.

Durchblick [dŏŏrċh'blik] *m* view; (*fig*) comprehension; **den ~ haben** (*fig umg*) know what's what.

durchblicken *vi* look through; (*umg: verste-*

hen) understand (*bei etw* sth); etw ~ **lassen** (*fig*) hint at sth.

Durchblutung [dōōrčhblōō:'tōong] *f* circulation (of blood) (*gen* to).

durch'bohren *vt untr* bore through, pierce.

durchboxen [dōōrčh'boksən] *vr* (*fig umg*) fight (one's way) through (*durch etw* sth).

durchbrechen [dōōrčh'brečhən] *vti unreg* break ♦ *vt unreg untr* [dōōrčhbre'čhən] (*Schranken*) break through.

durch- [dōōrčh'] *zW:* ~**brennen** *vi unreg* (*Draht, Sicherung*) burn through; (*umg*) run away; ~**bringen** *unreg vt* get through; (*Geld*) squander ♦ *vr* make a living.

Durchbruch [dōōrčh'brōōčh] *m* (*Öffnung*) opening; (*MIL*) breach; (*von Gefühlen etc*) eruption; (*der Zähne*) cutting; (*fig*) breakthrough; **zum** ~ **kommen** break through.

durchdacht [dōōrčhdáčht'] *a* well thought-out.

durchden'ken *vt unreg untr* think out.

durch- [dōōrčh'] *zW:* ~**diskutieren** *vt* talk over, discuss; ~**drängen** *vr* force one's way through; ~**drehen** *vt* (*Fleisch*) mince ♦ *vi* (*umg*) crack up.

durchdringen [dōōrčh'dringən] *vi unreg* penetrate, get through; **mit etw** ~ get one's way with sth ♦ *vt unreg untr* [dōōrčhdri'ngən] penetrate.

durchdringend *a* piercing; (*Kälte, Wind auch*) biting; (*Geruch*) pungent.

durchdrücken [dōōrčh'drükən] *vt* (*durch Presse*) press through; (*Creme, Teig*) pipe; (*fig: Gesetz, Reformen etc*) push through; (*seinen Willen*) get; (*Knie, Kreuz etc*) straighten.

durcheinander [dōōrčhīnán'dər] *ad* in a mess, in confusion; (*verwirrt*) confused; ~ **trinken** mix one's drinks; **D~** *nt* **-s** (*Verwirrung*) confusion; (*Unordnung*) mess; ~**bringen** *vt unreg* mess up; (*verwirren*) confuse; ~**reden** *vi* talk at the same time; ~**werfen** *vt unreg* muddle up.

durch- [dōōrčh'] *zW:* ~**fahren** *vi unreg:* **er ist bei Rot** ~**gefahren** he jumped the lights; **die Nacht** ~**fahren** travel through the night; **D~fahrt** *f* transit; (*Verkehr*) thoroughfare; **D~fahrt bitte freihalten!** please keep access free; **D~fahrt verboten!** no through road; **D~fall** *m* (*MED*) diarrhea (*US*), diarrhoea (*Brit*); ~**fallen** *vi unreg* fall through; (*in Prüfung*) fail; ~**finden** *vr unreg* find one's way through; ~**fliegen** *vi unreg* (*umg: in Prüfung*) fail (*durch etw, in etw* (*dat*) sth); **D~flug** *m:* **Passagiere auf dem D~flug** transit passengers.

durchforsch'en *vt untr* explore.

durchforsten [dōōrčhfors'tən] *vt untr* (*fig: Akten etc*) go through.

durch- [dōōrčh'] *zW:* ~**fragen** *vr* find one's way by asking; ~**fressen** *vt unreg* eat through.

durchführbar *a* feasible, practicable.

durchführen [dōōrčh'fü:rən] *vt* carry out; (*Gesetz*) implement; (*Kursus*) run.

Durchführung *f* execution, performance.

Durchgang [dōōrčh'gáng] *m* passage(way); (*bei Produktion, Versuch*) run; (*SPORT*) round; (*bei Wahl*) ballot; ~ **verboten** no thoroughfare.

durchgängig [dōōrčh'gengičh] *a* universal, general.

Durchgangs- *zW:* ~**handel** *m* transit trade; ~**lager** *nt* transit camp; ~**stadium** *nt* transitory stage; ~**verkehr** *m* through traffic.

durchgeben [dōōrčh'gā:bən] *vt unreg* (*RAD, TV: Hinweis, Wetter*) give; (*Lottozahlen*) announce.

durchgefallen [dōōrčh'gəfálən] *pp von* **durchfallen.**

durchgefroren [dōōrčh'gəfrō:rən] *a* (*See*) completely frozen; (*Mensch*) frozen stiff.

durchgehen [dōōrčh'gā:ən] *unreg vt* (*behandeln*) go over *od* through ♦ *vi* go through; (*ausreißen: Pferd*) break loose; (*Mensch*) run away; **mein Temperament ging mit mir durch** my temper got the better of me; **jdm etw** ~ **lassen** let sb get away with sth.

durchgehend *a* (*Zug*) through; (*Öffnungszeiten*) continuous.

durchgelesen [dōōrčh'gəlā:zən] *pp von* **durchlesen.**

durchgeschwitzt [dōōrčh'gəshvitst] *a* soaked in sweat.

durch- [dōōrčh'] *zW:* ~**greifen** *vi unreg* take strong action; ~**halten** *unreg vi* last out ♦ *vt* keep up; **D~haltevermögen** *nt* staying power; ~**hängen** *vi unreg* (*lit, fig*) sag; ~**hecheln** *vt* (*umg*) gossip about; ~**kommen** *vi unreg* get through; (*überleben*) pull through.

durchkreu'zen *vt untr* thwart, frustrate.

durch- [dōōrčh'] *zW:* ~**lassen** *vt unreg* (*Person*) let through; (*Wasser*) let in; ~**lässig** *a* leaky.

Durchlaucht [dōōrčh'loučht] *f* -, **-en:** (**Euer**) ~ Your Highness.

Durchlauf [dōōrčh'louf] *m* (*COMPUT*) run.

durchlau'fen *vt unreg untr* (*Schule, Phase*) go through.

Durchlauf(wasser)erhitzer *m* **-s, -** (water) heater.

Durchlaufzeit *f* (*COMPUT*) length of the run.

durch- *zW:* ~**le'ben** *vt untr* (*Zeit*) live *od* go through; (*Jugend, Gefühl*) experience; ~'**lesen** *vt unreg* read through; ~**leuch'ten** *vt untr* X-ray; ~**löchern** [-lœ'čhərn] *vt untr* perforate; (*mit Löchern*) punch holes in; (*mit Kugeln*) riddle; ~'**machen** *vt* go through; **die Nacht** ~**machen** make a night of it.

Durch- [dōōrčh'] *zW:* ~**marsch** *m* march through; ~**messer** *m* **-s, -** diameter.

durchnäs'sen *vt untr* soak (through).

durch- [dōōrčh'] *zW:* ~**nehmen** *vt unreg* go over; ~**numerieren** *vt* number consecutively; ~**organisieren** *vt* organize down to

the last detail; **~pausen** *vt* trace; **~peitschen** *vt* (*lit*) whip soundly; (*fig: Gesetzentwurf, Reform*) force through.
durchqueren [dŏŏrçkvä:'rən] *vt untr* cross.
durch- [dŏŏrç'] *zW*: **~rechnen** *vt* calculate; **~regnen** *vi unpers*: **es regnet durchs Dach** ~ the rain is coming through the roof; **D~reiche** *f* -, **-n** (serving) hatch, pass-through (*US*); **D~reise** *f* transit; **auf der D~reise** passing through; (*Güter*) in transit; **D~reisevisum** *nt* transit visa; **~ringen** *vr unreg* make up one's mind finally; **~rosten** *vi* rust through; **~rutschen** *vi* (*lit*) slip through (*durch etw* sth); (*bei Prüfung*) scrape through.
durchs [dŏŏrçhs] = *durch das*.
Durchsage [dŏŏrç'zägə] *f* intercom *od* radio announcement.
Durchsatz [dŏŏrç'zäts] *m* (*COMPUT, Produktion*) throughput.
durchschauen [dŏŏrç'shouən] *vti* (*lit*) look *od* see through ♦ *vt untr* [dŏŏrçhshou'ən] (*Person, Lüge*) see through.
durchscheinen [dŏŏrç'shinən] *vi unreg* shine through.
durchscheinend *a* translucent.
durchschlafen [dŏŏrç'shläfən] *vi unreg* sleep through.
Durchschlag [dŏŏrç'shläk] *m* (*Doppel*) carbon copy; (*Sieb*) strainer.
durchschlagen *unreg vt* (*entzweischlagen*) split (in two); (*sieben*) sieve ♦ *vi* (*zum Vorschein kommen*) emerge, come out ♦ *vr* get by.
durchschlagend *a* resounding; **(eine) ~e Wirkung haben** be totally effective.
Durchschlagpapier *nt* flimsy; (*Kohlepapier*) carbon paper.
Durchschlagskraft *f* (*von Geschoß*) penetration; (*fig: von Argument*) power.
durch- [dŏŏrç'] *zW*: **~schlängeln** *vr* (*durch etw: Mensch*) thread one's way through; **~schlüpfen** *vi* slip through; **~schneiden** *vt unreg* cut through.
Durchschnitt [dŏŏrçhsh'nit] *m* (*Mittelwert*) average; **über/unter dem ~** above/below average; **im ~** on average; **d~lich** *a* average ♦ *ad* on average; **d~lich begabt/groß** of average ability/height *etc*.
Durchschnitts- *zW*: **~geschwindigkeit** *f* average speed; **~mensch** *m* average man, man in the street; **~wert** *m* average.
durch- *zW*: **D~'schrift** *f* copy; **D~'schuß** *m* (*Loch*) bullet hole; **~schwim'men** *vt unreg untr* swim across; **~'segeln** *vi* (*umg: nicht bestehen*) fail, flunk (*umg*) (*durch etw, bei etw* sth); **~'sehen** *vt unreg* look through.
durchsetzen [dŏŏrç'zetsən] *vt* enforce; **seinen Kopf ~** get one's own way ♦ *vr* (*Erfolg haben*) succeed; (*sich behaupten*) get one's way [dŏŏrçhzes'tən] ♦ *vt untr* mix.
Durchsicht [dŏŏrçh'ziçht] *f* looking through, checking.
durchsichtig *a* transparent; **D~keit** *f*

transparency.
durch- *zW*: **~'sickern** *vi* seep through; (*fig*) leak out; **~'sieben** *vt* sieve; **~'sitzen** *vt unreg* (*Sessel etc*) wear out (the seat of); **~'spielen** *vt* go *od* run through; **~'sprechen** *vt unreg* talk over; **~'stehen** *vt unreg* live through; **D~'stehvermögen** *nt* endurance, staying power; **~'stellen** *vt* (*TEL*) put through; **~stöbern** [-shtœ'bərn] *vt untr* ransack, search through; **~'stoßen** *vti unreg* break through (*auch MIL*); **~'streichen** *vt unreg* cross out; **~'stylen** *vt* do, fix; **~su'chen** *vt untr* search; **D~su'chung** *f* search; **D~su'chungsbefehl** *m* search warrant; **~'trainieren** *vt* (*Sportler, Körper*): **(gut) ~trainiert** in superb condition; **~trän'ken** *vt untr* soak; **~'treten** *vt unreg* (*Pedal*) step on; (*Starter*) kick; **~trie'ben** *a* cunning, wily; **~wach'sen** *a* (*lit: Speck*) with fat running through; (*fig: mittelmäßig*) so-so.
Durchwahl [dŏŏrç'väl] *f* (*TEL*) direct dialling; (*bei Firma*) extension.
durch- *zW*: **~'weg** *ad* throughout, completely; **~'wursteln** *vr* (*umg*) muddle through; **~'zählen** *vt* count ♦ *vi* count off; **~zech'en** *vt untr*: **eine ~zechte Nacht** a night of drinking; **~'ziehen** *unreg vt* (*Faden*) draw through; **eine Sache ~ziehen** finish off sth ♦ *vi* pass through; **~zuck'en** *vt untr* shoot *od* flash through; **D~'zug** *m* (*Luft*) draft (*US*), draught (*Brit*); (*von Truppen, Vögeln*) passage; **~'zwängen** *vtr* squeeze *od* force through.
dürfen [dür'fən] *vi unreg* be allowed; **darf ich?** may I?; **es darf geraucht werden** you may smoke; **was darf es sein?** what can I do for you?; **das darf nicht geschehen** that must not happen; **das darf doch nicht wahr sein!** that can't be true!; **das ~ Sie mir glauben** you can believe me; **es dürfte Ihnen bekannt sein, daß ...** as you will probably know ...; (*Veranlassung haben, können*): **wir freuen uns, Ihnen mitteilen zu ~** we are pleased to be able to tell you.
durfte [dŏŏrf'tə] *imperf von* dürfen.
dürftig [dürf'tiçh] *a* (*ärmlich*) needy, poor; (*unzulänglich*) inadequate.
dürr [dür] *a* dried-up; (*Land*) arid; (*mager*) skinny, gaunt.
Dürre *f* -, **-n** aridity; (*Zeit*) drought.
Durst [dŏŏrst] *m* -(e)s thirst; **~ haben** be thirsty; **einen über den ~ getrunken haben** (*umg*) have had one too many.
durstig *a* thirsty.
Durststrecke *f* hard times *pl*.
Dusche [dŏŏ'shə] *f* -, **-n** shower; **das war eine kalte ~** (*fig*) that really brought him/her *etc* down with a bump.
duschen *vir* have a shower.
Duschgelegenheit *f* shower facilities *pl*.
Düse [dü:'zə] *f* -, **-n** nozzle; (*Flugzeug~*) jet.
Dusel [dŏŏ:'zəl] *m* (*umg*): **da hat er (einen) ~ gehabt** he was lucky.

Düsen- *zW*: **~antrieb** *m* jet propulsion; **~flugzeug** *nt* jet (plane); **~jäger** *m* jet fighter.

Dussel [dŏŏ'səl] *m* **-s, -** (*umg*) twit.

Düsseldorf [dü'səldorf] *nt* Dusseldorf.

dusselig, dußlig *a* (*umg*) stupid.

düster [dü:s'tər] *a* dark; (*Gedanken, Zukunft*) gloomy; **D~keit** *f* darkness, gloom; gloominess.

Dutzend [dŏŏ'tsənt] *nt* **-s, -e** dozen; **d~(e)mal** *ad* a dozen times; **~mensch** *m* man in the street; **~ware** *f* (*pej*) (cheap) mass-produced item; **d~weise** *ad* by the dozen.

duzen [dŏŏ:'tsən] *vtr* use the familiar form of address *od* "du" (*jdn* to *od* with sb).

Duzfreund *m* good friend.

DVA *f abk* = **Datenverarbeitungsanlage**.

Dynamik [dünä'mik] *f* (*PHYS*) dynamics; (*fig*: *Schwung*) momentum; (*von Mensch*) dynamism.

dynamisch [dünä'mish] *a* (*lit, fig*) dynamic; (*renten~*) index-linked.

Dynamit [dünämē:t'] *nt* **-s** dynamite.

Dynamo [dünä'mō] *m* **-s, -s** dynamo.

dz *abk* = **Doppelzentner**.

dz. *abk* = **derzeit**.

D-Zug [dä:'tsŏŏ:k] *m* express train; **ein alter Mann ist doch kein ~** (*umg*) I am going as fast as I can.

E

E, e [ā:] *nt* E, e.

E *abk* = **Eilzug; Europastraße**.

Ebbe [e'bə] *f* **-, -n** low tide; **~ und Flut** ebb and flow.

eben [ā:'bən] *a* level; (*glatt*) smooth ♦ *ad* just; (*bestätigend*) exactly; **das ist ~ so** that's just the way it is; **mein Bleistift war doch ~ noch da** my pencil was there (just) a minute ago; **~ deswegen** just because of that.

Ebenbild *nt*: **das genaue ~ seines Vaters** the spitting image of his father.

ebenbürtig *a*: **jdm ~ sein** be sb's peer.

Ebene *f* **-, -n** plain; (*MATH, PHYS*) plane; (*fig*) level.

eben- *zW*: **~erdig** *a* at ground level; **~falls** *ad* likewise; **E~heit** *f* levelness; (*Glätte*) smoothness; **E~holz** *nt* ebony; **~so** *ad* just as; **~sogut** *ad* just as well; **~sooft** *ad* just as often; **~soviel** *ad* just as much; **~soweit** *ad* just as far; **~sowenig** *ad* just as little.

Eber [ā:'bər] *m* **-s, -** boar.

Eberesche *f* mountain ash, rowan.

ebnen [ā:b'nən] *vt* level; **jdm den Weg ~** (*fig*) smooth the way for sb.

Echo [e'chō] *nt* **-s, -s** echo; **ein lebhaftes ~ finden** (*fig*) meet with a lively response (*bei* from).

Echolot [e'chōlō:t] *nt* (*NAUT*) echo-sounder, sonar.

Echse [ek'sə] *f* **-, -n** (*ZOOL*) lizard.

echt [echt] *a* genuine; (*typisch*) typical; **ich hab' ~ keine Zeit** (*umg*) I really don't have any time; **E~heit** *f* genuineness.

Eckball [ek'bál] *m* corner (kick).

Ecke [e'kə] *f* **-, -n** corner; (*MATH*) angle; **gleich um die ~** just around the corner; **an allen ~n und Enden sparen** (*umg*) pinch and scrape; **jdn um die ~ bringen** (*umg*) bump sb off; **mit jdm um ein paar ~n herum verwandt sein** (*umg*) be distantly related to sb, be sb's second cousin twice removed (*hum*).

eckig *a* angular.

Eckzahn *m* eye tooth; **E~ganove** *m* gentleman criminal; **E~gas** *nt* rare gas; **E~metall** *nt* rare metal; **E~stein** *m* precious stone.

Edinburg [ā:'dinbŏŏrk] *nt* Edinburgh.

EDV *f* **-** *abk* (= *elektronische Datenverarbeitung*) E.D.P., e.d.p.

EEG *nt* **-** *abk* (= *Elektroenzephalogramm*) EEG.

Efeu [ā:'foi] *m* **-s** ivy.

Effeff [efef'] *nt* **-** (*umg*): **etw aus dem ~ können** be able to do sth standing on one's head.

Effekten [efek'tən] *pl* stocks *pl*; **~börse** *f* Stock Exchange.

Effekthascherei [efekthåshərī'] *f* sensationalism.

effektiv [efektē:f'] *a* effective, actual.

Effet [efä:'] *m* **-s** spin.

EG *f* **-** *abk* (= *Europäische Gemeinschaft*) EC.

E.G., eG *abk* (= *eingetragene Genossenschaft*) registered cooperative *od* society.

egal [ägál'] *a* all the same; **das ist mir ganz ~** it's all the same to me.

egalitär [ägálēte:r'] *a* (*geh*) egalitarian.

Egge [e'gə] *f* **-n** (*AGR*) harrow.

EGKS *f* **-** *abk* (= *Europäische Gemeinschaft für Kohle und Stahl*) ECSC.

Egoismus [ägŏis'mŏŏs] *m* selfishness, egoism.

Egoist(in *f*) *m* egoist; **e~isch** *a* selfish, egoistic.

egozentrisch [ägōtsen'trish] *a* egocentric, self-centered.

eh [ā:] *ad*: **seit ~ und je** for ages, since the year dot (*umg*); **ich komme ~ nicht dazu** I won't get around to it anyway.

eh., e.h. *abk* = **ehrenhalber**.

ehe *kj* before.

Ehe [ā:'ə] *f* **-, -n** marriage; **die ~ eingehen** (*form*) enter into matrimony; **sie leben in wilder ~** (*veraltet*) they are living in sin; **~beratung** *f* marriage counseling; **~brecher** *m* **-s, -** adulterer; **~brecherin** *f* adulteress;

~**bruch** m adultery; ~**frau** f wife; ~**leute** pl married people pl; **e~lich** a matrimonial; (Kind) legitimate.
ehemalig a former.
ehemals ad formerly.
Ehe- zW: ~**mann** m married man; (Partner) husband; ~**paar** nt married couple; ~**partner(in** f) m husband; wife.
eher [ā:'ər] ad (früher) sooner; (lieber) rather, sooner; (mehr) more; **nicht** ~ **als** not before; **um so** ~, **als** the more so because.
Ehe- zW: ~**ring** m wedding ring; ~**scheidung** f divorce; ~**schließung** f marriage; ~**stand** m: **in den** ~**stand treten** (form) enter into matrimony.
eheste(r, s) [ā:'əstə(r, s)] a (früheste) first, earliest; **am** ~**n** (liebsten) soonest; (meist) most; (wahrscheinlichst) most probably.
Ehe- zW: ~**vermittlung** f (Büro) marriage bureau; ~**versprechen** nt (JUR) promise to marry.
ehrbar [ā:r'bár] a honorable (US), honourable (Brit), respectable.
Ehre f -, -n honor (US), honour (Brit); **etw in** ~**n halten** treasure od cherish sth.
ehren vt honor (US), honour (Brit).
Ehren- zW: **e~amtlich** a honorary; ~**bürgerrecht** nt: **die Stadt verlieh ihr das** ~**bürgerrecht** she was given the freedom of the city; ~**gast** m guest of honor; **e~haft** a honorable; **e~halber** ad: **er wurde e~halber zum Vorsitzenden auf Lebenszeit ernannt** he was made honorary president for life; ~**mann** m man of honor; ~**mitglied** nt honorary member; ~**platz** m place of honor; ~**rechte** pl civic rights pl; **e~rührig** a defamatory; ~**runde** f lap of honor; ~**sache** f point of honor; ~**sache!** (umg) you can count on me; ~**tag** m (Geburtstag) birthday; (großer Tag) big day; **e~voll** a honorable; ~**wort** nt word of honor; **Urlaub auf** ~**wort** parole.
Ehr- zW: **e~erbietig** a respectful; ~**furcht** f awe, deep respect; **e~furchtgebietend** a (Stimme) authoritative; ~**gefühl** nt sense of honor (US) od honour (Brit); ~**geiz** m ambition; **e~geizig** a ambitious; **e~lich** a honest; **e~lich verdientes Geld** hard-earned money; **e~lich gesagt** ... quite frankly od honestly ...; ~**lichkeit** f honesty; **e~los** a dishonorable.
Ehrung f honor(ing) (US), honour(ing) (Brit).
ehrwürdig a venerable.
ei interj well, well; (beschwichtigend) now, now.
Ei [ī] nt -(e)s, -er egg; **jdn wie ein rohes** ~ **behandeln** (fig) handle sb with kid gloves; **wie aus dem** ~ **gepellt aussehen** (umg) look spruce; **Eier** pl (umg!: Hoden) balls pl (!).
Eibe [ī'bə] f -, -n (BOT) yew.
Eichamt [ī'chámt] nt Office of Weights and

Measures.
Eiche f -, -n oak (tree).
Eichel f -, -n acorn; (KARTEN) club; (ANAT) glans.
eichen vt calibrate.
Eichhörnchen nt squirrel.
Eichmaß nt standard.
Eichung f standardization.
Eid [īt'] m -(e)s, -e oath; **eine Erklärung an** ~**es Statt abgeben** (JUR) make a solemn declaration.
Eidechse [ī'deksə] f -, -n lizard.
eidesstattlich a: ~**e Erklärung** affidavit.
Eid- zW: ~**genosse** m Swiss; ~**genossenschaft** f: **Schweizerische** ~**genossenschaft** Swiss Confederation; **e~lich** a (sworn) upon oath.
Eidotter nt egg yolk.
Eier- [ī'ər] zW: ~**becher** m eggcup; ~**kuchen** m omelet (US), omelette (Brit); pancake; ~**likör** m advocaat.
eiern [ī'ərn] vi (umg) wobble.
Eier- zW: ~**schale** f eggshell; ~**stock** m ovary; ~**uhr** f egg timer.
Eifel [ī'fəl] f - Eifel (Mountains).
Eifer [ī'fər] m -s zeal, enthusiasm; **mit großem** ~ **bei der Sache sein** put one's heart into it; **im** ~ **des Gefechts** (fig) in the heat of the moment; ~**sucht** f jealousy; **e~süchtig** a jealous (auf +akk of).
eifrig [ī'frich] a zealous, enthusiastic.
Eigelb [ī'gelp] nt -(e)s, - egg yolk.
eigen [ī'gən] a own; (~artig) peculiar; (ordentlich) particular; (übergenau) fussy; **ich möchte kurz in** ~**er Sache sprechen** I would like to say something on my own account; **mit dem ihm** ~**en Lächeln** with that smile peculiar to him; **sich** (dat) **etw zu** ~ **machen** make sth one's own; **E~art** f peculiarity; characteristic; ~**artig** a peculiar; **E~bau** m: **er fährt ein Fahrrad Marke E~bau** (hum umg) he rides a home-made bike; **E~bedarf** m one's own requirements pl; **E~brötler(in** f) m -, -s loner, lone wolf; (komischer Kauz) oddball (umg); **E~gewicht** nt net weight; ~**händig** a with one's own hand; **E~heim** nt owner-occupied house; **E~heit** f peculiarity; **E~initiative** f initiative of one's own; **E~kapital** nt personal capital; (von Firma) company capital; **E~lob** nt self-praise; ~**mächtig** a high-handed; (e~verantwortlich) taken/done etc on one's own authority; (unbefugt) unauthorized; **E~name** m proper name; **E~nutz** m self-interest.
eigens ad expressly, on purpose.
eigen- zW: **E~schaft** f quality, property, attribute; **E~schaftswort** nt adjective; **E~sinn** m obstinacy; ~**sinnig** a obstinate; ~**ständig** a independent; **E~ständigkeit** f independence.
eigentlich a actual, real ♦ ad actually, really; **was willst du** ~ **hier?** what do you want here anyway?

eigen- *zW*: **E~tor** *nt* own goal; **E~tum** *nt* property; **E~tümer(in** *f*) *m* **-s,** **-** owner, proprietor; **~tümlich** *a* peculiar; **E~tümlichkeit** *f* peculiarity.

Eigentums- *zW*: **~delikt** *nt* (*JUR*: *Diebstahl*) theft; **~wohnung** *f* condo(minium), freehold flat (*Brit*).

eigenwillig *a* with a mind of one's own.

eignen [ˈīgˈnən] *vr* be suited.

Eignung *f* suitability.

Eignungsprüfung *f*, **Eignungstest** *m* **-(e)s, -s** *od* **-e** aptitude test.

Eil- [ˈīl'] *zW*: **~bote** *m* courier; **per** *od* **durch ~boten** express; **~brief** *m* express letter.

Eile *f* **-** haste; **es hat keine ~** there's no hurry.

Eileiter [ˈīˈlītər] *m* (*ANAT*) Fallopian tube.

eilen *vi* (*Mensch*) hurry; (*dringend sein*) be urgent.

eilends *ad* hastily.

Eilgut *nt* express goods *pl*, fast freight.

eilig *a* hasty, hurried; (*dringlich*) urgent; **es ~ haben** be in a hurry.

Eil- *zW*: **~tempo** *nt*: **etw im ~tempo machen** do sth in a rush; **~zug** *m* fast stopping train; **~zustellung** *f* special delivery.

Eimer [ˈīˈmər] *m* **-s, -** bucket, pail; **im ~ sein** be down the tubes.

ein(e) [ˈīn'(ə)] *num* one ♦ *indef art* a, an ♦ *ad*: **nicht ~ noch aus wissen** not know what to do; **E~/Aus** (*an Geräten*) on/off; **er ist ihr ~ und alles** he means everything to her; **er geht bei uns ~ und aus** he is always round at our place.

einander [īnánˈdər] *pron* one another, each other.

einarbeiten [īnˈárbītən] *vr* familiarize o.s. (*in +akk* with).

Einarbeitungszeit *f* training period.

einarmig [īnˈármiçh] *a* one-armed.

einäschern [īnˈeshərn] *vt* (*Leichnam*) cremate; (*Stadt etc*) reduce to ashes.

einatmen [īnˈâtmən] *vti* inhale, breathe in.

einäugig [īnˈoigich] *a* one-eyed.

Einbahnstraße [īnˈbânshtrâsə] *f* one-way street.

Einband [īnˈbánt] *m* binding, cover.

einbändig [īnˈbendiçh] *a* one-volume.

einbauen [īnˈbouən] *vt* build in; (*Motor*) install, fit.

Einbau- *zW*: **~küche** *f* (fully-)fitted kitchen; **~möbel** *pl* built-in furniture; **~schrank** *f* fitted cupboard.

einbegriffen [īnˈbəgrifən] *a* included, inclusive.

einbehalten [īnˈbəhältən] *vt unreg* keep back.

einberufen *vt unreg* convene; (*MIL*) draft.

Einberufung *f* convocation; draft.

Einberufungsbescheid *m*, **Einberufungsbefehl** *m* (*MIL*) draft papers *pl*.

einbetten [īnˈbetən] *vt* embed.

Einbettzimmer *nt* single room.

einbeziehen [īnˈbətsē:ən] *vt unreg* include.

einbiegen [īnˈbē:gən] *vi unreg* turn.

einbilden [īnˈbildən] *vr*: **sich** (*dat*) **etw ~** imagine sth; **sich** (*dat*) **viel auf etw** (*akk*) **~** (*stolz sein*): be conceited about sth.

Einbildung *f* imagination; (*Dünkel*) conceit.

Einbildungskraft *f* imagination.

einbinden [īnˈbindən] *vt unreg* bind (up).

einblenden [īnˈblendən] *vt* fade in.

einbleuen [īnˈbloiən] *vt* (*umg*): **jdm etw ~** hammer sth into sb.

Einblick [īnˈblik] *m* insight; **~ in die Akten nehmen** examine the files; **jdm ~ in etw** (*akk*) **gewähren** allow sb to look at sth.

einbrechen [īnˈbreçhən] *vi unreg* (*einstürzen*) fall in; (*Einbruch verüben*) break in; **bei einbrechender Dunkelheit** at nightfall.

Einbrecher *m* **-s, -** burglar.

einbringen [īnˈbringən] *vt unreg* bring in; (*Geld, Vorteil*) yield; (*mitbringen*) contribute; **das bringt nichts ein** (*fig*) it's not worth it.

einbrocken [īnˈbrokən] *vt* (*umg*): **jdm/sich etwas ~** land sb/o.s. in it.

Einbruch [īnˈbrookh] *m* (*Haus~*) break-in, burglary; (*des Winters*) onset; (*Einsturz, FIN*) collapse; (*MIL*: *in Front*) breakthrough; **bei ~ der Nacht** at nightfall.

einbruchssicher *a* burglar-proof.

Einbuchtung [īnˈbookhtoong] *f* indentation; (*Bucht*) inlet, bay.

einbürgern [īnˈbürgərn] *vt* naturalize ♦ *vr* become adopted; **das hat sich so eingebürgert** that's become a custom.

Einbürgerung *f* naturalization.

Einbuße [īnˈbooːsə] *f* loss, forfeiture.

einbüßen [īnˈbüːsən] *vt* lose, forfeit.

einchecken [īnˈshekən] *vti* check in.

eincremen [īnˈkrāːmən] *vt* put cream on.

eindämmen [īnˈdemən] *vt* (*Fluß*) dam; (*fig*) check, contain.

eindecken [īnˈdekən] *vr* lay in stocks (*mit* of) ♦ *vt* (*umg*: *überhäufen*): **mit Arbeit eingedeckt sein** be inundated with work.

eindeutig [īnˈdoitiçh] *a* unequivocal.

eindeutschen [īnˈdoitshən] *vt* (*Fremdwort*) Germanize.

eindösen [īnˈdœzən] *vi* (*umg*) doze off.

eindringen [īnˈdringən] *vi unreg* (*in +akk*) force one's way in(to); (*in Haus*) break in(to); (*in Land*) invade; (*Gas, Wasser*) penetrate; (*mit Bitten*) pester (*auf jdn* sb).

eindring- *zW*: **~lich** *a* forcible, urgent; **ich habe ihn ~lich gebeten** ... I urged him ...; **E~ling** *m* intruder.

Eindruck [īnˈdrookh] *m* impression.

eindrücken [īnˈdrükən] *vt* press in.

Eindrucks- *zW*: **e~fähig** *a* impressionable; **e~voll** *a* impressive.

eine *siehe* **ein(e), eine(r,s).**

einebnen [īnˈāːbnən] *vt* (*lit*) level (off); (*fig*) level out.

Einehe [īnˈāːə] *f* monogamy.

eineiig [īnˈiiçh] *a* (*Zwillinge*) identical.

eineinhalb [ˈīnīnˈhálp] *num* one and a half.

einengen [īnˈengən] *vt* confine, restrict.

eine(r, s) *pron* one; *(jemand)* someone; **wie kann ~r nur so dumm sein** how could anybody be so stupid!; **es kam ~s zum anderen** it was (just) one thing after another; *(umg)*: **sich** *(dat)* **~n genehmigen** have a quick one.

Einer [ī'nər] *m* - *(MATH)* unit; *(Ruderboot)* single scull.

Einerlei ['īnər'lī] *nt* -s monotony; **e~** *a (gleichartig)* the same kind of; **es ist mir e~** it is all the same to me.

einerseits *ad* on the one hand.

Einf. *abk* = **Einführung.**

einfach [īn'fàkh] *a* simple; *(nicht mehrfach)* single ♦ *ad* simply; **E~heit** *f* simplicity.

einfädeln [īn'fe:dəln] *vt (Nadel)* thread; *(fig)* contrive.

einfahren [īn'fàrən] *unreg vt* bring in; *(Barriere)* knock down; *(Auto)* run in ♦ *vi* drive in; *(Zug)* pull in; *(MIN)* go down.

Einfahrt *f (Vorgang)* driving in; pulling in; *(MIN)* descent; *(Ort)* entrance; *(von Autobahn)* entrance ramp *(US)*, slip road *(Brit)*.

Einfall [īn'fàl] *m (Idee)* idea, notion; *(Licht~)* incidence; *(MIL)* raid.

einfallen *vi unreg (einstürzen)* fall in, collapse; *(Licht)* fall; *(MIL)* raid; *(einstimmen)* join in *(in +akk* with); **etw fällt jdm ein** sth occurs in sb; **das fällt mir gar nicht ein!** I wouldn't dream of it; **sich** *(dat)* **etwas ~ lassen** have a good idea; **dabei fällt mir mein Onkel ein, der ...** that reminds me of my uncle, who ...; **es fällt mir jetzt nicht ein** I can't think of it *od* it won't come to me at the moment.

einfallslos *a* unimaginative.

einfallsreich *a* imaginative.

einfältig [īn'feltiçh] *a* simple(-minded).

Einfaltspinsel [īn'fàltspinzəl] *m (umg)* simpleton.

Einfamilienhaus [īnfàmē:'lēənhous] *nt* family house.

einfangen [īn'fàngən] *vt unreg* catch.

einfarbig [īn'fàrbiçh] *a* all one color; *(Stoff etc)* self-colored.

einfassen [īn'fàsən] *vt (Edelstein)* set; *(Beet, Stoff)* edge.

Einfassung *f* setting; border.

einfetten [īn'fetən] *vt* grease.

einfinden [īn'findən] *vr unreg* come, turn up.

einfliegen [īn'flē:gən] *vt unreg* fly in.

einfließen [īn'flē:sən] *vi unreg* flow in.

einflößen [īn'flœsən] *vt*: **jdm etw ~** *(lit)* give sb sth; *(fig)* instil sth into sb.

Einfluß [īn'floos] *m* influence; **~ nehmen** bring an influence to bear; **~bereich** *m* sphere of influence; **e~reich** *a* influential.

einflüstern [īn'flüstərn] *vt*: **jdm etw ~** whisper sth to sb; *(fig)* insinuate sth to sb.

einförmig [īn'fœrmiçh] *a* uniform; *(eintönig)* monotonous; **E~keit** *f* uniformity; monotony.

einfrieren [īn'frē:rən] *unreg vi* freeze (in) ♦ *vt* freeze; *(POL: Beziehungen)* suspend.

einfügen [īn'fü:gən] *vt* fit in; *(zusätzlich)*

add; *(COMPUT)* insert.

einfühlen [īn'fü:lən] *vr*: **sich in jdn ~** empathize with sb.

Einfühlungsvermögen *nt*: **mit großem ~** with a great deal of sensitivity.

Einfuhr [īn'foo:r] *f* - import; **~artikel** *m* imported article.

einführen [īn'fü:rən] *vt* bring in; *(Mensch, Sitten)* introduce; *(Ware)* import; **jdn in sein Amt ~** install sb (in office).

Einfuhr- *zW*: **~genehmigung** *f* import permit; **~kontingent** *nt* import quota; **~sperre** *f*, **~stopp** *m* ban on imports.

Einführung *f* introduction.

Einführungspreis *m* introductory price.

Einfuhrzoll *m* import duty.

einfüllen [īn'fülən] *vt* pour in.

Eingabe [īn'gàbə] *f* petition; *(Daten~)* input; **~/Ausgabe** *(COMPUT)* input/output.

Eingang [īn'gàng] *m* entrance; *(COMM: Ankunft)* arrival; *(Sendung)* post; **wir bestätigen den ~ Ihres Schreibens vom ...** we acknowledge receipt of your letter of the ...

eingängig [īn'gengiçh] *a* catchy.

eingangs *ad, präp +gen* at the outset (of).

Eingangs- *zW*: **~bestätigung** *f* acknowledgement of receipt; **~halle** *f* entrance hall; **~stempel** *m (COMM)* receipt stamp.

eingeben [īn'gā:bən] *vt unreg (Arznei)* give; *(Daten etc)* feed; *(Gedanken)* inspire.

eingebettet [īn'gàbetət] *a*: **in od zwischen Hügeln ~** nestling among the hills.

eingebildet [īn'gàbildət] *a* imaginary; *(eitel)* conceited; **~er Kranker** hypochondriac.

Eingeborene(r) [īn'gàbō:rənə(r)] *mf dekl wie a* native.

Eingebung *f* inspiration.

eingedenk [īn'gədengk] *präp +gen* bearing in mind.

eingefahren [īn'gəfàrən] *a (Verhaltensweise)* well-worn.

eingefallen [īn'gəfàlən] *a (Gesicht)* gaunt.

eingefleischt [īn'gəflīsht] *a* inveterate; **~er Junggeselle** confirmed bachelor.

eingefroren [īn'gəfrō:rən] *a* frozen.

eingehen [īn'gā:ən] *unreg vi (Aufnahme finden)* come in; *(verständlich sein)* be comprehensible *(jdm* to sb); *(Sendung, Geld)* be received; *(Tier, Pflanze)* die; *(Firma)* fold; *(schrumpfen)* shrink; **auf etw** *(akk)* **~** go into sth; **auf jdn ~** respond to sb; **bei dieser Hitze/Kälte geht man ja ein!** *(umg)* this heat/cold is just too much; *(zustimmen)*: **auf einen Vorschlag/Plan ~** go along with a suggestion/plan ♦ *vt (abmachen)* enter into; *(Wette)* make.

eingehend *a* exhaustive, thorough.

eingekeilt [īn'gəkīlt] *a* hemmed in; *(fig)* trapped.

eingekesselt [īn'gəkesəlt] *a*: **~ sein** be encircled/surrounded.

Eingemachte(s) [īn'gəmàkhtə(s)] *nt* preserves *pl*.

eingemeinden [īn'gəmīndən] *vt* incorporate.

eingenommen [īn'gənomən] *a* (*von*) fond (of), partial (to); (*gegen*) prejudiced.

eingeschnappt [īn'gəshnápt] *a* (*umg*) cross; ~ **sein** be in a huff.

eingeschrieben [īn'gəshrē:bən] *a* registered.

eingeschworen [īn'gəshvō:rən] *a* confirmed; (*Gemeinschaft*) close.

eingesessen [īn'gəzesən] *a* old-established.

eingespannt [īn'gəshpánt] *a* busy.

eingespielt [īn'gəshpē:lt] *a*: **aufeinander** ~ **sein** be in tune with each other.

Eingeständnis [īn'gəshtentnis] *nt* admission, confession.

eingestehen [īn'gəshtā:ən] *vt unreg* confess.

eingestellt [īn'gəshtelt] *a*: **ich bin im Moment nicht auf Besuch** ~ I'm not prepared for visitors.

eingetragen [īn'gətrâgən] *a* (*COMM*) registered; ~**er Gesellschaftssitz** registered office; ~**es Warenzeichen** registered trademark.

Eingeweide [īn'gəvīdə] *nt* -**s**, - innards *pl*, intestines *pl*.

Eingeweihte(r) [īn'gəvītə(r)] *mf dekl wie a* initiate.

eingewöhnen [īn'gəvœnən] *vr* settle down (*in* +*dat* in).

eingezahlt [īn'gətsâlt] *a*: ~**es Kapital** paid-up capital.

eingießen [īn'gē:sən] *vt unreg* pour (out).

eingleisig [īn'glīzich] *a* single-track; **er denkt sehr** ~ (*fig*) he's completely single-minded.

eingliedern [īn'glē:dərn] *vt* integrate (*in* +*akk* into) ♦ *vr* integrate o.s. (*in* +*akk* into).

eingraben [īn'grâbən] *unreg vt* dig in ♦ *vr* dig o.s. in; **dieses Erlebnis hat sich seinem Gedächtnis eingegraben** this experience has engraved itself on his memory.

eingreifen [īn'grīfən] *vi unreg* intervene, interfere; (*Zahnrad*) mesh.

eingrenzen [īn'grentsən] *vt* enclose; (*fig: Problem*) delimit.

Eingriff [īn'grif] *m* intervention, interference; (*Operation*) operation.

einhaken [īn'hâkən] *vt* hook in ♦ *vr*: **sich bei jdm** ~ link arms with sb ♦ *vi* (*sich einmischen*) intervene.

Einhalt [īn'hált] *m*: ~ **gebieten** (+*dat*) put a stop to.

einhalten *unreg vt* (*Regel*) keep ♦ *vi* stop.

einhämmern [īn'hemərn] *vt*: **jdm etw** ~ (*fig*) hammer sth into sb.

einhandeln [īn'hándəln] *vt* trade (*gegen, für* for).

einhändig [īn'hendich] *a* one-handed.

einhändigen [īn'hendigən] *vt* hand in.

einhängen [īn'hengən] *vt* hang; (*Telefon: auch vi*) hang up; **sich bei jdm** ~ link arms with sb.

einheimisch [īn'hīmish] *a* native.

einheimsen *vt* (*umg*) bring home.

einheiraten [īn'hīrâtən] *vi*: **in einen Betrieb** ~ marry into a business.

Einheit [īn'hīt] *f* unity; (*Maß, MIL*) unit; **eine**

geschlossene ~ **bilden** form an integrated whole; **e**~**lich** *a* uniform.

Einheits- *zW*: ~**front** *f* (*POL*) united front; ~**liste** *f* (*POL*) single *od* unified list of candidates; ~**preis** *m* uniform price.

einheizen [īn'hītsən] *vi*: **jdm (tüchtig)** ~ (*umg: die Meinung sagen*) make things hot for sb.

einhellig [īn'helich] *a, ad* unanimous.

einholen [īn'hō:lən] *vt* (*Tau*) haul in; (*Fahne, Segel*) lower; (*Vorsprung aufholen*) catch up with; (*Verspätung*) make up; (*Rat, Erlaubnis*) ask ♦ *vi* (*einkaufen*) buy, shop.

Einhorn [īn'horn] *nt* unicorn.

einhüllen [īn'hülən] *vt* wrap up.

einig [ī'nich] *a* (*vereint*) united; **sich** (*dat*) ~ **sein** be in agreement; ~ **werden** agree.

einige *pl* some; (*mehrere*) several; *siehe* **einige(r, s)**.

einigemal *ad* a few times.

einigen *vt* unite ♦ *vr* agree (*auf* +*akk* on).

einige(r, s) [ī'nigə(r, s)] *a* some ♦ *pron*: **dazu ist noch** ~**s zu sagen** there are still one or two things to say about that; **mit Ausnahme** ~**r weniger** with a few exceptions; **vor** ~**n Tagen** the other day, a few days ago.

einigermaßen *ad* somewhat; (*leidlich*) reasonably.

einiges *siehe* **einige(r, s)**.

einiggehen *vi unreg* agree.

Einigkeit *f* unity; (*Übereinstimmung*) agreement.

Einigung *f* agreement; (*Vereinigung*) unification.

einimpfen [īn'impfən] *vt* inoculate (*jdm etw* sb with sth); (*fig*) impress (*jdm etw* sth upon sb).

einjagen [īn'yâgən] *vt*: **jdm Furcht/einen Schrecken** ~ give sb a fright.

einjährig [īn'ye:rich] *a* of *od* for one year; (*Alter*) one-year-old; (*Pflanze*) annual.

einkalkulieren [īn'kálkŏolē:rən] *vt* take into account, allow for.

einkassieren [īn'kásē:rən] *vt* (*Geld, Schulden*) collect.

Einkauf [īn'kouf] *m* purchase; (*COMM: Abteilung*) purchasing (department).

einkaufen *vt* buy ♦ *vi* shop; ~ **gehen** go shopping.

Einkäufer [īn'koifər] *m* (*COMM*) buyer.

Einkaufs- *zW*: ~**bummel** *m*: **einen** ~**bummel machen** go on a shopping spree; ~**leiter** *m* (*COMM*) chief buyer; ~**netz** *nt* shopping net (*US*), string bag (*Brit*); ~**preis** *m* cost price, wholesale price; ~**wagen** *m* cart (*US*), trolley (*Brit*); ~**zentrum** *nt* shopping center.

einkehren [īn'kā:rən] *vi* (*in Gasthof*) (make a) stop (*in* +*dat* at); (*geh: Ruhe, Frühling*) come.

einkerben [īn'kerbən] *vt* notch.

einklagen [īn'klâgən] *vt* (*Schulden*) sue for (the recovery of).

einklammern [īn'klámərn] *vt* put in brackets,

bracket.
Einklang [īn'klàng] *m* harmony.
einkleiden [īn'klīdən] *vt* clothe; *(fig)* express.
einklemmen [īn'klemən] *vt* jam.
einknicken [īn'knikən] *vt* bend in; *(Papier)* fold ♦ *vi (Knie)* give way.
einkochen [īn'koĸhən] *vt* boil down; *(Obst)* preserve, bottle.
Einkommen [īn'komən] *nt* **-s,** - income.
einkommens- *zW:* **~schwach** *a* low-income *attr;* **~stark** *a* high-income *attr.*
Einkommen(s)steuer *f* income tax; **~erklärung** *f* income tax return.
Einkommensverhältnisse *pl* (level of) income *sing.*
einkreisen [īn'krīzən] *vt* encircle.
einkriegen [īn'krē:gən] *vr (umg):* **sie konnte sich gar nicht mehr darüber ~, daß ...** she couldn't get over the fact that ...
Einkünfte [īn'künftə] *pl* income *sing*, revenue *sing.*
Einl. *abk* = **Einleitung.**
einladen [īn'lådən] *vt unreg (Person)* invite; *(Gegenstände)* load; **jdn ins Kino ~** take sb to the cinema.
Einladung *f* invitation.
Einlage [īn'lågə] *f (Programm~)* interlude; *(Spar~)* deposit; *(FIN: Kapital~)* investment; *(Schuh~)* insole; *(Fußstütze)* support; *(Zahn~)* temporary filling; *(KOCH)* noodles, vegetables *etc in clear soup.*
einlagern [īn'lågərn] *vt* store.
Einlaß [īn'làs] *m* **-sses, -lässe** admission; **jdm ~ gewähren** admit sb.
einlassen *unreg vt* let in; *(einsetzen)* set in ♦ *vr:* **sich mit jdm/auf etw** *(akk)* **~** get involved with sb/sth; **sich auf einen Kompromiß ~** agree to a compromise; **ich lasse mich auf keine Diskussion ein** I'm not having any discussion about it.
Einlauf [īn'louf] *m* arrival; *(von Pferden)* finish; *(MED)* enema.
einlaufen *unreg vi* arrive, come in; *(in Hafen)* enter; *(SPORT)* finish; *(Wasser)* run in; *(Stoff)* shrink ♦ *vt (Schuhe)* break in; **jdm das Haus ~** invade sb's house ♦ *vr (SPORT)* warm up; *(Motor, Maschine)* run in.
einläuten [īn'loitən] *vt (neues Jahr)* ring in; *(SPORT: Runde)* sound the bell for.
einleben [īn'lā:bən] *vr* settle in.
Einlegearbeit *f* inlay.
einlegen [īn'lā:gən] *vt (einfügen: Blatt, Sohle)* insert; *(KOCH)* pickle; *(in Holz etc)* inlay; *(Geld)* deposit; *(Pause)* have; *(Protest)* make; *(Veto)* use; *(Berufung)* lodge; **ein gutes Wort bei jdm ~** put in a good word with sb.
Einlegesohle *f* insole.
einleiten [īn'lītən] *vt* introduce, start; *(Geburt)* induce.
Einleitung *f* introduction; induction.
einlenken [īn'lengkən] *vi (fig)* yield, give way.
einlesen [īn'lā:zən] *unreg vr:* **sich in ein Ge-**

biet **~** get into a subject ♦ *vt (Daten)* feed *(in +akk* into).
einleuchten [īn'loiċhtən] *vi* be clear *od* evident *(jdm* to sb).
einleuchtend *a* clear.
einliefern [īn'lē:fərn] *vt* take *(in +akk* into); **jdn ins Krankenhaus ~** admit sb to hospital.
Einlieferungsschein *m* receipt *(for letter etc).*
einlochen [īn'loĸhən] *vt (umg: einsperren)* lock up.
einlösen [īn'lœzən] *vt (Scheck)* cash; *(Schuldschein, Pfand)* redeem; *(Versprechen)* keep.
einmachen [īn'màĸhən] *vt* preserve.
Einmachglas *nt* preserving jar.
einmal [īn'mål] *ad* once; *(erstens)* first of all, firstly; *(später)* one day; **nehmen wir ~ an** just let's suppose; **noch ~** once more; **nicht ~** not even; **auf ~** all at once; **es war ~** once upon a time there was *od* were; **~ ist keinmal** *(Sprichwort)* once doesn't count; **waren Sie schon ~ in Rom?** have you ever been to Rome?
Einmaleins' *nt* multiplication tables *pl;* *(fig)* ABC, basics *pl.*
einmalig *a* unique; *(einmal geschehend)* single; *(prima)* fantastic.
Einmann- [īnmán'] *zW:* **~betrieb** *m* one-man business; **~bus** *m* one-man-operated bus.
Einmarsch [īn'mársh] *m* entry; *(MIL)* invasion.
einmarschieren *vi* march in.
einmengen [īn'mengən] *vr* interfere *(in +akk* with).
einmieten [īn'mē:tən] *vr:* **sich bei jdm ~** take lodgings with sb.
einmischen [īn'mishən] *vr* interfere *(in +akk* with).
einmotten [īn'motən] *vt (Kleider etc)* put in mothballs.
einmünden [īn'mündən] *vi* run *(in +akk* into), join.
einmütig [īn'mü:tiċh] *a* unanimous.
einnähen [īn'ne:ən] *vt (enger machen)* take in.
Einnahme [īn'nåmə] *f* **-, -n** *(Geld)* takings *pl,* revenue; *(von Medizin)* taking; *(MIL)* capture, taking; **~n und Ausgaben** income and expenditure; **~quelle** *f* source of income.
einnehmen [īn'nå:mən] *vt unreg* take; *(Stellung, Raum)* take up; **~ für/gegen** persuade in favour of/against.
einnehmend *a* charming.
einnicken [īn'nikən] *vi* nod off.
einnisten [īn'nistən] *vr* nest; *(fig)* settle o.s.
Einöde [īn'œdə] *f* **-, -n** desert, wilderness.
einordnen [īn'ordnən] *vt* arrange, fit in ♦ *vr* adapt; *(AUT)* get into) lane.
einpacken [īn'påkən] *vt* pack (up).
einparken [īn'párkən] *vt* park.
einpauken [īn'poukən] *vt (umg):* **jdm etw ~** drum sth into sb.

einpendeln [īn'pɛndəln] vr even out.
einpennen [īn'pɛnən] vi (umg) drop off.
einpferchen [īn'pfɛrçhən] vt pen in; (fig) coop up.
einpflanzen [īn'pflántsən] vt plant; (MED) implant.
einplanen [īn'plânən] vt plan for.
einprägen [īn'prɛːgən] vt impress, imprint; (beibringen) impress (jdm on sb); **sich** (dat) **etw** ~ memorize sth.
einprägsam [īn'prɛːkzâm] a easy to remember; (Melodie) catchy.
einprogrammieren [īn'prŏgrámɛ̄ːrən] vt (COMPUT) feed in.
einprügeln [īn'prü:gəln] vt (umg): **jdm etw** ~ din sth into sb.
einquartieren [īnk'vártē:rən] vt (MIL auch) billet; **Gäste bei Freunden** ~ put visitors up with friends.
einrahmen [īn'râmən] vt frame.
einrasten [īn'rástən] vi engage.
einräumen [īn'roimən] vt (ordnend) put away; (überlassen: Platz) give up; (zugestehen) admit, concede.
einrechnen [īn'rɛçhnən] vt include; (berücksichtigen) take into account.
einreden [īn'rɑ̄:dən] vt: **jdm/sich etw** ~ talk sb/o.s. into believing sth ♦ vi: **auf jdn** ~ keep on and on at sb.
Einreibemittel nt liniment.
einreiben [īn'rībən] vt unreg rub in.
einreichen [īn'rɛ̄çhən] vt hand in; (Antrag) submit.
einreihen [īn'rīən] vt (einordnen, einfügen) put in (in +akk -to); (klassifizieren) classify ♦ vr (Auto: sich ~) get in lane.
Einreise [īn'rīzə] f entry; ~**bestimmungen** pl entry regulations pl; ~**er'laubnis** f, ~**genehmigung** f entry permit.
einreisen [īn'rīzən] vi enter (in ein Land a country).
Einreiseverbot nt refusal of entry.
einreißen [īn'rīsən] vt unreg (Papier) tear; (Gebäude) pull down ♦ vi tear; (Gewohnheit werden) catch on.
einrenken [īn'rɛngkən] vt (Gelenk, Knie) put back in place; (fig umg) sort out ♦ vr (fig umg) sort itself out.
einrichten [īn'rɛ̄çhtən] vt (Haus) furnish; (schaffen) establish, set up; (arrangieren) arrange; (möglich machen) manage ♦ vr (in Haus) furnish one's house; (sich vorbereiten) prepare o.s. (auf +akk for); (sich anpassen) adapt (auf +akk to).
Einrichtung f (Wohnungs~) furnishings pl; (öffentliche Anstalt) organization; (Dienste) service; (Labor~ etc) equipment; (Gewohnheit): **zur ständigen** ~ **werden** become an institution.
Einrichtungsgegenstand m item of furniture.
einrosten [īn'rostən] vi get rusty.
einrücken [īn'rükən] vi (MIL: Soldat) join up; (: in Land) move in ♦ vt (Anzeige) insert;

(Zeile, Text) indent.
Eins [īns] f -, -en one; **e**~ num one; **es ist mir alles e**~ it's all one to me; **e**~ **zu e**~ (SPORT) one all; **e**~ **a** (umg) first-rate.
einsalzen [īn'záltsən] vt salt.
einsam [īn'zâm] a lonely, lonesome, solitary; ~**e Klasse/Spitze** (umg) absolutely fantastic; **E**~**keit** f loneliness, solitude.
einsammeln [īn'zámoln] vt collect.
Einsatz [īn'záts] m (Teil) insert; (an Kleid) insertion; (Tisch) leaf; (Verwendung) use, employment; (Spiel~) stake; (Risiko) risk; (MIL) operation; (MUS) entry; **im** ~ **in action**; **etw unter** ~ **seines Lebens tun** risk one's life to do sth; ~**befehl** m order to go into action; **e**~**bereit** a ready for action; ~**kommando** nt (MIL) task force.
einschalten [īn'sháltən] vt (ELEK) switch on; (einfügen) insert; (Pause) make; (AUT: Gang) engage; (Anwalt) bring in ♦ vr (dazwischentreten) intervene.
Einschaltquote f (TV) ratings pl.
einschärfen [īn'sherfən] vt impress (jdm etw sth on sb).
einschätzen [īn'shetsən] vt estimate, assess ♦ vr rate o.s.
einschenken [īn'shengkən] vt pour out.
einscheren [īn'shâ:rən] vi get back (into lane).
einschicken [īn'shikən] vt send in.
einschieben [īn'shē:bən] vt unreg push in; (zusätzlich) insert; **eine Pause** ~ have a break.
einschiffen [īn'shifən] vt ship ♦ vr embark, go on board.
einschl. abk (= einschließlich) incl., inc.
einschlafen [īn'shlâfən] vi unreg fall asleep, go to sleep; (fig: Freundschaft) peter out.
einschläfern [īn'shle:fərn] vt (schläfrig machen) make sleepy; (Gewissen) soothe; (narkotisieren) give a soporific to; (töten: Tier) put to sleep.
einschläfernd a (MED) soporific; (langweilig) boring; (Stimme) lulling.
Einschlag [īn'shlâk] m impact; (AUT) lock; (fig: Beimischung) touch, hint.
einschlagen [īn'shlâgən] unreg vt knock in; (Fenster) smash, break; (Zähne, Schädel) smash in; (Steuer) turn; (kürzer machen) take up; (Ware) pack, wrap up; (Weg, Richtung) take ♦ vi hit (in etw (akk) sth, auf jdn sb); (sich einigen) agree; (Anklang finden) work, succeed; **es muß irgendwo eingeschlagen haben** something must have been struck by lightning; **gut** ~ (umg) go down well, be a big hit.
einschlägig [īn'shle:giç] a relevant; **er ist** ~ **vorbestraft** (JUR) he has a previous conviction for a similar offense.
einschleichen [īn'shlīçhən] vr unreg (in Haus: Fehler) creep in, steal in; (in Vertrauen) worm one's way in.
einschleppen [īn'shlepən] vt (fig: Krankheit etc) bring in.

einschleusen [īn'shloizən] *vt* smuggle in (*in* +*akk* -to).

einschließen [īn'shlē:sən] *unreg vt* (*Kind*) lock in; (*Häftling*) lock up; (*Gegenstand*) lock away; (*Bergleute*) cut off; (*umgeben*) surround; (*MIL*) encircle; (*fig*) include, comprise ♦ *vr* lock o.s. in.

einschließlich *ad* inclusive ♦ *präp* +*gen* inclusive of, including.

einschmeicheln [īnsh'mīċhəln] *vr* ingratiate o.s. (*bei* with).

einschmuggeln [īnsh'mōōgəln] *vt* smuggle in (*in* +*akk* -to).

einschnappen [īnsh'nåpən] *vi* (*Tür*) click to; (*fig*) be touchy; **eingeschnappt sein** be in a huff.

einschneidend [īnsh'nīdənt] *a* incisive.

einschneien [īnsh'nīən] *vi*: **eingeschneit sein** be snowed in.

Einschnitt [īnsh'nit] *m* (*MED*) incision; (*im Tal, Gebirge*) cleft; (*im Leben*) decisive point.

einschnüren [īnsh'nü:rən] *vt* (*einengen*) cut into; **dieser Kragen schnürt mir den Hals ein** this collar is strangling me.

einschränken [īn'shrengkən] *vt* limit, restrict; (*Kosten*) cut down, reduce; **einschränkend möchte ich sagen, daß** ... I'd like to qualify that by saying ... ♦ *vr* cut down (on expenditure).

einschränkend *a* restrictive.

Einschränkung *f* restriction, limitation; reduction; (*von Behauptung*) qualification.

Einschreib(e)brief *m* certified letter (*US*), recorded delivery letter (*Brit*).

einschreiben [īn'shrībən] *unreg vt* write in; (*POST*) send by certified mail (*US*), send recorded delivery (*Brit*) ♦ *vr* register; (*UNIV*) enrol; **E~** *nt* certified letter (*US*); recorded delivery letter (*Brit*).

Einschreib(e)sendung *f* certified (*US*) *od* recorded delivery (*Brit*) packet.

einschreiten [īn'shrītən] *vi unreg* step in, intervene; **~ gegen** take action against.

Einschub [īn'shōō:p] *m* **-s, ̈e** insertion.

einschüchtern [īn'shüċhtərn] *vt* intimidate.

einschulen [īn'shōō:lən] *vti*: **eingeschult werden** (*Kind*) start school.

einschweißen [īn'shvīsən] *vt* (*TECH*) weld in (*in* +*akk* -to); (*in Plastik*) shrink-wrap.

einschwenken [īn'shvengkən] *vi* turn *od* swing in (*in* +*akk* -to).

einsehen [īn'zā:ən] *vt unreg* (*prüfen*) inspect; (*Fehler etc*) recognize; (*verstehen*) see; **das sehe ich nicht ein** I don't see why; **E~** *nt* **-s** understanding; **ein E~ haben** show understanding.

einseifen [īn'zīfən] *vt* soap, lather; (*fig umg*) take in, con.

einseitig [īn'zītiċh] *a* one-sided; (*POL*) unilateral; (*Ernährung*) unbalanced; (*Diskette*) single-sided; **E~keit** *f* one-sidedness.

einsenden [īn'zendən] *vt unreg* send in.

Einsender(in *f*) *m* **-s,** - sender, contributor.

Einsendeschluß *m* closing date (for entries).

Einsendung *f* sending in.

einsetzen [īn'zetsən] *vt* put (in); (*in Amt*) appoint, install; (*Geld*) stake; (*verwenden*) use; (*MIL*) employ ♦ *vi* (*beginnen*) set in; (*MUS*) enter, come in ♦ *vr* work hard; **sich für jdn/etw ~** support sb/sth; **ich werde mich dafür ~, daß** ... I will do what I can to see that ...

Einsicht [īn'ziċht] *f* insight; (*in Akten*) look, inspection; **zu der ~ kommen, daß** ... come to the conclusion that ...

einsichtig *a* (*Mensch*) judicious; **jdm etw ~ machen** make sb understand *od* see sth.

Einsichtnahme *f* **-, -n** (*form*) perusal; **„zur ~"** "for attention".

einsichtslos *a* unreasonable.

einsichtsvoll *a* understanding.

Einsiedler [īn'zē:dlər] *m* **-s,** - hermit.

einsilbig [īn'zilbiċh] *a* (*lit, fig*) monosyllabic; **E~keit** *f* (*fig*) taciturnity.

einsinken [īn'zingkən] *vi unreg* sink in.

Einsitzer [īn'zitsər] *m* **-s,** - single-seater.

einspannen [īn'shpånən] *vt* (*Werkstück, Papier*) put (in), insert; (*Pferde*) harness; (*umg: Person*) rope in; **jdn für seine Zwecke ~** use sb for one's own ends.

einsparen [īn'shpårən] *vt* save, economize on; (*Kosten*) cut down on; (*Posten*) eliminate.

einspeichern [īn'shpīċhərn] *vt* (*COMPUT*) feed in (*in* +*akk* -to).

einsperren [īn'shperən] *vt* lock up.

einspielen [īn'shpē:lən] *vr* (*SPORT*) warm up; **sich aufeinander ~** become attuned to each other ♦ *vt* (*Film: Geld*) bring in; (*Instrument*) play in; **gut eingespielt** running smoothly.

einsprachig [īn'shpråkhiċh] *a* monolingual.

einspringen [īn'shpringən] *vi unreg* (*aushelfen*) stand in; (*mit Geld*) help out.

einspritzen [īn'shpritsən] *vt* inject.

Einspritzmotor *m* (*AUT*) injection engine.

Einspruch [īn'shprōōkh] *m* protest, objection; **~ einlegen** (*JUR*) file an objection.

Einspruchs- *zW*: **~frist** *f* (*JUR*) period for filing an objection; **~recht** *nt* veto.

einspurig [īn'shpōō:riċh] *a* single-lane; (*EISENB*) single track.

einst [īnst] *ad* once; (*zukünftig*) one *od* some day.

Einstand [īn'shtånt] *m* (*TENNIS*) deuce; (*Antritt*) entrance (to office); **er hat gestern seinen ~ gegeben** yesterday he celebrated starting his new job.

einstechen [īn'shteċhən] *vt unreg* pierce.

einstecken [īn'shtekən] *vt* stick in, insert; (*Brief*) post, mail; (*ELEK: Stecker*) plug in; (*Geld*) pocket; (*mitnehmen*) take; (*überlegen sein*) put in the shade; (*hinnehmen*) swallow.

einstehen [īn'shtā:ən] *vi unreg* guarantee (*für jdn/etw* sb/sth); (*verantworten*) answer (*für* for); (*Ersatz leisten*): **für etw ~** make

good sth.
einsteigen [ĭn'shtīgən] *vi unreg* get in *od* on; (*in Schiff*) go on board; (*sich beteiligen*) come in; (*hineinklettern*) climb in; ~! (*EISENB etc*) all aboard!
einstellbar *a* adjustable.
einstellen [ĭn'shtelən] *vti* (*in Firma*) employ, take on; (*aufhören*) stop; (*Geräte*) adjust (*auf* +*akk* to); (*Kamera etc*) focus (*auf* +*akk* on); (*Sender, Radio*) tune in to; (*unterstellen*) put; **Zahlungen** ~ suspend payment ♦ *vr* (*anfangen*) set in; (*kommen*) arrive; **sich auf jdn/etw** ~ adapt to sb/ prepare o.s. for sth.
einstellig *a* (*Zahl*) single-digit.
Einstellplatz *m* (*auf Hof*) carport; (*in Großgarage*) (covered) parking accommodation.
Einstellung *f* (*Aufhören*) suspension, cessation; adjustment; focusing; (*von Arbeiter etc*) appointment; (*Haltung*) attitude.
Einstellungs- *zW*: ~**gespräch** *nt* interview; ~**stopp** *m* halt in recruitment.
Einstieg [ĭn'shtē:k] *m* -**(e)s**, -**e** entry; (*fig*) approach; (*von Bus, Bahn*) door; **kein** ~ no entrance.
einstig [ĭns'tĭċh] *a* former.
einstimmen [ĭn'shtimən] *vi* join in ♦ *vt* (*MUS*) tune; (*in Stimmung bringen*) put in the mood.
einstimmig *a* unanimous; (*MUS*) for one voice; **E~keit** *f* unanimity.
einst- [ĭnst'] *zW*: ~**malig** *a* former; ~**mals** *ad* once, formerly.
einstöckig [ĭn'shtǣkiċh] *a* single-storied (*US*), single-storeyed (*Brit*).
einstöpseln [ĭn'shtǣpsəln] *vt* (*ELEK*) plug in (*in* +*akk* -to).
einstudieren [ĭn'shtōōdē:rən] *vt* study, rehearse.
einstufen [ĭn'shtōō:fən] *vt* classify.
Einstufung *f*: **nach seiner** ~ **in eine höhere Gehaltsklasse** after he was put on a higher salary grade.
einstündig [ĭn'shtündiċh] *a* one-hour.
einstürmen [ĭn'shtürmən] *vi*: **auf jdn** ~ rush at sb; (*Eindrücke*) overwhelm sb.
Einsturz [ĭn'shtōōrts] *m* collapse; ~**gefahr** *f* danger of collapse.
einstürzen [ĭn'shtürtsən] *vi* fall in, collapse; **auf jdn** ~ (*fig*) overwhelm sb.
einst- [ĭnst'] *zW*: ~**weilen** *ad* meanwhile; (*vorläufig*) temporarily, for the time being; ~**weilig** *a* temporary; ~**weilige Verfügung** (*JUR*) temporary *od* interim injunction.
eintägig [ĭn'te:giċh] *a* one-day.
Eintagsfliege [ĭn'tåksflē:gə] *f* (*ZOOL*) mayfly; (*fig*) nine days' wonder.
eintasten [ĭn'tåstən] *vt* (*Text*) key in.
eintauchen [ĭn'touҳhən] *vt* immerse, dip in ♦ *vi* dive.
eintauschen [ĭn'toushən] *vt* exchange.
eintausend [ĭn'touzənt] *num* one thousand.
einteilen [ĭn'tīlən] *vt* (*in Teile*) divide (up);

(*Menschen*) assign.
einteilig *a* one-piece.
eintönig [ĭn'tœniċh] *a* monotonous; **E~keit** *f* monotony.
Eintopf(gericht *nt*) [ĭn'topf(gəriċht)] *m* stew.
Eintracht [ĭn'tråҳht] *f* - concord, harmony.
einträchtig [ĭn'treċhtiċh] *a* harmonious.
Eintrag [ĭn'tråk] *m* -**(e)s**, ⁻**e** entry; **amtlicher** ~ entry in the register.
eintragen [ĭn'trågən] *unreg vt* (*in Buch*) enter; (*Profit*) yield; **jdm etw** ~ bring sb sth ♦ *vr* put one's name down.
einträglich [ĭn'tre:kliċh] *a* profitable.
Eintragung *f* entry (*in* +*akk* in).
eintreffen [ĭn'trefən] *vi unreg* happen; (*ankommen*) arrive; (*fig: wahr werden*) come true.
eintreiben [ĭn'trībən] *vt unreg* (*Geldbeträge*) collect.
eintreten [ĭn'trā:tən] *unreg vi* (*hineingehen*) enter (*in etw* (*akk*) sth); (*in Club, Partei*) join (*in etw* (*akk*) sth); (*sich ereignen*) occur; **für jdn/etw** ~ stand up for sb/sth ♦ *vt* (*Tür*) kick open.
eintrichtern [ĭn'triċhtərn] *vt* (*umg*): **jdm etw** ~ drum sth into sb.
Eintritt [ĭn'trit] *m* (*Betreten*) entrance; (*in Club etc*) joining; ~ **frei!** admission free; „~**verboten**" "no admittance"; **bei** ~ **der Dunkelheit** at nightfall.
Eintritts- *zW*: ~**geld** *nt*, ~**preis** *m* charge for admission; ~**karte** *f* (admission) ticket.
eintrocknen [ĭn'troknən] *vi* dry up.
eintrudeln [ĭn'trōō:dəln] *vi* (*umg*) drift in.
eintunken [ĭn'tōōngkən] *vt* (*Brot*) dunk (*in* +*akk* in).
einüben [ĭn'ü:bən] *vt* drill.
einverleiben [ĭn'ferlībən] *vt* incorporate; (*Gebiet*) annex; **sich** (*dat*) **etw** ~ (*fig: geistig*) assimilate sth.
Einvernehmen [ĭn'fernä:mən] *nt* -**s**, - agreement, understanding.
einverstanden [ĭn'fershtåndən] *interj* agreed ♦ *a*: ~ **sein** agree, be agreed **sich mit etw** ~ **erklären** give one's agreement to sth.
Einverständnis [ĭn'fershtentnis] *nt* -**ses** understanding; (*gleiche Meinung*) agreement; **im** ~ **mit jdm handeln** act with sb's consent.
Einwand [ĭn'vånt] *m* -**(e)s**, ⁻**e** objection; **einen** ~ **erheben** raise an objection.
Einwanderer [ĭn'våndərər] *m* immigrant.
einwandern *vi* immigrate.
Einwanderung *f* immigration.
einwandfrei *a* perfect; **etw** ~ **beweisen** prove sth beyond doubt.
einwärts [ĭn'verts] *ad* inwards.
einwecken [ĭn'vekən] *vt* bottle, preserve.
Einwegflasche [ĭn'vä:gflåshə] *f* non-returnable bottle.
einweichen [ĭn'viċhən] *vt* soak.
einweihen [ĭn'vīən] *vt* (*Kirche*) consecrate; (*Brücke*) open; (*Gebäude*) inaugurate; (*Person*) initiate (*in* +*akk* in); **er ist einge-**

weiht (*fig*) he knows all about it.
Einweihung *f* consecration; opening; inauguration; initiation.
einweisen [īn'vīzən] *vt unreg* (*in Amt*) install; (*in Arbeit*) introduce; (*in Anstalt*) send; (*in Krankenhaus*) admit (*in +akk -* to); (*AUT*) guide in (*in +akk -to*).
Einweisung *f* installation; introduction; sending.
einwenden [īn'vendən] *vt unreg* object, oppose (*gegen* to).
einwerfen [īn'verfən] *vt unreg* throw in; (*Brief*) post; (*Geld*) put in, insert; (*Fenster*) smash; (*äußern*) interpose.
einwickeln [īn'vikəln] *vt* wrap up; (*fig umg*) outsmart.
einwilligen [īn'viligən] *vi* consent, agree (*in +akk* to).
Einwilligung *f* consent.
einwirken [īn'virkən] *vi*: **auf jdn/etw** ~ influence sb/sth.
Einwirkung *f* influence.
Einwohner(in *f*) [īn'vō:nər(in)] *m* **-s,** - inhabitant; ~**mel'deamt** *nt* registration office; **sich beim** ~**meldeamt (an)melden** register with the police; ~**schaft** *f* population, inhabitants *pl*.
Einwurf [īn'vōōrf] *m* (*Öffnung*) slot; (*Einwand*) objection; (*SPORT*) throw-in.
Einzahl [īn'tsál] *f* singular.
einzahlen *vt* pay in.
Einzahlung *f* payment; (*auf Sparkonto auch*) deposit.
einzäunen [īn'tsoinən] *vt* fence in.
einzeichnen [īn'tsīçhnən] *vt* draw in.
Einzel [īn'tsəl] *nt* **-s,** - (*TENNIS*) singles *pl ♦ in zW* individual; single; ~**aufstellung** *f* (*COMM*) itemized list; ~**bett** *nt* single bed; ~**blattzuführung** *f* sheet feed; ~**fall** *m* single instance, individual case; ~**gänger(in** *f*) *m* loner; ~**haft** *f* solitary confinement; ~**handel** *m* retail trade; **im** ~**handel erhältlich** available retail.
Einzelhandels- *zW*: ~**geschäft** *nt* retail outlet; ~**preis** *m* retail price.
Einzel- *zW*: ~**händler** *m* retailer; ~**heit** *f* particular, detail; ~**kämpfermanier** *f* lone fighter manner; ~**kind** *nt* only child.
Einzeller [īn'tselər] *m* **-s,** - (*BIOL*) single-celled organism.
einzeln *a* single; (*von Paar*) odd ♦ *ad* singly; ~ **angeben** specify; ~**e** some (people), a few (people); **der/die** ~**e** the individual; **das** ~**e** the particular; **ins** ~**e gehen** go into detail(s); **etw im** ~**en besprechen** discuss sth in detail; ~ **aufführen** list separately *od* individually; **bitte** ~ **(eintreten)** please come in one (person) at a time.
Einzel- *zW*: ~**teil** *nt* individual part; (*Ersatzteil*) spare part; **etw in seine** ~**teile zerlegen** take sth to pieces, dismantle sth; ~**zimmer** *nt* single room.
einziehen [īn'tsē:ən] *unreg vt* draw in, take in; (*Kopf*) duck; (*Fühler, Antenne,*

Fahrgestell) retract; (*Steuern, Erkundigungen*) collect; (*MIL*) call up, draft (*US*); (*aus dem Verkehr ziehen*) withdraw; (*konfiszieren*) confiscate ♦ *vi* move in(to); (*Friede, Ruhe*) come; (*Flüssigkeit*) soak in (*in + akk* to).
einzig [īn'tsiçh] *a* only; (*ohnegleichen*) unique; **das** ~**e** the only thing; **der/die** ~**e** the only one; **kein** ~**es Mal** not once, not one single time; **kein** ~**er** nobody, not a single person ♦ *ad*: ~ **und allein** solely; ~**artig** *a* unique.
Einzug [īn'tsōō:k] *m* entry, moving in.
Einzugsbereich *m* catchment area.
Eis [īs] *nt* **-es,** - ice; (*Speise*~) ice cream; ~ **am Stiel** popsicle ® (*US*), ice(d)-lolly (*Brit*); ~**bahn** *f* ice *od* skating rink; ~**bär** *m* polar bear; ~**becher** *m* sundae; ~**bein** *nt* pig's feet *pl* (*US*) *od* trotters *pl* (*Brit*); ~**berg** *m* iceberg; ~**beutel** *m* ice pack.
Eischnee [īsh'nā:] *m* (*KOCH*) beaten white of egg.
Eis- *zW*: ~**decke** *f* sheet of ice; ~**diele** *f* ice-cream parlor.
Eisen [ī'zən] *nt* **-s,** - iron; **zum alten** ~ **gehören** (*fig*) be on the scrap heap; ~**bahn** *f* railroad (*US*), railway (*Brit*); **es ist (aller)höchste** ~**bahn** (*umg*) it's high time; ~**bahner** *m* **-s,** - railroader (*US*), railway employee (*Brit*); ~**bahnnetz** *nt* rail network; ~**bahnschaffner** *m* (railroad) conductor (*US*), railway guard (*Brit*); ~**bahnüberführung** *f* footbridge; ~**bahnübergang** *m* grade crossing (*US*), level crossing (*Brit*); ~**bahnwagen** *m* railroad carriage; ~**bahnwaggon** *m* (*Güterwagen*) goods wagon; ~**erz** *nt* iron ore; **e**~**haltig** *a* containing iron; ~**mangel** *m* iron deficiency; ~**warenhandlung** *f* hardware store.
eisern [ī'zərn] *a* iron; (*Gesundheit*) robust; (*Energie*) unrelenting; (*Reserve*) emergency; **der E**~**e Vorhang** the Iron Curtain; **in etw** ~ **sein** be adamant about sth; **er ist** ~ **bei seinem Entschluß geblieben** he stuck firmly to his decision.
Eis- *zW*: ~**fach** *nt* freezer compartment, icebox; **e**~**frei** *a* clear of ice; **e**~**gekühlt** *a* chilled; ~**hockey** *nt* ice hockey.
eisig [ī'ziçh] *a* icy.
Eis- *zW*: **e**~**kalt** *a* icy cold; ~**kunstlauf** *m* figure skating; ~**laufen** *nt* ice skating; ~**läufer** *m* ice-skater; ~**meer** *nt*: **Nördliches/Südliches** ~**meer** Arctic/Antarctic Ocean; ~**pickel** *m* ice-ax.
Eisprung [īsh'prōōng] *m* ovulation.
Eis- *zW*: ~**schießen** *nt* ≈ curling; ~**scholle** *f* ice floe; ~**schrank** *m* fridge, icebox (*US*); ~**zapfen** *m* icicle; ~**zeit** *f* Ice Age.
eitel [ī'təl] *a* vain; **E**~**keit** *f* vanity.
Eiter [ī'tər] *m* **-s** pus.
eiterig *a* suppurating.
eitern *vi* suppurate.
Ei- [ī] *zW*: ~**weiß** *nt* **-es,** **-e** white of an egg; (*CHEM*) protein; ~**weißgehalt** *m* protein

content; ~**zelle** f ovum.
EK nt abk (= Eisernes Kreuz) military honor.
EKD f abk = Evangelische Kirche In Deutschland.
Ekel [ā:'kəl] m -s nausea, disgust; **vor jdm/ etw einen ~ haben** loathe sb/sth ◆ nt -s, - (umg: Mensch) nauseating person; **e~erregend, e~haft, ek(e)lig** a nauseating, disgusting.
ekeln vt disgust; **es ekelt jdn** od **jdm** sb is disgusted ◆ vr loathe, be disgusted (vor +dat at).
EKG, Ekg nt - abk = Elektrokardiogramm.
Eklat [āklā'] m -s (geh: Aufsehen) sensation.
Ekstase [ekstā'zə] f -, -n ecstasy; **jdn in ~ versetzen** send sb into ecstasies.
Ekzem [ektsā:m'] nt -s, -e (MED) eczema.
Elan [ālân'] m -s elan.
elastisch [ālás'tish] a elastic.
Elastizität [ālástētsēte:t'] f elasticity.
Elbe [el'bə] f (Fluß) Elbe.
Elch [elċh] m -(e)s, -e elk.
Elefant [ālāfánt'] m elephant; **wie ein ~ im Porzellanladen** (umg) like a bull in a china shop.
elegant [ālāgánt'] a elegant.
Eleganz [ālāgánts'] f elegance.
Elektrifizierung [ālektrēfētsē:'rōong] f electrification.
Elektriker [ālek'trēkər] m -s, - electrician.
elektrisch [ālek'trish] a electric.
Elektrische f -n, -n (veraltet) streetcar (US), tram (Brit).
elektrisieren [ālektrēzē:'rən] vt (lit, fig) electrify; (Mensch) give an electric shock to ◆ vr get an electric shock.
Elektrizität [ālektrētsēte:t'] f electricity.
Elektrizitätswerk nt electric power station; (Gesellschaft) electric power company.
Elektroartikel [ālek'trōártikəl] m electrical appliance.
Elektrode [ālektrō:'də] f -, -n electrode.
Elektro- [ālektrō] zW: **~ge'rät** nt electrical appliance; **~'herd** m (electric) stove; **~kardio'gramm** nt (MED) electrocardiogram.
Elektrolyse [ālāktrōlü:'zə] f -, -n electrolysis.
Elektron [ālek'tron] nt -s, -en electron.
Elektronen- [ālektrō:'nən-] zW: **~(ge)hirn** nt electronic brain; **~rechner** m computer.
Elektronik [ālektrō:'nik] f electronics sing; (Teile) electronics pl.
elektronisch a electronic; **~e Post** electronic mail.
Elektro- zW: **~rasierer** m -s, - electric razor; **~schock** m (MED) electric shock, electroshock; **~techniker** m electrician; (Ingenieur) electrical engineer.
Element [ālāment'] nt -s, -e element; (ELEK) cell, battery.
elementar [ālāmentâr'] a elementary; (naturhaft) elemental; **E~teilchen** nt (PHYS) elementary particle.
Elend [ā:'lent] nt -(e)s misery; **da kann man**

das heulende ~ kriegen (umg) it's enough to make you scream; **e~** a miserable; **mir ist ganz e~** I feel really awful.
elendiglich [ā:'lendikliċh] ad miserably; **~ zugrunde gehen** come to a wretched end.
Elendsviertel nt slum.
elf [elf] num eleven; **E~** f -, -en (SPORT) eleven.
Elfe f -, -n elf.
Elfenbein nt ivory; **~küste** f Ivory Coast.
Elfmeter m (SPORT) penalty (kick).
eliminieren [ālēmēnē:'rən] vt eliminate.
elitär [ālēte:r'] a elitist ◆ ad in an elitist fashion.
Elite [ālē:'tə] f -, -n elite.
Elixier [āliksē:r'] nt -s, -e elixir.
Elle [e'lə] f -, -n ell; (Maß) ≈ yard.
Ell(en)bogen m elbow; **die ~ gebrauchen** (fig) be pushy (umg) od ruthless; **~freiheit** f (fig) elbow room; **~gesellschaft** f dog-eat-dog society.
Ellipse [elip'sə] f -, -n ellipse.
E-Lok [ā:'lok] f - abk (= elektrische Lokomotive) electric locomotive od engine.
Elsaß [el'zás] nt: **das ~** Alsace.
Elsässer(in f) [el'zesər(in)] m -s, - Alsatian, inhabitant of Alsace.
Elsässer, elsässisch a Alastian.
Elster [els'tər] f -, -n magpie.
elterlich a parental.
Eltern [el'tərn] pl parents pl; **nicht von schlechten ~ sein** (umg) be quite something; **~abend** m (SCH) parents' evening; **~haus** nt home; **e~los** a orphaned; **~sprechtag** m open house (for parents); **~teil** m parent.
Email [āmây'] nt -s, -s enamel.
emaillieren [āmáyē:'rən] vt enamel.
Emanze f -, -n (meist pej) women's libber (umg).
Emanzipation [āmántsēpátsēō:n'] f emancipation.
emanzipieren [āmántsēpē:'rən] vt emancipate.
Embargo [embár'gō] nt -s, -s embargo.
Embryo [em'brüō] m -s, -s od -nen embryo.
Emigrant(in f) [āmēgránt'(in)] m emigrant.
Emigration [āmēgrátsēō:n'] f emigration.
emigrieren [āmēgrē:'rən] vi emigrate.
Emissionskurs [āmisēō:ns'kōōrs] m (Aktien) issued price.
EMNID m abk (= Erforschung, Meinung, Nachrichten, Informationsdienst) ≈ Gallup od MORI poll.
emotional [āmōtsēōnâl'] a emotional; (Ausdrucksweise) emotive.
emotionsgeladen [āmōtsēō:ns'gəlâdən] a emotionally-charged.
Empf. abk = Empfänger.
empfahl [empfâl'] imperf von **empfehlen**.
empfand [empfánt'] imperf von **empfinden**.
Empfang [empfáng'] m -(e)s, ¨e reception; (Erhalten) receipt; **in ~ nehmen** receive; **(zahlbar) nach** od **bei ~** (+gen) (payable)

on receipt (of).

empfangen *unreg vt* receive ♦ *vi* (*schwanger werden*) conceive.

Empfänger(in *f*) |ɛmpfɛ'ngər(in)| *m* **-s,** - receiver; (*COMM*) addressee, consignee; ~ **unbekannt** (*auf Briefen*) not known at this address.

empfänglich *a* receptive, susceptible.

Empfängnis *f* -, **-se** conception; **e~verhütend** *a*: **e~verhütend Mittel** *pl* contraceptives *pl*; ~**verhütung** *f* contraception.

Empfangs- *zW*: ~**bestätigung** *f* (acknowledgement of) receipt; ~**chef** *m* (*von Hotel*) head porter; ~**dame** *f* receptionist; ~**schein** *m* receipt; ~**störung** *f* (*RAD, TV*) interference; ~**zimmer** *nt* reception room.

empfehlen |ɛmpfä:'lən| *unreg vt* recommend ♦ *vr* take one's leave.

empfehlenswert *a* recommendable.

Empfehlung *f* recommendation; **auf** ~ **von** on the recommendation of.

Empfehlungsschreiben *nt* letter of recommendation.

empfiehlt |ɛmpfē:lt'| *3. pers sing präs von* **empfehlen.**

empfinden |ɛmpfin'dən| *vt unreg* feel; **etw als Beleidigung** ~ find sth insulting; **E~** *nt* **-s: meinem E~ nach** to my mind.

empfindlich *a* sensitive; (*Stelle*) sore; (*reizbar*) touchy; **deine Kritik hat ihn** ~ **getroffen** your criticism cut him to the quick; **E~keit** *f* sensitiveness; (*Reizbarkeit*) touchiness.

empfindsam *a* sentimental; (*Mensch*) sensitive.

Empfindung *f* feeling, sentiment.

empfindungslos *a* unfeeling, insensitive.

empfing |ɛmpfing'| *imperf von* **empfangen.**

empfohlen |ɛmpfō:'lən| *a*: ~**er Einzelhandelspreis** recommended retail price ♦ *pp von* **empfehlen.**

empf. Rpr. *abk* (= *empfohlener Richtpreis*) RRP.

empfunden |ɛmpfoon'dən| *pp von* **empfinden.**

empor |ɛmpō:r'| *ad* up, upwards.

emporarbeiten *vr* (*geh*) work one's way up.

Empore |ɛmpō:'rə| *f* -, **-n** (*ARCHIT*) gallery.

empören |ɛmpœ'rən| *vt* make indignant; shock ♦ *vr* become indignant.

empörend *a* outrageous.

empor- *zW*: ~**kommen** *vi unreg* rise; (*vorankommen*) succeed; **E~kömmling** *m* upstart, parvenu.

empört *a* indignant, outraged (*über* +*akk* at).

Empörung *f* indignation.

emsig |ɛm'ziçh| *a* diligent, busy.

End- |ɛnt'| *in zW* final; ~**auswertung** *f* final analysis; ~**bahnhof** *m* terminus; ~**betrag** *m* final amount.

Ende |ɛn'də| *nt* **-s, -n** end; **am** ~ at the end;

(*schließlich*) in the end; **am** ~ **sein** be at the end of one's tether; ~ **Dezember** at the end of December; **zu** ~ **sein** be finished; **zu** ~ **gehen** come to an end; **etw zu** ~ **führen** finish (off) sth; **letzten** ~**s** in the end, at the end of the day (*auch fig*); **ein böses** ~ **nehmen** come to a bad end; **ich bin mit meiner Weisheit am** ~ I'm at my wits' end; **er wohnt am** ~ **der Welt** (*umg*) he lives at the end of the world.

enden *vi* end.

End- *zW*: ~**ergebnis** *nt* final result; **e~gültig** *a* final, definite.

Endivie |ɛndē:'vēə| *f* endive.

End- *zW*: ~**lagerung** *f* permanent disposal; **e~lich** *a* final; (*MATH*) finite ♦ *ad* finally; **e~lich!** at last!; **hör e~lich damit auf!** will you stop that!; **e~los** *a* endless, infinite; **E~lospapier** *nt* fan-fold paper; ~**produkt** *nt* end *od* final product; ~**spiel** *nt* final(s); ~**spurt** *m* (*SPORT*) final spurt; ~**station** *f* terminus; ~**ung** |ɛn'doong| *f* ending; ~**verbraucher** *m* consumer, end-user.

Energie |ānɛrgē:'| *f* energy; ~**aufwand** *m* energy expenditure; ~**einsparung** *f* energy saving; ~**gewinnung** *f* generation of energy; **e~los** *a* lacking in energy, weak; ~**versorgung** *f* supply of energy; ~**wirtschaft** *f* energy industry.

energisch |ānɛr'gish| *a* energetic; ~ **durchgreifen** take vigorous *od* firm action.

eng |ɛng| *a* narrow; (*Kleidung*) tight; (*fig: Horizont auch*) limited; (*Freundschaft, Verhältnis*) close; ~ **an etw** (*dat*) close to sth; **in die** ~**ere Wahl kommen** be on the short list.

Engagement |āṅgàzhəmâṅ'| *nt* **-s, -s** engagement; (*Verpflichtung*) commitment.

engagieren |āṅgàzhē:'rən| *vt* engage ♦ *vr* commit o.s.; **ein engagierter Schriftsteller** a committed writer.

Enge |ɛ'ngə| *f* -, **-n** (*lit, fig*) narrowness; (*Land~*) defile; (*Meer~*) straits *pl*; **jdn in die** ~ **treiben** drive sb into a corner.

Engel |ɛ'ngəl| *m* **-s,** - angel; **e~haft** *a* angelic; ~**macher(in** *f*) *m* **-s,** - (*umg*) backstreet abortionist.

Engels- *zW*: ~**geduld** *f*: **sie hat eine** ~**geduld** she has the patience of a saint; ~**zungen** *pl*: **(wie) mit** ~**zungen reden** use all one's own powers of persuasion.

engherzig *a* petty.

engl. *abk* = **englisch.**

England |ɛng'lànt| *nt* England.

Engländer |ɛng'lɛndər| *m* **-s,** - Englishman; English boy; **die** ~ *pl* the English; the British.

Engländerin *f* Englishwoman; English girl.

englisch |ɛng'lish| *a* English; **E~(e)** *nt* English.

engmaschig |ɛng'màshiçh| *a* close-meshed.

Engpaß *m* defile, pass; (*fig: Verkehr*) bottleneck.

en gros |āṅgrō'| *ad* wholesale.

engstirnig [eng'shtirnich] *a* narrow-minded.
Enkel [eng'kǝl] *m* **-s, -** grandson; ~**in** *f* granddaughter; ~**kind** *nt* grandchild.
en masse [ånmås'] *ad* en masse.
enorm [ānorm'] *a* enormous; (*umg:* *herrlich, kolossal*) tremendous.
en passant [ånpásån'] *ad* en passant, in passing.
Ensemble [ånsån'bǝl] *nt* **-s, -s** company, ensemble.
entarten [entår'tān] *vi* degenerate.
entbehren [entbā:'rǝn] *vt* do without, dispense with.
entbehrlich *a* superfluous.
Entbehrung *f* privation; ~**en auf sich** (*akk*) **nehmen** make sacrifices.
entbinden [entbin'dǝn] *unreg vt* release (*gen* from); (*MED*) deliver ♦ *vi* (*MED*) give birth.
Entbindung *f* release; (*MED*) confinement.
Entbindungs- *zW:* ~**heim** *nt* maternity hospital; ~**station** *f* maternity ward.
entblößen [entblœ'sǝn] *vt* denude, uncover; (*berauben*) deprive (*gen* of).
entbrennen [entbre'nǝn] *vi unreg* (*liter: Kampf, Streit*) flare up; (*Liebe*) be aroused.
entdecken [entde'kǝn] *vt* discover; **jdm etw** ~ disclose sth to sb.
Entdecker(in *f*) *m* **-s, -** discoverer.
Entdeckung *f* discovery.
Ente [en'tǝ] *f* **-, -n** duck; (*fig*) canard, false report; (*AUT*) Citroen 2CV, deux-chevaux.
entehren [entā:'rǝn] *vt* dishonor (*US*), dishonour (*Brit*), disgrace.
enteignen [entīg'nǝn] *vt* expropriate; (*Besitzer*) dispossess.
enteisen [entī'zǝn] *vt* de-ice; (*Kühlschrank*) defrost.
enterben [enter'bǝn] *vt* disinherit.
Enterhaken [en'tǝrhåkǝn] *m* grappling iron *od* hook.
entfachen [entfå'khǝn] *vt* kindle.
entfallen [entfál'lǝn] *vi unreg* drop, fall; (*wegfallen*) be dropped; **jdm** ~ (*vergessen*) slip sb's memory; **auf jdn** ~ be allotted to sb.
entfalten [entfál'tǝn] *vt* unfold; (*Talente*) develop ♦ *vr* open; (*Mensch*) develop one's potential.
Entfaltung *f* unfolding; (*von Talenten*) development.
entfernen [entfer'nǝn] *vt* remove; (*hinauswerfen*) expel ♦ *vr* go away, retire, withdraw.
entfernt *a* distant; **weit davon** ~ **sein, etw zu tun** be far from doing sth ♦ *ad*: **nicht im** ~**esten!** not in the slightest!
Entfernung *f* distance; (*Wegschaffen*) removal; **unerlaubte** ~ **von der Truppe** absence without leave.
Entfernungsmesser *m* (*PHOT*) rangefinder.
entfesseln [entfe'sǝln] *vt* (*fig*) arouse.
entfetten [entfe'tǝn] *vt* take the fat from.
entflammen [entflå'mǝn] *vt* (*fig*) (a)rouse ♦ *vi* burst into flames; (*fig: Streit*) flare up;

(*Leidenschaft*) be (a)roused *od* inflamed.
entfremden [entfrem'dǝn] *vt* estrange, alienate.
Entfremdung *f* estrangement, alienation.
entfrosten [entfros'tǝn] *vt* defrost.
Entfroster *m* **-s, -** (*AUT*) defroster.
entführen [entfü:'rǝn] *vt* abduct; kidnap; (*Flugzeug*) hijack.
Entführer *m* **-s, -** kidnaper (*US*), kidnapper (*Brit*); hijacker.
Entführung *f* abduction; kidnaping (*US*), kidnapping (*Brit*); hijacking.
entgegen [entgā:'gǝn] *präp* +*dat* contrary to, against ♦ *ad* towards; ~**bringen** *vt unreg* bring; (*fig*) show (*jdm etw* sb sth); ~**gehen** *vi unreg* (+*dat*) go to meet, go towards; **Schwierigkeiten** ~**gehen** be heading for difficulties; ~**gesetzt** *a* opposite; (*widersprechend*) opposed; ~**halten** *vt unreg* (*fig*) object; ~**kommen** *vi unreg* (+*dat*) come towards, approach; (*fig*) accommodate (*jdm* sb); **das kommt unseren Plänen sehr entgegen** that fits in very well with our plans; **E~kommen** *nt* obligingness; ~**kommend** *a* obliging; ~**laufen** *vi unreg* (+*dat*) run towards *od* to meet; (*fig*) run counter to; **E~nahme** *f* (*form: Empfang*) receipt; (*Annahme*) acceptance; ~**nehmen** *vt unreg* receive, accept; ~**sehen** *vi unreg* (+*dat*) await; ~**setzen** *vt* oppose (*dat* to); **dem habe ich entgegenzusetzen, daß** ... against that I'd like to say that ...; **jdm/einer Sache Widerstand** ~**setzen** put up resistance to sb/sth; ~**stehen** *vi unreg* (+*dat*): **dem steht nichts entgegen** there's no objection to that; ~**treten** *vi unreg* (+*dat*) (*lit*) step up to; (*fig*) oppose, counter; ~**wirken** *vi* (+*dat*) counteract.
entgegnen [entgā:g'nǝn] *vt* reply, retort.
Entgegnung *f* reply, retort.
entgehen [entgā:'ǝn] *vi unreg* (*fig*): **jdm** ~ escape sb's notice; **sich** (*dat*) **etw** ~ **lassen** miss sth.
entgeistert [entgīs'tǝrt] *a* thunderstruck.
Entgelt [entgelt'] *nt* **-(e)s, -e** remuneration.
entgelten *vt unreg*: **jdm etw** ~ repay sb for sth.
entgleisen [entglī'zǝn] *vi* (*EISENB*) be derailed; (*fig: Person*) misbehave; ~ **lassen** derail.
Entgleisung *f* derailment; (*fig*) faux pas, gaffe.
entgleiten [entglī'tǝn] *vi unreg* slip (*jdm* from sb's hand).
entgräten [åntgre:'tǝn] *vt* fillet, bone.
Enthaarungsmittel [enthå'rōōngsmitǝl] *nt* depilatory.
enthält [enthelt'] *3. pers sing präs von* **enthalten**.
enthalten [enthál'tǝn] *unreg vt* contain ♦ *vr* abstain, refrain (*gen* from); **sich (der Stimme)** ~ abstain.
enthaltsam [enthált'zåm] *a* abstinent, abstemious; **E~keit** *f* abstinence.

enthärten [enther'tən] *vt* (*Wasser*) soften; (*Metall*) anneal.
enthaupten [enthoup'tən] *vt* decapitate; (*als Hinrichtung auch*) behead.
enthäuten [enthoi'tən] *vt* skin.
entheben [enthä:'bən] *vt unreg*: **jdn einer Sache** (*gen*) ~ relieve sb of sth.
enthemmen [enthe'mən] *vt*: **jdn** ~ free sb from his inhibitions.
enthielt [enthē:lt'] *imperf von* **enthalten**.
enthüllen [enthü'lən] *vt* reveal, unveil.
Enthusiasmus [entōōzēās'mōōs] *m* enthusiasm.
entjungfern [entyōōng'fərn] *vt* deflower.
entkalken [entkál'kən] *vt* decalcify.
entkernen [entker'nən] *vt* core; stone.
entkleiden [entklī'dən] *vtr* (*geh*) undress.
entkommen [entko'mən] *vi unreg* get away, escape (*dat, aus* from).
entkorken [entkor'kən] *vt* uncork.
entkräften [entkref'tən] *vt* weaken, exhaust; (*Argument*) refute.
entkrampfen [entkrám'pfən] *vt* (*fig*) relax, ease.
entladen [entlâ'dən] *unreg vt* unload; (*ELEK*) discharge ♦ *vr* (*ELEK, Gewehr*) discharge; (*Ärger etc*) vent itself.
entlang [entlâng'] *präp +akk od dat, ad* along; ~ **dem Fluß, den Fluß** ~ along the river; **hier** ~ this way; ~**gehen** *vi unreg* walk along.
entlarven [entlár'fən] *vt* unmask, expose.
entlassen [entlá'sən] *vt unreg* discharge; (*Arbeiter*) dismiss; (*nach Stellenabbau*) make redundant.
entläßt [entlest'] *2./3. pers sing präs von* **entlassen**.
Entlassung *f* discharge; dismissal; **es gab 20** ~**en** there were 20 redundancies.
Entlassungs- *zW*: ~**abfindung** *f* lay-off/ redundancy payment; ~**zeugnis** *nt* (*SCH*) school leaving certificate.
entlasten [entlás'tən] *vt* relieve; (*Achse*) relieve the load on; (*Angeklagte*) exonerate; (*Konto*) clear.
Entlastung *f* relief; (*COMM*) crediting.
Entlastungs- *zW*: ~**zeuge** *m* defense (*US*) *od* defence (*Brit*) witness; ~**zug** *m* relief train.
entledigen [entlā:'digən] *vr*: **sich jds/einer Sache** ~ rid o.s. of sb/sth.
entleeren [entlā:'rən] *vt* empty; (*Darm*) evacuate.
entlegen [entlā:'gən] *a* remote.
entließ [entlē:s'] *imperf von* **entlassen**.
entlocken [entlo'kən] *vt* elicit (*jdm etw* sth from sb).
entlohnen *vt* pay; (*fig*) reward.
entlüften [entlüf'tən] *vt* ventilate.
entmachten [entmáḵh'tən] *vt* deprive of power.
entmenscht [entmensht'] *a* inhuman, bestial.
entmilitarisiert [entmēlētárēzē:rt'] *a* demilitarized.

entmündigen [entmün'digən] *vt* certify; (*JUR*) (legally) incapacitate, declare incapable of managing one's own affairs.
entmutigen [entmōō'tigən] *vt* discourage.
Entnahme [entnâ'mə] *f* -, -**n** removal, withdrawal.
Entnazifizierung [entnátsēfētsē:'rōōng] *f* denazification.
entnehmen [entnā:'mən] *vt unreg* (+*dat*) take out (of), take (from); (*folgern*) infer (from); **wie ich Ihren Worten entnehme, ...** I gather from what you say that ...
entpuppen [entpōō'pən] *vr* (*fig*) reveal o.s., turn out (*als* to be).
entrahmen [entrâ'mən] *vt* skim.
entreißen [entrī'sən] *vt unreg* snatch (away) (*jdm etw* sth from sb).
Entrepreneur [ántrəprənœr'] *m* entrepreneur.
entrichten [entriḵh'tən] *vt* (*form*) pay.
entrosten [entros'tən] *vt* derust.
entrüsten [entrüs'tən] *vt* incense, outrage ♦ *vr* be filled with indignation.
entrüstet *a* indignant, outraged.
Entrüstung *f* indignation.
Entsafter [entzáf'tər] *m* -**s**, - juice extractor.
entsagen [entzá'gən] *vi* renounce (*dat* sth).
entschädigen [entshe:'digən] *vt* compensate.
Entschädigung *f* compensation.
entschärfen [entsher'fən] *vt* defuse; (*Kritik*) tone down.
Entscheid [entshīt'] *m* -(**e**)**s**, -**e** (*form*) decision.
entscheiden *vtir unreg* decide; **darüber habe ich nicht zu** ~ that is not for me to decide; **sich für jdn/etw** ~ decide in favor of sb/sth, decide on sb/sth.
entscheidend *a* decisive; (*Stimme*) casting; **das E**~**e** the decisive *od* deciding factor.
Entscheidung *f* decision; **wie ist die** ~ **ausgefallen?** which way did the decision go?
Entscheidungs- *zW*: ~**befugnis** *f* decision-making powers *pl*; **e**~**fähig** *a* capable of deciding; ~**spiel** *nt* play-off.
entschied [entshē:t'] *imperf von* **entscheiden**.
entschieden [entshē:'dən] *a* decided; (*entschlossen*) resolute; **das geht** ~ **zu weit** that's definitely going too far ♦ *pp von* **entscheiden**; **E**~**heit** *f* firmness, determination.
entschlacken [entshlá'kən] *vt* (*MED: Körper*) purify.
entschließen [entshlē:'sən] *vr unreg* decide; **sich zu nichts** ~ **können** be unable to make up one's mind; **kurz entschlossen** straight away.
Entschließungsantrag *m* (*POL*) resolution proposal.
entschloß [entshlos'] *imperf von* **entschließen**.
entschlossen [entshlo'sən] *a* determined, resolute ♦ *pp von* **entschließen**; **E**~**heit** *f* determination.
entschlüpfen [entshlü'pfən] *vi* escape, slip away; (*fig: Wort etc*) slip out.

Entschluß [entshlōōs'] *m* decision; **aus eige-nem ~ handeln** act on one's own initiative; **es ist mein fester ~** it is my firm intention.
entschlüsseln [entshlü'səln] *vt* decipher; (*Funkspruch auch*) decode.
Entschluß- *zW*: **e~freudig** *a* decisive; **~kraft** *f* determination, decisiveness.
entschuldbar [entshōōlt'bår] *a* excusable.
entschuldigen [entshōōl'digən] *vt* excuse; **jdn bei jdm ~** make sb's excuses *od* apologies to sb ♦ *vr* apologize; **sich ~ lassen** send one's apologies ♦ *vi*: **~ Sie (bitte)!** excuse me; (*Verzeihung*) sorry.
Entschuldigung *f* apology; (*Grund*) excuse; **jdn um ~ bitten** apologize to sb; **~!** excuse me; (*Verzeihung*) sorry.
entschwefeln [entshve:'fəln] *vt* desulphurize.
entschwinden [entshvin'dən] *vi unreg* disappear.
entsetzen [entze'tsən] *vt* horrify ♦ *vr* be horrified *od* appalled; **E~** *nt* **-s** horror, dismay.
entsetzlich *a* dreadful, appalling.
entsetzt *a* horrified.
entsichern [entzi'çhərn] *vt* release the safety catch of.
entsinnen [entzi'nən] *vr unreg* remember (*gen* sth).
entsorgen [entzor'gən] *vt*: **eine Stadt ~** dispose of a town's refuse and sewage.
Entsorgungspark *m* (nuclear) waste dump.
entspannen [entshpá'nən] *vtr* (*Körper*) relax; (*POL: Lage*) ease.
Entspannung *f* relaxation, rest; (*POL*) détente.
Entspannungs- *zW*: **~politik** *f* policy of détente; **~übungen** *pl* relaxation exercises *pl*.
entspr. *abk* = **entsprechend.**
entsprach [entshpràkh'] *imperf von* **entsprechen.**
entsprechen [entshpre'çhən] *vi unreg* (+*dat*) correspond to; (*Anforderungen, Wünschen*) meet, comply with.
entsprechend *a* appropriate ♦ *ad* accordingly ♦ *präp* +*dat*: **er wird seiner Leistung ~ bezahlt** he is paid according to output.
entspricht [entshpriçht'] *3. pers sing präs von* **entsprechen.**
entspringen [entshpri'ngən] *vi unreg* spring (from).
entsprochen [entshpro'khən] *pp von* **entsprechen.**
entstaatlichen [entshtá'tliçhən] *vt* denationalize.
entstand [entshtánt'] *imperf von* **entstehen.**
entstanden [entshtán'dən] *pp von* **entstehen.**
entstehen [entshtā:'ən] *vi unreg* arise, result; **wir wollen nicht den Eindruck ~ lassen, ...** we don't want to give rise to the impression that ...; **für entstehenden** *od* **entstandenen Schaden** for damages incurred.
Entstehung *f* genesis, origin.
entstellen [entshte'lən] *vt* disfigure; (*Wahrheit*) distort.

Entstellung *f* distortion; disfigurement.
entstören [entshtœ'rən] *vt* (*RAD*) eliminate interference from; (*AUT*) suppress.
enttäuschen [enttoi'shən] *vt* disappoint.
Enttäuschung *f* disappointment.
entwachsen [entvàk'sən] *vi unreg* +*dat* outgrow, grow out of; (*geh: herauswachsen aus*) spring from.
entwaffnen [entváf'nən] *vt* (*lit, fig*) disarm.
Entwarnung [entvàr'nōōng] *f* all clear (signal).
entwässern [entve'sərn] *vt* drain.
Entwässerung *f* drainage.
entweder [entvā:'dər] *kj* either; **~ ... oder ...** either ... or ...
entweichen [entvī'çhən] *vi unreg* escape.
entweihen [entvī'ən] *vt unreg* desecrate.
entwenden [entven'dən] *vt unreg* purloin, steal.
entwerfen [entver'fən] *vt unreg* (*Zeichnung*) sketch; (*Modell*) design; (*Vortrag, Gesetz etc*) draft.
entwerten [entvā:r'tən] *vt* devalue; (*stempeln*) cancel.
Entwerter *m* **-s, -** ticket-validating machine.
entwickeln [entvi'kəln] *vtr* develop (*auch PHOT*); (*Mut, Energie*) show, display.
Entwickler *m* **-s, -** developer.
Entwicklung [entvi'klōōng] *f* development; (*PHOT*) developing; **in der ~** at the development stage; (*Jugendliche etc*) still developing.
Entwicklungs- *zW*: **~abschnitt** *m* stage of development; **~dienst** *m* ≈ Peace Corps (*US*); **~helfer(in** *f*) *m* Peace Corps worker; **~hilfe** *f* aid for developing countries; **~jahre** *pl* adolescence *sing*; **~land** *nt* developing country; **~zeit** *f* period of development; (*PHOT*) developing time.
entwirren [entvi'rən] *vt* disentangle.
entwischen [entvi'shən] *vi* escape.
entwöhnen [entvœ'nən] *vt* wean; (*Süchtige*) cure (*dat, von* of).
Entwöhnung *f* weaning; cure, curing.
entwürdigend [entvür'digənt] *a* degrading.
Entwurf [entvōōrf'] *m* outline, design; (*Vertrags~, Konzept*) draft.
entwurzeln [entvōōr'tsəln] *vt* uproot.
entziehen [enttsē:'ən] *unreg vt* withdraw, take away (*dat* from); (*Flüssigkeit*) draw, extract ♦ *vr* escape (*dat* from); (*jds Kenntnis*) be outside; (*der Pflicht*) shirk; **sich jds Blicken ~** be hidden from sight.
Entziehung *f* withdrawal.
Entziehungs- *zW*: **~anstalt** *f* drug addiction/alcoholism treatment unit; **~kur** *f* treatment for drug addiction/alcoholism.
entziffern [enttsi'fərn] *vt* decipher; (*Funkspruch*) decode.
entzücken [enttsü'kən] *vt* delight; **E~** *nt* **-s** delight.
entzückend *a* delightful, charming.
Entzug [enttsōō:k'] *m* **-(e)s** (*einer Lizenz etc, MED*) withdrawal.

Entzugserscheinung ƒ withdrawal symptom.

entzündbar a: **leicht ~** highly inflammable; (fig) easily roused.

entzünden [enttsün'dən] vt light, set light to; (fig, MED) inflame; (Streit) spark off ♦ vr (lit, fig) catch fire; (Streit) start; (MED) become inflamed.

Entzündung ƒ (MED) inflammation.

entzwei [enttsvī'] ad in two; broken; **~brechen** vti unreg break in two.

entzweien vt set at odds ♦ vr fall out.

entzweigehen vi unreg break (in two).

Enzian [en'tsēân] m -s, -e gentian.

Enzyklika [entsü:'klēkâ] ƒ -, -liken (REL) encyclical.

Enzyklopädie [entsüklōpedē:'] ƒ encyclopedia.

Enzym [entsü:m'] nt -s, -e enzyme.

Epidemie [āpēdāmē:'] ƒ epidemic.

Epilepsie [āpēlāpsē:'] ƒ epilepsy.

episch [ā:'pish] a epic.

Episode [āpēzō:'də] ƒ -, -n episode.

Epoche [āpo'қhə] ƒ -, -n epoch; **e~machend** a epoch-making.

Epos [ā:'pos] nt -, **Epen** epic (poem).

Equipe [ākip'] ƒ -, -n team.

er [ā:r] pron he; it.

erachten [eráқh'tən] vt (geh): **~ für** od **als** consider (to be); **meines E~s** in my opinion.

erarbeiten [erár'bītən] vt (auch **sich** (dat) **~**) work for, acquire; (Theorie) work out.

Erbanlage [erp'ánlâgə] ƒ hereditary factor(s pl).

erbarmen [erbár'mən] vr have pity od mercy (gen on); **Herr, erbarme dich (unser)!** Lord, have mercy (upon us)! ♦ vt: **er sieht zum E~ aus** he's a pitiful sight; **E~** nt -s pity.

erbärmlich [erberm'liқh] a wretched, pitiful; **E~keit** ƒ wretchedness.

Erbarmungs- [erbár'mŏŏngs] zW: **e~los** a pitiless, merciless; **e~voll** a compassionate; **e~würdig** a pitiable, wretched.

erbauen [erbou'ən] vt build, erect; (fig) edify; **er ist von meinem Plan nicht besonders erbaut** (umg) he isn't particularly enthusiastic about my plan.

Erbauer m -s, - builder.

erbaulich a edifying.

Erbauung ƒ construction; (fig) edification.

Erbbauzins [erp'boutsins] m ground rent.

erbberechtigt a entitled to inherit.

erbbiologisch a: **~es Gutachten** (JUR) blood test (to establish paternity).

Erbe [er'bə] m -n, -n heir; **jdn zum** od **als ~n einsetzen** make sb one's od sb's heir ♦ nt -s inheritance; (fig) heritage).

erben vt inherit; (umg: geschenkt bekommen) get, be given.

erbeuten [erboi'tən] vt carry off; (MIL) capture.

Erb- [erp'] zW: **~faktor** m gene; **~fehler** m hereditary defect; **~feind** m traditional od arch enemy; **~folge** ƒ (line of) succession.

Erbin ƒ heiress.

erbittern [erbi'tərn] vt embitter; (erzürnen) incense.

erbittert [erbi'tərt] a (Kampf) fierce, bitter.

erblassen [erblá'sən] vi siehe **erbleichen**.

Erblasser(in ƒ) m -s, - (JUR) person who leaves an inheritance.

erbleichen [erblī'қhən] vi unreg (turn) pale.

erblich [er'pliқh] a hereditary; **er ist ~ (vor)belastet** it runs in the family.

erblinden pp von **erbleichen**.

erblinden [erblin'dən] vi go blind.

Erbmasse [erp'másə] ƒ estate; (BIOL) genotype.

erbosen [erbō:'zən] vt (geh) anger ♦ vr grow angry.

erbrechen [erbre'қhən] vtr unreg vomit.

Erb- zW: **~recht** nt right of succession; hereditary right; law of inheritance; **~schaft** ƒ inheritance, legacy.

Erbschafts- zW: **~steuer** ƒ inheritance tax; **~-und Schenkungssteuer** ƒ capital transfer tax.

Erbschleicher(in ƒ) [erp'shlīқhər(in)] m -s, - legacy-hunter.

Erbse [erp'sə] ƒ -, -n pea.

Erb- zW: **~stück** nt heirloom; **~sünde** ƒ (REL) original sin; **~teil** nt inherited trait; (JUR) (portion of) inheritance.

Erd- [ā:rd'] zW: **~achse** ƒ earth's axis; **~atmosphäre** ƒ earth's atmosphere; **~bahn** ƒ orbit of the earth; **~beben** nt earthquake; **~beere** ƒ strawberry; **~boden** m ground; **etw dem ~boden gleichmachen** level sth, raze sth to the ground.

Erde ƒ -, -n earth; **zu ebener ~** at ground level; **auf der ganzen ~** all over the world; **du wirst mich noch unter die ~ bringen** (umg) you'll be the death of me yet.

erden vt (ELEK) ground (US), earth (Brit).

erdenkbar [erdengk'bâr], **erdenklich** [-liқh] a conceivable; **sich** (dat) **alle ~e Mühe geben** take the greatest (possible) pains.

Erdg. abk = **Erdgeschoß**.

Erd- zW: **~gas** nt natural gas; **~geschoß** nt first floor (US), ground floor (Brit); **~kunde** ƒ geography; **~nuß** ƒ peanut; **~oberfläche** ƒ surface of the earth; **~öl** nt (mineral) oil; **~ölfeld** nt oilfield; **~ölindustrie** ƒ oil industry; **~reich** nt soil, earth.

erdreisten [erdrīs'tən] vr dare, have the audacity (to do sth).

erdrosseln [erdro'səln] vt strangle, throttle.

erdrücken [erdrü'kən] vt crush; **erdrückende Übermacht/erdrückendes Beweismaterial** overwhelming superiority/evidence.

Erd- zW: **~rutsch** m landslide; (seismic) shock; **~teil** m continent.

erdulden [erdŏŏl'dən] vt endure, suffer.

ereifern [erī'farn] vr get excited.

ereignen [erīg'nən] vr happen.

Ereignis [erīg'nis] nt -ses, -se event; **e~reich** a eventful.

Eremit [ārāmē:t'] m -en, -en hermit.

erfahren |crfá'rən| *vt unreg* learn, find out; (*erleben*) experience ♦ *a* experienced.

Erfahrung *f* experience; ~**en sammeln** gain experience; **etw in** ~ **bringen** learn *od* find out sth.

Erfahrungs- *zW*: ~**austausch** *m* exchange of experiences; **e~gemäß** *ad* according to experience.

erfand |crfánt'| *imperf von* **erfinden**.

erfassen |crfá'sən| *vt* seize; (*fig*: *einbeziehen*) include, register; (*verstehen*) grasp.

erfinden |crfin'dən| *vt unreg* invent; **frei erfunden** completely fictitious.

Erfinder(in *f*) *m* **-s, -** inventor; **e~isch** *a* inventive.

Erfindung *f* invention.

Erfindungsgabe *f* inventiveness.

Erfolg |crfolk'| *m* **-(e)s, -e** success; (*Folge*) result; **viel ~!** good luck!

erfolgen |crfol'gən| *vi* follow; (*sich ergeben*) result; (*stattfinden*) take place; (*Zahlung*) be effected; **nach erfolgter Zahlung** when payment has been made.

Erfolg- *zW*: **e~los** *a* unsuccessful; ~**losigkeit** *f* lack of success; **e~reich** *a* successful.

Erfolgserlebnis *nt* feeling of success, sense of achievement.

erfolgversprechend *a* promising.

erforderlich *a* requisite, necessary.

erfordern |crfor'dərn| *vt* require, demand.

Erfordernis *nt* **-ses, -se** requirement, prerequisite.

erforschen |crfor'shən| *vt* (*Land*) explore; (*Problem*) investigate; (*Gewissen*) search.

Erforscher(in *f*) *m* **-s, -** explorer; investigator.

Erforschung *f* exploration; investigation; searching.

erfragen |crfrá'gən| *vt* inquire, ascertain.

erfreuen |crfroi'ən| *vr*: **sich ~ an** (+*dat*) enjoy; **sich einer Sache** (*gen*) ~ (*geh*) enjoy sth ♦ *vt* delight; **sehr erfreut!** (*form*: *bei Vorstellung*) pleased to meet you!

erfreulich |crfroi'liċh| *a* pleasing, gratifying.

erfreulicherweise *ad* happily, luckily.

erfrieren |crfrē'rən| *vi unreg* freeze (to death); (*Glieder*) get frostbitten; (*Pflanzen*) be killed by frost.

erfrischen |crfri'shən| *vt* refresh.

Erfrischung *f* refreshment.

Erfrischungsraum *m* snack bar, cafeteria.

erfüllen |crfü'lən| *vt* (*Raum etc*) fill; (*fig*: *Bitte etc*) fulfill (*US*), fulfil (*Brit*); **ein erfülltes Leben** a full life ♦ *vr* come true.

Erfüllung *f*: **in ~ gehen** be fulfilled.

erfunden |crfōōn'dən| *pp von* **erfinden**.

ergab |crgáp'| *imperf von* **ergeben**.

ergänzen |crgen'tsən| *vt* supplement, complete ♦ *vr* complement one another.

Ergänzung *f* completion; (*Zusatz*) supplement.

ergattern |crgá'tərn| *vt* (*umg*) get hold of, hunt up.

ergaunern |crgou'nərn| *vt* (*umg*): **sich** (*dat*)

etw ~ get hold of sth by underhand methods.

ergeben |crgā:'bən| *unreg vt* yield, produce ♦ *vr* surrender; (*sich hingeben*) give o.s. up, yield (*dat* to); (*folgen*) result; **es ergab sich, daß unsere Befürchtungen** ... it turned out that our fears ... ♦ *a* devoted; (*demütig*) humble; (*dem Trunk*) addicted (to); **E~heit** *f* devotion; humility.

Ergebnis |crgā:p'nis| *nt* **-ses, -se** result; **zu einem ~ kommen** come to *od* reach a conclusion; **e~los** *a* without result, fruitless; **e~los bleiben** *od* **verlaufen** come to nothing.

ergehen |crgā:'ən| *unreg vi* (*form*) be issued, go out; **etw über sich ~ lassen** put up with sth ♦ *vi unpers*: **es ergeht ihm gut/schlecht** he's faring *od* getting on well/badly ♦ *vr*: **sich in etw** (*dat*) ~ indulge in sth; **sich (in langen Reden) über ein Thema ~** (*fig*) hold forth at length on sth.

ergiebig |crgē:'biċh| *a* productive.

ergo |cr'gō| *kj* therefore, ergo (*liter*, *hum*).

Ergonomie |crgōnōmē:'| *f* ergonomics *pl*.

ergötzen |crgœ̈'tsən| *vt* amuse, delight.

ergrauen |crgrou'ən| *vi* turn *od* go gray (*US*) *od* grey (*Brit*).

ergreifen |crgrī'fən| *vt unreg* (*lit*, *fig*) seize; (*Beruf*) take up; (*Maßnahmen*) resort to; (*rühren*) move; **er ergriff das Wort** he began to speak.

ergreifend *a* moving, affecting.

ergriff |crgrif'| *imperf von* **ergreifen**.

ergriffen *a* deeply moved ♦ *pp von* **ergreifen**.

ergründen |crgrün'dən| *vt* (*Sinn etc*) fathom; (*Ursache*, *Motive*) discover.

Erguß |crgōōs'| *m* **-sses, -̈sse** discharge; (*fig*) outpouring, effusion.

erhaben |crhá'bən| *a* (*lit*) raised, embossed; (*fig*) exalted, lofty; **über etw** (*akk*) ~ **sein** be above sth.

Erhalt *m*: **bei** *od* **nach ~** on receipt.

erhält |crhelt'| *3. pers sing präs von* **erhalten**.

erhalten |crhál'tən| *vt unreg* receive; (*bewahren*) preserve, maintain; **das Wort ~** receive permission to speak; **jdn am Leben ~** keep sb alive; **gut ~** in good condition.

erhältlich |crhel'tliċh| *a* obtainable, available.

Erhaltung *f* maintenance, preservation.

erhängen |crhe'ngən| *vtr* hang.

erhärten |crher'tən| *vt* harden; (*These*) substantiate, corroborate.

erhaschen |crhá'shən| *vt* catch.

erheben |crhā:'bən| *unreg vt* raise; (*Protest*, *Forderungen*) make; (*Fakten*) ascertain ♦ *vr* rise (up); **sich über etw** (*akk*) ~ rise above sth.

erheblich |crhā:'pliċh| *a* considerable.

erheitern |crhī'tərn| *vt* amuse, cheer (up).

Erheiterung *f* exhilaration; **zur allgemeinen ~** to everybody's amusement.

erhellen |crhe'lən| *vt* (*lit*, *fig*) illuminate; (*Geheimnis*) shed light on ♦ *vr* brighten, light up.

erhielt |crhē:lt'| *imperf von* **erhalten**.

erhitzen [ɛrhi'tsən] *vt* heat ♦ *vr* heat up; (*fig*) become heated *od* aroused.

erhoffen [ɛrho'fən] *vt* hope for; **was erhoffst du dir davon?** what do you hope to gain from it?

erhöhen [ɛrhœ'ən] *vt* raise; (*verstärken*) increase; **erhöhte Temperatur haben** have a temperature. **Erhöhung** *f* (*Gehalt*) increment.

erholen [ɛrhō:'lən] *vr* recover; (*entspannen*) have a rest; (*fig*: *Preise, Aktien auch*) rally, pick up.

erholsam *a* restful.

Erholung *f* recovery; relaxation, rest.

Erholungs- *zW*: **e~bedürftig** *a* in need of a rest, run-down; **~heim** *nt* convalescent/rest home.

erhören [ɛrhœ'rən] *vt* (*Gebet etc*) hear; (*Bitte etc*) yield to.

Erika [ā:'rēkā] *f* -, **Eriken** heather.

erinnern [ɛri'nərn] *vt* remind (*an +akk* of) ♦ *vr* remember (*an etw (akk)* sth).

Erinnerung *f* memory; (*Andenken*) reminder; **~en** *pl* (*Lebens~*) reminiscences *pl*; (*LITER*) memoirs *pl*; **jdn/etw in guter ~ behalten** have pleasant memories of sb/sth.

Erinnerungs- *zW*: **~schreiben** *nt* (*COMM*) reminder; **~tafel** *f* commemorative plaque.

erkalten [ɛrkál'tən] *vi* go cold, cool (down).

erkälten [ɛrkel'tən] *vr* catch cold; **sich** (*dat*) **die Blase ~** catch a chill in one's bladder.

erkältet *a* with a cold; **~ sein** have a cold.

Erkältung *f* cold.

erkämpfen [ɛrkem'pfən] *vt* win, secure.

erkannt [ɛrkánt'] *pp von* **erkennen**.

erkannte *imperf von* **erkennen**.

erkennbar *a* recognizable.

erkennen [ɛrke'nən] *vt unreg* recognize; (*sehen, verstehen*) see; **jdm zu ~ geben, daß** ... give sb to understand that ...

erkenntlich *a*: **sich ~ zeigen** show one's appreciation; **E~keit** *f* gratitude; (*Geschenk*) token of one's gratitude.

Erkenntnis *f* -, **-se** knowledge; (*das Erkennen*) recognition; (*Einsicht*) insight; **zur ~ kommen** realize.

Erkennung *f* recognition.

Erkennungs- *zW*: **~dienst** *m* police records department; **~marke** *f* identity disc.

Erker [ɛr'kər] *m* -s, - bay; **~fenster** *nt* bay window.

erklärbar *a* explicable.

erklären [ɛrkle:'rən] *vt* explain; (*bekanntgeben*) declare (*als* to be); (*Rücktritt*) announce; (*Politiker, Pressesprecher etc*) say; **ich kann mir nicht ~, warum** ... I can't understand why ...

erklärlich *a* explicable; (*verständlich*) understandable.

erklärt *a attr* (*Gegner etc*) professed, avowed; (*Favorit, Liebling*) acknowledged.

Erklärung *f* explanation; (*Aussage*) declaration.

erklecklich [ɛrkle'kliçʰ] *a* considerable.

erklimmen [ɛrkli'mən] *vt unreg* to climb to.

erklingen [ɛrkli'ngən] *vi unreg* resound, ring out.

erklomm [ɛrklom'] *imperf von* **erklimmen**.

erklommen *pp von* **erklimmen**.

erkranken [ɛrkráng'kən] *vi* be taken ill (*an +dat* with); (*Organ, Pflanze, Tier*) become diseased (*an +dat* with).

Erkrankung *f* illness.

erkunden [ɛrkōōn'dən] *vt* find out, ascertain; (*bes MIL*) reconnoiter (*US*), reconnoitre (*Brit*), scout.

erkundigen *vr* inquire (*nach* about); **ich werde mich ~** I'll find out.

Erkundigung *f* inquiry; **~en einholen** make inquiries.

Erkundung *f* (*MIL*) reconnaissance, scouting.

erlahmen [ɛrlá'mən] *vi* tire; (*nachlassen*) flag, wane.

erlangen [ɛrlá'ngən] *vt* attain, achieve.

Erlaß [ɛrlás'] *m* **-sses**, **̄sse** decree; (*Aufhebung*) remission.

erlassen *vt unreg* (*Verfügung*) issue; (*Gesetz*) enact; (*Strafe*) remit; **jdm etw ~** release sb from sth.

erlauben [ɛrlou'bən] *vt* allow, permit (*jdm etw* sb to do sth); **~ Sie?** may I?; **~ Sie mal!** do you mind! ♦ *vr* permit o.s., venture; **was ~ Sie sich (eigentlich)!** how dare you!

Erlaubnis [ɛrloup'nis] *f* -, **-se** permission.

erläutern [ɛrloi'tərn] *vt* explain.

Erläuterung *f* explanation; **zur ~** in explanation.

Erle [ɛr'lə] *f* -, **-n** alder.

erleben [ɛrlā:'bən] *vt* experience; (*Zeit*) live through; (*mit~*) witness; (*noch mit~*) live to see; **so wütend habe ich ihn noch nie erlebt** I've never seen *od* known him so furious.

Erlebnis [ɛrlā:p'nis] *nt* **-ses**, **-se** experience.

erledigen [ɛrlā:'digən] *vt* take care of, deal with; (*Antrag etc*) process; (*umg: erschöpfen*) wear out; (*ruinieren*) finish; (*umbringen*) do in; **das ist erledigt** that's taken care of, that's been done; **ich habe noch einiges in der Stadt zu ~** I've still got a few things to do in town ♦ *vr*: **das hat sich erledigt** that's all settled.

erledigt *a* (*umg: erschöpft*) shattered, done in; (*ruiniert*) finished, ruined.

erlegen [ɛrlā:'gən] *vt* kill.

erleichtern [ɛrlīçʰ'tərn] *vt* make easier; (*fig: Last*) lighten; (*lindern, beruhigen*) relieve.

erleichtert *a* relieved; **~ aufatmen** breathe a sigh of relief.

Erleichterung *f* facilitation; lightening; relief.

erleiden [ɛrlī'dən] *vt unreg* suffer, endure.

erlernbar *a* learnable.

erlernen [ɛrler'nən] *vt* learn, acquire.

erlesen [ɛrlā:'zən] *a* select, choice.

erleuchten [ɛrloiçʰ'tən] *vt* illuminate; (*fig*) inspire.

Erleuchtung f (Einfall) inspiration.
erliegen [erlē:'gən] vi unreg (+dat) succumb to; (einem Irrtum) be the victim of; **zum E~ kommen** come to a standstill.
erlischt [erlisht'] 2./3. pers sing präs von **erlöschen**.
erlogen [erlō:'gən] a untrue, made-up.
Erlös [erlœs'] m **-es, -e** proceeds pl.
erlosch [erlosh'] imperf von **erlöschen**.
erlöschen [erlœ'shən] vi unreg (Feuer) go out; (Interesse) cease, die; (Vertrag, Recht) expire; **ein erloschener Vulkan** an extinct volcano.
erlösen [erlœ'zən] vt redeem, save.
Erlöser m **-s, -** (REL) Redeemer; (Befreier) savior (US), saviour (Brit).
Erlösung f release; (REL) redemption.
ermächtigen [ermeċh'tigən] vt authorize, empower.
Ermächtigung f authorization.
ermahnen [ermá'nən] vt admonish, exhort.
Ermahnung f admonition, exhortation.
Ermang(e)lung [ermá'ngəlōōng] f: **in ~** +gen because of the lack of.
ermäßigen [erme'sigən] vt reduce.
Ermäßigung f reduction.
ermessen [erme'sən] vt unreg estimate, gauge; **E~** nt **-s** estimation; discretion; **in jds E~ liegen** lie within sb's discretion; **nach meinem E~** in my judgement.
Ermessensfrage f matter of discretion.
ermitteln [ermi'təln] vt determine; (Täter) trace ♦ vi: **gegen jdn ~** investigate sb.
Ermittlung [ermi'tlōōng] f determination; (Polizei~) investigation; **~en anstellen** make inquiries (über +akk about).
Ermittlungsverfahren nt (JUR) pretrial examination (US), preliminary proceedings pl (Brit).
ermöglichen [ermœ'kliċhən] vt make possible (dat for).
ermorden [ermor'dən] vt murder.
Ermordung f murder.
ermüden [ermü:'dən] vti tire; (TECH) fatigue.
ermüdend a tiring; (fig) wearisome.
Ermüdung f fatigue.
Ermüdungserscheinung f sign of fatigue.
ermuntern [ermōōn'tərn] vt rouse; (ermutigen) encourage; (beleben) liven up; (aufmuntern) cheer up.
ermutigen [ermōō:'tigən] vt encourage.
ernähren [erne:'rən] vt feed, nourish; (Familie) support ♦ vr support o.s., earn a living; **sich ~ von** live on.
Ernährer(in f) m **-s, -** breadwinner.
Ernährung f nourishment; (MED) nutrition; (Unterhalt) maintenance.
ernennen [erne'nən] vt unreg appoint.
Ernennung f appointment.
erneuern [ernoi'ərn] vt renew; (restaurieren) restore; (renovieren) renovate.
Erneuerung f renewal; restoration; renovation.

erneut a renewed, fresh ♦ ad once more.
erniedrigen [ernē:'drigən] vt humiliate, degrade.
Ernst [ernst] m **-es** seriousness; **das ist mein ~** I'm quite serious; **im ~** in earnest; **~ machen mit etw** put sth into practice; **e~** a serious; **es steht e~ um ihn** things don't look too good for him; **~fall** m emergency; **e~gemeint** a meant in earnest, serious; **e~haft** a serious; **~haftigkeit** f seriousness; **e~lich** a serious.
Ernte [ern'tə] f **-, -n** harvest; **~dankfest** nt harvest festival.
ernten vt harvest; (Lob etc) earn.
ernüchtern [ernüċh'tərn] vt sober up; (fig) bring down to earth.
Ernüchterung f sobering up; (fig) disillusionment.
Eroberer [erō'bərər] m **-s, -** conqueror.
erobern vt conquer.
Eroberung f conquest.
eröffnen [erœf'nən] vt open; **jdm etw ~** (geh) disclose sth to sb ♦ vr present itself.
Eröffnung f opening.
Eröffnungsansprache f inaugural od opening address.
erogen [erōgā:n'] a erogenous.
erörtern [erœr'tərn] vt discuss (in detail).
Erörterung f discussion.
Erotik [ārō:'tik] f eroticism.
erotisch a erotic.
Erpel [er'pəl] m **-, -** drake.
erpicht [erpiċht'] a eager, keen (auf +akk on).
erpressen [erpre'sən] vt (Geld etc) extort; (Mensch) blackmail.
Erpresser m **-s, -** blackmailer.
Erpressung f blackmail; extortion.
erproben [erprō:'bən] vt test; **erprobt** tried and tested.
erraten [errá'tən] vt unreg guess.
errechnen [erreċh'nən] vt calculate, work out.
erregbar [errā:k'bâr] a excitable; (reizbar) irritable; **E~keit** f excitability; irritability.
erregen [errā:'gən] vt excite; (ärgern) infuriate; (hervorrufen) arouse, provoke ♦ vr get excited od worked up.
Erreger m **-s, -** causative agent.
Erregtheit f excitement; (Beunruhigung) agitation.
Erregung f excitement.
erreichbar a accessible, within reach.
erreichen [errī'ċhən] vt reach; (Zweck) achieve; (Zug) catch; **wann kann ich Sie morgen ~?** when can I get in touch with you tomorrow?; **vom Bahnhof leicht zu ~** within easy reach of the station.
errichten [erriċh'tən] vt erect, put up; (gründen) establish, set up.
erringen [erri'ngən] vt unreg gain, win.
erröten [errœ'tən] vi blush, flush.
Errungenschaft [errōō'ngənsháft] f achievement; (umg: Anschaffung) acquisition.
Ersatz [erzáts'] m **-es** substitute; replace-

ment; (*Schaden~*) compensation; (*MIL*) reinforcements *pl*; **als ~ für jdn einspringen** stand in for sb; **~befriedigung** *f* vicarious satisfaction; **~dienst** *m* (*MIL*) alternative service; **~kasse** *f* private health insurance; **~mann** *m* replacement; (*SPORT*) substitute; **~mutter** *f* foster mother; **e~pflichtig** *a* liable to pay compensation; **~reifen** *m* (*AUT*) spare tire (*US*) *od* tyre (*Brit*); **~teil** *nt* spare (part); **e~weise** *ad* as an alternative.

ersaufen [ɛrzou'fən] *vi unreg* (*umg*) drown.

ersäufen [ɛrzoi'fən] *vt* drown.

erschaffen [ɛrshȧ'fən] *vt unreg* create.

erscheinen [ɛrshī'nən] *vi unreg* appear.

Erscheinung *f* appearance; (*Geist*) apparition; (*Gegebenheit*) phenomenon; (*Gestalt*) figure; **in ~ treten** (*Merkmale*) appear; (*Gefühle*) show themselves.

Erscheinungs- *zW*: **~form** *f* manifestation; **~jahr** *nt* (*von Buch*) year of publication.

erschien [ɛrshē:n'] *imperf von* **erscheinen**.

erschienen *pp von* **erscheinen**.

erschießen [ɛrshē:'sən] *vt unreg* shoot (dead).

erschlaffen [ɛrshlȧ'fən] *vi* go limp; (*Mensch*) become exhausted.

erschlagen [ɛrshlȧ'gən] *vt unreg* strike dead ♦ *a* (*umg*: *todmüde*) worn out, dead beat (*umg*).

erschleichen [ɛrshlī'çhən] *vt unreg* obtain by stealth *od* dubious methods.

erschließen [ɛrshlē:'sən] *vt unreg* (*Gebiet, Absatzmarkt*) develop, open up; (*Bodenschätze*) tap.

erschlossen [ɛrshlo'sən] *a* (*Gebiet*) developed.

erschöpfen [ɛrshœ'pfən] *vt* exhaust.

erschöpfend *a* exhaustive, thorough.

erschöpft *a* exhausted.

Erschöpfung *f* exhaustion.

erschossen [ɛrsho'sən] *a* (*umg*): **(völlig) ~ sein** be whacked, be dead (beat).

erschrak [ɛrshrȧk'] *imperf von* **erschrecken**.

erschrecken [ɛrshre'kən] *vt* startle, frighten ♦ *vi unreg* be frightened *od* startled.

erschreckend *a* alarming, frightening.

erschrickt [ɛrshrikt'] *3. pers sing präs von* **erschrecken**.

erschrocken [ɛrshro'kən] *a* frightened, startled ♦ *pp von* **erschrecken**.

erschüttern [ɛrshü'tərn] *vt* shake; (*ergreifen*) move deeply; **ihn kann nichts ~** he's unflappable, he always keeps his cool (*umg*).

erschütternd *a* shattering.

Erschütterung *f* (*des Bodens*) tremor; (*tiefe Ergriffenheit*) shock.

erschweren [ɛrshvȧ:'rən] *vt* complicate; **erschwerende Umstände** (*JUR*) aggravating circumstances; **es kommt noch erschwerend hinzu, daß** .. to compound matters ...

erschwindeln [ɛrshvin'dəln] *vt* obtain by fraud.

erschwingen [ɛrshvi'ngən] *vt unreg* afford.

erschwinglich *a* within one's means.

ersehen [ɛrzā:'ən] *vt unreg*: **aus etw ~, daß...** gather from sth that...

ersehnt [ɛrzā:nt'] *a* longed-for.

ersetzbar *a* replaceable.

ersetzen [ɛrze'tsən] *vt* replace; **jdm Unkosten** *etc* **~** pay sb's expenses *etc*.

ersichtlich [ɛrziçh'tliçh] *a* evident, obvious.

ersparen [ɛrshpâ'rən] *vt* (*Ärger etc*) spare; (*Geld*) save; **ihr blieb auch nichts erspart** she was spared nothing.

Ersparnis *f* -, **-se** saving.

ersprießlich [ɛrshprē:s'liçh] *a* profitable, useful; (*angenehm*) pleasant.

erst [ā:rst] *ad* (at) first; (*nicht früher, nur*) only; (*nicht bis*) not till; **~ einmal** first; **wenn du das ~ einmal hinter dir hast** once you've got that behind you; **gerade ~** just; **da fange ich ~ gar nicht an** I simply won't bother to begin; **jetzt ~ recht!** that just makes me all the more determined; **da ging's ~ richtig los** then it really got going.

erstarren [ɛrshtȧ'rən] *vi* stiffen; (*vor Furcht*) grow rigid; (*Materie*) solidify.

erstatten [ɛrshtȧ'tən] *vt* (*Unkosten*) refund; **Anzeige** *etc* **gegen jdn ~** report sb; **Bericht ~** make a report.

Erstattung *f* (*von Unkosten*) reimbursement.

Erstaufführung [ā:rst'ouffü:rōōng] *f* first performance.

erstaunen [ɛrshtou'nən] *vt* astonish ♦ *vi* be astonished; **E~** *nt* **-s** astonishment.

erstaunlich *a* astonishing.

erst- [ā:rst'] *zW*: **E~ausgabe** *f* first edition; **~beste(r,s)** *a* first that comes along.

erstechen [ɛrshte'çhən] *vt unreg* stab (to death).

erstehen [ɛrshtā:'ən] *vt unreg* buy ♦ *vi* (a)rise.

ersteigen [ɛrshtī'gən] *vt unreg* climb, ascend.

ersteigern [ɛrshtī'gərn] *vt* buy at an auction.

erstellen [ɛrshte'lən] *vt* erect, build.

erstemal *ad*: **das ~** the first time.

erstens *ad* firstly, in the first place.

erste(r, s) *a* first; **als ~s** first of all; **in ~r Linie** first and foremost; **fürs ~** for the time being; **E~ Hilfe** first aid.

erstere(r, s) *pron* (the) former.

ersticken [ɛrshti'kən] *vt* (*lit, fig*) stifle; (*Mensch*) suffocate; (*Flammen*) smother; ♦ *vi* (*Mensch*) suffocate; (*Feuer*) be smothered; **mit erstickter Stimme** in a choked voice; **in Arbeit ~** be snowed under with work.

Erstickung *f* suffocation.

erst- *zW*: **~klassig** *a* first-class; **E~kommunion** *f* first communion; **~mals** *a* first; **~mals** *ad* for the first time; **~rangig** *a* first-rate.

erstrebenswert [ɛrshtrā:'bənsvā:rt] *a* desirable, worthwhile.

erstrecken [ɛrshtre'kən] *vr* extend, stretch.

Erststimme *f* first vote.

Ersttags- [ā:rst'tȧks] *zW*: **~brief** *m* first-day

cover; **~stempel** *m* first-day (date) stamp.
erstunken [ershtōōng'kən] *a*: **das ist ~ und erlogen** (*umg*) that's a pack of lies.
Erstwähler *m* **-s,-** first-time voter.
ersuchen [erzōō:'kłən] *vt* request.
ertappen [ertá'pən] *vt* catch, detect.
erteilen [ertī'lən] *vt* give.
ertönen [ertœ'nən] *vi* sound, ring out.
Ertrag [ertrák'] *m* **-(e)s,** ̈**e** yield; (*Gewinn*) proceeds *pl*.
ertragen *vt unreg* bear, stand.
erträglich [ertre:'klièh] *a* tolerable, bearable.
ertragreich *a* (*Geschäft*) profitable, lucrative.
ertrank [ertrángk'] *imperf von* **ertrinken**.
ertränken [ertreng'kən] *vt* drown.
erträumen [ertroi'mən] *vt*: **sich** (*dat*) **etw ~** dream of sth, imagine sth.
ertrinken [ertring'kən] *vi unreg* drown; **E~** *nt* **-s** drowning.
ertrunken [ertrōōng'kən] *pp von* **ertrinken**.
erübrigen [erü:'brigən] *vt* spare ♦ *vr* be unnecessary.
erwachen [ervá'khən] *vi* awake; **ein böses E~** (*fig*) a rude awakening.
erwachsen [ervák'sən] *a* grown-up ♦ *vi unreg*: **daraus erwuchsen ihm Unannehmlichkeiten** that caused him some trouble.
Erwachsene(r) *mf dekl wie a* adult.
Erwachsenenbildung *f* adult education.
erwägen [erve:'gən] *vt unreg* consider.
Erwägung *f* consideration; **etw in ~ ziehen** take sth into consideration.
erwähnen [erve:'nən] *vt* mention.
erwähnenswert *a* worth mentioning.
Erwähnung *f* mention.
erwarb [ervárp'] *imperf von* **erwerben**.
erwärmen [erver'mən] *vt* warm, heat ♦ *vr* get warm, warm up; **sich ~ für** warm to.
erwarten [ervár'tən] *vt* expect; (*warten auf*) wait for; **etw kaum ~ können** hardly be able to wait for sth.
Erwartung *f* expectation; **in ~ Ihrer baldigen Antwort** (*form*) in anticipation of your early reply.
Erwartungs- *zW*: **e~gemäß** *ad* as expected; **e~voll** *a* expectant.
erwecken [erve'kən] *vt* rouse, awake; **den Anschein ~** give the impression; **etw zu neuem Leben ~** resurrect sth.
erwehren [ervā:'rən] *vr* (*geh*) fend, ward (*gen* off); (*des Lachens etc*) refrain (*gen* from).
erweichen [ervī'èhən] *vt* soften; **sich nicht ~ lassen** be unmoved.
Erweis [ervī's'] *m* **-es, -e** proof.
erweisen [ervī'zən] *unreg vt* prove; (*Ehre, Dienst*) do (*jdm sb*) ♦ *vr* prove (*als* to be); **sich jdm gegenüber dankbar ~** show one's gratitude to sb.
erweitern [ervī'tərn] *vtr* widen, enlarge; (*Geschäft*) expand; (*MED*) dilate; (*fig: Kenntnisse*) broaden; (*Macht*) extend.
Erweiterung *f* expansion.

Erwerb [erverp'] *m* **-(e)s, -e** acquisition; (*Beruf*) trade.
erwerben [erver'bən] *vt unreg* acquire; **er hat sich** (*dat*) **große Verdienste um die Firma erworben** he has done great service for the firm.
Erwerbs- *zW*: **~gesellschaft** *f* acquisitive society; **e~los** *a* unemployed; **~quelle** *f* source of income; **e~tätig** *a* (gainfully) employed; **e~unfähig** *a* unable to work.
erwidern [ervē:'dərn] *vt* reply; (*vergelten*) return.
Erwiderung *f*: **in ~ Ihres Schreibens vom ...** (*form*) in reply to your letter of the ...
erwiesen [ervē:'zən] *a* proven.
erwirbt [ervirpt'] *3. pers sing präs von* **erwerben**.
erwirtschaften [ervirt'sháftən] *vt* (*Gewinn etc*) make by good management.
erwischen [ervi'shən] *vt* (*umg*) catch, get; **ihn hat's erwischt!** (*umg: verliebt*) he's got it bad; (*:krank*) he's got it; **kalt ~** (*umg*) catch off-balance.
erworben [ervor'bən] *pp von* **erwerben**.
erwünscht [ervünsht'] *a* desired.
erwürgen [ervür'gən] *vt* strangle.
Erz [ā:rts] *nt* **-es, -e** ore.
erzählen [ertse:'lən] *vti* tell; **dem werd' ich was ~!** (*umg*) I'll have something to say to him; **erzählende Dichtung** narrative fiction.
Erzähler(in *f*) *m* **-s, -** narrator.
Erzählung *f* story, tale.
Erz- *zW*: **~bischof** *m* archbishop; **~engel** *m* archangel.
erzeugen [ārtsoi'gən] *vt* produce; (*Strom*) generate.
Erzeugerpreis *m* producer's price.
Erzeugnis *nt* **-ses, -se** product, produce.
Erzeugung *f* production; generation.
Erzfeind *m* arch enemy.
erziehbar *a*: **ein Heim für schwer ~e Kinder** a home for difficult children.
erziehen [ertsē:'ən] *vt unreg* bring up; (*bilden*) educate, train.
Erziehung *f* bringing up; (*Bildung*) education.
Erziehungs- *zW*: **~beihilfe** *f* educational grant; **~berechtigte(r)** *mf dekl wie a* parent, legal guardian; **~heim** *nt* community home.
erzielen [ertsē:'lən] *vt* achieve, obtain; (*Tor*) score.
erzkonservativ ['ertskonzervá'tē:f] *a* ultraconservative.
erzog [ertsō:k'] *imperf von* **erziehen**.
erzogen [ārtsō:'gən] *pp von* **erziehen**.
erzürnen [ertsür'nən] *vt* (*geh*) anger, incense.
erzwingen [ertsvi'ngən] *vt unreg* force, obtain by force.
es [es] *pron nom, akk* it.
Es [es] *nt* - (*MUS: Dur*) E flat.
Esche [e'shə] *f* -, -n ash.
Esel [ā:'zəl] *m* **-s, -** donkey, ass; **ich ~!** (*umg*) silly me!
Esels- *zW*: **~brücke** *f* (*Gedächtnishilfe*) mne-

monic, aide-mémoire; ~**ohr** *nt* dog-ear.
Eskalation [eskálátsēō:n'] *f* escalation.
eskalieren [eskálē:'rən] *vti* escalate.
Eskimo [es'kēmō] *m* **-s, -s** eskimo.
Eskorte [eskor'tə] *f* -, **-n** (*MIL*) escort.
eskortieren [eskortē:'rən] *vt* (*geh*) escort.
Espenlaub [es'pənloup] *nt*: **zittern wie** ~ shake like a leaf.
eßbar [es'bár] *a* eatable, edible.
essen [e'sən] *vti unreg* eat; ~ **gehen** (*auswärts*) eat out; ~ **Sie gern Äpfel?** do you like apples?; **E**~ *nt* **-s, -** (*Mahlzeit*) meal; (*Nahrung*) food.
Essen(s)- *zW*: ~**ausgabe** *f* serving of meals; (*Stelle*) serving counter; ~**marke** *f* meal voucher; ~**zeit** *f* mealtime.
Eßgeschirr *nt* dinner service.
Essig [e'sich] *m* **-s, -e** vinegar; **damit ist es** ~ (*umg*) it's all off; ~**gurke** *f* gherkin.
Eßkastanie *f* sweet chestnut.
Eßl. *abk* (= *Eßlöffel*) tbs., tbsp.
Eß- [es'] *zW*: ~**löffel** *m* tablespoon; ~**tisch** *m* dining table; ~**waren** *pl* foodstuffs *pl*; ~**zimmer** *nt* dining room.
Establishment [iste'blishmənt] **-s, -s** *nt* establishment.
Estland [ā:s'tlánt] *nt* Estonia.
Estragon [e'trágon] *m* **-s** tarragon.
Estrich [es'trich] *m* **-s, -e** stone/clay *etc* floor.
etablieren [ātáblē:'rən] *vr* establish o.s.; (*COMM*) set up.
Etage [ātâ'zhə] *f* -, **-n** floor, story (*US*), storey (*Brit*).
Etagen- *zW*: ~**betten** *pl* bunk beds *pl*; ~**wohnung** *f* apartment, flat (*Brit*).
Etappe [ātá'pə] *f* -, **-n** stage.
etappenweise *ad* step by step, stage by stage.
Etat [ātâ'] *m* **-s, -s** budget; ~**jahr** *nt* financial year; ~**posten** *m* budget item.
etepetete [ā:təpātā:'tə] *a* (*umg*) fussy.
Ethik [ā:'tik] *f* ethics *sing*.
ethisch [ā:'tish] *a* ethical.
Etikett [ātēket'] *nt* **-(e)s, -e** (*lit, fig*) label.
Etikette *f* etiquette, manners *pl*.
Etikettenschwindel *m* (*POL*): **es ist reinster** ~, **wenn** ... it is just playing/juggling with names if ...
etikettieren [ātēketē:'rən] *vt* label.
etliche(r, s) [e'tlichə(r, s)] *pron* quite a lot of; ~ *pl* some, quite a few; ~**s** quite a lot.
Etüde [ātü:'də] *f* -, **-n** (*MUS*) étude.
Etui [etvē:'] *nt* **-s, -s** case.
etwa [et'vá] *ad* (*ungefähr*) about; (*vielleicht*) perhaps; (*beispielsweise*) for instance; **nicht** ~ by no means; (*entrüstet, erstaunt*): **hast du** ~ **schon wieder kein Geld dabei?** don't tell me you haven't got any money again!; **willst du** ~ **schon gehen?** (surely) you don't want to go already?; (*zur Bestätigung*): **Sie kommen doch, oder** ~ **nicht?** you are coming, aren't you?
etwaig [et'vich] *a* possible.
etwas *pron* something; (*fragend, verneinend*)

anything; (*ein wenig*) a little; **er kann** ~ he's good ♦ *ad* a little; **E**~ *nt*: **das gewisse E**~ that certain something.
Etymologie [ātümōlōgē:'] *f* etymology.
euch [oich] *pron* (*akk von* **ihr**) you; yourselves; (*dat von* **ihr**) (to/for) you ♦ *reflexiv* yourselves.
euer [oi'ər] *pron gen von* **ihr** of you ♦ *pron* your.
Eule [oi'lə] *f* -, **-n** owl.
Euphemismus [oifämis'mōōs] *m* euphemism.
Eurasien [oirâ'zēən] *nt* Eurasia.
Euratom [oirátō:m'] *f* - *abk* (= *Europäische Atomgemeinschaft*) Euratom.
eure(r, s) [oi'rə(r, s)] *pron* yours.
eurerseits *ad* on your part.
euresgleichen *pron* people like you.
euretwegen,   euretwillen   [oir'ətvā'gən, oir'ətvi'lən] *ad* (*für euch*) for your sakes; (*wegen euch*) on your account.
eurige *pron*: **der/die/das** ~ (*geh*) yours.
Eurokrat [oirōkrát'] *m* **-en, -en** eurocrat.
Europa [oirō:'pá] *nt* **-s** Europe.
Europäer(in *f*) [oirōpe:'ər(in)] *m* **-s, -** European.
europäisch *a* European; **das E**~**e Parlament** the European Parliament; **E**~**e (Wirtschafts)gemeinschaft** European (Economic) Community, Common Market.
Europa- *zW*: ~**meister** *m* European champion; ~**rat** *m* Council of Europe; ~**straße** *f* Euroroute.
Euroscheck [oirōshek'] *m* Eurocheque.
Euter [oi'tər] *nt* **-s, -** udder.
Euthanasie [oitánázē:'] *f* euthanasia.
ev. *abk* = **evangelisch**.
evakuieren [āvákōōē:'rən] *vt* evacuate.
evangelisch [āvánggā:'lish] *a* Protestant.
Evangelium [āvánggā:'lēōōm] *nt* Gospel.
Eva(s)kostüm [ā:'fá(s)kostü:m] *nt*: **im** ~ in her birthday suit.
eventuell [āventōōel'] *a* possible ♦ *ad* possibly, perhaps; **E**~**fall** *m* contingency.
Everest [e'vərest] *m* **-s** (Mount) Everest.
Evolutionstheorie [āvōlōōtsēō:ns'tāōrē:] *f* theory of evolution.
evtl. *abk* = **eventuell**.
EWG [ā:vā:gā:'] *f* - *abk* (= *Europäische Wirtschaftsgemeinschaft*) EEC, Common Market.
ewig [ā:'vich] *a* eternal ♦ *ad*: **auf** ~ forever; **ich habe Sie** ~ **lange nicht gesehen** (*umg*) I haven't seen you for ages; **E**~**keit** *f* eternity; **bis in alle E**~**keit** forever.
EWS *nt* *abk* (= *Europäisches Währungssystem*) EMS.
EWU *f* - *abk* (= *Europäische Währungsunion*) ECU.
ex [eks] *ad* (*umg*): **etw** ~ **trinken** drink sth in one gulp.
exakt [eksákt'] *a* exact.
exaltiert [eksáltē:rt'] *a* exaggerated, effusive.
Examen [eksá'mən] *nt* **-s, -** *od* **Examina** examination.

Examens- *zW*: **~angst** *f* exam nerves *pl*; **~arbeit** *f* dissertation.
Exekutionskommando [eksākōōtsēō:ns'-komándō] *nt* firing squad.
Exekutive [eksākōōtē:'və] *f* executive.
Exempel [eksem'pəl] *nt* **-s,** - example; **die Probe aufs ~ machen** put it to the test.
Exemplar [eksemplår'] *nt* **-s, -e** specimen; (*Buch~*) copy; **e~isch** *a* exemplary.
exerzieren [eksertsē:'rən] *vi* drill.
Exhibitionist [ekshēbētsēōnist'] *m* exhibitionist.
Exil [eksē:l'] *nt* **-s, -e** exile.
existentiell [eksistentsēel'] *a*: **von ~er Bedeutung** of vital significance.
Existenz [eksistents'] *f* existence; (*Unterhalt*) livelihood, living; (*pej: Mensch*) character; **~berechtigung** *f* right to exist; **~grundlage** *f* basis of one's livelihood; **~kampf** *m* struggle for existence; **~minimum** *nt* **-s, -ma** subsistence level.
existieren [eksistē:'rən] *vi* exist.
exkl. *abk* = **exklusive**.
exklusiv [eksklōōzē:f'] *a* exclusive; **E~bericht** *m* (*PRESSE*) exclusive report.
exklusive [eksklōōzē:'və] *ad, präp* +*gen* exclusive of, not including.
Exkursion [ekskōōrzēō:n'] *f* (study) trip.
Exmatrikulation [eksmátrēkōōlátsēō:n'] *f* (*UNIV*): **bei seiner ~** when he left university.
exorzieren [eksortsē:'rən] *vt* exorcize.
exotisch [eksō:'tish] *a* exotic.
Expansion [ekspánzēō:n'] *f* expansion.
expansiv [ekspánzē:f'] *a* expansionist; (*Wirtschaftszweige*) expanding.
Expedition [ekspādētsēō:n'] *f* expedition; (*COMM*) forwarding department.
Experiment [ekspārēment'] *nt* experiment.
experimentell [ekspārēmentel'] *a* experimental.
experimentieren [ekspārēmentē:'rən] *vi* experiment.
Experte [eksper'tə] *m* **-n, -n, Expertin** *f* expert, specialist.
explodieren [eksplōdē:'rən] *vi* explode.
Explosion [eksplōzēō:n'] *f* explosion.
explosiv [eksplōzē:f'] *a* explosive.
Exponent [ekspōnent'] *m* exponent.
exponieren [ekspōnē:'rən] *vt*: **an exponierter Stelle stehen** be in an exposed position.
Export [eksport'] *m* **-(e)s, -e** export.
Exporteur [eksportœr'] *m* exporter.
Export- *zW*: **~handel** *m* export trade; **~haus** *nt* export house.
exportieren [eksportē:'rən] *vt* export.
Export- *zW*: **~land** *nt* exporting country; **~vertreter** *m* export agent.
Expreßgut [ekspres'gōōt] *nt* express goods *pl od* freight.
Expressionismus [eksprɛsēōnis'mōōs] *m* expressionism.
Expreßzug *m* express (train).
extra [eks'trá] *a inv* (*umg: gesondert*)

separate; (*besondere*) extra ♦ *ad* (*gesondert*) separately; (*speziell*) specially; (*absichtlich*) on purpose; (*vor Adjektiven, zusätzlich*) extra; **E~** *nt* **-s, -s** extra; **E~ausgabe** *f*, **E~blatt** *nt* special edition.
Extrakt [ekstråkt'] *m* **-(e)s, -e** extract.
Extra- *zW*: **~tour** *f* (*fig umg*): **sich** (*dat*) **~touren leisten** do one's own thing; **~wurst** *f* (*umg: Sonderwunsch*): **er will immer eine ~wurst (gebraten haben)** he always wants something different.
extrem [eksträ:m'] *a* extreme; **E~fall** *m* extreme (case).
Extremist(in *f*) *m* extremist.
Extremistenerlaß [ekstrámis'tənerlås] *m* **-sses, -sse** (*Berufsverbot*) *law(s)* governing *extremism*.
extremistisch [ekstrámis'tish] *a* (*POL*) extremist.
Extremitäten [ekstrāmēte:'tən] *pl* extremities *pl*.
extrovertiert [ekstrōvertē:rt'] *a* extrovert.
Exzellenz [ekstselents'] *f* excellency.
exzentrisch [ekstsen'trish] *a* eccentric.
Exzeß [ekstses'] *m* **-sses, -sse** excess.
EZU *f* - *abk* (= *Europäische Zahlungsunion*) *European payments union*.

F

F, f [äf] *nt* **-,** - F, f; **nach Schema F** (*umg*) in the usual old way.
f *abk* (= *feminin*) fem.
Fa *abk* (= *Firma*) Co., co.
FA *abk* = **Finanzamt**.
Fabel [fá'bəl] *f* **-, -n** fable; **f~haft** *a* fabulous.
Fabrik [fábrē:k'] *f* factory; **~anlage** *f* plant; (*Gelände*) factory site.
Fabrikant [fábrē:kánt'] *m* (*Hersteller*) manufacturer; (*Besitzer*) industrialist.
Fabrikarbeiter(in *f*) *m* factory worker.
Fabrikat [fábrē:kåt'] *nt* **-(e)s, -e** manufacture, product.
Fabrikation [fábrē:kátsēō:n'] *f* manufacture, production.
Fabrik- *zW*: **~besetzung** *f* occupation (*by the workers*); **~besitzer** *m* factory owner; **~gelände** *nt* factory premises *pl*.
fabrizieren [fábrētsē:'rən] *vt* (*geistiges Produkt*) produce; (*Geschichte*) concoct, fabricate.
Fach [fáᴋh] *nt* **-(e)s, ̈er** compartment; (*in Schrank, Regal etc*) shelf; (*Sachgebiet*) subject; **ein Mann vom ~** an expert; **~arbeiter** *m* skilled worker; **~arzt** *m* (*medical*) specialist; **~ausdruck** *m* technical term; **~bereich** *m* (special) field; (*UNIV*) school,

faculty; **~buch** *nt* reference book.
Fächer [fe'çhər] *m* **-s,** - fan.
Fach- *zW*: **~frau** *f* expert; **~gebiet** *nt* (special) field; **~händler** *m* specialty dealer; **~hochschule** *f* technical/art college; **~idiot** *m* (*umg*) narrow-minded specialist; **~kreise** *pl*: **in ~kreisen** among experts; **f~kundig** *a* expert, specialist; **~lehrer** *m* specialist subject teacher; **f~lich** *a* technical; (*beruflich*) professional; **~mann** *m*, *pl* **-leute** specialist; **f~männisch** *a* professional; **~richtung** *f* subject area; **~schule** *f* technical college; **f~simpeln** *vi* talk shop; **f~spezifisch** *a* technical; **~verband** *m* trade association; **~welt** *f* profession; **~werk** *nt* timber frame; **~werkhaus** *nt* half-timbered house.
Fackel [fá'kəl] *f* **-,** **-n** torch.
fackeln *vi* (*umg*) dither.
Fackelzug *m* torchlight procession.
fad(e) [fât, fâ'də] *a* insipid; (*langweilig*) dull; (*Essen auch*) tasteless.
Faden [fâ'dən] *m* **-s,** ⁼ thread; **der rote ~** (*fig*) the central theme; **alle ~ laufen hier zusammen** this is the nerve center of the whole business; **~nudeln** *pl* vermicelli *sing*; **f~scheinig** *a* (*lit*, *fig*) threadbare.
Fagott [fágot'] *nt* **-s,** **-e** bassoon.
fähig [fe:'içh] *a* capable (*zu*, *gen* of); **zu allem ~ sein** be capable of anything; **F~keit** *f* ability.
Fähnchen [fe:n'çhən] *nt* pennon, streamer.
fahnden [fân'dən] *vi*: **~ nach** search for.
Fahndung *f* search.
Fahndungsliste *f* list of wanted criminals, wanted list.
Fahne [fâ'nə] *f* **-,** **-n** flag; standard; **mit fliegenden ~n zu jdm/etw überlaufen** go over to sb/sth; **eine ~ haben** (*umg*) smell of drink.
Fahnenflucht *f* desertion.
Fahrausweis *m* (*form*) ticket.
Fahrbahn *f* roadway.
fahrbar *a*: **~er Untersatz** (*hum*) wheels *pl*.
Fähre [fe:'rə] *f* **-,** **-n** ferry.
fahren [fâ'rən] *unreg vt* drive; (*Rad*) ride; (*befördern*) drive, take; (*Rennen*) drive in ♦ *vi* (*sich bewegen*) go; (*Schiff*) sail; (*ab~*) leave; **mit dem Auto/Zug ~** go *od* travel by car/train; **mit dem Aufzug ~** ride the elevator (*US*), take the lift (*Brit*); **links/rechts ~** drive on the left/right; **gegen einen Baum ~** drive *od* go into a tree; **der Bus fährt alle fünf Minuten** the bus goes *od* runs every five minutes; **mit der Hand ~ über** (+*akk*) pass one's hand over; **(bei etw) gut/schlecht ~** (*zurechtkommen*) do well/badly (with sth); **was ist (denn) in dich gefahren?** what's gotten into you?; **einen ~ lassen** (*umg*) fart (*!*).
fahrend *a*: **~es Volk** travel(l)ing people.
Fahrer(in *f*) [fâ'rər(in)] *m* **-s,** - driver; **~flucht** *f* hit-and-run.
Fahr- *zW*: **~gast** *m* passenger; **~geld** *nt*

fare; **~gelegenheit** *f* transport; **~gestell** *nt* chassis; (*AVIAT*) undercarriage.
fahrig [fâ'riçh] *a* nervous; (*unkonzentriert*) distracted.
Fahr- *zW*: **~karte** *f* ticket; **~kartenausgabe** *f* ticket office; **~kartenautomat** *m* ticket machine; **~kartenschalter** *m* ticket office; **f~lässig** *a* negligent; **f~lässige Tötung** manslaughter; **~lässigkeit** *f* negligence; **~lehrer** *m* driving instructor; **~plan** *m* timetable; **f~planmäßig** *a* (*EISENB*) scheduled; **~praxis** *f* driving experience; **~preis** *m* fare; **~prüfung** *f* driving test; **~rad** *nt* bicycle; **~rinne** (*NAUT*) shipping channel, fairway; **~schein** *m* ticket; **~schule** *f* driving school; **~schüler** *m* student driver (*US*), learner (driver) (*Brit*); **~spur** *f* lane; **~stuhl** *m* elevator (*US*), lift (*Brit*); **~stunde** *f* driving lesson.
Fahrt [fârt] *f* **-,** **-en** journey; (*kurz*) trip; (*AUT*) drive; (*Geschwindigkeit*) speed; **gute ~!** safe journey!; **volle ~ voraus!** (*NAUT*) full speed ahead!
fährt [fe:rt] *3. pers sing präs von* **fahren.**
fahrtauglich [fâr'touklichh] *a* fit to drive.
Fährte [fe:r'tə] *f* **-,** **-n** track, trail; **jdn auf eine falsche ~ locken** (*fig*) put sb off the scent.
Fahrtenschreiber *m* tachograph.
Fahrt- *zW*: **~kosten** *pl* travel(l)ing expenses *pl*; **~richtung** *f* course, direction.
fahrtüchtig [fâr'tüchhtichh] *a* fit to drive.
Fahr- *zW*: **~verhalten** *nt* (*von Fahrer*) behavior (*US*) *od* behaviour (*Brit*) behind the wheel; (*von Wagen*) road performance; **~zeug** *nt* vehicle; **~zeughalter** *m* **-s,** - owner of a vehicle; **~zeugpapiere** *pl* vehicle registration papers *pl*.
Faible [fe:bl'] *nt* **-s,** **-s** (*geh*) liking; (*Schwäche auch*) weakness; (*Vorliebe auch*) penchant.
Fäkalien [fekâ'lēən] *pl* feces *pl* (*US*), faeces *pl*.
Faksimile [fákzē:'mēlâ] *nt* **-s,-s** facsimile.
faktisch [fák'tish] *a* actual.
Faktor *m* factor.
Faktum *nt* **-s,** **-ten** fact.
fakturieren [fáktōōrē:'rən] *vt* (*COMM*) invoice.
Fakultät [fákōōlte:t'] *f* faculty.
Falke [fál'kə] *m* **-n,** **-n** falcon.
Fall [fál] *m* **-(e)s,** ⁼e (*Sturz*) fall; (*Sachverhalt*, *JUR*, *GRAM*) case; **auf jeden ~, auf alle ⁼e** in any case; (*bestimmt*) definitely; **gesetzt den ~** assuming (that); **jds ~ sein** (*umg*) be sb's cup of tea; **klarer ~!** (*umg*) sure thing!, you bet!; **das mache ich auf keinen ~** there's no way I'm going to do that.
Falle *f* **-,** **-n** trap; (*umg*: *Bett*) bed; **jdm eine ~ stellen** set a trap for sb.
fallen *vi unreg* fall; (*im Krieg*) fall, be killed; **etw ~ lassen** drop sth.
fällen [fe'lən] *vt* (*Baum*) fell; (*Urteil*) pass.
fallenlassen *vt unreg* (*Bemerkung*) make; (*Plan*) abandon, drop.

fällig [fɛ'liɕ] *a* due; (*Wechsel*) mature(d); **längst** ~ long overdue; **F~keit** *f* (*COMM*) maturity.
Fallobst *nt* fallen fruit, windfall.
falls *kj* in case, if.
Fall- *zW:* ~**schirm** *m* parachute; ~**schirmjäger** *pl,* ~**schirmtruppe** *f* paratroops *pl;* ~**schirmspringer**(**in** *f*) *m* parachutist; ~**strick** *m* (*fig*) trap, snare; ~**studie** *f* case study.
fällt [fɛlt] *3. pers sing präs von* **fallen.**
Falltür *f* trap door.
fallweise *a* from case to case.
falsch [falʃ] *a* false; (*unrichtig*) wrong; ~ **liegen** (*umg*) be wrong (*bei,* in +*dat* about, **mit** in); **ein** ~**es Spiel** (**mit jdm**) **treiben** play (sb) false; **etw** ~ **verstehen** misunderstand sth, get sth wrong.
fälschen [fɛl'ʃən] *vt* forge.
Fälscher(in *f*) *m* **-s,** - forger.
Falsch- *zW:* ~**geld** *nt* counterfeit money; ~**heit** *f* falsity, falseness; (*Unrichtigkeit*) wrongness.
fälsch- *zW:* ~**lich** *a* false; ~**licherweise** *ad* mistakenly.
Falschmeldung *f* (*PRESSE*) false report.
Fälschung *f* forgery.
fälschungssicher *a* forgery-proof.
Faltblatt *nt* leaflet; (*in Zeitschrift etc*) insert.
Fältchen [fɛlt'ɕən] *nt* crease, wrinkle.
Falte [fal'tə] *f* **-, -n** (*Knick*) fold, crease; (*Haut~*) wrinkle; (*Rock~*) pleat.
falten *vt* fold; (*Stirn*) wrinkle; **f~los** *a* without folds; without wrinkles.
Falter [fal'tər] *m* **-s,** - (*Tag~*) butterfly; (*Nacht~*) moth.
falzen [fal'tsən] *vt* (*Papierbogen*) fold.
Fam. *abk =* **Familie.**
familiär [famēlɛ̄:r'] *a* familiar.
Familie [famē:'lēə] *f* family; ~ **Otto Francke** (*als Anschrift*) Mr. & Mrs. Otto Francke and family; **zur** ~ **gehören** be one of the family.
Familien- *zW:* ~**ähnlichkeit** *f* family resemblance; ~**anschluß** *m:* **Unterkunft mit** ~**anschluß** *accommodation where one is treated as one of the family;* ~**kreis** *m* family circle; ~**name** *m* surname; ~**packung** *f* family(-size) pack; ~**planung** *f* family planning; ~**stand** *m* marital status; ~**vater** *m* head of the family; ~**verhältnisse** *pl* family circumstances *pl.*
Fanatiker(in *f*) [faná'tēkər(in)] *m* **-s,** - fanatic.
fanatisch *a* fanatical.
Fanatismus [fanátis'mōōs] *m* fanaticism.
fand [fant] *imperf von* **finden.**
Fang [faŋ] *m* **-(e)s, ⁼e** catch; (*Jagen*) hunting; (*Kralle*) talon, claw.
fangen *unreg vt* catch ♦ *vr* get caught; (*Flugzeug*) level out; (*Mensch: nicht fallen*) steady o.s.; (*fig*) compose o.s.; (*in Leistung*) get back on form.
Fang- *zW:* ~**frage** *f* catch *od* trick question; ~**gründe** *pl* fishing grounds *pl.*
fängt [fɛŋkt] *3. pers sing präs von* **fangen.**

Farb- [farp'] *zW:* ~**abzug** *m* colored print; ~**aufnahme** *f* color photograph; ~**band** *m* typewriter ribbon.
Farbe [far'bə] *f* **-, -n** color (*US*), colour (*Brit*); (*zum Malen etc*) paint; (*Stoff~*) dye; (*KARTEN*) suit.
farbecht [farp'ɛɕt] *a* colorfast.
färben [fer'bən] *vt* color; (*Stoff, Haar*) dye.
farben- [far'bən] *zW:* ~**blind** *a* color-blind; ~**froh,** ~**prächtig** *a* colorful.
Farb- [farp'] *zW:* ~**fernsehen** *nt* color television; ~**film** *m* color film.
farbig *a* black.
Farbige(r) *mf dekl wie a* black.
Farb- [farp'] *zW:* ~**kasten** *m* paint-box; **f~los** *a* colorless; ~**photographie** *f* color photography; ~**stift** *m* colored pencil; ~**stoff** *m* dye; (*Lebensmittel~*) (artificial) coloring; ~**ton** *m* hue, tone.
Färbung [fer'bōōŋ] *f* coloring; (*Tendenz*) bias.
Farn [farn] *m* **-(e)s, -e,** ~**kraut** *nt* fern; (*Adler~*) bracken.
Färöer [fɛrœ'ər] *pl* Faeroe Islands *pl.*
Fasan [fázán'] *m* **-(e)s, -e(n)** pheasant.
Fasching [fá'ʃiŋ] *m* **-s, -e** *od* **-s** carnival.
Faschismus [faʃis'mōōs] *m* fascism.
Faschist(in *f*) *m* fascist.
faschistisch [faʃis'tiʃ] *a* fascist.
faseln [fá'zəln] *vi* talk nonsense, drivel.
Faser [fá'zər] *f* **-, -n** fiber (*US*), fibre.
fasern *vi* fray.
Faß [fás] *nt* **-sses, Fässer** vat, barrel; (*für Öl*) drum; **Bier vom** ~ draught beer; **ein** ~ **ohne Boden** (*fig*) a bottomless pit.
Fassade [fásá'də] *f* (*lit, fig*) façade.
faßbar *a* comprehensible.
Faßbier *nt* draught beer.
fassen [fá'sən] *vt* (*ergreifen*) grasp, take; (*inhaltlich*) hold; (*Entschluß etc*) take; (*verstehen*) understand; (*Ring etc*) set; (*formulieren*) formulate, phrase; **nicht zu** ~ unbelievable ♦ *vr* calm down; **sich kurz** ~ be brief.
faßlich [fás'liɕ] *a* intelligible.
Fasson [fásõ'] *f* **-, -s** style; (*Art und Weise*) way; **aus der** ~ **geraten** (*lit*) lose its shape.
Fassung [fá'sōōŋ] *f* (*Umrahmung*) mounting; (*Lampen~*) socket; (*Wortlaut*) version; (*Beherrschung*) composure; **jdn aus der** ~ **bringen** upset sb; **völlig außer** ~ **geraten** lose all self-control.
Fassungs- *zW:* **f~los** *a* speechless; ~**vermögen** *nt* capacity; (*Verständnis*) comprehension.
fast [fást] *ad* almost, nearly; ~ **nie** hardly ever.
fasten [fás'tən] *vi* fast; **F~** *nt* **-s** fasting; **F~zeit** *f* Lent.
Fastnacht *f* Shrove Tuesday; Shrovetide carnival.
fatal [fátál'] *a* fatal; (*peinlich*) embarrassing.
fauchen [fou'khən] *vti* hiss.
faul [foul] *a* rotten; (*Person*) lazy; (*Ausreden*) lame; **daran ist etwas** ~ there's some-

thing fishy about it.
faulen vi rot.
faulenzen [fou'lentsən] vi idle.
Faulenzer(in f) m **-s,** - idler, loafer.
Faulheit f laziness.
faulig a putrid.
Fäulnis [foil'nis] f - decay, putrefaction.
Faulpelz m (umg) lazybones sing.
Faust [foust] f -, **Fäuste** fist; **das paßt wie die ~ aufs Auge** (paßt nicht) it's all wrong; **auf eigene ~** (fig) on one's own initiative.
Fäustchen [foist'çhən] nt: **sich** (dat) **ins ~ lachen** laugh up one's sleeve.
faustdick a (umg): **er hat es ~ hinter den Ohren** he's a crafty one.
Fausthandschuh m mitten.
Faustregel f rule of thumb.
Favorit(in f) [favōrē:t'(in)] m **-en, -en** favorite (US), favourite (Brit).
Faxen [fák'sən] pl: **~ machen** fool around.
Fazit [fá'tsit] nt **-s, -s** od **-e: wenn wir aus diesen vier Jahren das ~ ziehen** if we take stock of these four years.
FB m abk = **Fachbereich.**
FD m abk (= Fernschnellzug od Ferndurchgangszug) express train, long-distance train.
FdH abk (umg: = Friß die Hälfte) eat less.
FDJ f abk (= Freie Deutsche Jugend (DDR)) State-run youth organisation in the GDR.
FDP, F.D.P. f - abk (= Freie Demokratische Partei) Free Democratic Party.
Feb(r). abk (= Februar) Feb.
Februar [fā:'brōōár] m **-(s), -e** February; siehe **September.**
fechten [feçh'tən] vi unreg fence.
Feder [fā:'dər] f -, **-n** feather; (Schreib~) pen nib; (TECH) spring; **in den ~n liegen** (umg) be/stay in bed; **~ball** m shuttlecock; **~ballspiel** nt badminton; **~bett** nt continental quilt; **f~führend** a (Behörde) in overall charge (für of); **~halter** m penholder; pen; **f~leicht** a light as a feather; **~lesen** nt: **nicht viel ~lesens mit jdm/etw machen** make short work of sb/sth.
federn vi (nachgeben) be springy; (sich bewegen) bounce ♦ vt spring.
Federung f suspension.
Federvieh nt poultry.
Federweiße(r) m dekl wie a new wine.
Federzeichnung f pen-and-ink drawing.
Fee [fā:] f -, **-n** fairy.
feenhaft [fā:'ənhàft] a (liter) fairylike.
Fegefeuer [fā:'gəfoiər] nt purgatory.
fegen [fā:'gən] vt sweep.
fehl [fā:l] a: **~ am Platz** od **Ort** out of place; **F~anzeige** f (umg) dead loss.
fehlen vi be wanting od missing; (abwesend sein) be absent; **etw fehlt jdm** sb lacks sth; **du fehlst mir** I miss you; **was fehlt ihm?** what's wrong with him?; **der/das hat mir gerade noch gefehlt!** (ironisch) he/that was all I needed; **weit gefehlt!** (fig) you're way out! (umg); (ganz im Gegenteil) far from

it!; **mir ~ die Worte** words fail me ♦ vi unpers: **es fehlte nicht viel, und ich hätte ihn verprügelt** I almost hit him; **wo fehlt es?** what's the trouble?, what's up? (umg).
Fehlentscheidung f wrong decision.
Fehler m **-s,** - mistake, error; (Mangel, Schwäche) fault; **ihr ist ein ~ unterlaufen** she's made a mistake; **~beseitigung** f (COMPUT) debugging; **f~frei** a faultless; without any mistakes; **f~haft** a incorrect; faulty; **~meldung** f (COMPUT) error message; **~suchprogramm** nt (COMPUT) debugging program.
fehl- zW: **F~geburt** f miscarriage; **~gehen** vi unreg go astray; **F~griff** m blunder; **F~konstruktion** f: **F~konstruktion sein** be badly designed; **F~leistung** f: **Freudsche F~leistung** Freudian slip; **F~schlag** m failure; **~schlagen** vi unreg fail; **F~schluß** m wrong conclusion; **F~start** m (SPORT) false start; **F~tritt** m false move; (fig) blunder, slip; (fig: Affäre) indiscretion; **F~urteil** nt miscarriage of justice; **F~zündung** f (AUT) misfire, backfire.
Feier [fī'ər] f -, **-n** celebration; **~abend** m time to stop work; **~abend machen** stop, knock off; **was machst du am ~abend?** what are you doing after work?; **jetzt ist ~abend!** that's enough!
feierlich a solemn; **das ist ja nicht mehr ~** (umg) that's beyond a joke; **F~keit** f solemnity; **F~keiten** pl festivities pl.
feiern vti celebrate.
Feiertag m holiday.
feig(e) [fīk, fī'gə] a cowardly.
Feige f -, **-n** fig.
feig- zW: **F~heit** f cowardice; **F~ling** m coward.
Feile [fī'lə] f -, **-n** file.
feilen vti file.
feilschen [fīl'shən] vi haggle.
fein [fīn] a fine; (vornehm) refined; (Gehör etc) keen; **~!** great!; **er ist ~ raus** (umg) he's sitting pretty; **sich ~ machen** get all dressed up.
Feind(in f) [fīnt, fīn'din] m **-(e)s, -e** enemy; **~bild** nt concept of an/the enemy; **f~lich** a hostile; **~schaft** f enmity; **f~selig** a hostile; **~seligkeit** f hostility.
Fein- zW: **f~fühlend, f~fühlig** a sensitive; **~gefühl** nt delicacy, tact; **~heit** f fineness; refinement; keenness; **~kostgeschäft** nt delicatessen (shop); **~schmecker** m **-s,** - gourmet; **~waschmittel** nt mild(-action) detergent.
feist [fīst] a fat.
feixen [fīk'sən] vi (umg) smirk.
Feld [felt] nt **-(e)s, -er** field; (SCHACH) square; (SPORT) pitch; **Argumente ins ~ führen** bring arguments to bear; **das ~ räumen** (fig) bow out; **~arbeit** f (AGR) work in the fields; (GEOG etc) fieldwork; **~bett** nt cot (US), campbed (Brit); **~blume** f wild flower; **~herr** m commander; **~jäger** mpl

(*MIL*) the military police; ~**salat** *m* lamb's lettuce; ~**stecher** *m* (pair of) binoculars *pl od* field glasses *pl*.

Feld-Wald-und-Wiesen *in zW* (*umg*) common-or-garden.

Feld- *zW*: ~**webel** *m* **-s**, - sergeant; ~**weg** *m* path; ~**zug** *m* (*lit*, *fig*) campaign.

Felge [fɛl'gə] *f* -, **-n** (wheel) rim.

Felgenbremse *f* caliper brake.

Fell [fɛl] *nt* **-(e)s**, **-e** fur; coat; (*von Schaf*) fleece; (*von toten Tieren*) skin; **ein dickes ~ haben** be thickskinned, have a thick skin; **ihm sind die ~e weggeschwommen** (*fig*) all his hopes were dashed.

Fels [fɛls] *m* **-en**, **-en** = **Felsen**.

Felsen [fɛl'zən] *m* **-s**, - rock; (*von Dover etc*) cliff; **f~fest** *a* firm.

felsig *a* rocky.

Felsspalte *f* crevice.

Felsvorsprung *m* ledge.

feminin [fāmēnē:n'] *a* feminine; (*pej*) effeminate.

Feministin [fāmēnis'tin] *f* feminist.

Fenchel [fen'çəl] *m* **-s** fennel.

Fenster [fɛns'tər] *nt* **-s**, - window; **weg vom ~** (*umg*) out of the game, finished; ~**brett** *nt* windowsill; ~**laden** *m* shutter; ~**leder** *nt* chamois, shammy (leather); ~**putzer** *m* **-s**, - window cleaner; ~**scheibe** *f* windowpane; ~**sims** *m* windowsill.

Ferien [fā:'rēən] *pl* vacation (*US*), holidays *pl* (*Brit*); **die großen ~** the long vacation (*US UNIV*), the summer holidays (*Brit*); **~ haben** be on vacation; ~**gast** *m* vacationist (*US*), holiday-maker (*Brit*); ~**kurs** *m* ≈ summer school; ~**reise** *f* holiday; ~**zeit** *f* holiday period.

Ferkel [fer'kəl] *nt* **-s**, - piglet.

fern [fārn] *a*, *ad* far-off, distant; **~ von hier** a long way (away) from here; **F~amt** *nt* (*TEL*) exchange; **F~bedienung** *f* remote control.

Ferne *f* -, **-n** distance.

ferner *a*, *ad* further; (*weiterhin*) in future; **unter ~ liefen rangieren** (*umg*) be an also-ran.

fern- *zW*: **F~fahrer** *m* long-distance truck (*US*) *od* lorry (*Brit*) driver; **F~flug** *m* long-distance flight; **F~gespräch** *nt* long-distance call; ~**gesteuert** *a* remote-controlled; (*Rakete*) guided; **F~glas** *nt* binoculars *pl*; ~**halten** *vtr unreg* keep away; **F~kopierer** *m* facsimile machine; **F~kurs(us)** *m* correspondence course; **F~lenkung** *f* remote control; **F~licht** *nt* (*AUT*): **mit F~licht fahren** drive on full beam; ~**liegen** *vi unreg*: **jdm ~liegen** be far from sb's mind.

Fernmelde- *in zW* telecommunications; (*MIL*) signals.

fern- *zW*: **F~ost**: **aus/in F~ost** from/in the Far East; ~**östlich** *a* Far Eastern *attr*; **F~rohr** *nt* telescope; **F~schreiben** *nt* telex; **F~schreiber** *m* teleprinter; ~**schriftlich** *a* by telex.

Fernsehapparat *m* television set.

fernsehen [fārn'zā:ən] *vi unreg* watch television; **F~** *nt* **-s** television; **im F~** on television.

Fernseher *m* **-s**, - television.

Fernseh- *zW*: ~**gebühr** *f* television license (*US*) *od* licence (*Brit*) fee; ~**programm** *nt* (*Kanal*) channel, station; (*Sendung*) program (*US*), programme (*Brit*); (~*zeitschrift*) television guide; ~**überwachungsanlage** *f* closed-circuit television; ~**zuschauer** *m* (television) viewer.

fern- *zW*: **F~sprecher** *m* telephone; **F~sprechzelle** *f* telephone booth; **F~studium** *nt* multi-media course; **F~verkehr** *m* long-distance traffic; **F~weh** *m* wanderlust.

Ferse [fer'zə] *f* -, **-n** heel.

Fersengeld *nt*: **~ geben** take to one's heels.

fertig [fer'tiç] *a* (*bereit*) ready; (*beendet*) finished; (*gebrauchs~*) ready-made; **~ ausgebildet** fully qualified; **mit jdm/etw ~ werden** cope with sb/sth; **mit den Nerven ~ sein** be at the end of one's tether; **~ essen/lesen** finish eating/reading; **F~bau** *m* prefab(ricated house); ~**bringen** *vt unreg* (*fähig sein*) manage, be capable of; (*beenden*) finish; **F~gericht** *nt* ready-to-serve meal; **F~haus** *nt* prefab(ricated house); **F~keit** *f* skill; ~**machen** *vt* (*beenden*) finish; (*umg*: *Person*) finish; (*: körperlich*) exhaust; (*: moralisch*) get down ♦ *vr* get ready; ~**stellen** *vt* complete.

Fertigungs- *in zW* production; ~**straße** *f* production line.

Fertigware *f* finished product.

fesch [fesh] *a* (*umg*: *modisch*) smart; (*hübsch*) attractive.

Fessel [fe'səl] *f* -, **-n** fetter.

fesseln *vt* bind; (*mit Fesseln*) fetter; (*fig*) grip; **ans Bett gefesselt** (*fig*) confined to bed.

fesselnd *a* gripping.

fest [fest] *a* firm; (*Nahrung*) solid; (*Gehalt*) regular; (*Gewebe*, *Schuhe*) strong, sturdy; (*Freund(in)*) steady; **~ entschlossen sein** be absolutely determined; **~e Kosten** *pl* (*COMM*) fixed cost ♦ *ad* (*schlafen*) soundly.

Fest *nt* **-(e)s**, **-e** (*Feier*) celebration; (*Party*) party; **man soll die ~e feiern, wie sie fallen** (*Sprichwort*) make hay while the sun shines.

festangestellt *a* employed on a permanent basis.

Festbeleuchtung *f* illumination.

fest- [festklammern] *zW*: ~**binden** *vt unreg* tie, fasten; ~**bleiben** *vi unreg* stand firm.

Festessen *nt* banquet.

fest- *zW*: ~**fahren** *vr unreg* get stuck; ~**halten** ♦ *unreg vt* seize, hold fast; (*Ereignis*) record ♦ *vr* hold on (*an* +*dat* to).

festigen *vt* strengthen.

Festigkeit *f* strength.

fest- *zW*: ~**klammern** *vr* cling on (*an* +*dat*

to); **~klemmen** *vt* wedge fast; **F~komma** *nt* (*COMPUT*) fixed point; **F~land** *nt* mainland; **~legen** *vt* fix; **jdn auf etw** (*akk*) **~legen** (*~nageln*) tie sb (down) to sth; (*verpflichten*) commit sb to sth ♦ *vr* commit o.s.

festlich *a* festive.

fest- *zW*: **~liegen** *vi unreg* (*FIN*: *Geld*) be tied up; **~machen** *vt* fasten; (*Termin etc*) fix; **~nageln** *vt*: **jdn ~nageln** (*fig*, *umg*) pin sb down (*auf +akk* to); **F~nahme** *f* -, -n capture; **~nehmen** *vt unreg* capture, arrest; **F~platte** *f* (*COMPUT*) hard disk; **F~preis** *m* (*COMM*) fixed price.

Festrede *f* speech, address.

fest- *zW*: **~schnallen** *vt* strap down ♦ *vr* fasten one's seat belt; **~setzen** *vt* fix, settle; **F~spiel** *nt* festival; **~stehen** *vi unreg* be certain; **~stellbar** *a* (*herauszufinden*) ascertainable; **~stellen** *vt* establish; (*sagen*) remark; (*TECH*) lock (fast); **F~stellung** *f*: **die F~stellung machen, daß...** realize that...; (*bemerken*) remark *od* observe that...; **~umrissen** *a attr* clear-cut; **F~ung** *f* fortress; **~verzinslich** *a* fixed-interest *attr*; **F~wertspeicher** *m* (*COMPUT*) read-only memory.

Fete, Fête [fāː'tə] *f* -, -n party.

Fett [fɛt] *nt* -(e)s, -e fat, grease; **f~** *a* fat; (*Essen etc*) greasy; **f~arm** *a* low fat; **f~en** *vt* grease; **~fleck** *m* grease spot *od* stain; **f~gedruckt** *a* bold-type; **~gehalt** *m* fat content; **f~ig** *a* greasy, fatty; **~näpfchen** *nt*: **ins ~näpfchen treten** put one's foot in it; **~polster** *nt* (*hum umg*): **~polster haben** be well-padded.

Fetzen [fe'tsən] *m* -s, - scrap; ..., **daß die ~ fliegen** (*umg*) ... like mad.

feucht [foiçt] *a* damp; (*Luft*) humid; **~fröhlich** *a* (*hum*) boozy.

Feuchtigkeit *f* dampness; humidity.

Feuchtigkeitscreme *f* moisturizer.

feudal [foidâl'] *a* (*POL, HIST*) feudal; (*umg*) plush.

Feuer [foi'ər] *nt* -s, - fire; (*zum Rauchen*) a light; (*fig*: *Schwung*) spirit; **für jdn durchs ~ gehen** go through fire and water for sb; **~ und Flamme sein** (*umg*) be all fired up; **~ für etw/jdn fangen** (*fig*) develop a great interest in sth/sb; **~alarm** *nt* fire alarm; **~eifer** *m* zeal; **f~fest** *a* fireproof; **~gefahr** *f* danger of fire; **bei ~gefahr** in the event of fire; **f~gefährlich** *a* inflammable; **~leiter** *f* fire escape ladder; **~löscher** *m* -s, - fire extinguisher; **~melder** *m* -s, - fire alarm.

feuern *vti* (*lit, fig*) fire.

feuerpolizeilich *a* (*Bestimmungen*) laid down by the fire authorities.

Feuersbrunst *f* (*geh*) conflagration.

Feuer- *zW*: **~schlucker** *m* fire-eater; **~schutz** *m* (*Vorbeugung*) fire prevention; (*MIL*: *Deckung*) covering fire; **f~sicher** *a* fireproof; **~stein** *m* flint; **~stelle** *f* fireplace; **~versicherung** *f* fire insurance; **~wehr** *f* -,

-en fire brigade; **~wehrauto** *nt* fire engine; **~werk** *nt* fireworks *pl*; **~werkskörper** *m* firework; **~zangenbowle** *f* red wine punch containing rum which has been flamed off; **~zeug** *nt* (cigarette) lighter.

Feuilleton [fœyətõn'] *nt* -s, -s (*PRESSE*) feature section; (*Artikel*) feature (article).

feurig [foi'riç] *a* fiery.

FFF *abk* = Film, Funk, Fernsehen.

Fiche [fēːsh] *m od nt* -(s),-s (micro)fiche.

ficht [fiçt] 3. *pers sing präs von* fechten.

Fichte [fiç'tə] *f* -, -n spruce; pine.

ficken [fi'kən] *vti* (*umg!*) fuck (*!*).

fick(e)rig [fi'kriç] *a* (*umg*) fidgety.

fidel [fēdāːl'] *a* (*umg*) jolly.

Fidschiinseln [fid'zhēinzəln] *pl* Fiji Islands.

Fieber [fēː'bər] *nt* -s, - fever, temperature; (*Krankheit*) fever; **~ haben** have a temperature; **f~haft** *a* feverish; **~messer** *m*, **~thermometer** *nt* thermometer.

fiel [fēːl] *imperf von* fallen.

fies [fēːs] *a* (*umg*) nasty.

Figur [fēgōōːr'] *f* -, -en figure; (*Schach~*) chessman, chess piece; **eine gute/ schlechte/traurige ~ abgeben** cut a good/ poor/sorry figure.

fiktiv [fiktēːf'] *a* fictitious.

Fil. *abk* (= *Filiale*) br.

Filet [fēlā'] *nt* -s, -s (*KOCH*) fillet; (*Rinder~*) fillet steak; (*zum Braten*) piece of sirloin *od* tenderloin.

Filiale [fēlēâ'lə] *f* -, -n (*COMM*) branch.

Film [film] *m* -(e)s, -e movie, film; **da ist bei mir der ~ gerissen** (*umg*) I had a mental blackout; **~aufnahme** *f* shooting.

Filmemacher(in *f*) *m* film-maker.

filmen *vti* film.

Film- *zW*: **~festspiele** *pl* film festival *sing*; **~kamera** *f* movie camera; **~riß** *m* (*umg*) mental blackout; **~schauspieler(in** *f*) *m* movie *od* film actor/actress; **~verleih** *m* film distributors *pl*; **~vorführgerät** *nt* movie projector.

Filter [fil'tər] *m* -s, - filter; **~kaffee** *m* filter *od* drip (*US*) coffee; **~mundstück** *nt* filter tip.

filtern *vt* filter.

Filter- *zW*: **~papier** *nt* filter paper; **~zigarette** *f* filter cigarette.

Filz [filts] *m* -es, -e felt.

filzen *vt* (*umg*) frisk ♦ *vi* (*Wolle*) mat.

Filzstift *m* felt-tip (pen).

Fimmel [fi'məl] *m* -s, - (*umg*): **du hast wohl einen ~!** you're crazy!

Finale [fēnâ'lə] *nt* -s, -(s) finale; (*SPORT*) final (*s pl*).

Finanz [fēnänts'] *f* finance; **~amt** *nt* ≈ Internal Revenue Service (*US*), Inland Revenue Office (*Brit*); **~beamte(r)** *mf* revenue officer; **~en** *pl* finances *pl*; **das übersteigt meine ~en** that's beyond my means.

finanziell [fēnäntsēel'] *a* financial.

finanzieren [fēnäntsēː'rən] *vt* finance.

Finanz- *zW*: **~minister** *m* Minister of Finance; **f~schwach** *a* financially weak;

~wesen nt financial system; **~wirtschaft** f financial economy/system.

finden [fēn'dən] unreg vt find; (meinen) think; **ich finde nichts dabei, wenn...** I don't see what's wrong if ... ♦ vr be (found); (sich fassen) compose o.s.; **das wird sich ~ things will work out** ♦ vi: **ich finde schon allein hinaus** I can see myself out.

Finder(in f) m **-s,** - finder; **~lohn** m reward (for the finder).

findig a resourceful.

fing [fing] imperf von **fangen.**

Finger [fi'ngər] m **-s,** - finger; **mit ~n auf jdn zeigen** (fig) look askance at sb; **das kann sich jeder an den (fünf) ~n abzählen** (umg) it sticks out a mile; **sich** (dat) **etw aus den ~n saugen** conjure sth up; **lange ~ machen** (umg) be light-fingered; **~abdruck** m fingerprint; **~handschuh** m glove; **~hut** m thimble; (BOT) foxglove; **~ring** m ring; **~spitze** f fingertip; **~spitzengefühl** nt sensitivity; **~zeig** m **-(e)s, -e** hint, pointer.

fingieren [fingē:'rən] vt feign.

fingiert a made-up, fictitious.

Fink [fingk] m **-en, -en** finch.

Finne [fi'nə] m **-n, -n** Finn.

Finnin [fi'nin] f Finn.

finnisch a Finnish.

Finnland nt Finland.

finster [fin'stər] a dark, gloomy; (verdächtig) dubious; (verdrossen) grim; (Gedanke) dark; **jdn ~ ansehen** give sb a black look; **F~nis** f - darkness, gloom.

Finte [fin'tə] f **-, -n** feint, trick.

Firlefanz [fir'ləfánts] m (umg: Kram) frippery; (Albernheit): **mach keinen ~ don't clown around.**

firm [firm] a well-up.

Firma f **-, -men** firm; **die ~ dankt** (hum) much obliged (to you).

Firmen- zW: **~aufkauf** m acquisition; **~inhaber** m proprietor (of firm); **~register** nt register of companies; **~schild** nt (shop) sign; **~übernahme** f take-over; **~wagen** m company car; **F~zeichen** nt registered trademark.

Firmung f (REL) confirmation.

Firnis [fir'nis] m **-ses, -se** varnish.

Fis [fis] nt (MUS) F sharp.

Fisch [fish] m **-(e)s, -e** fish; **~e** pl (ASTROL) Pisces; **das sind kleine ~e** (fig umg) that's child's play; **~bestand** m fish population.

fischen vti fish.

Fischer m **-s,** - fisherman.

Fischerei [fishərī'] f fishing, fishery.

Fisch- zW: **~fang** m fishing; **~geschäft** nt fish store; **~gräte** f fishbone; **~gründe** pl fishing grounds pl, fisheries pl; **~stäbchen** nt fish stick (US), fish finger (Brit); **~zug** m catch of fish.

Fisimatenten [fēzēmáten'tən] pl (umg: Ausflüchte) excuses pl; (: Umstände) fuss sing.

Fiskus [fis'kŏōs] m (fig: Staatskasse) Treasury.

Fittich [fi'tich] m **-(e)s, -e** (liter): **jdn unter seine ~e nehmen** (hum) take sb under one's wing.

fix [fiks] a (flink) quick; (Person) alert, smart; **~e Idee** obsession, idée fixe; **~ und fertig** finished; (erschöpft) done in; **jdn ~ und fertig machen** (nervös machen) drive sb mad.

fixen vi (umg: Drogen spritzen) fix.

fixieren [fiksē:'rən] vt fix; (anstarren) stare at; **er ist zu stark auf seine Mutter fixiert** (PSYCH) he has a mother fixation.

Fixkosten pl (COMM) fixed costs pl.

FKK abk = **Freikörperkultur.**

flach [fláкh] a flat; (Gefäß) shallow; **auf dem ~en Land** in the middle of the country.

Fläche [fle'chə] f **-, -n** area; (Ober~) surface.

Flächeninhalt m surface area.

Flach- zW: **~heit** f flatness; shallowness; **~land** nt lowland; **f~liegen** vi unreg (umg) be laid up; **~mann** m, pl **-männer** (umg) hipflask.

flachsen [fláк'sən] vi (umg) kid around.

flackern [fláк'kərn] vi flare, flicker.

Fladen [flá'dən] m **-s,** - (KOCH) round flat dough-cake; (umg: Kuh~) cowpat.

Flagge [flá'gə] f **-, -n** flag; **~ zeigen** (fig) nail one's colors to the mast.

flaggen vi fly flags od a flag.

flagrant [flágránt'] a flagrant; **in flagranti** red-handed.

Flak [fláк] f **-s,** - (= Flug(zeug)abwehrkanone) anti-aircraft gun; (Einheit) anti-aircraft unit.

flambieren [flámbē:'rən] vt (KOCH) flambé.

Flame [flá'mə] m **-n, -n** Fleming.

Flämin [fle:'min] f Fleming.

flämisch a Flemish.

Flamme [flá'mə] f **-, -n** flame; **in ~n stehen/ aufgehen** be in flames/go up in flames.

Flandern [flán'dərn] nt Flanders sing.

Flanell [flánel'] m **-s, -e** flannel.

Flanke [fláng'kə] f **-, -n** flank; (SPORT: Seite) wing.

Flasche [flá'shə] f **-, -n** bottle; (umg: Versager) wash-out; **zur ~ greifen** (fig) hit the bottle.

Flaschen- zW: **~bier** nt bottled beer; **~öffner** m bottle opener; **~zug** m pulley.

flatterhaft a flighty, fickle.

flattern [flá'tərn] vi flutter.

flau [flou] a (Brise, COMM) slack; **jdm ist ~ (im Magen)** sb feels queasy.

Flaum [floum] m **-(e)s** (Feder) down; fluff.

flauschig [flou'shich] a fluffy.

Flausen [flou'zən] pl silly ideas pl; (Ausflüchte) weak excuses pl.

Flaute [flou'tə] f **-, -n** calm; (COMM) recession.

Flechte [flec'tə] f **-, -n** plait; (MED) dry scab; (BOT) lichen.

flechten vt unreg plait; (Kranz) twine.

Fleck [fleк] m **-(e)s, -e, Flecken** m **-s,** -

(*Schmutz~*) stain; (*Farb~*) patch; (*Stelle*) spot; **nicht vom ~ kommen** (*lit, fig*) not get any further; **sich nicht vom ~ rühren** not budge; **vom ~ weg** straight away.
Fleckchen *nt*: **ein schönes ~ (Erde)** a lovely little spot.
Flecken- *zW*: **f~los** *a* spotless; **~mittel** *nt*, **~wasser** *nt* stain remover.
fleckig *a* marked; stained.
Fledermaus [flä:'dərmous] *f* bat.
Flegel [flä:'gəl] *m* **-s, -** flail; (*Person*) lout; **f~haft** *a* loutish, unmannerly; **~jahre** *pl* adolescence.
flegeln *vr* loll, sprawl.
flehen [flä:'ən] *vi* (*geh*) implore.
flehentlich *a* imploring.
Fleisch [flīsh] *nt* **-(e)s** flesh; (*Essen*) meat; **sich** (*dat od akk*) **ins eigene ~ schneiden** cut off one's nose to spite one's face (*Sprichwort*); **es ist mir in ~ und Blut übergegangen** it has become second nature to me; **~brühe** *f* meat stock.
Fleischer *m* **-s, -** butcher.
Fleischerei [flīshərī'] *f* butcher's (shop).
fleischig *a* fleshy.
Fleisch- *zW*: **~käse** *m* meat loaf; **~kloß** *m*, **~klößchen** *nt* meat ball; **f~lich** *a* carnal; **~pastete** *f* meat pie; **~salat** *m* diced meat salad with mayonnaise; **~vergiftung** *f* food poisoning (*from meat*); **~wolf** *m* grinder (*US*), mincer (*Brit*); **~wunde** *f* flesh wound; **~wurst** *f* pork sausage.
Fleiß [flīs] *m* **-es** diligence, industry; **ohne ~ kein Preis** (*Sprichwort*) success never comes easily.
fleißig *a* diligent, industrious; **~ studieren/ arbeiten** study/work hard.
flektieren [flɛktē:'rən] *vt* inflect.
flennen [flɛ'nən] *vi* (*umg*) cry, blubber.
fletschen [flɛt'shən] *vt* (*Zähne*) show.
Fleurop [floi'rop] *f* ® ≈ Interflora ®.
flexibel [flɛksē:'bəl] *a* flexible.
flicht [flićht] *3. pers sing präs von* **flechten**.
flicken [fli'kən] *vt* mend.
Flicken *m* **-s, -** patch.
Flickschusterei [flik'shōō:stərī] *f*: **das ist ~** that's a patch-up job.
Flieder [flē:'dər] *m* **-s, -** lilac.
Fliege [flē:'gə] *f* **-, -n** fly; (*Schlips*) bow tie; **zwei ~n mit einer Klappe schlagen** (*Sprichwort*) kill two birds with one stone; **ihn stört die ~ an der Wand** every little thing irritates him.
fliegen *unreg vt* fly ♦ *vi* fly; **auf jdn/etw ~** (*umg*) be mad about sb/sth; **aus der Kurve ~** skid off the bend; **aus der Firma ~** (*umg*) get the sack.
fliegend *a attr* flying; **~e Hitze** hot flushes *pl*.
Fliegenklatsche [flē:'gənklåtshə] *f* fly-swat.
Fliegenpilz *m* fly agaric.
Flieger *m* **-s, -** flier, airman; **~alarm** *m* air-raid warning.
fliehen [flē:'ən] *vi unreg* flee.

Fliehkraft [flē:'kråft] *f* centrifugal force.
Fliese [flē:'zə] *f* **-, -n** tile.
Fließ- [flē:s'] *zW*: **~arbeit** *f* production-line work; **~band** *nt* production *od* assembly line; **am ~band arbeiten** work on the assembly *od* production line; **~band-produktion** *f* assembly-line production.
fließen *vi unreg* flow.
fließend *a* flowing; (*Rede, Deutsch*) fluent; (*Übergänge*) smooth.
Fließ- *zW*: **~heck** *nt* fastback; **~komma** *nt* (*COMPUT*) ≈ floating point; **~papier** *nt* blotter (*US*), blotting paper (*Brit*).
Flimmerkasten *m*, **Flimmerkiste** *f* (*umg*) TV, box.
flimmern [fli'mərn] *vi* glimmer; **es flimmert mir vor den Augen** my head's swimming.
flink [flingk] *a* nimble, lively; **mit etw ~ bei der Hand sein** be quick (off the mark) with sth; **F~heit** *f* nimbleness, liveliness.
Flinte [flin'tə] *f* **-, -n** shotgun; **die ~ ins Korn werfen** throw in the sponge.
flirten [flir'tən] *vi* flirt.
Flittchen *nt* **-s, -** (*pej umg*) slut.
Flitter [fli'tər] *m* **-s, -** (**~schmuck**) sequins *pl*.
Flitterwochen *pl* honeymoon.
flitzen [fli'tsən] *vi* flit.
Flitzer *m* **-s, -** (*umg; Auto*) sporty car.
floaten [flō:'tən] *vti* (*FIN*) float.
flocht [floḱht] *imperf von* **flechten**.
Flocke [flo'kə] *f* **-, -n** flake.
flockig *a* flaky.
flog [flō:k] *imperf von* **fliegen**.
floh [flō:] *imperf von* **fliehen**.
Floh *m* **-(e)s, ¨e** flea; **jdm einen ~ ins Ohr setzen** (*umg*) put an idea into sb's head; **~markt** *m* flea market.
Flora [flō:'rá] *f* **-, -ren** flora.
Florenz [flōrents'] *nt* Florence.
florieren [flōrē:'ārən] *vi* flourish.
Florist(in *f*) *m* florist.
Floskel [flos'kəl] *f* **-, -n** set phrase; **f~haft** *a* cliché-ridden, stereotyped.
floß [flos] *imperf von* **fließen**.
Floß [flō:s] *nt* **-es, ¨e** raft.
Flosse [flo'sə] *f* **-, -n** fin; (*Taucher~*) flipper; (*umg: Hand*) paw.
Flöte [flœ'tə] *f* **-, -n** flute; (*Block~*) recorder.
flötengehen [flœ'təngā:ən] *vi* (*umg*) be ruined.
Flötist(in *f*) [flœtist'(in)] *m* flautist.
flott [flot] *a* lively; (*elegant*) smart; (*NAUT*) afloat.
Flotte [flo'tə] *f* **-, -n** fleet.
Flottenstützpunkt *m* naval base.
Flöz [flœts] *nt* **-es, -e** layer, seam.
Fluch [flōō:ḱh] *m* **-(e)s, ¨e** curse; **f~en** *vi* curse, swear.
Flucht [flōō:ḱht] *f* **-, -en** flight; (*Fenster~*) row; (*Reihe*) range; (*Zimmer~*) suite; (*geglückt auch*) escape; **jdn/etw in die ~ schlagen** put sb/sth to flight.
fluchtartig *a* hasty.
flüchten [flüćh'tən] *vi* flee ♦ *vr* take refuge.

Fluchthilfe *f:* ~ **leisten** aid an escape.

flüchtig *a* fugitive; (*CHEM*) volatile; ΄(*oberflächlich*) cursory; (*eilig*) fleeting; ~**er Speicher** (*COMPUT*) volatile memory; **jdn** ~ **kennen** have met sb briefly; **F~keit** *f* transitoriness; volatility; cursoriness; **F~keitsfehler** *m* careless slip.

Flüchtling *m* refugee.

Flüchtlingslager *nt* refugee camp.

Flug [flōō:k] *m* -(e)s, ˉe flight; **im** ~ airborne, in flight; **wie im** ~(**e**) (*fig*) in a flash; ~**abwehr** [flōō:g'-] *f* anti-aircraft defense; ~**bahn** *f* flight path; (*von Rakete auch*) trajectory; (*Kreisbahn*) orbit; ~**begleiter** *m* (*AVIAT*) steward; ~**blatt** *nt* pamphlet.

Flügel [flü:'gəl] *m* -s, - wing; (*MUS*) grand piano; ~**tür** *f* double door.

flugfähig *a* able to fly; (*Flugzeug: in Ordnung*) airworthy.

Fluggast *m* airline passenger.

flügge [flü'gə] *a* (fully-)fledged; ~ **werden** (*lit*) be able to fly; (*fig*) leave the nest.

Flug- *zW:* ~**geschwindigkeit** *f* flying *od* air speed; ~**gesellschaft** *f* airline (company); ~**hafen** *m* airport; ~**höhe** *f* altitude (of flight); ~**lotse** *m* air traffic *od* flight controller; ~**plan** *m* flight schedule; ~**platz** *m* airport; (*klein*) airfield.

flugs [flōōks] *ad* speedily.

Flug- *zW:* ~**sand** *m* drifting sand; ~**schein** *m* pilot's license; ~**schreiber** *m* flight recorder; ~**schrift** *f* pamphlet; ~**steig** *m* gate; ~**strecke** *f* air route; ~**verkehr** *m* air traffic; ~**wesen** *nt* aviation.

Flugzeug *nt* -(e)s, -e plane, airplane (*US*), aeroplane (*Brit*); ~**entführung** *f* hijacking of a plane; ~**halle** *f* hangar; ~**träger** *m* aircraft carrier.

fluktuieren [flōōktōōē:'rən] *vi* fluctuate.

Flunder [flōōn'dər] *f* -, -n flounder.

flunkern [flōōng'kərn] *vi* fib, tell stories.

Fluor [flōō:'or] *nt* -s fluorine.

Flur [flōō:r] *m* -(e)s, -e hall; (*Treppen*~) staircase ♦ *f* -, -en (*geh*) open fields *pl;* **allein auf weiter** ~ **stehen** (*fig*) be out on a limb.

Fluß [flōōs] *m* -sses, ˉsse river; (*Fließen*) flow; **im** ~ **sein** (*fig*) be in progress; **etw in** ~ (*akk*) **bringen** get sth moving; ~**diagram** *nt* flow chart.

flüssig [flü'siċh] *a* liquid; (*Stil*) flowing; ~**es Vermögen** (*COMM*) liquid assets *pl;* **F~keit** *f* liquid; (*Zustand*) liquidity; ~**machen** *vt* (*Geld*) make available.

Fluß- *zW:* ~**mündung** *f* estuary; ~**pferd** *nt* hippopotamus.

flüstern [flüs'tərn] *vti* whisper.

Flüsterpropaganda *f* whispering campaign.

Flut [flōō:t] *f* -, -en (*lit, fig*) flood; (*Gezeiten*) high tide; **f~en** *vi* flood; ~**licht** *nt* floodlight.

flutschen [flōōt'shən] *vi* (*umg: rutschen*) slide; (*: funktionieren*) go well.

Flutwelle *f* tidal wave.

fl.W. *abk* = *fliessendes Wasser.*

focht [foķht] *imperf von* **fechten**.

föderativ [fœdārátē:f'] *a* federal.

Fohlen [fō:'lən] *nt* -s, - foal.

Föhn [fœn] *m* -(e)s, -e foehn, *warm dry alpine wind.*

Föhre [fœ'rə] *f* -, -n Scots pine.

Folge [fol'gə] *f* -, -n series, sequence; (*Fortsetzung*) installment (*US*), instalment (*Brit*); (*TV, RADIO*) episode; (*Auswirkung*) result; **in rascher** ~ in quick succession; **etw zur** ~ **haben** result in sth; ~**n haben** have consequences; **einer Sache** ~ **leisten** comply with sth; ~**erscheinung** *f* result, consequence.

folgen *vi* follow (*jdm* sb); (*gehorchen*) obey (*jdm* sb); **jdm** ~ **können** (*fig*) follow *od* understand sb; **daraus folgt, daß** ... it follows from this that...

folgend *a* following; **im** ~**en** in the following; (*schriftlich auch*) below.

folgendermaßen [fol'gəndərmá'sən] *ad* as follows, in the following way.

folgenreich, folgenschwer *a* momentous.

folgerichtig *a* logical.

folgern *vt* conclude (*aus* +*dat* from).

Folgerung *f* conclusion.

folgewidrig *a* illogical.

folglich [fol'kliċh] *ad* consequently.

folgsam [folk'zám] *a* obedient.

Folie [fō:'lēə] *f* -, -n foil.

Folienschweißgerät *nt* shrink-wrap machine.

Folklore [fol'klō:ər] *f* - folklore.

Folter [fol'tər] *f* -, -n torture; (*Gerät*) rack; **jdn auf die** ~ **spannen** (*fig*) keep sb on tenterhooks.

foltern *vt* torture.

Fön [fœn] *m* -(e)s, -e ® hair dryer; **f~en** *vt* (blow) dry.

Fonds [fōn] *m* -, - (*lit, fig*) fund; (*FIN: Schuldverschreibung*) government bond.

Fontäne [fonte:'nə] *f* -, -n fountain.

foppen [fo'pən] *vt* tease.

forcieren [forsē:'rən] *vt* push; (*Tempo*) force; (*Konsum, Produktion*) push *od* force up.

Förderband [fœr'dərbánt] *nt* conveyor belt.

Förderer *m* -s, - patron.

Förderin *f* patroness.

Fördergebiet *nt* development area.

Förderin *f* patroness.

Förderkorb *m* pit cage.

Förderleistung *f* (*MIN*) output.

förderlich *a* beneficial.

fordern [for'dərn] *vt* demand; (*fig: kosten: Opfer*) claim; (*: heraus*~) challenge.

fördern [fœr'dərn] *vt* promote; (*unterstützen*) help; (*Kohle*) extract; (*finanziell: Projekt*) sponsor; (*jds Talent, Neigung*) encourage, foster.

Förderplattform *f* production platform.

Förderstufe *f* (*SCH*) mixed-ability classes.

Förderturm *m* (*MIN*) winding tower; (*auf Bohrstelle*) derrick.

Forderung [for'dərōōng] *f* demand.

Förderung [fœr'dərōōng] *f* promotion; help; extraction.

Forelle [fōre'lə] f trout.

Form [form] f **-, -en** shape; (*Gestaltung*) form; (*Guß~*) mold (*US*), mould (*Brit*); (*Back~*) baking tin; **in ~ von** in the shape of; **in ~ sein** be in good form *od* shape; **die ~ wahren** observe the proprieties; **in aller ~** formally.

formal [formȧl'] a formal; (*Besitzer, Grund*) technical.

formalisieren [formȧlēzē:'rən] vt formalize.

Formalität [formȧlite:t'] f formality; **alle ~en erledigen** go through all the formalities.

Format [formȧt'] nt **-(e)s, -e** format; (*fig*) quality.

formatieren [formȧtē:'rən] vt (*Text, Diskette*) format.

Formation [formȧtsēō:n'] f formation.

formbar a malleable.

Formblatt nt form.

Formel f **-, -n** formula; (*von Eid etc*) wording; (*Floskel*) set phrase; **f~haft** a (*Sprache, Stil*) stereotyped.

formell [formel'] a formal.

formen vt form, shape.

Formfehler m faux pas, gaffe; (*JUR*) irregularity.

formieren [formē:'rən] vt form ♦ vr form up.

förmlich [fœrm'liċh] a formal; (*umg*) real; **F~keit** f formality.

formlos a shapeless; (*Benehmen etc*) informal; (*Antrag*) unaccompanied by a form *od* any forms.

Formsache f formality.

Formular [formōōlȧr'] nt **-s, -e** form.

formulieren [formōōlē:'rən] vt formulate.

Formulierung f wording.

formvollendet a perfect; (*Vase etc*) perfectly formed.

forsch [forsh] a energetic, vigorous.

forschen [for'shən] vi search (*nach* for); (*wissenschaftlich*) (do) research.

forschend a searching.

Forscher m **-s, -** research scientist; (*Natur~*) explorer.

Forschung [for'shōōng] f research; **~ und Lehre** research and teaching; **~ und Entwicklung** research and development (R&D).

Forschungsreise f scientific expedition.

Forst [forst] m **-(e)s, -e** forest; **~arbeiter** m forestry worker.

Förster [fœrs'tər] m **-s, -** forester; (*für Wild*) gamekeeper.

Forst- zW: **~wesen** nt, **~wirtschaft** f forestry.

fort [fort] ad away; (*verschwunden*) gone; (*vorwärts*) on; **und so ~** and so on; **in einem ~** incessantly; **~bestehen** vi *unreg* continue to exist; **~bewegen** vtr move away; **~bilden** vr continue one's education; **F~bildung** f further education; **~bleiben** vi *unreg* stay away; **~bringen** vt *unreg* take away; **F~dauer** f continuance; **~dauernd** a continuing; (*in der Vergangenheit*) continued ♦ ad constantly, continuously;

~fahren vi *unreg* depart; (*~setzen*) go on, continue; **~führen** vt continue, carry on; **F~gang** m (*Weggang*) departure (*aus* from); (*Verlauf*) progress; **~gehen** vi *unreg* go away; **~geschritten** a advanced; **~kommen** vi *unreg* get on; (*wegkommen*) get away; **~können** vi *unreg* be able to get away; **~lassen** vt (*auslassen*) leave out, omit; (*weggehen lassen*): **jdn ~lassen** let sb go; **~laufend** a: **~laufend numeriert** consecutively numbered; **~müssen** vi *unreg* have to go; **~pflanzen** vr reproduce; **F~pflanzung** f reproduction.

FORTRAN [for'trȧn] nt FORTRAN.

Forts. *abk* = **Fortsetzung.**

fort- zW: **~schaffen** vt remove; **~schreiten** vi *unreg* advance.

Fortschritt [fort'shrit] m advance; **~e machen** make progress; **dem ~ dienen** further progress; **f~lich** a progressive.

fortschrittsgläubig a believing in progress.

fort- zW: **~setzen** vt continue; **F~setzung** f continuation; (*folgender Teil*) installment (*US*), instalment (*Brit*); **F~setzung folgt** to be continued; **F~setzungsroman** m serialized novel; **~während** a incessant, continual; **~wirken** vi continue to have an effect; **~ziehen** *unreg* vr pull away ♦ vi move on; (*umziehen*) move away.

Foto [fō:'tō] nt **-s, -s** photo(graph); **ein ~ machen** take a photo(graph) ♦ m **-s, -s** (*~apparat*) camera; **~album** nt photograph album; **~apparat** m camera; **~graf('in** *f*) m **-en, -en** photographer; **~graphie** *f* photography; (*Bild*) photograph; **f~graphie'ren** vt photograph ♦ vi take photographs; **~kopie** f photocopy; **f~kopie'ren** vt photocopy; **~kopie'rer** m, **~kopier'gerät** nt photocopier.

Foul [foul] nt **-s, -s** foul.

Foyer [fōȧyā:'] nt **-s, -s** foyer; (*in Hotel auch*) lobby.

FPÖ *f* - *abk* (= *Freiheitliche Partei Österreichs*) Austrian Freedom Party.

Fr. *abk* (= **Frau**) Mrs.; Ms.

Fracht [frȧkht] *f* **-, -en** freight; (*NAUT*) cargo; (*Preis*) carriage; **~ zahlt Empfänger** (*COMM*) carriage forward; **~brief** m consignment note, waybill.

Frachter m **-s, -** freighter.

Fracht- zW: **f~frei** a (*COMM*) carriage paid *od* free; **~gut** nt freight; **~kosten** pl (*COMM*) freight charges pl.

Frack [frȧk] m **-(e)s, -e** tails pl.

Frage [frȧ'gə] *f* **-, -n** question; **etw in ~ stellen** question sth; **jdm eine ~ stellen** ask sb a question, put a question to sb; **das ist gar keine ~, das steht außer ~** there's no question about it; **in ~ kommend** possible; (*Bewerber*) worth considering; **nicht in ~ kommen** be out of the question; **~bogen** m questionnaire.

fragen vti ask; **nach Arbeit/Post ~** ask whether there is *od* was any work/mail; **da**

fragst du mich zuviel (*umg*) I really couldn't say; **nach** *od* **wegen** (*umg*) **jdm ~** ask for sb; (*nach jds Befinden*) ask after sb; **ohne lange zu ~** without asking a lot of questions ♦ *vr* wonder.

Fragerei [frågərī'] *f* questions *pl*.

Frage- *zW*: **~stunde** *f* (*PARL*) question time; **~zeichen** *nt* question mark.

frag- [fråk'] *zW*: **~lich** *a* questionable, doubtful; (*betreffend*) in question; **~los** *ad* unquestionably.

Fragment [fråg'ment'] *nt* fragment.

fragmentarisch [frågmentá'rish] *a* fragmentary.

fragwürdig [fråk'vürdiċh] *a* questionable, dubious.

Fraktion [fråktsēō:n'] *f* parliamentary party.

Fraktions- *zW*: **~vorsitzende(r)** *mf* (*POL*) party whip; **~zwang** *m* requirement to obey the party whip.

frank [frångk] *a* frank, candid.

Franken [frång'kən] *nt* Franconia ♦ *m* -, -: **(Schweizer) ~** (Swiss) franc.

Frankfurt [fr̊ångk'fōórt] *nt* **-s** Frankfurt.

frankieren [frångkē:'rən] *vt* stamp, frank.

Frankiermaschine *f* postage meter (*US*), franking machine (*Brit*).

franko *ad* free delivery; (*POST*) post-paid.

Franse [frán'zə] *f* -, **-n** fringe.

fransen *vi* fray.

franz. *abk* = **französisch**.

Franzbranntwein *m* alcoholic liniment.

Franzose [frántsō:'zə] *m* **-n**, **-n** Frenchman; French boy.

Französin [frántsœ'zin] *f* Frenchwoman; French girl.

französisch *a* French.

Fräse [fre:'zə] *f* -, **-n** (*Werkzeug*) milling cutter; (*für Holz*) molding cutter.

fraß [frås] *imperf von* **fressen**.

Fraß *m* **-es, -e** (*pej umg*: *Essen*) muck.

Fratze [frá'tsə] *f* -, **-n** grimace; **eine ~ schneiden** pull *od* make a face.

Frau [frou] *f* -, **-en** woman; (*Ehe~*) wife; (*Anrede*) Mrs; **~ Doktor** Doctor.

Frauen- *zW*: **~arzt** *m* gynecologist (*US*), gynaecologist (*Brit*); **~bewegung** *f* feminist movement; **f~feindlich** *a* anti-women, misogynous; **~rechtlerin** *f* feminist; **~zimmer** *nt* (*pej*) female, broad (*US*).

Fräulein [froi'līn] *nt* young lady; (*Anrede*) Miss; (*Verkäuferin*) sales clerk (*US*), assistant (*Brit*); (*Kellnerin*) waitress.

fraulich [frou'liċh] *a* womanly.

frech [freċh] *a* cheeky, impudent; **~ wie Oskar sein** (*umg*) be a little monkey; **F~dachs** *m* cheeky monkey; **F~heit** *f* cheek, impudence; **sich** (*dat*) **F~heiten erlauben** be a bit fresh *od* cheeky.

Fregatte [frågá'tə] *f* -, **-n** frigate.

frei [frī] *a* free; (*Stelle, Sitzplatz auch*) vacant; (*Mitarbeiter*) freelance; (*Geld*) available; (*unbekleidet*) bare; **aus ~en Stücken** *od* **~em Willen** of one's own free will; **~**

nach based on …; **für etw ~e Fahrt geben** (*fig*) give sth the go-ahead; **der Film ist ~ ab 16 (Jahren)** the film may be seen by people over (the age of) 16; **unter ~em Himmel** in the open (air); **morgen/ Mittwoch ist ~** tomorrow/Wednesday is a holiday; **"Zimmer ~"** "vacancies"; **auf ~er Strecke** (*EISENB*) between stations; (*AUT*) on the road; **sich ~ machen** (*beim Arzt*) take one's clothes off, strip; **~er Wettbewerb** fair/open competition; **~ Haus** (*COMM*) free delivery; **~ Schiff** (*COMM*) free on board; **~e Marktwirtschaft** free market economy; **sich** (*dat*) **einen Tag ~ nehmen** take a day off; **von etw ~ sein** be free of sth; **im F~en** in the open air; **~ sprechen** talk without notes; **F~bad** *nt* open-air swimming pool; **~bekommen** *vt unreg*: **jdn/einen Tag ~bekommen** get sb freed/get a day off; **~beruflich** *a* self-employed; **F~betrag** *m* tax allowance.

Freier *m* **-s, -** suitor.

Frei- *zW*: **~exemplar** *nt* free copy; **~gänger** *m* day-release/paroled prisoner; **f~geben** *vt unreg*: **etw zum Verkauf f~geben** allow sth to be sold on the open market; **f~gebig** *a* generous; **~gebigkeit** *f* generosity; **~hafen** *m* free port; **f~halten** *vt unreg* keep free; (*bezahlen*) pay for; **~handel** *m* free trade; **~handelszone** *f* free trade area; **f~händig** *ad* (*fahren*) with no hands.

Freiheit *f* freedom; **sich** (*dat*) **die ~ nehmen, etw zu tun** take the liberty of doing sth; **f~lich** *a* liberal; (*Verfassung*) based on the principle of liberty; (*Demokratie*) free.

Freiheits- *zW*: **~beraubung** *f* (*JUR*) wrongful deprivation of personal liberty; **~drang** *m* urge/desire for freedom; **~kampf** *m* fight for freedom; **~kämpfer(in** *f*) *m* freedom fighter; **~strafe** *f* prison sentence.

frei- *zW*: **~heraus** *ad* frankly; **F~karte** *f* free ticket; **~kaufen** *vt*: **jdn/sich ~kaufen** buy sb's/one's freedom; **~kommen** *vi unreg* get free; **F~körperkultur** *f* nudism; **~lassen** *vt unreg* (set) free; **F~lauf** *m* freewheeling; **~laufend** *a* (*Hühner*) free-range; **~legen** *vt* expose; **~lich** *ad* certainly, admittedly; **ja ~lich!** yes of course; **F~lichtbühne** *f* open-air theater (*US*) *od* theatre (*Brit*); **~machen** *vt* (*POST*) frank; (*AUT*) defog; **Tage ~machen** take days off ♦ *vr* arrange to be free; **F~maurer** *m* Mason, Freemason.

freimütig [frī'mü:tiċh] *a* frank, honest.

Frei- *zW*: **~raum** *m* (*fig*) freedom (*zu* for); **f~schaffend** *a attr* freelance; **~schärler** *m* **-s, -** guerrilla; **f~schwimmen** *vr* (*fig*) learn to stand on one's own two feet; **f~sinnig** *a* liberal; **f~sprechen** *vt unreg* acquit (*von* of); **~spruch** *m* acquittal; **f~stehen** *vi unreg*: **es steht dir frei, das zu tun** you are free to do so; **das steht Ihnen völlig frei** that is completely up to you; **f~stellen** *vt*: **jdm etw f~stellen** leave sth (up) to sb; **~stoß** *m* free kick; **~stunde** *f* free hour;

(*SCH*) free period.
Freitag m Friday: *siehe* **Dienstag.**
freitags *ad* on Fridays.
Frei- *zW*: **~tod** m suicide; **~übungen** *pl*
(physical) exercises *pl*; **~wild** *nt* (*fig*) fair
game; **f~willig** *a* voluntary; **~willige(r)** *mf*
volunteer; **~zeichen** *nt* (*TEL*) ringing tone;
~zeit *f* spare *od* free time; **~zeitgestaltung**
f organization of one's leisure time; **f~zügig**
a liberal, broad-minded; (*mit Geld*) generous.
fremd [fremt] *a* (*unvertraut*) strange;
(*ausländisch*) foreign; (*nicht eigen*) someone
else's; **etw ist jdm ~** sth is foreign to sb;
ich bin hier ~ I'm a stranger here; **sich ~**
fühlen feel like a stranger; **~artig** *a*
strange.
Fremde *f* - (*liter*): **die ~** foreign parts *pl*.
Fremden- *zW*: **~führer** m (tourist) guide;
(*Buch*) guide (book); **~legion** *f* foreign legion; **~verkehr** m tourism; **~zimmer** *nt*
guest room.
Fremde(r) [frɛm'də(r)] *mf dekl wie a*
stranger; (*Ausländer*) foreigner.
fremd- *zW*: **~gehen** *vi* unreg (*umg*) be unfaithful; **F~kapital** *nt* loan capital;
F~körper m foreign body; **~ländisch** *a*
foreign; **F~ling** m stranger; **F~sprache** *f*
foreign language.
Fremdsprachenkorrespondentin *f* bilingual secretary.
fremd- *zW*: **~sprachig** *a attr* foreign-
language; **F~wort** *nt* foreign word.
frenetisch [frānā:'tish] *a* frenetic.
Frequenz [frākvents'] *f* (*RAD*) frequency.
Fresse *f* -, **-n** (*umg!*: *Mund*) gob; (*Gesicht*)
mug.
fressen [frɛ'sən] *unreg vti* eat; **einen Narren**
an jdm/etw gefressen haben dote on sb/sth
♦ *vr*: **sich voll** *od* **satt ~** gorge o.s.
Freude [froi'də] *f* -, **-n** joy, delight; **~ an etw**
(*dat*) **haben** get *od* derive pleasure from
sth; **jdm eine ~ machen** *od* **bereiten** make
sb happy.
Freuden- *zW*: **~haus** *nt* (*veraltet*) house of
ill repute; **~tanz** m: **einen ~tanz aufführen**
dance with joy.
freudestrahlend *a* beaming with delight.
freudig *a* joyful, happy.
freudlos *a* joyless.
freuen [froi'ən] *vt unpers* make happy *od*
pleased ♦ *vr* be glad *od* happy; **sich auf etw**
(*akk*) **~** look forward to sth; **sich über etw**
(*akk*) **~** be pleased about sth; **sich zu früh**
~ get one's hopes up too soon.
Freund [froint] m **-(e)s, -e** friend; (*Liebha-*
ber) boyfriend; **ich bin kein ~ von so et-**
was I'm not one for that sort of thing; **~in**
[-din] *f* friend; girlfriend; **f~lich** *a* kind,
friendly; **bitte recht f~lich!** smile please!;
würden Sie bitte so f~lich sein und das
tun? would you be so kind as to do that?;
f~licherweise *ad* kindly; **~lichkeit** *f* friendliness, kindness; **~schaft** *f* friendship;

f~schaftlich *a* friendly.
Frevel [frā:'fəl] m **-s**, - crime, offense (*US*),
offence (*Brit*) (*an* +*dat* against); **f~haft** *a*
wicked.
Frhr. *abk* (= *Freiherr*) baron.
Frieden [frē:'dən] m **-s**, - peace; **im ~** in
peacetime; **~ schließen** make one's peace;
(*POL*) make peace; **um des lieben ~s wil-**
len (*umg*) for the sake of peace and quiet;
ich traue dem ~ nicht (*umg*) something
(fishy) is going on.
Friedens- *zW*: **~bewegung** *f* peace movement; **~richter** m justice of the peace;
~schluß m peace agreement; **~verhand-**
lungen *pl* peace negotiations *pl*; **~vertrag**
m peace treaty; **~zeit** *f* peacetime.
fried- [frē:t'] *zW*: **~fertig** *a* peaceable; **F~hof**
m cemetery; **~lich** *a* peaceful, law-abiding;
etw auf ~lichem Wege lösen solve sth by
peaceful means.
frieren [frē:'rən] *unreg vi, vt unpers* freeze;
ich friere, es friert mich I am freezing, I'm
cold; **wie ein Schneider ~** (*umg*) be *od* get
frozen to the marrow ♦ *vi unpers*: **heute**
nacht hat es gefroren it was below freezing
last night.
Fries [frē:s] m **-es, -e** (*ARCHIT*) frieze.
Friese [frē:'zə] m **-n, -n**, Friesin *f* Fri(e)sian.
frigid(e) [frēgē:t', frēgē:'də] *a* frigid.
Frikadelle [frēkáde'lə] *f* meatball.
frisch [frish] *a* fresh; (*lebhaft*) lively; **~ ge-**
strichen! wet paint!; **sich ~ machen**
freshen (o.s.) up; **jdn auf ~er Tat ertappen**
catch sb red-handed *od* in the act.
Frische *f* - freshness; liveliness; **in alter ~**
(*umg*) as always.
Frischhaltebeutel m airtight bag.
frischweg *ad* (*munter*) straight out.
Friseur [frēzœr'] m, **Friseuse** [frēzœ'zə] *f* hairdresser.
frisieren [frēzē:'rən] *vtr* do (one's hair); (*fig*:
Abrechnung) fiddle, doctor.
Frisier- *zW*: **~salon** m hairdressing
salon; **~tisch** m dressing table.
Frisör [frēzœr'] m **-s, -e** hairdresser.
frißt [frist] *2./3. pers sing präs von* **fressen.**
Frist [frist] *f* -, **-en** period; (*Termin*) deadline;
eine ~ einhalten/verstreichen lassen meet
a deadline/let a deadline pass; (*bei*
Rechnung) pay/not pay within the period
stipulated; **jdm eine ~ von vier Tagen ge-**
ben give sb four days' grace.
fristen *vt* (*Dasein*) lead; (*kümmerlich*) eke
out.
Frist- *zW*: **f~gerecht** *a* within the period
stipulated; **f~los** *a* (*Entlassung*) instant.
Frisur [frēzōō:r'] *f* hairdo, hairstyle.
Friteuse [frētœ'zə] *f* -, **-n** chip pan (*Brit*),
deep fat fryer.
fritieren [frētē:'rən] *vt* deep fry.
frivol [frēvō:l'] *a* frivolous.
Frl. *abk* (= *Fräulein*) Miss.
froh [frō:] *a* happy, cheerful; **ich bin ~, daß...**
I'm glad that ...

fröhlich [frœ'liĉ] *a* merry, happy; **F~keit** *f* merriment, gaiety.

froh- *zW*: **~lock'en** *vi* (*geh*) rejoice; (*pej*) gloat; **F~sinn** *m* cheerfulness.

fromm [from] *a* pious, good; (*Wunsch*) idle.

Frömmelei [frœmǝli'] *f* false piety.

Frömmigkeit *f* piety.

frönen [frœ'nǝn] *vi* indulge (*etw* (*dat*) in sth).

Fronleichnam [frō:nliĉ'nâm] *m* -(e)s Corpus Christi.

Front [front] *f* -, -en front; **klare ~en schaffen** (*fig*) clarify the position.

frontal [frontâl'] *a* frontal; **F~angriff** *m* frontal attack.

fror [frō:r] *imperf von* **frieren**.

Frosch [frosh] *m* -(e)s, ˸e frog; (*Feuerwerk*) squib; **sei kein ~!** (*umg*) be a sport!; **~mann** *m* frogman; **~perspektive** *f*: **etw aus der ~perspektive sehen** get a worm's-eye view of sth; **~schenkel** *m* frog's leg.

Frost [frost] *m* -(e)s, ˸e frost; **f~beständig** *a* frost-resistant; **~beule** *f* chilblain.

frösteln [frœs'tǝln] *vi* shiver.

frostig *a* frosty.

Frostschutzmittel *nt* anti-freeze.

Frottee [frotā:'] *nt od m* -(s), -s towelling.

frottieren [frotē:'rǝn] *vt* rub, towel.

Frottier(hand)tuch *nt* towel.

frotzeln [fro'tsǝln] *vti* (*umg*) tease.

Frucht [frōokht] *f* -, ˸e (*lit, fig*) fruit; (*Getreide*) corn; (*Embryo*) foetus; **f~bar** *a* fruitful, fertile; **~barkeit** *f* fertility; **~becher** *m* ice cream sundae with fresh fruit.

Früchtchen [früĉt'ĉǝn] *nt* (*umg*: *Tunichtgut*) good-for-nothing.

fruchten *vi* be of use.

Frucht- *zW*: **f~los** *a* fruitless; **~saft** *m* fruit juice.

früh [frü:] *a, ad* early; **heute ~** this morning; **~auf** *ad*: **von ~auf** from an early age; **F~aufsteher** *m* -s, - early riser; **F~dienst** *m*: **F~dienst haben** be on early shift.

Frühe *f* - early morning; **in aller ~** at the crack of dawn.

früher *komp von* **früh** ♦ *a* earlier; (*ehemalig*) former ♦ *ad* formerly; **~ war das anders** that used to be different; **~ oder später** sooner or later.

frühestens *ad* at the earliest.

früh- *zW*: **F~geburt** *f* premature birth/baby; **F~jahr** *nt* spring.

Frühjahrs- *zW*: **~müdigkeit** *f* springtime lethargy; **~putz** *m* spring-cleaning.

Frühling *m* spring; **im ~** in spring.

früh- *zW*: **~reif** *a* precocious; **F~rentner** *m* person who has retired early; **F~schicht** *f* early shift; **F~schoppen** *m* morning/lunchtime drink; **F~sport** *m* early morning exercise; **F~stück** *nt* breakfast; **~stücken** *vi* (have) breakfast; **F~warnsystem** *nt* early warning system; **~zeitig** *a* early; (*vorzeitig*) premature.

Frust *m* -(e)s (*umg*) frustration.

frustrieren [frōostrē:'rǝn] *vt* frustrate.

frz. *abk* = **französisch**.

FSV *abk* = *Fußball-Sportverein*.

FU *f* - *abk* = *Freie Universität* (*Berlin*).

Fuchs [fōoks] *m* -es, ˸e fox.

fuchsen (*umg*) *vt* rile, annoy ♦ *vr* be annoyed.

Füchsin [fük'sin] *f* vixen.

fuchsteufelswild *a* hopping mad.

Fuchtel [fōokh'tl'] *f* -, -n (*fig umg*): **unter jds ~** under sb's control *od* thumb.

fuchteln [fōokh'tǝln] *vi* gesticulate wildly.

Fuge [fōo:'gǝ] *f* -, -n joint; (*MUS*) fugue.

fügen [fü:'gǝn] *vt* place, join ♦ *vr* be obedient (*in* +*akk* to) ; (*anpassen*) adapt o.s. (*in* +*akk* to) ♦ *vr unpers* happen.

fügsam [fü:k'zâm] *a* obedient.

fühlbar *a* perceptible, noticeable.

fühlen [fü:'lǝn] *vtir* feel.

Fühler *m* -s, - feeler.

Fühlung *f*: **mit jdm in ~ bleiben/stehen** stay/be in contact *od* touch with sb.

fuhr [fōo:r] *imperf von* **fahren**.

Fuhre *f* -, -n (*Ladung*) load.

führen [fü:'rǝn] *vt* lead; (*Geschäft*) run; (*Name*) bear; (*Buch*) keep; (*im Angebot haben*) stock; **was führt Sie zu mir?** (*form*) what brings you to me?; **Geld/seine Papiere bei sich ~** (*form*) carry money/one's papers on one's person ♦ *vi* lead; **das führt zu nichts** that will come to nothing ♦ *vr* behave.

Führer(in *f*) [fü:'rǝr(in)] *m* -s, - leader; (*Fremden~*) guide; **~haus** *nt* cab; **~schein** *m* driver's license (*US*), driving licence (*Brit*); **den ~schein machen** (*AUT*) learn to drive; (*die Prüfung ablegen*) take one's (driving) test; **~scheinentzug** *m* disqualification from driving.

Fuhrmann [fōo:r'mán] *m, pl* -leute driver.

Führung [fü:'rōong] *f* leadership; (*eines Unternehmens*) management; (*MIL*) command; (*Benehmen*) conduct; (*Museums~*) conducted tour.

Führungs- *zW*: **~kraft** *f* executive; **~stab** *m* (*MIL*) command; (*COMM*) top management; **~stil** *m* management style; **~zeugnis** *nt* letter of recommendation.

Fuhrunternehmen *nt* trucking company (*US*), haulage business (*Brit*).

Fuhrwerk *nt* wagon, cart.

Fülle [fü'lǝ] *f* - wealth, abundance.

füllen *vtr* fill; (*KOCH*) stuff.

Füllen *nt* -s, - foal.

Füller *m* -s, -, **Füllfederhalter** *m* fountain pen.

Füllgewicht *nt* (*COMM*) weight at time of packing; (*auf Dosen*) net weight.

füllig [fü'liĉ] *a* (*Mensch*) corpulent, portly; (*Figur*) ample.

Füllung *f* filling; (*Holz~*) panel.

fummeln [fōo'mǝln] *vi* (*umg*) fumble.

Fund [fōont] *m* -(e)s, -e find.

Fundament [fōondáment'] *nt* foundation.

fundamental' *a* fundamental.

Fund- zW: ~**büro** nt lost and found (US), lost property (office) (Brit); ~**grube** f (fig) treasure trove.
fundieren [fŏŏndē:'rən] vt back up.
fundiert a sound.
fündig [fün'diċḥ] a (MIN) rich; ~ **werden** make a strike; (fig) strike it lucky.
Fundsachen pl lost and found (US), lost property sing (Brit).
fünf [fünf] num five; **seine** ~ **Sinne beisammen haben** have all one's wits about one; ~**(e) gerade sein lassen** (umg) turn a blind eye; ~**hundert** num five hundred; ~**jährig** a (Frist, Plan) five-year; (Kind) five-year-old; **F**~**prozentklausel** f clause debarring parties with less than 5% of the vote from Parliament.
Fünftel nt -s, - fifth.
fünfte(r, s) a fifth.
fünfzehn num fifteen.
fünfzig num fifty.
fungieren [fŏŏngē:'rən] vi function; (Person) act.
Funk [fŏŏngk] m -s radio; ~**ausstellung** f radio and television exhibition.
Funke m -ns, -n (lit, fig) spark.
funkeln vi sparkle.
funkelnagelneu a (umg) brand-new.
funken vt radio.
Funken m -s, - siehe **Funke**.
Funker m -s, - radio operator.
Funk- zW: ~**gerät** nt radio set; ~**haus** nt broadcasting center; ~**kolleg** nt educational radio broadcasts pl; ~**spot** m advertisement on the radio; ~**sprechgerät** nt radio telephone; ~**spruch** m radio message; ~**station** f radio station; ~**stille** f (fig) ominous silence; ~**streife** f police radio patrol.
Funktion [fŏŏngktsēō:n'] f function; **in** ~ **treten/sein** come into/be in operation.
Funktionär(in f) [fŏŏngktsēōne:r'(in)] m -s, -e functionary, official.
funktionieren [fŏŏngktsēōnē:'rən] vi work, function.
Funktions- zW: ~**taste** f (COMPUT) function key; **f**~**tüchtig** a in working order.
Funsel, Funzel [fŏŏn'zəl, -tsəl] f -, -n (umg) dim lamp.
für [fü:r] präp +akk for; **was** ~ what kind od sort of; ~**s erste** for the moment; **was Sie da sagen, hat etwas** ~ **sich** there's something in what you're saying; **Tag** ~ **Tag** day after day; **Schritt** ~ **Schritt** step by step; **das F**~ **und Wider** the pros and cons pl; **F**~**bitte** f intercession.
Furche [fŏŏr'ċḥə] f -, -n furrow.
furchen vt furrow.
Furcht [fŏŏrċḥt] f - fear; **f**~**bar** a terrible, awful.
fürchten [fürċḥ'tən] vt be afraid of, fear ♦ vr be afraid (vor +dat of).
fürchterlich a awful.
furcht- zW: ~**los** a fearless; ~**sam** a timorous.

füreinander [fü:rinán'dər] ad for each other.
Furie [fŏŏ:'rēə] f -, -n (MYTHOLOGIE) fury; (fig) hellcat.
Furnier [fŏŏrnē:r'] nt -s, -e veneer.
Furore [fŏŏrō:'rə] f od nt: ~ **machen** (umg) cause a sensation.
fürs [fü:rs] = **für das**.
Fürsorge [fü:r'zorgə] f care; (Sozial~) welfare; **von der** ~ **leben** live on welfare; ~**amt** nt welfare office.
Fürsorger(in f) m -s, - welfare worker.
Fürsorgeunterstützung f welfare benefit.
fürsorglich a caring.
Für- zW: ~**sprache** f recommendation; (um Gnade) intercession; ~**sprecher** m advocate.
Fürst [fürst] m -en, -en prince.
Fürstenum nt principality.
Fürstin f princess.
fürstlich a princely.
Furt [fŏŏrt] f -, -en ford.
Furunkel [fŏŏrŏŏng'kəl] nt od m -s, - boil.
Fürwort [fü:r'vort] nt pronoun.
furzen [fŏŏr'tsən] vi (umg!) fart (!).
Fusion [fŏŏzēō:n'] f amalgamation; (von Unternehmen) merger; (von Atomkernen, Zellen) fusion.
fusionieren [fŏŏzēōnē:'rən] vt amalgamate.
Fuß [fŏŏ:s] m -es, ⁼e foot; (von Glas, Säule etc) base; (von Möbel) leg; **zu** ~ on foot; **bei** ~! heel!; **jdm etw vor die** ~̃e **werfen** (lit) throw sth at sb; (fig) tell sb to keep sth; **(festen)** ~ **fassen** (lit, fig) gain a foothold; (sich niederlassen) settle down; **mit jdm auf gutem** ~ **stehen** be on good terms with sb; **auf großem** ~ **leben** live the high life.
Fußball m soccer, football; ~**spiel** nt soccer match; ~**spieler** m soccer player (US), footballer (Brit); ~**toto** m od nt soccer lottery (US), football pools pl (Brit).
Fußboden m floor.
Fußbremse f (AUT) footbrake.
fusselig [fŏŏ'səliċḥ] a: **sich** (dat) **den Mund** ~ **reden** (umg) talk till one is blue in the face.
fusseln [fŏŏ'səln] vi (Stoff, Kleid etc) shed fluff.
fußen vi rest, be based (auf +dat on).
Fuß- zW: ~**ende** nt foot; ~**gänger(in** f) m -s, - pedestrian; ~**gängerüberführung** f pedestrian bridge; ~**gängerüberweg** m crosswalk (US), pedestrian crossing (Brit); ~**gängerzone** f pedestrian zone; ~**leiste** f baseboard (US), skirting board (Brit); ~**note** f footnote; ~**pfleger** m chiropodist; ~**pilz** m (MED) athlete's foot; ~**spur** f footprint; ~**stapfen** m -s, -: **in jds** ~**stapfen treten** (fig) follow in sb's footsteps; ~**tritt** m kick; (Spur) footstep; ~**volk** nt (fig): **das** ~**volk** the rank and file; ~**weg** m footpath.
futsch [fŏŏtsh] a (umg: weg) gone, vanished.
Futter [fŏŏ'tər] nt -s, - fodder, feed; (Stoff) lining. ·

Futteral [fŏŏtərâl'] *nt* **-s, -e** case.
futtern [fŏŏ'tərn] *vi* (*hum umg*) stuff o.s. ♦ *vt* scoff.
füttern [fü'tərn] *vt* feed; (*Kleidung*) line; „**F~ verboten**" "do not feed the animals".
Futur [fŏŏtŏŏ:r'] *nt* **-s, -e** future.

G

G, g [gā:] *nt* G, g.
g *abk* = **Gramm; Groschen.**
gab [gáp] *imperf von* **geben.**
Gabe [gâ'bə] *f* -, **-n** gift.
Gabel [gâ'bəl] *f* -, **-n** fork; (*TEL*) rest, cradle; ~**frühstück** *nt* mid-morning snack; ~**stapler** *m* **-s, -** fork-lift truck.
Gabelung *f* fork.
Gabentisch [gâ'bəntish] *m* *table for Christmas or birthday presents.*
Gabun [gábŏŏ:n'] *nt* Gabon.
gackern [gâ'kərn] *vi* cackle.
gaffen [gâ'fən] *vi* gape.
Gag [gek] *m* **-s, -s** (*Film~*) gag; (*Werbe~*) gimmick.
Gage [gâ'zhə] *f* -, **-n** fee.
gähnen [ge:'nən] *vi* yawn; ~**de Leere** total emptiness.
GAL *f* - *abk* (= *Grün-Alternative Liste*) Greens' Alternative Party.
Gala [gâ'lâ] *f* - formal dress.
galant [gálánt'] *a* gallant, courteous.
Galavorstellung *f* (*THEAT*) gala performance.
Galerie [gálərē:'] *f* gallery.
Galgen [gál'gən] *m* **-s, -** gallows *pl*; ~**frist** *f* respite; ~**humor** *m* macabre humor; ~**strick** *m*, ~**vogel** *m* (*umg*) gallows bird.
Galionsfigur [gálēō:ns'fēgŏŏ:r] *f* figurehead.
gälisch [ge:'lish] *a* Gaelic.
Galle [gá'lə] *f* -, **-n** gall; (*Organ*) gall bladder; **jdm kommt die ~ hoch** sb's blood begins to boil.
Galopp [gálop'] *m* **-s, -s** *od* **-e** gallop; **im ~** (*lit*) at a gallop; (*fig*) at top speed.
galoppieren [gálopē:'rən] *vi* gallop.
galt [gált] *imperf von* **gelten.**
galvanisieren [gálvánēzē:'rən] *vt* galvanize.
Gamasche [gámá'shə] *f* -, **-n** gaiter; (*kurz*) spat.
Gammastrahlen [gá'máshtrâlən] *pl* gamma rays *pl*.
gamm(e)lig [gám'(ə)lich] *a* (*umg: Kleidung*) shabby.
gammeln [gá'məln] *vi* (*umg*) loaf about.
Gammler(in *f*) [gám'lər(in)] *m* **-s, -** drop-out.
Gang [gáng] *m* **-(e)s, ⁻e** walk; (*Boten~*) errand; (~*art*) gait; (*Abschnitt eines*

Vorgangs) operation; (*Essens~*, *Ablauf*) course; (*Flur etc*) corridor; (*Durch~*) passage; (*AUT. TECH*) gear; (*THEAT. AVIAT, in Kirche*) aisle; **den ersten ~ einlegen** shift into first (gear); **einen ~ machen/tun** go on an errand/go for a walk; **den ~ nach Canossa antreten** (*fig*) eat humble pie; **seinen gewohnten ~ gehen** (*fig*) run its usual course; **in ~ bringen** start up; (*fig*) get off the ground; **in ~ sein** be in operation; (*fig*) be underway ♦ *f* [geng] -, **-s** gang.
gang *a*: ~ **und gäbe** usual, normal.
Gangart *f* way of walking, walk; (*von Pferd*) gait; **eine härtere ~ einschlagen** (*fig*) apply harder tactics *od* tougher measures.
gangbar *a* passable; (*Methode*) practicable.
Gängelband [ge'ngəlbánt] *nt*: **jdn am ~ halten** (*fig*) spoonfeed sb.
gängeln *vt* spoonfeed; **jdn ~** treat sb like a child.
gängig [ge'ngich] *a* common, current; (*Ware*) in demand, selling well.
Gangschaltung *f* gearshift.
Gangway [geng'wā:] *f* (*NAUT*) gangway; (*AVIAT*) steps *pl*.
Ganove [gánō:'və] *m* **-n, -n** (*umg*) crook.
Gans [gáns] *f* -, ⁻**e** goose.
Gänse- [gen'zə] *zW*: ~**blümchen** *nt* daisy; ~**braten** *m* roast goose; ~**füßchen** *pl* (*umg*) quotes *pl*; ~**haut** *f* goose pimples *pl*; ~**marsch** *m*: **im ~marsch** in single file.
Gänserich *m* **-s, -e** gander.
ganz [gánts] *a* whole; (*vollständig*) complete; ~ **Europa** all Europe; **im (großen und) ~en** (*genommen*) on the whole, all in all; **etw wieder ~ machen** mend sth; **sein ~es Geld** all his money ♦ *ad* quite; (*völlig*) completely; (*sehr*) really; (*genau*) exactly; ~ **gewiß!** absolutely; **ein ~ klein wenig** just a tiny bit; **das mag ich ~ besonders gern(e)** I'm particularly fond of that; **sie ist ~ die Mutter** she's just *od* exactly like her mother; ~ **und gar nicht** not at all.
Ganze(s) *nt dekl wie a*: **es geht ums ~** everything's at stake; **aufs ~ gehen** go for it all.
Ganzheitsmethode [gánts'hītsmātō:də] *f* (*SCH*) look-and-say method.
gänzlich [gents'lich] *a, ad* complete(ly), entire(ly).
ganztägig [gánts'te:gich] *a* all-day *attr*.
ganztags *ad* (*arbeiten*) full time.
gar [gár] *a* cooked, done ♦ *ad* quite; ~ **nicht/ nichts/keiner** not/nothing/nobody at all; ~ **nicht schlecht** not bad at all; ~ **kein Grund** no reason whatsoever *od* at all; **er wäre ~ zu gern noch länger geblieben** he would really have liked to stay longer.
Garage [gárâ'zhə] *f* -, **-n** garage.
Garantie [gárántē:'] *f* guarantee; **das fällt noch unter die ~** that's covered by the guarantee.
garantieren *vt* guarantee.
garantiert *ad* guaranteed; (*umg*) I bet.

Garantieschein *m* guarantee.
Garaus [gâr'ous] *m* (*umg*): **jdm den ~ machen** do sb in.
Garbe [gár'bə] *f* -, **-n** sheaf; (*MIL*) burst of fire.
Garde [gár'də] *f* -, **-n** guard(s); **die alte ~** the old guard.
Garderobe [gárdərō:'bə] *f* -, **-n** wardrobe; (*Abgabe*) checkroom (*US*), cloakroom (*Brit*); (*Kleiderablage*) hallstand; (*THEAT*: *Umkleideraum*) dressing room.
Garderoben- *zW*: **~frau** *f* cloakroom attendant; **~ständer** *m* hallstand.
Gardine [gárdē:'nə] *f* -, **-n** curtain.
Gardinen- *zW*: **~predigt** *f* (*umg*): **jdm eine ~predigt halten** give sb a talking-to; **~stange** *f* curtain rail; (*zum Ziehen*) curtain rod.
garen [gâ'rən] *vti* (*KOCH*) cook.
gären [ge:'rən] *vi unreg* ferment.
Garn [gárn] *nt* **-(e)s, -e** thread; (*Häkel~*, *fig*) yarn.
Garnele [gárnā:'lə] *f* -, **-n** shrimp, prawn.
garnieren [gárnē:'rən] *vt* decorate; (*Speisen*) garnish.
Garnison [gárnēzō:n'] *f* -, **-en** garrison.
Garnitur [gárnētōō:r'] *f* (*Satz*) set; (*Unterwäsche*) set of (matching) underwear; **erste ~** (*fig*) top rank; **zweite ~** second rate.
garstig [gárs'tiçh] *a* nasty, horrid.
Garten [gár'tən] *m* **-s,** ̄ garden; **~arbeit** *f* gardening; **~bau** *m* horticulture; **~fest** *nt* garden party; **~gerät** *nt* gardening tool; **~haus** *nt* summerhouse; **~kresse** *f* cress; **~laube** *f* (*~häuschen*) summerhouse; **~lokal** *nt* beer garden; **~schere** *f* pruning shears *pl*; **~tür** *f* garden gate; **~zwerg** *m* garden gnome; (*pej umg*) squirt.
Gärtner(in *f*) [gert'nər(in)] *m* **-s,** - gardener.
Gärtnerei [gertnərī'] *f* nursery; (*Gemüse~*) truck farm (*US*), market garden (*Brit*).
gärtnern *vi* garden.
Gärung [ge:'rōōng] *f* fermentation.
Gas [gâs] *nt* **-es, -e** gas; **~ geben** (*AUT*) accelerate, step on the gas.
Gascogne [gáskon'yə] *f* Gascony.
Gas- *zW*: **~flasche** *f* bottle of gas, gas cylinder; **g~förmig** *a* gaseous; **~herd** *m*, **~kocher** *m* gas cooker; **~leitung** *f* gas pipeline; **~maske** *f* gasmask; **~pedal** *nt* accelerator, gas pedal (*US*); **~pistole** *f* gas pistol.
Gasse [gá'sə] *f* -, **-n** lane, alley.
Gassen- *zW*: **~hauer** *m* **-s,** - (*veraltet umg*) popular melody; **~junge** *m* street urchin.
Gast [gást] *m* **-es,** ̄**e** guest; **bei jdm zu ~ sein** be sb's guest(s); **~arbeiter** *m* foreign worker.
Gäste- [ges'tə] *zW*: **~buch** *nt* visitors' *od* guest book; **~zimmer** *nt* guest room.
Gast- *zW*: **g~freundlich** *a* hospitable; **~freundlichkeit** *f*, **~freundschaft** *f* hospitality; **~geber** *m* **-s,** - host; **~geberin** *f* hostess; **~haus** *nt*, **~hof** *m* hotel, inn;

~hörer(in *f*) *m* (*UNIV*) observer, auditor (*US*).
gastieren [gástē:'rən] *vi* (*THEAT*) (appear as a) guest.
Gast- *zW*: **~land** *nt* host country; **g~lich** *a* hospitable; **~lichkeit** *f* hospitality; **~rolle** *f* (*THEAT*) guest role; **eine ~rolle spielen** (*lit*) make a guest appearance.
Gastronomie [gástrōnōmē:'] *f* (*form*: *Gaststättengewerbe*) catering trade.
gastronomisch [gástrōnō:'mish] *a* gastronomic(al).
Gast- *zW*: **~spiel** *nt* (*SPORT*) away game; **ein ~spiel geben** (*THEAT*) give a guest performance; (*fig*) put in a brief appearance; **~stätte** *f* restaurant; (*Trinklokal*) pub; **~wirt** *m* innkeeper; **~wirtschaft** *f* hotel, inn; **~zimmer** *nt* guest room.
Gas- *zW*: **~vergiftung** *f* gas poisoning; **~versorgung** *f* (*System*) gas supply; **~werk** *nt* gasworks *sing od pl*; **~zähler** *m* gas meter.
Gatte [gá'tə] *m* **-n, -n** (*form*) husband, spouse; **die ~n** husband and wife.
Gatter [gá'tər] *nt* **-s,** - grating; (*Tür*) gate.
Gattin *f* (*form*) wife, spouse.
Gattung [gá'tōōng] *f* (*BIOL*) genus; (*Sorte*) kind.
GAU [gou] *m abk* (= *größter anzunehmender Unfall*) MCA, maximum credible accident.
Gaudi [gou'dē] *nt od f* (*umg*: *süddeutsch*, *österreichisch*) fun.
Gaukler [gou'klər] *m* **-s,** - juggler, conjurer.
Gaul [goul] *m* **-(e)s, Gäule** (*pej*) nag.
Gaumen [gou'mən] *m* **-s,** - palate.
Gauner [gou'nər] *m* **-s,** - rogue.
Gaunerei [gounərī'] *f* swindle.
Gaunersprache *f* underworld jargon.
Gaze [gá'zə] *f* -, **-n** gauze.
Gbf *abk* = **Güterbahnhof.**
GDA *f abk* (= *Gemeinschaft Deutsche Altershilfe*) ≈ Age Concern, Help The Aged.
Geäst [gɛst'] *nt* branches *pl*.
geb. *abk* = **geboren.**
Gebäck [gəbɛk'] *nt* **-(e)s, -e** (*Kekse*) cookies *pl* (*US*), biscuits *pl* (*Brit*); (*Teilchen*) pastries *pl*.
gebacken [gəbá'kən] *pp von* **backen.**
Gebälk [gəbɛlk'] *nt* **-(e)s** timberwork.
gebannt [gəbánt'] *a* spellbound.
gebar [gəbár'] *imperf von* **gebären.**
Gebärde [gəbɛ:r'də] *f* -, **-n** gesture.
gebärden *vr* behave.
Gebaren [gəbá'rən] *nt* **-s** behavior (*US*), behaviour (*Brit*); (*Geschäfts~*) conduct.
gebären [gəbɛ:'rən] *vt unreg* give birth to.
Gebärmutter *f* uterus, womb.
Gebäude [gəboi'də] *nt* **-s,** - building; **~komplex** *m* (*building*) complex; **~reinigung** *f* (*das Reinigen*) commercial cleaning; (*Firma*) cleaning contractors *pl*.
Gebein [gəbīn'] *nt* **-(e)s, -e** bones *pl*.
Gebell [gəbɛl'] *nt* **-(e)s** barking.
geben [gā:'bən] *unreg vti* give (*jdm etw* sb

sth *od* sth to sb); (*Karten*) deal; **in die Post
~ mail; das gibt keinen Sinn** that doesn't
make sense; **er gibt Englisch** he teaches
English; **viel/nicht viel auf etw** (*akk*) ~ set
great store/not much store by sth; **etw von
sich** ~ (*Laute etc*) utter; **ein Wort gab das
andere** one angry word led to another; **ein
gutes Beispiel** ~ set a good example; **~ Sie
mir bitte Herrn Braun** (*TEL*) can I speak to
Mr Braun please?; **ein Auto in Reparatur** ~
have a car repaired ♦ *vt unpers*: **es gibt**
there is/are; there will be; **was gibt's?**
what's the matter?, what's up?; **was gibt's
zum Mittagessen?** what's for lunch?; **das
gibt's doch nicht!** that's impossible ♦ *vr*
(*sich verhalten*) behave, act; (*aufhören*)
abate; **sich geschlagen** ~ admit defeat; **das
wird sich schon** ~ that'll soon sort itself
out.

Gebet [gəbã:t'] *nt* -(e)s, -e prayer; **jdn ins** ~
nehmen (*fig*) take sb to task.

gebeten [gəbã:'tən] *pp von* **bitten**.

gebeugt [gəboikt'] *a* (*Haltung*) stooped;
(*Kopf*) bowed; (*Schultern*) sloping.

gebiert [gəbē:rt'] 3. *pers sing präs von* **gebären**.

Gebiet [gəbē:t'] *nt* -(e)s, -e area; (*Hoheits~*)
territory; (*fig*) field.

gebieten *vt unreg* command, demand.

Gebieter *m* -s, - master; (*Herrscher*) ruler;
~in *f* mistress; **g~isch** *a* imperious.

Gebietshoheit *f* territorial sovereignty.

Gebilde [gəbil'də] *nt* -s, - object, structure.

gebildet *a* cultured, educated.

Gebimmel [gəbi'məl] *nt* -s (continual) ringing.

Gebirge [gəbir'gə] *nt* -s, - mountains *pl*.

gebirgig *a* mountainous.

Gebirgs- [gəbirks'-] *zW*: **~bahn** *f* railroad
crossing a mountain range; **~zug** *m*
mountain range.

Gebiß [gəbis'] *nt* **-sses, -sse** teeth *pl*;
(*künstlich*) dentures *pl*.

gebissen *pp von* **beißen**.

Gebläse [gəblɛ:'zə] *nt* - defogger (*US*), demister (*Brit*).

geblasen [gəblâ'zən] *pp von* **blasen**.

geblichen [gəbli'çhən] *pp von* **bleichen**.

geblieben [gəblē:'bən] *pp von* **bleiben**.

geblümt [gəblü:mt'] *a* flowered; (*Stil*) flowery.

Geblüt [gəblü:t'] *nt* -(e)s blood, race.

gebogen [gəbō:'gən] *pp von* **biegen**.

geboren [gəbō:'rən] *a* born; (*Frau*) née; **wo
sind Sie ~?** where were you born? ♦ *pp von*
gebären.

geborgen [gəbor'gən] *a* secure, safe ♦ *pp von*
bergen.

geborsten [gəbors'tən] *pp von* **bersten**.

gebot [gəbō:t'] *imperf von* **gebieten**.

Gebot *nt* -(e)s, -e command(ment *REL*); (*bei
Auktion*) bid; **das ~ der Stunde** the needs
of the moment.

geboten [gəbō:'tən] *a* (*geh: ratsam*) advis-

able; (: *notwendig*) necessary; (: *dringend*
~) imperative ♦ *pp von* **bieten; gebieten**.

Gebr. *abk* (= *Gebrüder*) Bros., bros.

gebracht [gəbráхht'] *pp von* **bringen**.

gebrannt [gəbránt'] *a*: **ein ~es Kind scheut
das Feuer** (*Sprichwort*) once bitten twice
shy (*Sprichwort*) ♦ *pp von* **brennen**.

gebraten [gəbrâ'tən] *pp von* **braten**.

Gebräu [gəbroi'] *nt* -(e)s, -e brew, concoction.

Gebrauch [gəbrouхh'] *m* -(e)s, **Gebräuche**
use; (*Sitte*) custom; **zum äußerlichen/
innerlichen** ~ to be taken externally/
internally.

gebrauchen *vt* use; **er/das ist zu nichts zu**
~ he's/that's (of) no use to anybody.

gebräuchlich [gəbroiçh'liçh] *a* usual, customary.

Gebrauchs- *zW*: **~anweisung** *f* directions *pl*
for use; **~artikel** *m* article of everyday use;
g~fertig *a* ready for use; **~gegenstand** *m*
commodity.

gebraucht [gəbrouхht'] *a* used; **G~wagen** *m*
secondhand *od* used car.

gebrechlich [gəbreçh'liçh] *a* frail; **G~keit** *f*
frailty.

gebrochen [gəbro'хhən] *pp von* **brechen**.

Gebrüder [gəbrü:'dər] *pl* brothers *pl*.

Gebrüll [gəbrül'] *nt* -(e)s (*von Mensch*) yell-
ing; (*von Löwe*) roar.

gebückt [gəbükt'] *a*: **eine ~e Haltung** a
stoop.

Gebühr [gəbü:r'] *f* -, -en charge; (*Post~*)
postage *no pl*; (*Honorar*) fee; **zu ermäßigter**
~ at a reduced rate; **~ (be)zahlt Empfänger**
postage to be paid by addressee; **nach** ~
suitably; **über** ~ excessively.

gebühren *vi* (*geh*): **jdm** ~ be sb's due *od*
due to sb ♦ *vr* be fitting.

gebührend *a* (*verdient*) due; (*angemessen*)
suitable.

Gebühren- *zW*: **~erlaß** *m* remission of fees;
~ermäßigung *f* reduction of fees; **g~frei** *a*
free of charge; **g~pflichtig** *a* subject to
charges; **g~pflichtige Verwarnung** (*JUR*)
fine.

gebunden [gəbōōn'dən] *a*: **vertraglich** ~ **sein**
be bound by contract ♦ *pp von* **binden**.

Geburt [gəbōō:rt'] *f* -, -en birth; **das war
eine schwere ~!** (*fig umg*) that took some
doing.

Geburten- *zW*: **~beschränkung** *f*,
~kontrolle *f*, **~reglung** *f* birth control;
~rückgang *m* drop in the birth rate;
g~schwach *a* (*Jahrgang*) with a low birth
rate; **~ziffer** *f* birth rate.

gebürtig [gəbür'tiçh] *a* born in, native of; **~e
Schweizerin** native of Switzerland, Swiss-
born woman.

Geburts- *zW*: **~anzeige** *f* birth notice;
~datum *nt* date of birth; **~fehler** *m* congenital defect; **~helfer** *m* (*Arzt*) obstetri-
cian; **~hilfe** *f* (*als Fach*) obstetrics *sing*;
(*von Hebamme auch*) midwifery; **~jahr** *nt*
year of birth; **~ort** *m* birthplace; **~tag** *m*

birthday; **herzlichen Glückwunsch zum ~tag!** happy birthday!, many happy returns (of the day)!; **~urkunde** f birth certificate.
Gebüsch [gəbüsh'] nt **-(e)s, -e** bushes pl.
gedacht[gədåkht']pp von **denken; gedenken.**
gedachte imperf von **gedenken.**
Gedächtnis [gədècht'nis] nt **-ses, -se** memory; **wenn mich mein ~ nicht trügt** if my memory serves me right; **~feier** f commemoration; **~hilfe** f memory aid, mnemonic; **~schwund** m loss of memory; **~verlust** m amnesia.
gedämpft [gədempft'] a (Geräusch) muffled; (Farben, Instrument, Stimmung) muted; (Licht, Freude) subdued.
Gedanke [gədáng'kə] m **-ns, -n** thought; (Idee, Plan, Einfall) idea; (Konzept) concept; **sich über etw** (akk) **~n machen** think about sth; **jdn auf andere ~n bringen** make sb think about other things; **etw ganz in ~n** (dat) **tun** do sth without thinking; **auf einen ~n kommen** have od get an idea.
Gedanken- zW: **~austausch** m exchange of ideas; **~freiheit** f freedom of thought; **g~los** a thoughtless; **~losigkeit** f thoughtlessness; **~sprung** m mental leap; **~strich** m dash; **~übertragung** f thought transference, telepathy; **g~verloren** a lost in thought; **g~voll** a thoughtful.
Gedärme [gədèr'mə] pl intestines pl.
Gedeck [gədek'] nt **-(e)s, -e** cover(ing); (Menü) set meal; **ein ~ auflegen** lay a place.
Gedeih m: **auf ~ und Verderb** for better or for worse.
gedeihen [gədî'ən] vi unreg thrive, prosper; **die Sache ist so weit gediehen, daß** ... the matter has reached the point od stage where ...
gedenken [gədeng'kən] vi unreg +gen (geh: denken an) remember; (beabsichtigen) intend.
Gedenken nt: **zum ~ an jdn** in memory od remembrance of sb.
Gedenk- zW: **~feier** f commemoration; **~minute** f minute's silence; **~stätte** f memorial; **~tag** m memorial day.
Gedicht [gədicht'] nt **-(e)s, -e** poem.
gediegen [gədē:'gən] a (good) quality; (Mensch) reliable; (rechtschaffen) honest; **G~heit** f quality; reliability; honesty.
gedieh [gədē:'] imperf von **gedeihen.**
gediehen pp von **gedeihen.**
gedr. abk (= gedruckt) printed.
Gedränge [gədre'ngə] nt **-s** crush, crowd; **ins ~ kommen** (fig) get into difficulties.
gedrängt a compressed; **~ voll** packed.
gedroschen [gədro'shən] pp von **dreschen.**
gedruckt [gədrõökt'] a: **lügen wie ~** (umg) lie right, left and center.
gedrungen [gədrõö'ngən] a thickset, stocky ♦ pp von **dringen.**
Geduld [gədõölt'] f - patience; **mir reißt die ~, ich verliere die ~** my patience is wear-

ing thin, I'm losing my patience.
gedulden [gədõöl'dən] vr be patient.
geduldig a patient.
Geduldsprobe f trial of (one's) patience.
gedungen [gədõö'ngən] a (pej geh: Mörder) hired.
gedunsen [gədõön'zən] a bloated.
gedurft [gədõörft'] pp von **dürfen.**
geehrt [gəã:rt'] a: **Sehr ~e Damen und Herren!** Ladies and Gentlemen!; (in Briefen) Dear Sir or Madam.
geeignet [gəîg'nət] a suitable; **im ~en Augenblick** at the right moment.
Gefahr [gəfår'] f -, **-en** danger; **~ laufen, etw zu tun** run the risk of doing sth; **auf eigene ~** at one's own risk; **außer ~** (nicht gefährdet) not in danger; (nicht mehr gefährdet) out of danger; (Patienten) off the danger list.
gefährden [gəfe:r'dən] vt endanger.
gefahren [gəfâ'rən] pp von **fahren.**
Gefahren- zW: **~quelle** f source of danger; **~schwelle** f threshold of danger; **~stelle** f danger spot; **~zulage** f hazardous pay (US), danger money (Brit).
gefährlich [gəfe:r'lich] a dangerous.
Gefährte [gəfe:r'tə] m **-n, -n, Gefährtin** f companion.
Gefälle [gəfe'lə] nt **-s, -** (von Land, Straße) slope; (Neigungsgrad) gradient; **starkes ~!** steep hill.
Gefallen [gəfâ'lən] m **-s, -** favor (US), favour (Brit) ♦ nt **-s** pleasure; **an etw** (dat) **~ finden** derive pleasure from sth; **an jdm ~ finden** take to sb; **jdm etw zu ~ tun** do sth to please sb.
gefallen vi unreg: **jdm ~** please sb; **er/es gefällt mir** I like him/it; **das gefällt mir an ihm** that's one thing I like about him; **sich** (dat) **etw ~ lassen** put up with sth ♦ pp von **fallen; gefällig.**
gefällig [gəfe'lich] a (hilfsbereit) obliging; (erfreulich) pleasant; **sonst noch etwas ~?** (veraltet, ironisch) will there be anything else?; **G~keit** f favor (US), favour (Brit); helpfulness; **etw aus G~keit tun** do sth as a favor (US) od favour (Brit).
gefälligst ad (umg) kindly; **sei ~ still!** will you kindly keep your mouth shut!
gefallsüchtig a eager to please.
gefällt [gəfelt'] 3. pers sing präs von **gefallen.**
gefangen [gəfâ'ngən] a captured; (fig) captivated ♦ pp von **fangen.**
Gefangene(r) mf dekl wie a prisoner, captive.
Gefangenenlager nt prisoner-of-war camp.
gefangen- zW: **~halten** vt unreg keep prisoner; **G~nahme** f **-, -n** capture; **G~schaft** f captivity.
Gefängnis [gəfeng'nis] nt **-ses, -se** prison; **zwei Jahre ~ bekommen** get two years' imprisonment; **~strafe** f prison sentence; **~wärter** m prison guard.
gefärbt [gəferpt'] a (fig: Bericht) biased; (Le-

bensmittel) colored (*US*), coloured (*Brit*).

Gefasel [gəfáˈzəl] *nt* **-s** twaddle, drivel.

Gefäß [gəfeːsˈ] *nt* **-es, -e** vessel (*auch* ANAT), container.

gefaßt [gəfást'] *a* composed, calm; **auf etw** (*akk*) ~ **sein** be prepared *od* ready for sth; **er kann sich auf etwas** ~ **machen** (*umg*) I'll give him something to think about.

Gefecht [gəfecht'] *nt* **-(e)s, -e** fight; (*MIL*) engagement; **jdn/etw außer** ~ **setzen** (*lit, fig*) put sb/sth out of action.

gefedert [gəfäːˈdərt] *a* (*Matratze*) sprung.

gefeiert [gəfiːˈərt] *a* celebrated.

gefeit [gəfiːt'] *a*: **gegen etw** ~ **sein** be immune to sth.

gefestigt [gəfesˈticht] *a* (*Charakter*) steadfast.

Gefieder [gəfeːˈdər] *nt* **-s, -** plumage, feathers *pl*.

gefiedert *a* feathered.

gefiel [gəfeːl'] *imperf von* **gefallen**.

Geflecht [gəflecht'] *nt* **-(e)s, -e** (*lit, fig*) network.

gefleckt [gəflekt'] *a* spotted; (*Blume, Vogel*) speckled.

Geflimmer [gəfliˈmər] *nt* **-s** shimmering; (*FILM, TV*) flicker(ing).

geflissentlich [gəfliˈsəntlich] *a, ad* (*geh*) intentional(ly).

geflochten [gəflokh'tən] *pp von* **flechten**.

geflogen [gəfloːˈgən] *pp von* **fliegen**.

geflohen [gəfloːˈən] *pp von* **fliehen**.

geflossen [gəfloˈsən] *pp von* **fließen**.

Geflügel [gəfluːˈgəl] *nt* **-s** poultry.

geflügelt *a*: ~**e Worte** familiar quotations.

Geflüster [gəflüsˈtər] *nt* **-s** whispering.

gefochten [gəfokh'tən] *pp von* **fechten**.

Gefolge [gəfolˈgə] *nt* **-s, -** retinue.

Gefolgschaft [gəfolkˈshaft] *f* following; (*Arbeiter*) personnel.

Gefolgsmann *m* **-(e)s, -leute** follower.

gefragt [gəfráktˈ] *a* in demand.

gefräßig [gəfreːˈsich] *a* voracious.

Gefreite(r) [gəfriˈtə(r)] *m dekl wie a* (*MIL*) private first class (*US*), lance corporal (*Brit*); (*NAUT*) seaman apprentice (*US*), able seaman (*Brit*); (*AVIAT*) airman first class (*US*), aircraftman (*Brit*).

gefressen [gəfreˈsən] *a*: **den hab(e) ich** ~ (*umg*) I'm sick of him ◆ *pp von* **fressen**.

gefrieren [gəfreːˈrən] *vi unreg aux sein* freeze (*chest*).

Gefrier- *zW*: ~**fach** *nt* freezer compartment; ~**fleisch** *nt* frozen meat; **g~getrocknet** *a* freeze-dried; ~**punkt** *m* freezing point; ~**schutzmittel** *nt* antifreeze; ~**truhe** *f* deep-freeze chest.

gefror [gəfroːr'] *imperf von* **gefrieren**.

gefroren *pp von* **gefrieren; gefrieren**.

Gefüge [gəfuːˈgə] *nt* **-s, -** structure.

gefügig *a* submissive; (*gehorsam*) obedient.

Gefühl [gəfuːl'] *nt* **-(e)s, -e** feeling; **etw im** ~ **haben** have a feel for sth; **g~los** *a* unfeeling; (*Glieder*) numb.

Gefühls- *zW*: **g~betont** *a* emotional;

~**duselei** [-zdoːːzəliˈ] *f* (*pej*) mawkishness; ~**leben** *nt* emotional life; **g~mäßig** *a* instinctive; ~**mensch** *m* emotional person.

gefühlvoll *a* (*empfindsam*) sensitive; (*ausdrucksvoll*) expressive; (*liebevoll*) loving.

gefüllt [gəfült'] *a* (*KOCH*) stuffed; (*Pralinen*) with soft centres.

gefunden [gəfoːn'dən] *a*: **das war ein** ~**es Fressen für ihn** that was handing it to him on a plate ◆ *pp von* **finden**.

gegangen [gəgáˈŋgən] *pp von* **gehen**.

gegeben [gəgəˈbən] *a* given; **zu** ~**er Zeit** in due course ◆ *pp von* **geben**.

gegebenenfalls [gəgəːˈbənənfáls] *ad* if need be.

gegen [gäːˈgən] *präp +akk* against; (*in Richtung auf, jdn betreffend, kurz vor*) towards; (*im Austausch für*) (in return) for; (*ungefähr*) (a)round about; (*verglichen mit*) compared with; **haben Sie ein Mittel** ~ **Schnupfen?** do you have anything for colds?; ~ **bar** for cash; **G~angriff** *m* counter-attack; **G~besuch** *m* return visit; **G~beweis** *m* counter-evidence.

Gegend [gäːˈgənt] *f* **-, -en** area, district.

Gegen- *zW*: ~**darstellung** *f* (*PRESSE*) reply; **g~einan'der** *ad* against one another; ~**fahrbahn** *f* opposite lane; ~**frage** *f* counterquestion; ~**gewicht** *nt* counterbalance; ~**gift** *nt* antidote; ~**kandidat** *m* rival candidate; **g~läufig** *a* contrary; ~**leistung** *f* service in return; ~**lichtaufnahme** *f* contre-jour photograph; ~**liebe** *f* requited love; (*fig: Zustimmung*) approval; ~**maßnahme** *f* countermeasure; ~**mittel** *nt* (*MED*) antidote (*gegen* to); ~**probe** *f* cross-check.

Gegensatz *m* **-es, ~e** contrast; ~**e überbrücken** overcome differences.

gegensätzlich *a* contrary, opposite; (*widersprüchlich*) contradictory.

Gegen- *zW*: ~**schlag** *m* counter-attack; ~**seite** *f* opposite side; (*Rückseite*) reverse; **g~seitig** *a* mutual, reciprocal; **sich g~seitig helfen** help each other; **in g~seitigem Einverständnis** by mutual agreement; ~**seitigkeit** *f* reciprocity; ~**spieler** *m* opponent; ~**sprechanlage** *f* (two-way) intercom; ~**stand** *m* object; **g~ständlich** *a* objective, concrete; (*KUNST*) representational; ~**stimme** *f* vote against; ~**stoß** *m* counterblow; ~**stück** *nt* counterpart; ~**teil** *nt* opposite; **im** ~**teil** on the contrary; **das** ~**teil bewirken** have the opposite effect; (*Mensch*) achieve the exact opposite; **ganz im** ~**teil** quite the reverse; **ins** ~**teil umschlagen** swing to the other extreme; **g~teilig** *a* opposite, contrary; **ich habe nichts** ~**teiliges gehört** I've heard nothing to the contrary.

gegenüber [gäːgənüːˈbər] *präp +dat* opposite; (*zu*) to(wards); (*in bezug auf*) with regard to; (*im Vergleich zu*) in comparison with; (*angesichts*) in the face of; **mir** ~ **hat er das nicht geäußert** he didn't say that to me ◆ *ad* opposite; **G~** *nt* **-s,** - (*bei Kampf*) opponent; (*bei Diskussion*) opposite number; **~liegen** *vr unreg* face each other; **~stehen** *vr unreg* be opposed (to each other); **~stellen** *vt* confront; (*fig*) contrast; **G~stellung** *f* confrontation; (*fig*) contrast; (*fig: Vergleich*) comparison; **~treten** *vi unreg* (+*dat*) face.

Gegen- *zW*: **~veranstaltung** *f* counter-meeting; **~verkehr** *m* oncoming traffic; **~vorschlag** *m* counterproposal.

Gegenwart [gā:'gənvàrt] *f* present; **in ~ von** in the presence of.

gegenwärtig *a* present; **das ist mir nicht mehr ~** that has slipped my mind ◆ *ad* at present.

gegenwartsbezogen *a* (*Roman etc*) relevant to present times.

Gegen- *zW*: **~wert** *m* equivalent; **~wind** *m* headwind; **~wirkung** *f* reaction; **g~zeichnen** *vt* countersign; **~zug** *m* counter-move; (*EISENB*) corresponding train in the other direction.

gegessen [gəge'sən] *pp von* **essen.**

geglichen [gəgli'çhən] *pp von* **gleichen.**

gegliedert [gəglē:'dərt] *a* jointed; (*fig*) structured.

geglitten [gəgli'tən] *pp von* **gleiten.**

geglommen [gəglo'mən] *pp von* **glimmen.**

geglückt [gəglükt'] *a* (*Feier*) successful; (*Überraschung*) real.

Gegner(in *f*) [gā:g'nər(in)] *m* **-s,** - opponent; **g~isch** *a* opposing; **~schaft** *f* opposition.

gegolten [gəgol'tən] *pp von* **gelten.**

gegoren [gəgō:'rən] *pp von* **gären.**

gegossen [gəgo'sən] *pp von* **gießen.**

gegr. *abk* (= *gegründet*) est., estab.

gegraben [gəgrà'bən] *pp von* **graben.**

gegriffen [gəgri'fən] *pp von* **greifen.**

geh. *abk* (= *geheim*) secret; (= *gehoben*) elevated; (= *geheftet*) stapled.

Gehabe [gəhá'bə] *nt* **-s** (*umg*) affected behavior (*US*) *od* behaviour (*Brit*).

gehabt [gəhàpt'] *pp von* **haben.**

Gehackte(s) [gāhák'tə(s)] *nt* ground meat (*US*), mince(d meat) (*Brit*).

Gehalt [gəhàlt'] *m* **-(e)s, -e** content ◆ *nt* **-(e)s, ̈-er** salary.

gehalten [gəhál'tən] *a*: **~sein, etw zu tun** (*form*) be required to do sth ◆ *pp von* **halten.**

Gehalts- *zW*: **~abrechnung** *f* salary statement; **~empfänger** *m* salary earner; **~erhöhung** *f* salary increase; **~klasse** *f* salary bracket; **~konto** *nt* checking account (*US*), current account (*Brit*); **~überprüfung** *f* salary review; **~zulage** *f* salary increment.

gehandikapt [gəhen'dēkept] *a* handicapped.

gehangen [gəhà'ngən] *pp von* **hängen.**

geharnischt [gəhár'nisht] *a* (*fig*) forceful, sharp.

gehässig [gəhe'siçh] *a* spiteful, nasty; **G~keit** *f* spite(fulness).

gehäuft [gəhoift'] *a* (*Löffel*) heaped.

Gehäuse [gəhoi'zə] *nt* **-s,** - case; (*Radio~, Uhr~*) casing; (*von Apfel etc*) core.

gehbehindert [gā:'bāhindərt] *a* disabled.

Gehege [gəhā:'gə] *nt* **-s,** - enclosure, preserve; **jdm ins ~ kommen** (*fig*) poach on sb's preserve.

geheim [gəhīm'] *a* secret; (*Dokumente*) classified; **streng ~** top secret; **G~dienst** *m* secret service, intelligence service; **G~fach** *nt* secret compartment; **~halten** *vt unreg* keep secret.

Geheimnis *nt* **-ses, -se** secret; (*rätselhaftes ~*) mystery; **~krämer** *m* mystery-monger; **g~voll** *a* mysterious.

Geheim- *zW*: **~nummer** *f* (*TEL*) unlisted (*US*) *od* ex-directory (*Brit*) number; **~polizei** *f* secret police; **~rat** *m* privy councillor; **~ratsecken** *pl*: **er hat ~ratsecken** he is going bald at the temples; **~schrift** *f* code, secret writing; **~tip** *m* (personal) tip.

Geheiß [gəhīs'] *nt* **-es** (*geh*) command; **auf jds ~** at sb's bidding.

geheißen [gəhī'sən] *pp von* **heißen.**

gehen [gā:'ən] *unreg vti* go; (*zu Fuß ~*) walk; (*funktionieren*) work; (*Auto, Uhr*) go; (*Teig*) rise; **~ nach** (*Fenster*) face; **in die** (*akk*) **~** think things over; **nach etw ~** (*urteilen*) go by sth; **wieviele Leute ~ in deinen Wagen?** how many people can you get in your car?; **nichts geht über** (+*akk*) ... there's nothing to beat ..., there's nothing better than ...; **schwimmen/schlafen ~** go swimming/to bed; **in die Tausende ~** run into (the) thousands ◆ *vi unpers*: **wie geht es dir?** how are you *od* things?; **mir/ihm geht es gut** I'm/he's (doing) fine; **geht das?** is that possible?; **geht's noch?** can you manage?; **es geht** not too bad, O.K.; **das geht nicht** that's not on; **es geht um etw** it concerns sth, it's about sth; **laß es dir gut ~** look after yourself, take care of yourself; **so geht das, das geht so** that/this is how it's done; **darum geht es (mir) nicht** that's not the point; (*spielt keine Rolle*) that's not important to me; **morgen geht es nicht** tomorrow's no good; **wenn es nach mir ginge** ... if it were *od* was up to me ...

gehenlassen *vr unreg* lose one's self-control; (*nachlässig sein*) let o.s. go.

gehetzt [gəhetst'] *a* harassed.

geheuer [gəhoi'ər] *a*: **nicht ~** eerie; (*fragwürdig*) dubious.

Geheul [gəhoil'] *nt* **-(e)s** howling.

Gehilfe [gəhil'fə] *m* **-n, -n, Gehilfin** *f* assistant.

Gehirn [gəhirn'] *nt* **-(e)s, -e** brain; **~erschütterung** *f* concussion; **~schlag** *m* stroke; **~wäsche** *f* brainwashing.

gehoben [gəhō:'bən] *a*: **~er Dienst** *professional and executive levels of the civil service* ◆ *pp von* **heben.**

geholfen [gəhol'fən] *pp von* **helfen.**

Gehör [gəhœr'] *nt* -(e)s hearing; **musikalisches** ~ ear; **absolutes** ~ perfect pitch; ~ **finden** gain a hearing; **jdm** ~ **schenken** give sb a hearing.

gehorchen [gəhor'çhən] *vi* obey (*jdm* sb).

gehören [gəhœ'rən] *vi* belong; **das gehört nicht zur Sache** that's irrelevant; **dazu gehört (schon) einiges** *od* **etwas** that takes some doing (*umg*); **er gehört ins Bett** he should be in bed ♦ *vr unpers* be right *od* proper.

gehörig *a* proper; ~ **zu** *od* +*dat* (*geh*) belonging to.

gehorsam [gəhō:r'zâm] *a* obedient; **G**~ *m* -s obedience.

Gehörsinn *m* sense of hearing.

Gehsteig [gā:'shtīk] *m*, **Gehweg** *m* sidewalk (*US*), pavement (*Brit*).

Geier [gī'ər] *m* -s, - vulture; **weiß der** ~ ~! (*umg*) God knows.

geifern [gī'fərn] *vi* slaver; (*fig*) be bursting with venom.

Geige [gī'gə] *f* -, -n violin; **die erste/zweite** ~ **spielen** (*lit*) play first/second violin; (*fig*) call the tune/play second fiddle.

Geiger(in *f*) *m* -s, - violinist.

Geigerzähler *m* geiger counter.

geil [gīl] *a* horny; (*pej*: *lüstern*) lecherous; (*umg*: *gut*) fantastic.

Geisel [gī'zəl] *f* -, -n hostage; ~**nahme** *f* taking of hostages.

Geißel [gī'səl] *f* -, -n scourge, whip.

geißeln *vt* scourge.

Geist [gīst] *m* -(e)s, -er spirit; (*Gespenst*) ghost; (*Verstand*) mind; **von allen guten** ~**ern verlassen sein** (*umg*) have taken leave of one's senses; **hier scheiden sich die** ~**er** this is the parting of the ways; **den** *od* **seinen** ~ **aufgeben** give up the ghost.

Geister- *zW*: ~**fahrer** *m* (*umg*) ghost-driver (*US*), *person driving in the wrong direction*; **g**~**haft** *a* ghostly; ~**hand** *f*: **wie von** ~**hand** as if by magic.

Geistes- *zW*: **g**~**abwesend** *a* absent-minded; ~**akrobat** *m* mental acrobat; ~**blitz** *m* brainwave; ~**gegenwart** *f* presence of mind; **g**~**gegenwärtig** *a* quick-witted; **g**~**gestört** *a* mentally disturbed *od* (*stärker*) deranged; ~**haltung** *f* mental attitude; **g**~**krank** *a* mentally ill; ~**kranke(r)** *mf* mentally ill person; ~**krankheit** *f* mental illness; ~**störung** *f* mental disturbance; ~**verfassung** *f* frame of mind; ~**wissenschaften** *pl* arts (subjects) *pl*, humanities *pl*; ~**zustand** *m* state of mind; **jdn auf seinen** ~**zustand untersuchen** give sb a psychiatric examination.

geistig *a* intellectual; (*PSYCH*) mental; (*Getränke*) alcoholic; ~ **behindert** mentally handicapped; ~**-seelisch** mental and spiritual.

geistl. *abk* = **geistlich**.

geistlich *a* spiritual; (*religiös*) religious; **G**~**e(r)** *m dekl wie a* clergyman; **G**~**keit** *f* clergy.

Geist- *zW*: **g**~**los** *a* uninspired, dull; **g**~**reich** *a* intelligent; (*witzig*) witty; **g**~**tötend** *a* soul-destroying; **g**~**voll** *a* intellectual; (*weise*) wise.

Geiz [gīts] *m* -es miserliness, meanness; **g**~**en** *vi* be miserly; ~**hals** *m*, ~**kragen** *m* miser.

geizig *a* miserly, mean.

gekannt [gəkánt'] *pp von* **kennen**.

Gekicher [gəki'çhər] *nt* -s giggling.

Geklapper [gəklá'pər] *nt* -s rattling.

Geklimper [gəklim'pər] *nt* -s (*umg*: *Klavier*~) tinkling; (*stümperhaft*) plunking (*umg*); (*von Geld*) jingling.

geklommen [gəklo'mən] *pp von* **klimmen**.

geklungen [gəklōō'ngən] *pp von* **klingen**.

geknickt [gəknikt'] *a* (*fig*) dejected.

gekniffen [gəkni'fən] *pp von* **kneifen**.

gekommen [gəko'mən] *pp von* **kommen**.

gekonnt [gəkont'] *a* skillful (*US*), skilful (*Brit*) ♦ *pp von* **können**.

gekoppelt [gəko'pəlt] *a* (*COMPUT*) on-line.

Gekritzel [gəkri'tsəl] *nt* -s scrawl, scribble.

gekrochen [gəkro'khən] *pp von* **kriechen**.

gekünstelt [gəküns'təlt] *a* artificial; (*Sprache*, *Benehmen*) affected.

Gelabere [gəlá'bərə] *nt* -(s) (*umg*) prattle.

Gelächter [gəlèçh'tər] *nt* -s, - laughter; **in** ~ **ausbrechen** burst out laughing.

gelackmeiert [gəlák'mīərt] *a* (*umg*) conned.

geladen [gəlá'dən] *a* loaded; (*ELEK*) live; (*fig*) furious ♦ *pp von* **laden**.

Gelage [gəlá'gə] *nt* -s, - feast, banquet.

gelagert [gəlá'gərt] *a*: **in anders/ähnlich** ~**en Fällen** in different/similar cases.

gelähmt [gəlɛ:mt'] *a* paralysed.

Gelände [gəlɛn'də] *nt* -s, - land, terrain; (*von Fabrik*, *Sport*~) grounds *pl*; (*Bau*~) site; ~**fahrzeug** *nt* cross-country vehicle; **g**~**gängig** *a* able to go cross-country; ~**lauf** *m* cross-country race.

Geländer [gəlɛn'dər] *nt* -s, - railing; (*Treppen*~) banister(s).

gelang *imperf von* **gelingen**.

gelangen [gəlá'ngən] *vi* (*an* +*akk od zu*) reach; (*erwerben*) attain; **in jds Besitz** ~ **to** come into sb's possession; **in die richtigen/ falschen Hände** ~ fall into the right/wrong hands.

gelangweilt *a* bored.

gelassen [gəlá'sən] *a* calm; (*gefasst*) composed ♦ *pp von* **lassen**; **G**~**heit** *f* calmness; composure.

Gelatine [zhälátē:'nə] *f* gelatine.

gelaufen [gəlou'fən] *pp von* **laufen**.

geläufig [gəloi'fiçh] *a* (*üblich*) common; **das ist mir nicht** ~ I'm not familiar with that; **G**~**keit** *f* commonness; familiarity.

gelaunt [gəlount'] *a*: **schlecht/gut** ~ in a bad/good mood; **wie ist er** ~**?** what sort of mood is he in?

Geläut(e) [gəloit'(ə)] *nt* -(e)s ringing; (*Läutwerk*) chime.

gelb [gɛlp] a yellow; (*Ampellicht*) yellow (*US*), amber (*Brit*); **~lich** a yellowish.

Gelbsucht f jaundice.

Geld [gɛlt] nt -(e)s, -er money; **etw zu ~ ma-chen** sell sth off; **er hat ~ wie Heu** (*umg*) he's stinking rich; **am ~ hängen** od **kleben** be tight with money; **staatliche/öffentliche ~er** state/public funds pl od money; **~adel** m: **der ~adel** the moneyed aristocracy; (*hum*: *die Reichen*) the rich; **~anlage** f investment; **~automat** m automated teller machine, cash dispenser (*Brit*); **~automatenkarte** f bank card (*for use with ATM*) (*US*), cash card (*Brit*); **~beutel** m, **~börse** f purse; **~einwurf** m slot; **~geber** m **-s,** - financial backer; **g~gierig** a avaricious; **~mittel** pl capital, means pl; **~quelle** f source of income; **~schein** m banknote; **~schrank** m safe, strongbox; **~strafe** f fine; **~stück** nt coin; **~verlegenheit** f: **in ~verlegenheit sein/kommen** to be/run short of money; **~verleiher** m **-s,** - moneylender; **~wechsel** m exchange (of money); **„~wechsel"** "(currency) exchange"; **~wert** m cash value; (*FIN*: *Kaufkraft*) currency value.

geleckt [gəlɛkt'] a: **wie ~ aussehen** be neat and tidy.

Gelee [zhālā:'] nt od m **-s, -s** jelly.

gelegen [gəlā:'gən] a situated; (*passend*) convenient, opportune; **etw kommt jdm ~** sth is convenient for sb; **mir ist viel/nichts daran ~** (*wichtig*) it matters a great deal/doesn't matter to me ♦ pp von **liegen**.

Gelegenheit [gəlā:'gənhīt] f opportunity; (*Anlaß*) occasion; **bei ~** some time (or other); **bei jeder ~** at every opportunity.

Gelegenheits- zW: **~arbeit** f casual work; **~arbeiter** m occasional (*US*) od casual (*Brit*) worker; **~kauf** m bargain.

gelegentlich [gəlā:'gəntlicḥ] a occasional ♦ ad occasionally; (*bei Gelegenheit*) some time (or other) ♦ präp +gen on the occasion of.

gelehrig [gəlā:'riċh] a quick to learn.

gelehrt a learned; **G~e(r)** mf dekl wie a scholar; **G~heit** f scholarliness.

Geleise [gəlī'zə] nt **-s,** track; *siehe* **Gleis.**

Geleit [gəlīt'] nt **-(e)s, -e** escort; **freies** od **sicheres ~** safe conduct; **g~en** vt escort; **~schutz** m escort.

Gelenk [gəlɛngk'] nt **-(e)s, -e** joint.

gelenkig a supple.

gelernt [gəlɛrnt'] a skilled.

gelesen [gəlā:'zən] pp von **lesen.**

Geliebte f dekl wie a sweetheart; (*Liebhaberin*) mistress.

Geliebte(r) [gəlē:p'tə(r)] m dekl wie a sweetheart; (*Liebhaber*) lover.

geliefert [gəlē:'fərt] a: **ich bin ~** (*umg*) I've had it.

geliehen [gəlē:'ən] pp von **leihen.**

gelind(e) [gə'lint, gə'lində] a (*geh*) mild; (*Wind, Frost, Regen*) light; (*col*: *Wut*) awful; **~e gesagt** to put it mildly.

gelingen [gəli'ngən] vi unreg succeed; **die Arbeit gelingt mir nicht** I'm not doing very well with this work; **es ist mir gelungen, etw zu tun** I succeeded in doing sth.

Gelingen nt (*geh*: *Glück*) success; (: *erfolgreiches Ergebnis*) successful outcome.

gelitten [gəli'tən] pp von **leiden.**

gellen [gɛ'lən] vi shrill.

gellend a shrill, piercing.

geloben [gəlō:'bən] vti vow, swear; **das Gelobte Land** (*REL*) the Promised Land.

gelogen [gəlō:'gən] pp von **lügen.**

gelten [gɛl'tən] unreg vt (*wert sein*) be worth; **was gilt die Wette?** do you want a bet? ♦ vi (*gültig sein*) be valid; (*erlaubt sein*) be allowed; **das gilt nicht!** that doesn't count!; (*nicht erlaubt*) that's not allowed; **etw gilt bei jdm viel/wenig** sb values sth highly/sb doesn't value sth very highly; **jdm viel/wenig ~** mean a lot/not mean much to sb; **jdm ~** (*gemünzt sein auf*) be meant for od aimed at sb; **etw ~ lassen** accept sth; **für diesmal lasse ich's ~** I'll let it go this time; **als** od **für etw ~** be considered to be sth; **jdm** od **für jdn ~** (*betreffen*) apply to sb ♦ vti unpers (*geh*): **es gilt, etw zu tun** it is necessary to do sth.

geltend a (*Preise*) current; (*Gesetz*) in force; (*Meinung*) prevailing; **etw ~ machen** to assert sth; **sich ~ machen** make itself/o.s. felt; **einen Einwand ~ machen** raise an objection.

Geltung [gɛl'tōōng] f: **~ haben** have validity; **sich/etw** (*dat*) **~ verschaffen** establish o.s./sth; **etw zur ~ bringen** show sth to its best advantage; **zur ~ kommen** be seen/heard etc to its best advantage.

Geltungs- zW: **~bedürfnis** nt desire for admiration; **g~süchtig** a craving admiration.

Gelübde [gəlüp'də] nt **-s,** - vow.

gelungen [gəlōō'ngən] a successful ♦ pp von **gelingen.**

Gem. abk = **Gemeinde.**

gemächlich [gəmɛ:ċh'liċh] a leisurely.

gemacht [gəmȧḳht'] a (*gewollt, gekünstelt*) false, contrived; **ein ~er Mann sein** be made; be a made man.

Gemahl [gəmȧl'] m **-(e)s, -e** (*geh, form*) spouse, husband; **~in** f (*geh, form*) spouse, wife.

gemahlen [gəmȧ'lən] pp von **mahlen.**

Gemälde [gəmɛ:l'də] nt **-s,** - picture, painting.

gemasert [gəmȧ'zərt] a (*Holz*) grained.

gemäß [gəmɛ:s'] präp +dat in accordance with ♦ a appropriate (dat to).

gemäßigt a moderate; (*Klima*) temperate.

Gemauschel [gəmou'shəl] nt **-s** (*umg*) scheming.

Gemecker [gəmɛ'kər] nt **-s** (*von Ziegen*) bleating; (*umg*: *Nörgelei*) moaning.

gemein [gəmīn'] a common; (*niederträchtig*) mean; **etw ~ haben** have sth in common (*mit* with).

Gemeinde [gəmīn'də] *f* -, -n district; (*Bewohner*) community; (*Pfarr~*) parish; (*Kirchen~*) congregation; ~**abgaben** *pl* local *od* municipal taxes *pl*; ~**ordnung** *f* by(e)laws *pl*, ordinances *pl* (*US*); ~**rat** *m* district council; (*Mitglied*) district councillor; ~**schwester** *f* district nurse; ~**steuer** *f* local rates *pl*; ~**verwaltung** *f* local administration; ~**vorstand** *m* local council; ~**wahl** *f* local election.

Gemein- *zW*: ~**eigentum** *nt* common property; **g~gefährlich** *a* dangerous to the public; ~**gut** *nt* public property; ~**heit** *f* (*Niedertracht*) meanness; **das war eine ~heit** that was a mean thing to do/to say; **g~hin** *ad* generally; ~**kosten** *pl* overhead (*US*), overheads *pl* (*Brit*); ~**nutz** *m* public good; **g~nützig** *a* of benefit to the public; (*wohltätig*) charitable; ~**platz** *m* commonplace, platitude; **g~sam** *a* joint, common (*auch MATH*); **g~same Sache mit jdm machen** be in cahoots with sb; **der g~same Markt** the Common Market; **g~sames Konto** joint account ♦ *ad* together, **etw g~sam haben** have sth in common; ~**samkeit** *f* common ground; ~**schaft** *f* community; **in ~schaft mit** jointly *od* together with; **eheliche ~schaft** (*JUR*) matrimony; **g~schaftlich** *a siehe* **g~sam**; ~**schaftsantenne** *f* party antenna (*US*) *od* aerial (*Brit*); ~**schaftsarbeit** *f* teamwork; team effort; ~**schaftsbesitz** *m* collective ownership; ~**schaftserziehung** *f* coeducation; ~**schaftskunde** *f* social studies *pl*; ~**schaftsraum** *m* recreation room; ~**sinn** *m* public spirit; **g~verständlich** *a* generally comprehensible; ~**wesen** *nt* community; ~**wohl** *nt* common good.

Gemenge [gəme'ngə] *nt* -s, - mixture; (*Hand~*) scuffle.

gemessen [gəme'sən] *a* measured ♦ *pp von* **messen**.

Gemetzel [gəme'tsəl] *nt* -s, - slaughter, carnage.

gemieden [gəmē:'dən] *pp von* **meiden**.

Gemisch [gəmish'] *nt* -es, -e mixture.

gemischt *a* mixed.

gemocht [gəmòkht'] *pp von* **mögen**.

gemolken [gəmol'kən] *pp von* **melken**.

Gemse [gem'zə] *f* -, -n chamois.

Gemunkel [gəmōōng'kəl] *nt* -s gossip.

Gemurmel [gəmōōr'məl] *nt* -s murmur(ing).

Gemüse [gəmü:'zə] *nt* -s, - vegetables *pl*; ~**garten** *m* vegetable garden; ~**händler** *m* vegetable dealer (*US*), greengrocer (*Brit*); ~**platte** *f* (*KOCH*): **eine ~platte** assorted vegetables *pl*.

gemußt [gəmōōst'] *pp von* **müssen**.

gemustert [gəmōōs'tərt] *a* patterned.

Gemüt [gəmü:t'] *nt* -(e)s, -er disposition, nature; (*fig: Mensch*) person; **sich** (*dat*) **etw zu ~e führen** (*umg*) indulge in sth; **die ~er erregen** arouse strong feelings; **wir müssen**

warten, bis sich die ~er beruhigt haben we must wait until feelings have cooled down.

gemütlich *a* comfortable, cozy (*US*), cosy (*Brit*); (*Person*) good-natured; **wir verbrachten einen ~en Abend** we spent a very pleasant evening; **G~keit** *f* comfortableness, coziness (*US*), cosiness (*Brit*); amiability.

Gemüts- *zW*: ~**bewegung** *f* emotion; **g~krank** *a* emotionally disturbed; ~**mensch** *m* sentimental person; ~**ruhe** *f* composure; **in aller ~ruhe** (*umg*) (as) cool as a cucumber; (*gemächlich*) at a leisurely pace; ~**zustand** *m* state of mind.

gemütvoll *a* warm, tender.

gen. *abk* (= *genannt*) named, called.

Gen [gā:n] *nt* -s, -e gene.

Gen. *abk* = **Genitiv; Genossenschaft**.

genannt [gənánt'] *pp von* **nennen**.

genas [gənás'] *imperf von* **genesen**.

genau [gənou'] *a*, *ad* exact(ly), precise(ly); **etw ~ nehmen** take sth seriously; **G~eres** further details *pl*; **etw ~ wissen** know sth for certain; ~ **auf die Minute, auf die Minute ~** exactly on time; ~**genommen** *ad* strictly speaking.

Genauigkeit *f* exactness, accuracy.

genauso [gənou'zō:] *ad* (*vor Adjektiv*) just as; (*alleinstehend*) just *od* exactly the same.

Gen.-Dir. *abk* = **Generaldirektor**.

genehm [gənā:m'] *a* agreeable, acceptable.

genehmigen *vt* approve, authorize; **sich** (*dat*) **etw ~** indulge in sth.

Genehmigung *f* approval, authorization.

geneigt [gənīkt'] *a* (*geh*) well-disposed, willing; ~ **sein, etw zu tun** be inclined to do sth.

General [gānārâl'] *m* -s, -e *od* ¨e general; ~**direktor** *m* president.

Generalist(in *f*) [gānərálist'(in)] *m* politician with no special abilities.

General- *zW*: ~**konsulat** *nt* consulate general; ~**probe** *f* dress rehearsal; ~**stabskarte** *f* ordnance survey map; ~**streik** *m* general strike; **g~überholen** *vt* overhaul thoroughly; ~**vertretung** *f* sole agency.

Generation [gānārátsēō:n'] *f* generation.

Generationskonflikt *m* generation gap.

Generator [gānārâ'tor] *m* generator, dynamo.

generell [gānərel'] *a* general.

genesen [gānā:'zən] *vi unreg* (*geh*) convalesce.

Genesende(r) *mf dekl wie a* convalescent.

Genesung *f* recovery, convalescence.

genetisch [gānā:'tish] *a* genetic.

Genf [genf] *nt* -s Geneva.

Genfer *a attr*: **der ~ See** Lake Geneva; **die ~ Konvention** the Geneva Convention.

genial [gānēâl'] *a* brilliant.

Genialität [gānēâlēte:t'] *f* brilliance, genius.

Genick [gənik'] *nt* -(e)s, -e (back of the) neck; **jdm/einer Sache das ~ brechen** (*fig*) finish sb/sth; ~**starre** *f* stiff neck.

Genie [zhānē:'] *nt* -s, -s genius.

genieren [zhānē:'rən] *vr* be embarrassed ♦ *vt* bother; **geniert es Sie, wenn ...?** do you mind if ...?
genießbar *a* edible; (*trinkbar*) drinkable.
genießen [gənē:'sən] *vt unreg* enjoy; (*essen*) eat; (*trinken*) drink; **er ist heute nicht zu ~** (*umg*) he is unbearable today.
Genießer(in *f*) *m* **-s,** - connoisseur; (*des Lebens*) pleasure-lover; **g~isch** *a* appreciative ♦ *ad* with relish.
Genitalien [gānētá'lēən] *pl* genitals *pl*.
Genitiv [gā:'nētē:f] *m* genitive.
genommen [gəno'mən] *pp von* **nehmen**.
genoß [gənos'] *imperf von* **genießen**.
Genosse [gəno'sə] *m* **-n,** **-n, Genossin** *f* comrade (*bes POL*), companion.
genossen *pp von* **genießen**.
Genossenschaft *f* cooperative (association).
genötigt [gənœ'tiçt] *a*: **sich ~ sehen, etw zu tun** feel obliged to do sth.
Genre [zhāń'rə] *nt* **-s,** **-s** genre.
Gentechnologie *f* genetic engineering.
Genua [gā:'nōoá] *nt* **-s** Genoa.
genug [gənōō:k'] *ad* enough; **jetzt ist('s) aber ~!** that's enough!
Genüge [gənü:'gə] *f* -: **jdm/etw ~ tun** *od* **leisten** satisfy sb/sth; **etw zur ~ kennen** know sth well enough; (*abwertender*) know sth only too well.
genügen *vi* be enough; (*Anforderungen*) satisfy.
genügend *a* enough, sufficient; (*befriedigend*) satisfactory.
genügsam [gənü:k'zȧm] *a* modest, easily satisfied; **G~keit** *f* moderation.
Genugtuung [gənōō:k'tōō:ōōng] *f* satisfaction.
Genus [gā:'nōōs] *nt* -, **-nera** [gā:'nȧrȧ] (*GRAM*) gender.
Genuß [gənōōs'] *m* **-sses,** -̈**sse** pleasure; (*Zusichnehmen*) consumption; **etw mit ~ essen** eat sth with relish; **in den ~ von etw kommen** receive the benefit of sth.
genüßlich [gənüs'liç] *ad* with relish.
Genußmittel *pl* (semi-)luxury items *pl*.
Geograph [gāōgráf'] *m* **-en,** **-en, Geographin** *f* geographer.
Geographie [gāōgráfē:'] *f* geography.
geographisch *a* geographical.
Geologe [gāōlō:'gə] *m* **-n,** **-n, Geologin** *f* geologist.
Geologie [gāōlō:gē:'] *f* geology.
Geometrie [gāōmātrē:'] *f* geometry.
geordnet [gəord'nət] *a*: **in ~en Verhältnissen leben** live a well-ordered life.
Gepäck [gəpɛk'] *nt* **-(e)s** baggage, luggage; **mit leichtem ~ reisen** travel light; **~abfertigung** *f*, **~annahme** *f*, **~ausgabe** *f* baggage desk/office; **~aufbewahrung** *f* baggage check (*US*), left-luggage office (*Brit*); **~netz** *nt* baggage rack; **~schein** *m* baggage ticket; **~träger** *m* porter; (*Fahrrad*) carrier; **~wagen** *m* baggage car (*US*), luggage van (*Brit*).

Gepard [gā:'párt] *m* **-(e)s,** **-e** cheetah.
gepfeffert [gəpfe'fərt] *a* (*umg*: *Preise*) steep; (: *Fragen, Prüfung*) tough; (: *Kritik*) biting.
gepfiffen [gəpfi'fən] *pp von* **pfeifen**.
gepflegt [gəpflā:kt'] *a* well-groomed; (*Park etc*) well looked after; (*Atmosphäre*) sophisticated; (*Ausdrucksweise, Sprache*) cultured.
Gepflogenheit [gəpflō:'gənhīt] *f* (*geh*) custom.
Geplapper [gəplá'pər] *nt* **-s** chatter.
Geplauder [gəplou'dər] *nt* **-s** chat(ting).
Gepolter [gəpol'tər] *nt* **-s** din.
gepr. *abk* (= *geprüft*) tested.
gepriesen [gəprē:'zən] *pp von* **preisen**.
gequält [gəkvɛlt'] *a* (*Lächeln*) forced; (*Miene, Ausdruck*) pained; (*Gesang, Stimme*) strained.
Gequatsche [gəkvát'shə] *nt* **-s** (*pej umg*) gabbing; (*Blödsinn*) twaddle.
gequollen [gəkvo'lən] *pp von* **quellen**.
gerade [gərȧ'də] *a* straight; (*Zahl*) even ♦ *ad* (*genau*) exactly; (*örtlich*) straight; (*eben*) just; **warum ~ ich?** why me?; **~ weil** just *od* precisely because; **nicht ~ schön** not exactly nice; **das ist es ja ~!** that's just it; **jetzt ~ nicht!** not now!; **~ noch** just; **~ neben** right next to; **~ du solltest dafür Verständnis haben** you especially should understand; **da wir ~ von Geld sprechen ...** talking of money ...
Gerade *f* **-n, -n** straight line.
gerade- *zW*: **~aus** *ad* straight ahead; **~biegen** *vt unreg* (*lit, fig*) straighten out; **~heraus** *ad* straight out, bluntly.
gerädert [gəre:'dərt] *a*: **wie ~ sein, sich wie ~ fühlen** be *od* feel dead tired *od* beat (*umg*).
geradeso *ad* just so; **~ dumm** *etc* just as stupid *etc*; **~ wie** just as.
geradestehen *vi unreg* (*aufrecht stehen*) stand up straight; **für jdn/etw ~** (*fig*) be answerable *od* answer for sb/sth.
geradezu *ad* (*beinahe*) virtually, almost.
geradlinig *a* straight.
gerammelt [gərá'məlt] *ad*: **~ voll** (*umg*) (jam-)packed.
Geranie [gərá'nēə] *f* geranium.
gerannt [gərȧnt'] *pp von* **rennen**.
gerät [gəre:t'] *3. pers sing präs von* **geraten**.
Gerät [gəre:t'] *nt* **-(e)s, -e** device; (*Apparat*) gadget; (*elektrisches ~*) appliance; (*Werkzeug*) tool; (*SPORT*) apparatus; (*Zubehör*) equipment *no pl*.
geraten [gərȧ'tən] *vi unreg* (*gelingen*) turn out well (*jdm* for sb); (*gedeihen*) thrive; (*zufällig gelangen*) get (*in +akk* into); **gut/ schlecht ~** turn out well/badly; **an jdn ~** come across sb; **an den Richtigen/Falschen ~** come to the right/wrong person; **in Angst ~** get frightened; **nach jdm ~** take after sb ♦ *pp von* **raten; geraten**.
Geräteturnen *nt* apparatus gymnastics.
Geratewohl [gərȧtəvō:l'] *nt*: **aufs ~** on the

off chance; (bei Wahl) at random.
geraum [gəroum'] a: **seit ~er Zeit** for some considerable time.
geräumig [gəroi'miçh] a roomy.
Geräusch [gəroish'] nt -(e)s, -e sound; (unangenehm) noise; **g~arm** a quiet; **~kulisse** f background noise; (FILM, RAD, TV) sound effects pl; **g~los** a silent; **~pegel** m sound level; **g~voll** a noisy.
gerben [ger'bən] vt tan.
Gerber m -s, - tanner.
Gerberei [gerbəri'] f tannery.
gerecht [gərecht'] a just, fair; **jdm/etw ~ werden** do justice to sb/sth; **~fertigt** a justified.
Gerechtigkeit f justice, fairness.
Gerechtigkeits- zW: **~fanatiker** m justice fanatic; **~gefühl** nt, **~sinn** m sense of justice.
Gerede [gərā:'də] nt -s talk; (Klatsch) gossip.
geregelt [gərā:'gəlt] a (Arbeit, Mahlzeiten) regular; (Leben) well-ordered.
gereizt [gərītst'] a irritable; **G~heit** f irritation.
Gericht [gəricht'] nt -(e)s, -e court; (Essen) dish; **jdm/einen Fall vor ~ bringen** take sb/a case to court; **mit jdm ins ~ gehen** (fig) judge sb harshly; **über jdn zu ~ sitzen** sit in judgement on sb; **das Letzte ~** the Last Judgement; **g~lich** a, ad judicial(ly), legal(ly); **ein g~liches Nachspiel haben** finish up in court; **g~lich gegen jdn vorgehen** take legal proceedings against sb.
Gerichts- zW: **~akten** pl court records pl; **~barkeit** f jurisdiction; **~hof** m court (of law); **~kosten** pl (legal) costs pl; **g~medizinisch** a forensic medical attr; **~saal** m courtroom; **~verfahren** nt legal proceedings pl; **~verhandlung** f court proceedings pl; **~vollzieher** m bailiff.
gerieben [gərē:'bən] a grated; (umg: schlau) smart, wily ♦ pp von **reiben**.
geriet [gərē:t'] imperf von **geraten**.
gering [gəring'] a slight, small; (niedrig) low; (Zeit) short; **~achten** vt think little of; **~fügig** a slight, trivial; **~schätzig** a disparaging; **G~schätzung** f disdain.
geringste(r, s) a slightest, least; **nicht im ~n** not in the least od slightest.
gerinnen [gəri'nən] vi unreg congeal; (Blut) clot; (Milch) curdle.
Gerinnsel [gərin'zəl] nt -s, - clot.
Gerippe [gəri'pə] nt -s, - skeleton.
gerissen [gəri'sən] a wily, smart ♦ pp von **reißen**.
geritten [gəri'tən] pp von **reiten**.
geritzt [gəritst'] a (umg): **die Sache ist ~** everything's fixed up od settled.
Germanist(in f) [germänist'(in)] m Germanist; (Student auch) German student; (Wissenschaftler auch) German specialist.
Germanistik f German (studies pl).
gern(e) [gern'(ə)] ad willingly, gladly; **(aber) ~!** of course!; **~ haben, ~ mögen** like; **~**

geschehen! you're welcome!, not at all!; **ein ~ gesehener Gast** a welcome visitor; **ich hätte** od **möchte ~ ...** I would like ...; **du kannst mich mal ~ haben!** (umg) (you can) go to hell!; **etw ~ tun** like doing sth.
Gernegroß m -, -e show-off.
gerochen [gəro'khən] pp von **riechen**.
Geröll [gərœl'] nt -(e)s, -e scree.
geronnen [gəro'nən] pp von **rinnen; gerinnen.**
Gerste [gers'tə] f -, -n barley.
Gerstenkorn nt (im Auge) stye.
Gerte [ger'tə] f -, -n switch, rod.
gertenschlank a willowy.
Geruch [gərōōkh'] m -(e)s, ⁻e smell, odor (US), odour (Brit); **g~los** a odorless (US), odourless (Brit).
Geruch(s)sinn m sense of smell.
Gerücht [gərücht'] nt -(e)s, -e rumor (US), rumour (Brit).
geruchtilgend a deodorant.
gerufen [gərōō:'fən] pp von **rufen**.
geruhen [gərōō:'ən] vi deign.
geruhsam [gərōō:'zám] a peaceful; (Spaziergang etc) leisurely.
Gerümpel [gərüm'pəl] nt -s junk.
gerungen [gərōō'ngən] pp von **ringen**.
Gerüst [gərüst'] nt -(e)s, -e (Bau~) scaffold(ing); (fig) framework.
Ges. abk (= Gesellschaft) Co., co.
gesalzen [gəzàl'tsən] a (fig umg: Preis, Rechnung) steep, stiff ♦ pp von **salzen**.
gesamt [gəzàmt'] a whole, entire; (Kosten) total; (Werke) complete; **im ~en** all in all; **G~auflage** f gross circulation; **G~ausgabe** f complete edition; **G~betrag** m total (amount); **~deutsch** a all-German; **G~eindruck** m general impression; **G~heit** f totality, whole; **G~hochschule** f polytechnic (Brit); **G~masse** f (COMM) total assets pl; **G~nachfrage** f (COMM) composite demand; **G~schaden** m total damage; **G~schule** f comprehensive school; **G~wertung** f (SPORT) overall standings pl (US) od placings pl (Brit).
gesandt pp von **senden**.
Gesandte(r) [gəzàn'tə(r)] mf dekl wie a envoy.
Gesandtschaft [gəzànt'shàft] f legation.
Gesang [gəzàng'] m -(e)s, ⁻e song; (Singen) singing; **~buch** nt (REL) hymn book; **~verein** m choral society.
Gesäß [gəze:s'] nt -es, -e seat, bottom.
gesättigt [gəze'tiçht] a (CHEM) saturated.
gesch. abk (= geschieden) div.
Geschädigte(r) [gəshe:'diçhtə(r)] mf dekl wie a victim.
geschaffen [gəshá'fən] pp von **schaffen**.
Geschäft [gəsheft'] nt -(e)s, -e business; (Laden) store (bes US), shop (bes Brit); (Geschäftsabschluß) deal; **mit jdm ins ~ kommen** do business with sb; **dabei hat er ein ~ gemacht** he made a profit by it; **im ~** at work; (im Laden) in the store; **sein ~**

verrichten do one's business (*euph*).
Geschäftemacher *m* **-s**, **-** profiteer;
wheeler-dealer.
geschäftig *a* active, busy; (*pej*) officious.
geschäftlich *a* commercial ♦ *ad* on business;
~ **unterwegs** away on business.
Geschäfts- *zW*: ~**abschluß** *m* business deal
od transaction; ~**aufgabe** *f*, ~**auflösung** *f*
closure of a/the business; ~**bereich** *m*
(*PARL*) responsibilities *pl*; **Minister ohne**
~**bereich** minister without portfolio;
~**bericht** *m* financial report; ~**computer** *m*
business computer; ~**essen** *nt* business
lunch; ~**führer** *m* manager; (*Klub*) secretary; ~**geheimnis** *nt* trade secret; ~**inhaber**
m owner; ~**jahr** *nt* financial year; ~**lage** *f*
business conditions *pl*; ~**leitung** *f* management; ~**mann** *m* **-(e)s, -leute** businessman;
g~mäßig *a* businesslike; ~**ordnung** *f* standing orders *pl*; **eine Frage zur** ~**ordnung** a
question on a point of order; ~**partner** *m*
partner; ~**reise** *f* business trip; ~**schluß** *m*
closing time; ~**sinn** *m* business sense;
~**stelle** *f* offices *pl*; **g~tüchtig** *a* business
minded; ~**viertel** *nt* business district;
~**wagen** *m* company car; ~**wesen** *nt* business; ~**zeiten** *pl* office/bank hours *pl*;
~**zweig** *m* branch (of a business).
geschah [gəshâ'] *imperf von* **geschehen**.
geschehen [gəshā:'ən] *vi unreg* happen; **das
geschieht ihm (ganz) recht** it serves him
(jolly well (*umg*)) right; **was soll mit ihm/
damit ~?** what is to be done with him/it?;
es war um ihn ~ that was the end of him.
gescheit [gəshīt'] *a* clever; (*vernünftig*) sensible.
Geschenk [gəshengk'] *nt* **-(e)s, -e** present,
gift; ~**artikel** *m* gift; ~**gutschein** *m* gift
voucher; ~**packung** *f* gift pack; ~**sendung** *f*
gift parcel.
Geschichte [gəshìç'tə] *f* **-**, **-n** story; (*Sache*)
affair; (*Historie*) history.
Geschichtenerzähler *m* **-s**, **-** storyteller.
geschichtlich *a* historical; (*bedeutungsvoll*)
historic.
Geschichts- *zW*: ~**fälschung** *f* falsification
of history; ~**schreiber** *m* historian.
Geschick [gəshik'] *nt* **-(e)s, -e** skill; (*geh*:
Schicksal) fate; ~**lichkeit** *f* skill, dexterity.
Geschicklichkeitsspiel *nt* game of skill.
geschickt *a* skillful (*US*), skilful (*Brit*); (*taktisch auch*) clever; (*beweglich*) agile.
geschieden [gəshē:'dən] *a* divorced ♦ *pp von*
scheiden.
geschieht [gəshē:t'] *3. pers sing präs von*
geschehen.
geschienen [gəshē:'nən] *pp von* **scheinen**.
Geschirr [gəshir'] *nt* **-(e)s, -e** tableware;
(*Küchen~*) pots and pans *pl*; (*Pferde~*) harness; ~**spülmaschine** *f* dishwasher; ~**tuch**
nt dishtowel (*US*), tea towel (*Brit*).
geschissen [gəshi'sən] *pp von* **scheißen**.
geschlafen [gəshlâ'fən] *pp von* **schlafen**.
geschlagen [gəshlâ'gən] *pp von* **schlagen**.

geschlaucht [gəshloukht'] *ad*: ~ **sein** (*umg*)
be exhausted *od* knackered.
Geschlecht [gəshleçt'] *nt* **-(e)s, -er** sex;
(*GRAM*) gender; (*Gattung*) race; (*Abstammung*) lineage; **g~lich** *a* sexual.
Geschlechts- *zW*: ~**krankheit** *f* venereal disease; sexually-transmitted disease; **g~reif** *a*
sexually mature; **g~spezifisch** *a* (*SOZIOLO-
GIE*) sex-specific; ~**teil** *nt od m* genitals *pl*;
~**verkehr** *m* sexual intercourse; ~**wort** *nt*
(*GRAM*) article.
geschlichen [gəshli'çən] *pp von* **schleichen**.
geschliffen [gəshli'fən] *pp von* **schleifen**.
geschlossen [gəshlo'sən] *a*: ~**e Gesellschaft**
closed society; (*Fest*) private party; ~**e
Ortschaft** built-up area ♦ *ad*: ~ **hinter jdm
stehen** stand solidly behind sb ♦ *pp von*
schließen.
geschlungen [gəshlōō'ngən] *pp von* **schlingen**.
Geschmack [gəshmàk'] *m* **-(e)s**, ⁻**e** taste;
nach jds ~ to sb's taste; ~ **finden an etw**
(*dat*) (come to) like sth; **je nach** ~ to one's
own taste; **er hat einen guten** ~ (*fig*) he
has good taste; **g~los** *a* tasteless; (*fig*) in
bad taste; ~**(s)sache** *f* matter of taste;
~**sinn** *m* sense of taste.
Geschmacksverirrung *f*: **unter** ~ **leiden**
(*ironisch*) have no taste.
geschmackvoll *a* tasteful.
Geschmeide [gəshmī'də] *nt* **-s**, **-** jewelry
(*US*), jewellery (*Brit*).
geschmeidig *a* supple; (*formbar*) malleable.
Geschmeiß [gəshmīs'] *nt* vermin *pl*.
Geschmiere [gəshmē:'rə] *nt* **-s** scrawl; (*Bild*)
daub.
geschmissen [gəshmi'sən] *pp von*
schmeißen.
geschmolzen [gəshmol'tsən] *pp von*
schmelzen.
Geschnetzelte(s) [gəshne'tsəltə(s)] *nt dekl
wie a* (*KOCH*) meat cut into strips and
stewed to produce a thick sauce.
geschnitten [gəshni'tən] *pp von* **schneiden**.
geschoben [gəshō:'bən] *pp von* **schieben**.
geschollen [gəsho'lən] *pp von* **schallen**.
gescholten [gəshol'tən] *pp von* **schelten**.
Geschöpf [gəshœpf'] *nt* **-(e)s, -e** creature.
geschoren [gəshō:'rən] *pp von* **scheren**.
Geschoß [gəshos'] *nt* **-sses, -sse** (*MIL*) projectile; (*Rakete*) missile; (*Stockwerk*) floor.
geschossen [gəsho'sən] *pp von* **schießen**.
geschraubt [gəshroupt'] *a* stilted, artificial.
Geschrei [gəshrī'] *nt* **-s** cries *pl*, shouting;
(*fig: Aufheben*) noise, fuss.
geschrieben [gəshrē:'bən] *pp von* **schreiben**.
geschrie(e)n [gəshrē:'(ə)n] *pp von* **schreien**.
geschritten [gəshri'tən] *pp von* **schreiten**.
geschunden [gəshōōn'dən] *pp von* **schinden**.
Geschütz [gəshüts'] *nt* **-es, -e** gun, piece of
artillery; **ein schweres** ~ **auffahren** (*fig*)
bring out the big guns; ~**feuer** *nt* artillery
fire, gunfire.
geschützt *a* protected; (*Winkel, Ecke*)

sheltered.
Geschw. *abk* = **Geschwister.**
Geschwader [gəshvá'dər] *nt* **-s,** - (*NAUT*) squadron; (*AVIAT*) group.
Geschwafel [gəshvá'fəl] *nt* **-s** silly talk.
Geschwätz [gəshvets'] *nt* **-es** chatter; (*Klatsch*) gossip.
geschwätzig *a* talkative; **G~keit** *f* talkativeness.
geschweige [gəshvī'gə] *ad*: ~ **(denn)** let alone, not to mention.
geschwiegen [gəshvē:'gən] *pp von* **schweigen.**
geschwind [gəshvint'] *a* quick, swift.
Geschwindigkeit [gəshvin'diċhkīt] *f* speed, velocity.
Geschwindigkeits- *zW*: **~begrenzung** *f* speed limit; **~beschränkung** *f* speed limit; **~messer** *m* (*AUT*) speedometer; **~überschreitung** *f* speeding.
Geschwister [gəshvis'tər] *pl* brothers and sisters *pl*.
geschwollen [gəshvo'lən] *a* pompous ♦ *pp von* **schwellen.**
geschwommen [gəshvo'mən] *pp von* **schwimmen.**
geschworen [gəshvō:'rən] *pp von* **schwören.**
Geschworene(r) *mf dekl wie a* juror; **~n** *pl* jury.
Geschwulst [gəshvōōlst'] *f* **-,** **-̈e** growth, tumor (*US*), tumour (*Brit*).
geschwunden [gəshvōōn'dən] *pp von* **schwinden.**
geschwungen [gəshvōō'ngən] *a* curved ♦ *pp von* **schwingen.**
Geschwür [gəshvü:r'] *nt* **-(e)s, -e** ulcer; (*Furunkel*) boil.
gesehen [gəzā:'ən] *pp von* **sehen.**
Geselle [gəze'lə] *m* **-n, -n** fellow; (*Handwerks~*) journeyman.
gesellen *vr*: **sich zu jdm** ~ join sb.
Gesellenprüfung *f* examination to become a journeyman.
gesellig *a* sociable; **~es Beisammensein** social gathering; **G~keit** *f* sociability.
Gesellschaft *f* society; (*Begleitung*, *COMM*) company; (*Abend~ etc*) party; (*pej*) crowd (*umg*); (*Kreis von Menschen*) group of people; **in schlechte** ~ **geraten** get into bad company; **geschlossene** ~ private party; **jdm** ~ **leisten** keep sb company; **g~lich** *a* social.
Gesellschafts- *zW*: **~anzug** *m* evening dress; **g~fähig** *a* socially acceptable; **~ordnung** *f* social structure; **~reise** *f* group tour; **~schicht** *f* social stratum; **~system** *nt* social system.
gesessen [gəze'sən] *pp von* **sitzen.**
Gesetz [gəzets'] *nt* **-es, -e** law; (*PARL*) act; (*Satzung, Regel*) rule; **vor dem** ~ in (the eyes of the) law; **nach dem** ~ under the law (*über +akk* on); **das oberste** ~ (**der Wirtschaft** *etc*) the golden rule (of industry *etc*); **~blatt** *nt* law gazette; **~buch** *nt* statute

book; **~entwurf** *m* bill.
Gesetzes- *zW*: **~hüter** *m* (*ironisch*) guardian of the law; **~vorlage** *f* bill.
Gesetz- *zW*: **g~gebend** *a* legislative; **~geber** *m* **-s,** - legislator; **~gebung** *f* legislation; **g~lich** *a* legal, lawful; **~lichkeit** *f* legality, lawfulness; **g~los** *a* lawless; **g~mäßig** *a* lawful.
gesetzt *a* (*Mensch*) sedate ♦ *kj*: ~ **den Fall** ... assuming (that) ...
gesetzwidrig *a* illegal; (*unrechtmäßig*) unlawful.
ges. gesch. *abk* (= *gesetzlich geschützt*) reg.
Gesicht [gəziċht'] *nt* **-(e)s, -er** face; **das Zweite** ~ second sight; **das ist mir nie zu** ~ **gekommen** I've never laid eyes on that; **jdn zu** ~ **bekommen** clap eyes on sb; **jdm etw ins** ~ **sagen** tell sb sth to his face; **sein wahres** ~ **zeigen** show (o.s. in) one's true colors; **jdm wie aus dem** ~ **geschnitten sein** be the spitting image of sb.
Gesichts- *zW*: **~ausdruck** *m* (facial) expression; **~farbe** *f* complexion; **~packung** *f* face pack; **~punkt** *m* point of view; **~wasser** *nt* face lotion; **~züge** *pl* features *pl*.
Gesindel [gəzin'dəl] *nt* **-s** rabble.
gesinnt [gəzint'] *a* disposed, minded.
Gesinnung [gəzi'nōōng] *f* disposition; (*Ansicht*) views *pl*.
Gesinnungs- *zW*: **~genosse** *m* like-minded person; **~losigkeit** *f* lack of conviction; **~schnüffelei** *f* (*pej*): **~schnüffelei betreiben** pry into people's political convictions; **~wandel** *m* change of opinion.
gesittet [gəzi'tət] *a* well-mannered.
gesoffen [gəzo'fən] *pp von* **saufen.**
gesogen [gəzō:'gən] *pp von* **saugen.**
gesollt [gəzolt'] *pp von* **sollen.**
gesondert [gəzon'dərt] *a* separate.
gesonnen [gəzo'nən] *pp von* **sinnen.**
gespalten [gəshpál'tən] *a* (*Bewußtsein*) split; (*Lippe*) cleft.
Gespann [gəshpán'] *nt* **-(e)s, -e** team; (*umg*) couple.
gespannt *a* tense, strained; (*neugierig*) curious; (*begierig*) eager; **ich bin ~, ob** I wonder if *od* whether; **auf etw/jdn** ~ **sein** look forward to sth/meeting sb; **ich bin ~ wie ein Flitzebogen** (*hum umg*) I'm on tenterhooks.
Gespenst [gəshpenst'] *nt* **-(e)s, -er** ghost; (*fig: Gefahr*) specter (*US*), spectre (*Brit*); **~er sehen** (*fig umg*) imagine things.
gespensterhaft *a* ghostly.
gespie(e)n [gəshpē:'(ə)n] *pp von* **speien.**
gespielt [gəshpē:lt'] *a* feigned.
gesponnen [gəshpo'nən] *pp von* **spinnen.**
Gespött [gəshpœt'] *nt* **-(e)s** mockery; **zum** ~ **werden** become a laughing stock.
Gespräch [gəshpre:ċh'] *nt* **-(e)s, -e** conversation; (*Diskussion*) discussion; (*Anruf*) call; **zum** ~ **werden** become a topic of conversation; **ein** ~ **unter vier Augen** a confidential

od private talk; **mit jdm ins ~ kommen** get into conversation with sb; (*fig*) establish a dialogue with sb.

gesprächig *a* talkative; **G~keit** *f* talkativeness.

Gesprächs- *zW:* **~einheit** *f* (*TEL*) unit; **~gegenstand** *m* topic; **~partner** *m:* **mein ~partner bei den Verhandlungen** my opposite number at the talks; **~stoff** *m* topics *pl;* **~thema** *nt* subject *od* topic (of conversation).

gesprochen [gəshpro'ḥən] *pp von* **sprechen.**
gesprossen [gəshpro'sən] *pp von* **sprießen.**
gesprungen [gəshprŏŏ'ngən] *pp von* **springen.**

Gespür [gəshpü:'r'] *nt* **-s** feeling.

gest. *abk* (= *gestorben*) dec.

Gestalt [gəshtált'] *f* **-, -en** form, shape; (*Person*) figure; (*LITER auch, pej:* *Mensch*) character; **in ~ von** in the form of; **~ annehmen** take shape.

gestalten *vt* (*formen*) shape, form; (*organisieren*) arrange, organize; **etw interessanter etc ~** make sth more interesting *etc* ♦ *vr* turn out (*zu* to be).

Gestaltung *f* formation; organization.

gestanden [gəshtán'dən] *pp von* **stehen; gestehen.**

geständig [gəshten'diḥ] *a:* **~ sein** have confessed.

Geständnis [gəshtent'nis] *nt* **-ses, -se** confession.

Gestank [gəshtángk'] *m* **-(e)s** stench.

gestatten [gəshtá'tən] *vt* permit, allow; **~ Sie?** may I?; **sich** (*dat*) **~, etw zu tun** take the liberty of doing sth.

Geste [ges'tə] *f* **-, -n** gesture.

Gesteck [gəshtek'] *nt* **-(e)s, -e** flower arrangement.

gestehen [gəshtā:'ən] *vt unreg* confess; **offen gestanden** quite frankly.

Gestein [gəshtīn'] *nt* **-(e)s, -e** rock.

Gestell [gəshtel'] *nt* **-(e)s, -e** stand; (*Regal*) shelf; (*Bett~, Brillen~*) frame.

gestellt *a* (*unecht*) posed.

gestern [ges'tərn] *ad* yesterday; **~ abend/ morgen** yesterday evening/morning; **er ist nicht von ~** (*umg*) he wasn't born yesterday.

gestiefelt [gəshtē:'fəlt] *a:* **der G~e Kater** Puss-in-Boots.

gestiegen [gəshtē:'gən] *pp von* **steigen.**

Gestik *f* **-** gestures *pl.*

gestikulieren [gestēkŏŏlē:'rən] *vi* gesticulate.

Gestirn [gəshtirn'] *nt* **-(e)s, -e** star.

gestoben [gəshtō:'bən] *pp von* **stieben.**

Gestöber [gəshtœ'bər] *nt* **-s, -** flurry; (*länger*) blizzard.

gestochen [gəshto'ḥən] *a* (*Handschrift*) clear, neat ♦ *pp von* **stechen.**

gestohlen [gəshtō:'lən] *a:* **der/das kann mir ~ bleiben** (*umg*) he/it can go hang ♦ *pp von* **stehlen.**

gestorben [gəshtor'bən] *pp von* **sterben.**

gestört [gəshtœrt'] *a* disturbed; (*Rundfunkempfang*) poor, with a lot of interference.

gestoßen [gəshtō:'sən] *pp von* **stoßen.**

Gestotter [gəshto'tər] *nt* **-s** stuttering, stammering.

Gesträuch [gəshtroiḥ'] *nt* **-(e)s, -e** shrubbery, bushes *pl.*

gestreift [gəshtrīft'] *a* striped.

gestrichen [gəshtri'ḥən] *a:* **~ voll** (*genau voll*) level; (*sehr voll*) full to the brim; **ein ~er Teelöffel voll** a level teaspoon(ful) ♦ *pp von* **streichen.**

gestrig [ges'triḥ] *a* yesterday's.

gestritten [gəshtri'tən] *pp von* **streiten.**

Gestrüpp [gəshtrüp'] *nt* **-(e)s, -e** undergrowth.

gestunken [gəshtŏŏng'kən] *pp von* **stinken.**

Gestüt [gəshtü:t'] *nt* **-(e)s, -e** stud farm.

gestylt [gəstīlt'] *a* (*Szene*) cool.

Gesuch [gəzŏŏ:ḥ'] *nt* **-(e)s, -e** petition; (*Antrag*) application.

gesucht *a* (*begehrt*) sought after.

gesund [gəzŏŏnt'] *a* healthy; **wieder ~ werden** get better; **~ und munter** hale and hearty; **jdn ~ schreiben** certify sb (as) fit; **G~heit** *f* health; (*Sportlichkeit, fig*) healthiness; **G~heit!** bless you!; **bei guter G~heit** in good health; **~heitlich** *a, ad* health *attr,* physical; **wie geht es Ihnen ~heitlich?** how's your health?

Gesundheits- *zW:* **~amt** *nt* public health department; **~apostel** *m* (*ironisch*) health freak (*umg*); **~fürsorge** *f* health care; **~risiko** *nt* health hazard; **g~schädlich** *a* unhealthy; **~wesen** *nt* health service; **~zeugnis** *nt* health certificate; **~zustand** *m* state of health.

gesungen [gəzŏŏ'ngən] *pp von* **singen.**

gesunken [gəzŏŏng'kən] *pp von* **sinken.**

getan [gətán'] *a:* **nach ~er Arbeit** when the day's work is done ♦ *pp von* **tun.**

Getier [gətē:'ər] *nt* **-(e)s, -e** (*Tiere, bes Insekten*) creatures *pl;* (*einzelnes*) creature.

Getöse [gətœ'zə] *nt* **-s** din, racket.

getragen [gətrá'gən] *pp von* **tragen.**

Getränk [gətrengk'] *nt* **-(e)s, -e** drink.

Getränke- *zW:* **~automat** *m* drinks machine *od* dispenser; **~karte** *f* (*in Café*) list of beverages; (*in Restaurant*) wine list.

getrauen [gətrou'ən] *vr* dare.

Getreide [gətrī'də] *nt* **-s, -** cereal, grain; **~speicher** *m* granary.

getrennt [gətrent'] *a* separate; **~ leben** be separated, live apart.

getreten [gətrā:'tən] *pp von* **treten.**

getreu [gətroi'] *a* faithful.

Getriebe [gətrē:'bə] *nt* **-s, -** (*Leute*) bustle; (*AUT*) gearbox.

getrieben *pp von* **treiben.**

Getriebeöl *nt* transmission oil.

getroffen [gətro'fən] *pp von* **treffen.**

getrogen [gətrō:'gən] *pp von* **trügen.**

getrost [gətrō:st'] *ad* confidently; **~ sterben** die in peace; **du kannst dich ~ auf ihn verlassen** you need have no fears about relying on him.

getrunken [gətrŏōng'kən] *pp von* **trinken**.

Getto [ge'tō] *nt* **-s, -s** ghetto.

Getue [gətōō:'ə] *nt* **-s** fuss.

Getümmel [gətü'məl] *nt* **-s** turmoil.

geübt [gəü:pt'] *a* experienced.

Gew. *abk* = **Gewerkschaft**.

GEW *f* - *abk* (= *Gewerkschaft Erziehung und Wissenschaft*) *union of employees in education and science.*

Gewächs [gəveks'] *nt* **-es, -e** growth; (*Pflanze*) plant.

gewachsen [gəvák'sən] *a:* **jdm/etw ~ sein** be sb's equal/equal to sth ♦ *pp von* **wachsen**.

Gewächshaus *nt* greenhouse.

gewagt [gəvâkt'] *a* daring, risky.

gewählt [gəve:lt'] *a* (*Sprache*) refined, elegant.

gewahr [gəvâr'] *a:* **eine(r) Sache ~ werden** become aware of sth.

Gewähr [gəve:r'] *f* - guarantee; **keine ~ übernehmen für** accept no responsibility for; **die Angabe erfolgt ohne ~** this information is supplied without liability.

gewähren *vt* grant; (*geben*) provide; **jdn ~ lassen** not stop sb.

gewährleisten *vt* guarantee.

Gewahrsam [gəvâr'zâm] *m* **-s, -e** safekeeping; (*Polizei~*) custody.

Gewährsmann *m* informant, source.

Gewährung *f* granting.

Gewalt [gəvâlt'] *f* -, **-en** power; (*große Kraft*) force; (*~taten*) violence; **mit aller ~** with all one's might; **die ausübende/ gesetzgebende/richterliche ~** the executive/legislature/judiciary; **elterliche ~** parental authority; **höhere ~** acts/an act of God; **~anwendung** *f* use of force.

Gewaltenteilung *f* separation of powers.

Gewaltherrschaft *f* tyranny.

gewaltig *a* tremendous; (*Irrtum*) huge; **sich ~ irren** be very much mistaken.

Gewalt- *zW:* **g~los** *a* non-violent ♦ *ad* without force/violence; **~marsch** *m* forced march; **~monopol** *nt* monopoly on violence; **g~sam** *a* forcible; **g~tätig** *a* violent; **~verbrechen** *nt* crime of violence; **~verzicht** *m* non-aggression.

Gewand [gəvânt'] *nt* **-(e)s, ̈er** garment.

gewandt [gəvânt'] *a* deft, skillful (*US*), skilful (*Brit*); (*erfahren*) experienced; ♦ *pp von* **wenden**; **G~heit** *f* dexterity, skill.

gewann [gəvân'] *imperf von* **gewinnen**.

gewaschen [gəvâ'shən] *pp von* **waschen**.

Gewässer [gəve'sər] *nt* **-s, -** waters *pl*.

Gewebe [gəvā:'bə] *nt* **-s, -** (*Stoff*) fabric; (*BIOL*) tissue.

Gewehr [gəvā:r'] *nt* **-(e)s, -e** (*Flinte*) rifle; (*Schrotbüchse*) shotgun; **~lauf** *m* rifle barrel; barrel of a shotgun.

Geweih [gəvī'] *nt* **-(e)s, -e** antlers *pl*.

Gewerbe [gəver'bə] *nt* **-s, -** trade, occupation; **Handel und ~** trade and industry; **fahrendes ~** mobile trade; **~schein** *m* trading

license; **~schule** *f* technical school; **g~treibend** *a* carrying on a trade.

gewerblich *a* industrial.

Gewerbs- *zW:* **g~mäßig** *a* professional; **~zweig** *m* line of trade.

Gewerkschaft [gəverk'shâft] *f* labor union (*US*), trade union.

Gewerkschaft(l)er(in *f*) *m* **-s, -** labor unionist (*US*), trade unionist.

gewerkschaftlich *a:* **wir haben uns ~ organisiert** we organized ourselves into a union.

Gewerkschaftsbund *m* federation of labor unions.

gewesen [gəvā:'zən] *pp von* **sein**.

gewichen [gəvi'çhən] *pp von* **weichen**.

Gewicht [gəviçht'] *nt* **-(e)s, -e** weight; (*fig*) importance.

gewichten *vt* evaluate.

Gewichtheben *nt* **-s** (*SPORT*) weight-lifting.

gewichtig *a* weighty.

Gewichtsklasse *f* (*SPORT*) weight (category).

gewieft [gəvē:ft'] (*umg*), **gewiegt** [gəvē:kt'] *a* (*umg*) shrewd, cunning.

gewiesen [gəvē:'zən] *pp von* **weisen**.

gewillt [gəvilt'] *a* willing, prepared.

Gewimmel [gəvi'məl] *nt* **-s** swarm.

Gewinde [gəvin'də] *nt* **-s, -** (*Kranz*) wreath; (*von Schraube*) thread.

Gewinn [gəvin'] *m* **-(e)s, -e** profit; (*bei Spiel*) winnings *pl*; **etw mit ~ verkaufen** sell sth at a profit; **aus etw ~ schlagen** (*umg*) make a profit out of sth; **~anteil** *m* (*COMM*) dividend; **~ausschüttung** *f* prize draw; **~beteiligung** *f* profit-sharing; **g~bringend** *a* profitable; **~chancen** *pl* (*beim Wetten*) odds *pl*.

gewinnen *unreg vt* win; (*erwerben*) gain; (*Kohle, Öl*) extract; **jdn ~** win sb over (*für etw* to sth) ♦ *vi* win; (*profitieren*) gain; **an etw** (*dat*) **~** gain in sth.

gewinnend *a* winning, attractive.

Gewinner(in *f*) *m* **-s, -** winner.

Gewinn- *zW:* **~spanne** *f* profit margin; **~sucht** *f* love of gain; **~(n)ummer** *f* winning number; **~- und Verlustrechnung** *f* profit and loss account.

Gewinnung *f* (*von Kohle etc*) mining; (*von Zucker etc*) extraction.

Gewirr [gəvir'] *nt* **-(e)s, -e** tangle; (*von Straßen*) maze.

gewiß [gəvis'] *a, ad* certain(ly); **in ~em Maße** to a certain extent.

Gewissen [gəvi'sən] *nt* **-s, -** conscience; **jdm ins ~ reden** have a serious talk with sb; **g~haft** *a* conscientious; **~haftigkeit** *f* conscientiousness; **g~los** *a* unscrupulous.

Gewissens- *zW:* **~bisse** *pl* pangs of conscience *pl*, qualms *pl*; **~frage** *f* matter of conscience; **~freiheit** *f* freedom of conscience; **~konflikt** *m* moral conflict.

gewissermaßen [gəvisərmâ'sən] *ad* more or less, in a way.

Gewiß- *zW:* **~heit** *f* certainty; **sich** (*dat*) **~heit verschaffen** find out for certain; **g~lich** *ad* surely.

Gewitter [gəvi'tər] *nt* **-s**, - thunderstorm.

gewittern *vi unpers:* **es gewittert** there's a thunderstorm.

Gewitter- *zW:* **g~schwül** *a* sultry and thundery; **~wolke** *f* thundercloud; (*fig umg*) storm cloud.

gewitzigt [gəvi'tsiçt] *a:* ~ **sein** have learned by experience.

gewitzt [gəvitst'] *a* shrewd, cunning.

gewoben [gəvō:'bən] *pp von* **weben**.

gewogen [gəvō:'gən] *a* well-disposed (+*dat* towards) ♦ *pp von* **wiegen**.

gewöhnen [gəvœ'nən] *vt:* **jdn an etw** (*akk*) ~ accustom sb to sth; (*erziehen zu*) teach sb sth ♦ *vr:* **sich an etw** (*akk*) ~ get used *od* accustomed to sth.

Gewohnheit [gəvō:n'hīt] *f* habit; (*Brauch*) custom; **aus** ~ from habit; **zur** ~ **werden** become a habit; **sich** (*dat*) **etw zur** ~ **machen** make a habit of sth.

Gewohnheits- *in zW* habitual; **~mensch** *m* creature of habit; **~recht** *nt* common law; **~tier** *nt* (*umg*) creature of habit.

gewöhnlich [gəvœn'liç] *a* usual; (*durchschnittlich*) ordinary; (*pej*) common; **wie** ~ as usual.

gewohnt [gəvō:nt'] *a* usual; **etw** ~ **sein** be used to sth.

Gewöhnung *f* getting accustomed (*an* +*akk* to); (*das Angewöhnen*) training (*an* +*akk* in).

Gewölbe [gəvœl'bə] *nt* **-s**, - vault.

gewollt [gəvolt'] *a* forced, artificial ♦ *pp von* **wollen**.

gewonnen [gəvo'nən] *pp von* **gewinnen**.

geworben [gəvor'bən] *pp von* **werben**.

geworden [gəvor'dən] *pp von* **werden**.

geworfen [gəvor'fən] *pp von* **werfen**.

gewrungen [gəvrōō'ngən] *pp von* **wringen**.

Gewühl [gəvü:l'] *nt* **-(e)s** throng.

gewunden [gəvōōn'dən] *pp von* **winden**.

gewunken [gəvōōng'kən] *pp von* **winken**.

Gewürz [gəvürts'] *nt* **-es**, **-e** spice; (*Pfeffer, Salz*) seasoning; **~gurke** *f* pickled gherkin; **~nelke** *f* clove.

gewußt [gəvōōst'] *pp von* **wissen**.

gez. *abk* (= *gezeichnet*) signed.

gezackt [gətsåkt'] *a* (*Fels*) jagged; (*Blatt*) serrated.

gezähnt [gətse:nt'] *a* serrated, toothed.

gezeichnet [gətsīç'nət] *a* marked.

Gezeiten [gətsī'tən] *pl* tides *pl*.

Gezeter [gətsā:'tər] *nt* **-s** nagging.

geziehen [gətsē:'ən] *pp von* **zeihen**.

gezielt [gətsē:lt'] *a* (*Frage, Maßnahme*) specific; (*Hilfe*) well-directed; (*Kritik*) pointed.

geziemen [gətsē:'mən] *vr unpers* be fitting.

geziemend *a* proper.

geziert [gətsē:rt'] *a* affected; **G~heit** *f* affectation.

gezogen [gətsō:'gən] *pp von* **ziehen**.

Gezwitscher [gətsvit'shər] *nt* **-s** twitter(ing), chirping.

gezwungen [gətsvōō'ngən] *a* forced; (*Atmosphäre*) strained ♦ *pp von* **zwingen**.

gezwungenermaßen *ad* of necessity; **etw** ~ **tun** be forced to do sth, do sth of necessity.

GG *abk* = **Grundgesetz**.

ggf. *abk* = **gegebenenfalls**.

Ghettoblaster [ge'tōblåstər] *m* **-s**, **-s** (*umg*) ghettoblaster.

gibst [gē:pst] *2. pers sing präs von* **geben**.

Gicht [giçht] *f* - gout; **g~isch** *a* gouty.

Giebel [gē:'bəl] *m* **-s**, - gable; **~dach** *nt* gable(d) roof; **~fenster** *nt* gable window.

Gier [gē:r] *f* - greed.

gierig *a* greedy.

Gießbach *m* torrent.

gießen [gē:'sən] *unreg vt* pour; (*Blumen*) water; (*Metall*) cast; (*Wachs*) mould (*US*), mould (*Brit*) ♦ *vi unpers:* **es gießt in Strömen** it's pouring down.

Gießerei [gē:sərī'] *f* foundry.

Gießkanne *f* watering can.

Gift [gift] *nt* **-(e)s**, **-e** poison; **das ist** ~ **für ihn** (*umg*) that is very bad for him; **darauf kannst du** ~ **nehmen** (*umg*) you can bet your life on it; **g~grün** *a* bilious green.

giftig *a* poisonous; (*fig: boshaft*) venomous.

Gift- *zW:* **~müll** *m* toxic waste; **~pilz** *m* poisonous toadstool; **~wolke** *f* poisonous cloud; **~zahn** *m* fang; **~zwerg** *m* (*umg*) spiteful little devil.

Gilde [gil'də] *f* -, **-n** guild.

gilt [gilt] *3. pers sing präs von* **gelten**.

ging [ging] *imperf von* **gehen**.

Ginster [gin'stər] *m* **-s**, - broom.

Gipfel [gip'fəl] *m* **-s**, - summit, peak; (*fig*) height; **das ist der** ~! (*umg*) that's the limit!; **~konferenz** *f* (*POL*) summit conference.

gipfeln *vi* culminate.

Gipfeltreffen *nt* summit (meeting).

Gips [gips] *m* **-es**, **-e** plaster; (*MED*) plaster (of Paris); **~abdruck** *m* plaster cast; **~bein** *nt* (*umg*) leg in plaster; **g~en** *vt* plaster; **~figur** *f* plaster figure; **~verband** *m* plaster (cast).

Giraffe [gērå'fə] *f* -, **-n** giraffe.

Girlande [girlån'də] *f* -, **-n** garland.

Giro [zhē:'rō] *nt* **-s**, **-s** giro; **~konto** *nt* checking account (*US*), current account (*Brit*).

girren [gi'rən] *vi* coo.

Gis [gis] *nt* -, - (*MUS*) G sharp.

Gischt [gisht] *m* **-(e)s**, **-e** spray, foam.

Gitarre [gētå'rə] *f* -, **-n** guitar.

Gitter [gi'tər] *nt* **-s**, - grating, bars *pl*; (*für Pflanzen*) trellis; (*Zaun*) railing(s); **~bett** *nt* crib (*US*), cot (*Brit*); **~fenster** *nt* barred window; **~zaun** *m* railing(s).

Glacéhandschuh [glåså:'håntshōō:] *m* kid

glove.
Gladiole [gládēō:'lə] *f* -, **-n** gladiolus.
Glanz [glánts] *m* **-es** shine, sheen; (*fig*) magnificence; **~abzug** *m* (*PHOT*) glossy *od* gloss print.
glänzen [glɛn'tsən] *vi* shine (*also fig*), gleam ♦ *vt* polish.
glänzend *a* shining; (*fig*) brilliant; **wir haben uns ~ amüsiert** we had a marvelous *od* great time.
Glanz- *zW*: **~lack** *m* gloss (paint); **~leistung** *f* brilliant achievement; **g~los** *a* dull; **~stück** *nt* pièce de résistance; **~zeit** *f* heyday.
Glas [glâs] *nt* **-es**, **⁻er** glass; (*Brillen~*) lens *sing*; **zwei ~ Wein** two glasses of wine; **~bläser** *m* **-s**, - glass blower; **~er** *m* **-s**, - glazier; **~faser** *f* fiberglass (*US*), fibreglass (*Brit*).
glasieren [glâzē:'rən] *vt* glaze.
glasig *a* glassy; (*Zwiebeln*) transparent.
Glas- *zW*: **g~klar** *a* crystal clear; **~scheibe** *f* pane.
Glasur [glázōō:r'] *f* glaze; (*KOCH*) icing, frosting.
glatt [glát] *a* smooth; (*rutschig*) slippery; (*Absage*) flat; (*Lüge*) downright; (*Haar*) straight; (*MED: Bruch*) clean; (*pej: allzu gewandt*) smooth, slick; **G~eis** *nt* (black) ice; „**Vorsicht G~eis!**" "danger, black ice!"; **jdn aufs G~eis führen** (*fig*) take sb for a ride.
Glätte [glɛ'tə] *f* -, **-n** smoothness; slipperiness.
glätten *vt* smooth out.
glatt- *zW*: **~gehen** *vi unreg* go smoothly; **~rasiert** *a* (*Mann, Kinn*) clean-shaven; **~streichen** *vt unreg* smooth out.
Glatze [glá'tsə] *f* -, **-n** bald head; **eine ~ bekommen** go bald.
glatzköpfig *a* bald.
Glaube [glou'bə] *m* **-ns**, **-n** faith (*an +akk* in); (*Überzeugung*) belief (*an +akk* in); **den ~n an jdn/etw verlieren** lose faith in sb/sth.
glauben *vti* believe (*an +akk* in, *jdm* sb); (*meinen*) think; **jdm (etw) aufs Wort ~** take sb's word (for sth); **wer's glaubt, wird selig** (*ironisch*) a likely story.
Glaubens- *zW*: **~bekenntnis** *nt* creed; **~freiheit** *f* religious freedom; **~gemeinschaft** *f* religious sect; (*christliche auch*) denomination.
glaubhaft [gloub'háft] *a* credible; **(jdm) etw ~ machen** satisfy sb of sth.
Glaubhaftigkeit *f* credibility.
gläubig [gloi'biçh] *a* (*REL*) devout; (*vertrauensvoll*) trustful; **G~e(r)** *mf dekl wie a* believer; **die G~en** the faithful.
Gläubiger(in *f*) *m* **-s**, - creditor.
glaubwürdig [gloub'vürdiçh] *a* credible; (*Mensch*) trustworthy; **G~keit** *f* credibility; trustworthiness.
gleich [glíçh] *a* equal; (*identisch*) (the) same, identical; **es ist mir ~** it's all the same to me; **zu ~en Teilen** in equal parts; **das ~e, aber nicht dasselbe Auto** a similar car, but not the same one; **ganz ~ wer/was** *etc* no matter who/what *etc*; **2 mal 2 ~ 4** 2 times 2 is *od* equals 4 ♦ *ad* equally; (*sofort*) straight away; (*bald*) in a minute; (*räumlich*): **~ hinter dem Haus** just behind the house; (*zeitlich*): **~ am Anfang** at the very beginning; **bis ~!** see you soon!; **wie war doch ~ Ihr Name?** what was your name again?; **es ist ~ drei Uhr** it's very nearly three o'clock; **sie sind ~ groß** they are the same size; **~ nach/an** right after/at; **~altrig** *a* of the same age; **~artig** *a* similar; **~bedeutend** *a* synonymous; **~berechtigt** *a* with equal rights; **G~berechtigung** *f* equal rights *pl*; **~bleibend** *a* constant; **bei ~bleibendem Gehalt** when one's salary stays the same.
gleichen *unreg vi*: **jdm/etw ~** be like sb/sth ♦ *vr* be alike.
gleichermaßen *ad* equally.
gleich- *zW*: **~falls** *ad* likewise; **danke ~falls!** the same to you; **G~förmigkeit** *f* uniformity; **~gesinnt** *a* like-minded; **~gestellt** *a*: **rechtlich ~gestellt** equal in law; **G~gewicht** *nt* equilibrium, balance; **jdm aus dem G~gewicht bringen** throw sb off balance; **~gültig** *a* indifferent; (*unbedeutend*) unimportant; **G~gültigkeit** *f* indifference; **G~heit** *f* equality; (*Identität*) identity; (*INDUSTRIE*) parity.
Gleichheits- *zW*: **~prinzip** *nt* principle of equality; **~zeichen** *nt* (*MATH*) equals sign.
gleich- *zW*: **~kommen** *vi unreg +dat* be equal to; **~lautend** *a* identical.
Gleichmacherei¹ *f* egalitarianism, levelling down (*pej*).
gleich- *zW*: **~mäßig** *a* even, equal; **G~mut** *m* equanimity.
Gleichnis *nt* **-ses**, **-se** parable.
gleich- *zW*: **~rangig** *a* (*Beamte etc*) equal in rank (*mit* to); at the same level (*mit* as); (*Probleme etc*) equally important; **~sam** *ad* as it were; **~schalten** *vt* (*pej*) bring into line; **G~schritt** *m*: **im G~schritt, marsch!** forward march!; **~sehen** *vi unreg* (*jdm*) be *od* look like (sb); **~stellen** *vt* (*rechtlich etc*) treat as equal; **G~strom** *m* (*ELEK*) direct current; **~tun** *vi unreg*: **es jdm ~tun** match sb; **G~ung** *f* equation; **~viel** *ad* no matter; **~wertig** *a* of the same value; (*Leistung, Qualität*) equal (*+dat* to); (*Gegner*) evenly matched; **~wohl** *ad* (*geh*) nevertheless; **~zeitig** *a* simultaneous.
Gleis [glīs] *nt* **-es**, **-e** track, rails *pl*; (*am Bahnhof*) track (*US*), platform (*Brit*).
gleißend [glī'sənt] *a* glistening, gleaming.
Gleit- [glīt'] *in zW* gliding; sliding.
gleiten *vi unreg* glide; (*rutschen*) slide.
gleitend *a*: **~e Arbeitszeit** flexible working hours *pl*, flex(i)time.
Gleit- *zW*: **~flug** *m* glide; gliding; **~klausel** *f* (*COMM*) escalator clause; **~komma** *nt*

floating point; ~**zeit** f flex(i)time.
Gletscher [glet'ʃər] m -s, - glacier; ~**spalte**
f crevasse.
glich [gliç] imperf von **gleichen**.
Glied [glē:t] nt -(e)s, -er member; (Arm,
Bein) limb; (Penis) penis; (von Kette) link;
(MIL) rank(s); **der Schreck steckt ihr noch
in den ~ern** she is still shaking with the
shock.
gliedern vt organize, structure.
Glieder- zW: ~**reißen** nt, ~**schmerz** m rheumatic pains pl.
Gliederung f structure, organization.
Gliedmaßen pl limbs pl.
glimmen [gli'mən] vi unreg glow.
Glimmer m -s, - (MINERAL) mica.
Glimmstengel m (umg) butt (US), fag
(Brit).
glimpflich [glimpf'liç] a mild, lenient; ~ **davonkommen** get off lightly.
glitschig [glit'ʃiç] a (umg) slippery, slippy.
glitt [glit] imperf von **gleiten**.
glitzern [gli'tsərn] vi glitter; (Stern) twinkle.
global [glōbâl'] a (weltweit) global, world-
wide; (ungefähr, pauschal) general.
Globus [glō:'bōōs] m - od -ses, Globen od -se
globe.
Glöckchen [glœk'çən] nt (little) bell.
Glocke [glo'kə] f -, -n bell; **etw an die große
~ hängen** (fig) shout sth from the rooftops.
Glocken- zW: ~**geläut** nt peal of bells;
~**schlag** m stroke (of the bell); (von Uhr)
chime; ~**spiel** nt chime(s); (MUS) glocken-
spiel.
glomm [glom] imperf von **glimmen**.
Glorie [glō:'rēə] f glory; (von Heiligen) halo.
glorreich [glō:r'rīç] a glorious.
Glossar [glosâr'] nt -s, -e glossary.
Glosse [glo'sə] f -, -n comment.
Glotze f -, -n (umg) box, TV set.
glotzen [glo'tsən] vi (umg) stare.
Glück [glük] nt -(e)s luck, fortune; (Freude)
happiness; ~ **haben** be lucky; **viel ~** good
luck; **zum ~** fortunately; **ein ~!** how
lucky!, what a stroke of luck!; **auf gut ~**
(aufs Geratewohl) on the off-chance; (unvorbereitet) trusting to luck; (wahllos) at
random; **sie weiß noch nichts von ihrem ~**
(ironisch) she doesn't know anything about
it yet; **er kann von ~ sagen, daß ...** he can
count himself lucky that ...; ~**auf** nt:
„~**auf!**" (Bergleute) (cry of) "good luck".
Glucke f -, -n (Bruthenne) broody hen; (mit
Jungen) mother hen.
glücken vi succeed; **es glückte ihm, es zu
bekommen** he succeeded in getting it.
gluckern [glōō'kərn] vi glug.
glücklich a fortunate; (froh) happy ♦ ad happily; (umg: endlich, zu guter Letzt) finally,
eventually; ~**erweise** ad fortunately.
Glücksbringer m -s, - lucky charm.
glückselig [glükzā'liç] a blissful.
Glücks- zW: ~**fall** m stroke of luck; ~**kind** nt
lucky person; ~**pilz** m lucky beggar (umg);

~**sache** f matter of luck; ~**spiel** nt game of
chance; ~**stern** m lucky star.
glückstrahlend a radiant (with happiness).
Glücks- zW: ~**strähne** f lucky streak; ~**zahl**
f lucky number.
Glückwunsch m congratulations pl (zu on),
best wishes pl.
Glühbirne f light bulb.
glühen [glü:'ən] vi glow.
glühend a glowing; (heiß~: Metall) red-hot;
(Hitze) blazing; (fig: leidenschaftlich)
ardent; (: Haß) burning; (Wangen) flushed,
burning.
Glüh- zW: ~**faden** m (ELEK) filament;
~**wein** m mulled wine; ~**würmchen** nt
glow-worm.
Glut [glōō:t] f -, -en (Röte) glow; (Feuers~)
fire; (Hitze) heat; (fig) ardor (US), ardour
(Brit).
GmbH f -, -s abk (= Gesellschaft mit beschränkter Haftung) Inc. (US), Ltd. (Brit),
plc (Brit).
Gnade [gnâ'də] f -, -n (Gunst) favor (US), favour (Brit); (Erbarmen) mercy; (Milde)
clemency; ~ **vor Recht ergehen lassen**
temper justice with mercy.
gnaden vi: **(dann) gnade dir Gott!** (then)
God help you od heaven have mercy on you!
Gnaden- zW: ~**brot** nt: **jdm/einem Tier das
~brot geben** keep sb/an animal in his/her/its
old age; ~**frist** f reprieve; ~**gesuch** nt petition for clemency; ~**stoß** m coup de grâce.
gnädig [gne:'diç] a gracious; (voll Erbarmen) merciful; ~**e Frau** (form) madam,
ma'am.
Gockel [go'kəl] m -s, - (bes süddeutsch) cock.
Gold [golt] nt -(e)s gold; **nicht mit ~ zu bezahlen** od **aufzuwiegen sein** be worth one's
weight in gold; **g~en** a golden; **g~ene Worte** words of wisdom; **der Tanz ums g~ene
Kalb** (fig) the worship of Mammon; ~**fisch**
m goldfish; ~**grube** f goldmine; ~**hamster**
m (golden) hamster.
goldig [gol'diç] a (fig umg: allerliebst)
sweet, cute.
Gold- zW: ~**regen** m laburnum; (fig) riches
pl; **g~richtig** a (umg) dead right; ~**schnitt**
m gilt edging; ~**standard** m gold standard;
~**stück** nt piece of gold; (fig umg) treasure;
~**waage** f: **jedes Wort auf die ~waage legen** (fig) weigh one's words; ~**währung** f
gold standard.
Golf [golf] m -(e)s, -e gulf ♦ nt -s golf; ~**platz**
m golf course; ~**schläger** m golf club;
~**spieler** m golfer; ~**staaten** pl: **die
~staaten** the Gulf States pl; ~**strom** m
(GEOG) Gulf Stream.
Gondel [gon'dəl] f -, -n gondola; (von
Seilbahn) cable car.
gondeln vi (umg): **durch die Welt ~** go
globetrotting.
Gong [gong] m -s, -s gong; (bei Boxkampf
etc) bell.
gönnen [gœ'nən] vt: **jdm etw ~** not be-

grudge sb sth; **sich** (*dat*) **etw** ~ allow o.s. sth.

Gönner *m* **-s,** - patron; **g~haft** *a* patronizing; **~in** *f* patroness; **~miene** *f* patronizing air.

gor [gō:r] *imperf von* **gären.**

Gorilla [gōri'lä] *m* **-s, -s** gorilla; (*umg*: *Leibwächter auch*) heavy.

goß [gos] *imperf von* **gießen.**

Gosse [go'sə] *f* -, -n gutter.

Gote [gō:'tə] *m* -n, -n, **Gotin** *f* Goth.

Gotik [gō:'tik] *f* (*KUNST*) Gothic (style); (*Epoche*) Gothic period.

Gott [got] *m* **-es,** ⁻er god; (*als Name*) God; **um ~es Willen!** for heaven's sake!; ~ **sei Dank!** thank God!; **grüß ~!** (*bes süddeutsch*, *österreichisch*) hello, good morning/afternoon/evening; **den lieben ~ einen guten Mann sein lassen** (*umg*) take things as they come; **ein Bild für ~er** (*hum umg*) a sight for sore eyes; **das wissen die ~er** (*umg*) God (only) knows; **über ~ und die Welt reden** (*fig*) talk about everything under the sun; **wie ~ in Frankreich leben** (*umg*) be in clover.

Götterspeise *f* (*KOCH*) jello (*US*), jelly (*Brit*).

Gottes- *zW*: **~dienst** *m* service; **~haus** *nt* place of worship; **~lästerung** *f* blasphemy.

Gottheit *f* deity.

Göttin [gœtin] *f* goddess.

göttlich *a* divine.

Gott- *zW*: **g~lob** *interj* thank heavens!; **g~los** *a* godless; **g~verlassen** *a* godforsaken; **~vertrauen** *nt* trust in God.

Götze [gœ'tsə] *m* -n, -n idol.

Grab [gráp] *nt* **-(e)s,** ⁻er grave.

grabbeln [grá'bəln] *vt* (*norddeutsch umg*) rummage.

graben [grá'bən] *vt unreg* dig; **G~** *m* **-s,** ⁻ ditch; (*MIL*) trench.

Grabesstille *f* (*liter*) deathly hush.

Grab- *zW*: **~mal** *nt* monument; (*~stein*) gravestone; **~rede** *f* funeral oration; **~stein** *m* gravestone.

gräbt *3. pers sing präs von* **graben.**

Gracht [gráxht] *f* -, -en canal.

Grad [grât] *m* **-(e)s,** -e degree; **im höchsten ~(e)** extremely; **Verbrennungen ersten ~es** (*MED*) first-degree burns; **~einteilung** *f* graduation; **g~linig** *a siehe* **geradlinig; g~weise** *ad* gradually.

Graf [gráf] *m* **-en,** -en count.

Gräfin [gre:'fin] *f* countess.

Grafschaft *f* county.

Grahambrot [grá'hámbrō:t] *nt* (type of) wholewheat bread.

Gralshüter [grálz'hü:tər] *m* **-s,** - (*fig*) guardian.

Gram [grám] *m* **-(e)s** (*geh*) grief, sorrow.

grämen [gre:'mən] *vr* grieve; **sich zu Tode ~** die of grief od sorrow.

Gramm [grám] *nt* **-s,** -e gram(me).

Grammatik [grámá'tik] *f* grammar.

grammatisch *a* grammatical.

Grammophon [grámōfō:n'] *nt* **-s, -e** phonograph (*US*), gramophone (*Brit*).

Granat [gránát'] *m* **-(e)s, -e** (*Stein*) garnet; **~apfel** *m* pomegranate.

Granate *f* -, -n (*MIL*) shell; (*Hand~*) grenade.

grandios [grándē'ō:s] *a* magnificent, superb.

Granit [gránē:t'] *m* **-s, -e** granite; **auf ~ beißen** (*bei …*) bang one's head against a brick wall (with …).

grantig [grán'tiçh] *a* (*umg*) grumpy.

Graphiker(in *f*) [grá'fikər(in)] *m* **-s,** - graphic artist; (*Illustrator*) illustrator.

graphisch [grá'fish] *a* graphic; **~e Darstellung** graph.

grapschen [gráp'shən] *vt* (*umg*) grab; **(sich** *dat*) **etw** ~ grab sth.

Gras [grás] *nt* **-es,** ⁻er grass; (*Drogen umg*: *Marihuana*) grass; **über etw** (*akk*) ~ **wachsen lassen** (*fig*) let the dust settle on sth; **g~en** *vi* graze; **~halm** *m* blade of grass.

grasig *a* grassy.

Grasnarbe *f* turf.

grassieren [gráse:'rən] *vi* be rampant, rage.

gräßlich [gres'liçh] *a* horrible.

Grat [grát] *m* **-(e)s, -e** ridge.

Gräte [gre:'tə] *f* -, -n fishbone.

Gratifikation [grátēfēkátsēō:n'] *f* bonus.

gratis [grá'tis] *a*, *ad* free (of charge); **G~probe** *f* free sample.

Grätsche [gre:t'shə] *f* -, -n (*SPORT*) straddle.

Gratulant(in *f*) [grátōōlánt'(in)] *m* wellwisher.

Gratulation [grátōōlátsēō:n'] *f* congratulation(s).

gratulieren [grátōōlē:'rən] *vi*: **jdm** ~ congratulate sb (*zu etw* on sth); **(ich) gratuliere!** congratulations!

Gratwanderung *f* (*fig*) tightrope walk.

grau [grou] *a* gray (*US*), grey (*Brit*); **der ~e Alltag** drab reality; **G~brot** *nt siehe* **Mischbrot.**

grauen *vi* (*Tag*) dawn ♦ *vi unpers*: **es graut jdm vor etw** sb dreads sth, sb is afraid of sth ♦ *vr*: **sich** ~ **vor** dread, have a horror of.

Grauen *nt* **-s** horror; **g~haft** *a* horrible.

grau- *zW*: **~haarig** *a* gray-haired; **~meliert** *a* gray-flecked.

Graupelregen [grou'pəlrā:gən] *m* sleet.

Graupelschauer *m* sleet.

Graupen [grou'pən] *pl* pearl barley *sing.*

grausam [grou'zám] *a* cruel; **G~keit** *f* cruelty.

Grausen [grou'zən] *nt* **-s** horror; **da kann man das kalte ~ kriegen** (*umg*) it's enough to give you the creeps; **g~** *vi unpers*, *vr siehe* **grauen.**

Grauzone *f* (*fig*) gray (*US*) od grey (*Brit*) area.

gravieren [grávē:'rən] *vt* engrave.

gravierend *a* grave.

Grazie [grå'tsēə] *f* grace.
graziös [grátsœes'] *a* graceful.
greifbar *a* tangible, concrete; **in ~er Nähe** within reach.
greifen [grī'fən] *unreg vt* (*nehmen*) grasp; (*grapschen*) seize, grab; **nach etw ~** reach for sth; **um sich ~** (*fig*) spread; **zu etw ~** (*fig*) turn to sth; **diese Zahl ist zu niedrig gegriffen** (*fig*) this figure is too low; **aus dem Leben gegriffen** taken from life ♦ *vi* (*nicht rutschen, einrasten*) grip.
Greifer *m* -s, - (*TECH*) grab.
Greifvogel *m* bird of prey.
Greis [grīs] *m* -es, -e old man.
Greisen- *zW:* **~alter** *nt* old age; **g~haft** *a* very old.
grell [grel] *a* harsh.
Gremium [grā:'mēōōm] *nt* body; (*Ausschuß*) committee.
Grenadier [gránádē:'ər] *m* -s, -e (*MIL: Infanterist*) infantryman.
Grenzbeamte(r) *m* frontier official.
Grenze *f* -, -n border; (*zwischen Grundstücken, fig*) boundary; (*Staats~*) frontier; (*Schranke*) limit; **über die ~ gehen/fahren** cross the border; **hart an der ~ des Erlaubten** bordering on the limits of what is permitted.
grenzen *vi* border (*an +akk* on).
grenzenlos *a* boundless.
Grenz- *zW:* **~fall** *m* borderline case; **~gänger** *m* (*Arbeiter*) international commuter (*across a local border*); **~gebiet** *nt* (*lit, fig*) border area; **~kosten** *pl* marginal cost; **~linie** *f* boundary; **~übergang** *m* frontier crossing; **~zwischenfall** *m* border incident.
Gretchenfrage [grā:t'çhənfrágə] *f* (*fig*) crucial question, sixty-four-thousand-dollar question (*umg*).
Greuel [groi'əl] *m* -s, - horror; (*~tat*) atrocity; **etw ist jdm ein ~** sb loathes sth; **~propaganda** *f* atrocity propaganda; **~tat** *f* atrocity.
greulich [groi'liçh] *a* horrible.
Grieche [grē:'çhə] *m* -n, -n, **Griechin** *f* Greek.
Griechenland *nt* Greece.
griechisch *a* Greek.
griesgrämig [grē:s'gre:miçh] *a* grumpy.
Grieß [grē:s] *m* -es, -e (*KOCH*) semolina; **~brei** *m* cooked semolina, cream of wheat (*US*).
griff *imperf von* **greifen.**
Griff [grif] *m* -(e)s, -e grip; (*Vorrichtung*) handle; (*das Greifen*): **der ~ nach etw** reaching for sth; **jdn/etw in den ~ bekommen** (*fig*) gain control of sb/sth; **etw in den ~ bekommen** (*geistig*) get a grasp of sth; **g~bereit** *a* handy.
Griffel [gri'fəl] *m* -s, - slate pencil; (*BOT*) style.
griffig [gri'fiçh] *a* (*Fahrbahn etc*) *that has a good grip*; (*fig: Ausdruck*) useful, handy.
Grille [gri'lə] *f* -, -n cricket; (*fig*) whim.

grillen *vt* grill.
Grimasse [grēmá'sə] *f* -, -n grimace; **~n schneiden** make faces.
Grimm [grim] *m* -(e)s fury.
grimmig *a* furious; (*heftig*) fierce, severe.
grinsen [grin'zən] *vi* grin; (*höhnisch auch*) smirk.
Grippe [gri'pə] *f* -, -n influenza, flu.
Grips [grips] *m* -es, -e (*umg*) sense.
grob [grō:p] *a* coarse, gross; (*Fehler, Verstoß*) gross; (*brutal, derb*) rough; (*unhöflich*) ill-mannered; **~ geschätzt** at a rough estimate; **G~heit** *f* coarseness; (*Beschimpfung*) coarse expression.
Grobian [grō:'bēán] *m* -s, -e ruffian.
grobknochig *a* large-boned.
groggy [gro'gi] *a* (*BOXEN*) groggy; (*umg: erschöpft*) all-in.
grölen [grœ'lən] *vti* (*pej*) bawl.
Groll [grol] *m* -(e)s resentment; **g~en** *vi* bear ill will (+*dat od mit* towards); (*Donner*) rumble.
Grönland [grœn'lánt] *nt* -s Greenland.
Grönländer(in *f*) *m* -s, - Greenlander.
Groschen [gro'shən] *m* -s, - (*umg*) 10-pfennig piece; (*Österreich*) groschen; (*fig*) penny, cent; **~roman** *m* (*pej*) cheap *od* dime novel.
groß [grō:s] *a* big, large; (*hoch*) tall; great; **im ~en und ganzen** on the whole; **wie ~ bist du?** how tall are you?; **die G~en** (*Erwachsene*) the grown-ups; **mit etw ~ geworden sein** have grown up with sth; **die G~en Seen** *pl* the Great Lakes *pl*; **~en Hunger haben** be very hungry; **~e Mode sein** be all the fashion ♦ *ad* greatly; **~ und breit** (*fig umg*) at great *od* enormous length; **ein Wort ~ schreiben** write a word with a capital; **G~abnehmer** *m* (*COMM*) bulk buyer; **G~alarm** *m* red alert; **~angelegt** *a attr* large-scale, on a large scale; **~artig** *a* great, splendid; **G~aufnahme** *f* (*FILM*) close-up; **G~britannien** *nt* (Great) Britain; **G~buchstabe** *m* capital (letter), upper case letter (*TYP*).
Größe [grœ'sə] *f* -, -n size; (*Länge*) height; (*fig*) greatness; **eine unbekannte ~** (*lit, fig*) an unknown quantity.
Groß- *zW:* **~einkauf** *m* bulk purchase; **~einsatz** *m:* **~einsatz der Polizei** *etc* large-scale operation by the police *etc*; **~eltern** *pl* grandparents *pl*.
Größenordnung *f* scale; (*Größe*) magnitude; (*MATH*) order (of magnitude).
großenteils *ad* for the most part.
Größen- *zW:* **~unterschied** *m* difference in size; **~wahn(sinn)** *m* megalomania, delusions *pl* of grandeur.
Groß- *zW:* **~format** *nt* large size; **~handel** *m* wholesale trade; **~handelspreisindex** *m* wholesale-price index; **~händler** *m* wholesaler; **g~herzig** *a* generous; **~hirn** *nt* cerebrum; **~industrielle(r)** *mf* major industrialist; **g~kotzig** ['grō:s'kotsiçh] *a* (*umg*) show-

offish, bragging; ~**kundgebung** *f* mass rally; ~**macht** *f* great power; ~**maul** *m* braggart; ~**mut** *f* - magnanimity; **g~mütig** *a* magnanimous; ~**mutter** *f* grandmother; ~**raum** *m*: **der** ~**raum München** the Munich area *od* conurbation, Greater Munich; ~**raumbüro** *nt* open-plan office; ~**rechner** *m* mainframe; ~**reinemachen** *nt* thorough cleaning, ≈ spring cleaning; ~**schreibung** *f* capitalization; **g~spurig** *a* pompous; ~**stadt** *f* city.

größtenteils *ad* for the most part.

größte(r, s) [grœs'tə(r, z)] *a superl von* **groß.**

Groß- *zW:* ~**tuer** *m* **-s,** - boaster; **g~tun** *vi unreg* boast; ~**vater** *m* grandfather; ~**verbraucher** *m* (*COMM*) heavy user; ~**verdiener** *m* big earner; ~**wild** *nt* big game; **g~ziehen** *vt unreg* raise; **g~zügig** *a* generous; (*Planung*) on a large scale.

grotesk [grōtesk'] *a* grotesque.

Grotte [gro'tə] *f* -, **-n** grotto.

grub [grōō:p] *imperf von* **graben.**

Grübchen [grü:p'çhən] *nt* dimple.

Grube [grōō:'bə] *f* -, **-n** pit; (*Bergwerk*) mine.

Gruben- *zW:* ~**arbeiter** *m* miner; ~**gas** *nt* firedamp.

grübeln [grü:'bəln] *vi* brood.

Grübler [grü:'blər] *m* **-s,** - brooder; **g~isch** *a* brooding, pensive.

Gruft [grōōft] *f* -, ⁓e tomb, vault.

grün [grü:n] *a* green; (*POL*): **die G~en** the Greens (*ecologist party*); **G~e Minna** (*umg*) police van; ~**e Welle** phased traffic lights; ~**e Versicherungskarte** (*AUT*) green card (*for international insurance*); **sich** ~ **und blau** *od* **gelb ärgern** (*umg*) be furious; **auf keinen** ~**en Zweig kommen** (*fig umg*) get nowhere; **G~anlage** *f* park.

Grund [grōōnt] *m* **-(e)s,** ⁓e ground; (*von See, Gefäß*) bottom; (*fig*) reason; **von** ~ **auf** entirely, completely; **auf** ~ **von** on the basis of; **aus gesundheitlichen** *etc* ~**en** for health *etc* reasons; **im** ~**e genommen** basically; **ich habe** ~ **zu der Annahme, daß** ... I have reason to believe that ...; **einer Sache** (*dat*) **auf den** ~ **gehen** (*fig*) get to the bottom of sth; **sich in** ~ **und Boden schämen** (*fig*) be utterly embarrassed; ~**ausbildung** *f* basic training; ~**bedeutung** *f* basic meaning; ~**bedingung** *f* fundamental condition; ~**besitz** *m* land(ed property), real estate; ~**buch** *nt* land register; **g~ehrlich** *a* thoroughly honest.

gründen [gründən] *vt* found; ~ **auf** (+*akk*) base on ♦ *vr* be based (*auf* +*dat* on).

Gründer(in *f*) *m* **-s,** - founder.

Grund- *zW:* **g~falsch** *a* utterly wrong; ~**gebühr** *f* basic charge; ~**gedanke** *m* basic idea; ~**gesetz** *nt* constitution; ~**kapital** *nt* nominal capital; ~**kurs** *m* basic course; ~**lage** *f* foundation; **jeder** ~**lage entbehren** be completely unfounded; **g~legend** *a* fundamental.

gründlich *a* thorough; **jdm** ~ **die Meinung**

sagen give sb a piece of one's mind.

Grund- *zW:* **g~los** *a* (*fig*) groundless; ~**mauer** *f* foundation wall; ~**nahrungsmittel** *nt* basic food(stuff).

Gründonnerstag *m* Maundy Thursday.

Grund- *zW:* ~**ordnung** *f:* **die freiheitlich-demokratische** ~**ordnung** (*POL BRD*) *the German Constitution based on democratic liberty;* ~**rechenart** *f* basic arithmetical operation; ~**recht** *nt* basic *od* constitutional right; ~**regel** *f* basic rule; ~**riß** *m* plan; (*fig*) outline; ~**satz** *m* principle; **g~sätzlich** *a, ad* fundamental(ly); (*Frage*) of principle; (*prinzipiell*) on principle; **das ist g~sätzlich verboten** it is absolutely forbidden; ~**satzurteil** *nt judgement that establishes a principle;* ~**schule** *f* elementary school; ~**stein** *m* foundation stone; ~**steuer** *f* (land) taxes *pl* (*US*), rates *pl* (*Brit*); ~**stück** *nt* plot (of land); (*Anwesen*) estate; ~**stück und Gebäude** premises *pl*.

Grundstücksmakler *m* real estate agent.

Grund- *zW:* ~**stufe** *f* first stage; (*SCH*) ≈ grade (*US*) *od* junior (*Brit*) school.

Gründung *f* foundation.

Gründungs- *zW:* ~**urkunde** *f* (*COMM*) certificate of incorporation; ~**versammlung** *f* (*Aktiengesellschaft*) statutory meeting.

Grund- *zW:* **g~verschieden** *a* utterly different; ~**wasserspiegel** *m* water table, ground-water level; ~**zug** *m* characteristic; **etw in seinen** ~**zügen darstellen** outline (the essentials of) sth.

Grüne *nt* **-n:** **im** ~**n** in the open air; **ins** ~ **fahren** go to the country.

Grüne(r) *mf dekl wie a* (*POL*) Ecologist, Green; **die** ~**n** (*als Partei*) the Greens.

Grün- *zW:* ~**kohl** *m* kale; ~**schnabel** *m* greenhorn; ~**span** *m* verdigris; ~**streifen** *m* median strip (*US*), central reservation (*Brit*).

grunzen [grōōn'tsən] *vi* grunt.

Gruppe [grōō'pə] *f* -, **-n** group.

Gruppen- *zW:* ~**arbeit** *f* teamwork; ~**dynamik** *f* group dynamics *pl*; ~**therapie** *f* group therapy; **g~weise** *ad* in groups.

gruppieren [grōōpē:'rən] *vtr* group.

gruselig *a* creepy.

gruseln [grōō:'zəln] *vi unpers:* **es gruselt jdm vor etw** sth gives sb the creeps ♦ *vr* have the creeps.

Gruß [grōō:s] *m* **-es,** ⁓e greeting; (*MIL*) salute; **viele** ~⁓e best wishes; ~⁓e **an** (+*akk*) regards to; **einen (schönen)** ~ **an Ihre Gattin!** (*geh*) my regards to your wife; **mit bestem** ~ *od* **besten** ~⁓**en** (*als Briefformel*) Yours, Yours sincerely, Yours truly; **mit freundlichen** ~⁓**en** (*als Briefformel*) Yours sincerely.

grüßen [grü:'sən] *vt* greet; (*MIL*) salute; **jdn von jdm** ~ give sb sb's regards; **jdn** ~ **lassen** send sb one's regards.

Grütze [grü'tsə] *f* -, **-n** (*Brei*) gruel; **rote** ~ red fruit and semolina dessert.

Guayana [gōōáyâ'ná] *nt* **-s** Guyana.
gucken [gōō'kən] *vi* look.
Guckloch *nt* peephole.
Gulasch [gōō:'lásh] *nt* **-(e)s**, **-e** goulash; **~kanone** *f* (*MIL*, *umg*) field kitchen.
gültig [gül'ti̧çh] *a* valid; **~ werden** become valid; (*Gesetz, Vertrag*) come into effect; (*Münze*) become legal tender; **G~keit** *f* validity; **G~keitsdauer** *f* period of validity.
Gummi [gōō'mē] *nt od m* **-s**, **-s** rubber; (*~harze*) gum; (*umg*: *Kondom*) rubber; (*auch*: **~band** *nt*) rubber *od* elastic band; (*Hosen~*) elastic; **~bärchen** *nt* gummi bear (*US*), jelly baby (*Brit*); **~paragraph** *m* ambiguous *od* meaningless law *od* statute; **~stiefel** *m* rubber boot, wellington (boot) (*Brit*); **~strumpf** *m* elastic stocking; **~zelle** *f* padded cell.
Gunst [gōōnst] *f* - favor (*US*), favour (*Brit*).
günstig [güns'ti̧çh] *a* favorable (*US*), favourable (*Brit*); (*Angebot, Preis etc*) reasonable, good; **bei ~er Witterung** weather permitting; **im ~sten Fall(e)** with luck.
Gurgel [gōōr'gəl] *f* -, **-n** throat.
gurgeln *vi* gurgle; (*im Rachen*) gargle.
Gurke [gōōr'kə] *f* -, **-n** cucumber; **saure ~** pickled cucumber, gherkin.
Gurt [gōōrt] *m* **-(e)s**, **-e**, **Gurte** *f* **-n -n** belt.
Gurtanlegepflicht *f* (*form*) obligation to *wear a safety belt in vehicles*.
Gürtel [gür'təl] *m* **-s**, - belt; (*GEOG*) zone; **~reifen** *m* radial tire; **~rose** *f* shingles *sing od pl*.
Guß [gōōs] *m* **-sses**, **Güsse** casting; (*Regen~*) downpour; (*KOCH*) glazing; **~eisen** *nt* cast iron.
gut *a* good; **das ist ~ gegen** *od* **für** (*umg*) **Husten** it's good for coughs; **sei so ~ (und) gib mir das** would you mind giving me that; **dafür ist er sich zu ~** he wouldn't stoop to that sort of thing; **das ist ja alles ~ und schön, aber ...** that's all very well but ...; **du bist ~!** (*umg*) you're a fine one! ♦ *ad* well; **du hast es ~!** you've got it made!; **~ und gern** easily; **laß es ~ sein** that'll do.
Gut [gōō:t] *nt* **-(e)s**, **¨er** (*Besitz*) possession; (*pl*: *Waren*) goods *pl*.
Gut- *zW*: **~achten** *nt* **-s**, - (expert) opinion; **~achter** *m* **-s**, - expert; **~achterkommission** *f* commission of independent experts; **g~artig** *a* good-natured; (*MED*) benign; **g~bürgerlich** *a* (*Küche*) (good) plain; **~dünken** *nt*: **nach ~dünken** at one's discretion.
Güte [gü:'tə] *f* - goodness, kindness; (*Qualität*) quality; **ach du liebe** *od* **meine ~!** (*umg*) goodness me!
Güteklasse *f* (*COMM*) grade.
Güteklasseneinteilung *f* (*COMM*) grading.
Güter- *zW*: **~abfertigung** *f* (*EISENB*) freight office; **~bahnhof** *m* freight station; **~trennung** *f* (*JUR*) separation of property; **~wagen** *m* freight car (*US*) *od* waggon (*Brit*); **~zug** *m* freight train.

Gütesiegel *nt* (*COMM*) stamp of quality.
gut- *zW*: **~gehen** *v unpers unreg* work, come off; **es geht jdm ~** sb's doing fine; **das ist noch einmal ~gegangen** it turned out all right; **~gehend** *a attr* thriving; **~gelaunt** *a* cheerful, in a good mood; **~gemeint** *a* well meant; **~gläubig** *a* trusting; **G~haben** *nt* **-s** credit; **~heißen** *vt unreg* approve (of); **~herzig** *a* kind(-hearted).
gütig [gü:'ti̧çh] *a* kind.
gütlich [gü:t'li̧çh] *a* amicable.
gut- *zW*: **~machen** *vt* (*in Ordnung bringen*: *Fehler*) put right, correct; (*Schaden*) make good; **~mütig** *a* good-natured; **G~mütigkeit** *f* good nature.
Gutsbesitzer(in *f*) *m* landowner.
Gut- *zW*: **~schein** *m* voucher, coupon; **g~schreiben** *vt unreg* credit; **~schrift** *f* credit.
Guts- *zW*: **~herr** *m* squire; **~hof** *m* estate.
gut- *zW*: **~situiert** *a attr* well-off; **~tun** *vi unreg*: **jdm ~tun** do sb good; **~unterrichtet** *a attr* well-informed; **~willig** *a* willing.
Gymnasiallehrer(in *f*) [gümnázēál'lā:rər(in)] *m* high school teacher.
Gymnasium [gümná'zēōōm] *nt* high school.
Gymnastik [gümnás'tik] *f* exercises *pl*, keep-fit; **~ machen** do keep-fit (exercises)/ gymnastics.
Gynäkologe [günekōlō:'gə] *m* **-n**, **-n**, **Gynäkologin** *f* gynecologist (*US*), gynaecologist (*Brit*).

H

H, h [hâ] *nt* H, h; (*MUS*) B.
ha *abk* = Hektar.
Haar [hár] *nt* **-(e)s**, **-e** hair; **um ein ~** nearly; **~e auf den Zähnen haben** be a tough customer; **sich die ~e raufen** (*umg*) tear one's hair; **sich** (*dat*) **in die ~e kriegen** (*umg*) quarrel; **das ist an den ~en herbeigezogen** that's rather far-fetched; **~ansatz** *m* hairline; **~bürste** *f* hairbrush.
haaren *vir* lose hair.
Haaresbreite *f*: **um ~** by a hair's-breadth.
Haar- *zW*: **~festiger** *m* setting lotion *od* gel; **h~genau** *ad* precisely.
haarig *a* hairy; (*fig*) nasty.
Haar- *zW*: **h~klein** *ad* in minute detail; **~klemme** *f* bobby pin (*US*), hair grip (*Brit*); **h~los** *a* hairless; **~nadel** *f* hairpin; **h~scharf** *ad* (*beobachten*) very sharply; (*daneben*) by a hair's breadth; **~schnitt** *m* haircut; **~schopf** *m* head of hair; **~sieb** *nt* fine sieve; **~spalterei'** *f* hair-splitting; **~spange** *f* barrette (*US*), hair slide (*Brit*);

h~sträubend *a* hair-raising; ~**teil** *nt* hairpiece; ~**waschmittel** *nt* shampoo; ~**wasser** *nt* hair lotion.

Hab [hâp] *nt*: ~ **und Gut** *sing* possessions *pl*, belongings *pl*, worldly goods *pl*.

Habe [hâ'bə] *f* - property.

haben [hâ'bən] *unreg vt, aux v* have; **Hunger/Angst** ~ be hungry/afraid; **da hast du 10 Mark** there is 10 Marks; **die** ~**'s (ja)** (*umg*) they can afford it; **Ferien** ~ be on vacation; **es am Herzen** ~ (*umg*) have heart trouble; **sie ist noch zu** ~ (*umg*: *nicht verheiratet*) she's still single; **für etw zu** ~ **sein** be keen on sth; **sie werden schon merken, was sie an ihm** ~ they'll see how valuable he is; **haste was, biste was** (*Sprichwort*) money brings status; **wie gehabt!** some things don't change; **das hast du jetzt davon** now see what's happened; **woher hast du das?** where did you get that from?; **was hast du denn?** what's the matter (with you)?; **ich habe zu tun** I'm busy ♦ *vr unpers*: **und damit hat es sich** (*umg*) and that's that.

Haben *nt* **-s,** - (*COMM*) credit; ~**seite** *f* (*COMM*) credit side.

Habgier *f* avarice.

habgierig *a* avaricious.

habhaft *a*: **jds/einer Sache** ~ **werden** (*geh*) get hold of sb/sth.

Habicht [hâ'biçht] *m* **-(e)s, -e** hawk.

Habilitation [hábēlētâtsēō:n'] *f* (*Lehrberechtigung*) postdoctoral lecturing qualification.

Habseligkeiten [hâp'zä:liçhkītən] *pl* belongings *pl*.

Hachse [hàk'sə] *f* **-, -n** (*KOCH*) knuckle.

Hack- *zW*: ~**braten** *m* meatloaf; ~**brett** *n* chopping board; (*MUS*) dulcimer.

Hacke [hà'kə] *f* **-, -n** hoe; (*Ferse*) heel.

hacken *vt* hack, chop; (*Erde*) hoe.

Hacker [hà'kər] *m* **-s,** - (*COMPUT*) hacker.

Hack- *zW*: ~**fleisch** *nt* ground meat (*US*), minced meat (*Brit*); ~**ordnung** *f* (*lit, fig*) pecking order.

Häcksel [hɛk'səl] *m od nt* **-s** chopped straw, chaff.

hadern [hâ'dərn] *vi* (*geh*) quarrel; (: *unzufrieden sein*) be at odds.

Hafen [hâ'fən] *m* **-s,** ⁼ harbor (*US*), harbour (*Brit*), port; (*fig*) haven; ~**anlagen** *pl* docks *pl*; ~**arbeiter** *m* longshoreman (*US*), docker (*Brit*); ~**damm** *m* jetty, mole; ~**gebühren** *pl* harbo(u)r dues *pl*; ~**stadt** *f* port.

Hafer [hâ'fər] *m* **-s,** - oats *pl*; **ihn sticht der** ~ (*umg*) he's feeling his oats; ~**brei** *m* oatmeal (*US*), porridge (*Brit*); ~**flocken** *pl* oatmeal (*US*), rolled oats *pl* (*Brit*); ~**schleim** *m* gruel.

Haff [hâf] *nt* **-s, -s** *od* **-e** lagoon.

Haft [hâft] *f* - custody; ~**anstalt** *f* detention center; **h**~**bar** *a* liable, responsible; ~**befehl** *m* warrant (for arrest); **einen** ~**befehl gegen jdn ausstellen** issue a warrant for sb's arrest.

haften *vi* stick, cling; ~ **für** be liable *od* responsible for; **für Garderobe kann nicht gehaftet werden** all articles are left at owner's risk; ~**bleiben** *vi unreg* stick (*an* +*dat* to).

Häftling [hɛft'ling] *m* prisoner; (*politisch auch*) detainee.

Haft- *zW*: ~**pflicht** *f* liability; ~**pflichtversicherung** *f* liability (*US*) *od* third party (*Brit*) insurance; ~**richter** *m* magistrate.

Haftschalen *pl* contact lenses *pl*.

Haftung *f* liability.

Hagebutte [hâ'gəbōōtə] *f* **-, -n** rose hip.

Hagedorn *m* hawthorn.

Hagel [hâ'gəl] *m* **-s** hail; ~**korn** *nt* hailstone; (*MED*) eye cyst.

hageln *vi unpers* hail.

Hagelschauer *m* (short) hailstorm.

hager [hâ'gər] *a* gaunt.

Häher [he:'ər] *m* **-s,** - jay.

Hahn [hân] *m* **-(e)s,** ⁼**e** cock; (*Wasser*~) faucet (*US*), tap; (*Abzug*) trigger; ~ **im Korb sein** (*umg*) be cock of the walk; **danach kräht kein** ~ **mehr** (*umg*) no one cares two hoots about that any more.

Hähnchen [he:n'çhən] *nt* cockerel; (*KOCH*) chicken.

Hai(fisch) [hī'(fish)] *m* **-(e)s, -e** shark.

Häkchen [he:k'çhən] *nt* small hook.

Häkelarbeit *f* crochet work.

häkeln [he:'kəln] *vt* crochet.

Häkelnadel *f* crochet hook.

Haken [hâ'kən] *m* **-s,** - hook; (*fig*) catch; **einen** ~ **schlagen** dart sideways; ~**kreuz** *nt* swastika; ~**nase** *f* hooked nose.

halb [hâlp] *a* half; ~ **eins** twelve thirty, half past twelve; **ein** ~**es Dutzend** half a dozen; **nichts H**~**es und nichts Ganzes** neither one thing nor the other; **(noch) ein** ~**es Kind sein** be scarcely more than a child ♦ *ad* (*beinahe*) almost; **das ist** ~ **so schlimm** it's not as bad as all that; **mit jdm** ~**e-**~**e machen** (*umg*) go halves with sb.

halb- *zW*: **H**~**blut** *nt* (*Tier*) crossbreed; **H**~**dunkel** *nt* semi-darkness.

halber [hâl'bər] *präp* +*gen* (*wegen*) on account of; (*für*) for the sake of.

Halb- *zW*: ~**finale** *nt* semi-final; ~**heit** *f* halfmeasure; **h**~**herzig** *a* half-heartedly.

halbieren [hâlbē:'rən] *vt* halve.

Halb- *zW*: ~**insel** *f* peninsula; **h**~**jährlich** *a* half-yearly, semiannual; ~**kreis** *m* semicircle; ~**kugel** *f* hemisphere; **h**~**lang** *a*: **nun mach mal h**~**lang!** (*umg*) now wait a minute!; **h**~**laut** *ad* in an undertone; ~**leiter** *m* (*PHYS*) semiconductor; ~**links** *m* -, - (*SPORT*) inside-left; **h**~**mast** *ad* at halfmast; ~**mond** *m* half-moon; (*fig*) crescent; **h**~**offen** *a* half-open; ~**pension** *f* room and one main meal; ~**rechts** *m* -, - (*SPORT*) inside-right; ~**schuh** *m* shoe; **h**~**seiden** *a* (*lit*) fifty per cent silk; (*fig*: *Dame*) fast; (*homosexuell*) gay; **h**~**seitig** *a* (*Anzeige*) half-page; **~starke(r)** *mf dekl wie a* hooligan, rowdy; **h~tags** *ad:* **h~tags arbeiten** work part-time; **~tagsarbeit** *f* part-time work; **~ton** *m* half-tone; (*MUS*) semitone; **~waise** *f child od person who has lost one parent*; **h~wegs** *ad* half-way; **h~wegs besser** more or less better; **~welt** *f* demimonde; **~wertzeit** *f* half-life; **~wüchsige(r)** *mf dekl wie a* adolescent; **~zeit** *f* (*SPORT*) half; (*Pause*) half-time.

Halde [hàl'də] *f* **-, -n** tip; (*Schlacken~*) slag heap.

half [hàlf] *imperf von* **helfen.**

Hälfte [helf'tə] **-, -n** *f* half; **um die ~ steigen** increase by half.

Halfter [hàlf'tər] *f* **-, -n** *od nt* **-s, -** halter; (*Pistolen~*) holster.

Hall [hàl] *m* **-(e)s, -e** sound.

Halle [hà'lə] *f* **-, -n** hall; (*AVIAT*) hangar.

hallen *vi* echo, resound.

Hallenbad *nt* indoor swimming pool.

hallo [hàlō:'] *interj* hallo.

Halluzination [hàlo͞otsēnátsēō:n'] *f* hallucination.

Halm [hàlm] *m* **-(e)s, -e** blade, stalk.

Hals [hàls] *m* **-es, ̈e** neck; (*Kehle*) throat; **sich** (*dat*) **nach jdm/etw den ~ verrenken** (*umg*) crane one's neck to see sb/sth; **jdm um den ~ fallen** fling one's arms around sb's neck; **aus vollem ~(e)** at the top of one's voice; **~ und Beinbruch!** good luck!; **~ über Kopf** in a rush; **jdn auf dem od am ~ haben** (*umg*) be saddled with sb; **das hängt mir zum ~ raus** (*umg*) I'm sick and tired of it; **sie hat es in den falschen ~ bekommen** (*falsch verstehen*) she took it wrongly; **~abschneider** *m* (*pej umg*) shark; **~band** *nt* (*Hunde*) collar; **h~brecherisch** *a* (*Tempo*) breakneck; (*Fahrt*) hair-raising; **~kette** *f* necklace; **~krause** *f* ruff: **~Nasen-Ohren-Arzt** *m* ear, nose and throat specialist; **~schlagader** *f* carotid artery; **~schmerzen** *pl* sore throat; **h~starrig** *a* stubborn, obstinate; **~tuch** *nt* scarf; **~weh** *nt* sore throat; **~wirbel** *m* cervical vertebra.

hält [helt] *3. pers sing präs von* **halten.**

Halt [hàlt] *m* **-(e)s, -e** stop; (*fester ~*) hold; (*innerer ~*) stability; **h~!** stop!, halt!; **h~bar** *a* durable; (*Lebensmittel*) nonperishable; (*MIL, fig*) tenable; **h~bar bis 6.11.** use by 6 Nov.; **~barkeit** *f* durability; (*non-*)perishability; tenability; (*von Lebensmitteln*) shelf life; **~barkeitsdatum** *nt* best before date.

halten [hàl'tən] *unreg vt* keep; (*fest~*) hold; **den Mund ~** (*umg*) keep one's mouth shut; **~ für** regard as; **~ von** think of; **das kannst du ~ wie du willst** that's completely up to you; **der Film hält nicht, was er verspricht** the film doesn't live up to expectations; **davon halt(e) ich nichts** I don't think much of it ♦ *vi* hold; (*frisch bleiben*) keep; (*stoppen*) stop; **zu jdm ~** stand *od* stick by sb; **an sich ~** restrain o.s.; **auf sich** (*akk*)

~ (*auf Äußeres achten*) take a pride in o.s. ♦ *vr* (*frisch bleiben*) keep; (*sich behaupten*) hold out; **er hat sich gut gehalten** (*umg*) he's well-preserved; **sich an ein Versprechen ~** keep a promise; **sich rechts/links ~** keep to the right/left.

Halter [hàl'tər] *m* **-s, -** (*Halterung*) holder.

Halte- *zW:* **~stelle** *f* stop; **~verbot** *nt:* **absolutes ~verbot** no stopping; **eingeschränktes ~verbot** no waiting.

Halt- *zW:* **h~los** *a* unstable; **~losigkeit** *f* instability; **h~machen** *vi* stop.

Haltung *f* posture; (*fig*) attitude; (*Selbstbeherrschung*) composure; **~ bewahren** keep one's composure.

Halunke [hàlo͞ong'kə] *m* **-n, -n** rascal.

Hamburg [hàm'bo͞ork] *nt* **-s** Hamburg.

Hamburger(in *f*) *m* **-s, -** native of Hamburg.

Hameln [hà'məln] *nt* Hamelin.

hämisch [he:'mish] *a* malicious.

Hammel [hà'məl] *m* **-s, ̈ od -** wether; **~fleisch** *nt* mutton; **~keule** *f* leg of mutton.

Hammelsprung *m* (*PARL*) division.

Hammer [hà'mər] *m* **-s, ̈** hammer; **das ist ein ~!** (*umg: unerhört*) that's absurd!

hämmern [he'mərn] *vti* hammer.

Hammondorgel [he'məndorgəl] *f* **-, -n** electric organ.

Hämorrhoiden [hemoroi:'dən] *pl* piles *pl*, hemorrhoids *pl* (*US*), haemorrhoids *pl* (*Brit*).

Hampelmann [hàm'pəlmán] *m* (*lit, fig*) puppet.

Hamster [hàms'tər] *m* **-s, -** hamster.

Hamsterei [hàmstərī'] *f* hoarding.

Hamsterer *m* **-s, -** hoarder.

hamstern *vi* hoard.

Hand [hànt] *f* **-, ̈e** hand; **etw zur ~ haben** have sth to hand; (*Ausrede, Erklärung*) have sth ready; **jdm zur ~ gehen** lend sb a helping hand; **zu ~en von jdm** for the attention of sb; **zu ~en sein** be spoken for; **die ~ für jdn ins Feuer legen** vouch for sb; **hinter vorgehaltener ~** on the quiet; **~ aufs Herz** cross your heart; **jdn auf ̈en tragen** cherish sb; **bei etw die** *od* **seine ~ im Spiel haben** have a hand in sth; **eine ~ wäscht die andere** (*Sprichwort*) if you scratch my back I'll scratch yours; **das hat weder ~ noch Fuß** that doesn't make sense; **das liegt auf der ~** (*umg*) that's obvious; **an ~ eines Beispiels** by means of an example; **~arbeit** *f* manual work; (*Nadelarbeit*) needlework; **~arbeiter** *m* manual worker; **~besen** *m* brush; **~betrieb** *m:* **mit ~betrieb** hand-operated; **~bibliothek** *f* reference library (*with open shelves*); **~bremse** *f* handbrake; **~buch** *nt* handbook, manual.

Hände- [hen'də] *zW:* **~druck** *m* handshake; **~klatschen** *nt* clapping, applause.

Handel [hàn'dəl] *m* **-s** trade; (*Geschäft*) transaction; **im ~ sein** be on the market; **(mit jdm) ~ treiben** trade (with sb); **etw in**

den ~ bringen/aus dem ~ ziehen put sth on/take sth off the market ♦ *m* **-s,** ⁼: ~ **haben** quarrel.

handeln [hán'dəln] *vi* trade; (*tätig werden*) act; ~ **von** be about; **ich lasse mit mir ~** I'm open to persuasion; (*in bezug auf Preis*) I'm open to offers ♦ *vr unpers:* **sich ~ um** be a question of, be about; **H~** *nt* **-s** action.

handelnd *a:* **die ~en Personen in einem Drama** the characters in a drama.

Handels- *zW:* ~**bank** *f* commercial bank; ~**bilanz** *f* balance of trade; **aktive/passive** ~**bilanz** balance of trade surplus/deficit; ~**delegation** *f* trade mission; **h~einig** *a:* **mit jdm h~einig werden** conclude a deal with sb; ~**gesellschaft** *f* commercial company; ~**kammer** *f* chamber of commerce; ~**klasse** *f* grade; ~**marine** *f* merchant marine (*US*) *od* navy (*Brit*); ~**marke** *f* trade name; ~**name** *m* trade name; ~**recht** *nt* commercial law; ~**register** *nt* register of companies; ~**reisende(r)** *m dekl wie a* traveling salesman (*US*), commercial traveller (*Brit*); ~**sanktionen** *pl* trade sanctions *pl*; ~**schule** *f* business school; ~**spanne** *f* gross margin, mark-up; **h~üblich** *a* customary; ~**vertreter** *m* sales representative; ~**vertretung** *f* trade mission.

händeringend [hɛn'dəringənd] *ad* wringing one's hands; (*fig*) imploringly.

Hand- *zW:* ~**feger** *m* **-s,** - brush; ~**fertigkeit** *f* dexterity; **h~fest** *a* hefty; ~**fläche** *f* palm *od* flat (of the *od* one's hand); **h~gearbeitet** *a* handmade; ~**gelenk** *nt* wrist; **aus dem** ~**gelenk** (*umg: ohne Mühe*) effortlessly; (: *improvisiert*) off the cuff; ~**gemenge** *nt* scuffle; ~**gepäck** *nt* hand baggage; **h~geschrieben** *a* handwritten; ~**granate** *f* hand grenade; **h~greiflich** *a* palpable; **h~greiflich werden** become violent; ~**griff** *m* flick of the wrist; ~**habe** *f:* **ich habe gegen ihn keine** ~**habe** (*fig*) I have no hold on him; **h~haben** *vt unreg untr* handle; ~**karren** *m* handcart; ~**käse** *m* strong-smelling, round German cheese; ~**kuß** *m* kiss on the hand; ~**langer** *m* **-s,** - odd-job man, handyman; (*fig: Untergeordneter*) gofer (*US*), dogsbody (*Brit*).

Händler [hen'dlər] *m* **-s,** - trader, dealer.

handlich [hán'tliċh] *a* handy.

Handlung [hán'dlŏng] *f* act(ion); (*in Buch*) plot; (*Geschäft*) store, shop.

Handlungs- *zW:* ~**ablauf** *m* plot; ~**bevollmächtige(r)** *mf dekl wie a* authorized agent; **h~fähig** *a* (*Regierung*) able to act; (*JUR*) empowered to act; ~**freiheit** *f* freedom of action; **h~orientiert** *a* action-orientated; ~**vollmacht** *f* proxy; ~**weise** *f* manner of dealing.

Hand- *zW:* ~**pflege** *f* manicure; ~**schelle** *f* handcuff; ~**schlag** *m* handshake; **keinen** ~**schlag tun** not do a stroke (of work); ~**schrift** *f* handwriting; (*Text*) manuscript; **h~schriftlich** *a* handwritten ♦ *ad* (*korrigie-*

ren, einfügen) by hand; ~**schuh** *m* glove; ~**schuhfach** *nt* (*AUT*) glove compartment; ~**tasche** *f* handbag; ~**tuch** *nt* towel; ~**umdrehen** *nt:* **im** ~**umdrehen** (*fig*) in the twinkling of an eye; ~**werk** *nt* trade, craft; **jdm das** ~**werk legen** (*fig*) put a stop to sb's game; ~**werker** *m* **-s** - craftsman, artisan; **wir haben seit Wochen die** ~**werker im Haus** we've had workmen in the house for weeks.

Handwerkskammer *f* trade corporation.

Hand- *zW:* ~**werkzeug** *nt* tools *pl*; ~**wörterbuch** *nt* concise dictionary; ~**zeichen** *nt* signal; (*Geste auch*) sign; (*bei Abstimmung*) show of hands; ~**zettel** *m* leaflet, handbill.

Hanf [hánf] *m* **-(e)s** hemp.

Hang [háng] *m* **-(e)s,** ⁼**e** inclination; (*Ab~*) slope.

Hänge- [he'ngə] *in zW* hanging; ~**brücke** *f* suspension bridge; ~**matte** *f* hammock; **soziale** ~**matte** social safety net.

hängen [he'ngən] *unreg vi* hang; ~ **an** (*fig*) be attached to; **den Kopf ~ lassen** (*fig*) be downcast; **die ganze Sache hängt an ihm** it all depends on him ♦ *vt* hang (*an* +*akk* on(to)); **sich ~ an** (+*akk*) hang on to, cling to.

Hängen *nt:* **mit ~ und Würgen** (*umg*) by the skin of one's teeth.

hängenbleiben *vi unreg* be caught (*an* +*dat* on); (*fig*) remain, stick; **es bleibt ja doch alles an mir hängen** (*fig umg*) in the end it's all down to me anyhow.

hängend *a:* **mit ~er Zunge kam er angelaufen** (*fig*) he came running up panting.

hängenlassen *vt unreg* (*vergessen*) leave behind ♦ *vr* let o.s. go.

Hängeschloß *nt* padlock.

Hanglage *f:* **in ~** situated on a slope.

Hannover [hánō:'fər] *nt* **-s** Hanover.

Hannoveraner(in *f*) [hánōvərá'nər(in)] *m* **-s,** - Hanoverian.

hänseln [hen'zəln] *vt* tease.

Hansestadt [hán'zəshtát] *f* Hanseatic *od* Hanse town.

Hanswurst [hánsvōörst'] *m* clown.

Hantel [hán'təl] *f* **-, -n** (*SPORT*) dumb-bell.

hantieren [hántē:'rən] *vi* work, be busy; **mit etw ~** handle sth.

hapern [há'pərn] *vi unpers:* **es hapert an etw** (*dat*) sth leaves something to be desired.

Happen [há'pən] *m* **-s,** - mouthful.

happig [há'piċh] *a* (*umg*) steep.

Hardware [há:rdweə] *f* **-, -s** hardware.

Harfe [hár'fə] *f* **-, -n** harp.

Harke [hár'kə] *f* **-, -n** rake.

harken *vti* rake.

harmlos [hárm'lō:s] *a* harmless.

Harmlosigkeit *f* harmlessness.

Harmonie [hármōnē:'] *f* harmony.

harmonieren *vi* harmonize.

Harmonika [hármō:'nēká] *f* **-, -s** (*Zieh~*) accordion.

harmonisch [hårmō:'nish] *a* harmonious.
Harmonium [hårmō:'nēōōm] *nt* **-s, -nien** *od* **-s** harmonium.
Harn [hårn'] *m* **-(e)s, -e** urine; **~blase** *f* bladder.
Harnisch [hår'nish] *m* **-(e)s, -e** armor (*US*), armour (*Brit*); **jdn in ~ bringen** infuriate sb; **in ~ geraten** become angry.
Harpune [hårpōō:'nə] *f* **-, -n** harpoon.
harren [hå'rən] *vi* wait (*auf* +*akk* for).
Harsch [hårsh] *m* **-(e)s** frozen snow.
harschig *a* (*Schnee*) frozen.
hart [hårt] *a* hard; (*fig*) harsh; **~e Währung** hard currency; **~ bleiben** stand firm; **es geht ~ auf ~** it's a tough fight ♦ *ad*: **das ist ~ an der Grenze** that's almost going too far.
Härte [her'tə] *f* **-, -n** hardness; (*fig*) harshness; **soziale ~n** social hardships; **~fall** *m* case of hardship; (*umg*: *Mensch*) hardship case; **~klausel** *f* hardship clause.
härten *vtr* harden.
hart- *zW*: **H~faserplatte** *f* fiberboard; **~gekocht** *a* hard-boiled; **~gesotten** *a* tough, hard-boiled; **~herzig** *a* hard-hearted; **~näckig** *a* stubborn; **H~näckigkeit** *f* stubbornness.
Harz [hårts] *nt* **-es, -e** resin ♦ *m* (*GEOG*) Harz Mountains *pl.*
Haschee [håshā:'] *nt* **-s, -s** hash.
haschen [hå'shən] *vt* catch, snatch ♦ *vi* (*umg*) smoke hash.
Haschisch [hå'shish] *nt* - hashish.
Hase [hå'zə] *m* **-n, -n** hare; **falscher ~** (*KOCH*) meat loaf; **wissen, wie der ~ läuft** (*fig umg*) know which way the wind blows; **mein Name ist ~(, ich weiß von nichts)** I don't know anything about anything.
Haselnuß [hå'zəlnōōs] *f* hazelnut.
Hasen- *zW*: **~fuß** *m* coward; **~scharte** *f* harelip.
Haspe [hås'pə] *f* **-, -n** hinge.
Haspel *f* **-, -n** reel, bobbin; (*Winde*) winch.
Haß [hås] *m* **-sses** hate, hatred; **einen ~ haben** (*umg*: *Wut*) be really mad (*auf jdn* with sb).
hassen [hå'sən] *vt* hate; **etw ~ wie die Pest** (*umg*) detest sth.
hassenswert *a* hateful.
häßlich [hes'liċh] *a* ugly; (*gemein*) nasty; **H~keit** *f* ugliness; nastiness.
hast [håst] *2. pers sing präs von* **haben**.
Hast *f* - haste.
hasten *vir* rush.
hastig *a* hasty.
hat [håt] *3. pers sing präs von* **haben**.
hätscheln [het'shəln] *vt* pamper; (*zärtlich*) cuddle.
hatte [hå'tə] *imperf von* **haben**.
hätte [he'tə] *Konjunktiv von* **haben**.
Haube [hou'bə] *f* **-, -n** hood; (*Mütze*) cap; (*AUT*) hood (*US*), bonnet (*Brit*); **unter der ~ sein/unter die ~ kommen** (*hum*) be/get married.

Hauch [houḳh] *m* **-(e)s, -e** breath; (*Luft~*) breeze; (*fig*) trace; **h~dünn** *a* extremely thin; (*Scheiben*) wafer-thin; (*fig*: *Mehrheit*) extremely narrow; **h~en** *vi* breathe; **h~fein** *a* very fine.
Haue [hou'ə] *f* **-, -n** hoe; (*Pickel*) pick; (*umg*) hiding.
hauen *vt unreg* hew, cut; (*umg*) thrash.
Hauer [hou'ər] *m* **-s, -** (*MIN*) underground worker, face-worker (*Brit*).
Häufchen [hoif'ċhən] *nt*: **ein ~ Unglück** *od* **Elend** a picture of misery.
Haufen [hou'fən] *m* **-s, -** heap; (*Leute*) crowd; **ein ~ (x)** (*umg*) loads *od* a lot (of x); **auf einem ~** in one heap; **etw** (*akk*) **über den ~ werfen** (*umg*: *verwerfen*) chuck sth out; **jdn über den ~ rennen** *od* **fahren** *etc* (*umg*) knock sb down.
häufen [hoi'fən] *vt* pile up ♦ *vr* accumulate.
haufenweise *ad* in heaps; in droves; **etw ~ haben** have piles of sth.
häufig [hoi'fiċh] *a*, *ad* frequent(ly); **H~keit** *f* frequency.
Haupt [houpt] *nt* **-(e)s, Häupter** head; (*Ober~*) chief ♦ *in zW* main; (*COMPUT*) master; **~akteur** *m* (*lit*, *fig*) leading light; (*pej*) main figure; **~aktionär** *m* major shareholder; **~bahnhof** *m* central station; **h~beruflich** *ad* as one's main occupation; **~buch** *nt* (*COMM*) ledger; **~darsteller(in** *f*) *m* leading actor/actress; **~eingang** *m* main entrance; **~fach** *nt* (*SCH. UNIV*) major (*US*), main subject; **etw im ~fach studieren** major in sth (*US*), study sth as one's main subject; **~film** *m* main *od* feature film; **~gericht** *nt* main course; **~geschäftsstelle** *f* head office; **~geschäftszeit** *f* peak (shopping) period; **~leitung** *f* mains gas (*od* water *od* electric) lines *pl*, mains *pl* (*Brit*).
Häuptling [hoip'tling] *m* chief(tain).
Haupt- *zW*: **~mahlzeit** *f* main meal; **~mann** *m*, *pl* **-leute** (*MIL*) captain; **~nahrungsmittel** *nt* staple food; **~postamt** *nt* main post office; **~quartier** *nt* headquarters *pl*; **~rolle** *f* leading part; **~sache** *f* main thing; **in der ~sache** in the main, mainly; **h~sächlich** *a*, *ad* chief(ly); **~saison** *f* peak *od* high season; **~satz** *m* main clause; **~schlagader** *f* aorta; **~schlüssel** *m* master key; **~schule** *f* junior high (school); **~sendezeit** *f* (*TV*) prime time; **~stadt** *f* capital; **~straße** *f* main street; **~verkehrsstraße** *f* (*in Stadt*) main street; (*Durchgangsstraße*) main thoroughfare; (*zwischen Städten*) main highway; **~verkehrszeit** *f* rush hour; **~versammlung** *f* general meeting; **~wohnsitz** *m* main place of residence; **~wort** *nt* noun.
hau ruck [hou' rōōk'] *interj* heave-ho.
Haus [hous] *nt* **-es, Häuser** house; **nach ~e** home; **zu ~e** at home; **fühl dich wie zu ~!** make yourself at home!; **ein Freund des ~es** a friend of the family; **wir liefern frei ~** (*COMM*) we offer free delivery; **das erste**

~ am Platze (*Hotel*) the best hotel in town; **~angestellte** *f* domestic servant; **~arbeit** *f* housework; (*SCH*) homework; **~arrest** *m* (*im Internat*) detention; (*JUR*) house arrest; **~arzt** *m* family doctor; **~aufgabe** *f* (*SCH*) homework; **~besetzung** *f* squatting; (*Haus*) squat; **~besitzer** *m* house-owner.

Häuschen [hois'çhən] *nt*: **ganz aus dem ~ sein** (*fig umg*) be out of one's mind (with excitement *od* fear *etc*).

Hauseigentümer *m* house-owner.

hausen [hou'zən] *vi* live (in poverty); (*pej*) wreak havoc.

Häuser- [hoi'zər] *zW*: **~block** *m* block (of houses); **~makler** *m* real estate agent (*US*), estate agent (*Brit*); **~reihe** *f*, **~zeile** *f* row of houses.

Haus- *zW*: **~frau** *f* housewife; **~freund** *m* family friend; (*umg*) lover; **~friedensbruch** *m* (*JUR*) trespass (*in sb's house*); **~gebrauch** *m*: **für den ~gebrauch** (*Gerät*) for domestic *od* household use; **h~gemacht** *a* home-made; **~gemeinschaft** *f* household (community); **~halt** *m* household; (*POL*) budget; **h~halten** *vi* unreg keep house; (*sparen*) economize; **~hälterin** *f* housekeeper.

Haushalts- *zW*: **~auflösung** *f* dissolution of the household; **~buch** *nt* housekeeping book; **~debatte** *f* (*PARL*) budget debate; **~geld** *nt* housekeeping (money); **~gerät** *nt* domestic appliance; **~hilfe** *f* domestic help; **~jahr** *nt* (*POL, WIRTSCHAFT*) financial *od* fiscal year; **~periode** *f* budget period; **~plan** *m* budget.

Haus- *zW*: **~haltung** *f* housekeeping; **~herr** *m* host; (*Vermieter*) landlord; **h~hoch** *ad*: **h~hoch verlieren** lose by a mile.

hausieren [houzē:'rən] *vi* peddle.

Hausierer *m* -s, - peddler.

hausintern [hous'intern] *a* internal company *attr*.

häuslich [hois'liçh] *a* domestic; **sich irgendwo ~ einrichten** *od* **niederlassen** settle in somewhere; **H~keit** *f* domesticity.

Hausmacherart [hous'mäkhərárt] *f*: **Wurst** *etc* **nach ~** home-made-style sausage *etc*.

Haus- *zW*: **~mann** *m*, *pl* **-männer** (*den Haushalt versorgender Mann*) man undertaking the role of housewife, house-husband; **~marke** *f* (*eigene Marke*) own brand; (*bevorzugte Marke*) favorite (*US*) *od* favourite (*Brit*) brand; **~meister** *m* caretaker, janitor; **~mittel** *nt* household remedy; **~ordnung** *f* house rules *pl*; **~putz** *m* house cleaning; **~ratversicherung** *f* (household) contents insurance; **~schlüssel** *m* front-door key; **~schuh** *m* slipper; **~schwamm** *m* dry rot.

Hausse [hō:'sə] *f* -, -n (*WIRTSCHAFT*) boom (*an +dat* in); (*BÖRSE*) bull market.

Haus- *zW*: **~segen** *m*: **bei ihnen hängt der ~segen schief** (*hum*) they're a bit short on domestic bliss; **~stand** *m*: **einen ~stand gründen** set up house *od* home; **~suchung** *f*

police raid; **~suchungsbefehl** *m* search warrant; **~tier** *nt* domestic animal; **~verbot** *nt*: **jdm ~verbot erteilen** ban sb from the house; **~verwalter** *m* caretaker; **~verwaltung** *f* property management; **~wirt** *m* landlord; **~wirtschaft** *f* domestic science; **~-zu-Haus-Verkauf** *m* door-to-door selling.

Haut [hout] *f* -, **Häute** skin; (*Tier~*) hide; **mit ~ und Haar(en)** (*umg*) completely; **aus der ~ fahren** (*umg*) go through the roof; **~arzt** *m* skin specialist, dermatologist.

häuten [hoi'tən] *vt* skin ♦ *vr* shed one's skin.

Haut- *zW*: **h~eng** *a* skintight; **~farbe** *f* complexion.

Havanna [hàvà'nà] *nt* **-s** Havana.

Havel [hâ'fəl] *f* - (*Fluß*) Havel.

Haxe [hàk'sə] *f* -, -n *siehe* **Hachse**.

Hbf. *abk* (= *Hauptbahnhof*) main *od* central station.

H-Bombe [hâ'bombə] *f* abk = **Wasserstoffbombe**.

hd. *abk* (= *hochdeutsch*) HG.

Hebamme [hā:p'àmə] *f* -, -n midwife.

Hebel [hā:'bəl] *m* -s, - lever; **alle ~ in Bewegung setzen** (*umg*) move heaven and earth; **am längeren ~ sitzen** (*umg*) have the whip hand.

heben [hā:'bən] *vt* unreg raise, lift; (*steigern*) increase; **einen ~ gehen** (*umg*) go for a drink.

Hebräer(in *f)* [hābre:'ər(in)] *m* **-s**, - Hebrew.

hebräisch [hābre:'ish] *a* Hebrew.

Hebriden [hābre:'dən] *pl*: **die ~** the Hebrides *pl*.

hecheln [he'çhəln] *vi* (*Hund*) pant.

Hecht [heçht] *m* **-(e)s, -e** pike; **~sprung** *m* (*beim Schwimmen*) racing dive; (*beim Turnen*) forward dive; (*FUSSBALL umg*) dive.

Heck [hek] *nt* **-(e)s, -e** stern; (*von Auto*) rear; **~fenster** *nt* (*AUT*) rear window.

Hecke [he'kə] *f* -, -n hedge.

Heckenrose *f* dog rose.

Heckenschütze *m* sniper.

heda [hā:'dà] *interj* hey there.

Heer [hā:r] *nt* **-(e)s, -e** army.

Hefe [hā:'fə] *f* -, -n yeast.

Heft [heft] *nt* **-(e)s, -e** exercise book; (*Zeitschrift*) number; (*von Messer*) haft; **jdm das ~ aus der Hand nehmen** (*fig*) seize control *od* power from sb.

Heftchen *nt* (*Fahrkarten~*) book of tickets; (*Briefmarken~*) book of stamps.

heften *vt* fasten (*an +akk* to); (*nähen*) baste, tack; (*mit Heftmaschine auch*) staple (*an +akk* to) ♦ *vr*: **sich an jds Fersen** *od* **Sohlen ~** (*fig*) dog sb's heels.

Hefter *m* -s, - folder.

heftig *a* fierce, violent; **H~keit** *f* fierceness, violence.

Heft- *zW*: **~klammer** *f* staple; **~maschine** *f* stapling machine; **~pflaster** *nt* adhesive tape (*US*), sticking plaster (*Brit*); **~zwecke**

f thumbtack (*US*), drawing pin (*Brit*).

hegen [hā:'gən] *vt* nurse; (*fig*) harbor (*US*), harbour (*Brit*), foster.

Hehl [hā:l] *m od nt*: **kein(en) ~ aus etw** (*dat*) **machen** make no secret of sth.

Hehler *m* **-s,** - receiver (of stolen goods), fence.

Heide [hī'də] *f* -, **-n** heath, moor; (*~kraut*) heather ♦ *m* **-n, -n, Heidin** *f* heathen, pagan; **~kraut** *nt* heather.

Heidelbeere *f* blueberry.

Heiden- *zW*: **~angst** *f* (*umg*): **eine ~angst vor etw/jdm** (*dat*) **haben** be scared stiff of sth/sb; **~arbeit** *f* (*umg*) real slog; **h~mäßig** *a* (*umg*) terrific; **~tum** *nt* paganism.

heidnisch [hīd'nish] *a* heathen, pagan.

heikel [hī'kəl] *a* awkward, thorny; (*wählerisch*) fussy.

heil [hīl] *a* in one piece, intact; **mit ~er Haut davonkommen** escape unscathed; **die ~e Welt** an ideal world (*without problems etc*).

Heil *nt* **-(e)s** well-being; (*Seelen~*) salvation ♦ *interj* hail; **Ski/Petri ~!** good skiing/fishing!

Heiland *m* **-(e)s, -e** savior (*US*), saviour (*Brit*).

Heil- *zW*: **~anstalt** *f* nursing home; (*für Sucht- oder Geisteskranke*) home; **~bad** *nt* (*Bad*) medicinal bath; (*Ort*) spa; **h~bar** *a* curable.

Heilbutt [hīl'boot] *m* **-s, -e** halibut.

heilen *vt* cure; **als geheilt entlassen werden** be discharged with a clean bill of health ♦ *vi* heal.

heilfroh *a* very relieved.

Heilgymnastin *f* physiotherapist.

heilig [hī'lich] *a* holy; **jdm ~ sein** (*lit, fig*) be sacred to sb; **die H~e Schrift** the Holy Scriptures *pl*; **es ist mein ~er Ernst I** am deadly serious; **H~abend** *m* Christmas Eve.

heiligen *vt* sanctify, hallow; **der Zweck heiligt die Mittel** the end justifies the means.

Heiligenschein *m* halo.

Heilige(r) *mf dekl wie a* saint.

heilig- *zW*: **H~keit** *f* holiness; **~sprechen** *vt unreg* canonize; **H~tum** *nt* shrine; (*Gegenstand*) relic.

Heilkunde *f* medicine.

heillos *a* unholy; (*Schreck*) terrible.

Heil- *zW*: **~mittel** *nt* remedy; **~praktiker(in** *f*) *m* non-medical practitioner; **h~sam** *a* (*fig*) salutary.

Heilsarmee *f* Salvation Army.

Heilung *f* cure.

heim [hīm] *ad* home.

Heim *nt* **-(e), -e** home; **~arbeit** *f* (*INDUSTRIE*) homework, outwork.

Heimat [hī'mât] *f* **-, -en** home (town *od* country *etc*); **~film** *m* sentimental film in idealized regional setting; **~kunde** *f* (*SCH*) local history; **~land** *nt* homeland; **h~lich** *a* native, home *attr*; (*Gefühle*) nostalgic; **h~los** *a* homeless; **~museum** *nt* local history museum; **~ort** *m* home town *od* area; **~vertriebene(r)** *mf dekl wie a* displaced

person.

heimbegleiten *vt* accompany home.

Heimchen *nt*: **~ (am Herd)** (*pej: Frau*) housewife.

heimelig [hī'məlich] *a* homely.

Heim- *zW*: **h~fahren** *vi unreg* drive *od* go home; **~fahrt** *f* journey home; **~gang** *m* return home; (*Tod*) decease; **h~gehen** *vi unreg* go home; (*sterben*) pass away; **h~isch** *a* (*gebürtig*) native; **sich h~isch fühlen** feel at home; **~kehr** *f* -, **-en** homecoming; **h~kehren** *vi* return home; **~kind** *nt* child brought up in a home; **~leiter** *m* warden of a home *od* hostel.

heimlich *a* secret ♦ *ad*: **~, still und leise** (*umg*) quietly, on the quiet; **H~keit** *f* secrecy; **H~tue'rei** *f* secrecy.

Heim- *zW*: **~reise** *f* journey home; **h~suchen** *vt* afflict; (*Geist*) haunt; **h~tückisch** *a* malicious; **h~wärts** *ad* homewards; **~weg** *m* way home; **~weh** *nt* homesickness; **~weh haben** be homesick; **~werker** *m* handyman; **h~zahlen** *vt*: **jdm etw h~zahlen** pay back sb for sth.

Heini [hī'nē] *m* **-s, -s**: **blöder ~** (*umg*) silly idiot.

Heirat [hī'rât] *f* -, **-en** marriage; **h~en** *vti* marry.

Heirats- *zW*: **~antrag** *m* proposal (of marriage); **~anzeige** *f* (*Annonce*) advertisement for a marriage partner; **~schwindler** *m* person who makes a marriage proposal in order to obtain money.

heiser [hī'zər] *a* hoarse; **H~keit** *f* hoarseness.

heiß [hīs] *a* hot; (*Thema*) hotly disputed; (*Diskussion, Kampf*) heated, fierce; (*Begierde, Liebe, Wunsch*) burning; **es wird nichts so ~ gegessen, wie es gekocht wird** (*Sprichwort*) things are never as bad as they seem; **~er Draht** hot line; **~es Geld** hot money; **ein ~es Eisen** (*umg*) a hot potato; **jdn/etw ~ und innig lieben** love sb/sth madly; **~blütig** *a* hot-blooded.

heißen [hī'sən] *unreg vi* be called; (*bedeuten*) mean; **wie ~ Sie?** what's your name?; ... **und wie sie alle ~** ... and the rest of them; **das will schon etwas ~** that's quite something ♦ *vt* command; (*nennen*) name; **jdn willkommen ~** bid sb welcome ♦ *vi unpers* it says; it is said; **das heißt** that is; (*mit anderen Worten*) that is to say.

Heiß- *zW*: **h~ersehnt** *a* longed for; **~hunger** *m* ravenous hunger; **h~laufen** *vir unreg* overheat; **~luft** *f* hot air; **h~umstritten** *a* attr hotly debated; **~wasserbereiter** *m* water heater.

heiter [hī'tər] *a* cheerful; (*Wetter*) bright; **aus ~em Himmel** (*fig*) out of the blue; **H~keit** *f* cheerfulness; (*Belustigung*) amusement.

Heiz- [hīts'] *zW*: **h~bar** *a* heated; (*Raum*) with heating; **leicht h~bar** easily heated; **~decke** *f* electric blanket.

heizen *vt* heat.

Heizer *m* **-s,** - stoker.
Heiz- *zW*: **~körper** *m* radiator; **~öl** *nt* fuel oil; **~sonne** *f* electric heater.
Heizung *f* heating.
Heizungsanlage *f* heating system.
Hektar [hɛktȧr'] *nt od m* **-s, -e** hectare.
hektisch [hɛk'tish] *a* hectic.
Hektoliter [hɛktȯlēː'tər] *m od nt* **-s,** - hectoliter (*US*), hectolitre (*Brit*).
Held [hɛlt] *m* **-en, -en** hero; **~in** *f* heroine.
helfen [hɛl'fən] *unreg vi* help (*jdm* sb, *bei* with); (*nützen*) be of use; **sich** (*dat*) **zu ~ wissen** be resourceful; **er weiß sich** (*dat*) **nicht mehr zu ~** he's at his wits' end ♦ *v unpers*: **es hilft nichts, du mußt ...** it's no use, you'll have to ...
Helfer(in *f*) *m* **-s,** - helper, assistant.
Helfershelfer *m* accomplice.
hell [hɛl] *a* clear; (*Licht, Himmel*) bright; (*Farbe*) light; **~es Bier** ≈ lager; **von etw ~ begeistert sein** be very enthusiastic about sth; **es wird ~** it's getting light; **~blau** *a* light blue; **~blond** *a* ash-blond.
Helle *f* - clearness; brightness.
Heller *m* **-s,** - farthing; **auf ~ und Pfennig** (down) to the last penny.
hellhörig *a* keen of hearing; (*Wand*) poorly soundproofed.
hellicht [hɛl'liçt] *a getrennt* **hell-licht: am ~en Tage** in broad daylight.
Helligkeit *f* clearness; brightness; lightness.
hell- *zW*: **~sehen** *vi*: **~sehen können** be clairvoyant; **H~seher** *m* clairvoyant; **~wach** *a* wide-awake.
Helm [hɛlm] *m* **-(e)s, -e** helmet.
Hemd [hɛmt] *nt* **-(e)s, -en** shirt; (*Unter~*) vest; **~bluse** *f* blouse.
Hemdenknopf *m* shirt button.
hemdsärmelig *a* shirt-sleeved; (*fig umg: salopp*) pally; (*Ausdrucksweise*) casual.
hemmen [hɛ'mən] *vt* check, hold up; **gehemmt sein** be inhibited.
Hemmschuh *m* (*fig*) impediment.
Hemmung *f* check; (*PSYCH*) inhibition; (*Bedenken*) scruple.
hemmungslos *a* unrestrained, without restraint.
Hengst [hɛŋst] *m* **-es, -e** stallion.
Henkel [hɛŋ'kəl] *m* **-s,** - handle; **~krug** *m* jug; **~mann** *m* (*umg: Gefäß*) canteen.
henken [hɛŋ'kən] *vt* hang.
Henker *m* **-s,** - hangman.
Henne [hɛ'nə] *f* **-, -n** hen.
her [hȧːr] *ad* here; (*Zeit*) ago; **von weit ~** from a long way off; **~ damit!** hand it over!
herab [hɛrȧp'] *ad* down(ward(s)); **~hängen** *vi unreg* hang down; **~lassen** *unreg vt* let down ♦ *vr* condescend; **~lassend** *a* condescending; **H~lassung** *f* condescension; **~sehen** *vi unreg* look down (*auf +akk* on); **~setzen** *vt* lower, reduce; (*fig*) belittle, disparage; **zu stark ~gesetzten Preisen** at greatly reduced prices; **H~setzung** *f* reduction; disparagement; **~stürzen** *vi* fall off

(*von etw* sth); (*Felsbrocken*) fall down (*von* from); **~würdigen** *vt* belittle, disparage.
heran [hɛrȧn'] *ad*: **näher ~!** come closer!; **~ zu mir!** come up to me!; **~bilden** *vt* train; **~bringen** *vt unreg* bring up (*an +akk* to); **~fahren** *vi unreg* drive up (*an +akk* to); **~gehen** *vi unreg*: **an etw ~gehen** (*an Problem, Aufgabe*) tackle sth; **~kommen** *vi unreg* (*an +akk*) approach, come near; **er läßt alle Probleme an sich ~kommen** he always adopts a wait-and-see attitude; **~machen** *vr*: **sich an jdn ~machen** make up to sb; (*umg*) approach sb; **~wachsen** *vi unreg* grow up; **H~wachsende(r)** *mf dekl wie a* adolescent; **~winken** *vt* beckon over; (*Taxi*) hail; **~ziehen** *vt unreg* pull nearer; (*aufziehen*) raise; (*ausbilden*) train; (*zu Hilfe holen*) call in; (*Literatur*) consult; **etw zum Vergleich ~ziehen** use sth by way of comparison; **jdn zu etw ~ziehen** call upon sb to help in sth.
herauf [hɛrouf'] *ad* up(ward(s)), up here; **~beschwören** *vt unreg* conjure up, evoke; **~bringen** *vt unreg* bring up; **~ziehen** *unreg vt* draw *od* pull up ♦ *vi* approach; (*Sturm*) gather.
heraus [hɛrous'] *ad* out; outside; from; **nach vorn ~ wohnen** live at the front (of the house); **~ mit der Sprache!** out with it!; **~arbeiten** *vt* work out; **~bekommen** *vt unreg* get out; (*fig*) find *od* figure out; (*Wechselgeld*) get back; **~bringen** *vt unreg* bring out; (*Geheimnis*) elicit; **jdn/etw ganz groß ~bringen** (*umg*) give sb/sth a big build-up; **aus ihm war kein Wort ~zubringen** they couldn't get a single word out of him; **~finden** *vt unreg* find out; **~fordern** *vt* challenge; **H~forderung** *f* challenge; provocation; **~geben** *unreg vt* give up, surrender; (*Geld*) give back; (*Buch*) edit; (*veröffentlichen*) publish ♦ *vi* (*Wechselgeld geben*): **können Sie (mir) ~geben?** can you give me change?; **H~geber** *m* **-s,** - editor; (*Verleger*) publisher; **~gehen** *vi unreg*: **aus sich** (*dat*) **~gehen** come out of one's shell; **~halten** *vr unreg*: **sich aus etw ~halten** keep out of sth; **~hängen** *vti unreg* hang out; **~holen** *vt* get out (*aus* of); **~hören** *vt* (*wahrnehmen*) hear; (*fühlen*) detect (*aus* in); **~kehren** *vt* (*lit*): **den Vorgesetzten ~kehren** act the boss; **~kommen** *vi unreg* come out; **dabei kommt nichts ~** nothing will come of it; **er kam aus dem Staunen nicht ~** he couldn't get over his astonishment; **es kommt auf dasselbe ~** it comes (down) to the same thing; **~nehmen** *vt unreg* take out; **sich** (*dat*) **Freiheiten ~nehmen** take liberties; **Sie nehmen sich zuviel ~** you're going too far; **~putzen** *vt*: **sich ~putzen** get dressed up; **~reden** *vr* talk one's way out of it (*umg*); **~reißen** *vt unreg* tear out; pull out; **~rücken** *vt* (*Geld*) fork out, hand over; **mit etw ~rücken** (*fig*)

come out with sth; ~**rutschen** *vi* slip out; ~**schieben** *vt* (*COMPUT*) scroll; ~**schlagen** *vt unreg* knock out; (*fig*) obtain; ~**sein** *vi unreg*: **aus dem Gröbsten** ~**sein** be over the worst; ~**stellen** *vr* turn out (*als* to be); **das muß sich erst** ~**stellen** that remains to be seen; ~**treten** *vi unreg* come out (*aus* of); ~**wachsen** *vi unreg* grow out (*aus* of); ~**winden** *vr unreg* (*fig*): **sich aus etw** ~**winden** wriggle out of sth; ~**wollen** *vi*: **nicht mit etw** ~**wollen** (*umg*: *sagen wollen*) not want to come out with sth; ~**ziehen** *vt unreg* pull out, extract.

herb [herp] *a* (slightly) bitter, acid; (*Wein*) dry; (*fig*: *schmerzlich*) bitter; (: *streng*) stern, austere.

herbei [herbi'] *ad* (over) here; ~**führen** *vt* bring about; ~**lassen** *vr unreg*: **sich** ~**lassen zu** condescend *od* deign to; ~**schaffen** *vt* procure; ~**sehnen** *vt* long for.

herbemühen [hā:r'bəmü:ən] *vr* take the trouble to come.

Herberge [her'bergə] *f* -, -n shelter; hostel.

Herbergsmutter *f*, **Herbergsvater** *m* warden.

her- [hā:r'] *zW*: ~**bitten** *vt unreg* ask to come (here); ~**bringen** *vt unreg* bring here.

Herbst [herpst] *m* -(e)s, -e fall (*US*), autumn; **im** ~ in the fall (*US*), in autumn; **h**~**lich** *a* autumnal.

Herd [hā:rt] *m* -(e)s, -e stove, cooker; (*fig*, *MED*) focus.

Herde [hā:r'də] *f* -, -n herd; (*Schaf*~) flock.

Herdentrieb *m* (*lit*, *fig pej*) herd instinct.

Herdplatte *f* (*von Elektroherd*) hotplate.

herein [herīn'] *ad* in (here), here; ~! come in!; ~**bitten** *vt unreg* ask in; ~**brechen** *vi unreg* set in; ~**bringen** *vt unreg* bring in; ~**dürfen** *vi unreg* have permission to enter; **H**~**fall** *m* letdown; ~**fallen** *vi unreg* be caught *od* taken in; ~**fallen auf** (+*akk*) fall for; ~**kommen** *vi unreg* come in; ~**lassen** *vt unreg* admit; ~**legen** *vt*: **jdn** ~**legen** take sb in; ~**platzen** *vi* burst in; ~**schneien** *vi* (*umg*) drop in; ~**spazieren** *vi*: ~**spaziert!** come right in!

her- [hā:r'] *zW*: **H**~**fahrt** *f* journey here; ~**fallen** *vi unreg*: ~**fallen über** fall upon; **H**~**gang** *m* course of events, circumstances *pl*; ~**geben** *vt unreg* give, hand (over); **sich zu etw** ~**geben** lend one's name to sth; **das Thema gibt viel/nichts** ~ there's a lot/ nothing to this topic; ~**gebracht** *a*: **in** ~**gebrachter Weise** in the traditional way; ~**gehen** *vi unreg*: **hinter jdm** ~**gehen** follow sb; **es geht hoch** ~ there are a lot of goings-on; ~**haben** *vt unreg* (*umg*): **wo hat er das** ~**?** where did he get that from?; ~**halten** *vt unreg* hold out; ~**halten müssen** (*umg*) have to suffer; ~**hören** *vi* listen; **hör mal** ~! listen here!

Hering [hā:'ring] *m* -s, -e herring; (*Zeltpflock*) (tent) peg.

her- [hā:r'] *zW*: ~**kommen** *vi unreg* come;

komm mal ~! come here!; ~**kömmlich** *a* traditional.

Herkunft *f* -, -künfte origin.

Herkunftsland *nt* (*COMM*) country of origin.

her- [hā:r'] *zW*: ~**laufen** *vi unreg*: ~**laufen hinter** (+*dat*) run after; ~**leiten** *vr* derive; ~**machen** *vr*: **sich** ~**machen über** (+*akk*) set about *od* upon ♦ *vt* (*umg*): **viel** ~**machen** look impressive.

Hermelin [herməlē:n'] *m od nt* -s, -e ermine.

hermetisch [hermā:'tish] *a* hermetic; ~ **ab-geriegelt** completely sealed off.

her- *zW*: ~**nach'** *ad* afterwards; ~'**nehmen** *vt unreg*: **wo soll ich das** ~**nehmen?** where am I supposed to get that from?; ~**nie'der** *ad* down.

Heroin [hāroi:n'] *nt* -s heroin.

heroisch [hārō:'ish] *a* heroic.

Herold [hā:'rolt] *m* -(e)s, -e herald.

Herr [her] *m* -(e)n, -en master; (*Mann*) gentleman; (*adliger*, *REL*) Lord; (*vor Namen*) Mr.; **mein** ~! sir!; **meine** ~**en!** gentlemen!; **Lieber** ~ **A, Sehr geehrter** ~ **A** (*in Brief*) Dear Mr. A; „~**en**" (*Toilette*) "men's room" (*US*), "gentlemen" (*Brit*); **die** ~**en der Schöpfung** (*hum*: *Männer*) the gentlemen.

Herrchen *nt* (*umg*: *von Hund*) master.

Herren- *zW*: ~**bekanntschaft** *f* gentleman friend; ~**bekleidung** *f* menswear; ~**besuch** *m* gentleman visitor *od* visitors; ~**doppel** *nt* men's doubles; ~**einzel** *nt* men's singles; ~**haus** *nt* mansion; **h**~**los** *a* ownerless; ~**magazin** *nt* men's magazine; ~**mensch** *m* member of master race.

Herrgott *m*: ~ **noch mal!** (*umg*) damn it all!

Herrgottsfrühe *f*: **in aller** ~ (*umg*) at the crack of dawn.

herrichten [hā:r'riҫhtən] *vt* prepare.

Herrin *f* mistress.

herrisch *a* domineering.

herrje, herrjemine [heryā:', heryā:'mēnā] *interj* goodness gracious!

Herr- *zW*: **h**~**lich** *a* wonderful, splendid; ~**lichkeit** *f* splendor (*US*), splendour (*Brit*), magnificence; ~**schaft** *f* power, rule; (*Herr und Herrin*) master and mistress; **meine** ~**schaften!** ladies and gentlemen!; ~**schaftsgebaren** *nt* delusions of grandeur *pl*.

herrschen [her'shən] *vi* rule; (*bestehen*) prevail, be; **hier** ~ **ja Zustände!** things are in a pretty state round here!

Herrscher(in *f*) *m* -s, - ruler.

Herrschsucht *f* domineeringness.

her- [hā:r'] *zW*: ~**rühren** *vi* arise, originate; ~**sagen** *vt* recite; ~**sehen** *vi unreg*: **hinter jdm/etw** ~**sehen** follow sb/sth with one's eyes; ~**sein** *vi unreg*: **das ist schon 5 Jahre** ~ that was 5 years ago; **hinter jdm/etw** ~**sein** be after sb/sth; ~**stammen** *vi* descend *od* come from; ~**stellen** *vt* make, manufacture; (*zustandebringen*) establish;

H~steller *m* **-s,** - manufacturer; **H~stellung** *f* manufacture; **H~stellungskosten** *pl* manufacturing costs *pl*; **~tragen** *vt unreg*: **etw hinter jdm ~tragen** carry sth behind sb.

herüber [herü:'bər] *ad* over (here), across.

herum [herōōm'] *ad* about, (a)round; **um etw ~** around sth; **~ärgern** *vr* get annoyed (*mit* with); **~blättern** *vi*: (in einem Buch) **~blättern** browse through a book; **~doktern** *vi* (*umg*) fiddle *od* tinker about; **~drehen** *vt*: **jdm das Wort im Mund ~drehen** twist sb's words; **~drücken** *vr* (*vermeiden*): **sich um etw ~drücken** dodge sth; **~fahren** *vi unreg* travel *od* (mit Auto) drive around; (*sich rasch umdrehen*) spin around; **~führen** *vt* show around; **~gammeln** *vi* (*umg*) bum around; **~gehen** *vi unreg* walk *od* go round (*um etw* sth); walk about; **etw ~gehen lassen** circulate sth; **~hacken** *vi* (*fig umg*): **auf jdm ~hacken** pick on sb; **~irren** *vi* wander about; **~kommen** *vi unreg* (*umg*): **um etw ~kommen** get out of sth; **er ist viel ~gekommen** he has been around a lot; **~kriegen** *vt* bring *od* talk round; **~lungern** *vi* lounge about; (*umg*) hang around; **~quälen** *vr*: **sich mit Rheuma ~quälen** be plagued by rheumatism; **~reißen** *vt unreg* swing around (hard); **~schleppen** *vt*: **etw mit sich ~schleppen** (*Sorge, Problem*) be troubled by sth; (*Krankheit*) have sth; **~sprechen** *vr unreg* get around, be spread; **~stochern** *vi* (*umg*): **im Essen ~stochern** pick at one's food; **~treiben** *vir unreg* drift about; **H~treiber(in** *f*) **-s,** - *m* (*pej*) tramp; **~ziehen** *vir unreg* wander about.

herunter [herōōn'tər] *ad* downward(s), down (there); **~gekommen** *a* run-down; **~handeln** *vt* (*umg*: *Preis*) beat down; **~hängen** *vi unreg* hang down; **~holen** *vt* bring down; **~kommen** *vi unreg* come down; (*fig*) come down in the world; **~leiern** *vt* (*umg*) reel off; **~machen** *vt* take down; (*schimpfen*) abuse, criticize severely; **~putzen** *vt* (*umg*): **jdn ~putzen** dress sb down; **~sein** *vi unreg* (*umg*): **mit den Nerven/der Gesundheit ~sein** be at the end of one's tether/be run-down; **~spielen** *vt* play down; **~wirtschaften** *vt* (*umg*) bring to the brink of ruin.

hervor [herfō:r'] *ad* out, forth; **~brechen** *vi unreg* burst forth, break out; **~bringen** *vt unreg* produce; (*Wort*) utter; **~gehen** *vi unreg* emerge, result; **daraus geht ~, daß ...** from this it follows that ...; **~heben** *vt unreg* stress; (*als Kontrast*) set off; **~ragend** *a* excellent; (*lit*) projecting; **~rufen** *vt unreg* cause; give rise to; **~stechen** *vi unreg* (*lit, fig*) stand out; **~stoßen** *vt unreg* (*Worte*) gasp (out); **~treten** *vi unreg* come out; **~tun** *vr unreg* distinguish o.s.; (*umg*: *sich wichtig tun*) show off (*mit etw* sth).

Herz [herts] *nt* **-ens, -en** heart; (*KARTEN*:

Farbe) hearts *pl*; **mit ganzem ~en** wholeheartedly; **etw auf dem ~en haben** have sth on one's mind; **sich** (*dat*) **etw zu ~en nehmen** take sth to heart; **du sprichst mir aus dem ~en** that's just what I feel; **es liegt mir am ~en** I am very concerned about it; **seinem ~en Luft machen** give vent to one's feelings; **sein ~ an jdn/etw hängen** commit o.s. heart and soul to sb/sth; **ein ~ und eine Seele sein** be the best of friends; **jdn/etw auf ~ und Nieren prüfen** examine sb/sth very thoroughly; **~anfall** *m* heart attack.

herzen *vt* caress, embrace.

Herzenslust *f*: **nach ~** to one's heart's content.

Herz- *zW*: **h~ergreifend** *a*, **h~erweichend** *a* heartrending; **~fehler** *m* heart defect; **h~haft** *a* hearty.

herziehen [hā:r'tsē:ən] *vi*: **über jdn/etw ~** (*umg*) pull sb/sth to pieces (*fig*).

Herz- *zW*: **~infarkt** *m* heart attack; **~klappe** *f* (heart) valve; **~klopfen** *nt* palpitation; **h~krank** *a* suffering from a heart condition; **h~lich** *a* cordial; **h~lichen Glückwunsch** congratulations *pl*; **h~liche Grüße** best wishes ♦ *ad* (*sehr*): **h~lich gern!** with the greatest of pleasure!; **~lichkeit** *f* cordiality; **h~los** *a* heartless; **~losigkeit** *f* heartlessness.

Herzog [her'tsō:k] *m* **-(e)s,** ̈**e** duke; **~in** *f* duchess; **h~lich** *a* ducal; **~tum** *nt* duchy.

Herz- *zW*: **~schlag** *m* heartbeat; (*MED*) heart attack; **~schrittmacher** *m* pacemaker; **h~zerreißend** *a* heartrending.

Hessen [he'sən] *nt* **-s** Hesse.

hessisch *a* Hessian.

heterogen [hātərōgā:n'] *a* heterogeneous.

heterosexuell [hātərōzeksōō'el] *a* heterosexual.

Hetze [he'tsə] *f* (*Eile*) rush.

hetzen *vt* hunt; (*verfolgen*) chase; **jdn/etw auf jdn/etw ~** set sb/sth on sb/sth ♦ *vi* (*eilen*) rush; **~ gegen** stir up feeling against; **~ zu** agitate for.

Hetzerei [hetsərī'] *f* agitation; (*Eile*) rush.

Hetzkampagne [hets'kámpányə] *f* **-, -n** smear campaign.

Heu [hoi] *nt* **-(e)s** hay; **~boden** *m* hayloft.

Heuchelei [hoichəlī'] *f* hypocrisy.

heucheln [hoi'chəln] *vt* pretend, feign ♦ *vi* be hypocritical.

Heuchler(in *f*) [hoichlər(in)] *m* **-s,** - hypocrite; **h~isch** *a* hypocritical.

heuer [hoi'ər] *ad* this year.

Heuer *f* **-, -n** (*NAUT*) pay.

heuern [hoi'ərn] *vt* sign on, hire.

Heu- *zW*: **~gabel** *f* pitchfork; **~haufen** *m* haystack.

heulen [hoi'lən] *vi* howl; cry; **das heulende Elend bekommen** get the blues.

heurig [hoi'rich] *a* this year's.

Heu- *zW*: **~schnupfen** *m* hay fever; **~schrecke** *f* grasshopper; (*in heißen Län-*

dern) locust.

heute [hɔi'tə] *ad* today; ~ **abend/früh** this evening/morning; ~ **morgen** this morning; ~ **in einer Woche** a week today, today week; **von** ~ **auf morgen** (*fig: plötzlich*) overnight, from one day to the next; **das H~** today.

heutig [hɔi'tiçh] *a* today's; **unser ~es Schreiben** (*COMM*) our letter of today('s date).

heutzutage [hɔit'tsoōtāgə] *ad* nowadays.

Hexe [hɛk'sə] *f* -, **-n** witch.

hexen *vi* practise witchcraft; **ich kann doch nicht** ~ I can't work miracles.

Hexen- *zW*: ~**häuschen** *nt* gingerbread house; ~**kessel** *m* (*lit, fig*) cauldron; ~**meister** *m* wizard; ~**schuß** *m* lumbago.

Hexerei [hɛksərī'] *f* witchcraft.

hg. *abk* (= *herausgegeben*) ed.

Hg. *abk* (= *Herausgeber*) ed.

HG *f abk* = **Handelsgesellschaft**.

HGB *nt* - *abk* (= *Handelsgesetzbuch*) *statutes of commercial law.*

hieb [hē:p] *imperf* (*veraltet*) *von* **hauen**.

Hieb *m* **-(e)s, -e** blow; (*Wunde*) cut, gash; (*Stichelei*) cutting remark; ~**e bekommen** get a thrashing.

hieb- und stichfest *a* (*fig*) watertight.

hielt [hē:lt] *imperf von* **halten**.

hier [hē:r] *ad* here; ~ **spricht Dr. Müller** (*TEL*) this is Dr Müller (speaking); **er ist von** ~ he's a local (man).

Hierarchie [hēārárchē:'] *f* -, **-n** hierarchy.

hier- *zW*: ~**auf** *ad* thereupon; (*danach*) after that; ~**aus** *ad*: ~**aus folgt, daß** ... from this it follows that ...; ~**behalten** *vt unreg* keep here; ~**bei** *ad* herewith, enclosed; ~**bleiben** *vi unreg* stay here; ~**durch** *ad* by this means; (*örtlich*) through here; ~**her** *ad* this way, here; ~**hergehören** *vi* belong here; (*fig: relevant sein*) be relevant; ~**lassen** *vt unreg* leave here; ~**mit** *ad* hereby; ~**mit erkläre ich** ... (*form*) I hereby declare ...; ~**nach** *ad* hereafter; ~**von** *ad* about this, hereof; ~**von abgesehen** apart from this; ~**zu** *ad* (*dafür*) for this; (*dazu*) with this; (*außerdem*) in addition to this, moreover; (*zu diesem Punkt*) about this; ~**zulande** *ad* in this country.

hiesig [hē:'ziçh] *a* of this place, local.

hieß [hē:s] *imperf von* **heißen**.

Hi-Fi-Anlage [hī'fēánlāgə] *f* -, **-n** hi-fi set *od* system.

High-Tech-Industrie [hī'tekindoōstrē:'] *f* hi(gh) tech industry.

Hilfe [hil'fə] *f* -, **-n** help; aid; **Erste** ~ first aid; **jdm** ~ **leisten** help sb; ~**!** help!; ~**leistung** *f*: **unterlassene** ~**leistung** (*JUR*) denial of assistance; ~**stellung** *f* (*SPORT, fig*) support.

Hilf- *zW*: **h~los** *a* helpless; ~**losigkeit** *f* helplessness; **h~reich** *a* helpful.

Hilfs- *zW*: ~**aktion** relief action, relief measures *pl*; ~**arbeiter** *m* laborer (*US*), labourer (*Brit*); **h~bedürftig** *a* needy;

h~**bereit** *a* ready to help; ~**kraft** *f* assistant, helper; ~**schule** *f* school for backward children; ~**zeitwort** *nt* auxiliary verb.

hilft [hilft] *3. pers sing präs von* **helfen**.

Himalaja [hēmâ'làyà] *m* **-s: der** ~ the Himalayas *pl*.

Himbeere [him'bā:rə] *f* -, **-n** raspberry.

Himmel [hi'məl] *m* **-s, -** sky; (*REL, liter*) heaven; **um ~s willen** (*umg*) for Heaven's sake; **zwischen ~ und Erde** in midair; **h~angst** *a*: **es ist mir h~angst** I'm scared to death; ~**bett** *nt* four-poster bed; **h~blau** *a* sky-blue; ~**fahrt** *f* Ascension.

Himmelfahrtskommando *nt* (*MIL umg*) suicide squad; (*Unternehmen*) suicide mission.

Himmel- *zW*: ~**reich** *nt* (*REL*) Kingdom of Heaven; **h~schreiend** *a* outrageous.

Himmelsrichtung *f* direction; **die vier ~en** the four points of the compass.

himmelweit *a*: **ein ~er Unterschied** a world of difference.

himmlisch [him'lish] *a* heavenly.

hin [hin] *ad* there; ~ **und her** to and fro; **etw** ~ **und her überlegen** think about sth a lot; ~ **und wieder** (every) now and again; **bis zur Mauer** ~ up to the wall; **Geld ~, Geld her** money or no money; **mein Glück ist** ~ my happiness has gone; **einmal München** ~ **und zurück** a roundtrip ticket to Munich (*US*), a return to Munich (*Brit*); **auf meinen Brief** ~ re my letter; **nichts wie** ~**!** (*umg*) let's go then!; **nach außen** ~ (*fig*) outwardly.

hinab [hinàp'] *ad* down; ~**gehen** *vi unreg* go down; ~**sehen** *vi unreg* look down.

hinarbeiten [hin'àrbītən] *vi*: **auf etw** (*akk*) ~ (*auf Ziel*) work towards sth.

hinauf [hinouf'] *ad* up; ~**arbeiten** *vr* work one's way up; ~**steigen** *vi unreg* climb.

hinaus [hinous'] *ad* out; **hinten/vorn** ~ at the back/front; **darüber** ~ over and above this; **auf Jahre** ~ for years to come; ~**befördern** *vt* kick *od* throw out; ~**führen** *vi*: **über etw** (*akk*) ~**führen** (*lit, fig*) go beyond sth; ~**gehen** *vi unreg* go out; ~**gehen über** (+*akk*) exceed; ~**laufen** *vi unreg* run out; ~**laufen auf** (+*akk*) come to, amount to; ~**schieben** *vt unreg* put off, postpone; ~**schießen** *vi unreg*: **über das Ziel** ~**schießen** (*fig*) overshoot the mark; ~**wachsen** *vi unreg*: **er wuchs über sich selbst** ~ he surpassed himself; ~**werfen** *vt unreg* throw out; ~**wollen** *vi* want to go out; **hoch** ~**wollen** aim high; ~**wollen auf** (+*akk*) drive at, get at; ~**ziehen** *unreg vt* draw out ♦ *vr* be protracted; ~**zögern** *vt* delay, put off ♦ *vr* be delayed, be put off.

hin- [hin'] *zW*: ~**bekommen** *vt unreg* (*umg*): **das hast du gut ~bekommen** you've made a good job of it; ~**blättern** *vt* (*umg*: *Geld*) fork out.

Hinblick [hin'blik] *m*: **in** *od* **im** ~ **auf** (+*akk*) in view of.

hinderlich [hin'dərliçh] *a* awkward; **jds Karriere** (*dat*) ~ **sein** be a hindrance to sb's career.

hindern *vt* hinder, hamper; **jdn an etw** (*dat*) ~ prevent sb from doing sth.

Hindernis *nt* **-ses, -se** obstacle; **~lauf** *m*, **~rennen** *nt* steeplechase.

Hinderungsgrund *m* obstacle.

hindeuten [hin'dɔitən] *vi* point (*auf* +*akk* to).

hindurch [hindōōrçh'] *ad* through; across; (*zeitlich*) over.

hindürfen [hindür'fən] *vi unreg* be allowed to go (*zu* to).

hinein [hinīn'] *ad* in; **bis tief in die Nacht** ~ well into the night; **~fallen** *vi unreg* fall in; **~fallen in** (+*akk*) fall into; **~finden** *vr unreg* (*fig: sich vertraut machen*) find one's feet; (*sich abfinden*) come to terms with it; **~gehen** *vi unreg* go in; **~gehen in** (+*akk*) go into, enter; **~geraten** *vi unreg:* **~geraten in** (+*akk*) get into; **~knien** *vr* (*fig umg*): **sich ~knien** (*akk*) **~knien** get into sth; **~lesen** *vt unreg:* **etw in etw** (*akk*) **~lesen** read sth into sth; **~passen** *vi* fit in; **~passen in** (+*akk*) fit into; **~prügeln** *vt:* **etw in jdn ~prügeln** cudgel sth into sb; **~reden** *vi:* **jdm ~reden** interfere in sb's affairs; **~stecken** *vt:* **Geld/Arbeit in etw** (*akk*) **~stecken** put money/some work into sth; **~steigern** *vr* get worked up; **~versetzen** *vr:* **sich ~versetzen in** (+*akk*) put o.s. in the position of.

hin- [hin'] *zW:* **~fahren** *unreg vi* go; drive ◊ *vt* take; drive; **H~fahrt** *f* journey there; **~fallen** *vi unreg* fall down; **~fällig** *a* (*Regel etc*) unnecessary; **~fliegen** *vi unreg* fly there; (*umg*: *~fallen*) fall down *od* over.

hing [hing] *imperf von* **hängen**.

hin- [hin'] *zW:* **H~gabe** *f* devotion; **mit H~gabe tanzen/singen** *etc* (*fig*) dance/sing *etc* with abandon; **~geben** *vr unreg* +*dat* give o.s. up to, devote o.s. to.

hingebungsvoll [hin'gā:bōōngsfol] *ad* (*begeistert*) with abandon; (*lauschen*) raptly.

hingegen [hingā:'gən] *kj* however.

hin- [hin'] *zW:* **~gehen** *vi unreg* go; (*Zeit*) pass; **gehst du auch ~?** are you going too?; **~gerissen** *a:* **~gerissen sein** be enraptured; **ich bin ganz ~ und hergerissen** that's absolutely great (*ironisch*); **~halten** *vt unreg* hold out; (*warten lassen*) put off, stall; **H~haltetaktik** *f* stalling *od* delaying tactics *pl.*

hinhauen [hin'houən] *vi unreg* (*umg:* *klappen*) work; (*ausreichen*) do.

hinhören [hin'hœrən] *vi* listen.

hinken [hing'kən] *vi* limp; (*Vergleich*) be unconvincing.

hin- [hin'] *zW:* **~kommen** *vi unreg* (*umg:* *auskommen*) manage; (: *ausreichen, stimmen*) be right; **~länglich** *a* adequate ◊ *ad* adequately; **~legen** *vt* put down ◊ *vr* lie down; **sich der Länge nach ~legen** (*umg*)

fall flat; **~nehmen** *vt unreg* (*fig*) put up with, take; **~reichen** *vi* be adequate ◊ *vt:* **jdm etw ~reichen** hand sb sth; **H~reise** *f* journey out; **~reißen** *vt unreg* carry away, enrapture; **sich ~reißen lassen, etw zu tun** get carried away and do sth; **~reißend** *a* (*Landschaft, Anblick*) enchanting; (*Schönheit, Mensch*) captivating; **~richten** *vt* execute; **H~richtung** *f* execution; **~sehen** *vi unreg:* **bei genauerem H~sehen** on closer inspection.

hinsein [hin'zīn] *vi unreg* (*umg: kaputt sein*) have had it; (*Ruhe*) be gone.

hin- [hin'] *zW:* **~setzen** *vr* sit down; **H~sicht** *f:* **in mancher** *od* **gewisser H~sicht** in some *od* many respects *od* ways; **~sichtlich** *präp* +*gen* with regard to; **~sollen** *vi* (*umg*): **wo soll ich/das Buch ~?** where do I/does the book go?; **H~spiel** *nt* (*SPORT*) first round; **~stellen** *vt* put (down) ◊ *vr* place o.s.

hintanstellen [hintän'shtelən] *vt* (*fig*) ignore.

hinten [hin'tən] *ad* at the back; behind; ~ **und vorn** (*fig: betrügen*) left, right and center; **das reicht ~ und vorn nicht** that's nowhere near enough; **~dran** *ad* (*umg*) at the back; **~herum** *ad* round the back; (*fig*) secretly.

hinter [hin'tər] *präp* +*dat od akk* behind; (*nach*) after; ~ **jdm hersein** be after sb; ~ **die Wahrheit kommen** get to the truth; **sich** ~ **jdn stellen** (*fig*) support sb; **etw** ~ **sich** (*dat*) **haben** (*zurückgelegt haben*) have got through sth; **sie hat viel** ~ **sich** she has been through a lot; **H~achse** *f* rear axle; **H~bänkler** *m* **-s, -** (*POL pej*) backbencher; **H~bein** *nt* hind leg; **sich auf die H~beine stellen** get tough; (*fig*) *wie* a surviving relative; **~drein'** *ad* afterwards; **~einan'der** *ad* one after the other; **zwei Tage ~einander** two days running.

hintere(r, s) *a* rear, back.

hinter- *zW:* **~fotzig** *a* (*umg*) underhanded; **~fra'gen** *vt untr* analyze; **H~gedanke** *m* ulterior motive; **~ge'hen** *vt unreg* deceive; **H~grund** *m* background; **~gründig** *a* cryptic, enigmatic; **H~grundprogramm** *nt* (*COMPUT*) background program; **H~halt** *m* ambush; **etw im H~halt haben** have sth in reserve; **~hältig** *a* underhand, sneaky; **~her'** *ad* afterwards, after; **~her'sein** *vi unreg:* **er ist ~her, daß** ... (*fig*) he sees to it that ...; **H~hof** *m* backyard; **H~kopf** *m* back of one's head; **H~land** *nt* hinterland; **~las'sen** *vt unreg* leave; **H~las'senschaft** *f* (*testator's*) estate; **~le'gen** *vt* deposit; **H~le'gungsstelle** *f* depository; **H~list** *f* cunning, trickery; (*Handlung*) trick, dodge; **~listig** *a* cunning, crafty; **H~mann** *m, pl* **-männer** person behind; **die H~männer des Skandals** the men behind the scandal.

Hintern [hin'tərn] *m* **-s, -** (*umg*): **jdm den** ~ **versohlen** smack sb's bottom.

hinter- *zW:* **H~rad** *nt* back wheel; **H~radantrieb** *m* (*AUT*) rear wheel drive;

~**rücks** *ad* from behind; **H~teil** *nt* behind; **H~treffen** *nt*: **ins H~treffen kommen** lose ground; ~**trei'ben** *vt unreg* prevent, frustrate; **H~treppe** *f* back stairs *pl*; **H~tür** *f* back door; (*fig: Ausweg*) escape, loophole; **H~wäldler** *m* -s, - (*umg*) backwoodsman, hillbilly (*bes US*); ~**zie'hen** *vt unreg* (*Steuern*) evade (paying).

hintun [hin'tōō:n] *vt unreg* (*umg*): **ich weiß nicht, wo ich ihn ~ soll** (*fig*) I can't (quite) place him.

hinüber [hinü:'bər] *ad* across, over; ~**gehen** *vi unreg* go over *od* across.

hinunter [hinōōn'tər] *ad* down; ~**bringen** *vt unreg* take down; ~**schlucken** *vt* (*lit, fig*) swallow; ~**spülen** *vt* flush away; (*Essen, Tablette*) wash down; (*fig: Ärger*) soothe; ~**steigen** *vi unreg* descend.

Hinweg [hin'vā:k] *m* journey out.

hinweg- [hinvek'] *zW*: ~**gehen** *vi unreg*: **über etw** (*akk*) ~**gehen** (*fig*) pass over sth; ~**helfen** *vi unreg*: **jdm über etw** (*akk*) ~**helfen** help sb to get over sth; ~**kommen** *vi unreg*: (*fig*) **über etw** (*akk*) ~**kommen** get over sth; ~**sehen** *vi unreg*: **darüber** ~**sehen, daß** ... overlook the fact that ...; ~**setzen** *vr*: **sich** ~**setzen über** (+*akk*) disregard.

Hinweis [hin'vīs] *m* -es, -e (*Andeutung*) hint; (*Anweisung*) instruction; (*Verweis*) reference; **sachdienliche** ~**e** relevant information.

hinweisen *vi unreg* (*auf* +*akk*) (*anzeigen*) point to; (*sagen*) point out, refer to.

Hinweisschild *nt*, **Hinweistafel** *f* sign.

hin- *zW*: ~**werfen** *vt unreg* throw down; **eine** ~**geworfene Bemerkung** a casual remark; ~**wirken** *vi*: **auf etw** (*akk*) ~**wirken** work towards sth.

Hinz [hints] *m*: ~ **und Kunz** (*umg*) every Tom, Dick and Harry.

hin- *zW*: ~**ziehen** *vr unreg* (*fig*) drag on; ~**zielen** *vi* aim (*auf* +*akk* at).

hinzu [hintsōō:'] *ad* in addition; ~**fügen** *vt* add; **H~fügung** *f*: **unter H~fügung von etw** (*form*) by adding sth; ~**kommen** *vi unreg*: **es kommt noch ~, daß** ... there is also the fact that ...; ~**ziehen** *vt unreg* consult.

Hiobsbotschaft [hē:'opsbō:tshäft] *f* bad news.

Hirn [hirn] *nt* -(e)s, -e brain(s); ~**gespinst** *nt* -(e)s, -e fantasy; ~**hautentzündung** *f* (*MED*) meningitis; **h~verbrannt** *a* half-baked, crazy; (*umg*) hare-brained.

Hirsch [hirsh] *m* -(e)s, -e stag.

Hirse [hir'zə] *f* -, -n millet.

Hirt [hirt] *m* -en, -en herdsman; (*Schaf~, fig*) shepherd.

hissen [hi'sən] *vt* hoist.

Historiker [histō:'rēkər] *m* -s, - historian.

historisch [histō:'rish] *a* historical.

Hit [hit] *m* -s, -s (*MUS, fig umg*) hit; ~**parade** [hit'párádə] *f* hit parade.

Hitze [hi'tsə] *f* - heat; **h~beständig** *a* heat-

resistant; **h~frei** *a*: **h~frei haben** *have time off from school on account of excessively hot weather*; ~**welle** *f* heatwave.

hitzig *a* hot-tempered; (*Debatte*) heated.

Hitz- *zW*: ~**kopf** *m* hothead; **h~köpfig** *a* fiery, hotheaded; ~**schlag** *m* heatstroke.

hl. *abk* = **heilig**.

H-Milch [hä'milℓĥ] *f* long-life milk, UHT milk.

HNO-Arzt *m* ear, nose and throat specialist.

hob [hō:p] *imperf von* **heben**.

Hobby [ho'bē] *nt* -s, -s hobby.

Hobel [hō:'bəl] *m* -s, - plane; ~**bank** *f* carpenter's bench.

hobeln *vti* plane.

Hobelspäne *pl* wood shavings *pl*.

hoch [hō:ℓĥ] *a*, *attr* **hohe(r, s)** high; **das ist mir zu ~** (*umg*) that's above my head; **ein hohes Tier** (*umg*) a big fish ♦ *ad*: **wenn es ~ kommt** (*umg*) at (the) most, at the outside; **es ging ~ her** (*umg*) we had a whale of a time; ~ **und heilig versprechen** promise faithfully.

Hoch *nt* -s, -s (*Ruf*) cheer; (*MET*) anticyclone.

hoch- *zW*: ~**achten** *vt* respect; **H~achtung** *f* respect, esteem; **mit vorzüglicher H~achtung** (*form: Briefschluß*) Yours faithfully; ~**achtungsvoll** *ad* yours faithfully; ~**aktuell** *a* highly topical; **H~amt** *nt* high mass; ~**arbeiten** *vr* work one's way up; ~**begabt** *a* extremely gifted; ~**betagt** *a* very old, aged; **H~betrieb** *m* intense activity; (*COMM*) peak time; **H~betrieb haben** be at one's *od* its busiest; ~**bringen** *vt unreg* bring up; **H~burg** *f* stronghold; **H~deutsch** *nt* High German; ~**dotiert** *a* highly paid; **H~druck** *m* high pressure; **H~ebene** *f* plateau; ~**entwickelt** *a attr* (*Kultur, Land*) highly developed; (*Geräte, Methoden*) sophisticated; ~**erfreut** *a* highly delighted; ~**fahren** *vi unreg* (*erschreckt*) jump; ~**fliegend** *a* ambitious; (*fig*) high-flown; **H~form** *f* top form; **H~gebirge** *nt* high mountains *pl*; **H~gefühl** *nt* elation; ~**gehen** *vi unreg* (*umg: explodieren*) blow up; (*Bombe*) go off; **H~genuß** *m* great *od* special treat; (*großes Vergnügen*) great pleasure; ~**geschlossen** *a* (*Kleid etc*) high-necked; ~**gestellt** *a attr* (*fig: Persönlichkeit*) high-ranking.

Hochglanz *m* high polish; (*PHOT*) gloss.

hoch- *zW*: ~**gradig** *a* intense, extreme; ~**halten** *vt unreg* hold up; (*fig*) uphold, cherish; **H~haus** *nt* multi-story (*US*) *od* -storey (*Brit*) building; ~**heben** *vt unreg* lift (up); ~**kant** *ad*: **jdn** ~**kant hinauswerfen** (*fig umg*) chuck sb out on his *od* her ear; **H~konjunktur** *f* boom; ~**krempeln** *vt* roll up; **H~land** *nt* highlands *pl*; ~**leben** *vi*: **jdn** ~**leben lassen** give sb three cheers; **H~leistungssport** *m* competitive sport; ~**modern** *a* very modern, ultra-modern; **H~mut** *m* pride; ~**mütig** *a* proud, haughty; ~**näsig** *a* stuck-up, snooty; **H~ofen** *m* blast

furnace; ~**prozentig** *a* (*Alkohol*) strong;
H~rechnung *f* projected result; **H~saison** *f*
high season; **H~schätzung** *f* high esteem.
Hochschul- *zW*: ~**abschluß** *m* degree;
~**bildung** *f* higher education.
Hochschule *f* college; (*Universität*) university.
Hochschulreife *f*: **er hat (die)** ~ he's
graduated from high school.
hoch- *zW*: ~**schwanger** *a* pregnant, well
advanced in pregnancy; **H~seefischerei** *f*
deep-sea fishing; **H~sitz** *m* (*Jagd*) (raised)
blind (*US*) *od* hide (*Brit*); **H~sommer** *m*
middle of summer; **H~spannung** *f* high tension; **H~sprache** *f* standard language;
~**spielen** *vt* (*fig*) blow up; ~**springen** *vi* *unreg* jump up; **H~sprung** *m* high jump.
höchst [hœçhst] *ad* highly, extremely.
Hochstapler [hō:kh'shtâplər] *m* **-s**, - swindler.
höchstens *ad* at the most.
höchste(r, s) *a* highest; (*äußerste*) extreme;
die ~ **Instanz** (*JUR*) the supreme court of
appeal.
Höchstgeschwindigkeit *f* maximum speed.
Höchstgew. *abk* (= *Höchstgewicht*) max.
weight.
Höchstgrenze *f* upper limit.
Hochstimmung *f* high spirits *pl*.
Höchst- *zW*: ~**leistung** *f* best performance;
(*bei Produktion*) maximum output;
h~persönlich *ad* personally, in person;
~**preis** *m* maximum price; ~**stand** *m* peak;
h~wahrscheinlich *ad* most probably.
Hoch- *zW*: ~**technologie** *f* high technology;
h~technologisch *a* high-tech; ~**tempera-
tur-Reaktor** *m* high-temperature reactor;
~**tour** *f*: **auf** ~**touren laufen** *od* **arbeiten** be
working flat out; **h~trabend** *a* pompous; ~**-
und Tiefbau** *m* structural and civil engineering; ~**verrat** *m* high treason; ~**wasser** *nt*
high water; (*Überschwemmung*) floods *pl*;
h~wertig *a* high-class, first-rate; ~**würden**
m Reverend; ~**zahl** *f* (*MATH*) exponent.
Hochzeit [hoxh'tsīt] *f* -, -**en** wedding; **man
kann nicht auf zwei** ~**en tanzen** (*Sprichwort*) you can't have your cake and eat it.
Hochzeits- *zW*: ~**reise** *f* honeymoon; ~**tag**
m wedding day; (*Jahrestag*) wedding anniversary.
Hocke [ho'kə] *f* -, -**n** squatting position; (*beim
Turnen*) squat vault; (*beim Skilaufen*)
crouch.
hocken [ho'kən] *vir* squat, crouch.
Hocker *m* -**s**, - stool.
Höcker [hœ'kər] *m* -**s**, - hump.
Hode [hō:'də] *m* -**n**, -**n** testicle.
Hodensack *m* scrotum.
Hof [hō:f] *m* -**(e)s**, ⁼e (*Hinter*~) yard;
(*Bauern*~) farm; (*Königs*~) court; **einem
Mädchen den** ~ **machen** (*veraltet*) court a
girl.
hoffen [ho'fən] *vi* hope (*auf* +*akk* for).
hoffentlich *ad* I hope, hopefully.
Hoffnung [hof'nōōng] *f* hope; **jdm** ~**en ma-**

chen raise sb's hopes; **sich** (*dat*) ~**en machen** have hopes; **sich** (*dat*) **keine** ~**en machen** not hold out any hope(s).
Hoffnungs- *zW*: **h~los** *a* hopeless;
~**losigkeit** *f* hopelessness; ~**schimmer** *m*
glimmer of hope; **h~voll** *a* hopeful.
höflich [hœf'liçh] *a* courteous, polite; **H~keit** *f*
courtesy, politeness.
Höhe [hœ'ə] *f* -, -**n** height; (*An*~) hill; **nicht
auf der** ~ **sein** (*fig umg*) feel below par; **ein
Scheck in** ~ **von ...** a check for the amount
of ...; **das ist doch die** ~ (*fig umg*) that's
the limit; **er geht immer gleich in die** ~
(*umg*) he always flares up; **auf der** ~ **der
Zeit sein** be in tune with the state-of-the-art.
Hoheit [hō:'hīt] *f* (*POL*) sovereignty; (*Titel*)
Highness.
Hoheits- *zW*: ~**gebiet** *nt* sovereign territory;
~**gewalt** *f* (national) jurisdiction;
~**gewässer** *nt* territorial waters *pl*;
~**zeichen** *nt* national emblem.
Höhen- [hœ'ən] *zW*: ~**angabe** *f* altitude reading; (*auf Karte*) height marking; ~**flug** *m*:
geistiger ~**flug** intellectual flight; ~**lage** *f*
altitude; ~**luft** *f* mountain air; ~**messer** *m*
altimeter; ~**sonne** *f* (*Lampe*) sun lamp;
~**unterschied** *m* difference in altitude;
~**zug** *m* mountain chain.
Höhepunkt *m* climax.
höher *a*, *ad* higher.
hohe(r, s) [hō:'ə(r, z)] *a* siehe **hoch.**
hohl [hō:l] *a* hollow; (*umg*: *dumm*) hollow(-
headed).
Höhle [hœ'lə] *f* -, -**n** cave, hole; (*Mund*~)
cavity; (*fig, ZOOL*) den.
Hohl- *zW*: ~**heit** *f* hollowness; ~**kreuz** *nt*
(*MED*) hollow back; ~**maß** *nt* measure of
volume; ~**raum** *m* hollow space; (*Gebäude
auch*) cavity; ~**saum** *m* hemstitch;
~**spiegel** *m* concave mirror.
Hohn [hō:n] *m* -**(e)s** scorn; **das ist der reinste** ~ it's sheer mockery.
höhnen [hœ'nən] *vt* taunt, scoff at.
höhnisch *a* scornful, taunting.
Hokuspokus [hō:kōōspō:'kōōs] *m* - (*Zau-
berformel*) hey presto; (*fig*: *Täuschung*)
hocus-pocus.
hold [holt] *a* charming, sweet.
holen [hō:'lən] *vt* get, fetch; (*Atem*) take;
jdn/etw ~ **lassen** send for sb/sth; **sich** (*dat*)
eine Erkältung ~ catch a cold.
Hölle [hœ'lə] *f* -, -**n** hell; **ich werde ihm die**
~ **heiß machen** (*umg*) I'll give him hell.
Höllen- *zW*: ~**angst** *f*: **eine** ~**angst haben**
be scared to death; ~**lärm** *m* infernal noise
(*umg*).
höllisch [hœ'lish] *a* hellish, infernal.
holperig [hol'pəriçh] *a* rough, bumpy.
holpern [hol'pərn] *vi* jolt.
Holunder [hōlōōn'dər] *m* -**s**, - elder.
Holz [holts] *nt* -**es**, ⁼er wood; **aus** ~ made of
wood, wooden; **aus einem anderen/
demselben** ~ **geschnitzt sein** (*fig*) be cast
in a different/the same mold; (*Kegel*): **gut**

~! have a good game!; **~bläser** m woodwind player.

hölzern [hœl'tsərn] a (lit, fig) wooden.

Holz- zW: **~fäller** m **-s,** - lumberjack, woodcutter; **~faserplatte** f (wood) fiberboard (US) od fibreboard (Brit); **h~frei** a (Papier) wood-free; **~hammermentalität** f sledgehammer mentality.

holzig a woody.

Holz- zW: **~klotz** m wooden block; **~kohle** f charcoal; **~kopf** m (fig umg) blockhead; **~scheit** nt log; **~schuh** m clog; **~weg** m (fig) wrong track; **~wolle** f excelsior ® (US), fine wood shavings pl; **~wurm** m woodworm.

Homecomputer [hōōōm'kompyōō:'tər] m **-s,** - home computer.

homogen [hōmōgā:n'] a homogenous.

Homöopath [hōmœōpåt'] m **-en,** -en homeopath (US), homoeopath (Brit).

homosexuell [hōmōzeksōōel'] a homosexual.

Hongkong [hongkong'] nt **-s** Hong Kong.

Honig [hō:'niċh] m **-s,** -e honey; **~lecken** nt (fig): **das ist kein ~lecken** it's no picnic; **~wabe** f honeycomb.

Honorar [hōnōrår'] nt **-s,** -e fee.

Honoratioren [hōnōråtsēō:'rən] pl dignitaries pl.

honorieren [hōnōrē:'rən] vt remunerate; (Scheck) honor (US), honour (Brit).

Hopfen [ho'pfən] m **-s,** - hops pl; **bei ihm ist ~ und Malz verloren** (umg) he's a total od dead loss.

hoppla [ho'plå] interj whoops.

hopsen [hop'sən] vi hop.

Hörapparat m hearing aid.

hörbar a audible.

horch [horċh] interj listen.

horchen vi listen; (pej) eavesdrop.

Horcher m **-s,** - listener; eavesdropper.

Horde [hor'də] f **-,** -n horde.

hören [hœ'rən] vti hear; **auf jdn/etw ~** listen to sb/sth; **ich lasse von mir ~** I'll be in touch; **etwas/nichts von sich ~ lassen** get/not get in touch; **H~ nt: es verging ihm H~ und Sehen** (umg) he didn't know whether he was coming or going; **H~sagen** nt: **vom H~sagen** from hearsay.

Hörer m **-s,** - hearer; (RAD) listener; (UNIV) student; (Telefon~) receiver.

Hör- zW: **~funk** m radio; **~gerät** nt hearing aid.

hörig [hœ'riċh] a: **sie ist ihm (sexuell) ~** he has (sexual) power over her.

Horizont [hōrētsont'] m **-(e)s,** -e horizon; **das geht über meinen ~** (fig) that is beyond me.

horizontal [hōrētsotål'] a horizontal.

Hormon [hormō:n'] nt **-s,** -e hormone.

Hörmuschel f (TEL) earpiece.

Horn [horn] nt **-(e)s,** ̈er horn; **ins gleiche** od **in jds ~ blasen** chime in; **sich** (dat) **die ~er abstoßen** (umg) sow one's wild oats; **~brille** f horn-rimmed spectacles pl.

Hörnchen [hœrn'ċhən] nt (Gebäck) croissant.

Hornhaut f horny skin.

Hornisse [horni'sə] f **-,** -n hornet.

Hornochs(e) [horn'oksə] m (fig umg) blockhead, idiot.

Horoskop [hōrōskō:p'] nt **-s,** -e horoscope.

Hör- zW: **~rohr** nt ear trumpet; (MED) stethoscope; **~saal** m lecture room; **~spiel** nt radio play.

Horst [horst] m **-(e)s,** -e (Nest) nest; (Adler~) aerie (US), eyrie (Brit).

Hort [hort] m **-(e)s,** -e hoard; (SCH) nursery school; **h~en** vt hoard.

Hörweite f: **in/außer ~** within/out of hearing od earshot.

Hose [hō:'zə] f **-,** -n pants pl (US), trousers pl (Brit); **in die ~ gehen** (umg) be a complete flop.

Hosen- zW: **~anzug** pantsuit; **~boden** m: **sich auf den ~boden setzen** (umg) get stuck in; **~rock** m culottes pl; **~tasche** f pants pocket; **~träger** m suspenders pl (US), braces pl (Brit).

Hostie [hos'tēə] f (REL) host.

Hotel [hōtel'] nt **-s,** -e hotel; **~fach** nt hotel management; **~ garni** nt bed and breakfast hotel.

Hotelier [hōtelēā:'] m **-s,** -s hotelkeeper, hotelier.

Hptst. abk = **Hauptstadt.**

Hr. abk (= Herr) Mr.

HR abk (= Hessischer Rundfunk) Hessen Radio.

hrsg. abk (= herausgegeben) ed.

Hrsg. abk (= Herausgeber) ed.

Hub [hōō:p] m **-(e)s,** ̈e lift; (TECH) stroke.

hüben [hü:'bən] ad on this side, over here; **~ und drüben** on both sides.

Hubraum m (AUT) cubic capacity.

hübsch [hüpsh] a pretty, nice; **immer ~ langsam!** (umg) nice and easy.

Hubschrauber m **-s,** - helicopter.

Hucke [hōō'kə] f **-,** -n: **jdm die ~ vollhauen** (umg) give sb a good hiding.

huckepack [hōō'kəpåk] ad piggy-back, pick-a-back.

hudeln [hōō:'dəln] vi be sloppy.

Huf [hōō:f] m **-(e)s,** -e hoof; **~eisen** nt horseshoe; **~nagel** m horseshoe nail.

Hüfte [hüf'tə] f **-,** -n hip.

Hüftgürtel m, **Hüfthalter** m girdle.

Huftier nt hoofed animal.

Hügel [hü:'gəl] m **-s,** - hill.

hug(e)lig a hilly.

Huhn [hōō:n] nt **-(e)s,** ̈er hen; (KOCH) chicken; **da lachen ja die ~er** (umg) it's enough to make a cat laugh; **sie sah aus wie ein gerupftes ~** (umg) she looked as though she'd been dragged through a hedge backwards.

Hühnchen [hü:n'ċhən] nt young chicken; **mit jdm ein ~ zu rupfen haben** (umg) have a bone to pick with sb.

Hühner- [hü:'nər] zW: **~auge** nt corn;

~**brühe** f chicken broth; ~**klein** nt (KOCH) chicken trimmings pl.
Huld [hŏŏlt] f - favor (US), favour (Brit).
huldigen [hŏŏl'digǝn] vi pay homage (jdm to sb).
Huldigung f homage.
Hülle [hü'lǝ] f -, -n cover(ing); (Cellophan~) wrapping; **in ~ und Fülle** galore; **die ~n fallen lassen** (fig) strip off.
hüllen vt cover; wrap (in +akk with).
Hülse [hül'zǝ] f -, -n husk, shell.
Hülsenfrucht f pulse.
human [hŏŏmán'] a humane.
humanistisch [hŏŏmánis'tish] a: ~**es Gymnasium** high school with bias on Latin and Greek.
humanitär [hŏŏmánēte:r'] a humanitarian.
Humanität f humanity.
Humanmedizin f (human) medicine.
Hummel [hŏŏ'mǝl] f -, -n bumblebee.
Hummer [hŏŏ'mǝr] m -s, - lobster.
Humor [hŏŏmō:r'] m -s, -e humor (US), humour (Brit); ~ **haben** have a sense of humor; ~**ist(in** f) [-rist'(in)] m humorist; **h~istisch** a, **h~voll** a humorous.
humpeln [hŏŏm'pǝln] vi hobble.
Humpen [hŏŏm'pǝn] m -s, - tankard.
Humus [hŏŏ:'mŏŏs] m -.
Hund [hŏŏnt] m -(e)s, -e dog; **auf den ~ kommen** (fig umg) od **vor die ~e gehen** (umg) go to the dogs; ~**e, die bellen, beißen nicht** (Sprichwort) empty vessels make most noise (Sprichwort); **er ist bekannt wie ein bunter ~** (umg) everybody knows him.
Hunde- zW: **h~elend** a (umg): **mir ist h~elend** I feel lousy; ~**hütte** f (dog) kennel; ~**kuchen** m dog biscuit; ~**marke** f dog tag; **h~müde** a (umg) dog-tired.
hundert [hŏŏn'dǝrt] num hundred; **H~** nt -s, -e hundred; **H~e von Menschen** hundreds of people.
Hunderter m -s, - hundred; (umg: Geldschein) hundred.
hundert- zW: **H~jahr'feier** f centenary; **H~meterlauf** m (SPORT): **der/ein H~meterlauf** the/a hundred meters sing; ~**prozentig** a, ad one hundred per cent.
hundertste(r, s) a hundredth; **von H~n ins Tausendste kommen** (fig) get carried away.
Hunde- zW: ~**steuer** f dog license fee; ~**wetter** nt (umg) filthy weather.
Hündin [hün'din] f bitch.
Hüne [hü:'nǝ] m -n, -n: **ein ~ von Mensch** a giant of a man.
Hünengrab nt megalithic tomb.
Hunger [hŏŏ'ngǝr] m -s hunger; ~ **haben** be hungry; **ich sterbe vor ~** (umg) I'm starving; ~**lohn** m starvation wages pl.
hungern vi starve.
Hungersnot f famine.
Hungerstreik m hunger strike.
Hungertuch nt: **am ~ nagen** (fig) be starving.
hungrig [hŏŏng'riċh] a hungry.

Hunsrück [hŏŏns'rük] m Hunsruck (Mountains).
Hupe [hŏŏ:'pǝ] f -, -n horn.
hupen vi hoot, sound one's horn.
hüpfen [hüp'fǝn], **hupfen** [hŏŏ:p'fǝn] vi hop, jump; **das ist gehupft wie gesprungen** (umg) it's six of one and half a dozen of the other.
Hupkonzert nt (umg) hooting (of car horns).
Hürde [hür'dǝ] f -, -n hurdle; (für Schafe) pen.
Hürdenlauf m hurdling.
Hure [hŏŏ:'rǝ] f -, -n whore.
Hurenbock m (pej) bastard (!), son of a bitch (!).
hurra [hŏŏrà'] interj hurray, hurrah.
hurtig [hŏŏr'tiċh] a, ad brisk(ly), quick(ly).
huschen [hŏŏ'shǝn] vi flit, scurry.
Husten [hŏŏ:s'tǝn] m -s cough; **h~** vi cough; **auf etw** (akk) **h~** (umg) not give a damn for sth; ~**anfall** m coughing fit; ~**bonbon** m od nt cough drop; ~**saft** m cough syrup.
Hut [hŏŏ:t] m -(e)s, ̈-e hat; **unter einen ~ bringen** (umg) reconcile; (Termine etc) fit in ♦ f - care; **auf der ~ sein** be on one's guard.
hüten [hü:'tǝn] vt guard; **das Bett/Haus ~** stay in bed/indoors ♦ vr watch out; **sich ~, zu** take care not to; **sich ~ vor** beware of; **ich werde mich ~!** not likely!
Hutschnur f: **das geht mir über die ~** (umg) that's going too far.
Hütte [hü'tǝ] f -, -n hut; cottage; (Eisen~) forge; (umg: Wohnung) pad; (TECH: Hüttenwerk) iron and steel works.
Hütten- zW: ~**industrie** f iron and steel industry; ~**werk** nt iron and steel works.
hutzelig [hŏŏ'tsǝliċh] a shrivelled.
Hyäne [hüe:'nǝ] f -, -n hyena.
Hyazinthe [hüätsin'tǝ] f -, -n hyacinth.
Hydrant [hüdrànt'] m hydrant.
hydraulisch [hüdrou'lish] a hydraulic.
Hydrierung [hüdrē:'rŏŏng] f hydrogenation.
Hygiene [hügēä:'nǝ] f - hygiene.
hygienisch [hügēä:'nish] a hygienic.
Hymne [hüm'nǝ] f -, -n hymn, anthem.
hyper- [hü'per] präf hyper-.
Hypnose [hüpnō:'zǝ] f -, -n hypnosis.
hypnotisch a hypnotic.
Hypnotiseur [hüpnōtēzœr'] m hypnotist.
hypnotisieren [hüpnōtēzē:rǝn] vt hypnotize.
Hypothek [hüpōtā:k'] f -, -en mortgage; **eine ~ aufnehmen** raise a mortgage; **etw mit einer ~ belasten** mortgage sth.
Hypothese [hüpōtā:'zǝ] f -, -n hypothesis.
hypothetisch [hüpōtā:'tish] a hypothetical.
Hysterie [hüstärē:'] f hysteria.
hysterisch [hüstä:'rish] a hysterical; **einen ~en Anfall bekommen** (fig) have hysterics.

I

I, i [ē:] *nt* I, i; **das Tüpfelchen auf dem I** (*fig*) the final touch.
i. *abk* = **in, im.**
i.A. *abk* (= *im Auftrag*) p.p.
iberisch [ēbā:'rish] *a* Iberian; **die ~e Halbinsel** the Iberian Peninsula.
IC *m - abk* = **Intercity-Zug.**
ich [iċh] *pron* I; **~ bin's!** it's me!; **I~** *nt* **-(s), -(s)** self; (*PSYCH*) ego; **I~form** *f* first person; **I~-Roman** *m* novel in the first person.
Ideal [ēdāāl'] *nt* **-s, -e** ideal; **i~** *a* ideal; **~fall** *m*: **im ~fall** ideally.
Idealismus [ēdāális'mŏŏs] *m* idealism.
Idealist(in *f*) *m* idealist; **i~isch** *a* idealistic.
Idealvorstellung *f* ideal.
Idee [ēdā:'] *f* **-, -n** [ēdā:'ən] idea; (*ein wenig*) shade, trifle; **jdn auf die ~ bringen, etw zu tun** give sb the idea of doing sth.
ideell [ēdāel'] *a* ideal.
identifizieren [ēdentēfētsē:'rən] *vt* identify.
identisch [ēden'tish] *a* identical.
Identität [ēdentēte:t'] *f* identity.
Ideologe [ēdāōlō:'gə] *m* **-n, -n, Ideologin** *f* ideologist.
Ideologie [ēdāōlōgē:'] *f* ideology.
ideologisch [ēdāōlō:'gish] *a* ideological.
idiomatisch [ēdēōmá'tish] *a* idiomatic.
Idiot [ēdēō:t'] *m* **-en, -en** idiot.
Idioten-: *zW*: **~hügel** *m* (*hum umg*) beginners' *od* nursery slope; **i~sicher** *a* (*umg*) foolproof.
Idiotin *f* idiot.
idiotisch *a* idiotic.
idyllisch [ēdü'lish] *a* idyllic.
IFO *abk* (= *Institut für Wirtschaftsforschung*) institute for economic research.
IG *abk* (= *Industriegewerkschaft*) industrial trade union.
IGB *m - abk* (= *Internationaler Gewerkschaftsbund*) International Trades Union Congress.
Igel [ē:'gəl] *m* **-s, -** hedgehog.
igitt(igitt) [ēgit'(ēgit')] *interj* ugh!, yuck!
Ignorant [ignōránt'] *m* **-en, -en** ignoramus.
ignorieren [ignōrē:'rən] *vt* ignore.
ihm [ē:m] *pers pron* (*dat von er, es*) (to) him, (to) it; **es ist ~ nicht gut** he doesn't feel well.
ihn [ē:n] *pers pron* (*akk von er*) him; (*bei Tieren, Dingen*) it.
ihnen [ē:'nən] *pers pron* (*dat von sie pl*) (to) them; (*nach Präpositionen*) them.
Ihnen *pers pron* (*dat von Sie*) (to) you;

ihr [ē:r] *pers pron* 2. *pers pl* (*nom*) you; (*dat von sie sing*) (*bei Personen*) (to) her; (*bei Tieren, Dingen*) (to) it; (*nach Prepositionen*) her; it ♦ *poss pron sing* her; its; *pl* their.
Ihr *poss pron* your.
ihrer [ē:'rər] *pers pron* (*gen von sie sing*) of her; *pl* of them.
Ihrer *pers pron* (*gen von Sie*) of you.
ihre(r, s) *poss pron sing* hers; (*eines Tiers*) its; (*von mehreren*) theirs; **sie taten das ~** (*geh*) they did their bit.
Ihre(r, s) *poss pron* yours; **tun Sie das ~** (*geh*) you do your bit.
ih'rerseits' *ad* for her/their part.
Ih'rerseits' *ad* for your part.
ih'resglei'chen *pron* people like her/them; (*von Dingen*) others like it; **eine Frechheit, die ~ sucht!** an incredible cheek!
ih'retwe'gen, ih'retwil'len *ad* (*für sie*) for her/its/their sake; (*wegen ihr, ihnen*) on her/its/their account; **sie sagte, ~ könnten wir gehen** she said that, as far as she was concerned, we could go.
ihrige [ē:'rigə] *pron*: **der/die/das ~** hers; its; theirs.
i.J. *abk* (= *im Jahre*) in (the year).
Ikone [ēkō:'nə] *f* **-, -n** icon.
illegal [i'lāgál] *a* illegal.
illegitim [i'lāgētē:m] *a* illegitimate.
Illusion [ilŏŏzēō:n'] *f* illusion; **sich** (*dat*) **~en machen** delude o.s.
illusorisch [ilŏŏzō:'rish] *a* illusory.
illustrieren [ilŏŏstrē:'rən] *vt* illustrate.
Illustrierte *f* **-n, -n** picture magazine.
Iltis [il'tis] *m* **-ses, -se** polecat.
im [im] = **in dem** ♦ *präp*: **etw ~ Liegen/Stehen tun** do sth lying down/standing up.
I.M. *abk* (= *Ihre Majestät*) H.M.
Imagepflege [i'mitshpflā:gə] *f* (*umg*) image-building.
imaginär [ēmàgēne:r'] *a* imaginary.
Imbiß [im'bis] *m* **-sses, -sse** snack; **~halle** *f*, **~stube** *f* snack bar.
imitieren [ēmētē:'rən] *vt* imitate.
Imker [im'kər] *m* **-s, -** beekeeper.
immanent [imánent'] *a* inherent, intrinsic.
Immatrikulation [imátrēkŏŏlátsēō:n'] *f* (*UNIV*) registration.
immatrikulieren [imátrēkŏŏlē:'rən] *vir* register.
immer [i'mər] *ad* always; **~ wieder** again and again; **etw ~ wieder tun** keep on doing sth; **~ noch** still; **~ noch nicht** still not; **für ~ forever**; **~ wenn ich ... every time I ...; ~ schöner/ trauriger** more and more beautiful/sadder and sadder; **was/wer (auch) ~** whatever/whoever; **~hin** *ad* all the same; **~zu** *ad* all the time.
Immigrant(in *f*) [imēgránt'(in)] *m* **-en, -en** immigrant.
Immobilien [imōbē:'lēən] *pl* real estate; (*in Zeitungsannoncen*) property *sing*; **~händler**

m real estate agent.

immun [imōō:n'] *a* immune.

Immunität [imōō:nētē:t'] *f* immunity.

imperativ [im'pārátē:f] *a:* ~es **Mandat** imperative mandate.

Imperativ *m* -s, -e imperative.

Imperfekt [im'perfekt] *nt* -s, -e imperfect (tense).

Imperialismus [impārĕális'mōōs] *m* - imperialism.

Imperialist [impārĕálist'] *m* imperialist; i~isch *a* imperialistic.

impfen [imp'fən] *vt* vaccinate.

Impf- *zW:* ~paß *m* vaccination card; ~schutz *m* protection given by vaccination; ~stoff *m* vaccine; ~ung *f* vaccination; ~zwang *m* compulsory vaccination.

implizieren [implētsē:'rən] *vt* imply (*mit* by).

imponieren [impōnē:'rən] *vi* impress (*jdm* sb).

Import [import'] *m* -(e)s, -e import.

importieren [importē:'rən] *vt* import.

imposant [impōzánt'] *a* imposing.

impotent [im'pōtent] *a* impotent.

Impotenz [im'pōtents] *f* impotence.

imprägnieren [impregnē:'rən] *vt* (water)proof.

Impressionismus [impresēōnis'mōōs] *m* impressionism.

Impressum [impre'sōōm] *nt* -s, -ssen imprint.

Improvisation [imprōvēzátsēō:n'] *f* improvisation.

improvisieren [imprōvēzē:'rən] *vti* improvise.

Impuls [impōōls'] *m* -es, -e impulse; **etw aus einem ~ heraus tun** do sth on impulse.

impulsiv [impōōlzē:f'] *a* impulsive.

imstande [imshtán'də] *a:* ~ **sein** be in a position; (*fähig*) be able; **er ist zu allem ~** he's capable of anything.

in [in] *präp* +*akk* in(to); to; +*dat* in; ~ **der/ die Stadt** in/into town; ~ **der/die Schule** at/ to school; ~ **diesem Jahr** (*laufendes Jahr*) this year; (*jenes Jahr*) in that year; **heute** ~ **zwei Wochen** two weeks today; **es** ~ **sich haben** (*umg: Text*) be tough; (: *Whisky*) have quite a kick; ~ **die Hunderte gehen** run into (the) hundreds.

inaktiv [in'áktē:f] *a* inactive; (*Mitglied*) nonactive.

Inangriffnahme [inán'grifnâmə] *f* -, -n (*form*) commencement.

Inanspruchnahme [inán'shprōōk͡hnâmə] *f* -, -n demands *pl* (*gen* on); **im Falle einer ~ der Arbeitslosenunterstützung** (*form*) where unemployment benefit has been sought.

Inbegriff [in'bəgrif] *m* embodiment, personification.

inbegriffen *ad* included.

Inbetriebnahme [in'bətrē:pnâmə] *f* -, -n (*form*) commissioning; (*von Gebäude*, *U-Bahn etc*) inauguration.

inbrünstig [in'brünstic͡h] *a* ardent.

indem [indā:m'] *kj* while; ~ **man etw macht**

(*dadurch*) by doing sth.

Inder(in *f*) [in'dər(in)] *m* -s, - Indian.

indes(sen) [indes'(ən)] *ad* meanwhile ♦ *kj* while.

Index [in'deks] *m* -es, -e *od* **Indizes** [in'dētsā:z]: **auf dem ~ stehen** (*fig*) be banned; ~zahl *f* index number.

Indianer(in *f*) [indēâ'nər(in)] *m* -s, - (Red *od* American) Indian.

indianisch *a* (Red *od* American) Indian.

Indien [in'dēən] *nt* -s India.

indigniert [indignē:rt'] *a* indignant.

Indikation [indēkátsēō:n'] *f:* **medizinische/ soziale ~** medical/social grounds for the termination of pregnancy.

Indikativ [in'dēkátē:f] *m* -s, -e indicative.

indirekt [in'dērekt] *a* indirect; ~e **Steuer** indirect tax.

indisch [in'dish] *a* Indian; I~er **Ozean** Indian Ocean.

indiskret [in'diskrā:t] *a* indiscreet.

Indiskretion [indiskrátsēō:n'] *f* indiscretion.

indiskutabel [in'diskōōtâbəl] *a* out of the question.

indisponiert [in'dispōnē:rt] *a* (*geh*) indisposed.

Individualist [indēvēdōōálist'] *m* individualist.

Individualität [indēvēdōōálētet'] *f* individuality.

individuell [indēvēdōōel'] *a* individual; **etw ~ gestalten** give sth a personal note.

Individuum [indēvē:'dōōōōm] *nt* -s, -en individual.

Indiz [indē:ts'] *nt* -es, -ien sign (*für* of); (*JUR*) clue.

Indizes [in'dētsā:z] *pl von* **Index**.

Indizienbeweis *m* circumstantial evidence.

indizieren [indētsē:'rən] *nt* (*COMPUT*) indexing.

indogermanisch ['indōgermâ'nish] *a* Indo-Germanic, Indo-European.

indoktrinieren [indoktrēnē:'rən] *vt* indoctrinate.

Indonesien [indōnā:'zēən] *nt* -s Indonesia.

Indonesier(in *f*) *m* Indonesian.

indonesisch [indōnā:'zish] *a* Indonesian.

Indossament [indosáment'] *nt* (*COMM*) endorsement.

Indossant [indosánt'] *m* endorser.

Indossat [indosât'] *nt* -en, -en endorsee.

indossieren *vt* endorse.

industrialisieren [indōōstrēálēzi':rən] *vt* industrialize.

Industrialisierung *f* industrialization.

Industrie [indōōstrē:'] *f* industry; **in der ~ arbeiten** be in industry ♦ *in zW* industrial; ~gebiet *nt* industrial area; ~gelände *nt* industrial park; ~kaufmann *m* industrial manager.

industriell [indōōstrēel'] *a* industrial; ~e **Revolution** industrial revolution.

Industrielle(r) *mf dekl wie a* industrialist.

Industrie- *zW:* ~staat *m* industrial nation; ~ **und Handelskammer** *f* chamber of industry and commerce; **~zweig** m branch of industry.

ineinander [inīnán'dər] ad in(to) one another od each other; ~ **übergehen** merge (into each other); **~greifen** vi unreg (lit) interlock; (Zahnräder) mesh; (fig: Ereignisse etc) overlap.

Infanterie [infántərē:'] f infantry.

Infarkt [infárkt'] m -(e)s, -e coronary (thrombosis).

Infektion [infektsēō:n'] f infection.

Infektions- zW: **~herd** m focus of infection; **~krankheit** f infectious disease.

Infinitiv [in'fēnētē:f] m -s, -e infinitive.

infizieren [infētsē:'rən] vt infect ♦ vr be infected (bei by).

in flagranti [in flàgrán'tē] ad in the act, redhanded.

Inflation [inflàtsēō:n'] f inflation.

Inflationsrate f rate of inflation.

inflatorisch [inflàtō:'rish] a inflationary.

infolge [infol'gə] präp +gen as a result of, owing to; **~dessen** [-de'sən] ad consequently.

Informatik [informâ'tik] f information science.

Information [informàtsēō:n'] f information no pl; **~en** pl (COMPUT) data; **zu Ihrer** ~ for your information.

Informations- zW: **~abruf** m (COMPUT) information retrieval; **~monopol** nt monopoly of information.

informativ [informàtē:f'] a informative.

informieren [informē:'rən] vt inform (über +akk about) ♦ vr find out (über +akk about).

Infrastruktur [in'fràshtrŏŏktŏŏ:r] f infrastructure.

Infusion [infŏŏzēō:n'] f infusion.

Ing. abk = **Ingenieur**.

Ingenieur [inzhānœ̄ər'] m engineer; **~schule** f school of engineering.

Ingwer [ing'vər] m -s ginger.

Inh. abk (= Inhaber(in)) prop.; (= Inhalt) cont.

Inhaber(in f) [in'hâbər(in)] m -s, - owner; (COMM) proprietor, (Haus~) occupier; (Lizenz~) licensee, holder; (FIN) bearer.

inhaftieren [inháftē:'rən] vt take into custody.

inhalieren [inhàlē:'rən] vti inhale.

Inhalt [in'hált] m -(e)s, -e contents pl; (eines Buchs etc) content; (MATH) area; volume; **i~lich** a as regards content.

Inhalts- zW: **~angabe** f summary; **i~los** a empty; **i~reich** a full; **~verzeichnis** nt table of contents; directory (auch COMPUT).

inhuman [in'hŏŏmàn] a inhuman.

initialisieren [ēnētsēàlēzē:'rən] vt (COMPUT) initialize.

Initialisierung f (COMPUT) initialization.

Initiative [ēnētsēàtē:'və] f initiative; **die** ~ **ergreifen** take the initiative.

Initiator(in f) [ēnētsēà'tor(in)] m (geh) initiator.

Injektion [inyektsēō:n'] f injection.

Inka [ing'kà] mf -(s), -s Inca.

Inkaufnahme [inkouf'nâmə] f (form): **unter** ~ **finanzieller Verluste** accepting the inevitable financial losses.

inkl. abk (= inklusive) incl., inc.

inklusive [inklŏŏzē:'və] präp, ad inclusive (gen of).

Inklusivpreis m all-inclusive rate.

inkognito [inkog'nētō] ad incognito.

inkonsequent [in'konzäkvent] a inconsistent.

inkorrekt [in'korekt] a incorrect.

Inkrafttreten [inkráft'trä:tən] nt -s coming into force.

Inland [in'lánt] nt -(e)s (GEOG) inland; (POL, COMM) home (country); **im** ~ **und Ausland** at home and abroad.

Inlandsporto nt domestic (US) od inland (Brit) postage.

inmitten [inmi'tən] präp +gen in the middle of; ~ **von** amongst.

innehaben [i'nəhâbən] vt unreg hold.

innehalten [i'nəhàltən] vi unreg pause, stop.

innen [i'nən] ad inside; **nach** ~ inwards; **von** ~ from the inside; **I~architekt** m interior designer; **I~aufnahme** f indoor photograph; **I~bahn** f (SPORT) inside lane; **I~dienst** m: **im I~dienst sein** work in the office; **I~einrichtung** f (interior) furnishings pl; **I~leben** nt (seelisch) emotional life; (umg: körperlich) insides pl; **I~minister** m minister of the interior; **I~politik** f domestic policy; **I~stadt** f town od city center.

inner- [i'nər] zW: **~betrieblich** a: **etw ~betrieblich regeln** settle sth within the company; **~deutsch** a: **~deutscher Handel** domestic trade in Germany.

Innereien [inərī'ən] pl innards pl.

innere(r, s) a inner; (im Körper, inländisch) internal.

Innere(s) nt dekl wie a inside; (Mitte) center (US), centre (Brit); (fig) heart.

inner- zW: **~halb** ad, präp +gen within; (räumlich) inside; **~lich** a internal; (geistig) inward; **I~lichkeit** f (LITER) inwardness; **~parteilich** a: **~parteiliche Demokratie** democracy (with)in the party structure.

innerste(r, s) a innermost.

Innerste(s) nt heart; **bis ins** ~ **getroffen** hurt to the quick.

innewohnen [i'nəvō:nən] vi +dat (geh) be inherent in.

innig [i'niç] a profound; (Freundschaft) intimate; **mein ~ster Wunsch** my dearest wish.

Innung [i'nŏŏng] f (trade) guild; **du blamierst die ganze** ~ (hum umg) you are letting the whole team down.

inoffiziell [in'ōfētsēēl] a unofficial.

ins [ins] = **in das**.

Insasse [in'zàsə] m -n, -n (Anstalt) inmate; (AUT) passenger.

insbesondere [insbəzon'dərə] ad

(e)specially.

Inschrift [in'shrift] *f* inscription.

Insekt [inzckt'] *nt* **-(e)s, -en** insect.

Insektenvertilgungsmittel *nt* insecticide.

Insel [in'zəl] *f* **-, -n** island.

Inserat [inzârât'] *nt* **-(e)s, -e** advertisement.

Inserent [inzârent'] *m* advertiser.

inserieren [inzârē:'rən] *vti* advertise.

insgeheim [insgəhīm'] *ad* secretly.

insgesamt [insgəzámt'] *ad* altogether, all in all.

insofern [inzōfern'], **insoweit** [inzōvīt'] *ad* in this respect; ~ **als** in so far as ♦ *kj* if; *(deshalb)* (and) so.

insolvent [in'zolvent] *a* bankrupt, insolvent.

Insolvenz *f* (*COMM*) insolvency.

insoweit = **insofern.**

in spe [inshpā:'] *a* (*umg*): **unser Schwiegersohn** ~ our son-in-law to be, our future son-in-law.

Inspektion [inspektsēō:n'] *f* inspection; (*AUT*) service.

inspirieren [inspērē:'rən] *vt* inspire; **sich von etw** ~ **lassen** get one's inspiration from sth.

inspizieren [inspētsē:'rən] *vt* inspect.

Installateur [instálátœr'] *m* plumber; (*Elektro*~) electrician.

installieren [instálē:'rən] *vt* (*fig auch*) install.

Instandhaltung [inshtánt'háltŏŏng] *f* maintenance.

inständig [inshten'diċh] *a* urgent; ~ **bitten** beg.

Instandsetzung *f* overhaul; (*eines Gebäudes*) restoration.

Instanz [instánts'] *f* authority; (*JUR*) court; **Verhandlung in erster/zweiter** ~ first/second court case.

Instanzenweg *m* official channels *pl.*

Instinkt [instinjkt'] *m* **-(e)s, -e** instinct.

instinktiv [instinjktē:f'] *a* instinctive.

Institut [instētŏŏ:t'] *nt* **-(e)s, -e** institute.

Institution [instētŏŏtsēō:n'] *f* institution.

Instrument [instrŏŏment'] *nt* instrument.

Insulin [inzŏŏlē:n'] *nt* **-s** insulin.

inszenieren [instsānē:'rən] *vt* direct; (*fig*) stage-manage.

Inszenierung *f* production.

Integralrechnung [intāgrál'reċhnŏŏng] *f* integral calculus.

integrieren [intāgrē:'rən] *vt* integrate; **integrierte Gesamtschule** non-selective school.

Intellekt [intelekt'] *m* **-(e)s** intellect.

intellektuell [intelektŏŏel'] *a* intellectual.

intelligent [intelēgent'] *a* intelligent.

Intelligenz [intelēgents'] *f* intelligence; (*Leute*) intelligentsia *pl*; ~**quotient** *m* IQ.

Intendant [intendánt'] *m* director.

intensiv [intenzē:f'] *a* intensive; **I~station** *f* intensive care unit.

Intercity-Zug [intərsi'tētsŏŏ:k] *m* inter-city train.

interessant [intāresánt'] *a* interesting; **sich** ~ **machen** attract attention.

interessanterweise *ad* interestingly enough.

Interesse [intāre'sə] *nt* **-s, -n** interest; ~ **haben** be interested (*an* +*dat* in).

Interessen- *zW*: ~**gebiet** *nt* field of interest; ~**gegensatz** *m* clash of interests.

Interessent(in *f*) [intāresent'(in)] *m* interested party; **es haben sich mehrere** ~**en gemeldet** several people have shown interest.

Interessenvertretung *f* representation of interests; (*Personen*) group representing (one's) interests.

interessieren [intāresē:'rən] *vt* interest (*für, an* +*dat* in); ~ ♦ *vr* be interested (*für* in).

interessiert *a*: **politisch** ~ interested in politics.

Interkontinentalrakete [intərkontēnentál'rākā:tə] *f* intercontinental missile.

intern [intern'] *a* internal.

Internat [internât'] *nt* **-(e)s, -e** boarding school.

international [internátsēōnál'] *a* international.

internieren [internē:'rən] *vt* intern.

Internist(in *f*) *m* internist.

Interpol [in'tərpō:l] *f* - *abk* (= *Internationale Polizei*) Interpol.

Interpret [intərprā:t'] *m* **-en, -en: Lieder verschiedener** ~**en** songs by various singers.

interpretieren [interprātē:'rən] *vt* interpret.

Interpretin *f siehe* **Interpret.**

Interpunktion [interpŏŏngktsēō:n'] *f* punctuation.

Intershop [in'tərshop] *m* **-s, -s** (*DDR*) international shop.

Intervall [intervál'] *nt* **-s, -e** interval.

Interview [intərvyŏŏ:'] *nt* **-s, -s** interview; **i~en** [-vyŏŏ:'ən] *vt* interview.

intim [intē:m'] *a* intimate; **I~bereich** *m* (*ANAT*) genital area.

Intimität [intēmēte:t'] *f* intimacy.

Intimsphäre *f*: **jds** ~ **verletzen** invade sb's privacy.

intolerant [in'tōlárânt] *a* intolerant.

intransitiv [in'tránzētē:f] *a* (*GRAM*) intransitive.

Intrige [intrē:'gə] *f* **-, -n** intrigue, plot.

intrinsisch [intrin'zish] *a*: ~**er Wert** intrinsic value.

introvertiert [intrōvertē:rt'] *a*: ~ **sein** be an introvert.

intuitiv [intŏŏētē:f'] *a* intuitive.

Invalide [inválē:'də] *m* **-n, -n** disabled person, invalid.

Invalidenrente *f* disability pension.

Invasion [inνázēō:n'] *f* invasion.

Inventar [inventâr'] *nt* **-s, -e** inventory; (*COMM*) assets and liabilities *pl.*

Inventur [inventŏŏ:r'] *f* stocktaking; ~ **machen** stocktake.

investieren [investē:'rən] *vt* invest.

investiert *a*: ~**es Kapital** capital employed.

Investition [investētsēō:n'] *f* investment.

Investitionszuschuß *m* investment grant.

Investmentgesellschaft [invest'məntgəzelsháft] *f* mutual fund (*US*), unit trust

(*Brit*).

inwiefern [invēfern'], **inwieweit** [invēvīt'] *ad* how far, to what extent.

Inzest [intsest'] *m* -(e)s, -e incest *no pl.*

inzwischen [intsvi'shən] *ad* meanwhile.

IOK *nt abk* (= *Internationales Olympisches Komitee*) IOC.

ionisch [ēō:'nish] *a* Ionian; **I~es Meer** Ionian Sea.

i.R. *abk* (= *im Ruhestand*) ret., retd.

Irak [ērâk'] *m* -s: **(der)** ~ Iraq.

Iraker(in *f*) *m* -s, - Iraqi.

irakisch *a* Iraqi.

Iran [ērân'] *m* -s: **(der)** ~ Iran.

Iraner(in *f*) *m* -s, - Iranian.

iranisch *a* Iranian.

irdisch [ir'dish] *a* earthly; **den Weg alles I~en gehen** go the way of all flesh.

Ire [ē:'rə] *m* -n, -n Irishman; Irish boy; **die ~n** the Irish.

irgend [ir'gənt] *ad* at all; **wann/was/wer** ~ whenever/whatever/whoever; ~ **jemand/ etwas** somebody/something; anybody/ anything; ~**ein(e, s)** *a* some, any; **haben Sie (sonst) noch ~einen Wunsch?** is there anything else you would like?; ~**einmal** *ad* sometime or other; (*fragend*) ever; ~**wann** *ad* sometime; ~**wie** *ad* somehow; ~**wo** *ad* somewhere, someplace; (*fragend, verneinend, bedingend*) anywhere, any place; ~**wohin** *ad* somewhere, someplace; (*fragend, verneinend, bedingend*) anywhere, any place.

Irin [ē:'rin] *f* Irishwoman; Irish girl.

irisch *a* Irish; **I~e See** Irish Sea.

IRK *nt abk* (= *Internationales Rotes Kreuz*) IRC.

Irland [ir'lânt] *nt* -s Ireland; (*Republik* ~) Eire.

Irländer(in *f*) [ir'lendər(in)] *m* -s, - *siehe* **Ire, Irin.**

Ironie [ērōnē:'] *f* irony.

ironisch [ērō:'nish] *a* ironic(al).

irre [i'rə] *a* crazy, mad; ~ **gut** (*umg*) way out (*umg*); ~**führen** *vt* mislead; **I~führung** *f* fraud.

irrelevant [i'rālāvànt] *a* irrelevant (*für* for, to).

irremachen *vt* confuse.

irren *vir* be mistaken; (*umher~*) wander, stray; **jeder kann sich mal** ~ anyone can make a mistake; **I~anstalt** *f* (*veraltet*) lunatic asylum; **I~haus** *nt*: **hier geht es zu wie im I~haus** (*umg*) this place is an absolute madhouse.

Irre(r) *mf dekl wie a* lunatic.

Irrfahrt [ir'fârt] *f* wandering.

irrig [i'rich] *a* incorrect, wrong.

irritieren [irētē:'rən] *vt* (*verwirren*) confuse, muddle; (*ärgern*) irritate.

Irr- *zW*: ~**licht** *nt* will-o'-the-wisp; **i~sinnig** *a* mad, crazy; (*umg*) terrific; **i~sinnig komisch** incredibly funny; ~**tum** *m* -s, -tümer mistake, error; **im ~tum sein** be wrong *od*

mistaken; ~**tum!** wrong!; **i~tümlich** *a* mistaken, taken.

i.Sa. *abk* (= *in Sachen*) in re.

ISBN *f abk* (= *Internationale Standardbuchnummer*) ISBN.

Ischias [i'shēàs] *m od nt* - sciatica.

Islam [is'làm] *m* -s Islam.

Island [ē:s'lânt] *nt* -s Iceland.

Isländer(in *f*) [ē:s'lendər(in)] *m* -s, - Icelander.

isländisch *a* Icelandic.

Isolation [ēzōlátsēō:n'] *f* isolation; (*ELEK*) insulation; (*von Häftlingen*) solitary confinement.

Isolator [ēzōlá'tor] *m* insulator.

Isolierband *nt* insulating tape.

isolieren [izōlē:'rən] *vt* isolate; (*ELEK*) insulate.

Isolierstation *f* (*MED*) isolation ward.

Isolierung *f* isolation; (*ELEK*) insulation.

Israel [is'rââ:l] *nt* -s Israel.

Israeli [isrâã:'lē] *m* -(s), -s Israeli ♦ *f* -s, -(s) Israeli.

israelisch *a* Israeli.

ißt [ist] *2./3. pers sing präs von* **essen.**

ist [ist] *3. pers sing präs von* **sein.**

Ist-Bestand *m* (*Geld*) cash in hand; (*Waren*) actual stock.

Italien [ētâ'lēən] *nt* -s Italy.

Italiener(in *f*) [ētâlēâ:'nər(in)] *m* -s, - Italian.

italienisch *a* Italian; **die ~e Schweiz** Italian-speaking Switzerland.

i.V. *abk* (= *in Vollmacht*) by proxy.

I.v. *abk* (= *Irrtum vorbehalten*) subject to correction.

i.V., I.V. *abk* (= *in Vertretung*) on behalf of.

IWF *m abk* (= *Internationaler Währungsfonds*) IMF.

J

J, j [yot] *nt* J, j.

ja [yâ] *ad* yes; **tu das** ~ **nicht!** don't do that!; ~ **und amen zu allem sagen** (*umg*) accept everything without question; **sie ist** ~ **erst fünf** (after all) she's only five; **Sie wissen** ~, **wie das so ist** you know how it is (, don't you?).

Jacht [yàḱht] *f* -, -en yacht.

Jacke [yà'kə] *f* -, -n jacket; (*Woll~*) cardigan.

Jacketkrone [zhàket'krō:nə] *f* (*Zahnkrone*) jacket crown.

Jackett [zhàket'] *nt* -s, -s *od* -e jacket.

Jagd [yâkt] *f* -, -en hunt; (*Jagen*) hunting; ~**beute** *f* kill; ~**flugzeug** *nt* fighter; ~**gewehr** *nt* sporting gun; ~**schein** *m* hunting license; ~**wurst** *f* smoked sausage.

jagen [yâ'gən] *vi* hunt; *(eilen)* race ♦ *vt* hunt; *(weg~)* drive (off); *(verfolgen)* chase; **mit diesem Essen kannst du mich ~** *(umg)* I wouldn't touch that food with a ten-foot pole.

Jäger [ye:'gər] *m* -s, - hunter; **~in** *f* huntress, huntswoman; **~latein** *nt* *(umg)* hunters' tales *pl*; **~schnitzel** *nt* *(KOCH)* cutlet served *with mushroom sauce.*

jäh [ye:] *a* abrupt, sudden; *(steil)* steep, precipitous; **~lings** *ad* abruptly.

Jahr [yâr] *nt* -(e)s, -e year; **im ~(e) 1776** in (the year) 1776; **die sechziger ~(e)** the sixties *sing od pl*; **mit dreißig ~en** at the age of thirty; **in den besten ~en sein** be in the prime of (one's) life; **nach ~ und Tag** after (many) years; **zwischen den ~en** *(umg)* between Christmas and New Year; **~buch** *nt* annual, year book.

jahrelang *ad* for years.

Jahres- *zW*: **~abonnement** *nt* annual subscription; **~abschluß** *m* end of the year; *(COMM)* annual statement of account; **~beitrag** *m* annual subscription; **~bericht** *m* annual report; **~hauptversammlung** *f* *(COMM)* annual general meeting, AGM; **~karte** *f* annual season ticket; **~tag** *m* anniversary; **~umsatz** *m* *(COMM)* yearly turnover; **~wechsel** *m* turn of the year; **~zahl** *f* date; year; **~zeit** *f* season.

Jahr- *zW*: **~gang** *m* age group; *(von Wein)* vintage; **er ist ~gang 1950** he was born in 1950; **~hun'dert** *nt* century; **~hun'dertfeier** *f* centenary; **~hun'dertwende** *f* turn of the century.

jährlich [ye:r'liċh] *a, ad* yearly; **zweimal ~** twice a year.

Jahr- *zW*: **~markt** *m* fair; **~zehnt'** *nt* decade.

Jähzorn [ye:'tsorn] *m* sudden anger; hot temper.

jähzornig *a* hot-tempered.

Jalousie [zhâlōōzē:'] *f* venetian blind.

Jamaika [yâmî'kâ] *nt* -s Jamaica.

Jammer [yâ'mər] *m* -s misery; **es ist ein ~, daß ...** it is a crying shame that ...

jämmerlich [ye'mərliċh] *a* wretched, pathetic; **J~keit** *f* wretchedness.

jammern *vi* wail ♦ *vt unpers*: **es jammert jdn** it makes sb feel sorry.

jammerschade *a*: **es ist ~** it is a crying shame.

Jan. *abk* (= *Januar*) Jan.

Januar [yâ'nōōâr] *m* -s, -e January; *siehe* **September**.

Japan [yâ'pán] *nt* -s Japan.

Japaner(in *f)* [yâpâ'nər(in)] *m* -s, - Japanese.

japanisch *a* Japanese.

Jargon [zhârgôn'] *m* -s, -s jargon.

Jasager [yâ'zâgər] *m* -s, - *(pej)* yes-man.

Jastimme *f* vote for; *(PARL auch)* yea *(US)*, aye *(Brit)*.

jäten [ye:'tən] *vti* weed.

Jauchegrube [you'ċhəgrōō:bə] *f* cesspool, cesspit.

jauchzen [youċh'tsən] *vi* rejoice, shout (with joy).

Jauchzer *m* -s, - shout of joy.

jaulen [you'lən] *vi* howl.

ja- *zW*: **~wohl'** *ad* yes (of course); **J~wort** *nt* consent; **jdm das J~wort geben** consent to marry sb; *(bei Trauung)* say "I do".

Jazz [dzhez] *m* - jazz; **~keller** *m* jazz club.

Jb. *abk* = **Jahrbuch**.

je [yā:] *ad* ever; *(jeweils)* each; **~ nach** depending on; **~ nachdem** it depends; **~ ... desto, ~ ... ~** the ... the.

Jeans [dzhē:nz] *pl* jeans *pl*; **~anzug** *m* denim suit.

jedenfalls *ad* in any case.

jede(r, s) [yā:'də(r, s)] *a (einzeln)* each; *(von zweien)* either; *(~ von allen)* every; **ohne ~ Anstrengung** without any effort ♦ *indef pron (einzeln)* each (one); *(~ von allen)* everyone, everybody; **~r zweite** every other one.

jedermann *pron* everyone; **das ist nicht ~s Sache** it's not everyone's cup of tea.

jederzeit *ad* at any time.

jedesmal *ad* every time, each time.

jedoch [yādoċh'] *ad* however.

jeher [yā:'hā:r] *ad*: **von ~** all along.

jein [yīn] *ad (hum)* yes no.

jemals [yā:'mâls] *ad* ever.

jemand [yā:'mánt] *indef pron* someone, somebody; *(bei Fragen, bedingenden Satzen, Negation)* anyone, anybody.

Jemen [yā:'mən] *m* -s Yemen.

Jenaer Glas [yā:'nâərglâs] *nt* ® heatproof glass, Pyrex ®.

jene(r, s) [yā:'nə(r, s)] *a* that; *pl* those ♦ *pron* that one; *pl* those; *(der Vorherige, die Vorherigen)* the former.

jenseits [yā:n'zîts] *ad* on the other side ♦ *präp* +*gen* on the other side of, beyond; **J~** *nt*: **das J~** the hereafter, the beyond; **jdn ins J~ befördern** *(umg)* send sb to kingdom come.

Jesus [yā:'zōōs] *m* **Jesu**: **~ Christus** Jesus Christ.

jetzig [ye'tsiċh] *a* present.

jetzt [yetst] *ad* now; **~ gleich** right now.

je'- *zW*: **~wei'lig** *a* respective; **die ~ weilige Regierung** the government of the day; **~weils'** *ad*: **~weils zwei zusammen** two at a time; **zu ~weils 5 DM** at 5 marks each; **~weils das erste** the first each time; **~weils am Monatsletzten** on the last day of each month.

Jg. *abk* = **Jahrgang**.

Jh. *abk* (= *Jahrhundert*) c., cent.

jiddisch [yi'dish] *a* Yiddish.

jobben [dzho'bən] *vi (umg)* work, have a job.

Joch [yoċh] *nt* -(e)s, -e yoke.

Jochbein *nt* cheekbone.

Jockei [dzho'kâ] *m* -s, -s jockey.

Jod [yō:t] *nt* -(e)s iodine.

jodeln [yō:'dəln] *vi* yodel.

joggen [dzho'gən] *vi* jog.

Jogging [dzho'ging] *nt* jogging.

Joghurt [yō:'gŏŏrt] *m od nt* **-s, -s** yog(h)urt.
Johannisbeere [yŏhá'nisbā:rə] *f* redcurrant; **schwarze ~** blackcurrant.
johlen [yō:'lən] *vi* yell.
Joint [dzhoint] *m* **-s, -s** (*umg*) joint.
Joint-venture [dzhoint'vāntshŏŏō] *nt* **-, -s** joint venture.
Jolle [yo'lə] *f* **-, -n** dinghy.
jonglieren [zhŏnglē:'rən] *vi* juggle.
Joppe [yo'pə] *f* **-, -n** jacket.
Jordanien [yordâ'nēən] *nt* **-s** Jordan.
Jordanier(in *f*) *m* **-s, -** Jordanian.
Journalismus [zhŏŏrnális'mŏŏs] *m* journalism.
Journalist(in *f*) [zhŏŏrnálist'(in)] *m* journalist; **j~isch** *a* journalistic.
jr. *abk* (= *junior*) jun., Jun.
Jubel [yōō:'bəl] *m* **-s** rejoicing; **~, Trubel, Heiterkeit** laughter and merriment; **~jahr** *nt*: **alle ~jahre (einmal)** (*umg*) once in a blue moon.
jubeln *vi* rejoice.
Jubilar(in *f*) [yōōbēlár'(in)] *m* **-s, -e** *person celebrating an anniversary.*
Jubiläum [yōōbēle:'ŏŏm] *nt* **-s, Jubiläen** anniversary; (*Jahrstag*) jubilee.
jucken [yōō'kən] *vi* itch ♦ *vt*: **es juckt mich am Arm** my arm is itching; **das juckt mich** that's itchy; **das juckt mich doch nicht** (*umg*) I don't care.
Juck- *zW*: **~pulver** *nt* itching powder; **~reiz** *m* itch.
Judaslohn [yōō:'dáslō:n] *m* (*liter*) blood money.
Jude [yōō:'də] *m* **-n, -n** Jew.
Juden- *zW*: **~stern** *m* star of David; **~tum** *nt* **-** Judaism; Jewry; **~verfolgung** *f* persecution of the Jews.
Jüdin [yü:'din] *f* Jewess.
jüdisch *a* Jewish.
Judo [yōō:'dō] *nt* **-s** (**-s**) judo.
Jugend [yōō:'gənt] *f* **-** youth; **~amt** *nt* youth welfare department; **j~frei** *a* suitable for young people; (*FILM*) G (*US*), U(-certificate) (*Brit*); **~herberge** *f* youth hostel; **~kriminalität** *f* juvenile crime; **j~lich** *a* youthful; **~liche(r)** *mf dekl wie a* teenager, young person; **~liebe** *f* (*Geliebte(r)*) love of one's youth; **~richter** *m* juvenile court judge; **~schutz** *m* protection of children and young people; **~stil** *m* (*KUNST*) Art Nouveau; **~strafanstalt** *f* juvenile detention home (*US*), youth custody centre (*Brit*); **~sünde** *f* youthful misdeed; **~zentrum** *nt* youth center.
Jugoslawe [yōōgōslá'və] *m* **-n, -n, Jugoslawin** *f* Yugoslav.
Jugoslawien [yōōgōslá'vēən] *nt* **-s** Yugoslavia.
jugoslawisch *a* Yugoslav(ian).
Juli [yōō:'lē] *m* **-(s), -s** July; *siehe* **September.**
jung [yōōng] *a* young.
Junge *m* **-n, -n** boy, lad.

jünger *a* younger.
Jünger [yü'ngər] *m* **-s, -** disciple.
Junge(s) *nt dekl wie a* young animal; (*pl*) young *pl.*
Jungfer *f* **-, -n: alte ~** old maid.
Jungfernfahrt *f* maiden voyage.
Jung- *zW*: **~frau** *f* virgin; (*ASTROL*) Virgo; **~geselle** *m* bachelor; **~gesellin** *f* bachelor girl; (*älter*) single woman.
Jüngling [yüng'ling] *m* youth.
Jungsozialist *m* (*BRD POL*) Young Socialist.
jüngst [yüngst] *ad* lately, recently.
jüngste(r, s) *a* youngest; (*neueste*) latest; **das J~ Gericht** the Last Judgement; **der J~ Tag** Doomsday, the Day of Judgement.
Jungwähler(in *f*) *m* young voter.
Juni [yōō:'nē] *m* **-(s), -s** June; *siehe* **September.**
Junior [yōō:'nēor] *m* **-s, -en** [yōōnēō:'rən] junior.
Junta [k̲hŏŏn'tá] *f* **-, -ten** (*POL*) junta.
jur. *abk* = **juristisch.**
Jura [yōō:'rá] *f* (*UNIV*) law.
Jurist(in *f*) [yōōrist'(in)] *m* jurist, lawyer; (*Student*) law student; **j~isch** *a* legal.
Juso [yōō:'zō] *m* **-s, -s** *abk* (= *Jungsozialist*) Young Socialist.
just [yōōst] *ad* just.
Justiz [yōōstē:ts'] *f* **-** justice; **~beamte(r)** *m* judicial officer; **~irrtum** *m* miscarriage of justice; **~mord** *m* judicial murder.
Juwel [yōōvā:l'] *nt od m* **-s, -en** jewel.
Juwelier [yōōválē:r'] *m* **-s, -e** jeweler (*US*), jeweller (*Brit*); **~geschäft** *nt* jeweler's (*US*), jeweller's (*Brit*).
Jux [yōōks] *m* **-es, -e** joke, lark; **etw aus ~ tun/sagen** (*umg*) do/say sth in fun.
jwd [yotwā:dā:'] *ad* (*hum*) at the end of the world (*fig*).

K

K, k [kâ] *nt* K, k.
Kabarett [kábáret'] *nt* **-s, -e** *od* **-s** cabaret; **~ist(in** *f*) [-tist'(in)] *m* cabaret artiste.
Kabel [kâ'bəl] *nt* **-s, -** (*ELEK*) wire; (*stark*) cable; **~fernsehen** *nt* cable television.
Kabeljau [kâ'bəlyou] *m* **-s, -e** *od* **-s** cod.
kabeln *vti* cable.
Kabelsalat *m* (*umg*) tangle of cable.
Kabine [kábē:'nə] *f* cabin; (*Zelle*) cubicle.
Kabinett [kábēnet'] *nt* **-s, -e** (*POL*) cabinet; (*kleines Zimmer*) small room ♦ *m* high-quality German white wine.
Kachel [kâ'k̲həl] *f* **-, -n** tile.
kacheln *vt* tile.

Kachelofen m tiled stove.
Kacke [kå'kə] f -; -n (umg!) crap (!).
Kadaver [kådå'vər] m -s, - carcass.
Kader [kå'dər] m -s, - (MIL, POL) cadre; (SPORT) squad; (DDR, Schweiz: Fachleute) group of specialists; ~**schmiede** f (POL) institution for the forming of cadre personnel.
Kadett [kådet'] m -en, -en cadet.
Käfer [ke:'fər] m -s, - beetle.
Kaff [kåf] nt -s, -s (umg) dump, hole.
Kaffee [kå'fā] m -s, -s coffee; **zwei ~, bitte!** two coffees, please; **das ist kalter ~** (umg) that's old hat; ~**kanne** f coffeepot; ~**klatsch** m, ~**kränzchen** nt hen party; coffee morning; ~**löffel** m coffee spoon; ~**maschine** f coffee machine; ~**mühle** f coffee grinder; ~**satz** m coffee grounds pl; ~**tante** f (hum) coffee addict; (in Café) old biddy; ~**wärmer** m cozy (US), cosy (Brit) (for coffeepot).
Käfig [ke:'fiçh] m -s, -e cage.
kahl [kål] a bald; ~**fressen** vt unreg strip bare; ~**geschoren** a shaven, shorn; **K~heit** f baldness; ~**köpfig** a bald-headed; **K~schlag** m (Wald) clearing.
Kahn [kån] m -(e)s, ⁻e boat, barge.
Kai [kī] m -s, -e od -s quay.
Kaiser [kī'zər] m -s, - emperor; ~**in** f empress; **k~lich** a imperial; ~**reich** nt empire; ~**schmarre(n)** [kī'zərshmårə(n)] m (KOCH) sugared, cut-up pancake with raisins; ~**schnitt** m (MED) Cesarean (US) od Caesarean (Brit) (section).
Kajüte [kåyü:'tə] f -, -n cabin.
Kakao [kåkå'ō] m -s, -s cocoa; **jdn durch den ~ ziehen** (umg: veralbern) make fun of sb; (boshaft reden) run sb down.
Kakerlak [kå'kərlåk] m -en, -en cockroach.
Kaktee [kåktā:'ə] f -, -n, **Kaktus** [kåk'tōōs] m -, -se cactus.
Kalabrien [kålå'brēən] nt -s Calabria.
Kalauer [kå'louər] m -s, - corny joke; (Wortspiel) corny pun.
Kalb [kålp] nt -(e)s, ⁻er calf; **k~en** [kål'bən] vi calve; ~**fleisch** nt veal.
Kalbsleder nt calf(skin).
Kalender [kålen'dər] m -s, - calendar; (Taschen~) diary.
Kali [kå'lē] nt -s, -s potash.
Kaliber [kålē:'bər] nt -s, - (lit, fig) caliber (US), calibre (Brit).
Kalifornien [kålēfor'nēən] nt -s California.
Kalk [kålk] m -(e)s, -e lime; (BIOL) calcium; ~**stein** m limestone.
Kalkül [kålkü:l'] m od nt -s, -e (geh) calculation.
Kalkulation [kålkōōlåtsēō:n'] f calculation.
Kalkulator [kålkōōlå'tor] m cost accountant.
kalkulieren [kålkōōlē:'rən] vt calculate.
kalkuliert a: ~**es Risiko** calculated risk.
Kalorie [kålōrē:'] f calorie.
kalorienarm a low-calorie.
kalt [kålt] a cold; **mir ist (es) ~** I am cold; ~**e Platte** cold meat; **der K~e Krieg** the Cold War; **etw ~ stellen** put sth to chill;

die Wohnung kostet ~ 480 DM the flat costs 480 DM without heating; ~**blütig** vi unreg be unmoved; ~**blütig** a cold-blooded; (ruhig) cool; **K~blütigkeit** f cold-bloodedness; coolness.
Kälte [kel'tə] f - cold; coldness; ~'**einbruch** m cold spell; ~**grad** m degree of frost od below zero; ~**welle** f cold spell.
kalt- zW: ~**herzig** a cold-hearted; ~**lächelnd** ad (ironisch) cool as you please; ~**machen** vt (umg) do in; **K~miete** f rent exclusive of heating; **K~schale** f (KOCH) cold sweet soup; ~**schnäuzig** a cold, unfeeling; ~**stellen** vt chill; (fig) leave out in the cold.
kam [kåm] imperf von **kommen**.
Kambodscha [kåmbod'zhå] nt Kampuchea.
Kamel [kåmā:l'] nt -(e)s, -e camel.
Kamera [kå'mårå] f -, -s camera.
Kamerad(in f) [kåməråt', -râ'din] m -en, -en comrade, friend; ~**schaft** f comradeship; **k~schaftlich** a comradely.
Kamera- zW: ~**führung** f camera work; ~**mann** m, pl -**männer** cameraman.
Kamerun [kå'mərōō:n] nt -s the Cameroons pl.
Kamille [kåmi'lə] f -, -n camomile.
Kamillentee m camomile tea.
Kamin [kåmē:n'] m -s, -e (außen) chimney; (innen) fireside; (Feuerstelle) fireplace; ~**feger**, ~**kehrer** m -s, - chimney sweep.
Kamm [kåm] m -(e)s, ⁻e comb; (Berg~) ridge; (Hahnen~) crest; **alle/alles über einen ~ scheren** (fig) lump everyone/everything together.
kämmen [ke'mən] vt comb.
Kammer [kå'mər] f -, -n chamber; small bedroom; ~**diener** m valet; ~**jäger** m (Schädlingsbekämpfer) pest controller; ~**musik** f chamber music; ~**zofe** f chambermaid.
Kammstück nt (KOCH) shoulder.
Kampagne [kåmpån'yə] f -, -n campaign.
Kampf [kåmpf] m -(e)s, ⁻e fight, battle; (Wettbewerb) contest; (fig: Anstrengung) struggle; **jdm/einer Sache den ~ ansagen** (fig) declare war on sb/sth; ~ **dem Atomtod!** fight the nuclear menace!; **k~bereit** a ready for action.
kämpfen [kem'pfən] vi fight; **ich habe lange mit mir ~ müssen, ehe ...** I had a long battle with myself before ...
Kampfer [kåm'pfər] m -s camphor.
Kämpfer(in f) m -s, - fighter, combatant.
Kampf- zW: ~**geist** m fighting spirit; ~**handlung** f action; **k~los** a without a fight; **k~lustig** a pugnacious; ~**platz** m battlefield; (SPORT) arena, stadium; ~**richter** m (SPORT) referee; (TENNIS) umpire.
Kanada [kå'nådå] nt -s Canada.
Kanadier [kånå'dēər] m -s, - Canadian man.
Kanadierin f Canadian woman; Canadian girl.
kanadisch [kånå'dish] a Canadian.

Kanal [kánâl'] *m* -s, **Kanäle** (*Fluß*) canal; (*Rinne*) channel; (*für Abfluß*) drain; **der ~** (*auch*: **der Ärmelkanal**) the (English) Channel.

Kanalisation [kánálēzátséō:n'] *f* sewage system.

kanalisieren [kánálēzē:'rən] *vt* provide with a sewage system; (*fig*: *Energie etc*) channel.

Kanarienvogel [kánâ'rēənfō:gəl] *m* canary.

Kanarische Inseln [ká'nárishə'inzəln] *pl* Canary Islands *pl*, Canaries *pl*.

Kandare [kándâ'rə] *f* -, -n: **jdn an die ~ nehmen** (*fig*) take sb in hand.

Kandidat(in *f*) [kándēdât'(in)] *m* -en, -en candidate; **jdn als ~en aufstellen** nominate sb.

Kandidatur [kándēdátōō:r'] *f* candidature, candidacy.

kandidieren [kándēdē:'rən] *vi* (*POL*) stand, run.

kandiert [kándē:rt'] *a* (*Frucht*) candied.

Kandis(zucker) [kán'dis(tsōōkər)] *m* - rock candy.

Känguruh [keng'gōōrōō] *nt* -s, -s kangaroo.

Kaninchen [kánē:n'ċhən] *nt* rabbit.

Kanister [kánis'tər] *m* -s, - can, canister.

kann [kán] *1./3. pers sing präs von* **können**.

Kännchen [ken'ċhən] *nt* pot; (*für Milch*) jug.

Kanne [ká'nə] *f* -, -n (*Krug*) jug; (*Kaffee~*) pot; (*Milch~*) churn; (*Gieß~*) watering can.

kannte [kán'tə] *imperf von* **kennen**.

Kanon [ká'non] *m* -s, -s canon.

Kanone [kánō:'nə] *f* -, -n gun; (*HIST*) cannon; (*fig*: *Mensch*) ace; **das ist unter aller ~** (*umg*) that defies description.

Kanonenfutter *nt* (*umg*) cannon fodder.

Kant. *abk* = **Kanton.**

Kantate [kántâ'tə] *f* -, -n cantata.

Kante [kán'tə] *f* -, -n edge; **Geld auf die hohe ~ legen** (*umg*) put money by.

kantig [kán'tiċh] *a* (*Holz*) edged; (*Gesicht*) angular.

Kantine [kántē:'nə] *f* canteen.

Kanton [kántō:n'] *m* -s, -e canton.

Kantor [kán'tor] *m* choirmaster.

Kanu [ká'nōō] *nt* -s, -s canoe.

Kanzel [kán'tsəl] *f* -, -n pulpit; (*AVIAT*) cockpit.

Kanzlei [kántslī'] *f* chancery; (*Büro*) chambers *pl*.

Kanzler [kánts'lər] *m* -s, - chancellor.

Kap [káp] *nt* -s, -s cape; **das ~ der guten Hoffnung** the Cape of Good Hope.

Kap. *abk* (= *Kapitel*) chap.

Kapazität [kápátsētē:t'] *f* capacity; (*Fachmann*) authority.

Kapelle [kápe'lə] *f* (*Gebäude*) chapel; (*MUS*) band.

Kapellmeister(in *f*) *m* director of music; (*MIL*, *von Tanzkapelle etc*) bandmaster, bandleader.

Kaper [ká'pər] *f* -, -n caper.

kapern *vt* capture.

kapieren [kápē:'rən] *vti* (*umg*) understand.

Kapital [kápētâl'] *nt* -s, -e *od* -ien capital; **aus etw ~ schlagen** (*pej*: *lit, fig*) make capital out of sth; **~anlage** *f* investment; **~aufwand** *m* capital expenditure; **~ertragssteuer** *f* capital gains tax; **~flucht** *f* flight of capital; **~gesellschaft** *f* (*COMM*) joint-stock company; **~güter** *pl* capital goods *pl*; **k~intensiv** *a* capital intensive.

Kapitalismus [kápētális'mōōs] *m* capitalism.

Kapitalist [kápētálist'] *m* capitalist.

Kapital- *zW*: **k~kräftig** *a* wealthy; **~markt** *m* money market; **~verbrechen** *nt* serious crime; (*mit Todesstrafe*) capital crime.

Kapitän [kápēte:n'] *m* -s, -e captain.

Kapitel [kápi'təl] *nt* -s, - chapter; **ein trauriges ~** (*Angelegenheit*) a sad story.

Kapitulation [kápētōōlátséō:n'] *f* capitulation.

kapitulieren [kápētōōlē:'rən] *vi* capitulate.

Kaplan [káplân'] *m* -s, **Kapläne** chaplain.

Kappe [ká'pə] *f* -, -n cap; (*Kapuze*) hood; **das nehme ich auf meine ~** (*fig umg*) I'll take the responsibility for that.

kappen *vt* cut.

Kapsel [káp'səl] *f* -, -n capsule.

Kapstadt [káp'shtát] *nt* Cape Town.

kaputt [kápōōt'] *a* (*umg*) smashed, broken; (*Person*) exhausted, finished; **der Fernseher ist ~** (*umg*) the TV's not working; **ein ~er Typ** (*umg*) a bum; **~gehen** *vi* unreg break; (*Schuhe*) fall apart; (*Firma*) go bust; (*Stoff*) wear out; (*sterben*) cop it (*umg*) ; **~lachen** *vr* laugh o.s. silly; **~machen** *vt* break; (*Mensch*) exhaust, wear out; **~schlagen** *vr* unreg (*umg*) smash.

Kapuze [kápōō:'tsə] *f* -, -n hood.

Karabiner [kárábē:'nər] *m* -s, - (*Gewehr*) carbine.

Karacho [kárá'ₓhō] *nt* -s: **mit ~** (*umg*) hell for leather.

Karaffe [kárá'fə] *f* -, -n carafe; (*geschliffen*) decanter.

Karambolage [kárámbōlâ'zhə] *f* -, -n (*Zusammenstoß*) crash.

Karamel [kárámel'] *m* -s caramel; **~bonbon** *m od nt* toffee.

Karat [kárât'] *nt* -(e)s, -e carat.

Karate *nt* -s karate.

Karawane [kárávâ'nə] *f* -, -n caravan.

Kardinal [kárdēnál'] *m* -s, **Kardinäle** cardinal; **~fehler** *m* cardinal error; **~zahl** *f* cardinal number.

Karenzzeit [kárents'tsīt] *f* waiting period; (*POL*) *period before the elections when campaigning is no longer allowed.*

Karfreitag [kárfrī'tâk] *m* Good Friday.

karg [kárk] *a* scanty, poor; (*Mahlzeit auch*) meager (*US*), meagre (*Brit*); **~ mit Worten sein** use few words; **K~heit** *f* poverty, scantiness; meagerness.

kärglich [ker'kliċh] *a* poor, scanty.

Kargo [kár'gō] *m* -s, -s (*COMM*) cargo.

Karibik [kárē:'bik] *f* -: **die ~** the Caribbean.

karibisch *a* Caribbean; **das K~e Meer** the Caribbean Sea.

kariert [kárē:rt'] a (Stoff) checkered (US), checked (Brit); (Papier) squared; ~ **reden** (umg) talk nonsense.
Karies [kå'rēes] f - caries.
Karikatur [kårēkátōō:r'] f caricature; ~**ist(in** f) [-rist'(in)] m cartoonist.
karikieren [kårēkē:'rən] vt caricature.
karitativ [kårētátē:f'] a charitable.
Karneval [kár'nəvál] m -s, -e od -s carnival.
Karnickel [kárni'kəl] nt -s, - (umg) rabbit.
Karo [kå'rō] nt -s, -s square; (KARTEN) diamonds; ~-**As** nt ace of diamonds.
Karosse [kåro'sə] f -, -n coach, carriage.
Karosserie [kårosərē:'] f (AUT) body(work).
Karotte [kåro'tə] f -, -n carrot.
Karpaten [kárpâ'tən] pl Carpathians pl.
Karpfen [kár'pfən] m -s, - carp.
Karre [kå'rə] f -, -n siehe **Karren**.
Karree [kårā:'] nt -s, -s: **einmal ums ~ gehen** (umg) walk around the block.
karren [kå'rən] vt cart, transport; **K~** m -s, - cart, barrow; **den K~ aus dem Dreck ziehen** (umg) get things sorted out.
Karriere [kårēe:'rə] f -, -n career; ~ **machen** get on, get to the top; ~**macher(in** f) m careerist.
Karsamstag [kårzáms'tâk] m Easter Saturday.
Karst [kårst] m -s, -e (GEOG, GEOL) karst, barren landscape.
Karte [kår'tə] f -, -n card; (Land~) map; (Speise~) menu; (Eintritts~, Fahr~) ticket; **mit offenen ~n spielen** (fig) put one's cards on the table; **alles auf eine ~ setzen** put all one's eggs in one basket.
Kartei [kártī'] f card index; ~**karte** f index card; ~**leiche** f (umg) sleeping od non-active member; ~**schrank** m filing cabinet.
Kartell [kártel'] nt -s, -e cartel; ~**amt** nt monopolies commission; ~**gesetzgebung** f anti-trust legislation.
Karten- zW: ~**haus** nt (lit, fig) house of cards; ~**legen** nt fortune-telling (using cards); ~**schlüssel** m key card; ~**spiel** nt card game; (KARTEN) deck (US), pack (Brit) of cards.
Kartoffel [kårto'fəl] f -, -n potato; ~**brei** m, ~**püree** nt mashed potatoes pl; ~**chips** pl potato chips pl (US), potato crisps pl (Brit); ~**salat** m potato salad.
Karton [kártōñ'] m -s, -s cardboard; (Schachtel) cardboard box.
kartoniert [kártōnē:rt'] a hardback.
Karussell [kårōōsel'] nt -s, -e merry-go-round.
Karwoche [kår'voḥə] f Holy Week.
Kaschemme [kåshe'mə] f -, -n dive.
kaschieren [kåshē:'rən] vt conceal, cover up.
Kaschmir [kåsh'mē:r] nt -s (GEOG) Kashmir.
Käse [ke:'zə] m -s, - cheese; (umg: Unsinn) nonsense; ~**blatt** nt (umg) (local) rag; ~**glocke** f cheese cover; ~**kuchen** m cheesecake.
Kaserne [kázer'nə] f -, -n barracks pl.
Kasernenhof m parade ground.

käsig [ke:'ziḥ] a (fig umg: Gesicht, Haut) pasty, pale; (vor Schreck) white; (lit) cheesy.
Kasino [kázē:'nō] nt -s, -s club; (MIL) officers' mess; (Spiel~) casino.
Kaskoversicherung [kås'kōferziḥərōōng] f (AUT: Teil~) ≈ third party, fire and theft insurance; (: Voll~) fully comprehensive insurance.
Kasper [kås'pər] m -s, - Punch; (fig) clown.
Kasperl(e)theater [kås'pərl(ə)tâātər] nt Punch and Judy (show).
Kaspisches Meer [kå'spishəsmā:r'] nt Caspian Sea.
Kasse [kå'sə] f -, -n (Geldkasten) cashbox; (in Geschäft) till, cash register; (Kino~, Theater~ etc) box office; ticket office; (Kranken~) health insurance; (Spar~) savings bank; **die ~ führen** be in charge of the money; **jdn zur ~ bitten** ask sb to pay up; ~ **machen** count the money; **getrennte ~ führen** pay separately; **an der ~** (in Geschäft) at the (cash) desk; **gut bei ~ sein** be in the money.
Kasseler [kå'sələr] nt -s, - lightly smoked pork loin.
Kassen- zW: ~**arzt** m doctor for insurance company; ~**bestand** m cash balance; ~**führer** m (COMM) cashier; ~**patient** m patient on insurance scheme; ~**prüfung** f audit; ~**schlager** m (umg: THEAT etc) box-office hit; (Ware) big seller; ~**sturz** m: ~**sturz machen** check one's money; ~**wart** m (Club etc) treasurer; ~**zettel** m sales slip.
Kasserolle [kåsəro'lə] f -, -n casserole.
Kassette [kåse'tə] f small box; (Tonband, PHOT) cassette; (COMPUT) cartridge, cassette; (Bücher~) case.
Kassettenrecorder m -s, - cassette recorder.
Kassiber [kåsē:'bər] m -s, - (in Gefängnis) secret message.
kassieren [kåsē:'rən] vt (Gelder etc) collect; (umg: wegnehmen) take (away) ♦ vi: **darf ich ~?** would you like to pay now?
Kassierer(in f) [kåsē:'rər(in)] m -s, - cashier; (von Klub) treasurer.
Kastanie [kåstå'nēə] f chestnut.
Kastanienbaum m chestnut tree.
Kästchen [kest'ḥən] nt small box, casket.
Kaste [kås'tə] f -, -n caste.
Kasten [kås'tən] m -s, - box (auch SPORT), case; (Truhe) chest; **er hat was auf dem ~** (umg) he's brainy; ~**form** f (KOCH) (square) baking tin; ~**wagen** m van.
kastrieren [kåstrē:'rən] vt castrate.
Katalog [kàtàlō:k'] m -(e)s, -e catalog (US), catalogue (Brit).
katalogisieren [kàtàlōgēzē:'rən] vt catalog (US), catalogue (Brit).
Katalysator [kàtàpōōlt'] m (lit, fig) catalyst.
Katapult [kàtàpōōlt'] m od nt -(e)s, -e cata-

pult.
katapultieren [kátápōōltē:'rən] *vt* catapult ♦ *vr* catapult o.s.; (*Pilot*) eject.
Katar [kå'tár] *nt* Qatar.
Katarrh [kátár'] *m* **-s, -e** catarrh.
Katasteramt [kátás'tərámt] *nt* land registry.
katastrophal [kátástrōfál'] *a* catastrophic.
Katastrophe [kátástrō:'fə] *f* **-, -n** catastrophe, disaster.
Katastrophen- [kátástrō:'fən-] *zW*: ~**alarm** *m* emergency alert; ~**medizin** *f* medical treatment in disasters; ~**schutz** *m* disaster control.
Kat-Auto [kát'outō] *nt vehicle fitted with catalytic converter.*
Kategorie [kátāgōrē:'] *f* category.
kategorisch [kátāgō:'rish] *a* categorical.
kategorisieren [kátāgōrēzē:'rən] *vt* categorize.
Kater [kå'tər] *m* **-s, -** tomcat; (*umg*) hangover; ~**frühstück** *nt breakfast (of pickled herring etc) to cure a hangover.*
kath. *abk* = **katholisch.**
Katheder [kátä:'dər] *nt* **-s, -** (*SCH*) teacher's desk; (*UNIV*) lectern.
Kathedrale [kátädrá'lə] *f* **-, -n** cathedral.
Katheter [kátä:'tər] *m* **-s, -** (*MED*) catheter.
Kathode [kátō:'də] *f* **-, -n** cathode.
Katholik(in *f*) [kátōlē:k'(in)] *m* **-en, -en** Catholic.
katholisch [kátō:'lish] *a* Catholic.
Katholizismus [kátōlētsis'mōōs] *m* Catholicism.
katzbuckeln [káts'bōōkəln] *vi* (*pej umg*) bow and scrape.
Kätzchen [kets'çhən] *nt* kitten.
Katze [ká'tsə] *f* **-, -n** cat; **die ~ im Sack kaufen** buy a pig in a poke; **für die Katz** (*umg*) in vain, for nothing.
Katzen- *zW*: ~**auge** *nt* cat's-eye (*Brit*); (*am Fahrrad*) rear light; ~**jammer** *m* (*umg*) hangover; ~**musik** *f* (*fig*) caterwauling; ~**sprung** *m* (*umg*) stone's throw, short distance; ~**wäsche** *f* lick and a promise.
Kauderwelsch [kou'dərvelsh] *nt* **-(s)** jargon; (*umg*) double Dutch (*Brit*).
kauen [kou'ən] *vti* chew.
kauern [kou'ərn] *vi* crouch.
Kauf [kouf] *m* **-(e)s, Käufe** purchase, buy; (*Kaufen*) buying; **ein guter ~** a bargain; **etw in ~ nehmen** put up with sth.
kaufen *vt* buy; **dafür kann ich mir nichts ~** (*ironisch*) what use is that to me!
Käufer(in *f*) [koi'fər(in)] *m* **-s, -** buyer.
Kauf- *zW*: ~**haus** *nt* department store; ~**kraft** *f* purchasing power; ~**laden** *m* shop, store.
käuflich [koi'fliçh] *a, ad* purchasable, for sale; (*pej*) venal; ~ **erwerben** purchase.
Kauf- *zW*: ~**lust** *f* desire to buy things; (*BÖRSE*) buying; **k~lustig** *a* interested in buying; ~**mann** *m, pl* **-leute** businessman; (*Einzelhandels~*) shopkeeper; **k~männisch** *a* commercial; **k~männischer Angestellter**

clerk; ~**vertrag** *m* bill of sale; ~**willige(r)** *mf dekl wie a* potential buyer; ~**zwang** *m*: **kein/ohne ~zwang** no/without obligation.
Kaugummi [kou'gōōmē] *m* chewing gum.
Kaukasus [kou'kázōōs] *m*: **der ~** (the) Caucasus.
Kaulquappe [koulk'vápə] *f* **-, -n** tadpole.
kaum [koum] *ad* hardly, scarcely; **wohl ~, ich glaube ~** I hardly think so.
Kausalzusammenhang [kouzál'tsōōzámənháng] *m* causal connection.
Kaution [koutsēō:n'] *f* deposit; (*JUR*) bail.
Kautschuk [kout'shōōk] *m* **-s, -e** India rubber.
Kauz [kouts] *m* **-es, Käuze** owl; (*fig*) queer fellow.
Kavalier [káválē:r'] *m* **-s, -e** gentleman.
Kavaliersdelikt *nt* peccadillo.
Kavallerie [káválərē:'] *f* cavalry.
Kavallerist [káválərist'] *m* cavalryman.
Kaviar [ká'vēár] *m* caviar.
KB *abk* = **Kilobyte.**
KDV *abk* = **Kriegsdienstverweigerer.**
keck [kek] *a* daring, bold; **K~heit** *f* daring, boldness.
Kegel [kā:'gəl] *m* **-s, -** ninepin (*US*), skittle (*Brit*); (*MATH*) cone; ~**bahn** *f* skittle alley, bowling alley; **k~förmig** *a* conical.
kegeln *vi* bowl (*US*), play skittles (*Brit*).
Kehle [kā:'lə] *f* **-, -n** throat; **er hat das in die falsche ~ bekommen** (*lit*) it went down the wrong way; (*fig*) he took it the wrong way; **aus voller ~** at the top of one's voice.
Kehl- *zW*: ~**kopf** *m* larynx; ~**kopfkrebs** *m* cancer of the throat; ~**laut** *m* guttural.
Kehre [kā:'rə] *f* **-, -n** turn(ing), bend.
kehren *vti* (*wenden*) turn; (*mit Besen*) sweep; **sich an etw** (*dat*) **nicht ~** not heed sth; **in sich** (*akk*) **gekehrt** (*versunken*) pensive; (*verschlossen*) introspective, introverted.
Kehricht *m* **-s** sweepings *pl*.
Kehr- *zW*: ~**maschine** *f* sweeper; ~**reim** *m* refrain; ~**seite** *f* reverse, other side; (*ungünstig*) wrong od bad side; **die ~seite der Medaille** the other side of the coin.
kehrtmachen *vi* turn about, about-turn.
Kehrtwendung *f* about-turn.
keifen [kī'fən] *vi* scold, nag.
Keil [kīl] *m* **-(e)s, -e** wedge; (*MIL*) arrowhead; **k~en** *vt* wedge ♦ *vr* fight.
Keilerei [kīlərī'] *f* (*umg*) brawl.
Keilriemen *m* (*AUT*) fan belt.
Keim [kīm] *m* **-(e)s, -e** bud; (*MED, fig*) germ; **etw im ~ ersticken** nip sth in the bud.
keimen *vi* germinate.
Keim- *zW*: **k~frei** *a* sterile; **k~tötend** *a* antiseptic, germicidal; ~**zelle** *f* (*fig*) nucleus.
kein, keine, kein [kīn] *indef pron* a no, none, not any; ~**e schlechte Idee** not a bad idea; ~**e Stunde/drei Monate** (*nicht einmal*) less than an hour/three months.
keine(r, s) *indef pron* no one, nobody; none.
keinerlei [kī'nərlī'] *a attr* no ... whatever.

keines- *zW*: **~falls** *ad* on no account; **~wegs** *ad* by no means.

keinmal *ad* not once.

Keks [kā:ks] *m od nt* **-es, -e** cookie (*US*), biscuit (*Brit*).

Kelch [kelçh] *m* **-(e)s, -e** cup, goblet, chalice.

Kelle [ke'lə] *f* **-, -n** ladle; (*Maurer~*) trowel.

Keller [ke'lər] *m* **-s, -** cellar; **~assel** *f* **-, -n** woodlouse.

Kellerei [kelərī'] *f* wine cellars *pl*; (*Firma*) wine producer.

Keller- *zW*: **~geschoß** *nt* basement; **~wohnung** *f* basement apartment.

Kellner [kel'nər] *m* **-s, -** waiter; **~in** *f* waitress.

kellnern *vi* (*umg*) wait on tables.

Kelter *f* **-, -n** winepress; (*Obst~*) press.

keltern [kel'tərn] *vt* press.

Kenia [kā:'nčā] *nt* **-s** Kenya.

kennen [ke'nən] *vt unreg* know; **~ Sie sich schon?** do you know each other (already)?; **kennst du mich noch?** do you remember me?; **~lernen** *vt* get to know; **sich ~lernen** get to know each other; (*zum erstenmal*) meet.

Kenner(in *f)* *m* **-s, -** connoisseur; expert (*von od gen* on).

Kennkarte *f* identification card, I.D. card.

kenntlich *a* distinguishable, discernible; **etw ~ machen** mark sth.

Kenntnis *f* **-, -se** knowledge *no pl*; **etw zur ~ nehmen** note sth; **von etw ~ nehmen** take notice of sth; **jdn in ~ setzen** inform sb; **über ~se von etw verfügen** be knowledgeable about sth.

Kenn- *zW*: **~wort** *nt* (*Chiffre*) code name; (*Losungswort*) password, code word; **~zeichen** *nt* mark, characteristic; **(amtliches/polizeiliches) ~zeichen** (*AUT*) license plate; **k~zeichnen** *vt untr* characterize; **k~zeichnenderweise** *ad* characteristically; **~ziffer** *f* (code) number; (*COMM*) reference number.

kentern [ken'tərn] *vi* capsize.

Keramik [kārâ'mik] *f* **-, -en** ceramics *pl*, (piece of) pottery.

Kerbe [ker'bə] *f* **-, -n** notch, groove.

Kerbel *m* **-s, -** chervil.

kerben *vt* notch.

Kerbholz *nt*: **etw auf dem ~ haben** have done sth wrong.

Kerker [ker'kər] *m* **-s, -** prison.

Kerl [kerl] *m* **-s, -e** (*umg*) fellow, guy; **du gemeiner ~!** (*umg*) you swine!

Kern [kern] *m* **-(e)s, -e** (*Obst~*) pip, pit (*US*), stone; (*Nuß~*) kernel; (*Atom~*) nucleus; (*fig*) heart, core; **~energie** *f* nuclear energy; **~fach** *nt* (*SCH*) core subject; **~forschung** *f* nuclear research; **~frage** *f* central issue; **~gehäuse** *nt* core; **k~gesund** *a* thoroughly healthy, fit as a fiddle.

kernig *a* robust; (*Ausspruch*) pithy.

Kern- *zW*: **~kraftwerk** *nt* nuclear power station; **k~los** *a* seedless, pipless; **~physik** *f*

nuclear physics; **~reaktion** *f* nuclear reaction; **~reaktor** *m* nuclear reactor; **~schmelze** *f* reactor meltdown; **~seife** *f* washing soap; **~spaltung** *f* nuclear fission; **~stück** *nt* (*fig*) main item; (*von Theorie etc*) central part, core; **~waffen** *pl* nuclear weapons *pl*; **k~waffenfrei** *a* nuclear-free; **~zeit** *f* core time.

Kerze [ker'tsə] *f* **-, -n** candle; (*Zünd~*) plug.

Kerzen- *zW*: **k~gerade** *a* straight as an arrow; **~halter** *m* candlestick; **~ständer** *m* candle holder.

keß [kes] *a* saucy.

Kessel [ke'səl] *m* **-s, -** kettle; (*von Lokomotive etc*) boiler; (*Mulde*) basin; (*GEOG*) depression; (*MIL*) encirclement; **~stein** *m* scale; **~treiben** *nt* (*fig*) witch hunt.

Kette [ke'tə] *f* **-, -n** chain; **jdn an die ~ legen** (*fig*) tie sb down.

ketten *vt* chain.

Ketten- *zW*: **~fahrzeug** *nt* tracked vehicle; **~hund** *m* watchdog; **~karussell** *nt* merry-go-round (*with gondolas suspended on chains*); **~laden** *m* chain store; **~rauchen** *nt* chain smoking; **~reaktion** *f* chain reaction.

Ketzer(in *f)* [ke'tsər(in)] *m* **-s, -** heretic; **k~isch** *a* heretical.

keuchen [koi'çhən] *vi* pant, gasp.

Keuchhusten *m* whooping cough.

Keule [koi'lə] *f* **-, -n** club; (*KOCH*) leg.

keusch [koish] *a* chaste; **K~heit** *f* chastity.

Kf. *abk* = **Kraftfahrer.**

kfm. *abk* = **kaufmännisch.**

Kfm. *abk* = **Kaufmann.**

Kfz *f* **-(s), -(s)** *abk* = **Kraftfahrzeug.**

KG *f* **-, -s** *abk* (= *Kommanditgesellschaft*) limited partnership.

k.g.V., kgV *abk* (= *kleinstes gemeinsames Vielfaches*) l.c.m., L.C.M.

k.H., kh. *abk* = **kurzerhand.**

kHz *abk* (= *Kilohertz*) kHz.

Kibbuz [kiboo:ts'] *m* **-, Kibbuzim** [kiboo:tsē:m'] *od* **-e** kibbutz.

kichern [ki'çhərn] *vi* giggle.

kicken [ki'kən] *vti* (*Fußball*) kick.

kidnappen [kit'nepən] *vt* kidnap.

Kidnapper(in *f)* *m* **-s, -** kidnapper.

Kiebitz [kē:'bits] *m* **-es, -e** lapwing, peewit.

Kiefer [kē:'fər] *m* **-s, -** jaw ♦ *f* **-, -n** pine.

Kiefern- *zW*: **~holz** *nt* pine(wood); **~zapfen** *m* pine cone.

Kieker [kē:'kər] *m* **-s, -**: **jdn auf dem ~ haben** (*umg*) have it in for sb.

Kiel [kē:l] *m* **-(e)s, -e** (*Feder~*) quill; (*NAUT*) keel; **k~holen** *vt* (*Person*) keelhaul; (*Schiff*) career; **~wasser** *nt* wake.

Kieme [kē:'mə] *f* **-, -n** gill.

Kies [kē:s] *m* **-es, -e** gravel; (*umg: Geld*) money, dough.

Kiesel [kē:'zəl] *m* **-s, -** pebble; **~stein** *m* pebble.

Kies- *zW*: **~grube** *f* gravel pit; **~weg** *m* gravel path.

kiffen [ki'fən] *vt* (*umg*) smoke pot *od* grass.

Kilimandscharo [kělěmándzhâ'rō] *m* -s Kilimanjaro.

Killer(in *f)* [ki'lər(in)] *m* -s, - (*umg*) killer, murderer; (*gedungener*) hit man.

Kilo [kě:'lō] *nt* -s, -(s) kilo; ~**byte** *nt* (*COMPUT*) kilobyte; ~**gramm** [kělōgrám'] *nt* -s, -e kilogram.

Kilometer [kělōmā:'tər] *m* kilometer (*US*), kilometre (*Brit*).

Kilometer- *zW:* ~**fresser** *m* (*umg*) long-haul driver; ~**geld** *nt* ≈ mileage (allowance); ~**stand** *m* ≈ mileage; ~**stein** *m* ≈ milestone; ~**zähler** *m* odometer (*US*), ≈ milometer (*Brit*).

Kimme [ki'mə] *f* -, -n notch; (*Gewehr*) back sight.

Kind [kint] *nt* -(e)s, -er [kin'dər] child; **sich freuen wie ein** ~ be as pleased as Punch; **mit** ~ **und Kegel** (*hum umg*) with the whole family; **von** ~ **auf** from childhood; **sich bei jdm lieb** ~ **machen** ingratiate o.s. with sb.

Kinder- *zW:* ~**arzt** *m* pediatrician (*US*), paediatrician (*Brit*); ~**bett** *nt* cot.

Kinderei [kindərī'] *f* childishness.

Kinder- *zW:* ~**erziehung** *f* bringing up of children; (*durch Schule*) education of children; **k~feindlich** *a* anti-children; (*Architektur, Planung*) not catering for children; ~**freibetrag** *m* child allowance; ~**garten** *m* nursery school, playgroup; ~**gärtner** *m* nursery-school teacher; ~**geld** *nt* child benefit (*Brit*); ~**laden** *m* (alternative) playgroup; ~**lähmung** *f* poliomyelitis; **k~leicht** *a* childishly easy; **k~lieb** *a* fond of children; ~**lied** *nt* nursery rhyme; **k~los** *a* childless; ~**mädchen** *nt* nursemaid; **k~reich** *a* with a lot of children; ~**schuh** *m*: **es steckt noch in den** ~**schuhen** (*fig*) it's still in its infancy; ~**spiel** *nt* child's play; ~**stube** *f*: **eine gute** ~**stube haben** be well-mannered.

Kindertagesstätte *f* day-nursery.

Kinderwagen *m* baby carriage (*US*), pram (*Brit*).

Kindes- *zW:* ~**alter** *nt* infancy; ~**beine** *pl*: **von** ~**beinen an** from early childhood; ~**mißhandlung** *f* child abuse.

Kind- *zW:* **k~gemäß** *a* suitable for a child *od* children; ~**heit** *f* childhood; **k~isch** *a* childish; **k~lich** *a* childlike.

kindsköpfig *a* childish.

Kinkerlitzchen [king'kərlitschən] *pl* (*umg*) knick-knacks *pl*.

Kinn [kin] *nt* -(e)s, -e chin; ~**haken** *m* (*BOXEN*) uppercut; ~**lade** *f* jaw.

Kino [kě:'nō] *nt* -s, -s movies, cinema (*Brit*); ~**besucher** *m* movie-goer (*US*), cinema-goer (*Brit*); ~**programm** *nt* movie program (*US*), film programme (*Brit*).

Kiosk [kěosk'] *m* -(e)s, -e kiosk.

Kippe [ki'pə] *f* -, -n cigarette butt (*US*) *od* end; (*umg*) cigarette, fag (*Brit*); **auf der** ~ **stehen** (*fig*) be touch and go.

kippen *vi* topple over, overturn ♦ *vt* tilt.

Kipper [ki'pər] *m* -s, - (*AUT*) tipper, dump(er) truck.

Kippschalter *m* toggle (*US*) *od* rocker (*Brit*) switch.

Kirche [kir'chə] *f* -, -n church.

Kirchen- *zW:* ~**diener** *m* churchwarden; ~**fest** *nt* church festival; ~**lied** *nt* hymn; ~**schiff** *nt* (*Längsschiff*) nave; (*Querschiff*) transept; ~**steuer** *f* church tax.

Kirch- *zW:* ~**gänger(in** *f)* *m* -s, - churchgoer; ~**hof** *m* churchyard; **k~lich** *a* ecclesiastical; ~**turm** *m* church tower, steeple; ~**weih** *f* fair, kermis (*US*).

Kirmes [kir'mes] *f* -, -sen (*Dialekt*) fair, kermis (*US*).

Kirsche [kir'shə] *f* -, -n cherry; **mit ihm ist nicht gut** ~**n essen** (*fig*) it's best not to tangle with him.

Kirsch- *zW:* ~**torte** *f*: **Schwarzwälder** ~**torte** Black Forest cherry-cake; ~**wasser** *nt* kirsch.

Kissen [ki'sən] *nt* -s, - cushion; (*Kopf*~) pillow; ~**bezug** *m* pillow case.

Kiste [kis'tə] *f* -, -n box; chest; (*umg: Sarg*) box.

Kita [ki'tá] *f abk* = **Kindertagesstätte.**

Kitsch [kitsh] *m* -(e)s trash.

kitschig *a* trashy.

Kitt [kit] *m* -(e)s, -e putty.

Kittchen *nt* (*umg*) can.

Kittel *m* -s, - overall; (*von Arzt, Laborant etc*) (white) coat.

kitten *vt* putty; cement; (*fig*) patch up.

Kitz [kits] *nt* -es, -e kid; (*Reh*~) fawn.

kitzelig [ki'tsəlich] *a* (*lit, fig*) ticklish.

kitzeln *vti* tickle.

k.J. *abk* (= *künftigen Jahres*) next year.

Kj. *abk* (= *Kalenderjahr*) calendar year.

KK *f abk* = **Krankenkasse.**

KKW *nt* -, -s *abk* = **Kernkraftwerk.**

Kl. *abk* (= *Klasse*) cl.

Klacks [kláks] *m* -es, -e (*umg: von Kartoffelbrei, Sahne*) dollop; (*von Senf, Farbe etc*) blob.

Kladde [klá'də] *f* -, -n rough book; (*Block*) scribbling pad.

klaffen [klá'fən] *vi* gape.

kläffen [kle'fən] *vi* yelp.

Klage [klâ'gə] *f* -, -n complaint; (*JUR*) action; **eine** ~ **gegen jdn einreichen** *od* **erheben** institute proceedings against sb; ~**lied** *nt*: **ein** ~**lied über jdn/etw anstimmen** (*fig*) complain about sb/sth; ~**mauer** *f*: **die** ~**mauer** the Wailing Wall.

klagen *vi* (*weh*~) lament, wail; (*sich beschweren*) complain; (*JUR*) take legal action; **jdm sein Leid/seine Not** ~ pour out one's sorrow/distress to sb.

Kläger(in *f)* [kle:'gər(in)] *m* -s, - plaintiff; (*JUR: in Scheidung*) petitioner; (*im Strafrecht auch*) prosecuting party.

Klageschrift *f* (*JUR*) charge; (*bei Scheidung*) petition.

kläglich [kle:'klich] *a* wretched.

Klamauk [klámouk'] *m* **-s** (*umg*: *Alberei*) tomfoolery; (*im Theater*) slapstick.

klamm [klám] *a* (*Finger*) numb; (*feucht*) damp.

Klamm *f* -, **-en** ravine.

Klammer [klá'mər] *f* -, **-n** clamp; (*in Text*) parenthesis, bracket; (*Büro~*) clip; (*Wäsche~*) pin (*US*), peg (*Brit*); (*Zahn~*) brace; ~ **auf/zu** open/close parentheses *od* brackets.

klammern *vr* cling (*an +akk* to).

klammheimlich [klámhīm'liċh] (*umg*) *a* secret ♦ *ad* on the quiet.

Klamotte [klámo'tə] *f* -, **-n** (*pej*: *Film etc*) rubbishy old film *etc*; (*Zeug*) stuff; ~**n** *pl* (*umg*: *Kleider*) clothes *pl*.

Klampfe [klámp'fə] *f* -, **-n** (*umg*) guitar.

klang [kláng] *imperf von* **klingen**.

Klang *m* **-(e)s**, ⁼**e** sound; **k~voll** *a* sonorous.

Klappbett *nt* folding bed.

Klappe [klá'pə] *f* -, **-n** valve; (*an Oboe etc*) key; (*FILM*) clapperboard; (*Ofen~*) damper; (*umg*: *Mund*) trap; **die** ~ **halten** shut one's trap.

klappen *vi* (*Geräusch*) click ♦ *vti* (*Sitz etc*) tip ♦ *vi unpers* work; **hat es mit den Karten/dem Job geklappt?** did you get the tickets/job O.K.?

Klappentext *m* blurb.

Klapper [klá'pər] *f* -, **-n** rattle.

klapperig *a* run-down, worn-out.

klappern *vi* clatter, rattle.

Klapper- *zW*: ~**schlange** *f* rattlesnake; ~**storch** *m* stork; **er glaubt noch an den** ~**storch** he still thinks babies are brought by the stork.

Klapp- *zW*: ~**messer** *nt* jackknife; ~**rad** *nt* collapsible bicycle; ~**stuhl** *m* folding chair.

Klaps [kláps] *m* **-es**, ⁼**e** slap; **einen** ~ **haben** (*umg*) have a screw loose; **k~en** *vt* slap.

klar [klár] *a* clear; (*NAUT*) ready to sail; (*MIL*) ready for action; **bei** ~**em Verstand sein** be in full possession of one's faculties; **sich** (*dat*) **im** ~**en sein über** (*+akk*) be clear about; **ins** ~**e kommen** get clear.

Klär- [kle:r'] *zW*: ~**anlage** *f* sewage plant, (*von Fabrik*) purification plant; **k~en** *vt* (*Flüßigkeit*) purify; (*Probleme*) clarify ♦ *vr* clear (itself) up.

Klare(r) *m* (*umg*) schnapps.

Klarheit *f* clarity; **sich** (*dat*) ~ **über etw** (*akk*) **verschaffen** get clear about sth.

Klarinette [klárēne'tə] *f* clarinet.

klar- *zW*: ~**kommen** *vi unreg* (*umg*): **mit jdm/etw** ~**kommen** be able to cope with sb/sth; ~**legen** *vt* clear up, explain; ~**machen** *vt* (*Schiff*) get ready for sea; **jdm etw** ~**machen** make sth clear to sb; ~**sehen** *vi unreg* see clearly; **K~sichtfolie** *f* transparent film; ~**stellen** *vt* clarify; **K~text** *m*: **im K~text** in clear; (*fig umg*) ≈ in plain English.

Klärung [kle:'rōōng] *f* purification; clarification.

klarwerden *vr unreg*: **sich** (*dat*) (**über etw** *akk*) ~ get (sth) clear in one's mind.

klasse [klá'sə] *a* (*umg*) smashing.

Klasse *f* -, **-n** class; (*SCH auch*) form; (*Steuer~ auch*) bracket; (*Güter~*) grade.

Klassen- *zW*: ~**arbeit** *f* test; ~**bewußtsein** *nt* class-consciousness; ~**buch** *nt* (*SCH*) (*class*) register; ~**gesellschaft** *f* class society; ~**kampf** *m* class conflict; ~**lehrer** *m* class teacher; **k~los** *a* classless; ~**sprecher(in** *f*) *m* ≈ class president (*US*), ≈ form prefect (*Brit*); ~**ziel** *nt*: **das** ~**ziel nicht erreichen** (*SCH*) not reach the required standard; (*fig*) not make the grade; ~**zimmer** *nt* classroom.

klassifizieren [klásēfētsē:'rən] *vt* classify.

Klassifizierung *f* classification.

Klassik [klá'sik] *f* (*Zeit*) classical period; (*Stil*) classicism; ~**er** *m* **-s**, - classic.

klassisch *a* (*lit*, *fig*) classical.

Klatsch [klátsh] *m* **-(e)s**, **-e** smack, crack; (*Gerede*) gossip; ~**base** *f* gossip(monger).

Klatsche *f* -, **-n** (*umg*) crib.

klatschen *vi* (*Geräusch*) clash; (*reden*) gossip; (*Beifall*) applaud, clap.

Klatsch- *zW*: ~**mohn** *m* (corn) poppy; **k~naß** *a* soaking wet; ~**spalte** *f* gossip column; ~**tante** *f* (*pej umg*) gossip(monger).

klauben [klou'bən] *vt* pick.

Klaue [klou'ə] *f* -, **-n** claw; (*umg*: *Schrift*) scrawl.

klauen *vt* claw; (*umg*) pinch.

Klause [klou'zə] *f* -, **-n** cell; (*von Mönch*) hermitage.

Klausel [klou'zəl] *f* -, **-n** clause; (*Vorbehalt*) proviso.

Klausur [klouzōō:r'] *f* seclusion; ~**arbeit** *f* examination paper.

Klaviatur [klávēátōō:r'] *f* keyboard.

Klavier [klávē:r'] *nt* **-s**, **-e** piano; ~**auszug** *m* piano score.

Klebemittel *nt* glue.

kleben [klā:'bən] *vt* stick (*an +akk* to); **jdm eine** ~ (*umg*) belt sb one.

Klebezettel *m* gummed label.

klebrig *a* sticky.

Kleb- *zW*: ~**stoff** *m* glue; ~**streifen** *m* adhesive tape.

kleckern [kle'kərn] *vi* spill.

Klecks [kleks] *m* **-es**, **-e** blot, stain; **k~en** *vi* blot; (*pej*) daub.

Klee [klā:] *m* **-s** clover; **jdn/etw über den grünen** ~ **loben** (*fig*) praise sb/sth to the skies; ~**blatt** *nt* cloverleaf; (*fig*) trio.

Kleid [klīt] *nt* **-(e)s**, **-er** garment; (*Frauen~*) dress; ~**er** *pl* clothes *pl*.

kleiden [klī'dən] *vt* clothe, dress; **jdn** ~ suit sb ♦ *vr* dress.

Kleider- *zW*: ~**bügel** *m* coathanger; ~**bürste** *f* clothes brush; ~**schrank** *m* wardrobe; ~**ständer** *m* coat-stand.

kleidsam *a* becoming.

Kleidung *f* clothing.

Kleidungsstück *nt* garment.
Kleie [klī'ə] *f* -, -n bran.
klein [klīn] *a* little, small; **haben Sie es nicht ~er?** haven't you got anything smaller?; **ein ~es Bier, ein K~es** (*umg*) ≈ half a pint, a half; **von ~ an** *od* **auf** (*von Kindheit an*) from childhood; (*von Anfang an*) from the very beginning; **das ~ere Übel** the lesser evil; **sein Vater war (ein) ~er Beamter** his father was a minor civil servant; **~ anfangen** start off in a small way; **ein Wort ~ schreiben** write a word with a small initial letter; **K~anzeige** *f* want ad (*US*), small ad (*Brit*); **K~anzeigen** *pl* classified advertising; **K~arbeit** *f*: **in zäher/mühseliger K~arbeit** with rigorous/painstaking attention to detail; **K~asien** *nt* Asia Minor; **K~bürgertum** *nt* petite bourgeoisie.
Kleine(r, s) *mf* little one.
klein- *zW*: **K~familie** *f* small family, nuclear family (*SOZIOLOGIE*); **K~format** *nt* small size; **im K~format** small-scale; **K~gedruckte(s)** *nt* small print; **K~geld** *nt* small change; **das nötige K~geld haben** (*fig*) have the necessary wherewithal (*umg*); **~gläubig** *a* of little faith; **~hacken** *vt* chop up; **K~holz** *nt* firewood; **K~holz aus jdm machen** make mincemeat of sb.
Kleinigkeit *f* trifle; **wegen** *od* **bei jeder ~** for the slightest reason; **eine ~ essen** have a bite to eat.
klein- *zW*: **~kariert** *a*: **~kariert denken** think small; **K~kind** *nt* infant; **K~kram** *m* details *pl*; **K~kredit** *m* personal loan; **~kriegen** *vt* (*umg: gefügig machen*) bring into line; (*unterkriegen*) get down; (*körperlich*) tire out; **~laut** *a* dejected, quiet; **~lich** *a* petty, paltry; **K~lichkeit** *f* pettiness, paltriness; **~mütig** *a* fainthearted.
Kleinod [klī'nō:t] *nt* -s, -odien [klīnō:'diən] gem, jewel; (*fig*) treasure.
klein- *zW*: **K~rechner** *m* minicomputer; **~schneiden** *vt* *unreg* chop up; **K~schreibung** *f* use of small initial letters; **~städtisch** *a* provincial.
kleinstmöglich *a* smallest possible.
Kleister [klīs'tər] *m* -s, - paste.
kleistern *vt* paste.
Klemme [kle'mə] *f* -, -n clip; (*MED*) clamp; (*fig*) jam; **in der ~ sitzen** *od* **sein** (*fig umg*) be in a fix.
klemmen *vt* (*festhalten*) jam; (*quetschen*) pinch, nip ♦ *vr* catch o.s.; (*sich hineinzwängen*) squeeze o.s.; **sich hinter jdn/etw ~** get on to sb/get down to sth ♦ *vi* (*Tür*) stick, jam.
Klempner [klemp'nər] *m* -s, - plumber.
Kleptomanie [kleptōmánē:'] *f* kleptomania.
Kleriker [klā:'rēkər] *m* -s, - cleric.
Klerus [klā:'rōōs] *m* - clergy.
Klette [kle'tə] *f* -, -n burr; **sich wie eine ~ an jdn hängen** cling to sb like a burr.
Kletterer [kle'tərər] *m* -s, - climber.
Klettergerüst *nt* climbing frame.

klettern *vi* climb.
Kletter- *zW*: **~pflanze** *f* creeper; **~seil** *nt* climbing rope.
klicken [kli'kən] *vi* click.
Klient(in *f*) [klēent'(in)] *m* client.
Klima [klē:'má] *nt* -s, -s *od* -te [klēmâ'tə] climate; **~'anlage** *f* air conditioning.
klimatisieren [klē:mátēzē:'rən] *vt* air-condition.
klimatisiert *a* air-conditioned.
Klimawechsel *m* change of air.
Klimbim [klimbim'] *m* -s (*umg*) odds and ends *pl*.
klimpern [klim'pərn] *vi* tinkle; (*mit Gitarre*) strum.
Klinge [kli'ngə] *f* -, -n blade, sword; **jdn über die ~ springen lassen** (*fig umg*) allow sb to run into trouble.
Klingel [kling'əl] *f* -, -n bell; **~beutel** *m* collection bag; **~knopf** *m* bell push.
klingeln *vi* ring; **es hat geklingelt** (*an Tür*) somebody just rang the doorbell.
klingen [kling'ən] *vi* *unreg* sound; (*Gläser*) clink.
Klinik [klē:'nik] *f* clinic.
klinisch [klē:'nish] *a* clinical.
Klinke [kling'kə] *f* -, -n handle.
Klinker [kling'kər] *m* -s, - clinker.
Klippe [kli'pə] *f* -, -n cliff; (*im Meer*) reef; (*fig*) hurdle.
klippenreich *a* rocky.
klipp und klar [klip'ōōntklâr] *a* clear and concise.
Klips [klips] *m* -es, -e clip; (*Ohr~*) earring.
klirren [kli'rən] *vi* clank, jangle; (*Gläser*) clink; **~de Kälte** biting cold.
Klischee [klishā:'] *nt* -s, -s (*Druckplatte*) plate, block; (*fig*) cliché; **~vorstellung** *f* stereotyped idea.
Klitoris [klē:'tōris] *f* -, - clitoris.
Klo [klō:] *nt* -s, -s (*umg*) john (*US*), loo (*Brit*).
Kloake [klōâ'kə] *f* -, -n sewer.
klobig [klō:'biç] *a* clumsy.
klopfen [klop'fən] *vi* knock; (*Herz*) thump; **es klopft** sb's knocking; **jdm auf die Finger ~** (*lit, fig*) give sb a rap on the knuckles; **jdm auf die Schulter ~** tap sb on the shoulder ♦ *vt* beat.
Klopfer *m* -s, - (*Teppich~*) beater; (*Tür~*) knocker.
Klöppel [klœ'pəl] *m* -s, - (*von Glocke*) clapper.
klöppeln *vi* make lace.
Klops [klops] *m* -es, -e meatball.
Klosett [klōzet'] *nt* -s, -e *od* -s lavatory, toilet; **~brille** *f* toilet seat; **~papier** *nt* toilet paper.
Kloß [klō:s] *m* -es, ̈e (*Erd~*) clod; (*im Hals*) lump; (*KOCH*) dumpling.
Kloster [klō:s'tər] *nt* -s, ̈ (*Männer~*) monastery; (*Frauen~*) convent; **ins ~ gehen** become a monk *od* nun.
klösterlich [klœs'tərliç] *a* monastic; convent.

Klotz [klots] *m* -es, ⁻e log; (*Hack~*) block; **jdm ein ~ am Bein** (*fig*) a millstone round sb's neck.

Klub [klōōp] *m* -s, -s club; **~jacke** *f* blazer; **~sessel** *m* easy chair.

Kluft [klōōft] *f* -, ⁻e cleft, gap; (*GEOG*) gorge, chasm; (*Uniform*) uniform; (*umg*: *Kleidung*) gear.

klug [klōō:k] *a* clever, intelligent; **ich werde daraus nicht ~** I can't make head or tail of it; **K~heit** *f* cleverness, intelligence; **K~schießer** *m* (*umg*) smart-ass.

Klümpchen [klümp'çhən] *nt* clot, blob.

klumpen [klōōm'pən] *vi* go lumpy, clot; **K~** *m* -s, - (*KOCH*) lump; (*Erd~*) clod; (*Blut~*) clot; (*Gold~*) nugget.

Klumpfuß [klōōmp'fōō:s] *m* club foot.

Klüngel [klü'ngəl] *m* -s, - (*umg*: *Clique*) clique.

Klunker [klōōng'kər] *m* -s, - (*umg*: *Schmuck*) rock(s).

km/h *abk* (= *Kilometer pro Stunde*) kph, km/h.

KMK *f abk* (= *Kultusministerkonferenz*) conference for ministers for education and the arts.

km/st *abk* (= *Kilometer pro Stunde*) kph, km/h.

knabbern [knå'bərn] *vti* nibble; **an etw ~** (*fig umg*) puzzle over sth.

Knabe [knå'bə] *m* -n, -n (*liter*) boy.

knabenhaft *a* boyish.

knackbraun [knåk'broun] *a* (*umg*) brown as a berry *od* nut.

Knäckebrot [kne'kəbrō:t] *nt* wheat *od* rye biscuit.

knacken [knå'kən] *vi* (*lit*, *fig*) crack ♦ *vt* (*umg*: *Auto*) break into.

knackfrisch *a* (*umg*) oven-fresh, crispy-fresh.

knackig *a* crisp.

Knacks [knåks] *m* -es, -e: **einen ~ weghaben** (*umg*) be uptight about sth.

Knackwurst *f type of frankfurter.*

Knall [knål] *m* -(e)s, -e bang; (*Peitschen~*) crack; **~ und Fall** (*umg*) unexpectedly; **einen ~ haben** (*umg*) be crazy *od* crackers; **~bonbon** *nt* (party) cracker; **~effekt** *m* surprise effect, spectacular effect; **k~en** *vi* bang; crack ♦ *vt*: **jdm eine k~en** (*umg*) clout sb; **~frosch** *m* jumping jack; **k~hart** *a* (*umg*) really hard; (*Film*) brutal; (*Porno*) hard-core; **k~rot** *a* bright red.

knapp [knåp] *a* (*Geld*) scarce; (*kurz*) short; (*Kleidungsstück etc*) tight; (*Mehrheit, Sieg*) narrow; (*Sprache*) concise; **meine Zeit ist ~ bemessen** I am short of time; **mit ~er Not** only just.

Knappe *m* -n, -n (*Edelmann*) young knight.

knapp- *zW*: **~halten** *vt unreg* stint; **K~heit** *f* tightness; scarcity; conciseness.

Knarre [knå'rə] *f* -, -n (*umg*: *Gewehr*) shooter.

knarren *vi* creak.

Knast [knåst] *m* -(e)s (*umg*) clink, can.

Knatsch [knåtsh] *m* -es (*umg*) trouble.

knattern [knå'tərn] *vi* rattle; (*Maschinengewehr*) chatter.

Knäuel [knoi'əl] *m od nt* -s, - (*Woll~*) ball; (*Menschen~*) knot.

Knauf [knouf] *m* -(e)s, **Knäufe** knob; (*Schwert~*) pommel.

Knauser [knou'zər] *m* -s, - miser.

knauserig *a* miserly.

knausern *vi* be mean.

knautschen [knout'shən] *vti* crumple.

Knebel [knā:'bəl] *m* -s, - gag.

knebeln *vt* gag; (*NAUT*) fasten.

Knebelvertrag *m unfairly binding contract, one-sided contract.*

Knecht [kneçht] *m* -(e)s, -e farm laborer (*US*) *od* labourer (*Brit*); servant.

knechten *vt* enslave.

Knechtschaft *f* servitude.

kneifen [knī'fən] *vti unreg* pinch; (*sich drücken*) back out; **vor etw ~** dodge sth.

Kneifzange *f* pliers *pl*; (*kleine*) pincers *pl*.

Kneipe [knī'pə] *f* -, -n (*umg*) bar, saloon (*US*).

Kneippkur [knīp'kōō:r] *f* Kneipp cure, *type of hydropathic treatment combined with diet, rest etc.*

Knete [knā:'tə] *f* (*umg*: *Geld*) dough.

kneten *vt* knead; (*Wachs*) mold (*US*), mould (*Brit*).

Knetgummi *m od nt*, **Knetmasse** *f* Plasticine ®, modeling clay.

Knick [knik] *m* -(e)s, -e (*Sprung*) crack; (*Kurve*) bend; (*Falte*) fold.

knicken *vti* (*springen*) crack; (*brechen*) break; (*Papier*) fold; **„nicht ~!"** "do not bend"; **geknickt sein** be downcast.

Knicks [kniks] *m* -es, -e curts(e)y; **k~en** *vi* curts(e)y.

Knie [knē:] *nt* -s, - knee; **in die ~ gehen** kneel; (*fig*) be brought to one's knees; **~beuge** *f* -, -n knee bend; **~fall** *m* genuflection; **~gelenk** *nt* knee joint; **~kehle** *f* back of the knee.

knien *vi* kneel ♦ *vr*: **sich in die Arbeit ~** (*fig*) get down to one's work.

Knie- *zW*: **~scheibe** *f* kneecap; **~strumpf** *m* knee-length sock.

kniff [knif] *imperf von* **kneifen.**

Kniff *m* -(e)s, -e (*Zwicken*) pinch; (*Falte*) fold; (*fig*) trick, knack.

kniffelig *a* tricky.

knipsen [knip'sən] *vti* (*Fahrkarte*) punch; (*PHOT*) take a snap (of), snap.

Knirps [knirps] *m* -es, -e little chap; (®: *Schirm*) telescopic umbrella.

knirschen [knir'shən] *vi* crunch; **mit den Zähnen ~** grind one's teeth.

knistern [knis'tərn] *vi* crackle; (*Papier, Seide*) rustle.

Knitter- [kni'tər] *zW*: **~falte** *f* crease; **k~frei** *a* non-crease.

knittern *vi* crease.

knobeln [knō:'bəln] *vi* (*würfeln*) play dice; (*um eine Entscheidung*) toss *od* flip for it.
Knoblauch [knō:p'loukh] *m* -(e)s garlic.
Knöchel [knœ'chəl] *m* -s, - knuckle; (*Fuß~*) ankle.
Knochen [kno'khən] *m* -s, - bone; **~arbeit** *f* (*umg*) hard work; **~bau** *m* bone structure; **~bruch** *m* fracture; **~gerüst** *nt* skeleton; **~mark** *nt* bone marrow.
knöchern [knœ'chərn] *a* bone.
knochig [kno'khich] *a* bony.
Knödel [knœ'dəl] *m* -s, - dumpling.
Knolle [kno'lə] *f* -, -n bulb.
Knopf [knopf] *m* -(e)s, ¨e button; (*Kragen~*) stud.
knöpfen [knœp'fən] *vt* button.
Knopfloch *nt* buttonhole.
Knorpel [knor'pəl] *m* -s, - cartilage, gristle.
knorpelig *a* gristly.
knorrig [kno'rich] *a* gnarled, knotted.
Knospe [knos'pə] *f* -, -n bud.
knospen *vi* bud.
knoten [knō:'tən] *vt* knot; **K~** *m* -s, - knot; (*Haar auch*) bun; (*BOT*) node; (*MED*) lump; **~punkt** *m* junction.
knuffen [knoo'fən] *vt* (*umg*) cuff.
Knüller [knü'lər] *m* -s, - (*umg*) hit; (*Reportage*) scoop.
knüpfen [knüp'fən] *vt* tie; (*Teppich*) knot; (*Freundschaft*) form.
Knüppel [knü'pəl] *m* -s, - cudgel; (*Polizei~*) baton, truncheon; (*AVIAT*) (joy)stick; **jdm ~ zwischen die Beine werfen** (*fig*) put a spoke in sb's wheel; **k~dick** *a* (*umg*) very thick; (*fig*) thick and fast; **~schaltung** *f* (*AUT*) floor-mounted gearshift.
knurren [knoo'rən] *vi* (*und Hund*) snarl, growl; (*Magen*) rumble; (*Mensch*) mutter.
knusperig [knoos'pərich] *a* crisp; (*Keks*) crunchy.
knutschen [knoo:t'shən] *vt* (*umg*) neck with ♦ *vir* neck.
k.o. *a* (*SPORT*) knocked out; (*fig umg*) whacked.
Koalition [kōálētsēō:n'] *f* coalition.
Kobalt [kō:'bált] *nt* -s cobalt.
Kobold [kō:'bolt] *m* -(e)s, -e goblin, imp.
Kobra [kō:'brà] *f* -, -s cobra.
Koch [kokh] *m* -(e)s, ¨e cook; **~buch** *nt* cookery book; **k~echt** *a* (*Farbe*) fast.
kochen *vi* cook; (*Wasser*) boil; **er kochte vor Wut** (*umg*) he was seething ♦ *vt* (*Essen*) to cook; **etw auf kleiner Flamme ~** simmer sth over a low heat.
Kocher *m* -s, - stove, cooker.
Köcher [kœ'chər] *m* -s, - quiver.
Kochgelegenheit *f* cooking facilities *pl*.
Köchin [kœ'chin] *f* cook.
Koch- *zW:* **~kunst** *f* cooking; **~löffel** *m* kitchen spoon; **~nische** *f* kitchenette; **~platte** *f* hotplate; **~salz** *nt* cooking salt; **~topf** *m* saucepan, pot; **~wäsche** *f* washing that can be boiled.
Köder [kœ'dər] *m* -s, - bait, lure.

ködern *vt* lure, entice.
Koexistenz [kōeksistents'] *f* coexistence.
Koffein [kofáē:n'] *nt* -s caffeine; **k~frei** *a* decaffeinated.
Koffer [ko'fər] *m* -s, - suitcase; (*Schrank~*) trunk; **die ~ packen** (*lit, fig*) pack one's bags; **~kuli** *m* cart (*US*), (luggage) trolley (*Brit*); **~radio** *nt* portable radio; **~raum** *m* (*AUT*) trunk (*US*), boot (*Brit*).
Kognak [kon'yák] *m* -s, -s brandy, cognac.
Kohl [kō:l] *m* -(e)s, -e cabbage.
Kohldampf *m* (*umg*): **~ haben** be famished.
Kohle [kō:'lə] *f* -, -n coal; (*Holz~*) charcoal; (*CHEM*) carbon; (*umg*: *Geld*): **die ~n stimmen** the money's right; (*CHEM*) **~hydrat** *nt* -(e)s, -e carbohydrate; **~kraftwerk** *nt* coal-fired power station.
kohlen [kō:'lən] *vi* (*umg*) tell white lies.
Kohlen- *zW:* **~bergwerk** *nt* coal mine, pit; **~dioxyd** *nt* -(e)s, -e carbon dioxide; **~grube** *f* coal mine, pit; **~händler** *m* coal merchant, coalman; **~säure** *f* carbon dioxide; **ein Getränk ohne ~säure** a non-carbonated *od* still drink; **~stoff** *m* carbon.
Kohlepapier *nt* carbon paper.
Köhler [kœ'lər] *m* -s, - charcoal burner.
Kohle- *zW:* **~stift** *m* charcoal pencil; **~zeichnung** *f* charcoal drawing.
Kohl- *zW:* **k~(pech)rabenschwarz** *a* (*Haar*) jet-black; (*Nacht*) pitch-black; **~rübe** *f* rutabaga (*US*), (Swedish) turnip; **k~schwarz** *a* coal-black.
Koitus [kō:'ētoōs] *m* -, -*od* -se coitus.
Koje [kō:'yə] *f* -, -n cabin; (*Bett*) bunk.
Kokain [kōkī:n'] *nt* -s cocaine.
kokett [kōket'] *a* coquettish, flirtatious.
kokettieren [kōketē:'rən] *vi* flirt.
Kokosnuß [kō:'kosnoōs] *f* coconut.
Koks [kō:ks] *m* -es, -e coke.
Kolben [kol'bən] *m* -s, - (*Gewehr~*) rifle butt; (*Keule*) club; (*CHEM*) flask; (*TECH*) piston; (*Mais~*) cob.
Kolchose [kolchō:'zə] *f* -, -n collective farm.
Kolik [kō:'lik] *f* colic, gripe.
Kollaborateur(in *f*) [kolábōrátœr'(in)] *m* (*POL*) collaborator.
Kollaps [koláps'] *m* -es, -e collapse.
Kolleg [kolā:k'] *nt* -s, -s *od* -ien lecture course.
Kollege [kolā:'gə] *m* -n, -n, **Kollegin** *f* colleague.
kollegial [kolāgēál'] *a* cooperative.
Kollegium *nt* board; (*SCH*) staff.
Kollekte [kolek'tə] *f* -, -n (*REL*) collection.
Kollektion [kolektsēō:n'] *f* collection; (*Sortiment*) range.
kollektiv [kolektē:f'] *a* collective.
Koller [ko'lər] *m* -s, - (*umg*: *Anfall*) funny mood; (*Wutanfall*) rage; (*Tropen~*) tropical madness; (*Gefängnis~*) prison madness.
kollidieren [kolēdē:'rən] *vi* collide; (*zeitlich*) clash.
Kollier [kolēā:'] *nt* -s, -s necklet, necklace.
Kollision [kolēzēō:n'] *f* collision; (*zeitlich*)

clash.

Kollisionskurs *m*: **auf ~ gehen** (*fig*) be heading for trouble.

kolonial [kŏlŏnĕål'] *a* colonial; **K~macht** *f* colonial power; **K~warenhändler** *m* grocer.

Kolonie [kŏlŏnĕː'] *f* colony.

kolonisieren [kŏlŏnĕzĕː'rən] *vt* colonize.

Kolonist(in *f*) [kŏlŏnist'(in)] *m* colonist.

Kolonne [kŏlo'nə] *f* -, **-n** column; (*von Fahrzeugen*) convoy.

Koloß [kŏlos'] *m* **-sses, -sse** colossus.

kolossal [kŏlosål'] *a* colossal.

Koma [kŏː'mȧ] *nt* -s, -s *od* -ta [-tȧ] (*MED*) coma.

Kombi [kom'bĕ] *m* -s, -s (*AUT*) station wagon (*US*), estate (car) (*Brit*).

Kombination [kombĕnátsĕŏːn'] *f* combination; (*Vermutung*) conjecture; (*Hemdhose*) combinations *pl*; (*AVIAT*) flying suit.

Kombinationsschloß *nt* combination lock.

kombinieren [kombĕnĕː'rən] *vt* combine ♦ *vi* deduce, work out; (*vermuten*) guess.

Kombi- *zW*: **~wagen** *m* (*AUT*) station wagon (*US*), estate (car) (*Brit*); **~zange** *f* (pair of) pliers.

Komet [kŏmȧː't] *m* **-en, -en** comet.

kometenhaft *a* (*fig*: *Aufstieg*) meteoric.

Komfort [komfŏːr'] *m* **-s** luxury; (*von Möbel etc*) comfort; (*von Wohnung*) amenities *pl*; (*von Auto*) luxury features *pl*; (*von Gerät*) extras *pl*.

Komik [kŏː'mik] *f* humor (*US*), humour (*Brit*), comedy; **~er** *m* -s, - comedian.

komisch [kŏː'mish] *a* funny; **mir ist so ~** (*umg*) I feel funny *od* strange *od* odd.

Komitee [kŏmĕtȧː'] *nt* -s, -s committee.

Komm. *abk* (= *Kommission*) comm.

Komma [ko'mȧ] *nt* -s, -s *od* -ta [-tȧ] comma; (*MATH*) decimal point; **fünf ~ drei** five point three.

Kommandant [komȧndȧnt'] *m* commander, commanding officer.

Kommandeur [komȧndœr'] *m* commanding officer.

kommandieren [komȧndĕː'rən] *vt* command ♦ *vi* command; (*Befehle geben*) give orders.

Kommando [komȧn'dŏ] *nt* -s, -s command, order; (*Truppe*) detachment, squad; **auf ~** to order; **~brücke** *f* (*NAUT*) bridge.

kommen [ko'mən] *unreg vi* come; (*näher ~*) approach; (*passieren*) happen; (*sich verschaffen*) get hold of; (*gelangen, geraten*) get; (*Blumen, Zähne, Tränen etc*) appear; (*in die Schule, ins Zuchthaus etc*) go; **~ lassen** send for; **in Bewegung ~** start moving; **jdn besuchen ~** come and visit sb; (*stattfinden*): **was kommt diese Woche im Kino?** what's on at the movies this week?; **das kommt davon!** see what happens?; **du kommst mir gerade recht** (*ironisch*) you're just what I need; **das kommt in den Schrank** that goes in the closet; **an etw** (*akk*) **~** (*berühren*) touch sth; **auf etw** (*akk*) **~** (*sich erinnern*) think of sth; (*spre-*

chen über) get onto sth; **das kommt auf die Rechnung** that goes onto the bill; **hinter etw** (*akk*) **~** (*herausfinden*) find sth out; **zu sich ~** come round *od* to; **zu etw ~** acquire sth; **um etw ~** lose sth; **nichts auf jdn/etw ~ lassen** have nothing said against sb/sth; **jdm frech ~** get cheeky with sb; **auf jeden vierten kommt ein Platz** there's one place to every fourth person; **mit einem Anliegen ~** have a request (to make); **wer kommt zuerst?** who's first?; **wer zuerst kommt, mahlt zuerst** (*Sprichwort*) first come first served; **unter ein Auto ~** be run over by a car; **wie hoch kommt das?** what does that cost? ♦ *vi unpers*: **es kam eins zum anderen** one thing led to another; **und so kam es, daß ...** and that is how it happened that ...; **daher kommt es, daß ...** that's why ...

Kommen *nt* -s coming.

kommend *a* (*Jahr, Woche, Generation*) coming; (*Ereignisse, Mode*) future; **(am) ~en Montag** next Monday.

Kommentar [komentȧr'] *m* commentary; **kein ~** no comment; **k~los** *a* without comment.

Kommentator [komentȧ'tor] *m* (*TV*) commentator.

kommentieren [komentĕː'rən] *vt* comment on; **kommentierte Ausgabe** annotated edition.

kommerziell [komertsĕel'] *a* commercial.

Kommilitone [komĕlĕtŏː'nə] *m* -n, -n, **Kommilitonin** *f* fellow student.

Kommiß [komis'] *m* **-sses** (life in the) army.

Kommissar [komisȧr'] *m* police inspector.

Kommißbrot *nt* army bread.

Kommission [komisĕŏːn'] *f* (*COMM*) commission; (*Ausschuß*) committee; **etw in ~ geben** give (to a dealer) for sale on commission.

Kommode [komŏː'də] *f* -, **-n** (chest of) drawers.

kommunal [komŏŏnȧl'] *a* local; (*von Stadt auch*) municipal; **K~abgaben** *pl* local rates and taxes *pl*; **K~wahlen** *pl* local (government) elections *pl*.

Kommune [komŏŏː'nə] *f* -, **-n** commune.

Kommunikation [komŏŏnikátsĕŏːn'] *f* communication.

Kommunion [komŏŏnĕŏːn'] *f* communion.

Kommuniqué [komünĕkȧː'] *nt* -s, -s communiqué.

Kommunismus [komŏŏnis'mŏŏs] *m* communism.

Kommunist(in *f*) [komŏŏnist'(in)] *m* communist; **k~isch** *a* communist.

kommunizieren [komŏŏnĕtsĕː'rən] *vi* communicate; (*ECCL*) receive communion.

Komödiant [kŏmœdĕȧnt'] *m* comedian; **~in** *f* comedienne.

Komödie [kŏmœ'dĕə] *f* comedy; **~ spielen** (*fig*) put on an act.

Kompagnon [kompȧnyŏn'] *m* -s, -s (*COMM*) partner.

kompakt [kompákt'] *a* compact.
Kompaktanlage *f* (*RAD*) audio system.
Kompanie [kompánē:'] *f* company.
Komparativ [kom'párátē:f] *m* **-s, -e** comparative.
Kompaß [kom'pás] *m* **-sses, -sse** compass.
Kompatibilität [kompátēbēlēte:t'] *f* (*auch* COMPUT) compatibility.
kompensieren [kompenzē:'rən] *vt* compensate for, offset.
kompetent [kompātent'] *a* competent.
Kompetenz *f* competence, authority.
Kompetenzstreitigkeiten *pl* dispute over respective areas of responsibility.
komplett [komplet'] *a* complete.
Komplikation [komplēkátsēō:n'] *f* complication.
Kompliment [komplēment'] *nt* compliment.
Komplize [komplē:'tsə] *m* **-n, -n, Komplizin** *f* accomplice.
komplizieren [komplētsē:'rən] *vt* complicate.
kompliziert *a* complicated; (MED: *Bruch*) compound.
Komplott [komplot'] *nt* **-(e)s, -e** plot.
komponieren [kompōnē:'rən] *vt* compose.
Komponist(in *f*) [kompōnist'(in)] *m* composer.
Komposition [kompōzētsēō:n'] *f* composition.
Kompost [kompost'] *m* **-(e)s, -e** compost; ~**haufen** *m* compost heap.
Kompott [kompot'] *nt* **-(e)s, -e** stewed fruit.
Kompresse [kompre'sə] *f* **-, -n** compress.
Kompressor [kompre'sor] *m* compressor.
Kompromiß [komprōmis'] *m* **-sses, -sse** compromise; **einen ~ schließen** compromise; **k~bereit** *a* willing to compromise; ~**lösung** *f* compromise solution.
kompromittieren [komprōmitē:'rən] *vt* compromise.
Kondensation [kondenzátsēō:n'] *f* condensation.
Kondensator [kondenzá'tor] *m* condenser.
kondensieren [kondenzē:'rən] *vt* condense; (*fig auch*) distill (*US*), distil (*Brit*).
Kondens- *zW:* ~**milch** *f* condensed milk; ~**streifen** *m* vapor trail.
Kondition [kondētsēō:n'] *f* condition, shape; (*Durchhaltevermögen*) stamina.
Konditionalsatz [kondētsēōnál'záts] *m* conditional clause.
Konditionstraining *nt* fitness training.
Konditor [kondē:'tor] *m* pastrycook.
Konditorei [kondētōrī'] *f* cake shop; (*mit Café*) café.
kondolieren [kondōlē:'rən] *vi* condole (*jdm* with sb).
Kondom [kondō:m'] *nt* **-s, -e** condom.
Konfektion [konfektsēō:n'] *f* production of ready-made clothing.
Konfektionskleidung *f* ready-made clothing.
Konferenz [konfārents'] *f* conference; meeting; ~**schaltung** *f* (TEL) conference circuit; (RAD, TV) television *od* radio link-up.

konferieren [konfārē:'rən] *vi* confer; have a meeting.
Konfession [konfesēō:n'] *f* religion; (*christlich*) denomination; **k~ell** [-nel'] *a* denominational.
Konfessions- *zW:* **k~gebunden** *a* denominational; **k~los** *a* non-denominational; ~**schule** *f* denominational school.
Konfetti [konfe'tē] *nt* **-(s)** confetti.
Konfiguration [konfēgōōrátsēō:n'] *f* (COMPUT) configuration.
Konfirmand(in *f*) [konfirmánt', -mán'din] *m* candidate for confirmation.
Konfirmation [konfirmátsēō:n'] *f* (ECCL) confirmation.
konfirmieren [konfirmē:'rən] *vt* confirm.
konfiszieren [konfistsē:'rən] *vt* confiscate.
Konfitüre [konfētü:'rə] *f* **-, -n** jam.
Konflikt [konflikt'] *m* **-(e)s, -e** conflict; ~**herd** *m* (POL) center of conflict; ~**stoff** *m* cause of conflict.
konform [konform'] *a* concurring; ~ **gehen** be in agreement.
konfrontieren [konfrontē:'rən] *vt* confront.
konfus [konfōō:s'] *a* confused.
Kongo [kong'gō] *m* **-(s)** Congo.
Kongreß [kongres'] *m* **-sses, -sse** congress.
Kongruenz [kongrōōents'] *f* agreement, congruence.
König [kœ'niċh] *m* **-(e)s, -e** king.
Königin [kœ'nigin] *f* queen.
König- *zW:* **k~lich** *a* royal ♦ *ad:* **sich k~lich amüsieren** (*umg*) have the time of one's life; ~**reich** *nt* kingdom.
Königtum [kœ'niċhtōō:m] *nt* **-(e)s, -tümer** kingship.
konisch [kō:'nish] *a* conical.
Konj. *abk* = **Konjunktiv.**
Konjugation [konyōōgátsēō:n'] *f* conjugation.
konjugieren [konyōōgē:'rən] *vt* conjugate.
Konjunktion [konyōōngktsēō:n'] *f* conjunction.
Konjunktiv [kon'yōōngktē:f] *m* **-s, -e** subjunctive.
Konjunktur [konyōōngktōō:r'] *f* economic situation; (*Hoch~*) boom; **steigende/fallende ~** upward/downward economic trend; ~**loch** *nt* temporary economic dip; ~**politik** *f* policies aimed at preventing economic fluctuation.
konkav [konkáf'] *a* concave.
konkret [konkrā:t'] *a* concrete.
Konkurrent(in *f*) [konkōōrent'(in)] *m* competitor.
Konkurrenz [konkōōrents'] *f* competition; **jdm ~ machen** (COMM, *fig*) compete with sb; **k~fähig** *a* competitive; ~**kampf** *m* competition; (*umg*) rat race.
konkurrieren [konkōōrē:'rən] *vi* compete.
Konkurs [konkōōrs'] *m* **-es, -e** bankruptcy; **in ~ gehen, ~ machen** (*umg*) go bankrupt; ~**verfahren** *nt* bankruptcy proceedings *pl*; ~**verwalter** *m* receiver; (*von Gläubigern bevollmächtigt*) trustee.

können [kœ'nən] *vti unreg* be able to, can; (*wissen*) know; **was ~ Sie?** what can you do?; **~ Sie Deutsch?** can you speak German?; **ich kann nicht ...** I can't *od* cannot ...; **kann ich gehen?** can I go?; **das kann sein** that's possible; **ich kann nicht mehr** I can't go on; **ich kann nichts dafür** it's not my fault; **du kannst mich (mal)!** (*umg*) get lost!
Können *nt* -s ability.
Konnossement [konosəment'] *nt* (*COMM*) bill of lading.
konnte [kon'tə] *imperf von* **können**.
konsequent [konzäkvent'] *a* consistent; **ein Ziel ~ verfolgen** pursue an objective single-mindedly.
Konsequenz [konzäkvents'] *f* consistency; (*Folgerung*) conclusion; **die ~en tragen** take the consequences; (**aus etw) die ~en ziehen** take the appropriate steps.
konservativ [konzervátē:f'] *a* conservative.
Konservatorium [konzervátō:'rēōōm] *nt* academy of music, conservatory.
Konserve [konzer'və] *f* -, **-n** canned food.
Konservenbüchse *f*, **Konservendose** *f* can.
konservieren [konzervē:'rən] *vt* preserve.
Konservierung *f* preservation.
Konservierungsmittel *nt* preservative.
konsolidiert [konzōlēdē:rt'] *a* consolidated.
Konsolidierung *f* consolidation.
Konsonant [konzonánt'] *m* consonant.
Konsortium [konzor'tsēōōm] *nt* consortium, syndicate.
konspirativ [konspērátē:f'] *a*: **~e Wohnung** house of conspirators.
konstant [konstánt'] *a* constant.
Konstellation [konstelátsēō:n'] *f* constellation; (*fig*) line-up; (*von Faktoren etc*) combination.
Konstitution [konstētōōtsēō:n'] *f* constitution.
konstitutionell [konstētōōtsēōnel'] *a* constitutional.
konstruieren [konstrōōē:'rən] *vt* construct.
Konstrukteur(in *f*) [konstrōōktœr'(in)] *m* designer.
Konstruktion [konstrōōktsēōn'] *f* construction.
Konstruktionsfehler *m* (*im Entwurf*) design fault; (*im Aufbau*) structural defect.
konstruktiv [konstrōōktē:f'] *a* constructive.
Konsul [kon'zōōl] *m* -s, **-n** consul.
Konsulat [konzōōlát'] *nt* consulate.
konsultieren [konzōōltē:'rən] *vt* consult.
Konsum [konzōō:m'] *m* -s, -s consumption; [kon'zōō:m] (*Genossenschaft*) cooperative society; (*Laden*) cooperative store, co-op (*umg*); **~artikel** *m* consumer article.
Konsument [konzōōment'] *m* consumer.
Konsumgesellschaft *f* consumer society.
konsumieren [konzōōmē:'rən] *vt* consume.
Konsumterror *m* pressure of the materialistic society.
Kontakt [kontákt'] *m* -(e)s, -e contact; **mit jdm ~ aufnehmen** get in touch with sb;

k~arm *a* unsociable; **k~freudig** *a* sociable.
kontaktieren [kontáktē:'rən] *vt* contact.
Kontakt- *zW*: **~linsen** *pl* contact lenses *pl*; **~mann** *m*, *pl* **-männer** (*Agent*) contact.
Konterfei [kon'tərfī] *nt* -s, -s likeness, portrait.
kontern [kon'tərn] *vti* counter.
Konterrevolution [kon'tərrävōlōōtsēō:n] *f* counter-revolution.
Kontinent [kontēnent'] *m* continent.
Kontingent [kontinggent'] *nt* -(e)s, -e quota; (*Truppen~*) contingent.
kontinuierlich [kontēnōōē:r'liçh] *a* continuous.
Kontinuität [kontēnōōēte:t'] *f* continuity.
Konto [kon'tō] *nt* -s, **Konten** account; **das geht auf mein ~** (*umg*: **ich bin schuldig**) I am to blame for this; (*ich zahle*) this is on me (*umg*); **~'auszug** *m* statement (of account); **~'inhaber(in** *f*) *m* account holder.
Kontor [kontō:r'] *nt* -s, -e office.
Kontorist(in *f*) [kontō'rist'(in)] *m* clerk, office worker.
Kontostand *m* state of account.
kontra [kon'trá] *präp* +*akk* against; (*JUR*) versus.
Kontra *nt* -s, -s (*KARTEN*) double; **jdm ~ geben** (*fig*) contradict sb; **~baß** *m* double bass.
Kontrahent [-hent'] *m* contracting party, opponent.
Kontrapunkt *m* counterpoint.
Kontrast [kontrást'] *m* -(e)s, -e contrast.
Kontrollabschnitt *m* (*COMM*) counterfoil, stub.
Kontrollampe [kontrol'lámpə] *f* pilot lamp; (*AUT*: *für Olstand etc*) warning light.
Kontrolle [kontro'lə] *f* -, **-n** control, supervision; (*Paß~*) passport control.
Kontrolleur [kontrolœr'] *m* inspector.
kontrollieren [kontrolē:'rən] *vt* control, supervise; (*nachprüfen*) check.
Kontrollturm *m* control tower.
Kontroverse [kontrōver'zə] *f* -, **-n** controversy.
Kontur [kontōō:r'] *f* contour.
Konvention [konventsēō:n'] *f* convention.
Konventionalstrafe [konventsēōnál'shtráfə] *f* penalty *od* fine (*for breach of contract*).
konventionell [konventsēōnel'] *a* conventional.
Konversation [konverzátsēō:n'] *f* conversation.
Konversationslexikon *nt* encyclopaedia.
konvex [konveks'] *a* convex.
Konvoi [kon'voi] *m* -s, -s convoy.
Konzentration [kontsentrátsēō:n'] *f* concentration.
Konzentrations- *zW*: **~fähigkeit** *f* power of concentration; **~lager** *nt* concentration camp.
konzentrieren [kontsentrē:'rən] *vtr* concentrate.
konzentriert *a* concentrated ♦ *ad* (*zuhören*,

arbeiten) intently.
Konzept [kontsept'] *nt* -(e)s, -e rough draft; (*Plan, Programm*) plan; (*Begriff, Vorstellung*) concept; **jdn aus dem ~ bringen** confuse sb; **~papier** *nt* rough paper.
Konzern [kontsern'] *m* -s, -e combine.
Konzert [kontsert'] *nt* -(e)s, -e concert; (*Stück*) concerto; **~saal** *m* concert hall.
Konzession [kontseseō:n'] *f* license (*US*), licence (*Brit*); (*Zugeständnis*) concession; **~ entziehen** (*COMM*) disenfranchise.
Konzessionär [kontseseōne:r'] *m* -s, -e concessionaire.
konzessionieren [kontseseōnē:'rən] *vt* license.
Konzil [kontse:l'] *nt* -s, -e *od* -ien council.
konzipieren [kontsēpē:'rən] *vt* conceive; (*entwerfen auch*) design.
kooperativ [kōōpārátē:f'] *a* cooperative.
kooperieren [kōōpārē:'rən] *vi* cooperate.
Kopenhagen [kō:pənhá'gən] *nt* -s Copenhagen.
Kopf [kopf] *m* -(e)s, ⁼e head; **~ hoch!** chin up!; **~ an ~** shoulder to shoulder; (*Pferderennen, SPORT*) neck and neck; **pro ~** per person *od* head; **~ oder Zahl?** heads or tails?; **jdm den ~ waschen** (*fig umg*) give sb a piece of one's mind; **jdm über den ~ wachsen** (*lit*) outgrow sb; (*fig: Sorgen etc*) be more than sb can cope with; **jdn vor den ~ stoßen** antagonize sb; **sich** (*dat*) **an den ~ fassen** (*fig*) be speechless; **sich** (*dat*) **über etw** (*akk*) **den ~ zerbrechen** rack one's brains over sth; **sich** (*dat*) **etw durch den ~ gehen lassen** think about sth; **sich** (*dat*) **etw aus dem ~ schlagen** put sth out of one's mind; **... und wenn du dich auf den ~ stellst!** (*umg*) ... no matter what you say *od* do!; **er ist nicht auf den ~ gefallen** he's no fool; **~bahnhof** *m* terminus station; **~bedeckung** *f* headgear.
Köpfchen [kœpf'çhən] *nt*: **~ haben** be brainy.
köpfen [kœ'pfən] *vt* behead; (*Baum*) lop; (*Ei*) take the top off; (*Ball*) head.
Kopf- *zW*: **~ende** *nt* head; **~haut** *f* scalp; **~hörer** *m* headphone; **~kissen** *nt* pillow; **k~lastig** *a* completely rational; **k~los** *a* panic-stricken; **~losigkeit** *f* panic; **k~rechnen** *vi* do mental arithmetic; **~salat** *m* lettuce; **k~scheu** *a*: **jdn k~scheu machen** intimidate sb; **~schmerzen** *pl* headache *sing*; **~sprung** *m* header, dive; **~stand** *m* headstand; **~steinpflaster** *nt*: **eine Straße mit ~steinpflaster** a cobbled street; **~tuch** *nt* headscarf; **k~über** *ad* head over heels; **~weh** *nt* headache; **~zerbrechen** *nt*: **jdm ~zerbrechen machen** give sb a lot of headaches.
Kopie [kōpē:'] *f* copy.
kopieren [kōpē:'rən] *vt* copy.
Kopierer *m* -s, - (photo)copier.
Koppel [ko'pəl] *f* -, -n (*Weide*) enclosure ♦ *nt* -s, - (*Gürtel*) belt.

koppeln *vt* couple.
Koppelung *f* coupling.
Koppelungsmanöver *nt* docking maneuver (*US*) *od* manoeuvre (*Brit*).
Koralle [kōrá'lə] *f* -, -n coral.
Korallen- *zW*: **~kette** *f* coral necklace; **~riff** *nt* coral reef.
Korb [korp] *m* -(e)s, ⁼e basket; **jdm einen ~ geben** (*fig*) turn sb down; **~ball** *m* basketball.
Körbchen [kœrp'çhən] *nt* (*von Büstenhalter*) cup.
Korbstuhl *m* wicker chair.
Kord [kort] *m* -(e)s, -e corduroy.
Kordel [kor'dəl] *f* -, -n cord, string.
Korea [kōrā:'á] *nt* -s Korea.
Koreaner(in *f*) *m* -s, - Korean.
Korinthe [kōrin'tə] *f* -, -n currant.
Korinthenkacker [kōrin'tənkákər] *m* -s, - (*umg*) fusspot, hair-splitter.
Kork [kork] *m* -(e)s, -e cork.
Korken *m* -s, - stopper, cork; **~zieher** *m* -s, - corkscrew.
Korn [korn] *nt* -(e)s, ⁼er corn, grain; (*Gewehr*) sight; **etw aufs ~ nehmen** (*fig umg*) hit out at sth ♦ *m* -, -s (*Kornbranntwein*) corn schnapps; **~blume** *f* cornflower.
Körnchen [kœrn'çhən] *nt* grain, granule.
Körnerfresser [kœr'nərfresər] *m* (*umg*) seed-eater, nature freak.
Kornkammer *f* granary.
Körnung [kœr'nōōng] *f* (*TECH*) grain size; (*PHOT*) granularity.
Körper [kœr'pār] *m* -s, - body; **~bau** *m* build; **k~behindert** *a* disabled; **~gewicht** *nt* weight; **~größe** *f* height; **~haltung** *f* carriage, deportment; **k~lich** *a* physical; **k~liche Arbeit** manual work; **~pflege** *f* personal hygiene; **~schaft** *f* corporation; **~schaft des öffentlichen Rechts** public corporation *od* body; **~schaftssteuer** *f* corporation tax; **~teil** *m* part of the body.
Korps [kō:r] *nt* -, - (*MIL*) corps; (*UNIV*) students' club.
korpulent [korpōōlent'] *a* corpulent.
korrekt [korekt'] *a* correct; **K~heit** *f* correctness.
Korrektor(in *f*) [korek'tor, -tō:'rin] *m* -s, - proofreader.
Korrektur [korektōō:r'] *f* (*eines Textes*) proofreading; (*Text*) proof; (*SCH*) marking, correction; **~ lesen** proofread (*bei etw* sth); **~fahne** *f* (*TYP*) proof.
Korrespondent(in *f*) [korespondent'(in)] *m* correspondent.
Korrespondenz [korespondents'] *f* correspondence; **~qualität** *f* (*Drucker*) letter quality.
korrespondieren [korespondē:'rən] *vi* correspond.
Korridor [ko'rēdō:r] *m* -s, -e corridor.
korrigieren [korēgē:'rən] *vt* correct; (*Aufsätze etc auch*) mark; (*Meinung, Einstellung*) change.

Korrosionsschutz [korōzēō:ns'shōōts] *m* corrosion prevention.

korrumpieren [korōōmpē:'rən] *vt* (*auch* COMPUT) corrupt.

Korruption [korōōptsēō:n'] *f* corruption.

Korsett [korzet'] *nt* -(e)s, -e corset.

Korsika [kor'zēkä] *nt* -s Corsica.

Koseform [kō:'zəform] *f* pet form.

kosen *vt* caress ♦ *vi* bill and coo.

Kose- *zW:* ~**name** *m* nickname, pet name (*Brit*); ~**wort** *nt* term of endearment.

Kosmetik [kosmā:'tik] *f* cosmetics *pl.*

Kosmetikerin *f* beautician.

kosmetisch *a* cosmetic; (*Chirurgie*) plastic.

kosmisch [kos'mish] *a* cosmic.

Kosmonaut [kosmōnout'] *m* -en, -en cosmonaut.

Kosmopolit *m* -en, -en cosmopolitan; **k~isch** [-pōlē:'tish] *a* cosmopolitan.

Kosmos [kos'mos] *m* - cosmos.

Kost [kost] *f* - (*Nahrung*) food; (*Verpflegung*) board; ~ **und Logis** board and lodging.

kostbar *a* precious; (*teuer*) costly, expensive; **K~keit** *f* preciousness; costliness, expensiveness; (*Wertstück*) valuable.

kosten *vt* cost ♦ *vti* (*versuchen*) taste; **koste es, was es wolle** whatever the cost.

Kosten *pl* cost(s); (*Ausgaben*) expenses *pl*; **auf** ~ **von** at the expense of; **auf seine** ~ **kommen** (*fig*) get one's money's worth; ~**anschlag** *m* estimate; **k~deckend** *a* self-liquidating; ~**erstattung** *f* reimbursement of expenses; ~**kontrolle** *f* cost control; **k~los** *a* free (of charge); **k~pflichtig** *a*: **ein Auto k~pflichtig abschleppen** tow away a car at the owner's expense; ~**nutzenanalyse** *f* cost-benefit analysis; ~**stelle** *f* (*COMM*) cost center; ~**voranschlag** *m* (costs) estimate.

Kostgeld *nt* board.

köstlich [kœs'tlich] *a* precious; (*Einfall*) delightful; (*Essen*) delicious; **sich** ~ **amüsieren** have a marvelous time.

Kost- *zW:* ~**probe** *f* taste; (*fig*) sample; **k~spielig** *a* expensive.

Kostüm [kostü:m'] *nt* -s, -e costume; (*Damen*~) suit; ~**fest** *nt* fancy-dress party.

kostümieren [kostümē:'rən] *vtr* dress up.

Kostüm- *zW:* ~**probe** *f* (*THEAT*) dress rehearsal; ~**verleih** *m* costume agency.

Kot [kō:t] *m* -(e)s excrement.

Kotelett [kōtəlet'] *nt* -(e)s, -e *od* -s cutlet, chop.

Koteletten *pl* sideburns.

Köter [kœ'tər] *m* -s, - cur.

Kotflügel *m* (*AUT*) fender (*US*), wing (*Brit*).

kotzen [ko'tsən] *vi* (*umg!*) puke (*!*), throw up; **das ist zum K~** it makes you sick.

KP *f* -, -s *abk* (= *Kommunistische Partei*) C.P.

KPD *f* - *abk* (= *Kommunistische Partei Deutschlands*) West German communist party.

KPdSU *f* - *abk* (= *Kommunistische Partei der Sowjetunion*) C.P.S.U.

KPÖ *f* - *abk* (= *Kommunistische Partei Österreichs*) Austrian communist party.

Kr., Krs. *abk* = **Kreis.**

Krabbe [krä'bə] *f* -, -n shrimp.

krabbeln *vi* crawl.

Krach [kräkh] *m* -(e)s, -s *od* -e crash; (*andauernd*) noise; (*umg: Streit*) quarrel, argument; ~ **schlagen** make a fuss; **k~en** *vi* crash; (*beim Brechen*) crack ♦ *vr* (*umg*) argue, quarrel.

krächzen [krech'tsən] *vi* croak.

Kräcker [kre'kər] *m* -s, - (*KOCH*) cracker.

kraft [kräft] *präp* +*gen* by virtue of.

Kraft *f* -, ¨e strength; power; force; (*Arbeits*~) worker; **mit vereinten ~en werden wir ...** if we combine our efforts we will ...; **nach (besten) ~en** to the best of one's abilities; (*JUR: Geltung*): **außer** ~ **sein** be no longer in force; **in** ~ **treten** come into effect; ~**aufwand** *m* effort; ~**ausdruck** *m* swearword; ~**brühe** *f* beef bouillon.

Kräfteverhältnis [kref'tərheltnis] *nt* (*POL*) balance of power; (*von Mannschaften etc*) relative strength.

Kraft- *zW:* ~**fahrer** *m* (motor) driver; ~**fahrzeug** *nt* motor vehicle.

Kraftfahrzeug- *zW:* ~**brief** *m* (*AUT*) motor-vehicle registration certificate; ~**schein** *m* (*AUT*) car license; ~**steuer** *f* motor vehicle tax.

kräftig [kref'tich] *a* strong; (*Suppe, Essen*) nourishing; ~**en** [kref'tigən] *vt* strengthen.

Kraft- *zW:* **k~los** *a* weak; powerless; (*JUR*) invalid; ~**meierei** [-mīərī'] *f* (*umg*) showing off of physical strength; ~**probe** *f* trial of strength; ~**rad** *nt* motorcycle; ~**stoff** *m* fuel; **k~voll** *a* vigorous; ~**wagen** *m* motor vehicle; ~**werk** *nt* power station; ~**werker** *m* power station worker.

Kragen [krä'gən] *m* -s, - collar; **da ist mir der** ~ **geplatzt** (*umg*) I blew my top; **es geht ihm an den** ~ (*umg*) he's in for it; ~**weite** *f* collar size; **das ist nicht meine** ~**weite** (*fig umg*) that's not my cup of tea.

Krähe [kre:'ə] *f* -, -n crow.

krähen *vi* crow.

krakeelen [krakā:'lən] *vi* (*umg*) make a din.

krakelig [krä'kəlich] *a* (*umg: Schrift*) scrawly, spidery.

Kralle [krä'lə] *f* -, -n claw; (*Vogel*~) talon.

krallen *vt* clutch; (*krampfhaft*) claw.

Kram [kräm] *m* -(e)s stuff, rubbish; **den** ~ **hinschmeißen** (*umg*) chuck the whole thing; **k~en** *vi* rummage; ~**laden** *m* (*pej*) small store.

Krampf [krämpf] *m* -(e)s, ¨e cramp; (*zuckend*) spasm; (*Unsinn*) rubbish; ~**ader** *f* varicose vein; **k~haft** *a* convulsive; (*fig: Versuche*) desperate.

Kran [krän] *m* -(e)s, ¨e crane; (*Wasser*~) faucet (*US*), tap.

Kranich [krä'nich] *m* -s, -e (*ZOOL*) crane.

krank [krängk] *a* ill, sick; **sich** ~ **melden** let one's boss *etc* know that one is ill; (*telefo-*

nisch) phone in sick; (*bes MIL*) report sick; **jdn ~ schreiben** give sb a medical certificate; (*bes MIL*) put sb on the sicklist; **das macht mich ~!** (*umg*) it gets on my nerves!, it drives me round the bend!; **sich ~ stellen** pretend to be ill, malinger.

kränkeln [kreng'kəln] *vi* be in bad health.

kranken [kràng'kən] *vi*: **an etw** (*dat*) **~** (*fig*) suffer from sth.

kränken [kreng'kən] *vt* hurt.

Kranken- *zW*: **~bericht** *m* medical report; **~geld** *nt* sick pay; **~geschichte** *f* medical history; **~haus** *nt* hospital; **~kasse** *f* health insurance; **~pfleger** *m* orderly; (*mit Schwesternausbildung*) male nurse; **~pflegerin** *f* nurse; **~schein** *m* medical insurance card; **~schwester** *f* nurse; **~versicherung** *f* health insurance; **~wagen** *m* ambulance.

Kranke(r) *mf dekl wie a* sick person, invalid; (*Patient*) patient.

krankfeiern *vi* (*umg*) be off "sick"; (*vortäuschend*) call in "sick".

Krank- *zW*: **k~haft** *a* diseased; (*Angst etc*) morbid; **sein Geiz ist schon k~haft** his meanness is almost pathological; **~heit** *f* illness; disease; **nach langer schwerer ~heit** after a long serious illness.

Krankheitserreger *m* **-s, -** disease-causing agent.

kränklich [kreng'kliĊħ] *a* sickly.

Kränkung *f* insult.

Kranz [krànts] *m* **-es, ⁻e** wreath, garland.

Kränzchen [krents'ċħən] *nt* small wreath; (*fig*) ladies' party.

Krapfen [kràp'fən] *m* **-s, -** fritter; (*Berliner*) donut (*US*), doughnut (*Brit*).

kraß [kràs] *a* crass; (*Unterschied*) extreme.

Krater [krà'tər] *m* **-s, -** crater.

Kratzbürste [kràts'bürstə] *f* (*fig*) crosspatch.

Krätze [kre'tsə] *f* (*MED*) scabies.

krätzen *vti* scratch.

Krätzer *m* **-s, -** scratch; (*Werkzeug*) scraper.

Kraul [kroul] *m* ' **-s** (*auch*: **~schwimmen**) crawl; **k~en** *vi* (*schwimmen*) do the crawl ♦ *vt* (*streicheln*) tickle.

kraus [krous] *a* crinkly; (*Haar*) frizzy; (*Stirn*) wrinkled.

Krause [krou'zə] *f* **-, -n** frill, ruffle.

kräuseln [kroi'zəln] *vt* (*Haar*) make frizzy; (*Stoff*) gather; (*Stirn*) wrinkle ♦ *vr* (*Haar*) go frizzy; (*Stirn*) wrinkle; (*Wasser*) ripple.

Kraut [krout] *nt* **-(e)s, Kräuter** plant; (*Gewürz*) herb; (*Gemüse*) cabbage; **dagegen ist kein ~ gewachsen** (*fig*) there's nothing anyone can do about that; **ins ~ schießen** (*lit*) run to seed; (*fig*) get out of control; **wie ~ und Rüben** (*umg*) extremely untidy.

Krawall [kràvàl'] *m* **-s, -e** row, uproar.

Krawatte [kràvà'tə] *f* **-, -n** (neck)tie.

Krawattennadel *f* tie tack (*US*), tie pin (*Brit*).

kreativ [krāàtē:f'] *a* creative.

Kreatur [krāàtōō:r'] *f* creature.

Krebs [krā:ps] *m* **-es, -e** crab; (*MED*) cancer; (*ASTROL*) Cancer; **k~erregend** *a* carcinogenic; **k~rot** *a* red as a lobster.

Kredit [krādē:t'] *m* **-(e)s, -e** credit; (*Darlehen*) loan; (*fig auch*) standing; **~drosselung** [krādē:t'drosəlōōng] *f* credit squeeze; **k~fähig** *a* credit-worthy; **~hai** *m* (*umg*) loan shark; **~karte** *f* credit card; **~konto** *nt* credit account; **~würdigkeit** *f* credit rating.

Kreide [krī'də] *f* **-, -n** chalk; **bei jdm (tief) in der ~ stehen** be (deep) in debt to sb; **k~bleich** *a* as white as a sheet.

Kreis [krīs] *m* **-es, -e** circle; (*Stadt~ etc*) district; **im ~ gehen** (*lit, fig*) go round in circles; **(weite) ~e ziehen** (*fig*) have (wide) repercussions; **weite ~e der Bevölkerung** wide sections of the population; **eine Feier im kleinen ~e** a celebration for a few close friends and relatives.

kreischen [krī'shən] *vi* shriek, screech.

Kreisel [krī'zəl] *m* **-s, -** top; (*Verkehrs~*) traffic circle (*US*), roundabout (*Brit*).

kreisen [krī'zən] *vi* spin; (*fig*: *Gedanken, Gespräch*) revolve (*um* around).

Kreis- *zW*: **k~förmig** *a* circular; **~lauf** *m* (*MED*) circulation; (*fig*: *der Natur etc*) cycle; **~laufstörungen** *pl* circulatory disorders; **~säge** *f* circular saw.

Kreißsaal [krīs'zál] *m* delivery room.

Kreis- *zW*: **~stadt** *f* county town; **~verkehr** *m* traffic circle (*US*), roundabout (*Brit*).

Krem [krā:m] *f* **-, -s** cream, mousse.

Krematorium [krāmàtō:'rēōōm] *nt* crematorium.

Kreml [krā:ml'] *m* **-s**: **der ~** the Kremlin.

Krempe [krem'pə] *f* **-, -n** brim.

Krempel *m* **-s** (*umg*) rubbish.

krepieren [krāpē:'rən] *vi* (*umg*: *sterben*) die, kick the bucket.

Krepp [krep] *m* **-s, -s** *od* **-e** crêpe.

Kreppapier *nt* crêpe paper.

Kreppsohle *f* crêpe sole.

Kresse [kre'sə] *f* **-, -n** cress.

Kreta [krā:'tà] *nt* **-s** Crete.

kreuz [kroits] *a*: **~ und quer** all over.

Kreuz *nt* **-es, -e** cross; (*ANAT*) small of the back; (*KARTEN*) clubs; (*MUS*) sharp; (*Autobahn~*) intersection; **zu ~e kriechen** (*fig*) eat humble pie, eat crow (*US*); **jdn aufs ~ legen** throw sb on his back; (*fig umg*) take sb for a ride.

kreuzen *vt* cross; **die Arme ~** fold one's arms ♦ *vr* cross; (*Meinungen etc*) clash ♦ *vi* (*NAUT*) cruise.

Kreuzer *m* **-s, -** (*Schiff*) cruiser.

Kreuz- *zW*: **~fahrt** *f* cruise; **~feuer** *nt* (*fig*): **im ~feuer stehen** be caught in the crossfire; **~gang** *m* cloisters *pl*.

kreuzigen *vt* crucify.

Kreuzigung *f* crucifixion.

Kreuz- *zW*: **~otter** *f* adder; **~schmerzen** *pl* backache *sing*.

Kreuzung *f* (*Verkehrs~*) crossing, junction; (*Züchtung*) cross.

Kreuz- *zW*: **k~unglücklich** *a* absolutely miserable; **~verhör** *nt* cross-examination; **~weg** *m* crossroads; (*REL*) Way of the Cross; **~worträtsel** *nt* crossword puzzle; **~zeichen** *nt* sign of the cross; **~zug** *m* crusade.

kribb(e)lig [krib'(ə)liç] *a* (*umg*) fidgety; (*kribbelnd*) tingly.

kribbeln [kri'bəln] *vi* (*jucken*) itch; (*prickeln*) tingle.

kriechen [krē:'çən] *vi unreg* crawl, creep; (*pej*) grovel, crawl.

Kriecher *m* **-s**, - crawler.

Kriech- *zW*: **~spur** *f* slow lane (*for trucks*); **~tier** *nt* reptile.

Krieg [krē:k] *m* **-(e)s**, **-e** war; **~ führen** wage war (*mit*, *gegen* on).

kriegen [krē:'gən] *vt* (*umg*) get.

Krieger *m* **-s**, - warrior; **~denkmal** *nt* war memorial; **k~isch** warlike.

Kriegführung *f* warfare.

Kriegs- *zW*: **~beil** *nt*: **das ~beil begraben** (*fig*) bury the hatchet; **~bemalung** *f* war paint; **~dienstverweigerer** *m* conscientious objector; **~erklärung** *f* declaration of war; **~fuß** *m*: **mit jdm/etw auf ~fuß stehen** be at loggerheads with sb/not get on with sth; **~gefangene(r)** *mf* prisoner of war; **~gefangenschaft** *f* captivity; **~gericht** *nt* court-martial; **~rat** *m* council of war; **~recht** *nt* (*MIL*) martial law; **~schauplatz** *m* theater of war; **~schiff** *nt* warship; **~schuld** *f* war guilt; **~verbrecher** *m* war criminal; **~versehrte(r)** *mf* person disabled in the war; **~zustand** *m* state of war.

Krim [krim] *f*: **die ~** the Crimea.

Krimi [krē:'mē] *m* **-s**, **-s** (*umg*) thriller.

kriminal [krēmēnâl'] *a* criminal; **K~beamte(r)** *m* detective; **K~film** *m* crime thriller *od* movie.

Kriminalität [krēmēnälēte:t'] *f* criminality.

Kriminal- *zW*: **~polizei** *f* ≈ Federal Bureau of Investigation (*US*); ≈ Criminal Investigation Department (*Brit*); **~roman** *m* detective story.

kriminell [krēmēnel'] *a* criminal.

Kriminelle(r) *mf dekl wie a* criminal.

Krimskrams [krims'kráms] *m* **-es** (*umg*) odds and ends *pl*.

Kringel [kri'ngəl] *m* **-s**, - (*der Schrift*) squiggle; (*KOCH*) ring.

kringelig *a*: **sich ~ lachen** (*umg*) kill o.s. laughing.

Kripo [krē:'pō] *f* **-**, **-s** *abk* = **Kriminalpolizei.**

Krippe [kri'pə] *f* **-**, **-n** manger, crib; (*Kinder~*) crèche.

Krippenspiel *nt* nativity play.

Krise [krē:'zə] *f* **-**, **-n** crisis.

kriseln *vi*: **es kriselt** there's a crisis, there is trouble brewing.

Krisen- *zW*: **k~fest** *a* stable; **~herd** *m* flash point; trouble spot; **~stab** *m* action *od* crisis committee.

Kristall [kristál'] *m* **-s**, **-e** crystal ♦ *nt* **-s**

(*Glas*) crystal.

Kriterium [krētā:'rēōōm] *nt* criterion.

Kritik [krētē:k'] *f* criticism; (*Zeitungs~*) review, write-up; **an jdm/etw ~ üben** criticize sb/sth; **unter aller ~ sein** (*umg*) be beneath contempt.

Kritikaster(in *f*) [krētēkás'tər(in)] *m* **-s**, - fault-finder.

Kritiker(in *f*) [krē:'tēkər(in)] *m* **-s**, - critic.

kritiklos *a* uncritical.

kritisch [krē:'tish] *a* critical.

kritisieren [krētēzē:'rən] *vti* criticize.

kritteln [kri'təln] *vi* find fault, carp.

kritzeln [kri'tsəln] *vti* scribble, scrawl.

kroch [kroḵḥ] *imperf von* **kriechen.**

Krokodil [krōkōdē:l'] *nt* **-s**, **-e** crocodile.

Krokodilstränen *pl* crocodile tears *pl*.

Krokus [krō:'kōōs] *m* **-**, - *od* **-se** crocus.

Krone [krō:'nə] *f* **-**, **-n** crown; (*Baum~*) top; **einen in der ~ haben** (*umg*) be tipsy.

krönen [krœ'nən] *vt* crown.

Kron- *zW*: **~korken** *m* bottle top; **~leuchter** *m* chandelier; **~prinz** *m* crown prince.

Krönung [krœ'nōōng] *f* coronation.

Kronzeuge *m* (*JUR*) person who turns State's evidence (*US*) *od* Queen's evidence (*Brit*); (*Hauptzeuge*) principal witness.

Kropf [kropf] *m* **-(e)s**, **-̈e** (*MED*) goiter (*US*), goitre (*Brit*); (*von Vogel*) crop.

Krösus [krœ'zōōs] *m* **-ses**, **-se**: **ich bin doch kein ~** (*umg*) I'm not made of money.

Kröte [krœ'tə] *f* **-**, **-n** toad; **~n** *pl* (*umg*: *Geld*) pennies *pl*.

Krücke [krü'kə] *f* **-**, **-n** crutch.

Krug [krōō:k] *m* **-(e)s**, **-̈e** jug; (*Bier~*) mug.

Krümel [krü:'məl] *m* **-s**, - crumb.

krümeln *vti* crumble.

krumm [krōōm] *a* (*lit*, *fig*) crooked; (*kurvig*) curved; **sich ~ und schief lachen** (*umg*) fall about laughing; **keinen Finger ~ machen** (*umg*) not lift a finger; **ein ~es Ding drehen** (*umg*) do something crooked; **~beinig** *a* bandy-legged.

krümmen [krü'mən] *vtr* curve, bend.

krumm- *zW*: **~lachen** *vr* (*umg*) laugh o.s. silly; **~nehmen** *vt unreg*: **jdm etw ~nehmen** (*umg*) take sth amiss.

Krümmung *f* bend, curve.

Krüppel [krü'pəl] *m* **-s**, - cripple.

Kruste [krōōs'tə] *f* **-**, **-n** crust.

Kruzifix [krōōtsēfiks'] *nt* **-es**, **-e** crucifix.

KSZE *f abk* (= *Konferenz über Sicherheit und Zusammenarbeit in Europa*) Conference on Security and Cooperation in Europe.

Kt. *abk* = **Kanton.**

Kto. *abk* (= *Konto*) a/c.

Kuba [kōō:'bá] *nt* **-s** Cuba.

Kubaner(in *f*) [kōōbá'nər(in)] *m* **-s**, - Cuban.

kubanisch [kōōbá'nish] *a* Cuban.

Kübel [kü:'bəl] *m* **-s**, - tub; (*Eimer*) pail.

Küche [kü'çə] *f* **-**, **-n** kitchen; (*Kochen*) cooking, cuisine.

Kuchen [kōō:'ḵḥən] *m* **-s**, - cake; **~blech** *nt* baking sheet; **~form** *f* baking pan (*US*) *od* tin (*Brit*); ~**gabel** *f* pastry fork.

Küchen- *zW*: ~**gerät** *nt* kitchen utensil; (*elektrisch*) kitchen appliance; ~**herd** *m* range; (*Gas*, ELEK) cooker, stove; ~**messer** *nt* kitchen knife; ~**schabe** *f* cockroach; ~**schrank** *m* kitchen cabinet.

Kuchenteig *m* cake mixture.

Kuckuck [kōō'kōōk] *m* -s, -e cuckoo; (*umg*: *Siegel des Gerichtsvollziehers*) bailiff's seal (for distraint of goods); **das weiß der ~** heaven (only) knows.

Kuddelmuddel [kōō'dəlmōōdəl] *m od nt* -s (*umg*) mess.

Kufe [kōō:'fə] *f* -, -n (*Faß*~) vat; (*Schlitten*~) runner; (AVIAT) skid.

Kugel [kōō:'gəl] *f* -, -n ball; (MATH) sphere; (MIL) bullet; (*Erd*~) globe; (SPORT) shot; **eine ruhige ~ schieben** (*umg*) have an easy life *od* a cushy time; **k~förmig** *a* spherical; ~**kopf** *m* (*Schreibmaschine*) golf ball; ~**kopfschreibmaschine** *f* golf-ball typewriter; ~**lager** *nt* ball bearing.

kugeln *vt* roll; (SPORT) bowl ♦ *vr* (*vor Lachen*) double up.

Kugel- *zW*: **k~rund** *a* (*Gegenstand*) round; (*umg*: *Person*) tubby; ~**schreiber** *m* ballpoint (pen); **k~sicher** *a* bulletproof; ~**stoßen** *nt* -s shot put.

Kuh [kōō:] *f* -, ̈e cow; ~**dorf** *nt* (*pej umg*) one-horse town; ~**handel** *m* (*pej umg*) horse-trading; ~**haut** *f*: **das geht auf keine ~haut** (*fig umg*) that's absolutely incredible.

kühl [kü:l] *a* (*lit*, *fig*) cool; **K~anlage** *f* refrigeration plant.

Kühle *f* - coolness.

kühlen *vt* cool.

Kühler *m* -s, - (AUT) radiator; ~**haube** (AUT) hood (US), bonnet (*Brit*).

Kühl- *zW*: ~**haus** *nt* cold-storage depot; ~**raum** *m* cold-storage chamber; ~**schrank** *m* refrigerator; ~**tasche** *f* cool bag; ~**truhe** *f* (chest) freezer; ~**ung** *f* cooling; ~**wagen** *m* (EISENB. *Lastwagen*) refrigerator car (US) *od* van (*Brit*); ~**wasser** *nt* cooling water.

kühn [kü:n] *a* bold, daring; **K~heit** *f* boldness.

k.u.k. *abk* (= *kaiserlich und königlich*) imperial and royal.

Küken [kü:'kən] *nt* -s, - chicken; (*umg*: *Nesthäkchen*) baby of the family.

kulant [kōōlànt'] *a* obliging.

Kulanz [kōōlànts'] *f* accommodating attitude, generousness.

Kuli [kōō:'lē] *m* -s, -s coolie; (*umg*: *Kugelschreiber*) ballpoint (pen).

kulinarisch [kōōlēnä'rish] *a* culinary.

Kulisse [kōōli'sə] *f* -, -n scene.

Kulissenschieber(in *f***)** *m* stagehand.

Kulleraugen [kōō'lərougən] *pl* (*umg*) wide eyes *pl*.

kullern [kōō'lərn] *vi* roll.

Kult [kōōlt] *m* -(e)s, -e worship, cult; **mit etw ~ treiben** make a cult out of sth.

kultivieren [kōōltēvē:'rən] *vt* cultivate.

kultiviert *a* cultivated, refined.

Kultstätte *f* place of worship.

Kultur [kōōltōō:r'] *f* culture; (*Lebensform*) civilization; (*des Bodens*) cultivation; ~**banause** *m* (*umg*) philistine, low-brow; ~**betrieb** *m* culture industry; ~**beutel** *m* washbag.

kulturell [kōōltōōrel'] *a* cultural.

Kultur- *zW*: ~**film** *m* documentary film; ~**teil** *m* (*von Zeitung*) arts section.

Kultusminister [kōōl'tōōsmēnistər] *m* minister of education and the arts.

Kümmel [kü'məl] *m* -s, - caraway seed; (*Branntwein*) kümmel.

Kummer [kōō'mər] *m* -s grief, sorrow.

kümmerlich [kü'mərlich] *a* miserable, wretched.

kümmern *vr*: **sich um jdn ~** look after sb; **sich um etw ~** see to sth ♦ *vt* concern; **das kümmert mich nicht** that doesn't worry me.

Kumpan(in *f***)** [kōōmpän'(in)] *m* -s, -e mate, buddy; (*pej*) accomplice.

Kumpel [kōōm'pəl] *m* -s, - (*umg*) mate.

kündbar [künt'bàr] *a* redeemable, recallable; (*Vertrag*) terminable.

Kunde [kōōn'də] *m* -n, -n, **Kundin** *f* customer ♦ *f* -, -n (*Botschaft*) news.

Kunden- *zW*: ~**dienst** *m* customer service; ~**fang** *m* (*pej*): **auf ~fang sein** to be touting for customers; ~**fänger** *m* tout (*umg*); ~**konto** *nt* charge account; ~**kreis** *m* customers *pl*, clientele; ~**werbung** *f* publicity (*aimed at attracting custom or customers*).

Kund- *zW*: ~**gabe** *f* announcement; **k~geben** *vt unreg* announce; ~**gebung** *f* announcement; (*Versammlung*) rally.

kundig *a* expert, experienced.

kündigen [kün'digən] *vi* give in one's notice; **jdm ~** give sb his notice; **zum 1. April ~** give one's notice for April 1st; (*Mieter*) give notice for April 1st; (*bei Mitgliedschaft*) cancel one's membership as of April 1st ♦ *vt* cancel; **(jdm) die Stellung ~** give (sb) notice; **sie hat ihm die Freundschaft gekündigt** she has broken off their friendship.

Kündigung *f* notice.

Kündigungs- *zW*: ~**frist** *f* period of notice; ~**schutz** *m* protection against wrongful dismissal.

Kundin *f siehe* **Kunde**.

Kundschaft *f* customers *pl*, clientele.

Kundschafter *m* -s, - spy; (MIL) scout.

künftig [künf'tich] *a* future ♦ *ad* in future.

Kunst [kōōnst] *f* -, ̈e art; (*Können*) skill; **das ist doch keine ~** it's easy; **mit seiner ~ am Ende sein** be at one's wits' end; **das ist eine brotlose ~** there's no money in that; ~**akademie** *f* academy of art; ~**druck** *m* art print; ~**dünger** *m* artificial fertilizer *od* manure; ~**(erziehung)** *f* (SCH) art; ~**faser** *f* synthetic fiber; ~**fehler** *m* professional error; (*weniger ernst*) slip; ~**fertigkeit** *f* skillfulness; ~**flieger** *m* stunt flyer;

~geschichte f history of art; **~gewerbe** nt arts and crafts pl; **~griff** m trick, knack; **~händler** m art dealer; **~harz** nt artificial resin.

Künstler(in f) [künst'lər(in)] m **-s**, - artist; **k~isch** a artistic; **~name** m pseudonym; (von Schauspieler) stage name; **~pech** nt (umg) hard luck.

künstlich [künst'liç] a artificial; **~e Intelligenz** (COMPUT) artificial intelligence; **sich ~ aufregen** (umg) get all worked up about nothing.

Kunst- zW: **~sammler** m **-s**, - art collector; **~seide** f artificial silk; **~stoff** m synthetic material; **~stopfen** nt **-s** invisible mending; **~stück** nt trick; **das ist kein ~stück** (fig) there's nothing to it; **~turnen** nt gymnastics sing; **k~voll** a artistic; **~werk** nt work of art.

kunterbunt [koon'tərboont] a higgledy-piggledy.

Kupfer [koop'fər] nt **-s**, - copper; **~geld** nt ≈ pennies.

kupfern a copper ♦ vt (fig umg) plagiarize, copy, imitate.

Kupferstich m copperplate engraving.

Kuppe [koo'pə] f **-**, **-n** (Berg~) top; (Finger~) tip.

Kuppel f **-**, **-n** cupola, dome.

Kuppelei [koopəli'] f (JUR) procuring.

kuppeln vi (JUR) procure; (AUT) declutch ♦ vt join.

Kuppler [koop'lər] m **-s**, - pimp; **~in** f matchmaker.

Kupplung f (TECH auch) coupling; (AUT etc) clutch; **die ~ (durch)treten** disengage the clutch.

Kur [koo:r] f **-**, **-en** cure, treatment; (Schlankheits~) diet; **eine ~ machen** take a cure.

Kür [kü:r] f **-**, **-en** (SPORT) free exercises pl.

Kuratorium [koorātō:'reoom] nt (Vereinigung) committee.

Kurbel [koor'bəl] f **-**, **-n** crank, winch; (AUT) starting handle; **~welle** f crankshaft.

Kürbis [kür'bis] m **-ses**, **-se** pumpkin; (exotisch) gourd.

Kurfürst [koo:r'fürst] m Elector, electoral prince.

Kurgast m visitor (to a health resort).

Kurier [koorē:r'] m **-s**, **-e** courier, messenger.

kurieren [koorē:'rən] vt cure.

kurios [koorēō:s'] a curious, odd.

Kuriosität [koorēōzēte:t'] f curiosity.

Kur- zW: **~konzert** nt concert (at a health resort); **~ort** m health resort; **~pfuscher** m quack.

Kurs [koors] m **-es**, **-e** course; (FIN) rate; **hoch im ~ stehen** (fig) be highly thought of; **einen ~ besuchen** od **mitmachen** attend a class; **harter/weicher ~** (POL) hard/soft line; **~änderung** f (lit, fig) change of course; **~buch** nt timetable.

Kurschatten m (umg) temporary partner

during a recuperative cure at a spa.

Kürschner(in f) [kürsh'nər(in)] m **-s**, - furrier.

kursieren [koorzē:'rən] vi circulate.

kursiv ad in italics.

Kursnotierung f quotation.

Kursus [koor'zoos] m **-**, **Kurse** course.

Kurswagen m (EISENB) through coach.

Kurswert m (FIN) market value.

Kurve [koor'və] f **-**, **-n** curve; (Straßen~ auch) bend; (statistisch, Fieber~ etc) graph; **die ~ nicht kriegen** (umg) not get around to it.

kurvenreich a: **„~e Strecke"** "winding road".

kurvig a (Straße) bendy.

kurz [koorts] a short; **zu ~ kommen** come off badly; **den ~eren ziehen** get the worst of it ♦ ad: **~ und bündig** concisely; **~ und gut** in short; **über ~ oder lang** sooner or later; **eine Sache ~ abtun** dismiss sth out of hand; **sich ~ fassen** be brief; **darf ich mal ~ stören?** could I just interrupt for a moment?; **K~arbeit** f reduced working hours; **~ärm(e)lig** a short-sleeved; **~atmig** a (fig) feeble, lame; (MED) short-winded.

Kürze [kür'tsə] f **-**, **-n** shortness, brevity.

kürzen vt cut short; (in der Länge) shorten; (Gehalt) reduce.

kurzerhand [koor'tsərhànt'] ad without further ado; (entlassen) on the spot.

kurz- zW: **K~fassung** f shortened version; **~fristig** a short-term; **~fristige Verbindlichkeiten** pl current liabilities pl; **~gefaßt** a concise; **K~geschichte** f short story; **~halten** vt unreg keep short; **~lebig** a short-lived.

kürzlich [kürts'liç] ad lately, recently.

Kurz- zW: **~meldung** f news flash; **~schluß** m (ELEK) short circuit; **~schlußhandlung** f (fig) rash action; **~schrift** f shorthand; **k~sichtig** a short-sighted; **k~treten** vi unreg (fig umg) go easy; **k~um'** ad in a word.

Kürzung f cutback.

Kurz- zW: **~waren** pl notions pl (US), haberdashery (Brit), dry goods pl; **~welle** f short wave.

kuschelig a cuddly.

kuscheln [koo'shəln] vr snuggle up.

kuschen [koo'shən] vir (Hund etc) get down; (fig) knuckle under.

Kusine [koozē:'nə] f cousin.

Kuß [koos] m **-sses**, **-sse** kiss.

küssen [kü'sən] vtr kiss.

Küste [küs'tə] f **-**, **-n** coast, shore.

Küsten- zW: **~gewässer** pl coastal waters pl; **~schiff** nt coaster; **~wache** f coastguard (station).

Küster [küs'tər] m **-s**, - sexton, verger.

Kutsche [koot'shə] f **-**, **-n** coach, carriage.

Kutscher m **-s**, - coachman.

kutschieren [kootshē:'rən] vi: **durch die Gegend ~** (umg) drive around.

Kutte [koo'tə] f **-**, **-n** cowl.

Kuvert [koovert'] *nt* **-s, -e** *od* **-s** envelope; (*Gedeck*) cover.
KV *abk* (*MUS*: = *Köchelverzeichnis*) Köchel index.
KW *abk* (= *Kurzwelle*) SW.
Kybernetik [kübernä:'tik] *f* cybernetics *sing*.
kybernetisch [kübernä:'tish] *a* cybernetic.
KZ *nt* **-s, -s** *abk* = **Konzentrationslager.**

L

L, l [el] *nt* L, l.
laben [lå'bən] *vtr* refresh (o.s.); (*fig*) relish (*an etw* (*dat*) sth).
labern [lå'bərn] *vi* (*umg*) prattle (on) ♦ *vt* talk.
labil [låbē:l'] *a* (*physisch: Gesundheit*) delicate; (: *Kreislauf*) poor; (*psychisch*) weak.
Labor [låbō:r'] *nt* **-s, -e** *od* **-s** lab(oratory).
Laborant(in *f*) [låbōrånt'(in)] *m* lab(oratory) assistant.
Laboratorium [låbōråtō:'rēŏŏm] *nt* lab(oratory).
Labyrinth [låbürint'] *nt* **-s, -e** labyrinth.
Lache [lå'khə] *f* **-, -n** (*Wasser*) pool, puddle; (*umg: Gelächter*) laugh.
lächeln [le'cḥəln] *vi* smile; **L~** *nt* **-s** smile.
lachen [lå'khən] *vi* laugh; **mir ist nicht zum L~ (zumute)** I'm in no laughing mood; **daß ich nicht lache!** (*umg*) don't make me laugh!; **das wäre doch gelacht** it would be ridiculous.
Lachen *nt*: **dir wird das ~ schon noch vergehen!** you'll soon be laughing on the other side of your face.
Lacher *m* **-s, -:** **die ~ auf seiner Seite haben** have the last laugh.
lächerlich [le'cḥərlicḥ] *a* ridiculous; **L~keit** *f* absurdity.
Lach- *zW*: **~gas** *nt* laughing gas; **l~haft** *a* laughable; **~krampf** *m*: **einen ~krampf bekommen** go into fits of laughter.
Lachs [låks] *m* **-es, -e** salmon.
Lachsalve [låkh'zålvə] *f* burst *od* roar of laughter.
Lachsschinken *m* smoked, rolled fillet of ham.
Lack [låk] *m* **-(e)s, -e** lacquer, varnish; (*von Auto*) paint.
lackieren [låkē:'rən] *vt* varnish; (*Auto*) spray.
Lackierer [låkē:'rər] *m* **-s, -** varnisher.
Lackleder *nt* patent leather.
Lackmus [låk'mŏŏs] *m od nt* **-** litmus.
Lade [lå'də] *f* **-, -n** box, chest; **~baum** *m* derrick; **~fähigkeit** *f* load capacity; **~fläche** *f* load area; **~gewicht** *nt* tonnage;

~hemmung *f*: **das Gewehr hat ~hemmung** the gun is jammed.
laden [lå'dən] *vt unreg* (*Lasten, COMPUT*) load; (*JUR*) summon; (*einladen*) invite; **eine schwere Schuld auf sich** (*akk*) **~** place o.s. under a heavy burden of guilt.
Laden [lå'dən] *m* **-s, ⁼** shop; (*Fenster~*) shutter; (*umg: Betrieb*) outfit; **der ~ läuft** (*umg*) business is good; **~aufsicht** *f* floorwalker (*US*), shopwalker (*Brit*); **~besitzer** *m* shopkeeper; **~dieb** *m* shoplifter; **~diebstahl** *m* shoplifting; **~hüter** *m* **-s, -** unsaleable item; **~preis** *m* retail price; **~schluß** *m* closing time; **~tisch** *m* counter.
Laderampe *f* loading ramp.
Laderaum *m* (*NAUT*) hold.
lädt [le:t] *3. pers sing präs von* **laden.**
Ladung [lå'dŏŏng] *f* (*Last*) cargo, load; (*Beladen*) loading; (*JUR*) summons; (*Einladung*) invitation; (*Sprengladung*) charge.
lag [låk] *imperf von* **liegen.**
LAG *abk* = **Lastenausgleichsgesetz.**
Lage [lå'gə] *f* **-, -n** position, situation; (*Schicht*) layer; **in der ~ sein** be in a position; **eine gute/ruhige ~ haben** be in a good/peaceful location; **Herr der ~ sein** be in control of the situation.
Lage- *zW*: **~bericht** *m* report; (*MIL*) situation report; **~beurteilung** *f* situation assessment.
lagenweise *ad* in layers.
Lager [lå'gər] *nt* **-s, -** camp; (*COMM*) warehouse; (*Schlaf~*) bed; (*von Tier*) lair; (*TECH*) bearing; **etw auf ~ haben** have sth in stock; **~arbeiter** *m* warehouseman; **~bestand** *m* stocks *pl*; **~geld** *nt* storage (charges *pl*); **~haus** *nt* warehouse, store.
Lagerist(in *f*) [lågərist'(in)] *m* warehouse clerk (*US*), storeman/woman (*Brit*).
lagern [lå'gərn] *vi* (*Dinge*) be stored; (*Menschen*) camp; (*auch vr: rasten*) lie down ♦ *vt* store; (*betten*) lay down; (*Maschine*) bed.
Lager- *zW*: **~raum** *m* storeroom; (*in Geschäft*) stockroom; **~schuppen** *m* storage shed; **~stätte** *f* resting place; (*GEOL*) deposit.
Lagerung *f* storage.
Lagune [lågōō:'nə] *f* **-, -n** lagoon.
lahm [lâm] *a* lame; (*umg: langsam, langweilig*) dreary, dull; (*Geschäftsgang*) slow, sluggish; **eine ~e Ente sein** (*umg*) have no zip.
lahmarschig [lâm'årshicḥ] *a* (*umg*) bloody *od* damn (!) slow.
lahmen *vi* be lame, limp.
lähmen [le:'mən], **lahmlegen** *vt* paralyze.
Lähmung *f* paralysis.
Lahn [lân] *f* **-** (*Fluß*) Lahn.
Laib [lîp] *m* **-s, -e** loaf.
Laich [lîcḥ] *m* **-(e)s, -e** spawn; **l~en** *vi* spawn.
Laie [lî'ə] *m* **-n, -n** layman; (*fig auch, THEAT*) amateur.
laienhaft *a* amateurish.

Lakai [lákī'] *m* **-en, -en** lackey.
Laken [lå'kən] *nt* **-s**, - sheet.
Lakritze [låkrit'sə] *f* **-, -n** licorice.
lala [lå'lå'] *ad* (*umg*): **so ~** so-so, not too bad.
lallen [lå'lən] *vti* slur; (*Baby*) babble.
Lamelle [låme'lə] *f* lamella; (*ELEK*) lamina; (*TECH*) plate.
lamentieren [låmentē:'rən] *vi* lament.
Lametta [låme'tå] *nt* **-s** tinsel.
Lamm [låm] *nt* **-(e)s, ⁻er** lamb; **~fell** *nt* lambskin; **l~fromm** *a* like a lamb; **~wolle** *f* lambswool.
Lampe [låm'pə] *f* **-, -n** lamp.
Lampen- *zW*: **~fieber** *nt* stage fright; **~schirm** *m* lampshade.
Lampion [låmpēōń'] *m* **-s, -s** Chinese lantern.
Land [lånt] *nt* **-(e)s, ⁻er** land; (*Nation, nicht Stadt*) country; (*Bundes~*) state; **auf dem ~(e)** in the country; **an ~ gehen** go ashore; **endlich sehe ich ~** (*fig*) at last I can see the light at the end of the tunnel; **einen Auftrag an ~ ziehen** (*umg*) land an order; **aus aller Herren ~⁻er** from all over the world; **~arbeiter** *m* farm *od* agricultural worker; **~besitz** *m* landed property; **~besitzer** *m* landowner.
Landebahn *f* runway.
landeinwärts [låntīn'verts] *ad* inland.
landen [lån'dən] *vti* land; **mit deinen Komplimenten kannst du bei mir nicht ~** your compliments won't get you anywhere with me.
Ländereien [lendərī'ən] *pl* estates *pl*.
Länderspiel *nt* international (match).
Landes- [lån'dəs] *zW*: **~farben** *pl* national colors *pl*; **~innere(s)** *nt* inland region; **~kind** *nt* native of a state of the FRG; **~kunde** *f* regional studies *pl*; **~tracht** *f* national costume; **l~üblich** *a* customary; **~verrat** *m* high treason; **~verweisung** *f* banishment; **~währung** *f* national currency.
Land- *zW*: **~flucht** *f* emigration to the cities; **~gut** *nt* estate; **~haus** *nt* country house; **~karte** *f* map; **~kreis** *m* administrative region; **l~läufig** *a* customary.
ländlich [lent'liçh] *a* rural.
Land- *zW*: **~rat** *m* head of administration of a Landkreis; **~schaft** *f* countryside; (*KUNST*) landscape; **die politische ~schaft** the political scene; **l~schaftlich** *a* scenic; (*Besonderheiten*) regional.
Landsmann *m*, **Landsmännin** *f*, *pl* **Landsleute** compatriot, fellow countryman *od* countrywoman.
Land- *zW*: **~straße** *f* country road; **~streicher** *m* **-s**, - tramp, hobo (*US*); **~strich** *m* region; **~tag** *m* (*POL*) regional parliament.
Landung [lån'doong] *f* landing.
Landungs- *zW*: **~boot** *nt* landing craft; **~brücke** *f* jetty, pier; **~stelle** *f* landing place.
Land- *zW*: **~urlaub** *m* shore leave;

~vermesser *m* surveyor.
landw. *abk* (= *landwirtschaftlich*) agric., agr.
Land- *zW*: **~wirt** *m* farmer; **~wirtschaft** *f* agriculture; **~wirtschaft betreiben** farm; **~zunge** *f* spit.
lang [lång] *a* long; (*umg: Mensch*) tall; **hier wird mir die Zeit nicht ~** I won't get bored here; **er machte ein ~es Gesicht** his face fell ♦ *ad*: **~ anhaltender Beifall** prolonged applause; **~ und breit** at great length; **~atmig** *a* long-winded.
lange *ad* for a long time; (*dauern, brauchen*) a long time; **~ nicht so ...** not nearly as ...; **wenn der das schafft, kannst du das schon ~** if he can do it, you can do it easily.
Länge [leng'ə] *f* **-, -n** length; (*GEOG*) longitude; **etw der ~ nach falten** fold sth lengthways; **etw in die ~ ziehen** drag sth out (*umg*); **der ~ nach hinfallen** fall flat (on one's face).
langen [lång'ən] *vi* (*ausreichen*) do, suffice; (*fassen*) reach (*nach* for); **es langt mir** I've had enough; **jdm eine ~** (*umg*) give sb a clip on the ear.
Längen- *zW*: **~grad** *m* longitude; **~maß** *nt* linear measure.
langersehnt [lång'erzā:nt] *a attr* longed-for.
Langeweile *f* boredom.
lang- *zW*: **~fristig** *a* long-term; **~fristige Verbindlichkeiten** *pl* long-term liabilities *pl* ♦ *ad* in the long term; (*planen*) for the long term; **~jährig** *a* (*Freundschaft, Gewohnheit*) long-standing; (*Erfahrung, Verhandlungen*) many years of; (*Mitarbeiter*) of many years' standing; **L~lauf** *m* (*SKI*) cross-country ski-ing; **~lebig** *a* long-lived; **~lebige Gebrauchsgüter** *pl* durable goods *pl*.
länglich *a* longish.
lang- *zW*: **L~mut** *f* forbearance, patience; **~mütig** *a* forbearing.
längs [lengs] *präp* +*gen od dat* along ♦ *ad* lengthways.
langsam *a* slow; **immer schön ~!** (*umg*) easy does it!; **ich muß jetzt ~ gehen** I must be getting on my way; **~ (aber sicher) reicht es mir** I've just about had enough; **L~keit** *f* slowness.
lang- *zW*: **L~schläfer** *m* late riser; **L~spielplatte** *f* long-playing record.
längsseit(s) *ad, präp* +*gen* alongside.
längst [lengst] *ad*: **das ist ~ fertig** that was finished a long time ago, that has been finished for a long time.
längste(r, s) *a* longest.
Langstreckenläufer *m* long-distance runner.
Languste [lång(g)oō'stə] *f* **-, -n** crayfish, crawfish (*US*).
lang- *zW*: **~weilen** *untr vt* bore ♦ *vr* be *od* get bored; **L~weiler** *m* **-s**, - bore; **~weilig** *a* boring, tedious; **L~welle** *f* long wave; **~wierig** *a* lengthy, long-drawn-out.
Lanze [lån'tsə] *f* **-, -n** lance.

Lanzette [lántse'tə] f lancet.
lapidar [lápēdár'] a terse, pithy.
Lappalie [lápâ'lēə] f trifle.
Lappe [lá'pə] m **-n, -n, Lappin** f Lapp, Laplander.
Lappen m **-s,** - cloth, rag; (ANAT) lobe; **jdm durch die ~ gehen** (umg) slip through sb's fingers.
läppern [le'pərn] vr unpers (umg): **es läppert sich zusammen** it (all) mounts up.
läppisch [le'pish] a foolish.
Lappland [láp'lánt] nt -s Lapland.
Lapsus [láp'sōōs] m -, - slip.
LAR abk (= Lehramtsreferendar) trainee teacher.
LArbG abk (= Landesarbeitsgericht) labor relations board.
Lärche [ler'çhə] f -, -n larch.
Lärm [lerm] m **-(e)s** noise; **~belästigung** f noise nuisance; **l~en** vi be noisy, make a noise.
Larve [lár'fə] f -, -n mask; (BIOL) larva.
las [lás] imperf von **lesen.**
lasch [lásh] a slack; (Geschmack) tasteless.
Lasche [lá'shə] f -, -n (Schuh~) tongue; (EISENB) fishplate.
Laser [lā:'zər] m **-s,** - laser; **~drucker** m laser printer.
lassen [lá'sən] vti unreg leave; (erlauben) let; (aufhören mit) stop; (veranlassen) make; **etw machen ~** have sth done; **es läßt sich machen** it can be done; **es läßt sich öffnen** it can be opened, it opens; **er kann es nicht ~!** he will keep on doing it!; **tu, was du nicht ~ kannst!** if you must, you must!; **das muß man ihr ~** (zugestehen) you've got to grant her that; **mein Vater wollte mich studieren ~** my father wanted me to study; **einen Bart wachsen ~** grow a beard; **jdn warten ~** keep sb waiting; **laß es dir gutgehen!** take care of yourself!
lässig [le'siçh] a casual; **L~keit** f casualness.
läßlich [les'liçh] a pardonable, venial.
läßt [lest] 2./3. pers sing präs von **lassen.**
Last [lást] f -, **-en** load; (Trag~) burden; (NAUT, AVIAT) cargo; (meist pl: Gebühr) charge; **jdm zur ~ fallen** be a burden to sb; **~auto** nt truck.
lasten vi weigh on (auf +dat).
Lastenaufzug m hoist, freight elevator (US).
Lastenausgleichsgesetz nt law on financial compensation for losses suffered in WWII.
Laster [lá'stər] nt **-s,** - vice ♦ m **-s,** - (umg) truck.
Lästerer [le'stərər] m **-s,** - mocker; (Gottes~) blasphemer.
lasterhaft a immoral.
lästerlich a scandalous.
lästern [le'stərn] vti (Gott) blaspheme; (schlecht sprechen) mock.
Lästerung f jibe; (Gottes~) blasphemy.
lästig [le'stiçh] a troublesome, tiresome; **jdm ~ werden** become a nuisance (to sb); (zum

Ärgernis werden) get annoying (to sb).
Last- zW: **~kahn** m barge; **~kraftwagen** m heavy goods truck; **~schrift** f debiting; (Eintrag) debit item; **~tier** nt beast of burden; **~träger** m porter; **~wagen** m truck.
Latein [látīn'] nt -s Latin; **mit seinem ~ am Ende sein** (fig) be stumped (umg); **~amerika** nt Latin America; **l~-amerikanisch** a Latin-American.
lateinisch a Latin.
latent [látent'] a latent.
Laterne [láter'nə] f -, -n lantern; (Straßen~) lamp, light.
Laternenpfahl m lamppost.
Latinum [látē:'nōōm] nt **-s: kleines/großes ~** Latin certificate taken at 16/18.
Latrine [látrē:'nə] f latrine.
Latsche [lát'shə] f -, -n dwarf pine.
latschen [lát'shən] vi (umg: gehen) wander, go; (lässig) slouch.
Latschen m (umg: Hausschuh) slipper; (pej: Schuh) worn-out shoe.
Latte [lá'tə] f -, -n lath; (SPORT) goalpost; (quer) crossbar.
Lattenzaun m lattice fence.
Latz [láts] m **-es, ̈-e** bib; (Hosen~) front flap.
Lätzchen [lets'çhən] nt bib.
Latzhose f dungarees pl.
lau [lou] a (Nacht) balmy; (Wasser) lukewarm; (fig: Haltung) half-hearted.
Laub [loup] nt **-(e)s** foliage; **~baum** m deciduous tree.
Laube [lou'bə] f -, -n arbor (US), arbour (Brit); (Gartenhäuschen) summerhouse.
Laub- zW: **~frosch** m tree frog; **~säge** f fretsaw; **~wald** m deciduous forest.
Lauch [loukh] m **-(e)s, -e** leek.
Lauer [lou'ər] f: **auf der ~ sein** od **liegen** lie in wait.
lauern vi lie in wait; (Gefahr) lurk.
Lauf [louf] m **-(e)s, Läufe** run; (Wett~) race; (Entwicklung, ASTRON) course; (Gewehr~) barrel; **im ~e des Gesprächs** during the conversation; **sie ließ ihren Gefühlen freien ~** she gave way to her feelings; **einer Sache ihren ~ lassen** let sth take its course; **~bahn** f career; **eine ~bahn einschlagen** embark on a career; **~bursche** m errand boy.
laufen [lou'fən] unreg vi run; (umg: gehen) walk; (Uhr) go; (funktionieren) work; (fließen) run; (Elektrogerät: eingeschaltet sein) be on; (gezeigt werden: Film, Stück) be on; (Bewerbung, Antrag) be under consideration; **es lief mir eiskalt über den Rücken** a chill ran up my spine; **ihm läuft die Nase** he's got a runny nose; **die Dinge ~ lassen** let things slide; **die Sache ist gelaufen** (umg) it's in the bag; **das Auto läuft auf meinen Namen** the car is in my name ♦ vt run; **Ski/Schlittschuh/Rollschuh** etc **~** ski/skate/rollerskate etc.
laufend a running; (Monat, Ausgaben)

current; **auf dem ~en sein/halten** be/keep up to date; **am ~en Band** (*fig*) continuously; **~e Nummer** serial number; (*von Konto*) number; **~e Kosten** *pl* running costs *pl*.

laufenlassen *vt unreg* (*Person*) let go.

Läufer [loi'fər] *m* **-s, -** (*Teppich*, *SPORT*) runner; (*Fußball*) half-back; (*Schach*) bishop.

Lauferei [loufərī'] *f* (*umg*) running about.

Läuferin *f* (*SPORT*) runner.

Lauf- *zW*: **~feuer** *nt*: **sich wie ein ~feuer verbreiten** spread like wildfire; **~kundschaft** *f* passing trade; **~masche** *f* run, ladder (*Brit*); **~paß** *m*: **jdm den ~paß geben** (*umg*) give sb his *od* her marching orders; **~schritt** *m*: **im ~schritt** at a run; (*MIL*) on the double; **~stall** *m* playpen; **~steg** *m* catwalk.

läuft [loift] *3. pers sing präs von* **laufen**.

Lauf- *zW*: **~werk** *nt* running gear; (*COMPUT*) drive; **~zeit** *f* (*von Wechsel*, *Vertrag*) period of validity; (*von Maschine*) life; **~zettel** *m* circular.

Lauge [lou'gə] *f* **-, -n** soapy water; (*CHEM*) alkaline solution.

Laune [lou'nə] *f* **-, -n** mood; (*Einfall*) caprice; (*schlechte*) temper.

launenhaft *a* capricious, changeable.

launisch *a* moody.

Laus [lous] *f* **-, Läuse** louse; **ihm ist (wohl) eine ~ über die Leber gelaufen** (*umg*) something's eating him; **~bub** *m* rascal, imp.

Lauschangriff *m* bugging operation (*gegen* on).

lauschen [lou'shən] *vi* eavesdrop, listen in.

Lauscher(in *f*) *m* **-s, -** eavesdropper.

lauschig [lou'shich] *a* snug.

Lausejunge *m* (*umg*) little devil; (*wohlwollend*) rascal.

lausen [lou'zən] *vt* delouse; **ich denk', mich laust der Affe!** (*umg*) well blow me down!

lausig [lou'zich] *a* (*umg*) lousy; (*Kälte*) perishing ♦ *ad* awfully.

laut [lout] *a* loud ♦ *ad* loudly; (*lesen*) aloud ♦ *präp* +*gen od dat* according to.

Laut *m* **-(e)s, -e** sound.

Laute [lou'tə] *f* **-, -n** lute.

lauten [lou'tən] *vi* say; (*Urteil*) be.

läuten [loi'tən] *vti* ring, sound; **er hat davon (etwas) ~ hören** (*umg*) he has heard something about it.

lauter [lou'tər] *a* (*Wasser*) clear, pure; (*Wahrheit*, *Charakter*) honest; *inv* (*Freude*, *Dummheit etc*) sheer ♦ *ad* (*nur*) nothing but, only; **L~keit** *f* purity; honesty, integrity.

läutern [loi'tərn] *vt* purify.

Läuterung *f* purification.

laut- *zW*: **~hals** *ad* at the top of one's voice; **~los** *a* noiseless, silent; **~malend** *a* onomatopoeic; **L~schrift** *f* phonetics *pl*; **L~sprecher** *m* loudspeaker; **L~sprecheranlage** *f*: **öffentliche L~sprecher-**

anlage public-address *od* PA system; **L~sprecherwagen** *m* loudspeaker van; **~stark** *a* vociferous; **L~stärke** *f* (*RAD*) volume.

lauwarm [lou'vàrm] *a* (*lit*, *fig*) lukewarm.

Lava [lå'vå] *f* **-, Laven** lava.

Lavendel [làven'dəl] *m* **-s, -** lavender.

Lawine [làvē:'nə] *f* avalanche.

Lawinengefahr *f* danger of avalanches.

lax [làks] *a* lax.

Layout [lā:'out] *nt* **-s, -s** layout.

Lazarett [làtsáret'] *nt* **-(e)s, -e** (*MIL*) hospital, infirmary.

Ld. *abk* = **Land**.

Ldkrs. *abk* = **Landkreis**.

Ldw. *abk* = **Landwirt**.

Leasing [lē:'zing] *nt* **-s, -s** (*COMM*) leasing.

Lebehoch *nt* three cheers *pl*.

Lebemann *m*, *pl* **-männer** man about town.

leben [lā:'bən] *vti* live.

Leben *nt* **-s, -** life; **am ~ sein/bleiben** be/stay alive; **ums ~ kommen** die; **etw ins ~ rufen** bring sth into being; **seines ~s nicht mehr sicher sein** fear for one's life; **etw für sein ~ gern tun** love doing sth.

lebend *a* living; **~es Inventar** livestock.

lebendig [lāben'dich] *a* living, alive; (*lebhaft*) lively; **L~keit** *f* liveliness.

Lebens- *zW*: **~abend** *m* old age; **~alter** *nt* age; **~anschauung** *f* philosophy of life; **~art** *f* way of life; **l~bejahend** *a* positive; **~dauer** *f* life (span); (*von Maschine*) life; **~erfahrung** *f* experience of life; **~erwartung** *f* life expectancy; **l~fähig** *a* able to live; **l~froh** *a* full of the joys of life; **~gefahr** *f*: **~gefahr!** danger!; **in ~gefahr** dangerously ill; **l~gefährlich** *a* dangerous; (*Krankheit*, *Verletzung*) critical; **~gefährte** *m*, **~gefährtin** *f*: **ihr ~gefährte** the man she lives with; **~größe** *f*: **in ~größe** lifesize; **~haltungskosten** *pl* cost of living *sing*; **~inhalt** *m* purpose in life; **~jahr** *nt* year of life; **~künstler** *m* master in the art of living; **~lage** *f* situation in life; **l~länglich** *a* (*Strafe*) for life; **~lauf** *m* curriculum vitae, CV, résumé (*US*); **l~lustig** *a* cheerful, lively; **~mittel** *pl* food *sing*; **~mittelgeschäft** *nt* grocery store; **~müde** *a* tired of life; **~raum** *m* (*POL*) Lebensraum; (*BIOL*) biosphere; **~retter** *m* lifesaver; **~standard** *m* standard of living; **~stellung** *f* permanent post; **~stil** *m* life style; **~unterhalt** *m* livelihood; **~versicherung** *f* life insurance; **~wandel** *m* way of life; **~weise** *f* way of life, habits *pl*; **~weisheit** *f* maxim; (*~erfahrung*) wisdom; **~zeichen** *nt* sign of life; **~zeit** *f* lifetime; **Beamter auf ~zeit** permanent civil servant.

Leber [lā:'bər] *f* **-, -n** liver; **frei** *od* **frisch von der ~ weg reden** (*umg*) speak out frankly; **~fleck** *m* mole; **~käse** *m* ≈ meat loaf; **~tran** *m* cod-liver oil; **~wurst** *f* liver sausage.

Lebe- *zW*: **~wesen** *nt* creature; **~wohl** *nt*

farewell, goodbye.

leb- [lā:p'] *zW*: **~haft** *a* lively, vivacious; **L~haftigkeit** *f* liveliness, vivacity; **L~kuchen** *m* gingerbread; **~los** *a* lifeless; **L~tag** *m* (*fig*): **das werde ich mein L~tag nicht vergessen** I'll never forget that as long as I live; **L~zeiten** *pl*: **zu jds L~zeiten** (*Leben*) in sb's lifetime.

lechzen [leçh'tsən] *vi*: **nach etw ~** long for sth.

leck [lɛk] *a* leaky, leaking; **L~** *nt* -(e)s, -e leak; **~en** *vi* (*Loch haben*) leak ♦ *vti* (*schlecken*) lick.

lecker [le'kər] *a* delicious, tasty; **L~bissen** *m* dainty morsel; **L~maul** *nt*: **ein L~maul sein** enjoy one's food.

led. *abk* = **ledig.**

Leder [lā:'dər] *nt* -s, - leather; (*umg*: *Fußball*) ball; **~hose** *f* leather trousers *pl*; (*von Tracht*) leather shorts *pl*.

ledern *a* leather.

Lederwaren *pl* leather goods *pl*.

ledig [lā:'diçh] *a* single; **einer Sache ~ sein** be free of sth; **~lich** *ad* merely, solely.

leer [lā:r] *a* empty; (*Blick*) vacant.

Leere *f* - emptiness; **(eine) gähnende ~** a gaping void.

leeren *vt* empty ♦ *vr* (become) empty.

leer- *zW*: **~gefegt** *a* (*Straße*) deserted; **L~gewicht** *nt* unladen weight; **L~gut** *nt* empties *pl*; **L~lauf** *m* (*AUT*) neutral; **~stehend** *a* empty; **L~taste** *f* (*Schreibmaschine*) space-bar.

Leerung *f* emptying; (*POST*) collection.

legal [lāgál'] *a* legal, lawful.

legalisieren [lāgálēzē:'rən] *vt* legalize.

Legalität [lāgálēte:t'] *f* legality; **(etwas) außerhalb der ~** (*euph*) (slightly) outside the law.

Legasthenie [lāgástēnē:'] *f* dyslexia.

legen [lā:'gən] *vt* lay, put, place; (*Ei*) lay ♦ *vr* lie down; (*fig*) subside; **sich ins Bett ~** go to bed.

Legende [lāgen'də] *f* -, -n legend.

leger [lāzhe:r'] *a* casual.

legieren [lāgē:'rən] *vt* alloy.

Legierung *f* alloy.

Legislative [lāgislátē:'və] *f* legislature.

Legislaturperiode [lāgislátōō:r'pārēō:də] *f* ≈ congressional (*US*) *od* parliamentary (*Brit*) term.

legitim [lāgētē:m'] *a* legitimate.

Legitimation [lāgētē:mátsēō:n'] *f* legitimation.

legitimieren [lāgētē:mē:'rən] *vt* legitimate ♦ *vr* prove one's identity.

Legitimität [lāgētēmēte:t'] *f* legitimacy.

Lehm [lā:m] *m* -(e)s, -e loam; **l~ig** *a* loamy.

Lehne [lā:'nə] *f* -, -n arm; (*Rücken~*) back.

lehnen *vtr* lean.

Lehnstuhl *m* armchair.

Lehr- *zW*: **~amt** *nt* teaching profession; **~befähigung** *f* teaching qualification; **~brief** *m* certificate of apprenticeship; **~buch** *nt*

textbook.

Lehre [lā:'rə] *f* -, -n teaching, doctrine; (*beruflich*) apprenticeship *sing*; (*moralisch*) lesson; (*TECH*) gauge; **bei jdm in die ~ gehen** serve one's apprenticeship with sb.

lehren *vt* teach.

Lehrer(in *f*) *m* -s, - teacher; **~ausbildung** *f* teacher training; **~feuerwehr** *f* supply teachers *pl*.

Lehr- *zW*: **~gang** *m* course; **~geld** *nt*: **~geld für etw zahlen müssen** (*fig*) pay dearly for sth; **~jahre** *pl* apprenticeship *sing*; **~kraft** *f* (*form*) teacher; **~ling** *m* apprentice; trainee; **~mittel** *nt* teaching aid; **~plan** *m* syllabus; **~probe** *f* demonstration lesson; **l~reich** *a* instructive; **~satz** *m* proposition; **~stelle** *f* apprenticeship; **~stuhl** *m* chair; **~zeit** *f* apprenticeship.

Leib [līp] *m* -(e)s, -er body; **halt ihn mir vom ~!** keep him away from me; **etw am eigenen ~(e) spüren** experience sth for o.s.

leiben [lī'bən] *vi*: **wie er leibt und lebt** to a T (*umg*).

Leibes- [lī'bəs-] *zW*: **~erziehung** *f* physical education; **~kraft** *f*: **aus ~kräften schreien** *etc* shout *etc* with all one's might; **~übung** *f* physical exercise; **~visitation** *f* body check.

Leibgericht *nt* favorite meal.

Leib- *zW*: **l~haftig** *a* personified; (*Teufel*) incarnate; **l~lich** *a* bodily; (*Vater etc*) own; **~rente** *f* life annuity; **~halle** *f* bodyguard.

Leiche [lī'çhə] *f* -, -n corpse; **er geht über ~n** (*umg*) he'd stop at nothing.

Leichen- *zW*: **~beschauer** *m* -s, - doctor conducting an autopsy; **~halle** *f* mortuary; **~hemd** *nt* shroud; **~träger** *m* bearer; **~wagen** *m* hearse.

Leichnam [līçh'nám] *m* -(e)s, -e corpse.

leicht [līçt] *a* light; (*einfach*) easy; **nichts ~er als das!** nothing (could be) simpler! ♦ *ad*: **~ zerbrechlich** very fragile; **L~athletik** *f* athletics *sing*; **~fallen** *vi unreg*: **jdm ~fallen** be easy for sb; **~fertig** *a* thoughtless; **~gläubig** *a* gullible, credulous; **L~gläubigkeit** *f* gullibility, credulity; **~hin** *ad* lightly.

Leichtigkeit *f* easiness; **mit ~** with ease.

leicht- *zW*: **~lebig** *a* easy-going; **~machen** *vt*: **es sich** (*dat*) **~machen** make things easy for o.s.; (*nicht gewissenhaft sein*) take the easy way out; **L~matrose** *m* ordinary seaman; **~nehmen** *vt unreg* take lightly; **L~sinn** *m* carelessness; **sträflicher L~sinn** criminal negligence; **~sinnig** *a* careless; **~verletzt** *a attr* slightly injured.

leid [līt] *a*: **etw ~ haben** *od* **sein** be tired of sth; **es tut mir/ihm ~** I am/he is sorry; **er/ das tut mir ~** I am sorry for him/about it; **sie kann einem ~ tun** you can't help feeling sorry for her.

Leid *nt* -(e)s grief, sorrow; **jdm sein ~ klagen** tell sb one's troubles.

leiden [lī'dən] *unreg vt* suffer; (*erlauben*) permit; **jdn/etw nicht ~ können** not be able to stand sb/sth ♦ *vi* suffer; **L∼** *nt* **-s,** - suffering; (*Krankheit*) complaint.

Leidenschaft *f* passion; **l∼lich** *a* passionate.

Leidens- *zW*: **∼genosse** *m*, **∼genossin** *f* fellow sufferer; **∼geschichte** *f*: **die ∼geschichte (Christi)** (*REL*) Christ's Passion.

leider [lī'dər] *ad* unfortunately; **ja,** ∼ yes, I'm afraid so; ∼ **nicht** I'm afraid not.

leidig [lī'dic̦] *a* miserable, tiresome.

leidlich [līt'lic̦] *a* tolerable ♦ *ad* tolerably.

Leid- *zW*: **∼tragende(r)** *mf dekl wie a* bereaved; (*Benachteiligter*) one who suffers; **∼wesen** *nt*: **zu jds ∼wesen** to sb's dismay.

Leier [lī'ər] *f* **-,** **-n** lyre; (*fig*) old story.

Leierkasten *m* barrel organ.

leiern *vti* (*Kurbel*) turn; (*umg*: *Gedicht*) rattle off.

Leiharbeiter(in *f*) *m* temp.

Leihbibliothek *f* lending library.

leihen [lī'ən] *vt unreg* lend; **sich** (*dat*) **etw** ∼ borrow sth.

Leih- *zW*: **∼gabe** *f* loan; **∼gebühr** *f* rental fee; **∼haus** *nt* pawnshop; **∼mutter** *f* surrogate mother; **∼schein** *m* pawn ticket; (*in der Bibliothek*) borrowing slip; **∼unternehmen** *nt* hire service; (*Arbeitsmarkt*) temp service; **∼wagen** *m* rental car (*US*), hired car (*Brit*).

Leim [līm] *m* **-(e)s,** **-e** glue; **jdm auf den** ∼ **gehen** be taken in by sb; **l∼en** *vt* glue.

Leine [lī'nə] *f* **-,** **-n** line, cord; (*Hunde∼*) leash, lead; ∼ **ziehen** (*umg*) clear out.

leinen *a* linen.

Leinen *nt* **-s,** - linen; (*grob, segeltuchartig*) canvas; (*als Bucheinband*) cloth.

Lein- *zW*: **∼samen** *m* linseed; **∼tuch** *nt* linen cloth; (*Bettuch*) sheet; **∼wand** *f* (*KUNST*) canvas; (*FILM*) screen.

leise [lī'zə] *a* quiet; (*sanft*) soft, gentle; **mit** ∼**r Stimme** in a low voice; **nicht die** ∼**ste Ahnung haben** not have the slightest (idea).

Leisetreter *m* (*pej umg*) pussyfoot(er).

Leiste [lī'stə] *f* **-,** **-n** ledge; (*Zier∼*) strip; (*ANAT*) groin.

leisten [lī'stən] *vt* (*Arbeit*) do; (*Gesellschaft*) keep; (*Ersatz*) supply; (*vollbringen*) achieve; **sich** (*dat*) **etw** ∼ allow o.s. sth; (*sich gönnen*) treat o.s. to sth; **sich** (*dat*) **etw** ∼ **können** be able to afford sth.

Leistenbruch *m* (*MED*) hernia, rupture.

Leistung *f* performance; (*gute*) achievement; (*eines Motors*) power; (*von Krankenkasse etc*) benefit; (*Zahlung*) payment.

Leistungs- *zW*: **∼abfall** *m* (*in bezug auf Qualität*) drop in performance; (*in bezug auf Quantität*) drop in productivity; **∼beurteilung** *f* performance appraisal, rating; **∼druck** *m* pressure; **l∼fähig** *a* efficient; **∼fähigkeit** *f* efficiency; **∼gesellschaft** *f* meritocracy; **∼kurs** *m* (*SCH*) set; **l∼orientiert** *a* performance-orientated; **∼prinzip** *nt* achievement principle; **∼sport** *m* competitive sport; **∼zulage** *f* productivity bonus.

Leit- *zW*: **∼artikel** *m* editorial, leading article; **∼bild** *nt* model.

leiten [lī'tən] *vt* lead; (*Firma*) manage; (*in eine Richtung*) direct; (*ELEK*) conduct; **sich von jdm/etw** ∼ **lassen** (*lit, fig*) (let o.s.) be guided by sb/sth.

leitend *a* leading; (*Gedanke, Idee*) dominant; (*Stellung, Position*) managerial; (*Ingenieur, Beamter*) in charge; (*PHYS*) conductive; **∼er Angestellter** executive.

Leiter [lī'tər] *m* **-s,** - leader, head; (*ELEK*) conductor ♦ *f* **-,** **-n** ladder.

Leiterin *f* leader, head.

Leiterplatte *f* (*COMPUT*) board, breadboard.

Leit- *zW*: **∼faden** *m* guide; **∼fähigkeit** *f* conductivity; **∼gedanke** *m* central idea; **∼motiv** *nt* leitmotiv; **∼planke** *f* guardrail, crash barrier (*Brit*); **∼spruch** *m* motto.

Leitung *f* (*Führung*) direction; (*FILM, THEAT etc*) production; (*von Firma*) management; directors *pl*; (*Wasser∼*) pipe; (*Kabel*) cable; **eine lange** ∼ **haben** be slow on the uptake; **da ist jemand in der** ∼ (*umg*) there's somebody else on the line.

Leitungs- *zW*: **∼draht** *m* wire; **∼mast** *m* telegraph pole; **∼rohr** *nt* pipe; **∼wasser** *nt* tap water.

Leitwerk *nt* (*AVIAT*) tail unit.

Lektion [lektsēō:n'] *f* lesson; **jdm eine** ∼ **erteilen** (*fig*) teach sb a lesson.

Lektor(in *f*) [lek'tor, lektō:'rin] *m* (*UNIV*) lector; (*Verlag*) editor.

Lektüre [lektü:'rə] *f* **-,** **-n** (*Lesen*) reading; (*Lesestoff*) reading matter.

Lende [len'də] *f* **-,** **-n** loin.

Lenden- *zW*: **∼braten** *m* roast sirloin; **∼stück** *nt* fillet.

lenkbar [lengk'bâr] *a* (*Fahrzeug*) steerable; (*Kind*) manageable.

lenken *vt* steer; (*Kind*) guide; (*Blick, Aufmerksamkeit*) direct (*auf* +*akk* at); (*Verdacht*) throw; (*auf sich*) draw (*auf* +*akk* onto); (*Gespräch*) lead.

Lenk- *zW*: **∼rad** *nt* steering wheel; **∼stange** *f* handlebars *pl*.

Lenz [lents] *m* **-es,** **-e** (*liter*) spring; **sich** (*dat*) **einen (faulen)** ∼ **machen** (*umg*) laze around.

Leopard [lāōpàrt'] *m* **-en,** **-en** leopard.

Lepra [lā:'prà] *f* - leprosy; **∼kranke(r)** *mf* leper.

Lerche [ler'c̦ə] *f* **-,** **-n** lark.

lern- [lern] *zW*: **∼begierig** *a* eager to learn; **∼behindert** *a* educationally handicaped.

lernen *vt* learn ♦ *vi*: **er lernt bei der Firma Braun** he's training at Braun's.

Lernhilfe *f* educational aid.

lesbar [lā:s'bâr] *a* legible.

Lesbierin [les'bēərin] *f* lesbian.

lesbisch *a* lesbian.

Lese [lā:'zə] *f* **-,** **-n** gleaning; (*Wein∼*) harvest.

Lesebuch *nt* reading book, reader.

lesen *vti unreg* read; (*ernten*) gather, pick;

~/schreiben (*COMPUT*) read/write.
Leser(in *f*) *m* **-s,** - reader.
Leseratte [lä:'zərátə] *f* **-,** **-n** (*umg*) bookworm.
Leser- *zW*: **~brief** *m* reader's letter; „**~briefe**" "letters to the editor"; **~kreis** *m* readership; **l~lich** *a* legible.
Lese- *zW*: **~saal** *m* reading room; **~stoff** *m* reading material; **~zeichen** *nt* bookmark; **~zirkel** *m* magazine club.
Lesung [lä:'zōōng] *f* (*PARL*) reading; (*ECCL*) lesson.
lethargisch [lätár'gish] *a* (*MED, fig*) lethargic.
Lettland [let'lánt] *nt* **-s** Latvia.
Letzt *f:* **zu guter** ~ finally, in the end.
letztenmal *ad:* **zum** ~ for the last time.
letztens *ad* lately.
letzte(r, s) [lets'tə(r, s)] *a* last; (*neueste*) latest; **der L~ Wille** last will and testament; **bis zum ~n** to the utmost; **in ~r Zeit** recently.
letztere(r, s) *a* the latter.
Letzte(s) *n:* **das ist ja das ~!** (*umg*) that really is the limit!
letztlich in the end.
Leuchte [loiċh'tə] *f* **-,** **-n** lamp, light; (*umg: Mensch*) genius.
leuchten *vi* shine, gleam.
Leuchter *m* **-s,** - candlestick.
Leucht- *zW*: **~farbe** *f* fluorescent color; **~feuer** *nt* beacon; **~käfer** *m* glow-worm; **~kugel** *f,* **~rakete** *f* flare; **~pistole** *f* flare pistol; **~reklame** *f* neon sign; **~röhre** *f* fluorescent light; **~turm** *m* lighthouse; **~zifferblatt** *nt* luminous dial.
leugnen [loig'nən] *vti* deny.
Leugnung *f* denial.
Leukämie [loikemē:'] *f* leukemia (*US*), leukaemia (*Brit*).
Leukoplast [loikōplást'] *nt* **-(e)s, -e** ® Elastoplast ®.
Leumund [loi'mōōnt] *m* **-(e)s, -e** reputation.
Leumundszeugnis *nt* character reference.
Leute [loi'tə] *pl* people *pl*; **kleine** ~ (*fig*) ordinary people; **etw unter die** ~ **bringen** (*umg: Gerücht etc*) spread sth around.
Leutnant [loit'nánt] *m* **-s, -s** *od* **-e** lieutenant.
leutselig [loit'zā:liċh] *a* affable; **L~keit** *f* affability.
Leviten [lävē:'tən] *pl:* **jdm die** ~ **lesen** (*umg*) read sb the riot act.
lexikalisch [leksēkä'lish] *a* lexical.
Lexikon [lek'sēkon] *nt* **-s, Lexiken** *od* **Lexika** encyclopedia.
lfd. *abk* = **laufend.**
LFZG *nt abk* = **Lohnfortzahlungsgesetz.**
LG *nt abk* (= *Landgericht*) district court.
Libelle [lēbe'lə] *f* **-,** **-n** dragonfly; (*TECH*) spirit level.
liberal [lēbārál'] *a* liberal.
Liberale(r) *mf dekl wie a* (*POL*) Liberal.
Liberalisierung [lēbārálēzē:'rōōng] *f* liberalization.
Liberalismus [lēbārális'mōōs] *m* liberalism.
Libero [lē:'bārō] *m* **-s, -s** (*FUSSBALL*) sweep-

er.
licht [liċht] *a* light, bright.
Licht *nt* **-(e)s, -er** light; ~ **machen** (*anschalten*) turn on a light; (*anzünden*) light a candle *etc*; **mir geht ein** ~ **auf** it's dawned on me; **jdn hinters** ~ **führen** (*fig*) lead sb up the garden path; **~bild** *nt* photograph; (*Dia*) slide; **~blick** *m* cheering prospect; **l~empfindlich** *a* sensitive to light.
lichten [liċh'tən] *vt* clear; (*Anker*) weigh ♦ *vr* clear up; (*Haar*) thin.
lichterloh [liċh'tərlō:'] *ad:* ~ **brennen** blaze.
Licht- *zW*: **~geschwindigkeit** *f* speed of light; **~griffel** *m* (*COMPUT*) light pen; **~hupe** *f* flashing of headlights; **~jahr** *nt* light year; **~maschine** *f* dynamo; **~meß** *f* - Candlemas; **~pause** *f* photocopy; (*bei Blaupausverfahren*) blueprint; **~schalter** *m* light switch; **l~scheu** *a* averse to light; (*fig: Gesindel*) shady; **~setzmaschine** *f* (*TYP*) photosetting machine.
Lichtung *f* clearing, glade.
Lid [lē:t] *nt* **-(e)s, -er** eyelid; **~schatten** *m* eyeshadow.
lieb [lē:p] *a* dear; **(viele)** **~e Grüße Deine Silvia** love Silvia; **L~e Anna, ~er Klaus!** ... Dear Anna and Klaus, ...; **am ~sten lese ich Kriminalromane** best of all I like detective novels; **den ~en langen Tag** (*umg*) the whole livelong day; **sich bei jdm** ~ **Kind machen** (*pej*) suck up to sb (*umg*).
liebäugeln [lē:p'oigəln] *vi untr:* **mit dem Gedanken** ~, **etw zu tun** toy with the idea of doing sth.
Liebe [lē:'bə] *f* **-,** **-n** love; (*Sex*) love-making; **l~bedürftig** *a:* **l~bedürftig sein** need love.
Liebelei *f* flirtation.
lieben [lē:'bən] *vt* love; (*weniger stark*) like; **etw liebend gern tun** love to do sth.
liebens- *zW*: **~wert** *a* loveable; **~würdig** *a* kind; **~würdigerweise** *ad* kindly; **L~würdigkeit** *f* kindness.
lieber [lē:'bər] *ad* rather, preferably; **ich gehe ~ nicht** I'd rather not go; **ich trinke ~ Wein als Bier** I prefer wine to beer; **bleib ~ im Bett** you'd better stay in bed.
Liebes- *zW*: **~brief** *m* love letter; **~dienst** *m* good turn; **~kummer** *m:* **~kummer haben** be lovesick; **~paar** *nt* courting couple, lovers *pl*; **~roman** *m* romantic novel.
liebevoll *a* loving.
lieb- [lē:p'] *zW*: **~gewinnen** *vt unreg* get fond of; **~haben** *vt unreg* love; (*weniger stark*) be (very) fond of; **L~haber(in** *f*) *m* **-s, -** lover; (*Sammler*) collector; **L~haberei'** *f* hobby; **~kosen** [lē:pkō:'zən] *vt untr* caress; **~lich** *a* lovely, charming; (*Duft, Wein*) sweet.
Liebling *m* darling.
Lieblings- *in zW* favorite (*US*), favourite (*Brit*); **l~los** *a* unloving; **~schaft** *f* love affair.
Liechtenstein [liċh'tənshtīn] *nt* **-s** Liechtenstein.

Lied [lēːt] *nt* -(e)s, -er song; (*ECCL*) hymn; **davon kann ich ein ~ singen** (*fig*) I could tell you a thing or two about that (*umg*).

Liederbuch *nt* songbook; (*REL*) hymn book.

liederlich [lēːˈdərlɪçh] *a* slovenly; (*Lebenswandel*) loose, immoral; **L~keit** *f* slovenliness; immorality.

lief [lēːf] *imperf von* **laufen**.

Lieferant [lēːfəránt'] *m* supplier.

Lieferanteneingang *m* tradesmen's entrance; (*von Warenhaus etc*) deliveries *pl*.

Liefer- *zW*: **l~bar** *a* (*vorrätig*) available; **~frist** *f* delivery period.

liefern [lēːˈfərn] *vt* deliver; (*versorgen mit*) supply; (*Beweis*) produce.

Liefer- *zW*: **~schein** *m* delivery slip; **~termin** *m* delivery date; **~ung** *f* delivery; (*Versorgung*) supply; **~wagen** *m* delivery truck.

Liege [lēːˈgə] *f* -, -n bed; (*Camping~*) cot (*US*), camp bed (*Brit*); **~geld** *nt* (*Hafen, Flughafen*) demurrage.

liegen [lēːˈgən] *vi unreg* lie; (*sich befinden*) be (situated); **mir liegt nichts/viel daran** it doesn't matter to me/it matters a lot to me; **es liegt bei Ihnen, ob ...** it rests with you whether ...; **Sprachen ~ mir nicht** languages are not my line; **woran liegt es?** what's the cause?; **so, wie die Dinge jetzt ~** as things stand at the moment; **an mir soll es nicht ~, wenn die Sache schiefgeht** it won't be my fault if things go wrong; **einen Ort links** *od* **rechts ~ lassen** pass by a place; **~bleiben** *vi unreg* (*Person*) stay in bed; (*nicht aufstehen*) stay lying down; (*Ding*) be left (behind); (*nicht ausgeführt werden*) be left (undone); **~lassen** *vt unreg* (*vergessen*) leave behind; **L~schaft** *f* real estate.

Liege- *zW*: **~platz** *m* (*auf Schiff, in Zug etc*) berth; (*Ankerplatz*) moorings *pl*; **~sitz** *m* (*AUT*) reclining seat; **~stuhl** *m* deck chair; **~stütz** *m* (*SPORT*) push-up; **~wagen** *m* (*EISENB*) couchette car; **~wiese** *f* lawn (*for sunbathing*).

lieh [lēː] *imperf von* **leihen**.

ließ [lēːs] *imperf von* **lassen**.

liest [lēːst] *2./3. pers sing präs von* **lesen**.

Lift [lɪft] *m* -(e)s, -e *od* -s elevator (*US*), lift (*Brit*).

liieren [lēːˈrən] *vt*: **liiert sein** (*Firmen etc*) be working together; (*ein Verhältnis haben*) have a relationship.

Likör [lēkœr'] *m* -s, -e liqueur.

lila [lēːˈlá] *a inv* purple; lilac; **L~** *nt* -s, -s (*Farbe*) purple; lilac.

Lilie [lēːˈlēə] *f* lily.

Liliputaner(in *f*) [lēlēpōōtáˈnər(in)] *m* -s, - midget.

Limit [liˈmit] *nt* -s, -s *od* -e limit; (*FIN*) ceiling.

Limonade [lēmōnáˈdə] *f* lemonade.

Limousine [lēmōōzēːˈnə] *f* sedan (*US*), saloon (*Brit*).

lind [lɪnt] *a* gentle, mild.

Linde [lɪn'də] *f* -, -n lime tree, linden.

lindern [lɪn'dərn] *vt* alleviate, soothe.

Linderung *f* alleviation.

lindgrün *a* lime green.

Lineal [lēnāál'] *nt* -s, -e ruler.

linear [lēnāár'] *a* linear.

Linguist(in *f*) [linggōōist'(in)] *m* linguist.

Linguistik *f* linguistics *sing*.

Linie [lēːˈnēə] *f* line; **in erster ~** first and foremost; **auf die ~ achten** watch one's figure; **fahren Sie mit der ~ 2** take the number 2 (*bus etc*).

Linien- *zW*: **~blatt** *nt* ruled sheet; **~bus** *m* regular bus; **~flug** *m* scheduled flight; **~richter** *m* (*SPORT*) linesman; **l~treu** *a* loyal to the (party) line.

liniieren [lēnēēˈrən] *vt* line.

Linke [liŋ'kə] *f* -, -n left side; left hand; (*POL*) left.

Linke(r) *mf dekl wie a* (*POL*) left-winger, leftist (*pej*).

linke(r, s) *a* left; **~ Masche** purl; **das mache ich mit der ~n Hand** (*umg*) I can do that with my eyes shut.

linkisch *a* awkward, gauche.

links *ad* left; to *od* on the left; **~ von mir** on *od* to my left; **~ von der Mitte** left of center; **jdn ~ liegenlassen** (*fig umg*) ignore sb; **L~abbieger** *m* motorist *od* vehicle turning left; **L~außen** [liŋksouˈsən] *m* -s, - (*SPORT*) outside left; **L~händer(in** *f*) *m* -s, - left-handed person; **L~kurve** *f* left curve (*US*), left-hand bend (*Brit*); **~lastig** *a*: **~lastig sein** list *od* lean to the left; **~radikal** *a* (*POL*) radically left-wing; **L~rutsch** *m* (*POL*) swing to the left; **L~verkehr** *m* driving on the left.

Linoleum [lēnōːˈláōōm] *nt* -s lino(leum).

Linse [lin'zə] *f* -, -n lentil; (*optisch*) lens.

linsen *vi* (*umg*) peak.

Lippe [li'pə] *f* -, -n lip.

Lippen- *zW*: **~bekenntnis** *nt* lip service; **~stift** *m* lipstick.

Liquidationswert [lēkvēdátsēōːns'vāːrt] *m* break-up value.

Liquidator [lēkvēdâ'tor] *m* liquidator.

liquid(e) [lēkvēːt', lēkvēːˈdə] *a* (*Firma*) solvent.

liquidieren [lēkvēdēˈrən] *vt* liquidate.

Liquidität [lēkvēdēteːt'] *f* liquidity.

lispeln [lisˈpəln] *vi* lisp.

Lissabon [liˈsábon] *nt* Lisbon.

List [list] *f* -, -en cunning; (*Plan*) trick, ruse; **mit ~ und Tücke** (*umg*) with a lot of coaxing.

Liste [liˈstə] *f* -, -n list.

Listen- *zW*: **~platz** *m* (*POL*) place on the party list; **~preis** *m* list price.

listig *a* cunning, sly.

Litanei [lētáni'] *f* litany.

Litauen [lēːˈtouən] *nt* -s Lithuania.

litauisch *a* Lithuanian.

Liter [lēːˈtər] *nt od m* -s, - liter (*US*), litre

(*Brit*).

literarisch [litārâ'rish] *a* literary.

Literatur [litārátōō:r'] *f* literature; ~**preis** *m* award for literature; ~**wissenschaft** *f* literary criticism *od* studies *pl*.

literweise [lē:'tərvīzə] *ad* (*lit*) by the liter; (*fig*) by the gallon.

Litfaßsäule [lit'fászoilə] *f* advertizing pillar.

Lithographie [lētōgráfē:'] *f* lithography.

litt [lit] *imperf von* **leiden**.

Liturgie [lētōōrgē:'] *f* liturgy.

liturgisch [lētōōr'gish] *a* liturgical.

Litze [lit'sə] *f* -, -**n** braid; (*ELEK*) cord (*US*), flex (*Brit*).

live [līf] *a*, *ad* (*RAD*, *TV*) live.

Livree [lēvrā:'] *f* -, -**n** livery.

Lizenz [lētsents'] *f* license (*US*), licence (*Brit*); ~**ausgabe** *f* licensed edition; ~**gebühr** *f* license fee; (*im Verlagswesen*) royalty.

I.J. *abk* (= *laufenden Jahres*) current year.

Lkw, LKW *m* -(**s**), -(**s**) *abk* = **Lastkraftwagen**.

I.M. *abk* (= *laufenden Monats*) inst.

Lob [lō:p] *nt* -(**e**)**s** praise.

Lobby [lo'bē] *f* -, -**s** *od* **Lobbies** lobby.

loben [lō:'bən] *vt* praise; **das lob ich mir** that's what I like (*to see/hear etc*).

lobenswert *a* praiseworthy.

löblich [lœ'plich] *a* praiseworthy, laudable.

Lobrede *f* eulogy.

Loch [loh] *nt* -(**e**)**s**, ⁻**er** hole; **l~en** *vt* punch holes in; ~**er** *m* -**s**, - punch.

löcherig [lœ'chərich] *a* full of holes.

löchern *vt* (*umg*): **jdn** ~ pester sb with questions.

Loch- *zW*: ~**karte** *f* punch card; ~**streifen** *m* punch tape; ~**zange** *f* punch.

Locke [lo'kə] *f* -, -**n** lock, curl.

locken *vt* entice; (*Haare*) curl.

lockend *a* tempting.

Lockenwickler *m* -**s**, - curler.

locker [lo'kər] *a* loose; (*Kuchen, Schaum*) light; (*umg*) cool; ~**lassen** *vi unreg*: **nicht** ~**lassen** not let up.

lockern *vt* loosen ♦ *vr* (*Atmosphäre*) get more relaxed.

Lockerungsübung *f* loosening-up exercise; (*zur Warmwerden*) limbering-up exercise.

lockig [lo'kich] *a* curly.

Lock- *zW*: ~**mittel** *nt* lure; ~**ruf** *m* call.

Lockung *f* enticement.

Lockvogel *m* decoy, bait; ~**angebot** *nt* (*COMM*) loss leader.

Lodenmantel [lō:'dənmántəl] *m* thick woollen coat.

lodern [lō:'dərn] *vi* blaze.

Löffel [lœ'fəl] *m* -**s**, - spoon.

löffeln *vt* (eat with a) spoon.

löffelweise *ad* by the spoonful.

log [lō:k] *imperf von* **lügen**.

Logarithmentafel [lōgárit'məntáfəl] *f* log(arithm) tables *pl*.

Logarithmus [lōgárit'mōōs] *m* logarithm.

Loge [lō:'zhə] *f* -, -**n** (*THEAT*) box; (*Freimau-

rer*) (masonic) lodge; (*Pförtner*~) office.

logieren [lōzhē:'rən] *vi* lodge, stay.

Logik [lō:'gik] *f* logic.

Logis [lōzhē:'] *nt* -, -: **Kost und** ~ board and lodging.

logisch [lō:'gish] *a* logical; (*umg*: *selbstverständlich*) of course.

logo [lō'gō] *interj* (*umg*) obvious!

Logopäde [lōgōpe:'də] *m* -**n**, -**n**, **Logopädin** *f* speech therapist.

Lohn [lō:n] *m* -(**e**)**s**, ⁻**e** reward; (*Arbeits*~) pay, wages *pl*; ~**abrechnung** *f* statement of earnings, wages slip; ~**ausfall** *m* loss of earnings; ~**büro** *nt* wages office; ~**diktat** *nt* wage dictate; ~**empfänger** *m* wage earner.

lohnen [lō:'nən] *vt* (*liter*) reward (*jdm etw* sb for sth) ♦ *vr unpers* be worth it.

lohnend *a* worthwhile.

Lohn- *zW*: ~**forderung** *f* wage claim; ~**fortzahlung** *f* continued payment of wages; ~**fortzahlungsgesetz** *nt* law on continued payment of wages; ~**gefälle** *nt* wage differential; ~**kosten** *pl* labor costs; ~**politik** *f* wages policy; ~**steuer** *f* income tax.

Lohnsteuer- *zW*: ~**jahresausgleich** *m* income tax return; ~**karte** *f* (income) tax card.

Lohn- *zW*: ~**stopp** *m* pay freeze; ~**streifen** *m* pay slip; ~**tüte** *f* pay envelope (*US*) *od* packet (*Brit*).

Lok [lok] *f* -, -**s** *abk* (= *Lokomotive*) loco (*umg*).

lokal [lōkâl'] *a* local.

Lokal *nt* -(**e**)**s**, -**e** bar.

lokalisieren [lōkâlēzē:'rən] *vt* localize.

Lokalisierung *f* localization.

Lokalität [lōkálēte:t'] *f* locality; (*Raum*) facilities *pl*.

Lokal- *zW*: ~**presse** *f* local press; ~**teil** *m* (*Zeitung*) local section; ~**termin** *m* (*JUR*) visit to the scene of the crime.

Lokomotive [lōkōmōtē:'və] *f* -, -**n** locomotive.

Lokomotivführer *m* engineer (*US*), engine driver (*Brit*).

Lombardei [lombárdī'] *f* Lombardy.

London [lon'don] *nt* -**s** London.

Lorbeer [lor'bā:r] *m* -**s**, -**en** (*lit*, *fig*) laurel; ~**blatt** *nt* (*KOCH*) bay leaf.

Lore [lō:'rə] *f* -, -**n** (*MIN*) truck.

los [lō:s] *a* loose; **etw** ~ **sein** be rid of sth; **was ist** ~? what's the matter?; **dort ist nichts/viel** ~ there's nothing/a lot going on there; **ich bin mein ganzes Geld** ~ (*umg*) I'm cleaned out; **irgendwas ist mit ihm** ~ there's something wrong with him ♦ *ad*: ~! go on!; **wir wollen früh** ~ we want to be off early; **nichts wie** ~! let's get going.

Los [lō:s] *nt* -**es**, -**e** (*Schicksal*) lot, fate; (*in der Lotterie*) lottery ticket; **das große** ~ **ziehen** (*lit*, *fig*) hit the jackpot; **etw durch das** ~ **entscheiden** decide sth by drawing lots.

los- *zW*: ~**binden** *vt unreg* untie; ~**brechen** *vi unreg* (*Sturm, Gewitter*) break.

losch [losh] *imperf von* **löschen**.

Löschblatt [lœsh'blát] *nt* blotter, sheet of blotting paper.

löschen [lœ'shən] *vt* (*Feuer, Licht*) put out, extinguish; (*Durst*) quench; (*COMM*) cancel; (*Tonband*) erase; (*Fracht*) unload; (*COMPUT*) delete ♦ *vi* (*Feuerwehr*) put out a fire; (*Papier*) blot.

Lösch- *zW:* ~**fahrzeug** *nt* fire engine; ~**gerät** *nt* fire extinguisher; ~**papier** *nt* blotting paper.

Löschung *f* extinguishing; (*COMM*) cancellation; (*Fracht*) unloading.

lose [lō:'zə] *a* loose.

Lösegeld *nt* ransom.

losen [lō:'zən] *vi* draw lots.

lösen [lœ'zən] *vt* loosen; (*Handbremse*) release; (*Husten, Krampf*) ease; (*Rätsel etc*) solve; (*Verlobung*) call off; (*CHEM*) dissolve; (*Partnerschaft*) break up; (*Fahrkarte*) buy ♦ *vr* (*aufgehen*) come loose; (*Schuß*) go off; (*Zucker etc*) dissolve; (*Problem, Schwierigkeit*) (re)solve itself.

los- *zW:* ~**fahren** *vi unreg* leave; ~**gehen** *vi unreg* set out; (*anfangen*) start; (*Bombe*) go off; **jetzt geht's** ~! here we go!; **nach hinten** ~**gehen** (*umg*) backfire; **auf jdn** ~**gehen** go for sb; ~**kaufen** *vt* (*Gefangene, Geißeln*) pay ransom for; ~**kommen** *vi unreg* (*sich befreien*) free o.s. (*von* from); **von etw** ~**kommen** get away from sth; ~**lassen** *vt unreg* (*Seil*) let go of; (*Schimpfe*) let loose; **der Gedanke läßt mich nicht mehr** ~ the thought haunts me; ~**laufen** *vi unreg* run off; ~**legen** *vi* (*umg*): **nun leg mal** ~ **und erzähl(e)** ... now come on and tell me *od* us ...

löslich [lœs'liçh] *a* soluble; **L**~**keit** *f* solubility.

los- *zW:* ~**lösen** *vt* free ♦ *vr* detach o.s. (*von* from); ~**machen** *vt* loosen; (*Boot*) unmoor ♦ *vr* get free.

Losnummer *f* ticket number.

los- *zW:* ~**sagen** *vr* renounce (*von jdm/etw* sb/sth); ~**schießen** *vi unreg*: **schieß** ~! (*fig umg*) fire away!; ~**schrauben** *vt* unscrew; ~**sprechen** *vt unreg* absolve; ~**stürzen** *vi*: **auf jdn/etw** ~**stürzen** pounce on sb/sth.

Losung [lō:'zōōng] *f* watchword, slogan.

Lösung [lœ'zōōng] *f* (*Lockermachen*) loosening; (*eines Rätsels, CHEM*) solution.

Lösungsmittel *nt* solvent.

los- *zW:* ~**werden** *vt unreg* get rid of; ~**ziehen** *vi unreg* (*sich aufmachen*) set out; **gegen jdn** ~**ziehen** (*fig*) run sb down.

Lot [lō:t] *nt* **-(e)s, -e** plumbline; (*MATH*) perpendicular; **im** ~ vertical; (*fig*) on an even keel; **die Sache ist wieder im** ~ things have been straightened out; **l**~**en** *vti* plumb, sound.

löten [lœ'tən] *vt* solder.

Lötkolben *m* soldering iron.

Lotse [lō:'tsə] *m* **-n, -n** pilot; (*AVIAT*) air traffic controller.

lotsen *vt* pilot; (*umg*) lure.

Lotterie [lotərē:'] *f* lottery.

Lotterleben [lo'tərlā:bən] *nt* (*umg*) dissolute life.

Lotto [lo'tō] *nt* **-s, -s** national lottery; ~**zahlen** *pl* winning Lotto numbers *pl*.

Löwe [lœ'və] *m* **-n, -n** lion; (*ASTROL*) Leo.

Löwen- *zW:* ~**anteil** *m* lion's share; ~**maul** *nt* snapdragon; ~**zahn** *m* dandelion.

Löwin [lœ'vin] *f* lioness.

loyal [lōáyâl'] *a* loyal.

Loyalität [lōáyálēte:t'] *f* loyalty.

LP *f* **-, -s** *abk* (= *Langspielplatte*) LP.

LPG *f* *abk* (*DDR*: = *Landwirtschaftliche Produktionsgenossenschaft*) agricultural production cooperative.

lt. *abk* = **laut.**

Lt. *abk* (= *Leutnant*) Lt.

Luchs [lŏŏks] *m* **-es, -e** lynx.

Lücke [lü'kə] *f* **-, -n** gap; (*Gesetzes*~) loophole; (*in Versorgung*) break.

Lücken- *zW:* ~**büßer** *m* **-s, -** stopgap; **l**~**haft** *a* full of gaps; (*Versorgung*) deficient; **l**~**los** *a* complete; ~**test** *m* (*SCH*) completion test.

lud [lŏŏt] *imperf von* **laden.**

Luder [lŏŏ:'dər] *nt* **-s, -** (*pej: Frau*) hussy; (*bedauernswert*) poor wretch.

Luft [lŏŏft] *f* **-, :-e** air; (*Atem*) breath; **die** ~ **anhalten** (*lit*) hold one's breath; **seinem Herzen** ~ **machen** get everything off one's chest; **in der** ~ **liegen** be in the air; **dicke** ~ (*umg*) a bad atmosphere; (**frische**) ~ **schnappen** (*umg*) get some fresh air; **in die** ~ **fliegen** (*umg*) explode; **die Behauptung ist aus der** ~ **gegriffen** this statement is (a) pure invention; **die** ~ **ist rein** (*umg*) the coast is clear; **jdn an die (frische)** ~ **setzen** (*umg*) show sb the door; **er ist** ~ **für mich** I'm not speaking to him; **jdn wie** ~ **behandeln** ignore sb; ~**angriff** *m* air raid; ~**aufnahme** *f* aerial photo; ~**ballon** *m* balloon; ~**blase** *f* air bubble; ~**brücke** *f* airlift; **l**~**dicht** *a* airtight; ~**druck** *m* atmospheric pressure; **l**~**durchlässig** *a* pervious to air.

lüften [lüf'tən] *vti* air; (*Hut*) lift, raise.

Luft- *zW:* ~**fahrt** *f* aviation; ~**feuchtigkeit** *f* humidity; ~**fracht** *f* air cargo; **l**~**gekühlt** *a* air-cooled.

luftig *a* (*Ort*) breezy; (*Raum*) airy; (*Kleider*) summery.

Luft- *zW:* ~**kissenfahrzeug** *nt* hovercraft; ~**krieg** *m* war in the air, aerial warfare; ~**kurort** *m* health resort; **l**~**leer** *a*: **l**~**leerer Raum** vacuum; ~**linie** *f*: **in der** ~**linie** as the crow flies; ~**loch** *nt* air hole; (*AVIAT*) air pocket; ~**matratze** *f* air mattress; ~**pirat** *m* hijacker; ~**post** *f* airmail; ~**pumpe** *f* (*für Fahrrad*) (bicycle) pump; ~**röhre** *f* (*ANAT*) windpipe; ~**schlange** *f* streamer; ~**schloß** *nt* (*fig*) castle in the air; ~**schutz** *m* anti-aircraft defense; ~**schutzbunker** *m*, ~**schutzkeller** *m* air-raid shelter; ~**sprung** *m*: (*fig*) **einen** ~**sprung machen** jump for joy.

Lüftung [lüf'tōōng] *f* ventilation.

Luft- *zW:* **~veränderung** *f* change of air; **~verkehr** *m* air traffic; **~waffe** *f* air force; **~weg** *m:* **etw auf dem ~weg befördern** transport sth by air; **~zufuhr** *f* air supply; **~zug** *m* draft (*US*), draught (*Brit*).

Lüge [lü:'gə] *f* -, **-n** lie; **jdn/etw ~n strafen** give the lie to sb/sth.

lügen [lü:'gən] *vi unreg* lie; **wie gedruckt ~** (*umg*) lie like mad.

Lügner(in *f*) *m* **-s,** - liar.

Luke [lōō:'kə] *f* -, **-n** skylight; (*NAUT*) hatch.

lukrativ [lōōkrátē:f'] *a* lucrative.

Lümmel [lü'məl] *m* **-s,** - lout.

lümmeln *vr* lounge (about).

Lump [lōōmp] *m* **-en,** **-en** scamp, rascal.

lumpen [lōōm'pən] *vt:* **sich nicht ~ lassen** not be mean, be generous.

Lumpen *m* **-s,** - rag; **~sammler** *m* ragman.

lumpig [lōōm'pich] *a* shabby; **~e 10 Mark** (*umg*) 10 measly marks.

Lüneburger Heide ['lü:nəbōōrgər 'hīdə] *f* Heath of Lüneburg.

Lunge [lōō'ngə] *f* -, **-n** lung.

Lungen- *zW:* **~entzündung** *f* pneumonia; **l~krank** *a* consumptive.

lungern [lōōng'ərn] *vi* hang about.

Lunte [lōōn'tə] *f* -, **-n** fuse; **~ riechen** smell a rat.

Lupe [lōō:'pə] *f* -, **-n** magnifying glass; **unter die ~ nehmen** (*fig*) scrutinize.

lupenrein *a* (*lit: Edelstein*) flawless.

Lupine [lōōpē:'nə] *f* lupin.

Lurch [lōōrch] *m* **-(e)s,** **-e** amphibian.

Lust [lōōst] *f* -, **ͤe** joy, delight; (*Neigung*) desire; (*sexuell auch*) lust (*pej*); **~ haben zu od auf etw** (*akk*)**/etw zu tun** feel like sth/ doing sth; **hast du ~?** how about it?; **er hat die ~ daran verloren** he has lost all interest in it; **je nach ~ und Laune** just depending on how I *od* you *etc* feel; **l~betont** *a* pleasure-orientated.

lüstern [lü'stərn] *a* lustful, lecherous.

Lust- *zW:* **~gefühl** *nt* pleasurable feeling; **~gewinn** *m* pleasure.

lustig [lōō'stich] *a* (*komisch*) amusing, funny; (*fröhlich*) cheerful; **sich über jdn/etw ~ machen** make fun of sb/sth.

Lüstling *m* lecher.

Lust- *zW:* **l~los** *a* unenthusiastic; **~mord** *m* sex(ual) murder; **~prinzip** *nt* (*PSYCH*) pleasure principle; **~spiel** *nt* comedy; **l~wandeln** *vi* stroll about.

lutschen [lōōt'shən] *vti* suck; **am Daumen ~** suck one's thumb.

luth. *abk* (= *lutherisch*) Lutheran.

Lutscher *m* **-s,** - lollipop.

Luxemburg [lōōk'səmbōōrk] *nt* **-s** Luxembourg.

luxemburgisch [lōōk'səmbōōrgish] *a* Luxembourgian.

luxuriös [lōōksōōrēœs'] *a* luxurious.

Luxus [lōōk'sōōs] *m* - luxury; **~artikel** *pl* luxury goods *pl*; **~ausführung** *f* de luxe model; **~dampfer** *m* luxury cruise ship;

~hotel *nt* luxury hotel; **~steuer** *f* tax on luxuries.

LVA *f* - *abk* (= *Landesversicherungsanstalt*) *county insurance company*.

Lymphe [lüm'fə] *f* -, **-n** lymph.

Lymphknoten *m* lymph(atic) gland.

lynchen [lün'chən] *vt* lynch.

Lynchjustiz *f* lynch law.

Lyrik [lü:'rik] *f* lyric poetry; **~er(in** *f*) *m* **-s,** - lyric poet.

lyrisch [lü:'rish] *a* lyrical.

M

M, m [em] *nt* M, m.

m *abk* (= *Meter; männlich*) m.

M. *abk* = **Mitglied; Monat.**

MA. *abk* = **Mittelalter.**

Maat [mât] *m* **-s,** **-e** *od* **-en** (*NAUT*) (ship's) mate.

Mach- [màkh] *zW:* **~art** *f* make; **m~bar** *a* feasible.

Mache *f* - (*umg*) show, sham; **jdn in der ~ haben** be having a go at sb.

machen [mà'khən] *vt* make; (*tun*) do; (*umg: reparieren*) fix; (*betragen*) be; **was machst du denn hier?** what (on earth) are you doing here?; **was ~ Sie (beruflich)?** what do you do for a living?; **das Essen ~** get the meal; **wieviel macht das (alles zusammen)?** how much is that (altogether)?; **mach's gut!** take care, all the best; **mach, daß du hier verschwindest!** (you just) get out of here!; **mit mir kann man's ja ~!** (*umg*) the things I put up with!; **das läßt er nicht mit sich ~** he won't stand for that; **eine Prüfung ~** take an exam; **groß/klein ~** (*umg: Notdurft*) do a big/little job (*Kindersprache*); **das macht nichts** that doesn't matter ♦ *vr* come along (nicely); **sich** (*dat*) **viel aus jdm/etw ~** like sb/sth; **mach dir nichts daraus** don't let it bother you; **sich auf den Weg ~** get going; **sich an etw** (*akk*) **~** set about sth ♦ *vi:* **mach schon** *od* **schneller!** (*umg*) get a move on!, hurry up!; **jetzt macht sie auf große Dame** (*umg*) she's playing the lady now; **(sich** *dat*) **in die Hosen ~** (*lit, fig*) wet o.s., wet one's pants; **laß mich mal ~** (*umg*) let me do it; (*ich bringe das in Ordnung*) let me see to that; **in etw** (*dat*) **~** (*COMM*) be *od* deal in sth.

Machenschaften *pl* wheelings and dealings *pl*, machinations *pl*.

Macher *m* **-s,** - (*umg*) man of action.

Macht [màkht] *f* **-s,** **ͤe** power; **mit aller ~** with all one's might; **an der ~ sein** be in power; **alles in unserer ~ Stehende** everything in our power; ~**ergreifung** *f* seizure of power; ~**haber** *m* -**s**, - ruler.

mächtig [mečh'tiċh] *a* powerful, mighty; (*umg*: *ungeheuer*) enormous.

Macht- *zW*: **m~los** *a* powerless; ~**probe** *f* trial of strength; ~**stellung** *f* position of power; ~**wort** *nt*: **ein ~wort sprechen** lay down the law.

Machwerk *nt* work; (*schlechte Arbeit*) poor *od* sorry effort.

Macke [má'kə] *f* -, -**n** (*umg*: *Tick, Knall*) quirk; (*Fehler*) fault.

Macker *m* -**s**, - (*umg*) fellow, guy.

MAD *m* - *abk* (= *Militärischer Abschirmdienst*) ≈ MI5.

Mädchen [me:t'chən] *nt* girl; **ein ~ für alles** (*umg*) a gofer (*US*), a dogsbody (*Brit*); **m~haft** *a* girlish; ~**name** *m* maiden name.

Made [má'də] *f* -, -**n** maggot.

Mädel [me:dl'] *nt* -**s**, -**(s)** (*Dialekt*) lass, girl.

madig [má'diċh] *a* maggoty; **jdm etw ~ machen** spoil sth for sb.

Madrid [mádrit'] *nt* -**s** Madrid.

mag [mâk] *1./3. pers sing präs von* **mögen**.

Mag. *abk* = **Magister**.

Magazin [mágátsē:n'] *nt* -**s**, -**e** (*Zeitschrift, am Gewehr*) magazine; (*Lager*) storeroom; (*Bibliotheks~*) stockroom.

Magd [mâkt] *f* -, ¨-**e** maid(servant).

Magen [má'gən] *m* -**s**, - *od* ¨ stomach; **jdm auf den ~ schlagen** (*umg*) upset sb's stomach; (*fig*) upset sb; **sich** (*dat*) **den ~ verderben** upset one's stomach; ~**bitter** *m* bitters *pl*; ~**schmerzen** *pl* stomach-ache *sing*; ~**verstimmung** *f* stomach upset.

mager [má'gər] *a* lean; (*dünn*) thin; **M~keit** *f* leanness; thinness; **M~milch** *f* skimmed milk; **M~quark** *m* low-fat soft cheese.

Magie [mágē:'] *f* magic.

Magier [má'gēər] *m* -**s**, - magician.

magisch [má'gish] *a* magical.

Magister [mági'stər] *m* -**s**, - (*UNIV*) M.A., Master of Arts.

Magistrat [mágistrât'] *m* -**(e)s**, -**e** municipal authorities *pl*.

Magnat [mágnât'] *m* -**en**, -**en** magnate.

Magnet [mágnā:t'] *m* -**s** *od* -**en**, -**en** magnet; ~**band** *nt* (*COMPUT*) magnetic tape; **m~isch** *a* magnetic.

magnetisieren [mágnātēzē:'rən] *vt* magnetize.

Magnet- *zW*: ~**nadel** *f* magnetic needle; ~**tafel** *f* magnetic board.

Mahagoni [máhágō:'nē] *nt* -**s** mahogany.

Mähdrescher *m* -**s**, - combine (harvester).

mähen [me:'ən] *vti* mow.

Mahl [mâl] *nt* -**(e)s**, -**e** meal.

mahlen *vt unreg* grind.

Mahlstein *m* grindstone.

Mahlzeit *f* meal ♦ *interj* enjoy your meal!

Mahnbrief *m* reminder.

Mähne [me:'nə] *f* -, -**n** mane.

mahnen [má'nən] *vt* remind; (*warnend*) warn; (*wegen Schuld*) demand payment

from; **jdn zur Eile/Geduld** *etc* ~ (*auffordern*) urge sb to hurry/be patient *etc.*

Mahn- *zW*: ~**mal** *nt* memorial; ~**schreiben** *nt* reminder.

Mahnung *f* reminder; admonition, warning.

Mähre [me:'rə] *f* -, -**n** mare.

Mai [mī] *m* -**(e)s**, -**e** May; *siehe* **September**.

Mai- *zW*: ~**baum** *m* maypole; ~**bowle** *f* white wine punch (*flavored with woodruff*); ~**glöckchen** *nt* lily of the valley; ~**käfer** *m* cockchafer.

Mailand [mī'lánt] *nt* -**s** Milan.

Main [mīn] *m* -**(e)s** (*Fluß*) Main.

Mais [mís] *m* -**es**, -**e** maize, corn (*US*); ~**kolben** *m* corncob.

Majestät [máyeste:t'] *f* majesty.

majestätisch *a* majestic.

Majestätsbeleidigung *f* lese-majesty.

Major [máyō:r'] *m* -**s**, -**e** (*MIL*) major; (*AVIAT*) squadron leader.

Majoran [máyōrân'] *m* -**s**, -**e** marjoram.

makaber [máká'bər] *a* macabre.

Makel [má'kəl] *m* -**s**, - blemish; (*moralisch*) stain; **ohne ~** flawless; **m~los** *a* immaculate, spotless.

mäkeln [me:'kəln] *vi* find fault.

Make-up [mā:káp'] *nt* -**s**, -**s** make-up; (*flüssig*) foundation.

Makkaroni [mákárō:'nē] *pl* macaroni *sing*.

Makler [má'klər] *m* -**s**, - broker; (*Grundstücks~*) real estate agent; ~**gebühr** *f* broker's commission, brokerage.

Makrele [mákrā:'lə] *f* -, -**n** mackerel.

Makro- *in zW* macro-.

Makrone [mákrō:'nə] *f* -, -**n** macaroon.

Makroö'konomie *f* macroeconomics *sing*.

mal [mál] *ad* times.

Mal *nt* -**(e)s**, -**e** mark, sign; (*Zeitpunkt*) time; **ein für alle ~** once and for all; **mit einem ~(e)** all of a sudden.

Malaysia [máli'zēá] *nt* -**s** Malaysia.

malen *vti* paint.

Maler *m* -**s**, - painter.

Malerei [málərī'] *f* painting.

malerisch *a* picturesque.

Malkasten *m* paintbox.

Mallorca [málor'ká] *nt* -**s** Majorca, Mallorca.

malnehmen *vti unreg* multiply.

Malta [mál'tá] *nt* -**s** Malta.

Malteser(in *f*) [máltā:'zər(in)] *m* -**s**, - Maltese.

Malteser-Hilfsdienst *m* ≈ St. John's Ambulance Brigade (*Brit*).

malträtieren [máltretē:'rən] *vt* ill-treat, maltreat.

Malz [málts] *nt* -**es** malt; ~**bonbon** *nt* cough drop; ~**kaffee** *m* coffee substitute made from malt barley.

Mama [má'má] *f* -, -**s**, **Mami** [má'mē] *f* -, -**s** (*umg*) mommy (*US*), mummy (*Brit*).

Mammographie [mámográfē:'] *f* (*MED*) mammography.

Mammut [má'mōōt] *nt* -**s**, -**e** *od* -**s** mammoth; ~**anlagen** *pl* (*INDUSTRIE*) mammoth plants.

mampfen [mám'pfən] *vti* (*umg*) munch, chomp.

man [mán] *pron* one, you, people *pl*; ~ **hat mir gesagt ...** I was told ...

managen [me'nidzhən] *vt*: **ich manage das schon!** (*umg*) I'll fix it somehow!

Manager *m* **-s, -** manager.

manche(r, s) [mán'çhə(r, s)] *a* many a; (*pl*) a number of ♦ *pron* some.

mancherlei [mánçhərlī'] *a inv* various ♦ *pron* a variety of things.

manchmal *ad* sometimes.

Mandant(in *f*) [mándánt'(in)] *m* (*JUR*) client.

Mandarine [mándárē:'nə] *f* mandarin, tangerine.

Mandat [mándât'] *nt* **-(e)s, -e** mandate; **sein ~ niederlegen** (*PARL*) resign one's seat.

Mandel [mán'dəl] *f* **-, -n** almond; (*ANAT*) tonsil; ~**entzündung** *f* tonsillitis.

Manege [mánā:'zhə] *f* **-, -n** ring, arena.

Mangel [máng'əl] *f* **-, -n** mangle; **durch die ~ drehen** (*fig umg*) put through it; (*Prüfling etc auch*) put through the mill ♦ *m* **-s, -** lack; (*Knappheit*) shortage (*an* +*dat* of); (*Fehler*) defect, fault.

Mängelbericht [meng'əlbəriçht] *m* list of faults.

Mangel- *zW*: ~**erscheinung** *f* deficiency symptom; **m~haft** *a* poor; (*fehlerhaft*) defective, faulty; (*Schulnote auch*) unsatisfactory.

mangeln *vi unpers*: **es mangelt jdm an etw** (*dat*) sb lacks sth ♦ *vt* (*Wäsche*) mangle.

mangels *präp* +*gen* for lack of.

Mangelware *f* scarce commodity.

Manie [mánē:'] *f* mania.

Manier [mánē:'r'] *f* **-** manner; style; (*pej*) mannerism.

Manieren *pl* manners *pl*; mannerisms *pl*.

manieriert [mánērē:rt'] *a* mannered, affected.

manierlich *a* well-mannered.

Manifest [mánēfest'] *nt* **-es, -e** manifesto.

Maniküre [mánēkü:'rə] *f* **-, -n** manicure.

maniküren *vt* manicure.

manipulieren [mánēpōōlē:'rən] *vt* manipulate.

Manko [máng'kō] *nt* **-s, -s** deficiency; (*COMM*) deficit.

Mann [mán] *m* **-(e)s, ¨er** man; (*Ehe~*) husband; (*NAUT*: *pl* **Leute**) hand; **pro ~** per head; **mit ~ und Maus untergehen** go down with all hands; (*Passagierschiff*) go down with no survivors; **seinen ~ stehen** hold one's own; **etw an den ~ bringen** (*umg*) get rid of sth; **einen kleinen ~ im Ohr haben** (*hum umg*) be crazy.

Männchen [men'çhən] *nt* little man; (*Tier*) male; ~ **machen** (*Hund*) (sit up and) beg.

Mannequin [mánəkań:'] *nt* **-s, -s** fashion model.

Männersache [me'nərzáhhə] *f* (*Angelegenheit*) man's business; (*Arbeit*) man's job.

mannigfaltig [má'niçhfáltiçh] *a* various, varied; **M~keit** *f* variety.

männlich [men'liçh] *a* (*BIOL*) male; (*fig, GRAM*) masculine.

Mannsbild *nt* (*veraltet pej*) fellow.

Mannschaft *f* (*SPORT, fig*) team; (*NAUT, AVIAT*) crew; (*MIL*) other ranks *pl*.

Mannsleute *pl* (*umg*) menfolk *pl*.

Mannweib *nt* (*pej*) mannish woman.

Manometer [mánōmā:'tər] *nt* (*TECH*) pressure gage; ~! (*umg*) wow!

Manöver [mánœ'vər] *nt* **-s, -** maneuver (*US*), manoeuvre (*Brit*).

manövrieren [mánœvrē:'rən] *vti* maneuver (*US*), manoeuvre (*Brit*).

Mansarde [mánzár'də] *f* **-, -n** attic.

Manschette [mánshe'tə] *f* cuff; (*Papier*~) paper frill; (*TECH*) sleeve.

Manschettenknopf *m* cufflink.

Mantel [mán'təl] *m* **-s, ¨** coat; (*TECH*) casing, jacket; ~**tarifvertrag** *m* general agreement on conditions of employment.

Manuskript [mánōōskript'] *nt* **-(e)s, -e** manuscript.

Mappe [má'pə] *f* **-, -n** briefcase; (*Akten*~) folder.

Marathonlauf [má'rátonlouf] *m* marathon.

Märchen [me:r'çhən] *nt* fairy tale; **m~haft** *a* fabulous; ~**prinz** *m* prince charming.

Marder [már'dər] *m* **-s, -** marten.

Margarine [márgárē:'nə] *f* margarine.

Marge [már'zhə] *f* **-, -n** (*COMM*) margin.

Maria [márē:'á] *f* - Mary.

Marien- [márē:'ən-] *zW*: ~**bild** *nt* picture of the Virgin Mary; ~**käfer** *m* ladybug (*US*), ladybird (*Brit*).

Marihuana [márēhōōá'ná] *nt* **-s** marijuana.

Marinade [márēná'də] *f* **-, -n** (*KOCH*) marinade; (*Soße*) mayonnaise-based sauce.

Marine [márē:'nə] *f* navy; **m~blau** *a* navy-blue.

marinieren [márēnē:'rən] *vt* marinate.

Marionette [márēōne'tə] *f* puppet.

Mark [márk] *f* **-, -** (*Geld*) mark ♦ *nt* **-(e)s** (*Knochen*~) marrow; **jdn bis ins ~ treffen** (*fig*) cut sb to the quick; **durch ~ und Bein gehen** go right through sb.

markant [márkánt'] *a* striking.

Marke [már'kə] *f* **-, -n** mark; (*Warensorte*) brand; (*Fabrikat*) make; (*Rabatt~, Brief~*) stamp; (*Essen(s)*~) meal ticket; (*aus Metall etc*) token, disc.

Marken- *zW*: ~**artikel** *m* registered brand article; ~**butter** *f* best quality butter.

Marketing [már'kəting] *nt* **-s** marketing.

markieren [márkē:'rən] *vt* mark ♦ *vti* (*umg*) act.

Markierung *f* marking.

markig [már'kiçh] *a* (*fig*) pithy.

Markise [márkē:'zə] *f* **-, -n** awning.

Markstück *nt* one-mark piece.

Markt [márkt] *m* **-(e)s, ¨e** market; ~**analyse** *f* market analysis; ~**anteil** *m* market share; **m~fähig** *a* marketable; ~**forschung** *f* market research; **m~gängig** *a* marketable; **m~gerecht** *a* geared to market requirements; **~platz** *m* market place; **~preis** *m* market price; **~wert** *m* market value; **~wirtschaft** *f* market economy; **m~wirtschaftlich** *a* free enterprise.

Marmelade [mármǝlâ'dǝ] *f* -, **-n** jam.

Marmor [már'mor] *m* **-s, -e** marble.

marmorieren [mármōrē:'rǝn] *vt* marble.

Marmorkuchen *m* marble cake.

marmorn *a* marble.

marokkanisch [mároká'nish] *a* Moroccan.

Marokko [máro'kō] *nt* **-s** Morocco.

Marone [márō:'nǝ] *f* -, **-n** *od* **Maroni** chestnut.

Marotte [máro'tǝ] *f* -, **-n** fad, quirk.

marsch [mársh] *interj* march; **~ ins Bett!** off to bed with you!

Marsch *m* **-(e)s,** ¨**e** march; **jdm den ~ blasen** *(umg)* give sb a piece of one's mind ♦ *f* -, **-en** marsh; **~befehl** *m* marching orders *pl*; **m~bereit** *a* ready to move.

marschieren [márshē:'rǝn] *vi* march.

Marschverpflegung *f* rations *pl*; *(MIL)* field rations *pl*.

Marseille [márze:y'] *nt* **-s** Marseilles.

Marsmensch [márs'mensh] *m* Martian.

Marter [már'tǝr] *f* -, **-n** torment.

martern *vt* torture.

Martinshorn [már'tē:nshorn] *nt* siren *(of police etc)*.

Märtyrer(in *f)* [mer'türǝr(in)] *m* **-s, -** martyr.

Martyrium [màrtü:'rēōōm] *nt* *(fig)* ordeal.

Marxismus [màrksis'mōōs] *m* Marxism.

März [merts] *m* **-(es),** **-e** March; *siehe* **September.**

Marzipan [mártsēpân'] *nt* **-s, -e** marzipan.

Masche [má'shǝ] *f* -, **-n** mesh; *(Strick~)* stitch; **das ist die neueste ~** that's the latest thing *or* trick; **durch die ~n schlüpfen** slip through the net.

Maschen- *zW:* **~draht** *m* wire mesh; **m~fest** *a* runproof.

Maschine [máshē:'nǝ] *f* machine; *(Motor)* engine.

maschinell [máshēnel'] *a* machine(-), mechanical.

Maschinen- *zW:* **~ausfallzeit** *f* machine down time; **~bauer** *m* mechanical engineer; **~befehl** *m* *(COMPUT)* machine code instruction; **~führer** *m* machinist; **~gewehr** *nt* machine gun; **m~lesbar** *a* *(COMPUT)* machine-readable; **~pistole** *f* submachine gun; **~raum** *m* plant room; *(NAUT)* engine room; **~saal** *m* machine shop; **~schaden** *m* mechanical fault; **~schlosser** *m* fitter; **~schrift** *f* typescript; **~sprache** *f* *(COMPUT)* machine language.

Maschinerie [máshēnǝrē:'] *f* *(fig)* machinery.

maschineschreiben *vi unreg* type.

Maschinist(in *f)* [máshēnist'(in)] *m* engineer.

Maser [má'zǝr] *f* -, **-n** (wood) grain.

Masern *pl* *(MED)* measles *sing.*

Maserung *f* grain(ing).

Maske [más'kǝ] *f* -, **-n** mask.

Masken- *zW:* **~ball** *m* masked *od* fancy-dress ball; **~bildner(in** *f)* *m* make-up artist.

Maskerade [máskǝrâ'dǝ] *f* masquerade.

maskieren [máskē:'rǝn] *vt* mask; *(verkleiden)* dress up ♦ *vr* disguise o.s., dress up.

Maskottchen [máskot'çhǝn] *nt* (lucky) mascot.

Maskulinum [máskōōlē:'nōōm] *nt* **-s, Maskulina** *(GRAM)* masculine noun.

maß [mâs] *imperf von* **messen.**

Maß *nt* **-es, -e** measure; *(Mäßigung)* moderation; *(Grad)* degree, extent; **über alle ~en** *(liter)* extremely, beyond measure; **mit zweierlei ~ messen** *(fig)* operate a double standard; **sich** *(dat)* **etw nach ~ anfertigen lassen** have sth made to order *(US)* *od* measure *(Brit)*; **in besonderem ~e** especially; **das ~ ist voll** *(fig)* that's enough (of that) ♦ *f* -, **-(e)** liter of beer.

Massage [màsâ'zhǝ] *f* -, **-n** massage.

Massaker [màsâ'kǝr] *nt* **-s, -** massacre.

Maß- *zW:* **~anzug** *m* made-to-order *(US)* *od* made-to-measure suit *(Brit)*; **~arbeit** *f* *(fig)* neat piece of work.

Masse [má'sǝ] *f* -, **-n** mass; **eine ganze ~** *(umg)* a great deal.

Maßeinheit *f* unit of measurement.

Massen- *zW:* **~artikel** *m* mass-produced article; **~blatt** *nt* tabloid; **~grab** *nt* mass grave; **m~haft** *a* loads of; **~medien** *pl* mass media *pl*; **~produktion** *f* mass production; **~veranstaltung** *f* mass meeting; **~vernichtungswaffen** *pl* weapons of mass destruction *od* extermination; **~ware** *f* mass-produced article.

Masseur [máscœr'] *m* masseur.

Masseuse [máscœ'zǝ] *f* masseuse.

Maß- *zW:* **m~gebend** *a* authoritative; **m~gebende Kreise** influential circles; **m~geblich** *a* definitive; **m~geschneidert** *a* *(Anzug)* made-to-order *(US)*, custom *attr* *(US)*, made-to-measure *(Brit)*; **m~halten** *vi* unreg exercise moderation; **~halteparole** *f* appeal for moderation.

massieren [máse:'rǝn] *vt* massage; *(MIL)* mass.

massig [má'siçh] *a* massive; *(umg)* a massive amount of.

mäßig [me:'siçh] *a* moderate; **~en** [me:'sigǝn] *vt* restrain, moderate; **sein Tempo ~en** slacken one's pace; **M~keit** *f* moderation.

massiv [máse:'f'] *a* solid; *(fig)* heavy, rough; **~ werden** *(umg)* turn nasty; **M~** *nt* **-s, -e** massif.

Maß- *zW:* **~krug** *m* tankard; **m~los** *a* extreme; **~nahme** *f* -, **-n** measure, step; **m~regeln** *vt* unt̸r reprimand; **~stab** *m* rule, measure; *(fig)* standard; *(GEOG)* scale; **als ~stab dienen** serve as a model.

maßstab(s)getreu *a* (true) to scale.

maßvoll *a* moderate.

Mast [mást] *m* **-(e)s, -e(n)** mast; *(ELEK)* pylon.

Mastdarm *m* rectum.

mästen [me'stǝn] *vt* fatten.

masturbieren [mástōōrbē:'rǝn] *vi*

masturbate.

Material [mátārēál'] *nt* **-s, -ien** material(s); **~fehler** *m* material defect.

Materialismus [mátārēálēs'mōōs] *m* materialism.

Materialist(in *f)* *m* materialist; **m~isch** *a* materialistic.

Material- *zW*: **~kosten** *pl* cost of materials *sing*; **~prüfung** *f* material(s) control.

Materie [mátā:'rēə] *f* matter, substance.

materiell [mátārēēl'] *a* material.

Mathe [má'tə] *f* - (*SCH umg*) math (*US*), maths (*Brit*).

Mathematik [mátāmátē:k'] *f* mathematics *sing*; **~er(in** *f)* [mátāmā'tēkər(in)] *m* **-s,** - mathematician.

mathematisch [mátāmā'tish] *a* mathematical.

Matjeshering [mát'yəshā:ring] *m* (*umg*) young herring.

Matratze [mátrá'tsə] *f* -, **-n** mattress.

Matrix- [má'triks-] *zW*: **~drucker** *m* dotmatrix printer; **~zeichen** *nt* matrix character.

Matrize [mátrē:'tsə] *f* -, **-n** matrix; (*zum Abziehen*) stencil.

Matrose [mátrō:'zə] *m* **-n, -n** sailor.

Matsch [mátsh] *m* **-(e)s** mud; (*Schnee~*) slush.

matschig *a* muddy; slushy.

matt [mát] *a* weak; (*glanzlos*) dull; (*PHOT*) matt; (*SCHACH*) mate; **jdn ~ setzen** (*auch fig*) checkmate sb.

Matte [má'tə] *f* -, **-n** mat; **auf der ~ stehen** (*am Arbeitsplatz etc*) be in.

Mattigkeit *f* weakness; dullness.

Mattscheibe *f* (*TV*) screen; **~ haben** (*umg*) be not quite with it.

Mätzchen [mets'çhən] *nt* (*umg*) antics *pl*; **~ machen** fool around.

mau [mou] *a* (*umg*) lousy (*umg*), poor, bad.

Mauer [mou'ər] *f* -, **-n** wall; **~blümchen** *nt* (*fig umg*) wallflower.

mauern *vi* build; lay bricks ♦ *vt* build.

Mauer- *zW*: **~schwalbe** *f*, **~segler** *m* swift; **~werk** *nt* brickwork; (*Stein*) masonry.

Maul [moul] *nt* **-(e)s, Mäuler** mouth; **ein loses od lockeres ~ haben** (*umg: frech sein*) be an impudent so-and-so; (: *indiskret sein*) be a blabbermouth; **halt's ~!** (*umg*) shut your mouth (!); **darüber werden sich die Leute das ~ zerreißen** (*umg*) that will start people's tongues wagging; **dem Volk od den Leuten aufs ~ schauen** (*umg*) listen to what ordinary people say; **m~en** *vi* (*umg*) grumble; **~esel** *m* mule; **~korb** *m* muzzle; **~sperre** *f* lockjaw; **~tier** *nt* mule; **~- und Klauenseuche** *f* (*Tiere*) foot-and-mouth disease.

Maulwurf *m* mole.

Maulwurfshaufen *m* molehill.

Maurer [mou'rər] *m* **-s,** - bricklayer; **pünktlich wie die ~** (*hum*) super-punctual.

Maus [mous] *f* -, **Mäuse** (*auch COMPUT*)

mouse; **Mäuse** *pl* (*umg*: *Geld*) bread *sing*, dough *sing*.

mauscheln [mou'shəln] *vti* (*umg*: *manipulieren*) fiddle.

mäuschenstill [mois'çhənshtil'] *a* very quiet.

Mausefalle *f* mousetrap.

mausen *vt* (*umg*) flinch ♦ *vi* catch mice.

mausern *vr* molt (*US*), moult (*Brit*).

maus(e)tot *a* stone dead.

Maut [mout] *f* -, **-en** (*veraltet*) toll.

m.a.W. *abk* (= *mit anderen Worten*) in other words.

max. *abk* (= *maximal*) max.

maximal [máksēmál'] *a* maximum.

Maxime [máksē:'mə] *f* -, **-n** maxim.

Maximierung [máksēmē:'rōōng] *f* (*WIRTSCHAFT*) maximization.

Maxi-Single [mák'sēsinggəl] *f* -, **-(s)** twelveinch single, maxisingle.

Mayonnaise [máyone:'zə] *f* -, **-n** mayonnaise.

Mäzen [metsä:n'] *m* **-s, -e** (*gen*) patron, sponsor.

Md. *abk* = **Milliarde.**

MdA *nt abk* (= *Mitglied des Abgeordnetenhauses*) member of state parliament.

M.d.B., MdB *nt abk* (= *Mitglied des Bundestages*) ≈ Member of Congress (*US*), ≈ MP (*Brit*).

M.d.L., MdL *nt abk* (= *Mitglied des Landtages*) *member of the Landtag*.

m.d.W.d.G.b. *abk* (= *mit der Wahrnehmung der Geschäfte beauftragt*) entrusted with the care of sb's business.

m.E. *abk* = **meines Erachtens.**

Mechanik [meçhá'nik] *f* mechanics *sing*; (*Getriebe*) mechanics *pl*; **~er** *m* **-s,** - mechanic, engineer.

mechanisch *a* mechanical.

mechanisieren [meçhánēzē:'rən] *vt* mechanize.

Mechanisierung *f* mechanization.

Mechanismus [meçhánis'mōōs] *m* mechanism.

meckern [me'kərn] *vi* bleat; (*umg*) grouse, moan.

Medaille [mádál'yə] *f* -, **-n** medal.

Medaillengewinner *m* medalist (*US*), medallist (*Brit*).

Medaillon [mádályōñ'] *nt* **-s, -s** (*Schmuck*) locket.

Medien [mā:'dēən] *pl* media *pl*; **~forschung** *f* media research.

Medikament [mádēkáment'] *nt* medicine.

meditieren [mádētē:'rən] *vi* meditate.

Medium [mā:'dēōōm] *nt* medium.

Medizin [mádētsē:n'] *f* -, **-en** medicine.

Mediziner(in *f)* *m* **-s,** - doctor; (*UNIV*) medic (*umg*).

medizinisch *a* medical; **~-technische Assistentin** medical assistant.

Med.R., MedR *abk* (= *Medizinalrat*) medical officer of health.

Meer [mā:r] *nt* **-(e)s, -e** sea; **am ~(e)** by the sea; **ans ~ fahren** go to the sea(side);

~busen m bay, gulf; **~enge** f straits pl.
Meeres- zW: **~klima** nt maritime climate; **~spiegel** m sea level.
Meer- zW: **~jungfrau** f mermaid; **~rettich** m horseradish; **~schweinchen** nt guinea pig.
mega-, Mega- in zW mega-.
Megaphon [māgáfōːnˈ] nt **-s, -e** megaphone.
Mehl [māːl] nt **-(e)s, -e** flour.
mehlig a floury.
Mehlschwitze f (KOCH) roux.

mehr [māːr] ad more; **nie** ~ never again, nevermore (liter); **es war niemand** ~ **da** there was no-one left; **nicht** ~ **lange** not much longer; **M~aufwand** m additional expenditure; **M~belastung** f excess load; (fig) additional burden; **~deutig** a ambiguous.
mehrere indef pron several; (verschiedene) various.
mehrfach a multiple; (wiederholt) repeated; **~drucken** vt (COMPUT) overstrike.
Mehrheit f majority.
Mehrheitsprinzip nt principle of majority rule.
mehr- zW: **~jährig** a attr of several years; **M~kosten** pl additional costs pl; **~malig** a repeated; **~mals** ad repeatedly; **M~parteiensystem** nt multi-party system; **M~platzsystem** nt (COMPUT) multi-user system; **M~programmbetrieb** m (COMPUT) multiprogramming; **~sprachig** a multilingual; **~stimmig** a for several voices; **~stimmig singen** harmonize; **~stöckig** a multistory (US), multistorey (Brit); **M~wertsteuer** f value added tax, VAT; **M~zahl** f majority; (GRAM) plural.
Mehrzweck- in zW multipurpose.
meiden [miˈdən] vt unreg avoid.
Meile [miˈlə] f **-, -n** mile; **das riecht man drei ~n gegen den Wind** (umg) you can smell that a mile off.
Meilen- zW: **~stein** m milestone; **m~weit** a for miles.
mein [min] pron my.
Meineid [minˈit] m perjury.
meinen [miˈnən] vti think; (sagen) say; (sagen wollen) mean; **wie Sie ~!** as you wish; (drohend auch) have it your own way; **damit bin ich gemeint** that refers to me; **das will ich** ~ I should think so.
meiner pron (gen von **ich**) of me.
meine(r, s) poss pron mine.
meinerseits ad for my part.
meinesgleichen [miˈnəsgliˈçhən] pron people like me.
meinetwegen [miˈnətvāːˈgən], **meinetwillen** [miˈnətviˈlən] ad (für mich) for my sake; (wegen mir) on my account; (von mir aus) as far as I'm concerned; (nichts dagegen) I don't care od mind.
meinige pron: **der/die/das** ~ mine.
meins [mins] pron mine.
Meinung [miˈnōōng] f opinion; **meiner ~ nach** in my opinion; **einer ~ sein** think the same; **jdm die** ~ **sagen** give sb a piece of one's mind.
Meinungs- zW: **~austausch** m exchange of views; **~forschungsinstitut** nt opinion research institute; **~freiheit** f freedom of speech; **~umfrage** f opinion poll; **~verschiedenheit** f difference of opinion.
Meise [miˈzə] f **-, -n** tit(mouse); **eine ~ haben** (umg) be crazy.
Meißel [miˈsəl] m **-s, -** chisel.
meißeln vt chisel.
meist [mist] a most ♦ ad siehe **meistens**; **M~begünstigungsklausel** f (COMM) most-favored-nation clause; **~bietend** a: **~bietend versteigern** sell to the highest bidder.
meistens ad mostly.
meiste(r, s) superl von **viel**.
Meister [miˈstər] m **-s, -** master; (SPORT) champion; **seinen** ~ **machen** take one's master craftsman's certificate; **es ist noch kein** ~ **vom Himmel gefallen** (Sprichwort) no-one is born an expert; **~brief** m master craftsman's certificate; **m~haft** a masterly.
meistern vt master; **sein Leben** ~ come to grips with one's life.
Meister- zW: **~schaft** f mastery; (SPORT) championship; **~stück** nt, **~werk** nt masterpiece.
meistgekauft a attr best-selling.
Mekka [meˈká] nt **-s, -s** (GEOG, fig) Mecca.
Melancholie [mālángkōlēːˈ] f melancholy.
melancholisch [mālángkōˈlish] a melancholy.
Melde- [melˈdə] zW: **~behörde** f registration authorities pl; **~frist** f registration period.
melden vt report; (registrieren) register; (MIL) sign up; **nichts zu ~ haben** (umg) have no say; **wen darf ich ~?** who shall I say (is here)? ♦ vr report, register (bei to); (SCH) put one's hand up; (freiwillig) volunteer; (auf etw, am Telefon) answer; **sich auf eine Anzeige** ~ answer an advertisement; **es meldet sich niemand** there's no answer; **sich zu Wort** ~ ask to speak.
Melde- zW: **~pflicht** f obligation to register with the police; **~stelle** f registration office.
Meldung [melˈdōōng] f announcement; (Bericht) report.
meliert [mālēˈrt] a mottled, speckled.
melken [melˈkən] vt unreg milk.
Melodie [mālōdēːˈ] f melody, tune.
melodisch [mālōˈdish] a melodious, tuneful.
melodramatisch [mālōdrámáˈtish] a (auch fig) melodramatic.
Melone [mālōˈnə] f **-, -n** melon; (Hut) bowler (hat).
Membran [mämbrânˈ] f **-, -en** (TECH) diaphragm; (ANAT) membrane.
Memme [meˈmə] f **-, -n** (umg) cissy, yellowbelly (umg).
Memoiren [māmōáˈrən] pl memoirs pl.
Menge [meˈngə] f **-, -n** quantity;

(*Menschen~*) crowd; (*große Anzahl*) lot (of); **jede ~** (*umg*) masses *pl*, loads *pl*.

mengen *vt* mix ♦ *vr*: **sich ~ in** (+*akk*) meddle with.

Mengen- *zW*: **~einkauf** *m* bulk buying; **~lehre** *f* (*MATH*) set theory; **~rabatt** *m* bulk discount.

Mensa [men'zå] *f* -, **-s** *od* **Mensen** (*UNIV*) cafeteria.

Mensch [mensh] *m* **-en, -en** human being, man; (*Person*) person; **kein ~** nobody; **ich bin auch nur ein ~!** I'm only human ♦ *nt* **-(e)s, -er** hussy; **~ ärgere dich nicht** *nt* (*Spiel*) Sorry (*US*), Ludo (*Brit*).

Menschen- *zW*: **~alter** *nt* generation; **~feind** *m* misanthrope; **m~freundlich** *a* philanthropical; **~gedenken** *nt*: **der kälteste Winter seit ~gedenken** the coldest winter in living memory; **~handel** *m* slave trade; (*JUR*) trafficking in human beings; **~kenner** *m* judge of human nature; **~liebe** *f* philanthropy; **~masse** *f*, **~menge** *f* crowd (of people); **m~möglich** *a* humanly possible; **~recht** *nt* human rights *pl*; **m~scheu** *a* shy; **~schlag** *m* (*umg*) kind of people; **~seele** *f*: **keine ~seele** (*fig*) not a soul.

Menschenskind *interj* good heavens!

Menschen- *zW*: **m~unwürdig** *a* degrading; **~verachtung** *f* contempt for mankind *od* human life, misanthropy; **~verstand** *m*: **gesunder ~verstand** common sense; **~würde** *f* human dignity.

Mensch- *zW*: **~heit** *f* humanity, mankind; **m~lich** *a* human; (*human*) humane; **~lichkeit** *f* humanity.

Menstruation [menstrōōátsēō:n'] *f* menstruation.

Mentalität [mentálēte:t'] *f* mentality.

Menü [mānü:'] *nt* **-s, -s** (*auch* COMPUT) menu; **m~gesteuert** *a* (COMPUT) menu-driven.

Merkblatt *nt* instruction sheet *od* leaflet.

merken [mer'kən] *vt* notice; **sich** (*dat*) **etw ~** remember sth; **sich** (*dat*) **eine Nummer ~** make a (mental) note of a number.

merklich *a* noticeable.

Merkmal *nt* sign, characteristic.

merkwürdig *a* odd.

meschugge [måshōō'gə] *a* (*umg*) nuts, meshuga (*US*).

Meß- [mes] *zW*: **~band** *nt* tape measure; **m~bar** *a* measurable; **~becher** *m* measuring cup; **~buch** *nt* missal; **~diener** *m* (*REL*) server, acolyte (*form*).

Messe [me'sə] *f* -, **-n** fair; (*ECCL*) mass; (*MIL*) mess; **auf der ~** at the fair; **~gelände** *nt* exhibition center.

messen *unreg vt* measure ♦ *vr* compete.

Messer *nt* **-s,** - knife; **auf des ~s Schneide stehen** (*fig*) hang in the balance; **jdm ins offene ~ laufen** (*fig*) walk into a trap; **m~scharf** *a* (*fig*): **m~scharf schließen** conclude with incredible logic (*ironisch*); **~spitze** *f* knife point; (*in Rezept*) pinch;

~stecherei *f* knife fight.

Messe- *zW*: **~stadt** *f* (town with an) exhibition center; **~stand** *m* exhibition stand.

Meßgerät *nt* measuring device, gage.

Meßgewand *nt* chasuble.

Messing [me'sing] *nt* **-s** brass.

Meßstab *m* (*AUT*: *Öl~ etc*) dipstick.

Messung *f* (*das Messen*) measuring; (*von Blutdruck*) taking; (*Meßergebnis*) measurement.

Meßwert *m* measurement; (*Ableseergebnis*) reading.

Metall [mātál'] *nt* **-s, -e** metal; **m~en,** **m~isch** *a* metallic; **m~verarbeitend** *a*: **die m~verarbeitende Industrie** the metal-processing industry.

Metaphysik [mātáfüzē:k'] *f* metaphysics *sing*.

Metastase [mātástâ'zə] *f* -, **-n** (*MED*) secondary growth.

Meteor [mātāō:r'] *nt* **-s, -e** meteor.

Meter [mā:'tər] *nt od m* **-s,** - meter (*US*), metre (*Brit*); **in 500 ~ Höhe** at a height of 500 meters; **~maß** *nt* tape measure; **~tonne** *f* metric ton; **~ware** *f* (*TEXTIL*) piece goods.

Methode [mātō:'də] *f* -, **-n** method.

Methodik [mātō:'dik] *f* methodology.

methodisch [mātō:'dish] *a* methodical.

Metier [mātēā:'] *nt* **-s, -s** (*hum*) job, profession.

metrisch [mā:'trish] *a* metric, metrical.

Metropole [mātrōpō:'lə] *f* -, **-n** metropolis.

Mettwurst [met'vōōrst] *f* (smoked) pork *od* beef sausage.

Metzger [mets'gər] *m* **-s,** - butcher.

Metzgerei [metsgərī'] *f* butcher's (shop).

Meuchelmord [moi'çhəlmort] *m* assassination.

Meute [moi'tə] *f* -, **-n** pack.

Meuterei [moitərī'] *f* mutiny.

Meuterer *m* **-s,** - mutineer.

meutern *vi* mutiny.

Mexikaner(in *f*) [meksēkå'nər(in)] *m* **-s,** - Mexican.

mexikanisch *a* Mexican.

Mexiko [mek'sēkō] *nt* **-s** Mexico.

MEZ *abk* (= *Mitteleuropäische Zeit*) C.E.T.

MFG *abk* = **Mitfahrgelegenheit.**

MfS *abk* (*DDR*: = *Ministerium für Staatssicherheit*) *abk* = ministry of state security.

MG *nt* **-(s), -(s)** *abk* = **Maschinengewehr.**

mhd. *abk* (= *mittelhochdeutsch*) MHG.

miauen [mēou'ən] *vi* meow (*US*), miaow (*Brit*).

mich [miçh] *pron* (*akk von* **ich**) me; (*reflexiv*) myself.

mick(e)rig [mik'(ə)riçh] *a* (*umg*) pathetic; (*Betrag auch*) paltry; (*altes Männchen*) puny.

mied [mē:t] *imperf von* **meiden.**

Miederwaren [mē:'dərvårən] *pl* foundation garments *pl*.

Mief [mē:f] *m* **-s** (*umg*) fug; (*muffig*) stale air; (*Gestank*) stink.

miefig a (umg) smelly.
Miene [mē:'nə] f -, -n look, expression; **gute ~ zum bösen Spiel machen** grin and bear it.
Mienenspiel nt facial expressions pl.
mies [mē:s] a (umg) lousy.
Miese [mē:'zə] pl (umg): **in den ~n sein** be in the red.
Miesmacher(in f) m (umg) killjoy.
Mietauto nt rental car (US), hired car (Brit).
Miete [mē:'tə] f -, -n rent; **zur ~ wohnen** live in rented accommodation.
mieten vt rent; (Auto) hire.
Mieter(in f) m -s, - tenant; **~schutz** m rent control.
Mietshaus nt tenement, apartment block.
Miet- zW: **~verhältnis** nt tenancy; **~vertrag** m tenancy agreement; rental agreement; **~wagen** m = **~auto**; **~wucher** m the charging of exorbitant rent(s).
Mieze [mē:'tsə] f -, -n (umg: Katze) pussy; (: Mädchen) chick.
Migräne [mēgre:'nə] f -, -n migraine.
Mikado [mēkā'dō] nt -s (Spiel) pick-up-sticks.
Mikro- [mē'krō] in zW micro-.
Mikrobe [mēkrō:'bə] f -, -n microbe.
Mikro- zW: **~computer** m microcomputer; **~fiche** m od nt microfiche; **~film** m microfilm.
Mikrofon, Mikrophon [mēkrōfō:n'] nt -s, -e microphone.
Mikro- zW: **~'ökonomie** f microeconomics pl; **~prozessor** m microprocessor.
Mikroskop [mēkrōskō:p'] nt -s, -e microscope; **m~isch** a microscopic.
Mikrowellenherd [mē:'krōvelənhā:rt] m microwave oven.
Milbe [mil'bə] f -, -n mite.
Milch [milç] f - milk; (Fisch~) milt, roe; **~drüse** f mammary gland; **~glas** nt frosted glass.
milchig a milky.
Milch- zW: **~kaffee** m white coffee; **~pulver** nt powdered milk; **~straße** f Milky Way; **~tüte** f milk carton; plastic bag of milk; **~zahn** m milk tooth.
mild [milt] a mild; (Richter) lenient; (freundlich) kind, charitable.
Milde [mil'də] f -, -n mildness; leniency.
mildern vt mitigate, soften; (Schmerz) alleviate; **mildernde Umstände** extenuating circumstances.
Milieu [mēlēœ'] nt -s, -s background, environment; **m~geschädigt** a maladjusted.
militant [mēlētánt'] a militant.
Militär [mēlēte:r'] nt -s military, army; **~dienst** m military service; **~gericht** nt military court; **m~isch** a military.
Militarismus [mēlētáris'mŏŏs] m militarism.
militaristisch a militaristic.
Militärpflicht f (compulsory) military service.
Mill. abk = **Million(en)**.

Milli- in zW milli-.
Milliardär(in f) [milēárde:r'(in)] m -s, -e multimillionaire.
Milliarde [milēár'də] f -, -n milliard, billion (bes US).
Millimeter m millimeter (US), millimetre (Brit); **~papier** nt graph paper.
Million [milēō:n'] f -, -en million.
Millionär(in f) [milēōne:r'(in)] m -s, -e millionaire.
millionenschwer a (umg) worth a few million.
Milz [milts] f -, -en spleen.
Mimik [mē:'mik] f mime.
Mimose [mēmō:'zə] f -, -n mimosa; (fig) sensitive person.
minder [min'dər] a inferior ♦ ad less; **~bemittelt** a: **geistig ~bemittelt** (ironisch) mentally less gifted.
Minderheit f minority.
Minderheits- zW: **~beteiligung** f (Aktien) minority interest; **~regierung** f minority government.
minder- zW: **~jährig** a minor; **M~jährigkeit** f minority.
mindern vtr decrease, diminish.
Minderung f decrease.
minder- zW: **~wertig** a inferior; **M~wertigkeitsgefühl** nt, **M~wertigkeitskomplex** m -es, -e inferiority complex.
Mindest- [min'dəst] zW: **~alter** nt minimum age; **~betrag** m minimum amount.
mindestens, zum mindesten ad at least.
mindeste(r, s) a least.
Mindest- zW: **~lohn** m minimum wage; **~maß** nt minimum; **~stand** m (COMM) minimum stock; **~umtausch** m minimum obligatory exchange.
Min.-Dir., MinDir. abk (= Ministerialdirektor) permanent secretary in the civil service.
Mine [mē:'nə] f -, -n mine; (Bleistift~) lead; (Kugelschreiber~) refill.
Minen- zW: **~feld** nt minefield; **~suchboot** nt minesweeper.
Mineral [mēnárál'] nt -s, -e od -ien mineral; **m~isch** a mineral; **~ölsteuer** f tax on oil; **~wasser** nt mineral water.
Miniatur [mēnēátŏŏ:r'] f miniature.
Minigolf [mi'nēgolf] nt miniature golf.
minimal [mēnēmál'] a minimal.
Minister(in f) [mēni'stər(in)] m -s, - (POL) minister.
ministeriell [mēnistāréèl'] a ministerial.
Ministerium [mēnistä:'rēŏŏm] nt ministry.
Ministerpräsident m prime minister.
Minna [mi'ná] f: **jdn zur ~ machen** (umg) give sb a piece of one's mind.
Min.-Rat, MinR abk (= Ministerialrat) assistant secretary in the civil service.
minus [mē:'nŏŏs] ad minus; **M~** nt -, -deficit; **M~pol** m negative pole; **M~zeichen** nt minus sign.
Minute [mēnŏŏ:'tə] f -, -n minute; **auf die ~**

(genau *od* **pünktlich)** (right) on the dot.
Minutenzeiger *m* minute hand.
Mio [mē:'ō] *abk* (= *Million(en)*) M.
mir [mē:r] *pron* (*dat von* **ich**) (to) me; **von** ~
aus! I don't mind; **wie du** ~, **so ich dir**
(*Sprichwort*) tit for tat (*umg*); (*als Drohung*) I'll get my own back; ~ **nichts, dir**
nichts just like that.
Mirabelle [mērábe'lə] *f* -, -n mirabelle, *small*
yellow plum.
Misch- [mish] *zW:* ~**brot** *nt* bread made *from*
more than one kind of flour; ~**ehe** *f* mixed
marriage.
mischen *vt* mix; (*COMPUT: Datei, Text*)
merge ♦ *vi* (*Karten*) shuffle.
Misch- *zW:* ~**konzern** *m* conglomerate;
~**ling** *m* half-caste; ~**masch** *m* (*umg*)
mixture, concoction; (*Essen auch*) concoction; ~**pult** *nt* (*RAD., TV*) mixing panel;
~**ung** *f* mixture; ~**wald** *m* mixed (deciduous and coniferous) woodland.
miserabel [mēzərá'bəl] *a* (*umg*) lousy;
(*Gesundheit*) wretched; (*Benehmen*) dreadful.
Misere [mēzā:'rə] *f* -, -n (*von Leuten, Wirtschaft etc*) plight; (*von Hunger, Krieg etc*)
misery, miseries *pl.*
Miß- [mis] *zW:* m~**ach'ten** *vt untr* disregard;
~**ach'tung** *f* disregard; ~**behagen** *nt* discontent; (~*fallen*) uneasiness; ~**bildung** *f*
deformity; m~**bil'ligen** *vt untr* disapprove
of; ~**billigung** *f* disapproval; ~**brauch** *m*
abuse; (*falscher Gebrauch*) misuse;
m~**brau'chen** *vt untr* abuse; misuse (*zu*
for); (*vergewaltigen*) assault; m~**deu'ten**
vt untr misinterpret.
missen *vt* do without; (*Erfahrung*) miss.
Mißerfolg *m* failure.
Missetat [mi'sətât] *f* misdeed.
Missetäter *m* criminal; (*umg*) scoundrel.
Miß- *zW:* m~**fal'len** *vi unreg untr* displease
(*jdm* sb); ~**fallen** *nt* -s displeasure;
~**geburt** *f* freak; (*fig*) failure; ~**geschick** *nt*
misfortune; m~**glücken** [misglü'kən] *vi untr*
fail; **jdm** m~**glückt etw** sb does not succeed
with sth; m~**gön'nen** *vt untr:* **jdm etw**
m~**gönnen** (be)grudge sb sth; ~**griff** *m*
mistake; ~**gunst** *f* envy; m~**günstig** *a* envious; m~**han'deln** *vt untr* ill-treat;
~**hand'lung** *f* ill-treatment; ~**helligkeit** *f:*
~**helligkeiten haben** be at variance.
Mission [misēō:n'] *f* mission.
Missionar(in *f*) [misēōnár'(in)] *m* missionary.
Miß- *zW:* ~**klang** *m* discord; ~**kredit** *m* discredit.
mißlang [mislàng'] *imperf von* **mißlingen.**
mißliebig *a* unpopular.
mißlingen [misling'ən] *vi unreg untr* fail; **M**~
nt -s failure.
mißlungen [mislōōng'ən] *pp von* **mißlingen.**
Miß- *zW:* m~**mut** *m* bad temper; m~**mutig** *a*
cross; m~**ra'ten** *vi unreg untr* turn out
badly ♦ *a* ill-bred; ~**stand** *m* deplorable
state of affairs; ~**stimmung** *f* ill humor, dis-

cord.
mißt *2./3. pers sing präs von* **messen.**
Miß- *zW:* m~**trau'en** *vi untr* mistrust;
~**trauen** *nt* -s distrust, suspicion (*gegenüber*
of); ~**trauensantrag** *m* (*POL*) motion of no
confidence; ~**trauensvotum** *nt* -s, -**voten**
(*POL*) vote of no confidence; m~**trauisch** *a*
distrustful, suspicious; ~**verhältnis** *nt* disproportion; m~**verständlich** *a* unclear;
~**verständnis** *nt* misunderstanding;
m~**verstehen** *vt unreg untr* misunderstand.
Mißwahl, Misswahl [mis'vâl] *f* beauty contest.
Mist [mist] *m* -(e)s dung; (*umg*) rubbish; ~!
(*umg*) blast!; **das ist nicht auf seinem** ~
gewachsen (*umg*) he didn't think that up
himself.
Mistel *f* -, -n mistletoe.
Mist- *zW:* ~**gabel** *f* pitchfork (*used for shift-
ing manure*); ~**haufen** *m* dungheap; ~**stück**
nt, ~**vieh** *nt* (*umg!: Mann*) bastard (*!*); (:
Frau auch) bitch (*!*).
mit [mit] *präp* +*dat* with; (*mittels*) by; ~ **der**
Bahn by train; ~ **dem nächsten Flugzeug/**
Bus kommen come on the next plane/bus; ~
Bleistift schreiben write in pencil; ~ **Ver-**
lust at a loss; **er ist** ~ **der Beste in der**
Gruppe he is among the best in the group;
wie wär's ~ **einem Bier?** (*umg*) how about
a beer?; ~ **10 Jahren** at the age of 10 ♦ *ad*
along, too; **wollen Sie** ~? do you want to
come along?
Mitarbeit [mēt'árbīt] *f* cooperation; m~**en** *vi*
cooperate, collaborate; **seine Frau arbeitet**
mit his wife works too.
Mitarbeiter(in *f*) *m* collaborator; co-worker
♦ *pl* staff.
Mitarbeiterstab *m* staff.
mit- *zW:* ~**bekommen** *vt unreg* get *od* be giv-
en; (*umg: verstehen*) get; ~**bestimmen** *vi*
have a say (*bei* in); participate (*bei* in) ♦ *vt*
have an influence on; **M**~**bestimmung** *f*
participation in decision-making; (*POL*) determination; ~**bringen** *vt unreg* bring along.
Mitbringsel [mit'bringzəl] *nt* -s, - (*Geschenk*)
small present; (*Andenken*) souvenir.
mit- *zW:* **M**~**bürger** *m* fellow citizen;
~**denken** *vi unreg* follow; **du hast ja mitge-**
dacht! good thinking!; ~**dürfen** *vi unreg:*
wir durften nicht ~ we weren't allowed to
go along; **M**~**eigentümer** *m* joint owner.
miteinander [mitinán'dər] *ad* together, with
one another.
miterleben *vt* see, witness.
Mitesser [mit'esər] *m* -s, - blackhead.
mit- *zW:* ~**fahren** *vi unreg:* **(mit jdm)**
~**fahren** go (with sb); (*auf Reise auch*)
travel (with sb); **M**~**fahrzentrale** *f* agency
for arranging rides (*to work etc*);
M~**fahrgelegenheit** *f* ride, lift (*Brit*);
~**führen** *vt* (*Papiere, Ware etc*) carry (with
one); (*Fluß*) carry along; ~**geben** *vt unreg*
give; **M**~**gefühl** *nt* sympathy; ~**gehen** *vi*
unreg go *od* come along; **etw** ~**gehen las-**

sen (*umg*) pinch sth; **~genommen** *a* done in, in a bad way; **M~gift** *f* dowry.

Mitgl. *abk* = **Mitglied.**

Mitglied [mit'glē:t] *nt* member.

Mitgliedsbetrag *m* membership fee.

Mitgliedschaft *f* membership.

mit- *zW*: **~haben** *vt unreg*: **etw ~haben** have sth (with one); **~halten** *vi unreg* keep up; **M~hilfe** *f* help, assistance; **~hören** *vt* listen in to; **~kommen** *vi unreg* come along; (*verstehen*) keep up, follow; **M~läufer** *m* hanger-on; (*POL*) fellow traveler (*US*) od traveller (*Brit*).

Mitleid *nt* sympathy; (*Erbarmen*) compassion.

Mitleidenschaft *f*: **in ~ ziehen** affect.

mitleidig *a* sympathetic.

mitleidslos *a* pitiless, merciless.

mit- *zW*: **~machen** *vt* join in, take part in; **da macht mein Chef nicht ~** (*umg*: *einverstanden sein*) my boss won't go along with that; **M~mensch** *m* fellow man; **~mischen** *vi* (*umg*: *sich beteiligen*) be involved (*in +dat, bei* in); (: *sich einmischen*) interfere (*in +dat, bei* in); **~nehmen** *vt unreg* take along od away; (*anstrengen*) wear out, exhaust; **mitgenommen aussehen** look the worse for wear; **~reden** *vi* (*Meinung äußern*) join in (*bei etw* sth); (*~bestimmen*) have a say (*bei* in) ♦ *vt*: **Sie haben hier nichts mitzureden** this is none of your concern; **~reißen** *a* (*Rhythmus*) infectious; (*Reden*) rousing; (*Film, Fußballspiel*) thrilling, exciting.

mitsamt [mitzämt'] *präp +dat* together with.

Mitschnitt [mit'shnit] *m* -(e)s, -e recording.

mitschreiben *vt unreg* write od take down ♦ *vi* take notes.

Mitschuld *f* complicity.

mitschuldig *a* implicated (*an +dat* in); (*an Unfall*) partly responsible (*an +dat* for).

Mitschuldige(r) *mf dekl wie a* accomplice.

mit- *zW*: **M~schüler** *m* schoolmate; **~spielen** *vi* join in, take part; **er hat ihr übel** od **hart mitgespielt** (*Schaden zufügen*) he has treated her badly; **M~spieler** *m* partner; **M~spracherecht** *nt* voice, say.

mittag [mi'täk] *ad* at lunchtime od noon; **M~** *m* -(e)s, -e midday, noon, lunchtime; **M~ machen** take one's lunch hour; (**zu**) **M~ essen** have lunch; (**essen** *nt* lunch, dinner.

mittags *ad* at lunchtime od noon.

Mittags- *zW*: **~pause** *f* lunch break; **~ruhe** *f* period of quiet (after lunch); (*in Geschäft*) midday closing; **~schlaf** *m* early afternoon nap, siesta; **~zeit** *f*: **während** od **in der ~zeit** at lunchtime.

Mittäter(in *f*) [mit'te:tər(in)] *m* accomplice.

Mitte [mi'tə] *f* -, -n middle; **aus unserer ~** from our midst.

mitteilen [mit'tīlən] *vt*: **jdm etw ~** inform sb of sth, communicate sth to sb ♦ *vr* communicate (*jdm* with sb).

mitteilsam *a* communicative.

Mitteilung *f* communication; **jdm (eine) ~ (von etw) machen** (*form*) inform sb (of sth); (*bekanntgeben*) announce (sth) to sb.

Mitteilungsbedürfnis *nt* need to talk to other people.

Mittel [mi'təl] *nt* -s - means; (*Methode*) method; (*MATH*) average; (*MED*) medicine; **kein ~ unversucht lassen** try everything; **als letztes ~** as a last resort; **ein ~ zum Zweck** a means to an end; **~alter** *nt* Middle Ages *pl*; **m~alterlich** *a* medieval; **~amerika** *nt* Central America (and the Caribbean); **m~amerikanisch** *a* Central American; **m~bar** *a* indirect; **~deutschland** *nt* (*BRD: als Land*) East Germany; **~ding** *nt* (*Mischung*) cross; **~europa** *nt* Central Europe; **~europäer** *m* Central European; **m~europäisch** *a* Central European; **m~fristig** *a* (*Finanzplanung, Kredite*) medium-term; **~gebirge** *nt* low mountain range; **m~los** *a* without means; **~maß** *nt*: **das (gesunde) ~maß** the happy medium; **m~mäßig** *a* mediocre, middling; **~mäßigkeit** *f* mediocrity; **~meer** *nt* Mediterranean (Sea); **m~prächtig** *a* not bad; **~punkt** *m* center (*US*), centre (*Brit*).

mittels *präp +gen* by means of.

Mittelschicht *f* middle class.

Mittelsmann *m* -(e)s, *pl* -männer od -leute intermediary.

Mittel- *zW*: **~stand** *m* middle class; **~streckenrakete** *f* medium-range missile; **~streifen** *m* median strip (*US*), central reservation (*Brit*); **~stufe** *f* (*SCH*) junior high (*US*), middle school (*Brit*); **~stürmer** *m* center forward; **~weg** *m* middle course; **~welle** *f* (*RAD*) medium wave; **~wert** *m* average value, mean.

mitten [mi'tən] *ad* in the middle; **~ auf der Straße/in der Nacht** in the middle of the street/night; **~drin** *ad* (right) in the middle of it; **~hindurch** [-hindōōrċh'] *ad* through the middle.

Mitternacht [mi'tərnàḳht] *f* midnight.

mitternachts *ad* at midnight; **M~schlosser** *m* (*umg*: *Einbrecher*) burglar.

mittlere(r, s) [mit'lərə(r, s)] *a* middle; (*durchschnittlich*) medium, average; **der M~ Osten** the Middle East; **~s Management** middle management.

Mittlerstellung *f* mediatory position.

mittlerweile [mit'lərvī'lə] *ad* meanwhile.

Mittwoch [mit'voḳh] *m* -(e)s, -e Wednesday; *siehe* **Dienstag.**

mittwochs *ad* on Wednesdays.

mitunter [mitōōn'tər] *ad* occasionally, sometimes.

mit- *zW*: **~verantwortlich** *a* also responsible; **~verdienen** *vi* (go out to) work as well; **M~verfasser** *m* co-author; **M~verschulden** *nt* contributory negligence; **~wirken** *vi* contribute (*bei* to); (*THEAT*) take part (*bei* in); **M~wirkende(r)** *mf dekl wie a*: **die M~wirkenden** (*THEAT*) the cast;

M~wirkung *f* contribution; participation; unter **M~wirkung von** with the help of; **M~wisser** *m* -s, - somebody in the know.

Mixer [mik'sər] *m* -s, - (*Bar~*) cocktail waiter; (*Küchen~*) blender; (*Rührmaschine, RAD, TV*) mixer.

ml *abk* (= *Milliliter*) ml.

mm *abk* (= *Millimeter*) mm.

Mnemonik [mnāmō:'nik] *f* (*auch COMPUT*) mnemonic.

Möbel [mœ'bəl] *nt* -s, - (piece of) furniture; **~packer** *m* mover (*US*), removal man; **~wagen** *m* moving van (*US*), furniture *od* removal van (*Brit*).

mobil [mōbē:l'] *a* mobile; (*MIL*) mobilized.

Mobiliar [mōbēlēâr'] *nt* -s, -e movable assets *pl*.

Mobilmachung *f* mobilization.

möbl. *abk* = *möbliert*.

möblieren [mœblē:'rən] *vt* furnish; **möbliert wohnen** live in furnished *od* rented accommodation.

mochte [moḵh'tə] *imperf von* **mögen**.

Möchtegern- [mœḵh'təgern] *in zW* (*ironisch*) would-be.

Modalität [mōdálēte:t'] *f* (*von Plan, Vertrag etc*) arrangement.

Mode [mō:'də] *f* -, -n fashion; **~farbe** *f* fashionable color; **~heft** *nt*, **~journal** *nt* fashion magazine.

Modell [mōdel'] *nt* -s, -e model; **~eisenbahn** *f* model train; (*als Spielzeug*) train set.

modellieren [mōdelē:'rən] *vt* model.

Modellversuch *m* (*bes SCH*) experiment.

Mode(n)schau *f* fashion show.

Modepapst *m* high priest of fashion.

Moder [mō:'dər] *m* -s mustiness; (*Schimmel*) mildew.

moderat [mōdárát'] *a* moderate.

Moderator(in *f*) [mōdárá'tor, -átō:'rin] *m* presenter.

moderieren [mōdárē:'rən] *vti* (*RAD, TV*) present.

modern [mōdern'] *a* modern; (*modisch*) fashionable.

modernisieren [mōdernēzē:'rən] *vt* modernize.

Mode- *zW:* **~schmuck** *m* fashion jewelry; **~schöpfer(in** *f*) *m* fashion designer; **~wort** *nt* fashionable word.

modifizieren [mōdēfētsē:'rən] *vt* modify.

modisch [mō:'dish] *a* fashionable.

Modul [mō:'dool] *nt* -s, -n (*COMPUT*) module.

Modus [mō:'doos] *m* -, **Modi** way; (*GRAM*) mood; (*COMPUT*) mode.

Mofa [mō:'fá] *nt* -s, -s (= *Motorfahrrad*) small moped.

mogeln [mō:'gəln] *vi* (*umg*) cheat.

mögen [mœ'gən] *vti unreg* like; **ich möchte ... I** would like ...; **ich mag nicht mehr** I've had enough; (*bin am Ende*) I can't take any more; **man möchte meinen, daß** ... you

would think that ...; **das mag wohl sein** that may well be so.

möglich [mœk'liḵh] *a* possible; **er tat sein ~stes** he did his utmost.

möglicherweise *ad* possibly.

Möglichkeit *f* possibility; **nach ~** if possible.

möglichst *ad* as ... as possible.

Mohammedaner(in *f*) [mōhámádá'nər(in)] *m* -s, - Mohammedan, Muslim.

Mohikaner [mōhēkâ'nər] *m* -s, -: **der letzte ~** (*hum umg*) the very last one.

Mohn [mō:n] *m* -(e)s, -e (*~blume*) poppy; (*~samen*) poppy seed.

Möhre [mœ'rə] *f* -, -n carrot.

Mohrenkopf [mō:'rənkopf] *m* small chocolate-covered cream cake or confectionery.

Mohrrübe *f* carrot.

mokieren [mōkē:'rən] *vr* make fun (*über +akk* of).

Mokka [mo'ká] *m* -s mocha, *strong coffee*.

Mole [mō:'lə] *f* -, -n (*NAUT*) mole, breakwater.

Molekül [mōlākü:l'] *nt* -s, -e molecule.

molk [molk] *imperf von* **melken**.

Molkerei [molkərī'] *f* dairy; **~butter** *f* blended butter.

Moll [mol] *m* -, - (*MUS*) minor (key).

mollig *a* cozy (*US*), cosy (*Brit*); (*dicklich*) plump.

Moment [mōment'] *m* -(e)s, -e moment; **im ~** at the moment; **~ mal!** just a minute!; **im ersten ~** for a moment ♦ *nt* -(e)s, -e factor, element.

momentan [mōmentân'] *a* momentary ♦ *ad* at the moment.

Monaco [mō:'nákō] *nt* -s Monaco.

Monarch [mōnárḵh'] *m* -en, -en monarch.

Monarchie [mōnárḵhē:'] *f* monarchy.

Monat [mō:'nát] *m* -(e)s, -e month; **sie ist im sechsten ~** (*schwanger*) she's five months pregnant; **was verdient er im ~?** how much does he earn a month?

monatelang *ad* for months.

monatlich *a* monthly.

Monats- *zW:* **~blutung** *f* menstrual period; **~karte** *f* monthly ticket *od* pass; **~rate** *f* monthly installment.

Mönch [mœnḵh] *m* -(e)s, -e monk.

Mond [mō:nt] *m* -(e)s, -e moon; **auf** *od* **hinter dem ~ leben** (*umg*) be behind the times; **~fähre** *f* lunar (excursion) module; **~finsternis** *f* eclipse of the moon; **m~hell** *a* moonlit; **~landung** *f* moon landing; **~schein** *m* moonlight; **~sonde** *f* moon probe.

Monegasse [mōnāgá'sə] *m* -n, -n, **Monegassin** *f* Monegasque.

Monetarismus [mōnātáris'moos] *m* (*WIRTSCHAFT*) monetarism.

Monetarist *m* monetarist.

Moneten [mōnā:'tən] *pl* (*umg*: *Geld*) bread *sing*, dough *sing*.

Mongole [monggō:'lə] *m* -n, -n, **Mongolin** *f* Mongolian, Mongol.

Mongolei [monggōli'] f: **die ~** Mongolia.
mongoloid [monggōloi:t'] a (MED) mongoloid.
monieren [mōnē:'rən] vt complain about ♦ vi complain.
Monitor [mō:'nētor] m (Bildschirm) monitor.
Mono- [mōnō] in zW mono.
Monolog [mōnōlō:k'] m **-s, -e** monologue.
Monopol nt **-s, -e** monopoly.
monopolisieren [mōnōpōlēzē:'rən] vt monopolize.
Monopolstellung f monopoly.
monoton [mōnōtō:n'] a monotonous.
Monotonie [mōnōtōnē:'] f monotony.
Monsun [monzōō:n'] m **-s, -e** monsoon.
Montag [mō:n'tâk] m **-(e)s, -e** Monday; siehe **Dienstag.**
Montage [montâ'zhə] f **-, -n** (PHOT etc) montage; (TECH) assembly; (Einbauen) fitting.
montags ad on Mondays.
Montanindustrie [montân'indōōstrē:] f coal and steel industry.
Montblanc [mōnblân'] m Mont Blanc.
Monteur [montœr'] m fitter, assembly man.
montieren [montē:'rən] vt assemble, set up.
Montur [montōō:r'] f (umg: Spezialkleidung) gear, rig(-out).
Monument [mōnōōment'] nt monument.
monumental [mōnōōmentâl'] a monumental.
Moor [mō:r] nt **-(e)s, -e** moor; **~bad** nt mud bath.
Moos [mō:s] nt **-es, -e** moss.
Moped [mō:'pet] nt **-s, -s** moped.
Mops [mops] m **-es, ≔e** (Hund) pug.
Moral [mōrâl'] f **-, -en** morality; (einer Geschichte) moral; (Disziplin: von Volk, Soldaten) morale; **~apostel** m upholder of moral standards; **m~isch** a moral; **den ~ischen haben** (umg) have (a fit of) the blues.
Moräne [mōre:'nə] f **-, -n** moraine.
Morast [mōrâst'] m **-(e)s, -e** morass, mire.
morastig a boggy.
Mord [mort] m **-(e)s, -e** murder; **dann gibt es ~ und Totschlag** (umg) there'll be hell to pay; **~anschlag** m murder attempt.
Mörder [mœr'dər] m **-s, -** murderer; **~in** f murderess.
mörderisch a (fig: schrecklich) dreadful, terrible; (Preise) exorbitant; (Konkurrenzkampf) cut-throat ♦ ad (umg: entsetzlich) dreadfully, terribly.
Mordkommission f homicide squad (US), murder squad (Brit).
Mords- zW: **~glück** nt (umg) amazing luck; **~kerl** m (umg: verwegen) hell of a guy; **m~mäßig** a (umg) terrific, enormous; **~schreck** m (umg) terrible fright.
Mord- zW: **~verdacht** m suspicion of murder; **~waffe** f murder weapon.
morgen [mor'gən] ad tomorrow; **bis ~!** see you tomorrrow!; **~ in acht Tagen** a week (from) tomorrow; **~ um diese Zeit** this time tomorrow; **~ früh** tomorrow morning;

M~ m **-s, -** morning; (Maß) ≈ acre; **am M~** in the morning; **guten M~!** good morning!; **M~grauen** nt dawn, daybreak; **M~mantel** m, **M~rock** m housecoat; **M~röte** f dawn.
morgens ad in the morning; **von ~ bis abends** from morning to night.
Morgenstunde f: **Morgenstund(e) hat Gold im Mund(e)** (Sprichwort) the early bird catches the worm (Sprichwort).
morgig [mor'giĉh] a tomorrow's; **der ~e Tag** tomorrow.
Morphium [mor'fēōōm] nt morphine.
morsch [morsh] a rotten.
Morsealphabet [mor'zəálfâbā:t] nt Morse code.
morsen vi send a message by Morse code.
Mörser [mœr'zər] m **-** mortar (auch MIL).
Mörtel [mœr'təl] m **-s, -** mortar.
Mosaik [mōzî:k'] nt **-s, -en** od **-e** mosaic.
Moschee [moshā:'] f **-, -n** [moshā:'ən] mosque.
Mosel [mō:'zəl] f (GEOG) Moselle; **~(wein)** m Moselle (wine).
mosern [mō:'zərn] vi (umg) gripe, bellyache.
Moskau [mos'kou] nt **-s** Moscow.
Moskito [moskē:'tō] m **-s, -s** mosquito.
Moslem [mos'lem] m **-s, -s** Moslem, Muslim.
Most [most] m **-(e)s, -e** (unfermented) fruit juice; (Apfelwein) cider.
Motel [mōtāl'] nt **-s, -s** motel.
Motiv [mōtē:f'] nt **-s, -e** motive; (MUS) theme.
motivieren [mōtēvē:'rən] vt motivate.
Motivierung f motivation.
Motor [mō:'tor] m **-s, -en** [mōtō:'rən] engine; (bes ELEK) motor; **~boot** nt motorboat.
Motorenöl nt motor oil.
motorisch a (PHYSIOLOGIE) motor attr.
motorisieren [mōtōrēzē:'rən] vt motorize.
Motor- zW: **~rad** nt motorcycle; **~roller** m motor scooter; **~schaden** m engine trouble od failure.
Motte [mo'tə] f **-, -n** moth.
Motten- zW: **~kiste** f: **etw aus der ~kiste hervorholen** (fig) dig sth out; **~kugel** f, **~pulver** nt mothball(s).
Motto [mo'tō] nt **-s, -s** motto.
motzen [mot'sən] vi (umg) grouse, beef.
Möwe [mœ'və] f **-, -n** seagull.
Mozambique [mōzàmbik'] nt **-s** Mozambique.
MP f - abk = **Maschinenpistole.**
Mrd. abk = **Milliarde.**
MS abk (= Motorschiff) vessel.
MSchr., Mschr. abk (= Monatsschrift) monthly (journal od periodical).
Mskr. abk (= Manuskript) MS.
MTA f -, **-s** abk (= medizinisch-technische Assistentin) medical assistant.
mtl. abk = **monatlich.**
Mucke [mōō'kə] f **-, -n** (meist pl) caprice; (von Ding) snag, bug; **seine ~n haben** be temperamental.
Mücke [mü'kə] f **-, -n** midge, gnat; **aus einer ~ einen Elefanten machen** (umg) make a

mountain out of a molehill.

Muckefuck [mōō'kəfōōk] *m* **-s** (*umg*) coffee substitute.

mucken *vi*: **ohne zu** ~ without a murmur.

Mückenstich *m* midge *od* gnat bite.

Mucks [mōōks] *m* **-es, -e: keinen** ~ **sagen** not make a sound; (*widersprechend*) not say a word.

mucksen *vr* (*umg*) budge; (*Laut geben*) open one's mouth.

mucksmäuschenstill [mōōks'mois'çhənshtil] *a* (*umg*) (as) quiet as a mouse.

müde [mü:'də] *a* tired.

Müdigkeit [mü:'diçhkit] *f* tiredness; **nur keine** ~ **vorschützen!** (*umg*) don't (you) tell me you're tired.

Muff [mōōf] *m* **-(e)s, -e** (*Handwärmer*) muff ♦ *m* **-s,** *no pl* (*Geruch*) musty smell.

Muffel *m* **-s, -** (*umg*) killjoy, sourpuss.

muffig *a* (*Luft*) musty.

Mühe [mü:'ə] *f* **-, -n** trouble, pains *pl*; **mit Müh und Not** with great difficulty; **sich** (*dat*) ~ **geben** go to a lot of trouble; **m~los** *a* effortless, easy.

muhen [mōō:'ən] *vi* low, moo.

mühevoll *a* laborious, arduous.

Mühle [mü:'lə] *f* **-, -n** mill; (*Kaffee*~) grinder; (~*spiel*) nine men's morris.

Mühsal *f* **-, -e** tribulation.

mühsam *a* arduous, troublesome ♦ *ad* with difficulty.

mühselig *a* arduous, laborious.

Mulatte [mōōlà'tə] *m* **-, -n, Mulattin** *f* mulatto.

Mulde [mōōl'də] *f* **-, -n** hollow, depression.

Mull [mōōl] *m* **-(e)s, -e** thin muslin.

Müll [mül] *m* **-(e)s** garbage, refuse, rubbish; ~**abfuhr** *f* garbage disposal; (*Leute*) garbagemen *pl* (*US*), dustmen *pl* (*Brit*); ~**abladeplatz** *m* garbage dump.

Mullbinde *f* gauze bandage.

Müll- *zW*: ~**deponie** *f* waste disposal site, rubbish tip (*Brit*); ~**eimer** *m* garbage can (*US*), dustbin (*Brit*).

Müller *m* **-s, -** miller.

Müll- *zW*: ~**haufen** *m* garbage heap; ~**schlucker** *m* **-s, -** garbage (*US*) *od* waste (*Brit*) disposal unit; ~**tonne** *f* trash can (*US*), dustbin (*Brit*); ~**wagen** *m* garbage truck (*US*), dustcart (*Brit*).

mulmig [mōōl'miçh] *a* rotten; (*umg*) uncomfortable; **jdm ist** ~ sb feels funny.

Multi [mōōl'tē] *m* **-s, -s** (*umg*) multinational (organization).

multi- *in zW* multi; ~**lateral** *a*: ~**lateraler Handel** multilateral trade; ~**national** *a* multinational; ~**nationaler Konzern** multinational organization.

multiple Sklerose [mōōltē:'plə sklärō:'zə] *f* multiple sclerosis.

multiplizieren [mōōltēplētsē:'rən] *vt* multiply.

m.ü.M. *abk* (= *Meter über dem Meeresspiegel*) meters above sea level.

Mumie [mōō:'mēə] *f* (*Leiche*) mummy.

Mumm [mōōm] *m* **-s** (*umg*) gumption, nerve.

Mumps [mōōmps] *m od f* - (the) mumps *sing*.

München [mün'çhən] *nt* Munich.

Münchner(in *f*) *m* **-s, -** person from Munich.

Mund [mōōnt] *m* **-(e)s, -er** mouth; **den** ~ **aufmachen** (*fig*: *seine Meinung sagen*) speak up; **sie ist nicht auf den** ~ **gefallen** (*umg*) she's never at a loss for words; ~**art** *f* dialect.

Mündel [mün'dəl] *nt* **-s, -** (*JUR*) ward.

münden [mün'dən] *vi* flow (*in* +*akk* into).

Mund- *zW*: **m~faul** *a* uncommunicative; **m~gerecht** *a* bite-sized; ~**geruch** *m* bad breath; ~**harmonika** *f* mouth organ.

mündig [mün'diçh] *a* of age; **M~keit** *f* majority.

mündlich [münt'liçh] *a* oral; ~**e Verhandlung** (*JUR*) hearing; **alles weitere** ~**!** let's talk about it more when I see you.

Mund- *zW*: ~**raub** *m* (*JUR*) theft of food for personal consumption; ~**stück** *nt* mouthpiece; (*von Zigarette*) tip; **m~tot** *a*: **jdn m~tot machen** muzzle sb.

Mündung [mün'dōōng] *f* estuary; (*von Fluß, Rohr etc*) mouth; (*Gewehr*~) muzzle.

Mund- *zW*: ~**wasser** *nt* mouthwash; ~**werk** *nt*: **ein großes** ~**werk haben** have a big mouth; ~**winkel** *m* corner of the mouth; ~**zu-**~**-Beatmung** *f* mouth-to-mouth resuscitation.

Munition [mōōnētsēō:n'] *f* ammunition.

Munitionslager *nt* ammunition dump.

munkeln [mōōng'kəln] *vi* whisper, mutter; **man munkelt, daß** ... there's a rumor that ...

Münster [mün'stər] *nt* **-s, -** minster, cathedral.

munter [mōōn'tər] *a* lively; (*wach*) awake; (*aufgestanden*) up and about; **M~keit** *f* liveliness.

Münzanstalt *f* mint.

Münzautomat *m* vending machine.

Münze [mün'tsə] *f* **-, -n** coin.

münzen *vt* coin, mint; **auf jdn gemünzt sein** be aimed at sb.

Münzfernsprecher [münts'fernshpreçhər] *m* pay phone.

mürb(e) [mürb'(ə)] *a* (*Gestein*) crumbly; (*Holz*) rotten; (*Gebäck*) crisp; **jdn** ~ **machen** wear sb down.

Mürb(e)teig *m* shortcrust pastry.

Murmel [mōōr'məl] *f* **-, -n** marble.

murmeln *vti* murmur, mutter.

Murmeltier [mōōr'məltē:r] *nt* marmot; **schlafen wie ein** ~ sleep like a log.

murren [mōō'rən] *vi* grumble, grouse.

mürrisch [mü'rish] *a* sullen.

Mus [mōō:s] *nt* **-es, -e** purée.

Muschel [mōō'shəl] *f* **-, -n** mussel; (~*schale*) shell; (*Telefon*~) receiver.

Muse [mōō:'zə] *f* **-, -n** muse.

Museum [mōōzā:'ōōm] *nt* **-s, Museen** museum.

museumsreif *a*: ~ **sein** be almost a mu-

seum piece.
Musik [mōōzēːk'] *f* music; (*Kapelle*) band.
musikalisch [mōōzēːkáʼlish] *a* musical.
Musikbox *f* jukebox.
Musiker(in *f*) [mōō:'zēkər(in)] *m* **-s**, - musician.
Musik- *zW*: ~**hochschule** *f* music school; ~**instrument** *nt* musical instrument; ~**kapelle** *f* band; ~**stunde** *f* music lesson.
musizieren [mōōzētsēː'rən] *vi* make music.
Muskat [mōōskát'] *m* **-(e)s**, **-e** nutmeg.
Muskel [mōōs'kəl] *m* **-s**, **-n** muscle; ~**kater** *m*: **einen** ~**kater haben** be stiff.
Muskulatur [mōōskōōlátōō:r'] *f* muscular system.
muskulös [mōōskōōlœs'] *a* muscular.
Müsli [müːs'lē] *nt* **-s**, - muesli.
muß [mōōs] *1./3. pers sing präs von* **müssen**.
Muß *nt* - necessity, must.
Muße [mōō:'sə] *f* - leisure.
müssen [mü'sən] *vi unreg* must, have to; **wenn es (unbedingt) sein muß** if it's absolutely necessary; (*sollen*): **das müßtest du eigentlich wissen** you ought to *od* you should know that; **der Brief muß heute noch zur Post** the letter must be mailed today; **ich muß mal** (*umg*) I need to go to the bathroom; **er hat gehen** ~ he (has) had to go.
Mußheirat *f* (*umg*) shotgun wedding.
müßig [müː'sich] *a* idle; **M**~**gang** *m* idleness.
mußt [mōōst] *2. pers sing präs von* **müssen**.
mußte [mōōs'tə] *imperf von* **müssen**.
Muster [mōō'stər] *nt* **-s**, - model; (*Dessin*) pattern; (*Probe*) sample; ~ **ohne Wert** free sample; ~**beispiel** *nt* classic example; **m**~**gültig**, **m**~**haft** *a* exemplary.
mustern *vt* (*Tapete*) pattern; (*fig*, *MIL*) examine; (*Truppen*) inspect.
Muster- *zW*: ~**prozeß** *m* test case; ~**schüler** *m* model pupil.
Musterung *f* (*von Stoff*) pattern; (*MIL*) inspection.
Mut [mōō:t] *m* courage; **nur** ~! cheer up!; **jdm** ~ **machen** encourage sb; ~ **fassen** pluck up courage.
mutig *a* courageous.
mutlos *a* discouraged, despondent.
mutmaßen *vti untr* conjecture.
mutmaßlich [mōō:t'máslich] *a* presumed ♦ *ad* probably.
Mutprobe *f* test of courage.
Mutter [mōō'tər] *f* -, ⁼ mother; *pl* ~**n** (*Schrauben*~) nut; ~**freuden** *pl* the joys of motherhood *pl*; ~**gesellschaft** *f* (*COMM*) parent company; ~**kuchen** *m* (*ANAT*) placenta; ~**land** *nt* mother country; ~**leib** *m* womb.
mütterlich [mü'tərlich] *a* motherly.
mütterlicherseits *ad* on the mother's side.
Mutter- *zW*: ~**liebe** *f* motherly love; ~**mal** *nt* birthmark; ~**schaft** *f* motherhood.
Mutterschafts- *zW*: ~**geld** *nt* maternity benefit; ~**urlaub** *m* maternity leave.
Mutter- *zW*: ~**schutz** *m* maternity regula-

tions *pl*; **mut'tersee'lenallein'** *a* all alone; ~**sprache** *f* native language; ~**tag** *m* Mother's Day.
Mutti *f* -, **-s** (*umg*) mom(my) (*US*), mum(my) (*Brit*).
mutwillig [mōō:t'vilich] *a* malicious, deliberate.
Mütze [müʼtsə] *f* -, **-n** cap.
MV *f abk* (= *Mitgliederversammlung*) general meeting.
MVA *f abk* (= *Müllverbrennungsanlage*) incinerating plant.
m.W. *abk* (= *meines Wissens*) to my knowledge.
MW *abk* (= *Mittelwelle*) MW.
MwSt, MWSt *abk* (= *Mehrwertsteuer*) VAT.
mysteriös [müstārēœs'] *a* mysterious.
Mystik [mü'stik] *f* mysticism; ~**er(in** *f*) *m* **-s**, - mystic.
Mythologie [mütōlōgēː'] *f* mythology.
Mythos [müː'tos] *m* -, **Mythen** myth.

N

N, n [en] *nt* N, n.
N *abk* (= *Norden*) N.
na [nà] *interj* well; ~ **gut** (*umg*) all right, OK; ~ **also!** (well,) there you are (then)!; ~ **so was!** well, I never!; ~ **und?** so what?
NA *abk* = **Notausgang**.
Nabel [nàʼbəl] *m* **-s**, - navel; **der** ~ **der Welt** (*fig*) the hub of the universe; ~**schnur** *f* umbilical cord.
nach [nàkh] *präp* +*dat* after; (*in Richtung*) to; (*gemäß*) according to; ~ **oben/hinten** up/back; ~ **links/rechts** (to the) left/right; **fünf (Minuten)** ~ **drei** five (minutes) after (*US*) *od* past (*Brit*) three; **er ist schon** ~ **Chicago abgefahren** he has already left for Chicago; **ich fuhr mit dem Zug** ~ **Mailand** I took the train to Milan; **die Uhr** ~ **dem Radio stellen** put a clock right *od* set a clock by the radio; **ihrer Sprache** ~ **(zu urteilen)** judging by her language; **dem Namen** ~ judging by his name ♦ *ad*: **ihm** ~! after him!; ~ **wie vor** still; ~ **und** ~ gradually.
nachäffen [nàkh'efən] *vt* ape.
nachahmen [nàkh'àmən] *vt* imitate.
nachah'menswert *a* exemplary.
Nachah'mung *f* imitation; **etw zur** ~ **empfehlen** recommend sth as an example.
Nachbar(in *f*) [nàkh'bár(in)] *m* **-n** *od* **-s**, **-n** neighbor (*US*), neighbour (*Brit*); ~**haus** *nt*: **im** ~**haus** next door; **n**~**lich** *a* neighborly; ~**schaft** *f* neighborhood; ~**staat** *m* neighboring state.
nach- *zW*: **N**~**behandlung** *f* (*MED*) follow-up

treatment; ~**bestellen** vt order again;
N~bestellung f (COMM) repeat order;
~**beten** vt (pej umg) repeat parrot-fashion;
~**bezahlen** vt pay; (später) pay later;
~**bilden** vt copy; **N~bildung** f imitation,
copy; ~**blicken** vi look od gaze after;
~**datieren** vt postdate.
nachdem [nâĥdā:m'] kj after; (weil) since;
je ~ (ob) it depends (whether).
nach- zW: ~**denken** vi unreg think (über
+akk about); **darüber darf man gar nicht
~denken** it doesn't bear thinking about;
N~denken nt reflection, meditation;
~**denklich** a thoughtful, pensive; ~**denklich
gestimmt sein** be in a thoughtful mood.
Nachdr. abk = **Nachdruck.**
Nachdruck [nâĥ'drōōk] m emphasis; (TYP)
reprint, reproduction; **besonderen ~ darauf
legen, daß** ... stress od emphasize particularly that ...
nachdrücklich [nâĥ'drükliĥ] a emphatic; ~
auf etw (dat) **bestehen** insist firmly (up)on
sth.
nacheifern [nâĥ'īfərn] vi emulate (jdm sb).
nacheinander [nâĥīnán'dər] ad one after the
other; **kurz ~** shortly after each other; **drei
Tage ~** three days running.
nachempfinden [nâĥ'empfindən] vt unreg:
jdm etw ~ feel sth with sb.
nacherzählen [nâĥ'ertsɛ:lən] vt retell.
Nacher'zählung f reproduction (of a story).
Nachf. abk = **Nachfolger.**
Nachfahr [nâĥ'fâr] m -s, -en descendant.
Nachfolge [nâĥ'folgə] f succession; **jds/die
~ antreten** succeed sb/succeed.
nachfolgen vi (lit) follow (jdm/etw sb/sth).
nachfolgend a following.
Nachfolger(in f) m -s, - successor.
nach- zW: ~**forschen** vti investigate;
N~forschung f investigation; **N~
forschungen anstellen** make enquiries.
Nachfrage [nâĥ'frâgə] f inquiry; (COMM) demand; **es besteht eine rege ~** (COMM)
there is a great demand; **danke der ~**
(form) thank you for your concern; (umg)
nice of you to ask; **n~mäßig** a according to
demand.
nachfragen vi inquire.
nach- zW: ~**fühlen** vt siehe ~**empfinden;**
~**füllen** vt refill; ~**geben** vi unreg give way,
yield.
Nach- zW: ~**gebühr** f surcharge; (POST)
postage due; ~**geburt** f afterbirth.
nachgehen [nâĥ'gā:ən] vi unreg follow (jdm
sb); (erforschen) inquire (einer Sache into
sth); (Uhr) be slow; **einer geregelten Arbeit ~** have a steady job.
Nachgeschmack [nâĥ'gəshmák] m aftertaste.
nachgiebig [nâĥ'gē:biĥ] a soft, accommodating; **N~keit** f softness.
nachgrübeln [nâĥ'grü:bəln] vi think (über
+akk about); (sich Gedanken machen)
ponder (über +akk on).

nachgucken [nâĥ'gōōkən] vti siehe **nachsehen.**
nachhaken [nâĥ'hâkən] vi (umg) dig deep-
er.
Nachhall [nâĥ'hál] m resonance.
nachhallen vi resound.
nachhaltig [nâĥ'háltiĥ] a lasting; (Widerstand) persistent.
nachhängen [nâĥ'hɛngən] vi unreg: **seinen
Erinnerungen ~** lose o.s. in one's memories.
Nachhauseweg [nâĥhou'zəvā:k] m way
home.
nachhelfen [nâĥ'helfən] vi unreg assist, help
(jdm sb); **er hat dem Glück ein bißchen
nachgeholfen** he engineered himself a little
luck.
nachher [nâĥhā:r'] ad afterwards; **bis ~** see
you later!
Nachhilfeunterricht [nâĥ'hilfəōōntərriĥt]
m extra tutoring.
nachhinein [nâĥ'hinīn] ad: **im ~** afterwards; (rückblickend) in retrospect.
Nachholbedarf m: **einen ~ an etw** (dat)
haben have a lot of sth to catch up on.
nachholen [nâĥ'hō:lən] vt catch up with;
(Versäumtes) make up for.
Nachkomme [nâĥ'komə] m -n, -n
descendant.
nachkommen vi unreg follow; (einer
Verpflichtung) fulfill (US), fulfil (Brit); **Sie
können Ihr Gepäck ~ lassen** you can have
your baggage sent on (after).
Nachkommenschaft f descendants pl.
Nachkriegs- [nâĥ'krē:ks] in zW postwar;
~**zeit** f postwar period.
Nach- zW: ~**laß** m -lasses, -lässe (COMM)
discount, rebate; (Erbe) estate; **n~lassen**
unreg vt (Strafe) remit; (Summe) take off;
(Schulden) cancel ♦ vi decrease, ease off;
(Sturm auch) die down; (schlechter werden)
deteriorate; **er hat nachgelassen** he has got
worse; **n~lässig** a negligent, careless;
~**lässigkeit** f negligence, carelessness;
~**laßsteuer** f inheritance tax; ~**laß-
verwalter** m executor.
nachlaufen [nâĥ'loufən] vi unreg run after,
chase (jdm sb).
nachliefern [nâĥ'lē:fərn] vt (später liefern)
deliver at a later date; (zuzüglich liefern)
make a further delivery of.
nachlösen [nâĥ'lœzən] vi pay on the train
od on arrival; (zur Weiterfahrt) pay the
extra.
nachm. abk (= nachmittags) p.m.
nachmachen [nâĥ'máĥən] vt imitate, copy
(jdm etw sth from sb); (fälschen) counterfeit; **das soll erst mal einer ~!** I'd like to
see anyone else do that!
Nachmieter(in f) [nâĥ'mē:tər(in)] m: **wir
müssen einen ~ finden** we have to find
someone to take over the apartment etc.
nachmittag [nâĥ'miták] ad: **gestern/heute
~** yesterday/this afternoon; **N~** m afternoon; **am N~** in the afternoon.

nachmittags *ad* in the afternoon.
Nachmittagsvorstellung *f* matinée (performance).
Nachn. *abk* = **Nachnahme.**
Nachnahme *f* -, -n collect (*US*) *od* cash (*Brit*) on delivery; **per** ~ C.O.D.
Nach- *zW:* ~**name** *m* surname; ~**porto** *nt* postage due.
nachprüfbar [nâ̱ḵẖ'prü:fbâr] *a* verifiable.
nachprüfen [nâ̱ḵẖ'prü:fən] *vt* check, verify.
nachrechnen [nâ̱ḵẖ'rec̱hnən] *vt* check.
Nachrede [nâ̱ḵẖ'rā:də] *f:* **üble** ~ (*JUR*) defamation of character.
nachreichen [nâ̱ḵẖ'ric̱hən] *vt* hand in later.
Nachricht [nâ̱ḵẖ'ric̱ht] *f* -, -en (piece of) news; (*Mitteilung*) message.
Nachrichten *pl* news; ~**agentur** *f* news agency; ~**dienst** *m* (*MIL*) intelligence service; ~**satellit** *m* (tele)communications satellite; ~**sperre** *f* news blackout; ~**sprecher** *m* newscaster; ~**technik** *f* telecommunications *sing.*
nachrücken [nâ̱ḵẖ'rükən] *vi* move up.
Nachruf [nâ̱ḵẖ'rōō:f] *m* obituary (notice).
nachrüsten [nâ̱ḵẖ'rüstən] *vti* fit with more modern components; (*Waffen*) keep up to date.
nachsagen [nâ̱ḵẖ'zâgən] *vt* repeat; **jdm etw** ~ say sth of sb; **das lasse ich mir nicht** ~**!** I'm not having that said of me!
Nachsaison [nâ̱ḵẖ'zezôn] *f* off season.
nachschenken [nâ̱ḵẖ'shengkən] *vti:* **darf ich Ihnen noch (etwas)** ~**?** may I top up your glass?
nachschicken [nâ̱ḵẖ'shikən] *vt* forward.
nachschlagen [nâ̱ḵẖ'shlâgən] *unreg vt* look up ♦ *vi:* **jdm** ~ take after sb.
Nachschlagewerk *nt* reference book.
Nachschlüssel *m* master key.
nachschmeißen [nâ̱ḵẖ'shmīsən] *vt* *unreg* (*umg*): **das ist ja nachgeschmissen!** it's a real bargain!
Nachschrift [nâ̱ḵẖ'shrift] *f* postscript.
Nachschub [nâ̱ḵẖ'shōō:p] *m* supplies *pl*; (*Truppen*) reinforcements *pl.*
nachsehen [nâ̱ḵẖ'zā:ən] *unreg vt* (*prüfen*) check; **jdm etw** ~ forgive sb sth ♦ *vi* look after (*jdm* sb); (*erforschen*) look and see.
Nachsehen *nt:* **das** ~ **haben** be left empty-handed.
nachsenden [nâ̱ḵẖ'zendən] *vt* *unreg* send on, forward.
Nachsicht [nâ̱ḵẖ'zic̱ht] *f* - indulgence, leniency.
nachsichtig *a* indulgent, lenient.
Nachsilbe [nâ̱ḵẖ'zilbə] *f* suffix.
nachsitzen [nâ̱ḵẖ'zitsən] *vi* *unreg* (*SCH*) be kept in.
Nachspann [nâ̱ḵẖ'shpán] *m* credits *pl.*
Nachspeise [nâ̱ḵẖ'shpīzə] *f* dessert.
Nachspiel [nâ̱ḵẖ'shpē:l] *nt* epilogue; (*fig*) sequel.
nachspionieren [nâ̱ḵẖ'shpēōnē:rən] *vi* (*umg*): **jdm** ~ spy on sb.

nachsprechen [nâ̱ḵẖ'shprec̱hən] *vt* *unreg* repeat (*jdm* after sb).
nächst [ne:c̱hst] *präp* +*dat* (*räumlich*) next to; (*außer*) apart from; ~**beste(r, s)** *a* first that comes along; (*zweitbeste*) next best.
nachstehen [nâ̱ḵẖ'shtā:ən] *vi* *unreg:* **jdm in nichts** (*dat*) ~ be sb's equal in every way.
nachstehend *a* *attr* following.
nachstellen [nâ̱ḵẖ'shtelən] *vi:* **jdm** ~ follow sb; (*aufdringlich umwerben*) pester sb.
Nächstenliebe *f* love for one's fellow men.
nächstens *ad* shortly, soon.
nächste(r, s) *a* next; (*nächstgelegen*) nearest; **aus** ~**r Nähe** from close by; (*betrachten*) at close quarters; **Ende** ~**n Monats** at the end of next month; **am** ~**n Tag** (the) next day; **bei** ~**r Gelegenheit** at the earliest opportunity; **in** ~**r Zeit** some time soon; **der** ~ **Angehörige** the next of kin.
Nächste(r, s) *mf* neighbor (*US*), neighbour (*Brit*).
nächst- *zW:* ~**liegend** *a* (*lit*) nearest; (*fig*) obvious; ~**möglich** *a* next possible.
nachsuchen [nâ̱ḵẖ'zōō:ḵhən] *vi:* **um etw** ~ ask *od* apply for sth.
nacht [nâ̱ḵẖt] *ad:* **heute** ~ tonight.
Nacht *f* -, -̈e night; **gute** ~**!** good night!; **in der** ~ at night; **in der** ~ **auf Dienstag** during Monday night; **in der** ~ **vom 12. zum 13. April** during the night of April 12th to 13th; **über** ~ (*lit*, *fig*) overnight; **bei** ~ **und Nebel** (*umg*) at dead of night; **sich** (*dat*) **die** ~ **um die Ohren schlagen** (*umg*) stay up all night; (*mit Feiern, arbeiten*) make a night of it; ~**dienst** *m* night duty.
Nachteil [nâ̱ḵẖ'tīl] *m* disadvantage; **im** ~ **sein** be at a disadvantage.
nachteilig *a* disadvantageous.
Nachthemd *nt* nightgown.
Nachtigall [nâ̱ḵẖ'tigál] *f* -, -en nightingale.
Nachtisch [nâ̱ḵẖ'tish] *m* = **Nachspeise.**
nächtlich [nec̱ht'lic̱h] *a* (*jede Nacht*) nightly; (*in der Nacht*) nocturnal.
Nachtmensch [nâ̱ḵẖt'mensh] *m* night person.
Nachtrag [nâ̱ḵẖ'trák] *m* -(e)s, -träge supplement.
nach- *zW:* ~**tragen** *vt* *unreg* carry (*jdm* after sb); (*zufügen*) add; **jdm etw** ~**tragen** hold sth against sb; ~**tragend** *a* resentful; ~**träglich** *a* later, subsequent(ly); (*zusätzlich*) additional(ly); ~**trauern** *vi:* **jdm/etw** ~**trauern** mourn the loss of sb/sth.
Nachtruhe [nâ̱ḵẖ'trōō:ə] *f* sleep.
nachts *ad* by night.
Nachtschicht *f* nightshift.
nachtsüber *ad* during the night.
Nacht- *zW:* ~**tarif** *m* off-peak tariff; ~**tisch** *m* bedside table; ~**topf** *m* chamberpot; ~**wache** *f* night watch; (*im Krankenhaus*) night duty; ~**wächter** *m* night watchman.
Nach- *zW:* ~**untersuchung** *f* checkup; **n**~**vollziehen** *vt* *unreg* understand, comprehend; **n**~**wachsen** *vi* *unreg* grow again; ~**wehen** *pl* afterpains *pl*; (*fig*) after-effects

pl; **n~weinen** *vi* + *dat*: **dieser Sache weine ich keine Träne** ~ I won't shed any tears over that.

Nachweis [nâk̦h'vīs] *m* **-es, -e** proof; **den** ~ **für etw erbringen** *od* **liefern** furnish proof of sth; **n~bar** *a* provable, demonstrable; **n~en** [nâk̦h'vīzən] *vt unreg* prove; **jdm etw n~en** point sth out to sb; **n~lich** *a* evident, demonstrable.

Nachwelt [nâk̦h'velt] *f*: **die** ~ posterity.

nach- *zW*: **~winken** *vi* wave (*jdm* after sb); **~wirken** *vi* have after-effects; **N~wirkung** *f* after-effect; **N~wort** *nt* appendix; **N~wuchs** *m* offspring; (*beruflich etc*) new recruits *pl*; **~zahlen** *vti* pay extra; **N~zahlung** *f* additional payment; (*zurückdatiert*) back pay; **~zählen** *vt* count again.

nachziehen [nâk̦h'tsē:ən] *vt unreg* (*Linie*) go over; (*Lippen*) paint; (*Augenbrauen*) pencil in; (*hinterherziehen*): **etw** ~ drag sth behind one.

Nachzügler *m* **-s, -** straggler.

Nackedei [ná'kədī] *m* **-(e)s, -e** *od* **-s** (*hum umg*: *Kind*) little bare monkey.

Nacken [ná'kən] *m* **-s, -** nape of the neck; **jdm im** ~ **sitzen** (*umg*) breathe down sb's neck.

nackt [nâkt] *a* naked; (*Tatsachen*) plain, bare; **N~heit** *f* nakedness; **N~kultur** *f* nudism.

Nadel [ná'dəl] *f* **-, -n** needle; (*Steck~*) pin; **~baum** *m* conifer; **~kissen** *nt* pincushion; **~öhr** *nt* eye of a needle; **~wald** *m* coniferous forest.

Nagel [ná'gəl] *m* **-s, -̈** nail; **sich** (*dat*) **etw unter den** ~ **reißen** (*umg*) pinch sth; **etw an den** ~ **hängen** (*fig*) chuck sth in (*umg*); **-̈ mit Köpfen machen** (*umg*) do the job properly; **~feile** *f* nailfile; **~haut** *f* cuticle; **~lack** *m* nail polish; **~lackentferner** *m* **-s, -** nail polish remover.

nageln *vti* nail.

Nagel- *zW*: **n~neu** *a* brand-new; **~schere** *f* nail scissors *pl*.

nagen [ná'gən] *vti* gnaw.

Nagetier [ná'gətē:r] *nt* rodent.

nah *a siehe* **nah(e)**.

Nahaufnahme *f* close-up.

nah(e) [ná'(ə)] *a* (*räumlich*) near(by); (*Verwandte*) near, close; (*Freunde*) close; (*zeitlich*) near, close; **von ~em** at close quarters; **der N~e Osten** the Middle East ♦ *ad*: **von** ~ **und fern** from near and far; **jdm zu ~(e) treten** (*fig*) offend sb; **mit jdm** ~ **verwandt sein** be closely related to sb ♦ *präp* +*dat* near (to), close to.

Nahe *f* (*Fluß*) Nahe.

Nähe [ne:'ə] *f* - nearness, proximity; (*Umgebung*) vicinity; **in der** ~ close by; at hand; **aus der** ~ from close to.

nahe- *zW*: **~bei** *ad* nearby; **~bringen** *vt unreg* +*dat* (*fig*): **jdm etw ~bringen** bring sth home to sb; **~gehen** *vi unreg* grieve (*jdm*

sb); **~kommen** *vi unreg* get close (*jdm* to sb); **~legen** *vt*: **jdm etw ~legen** suggest sth to sb; **~liegen** *vi unreg* be obvious; **der Verdacht liegt** ~, **daß** ... it seems reasonable to suspect that ...; **~liegend** *a* obvious.

nahen *vir* approach, draw near.

nähen [ne:'ən] *vti* sew.

näher *a*, *ad* nearer; (*Erklärung, Erkundigung*) more detailed; **ich kenne ihn nicht** ~ I don't know him well.

Näherei [ne:ərī'] *f* sewing, needlework.

Nähere(s) *nt dekl wie a* details *pl*, particulars *pl*.

Näherin *f* seamstress.

näherkommen *vir unreg* get closer.

nähern *vr* approach.

Näherungswert *m* approximate value.

nahe- *zW*: **~stehen** *vi unreg* be close (*jdm* to sb); **einer Sache ~stehen** sympathize with sth; **~stehend** *a* close; **~treten** *vi unreg*: **jdm (zu) ~treten** offend sb; **~zu** *ad* nearly.

Näh- *zW*: **~garn** *nt* thread; **~kasten** *m* workbox.

nahm [nâm] *imperf von* **nehmen**.

Näh- *zW*: **~maschine** *f* sewing machine; **~nadel** *f* needle.

Nährboden *m* (*lit*) fertile soil; (*fig*) breeding-ground.

nähren [ne:'rən] *vtr* feed; **er sieht gut genährt aus** he looks well fed.

Nähr- [ne:r'] *zW*: **~gehalt** *m* nutritional value; **~stoffe** *pl* nutrients *pl*.

Nahrung [ná'rōōng] *f* food; (*fig auch*) sustenance.

Nahrungs- *zW*: **~aufnahme** *f*: **die ~aufnahme verweigern** refuse food; **~mittel** *nt* foodstuffs *pl*; **~mittelindustrie** *f* food industry; **~suche** *f* search for food.

Nährwert *m* nutritional value.

Naht [nât] *f* **-, -̈e** seam; (*MED*) suture; (*TECH*) join; **aus allen -̈en platzen** (*umg*) be bursting at the seams; **n~los** *a* seamless; **n~los ineinander übergehen** follow without a gap.

Nah- *zW*: **~verkehr** *m* local traffic; **~verkehrszug** *m* local train.

Nähzeug *nt* sewing kit, sewing things *pl*.

Nahziel *nt* immediate objective.

naiv [ni:f'] *a* naïve.

Naivität [nīvētē:t'] *f* naïvety.

Name [ná'mə] *m* **-ns, -n** name; **im ~n von** on behalf of; **dem ~n nach müßte sie Jugoslawin sein** judging by her name she must be Yugoslavian; **die Dinge beim ~n nennen** (*fig*) call a spade a spade; **ich kenne das Stück nur dem ~n nach** I've heard of the play but that's all.

namens *ad* by the name of.

Namens- *zW*: **~änderung** *f* change of name; **~tag** *m* name day, Saint's day.

namentlich [ná'məntlik̦h] *a* by name ♦ *ad* particularly, especially.

namhaft [nâm'hâft] *a* (*berühmt*) famed, renowned; (*beträchtlich*) considerable; ~ **ma-**

chen name, identify.

nämlich [nɛːmˈliç] *ad* that is to say, namely; (*denn*) since; **der/die/das ~e** the same.

nannte [nánˈtə] *imperf von* **nennen**.

nanu [nánoōˈ] *interj* well I never!

Napalm [náˈpálm] *nt* **-s** napalm.

Napf [nápf] *m* **-(e)s, ⁻e** bowl, dish; **~kuchen** *m* ≈ ring-shaped pound cake.

Narbe [nárˈbə] *f* **-, -n** scar.

narbig [nárˈbiç] *a* scarred.

Narkose [nárkōːˈzā] *f* **-, -n** anesthetic (*US*), anaesthetic (*Brit*).

Narr [nár] *m* **-en, -en** fool; **jdn zum ~en halten** make a fool of sb; **n~en** *vt* fool.

Narrenfreiheit *f*: **sie hat bei ihm ~** he gives her (a) free rein.

Narrheit *f* foolishness.

Närrin [nɛˈrin] *f* fool.

närrisch *a* foolish, crazy; **die ~en Tage** *Fasching and the period leading up to it*.

Narzisse [nártsiˈsə] *f* **-, -n** narcissus; daffodil.

narzißtisch [nártsisˈtish] *a* narcissistic.

NASA [náˈzá] *f* **-** *abk* (= *National Aeronautics and Space Administration*) NASA.

naschen [náˈshən] *vti* nibble; (*heimlich*) eat secretly.

naschhaft *a* sweet-toothed.

Nase [náˈzə] *f* **-, -n** nose; **sich die ~ putzen** wipe one's nose; (*sich schnäuzen*) blow one's nose; **jdm auf der ~ herumtanzen** (*umg*) play sb up; **jdm etw vor der ~ wegschnappen** (*umg*) just beat sb to sth; **die ~ voll haben** (*umg*) have had enough; **jdm etw auf die ~ binden** (*umg*) tell sb all about sth; **(immer) der ~ nachgehen** (*umg*) follow one's nose; **jdn an der ~ herumführen** (*als Täuschung*) lead sb by the nose; (*als Scherz*) pull sb's leg; **in die ~ fahren** get up one's nose.

Nasen- *zW*: **~bluten** *nt* **-s** nosebleed; **~loch** *nt* nostril; **~rücken** *m* bridge of the nose; **~tropfen** *pl* nose drops *pl*.

naseweis *a* pert, cheeky; (*neugierig*) nosey.

Nashorn [násˈhorn] *nt* rhinoceros.

naß [nás] *a* wet.

Nassauer [náˈsouər] *m* **-s, -** (*umg*) scrounger.

Nässe [nɛˈsə] *f* **-** wetness.

nässen *vt* wet.

naß- *zW*: **~kalt** *a* wet and cold; **N~rasur** *f* wet shave.

Nation [nátsēōːn] *f* nation.

national [nátsēōnálˈ] *a* national; **N~elf** *f* international (soccer) team; **N~hymne** *f* national anthem.

nationalisieren [nátsēōnálēzēːrən] *vt* nationalize.

Nationalisierung *f* nationalization.

Nationalismus [nátsēōnálisˈmoōs] *m* nationalism.

nationalistisch [nátsēōnálisˈtish] *a* nationalistic.

Nationalität [nátsēōnálētɛːtˈ] *f* nationality.

National- *zW*: **~mannschaft** *f* national team; **~sozialismus** *m* National Socialism;

~sozialist *m* National Socialist.

Natrium [náˈtrēoōm] *nt* **-s** sodium.

Natron [náˈtron] *nt* **-s** soda.

Natter [náˈtər] *f* **-, -n** adder.

Natur [nátōōːr] *f* nature; (*körperlich*) constitution; (*freies Land*) countryside; **das geht gegen meine ~** it goes against the grain.

Naturalien [nátōōráˈlēən] *pl* natural produce; **in ~** in kind.

Naturalismus [nátōōːrálisˈmoōs] *m* naturalism.

Naturell [nátōōrelˈ] *nt* **-s, -e** temperament, disposition.

Natur- *zW*: **~erscheinung** *f* natural phenomenon *od* event; **n~farben** *a* natural-colored; **~forscher** *m* natural scientist; **~freak** *m* **-s, -s** (*umg*) back-to-nature freak; **n~gemäß** *a* natural; **~geschichte** *f* natural history; **~gesetz** *nt* law of nature; **~heilverfahren** *nt* natural cure; **~katastrophe** *f* natural disaster; **~kunde** *f* natural history.

natürlich [nátüːrˈliç] *a* natural; **eines ~en Todes sterben** die of natural causes ◊ *ad* naturally.

natürlicherweise [nátüːrliçərvīˈzə] *ad* naturally, of course.

Natürlichkeit *f* naturalness.

Natur- *zW*: **~produkt** *nt* natural product; **n~rein** *a* natural, pure; **~schutz** *m*: **unter ~schutz stehen** be legally protected; **~schutzgebiet** *nt* national park (*US*), nature reserve (*Brit*); **~talent** *nt* natural prodigy; **n~verbunden** *a* nature-loving; **~wissenschaft** *f* natural science; **~wissenschaftler** *m* scientist; **~zustand** *m* natural state.

Nautik [nouˈtik] *f* nautical science, navigation.

nautisch [nouˈtish] *a* nautical.

Navelorange [náˈvəlōránzhə] *f* navel orange.

Navigation [návēgátsēōːnˈ] *f* navigation.

Navigations- *zW*: **~fehler** *m* navigational error; **~instrumente** *pl* navigation instruments *pl*.

Nazi [náˈtsē] *m* **-s, -s** Nazi.

n.Br. *abk* (= *nördlicher Breite*) northern latitude.

Nchf. *abk* = **Nachfolger**.

n.Chr. *abk* (= *nach Christus*) A.D.

NDP *f* - *abk* (= *Nationaldemokratische Partei*) National Democratic Party.

NDR *m* - *abk* (= *Norddeutscher Rundfunk*) North German Radio.

Ndrh. *abk* = **Niederrhein**.

Neapel [nāāˈpəl] *nt* **-s** Naples.

Neapolitaner(in *f*) [nāápōlētáˈnər(in)] *m* **-s, -** Neapolitan.

Nebel [nāːˈbəl] *m* **-s, -** fog, mist.

neb(e)lig *a* foggy, misty.

Nebel- *zW*: **~scheinwerfer** *m* fog light; **~(schluß)leuchte** *f* (*AUT*) rear fog light.

neben [nāːˈbən] *präp* +*akk od dat* next to; (*außer*) apart from, besides; **~an** [nāːbənánˈ] *ad* next door; **N~anschluß** *m*

(*TEL*) extension; **N~ausgaben** *pl* incidental expenses *pl*; **~bei** [nā:bənbī'] *ad* at the same time; (*außerdem*) additionally; (*beiläufig*) incidentally; **~bei bemerkt** *od* **gesagt** by the way, incidentally; **N~beschäftigung** *f* sideline; (*Zweitberuf*) extra job; (*abends, nachts*) moonlighting (*umg*); **N~buhler(in** *f*) *m* **-s,** - rival; **~einander** [nā:bənīnán'dər] *ad* side by side; **~einanderlegen** *vt* put next to each other; **N~eingang** *m* side entrance; **N~einkünfte, N~einnahmen** *pl* supplementary income; **N~erscheinung** *f* side effect; **N~fach** *nt* minor (*US*), subsidiary subject (*Brit*); **N~fluß** *m* tributary; **N~geräusch** *nt* (*RAD*) atmospherics *pl*, interference; **N~handlung** *f* (*LITER*) subplot; **~her** [nā:bənhā:r'] *ad* (*zusätzlich*) besides; (*gleichzeitig*) at the same time; (*daneben*) alongside; **~herfahren** *vi unreg* drive alongside; **N~kläger** *m* (*JUR*) joint plaintiff; **N~kosten** *pl* extra charges *pl*, extras *pl*; **N~mann** *m, pl* **N~männer: Ihr N~mann** the person next to you; **N~produkt** *nt* byproduct; **N~rolle** *f* minor part; **N~sache** *f* trifle, side issue; **~sächlich** *a* minor, peripheral; **N~satz** *m* (*GRAM*) subordinate clause; **~stehend** *a:* **~stehende Abbildung** illustration opposite; **N~straße** *f* side street; **N~strecke** *f* (*EISENB*) branch *od* local line; **N~zimmer** *nt* adjoining room.

Necessaire [nāsese:r'] *nt* **-s, -s** (*Näh~*) needlework box; (*Nagel~*) manicure case.

Neckar [ne'kár] *m* **-s** (*Fluß*) Neckar.

necken [ne'kən] *vt* tease.

Neckerei [nekərī'] *f* teasing.

neckisch *a* coy; (*Einfall, Lied*) amusing.

nee [nā:] *ad* (*umg*) no, nope.

Neffe [ne'fə] *m* **-n, -n** nephew.

negativ [nā:'gátē:f] *a* negative; **N~** *nt* **-s, -e** (*PHOT*) negative.

Neger [nā:'gər] *m* **-s,** - negro; **~in** *f* negress; **~kuß** *m* chocolate marshmallow.

negieren [nāgē:'rən] *vt* (*bestreiten*) deny; (*verneinen*) negate.

nehmen [nā:'mən] *vti unreg* take; **etw zu sich ~** take sth, partake of sth (*liter*); **jdm etw ~** take sth (away) from sb; **sich ernst ~** take o.s. seriously; **~ Sie sich doch bitte** help yourself; **man nehme ...** (*KOCH*) take ...; **wie man's nimmt** depending on your point of view; **die Mauer nimmt einem die ganze Sicht** the wall blocks the whole view; **er ließ es sich** (*dat*) **nicht ~, mich persönlich hinauszubegleiten** he insisted on showing me out himself.

Nehrung [nā:'rōōng] *f* (*GEOG*) spit (of land).

Neid [nīt] *m* **-(e)s** envy.

Neider [nī'dər] *m* **-s,** - envier.

Neidhammel *m* (*umg*) envious person.

neidisch *a* envious, jealous.

Neige *f* **-, -n** (*geh: Ende*): **die Vorräte gehen zur ~** the provisions are fast becoming exhausted.

neigen [nī'gən] *vt* incline, lean; (*Kopf*) bow ♦

vi: **zu etw ~** tend to sth.

Neigung *f* (*des Geländes*) slope; (*Tendenz*) tendency, inclination; (*Vorliebe*) liking; (*Zuneigung*) affection.

Neigungswinkel *m* angle of inclination.

nein [nīn] *ad* no.

Nelke [nel'kə] *f* **-, -n** carnation, pink; (*Gewürz~*) clove.

nennen [ne'nən] *vt unreg* name; (*mit Namen*) call; **das nenne ich Mut!** that's what I call courage!

nennenswert *a* worth mentioning.

Nenner *m* **-s,** - denominator; **etw auf einen ~ bringen** (*lit, fig*) reduce sth to a common denominator.

Nennung *f* naming.

Nennwert *m* nominal value; (*COMM*) par.

Neon [nā:'on] *nt* **-s** neon.

Neo-Nazi [nāōnā'tsē] *m* Neo-Nazi.

Neon- *zW:* **~licht** *nt* neon light; **~reklame** *f* neon sign; **~röhre** *f* neon tube.

Nepp [nep] *m* **-s** (*umg*): **der reinste ~** daylight robbery, a rip-off.

Nerv [nerf] *m* **-s, -en** nerve; **die ~en sind mit ihm durchgegangen** he lost control, he snapped (*umg*); **jdm auf die ~en gehen** get on sb's nerves.

nerven *vt* (*umg*): **jdn ~** get on sb's nerves.

Nerven- *zW:* **n~aufreibend** *a* nerve-racking; **~bündel** *nt* bundle of nerves; **~gas** *nt* (*MIL*) nerve gas; **~heilanstalt** *f* mental home; **~klinik** *f* psychiatric clinic; **n~krank** *a* mentally ill; **~säge** *f* (*umg*) pain (in the neck); **~schwäche** *f* neurasthenia; **~system** *nt* nervous system; **~zusammenbruch** *m* nervous breakdown.

nervig [ner'vi¢h] *a* (*umg*) exasperating, annoying.

nervös [nervœs'] *a* nervous.

Nervosität [nervōzēte:t'] *f* nervousness.

nervtötend *a* nerve-racking; (*Arbeit*) soul-destroying.

Nerz [nerts] *m* **-es, -e** mink.

Nessel [ne'səl] *f* **-, -n** nettle; **sich in die ~n setzen** (*fig umg*) put o.s. in a spot.

Nest [nest] *nt* **-(e)s, -er** nest; (*umg: Ort*) dump; (*fig: Bett*) bed; (*fig: Schlupfwinkel*) hideout, lair; **da hat er sich ins warme ~ gesetzt** (*umg*) he's got it made; **~beschmutzung** *f* (*pej*) running-down (*umg*), denigration (*of one's family od country*).

nesteln *vi* fumble *od* fiddle about (*an +dat* with).

Nesthäkchen [nest'he:k¢hən] *nt* baby of the family.

nett [net] *a* nice; (*freundlich auch*) kind; **sei so ~ und räum auf!** would you mind clearing up?

netterweise [ne'tərvī'zə] *ad* kindly.

netto *ad* net; **N~einkommen** *nt* net income; **N~gewicht** *nt* net weight; **N~gewinn** *m* net profit; **N~gewinnspanne** *f* net margin; **N~lohn** *m* take-home pay, nominal wages *pl.*

Netz [nets] *nt* **-es, -e** net; (*Gepäck~*) rack; (*Einkaufs~*) shopping net (*US*), string bag (*Brit*); (*Spinnen~*) web; (*System*) network; (*Strom~*) main electric lines *pl*; **jdm ins ~ gehen** (*fig*) fall into sb's trap; **~anschluß** *m* mains connection; **~haut** *f* retina; **~karte** *f* (*EISENB*) zone pass (*US*), runabout ticket (*Brit*); **~plantechnik** *f* network analysis.

neu [noi] *a* new; (*Sprache, Geschichte*) modern; **seit ~estem** (since) recently; **~ schreiben** rewrite, write again; **auf ein ~es!** (*Aufmunterung*) let's try again; **was gibt's N~es?** (*umg*) what's the latest?; **von ~em** (*von vorn*) from the beginning; (*wieder*) again; **sich ~ einkleiden** buy o.s. a new set of clothes; **N~anschaffung** *f* new purchase *od* acquisition; **~artig** *a* new kind of; **N~auflage** *f*, **N~ausgabe** *f* new edition; **N~bau** *m* **-(e)s, -ten** new building; **N~bauwohnung** *f* newly-built apartment; **N~bearbeitung** *f* revised edition; (*das N~bearbeiten*) revision, reworking.

Neudr. *abk* = **Neudruck.**

Neudruck *m* reprint.

Neuemission *f* (*Aktien*) new issue.

neuerdings *ad* (*kürzlich*) (since) recently; (*von neuem*) again.

neu- *zW*: **~eröffnet** *a attr* newly-opened; (*wiedergeöffnet*) reopened; **N~erscheinung** *f* (*Buch*) new publication; (*Schallplatte*) new release.

Neuerung *f* innovation, new departure.

Neu- *zW*: **~fassung** *f* revised version; **~fund'land** *nt* Newfoundland.

neugeboren *a* newborn; **sich wie ~ fühlen** feel (like) a new man *od* woman.

Neugier *f* curiosity.

Neugierde *f* -: **aus ~** out of curiosity.

neugierig *a* curious.

Neuheit *f* newness; novelty; (*neuartige Ware*) new thing.

Neuigkeit *f* news.

neu- *zW*: **N~jahr** *nt* New Year; **N~land** *nt* virgin land; (*fig*) new ground; **~lich** *ad* recently, the other day; **N~ling** *m* novice; **~modisch** *a* fashionable; (*pej*) new-fangled; **N~mond** *m* new moon.

neun [noin] *num* nine.

Neun *f* -, **-en: ach du grüne ~e!** (*umg*) well I'm blowed!

neunmalklug *a* (*ironisch*) smart-aleck *attr*.

neunzehn *num* nineteen.

neunzig *num* ninety.

Neureg(e)lung *f* adjustment.

neureich *a* nouveau riche; **N~e(r)** *mf dekl wie a* nouveau riche.

Neurose [noiroː'zə] *f* -, **-n** neurosis.

Neurotiker(in *f*) [noiroː'tēkər(in)] *m* **-s,** - neurotic.

neurotisch *a* neurotic.

Neu- *zW*: **~schnee** *m* fresh snow; **~seeland** *nt* New Zealand; **n~seeländisch** *a* New Zealand; **n~sprachlich** *a*: **n~sprachliches**

Gymnasium high school stressing modern languages.

Neutr. *abk* (= *Neutrum*) neut.

neutral [noitrál'] *a* neutral.

Neutralität [noitrálitɛː't] *f* neutrality.

neutralisieren [noitrálēzē:'rən] *vt* neutralize.

Neutron [noi'tron] *nt* **-s, -en** neutron.

Neutrum [noi'trōōm] *nt* **-s, Neutra** *od* **Neutren** neuter.

Neu- *zW*: **~wert** *m* purchase price; **~zeit** *f* modern age; **n~zeitlich** *a* modern, recent.

ngr. *abk* (= *neugriechisch*) modern Greek.

N.H. *abk* (= *Normalhöhenpunkt*) normal peak (level).

nhd. *abk* = *neuhochdeutsch.*

Nicaragua [nēkárá'gōōá] *nt* **-s** Nicaragua.

nicht [nièt] *ad* not ♦ *präf* non-; **~ wahr?** isn't it *od* he?, don't you? *etc*; **~ doch!** don't!; **~ berühren!** do not touch!; **was du ~ sagst!** the things you say!; **~ mehr als** no more than; **N~achtung** *f* disregard; **N~anerkennung** *f* repudiation; **N~angriffspakt** *m* non-aggression pact.

Nichte [nièh'tə] *f* -, **-n** niece.

Nicht- *zW*: **~einhaltung** *f* non-compliance (+*gen* with); **~einmischung** *f* (*POL*) nonintervention; **~gefallen** *nt*: **bei ~gefallen (zurück)** if not satisfied (return).

nichtig [nièh'tièh] *a* (*ungültig*) null, void; (*wertlos*) futile; **N~keit** *f* nullity, invalidity; (*Sinnlosigkeit*) futility.

Nicht- *zW*: **~raucher** *m* non-smoker; **ich bin ~raucher** I don't smoke; **n~rostend** *a* stainless.

nichts [nièhts] *pron* nothing; **~ als** nothing but; **~ da!** (*ausgeschlossen*) nothing doing (*umg*); **~ wie raus/hin** *etc* (*umg*) let's get out/over there *etc* (on the double); **für ~ und wieder ~** for nothing at all; **N~** *nt* **-s** nothingness; (*pej: Person*) nonentity; **~ahnend** *a* unsuspecting; **~destotrotz'** *ad* notwithstanding (*form*), nonetheless; **~destowe'niger** *ad* nevertheless; **N~nutz** *m* **-es, -e** good-for-nothing; **~nutzig** *a* worthless, useless; **~sagend** *a* meaningless; **N~tun** *nt* **-s** idleness.

Nichtzutreffende(s) *nt*: **~ (bitte) streichen!** (please) delete as applicable.

Nickel [ni'kəl] *nt* **-s** nickel; **~brille** *f* metalrimmed glasses *pl.*

nicken [ni'kən] *vi* nod.

Nickerchen [ni'karèhən] *nt* nap; **ein ~ machen** (*umg*) have forty winks.

Nicki [ni'kē] *m* **-s, -s** velour pullover.

nie [nē:] *ad* never; **~ wieder** *od* **mehr** never again; **~ und nimmer** never ever; **fast ~** hardly ever.

nieder [nē:'dər] *a* low; (*gering*) inferior ♦ *ad* down; **~deutsch** *a* (*LING*) Low German; **N~gang** *m* decline; **~gehen** *vi unreg* descend; (*AVIAT*) come down; (*Regen*) fall; (*Boxer*) go down; **~geschlagen** *a* depressed, dejected; **N~geschlagenheit** *f* depression, dejection; **~kunft** *f* (*veraltet*) delivery, giv-

ing birth; **N~lage** *f* defeat; (*Lager*) depot; (*Filiale*) branch.
Niederlande [nē:'dərländə] *pl*: **die ~** the Netherlands *pl*, the Low Countries *pl*.
Niederländer(in *f*) [nē:'dərlendər(in)] *m* **-s,** - Netherlander, Dutchman/Dutchwoman.
niederländisch *a* Dutch, Netherlands.
nieder- *zW*: **~lassen** *vr unreg* (*sich setzen*) sit down; (*an Ort*) settle (down); (*Arzt, Rechtsanwalt*) set up a practice; **N~lassung** *f* settlement; (*COMM*) branch; **~legen** *vt* lay down; (*Arbeit*) stop; (*Amt*) resign; **~machen** *vt* mow down; **N~rhein** *m* Lower Rhine; **~rheinisch** *a* Lower Rhine; **N~sachsen** *nt* Lower Saxony; **N~schlag** *m* (*CHEM*) precipitate; (*Bodensatz*) sediment; (*MET*) precipitation (*form*), rainfall; (*BOXEN*) knockdown; **radioaktiver N~schlag** (radioactive) fallout; **~schlagen** *unreg vt* (*Gegner*) beat down; (*Gegenstand*) knock down; (*Augen*) lower; (*JUR*: *Prozeß*) dismiss; (*Aufstand*) put down ♦ *vr* (*CHEM*) precipitate; **sich in etw** (*dat*) **~schlagen** (*Erfahrungen etc*) find expression in sth.
niederschlagsfrei [nē:'dərshläksfrī] *a* dry, without precipitation (*form*).
nieder- *zW*: **~schmetternd** *a* (*Nachricht, Ergebnis*) shattering; **N~schrift** *f* transcription; **~tourig** *a* (*Motor*) low-revving; **~trächtig** *a* base, mean; **N~trächtigkeit** *f* despicable *od* malicious behavior.
Niederung *f* (*GEOG*) depression.
niederwalzen [nē:'dərvältsən] *vt*: **jdn/etw ~** (*umg*) mow sb/sth down.
niederwerfen [nē:'dərverfən] *vt unreg* throw down; (*fig*) overcome; (*Aufstand*) suppress; (*lit*: *Gegner*) floor.
niedlich [nē:'tlich] *a* sweet, nice, cute.
niedrig [nē:'drich] *a* low; (*Stand*) lowly, humble; (*Gesinnung*) mean.
niemals [nē:'mâls] *ad* never.
niemand [nē:'mánt] *pron* nobody, no-one.
Niemandsland [nē:'mántslánt] *nt* no-man's-land.
Niere [nē:'rə] *f* **-, -n** kidney; **künstliche ~** kidney machine.
Nierenentzündung *f* kidney infection.
nieseln [nē:'zəln] *vi* drizzle.
Nieselregen *m* drizzle.
niesen [nē:'zən] *vi* sneeze.
Niespulver *nt* sneezing powder.
Niet [nē:t] *m* **-(e)s, -e** (*TECH*) rivet.
Niete *f* **-, -n** (*TECH*) rivet; (*Los*) blank; (*Reinfall*) flop; (*Mensch*) failure.
nieten *vt* rivet.
Nietenhose *f* (pair of) studded jeans *pl*.
niet- und nagelfest *a* (*umg*) nailed down.
Nigeria [nēgä:'rēä] *nt* **-s** Nigeria.
Nihilismus [nēhēlis'môōs] *m* nihilism.
Nihilist [nēhēlist'] *m* nihilist; **n~isch** *a* nihilistic.
Nikolaus [nē:'kōlous] *m* **-, -e** *od* (*hum umg*) **Nikoläuse** St Nicholas.
Nikosia [nēkōzē:'á] *nt* **-s** Nicosia.

Nikotin [nēkōtē:n'] *nt* **-s** nicotine; **n~arm** *a* low-nicotine.
Nil [nē:l] *m* **-s** Nile; **~pferd** *nt* hippopotamus.
Nimbus [nim'bōōs] *m* **-, -se** (*Heiligenschein*) halo; (*fig*) aura.
nimmersatt [ni'mərzàt] *a* insatiable; **N~** *m* **-(e)s, -e** glutton.
Nimmerwie'dersehen *nt* (*umg*): **auf ~!** I never want to see you again.
nimmt [nimt] *3. pers sing präs von* **nehmen**.
nippen [ni'pən] *vti* sip.
Nippes [ni'pəs] *pl* knick-knacks *pl*, bric-a-brac *sing*.
Nippsachen [nip'zàkhən] *pl* knick-knacks *pl*.
nirgends [nir'gənts], **nirgendwo** [nir'gəntvō:] *ad* nowhere; **überall und nirgends** here, there and everywhere.
Nische [nē:'shə] *f* **-, -n** niche.
nisten [nis'tən] *vi* nest.
Nitrat [nētrât'] *nt* **-(e)s, -e** nitrate.
Niveau [nēvō:'] *nt* **-s, -s** level; **diese Schule hat ein hohes ~** this school has high standards; **unter meinem ~** beneath me.
Nivellierung [nēvelē:'rōōng] *f* (*Ausgleichung*) levelling out.
nix [niks] *pron* (*umg*) *siehe* **nichts**.
Nixe [nik'sə] *f* **-, -n** water nymph.
Nizza [ni'tsá] *nt* **-s** Nice.
n.J. *abk* (= *nächsten Jahres*) next year.
n.M. *abk* (= *nächsten Monats*) next month.
NN, N.N. *abk* (= *Normalnull*) m.s.l.
no. *abk* (= *netto*) net.
NO *abk* (= *Nordost*) NE.
nobel [nō:'bəl] *a* (*großzügig*) generous; (*elegant*) posh (*umg*).
Nobelpreisträger(in *f*) [nōbel'prīstre:gər(in)] *m* Nobel prize winner.
noch [nokh] *ad* still; (*in Zukunft*) still, yet; (*irgendwann*) one day; (*außerdem*) else ♦ *kj* nor; **~ nie** never (yet); **~ nicht** not yet; **immer ~** still; **~ heute** today; **~ vor einer Woche** only a week ago; **und wenn es ~ so schwer ist** however hard it is; **~ einmal** again; **~ dreimal** three more times; **~ und ~** heaps of; (*mit Verb*) again and again; **ich gehe kaum ~ aus** I hardly go out any more; **und es regnete auch ~** and on top of that it was raining; **ich möchte gern(e) ~ bleiben** I'd like to stay on longer; **können Sie das heute ~ erledigen?** can you do it (for) today?; **~mal(s)** *ad* again, once more; **~malig** *a* repeated.
Nockenwelle [no'kənvelə] *f* camshaft.
NOK *abk* (= *Nationales Olympisches Komitee*) National Olympic Committee.
Nom. *abk* = **Nominativ**.
Nominalwert [nōmēnâl'vä:rt] *m* (*FIN*) nominal *od* par value.
Nominativ [nō:'mēnátē:f] *m* **-s, -e** nominative.
nominell [nōmēnel'] *a* nominal.
nominieren [nōmēnē:'rən] *vt* nominate.
Nonne [no'nə] *f* **-, -n** nun.
Nonnenkloster *nt* convent.

Nonplusultra [nonplōosōōl'trà] *nt* **-s** ultimate.
Nord [nort] *m* **-s** north; ~**amerika** *nt* North America.
nordd. *abk* = **norddeutsch.**
Nord- *zW*: **n**~**deutsch** *a* North German; ~**deutschland** *nt* North(ern) Germany.
Norden [nor'dən] *m* north.
Nord- *zW*: ~**england** *nt* the North of England; ~**irland** *nt* Northern Ireland, Ulster; **n**~**isch** *a* northern; **n**~**ische Kombination** (*SKI*) nordic combination; ~**kap** *nt* North Cape.
nördlich [nœrt'liçh] *a* northerly, northern; **der** ~**e Polarkreis** the Arctic Circle; **N**~**es Eismeer** Arctic Ocean; ~ **von** north of ♦ *präp* +*gen* (to the) north of.
Nord- *zW*: ~**licht** *nt* northern lights *pl*, aurora borealis; ~**-Ostsee-Kanal** *m* Kiel Canal; ~**pol** *m* North Pole; ~**polargebiet** *nt* Arctic (Zone).
Nordrhein-Westfalen [nort'rīnvestfà'lən] *nt* **-s** North Rhine-Westphalia.
Nord- *zW*: ~**see** *f* North Sea; **n**~**wärts** *ad* northwards.
Nörgelei [nœrgəlī'] *f* grumbling.
nörgeln *vi* grumble.
Nörgler(in *f*) *m* **-s**, - grumbler.
Norm [norm] *f* -, **-en** norm; (*Leistungssoll*) quota; (*Größenvorschrift*) standard (specification).
normal [normál'] *a* normal; **bist du noch** ~? (*umg*) have you gone mad?
normalerwei'se *ad* normally.
Normal- *zW*: ~**fall** *m*: **im** ~**fall** normally; ~**gewicht** *nt* normal weight; (*genormt*) standard weight.
normalisieren [normálēzē:'rən] *vt* normalize ♦ *vr* return to normal.
Normalzeit *f* (*GEOG*) standard time.
Normandie [normàndē:'] *f* Normandy.
normen *vt* standardize.
Norwegen [nor'vā:gən] *nt* **-s** Norway.
Norweger(in *f*) *m* **-s**, - Norwegian.
norwegisch *a* Norwegian.
Nostalgie [nostálgē:'] *f* nostalgia.
Not [nō:t] *f* -, **-̈e** need; (*Mangel*) want; (*Mühe*) trouble; (*Zwang*) necessity; **zur** ~ if necessary; (*gerade noch*) just about; **wenn** ~ **am Mann ist** if you *od* they *etc* are short (*umg*); (*im Notfall*) in an emergency; **er hat seine liebe** ~ **mit ihr/damit** he really has problems with her/it; **in seiner** ~ is in his hour of need.
Notar(in *f*) [nōtár'(in)] *m* **-s**, **-e** notary; **n**~**i'ell** *a* notarial; **n**~**iell beglaubigt** attested by a notary.
Not- *zW*: ~**arzt** *m* doctor on emergency call; ~**ausgang** *m* emergency exit; ~**behelf** *m* stopgap; ~**bremse** *f* emergency brake; **n**~**dürftig** *a* scanty; (*behelfsmäßig*) makeshift; **sich n**~**dürftig verständigen** just about understand each other.
Note [nō:'tə] *f* -, **-n** note; (*SCH*) grade (*US*), mark (*Brit*); ~**n** *pl* music; **eine persönliche**

~ a personal touch.
Noten- *zW*: ~**bank** *f* issuing bank; ~**blatt** *nt* sheet of music; ~**schlüssel** *m* clef; ~**ständer** *m* music stand.
Not- *zW*: ~**fall** *m* (case of) emergency; **n**~**falls** *ad* if need be; **n**~**gedrungen** *a* necessary, unavoidable; **etw n**~**gedrungen machen** be forced to do sth.
Notgroschen [nō:t'groshən] *m* nest egg.
notieren [nōtē:'rən] *vt* note; (*COMM*) quote.
Notierung *f* (*COMM*) quotation.
nötig [nœ'tiçh] *a* necessary; **etw** ~ **haben** need sth; **das habe ich nicht** ~! I can do without that ♦ *ad* (*dringend*): **etw** ~ **brauchen** need sth urgently.
nötigen *vt* compel, force; ~**falls** *ad* if necessary.
Nötigung *f* compulsion, coercion (*JUR*).
Notiz [nōtē:ts'] *f* -, **-en** note; (*Zeitungs*~) item; ~ **nehmen** take notice; ~**buch** *nt* notebook; ~**zettel** *m* piece of paper.
Not- *zW*: ~**lage** *f* crisis, emergency; **n**~**landen** *vi* make a forced *od* emergency landing; ~**landung** *f* emergency landing; **n**~**leidend** *a* needy; ~**lösung** *f* temporary solution; ~**lüge** *f* white lie.
notorisch [nōtō:'rish] *a* notorious.
Not- *zW*: ~**ruf** *m* emergency call; ~**rufsäule** *f* emergency telephone; **n**~**schlachten** *vt* (*Tiere*) destroy; ~**stand** *m* state of emergency; ~**standsgebiet** *nt* (*wirtschaftlich*) depressed area; (*bei Katastrophen*) disaster area; ~**standsgesetz** *nt* emergency law; ~**unterkunft** *f* emergency accommodation; ~**verband** *m* emergency dressing; ~**wehr** *f* - self-defense (*US*), self-defence (*Brit*); **n**~**wendig** *a* necessary; ~**wendigkeit** *f* necessity; ~**zucht** *f* rape.
Nov. *abk* (= *November*) Nov.
Novelle [nōve'lə] *f* -, **-n** short story; (*JUR*) amendment.
November [nōvem'bər] *m* **-(s)**, - November; *siehe* **September**.
Novum [nō:'vōōm] *nt* **-s, Nova** novelty.
NPD *f* - *abk* (= *Nationaldemokratische Partei Deutschlands*) National Democratic Party.
Nr. *abk* (= *Nummer*) No., no.
NRW *abk* = **Nordrhein-Westfalen.**
NS *abk* = **Nachschrift; Nationalsozialismus.**
NS- *in zW* Nazi.
N.T. *abk* (= *Neues Testament*) N.T.
Nu [nōō:] *m*: **im** ~ in an instant.
Nuance [nüáṅ'sə] *f* -, **-n** nuance; (*Kleinigkeit*) shade.
nüchtern [nüçh'tərn] *a* sober; (*Magen*) empty; (*Urteil*) prudent; **N**~**heit** *f* sobriety.
Nudel [nōō:'dəl] *f* -, **-n** noodle; (*umg*: *Mensch*: *dick*) dumpling; (: *komisch*) character; ~**holz** *nt* rolling pin.
Nugat [nōō:'gát] *m od nt* **-s, -s** nougat.
nuklear [nōōkláär'] *a attr* nuclear.
null [nōōl] *num* zero; (*Fehler*) no; ~ **Uhr** midnight; ~ **und nichtig** null and void; **N**~ *f* -, **-en** nought, zero; (*pej*: *Mensch*) dead

loss; **in N~ Komma nichts** (*umg*) in less than no time; **die Stunde N~** the new starting point; **gleich N~ sein** be absolutely nil.

nullachtfünfzehn [nōōl'åk̦ht'fünf'tsā:n] *a* (*umg*) run-of-the-mill.

Nullösung [nōōl'lœzōōng] *f* (*POL*) zero option.

Null- *zW:* **~punkt** *m* zero; **auf dem ~punkt** at zero; **~tarif** *m* (*für Verkehrsmittel*) free travel.

numerieren [nōōmārē:'rən] *vt* number.

numerisch [nōōmā:'rish] *a* numerical; **~es Tastenfeld** (*COMPUT*) numeric pad.

Numerus [nōō:'mårōōs] *m* -, **Numeri** (*GRAM*) number; **~ clausus** (*UNIV*) restricted entry.

Nummer [nōō'mər] *f* -, **-n** number; **auf ~ Sicher gehen** (*umg*) play (it) safe.

Nummern- *zW:* **~konto** *nt* numbered bank account; **~-scheibe** *f* telephone dial; **~schild** *nt* (*AUT*) license plate.

nun [nōō:n] *ad* now ♦ *interj* well.

nur [nōō:r] *ad* just, only; **nicht ~ ..., sondern auch ...** not only ... but also ...; **alle, ~ ich nicht** everyone but me; **ich hab' das ~ so gesagt** I was just talking.

Nürnberg [nürn'berk] *nt* **-s** Nuremberg.

nuscheln [nōō'shəln] *vti* (*umg*) mutter, mumble.

Nuß [nōōs] *f* -, **Nüsse** nut; **eine doofe ~** (*umg*) a stupid clod; **eine harte ~** a hard nut (to crack); **~baum** *m* walnut tree; **~knacker** *m* **-s,** - nutcracker.

Nüster [nü:'stər] *f* -, **-n** nostril.

Nutte [nōō'tə] *f* -, **-n** hooker.

nutz [nōōts], **nütze** [nüt'sə] *a:* **zu nichts ~ sein** be useless; **~bar** *a:* **~bar machen** utilize; **N~barmachung** *f* utilization; **~bringend** *a* profitable; **etw ~bringend anwenden** use sth to good effect, put sth to good use.

nutzen, nützen *vt* use (*zu etw* for sth) ♦ *vi* be of use; **was nützt es?** what's the use?, what use is it?; **Nutzen** *m* **-s** usefulness; (*Gewinn*) profit; **von Nutzen** useful.

Nutz- *zW:* **~fahrzeug** *nt* farm *od* military vehicle *etc*; (*COMM*) commercial vehicle; **~fläche** *f* us(e)able floor space; (*AGR*) productive land; **~last** *f* maximum load, payload.

nützlich [nüts'lic̦h] *a* useful; **N~keit** *f* usefulness.

Nutz- *zW:* **n~los** *a* useless; (*unnötig*) needless; **~losigkeit** *f* uselessness; **~nießer** *m* **-s,** - beneficiary.

Nutzung *f* (*Gebrauch*) use; (*das Ausnutzen*) exploitation.

NWDR *m* - *abk* (= *Nordwestdeutscher Rundfunk*) North West German Radio.

Nymphe [nüm'fə] *f* -, **-n** nymph.

O, o [ō:] *nt* O, o.

O *abbr* (= *Osten*) E.

Oase [ōå'zə] *f* -, **-n** oasis.

ob [op] *kj* if, whether; **~ das wohl wahr ist?** can that be true?; **~ ich (nicht) lieber gehe?** maybe I'd better go; **(so) tun als ~** (*umg*) pretend; **und ~!** you bet!

OB *m* **-s, -s** *abk* = **Oberbürgermeister**.

Obacht [ō:'bak̦ht] *f:* **~ geben** pay attention.

Obdach [op'dåk̦h] *nt* **-(e)s** shelter, lodging; **o~los** *a* homeless; **~losenasyl** *nt*, **~losenheim** *nt* hostel *od* shelter for the homeless; **~lose(r)** *mf dekl wie a* homeless person.

Obduktion [opdōōktsēō:n'] *f* autopsy.

obduzieren [opdōōtsē:'rən] *vt* do an autopsy on.

O-Beine [ō:'bīnə] *pl* bow *od* bandy legs *pl*.

oben [ō:'bən] *ad* above; (*in Haus*) upstairs; (*am oberen Ende*) at the top; **nach ~** up; **von ~** down; **siehe ~** see above; **ganz ~** right at the top; **~ ohne** topless; **die Abbildung ~ links** *od* **links ~** the illustration in the top left-hand corner; **jdn von ~ herab behandeln** treat sb condescendingly; **jdn von ~ bis unten ansehen** look sb up and down; **Befehl von ~** orders from above; (*umg: die Vorgesetzten*): **die da ~** the powers that be; **~an'** *ad* at the top; **~auf'** *ad* up above, on the top ♦ *a* (*munter*) in form; **~drein** *ad* into the bargain; **~erwähnt** *a*, **~genannt** *a* above-mentioned; **~hin** *ad* cursorily, superficially.

Ober [ō:'bər] *m* **-s,** - waiter.

Ober- *zW:* **~arm** *m* upper arm; **~arzt** *m* senior physician; **~aufsicht** *f* supervision; **~befehl** *m* supreme command; **~befehlshaber** *m* commander-in-chief; **~begriff** *m* generic term; **~bekleidung** *f* outer clothing; **~bett** *nt* quilt; **~bür'germeister** *m* lord mayor; **~deck** *nt* upper *od* top deck.

obere(r, s) *a* upper; **die O~n** the bosses; (*ECCL*) the superiors; **die ~n Zehntausend** (*umg*) high society.

Ober- *zW:* **~fläche** *f* surface; **o~flächlich** *a* superficial; **bei o~flächlicher Betrachtung** at a quick glance; **jdn (nur) o~flächlich kennen** know sb (only) slightly; **~geschoß** *nt* upper floor; **im zweiten ~geschoß** on the third (*US*) *od* second (*Brit*) floor; **o~halb** *ad*, *präp* +*gen* above; **~hand** *f* (*fig*): **die ~hand gewinnen** get the upper hand (*über* +*akk* over); **~haupt** *nt* head, chief; **~haus**

nt (*POL*) upper house; ~**hemd** *nt* shirt; ~**herrschaft** *f* supremacy, sovereignty.

Oberin *f* matron; (*ECCL*) Mother Superior.

Ober- *zW:* **o~irdisch** *a* above ground; (*Leitung*) overhead; ~**kellner** *m* head waiter; ~**kiefer** *m* upper jaw; ~**kommando** *nt* supreme command; ~**körper** *m* trunk, upper part of body; ~**lauf** *m:* **am ~lauf des Rheins** in the upper reaches of the Rhine; ~**leitung** *f* direction; (*ELEK*) overhead cable; ~**licht** *nt* skylight; ~**lippe** *f* upper lip; ~**prima** *f* final year of German high school; ~**schenkel** *m* thigh; ~**schicht** *f* upper classes *pl*; ~**schule** *f* high school; ~**schwester** *f* (*MED*) matron; ~**seite** *f* top (side); ~**sekunda** *f* -, **-sekunden** seventh year of German high school.

Oberst [ō:'bərst] *m* -en *od* -s, -en *od* -e colonel.

oberste(r, s) *a* very top, topmost.

Ober- *zW:* ~**stübchen** *nt* (*umg*): **er ist nicht ganz richtig im ~stübchen** he's not quite right up top; ~**stufe** *f* upper school; ~**teil** *nt* upper part; ~**tertia** [-ter'tsēä] *f* -, **-tertien** fifth year of German high school; ~**wasser** *nt:* ~**wasser haben/bekommen** be/get on top (of things); ~**weite** *f* bust *od* chest measurement.

obgleich [opglīċḥ'] *kj* although.

Obhut [op'hōō:t] *f* - care, protection; **in jds ~ sein** be in sb's care.

obig [ō:'bíċḥ] *a* above.

Objekt [opyekt'] *nt* -(e)s, -e object.

objektiv [opyektē:f'] *a* objective.

Objektiv *nt* -s, -e lens.

Objektivität [opyektēvētē:t'] *f* objectivity.

Oblate [ōblá'tə] *f* -, -n (*Gebäck*) wafer; (*ECCL*) host.

obligatorisch [ōblēgátō:'rish] *a* compulsory, obligatory.

Oboe [ōbō:'ə] *f* -, -n oboe.

Obrigkeit [ō:'briċḥkīt] *f* (*Behörden*) authorities *pl*, administration; (*Regierung*) government.

Obrigkeitsdenken *nt* acceptance of authority.

obschon [opshō:n'] *kj* although.

Observatorium [opzervátō:'rēōōm] *nt* observatory.

obskur [opskōō:r'] *a* obscure; (*verdächtig*) dubious.

Obst [ō:pst] *nt* -(e)s fruit; ~**bau** *m* fruitgrowing; ~**baum** *m* fruit tree; ~**garten** *m* orchard; ~**händler** *m* fruit merchant; ~**kuchen** *m* fruit tart; ~**saft** *m* fruit juice.

obszön [opstsœn'] *a* obscene.

Obszönität [opstœnētē:t'] *f* obscenity.

Obus [ō:'bōōs] *m* -ses, -se (*umg*) trolley bus.

obwohl [opvō:l'] *kj* although.

Ochse [ok'sə] *m* -n, -n ox; (*umg: Dummkopf*) twit; **er stand da wie der ~ vorm Berg** (*umg*) he stood there utterly bewildered.

ochsen *vti* (*umg*) cram, swot (*Brit*).

Ochsen- *zW:* ~**schwanzsuppe** *f* oxtail soup; ~**zunge** *f* oxtongue.

Ocker [o'kər] *m* *od* *nt* -s, - ocher (*US*), ochre (*Brit*).

öd(e) [œt, œ'də] *a* (*Land*) waste, barren; (*fig*) dull; **öd und leer** dreary and desolate.

Öde *f* -, -n desert, waste(land); (*fig*) tedium.

oder [ō:'dər] *kj* or; **entweder ...** ~ either ... or; **du kommst doch,** ~? you're coming, aren't you?

Ofen [ō:'fən] *m* -s, ⁼ oven; (*Heiz~*) fire, heater; (*Kohle~*) stove; (*Hoch~*) furnace; (*Herd*) cooker, stove; **jetzt ist der ~ aus** (*umg*) that does it!; ~**rohr** *nt* stovepipe.

offen [o'fən] *a* open; (*aufrichtig*) frank; (*Stelle*) vacant; (*Bein*) ulcerated; (*Haare*) loose; ~**er Wein** wine by the carafe *od* glass; **auf ~er Strecke** (*Straße*) on the open road; (*EISENB*) between stations; **Tag der ~en Tür** open house; ~**e Handelsgesellschaft** (*COMM*) partnership; **seine Meinung ~ sagen** speak one's mind; **ein ~es Wort mit jdm reden** have a frank talk with sb; ~ **gesagt** to be honest; ~**bar** *a* obvious; (*vermutlich*) apparently.

offenbaren [ofənbâ'rən] *vt* reveal, manifest.

Offenbarung *f* (*REL*) revelation.

Offenbarungseid *m* (*JUR*) oath of disclosure.

offen- *zW:* ~**bleiben** *vi* unreg (*Fenster*) stay open; (*Frage, Entscheidung*) remain open; ~**halten** *vt* unreg keep open; **O~heit** *f* candor (*US*), candour (*Brit*), frankness; ~**herzig** *a* candid, frank; (*hum: Kleid*) revealing; **O~herzigkeit** *f* frankness; ~**kundig** *a* well-known; (*klar*) evident; ~**lassen** *vt* unreg leave open; ~**sichtlich** *a* evident, obvious.

offensiv [ofenzē:f'] *a* offensive.

Offensive *f* -, -n offensive.

offenstehen *vi* unreg be open; (*Rechnung*) be unpaid; **es steht Ihnen offen, es zu tun** you are at liberty to do it; **die (ganze) Welt steht ihm offen** he has the (whole) world at his feet.

öffentlich [œ'fəntliċḥ] *a* public; **die ~e Hand** (central *od* local) government; **Anstalt des ~en Rechts** public institution; **Ausgaben der ~en Hand** public spending; **Ö~keit** *f* (*Leute*) public; (*einer Versammlung etc*) public nature; **in aller Ö~keit** in public; **an die Ö~keit dringen** reach the public ear; **unter Ausschluß der Ö~keit** in secret; (*JUR*) in camera.

Öffentlichkeitsarbeit *f* public relations work.

öffentlich-rechtlich *a* attr (under) public law.

offerieren [ofārē:'rən] *vt* offer.

Offerte [ofer'tə] *f* -, -n offer.

offiziell [ofētsēel'] *a* official.

Offizier [ofētsē:r'] *m* -s, -e officer.

Offizierskasino *nt* officers' mess.

öffnen [œf'nən] *vtr* open; **jdm die Tür ~** open

the door for sb.
Öffner [œf'nər] *m* **-s,** - opener.
Öffnung [œf'nōōŋ] *f* opening.
Öffnungszeiten *pl* business hours *pl*.
Offsetdruck [of'setdrōōk] *m* offset (printing).
oft [oft] *ad* often.
öfter [œf'tər] *ad* more often *od* frequently;
des ~en quite frequently.
öfter(s) *ad* often, frequently; ~ **mal was
Neues** (*umg*) variety is the spice of life
(*Sprichwort*).
oftmals *ad* often, frequently.
o.G. *abk* (= *ohne Gewähr*) subject to change,
without liability.
OHG *f abk* (= *offene Handelsgesellschaft*)
general *od* ordinary (*US*) partnership.

ohne [ō:'nə] *präp* +*akk, kj* without; **das Darlehen ist** ~ **weiteres bewilligt worden** the
loan was granted without any problem; **das
kann man nicht** ~ **weiteres voraussetzen**
you can't just assume that automatically;
das ist nicht ~ (*umg*) it's not bad; ~ **weiteres** without a second thought; (*sofort*)
immediately.
ohne- *zW*: ~**dies'** *ad* anyway; ~**einander**
[ō:nəīnán'dər] *ad* without each other;
~**glei'chen** *a* unsurpassed, without equal;
~**hin'** *ad* anyway, in any case; **es ist** ~**hin
schon spät** it's late enough already.
Ohnmacht [ō:n'máƙht] *f* faint; (*fig*) impotence; **in** ~ **fallen** faint.
ohnmächtig [ō:n'mecħtiçh] *a* in a faint, unconscious; (*fig*) weak, impotent; **sie ist** ~
she has fainted; ~**e Wut** *od* ~**er Zorn** helpless rage; **einer Sache** (*dat*) ~ **gegenüberstehen** be helpless in the face of sth.
Ohr [ō:r] *nt* **-(e)s, -en** ear; (*Gehör*) hearing;
sich aufs ~ **legen** *od* **hauen** (*umg*) take a
nap; **jdm die** ~**en langziehen** (*umg*) tweak
sb's ear(s); **jdm in den** ~**en liegen** keep on
at sb; **jdn übers** ~ **hauen** (*umg*) pull a fast
one on sb; **auf dem** ~ **bin ich taub** (*fig*)
nothing doing (*umg*); **schreib es dir hinter
die** ~**en** (*umg*) will you (finally) get that
into your (thick) head!; **bis über die** *od* **beide** ~**en verliebt sein** be head over heels in
love; **viel um die** ~**en haben** (*umg*) have a
lot on (one's plate); **halt die** ~**en steif!** keep
a stiff upper lip!
Öhr [œr] *nt* **-(e)s, -e** eye.
Ohren- *zW*: ~**arzt** *m* ear specialist;
o~**betäubend** *a* deafening; ~**sausen** *nt*
(*MED*) buzzing in one's ears; ~**schmalz** *nt*
earwax; ~**schmerzen** *pl* earache *sing*;
~**schützer** *m* **-s,** - earmuff.
Ohr- *zW*: ~**feige** *f* slap on the face; box on
the ears; **o**~**feigen** *vt untr* slap sb's face;
box sb's ears; **ich könnte mich selbst
o**~**feigen, daß ich das gemacht habe** I
could kick myself for doing that; ~**läppchen**
nt ear lobe; ~**ringe** *pl* earrings *pl*; ~**wurm**
m earwig; (*MUS*) catchy tune.
o.J. *abk* (= *ohne Jahr*) no year given.
okkupieren [okōōpē:'rən] *vt* occupy.

Ökologie [œkōlōgē:'] *f* ecology.
ökologisch [œkōlō:'gish] *a* ecological, envi-
ronmental.
Ökonometrie [œkōnōmātrē:'] *f* econometrics
pl.
Ökonomie [œkōnōmē:'] *f* economy; (*als
Wissenschaft*) economics *sing*.
ökonomisch [œkōnō:'mish] *a* economical.
Ökopaxe [œkōpák'sə] *m* **-n, -n** (*umg*) envi-
ronmentalist.
OKR *m abk* (= *Oberkirchenrat*) church
assembly.
Okt. *abk* (= *Oktober*) Oct.
Oktanzahl [oktán'tsál] *f* (*bei Benzin*) octane.
Oktave [oktá'və] *f* **-, -n** octave.
Oktober [oktō:'bər] *m* **-(s),** - October; *siehe*
September.
ökumenisch [œkōōmā:'nish] *a* ecumenical.
ö.L. *abk* (= *östliche(r) Länge*) eastern longitude.
Öl [œl] *nt* **-(e)s, -e** oil; **auf** ~ **stoßen** strike
oil; ~**baum** *m* olive tree; **ö**~**en** *vt* oil;
(*TECH*) lubricate; **wie ein geölter Blitz**
(*umg*) like greased lightning; ~**farbe** *f* oil
paint; ~**feld** *nt* oilfield; ~**film** *m* film of oil;
~**heizung** *f* oil-fired central heating.
ölig *a* oily.
Oligopol [ōlēgōpō:l'] *nt* **-s, -e** oligopoly.
oliv [ōlē:f'] *a* olive green.
Olive [ōlē:'və] *f* **-, -n** olive.
Öljacke *f* oilskin jacket.
oll [ol] *a* (*umg*): **das sind** ~**e Kamellen** that's
old hat.
Öl- *zW*: ~**meßstab** *m* dipstick; ~**pest** *f* oil
pollution; ~**platform** *f* oil rig; ~**sardine** *f*
sardine; ~**scheich** *m* oil sheik;
~**standanzeiger** *m* (*AUT*) oil gage; ~**tanker**
m oil tanker; ~**teppich** *m* oil slick.
Ölung *f* oiling; (*ECCL*) anointment; **die Letz-
te** ~ Extreme Unction.
Öl- *zW*: ~**wanne** *f* (*AUT*) oil pan (*US*), sump
(*Brit*); ~**wechsel** *m* oil change; ~**zeug** *nt*
oilskins *pl*.
Olymp [ōlümp'] *m* **-s** (*Berg*) Mount Olympus.
Olympiade [ōlümpēá'də] *f* **-, -n** Olympic
Games *pl*.
Olympiasieger(in *f*) [ōlüm'pēázē:gər(in)] *m*
Olympic champion.
Olympiateilnehmer(in *f*) *m* Olympic
competitor.
Olympionike [ōlümpēōnē:'kə] *m*, **Olympio-
ni'kin** *f* Olympic competitor.
olympisch [ōlüm'pish] *a* Olympic.
Oma [ō:'má] *f* **-, -s** (*umg*) granny, grandma.
Omelett [om(ə)let'] *nt* **-(e)s, -s, Omelette** *f*
omelet, omelette (*Brit*).
Omen [ō:'men] *nt* **-s,** - *od* **Omina** omen.
Omnibus [om'nēbōōs] *m* (omni)bus.
Onanie [ōnánē:'] *f* masturbation.
onanieren *vi* masturbate.
ondulieren [ondōōlē:'rən] *vtr* crimp.
Onkel [ong'kəl] *m* **-s,** - uncle.
o.P. *abk* = **ordentlicher Professor**.
OP *m abk* = **Operationssaal**.

Opa [ō:'pá] *m* **-s, -s** (*umg*) grandpa.
Opal [ōpál'] *m* **-s, -e** opal.
ÖPD *m* - *abk* = *Österreichischer Pressedienst.*
Oper [ō:'pər] *f* **-, -n** opera; (*Opernhaus*) opera house.
Operation [ōpārátsē̄o:n'] *f* operation.
Operationssaal *m* operating room.
operativ [ōpərátē:f'] *a* (*MED*): **eine Geschwulst ~ entfernen** remove a growth by surgery.
Operette [ōpāre'tə] *f* operetta.
operieren [ōpārē:'rən] *vti* operate; **sich ~ lassen** have an operation.
Opern- *zW*: **~glas** *nt* opera glasses *pl*; **~haus** *nt* opera house; **~sänger** *m* opera singer.
Opfer [o'pfər] *nt* **-s,** - sacrifice; (*Mensch*) victim; **~bereitschaft** *f* readiness to make sacrifices.
opfern *vt* sacrifice.
Opfer- *zW*: **~stock** *m* (*ECCL*) offertory box; **~ung** *f* sacrifice; (*ECCL*) offertory.
Opium [ō:'pēōōm] *nt* **-s** opium.
opponieren [opōnē:'rən] *vi* oppose (*gegen jdn/etw* sb/sth).
opportun [oportōō:n'] *a* opportune; **O~ismus** [-nis'mōōs] *m* opportunism; **O~ist(in** *f*) [-nist'(in)] *m* opportunist.
Opposition [opōzētsē̄o:n'] *f* opposition.
oppositionell [opōzētsēō:nel'] *a* opposing.
Oppositionsführer *m* leader of the opposition.
optieren [optē:'rən] *vi* (*POL form*): **~ für** opt for.
Optik [op'tik] *f* optics *sing*; **du hast wohl einen Knick in der ~!** (*umg*) can't you see straight?!
Optiker(in *f*) *m* **-s,** - optician.
optimal [optēmál'] *a* optimal, optimum.
Optimismus [optēmis'mōōs] *m* optimism.
Optimist(in *f*) [optēmist'(in)] *m* optimist; **o~isch** *a* optimistic.
optisch [op'tish] *a* optical; **~e Täuschung** optical illusion.
Orakel [ōrá'kəl] *nt* **-s,** - oracle.
orange [ōráñ'zhə] *a* orange; **O~** *f* **-, -n** orange.
Orangeade [ōráñzhá'də] *f* **-, -n** orangeade.
Orangeat [ōráñzhát'] *nt* **-s, -e** candied peel.
Orangen- *zW*: **~marmelade** *f* marmelade; **~saft** *m* orange juice; **~schale** *f* orange peel.
Oratorium [ōrátō:'rēōōm] *nt* (*MUS*) oratorio.
Orchester [orke'stər] *nt* **-s,** - orchestra.
Orchidee [orċhēdā:'ə] *f* **-, -n** orchid.
Orden [or'dən] *m* **-s,** - (*ECCL*) order; (*MIL*) decoration.
Ordens- *zW*: **~gemeinschaft** *f* religious order; **~schwester** *f* nun.
ordentlich [or'dəntliċh] *a* (*anständig*) decent, respectable; (*geordnet*) tidy, neat; (*umg*: *annehmbar*) not bad; (: *tüchtig*) real, proper; (*Leistung*) reasonable; **~es Mitglied** full

member; **~er Professor** (full) professor; **eine ~e Tracht Prügel** a proper hiding; **~ arbeiten** be a thorough and precise worker; **O~keit** *f* respectability; tidiness, neatness.
Order *f* **-, -s** *od* **-n** (*COMM*: *Auftrag*) order.
ordern *vt* (*COMM*) order.
Ordinalzahl [ordēnál'tsāl] *f* ordinal number.
ordinär [ordēne:r'] *a* common, vulgar.
Ordinarius [ordēná'rēōōs] *m* **-,** **Ordinarien** (*UNIV*) professor (*für* of).
ordnen [ord'nən] *vt* order, put in order.
Ordner *m* **-s,** - steward; (*COMM*) file.
Ordnung *f* order; (*Ordnen*) ordering; (*Geordnetsein*) tidiness; **geht in ~** (*umg*) that's all right *od* OK (*umg*); **~ schaffen, für ~ sorgen** put things in order, tidy things up; **jdn zur ~ rufen** call sb to order; **bei ihm muß alles seine ~ haben** (*räumlich*) he has to have everything in its proper place; (*zeitlich*) he has to do everything according to a fixed schedule; **das Kind braucht seine ~** the child needs a routine.
Ordnungs- *zW*: **~amt** *nt* ≈ town *od* county clerk's office; **o~gemäß** *a* proper, according to the rules; **o~halber** *ad* as a matter of form; **~liebe** *f* tidiness, orderliness; **~strafe** *f* fine; **o~widrig** *a* contrary to the rules, irregular; **~widrigkeit** *f* infringement (*of law or rule*); **~zahl** *f* ordinal number.
ORF *m* - *abk* = *Österreichischer Rundfunk.*
Organ [orgán'] *nt* **-s, -e** organ; (*Stimme*) voice.
Organisation [organēzátsē̄o:n'] *f* organization.
Organisationstalent *nt* organizing ability; (*Person*) good organizer.
Organisator [organēzá'tor] *m* organizer.
organisch [orgá'nish] *a* organic; (*Erkrankung, Leiden*) physical.
organisieren [organēzē:'rən] *vt* organize, arrange; (*umg*: *beschaffen*) acquire ♦ *vr* organize.
Organismus [organis'mōōs] *m* organism.
Organist [organist'] *m* organist.
Organ- *zW*: **~spender** *m* donor (of an organ); **~verpflanzung** *f* transplantation (of an organ).
Orgasmus [orgás'mōōs] *m* orgasm.
Orgel [or'gəl] *f* **-, -n** organ; **~pfeife** *f* organ pipe; **wie die ~pfeifen stehen** stand in order of height.
Orgie [or'gēə] *f* orgy.
Orient [ō:'rēent] *m* **-s** Orient, east; **der Vordere ~** the Near East.
Orientale [ō:rēentá'lə] *m* **-n, -n, Orientalin** *f* Oriental.
orientalisch *a* oriental.
orientieren [ō:rēentē:'rən] *vt* (*örtlich*) locate; (*fig*) inform ♦ *vr* find one's way *od* bearings; inform o.s.
Orientierung [ō:rēentē:'rōōng] *f* orientation; (*fig*) information; **die ~ verlieren** lose one's

bearings.
Orientierungs- *zW*: **~sinn** *m* sense of direction; **~stufe** *f* (*SCH*) *transitional stage between grade and high schools in the FRG in order to ascertain abilities.*
original [ōrēgēnȧl'] *a* original; **~ Meißener Porzellan** genuine Meissen porcelain; **O~** *nt* **-s, -e** original; (*Mensch*) character; **O~ausgabe** *f* first edition; **O~fassung** *f* original version.
Originalität [ōrēgēnȧlēte:t'] *f* originality.
originell [ōrēgēnel'] *a* original.
Orkan [orkȧn'] *m* **-(e)s, -e** hurricane; **o~artig** *a* (*Wind*) gale-force; (*Beifall*) thunderous.
Orkneyinseln [or'kniinzəln] *pl* Orkney Islands *pl*, Orkneys *pl*.
Ornament [ornȧment'] *nt* decoration, ornament.
ornamental [ornȧmentȧl'] *a* decorative, ornamental.
Ornithologe [ornētōlō:'gə] *m* **-n, -n, Ornithologin** *f* ornithologist.
Ort [ort] *m* **-(e)s, -e** place; **an ~ und Stelle** on the spot; **am ~** in the place; **am angegebenen ~** in the place quoted, loc.cit.; **~ der Handlung** (*THEAT*) scene of the action; **das ist höheren ~s entschieden worden** (*hum, form*) the decision came from above ♦ *m* **-(e)s, ¨er: vor ~** at the (coal) face; (*lit, fig*) on the spot.
Örtchen [œrt'çhən] *nt* (*umg*) john (*US*), loo (*Brit*).
orten *vt* locate.
orthodox [ortōdoks'] *a* orthodox.
Orthographie [ortōgrȧfē:'] *f* spelling, orthography.
orthographisch [ortōgrȧ'fish] *a* orthographic.
Orthopäde [ortōpe:'də] *m* **-n, -n** orthopedist (*US*), orthopaedist (*Brit*).
Orthopädie [ortōpedē:'] *f* orthopedics (*US*), orthopaedics (*Brit*) *sing*.
orthopädisch *a* orthopedic (*US*), orthopaedic (*Brit*).
örtlich [œrt'liçh] *a* local; **jdn ~ betäuben** give sb a local anesthetic (*US*) *od* anaesthetic (*Brit*); **Ö~keit** *f* locality; **sich mit den Ö~keiten vertraut machen** get to know the place.
Orts- *zW*: **~angabe** *f* (name of the) town; **ohne ~angabe** no place of publication indicated; **o~ansässig** *a* local.
Ortschaft *f* village, small town; **geschlossene ~** built-up area.
Orts- *zW*: **o~fremd** *a* non-local; **~fremde(r)** *mf* stranger; **~gespräch** *nt* local (phone) call; **~gruppe** *f* local branch *od* group; **~kenntnis** *f*: **(gute) ~kenntnisse haben** know one's way around (well); **~krankenkasse** *f*: **Allgemeine ~krankenkasse** *compulsory medical insurance scheme*; **~name** *m* place name; **~netz** *nt* (*TEL*) local telephone exchange area; **~netzkennzahl** *f* (*TEL*) area code; **~schild** *nt* place name sign; **~sinn** *m* sense of direc-

tion; **~tarif** *m* (*TEL*) charge for local calls; **~vorschriften** *pl* by(e)laws *pl*; **~zeit** *f* local time; **~zuschlag** *m* living allowance.
Ortung *f* locating.
öS. *abk* = *österreichischer Schilling*.
Öse [œ'zə] *f* **-, -n** loop; (*an Kleidung*) eye.
öst *abk* (= *österreichisch*) Aust.
OStA *abk* (= *Oberstaatsanwalt*) public prosecutor.
Ost- [ost] *zW*: **~afrika** *nt* East Africa; **~Berlin** *nt* East Berlin; **~block** *m* (*POL*) Eastern bloc; **o~deutsch** *a* East German; **~deutschland** *nt* (*POL*) East Germany; (*GEOG*) Eastern Germany.
Osten *m* **-s** east; **der Ferne ~** the Far East; **der Nahe ~** the Middle East, the Near East.
ostentativ [ostentȧtē:f'] *a* pointed, ostentatious.
Oster- [ō:'stər] *zW*: **~ei** *nt* Easter egg; **~fest** *nt* Easter; **~glocke** *f* daffodil; **~hase** *m* Easter bunny; **~marsch** *m* Easter demonstration; **~montag** *m* Easter Monday.
Ostern *nt* **-s, -** Easter; **frohe** *od* **fröhliche ~!** Happy Easter!; **zu ~** at Easter.
Österreich [œ'stəriçh] *nt* **-s** Austria.
Österreicher(in *f*) *m* **-s, -** Austrian.
österreichisch *a* Austrian.
Ostersonntag *m* Easter Day *od* Sunday.
Ost- *zW*: **~europa** *nt* East(ern) Europe; **o~europäisch** *a* East European.
östlich [œst'liçh] *a* eastern, easterly.
Ost- *zW*: **~mark** *f* (*umg*) East German Mark; **~politik** *f* Ostpolitik, *foreign policy regarding the Eastern bloc.*
OStR *abk* (= *Oberstudienrat*) senior teacher.
Östrogen [œstrōgā:n'] *nt* **-s, -e** estrogen (*US*), oestrogen (*Brit*).
Ost- *zW*: **~see** *f* Baltic Sea; **~verträge** *pl* (*POL*) state contracts between FRG and GDR; **o~wärts** *ad* eastwards; **~wind** *m* east wind.
oszillieren [ostsilē:'rən] *vi* oscillate.
Otter [o'tər] *m* **-s, -** otter ♦ *f* **-, -n** (*Schlange*) adder.
ÖTV *f* **-** *abk* (= *Gewerkschaft öffentliche Dienste, Transport und Verkehr*) labor union.
Ouvertüre [ōōvertü:'rə] *f* **-, -n** overture.
oval [ōvȧl'] *a* oval.
Ovation [ōvȧtsēō:n'] *f* ovation.
Overall [ō'ōōvərorl] *m* **-s, -s** (*Schutzanzug*) overalls *pl*.
ÖVP *f* **-** *abk* (= *österreichische Volkspartei*) Austrian People's Party.
Ovulation [ōvōōlȧtsēō:n'] *f* ovulation.
Oxyd [oksü:t'] *nt* **-(e)s, -e** oxide.
oxydieren [oksüdē:'rən] *vti* oxidize.
Oxydierung *f* oxidization.
Ozean [ō:'tsȧȧn] *m* **-s, -e** ocean; **~dampfer** *m* (ocean-going) liner.
Ozeanien [ōtsȧȧ'nēən] *nt* **-s** Oceania.
ozeanisch [ōtsȧȧ'nish] *a* oceanic; (*Sprachen*) Oceanic.
Ozeanriese *m* (*umg*) ocean liner.

Ozon [ōtsō:n'] *nt* **-s** ozone.

P

P, p [pā:] *nt* P, p.
P. *abk* = **Pastor; Pater.**
p.A. *abk* (= *per Adresse*) c/o.
paar *a inv*: **ein ~** a few; (*zwei oder drei*) a couple of.
Paar [pår] *nt* **-(e)s, -e** pair; (*Ehe~*) couple.
paaren *vtr* (*Tiere*) mate, pair.
Paar- *zW*: **~hufer** *pl* (*ZOOL*) cloven-hoofed animals *pl*; **~lauf** *m* pair skating; **p~mal** *ad*: **ein p~mal** a few times.
Paarung *f* combination; mating.
paarweise *ad* in pairs; in couples.
Pacht [påkht] *f* **-, -en** lease; (*Entgelt*) rent; **p~en** *vt* lease; **du hast das Sofa doch nicht für dich gepachtet** (*umg*) don't hog the sofa.
Pächter(in *f*) [pecħ'tər(in)] *m* **-s, -** leaseholder, tenant.
Pachtvertrag *m* lease.
Pack [påk] *m* **-(e)s, -e** *od* *:-*e bundle, pack ♦ *nt* **-(e)s** (*pej*) mob, rabble.
Päckchen [pɛk'çhən] *nt* small package; (*Zigaretten*) packet; (*Post~*) small parcel.
Packeis *nt* pack ice.
packen *vti* (*auch COMPUT*) pack; (*fassen*) grasp, seize; (*umg: schaffen*) manage; (*fig: fesseln*) grip; **~ wir's!** (*umg: gehen*) let's go.
Packen *m* **-s, -** bundle; (*fig: Menge*) heaps of.
Packer(in *f*) *m* **-s, -** packer.
Pack- *zW*: **~esel** *m* pack mule; (*fig*) packhorse; **~papier** *nt* brown paper, wrapping paper.
Packung *f* packet; (*Pralinen~*) box; (*MED*) compress.
Pädagoge [pɛdågō:'gə] *m* **-n, -n, Pädagogin** *f* educationalist.
Pädagogik *f* education.
pädagogisch *a* educational, pedagogical; **P~e Hochschule** college of education.
Paddel [på'dəl] *nt* **-s, -** paddle; **~boot** *nt* canoe.
paddeln *vi* paddle.
paffen [på'fən] *vti* puff.
Page [på'zhə] *m* **-n, -n** page(boy).
Pagenkopf *m* pageboy cut.
paginieren [pågēnē:'rən] *vt* paginate.
Paginierung *f* pagination.
Paillette [pīye'tə] *f* sequin.
Paket [påkā:t'] *nt* **-(e)s, -e** packet; (*Post~*) parcel; **~annahme** *f*, **~ausgabe** *f* parcels office; **~karte** *f* dispatch note; **~post** *f*

parcel post; **~schalter** *m* parcels counter.
Pakistan [på'kistân] *nt* **-s** Pakistan.
Pakistaner(in *f*) [påkistå'nər(in)] *m* **-s, -, Pakistani** *m* **-(s), -(s)** Pakistani.
Pakt [påkt] *m* **-(e)s, -e** pact.
Palast [pålåst'] *m* **-es, Paläste** palace.
Palästina [pålɛstē:'nå] *nt* **-s** Palestine.
Palästinenser(in *f*) [pålɛstēnen'zər(in)] *m* **-s, - Palestinian.**
Palaver [pålå'vər] *nt* **-s, -** (*lit, fig umg*) palaver.
Palette [pålɛ'tə] *f* palette; (*fig*) range; (*Lade~*) pallet.
Palme [pål'mə] *f* **-, -n** palm (tree); **jdn auf die ~ bringen** (*umg*) make sb see red.
Palmsonntag *m* Palm Sunday.
Pampelmuse [påm'pəlmōō:zə] *f* **-, -n** grapefruit.
pampig [påm'piçh] *a* (*umg: frech*) fresh.
Panama [på'nåmå] *nt* **-s** Panama; **~kanal** *m* Panama Canal.
Panflöte [pån'flœtə] *f* panpipes *pl*, Pan's pipes *pl*.
panieren [pånē:'rən] *vt* (*KOCH*) coat with egg and breadcrumbs.
Paniermehl [pånē:r'mā:l] *nt* breadcrumbs *pl*.
Panik [på'nik] *f* panic; **nur keine ~!** don't panic!; **in ~ ausbrechen** panic; **~mache** *f* (*umg*) panicmongering.
panisch [på'nish] *a* panic-stricken.
Panne [på'nə] *f* **-, -n** (*AUT etc*) breakdown; (*Mißgeschick*) slip; **uns ist eine ~ passiert** there's been a slip-up, we've goofed (*umg*).
Pannendienst *m*, **Pannenhilfe** *f* breakdown service.
panschen [pån'shən] *vi* splash about ♦ *vt* water down.
Panther [pån'tər] *m* **-s, -** panther.
Pantoffel [pånto'fəl] *m* **-s, -n** slipper; **~held** *m* (*umg*) henpecked husband.
Pantomime [påntōmē:'mə] *f* **-, -n** mime.
Panzer [pån'tsər] *m* **-s, -** armor (*US*), armour (*Brit*); (*fig*) shield; (*Platte*) armor plate; (*Fahrzeug*) tank; **~faust** *f* bazooka; **~glas** *nt* bulletproof glass; **~grenadier** *m* armored infantryman.
panzern *vtr* armor plate; (*fig*) arm o.s.
Panzer- *zW*: **~schrank** *m* strongbox; **~wagen** *m* armored car.
Papa [påpå'] *m* **-s, -s** (*umg*) pa, dad(dy).
Papagei [påpågī'] *m* **-s, -en** parrot.
Papier [påpē:r'] *nt* **-s, -e** paper; (*Wert~*) share; **~e** *pl* (identity) papers *pl*; (*Urkunden*) documents *pl*; **seine ~e bekommen** (*entlassen werden*) get one's walking papers (*US*) *od* one's cards (*Brit*); **~fabrik** *f* paper mill; **~geld** *nt* paper money; **~korb** *m* wastepaper basket; **~kram** *m* (*umg*) useless papers; **~krieg** *m* red tape; **~tüte** *f* paper bag; **~vorschub** *m* (*Drucker*) paper advance.
Pappdeckel *f* **-, -n** cardboard.
Pappe [på'pə] *m* cardboard; **das ist nicht von ~** (*umg*) that is really something.

Pappeinband m pasteboard.
Pappel f -, -n poplar.
pappen vti (umg) stick.
Pappen- zW: **~heimer** pl: **ich kenne meine ~heimer** (umg) I know you lot od that lot (inside out); **~stiel** m (umg): **keinen ~stiel wert sein** not be worth a thing; **für einen ~stiel bekommen** get for a song.
papperlapapp [pápərlápáp'] interj rubbish!
pappig a sticky.
Pappmaché [pápmáshā:'] nt -s, -s papier-mâché.
Paprika [pá'prēká] m -s, -s (Gewürz) paprika; (~schote) pepper; **~schote** f: **gefüllte ~schoten** stuffed peppers.
Papst [pâpst] m -(e)s, ⁻e pope.
päpstlich [pe:pst'liċh] a papal; **~er als der Papst sein** be more Catholic than the Pope.
Parabel [párá'bəl] f -, -n parable; (MATH) parabola.
Parade [párá'də] f -, -n (MIL) parade, review; (SPORT) parry; **~beispiel** nt prime example; **~marsch** m march past; **~schritt** m goose step.
Paradies [párádē:s'] nt -es, -e paradise; **p~isch** a heavenly.
paradox [párádoks'] a paradoxical; **P~** nt -es, -e paradox.
Paraffin [páráfē:n'] nt -s, -e (CHEM: ~öl) kerosene (US), paraffin (Brit); (~wachs) paraffin wax.
Paragraph [párágrâf'] m -en, -en paragraph; (JUR) section.
Paragraphenreiter m (umg) pedant.
Paraguay [párágōōá'ē] nt -s Paraguay.
parallel [párálā:l'] a parallel; **~ schalten** (ELEK) connect in parallel.
Parallele f parallel.
Parameter [párá'mātər] m parameter.
paramilitärisch [párámēlēte:'rish] a paramilitary.
Paranuß [pá'ránōōs] f Brazil nut.
paraphieren [páráfē:'rən] vt (Vertrag) initial.
Parasit [párázē:t'] m -en, -en (lit, fig) parasite.
parat [párât'] a ready.
Pärchen [pe:r'ċhən] nt couple.
Parcours [párkōō:r'] m -, - show-jumping course; (Sportart) show-jumping.
Pardon [párdōn'] m od nt -s (umg): **~!** (Verzeihung) sorry!; **kein ~ kennen** be ruthless.
Parfüm [párfü:m'] nt -s, -s od -e perfume.
Parfümerie [párfümərē:'] f perfumery.
Parfümflasche f scent bottle.
parfümieren [párfümē:'rən] vt scent, perfume.
parieren [párē:'rən] vt parry ♦ vi (umg) obey.
Pariser [párē:'zər] m -s, - Parisian; (umg: Kondom) rubber ♦ a attr Parisian, Paris.
Pariserin f Parisienne.
Parität [párēte:t'] f parity; **p~isch** a: **p~ische Mitbestimmung** equal representation.

Pariwert [pâ'rēvā:rt] m par value, parity.
Park [párk] m -s, -s park.
Parka [pár'ká] m -(s), -s parka.
Parkanlage f park; (um Gebäude) grounds pl.
Parkbucht f parking bay.
parken vti park; **„P~ verboten!"** "No Parking".
Parkett [párket'] nt -(e)s, -e parquet (floor); (THEAT) orchestra (US), stalls pl (Brit).
Park- zW: **~haus** nt multi-story car park; **~lücke** f parking space; **~platz** m parking lot (US), car park (Brit); parking place; **~scheibe** f parking disc; **~uhr** f parking meter; **~verbot** nt parking ban.
Parlament [párláment'] nt parliament.
Parlamentarier [párlámentá'rēər] m -s, - parliamentarian.
parlamentarisch a parliamentary.
Parlaments- zW: **~ausschuß** m parliamentary committee; **~beschluß** m vote of parliament; **~ferien** pl recess; **~mitglied** nt ≈ Congressman (US), ≈ member of parliament (Brit); **~sitzung** f sitting (of parliament).
Parodie [párōdē:'] f parody.
parodieren vt parody.
Parodontose [párōdontō:'zə] f -, -n shrinking gums.
Parole [párō:'lə] f -, -n password; (Wahlspruch) motto.
Partei [pártī'] f party; (im Mietshaus) tenant, party (form); **~ ergreifen für jdn** take sb's side; **~buch** nt party membership book; **~führung** f party leadership; **~genosse** m party member; **p~isch** a partial, biased; **~linie** f party line; **p~los** a neutral; **~nahme** f -, -n partisanship; **p~politisch** a party political; **~programm** nt (party) manifesto; **~tag** m party conference; **~vorsitzende(r)** mf party leader.
Parterre [párter'] nt -s, -s first (US) od ground (Brit) floor; (THEAT) orchestra (US), stalls pl (Brit).
Partie [pártē:'] f part; (Spiel) game; (Ausflug) outing; (Mann, Frau) catch; (COMM) lot; **mit von der ~ sein** join in.
partiell [pártsēel'] a partial.
Partikel [pártē:'kəl] f -, -n particle.
Partisan(in f) [pártēzán'(in)] m -s od -en, -en partisan.
Partitur [pártētōō:r'] f (MUS) score.
Partizip [pártētsē:p'] nt -s, -ien participle; **~ Präsens/Perfekt** (GRAM) present/past participle.
Partner(in f) [párt'nər(in)] m -s, - partner; **p~schaftlich** a as partners.
partout [pártōō:'] ad: **er will ~ ins Kino gehen** he insists on going to the movies.
Party [pár'tē] f -, -s od **Parties** party.
Parzelle [pártse'lə] f plot, lot.
Pascha [pá'shá] m -s, -s: **wie ein ~** like a Lord.
Paß [pás] m -sses, ⁻sse pass; (Ausweis) pass-

port.

passabel [pásá'bəl] *a* passable, reasonable.

Passage [pásá'zhə] *f* -, **-n** passage; *(Ladenstraße)* arcade.

Passagier [pásázhē:r'] *m* **-s, -e** passenger; ~**dampfer** *m* passenger steamer; ~**flugzeug** *nt* airliner.

Passah, Passahfest [pá'sá(fest)] *nt* **-s** (Feast of the) Passover.

Paßamt *nt* passport office.

Passant(in *f)* [pásánt'(in)] *m* passer-by.

Paßbild *nt* passport photograph.

passé [pásá:'] *a*: **diese Mode ist längst ~** this fashion went out long ago.

passen [pá'sən] *vi* fit; *(Farbe)* go *(zu* with); *(auf Frage, KARTEN, SPORT)* pass; **Sonntag paßt uns nicht** *(genehm sein)* Sunday is no good for us; **die Schuhe ~ (mir) gut** the shoes are a good fit (for me); **zu jdm ~** *(Mensch)* suit sb; **das paßt mir nicht** that doesn't suit me; **er paßt nicht zu dir** he's not right for you; **das könnte dir so ~!** *(umg)* you'd like that, wouldn't you?

passend *a* suitable; *(zusammen~)* matching; *(angebracht)* fitting; *(Zeit)* convenient; **haben Sie es ~?** *(Geld)* have you got the right money?

Paßfoto *nt* passport photo(graph).

passierbar [pásē:r'bár] *a* passable; *(Fluß, Kanal)* negotiable.

passieren *vt* pass; *(durch Sieb)* strain ♦ *vi aux sein* happen; **es ist ein Unfall passiert** there has been an accident.

Passierschein *m* pass, permit.

Passion [pásēō:n'] *f* passion.

passioniert [pásēō:nē:rt'] *a* enthusiastic, passionate.

Passions- *zW*: ~**spiel** *nt* Passion Play; ~**zeit** *f* Passiontide.

passiv [pá'sē:f] *a* passive; **P~** *nt* **-s, -e** passive.

Passiva [pásē:'vá] *pl* (COMM) liabilities *pl*.

Passivität [pásēvētè:t'] *f* passiveness.

Passivposten *m* **-s, -** (COMM) debit entry.

Paß- *zW*: ~**kontrolle** *f* passport control; ~**stelle** *f* passport office; ~**straße** *f* (mountain) pass; ~**zwang** *m* requirement to carry a passport.

Paste [pá'stə] *f* -, **-n** paste.

Pastell [pástel'] *nt* **-(e)s, -e** pastel.

Pastete [pástā:'tə] *f* -, **-n** pie; *(Pastetchen)* vol-au-vent; *(ungefüllt)* vol-au-vent case.

pasteurisieren [pástœrēzē:'rən] *vt* pasteurize.

Pastor [pá'stor] *m* vicar; pastor, minister.

Pate [pá'tə] *m* **-n, -n** godfather; **bei etw ~ gestanden haben** *(fig)* be the force behind sth.

Paten- *zW*: ~**kind** *nt* godchild; ~**stadt** *f* sister city (US), twin(ned) town (Brit).

patent [pátent'] *a* clever.

Patent *nt* **-(e)s, -e** patent; (MIL) commission; **etw als** *od* **zum ~ anmelden** apply for a patent on sth; ~**amt** *nt* patent office.

patentieren [pátentē:'rən] *vt* patent.

Patent- *zW*: ~**inhaber** *m* patentee; ~**lösung** *f* *(fig)* patent remedy; ~**schutz** *m* patent right; ~**urkunde** *f* letters patent.

Pater [pá'tər] *m* **-s, -** *od* **Patres** (ECCL) Father.

Paternoster [pátərno'stər] *m* **-s, -** *(Aufzug)* paternoster.

pathetisch [pátā:'tish] *a* emotional.

Pathologe [pátōlō:'gə] *m* **-n, -n, Pathologin** *f* pathologist.

pathologisch *a* pathological.

Pathos [pá'tos] *nt* - emotiveness, emotionalism.

Patience [pásēáns'] *f* -, **-n:** ~**n legen** play patience.

Patient(in *f)* [pátsēent'(in)] *m* patient.

Patin [pá'tin] *f* godmother.

Patina [pá'tēná] *f* - patina.

Patriarch [pátrēárch'] *m* **-en, -en** patriarch.

patriarchalisch [pátrēárchá'lish] *a* patriarchal.

Patriot(in *f)* [pátrēō:t'(in)] *m* **-en, -en** patriot; **p~isch** *a* patriotic.

Patriotismus [pátrēō:tis'mōōs] *m* patriotism.

Patron [pátrō:n'] *m* **-s, -e** patron; (ECCL) patron saint; *(pej)* beggar.

Patrone *f* -, **-n** cartridge.

Patronenhülse *f* cartridge case.

Patronin *f* patroness; (ECCL) patron saint.

Patrouille [pátrōōl'yə] *f* -, **-n** patrol.

patrouillieren [pátrōōlyē:'rən] *vi* patrol.

patsch [pátsh] *interj* splash!

Patsche *f* -, **-n** *(umg: Händchen)* paw; *(Fliegen~)* swat(ter); *(Feuer~)* beater; *(Bedrängnis)* mess, jam.

patschen *vti* smack, slap; *(im Wasser)* splash.

patschnaß *a* soaking wet.

Patt [pát] *nt* **-s, -s** *(lit, fig)* stalemate.

patzen [pát'sən] *vi* *(umg)* goof (US), boob (Brit).

patzig [pát'siċh] *a* *(umg)* cheeky, saucy.

Pauke [pou'kə] *f* -, **-n** kettledrum; **auf die ~ hauen** live it up; **mit ~n und Trompeten durchfallen** *(umg)* fail dismally.

pauken *vti* (SCH) cram.

Pauker *m* **-s, -** *(umg)* teacher.

pausbäckig [pous'bekiċh] *a* chubby-cheeked.

pauschal [poushál'] *a* *(Kosten)* inclusive; *(einheitlich)* flat-rate *attr*; *(Urteil)* sweeping; **die Werkstatt rechnet ~ pro Inspektion 250 DM** the garage has a flat rate of DM250 per service.

Pauschale *f* -, **-n,** *f* flat rate; *(vorläufig geschätzter Betrag)* estimated amount.

Pauschal- *zW*: ~**gebühr** *f* flat rate; ~**preis** *m* all-inclusive price; ~**reise** *f* package tour; ~**summe** *f* lump sum; ~**versicherung** *f* comprehensive insurance.

Pause [pou'zə] *f* -, **-n** break; (THEAT) interval; *(innehalten)* pause; *(Kopie)* tracing.

pausen *vt* trace.

Pausen- *zW*: ~**brot** *nt* something to eat at break; ~**hof** *m* schoolyard; **p~los** *a* nonstop; ~**zeichen** *nt* (*RAD*) call sign; (*MUS*) rest.

pausieren [pousē:'rən] *vi* make a break.

Pauspapier [pous'pápē:r] *nt* tracing paper.

Pavian [pâ'vēån] *m* -s, -e baboon.

Pazifik [pâtsē:'fik] *m* -s Pacific.

pazifisch *a* Pacific; **der P~e Ozean** the Pacific (Ocean).

Pazifist(in *f)* [pátsēfist'(in)] *m* pacifist; **p~isch** *a* pacifist.

PC *abk* = **Personal-Computer.**

Pech [pcçh] *nt* -s, -e pitch; (*fig*) bad luck; ~ **haben** be unlucky; **die beiden halten zusammen wie ~ und Schwefel** (*umg*) the two are inseparable; ~ **gehabt!** tough! (*umg*); **p~schwarz** *a* pitch-black; ~**strähne** *f* (*umg*) unlucky streak; ~**vogel** *m* (*umg*) unlucky person.

Pedal [pādål'] *nt* -s, -e pedal; **in die ~e treten** pedal (hard).

Pedant [pādánt'] *m* pedant.

Pedanterie [pādántərē:'] *f* pedantry.

pedantisch *a* pedantic.

Peddigrohr [pe'diçhrō:r] *nt* cane.

Pediküre [pādēkü:'rə] *f* -, -n (*Fußpflege*) pedicure; (*Fußpflegerin*) chiropodist.

Pegel [pā:'gəl] *m* -s, - water gage; (*Geräusch~*) noise level; ~**stand** *m* water level.

peilen [pī'lən] *vt* get a fix on; **die Lage ~** (*umg*) see how the land lies.

Pein [pīn] *f* - agony, suffering.

peinigen *vt* torture; (*plagen*) torment.

Pein- *zW:* **p~lich** *a* (*unangenehm*) embarrassing, awkward, painful; (*genau*) painstaking; **in seinem Zimmer herrschte p~liche Ordnung** his room was meticulously tidy; **er vermied es p~lichst, davon zu sprechen** he was at pains not to talk about it; ~**lichkeit** *f* painfulness, awkwardness; scrupulousness.

Peitsche [pīt'shə] *f* -, -n whip.

peitschen *vt* whip; (*Regen*) lash.

Peitschenhieb *m* lash.

Pekinese [pākēnā:'zə] *m* -n, -n Pekinese, peke (*umg*).

Pelikan [pā:'lēkån] *m* -s, -e pelican.

Pelle [pe'lə] *f* -, -n skin; **der Chef sitzt mir auf der ~** (*umg*) I've got the boss on my back.

pellen *vt* skin, peel.

Pellkartoffeln *pl* baked potatoes *pl.*

Pelz [pelts] *m* -es, -e fur.

Pendel [pen'dəl] *nt* -s, - pendulum.

pendeln *vi* (*schwingen*) swing (to and fro); (*Zug, Fähre etc*) shuttle; (*Mensch*) commute; (*fig*) fluctuate.

Pendelverkehr *m* shuttle service; (*für Pendler*) commuter traffic.

Pendler(in *f)* [pend'lər(in)] *m* -s, - commuter.

penetrant [pānātránt'] *a* sharp; (*Person*) pushing; **das schmeckt/riecht ~ nach Knoblauch** it has a very strong taste/smell of garlic.

penibel [pānē:'bəl] *a* persnickety (*umg*), precise.

Penis [pā:'nis] *m* -, -se penis.

Pennbruder [pen'broo:dər] *m* (*umg*) tramp, hobo (*US*).

Penne *f* -, -n (*umg: SCH*) school.

pennen *vi* (*umg*) nap.

Penner *m* -s, - (*pej umg*) tramp, hobo (*US*).

Pension [penzēō:n'] *f* (*Geld*) pension; (*Ruhestand*) retirement; (*für Gäste*) boarding *od* guest house; **halbe/volle ~** half/full board; **in ~ gehen** retire.

Pensionär(in *f)* [penzēōne:r'(in)] *m* -s, -e pensioner.

Pensionat *nt* -(e)s, -e boarding school.

pensionieren [penzēōnē:'rən] *vt* pension (off); **sich ~ lassen** retire.

pensioniert *a* retired.

Pensionierung *f* retirement.

Pensions- *zW:* **p~berechtigt** *a* entitled to a pension; ~**gast** *m* boarder, paying guest; **p~reif** *a* (*umg*) ready for retirement.

Pensum [pen'zoom] *nt* -s, **Pensen** quota; (*SCH*) curriculum.

Peperoni [pāpārō:'nē] *pl* cayenne peppers *pl* (*US*), chillies *pl* (*Brit*).

per [per] *präp* +*akk* by, per; (*pro*) per; (*bis*) by; ~ **Adresse** (*COMM*) care of, c/o; **mit jdm ~ du sein** (*umg*) be on first-name terms with sb.

perfekt [perfekt'] *a* perfect; (*abgemacht*) settled; **die Sache ~ machen** clinch the deal; **der Vertrag ist ~** the contract is all settled.

Perfekt [per'fekt] *nt* -(e)s, -e perfect.

perfektionieren [perfektsēōnē:'rən] *vt* perfect.

Perfektionismus [perfektsēōnis'moos] *m* perfectionism.

perforieren [perfōrē:'rən] *vt* perforate.

Pergament [pergáment'] *nt* parchment; ~**papier** *nt* greaseproof paper.

Pergola [per'gōlà] *f* -, **Pergolen** bower.

Periode [pārēō:'də] *f* -, -n period; **0,33 ~ 0.33** recurring.

periodisch [pārēō:'dish] *a* periodic; (*dezimal*) recurring.

Peripherie [pārēfārē:'] *f* periphery; (*um Stadt*) outskirts *pl*; (*MATH*) circumference; ~**gerät** *nt* (*COMPUT*) peripheral.

Perle [per'lə] *f* -, -n (*lit, fig*) pearl; (*Glas~, Holz~, Tropfen*) bead; (*veraltet umg: Hausgehilfin*) maid.

perlen *vi* sparkle; (*Tropfen*) trickle.

Perlhuhn *nt* guinea fowl.

Perlmutt [perl'moot] *nt* -s mother-of-pearl.

Perlon [per'lon] *nt* -s ® ≈ nylon.

perplex [perpleks'] *a* dumbfounded.

Perser [per'zər] *m* -s, - (*Person*) Persian; (*umg: Teppich*) Persian carpet.

Perserin *f* Persian.

Persianer [perzēå'nər] *m* -s, - Persian lamb (coat).

Persien [per'zēən] *nt* -s Persia.

Persiflage [perzēflà'zhə] *f* -, -n pastiche, sat-

ire (gen, auf +akk on, of).
persisch a Persian; **P~er Golf** Persian Gulf.
Person [perzõ:n'] f -, -en person; (pej: Frau) female; **er ist Mutter und Vater in einer ~** he's mother and father rolled into one; **ich für meine ~** personally I.
Personal [perzõnál'] nt -s personnel; (Bedienung) servants pl; **~abbau** m staff cuts pl; **~akte** f personal file; **~angaben** pl personal information; **~ausweis** m identity card; **~bogen** m personal record; **~büro** nt personnel (department); **~-Computer** m personal computer.
Personalien [perzõná'lēən] pl personal information.
Personalität [perzõnálēte:t'] f personality.
Personalmangel m undermanning.
Personalpronomen nt personal pronoun.
Personalreduzierung f natural wastage.
Personen- zW: **~aufzug** m elevator (US), lift (Brit); **~beschreibung** f (personal) description; **~gedächtnis** nt memory for faces; **~gesellschaft** f partnership; **~kraftwagen** m private motorcar; **~kreis** m group of people; **~kult** m personality cult; **~schaden** m injury to persons; **~waage** f scales pl; **~zug** m stopping train; passenger train.
personifizieren [perzõnēfētsē:'rən] vt personify.
persönlich [perzœn'liċh] a personal ♦ ad in person; personally; (auf Briefen) private (and confidential); **~ haften** (COMM) be personally liable; **P~keit** f personality; **P~keiten des öffentlichen Lebens** public figures.
Perspektive [perspektē:'və] f perspective; **das eröffnet ganz neue ~n für uns** that opens new horizons for us.
Pers. Ref. abk (= Persönlicher Referent) personal representative.
Peru [pārõõ:'] nt -s Peru.
Peruaner(in f) [pārõõá'nər(in)] m -s, - Peruvian.
Perücke [pārü'kə] f -, -n wig.
pervers [pervers'] a perverse.
Perversität [perverzēte:t'] f perversity.
Pessar [pesár'] nt -s, -e pessary; (zur Empfängnisverhütung) cap, diaphragm.
Pessimismus [pesēmis'mõõs] m pessimism.
Pessimist(in f) [pesēmist'(in)] m pessimist; **p~isch** a pessimistic.
Pest [pest] f - plague; **jdn/etw wie die ~ hassen** (umg) loathe (and detest) sb/sth.
Petersilie [pātərzē:'lēə] f parsley.
Petrodollar [pātrõdo'lár] m petrodollar.
Petro(l)chemie [pātrõ:(l)ċhāmē:'] f petrochemistry.
Petroleum [pātrõ:'lāõõm] nt -s kerosene (US), paraffin (Brit).
petzen [pet'sən] vi (umg) tell tales; **der petzt alles** he always tells.
Pf abk = **Pfennig**.
Pfad [pfât] m -(e)s, -e path; **~finder** m Boy

Scout; **er ist bei den ~findern** he's in the (Boy) Scouts; **~finderin** f Girl Guide.
Pfaffe [pfá'fə] m -n, -n (pej) cleric, parson.
Pfahl [pfâl] m -(e)s, ¨e post, stake; **~bau** m pile dwelling.
Pfalz [pfálts] f -, -en (GEOG) Palatinate.
Pfälzer(in f) [pfel'tsər(in)] m -s, - person from the Palatinate.
pfälzisch a Palatine, of the (Rhineland) Palatinate.
Pfand [pfánt] nt -(e)s, ¨er pledge, security; (Flaschen~) deposit; (im Spiel) forfeit; (fig: der Liebe etc) pledge; **~brief** m bond.
pfänden [pfen'dən] vt seize, impound.
Pfänderspiel nt game of forfeits.
Pfand- zW: **~haus** nt pawnshop; **~leiher** m -s, - pawnbroker; **~recht** nt lien; **~schein** m pawn ticket.
Pfändung [pfen'dõõng] f seizure, distraint (form).
Pfanne [pfá'nə] f -, -n (frying) pan; **jdn in die ~ hauen** (umg) bawl sb out.
Pfannkuchen m pancake; (Berliner) donut (US), doughnut (Brit).
Pfarrei [pfárrī'] f parish.
Pfarrer m -s, - priest; (evangelisch) vicar; (von Freikirchen) minister.
Pfarrhaus nt vicarage; manse.
Pfau [pfou] m -(e)s, -en peacock.
Pfauenauge nt peacock butterfly.
Pfd. abk (= Pfund) lb.
Pfeffer [pfe'fər] m -s, - pepper; **er soll bleiben, wo der ~ wächst!** (umg) he can take a running jump; **~korn** nt peppercorn; **~kuchen** m gingerbread; **~minz** nt -es, -e peppermint; **~mühle** f pepper mill.
pfeffern vt pepper; (umg: werfen) fling; **gepfefferte Preise/Witze** steep prices/spicy jokes.
Pfeife [pfī'fə] f -, -n whistle; (Tabak~, Orgel~) pipe; **nach jds ~ tanzen** dance to sb's tune.
pfeifen vti unreg whistle; **auf dem letzten Loch ~** (umg: erschöpft sein) be on one's last legs; (: finanziell) be broke; **ich pfeif(e) drauf!** (umg) I don't give a damn!; **P~stopfer** m tamper.
Pfeifer m -s, - piper.
Pfeifkonzert nt catcalls pl.
Pfeil [pfīl] m -(e)s, -e arrow.
Pfeiler [pfī'lər] m -s, - pillar, prop; (Brücken~) pier.
Pfennig [pfe'niċh] m -(e)s, -e pfennig (hundredth part of a mark); **~absatz** m stiletto heel; **~fuchser** m -s, - (umg) skinflint.
pferchen [pfer'ċhən] vt cram, pack.
Pferd [pfā:rt] nt -(e)s, -e horse; **wie ein ~ arbeiten** (umg) work like a Trojan; **mit ihm kann man ~e stehlen** (umg) he's a great sport; **auf das falsche/richtige ~ setzen** (lit, fig) back the wrong/right horse.
Pferde- [pfā:r'də] zW: **~äpfel** pl horse droppings pl od dung sing; **~fuß** m: **die Sache hat aber einen ~fuß** there's just one snag;

~rennen *nt* horse-race; (*Sportart*) horse-racing; **~schwanz** *m* (*Frisur*) ponytail; **~stall** *m* stable; **~stärke** *f* horsepower.

pfiff [pfif] *imperf von* **pfeifen.**

Pfiff *m* -(e)s, -e whistle; (*Kniff*) trick.

Pfifferling [pfi'fərliŋ] *m* yellow chanterelle; **keinen ~ wert** not worth a thing.

pfiffig *a* sly, sharp.

Pfingsten [pfiŋ'stən] *nt* -, - Whitsun.

Pfingst- *zW:* **~rose** *f* peony; **~sonntag** *m* Whit Sunday, Pentecost (*REL*).

Pfirsich [pfir'ziç] *m* -s, -e peach.

Pflanze [pflån'tsə] *f* -, -n plant.

pflanzen *vt* plant.

Pflanzen- *zW:* **~fett** *nt* vegetable fat; **~schutzmittel** *nt* pesticide.

Pflanzung *f* plantation.

Pflaster [pflå'stər] *nt* -s, - plaster; (*Straßen~*) sidewalk (*US*), pavement (*Brit*); **ein teures ~** (*umg*) a pricey place; **ein heißes ~** a dangerous *od* unsafe place; **p~müde** *a* dead on one's feet.

pflastern *vt* pave.

Pflasterstein *m* paving stone.

Pflaume [pflou'mə] *f* -, -n plum; (*umg: Mensch*) clod (*umg*), nitwit (*umg*).

Pflaumenmus *nt* plum jam.

Pflege [pflä:'gə] *f* -, -n care; (*von Idee*) cultivation; (*Kranken~*) nursing; **jdn/etw in ~ nehmen** look after sb/sth; **in ~ sein** (*Kind*) be fostered out; **p~bedürftig** *a* needing care; **~eltern** *pl* foster parents *pl*; **~fall** *m* case for nursing; **~geld** *nt* (*für ~kinder*) payment to foster parents; (*für Kranke*) attendance allowance; **~kind** *nt* foster child; **p~leicht** *a* easy-care; **~mutter** *f* foster mother.

pflegen *vt* look after; (*Kranke*) nurse; (*Beziehungen*) foster ♦ *vi* (*gewöhnlich tun*): **sie pflegte zu sagen** she used to say.

Pfleger *m* -s, - (*im Krankenhaus*) orderly; (*voll qualifiziert*) male nurse; **~in** *f* nurse.

Pflege- *zW:* **~satz** *m* hospital and nursing charges *pl*; **~vater** *m* foster father.

Pflicht [pfliçt] *f* -, -en duty; (*SPORT*) compulsory section; **Rechte und ~en** rights and responsibilities; **p~bewußt** *a* conscientious; **~bewußtsein** *nt* sense of duty; **~fach** *nt* (*SCH*) compulsory subject; **~gefühl** *nt* sense of duty; **p~gemäß** *a* dutiful ♦ *ad* as in duty bound; **p~vergessen** *a* irresponsible; **~versicherung** *f* compulsory insurance.

Pflock [pflok] *m* -(e)s, ⁿe peg; (*für Tiere*) stake.

pflog [pflō:k] *imperf* (*veraltet*) *von* **pflegen.**

pflücken [pflü'kən] *vt* pick; (*Blumen auch*) pluck.

Pflug [pflōo:k] *m* -(e)s, ⁿe plow (*US*), plough (*Brit*).

pflügen [pflü:'gən] *vt* plow (*US*), plough (*Brit*).

Pflugschar *f* plowshare (*US*), ploughshare (*Brit*).

Pforte [pfor'tə] *f* -, -n (*Tor*) gate.

Pförtner(in *f*) [pfœrt'nər(in)] *m* -s, - porter, doorkeeper, doorman.

Pfosten [pfo'stən] *m* -s, - post; (*senkrechter Balken*) upright.

Pfote [pfō:'tə] *f* -, -n paw; (*umg: Schrift*) scrawl.

Pfropf [pfropf] *m* -(e)s, -e (*Flaschen~*) stopper; (*Blut~*) clot.

pfropfen *vt* (*stopfen*) cram; (*Baum*) graft; **gepfropft voll** crammed full; **P~** *m* -s, -e *siehe* **Pfropf.**

pfui [pfōoi] *interj* ugh!; (*na na*) tut tut; (*Buhruf*) boo!; **~ Teufel** (*umg*) ugh!, yuck!

Pfund [pfōont] *nt* -(e)s, -e (*Gewicht, FIN*) pound; **das ~ sinkt** sterling *od* the pound is falling.

pfundig *a* (*umg*) great.

Pfundskerl [pfōonts'kerl] *m* (*umg*) great guy.

pfundweise *ad* by the pound.

pfuschen [pfōo'shən] *vi* bungle; (*einen Fehler machen*) slip up.

Pfuscher(in *f*) [pfōo'shər(in)] *m* -s, - (*umg*) sloppy worker; (*Kur~*) quack.

Pfuscherei [pfōoshəri'] *f* (*umg*) sloppy work; (*Kur~*) malpractice.

Pfütze [pfü'tsə] *f* -, -n puddle.

PH *f* -, -s *abk* = **Pädagogische Hochschule.**

Phänomen [fenōmä:n'] *nt* -s, -e phenomenon; **p~al** [-nâl'] *a* phenomenal.

Phantasie [fåntåzē:'] *f* imagination; **in seiner ~** in his mind; **~gebilde** *nt* (*Einbildung*) figment of the imagination; **p~los** *a* unimaginative.

phantasieren [fåntåzē:'rən] *vi* fantasize; (*MED*) be delirious.

phantasievoll *a* imaginative.

Phantast [fåntåst'] *m* -en, -en dreamer, visionary.

phantastisch *a* fantastic.

Phantom [fåntō:m'] *nt* -s, -e (*Trugbild*) phantom; **einem ~ nachjagen** (*fig*) tilt at windmills.

Pharisäer [fårēze:'ər] *m* -s, - (*lit, fig*) pharisee.

Pharmazeut(in *f*) [fårmåtsoit'(in)] *m* -en, -en pharmacist.

Pharmazie *f* pharmacy, pharmaceutics *sing.*

Phase [få'zə] *f* -, -n phase.

Philanthrop [fēlåntrō:p'] *m* -en, -en philanthropist; **p~isch** *a* philanthropic.

Philharmoniker [filhårmō:'nēkər] *m* -s, -: **die ~** the philharmonic (orchestra) *sing.*

Philippine [filipē:'nə] *m* -n, -n, **Philippinin** *f* Filipino.

Philippinen *pl* Philippines *pl*, Philippine Islands *pl.*

Philologe [fēlōlō:'gə] *m* -n, -n philologist.

Philologie [fēlōlōgē:'] *f* philology.

Philologin *f* philologist.

Philosoph(in *f*) [fēlōzō:f'(in)] *m* -en, -en philosopher.

Philosophie [fēlōzōfē:'] *f* philosophy.

philosophieren [fēlōzōfē:'rən] *vi* philosophize

(*über* +*akk* about).
philosophisch *a* philosophical.
Phlegma [fleg'má] *nt* -s lethargy.
phlegmatisch [flegmá'tish] *a* lethargic.
Phobie [fōbē:'] *f* phobia (*vor* about).
Phonetik [fōnā:'tik] *f* phonetics *sing*.
phonetisch *a* phonetic.
Phonotypistin [fōnōtüpi'stin] *f* secretary (*using Dictaphone*), audiotypist (*Brit*).
Phosphor [fos'for] *m* -s phosphorus.
phosphoreszieren [fosfōrestsē:'rən] *vt* phosphoresce.
Photo [fō:'tō] *nt* -s, -s *etc* = **Foto** *etc*.
Phrase [frâ'zə] *f* -, -n phrase; (*pej*) hollow phrase; ~**n dreschen** (*umg*) churn out one cliché after another.
Physik [füzē:k'] *f* physics *sing*.
physikalisch [füzēkâ'lish] *a* of physics.
Physiker(in *f)* [fü:'zēkər(in)] *m* -s, - physicist.
Physikum [fü:'zēkōōm] *nt* -s (*UNIV*) *preliminary examination in medicine.*
Physiologe [füzēōlō:'gə] *m* -n, -n, **Physiologin** *f* physiologist.
Physiologie [füzēōlōgē:'] *f* physiology.
physisch [fü:'zish] *a* physical.
Pianist(in *f)* [pēánist'(in)] *m* pianist.
picheln [pi'çhəln] *vi* (*umg*) booze.
Pickel [pi'kəl] *m* -s, - pimple; (*Werkzeug*) pickaxe; (*Berg*~) ice axe.
pick(e)lig *a* pimply.
picken [pi'kən] *vti* peck (*nach* at).
Picknick [pi'knik] *nt* -s, -e *od* -s picnic; ~ **machen** have a picnic.
piekfein [pē:k'fīn'] *a* (*umg*) posh.
Piemont [pēámont'] *nt* -s Piedmont.
piepen [pē:'pən], **piepsen** [pē:p'sən] *vi* chirp; (*Funkgerät etc*) bleep; **bei dir piept's wohl!** (*umg*) are you off your head?; **es war zum P~!** (*umg*) it was a scream.
Piepsstimme *f* squeaky voice.
Pier [pē:ər] *m* -s, -s *od* -e jetty, pier.
piesacken [pē:'zákən] *vt* (*umg*) torment.
Pietät [pēáte:t'] *f* piety; reverence; **p~los** *a* impious, irreverent.
Pigment [pigment'] *nt* -(e)s, -e pigment.
Pik [pē:k] *nt* -s, -s (*KARTEN*) spades; **einen ~ auf jdn haben** (*umg*) have it in for sb.
pikant [pēkánt'] *a* spicy, piquant; (*anzüglich*) suggestive.
Pike *f* -, -n: **etw von der ~ auf lernen** (*fig*) learn sth from the bottom up.
pikiert [pēkē:rt'] *a* offended.
Pikkolo [pi'kōlō] *m* -s, -s trainee waiter; (*auch*: ~**flasche**) *quarter bottle of champagne*; (*MUS auch*: ~**flöte**) piccolo.
Piktogramm [piktōgrám'] *nt* pictogram.
Pilger(in *f)* [pil'gər(in)] *m* -s, - pilgrim; ~**fahrt** *f* pilgrimage.
pilgern *vi* make a pilgrimage; (*umg*: *gehen*) wend one's way.
Pille [pi'lə] *f* -, -n pill.
Pilot(in *f)* [pēlō:t'(in)] *m* -en, -en pilot.
Pils [pils] *nt* -, -, **Pils(e)ner** [pilz(ə)nər] *nt* -s, - Pilsner (lager).

Pilz [pilts] *m* -es, -e fungus; (*eßbar*) mushroom; (*giftig*) toadstool; **wie** ~**e aus dem Boden schießen** (*fig*) mushroom; ~**krankheit** *f* fungal disease.
Pimmel [pi'məl] *m* -s, - (*umg*: *Penis*) dick (*umg*), peter (*umg*).
pingelig [pi'ngəliçh] *a* (*umg*) fussy.
Pinguin [ping'gōōē:n] *m* -s, -e penguin.
Pinie [pē:'nēə] *f* pine.
Pinkel *m* -s, - (*umg*): **ein feiner** *od* **vornehmer** ~ a swell.
pinkeln [ping'kəln] *vi* (*umg*) pee.
Pinsel [pin'zəl] *m* -s, - paintbrush.
pinseln *vti* (*umg*) paint; (*pej*: *malen*) daub.
Pinte [pin'tə] *f* -, -n (*umg*: *Lokal*) bar.
Pinzette [pintse'tə] *f* tweezers *pl*.
Pionier [pēōnē:r'] *m* -s, -e pioneer; (*MIL*) sapper, engineer; ~**unternehmen** *nt* pioneer company.
Pipi [pēpē:'] *nt od m* -s, -s (*Kindersprache*) wee(-wee).
Pirat [pērât'] *m* -en, -en pirate.
Piratensender *m* pirate radio station.
Pirsch [pirsh] *f* - stalking.
pissen [pi'sən] *vi* (*umg!*) (have a) piss (!); (: *regnen*) piss down (!).
Pistazie [pistá'tsēə] *f* -, -n pistachio.
Piste [pi'stə] *f* -, -n (*SKI*) run, piste; (*AVIAT*) runway.
Pistole [pistō:'lə] *f* -, -n pistol; **wie aus der ~ geschossen** (*fig*) like a shot; **jdm die ~ auf die Brust setzen** (*fig*) hold a pistol to sb's head.
pitsch(e)naß [pitsh'(ə)nás'] *a* (*umg*) soaking (wet).
Pizza [pi'tsá] *f* -, -s pizza.
Pkw, PKW *m* -(s), -(s) *abk* = **Personenkraftwagen**.
pl., Pl. *abk* (= *Plural*) pl.
Pl. *abk* (= *Platz*) Sq.
Plackerei [plákəri'] *f* drudgery.
plädieren [pledē:'rən] *vi* plead.
Plädoyer [pledōáyā:'] *nt* -s, -s summing-up for the defense; (*fig*) plea.
Plage [plâ'gə] *f* -, -n plague; (*Mühe*) nuisance; ~**geist** *m* pest, nuisance.
plagen *vt* torment ♦ *vr* toil, slave.
Plagiat [plágēát'] *nt* plagiarism.
Plakat [plákât'] *nt* -(e)s, -e poster; (*aus Pappe*) placard.
plakativ [plákátē:f'] *a* striking, bold.
Plakatwand *f* hoarding, billboard.
Plakette [pláke'tə] *f* -, -n (*Abzeichen*) badge; (*Münze*) commemorative coin; (*an Wänden*) plaque.
Plan [plân] *m* -(e)s, ˜e plan; (*Karte*) map; ˜**e schmieden** make plans; **nach** ~ **verlaufen** go according to plan; **jdn auf den** ~ **rufen** (*fig*) bring sb into the arena.
Plane *f* -, -n tarpaulin.
planen *vt* plan; (*Mord etc*) plot.
Planer(in *f)* *m* -s, - planner.
Planet [plánā:t'] *m* -en -en planet.
Planetenbahn *f* orbit (of a planet).

planieren [planē:'rən] *vt* level off.
Planierraupe *f* bulldozer.
Planke [plång'kə] *f* -, **-n** plank.
Plänkelei [plengkəlī'] *f* skirmish(ing).
plänkeln [pleng'kəln] *vi* skirmish.
Plankton [plångk'ton] *nt* **-s** plankton.
Plan- *zW*: **p~los** *a* (*Vorgehen*) unsystematic; (*Umherlaufen*) aimless; **p~mäßig** *a* according to plan; (*methodisch*) systematic; (*EISENB*) scheduled.
Planschbecken [plånsh'bekən] *nt* wading (*US*) *od* paddling pool (*Brit*).
planschen *vi* splash.
Plan- *zW*: **~soll** *nt* output target; **~stelle** *f* post.
Plantage [plåntá'zhə] *f* -, **-n** plantation.
Planung *f* planning.
Plan- *zW*: **~wagen** *m* covered wagon; **~wirtschaft** *f* planned economy.
Plappermaul *nt* (*umg*: *Kind*) chatterbox.
plappern [plå'pərn] *vi* chatter.
plärren [ple'rən] *vi* (*Mensch*) cry, whine; (*Radio*) blare.
Plasma [plås'må] *nt* **-s, Plasmen** plasma.
Plastik [plås'stik] *f* sculpture ♦ *nt* **-s** (*Kunststoff*) plastic; **~folie** *f* plastic film; **~mensch** *m* (*umg*) somebody showing little emotion.
Plastilin [plåstēlē:n'] *nt* **-s** Plasticine ®.
plastisch [plås'stish] *a* plastic; **stell dir das ~ vor!** just picture it!
Platane [plåtá'nə] *f* -, **-n** plane (tree).
Platin [plå'tē:n] *nt* **-s** platinum.
Platitüde [plåtētü:'də] *f* -, **-n** platitude.
platonisch [plåtō:'nish] *a* platonic.
platsch [plåtsh] *interj* splash!
platschen *vi* splash.
plätschern [plet'shərn] *vi* babble.
platschnaß *a* drenched.
platt [plåt] *a* flat; (*umg*: *überrascht*) flabbergasted; (*fig*: *geistlos*) flat, boring; **einen P~en haben** (*umg*) have a flat.
plattdeutsch *a* Low German.
Platte *f* -, **-n** (*Speisen~, PHOT, TECH*) plate; (*Stein~*) flag; (*Kachel*) tile; (*Schall~*) record; **kalte ~** cold dish; **die ~ kenne ich schon** (*umg*) I've heard all that before.
Plätt- [plet'] *zW*: **~eisen** *nt* iron; **p~en** *vti* iron.
Platten- *zW*: **~leger** *m* **-s, -** paver; **~spieler** *m* record player; **~teller** *m* turntable.
Platt- *zW*: **~form** *f* platform; (*fig*: *Grundlage*) basis; **~fuß** *m* flat foot; (*Reifen*) flat.
Platz [plåts] *m* **-es, ¨e** place; (*Sitz~*) seat; (*Raum*) space, room; (*in Stadt*) square; (*Sport~*) playing field; **jdm ~ machen** make room for sb; **~ nehmen** take a seat; **~ machen** get out of the way; **auf ~ zwei** in second place; **fehl am ~e sein** be out of place; **seinen ~ behaupten** stand one's ground; **das erste Hotel am ~** the best hotel in town; **auf die ¨e, fertig, los!** (*beim Sport*) on your marks, get set, go!; **einen Spieler vom ~ stellen** *od* **verweisen** (*SPORT*) send a player off; **~angst** *f* (*MED*) agoraphobia; (*umg*) claustrophobia; **~anweiser(in** *f*) *m* **-s, -** usher(ette).
Plätzchen [plets'chən] *nt* spot; (*Gebäck*) cookie (*US*), biscuit (*Brit*).
platzen *vi* *aux sein* burst; (*Bombe*) explode; (*Naht, Hose, Haut*) split; (*umg*: *scheitern*: *Geschäft*) fall through; (: *Freundschaft*) break up; (: *Theorie, Verschwörung*) collapse; (*umg*: *Wechsel*) bounce; **vor Wut ~** (*umg*) be bursting with anger.
Platz- *zW*: **~karte** *f* seat reservation; **~konzert** *nt* open-air concert; **~mangel** *m* lack of space; **~patrone** *f* blank cartridge; **~regen** *m* downpour; **~verweis** *m* sending-off; **~wart** *m* (*SPORT*) groundsman; **~wunde** *f* cut.
Plauderei [ploudərī'] *f* chat, conversation; (*RAD*) talk.
plaudern [plou'dərn] *vi* chat, talk.
Plausch [ploush] *m* **-(e)s, -e** (*umg*) chat.
plausibel [plouzē:'bəl] *a* plausible.
Playback [plā:'bek] *nt* **-s, -s** (*Verfahren*: *Schallplatte*) double-tracking; (*TV*) miming.
plazieren [plåtsē:'rən] *vt* place ♦ *vr* (*SPORT*) be placed; (*TENNIS*) be seeded; (*umg*: *sich setzen, stellen*) plant o.s.
Plebejer(in *f*) [plābā:'yər(in)] *m* **-s, -** plebeian.
plebejisch [plābā:'yish] *a* plebeian.
pleite [plī'tə] *a* (*umg*) broke; **P~** *f* -, **-n** bankruptcy; (*umg*: *Reinfall*) flop; **P~ machen** go bust.
Pleitegeier *m* (*umg*: *drohende Pleite*) vulture; (*Bankrotteur*) bankrupt.
plemplem [plemplem'] *a* (*umg*) nuts.
Plenarsitzung [plānár'zitsōōng] *f* plenary session.
Plenum [plā:'nōōm] *nt* **-s, Plenen** plenum.
Pleuelstange [ploi'əlshtångə] *f* connecting rod.
Plissee [plisā:'] *nt* **-s, -s** pleat.
Plombe [plom'bə] *f* -, **-n** lead seal; (*Zahn~*) filling.
plombieren [plombē:'rən] *vt* seal; (*Zahn*) fill.
Plotter [plo'tər] *m* **-s, -s** (*COMPUT*) plotter.
plötzlich [plēts'lich] *a* sudden ♦ *ad* suddenly.
Pluderhose [plōō:'dərhō:zə] *f* harem trousers *pl*.
plump [plōōmp] *a* clumsy; (*Hände*) coarse; (*Körper*) shapeless; **~e Annäherungsversuche** very obvious advances.
plumpsen *vi* (*umg*) plump down, fall.
Plunder [plōōn'dər] *m* **-s** junk.
Plundergebäck *nt* French (*US*) *od* flaky (*Brit*) pastry.
plündern [plün'dərn] *vti* plunder; (*Stadt*) sack.
Plünderung [plün'dərōōng] *f* plundering, sack, pillage.
Plural [plōō:'rål] *m* **-s, -e** plural; **im ~ stehen** be (in the) plural.
pluralistisch [plōōráli'stish] *a* pluralistic.
plus [plōōs] *ad* plus; **P~** *nt* -, - plus; (*FIN*) profit; (*Vorteil*) advantage.

Plüsch [plü:sh] *m* -(e)s, -e plush; ~**tier** *nt* ≈ soft toy.

plus-minus-null *ad*: ~ **abschließen** (*COMM*) break even.

Plus- *zW*: ~**pol** *m* (*ELEK*) positive pole; ~**punkt** *m* (*SPORT*) point; (*fig*) point in sb's favour; ~**quamperfekt** *nt* pluperfect.

Plutonium [plōōtō:'nēōōm] *nt* -s plutonium.

PLZ *abk* = **Postleitzahl**.

Pneu [pnoi] *m* -s, -s *abk* (= *Pneumatik*) tire (*US*), tyre (*Brit*).

Po [pō:] *m* -s, -s (*umg*) bottom, ass.

Pöbel [pœ'bəl] *m* -s mob, rabble.

Pöbelei [pœbəlī'] *f* vulgarity.

pöbelhaft *a* low, vulgar.

pochen [po'Khən] *vi* knock; (*Herz*) pound; **auf etw** (*akk*) ~ (*fig*) insist on sth.

Pocken [po'kən] *pl* smallpox.

Pocken(schutz)impfung *f* smallpox vaccination.

Podest [podest'] *nt od m* -(e)s, -e (*Sockel*) pedestal (*auch fig*); (*Podium*) platform.

Podium [pō:'dēōōm] *nt* podium.

Podiumsdiskussion *f* panel discussion.

Poesie [pōāzē:'] *f* poetry.

Poet [pōā:t'] *m* -en, -en poet; **p~isch** *a* poetic.

pofen [pō:'fən] *vi* (*umg*) sleep.

Pointe [pōań:'tə] *f* -, -n point; (*eines Witzes*) punch line.

pointiert [pōańtē:rt'] *a* trenchant, pithy.

Pokal [pōkál'] *m* -s, -e goblet; (*SPORT*) cup; ~**spiel** *nt* cup competition (*US*) *od* tie (*Brit*).

Pökelfleisch [pœ'kəlflīsh] *nt* salt meat.

pökeln *vt* (*Fleisch, Fisch*) pickle, salt.

pokern [pō:'kərn] *vi* play poker.

pol. *abk* = **politisch; polizeilich**.

Pol [pō:l] *m* -s, -e pole; **der ruhende** ~ (*fig*) the calming influence.

Pol. *abk* = **Polizei**.

polar [pōlár'] *a* polar.

polarisieren [pōlárēzē:'rən] *vtr* polarize.

Polarkreis *m* polar circle.

Pole [pō:'lə] *m* -n, -n Pole.

Polemik [pōlā:'mik] *f* polemics *sing*.

polemisch *a* polemical.

polemisieren [pōlāmēzē:'rən] *vi* polemicize.

Polen [pō:'lən] *nt* -s Poland.

Polente *f* - (*veraltet umg*) cops *pl*.

Police [pōlē:s'(ə)] *f* -, -n insurance policy.

Polier [pōlē:r'] *m* -s, -e foreman.

polieren *vt* polish.

Poliklinik [pōlēklē:'nik] *f* outpatients dept.

Polin *f* Pole, Polish woman.

Politesse [pōlēte'sə] *f* -, -n (*Frau*) ≈ meter maid (*US*), ≈ traffic warden (*Brit*).

Politik [pōlētē:k'] *f* politics *sing*; (*eine bestimmte*) policy; **in die** ~ **gehen** go into politics; **eine** ~ **verfolgen** pursue a policy.

Politiker(in *f*) [pōlē:'tēkər(in)] *m* -s, - politician.

politisch [pōlē:'tish] *a* political.

politisieren [pōlētēzē:'rən] *vi* talk politics ♦

vt politicize; **jdn** ~ make sb politically aware.

Politur [pōlētōō:r'] *f* polish.

Polizei [pōlētsī'] *f* police; ~**aufsicht** *f*: **unter** ~**aufsicht stehen** have to report regularly to the police; ~**beamte(r)** *m* police officer; **p~lich** *a* police *attr*; **sich p~lich melden** register with the police; **p~liches Führungszeugnis** *certificate issued by the police, stating that the holder has no criminal record*; ~**präsidium** *nt* police headquarters *pl*; ~**revier** *nt* police station; ~**spitzel** *m* police spy *od* informer; ~**staat** *m* police state; ~**streife** *f* police patrol; ~**stunde** *f* closing time; ~**wache** *f* police station; **p~widrig** *a* illegal.

Polizist [pōlētsist'] *m* -en, -en policeman.

Polizistin *f* policewoman.

Pollen [po'lən] *m* -s, - pollen.

poln. *abk* = **polnisch**.

polnisch [pol'nish] *a* Polish.

Polohemd [pō:'lōhemt] *nt* sports *od* polo shirt; (*für Frau*) casual blouse.

Polster [pol'stər] *nt* -s, - cushion; (*Polsterung*) upholstery; (*in Kleidung*) padding; (*fig: Geld*) reserves *pl*; ~**er** *m* -s, - upholsterer; ~**garnitur** *f* three-piece suite; ~**möbel** *pl* upholstered furniture.

polstern *vt* upholster; (*Kleidung*) pad; **sie ist gut gepolstert** (*umg*) she's well-padded; (: *finanziell*) she's well-heeled.

Polsterung *f* upholstery.

Polterabend [pol'tərâbənt] *m* party on eve of wedding.

poltern *vi* (*Krach machen*) crash; (*schimpfen*) rant.

Polygamie [pōlügámē:'] *f* polygamy.

Polynesien [pōlünä:'zēən] *nt* -s Polynesia.

Polyp [pōlü:p'] *m* -en -en polyp; (*pl*: *MED*) adenoids *pl*; (*umg*) cop.

Polytechnikum [pōlüteċh'nēkōōm] *nt* -s, -**Polytechnika** polytechnic, poly (*umg*).

Pomade [pōmá'də] *f* hair cream.

Pommern [po'mərn] *nt* -s Pomerania.

Pommes frites [pomfrit'] *pl* French fries *pl*.

Pomp [pomp] *m* -(e)s pomp.

pompös [pompœs'] *a* grandiose.

Pontius [pon'tsēōōs] *m*: **von** ~ **zu Pilatus** from pillar to post.

Pony [po'nē] *m* -s, -s (*Frisur*) bangs *pl* (*US*), fringe (*Brit*) ♦ *nt* -s, -s (*Pferd*) pony.

Pop [pop] *m* -s (*MUS*) pop; (*KUNST*) pop art.

Popelin [pōpəlē:n'] *m* -s, -e poplin.

Popeline *f* -, -n poplin.

Popo [pōpō:'] *m* -s, -s (*umg*) bottom, ass.

populär [pōpōōlɛ:r'] *a* popular.

Popularität [pōpōōlárēte:t'] *f* popularity.

populärwissenschaftlich *a* popular science.

Pore [po:'rə] *f* -, -n pore.

Pornographie [pornōgráfē:'] *f* pornography.

porös [pōrœs'] *a* porous.

Porree [po'rā] *m* -s, -s leek.

Portal [portál'] *nt* -s, -e portal.

Portefeuille [port(ə)fœy'] *nt* -s, -s (*POL, FIN*) portfolio.

Portemonnaie [portmone:'] *nt* -s, -s purse.

Portier [portēā:'] *m* -s, -s porter; = **Pförtner.**

Portion [portsēō:n'] *f* portion, helping; (*umg: Anteil*) amount; **eine halbe** ~ (*fig umg: Person*) a half-pint; **eine** ~ **Kaffee** a pot of coffee.

Porto [por'tō] *nt* -s, -s *od* **Porti** postage; ~ **zahlt Empfänger** postage paid; **p~frei** *a* (postage) prepaid.

Porträt [portre:'] *nt* -s, -s portrait.

porträtieren [portretē:'rən] *vt* paint (a portrait of), portray.

Portugal [por'tōōgál] *nt* -s Portugal.

Portugiese [portōōgē:'zə] *m* -n, -n, **Portugiesin** *f* Portuguese.

portugiesisch *a* Portuguese.

Portwein [port'vīn] *m* port.

Porzellan [portselán'] *nt* -s, -e china, porcelain; (*Geschirr*) china.

Posaune [pōzou'nə] *f* -, -n trombone; (*fig*) trumpet.

Pose [pō:'zə] *f* -, -n pose.

posieren [pōzē:'rən] *vi* pose.

Position [pōzētsēō:n'] *f* position; (*COMM: auf Liste*) item.

Positionslichter *pl* navigation lights *pl*.

positiv [pō:'zētē:f] *a* positive; ~ **zu etw stehen** be in favor of sth; **P~** *nt* -s, -e (*PHOT*) positive.

Positur [pōzētōō:r'] *f* posture, attitude; **sich in** ~ **setzen** *od* **stellen** adopt a posture.

Posse [po'sə] *f* -, -n farce.

possessiv [po'sesē:f] *a* possessive; **P~(pronomen)** *nt* -s, -e possessive pronoun.

possierlich [posē:r'liċh] *a* funny.

Post [post] *f* -, -en post (office); (*Briefe*) mail; **ist** ~ **für mich da?** are there any letters for me?; **mit getrennter** ~ under separate cover; **etw auf die** ~ **geben** mail *od* post (*Brit*) sth; **auf die** *od* **zur** ~ **gehen** go to the post office; **~amt** *nt* post office; **~anweisung** *f* money order; **~bote** *m* mailman (*US*), postman (*Brit*).

Posten *m* -s, - post, position; (*COMM*) item; (: *Warenmenge*) quantity, lot; (*auf Liste*) entry; (*MIL*) sentry; (*Streik~*) picket; ~ **beziehen** take up one's post; **nicht ganz auf dem** ~ **sein** (*nicht gesund sein*) be off-color.

Poster [po'stər] *nt* -s, -(s) poster.

Postf. *abk* (= *Postfach*) PO Box.

Post- *zW*: **~fach** *nt* post office box; **~karte** *f* postcard; **p~lagernd** *ad* general delivery (*US*), poste restante (*Brit*); **~leitzahl** *f* zip code (*US*), post code (*Brit*).

postmodern [postmōdern'] *a* post-modern.

Post- *zW*: **~scheckkonto** *nt* Post Office account; **~sparkasse** *f* post office savings bank; **~stempel** *m* postmark; **p~wendend** *ad* by return mail (*US*), by return (of post) (*Brit*); **~wertzeichen** *nt* (*form*) postage stamp; **~wurfsendung** *f* postal door-to-door delivery.

potent [pōtent'] *a* potent; (*fig*) high-powered.

Potential [pōtentsēál'] *nt* -s, -e potential.

potentiell [pōtentsēel'] *a* potential.

Potenz [pōtents'] *f* power; (*eines Mannes*) potency.

potenzieren [pōtentsē:'rən] *vt* (*MATH*) raise to the power of.

Potpourri [pot'pōōrē] *nt* -s, -s (*MUS*) medley (*aus* +*dat* of); (*fig*) assortment.

Pott [pot] *m* -(e)s, -̈e (*umg*) pot; **p~häßlich** *a* (*umg*) ugly as sin.

pp., ppa. *abk* (= *per procura*) p.p.

Präambel [preám'bəl] *f* -, -n preamble (*gen* to).

Pracht [práḱht] *f* - splendor (*US*), splendour (*Brit*), magnificence; **es ist eine wahre** ~ it's (really) magnificent; **~exemplar** *nt* beauty (*umg*); (*fig: Mensch*) fine specimen.

prächtig [preċh'tiċh] *a* splendid.

Pracht- *zW*: **~stück** *nt* showpiece; **p~voll** *a* splendid, magnificent.

prädestinieren [predestēnē:'rən] *vt* predestine.

Prädikat [predēkát'] *nt* -(e)s, -e title; (*GRAM*) predicate; (*Zensur*) distinction; **Wein mit** ~ special quality wine.

Prag [prák] *nt* -s Prague.

prägen [pre:'gən] *vt* stamp; (*Münze*) mint; (*Ausdruck*) coin; (*Charakter*) form; (*kennzeichnen: Stadtbild*) characterize; **das Erlebnis prägte ihn** the experience left its mark on him.

prägend *a* forming *od* shaping in influence.

pragmatisch [prágmá'tish] *a* pragmatic.

prägnant [pregnánt'] *a* concise, terse.

Prägnanz *f* conciseness, terseness.

Prägung [pre:'gōōng] *f* minting; forming; (*Eigenart*) character, stamp.

prahlen [prá'lən] *vi* boast, brag.

Prahlerei [prálərī'] *f* boasting.

prahlerisch *a* boastful.

Praktik [prák'tik] *f* practice.

praktikabel [práktiká'bəl] *a* practicable.

Praktikant(in *f***)** [práktikánt'(in)] *m* trainee.

Praktikum *nt* -s, **Praktika** *od* **Praktiken** practical training.

praktisch [prák'tish] *a* practical, handy; **~er Arzt** general practitioner; **~es Beispiel** concrete example.

praktizieren [práktētsē:'rən] *vti* practice (*US*), practise (*Brit*).

Praline [prálē:'nə] *f* chocolate.

prall [prál] *a* firmly rounded; (*Segel*) taut; (*Arme*) plump; (*Sonne*) blazing.

prallen *vi* bounce, rebound; (*Sonne*) blaze.

prallvoll *a* full to bursting; (*Brieftasche*) bulging.

Prämie [pre:'mēə] *f* premium; (*Belohnung*) award, prize.

prämien- *zW*: **~begünstigt** *a* with benefit of premiums; **~sparen** *vi* save in a bonus scheme.

prämieren [premē:'rən] *vt* give an award to.

Pranger [prá'ngər] *m* -s, - (*HIST*) pillory; **jdn**

an den ~ stellen (*fig*) pillory sb.
Pranke |pràng'kə| *f* -, **-n** (*Tier*~, *umg*: *Hand*) paw.
Präparat |prepárát'| *nt* -(e)s, **-e** (*BIOL*) preparation; (*MED*) medicine.
präparieren *vt* (*konservieren*) preserve; (*MED*: *zerlegen*) dissect.
Präposition |prepōzētsēō:n'| *f* preposition.
Prärie |prcrē:'| *f* prairie.
Präs. *abk* = **Präsens; Präsident.**
Präsens |prc:'zens| *nt* - present tense.
präsent *a*: **etw ~ haben** have sth at hand.
präsentieren |prezentē:'rən| *vt* present.
Präsenzbibliothek *f* reference library.
Präservativ |prezervátē:f'| *nt* -s, **-e** contraceptive.
Präsident(in *f*) |prezēdent'(in)| *m* president; **~schaft** *f* presidency; **~schaftskandidat** *m* presidential candidate.
Präsidium |prezē:'dēōōm| *nt* presidency, chairmanship; (*Polizei*~) police headquarters *pl*.
prasseln |prà'səln| *vi* (*Feuer*) crackle; (*Hagel*) drum; (*Wörter*) rain down.
prassen |prà'sən| *vi* live it up.
Präteritum |pretä:'rētōōm| *nt* -s, **Präterita** preterite.
Pratze |prà'tsə| *f* -, **-n** paw.
Präventiv- |preventē:f'| *in zW* preventive.
Praxis |pràk'sis| *f* -, **Praxen** practice; (*Erfahrung*) experience; (*Behandlungsraum*) doctor's office (*US*), surgery (*Brit*); (*von Anwalt*) office; **die ~ sieht anders aus** the reality is different; **ein Beispiel aus der ~** an example from real life.
Präzedenzfall |pretsā:dents'fál| *m* precedent.
präzis |pretsē:s'| *a* precise.
Präzision |pretsēzēō:n'| *f* precision.
PR-Chef *m* -s, **-s** PR officer.
predigen |prä:'digən| *vti* preach.
Prediger *m* -s, - preacher.
Predigt |prä:'diçht| *f* -, **-en** sermon.
Preis |prīs| *m* -es, **-e** price; (*Sieges*~) prize; (*Auszeichnung*) award; **~ pro Maßeinheit** unit price; **um keinen ~** not at any price; **~angebot** *nt* quotation; **~ausschreiben** *nt* competition; **~bindung** *f* price fixing; **~brecher** *m* (*Firma*) undercutter.
Preiselbeere *f* cranberry.
preisempfindlich *a* price-sensitive.
preisen |prī'zən| *vt unreg* praise; **sich glücklich ~** (*geh*) count o.s. lucky.
Preis- *zW*: **~entwicklung** *f* price trend; **~frage** *f* question of price; (*Wettbewerb*) prize question.
preisgeben *vt unreg* abandon; (*opfern*) sacrifice; (*zeigen*) expose.
Preis- *zW*: **~gefälle** *nt* price gap; **p~gekrönt** *a* prize-winning; **~gericht** *nt* jury; **p~günstig** *a* inexpensive; **~index** *m* price index; **~krieg** *m* price war; **~lage** *f* price range; **p~lich** *a* price, in price; **~liste** *f* price list, tariff; **~nachlaß** *m* discount; **~schild** *nt* price tag; **~spanne** *f* price

range; **~sturz** *m* slump; **~träger** *m* prizewinner; **p~wert** *a* inexpensive.
prekär |prāke:r'| *a* precarious.
Prellbock |prel'bok| *m* buffers *pl*.
prellen *vt* bump; (*fig*) cheat, swindle.
Prellung *f* bruise.
Premiere |prəmēē:'rə| *f* -, **-n** premiere.
Premierminister(in *f*) |prəmiä:'ministər(in)| *m* prime minister, premier.
Presse |prc'sə| *f* -, **-n** press; **~erklärung** *f* press release; **~freiheit** *f* freedom of the press; **~konferenz** *f* press conference; **~meldung** *f* press report.
pressen *vt* press.
Presse- *zW*: **~stelle** *f* press office; **~verlautbarung** *f* press release.
pressieren |presē:'rən| *vi* (be in a) hurry; **es pressiert** it's urgent.
Preßluft |pres'lōōft| *f* compressed air; **~bohrer** *m* pneumatic drill.
Prestige |prestē:'zhə| *nt* -s prestige; **~verlust** *m* loss of prestige.
Preuße |proi'sə| *m* -n, **-n**, **Preußin** *f* Prussian.
Preußen *nt* -s Prussia.
preußisch *a* Prussian.
prickeln |pri'kəln| *vti* tingle, tickle; (*Bläschen bilden*) sparkle, bubble.
pries |prē:s| *imperf von* **preisen.**
Priester |prē:'stər| *m* -s, - priest.
Priesterin *f* priestess.
Priesterweihe *f* ordination (to the priesthood).
prima |prē:'má| *a inv* first-class, excellent.
Prima *f* -, **Primen** *eighth and ninth year of German high school.*
primär |prēme:r'| *a* primary; **P~daten** *pl* primary data.
Primel |prē:'məl| *f* -, **-n** primrose.
primitiv |prēmētē:f'| *a* primitive.
Primzahl |prē:m'tsál| *f* prime (number).
Prinz |prints| *m* -en, **-en** prince.
Prinzessin |printse'sin| *f* princess.
Prinzip |printsē:p'| *nt* -s, **-ien** principle; **aus ~** on principle; **im ~** in principle.
prinzipiell |printsēpē'el| *a* on principle.
prinzipienlos *a* unprincipled.
Priorität |prēōrēte:t'| *f* priority; **~en** *pl* (*COMM*) preferred stock (*US*), preference shares *pl* (*Brit*); **~en setzen** establish one's priorities.
Prise |prē:'zə| *f* -, **-n** pinch.
Prisma |pris'má| *nt* -s, **Prismen** prism.
privat |prēvát'| *a* private; **jdn ~ sprechen** speak to sb in private; **P~** *in zW* private; **P~besitz** *m* private property; **P~dozent** *m* outside lecturer; **P~gespräch** *nt* private conversation; (*am Telefon*) private call.
privatisieren |prēvátēzē:'rən| *vt* privatize.
Privatwirtschaft *f* private industry.
Priv. Doz. *abk* = **Privatdozent.**
Privileg |prēvēlā:k'| *nt* -(e)s, **-ien** privilege.
pro |prō:| *präp* +*akk* per; **~ Stück** each, apiece.
Pro *nt* - pro.

Probe [prō:'bə] ƒ -, -n test; (Teststück) sample; (THEAT) rehearsal; **jdn auf die ~ stellen** put sb to the test; **er ist auf ~ angestellt** he's employed for a probationary period; **zur ~** to try out; **~bohrung** ƒ (Öl) exploration well; **~exemplar** nt specimen copy; **~fahrt** ƒ test drive; **~lauf** m trial run.
proben vt try; (THEAT) rehearse.
Probe- zW: **~stück** nt specimen; **p~weise** ad on approval; **~zeit** ƒ probationary period.
probieren [prōbē:'rən] vti try; (Wein, Speise) taste, sample.
Problem [prōblā:m'] nt -s, -e problem; **vor einem ~ stehen** be faced with a problem.
Problematik [prōblā:mâ'tik] ƒ problem.
problematisch [prōblā:mâ'tish] a problematic.
Problem- zW: **p~los** a problem-free; **~stellung** ƒ way of looking at a problem.
Produkt [prōdōōkt'] nt -(e)s, -e product; (AGR) produce no pl.
Produktion [prōdōōktsēō:n'] ƒ production.
Produktions- zW: **~manager** m production manager; **~stätte** ƒ (Halle) shop floor.
produktiv [prōdōōktē:f'] a productive.
Produktivität [prōdōōktēvētе:t'] ƒ productivity.
Produzent [prōdōōtsent'] m manufacturer; (FILM) producer.
produzieren [prōdōōtsē:'rən] vt produce ♦ vr show off.
Prof. [prōf] abk (= Professor) Prof.
profan [prōfân'] a (weltlich) secular, profane; (gewöhnlich) mundane.
professionell [prōfesēōnel'] a professional.
Professor(in ƒ) [prōfe'sor(in)] m professor; (Österreich: Gymnasiallehrer) high school teacher.
Professur [prōfesōō:r'] ƒ professorship (für in, of).
Profi [prō:'fē] m -s, -s abk (= Professional) pro.
Profil [prōfē:l'] nt -s, -e profile; (fig) image; (Querschnitt) cross section; (Längsschnitt) vertical section; (von Reifen, Schuhsohle) tread.
profilieren [prōfēlē:'rən] vr create an image for o.s.
Profilsohle ƒ sole with a tread.
Profit [prōfē:t'] m -(e)s, -e profit.
profitieren [prōfētē:'rən] vi profit (von from).
Profitmacherei ƒ (umg) profiteering.
pro forma ad as a matter of form.
Pro-forma-Rechnung ƒ pro forma invoice.
Prognose [prōgnō:'zə] ƒ -, -n prediction, prognosis.
Programm [prōgrám'] nt -s, -e program (US), programme (Brit); (COMPUT) program; (TV: Sender) channel; (Kollektion) range; **nach ~** as planned; **p~(m)äßig** a according to plan; **~fehler** m (COMPUT) bug; **~hinweis** m (RAD, TV) program announcement.
programmieren [prōgrámē:'rən] vt program

(US), programme (Brit); **auf etw** (akk) **programmiert sein** (fig) be geared to sth.
Programmierer(in ƒ) m -s, - programmer.
Programmiersprache ƒ (COMPUT) programing language.
programmiert a: **~er Unterricht** programmed instruction.
Programmierung ƒ (COMPUT) programing (US), programming (Brit).
Programmvorschau ƒ preview (für of); (FILM) trailer.
progressiv [prōgresē:f'] a progressive.
Projekt [prōyekt'] nt -(e)s, -e project.
Projektleiter(in ƒ) m project manager(ess).
Projektor [prōyek'tor] m projector.
projizieren [prōyētsē:'rən] vt project.
proklamieren [prōklámē:'rən] vt proclaim.
Pro-Kopf-Einkommen nt per capita income.
Prokura [prōkōō:'rà] ƒ -, **Prokuren** (form) power of attorney.
Prokurist(in ƒ) [prōkōōrist'(in)] m attorney.
Prolet [prōlā:t'] m -en, -en prole, pleb.
Proletariat [prōlätárēât'] nt -(e)s, -e proletariat.
Proletarier [prōlätá'rēər] m -s, - proletarian.
Prolog [prōlō:k'] m -(e)s, -e prolog (US), prologue (Brit).
Promenade [prōmənâ'də] ƒ -, -n promenade.
Promenadenmischung ƒ (hum) mongrel.
Promille [prōmi'lä] nt -(s), - alcohol level.
prominent [prōmēnent'] a prominent.
Prominenz [prōmēnents'] ƒ VIPs pl.
Promoter [prōmō:'tər] m -s, - promoter.
Promotion [prōmōtsēō:n'] ƒ doctorate, Ph.D.
promovieren [prōmōvē:'rən] vi receive a doctorate etc.
prompt [prompt] a prompt.
Pronomen [prōnō:'men] nt -s, - pronoun.
Propaganda [prōpágán'dà] ƒ - propaganda.
propagieren [prōpágē:'rən] vt propagate.
Propangas [prōpán'gâs] nt propane gas.
Propeller [prōpe'lər] m -s, - propeller.
proper [pro'pər] a (umg) neat, tidy.
Prophet [prōfā:t'] m -en, -en prophet.
Prophetin ƒ prophetess.
prophezeien [prōfâtsī'ən] vt prophesy.
Prophezeiung ƒ prophecy.
prophylaktisch [prōfülák'tish] a prophylactic (form), preventive.
Proportion [prōportsēō:n'] ƒ proportion.
proportional [prōportsēōnál'] a proportional; **P~schrift** ƒ (COMPUT) proportional printing.
Proporz [prōports'] m -es, -e proportional representation.
Prosa [prō:'zà] ƒ - prose.
prosaisch [prōzâ'ish] a prosaic.
prosit [prō:'zit] interj cheers; **P~ Neujahr!** happy New Year!
Prospekt [prōspekt'] m -(e)s, -e leaflet, brochure.
prost [prō:st] interj cheers!
Prostata [pro'státá] ƒ - prostate gland.
Prostituierte [prōstētōōē:r'tə] ƒ -n, -n prosti-

tute.
Prostitution [prŏstētōōtsēō:n'] *f* prostitution.
prot. [prŏt] *abk* = **protestantisch.**
Protektionismus [prŏtektsēōnis'mōōs] *m* protectionism.
Protektorat [prŏtektōrât'] *nt* **-(e)s, -e** (*Schirmherrschaft*) patronage; (*Schutzgebiet*) protectorate.
Protest [prŏtest'] *m* **-(e)s, -e** protest.
Protestant(in *f*) [prŏtestánt'(in)] *m* Protestant; **p~isch** a Protestant.
Protestbewegung *f* protest movement.
protestieren [prŏtestē:'rən] *vi* protest.
Protestkundgebung *f* (protest) rally.
Prothese [prŏtā:'zə] *f* **-, -n** artificial limb; (*Zahn~*) dentures *pl*.
Protokoll [prŏtōkol'] *nt* **-s, -e** register; (*Niederschrift*) record; (*von Sitzung*) minutes *pl*; (*diplomatisch*) protocol; (*Polizei~*) statement; (*Strafzettel*) ticket; **(das)** ~ **führen** (*bei Sitzung*) take the minutes; (*bei Gericht*) make a transcript of the proceedings; **etw zu** ~ **geben** have sth put on record; (*bei Polizei*) say sth in one's statement; **~führer** *m* secretary; (*JUR*) clerk (of the court).
protokollieren [prŏtōkolē:'rən] *vt* take down; (*Bemerkung*) enter in the minutes.
Proton [prŏ:'ton] *nt* **-s, -en** proton.
Prototyp *m* prototype.
Protz [prots'] *m* **-en, -e(n)** swank; **p~en** *vi* show off.
protzig *a* ostentatious.
Proviant [prŏvēánt'] *m* **-s, -e** provisions *pl*, supplies *pl*.
Provinz [prŏvints'] *f* **-, -en** province; **das ist finsterste** ~ (*pej*) it's a cultural backwater.
provinziell [prŏvintsē'el] *a* provincial.
Provision [prŏvēzēō:n'] *f* (*COMM*) commission.
provisorisch [prŏvēzō:'rish] *a* provisional.
Provokation [prŏvŏkátsēō:n'] *f* provocation.
provokativ [prŏvŏkátē:f'], **provokatorisch** [prŏvŏkátō:'rish] *a* provocative, provoking.
provozieren [prŏvōtsē:'rən] *vt* provoke.
Proz. *abk* (= *Prozent*) p.c.
Prozedur [prŏtsádōō:r'] *f* procedure; (*pej*) carry-on; **die** ~ **beim Zahnarzt** the ordeal at the dentist's.
Prozent [prŏtsent'] *nt* **-(e)s, -e** per cent, percentage; **~rechnung** *f* percentage calculation; **~satz** *m* percentage.
prozentual [prŏtsentōōál'] *a* percentage; as a percentage.
Prozeß [prŏtses'] *m* **-sses, -sse** trial, case; (*Vorgang*) process; **es zum** ~ **kommen lassen** go to court; **mit jdm/etw kurzen** ~ **machen** (*fig umg*) make short work of sb/sth; **~anwalt** *m* counsel; **~führung** *f* handling of a case.
prozessieren [prŏtsesē:'rən] *vi* bring an action, go to law (*mit* against).
Prozession [prŏtsesēō:n'] *f* procession.
Prozeßkosten *pl* (legal) costs *pl*.
prüde [prü:'də] *a* prudish.

Prüderie [prü:dərē:'] *f* prudery.
prüfen [prü:'fən] *vt* examine, test; (*nach~*) check; (*erwägen*) consider; (*Geschäftsbücher*) audit; (*mustern*) scrutinize.
Prüfer(in *f*) *m* **-s, -** examiner.
Prüfling *m* examinee.
Prüfstein *m* touchstone.
Prüfung *f* (*SCH, UNIV*) examination; (*Über~*) checking; **eine** ~ **machen** take an exam; **durch eine** ~ **fallen** fail an examination.
Prüfungs- *zW*: **~ausschuß** *m*, **~kommission** *f* examining board; **~ordnung** *f* exam(ination) regulations *pl*.
Prügel [prü:'gəl] *m* **-s, -** cudgel; *pl* beating.
Prügelei [prü:gəlī'] *f* fight.
Prügelknabe *m* scapegoat.
prügeln *vt* beat ♦ *vr* fight.
Prügelstrafe *f* corporal punishment.
Prunk [prŏŏngk] *m* **-(e)s** pomp, show; **p~voll** *a* splendid, magnificent.
prusten [prŏŏ:'stən] *vi* (*umg*) snort.
PS *abk* (= *Pferdestärke*) HP, hp.
Psalm [psálm] *m* **-s, -en** psalm.
PSchA *nt abk* (= *Postscheckamt*) ≈ National Giro Office.
pseudo- [psoidō] *in* *zW* pseudo.
Psychiater [psüchē'átər] *m* **-s, -** psychiatrist.
Psychiatrie [psüchēátrē:'] *f* psychiatry.
psychisch [psü:'chish] *a* psychological; ~ **gestört** emotionally *od* psychologically disturbed.
Psychoanalyse [psüchōánálü:'zə] *f* psychoanalysis.
Psychologe [psüchōlō:'gə] *m* **-n, -n, Psychologin** *f* psychologist.
Psychologie' *f* psychology.
psychologisch *a* psychological.
Psychotherapie' *f* psychotherapy.
Pubertät [pŏŏberte:t'] *f* puberty.
publik [pŏŏblē:k'] *a*: ~ **werden** become public knowledge.
Publikum [pŏŏ:'blēkŏŏm] *nt* **-s** audience; (*SPORT*) crowd; **in diesem Lokal verkehrt ein schlechtes** ~ this pub attracts a bad type of customer.
Publikums- *zW*: **~erfolg** *m* popular success; **~verkehr** *m*: „**heute kein ~verkehr**" "closed today for public business".
publizieren [pŏŏblētsē:'rən] *vt* publish.
Pudding [pŏŏ'ding] *m* **-s, -e** *od* **-s** blancmange; **~pulver** *nt* custard powder.
Pudel [pŏŏ:'dəl] *m* **-s** poodle; **das also ist des ~s Kern** (*fig*) that's what it's really all about.
pudelwohl *a* (*umg*): **sich** ~ **fühlen** feel on top of the world.
Puder [pŏŏ:'dər] *m* **-s, -** powder; **~dose** *f* powder compact.
pudern *vt* powder.
Puderzucker *m* confectioner's (*US*) *od* icing (*Brit*) sugar.
Puff [pŏŏf'] *m* **-s, -e** (*Wäsche~*) linen basket; (*Sitz~*) pouf; *pl* **-e** (*umg: Stoß*) push; *pl* **-s** (*umg: Bordell*) brothel.

Puffer *m* **-s, -** (*auch* COMPUT) buffer; ~**speicher** *m* (COMPUT) cache; ~**staat** *m* buffer state.

Puffreis *m* puffed rice.

Pulle [pōō'lə] *f* **-, -n** (*umg*) bottle; **volle** ~ **fahren** (*umg*) drive flat out.

Pulli [pōō'lē] *m* **-s, -s** (*umg*), **Pullover** [pōōlō:'vər] *m* **-s, -** sweater, jumper (*Brit*).

Pullunder [pōōlōōn'dər] *m* **-s, -** slipover.

Puls [pōōls] *m* **-es, -e** pulse; ~**ader** *f* artery; **sich** (*dat*) **die** ~**ader(n) aufschneiden** slash one's wrists.

pulsieren [pōōlzē:'rən] *vi* throb, pulsate.

Pult [pōōlt] *nt* **-(e)s, -e** desk.

Pulver [pōōl'fər] *nt* **-s, -** powder; ~**faß** *nt*: **(wie) auf einem** ~**faß sitzen** (*fig*) be sitting on (top of) a volcano.

pulverig *a* powdery.

pulverisieren [pōōlvārēzē:'rən] *vt* pulverize.

Pulver- *zW*: ~**kaffee** *m* instant coffee; ~**schnee** *m* powdery snow.

pummelig [pōō'məlich] *a* chubby.

Pump *m* **-(e)s** (*umg*): **auf** ~ **kaufen** buy on credit.

Pumpe [pōōm'pə] *f* **-, -n** pump; (*umg*: *Herz*) ticker.

pumpen *vt* pump; (*umg*) lend; (*entleihen*) borrow.

Pumphose *f* knickerbockers *pl*.

puncto [pōōngk'tō] *präp* +*gen*: **in** ~ **X** where X is concerned.

Punkt [pōōngkt] *m* **-(e)s, -e** point; (*bei Muster*) dot; (*Satzzeichen*) period, full stop; ~ **12 Uhr** at 12 o'clock on the dot; **nun mach aber mal einen** ~**!** (*umg*) come off it!; **p**~**gleich** *a* (SPORT) even, level.

punktieren [pōōngktē:'rən] *vt* dot; (MED) aspirate.

pünktlich [püngkt'lich] *a* punctual; **P**~**keit** *f* punctuality.

Punkt- *zW*: ~**matrix** *f* dot matrix; ~**richter** *m* (SPORT) judge; ~**sieg** *m* victory on points; ~**wertung** *f* points system; ~**zahl** *f* score.

Punsch [pōōnsh] *m* **-(e)s, -e** (hot) punch.

Pupille [pōōpi'lə] *f* **-, -n** (*im Auge*) pupil.

Puppe [pōō'pə] *f* **-, -n** doll; (*Marionette*) puppet; (*Insekten*~) pupa, chrysalis; (*Schaufenster*~, MIL: *Übungs*~) dummy; (*umg*: *Mädchen*) doll, chick.

Puppen- *zW*: ~**spieler** *m* puppeteer; ~**stube** *f* doll's house; ~**wagen** *m* doll carriage (*US*), doll's pram (*Brit*).

pupsen [pōō:p'sən] *vi* (*umg*) make a rude noise *od* smell.

pur [pōō:r] *a* pure; (*völlig*) sheer; (*Whisky*) straight.

Püree [pürā:'] *nt* **-s, -s** purée; (*Kartoffel*~) mashed potatoes *pl*.

Purpur [pōōr'pōōr] *m* **-s** crimson.

Purzelbaum [pōōr'tsəlboum] *m* somersault.

purzeln *vi* tumble.

Puste [pōō:'stə] *f* **-** (*umg*) puff; (*fig*) steam.

Pusteblume *f* (*umg*) dandelion.

Pustel [pōō'stəl] *f* **-, -n** pustule.

pusteln *vi* puff, blow.

Pute [pōō:'tə] *f* **-, -n** turkey hen.

Puter *m* **-s, -** turkey cock; **p**~**rot** *a* scarlet.

Putsch [pōōtsh] *m* **-(e)s, -e** revolt, putsch; **p**~**en** *vi* revolt; ~**ist** [pōōtshist'] *m* rebel; ~**versuch** *m* attempted coup (d'état).

Putte [pōō'tə] *f* **-, -n** (KUNST) cherub.

Putz [pōōts] *m* **-es** (*Mörtel*) plaster, roughcast; **eine Mauer mit** ~ **verkleiden** roughcast a wall.

putzen *vt* clean; (*Nase*) wipe, blow ♦ *vr* clean o.s.; (*veraltet*: *sich schmücken*) dress o.s. up.

Putzfrau *f* cleaning woman.

putzig *a* quaint, funny.

Putzlappen *m* cloth.

putzmunter *a* (*umg*) full of beans.

Putz- *zW*: ~**tag** *m* cleaning day; ~**teufel** *m* (*umg*: *Frau*) maniac for housework; ~**zeug** *nt* cleaning things *pl*.

Puzzle [pá'səl] *nt* **-s, -s** jigsaw (puzzle).

Pygmäe [pügme:'ə] *m* **-n, -n** Pygmy.

Pyjama [pēdzhá'má] *m* **-s, -s** pajamas *pl* (*US*), pyjamas *pl* (*Brit*).

Pyramide [pürámē:'də] *f* **-, -n** pyramid.

Pyrenäen [pürānē:'ən] *pl*: **die** ~ the Pyrenees *pl*.

Python [pü:'ton] *m* **-s, -s** *od* **Pythonen** [pütō:'nən], **Pythonschlange** *f* python.

Q

Q, q [kōō:] *nt* Q, q.

qcm *abk* (= *Quadratzentimeter*) cm².

qkm *abk* (= *Quadratkilometer*) km².

qm *abk* (= *Quadratmeter*) m².

quabb(e)lig [kváb'(ə)lich] *a* wobbly; (*Frosch*) slimy.

Quacksalber [kvák'zálbər] *m* **-s, -** quack (doctor).

Quader [kvá'dər] *m* **-s, -** square stone block; (MATH) cuboid.

Quadrat [kvádrát'] *nt* **-(e)s, -e** square; **q**~**isch** *a* square; ~**latschen** *pl* (*hum umg*: *Schuhe*) clodhoppers; ~**meter** *m* square meter.

quadrieren [kvádrē:'rən] *vt* square.

quaken [kvá'kən] *vi* croak; (*Ente*) quack.

quäken [kve:'kən] *vi* screech.

quäkend *a* screeching.

Quäker(in *f*) *m* **-s, -** Quaker.

Qual [kvál] *f* **-, -en** pain, agony; (*seelisch*) anguish; **er machte ihr das Leben zur** ~ he made her life a misery.

quälen [kve:'lən] *vt* torment; **quälende Ungewißheit** agonizing uncertainty ♦ *vr* (*sich abmühen*) struggle; (*geistig*) torment o.s.

Quälerei [kvɛ:ləri̅'] f torture, torment.
Quälgeist m (umg) pest.
Qualifikation [kvälēfēkátsē̅ō:n'] f qualification.
qualifizieren [kválēfētsē̅:'rən] vtr qualify; (einstufen) label.
qualifiziert a (Arbeiter, Nachwuchs) qualified; (Arbeit) professional; (POL: Mehrheit) requisite.
Qualität [kválēte:t'] f quality; **von ausgezeichneter** ~ (of) top quality.
qualitativ [kválētátē̅:f'] a qualitative.
Qualitäts- zW: ~**kontrolle** f quality control; ~**ware** f article of high quality.
Qualle [kvá'lə] f -, -n jellyfish.
Qualm [kválm] m -(e)s thick smoke.
qualmen vti smoke.
qualvoll [kvál'fol] a painful; (Schmerzen) excruciating, agonizing.
Quantentheorie [kvàn'təntǎōrē:] f quantum theory.
Quantität [kvántē̅te:t'] f quantity.
quantitativ [kvántētátē̅:f'] a quantitative.
Quantum [kván'tōōm] nt -s, **Quanten** quantity, amount.
Quarantäne [kvárànte:'nə] f -, -n quarantine.
Quark [kvárk] m -s curd cheese; (umg) rubbish.
Quarta [kvár'tá] f -, **Quarten** third year of German high school.
Quartal [kvártál'] nt -s, -e quarter (year); **Kündigung zum** ~ quarterly notice date.
Quartett [kvártet'] nt -s, -e (MUS) quartet; (Kartenspiel) ≈ happy families; (KARTEN) set of four cards.
Quartier [kvàrtē:r'] nt -s, -e accommodations (US), accommodation (Brit); (MIL) quarters pl; (Stadt~) district.
Quarz [kvárts] m -es, -e quartz.
quasi [kvá'zē] ad virtually ♦ präf quasi.
quasseln [kvá'səln] vi (umg) natter.
Quaste [kvás'tə] f -, -n (Troddel) tassle; (von Pinsel) bristles pl.
Quästur [kvestōō:r'] f -, -en (UNIV) treasurer's (US) od bursar's (Brit) office.
Quatsch [kvátsh] m -es rubbish; (umg: Dummheiten): **hört doch endlich auf mit dem** ~! stop being so stupid!; ~ **machen** mess about.
quatschen vi chat, natter.
Quatschkopf m (pej umg: Schwätzer) windbag; (umg: Dummkopf) blockhead, knucklehead (US).
Quecksilber [kvek'zilbər] nt mercury.
Quelle [kve'lə] f -, -n spring; (eines Flusses: auch COMPUT) source; **an der** ~ **sitzen** (fig) be well-placed; **aus zuverlässiger** ~ from a reliable source.
quellen vi (hervor~) pour od gush forth; (schwellen) swell.
Quellenangabe f reference.
Quellsprache f source language.
Quengelei [kvengəli̅'] f (umg) whining.
quengelig a (umg) whining.

quengeln vi (umg) whine.
quer [kvā:r] ad crossways, diagonally; (rechtwinklig) at right angles; ~ **auf dem Bett** across the bed; **Q**~**balken** m crossbeam.
Quere [kvā:'rə] f -: **jdm in die** ~ **kommen** cross sb's path.
quer- zW: ~**feld'ein** ad across country; **Q**~**feld'einrennen** nt cross-country; (mit Motorrädern) motocross; (Radrennen) cyclo-cross; **Q**~**flöte** f flute; **Q**~**format** nt oblong format; ~**gestreift** a attr horizontally striped; **Q**~**kopf** m awkward customer; ~**legen** vr (fig umg) be awkward; **Q**~**schiff** nt transept; **Q**~**schläger** m (umg) ricochet; **Q**~**schnitt** m cross section; ~**schnittsgelähmt** a paraplegic, paralysed below the waist; **Q**~**straße** f intersecting road; **Q**~**strich** m (horizontal) stroke od line; **Q**~**summe** f (MATH) sum of digits of a number; **Q**~**treiber** m -s, - obstructionist.
Querulant(in f) [kvǎrōōlánt'(in)] m -en, -en grumbler.
quer- zW: **Q**~**verbindung** f connection, link; **Q**~**verweis** m cross-reference.
quetschen [kvet'shən] vt squash, crush; (MED) bruise ♦ vr (sich klemmen) be caught; (sich zwängen) squeeze (o.s.).
Quetschung f bruise, contusion (form).
Queue [kœ] nt -s, -s (BILLIARD) cue.
quicklebendig [kvik'lāben'diċh] a (umg: Kind) lively, active; (: ältere Person auch) spry.
quieken [kvē̅:'kən] vi squeak.
quietschen [kvē̅:t'shən] vi squeak.
quietschvergnügt [kvē̅:tsh'fergnü:kt] a (umg) blissfully happy.
quillt [kvilt] 3. pers sing präs von **quellen**.
Quinta [kvin'tá] f -, **Quinten** second year in German secondary school.
Quintessenz [kvin'tesents] f quintessence.
Quintett [kvintet'] nt -(e)s, -e quintet.
Quirl [kvirl] m -(e)s, -e whisk.
quirlig [kvir'liċh] a lively, frisky.
quitt [kvit] a quits, even.
Quitte f -, -n quince.
quittieren [kvitē:'rən] vt give a receipt for; (Dienst) leave.
Quittung f receipt; **er hat seine** ~ **bekommen** he's paid the penalty od price.
Quiz [kvis] nt -, - quiz.
quoll [kvol] imperf von **quellen**.
Quote [kvō:'tə] f -, -n proportion; rate.
Quotierung [kvōtē:'rōōng] f (COMM) quotation.

R

R, r [er] *nt* R, r.
r. *abk* (= *rechts*) r.
r, R *abk* (= *Radius*) r.
Rabatt [rábát'] *m* -(e)s, -e discount.
Rabatte *f* -, -n flower bed, border.
Rabattmarke *f* trading stamp.
Rabatz [rábáts'] *m* -es (*umg*) row, din.
Rabe [rá'bə] *m* -n, -n raven.
Raben- *zW*: ~mutter *f* bad mother;
r~schwarz *a* pitch-black.
rabiat [rábēát'] *a* furious.
Rache [rá'xə] *f* - revenge, vengeance.
Rachen *m* -s, - throat.
rächen [re'çhən] *vt* avenge, revenge ♦ *vr* take
(one's) revenge; **das wird sich** ~ you'll pay
for that.
Rachitis [ráxhē:'tis] *f* - rickets *sing*.
Rachsucht *f* vindictiveness.
rachsüchtig *a* vindictive.
Racker [rá'kər] *m* -s, - rascal, scamp.
Rad [rát] *nt* -(e)s, ̈er wheel; (*Fahr*~) bike;
unter die ~er **kommen** (*umg*) fall into bad
ways; **das fünfte** ~ **am Wagen sein** (*umg*)
be in the way.
Radar [rá'dár] *m od nt* -s radar; ~falle *f*
speed trap; ~kontrolle *f* radar-controlled
speed trap.
Radau [rádou'] *m* -s (*umg*) row; ~ **machen**
kick up a row; (*Unruhe stiften*) cause
trouble.
Raddampfer *m* paddle steamer.
radebrechen [rá'dəbreçhən] *vi untr*: **deutsch**
etc ~ speak broken German *etc*.
radeln *vi aux sein* cycle.
Rädelsführer [re:'dəlsfü:rər] *m* -s, - ringleader.
Rad- *zW*: r~fahren *vi unreg* cycle; ~fahrer
m cyclist; (*pej umg*) brownnose(r) (*US*),
crawler (*Brit*); ~fahrweg *m* cycle track *od*
path.
radieren [rádē:'rən] *vt* rub out, erase; (*ART*)
etch.
Radier- *zW*: ~gummi *m* eraser; ~ung *f*
etching.
Radieschen [rádē:s'çhən] *nt* radish.
radikal [rádēkál'] *a* radical; ~ **gegen etw**
vorgehen take radical steps against sth.
Radikale(r) *mf dekl wie a* radical.
Radikalisierung [rádēkálēzē:'rōōng] *f* radi-
calization.
Radikalkur *f* (*umg*) drastic remedy.
Radio [rá'dēō] *nt* -s, -s radio; **im** ~ on the
radio; r~aktiv' *a* radioactive; r~aktiver
Niederschlag (radioactive) fallout;

~aktivität' *f* radioactivity; ~apparat *m*
radio (set).
Radium [rá'dēōōm] *nt* -s radium.
Radius [rá'dēōōs] *m* -, **Radien** radius.
Radkappe *f* (*AUT*) hub cap.
Radler(in *f*) *m* -s, - cyclist.
Rad- *zW*: ~rennbahn *f* cycling (race)track;
~rennen *nt* cycle race; (*Sportart*) cycle rac-
ing; ~sport *m* cycling.
RAF *f* - *abk* (= *Rote-Armee-Fraktion*) Red
Army Faction.
raffen [rá'fən] *vt* snatch, pick up; (*Stoff*)
gather (up); (*Geld*) pile up, rake in.
Raffgier *f* greed, avarice.
Raffinade [ráfēná'də] *f* refined sugar.
Raffinesse [ráfēne'sə] *f* - (*Feinheit*) refinement; (*Schlauheit*) cunning.
raffinieren [ráfēnē:'rən] *vt* refine.
raffiniert *a* crafty, cunning; (*Zucker*) refined.
Rage [rá'zhə] *f* - (*Wut*) rage, fury.
ragen [rá'gən] *vi* tower, rise.
Rahm [rám] *m* -s cream.
rahmen *vt* frame.
Rahmen *m* -s, - frame(work); **aus dem** ~
fallen go too far; **im** ~ **des Möglichen** within the bounds of possibility; ~handlung *f*
(*LITER*) background story; ~plan *m* outline
plan; ~richtlinien *pl* guidelines *pl*.
rahmig *a* creamy.
Rakete [ráká:'tə] *f* -, -n rocket; **ferngelenkte**
~ guided missile.
Raketenstützpunkt *m* missile base.
rammdösig [rám'dœziçh] *a* (*umg*) giddy,
dizzy.
rammen [rá'mən] *vt* ram.
Rampe [rám'pə] *f* -, -n ramp.
Rampenlicht *nt* (*THEAT*) footlights *pl*; **sie**
möchte immer im ~ **stehen** (*fig*) she
always wants to be in the limelight.
ramponieren [rámpōnē:'rən] *vt* (*umg*) damage.
Ramsch [rámsh] *m* -(e)s, -e junk.
ran [rán] *ad* (*umg*) = **heran.**
Rand [ránt] *m* -(e)s, ̈er edge; (*von Brille,*
Tasse etc) rim; (*Hut*~) brim; (*auf Papier*)
margin; (*Schmutz*~, *unter Augen*) ring;
(*fig*) verge, brink; **außer** ~ **und Band** wild;
am ~e **bemerkt** mentioned in passing; **am**
~e **der Stadt** on the outskirts of the town;
etw am ~e **miterleben** experience sth from
the sidelines.
randalieren [rándálē:'rən] *vi* (go on the)
rampage.
Rand- *zW*: ~bemerkung *f* marginal note;
(*fig*) odd comment; ~erscheinung *f*
unimportant side effect, marginal phenomenon; ~figur *f* minor figure; ~gebiet *nt*
(*GEOG*) fringe; (*POL*) border territory; (*fig*)
subsidiary; r~voll *a* full to the brim.
rang [ráng] *imperf von* **ringen.**
Rang *m* -(e)s, ̈e rank; (*Stand*) standing;
(*Wert*) quality; (*THEAT*) balcony (*US*),
circle (*Brit*); **ein Mann ohne** ~ **und Namen**
a man without any standing; **erster/zweiter**

~ first/second balcony (*US*), dress/upper circle (*Brit*); **~abzeichen** *nt* badge *od* insignia of rank; **~älteste(r)** *m dekl wie a* senior officer.

rangeln [rá'ngəln] *vi* (*umg*) scrap; (*um Posten*) wrangle (*um* for).

Rangfolge *f* order of rank (*bes MIL*).

Rangierbahnhof [rànzhē:r'bánhō:f] *m* switch yard (*US*), marshal(l)ing yard.

rangieren *vt* (*EISENB*) shunt, switch (*US*) ♦ *vi* rank, be classed.

Rangiergleis *nt* siding.

Rang- *zW*: **~ordnung** *f* hierarchy; (*MIL*) rank; **~unterschied** *m* social distinction; (*MIL*) difference in rank.

rank [ràngk] *a*: ~ **und schlank** (*liter*) slender and supple.

Ranke [ráng'kə] *f* -, -**n** tendril, shoot.

Ränke [reng'kə] *pl* intrigues *pl*; **~schmied** *m* (*liter*) intriguer; **r~voll** *a* scheming.

ranklotzen [rán'klotsən] *vi* (*umg*) put one's nose to the grindstone.

ranlassen *vt unreg* (*umg*): **jdn** ~ let sb have a go.

rann [rán] *imperf von* **rinnen**.

rannte [rán'tə] *imperf von* **rennen**.

Ranzen [rán'tsən] *m* -**s**, - school bag, satchel; (*umg: Bauch*) gut, belly.

ranzig [rán'tsiç] *a* rancid.

Rappe [rá'pə] *m* -**n**, -**n** black horse.

Rappel [rá'pəl] *m* -**s**, - (*umg: Fimmel*) craze; (*Wutanfall*): **einen** ~ **kriegen** throw a fit.

Rappen [rá'pən] *m* -**s**, - (*Schweiz: Geld*) centime, rappen.

Raps [ráps] *m* -**es**, -**e** (*BOT*) rape.

rar [rár] *a* rare; **sich** ~ **machen** (*umg*) keep o.s. to o.s.

Rarität [rárēte:t'] *f* rarity; (*Sammelobjekt*) curio.

rasant [rázánt'] *a* quick, rapid.

rasch [ràsh] *a* quick.

rascheln *vi* rustle.

rasen [rá'zən] *vi* rave; (*sich schnell bewegen*) race.

Rasen *m* -**s**, - grass; (*gepflegt*) lawn.

rasend *a* furious; **~e Kopfschmerzen** a splitting headache.

Rasen- *zW*: **~mäher** *m* -**s**, -, **~mähmaschine** *f* lawnmower; **~platz** *m* lawn; **~sprenger** *m* (lawn) sprinkler.

Raserei [rázərī'] *f* raving, ranting; (*Schnelle*) reckless speeding.

Rasier- [ràzē:r'] *zW*: **~apparat** *m* shaver; **~creme** *f* shaving cream; **r~en** *vtr* shave; **~klinge** *f* razor blade; **~messer** *nt* razor; **~pinsel** *m* shaving brush; **~seife** *f* shaving soap *od* stick; **~wasser** *nt* aftershave.

raspeln [rás'pəln] *vt* grate; (*Holz*) rasp.

Rasse [rá'sə] *f* -, -**n** race; (*Tier~*) breed; **~hund** *m* thoroughbred dog.

Rassel *f* -, -**n** rattle.

rasseln *vi* rattle, clatter.

Rassen- *zW*: **~haß** *m* race *od* racial hatred; **~trennung** *f* racial segregation.

rassig [rá'siçh] *a* (*Pferd, Auto*) sleek; (*Frau*) vivacious; (*Wein*) spirited, lively.

Rassismus [rásis'mōōs] *m* - racialism, racism.

Rast [ràst] *f* -, -**en** rest; **r~en** *vi* rest.

Raster [rás'tər] *m* -**s**, - (*ARCHIT*) grid; (*PHOT: Gitter*) screen; (*TV*) raster; (*fig*) framework.

Rast- *zW*: **~haus** *nt* (*AUT*) service station; **r~los** *a* tireless; (*unruhig*) restless; **~platz** *m* (*AUT*) rest stop (*US*), lay-by (*Brit*); **~stätte** *f* service area, services *pl*.

Rasur [rázōō:r'] *f* shaving; (*Radieren*) erasure.

rät [re:t] *3. pers sing präs von* **raten**.

Rat [ràt] *m* -**(e)s, -schläge** (piece of) advice; **jdn zu ~e ziehen** consult sb; **jdm mit ~ und Tat zur Seite stehen** support sb in (both) word and deed; **keinen ~ wissen** not know what to do.

Rate *f* -, -**n** installment (*US*), instalment (*Brit*); **auf ~n kaufen** to buy on the installment plan (*US*) *od* on hire purchase (*Brit*).

raten *vti unreg* guess; (*empfehlen*) advise (*jdm* sb); **dreimal darfst du** ~ I'll give you three guesses (*auch ironisch*).

Raten- *zW*: **r~weise** *ad* by installments; **~zahlung** *f* installment plan (*US*), hire purchase (*Brit*).

Ratespiel *nt* guessing game; (*TV*) quiz; (*Beruferaten etc auch*) panel game.

Rat- *zW*: **~geber** *m* -**s**, - adviser; **~haus** *nt* town hall.

ratifizieren [rátēfētsē:'rən] *vt* ratify.

Ratifizierung *f* ratification.

Ration [rátsēō:n'] *f* ration.

rational [rátsēōnál'] *a* rational.

rationalisieren [rátsēōnálēzē:'rən] *vt* rationalize.

rationell [rátsēōnel'] *a* efficient.

rationieren [rátsēōnē:'rən] *vt* ration.

Rat- *zW*: **r~los** *a* at a loss, helpless; **~losigkeit** *f* helplessness; **r~sam** *a* advisable; **~schlag** *m* (piece of) advice.

Rätsel [re:'tsəl] *nt* -**s**, - puzzle; (*Wort~*) riddle; **vor einem** ~ **stehen** be baffled; **r~haft** *a* mysterious; **es ist mir r~haft** it's a mystery to me; **~raten** *nt* guessing game.

Rats- *zW*: **~herr** *m* councilor (*US*), councillor (*Brit*); **~keller** *m* town-hall restaurant.

ratsuchend *a*: **sich** ~ **an jdn wenden** turn to sb for advice.

Ratte [rá'tə] *f* -, -**n** rat.

Rattenfänger *m* -**s**, - ratcatcher.

rattern [rá'tərn] *vi* rattle, clatter.

Raub [roup] *m* -**(e)s** robbery; (*Beute*) loot, booty; **~bau** *m* overexploitation; **~cassette** *f* pirate cassette; **~druck** *m* pirate(d) edition; **r~en** [rou'bən] *vt* rob; (*Mensch*) kidnap, abduct.

Räuber [roi'bər] *m* -**s**, - robber; **r~isch** *a* thieving.

Raub- *zW*: **~fisch** *m* predatory fish; **r~gierig** *a* rapacious; **~mord** *m* robbery with murder; ~**tier** *nt* predator; ~**überfall** *m* robbery with violence; ~**vogel** *m* bird of prey.

Rauch [rouкh] *m* -(e)s smoke; ~**abzug** *m* smoke outlet.

rauchen *vti* smoke; **mir raucht der Kopf** (*fig*) my head's spinning; „**R**~ **verboten**" "no smoking".

Raucher(in *f*) *m* -s, - smoker; ~**abteil** *nt* (*EISENB*) smoker.

räuchern [roi'çhərn] *vt* smoke, cure.

Räucher- *zW*: ~**speck** *m* ≈ smoked bacon; ~**stäbchen** *nt* joss stick.

Rauch- *zW*: ~**fahne** *f* smoke trail; ~**fang** *m* (~*abzug*) chimney hood; ~**fleisch** *nt* smoked meat.

rauchig *a* smoky.

Rauchschwaden *pl* drifts of smoke *pl*.

räudig [roi'diçh] *a* mangy.

rauf [rouf] *ad* (*umg*) = **herauf**.

Raufbold *m* -(e)s, -e rowdy, hooligan.

raufen *vt* (*Haare*) pull out ♦ *vir* fight.

Rauferei [roufərī'] *f* brawl, fight.

rauflustig *a* spoiling for a fight, rowdy.

rauh [rou] *a* rough, coarse; (*Wetter*) harsh; **in** ~**en Mengen** (*umg*) by the ton, galore; ~**beinig** *a* rough-and-ready; **R**~**fasertapete** *f* woodchip paper; ~**haarig** *a* wire-haired; **R**~**reif** *m* hoarfrost.

Raum [roum] *m* -(e)s, **Räume** space; (*Zimmer, Platz*) room; (*Gebiet*) area; **eine Frage im** ~ **stehen lassen** leave a question unresolved; ~**ausstatter(in** *f*) *m* interior decorator; ~**bild** *nt* 3-D picture.

räumen [roi'mən] *vt* clear; (*Wohnung, Platz*) vacate, move out of; (*Gebäude, Lager*) clear (*von* of); (*verlassen: Gebiet*) evacuate; (*wegbringen*) shift, move; (*in Schrank etc*) put away.

Raum- *zW*: ~**fähre** *f* space shuttle; ~**fahrer** *m* astronaut; (*sowjetisch*) cosmonaut; ~**fahrt** *f* space travel.

Räumfahrzeug [roim'fårtsoik] *nt* bulldozer; (*für Schnee*) snow-clearer.

Raum- *zW*: ~**inhalt** *m* cubic capacity, volume; ~**kapsel** *f* space capsule.

räumlich [roim'liçh] *a* spatial; **R**~**keiten** *pl* premises *pl*.

Raum- *zW*: ~**mangel** *m* lack of space; ~**maß** *nt* unit of volume; cubic measurement; ~**meter** *m* cubic meter; ~**pflegerin** *f* cleaner; ~**schiff** *nt* spaceship; ~**schiffahrt** *f* space travel; **r**~**sparend** *a* space-saving; ~**station** *f* space station.

Räumung [roi'mŏŏng] *f* vacating, evacuation; clearing (away); (*unter Zwang*) eviction.

Räumungs- *zW*: ~**befehl** *m* eviction order; ~**klage** *f* action for eviction; ~**verkauf** *m* clearance sale.

raunen [rou'nən] *vti* whisper.

Raupe [rou'pə] *f* -, -n caterpillar; (*Raupenkette*) track.

Raupenschlepper *m* -s, - caterpillar tractor.

raus [rous] *ad* (*umg*) = **heraus, hinaus.**

Rausch [roush] *m* -(e)s, **Räusche** intoxication; **einen** ~ **haben** be drunk.

rauschen *vi* (*Wasser*) rush; (*Baum*) rustle; (*Radio etc*) hiss; (*Mensch*) sweep, sail.

rauschend *a* (*Beifall*) thunderous; (*Fest*) sumptuous.

Rausch- *zW*: ~**gift** *nt* drug; ~**gifthandel** *m* drug traffic; ~**giftsüchtige(r)** *mf dekl wie a* drug addict.

rausfliegen *vi unreg* (*umg*) be thrown out.

räuspern [rois'pərn] *vr* clear one's throat.

Rausschmeißer [roussh'mīsər] *m* -s, - (*umg*) bouncer.

Raute [rou'tə] *f* -, -n diamond; (*MATH*) rhombus.

rautenförmig *a* rhombic.

Razzia [rá'tsēá] *f* -, **Razzien** raid.

rd. *abk* = **rund.**

Rdsch. *abk* (= *Rundschau*) review.

Rdschr. *abk* = **Rundschreiben.**

Reagenzglas [rāāgents'glås] *nt* test tube.

reagieren [rāāgē:'rən] *vi* react (*auf* +*akk* to).

Reaktion [rāāktsēō:n'] *f* reaction.

reaktionär [rāāktsēōnɛ:r'] *a* reactionary.

Reaktions- *zW*: ~**fähigkeit** *f* reactions *pl*; ~**geschwindigkeit** *f* speed of reaction.

Reaktor [rāāk'tor] *m* reactor; ~**block** *m* reactor building *od* housing; ~**katastrophe** *f* nuclear catastrophe; ~**schmelze** *f* reactor meltdown.

real [rāāl'] *a* real, material; **R**~**einkommen** *nt* real income.

realisierbar [rāālēzē:r'bår] *a* practicable, feasible.

Realismus [rāālis'mŏŏs] *m* realism.

Realist(in *f*) [rāālist'(in)] *m* realist; **r**~**isch** *a* realistic.

Realität [rāālɛte:t'] *f* reality; ~**en** *pl* (*Gegebenheiten*) facts *pl*.

realitätsfremd *a* out of touch with reality.

Real- *zW*: ~**politik** *f* political realism; ~**schule** *f* ≈ junior high school; ~**zeit** *f* real time.

Rebe [rā:'bə] *f* -, -n vine.

Rebell(in *f*) [rābel'(in)] *m* -en, -en rebel.

Rebellion [rābelēō:n'] *f* rebellion.

rebellisch [rābe'lish] *a* rebellious.

Rebensaft *m* grape juice.

Reb- [rep] *zW*: ~**huhn** *nt* partridge; ~**laus** *f* vine pest; ~**stock** *m* vine.

rechen [re'çhən] *vti* rake; **R**~ *m* -s, - rake.

Rechen- *zW*: ~**aufgabe** *f* sum, mathematical problem; ~**fehler** *m* miscalculation; ~**maschine** *f* adding machine.

Rechenschaft *f* account; **jdm über etw** (*akk*) ~ **ablegen** account to sb for sth; **jdn zur** ~ **ziehen** call sb to account (*fur etw* for *od* over sth); **jdm** ~ **schulden** be accountable to sb.

Rechenschaftsbericht *m* report.

Rechen- *zW*: ~**schieber** *m* slide rule; ~**zentrum** *nt* computer center.

recherchieren [rāshershē:'rən] *vti* investigate.

rechnen [reçh'nən] *vti* calculate; (*veranschlagen*) estimate, reckon; **jdn/etw** ~ **zu** *od* **unter** (+*akk*) count sb/sth among; ~ **mit** reckon with; ~ **auf** (+*akk*) count on; **R**~ *nt* arithmetic; (*bes SCH*) sums *pl*.

Rechner *m* **-s**, - calculator; **r**~**abhängig** *a* (*COMPUT*) on line; **r**~**fern** *a* (*COMPUT*) remote; **r**~**isch** *a* arithmetical; **r**~**unabhängig** *a* (*COMPUT*) off line.

Rechnung *f* calculation(s); (*COMM*) check, bill (*Brit*); **auf eigene** ~ on one's own account; (**jdm**) **etw in** ~ **stellen** charge (sb) for sth; **jdm/etw** ~ **tragen** take sb/sth into account.

Rechnungs- *zW*: ~**aufstellung** *f* statement; ~**buch** *nt* account book; ~**hof** *m* general accounting office; ~**jahr** *nt* financial year; ~**prüfer** *m* auditor; ~**prüfung** *f* audit(ing).

recht [reçht] *a*, *ad* right; (*vor Adjektiv*) really, quite; **das ist mir** ~ that suits me; **jetzt erst** ~ now more than ever; **alles, was** ~ **ist** (*empört*) fair's fair; (*anerkennend*) you can't deny it; **nach dem R**~**en sehen** see that everything's O.K.; ~ **haben** be right; **jdm** ~ **geben** agree with sb, admit that sb is right; **du kommst gerade** ~, **um** ... you're just in time to ...; **gehe ich** ~ **in der Annahme, daß** ...? am I correct in assuming that ...?; ~ **herzlichen Dank** thank you very much indeed.

Recht *nt* **-(e)s**, **-e** right; (*JUR*) law; ~ **sprechen** administer justice; **mit** *od* **zu** ~ rightly, justly; **von** ~**s wegen** by rights; **zu seinem** ~ **kommen** (*lit*) gain one's rights; (*fig*) come into one's own; **gleiches** ~ **für alle!** equal rights for all!

Rechte *f* **-n**, **-n** right (hand); (*POL*) Right.

recht- *zW*: **R**~**eck** *nt* **-s**, **-e** rectangle; ~**eckig** *a* rectangular.

rechte(r, s) *a* right; (*POL*) right-wing; **R**~**(r)** *mf dekl wie a* right person; **R**~**(s)** *nt* right thing; **etwas/nichts R**~**s** something/nothing proper.

recht- *zW*: ~**fertigen** *vtr untr* justify (o.s.); **R**~**fertigung** *f* justification; ~**haberisch** *a* dogmatic; ~**lich** *a*, ~**mäßig** *a* legal, lawful; ~**lich nicht zulässig** not permissible in law, illegal.

rechts [reçhts] *ad* on *od* to the right; ~ **stehen** *od* **sein** (*POL*) be right-wing; ~ **stricken** knit (plain); **R**~**abbieger** *m*: **die Spur für R**~**abbieger** the right-turn lane; **R**~**anspruch** *m*: **einen R**~**anspruch auf etw** (*akk*) **haben** be legally entitled to sth; **R**~**anwalt** *m* lawyer, attorney (*US*); **R**~**au'ßen** *m* -, - (*SPORT*) outside right; **R**~**beistand** *m* legal adviser.

Recht- *zW*: **r**~**schaffen** *a* upright; ~**schreibung** *f* spelling.

Rechts- *zW*: ~**drehung** *f* clockwise rotation; ~**extremist** *m* right-wing extremist; ~**fall** *m* (law) case; ~**frage** *f* legal question; **r**~**gültig** *a* legally valid; ~**händer(in** *f*) *m* **-s**, - right-handed person; **r**~**kräftig** *a* valid, legal; ~**kurve** *f* right-hand bend; ~**lage** *f* legal position; **r**~**lastig** *a* listing to the right; (*fig*) leaning to the right; ~**pflege** *f* administration of justice; ~**pfleger** *m* *official with certain judicial powers*.

Rechtsprechung [reçht'shpreçhōōng] *f* (*Gerichtsbarkeit*) jurisdiction; (*richterliche Tätigkeit*) dispensation of justice.

Rechts- *zW*: **r**~**radikal** *a* (*POL*) extreme right-wing; ~**schutz** *m* legal protection; ~**spruch** *m* verdict; ~**staat** *m* state under the rule of law; ~**streit** *m* lawsuit; ~**titel** *m* title; **r**~**verbindlich** *a* legally binding; ~**verkehr** *m* driving on the right; ~**weg** *m*: **der** ~**weg ist ausgeschlossen** ≈ the judges' decision is final; **r**~**widrig** *a* illegal; ~**wissenschaft** *f* jurisprudence.

recht- *zW*: ~**winklig** *a* right-angled; ~**zeitig** *a* timely ♦ *ad* in time.

Reck [rek] *nt* **-(e)s**, **-e** horizontal bar.

recken *vtr* stretch.

Red. *abk* = **Redaktion**; (= *Redakteur(in)*) ed.

Redakteur(in *f*) [rādáktœr'(in)'] *m* editor.

Redaktion [rādáktsēō:n'] *f* editing; (*Leute*) editorial staff; (*Büro*) editorial office(s).

Redaktionsschluß *m* time of going to press; (*Einsendeschluß*) copy deadline.

Rede [rā:'də] *f* -, **-n** speech; (*Gespräch*) talk; **jdn zur** ~ **stellen** take sb to task; **eine** ~ **halten** make a speech; **das ist nicht der** ~ **wert** it's not worth mentioning; **davon kann keine** ~ **sein** it's out of the question; ~**freiheit** *f* freedom of speech; **r**~**gewandt** *a* eloquent.

reden *vi* talk, speak ♦ *vt* say; (*Unsinn etc*) talk; (**viel**) **von sich** ~ **machen** become (very much) a talking point; **darüber läßt sich** ~ that's a possibility; (*über Preis, Bedingungen*) I think we could discuss that; **er läßt mit sich** ~ he could be persuaded; (*in bezug auf Preis*) he's open to offers; (*gesprächsbereit*) he's open to discussion; **R**~ *nt* **-s** talking, speech.

Redensart *f* expression.

Rede- *zW*: ~**schwall** *m* torrent of words; ~**wendung** *f* expression, idiom.

redlich [rā:'tliçh] *a* honest; **R**~**keit** *f* honesty.

Redner(in *f*) *m* **-s**, - speaker, orator.

redselig [rā:t'zā:liçh] *a* talkative, loquacious; **R**~**keit** *f* talkativeness.

redundant [rādōōndánt'] *a* redundant.

Redundanz [rādōōndánts'] *f* - redundancy.

reduzieren [rādōōtsē:'rən] *vt* reduce.

Reduzierung *f* reduction.

Reede [rā:'də] *f* -, **-n** protected anchorage.

Reeder *m* **-s**, - shipowner.

Reederei [rā:dərī'] *f* shipping line *od* firm.

reell [rāel'] *a* fair, honest; (*Preis*) fair; (*COMM: Geschäft*) sound; (*MATH*) real.

Reetdach [rā:t'dákh] *nt* thatched roof.

Ref. *abk* = **Referendar; Referent.**

Referat [rāfārát'] *nt* **-(e)s**, **-e** report; (*Vortrag*) paper; (*Gebiet*) section; (*VERWALTUNG*:

Ressort) department; **ein ~ halten** present a seminar paper.

Referendar(in *f*) [räfärendàr'(in)] *m* trainee (in civil service); (*Studien~*) trainee teacher; (*Gerichts~*) articled clerk.

Referendum [räfären'dōōm] *nt* **-s, Referenden** referendum.

Referent(in *f*) [räfärent'(in)] *m* speaker; (*Berichterstatter*) reporter; (*Sachbearbeiter*) expert.

Referenz [räfärents'] *f* reference.

referieren [räfärē:'rən] *vi*: **~ über** (+*akk*) speak *od* talk on.

reflektieren [räfläktē:'rən] *vti* reflect; **~ auf** (+*akk*) be interested in.

Reflex [räfleks'] *m* **-es, -e** reflex; **~bewegung** *f* reflex action.

reflexiv [räfleksē:f'] *a* (*GRAM*) reflexive.

Reform [räform'] *f* **-, -en** reform.

Reformation [räformátsēō:n'] *f* reformation.

Reformator [räformá'tor] *m* reformer; **r~isch** *a* reformatory, reforming.

reform- *zW*: **~bedürftig** *a* in need of reform; **~freudig** *a* avid for reform; **R~haus** *nt* health food store.

reformieren [räformē:'rən] *vt* reform.

Refrain [rəfrań'] *m* **-s, -s** refrain, chorus.

Reg. *abk* (= *Regierungs-*) Gov., gov.; (= *Register*) reg.

Regal [rägál'] *nt* **-s, -e** (book)shelves *pl*, bookcase; (*TYP*) stand, rack.

Reg.-Bez. *abk* (= *Regierungsbezirk*) governmental *od* federal district.

rege [rā:'gə] *a* lively, active; (*Geschäft*) brisk.

Regel [rā:'gəl] *f* **-, -n** rule; (*MED*) period; **in der ~** as a rule; **nach allen ~n der Kunst** (*fig*) thoroughly; (*Gewohnheit*): **sich** (*dat*) **etw zur ~ machen** make a habit of sth; **r~los** *a* irregular, unsystematic; **r~mäßig** *a* regular; **~mäßigkeit** *f* regularity.

regeln *vt* regulate, control; (*Angelegenheit*) settle; **gesetzlich geregelt sein** be laid down by law ♦ *vr*: **sich von selbst ~** take care of itself.

Regel- *zW*: **r~recht** *a* proper, thorough; **~ung** *f* regulation; settlement; **r~widrig** *a* irregular, against the rules.

regen [rā:'gən] *vtr* move, stir.

Regen *m* **-s, -** rain; **Saurer ~** acid rain; **vom ~ in die Traufe kommen** (*Sprichwort*) jump out of the frying pan into the fire (*Sprichwort*); **~bogen** *m* rainbow; **~bogenhaut** *f* (*ANAT*) iris; **~bogenpresse** *f* trashy magazines *pl*.

regenerieren [rägänärē:'rən] *vr* (*BIOL*) regenerate; (*fig*) revitalize *od* regenerate o.s. *od* itself; (*nach Anstrengung, Schock etc*) recover.

Regen- *zW*: **~guß** *m* downpour; **~mantel** *m* raincoat; **~menge** *f* rainfall; **~schauer** *m* shower (of rain); **~schirm** *m* umbrella.

Regent(in *f*) [rägent'(in)] *m* regent.

Regentag *m* rainy day.

Regentschaft *f* regency.

Regen- *zW*: **~wald** *m* (*GEOG*) rain forest; **~wetter** *nt*: **er macht ein Gesicht wie drei** *od* **sieben Tage ~wetter** (*umg*) he's got a face as long as a month of Sundays; **~wurm** *m* earthworm; **~zeit** *f* rainy season, rains *pl*.

Regie[rāzhē:'] *f* (*FILM etc*) direction; (*THEAT*) production; **unter der ~ von** directed *od* produced by; **~anweisung** *f* (stage) direction.

regieren [rägē:'rən] *vti* govern, rule.

Regierung *f* government; (*Monarchie*) reign; **an die ~ kommen** come to power; (*durch Wahl auch*) come into *od* take office.

Regierungs- *zW*: **~bezirk** *m* ≈ county; **~erklärung** *f* inaugural speech; (*in Großbritannien*) King's *od* Queen's Speech; **~sprecher** *m* government spokesman; **~vorlage** *f* government bill; **~wechsel** *m* change of government; **~zeit** *f* period in government; (*von König*) reign.

Regiment [rägēment'] *nt* **-s, -er** regiment.

Region [rägēō:n'] *f* region.

Regionalplanung [rägēōnàl'plànōōng] *f* regional planning.

Regisseur(in *f*) [rāzhiscer'(in)] *m* director; (*THEAT*) (stage) producer.

Register [rägis'tər] *nt* **-s, -** register; (*in Buch*) table of contents, index; **alle ~ ziehen** (*fig*) pull out all the stops; **~führer** *m* registrar.

Registratur [rägistrátōō:r'] *f* registry, records office.

registrieren [rägistrē:'rən] *vti* register; (*umg*: *zur Kenntnis nehmen*) note.

Registrierkasse *f* cash register.

Regler [rā:'glər] *m* **-s, -** regulator, governor.

reglos [rā:'klō:s] *a* motionless.

regnen [rā:g'nən] *vti unpers* rain; **es regnet in Strömen** it's pouring (with rain).

regnerisch *a* rainy.

Reg.-Präs *abk* (= *Regierungspräsident*) ≈ Chairman of Regional Council.

Reg.-Rat *abk* (= *Regierungsrat*) senior civil servant.

Regreß [rägres'] *m* **-sses, -sse** (*JUR*) recourse, redress; **~anspruch** *m* (*JUR*) claim for compensation.

regsam [rā:k'zám] *a* active.

regulär [rägōōle:r'] *a* regular.

regulieren [rägōōlē:'rən] *vt* regulate; (*COMM*) settle; **sich von selbst ~** be self-regulating.

Regung [rā:'gōōng] *f* motion; (*Gefühl*) feeling, impulse.

regungslos *a* motionless.

Reh [rā:] *nt* **-(e)s, -e** deer, roe deer.

rehabilitieren [rähábēlētē:'rən] *vt* rehabilitate; (*Ruf, Ehre*) vindicate ♦ *vr* rehabilitate (*form*) *od* vindicate o.s.

Reh- *zW*: **~bock** *m* roebuck; **~braten** *m* roast venison; **~kalb** *nt*, **~kitz** *nt* fawn.

Reibach [rī'bàkh] *m* **-s**: **einen ~ machen** (*umg*) make a killing.

Reibe [rī'bə] *f* **-, -n, Reibeisen** *nt* grater.

Reibekuchen *m* (*KOCH*) ≈ potato waffle.
reiben *vt unreg* rub; (*KOCH*) grate.
Reiberei |rībərī'| *f* friction *no pl.*
Reibfläche *f* rough surface.
Reibung *f* friction.
reibungslos *a* smooth; ~ **verlaufen** go off smoothly.
reich [rīċh] *a* rich; **eine ~ ausgestattete Bibliothek** a well-stocked library.
Reich *nt* **-(e)s, -e** empire, kingdom; (*fig*) realm; **das Dritte ~** the Third Reich.
reichen *vi* reach; (*genügen*) be enough *od* sufficient (*jdm* for sb); **so weit das Auge reicht** as far as the eye can see ♦ *vt* hold out; (*geben*) pass, hand; (*anbieten*) offer.
reich- *zW:* ~**haltig** *a* ample, rich; ~**lich** *a* ample, plenty of; **R~tum** *m* **-s, -tümer** wealth; **R~weite** *f* range; **jd ist in R~weite** sb is nearby.
reif [rīf] *a* ripe; (*Mensch, Urteil*) mature; **für etw ~ sein** (*umg*) be ready for sth.
Reif *m* **-(e)s** hoarfrost ♦ *m* **-(e)s, -e** (*Ring*) ring, hoop.
Reife *f* - ripeness; maturity; **mittlere ~** (*SCH*) *first public examination in high school.*
reifen *vi* mature; (*Obst*) ripen.
Reifen *m* **-s,** - ring, hoop; (*Fahrzeug~*) tire (*US*), tyre (*Brit*); ~**panne** *f* puncture, flat; ~**profil** *nt* tire tread; ~**schaden** *m* puncture, flat.
Reife- *zW:* ~**prüfung** *f* school-leaving exam, ≈ final exams at graduation (*US*); ~**zeugnis** *nt* ≈ certificate of graduation (*US*), ≈ school-leaving certificate (*Brit*).
reiflich [rī'flich] *a* thorough, careful.
Reihe [rī'ə] *f* -, **-n** row; (*von Tagen etc, umg: Anzahl*) series *sing*; (*unbestimmte Anzahl*): **eine ganze ~ (von)** a whole lot (of); **der ~ nach** in turn; **er ist an der ~** it's his turn; **an die ~ kommen** have one's turn; **außer der ~** out of turn; (*ausnahmsweise*) out of the usual way of things; **etw auf die ~ kriegen** (*umg*) bring sth into perspective; **aus der ~ tanzen** (*fig umg*) be different; (*gegen Konventionen verstoßen*) step out of line.
reihen *vt* set in a row; arrange in series; (*Perlen*) string.
Reihen- *zW:* ~**folge** *f* sequence; **alphabetische ~folge** alphabetical order; ~**haus** *nt* row (*US*) *od* town house; ~**untersuchung** *f* mass screening; **r~weise** *ad* (*in Reihen*) in rows; (*fig: in großer Anzahl*) by the dozen.
Reiher *m* **-s,** - heron.
reihum [rīōōm'] *ad:* **etw ~ gehen lassen** pass sth around.
Reim [rīm] *m* **-(e)s, -e** rhyme; **sich** (*dat*) **einen ~ auf etw** (*akk*) **machen** (*umg*) make sense of sth; **r~en** *vt* rhyme.
rein [rīn] *ad* (*umg*) = **herein, hinein** ♦ *a, ad* pure(ly); (*sauber*) clean; **das ist die ~ste Freude/der ~ste Hohn** *etc* it's pure *od* sheer joy/mockery *etc*; **~ unmöglich** (*umg: ganz, völlig*) absolutely impossible; **etw ins**

~**e schreiben** make a fair copy of sth; **etw ins ~e bringen** clear sth up; ~**en Tisch machen** (*fig*) get things straight.
Rein- *in zW* (*COMM*) net(t).
Rein(e)machefrau *f* cleaning woman.
rein(e)weg *ad* (*umg*) completely, absolutely.
rein- *zW:* **R~fall** *m* (*umg*) let-down; ~**fallen** *vi:* **auf jdn/etw ~fallen** be taken in by sb/sth; **R~gewinn** *m* net profit; **R~heit** *f* purity; cleanness.
reinigen *vt* clean; (*Wasser*) purify.
Reinigung *f* cleaning; purification; (*Geschäft*) cleaner's; **chemische ~** dry-cleaning; dry-cleaner's.
Reinigungsmittel *nt* cleansing agent.
rein- *zW:* ~**lich** *a* clean; **R~lichkeit** *f* cleanliness; ~**rassig** *a* pedigree; ~**reiten** *vt unreg:* **jdn ~reiten** (*umg*) get sb into a mess; **R~schrift** *f* final copy; **R~vermögen** *f* net assets *pl;* ~**waschen** *vr unreg* clear o.s.
Reis [rīs] *m* **-es, -e** rice ♦ *nt* **-es, -er** twig, sprig.
Reise [rī'zə] *f* -, **-n** journey; (*Schiff~*) voyage; **gute ~!** bon voyage!, have a good journey!; ~**n** *pl* travels *pl;* **auf ~n sein** be away traveling; **er ist viel auf ~n** he does a lot of traveling; ~**andenken** *nt* souvenir; ~**apotheke** *f* first-aid kit; ~**bericht** *m* account of one's journey; (*Buch*) travel story; (*Film*) travelog (*US*), travelogue (*Brit*); ~**büro** *nt* travel agency; ~**erleichterungen** *pl* easing of travel restrictions; **r~fertig** *a* ready to start; ~**fieber** *nt* (*fig*) travel nerves *pl;* ~**führer** *m* guide(book); (*Mensch*) (travel) guide; ~**gepäck** *nt* luggage; ~**gesellschaft** *f* tour group; ~**kosten** *pl* traveling expenses *pl;* ~**leiter** *m* tour guide (*US*), courier (*Brit*); ~**lektüre** *f* reading for the journey; ~**lust** *f* wanderlust.
reisen *vi* travel; go (*nach* to).
Reisende(r) *mf dekl wie a* traveler (*US*), traveller (*Brit*).
Reise- *zW:* ~**paß** *m* passport; ~**pläne** *pl* plans *pl* for a *od* the journey; ~**proviant** *m* provisions *pl* for the journey; ~**scheck** *m* traveler's check (*US*), traveller's cheque (*Brit*); ~**schreibmaschine** *f* portable typewriter; ~**tasche** *f* carryall, tote bag; ~**verkehr** *m* tourist *od* holiday traffic; ~**wetter** *nt* holiday weather; ~**ziel** *nt* destination.
Reisig [rī'ziċh] *nt* **-s** brushwood.
Reißaus' *m:* ~ **nehmen** run away, flee.
Reiß- *zW:* ~**brett** *nt* drawing board; ~**brettstift** *m* thumbtack (*US*), drawing pin (*Brit*).
reißen *vti unreg* tear; (*ziehen*) pull, drag; (*Witz*) crack; **etw an sich ~** snatch sth up; (*fig*) take sth over; **sich um etw ~** scramble for sth; **hin und her gerissen sein** (*fig*) be torn; **wenn alle Stricke ~** (*fig umg*) if the worst happens.
Reißen [rī'sən] *nt* (*Gewichtheben: Disziplin*)

snatch; (*umg*: *Glieder~*) ache.

reißend *a* (*Fluß*) torrential; (*COMM*) rapid; **~en Absatz finden** sell like hot cakes (*umg*).

Reißer *m* **-s,** **-** (*umg*) thriller; **r~isch** *a* sensational.

Reiß- *zW*: **~leine** *f* (*AVIAT*) ripcord; **~nagel** *m* thumbtack (*US*), drawing pin (*Brit*); **~schiene** *f* T-square; **~verschluß** *m* zipper, zip (fastener) (*Brit*); **~wolf** *m* shredder; **durch den ~wolf geben** (*Dokumente*) shred; **~zeug** *nt* geometry set; **~zwecke** *f* = **~nagel**.

reiten [rī'tən] *vti unreg* ride.

Reiter(in *f)* *m* **-s,** **-** rider; (*MIL*) cavalryman, trooper.

Reiterei [rītərī'] *f* cavalry.

Reit- *zW*: **~hose** *f* riding breeches *pl*; **~pferd** *nt* saddle horse; **~stiefel** *m* riding boot; **~turnier** *nt* horse show; **~zeug** *nt* riding outfit.

Reiz [rīts] *m* **-es,** **-e** stimulus; (*angenehm*) charm; (*Verlockung*) attraction.

reizbar *a* irritable; **R~keit** *f* irritability.

reizen *vt* stimulate; (*unangenehm*) irritate; (*verlocken*) appeal to, attract; (*KARTEN*) bid ♦ *vi*: **zum Widerspruch ~** invite contradiction.

reizend *a* charming.

Reiz- *zW*: **~gas** *nt* tear gas, CS gas; **~husten** *m* constant chesty cough; **r~los** *a* unattractive; **r~voll** *a* attractive; **~wäsche** *f* sexy underwear; **~wort** *nt* emotive word.

rekapitulieren [rākápētōōlē:'rən] *vt* recapitulate.

rekeln [rā:'kəln] *vr* stretch out; (*lümmeln*) lounge *od* loll about.

Reklamation [rāklámátsēō:n'] *f* complaint.

Reklame [rāklä'mə] *f* **-,** **-n** advertising; (*Anzeige*) advertisement; **mit etw ~ machen** (*pej*) show off about sth; **~ machen für etw** advertise sth; **~trommel** *f*: **die ~trommel für jdn/etw rühren** (*umg*) beat the (big) drum for sb/sth; **~wand** *f* billboard.

reklamieren [rāklámē:'rən] *vti* complain (about); (*zurückfordern*) reclaim.

rekonstruieren [rākonstrōōē:'rən] *vt* reconstruct.

Rekonvaleszenz [rākonválestsents'] *f* convalescence.

Rekord [rākort'] *m* **-(e)s,** **-e** record; **~leistung** *f* record performance.

Rekrut [rākrōō:t'] *m* **-en,** **-en** recruit.

rekrutieren [rākrōōtē:'rən] *vt* recruit ♦ *vr* be recruited.

Rektor [rek'tor] *m* (*UNIV*) rector, vicechancellor; (*SCH*) principal.

Rektorat [rektorát'] *nt* **-(e)s,** **-e** rectorate, vice-chancellorship; principalship; (*Zimmer*) rector's *etc* office.

Rektorin [rektō:'rin] *f* (*SCH*) principal.

Rel. *abk* (= *Religion*) rel.

Relais [rəle:'] *nt* **-,** **-** relay.

Relation [rālátsēō:n'] *f* **-,** **-en** relation.

relativ [rālátē:f'] *a* relative.

Relativität [rālátēvēte:t'] *f* relativity.

Relativpronomen *nt* (*GRAM*) relative pronoun.

relevant [rālāvánt'] *a* relevant.

Relevanz *f* relevance.

Relief [rālēef'] *nt* **-s,** **-s** relief.

Religion [rālēgēō:n'] *f* religion.

Religions- *zW*: **~freiheit** *f* freedom of worship; **~lehre** *f,* **~unterricht** *m* religious instruction.

religiös [rālēgēœs'] *a* religious.

Relikt [rālikt'] *nt* **-(e)s,** **-e** relic.

Reling [rā:'ling] *f* **-,** **-s** (*NAUT*) rail.

Reliquie [rālē:k'vēə] *f* relic.

Reminiszenz [rāmēnistsents'] *f* reminiscence, recollection.

Remis [rəmē:'] *nt* **-,** **-** *od* **-en** (*SCHACH, SPORT*) draw.

Remittende [rāmiten'də] *f* **-,** **-n** (*COMM*) return.

Remittent *m* (*FIN*) payee.

remittieren *vt* (*COMM*: *Waren*) return; (*Geld*) remit.

Remmidemmi ['remē'demē] *nt* **-s** (*umg*: *Krach*) row, rumpus.

Remoulade [rāmōōlá'də] *f* remoulade.

rempeln [rem'pəln] *vti* (*umg*) jostle, elbow; (*SPORT*) barge (*jdn* into sb); (*foulen*) push.

Ren [ren] *nt* **-s,** **-s** *od* **-e** reindeer.

Renaissance [rənesâns'] *f* **-,** **-n** (*HIST*) renaissance; (*fig*) revival, rebirth.

Rendezvous [râñdāvōō:'] *nt* **-,** **-** rendezvous.

Rendite [rendē:'tə] *f* **-,** **-n** (*FIN*) yield, return on capital.

Rennbahn *f* racecourse; (*AUT*) circuit, racetrack.

rennen [re'nən] *vti unreg* run, race; **um die Wette ~** have a race; **R~** *nt* **-s,** **-** running; (*Wettbewerb*) race; **das R~ machen** (*lit, fig*) win (the race).

Renner *m* **-s,** **-** (*umg*) winner.

Renn- *zW*: **~fahrer** *m* race car driver (*US*), racing driver (*Brit*); **~pferd** *nt* racehorse; **~platz** *m* racecourse; **~sport** *m* racing; **~wagen** *m* race car (*US*), racing car (*Brit*).

renommiert [rānomē:rt'] *a* renowned, famous (*wegen* for).

renovieren [rānōvē:'rən] *vt* renovate.

Renovierung *f* renovation.

rentabel [rentá'bəl] *a* profitable, lucrative.

Rentabilität [rentábēlēte:t'] *f* profitability.

Rente [ren'tə] *f* **-,** **-n** pension.

Renten- *zW*: **~basis** *f* annuity basis; **~empfänger** *m* pensioner; **~papier** *nt* (*FIN*) fixed-interest security; **~versicherung** *f* pension plan.

Rentier [ren'tē:r] *nt* reindeer.

rentieren [rentē:'rən] *vir* pay, be profitable; **das rentiert (sich) nicht** it's not worth it.

Rentner(in *f)* [rent'nər(in)] *m* **-s,** **-** pensioner.

Reparation [rāpárátsēō:n'] *f* reparation.

Reparatur [räpárátōō:r'] *f* repairing; repair; **etw in ~ geben** have sth repaired; **r~bedürftig** *a* in need of repair; **~werkstatt** *f* repair shop; (*AUT*) garage.

reparieren [räpárē:'rən] *vt* repair.

Repertoire [räpertōár'] *nt* **-s, -s** repertoire.

Reportage [räportá'zhə] *f* **-, -n** (on-the-spot) report; (*TV, RAD*) live commentary *od* coverage.

Reporter [räpor'tər] *m* **-s,** - reporter, commentator.

Repräsentant(in *f***)** [räprezentánt'(in)] *m* representative.

repräsentativ [räprezentátē:f'] *a* representative; (*Geschenk etc*) prestigious; **die ~en Pflichten eines Botschafters** the social duties of an ambassador.

repräsentieren [räprezentē:'rən] *vti* represent.

Repressalien [räpresá'lēən] *pl* reprisals *pl*.

reprivatisieren [räprēvátēzē:'rən] *vt* denationalize.

Reprivatisierung *f* denationalization.

Reproduktion [räprōdōōktsēō:n'] *f* reproduction.

reproduzieren [räprōdōōtsē:'rən] *vt* reproduce.

Reptil [reptē:l'] *nt* **-s, -ien** reptile.

Republik [räpōōblē:k'] *f* republic.

Republikaner [räpōōblēká'nər] *m* **-s,** - republican.

republikanisch *a* republican.

Republikflucht *f* (*DDR*) *illegal crossing of the border*.

Requisit [räkvēzē:t'] *nt* **-en, -en: ~en** (*THEAT*) props, properties (*form*).

Reservat [räzervát'] *nt* **-(e)s, -e** reservation.

Reserve [räzer'və] *f* **-, -n** reserve; **jdn aus der ~ locken** bring sb out of his *od* her shell; **~rad** *nt* (*AUT*) spare wheel; **~spieler** *m* substitute; **~tank** *m* reserve tank.

reservieren [räzervē:'rən] *vt* reserve.

reserviert *a* (*Platz, Mensch*) reserved.

Reservist [räzervist'] *m* reservist.

Reservoir [räzervōár'] *nt* **-s, -e** reservoir.

Residenz [räzēdents'] *f* residence, seat.

residieren [räzēdē:'rən] *vi* reside.

Resignation [räzignátsēō:n'] *f* resignation.

resignieren [räzignē:'rən] *vi* resign.

resolut [räzōlōō:t'] *a* resolute.

Resolution [räzōlōōtsēō:n'] *f* resolution; (*Bittschrift*) petition.

Resonanz [räzōnánts'] *f* (*lit, fig*) resonance; **~boden** *m* sounding board; **~kasten** *m* soundbox.

Resopal [räzōpál'] *nt* **-s** ® Formica ®.

resozialisieren [räzōtsēálēzē:'rən] *vt* rehabilitate.

Resozialisierung *f* rehabilitation.

Respekt [respekt'] *m* **-(e)s** respect; (*Angst*) fear; **bei allem ~** with all due respect (*vor jdm/etw* to sb/for sth).

respektabel [respektá'bəl] *a* respectable.

respektieren [respektē:'rən] *vt* respect.

respektlos *a* disrespectful.

Respektsperson *f* person commanding respect.

Respekttage *pl* days of grace.

respektvoll *a* respectful.

Ressentiment [resántēmáṅ'] *nt* **-s, -s** resentment (*gegen* against).

Ressort [resō:r'] *nt* **-s, -s** department; **in das ~ von jdm fallen** (*lit, fig*) be sb's department.

Ressourcen [resōōr'sən] *pl* resources *pl*.

Rest [rest] *m* **-(e)s, -e** remainder, rest; (*Über~*) remains *pl*; **das hat mir den ~ gegeben** (*umg*) that finished me off; **~e** *pl* (*COMM*) remnants *pl*.

Restaurant [restōráṅ'] *nt* **-s, -s** restaurant.

Restauration [rästourátsēō:n'] *f* restoration.

restaurieren [rästourē:'rən] *vt* restore.

Rest- *zW:* **~betrag** *m* remainder, outstanding amount; **r~lich** *a* remaining; **r~los** *a* complete; **~posten** *m* (*COMM*) remaining stock.

Resultat [räzōōltát'] *nt* **-(e)s, -e** result.

Retorte [rätor'tə] *f* **-, -n** retort; **aus der ~** (*umg*) synthetic.

Retortenbaby *nt* test-tube baby.

retour [rätōō:r'] *ad* (*veraltet*) back.

Retouren *pl* (*Waren*) returns.

retten [re'tən] *vtr* save, rescue; **bist du noch zu ~?** (*umg*) are you out of your mind?; **sich vor etw nicht mehr ~ können** (*fig*) be swamped with sth.

Retter(in *f***)** *m* **-s,** - rescuer, savior (*US*), saviour (*Brit*).

Rettich [re'tiċh] *m* **-s, -e** radish.

Rettung *f* rescue; (*Hilfe*) help; **seine letzte ~** his last hope.

Rettungs- *zW:* **~aktion** *f* rescue operation; **~boot** *nt* lifeboat; **~gürtel** *m*, **~ring** *m* lifebelt, life preserver; **r~los** *a* hopeless; **~schwimmer** *m* lifesaver; (*am Strand*) lifeguard.

Return-Taste [rētœrn'tástə] *f* (*COMPUT*) return key.

retuschieren [rätōōshē:'rən] *vt* (*PHOT*) retouch.

Reue [roi'ə] *f* - remorse; (*Bedauern*) regret.

reuen *vt:* **es reut ihn** he regrets (it), he is sorry (about it).

reuig [roi'iċh] *a* penitent.

reumütig *a* remorseful; (*Sünder*) contrite.

Reuse [roi'zə] *f* **-, -n** fish trap.

Revanche [rävan'shə] *f* **-, -n** revenge; (*SPORT*) return match.

revanchieren [rävánshē:'rən] *vr* (*sich rächen*) get one's own back, have one's revenge; (*erwidern*) reciprocate, return the compliment.

Revers [rävē:r'] *m od nt* **-,** - lapel.

revidieren [rävēdē:'rən] *vt* revise; (*COMM*) audit.

Revier [rävē:r'] *nt* **-s, -e** district; (*MIN: Kohlen~*) (coal)mine; (*Jagd~*) preserve; (*Polizei~*) station house (*US*), police station (*Brit*); (*Dienstbereich*) precinct (*US*), beat

(*Brit*); (*MIL*) sick bay.
Revision [rävēzēō:n'] *f* revision; (*COMM*) auditing; (*JUR*) appeal.
Revisionsverhandlung *f* appeal hearing.
Revisor [rävē:'zor] *m* **-s, -en** (*COMM*) auditor.
Revolte [rävol'tə] *f* **-, -n** revolt.
Revolution [rävōlōōtsēō:n'] *f* revolution.
Revolutionär(in *f*) [rävōlōōtsēōne:r'(in)] *m* **-s, -e** revolutionary.
revolutionieren [rävōlōōtsēōnē:'rən] *vt* revolutionize.
Revoluzzer [rävōlōō'tsər] *m* **-s, -** (*pej*) would-be revolutionary.
Revolver [rävol'vər] *m* **-s, -** revolver.
Revue [rəvü:'] *f* **-, -n**: **etw ~ passieren lassen** (*fig*) pass sth in review.
Rezensent [rätsenzent'] *m* reviewer, critic.
rezensieren [rätsenzē:'rən] *vt* review.
Rezension *f* review, criticism.
Rezept [rätsept'] *nt* **-(e)s, -e** recipe; (*MED*) prescription.
Rezeption [rätseptsēō:n'] *f* (*von Hotel: Empfang*) reception.
rezeptpflichtig *a* available only on prescription.
Rezession [rätsesēō:n'] *f* (*FIN*) recession.
rezitieren [rätsētē:'rən] *vt* recite.
RGW *m* *abk* (= *Rat für gegenseitige Wirtschaftshilfe*) COMECON.
rh *abk* (= *Rhesus(faktor) negativ*) Rh negative.
Rh *abk* (= *Rhesus(faktor) positiv*) Rh positive.
Rh. *abk* = **Rhein**.
Rhabarber [rábár'bər] *m* **-s** rhubarb.
rhein. *abk* = **rheinisch**.
Rhein [rīn] *m* **-(e)s** Rhine; **~gau** *m* wine-growing area along the Rhine; **~hessen** *nt* wine-growing area along the Rhine.
rheinisch *a attr* Rhenish, Rhineland.
Rhein- *zW*: **~länder(in** *f*) *m* Rhinelander; **~land-Pfalz** *nt* Rhineland-Palatinate.
Rhesusfaktor [rā:'zōōsfáktor] *m* rhesus factor.
Rhetorik [rätō:'rik] *f* rhetoric.
rhetorisch [rätō:'rish] *a* rhetorical.
Rheuma [roi'má] *nt* **-s, Rheumatismus** [roimátis'mōōs] *m* rheumatism.
Rhinozeros [rēnō:'tsáros] *nt* - *od* **-ses, -se** rhinoceros; (*umg: Dummkopf*) fool.
Rhld. *abk* = *Rheinland*.
Rhodesien [rōdā:'zēən] *nt* **-s** Rhodesia.
Rhodos [rō:'dos] *nt* - Rhodes.
rhythmisch [rüt'mish] *a* rythmical.
Rhythmus *m* rhythm.
RIAS [rē:'ás] *m* - *abk* (= *Rundfunksender im amerikanischen Sektor (Berlin)*) *radio in the American sector of Berlin*.
Richtantenne [riçht'ántenə] *f* **-, -n** directional antenna *od* aerial (*bes Brit*).
richten [riçh'tən] *vt* direct (*an +akk* at; (*fig*) to); (*Waffe*) aim (*auf +akk* at); (*einstellen*) adjust; (*instand setzen*) repair; (*zurechtmachen*) prepare, get ready; (*adressie-

ren: *Briefe, Anfragen*) address (*an +akk* to); (*Bitten, Forderungen*) make (*an +akk* to); (*in Ordnung bringen*) do, fix; (*bestrafen*) pass judgement on ♦ *vr*: **sich ~ nach** go by; **wir ~ uns ganz nach unseren Kunden** we are guided entirely by our customers' wishes.
Richter(in *f*) *m* **-s, -** judge; **sich zum ~ machen** (*fig*) set (o.s.) up in judgement; **r~lich** *a* judicial.
Richtgeschwindigkeit *f* recommended speed.
richtig *a* right, correct; (*echt*) proper ♦ *ad* correctly, right; (*umg: sehr*) really; **der/die R~e** the right one *od* person; **das R~e** the right thing; **die Uhr geht ~** the clock is right; **R~keit** *f* correctness; **das hat schon seine R~keit** it's right enough; **R~stellung** *f* correction, rectification.
Richt- *zW*: **~linie** *f* guideline; **~preis** *m* recommended price; **~schnur** *f* (*fig: Grundsatz*) guiding principle.
Richtung *f* direction; (*Tendenz*) tendency, orientation; **in jeder ~** each way.
richtungsweisend *a*: **~ sein** point the way (ahead).
rieb [rē:p] *imperf von* **reiben**.
riechen [rē:'çhən] *vti unreg* smell (*an etw dat* sth); **es riecht nach Gas** there's a smell of gas; **ich kann das/ihn nicht ~** (*umg*) I can't stand it/him; **das konnte ich doch nicht ~!** (*umg*) how was I (supposed) to know?
Riecher *m* **-s, -**: **einen guten** *od* **den richtigen ~ haben** (*umg*) have a nose (*für etw* for sth).
Ried [rē:t] *nt* **-(e)s, -e** reed; (*Moor*) marsh.
rief [rē:f] *imperf von* **rufen**.
Riege [rē:'gə] *f* **-, -n** team, squad.
Riegel [rē:'gəl] *m* **-s, -** bolt, bar; **einer Sache** (*dat*) **einen ~ vorschieben** (*fig*) clamp down on sth.
Riemen [rē:'mən] *m* **-s, -** strap; (*Gürtel, TECH*) belt; (*NAUT*) oar; **sich am ~ reißen** (*fig umg*) get a grip on o.s.; **~antrieb** *m* belt drive.
Riese [rē:'zə] *m* **-n, -n** giant.
rieseln *vi* trickle; (*Schnee*) fall gently.
Riesen- *zW*: **~erfolg** *m* enormous success; **~gebirge** *nt* (*GEOG*) Sudeten Mountains *pl*; **r~groß** *a*, **r~haft** *a* colossal, gigantic, huge; **~rad** *nt* big *od* Ferris wheel; **~schritt** *m*: **sich mit ~schritten nähern** (*fig*) be drawing on apace.
riesig [rē:'ziçh] *a* enormous, huge, vast.
Riesin *f* giantess.
riet [rē:t] *imperf von* **raten**.
Riff [rif] *nt* **-(e)s, -e** reef.
rigoros [rēgōrō:s'] *a* rigorous.
Rille [ri'lə] *f* **-, -n** groove.
Rind [rint] *nt* **-(e)s, -er** ox; cow; (*KOCH*) beef; **~er** cattle *pl*; **vom ~** beef.
Rinde [rin'də] *f* **-, -n** rind; (*Baum~*) bark; (*Brot~*) crust.

Rindfleisch *nt* beef.
Rindsbraten *m* roast beef.
Rindvieh *nt* cattle *pl*; (*umg*) blockhead, stupid oaf.
Ring [riŋ] *m* -(e)s, -e ring; ~**buch** *nt* ring binder.
ringeln [ˈriŋəln] *vt* (*Pflanze*) (en)twine; (*Schwanz etc auch*) curl ♦ *vr* go curly, curl; (*Rauch*) curl up(wards).
Ringel- *zW*: ~**natter** *f* grass snake; ~**taube** *f* wood pigeon.
ringen *vi unreg* wrestle; (*streben*) **nach** *od* **um etw** ~ struggle for sth; **R~** *nt* -s wrestling.
Ring- *zW*: ~**finger** *m* ring finger; **r~förmig** *a* ring-shaped; ~**kampf** *m* wrestling match; ~**richter** *m* referee.
rings *ad*: ~ **um** round; ~**herum** *ad* round about.
Ringstraße *f* ring road.
ringsum(her) [ˈriŋsˈʊm, ˈriŋsʊmˈhɛːr] *ad* (*rundherum*) round about; (*überall*) all round.
Rinne [ˈrinə] *f* -, -n gutter, drain.
rinnen *vi unreg* run, trickle.
Rinn- *zW*: ~**sal** *nt* -s, -e trickle of water; ~**stein** *m* gutter.
Rippchen [ˈripçən] *nt* small rib; cutlet.
Rippe [ˈripə] *f* -, -n rib.
Rippen- *zW*: ~**fellentzündung** *f* pleurisy; ~**speer** *m od nt* (*KOCH*): **Kasseler ~speer** *slightly cured pork spare rib*; ~**stoß** *m* jab in the ribs.
Risiko [ˈriːzikoː] *nt* -s, -s *od* **Risiken** risk; **r~behaftet** *a* fraught with risk; ~**investition** *f* sunk cost.
riskant [risˈkant] *a* risky, hazardous.
riskieren [risˈkiːrən] *vt* risk.
riß [ris] *imperf von* **reißen**.
Riß *m* -sses, -sse tear; (*in Mauer, Tasse etc*) crack; (*in Haut*) scratch; (*TECH*) design.
rissig [ˈrisiç] *a* torn; cracked; scratched.
ritt [rit] *imperf von* **reiten**.
Ritt *m* -(e)s, -e ride.
Ritter *m* -s, - knight; **jdn zum** ~ **schlagen** knight sb; **arme** ~ *pl* (*KOCH*) *sweet French toast soaked in milk*; **r~lich** *a* chivalrous; ~**schlag** *m* knighting; ~**tum** *nt* -s chivalry; ~**zeit** *f* age of chivalry.
rittlings *ad* astride.
Ritual [ritoˈaːl] *nt* -s, -e *od* -ien (*lit, fig*) ritual.
Ritus [ˈriːtus] *m* -, **Riten** rite.
Ritze [ˈritsə] *f* -, -n crack, chink.
ritzen *vt* scratch; **die Sache ist geritzt** (*umg*) it's all fixed up.
Rivale [riˈvaːlə] *m* -n, -n rival.
rivalisieren [rivaliˈziːrən] *vi*: **mit jdm** ~ compete with sb.
Rivalität [rivaliːtɛˈtiː] *f* rivalry.
Rizinusöl [ˈriːtsinusˈøːl] *nt* castor oil.
Rj. *abk* = **Rechnungsjahr**.
r.-k., röm.-kath. *abk* (= *römisch-katholisch*) R.C.

Robbe [ˈrobə] *f* -, -n seal.
robben [ˈrobən] *vi aux sein* (*MIL auch*) crawl.
Robbenfang *m* seal hunting.
Robe [ˈroːbə] *f* -, -n robe.
Roboter [roˈbotər] *m* -s, - robot; ~**technik** *f* robotics *sing*.
Robotik [roˈbotik] *f* robotics *sing*.
robust [roˈbʊst'] *a* (*Mensch, Gesundheit*) robust; (*Material*) tough.
roch [rox] *imperf von* **riechen**.
Rochade [roˈxaːdə] *f* -, -n (*SCHACH*): **die kleine/große** ~ castling king's side/queen's side.
röcheln [ˈrœçəln] *vi* wheeze; (*Sterbender*) give the death rattle.
Rock [rok] *m* -(e)s, ¨e skirt; (*Jackett*) jacket; (*Uniform~*) tunic; ~**zipfel** *m*: **an Mutters ~zipfel hängen** (*umg*) cling to (one's) mother's apron strings.
Rodel [ˈroːdəl] *m* -s, - toboggan; ~**bahn** *f* toboggan run.
rodeln *vi* toboggan.
roden [ˈroːdən] *vti* clear.
Rogen [ˈroːgən] *m* -s, - roe.
Roggen [ˈrogən] *m* -s, - rye; ~**brot** *nt* rye bread, black bread.
roh [roː] *a* raw; (*Mensch*) coarse, crude; ~**e Gewalt** brute force; **R~bau** *m* shell of a building; **R~eisen** *nt* pig iron; **R~fassung** *f* rough draft; **R~kost** *f* raw fruit and vegetables *pl*; **R~ling** *m* ruffian; **R~material** *nt* raw material; **R~öl** *nt* crude oil.
Rohr [roːr] *nt* -(e)s, -e pipe, tube; (*BOT*) cane; (*Schilf*) reed; (*Gewehr~*) barrel; ~**bruch** *m* burst pipe.
Röhre [ˈrœːrə] *f* -, -n tube, pipe; (*RAD etc*) valve; (*Back~*) oven.
Rohr- *zW*: ~**geflecht** *nt* wickerwork; ~**leger** *m* -s, - plumber; ~**leitung** *f* pipeline; ~**post** *f* pneumatic post; ~**spatz** *m*: **schimpfen wie ein ~spatz** (*umg*) curse and swear; ~**stock** *m* cane; ~**stuhl** *m* basket chair; ~**zucker** *m* cane sugar.
Roh- *zW*: ~**seide** *f* raw silk; ~**stoff** *m* raw material.
Rokoko [roˈkokoː] *nt* -s rococo.
Roll- [rol'] *zW*: ~**(l)aden** *m* shutter; ~**bahn** *f* (*AVIAT*) runway.
Rolle [ˈrolə] *f* -, -n roll; (*THEAT, SOZIOLOGIE*) role; (*Garn~ etc*) reel, spool; (*Walze*) roller; (*Wäsche~*) mangle; **bei** *od* **in etw** (*dat*) **eine** ~ **spielen** play a part in sth; (*Mensch auch*) play a role in sth; **aus der** ~ **fallen** (*fig*) forget o.s.; **keine** ~ **spielen** not matter.
rollen *vti* roll; (*AVIAT*) taxi; (*Wäsche*) mangle; **den Stein ins R~ bringen** (*fig*) start the ball rolling.
Rollen- *zW*: ~**besetzung** *f* (*THEAT*) cast; ~**konflikt** *m* (*PSYCH*) role conflict; ~**spiel** *nt* role-play exercise; ~**tausch** *m* exchange of roles; (*SOZIOLOGIE auch*) role reversal.
Roller *m* -s, - scooter; (*Welle*) roller.
Roll- *zW*: ~**feld** *nt* runway; ~**kragen** *m* roll *od* polo neck; ~**mops** *m* pickled herring.

Rollo |ro'lō| *nt* -, -s (roller) blind.

Roll- *zW:* ~**schrank** *m* roll-fronted cupboard; ~**schuh** *m* roller skate; ~**splitt** *m* grit; ~**stuhl** *m* wheelchair; ~**treppe** *f* escalator.

röm. *abk* = **römisch.**

Rom |rō:m| *nt* -s Rome; **das sind Zustände wie im alten** ~ (*umg:* unmoralisch) it's disgraceful; (: *primitiv*) it's medieval (*umg*).

Roman |rōmán'| *m* -s, -e novel; **(jdm) einen ganzen** ~ **erzählen** (*umg*) give (sb) a long rigmarole; ~**heft** *nt* pulp novel.

romanisch *a* (*Volk, Sprache*) Romance; (*KUNST*) Romanesque.

Romanistik |rōmánis'tik| *f* (*UNIV*) Romance languages and literature.

Romanschreiber *m*, **Romanschriftsteller** *m* novelist.

Romantik |rōmán'tik| *f* romanticism.

Romantiker(in *f*) *m* -s, - romanticist.

romantisch *a* romantic.

Romanze |rōmán'tsə| *f* -, -n romance.

Römer |rœ'mər| *m* -s, - wineglass; (*Mensch*) Roman; ~**topf** *m* ℝ (*KOCH*) ≈ (chicken) brick.

römisch |rœ'mish| *a* Roman.

Rommé |romā:'| *nt* -s, -s rummy.

röntgen |rœnt'gən| *vt* X-ray; **R**~**aufnahme** *f*, **R**~**bild** *nt* X-ray; **R**~**strahlen** *pl* X-rays *pl*.

rosa |rō:'zà| *a inv* pink, rose(-coloured).

Rose |rō:'zə| *f* -, -n rose.

Rosenkohl *m* Brussels sprouts *pl*.

Rosen- *zW:* ~**kranz** *m* rosary; ~**montag** *m* Monday of Shrovetide.

Rosette |rōzε'tə| *f* rosette.

rosig |rō:'zich| *a* rosy.

Rosine |rōzē:'nə| *f* raisin; **(große)** ~**n im Kopf haben** (*umg*) have big ideas.

Rosmarin |rō:s'márē:n| *m* -s rosemary.

Roß |ros| *nt* -sses, -sse horse, steed; **auf dem hohen** ~ **sitzen** (*fig*) be on one's high horse; ~**kastanie** *f* horse chestnut; ~**kur** *f* (*umg*) kill-or-cure remedy.

Rost |rost| *m* -(e)s, -e rust; (*Gitter*) grill, gridiron; (*Bett*~) springs *pl;* ~**braten** *m* roast(ed) meat, joint; ~**bratwurst** *f* grilled *od* barbecued sausage.

rosten *vi* rust.

rösten |rœs'tən| *vt* roast; toast; broil (*US*), grill (*Brit*).

rostfrei *a* (*Stahl*) stainless.

rostig *a* rusty.

Röstkartoffeln *pl* fried potatoes *pl*.

Rostschutz *m* rustproofing.

rot |rō:t| *a* red; ~ **werden, einen** ~**en Kopf bekommen** blush, go red; ~ **sehen** (*umg*) see red, become angry; **die R**~**e Armee** the Red Army; **das R**~**e Kreuz** the Red Cross; **das R**~**e Meer** the Red Sea.

Rotation |rōtátsēō:n'| *f* rotation.

rot- *zW:* ~**bäckig** *a* red-cheeked; **R**~**barsch** *m* rosefish, ocean perch (*US*); ~**blond** *a* strawberry blond.

Röte |rœ'tə| *f* - redness.

Röteln *pl* German measles *sing*.

röten *vtr* redden.

rothaarig *a* red-haired.

rotieren |rōtē:'rən| *vi* rotate.

Rot- *zW:* ~**käppchen** *nt* Little Red Riding Hood; ~**kehlchen** *nt* robin; ~**kohl** *m,* ~**kraut** *nt* red cabbage; ~**stift** *m* red pencil; ~**wein** *m* red wine.

Rotz |rots| *m* -es, -e (*umg*) snot; **r**~**frech** *a* (*umg*) cocky; **r**~**näsig** *a* (*umg*) snotty-nosed.

Roulade |rōōlá'də| *f* (*KOCH*) filled roll of beef.

Route |rōō:'tə| *f* -, -n route.

Routine |rōōtē:'nə| *f* experience; (*Gewohnheit*) routine.

routiniert |rōōtēnē:'ərt| *a* experienced.

Rowdy |rou'di| *m* -s, -s *od* **Rowdies** hooligan; (*zerstörerisch*) vandal; (*lärmend*) rowdy (type).

rubbeln |rōō'bəln| *vti* (*umg*) rub.

Rübe |rü:'bə| *f* -, -n turnip; **gelbe** ~ carrot; **rote** ~ beet (*US*), beetroot (*Brit*).

Rübenzucker *m* beet sugar.

Rubin |rōōbē:n'| *m* -s, -e ruby.

Rubrik |rōōbrē:k'| *f* heading; (*Spalte*) column.

Ruck |rōōk| *m* -(e)s, -e jerk, jolt; **sich** (*dat*) **einen** ~ **geben** (*fig umg*) make an effort; **r**~, **zuck** *ad:* **das geht r**~, **zuck** it won't take a second.

Rückantwort *f* reply, answer; **um** ~ **wird gebeten** please reply.

ruckartig *a:* **er stand** ~ **auf** he shot to his feet.

Rück- |rük'| *zW:* ~**besinnung** *f* recollection; **r**~**bezüglich** *a* reflexive; **r**~**blenden** *vi* flash back; ~**blick** *m:* **im** ~**blick auf etw** (*akk*) looking back on sth; **r**~**blickend** *a* retrospective; **r**~**datieren** *vt* backdate.

rücken *vti* move.

Rücken *m* -s, - back; (*Berg*~) ridge; **jdm in den** ~ **fallen** (*fig*) stab sb in the back; ~**deckung** *f* backing; ~**lage** *f* supine position; ~**lehne** *f* back (of chair); ~**mark** *nt* spinal cord; ~**schwimmen** *nt* backstroke; ~**stärkung** *f* (*fig*) moral support; ~**wind** *m* following wind.

Rück- *zW:* ~**erstattung** *f* return, restitution; ~**fahrscheinwerfer** *npl* back-up lights (*US*), reversing lights (*Brit*); ~**fahrt** *f* return journey; ~**fall** *m* relapse; **r**~**fällig** *a* relapsed; **r**~**fällig werden** relapse; ~**flug** *m* return flight; ~**frage** *f* question; **nach** ~**frage bei der zuständigen Behörde** ... after checking this with the appropriate authority ...; ~**führung** *f* (*von Menschen*) repatriation, return; ~**gabe** *f* return; **gegen** ~**gabe** on return; ~**gang** *m* decline, fall; **r**~**gängig** *a:* **etw r**~**gängig machen** cancel sth; ~**gewinnung** *f* recovery; (*von Land, Gebiet*) reclaiming; (*aus verbrauchten Stoffen*) recycling.

Rückgrat *nt* -(e)s, -e spine, backbone.

Rück- *zW:* ~**griff** *m* recourse; ~**halt** *m* backing; (*Einschränkung*) reserve; **r**~**haltlos** *a*

unreserved; **r~kaufbar** _a_ redeemable;
~kehr _f_ -, **-en** return; **~koppelung** _f_ feedback; **~lage** _f_ reserve, savings _pl_; **~lauf** _m_
reverse running; (_beim Tonband_) fast rewind; (_von Maschinenteil_) return travel;
r~läufig _a_ declining, falling; **eine r~läufige
Entwicklung** a decline; **~licht** _nt_ back light;
r~lings _ad_ from behind; (_rückwärts_) backwards; **~meldung** _f_ (_UNIV_) reregistration;
~nahme _f_ -, **-n** taking back; **~porto** _nt_ return postage; **~reise** _f_ return journey;
(_NAUT_) home voyage; **~ruf** _m_ recall.
Rucksack [rōōk'zak] _m_ rucksack.
Rück- _zW:_ **~schau** _f_ reflection; **r~schauend**
_a_ retrospective, in retrospect; **~schluß** _m_
conclusion; **~schritt** _m_ retrogression;
r~schrittlich _a_ reactionary; retrograde;
~seite _f_ back; (_von Münze etc_) reverse;
siehe ~seite see over(leaf); **r~setzen** _vt_
(_COMPUT_) reset; **~sicht** _f_ consideration;
~sicht nehmen auf (+_akk_) show consideration for; **~sichtnahme** _f_ consideration.
rücksichts- _zW:_ **~los** _a_ inconsiderate;
(_Fahren_) reckless; (_unbarmherzig_) ruthless;
~voll _a_ considerate.
Rück- _zW:_ **~sitz** _m_ back seat; **~spiegel** _m_
(_AUT_) rear-view mirror; **~spiel** _nt_ return
match; **~sprache** _f_ further discussion _od_
talk; **~sprache mit jdm nehmen** confer
with sb; **~stand** _m_ arrears _pl_; (_Verzug_) delay; **r~ständig** _a_ backward, out-of-date;
(_Zahlungen_) in arrears; **~stoß** _m_ recoil;
~strahler _m_ **-s**, - rear reflector; **~strom** _m_
(_von Menschen, Fahrzeugen_) return (_from
vacation etc_); **~taste** _f_ (_an Schreib-
maschine_) backspace key; **~tritt** _m_ resignation; **~trittbremse** _f_ backpedal brake.
Rücktrittsklausel _f_ (_Vertrag_) escape clause.
Rück- _zW:_ **~vergütung** _f_ repayment;
(_COMM_) refund; **r~versichern** _vti_ reinsure ♦
_vr_ check (up _od_ back); **~versicherung** _f_ re-
insurance; **r~wärtig** _a_ rear; **r~wärts** _ad_
backward(s), back; **~wärtsgang** _m_ (_AUT_)
reverse gear; **im ~wärtsgang fahren** reverse; **~weg** _m_ return journey, way back;
r~wirkend _a_ retroactive; **~wirkung** _f_ repercussion; **eine Zahlung/Gesetzesände-
rung mit ~wirkung vom** ... a payment
backdated to/an amendment made retrospective to ...; **~zahlung** _f_ repayment; **~zieher**
_m_ (_umg_): **einen ~zieher machen** back out;
~zug _m_ retreat; **~zugsgefecht** _nt_ (_MIL, fig_)
rearguard action.
rüde [rü'də] _a_ blunt, gruff.
Rüde _m_ **-n**, **-n** male dog _od_ fox _od_ wolf.
Rudel [rōō'dəl] _nt_ **-s**, - pack; (_von Hirschen_)
herd.
Ruder [rōō'dər] _nt_ **-s**, - oar; (_Steuer_) rudder;
das ~ fest in der Hand haben (_fig_) be in
control of the situation; **~boot** _nt_ rowing
boat; **~er** _m_ **-s**, - rower.
rudern _vti_ row; **mit den Armen ~** (_fig_) flail
one's arms about.
Ruf [rōō:f] _m_ **-(e)s**, **-e** call, cry; (_Ansehen_)

reputation; (_UNIV_: _Berufung_) offer of a
chair.
rufen _vti_ _unreg_ call; (_aus~_) cry; **um Hilfe ~**
call for help; **das kommt mir wie gerufen**
that's just what I needed.
Rüffel [rü'fəl] _m_ **-s**, - (_umg_) telling- _od_
ticking-off.
Ruf- _zW:_ **~mord** _m_ character assassination;
~name _m_ usual (first) name; **~nummer** _f_
(tele)phone number; **~säule** _f_ (_für Taxi_)
telephone; (_an Autobahn_) emergency telephone; **~zeichen** _nt_ (_RAD_) call sign; (_TEL_)
ringing tone.
Rüge [rü'gə] _f_ -, **-n** reprimand, rebuke.
rügen _vt_ reprimand.
Ruhe [rōō:'ə] _f_ - rest; (_Ungestörtheit_) peace,
quiet; (_Gelassenheit, Stille_) calm; (_Schwei-
gen_) silence; **~!** be quiet!, silence!; **angenehme ~!** sleep well!; **~bewahren** stay
cool _od_ calm; **das läßt ihm keine ~** he
can't stop thinking about it; **sich zur ~ setzen** retire; **die ~ weghaben** (_umg_) be unflappable; **immer mit der ~** (_umg_) don't
panic; **die letzte ~ finden** (_liter_) be laid to
rest; **~lage** _f_ (_von Mensch_) reclining position; (_MED: bei Bruch_) immobile position;
r~los _a_ restless.
ruhen _vi_ rest; (_Arbeit auch, Verkehr_) cease;
(_Waffen_) be laid down; (_begraben sein_) lie,
be buried.
Ruhe- _zW:_ **~pause** _f_ break; **~platz** _m_ resting
place; **~stand** _m_ retirement; **~stätte** _f_:
letzte ~stätte final resting place; **~störung**
_f_ breach of the peace; **~tag** _m_ closing day.
ruhig [rōō:'iç] _a_ quiet; (_bewegungslos_) still;
(_Hand_) steady; (_gelassen, friedlich_) calm;
(_Gewissen_) clear; **tu das ~** feel free to do
that; **etw ~ mitansehen** (_gleichgültig_)
stand by and watch sth; **du könntest ~ mal
etwas für mich tun!** it's about time you did
something for me!
Ruhm [rōō:m] _m_ **-(e)s** fame, glory.
rühmen [rü'mən] _vt_ praise ♦ _vr_ boast.
rühmlich _a_ praiseworthy; (_Ausnahme_) notable.
ruhm- _zW:_ **~los** _a_ inglorious; **~reich** _a_ glorious.
Ruhr [rōō:r] _f_ - dysentery.
Rührei [rü:r'ī] _nt_ scrambled egg.
rühren _vtr_ (_lit, fig_) move, stir (_auch KOCH_) ♦
_vi_: **~von** come _od_ stem from; **~ an** (+_akk_)
touch; (_fig_) touch on.
rührend _a_ touching, moving; **das ist ~ von
Ihnen** that is sweet of you.
Ruhrgebiet _nt_ Ruhr (area).
rührig _a_ active, lively.
rührselig _a_ sentimental, emotional.
Rührung _f_ emotion.
Ruin [rōōē:n'] _m_ **-s** ruin; **vor dem ~ stehen**
be on the brink _od_ verge of ruin.
Ruine _f_ -, **-n** (_lit, fig_) ruin.
ruinieren [rōōēnē:'rən] _vt_ ruin.
rülpsen [rülp'sən] _vti_ burp, belch.
rum _ad_ (_umg_) = **herum**.

Rum [rōōm] *m* **-s, -s** rum.
Rumäne [rōōme:'nə] *m* **-n, -n, Rumänin** *f* Romanian.
Rumänien *nt* **-s** Romania.
rumänisch *a* Romanian.
rumfuhrwerken [rōōm'fōō:rverkən] *vt* (*umg*) bustle around.
Rummel [rōōm'əl] *m* **-s** (*umg*) hubbub; (*Jahrmarkt*) fair; ~**platz** *m* fairground, fair.
rumoren [rōōmō:'rən] *vi* be noisy, make a noise.
Rumpelkammer [rōōm'pəlkâmər] *f* junk room.
rumpeln *vi* rumble; (*holpern*) jolt.
Rumpf [rōōmpf] *m* **-(e)s, ⁼e** trunk, torso; (*AVIAT*) fuselage; (*NAUT*) hull.
rümpfen [rümp'fən] *vt* (*Nase*) turn up.
Rumtopf *m* soft fruit in rum.
rund [rōōnt] *a* round ◆ *ad* (*etwa*) around; ~ **um etw** round sth; **jetzt geht's** ~ (*umg*) this is where the fun starts; **wenn der das erfährt, geht's** ~ (*umg*) there'll be a to-do when he finds out; **R~bogen** *m* Norman *od* Romanesque arch; **R~brief** *m* circular.
Runde [rōōn'də] *f* **-, -n** round; (*in Rennen*) lap; (*Gesellschaft*) circle; **die** ~ **machen** do the rounds; (*herumgegeben werden*) be passed round; **über die** ~ **kommen** (*SPORT, fig*) pull through; **eine** ~ **spendieren** *od* **schmeißen** (*umg*: *Getränke*) stand a round.
runden *vt* make round ◆ *vr* (*fig*) take shape.
rund- *zW*: ~**erneuert** *a* (*Reifen*) retreaded (*US*), remoulded (*Brit*); **R~fahrt** *f* (round) trip; ~**frage** *f* survey (*an +akk, unter +dat* of).
Rundfunk [rōōnt'fōōngk] *m* **-(e)s** broadcasting; (*bes Hörfunk*) radio; (~*anstalt*) broadcasting service; **im** ~ on the radio; ~**anstalt** *f* broadcasting corporation; ~**empfang** *m* reception; ~**gebühr** *f* license (*US*), licence (*Brit*); ~**gerät** *nt* radio set; ~**sendung** *f* broadcast, radio program.
Rund- *zW*: ~**gang** *m* (*Spaziergang*) walk; (*von Wachmann*) rounds *pl*; (*von Briefträger etc*) round; (*zur Besichtigung*) tour (*durch* of); **r~heraus** *ad* straight out, bluntly; **r~herum** *ad* all round; (*fig umg: völlig*) totally; **r~lich** *a* plump, rounded; ~**reise** *f* round trip; ~**schreiben** *nt* (*COMM*) circular; **r~um** *ad* all around; (*fig*) completely; ~**ung** *f* curve, roundness; **r~weg** *ad* straight out.
runter [rōōn'tər] *ad* (*umg*) = herunter, hinunter; ~**würgen** *vt* (*umg*: *Ärger*) swallow.
Runzel [rōōn'tsəl] *f* **-, -n** wrinkle.
runz(e)lig *a* wrinkled.
runzeln *vt* wrinkle; **die Stirn** ~ frown.
Rüpel [rü:'pəl] *m* **-s, -** lout; **r~haft** *a* loutish.
rupfen [rōōp'fən] *vt* pluck; **wie ein gerupftes Huhn aussehen** look like a shorn sheep.
Rupfen *m* **-s, -** sackcloth.
ruppig [rōō'piçh] *a* rough, gruff.

Rüsche [rü:'shə] *f* **-, -n** frill.
Ruß [rōō:s] *m* **-es** soot.
Russe [rōō'sə] *m* **-n, -n** Russian, Russian man *od* boy.
Rüssel [rü:'səl] *m* **-s, -** snout; (*Elefanten~*) trunk.
rußen *vi* smoke; (*Ofen*) be sooty.
rußig *a* sooty.
Russin *f* Russian, Russian woman *od* girl.
russisch *a* Russian; ~**e Eier** (*KOCH*) egg(s) mayonnaise.
Rußland *nt* **-s** Russia.
rüsten [rü:'stən] *vtir* prepare; (*MIL*) arm.
rüstig [rü:'stiçh] *a* sprightly, vigorous; **R~keit** *f* sprightliness, vigor (*US*), vigour (*Brit*).
rustikal [rōōstēkâl'] *a*: **sich** ~ **einrichten** furnish one's home in a rustic style.
Rüstung [rü:'stōōng] *f* preparation; (*MIL*) arming; (*Ritter~*) armor (*US*), armour (*Brit*); (*Waffen etc*) armaments *pl*.
Rüstungs- *zW*: ~**gegner** *m* opponent of the arms race; ~**kontrolle** *f* arms control; ~**wettlauf** *m* arms race.
Rüstzeug *nt* tools *pl*; (*fig*) capacity.
Rute [rōō:'tə] *f* **-, -n** rod, switch.
Rutsch [rōōtsh] *m* **-(e)s, -e** slide; (*Erd~*) landslide; **guten** ~! (*umg*) have a good New Year!; ~**bahn** *f* slide.
rutschen *vi* slide; (*aus~*) slip; **auf dem Stuhl hin und her** ~ fidget around on one's chair.
rutschfest *a* non-slip.
rutschig *a* slippery.
rütteln [rü:'təln] *vti* shake, jolt; **daran ist nicht zu** ~ (*fig umg*: *an Grundsätzen*) there's no doubt about that.

S

S, s [es] *nt* S, s.
s *abk* (= *Sekunde*) sec.; (= *siehe*) v., vid.
S *abk* (= *Süden*) S; (= *Seite*) p.
s.a. *abk* (= *siehe auch*) see also.
SA *f* - *abk* (= *Sturmabteilung*) SA.
Saal [zâl] *m* **-(e)s, Säle** hall; (*für Sitzungen etc*) room.
Saarland [zâr'lânt] *nt* **-s** Saarland.
Saat [zât] *f* **-, -en** seed; (*Pflanzen*) crop; (*Säen*) sowing; ~**gut** *nt* seed(s *pl*).
sabbern [zä'bərn] *vi* (*umg*) dribble.
Säbel [ze:'bəl] *m* **-s, -** saber (*US*), sabre (*Brit*), sword.
Sabotage [zäbōtä'zhə] *f* **-, -n** sabotage.
sabotieren [zäbōtē:'rən] *vt* sabotage.
Sachanlagen [zäḥ'ânlâgən] *pl* tangible assets *pl*.
Sachbearbeiter(in *f)* *m* specialist;

(Beamter) official in charge *(für* of).
Sachbuch *nt* non-fiction book.
sachdienlich *a* relevant, helpful.
Sache [zá'ʞʰə] *f* -, -n thing; *(Angelegenheit)* affair, business; *(Frage)* matter; *(Pflicht)* task; *(Thema)* subject; *(JUR)* case; *(Aufgabe)* job; *(Ideal)* cause; **ich habe mir die ~ anders vorgestellt** I had imagined things differently; **er versteht seine ~** he knows what he's doing; **das ist so eine ~** *(umg)* it's a bit tricky; **mach keine ~n!** *(umg)* don't be daft!; **bei der ~ bleiben** *(bei Diskussion)* keep to the point; **bei der ~ sein** be with it *(umg)*; **das ist ~ der Polizei** this is a matter for the police; **zur ~** to the point; *(Tempo)*: **mit 60/100 ~n** *(umg)* at 60/100; **das ist eine runde ~** that is well-balanced *od* rounded-off.
Sachertorte [zá'ʞʰərtortə] *f* -, -n *a* rich chocolate cake, sachertorte.
Sach- *zW*: **s~gemäß** *a* appropriate, suitable; **~kenntnis** *f* *(in bezug auf Wissensgebiet)* knowledge of the *od* his *etc* subject; *(in bezug auf ~lage)* knowledge of the facts; **s~kundig** *a* expert; **~lage** *f* situation, state of affairs; **~leistung** *f* payment in kind; **s~lich** *a* matter-of-fact; *(Kritik etc)* objective; *(Irrtum, Angabe)* factual; **bleiben Sie bitte s~lich** don't get carried away *(umg)*; *(nicht persönlich werden)* please stay objective.
sächlich [zeʞʰ'liʞʰ] *a* neuter.
Sach- *zW*: **~register** *nt* subject index; **~schaden** *m* damage to property.
Sachse [zák'sə] *m* -n, -n, **Sächsin** *f* Saxon.
Sachsen *nt* -s Saxony.
sächsisch [zek'sish] *a* Saxon.
sacht(e) *ad* softly, gently.
Sach- *zW*: **~verhalt** *m* -(e), -e facts *pl* (of the case); **~verständige(r)** *mf dekl wie a* expert; **~zwang** *m* force of circumstances.
Sack [zák] *m* -(e)s, -̈e sack; *(aus Papier, Plastik)* bag; *(ANAT, ZOOL)* sac; *(umg!: Hoden)* balls *pl* (!); *(: Kerl, Bursche)* bastard *(!)*; **mit ~ und Pack** *(umg)* with bag and baggage.
sacken *vi* sag, sink.
Sack- *zW*: **~gasse** *f* cul-de-sac, dead-end street *(US)*; **~hüpfen** *nt* sack race.
Sadismus [zádis'moos] *m* sadism.
Sadist(in *f)* [zádist'(in)] *m* sadist; **s~isch** *a* sadistic.
säen [ze:'ən] *vti* sow; **dünn gesät** *(fig)* thin on the ground, few and far between.
Saft [záft] *m* -(e)s, -̈e juice; *(BOT)* sap; **ohne ~ und Kraft** *(fig)* wishy-washy *(umg)*, effete.
saftig *a* juicy; *(Grün)* lush; *(umg: Rechnung, Ohrfeige)* hefty; *(Brief, Antwort)* potent.
Saft- *zW*: **~laden** *m* *(pej, umg)* rum joint; **s~los** *a* dry.
Sage [zá'gə] *f* -, -n saga.
Säge [ze:'gə] *f* -, -n saw; **~blatt** *nt* saw blade; **~mehl** *nt* sawdust.

sagen [zá'gən] *vti* say *(jdm* to sb), tell *(jdm* sb); **unter uns gesagt** between you and me (and the gatepost *hum umg)*; **laß dir das gesagt sein** take it from me; **das hat nichts zu ~** that doesn't mean anything; **sagt dir der Name etwas?** does the name mean anything to you?; **das ist nicht gesagt** that's by no means certain; **sage und schreibe** (whether you) believe it or not.
sägen *vti* saw; *(hum umg: schnarchen)* snore, saw wood *(US)*.
sagen- *zW*: **~haft** *a* legendary; *(umg)* great, smashing; **~umwoben** *a* legendary.
Säge- *zW*: **~späne** *pl* wood shavings *pl*; **~werk** *nt* sawmill.
sah [zá] *imperf von* **sehen**.
Sahara [záhá'rá] *f* Sahara (Desert).
Sahne [zá'nə] *f* - cream.
Saison [zezõn'] *f* -, -s season.
saisonal [zezõnál'] *a* seasonal.
Saison- *zW*: **~arbeiter** *m* seasonal worker; **s~bedingt** *a* seasonal.
Saite [zī'tə] *f* -, -n string; **andere ~n aufziehen** *(umg)* get tough.
Saiteninstrument *nt* string(ed) instrument.
Sakko [zá'kõ] *m od nt* -s, -s jacket.
Sakrament [zákráment'] *nt* sacrament.
Sakristei [zákristī'] *f* sacristy.
Salami [zálá'mē] *f* -, -s salami.
Salat [zálát'] *m* -(e)s, -e salad; *(Kopf~)* lettuce; **da haben wir den ~!** *(umg)* now we're in a fine mess; **~besteck** *nt* salad servers *pl*; **~platte** *f* salad; **~soße** *f* salad dressing.
Salbe [zál'bə] *f* -, -n ointment.
Salbei [zálbī'] *m od f* -s *od* - sage.
salben *vt* anoint.
Salbung *f* anointing.
salbungsvoll *a* unctuous.
saldieren [záldē:'rən] *vt* *(COMM)* balance.
Saldo [zál'dõ] *m* -s, **Salden** balance; **~übertrag** *m*, **~vortrag** *m* balance brought *od* carried forward.
Salmiak [zálmēák'] *m* -s sal ammoniac; **~geist** *m* liquid ammonia.
Salmonellen [zálmõne'lən] *pl* salmonellae.
Salon [zálõn'] *m* -s, -s salon; **~löwe** *m* lounge lizard.
salopp [zálop'] *a* casual; *(Manieren)* slovenly; *(Sprache)* slangy.
Salpeter [zálpā:'tər] *m* -s saltpeter *(US)*, saltpetre *(Brit)*; **~säure** *f* nitric acid.
Salto [zál'tõ] *m* -s, -s *od* **Salti** somersault.
Salut [zálōō:t'] *m* -(e)s, -e salute.
salutieren [zálōōtē:'rən] *vi* salute.
Salve [zál'və] *f* -, -n salvo.
Salz [zálts] *nt* -es, -e salt; **s~arm** *a* *(KOCH)* low-salt.
salzen *vt unreg* salt.
salzig *a* salty.
Salz- *zW*: **~kartoffeln** *pl* boiled potatoes *pl*; **~säule** *f*: **zur ~säule erstarren** *(fig)* stand (as though) rooted to the spot; **~säure** *f* hydrochloric acid; **~stange** *f* pretzel stick.

Sambia [zàm'bëà] *nt* **-s** Zambia.
sambisch *a* Zambian.
Samen [zà'mən] *m* **-s, -** seed; (*ANAT*) sperm; **~bank** *f* sperm bank; **~handlung** *f* seed shop.
sämig [ze:'miċh] *a* thick, creamy.
Sammel- [zà'məl] *zW:* **~anschluß** *m* (*TEL*) private (branch) exchange; (*von Privathäusern*) party line; **~antrag** *m* composite motion; **~band** *m* anthology; **~becken** *nt* reservoir; (*fig*) melting pot (*von* for); **~begriff** *m* collective term; **~bestellung** *f* collective order; **~büchse** *f* collecting can; **~mappe** *f* folder.
sammeln *vt* collect ♦ *vr* assemble, gather; (*sich konzentrieren*) collect one's thoughts.
Sammel- *zW:* **~name** *m* collective term; **~nummer** *f* (*TEL*) private exchange number, switchboard number.
Sammelsurium [zàməlzōō:'rēōōm] *nt* hodgepodge (*US*), hotchpotch (*Brit*).
Sammler(in *f*) *m* **-s, -** collector.
Sammlung [zàm'lōōng] *f* collection; assembly, gathering; composure.
Samstag [zàms'tàk] *m* Saturday; *siehe* **Dienstag.**
samstags *ad* (on) Saturdays.
samt [zàmt] *präp* +*dat* (along) with, together with; **~ und sonders** each and every one (of them).
Samt *m* **-(e)s, -e** velvet; **in ~ und Seide** (*liter*) in silks and satins; **~handschuh** *m*: **jdn mit ~handschuhen anfassen** (*umg*) handle sb with kid gloves.
sämtlich [zem'tlich] *a* all (the), entire; **Schillers ~e Werke** the complete works of Schiller.
Sand [zànt] *m* **-(e)s, -e** sand; **das** *od* **die gibt's wie ~ am Meer** (*umg*) there are heaps of them; **im ~e verlaufen** peter out.
Sandale [zàndà'lə] *f* **-, -n** sandal.
Sandbank *f* sandbank.
Sandelholz [zàn'dəlholts] *nt* **-es** sandalwood.
sandig [zàn'diċh] *a* sandy.
Sand- *zW:* **~kasten** *m* sandbox (*US*), sandpit (*Brit*); **~kastenspiele** *pl* (*MIL*) sand-table exercises *pl*; (*fig*) tactical maneuverings *pl* ; **~kuchen** *m* Madeira cake; **~mann** *m*, **~männchen** *nt* (*in Geschichten*) sandman; **~papier** *nt* sandpaper; **~stein** *m* sandstone; **s~strahlen** *vti untr* sandblast.
sandte [zàn'tə] *imperf von* **senden.**
Sanduhr *f* hourglass; (*Eieruhr*) egg timer.
sanft [zànft] *a* soft, gentle; **~mütig** *a* gentle, meek.
sang [zàng] *imperf von* **singen.**
Sänger(in *f*) [ze'ngər(in)] *m* **-s, -** singer.
sang'- und klang'los *ad* (*umg*) without any ado, quietly.
Sani [zà'nē] *m* **-s, -s** (*umg*) = **Sanitäter.**
sanieren [zànē:'rən] *vt* redevelop; (*Betrieb*) make financially sound; (*Haus*) renovate ♦ *vr* line one's pockets; (*Unternehmen*) become financially sound.

Sanierung *f* redevelopment; renovation.
sanitär [zànēte:r'] *a* sanitary; **~e Anlagen** sanitation.
Sanitäter [zànēte:'tər] *m* **-s, -** first-aid attendant; (*in Krankenwagen*) ambulance man; (*MIL*) (medical) orderly.
Sanitätsauto *nt* ambulance.
sank [zàngk] *imperf von* **sinken.**
Sanka [zàng'kà] *m* **-s, -s** *abk* (*umg*: = *Sanitätskraftwagen*) ambulance.
sanktionieren [zàngktsēōnē:'rən] *vt* sanction.
sann [zàn] *imperf von* **sinnen.**
Saphir [zà'fē:r] *m* **-s, -e** sapphire.
Sardelle [zàrde'lə] *f* anchovy.
Sardine [zàrdē:'nə] *f* sardine.
Sardinien [zàrdē:'nēən] *nt* **-s** Sardinia.
sardinisch, sardisch *a* Sardinian.
Sarg [zàrk] *m* **-(e)s, ⁼e** coffin; **~nagel** *m* (*umg*: *Zigarette*) coffin nail.
Sarkasmus [zàrkàs'mōōs] *m* sarcasm.
sarkastisch [zàrkàs'tish] *a* sarcastic.
saß [zàs] *imperf von* **sitzen.**
Satan [zà'tàn] *m* **-s, -e** Satan; (*fig*) devil.
Satansbraten *m* **-s, -** (*hum umg*) young devil.
Satellit [zàtelē:t'] *m* **-en, -en** satellite.
Satelliten- *zW:* **~foto** *nt* satellite picture; **~station** *f* space station.
Satire [zàtē:'rə] *f* **-, -n** satire (*auf* +*akk* on).
satirisch [zàtē:'rish] *a* satirical.
satt [zàt] *a* full; (*Farbe*) rich, deep; (*blasiert, übersättigt*) well-fed; (*selbstgefällig*) smug; **jdn/etw ~ sein** *od* **haben** be fed-up with sb/sth; **sich ~ hören/sehen an** (+*dat*) see/hear enough of; **sich ~ essen** eat one's fill; **~ machen** be filling.
Sattel [zà'təl] *m* **-s, ⁼** saddle; (*Berg*) ridge; **s~fest** *a* (*fig*) proficient.
satteln *vt* saddle.
Sattel- *zW:* **~schlepper** *m* semitrailer (*US*), semi (*US umg*), articulated lorry (*Brit*), artic (*Brit umg*); **~tasche** *f* saddlebag; (*Gepäcktasche am Fahrrad*) pannier.
sättigen [ze'tigən] *vt* satisfy; (*CHEM*) saturate.
Sattler *m* **-s, -** saddler; (*Polsterer*) upholsterer.
Satz [zàts] *m* **-es, ⁼e** (*GRAM*) sentence; (*Nebene~, Adverbial~*) clause; (*Theorem*) theorem; (*der gesetzte Text*) type; (*MUS*) movement; (*COMPUT*) record; (*TENNIS, Briefmarken, Zusammengehöriges*) set; (*Kaffee~*) grounds *pl*; (*Boden~*) dregs *pl*; (*Spesen~*) allowance; (*COMM*) rate; (*Sprung*) jump; **~bau** *m* sentence construction; **~gegenstand** *m* (*GRAM*) subject; **~lehre** *f* syntax; **~teil** *m* constituent (of a sentence).
Satzung *f* statute, rule; (*Firma*) articles of association, memorandum and articles of association.
satzungsgemäß *a* statutory.
Satzzeichen *nt* punctuation mark.
Sau [zou] *f* **-, Säue** sow; (*umg*) dirty pig; **die**

~ **rauslassen** (*fig umg*) let it all hang out.

sauber [zou'bər] *a* clean; (*ironisch*) fine; (*anständig*) honest, upstanding; (*umg*: *großartig*) fantastic, great; ~ **sein** (*Kind*) be (potty-)trained; (*Hund etc*) be housetrained; ~**halten** *vt unreg* keep clean; **S~keit** *f* cleanness; (*einer Person*) cleanliness.

säuberlich [zoi'bərlich] *ad* neatly.

saubermachen *vt* clean.

säubern *vt* clean; (*POL etc*) purge.

Säuberung *f* cleaning; purge.

Säuberungsaktion *f* cleaning-up operation; (*POL*) purge.

Sau- *zW*: **s~blöd** *a* (*umg*) damn (*!*) stupid; ~**bohne** *f* broad bean.

Sauce [zō:'sə] *f* -, -n = **Soße**.

Sauciere [zōsēā:'rə] *f* -, -n sauce boat.

Saudi-Arabien [zoudēārā'bēən] *nt* -s Saudi Arabia.

sauer [zou'ər] *a* sour; (*CHEM*) acid; (*umg*) cross; **Saurer Regen** acid rain; ~ **werden** (*Milch, Sahne*) go sour, turn; **jdm das Leben** ~ **machen** make sb's life a misery; **S~braten** *m* braised beef (*marinaded in vinegar*), sauerbraten (*US*).

Sauerei [zouərī'] *f* (*umg*) rotten state of affairs, scandal; (*Schmutz etc*) mess; (*Unanständigkeit*) obscenity.

Sauerkraut *nt* -(e)s sauerkraut, pickled cabbage.

säuerlich [zoi'ərlich] *a* sourish, tart.

Sauer- *zW*: ~**milch** *f* sour milk; ~**stoff** *m* oxygen; ~**stoffgerät** *nt* breathing apparatus; ~**teig** *m* leaven.

saufen [zou'fən] *vti unreg* (*umg*) drink, booze; **wie ein Loch** ~ (*umg*) drink like a fish.

Säufer(in *f*) [zoi'fər(in)] *m* -s, - (*umg*) boozer, drunkard.

Sauferei [zoufərī'] *f* drinking, boozing; (*Saufgelage*) booze-up.

Saufgelage *nt* (*pej umg*) drinking bout, booze-up.

säuft [zoift] *3. pers sing präs von* **saufen**.

saugen [zou'gən] *vti unreg* suck.

säugen [zoi'gən] *vt* suckle.

Sauger [zou'gər] *m* -s, - pacifier (*US*), dummy (*Brit*); (*auf Flasche*) teat; (*Staub~*) vacuum cleaner, Hoover ®.

Säugetier *nt* mammal.

saugfähig *a* absorbent.

Säugling *m* infant, baby.

Säuglingsschwester *f* nurse (*for newborn babies*).

Sau- *zW*: ~**haufen** *m* (*umg*) bunch of layabouts; **s~kalt** *a* (*umg*) damn (*!*) cold; ~**klaue** *f* (*umg*) scrawl.

Säule [zoi'lə] *f* -, -n column, pillar.

Säulengang *m* arcade.

Saum [zoum] *m* -(e)s, **Säume** hem; (*Naht*) seam.

saumäßig *a*, *ad* (*umg*) lousy.

säumen [zoi'mən] *vt* hem; seam ♦ *vi* delay,

hesitate.

säumig [zoi'mich] *a* (*geh*: *Schuldner*) defaulting; (*Zahlung*) outstanding, overdue.

Sauna [zou'nå] *f* -, -s sauna.

Säure [zoi'rə] *f* -, -n acid; (*Geschmack*) sourness, acidity; **s~beständig** *a* acid-proof.

Sauregur'kenzeit *f* - (*hum umg*) bad time *od* period; (*in den Medien*) silly season.

säurehaltig *a* acidic.

Saus [zous] *m* -es: **in** ~ **und Braus leben** live like a lord.

säuseln [zoi'zəln] *vti* murmur; (*Blätter*) rustle.

sausen [zou'zən] *vi* blow; (*umg*: *eilen*) rush; (*Ohren*) buzz; **etw** ~ **lassen** (*umg*) not bother with sth.

Sau- *zW*: ~**stall** *m* (*umg*) pigsty; ~**wetter** *nt* (*umg*) damn (*!*) awful weather; **s~wohl** *a* (*umg*): **ich fühle mich s~wohl** I feel really good.

Saxophon [zåksōfō:n'] *nt* -s, -e saxophone.

SB *abk* = **Selbstbedienung**.

S-Bahn *f* *abk* (= *Schnellbahn*) high-speed suburban railroad.

SBB *abk* (= *Schweizerische Bundesbahnen*) Swiss Railways.

s. Br. *abk* (= *südlicher Breite*) southern latitude.

Schabe [shå'bə] *f* -, -n cockroach.

schaben *vt* scrape.

Schaber *m* -s, - scraper.

Schabernack *m* -(e)s, -e trick, prank.

schäbig [she:'bich] *a* shabby; (*Mensch*) mean; **S~keit** *f* shabbiness.

Schablone [shåblō:'nə] *f* -, -n stencil; (*Muster*) pattern; (*fig*) convention.

schablonenhaft *a* stereotyped, conventional.

Schach [shåkh] *nt* -s, -s chess; (*Stellung*) check; **im** ~ **stehen** be in check; **jdn in** ~ **halten** (*fig*) stall sb; ~**brett** *nt* chessboard.

schachern *vi* (*pej*): **um etw** ~ haggle over sth.

Schach- *zW*: ~**figur** *f* chessman; **s~'matt'** *a* checkmate; **jdn s~matt setzen** (*lit*) (check)mate sb; (*fig*) snooker sb (*umg*); ~**partie** *f*, ~**spiel** *nt* game of chess.

Schacht [shåkht] *m* -(e)s, -e shaft.

Schachtel *f* -, -n box; (*pej*: *Frau*) bag, cow (*Brit*); ~**satz** *m* complicated *od* multi-clause sentence.

schade [shå'də] *a* a pity *od* shame; **sich** (*dat*) **zu** ~ **sein für** etw consider o.s. too good for sth; **um sie ist es nicht** ~ she's no great loss ♦ *interj* (what a) pity *od* shame.

Schädel [she:'dəl] *m* -s, - skull; **einen dicken** ~ **haben** (*fig umg*) be stubborn; ~**bruch** *m* fractured skull.

schaden [shå'dən] *vi* (+*dat*) hurt; **einer Sache** ~ damage sth; **S~** *m* -s, - damage; (*Verletzung*) injury; (*Nachteil*) disadvantage; **zu S~ kommen** suffer; (*physisch*) be injured; **jdm S~ zufügen** harm sb; **S~ersatz** *m* compensation, damages *pl*; **S~ersatz leisten** pay compensation;

S~ersatzanspruch *m* claim for compensation; **~ersatzpflichtig** *a* liable for damages; **S~freude** *f* malicious delight; **~froh** *a* gloating.

Schadenfreiheitsrabatt *m* -(e)s, -e *(Versicherung)* accident-free discount *(US)*, no-claim(s) bonus *(Brit)*.

schadhaft [shât'hâft] *a* faulty, damaged.

schädigen [she'digən] *vt* damage; *(Person)* do harm to, harm.

Schädigung *f* damage; harm.

schädlich *a* harmful *(für* to); **S~keit** *f* harmfulness.

Schädling *m* pest.

Schädlingsbekämpfungsmittel *nt* pesticide.

schadlos [shâ'tlōs] *a*: **sich ~ halten an** (+*dat*) take advantage of.

Schadstoff *m* -(e)s, -e harmful substance; **s~arm** *a* free from harmful substances; **s~haltig** *a* containing harmful substances.

Schaf [shâf] *nt* -(e)s, -e sheep; *(umg: Dummkopf)* clod, dope; **~bock** *m* ram.

Schäfchen [she:f'çhən] *nt* lamb; **sein ~ ins trockene bringen** *(Sprichwort)* look after one's own interests; **~wolken** *pl* fleecy clouds *pl*.

Schäfer [she:'fər] *m* -s, -e shepherd; **~hund** *m* German shepherd (dog) *(US)*, Alsatian *(Brit)*; **~in** *f* shepherdess.

schaffen [shâ'fən] *vt unreg* create; *(Platz)* make; **sich** *(dat)* **etw ~** get o.s. sth; **dafür ist er wie geschaffen** he's just made for it ♦ *vt (erreichen)* manage, do; *(erledigen)* finish; *(Prüfung)* pass; *(transportieren)* take; **das ist nicht zu ~** that can't be done; **das hat mich geschafft** it took it out of me; *(nervlich)* it got on top of me ♦ *vi (tun)* do; *(umg: arbeiten)* work; **ich habe damit nichts zu ~** that has nothing to do with me; **jdm (schwer) zu ~ machen** *(zusetzen)* cause sb (a lot of) trouble; *(bekümmern)* worry sb (a lot); **sich** *(dat)* **an etw** *(dat)* **zu ~ machen** busy o.s. with sth.

Schaffen *nt* -s (creative) activity.

Schaffens- *zW*: **~drang** *m* energy; *(von Künstler)* creative urge; **~kraft** *f* creativity.

Schaffner(in *f*) [shâf'nər(in)] *m* -s, - conductor; conductress.

Schafskäse *m* sheep's milk cheese.

Schaft [shâft] *m* -(e)s, -e shaft; *(von Gewehr)* stock; *(von Stiefel)* leg; *(BOT)* stalk; *(von Baum)* tree trunk; **~stiefel** *m* high boot.

Schakal [shâkâl'] *m* -s, -e jackal.

Schäker(in *f*) [she:'kər(in)] *m* -s, - flirt; *(Witzbold)* joker.

schäkern *vi* flirt; joke.

schal [shâl] *a* flat; *(fig)* insipid.

Schal *m* -s, -s *od* -e scarf.

Schälchen [she:l'çhən] *nt* bowl.

Schale [shâ'lə] *f* -, -n skin; *(abgeschält)* peel; *(Nuß~, Muschel~, Ei~)* shell; *(Geschirr)* dish, bowl; **sich in ~ werfen** *(umg)* get dressed up.

schälen [she:'lən] *vt* peel; shell ♦ *vr* peel.

Schalk [shâlk] *m* -s, -e *od* -̈e *(veraltet)* joker.

Schall [shâl] *m* -(e)s, -e sound; **Name ist ~ und Rauch** what's in a name?; **s~dämmend** *a* sound-deadening; **~dämpfer** *m* *(AUT)* muffler *(US)*, silencer *(Brit)*; **s~dicht** *a* soundproof.

schallen *vi* (re)sound.

schallend *a* resounding, loud.

Schall- *zW*: **~geschwindigkeit** *f* speed of sound; **~grenze** *f*, **~mauer** *f* sound barrier; **~platte** *f* record.

schalt [shâlt] *imperf von* **schelten**.

Schalt- *zW*: **~bild** *nt* circuit diagram; **~brett** *nt* switchboard.

schalten [shâl'tən] *vt* switch, turn; **in Reihe/ parallel ~** *(ELEK)* connect in series/in parallel ♦ *vi (AUT)* change (gear); *(umg: begreifen)* catch on; *(reagieren)* react; **~ und walten** do as one pleases.

Schalter *m* -s, - counter; *(an Gerät)* switch; **~beamte(r)** *m* counter clerk; **~stunden** *pl* hours of business *pl*.

Schalt- *zW*: **~hebel** *m* switch; *(AUT)* gearshift; **~jahr** *nt* leap year; **~knüppel** *m* *(AUT)* gearshift; *(AVIAT, COMPUT)* joystick; **~pult** *nt* control desk; **~stelle** *f* *(fig)* coordinating point.

Schaltung *f* switching; *(ELEK)* circuit; *(AUT)* gearshift.

Scham [shâm] *f* - shame; *(~gefühl)* modesty; *(Organe)* private parts *pl*.

schämen [she:'mən] *vr* be ashamed.

Scham- *zW*: **~gefühl** *nt* sense of shame; **~haare** *pl* pubic hair *sing*; **s~haft** *a* modest, bashful; **~lippen** *pl* labia *pl*, lips *pl* of the vulva; **s~los** *a* shameless; *(unanständig)* indecent; *(Lüge)* brazen, barefaced.

Schande [shân'də] *f* - disgrace; **zu meiner ~ muß ich gestehen, daß ...** to my shame I have to admit that ...

schänden [shen'dən] *vt* violate.

Schandfleck [shânt'flek] *m* -(e)s, -e: **er war der ~ der Familie** he was the disgrace of his family.

schändlich [shen'tliçh] *a* disgraceful, shameful; **S~keit** *f* disgracefulness.

Schand- *zW*: **~mauer** *f* *(Berlin)* the wall of shame; **~tat** *f* *(umg)* escapade, shenanigan.

Schändung *f* violation, defilement.

Schank- [shângk'] *zW*: **~erlaubnis** *f*, **~konzession** *f* liquor license *(US)*, (publican's) licence *(Brit)*; **~tisch** *m* bar.

Schanze [shân'tsə] *f* -, -n *(MIL)* fieldwork, earthworks *pl*; *(Sprung~)* ski jump.

Schar [shâr] *f* -, -en band, company; *(Vögel)* flock; *(Menge)* crowd; **in ~en** in droves.

Scharade [shârâ'də] *f* -, -n charade.

scharen *vr* assemble, rally.

scharenweise *ad* in droves.

scharf [shârf] *a* sharp; *(Verstand, Augen)* keen; *(Kälte, Wind)* biting; *(Protest)* fierce; *(Ton)* piercing, shrill; *(Essen)* hot, spicy; *(Munition)* live; *(Maßnahmen)* severe; *(Be-*

wachung) close, tight; (*Geruch, Geschmack*) pungent, acrid; (*umg: geil*) horny; (*Film*) sexy, blue *attr*; ~ **nachdenken** think hard; ~ **aufpassen/zuhören** pay close attention/ listen closely; **etw** ~ **einstellen** (*Bild, Dia-projektor etc*) bring sth into focus; **mit** ~**em Blick** (*fig*) with penetrating insight; **auf etw** (*akk*) ~ **sein** (*umg*) be keen on sth; ~**e Sachen** (*umg*) hard stuff.

Scharfblick *m* (*fig*) penetration.

Schärfe [sher'fə] *f* -, -**n** sharpness; (*Strenge*) rigor (*US*), rigour (*Brit*); (*an Kamera, Fernsehen*) focus.

schärfen *vt* sharpen.

Schärfentiefe *f* (*PHOT*) depth of focus.

Scharf- *zW*: **s~machen** *vt* (*umg*) stir up; ~**richter** *m* executioner; ~**schießen** *nt* firing live ammunition; ~**schütze** *m* marksman, sharpshooter; ~**sinn** *m* astuteness, shrewdness; **s~sinnig** *a* astute, shrewd.

Scharlach [shár'lák̬h] *m* -**s**, -**e** scarlet; (*auch*: ~**fieber** *nt*) scarlet fever.

Scharlatan [shár'látàn] *m* -**s**, -**e** charlatan; (*Arzt auch*) quack.

Scharmützel [shàrmü'tsəl] *nt* -**s**, - skirmish.

Scharnier [shàrnē:r'] *nt* -**s**, -**e** hinge.

Schärpe [sher'pə] *f* -, -**n** sash.

scharren [shá'rən] *vti* scrape, scratch.

Scharte [shár'tə] *f* -, -**n** notch, nick; (*Berg*) wind gap.

schartig [shár'tik̬h] *a* jagged.

Schaschlik [shà'shlik] *m od nt* -**s**, -**s** (shish) kebab.

Schatten [shá'tən] *m* -**s**, - shadow; (*schattige Stelle*) shade; **jdn/etw in den** ~ **stellen** (*fig*) overshadow sb/sth; ~**bild** *nt* silhouette.

Schattenmorelle *f* -, -**n** morello cherry.

Schatten- *zW*: ~**riß** *m* silhouette; ~**seite** *f* shady side; (*von Planeten*) dark side; (*fig*: *Nachteil*) drawback; ~**wirtschaft** *f* black economy.

schattieren [shàtē:'rən] *vti* shade.

Schattierung *f* shading.

schattig [shá'tik̬h] *a* shady.

Schatulle [shàtoo'lə] *f* -, -**n** casket; (*Geld~*) coffer.

Schatz [sháts] *m* -**es**, ̈-**e** treasure; (*Person*) darling; ~**amt** *nt* treasury.

schätzbar [shets'bâr] *a* assessable.

Schätzchen *nt* darling, love.

schätzen *vt* (*ab~*) estimate; (*Gegenstand*) value; (*würdigen*) value, esteem; (*vermuten*) reckon; **etw zu** ~ **wissen** appreciate sth; **sich glücklich** ~ consider o.s. lucky; ~**lernen** *vt* learn to appreciate.

Schatzkammer *f* treasure chamber *od* vault.

Schätzung *f* estimate; estimation; valuation; **nach meiner** ~ ... I reckon that ...

schätzungsweise *ad* (*ungefähr*) approximately; (*so vermutet man*) it is thought.

Schätzwert *m* estimated value.

Schau [shou] *f* - show; (*Ausstellung*) display, exhibition; **etw zur** ~ **stellen** make a show

of sth, show sth off; **eine** ~ **abziehen** (*umg*) put on a show; ~**bild** *nt* diagram.

Schauder [shou'dər] *m* -**s**, - shudder; (*wegen Kälte*) shiver; **s~haft** *a* horrible.

schaudern *vi* shudder; shiver.

schauen [shou'ən] *vi* look; **da schau her!** well, well!

Schauer [shou'ər] *m* -**s**, - (*Regen~*) shower; (*Schreck*) shudder; ~**geschichte** *f* horror story; **s~lich** *a* horrific, spine-chilling; ~**märchen** *nt* (*umg*) horror story.

Schaufel [shou'fəl] *f* -, -**n** shovel; (*Kehricht~*) dustpan; (*von Turbine*) vane; (*NAUT*) paddle; (*TECH*) scoop.

schaufeln *vt* shovel; (*Grab, Grube*) dig ♦ *vi* shovel.

Schaufenster *nt* store (*US*) *od* shop (*Brit*) window; ~**auslage** *f* window display; ~**bummel** *m* window-shopping (expedition); ~**dekorateur** *m* window dresser; ~**puppe** *f* display dummy.

Schau- *zW*: ~**geschäft** *nt* show business; ~**kasten** *m* showcase.

Schaukel [shou'kəl] *f* -, -**n** swing.

schaukeln *vi* swing, rock ♦ *vt* rock; **wir werden das Kind** *od* **das schon** ~ (*fig umg*) we'll manage it.

Schaukel- *zW*: ~**pferd** *nt* rocking horse; ~**stuhl** *m* rocking chair.

Schaulustige(r) [shou'loostigə(r)] *mf dekl wie a* (curious) onlooker.

Schaum [shoum] *m* -**(e)s, Schäume** foam; (*Seifen~*) lather; (*von Getränken*) froth; (*von Bier*) head; ~**bad** *nt* bubble bath.

schäumen [shoi'mən] *vi* foam.

Schaumgummi *m* foam (rubber).

schaumig *a* frothy, foamy.

Schaum- *zW*: ~**festiger** *m* (hair) mousse; ~**krone** *f* whitecap; ~**schläger** *m* (*fig*) windbag; ~**schlägerei** *f* (*fig umg*) hot air; ~**stoff** *m* foam material; ~**wein** *m* sparkling wine.

Schauplatz *m* scene.

schaurig *a* horrific, dreadful.

Schauspiel *nt* spectacle; (*THEAT*) play.

Schauspieler *m* actor; ~**in** *f* actress.

schauspielern *vi untr* act.

Schauspiel- *zW*: ~**haus** *nt* playhouse, theater (*US*), theatre (*Brit*); ~**schule** *f* drama school.

Scheck [shek] *m* -**s**, -**s** check (*US*), cheque (*Brit*); ~**buch** *nt*, ~**heft** *nt* checkbook (*US*), chequebook (*Brit*).

scheckig *a* dappled, piebald.

Scheckkarte *f* -, -**n** check (*US*) *od* cheque (*Brit*) card.

scheel [shā:l] *a* (*umg*) dirty; **jdn** ~ **ansehen** give sb a dirty look.

scheffeln [she'fəln] *vt* amass.

Scheibe [shī'bə] *f* -, -**n** disk; (*Brot etc*) slice; (*Glas~*) pane; (*MIL*) target; (*Eishockey*) puck; (*Töpfer~*) wheel; (*umg: Schallplatte*) disk; **von ihm könntest du dir eine** ~ **abschneiden** (*fig umg*) you could take a leaf out of his book.

Scheiben- zW: ~**bremse** f (AUT) disk brake; ~**kleister** interj (euph umg) shoot! (US), sugar! (Brit); ~**waschanlage** f (AUT) windshield (US) od windscreen (Brit) washers pl; ~**wischer** m (AUT) windshield (US) od windscreen (Brit) wiper.

Scheich [shīċh] m -s, -e od -s sheik(h).

Scheide [shī'də] f -, -n sheath; (Grenze) boundary; (ANAT) vagina.

scheiden unreg vt separate; (Ehe) dissolve; **sich ~ lassen** get a divorce; **von dem Moment an waren wir (zwei) geschiedene Leute** (umg) after that it was the parting of the ways for us ♦ vi depart; (sich trennen) part; **aus dem Leben ~** depart this life ♦ vr (Wege) divide; (Meinungen) diverge.

Scheideweg m (fig) crossroads sing.

Scheidung f (Ehe~) divorce; **die ~ einreichen** file a petition for divorce.

Scheidungs- zW: ~**grund** m grounds pl for divorce; ~**klage** f divorce suit.

Schein [shīn] m -(e)s, -e light; (An~) appearance; (Geld~) (bank)note; (Bescheinigung) certificate; **den ~ wahren** keep up appearances; **zum ~** in pretense; **s~bar** a apparent.

scheinen vi unreg shine; (Anschein haben) seem.

Schein- zW: **s~heilig** a hypocritical; ~**student** m student in name only, mock-student; ~**tod** m apparent death; ~**werfer** m -s, - floodlight; (THEAT) spotlight; (Suchscheinwerfer) searchlight; (AUT) headlight.

Scheiß [shīs'] in zW (umg!) bloody (Brit!); ~**dreck** m (umg!) shit (!), crap (!); **das geht dich einen ~dreck an** what the hell has it got to do with you?.

Scheiße f - (umg) shit (!).

scheißegal a (umg!): **das ist mir doch ~!** I don't give a shit (!).

scheißen vi (umg!) shit (!).

Scheiß- zW: **s~freundlich** a (pej umg) as nice as pie (ironisch); ~**kerl** m (umg!) bastard (!), son-of-a-bitch (US!).

Scheit [shīt] nt -(e)s, -e od -er log.

Scheitel [shī'təl] m -s, - top; (Haar) part (US), parting (Brit).

scheiteln vt part.

Scheitelpunkt m zenith, apex.

Scheiterhaufen [shī'tərhoufən] m (funeral) pyre; (HIST: zur Hinrichtung) stake.

scheitern [shī'tərn] vi fail.

Schelle [she'lə] f -, -n small bell.

schellen vi ring; **es hat geschellt** the bell has gone.

Schellfisch [shel'fish] m haddock.

Schelm [shelm] m -(e)s, -e rogue.

Schelmenroman m picaresque novel.

schelmisch a mischievous, roguish.

Schelte [shel'tə] f -, -n scolding.

schelten vt unreg scold.

Schema [shā:'má] nt -s, -s od -ta scheme, plan; (Darstellung) schema; **nach ~ F** quite

mechanically.

schematisch [shāmá'tish] a schematic; (pej) mechanical.

Schemel [shā:'məl] m -s, - (foot)stool.

schemenhaft a shadowy.

Schenke f -, -n tavern, inn.

Schenkel [sheng'kəl] m -s, - thigh; (MATH: von Winkel) side.

schenken [sheng'kən] vt (lit, fig) give; (Getränk) pour; **ich möchte nichts geschenkt haben!** (lit) I don't want any presents!; (fig: bevorzugt werden) I don't want any special treatment!; **sich** (dat) **etw ~** (umg) skip sth; **jdm etw ~** (erlassen) let sb off sth; **ihm ist nie etwas geschenkt worden** (fig) he never had it easy; **das ist geschenkt!** (billig) that's a giveaway!; (nichts wert) that's worthless!

Schenkung f gift.

Schenkungsurkunde f -, -n deed of gift.

scheppern [she'pərn] vi (umg) clatter.

Scherbe [sher'bə] f -, -n broken piece, fragment; (archäologisch) potsherd.

Schere [shā:'rə] f -, -n scissors pl; (groß) shears pl; (ZOOL) pincer; (von Hummer, Krebs etc auch) claw; **eine ~** a pair of scissors.

scheren vt unreg cut; (Schaf) shear; (sich kümmern) bother ♦ vr care; **scher dich (zum Teufel)!** get lost!

Scheren- zW: ~**schleifer** m -s, - knife-grinder; ~**schnitt** m silhouette.

Schererei [shā:rərī'] f (umg) bother, trouble.

Scherflein [sher'flīn] nt mite, bit.

Scherz [sherts] m -es, -e joke; fun; **s~en** vi (albern) banter; ~**frage** f conundrum; **s~haft** a joking, jocular.

scheu [shoi] a shy; **S~** f - shyness; (Angst) fear (vor +dat of); (Ehrfurcht) awe.

Scheuche f -, -n scarecrow.

scheuchen [shoi'ċhən] vt scare (off).

scheuen vr: **sich ~ vor** (+dat) be afraid of, shrink from ♦ vt shun; **weder Kosten noch Mühe ~** spare neither trouble nor expense ♦ vi (Pferd) shy.

Scheuer [shoi'ər] f -, -n barn.

Scheuer- zW: ~**bürste** f scrubbing brush; ~**lappen** m scrubbing rag (US), floorcloth (Brit); ~**leiste** f skirting board.

scheuern vt scour; (mit Bürste) scrub; **jdm eine ~** (umg) clout sb one ♦ vr: **sich** (akk) **(wund)** ~ chafe o.s.

Scheuklappe f blinder (US), blinker (Brit).

Scheune [shoi'nə] f -, -n barn.

Scheunendrescher m -s, -: **er frißt wie ein ~** (umg) he eats like a horse.

Scheusal [shoi'zál] nt -s, -e monster.

scheußlich [shois'liċh] a dreadful, frightful; **S~keit** f dreadfulness.

Schi [shē:] m = **Ski.**

Schicht [shiċht] f -, -en layer; (Klasse) class, level; (in Fabrik etc) shift; ~**arbeit** f shift work; **s~en** vt layer, stack; ~**wechsel** m change of shifts.

schick [shik] *a* stylish, chic.
schicken *vt* send ♦ *vr* resign o.s. (*in* +*akk* to) ♦ *v unpers* (*anständig sein*) be fitting.
Schickeria [shikərē:'á] *f* (*ironisch*) in-people *pl*.
schicklich *a* proper, fitting.
Schicksal *nt* **-s, -e** fate.
Schicksalsschlag *m* great misfortune, blow.
Schickse [shik'sə] *f* - (*umg*) floozy, shiksa (*US*).
Schiebedach *nt* (*AUT*) sunroof.
schieben [shē:'bən] *vti unreg* push; (*Schuld*) put (*auf jdn* on sb); (*umg: handeln mit*) traffic in; (: *Drogen*) push; **etw vor sich** (*dat*) **her** ~ (*fig*) put off sth.
Schieber *m* **-s, -** slide; (*Besteckteil*) pusher; (*Person*) profiteer; (*umg: Schwarzhändler*) black marketeer; (: *Waffen*~) gunrunner; (: *Drogen*~) pusher.
Schiebetür *f* sliding door.
Schieblehre *f* (*MATH*) caliper (*US*) *od* calliper (*Brit*) rule.
Schiebung *f* fiddle; **das war doch** ~ (*umg*) that was rigged *od* a fix.
schied [shē:t] *imperf von* **scheiden**.
Schieds- [shē:ts'] *zW*: ~**gericht** *nt* court of arbitration; ~**mann** *m, pl* **-männer** arbitrator; ~**richter** *m* referee, umpire; (*Schlichter*) arbitrator; **s**~**richtern** *vti untr* referee, umpire; arbitrate; ~**spruch** *m* (arbitration) award; ~**verfahren** *nt* arbitration.
schief [shē:f] *a* crooked; (*Ebene*) sloping; (*Turm*) leaning; (*Winkel*) oblique; (*Blick*) wry; (*Vergleich*) distorted; **auf die** ~**e Bahn geraten** (*fig*) leave the straight and narrow ♦ *ad* crookedly; (*ansehen*) askance; **etw** ~ **stellen** slope sth.
Schiefer [shē:'fər] *m* **-s, -** slate; ~**dach** *nt* slate roof; ~**tafel** *f* (child's) slate.
schief- *zW*: ~**gehen** *vi unreg* (*umg*) go wrong; **es wird schon** ~**gehen!** (*hum*) it'll be O.K.; ~**lachen** *vr* (*umg*) kill o.s. laughing; ~**liegen** *vi unreg* (*umg*) be wrong, be on the wrong track (*umg*).
schielen [shē:'lən] *vi* squint; **nach etw** ~ (*fig*) eye sth up.
schien [shē:n] *imperf von* **scheinen**.
Schienbein *nt* shinbone.
Schiene [shē:'nə] *f* -, **-n** rail; (*MED*) splint.
schienen *vt* put in splints.
Schienen- *zW*: ~**bus** *m* rail bus; ~**strang** *m* (*EISENB etc*) (section of) track.
schier [shē:r] *a* pure; (*Fleisch*) lean and boneless; (*fig*) sheer ♦ *ad* nearly, almost.
Schieß- *zW*: ~**bude** *f* shooting gallery; ~**budenfigur** *f* (*umg*) clown, ludicrous figure.
schießen [shē:'sən] *vti unreg* shoot (*auf* +*akk* at); (*Salat etc*) run to seed; (*Ball*) kick; (*Geschoß*) fire; **aus dem Boden** ~ (*lit, fig*) spring *od* sprout up; **jdm durch den Kopf** ~ (*fig*) flash through sb's mind.
Schießerei [shē:sərī'] *f* shooting incident,

shoot-out.
Schieß- *zW*: ~**gewehr** *nt* (*hum*) gun; ~**hund** *m*: **wie ein** ~**hund aufpassen** (*umg*) watch like a hawk; ~**platz** *m* firing range; ~**pulver** *nt* gunpowder; ~**scharte** *f* embrasure; ~**stand** *m* rifle *od* shooting range.
Schiff [shif] *nt* **-(e)s, -e** ship, vessel; (*Kirchen*~) nave; **s**~**bar** *a* navigable; ~**bau** *m* shipbuilding; ~**bruch** *m* shipwreck; ~**bruch erleiden** (*lit*) be shipwrecked; (*fig*) fail; (*Unternehmen*) founder; **s**~**brüchig** *a* shipwrecked.
Schiffchen *nt* small boat; (*Weben*) shuttle; (*Mütze*) soldier's undress cap, forage cap (*Brit*).
Schiffer *m* **-s, -** boatman, sailor; (*von Lastkahn*) bargee.
Schiff- *zW*: ~**(f)ahrt** *f* shipping; (*Reise*) voyage; ~**(f)ahrtslinie** *f* shipping route; ~**schaukel** *f* swing boat.
Schiffs- *zW*: ~**junge** *m* cabin boy; ~**körper** *m* hull; ~**ladung** *f* cargo, shipload; ~**planke** *f* gangplank; ~**schraube** *f* ship's propeller.
Schikane [shēká'nə] *f* -, **-n** harassment; dirty trick; **mit allen** ~**n** with all the trimmings; **das hat er aus reiner** ~ **gemacht** he did it just to be mean.
schikanieren [shēkánē:'rən] *vt* harass; (*Ehepartner*) mess around; (*Mitschüler*) bully.
schikanös [shēkánœs'] *a* (*Mensch*) bloodyminded; (*Maßnahme etc*) harassing.
Schild [shilt] *m* **-(e)s, -e** shield; (*Mützen*~) peak, visor; **etw im** ~ **führen** be up to sth ♦ *nt* **-(e)s, -er** sign; (*Namens*~) nameplate; (*an Monument, Haus, Grab*) plaque; (*Etikett*) label.
Schildbürger *m* duffer, blockhead.
Schilddrüse *f* thyroid gland.
schildern [shil'dərn] *vt* describe; (*Menschen etc*) portray; (*skizzieren*) outline.
Schilderung *f* description; portrayal.
Schild- *zW*: ~**kröte** *f* tortoise; (*Wasserschildkröte*) turtle; ~**krötensuppe** *f* turtle soup.
Schilf [shilf] *nt* **-(e)s, -e, Schilfrohr** *nt* (*Pflanze*) reed; (*Material*) reeds *pl*, rushes *pl*.
Schillerlocke [shi'lərlokə] *f* -, **-n** (*Gebäck*) cream horn; (*Räucherfisch*) strip of smoked rock salmon.
schillern [shi'lərn] *vi* shimmer.
schillernd *a* iridescent; (*fig: Charakter*) enigmatic.
schilt [shilt] *3. pers sing präs von* **schelten**.
Schimmel [shi'məl] *m* **-s, -** mold (*US*), mould (*Brit*); (*Pferd*) white horse, gray (*US*), grey (*Brit*).
schimm(e)lig *a* moldy (*US*), mouldy (*Brit*).
schimmeln *vi* go moldy.
Schimmer [shi'mər] *m* **-s** glimmer; **keinen (blassen)** ~ **von etw haben** (*umg*) not have the slightest idea about sth.
schimmern *vi* glimmer; (*Seide, Perlen*) shimmer.

Schimpanse [shimpán'zə] *m* **-n, -n** chimpanzee.

Schimpf [shimpf] *m* **-(e)s, -e** disgrace; **mit ~ und Schande** in disgrace.

schimpfen *vti* scold ♦ *vi* curse, complain.

Schimpf- *zW*: **~kanonade** *f* barrage of abuse; **~wort** *nt* term of abuse.

Schindel [shin'dəl] *f* -, **-n** shingle.

schinden [shin'dən] *unreg vt* maltreat, drive too hard; **Eindruck ~** (*umg*) create an impression ♦ *vr* sweat and strain, toil away (*mit* at).

Schinder *m* **-s,** - knacker; (*fig*) slave driver.

Schinderei [shindəri'] *f* grind, drudgery.

Schindluder [shin'tloo:dər] *nt*: **mit etw ~ treiben** muck *od* mess sth about; (*Vorrecht*) abuse sth.

Schinken [shing'kən] *m* **-s,** - ham; (*gekocht und geräuchert auch*) gammon; (*pej umg*) hackneyed and clichéd play *etc*; **~speck** *m* bacon.

Schippe [shi'pə] *f* -, **-n** shovel; **jdn auf die ~ nehmen** (*fig umg*) pull sb's leg.

schippen *vt* shovel.

Schirm [shirm] *m* **-(e)s, -e** (*Regen~*) umbrella; (*Sonnen~*) parasol, sunshade; (*Wand~*, *Bild~*) screen; (*Lampen~*) (lamp)shade; (*Mützen~*) peak; (*Pilz~*) cap; **~bildaufnahme** *f* X-ray; **~herr(in** *f*) *m* patron; patroness; **~mütze** *f* peaked cap; **~ständer** *m* umbrella stand.

schiß [shis] *imperf von* **scheißen**.

Schiß *m*: **~ haben** (*umg*) be shit scared (*!*).

schizophren [shētsōfrä:n'] *a* schizophrenic.

schlabbern [shlä'bərn] *vti* (*umg*) slurp.

Schlacht [shläₓht] *f* -, **-en** battle.

schlachten *vt* slaughter, kill.

Schlachtenbummler *m* (*umg*) visiting soccer fan.

Schlachter *m* **-s,** - butcher.

Schlacht- *zW*: **~feld** *nt* battlefield; **~fest** *nt* a country feast to eat up meat from freshly slaughtered pigs; **~haus** *nt*, **~hof** *m* slaughterhouse; **~opfer** *nt* sacrifice; (*Mensch*) human sacrifice; **~plan** *m* battle plan; (*fig*) plan of action; **~ruf** *m* battle cry, war cry; **~schiff** *nt* battleship; **~vieh** *nt* animals kept for meat.

Schlacke [shlä'kə] *f* -, **-n** slag.

schlackern *vi* (*umg*) tremble; (*Kleidung*) hang loosely, be baggy; **mit den Ohren ~** (*fig*) be (left) speechless.

Schlaf [shläf] *m* **-(e)s** sleep; **um seinen ~ kommen** *od* **gebracht werden** lose sleep; **~anzug** *m* pajamas *pl* (*US*), pyjamas *pl* (*Brit*).

Schläfchen [shle:f'ₓhən] *nt* nap.

Schläfe *f* -, **-n** (*ANAT*) temple.

schlafen *vi unreg* sleep; (*umg: nicht aufpassen*) be asleep; **bei jdm ~** stay overnight with sb; **S~gehen** *nt* going to bed.

Schlafenszeit *f* bedtime.

Schläfer(in *f*) [shle:'fər(in)] *m* **-s,** - sleeper.

schlaff [shläf] *a* slack; (*Haut*) loose;

(*Muskeln*) flabby; (*energielos*) limp; (*erschöpft*) exhausted; **S~heit** *f* slackness; looseness; flabbiness; limpness; exhaustion.

Schlafgelegenheit *f* sleeping accommodation.

Schlafittchen [shläfit'ₓhən] *nt* (*umg*): **jdn am** *od* **beim ~ nehmen** take sb by the scruff of the neck.

Schlaf- *zW*: **~lied** *nt* lullaby; **s~los** *a* sleepless; **~losigkeit** *f* sleeplessness, insomnia; **~mittel** *nt* sleeping drug; (*fig, ironisch*) soporific; **~mütze** *f* (*umg*) dope.

schläfrig [shle:'friₓh] *a* sleepy.

Schlaf- *zW*: **~rock** *m* dressing gown; **Apfel im ~rock** baked apple in puff pastry; **~saal** *m* dormitory; **~sack** *m* sleeping bag.

schläft [shle:ft] *3. pers sing präs von* **schlafen**.

Schlaf- *zW*: **~tablette** *f* sleeping pill; **s~trunken** *a* drowsy, half-asleep; **~wagen** *m* sleeping car, sleeper; **s~wandeln** *vi untr* sleepwalk; **~wandler(in** *f*) *m* **-s,** - sleepwalker; **~zimmer** *nt* bedroom.

Schlag [shläk] *m* **-(e)s, ⁻e** (*lit, fig*) blow; (*auch MED*) stroke; (*Puls~*, *Herz~*) beat; (*pl: Tracht Prügel*) beating; (*ELEK*) shock; (*Blitz~*) bolt, stroke; (*Glocken~*) chime; (*Autotür*) car door; (*umg: Portion*) helping; (*: Art*) kind, type; **~ acht Uhr** (*umg*) on the stroke of eight; **mit einem ~** all at once; **~ auf ~** in rapid succession; **die haben keinen ~ getan** (*umg*) they haven't done a stroke (of work); **ich dachte, mich trifft der ~** (*umg*) I was thunderstruck; **vom gleichen ~ sein** be cast in the same mold; (*pej*) be tarred with the same brush; **ein ~ ins Wasser** (*umg*) a wash-out; **~abtausch** *m* (*BOXEN*) exchange of blows; (*fig*) (verbal) exchange; **~ader** *f* artery; **~anfall** *m* stroke; **s~artig** *a* sudden, without warning; **~baum** *m* barrier; **~bohrer** *m* percussion drill.

schlagen [shlä'gən] *unreg vti* strike, hit; (*wiederholt ~, besiegen*) beat; (*Glocke*) ring; (*Stunde*) strike; (*Kreis, Bogen*) describe; (*Purzelbaum*) do; (*Sahne*) whip; (*Schlacht*) fight; (*einwickeln*) wrap; **um sich ~** lash out; **ein Ei in die Pfanne ~** crack an egg into the pan; **eine geschlagene Stunde** a full hour; **na ja, ehe ich mich ~ lasse!** (*hum umg*) yes, I don't mind if I do; **nach jdm ~** (*fig*) take after sb ♦ *vr* fight; **sich gut ~** (*fig*) do well; **sich nach links/ Norden ~** strike out to the left/for the north; **sich auf jds Seite ~** side with sb; (*die Fronten wechseln*) go over to sb.

schlagend *a* (*Beweis*) convincing; **~e Wetter** (*MIN*) firedamp.

Schlager [shlä'gər] *m* **-s,** - (*lit, fig*) hit.

Schläger [shle:'gər] *m* **-s,** - brawler; (*SPORT*) bat; (*TENNIS*) racket; (*TISCHTENNIS*) paddle (*US*), bat (*Brit*); (*GOLF*) club; (*Hockey~*) hockey stick; (*Waffe*) rapier.

Schlägerei [shle:gəri'] *f* fight, brawl.

Schlagersänger *m* pop singer.
Schlägertyp *m* (*umg*) thug.
Schlag- *zW:* **s~fertig** *a* quick-witted; **~fertigkeit** *f* ready wit, quickness of repartee; **~instrument** *nt* percussion instrument; **~kraft** *f* (*lit, fig*) power; (*MIL*) strike power; (*BOXEN*) punch(ing power); **s~kräftig** *a* powerful; (*Beweise*) clear-cut; **~loch** *nt* pothole; **~rahm** *m*, **~sahne** *f* (whipped) cream; **~seite** *f* (*NAUT*) list; **~stock** *m* (*form*) nightstick (*US*), truncheon (*Brit*).
schlägt [shle:kt] *3. pers sing präs von* **schlagen.**
Schlag- *zW:* **~wort** *nt* slogan, catch phrase; **~zeile** *f* headline; **~zeilen machen** (*umg*) hit the headlines; **~zeug** *nt* drums *pl;* (*in Orchester*) percussion; **~zeuger** *m* **-s,** **-** drummer.
schlaksig [shlák'sich] *a* (*umg*) gangling, gawky.
Schlamassel [shlámá'səl] *m* **-s,** **-** (*umg*) mess.
Schlamm [shlám] *m* **-(e)s, -e** mud.
schlammig *a* muddy.
Schlampe [shlám'pə] *f* **-, -n** (*umg*) slattern, slut.
schlampen *vi* (*umg*) be sloppy.
Schlamperei [shlámpərī'] *f* (*umg*) disorder, untidiness; (*schlechte Arbeit*) sloppy work.
schlampig *a* (*umg*) slovenly, sloppy.
schlang [shláng] *imperf von* **schlingen.**
Schlange [shlá'ngə] *f* **-, -n** snake; (*Menschen~*) line (*US*), queue (*Brit*); **~ stehen** stand in line (*US*), (form a) queue (*Brit*); **eine falsche ~** a snake in the grass.
schlängeln [shle'ngəln] *vr* twist, wind; (*Fluß*) meander.
Schlangen- *zW:* **~biß** *m* snake bite; **~gift** *nt* snake venom; **~linie** *f* wavy line.
schlank [shlángk] *a* slim, slender; **S~heit** *f* slimness, slenderness; **S~heitskur** *f* diet.
schlapp [shláp] *a* limp; (*locker*) slack; (*umg: energielos*) listless; (*nach Krankheit etc*) run-down.
Schlappe *f* **-, -n** (*umg*) setback.
Schlappen *m* **-s, -** (*umg*) slipper.
schlapp- *zW:* **S~heit** *f* limpness; slackness; **S~hut** *m* slouch hat; **~machen** *vi* (*umg*) wilt, droop; **S~schwanz** *m* (*pej umg*) weakling, softy.
Schlaraffenland [shlárá'fənlànt] *nt* land of milk and honey.
schlau [shlou] *a* crafty, cunning; **ich werde nicht ~ aus ihm** I don't know what to make of him; **S~berger** *m* **-s, -** (*umg*) smart-ass.
Schlauch [shloukh] *m* **-(e)s, Schläuche** hose; (*in Reifen*) inner tube; (*umg: Anstrengung*) grind; **auf dem ~ stehen** (*umg*) be in a jam *od* fix; **~boot** *nt* rubber dinghy.
schlauchen *vt* (*umg*) tell on, exhaust.
schlauchlos *a* (*Reifen*) tubeless.
Schläue [shloi'ə] *f* - cunning.
Schlaufe [shlou'fə] *f* **-, -n** loop; (*Aufhänger*)

hanger.
Schlau- *zW:* **~heit** *f* cunning; **~kopf** *m* smart-ass.
Schlawiner [shlávē:'nər] *m* **-s, -** (*hum umg*) villain, rogue.
schlecht [shlecht] *a* bad; **jdm ist ~** sb feels sick *od* ill **♦** *ad:* **er kann ~ nein sagen** he finds it hard to say no, he can't say no; **~ und recht** after a fashion; **auf jdn ~ zu sprechen sein** not have a good word to say for sb; **er hat nicht ~ gestaunt** (*umg*) he wasn't half surprised.
schlechterdings *ad* simply.
schlecht- *zW:* **~gehen** *vi unpers unreg:* **jdm geht es ~** sb is in a bad way; **heute geht es ~** today is not very convenient; **S~heit** *f* badness; **~'hin** *ad* simply; **der Dramatiker ~hin** THE playwright.
Schlechtigkeit *f* badness; (*Tat*) bad deed.
schlecht- *zW:* **~machen** *vt* run down, denigrate; **~weg** *ad* simply.
schlecken [shle'kən] *vti* lick.
Schlegel [shlā:'gəl] *m* **-s, -** (drum)stick; (*Hammer*) hammer; (*KOCH*) leg.
schleichen [shlī'chən] *vi unreg* creep, crawl.
schleichend *a* creeping; (*Krankheit, Gift*) insidious.
Schleich- *zW:* **~weg** *m:* **auf ~wegen** (*fig*) on the quiet; **~werbung** *f* a plug.
Schleie [shlī'ə] *f* **-, -n** tench.
Schleier [shlī'ər] *m* **-s, -** veil; **~eule** *f* barn owl; **s~haft** *a* (*umg*): **jdm s~haft sein** be a mystery to sb.
Schleife [shlī'fə] *f* **-, -n** (*auch COMPUT*) loop; (*Band*) bow; (*Kranz~*) ribbon.
schleifen *vt* drag; (*MIL: Festung*) raze **♦** *vi* drag; **die Kupplung ~ lassen** (*AUT*) slip the clutch **♦** *vt unreg* grind; (*Edelstein*) cut; (*MIL: Soldaten*) drill.
Schleif- *zW:* **~maschine** *f* grinding machine; **~stein** *m* grindstone.
Schleim [shlīm] *m* **-(e)s, -e** slime; (*MED*) mucus; (*KOCH*) gruel; **~haut** *f* mucous membrane.
schleimig *a* slimy.
schlemmen [shle'mən] *vi* feast.
Schlemmer(in *f)* *m* **-s, -** gourmet, bon vivant.
Schlemmerei [shlemərī'] *f* gluttony, feasting.
schlendern [shlen'dərn] *vi* stroll.
Schlendrian [shlen'drēàn] *m* **-(e)s** sloppy way of working.
Schlenker [shleng'kər] *m* **-s, -** swerve.
schlenkern *vti* swing, dangle.
Schleppe [shle'pə] *f* **-, -n** train.
schleppen *vt* drag; (*Auto, Schiff*) tow; (*tragen*) lug.
schleppend *a* dragging; (*Bedienung, Abfertigung*) sluggish, slow.
Schlepper *m* **-s, -** tractor; (*Schiff*) tug.
Schlepp- *zW:* **~kahn** *m* (canal) barge; **~tau** *nt* towrope; **jdn ins ~tau nehmen** (*fig*) take sb in tow.
Schlesien [shlā:'zēən] *nt* **-s** Silesia.

Schlesier(in *f*) *m* **-s,** - Silesian.
schlesisch *a* Silesian.
Schleswig-Holstein [shlā:s'vichhol'shtīn] *nt* **-s** Schleswig-Holstein.
Schleuder [shloi'dər] *f* **-,** **-n** catapult; (*Wäsche~*) spin-dryer; (*Butter~ etc*) centrifuge; **~honig** *m* extracted honey.
schleudern *vt* hurl; (*Wäsche*) spin-dry ♦ *vi* (*AUT*) skid; **ins S~ kommen** (*AUT*) go into a skid; (*fig umg*) run into trouble.
Schleuder- *zW*: **~preis** *m* give-away price; **~sitz** *m* (*AVIAT*) ejector seat; (*fig*) hot seat; **~ware** *f* cheap goods *pl*, cut-rate goods *pl*.
schleunig [shloi'nich] *a* prompt, speedy; (*Schritte*) quick.
schleunigst *ad* straight away.
Schleuse [shloi'zə] *f* **-,** **-n** lock; (*Schleusentor*) sluice.
schleusen *vt* (*Schiffe*) pass through a lock, lock; (*Wasser*) channel; (*Menschen*) filter; (*fig: heimlich*) smuggle.
schlich [shlich] *imperf von* **schleichen.**
Schlich *m* **-(e)s,** **-e** dodge, trick; **jdm auf die ~e kommen** get wise to sb.
schlicht [shlicht] *a* simple, plain.
schlichten *vt* smooth; (*beilegen*) settle; (*Streit: vermitteln*) mediate, arbitrate.
Schlichter(in *f*) *m* **-s,** - mediator, arbitrator.
Schlichtung *f* settlement; arbitration.
Schlick [shlik] *m* **-(e)s,** **-e** mud; (*Öl~*) slick.
schlief [shlē:f] *imperf von* **schlafen.**
Schließe [shlē:'sə] *f* **-,** **-n** fastener.
schließen [shlē:'sən] *unreg vtir* close, shut; (*beenden*) close; (*Freundschaft, Bündnis, Ehe*) enter into; (*folgern*) infer (*aus* from); (*COMPUT: Datei*) close; **auf etw** (*akk*) **~ lassen** suggest sth; **jdn/etw in sein Herz ~** take sb/sth to one's heart; **etw in sich ~** include sth; **„geschlossen"** "closed".
Schließfach *nt* locker.
schließlich *ad* finally; (**~** *doch*) after all.
schliff [shlif] *imperf von* **schleifen.**
Schliff *m* **-(e)s,** **-e** cut(ting); (*fig*) polish; **einer Sache den letzten ~ geben** (*fig*) put the finishing touch(es) to sth.
schlimm [shlim] *a* bad; **das war ~ that was terrible; das ist halb so ~!** that's not so bad!; **~er** *a* worse; **~ste(r,s)** *a* worst.
schlimmstenfalls *ad* at (the) worst.
Schlinge [shli'ngə] *f* **-,** **-n** loop; (*an Galgen*) noose; (*Falle*) snare; (*MED*) sling.
Schlingel *m* **-s,** - rascal.
schlingen *unreg vt* wind ♦ *vi* (*essen*) bolt one's food, gobble.
schlingern *vi* roll.
Schlips [shlips] *m* **-es,** **-e** necktie (*US*), tie; **sich auf den ~ getreten fühlen** (*fig umg*) feel offended.
Schlitten [shli'tən] *m* **-s,** - sledge, sled; (*Pferde~*) sleigh; **mit jdm ~ fahren** (*umg*) give sb a rough time; **~bahn** *f* toboggan run; **~fahren** *nt* **-s** tobogganing.
schlittern [shli'tərn] *vi* slide; (*Wagen*) skid.
Schlittschuh [shlit'shōō:] *m* skate; **~ laufen**

skate; **~bahn** *f* skating rink; **~läufer** *m* skater.
Schlitz [shlits] *m* **-es,** **-e** slit; (*für Münze*) slot; (*Hosen~*) flies *pl*; **s~äugig** *a* slant-eyed; **s~en** *vt* slit; **~ohr** *nt* (*fig*) sly fox.
schlohweiß [shlō:'vīs'] *a* snow-white.
schloß [shlos] *imperf von* **schließen.**
Schloß *nt* **-sses,** **-̈sser** lock, padlock; (*an Schmuck etc*) clasp; (*Bau*) castle; (*Palast*) palace; **ins ~ fallen** lock (itself).
Schlosser [shlo'sər] *m* **-s,** - fitter; (*für Schlüssel etc*) locksmith.
Schlosserei [slosərī'] *f* metal(working) shop.
Schloßhund *m* **-(e)s -e: heulen wie ein ~** (*umg*) howl one's head off.
Schlot [shlō:t] *m* **-(e)s,** **-e** chimney; (*NAUT*) funnel.
schlottern [shlo'tərn] *vi* shake; (*vor Angst*) tremble; (*Kleidung*) be baggy.
Schlucht [shlōōkht] *f* **-,** **-en** gorge, ravine.
schluchzen [shlōōkh'tsən] *vi* sob.
Schluck [shlōōk] *m* **-(e)s,** **-e** swallow; (*größer*) gulp; (*kleiner*) sip; (*ein bißchen*) drop.
Schluckauf *m* **-s, Schlucken** *m* **-s** hiccups *pl*.
schlucken *vt* swallow; (*umg: Alkohol, Benzin*) guzzle; (: *verschlingen*) swallow up ♦ *vi* swallow.
Schlucker *m* **-s,** - (*umg*): **armer ~** poor devil.
Schluckimpfung *f* oral vaccination.
schludern [shlōō:'dərn] *vi* skimp; do sloppy work.
schlug [shlōō:k] *imperf von* **schlagen.**
Schlummer [shlōō'mər] *m* **-s** slumber.
schlummern *vi* slumber.
Schlund [shlōōnt] *m* **-(e)s,** **-̈e** gullet; (*fig*) jaw.
schlüpfen [shlü'pfən] *vi* slip; (*Vogel etc*) hatch (out).
Schlüpfer [shlü'pfər] *m* **-s,** - panties *pl*.
Schlupfloch [shlōōpf'lokh] *nt* hole; (*Versteck*) hide-out; (*fig*) loophole.
schlüpfrig [shlüp'frich] *a* slippery; (*fig*) lewd; **S~keit** *f* slipperiness; lewdness.
Schlupfwinkel *m* **-s,** - hiding place; (*fig*) quiet corner.
schlurfen [shlōōr'fən] *vi* shuffle.
schlürfen [shlür'fən] *vti* slurp.
Schluß [shlōōs] *m* **-sses,** **-̈sse** end; (**~***folgerung*) conclusion; **am ~** at the end; **~ für heute!** that'll do for today; **~ jetzt!** that's enough now!; **~ machen mit** finish with.
Schlüssel [shlü'səl] *m* **-s,** - (*lit, fig*) key; (*Schraub~*) spanner, wrench; (*MUS*) clef; **~bein** *nt* collarbone; **~blume** *f* cowslip, primrose; **~bund** *m* bunch of keys; **~erlebnis** *nt* (*PSYCH*) crucial experience; **~kind** *nt* latchkey child; **~loch** *nt* keyhole; **~position** *f* key position; **~wort** *f* safe combination; (*COMPUT*) keyword.
Schluß- *zW*: **~folgerung** *f* conclusion, inference; **~formel** *f* (*in Brief*) closing formula;

(*bei Vertrag*) final clause.

schlüssig [schlü'siĉh] *a* conclusive; **sich** (*dat*) ~ **sein** have made up one's mind (*über etw akk* about sth).

Schluß- *zW:* ~**licht** *nt* taillight; (*fig*) cellar dweller (*US umg*), tail ender (*Brit*); ~**strich** *m* (*fig*) final stroke; **einen** ~**strich unter etw** (*akk*) **ziehen** consider sth finished; ~**verkauf** *m* clearance sale; ~**wort** *nt* concluding words *pl*.

Schmach [schmâĉh] *f* - disgrace, ignominy.

schmachten [schmâĉh'tən] *vi* languish; **nach jdm** ~ pine for sb.

schmächtig [schmeĉh'tiĉh] *a* slight.

schmachvoll *a* ignominious, humiliating.

schmackhaft [schmâk'hâft] *a* tasty; **jdm etw** ~ **machen** (*fig*) make sth palatable to sb.

schmähen [schme:'ən] *vt* abuse, revile.

schmäh- *zW:* ~**lich** *a* ignominious, shameful; **S**~**ung** *f* abuse.

schmal [schmâl] *a* narrow; (*Person, Buch etc*) slender, slim; (*karg*) meager (*US*), meagre (*Brit*); ~**brüstig** *a* narrow-chested.

schmälern [schme:'lərn] *vt* diminish; (*fig*) belittle.

Schmal- *zW:* ~**film** *m* movie film; ~**spur** *f* narrow gauge.

Schmalspur- *in zW* (*pej*) small-time.

Schmalz [schmâlts] *nt* -**es**, -**e** dripping; (*Schweine*~) lard; (*fig*) sentiment, schmaltz.

schmalzig *a* (*fig*) schmaltzy, slushy.

schmarotzen [schmâro'tsən] *vi* (*BIOL*) be parasitic; (*fig*) sponge.

Schmarotzer *m* -**s**, - (*BIOL*) parasite; (*fig auch*) sponger, freeloader.

Schmarren [schmâ'rən] *m* -**s**, - (*Österreich*) small piece of pancake; (*fig*) rubbish, tripe.

schmatzen [schmâ'tsən] *vi* eat noisily.

Schmaus [schmous] *m* -**es**, **Schmäuse** feast; **s**~**en** *vi* feast.

schmecken [schme'kən] *vti* taste; **es schmeckt ihm** he likes it; **schmeckt es Ihnen?** is it good?, are you enjoying your food *od* meal?; **das schmeckt nach mehr!** (*umg*) it's very more-ish (*hum*); **es sich** ~ **lassen** dig in.

Schmeichelei [schmîĉhəlî'] *f* flattery.

schmeichelhaft [schmî'ĉhəlhâft] *a* flattering.

schmeicheln *vi* flatter.

Schmeichler(in *f)* *m* -**s**, - flatterer.

schmeißen [schmî'sən] *vt unreg* (*umg*) throw, chuck; (*spendieren*): **eine Runde** *od* **Lage** ~ stand a round.

Schmeißfliege *f* bluebottle.

Schmelz [schmelts] *m* -**es**, -**e** enamel; (*Glasur*) glaze; (*von Stimme*) melodiousness; **s**~**bar** *a* fusible.

schmelzen [schmel'tsən] *vti unreg* melt; (*Erz*) smelt.

Schmelz- *zW:* ~**hütte** *f* smelting works *pl*; ~**käse** *m* cheese spread; (*in Scheiben*) processed cheese; ~**ofen** *m* melting furnace; (*für Erze*) smelting furnace; ~**punkt** *m* melting point; ~**spalte** *f* (*umg*) agony column; ~**tiegel** *m* (*lit, fig*) melting pot;

~**wasser** *nt* melted snow.

Schmerbauch [schmâ:r'boukh] *m* (*umg*) paunch, potbelly.

Schmerz [schmerts] *m* -**es**, -**en** pain; (*Trauer*) grief *no pl*; ~**en haben** be in pain; **s**~**empfindlich** *a* sensitive to pain.

schmerzen *vti* hurt.

Schmerzensgeld *nt* compensation.

Schmerz- *zW:* **s**~**haft**, **s**~**lich** *a* painful; **s**~**lindernd** *a* pain-relieving; **s**~**los** *a* painless; **s**~**stillend** *a* soothing.

Schmetterling [schme'tərling] *m* butterfly.

Schmetterlingsstil *m* (*SCHWIMMEN*) butterfly stroke.

schmettern [schme'tərn] *vti* smash; (*Melodie*) sing loudly, bellow out; (*Trompete*) blare.

Schmied [schmē:t] *m* -**(e)s**, -**e** blacksmith.

Schmiede [schmē:'də] *f* -, -**n** smithy, forge; ~**'eisen** *nt* wrought iron.

schmieden *vt* forge; (*Pläne*) devise, concoct.

schmiegen [schmē:'gən] *vt* press, nestle ♦ *vr* cuddle, nestle (*an* +*akk* up to).

schmiegsam [schmē:k'zâm] *a* flexible, pliable.

Schmiere [schmē:'rə] *f* -, -**n** grease; (*THEAT*) greasepaint, make-up; (*pej: schlechtes Theater*) fleapit; ~ **stehen** (*umg*) be the look-out.

schmieren *vt* smear; (*ölen*) lubricate, grease; (*bestechen*) bribe; **es läuft wie geschmiert** it's going like clockwork; **jdm eine** ~ (*umg*) clout sb one ♦ *vi* (*schreiben*) scrawl; **S**~**komödiant** *m* (*pej*) ham (actor).

Schmier- *zW:* ~**fett** *nt* grease; ~**fink** *m* messy person; ~**geld** *nt* bribe; ~**heft** *nt* notebook.

schmierig *a* greasy.

Schmier- *zW:* ~**mittel** *nt* lubricant; ~**seife** *f* soft soap.

schmilzt [schmilst] *2./3. pers sing präs von* **schmelzen.**

Schminke [schming'kə] *f* -, -**n** make-up.

schminken *vtr* make up.

schmirgeln [schmir'gəln] *vt* sand (down).

Schmirgelpapier *nt* -**s** emery paper.

schmiß [schmis] *imperf von* **schmeißen.**

Schmiß *m* -**sses**, -**sse** (*Narbe*) scar; (*veraltet: Schwung*) dash, élan.

Schmöker [schmœ'kər] *m* -**s**, - (*umg*) (trashy) old book.

schmökern *vi* bury o.s. in a book; (*umg*) browse.

schmollen [schmo'lən] *vi* pout; (*gekränkt*) sulk.

schmollend *a* sulky.

Schmollmund *m* pout.

schmolz [schmolts] *imperf von* **schmelzen.**

Schmor- [schmō:r'] *zW:* ~**braten** *m* stewed *od* braised meat; **s**~**en** *vt* braise.

Schmu [schmō̄:] *m* -**s**, - (*umg*) cheating.

Schmuck [schmŏŏk] *m* -**(e)s**, -**e** jewelry (*US*), jewellery (*Brit*); (*Verzierung*) decoration.

schmücken [schmü'kən] *vt* decorate.

Schmuck- *zW:* **s**~**los** *a* unadorned, plain;

~**losigkeit** *f* simplicity; ~**sachen** *pl* jewels *pl*, jewelry *sing* (*US*), jewellery *sing* (*Brit*); ~**stück** *nt* (*Ring etc*) piece of jewelry; (*fig*: *Prachtstück*) gem.

schmudd(e)lig [shmŏŏd'(ə)licĥ] *a* messy; (*schmutzig*) dirty; (*schmierig, unsauber*) filthy.

Schmuggel [shmŏŏ'gəl] *m* -s smuggling.

schmuggeln *vti* smuggle.

Schmuggelware *f* -, -n contraband.

Schmuggler(in *f*) *m* -s, - smuggler.

schmunzeln [shmŏŏn'tsəln] *vi* smile benignly.

schmusen [shmŏŏ:'zən] *vi* (*umg*: *zärtlich sein*) cuddle; **mit jdm** ~ cuddle sb.

Schmutz [shmŏŏts] *m* -es dirt; (*fig auch*) filth; **s~en** *vi* get dirty; ~**fink** *m* filthy creature; ~**fleck** *m* stain.

schmutzig *a* dirty; ~**e Wäsche waschen** (*fig*) wash one's dirty linen in public.

Schnabel [shnà'bəl] *m* -s, ⁼ beak, bill; (*Ausguß*) spout; (*umg*: *Mund*) mouth; **reden, wie einem der** ~ **gewachsen ist** say exactly what comes into one's head; (*unaffektiert*) talk naturally.

schnacken [shnà'kən] *vi* (*norddeutsch umg*) chat.

Schnake [shnà'kə] *f* -, -n crane fly; (*Stechmücke*) gnat.

Schnalle [shnà'lə] *f* -, -n buckle; (*an Handtasche, Buch*) clasp.

schnallen *vt* buckle.

schnalzen [shnàl'tsən] *vi* snap; (*mit Zunge*) click.

schnappen [shnà'pən] *vt* grab, catch; (*umg*: *ergreifen*) snatch ♦ *vi* snap.

Schnapp- *zW*: ~**schloß** *nt* spring lock; ~**schuß** *m* (*PHOT*) snapshot.

Schnaps [shnàps] *m* -es, ⁼e schnapps; (*umg*: *Branntwein*) spirits *pl*; ~**idee** *f* (*umg*) crackpot idea; ~**leiche** *f* (*umg*) drunk.

schnarchen [shnàr'cĥən] *vi* snore.

schnattern [shnà'tərn] *vi* chatter; (*zittern*) shiver.

schnauben [shnou'bən] *vi* snort ♦ *vr* blow one's nose.

schnaufen [shnou'fən] *vi* puff, pant.

Schnaufer *m* -s, - (*umg*) breath.

Schnauzbart [shnouts'bárt] *m* mustache (*US*), moustache (*Brit*).

Schnauze *f* -, -n snout, muzzle; (*Ausguß*) spout; (*umg*) gob; **auf die** ~ **fallen** (*fig*) fail completely; **etw frei nach** ~ **machen** do sth any old how.

Schnecke [shne'kə] *f* -, -n snail; (*Nackt*~) slug; (: *Gebäck*) ≈ cinnamon roll (*US*), Chelsea bun (*Brit*); **jdn zur** ~ **machen** (*umg*) give sb a real bawling out.

Schnecken- *zW*: ~**haus** *nt* snail's shell; ~**tempo** *nt* (*umg*): **im** ~**tempo** at a snail's pace.

Schnee [shnā:] *m* -s snow; (*Ei*~) beaten egg white; ~ **von gestern** old hat; water under the bridge; ~**ball** *m* snowball; ~**besen** *m* (*KOCH*) whisk; ~**flocke** *f* snowflake;

~**gestöber** *nt* snowstorm; ~**glöckchen** *nt* snowdrop; ~**grenze** *f* snowline; ~**kette** *f* (*AUT*) snow chain; ~**könig** *m*: **sich freuen wie ein** ~**könig** be as pleased as Punch; ~**mann** *m* snowman; ~**pflug** *m* snowplow (*US*), snowplough (*Brit*); ~**regen** *m* sleet; ~**schmelze** *f* -, -n thaw; ~**treiben** *nt* driving snow; ~**wehe** *f* snowdrift; ~**wittchen** *nt* Snow White.

Schneid [shnīt] *m* -(e)s (*umg*) pluck.

Schneidbrenner *m* -s, - (*TECH*) oxyacetylene torch.

Schneide [shnī'də] *f* -, -n edge; (*Klinge*) blade.

schneiden *vt unreg* cut; (*Film, Tonband*) edit; (*kreuzen*) cross, intersect; (*umg*: *sich täuschen*): **da hat er sich aber geschnitten!** he's very much mistaken; **die Luft ist zum S~** (*fig umg*) the air is very bad ♦ *vr* cut o.s.

schneidend *a* cutting.

Schneider *m* -s, - tailor; **frieren wie ein** ~ (*umg*) be frozen to the marrow; **aus dem** ~ **sein** (*fig*) be out of the woods.

Schneiderin *f* dressmaker.

schneidern *vt* make ♦ *vi* be a tailor.

Schneidersitz *m* -es: **im** ~ **sitzen** sit cross-legged.

Schneidezahn *m* incisor.

schneidig *a* dashing; (*mutig*) plucky.

schneien [shnī'ən] *vi* snow; **jdm ins Haus** ~ (*umg*: *Besuch*) drop in on sb; (: *Rechnung, Brief*) arrive through sb's letterbox *od* in the mail.

Schneise [shnī'zə] *f* -, -n (*Wald*~) clearing.

schnell [shnel] *a, ad* quick(ly), fast; **das ging** ~ that was quick; **S~boot** *nt* speedboat.

Schnelle *f* -: **etw auf die** ~ **machen** do sth in a rush.

schnellen *vi* shoot.

Schnell- *zW*: ~**gericht** *nt* (*JUR*) summary court; (*KOCH*) convenience food; ~**hefter** *m* loose-leaf binder.

Schnelligkeit *f* speed.

Schnell- *zW*: ~**imbiß** *m* (*Essen*) (quick) snack; (*Raum*) snack bar; ~**kochtopf** *m* (*Dampfkochtopf*) pressure cooker.

schnellstens *ad* as quickly as possible.

Schnell- *zW*: ~**straße** *f* expressway; ~**zug** *m* fast *od* express train.

schneuzen [shnoi'tsən] *vr* blow one's nose.

Schnickschnack [shniksh'nák] *m* -(e)s (*umg*) twaddle.

Schnippchen [shnip'cĥən] *nt*: **jdm ein** ~ **schlagen** play a trick on sb.

schnippeln [shni'pəln] *vti* (*umg*) snip (*an* +*dat* at); (*mit Messer*) hack (*an* +*dat* at).

schnippen [shni'pən] *vi*: **mit den Fingern** ~ snap one's fingers.

schnippisch [shni'pish] *a* sharp-tongued.

Schnipsel [shnip'səl] *m od nt* -s, - (*umg*) scrap; (*Papier*~) scrap of paper.

schnitt [shnit] *imperf von* schneiden.

Schnitt *m* -(e)s, -e cut(ting); (~*punkt*) intersection; (*Quer~*) (cross) section; (*Durch~*) average; (*~muster*) pattern; (*Ernte*) crop; (*an Buch*) edge; (*umg: Gewinn*) profit; ~: **L. Schwarz** (*FILM*) editor – L. Schwarz; **im** ~ on average.

Schnitt- *zW*: **~blumen** *pl* cut flowers *pl*; **~bohnen** *pl* French *od* green beans *pl*.

Schnitte *f* -, **-n** slice; (*belegt*) sandwich.

Schnitt- *zW*: **s~fest** *a* (*Tomaten*) firm; **~fläche** *f* section.

schnittig [ʃni'tiç] *a* smart; (*Auto, Formen*) stylish.

Schnitt- *zW*: **~lauch** *m* chive; **~muster** *nt* pattern; **~punkt** *m* (point of) intersection; **~stelle** *f* (*COMPUT*) interface; **~wunde** *f* cut.

Schnitzarbeit *f* wood carving.

Schnitzel *nt* **-s**, - scrap; (*KOCH*) escalope; **~jagd** *f* paperchase.

schnitzen [ʃni'tsən] *vt* carve.

Schnitzer *m* **-s**, - carver; (*umg*) blunder.

Schnitzerei [ʃnitsəri'] *f* wood carving.

schnodderig [ʃno'dəriç] *a* (*umg*) snotty.

schnöde [ʃnœ'də] *a* base, mean.

Schnorchel [ʃnor'çəl] *m* **-s**, - snorkel.

Schnörkel [ʃnœr'kəl] *m* **-s**, - flourish; (*ARCHIT*) scroll.

schnorren [ʃno'rən] *vti* scrounge.

Schnorrer *m* **-s**, - (*umg*) scrounger.

Schnösel [ʃnœ'zəl] *m* **-s**, - (*umg*) snotty-(-nosed) little upstart.

schnuckelig [ʃnô̄o'kəliç] *a* (*umg*: gemütlich*) snug, cosy; (*Person*) sweet.

schnüffeln [ʃnü'fəln] *vi* sniff; (*fig umg*: *spionieren*) snoop around; **S~** *nt* (*Klebstoff etc*) glue-sniffing.

Schnüffler(in *f*) *m* **-s**, - snooper.

Schnuller [ʃnô̄o'lər] *m* **-s**, - pacifier (*US*), dummy (*Brit*).

Schnulze [ʃnô̄ol'tsə] *f* -, **-n** (*umg*) schmaltzy film *od* book *od* song.

Schnupfen [ʃnô̄op'fən] *m* **-s**, - cold.

Schnupftabak *m* snuff.

schnuppe [ʃnô̄o'pə] *a* (*umg*): **jdm** ~ **sein** be all the same to sb.

schnuppern [ʃnô̄o'pərn] *vi* sniff.

Schnur [ʃnô̄o:r] *f* -, **-̈e** string; (*Kordel*) cord; (*ELEK*) cord (*US*), flex (*Brit*).

Schnürchen [ʃnü:r'çən] *nt*: **es läuft** *od* **klappt (alles) wie am** ~ everything's going like clockwork.

schnüren [ʃnü:'rən] *vt* tie.

schnurgerade *a* straight (as a die *od* an arrow).

Schnurrbart [ʃnô̄or'bârt] *m* mustache (*US*), moustache (*Brit*).

schnurren [ʃnô̄o'rən] *vi* purr; (*Kreisel*) hum.

Schnür- *zW*: **~schuh** *m* lace-up (shoe); **~senkel** *m* shoelace.

schnurstracks *ad* straight (away); ~ **auf jdn/etw zugehen** make a beeline for sb/sth (*umg*).

schob [ʃô̄o:p] *imperf von* **schieben**.

Schock [ʃok] *m* **-(e)s**, **-e** shock; **unter** ~ **stehen** be in (a state of) shock.

shocken *vt* (*umg*) shock.

shockieren [ʃokē:'rən] *vt* shock, outrage.

Schöffe [ʃœ'fə] *m* **-n**, **-n** lay magistrate.

Schöffengericht *nt* magistrates' court.

Schöffin *f* lay magistrate.

Schokolade [ʃōkōlá'də] *f* -, **-n** chocolate.

scholl [ʃol] *imperf von* **schallen**.

Scholle [ʃo'lə] *f* -, **-n** clod; (*Eis~*) ice floe; (*Fisch*) plaice.

Scholli [ʃo'li] *m* (*umg*): **mein lieber** ~! (*drohend*) now look here!

schon [ʃō:n] *ad* already; (*zwar*) certainly; ~ **vor 100 Jahren** as far back as 100 years ago; **er wollte** ~ **die Hoffnung aufgeben, als** ... he was just about to give up hope when ...; **wartest du** ~ **lange?** have you been waiting (for) long?; **wie** ~ **so oft** as so often (before); **warst du** ~ **einmal da?** have you ever been there?; **ich war** ~ **einmal da** I've been there before; **das ist** ~ **immer so** that has always been the case; **das wird** ~ **(noch) gut** that'll be O.K.; **was,** ~ **wieder?** what – again?; **das ist** ~ **möglich** that's quite possible; **hör** ~ **auf damit!** will you stop that!; **was macht das** ~, **wenn** ...? what does it matter if ...?; **und wenn** ~! (*umg*) so what?; ~ **gut** all right, okay; **wenn ich das** ~ **höre** ... I only have to hear that ...; **ich habe das** ~ **mal gehört** I've heard that before; ~ **der Gedanke** the very thought.

schön [ʃœn] *a* beautiful; (*nett*) nice; (*Mann*) handsome; **da hast du etwas S~es angerichtet** you've made a fine *od* nice mess; **~e Grüße** best wishes; **~en Dank** (many) thanks ♦ *ad*: **sich ganz** ~ **ärgern** be very angry; ~ **weich/warm** nice and soft/warm.

schonen [ʃō:'nən] *vt* look after; (*jds Nerven*) spare; (*Gegner, Kind*) be easy on; (*Teppich, Füße*) save ♦ *vr* take it easy.

schonend *a* careful, gentle; **jdm etw** ~ **beibringen** break sth to sb gently.

Schoner [ʃō:'nər] *m* **-s**, - (*NAUT*) schooner; (*Sessel~*) cover.

Schönfärberei' *f* (*fig*) glossing things over.

Schonfrist *f* period of grace.

Schön- *zW*: **~geist** *m* cultured person; **~heit** *f* beauty.

Schönheits- *zW*: **~fehler** *m* blemish, flaw; **~operation** *f* cosmetic plastic surgery; ~ **wettbewerb** *m* beauty contest.

Schonkost *f* - light diet.

schönmachen *vr* make o.s. look nice.

Schön- *zW*: **~schrift** *f*: **in ~schrift** in one's best (hand)writing; **s~tun** *vi unreg*: **jdm s~tun** (*schmeicheln*) flatter *od* soft-soap sb, play up to sb.

Schonung *f* good care; (*Nachsicht*) consideration; (*Forst*) plantation of young trees.

schonungslos *a* ruthless, harsh.

Schonzeit *f* closed season.

Schopf [ʃopf] *m* **-(e)s**, **-̈e**: **eine Gelegenheit**

beim ~ ergreifen od **fassen** seize od grasp an opportunity with both hands.

schöpfen [shœˈpfən] vt scoop; (Suppe) ladle; (Mut) summon up; (Luft) breathe in; (Hoffnung) find.

Schöpfer m -s, - creator; (Gott) Creator; (umg: Schöpflöffel) ladle; **s~isch** a creative.

Schöpf- zW: **~kelle** f ladle; **~löffel** m skimmer, scoop.

Schöpfung f creation.

Schoppen [shoˈpən] m -s, - (Glas Wein) glass of wine.

schor [shoːr] imperf von **scheren**.

Schorf [shorf] m -(e)s, -e scab.

Schorle [shorˈlə] f -, -n wine and soda water od lemonade mix.

Schornstein [shornˈshtīn] m chimney; (NAUT) funnel; **~feger** m -s, - chimney sweep.

schoß [shos] imperf von **schießen**.

Schoß [shoːs] m -es, �¨e lap; (Rock~) coat tail; **im ~e der Familie** in the bosom of one's family; **~hund** m lapdog.

Schößling [shœsˈling] m (BOT) shoot.

Schote [shoːˈtə] f -, -n pod.

Schotte [shoˈtə] m -n, -n Scot, Scotsman.

Schottenrock [shoˈtənrok] m tartan skirt; kilt.

Schotter [shoˈtər] m -s gravel; (im Straßenbau) road metal; (EISENB) ballast.

Schottin [shoˈtin] f Scot, Scotswoman.

schottisch [shoˈtish] a Scottish, Scots; **das ~e Hochland** the Scottish Highlands pl.

Schottland nt -s Scotland.

schraffieren [shráfēˈrən] vt hatch.

schräg [shreːk] a slanting; (schief, geneigt) sloping; (nicht gerade od parallel) oblique ♦ ad: **~ gedruckt** in italics; **etw ~ stellen** put sth at an angle; **~ gegenüber** diagonally opposite.

Schräge [shreːˈgə] f -, -n slant.

Schräg- zW: **~kante** f beveled (US) od bevelled (Brit) edge; **~schrift** f italics pl; **~streifen** m bias binding; **~strich** m slash.

Schramme [shráˈmə] f -, -n scratch.

schrammen vt scratch.

Schrank [shrángk] m -(e)s, ¨e closet (US), cupboard (Brit); (Kleider~) wardrobe.

Schranke f -, -n barrier; (fig: Grenze) limit; (: Hindernis) barrier; **jdn in seine ~n (ver)weisen** (fig) put sb in his place.

Schranken- zW: **s~los** a boundless; (zügellos) unrestrained; **~wärter** m (EISENB) grade-crossing (US) od level-crossing (Brit) attendant.

Schrank- zW: **~koffer** m wardrobe trunk; **~wand** f wall unit.

Schraube [shrouˈbə] f -, -n screw.

schrauben vt screw; **etw in die Höhe ~** (fig: Preise, Rekorde) push sth up; (: Ansprüche) raise sth.

Schrauben- zW: **~schlüssel** m wrench (US), spanner (Brit); **~zieher** m -s, - screwdriver.

Schraubstock [shroupˈshtok] m (TECH) vise

(US), vice (Brit).

Schrebergarten [shráːˈbərgártən] m separate garden plot, allotment (Brit).

Schreck [shrek] m -(e)s, -e terror; **o ~ laß nach** (hum umg) for goodness' sake!

schrecken vt frighten, scare; **aus dem Schlaf ~** be startled out of one's sleep; **S~** m -s, - terror; (Schreck) fright.

Schreckens- zW: **s~bleich** a as white as a sheet od ghost; **~herrschaft** f (reign of) terror.

Schreck- zW: **~gespenst** nt nightmare; **s~haft** a jumpy, easily frightened; **s~lich** a terrible, dreadful; **s~lich gerne!** (umg) I'd absolutely love to; **~schraube** f (pej, umg) (old) battle-axe; **~schuß** m shot fired in the air; **~sekunde** f moment of shock.

Schrei [shrī] m -(e)s, -e scream; (Ruf) shout; **der letzte ~** (umg) the latest thing, all the rage.

Schreib- [shrīp] zW: **~bedarf** m writing materials pl, stationery; **~block** m writing pad.

schreiben [shrīˈbən] vti unreg write; (mit Schreibmaschine) type (out); (berichten: Zeitung etc) say; (buchstabieren) spell ♦ vr: **wie schreibt sich das?** how is that spelt?; **S~** nt -s, - letter, communication.

Schreiber(in f) m -s, - writer; (Büro~) clerk.

Schreib- zW: **s~faul** a lazy about writing letters; **~fehler** m spelling mistake; **~kraft** f typist; **~maschine** f typewriter; **~papier** nt notepaper, writing paper; **~schutz** m (COMPUT) write protect; **~stube** f orderly room; **~tisch** m desk; **~tischtäter** m wire od string puller; **~unterlage** f pad; **~waren** pl stationery sing; **~weise** f spelling; (Stil) style; **s~wütig** a crazy about writing; **~zentrale** f typing pool; **~zeug** nt writing materials pl.

schreien [shriˈən] vti unreg scream; (rufen) shout; **es war zum S~** (umg) it was a scream od a hoot; **nach etw ~** (fig) cry out for sth.

schreiend a (fig) glaring; (: Farbe) loud.

Schrei- zW: **~hals** m (umg: Baby) bawler; (Unruhestifter) noisy troublemaker; **~krampf** m screaming fit.

Schreiner [shrīˈnər] m -s, - joiner; (Zimmermann) carpenter; (Möbel~) cabinetmaker.

Schreinerei [shrīnərīˈ] f joiner's workshop.

schreiten [shrīˈtən] vi unreg stride.

schrie [shrē] imperf von **schreien**.

schrieb [shrēp] imperf von **schreiben**.

Schrieb m -(e)s, -e (umg) missive (hum).

Schrift [shrift] f - en writing; (Hand~) handwriting; (~art) script; (Buch) work; **~art** f (Hand~) script; (TYP) typeface; **~bild** nt script; (COMPUT) typeface; **~deutsch** nt written German; **~führer** m secretary; **s~lich** a written; **das kann ich Ihnen s~lich geben** (fig umg) I can tell you that for free ♦ ad in writing; **~probe** f (Hand~) specimen of one's handwriting; ~**satz** m (TYP) font; ~**setzer** m compositor, typesetter; ~**sprache** f written language.

Schriftsteller(in f) m -**s**, - writer; **s**~**isch** a literary.

Schrift- zW: ~**stück** nt document; ~**verkehr** m, ~**wechsel** m correspondence.

schrill [ʃrɪl] a shrill; ~**en** vi (Stimme) sound shrilly; (Telefon) ring shrilly.

schritt [ʃrɪt] imperf von **schreiten**.

Schritt m -(e)s, -e step; (Gangart) walk; (Tempo) pace; (von Hose) crotch; **auf ~ und Tritt** (lit, fig) wherever od everywhere one goes; „~ **fahren"** "drive at a walking pace"; **mit zehn ~en Abstand** at a distance of ten paces; **den ersten ~ tun** (fig) make the first move; (: etw beginnen) take the first step; ~**macher** m pacemaker; ~**(t)empo** nt: **im ~(t)empo** at a walking pace; **s**~**weise** ad gradually, little by little.

schroff [ʃrɔf] a steep; (zackig) jagged; (fig) brusque; (ungeduldig) abrupt.

schröpfen [ˈʃrœpfən] vt (fig) fleece.

Schrot [ʃroːt] m od nt -(e)s, -e (Blei) (small) shot; (Getreide) coarsely ground grain, groats pl; ~**flinte** f shotgun.

Schrott [ʃrɔt] m -(e)s, -e scrap metal; **ein Auto zu ~ fahren** (durch Unfall) write off a car; ~**haufen** m scrap heap; ~**reif** a ready for the scrap heap; ~**wert** m scrap value.

schrubben [ˈʃrʊbən] vt scrub.

Schrubber m -**s**, - scrubbing brush.

Schrulle [ˈʃrʊlə] f -, -n eccentricity, queer idea od habit.

schrumpfen [ˈʃrʊmpfən] vi aux sein shrink; (Apfel) shrivel; (Leber, Niere) atrophy.

Schub [ʃuːp] m -**s**, -̈e (Stoß) push, shove; (Gruppe, Anzahl) batch.

Schub- zW: ~**fach** nt drawer; ~**karren** m wheelbarrow; ~**lade** f drawer.

Schubladendenken nt -**s** thinking in categories.

Schubs [ʃuːps] m -**es**, -e (umg) shove, push; **s**~**en** vti (umg) shove, push.

schüchtern [ˈʃʏçtərn] a shy; **S**~**heit** f shyness.

schuf [ʃuːf] imperf von **schaffen**.

Schuft [ʃʊft] m -(e)s, -e scoundrel.

schuften vi (umg) graft, slave away.

Schuh [ʃuː] m -(e)s, -e shoe; **jdm etw in die ~ schieben** (fig umg) put the blame for sth on sb; **wo drückt der ~?** (fig) what's troubling you?; ~**band** nt shoelace; ~**creme** f shoe polish; ~**löffel** m shoehorn; ~**macher** m shoemaker; ~**werk** nt footwear.

Schukosteckdose [ˈʃuːkoˌʃtɛkdoːzə] f -, -n ® grounded outlet (US), safety socket (Brit).

Schul- [ʃuːl'] zW: ~**aufgaben** pl homework sing; ~**bank** f: **die ~bank drücken** (umg) go to school; ~**behörde** f education authority; ~**besuch** m school attendance; ~**buchverlag** m educational publishing

company.

schuld [ʃʊlt] a: ~ **sein** od **haben** be to blame (an +dat for); **er ist** od **hat ~** it's his fault; **jdm ~ geben** blame sb.

Schuld f -, -**en** guilt; (FIN) debt; (Verschulden) fault; **jdm die ~ geben** od **zuschieben** blame sb; **ich bin mir keiner ~ bewußt** I'm not aware of having done anything wrong; ~ **und Sühne** crime and punishment; **ich stehe tief in seiner ~** (fig) I'm deeply indebted to him; ~**en machen** run up debts.

schuldbewußt a (Mensch) feeling guilty; (Miene) guilty.

schulden [ˈʃʊldən] vt owe; ~**frei** a free from debt.

Schuld- zW: ~**gefühl** nt feeling of guilt; **s**~**haft** a (JUR) culpable.

Schuldienst m -(e)s (school-)teaching.

schuldig a guilty (an +dat of); (gebührend) due; **jdm etw ~ sein** od **bleiben** owe sb sth; **jdn ~ sprechen** find sb guilty; ~ **geschieden sein** be the guilty party in a divorce; **S**~**keit** f duty.

schuldlos a innocent, blameless.

Schuldner(in f) m -**s**, - debtor.

Schuld- zW: ~**prinzip** nt (JUR) principle of the guilty party; ~**schein** m promissory note, IOU; ~**spruch** m verdict of guilty.

Schule [ˈʃuːlə] f -, -**n** school; **auf** od **in der ~** at school; **in die ~ kommen/gehen** start school/go to school; ~ **machen** (fig) become the accepted thing.

schulen vt train, school.

Schüler(in f) [ˈʃyːlər(ɪn)] m -**s**, - pupil; ~**ausweis** m (school) student card; ~**lotse** m pupil acting as a road-crossing guard; ~**mitverwaltung** f school od student council.

Schul- zW: ~**ferien** pl school vacation; ~**fernsehen** nt schools' od educational television; **s**~**frei** a: **die Kinder haben morgen s**~**frei** the children don't have to go to school tomorrow; ~**funk** m schools' broadcasts pl; ~**geld** nt registration (US) od school fees pl; ~**heft** nt exercise book; ~**hof** m playground.

schulisch [ˈʃuːlɪʃ] a (Leistungen, Probleme) at school; (Angelegenheiten) school attr.

Schul- zW: ~**jahr** nt school year; ~**junge** m schoolboy; ~**leiter(in** f) m principal; ~**mädchen** nt schoolgirl; ~**medizin** f orthodox medicine; ~**pflicht** f compulsory school attendance; **s**~**pflichtig** a of school age; ~**reife** f: **die ~reife haben** be ready to go to school; ~**schiff** nt (NAUT) training ship; ~**sprecher(in** f) m student president (US), head boy/head girl (Brit); ~**stunde** f period, lesson; ~**tasche** f school bag.

Schulter [ˈʃʊltər] f -, -**n** shoulder; **auf die leichte ~ nehmen** take lightly; ~**blatt** nt shoulder blade.

schultern vt shoulder.

Schultüte f large conical bag of sweets given to children on their first day at school.

Schulung *f* education, schooling.
Schul- *zW*: **~wesen** *nt* educational system; **~zeugnis** *nt* report card (*US*), school report (*Brit*).
schummeln [shōō'məln] *vi* (*umg*) cheat (*bei etw* at sth).
schumm(e)rig [shōōm'(ə)riċh] *a* (*Beleuchtung*) dim; (*Raum*) dimly-lit.
schund [shōōnt] *imperf von* **schinden.**
Schund *m* **-(e)s** trash, garbage; **~roman** *m* trashy novel.
Schupo [shōō:'pō] *m* **-s, -s** *abk* (*veraltet*: = *Schutzpolizist*) cop.
Schuppe [shōō'pə] *f* **-, -n** scale; **~n** *pl* (*Haarschuppen*) dandruff.
schuppen *vt* scale ♦ *vr* peel.
Schuppen *m* **-s, -** shed; (*umg: übles Lokal*) dive.
schuppig [shōō'piċh] *a* scaly.
Schur [shōō:r] *f* **-, -en** shearing.
Schüreisen *nt* poker.
schüren [shü:'rən] *vt* rake; (*fig*) stir up.
schürfen [shür'fən] *vti* scrape, scratch; (*MIN*) prospect; dig.
Schürfung *f* abrasion; (*MIN*) prospecting.
Schürhaken *m* **-s, -** poker.
Schurke [shōōr'kə] *m* **-n, -n** rogue.
Schurwolle *f*: **„reine ~"** "virgin wool".
Schurz [shōōrts] *m* **-es, -e, Schürze** [shür'tsə] *f* **-, -n** apron.
Schürzenjäger *m* (*umg*) philanderer, one for the girls.
Schuß [shōōs] *m* **-sses, ⁻sse** shot; (*FUSSBALL*) kick; (*Spritzer: von Wein, Essig etc*) dash; (*WEBEN*) woof; **(gut) in ~ sein** (*umg*) be in good shape *od* nick; (*Mensch*) be in form; **etw in ~ halten** keep sth in good shape; **weitab vom ~ sein** (*fig umg*) be miles from where the action is; **der goldene ~** a lethal dose of a drug; **ein ~ in den Ofen** (*umg*) a complete waste of time, a failure; **~bereich** *m* effective range.
Schüssel [shü'səl] *f* **-, -n** bowl; basin; (*Servier~ auch*) dish; (*Wasch~*) basin.
schusselig [shōō'səliċh] *a* (*umg*) daft (*Brit*); (*zerstreut*) scatterbrained, muddle-headed (*umg*).
Schuß- *zW*: **~linie** *f* line of fire; **~verletzung** *f* bullet wound; **~waffe** *f* firearm; **~waffengebrauch** *m* (*form*) use of firearms; **~weite** *f* range (of fire).
Schuster [shōō:s'tər] *m* **-s, -** cobbler, shoemaker.
Schutt [shōōt] *m* **-(e)s** rubbish; (*Bau~*) rubble; **„~ abladen verboten"** "no dumping"; **~abladeplatz** *m* refuse dump.
Schüttelfrost *m* shivering.
schütteln [shü'təln] *vt* shake ♦ *vr* shake o.s.; (*vor Kälte*) shiver (*vor* with); (*vor Ekel*) shudder (*vor* with, in).
schütten [shü'tən] *vt* pour; (*Zucker, Kies etc*) tip; (*verschütten*) spill ♦ *vi unpers* pour (down).
schütter *a* (*Haare*) sparse, thin.

Schutt- *zW*: **~halde** *f* dump; **~haufen** *m* heap of rubble.
Schutz [shōōts] *m* **-es** protection; (*Unterschlupf*) shelter; **jdn in ~ nehmen** stand up for sb; **~anzug** *m* overalls *pl*; **s~bedürftig** *a* in need of protection; **~befohlene(r)** *mf dekl wie a* charge; **~blech** *nt* fender (*US*), mudguard (*Brit*); **~brief** *m* (*Versicherung*) = **Auslandsschutzbrief**; **~brille** *f* goggles *pl*.
Schütze [shü'tsə] *m* **-n, -n** gunman; (*Gewehr~*) rifleman; (*Scharf~, Sport~*) marksman; (*ASTROL*) Sagittarius.
schützen [shü'tsən] *vt* protect (*vor +dat, gegen* from, against) ♦ *vr* protect o.s.; **gesetzlich/urheberrechtlich geschützt** registered/protected by copyright; **vor Nässe ~!** keep dry.
Schützenfest *nt* fair featuring shooting matches.
Schutzengel *m* guardian angel.
Schützen- *zW*: **~graben** *m* trench; **~hilfe** *f* (*fig*) support.
Schutz- *zW*: **~gebiet** *nt* protectorate; (*Natur- ~*) reserve; **~gebühr** *f* (token) fee; **~haft** *f* protective custody; **~heilige(r)** *mf* patron saint; **~impfung** *f* immunization.
Schützling [shüts'ling] *m* protégé; (*bes Kind*) charge.
Schutz- *zW*: **s~los** *a* defenseless (*US*), defenceless (*Brit*); **~mann** *m, pl* **-leute** *od* **-männer** policeman; **~marke** *f* trademark; **~maßnahme** *f* precaution; **~patron** *m* patron saint; **~schirm** *m* (*TECH*) protective screen; **~umschlag** *m* (book) jacket; **~verband** *m* (*MED*) protective bandage *od* dressing; **~vorrichtung** *f* safety device.
Schw. *abk* = **Schwester.**
schwäb. *abk* = **schwäbisch.**
schwabbelig [shväb'(ə)liċh] *a* (*umg: Körperteil*) flabby; (*Gelee*) wobbly.
Schwabe [shvá'bə] *m* **-n, -n, Schwäbin** [shve:'bin] *f* Swabian.
Schwaben *nt* **-s** Swabia.
schwäbisch [shve:'bish] *a* Swabian.
schwach [shväḥ] *a* weak, feeble; (*Gedächtnis, Gesundheit*) poor; (*Hoffnung*) faint; **~ werden** weaken; **das ist ein ~es Bild** (*umg*) *od* **eine ~e Leistung** (*umg*) that's a poor show; **ein ~er Trost** cold *od* small comfort; **mach mich nicht ~!** (*umg*) don't say that!; **auf ~en Beinen** *od* **Füßen stehen** (*fig*) be on shaky ground; (: *Theorie*) be shaky.
Schwäche [shve:'ċhə] *f* **-, -n** weakness.
schwächen *vt* weaken.
schwach- *zW*: **S~heit** *f* weakness; **S~kopf** *m* (*umg*) dimwit, idiot; **~köpfig** *a* silly, daft.
Schwäch- *zW*: **s~lich** *a* weakly, delicate; **~ling** *m* weakling.
Schwach- *zW*: **~sinn** *m* (*MED*) mental deficiency, feeble-mindedness (*veraltet*); (*umg: Quatsch*) rubbish; (*fig umg: unsinnige Tat*) idiocy; **s~sinnig** *a* mentally

deficient; (*Idee*) idiotic; ~**stelle** *f* weak point; ~**strom** *m* weak current.

Schwächung [shve'çhōōng] *f* weakening.

Schwaden [shvâ'dən] *m* -**s**, - cloud.

schwafeln [shvâ'fəln] *vi* (*umg*) blather, drivel; (*in einer Prüfung*) waffle.

Schwager [shvâ'gər] *m* -**s**, ⁼ brother-in-law.

Schwägerin [shve:'gərin] *f* sister-in-law.

Schwalbe [shvâl'bə] *f* -, -**n** swallow.

Schwall [shvál] *m* -**(e)s**, -**e** surge; (*Worte*) flood, torrent.

schwamm [shvám] *imperf von* **schwimmen**.

Schwamm *m* -**(e)s**, ⁼**e** sponge; (*Pilz*) fungus; ~ **drüber!** (*umg*) (let's) forget it!

schwammig *a* spongy; (*Gesicht*) puffy; (*vage: Begriff*) wooly (*US*), woolly (*Brit*).

Schwan [shvân] *m* -**(e)s**, ⁼**e** swan.

schwand [shvánt] *imperf von* **schwinden**.

schwanen *vi unpers*: **jdm schwant etwas** sb has a foreboding of sth.

schwang [shvángg] *imperf von* **schwingen**.

schwanger [shván'gər] *a* pregnant.

schwängern [shve'ngərn] *vt* make pregnant.

Schwangerschaft *f* pregnancy.

Schwangerschaftsabbruch *m* termination of pregnancy, abortion.

Schwank [shvángk] *m* -**(e)s**, ⁼**e** funny story; (*LITER*) merry *od* comical tale; (*THEAT*) farce.

schwanken *vi* sway; (*taumeln*) stagger, reel; (*Preise, Zahlen*) fluctuate; (*zögern*) hesitate; vacillate; (*Überzeugung etc*) begin to waver; **ins S~ kommen** (*Baum, Gebäude etc*) start to sway; (*Preise, Kurs etc*) start to fluctuate *od* vary.

Schwankung *f* fluctuation.

Schwanz [shvánts] *m* -**es**, ⁼**e** tail; (*umg!: Penis*) prick (*!*); **kein ~** (*umg*) not a (blessed) soul.

schwänzen [shven'tsən] (*umg*) *vt* (*Stunde, Vorlesung*) skip ♦ *vi* play truant.

Schwänzer [shven'tsər] *m* -**s**, - (*umg*) truant.

schwappen [shvá'pən] *vi* (*über~*) splash, slosh.

Schwarm [shvárm] *m* -**(e)s**, ⁼**e** swarm; (*umg*) heart-throb, idol.

schwärmen [shver'mən] *vi* swarm; ~ **für** be mad *od* wild about.

Schwärmerei [shvermərî'] *f* enthusiasm.

schwärmerisch *a* impassioned, effusive.

Schwarte [shvár'tə] *f* -, -**n** hard skin; (*Speck~*) rind; (*umg: Buch*) old book, tome (*hum*).

Schwartenmagen *m* -**s** (*KOCH*) brawn.

schwarz [shvárts] *a* black; (*umg: ungesetzlich*) illicit; (: *katholisch*) Catholic, Papist (*pej*); **ins S~e treffen** (*lit, fig*) hit the bull's-eye; **das S~e Brett** the bulletin board; ~**e Liste** blacklist; **das S~e Meer** the Black Sea; **S~er Peter** (*KARTEN*) *children's card game*; **jdm den S~en Peter zuschieben** (*fig: die Verantwortung abschieben*) pass the buck to sb (*umg*); **sich ~ ärgern** get extremely annoyed; **dort wählen**

alle ~ they all vote conservative there; **in den ~en Zahlen** in the black; **S~arbeit** *f* illicit work, moonlighting; **S~brot** *nt* (*Pumpernickel*) black bread, pumpernickel; (*braun*) brown rye bread.

Schwärze [shver'tsə] *f* -, -**n** blackness; (*Farbe*) blacking; (*Drucker~*) printer's ink.

schwärzen *vt* blacken.

Schwarz- *zW*: **s~fahren** *vi unreg* travel without paying; (*ohne Führerschein*) drive without a license; ~**fahrer** *m* (*Bus etc*) fare dodger (*umg*); ~**handel** *m* blackmarket (trade); ~**händler** *m* black-market operator; **s~hören** *vi* listen to the radio without a license.

schwärzlich [shverts'liçh] *a* blackish, darkish.

Schwarz- *zW*: **s~malen** *vti* be pessimistic (about); ~**markt** *m* black market; **s~sehen** *vi unreg* see the gloomy side of things; (*TV*) watch TV without a license; ~**seher** *m* pessimist; (*TV*) viewer without a license; ~**wald** *m* Black Forest; ~**wälder Kirschtorte** *f* Black Forest cherry-cake; **s~weiß** *a* black and white; ~**wurzel** *f* (*KOCH*) salsify.

schwatzen [shvát'sən], **schwätzen** [shvet'sən] *vi* chatter; (*über belanglose Dinge*) prattle; (*Unsinn reden*) blether (*umg*).

Schwätzer(in *f*) [shve'tsər(in)] *m* -**s**, - windbag (*umg*); chatterbox, gossip.

schwatzhaft *a* talkative, gossipy.

Schwebe [shvā:'bə] *f*: **in der ~** (*fig*) in abeyance; (*JUR, COMM*) be pending.

Schwebe- *zW*: ~**bahn** *f* overhead railroad (*US*) *od* railway (*Brit*); ~**balken** *m* (*SPORT*) beam.

schweben *vi* drift, float; (*hoch*) soar; (*unentschieden sein*) be in the balance; **es schwebte mir vor Augen** (*Bild*) I saw it in my mind's eye.

schwebend *a* (*TECH, CHEM*) suspended; (*fig*) undecided, unresolved; ~**es Verfahren** (*JUR*) pending case.

schwed. *abk* = **schwedisch**.

Schwede [shvā:'də] *m* -**n**, -**n**, **Schwedin** *f* Swede.

Schweden *nt* -**s** Sweden.

schwedisch *a* Swedish.

Schwefel [shvā:'fəl] *m* -**s** sulfur (*US*), sulphur (*Brit*).

schwefelig *a* sulfurous (*US*), sulphurous (*Brit*).

Schwefelsäure *f* sulfuric (*US*) *od* sulphuric (*Brit*) acid.

Schweif [shvîf] *m* -**(e)s**, -**e** tail.

schweifen *vi* wander, roam.

Schweige- *zW*: ~**geld** *nt* hush money; ~**minute** *f* one minute('s) silence.

schweigen [shvî'gən] *vi unreg* be silent; (*still sein*) keep quiet; **kannst du ~?** can you keep a secret?; **ganz zu ~ von ...** to say nothing of ...; **S~** *nt* -**s** silence.

Schweigepflicht *f* pledge of secrecy; (*von Anwalt etc*) requirement of confidentiality.

schweigsam [shvīk'zâm] *a* silent, taciturn; **S~keit** *f* taciturnity, quietness.

Schwein [shvīn] *nt* **-(e)s, -e** pig; (*fig umg*) (good) luck; **kein ~** (*umg*) nobody, not a single person.

Schweine- *zW:* **~braten** *m* joint of pork; (*gekocht*) roast pork; **~fleisch** *nt* pork; **~geld** *nt* (*umg*): **ein ~geld** a bundle (*US*) *od* packet (*Brit*); **~hund** *m* (*umg*) stinker, swine.

Schweinerei [shvīnərī'] *f* mess; (*Gemeinheit*) dirty trick; **so eine ~!** (*umg*) how disgusting!

Schweine- *zW:* **~schmalz** *nt* dripping; (*als Kochfett*) lard; **~stall** *m* pigsty.

schweinisch *a* filthy.

Schweins- *zW:* **~leder** *nt* pigskin; **~ohr** *nt* pig's ear; (*Gebäck*) (*kidney-shaped*) pastry.

Schweiß [shvīs] *m* **-es** sweat, perspiration; **~band** *nt* sweatband.

Schweißbrenner *m* **-s, -** (*TECH*) welding torch.

schweißen *vti* weld.

Schweißer *m* **-s, -** welder.

Schweißfüße *pl* sweaty feet *pl*.

Schweißnaht *f* weld.

schweißnaß *a* sweaty.

Schweiz [shvīts] *f:* **die ~** Switzerland.

schweiz. *abk* = **schweizerisch.**

Schweizer [shvī'tsər] *a attr* Swiss ♦ *m* **-s, -** Swiss; **~deutsch** *nt* Swiss German; **~in** *f* Swiss; **s~isch** *a* Swiss.

schwelen [shvā:'lən] *vi* smolder (*US*), smoulder (*Brit*).

schwelgen [shvɛl'gən] *vi* indulge o.s. (*in* +*dat* in).

Schwelle [shvɛ'lə] *f* **-, -n** threshold (*auch fig*); doorstep; (*EISENB*) railroad tie (*US*), sleeper (*Brit*).

schwellen *vi unreg* swell.

Schwellenstaat *m* threshold country.

Schwellung *f* swelling.

schwemmen [shvɛ'mən] *vt* (*treiben: Sand etc*) wash.

Schwengel [shvɛ'ngəl] *m* **-s, -** pump handle; (*Glocken~*) clapper.

Schwenk [shvɛngk] *m* **-s, -s** (*FILM*) pan, panning shot.

Schwenk- *zW:* **~arm** *m* swivel arm; **s~bar** *a* swivel-mounted.

schwenken *vt* swing; (*Kamera*) pan; (*Fahne*) wave; (*Kartoffeln*) toss; (*abspülen*) rinse ♦ *vi* turn, swivel; (*MIL*) wheel.

Schwenkung *f* turn; (*MIL*) wheel.

schwer [shvā:r] *a* heavy; (*schwierig*) difficult, hard; (*schlimm*) serious, bad ♦ *ad* (*sehr*) very (much); (*verletzt etc*) seriously, badly; **~ erkältet sein** have a heavy cold; **er lernt ~** he's a slow learner; **er ist ~ in Ordnung** (*umg*) he's a good bloke (*Brit*) *od* guy; **~ hören** be hard of hearing; **S~arbeiter** *m* manual worker, laborer (*US*), labourer (*Brit*); **S~beschädigte(r)** *mf dekl wie a* (severely) disabled person.

Schwere *f* **-, -n** weight; heaviness; (*PHYS*) gravity; **s~los** *a* weightless; (*Kammer*) zero-G; **~losigkeit** *f* weightlessness.

schwer- *zW:* **~erziehbar** *a* difficult (to bring up); **~fallen** *vi unreg:* **jdm ~fallen** be difficult for sb; **~fällig** *a* (*auch Stil*) ponderous; (*Gang*) clumsy, awkward; (*Verstand*) slow; **S~gewicht** *nt* heavyweight; (*fig*) emphasis; **~gewichtig** *a* heavyweight; **~hörig** *a* hard of hearing; **S~industrie** *f* heavy industry; **S~kraft** *f* gravity; **S~kranke(r)** *mf* person who is seriously ill; **~lich** *ad* hardly; **~machen** *vt:* **jdm/sich etw ~machen** make sth difficult for sb/o.s.; **S~metall** *nt* heavy metal; **~mütig** *a* melancholy; **~nehmen** *vt unreg* take to heart; **S~punkt** *m* center of gravity; (*fig*) emphasis, crucial point; **S~punktstreik** *m* pinpoint strike; **~reich** *a attr* (*umg*) stinking rich.

Schwert [shvā:rt] *nt* **-(e)s, -er** sword; **~lilie** *f* iris.

schwer- *zW:* **~tun** *vi unreg:* **sich** (*dat od akk*) **~tun** have difficulties; **S~verbrecher** *m* (dangerous) criminal; **~verdaulich** *a* indigestible; (*fig*) heavy; **~verdient** *a attr* (*Geld*) hard-earned; **~verletzt** *a* seriously *od* badly injured; **S~verletzte(r)** *mf* serious casualty; (*bei Unfall etc auch*) seriously injured person; **~verwundet** *a* seriously wounded; **~wiegend** *a* weighty, important.

Schwester [shvɛs'tər] *f* **-, -n** sister; (*MED*) nurse; **s~lich** *a* sisterly.

schwieg [shvē:k] *imperf von* **schweigen.**

Schwieger- [shvē:'gər] *zW:* **~eltern** *pl* parents-in-law *pl*; **~mutter** *f* mother-in-law; **~sohn** *m* son-in-law; **~tochter** *f* daughter-in-law; **~vater** *m* father-in-law.

Schwiele [shvē:'lə] *f* **-, -n** callus.

schwierig [shvē:'rich] *a* difficult, hard; **S~keit** *f* difficulty; **S~keitsgrad** *m* degree of difficulty.

schwillt [shvilt] *3. pers sing präs von* **schwellen.**

Schwimm- [shvim'] *zW:* **~bad** *nt* swimming pool; **~becken** *nt* swimming pool.

schwimmen *vi unreg* swim; (*treiben, nicht sinken*) float; (*fig: unsicher sein*) be all at sea; **im Geld ~** (*umg*) be rolling in money; **mir schwimmt es vor den Augen** I feel dizzy.

Schwimmer *m* **-s, -** swimmer; (*Angeln*) float.

Schwimmerin *f* swimmer.

Schwimm- *zW:* **~flosse** *f* (*von Taucher*) flipper; **~haut** *f* (*ORNITHOLOGIE*) web; **~lehrer** *m* swimming instructor; **~sport** *m* swimming; **~weste** *f* life jacket.

Schwindel [shvin'dəl] *m* **-s** giddiness; dizzy spell; (*Betrug*) swindle, fraud; (*Zeug*) stuff; **s~erregend** *a:* **in s~erregender Höhe** at a dizzy height; **s~frei** *a* free from giddiness.

schwindeln *vi* (*umg: lügen*) fib; **mir schwindelt** I feel dizzy; **jdm schwindelt es** sb feels dizzy.

schwinden [ʃvin'dən] *vi unreg* disappear; fade, fail; (*sich verringern*) decrease; (*Kräfte*) decline.
Schwindler *m* **-s,** - swindler; con man, fraud; (*Lügner*) liar.
schwindlig *a* dizzy; **mir ist** ~ I feel dizzy.
Schwindsucht *f* (*veraltet*) consumption.
schwingen [ʃvi'ŋən] *vti unreg* swing; (*Waffe etc*) brandish; (*vibrieren*) vibrate; (*klingen*) sound.
Schwinger *m* **-s,** - (*BOXEN*) swing.
Schwingtür *f* swinging (*US*) *od* swing (*Brit*) door(s *pl*).
Schwingung *f* vibration; (*PHYS*) oscillation.
Schwips [ʃvips] *m* **-es, -e: einen** ~ **haben** be tipsy.
schwirren [ʃvi'rən] *vi* buzz.
Schwitze [ʃvi'tsə] *f* **-n, -n** (*KOCH*) roux.
schwitzen *vi* sweat, perspire.
schwofen [ʃvoː'fən] *vi* (*umg*) dance.
schwoll [ʃvɔl] *imperf von* **schwellen.**
schwor [ʃvoːr] *imperf von* **schwören.**
schwören [ʃvœ'rən] *vti unreg* swear; **auf jdn/etw** ~ (*fig*) swear by sb/sth.
schwul [ʃvo͞oːl] *a* (*umg*) gay, queer (*pej*).
schwül [ʃvüːl] *a* sultry, close.
Schwüle *f* - sultriness, closeness.
Schwule(r) *mf dekl wie a* (*umg*) gay, queer (*pej*).
Schwulität [ʃvo͞olɛːt'] *f* (*umg*) trouble, difficulty.
Schwulst [ʃvo͞olst] *f* **-(e)s, ⁼e** bombast.
schwülstig [ʃvüls'tiç] *a* pompous.
Schwund [ʃvo͞ont] *m* **-(e)s** decrease (*gen* in), decline (*gen* in), dwindling (*gen* of); (*MED*) atrophy; (*Schrumpfen*) shrinkage.
Schwung [ʃvo͞oŋ] *m* **-(e)s, ⁼e** swing; (*Triebkraft*) momentum; (*fig: Energie*) verve, energy; (*umg: Menge*) batch; **in** ~ **sein** (*fig*) be in full swing; ~ **in die Sache bringen** (*umg*) liven things up; **s~haft** *a* brisk, lively; ~**rad** *nt* flywheel; **s~voll** *a* vigorous.
Schwur *m* **-(e)s, ⁼e** oath; ~**gericht** *nt* court with a jury.
SDR *m* - *abk* (= *Süddeutscher Rundfunk*) South German Radio.
sechs [zɛks] *num* six; **S~eck** *nt* hexagon; ~**hundert** *num* six hundred; ~**te(r, s)** *a* sixth.
Sechstel [zɛks'təl] *nt* **-s,** - sixth.
sechzehn [zɛç'tsaːn] *num* sixteen.
sechzig [zɛç'tsiç] *num* sixty.
SED *f* - *abk* (*DDR*: = *Sozialistische Einheitspartei Deutschlands*) Socialist Unity Party.
See [zɛː] *f* **-, -n** sea; **an der** ~ by the sea, at the seaside; **in** ~ **stechen** put to sea; **auf hoher** ~ on the high seas ♦ *m* **-s, -n** lake; ~**bad** *nt* seaside resort; ~**bär** *m* (*hum umg*) seadog; (*ZOOL*) fur seal; ~**fahrt** *f* seafaring; (*Reise*) voyage; **s~fest** *a* (*Mensch*) not subject to seasickness; ~**gang** *m* (motion of the) sea; ~**gras** *nt* seaweed; ~**hund** *m* seal; ~**igel** [zɛː'ēːgəl] *m* sea urchin; **s~krank** *a*

seasick; ~**krankheit** *f* seasickness; ~**lachs** *m* rock salmon.
Seele [zɛː'lə] *f* **-, -n** soul; (*Mittelpunkt*) life and soul; **jdm aus der** ~ **sprechen** express exactly what sb feels; **das liegt mir auf der** ~ it weighs heavily on my mind; **eine** ~ **von Mensch** a good soul.
Seelen- *zW*: ~**amt** *nt* (*REL*) requiem; ~**friede(n)** *m* peace of mind; ~**heil** *nt* salvation of one's soul; (*fig*) spiritual welfare; ~**ruhe** *f*: **in aller** ~**ruhe** calmly; (*kaltblütig*) as cool as you please; **s~ruhig** *ad* calmly.
Seeleute [zɛː'loitə] *pl* seamen *pl*.
Seel- *zW*: **s~isch** *a* mental; (*REL*) spiritual; (*Belastung*) emotional; ~**sorge** *f* pastoral duties *pl*; ~**sorger** *m* **-s,** - clergyman.
See- *zW*: ~**macht** *f* naval power; ~**mann** *m*, *pl* **-leute** seaman, sailor; ~**meile** *f* nautical mile.
Seengebiet [zɛː'əngəbēːt] *nt* **-(e)s, -e** lakeland district.
See- *zW*: ~**not** *f*: **in** ~**not** (*Schiff etc*) in distress; ~**pferd(chen)** *nt* sea horse; ~**räuber** *m* pirate; ~**recht** *nt* maritime law; ~**rose** *f* waterlily; ~**stern** *m* starfish; ~**tang** *m* seaweed; **s~tüchtig** *a* seaworthy; ~**versicherung** *f* marine insurance; ~**weg** *m* sea route; **auf dem** ~**weg** by sea; ~**zunge** *f* sole.
Segel [zɛː'gəl] *nt* **-s,** - sail; **mit vollen** ~**n** under full sail *od* canvas; (*fig*) with gusto; **die** ~ **streichen** (*fig*) give in; ~**boot** *nt* yacht; ~**fliegen** *nt* **-s** gliding; ~**flieger** *m* glider pilot; ~**flugzeug** *nt* glider.
segeln *vti* sail; **durch eine Prüfung** ~ (*umg*) flop in an exam, fail (in) an exam.
Segel- *zW*: ~**schiff** *nt* sailing vessel; ~**sport** *m* sailing; ~**tuch** *nt* canvas.
Segen [zɛː'gən] *m* **-s,** - blessing.
segensreich *a* beneficial.
Segler [zɛː'glər] *m* **-s,** - sailor, yachtsman; (*Boot*) sailing boat.
Seglerin *f* yachtswoman.
segnen [zɛː'g'nən] *vt* bless.
sehen [zɛː'ən] *vti unreg* see; (*in bestimmte Richtung*) look; (*Fernsehsendung auch*) watch; **sieht man das?** does it show?; **da sieht man('s) mal wieder!** that's typical!; **du siehst das nicht richtig** you've got it wrong; **so gesehen** looked at in this way; **sich** ~ **lassen** put in an appearance, appear; **das neue Rathaus kann sich** ~ **lassen** the new town hall is certainly something to be proud of; **siehe oben/unten** see above/below; **da kann man mal** ~ that just shows (you) *od* goes to show (*umg*); **mal** ~! we'll see; **darauf** ~, **daß** ... make sure (that) ...; **jdn kommen** ~ see sb coming.
sehens- *zW*: ~**wert** *a* worth seeing; **S~würdigkeiten** *pl* sights *pl* (of a town).
Seher *m* **-s,** - seer.
Seh- *zW*: ~**fehler** *m* sight defect; ~**kraft** *f* (eye)sight.
Sehne [zɛː'nə] *f* **-, -n** sinew; (*an Bogen*)

string.

sehnen *vr* long *od* yearn (*nach* for).

Sehnerv *m* optic nerve.

sehnig *a* sinewy.

sehnlich *a* ardent.

Sehnsucht *f* longing.

sehnsüchtig *a* longing; (*Erwartung*) eager.

sehnsuchtsvoll *ad* longingly, yearningly.

sehr [zā:r] *ad* (*vor a, ad*) very; (*mit Verben*) a lot, (very) much; **zu ~** too much; **er ist ~ dafür/dagegen** he is all for it/very much against it; **wie ~ er sich auch bemühte ...** however much he tried ...

Sehvermögen [zā:'fɛrmœgən] *nt* **-s** powers of vision *pl*.

seicht [zɪçt] *a* (*lit, fig*) shallow.

seid [zɪt] *2. pers pl präs von* **sein**.

Seide [zɪ'də] *f* -, **-n** silk.

Seidel *nt* **-s**, - tankard, beer mug.

seiden *a* silk; **S~papier** *nt* tissue paper.

seidig [zɪ'dɪç] *a* silky.

Seife [zɪ'fə] *f* -, **-n** soap.

Seifen- *zW*: **~blase** *f* soap bubble; (*fig*) bubble; **~lauge** *f* soapsuds *pl*; **~schale** *f* soap dish; **~schaum** *m* lather.

seifig [zɪ'fɪç] *a* soapy.

seihen [zɪ'ən] *vt* strain, filter.

Seil [zɪl] *nt* **-(e)s, -e** rope; (*Kabel*) cable; **~bahn** *f* cable railway; **~hüpfen** *nt* **-s**, **~springen** *nt* **-s** jump (the) rope (*US*), skipping (*Brit*); **~tänzer(in** *f*) *m* tightrope walker; **~zug** *m* tackle.

sein [zɪn] *vi unreg* be; **laß das ~!** leave that!; stop that!; **es ist an dir, zu ...** it's up to you to ...; **seien Sie nicht böse, aber ...** don't be angry but ...; **was sind Sie (beruflich)?** what do you do?; **das kann schon ~** that may well be; **ist was?** what is it?; (*umg*: *paßt dir was nicht?*) is something the matter?; **mir ist kalt** I'm cold; **mir ist, als hätte ich ihn früher schon einmal gesehen** I have a feeling I've seen him before ♦ *pron* his; its.

Sein *nt* **-s**: **~ oder Nichtsein** to be or not to be.

seiner *pron* (*gen von* **er** *und* **es**) of him; of it.

seine(r, s) *poss pron* his; its; **er ist gut ~ zwei Meter** (*umg*) he's over six feet; **die S~n** (*geh*) his family, his people; **jedem das S~** to each his own.

seiner- *zW*: **~seits** *ad* for his part; **~zeit** *ad* in those days, formerly.

sei'nesglei'chen *pron* people like him.

sei'netwe'gen, sei'netwil'len *ad* (*für ihn*) for his sake; (*wegen ihm*) on his account; (*von ihm aus*) as far as he is concerned.

seinige *pron*: **der/die/das ~** his.

seinlassen *vt unreg*: **etw ~** (*aufhören*) stop (doing) sth; (*nicht tun*) drop sth, leave sth.

Seismograph [zɪsmōgrāf'] *m* **-en, -en** seismograph.

seit [zɪt] *präp, kj* since; (*Zeitdauer*) for, in; **er ist ~ einer Woche hier** he has been here for a week; **~ langem** for a long time; **~dem**

[zɪtdā:m'] *ad, kj* since.

Seite [zɪ'tə] *f* -, **-n** side; (*Buch~*) page; (*MIL*) flank; **~ an ~** side by side; **jdm zur ~ stehen** (*fig*) stand by sb's side; **jdn zur ~ nehmen** take sb aside *od* on one side; **auf der einen ~ ..., auf der anderen (~) ...** on the one hand ..., on the other (hand) ...; **einer Sache** (*dat*) **die beste ~ abgewinnen** make the best *od* most of sth.

seiten *präp* +*gen*: **auf** *od* **von ~** on the part of.

Seiten- *zW*: **~ansicht** *f* side view; **~hieb** *m* (*fig*) passing shot, dig; **s~lang** *a* several pages long, going on for pages; **~ruder** *nt* (*AVIAT*) rudder.

seitens *präp* (+*gen*) on the part of.

Seiten- *zW*: **~schiff** *nt* aisle; **~sprung** *m* extramarital escapade; **~stechen** *nt* (a) stitch; **~straße** *f* side road; **~streifen** *m* verge; (*der Autobahn*) shoulder (*US*), emergency lane (*US*), hard shoulder (*Brit*); **~wagen** *m* sidecar; **~wind** *m* crosswind; **~zahl** *f* page number; (*Gesamtzahl*) number of pages.

seit- *zW*: **~her** [zɪthā:r'] *ad, kj* since (then); **~lich** *ad* on one *od* the side ♦ *a* side *attr*; **~wärts** *ad* sideways.

sek, Sek. *abk* (= *Sekunde*) sec.

Sekretär [zākrāte:r'] *m* secretary; (*Möbel*) bureau.

Sekretariat [zākrātārēat'] *nt* **-(e)s, -e** secretary's office, secretariat.

Sekretärin *f* secretary.

Sekt [zekt] *m* **-(e)s, -e** champagne, sparkling wine.

Sekte *f* -, **-n** sect.

Sektor [zek'tor] *m* sector; (*Sachgebiet*) field.

Sekunda [zākōōn'dá] *f* -, **Sekunden** (*SCH*: *Unter~/Ober~*) sixth and seventh year of German high school.

sekundär [zākōōnde:r'] *a* secondary; **S~literatur** *f* secondary literature.

Sekunde [zākōōn'də] *f* -, **-n** second.

Sekunden- *zW*: **~schnelle** *f*: **in ~schnelle** in a matter of seconds; **~zeiger** *m* second hand.

sel. *abk* = **selig**.

selber [zel'bər] *demonstrativ pron* = **selbst**; **S~machen** *nt* do-it-yourself; (*von Kleidern etc*) making one's own.

selbst [zelpst] *pron* myself; itself; themselves *etc*; **~ ist der Mann** *od* **die Frau!** self-reliance is the name of the game (*umg*); **das muß er ~ wissen** it's up to him; **von ~** by itself *etc*; **er kam ganz von ~** he came of his own accord ♦ *ad* even; **S~** *nt* - self; **S~achtung** *f* self-respect.

selbständig [zelp'shtɛndɪç] *a* independent; **sich ~ machen** (*beruflich*) set up on one's own, start one's own business; **S~keit** *f* independence.

Selbst- *zW*: **~anzeige** *f*: **~anzeige erstatten** come forward o.s.; **~auslöser** *m* (*PHOT*) delayed-action shutter release; **~bedienung**

f self-service; **~befriedigung** *f* masturbation; (*fig*) self-gratification; **~beherrschung** *f* self-control; **~bestätigung** *f* self-affirmation; **s~bewußt** *a* self-confident; (*s~sicher*) self-assured; **~bewußtsein** *nt* self-confidence; **~erhaltung** *f* self-preservation; **~erkenntnis** *f* self-knowledge; **~fahrer** *m* (*AUT*): **Autovermietung für ~fahrer** self-drive car rental *od* hire (*Brit*); **s~gefällig** *a* smug, self-satisfied; **s~gemacht** *a* home-made; **s~gerecht** *a* self-righteous; **~gespräch** *nt* conversation with o.s.; **s~gestrickt** *a* hand-knitted; (*umg: Methode etc*) homespun, amateurish; **s~gewiß** *a* confident; **s~herrlich** *a* high-handed; (*s~gerecht*) self-satisfied; **~hilfe** *f* self-help; **zur ~hilfe greifen** take matters into one's own hands; **~kostenpreis** *m* cost price; **s~los** *a* unselfish, selfless; **~mord** *m* suicide; **~mörder(in** *f*) *m* (*Person*) suicide; **s~mörderisch** *a* suicidal; **s~sicher** *a* self-assured; **~studium** *nt* private study; **s~süchtig** *a* selfish; **s~tätig** *a* automatic; **~überwindung** *f* will power; **s~verdient** *a*: **s~verdientes Geld** money one has earned o.s.; **s~vergessen** *a* absent-minded; (*Blick*) faraway; **s~verschuldet** *a*: **wenn der Unfall s~verschuldet ist** if there is personal responsibility for the accident; **~versorger** *m*: **~versorger sein** be self-sufficient *od* self-reliant; **Urlaub für ~versorger** self-catering holiday.

selbstverständlich *a* obvious ♦ *ad* naturally; **ich halte das für ~** I take that for granted.

Selbst- *zW*: **~verständnis** *nt*: **nach seinem eigenen ~verständnis** as he sees himself; **~vertrauen** *nt* self-confidence; **~verwaltung** *f* autonomy, self-government; **~wählferndienst** *m* (*TEL*) automatic dialing service; **~wertgefühl** *nt* feeling of one's own worth *od* value, self-esteem; **s~zufrieden** *a* self-satisfied; **~zweck** *m* end in itself.

selig [zā:'liċh] *a* happy, blissful; (*REL*) blessed; (*tot*) late; **S~keit** *f* bliss.

Sellerie [ze'lərē:] *m* **-s, -(s)** *od f* **-, -n** celery.

selten [zel'tən] *a* rare ♦ *ad* seldom, rarely; **S~heit** *f* rarity.

Seltenheitswert *m* **-(e)s** rarity value.

Selterswasser [zel'tərsvásər] *nt* soda water.

seltsam [zelt'zâm] *a* curious, strange.

selt'samerwei'se *ad* curiously, strangely.

Seltsamkeit *f* strangeness.

Semester [zāmes'tər] *nt* **-s, -** semester; **ein älteres ~** a senior student.

Semi- [zāmē] *in zW* semi-; **~kolon** [-kō:'lon] *nt* **-s, -s** semicolon.

Seminar [zāmēnár'] *nt* **-s, -e** seminary; (*Kurs*) seminar; (*UNIV: Ort*) department building.

semitisch [zāmē:'tish] *a* Semitic.

Semmel [ze'məl] *f* **-, -n** roll; **~brösel(n)** *pl* breadcrumbs *pl*; **~knödel** *m* (*süddeutsch, österreichisch*) bread dumpling.

sen. *abk* (= *senior*) sen.

Senat [zānât'] *m* **-(e)s, -e** senate.

Sende- [zen'də] *zW*: **~bereich** *m* transmission range; **~folge** *f* (*Serie*) series.

senden *vt unreg* send ♦ *vti* (*RAD, TV*) transmit, broadcast.

Sende- *zW*: **~netz** *nt* network; **~pause** *f* (*RAD, TV*) interlude (*US*), interval (*Brit*).

Sender *m* **-s, -** station; (*Anlage*) transmitter.

Sende- *zW*: **~reihe** *f* series (of broadcasts); **~schluß** *m* (*RAD, TV*) end of the day's broadcasting, closedown (*Brit*); **~station** *f*, **~stelle** *f* transmitting station; **~zeit** *f* broadcasting time.

Sendung [zen'dŏŏng] *f* consignment; (*Aufgabe*) mission; (*RAD, TV*) transmission; (*Programm*) program (*US*), programme (*Brit*).

Senf [zenf] *m* **-(e)s, -e** mustard; **seinen ~ dazugeben** (*umg*) put one's oar in.

sengen [ze'ngən] *vt* singe ♦ *vi* scorch.

senil [zānē:l'] *a* (*pej*) senile.

Seniorenpaß [zānēō:'rənpás] *m* senior citizen's travel card.

Senkblei [zengk'blī] *nt* plumb.

Senke *f* **-, -n** depression.

Senkel *m* **-s, -** (shoe)lace.

senken *vt* lower; (*Kopf*) bow; (*TECH*) sink ♦ *vr* sink; (*Stimme*) drop.

Senk- *zW*: **~fuß** *m* flat foot; **~grube** *f* cesspit; **s~recht** *a* vertical, perpendicular; **~rechte** *f* perpendicular; **~rechtstarter** *m* (*AVIAT*) jump jet; (*fig: Person*) high-flier.

Senner(in *f*) [ze'nər(in)] *m* **-s, -** (Alpine) dairyman *od* dairymaid.

Sensation [zānzátsēō:n'] *f* sensation.

sensationell [zenzátsēōnel'] *a* sensational.

Sensations- *zW*: **~blatt** *nt* sensational paper; **~sucht** *f* sensationalism.

Sense [zen'zə] *f* **-, -n** scythe; **dann ist ~!** (*umg*) that's the end!

sensibel [zenzē:'bəl] *a* sensitive.

sensibilisieren [zenzēbēlēzē:'rən] *vt* sensitize.

Sensibilität [zenzēbēlēte:t'] *f* sensitivity.

sentimental [zentēmentál'] *a* sentimental.

Sentimentalität [zentēmentálēte:t'] *f* sentimentality.

separat [zāpárât'] *a* separate; (*Wohnung, Zimmer*) self-contained.

Sept. *abk* (= *September*) Sept.

September [zeptem'bər] *m* **-(s), -** September; **im ~** in September; **im Monat ~** in the month of September; **heute ist der zweite ~** today is the second of September *od* September second (*US*); (*geschrieben*) today is 2nd September; **in diesem ~** this September; **Anfang/Ende/Mitte ~** at the beginning/end/in the middle of September.

septisch [zep'tish] *a* septic.

sequentiell [zākventsēel'] *a*: **~e Datei** (*COMPUT*) sequential file; **~er Zugriff** (*COMPUT*) sequential access.

Sequenz [zākvents'] *f* sequence.

Serbe [zer'bə] *m* **-n, -n** Serbian, Serbian man

od boy.
Serbien *nt* -s Serbia.
Serbin *f* Serbian, Serbian woman *od* girl.
serbisch *a* Serbian.
Serie [zä:'rēə] *f* series.
seriell [zārēel'] *a* (*COMPUT*) serial; ~**er An-schluß** serial port; ~**e Daten** *pl* serial data *pl*; ~**er Drucker** serial printer.
Serien- *zW*: ~**herstellung** *f* mass production; **s~mäßig** *a* (*Ausstattung*) standard; (*Herstellung*) series *attr* ♦ *ad* (*herstellen*) in series; ~**nummer** *f* serial number; **s~weise** *ad* in series.
seriös [zārēœs'] *a* serious; (*anständig*) respectable.
Serpentine [zerpentē:'nə] *f* hairpin (bend).
Serum [zā:'rōōm] *nt* -s, **Seren** serum.
Service [zervē:s'] *nt* -(**s**), - (*Gläser*~) set; (*Geschirr*) service ♦ *m* [ze:r'vis] -, -s (*COMM, SPORT*) service.
servieren [zervē:'rən] *vti* serve.
Serviererin [zervē:'rərin] *f* waitress.
Servierwagen *m* -s, - serving cart (*US*), trolley (*Brit*).
Serviette [zervēe'tə] *f* napkin, serviette.
Servus [zer'vōōs] *interj* (*österreichisch, süddeutsch*) hello; (*beim Abschied*) goodbye, so long (*umg*).
Sesam [zā:'zàm] *m* -s, -s sesame.
Sessel [ze'səl] *m* -s, - armchair; ~**lift** *m* chairlift.
seßhaft [zes'hàft] *a* settled; (*ansässig*) resident.
Sets [zets] *pl* tablemats *pl*.
setzen [ze'tsən] *vt* put, place, set; (*Baum etc*) plant; (*Segel, TYP*) set; **jdm ein Denkmal ~** build a monument to sb ♦ *vr* (*Platz nehmen*) sit down; (*Kaffee, Tee*) settle; **sich zu jdm ~** sit with sb ♦ *vi* leap; (*wetten*) bet; (*TYP*) set.
Setzer [ze'tsər] *m* -s, - (*TYP*) typesetter, compositor.
Setzerei [zetsəri'] *f* caseroom.
Setz- *zW*: ~**kasten** *m* (*TYP*) case; (*an Wand*) ornament shelf; ~**ling** *m* young plant; ~**maschine** *f* (*TYP*) typesetting machine.
Seuche [zoi'çhə] *f* -, -n epidemic.
Seuchengebiet *nt* infected area.
seufzen [zoif'tsən] *vti* sigh.
Seufzer [zoif'tsər] *m* -s, - sigh.
Sex [zeks] *m* -(**es**) sex.
Sexta [zeks'tà] *f* -, **Sexten** first year of German high school.
Sexualität [zeksōōàlēte:t'] *f* sex, sexuality.
sexuell [zeksōōel'] *a* sexual.
Seychellen [zäshe'lən] *pl* Seychelles *pl*.
sezieren [zātsē:'rən] *vt* dissect.
SFB *m* - *abk* (= *Sender Freies Berlin*) Radio Free Berlin.
sfr *abk* (= *Schweizer Franken*) sfr.
S.H. *abk* (= *Seine Hoheit*) H.H.
Shampoo(n) [shempōō:(n)'] *nt* -s, -s shampoo.
Shetlandinseln [she'tlàntinzəln] *pl* Shetland,

Shetland Isles *pl*.
SHG *nt abk* = **Soforthilfegesetz**.
Showmaster [shō'ōōmàstər] *m* -s, - compère, emcee.
siamesisch [zēàmà:'zish] *a*: ~**e Zwillinge** Siamese twins.
Siamkatze *f* Siamese (cat).
Sibirien [zēbē:'rēən] *nt* -s Siberia.
sibirisch *a* Siberian.
sich [ziçh] *pron* himself; herself; itself; oneself; yourself; yourselves; themselves; each other; (*unpers*): **hier sitzt es ~ gut** it's good to sit here; ~ **die Haare waschen** wash one's hair.
Sichel [zi'çhəl] *f* -, -n sickle; (*Mond*~) crescent.
sicher [zi'çhər] *a* safe (*vor +dat* from); (*gewiß*) certain (*+gen* of); (*Hand, Job*) steady; (*zuverlässig*) secure, reliable; (*selbst*~) confident; (*Stellung*) secure; **sich** (*dat*) **einer Sache/jds ~ sein** be sure of sth/sb; ~ **ist** ~ you can't be too sure ♦ *ad* (*natürlich*): **du hast dich ~ verrechnet** you must have counted wrongly.
sichergehen *vi unreg* make sure.
Sicherheit [zi'çhərhīt] *f* safety; (*auch FIN*) security; (*Gewißheit*) certainty; (*Selbst*~) confidence; **die öffentliche ~** public security; ~ **im Straßenverkehr** road safety; ~ **leisten** (*COMM*) offer security.
Sicherheits- *zW*: ~**abstand** *m* safe distance; ~**bestimmungen** *pl* safety regulations *pl*; (*betrieblich, POL etc*) security controls *pl*; ~**einrichtungen** *pl* safety equipment *sing*, security devices *pl*; ~**glas** *nt* safety glass; ~**gurt** *m* seat belt; **s~halber** *ad* for safety; to be on the safe side; ~**nadel** *f* safety pin; ~**schloß** *nt* safety lock; ~**spanne** *f* (*COMM*) margin of safety; ~**verschluß** *m* safety clasp; ~**vorkehrung** *f* safety precaution.
sicherlich *ad* certainly; surely.
sichern *vt* secure; (*schützen*) protect; (*Bergsteiger etc*) belay; (*Waffe*) put the safety catch on; **jdm/sich etw ~** secure sth for sb/ for o.s.
sicherstellen *vt* impound; (*COMPUT*) save.
Sicherung *f* (*Sichern*) securing; (*Vorrichtung*) safety device; (*an Waffen*) safety catch; (*ELEK*) fuse; **da ist (bei) ihm die ~ durchgebrannt** (*fig umg*) he blew a fuse.
Sicherungskopie *f* backup copy.
Sicht [ziçht] *f* - sight; (*Aus*~) view; (*Sehweite*) visibility; **auf** *od* **nach ~** (*FIN*) at sight; **auf lange ~** on a long-term basis; **s~bar** *a* visible; ~**barkeit** *f* visibility.
sichten *vt* sight; (*auswählen*) sort out; (*ordnen*) sift through.
Sicht- *zW*: **s~lich** *a* evident, obvious; ~**verhältnisse** *pl* visibility *sing*; ~**vermerk** *m* visa; ~**weite** *f* visibility; **außer ~weite** out of sight.
sickern [zi'kərn] *vi aux sein* seep; (*in Tropfen*) drip.

sie [zē:] *pron* (*sing*: *nom*) she; (: *akk*) her; (*pl*: *nom*) they; (: *akk*) them.
Sie *pron sing/pl, nom/akk* you.
Sieb [zē:p] *nt* **-(e)s, -e** sieve; (*KOCH*) strainer; (*Gemüse~*) colander; **s~en** [zē:'bən] *vt* sieve, sift; (*Flüssigkeit*) strain ♦ *vi*: **bei der Prüfung wird stark gesiebt** (*fig umg*) the exam will weed a lot of people out.
sieben [zē:'bən] *vt siehe* **Sieb** ♦ *num* seven; **S~gebirge** *nt*: **das S~gebirge** the Seven Mountains *pl* (*near Bonn*); **~hundert** *num* seven hundred; **S~meter** *m* (*SPORT*) penalty; **S~sachen** *pl* belongings *pl*; **S~schläfer** *m* (*ZOOL*) dormouse.
Siebtel *nt* **-s, -** seventh.
siebte(r, s) [zē:p'tə(r, z)] *a* seventh.
siebzehn [zē:p'tsā:n] *num* seventeen.
siebzig [zē:p'tsiç] *num* seventy.
siedeln [zē:'dəln] *vi* settle.
sieden [zē:'dən] *vti* boil; simmer.
Siedepunkt *m* boiling point.
Siedler *m* **-s, -** settler.
Siedlung *f* settlement; (*Häuser~*) housing development.
Sieg [zē:k] *m* **-(e)s, -** victory.
Siegel [zē:'gəl] *nt* **-s, -** seal; **~lack** *m* sealing wax; **~ring** *m* signet ring.
siegen [zē:'gən] *vi* be victorious; (*SPORT*) win; **über jdn/etw ~** (*fig*) triumph over sb/ sth; (*in Wettkampf*) beat sb/sth.
Sieger(in *f*) *m* **-s, -** victor; (*SPORT etc*) winner; **~ehrung** *f* (*SPORT*) presentation ceremony.
Sieges- *zW*: **s~sicher** *a* sure of victory; **~zug** *m* triumphal procession.
siegreich *a* victorious.
siehe [zē:'ə] *Imperativ sing von* **sehen** see; (**~ da**) behold.
siehst [zē:st] *2. pers sing präs von* **sehen**.
sieht [zē:t] *3. pers sing präs von* **sehen**.
Siel [zē:l] *nt od m* **-(e)s, -e** (*Schleuse*) sluice; (*Abwasserkanal*) sewer.
siezen [zē:'tsən] *vt* address as 'Sie'.
Signal [zignâl'] *nt* **-s, -e** signal; **~anlage** *f* signals *pl*, set of signals.
signalisieren [zignálēzē:'rən] *vt* (*lit, fig*) signal.
Signatur [zignátōō:r'] *f* signature; (*Bibliotheks~*) shelf mark.
Silbe [zil'bə] *f* **-, -n** syllable; **er hat es mit keiner ~ erwähnt** he didn't say a word about it.
Silber [zil'bər] *nt* **-s** silver; **~bergwerk** *nt* silver mine; **~blick** *m*: **einen ~blick haben** have a slight squint.
silbern *a* silver.
Silberpapier *nt* silver paper.
Silhouette [zēlōōe'tə] *f* silhouette.
Silikonchip [zēlēkō:n'tship] *m*, **Silikonplättchen** [zēlēkō:n'pletçhən] *nt* silicon chip.
Silo [zē:'lō] *nt od m* **-s, -s** silo.
Silvester [zilves'tər] *nt* **-s, -**, **Silvesterabend** *m* [zilves'tərâbənt] New Year's Eve, Hogmanay (*Scot*).

simpel [zim'pəl] *a* simple; **S~** *m* **-s, -** (*umg*) simpleton.
Sims [zims] *nt od m* **-es, -e** (*Kamin~*) mantelpiece; (*Fenster~*) (window)sill.
Simulant(in *f*) [zēmōōlánt'(in)] *m* **-en, -en** malingerer.
simulieren [zēmōōlē:'rən] *vti* simulate; (*vortäuschen*) feign.
simultan [zēmōōltân'] *a* simultaneous; **S~dolmetscher** *m* simultaneous interpreter.
sind [zint] *1./3. pers pl präs von* **sein**.
Sinfonie [zinfōnē:'] *f* symphony.
Singapur [zing'gápōō:r] *nt* **-s** Singapore.
singen [zi'ngən] *vti unreg* sing.
Single [sing'gəl] *m* **-s, -s** (*Alleinlebender*) single person.
Sing- *zW*: **~sang** *m* (*Gesang*) monotonous singing; **~stimme** *f* vocal part.
Singular [zing'gōōlár] *m* singular.
Singvogel [zing'fō:gəl] *m* songbird.
sinken [zing'kən] *vi unreg* sink; (*Boden, Gebäude*) subside; (*Fundament*) settle; (*Preise etc*) fall, go down; **den Mut/die Hoffnung ~ lassen** lose courage/hope.
Sinn [zin] *m* **-(e)s, -e** mind; (*Wahrnehmungs~*) sense; (*Bedeutung*) sense, meaning; **~ für etw** sense of sth; (*Geist*): **im ~e des Gesetzes** according to the spirit of the law; **im ~e des Verstorbenen** in accordance with the wishes of the deceased; **von ~en sein** be out of one's mind; **das ist nicht der ~ der Sache** that is not the point; **das hat keinen ~** there is no point in that; **~bild** *nt* symbol; **s~bildlich** *a* symbolic.
sinnen [zi'nən] *vi unreg* ponder; **auf etw** (*akk*) **~** contemplate sth.
Sinnenmensch *m* sensualist.
Sinnes- *zW*: **~organ** *nt* sense organ; **~täuschung** *f* illusion; **~wandel** *m* change of mind.
sinngemäß *a* faithful; (*Wiedergabe*) in one's own words.
sinnig *a* apt; (*ironisch*) clever.
Sinn- *zW*: **s~lich** *a* sensual, sensuous; (*Wahrnehmung*) sensory; **~lichkeit** *f* sensuality; **s~los** *a* senseless, meaningless; **s~los betrunken** blind drunk; **~losigkeit** *f* senselessness, meaninglessness; **s~verwandt** *a* synonymous; **s~voll** *a* meaningful; (*vernünftig*) sensible.
Sinologe [zēnōlō:'gə] *m* **-n, -n**, **Sinologin** *f* Sinologist.
Sintflut [zint'flōō:t] *f* Flood; **nach uns die ~** (*umg*) it doesn't matter what happens after we've gone; **s~artig** *a*: **s~artige Regenfälle** *pl* torrential rain *sing*.
Sinus [zē:'nōōs] *m* **-, - od -se** (*ANAT*) sinus; (*MATH*) sine.
Siphon [zēfō̄n'] *m* **-s, -s** siphon.
Sippe [zi'pə] *f* **-, -n** (extended) family; (*umg*: *Verwandtschaft*) clan.
Sippschaft [zip'sháft] *f* (*pej*) tribe; (*Bande*) gang.

Sirene [zērā:'nə] *f* -, -n siren.
Sirup [zē:'rōŏp] *m* -s, -e syrup.
Sit-in [sitin'] *nt* -(s), -s: **ein ~ machen** stage a sit-in.
Sitte [zi'tə] *f* -, -n custom; *pl* morals *pl*; **was sind denn das für ~n?** what sort of way is that to behave!
Sitten- *zW*: **~polizei** *f* vice squad; **~strolch** *m* (*umg*) sex fiend; **~wächter** *m* (*ironisch*) guardian of public morals; **s~widrig** *a* (*form*) immoral.
Sittich [zi'tiçh] *m* -(e)s, -e parakeet.
Sitt- *zW*: **s~lich** *a* moral; **~lichkeit** *f* morality; **~lichkeitsverbrechen** *nt* sex offense (*US*) *od* offence (*Brit*); **s~sam** *a* modest, demure.
Situation [zētōŏátsēō:n'] *f* situation.
situiert [zētōŏē:rt'] *a*: **gut ~ sein** be well situated financially.
Sitz [zits] *m* -es, -e seat; (*von Firma, Verwaltung*) headquarters *pl*; **der Anzug hat einen guten ~** the suit sits well.
sitzen *vi unreg* sit; (*Bemerkung, Schlag*) strike home; (*Gelerntes*) have sunk in; (*umg*: **im Gefängnis ~**) be inside; **locker ~** be loose; **~ Sie bequem?** are you comfortable?; **einen ~ haben** (*umg*) have had one too many; **er sitzt im Kultusministerium** (*umg*: *sein*) he's in the Ministry of Education; **~ bleiben** remain seated.
sitzenbleiben *vi unreg* (*SCH*) have to repeat a year; **auf etw** (*dat*) **~ be saddled with** sth.
sitzend *a* (*Tätigkeit*) sedentary.
sitzenlassen *vt unreg* (*SCH*) make (sb) repeat a year; (*Mädchen*) jilt; (*Wartenden*) stand up; **etw auf sich** (*dat*) **~ take sth** lying down.
Sitz- *zW*: **~fleisch** *nt* (*umg*): **~fleisch haben** be able to sit still; **~gelegenheit** *f* seats *pl*; **~ordnung** *f* seating plan; **~platz** *m* seat; **~streik** *m* sit-down strike.
Sitzung *f* meeting.
Sizilianer(in *f*) [zētsēlēâ'nər(in)] *m* -s, - Sicilian.
sizilianisch *a* Sicilian.
Sizilien [zētsē:'lēən] *nt* -s Sicily.
SK *m* -s, -s *abk* = Sportklub.
Skala [skâ'lá] *f* -, Skalen scale; (*fig*) range.
Skalpell [skálpel'] *nt* -s, -e scalpel.
skalpieren [skálpē:'rən] *vt* scalp.
Skandal [skándâl'] *m* -s, -e scandal.
skandalös [skándálœs'] *a* scandalous.
Skandinavien [skándēnâ'vēən] *nt* -s Scandinavia.
Skandinavier(in *f*) *m* -s, - Scandinavian.
skandinavisch *a* Scandinavian.
Skat [skât] *m* -(e)s, -e *od* -s (*KARTEN*) skat.
Skelett [skálet'] *nt* -(e)s, -e skeleton.
Skepsis [skep'sis] *f* - skepticism (*US*), scepticism (*Brit*).
skeptisch [skep'tish] *a* skeptical (*US*), sceptical (*Brit*).
Ski [shē:] *m* -s, -er ski; **~ laufen** *od* **fahren**

ski; **~fahrer** *m* skier; **~hütte** *f* ski hut *od* lodge (*US*); **~läufer** *m* skier; **~lehrer** *m* ski instructor; **~lift** *m* ski lift; **~springen** *nt* ski jumping.
Skizze [ski'tsə] *f* -, -n sketch.
skizzieren [skitsē:'rən] *vti* sketch; (*fig*: *Plan etc*) outline.
Sklave [sklâ'və] *m* -n, -n, **Sklavin** *f* slave.
Sklaventreiber *m* -s, - (*pej*) slave-driver.
Sklaverei [sklâvərī'] *f* slavery.
sklavisch *a* slavish.
Skonto [skon'tō] *m od nt* -s, -s discount.
Skorbut [skorbōō:t'] *m* -(e)s scurvy.
Skorpion [skorpēō:n'] *m* -s, -e scorpion; (*ASTROL*) Scorpio.
Skrupel [skrōō:'pəl] *m* -s, - scruple; **s~los** *a* unscrupulous.
Skulptur [skōŏlptōō:r'] *f* sculpture.
skurril [skōŏrē:l'] *a* (*geh*) droll, comical.
Slalom [slâ'lom] *m* -s, -s slalom.
Slawe [slâ'və] *m* -n, -n, **Slawine** [slâvē:'nə] *f* Slav.
slawisch *a* Slavonic, Slavic.
Slip [slip] *m* -s, -s (pair of) briefs *pl*.
S.M. *abk* (= *Seine Majestät*) H.M.
Smaragd [smárákt'] *m* -(e)s, -e emerald.
Smoking [smō:'king] *m* -s, -s tuxedo, dinner jacket (*Brit*).
SMV *f* -, -s *abk* = Schülermitverwaltung.
so [zō:] *ad* so; (*auf diese Weise*) like this; (*etwa*) roughly; **~ ein ... such a ...**; **~, das ist fertig** well, that's finished; **~ etwas!** well, well!; **na ~ was!** well I never!; **das hat ihn ~ geärgert, daß ...** that annoyed him so much that ...; **~ ist sie nun einmal** that's the way she is; **das ist gut ~** that's fine; **das habe ich nur ~ gesagt** I didn't really mean it; **~ gut es geht** as best as I *etc* can; **~ ... wie ...** as ... as ... ◊ (*als Füllwort*: *nicht übersetzt*): **~ mancher** a number of people *pl* ◊ *kj* so; **~ daß** so that, with the result that.
SO *abk* (= *Südost(en)*) SE.
s.o. *abk* = siehe oben.
sobald [zōbált'] *kj* as soon as.
Socke [zo'kə] *f* -, -n sock; **sich auf die ~n machen** (*umg*) get going.
Sockel [zo'kəl] *m* -s, - pedestal, base.
Sodawasser [zō:'dávəsər] *nt* soda water.
Sodbrennen [zō:t'brenən] *nt* -s, - heartburn.
Sodomie [zōdōmē:'] *f* buggery; bestiality.
soeben [zōā:'bən] *ad* just (now).
Sofa [zō:'fá] *nt* -s, -s sofa.
sofern [zōfern'] *kj* if, provided (that).
soff [zof] *imperf von* saufen.
sofort [zōfort'] *ad* immediately, at once; (**ich**) **komme ~!** (I'm) just coming!; **S~hilfe** *f* emergency relief *od* aid; **S~hilfegesetz** *nt* law on emergency aid.
sofortig *a* immediate.
Sofortmaßnahme *f* immediate measure.
Softeis [soft'īs] *nt* -es soft ice-cream.
Softie [zof'tē:] *m* (*umg*) softy.
Software [zoft'we:ər] *f* software;

s~kompatibel *a* software compatible; ~-
Paket *nt* software package.
sog [zō:k] *imperf von* **saugen.**
Sog *m* -(e)s, -e suction; (*von Strudel*) vortex;
(*fig*) maelstrom.
sog. *abk* = **sogenannt.**
sogar [zōgắr'] *a* even.
so- *zW:* **~genannt** [zō:'gənánt] *a* so-called;
~gleich [zōglìċh'] *ad* straight away, at once.
Sogwirkung *f* effect of magnetism; slipstream.
Sohle [zō:'lə] *f* -, -n (*Fuß~*) sole; (*Tal~ etc*)
bottom; (*MIN*) level; **auf leisen ~n** (*fig*)
softly, noiselessly.
Sohn [zō:n] *m* -(e)s, ⁻e son.
Sojasoße [zō:'yázō:sə] *f* soya sauce.
solang(e) [zōláng'(ə)] *kj* as *od* so long as.
Solar- [zōlár'] *in zW* solar; **~energie** *f* solar
energy.
Solbad [zō:l'bât] *nt* saltwater bath.
solch [zolċh] *a inv,* **solche(r, s)** *a* such; **ein
~er Mensch** such a person.
Sold [zolt] *m* -(e)s, -e pay.
Soldat [zoldât'] *m* -en, -en soldier; **s~isch** *a*
soldierly.
Söldner [zœld'nər] *m* -s, - mercenary.
Sole [zō:'lə] *f* -, -n brine, salt water.
Solei [zō:'lī] *nt* pickled egg.
Soli [zō:'lē] *pl von* **Solo.**
solidarisch [zōlēdá'rish] *a* in *od* with solidarity; **sich ~ erklären** declare one's solidarity.
solidarisieren [zōlēdárēzē:'rən] *vr:* **sich ~
mit** show (one's) solidarity with.
Solidaritätsstreik [zōlēdárēte:ts'shtrīk] *m*
sympathy strike.
solid(e) [zōlē:d'(ə)] *a* solid; (*Arbeit, Wissen*)
sound; (*Leben, Person*) staid, respectable.
Solist(in *f)* [zōlist'(in)] *m* (*MUS*) soloist; (*fig*)
lone wolf.
soll [zol] *1./3. pers sing präs von* **sollen.**
Soll *nt* -(s), -(s) (*FIN*) debit (side);
(*Arbeitsmenge*) quota, target; **~ und Haben**
debit and credit.
sollen [zo'lən] *vi* be supposed to;
(*Verpflichtung*) should, ought to; **du hättest
nicht gehen ~** you shouldn't have gone; **das
hättest du nicht tun ~** you shouldn't have
od oughtn't to have done that; **mir soll es
gleich sein** it's all the same to me; **er sollte
sie nie wiedersehen** he was never to see
her again; **soll ich?** shall I?; **was soll das?**
what's that supposed to mean?; **was soll's?**
what the hell? (*umg*).
sollte [zol'tə] *imperf von* **sollen.**
solo [zō:'lō] *ad* (*MUS*) solo; (*fig umg*) on one's
own, alone.
Solo *nt* -s, -s *od* **Soli** solo.
solvent [zolvent'] *a* (*FIN*) solvent.
Solvenz [zolvents'] *f* (*FIN*) solvency.
somit [zōmit'] *kj* and so, therefore.
Sommer [zo'mər] *m* -s, - summer; **~ wie
Winter** all year round; **~ferien** *pl* summer
vacation *sing*; (*JUR. PARL*) summer recess;
s~lich *a* summery; (*Sommer~*) summer

attr; **~loch** *nt* period of slack time during
the summer vacation; **~reifen** *m* normal
tire (*US*) *od* tyre (*Brit*); **~schlußverkauf** *m*
summer sale; **~semester** *nt* (*UNIV*) summer
semester; **~sprossen** *pl* freckles *pl;* **~zeit** *f*
summertime.
Sonate [zōnă'tə] *f* -, -n sonata.
Sonde [zon'də] *f* -, -n probe.
Sonder- [zon'dər] *in zW* special;
~anfertigung *f* special model; **~angebot** *nt*
special offer; **~ausgabe** *f* special edition;
s~bar *a* strange, odd; **~beauftragte(r)** *mf*
(*POL*) special emissary; **~beitrag** *m*
(special) feature; **~fahrt** *f* special trip;
~fall *m* special case; **s~gleichen** *a inv* without parallel, unparalleled; **eine Frechheit
s~gleichen** the height of cheek; **s~lich** *a*
particular; (*außergewöhnlich*) remarkable;
(*eigenartig*) peculiar; **~ling** *m* eccentric;
~marke *f* special issue (stamp).
sondern *kj* but; **nicht nur ..., ~ auch** not
only ..., but also ♦ *vt* separate.
Sonder- *zW:* **~regelung** *f* special provision;
~schule *f* special school; **~vergünstigungen**
pl perquisites *pl,* perks *pl* (*bes Brit*);
~wünsche *pl* special requests *pl;* **~zug** *m*
special train.
sondieren [zondē:'rən] *vt* suss out; (*Gelände*)
scout out.
Sonett [zōnet'] *nt* -(e)s, -e sonnet.
Sonnabend [zon'ábənt] *m* Saturday; *siehe*
Dienstag.
Sonne [zo'nə] *f* -, -n sun; **an die ~ gehen** go
out in the sun.
sonnen *vt* put out in the sun ♦ *vr* sun o.s.
Sonnen- *zW:* **~aufgang** *m* sunrise; **s~baden**
vi sunbathe; **~blume** *f* sunflower; **~brand**
m sunburn; **~brille** *f* sunglasses *pl;*
~energie *f* solar energy; **~finsternis** *f* solar
eclipse; **s~gebräunt** *a* suntanned; **s~klar** *a*
crystal-clear; **~öl** *nt* suntan oil; **~schein** *m*
sunshine; **~schirm** *m* parasol; sunshade;
~stich *m* sunstroke; **du hast wohl einen
~stich!** (*hum umg*) you must have been out
in the sun too long!; **~uhr** *f* sundial;
~untergang *m* sunset; **~wende** *f* solstice.
sonnig [zo'niċh] *a* sunny.
Sonntag [zon'tâk] *m* Sunday; *siehe* **Dienstag.**
sonntäglich *a attr:* **~ gekleidet** dressed in
one's Sunday best.
sonntags *ad* (on) Sundays.
Sonntags- *zW:* **~dienst** *m:* **~dienst haben**
(*Apotheke*) be open on Sundays; **~fahrer** *m*
(*pej*) Sunday driver.
sonst [zonst] *ad* otherwise; (*mit pron, in Fragen*) else; (*zu anderer Zeit*) at other times;
(*gewöhnlich*) usually, normally ♦ *kj* otherwise; **er denkt, er ist ~ wer** (*umg*) he
thinks he's somebody special; **~ geht's dir
gut?** (*ironisch umg*) are you feeling okay?;
wenn ich Ihnen ~ noch behilflich sein kann
if I can help you in any other way; **~ noch
etwas?** anything else?; **~ nichts** nothing
else.

sonstig *a* other; „**S~es**" "other".

sonst- *zW:* ~**jemand** *pron* (*umg*) anybody (at all); ~**was** *pron* (*umg*): **da kann ja** ~**was passieren** anything could happen; ~**wo** *ad* (*umg*) somewhere else; ~**woher** *ad* (*umg*) from somewhere else; ~**wohin** *ad* = ~**wo**.

sooft [zōoft'] *kj* whenever.

Sopran [zōprán'] *m* **-s, -e** soprano (voice).

Sopranistin [zōprănis'tin] *f* soprano (singer).

Sorge [zor'gə] *f* **-, -n** care, worry; **dafür** ~ **tragen, daß ...** (*geh*) see to it that ...

sorgen *vi:* **für jdn** ~ look after sb; **für etw** ~ take care of *od* see to sth; **dafür** ~, **daß ...** see to it that ...; **dafür ist gesorgt** that's taken care of ♦ *vr* worry (*um* about).

Sorgen- *zW:* **s~frei** *a* carefree; ~**kind** *nt* problem child; **s~voll** *a* troubled, worried.

Sorgerecht *nt* **-(e)s** custody (of a child).

Sorgfalt [zork'fált] *f* **-** care(fulness); **viel** ~ **auf etw** (*akk*) **verwenden** take a lot of care over sth.

sorgfältig *a* careful.

Sorg- *zW:* **s~los** *a* careless; (*ohne Sorgen*) carefree; **s~sam** *a* careful.

Sorte [zor'tə] *f* **-, -n** sort; (*Waren~*) brand; ~**n** *pl* (*FIN*) foreign currency.

sortieren [zortē:'rən] *vt* sort (out); (*auch COMPUT*) sort.

Sortiermaschine *f* sorting machine.

Sortiment [zortēment'] *nt* assortment.

sosehr [zōzá:r'] *kj* as much as.

soso [zōzō:'] *interj:* ~**!** I see!; (*erstaunt*) well, well!; (*drohend*) well!

Soße [zō:'sə] *f* **-, -n** sauce; (*Braten~*) gravy.

Souffleur [zōōflœr'] *m*, **Souffleuse** [zōōflœ'zə] *f* prompter.

soufflieren [zōōflē:'rən] *vti* prompt.

soundso [zō:'ōōntzō:'] *ad:* ~ **lange** for such and such a time.

soundsovielte(r, s) *a*: **am S~n** (*Datum*) on such and such a date.

Souterrain [zōōteraŋ:'] *nt* **-s, -s** basement.

Souvenir [zōōvənē:r'] *nt* **-s, -s** souvenir.

souverän [zōōvərɛ:n'] *a* sovereign; (*überlegen*) superior; (*fig*) supremely good.

soviel [zōfē:l'] *kj* as far as ♦ *pron* as much (*wie* as); **rede nicht** ~ don't talk so much.

soweit [zōvīt'] *kj* as far as ♦ *ad:* ~ **sein** be ready; ~ **wie** *od* **als möglich** as far as possible; **ich bin** ~ **zufrieden** by and large I'm quite satisfied; **es ist bald** ~ it's nearly time.

sowenig [zōvá:'nich] *ad* no more, not any more (*wie* than); ~ **wie möglich** as little as possible ♦ *kj* however little.

sowie [zōvē:'] *kj* (*sobald*) as soon as; (*ebenso*) as well as.

sowieso [zōvēzō:'] *ad* anyway.

sowj., sowjet. *abk* = **sowjetisch**.

sowjetisch [zovye'tish] *a* Soviet.

Sowjet- *zW:* ~**republik** *f* Soviet Republic; ~**russe** *m* Soviet Russian; ~**union** *f* Soviet Union.

sowohl [zōvō:l'] *kj:* ~ **. . . als** *od* **wie auch** both . . . and.

soz. *abk* = **sozial; sozialistisch**.

sozial [zōtsēál'] *a* social; ~ **eingestellt** public-spirited; ~**er Wohnungsbau** government housing; **S~abbau** *m* public-spending cuts; **S~abgaben** *pl* Social Security contributions *pl*; **S~amt** *nt* (social) welfare office; **S~arbeiter** *m* social worker; **S~beruf** *m* caring profession; **S~demokrat** *m* social democrat; **S~hilfe** *f* welfare (aid).

Sozialisation [zōtsēálēzàtsēō:n'] *f* (*PSYCH, SOZIOLOGIE*) socialization.

sozialisieren [zōtsēálēzē:'rən] *vt* socialize.

Sozialismus [zōtsēális'mōōs] *m* socialism.

Sozialist(in *f)* [zōtsēálist'(in)] *m* socialist; **s~isch** *a* socialist.

sozial- *zW:* **S~politik** *f* social welfare policy; **S~produkt** *nt* (gross *od* net) national product; **S~staat** *m* welfare state; **S~wohnung** *f* ≈ state-subsidized apartment.

Soziologe [zōtsēōlō:'gə] *m* **-n, -n, Soziologin** *f* sociologist.

Soziologie [zōtsēōlōgē:'] *f* sociology.

soziologisch [zōtsēōlō:'gish] *arr* sociological.

Sozius [zō:'tsēōōs] *m* **-, -se** (*COMM*) partner; (*Motorrad*) pillion rider; ~**sitz** *m* pillion (seat).

sozusagen [zōtsōōzá'gən] *ad* so to speak.

Spachtel [shpákh'təl] *m* **-s, -** spatula.

spachteln *vt* (*Mauerfugen, Ritzen*) fill (in) ♦ *vi* (*umg: essen*) dig in.

Spagat [shpágát'] *m* *od nt* **-s, -e** splits *pl*.

spähen [shpe:'ən] *vi* peep, peek.

Spalier [shpálē:r'] *nt* **-s, -e** (*Gerüst*) trellis; (*Leute*) guard of honor; ~ **stehen** *od* **ein** ~ **bilden** form a guard of honour.

Spalt [shpált] *m* **-(e)s, -e** crack; (*Tür~*) chink; (*fig: Kluft*) split.

Spalte *f* **-, -n** crack, fissure; (*Gletscher~*) crevasse; (*in Text*) column.

spalten *vtr* (*lit, fig*) split.

Spaltung *f* splitting.

Span [shpán] *m* **-(e)s, -̈e** shaving.

Spanferkel *nt* **-s, -** sucking pig.

Spange [shpá'ngə] *f* **-, -n** clasp; (*Haar~*) hair slide; (*Schnalle*) buckle; (*Arm~*) bangle.

Spanien [shpá'nēən] *nt* **-s** Spain.

Spanier(in *f)* *m* **-s, -** Spaniard.

spanisch *a* Spanish; **das kommt mir** ~ **vor** (*umg*) that seems odd to me; ~**e Wand** (folding) screen.

spann [shpán] *imperf von* **spinnen**.

Spann *m* **-(e)s, -e** instep.

Spannbeton *m* **-s** prestressed concrete.

Spanne *f* **-, -n** (*Zeit~*) space; (*Differenz*) gap.

spannen *vt* (*straffen*) tighten, tauten; (*befestigen*) brace ♦ *vi* be tight.

spannend *a* exciting, gripping; **mach's nicht so** ~**!** (*umg*) don't keep me *etc* in suspense.

Spanner *m* **-s, -** (*umg: Voyeur*) peeping Tom.

Spannkraft *f* elasticity; (*fig*) energy.

Spannung f tension; (*ELEK*) voltage; (*fig*) suspense; (*unangenehm*) tension.
Spannungs- zW: ~**gebiet** nt (*POL*) flashpoint, area of tension; ~**prüfer** m voltage detector.
Spannweite f (*von Flügeln*, *AVIAT*) (wing)span.
Spanplatte f chipboard.
Spar- zW: ~**buch** nt savings book; ~**büchse** f (piggy) bank.
sparen [shpá'rən] vti save; **sich** (*dat*) **etw** ~ save o.s. sth; (*Bemerkung*) keep sth to o.s.; **mit etw** (*dat*) ~ be sparing with sth; **an etw** (*dat*) ~ economize on sth.
Sparer(in f) m -s, - (*bei Bank etc*) saver.
Sparflamme f low flame; **auf** ~ (*fig umg*) just ticking over.
Spargel [shpár'gəl] m -s, - asparagus.
Spar- zW: ~**groschen** m nest egg; ~**kasse** f savings bank; ~**konto** nt savings account.
spärlich [shpe:r'liçh] a meager (*US*), meagre (*Brit*); (*Bekleidung*) scanty; (*Beleuchtung*) poor.
Spar- zW: ~**maßnahme** f economy measure; ~**packung** f economy size; **s~sam** a economical, thrifty; **s~sam im Verbrauch** economical; ~**samkeit** f thrift, economizing; ~**schwein** nt piggy bank.
Sparte [shpár'tə] f -, -n field; (*COMM*) line of business; (*PRESSE*) column.
Sparvertrag m savings agreement.
Spaß [shpás] m -es, ²e joke; (*Freude*) fun; ~ **muß sein** there's no harm in a joke; **jdm** ~ **machen** be fun (for sb); **s~en** vi joke; **mit ihm ist nicht zu s~en** you can't take liberties with him.
spaßeshalber ad for the fun of it.
spaßig a funny, droll.
Spaß- zW: ~**macher** m joker, funny man; ~**verderber** m -s, - spoilsport; ~**vogel** m joker.
spät [shpe:t] a, ad late; **heute abend wird es** ~ it'll be a late night tonight.
Spaten [shpá'tən] m -s, - spade; ~**stich** m: **den ersten** ~**stich tun** turn the first sod.
Spätentwickler m late developer.
später a, ad later; **an** ~ **denken** think of the future; **bis** ~! see you later!
spätestens ad at the latest.
Spätlese f late vintage.
Spatz [shpáts] m -en, -en sparrow.
spazieren [shpàtsē:'rən] vi aux sein stroll; ~**fahren** vi unreg go for a drive; ~**gehen** vi unreg go for a walk.
Spazier- zW: ~**gang** m walk; **einen** ~**gang machen** go for a walk; ~**gänger(in** f) m stroller; ~**stock** m walking stick; ~**weg** m path, walk.
SPD f - abk (= *Sozialdemokratische Partei Deutschlands*) German Social Democratic Party.
Specht [shpeçht] m -(e)s, -e woodpecker.
Speck [shpek] m -(e)s, -e bacon; **mit** ~ **fängt man Mäuse** (*Sprichwort*) good bait catches

fine fish; **'ran an den** ~ (*umg*) let's get stuck in.
Spediteur [shpädētœr'] m carrier; (*Möbel*~) furniture remover.
Spedition [shpädētsēō:n'] f carriage; (*Speditionsfirma*) road haulage contractor; (*Umzugsfirma*) removal firm.
Speer [shpä:r] m -(e)s, -e spear; (*SPORT*) javelin; ~**werfen** nt: **das** ~**werfen** throwing the javelin.
Speiche [shpī'çhə] f -, -n spoke.
Speichel [shpī'çhəl] m -s saliva, spit(tle); ~**lecker** m (*pej umg*) bootlicker.
Speicher [shpī'çhər] m -s, - storehouse; (*Dach*~) attic, loft; (*Korn*~) granary; (*Wasser*~) tank; (*TECH*) store; (*COMPUT*) memory; ~**auszug** m (*COMPUT*) dump; ~**bereinigung** f (*COMPUT*) clearing the memory.
speichern vt (*auch COMPUT*) store.
speien [shpī'ən] vti unreg spit; (*erbrechen*) vomit; (*Vulkan*) spew.
Speise [shpī'zə] f -, -n food; **kalte und warme** ~**n** hot and cold meals; ~**eis** [-īs'] nt ice-cream; ~**fett** nt cooking fat; ~**kammer** f larder, pantry; ~**karte** f menu.
speisen vt feed; eat ♦ vi dine.
Speise- zW: ~**öl** nt salad oil; (*zum Braten*) cooking oil; ~**röhre** f (*ANAT*) gullet, esophagus (*US*), oesophagus (*Brit*); ~**saal** m dining room; ~**wagen** m dining car; ~**zettel** m menu.
Spektakel [shpektá'kəl] m -s, - (*umg*: *Lärm*) row ♦ nt -s, - spectacle.
spektakulär [shpektákōōle:r'] a spectacular.
Spekulant(in f) [shpākōōlànt'(in)] m speculator.
Spekulation [shpākōōlàtsēō:n'] f speculation.
Spekulatius [shpākōōlá'tsēōōs] m -, - spiced cookie (*US*) od biscuit (*Brit*).
spekulieren [shpākōōlē:'rən] vi (*fig*) speculate; **auf etw** (*akk*) ~ have hopes of sth.
Spelunke [shpālōōng'kə] f -, -n dive.
spendabel [shpendá'bəl] a (*umg*) generous, open-handed.
Spende [shpen'də] f -, -n donation.
spenden vt donate, give; **S~konto** nt donations account; **S~sumpf** m (*POL*) party-donation fund; **S~waschanlage** f laundering operation.
Spender(in f) m -s, - donator; (*auch MED*) donor.
spendieren [shpendē:'rən] vt pay for, buy; **jdm etw** ~ treat sb to sth, stand sb sth.
Sperling [shper'ling] m sparrow.
Sperma [sper'má] nt -s, **Spermen** sperm.
sperrangelweit [shper'áng'əlvīt'] a wide-open.
Sperrbezirk m restricted area.
Sperre f -, -n barrier; (*Verbot*) ban; (*Polizei*~) roadblock.
sperren [shpe'rən] vt block; (*COMM*: *Konto*) freeze; (*COMPUT*: *Daten*) disable; (*SPORT*) suspend; bar; (*vom Ball*) obstruct;

(einschließen) lock; *(verbieten)* ban ♦ *vr* baulk, jib(e).

Sperr- *zW:* ~**feuer** *nt* (*MIL. fig*) barrage; ~**frist** *f* (*auch JUR*) waiting period; (*SPORT*) (period of) suspension; ~**gebiet** *nt* prohibited area; ~**gut** *nt* bulky freight; ~**holz** *nt* plywood.

sperrig *a* bulky.

Sperr- *zW:* ~**konto** *nt* blocked account; ~**müll** *m* bulky refuse; ~**sitz** *m* (*THEAT*) orchestra (*US*), stalls *pl* (*Brit*); ~**stunde** *f*, ~**zeit** *f* closing time.

Spesen [shpā:'zən] *pl* expenses *pl*; ~**abrechnung** *f* expense account.

Spessart [shpe'sárt] *m* -s Spessart (Mountains).

Spezi [shpā:'tsē] *m* -s, -s (*umg*) pal.

Spezial- [shpātsēál'] *in zW* special; s~**angefertigt** *a* custom-built; ~**ausbildung** *f* specialized training.

spezialisieren [shpātsēálēzē:'rən] *vr* specialize.

Spezialisierung *f* specialization.

Spezialist(in *f)* [shpātsēálist'(in)] *m* specialist *(für* in).

Spezialität [shpātsēálēte:t'] *f* specialty.

speziell [shpātsēcl'] *a* special.

Spezifikation [shpātsēfēkátsēō:n'] *f* specification.

spezifisch [shpātsē:'fish] *a* specific.

Sphäre [sfe:'rə] *f* -, -n sphere.

spicken [shpi'kən] *vt* lard ♦ *vi* (*SCH*) copy, crib.

Spickzettel *m* -s, - (*SCH umg*) crib.

spie [shpē:] *imperf von* **speien.**

Spiegel [shpē:'gəl] *m* -s, - mirror; (*Wasser~*) level; (*MIL*) tab; ~**bild** *nt* reflection; s~**bildlich** *a* reversed.

Spiegelei [shpē:'gəlī] *nt* fried egg.

spiegeln *vt* mirror, reflect ♦ *vr* be reflected ♦ *vi* gleam; *(wider~)* be reflective.

Spiegel- *zW:* ~**reflexkamera** *f* reflex camera; ~**schrift** *f* mirror writing.

Spiegelung *f* reflection.

Spiel [shpē:l] *nt* -(e)s, -e game; *(Schau~)* play; *(Tätigkeit)* play(ing); (*KARTEN*) deck (*US*), pack (*Brit*); (*TECH*) (free) play; **leichtes ~ haben** have an easy job of it (*mit od bei jdm* with sb); **die Hand** *od* **Finger im ~ haben** have a hand in affairs; **jdn/etw aus dem ~ lassen** leave sb/sth out of it; **auf dem ~(e) stehen** be at stake; ~**automat** *m* gambling machine; *(zum Geldgewinnen)* slot machine; ~**bank** *f* casino; ~**dose** *f* music box.

spielen *vti* play; *(um Geld)* gamble; (*THEAT*) perform, act; **was wird hier gespielt?** (*umg*) what's going on here?

spielend *ad* easily.

Spieler(in *f)* *m* -s, - player; *(um Geld)* gambler.

Spielerei [shpē:lərī'] *f* trifling pastime.

spielerisch *a* playful; *(Leichtigkeit)* effortless; ~**es Können** skill as a player;

(THEAT) acting ability.

Spiel- *zW:* ~**feld** *nt* pitch, field; ~**film** *m* feature film; ~**geld** *nt* (*Einsatz*) stake; *(unechtes Geld)* toy money; ~**karte** *f* playing card; ~**mannszug** *m* (brass) band; ~**plan** *m* (*THEAT*) program (*US*), programme (*Brit*); ~**platz** *m* playground; ~**raum** *m* room to maneuver, scope; ~**regel** *f* (*lit, fig*) rule of the game; ~**sachen** *pl* toys *pl*; ~**stand** *m* score; ~**verderber** *m* -s, - spoilsport; ~**waren** *pl* toys *pl*; ~**zeit** *f* (*Saison*) season; *(~dauer)* playing time; ~**zeug** *nt* toys *pl*.

Spieß [shpē:s] *m* -es, -e spear; (*Brat~*) spit; (*MIL umg*) sarge; **den ~ umdrehen** *(fig)* turn the tables; **wie am ~(e) schreien** (*umg*) squeal like a stuck pig; ~**braten** *m* joint roasted on a spit.

Spießbürger *m, Spießer m* -s, - bourgeois.

Spikes [spīks] *pl* (*SPORT*) spikes *pl*; (*AUT*) studs *pl*.

Spinat [shpēnât'] *m* -(e)s, -e spinach.

Spind [shpint] *m od nt* -(e)s, -e locker.

spindeldürr [shpin'dəldür'] *a* (*pej*) spindly, thin as a rake.

Spinne [shpi'nə] *f* -, -n spider; s~**feind** *a* (*umg*): **sich** *od* **einander** *(dat)* s~**feind sein** be deadly enemies.

spinnen *vti unreg* spin; (*umg*) talk rubbish; *(verrückt)* be crazy *od* mad; **ich denk' ich spinne** (*umg*) I don't believe it.

Spinnengewebe *nt =* **Spinngewebe.**

Spinner(in *f)* *m* -s, - *(fig umg)* screwball.

Spinnerei [shpinərī'] *f* spinning mill.

Spinn- *zW:* ~**gewebe** *nt* cobweb; ~**rad** *nt* spinning wheel; ~**webe** *f* cobweb.

Spion [shpēō:n'] *m* -s, -e spy; *(in Tür)* spyhole.

Spionage [shpēōnâ'zhə] *f* -, -n espionage; ~**abwehr** *f* counter-intelligence; ~**satellit** *m* spy satellite.

spionieren [shpēōnē:'rən] *vi* spy.

Spionin *f* (woman) spy.

Spirale [shpērâ'lə] *f* -, -n spiral; (*MED*) coil.

Spirituosen [shpērētōōō:'zən] *pl* spirits *pl*.

Spiritus [shpē:'rētōōs] *m* -, -se (methylated) spirits; ~**kocher** *m* spirit stove.

spitz [shpits] *a* pointed; *(Winkel)* acute; *(fig: Zunge)* sharp; (: *Bemerkung*) caustic.

Spitz *m* -es, -e *(Hund)* spitz.

Spitz- *zW:* s~**bekommen** *vt unreg* (*umg*): **etw** s~**bekommen** get wise to sth; ~**bogen** *m* pointed arch; ~**bube** *m* rogue.

Spitze *f* -, -n point, tip; *(Berg~)* peak; *(Bemerkung)* taunt; *(fig: Stichelei)* dig; *(erster Platz)* lead, top; *(meist pl: Gewebe)* lace; (*umg: prima*) great; **etw auf die ~ treiben** carry sth too far.

Spitzel *m* -s, - police informer.

spitzen *vt* sharpen; *(Lippen, Mund)* purse; *(lit, fig: Ohren)* prick up.

Spitzen- *in zW* top; ~**leistung** *f* top performance; ~**lohn** *m* top wages *pl*; ~**marke** *f* brand leader; s~**mäßig** *a* really great; **~position** *f* leading position; **~reiter** *m* (*SPORT*) leader; (*fig*: *Kandidat*) frontrunner; (*Ware*) top seller; (*Schlager*) number one; **~sportler** *m* top-class sportsman; **~verband** *m* leading organization.

Spitzer *m* **-s**, - sharpener.

spitzfindig *a* (over)subtle.

spitzig *a* = **spitz**.

Spitz- *zW*: **~maus** *f* shrew; **~name** *m* nickname.

Spleen [shplē:n] *m* **-s**, **-e** *od* **-s** (*umg*: *Angewohnheit*) crazy habit; (: *Idee*) crazy idea; (*Fimmel*) obsession.

Splitt [shplit] *m* **-s**, **-e** stone chippings *pl*; (*Streumittel*) grit.

Splitter *m* **-s**, - splinter; **~gruppe** *f* (*POL*) splinter group; **s~nackt** *a* stark naked.

SPÖ *f* - *abk* (= *Sozialistische Partei Österreichs*) Austrian Socialist Party.

sponsern [shpon'zərn] *vt* sponsor.

Sponsor [shpon'zɔr] *m* **-s**, **-s** sponsor.

spontan [shpontân'] *a* spontaneous.

sporadisch [shpōrá'dish] *a* sporadic.

Sporen [shpō:'rən] *pl* (*auch BOT. ZOOL*) spurs *pl*.

Sport [shport] *m* **-(e)s**, **-e** sport; (*fig*) hobby; **treiben Sie ~?** do you do any sport?; **~abzeichen** *nt* sports certificate; **~artikel** *pl* sports equipment *sing*; **~klub** *m* sports club; **~lehrer** *m* games *od* P.E. teacher.

Sportler(in *f*) *m* **-s**, - sportsman; sportswoman.

Sport- *zW*: **s~lich** *a* sporting; (*Mensch*) sporty; (*durchtrainiert*) athletic; (*Kleidung*) smart but casual; **~medizin** *f* sports medicine; **~platz** *m* playing *od* sports field.

Sportsfreund *m* (*fig umg*) buddy.

Sport- *zW*: **~verein** *m* sports club; **~wagen** *m* sports car; (*für Baby*) stroller; **~zeug** *nt* sports gear.

Spot [spot] *m* **-s**, **-s** commercial, advertisement.

Spott [shpot] *m* **-(e)s** mockery, ridicule; **s~billig** *a* dirt cheap; **s~en** *vi* mock (*über* +*akk* at), ridicule; **das spottet jeder Beschreibung** that simply defies description.

spöttisch [shpœ'tish] *a* mocking.

Spottpreis *m* **-es**, **-e** ridiculously low price.

sprach [shprâkh] *imperf von* **sprechen**.

sprachbegabt *a* good at languages.

Sprache *f* -, **-n** language; **heraus mit der ~!** (*umg*) come on, out with it!; **zur ~ kommen** be mentioned; **in französischer ~** in French.

Sprach- *zW*: **~fehler** *m* speech defect; **~fertigkeit** *f* fluency; **~führer** *m* phrase book; **~gebrauch** *m* (linguistic) usage; **~gefühl** *nt* feeling for language; **~kenntnisse** *pl*: **mit englischen ~kenntnissen** with a knowledge of English; **~labor** *nt* language lab(oratory); **s~lich** *a* linguistic; **s~los** *a* speechless; **~rohr** *nt* megaphone; (*fig*) mouthpiece; **~störung** *f* speech disorder; **~wissenschaft** *f* linguistics

sing.

sprang [shprâng] *imperf von* **springen**.

Spray [sprā:] *m od nt* **-s**, **-s** spray; **~dose** *f* aerosol (can), spray.

sprayen *vti* spray.

Sprechan'lage *f* -, **-n** intercom.

sprechen [shpre'çhən] *unreg vi* speak, talk (*mit* to); **das spricht für ihn** that's a point in his favour; **frei ~** extemporize; **nicht gut auf jdn zu ~ sein** be on bad terms with sb; **es spricht vieles dafür, daß ...** there is every reason to believe that ... ♦ *vt* say; (*Sprache*) speak; (*Person*) speak to; **hier spricht man Spanisch** Spanish spoken; **wir ~ uns noch!** you haven't heard the last of this!

Sprecher(in *f*) *m* **-s**, - speaker; (*für Gruppe*) spokesman; (*RAD. TV*) announcer.

Sprech- *zW*: **~funkgerät** *nt* radio telephone; **~rolle** *f* speaking part; **~stunde** *f* consultation (hour); **~stundenhilfe** *f* (doctor's) receptionist; **~zimmer** *nt* consulting room, surgery (*Brit*).

spreizen [shprī'tsən] *vt* spread ♦ *vr* put on airs.

Sprengarbeiten *pl* blasting operations *pl*.

sprengen [shpre'ngən] *vt* sprinkle; (*mit Sprengstoff*) blow up; (*Gestein*) blast; (*Versammlung*) break up.

Spreng- *zW*: **~ladung** *f* explosive charge; **~satz** *m* explosive device; **~stoff** *m* explosive(s *pl*); **~stoffanschlag** *m* bomb attack.

Spreu [shproi] *f* - chaff.

spricht [shpriçht] 3. *pers sing präs von* **sprechen**.

Sprich- [shpriçh'] *zW*: **~wort** *nt* proverb; **s~wörtlich** *a* proverbial.

sprießen [shprē:'sən] *vi* (*aus der Erde*) spring up; (*Knospen*) shoot.

Springbrunnen *m* fountain.

springen [shpri'ngən] *vi unreg* jump, leap; (*Glas*) crack; (*mit Kopfsprung*) dive; **etw ~ lassen** (*umg*) fork out for sth.

springend *a*: **der ~e Punkt** the crucial point.

Springer *m* **-s**, - jumper; (*SCHACH*) knight.

Sprinkler [shpring'klər] *m* **-s**, - sprinkler.

Sprit [shprit] *m* **-(e)s**, **-e** (*umg*) gas(oline) (*US*), fuel.

Spritzbeutel *m* **-s**, - icing bag.

Spritze [shpri'tsə] *f* -, **-n** syringe; (*Injektion*) injection; (*an Schlauch*) nozzle.

spritzen *vt* spray; (*Wein*) dilute with soda water *od* lemonade; (*MED*) inject ♦ *vi* splash; (*heißes Fett*) spit; (*heraus~*) spurt; (*aus einer Tube etc*) squirt; (*MED*) give injections.

Spritzer *m* **-s**, - (*Farb~, Wasser~*) splash.

Spritz- *zW*: **~pistole** *f* spray gun; **~tour** *f* (*umg*) spin.

spröde [shprœ'də] *a* brittle; (*Person*) reserved; (*Haut*) rough.

sproß [shpros] *imperf von* **sprießen**.

Sproß *m* **-sses**, **-sse** shoot.

Sprosse [shpro'sə] *f* -, -n rung.
Sprossenwand *f* (*SPORT*) wall bars *pl*.
SpRÖßling [shprœs'ling] *m* offspring *no pl*.
Spruch [shprōōkh] *m* -(e)s, ꞊e saying, maxim; (*JUR*) judgement; ~e **klopfen** (*umg*) talk fancy; ~**band** *nt* banner.
Sprüchemacher [shprü'chəmákhər] *m* -s, - (*umg*) big talker.
spruchreif *a*: **die Sache ist noch nicht** ~ it's not definite yet.
Sprudel [shprōō:'dəl] *m* -s, - mineral water; (*süß*) lemonade.
sprudeln *vi* bubble.
Sprüh- [shprü:'] *zW*: ~**dose** *f* aerosol (can); **s~en** *vti* spray; (*fig*) sparkle; ~**regen** *m* drizzle.
Sprung [shprōōng] *m* -(e)s, ꞊e jump; (*Riß*) crack; (*schwungvoll, fig*: *Gedanken*~) leap; **immer auf dem** ~ **sein** (*umg*) always be on the go; **jdm auf die** ꞊e **helfen** (*wohlwollend*) give sb a (helping) hand; **auf einen** ~ **bei jdm vorbeikommen** (*umg*) drop in to see sb; **damit kann man keine großen** ꞊e **machen** (*umg*) you can't exactly live it up on that; ~**brett** *nt* springboard; ~**feder** *f* spring; **s~haft** *a* erratic; (*Aufstieg*) rapid; ~**schanze** *f* ski jump; ~**turm** *m* diving platform.
Spucke [shpōō'kə] *f* - spit.
spucken *vti* spit; **in die Hände** ~ (*fig*) roll up one's sleeves.
Spucknapf *m* -(e)s, ꞊e spittoon.
Spuk [shpōō:k] *m* -(e)s, -e haunting; (*fig*) nightmare; **s~en** *vi* haunt; **hier spukt es** this place is haunted.
Spule [shpōō:'lə] *f* -, -n spool; (*ELEK*) coil.
Spüle [shpü:'lə] *f* -, -n (kitchen) sink.
spülen *vti* rinse; (*Geschirr*) do the dishes; (*Toilette*) flush; **etw an Land** ~ wash sth ashore.
Spül- *zW*: ~**maschine** *f* dishwasher; ~**mittel** *nt* dishwashing liquid; ~**stein** *m* sink.
Spülung *f* rinsing; (*Wasser*~) flush; (*MED*) irrigation.
Spund [shpōōnt] *m* -(e)s, -e: **junger** ~ (*veraltet umg*) young pup.
Spur [shpōō:r] *f* -, -en trace; (*Fuß*~, *Rad*~, *Tonband*~) track; (*Fährte*) trail; (*Fahr*~) lane; **jdm auf die** ~ **kommen** get onto sb; **(seine)** ~**en hinterlassen** (*fig*) leave its mark; **keine** ~ (*umg*) not *od* nothing at all.
spürbar *a* noticeable, perceptible.
spuren *vi* (*umg*) obey; (*sich fügen*) toe the line.
spüren [shpü:'rən] *vt* feel; **etw zu** ~ **bekommen** (*lit*) feel sth; (*fig*) feel the (full) force of sth.
Spuren- *zW*: ~**element** *nt* trace element; ~**sicherung** *f* securing of evidence.
Spürhund *m* hunting dog; (*fig*) sleuth.
spurlos *ad* without (a) trace; ~ **an jdm vorübergehen** have no effect on sb.
Spurt [shpōōrt] *m* -(e)s, -s *od* -e spurt.
sputen [shpōō:'tən] *vr* make haste.

s. S. *abk* = **siehe Seite** .
SS *f* - *abk* (= *Schutzstaffel*) SS *nt*; = **Sommersemester**.
SSD *m* - *abk* (*DDR*: = *Staatssicherheitsdienst*) state security service.
SSV *abk* = **Sommerschlußverkauf**.
st *abk* (= *Stunde*) h.
St. *abk* = **Stück; Stunde; Sankt**.
StA *abk* = **Staatsanwalt; Stammaktie(n)**.
Staat [shtát] *m* -(e)s, -en state; (*Prunk*) show; (*Kleidung*) finery; **mit etw** ~ **machen** show off *od* parade sth.
staatenlos *a* stateless.
staatl. *abk* = **staatlich**.
staatlich *a* state *attr*; state-run ♦ *ad*: ~ **geprüft** state-certified.
Staats- *zW*: ~**affäre** *f* (*lit*) affair of state; (*fig*) major operation; ~**angehörigkeit** *f* nationality; ~**anleihe** *f* government bond; ~**anwalt** *m* public prosecutor; ~**bürger** *m* citizen; ~**dienst** *m* civil service; **s~eigen** *a* state-owned; ~**eigentum** *nt* public ownership; ~**examen** *nt* (*UNIV*) degree; **s~feindlich** *a* subversive; ~**geheimnis** *nt* (*lit, fig hum*) state secret; ~**haushalt** *m* budget; ~**kosten** *pl* public expenses *pl*; ~**mann** *m*, *pl* -**männer** statesman; **s~männisch** *a* statesmanlike; ~**schuld** *f* (*FIN*) national debt; ~**sekretär** *m* secretary of state; ~**streich** *m* coup (d'état).
Stab [shtáp] *m* -(e)s, ꞊e rod; (*für* ~*hochsprung*) pole; (*für Staffellauf*) baton; (*Gitter*~) bar; (*Menschen*) staff; (*von Experten*) panel.
Stäbchen [shte:t'çhən] *nt* (*Eß*~) chopstick.
Stabhochsprung *m* pole vault.
stabil [shtábē:l'] *a* stable; (*Möbel*) sturdy.
Stabilisator [shtábēlēzá'tor] *m* stabilizer.
stabilisieren [shtábēlēzē:'rən] *vt* stabilize.
Stabilisierung *f* stabilization.
Stabreim *m* alliteration.
Stabsarzt *m* (*MIL*) captain in the medical corps.
stach [shtákh] *imperf von* **stechen**.
Stachel [shtá'khəl] *m* -s, -n spike; (*von Tier*) spine; (*von Insekten*) sting; ~**beere** *f* gooseberry; ~**draht** *m* barbed wire.
stach(e)lig *a* prickly.
Stachelschwein *nt* porcupine.
Stadion [shtá'dēon] *nt* -s, **Stadien** stadium.
Stadium [shtá'dēōōm] *nt* stage, phase.
Stadt [shtát] *f* -, ꞊e town; (*Groß*~) city; (~*verwaltung*) (town) council; ~**bad** *nt* municipal swimming pool; **s~bekannt** *a* known all over town; ~**bezirk** *m* municipal district.
Städtchen [shte:t'çhən] *nt* small town.
Städtebau *m* -(e)s town planning.
Städter(in *f*) *m* -s, - town *od* city dweller.
Stadt- *zW*: ~**gespräch** *nt*: (**das**) ~**gespräch sein** be the talk of the town; ~**gue(r)rilla** *f* urban guerrilla.
städtisch *a* municipal; (*nicht ländlich*) urban.
Stadt- *zW*: ~**kasse** *f* town *od* city treasury;

~kreis m town od city borough; **~mauer** f city wall(s pl); **~mitte** f town od city center (US) od centre (Brit); **~park** m municipal park; **~plan** m street map; **~rand** m outskirts pl; **~rat** m (Behörde) (town od city) council; **~teil** m district, part of town; **~verwaltung** f (Behörde) municipal authority.

Staffel [shtá'fəl] f -, -n rung; (SPORT) relay (team); (AVIAT) squadron.

Staffelei [shtáfəlī'] f easel.

staffeln vt graduate.

Staffeltarif m (Steuer) sliding scale.

Staffelung f graduation.

Stagnation [shtágnátsēō:n'] f stagnation.

stagnieren [shtágnē:'rən] vi stagnate.

stahl [shtál] imperf von **stehlen**.

Stahl m -(e)s, ¨e steel; **~helm** m steel helmet.

stak [shták] imperf von **stecken**.

Stalag [shtá'lák] abk (= Stammlager für Kriegsgefangene) stalag.

Stall [shtál] m -(e)s, ¨e stable; (Kaninchen~) hutch; (Schweine~) sty; (Hühner~) henhouse.

Stallung f stables pl.

Stamm [shtám] m -(e)s, ¨e (Baum~) trunk; (Menschen~) tribe; (GRAM) stem; (Bakterien~) strain; **~aktie** f ordinary share, common stock (US); **~baum** m family tree; (von Tier) pedigree; **~buch** nt book of family events with legal documents, ≈ family bible.

stammeln vti stammer.

stammen vi: ~ **von** od **aus** come from.

Stamm- zW: **~form** f base form; **~gast** m regular (customer); **~halter** m son and heir.

stämmig [shte'miċh] a sturdy; (Mensch) stocky; **S~keit** f sturdiness; stockiness.

Stamm- zW: **~kapital** nt (FIN) ordinary share od common stock (US) capital; **~kunde** m, **~kundin** f regular (customer); **~lokal** nt favorite café od restaurant etc; (Kneipe) local bar; **~platz** m usual seat; **~tisch** m (Tisch in Gasthaus) table reserved for the regulars.

stampfen [shtám'pfən] vi stamp; (stapfen) tramp ♦ vt (mit Stampfer) mash.

Stampfer m -s, - (Stampfgerät) pounder.

stand [shtánt] imperf von **stehen**.

Stand m -(e)s, ¨e position; (Wasser~, Benzin~ etc) level; (Zähler~ etc) reading; (Stehen) standing position; (Zustand) state; (Spiel~) score; (Messe~ etc) stand; (Klasse) class; (Beruf) profession; **bei jdm** od **gegen jdn einen schweren ~ haben** (fig) have a hard time of it with sb; **etw auf den neuesten ~ bringen** bring sth up to date.

Standard [shtán'dárt] m -s, -s standard; **~ausführung** f standard design.

standardisieren [shtándárdēzē:'rən] vt standardize.

Standarte f -, -n (MIL. POL) standard.

Standbild nt statue.

Ständchen [shtent'ċhən] nt serenade.

Ständer m -s, - stand.

Standes- [shtán'dəs] zW: **~amt** nt city od county clerk's office (US), registry office (Brit); **s~amtlich** a: **s~amtliche Trauung** civil marriage ceremony; **~beamte(r)** m registrar; **~bewußtsein** nt status consciousness; **~dünkel** m snobbery; **s~gemäß** a, ad according to one's social position; **~unterschied** m social difference.

Stand- zW: **s~fest** a (Tisch, Leiter) stable, steady; (fig) steadfast; **s~haft** a steadfast; **~haftigkeit** f steadfastness; **s~halten** vi unreg stand firm (jdm/etw against sb/sth), resist (jdm/etw sb/sth).

ständig [shten'diċh] a permanent; (ununterbrochen) constant, continual.

Stand- zW: **~licht** nt parking lights pl (US), sidelights pl (Brit); **~ort** m location; (MIL) garrison; **~pauke** f (umg): **jdm eine ~pauke halten** give sb a lecture; **~punkt** m standpoint; **s~rechtlich** a: **s~rechtlich erschießen** put before a firing squad; **~spur** f (AUT) shoulder (US), hard shoulder (Brit).

Stange [shtá'ngə] f -, -n stick; (Stab) pole, bar; rod; (Zigaretten) carton; **von der ~** (COMM) ready-made, off the rack (US), off the peg; **eine ~ Geld** quite a packet; **jdm die ~ halten** (umg) stick up for sb; **bei der ~ bleiben** (umg) stick at od to sth.

Stangenbohne f -, -n pole bean (US), runner bean (Brit).

stank [shtángk] imperf von **stinken**.

stänkern [shteng'kərn] vi (umg) stir things up.

Stanniol [shtánēō:l'] nt -s, -e tinfoil.

St.-Anw m - abk (= Staatsanwalt) Prosecuting Attorney.

Stanze [shtán'tsə] f -, -n stanza; (TECH) stamp.

stanzen vt stamp; (Löcher) punch.

Stapel [shtá'pəl] m -s, - pile; (NAUT) stocks pl; **~lauf** m launch.

stapeln vt pile (up).

Stapelverarbeitung f (COMPUT) batch processing.

stapfen [shtá'pfən] vi trudge, plod.

Star [shtár] m -(e)s, -e starling; (MED) cataract ♦ m -s, -s (Film~ etc) star.

starb [shtárp] imperf von **sterben**.

stark [shtárk] a strong; (heftig, groß) heavy; (Maßangabe) thick; (umg: hervorragend) great; **das ist ein ~es Stück!** (umg) that's a bit much!; **sich für etw ~ machen** (umg) stand up for sth ♦ ad very; (beschädigt etc) badly; (vergrößert, verkleinert) greatly; **er ist ~ erkältet** he has a bad cold.

Stärke [shter'kə] f -, -n strength (auch fig); heaviness; thickness; (von Mannschaft) size; (KOCH, Wäsche) starch; **~mehl** nt (KOCH) thickening agent.

stärken vt (lit, fig) strengthen; (Wäsche)

starch; (*Selbstbewußtsein*) boost; (*Gesundheit*) improve; (*erfrischen*) fortify ♦ *vi* be fortifying; **stärkendes Mittel** tonic.

Starkstrom *m* heavy current.

Stärkung [shter'kōōng] *f* strengthening; (*Essen*) refreshment.

starr [shtár] *a* stiff; (*unnachgiebig*) rigid; (*Blick*) staring.

starren *vi* stare; ~ **vor** *od* **von** (*voll von*) be covered in; (*Waffen*) be bristling with; **vor sich** (*akk*) **hin** ~ stare straight ahead.

Starrheit *f* rigidity.

starr- *zW*: ~**köpfig** *a* stubborn; **S~sinn** *m* obstinacy.

Start [shtárt] *m* -(e)s, -e start; (*AVIAT*) takeoff; ~**automatik** *f* (*AUT*) automatic choke; ~**bahn** *f* runway; **s~en** *vti* start; (*AVIAT*) take off; ~**er** *m* -s, - starter; ~**erlaubnis** *f* takeoff clearance; ~**hilfe** *f* (*AVIAT*) rocket-assisted takeoff; (*fig*) initial aid; **jdm** ~**hilfe geben** help sb get off the ground; ~**hilfekabel** *nt* jumper cables *pl* (*US*), jump leads *pl* (*Brit*); **s~klar** *a* (*AVIAT*) clear for takeoff; (*SPORT*) ready to start; ~**kommando** *nt* (*SPORT*) starting signal; ~**zeichen** *nt* start signal.

Station [shtátsēō:n'] *f* station; (*Kranken~*) hospital ward; (*Haltestelle*) stop; ~ **machen** stop off.

stationär [shtátsēōne:r'] *a* stationary; (*MED*) in-patient *attr*.

stationieren [shtátsēōnē:'rən] *vt* station; (*Atomwaffen etc*) deploy.

Stations- *zW*: ~**arzt** *m*, ~**ärztin** *f* ward doctor; ~**vorsteher** *m* (*EISENB*) stationmaster.

Statist(in *f*) [shtátist'(in)] *m* (*FILM*) extra; supernumerary.

Statistik *f* statistics *sing*; ~**er(in** *f*) *m* -s, - statistician.

statistisch *a* statistical.

Stativ [shtátē:f'] *nt* -s, -e tripod.

statt [shtát] *kj*, *präp* +*gen od dat* instead of; ~ **dessen** instead.

Statt *f* - place.

Stätte [shte'tə] *f* -, -n place.

statt- *zW*: ~**finden** *vi unreg* take place; ~**haft** *a* admissible; **S~halter** *m* governor; ~**lich** *a* imposing, handsome; (*Bursche*) strapping; (*Sammlung*) impressive; (*Familie*) large; (*Summe*) handsome.

Statue [shtá'tōōə] *f* -, -n statue.

Statur [shtátōō:r'] *f* build.

Status [shtá'tōōs] *m* -, - status; ~**symbol** *nt* status symbol.

Statuten [shtátōō:'tən] *pl* by-law(s *pl*).

Stau [shtou] *m* -(e)s, -e blockage; (*Verkehrs~*) (traffic) jam.

Staub [shtoup] *m* -(e)s dust; ~ **wischen** dust; **sich aus dem** ~ **machen** (*umg*) clear off.

stauben [shtou'bən] *vi* be dusty.

Staubfaden *m* (*BOT*) stamen.

staubig [stou'biçh] *a* dusty.

Staub- *zW*: ~**lappen** *m* duster; ~**lunge** *f*

(*MED*) dust on the lung; **s~saugen** *vi untr* vacuum; ~**sauger** *m* vacuum cleaner; ~**tuch** *nt* duster.

Staudamm *m* dam.

Staude [shtou'də] *f* -, -n shrub.

stauen [shtou'ən] *vt* (*Wasser*) dam up; (*Blut*) stop the flow of ♦ *vr* (*Wasser*) become dammed up; (*MED*, *Verkehr*) become congested; (*Menschen*) collect together; (*Gefühle*) build up.

staunen [shtou'nən] *vi* be astonished; **da kann man nur noch** ~ it's just amazing; **S~** *nt* -s amazement.

Stausee [shtou'zā:] *m* -s, -n reservoir; artificial lake.

Stauung [shtou'ōōng] *f* (*von Wasser*) damming-up; (*von Blut*, *Verkehr*) congestion.

Std., **Stde.** *abk* (= *Stunde*) h.

stdl. *abk* = **stündlich**.

Stechbecken *nt* bedpan.

stechen [shtc'çhən] *unreg vt* (*mit Nadel etc*) prick; (*mit Messer*) stab; (*mit Finger*) poke; (*Biene etc*) sting; (*Mücke*) bite; (*KARTEN*) take; (*KUNST*) engrave; (*Torf*, *Spargel*) cut ♦ *vi* (*Sonne*) beat down; (*mit Stechkarte*) clock in; **in See** ~ put to sea ♦ *vr*: **sich** (*akk od dat*) **in den Finger** ~ prick one's finger ♦ *vti unpers*: **es sticht** it is prickly.

Stechen *nt* -s, - (*SPORT*) play-off; jump-off; (*Schmerz*) sharp pain.

stechend *a* piercing, stabbing; (*Geruch*) pungent.

Stech- *zW*: ~**karte** *f* time *od* clocking-in (*Brit*) card; ~**mücke** *f* gnat; ~**palme** *f* holly; ~**uhr** *f* time clock.

Steck- *zW*: ~**brief** *m* "wanted" poster; **s~brieflich** *ad*: **s~brieflich gesucht werden** be wanted; ~**dose** *f* outlet (*US*), (wall) socket (*Brit*).

stecken [shtc'kən] *vt* put; insert; (*Nadel*) stick; (*Pflanzen*) plant; (*beim Nähen*) pin; (*umg: investieren: Geld*, *Mühe*) put (*in* +*akk* into); (: *Zeit*) devote (*in* +*akk* to) ♦ *vi* unreg be; (*festsitzen*) be stuck; (*Nadeln*) stick; **der Schlüssel steckt** the key is in the lock; **wo steckt er?** where has he got to?; **zeigen, was in einem steckt** show what one is made of; ~**bleiben** *vi unreg* get stuck; ~**lassen** *vt unreg* leave in.

Steckenpferd *nt* hobbyhorse.

Stecker *m* -s, - (*ELEK*) plug.

Steck- *zW*: ~**nadel** *f* pin; ~**rübe** *f* swede, turnip; ~**schlüssel** *m* box wrench (*US*) *od* spanner (*Brit*); ~**zwiebel** *f* bulb.

Steg [shtā:k] *m* -(e)s, -e small bridge; (*Anlege~*) landing stage.

Stegreif *m*: **aus dem** ~ just like that.

Stehaufmännchen [shtā:'oufmençhən] *nt* (*Spielzeug*) tumbler.

stehen [shtā:'ən] *unreg vi* stand (*zu* by); (*sich befinden*) be; (*in Zeitung*) say; (*angehalten haben*) have stopped; **jdm** ~ suit sb;

ich tue, was in meinen Kräften steht I'll do everything I can; **es steht 2:1 für München** the score is 2-1 to Munich; **mit dem Dativ ~** (*GRAM*) take the dative; **auf Betrug steht eine Gefängnisstrafe** the penalty for fraud is imprisonment; **wie ~ Sie dazu?** what are your views on that? ♦ *vi unpers:* **es steht schlecht um ...** things are bad for ...; **wie steht's?** how are things?; (*SPORT*) what's the score?; **wie steht es damit?** how about it? ♦ *vr:* **sich gut/schlecht ~** be well-off/ badly off; **~bleiben** *vi unreg* (*Uhr*) stop; (*Zeit*) stand still; (*Auto, Zug*) stand; (*Fehler*) stay as it is.

stehend *a attr* (*Fahrzeug*) stationary; (*Gewässer*) stagnant; (*ständig:* *Heer*) regular.

stehenlassen *vt unreg* leave; (*Bart*) grow; **alles stehen- und liegenlassen** drop everything.

Stehlampe *f* floor lamp.

stehlen [ʃtäː'lən] *vt unreg* steal.

Steh- *zW:* **~platz** *m:* **ein ~platz kostet 10 Mark** a ticket for standing room costs 10 marks; **~vermögen** *nt* staying power, stamina.

steif [ʃtīf] *a* stiff; **~ und fest auf etw** (*dat*) **beharren** insist stubbornly on sth; **S~heit** *f* stiffness; **S~tier** *nt* ® soft toy animal.

Steigbügel [ʃtīk'büːgəl] *m* stirrup.

Steige [ʃtī'gə] *f* -, -n (*Straße*) steep road; (*Kiste*) crate.

Steigei'sen *nt* crampon.

steigen *vi unreg* rise; (*klettern*) climb; **das Blut stieg ihm in den Kopf** the blood rushed to his head; **~ in** (+*akk*)/**auf** (+*akk*) get in/ on ♦ *vt* (*Treppen, Stufen*) climb (up).

Steiger *m* -s, - (*MIN*) pit foreman.

steigern *vt* raise; (*GRAM*) compare ♦ *vi* (*Auktion*) bid ♦ *vr* increase.

Steigerung *f* raising; (*GRAM*) comparison.

Steigung *f* incline, gradient, rise.

steil [ʃtīl] *a* steep; **S~hang** *m* steep slope; **S~paß** *m* (*SPORT*) long pass.

Stein [ʃtīn] *m* -(e)s, -e stone; (*in Uhr*) jewel; **mir fällt ein ~ vom Herzen!** (*fig*) that's a load off my mind!; **bei jdm einen ~ im Brett haben** (*fig umg*) be well in with sb; **jdm ~e in den Weg legen** make things difficult for sb; **~adler** *m* golden eagle; **s~alt** *a* ancient; **~bock** *m* (*ASTROL*) Capricorn; **~bruch** *m* quarry.

steinern *a* (made of) stone; (*fig*) stony.

Stein- *zW:* **~erweichen** *nt:* **zum ~erweichen weinen** cry heartbreakingly; **~garten** *m* rockery; **~gut** *nt* stoneware; **s~hart** *a* hard as stone.

steinig *a* stony; **~en** *vt* stone.

Stein- *zW:* **~metz** *m* -es, -e stonemason; **s~reich** *a* (*umg*) stinking rich; **~schlag** *m:* „**Achtung ~schlag**" "danger – falling rock"; **~wurf** *m* (*fig*) stone's throw.

Steiß [ʃtīs] *m* -es, -e rump; **~bein** *nt* (*ANAT*) coccyx.

Stelle [ʃte'lə] *f* -, -n place; (*Arbeit*) post,

job; (*Amt*) office; (*Abschnitt*) passage; (*Text~, bes beim Zitieren*) reference; **drei ~n hinter dem Komma** (*MATH*) three decimal places; **eine freie** *od* **offene ~** a vacancy; **an dieser ~** in this place, here; **an anderer ~** elsewhere; **nicht von der ~ kommen** not make any progress; **auf der ~** (*fig: sofort*) on the spot.

stellen *vt* put; (*Uhr etc*) set; (*zur Verfügung ~*) supply; (*fassen: Dieb*) apprehend; (*Antrag, Forderung*) make; (*Aufnahme*) pose; (*arrangieren: Szene*) arrange; **das Radio lauter/leiser ~** turn the radio up/down; **auf sich** (*akk*) **selbst gestellt sein** (*fig*) have to fend for o.s. ♦ *vr* (*sich auf~*) stand; (*sich einfinden*) present o.s.; (*bei Polizei*) give o.s. up; (*vorgeben*) pretend (to be); **sich hinter jdn/etw ~** (*fig*) support sb/sth; **sich einer Herausforderung ~** take up a challenge; **sich zu etw ~** have an opinion of sth.

Stellen- *zW:* **~angebot** *nt* offer of a post; (*Zeitung*) vacancies; **~anzeige** *f* job advertisement *od* ad (*umg*); **~gesuch** *nt* application for a post; „**~gesuche**" "work wanted"; **~markt** *m* job market; (*in Zeitung*) appointments section; **~nachweis** *m*, **~vermittlung** *f* employment agency; **s~weise** *ad* in places; **~wert** *m* (*fig*) status.

Stellung *f* position; (*MIL*) line; **~ nehmen zu** comment on.

Stellungnahme *f* comment.

stellv. *abk* = **stellvertretend.**

Stell- *zW:* **s~vertretend** *a* deputy *attr*, acting *attr*; **~vertreter** *m* (*von Amts wegen*) deputy, (acting) representative; **~werk** *nt* (*EISENB*) switch tower (*US*), signal box (*Brit*).

Stelze [ʃtel'tsə] *f* -, -n stilt.

stelzen *vi* (*umg*) stalk.

Stemm- [ʃtem'] *zW:* **~bogen** *m* (*SKI*) stem turn; **~eisen** *nt* crowbar.

stemmen *vt* lift (up); (*drücken*) press; **sich ~ gegen** (*fig*) resist, oppose.

Stempel [ʃtem'pəl] *m* -s, - stamp; (*Post~*) postmark; (*TECH*: *Präge~*) die; (*BOT*) pistil; **~gebühr** *f* stamp duty; **~kissen** *nt* inkpad.

stempeln *vt* stamp; (*Briefmarke*) cancel ♦ *vi* (*umg: Stempeluhr betätigen*) clock in *od* out; **~ gehen** (*umg*) be *od* go on welfare.

Stengel [ʃte'ngəl] *m* -s, - stalk; **vom ~ fallen** (*umg: überrascht sein*) be staggered.

Steno [ʃtä'nō] *f* (*umg*) shorthand.

Steno- [ʃtänō] *zW:* **~gramm** [-gràm'] *nt* shorthand report; **~graph(in** *f*) [-gràf'(in)] *m* (*im Büro*) shorthand secretary; **~graphie** [-gràfēː'] *f* shorthand; **s~graphieren** [-gràfēː'rən] *vti* write (in) shorthand; **~typist(in** *f*) [-tüpist'(in)] *m* stenographer (*US*), shorthand typist (*Brit*).

Steppdecke *f* quilt.

Steppe *f* -, -n steppe.

steppen [ʃte'pən] *vt* stitch ♦ *vi* tap-dance.

Steptanz *m* tap-dance.

Sterbe- *zW:* **~bett** *nt* deathbed; **~fall** *m*

death; ~**hilfe** f euthanasia; ~**kasse** f death benefit fund.

sterben [shter'bən] vi unreg die; **an einer Krankheit/Verletzung** ~ to die of an illness/from an injury; **er ist für mich gestorben** (fig umg) he might as well be dead.

Sterben nt: **im** ~ **liegen** be dying.

Sterbens- zW: **s~langweilig** a (umg) deadly boring; ~**wörtchen** nt (umg): **er hat kein** ~**wörtchen gesagt** he didn't say a word.

Sterbeur'kunde f -, -n death certificate.

sterblich [shter'pliçh] a mortal; **S~keit** f mortality; **S~keitsziffer** f death rate.

stereo- [stā:'rāō] in zW stereo(-); **S~anlage** f stereo unit; ~**typ** [stārāōtü:p'] a stereotyped.

steril [shtārē:l'] a sterile.

sterilisieren [shtārēlēzē:'rən] vt sterilize.

Sterilisierung f sterilization.

Stern [shtern] m -(e)s, -e star; **das steht (noch) in den** ~**en** (fig) it's in the lap of the gods; ~**bild** nt constellation; ~**chen** nt asterisk; ~**schnuppe** f -, -n meteor, falling star; ~**stunde** f historic moment; ~**warte** f observatory; ~**zeichen** nt (ASTROL) sign of the zodiac.

stet [shtā:t] a steady.

Stethoskop [shtātōskō:p'] nt -(e)s, -e stethoscope.

stetig a constant, continual; (MATH: Funktion) continuous.

stets ad continually, always.

Steuer [shtoi'ər] nt -s, - (NAUT) helm; (~**ruder**) rudder; (AUT) steering wheel; **am** ~ **sitzen** (umg: AUT) be at the wheel; (: AVIAT) be at the controls ♦ f -, -n tax; ~**befreiung** f tax exemption; **s~begünstigt** a (Investitionen, Hypothek) tax-deductible; (Waren) taxed at a lower rate; ~**berater(in** f) m tax consultant; ~**bescheid** m tax assessment; ~**bord** nt starboard; ~**erklärung** f tax return; ~**frei** a tax-free; ~**freibetrag** m tax allowance; ~**hinterziehung** f tax evasion; ~**jahr** nt fiscal od tax year; ~**karte** f tax notice; ~**klasse** f tax band; ~**knüppel** m control column; (AVIAT, COMPUT) joystick; **s~lich** a tax attr; ~**mann** m, pl -**männer** od -**leute** helmsman.

steuern vti steer; (Flugzeug) pilot; (Entwicklung, Tonstärke) control.

Steuer- zW: ~**nummer** nt ≈ Social Security Number; ~**paradies** nt tax haven; **s~pflichtig** a taxable; (Person) liable to pay tax; ~**progression** f progressive taxation; ~**prüfung** f I.R.S. audit (US), Inland Revenue investigation (Brit); ~**rad** nt steering wheel; ~**rückvergütung** f tax rebate.

Steuerung f (auch AUT) steering; piloting; control; (Vorrichtung) controls pl; **automatische** ~ (AVIAT) autopilot; (TECH) automatic steering (device).

Steuer- zW: ~**vergünstigung** f tax relief; ~**zahler** m taxpayer; ~**zuschlag** m additional tax.

Steward [styōō:'ərt] m -s, -s steward.

Stewardeß [styōō:'ərdes] f -, -**essen** stewardess, air hostess.

StGB nt -s abk = **Strafgesetzbuch**.

stibitzen [shtēbi'tsən] vt (umg) pilfer, pinch (umg).

Stich [shtiçh] m -(e)s, -e (Insekten~) sting; (Messer~) stab; (beim Nähen) stitch; (Färbung) tinge; (KARTEN) trick; (ART) engraving; (fig) pang; **ein** ~ **ins Rote** a tinge of red; **einen** ~ **haben** (Eßwaren) be bad; (umg: Mensch: verrückt sein) be nuts; **jdn im** ~ **lassen** leave sb in the lurch.

Stichel m -s, - engraving tool, style.

Stichelei [shtiçhəlī'] f jibe, taunt.

sticheln vi (fig) jibe; (pej umg) make snide remarks.

Stich- zW: ~**flamme** f tongue of flame; **s~haltig** a valid; (Beweis) conclusive; ~**probe** f spot check.

sticht [shtiçht] 3. pers sing präs von **stechen**.

Stich- zW: ~**tag** m qualifying date, deadline; ~**wahl** f run-off election (US), final ballot.

Stichwort nt -s, -**worte** cue; pl -**wörter** (in Wörterbuch) headword; pl -**worte** (für Vortrag) note; ~**katalog** m classified catalog; ~**verzeichnis** nt index.

Stichwunde f stab wound.

sticken [shti'kən] vti embroider.

Stickerei' f embroidery.

stickig a stuffy, close.

Stickstoff m nitrogen.

stieben [shtē:'bən] vi (geh: sprühen) fly.

Stiefel [shtē:'fəl] m -s, - boot; (Trinkgefäß) large boot-shaped beer glass.

Stief- [shtē:f'] in zW step; **s~kind** nt stepchild; (fig) Cinderella; ~**mutter** f stepmother; ~**mütterchen** nt pansy; **s~mütterlich** a (fig): **jdn/etw s~mütterlich behandeln** pay little attention to sb/sth.

stieg [shtē:k] imperf von **steigen**.

Stiege [shtē:'gə] f -, -n staircase.

Stieglitz [shtē:'glits] m -es, -e goldfinch.

stiehlt [shtē:lt] 3. pers sing präs von **stehlen**.

Stiel [shtē:l] m -(e)s, -e handle; (BOT) stalk.

Stielau'gen pl (fig umg): **er machte** ~ his eyes (nearly) popped out of his head.

stier [shtē:r] a staring, fixed.

Stier m -(e)s, -e bull; (ASTROL) Taurus.

stieren vi stare.

stieß [shtē:s] imperf von **stoßen**.

Stift [shtift] m -(e)s, -e peg; (Nagel) tack; (Farb~) crayon; (Blei~) pencil; (umg: Lehrling) apprentice (boy).

stiften vt found; (Unruhe) cause; (spenden) contribute; ~**gehen** vi unreg (umg) take off.

Stifter(in f) m -s, - founder.

Stiftung f donation; (Organisation) foundation.

Stiftzahn m post crown.

Stil [shtē:l] m -(e)s, -e style; (Eigenart) way, manner; ~**blüte** f real boner (US), howler; ~**bruch** m stylistic incongruity.

stilistisch [shtēlis'tish] a stylistic.

still [shtil] a quiet; (unbewegt) still;

(*heimlich*) secret; **ich dachte mir im ~en** I thought to myself; **er ist ein ~es Wasser** he's a deep one; **~er Teilhaber** (*COMM*) silent (*US*) *od* sleeping (*Brit*) partner; **der S~e Ozean** the Pacific (Ocean).

Stille *f* -, **-n** stillness; quietness; **in aller ~** quietly.

Stilleben = **Still(l)eben**.

Stillegung = **Still(l)egung**.

stillen *vt* stop; (*befriedigen*) satisfy; (*Säugling*) breast-feed.

still- *zW*: **~gestanden** *interj* attention; **S~halteabkommen** *nt* (*FIN, fig*) moratorium; **~halten** *vi unreg* keep still; **S~(l)eben** *nt* still life; **~(l)egen** *vt* close down; **S~(l)egung** *f* (*Betrieb*) shut-down, closure.

still(l)iegen *vi unreg* (*außer Betrieb sein*) be shut down; (*lahmliegen*) be at a standstill.

still- *zW*: **~schweigen** *vi unreg* be silent; **S~schweigen** *nt* silence; **~schweigend** *a, ad* silent(ly); (*Einverständnis*) tacit(ly); **S~stand** *m* standstill; **~stehen** *vi unreg* stand still.

Stilmöbel *pl* period furniture *sing*.

Stimm- *zW*: **~abgabe** *f* voting; **~bänder** *pl* vocal cords *pl*; **s~berechtigt** *a* entitled to vote; **~bruch** *m*: **er ist im ~bruch** his voice is breaking.

Stimme [ʃtɪˈmə] *f* -, **-n** voice; (*Wahl~*) vote; (*MUS: Rolle*) part; **mit leiser/lauter ~** in a soft/loud voice; **seine ~ abgeben** vote.

stimmen *vi* (*richtig sein*) be right; (*wählen*) vote; **stimmt so!** that's all right; **für/gegen etw ~** vote for/against sth ♦ *vt* (*Instrument*) tune; **jdn traurig ~** make sb feel sad.

Stimmen- *zW*: **~gewirr** *nt* babble of voices; **~gleichheit** *f* tied vote; **~mehrheit** *f* majority (of votes).

Stimm- *zW*: **~enthaltung** *f* abstention; **~gabel** *f* tuning fork; **s~haft** *a* voiced.

stimmig *a* harmonious.

Stimm- *zW*: **s~los** *a* (*LING*) unvoiced; **~recht** *nt* right to vote; **s~rechtslos** *a*: **s~rechtslose Aktien** non-voting shares.

Stimmung *f* mood; (*Atmosphäre*) atmosphere; (*Moral*) morale; **in ~ kommen** liven up; **~ gegen/für jdn/etw machen** stir up (public) opinion against/in favour of sb/sth.

Stimmungs- *zW*: **~kanone** *f* (*umg*) life and soul of the party; **~mache** *f* (*pej*) cheap propaganda; **s~voll** *a* (*Atmosphäre*) enjoyable; (*Gedicht*) full of atmosphere.

Stimmzettel *m* ballot paper.

stinken [ʃtɪŋkən] *vi unreg* stink; **die Sache stinkt mir** (*umg*) I'm fed-up to the back teeth (with it).

Stink- *zW*: **s~faul** *a* (*umg*) bone-lazy; **s~langweilig** *a* (*umg*) deadly boring; **~tier** *nt* skunk; **~wut** *f* (*umg*): **eine ~wut haben** be livid (*auf jdn* with sb).

Stipendium [ʃtɪˈpɛndiˌoːm] *nt* grant; (*als Auszeichnung erhalten*) scholarship.

stirbt [ʃtɪrpt] *3. pers sing präs von* **sterben**.

Stirn [ʃtɪrn] *f* -, **-en** forehead, brow; (*Frechheit*) impudence; **die ~ haben zu ...** have the nerve to ...; **~höhle** *f* sinus; **~runzeln** *nt* -s frown.

St.-Nr. *abk* (= *Steuernummer*) ≈ Social Security Number.

stob [ʃtoːp] *imperf von* **stieben**.

stöbern [ʃtœˈbərn] *vi* rummage.

stochern [ʃtoˈxərn] *vi* poke (about).

Stock [ʃtɔk] *m* **-(e)s,** ⁼e stick; (*Rohr~*) cane; (*Zeige~*) pointer; (*BOT*) stock; **über ~ und Stein** up hill and down dale; *pl* **-werke** story (*US*), storey (*Brit*); **im ersten ~** on the second (*US*) *od* first (*Brit*) floor.

stock- *in zW vor a* (*umg*) completely.

Stöckelschuh [ʃtœˈkəlʃoː] *m* stiletto-heeled shoe.

stocken *vi* stop, pause; (*Arbeit, Entwicklung*) make no progress; (*im Satz*) break off; (*Verkehr*) be held up.

stockend *a* halting.

stock'fin'ster *a* (*umg*) pitch-dark.

Stockholm [ʃtɔkˈhɔlm] *nt* -s Stockholm.

Stock'- *zW*: **s~sauer** *a* (*umg*) pissed-off (*!*); **s~taub** *a* stone-deaf; **~ung** *f* stoppage; **~werk** *nt* story (*US*), storey (*Brit*), floor.

Stoff [ʃtɔf] *m* **-(e)s, -e** (*Gewebe*) material, cloth; (*Materie*) matter; (*von Buch etc*) subject (matter); (*umg: Rauschgift*) dope.

Stoffel *m* -s, - (*pej umg*) lout, boor.

stofflich *a* with regard to subject matter.

Stoffrest *m* remnant.

Stoffwechsel *m* metabolism.

stöhnen [ʃtœˈnən] *vi* groan.

stoisch [ʃtoːˈɪʃ] *a* stoical.

Stola [ʃtoːˈlà] *f* -, **Stolen** stole.

Stollen [ʃtoˈlən] *m* -s, - (*MIN*) gallery; (*KOCH*) stollen, *cake eaten at Christmas*; (*von Schuhen*) stud.

stolpern [ʃtɔlˈpərn] *vi* stumble, trip; (*fig: zu Fall kommen*) fall on one's face.

stolz [ʃtɔlts] *a* proud; (*imposant: Bauwerk*) majestic; (*ironisch: Preis*) princely; **S~** *m* **-es** pride.

stolzieren [ʃtɔltsɛːˈrən] *vi* strut.

stopfen [ʃtoˈpfən] *vt* (*hinein~*) stuff; (*voll~*) fill (up); (*nähen*) darn; **jdm das Maul ~** (*umg*) silence sb ♦ *vi* (*MED*) cause constipation.

Stopfgarn *nt* darning thread.

Stopp [ʃtɔp] *m* -s, -s stop, halt; (*Lohn~*) freeze.

Stoppel [ʃtoˈpəl] *f* -, **-n** stubble.

stoppen *vti* stop; (*mit Uhr*) time.

Stopp- *zW*: **~schild** *nt* stop sign; **~uhr** *f* stopwatch.

Stöpsel [ʃtɛpˈsəl] *m* **-s,** - plug; (*für Flaschen*) stopper.

Stör [ʃtœr] *m* **-(e)s, -e** sturgeon.

Stör- *zW*: **~aktion** *f* disruptive action; **s~anfällig** *a* susceptible to interference *od* breakdown.

Storch [ʃtɔrç] *m* **-(e)s,** ⁼e stork.

Store [ʃtoːr] *m* -s, -s net curtain.

stören [shtœ'rən] *vt* disturb; (*behindern*, *RAD*) interfere with; **was mich an ihm/ daran stört** what I don't like about him/it; **stört es Sie, wenn ich rauche?** do you mind if I smoke? ♦ *vr*: **sich an etw** (*dat*) ~ let sth bother one ♦ *vi* get in the way; **ich möchte nicht** ~ I don't want to be in the way.

störend *a* disturbing, annoying.

Störenfried *m* -(e)s, -e troublemaker.

Störfall *m* case *od* incidence of interference *od* breakdown.

stornieren [shtornē:'rən] *vti* (*COMM: Auftrag*) cancel; (: *Buchungsfehler*) reverse.

Storno [shtor'nō] *m od nt* -s (*COMM: von Buchungsfehler*) reversal; (: *von Auftrag*) cancelation (*US*), cancellation (*Brit*).

störrig [shtœ'riçh], **störrisch** [shtœ'rish] *a* stubborn, perverse.

Störsender *m* jammer, transmitter.

Störung *f* disturbance; interference; (*TECH*) fault; (*MED*) disorder.

Störungsstelle *f* (*TEL*) repair service.

Stoß [shtō:s] *m* -es, ⁼e (*Schub*) push; (*leicht*) poke; (*Schlag*) blow; knock; (*mit Schwert*) thrust; (*mit Ellbogen*) nudge; (*mit Fuß*) kick; (*Erd*~) shock; (*Haufen*) pile; **seinem Herzen einen** ~ **geben** pluck up courage; ~**dämpfer** *m* shock absorber.

Stößel [shtœ'səl] *m* -s, - pestle; (*AUT*: *Ventil*~) tappet.

stoßen *unreg vt* (*mit Druck*) shove, push; (*mit Schlag*) knock, bump; (*mit Ellbogen*) nudge; (*mit Fuß*) kick; (*mit Schwert*) thrust; (*an*~: *Kopf etc*) bump; (*zerkleinern*) pulverize ♦ *vr* get a knock; **sich** ~ **an** (+*dat*) (*fig*) take exception to ♦ *vi*: ~ **an** *od* **auf** (+*akk*) bump into; (*finden*) come across; (*angrenzen*) be next to; **zu jdm** ~ meet up with sb.

Stoß- *zW*: ~**gebet** *nt* quick prayer; ~**stange** *f* (*AUT*) bumper.

stößt [shtœst] *2./3. pers sing präs von* **stoßen**.

Stoßzeit *f* (*im Verkehr*) rush hour; (*in Geschäft etc*) peak period.

Stotterer *m* -s, -, **Stotterin** *f* stutterer.

stottern [shto'tərn] *vti* stutter.

Stövchen [shtœf'çhən] *nt* -s, - (teapot- *etc*) warmer.

StPO *abk* = **Strafprozeßordnung**.

Str. *abk* (= *Straße*) St.

StR *abk* = **Studienrat**.

stracks [shtráks] *ad* straight.

Straf- *zW*: ~**anstalt** *f* penal institution; ~**arbeit** *f* (*SCH*) punishment exercise; ~**bank** *f* (*SPORT*) penalty box *od* bench; s~**bar** *a* punishable; **sich s~bar machen** commit an offense; ~**barkeit** *f* criminal nature.

Strafe [shtrâ'fə] *f* -, -n punishment; (*JUR*) penalty; (*Gefängnis*~) sentence; (*Geld*~) fine; **... bei** ~ **verboten** ... forbidden; **100 Dollar** ~ **zahlen** pay a $100 fine; **er hat seine** ~ **weg** (*umg*) he's had his punishment.

strafen *vti* punish; **mit etw gestraft sein** be cursed with sth.

strafend *a attr* punitive; (*Blick*) reproachful.

straff [shtráf] *a* tight; (*streng*) strict; (*Stil etc*) concise; (*Haltung*) erect.

straffällig [shtráf'felíçh] *a*: ~ **werden** commit a criminal offense.

straffen *vt* tighten; tauten.

Straf- *zW*: s~**frei** *a*: s~**frei ausgehen** go unpunished; ~**gefangene(r)** *mf* prisoner, convict; ~**gesetzbuch** *nt* penal code; ~**kolonie** *f* penal colony.

Sträf- [shtre:f'] *zW*: s~**lich** *a* criminal ♦ *ad* (*vernachlässigen etc*) criminally; ~**ling** *m* convict.

Straf- *zW*: ~**mandat** *nt* ticket; ~**maß** *nt* sentence; s~**mildernd** *a* mitigating; ~**porto** *nt* excess postage (charge); ~**predigt** *f* severe lecture; ~**prozeßordnung** *f* code of criminal procedure; ~**raum** *m* (*FUSSBALL*) penalty area; ~**recht** *nt* criminal law; s~**rechtlich** *a* criminal; ~**stoß** *m* (*SPORT*) penalty (kick); ~**tat** *f* punishable act; s~**versetzen** *vt untr* (*Beamte*) transfer for disciplinary reasons; ~**vollzug** *m* penal system; ~**zettel** *m* (*umg*) ticket.

Strahl [shtrál] *m* -(e)s, -en ray, beam; (*Wasser*~) jet.

strahlen *vi* (*Kernreaktor*) radiate; (*Sonne*, *Licht*) shine; (*fig*) beam.

Strahlen- *zW*: ~**behandlung** *f* radiotherapy; ~**dosis** *f* radiation dose; ~**furcht** *f* fear of radiation; s~**geschädigt** *a* suffering from radiation damage; ~**opfer** *nt* victim of radiation; ~**schutz** *m* radiation protection; ~**therapie** *f* radiotherapy.

Strahlung *f* radiation.

Strähnchen [shtre:n'çhən] *pl* strands (of hair).

Strähne *f* -, -n strand.

strähnig *a* (*Haar*) straggly.

stramm [shtrám] *a* tight; (*Haltung*) erect; (*Mensch*) robust; ~**stehen** *vi unreg* (*MIL*) stand to attention.

Strampelhöschen *nt* rompers *pl*.

strampeln [shtrám'pəln] *vi* kick (about), fidget.

Strand [shtránt] *m* -(e)s, ⁼e shore; (*Meeres*~) beach; **am** ~ on the beach; ~**bad** *nt* open-air swimming pool; (*Badeort*) bathing resort.

stranden [shtrán'dən] *vi* run aground; (*fig*: *Mensch*) fail.

Strand- *zW*: ~**gut** *nt* flotsam; ~**korb** *m* beach chair.

Strang [shtráng] *m* -(e)s, ⁼e (*Nerven*~, *Muskel*~) cord; (*Schienen*~) track; **über die** ⁼**e schlagen** run riot (*umg*); **an einem** ~ **ziehen** (*fig*) be in the same boat.

strangulieren [shtránggōōlē:'rən] *vt* strangle.

Strapaze [shtrápá'tsə] *f* -, -n strain.

strapazieren [shtrápátsē:'rən] *vt* (*Material*) treat roughly; punish; (*Mensch*, *Kräfte*) wear out, exhaust.

strapazierfähig a hard-wearing.
strapaziös [shtrápátsœœs'] a exhausting, tough.
Straßburg [shtrâs'bŏŏrk] nt -s Strasbourg.
Straße [shtrâ'sə] f -, -n street; road; **auf der ~ in** the street; **auf der ~ liegen** (fig umg) be out of work; **auf die ~ gesetzt werden** (umg) be turned out (onto the streets).
Straßen- zW: **~bahn** f streetcar (US), tram (Brit); **~bauarbeiten** pl roadwork sing (US), roadworks pl (Brit); **~beleuchtung** f street lighting; **~feger** m -s, - roadsweeper; **~glätte** f slippery road surface; **~junge** m (pej) street urchin; **~kehrer** m -s, - roadsweeper; **~kreuzer** m (umg) limousine; **~mädchen** nt streetwalker; **~rand** m road side; **~sperre** f roadblock; **~überführung** f footbridge; **~verkehrsordnung** f traffic regulations; **~zustandsbericht** m road report.
Stratege [shtrátä:'gə] m -n, -n strategist.
Strategie [shtrátägē:'] f strategy.
strategisch a strategic.
Stratosphäre [shtrátōsfe:'rə] f - stratosphere.
sträuben [shtroi'bən] vt ruffle ♦ vr bristle; (Mensch) resist (gegen etw sth).
Strauch [shtroukh] m -(e)s, Sträucher bush, shrub.
straucheln [shtrou'khəln] vi stumble, stagger.
Strauß [shtrous] m -es, Sträuße (Blumen~) bouquet, bunch; pl -e ostrich.
Strebe [shträ:'bə] f -, -n strut.
Strebebalken m buttress.
streben vi strive (nach for), endeavor (US), endeavour (Brit); **~ zu** od **nach** (sich bewegen) make for.
Strebepfeiler m buttress.
Streber m -s, - (pej) pushy person; (SCH) crammer.
strebsam a industrious; **S~keit** f industry.
Strecke [shtre'kə] f -, -n stretch; (Entfernung) distance; (EISENB, MATH) line; **auf der ~ Paris-Brüssel** on the way from Paris to Brussels; **auf der ~ bleiben** (fig) fall by the wayside; **zur ~ bringen** (Jagd) bag.
strecken vt stretch; (Waffen) lay down; (KOCH) eke out ♦ vr stretch (o.s.) ♦ vi (SCH) put one's hand up; **~weise** ad in parts.
Streich [shtrīkh] m -(e)s, -e trick, prank; (Hieb) blow; **jdm einen ~ spielen** (lit) play a trick on sb.
streicheln vt stroke.
streichen unreg vt (berühren) stroke; (auftragen) spread; (anmalen) paint; (durch~) delete; (nicht genehmigen) cancel; (Schulden) write off; (Zuschuß etc) cut; **etw glatt ~** smooth sth (out) ♦ vi (berühren) brush; (schleichen) prowl.
Streicher pl (MUS) strings pl.
Streich- zW: **~holz** nt match; **~instrument** nt string instrument; **~käse** m cheese spread.
Streif- zW: **~band** nt wrapper; **~bandzeitung** f newspaper sent at printed

paper rate.
Streife f -, -n patrol.
streifen [shtri'fən] vt (leicht berühren) brush against, graze; (Blick) skim over; (Thema, Problem) touch on; (ab~) take off ♦ vi (gehen) roam.
Streifen m -s, - (Linie) stripe; (Stück) strip; (Film) film; **~dienst** m patrol duty; **~wagen** m patrol car.
Streif- zW: **~schuß** m graze, grazing shot; **~zug** m scouting trip; (Bummel) expedition; (fig: kurzer Überblick) brief survey (durch of).
Streik [shtrīk] m -(e)s, -s strike; **in den ~ treten** come out on strike, strike; **~brecher** m strikebreaker; **s~en** vi strike; **der Computer streikt** the computer's packed up (umg) od on the blink (umg); **da streike ich** (umg) no way!; **~kasse** f strike fund; **~maßnahmen** pl industrial action sing; **~posten** m (peaceful) picket.
Streit [shtrīt] m -(e)s, -e argument; (Auseinandersetzung) dispute.
streiten vir unreg argue; dispute; **darüber läßt sich ~** that's debatable.
Streit- zW: **~frage** f point at issue; **~gespräch** nt debate.
streitig a: **jdm etw ~ machen** dispute sb's right to sth; **S~keiten** pl quarrel sing, dispute sing.
Streit- zW: **~kräfte** pl (MIL) armed forces pl; **s~lustig** a quarrelsome; **~punkt** m contentious issue; **~sucht** f quarrelsomeness.
streng [shtreng] a severe; (Lehrer, Maßnahme) strict; (Geruch etc) sharp; **~ geheim** top-secret; **~ verboten!** strictly prohibited.
Strenge f - severity; strictness; sharpness.
streng- zW: **~genommen** ad strictly speaking; **~gläubig** a strict.
Streß [shtres] m -sses, -sse stress.
stressen vt put under stress.
streßfrei a without stress.
Streu [shtroi] f -, -en litter, bed of straw.
streuen vt strew, scatter, spread ♦ vi (mit Streupulver) grit; (mit Salz) put down salt.
Streuer m -s, - shaker; (Salz~) cellar; (Pfeffer~) pot.
Streufahrzeug nt sander.
streunen vi roam about; (Hund, Katze) stray.
Streupulver nt -s grit od sand for road.
Streuselkuchen [shtroi'zəlkŏŏ:khən] m cake with crumble topping.
Streuung f dispersion; (Statistik) mean variation; (PHYS) scattering.
strich [shtrikh] imperf von **streichen**.
Strich m -(e)s, -e (Linie) line; (Feder~, Pinsel~) stroke; (von Geweben) nap; (von Fell) pile; (Quer~) dash; (Schräg~) slash; **jdm einen ~ durch die Rechnung machen** thwart sb's plans; **einen ~ (unter etw akk) machen** (fig) forget sth; **nach ~ und Faden** (umg) good and proper; **auf den ~ gehen**

(*umg*) walk the streets; **jdm gegen den ~ gehen** rub sb up the wrong way; **einen ~ machen durch** (*lit*) cross out; (*fig*) foil; ~**einteilung** *f* calibration.

stricheln [ʃtriˈçəln] *vti*: **eine gestrichelte Linie** a broken line.

Strich- *zW*: ~**junge** *m* (*umg*) male prostitute; ~**mädchen** *nt* streetwalker; ~**punkt** *m* semicolon; **s~weise** *ad* here and there; **s~weise Regen** (*MET*) rain in places.

Strick [ʃtrik] *m* **-(e)s, -e** rope; **jdm aus etw einen ~ drehen** use sth against sb.

stricken *vti* knit.

Strick- *zW*: ~**jacke** *f* cardigan; ~**leiter** *f* rope ladder; ~**nadel** *f* knitting needle; ~**waren** *pl* knitwear *sing*.

striegeln [ʃtrɛːˈgəln] *vr* (*umg*) spruce o.s. up.

Strieme [ʃtrɛːˈmə] *f* **-, -n** welt, weal.

strikt [ʃtrikt] *a* strict.

Strippe [ʃtriˈpə] *f* **-, -n** (*TEL umg*): **jdn an der ~ haben** have sb on the line.

Stripper(in *f*) *m* **-s, -** stripper.

stritt [ʃtrit] *imperf von* **streiten**.

strittig [ʃtriˈtiç] *a* disputed, in dispute.

Stroh [ʃtroː] *nt* **-(e)s** straw; ~**blume** *f* everlasting flower; ~**dach** *nt* thatched roof; **s~dumm** *a* (*umg*) thick; ~**feuer** *nt*: **ein ~feuer sein** (*fig*) be a passing fancy; ~**halm** *m* (drinking) straw; ~**mann** *m*, *pl* **-männer** (*COMM, KARTEN*) dummy; front man; ~**witwe** *f* grass widow; ~**witwer** *m* grass widower.

Strolch [ʃtrɔlç] *m* **-(e)s, -e** (*pej*) rogue, rascal.

Strom [ʃtroːm] *m* **-(e)s, ⁼e** river; (*fig*) stream; (*ELEK*) current; **unter ~ stehen** (*ELEK*) be live; (*fig*) be excited; **der Wein floß in ⁼en** the wine flowed like water; **in ⁼en regnen** be pouring with rain; **s~abwärts** [-ˈápˈvɛrts] *ad* downstream; ~**anschluß** *m*: ~**anschluß haben** be connected to the electricity mains; **s~aufwärts** [-ˈoufˈvɛrts] *ad* upstream; ~**ausfall** *m* power failure; ~**bedarf** *m* electricity consumption.

strömen [ʃtrœˈmən] *vi* stream, pour.

Strom- *zW*: ~**kabel** *nt* electric cable; ~**kreis** *m* (electrical) circuit; **s~linienförmig** *a* streamlined; ~**netz** *nt* power supply system; ~**rechnung** *f* electricity bill; ~**schnelle** *f* rapids *pl*; ~**sperre** *f* power cut; ~**stärke** *f* amperage.

Strömung [ʃtrœˈmoːŋg] *f* current.

Stromzähler *m* electricity meter.

Strophe [ʃtroːˈfə] *f* **-, -n** verse.

strotzen [ʃtroˈtsən] *vi:* ~ **vor** *od* **von** abound in, be full of.

Strudel [ʃtruːˈdəl] *m* **-s, -** whirlpool, vortex; (*KOCH*) strudel.

strudeln *vi* swirl, eddy.

Struktur [ʃtrukˈtoːr'] *f* structure.

strukturell [ʃtruktoːˈrɛl'] *a* structural.

strukturieren [ʃtruktoːrɛːˈrən] *vt* structure.

Strumpf [ʃtroːmpf] *m* **-(e)s, ⁼e** stocking;

~**band** *nt* garter; ~**halter** *m* garter (*US*), suspender (*Brit*); ~**hose** *f* (pair of) pantihose *pl* (*US*) *od* tights *pl* (*Brit*).

Strunk [ʃtroːŋk] *m* **-(e)s, ⁼e** stump.

struppig [ʃtruːˈpiç] *a* shaggy, unkempt.

Stube [ʃtoːˈbə] *f* **-, -n** room; **die gute ~** the parlor (*veraltet: US*) *od* parlour (: *Brit*).

Stuben- *zW*: ~**arrest** *m* confinement to one's room; (*MIL*) confinement to quarters; ~**fliege** *f* (common) housefly; ~**hocker** *m* (*umg*) stay-at-home; **s~rein** *a* house-trained.

Stuck [ʃtoːk] *m* **-(e)s** stucco.

Stück [ʃtük] *nt* **-(e)s, -e** piece; (*etwas*) bit; (*THEAT*) play; **am ~** in one piece; **das ist ein starkes ~!** (*umg*) that's a bit much!; **große ~e auf jdn halten** think highly of sb; ~**arbeit** *f* piecework; ~**gut** *nt* (*EISENB*) freight *od* parcel service; ~**kosten** *pl* unit cost *sing*; ~**lohn** *m* piecework rates *pl*; **s~weise** *ad* bit by bit, piecemeal; (*COMM*) individually; ~**werk** *nt* bits and pieces *pl*.

Student(in *f*) *m* [ʃtuˈdɛnt'(in)] *m* student.

Studenten- *zW*: ~**ausweis** *m* student identification card; ~**futter** *nt* nuts and raisins *pl*; ~**werk** *nt* student administration; ~**wohnheim** *nt* dormitory (*US*), hall of residence (*Brit*).

studentisch *a* student *attr*, academic.

Studie [ʃtuːˈdɛə] *f* study.

Studien- *zW*: ~**beratung** *f* course counseling (*US*) *od* guidance (*Brit*) service; ~**buch** *nt* (*UNIV*) book in which the courses one has attended are entered; ~**fahrt** *f* study trip; ~**platz** *m* university place; ~**rat** *m*, ~**rätin** *f* teacher at a high school.

studieren [ʃtuˈdɛːˈrən] *vti* study; **bei jdm ~** study under sb.

Studio [ʃtuːˈdɛoː] *nt* **-s, -s** studio.

Studium [ʃtuːˈdɛoːm] *nt* studies *pl*.

Stufe [ʃtuːˈfə] *f* **-, -n** step; (*Entwicklungs~*) stage; (*Niveau*) level.

Stufen- *zW*: ~**leiter** *f* (*fig*) ladder; ~**plan** *m* graduated plan (*zu* for); ~**schnitt** *m* (*Frisur*) layer cut; **s~weise** *ad* gradually.

Stuhl [ʃtoːl] *m* **-(e)s, ⁼e** chair; **zwischen zwei ⁼en sitzen** (*fig*) fall between two stools.

Stuhlgang *m* bowel movement.

Stuka [ʃtuːˈká] *m* **-s, -s** *abk* (= *Sturzkampfflugzeug*) Stuka, dive bomber.

Stukkateur [ʃtukaˈtœr'] *m* ornamental plasterer.

stülpen [ʃtülˈpən] *vt* (*bedecken*) put; **etw über etw** (*akk*) ~ put sth over sth; **den Kragen nach oben ~** turn up one's collar.

stumm [ʃtoːm] *a* silent; (*MED*) dumb.

Stummel *m* **-s, -** stump; (*Zigaretten~*) stub.

Stummfilm *m* silent movie.

Stümper(in *f*) *m* [ʃtümˈpər(in)] *m* **-s, -** incompetent, duffer; **s~haft** *a* bungling, incompetent.

stümpern *vi* (*umg*) bungle.

stumpf [ʃtoːmpf] *a* blunt; (*teilnahmslos, glanzlos*) dull; (*Winkel*) obtuse.

Stumpf *m* -(e)s, ̈e stump; **etw mit ~ und Stiel ausrotten** eradicate sth root and branch.

Stumpfsinn *m* -(e)s tediousness.

stumpfsinnig *a* dull.

Stunde [shtoͦon'də] *f* -, -n hour; (*Augenblick, Zeitpunkt*) time; (*SCH*) lesson, period (*Brit*); **~ um ~** hour after hour; **90 Meilen in der ~** 90 miles per hour.

stunden *vt*: **jdm etw ~** give sb time to pay sth.

Stunden- *zW*: **~geschwindigkeit** *f* average speed per hour; **~kilometer** *pl* kilometers per hour; **s~lang** *a* for hours; **~lohn** *m* hourly wage; **~plan** *m* timetable, schedule; **s~weise** *a* by the hour; (*stündlich*) every hour.

stündlich [shtün'tlicḥ] *a* hourly.

stupide [shtoͦopēː'də] *a* mindless.

Stups [shtoͦops] *m* -es, -e (*umg*) push.

stupsen *vt* nudge.

Stupsnase *f* snub nose.

stur [shtoͦoːr] *a* obstinate, stubborn; (*Nein, Arbeiten*) dogged; **er fuhr ~ geradeaus** he just carried straight on; **sich ~ stellen, auf ~ stellen** (*umg*) dig one's heels in; **ein ~er Bock** (*umg*) a pig-headed fellow.

Sturm [shtoͦorm] *m* -(e)s, ̈e storm, gale; (*MIL etc*) attack, assault; **~ läuten** keep one's finger on the doorbell; **gegen etw ~ laufen** (*fig*) be up in arms against sth.

stürmen [shtür'mən] *vi* (*Wind*) blow hard, rage; (*rennen*) storm ♦ *vt* (*MIL, fig*) storm ♦ *vi unpers*: **es stürmt** there's a gale blowing.

Stürmer *m* -s, - (*SPORT*) forward.

sturmfrei *a* (*MIL*) unassailable; **eine ~e Bude** (*umg*) a room free from disturbance.

stürmisch *a* stormy; (*fig*) tempestuous; (*Entwicklung*) rapid; (*Liebhaber*) passionate; (*Beifall*) tumultuous; **nicht so ~** take it easy.

Sturm- *zW*: **~schritt** *m* (*MIL, fig*): **im ~schritt** on the double; **~warnung** *f* gale warning; **~wind** *m* storm, gale.

Sturz [shtoͦorts] *m* -es, ̈e fall; (*POL*) overthrow; (*in Temperatur, Preis*) drop.

stürzen [shtür'tsən] *vt* (*werfen*) hurl; (*POL*) overthrow; (*umkehren*) overturn; **jdn ins Unglück ~** bring disaster upon sb; **„nicht ~!"** "this side up" ♦ *vr* rush; (*hinein~*) plunge; **sich auf jdn/etw ~** pounce on sb/sth; **sich in Unkosten ~** go to great expense ♦ *vi* fall; (*AVIAT*) dive; (*rennen*) dash.

Sturz- *zW*: **~flug** *m* nose dive; **~helm** *m* crash helmet.

Stuß [shtoͦos] *m* **Stusses** (*umg*) nonsense, rubbish.

Stute [shtoͦoː'tə] *f* -, -n mare.

Stuttgart [shtoͦoːt'gárt] *nt* -s Stuttgart.

Stützbalken *m* brace, joist.

Stütze [shtü'tsə] *f* -, -n support; (*Hilfe*) help; **die ~n der Gesellschaft** the pillars of society.

stutzen [shtoͦo'tsən] *vt* trim; (*Ohr, Schwanz*)

dock; (*Flügel*) clip ♦ *vi* hesitate; (*argwöhnisch werden*) become suspicious.

stützen *vt* (*lit, fig*) support; (*Ellbogen etc*) prop up ♦ *vr*: **sich auf jdn/etw ~** (*lit*) lean on sb/sth; (*Beweise, Theorie*) be based on sb/sth.

stutzig *a* perplexed, puzzled; (*mißtrauisch*) suspicious.

Stütz- *zW*: **~mauer** *f* supporting wall; **~punkt** *m* point of support; (*von Hebel*) fulcrum; (*MIL, fig*) base.

Stützungskäufe *pl* (*FIN*) support buying sing.

StV *abk* = **Stadtverwaltung; Stellvertreter.**

Stv., StV *abk* (= *Stellvertreter*) dep.

StVO *abk* = **Straßenverkehrsordnung.**

stylen [stī'lən] *vt* style.

Styropor [shtürōpōː'r] *nt* -s ® polystyrene.

SU *abk* (= *Sowjetunion*) SU.

s.u. *abk* (= *siehe unten*) see below.

Subjekt [zoͦopyekt'] *nt* -(e)s, -e subject; (*pej: Mensch*) character (*umg*).

subjektiv [zoͦopyektēːf'] *a* subjective.

Subjektivität [zoͦopyektēvēːtɛ:t'] *f* subjectivity.

Subkultur [zoͦop'koͦoltoͦoːr] *f* subculture.

sublimieren [zoͦoblēmēː'rən] *vt* (*CHEM, PSYCH*) sublimate.

Submissionsangebot [zoͦopmisēō:ns'-ángəbō:t] *nt* sealed-bid tender.

Subroutine [zoͦo'prōōtē:nə] *f* (*COMPUT*) subroutine.

Substantiv [zoͦopstántē:f'] *nt* -s, -e noun.

Substanz [zoͦopstánts'] *f* substance; **von der ~ zehren** live on one's capital.

subtil [zoͦoptē:l'] *a* subtle.

subtrahieren [zoͦoptráhēː'rən] *vt* subtract.

subtropisch [zoͦop'trō:pish] *a* subtropical.

Subunternehmer *m* subcontractor.

Subvention [zoͦopventsēō:n'] *f* subsidy.

subventionieren [zoͦopventsēōnēː'rən] *vt* subsidize.

subversiv [zoͦopverzē:f'] *a* subversive.

Such- *zW*: **~aktion** *f* search; **~dienst** *m* missing persons tracing service.

Suche *f* -, -n search.

suchen [zoͦoː'kḥən] *vti* look (for), seek; (*versuchen*) try; **du hast hier nichts zu ~** you have no business being here; **nach Worten ~** search for words; (*sprachlos sein*) be at a loss for words; **such!** (*zu Hund*) seek!, find!; **~ und ersetzen** (*COMPUT*) search and replace.

Sucher *m* -s, - seeker, searcher; (*PHOT*) viewfinder.

Suchscheinwerfer *m* searchlight.

Sucht [zoͦokḥt] *f* -, ̈e mania; (*MED*) addiction, craving.

süchtig [züchʹticḥ] *a* addicted; **S~e(r)** *mf dekl wie a* addict.

Süd [zü:t] *m* -(e)s south; **~afrika** *nt* South Africa; **~amerika** *nt* South America.

Sudan [zoͦodán'] *m* -s: **der ~** the Sudan.

Sudanese [zoͦodánäː'zə] *m* -n, -n, **Sudanesin** *f* Sudanese.

südd. *abk* = **süddeutsch.**
Süd- *zW*: **s~deutsch** *a* South German;
~deutschland *nt* South(ern) Germany.
Süden [zü:'dən] *m* **-s** south.
Süd- *zW*: **~europa** *nt* Southern Europe;
~früchte *pl* (sub)tropical fruit; **s~ländisch**
a southern; (*italienisch, spanisch etc*) Latin;
s~lich *a* southern; **s~lich von** (to the) south
of; **~ostasien** *nt* South-East Asia; **~pol** *m*
South Pole; **~polarmeer** *nt* Antarctic
Ocean; **~see** *f* South Seas *pl*, South Pacific;
s~wärts *ad* southwards; **~westafrika** *nt*
South West Africa, Namibia.
Suezkanal [zoo:'eskånàl] *m* **-s** Suez Canal.
Suff [zoof] *m*: **etw im ~ sagen** (*umg*) say
sth while under the influence.
süffig [zü'fĭçh] *a* (*Wein*) pleasant to the taste.
süffisant [züfēzànt'] *a* smug.
suggerieren [zoogārē:'rən] *vt* suggest (*jdm
etw* sth to sb).
Suggestivfrage [zoogestē:f'frågə] *f* **-**, **-n** lead-
ing question.
suhlen [zoo:'lən] *vr* (*lit, fig*) wallow.
Sühne [zü:'nə] *f* **-**, **-n** atonement, expiation.
sühnen *vt* atone for, expiate.
Sühnetermin *m* (*JUR*) conciliatory hearing.
Sultan [zool'tán] *m* **-s**, **-e** sultan.
Sultanine [zooltánē:'nə] *f* sultana.
Sülze [zül'tsə] *f* **-**, **-n** headcheese (*US*), brawn
(*Brit*).
summarisch [zoomá'rish] *a* summary.
Summe *f* **-**, **-n** sum, total.
summen *vti* buzz; (*Lied*) hum.
Summer *m* **-s**, **-** buzzer.
summieren [zoomē:'rən] *vtr* add up (to).
Sumpf [zoompf] *m* **-(e)s**, **̈e** swamp, marsh.
sumpfig *a* marshy.
Sund [zoont] *m* **-(e)s**, **-e** sound, straits *pl*.
Sünde [zün'də] *f* **-**, **-n** sin.
Sünden- *zW*: **~bock** *m* (*fig*) scapegoat; **~fall**
m (*REL*) Fall; **~register** *nt* (*fig*) list of sins.
Sünder(in *f*) *m* **-s**, **-** sinner.
sündhaft *a* (*lit*) sinful; (*fig umg: Preise*)
wicked.
sündigen [zün'digən] *vi* sin (*an* +*dat*
against); (*hum*) indulge.
super [zoo:'pər] *a* (*umg*) super ♦ *ad* incredibly well.
Super *nt* **-s** (*Benzin*) premium (gasoline).
Superlativ [zoo:'pərlátē:f] *m* **-s**, **-e** superlative.
Supermarkt *m* supermarket.
Suppe [zoo'pə] *f* **-**, **-n** soup; (*mit Einlage*)
broth; (*klare Brühe*) bouillon; (*fig umg: Nebel*) peasouper, pea soup (*US*); **jdm die ~
versalzen** (*umg*) put a spoke in sb's wheel.
Suppen- *zW*: **~fleisch** *nt* meat for making
soup; **~grün** *nt herbs and vegetables for
making soup*; **~kasper** *m* (*umg*) poor eater.
surfen [zœr'fən] *vi* surf.
Surrealismus [zoorǟális'moos] *m* surrealism.
surren [zoo'rən] *vi* buzz; (*Insekt auch*) hum.
Surrogat [zoorōgât'] *nt* **-(e)s**, **-e** substitute,
surrogate.

suspekt [zoospekt'] *a* suspect.
suspendieren [zoospendē:'rən] *vt* suspend
(*von* from).
Suspendierung *f* suspension.
süß [zü:s] *a* sweet.
Süße *f* **-** sweetness.
süßen *vt* sweeten.
Süßholz *nt*: **~ raspeln** (*fig*) turn on the
blarney.
Süßigkeit *f* sweetness; (*Bonbon etc*) candy
(*US*), sweet (*Brit*).
süß- *zW*: **~lich** *a* sweetish; (*fig*) sugary;
~sauer *a* sweet-and-sour; (*fig: gezwungen*)
forced; (*Gurken etc*) pickled; (*Miene*)
artificially friendly; **S~speise** *f* pudding,
dessert; **S~stoff** *m* sweetener; **S~wasser** *nt*
fresh water.
SV *m* **-** *abk* = **Sportverein.**
SW *abk* (= *Südwest(en)*) SW.
Swasiland [svâ'zēlánt] *nt* **-s** Swaziland.
SWF *m* **-** *abk* (= *Südwestfunk*) South West
Radio.
s.w.u. *abk* (= *siehe weiter unten*) see further
below.
Sylvester [zülves'tər] *nt* **-s**, **-** = **Silvester.**
Symbol [zümbō:l'] *nt* **-s**, **-e** symbol.
Symbolik *f* symbolism.
symbolisch *a* symbolic(al).
symbolisieren [zümbōlizē:'rən] *vt* symbolize.
Symmetrie [zümātrē:'] *f* symmetry; **~achse**
f symmetric axis.
symmetrisch [zümā:'trish] *a* symmetrical.
Sympathie [zümpátē:'] *f* liking; sympathy;
er hat sich (*dat*) **alle ~(n) verscherzt** he
has turned everyone against him;
~kundgebung *f* demonstration of support;
~streik *m* sympathy strike.
Sympathisant(in *f*) *m* sympathizer.
sympathisch [zümpá'tish] *a* likeable, congenial; **er ist mir ~** I like him.
sympathisieren [zümpátēzē:'rən] *vi*
sympathize.
Symphonie [zümfōnē:'] *f* symphony.
Symptom [zümptō:m'] *nt* **-s**, **-e** symptom.
symptomatisch [zümptōmá'tish] *a* symptomatic.
Synagoge [zünágō:'gə] *f* **-**, **-n** synagogue.
synchron [zünkrō:n'] *a* synchronous;
S~getriebe *nt* synchromesh (gears *pl*).
synchronisieren [zünkrōnēzē:'rən] *vt*
synchronize; (*Film*) dub.
Syndikat [zündēkât'] *nt* **-(e)s**, **-e** combine,
syndicate.
Syndrom [zündrō:m'] *nt* **-s**, **-e** syndrome.
Synkope [zünko:'pə] *f* **-**, **-n** (*MUS*) syncopa-
tion.
Synode [zünō:'də] *f* **-**, **-n** (*REL*) synod.
synonym [zünōnü:m'] *a* synonymous; **S~** *nt*
-s, **-e** synonym.
Syntax [zün'táks] *f* **-**, **-en** syntax.
Synthese [züntä:'zə] *f* **-**, **-n** synthesis.
synthetisch *a* synthetic.
Syphilis [zü:'fēlis] *f* syphilis.
Syrer(in *f*) [zü:'rər(in)] *m* **-s**, **-** Syrian.

Syrien nt -s Syria.
syrisch a Syrian.
System [züstä:m'] nt -s, -e system; ~**analyse** f systems analysis.
Systematik f system.
systematisch [züstämá'tish] a systematic.
systematisieren [züstämátēzē:'rən] vt systematize.
System- zW: ~**kritiker** m critic of the system; ~**platte** f (COMPUT) system disk.
s.Z. abk (= seinerzeit) at that time.
Szenarium [stsänä'rēōōm] nt scenario.
Szene [stsä:'nə] f -, -n scene; **sich in der** ~ **auskennen** (umg) know the scene; **sich in** ~ **setzen** play to the gallery.
Szenenwechsel m scene change.
Szenerie [stsänərē:'] f scenery.

T

T, t [tä:] nt T, t.
t abk = Tempo; Tonne.
Tab. abk = Tabelle.
Tabak [tâ'bák] m -s, -e tobacco; ~**laden** m tobacco store (US), tobacconist's (Brit).
tabellarisch [tábelä'rish] a tabular.
Tabelle f -, -n table.
Tabellenführer m (SPORT) top of the table, league leader.
Tabernakel [tábernä'kəl] m -s, - tabernacle.
Tabl. abk = Tablette(n).
Tablett nt -(e)s, -s od -e tray.
Tablette [táble'tə] f -, -n tablet, pill.
Tabu [tábōō:'] nt -s, -s taboo.
tabuisieren [tábōōēzē:'rən] vt make taboo.
Tabulator [tábōōlá'tor] m tabulator, tab (umg).
tabulieren vt tab.
Tachometer [tákḥōmä:'tər] m -s, - (AUT) speedometer.
Tadel [tâ'dəl] m -s, - censure, scolding; (Fehler) fault; (Makel) blemish; **t~los** a faultless, irreproachable.
tadeln vt scold.
tadelnswert a blameworthy.
Tafel [tâ'fəl] f -, -n (form: festlicher Speisetisch, MATH) table; (Festmahl) meal; (Anschlag~) board; (Wand~) blackboard; (Schiefer~) slate; (Gedenk~) plaque; (Illustration) plate; (Schalt~) panel; (Schokoladen~ etc) bar.
täfeln [te:'fəln] vt panel.
Tafelöl nt cooking od salad oil.
Täfelung f paneling (US), panelling (Brit).
Taft [táft] m -(e)s, -e taffeta.
Tag [tâk] m -(e)s, -e day; (Tageslicht) daylight; **am** ~ during the day; **für** od **auf ein**

paar ~**e** for a few days; **in den** ~ **hinein leben** take each day as it comes; **bei** ~(**e**) (ankommen) while it's light; (arbeiten, reisen) during the day; **unter** ~ (MIN) underground; **über** ~ on the surface; **an den** ~ **kommen** come to light; **er legte großes Interesse an den** ~ he showed great interest; **auf den** ~ (**genau**) to the day; **auf seine alten** ~**e** at his age; **guten** ~! good morning od afternoon!; **t~aus** ad: **t~aus tagein** day in, day out; ~**dienst** m day duty.
Tage- [tâ'gə] zW: ~**bau** m (MIN) open-pit (US) od open-cast (Brit) mining; ~**buch** nt diary; ~**dieb** m idler; ~**geld** nt daily allowance; **t~lang** ad for days.
tagen vi sit, meet ♦ vi unpers: **es tagt** dawn is breaking.
Tages- zW: ~**ablauf** m course of the day; ~**anbruch** m dawn; ~**ausflug** m day trip; ~**decke** f bedspread; ~**kasse** f (COMM) day's receipts pl; (THEAT) box office; ~**licht** nt daylight; ~**mutter** f baby tender (US), child minder (Brit); ~**ordnung** f agenda; **an der** ~**ordnung sein** (fig) be the order of the day; ~**satz** m daily rate; ~**wert** m (FIN) present value; ~**zeit** f time of day; **zu jeder** ~-**und Nachtzeit** at all hours of the day and night; ~**zeitung** f daily (paper).
tägl. abk = täglich.
täglich [te:'kliĉh] a, ad daily; **einmal** ~ once a day.
tags [táks] ad: ~ **darauf** od **danach** the next od following day; ~**über** ad during the day.
tagtäglich a daily ♦ ad every (single) day.
Tagung f conference.
Tagungsort m venue (of a conference).
Taifun [tifōō:n'] m -s, -e typhoon.
Taille [tál'yə] f -, -n waist.
Takel [tâ'kəl] nt -s, - tackle.
takeln vt rig.
Takt [tákt] m -(e)s, -e tact; (MUS) time; ~**gefühl** nt tact.
Taktik f tactics pl.
taktisch a tactical.
Takt- zW: **t~los** a tactless; ~**losigkeit** f tactlessness; ~**stock** m (conductor's) baton; ~**strich** m (MUS) bar (line); **t~voll** a tactful.
Tal [tâl] nt -(e)s, "-er valley.
Talar [tálár'] m -s, -e (JUR) robe; (UNIV) gown.
Talbrücke f bridge over a valley.
Talent [tálent'] nt -(e)s, -e talent.
talentiert [tálentē:rt'], **talentvoll** a talented, gifted.
Talfahrt f descent; (fig) decline.
Talg [tálk] m -(e)s, -e tallow.
Talgdrüse f sebaceous gland.
Talisman [tâ'lismán] m -s, -e talisman.
Tal- zW: ~**sohle** f bottom of a valley; ~**sperre** f dam; **t~wärts** ad down to the valley.
Tamburin [támbōōrē:n'] nt -s, -e tambourine.
Tampon [tám'pon] m -s, -s tampon.

Tamtam [támtâm'] *nt* **-s, -s** (*MUS*) tomtom; (*umg*: *Wirbel*) fuss, ballyhoo; (*Lärm*) din.
Tang [tâng] *m* **-(e)s, -e** seaweed.
Tangente [tânggen'tə] *f* **-, -n** tangent.
tangieren [tânggē:'rən] *vt* (*Problem*) touch on; (*fig*) affect.
Tank [tângk] *m* **-s, -s** tank.
tanken *vti* fill up; (*AVIAT*) (re)fuel; (*umg*: *frische Luft, neue Kräfte*) get.
Tanker *m* **-s,** - tanker.
Tank- *zW:* **~laster** *m* tanker; **~schiff** *nt* tanker; **~stelle** *f* gas (*US*) *od* petrol (*Brit*) station; **~uhr** *f* fuel gauge; **~wart** *m* gas station (*US*) *od* petrol pump (*Brit*) attendant.
Tanne [tá'nə] *f* **-, -n** fir.
Tannen- *zW:* **~baum** *m* fir tree; **~zapfen** *m* fir cone.
Tansania [tânzâ'nēâ] *nt* **-s** Tanzania.
Tante [tán'tə] *f* **-, -n** aunt; **~-Emma-Laden** *m* (*umg*) corner shop.
Tantieme [tâṅtēâ:'mə] *f* **-, -n** fee; (*für Künstler etc*) royalty.
Tanz [tânts] *m* **-es,** ⁻**e** dance.
tänzeln [ten'tsəln] *vi* dance along.
tanzen *vti* dance.
Tänzer(in *f)* *m* **-s,** - dancer.
Tanz- *zW:* **~fläche** *f* (dance) floor; **~schule** *f* dancing school.
Tapet *nt* (*umg*): **etw aufs ~ bringen** bring sth up.
Tapete [tápā:'tə] *f* **-, -n** wallpaper.
Tapetenwechsel *m* (*fig*) change of scenery.
tapezieren [tápâtsē:'rən] *vt* (wall)paper.
Tapezierer *m* **-s,** - (interior) decorator.
tapfer [táp'fər] *a* brave; **sich ~ schlagen** (*umg*) put on a brave show; **T~keit** *f* courage, bravery.
tappen [tá'pən] *vi* walk uncertainly *od* clumsily; **im dunklen ~** (*fig*) grope in the dark.
täppisch [te'pish] *a* clumsy.
Tara [tá'râ] *f* **-,** **Taren** tare.
Tarantel [tárán'təl] *f* **-, -n:** **wie von der ~ gestochen** as if stung by a bee.
Tarif [tárē:f'] *m* **-s, -e** tariff, (scale of) fares *od* charges; **nach/über/unter ~ bezahlen** pay according to/above/below the (union) rate(s); **~autonomie** *f* free collective bargaining; **~gruppe** *f* grade; **t~lich** *a* agreed, union; **~lohn** *m* standard wage rate; **~ordnung** *f* wage *od* salary scale; **~partner** *m*: **die ~partner** *pl* union and management; **~vereinbarung** *f* labor agreement; **~verhandlungen** *pl* collective bargaining *sing*; **~vertrag** *m* pay agreement.
tarnen [tár'nən] *vt* camouflage; (*Person, Absicht*) disguise.
Tarn- *zW:* **~farbe** *f* camouflage paint; **~manöver** *nt* (*lit, fig*) feint, covering ploy.
Tarnung *f* camouflaging; disguising.
Tasche [tá'shə] *f* **-, -n** pocket; (*Hand~*) handbag; **in die eigene ~ wirtschaften** line one's own pockets; **jdm auf der ~ liegen** (*umg*) live off sb.
Taschen- *zW:* **~buch** *nt* paperback; **~dieb** *m* pickpocket; **~geld** *nt* pocket money; **~lampe** *f* (electric) torch, flashlight; **~messer** *nt* penknife; **~rechner** *m* pocket calculator; **~spieler** *m* conjurer; **~tuch** *nt* handkerchief.
Tasmanien [tàsmâ'nēən] *nt* **-s** Tasmania.
Tasse [tá'sə] *f* **-, -n** cup; **er hat nicht alle ~n im Schrank** (*umg*) he's not all there.
Tastatur [tástâtōō:r'] *f* keyboard.
Taste [tá'stə] *f* **-, -n** push-button control; (*an Schreibmaschine*) key.
tasten *vt* feel, touch; (*drücken*) press ♦ *vi* feel, grope ♦ *vr* feel one's way; **T~telefon** *nt* pushbutton telephone.
Tastsinn *m* sense of touch.
tat [tât] *imperf von* **tun.**
Tat *f* **-, -en** act, deed, action; **in der ~** indeed, as a matter of fact; **etw in die ~ umsetzen** put sth into action; **~bestand** *m* facts *pl* of the case.
Taten- *zW:* **~drang** *m* energy; **t~los** *a* inactive.
Täter(in *f)* [te:'tər(in)] *m* **-s,** - perpetrator, culprit; **~schaft** *f* guilt.
tätig *a* active; **~er Teilhaber** active partner; **in einer Firma ~ sein** work for a firm.
tätigen *vt* (*COMM*) conclude; (*geh: Einkäufe, Anruf*) make.
Tätigkeit *f* activity; (*Beruf*) occupation.
Tätigkeitsbereich *m* field of activity.
tatkräftig *a* energetic; (*Hilfe*) active.
tätlich *a* violent; **T~keit** *f* violence; **T~keiten** blows *pl*.
Tat'ort *m* **-(e)s, -e** scene of the crime.
tätowieren [tetōvē:'rən] *vt* tattoo.
Tat- *zW:* **~sache** *f* fact; **jdn vor vollendete ~sachen stellen** present sb with a fait accompli; **~sachenbericht** *m* documentary (report); **t~sächlich** *a* actual ♦ *ad* really; **t~verdächtig** *a* suspected.
Tatze [tá'tsə] *f* **-, -n** paw.
Tau [tou] *nt* **-(e)s, -e** rope ♦ *m* **-(e)s** dew.
taub [toup] *a* deaf; (*Nuß*) hollow; **sich ~ stellen** pretend not to hear.
Taube [tou'bə] *f* **-, -n** (*ZOOL*) pigeon; (*fig*) dove.
Taubenschlag *m* dovecote; **hier geht es zu wie im ~** (*fig umg*) it's like Grand Central Station here.
Taubheit *f* deafness.
taubstumm *a* deaf-mute.
tauchen [tou'khən] *vt* dip ♦ *vi* dive; (*NAUT*) submerge.
Taucher *m* **-s,** - diver; **~anzug** *m* diving suit.
Tauch- *zW:* **~sieder** *m* **-s,** - portable immersion heater; **~station** *f*: **auf ~station gehen** (*U-Boot*) dive.
tauen [tou'ən] *vti, vi unpers* thaw.
Taufbecken *nt* font.
Taufe [tou'fə] *f* **-, -n** baptism.
taufen *vt* baptize; (*nennen*) christen.

Tauf- *zW:* **~name** *m* Christian name; **~pate** *m* godfather; **~patin** *f* godmother; **~schein** *m* certificate of baptism.

taugen [tou'gən] *vi* be of use; **~ für** do *od* be good for; **nicht ~** be no good *od* useless.

Taugenichts *m* **-es, -e** good-for-nothing.

tauglich [touk'lich] *a* suitable; (*MIL*) fit (for service); **T~keit** *f* suitability; fitness.

Taumel [tou'məl] *m* **-s** dizziness; (*fig*) frenzy.

taumelig *a* giddy, reeling.

taumeln *vi* reel, stagger.

Taunus [tou'nŏŏs] *m* - Taunus (Mountains *pl*).

Tausch [toush] *m* **-(e)s, -e** exchange; **einen guten/schlechten ~ machen** get a good/bad deal.

tauschen *vt* exchange, swap ♦ *vi:* **ich möchte nicht mit ihm ~** I wouldn't like to be in his place.

täuschen [toi'shən] *vt* deceive; **wenn mich nicht alles täuscht** unless I'm completely wrong ♦ *vi* be deceptive ♦ *vr* be wrong.

täuschend *a* deceptive.

Tauschhandel *m* barter.

Täuschung *f* deception; (*optisch*) illusion.

Täuschungsmanöver *nt* (*SPORT*) feint; (*fig*) ploy.

tausend [tou'zənt] *num* a *od* one thousand; **T~** *f* **-, -en** (*Zahl*) thousand.

Tausender *m* **-s, -** (*Geldschein*) thousand.

Tausendfüßler *m* **-s, -** centipede.

Tau- *zW:* **~tropfen** *m* dew drop; **~wetter** *nt* thaw; **~ziehen** *nt* tug-of-war.

Taxe [ták'sə] *f* **-, -n** taxi, cab.

Taxi [ták'sē] *nt* **-(s), -(s)** taxi, cab; **~fahrer** *m* taxi driver; **~stand** *m* taxi stand.

Teamarbeit [tē:m'árbīt] *f* teamwork.

Technik [tech'nik] *f* technology; (*Methode, Kunstfertigkeit*) technique.

Techniker(in *f*) *m* **-s -** technician.

technisch *a* technical; **T~e Hochschule** ≈ polytechnic.

Technologie [technōlōgē:'] *f* technology.

technologisch [technōlō:'gish] *a* technological.

Techtelmechtel [techtəlmech'təl] *nt* **-s, -** (*umg: Liebschaft*) affair, carry-on.

Tee [tā:] *m* **-s, -s** tea.

TEE *abk* (= *Trans-Europ-Express*) Trans-Europe-Express.

Tee- *zW:* **~kanne** *f* teapot; **~licht** *nt* nightlight; **~löffel** *m* teaspoon; **~mischung** *f* blend of tea.

Teer [tā:r] *m* **-(e)s, -e** tar; **t~en** *vt* tar.

Tee- *zW:* **~sieb** *nt* tea strainer; **~wagen** *m* cart (*US*), tea trolley (*Brit*).

Teheran [tā:'hərán] *nt* **-s** Teheran.

Teich [tīch] *m* **-(e)s, -e** pond.

Teig [tīk] *m* **-(e)s, -e** dough.

teigig [tī'gich] *a* doughy.

Teigwaren *pl* pasta *sing*.

Teil [tīl] *m od nt* **-(e)s, -e** part; (*Anteil*) share; (*Bestand~*) component; **zum ~** partly; **ich für meinen ~** ... I, for my part ...; **sich**

(*dat*) **sein ~ denken** (*umg*) draw one's own conclusions; **er hat seinen ~ dazu beigetragen** he did his bit *od* share; **t~bar** *a* divisible; **~betrag** *m* installment (*US*), instalment (*Brit*); **~chen** *nt* (atomic) particle.

teilen *vtr* divide; (*mit jdm*) share.

Teil- *zW:* **~gebiet** *nt* (*Bereich*) branch; (*räumlich*) area; **t~haben** *vi unreg* share (*an +dat* in); **~haber** *m* **-s, -** partner; **~kaskoversicherung** *f* third party, fire and theft insurance.

Teilnahme *f* **-, -n** participation; (*Mitleid*) sympathy; **jdm seine herzliche ~ aussprechen** offer sb one's heartfelt sympathy.

teilnahmslos *a* disinterested, apathetic.

teilnehmen *vi unreg* take part (*an +dat* in).

Teilnehmer *m* **-s, -** participant.

teils *ad* partly.

Teil- *zW:* **~schaden** *m* partial loss; **~strecke** *f* stage; (*von Straße*) stretch; (*bei Bus etc*) fare zone.

Teilung *f* division.

Teil- *zW:* **t~weise** *ad* partially, in part; **~zahlung** *f* payment by installments; **~zeitarbeit** *f* part-time job *od* work.

Teint [tań:] *m* **-s, -s** complexion.

Tel.Adr. *abk* (= *Telegramm-Adresse*) telegram address.

Telebrief [tā:'läbrē:f] *m* facsimile, fax.

Telefax [tā:'läfáks] *nt* telefax.

Telefon [tālāfō:n'] *nt* **-s, -e** (tele)phone; **ans ~ gehen** answer the phone; **~amt** *nt* (tele)phone exchange; **~anruf** *m* (tele)phone call.

Telefonat [tālāfōnát'] *nt* **-(e)s, -e** (tele)phone call.

Telefon- *zW:* **~buch** *nt* (tele)phone directory; **~gebühr** *f* call charge; (*Grundgebühr*) (tele)phone rental; **~gespräch** *nt* (tele)phone call.

telefonieren [tālāfōnē:'rən] *vi* (tele)phone; **bei jdm ~** use sb's phone; **mit jdm ~ speak** to sb on the phone.

telefonisch [tālāfō:'nish] *a* telephone; (*Benachrichtigung*) by telephone; **ich bin ~ zu erreichen** I can be reached by phone.

Telefonist(in *f*) [tālāfōnist'(in)] *m* (telephone) operator.

Telefon- *zW:* **~nummer** *f* (tele)phone number; **~verbindung** *f* telephone connection; **~zelle** *f* telephone booth (*US*) *od* box (*Brit*); **~zentrale** *f* telephone exchange.

Telegraf [tālāgráf'] *m* **-en, -en** telegraph.

Telegrafen- *zW:* **~leitung** *f* telegraph line; **~mast** *m* telegraph pole.

Telegrafie [tālāgráfē:'] *f* telegraphy.

telegrafieren [tālāgráfē:'rən] *vti* telegraph, cable.

telegrafisch [tālāgrá'fish] *a* telegraphic; **jdm ~ Geld überweisen** cable sb money.

Telegramm [tālāgrám'] *nt* **-s, -e** telegram, cable; **~adresse** *f* telegraphic address; **~formular** *nt* telegram form.

Telegraph *m* = **Telegraf**.

Telekolleg [tä:'ləkolä:k] *nt TV courses for credit.*
Teleobjektiv [tä:'ləopyektē:f] *nt* telephoto lens.
Telepathie [tälápátē:'] *f* telepathy.
telepathisch [tälápá'tish] *a* telepathic.
Telephon *nt* = **Telefon.**
Teleskop [tälāskō:p'] *nt* **-s, -e** telescope.
Telex [tä:'leks] *nt* **-(e)** telex.
Teller [te'lər] *m* **-s, -** plate.
Tempel [tem'pəl] *m* **-s, -** temple.
Temperafarbe [tem'pä́ráfárbə] *f* distemper.
Temperament [tempärámént'] *nt* temperament; *(Schwung)* vivacity, vitality; **sein ~ ist mit ihm durchgegangen** he went over the top; **t~los** *a* spiritless; **t~voll** *a* highspirited, lively.
Temperatur [tempärátōō:r'] *f* temperature; **erhöhte ~ haben** have a temperature.
Tempo [tem'pō] *nt* **-s, -s** speed, pace; **~!** get a move on!; *pl* **Tempi** *(MUS)* tempo; **das ~ angeben** *(fig)* set the pace.
temporär [tempōre:r'] *a* temporary.
Tempotaschentuch *nt* ® Kleenex ®.
Tendenz [tendents'] *f* tendency; *(Absicht)* intention.
tendenziell [tendentsēel'] *a:* **nur ~e Unterschiede** merely differences in emphasis.
tendenziös [tendentsēœs'] *a* biased, tendentious.
tendieren [tendē:'rən] *vi* show a tendency, incline *(zu* to(wards)).
Tenne [te'nə] *f* **-, -n** threshing floor.
Tennis [te'nis] *nt* **-** tennis; **~platz** *m* tennis court; **~schläger** *m* tennis racket; **~spieler** *m* tennis player.
Tenor [tānō:r'] *m* **-s, -̈e** tenor.
Teppich [te'piċh] *m* **-s, -e** carpet; **~boden** *m* wall-to-wall carpeting; **~kehrmaschine** *f* carpet sweeper; **~klopfer** *m* carpet beater.
Termin [termē:n'] *m* **-s, -e** *(Zeitpunkt)* date; *(Frist)* deadline; *(Arzt~ etc)* appointment; *(JUR: Verhandlung)* hearing; **sich** *(dat)* **einen ~ geben lassen** make an appointment; **t~gerecht** *a* on schedule.
terminieren [termēnē:'rən] *vt (befristen)* limit; *(Termine)* make appointments.
Terminkalender *m* diary, appointments book.
Terminologie [termēnōlōgē:'] *f* terminology.
Termite [termē:'tə] *f* **-, -n** termite.
Terpentin [terpentē:n'] *nt* **-s, -e** turpentine, turps *sing.*
Terrain [terȧn̂:'] *nt* **-s, -s** land, terrain; *(fig)* territory; **das ~ sondieren** *(MIL)* reconnoiter the terrain; *(fig)* see how the land lies.
Terrasse [terȧ'sə] *f* **-, -n** terrace.
Terrine [terē:'nə] *f* **-, -n** tureen.
territorial [teretōrēȧl'] *a* territorial.
Territorium [teretō:'rēōōm] *nt* territory.
Terror [te'ror] *m* **-s** terror; *(~herrschaft)* reign of terror; **blanker ~** sheer terror; **~anschlag** *m* terrorist attack.

terrorisieren [terōrēzē:'rən] *vt* terrorize.
Terrorismus [terōris'mōōs] *m* terrorism.
Terrorist(in *f)* *m* terrorist.
Terrororganisation *f* terrorist organization.
Tertia [ter'tsēä] *f* **-, Tertien** *(SCH: Unter~/ Ober~) fourth/fifth year of German high school.*
Terz [terts] *f* **-, -en** *(MUS)* third; **einen ~ machen** *(umg)* play merry hell.
Terzett [tertset'] *nt* **-(e)s, -e** *(MUS)* trio.
Tesafilm [tä:'záfilm] *m* ® Scotch tape ® *(US)*, Sellotape ® *(Brit)*.
Testament [testámént'] *nt* will, testament; *(REL)* Testament; **Altes/Neues ~** Old/New Testament.
testamentarisch [testámentá'rish] *a* testamentary.
Testamentsvollstrecker(in *f)* *m* **-s, -** executor (of a will).
Testat [testȧt'] *nt* **-(e)s, -e** certificate.
Testator [testȧ'tor] *m* testator.
Test- *zW:* **~bild** *nt* *(TV)* test card; **t~en** *vt* test; **~fall** *m* test case; **~person** *f* subject (of a test); **~stoppabkommen** *nt* nuclear test ban agreement.
Tetanus [tä:'tȧnōōs] *m* **-** tetanus; **~impfung** *f* (anti-)tetanus injection.
teuer [toi'ər] *a* expensive; **~es Geld** good money; **das wird ihn ~ zu stehen kommen** *(fig)* that will cost him dear.
Teuerung *f* increase in prices.
Teuerungszulage *f* cost-of-living bonus.
Teufel [toi'fəl] *m* **-s, -** devil; **den ~ an die Wand malen** *(schwarzmalen)* imagine the worst; *(Unheil heraufbeschwören)* tempt fate *od* providence; **in ~s Küche kommen** get into a mess; **jdn zum ~ jagen** *(umg)* send sb packing.
Teufelei [toifəlī'] *f* devilment.
Teufels- *zW:* **~austreibung** *f* exorcism; **~brut** *f* *(umg)* devil's brood; **~kreis** *m* vicious circle.
teuflisch [toif'lish] *a* fiendish, diabolic.
Text [tekst] *m* **-(e)s, -e** text; *(Lieder~)* words *pl;* **~dichter** *m* songwriter; **t~en** *vi* write the words.
textil [tekstē:l'] *a* textile; **T~branche** *f* textile trade.
Textilien *pl* textiles *pl.*
Textil- *zW:* **~industrie** *f* textile industry; **~waren** *pl* textiles *pl.*
Text- *zW:* **~stelle** *f* passage; **~verarbeitungssystem** *nt* word processor.
Tgb. *abk* = **Tagebuch.**
TH *f* **-, -s** *abk* = **Technische Hochschule.**
Thailand [tī'lȧnt] *nt* **-s** Thailand.
Thailänder(in *f)* [tī'lendər(in)] *m* **-s, -** Thai.
Theater [tä́ä'tər] *nt* **-s, -** theater *(US)*; theatre *(Brit)*; *(umg)* fuss; **(ein) ~ machen** make a (big) fuss *(mit jdm* of sb); **~ spielen** *(lit, fig)* playact; **~besucher** *m* playgoer; **~kasse** *f* box office; **~stück** *nt* (stage) play.
theatralisch [tä́ätrȧ'lish] *a* theatrical.
Theke [tä:'kə] *f* **-, -n** *(Schanktisch)* bar; *(La-*

dentisch) counter.
Thema [tā:'má] *nt* **-s, Themen** *od* **-ta** *(MUS, Leitgedanke)* theme; topic, subject; **beim ~ bleiben/vom ~ abschweifen** stick to/wander off the subject.
thematisch [tāmá'tish] *a* thematic.
Themenkreis *m* topic.
Themse [tem'zə] *f (Fluß)* Thames.
Theologe [tāōlō:'gə] *m* **-n, -n, Theologin** *f* theologian.
Theologie [tāōlōgē:'] *f* theology.
theologisch [tāōlō:'gish] *a* theological.
Theoretiker(in *f)* [tāōrā:'tēkər(in)] *m* **-s, -** theorist.
theoretisch *a* theoretical; **~ gesehen** in theory, theoretically.
Theorie [tāōrē:'] *f* theory.
Therapeut [tārápoit'] *m* **-en, -en** therapist.
therapeutisch *a* therapeutic.
Therapie [tārápē:'] *f* therapy.
Thermal- [termál'] *zW:* **~bad** *nt* thermal bath; *(Badeort)* thermal spa; **~quelle** *f* thermal spring.
Thermometer [termōmā:'tər] *nt* **-s, -** thermometer.
Thermosflasche [ter'mosflàshə] *f* Thermos ®.
Thermostat [termōstàt'] *m* **-(e)s** *od* **-en, -e(n)** thermostat.
These [tā:'zə] *f* **-, -n** thesis.
Thrombose [trombō:'sə] *f* **-, -n** thrombosis.
Thron [trō:n] *m* **-(e)s, -e** throne; **~besteigung** *f* accession (to the throne).
thronen *vi* sit enthroned; *(fig)* sit in state.
Thron- *zW:* **~erbe** *m* heir to the throne; **~folge** *f* succession (to the throne).
Thunfisch [tōō:n'fish] *m* tuna (fish).
Thymian [tü:'mēàn] *m* **-s, -e** thyme.
Tick [tik] *m* **-(e)s, -s** tic; *(Eigenart)* quirk; *(Fimmel)* craze.
ticken *vi* tick; **nicht richtig ~** *(umg)* be off one's rocker.
tief [tē:f] *a* deep; *(~sinnig)* profound; *(Ausschnitt, Ton)* low; **~er Teller** soup plate; **bis ~ in die Nacht hinein** late into the night; **T~** *nt* **-s, -s** *(MET)* depression; *(fig)* low; **T~bau** *m* civil engineering *(excluding the construction of buildings)*; **T~druck** *m* low pressure.
Tiefe *f* **-, -n** depth.
Tiefebene [tē:f'ā:bənə] *f* plain.
Tiefen- *zW:* **~psychologie** *f* depth psychology; **~schärfe** *f (PHOT)* depth of focus.
tief- *zW:* **~ernst** *a* very grave *od* solemn; **T~flug** *m* low-level *od* low-altitude flight; **T~gang** *m (NAUT)* draft *(US)*, draught *(Brit)*; *(geistig)* depth; **T~garage** *f* underground parking lot *(US)* *od* car park *(Brit)*; **~gekühlt** *a* frozen; **~greifend** *a* far-reaching; **T~kühlfach** *nt* deepfreeze compartment; **T~kühltruhe** *f* freezer; **T~lader** *m* **-s, -** low-loader; **T~land** *nt* lowlands *pl*; **T~parterre** *f* basement; **T~punkt** *m* low point; *(fig)* low ebb; **T~schlag** *m*

(BOXEN, fig) blow below the belt;
~schürfend *a* profound; **T~see** *f* deep parts of the sea; **T~sinn** *m* profundity; **~sinnig** *a* profound; *(umg)* melancholy; **T~stand** *m* low level; **~stapeln** *vi* be overmodest; **T~start** *m (SPORT)* crouch start.
Tiefstwert *m* minimum *od* lowest value.
Tiegel [tē:'gəl] *m* **-s, -** saucepan; *(CHEM)* crucible.
Tier [tē:r] *nt* **-(e)s, -e** animal; **~arzt** *m* vet(erinarian) *(US)*, vet(erinary surgeon) *(Brit)*; **~freund** *m* animal lover; **~garten** *m* zoo(logical gardens *pl)*; **~handlung** *f* pet store; **t~isch** *a* animal *attr*; *(lit, fig)* brutish; *(fig: Ernst etc)* deadly; **~kreis** *m* zodiac; **~kunde** *f* zoology; **t~liebend** *a* fond of animals; **~quälerei** *f* cruelty to animals; **~reich** *nt* animal kingdom; **~schutzverein** *m* society for the prevention of cruelty to animals; **~versuch** *m* animal experiment.
Tiger [tē:'gər] *m* **-s, -** tiger; **~in** *f* tigress.
tilgen [til'gən] *vt* erase; *(Sünden)* expiate; *(Schulden)* pay off.
Tilgung *f* erasing, blotting out; expiation; repayment.
Tilgungsfonds *m (COMM)* sinking fund.
tingeln [ting'əln] *vi (umg)* appear in small night clubs.
Tinktur [tingktōō:r'] *f* tincture.
Tinte [tin'tə] *f* **-, -n** ink.
Tinten- *zW:* **~faß** *nt* inkwell; **~fisch** *m* cuttlefish; *(achtarmig)* octopus; **~fleck** *m* ink stain *od* blot; **~spritzdrucker** *m* ink-jet printer; **~stift** *m* indelible pencil.
Tip [tip] *m* **-s, -s** *(SPORT, BÖRSE)* tip; *(Andeutung)* hint; *(an Polizei)* tip-off.
Tippelbruder *m (umg)* tramp, hobo *(US)*.
tippen [ti'pən] *vti* tap, touch; *(umg: schreiben)* type; *(: raten)* tip *(auf jdn* sb); *(im Lotto etc)* bet (on).
Tippfehler *m (umg)* typing error.
Tippse *f* **-, -n** *(umg)* typist.
tipptopp [tip'top'] *a (umg)* tip-top.
Tippzettel *m* ≈ lottery ticket.
Tirol [tērō:l'] *nt* **-s** the Tyrol.
Tiroler(in *f)* *m* **-s, -** Tyrolese, Tyrolean.
Tisch [tish] *m* **-(e)s, -e** table; **bitte zu ~!** lunch *od* dinner is served; **bei ~** at table; **vor/nach ~** before/after eating; **unter den ~ fallen** *(fig)* be dropped; **~decke** *f* tablecloth.
Tischler *m* **-s, -** carpenter, joiner.
Tischlerei [tishlərī'] *f* joiner's workshop; *(Arbeit)* carpentry, joinery.
Tischlerhandwerk *nt* cabinetmaking.
tischlern *vi* do carpentry *etc*.
Tisch- *zW:* **~nachbar** *m* neighbor (at table); **~rechner** *m* desk calculator; **~rede** *f* after-dinner speech; **~tennis** *nt* table tennis; **~tuch** *nt* tablecloth.
Titel [tē:'təl] *m* **-s, -** title; **~anwärter** *m (SPORT)* challenger; **~bild** *nt* cover (picture); *(von Buch)* frontispiece; **~geschichte** *f* headline story; **~rolle** *f* title

role; ~**seite** f cover; (*Buch*~) title page;
~**verteidiger** m defending champion, title
holder.
Titte [ti'tə] f -, -n (*umg: weibliche Brust*)
boob, tit (*umg*).
titulieren [tētōōlē:'rən] vt entitle; (*anreden*)
address.
tja [tyà] *interj* well!
TO f *abk* (= *Tarifordnung*) *regulations of pay*
scale.
Toast [tō:st] m -(e)s, -s *od* -e toast.
toasten vi drink a toast (*auf* +*akk* to) ♦ vt
(*Brot*) toast.
Toaster m -s, - toaster.
toben [tō:'bən] vi rage; (*Kinder*) romp about.
tob- zW: **T~sucht** f raving madness;
~**süchtig** a maniacal; **T~suchtsanfall** m
maniacal fit.
Tochter [toxh'tər] f -, ⁼ daughter;
~**gesellschaft** f subsidiary (company).
Tod [tō:t] m -(e)s, -e death; **zu ~e betrübt**
sein be in the depths of despair; eines
natürlichen/gewaltsamen ~es sterben die
of natural causes/die a violent death;
t~ernst a (*umg*) deadly serious ♦ *ad* in
dead earnest.
Todes- [tō:'dəs] zW: ~**angst** f mortal fear;
~**ängste ausstehen** (*umg*) be scared to
death; ~**anzeige** f obituary (notice); ~**fall**
m death; ~**kampf** m death throes *pl*;
~**opfer** nt death, casualty, fatality; ~**qualen**
pl: ~**qualen ausstehen** (*fig*) suffer agonies;
~**stoß** m deathblow; ~**strafe** f death penalty; ~**tag** m anniversary of death;
~**ursache** f cause of death; ~**urteil** nt death
sentence; ~**verachtung** f utter disgust.
Tod- zW: ~**feind** m deadly *od* mortal enemy;
t~krank a dangerously ill.
tödlich [tœt'lixh] a fatal; (*Gift*) deadly, lethal.
tod- zW: ~**müde** a dead tired; ~**schick** a
(*umg*) smart, classy; ~**sicher** a (*umg*) absolutely *od* dead certain; **T~sünde** f deadly
sin; ~**traurig** a extremely sad.
Toilette [tōàlε'tə] f toilet, bathroom; (*Fri-*
siertisch) dressing table; (*Kleidung*) outfit;
auf die ~ gehen/auf der ~ sein go to/be in
the toilet.
Toiletten- zW: ~**artikel** *pl* toiletries *pl*, toilet
articles *pl*; ~**papier** nt toilet paper; ~**tisch**
m dressing table.
Tokio [tō:'kyō] nt -s **Tokyo.
tolerant [tōlàrànt'] a tolerant.
Toleranz f tolerance.
tolerieren [tōlàrē:'rən] vt tolerate.
toll [tol] a mad; (*Treiben*) wild; (*umg*)
terrific.
tollen vi romp.
toll- zW: **T~heit** f madness, wildness;
T~kirsche f deadly nightshade; ~**kühn** a
daring; **T~wut** f rabies.
Tölpel [tœl'pəl] m -s, - oaf, clod.
Tomate [tōmâ'tə] f -, -n tomato; **du treulose**
~**!** (*umg*) you're a fine friend!
Tomatenmark nt -(e)s tomato purée.

Ton [tō:n] m -(e)s, -e (*Erde*) clay; *pl* ⁼e
(*Laut*) sound; (*MUS*) note; (*Redeweise*)
tone; (*Farb*~, *Nuance*) shade; (*Betonung*)
stress; **keinen ~ herausbringen** not be able
to say a word; **den ~ angeben** (*MUS*) give
an A; (*fig: Mensch*) set the tone;
~**abnehmer** m pickup; **t~angebend** a leading; ~**arm** m pickup arm; ~**art** f (musical)
key; ~**band** nt tape; ~**bandaufnahme** f
tape recording; ~**bandgerät** nt tape recorder.
tönen [tœ'nən] vi sound ♦ vt shade; (*Haare*)
tint.
tönern [tœ'nərn] a clay.
Ton- zW: ~**fall** m intonation; ~**film** m sound
film; ~**höhe** f pitch.
Tonika [tō:'nēkà] f -, -iken (*MUS*) tonic.
Tonikum nt -s, -ika (*MED*) tonic.
Ton- zW: ~**ingenieur** m sound engineer;
~**kopf** m recording head; ~**künstler** m musician; ~**leiter** f (*MUS*) scale; **t~los** a sound-
less.
Tonne [to'nə] f -, -n barrel; (*Maß*) ton.
Tonspur f soundtrack.
Ton- zW: ~**taube** f clay pigeon; ~**waren** *pl*
pottery *sing*, earthenware *sing*.
Topf [topf] m -(e)s, ⁼e pot; **alles in einen ~**
werfen (*fig*) lump everything together;
~**blume** f pot plant.
Töpfer(in f) [tœp'fər(in)] m -s, - potter.
Töpferei [tœpfərī'] f piece of pottery.
töpfern vi do pottery.
Töpferscheibe f -, -n potter's wheel.
topfit [top'fit'] a in top form.
Topflappen m potholder.
topographisch [tōpōgrà'fish] a topographic.
topp [top] *interj* O.K.
Tor [tō:r] m -en, -en fool ♦ nt -(e)s, -e gate;
(*SPORT*) goal; ~**bogen** m archway;
~**einfahrt** f entrance gate.
Toresschluß m: (**kurz**) **vor ~** right at the
last minute.
Torf [torf] m -(e)s peat; ~**stechen** nt peat-
cutting.
Torheit f foolishness; (*törichte Handlung*)
foolish deed.
Torhüter m -s, - goalkeeper.
töricht [tœ'rixht] a foolish.
torkeln [tor'kəln] vi stagger, reel.
torpedieren [torpādē:'rən] vt (*lit, fig*) torpedo.
Torpedo [torpà:'dō] m -s, -s torpedo.
Torschlußpanik [tō:r'shlōōspânik] f (*umg*:
von Unverheirateten) *fear of being left on*
the shelf.
Torte [tor'tə] f -, -n cake; (*Obst*~) flan, tart.
Torten- zW: ~**guß** m glaze; ~**heber** m cake
server.
Tortur [tortōō:r'] f ordeal.
Tor- zW: ~**verhältnis** nt goal average; ~**wart**
m -(e)s, -e goalkeeper.
tosen [tō:'zən] vi roar.
Toskana [toskâ'nà] f Tuscany.
tot [tō:t] a dead; **er war auf der Stelle ~** he

died instantly; **der ~e Winkel** the blind spot; **einen ~en Punkt haben** be at one's lowest; **das T~e Meer** the Dead Sea.
total [tōtál'] *a* total; **T~ausverkauf** *m* clearance sale.
totalitär [totálē:te:r'] *a* totalitarian.
Total- *zW*: **~operation** *f* extirpation; (*von Gebärmutter*) hysterectomy; **~schaden** *m* (*AUT*) total loss (*US*), complete write-off (*Brit*).
tot- *zW*: **~arbeiten** *vr* work o.s. to death; **~ärgern** *vr* (*umg*) get really annoyed.
töten [tœ'tən] *vti* kill.
Toten- *zW*: **~bett** *nt* death bed; **t~blaß** *a* deathly pale, white as a sheet; **~gräber** *m* **-s, -** gravedigger; **~hemd** *nt* shroud; **~kopf** *m* skull; **~messe** *f* requiem mass; **~schein** *m* death certificate; **~stille** *f* deathly silence; **~tanz** *m* danse macabre; **~wache** *f* wake.
Tote(r) *mf dekl wie a* dead person.
tot- *zW*: **~fahren** *vt unreg* run over; **~geboren** *a* stillborn; **~kriegen** *vt* (*umg*): **nicht totzukriegen sein** go on for ever; **~lachen** *vr* (*umg*) laugh one's head off.
Toto [tō:'tō] *m od nt* **-s, -s** (= *Totalisator*) ≈ lottery; **~schein** *m* ≈ lottery ticket.
tot- *zW*: **~sagen** *vt*: **jdn ~sagen** say that sb is dead; **T~schlag** *m* (*JUR*) manslaughter, second degree murder (*US*); **~schlagen** *vt unreg* (*lit, fig*) kill; **T~schläger** *m* (*Waffe*) blackjack (*US*), cosh (*Brit*); **~schweigen** *vt unreg* hush up; **~stellen** *vr* pretend to be dead; **~treten** *vt unreg* trample to death.
Tötung [tœ'toong] *f* killing.
Toupet [tōōpā:'] *nt* **-s, -s** toupee.
toupieren [tōōpē:'rən] *vt* tease.
Tour [tōō:r] *f* **-, -en** tour, trip; (*Umdrehung*) revolution; (*Verhaltensart*) way; **auf ~en kommen** (*AUT*) reach top speed; (*fig*) get into top gear; **auf vollen ~en laufen** (*lit*) run at full speed; (*fig*) be in full swing; **auf die krumme ~** by dishonest means; **in einer ~** incessantly.
Touren- *zW*: **~zahl** *f* number of revolutions; **~zähler** *m* tachometer.
Tourismus [tōōris'mōōs] *m* tourism.
Tourist(in *f*) *m* tourist.
Touristenklasse *f* tourist class.
Tournee [tōōrnā:'] *f* **-, -s** *od* **-n** (*THEAT etc*) tour; **auf ~ gehen** go on tour.
Trab [tráp] *m* **-(e)s** trot; **auf ~ sein** (*umg*) be on the go.
Trabant [trábánt'] *m* satellite.
Trabantenstadt *f* satellite town.
traben *vi* trot.
Tracht [trákht] *f* **-, -en** (*Kleidung*) costume, dress; **eine ~ Prügel** a sound thrashing.
trachten *vi* strive (*nach* for), endeavor (*US*), endeavour (*Brit*); **jdm nach dem Leben ~** seek to kill sb.
trächtig [treçh'tiçh] *a* (*Tier*) pregnant; (*fig*) rich, fertile.
Tradition [trádētsēō:n'] *f* tradition.

traditionell [trádētsēō:nel'] *a* traditional.
traf [tráf] *imperf von* **treffen**.
Trag- [trág] *zW*: **~bahre** *f* stretcher; **t~bar** *a* (*Gerät*) portable; (*Kleidung*) wearable; (*erträglich*) bearable.
träge [tre:'gə] *a* sluggish, slow; (*PHYS*) inert.
tragen [trá'gən] *unreg vt* carry; (*Kleidung, Brille*) wear; (*Namen, Früchte*) bear; (*erdulden*) endure ♦ *vi* (*schwanger sein*) be pregnant; (*Eis*) hold; **schwer an etw** (*dat*) **~** (*lit*) have a job carrying sth; (*fig*) find sth hard to bear; **zum T~ kommen** come to fruition; (*nützlich werden*) come in useful.
tragend *a* (*Säule, Bauteil*) load-bearing; (*Idee, Motiv*) fundamental.
Träger [tre:'gər] *m* **-s, -** carrier; wearer; bearer; (*Ordens~*) holder; (*an Kleidung*) (shoulder) strap; (*Körperschaft etc*) sponsor; (*Holz~, Beton~*) (supporting) beam; (*Stahl~, Eisen~*) girder; (*TECH*: *Stütze von Brücken etc*) support.
Trägerin *f siehe* **Träger**.
Träger- *zW*: **~kleid** *nt* jumper (*US*), pinafore dress (*Brit*); **~rakete** *f* launch vehicle; **~rock** *m* skirt with shoulder straps.
Tragetasche *f* carry-all (*US*), carrier bag (*Brit*).
Trag- [trák'] *zW*: **~fähigkeit** *f* load-bearing capacity; **~fläche** *f* (*AVIAT*) wing; **~flügelboot** *nt* hydrofoil.
Trägheit [tre:k'hīt] *f* laziness; (*PHYS*) inertia.
Tragik [trá'gik] *f* tragedy.
tragikomisch [trágēkō:'mish] *a* tragi-comic.
tragisch *a* tragic; **etw ~ nehmen** (*umg*) take sth to heart.
Traglast *f* load.
Tragödie [trágœ'dēə] *f* tragedy.
trägt [tre:kt] *3. pers sing präs von* **tragen**.
Trag- [trák'] *zW*: **~weite** *f* range; (*fig*) scope; **von großer ~weite sein** have far-reaching consequences; **~werk** *nt* wing assembly.
Trainer(in *f*) [tre:'nər(in)] *m* **-s, -** (*SPORT*) trainer, coach; (*FUSSBALL*) manager.
trainieren [trenē:'rən] *vti* train; (*Mensch auch*) coach; (*Übung*) practice (*US*), practise (*Brit*); **Fußball ~** do soccer practice.
Training *nt* **-s, -s** training.
Trainingsanzug *m* sweat suit (*US*), tracksuit (*Brit*).
Trakt [trákt] *m* **-(e)s, -e** (*Gebäudeteil*) section; (*Flügel*) wing.
Traktat [tráktát'] *m od nt* **-(e)s, -e** (*Abhandlung*) treatise; (*Flugschrift, religiöse Schrift*) tract.
traktieren *vt* (*umg: schlecht behandeln*) maltreat; (*quälen*) torment.
Traktor [trák'tor] *m* tractor; (*von Drucker*) tractor feed.
trällern [tre'lərn] *vti* warble; (*Vogel*) trill.
trampeln [trám'pəln] *vt* trample; (*abschütteln*) stamp ♦ *vi* stamp.
Trampel- *zW*: **~pfad** *m* track, path; **~tier** *nt* (*ZOOL*) (Bactrian) camel; (*fig umg*) clumsy

oaf.
trampen |tràm'pən| *vi* hitch-hike.
Tranchierbesteck *nt* (pair of) carvers.
tranchieren |trànshē:'rən| *vt* carve.
Träne |trɛ:'nə| *f* -, -n tear.
tränen *vi* water.
Tränengas *nt* tear gas.
tranig |trà'niˈʦˈ| *a* (*umg*) slow, sluggish.
trank |tràngk| *imperf von* **trinken**.
Tränke |trɛng'kə| *f* -, -n watering place.
tränken *vt* (*naß machen*) soak; (*Tiere*) water.
Transaktion |trànsàktsˈēō:n'| *f* transaction.
Transformator |trànsformà'tor| *m* transformer.
Transfusion |trànsfōōzˈēō:n'| *f* transfusion.
Transistor |trànzē'stor| *m* transistor.
transitiv |tràn'zētē:f| *a* transitive.
Transitverkehr |trànzē:t'fɛrkā:r| *m* transit traffic.
transparent |trànspàrɛnt'| *a* transparent; **T~** *nt* **-(e)s, -e** (*Bild*) transparency; (*Spruchband*) banner.
transpirieren |trànspērē:'rən| *vi* perspire.
Transplantation |trànsplàntàtsˈēō:n'| *f* transplantation; (*Haut~*) graft(ing).
Transport |trànsport'| *m* **-(e)s, -e** transport; (*Fracht*) consignment, shipment; **t~fähig** *a* moveable.
transportieren |trànsportē:'rən| *vt* transport.
Transport- *zW:* **~kosten** *pl* transportation costs *pl*, carriage *sing*; **~mittel** *nt* means of transport (*sing*); **~unternehmen** *nt* carrier.
transusig |tràns'ōō:ziˈʦˈ| *a* (*umg*) sluggish.
Transvestit |trànsvɛstē:t'| *m* **-en, -en** transvestite.
Trapez |tràpā:ts'| *nt* **-es, -e** trapeze; (*MATH*) trapezium.
Trara |tràrà'| *nt* **-s: mit viel ~** (*fig umg*) with a great hullabaloo (*um* about).
trat |tràt| *imperf von* **treten**.
tratschen |tràt'shən| *vi* (*umg*) gossip.
Tratte |trà'tə| *f* -, -n (*FIN*) draft.
Traube |trou'bə| *f* -, -n grape; (*ganze Frucht*) bunch (of grapes).
Trauben- *zW:* **~lese** *f* vintage; **~zucker** *m* glucose.
trauen |trou'ən| *vi* (*+dat*) trust; **jdm/etw ~** trust sb/sth ♦ *vr* dare ♦ *vt* marry.
Trauer |trou'ər| *f* - sorrow; (*für Verstorbenen*) mourning; (*~fall* *m* death, bereavement; **~flor** *m* **-s, -e** black ribbon; **~gemeinde** *f* mourners *pl*; **~marsch** *m* funeral march.
trauern *vi* mourn (*um* for).
Trauer- *zW:* **~rand** *m* black border; **~spiel** *nt* tragedy; **~weide** *f* weeping willow.
Traufe |trou'fə| *f* -, -n eaves *pl*.
träufeln |troi'fəln| *vti* drip.
traulich |trou'liˈʦˈ| *a* cosy, intimate.
Traum |troum| *m* **-(e)s, Träume** dream; **aus der ~!** it's all over!
Trauma *nt* **-s, -men** trauma.
Traum- *zW:* **~bild** *nt* vision; **~deutung** *f*

interpretation of dreams.
träumen |troi'mən| *vti* dream; **das hätte ich mir nicht ~ lassen** I'd never have thought it possible.
Träumer(in *f*) *m* **-s, -** dreamer.
Träumerei |troimərī'| *f* dreaming.
träumerisch *a* dreamy.
traumhaft *a* dreamlike; (*fig*) wonderful.
Traumtänzer *m* dreamer.
traurig |trou'riˈʦˈ| *a* sad; **T~keit** *f* sadness.
Trau- *zW:* **~ring** *m* wedding ring; **~schein** *m* marriage certificate.
Trauung *f* wedding ceremony.
Trauzeuge *m* witness (to a marriage).
treffen |trɛ'fən| *unreg vti* strike, hit; (*Bemerkung*) hurt; (*begegnen*) meet; (*Entscheidung etc*) make; (*Maßnahmen*) take; **er hat es gut getroffen** he did well; **er fühlte sich getroffen** he took it personally; **~ auf** (+ *akk*) come across, meet ♦ *vr* meet; **es traf sich, daß ...** it so happened that ...; **es trifft sich gut** it's convenient.
Treffen *nt* **-s, -** meeting.
treffend *a* pertinent, apposite.
Treffer *m* **-s, -** hit; (*Tor*) goal; (*Los*) winner.
trefflich *a* excellent.
Treffpunkt *m* meeting place.
Treib'eis *nt* drift ice.
treiben |trī'bən| *unreg vt* drive; (*Studien etc*) pursue; (*SPORT*) do, go in for; **die treibende Kraft** (*fig*) the driving force; **Handel mit etw/jdm ~** trade in sth/with sb; **es zu weit ~** go too far; **Unsinn ~** fool around ♦ *vi* (*Schiff etc*) drift; (*Pflanzen*) sprout; (*KOCH: aufgehen*) rise; (*Medikamente*) be diuretic.
Treiben *nt* **-s** activity.
Treib- *zW:* **~gut** *nt* flotsam; **~haus** *nt* greenhouse; **~jagd** *f* drive, shoot (*in which game is sent up by beaters*); (*fig*) witchhunt; **~sand** *m* quicksand; **~stoff** *m* fuel.
Trend |trɛnt| *m* **-s, -s** trend; **~wende** *f* trend away from.
trennbar *a* separable.
trennen |trɛ'nən| *vt* separate; (*teilen*) divide ♦ *vr* separate; **sich ~ von** part with.
Trennschärfe *f* (*RAD*) selectivity.
Trennung *f* separation.
Trennungsstrich *m* hyphen.
Trennwand *f* partition (wall).
treppab' *ad* downstairs.
treppauf' *ad* upstairs.
Treppe |trɛ'pə| *f* -, -n stairs *pl*, staircase; (*im Freien*) steps *pl*; **eine ~** a staircase, a flight of stairs *od* steps; **sie wohnt zwei ~n höher** she lives two flights up.
Treppen- *zW:* **~geländer** *nt* banister; **~haus** *nt* staircase.
Tresen |trā:'zən| *m* **-s -** (*Theke*) bar; (*Ladentisch*) counter.
Tresor |trāzō:r'| *m* **-s, -e** safe.
Tretboot *nt* pedal boat, pedalo.
treten |trā:'tən| *unreg vi* step; (*Tränen, Schweiß*) appear; **~ nach** kick at; **~ in** (+*akk*) step in(to); **in Verbindung ~** get in

contact; **in Erscheinung** ~ appear; **der Fluß trat über die Ufer** the river overflowed its banks; **in Streik** ~ go on strike ♦ *vt* (*mit Fußtritt*) kick; (*nieder*~) tread, trample.

Treter [trä:'tər] *pl* (*umg: Schuhe*) casual shoes *pl.*

Tret- *zW:* ~**mine** *f* (*MIL*) (anti-personnel) mine; ~**mühle** *f* (*fig*) daily grind.

treu [troi] *a* faithful, true; ~**doof** *a* (*umg*) naïve.

Treue *f* - loyalty, faithfulness.

treu- *zW:* **T**~**händer** *m* **-s,** - trustee; **T**~**handgesellschaft** *f* trust company; ~**herzig** *a* innocent; ~**lich** *ad* faithfully; ~**los** *a* faithless; ~**los an jdm handeln** fail sb.

Tribüne [trēbü:'nə] *f* -, **-n** grandstand; (*Redner*~) platform.

Tribut [trēbōō:t'] *nt* -(e)s, -e tribute.

Trichter [trièh'tər] *m* **-s,** - funnel; (*Bomben*~) crater.

Trick [trik] *m* **-s, -e** *od* **-s** trick; ~**film** *m* cartoon.

trieb [trē:p] *imperf von* **treiben**.

Trieb *m* **-(e)s, -e** urge, drive; (*Neigung*) inclination; (*BOT*) shoot; ~**feder** *f* (*fig*) motivating force; ~**haft** *a* impulsive; ~**kraft** *f* (*fig*) drive; ~**täter** *m* sex offender; ~**wagen** *m* (*EISENB*) railcar; ~**werk** *nt* engine.

triefen [trē:'fən] *vi* drip.

trifft [trift] *3. pers sing präs von* **treffen**.

triftig [trif'tièh] *a* convincing; (*Grund etc*) good.

Trigonometrie [trēgōnōmātrē:'] *f* trigonometry.

Trikot [trēkō:'] *nt* **-s, -s** vest; (*SPORT*) shirt ♦ *m* **-s, -s** (*Gewebe*) tricot.

Triller [tri'lər] *m* **-s,** - (*MUS*) trill.

trillern *vi* trill, warble.

Trillpfeife *f* whistle.

Trilogie [trēlōgē:'] *f* trilogy.

Trimester [trēme'stər] *nt* **-s,** - term.

Trimm- [trim] *zW:* ~**-Aktion** *f* keep-fit campaign; ~**-dich-Pfad** *m* keep-fit trail.

trimmen *vt* (*Hund*) trim; (*umg: Mensch, Tier*) teach, train ♦ *vr* keep fit.

trinkbar *a* drinkable.

trinken [tring'kən] *vti unreg* drink.

Trinker(in *f*) *m* **-s,** - drinker.

Trink- *zW:* **t**~**fest** *a:* **ich bin nicht sehr t**~**fest** I can't hold my drink very well; ~**geld** *nt* tip; ~**halle** *f* (*Kiosk*) refreshment stand; ~**halm** *m* (drinking) straw; ~**milch** *f* milk; ~**spruch** *m* toast; ~**wasser** *nt* drinking water.

trippeln [tri'pəln] *vi* toddle.

Tripper [tri'pər] *m* **-s,** - gonorrhea (*US*), gonorrhoea (*Brit*).

trist [trist] *a* dreary, dismal; (*Farbe*) dull.

tritt [trit] *3. pers sing präs von* **treten**.

Tritt *m* **-(e)s, -e** step; (*Fuß*~) kick; ~**brett** *nt* (*EISENB*) step; (*AUT*) running board; ~**leiter** *f* stepladder.

Triumph [trēōōmf'] *m* **-(e)s, -e** triumph;

~**bogen** *m* triumphal arch.

triumphieren [trēōōmfē:'rən] *vi* triumph; (*jubeln*) exult.

trivial [trēvēàl'] *a* trivial; **T**~**literatur** *f* light fiction.

trocken [tro'kən] *a* dry; **sich** ~ **rasieren** use an electric razor; **T**~**automat** *m* tumble dryer; **T**~**dock** *nt* dry dock; **T**~**element** *nt* dry cell; **T**~**haube** *f* hair dryer; **T**~**heit** *f* dryness; ~**legen** *vt* (*Sumpf*) drain; (*Kind*) put a clean diaper (*US*) *od* nappy (*Brit*) on; **T**~**milch** *f* dried milk; **T**~**zeit** *f* (*Jahreszeit*) dry season.

trocknen *vti* dry.

Troddel [tro'dəl] *f* -, **-n** tassel.

Trödel [trœ'dəl] *m* **-s** (*umg*) junk.

trödeln *vi* (*umg*) dawdle.

Trödler *m* **-s,** - secondhand dealer.

troff [trof] *imperf* (*veraltet*) *von* **triefen**.

trog [trō:k] *imperf von* **trügen**.

Trog *m* **-(e)s,** ̈**e** trough.

trollen [tro'lən] *vr* (*umg*) push off.

Trommel [tro'məl] *f* -, **-n** drum; **die** ~ **rühren** (*fig umg*) drum up support; ~**fell** *nt* eardrum; ~**feuer** *nt* drumfire, heavy barrage.

trommeln *vti* drum.

Trommel- *zW:* ~**revolver** *m* revolver; ~**waschmaschine** *f* tumble-action washing machine.

Trommler(in *f*) [trom'lər(in)] *m* **-s,** - drummer.

Trompete [trompā:'tə] *f* -, **-n** trumpet.

Trompeter *m* **-s,** - trumpeter.

Tropen [trō:'pən] *pl* tropics *pl;* **t**~**beständig** *a* suitable for the tropics; ~**helm** *m* topee, sun helmet.

Tropf [tropf] *m* **-(e)s,** ̈**e** (*umg*) rogue; (*kein pl: Infusion*) drip (*umg*); **armer** ~ poor devil.

tröpfeln [trœp'fəln] *vi* drip, trickle.

tropfen *vti* drip ♦ *vi unpers:* **es tropft** a few raindrops are falling.

Tropfen *m* **-s,** - drop; **ein guter** *od* **edler** ~ a good wine; **ein** ~ **auf den heißen Stein** (*fig umg*) a drop in the ocean.

tropfenweise *ad* in drops.

Tropfsteinhöhle *f* stalactite cave.

Trophäe [trōfe:'ə] *f* -, **-n** trophy.

tropisch [trō:'pish] *a* tropical.

Trost [trō:st] *m* **-es** consolation, comfort; **t**~**bedürftig** *a* in need of consolation.

trösten [trœ'stən] *vt* console, comfort.

Tröster(in *f*) *m* **-s,** - comfort(er).

tröstlich *a* comforting.

trost- *zW:* ~**los** *a* bleak; (*Verhältnisse*) wretched; **T**~**pflaster** *nt* (*fig*) consolation; **T**~**preis** *m* consolation prize; ~**reich** *a* comforting.

Tröstung [trœ'stōōng] *f* comfort, consolation.

Trott [trot] *m* **-(e)s, -e** trot; (*Routine*) routine.

Trottel *m* **-s,** - (*umg*) fool, dope.

trotten *vi* trot.

Trottoir [trotôàr'] *nt* **-s, -s** *od* **-e** (*veraltet*) sidewalk (*US*), pavement (*Brit*).

trotz [trots] *präp* +*gen od dat* in spite of.
Trotz *m* **-es** pig-headedness; **etw aus** ~ **tun** do sth just to show them; **jdm zum** ~ in defiance of sb; ~**alter** *nt* obstinate phase.
trotzdem *ad* nevertheless ♦ *kj* although.
trotzen *vi* (+*dat*) defy; (*der Kälte, Klima etc*) withstand; (*der Gefahr*) brave; (*trotzig sein*) be awkward.
trotzig *a* defiant; (*Kind*) difficult, awkward.
Trotz- *zW*: ~**kopf** *m* obstinate child; ~**reaktion** *f* fit of pique.
trüb [trü:p] *a* dull; (*Flüssigkeit, Glas*) cloudy; (*fig*) gloomy; ~**e Tasse** (*umg*) drip.
Trubel [troo:'bəl] *m* **-s** hurly-burly.
trüben [trü:'bən] *vt* cloud ♦ *vr* become clouded.
Trübheit *f* dullness; cloudiness; gloom.
Trübsal *f* **-**, **-e** distress; ~ **blasen** (*umg*) mope.
trüb- *zW*: ~**selig** *a* sad, melancholy; **T**~**sinn** *m* depression; ~**sinnig** *a* depressed, gloomy.
trudeln [troo:'dəln] *vi* (*AVIAT*) (go into a) spin.
Trüffel [trü'fəl] *f* **-**, **-n** truffle.
trug [troo:k] *imperf von* **tragen**.
Trug *m* **-(e)s** (*liter*) deception; (*der Sinne*) illusion.
trügen [trü:'gən] *unreg vt* deceive; **wenn mich nicht alles trügt** unless I am very much mistaken; ♦ *vi* be deceptive.
trügerisch *a* deceptive.
Trugschluß [troo:g'shloos] *m* false conclusion.
Truhe [troo:'ə] *f* **-**, **-n** chest.
Trümmer [trü'mər] *pl* wreckage *sing*; (*Bau*~) ruins *pl*; ~**feld** *nt* expanse of rubble *od* ruins; (*fig*) scene of devastation; ~**frauen** *pl* women who cleared the rubble in Germany after the end of the war; ~**haufen** *m* heap of rubble.
Trumpf [troompf] *m* **-(e)s**, **-e** (*lit, fig*) trump; **t**~**en** *vti* trump.
Trunk [troongk] *m* **-(e)s**, **-e** drink.
trunken *a* intoxicated; **T**~**bold** *m* **-(e)s**, **-e** drunkard; **T**~**heit** *f* intoxication; **T**~**heit am Steuer** drunken driving.
Trunksucht *f* alcoholism.
Trupp [troop] *m* **-s**, **-s** troop.
Truppe *f* **-**, **-n** troop; (*Waffengattung*) force; (*Schauspiel*~) troupe; **nicht von der schnellen** ~ **sein** (*umg*) be slow.
Truppen *pl* troops *pl*; ~**führer** *m* (military) commander; ~**teil** *m* unit; ~**übungsplatz** *m* training area.
Trust [träst] *m* **-(e)s**, **-e** *od* **-s** trust.
Truthahn [troo:t'hân] *m* turkey.
Tschad [tshât] *m* **-s**: **der** ~ Chad.
Tscheche [tshe'çhə] *m* **-n**, **-n**, **Tschechin** *f* Czech.
tschechisch *a* Czech.
Tschechoslowake [tsheçhōslōvâ'kə] *m* **-n**, **-n**, **Tschechoslowakin** *f* Czechoslovak.
Tschechoslowakei [tsheçhōslōváki'] *f*: **die** ~ Czechoslovakia.

tschüs [tshüs] *interj* (*umg*) so long.
Tsd. *abk* = **Tausend**.
TSG *nt abk* (= *Tierschutzgesetz*) animal protection law.
TSV *m abk* (= *Turn- Und Sportverein(igung)*) gymnastics and sport organization.
TU *f - abk* (= *Technische Universität*) ≈ polytechnic.
Tube [too:'bə] *f* **-**, **-n** tube.
Tuberkulose [too:bərkoo:lō:'zə] *f* **-**, **-n** tuberculosis.
Tuch [too:kh] *nt* **-(e)s**, **-er** cloth; (*Hals*~) scarf; (*Kopf*~) (head)scarf; (*Hand*~) towel; ~**fühlung** *f* physical contact.
tüchtig [tüçh'tiçh] *a* efficient; (*fähig*) able, capable; (*umg*: *kräftig*) good, sound; **etwas T**~**es lernen/werden** (*umg*) get a proper training/job; **T**~**keit** *f* efficiency; ability.
Tücke [tü'kə] *f* **-**, **-n** (*Arglist*) malice; (*Trick*) trick; (*Schwierigkeit*) difficulty, problem; **seine** ~**n haben** be temperamental.
tückisch *a* treacherous; (*böswillig*) malicious.
tüfteln [tüf'təln] *vi* (*umg*) puzzle; (*basteln*) fiddle about.
Tugend [too:'gənt] *f* **-**, **-en** virtue; **t**~**haft** *a* virtuous.
Tüll [tül] *m* **-s**, **-e** tulle.
Tülle *f* **-**, **-n** spout.
Tulpe [tool'pə] *f* **-**, **-n** tulip.
tummeln [too'məln] *vr* romp (about); (*sich beeilen*) hurry.
Tummelplatz *m* play area; (*fig*) hotbed.
Tumor [too:'mor] *m* **-s**, **-e** tumor (*US*), tumour (*Brit*).
Tümpel [tüm'pəl] *m* **-s**, **-** pond.
Tumult [too:moolt'] *m* **-(e)s**, **-e** tumult.
tun [too:n] *unreg vt* (*machen*) do; (*legen*) put; **jdm etw** ~ do sth to sb; **etw tut es auch** sth will do; **das tut nichts** that doesn't matter; **das tut nichts zur Sache** that's neither here nor there; **du kannst** ~ **und lassen, was du willst** you can do as you please ♦ *vi* act; **so** ~, **als ob** act as if; **zu** ~ **haben** (*beschäftigt sein*) be busy, have work to do ♦ *vr*: **es tut sich etwas/viel** something/a lot is happening.
Tünche [tün'çhə] *f* **-**, **-n** whitewash.
tünchen *vt* whitewash.
Tunesien [too:nä:'zēən] *nt* **-s** Tunisia.
tunesisch *a* Tunisian.
Tunke [toong'kə] *f* **-**, **-n** sauce.
tunken *vt* dip, dunk.
tunlichst [too:n'liçhst] *ad* if at all possible; ~ **bald** as soon as possible.
Tunnel [too:'nəl] *m* **-s**, **-s** *od* **-** tunnel.
Tunte [toon'tə] *f* **-**, **-n** (*pej umg*) fairy (*pej*).
Tüpfel [tüp'fəl] *m* **-s**, **-** dot; ~**chen** *nt* (small) dot.
tüpfeln *vt* dab.
tupfen [too:p'fən] *vti* dab; (*mit Farbe*) dot; **T**~ *m* **-s**, **-** dot, spot.
Tupfer *m* **-s**, **-** swab.
Tür [tü:r] *f* **-**, **-en** door; **an die** ~ **gehen**

answer the door; **zwischen ~ und Angel** in passing; **Weihnachten steht vor der ~** (*fig*) Christmas is just around the corner; **mit der ~ ins Haus fallen** (*umg*) blurt it *od* things out; **~angel** *f* (door) hinge.

Turbine [tŏŏrbē:'nə] *f* turbine.

turbulent [tŏŏrbŏŏlent'] *a* turbulent.

Türke [tür'kə] *m* **-n, -n, Türkin** *f* Turk.

Türkei [türkī'] *f*: **die ~** Turkey.

türkis [türkē:s'] *a* turquoise; **T~** *m* **-es, -e** turquoise.

türkisch *a* Turkish.

Turm [tŏŏrm] *m* **-(e)s, ⁻e** tower; (*Kirch~*) steeple; (*Sprung~*) diving platform; (*SCHACH*) castle, rook.

türmen [tür'mən] *vr* tower up ♦ *vt* heap up ♦ *vi* (*umg*) scarper, bolt.

Turm'uhr *f* clock (on a tower); (*Kirch~*) church clock.

Turn'anzug *m* gymnastics outfit.

turnen [tŏŏr'nən] *vi* do gymnastic exercises; (*herumklettern*) climb about; (*Kind*) romp ♦ *vt* perform; **T~** *nt* **-s** gymnastics *sing*; (*SCH*) physical education, P.E.

Turner(in *f*) *m* **-s, -** gymnast.

Turn- *zW*: **~halle** *f* gym(nasium); **~hose** *f* gym shorts *pl*.

Turnier [tŏŏrnē:r'] *nt* **-s, -e** tournament.

Turnschuh *m* gym shoe.

Turnus [tŏŏr'nŏŏs] *m* **-, -se** rota; **im ~** in rotation.

Turn- *zW*: **~verein** *m* gymnastics club; **~zeug** *nt* gym kit.

Tür'öffner *m* buzzer.

turteln [tŏŏr'təln] *vi* (*umg*) bill and coo; (*fig*) whisper sweet nothings.

Tusch [tŏŏsh] *m* **-(e)s, -e** (*MUS*) flourish.

Tusche [tŏŏ'shə] *f* **-, -n** Indian ink.

tuscheln [tŏŏ'shəln] *vti* whisper.

Tuschkasten *m* paintbox.

Tussi [tŏŏ'si] *f* **-, -s** (*umg*: *Frau, Freundin*) doll, chick.

tust [tŏŏːst] *2. pers sing präs von* **tun**.

tut [tŏŏːt] *3. pers sing präs von* **tun**.

Tüte [tü:'tə] *f* **-, -n** bag; **in die ~ blasen** (*umg*) be checked for intoxication (*US*), be breathalyzed; **das kommt nicht in die ~!** (*umg*) no way!

tuten [tŏŏː'tən] *vi* (*AUT*) honk; **von T~ und Blasen keine Ahnung haben** (*umg*) not have a clue.

TÜV [tüf] *m* (= *Technischer Überwachungs-Verein*) annual government car-safety check.

Twen [tven] *m* **-(s), -s** person in his or her twenties.

Typ [tü:p] *m* **-s, -en** type.

Type *f* **-, -n** (*TYP*) type.

Typenrad *nt* (*Drucker*) daisywheel; **~drucker** *m* daisywheel printer.

Typhus [tü:'fŏŏs] *m* **-** typhoid (fever).

typisch [tü:'pish] *a* typical (*für od*).

Tyrann(in *f*) [türán'(in)] *m* **-en, -en** tyrant.

Tyrannei [türánī'] *f* tyranny.

tyrannisch *a* tyrannical.

tyrannisieren [türánēzē:'rən] *vt* tyrannize.

tyrrhenisch [türā:'nish] *a* Tyrrhenian; **T~es Meer** Tyrrhenian Sea.

U

U, u [ŏŏː] *nt* U, u.

u. *abk* = **und**.

U *abk* = **Unterseeboot**.

u.a. *abk* (= *und andere(s)*) et al, and others; (= *unter anderem/anderen*) amongst other things.

u.ä. *abk* (= *und ähnliche(s)*) and similar.

u.A.w.g. *abk* (= *um Antwort wird gebeten*) R.S.V.P.

UB *f* **-, -s** *abk* (= *Universitätsbibliothek*) university library.

U-Bahn [ŏŏː'bán] *f abk* (= *Untergrundbahn*) subway (*US*), underground (*Brit*).

übel [ü:'bəl] *a* bad; (*moralisch auch*) wicked; **jdm ist ~** sb feels sick; **Ü~** *nt* **-s, -** evil; (*Krankheit*) disease; **zu allem Ü~** ... to make matters worse ...; **~gelaunt** *a attr* bad-tempered, sullen; **Ü~keit** *f* nausea; **~nehmen** *vt unreg*: **jdm eine Bemerkung** *etc* **~nehmen** be offended at sb's remark *etc*; **Ü~stand** *m* bad state of affairs; **Ü~täter** *m* wrongdoer; **~wollend** *a* malevolent.

üben [ü:'bən] *vtir* practice (*US*), practise (*Brit*); (*Gedächtnis, Muskeln*) exercise; **Kritik an etw** (*dat*) **~** criticize sth.

über [ü:'bər] *präp +dat od akk* over; (*hoch ~ auch*) above; (*quer ~ auch*) across; (*Route*) via; (*betreffend*) about; **sie liebt ihn ~ alles** she loves him more than anything; **~ kurz oder lang** sooner or later; **ein Scheck ~ DM 20** a check for 20 DM; **Fehler ~ Fehler** mistake upon *od* after mistake; **er lachte ~ das ganze Gesicht** he was beaming all over his face; **den ganzen Tag ~** all day long; **die ganze Zeit ~** all the time; **jdm in etw** (*dat*) **~ sein** (*umg*) be superior to sb in sth ♦ *ad* over; **~ und ~** all over.

überall [ü:bərál'] *ad* everywhere; **~hin'** *ad* everywhere.

überaltert [ü:bərál'tərt] *a* obsolete.

Überangebot [ü:'bərángəbō:t] *nt* surplus (*an +dat* of).

überanstrengen [ü:bərán'shtrengən] *vtr untr* overexert (o.s.).

überantworten [ü:bəránt'vortən] *vt untr* hand over, deliver (up).

überarbeiten [ü:bərár'bītən] *vt untr* revise, rework ♦ *vr* overwork (o.s.).

überaus [ü:'bərous] *ad* exceedingly.

überbacken |ü:bərbá'kən| vt unreg untr put in the oven/under the grill.

Überbau |ü:bərbou| m (Gebäude, Philosophie) superstructure.

überbeanspruchen |ü:'bərbəánshprōōk]hən| vt untr (Menschen, Körper, Maschine) overtax.

überbelichten |ü:'bərbəlichtən| vt untr (PHOT) overexpose.

Überbesetzung |ü:'bərbəzctsōōng| f overmanning.

überbewerten |ü:'bərbəvā:rtən| vt untr (fig) overrate; (Äußerungen) attach too much importance to.

überbieten |ü:bərbē:'tən| vt unreg untr outbid; (übertreffen) surpass; (Rekord) break ♦ vr: **sich in etw** (dat) **(gegenseitig)** ~ **vie** with each other in sth.

Überbleibsel |ü:'bərblīpsəl| nt -s, - residue, remainder.

Überblick |ü:'bərblik| m view; (fig: Darstellung) survey, overview; (Fähigkeit) overall view, grasp (über +akk of); **den** ~ **verlieren** lose track (of things); **sich** (dat) **einen** ~ **verschaffen** get a general idea.

überblicken |ü:'bərbli'kən| vt untr survey; (fig) see; (Lage etc auch) grasp.

überbringen |ü:'bərbring'ən| vt unreg untr deliver, hand over.

Überbringer m -s, - bearer.

Überbringung f delivery.

überbrücken |ü:bərbrü'kən| vt untr bridge (over).

Überbrückung f: **100 Mark zur** ~ 100 marks to tide me od him etc over.

Überbrückungsdarlehen nt bridging loan.

überbuchen |ü:'bərbōō:k]hən| vt overbook.

überdauern |ü:bərdou'ərn| vt untr outlast.

überdenken |ü:bərdcng'kən| vt unreg untr think over.

überdies |ü:bərdē:'s| ad besides.

überdimensional |ü:'bərdēmcnzēōnál| a oversize.

Überdosis |ü:bərdō:zis| f overdose, OD (umg); (zu große Zumessung) excessive amount.

überdrehen |ü:bərdrā:'ən| vt untr (Uhr etc) overwind.

überdreht a: ~ **sein** (fig) be hyped up, be over-excited.

Überdruck |ü:'bərdrōōk| m (TECH) excess pressure.

Überdruß |ü:'bərdrōōs| m **-sses** weariness; **bis zum** ~ ad nauseam.

überdrüssig |ü:'bərdrüsi]h| a tired, sick (gen of).

überdurchschnittlich |ü:'bərdōōrc]hshnitli]h| a above-average ♦ ad exceptionally.

übereifrig |ü:'bərīfrich| a overzealous.

übereignen |ü:bərīg'nən| vt untr: **jdm etw** ~ (geh) make sth over to sb.

übereilen |ü:bərī'lən| vt untr hurry.

übereilt a (over)hasty.

übereinander |ü:bərīnán'dər| ad one upon the other; (sprechen) about each other; ~**schlagen** vt unreg (Arme) fold; (Beine) cross.

übereinkommen |ü:bərīn'komən| vi unreg agree.

Übereinkunft |ü:bərīn'kōōnft| f -, **-künfte** agreement.

übereinstimmen |ü:bərīn'shtimən| vi agree; (Angaben, Meßwerte etc) tally; (mit Tatsachen) fit.

Übereinstimmung f agreement.

überempfindlich |ü:'bərcmpfintli]h| a hypersensitive.

überfahren |ü:'bərfārən| unreg vt take across ♦ vi cross, go across ♦ |ü:bərfá'rən| vt untr (AUT) run over; (fig) walk all over.

Überfahrt |ü:'bərfárt| f crossing.

Überfall |ü:'bərfál| m (Bank~, MIL) raid; (auf jdn) assault.

überfallen |ü:bərfá'lən| vt unreg untr attack; (Bank) raid; (besuchen) surprise.

überfällig |ü:'bərfcli]h| a overdue.

Überfallkommando nt flying squad.

überfliegen |ü:bərflē:'gən| vt unreg untr fly over, overfly; (Buch) skim through.

Überflie'ger m (SCH) academic genius.

überflügeln |ü:bərflü:'gəln| vt untr outdo.

Überfluß |ü:'bərflōōs| m (super)abundance, excess (an +dat of); **zu allem** od **zum** ~ (unnötigerweise) superfluously; (obendrein) to crown it all (umg).

überflüssig |ü:'bərflüsi]h| a superfluous.

überfluten |ü:bərflōō:'tən| vt untr (lit, fig) flood; (fig auch) inundate.

überfordern |ü:bərfor'dərn| vt untr demand too much of; (Kräfte etc) overtax.

überfragt |ü:bərfrákt| a: **da bin ich** ~ there you've got me.

überführen |ü:'bərfü:rən| vt transfer; (Leiche etc) transport ♦ |ü:bərfü:'rən| vt untr (Täter) have convicted (gen of).

Überfüh'rung f transport; conviction; (Brücke) bridge, overpass.

Übergabe |ü:'bərgábə| f handing over; (MIL) surrender.

Übergang |ü:'bərgàng| m crossing; (Wandel, Überleitung) transition.

Übergangs- zW: ~**erscheinung** f transitory phenomenon; ~**finanzierung** f (FIN) accommodation; **ü~los** a without a transition; ~**lösung** f provisional solution, stopgap; ~**stadium** nt state of transition; ~**zeit** f transitional period.

übergeben |ü:bərgē:'bən| unreg untr vt hand over; (MIL) surrender; **dem Verkehr** ~ open to traffic ♦ vr be sick.

übergehen |ü:'bərgā:ən| unreg vi (Besitz) pass; (zum Feind etc) go over, defect; (überleiten) go on (zu to); (sich verwandeln) turn (in +akk into) |ü:bərgā:'ən| ♦ vt untr pass over, omit.

übergeordnet |ü:'bərgeordnət| a (Behörde) higher.

übergeschnappt |ü:'bərgəshnápt| a (umg)

crazy.

Übergewicht |üːˈbərgəvi̇çht| *nt* excess weight; (*fig*) preponderance.

übergießen |üːbərgēːˈsən| *vt unreg untr* pour over; (*Braten*) baste.

überglücklich |üːˈbərglüklı̇çh| *a* overjoyed.

übergreifen |üːˈbərgrı̇fən| *vt unreg* (*auf Rechte etc*) encroach (*auf +akk* on); (*Feuer, Streik, Krankheit etc*) spread (*auf +akk* to); **ineinander** ~ overlap.

übergroß |üːˈbərgrōːs| *a* outsize, oversize.

überhaben |üːbərhábən| *vt unreg* (*umg*) be fed up with.

überhandnehmen |üːbərhántˈnāːmən| *vi unreg* gain the ascendancy.

überhängen |üːˈbərhɛngən| *vi unreg* overhang.

überhäufen |üːbərhoiˈfən| *vt untr*: **jdn mit Geschenken/Vorwürfen** ~ heap presents/reproaches on sb.

überhaupt |üːbərhoupt'| *ad* at all; (*im allgemeinen*) in general; (*besonders*) especially; ~ **nicht** not at all; **wer sind Sie** ~? who do you think you are?

überheblich |üːbərhāːpˈlı̇çh| *a* arrogant; **Ü~keit** *f* arrogance.

überhöht |üːbərhœt'| *a* (*Forderungen, Preise*) exorbitant, excessive.

überholen |üːbərhōːˈlən| *vt untr* overtake; (*TECH*) overhaul.

Überholspur *f* passing (*US*) *od* fast (*Brit*) lane.

überholt *a* out-of-date, obsolete.

überhören |üːbərhœˈrən| *vt untr* not hear; (*absichtlich*) ignore; **das möchte ich überhört haben!** (I'll pretend) I didn't hear that!

Über-Ich |üːˈbərı̇çh| *nt* **-s** superego.

überirdisch |üːˈbərirdish| *a* supernatural, unearthly.

überkapitalisieren |üːˈbərkápētálēˈzēːrən| *vt* overcapitalize.

überkochen |üːˈbərkokhən| *vi* boil over.

überkompensieren |üːˈbərkompɛnzēːrən| *vt untr* overcompensate for.

überladen |üːbərláˈdən|/*vt unreg untr* overload ◆ *a* (*fig*) cluttered.

überlassen |üːbərláˈsən| *unreg untr vt*: **jdm etw** ~ leave sth to sb; **das bleibt Ihnen** ~ that's up to you; **jdn sich** (*dat*) **selbst** ~ leave sb to his *od* her own devices ◆ *vr*: **sich etw** (*dat*) ~ give o.s. over to sth.

überlasten |üːbərláˈstən| *vt untr* overload; (*Mensch*) overtax.

überlaufen |üːˈbərloufən| *unreg vi* (*Flüssigkeit*) flow over; (*zum Feind etc*) go over, defect ◆ |üːbərlouˈfən| *untr vt* (*Schauer etc*) come over ◆ *a* overcrowded; ~ **sein** be inundated *od* besieged.

Überläufer |üːbərloifər| *m* deserter.

überleben |üːbərláːˈbən| *vt untr* survive.

Überlebende(r) *mf dekl wie a* survivor.

überlebensgroß *a* larger-than-life.

überlegen |üːbərláːˈgən| *vt untr* consider; **ich habe es mir anders** *od* **noch einmal über-**

legt I've changed my mind ◆ *a* superior; **Ü~heit** *f* superiority.

Überlegung *f* consideration, deliberation.

überleiten |üːbərlītən| *vt* (*Abschnitt etc*) link up (*in +akk* with).

überlesen |üːbərláːˈzən| *vt unreg untr* (*übersehen*) overlook, miss.

überliefern |üːbərlēːˈfərn| *vt untr* hand down, transmit.

Überlieferung *f* tradition; **schriftliche** ~**en** (written) records.

überlisten |üːbərlisˈtən| *vt untr* outwit.

überm |üːˈbərm| = **über dem**.

Übermacht |üːˈbərmákht| *f* superior force, superiority.

übermächtig |üːˈbərmɛçhtı̇çh| *a* superior (in strength); (*Gefühl etc*) overwhelming.

übermannen |üːbərmáˈnən| *vt untr* overcome.

Übermaß |üːˈbərmás| *nt* excess (*an +dat* of).

übermäßig |üːˈbərmɛːsı̇çh| *a* excessive.

Übermensch |üːˈbərmɛnsh| *m* superman; **ü~lich** *a* superhuman.

übermitteln |üːbərmiˈtəln| *vt untr* convey.

übermorgen |üːˈbərmorgən| *ad* the day after tomorrow.

Übermüdung |üːbərmüːˈdōōng| *f* fatigue, overtiredness.

Übermut |üːˈbərmōōːt| *m* exuberance.

übermütig |üːˈbərmüːtı̇çh| *a* exuberant, high-spirited; ~ **werden** get overconfident.

übernachten |üːbərnákhˈtən| *vi untr* spend the night (*bei jdm* at sb's place).

übernächtigt |üːbərnɛçhˈtı̇çht| *a* sleepy, tired.

Übernachtung *f*: ~ **mit Frühstück** bed and breakfast.

Übernahme |üːˈbərnáməˈ| *f* **-**, **-n** taking over *od* on; (*von Verantwortung*) acceptance; ~**angebot** *nt* takeover bid.

übernatürlich |üːˈbərnátüːrlı̇çh| *a* supernatural.

übernehmen |üːbərnāːˈmən| *unreg untr vt* take on, accept; (*Amt, Geschäft*) take over ◆ *vr* take on too much; (*sich überanstrengen*) overdo it.

überparteilich |üːˈbərpártı̇lı̇çh| *a* (*Zeitung*) independent; (*Amt, Präsident etc*) above party politics.

überprüfen |üːbərprüːˈfən| *vt untr* examine, check; (*POL: jdn*) screen.

Überprüfung *f* examination.

überqueren |üːbərkváːˈrən| *vt untr* cross.

überragen |üːbərráˈgən| *vt untr* tower above; (*fig*) surpass ◆ |üːˈbərrágən| *vi* project, stick out.

überra'gend *a* outstanding; (*Bedeutung*) paramount.

überraschen |üːbərráˈshən| *vt untr* surprise.

Überraschung *f* surprise.

überreden |üːbərráːˈdən| *vt untr* persuade; **jdn zu etw** ~ talk sb into sth.

Überredungskunst *f* powers of persuasion *pl*.

überregional |üːˈbərrāgēōnál| *a* national;

(*Zeitung, Sender*) nationwide.
überreichen [ü:bərrī'ċɦən] *vt untr* hand over; (*feierlich*) present.
überreichlich *a, ad* (more than) ample.
überreizt [ü:bərrītst'] *a* overwrought (*Brit*).
Überreste [ü:'bərrestə] *pl* remains *pl*, remnants *pl*.
überrumpeln [ü:bərrōōm'pəln] *vt untr* take by surprise; (*umg*: *überwältigen*) overpower.
überrunden [ü:bərrōōn'dən] *vt untr* (*SPORT*) lap.
übers [ü:'bərs] = **über das**.
übers. *abk* (= *Übersetzung*) trans., transl.
übersättigen [ü:bərze'tigən] *vt untr* satiate.
Überschall- [ü:'bərshál] *in zW* supersonic; **~flugzeug** *nt* supersonic jet; **~geschwindigkeit** *f* supersonic speed.
überschätzen [ü:bərshc'tsən] *vtr untr* overestimate.
überschaubar [ü:bərshou'bâr] *a* (*Plan*) easily comprehensible, clear.
überschäumen [ü:'bərshoimən] *vi* froth over; (*fig*) bubble over.
überschlafen [ü:bərshlâ'fən] *vt unreg untr* (*Problem*) sleep on.
Überschlag [ü:'bərshlâk] *m* (*FIN*) estimate; (*SPORT*) somersault.
überschlagen [ü:bərshlâ'gən] *unreg untr vt* (*berechnen*) estimate; (*auslassen: Seite*) omit ♦ *vr* somersault; (*Stimme*) crack; (*AVIAT*) loop the loop ♦ [ü:'bərshlâgən] *unreg vt* (*Beine*) cross; (*Arme*) fold ♦ *vi aux sein* (*Wellen*) break over; (*Funken*) flash over; **in etw** (*akk*) ~ (*Stimmung etc*) turn into sth ♦ *a* lukewarm, tepid.
überschnappen [ü:'bərshnápən] *vi* (*Stimme*) crack; (*umg: Mensch*) flip one's lid.
überschneiden [ü:bərshnī'dən] *vr unreg untr* (*lit, fig*) overlap; (*Linien*) intersect.
überschreiben [ü:bərshrī'bən] *vt unreg untr* provide with a heading; (*COMPUT*) overwrite; **jdm etw** ~ transfer *od* make over sth to sb.
überschreiten [ü:bərshrī'tən] *vt unreg untr* cross over; (*fig*) exceed; (*verletzen*) transgress.
Überschrift [ü:'bərshrift] *f* heading, title.
überschuldet [ü:bərshōōl'dət] *a* heavily in debt; (*Grundstück*) heavily mortgaged.
Überschuß [ü:'bərshōōs] *m* surplus (*an +dat* of).
überschüssig [ü:'bərshüsiċɦ] *a* surplus, excess.
überschütten [ü:bərshü'tən] *vt untr*: **jdn/etw mit etw** ~ (*lit*) pour sth over sb/sth; **jdn mit etw** ~ (*fig*) shower sb with sth.
Überschwang [ü:'bərshváng] *m* exuberance.
überschwappen [ü:'bərshvápən] *vi* splash over.
überschwemmen [ü:bərshvc'mən] *vt untr* flood.
Überschwemmung *f* flood.
überschwenglich [ü:'bərshvcngliċɦ] *a* effu-

sive; **Ü~keit** *f* effusion.
Übersee [ü:'bərzä:] *f*: **nach** *od* **in** ~ overseas.
überseeisch *a* overseas.
übersehbar [ü:bərzä:'bâr] *a* (*fig*: Folgen, Zusammenhänge etc) clear; (*Kosten, Dauer etc*) assessable.
übersehen [ü:bərzä:'ən] *vt unreg untr* look (out) over; (*fig: Folgen*) see, get an overall view of; (: *nicht beachten*) overlook.
übersenden [ü:bərzen'dən] *vt unreg untr* send, forward.
übersetzen [ü:bərze'tsən] *vti untr* translate ♦ [ü:'bərzetsən] *vi aux sein* cross.
Übersetzer(in *f*) [ü:bərze'tsər(in)] *m* **-s, -** translator.
Übersetzung [ü:bərze'tsōōng] *f* translation; (*TECH*) gear ratio.
Übersicht [ü:'bərziċɦt] *f* overall view; (*Darstellung*) survey; **die** ~ **verlieren** lose track; **ü~lich** *a* clear; (*Gelände*) open; **~lichkeit** *f* clarity, lucidity.
übersiedeln [ü:'bərzē:dəln] *od* [ü:bərzē:'dəln] *vi trennbar od untr* move.
überspannen [ü:bərshpá'nən] *vt untr* (*zu sehr spannen*) overstretch; (*überdecken*) cover.
überspannt *a* eccentric; (*Idee*) wild, crazy; **Ü~heit** *f* eccentricity.
überspielen [ü:bərshpē:'lən] *vt untr* (*verbergen*) cover (up); (*übertragen: Aufnahme*) transfer.
überspitzt [ü:bərshpitst'] *a* exaggerated.
überspringen [ü:bərshpring'ən] *vt unreg untr* jump over; (*fig*) skip.
übersprudeln [ü:'bərshprōō:dəln] *vi* bubble over.
überstehen [ü:bərshtä:'ən] *unreg untr vt* overcome, get over; (*Winter etc*) survive, get through ♦ [ü:'bərshtä:ən] *vi* project.
übersteigen [ü:bərshtī'gən] *vt unreg untr* climb over; (*fig*) exceed.
übersteigert [ü:bərshtī'gərt] *a* excessive.
überstimmen [ü:bärshti'mən] *vt untr* outvote.
überstrapazieren [ü:'bərshträpátsē:rən] *vtr untr* wear out.
überstreifen [ü:'bərshtrīfən] *vt*: (**sich** *dat*) **etw** ~ slip sth on.
überströmen [ü:bərshtrœmən] *untr vt*: **von Blut überströmt sein** be streaming with blood ♦ *vi* (*lit, fig*) overflow (*vor +dat* with).
Überstunden [ü:'bərshtōōndən] *pl* overtime *sing*.
überstürzen [ü:bərshtür'tsən] *untr vt* rush ♦ *vr* follow (one another) in rapid succession.
überstürzt *a* (over)hasty.
übertariflich [ü:'bərtarēfliċɦ] *a, ad* above the agreed *od* union rate.
übertölpeln [ü:bərtœl'pəln] *vt untr* dupe.
übertönen [ü:bərtœ'nən] *vt untr* drown (out).
Übertrag [ü:'bərträk] *m* **-(e)s, -träge** (*COMM*) amount brought forward; **ü~bar** [ü:bərträk'bâr] *a* transferable; (*MED*) infectious.
übertragen [ü:bərträ'gən] *unreg untr vt* transfer (*auf +akk* to); (*RAD*) broadcast;

(anwenden: Methode) apply (auf +akk to); (Verantwortung etc) give (jdm sb); (übersetzen) render; (Krankheit) transmit; **jdm etw** ~ assign sth to sb ♦ vr spread (auf +akk to) ♦ a figurative.

Übertragung f transference; broadcast; rendering; transmission.

übertreffen |ü:bərtre'fən| vt unreg untr surpass.

übertreiben |ü:bərtrī'bən| vt unreg untr exaggerate; **man kann es auch** ~ you can overdo things.

Übertreibung f exaggeration.

übertreten |ü:bərträ:'tən| unreg untr vt cross; (Gebot etc) break ♦ |ü:'bərträ:tən| vi (über Linie, Gebiet) step (over); (SPORT) overstep; (in andere Partei) go over (in +akk to); (zu anderem Glauben) be converted.

Übertre'tung f violation, transgression.

übertrieben |ü:bərtrē:'bən| a exaggerated, excessive.

Übertritt |ü:'bərtrit| m (zu anderem Glauben) conversion; (bes zu anderer Partei) defection.

übertrumpfen |ü:bərtroōm'pfən| vt untr outdo; (KARTEN) overtrump.

übertünchen |ü:bərtün'çhən| vt untr whitewash; (fig) cover up, whitewash.

übervölkert |ü:bərfœl'kərt| a overpopulated.

übervoll |ü:'bərfol| a overfull.

übervorteilen |ü:bərfor'tīlən| vt untr dupe, cheat.

überwachen |ü:bərvá'ќhən| vt untr supervise; (Verdächtigen) keep under surveillance.

Überwachung f supervision; surveillance.

überwältigen |ü:bərvel'tigən| vt untr overpower.

überwältigend a overwhelming.

überwechseln |ü:'bərvекsəln| vi move (in +akk to); (zu Partei etc) go over (zu to).

überweisen |ü:bərvī'zən| vt unreg untr transfer; (Patienten) refer.

Überweisung f transfer.

überwerfen |ü:'bərverfən| unreg vt (Kleidungsstück) put on; (sehr rasch) throw on ♦ |ü:bərver'fən| untr vr: **sich (mit jdm)** ~ fall out (with sb).

überwiegen |ü:bərvē:'gən| vi unreg untr predominate.

überwiegend a predominant.

überwinden |ü:bərvin'dən| unreg untr vt overcome ♦ vr: **sich** ~, **etw zu tun** make an effort to do sth, bring o.s. to do sth.

Überwindung f effort; strength of mind.

überwintern |ü:bərvin'tərn| vi untr (spend the) winter; (umg: Winterschlaf halten) hibernate.

Überwurf |ü:'bərvoōrf| m wrap; shawl.

Überzahl |ü:'bərtsäl| f superior numbers pl, superiority; **in der** ~ **sein** be numerically superior.

überzählig |ü:'bərtse:liçh| a surplus.

überzeugen |ü:bərtsoi'gən| vt untr convince.

überzeugend a convincing.

überzeugt a attr (Anhänger, Vegetarier etc) dedicated; (Christ, Moslem) devout.

Überzeugung f conviction; **zu der** ~ **gelangen, daß** ... become convinced that ...

Überzeugungskraft f power of persuasion.

überziehen |ü:'bərtsē:ən| unreg vt put on ♦ |ü:bərtse:'ən| vt untr cover; (Konto) overdraw; (Redezeit etc) overrun; **ein Bett frisch** ~ change the sheets ♦ vr (Himmel) cloud over.

Überziehungskredit m overdraft.

überzüchten |ü:bərtsüçh'tən| vt untr overbreed.

Überzug |ü:'bərtsoō:k| m cover; (Belag) coating.

üblich |ü:p'liçh| a usual; **allgemein** ~ **sein** be common practice.

U-Boot |oō:'bō:t| nt U-boat, submarine.

übrig |ü:b'riçh| a remaining; **für jdn etwas** ~ **haben** (umg) be fond of sb; **die** ~**en** |ü:b'rigən| the others; **das** ~**e** the rest; **im** ~**en** besides; ~**bleiben** vi unreg remain, be left (over).

übrigens |ü:b'rigəns| ad besides; (nebenbei bemerkt) by the way.

übriglassen |ü:b'riglásən| vt unreg leave (over); **einiges/viel zu wünschen** ~ (umg) leave something/a lot to be desired.

Übung |ü:'boōng| f practice; (Turn~, Aufgabe etc) exercise; ~ **macht den Meister** (Sprichwort) practice makes perfect.

Übungs- zW: ~**arbeit** f (SCH) practice od mock test; ~**platz** m training ground; (MIL) drill ground.

u. desgl. (m.) abk (= und desgleichen (mehr)) and the like.

u. dgl. (m.) abk (= und dergleichen (mehr)) and the like.

u.d.M. abk (= unter dem Meeresspiegel) below sea level.

ü.d.M. abk (= über dem Meeresspiegel) above sea level.

UdSSR f - abk (= Union der Sozialistischen Sowjetrepubliken) USSR; **die** ~ the USSR.

u.E. abk (= unseres Erachtens) in our opinion.

Ufer |oō:'fər| nt -s, - bank; (Meeres~) shore; ~**befestigung** f embankment; **u**~**los** a endless; (grenzenlos) boundless; **ins u**~**lose gehen** (Kosten) go up and up; (Debatte etc) go on forever.

u.ff. abk (= und folgende (Seiten)) ff.

Uffz. abk = Unteroffizier.

Uganda |oōgán'dà| nt -s Uganda.

Ugander(in f) m -s, - Ugandan.

ugs. abk (= umgangssprachlich) colloquial.

U-Haft |oō:'háft| f abk = **Untersuchungshaft.**

UHF abk (= Ultrahochfrequenz) UHF.

Uhr |oō:r| f -, -en clock; (Armband~) watch; **wieviel** ~ **ist es?** what time is it?; **um wieviel** ~**?** at what time?; **1** ~ 1 o'clock; **20** ~

8 o'clock, 20.00 (twenty hundred) hours;
~**band** *nt* watch strap; ~**(en)gehäuse** *nt*
clock/watch case; ~**kette** *f* watch chain;
~**macher** *m* watchmaker; ~**werk** *nt* clockwork mechanism (*auch fig*); works of a
watch; ~**zeiger** *m* hand; ~**zeigersinn** *m*: im
~**zeigersinn** clockwise; **entgegen dem**
~**zeigersinn** counterclockwise, anticlockwise
(*Brit*); ~**zeit** *f* time (of day).
Uhu [ōō:'hōō] *m* **-s, -s** eagle owl.
Ukrainer(in *f*) [ōōkrī:'nər(in)] *m* **-s, -** Ukrain-
ian.
UKW *abk* (= *Ultrakurzwelle*) VHF.
Ulk [ōōlk] *m* **-s, -e** lark.
ulkig [ōōl'kičh] *a* funny.
Ulme [ōōl'mə] *f* **-, -n** elm.
Ulster [ōōl'stər] *nt* **-s** Ulster.
Ultimatum [ōōltēmá'tōōm] *nt* **-s, Ultimaten**
ultimatum; **jdm ein** ~ **stellen** give sb an
ultimatum.
Ultra- [ōōl'trá] *zW*: ~**kurz'wellen** *pl* very high
frequency; ~**schall** *m* (*PHYS*) ultrasound;
u~violett *a* ultraviolet.
um [ōōm] *präp* +*akk* (a)round; (*zeitlich*) at;
(*mit Größenangabe*) by; (*für*) for; **es geht**
~ **das Prinzip** it's a question of principles;
~ **10% teurer** 10% more expensive; **jdn** ~
etw bringen deprive sb of sth; **er schlug** ~
sich he hit out about him; **Stunde** ~ **Stunde**
hour after hour; **Auge** ~ **Auge** an eye for
an eye; ~ **vieles (besser)** (better) by far; ~
nichts besser not in the least better ♦ *präp*
+*gen*: ~ ... **willen** for the sake of ... ♦ *kj*
(*damit*) (in order) to; ~ **so besser** so much
the better; ~ **so mehr, als** ... all the more
considering ...; **zu klug,** ~ **zu** ... too clever
to ... ♦ *ad* (*ungefähr*) about; **die zwei Stunden sind jetzt** ~ the two hours are now up.
umadressieren [ōōm'ádresē:rən] *vt* re-
address.
umändern [ōōm'endərn] *vt* alter.
Umänderung *f* alteration.
umarbeiten [ōōm'árbītən] *vt* remodel; (*Buch
etc*) revise, rework.
umarmen [ōōmár'mən] *vt untr* embrace.
Umbau [ōōm'bou] *m* **-(e)s, -e** *od* **-ten** reconstruction, alteration(s).
umbauen [ōōm'bouən] *vt* rebuild, reconstruct.
umbenennen [ōōm'bənenən] *vt unreg* rename.
umbesetzen [ōōm'bəzetsən] *vt* (*THEAT*) re-
cast; (*Mannschaft*) change; (*Posten, Stelle*)
find someone else for.
umbiegen [ōōm'bē:gən] *vt unreg* bend
(over).
umbilden [ōōm'bildən] *vt* reorganize; (*POL*:
Kabinett) reshuffle.
umbinden [ōōm'bindən] *unreg vt* (*Krawatte
etc*) put on ♦ [ōōmbin'dən] *vt unreg untr* tie
(sth) round.
umblättern [ōōm'bletərn] *vt* turn over.
umblicken [ōōm'blikən] *vr* look around.
umbringen [ōōm'bringən] *vt unreg* kill.

Umbruch [ōōm'brōōкh] *m* radical change;
(*TYP*) make-up.
umbuchen [ōōm'bōō:кhən] *vti* change one's
reservation *od* flight *etc*.
umdenken [ōōm'dengkən] *vi unreg* adjust
one's views.
umdisponieren [ōōm'dispōnē:rən] *vi* change
one's plans.
umdrängen [ōōmdreng'ən] *vt untr* crowd
round.
umdrehen [ōōm'drā:ən] *vtr* turn (round);
(*Hals*) wring; **jdm den Arm** ~ twist sb's
arm.
Umdre'hung *f* turn; (*PHYS*) revolution, rotation.
umeinander [ōōmīnán'dər] *ad* round one
another; (*füreinander*) for one another.
umerziehen [ōōm'ertsē:ən] *vt unreg* (*POL
euph*) re-educate (*zu* to become).
umfahren [ōōm'fárən] *unreg vt* run over ♦
[ōōmfá'rən] *vt untr* drive around; (*die Welt*)
sail round.
umfallen [ōōm'fálən] *vi unreg* fall down *od*
over; (*fig umg*: *nachgeben*) give in.
Umfang [ōōm'fáng] *m* extent; (*von Buch*)
size; (*Reichweite*) range; (*Fläche*) area;
(*MATH*) circumference; **in großem** ~ on a
large scale; **u~reich** *a* extensive; (*Buch
etc*) voluminous.
umfassen [ōōmfá'sən] *vt untr* embrace;
(*umgeben*) surround; (*enthalten*) include.
umfassend *a* comprehensive; (*umfangreich*)
extensive.
Umfeld [ōōm'felt] *nt*: **zum** ~ **von etw gehören** be associated with sth.
umformatieren [ōōm'formátē:rən] *vt*
(*COMPUT*) reformat.
umformen [ōōm'formən] *vi* transform.
Umformer *m* **-s, -** (*ELEK*) converter.
umformulieren [ōōm'formōōlē:rən] *vt* redraft.
Umfrage [ōōm'frágə] *f* poll; ~ **halten** ask
around.
umfüllen [ōōm'fülən] *vt* transfer; (*Wein*) decant.
umfunktionieren [ōōm'fōōngktsēōnē:rən] *vt*
convert; transform.
umg *abk* (= *umgangssprachlich*) colloquial.
Umgang [ōōm'gáng] *m* company; (*mit jdm*)
dealings *pl*; (*Behandlung*) way of behaving.
umgänglich [ōōm'genglichh] *a* sociable.
Umgangs- *zW*: ~**formen** *pl* manners *pl*;
~**sprache** *f* colloquial language; **u~sprach-
lich** *a* colloquial.
umgeben [ōōmgā:'bən] *vt unreg untr*
surround.
Umgebung *f* surroundings *pl*; (*Milieu*) environment; (*Personen*) people in one's
circle; **in der näheren/weiteren** ~ **Mün-
chens** on the outskirts/in the environs of Munich.
umgehen [ōōm'gā:ən] *unreg vi* go (a)round;
im Schlosse ~ haunt the castle; **mit jdm/
etw** ~ **können** know how to handle sb/sth;

mit jdm grob *etc* ~ treat sb roughly *etc*;
mit Geld sparsam ~ be careful with one's
money ◆ |ōōmgā:'ən| *vt untr* bypass; (*MIL*)
outflank; (*Steuer*) evade; (*Gesetz etc*)
circumvent; (*vermeiden*) avoid.
um'gehend *a* immediate.
Umge'hung *f* bypassing; outflanking;
circumvention; avoidance.
Umgehungsstraße *f* bypass.
umgekehrt |ōōm'gəkä:rt| *a* reverse(d); (*ge-
genteilig*) opposite ◆ *ad* the other way
around; **und** ~ and vice versa.
umgestalten |ōōm'gəshtáltən| *vt* alter; (*re-
organisieren*) reorganize; (*umordnen*) rearrange.
umgewöhnen |ōōm'gəvœnən| *vr* readapt.
umgraben |ōōm'grábən| *vt unreg* dig up.
umgruppieren |ōōm'grōōpē:rən| *vt* regroup.
Umhang |ōōm'háng| *m* wrap, cape.
umhängen |ōōm'hengən| *vt* (*Bild*) hang
somewhere else; **jdm etw** ~ put sth on sb.
Umhängetasche *f* shoulder bag.
umhauen |ōōm'houən| *vt* fell; (*fig*) bowl
over.
umher |ōōmhā:r'| *ad* about, around; ~**gehen**
vi unreg walk about; ~**irren** *vi* wander
around; (*Blick, Augen*) roam about;
~**reisen** *vi* travel about; ~**schweifen** *vi*
roam about; ~**ziehen** *vi unreg* wander from
place to place.
umhinkönnen |ōōmhin'kœnən| *vi unreg*: **ich
kann nicht umhin, das zu tun** I can't help
doing it.
umhören |ōōm'hœrən| *vr* ask around.
umkämpfen |ōōmkem'pfən| *vt untr* (*Ent-
scheidung*) dispute; (*Wahlkreis, Sieg*) contest.
Umkehr |ōōm'kā:r| *f* - turning back; (*Ände-
rung*) change.
umkehren *vi* turn back; (*fig*) change one's
ways ◆ *vt* turn round, reverse; (*Tasche etc*)
turn inside out; (*Gefäß etc*) turn upside
down.
umkippen |ōōm'kipən| *vt* tip over ◆ *vi* over-
turn; (*fig: Meinung ändern*) change one's
mind; (*umg: Mensch*) keel over.
umklammern |ōōmklá'mərn| *vt untr* (*mit
Händen*) clasp; (*festhalten*) cling to.
umklappen |ōōm'klápən| *vt* fold down.
Umkleideraum |ōōm'klīdəroum| *m* changing
room; (*THEAT*) dressing room.
umknicken |ōōm'knikən| *vt* (*Ast*) snap;
(*Papier*) fold (over) ◆ *vi*: **mit dem Fuß** ~
twist one's ankle.
umkommen |ōōm'komən| *vi unreg* die,
perish; (*Lebensmittel*) go bad.
Umkreis |ōōm'krīs| *m* neighborhood (*US*),
neighbourhood (*Brit*); **im** ~ **von** within a radius of.
umkreisen |ōōmkrī'zən| *vt untr* circle
(round); (*Satellit*) orbit.
umkrempeln |ōōm'krempəln| *vt* turn up;
(*mehrmals*) roll up; (*umg: Betrieb*) shake
up.

umladen |ōōm'lâdən| *vt unreg* transfer, re-
load.
Umlage |ōōm'lágə| *f* share of the costs.
Umlauf *m* (*Geld*~) circulation; (*von Gestirn*)
revolution; (*Schreiben*) circular; **in** ~ **bring-
en** circulate; ~**bahn** *f* orbit.
umlaufen |ōōm'loufən| *vi unreg* circulate.
Umlauf- *zW*: ~**kapital** *nt* working capital;
~**vermögen** *nt* current assets *pl.*
Umlaut |ōōm'lout| *m* umlaut.
umlegen |ōōm'lā:gən| *vt* put on; (*verlegen*)
move, shift; (*Kosten*) share out; (*umkippen*)
tip over; (*umg: töten*) bump off.
umleiten |ōōm'lītən| *vt* detour (*US*), divert
(*Brit*).
Umleitung *f* detour (*US*), diversion (*Brit*).
umlernen |ōōm'lernən| *vi* learn something
new; (*fig*) adjust one's views.
umliegend |ōōm'lē:gənt| *a* surrounding.
ummelden |ōōm'meldən| *vtr*: **jdn/sich** ~ no-
tify (the police of) a change in sb's/one's address.
Umnachtung |ōōmnāk̬h'tōōng| *f* mental de-
rangement.
umorganisieren |ōōm'orgánēzē:rən| *vt* re-
organize.
umpflanzen |ōōm'pflántsən| *vt* transplant.
umquartieren |ōōmk'vàrtē:rən| *vt* move;
(*Truppen*) requarter.
umrahmen |ōōmrá'mən| *vt untr* frame.
umranden |ōōmrán'dən| *vt untr* border, edge.
umräumen |ōōm'roimən| *vti* (*anders
anordnen*) rearrange.
umrechnen |ōōm'reċhnən| *vt* convert.
Umrechnung *f* conversion.
Umrechnungskurs *m* rate of exchange.
umreißen |ōōmrī'sən| *vt unreg untr* outline.
umrennen |ōōm'rcnən| *vt unreg* (run into
and) knock down.
umringen |ōōmri'ngən| *vt untr* surround.
Umriß |ōōm'ris| *m* outline.
umrühren |ōōm'rü:rən| *vti* stir.
umrüsten |ōōm'rüstən| *vt* (*TECH*) adapt (*auf
+akk* to); (*MIL*) re-equip.
ums |ōōms| = **um das.**
umsatteln |ōōm'zátəln| *vi* (*umg*) change
one's occupation, switch jobs.
Umsatz |ōōm'záts| *m* turnover; ~**beteiligung**
f commission; ~**einbuße** *f* loss of profit;
~**steuer** *f* turnover *od* sales tax.
umschalten |ōōm'shàltən| *vt* switch ◆ *vi*
push/pull a lever; (*auf anderen Sender*)
change over (*auf +akk* to); (*AUT*) shift (*in
+akk* in)to); „**wir schalten jetzt um nach
Hamburg"** "and now we go over to Hamburg".
Umschalttaste *f* shift-key.
Umschau *f* look(ing) round; ~ **halten nach**
look around for.
umschauen |ōōm'shouən| *vr* look round.
Umschlag |ōōm'shlàk| *m* cover; (*Buch~
auch*) jacket; (*MED*) compress; (*Brief*~) envelope; (*Gütermenge*) volume of traffic;
(*Wechsel*) change; (*von Hose*) turn-up.

umschlagen |ōōm'shlágən| *unreg vi* change; (*NAUT*) capsize ♦ *vt* knock over; (*Ärmel*) turn up; (*Seite*) turn over; (*Waren*) transfer.

Umschlag- *zW:* ~**hafen** *m* port of transshipment; ~**platz** *m* (*COMM*) distribution center; ~**seite** *f* cover page.

umschlingen |ōōmshli'ngən| *vt unreg untr* (*Pflanze*) twine around; embrace.

umschreiben |ōōm'shrībən| *unreg vt* (*neu* ~) rewrite; (*übertragen*) transfer (*auf* +*akk* to) ♦ |ōōmshrī'bən| *vt untr* paraphrase; (*abgrenzen*) circumscribe, define.

Umschuldung |ōōm'shōōldōōng| *f* rescheduling (of debts).

umschulen |ōōm'shōō:lən| *vt* retrain; (*Kind*) send to another school.

umschwärmen |ōōmshvcr'mən| *vt untr* swarm round; (*fig*) surround, idolize.

Umschweife |ōōm'shvīfə| *pl:* **ohne** ~ without beating about the bush, straight out.

umschwenken |ōōm'shvcnkən| *vi* (*Kran*) swing out; (*fig*) do an about-turn; (*Wind*) veer.

Umschwung |ōōm'shvōōng| *m* (*Gymnastik*) circle; (*fig: ins Gegenteil*) change (around).

umsegeln |ōōm'zā:gəln| *vt untr* sail around; (*Erde*) circumnavigate.

umsehen |ōōm'zā:ən| *vr unreg* look around *od* about; (*suchen*) look out (*nach* for); **ich möchte mich nur mal** ~ (*in Geschäft*) I'm just looking.

umseitig |ōōm'zītiċh| *ad* overleaf.

umsetzen |ōōm'zctsən| *vt* (*Waren*) turn over; **etw in die Tat** ~ translate sth into action ♦ *vr* (*Schüler*) change places.

Umsicht |ōōm'ziċht| *f* prudence, caution.

umsichtig *a* prudent, cautious.

Umsiedler(in *f*) |ōōm'zē:dlər(in)| *m* **-s,** - resettler.

umsonst |ōōmzonst'| *ad* in vain; (*gratis*) for nothing.

umspringen |ōōm'shpringən| *vi unreg* change; (*Wind auch*) veer; **mit jdm** ~ treat sb badly.

Umstand |ōōm'shtánt| *m* circumstance; **Umstände** *pl* (*fig: Schwierigkeiten*) fuss *sing*; **in anderen Umständen sein** be pregnant; **Umstände machen** go to a lot of trouble; **den Umständen entsprechend** much as one would expect (under the circumstances); **die näheren Umstände** further details; **unter Umständen** possibly; **mildernde Umstände** (*JUR*) extenuating circumstances.

umständehalber *ad* owing to circumstances.

umständlich |ōōm'shtcntliċh| *a* (*Methode*) cumbersome, complicated; (*Ausdrucksweise, Erklärung auch*) long-winded; (*ungeschickt*) ponderous; **etw** ~ **machen** make sth complicated, make heavy weather of sth (*Brit*).

Umstandskleid *nt* maternity dress.

Umstandswort *nt* adverb.

umstehend |ōōm'shtā:ənt| *a attr* (*umseitig*) overleaf.

Umstehende(n) |ōōm'shtā:əndə(n)| *pl* bystanders *pl*.

Umsteigekarte *f* transfer ticket.

umsteigen |ōōm'shtīgən| *vi unreg* (*EISENB*) change; (*fig umg*) change over, switch (over) (*auf* +*akk* to).

umstellen |ōōm'shtelən| *vt* (*an anderen Ort*) change round, rearrange; (*TECH*) convert ♦ *vr* adapt o.s. (*auf* +*akk* to) ♦ |ōōmshtc'lən| *vt untr* surround.

Um'stellung *f* change; (*Umgewöhnung*) adjustment; (*TECH*) conversion.

umstimmen |ōōm'shtimən| *vt* (*MUS*) retune; **jdn** ~ make sb change his mind.

umstoßen |ōōm'shtō:sən| *vt unreg* (*lit*) overturn; (*Plan etc*) change, upset.

umstritten |ōōmshtri'tən| *a* disputed; (*fraglich*) controversial.

Umsturz |ōōm'shtōōrts| *m* overthrow.

umstürzen |ōōm'shtürtsən| *vt* (*umwerfen*) overturn ♦ *vi* collapse, fall down; (*Wagen*) overturn.

umstürzlerisch *a* revolutionary.

Umtausch |ōōm'toush| *m* exchange; **diese Waren sind vom** ~ **ausgeschlossen** these goods cannot be exchanged.

umtauschen *vt* exchange.

Umtriebe |ōōm'trē:bə| *pl* machinations *pl*, intrigues *pl*.

umtun |ōōm'tōō:n| *vr unreg* see; **sich nach etw** ~ look for sth.

umverteilen |ōōm'fcrtīlən| *vt* redistribute.

umwälzend |ōōm'vcltsənt| *a* (*fig*) radical; (*Veränderungen*) sweeping; (*Ereignisse*) revolutionary.

Umwälzung *f* (*fig*) radical change.

umwandeln |ōōm'vándəln| *vt* change, convert; (*ELEK*) transform.

umwechseln |ōōm'vcksəln| *vt* change.

Umweg |ōōm'vā:k| *m* detour; (*fig*) roundabout way.

Umwelt |ōōm'vclt| *f* environment; ~**auto** *nt* (*umg*) vehicle which does not harm the environment; ~**bewußtsein** *nt* consciousness of environmental problems; **u~freundlich** *a* ecologically harmless, pollution-free; ~**ministerium** *nt* Ministry for the Environment; **u~schädlich** *a* harmful to the environment; ~**schutz** *m* conservation; ~**schützer** *m* **-s,** - environmentalist; ~**verschmutzung** *f* environmental pollution.

umwenden |ōōm'vcndən| *vtr unreg* turn (round).

umwerben |ōōmvcr'bən| *vt unreg untr* court, woo.

umwerfen |ōōm'vcrfən| *vt unreg* (*lit*) upset, overturn; (*Mantel*) throw on; (*fig: erschüttern*) upset, throw.

umwerfend *a* (*umg*) fantastic.

umziehen |ōōm'tsē:ən| *unreg vtr* change ♦ *vi* move.

umzingeln |ōōmtsi'ngəln| *vt untr* surround,

encircle.

Umzug [ōōm'tsōō:k] *m* procession; (*Wohnungs~*) move, removal.

UN *pl abk* (= *United Nations*) UN.

un- [ōōn'] *zW*: **~abän'derlich** *a* irreversible, unalterable; **~abänderlich feststehen** be absolutely certain; **~abding'bar** *a* indispensable, essential; (*Recht*) inalienable; **~abhängig** *a* independent; **U~abhängigkeit** *f* independence; **~abköm'mlich** *a* indispensable; **zur Zeit ~abkömmlich** not free at the moment; **~abläs'sig** *a* incessant, constant; **~abseh'bar** *a* immeasurable; (*Folgen*) unforeseeable; (*Kosten*) incalculable; **~absichtlich** *a* unintentional; **~abwend'bar** *a* inevitable.

unachtsam [ōōn'ákhtzâm] *a* careless; **U~keit** *f* carelessness.

un- [ōōn'] *zW*: **~anfecht'bar** *a* indisputable; **~angebracht** *a* uncalled-for; **~angefochten** *a* unchallenged; (*Testament, Wahlkandidat, Urteil*) uncontested; **~angemeldet** *a* unannounced; (*Besucher*) unexpected; **~angemessen** *a* inadequate; **~angenehm** *a* unpleasant; (*peinlich*) embarrassing; **~angepaßt** *a* non-conformist; **U~annehmlichkeit** *f* inconvenience; **U~annehmlichkeiten** *pl* trouble; **~ansehnlich** *a* unsightly; **~anständig** *a* indecent, improper; **U~anständigkeit** *f* indecency, impropriety; **~antast'bar** *a* inviolable, sacrosanct.

unappetitlich [ōōn'ápätē:tlich] *a* unsavory (*US*), unsavoury (*Brit*).

Unart [ōōn'ârt] *f* bad manners *pl*; (*Angewohnheit*) bad habit.

unartig *a* naughty, badly behaved.

un- [ōōn'] *zW*: **~aufdringlich** *a* unobtrusive; (*Parfüm*) discreet; (*Mensch*) unassuming; **~auffällig** *a* unobtrusive; (*Kleidung*) inconspicuous; **~auffind'bar** *a* not to be found; **~aufgefordert** *a* unasked ♦ *ad* spontaneously; **~aufgefordert zugesandte Manuskripte** unsolicited manuscripts; **~aufhalt'sam** *a* irresistible; **~aufhör'lich** *a* incessant, continuous; **~aufmerksam** *a* inattentive; **~aufrichtig** *a* insincere.

un- [ōōn'] *zW*: **~ausbleib'lich** *a* inevitable, unavoidable; **~ausgeglichen** *a* volatile; **~ausgegoren** *a* immature; (*Idee, Plan*) half-baked; **~ausgesetzt** *a* incessant, constant; **~ausgewogen** *a* unbalanced; **~aussprech'lich** *a* inexpressible; **~aussteh'lich** *a* intolerable; **~ausweich'lich** *a* inescapable, ineluctable.

unbändig [ōōn'bendich] *a* extreme, excessive.

unbarmherzig [ōōn'bârmhertsich] *a* pitiless, merciless.

unbeabsichtigt [ōōn'bəápzichticht] *a* unintentional.

unbeachtet [ōōn'bəákhtət] *a* unnoticed; (*Warnung*) ignored.

unbedacht [ōōn'bədákht] *a* rash.

unbedarft [ōōn'bədârft] *a* (*umg*) clueless.

unbedenklich [ōōn'bədengklich] *a* unhesi-

tating; (*Plan*) unobjectionable ♦ *ad* without hesitation.

unbedeutend [ōōn'bədoitənt] *a* insignificant, unimportant; (*Fehler*) slight.

unbedingt [ōōn'bədingt] *a* unconditional ♦ *ad* absolutely; **mußt du ~ gehen?** do you really have to go?; **nicht ~** not necessarily.

unbefangen [ōōn'bəfángən] *a* impartial, unprejudiced; (*ohne Hemmungen*) uninhibited; **U~heit** *f* impartiality; uninhibitedness.

unbefriedigend [ōōn'bəfrē:digənd] *a* unsatisfactory.

unbefriedigt [ōōn'bəfrē:dicht] *a* unsatisfied; (*unzufrieden*) dissatisfied; (*unerfüllt*) unfulfilled.

unbefugt [ōōn'bəfōō:kt] *a* unauthorized; **U~en ist der Eintritt verboten** no admittance to unauthorized persons.

unbegabt [ōōn'bəgápt] *a* untalented.

unbegreiflich [ōōnbəgrī'flich] *a* inconceivable.

unbegrenzt [ōōn'bəgrentst] *a* unlimited.

unbegründet [ōōn'bəgründət] *a* unfounded.

Unbehagen [ōōn'bəhágən] *nt* discomfort.

unbehaglich [ōōn'bəháklich] *a* uncomfortable; (*Gefühl*) uneasy.

unbeherrscht [ōōn'bəhersht] *a* uncontrolled; (*Mensch*) lacking self-control.

unbeholfen [ōōn'bəholfən] *a* awkward, clumsy; **U~heit** *f* awkwardness, clumsiness.

unbeirrt [ōōn'bəirt] *a* imperturbable.

unbekannt [ōōn'bəkánt] *a* unknown; **~e Größe** (*MATH, fig*) unknown quantity.

un'bekannterwei'se *ad*: **grüß(e) sie ~ von mir** give her my regards although I don't known her.

unbekümmert [ōōn'bəkümərt] *a* unconcerned.

unbelehrbar [ōōnbəlā:r'bár] *a* fixed in one's views; (*Rassist etc*) dyed-in-the-wool *attr*.

unbeliebt [ōōn'bəlē:pt] *a* unpopular; **U~heit** *f* unpopularity.

unbemannt [ōōn'bəmánt] *a* (*Raumflug*) unmanned; (*Flugzeug*) pilotless.

unbemerkt [ōōn'bəmerkt] *a* unnoticed.

unbenommen [ōōn'bəno'mən] *a* (*form*): **es bleibt** *od* **ist Ihnen ~, zu ...** you are at liberty to ...

unbequem [ōōn'bəkvä:m] *a* (*Stuhl*) uncomfortable; (*Mensch*) bothersome; (*Regelung*) inconvenient.

unberechenbar [ōōnbəre'chənbár] *a* incalculable; (*Mensch, Verhalten*) unpredictable.

unberechtigt [ōōn'bərechticht] *a* unjustified; (*nicht erlaubt*) unauthorized.

unberücksichtigt [ōōnbərük'zichticht] *a*: **etw ~ lassen** not consider sth.

unberufen [ōōnbərōō:'fən] *interj* knock on wood! (*US*), touch wood! (*Brit*).

unberührt [ōōn'bərü:rt] *a* untouched; (*Natur*) unspoiled; **sie ist noch ~** she is still a virgin.

unbeschadet [ōōnbəshâ'dət] *präp* +*gen* (*form*) regardless of.

unbescheiden [ōōn'bəshīdən] *a* presumptuous.

unbescholten [ōōn'bəsholtən] a respectable; (Ruf) spotless.

unbeschränkt [ōōnbəshrengkt'] a: ~e **Haftung** unlimited liability.

unbeschreiblich [ōōnbəshrī'pliçh] a indescribable.

unbeschwert [ōōn'bəshvā:rt] a (sorgenfrei) carefree; (Melodien) light.

unbesehen [ōōnbəzā:'ən] ad indiscriminately; (ohne es anzusehen) without looking at it.

unbesonnen [ōōn'bəzonən] a unwise, rash, imprudent.

unbesorgt [ōōn'bəzorkt] a unconcerned; **Sie können ganz ~ sein** you can set your mind at rest.

unbest. abk = **unbestimmt.**

unbeständig [ōōn'bəshtendiçh] a (Mensch) inconstant; (Wetter) unsettled; (Lage) unstable.

unbestechlich [ōōnbəshteçh'liçh] a incorruptible.

unbestimmt [ōōn'bəshtimt] a indefinite; (Zukunft auch) uncertain; **U~heit** f vagueness.

unbestritten [ōōn'bəshtritən] a undisputed, indisputable.

unbeteiligt [ōōn'bətī'liçht] a unconcerned; (uninteressiert) indifferent.

unbeugsam [ōōn'boikzâm] a stubborn, inflexible; (Wille auch) unbending.

unbewacht [ōōn'bəvàḳht] a unguarded, unwatched.

unbewaffnet [ōōn'bəváfnət] a unarmed.

unbeweglich [ōōn'bəvä:kliçh] a immovable.

unbewegt a motionless; (fig: unberührt) unmoved.

unbewohnt [ōōn'bəvō:nt] a (Gegend) uninhabited; (Haus) unoccupied.

unbewußt [ōōn'bəvōōst] a unconscious.

unbezahlbar [ōōnbətsál'bár] a prohibitively expensive; (fig) priceless; (nützlich) invaluable.

unbrauchbar [ōōn'broukḥbâr] a (Arbeit) useless; (Gerät auch) unusable; **U~keit** f uselessness.

unbürokratisch [ōōn'bürōkrátish] a without any red tape.

und [ōōnt] kj and; ~ **so weiter** and so on.

Undank [ōōn'dángk] m ingratitude; **u~bar** a ungrateful; **~barkeit** f ingratitude.

undefinierbar [ōōndāfēnē:r'bár] a indefinable.

undenkbar [ōōndengk'bâr] a inconceivable.

undeutlich [ōōn'doitliçh] a indistinct; (Schrift) illegible; (Ausdrucksweise) unclear.

undicht [ōōn'diçht] a leaky.

undifferenziert [ōōn'difərentsē:rt] a simplistic.

Unding [ōōn'ding] nt absurdity.

unduldsam [ōōn'bdldsâm] a intolerant.

un- [ōōn'] zW: ~**durchdring'lich** a (Urwald) impenetrable; (Gesicht) inscrutable; ~**durchführ'bar** a impracticable; ~**durchläs-**

sig a waterproof, impermeable; ~**durchsichtig** a opaque; (Motive) obscure; (fig pej: Mensch, Methoden) devious.

uneben [ōōn'ā:bən] a uneven.

unehelich [ōōn'ā:əliçh] a illegitimate.

uneigennützig [ōōn'īgənnütsiçh] a unselfish.

uneinbringlich [ōōnīnbring'liçh] a: ~e **Forderungen** pl (COMM) bad debts pl.

uneingeschränkt [ōōn'īngəshrengkt] a absolute, total; (Rechte, Handel) unrestricted; (Zustimmung) unqualified.

uneinig [ōōn'īniçh] a divided; ~ **sein** disagree; **U~keit** f discord, dissension.

uneinnehmbar [ōōnīnnā:m'bár] a impregnable.

uneins [ōōn'īns] a at variance, at odds.

unempfänglich [ōōn'empfengliçh] a not susceptible (für to).

unempfindlich [ōōn'empfintliçh] a insensitive; **U~keit** f insensitivity.

unendlich [ōōnen'tliçh] a infinite ♦ ad endlessly; (fig: sehr) terribly; **U~keit** f infinity.

un- [ōōn'] zW: ~**entbehr'lich** a indispensable; ~**entgelt'lich** a free (of charge); ~**entschieden** a undecided; ~**entschieden enden** (SPORT) end in a draw; ~**entschlossen** a undecided; irresolute; ~**entwegt'** a unswerving; (unaufhörlich) incessant.

un- [ōōn'] zW: ~**erbitt'lich** a unyielding, inexorable; ~**erfahren** a inexperienced; ~**erfreulich** a unpleasant; **U~erfreuliches** (schlechte Nachrichten) bad news sing; (Übles) bad things pl; ~**erfüllt** a unfulfilled; ~**ergiebig** a (Quelle, Thema) unproductive; (Ernte, Nachschlagewerk) poor; ~**ergründ'lich** a unfathomable; ~**erheblich** a unimportant; ~**erhört'** a unheard-of; (unverschämt) outrageous; (Bitte) unanswered; ~**erläß'lich** a indispensable; ~**erlaubt** a unauthorized; ~**erledigt** a unfinished; (Post) unanswered; (Rechnung) outstanding; (schwebend) pending; ~**ermeß'lich** a immeasurable, immense; ~**ermüd'lich** a indefatigable; ~**ersätt'lich** a insatiable; ~**erschlossen** a (Land) undeveloped; (Boden) unexploited; (Vorkommen, Markt) untapped; ~**erschöpf'lich** a inexhaustible; ~**erschrocken** a intrepid, courageous; ~**erschüt'terlich** a unshakeable; ~**erschwing'lich** a (Preis) exorbitant, prohibitive; ~**ersetz'lich** a irreplaceable; ~**erträg'lich** a unbearable; (Frechheit) insufferable; ~**erwartet** a unexpected; ~**erwünscht** a undesirable, unwelcome; ~**erzogen** a ill-bred, rude.

unfähig [ōōn'fe:içh] a incapable (zu of); (attr) incompetent; **U~keit** f inability; incompetence.

unfair [ōōn'fe:r] a unfair.

Unfall [ōōn'fál] m accident; ~**flucht** f hit-and-run (driving); ~**geld** nt injury benefit; ~**opfer** nt casualty; ~**stelle** f scene of the accident; ~**versicherung** f accident insur-

ance; ~**wagen** *m* *car involved in an accident*; (*umg: Rettungswagen*) ambulance.
unfaßbar [ōōnfás'bâr] *a* inconceivable.
unfehlbar [ōōnfā:l'bâr] *a* infallible ♦ *ad* without fail; **U~keit** *f* infallibility.
unfertig [ōōn'fertiċḣ] *a* unfinished, incomplete; (*Mensch*) immature.
unflätig [ōōn'fle:tiċḣ] *a* rude. -
unfolgsam [ōōn'folkzâm] *a* disobedient.
unförmig [ōōn'fœrmiċḣ] *a* (*formlos*) shapeless; (*groß*) cumbersome; (*Füße, Gesicht*) unshapely.
unfrankiert [ōōn'frángkē:rt] *a* unfranked.
unfrei [ōōn'frī] *a* not free.
unfreiwillig *a* involuntary, against one's will.
unfreundlich [ōōn'frointliċḣ] *a* unfriendly; **U~keit** *f* unfriendliness.
Unfriede(n) [ōōn'frē:də(n)] *m* dissension, strife.
unfruchtbar [ōōn'frōōkḣtbâr] *a* infertile; (*Gespräche*) unfruitful; fruitless; **U~keit** *f* infertility; unfruitfulness.
Unfug [ōōn'fōō:k] *m* **-s** (*Benehmen*) mischief; (*Unsinn*) nonsense; **grober** ~ (*JUR*) gross misconduct; malicious damage.
Ungar(in *f*) [ōōng'gár(in)] *m* **-n, -n** Hungarian; **u~isch** *a* Hungarian.
Ungarn *nt* **-s** Hungary.
ungeachtet [ōōn'gəákḣtət] *präp* +*gen* notwithstanding.
ungeahndet [ōōn'gəândət] *a* (*JUR*) unpunished.
ungeahnt [ōōn'gəânt] *a* unsuspected, undreamt-of.
ungebeten [ōōn'gəbā:tən] *a* uninvited.
ungebildet [ōōn'gəbildət] *a* uncultured; (*ohne Bildung*) uneducated.
ungeboren [ōōn'gəbō:rən] *a* unborn.
ungebräuchlich [ōōn'gəbroiċḣliċḣ] *a* unusual, uncommon.
ungebührlich [ōōn'gəbü:rliċḣ] *a*: **sich** ~ **aufregen** get unduly excited.
ungebunden [ōōn'gəbōōndən] *a* (*Buch*) unbound; (*Leben*) (fancy-)free; (*unverheiratet*) unattached; (*POL*) independent.
ungedeckt [ōōn'gədekt] *a* (*schutzlos*) unprotected; (*Scheck*) uncovered.
Ungeduld [ōōn'gədōōlt] *f* impatience.
ungeduldig [ōōn'gədōōldiċḣ] *a* impatient.
ungeeignet [ōōn'gəîgnət] *a* unsuitable.
ungefähr [ōōn'gəfe:r] *a* rough, approximate ♦ *ad* roughly, approximately; **so** ~! more or less!; **das kommt nicht von** ~ that's hardly surprising.
ungefährlich [ōōn'gəfe:rliċḣ] *a* not dangerous, harmless.
ungehalten [ōōn'gəháltən] *a* indignant.
ungeheuer [ōōn'gəhoiər] *a* huge ♦ *ad* (*umg*) enormously; **U~** *nt* **-s, -** monster; **~lich** [ōōngəhoi'ərliċḣ] *a* monstrous.
ungehindert [ōōn'gəhindərt] *a* unimpeded.
ungehobelt [ōōn'gəhō:bəlt] *a* (*fig*) uncouth.
ungehörig [ōōn'gəhœriċḣ] *a* impertinent, improper; **U~keit** *f* impertinence.

ungehorsam [ōōn'gəhō:rzâm] *a* disobedient; **U~** *m* disobedience.
ungeklärt [ōōn'gəkle:rt] *a* not cleared up; (*Rätsel*) unsolved; (*Abwasser*) untreated.
ungekürzt [ōōn'gəkürtst] *a* not shortened; (*Film*) uncut.
ungeladen [ōōn'gəlâdən] *a* not loaded; (*ELEK*) uncharged; (*Gast*) uninvited.
ungelegen [ōōn'gəlā:gən] *a* inconvenient; **komme ich (Ihnen)** ~? is this an inconvenient time for you?
ungelernt [ōōn'gəlernt] *a* unskilled.
ungelogen [ōōn'gəlō:gən] *ad* really, honestly.
ungemein [ōōn'gəmīn] *a* uncommon.
ungemütlich [ōōn'gəmü:tliċḣ] *a* uncomfortable; (*Person*) disagreeable; **er kann** ~ **werden** he can get nasty.
ungenau [ōōn'gənou] *a* inaccurate.
Ungenauigkeit *f* inaccuracy.
ungeniert [ōōn'zhānē:rt] *a* free and easy; (*bedenkenlos, taktlos*) uninhibited ♦ *ad* without embarrassment, freely.
ungenießbar [ōōn'gənē:sbâr] *a* inedible; (*nicht zu trinken*) undrinkable; (*umg*) unbearable.
ungenügend [ōōn'gənü:gənt] *a* insufficient, inadequate; (*SCH*) unsatisfactory.
ungenutzt [ōōn'gənōōtst] *a*: **eine Chance** ~ **lassen** miss an opportunity.
ungepflegt [ōōn'gəpflā:kt] *a* (*Garten etc*) untended; (*Person*) unkempt; (*Hände*) neglected.
ungerade [ōōn'gərâdə] *a* uneven, odd.
ungerecht [ōōn'gəreċḣt] *a* unjust.
ungerechtfertigt *a* unjustified.
Ungerechtigkeit *f* unfairness, injustice.
ungeregelt [ōōn'gərā:gəlt] *a* irregular.
ungereimt [ōōn'gərīmt] *a* (*Verse*) unrhymed; (*fig*) inconsistent.
ungern [ōōn'gern] *ad* unwillingly, reluctantly.
ungerufen [ōōn'gərōō:fən] *a* without being called.
ungeschehen [ōōn'gəshā:ən] *a*: ~ **machen** undo.
Ungeschicklichkeit [ōōn'gəshikliċḣkīt] *f* clumsiness.
ungeschickt *a* awkward, clumsy.
ungeschliffen [ōōn'gəshlifən] *a* (*Edelstein*) uncut; (*Messer etc*) blunt; (*fig: Benehmen*) uncouth.
ungeschmälert [ōōn'gəshme:lərt] *a* undiminished.
ungeschminkt [ōōn'gəshmingkt] *a* without make-up; (*fig*) unvarnished.
ungeschoren [ōōn'gəshō:rən] *a*: **jdn** ~ **lassen** (*umg*) spare sb; (*ungestraft*) let sb off.
ungesetzlich [ōōn'gəzetsliċḣ] *a* illegal.
ungestempelt [ōōn'gəshtempəlt] *a* (*Briefmarke*) unfranked, uncancelled.
ungestört [ōōn'gəshtœrt] *a* undisturbed.
ungestraft [ōōn'gəshtráft] *ad* with impunity.
ungestüm [ōōn'gəshtü:m] *a* impetuous; **U~** *nt* **-(e)s** impetuosity.
ungesund [ōōn'gəzōōnt] *a* unhealthy.

ungetrübt [ōōn'gətrü:pt] *a* clear; *(fig)* untroubled; *(Freude)* unalloyed.

Ungetüm [ōōn'gətü:m] *nt* **-(e)s, -e** monster.

ungeübt [ōōn'gəü:pt] *a* unpracticed *(US)*, unpractised *(Brit)*; *(Mensch)* out of practice.

ungewiß [ōōn'gəvis] *a* uncertain; **U~heit** *f* uncertainty.

ungewöhnlich [ōōn'gəvœnlich] *a* unusual.

ungewohnt [ōōn'gəvō:nt] *a* unaccustomed.

ungewollt [ōōn'gəvolt] *a* unintentional.

Ungeziefer [ōōn'gətsē:fər] *nt* **-s** vermin.

ungezogen [ōōn'gətsō:gən] *a* rude, impertinent; **U~heit** *f* rudeness, impertinence.

ungezwungen [ōōn'gətsvōōngən] *a* natural, unconstrained.

ungläubig [ōōn'gloibich] *a* unbelieving; **ein ~er Thomas** a doubting Thomas; **die U~en** the infidel(s *pl*).

unglaub- *zW:* **~lich** [ōōngloup'lich] *a* incredible; **~würdig** [ōōn'gloupvürdich] *a* untrustworthy, unreliable; *(Geschichte)* improbable; **sich ~würdig machen** lose credibility.

ungleich [ōōn'glich] *a* dissimilar; *(Mittel, Waffen)* unequal ♦ *ad* incomparably; **~artig** *a* different; **U~behandlung** *f* *(von Frauen, Ausländer)* unequal treatment; **U~heit** *f* dissimilarity; inequality; **~mäßig** *a* uneven; *(Atemzüge, Gesichtszüge, Puls)* irregular.

Unglück [ōōn'glük] *nt* misfortune; *(Pech)* bad luck; *(Unglücksfall)* calamity, disaster; *(Verkehrs~)* accident; **zu allem ~** to make matters worse; **u~lich** *a* unhappy; *(erfolglos)* unlucky; *(unerfreulich)* unfortunate; **u~licherweise** [-vī'zə] *ad* unfortunately; **u~selig** *a* calamitous; *(Person)* unfortunate.

Unglücks- *zW:* **~fall** *m* accident, mishap; **~rabe** *m* *(umg)* poor devil.

Ungnade [ōōn'gnâdə] *f:* **bei jdm in ~ fallen** fall out of favor with sb.

ungültig [ōōn'gültich] *a* invalid; **etw für ~ erklären** declare sth null and void; **U~keit** *f* invalidity.

ungünstig [ōōn'günstich] *a* unfavorable *(US)*, unfavourable *(Brit)*; *(Termin)* inconvenient; *(Augenblick, Wetter)* bad; *(nicht preiswert)* expensive.

ungut [ōōn'gōō:t] *a* *(Gefühl)* uneasy; **nichts für ~!** no offence!

unhaltbar [ōōn'hâltbâr] *a* untenable.

unhandlich [ōōn'hântlich] *a* unwieldy.

Unheil [ōōn'hīl] *nt* evil; *(Unglück)* misfortune; **~ anrichten** cause mischief; **u~bringend** *a* fatal, fateful; **u~voll** *a* disastrous.

unheimlich [ōōn'hīmlich] *a* weird, uncanny; **das/er ist mir ~** it/he gives me the creeps *(umg)* ♦ *ad* *(umg)* tremendously.

unhöflich [ōōn'hœflich] *a* impolite; **U~keit** *f* impoliteness.

unhörbar [ōōnhœr'bâr] *a* silent; *(Frequenzen)* inaudible.

unhygienisch [ōōn'hügēā:nish] *a* unhygienic.

uni [ōōnē:'] *a* unicolor *(US)*, self-coloured *(Brit)*.

Uni [ōō'nē] *f* **-, -s** university.

Uniform [ōōnēform'] *f* **-, -en** uniform.

uniformiert [ōōnēformē:rt'] *a* uniformed.

uninteressant [ōōn'intāresánt] *a* uninteresting.

Union [ōōnēō:n'] *f* **-, -en** union.

Unionsparteien *pl* *(BRD POL)* CDU and CSU parties *pl*.

universal [ōōnēverzâl'], **universell** [ōōnēverzel'] *a* universal.

Universität [ōōnēverzēte:t'] *f* **-, -en** university; **auf die ~ gehen, die ~ besuchen** go to university.

Universum [ōōnēver'zōōm] *nt* **-s** universe.

unkenntlich [ōōn'kentlich] *a* unrecognizable; **U~keit** *f:* **bis zur U~keit** beyond recognition.

Unkenntnis [ōōn'kentnis] *f* ignorance.

unklar [ōōn'klâr] *a* unclear; **im ~en sein über** *(+akk)* be in the dark about; **U~heit** *f* unclarity; *(Unentschiedenheit)* uncertainty.

unklug [ōōn'klōō:k] *a* unwise.

unkompliziert [ōōn'komplētsē:rt] *a* straightforward, uncomplicated.

Unkosten [ōōn'kostən] *pl* expense(s *pl*); **sich in ~ stürzen** *(umg)* go to a lot of expense.

Unkraut [ōōn'krout] *nt* weed, weeds *pl*; **~ vergeht nicht** *(Sprichwort)* it would take more than that to finish me *od* him *etc* off; **~vertilgungsmittel** *nt* weed killer.

unlängst [ōōn'lengst] *ad* not long ago.

unlauter [ōōn'loutər] *a* unfair.

unleserlich [ōōn'lā:zərlich] *a* illegible.

unleugbar [ōōn'loikbâr] *a* undeniable, indisputable.

unlogisch [ōōn'lō:gish] *a* illogical.

unlösbar [ōōnlœs'bâr], **unlöslich** [ōōnlœs'lich] *a* insoluble.

Unlust [ōōn'lōōst] *f* lack of enthusiasm.

unlustig [ōōn'lustich] *a* unenthusiastic.

Unmasse [ōōn'másə] *f* *(umg)* load.

unmäßig [ōōn'me:sich] *a* immoderate.

Unmenge [ōōn'mengə] *f* tremendous number, vast number.

Unmensch [ōōn'mensh] *m* ogre, brute; **u~lich** *a* inhuman, brutal; *(ungeheuer)* awful.

unmerklich [ōōnmerk'lich] *a* imperceptible.

unmißverständlich [ōōn'misfershtentlich] *a* unmistakable.

unmittelbar [ōōn'mitəlbâr] *a* immediate; direct; **~e Kostenaufwand** direct expense.

unmöbliert [ōōn'mœblē:rt] *a* unfurnished.

unmöglich [ōōn'mœklich] *a* impossible; **~ aussehen** *(umg)* look ridiculous; **U~keit** *f* impossibility.

unmoralisch [ōōn'mōrálish] *a* immoral.

unmotiviert [ōōn'mōtēvē:rt] *a* unmotivated.

unmündig [ōōn'mündich] *a* *(minderjährig)* underage.

Unmut [ōōn'mōō:t] *m* ill humor *(US)* *od* humour *(Brit)*.

unnachahmlich [ōōn'náк̣hȧmliсh] *a* inimitable.

unnachgiebig [ōōn'náк̣hge̅:biсh] *a* unyielding.

unnahbar [ōōnná'bȧr] *a* unapproachable.

unnormal [ōōn'normȧl] *a* abnormal.

unnötig [ōōn'nœtiсh] *a* unnecessary.

unnötigerwei'se *ad* unnecessarily.

unnütz [ōōn'nüts] *a* useless.

UNO [ōō:'nō] *f abk* (= *United Nations Organization*) **die ~** the UN.

unordentlich [ōōn'ordəntliсh] *a* untidy.

Unordnung [ōōn'ordnōōng] *f* disorder; (*Durcheinander*) mess.

unorganisiert [ōōn'orgánēzē:rt] *a* disorganized.

unparteiisch [ōōn'pȧrtīish] *a* impartial.

Unparteiische(r) *m dekl wie a* umpire; (*FUSSBALL*) referee.

unpassend [ōōn'pásənt] *a* inappropriate; (*Zeit*) inopportune.

unpäßlich [ōōn'pesliсh] *a* unwell.

unpersönlich [ōōn'perzœnliсh] *a* impersonal.

unpolitisch [ōōn'pōlē:tish] *a* apolitical.

unpraktisch [ōōn'prȧktish] *a* unpractical.

unproduktiv [ōōn'prōdōōktē:f] *a* unproductive.

unproportioniert [ōōn'prōportsēōnē:rt] *a* out of proportion.

unpünktlich [ōōn'püngktliсh] *a* unpunctual.

unqualifiziert [ōōn'kvȧlēfētsē:rt] *a* unqualified; (*Äußerung*) incompetent.

Unrat [ōōn'rȧt] *m* **-(e)s** (*geh*) refuse; (*fig*) filth.

unrationell [ōōn'rȧtsēōnel] *a* inefficient.

unrecht [ōōn'reсht] *a* wrong; **das ist mir gar nicht so ~** I don't really mind; **U~** *nt* wrong; **zu U~** wrongly; **nicht zu U~** not without good reason; **U~ haben, im U~ sein** be wrong; **~mäßig** *a* unlawful, illegal.

unredlich [ōōn'rā:liсh] *a* dishonest; **U~keit** *f* dishonesty.

unreell [ōōn'rāel] *a* unfair; (*unredlich*) dishonest; (*Preis*) unreasonable.

unregelmäßig [ōōn'rā:gəlmesiсh] *a* irregular; **U~keit** *f* irregularity.

unreif [ōōn'rīf] *a* (*Obst*) unripe; (*fig*) immature.

unrein [ōōn'rīn] *a* not clean; (*Ton*) impure; (*Atem, Haut*) bad; (*Gedanken, Taten*) impure.

unrentabel [ōōn'rentȧbəl] *a* unprofitable.

unrichtig [ōōn'riсhtiсh] *a* incorrect, wrong.

Unruh [ōōn'rōō:] *f* **-, -en** (*von Uhr*) balance.

Unruhe *f* **-, -n** unrest; **~stifter** *m* troublemaker.

unruhig *a* restless; (*nervös*) fidgety; (*belebt*) noisy; (*Schlaf*) fitful; (*Zeit etc, Meer*) troubled.

unrühmlich [ōōn'rü:mliсh] *a* inglorious.

uns [ōōns] *pron* (*akk, dat von* **wir**) us; (*reflexiv*) ourselves.

unsachgemäß [ōōn'záк̣hgəmes] *a* improper.

unsachlich [ōōn'záк̣hliсh] *a* not to the point, irrelevant; (*persönlich*) personal.

unsagbar [ōōnzȧk'bȧr], **unsäglich** [ōōnze:k'liсh] *a* indescribable.

unsanft [ōōn'zȧnft] *a* rough.

unsauber [ōōn'zoubər] *a* (*schmutzig*) dirty; (*fig*) crooked; (*Klang*) impure.

unschädlich [ōōn'she:dliсh] *a* harmless; **jdn/ etw ~ machen** render sb/sth harmless.

unscharf [ōōn'shȧrf] *a* indistinct; (*Bild etc*) out of focus, blurred.

unschätzbar [ōōnshets'bȧr] *a* incalculable; (*Hilfe*) invaluable.

unscheinbar [ōōn'shīnbȧr] *a* insignificant; (*Aussehen, Haus etc*) unprepossessing.

unschlagbar [ōōnshlȧk'bȧr] *a* invincible.

unschlüssig [ōōn'shlüsiсh] *a* undecided.

Unschuld [ōōn'shōōlt] *f* innocence.

unschuldig [ōōn'shōōldiсh] *a* innocent.

unschwer [ōōn'shvā:r] *ad* easily, without difficulty.

unselbständig [ōōn'zelpshtendiсh] *a* dependent, over-reliant on others.

unselig [ōōn'zā:liсh] *a* unfortunate; (*verhängnisvoll*) ill-fated.

unser [ōōn'zər] *poss pron* our ♦ *gen von* **wir** of us.

unserei'ner, unsereins', un's(e)resglei'chen *pron* people like us.

uns(e)re(r, s) *poss pron* ours; **wir tun das U~** (*geh*) we are doing our bit.

uns(e)rige(r, s) *poss pron:* **der/die/das ~** ours.

unseriös [ōōn'zārœœs] *a* (*unehrlich*) not straight, untrustworthy.

uns(e)rseits *ad* on our part.

unsertwegen [ōōn'zərtvā:'gən], **unsertwillen** [ōōn'zərtvi'lən] *ad* (*für uns*) for our sake; (*wegen uns*) on our account.

unsicher [ōōn'ziсhər] *a* uncertain; (*Mensch*) insecure; **die Gegend ~ machen** (*fig umg*) hang out in the district; **U~heit** *f* uncertainty; insecurity.

unsichtbar [ōōn'ziсhtbȧr] *a* invisible; **U~keit** *f* invisibility.

Unsinn [ōōn'zin] *m* nonsense.

unsinnig *a* nonsensical.

Unsitte [ōōn'zitə] *f* deplorable habit.

unsittlich [ōōn'zitliсh] *a* indecent; **U~keit** *f* indecency.

unsozial [ōōn'zōtsēȧl] *a* (*Verhalten*) antisocial; (*Politik*) unsocial.

unsportlich [ōōn'shportliсh] *a* not sporty; (*Verhalten*) unsporting.

unsre [ōōn'zrə] = **unsere**; *siehe* **unser**; **unsre(r, s)**.

unsrige(r, s) [ōōn'zrigə(r, s)] = **unserige**.

unsterblich [ōōn'shterpliсh] *a* immortal; **U~keit** *f* immortality.

unstet [ōōn'shtā:t] *a* (*Mensch*) restless; (*wankelmütig*) changeable; (*Leben*) unsettled.

Unstimmigkeit [ōōn'shtimiсhkīt] *f* inconsistency; (*Streit*) disagreement.

Unsumme [ōōn'zōōmə] *f* vast sum.

unsympathisch [ōōn'zümpȧtish] *a* unpleas-

ant; **er ist mir ~** I don't like him.
untad(e)lig [o͞on'tåd(ə)lich] *a* impeccable;
(*Mensch*) beyond reproach.
Untat [o͞on'tát] *f* atrocity.
untätig [o͞on'te:tich] *a* idle.
untauglich [o͞on'touglich] *a* unsuitable; (*MIL*)
unfit; **U~keit** *f* unsuitability; unfitness.
unteilbar [o͞ontīl'bár] *a* indivisible.
unten [o͞on'tən] *ad* below; (*im Haus*) downstairs; (*an der Treppe etc*) at the bottom;
siehe ~ see below; **nach ~** down; **~ am
Berg** at the bottom of the mountain *etc*;
er ist bei mir ~ durch (*umg*) I'm through
with him; **~an** *ad* (*am unteren Ende*) at the
far end; (*lit*, *fig*) at the bottom; **~genannt** *a*
undermentioned.
unter [o͞on'tər] *präp* +*akk od dat* under, below; (*bei Menschen*) among; (*während*) during; **sie waren ~ sich** (*dat*) they were by
themselves ♦ *ad* under.
Unter- *zW*: **~abteilung** *f* subdivision; **~arm**
m forearm; **u~belegt** *a* (*Kurs*) under-
subscribed; (*Hotel etc*) not full.
unterbelichten [o͞on'tərbəlichtən] *vt* (*PHOT*)
underexpose.
Unterbeschäftigung [o͞on'tərbəsheftigo͞ong] *f*
underemployment.
unterbesetzt [o͞on'tərbəzetst] *a* understaffed.
Unterbewußtsein [o͞on'tərbəvo͞ostzīn] *nt* subconscious.
unterbezahlt [o͞on'tərbəzált] *a* underpaid.
unterbieten [o͞on'tərbē:'tən] *vt unreg untr*
(*COMM*) undercut; (*fig*) surpass.
unterbinden [o͞ontərbin'dən] *vt unreg untr*
stop, call a halt to.
unterbleiben [o͞ontərblī'bən] *vi unreg untr*
(*aufhören*) stop; (*versäumt werden*) be
omitted.
Unterbodenschutz [o͞ontərbo͞o:'dənsho͞ots] *m*
(*AUT*) underseal.
unterbrechen [o͞ontərbre'chən] *vt unreg untr*
interrupt.
Unterbrechung *f* interruption.
unterbreiten [o͞ontərbrī'tən] *vt untr* (*Plan*)
present.
unterbringen [o͞on'tərbringən] *vt unreg* (*in
Koffer*) stow; (*in Zeitung*) place; (*Person:
in Hotel etc*) accommodate, put up; (: *beruflich*) fix up (*bei* with).
unterbuttern [o͞on'tərbo͞otərn] *vt* (*umg*:
zuschießen) throw in; (: *unterdrücken*) ride
roughshod over.
unterderhand [o͞ontərdárhánt'] *ad* secretly;
(*verkaufen*) privately.
unterdessen [o͞ontərde'sən] *ad* meanwhile.
Unterdruck [o͞on'tərdro͞ok] *m* low pressure.
unterdrücken [o͞ontərdrü'kən] *vt untr*
suppress; (*Leute*) oppress.
untereinander [o͞ontərīnán'dər] *ad* (*gegenseitig*) each other; (*miteinander*) among
themselves *etc*.
unterentwickelt [o͞on'tərentvikəlt] *a* underdeveloped.
untere(r, s) [o͞on'tərə(r, s)] *a* lower.

unterernährt [o͞on'tərerne:rt] *a* undernourished; underfed.
Unterernährung *f* malnutrition.
Unterführung [o͞ontərfü:'ro͞ong] *f* subway,
underpass.
Untergang [o͞on'tərgáng] *m* (down)fall, decline; (*NAUT*) sinking; (*von Gestirn*)
setting; **dem ~ geweiht sein** be doomed.
untergeben [o͞ontərgä:'bən] *a* subordinate.
Untergebene(r) *mf dekl wie a* subordinate.
untergehen [o͞on'tərgä:ən] *vi unreg* go down;
(*Sonne auch*) set; (*Staat*) fall; (*Volk*)
perish; (*Welt*) come to an end; (*im Lärm*)
be drowned.
untergeordnet [o͞on'tərgəordnət] *a* (*Dienststelle*) subordinate; (*Bedeutung*) secondary.
Untergeschoß [o͞on'tərgəshos] *nt* basement.
untergliedern [o͞ontərglē:'dərn] *vt untr* subdivide.
untergraben [o͞ontərgrá'bən] *vt unreg untr*
undermine.
Untergrund [o͞on'tərgro͞ont] *m* foundation;
(*POL*) underground; **~bahn** *f* subway (*US*),
underground (*Brit*); **~bewegung** *f* underground (movement).
unterhaken [o͞on'tərhákən] *vr*: **sich bei jdm
~** link arms with sb.
unterhalb [o͞on'tərhálp] *präp* +*gen*, *ad* below;
~ von below.
Unterhalt [o͞on'tərhált] *m* maintenance; **seinen ~ verdienen** earn one's living.
unterhalten [o͞ontərhál'tən] *unreg untr vt*
maintain; (*belustigen*) entertain; (*versorgen*) support; (*Geschäft*, *Kfz*) run; (*Konto*)
have ♦ *vr* talk; (*sich belustigen*) enjoy o.s.
unterhaltend *a* entertaining.
Unterhalts- *zW*: **~kosten** *pl* maintenance
costs *pl*; **~zuschuß** *m* subsistence; living
allowance.
Unterhaltung *f* maintenance; (*Belustigung*)
entertainment, amusement; (*Gespräch*) talk.
Unterhaltungskosten *pl* running costs *pl*.
Unterhändler [o͞on'tərhentlər] *m* negotiator.
Unterhaus [o͞on'tərhous] *nt* lower house.
Unterhemd [o͞on'tərhemt] *nt* undershirt (*US*),
vest (*Brit*).
Unterholz [o͞on'tərholts] *nt* undergrowth.
Unterhose [o͞on'tərho͞o:zə] *f* underpants *pl*.
unterirdisch [o͞on'tərirdish] *a* underground.
unterkapitalisiert [o͞on'tərkápētálēzē:'ərt] *a*
undercapitalised.
unterkellern [o͞ontərke'lərn] *vt untr* build
with a cellar.
Unterkiefer [o͞on'tərkē:fər] *m* lower jaw.
unterkommen [o͞on'tərkomən] *vi unreg* find
shelter; (*Stelle finden*) find work; **das ist
mir noch nie untergekommen** I've never
met with that; **bei jdm ~** stay at sb's
(place).
unterkühlt [o͞ontərkü:lt] *a* (*Körper*) affected
by hypothermia; (*fig*: *Mensch*, *Atmosphäre*)
cool.
Unterkunft [o͞on'tərko͞onft] *f* **-**, **-künfte**
accommodations *pl* (*US*), accommodation

(Brit); ~ **und Verpflegung** room and board.
Unterlage [ōōn'tərlågə] *f* foundation; *(Beleg)* document; *(Schreib~ etc)* pad.
unterlassen [ōōntərlá'sən] *vt unreg untr (versäumen)* fail (to do); *(sich enthalten)* refrain from.
unterlaufen [ōōntərlou'fən] *vi unreg untr* happen; **mir ist ein Fehler** ~ I made a mistake ♦ *a*: **mit Blut** ~ suffused with blood; *(Augen)* bloodshot.
unterlegen [ōōn'tərlā:gən] *vt* lay *od* put under ♦ [ōōntərlā:'gən] *a* inferior *(dat* to); *(besiegt)* defeated.
Unterleib [ōōn'tərlīp] *m* abdomen.
Unterleibskrebs *m* cancer of the abdomen *od* the womb.
unterliegen [ōōntərlē:'gən] *vi unreg untr* be defeated *od* overcome *(jdm* by sb); *(unterworfen sein)* be subject to.
Unterlippe [ōōn'tərlipə] *f* bottom *od* lower lip.
untermalen [ōōntərmá'lən] *vt untr (mit Musik)* provide with background music.
untermauern [ōōntərmou'ərn] *vt untr (Gebäude, fig)* underpin.
Untermiete [ōōn'tərmē:tə] *f* subtenancy; **bei jdm zur ~ wohnen** rent a room from sb.
Untermieter(in *f)* *m* lodger.
unternehmen [ōōntərnā:'mən] *vt unreg untr* do; *(durchführen)* undertake; *(Versuch, Reise)* make; **U~** *nt* **-s, -** undertaking, enterprise *(auch COMM)*; *(Firma)* business.
unternehmend *a* enterprising, daring.
Unternehmens- *zW*: **~berater** *m* management consultant; **~planung** *f* corporate planning, management planning.
Unternehmer(in *f)* [ōōntərnā:'mər(in)] *m* **-s, -** (business) employer; *(alten Stils)* entrepreneur; **~verband** *m* employers' association.
unternehmungslustig *a* enterprising.
Unteroffizier [ōōn'tərofitsē:r] *m* noncommissioned officer, NCO.
Unterprima [ōōn'tərprē:má] *f* **-, -primen** *eighth year of German high school.*
Unterprogramm [ōōn'tərprōgrám] *nt (COMPUT)* subroutine.
Unterredung [ōōntərrā:'dōōng] *f* discussion, talk.
Unterricht [ōōn'tərricht] *m* **-(e)s** instruction, lessons *pl*.
unterrichten [ōōntərrich'tən] *untr vt* instruct; *(SCH)* teach ♦ *vr* inform o.s. *(über +akk* about).
Unterrichts- *zW*: **~gegenstand** *m* topic, subject; **~zwecke** *pl*: **zu ~zwecken** for teaching purposes.
Unterrock [ōōn'tərrok] *m* petticoat, slip.
untersagen [ōōntərzá'gən] *vt untr* forbid *(jdm etw* sb (to do) sth).
Untersatz [ōōn'tərzáts] *m* mat; *(für Blumentöpfe etc)* base.
unterschätzen [ōōntərshe'tsən] *vt untr* underestimate.
unterscheiden [ōōntərshī'dən] *unreg untr vt*

distinguish ♦ *vr* differ.
Unterscheidung *f (Unterschied)* distinction; *(Unterscheiden)* differentiation.
Unterschicht [ōōn'tərshicht] *f* lower class.
unterschieben [ōōntərshē:'bən] *vt unreg (fig)*: **jdm etw** ~ foist sth on sb.
Unterschied [ōōn'tərshē:t] *m* **-(e)s, -e** difference, distinction; **im** ~ **zu** as distinct from; **u~lich** *a* varying, differing; *(diskriminierend)* discriminatory.
unterschiedslos *ad* indiscriminately.
unterschlagen [ōōntərshlá'gən] *vt unreg untr* embezzle; *(verheimlichen)* suppress.
Unterschlagung *f* embezzlement; *(von Briefen, Beweis)* withholding.
Unterschlupf [ōōn'tərshlōōpf] *m* **-(e)s, -schlüpfe** refuge.
unterschlüpfen [ōōn'tərshlüpfən] *vi (umg)* take cover *od* shelter; *(Versteck finden)* hide out *(umg) (bei jdm* at sb's).
unterschreiben [ōōntərshrī'bən] *vt unreg untr* sign.
Unterschrift [ōōn'tərshrift] *f* signature; *(Bild~)* caption.
unterschwellig [ōōn'tərshvelich] *a* subliminal.
Unterseeboot [ōōn'tərzā:bō:t] *nt* submarine.
Untersekunda [ōōn'tərzākōōndá] *f* **-, -sekunden** *sixth year of German high school.*
Untersetzer [ōōn'tərzetsər] *m* tablemat; *(für Gläser)* coaster.
untersetzt [ōōntərzetst'] *a* stocky.
unterstehen [ōōntərshtā:'ən] *unreg untr vi* be under *(jdm* sb) ♦ *vr* dare [ōōn'tərshtā:ən] ♦ *vi* shelter.
unterstellen [ōōntərshte'lən] *vt untr* subordinate *(dat* to); *(fig)* impute *(jdm etw* sth to sb); **jdm/etw unterstellt sein** be under sb/ sth; *(in Firma)* report to sb/sth ♦ [ōōn'tərshtelən] *vt (Auto)* garage, park ♦ *vr* take shelter.
Unterstel'lung *f (falsche Behauptung)* misrepresentation; *(Andeutung)* insinuation.
unterste(r, s) [ōōn'tərstə(r, s)] *a* lowest, bottom.
unterstreichen [ōōntərshtrī'chən] *vt unreg untr (lit, fig)* underline.
Unterstufe [ōōn'tərshtōō:fə] *f* lower grade.
unterstützen [ōōntərshtü'tsən] *vt untr* support.
Unterstützung *f* support, assistance.
untersuchen [ōōntərzōō:'chən] *vt untr (MED)* examine; *(Polizei)* investigate; **sich ärztlich** ~ **lassen** have a medical *od* a check-up.
Untersuchung *f* examination; investigation, inquiry.
Untersuchungs- *zW*: **~ausschuß** *m* committee of inquiry; **~ergebnis** *nt (JUR)* findings *pl*; *(MED)* result of an examination; **~haft** *f* imprisonment *od* detention while awaiting trial; **~richter** *m* examining magistrate.
Untertagebau [ōōntərtá'gəbou] *m* underground mining.

Untertan [ōōn'tərtân] m **-s**, **-en** subject.
untertänig [ōōn'tərte:niĊħ] a submissive, humble.
Untertasse [ōōn'tərtásə] f saucer.
untertauchen [ōōn'tərtouĊħən] vi dive; (fig) disappear, go underground.
Unterteil [ōōn'tərtīl] nt od m lower part, bottom.
unterteilen [ōōntərtī'lən] vt untr divide up.
Untertertia [ōōn'tərtertsēâ] f -, **-tertien** fourth year of German high school.
Untertitel [ōōn'tərtē:təl] m subtitle; (für Bild) caption.
Unterwäsche [ōōn'tərveshə] f underwear.
unterwegs [ōōntərvā:ks'] ad on the way; (auf Reisen) away.
unterweisen [ōōntərvī'zən] vt unreg untr instruct.
Unterwelt [ōōn'tərvelt] f (lit, fig) underworld.
unterwerfen [ōōntərver'fən] unreg untr vt subject; (Volk) subjugate ♦ vr submit (dat to).
unterwürfig [ōōntərvür'fiĊħ] a obsequious.
unterzeichnen [ōōntərtsīĊħ'nən] vt untr sign; (Aktien) subscribe.
Unterzeichner m signatory.
unterziehen [ōōntərzē:'ən] unreg untr vt subject (dat to) ♦ vr undergo (etw (dat) sth); (einer Prüfung) take.
Untier [ōōn'tē:r] nt monster.
untragbar [ōōntrâk'bâr] a intolerable, unbearable.
untreu [ōōn'troi] a unfaithful; **sich** (dat) **selbst ~ werden** be untrue to o.s.
Untreue f unfaithfulness.
untröstlich [ōōntrœs'tliĊħ] a inconsolable.
Untugend [ōōn'tōō:gənt] f vice; (Angewohnheit) bad habit.
un- [ōōn] zW: **~überbrück'bar** a (fig: Gegensätze etc) irreconcilable; (Kluft) unbridgeable; **~'überlegt** a ill-considered ♦ ad without thinking; **~überseh'bar** a (Schaden etc) incalculable; (Menge) vast, immense; (auffällig: Fehler etc) obvious; **~'übersichtlich** a (Gelände) broken; (Kurve) blind; (System, Plan) confused; **~übertrof'fen** a unsurpassed.
un- [ōōn] zW: **~umgäng'lich** a indispensable, vital; **~umstöß'lich** a (Tatsache) incontrovertible; (Entschluß) rrevocable; **~umstrit'ten** a indisputable, undisputed; **~umwunden** [-ōōmvōōn'dən] a candid ♦ ad straight out.
ununterbrochen [ōōn'ōōntərbroĊħən] a uninterrupted.
un- [ōōn'] zW: **~verän'derlich** a unchangeable; **~verant'wortlich** a irresponsible; (~entschuldbar) inexcusable; **~verarbeitet** a (lit, fig) raw; **~veräußerlich** [feroi'sərliĊħ] a inalienable; (Besitz) unmarketable; **~verbes'serlich** a incorrigible; **~verbindlich** a not binding; (Antwort) curt ♦ ad (COMM) without obligation; **~verbleit** [-ferblīt] a (Benzin) unleaded; **~verblümt**

[-ferblü:mt'] a, ad plain(ly), blunt(ly); **~verdaulich** a indigestible; **~verdorben** a unspoilt; **~verdrossen** a undeterred; (~ermüdlich) untiring; **~verein'bar** a incompatible; **~verfälscht** [-ferfelsht] a (lit, fig) unadulterated; (Dialekt) pure; (Natürlichkeit) unaffected; **~verfänglich** a harmless; **~verfroren** a impudent; **~vergänglich** a immortal; (Eindruck, Erinnerung) everlasting; **~vergleich'lich** a unique, incomparable; **~verheiratet** a unmarried; **~verhofft** a unexpected; **~verhohlen** [-ferhō:lən] a open, unconcealed; **~verkäuflich** a: „**~verkäuflich**" "not for sale"; **~verkenn'bar** a unmistakable; **~verletz'lich** a (fig: Rechte) inviolable; (lit) invulnerable; **~vermeid'lich** a unavoidable; **~vermittelt** a (plötzlich) sudden, unexpected; **U~vermögen** nt inability; **~vermutet** a unexpected; **~vernünftig** a foolish; **~verrichtet** a: **~verrichteter Dinge** empty-handed; **~verschämt** a impudent; **U~verschämtheit** f impudence, insolence; **~verschuldet** a occurring through no fault of one's own; **~versehens** ad all of a sudden; **~versehrt** [-ferzā:rt] a uninjured; **~versöhnlich** a irreconcilable; **U~verstand** m lack of judgement; (Torheit) folly; **~verständlich** a unintelligible; **~versucht** a: **nichts ~versucht lassen** try everything; **~verträglich** a quarrelsome; (Meinungen, MED) incompatible; **~verwech'selbar** a unmistakable, distinctive; **~verwüst'lich** a indestructible; (Mensch) irrepressible; **~verzeih'lich** a unpardonable; **~verzins'lich** a interest-free; **~verzüglich** [-fertsü:k'liĊħ] a immediate.
un- [ōōn'] zW: **~vollendet** a unfinished; **~vollkommen** a imperfect; **~vollständig** a incomplete.
un- [ōōn'] zW: **~vorbereitet** a unprepared; **~voreingenommen** a unbiased; **~vorhergesehen** a unforeseen; **~vorsichtig** a careless, imprudent; **~vorstell'bar** a inconceivable; **~vorteilhaft** a disadvantageous.
unwahr [ōōn'vâr] a untrue; **~haftig** a untruthful; **~scheinlich** a improbable, unlikely ♦ ad (umg) incredibly; **U~scheinlichkeit** f improbability, unlikelihood.
unwegsam [ōōn'vā:kzâm] a (Gelände etc) rough.
unweigerlich [ōōnvī'gərliĊħ] a unquestioning ♦ ad without fail.
unweit [ōōn'vīt] präp +gen, ad not far from.
Unwesen [ōōn'vā:zən] nt nuisance; (Unfug) mischief; **sein ~ treiben** wreak havoc; (Mörder etc) be at large.
unwesentlich a inessential, unimportant; **~ besser** marginally better.
Unwetter [ōōn'vetər] nt thunderstorm.
unwichtig [ōōn'viĊħtiĊħ] a unimportant.
un- [ōōn'] zW: **~widerleg'bar** a irrefutable; **~widerruf'lich** a irrevocable; **~widerstehlich** [-vē:dərshtā:'liĊħ] a irresistible.

unwiederbringlich [ŏŏnvē:dərbring'liċh] *a* (*geh*) irretrievable.

Unwillen [ŏŏn'vilən] *m* indignation.

unwillig *a* indignant; (*widerwillig*) reluctant.

unwillkürlich [ŏŏn'vilkü:rliċh] *a* involuntary ♦ *ad* instinctively; (*lachen*) involuntarily.

unwirklich [ŏŏn'virkliċh] *a* unreal.

unwirsch [ŏŏn'virsh] *a* cross, surly.

unwirtlich [ŏŏn'virtliċh] *a* inhospitable.

unwirtschaftlich [ŏŏn'virtsháftliċh] *a* uneconomical.

unwissend [ŏŏn'visənt] *a* ignorant.

Unwissenheit *f* ignorance.

unwissenschaftlich *a* unscientific.

unwissentlich *ad* unwittingly, unknowingly.

unwohl [ŏŏn'vō:l] *a* unwell, ill; **U~sein** *nt* **-s** indisposition.

unwürdig [ŏŏn'vürdiċh] *a* unworthy (*jds* of sb).

unzählig [ŏŏntse:'liċh] *a* innumerable, countless.

unzeitgemäß [ŏŏn'tsītgəme:s] *a* (*altmodisch*) old-fashioned.

un- [ŏŏn] *zW*: **~zerbrech'lich** *a* unbreakable; **~zerreiß'bar** *a* untearable; **~zerstör'bar** *a* indestructible; **~zertrenn'lich** *a* inseparable.

Unzucht [ŏŏn'tsŏŏkht] *f* sexual offence.

unzüchtig [ŏŏn'tsüċhtiċh] *a* immoral.

un- [ŏŏn'] *zW*: **~zufrieden** *a* dissatisfied; **U~zufriedenheit** *f* discontent; **~zugänglich** *a* (*Gegend*) inaccessible; (*Mensch*) inapproachable; (: *unaufgeschlossen gegen*) deaf (+*dat* to); **~zulänglich** [-tsŏŏ:lengliċh] *a* inadequate; **~zulässig** *a* inadmissible; **~zumutbar** *a* unreasonable; **~zurechnungsfähig** *a* irresponsible; **jdn für ~zurechnungsfähig erklären lassen** (*JUR*) have sb certified (insane); **~zusammenhängend** *a* disconnected; (*Äußerung*) incoherent; **~zutreffend** *a* incorrect; **~zutreffendes bitte streichen** delete as applicable; **~zuverlässig** *a* unreliable.

unzweckmäßig [ŏŏn'tsvekme:siċh] *a* (*nicht ratsam*) inadvisable; (*unpraktisch*) impractical; (*ungeeignet*) unsuitable.

unzweideutig [ŏŏn'tsvīdoitiċh] *a* unambiguous.

üppig [ü'piċh] *a* (*Frau*) curvaceous; (*Essen*) sumptuous, lavish; (*Vegetation*) luxuriant, lush; (*Haar*) thick.

Urabstimmung [ŏŏ:r'ápshtimŏŏng] *f* strike ballot.

Ural [ŏŏrál'] *m* **-s: der ~** the Ural mountains *pl*, the Urals *pl*; **~gebirge** *nt* the Ural mountains.

uralt [ŏŏ:r'ált] *a* ancient, very old.

Uran [ŏŏrân'] *nt* **-s** uranium.

Ur- [ŏŏ:r'] *in zW* original; **~aufführung** *f* first performance.

urbar *a*: **die Wüste/Land ~ machen** reclaim the desert/cultivate land.

Ur- *zW*: **~einwohner** *m* original inhabitant; **~eltern** *pl* ancestors *pl*; **~enkel(in** *f*) *m* great-grandchild; **~fassung** *f* original ver-

sion; **~großmutter** *f* great-grandmother; **~großvater** *m* great-grandfather.

Urheber *m* **-s**, **-** originator; (*Autor*) author; **~recht** *nt* copyright (*an* +*dat* on); **u~rechtlich** *a*: **u~rechtlich geschützt** copyright.

urig [ŏŏ:'riċh] *a* (*umg*: *Mensch, Atmosphäre*) earthy.

Urin [ŏŏrē:n'] *m* **-s**, **-e** urine.

urkomisch *a* incredibly funny.

Urkunde *f* document; (*Kauf~*) deed.

urkundlich [ŏŏ:r'kŏŏntliċh] *a* documentary.

urladen [ŏŏ:r'ládən] *vt* (*COMPUT*) boot (up).

Urlader *m* (*COMPUT*) bootstrap.

Urlaub [ŏŏ:r'loup] *m* **-(e)s**, **-e** vacation (*US*), holiday(s *pl*) (*Brit*); (*MIL etc*) leave; **~er** *m* **-s**, **-** vacationer (*US*), holiday-maker (*Brit*).

Urlaubsgeld *nt* vacation (*US*) *od* holiday (*Brit*) money.

Urmensch *m* primitive man.

Urne [ŏŏr'nə] *f* **-**, **-n** urn; **zur ~ gehen** go to the polls.

urplötzlich [ŏŏ:r'plœts'liċh] *ad* (*umg*) all of a sudden.

Ursache [ŏŏ:r'zákhə] *f* cause; **keine ~!** (*auf Dank*) don't mention it, you're welcome; (*auf Entschuldigung*) that's all right.

ursächlich [ŏŏ:r'zeċhliċh] *a* casual.

Urschrei [ŏŏ:r'shrī] *m* (*PSYCH*) primal scream.

Ursprung [ŏŏ:r'shprŏŏng] *m* origin, source; (*von Fluß*) source.

ursprünglich [ŏŏ:r'shprüngliċh] *a*, *ad* original(ly).

Ursprungs- *zW*: **~land** *nt* (*COMM*) country of origin; **~zeugnis** *nt* certificate of origin.

Urteil [ŏŏr'tīl] *nt* **-s**, **-e** opinion; (*JUR*) sentence, judgement; **sich** (*dat*) **ein ~ über etw** (*akk*) **erlauben** *od* **sich** (*dat*) **ein ~ über etw fällen** pass judgement on sth; **u~en** *vi* judge.

Urteils- *zW*: **~begründung** *f* (*JUR*) opinion; **~spruch** *m* sentence; verdict.

Urtrieb [ŏŏ:r'trē:p] *m* **-(e)s** basic drive.

Uruguay [ŏŏrŏŏgŏŏâ'ē] *nt* **-s** Uruguay.

Ur- *zW*: **~wald** *m* jungle; **~zeit** *f* prehistoric times *pl*.

usf. *abk* (= *und so fort*) and so on.

USt *abk* = **Umsatzsteuer.**

usw *abk* (= *und so weiter*) etc.

Utensilien [ŏŏtenzē:'lēən] *pl* utensils *pl*.

Utopie [ŏŏtōpē:'] *f* pipedream.

utopisch [ŏŏtō:'pish] *a* utopian.

u.U. *abk* (= *unter Umständen*) possibly.

UV *abk* (= *ultraviolett*) U.V.

u.v.a. *abk* (= *und viele(s) andere*) and much/many more.

u.v.a.m. *abk* (= *und viele(s) andere mehr*) and much/many more.

U.v.D. *abk* (= *Unteroffizier vom Dienst*) duty NCO.

u.W. *abk* (= *unseres Wissens*) to our knowledge.

Ü-Wagen *m* (*RAD, TV*) outside broadcast ve-

hicle.
uzen [ōō:'tsən] *vti* (*umg*) tease, kid.
u.zw. *abk* = *und zwar*.

V

V, v [fou] *nt* V, v.
V.a.G. *abk* (= *Verein auf Gegenseitigkeit*) ≈ mutual company.
vag(e) [vâk, vâgə] *a* vague.
Vagina [vágē:'nà] *f* -, **Vaginen** vagina.
Vakuum [vâ'kōōōōm] *nt* -s, **Vakua** *od* **Vakuen** vacuum; **v~verpackt** *a* vacuum-packed.
Vandalismus [vàndàlis'mōōs] *m* vandalism.
Vanille [vánil'yə] *f* - vanilla; **~zucker** *m*, **Vanillinzucker** *m* vanilla sugar.
variabel [vârēá'bəl] *a*: **variable Kosten** *pl* variable costs *pl*.
Variable [vârēá'blə] *f* -, **-n** variable.
Variante [vârēán'tə] *f* -, **-n** variant (*zu* on).
Variation [vârēátsēō:n'] *f* variation.
variieren [vârēē:'rən] *vti* vary.
Vase [vâ'zə] *f* -, **-n** vase.
Vater [fâ'tər] *m* -s, ⸚ father; **~ Staat** (*umg*) the State; **~land** *nt* native country; (*bes Deutschland*) Fatherland; **~landsliebe** *f* patriotism.
väterlich [fe:'tərliçh] *a* fatherly.
väterlicherseits *ad* on the father's side.
Vaterschaft *f* paternity.
Vaterschaftsklage *f* paternity suit.
Vater- *zW*: **~stelle** *f*: **~stelle bei jdm vertreten** take the place of sb's father; **~unser** *nt* -s, - Lord's Prayer.
Vati [fâ'tē] *m* -s, -s (*umg*) dad(dy).
V-Ausschnitt [fou'oussnit] *m* V-neck.
VBL *abk* = *Versorgungsanstalt des Bundes und der Länder*.
v. Chr. *abk* (= *vor Christus*) B.C.
VDP *m abk* (= *Verband Deutscher Presse*) German Press Association.
VE *abk* (= *Verrechnungseinheiten*) clearing *od* accounting units.
VEB *m abk* (*DDR*: = *volkseigener Betrieb*) state-owned cooperative.
Vegetarier(in *f*) [vāgátá'rēər(in)] *m* -s, - vegetarian.
vegetieren [vāgātē:'rən] *vi* vegetate; (*kärglich leben*) eke out a bare existence.
Vehikel [vāhē:'kəl] *nt* -s, - (*pej umg*) boneshaker.
Veilchen [fïl'çhən] *nt* violet; (*umg*: *blaues Auge*) shiner, black eye.
Velours(leder) [vəlōō:rs'(lā:dər)] *nt* suede.
Vene [vā:'nə] *f* -, **-n** vein.
Venedig [vānā:'diçh] *nt* -s Venice.
Venezolaner(in *f*) [vānātsōlá'nər(in)] *m* -s, -

Venezuelan.
venezolanisch *a* Venezuelan.
Venezuela [vānātsōōā:'là] *nt* -s Venezuela.
Ventil [ventē:l'] *nt* -s, **-e** valve.
Ventilator [ventēlâ'tor] *m* ventilator.
Ver. *abk* (= *Verein*) Soc., soc.
verabreden [ferá'prä:dən] *vt* arrange; (*Termin*) agree upon; **schon verabredet sein** have a prior engagement (*form*), have something else on ♦ *vr* arrange to meet (*mit jdm* sb).
Verabredung *f* arrangement; (*Treffen*) appointment; **ich habe eine ~** I'm meeting somebody.
verabreichen [feráp'rïçhən] *vt* (*Tracht Prügel etc*) give; (*Arznei*) administer (*form*) (*jdm* to sb).
verabscheuen [feráp'shoiən] *vt* detest, abhor.
verabschieden [feráp'shē:dən] *vt* (*Gäste*) say goodbye to; (*entlassen*) discharge; (*Gesetz*) pass ♦ *vr* take one's leave (*von* of).
Verabschiedung *f* leave-taking; discharge; passing.
verachten [feráḳh'tən] *vt* despise; **nicht zu ~** (*umg*) not to be scoffed at.
verächtlich [fereçh'tliçh] *a* contemptuous; (*verachtenswert*) contemptible; **jdn ~ machen** run sb down.
Verachtung *f* contempt; **jdn mit ~ strafen** treat sb with contempt.
veralbern [ferál'bərn] *vt* (*umg*) make fun of.
verallgemeinern [ferálgəmī'nərn] *vt* generalize.
Verallgemeinerung *f* generalization.
veralten [ferál'tən] *vi* become obsolete *od* out-of-date.
Veranda [vārán'dà] *f* -, **Veranden** veranda.
veränderlich [feren'dərliçh] *a* changeable; **V~keit** *f* variability; changeability.
verändern *vtr* change.
Veränderung *f* change; **eine berufliche ~** a change of job.
verängstigen [ferengs'tigən] *vt* (*erschrecken*) frighten; (*einschüchtern*) intimidate.
verankern [feráng'kərn] *vt* (*NAUT. TECH*) anchor; (*fig*) embed (*in* +*dat* in).
veranlagen [ferán'lâgən] *vt* assess (*mit* at).
veranlagt *a* with a ... nature; **praktisch ~ sein** be practically minded; **zu** *od* **für etw ~ sein** be cut out for sth.
Veranlagung *f* disposition, aptitude.
veranlassen [ferán'lásən] *vt* cause; **Maßnahmen ~** take measures; **sich veranlaßt sehen** feel prompted; **etw ~** arrange for sth; (*befehlen*) order sth.
Veranlassung *f* cause; motive; **auf jds ~ (hin)** at sb's instigation.
veranschaulichen [ferán'shouliçhən] *vt* illustrate.
veranschlagen [ferán'shlâgən] *vt* estimate.
veranstalten [ferán'shtáltən] *vt* organize, arrange.
Veranstalter(in *f*) *m* -s, - organizer; (*COMM*: *von Konzerten etc*) promoter.

Veranstaltung *f* (*Veranstalten*) organizing; (*Veranstaltetes*) event; (*feierlich, öffentlich*) function.

verantworten [feránt'vortən] *vt* accept responsibility for; (*Folgen etc*) answer for (*vor +dat* to) ♦ *vr* justify o.s.

verantwortlich *a* responsible.

Verantwortung *f* responsibility; **jdn zur ~ ziehen** call sb to account.

verantwortungs- *zW*: **~bewußt** *a* responsible; **~los** *a* irresponsible.

verarbeiten [ferár'bītən] *vt* process; (*geistig*) assimilate; (*Erlebnis etc*) digest; **etw zu etw ~** make sth into sth; **verarbeitende Industrie** processing industries *pl*.

verarbeitet *a*: **gut ~** (*Kleid etc*) well finished.

Verarbeitung *f* processing; assimilation.

verärgern [ferer'gərn] *vt* annoy.

verarmen [ferár'mən] *vi* (*lit, fig*) become impoverished.

verarschen [ferár'shən] *vt* (*umg!*): **jdn ~** poke fun at sb.

verarzten [ferârts'tən] *vt* fix up (*umg*).

verausgaben [ferous'gâbən] *vr* run out of money; (*fig*) exhaust o.s.

veräußern [feroi'sərn] *vt* (*form: verkaufen*) dispose of.

verb. *abk* = **verbessert.**

Verb [verp] *nt* **-s, -en** verb.

Verb. *abk* (= *Verband*) Assoc., assoc.

verballern [ferbá'lərn] *vt* (*umg*) use up, spend.

verbalradikal [verbâl'rádēkâl] *a* radical with words.

verband [ferbánt'] *imperf von* **verbinden.**

Verband *m* **-(e)s, ⁻e** (*MED*) bandage, dressing; (*Bund*) association, society; (*MIL*) unit; **~(s)kasten** *m* medicine chest, first aid kit; **~(s)päckchen** *nt* gauze bandage; **~stoff** *m*, **~zeug** *nt* bandage, dressing material.

verbannen [ferbá'nən] *vt* banish.

Verbannung *f* exile.

verbarrikadieren [ferbárēkádē:'rən] *vtr* barricade.

verbauen [ferbou'ən] *vt*: **sich** (*dat*) **alle Chancen ~** spoil one's chances.

verbergen [ferber'gən] *vtr unreg* hide (*vor +dat* from).

verbessern [ferbe'sərn] *vtr* improve; (*berichtigen*) correct (o.s.).

verbessert *a* revised; improved; **eine neue, ~e Auflage** a new revised edition.

Verbesserung *f* improvement; correction.

verbeugen [ferboi'gən] *vr* bow.

Verbeugung *f* bow.

verbiegen [ferbē:'gən] *vi unreg* bend.

verbiestert [ferbē:'stərt] *a* (*umg*) crotchety.

verbieten [ferbē:'tən] *vt unreg* forbid (*jdm etw* sb to do sth); (*amtlich auch*) prohibit; (*Zeitung, Partei*) ban.

verbilligen [ferbi'ligən] *vtr* reduce.

verbinden [ferbin'dən] *unreg vt* connect; (*kombinieren*) combine; (*MED*) bandage;

jdm die Augen ~ blindfold sb ♦ *vr* combine (*auch CHEM*), join (*together*).

verbindlich [ferbin'tlich] *a* binding; (*freundlich*) friendly; obliging; **~ zusagen** accept definitely; **V~keit** *f* obligation; (*Höflichkeit*) civility; **V~keiten** *pl* (*JUR*) obligations *pl*; (*COMM*) liabilities *pl*.

Verbindung *f* connection; (*Zusammensetzung*) combination; (*CHEM*) compound; (*UNIV*) club; (*TEL: Anschluß*) line; **mit jdm in ~ stehen** be in touch *od* contact with sb; **~ mit jdm aufnehmen** contact sb.

Verbindungsmann *m* **-s, -männer** *od* **-leute** intermediary; (*Agent*) contact.

verbissen [ferbi'sən] *a* grim; (*Arbeiter*) dogged; **V~heit** *f* grimness; doggedness.

verbitten [ferbi'tən] *vt unreg*: **sich** (*dat*) **etw ~** not tolerate sth, not stand for sth.

verbittern [ferbi'tərn] *vt* embitter ♦ *vi* get bitter.

verblassen [ferblá'sən] *vi* fade.

Verbleib [ferblīp'] *m* **-(e)s** whereabouts.

verbleiben [ferblī'bən] *vi unreg* remain; **wir sind so verblieben, daß wir ...** we agreed to ...

Verblendung [ferblen'dōong] *f* (*fig*) delusion.

verblöden [ferblœ'dən] *vi aux sein* get stupid.

verblüffen [ferblü'fən] *vt* amaze; (*verwirren*) baffle.

Verblüffung *f* stupefaction.

verblühen [ferblü:'ən] *vi* wither, fade.

verbluten [ferblōō:'tən] *vi* bleed to death.

verbohren [ferbō:'rən] *vr* (*umg*): **sich in etw ~** become obsessed with sth.

verbohrt *a* (*Haltung*) stubborn, obstinate.

verborgen [ferbor'gən] *a* hidden; **~e Mängel** *pl* latent defects *pl*.

Verbot [ferbō:t'] *nt* **-(e)s, -e** prohibition, ban.

verboten *a* forbidden; **Rauchen ~!** no smoking; **er sah ~ aus** (*umg*) he looked a real sight.

verbo'tenerwei'se *ad* though it is forbidden.

Verbotsschild *nt* prohibitory sign.

verbrämen [ferbre:'mən] *vt* (*fig*) gloss over; (*Kritik*) veil (*mit* in).

Verbrauch [ferbroukh'] *m* **-(e)s** consumption.

verbrauchen *vt* use up; **der Wagen verbraucht 10 Liter Benzin auf 100 km** the car does 10 kms to the liter.

Verbraucher(in *f*) *m* **-s, -** consumer; **~markt** *m* consumer market; **v~nah** *a* consumer-friendly; **~schutz** *m* consumer protection; **~verband** *m* consumer council.

Verbrauchsgüter *pl* consumer goods *pl*.

verbraucht *a* used up, finished; (*Luft*) stale; (*Mensch*) worn-out.

verbrechen [ferbre'chən] *vt unreg* perpetrate.

Verbrechen *nt* **-s, -** crime.

Verbrecher(in *f*) *m* **-s, -** criminal; **v~isch** *a* criminal; **~kartei** *f* criminal records *pl*; **~tum** *nt* **-s** criminality.

verbreiten [ferbrī'tən] *vt* spread; (*Licht*) shed; (*Wärme, Ruhe*) radiate; **eine (weit)**

verbreitete Ansicht a widely held opinion; **sich über etw** (akk) ~ expound on sth ♦ vr spread.
verbreitern [ferbrī'tərn] vt broaden.
Verbreitung f spread(ing); propagation.
verbrennbar a combustible.
verbrennen [ferbre'nən] vt unreg burn; (Leiche) cremate; (versengen) scorch; (Haar) singe; (verbrühen) scald.
Verbrennung f burning; (in Motor) combustion; (von Leiche) cremation.
Verbrennungs- zW: ~anlage f incineration plant; ~motor m internal-combustion engine.
verbriefen [ferbrē:'fən] vt document.
verbringen [ferbri'ngən] vt unreg spend.
Verbrüderung [ferbrü:'dərōōng] f fraternization.
verbrühen [ferbrü:'ən] vt scald.
verbuchen [ferbōō:'khən] vt (FIN) register; (Erfolg) enjoy; (Mißerfolg) suffer.
verbummeln [ferbōō'məln] vt (umg: verlieren) lose; (Zeit) waste, fritter away; (Verabredung) miss.
verbunden [ferbōōn'dən] a connected; **jdm** ~ **sein** be obliged od indebted to sb; **ich/er** etc **war falsch** ~ (TEL) it was a wrong number.
verbünden [ferbün'dən] vr form an alliance.
Verbundenheit f bond, relationship.
Verbündete(r) mf dekl wie a ally.
verbürgen [ferbür'gən] vr: **sich** ~ **für** vouch for; **ein verbürgtes Recht** an established right.
verbüßen [ferbü:'sən] vt: **eine Strafe** ~ serve a sentence.
verchromt [ferkrō:mt'] a chromium-plated.
Verdacht [ferdåkht'] m -(e)s suspicion; ~ **schöpfen** become suspicious (gegen jdn of sb); **jdn in** ~ **haben** suspect sb; **es besteht** ~ **auf Krebs** (akk) cancer is suspected.
verdächtig a suspicious.
verdächtigen [ferdeçh'tigən] vt suspect.
verdammen [ferdå'mən] vt damn, condemn.
Verdammnis f -, -se perdition, damnation.
verdammt a, ad (umg) damned; ~ **noch mal!** damn (it) (!).
verdampfen [ferdåmp'fən] vti (vi aux sein) vaporize; (KOCH) boil away.
verdanken [ferdång'kən] vt: **jdm etw** ~ owe sb sth.
verdarb [ferdårp'] imperf von **verderben**.
verdattert [ferdå'tərt] a, ad (umg) flabbergasted.
verdauen [ferdou'ən] vt (lit, fig) digest.
verdaulich [ferdou'liçh] a digestible; **das ist schwer** ~ that is hard to digest.
Verdauung f digestion.
Verdauungs- zW: ~spaziergang m constitutional; ~störung f indigestion.
Verdeck [ferdek'] nt -(e)s, -e (AUT) soft top; (NAUT) deck.
verdecken vt cover (up); (verbergen) hide.
verdenken [ferdeng'kən] vt unreg: **jdm etw** ~ blame sb for sth, hold sth against sb.

verderben [ferder'bən] unreg vt spoil; (schädigen) ruin; (moralisch) corrupt; **es mit jdm** ~ get into sb's bad books ♦ vi (Essen) spoil, rot; (Mensch) go to the bad; **V**~ nt -s ruin.
verderblich a (Einfluß) pernicious; (Lebensmittel) perishable.
verderbt a (veraltet) depraved; **V~heit** f depravity.
verdeutlichen [ferdoi'tliçhən] vt make clear.
verdichten [ferdiçh'tən] vt (PHYS, fig) compress ♦ vr thicken; (Verdacht, Eindruck) deepen.
verdienen [ferdē:'nən] vt earn; (moralisch) deserve ♦ vi (Gewinn machen) make (a profit) (an +dat on).
Verdienst [ferdē:nst'] m earnings pl ♦ nt -(e)s, -e merit; (Leistung) service (um to), contribution; (Dank) credit; **v~voll** a commendable.
verdient [ferdē:nt'] a well-earned; (Person) deserving of esteem; (Lohn, Strafe) rightful; **sich um etw** ~ **machen** do a lot for sth.
verdirbst [ferdirpst'] 2. pers sing präs von **verderben**.
verdirbt [ferdirpt'] 3. pers sing präs von **verderben**.
verdonnern [ferdo'nərn] vt (umg: zu Haft etc) sentence (zu to); **jdn zu etw** ~ order sb to do sth.
verdoppeln [ferdo'pəln] vt double.
Verdopp(e)lung f doubling.
verdorben [ferdor'bən] a spoilt; (geschädigt) ruined; (moralisch) corrupt ♦ pp von **verderben**.
verdorren [ferdo'rən] vi wither.
verdrängen [ferdreng'ən] vt oust; (auch PHYS) displace; (PSYCH) repress.
Verdrängung f displacement; (PSYCH) repression.
verdrehen [ferdrā:'ən] vt (lit, fig) twist; (Augen) roll; **jdm den Kopf** ~ (fig) turn sb's head.
verdreht a (umg) crazy; (Bericht) confused.
verdreifachen [ferdrī'fåkhən] vt treble.
verdrießen [ferdrē:'sən] vt unreg annoy.
verdrießlich [ferdrē:s'liçh] a peevish, annoyed.
verdroß [ferdros'] imperf von **verdrießen**.
verdrossen [ferdro'sən] a cross, sulky ♦ pp von **verdrießen**.
verdrücken [ferdrü'kən] vt (umg) put away, eat ♦ vr (umg) disappear.
Verdruß [ferdrōōs'] m -sses, -sse frustration; **zu jds** ~ to sb's annoyance.
verduften [ferdōōf'tən] vi evaporate; (umg) disappear.
verdummen [ferdōō'mən] vt make stupid ♦ vi grow stupid.
verdunkeln [ferdōōng'kəln] vtr darken; (fig) obscure.
Verdunk(e)lung f blackout; (fig) obscuring.
verdünnen [ferdü'nən] vt dilute.
Verdünner m -s, - thinner.

verdünnisieren [ferdünēzē:'rən] *vr* (*umg*) make o.s. scarce.
verdunsten [ferdŏŏns'tən] *vi* evaporate.
verdursten [ferdŏŏrs'tən] *vi* die of thirst.
verdutzt [ferdŏŏtst'] *a* taken aback.
verebben [fere'bən] *vi* subside.
veredeln [ferā:'dəln] *vt* (*Metalle, Erdöl*) refine; (*Fasern*) finish; (*BOT*) graft.
verehren [ferā:'rən] *vt* venerate, worship (*auch REL*); **jdm etw ~** present sb with sth.
Verehrer(in *f*) *m* **-s**, - admirer.
verehrt *a* esteemed; **(sehr) ~e Anwesende** *od* **Gäste/~es Publikum** Ladies and Gentlemen.
Verehrung *f* respect; (*REL*) worship.
vereidigen [ferī'digən] *vt* put on oath; **jdn auf etw** (*akk*) **~** make sb swear on sth.
Vereidigung *f* swearing in.
Verein [ferīn'] *m* **-(e)s**, **-e** club, association; **ein wohltätiger ~** a charity; **v~bar** *a* compatible.
vereinbaren [ferīn'bârən] *vt* agree upon.
Vereinbarkeit *f* compatibility.
Vereinbarung *f* agreement.
vereinfachen [ferīn'fákhən] *vt* simplify.
vereinheitlichen [ferīn'hītlichən] *vt* standardize.
vereinigen [ferī'nigən] *vtr* unite.
Vereinigtes Königreich [ferī'nichtəskœ'-nikrich] *nt* United Kingdom.
Vereinigte Staaten *pl* United States.
Vereinigung *f* union; (*Verein*) association.
vereinnahmen [ferīn'nâmən] *vt* (*geh*) take; **jdn ~** (*fig*) make demands on sb.
vereinsamen [ferīn'zâmən] *vi* become lonely.
vereinsamt *a* united.
Vereinte Nationen *pl* United Nations.
vereinzelt [ferīn'tsəlt] *a* isolated.
vereisen [ferī'zən] *vi* freeze, ice over ♦ *vt* (*MED*) freeze.
vereiteln [ferī'təln] *vt* frustrate.
vereitern [ferī'tərn] *vi* suppurate, fester.
Verelendung [ferā:'lendŏŏng] *f*: **soziale ~** social impoverishment.
verenden [feren'dən] *vi* perish, die.
verengen [fere'ngən] *vr* narrow.
vererben [ferer'bən] *vt* bequeath; (*BIOL*) transmit ♦ *vr* be hereditary.
vererblich [ferer'plich] *a* hereditary.
Vererbung *f* bequeathing; (*BIOL*) transmission; (*Lehre*) heredity.
verewigen [ferā:'vigən] *vt* immortalize ♦ *vr* (*umg*) leave one's name.
Verf. *abk* = **Verfasser.**
verfahren [ferfâ'rən] *unreg vi* act; **~ mit** deal with ♦ *vr* get lost ♦ *a* tangled.
Verfahren *nt* **-s**, - procedure; (*TECH*) process; (*JUR*) proceedings *pl*.
Verfahrens- *zW*: **~technik** *f* (*Methode*) process; **~weise** *f* procedure.
Verfall [ferfál'] *m* **-(e)s** decline; (*von Haus*) dilapidation; (*FIN*) expiry.
verfallen *vi unreg* decline; (*Haus*) be falling down; (*FIN*) lapse; **~ in** (+*akk*) lapse into;

~ auf (+*akk*) hit upon; **einem Laster ~ sein** be addicted to a vice; **jdm völlig ~ sein** be completely under sb's spell ♦ *a* (*Gebäude*) dilapidated, ruined; (*Karten, Briefmarken*) invalid; (*Strafe*) lapsed; (*Paß*) expired.
Verfallsdatum *nt* expiration (*US*) *od* expiry (*Brit*) date; (*der Haltbarkeit*) sell-by date.
verfänglich [ferfeng'lich] *a* awkward, tricky; (*Aussage, Beweismaterial etc*) incriminating; (*gefährlich*) dangerous.
verfärben [ferfer'bən] *vr* change color.
verfassen [ferfá'sən] *vt* write; (*Gesetz, Urkunde*) draw up.
Verfasser(in *f*) *m* **-s**, - author, writer.
Verfassung *f* constitution (*auch POL*); (*körperlich*) state of health; (*seelisch*) state of mind; **sie ist in guter/schlechter ~** she is in good/bad shape.
Verfassungs- *zW*: **v~feindlich** *a* anticonstitutional; **~gericht** *nt* constitutional court; **v~mäßig** *a* constitutional; **~schutz** *m* (*Aufgabe*) defence of the constitution; (*Amt*) *office responsible for defending the constitution*; **~schützer(in** *f*) *m* defender of the constitution; **v~widrig** *a* unconstitutional.
verfaulen [ferfou'lən] *vi* rot.
verfechten [ferfech'tən] *vt unreg* defend; (*Lehre*) advocate.
Verfechter(in *f*) [ferfech'tər(in)] *m* **-s**, - champion; defender.
verfehlen [ferfā:'lən] *vt* miss; **das Thema ~** be completely off the subject.
verfehlt *a* unsuccessful; (*unangebracht*) inappropriate; **etw für ~ halten** regard sth as mistaken.
Verfehlung *f* (*Vergehen*) misdemeanor (*US*), misdemeanour (*Brit*); (*Sünde*) transgression.
verfeinern [ferfī'nərn] *vt* refine.
Verfettung [ferfe'tŏŏng] *f* (*von Organ, Muskeln*) fatty degeneration.
verfeuern [ferfoi'ərn] *vt* burn; (*Munition*) fire; (*umg*) use up.
verfilmen [ferfil'mən] *vt* film, make a film of.
Verfilmung *f* film (version).
Verfilzung [ferfil'tsŏŏng] *f* (*fig: Wirtschaft, Politik*) entanglements *pl*.
verflachen [ferflá'khən] *vi* flatten out; (*fig: Diskussion*) become superficial.
verfliegen [ferflē:'gən] *vi unreg* evaporate; (*Zeit*) pass, fly ♦ *vr* stray (past).
verflixt [ferflikst'] *a, ad* (*umg*) darned.
verflossen [ferflo'sən] *a* past, former.
verfluchen [ferflŏŏ:'khən] *vt* curse.
verflüchtigen [ferflüch'tigən] *vr* evaporate; (*Geruch*) fade.
verflüssigen [ferflü'sigən] *vr* become liquid.
verfolgen [ferfol'gən] *vt* pursue; (*gerichtlich*) prosecute; (*grausam, bes POL*) persecute.
Verfolger(in *f*) *m* **-s**, - pursuer.
Verfolgte(r) *mf dekl wie a* (*politisch*) victim of persecution.
Verfolgung *f* pursuit; persecution; **straf-**

rechtliche ~ prosecution.
Verfolgungswahn *m* persecution mania.
verfrachten [ferfràẋ'tən] *vt* ship.
verfremden [ferfrem'dən] *vt* alienate, distance.
verfressen [ferfre'sən] *a* *(umg)* greedy.
verfrüht [ferfrü:t'] *a* premature.
verfügbar *a* available.
verfügen [ferfü:'gən] *vt* direct, order ♦ *vr* proceed ♦ *vi*: ~ **über** (+*akk*) have at one's disposal; **über etw** *(akk)* **frei** ~ **können** be able to do as one wants with sth.
Verfügung *f* direction, order; *(JUR)* writ; **zur** ~ at one's disposal; **jdm zur** ~ **stehen** be available to sb.
Verfügungsgewalt *f* (*JUR*) right of disposal.
verführen [ferfü:'rən] *vt* tempt; *(sexuell)* seduce; *(die Jugend, das Volk etc)* lead astray.
Verführer *m* tempter; seducer.
Verführerin *f* temptress; seductress.
verführerisch *a* seductive.
Verführung *f* seduction; *(Versuchung)* temptation.
Vergabe [fergà'bə] *f* *(von Arbeiten)* allocation; *(von Stipendium, Auftrag etc)* award.
vergällen [ferge'lən] *vt* *(geh)*: **jdm die Freude/das Leben** ~ spoil sb's fun/sour sb's life.
vergaloppieren [fergàlopē:'rən] *vr* *(umg: sich irren)* be on the wrong track.
vergammeln [fergà'məln] *vi* *(umg)* go to seed; *(Nahrung)* go off; *(umg: Zeit)* waste.
vergangen [fergàng'ən] *a* past; **V~heit** *f* past.
Vergangenheitsbewältigung *f* coming to terms with the past.
vergänglich [fergeng'liẋ] *a* transitory; **V~keit** *f* transitoriness, impermanence.
vergasen [fergà'zən] *vt* gasify; *(töten)* gas.
Vergaser *m* **-s, -** *(AUT)* carburetor *(US)*, carburettor *(Brit)*.
vergaß [fergàs'] *imperf von* **vergessen**.
vergeben [fergā:'bən] *vt unreg* forgive *(jdm etw* sb for sth); *(weggeben)* give away; *(fig: Chance)* throw away; *(Auftrag, Preis)* award *(an* +*akk* to); *(Studienplätze, Stellen)* allocate; ~ **sein** be occupied; *(umg: Mädchen)* be spoken for.
vergebens *ad* in vain.
vergeblich [fergā:'pliẋ] *ad* in vain ♦ *a* vain, futile.
Vergebung *f* forgiveness.
vergegenwärtigen [fergā:'gənvertigən] *vr*: **sich** *(dat)* **etw** ~ recall *od* visualize sth.
vergehen [fergā:'ən] *unreg vi* pass by *od* away; **vor Angst** ~ be scared to death; **jdm vergeht etw** sb loses sth ♦ *vr* commit an offense *(gegen etw* against sth); **sich an jdm** ~ *(sexually)* assault sb; **V~** *nt* **-s, -** offense *(US)*, offence *(Brit)*.
vergeigen [fergī'gən] *vt* *(umg)* mess up.
vergeistigt [fergīs'tiẋt] *a* spiritual.
vergelten [fergel'tən] *vt unreg* repay *(jdm*

etw sb for sth).
Vergeltung *f* retaliation, reprisal.
Vergeltungs- *zW*: ~**maßnahme** *f* retaliatory measure; ~**schlag** *m* (*MIL*) reprisal.
vergesellschaften [fergəzel'sháftən] *vt* *(POL)* nationalize.
vergessen [ferge'sən] *vt unreg* forget; **V~heit** *f* oblivion; **in V~heit geraten** fall into oblivion.
vergeßlich [ferges'liẋ] *a* forgetful; **V~heit** *f* forgetfulness.
vergeuden [fergoi'dən] *vt* squander, waste.
vergewaltigen [fergəvàl'tigən] *vt* rape; *(fig)* violate.
Vergewaltigung *f* rape.
vergewissern [fergəvi'sərn] *vr* make sure; **sich einer Sache** *(gen)* *od* **über etw** *(akk)* ~ make sure of sth.
vergießen [fergē:'sən] *vt unreg* shed.
vergiften [fergif'tən] *vt* poison.
Vergiftung *f* poisoning.
vergilbt [fergilpt'] *a* yellowed.
Vergißmeinnicht [fergis'mïnniẋt] *nt* **-(e)s, -e** forget-me-not.
vergißt [fergist'] *2./3. pers sing präs von* **vergessen**.
vergittert [fergi'tərt] *a*: ~**e Fenster** barred windows.
verglasen [ferglà'zən] *vt* glaze.
Vergleich [fergliẋ'] *m* **-(e)s, -e** comparison; *(JUR)* settlement; **einen** ~ **schließen** *(JUR)* reach a settlement; **in keinem** ~ **zu etw stehen** be out of all proportion to sth; **im** ~ **mit** *od* **zu** compared with *od* to; **v~bar** *a* comparable.
vergleichen *unreg vt* compare ♦ *vr* reach a settlement.
vergleichsweise *ad* comparatively.
verglühen [ferglü:'ən] *vi* *(Feuer)* die away; *(Draht)* burn out; *(Raumkapsel, Meteor etc)* burn up.
vergnügen [fergnü:'gən] *vr* enjoy *od* amuse o.s.; **V~** *nt* **-s, -** pleasure; **das war ein teures V~** *(umg)* that was an expensive bit of fun; **viel V~!** enjoy yourself!
vergnüglich *a* enjoyable.
vergnügt [fergnü:kt'] *a* cheerful.
Vergnügung *f* pleasure, amusement.
Vergnügungs- *zW*: ~**park** *m* amusement park; **v~süchtig** *a* pleasure-loving; ~**viertel** *nt* entertainments district.
vergolden [fergol'dən] *vt* gild.
vergönnen [fergœ'nən] *vt* grant.
vergöttern [fergœ'tərn] *vt* idolize.
vergraben [fergrà'bən] *vt* bury.
vergrämt [fergre:mt'] *a* *(Gesicht)* troubled.
vergreifen [fergrī'fən] *vr unreg*: **sich an jdm** ~ lay hands on sb; **sich an etw** ~ misappropriate sth; **sich im Ton** ~ say the wrong thing.
vergriffen [fergri'fən] *a* *(Buch)* out of print; *(Ware)* out of stock.
vergrößern [fergrœ'sərn] *vt* enlarge; *(mengenmäßig)* increase; *(Lupe)* magnify.

Vergrößerung *f* enlargement; increase; magnification.

Vergrößerungsglas *nt* magnifying glass.

vergünstigt *a* (*Lage*) improved; (*Preis*) reduced.

Vergünstigung |fɛrgüns'tigoͦong| *f* concession; (*Vorteil*) privilege.

vergüten |fɛrgü:'tən| *vt*: **jdm etw** ~ compensate sb for sth; (*Arbeit, Leistung*) pay sb for sth.

Vergütung *f* compensation.

verh. *abk* = **verheiratet.**

verhaften |fɛrháf'tən| *vt* arrest.

Verhaftete(r) *mf dekl wie a* prisoner.

Verhaftung *f* arrest.

Verhaftungsbefehl *m* warrant (for arrest).

verhallen |fɛrhä'lən| *vi* die away.

verhalten |fɛrhál'tən| *unreg vr* (*Sachen*) be, stand; (*sich benehmen*) behave; (*MATH*) be in proportion to; **sich ruhig** ~ keep quiet; (*sich nicht bewegen*) keep still ♦ *vr unpers*: **wie verhält es sich damit?** (*wie ist die Lage?*) how do things stand?; (*wie wird das gehandhabt?*) how do you go about it?; **wenn sich das so verhält** ... if that is the case ... ♦ *vt* hold *od* keep back; (*Schritt*) check ♦ *a* restrained.

Verhalten *nt* **-s** behavior (*US*), behaviour (*Brit*).

Verhaltens- *zW*: ~**forschung** *f* behavioral (*US*) *od* behavioural (*Brit*) science; **v~gestört** *a* disturbed; ~**maßregel** *f* rule of conduct.

Verhältnis |fɛrhɛlt'nis| *nt* **-ses, -se** relationship; (*Einstellung*) attitude (*zu* to); (*Liebes*~) affair; (*MATH*) proportion, ratio; ~**se** *pl* (*Umstände*) conditions *pl*; **aus was für** ~**sen kommt er?** what sort of background does he come from?; **für klare** ~**se sorgen, klare** ~**se schaffen** get things straight; **über seine** ~**se leben** live beyond one's means; ~**mäßig** *a*, *ad* relative(ly), comparative(ly); ~**wahl(recht** *nt*) *f* proportional representation.

verhandeln |fɛrhán'dəln| *vi* negotiate (*über etw* (*akk*) sth); (*JUR*) hold proceedings ♦ *vt* discuss; (*JUR*) hear.

Verhandlung *f* negotiation; (*JUR*) proceedings *pl*; ~**en führen** negotiate.

Verhandlungspaket *nt* (*COMM*) package deal.

verhangen |fɛrhä'ngən| *a* overcast.

verhängen |fɛrhe'ngən| *vt* (*fig*) impose, inflict.

Verhängnis |fɛrheng'nis| *nt* **-ses, -se** fate; doom; **jdm zum** ~ **werden** be sb's undoing; **v~voll** *a* fatal, disastrous.

verharmlosen |fɛrhárm'lō:zən| *vt* make light of, play down.

verharren |fɛrhá'rən| *vi* remain; (*hartnäckig*) persist.

verhärten |fɛrher'tən| *vr* harden.

verhaspeln |fɛrhás'pəln| *vr* (*umg*) get into a muddle *od* tangle.

verhaßt |fɛrhást'| *a* odious, hateful.

verhätscheln |fɛrhɛ:t'shəln| *vt* spoil, pamper.

Verhau |fɛrhou'| *m* **-(e)s, -e** (*zur Absperrung*) barrier; (*Käfig*) coop.

verhauen *vt unreg* (*umg*: *verprügeln*) beat up; (: *Prüfung etc*) muff.

verheben |fɛrhä:'bən| *vr unreg* hurt o.s. lifting sth.

verheerend |fɛrhä:'rənt| *a* disastrous, devastating.

verhehlen |fɛrhä:'lən| *vt* conceal.

verheilen |fɛrhī'lən| *vi* heal.

verheimlichen |fɛrhīm'lichən| *vt* keep secret (*jdm* from sb).

verheiratet |fɛrhī'rátət| *a* married.

verheißen |fɛrhī'sən| *vt unreg*: **jdm etw** ~ promise sb sth.

verheizen |fɛrhī'tsən| *vt* burn, use as fuel.

verhelfen |fɛrhɛl'fən| *vi unreg*: **jdm zu etw** ~ help sb to get sth.

verherrlichen |fɛrher'lichən| *vt* glorify.

verheult |fɛrhoilt'| *a* (*Augen, Gesicht*) puffy.

verhexen |fɛrhɛk'sən| *vt* bewitch; **es ist wie verhext** it's jinxed.

verhindern |fɛrhin'dərn| *vt* prevent; **verhindert sein** be unable to make it; **das läßt sich leider nicht** ~ it can't be helped, unfortunately; **ein verhinderter Politiker** (*umg*) a would-be politician.

Verhinderung *f* prevention.

verhöhnen |fɛrhœ'nən| *vt* mock, sneer at.

verhohnepipeln |fɛrhō:'nəpe:pəln| *vt* (*umg*) ridicule.

verhökern |fɛrhœ'kərn| *vt* (*umg*) turn into cash.

Verhör |fɛrhœr'| *nt* **-(e)s, -e** interrogation; (*gerichtlich*) (cross-)examination.

verhören *vt* interrogate; (cross-)examine ♦ *vr* mishear.

verhüllen |fɛrhü'lən| *vt* veil; (*Haupt, Körperteil*) cover.

verhungern |fɛrhoͦong'ərn| *vi* starve, die of hunger.

verhunzen |fɛrhoͦon'tsən| *vt* (*umg*) ruin.

verhüten |fɛrhü:'tən| *vt* prevent, avert.

Verhütung *f* prevention.

Verhütungsmittel *nt* contraceptive.

verifizieren |vārēfētsē:'rən| *vt* verify.

verinnerlichen |fɛri'nərlichən| *vt* internalize.

verirren |fɛri'rən| *vr* get lost, lose one's way; (*fig*) go astray; (*Tier, Kugel*) stray.

verjagen |fɛryá'gən| *vt* drive away *od* out.

verjähren |fɛrye:'rən| *vi* come under the statute of limitations; (*Anspruch*) lapse.

Verjährungsfrist *f* limitation period.

verjubeln |fɛryōō:'bəln| *vt* (*umg*: *Geld*) blow.

verjüngen |fɛryü'ngən| *vt* rejuvenate ♦ *vr* taper.

verkabeln |fɛrkä'bəln| *vt* (*Stadtteil*) connect up for cable TV.

Verkabelung *f* connection for cable TV.

verkalken |fɛrkál'kən| *vi* calcify; (*umg*) become senile.

verkalkulieren |fɛrkálkōōlē:'rən| *vr* miscalculate.

verkannt [fɛrkánt'] *a* unappreciated.

verkatert [fɛrkâ'tərt] *a* (*umg*) hung-over.

Verkauf [fɛrkouf'] *m* sale; **zum ~ stehen** be up for sale.

verkaufen *vti* sell; „**zu ~**" "for sale".

Verkäufer(in *f*) [fɛrkoi'fər(in)] *m* **-s,** - seller; (*im Außendienst*) salesman; saleswoman; (*in Laden*) sales clerk (*US*), shop assistant (*Brit*).

verkäuflich [fɛrkoi'fliç] *a* saleable.

Verkaufs- *zW*: **~abteilung** *f* sales department; **~automat** *m* vending machine; **~bedingungen** *pl* (*COMM*) terms and conditions of sale; **~ingenieur** *m* sales engineer; **~kampagne** *f* sales drive; **~leiter** *m* sales manager; **v~offen** *a*: **v~offener Samstag** open for business all day Saturday; **~schlager** *m* big seller, moneymaker; **~stelle** *f* outlet; **~tüchtigkeit** *f* salesmanship.

Verkehr [fɛrkā:r'] *m* **-s, -e** traffic; (*Umgang, bes sexuell*) intercourse; (*Umlauf*) circulation; **aus dem ~ ziehen** withdraw from service; **für den ~ freigeben** (*Straße etc*) open to traffic; (*Transportmittel*) bring into service.

verkehren *vi* (*Fahrzeug*) ply, run; (*besuchen*) visit regularly (*bei jdm* sb); **~ mit** associate with; **mit jdm brieflich** *od* **schriftlich ~** (*form*) correspond with sb ♦ *vtr* turn, transform.

Verkehrs- *zW*: **~ampel** *f* traffic lights *pl*; **~aufkommen** *nt* volume of traffic; **~betriebe** *pl* transport services *pl*; **~delikt** *nt* traffic violation (*US*) *od* offence (*Brit*); **~erziehung** *f* road safety training; **v~günstig** *a* convenient; **~insel** *f* traffic island; **~knotenpunkt** *m* traffic junction; **~mittel** *nt*: **öffentliche/private ~mittel** public/private transport; **~stockung** *f* traffic jam, stoppage; **~sünder** *m* (*umg*) traffic offender; **~teilnehmer** *m* road user; **v~tüchtig** *a* (*Fahrzeug*) roadworthy; (*Mensch*) fit to drive; **~unfall** *m* traffic accident; **~verein** *m* tourist information office; **v~widrig** *a* contrary to traffic regulations; **~zeichen** *nt* road sign.

verkehrt *a* wrong; (*umgekehrt*) the wrong way round.

verkennen [fɛrke'nən] *vt unreg* misjudge; (*unterschätzen*) underestimate.

Verkettung [fɛrke'tōōŋ] *f*: **eine ~ unglücklicher Umstände** an unfortunate chain of events.

verklagen [fɛrklâ'gən] *vt* take to court.

verklären [fɛrkle:'rən] *vt* transfigure; **verklärt lächeln** smile radiantly.

verklausulieren [fɛrklouzōōlē:'rən] *vt* (*Vertrag*) hedge in with (restrictive) clauses.

verkleben [fɛrklā:'bən] *vt* glue up, stick ♦ *vi* stick together.

verkleiden [fɛrklī'dən] *vtr* disguise (o.s.); (*kostümieren*) dress up; (*Schacht, Tunnel*)

line; (*vertäfeln*) panel; (*Heizkörper*) cover in.

Verkleidung *f* disguise; (*ARCHIT*) wainscoting.

verkleinern [fɛrklī'nərn] *vt* make smaller, reduce in size.

verklemmt [fɛrklemt'] *a* (*fig*) inhibited.

verklickern [fɛrkli'kərn] *vt* (*umg*): **jdm etw ~** make sth clear to sb.

verklingen [fɛrkli'ŋgən] *vi unreg* die away.

verknacksen [fɛrknák'sən] *vt* (*umg*): **sich** (*dat*) **den Fuß ~** twist one's ankle.

verknallen [fɛrknâ'lən] *vr* (*umg*): **sich in jdn ~** fall for sb.

verkneifen [fɛrknī'fən] *vt* (*umg*): **sich** (*dat*) **etw ~** stop o.s. from doing sth; **ich konnte mir das Lachen nicht ~** I couldn't help laughing.

verknöchert [fɛrknœ'çərt] *a* (*fig*) fossilized.

verknüpfen [fɛrknüp'fən] *vt* tie (up), knot; (*fig*) connect.

Verknüpfung *f* connection.

verkochen [fɛrko'khən] *vti* (*Flüssigkeit*) boil away.

verkohlen [fɛrkō:'lən] *vti* carbonize ♦ *vt* (*umg*): **jdn ~** put sb on.

verkommen [fɛrko'mən] *vi unreg* deteriorate, decay; (*Mensch*) go downhill, come down in the world ♦ *a* (*moralisch*) dissolute, depraved; **V~heit** *f* depravity.

verkorksen [fɛrkork'sən] *vt* (*umg*) ruin, mess up.

verkörpern [fɛrkœr'pərn] *vt* embody, personify.

verköstigen [fɛrkœs'tigən] *vt* feed.

verkrachen [fɛrkrâ'khən] *vr* (*umg*): **sich (mit jdm) ~** fall out (with sb).

verkracht *a* (*umg*: *Leben*) ruined.

verkraften [fɛrkráf'tən] *vt* cope with.

verkrampft [fɛrkrámpft'] *a* (*fig*) tense.

verkriechen [fɛrkrē:'çhən] *vr unreg* creep away, creep into a corner.

verkrümeln [fɛrkrü:'məln] *vr* (*umg*) disappear.

verkrümmt [fɛrkrümt'] *a* crooked.

Verkrümmung *f* bend, warp; (*ANAT*) curvature.

verkrüppelt [fɛrkrü'pəlt] *a* crippled.

verkrustet [fɛrkrōōs'tət] *a* encrusted.

verkühlen [fɛrkü:'lən] *vr* get a chill.

verkümmern [fɛrkü'mərn] *vi* waste away; **emotionell/geistig ~** become emotionally/ intellectually stunted.

verkünden [fɛrkün'dən] *vt* proclaim; (*Urteil*) pronounce.

verkündigen [fɛrkün'digən] *vt* proclaim; (*ironisch*) announce; (*Evangelium*) preach.

verkuppeln [fɛrku'pəln] *vt*: **jdn an jdn ~** (*Zuhälter*) procure sb for sb.

verkürzen [fɛrkür'tsən] *vt* shorten; (*Wort*) abbreviate; **sich** (*dat*) **die Zeit ~** while away the time; **verkürzte Arbeitszeit** shorter working hours *pl*.

Verkürzung *f* shortening; abbreviation.

Verl. abk (= Verlag; Verleger) publ.
verladen [ferlā'dən] vt unreg load.
Verlag [ferlāk'] m -(e)s, -e publishing firm.
verlagern [ferlā'gərn] vtr (lit, fig) shift.
Verlags- zW: ~**anstalt** f publishing firm; ~**wesen** nt publishing.
verlangen [ferlàng'ən] vt demand; (wollen) want; **Sie werden am Telefon verlangt** you are wanted on the phone; ~ **Sie Herrn X** ask for Mr X ♦ vi: ~ **nach** ask for; **V~** nt -s, - desire (nach for); **auf jds V~ (hin)** at sb's request.
verlängern [ferleng'ərn] vt extend; (länger machen) lengthen; (zeitlich) prolong; (Paß, Abonnement etc) renew; **ein verlängertes Wochenende** a long weekend.
Verlängerung f extension; (SPORT) overtime (US), extra time (Brit).
Verlängerungsschnur f extension cord (US) od cable (Brit).
verlangsamen [ferlàng'zâmən] vtr decelerate, slow down.
Verlaß [ferlàs'] m: **auf ihn/das ist kein ~** he/it cannot be relied upon.
verlassen [ferlà'sən] unreg vt leave ♦ vr depend (auf +akk on) ♦ a desolate; (Mensch) abandoned; **einsam und ~** so all alone; **V~heit** f loneliness, lonesomeness.
verläßlich [ferles'liċh] a reliable.
Verlauf [ferlouf'] m course; **einen guten/ schlechten ~ nehmen** go well/badly.
verlaufen unreg vi (zeitlich) pass; (Farben) run ♦ vr get lost; (Menschenmenge) disperse.
Verlautbarung f announcement.
verlauten [ferlou'tən] vi: **etw ~ lassen** disclose sth; **wie verlautet** as reported.
verleben [ferlā'bən] vt spend.
verlebt [ferlā:pt'] a dissipated, worn-out.
verlegen [ferlā:'gən] vt move; (verlieren) mislay; (verschieben) postpone (auf +akk until); (Kabel, Fliesen etc) lay; (abspielen lassen: Handlung) set (nach in); (Buch) publish ♦ vr: **sich auf etw** (akk) ~ resort to sth ♦ a embarrassed; **nicht ~ um** never at a loss for; **V~heit** f embarrassment; (Situation) difficulty, scrape.
Verleger [ferlā:'gər] m -s, - publisher.
verleiden [ferlī'dən] vt: **jdm etw ~** put sb off sth.
Verleih [ferlī'] m -(e)s, -e hire service; (das ~en) renting (out), hiring (out) (Brit); (Film~) distribution.
verleihen vt unreg lend (an jdn to sb); (gegen Gebühr) rent, hire (Brit); (Kraft, Anschein) confer, bestow; (Preis, Medaille) award.
Verleiher m -s, - rental od hire (Brit) firm; (von Filmen) distributor; (von Büchern) lender.
Verleihung f lending; bestowal; award.
verleiten [ferlī'tən] vt lead astray; ~ **zu** talk into, tempt into.
verlernen [ferler'nən] vt forget, unlearn.

verlesen [ferlā:'zən] unreg vt read out; (aussondern) sort out ♦ vr make a mistake in reading.
verletzbar a vulnerable.
verletzen [ferlet'sən] vt (lit, fig) injure, hurt; (Gesetz etc) violate.
verletzend a (fig: Worte) hurtful.
verletzlich a vulnerable.
Verletzte(r) mf dekl wie a injured person.
Verletzung f injury; (Verstoß) violation, infringement.
verleugnen [ferloig'nən] vt deny; (Menschen) disown; **er läßt sich immer ~** he always pretends not to be there.
Verleugnung f denial.
verleumden [ferloim'dən] vt slander; (schriftlich) libel.
verleumderisch a slanderous; libellous (US), libellous (Brit).
Verleumdung f slander; libel.
verlieben vr fall in love (in jdn with sb).
verliebt [ferlē:pt'] a in love; **V~heit** f being in love.
verlieren [ferlē:'rən] unreg vti lose; **das/er hat hier nichts verloren** (umg) that/he has no business to be here ♦ vr get lost; (verschwinden) disappear.
Verlies [ferlē:s'] nt -es, -e dungeon.
verloben [ferlō:'bən] vr get engaged (mit to); **verlobt sein** to be engaged.
Verlobte(r) [ferlō:p'tə(r)] mf dekl wie a fiancé(e).
Verlobung f engagement.
verlocken [ferlo'kən] vt entice, lure.
Verlockung f temptation, attraction.
verlogen [ferlō:'gən] a untruthful; (Komplimente, Versprechungen) false; (Moral, Gesellschaft) hypocritical; **V~heit** f untruthfulness.
verlor [ferlō:r'] imperf von **verlieren**.
verloren pp von **verlieren** ♦ a lost; (Eier) poached; **der ~e Sohn** the prodigal son; **auf ~em Posten kämpfen** od **stehen** be fighting a losing battle; **etw ~ geben** give sth up for lost; ~**gehen** vi unreg get lost; **an ihm ist ein Sänger verlorengegangen** he would have made a (good) singer.
verlöschen [ferlœ'shən] vi aux sein go out; (Inschrift, Farbe, Erinnerung) fade.
verlosen [ferlō:'zən] vt raffle (off), draw lots for.
Verlosung f raffle, lottery.
verlottern [ferlo'tərn], **verludern** [ferlōō:'dərn] vi (umg) go to the dogs.
Verlust [ferlōōst'] m -(e)s, -e loss; (MIL) casualty; **mit ~ verkaufen** sell at a loss; ~**anzeige** f "lost (and found)" notice; ~**geschäft** nt: **das war ein ~geschäft** I/he etc made a loss; ~**zeit** f (INDUSTRIE) idle time.
verm. abk (= vermißt) MIA.
vermachen [fermà'ḣən] vt bequeath, leave.
Vermächtnis [fermeċht'nis] nt -ses, -se legacy.

vermählen [fermeː'lən] *vr* marry.
Vermählung *f* wedding, marriage.
Vermarktung [fermárk'tōōng] *f* marketing.
vermasseln [fermá'səln] *vt* (*umg*) mess up.
vermehren [fermäː'rən] *vtr* multiply; (*Menge*) increase.
Vermehrung *f* multiplying; increase.
vermeiden [fermī'dən] *vt unreg* avoid.
vermeidlich *a* avoidable.
vermeintlich [fermīn'tlich] *a* supposed.
vermengen [fermeng'ən] *vtr* mix; (*fig*) mix up, confuse.
Vermenschlichung [fermen'shlichōōng] *f* humanization.
Vermerk [fermerk'] *m* -(e)s, -e note; (*in Ausweis*) endorsement.
vermerken *vt* note.
vermessen [ferme'sən] *unreg vt* survey ♦ *vr* (*falsch messen*) measure incorrectly ♦ *a* presumptuous, bold; **V~heit** *f* presumptuousness; recklessness.
Vermessung *f* survey(ing).
Vermessungs- *zW*: **~amt** *nt* land survey(ing) office; **~ingenieur** *m* land surveyor.
vermiesen [fermēː'zən] *vt* (*umg*) spoil.
vermieten [fermēː'tən] *vt* rent (out); (*Auto*) hire out, rent.
Vermieter(in *f*) *m* -s, - landlord; landlady.
Vermietung *f* letting, renting (out); (*von Autos*) hiring (out), rental.
vermindern [fermin'dərn] *vtr* lessen, decrease; (*Preise*) reduce.
Verminderung *f* reduction.
verminen [fermēː'nən] *vt* mine.
vermischen [fermi'shən] *vtr* mix; (*Teesorten etc*) blend; **vermischte Schriften** miscellaneous writings.
vermissen [fermi'sən] *vt* miss; **vermißt sein** *od* **als vermißt gemeldet sein** be reported missing; **wir haben dich bei der Party vermißt** we didn't see you at the party.
Vermißtenanzeige *f* missing persons report.
vermitteln [fermi'təln] *vi* mediate; **vermittelnde Worte** conciliatory words ♦ *vt* arrange (*jdm* for sb); (*Gespräch*) (*Stelle*) find (*jdm* for sb); (*Gefühl, Bild, Idee etc*) convey; (*Wissen*) impart (*jdm* to sb); **jdm etw ~** help sb to obtain sth.
Vermittler(in *f*) [fermi'tlər(in)] *m* -s, - (*COMM*) agent; (*Schlichter*) mediator.
Vermittlung *f* procurement; (*Stellen~*) agency; (*TEL*) exchange; (*Schlichtung*) mediation.
Vermittlungsgebühr *f* brokerage, (broker's) commission.
vermögen [fermœ'gən] *vt unreg* be capable of; **~ zu** be able to.
Vermögen *nt* -s, - wealth; (*Fähigkeit*) ability; **mein ganzes ~ besteht aus** ... my entire assets consist of ...; **ein ~ kosten** cost a fortune.
vermögend *a* wealthy.

Vermögens- *zW*: **~steuer** *f* property tax, wealth tax; **~wert** *m* asset; **v~wirksam** *a*: **sein Geld v~wirksam anlegen** invest one's money profitably; **v~wirksame Leistungen** employers' contributions to tax-deductible savings scheme.
vermummen [fermōō'mən] *vr* wrap up (warm); (*sich verkleiden*) disguise.
Vermummungsverbot *nt* -(e)s *law against disguising o.s. at demonstrations in the FRG.*
vermurksen [fermōōrk'sən] *vt* (*umg*): **etw ~** make a mess of sth.
vermuten [fermōō:'tən] *vt* suppose; (*argwöhnen*) suspect.
vermutlich *a* supposed, presumed ♦ *ad* probably.
Vermutung *f* supposition; suspicion; **die ~ liegt nahe, daß** ... there are grounds for assuming that ...
vernachlässigen [fernákh'lesigən] *vt* neglect ♦ *vr* neglect o.s. *od* one's appearance.
vernarben [fernár'bən] *vi* heal up.
vernarren [ferná'rən] *vr* (*umg*): **in jdn/etw vernarrt sein** be crazy about sb/sth.
vernaschen [ferná'shən] *vt* (*Geld*) spend on sweets; (*umg*: *Mädchen, Mann*) make it with.
vernehmen [fernäː'mən] *vt unreg* hear, perceive; (*erfahren*) learn; (*JUR*) (cross-) examine; (*Polizei*) question; **V~** *nt*: **dem V~ nach** from what I *od* we *etc* hear.
vernehmlich *a* audible.
Vernehmung *f* (cross-)examination.
vernehmungsfähig *a* in a condition to be (cross-)examined.
verneigen [fernī'gən] *vr* bow.
verneinen [fernī'nən] *vt* (*Frage*) answer in the negative; (*ablehnen*) deny; (*GRAM*) negate.
verneinend *a* negative.
Verneinung *f* negation.
vernichten [ferni'tən] *vt* destroy, annihilate.
vernichtend *a* (*fig*) crushing; (*Blick*) withering; (*Kritik*) scathing.
Vernichtung *f* destruction, annihilation.
Vernichtungsschlag *m* devastating blow.
verniedlichen [fernēː'tlichən] *vt* play down.
Vernunft [fernōōnft'] *f* - reason; **~ annehmen** see reason; **~heirat** *f* marriage of convenience.
vernünftig [fernünf'tich] *a* sensible, reasonable.
Vernunftmensch *m* rational person.
veröden [ferœ'dən] *vi* become desolate ♦ *vt* (*MED*) obliterate.
veröffentlichen [ferœ'fəntlichən] *vt* publish.
Veröffentlichung *f* publication.
verordnen [ferord'nən] *vt* (*MED*) prescribe.
Verordnung *f* order, decree; (*MED*) prescription.
verpachten [ferpákh'tən] *vt* lease (out).
verpacken [ferpá'kən] *vt* pack; (*ver-*

brauchergerecht) package; (*einwickeln*) wrap.

Verpackung *f* packing, wrapping.

verpassen [ferpá'sən] *vt* miss; **jdm eine Ohrfeige** ~ (*umg*) give sb a clip round the ear.

verpatzen [ferpá'tsən] *vt* (*umg*) spoil, mess up.

verpennen [ferpe'nən] *vir* (*umg*) oversleep.

verpesten [ferpes'tən] *vt* pollute.

verpetzen [ferpe'tsən] *vt* (*umg*) tell on (*bei* to).

verpfänden [ferpfen'dən] *vt* pawn; (*JUR*) mortgage.

verpfeifen [ferpfī'fən] *vt* unreg (*umg*) tell on (*bei* to).

verpflanzen [ferpflán'tsən] *vt* transplant.

Verpflanzung *f* transplanting; (*MED*) transplant.

verpflegen [ferpflā:'gən] *vt* feed, cater for.

Verpflegung *f* feeding; catering; (*Kost*) food; (*in Hotel*) board.

verpflichten [ferpflích'tən] *vt* oblige, bind; (*anstellen*) engage; **jdm verpflichtet sein** be under an obligation to sb; **verpflichtend** (*Zusage*) binding ♦ *vr* undertake; (*MIL*) sign on; **sich zu etw** ~ commit o.s. to doing sth ♦ *vi* carry obligations; **jdm zu Dank verpflichtet sein** be obliged to sb.

Verpflichtung *f* obligation; (*Aufgabe*) duty.

verpfuschen [ferpfōō'shən] *vt* (*umg*) bungle, make a mess of.

verplanen [ferplá'nən] *vt* (*Zeit*) book up; (*Geld*) budget.

verplappern [ferplá'pərn] *vr* (*umg*) open one's big mouth.

verplempern [ferplem'pərn] *vt* (*umg*) waste.

verpönt [ferpœnt'] *a* frowned upon (*bei* by).

verprassen [ferprá'sən] *vt* squander.

verprügeln [ferprü:'gəln] *vt* (*umg*) beat up.

verpuffen [ferpōō'fən] *vi* (go) pop; (*fig*) fall flat.

Verputz [ferpōōts'] *m* plaster; (*Rauhputz*) roughcast; **v~en** *vt* plaster; (*umg: Essen*) put away.

verqualmen [ferkvál'mən] *vt* (*Zimmer*) fill with smoke.

verquollen [ferkvo'lən] *a* swollen; (*Holz*) warped.

verrammeln [ferrá'məln] *vt* barricade.

Verrat [ferrát'] *m* **-(e)s** treachery; (*POL*) treason; ~ **an jdm üben** betray sb.

verraten *unreg vt* betray; (*fig: erkennen lassen*) show; (*Geheimnis*) divulge ♦ *vr* give o.s. away.

Verräter [ferre:'tər] *m* **-s**, - traitor; ~**in** *f* traitress; **v~isch** *a* treacherous.

verrauchen [ferrou'khən] *vi* (*fig: Zorn*) blow over.

verrechnen [ferréch'nən] *vt*: ~ **mit** set off against ♦ *vr* miscalculate.

Verrechnungsscheck *m* non-negotiable check.

verregnet [ferrā:g'nət] *a* rainy, spoiled by rain.

verreisen [ferrī'zən] *vi* go away (on a journey); **er ist geschäftlich verreist** he's away on business.

verreißen [ferrī'sən] *vt* unreg pull to pieces.

verrenken [ferreng'kən] *vt* contort; (*MED*) dislocate; **sich** (*dat*) **den Knöchel** ~ sprain one's ankle.

Verrenkung *f* contortion; (*MED*) dislocation.

verrennen [ferre'nən] *vr* unreg: **sich in etw** (*akk*) ~ get stuck on sth.

verrichten [ferrich'tən] *vt* (*Arbeit*) do, perform.

verriegeln [ferre:'gəln] *vt* bolt.

verringern [ferri'ngərn] *vt* reduce ♦ *vr* decrease.

Verringerung *f* reduction; lessening.

verrinnen [ferri'nən] *vi* unreg run out *od* away; (*Zeit*) elapse.

Verriß [ferris'] *m* scathing review.

verrohen [ferrō:'ən] *vi* become brutalized.

verrosten [ferros'tən] *vi* rust.

verrotten [ferro'tən] *vi* rot.

verrucht [ferrōō:kht'] *a* despicable; (*verrufen*) disreputable.

verrücken [ferrü'kən] *vt* move, shift.

verrückt *a* crazy, mad; **V~e(r)** *mf dekl wie a* lunatic; **V~heit** *f* madness, lunacy.

Verruf [ferrōō:f'] *m*: **in** ~ **geraten/bringen** fall/bring into disrepute.

verrufen *a* disreputable.

verrutschen [ferrōōt'shən] *vi* slip.

Vers [fers] *m* **-es**, **-e** verse.

versacken [ferzá'kən] *vi* (*lit*) sink; (*fig ung: herunterkommen*) go downhill; (*umg: lange zechen*) get involved in a drinking spree.

versagen [ferzá'gən] *vt*: **jdm/sich** (*dat*) **etw** ~ deny sb/o.s. sth ♦ *vi* fail.

Versagen *nt* **-s** failure; **menschliches** ~ human error.

Versager *m* **-s**, - failure.

versalzen [ferzál'tsən] *vt* put too much salt in; (*fig*) spoil.

versammeln [ferzá'məln] *vtr* assemble, gather.

Versammlung *f* meeting, gathering.

Versammlungsfreiheit *f* freedom of assembly.

Versand [ferzánt'] *m* **-(e)s** forwarding; dispatch; (~*abteilung*) dispatch department; ~**bahnhof** *m* dispatch station; ~**haus** *nt* mail-order firm; ~**kosten** *pl* transport(ation) costs *pl*; ~**weg** *m*: **auf dem** ~**weg** by mail order.

versäumen [ferzoi'mən] *vt* miss; (*unterlassen*) neglect; (*Zeit*) lose.

Versäumnis *f* **-**, **-se** neglect; omission.

verschachern [fershá'khərn] *vt* (*umg*) sell off.

verschachtelt [fershákh'təlt] *a* (*Satz*) complex.

verschaffen [fershá'fən] *vt*: **jdm/sich etw** ~ get *od* procure sth for sb/o.s.

verschämt [fershe:mt'] *a* bashful.

verschandeln [fershán'dəln] *vt* (*umg*) spoil.

verschanzen [fershán'tsən] *vr*: **sich hinter etw** (*dat*) ~ dig in behind sth; (*fig*) take refuge behind sth.

verschärfen [fersher'fən] *vtr* intensify; (*Lage*) aggravate; (*strenger machen*: *Kontrollen*, *Gesetze*) tighten up.

verscharren [fershá'rən] *vt* bury.

verschätzen [fershe'tsən] *vr* be out in one's reckoning.

verschenken [fersheng'kən] *vt* give away.

verscherzen [fersher'tsən] *vt*: **sich** (*dat*) **etw** ~ lose sth, throw sth away.

verscheuchen [fershoi'çhən] *vt* frighten away.

verschicken [fershi'kən] *vt* send off; (*Sträfling*) transport, deport.

verschieben [fershē:'bən] *vt unreg* shift; (*EISENB*) shunt; (*Termin*) postpone; (*umg*: *Waren*, *Devisen*) traffic in; (*COMM*) push.

Verschiebung *f* shift, displacement; shunting; postponement.

verschieden [fershē:'dən] *a* different; **das ist ganz** ~ (*wird* ~ *gehandhabt*) that varies, that just depends; **sie sind** ~ **groß** they are of different sizes; **~e** *pl* various people; **~es** *pron* various things *pl*; **etwas V~es** something different; **~artig** *a* various, of different kinds; **zwei so ~artige ...** two such differing ...; **V~heit** *f* difference.

verschiedentlich *ad* several times.

verschiffen [fershi'fən] *vt* ship; (*Sträfling*) transport.

verschimmeln [fershi'məln] *vi* (*Nahrungsmittel*) go moldy (*US*) *od* mouldy (*Brit*); (*Leder*, *Papier etc*) become mildewed.

verschlafen [fershlâ'fən] *unreg vt* sleep through; (*fig*: *versäumen*) miss ♦ *vir* oversleep ♦ *a* sleepy.

Verschlag [fershlâk'] *m* shed.

verschlagen [fershlâ'gən] *vt unreg* board up; (*TENNIS*) hit out of play; (*Buchseite*) lose; **jdm den Atem** ~ take sb's breath away; **an einen Ort** ~ **werden** wind up in a place ♦ *a* cunning.

verschlampen [fershlám'pən] *vi aux sein* (*Mensch*) go to seed (*umg*) ♦ *vt* lose, mislay.

verschlechtern [fershleçh'tərn] *vt* make worse ♦ *vr* deteriorate, get worse; (*gehaltlich*) take a lower-paid job.

Verschlechterung *f* deterioration.

Verschleierung [fershlī'əroong] *f* veiling; (*fig*) concealment; (*MIL*) screening.

Verschleierungstaktik *f* smoke-screen tactics *pl*.

Verschleiß [fershlīs'] *m* **-es**, **-e** wear and tear.

verschleißen *unreg vtir* wear out.

verschleppen [fershle'pən] *vt* carry off, abduct; (*zeitlich*) drag out, delay; (*verbreiten*: *Seuche*) spread.

verschleudern [fershloi'dərn] *vt* squander; (*COMM*) sell dirt-cheap.

verschließbar *a* lockable.

verschließen [fershlē:'sən] *unreg vt* close; lock ♦ *vr*: **sich einer Sache** ~ close one's mind to sth.

verschlimmern [fershli'mərn] *vt* make worse, aggravate ♦ *vr* get worse, deteriorate.

Verschlimmerung *f* deterioration.

verschlingen [fershli'ngən] *vt unreg* devour, swallow up; (*Fäden*) twist.

verschliß [fershlis'] *imperf von* **verschleißen**.

verschlissen [fershli'sən] *a* worn(-out) ♦ *pp von* **verschleißen**.

verschlossen [fershlo'sən] *a* locked; (*fig*) reserved; **V~heit** *f* reserve.

verschlucken [fershlōō'kən] *vt* swallow ♦ *vr* choke.

Verschluß [fershlōōs'] *m* lock; (*von Kleid etc*) fastener; (*PHOT*) shutter; (*Stöpsel*) plug; **unter** ~ **halten** keep under lock and key.

verschlüsseln [fershlü'səln] *vt* encode.

verschmachten [fershmákh'tən] *vi* languish (*vor* +*dat* for).

verschmähen [fershme:'ən] *vt* scorn, disdain.

verschmelzen [fershmel'tsən] *vti unreg* merge, blend.

verschmerzen [fershmer'tsən] *vt* get over.

verschmiert [fershmē:rt'] *a* (*Hände*) smeary; (*Schminke*) smudged.

verschmitzt [fershmitst'] *a* mischievous.

verschmutzen [fershmōō'tsən] *vt* soil; (*Umwelt*) pollute.

verschnaufen [fershnou'fən] *vir* (*umg*) have a breather.

verschneiden [fershnī'dən] *vt* (*Whisky etc*) blend.

verschneit [fershnīt'] *a* snowed in, covered in snow.

Verschnitt [fershnit'] *m* (*von Whisky etc*) blend.

verschnörkelt [fershnœr'kəlt] *a* ornate.

verschnupft [fershnōōpft'] *a* (*umg*): ~ **sein** have a cold; (*beleidigt*) be peeved (*umg*).

verschnüren [fershnü:'rən] *vt* tie up.

verschollen [fersho'lən] *a* lost, missing.

verschonen [fershō:'nən] *vt* spare (*jdn mit etw* sb sth); **von etw verschont bleiben** escape sth.

verschönern [fershœ'nərn] *vt* decorate; (*verbessern*) improve.

verschossen [fersho'sən] *a*: ~ **sein** (*fig umg*) be in love.

verschränken [fershreng'kən] *vt* cross; (*Arme*) fold.

verschreckt [fershrekt'] *a* frightened, scared.

verschreiben [fershrī'bən] *unreg vt* (*Papier*) use up; (*MED*) prescribe ♦ *vr* make a mistake (in writing); **sich einer Sache** ~ devote o.s. to sth.

verschrie(e)n [fershrē:'(ə)n] *a* notorious.

verschroben [fershrō:'bən] *a* eccentric, odd.

verschrotten [fershro'tən] *vt* scrap.

verschüchtert [fershüçh'tərt] *a* subdued, intimidated.

verschulden [fershool'dən] *vt* be guilty of ♦ *vi* (*in Schulden geraten*) get into debt; **V~** *nt* -s fault.

verschuldet *a* in debt.

Verschuldung *f* fault; (*Geld*) debts *pl*.

verschütten [fershü'tən] *vt* spill; (*zuschütten*) fill; (*unter Trümmer*) bury.

verschwand [fershvànt'] *imperf von* **verschwinden**.

verschweigen [fershvī'gən] *vt unreg* keep secret; **jdm etw ~** keep sth from sb.

verschwenden [fershven'dən] *vt* squander.

Verschwender(in *f*) *m* -s, - spendthrift; **v~isch** *a* wasteful; (*Leben*) extravagant.

Verschwendung *f* waste; extravagance.

verschwiegen [fershvē:'gən] *a* discreet; (*Ort*) secluded; **V~heit** *f* discretion; seclusion; **zur V~heit verpflichtet** bound to secrecy.

verschwimmen [fershvi'mən] *vi unreg* grow hazy, become blurred.

verschwinden [fershvin'dən] *vi unreg* disappear, vanish; **verschwinde!** clear off! (*umg*); **V~** *nt* -s disappearance.

verschwindend *a* (*Anzahl, Menge*) insignificant.

verschwitzen [fershvi'tsən] *vt* stain with sweat; (*umg*) forget.

verschwitzt *a* (*Kleidung*) sweat-stained; (*Mensch*) sweaty.

verschwommen [fershvo'mən] *a* hazy, vague.

verschworen [fershvō:'rən] *a* (*Gesellschaft*) sworn.

verschwören [fershvœ'rən] *vr unreg* conspire, plot.

Verschwörer(in *f*) *m* -s, - conspirator.

Verschwörung *f* conspiracy, plot.

verschwunden [fershvoon'dən] *pp von* **verschwinden** ♦ *a* missing.

versehen [ferzä:'ən] *unreg vt* supply, provide; (*Pflicht*) carry out; (*Amt*) fill; (*Haushalt*) keep ♦ *vr* (*fig*) make a mistake; **ehe er (es) sich ~ hatte ...** before he knew it ...

Versehen *nt* -s, - oversight; **aus ~** by mistake.

versehentlich *ad* by mistake.

Versehrte(r) [ferzä:r'tə(r)] *mf dekl wie a* disabled person.

verselbständigen [ferzelp'shtendigən] *vr* become independent.

versenden [ferzen'dən] *vt unreg* send; (*COMM*) forward.

versengen [ferzeng'ən] *vt* scorch; (*Feuer*) singe; (*umg: verprügeln*) wallop.

versenken [ferzeng'kən] *vt* sink ♦ *vr* become engrossed (*in +akk* in).

versessen [ferze'sən] *a*: **~ auf** (*+akk*) mad about.

versetzen [ferze'tsən] *vt* transfer; (*verpfänden*) pawn; (*umg: vergeblich warten lassen*) stand up; (*nicht geradlinig anordnen*) stagger; (*SCH: in höhere Klasse*) move up; **jdm einen Tritt/Schlag ~** kick/hit

sb; **etw mit etw ~** mix sth with sth; **jdm einen Stich ~** (*fig*) cut sb to the quick, wound sb (deeply); **jdn in gute Laune ~** put sb in a good mood ♦ *vr*: **sich in jdn** *od* **in jds Lage ~** put o.s. in sb's place.

Versetzung *f* transfer; **seine ~ ist gefährdet** (*SCH*) he's in danger of having to repeat a year.

verseuchen [ferzoi'çhən] *vt* contaminate.

Versicherer *m* -s, - insurer; (*bei Schiffen*) underwriter.

versichern [ferzi'çhərn] *vt* assure; (*mit Geld*) insure ♦ *vr*: **sich ~** (*+gen*) make sure of.

Versicherung *f* assurance; insurance.

Versicherungs- *zW*: **~beitrag** *m* insurance premium; (*bei staatlicher Versicherung etc*) social security contribution; **~gesellschaft** *f* insurance company; **~nehmer** *m* -s, - (*form*) insured, policy holder; **~police** *f* insurance policy; **~schutz** *m* insurance cover; **~summe** *f* sum insured; **~träger** *m* insurer.

versickern [ferzi'kərn] *vi* seep away; (*fig: Interesse etc*) peter out.

versiegeln [ferzē:'gəln] *vt* seal (up).

versiegen [ferzē:'gən] *vi* dry up.

versiert [verzē:rt'] *a*: **in etw** (*dat*) **~ sein** be experienced *od* well versed in sth.

versinken [ferzing'kən] *vi unreg* sink; **ich hätte im Boden/vor Scham ~ mögen** I wished the ground would swallow me up.

versinnbildlichen [ferzin'biltliçhən] *vt* symbolize.

Version [verzēō:n'] *f* version.

Versmaß [fers'mâs] *nt* meter (*US*), metre (*Brit*).

versohlen [ferzō:'lən] *vt* (*umg*) leather.

versöhnen [ferzœ'nən] *vt* reconcile ♦ *vr* become reconciled.

Versöhnung *f* reconciliation.

versonnen [ferzo'nən] *a* (*Gesichtsausdruck*) pensive, thoughtful; (*träumerisch: Blick*) dreamy.

versorgen [ferzor'gən] *vt* provide, supply (*mit* with); (*Familie etc*) look after ♦ *vr* look after o.s.

Versorger(in *f*) *m* -s, - (*Ernährer*) provider, breadwinner; (*Belieferer*) supplier.

Versorgung *f* provision; (*Unterhalt*) maintenance; (*Alters~ etc*) benefit, assistance.

Versorgungs- *zW*: **~amt** *nt* pension office; **~betrieb** *m* public utility; **~netz** *nt* (*Wasserversorgung etc*) (supply) grid; (*von Waren*) supply network.

verspannen [fershpà'nən] *vr* (*Muskeln*) tense up.

verspäten [fershpe:'tən] *vr* be late.

Verspätung *f* delay; **~ haben** be late; **mit zwanzig Minuten ~** twenty minutes late.

versperren [fershpe'rən] *vt* bar, obstruct.

Versperrung *f* barrier.

verspielen [fershpē:'lən] *vti* lose; **jetzt hast du (bei ihr) verspielt** you've had it now (with her) (*umg*).

verspielt [fershpē:lt'] *a* playful; **bei jdm ~**

haben be on sb's bad side (US) od in sb's bad books (Brit).

versponnen |fershpo'nən| a wild, unrealistic.

verspotten [fershpo'tən] vt ridicule, scoff at.

versprach [fershpráƙh'] imperf von **versprechen**.

versprechen [fershpre'čhən] unreg vt promise; **sich** (dat) **etw von etw** ~ expect sth from sth ♦ vr (etwas Nicht-Gemeintes sagen) make a slip of the tongue; **V~** nt **-s, -** promise.

Versprecher m **-s, -** (umg) slip (of the tongue).

verspricht [fershpričht'] 3. pers sing präs von **versprechen**.

verspüren [fershpü:'rən] vt feel, be conscious of.

verstaatlichen [fershtá'tličhən] vt nationalize.

verstaatlicht a: ~**er Industriezweig** nationalized industry.

Verstaatlichung f nationalization.

verstand imperf von **verstehen**.

Verstand [fershtánt'] m intelligence; (Intellekt) mind; (Fähigkeit zu denken) reason; **den** ~ **verlieren** go out of one's mind; **über jds** ~ **gehen** be beyond sb.

verstanden [fershtán'dən] pp von **verstehen**.

verstandesmäßig a rational.

verständig [fershten'dičh] a sensible.

verständigen [fershten'digən] vt inform ♦ vr communicate; (sich einigen) come to an understanding.

Verständigkeit f good sense.

Verständigung f communication; (Benachrichtigung) informing; (Einigung) agreement.

verständlich [fershtent'ličh] a understandable, comprehensible; (hörbar) audible; **sich** ~ **machen** make o.s. understood; (sich klar ausdrücken) make o.s. clear.

verständlicherweise ad understandably (enough).

Verständlichkeit f clarity, intelligibility.

Verständnis nt **-ses, -se** understanding; **für etw kein** ~ **haben** have no understanding od sympathy for sth; (für Kunst etc) have no appreciation of sth; **v~los** a uncomprehending; **v~voll** a understanding, sympathetic.

verstärken [fershter'kən] vt strengthen; (Ton) amplify; (erhöhen) intensify ♦ vr intensify.

Verstärker m **-s, -** amplifier.

Verstärkung f strengthening; (Hilfe) reinforcements pl; (von Ton) amplification.

verstaubt [fershtoupt'] a dusty; (fig: Ansichten) fuddy-duddy (umg).

verstauchen [fershtou'ƙhən] vt sprain.

verstauen [fershtou'ən] vt stow away.

Versteck [fershtek'] nt **-(e)s, -e** hiding (place).

verstecken vtr hide.

versteckt a hidden; (Tür) concealed; (fig: Lächeln, Blick) furtive; (Andeutung) veiled.

verstehen [fershtä:'ən] unreg vti understand;

(können, beherrschen) know; **das ist nicht wörtlich zu** ~ that isn't to be taken literally ♦ vr (auskommen) get on; **das versteht sich von selbst** that goes without saying; **die Preise** ~ **sich einschließlich Lieferung** prices are inclusive of delivery; **sich auf etw** (akk) ~ be an expert at sth.

versteifen [fershtī'fən] vt stiffen, brace ♦ vr (fig) insist (auf +akk on).

versteigen [fershtī'gən] vr unreg: **sie hat sich zu der Behauptung verstiegen, daß ...** she presumed to claim that ...

versteigern [fershtī'gərn] vt auction.

Versteigerung f auction.

verstellbar a adjustable, variable.

verstellen [fershte'lən] vt move, shift; (Uhr) adjust; (versperren) block; (fig) disguise ♦ vr pretend, put on an act.

Verstellung f pretense (US), pretence (Brit).

versteuern [fershtoi'ərn] vt pay tax on; **zu** ~ taxable.

verstiegen [fershtē:'gən] a exaggerated.

verstimmt [fershtimt'] a out of tune; (fig) cross, put out; (: Magen) upset.

verstockt [fershtokt'] a stubborn; **V~heit** f stubbornness.

verstohlen [fershtō:'lən] a stealthy.

verstopfen [fershtop'fən] vt block, stop up; (MED) constipate.

Verstopfung f obstruction; (MED) constipation.

verstorben [fershtor'bən] a deceased, late.

Verstorbene(r) mf dekl wie a deceased.

verstört [fershtœrt'] a (Mensch) distraught.

Verstoß [fershtō:s'] m infringement, violation (gegen of).

verstoßen unreg vt disown, reject ♦ vi: ~ **gegen** offend against.

Verstrebung [fershträ:'bōōng] f (Strebebalken) support(ing beam).

verstreichen [fershtrī'čhən] unreg vt spread ♦ vi elapse; (Zeit) pass (by); (Frist) expire.

verstreuen [fershtroi'ən] vt scatter (about).

verstricken [fershtri'kən] vt (fig) entangle, ensnare ♦ vr get entangled (in +akk in).

verströmen [fershtrœ'mən] vt exude.

verstümmeln [fershtü'məln] vt maim, mutilate (auch fig).

verstummen [fershtōō'mən] vi go silent; (Lärm) die away.

Versuch [ferzōō'ƙh'] m **-(e)s, -e** attempt; (CHEM etc) experiment; **das käme auf einen** ~ **an** we'll have to have a try.

versuchen vt try; (verlocken) tempt ♦ vr: **sich an etw** (dat) ~ try one's hand at sth.

Versuchs- zW: ~**anstalt** f research institute; ~**bohrung** f test drilling; ~**kaninchen** nt guinea pig; ~**objekt** nt test object; (fig: Mensch) guinea pig; ~**reihe** f series of experiments; **v~weise** ad tentatively.

Versuchung f temptation.

versumpfen [ferzōōmp'fən] vi (Gebiet) become marshy; (fig umg) go to pot; (lange zechen) get involved in a drinking spree.

versündigen |ferzün'digən| *vr* (*geh*): **sich an jdm/etw** ~ sin against sb/sth.

versunken |ferzŏŏng'kən| *a* sunken; ~ **sein in** (+*akk*) be absorbed *od* engrossed in.

versüßen |ferzü:'sən| *vt*: **jdm etw** ~ (*fig*) make sth more pleasant for sb.

vertagen |fertâ'gən| *vti* adjourn. **Vertagung** *f* adjournment.

vertauschen |fertou'shən| *vt* exchange; (*versehentlich*) mix up; **vertauschte Rollen** reversed roles.

verteidigen |fertī'digən| *vt* defend ♦ *vr* defend o.s.; (*vor Gericht*) conduct one's own defense.

Verteidiger(in *f*) *m* -**s**, - defender; (*Anwalt*) defense lawyer.

Verteidigung *f* defense (*US*), defence (*Brit*).

Verteidigungs- *zW*: ~**fähigkeit** *f* ability to defend; ~**minister** *m* Secretary of Defense.

verteilen |fertī'lən| *vt* distribute; (*Rollen*) assign; (*Salbe*) spread.

Verteiler *m* -**s**, - (*COMM. AUT*) distributor. **Verteilung** *f* distribution.

Verteuerung |fertoi'ərŏŏng| *f* increase in price.

verteufeln |fertoi'fəln| *vt* condemn.

verteufelt *a*, *ad* (*umg*) awful(ly), devilish(ly).

vertiefen |fertē:'fən| *vt* deepen; (*SCH*) consolidate ♦ *vr*: **sich in etw** (*akk*) ~ become engrossed *od* absorbed in sth.

Vertiefung *f* depression.

vertikal |vertēkâl'| *a* vertical.

vertilgen |fertil'gən| *vt* exterminate; (*umg*) eat up, consume.

Vertilgungsmittel *nt* weedkiller; (*Insekten*~) pesticide.

vertippen |ferti'pən| *vr* make a typing mistake.

vertonen |fertō:'nən| *vt* set to music; (*Film etc*) add a sound-track to.

Vertrag |fertrâk'| *m* -**(e)s**, -̈e contract, agreement; (*POL*) treaty.

vertragen |fertrâ'gən| *unreg vt* tolerate, stand; **viel** ~ **können** (*umg*: *Alkohol*) be able to hold one's drink ♦ *vr* get along; (*sich aussöhnen*) become reconciled; **sich mit etw** ~ (*Nahrungsmittel*, *Farbe*) go with sth; (*Aussage*, *Verhalten*) be consistent with sth.

vertraglich *a* contractual.

verträglich |fertre:k'liċh| *a* good-natured, sociable; (*Speisen*) easily digested; (*MED*) easily tolerated; **V**~**keit** *f* sociability; good nature; digestibility.

Vertrags- *zW*: ~**bruch** *m* breach of contract; **v**~**brüchig** *a* in breach of contract; **v**~**fähig** *a* (*JUR*) competent to contract; **v**~**mäßig** *a*, *ad* stipulated, according to contract; ~**partner** *m* party to a contract; ~**spieler** *m* (*SPORT*) player under contract; **v**~**widrig** *a*, *ad* contrary to contract.

vertrakt |fertrákt'| *a* awkward, tricky, complex.

vertrauen |fertrou'ən| *vi* trust (*jdm* sb); ~

auf (+*akk*) rely on; **V**~ *nt* -**s** confidence; **jdn ins V**~ **ziehen** take sb into one's confidence; **V**~ **zu jdm fassen** gain confidence in sb; ~**erweckend** *a* inspiring trust.

Vertrauens- *zW*: ~**mann** *m*, *pl* -**männer** *od* -**leute** intermediary; ~**sache** *f* (*vertrauliche Angelegenheit*) confidential matter; (*Frage des Vertrauens*) question of trust; **v**~**selig** *a* trusting; **v**~**voll** *a* trustful; ~**votum** *nt* (*PARL*) vote of confidence; **v**~**würdig** *a* trustworthy.

vertraulich |fertrou'liċh| *a* familiar; (*geheim*) confidential; **V**~**keit** *f* familiarity; confidentiality.

verträumt |fertroimt'| *a* dreamy; (*Städtchen etc*) sleepy.

vertraut |fertrout'| *a* familiar; **sich mit dem Gedanken** ~ **machen, daß** ... get used to the idea that ...

Vertraute(r) *mf dekl wie a* confidant(e), close friend.

Vertrautheit *f* familiarity.

vertreiben |fertrī'bən| *vt unreg* drive away; (*aus Land*) expel; (*COMM*) sell; (*Zeit*) pass. **Vertreibung** *f* expulsion.

vertretbar *a* justifiable; (*Theorie*, *Argument*) tenable.

vertreten |fertrā:'tən| *vt unreg* represent; (*Ansicht*) hold, advocate; (*ersetzen*) replace; (*Kollegen*) stand in for; (*COMM*) be the agent for; **sich** (*dat*) **die Beine** ~ stretch one's legs.

Vertreter(in *f*) *m* -**s**, - representative; (*Verfechter*) advocate; (*COMM*: *Firma*) agent; ~**provision** *f* agent's commission.

Vertretung *f* representation; advocacy; **die** ~ **übernehmen** stand in (*für jdn* for sb).

Vertretungsstunde *f* (*SCH*) lesson taken by a substitute teacher.

Vertrieb |fertrē:p'| *m* -**(e)s**, -**e** marketing; **den** ~ **für eine Firma haben** have the (selling) agency for a firm.

Vertriebene(r) |fertrē:'bənə(r)| *mf dekl wie a* exile.

Vertriebskosten *pl* marketing costs *pl*.

vertrocknen |fertro'knən| *vi* dry up.

vertrödeln |fertrœ'dəln| *vt* (*umg*) fritter away.

vertrösten |fertrœs'tən| *vt* put off.

vertun |fertŏŏ:n'| *unreg vt* (*umg*) waste ♦ *vr* make a mistake.

vertuschen |fertŏŏ'shən| *vt* hush *od* cover up.

verübeln |ferü'bəln| *vt*: **jdm etw** ~ be cross *od* offended with sb on account of sth.

verüben |ferü:'bən| *vt* commit.

verulken |ferŏŏl'kən| *vt* (*umg*) make fun of.

verunglimpfen |ferŏŏn'glimpfən| *vt* disparage.

verunglücken |ferŏŏn'glükən| *vi* have an accident; (*fig umg*: *mißlingen*) go wrong; **tödlich** ~ be killed in an accident.

verunreinigen |ferŏŏn'rīnigən| *vt* soil; (*Umwelt*) pollute.

verunsichern |ferŏŏn'ziċhərn| *vt* rattle (*fig*).

verunstalten [ferōōn'shtáltən] *vt* disfigure; (*Gebäude etc*) deface.
veruntreuen [ferōōn'troiən] *vt* embezzle.
verursachen [ferōō:r'zákhən] *vt* cause.
verurteilen [ferōō:r'tīlən] *vt* condemn; (*für schuldig befinden*) convict (*für* of); (*zu Strafe*) sentence.
Verurteilung *f* condemnation; (*JUR*) conviction; sentence.
vervielfachen [ferfē:l'fákhən] *vt* multiply.
vervielfältigen [ferfē:l'feltigən] *vt* duplicate, copy.
Vervielfältigung *f* duplication, copying.
vervollkommnen [ferfol'komnən] *vt* perfect.
vervollständigen [ferfol'shtendigən] *vt* complete.
verw. *abk* = **verwitwet.**
Verw. *abk* = **Verwaltung.**
verwachsen [fervák'sən] *a* (*Mensch*) deformed; (*verkümmert*) stunted; (*überwuchert*) overgrown.
verwackeln [fervá'kəln] *vt* (*Photo*) blur.
verwählen [ferve:'lən] *vr* (*TEL*) dial the wrong number.
verwahren [fervâ'rən] *vt* keep (safe) ♦ *vr* protest.
verwahrlosen *vi* become neglected; (*moralisch*) go to the bad.
verwahrlost *a* neglected; (*moralisch*) wayward.
Verwahrung *f* (*von Geld etc*) keeping; (*von Täter*) custody, detention; **jdn in ~ nehmen** take sb into custody.
verwaist [fervīst'] *a* orphaned.
verwalten [fervál'tən] *vt* manage; administer.
Verwalter(in *f*) *m* **-s,** - adminstrator; (*Vermögens~*) trustee.
Verwaltung *f* administration; management.
Verwaltungs- *zW*: **~apparat** *m* administrative machinery; **~bezirk** *m* administrative district; **~gericht** *nt* Administrative Court.
verwandeln [fervàn'dəln] *vtr* change, transform.
Verwandlung *f* change, transformation.
verwandt [fervánt'] *a* related (*mit* to); **geistig ~ sein** (*fig*) be kindred spirits.
Verwandte(r) *mf dekl wie a* relative, relation.
Verwandtschaft *f* relationship; (*Menschen*) relatives, relations *pl*; (*fig*) affinity.
verwarnen [fervár'nən] *vt* caution.
Verwarnung *f* caution.
verwaschen [fervá'shən] *a* faded; (*fig*) vague.
verwässern [ferve'sərn] *vt* dilute, water down.
verwechseln [fervek'səln] *vt* confuse (*mit* with); mistake (*mit* for); **zum V~ ähnlich** as like as two peas.
Verwechslung *f* confusion, mixing up; **das muß eine ~ sein** there must be some mistake.
verwegen [fervā:'gən] *a* daring, bold; **V~heit**

f daring, audacity, boldness.
verwehren [fervā:'rən] *vt* (*geh*): **jdm etw ~** refuse *od* deny sb sth.
Verwehung [fervā:'ōōng] *f* snowdrift; sand drift.
verweichlichen [fervīch'lichən] *vt* mollycoddle.
verweichlicht *a* effeminate, soft.
verweigern [fervī'gərn] *vt* refuse (*jdm etw* sb sth); **den Gehorsam/die Aussage ~** refuse to obey/testify.
Verweigerung *f* refusal.
verweilen [fervī'lən] *vi* stay; (*fig*) dwell (*bei* on).
verweint [fervīnt'] *a* (*Augen*) tear-swollen; (*Gesicht*) tear-stained.
Verweis [fervīs'] *m* **-es, -e** reprimand, rebuke; (*Hinweis*) reference.
verweisen [fervī'zən] *vt unreg* refer; **jdn auf etw** (*akk*)**/an jdn ~** (*hinweisen*) refer sb to sth/sb; **jdn vom Platz** *od* **des Spielfeldes ~** (*SPORT*) send sb off; **jdm etw ~** (*tadeln*) scold sb for sth; **jdn von der Schule ~** expel sb (from school); **jdn des Landes ~** deport sb.
Verweisung *f* reference; (*Tadel*) reprimand; (*Landes~*) deportation.
verwelken [fervel'kən] *vi* fade; (*Blumen*) wilt.
verweltlichen [fervel'tlichən] *vt* secularize.
verwenden [ferven'dən] *unreg vt* use; (*Mühe, Zeit, Arbeit*) spend ♦ *vr* intercede.
Verwendung *f* use.
Verwendungsmöglichkeit *f* (possible) use.
verwerfen [ferver'fən] *vt unreg* reject; (*Urteil*) quash; (*kritisieren: Handlungsweise*) condemn.
verwerflich [ferver'flich] *a* reprehensible.
verwertbar *a* usable.
verwerten [fervā:r'tən] *vt* utilize.
Verwertung *f* utilization.
verwesen [fervā:'zən] *vi* decay.
Verwesung *f* decomposition.
verwickeln [fervi'kəln] *vt* tangle (up); (*fig*) involve (*in* +*akk*) ♦ *vr* get tangled (up); **sich ~ in** (+*akk*) get involved in.
Verwicklung *f* entanglement, complication.
verwildern [fervil'dərn] *vi* run wild.
verwildert *a* wild; (*Garten*) overgrown; (*jds Aussehen*) unkempt.
verwinden [fervin'dən] *vt unreg* get over.
verwirken [fervir'kən] *vt* (*geh*) forfeit.
verwirklichen [fervir'klichən] *vt* realize, put into effect.
Verwirklichung *f* realization.
verwirren [fervi'rən] *vt* tangle (up); (*fig*) confuse.
Verwirrspiel *nt* confusing tactics *pl*.
Verwirrung *f* confusion.
verwischen [fervi'shən] *vt* (*verschmieren*) smudge; (*lit, fig: Spuren*) cover over; (*fig: Erinnerungen*) blur.
verwittern [fervi'tərn] *vi* weather.
verwitwet [fervit'vət] *a* widowed.

verwöhnen |fɛrvœ'nən| *vt* spoil, pamper.
Verwöhnung *f* spoiling, pampering.
verworfen |fɛrvor'fən| *a* depraved; **V~heit** *f* depravity.
verworren |fɛrvo'rən| *a* confused.
verwundbar |fɛrvōōnt'bár| *a* vulnerable.
verwunden |fɛrvōōn'dən| *vt* wound.
verwunderlich |fɛrvōōn'dərliċh| *a* surprising; (*stärker*) astonishing.
verwundern *vt* astonish ♦ *vr* be astonished (*über* +*akk* at).
Verwunderung *f* astonishment.
Verwundete(r) *mf* *dekl* *wie* *a* injured (person).
Verwundung *f* wound, injury.
verwünschen |fɛrwün'shən| *vt* curse.
verwurzelt |fɛrvōōr'tsəlt| *a*: **(fest) in** *od* **mit etw** (*dat*) ~ (*fig*) deeply rooted in sth.
verwüsten |fɛrvü:s'tən| *vt* devastate.
Verwüstung *f* devastation.
Verz. *abk* = **Verzeichnis**.
verzagen |fɛrtsâ'gən| *vi* despair.
verzagt |fɛrtsâkt'| *a* disheartened.
verzählen |fɛrtsɛ:'lən| *vr* miscount.
verzahnen |fɛrtsâ'nən| *vt* dovetail; (*Zahnräder*) cut teeth in.
verzapfen |fɛrtsá'pfən| *vt* (*umg*): **Unsinn** ~ talk nonsense.
verzaubern |fɛrtsou'bərn| *vt* (*lit*) cast a spell on; (*fig: Mensch*) enchant.
verzehren |fɛrtsâ:'rən| *vt* consume.
verzeichnen |fɛrtsiċh'nən| *vt* list; (*Niederlage, Verlust*) register.
Verzeichnis *nt* **-ses, -se** list, catalog (*US*), catalogue (*Brit*); (*in Buch*) index.
verzeihen |fɛrtsī'ən| *vti* *unreg* forgive (*jdm etw* sb for sth); ~ **Sie!** excuse me!
verzeihlich *a* pardonable.
Verzeihung *f* forgiveness, pardon; ~! sorry!, excuse me!; **um** ~ **bitten** apologize (*jdn* to sb).
verzerren |fɛrtsɛ'rən| *vt* distort; (*Sehne, Muskel*) strain, pull.
verzetteln |fɛrtse'təln| *vr* waste a lot of time.
Verzicht |fɛrtsiċht'| *m* **-(e)s, -e** renunciation (*auf* +*akk* of); **v~en** *vi* forego, give up (*auf etw* (*akk*) sth).
verziehen |fɛrtsē:'ən| *unreg* *vi* *aux sein* move; **verzogen** (*Vermerk*) no longer at this address ♦ *vt* put out of shape; (*Kind*) spoil; (*Pflanzen*) thin out; **kein Miene** ~ not turn a hair; **das Gesicht** ~ pull a face ♦ *vr* go out of shape; (*Gesicht*) contort; (*verschwinden*) disappear.
verzieren |fɛrtsē:'rən| *vt* decorate.
verzinsen |fɛrtsin'zən| *vt* pay interest on.
verzinslich *a*: ~/**fest** ~ **sein** yield interest/a fixed rate of interest.
verzogen |fɛrtsō:'gən| *a* (*Kind*) spoiled; *siehe auch* **verziehen**.
verzögern |fɛrtsœ'gərn| *vt* delay.
Verzögerung *f* delay.
Verzögerungstaktik *f* delaying tactics *pl*.
verzollen |fɛrtso'lən| *vt* pay duty on; **haben**

Sie etwas zu ~? have you anything to declare?
verzücken |fɛrtsü'kən| *vt* send into ecstasies, enrapture.
Verzug |fɛrtsōō:k'| *m* delay; (*FIN*) arrears *pl*; **mit etw in** ~ **geraten** fall behind with sth; (*mit Zahlungen*) fall into arrears with sth.
verzweifeln |fɛrtsvī'fəln| *vi* despair.
verzweifelt *a* desperate.
Verzweiflung *f* despair.
verzweigen |fɛrtsvī'gən| *vr* branch out.
verzwickt |fɛrtsvikt'| *a* (*umg*) awkward, complicated.
Vesper |fes'pər| *f* **-, -n** vespers *pl*.
Vesuv |vāzōō:f'| *m* **-(s)** Vesuvius.
Veto |vā:'tō| *nt* **-s, -s** veto.
Vetter |fe'tər| *m* **-s, -n** cousin.
vgl. *abk* (= *vergleiche*) cf.
v.g.u. *abk* (= *vorgelesen, genehmigt, unterschrieben*) read, approved, signed.
v.H. *abk* (= *vom Hundert*) p.c.
VHS *f* - *abk* = **Volkshochschule**.
Viadukt |vēádōōkt'| *m* **-(e)s, -e** viaduct.
vibrieren |vēbrē:'rən| *vi* vibrate.
Video |vē:'dāō| *nt* **-s, -s** video; ~**aufnahme** *f* video (recording); ~**recorder** *m* video recorder; ~**text** *m* teletext.
Vieh [fē:] *nt* **-(e)s** cattle *pl*; (*Nutztiere*) livestock; (*umg: Tier*) animal; **v~isch** *a* bestial; ~**zucht** *f* (live)stock *od* cattle breeding.
viel [fē:l] *a* a lot of, much; **in** ~**em** in many respects; **noch (ein)mal so** ~ (*Zeit etc*) as much (time *etc*) again; **einer zu** ~ one too many; ~**e** *pl* a lot of, many; **gleich** ~**e (Angestellte/Anteile** *etc*) the same number (of employees/shares *etc*) ♦ *ad* a lot, much; ~ **zuwenig** much too little; ~**beschäftigt** *a* attr very busy.
vie'lerlei *a* a great variety of.
vie'lerorts' *ad* in many places.
viel- *zW*: ~**fach** *a*, *ad* many times; **auf** ~**fachen Wunsch** at the request of many people; **V~fache(s)** *nt* *dekl* *wie* *a* (*MATH*) multiple; **um ein V~faches** many times over; **V~falt** *f* - variety; ~**fältig** *a* varied, many-sided; **V~fraß** *m* glutton; ~**geprüft** *a* attr (*hum*) sorely tried.
vielleicht [fēliċht'] *ad* perhaps; (*in Bitten*) by any chance; **du bist** ~ **ein Idiot!** (*umg*) you really are an idiot!
viel- *zW*: ~**mal(s)** *ad* many times; **danke** ~**mals** many thanks; **ich bitte** ~**mals um Entschuldigung!** I do apologize!; ~**mehr** *ad* rather, on the contrary; ~**sagend** *a* significant; ~**schichtig** *a* (*fig*) complex; ~**seitig** *a* many-sided; (*Ausbildung*) all-round *attr*; (*Interessen*) varied; (*Mensch, Gerät*) versatile; ~**versprechend** *a* promising; **V~völkerstaat** [fē:lfœl'kərshtât] *m* multinational state.
vier [fē:r] *num* four; **alle** ~**e von sich strecken** (*umg*) stretch out; **V~beiner** *m* (*hum*) four-legged friend; **V~eck** *nt* **-(e)s, -e**

four-sided figure; (*gleichseitig*) square; **~eckig** *a* four-sided; square; **~hundert** *num* four hundred; **~kant** *a, ad* (*NAUT*) square; **~köpfig** *a*: **eine ~köpfige Familie** a family of four; **V~mächteabkommen** *nt* four-power agreement.

viert *a*: **wir gingen zu ~** four of us went.

Viertaktmotor *m* four-stroke engine.

vierteilen *vt* quarter.

Viertel [fir'təl] *nt* **-s, -** quarter; **ein ~ Leberwurst** a quarter of liver sausage; **~finale** *nt* quarter finals *pl*; **~jahr** *nt* three months *pl*, quarter (*COMM, FIN*); **~jahresschrift** *f* quarterly; **v~jährlich** *a* quarterly; **~note** *f* quarter note (*US*), crotchet (*Brit*); **~stun'de** *f* quarter of an hour.

vierte(r, s) [fē:r'tə(r, s)] *a* fourth.

vier- *zW*: **~türig** *a* four-door *attr*; **V~waldstättersee** *m* Lake Lucerne; **~zehn** [fir'tsä:n] *num* fourteen; **in ~zehn Tagen** in two weeks; **~zehntägig** *ad* every two weeks; **~zehnte(r, s)** *a* fourteenth.

vierzig [fir'tsiċh] *num* forty; **V~stundenwoche** *f* forty-hour week.

Vierzim'merwohnung *f* four-room apartment.

Vietnam [vēetnám'] *nt* **-s** Vietnam.

Vietnamese [vēetnámä:'zə] *m* **-n, -n, Vietnamesin** *f* Vietnamese.

Vikar [vēkår'] *m* **-s, -e** curate.

Villa [vi'lá] *f* **-, Villen** villa.

Villenviertel *nt* (prosperous) residential area.

violett [vēōlet'] *a* violet.

Violinbogen *m* violin bow.

Violine [vēōlē:'nə] *f* **-, -n** violin.

Violin- *zW*: **~konzert** *nt* violin concerto; **~schlüssel** *m* treble clef.

virtuell [virtōōel'] *a*: **~e Adresse** (*COMPUT*) virtual address; **~er Speicher** (*COMPUT*) virtual memory.

Virtuose [virtōōō:'zə] *m* **-n, -n, Virtuosin** *f* virtuoso.

Virus [vē:'rōōs] *m od nt* **-, Viren** virus.

Visage [vēzá'zhə] *f* **-, -n** (*pej*) face, (ugly) mug (*umg*).

Visagist(in *f*) [vēzázhist'(in)] *m* make-up artist.

vis-à-vis [vēzávē:'] *ad* (*veraltet*) opposite (*von* to) ♦ *präp +dat* opposite (to).

Visier [vēzē:r'] *nt* **-s, -e** gunsight; (*am Helm*) visor.

Visite [vēzē:'tə] *f* **-, -n** (*MED*) visit.

Visitenkarte *f* visiting card.

visuell [vēzōōel'] *a* visual.

Visum [vē:'zōōm] *nt* **-s, Visa** *od* **Visen** visa; **~zwang** *m* obligation to hold a visa.

vital [vētál'] *a* lively, full of life; (*lebenswichtig*) vital.

Vitamin [vētámē:n'] *nt* **-s, -e** vitamin; **~mangel** *m* vitamin deficiency.

Vitrine [vētrē:'nə] *f* **-, -n** (*Schrank*) glass cabinet; (*Schaukasten*) showcase, display case.

Vivisektion [vēvēzektsēō:n'] *f* vivisection.

Vize [fē:'tsə] *m* (*umg*) number two; (**~meister**) runner-up ♦ *in zW* vice-.

v.J. *abk* (= *vorigen Jahres*) of the previous *od* last year.

Vj. *abk* (= *Vierteljahr*) quarter.

Vkz *abk* (= *Vertriebskennzeichen*) distribution indices.

Vlies [flē:s] *nt* **-es, -e** fleece.

vm. *abk* (= *vormittags*) a.m.

v.M. *abk* (= *vorigen Monats*) ult.

V-Mann *m abk* = **Verbindungsmann; Vertrauensmann.**

VN *pl abk* (= *Vereinte Nationen*) UN.

VO *abk* = **Verordnung.**

Vogel [fō:'gəl] *m* **-s, ⁻** bird; **einen ~ haben** (*umg*) have bats in the belfry; **den ~ abschießen** (*umg*) surpass everyone (*ironisch*); **~bauer** *nt* birdcage; **~beerbaum** *m* rowan tree; **~dreck** *m* bird droppings *pl*; **~perspektive** *f*, **~schau** *f* bird's-eye view; **~scheuche** *f* scarecrow; **~-Strauß-Politik** *f* head-in-the-sand policy.

Vogesen [vōgā:'zən] *pl* Vosges *pl*.

Vokabel [vōká'bəl] *f* **-, -n** word.

Vokabular [vōkábōōlår'] *nt* **-s, -e** vocabulary.

Vokal [vōkál'] *m* **-s, -e** vowel.

Volk [folk] *nt* **-(e)s, ⁻er** people; (*Nation*) nation; **etw unters ~ bringen** (*Nachricht*) spread sth.

Völker- [fœl'kər] *zW*: **~bund** *m* League of Nations; **~kunde** *f* ethnology; **~mord** *m* genocide; **~recht** *nt* international law; **v~rechtlich** *a* according to international law; **~verständigung** *f* international understanding; **~wanderung** *f* migration.

Volks- *zW*: **~abstimmung** *f* referendum; **~armee** *f* (*DDR*) People's Army; **v~eigen** *a* (*DDR*) nationally-owned; **~feind** *m* enemy of the people; **~hochschule** *f* adult education classes *pl*; **~lied** *nt* folksong; **~mund** *m* vernacular; **~polizei** *f* (*DDR*) People's Police; **~republik** *f* people's republic; **~schule** *f* elementary school; **~seuche** *f* epidemic; **~stamm** *m* tribe; **~stück** *nt* folk play in dialect; **~tanz** *m* folk dance; **v~tümlich** [folks'tü:mliċh] *a* popular; **~wirtschaft** *f* national economy; (*Fach*) economics *sing*, political economy; **~wirtschaftler** *m* economist; **~zählung** *f* (national) census.

voll [fol] *a* full; **jdn für ~ nehmen** (*umg*) take sb seriously; **aus dem ~en schöpfen** draw on unlimited resources; **in ~er Größe** (*Bild*) life-size; (*bei plötzlicher Erscheinung etc*) large as life; **~ sein** (*umg*: *satt*) be full (up); (: *betrunken*) be plastered ♦ *ad* fully; **~ und ganz** completely.

vollauf [folouf'] *ad* amply; **~ zu tun haben** have quite enough to do.

voll(l)aufen [fol'loufən] *vi unreg*: **etw ~ lassen** fill sth (up).

voll- *zW*: **V~bad** *nt* (full-length) bath; **V~beschäftigung** *f* full employment; **V~besitz** *m*: **im V~besitz** +*gen* in full possession of; **V~blut** *nt* thoroughbred; **~blütig** *a* full-blooded; **V~bremsung** *f* emergency braking; **~bring'en** *vt unreg untr* accomplish; **V~dampf** *m* (*NAUT*): **mit V~dampf** at full steam; **~en'den** *vt untr* finish, complete; **~ends** [fol'ɛnts] *ad* completely; **V~en'dung** *f* completion.

voller *a* fuller; (+*gen*) full of.

Völlerei [fœ̈lərī'] *f* gluttony.

Volleyball [vo'lēbál] *m* volleyball.

Vollgas *nt*: **mit ~** at full throttle; **~ geben** step on it.

völlig [fœ̈'liç] *a*, *ad* complete(ly).

voll- *zW*: **~jährig** *a* of age; **V~kaskoversicherung** *f* fully comprehensive insurance; **~kom'men** *a* perfect; (*völlig*) complete, absolute; **V~kom'menheit** *f* perfection; **V~kornbrot** *nt* whole-wheat bread; **~machen** *vt* fill (up); **V~macht** *f* authority, full powers *pl*; **V~matrose** *m* able-bodied seaman; **V~milch** *f* whole (*US*) *od* full-cream (*Brit*) milk; **V~mond** *m* full moon; **V~narkose** *f* general anesthetic (*US*) *od* anaesthetic (*Brit*); **V~pension** *f* full board; **~schlank** *a* plump, stout; **~schreiben** *vt unreg* (*Heft, Seite*) fill; (*Tafel*) cover (with writing); **~ständig** *a* complete; **~streck'en** *vt untr* execute; **~tanken** *vti* fill (up); **V~treffer** *m* (*lit, fig*) bull's-eye; **V~versammlung** *f* general meeting; **V~waise** *f* orphan; **~wertig** *a* full *attr*; (*Stellung*) equal; **~zählig** *a* complete; (*anwesend*) in full number; **~zie'hen** *vt unreg untr* carry out ♦ *vr* happen; **V~zug'** *m* execution.

Volontär(in *f*) [vŏlonte:r'(in)] *m* **-s, -e** trainee.

Volt [volt] *nt* **- *od* -(e)s, -** volt.

Volumen [vŏlōō:'mən] *nt* **-s, - *od* Volumina** volume.

vom [fom] = **von dem.**

von [fon] *präp* +*dat* from; (*über*) about; (*statt Genitiv, bestehend aus*) of; (*im Passiv*) by; **er erzählte vom Urlaub** he talked about his vacation; **ein Freund ~ mir** a friend of mine; **~ mir aus** (*umg*) O.K. by me; **~ wegen!** no way!

vonei'nan'der *ad* from each other.

vonstatten [fonshtá'tən] *ad*: **~ gehen** proceed, go.

Vopo [fŏ:'pŏ] *f* - *abk* = **Volkspolizei.**

vor [fŏ:r] *präp* +*dat od akk* before; (*räumlich*) in front of; **~ sich hin summen** hum to o.s.; **~ lauter Arbeit** because of work; **~ Wut/Liebe** with rage/love; **~ 2 Tagen** 2 days ago; **~ allem** above all ♦ *ad*: **~ und zurück** backwards and forwards; **V~abdruck** *m* preprint; **V~abend** *m* evening before, eve; **V~ahnung** *f* presentiment, premonition.

voran [fŏrán'] *ad* before, ahead; **~bringen** *vt unreg* make progress with; **~gehen** *vi unreg* go ahead; **einer Sache** (*dat*) **~gehen** precede sth; **~gehend** *a* previous; **~kommen** *vi unreg* make progress, come along.

Voranschlag [fŏ:r'ánshlâk] *m* estimate.

voranstellen [fŏrán'shtelən] *vt* put in front (*dat* of); (*fig*) give precedence (*dat* over).

Vorarbeiter [fŏ:r'árbītər] *m* foreman.

voraus [fŏrous'] *ad* ahead; (*zeitlich*) in advance; **jdm ~ sein** be ahead of sb; **im ~** in advance; **~bezahlen** *vt* pay in advance; **~gehen** *vi unreg* go (on) ahead; (*fig*) precede; **~haben** *vt unreg*: **jdm etw ~haben** have the edge on sb in sth; **V~sage** *f* prediction; **~sagen** *vt* predict; **~sehen** *vt unreg* foresee; **~setzen** *vt* assume; (*sicher annehmen*) take for granted; (*erfordern*: *Kenntnisse, Geduld*) require, demand; **~gesetzt, daß ...** provided that ...; **V~setzung** *f* requirement, prerequisite; **unter der V~setzung, daß ...** on condition that ...; **V~sicht** *f* foresight; **aller V~sicht nach** in all probability; **in der V~sicht, daß ...** anticipating that ...; **~sichtlich** *ad* probably; **V~zahlung** *f* advance payment.

vorbauen [fŏ:r'bouən] *vt* build up in front ♦ *vi* take precautions (*dat* against).

Vorbedacht [fŏ:r'bədákht] *m*: **mit/ohne ~** (*Überlegung*) with/without due consideration; (*Absicht*) intentionally/unintentionally.

Vorbedingung [fŏ:r'bədingōōng] *f* precondition.

Vorbehalt [fŏ:r'bəhált] *m* reservation, proviso; **unter dem ~, daß ...** with the reservation that ...

vorbehalten *vt unreg*: **sich/jdm etw ~** reserve sth (for o.s.)/for sb; **alle Rechte ~** all rights reserved.

vorbehaltlich *präp* +*gen* (*form*) subject to.

vorbehaltlos *a*, *ad* unconditional(ly).

vorbei [forbī'] *ad* by, past; **aus und ~ over** and done with; **damit ist es nun ~** that's all over now; **~bringen** *vt unreg* (*umg*) drop off; **~gehen** *vi unreg* pass by, go past; **~kommen** *vi unreg*: **bei jdm ~kommen** drop *od* call in on sb; **~reden** *vi*: **an etw** (*dat*) **~reden** talk around sth.

vorbelastet [fŏ:r'bəlàstət] *a* (*fig*) handicaped (*US*), handicapped (*Brit*).

Vorbemerkung [fŏ:r'bəmerkōōng] *f* introductory remark.

vorbereiten [fŏ:r'bərītən] *vt* prepare.

Vorbereitung *f* preparation.

vorbestellen [fŏ:r'bəshtelən] *vt* book (in advance), reserve.

vorbestraft [fŏ:r'bəshtráft] *a* previously convicted, with a record.

Vorbeugehaft *f* preventive custody.

vorbeugen [fŏ:r'boigən] *vtr* lean forward ♦ *vi* prevent (*einer Sache* (*dat*) sth).

vorbeugend *a* preventive.

Vorbeugung *f* prevention; **zur ~ gegen** for the prevention of.

Vorbild [fŏ:r'bilt] *nt* model; **sich** (*dat*) **jdn zum ~ nehmen** model o.s. on sb; **v~lich** *a* model, ideal.

Vorbildung [fŏ:r'bildōōng] *f* educational background.

Vorbote [fō:r'bō:tə] *m* (*fig*) herald.

vorbringen [fō:r'bringən] *vt unreg* voice; (*Meinung etc*) advance, state; (*umg: nach vorne*) bring to the front.

vordatieren [fō:r'dátē:rən] *vt* (*Schreiben*) postdate.

Vorder- [for'dər] *zW:* ~**achse** *f* front axle; ~**ansicht** *f* front view; ~**asien** *nt* Near East.

vordere(r, s) *a* front.

Vorder- *zW:* ~**grund** *m* foreground; **im** ~**grund stehen** (*fig*) be to the fore; ~**grundprogramm** *nt* (*COMPUT*) foreground program; **v**~**hand** *ad* for the present; ~**mann** *m*, *pl* -**männer** man in front; **jdn auf** ~**mann bringen** (*umg*) get sb to shape up; ~**seite** *f* front (side); ~**sitz** *m* front seat.

vorderste(r, s) *a* front.

vordrängen [fō:r'drengən] *vr* push to the front.

vordringen [fō:r'dringən] *vi unreg:* **bis zu jdm/etw** ~ get as far as sb/sth.

Vordruck [fō:r'drōōk] *m* form.

vorehelich [fō:r'ā:əlich] *a* premarital.

voreilig [fō:r'īlich] *a* hasty, rash; ~**e Schlüsse ziehen** jump to conclusions.

voreinander [fō:rīnán'dər] *ad* (*räumlich*) in front of each other; (*einander gegenüber*) face to face.

voreingenommen [fō:r'īngənomən] *a* bias(s)ed; **V**~**heit** *f* bias.

voreingestellt [fō:r'īngəshtelt] *a:* ~**er Parameter** (*COMPUT*) default (parameter).

vorenthalten [fō:r'entháltən] *vt unreg:* **jdm etw** ~ withhold sth from sb.

Vorentscheidung [fō:r'entshīdōōng] *f* preliminary decision.

vorerst [fō:r'ā:rst] *ad* for the moment *od* present.

Vorfahr [fō:r'fár] *m* -**en**, -**en** ancestor.

vorfahren *vi unreg* drive (on) ahead; (*vors Haus etc*) drive up.

Vorfahrt *f* (*AUT*) right of way; „~" (**be)achten"** "yield" (*US*), "give way" (*Brit*).

Vorfahrts- *zW:* ~**regel** *f* right of way; ~**schild** *nt* yield (*US*) *od* give way (*Brit*) sign; ~**straße** *f* major road.

Vorfall [fō:r'fál] *m* incident.

vorfallen *vi unreg* occur.

Vorfeld [fō:r'felt] *nt* (*fig*) run-up (+*gen* to).

Vorfilm [fō:r'film] *m* short.

vorfinden [fō:r'findən] *vt unreg* find.

Vorfreude [fō:r'froidə] *f* anticipation.

vorfühlen [fō:r'fü:lən] *vi* (*fig*) put out feelers.

vorführen [fō:r'fü:rən] *vt* show. display; (*Theaterstück, Kunststücke*) perform (*dat* to *od* in front of); **dem Gericht** ~ bring before the court.

Vorgabe [fō:r'gâbə] *f* (*SPORT*) handicap.

Vorgabe- *in zW* (*COMPUT*) default.

Vorgang [fō:r'gàng] *m* course of events; (*CHEM etc*) process; **der** ~ **von etw** how sth

happens.

Vorgänger(in *f*) [fō:r'gengər(in)] *m* -**s**, - predecessor.

vorgaukeln [fō:r'goukəln] *vt:* **jdm etw** ~ lead sb to believe in sth.

vorgeben [fō:r'gā:bən] *vt unreg* pretend, use as a pretext; (*SPORT*) give an advantage *od* a start of.

Vorgebirge [fō:r'gəbirgə] *nt* foothills *pl*.

vorgefaßt [fō:r'gəfást] *a* preconceived.

vorgefertigt [fō:r'gəferticht] *a* prefabricated.

Vorgefühl [fō:r'gəfül] *nt* anticipation; (*etwas Böses*) presentiment.

vorgehen [fō:r'gā:ən] *vi unreg* (*voraus*) go (on) ahead; (*nach vorn*) go forward; (*handeln*) act, proceed; (*Uhr*) be fast; (*Vorrang haben*) take precedence; (*passieren*) go on.

Vorgehen *nt* -**s** action.

Vorgehensweise *f* proceedings.

vorgerückt [fō:r'gərükt] *a* (*Stunde*) late; (*Alter*) advanced.

Vorgeschmack [fō:r'gəshmák] *m* foretaste.

Vorgesetzte(r) [fō:r'gəzetstə(r)] *mf dekl wie a* superior.

vorgestern [fō:r'gestərn] *ad* the day before yesterday; **von** ~ (*fig*) antiquated.

vorgreifen [fō:r'grīfən] *vi unreg* anticipate; **jdm** ~ forestall sb.

vorhaben [fō:r'hâbən] *vt unreg* intend; **hast du schon was vor?** do you have anything planned?

Vorhaben *nt* -**s**, - intention.

Vorhalle [fō:r'hálə] *f* (*Diele*) entrance hall; (*von Parlament*) lobby.

vorhalten [fō:r'háltən] *unreg vt* hold *od* put up; (*fig*) reproach (*jdm etw* sb for sth) ♦ *vi* last.

Vorhaltung *f* reproach.

vorhanden [fō:rhán'dən] *a* existing; (*erhältlich*) available; **V**~**sein** *nt* -**s** existence, presence.

Vorhang [fō:r'háng] *m* curtain.

Vorhängeschloß [fō:r'hengəshlos] *nt* padlock.

Vorhaut [fō:r'hout] *f* (*ANAT*) foreskin.

vorher [fō:rhā:r'] *ad* before(hand); ~**bestimmen** *vt* (*Schicksal*) preordain; ~**gehen** *vi unreg* precede.

vorherig [fō:rhā:'rich] *a* previous.

Vorherrschaft [fō:r'hersháft] *f* predominance, supremacy.

vorherrschen *vi* predominate.

vorher- [fō:rhā:r] *zW:* **V**~**sage** *f* forecast; ~**sagen** *vt* forecast, predict; ~**sehbar** *a* predictable; ~**sehen** *vt unreg* foresee.

vorhin [fō:rhin'] *ad* not long ago, just now.

vorhinein [fō:rhinin'] *ad:* **im** ~ beforehand.

Vorhof [fō:r'hō:f] *m* forecourt.

vorig [fō:'rich] *a* previous, last.

Vorjahr [fō:r'yâr] *nt* previous year, year before.

vorjährig [fō:r'ye:rich] *a* of the previous year; last year's.

vorjammern [fō:r'yámərn] *vti:* **jdm (etwas)**

~ moan to sb (von about).

Vorkämpfer(in f) [fō:r'kempfər(in)] m pioneer.

Vorkaufsrecht [fō:r'koufsreçht] nt option to buy.

Vorkehrung [fō:r'kā:rōōng] f precaution.

Vorkenntnis [fō:r'kentnis] f previous knowledge.

vorknöpfen [fō:r'knœpfən] vt (fig umg): **sich** (dat) **jdn** ~ take sb to task.

vorkommen [fō:r'komən] vi unreg come forward; (geschehen, sich finden) occur; (scheinen) seem (to be); **so was soll** ~! that's life!; **sich** (dat) **dumm** etc ~ feel stupid etc.

Vorkommen nt occurrence; (MIN) deposit.

Vorkommnis [fō:r'komnis] nt -ses, -se occurrence.

Vorkriegs- [fō:r'krē:ks] in zW pre-war.

vorladen [fō:r'lādən] vt unreg (bei Gericht) summons.

Vorladung f summons.

Vorlage [fō:r'lāgə] f model, pattern; (das Vorlegen) presentation; (von Beweismaterial) submission; (Gesetzes~) bill; (SPORT) pass.

vorlassen [fō:r'lásən] vti unreg admit; (überholen lassen) let pass; (vorgehen lassen) allow to go in front.

Vorläufer m forerunner.

vorläufig [fō:r'loifiçh] a temporary; (provisorisch) provisional.

vorlaut [fō:r'lout] a impertinent, cheeky.

Vorleben [fō:r'lā:bən] nt past (life).

vorlegen [fō:r'lā:gən] vt put in front; (fig) produce, submit; **jdm etw** ~ put sth before sb.

Vorleger m -s, - mat.

Vorleistung [fō:r'listōōng] f (FIN: Vorausbezahlung) advance (payment); (Vorarbeit) preliminary work; (POL) prior concession.

vorlesen [fō:r'lā:zən] vt unreg read (out).

Vorlesung f (UNIV) lecture.

Vorlesungsverzeichnis nt lecture timetable.

vorletzte(r, s) [fō:r'letstə(r, s)] a last but one, next to last, penultimate.

Vorliebe [fō:r'lē:bə] f preference, special liking; **etw mit** ~ **tun** particularly like doing sth.

vorliebnehmen [fō:rlē:p'nā:mən] vi unreg: ~ **mit** make do with.

vorliegen [fō:r'lē:gən] vi unreg be (here); **etw liegt jdm vor** sb has sth; **etw liegt gegen jdn vor** sb is charged with sth.

vorliegend a present, at issue.

vorm. abk (= vormittags) a.m.

vormachen [fō:r'mákhən] vt: **jdm etw** ~ show sb how to do sth; **jdm etwas** ~ (fig) fool sb; **mach mir doch nichts vor** don't try and fool me.

Vormachtstellung [fō:r'mákhtshtelōōng] f supremacy.

Vormarsch [fō:r'mársh] m advance.

vormerken [fō:r'merkən] vt book; (notieren) make note of; (bei Bestellung) take an order for.

Vormittag [fō:r'mitâk] m morning; **am** ~ in the morning.

vormittags ad in the morning, before noon.

Vormund [fō:r'mōōnt] m -(e)s, -e od -münder guardian.

vorn [forn] ad in front; **von** ~ **anfangen** start at the beginning; **nach** ~ to the front; **er betrügt sie von** ~ **bis hinten** he deceives her right, left and centre.

Vorname [fō:r'nâmə] m first od Christian name.

vornan [fornán'] ad at the front.

vorne [for'nə] = **vorn.**

vornehm [fō:r'nā:m] a distinguished; (Manieren etc) refined; (Kleid) elegant; **in** ~**en Kreisen** in polite society.

vornehmen vt unreg (fig) carry out; **sich** (dat) **etw** ~ start on sth; (beschließen) decide to do sth; **sich** (dat) **zuviel** ~ take on too much; **sich** (dat) **jdn** ~ tell sb off.

vornehmlich ad chiefly, specially.

vorn(e)weg [forn'(ə)vek] ad in front; (als erstes) first.

vornherein [forn'herīn] ad: **von** ~ from the start.

Vorort [fō:r'ort] m suburb; ~**zug** m commuter train.

vorprogrammiert [fō:r'prōgrámē:rt] a (Erfolg, Antwort) automatic.

Vorrang [fō:r'ráng] m precedence, priority.

vorrangig a of prime importance, primary.

Vorrat [fō:r'rât] m stock, supply; **solange der** ~ **reicht** (COMM) while stocks last.

vorrätig [fō:r're:tiçh] a in stock.

Vorraum m anteroom; (Büro) outer office.

vorrechnen [fō:r'reçhnən] vt: **jdm etw** ~ calculate sth for sb; (als Kritik) point sth out to sb.

Vorrecht [fō:r'reçht] nt privilege.

Vorrede [fō:r'rā:də] f introductory speech; (THEAT) prolog (US), prologue (Brit).

Vorrichtung [fō:r'riçhtōōng] f device, gadget.

vorrücken [fō:r'rükən] vi advance ♦ vt move forward.

Vorruhestand [fō:r'rōō:əshtánt] m early retirement.

Vorrunde [fō:r'rōōndə] f (SPORT) preliminary round.

Vors. abk = **Vorsitzende(r).**

vorsagen [fō:r'zágən] vt recite; (SCH: zuflüstern) tell secretly, prompt.

Vorsaison [fō:r'zezôň] f low season, early season.

Vorsatz [fō:r'záts] m intention; (JUR) intent; **einen** ~ **fassen** make a resolution.

vorsätzlich [fō:r'zetsliçh] a intentional; (JUR) premeditated ♦ ad intentionally.

Vorschau [fō:r'shou] f (RAD, TV) (program (US) od programme (Brit)) preview; (Film) trailer.

Vorschein [fō:r'shīn] m: **zum** ~ **kommen**

(lit: sichtbar werden) appear; *(fig: entdeckt werden)* come to light.

vorschieben |fō:r'shē:bən| *vt unreg* push forward; *(vor etw)* push across; *(fig)* put forward as an excuse; **jdn ~ use** sb as a front.

vorschießen |fō:r'shē:sən| *vt unreg (umg)*: **jdm Geld ~** advance sb money.

Vorschlag |fō:r'shläk| *m* suggestion, proposal.

vorschlagen |fō:r'shlägən| *vt unreg* suggest, propose.

Vorschlaghammer *m* sledgehammer.

vorschnell |fō:rsh'nel| *a* hasty, too quick.

vorschreiben |fō:r'shrībən| *vt unreg (lit)* write out *(dat* for); *(Dosis)* prescribe; *(befehlen)* specify; **ich lasse mir nichts ~** I won't be dictated to.

Vorschrift |fō:r'shrift| *f* regulation(s *pl)*, rule(s *pl)*; *(Anweisungen)* instruction(s *pl)*; **jdm ~en machen** give sb orders; **Dienst nach ~** slowdown *(US)*, work-to-rule *(Brit)*.

vorschriftsmäßig *ad* as per regulations/ instructions.

Vorschub |fō:r'shōō:p| *m*: **jdm/einer Sache ~ leisten** encourage sb/sth.

vorschulisch |fō:r'shōō:lish| *a* preschool *attr*.

Vorschuß |fō:r'shōōs| *m* advance.

vorschützen |fō:r'shütsən| *vt* put forward as a pretext; *(Unwissenheit)* plead.

vorschweben |fō:r'shvä:bən| *vi*: **jdm schwebt etw vor** sb has sth in mind.

vorsehen |fō:r'zā:ən| *unreg vt* provide for; *(planen)* plan ♦ *vr* take care, be careful ♦ *vi* be visible.

Vorsehung *f* providence.

vorsetzen |fō:r'zetsən| *vt* move forward; *(davorsetzen)* put in front *(vor +akk* of); *(anbieten)* offer.

Vorsicht |fō:r'zicht| *f* caution, care; **~!** look out!, take care!; *(auf Schildern)* caution!, danger!; **~, Stufe!** watch your step!; **etw mit ~ genießen** *(umg)* take sth with a pinch of salt.

vorsichtig *a* cautious, careful.

Vorsichts- *zW*: **v~halber** *ad* just in case; **~maßnahme** *f* precaution.

Vorsilbe |fō:r'zilbə| *f* prefix.

vorsintflutlich |fō:r'zintflōō:tlich| *a (umg)* antiquated.

Vorsitz |fō:r'zits| *m* chair(manship); **den ~ führen** chair the meeting.

Vorsitzende(r) *mf dekl wie a* chairman; chairwoman; chairperson.

Vorsorge |fō:r'zorgə| *f* precaution(s *pl)*; *(Fürsorge)* provision(s *pl)*.

vorsorgen *vi*: **~ für** make provision(s *pl)* for.

Vorsorgeuntersuchung |fō:r'zorgəōōntər-zōō:khōōng| *f medical checkup (for the detection of cancer)*.

vorsorglich |fō:r'zorklich| *ad* as a precaution.

Vorspann |vō:r'shpän| *m* **-(e)s, -e** *(FILM, TV)* opening credits *pl*; *(PRESSE)* opening paragraph.

vorspannen *vt (Pferde)* harness.

Vorspeise |fō:r'shpīzə| *f* hors d'œuvre, starter.

Vorspiegelung |fō:r'shpē:gəlōōng| *f*: **das ist (eine) ~ falscher Tatsachen** it's all sham.

Vorspiel |fō:r'shpē:l| *nt* prelude; *(bei Geschlechtsverkehr)* foreplay.

vorspielen *vt*: **jdm etw ~** *(MUS)* play sth to sb; *(THEAT)* act sth to sb; *(fig)* act out a sham of sth in front of sb.

vorsprechen |fō:r'shprechən| *unreg vt* say out loud; *(vortragen)* recite ♦ *vi (THEAT)* audition; **bei jdm ~** call on sb.

vorspringend |fō:r'shpringənt| *a* projecting; *(Nase, Kinn)* prominent.

Vorsprung |fō:r'shprōōng| *m* projection; *(Fels~)* ledge; *(fig)* advantage, start.

Vorst. *abk* = **Vorstand; Vorstands-.**

Vorstadt |fō:r'shtät| *f* suburbs *pl.*

Vorstand |fō:r'shtänt| *m* executive committee; *(COMM)* board (of directors); *(Person)* director; *(Leiter)* head.

Vorstands- *zW*: **~sitzung** *f (von Firma)* board meeting; **~vorsitzende(r)** *mf dekl wie a* chairperson.

vorstehen |fō:r'shtä:ən| *vi unreg* project; **etw** *(dat)* **~** *(fig)* be the head of sth.

Vorsteher(in *f)* *m* **-s, -** *(von Abteilung)* head; *(von Gefängnis)* governor; *(Bahnhofs~)* stationmaster.

vorstellbar *a* conceivable.

vorstellen |fō:r'shtelən| *vt* put forward; *(vor etw)* put in front; *(bekannt machen)* introduce; *(darstellen)* represent ♦ *vr* introduce o.s. *(jdm* to sb); *(bei Bewerbung)* go for an interview; **sich** *(dat)* **etw ~** imagine sth; **stell dir das nicht so einfach vor** don't think it's so easy.

Vorstellung *f (Bekanntmachen)* introduction; *(THEAT etc)* performance; *(Gedanke)* idea, thought.

Vorstellungs- *zW*: **~gespräch** *nt* interview; **~vermögen** *nt* powers of imagination *pl.*

Vorstoß |fō:r'shtō:s| *m* advance; *(fig: Versuch)* attempt.

vorstoßen *vti unreg* push forward.

Vorstrafe |fō:r'shträfə| *f* previous conviction.

vorstrecken |fō:r'shtrekən| *vt* stretch out; *(Geld)* advance.

Vorstufe |fō:r'shtōō:fə| *f* first step(s).

Vortag |fō:r'täk| *m* day before *(einer Sache* sth).

vortasten |fō:r'tästən| *vr*: **sich langsam zu etw ~** approach sth carefully.

vortäuschen |fō:r'toishən| *vt* pretend, feign.

Vortäuschung *f*: **unter ~ falscher Tatsachen** under false pretenses.

Vorteil |fō:r'tīl| *m* **-s, -e** advantage *(gegenüber* over); **im ~ sein** have the advantage; **die Vor- und Nachteile** the pros and cons; **v~haft** *a* advantageous; *(Kleider)* flattering; *(Geschäft)* lucrative.

Vortr. *abk* = **Vortrag.**

Vortrag |fō:r'träk| *m* **-(e)s, Vorträge** talk,

lecture; (*Vortragsart*) delivery; (*von Gedicht*) rendering; (*COMM*) balance carried forward; **einen ~ halten** give a lecture *od* talk.

vortragen |fō:r'trâgən| *vt unreg* carry forward (*auch COMM*); (*fig*) recite; (*Rede*) deliver; (*Lied*) perform; (*Meinung etc*) express.

Vortrags- *zW:* **~abend** *m* lecture evening; (*mit Musik*) recital; (*mit Gedichten*) poetry reading; **~reihe** *f* series of lectures.

vortrefflich |fō:rtref'lìʧ| *a* excellent.

vortreten |fō:r'trä:tən| *vi unreg* step forward; (*Augen etc*) protrude.

Vortritt |fō:r'trit| *m:* **jdm den ~ lassen** (*lit, fig*) let sb go first.

vorüber |fōrü:'bər| *ad* past, over; **~gehen** *vi unreg* pass (by); **~gehen an** (+*dat*) (*fig*) pass over; **~gehend** *a* temporary, passing.

Voruntersuchung |fō:r'ōōntərzōō:kʰōōng| *f* (*MED*) preliminary examination; (*JUR*) preliminary investigation.

Vorurteil |fō:r'ōōrtìl| *nt* prejudice.

vorurteilsfrei *a* unprejudiced, open-minded.

Vorverkauf |fō:r'ferkouf| *m* advance booking.

vorverlegen |fō:r'ferlä:gən| *vt* (*Termin*) bring forward.

Vorw. *abk* = **Vorwort**.

vorwagen |fō:r'vâgən| *vr* venture forward.

Vorwahl |fō:r'vâl| *f* preliminary election; (*TEL*) area code.

Vorwand |fō:r'vânt| *m* **-(e)s, Vorwände** pretext.

vorwärts |fō:r'verts| *ad* forward; **~** (*umg*) let's go!; (*MIL*) forward march!; **V~gang** *m* (*AUT etc*) forward gear; **~gehen** *vi unreg* progress; **~kommen** *vi unreg* get on, make progress.

Vorwäsche *f,* **Vorwaschgang** *m* prewash.

vorweg |fō:rvek'| *ad* in advance; **V~nahme** *f* **-, -n** anticipation; **~nehmen** *vt unreg* anticipate.

vorweisen |fō:r'vīzən| *vt unreg* show, produce.

vorwerfen |fō:r'verfən| *vt unreg:* **jdm etw ~** reproach sb for sth, accuse sb of sth; **sich** (*dat*) **nichts vorzuwerfen haben** have nothing to reproach o.s. with; **das wirft er mir heute noch vor** he still holds it against me; **Tieren/Gefangenen etw ~** (*lit*) throw sth down for the animals/prisoners.

vorwiegend |fō:r'vē:gənt| *a, ad* predominant(ly).

Vorwitz |fō:r'vits| *m* impertinence.

vorwitzig *a* saucy, cheeky.

Vorwort |fō:r'vort| *nt* **-(e)s, -e** preface.

Vorwurf |fō:r'vōōrf| *m* **-(e)s, ⁻e** reproach; **jdm/sich Vorwürfe machen** reproach sb/o.s.

vorwurfsvoll *a* reproachful.

Vorzeichen |fō:r'tsìʧən| *nt* (*Omen*) omen; (*MED*) early symptom; (*MATH*) sign.

vorzeigen |fō:r'tsīgən| *vt* show, produce.

Vorzeit |fō:r'tsīt| *f* prehistoric times *pl.*

vorzeitig *a* premature.

vorziehen |fō:r'tsē:ən| *vt unreg* pull forward; (*Gardinen*) draw; (*zuerst behandeln, abfertigen*) give priority to; (*lieber haben*) prefer.

Vorzimmer |fō:r'tsimər| *nt* anteroom; (*Büro*) outer office.

Vorzug |fō:r'tsōō:k| *m* preference; (*gute Eigenschaft*) merit, good quality; (*Vorteil*) advantage; (*EISENB*) relief train; **einer Sache** (*dat*) **den ~ geben** (*form*) prefer sth; (*Vorrang geben*) give sth precedence.

vorzüglich |fō:rtsü:k'lìʧ| *a* excellent, firstrate.

Vorzugsaktie *f* preferred stock (*US*), preference share (*Brit*).

vorzugsweise *ad* preferably; (*hauptsächlich*) chiefly.

Votum |vō:'tōōm| *nt* **-s, Voten** vote.

v.R.w. *abk* (= *von Rechts wegen*) legally, as of right.

v.T. *abk* (= *vom Tausend*) per thousand.

v.u. *abk* = *von unten*.

vulgär |vōōlgɛ:r'| *a* vulgar.

Vulkan |vōōlkán'| *m* **-s, -e** volcano; **~ausbruch** *m* volcanic eruption.

vulkanisieren |vōōlkánēzē:'rən| *vt* vulcanize.

v.u.Z. *abk* (= *vor unserer Zeitrechnung*) B.C.

v.v. *abk* (= *vice versa*) v.v.

VV *abk* = **Vollversammlung;** (= *Verschönerungsverein*) association for environmental improvement.

W

W, w |vä:| *nt* W, w.

w. = **wenden; werktags; westlich;** (= *weiblich*) f.

W. *abk* (= *West(en)*) W.

WAA *f abk* = **Wiederaufbereitungsanlage.**

Waage |vä'gə| *f* **-, -n** scales *pl*; (*ASTROL*) Libra; **sich** (*dat*) **die ~ halten** (*fig*) balance one another; **w~recht** *a* horizontal.

Waagschale *f* (scale) pan; **(schwer) in die ~ fallen** (*fig*) carry weight.

wabb(e)lig |vâb'(ə)lìʧ| *a* wobbly.

Wabe |vä'bə| *f* **-, -n** honeycomb.

wach |vâkʰ| *a* awake; (*fig*) alert; **~ werden** wake up.

Wachablösung *f* changing of the guard; (*Mensch*) relief guard; (*fig: Regierungswechsel*) change of government.

Wache *f* **-, -n** guard, watch; **~ halten** keep watch; **~ stehen** *od* **schieben** (*umg*) be on guard (duty).

wachen *vi* be awake; (*Wache halten*) keep watch; **bei jdm ~** sit up with sb.

Wach- *zW*: **w~habend** *a attr* duty; **~hund** *m* watchdog, guard dog; (*fig*) watchdog.
Wacholder [vàkhol'dər] *m* **-s**, **-** juniper.
wachrütteln [vàkh'rütəln] *vt* (*fig*) (a)rouse.
Wachs [vàks] *nt* **-es**, **-e** wax.
wachsam [vàkh'zâm] *a* watchful, vigilant, alert; **W~keit** *f* vigilance.
wachsen *vi unreg* grow ♦ *vt* (*Skier*) wax.
Wachsstift *m* wax crayon.
wächst [vekst] *2./3. pers sing präs von* **wachsen.**
Wachstuch [vàks'tōō:kh] *nt* oilcloth.
Wachstum [vàks'tōō:m] *nt* **-s** growth.
Wachstums- *zW*: **~grenze** *f* limits of growth; **w~hemmend** *a* growth-inhibiting; **~rate** *f* growth rate; **~störung** *f* disturbance of growth.
Wachtel [vàkh'təl] *f* **-**, **-n** quail.
Wächter [vechh'tər] *m* **-s**, **-** guard; (*Park~*) warden, keeper; (*Museums~, Parkplatz~*) attendant.
Wacht- [vàkht] *zW*: **~meister** *m* officer; **~posten** *m* guard, sentry.
Wach(t)turm *m* watchtower.
Wach- und Schließgesellschaft *f* security corps.
wack(e)lig [vàk'(ə)lichh] *a* shaky, wobbly; **auf ~en Beinen stehen** be wobbly on one's legs; (*fig*) be unsteady.
Wackelkontakt *m* loose connection.
wackeln *vi* shake; (*fig: Position*) be shaky; **mit dem Kopf/Schwanz ~** wag one's head/ its tail.
wacker [và'kər] *a* valiant, stout; **sich ~ schlagen** (*umg*) put up a brave fight.
Wade [và'də] *f* **-**, **-n** (*ANAT*) calf.
Waffe [và'fə] *f* **-**, **-n** weapon; **jdn mit seinen eigenen ~n schlagen** (*fig*) beat sb at his own game.
Waffel [và'fəl] *f* **-**, **-n** waffle; (*Eis~*) wafer.
Waffen- *zW*: **~gewalt** *f*: **mit ~gewalt** by force of arms; **~lager** *nt* (*von Armee*) ordnance depot; (*von Terroristen*) cache; **~schein** *m* firearms license; **~schmuggel** *m* gunrunning, arms smuggling; **~stillstand** *m* armistice, truce.
Wagemut [và'gəmōō:t] *m* daring.
wagen [và'gən] *vt* venture, dare.
Wagen [và'gən] *m* **-s**, **-** vehicle; (*Auto*) car, automobile (*US*); (*EISENB*) car, carriage (*Brit*); (*Pferde~*) cart wagon (*US*), waggon (*Brit*); **~führer** *m* driver; **~heber** *m* **-s**, **-** jack; **~park** *m* fleet of cars; **~rückholtaste** *f* (*Schreibmaschine*) carriage return (key); **~rücklauf** *m* carriage return.
Waggon [vágōñ'] *m* **-s**, **-s** wagon (*US*), waggon (*Brit*); (*Güter~*) freight car (*US*), goods van (*Brit*).
waghalsig [vàk'hàlzichh] *a* foolhardy.
Wagnis [vàk'nis] *nt* **-ses**, **-se** risk.
Wahl [vâl] *f* **-**, **-en** choice; (*POL*) election; (*Gemüse, Eier*) grade one; **erste ~** (*Qualität*) top quality; **aus freier ~** of one's own free choice; **wer die ~ hat, hat die Qual**

(*Sprichwort*) he is *od* you are *etc* spoiled for choice; **die ~ fiel auf ihn** he was chosen; **sich zur ~ stellen** (*POL etc*) run (for congress *etc*).
wählbar *a* eligible.
Wahl- *zW*: **w~berechtigt** *a* entitled to vote; **~beteiligung** *f* poll, turnout; **~bezirk** *m* (*POL*) district.
wählen [ve:'lən] *vti* choose; (*POL*) elect, vote (for); (*TEL*) dial.
Wähler(in *f*) *m* **-s**, **-** voter; **~abwanderung** *f* voter drift; **w~isch** *a* fastidious, particular; **~schaft** *f* electorate.
Wahl- *zW*: **~fach** *nt* elective (*US*), optional subject; **w~frei** *a*: **w~freier Zugriff** (*COMPUT*) random access; **~gang** *m* ballot; **~geschenk** *nt* pre-election vote-catching gimmick; **~heimat** *f* country of adoption; **~helfer** *m* (*im ~kampf*) election assistant; (*bei der Wahl*) polling officer; **~kabine** *f* polling booth; **~kampf** *m* election campaign; **~kreis** *m* constituency; **~liste** *f* electoral register; **~lokal** *nt* polling station; **w~los** *ad* at random; (*nicht wählerisch*) indiscriminately; **~recht** *nt* franchise; **allgemeines ~recht** universal franchise; **das aktive ~recht** the right to vote; **das passive ~recht** eligibility (for political office); **~spruch** *m* motto; **~urne** *f* ballot box; **w~weise** *ad* alternatively.
Wählzeichen *nt* (*TEL*) dial tone (*US*), dialling tone (*Brit*).
Wahn [vân] *m* **-(e)s** delusion; **~sinn** *m* madness; **w~sinnig** *a* insane, mad ♦ *ad* (*umg*) incredibly; **w~witzig** *a* crazy *attr* ♦ *ad* terribly.
wahr [vâr] *a* true; **da ist (et)was W~es dran** there's some truth in that.
wahren *vt* maintain, keep.
während [ve:'rən] *vi* last.
während *präp* +*gen* during ♦ *kj* while; **~dessen** [ve:rəndes'sən] *ad* meanwhile.
wahr- *zW*: **~haben** *vt unreg*: **etw nicht ~haben wollen** refuse to admit sth; **~haft** *ad* (*tatsächlich*) truly; **~haftig** [vârhàf'tichh] *a* true, real ♦ *ad* really; **W~heit** *f* truth; **die W~heit sagen** tell the truth.
wahrheitsgetreu *a* (*Bericht*) truthful; (*Darstellung*) faithful.
wahrnehmen *vt unreg* perceive; (*Frist*) observe; (*Veränderungen etc*) be aware of; (*Gelegenheit*) take; (*Interessen, Rechte*) look after.
Wahrnehmung *f* perception; observing; awareness; taking; looking after.
wahr- *zW*: **~sagen** *vi* predict the future, tell fortunes; **W~sager** *m* fortune teller.
wahrscheinlich [vârshīn'lichh] *a* probable ♦ *ad* probably; **W~keit** *f* probability; **aller W~keit nach** in all probability.
Währung [ve:'rōōng] *f* currency.
Währungs- *zW*: **~einheit** *f* monetary unit; **~politik** *f* monetary policy; **~reserven** *pl* official reserves *pl*.

Wahrzeichen *nt* (*Gebäude, Turm etc*) symbol; (*von Stadt, Verein*) emblem.
Waise [vḯzə] *f* -, **-n** orphan.
Waisen- *zW:* ~**haus** *nt* orphanage; ~**kind** *nt* orphan; ~**knabe** *m*: **gegen dich ist er ein** ~**knabe** (*umg*) he's no match for you; ~**rente** *f* orphan's allowance.
Wal [vâl] *m* **-(e)s, -e** whale.
Wald [vâlt] *m* **-(e)s,** ̈**er** wood(s *pl*); (*groß*) forest.
Wäldchen [velt'çhən] *nt* copse, grove.
waldig [vál'diçh] *a* wooded.
Wald- *zW:* ~**lehrpfad** *m* nature trail; ~**meister** *m* (*BOT*) woodruff; ~**sterben** *nt* loss of trees due to pollution.
Wald- und Wiesen- in *zW* (*umg*) common-or-garden.
Waldweg *m* woodland *od* forest path.
Wales [wä:lz] *nt* Wales.
Walfang [vâl'fâng] *m* whaling.
Waliser(in *f)* [vâlē:'zər(in)] *m* -s, - Welshman; Welshwoman.
walisisch *a* Welsh.
Wall [vâl] *m* **-(e)s,** ̈**e** embankment; (*Bollwerk*) rampart.
wallfahren *vi untr* go on a pilgrimage.
Wallfahrer(in *f)* *m* pilgrim.
Wallfahrt *f* pilgrimage.
Wallone [vâlō:'nə] *m* **-n, -n, Wallonin** *f* Walloon.
Walnuß [vâl'nōōs] *f* walnut.
Walroß [vâl'ros] *nt* walrus.
walten [vâl'tən] *vi* (*geh*): **Vernunft** ~ **lassen** let reason prevail.
Walzblech *nt* **-(e)s** sheet metal.
Walze [vâl'tsə] *f* -, **-n** (*Gerät*) cylinder; (*Fahrzeug*) roller.
walzen *vt* roll (out).
wälzen [vel'tsən] *vt* roll (over); (*Bücher*) hunt through; (*Probleme*) deliberate on ♦ *vr* wallow; (*vor Schmerzen*) roll about; (*im Bett*) toss and turn.
Walzer [vâl'tsər] *m* **-s,** - waltz.
Wälzer [vel'tsər] *m* **-s,** - (*umg*) tome.
Wampe [vám'pə] *f* -, **-n** (*umg*) paunch.
wand [vânt] *imperf von* **winden**.
Wand *f* -, ̈**e** wall; (*Trenn*~) partition; (*Berg*~) precipice; (*Fels*~) (rock) face; (*fig*) barrier; **weiß wie die** ~ as white as a sheet; **jdn an die** ~ **spielen** put sb in the shade; (*SPORT*) outplay sb.
Wandel [vân'dəl] *m* **-s** change; **w**~**bar** *a* changeable, variable; ~**halle** *f* foyer; (*im Parlament*) lobby.
wandeln *vtr* change ♦ *vi* (*gehen*) walk.
Wander- [vân'dər] *zW:* ~**ausstellung** *f* touring exhibition; ~**bühne** *f* touring theater (*US*) *od* theatre (*Brit*).
Wanderer *m* **-s, -, Wanderin** *f* hiker, rambler.
Wander- *zW:* ~**karte** *f* map of walks; ~**lied** *nt* hiking song.
wandern *vi* hike; (*Blick*) wander; (*Gedanken*) stray; (*umg: in den Papierkorb*) land.

Wander- *zW:* ~**preis** *m* challenge trophy; ~**schaft** *f* traveling (*US*), travelling (*Brit*).
Wanderung *f* walking tour, hike; (*von Tieren, Völkern*) migration.
Wanderweg *m* trail, (foot)path.
Wandlung *f* change; transformation; (*REL*) transubstantiation.
Wand- *zW:* ~**malerei** *f* mural painting; ~**schirm** *m* (folding) screen; ~**schrank** *m* cupboard.
wandte [vân'tə] *imperf von* **wenden**.
Wand- *zW:* ~**teppich** *m* tapestry; ~**verkleidung** *f* wainscoting.
Wange [vâng'ə] *f* -, **-n** cheek.
wankelmütig [vâng'kəlmü:tiçh] *a* fickle, inconstant.
wanken [vân'kən] *vi* stagger; (*fig*) waver.
wann [vân] *ad* when; **seit** ~ **bist/hast du** ...? how long have you been/have you had ...?
Wanne [vá'nə] *f* -, **-n** tub.
Wanze [vân'tsə] *f* -, **-n** (*ZOOL, Abhörgerät*) bug.
Wappen [vá'pən] *nt* **-s,** - coat of arms, crest; ~**kunde** *f* heraldry.
wappnen *vr* (*fig*): **gewappnet sein** be forearmed.
war [vâr] *imperf von* **sein**.
warb [vârp] *imperf von* **werben**.
Ware [vâ'rə] *f* -, **-n** ware; ~**n** *pl* goods *pl*.
wäre [ve:'rə] *Konjunktiv imperf von* **sein**.
Waren- *zW:* ~**bestand** *m* inventory, stock-intrade; ~**haus** *nt* department store; ~**lager** *nt* stock, store; ~**muster** *nt*, ~**probe** *f* sample; ~**rückstände** *pl* backlog *sing*; ~**sendung** *f* trade sample (sent by post); ~**zeichen** *nt* trademark.
warf [vârf] *imperf von* **werfen**.
warm [vârm] *a* warm; (*Essen*) hot; (*umg: homosexuell*) queer; **mir ist** ~ I'm warm; **mit jdm** ~ **werden** (*umg*) get close to sb.
Wärme [ver'mə] *f* -, **-n** warmth; **10 Grad** ~ 10 degrees above zero.
wärmen *vtr* warm, heat.
Wärmflasche *f* hot-water bottle.
warm- *zW:* **W**~**front** *f* (*MET*) warm front; ~**halten** *vtr*: **sich jdn** ~**halten** (*fig*) stay on sb's good side (*US*) *od* in sb's good books (*Brit*); ~**herzig** *a* warm-hearted; ~**laufen** *vi unreg* (*AUT*) warm up; **W**~**wassertank** *m* hot-water tank.
Warn- *zW:* ~**blinkanlage** *f* (*AUT*) hazard warning lights *pl*; ~**dreieck** *nt* warning triangle.
warnen [vár'nən] *vt* warn.
Warnstreik *m* token strike.
Warnung *f* warning.
Warschau [vár'shou] *nt* **-s** Warsaw; ~**er Pakt** *m* Warsaw Pact.
Warte *f* -, **-n** observation point; (*fig*) viewpoint.
warten [vár'tən] *vi* wait (*auf +akk* for); **auf sich** ~ **lassen** take a long time; **warte mal!** wait a minute!; (*überlegend*) let me see; **mit dem Essen auf jdn** ~ wait for sb before

eating ♦ *vt* (*Auto, Maschine*) service.

Wärter(in *f*) [ver'tər(in)] *m* **-s, -** attendant.

Wartesaal *m* (*EISENB*) waiting room.

Wartezimmer *nt* (*bes beim Arzt*) waiting room.

Wartung *f* (*von Auto, Maschine*) servicing; ~ **und Instandhaltung** maintenance.

warum [vàrōōm'] *ad* why; ~ **nicht gleich so!** that's better.

Warze [vár'tsə] *f* **-, -n** wart.

was [vàs] *pron* what; which; (*umg: etwas*) something; ~ **für ...?** what sort *od* kind of ...?

Wasch- [vàsh'] *zW*: ~**anlage** *f* (*für Autos*) car wash; **w~bar** *a* washable; ~**becken** *nt* washbasin; ~**beutel** *m* washbag.

Wäsche [ve'shə] *f* **-, -n** wash(ing); (*Bett~*) linen; (*Unter~*) underwear; **dumm aus der** ~ **gucken** (*umg*) look stupid.

waschecht *a* (*Farbe*) fast; (*fig*) genuine.

Wäsche- *zW*: ~**klammer** *f* clothes pin (*US*), clothes peg (*Brit*); ~**korb** *m* dirty clothes basket; ~**leine** *f* clothes line.

waschen [vá'shən] *unreg vti* wash ♦ *vr* (have a) wash; **sich** (*dat*) **die Hände** ~ wash one's hands; ~ **und legen** (*Haare*) shampoo and set.

Wäscherei [veshərī'] *f* laundry.

Wäscheschleuder *f* spin-dryer.

Wasch- *zW*: ~**gang** *m* stage of the washing program; ~**küche** *f* laundry room; ~**lappen** *m* washcloth; (*umg*) softy; ~**maschine** *f* washing machine; **w~maschinenfest** *a* machine-washable; ~**mittel** *nt* detergent; ~**pulver** *nt* washing powder; ~**salon** *m* laundromat (*US*), launderette (*Brit*).

wäscht [vesht] *3. pers sing präs von* **waschen.**

Waschtisch *m* wash stand.

Washington [wo'shingtən] *nt* **-s** Washington.

Wasser [và'sər] *nt* **-s, -** water; **dort wird auch nur mit** ~ **gekocht** (*fig*) they're no different from anybody else (there); **ins** ~ **fallen** (*fig*) fall through; **mit allen** ~**n gewaschen sein** (*umg*) be a shrewd customer; ~ **lassen** (*euph*) pass water; **jdm das** ~ **abgraben** (*fig*) take the bread from sb's mouth, take away sb's livelihood ♦ *nt* **-s, -** (*Flüssigkeit*) water; (*MED*) lotion; (*Parfüm*) cologne; (*Mineral~*) mineral water; **w~abstoßend** *a* water-repellent.

Wässerchen *nt*: **er sieht aus, als ob er kein** ~ **trüben könnte** he looks as if butter wouldn't melt in his mouth.

Wasser- *zW*: **w~dicht** *a* watertight; (*Stoff, Uhr*) waterproof; ~**fall** *m* waterfall; ~**farbe** *f* watercolor (*US*), watercolour (*Brit*); **w~gekühlt** *a* (*AUT*) water-cooled; ~**graben** *m* (*SPORT*) water jump; (*um Burg*) moat; ~**hahn** *m* tap, faucet (*US*).

wässerig [ve'sərich] *a* watery.

Wasser- *zW*: ~**kessel** *m* kettle; (*TECH*) boiler; ~**kraftwerk** *nt* hydroelectric power station; ~**leitung** *f* water pipe; (*Anlagen*)

plumbing; ~**mann** *m* (*ASTROL*) Aquarius.

wassern *vi* land on the water.

wässern [ve'sərn] *vti* water.

Wasser- *zW*: ~**scheide** *f* watershed; **w~scheu** *a* afraid of water; ~**schi** *nt* water-skiing; ~**schutzpolizei** *f* (*auf Flüssen*) river police; (*im Hafen*) harbor police; (*auf der See*) coastguard service; ~**spiegel** *m* (*Oberfläche*) surface of the water; (*~stand*) water level; ~**stand** *m* water level; ~**stoff** *m* hydrogen; ~**stoffbombe** *f* hydrogen bomb; ~**verbrauch** *m* water consumption; ~**waage** *f* spirit level; ~**welle** *f* shampoo and set; ~**werfer** *m* water cannon; ~**werk** *nt* waterworks *sing od pl*; ~**zeichen** *nt* watermark.

waten [và'tən] *vi* wade.

watscheln [vàt'shəln] *vi* waddle.

Watt [vàt] *nt* **-(e)s, -en** mud flats *pl* ♦ *nt* **-s, -** (*ELEK*) watt.

Watte *f* **-, -n** (absorbent) cotton (*US*), cotton wool (*Brit*).

Wattenmeer *nt* **-(e)s** mud flats *pl*.

Wattestäbchen *nt* cotton(-wool) swab.

wattieren [vàtē:'rən] *vt* pad.

WDR *m* - *abk* (= *Westdeutscher Rundfunk*) *West German Radio.*

WE *abk* (= *Wärmeeinheit*) unit of heat.

weben [vā:'bən] *vt unreg* weave.

Weber(in *f*) *m* **-s, -** weaver.

Weberei [vā:bərī'] *f* (*Betrieb*) weaving mill.

Webstuhl [vā:p'shtōō:l] *m* loom.

Wechsel [vek'səl] *m* **-s, -** change; (*Geld~*) exchange; (*COMM*) bill of exchange; ~**bäder** *pl* alternating hot and cold baths *pl*; ~**beziehung** *f* correlation; ~**forderungen** *pl* (*COMM*) bills receivable *pl*; ~**geld** *nt* change; **w~haft** *a* (*Wetter*) variable; ~**inhaber** *m* bearer; ~**jahre** *pl* change of life, menopause; **in die** ~**jahre kommen** start the change; ~**kurs** *m* rate of exchange.

wechseln *vt* change; (*Blicke*) exchange ♦ *vi* change; (*einander ablösen*) alternate.

wechselnd *a* changing; (*Stimmungen*) changeable; (*Winde, Bewölkung*) variable.

Wechsel- *zW*: **w~seitig** *a* reciprocal; ~**sprechanlage** *f* two-way intercom; ~**strom** *m* alternating current; ~**stube** *f* currency exchange, bureau de change; ~**verbindlichkeiten** *pl* bills payable *pl*; ~**wirkung** *f* interaction.

wecken [ve'kən] *vt* wake (up); (*fig*) arouse; (*Bedarf*) create; (*Erinnerungen*) revive.

Wecker *m* **-s, -** alarm clock; **jdm auf den** ~ **fallen** (*umg*) get on sb's nerves.

Weck- *zW*: ~**glas** *nt* ® preserving jar; ~**ruf** *m* (*TEL*) alarm call.

wedeln [vā:'dəln] *vi* (*mit Schwanz*) wag; (*mit Fächer*) fan; (*SKI*) wedeln.

weder [vā:'dər] *kj* neither; ~ ... **noch** ... neither ... nor ...

weg [vek] *ad* away, off; **über etw** (*akk*) ~ **sein** be over sth; **er war schon** ~ he had already left; **nichts wie** *od* **nur** ~ **von hier!**

let's get out of here!; ~ **damit!** (*mit Schere etc*) put them away!; **Finger ~!** hands off!

Weg [vãːk] *m* **-(e)s, -e** way; (*Pfad*) path; (*Route*) route; **sich auf den ~ machen** be on one's way; **jdm aus dem ~ gehen** keep out of sb's way; **jdm nicht über den ~ trauen** (*fig*) not to trust sb an inch; **den ~ des geringsten Widerstandes gehen** follow the line of least resistance; **etw in die ~e leiten** arrange sth; **jdm Steine in den ~ legen** (*fig*) put obstacles in sb's way; **~bereiter** *m* **-s, -** pioneer.

weg- [vɛk'] *zW:* **~blasen** *vt unreg* blow away; **wie ~geblasen sein** (*fig*) have vanished; **~bleiben** *vi unreg* stay away; **mir bleibt die Spucke ~!** (*umg*) I am absolutely flabbergasted!

wegen [vãː'ɡən] *präp* +*gen od* (*umg*) *dat* because of; **von ~!** (*umg*) you must be joking!

weg- [vɛk'] *zW:* **~fahren** *vi unreg* drive away; (*abfahren*) leave; **~fallen** *vi unreg* be left out; (*Ferien, Bezahlung*) be cancelled; (*aufhören*) cease; **~gehen** *vi unreg* go away, leave; (*umg: Ware*) sell; **~jagen** *vt* chase away; **~kommen** *vi unreg:* **gut/ schlecht ~kommen** (*umg*) come off well/ badly (*bei etw* with sth); **~lassen** *vt unreg* leave out; **~laufen** *vi unreg* run away *od* off; **das läuft (dir) nicht ~!** (*fig hum*) that can wait; **~legen** *vt* put aside; **~machen** *vt* (*umg*) get rid of; **~müssen** *vi unreg* (*umg*) have to go; **~nehmen** *vt unreg* take away.

Wegrand [vãː'krant] *m* wayside.

weg- [vɛk'] *zW:* **~räumen** *vt,* **~schaffen** *vt* clear away; **~schließen** *vt unreg* lock away; **~schnappen** *vt* snatch away (*jdm etw* sth from sb); **~stecken** *vt* put away; (*umg: verkraften*) cope with; **~treten** *vi unreg* (*MIL*): **~treten!** dismiss!; **geistig ~getreten sein** (*umg: geistesabwesend*) be away with the fairies; **~tun** *vt unreg* put away.

wegweisend [vãːg'vɪzənt] *a* pioneering *attr,* revolutionary.

Wegweiser [vãːg'vɪzər] *m* **-s, -** road sign, signpost; (*fig: Buch etc*) guide.

Wegwerf- [vɛk'vɛrf] *in zW* disposable.

weg- [vɛk'] *zW:* **~werfen** *vt unreg* throw away; **~werfend** *a* disparaging; **W~werfgesellschaft** *f* throw-away society; **~wollen** *vi unreg* (*verreisen*) want to go away; **~ziehen** *vi unreg* move away.

weh [vãː] *a* sore; **~ tun** hurt, be sore; **jdm/ sich ~ tun** hurt sb/o.s.

wehe [vãː'ə] *interj:* **~, wenn du ...** woe betide you if ...; **o ~!** oh dear!

Wehe *f* **-, -n** drift.

wehen *vti* blow; (*Fahnen*) flutter.

Wehen *pl* (*MED*) contractions *pl;* **in den ~ liegen** be in labor.

weh- *zW:* **~klagen** *vi untr* wail; **~leidig** *a* oversensitive to pain; (*jämmernd*) whiny, whining; **W~mut** *f* melancholy; **~mütig** *a* melancholy.

Wehr [vãːr] *nt* **-(e)s, -e** weir ♦ *f* **-, -en** (*Feuer~*) fire department; **sich zur ~ setzen** defend o.s. ♦ *in zW* defense (*US*), defence (*Brit*); **~dienst** *m* military service; **~dienstverweigerer** *m* ≈ conscientious objector.

wehren *vr* defend o.s.

Wehr- *zW:* **w~los** *a* defenseless (*US*), defenceless (*Brit*); **jdm w~los ausgeliefert sein** be at sb's mercy; **~macht** *f* armed forces *pl;* **~pflicht** *f* compulsory military service; **w~pflichtig** *a* liable for military service; **~übung** *f* reserve duty training exercise.

Wehwehchen *nt* (*umg*) (minor) complaint.

Weib [vɪp] *nt* **-(e)s, -er** woman, female (*pej*).

Weibchen *nt* (*Ehefrau*) little woman; (*ZOOL*) female.

weibisch [vɪ'bish] *a* effeminate.

weiblich *a* feminine.

weich [vɪçh] *a* soft; (*Ei*) soft-boiled; **~e Währung** soft currency.

Weiche *f* **-, -n** (*EISENB*) points *pl;* **die ~n stellen** (*lit*) switch the points; (*fig*) set the course.

weichen *vi unreg* yield, give way; **(nicht) von jdm** *od* **jds Seite ~** (not) leave sb's side.

Weichensteller *m* **-s, -** switchman (*US*), pointsman (*Brit*).

weich- *zW:* **W~heit** *f* softness; **W~käse** *m* soft cheese; **~lich** *a* soft, namby-pamby; **W~ling** *m* weakling; **W~spüler** *m* fabric conditioner; **W~teile** *pl* soft parts *pl;* **W~tier** *nt* mollusk (*US*), mollusc (*Brit*).

Weide [vɪ'də] *f* **-, -n** (*Baum*) willow; (*Gras*) pasture.

weiden *vi* graze ♦ *vr:* **sich an etw** (*dat*) **~** delight in sth.

Weidenkätzchen *nt* willow catkin.

weidlich [vɪt'lichh] *ad* thoroughly.

weigern [vɪ'ɡərn] *vr* refuse.

Weigerung [vɪ'ɡərŏŏng] *f* refusal.

Weihe [vɪ'ə] *f* **-, -n** consecration; (*Priester~*) ordination.

weihen *vt* consecrate; (*widmen*) dedicate; **dem Untergang geweiht** (*liter*) doomed.

Weiher *m* **-s, -** pond.

Weihnachten *nt* - Christmas; **fröhliche ~!** happy *od* merry Christmas!; **w~** *vi unpers:* **es weihnachtet sehr** (*poetisch, ironisch*) Christmas is very much in evidence.

weihnachtlich *a* Christmas(sy).

Weihnachts- *zW:* **~abend** *m* Christmas Eve; **~geld** *nt* Christmas bonus; **~lied** *nt* Christmas carol; **~mann** *m* Father Christmas (*Brit*), Santa Claus; **~markt** *m* Christmas fair.

Weih- *zW:* **~rauch** *m* incense; **~wasser** *nt* holy water.

weil [vɪl] *kj* because.

Weile [vɪ'lə] *f* - while, short time.

Weiler [vɪ'lər] *m* **-s, -** hamlet.

Weimarer Republik [vɪ'mãrər rãpŏŏblēːk'] *f*

Weimar Republic.

Wein [vīn] *m* **-(e)s, -e** wine; (*Pflanze*) vine; **jdm reinen ~ einschenken** (*fig*) tell sb the truth; **~bau** *m* cultivation of vines; **~bauer** *m* wine-grower; **~beere** *f* grape; **~berg** *m* vineyard; **~bergschnecke** *f* snail; **~brand** *m* brandy.

weinen *vti* cry; **das ist zum W~** it's enough to make you cry *od* weep.

weinerlich *a* tearful.

Wein- *zW:* **~gegend** *f* wine-growing area; **~geist** *m* (ethyl) alcohol; **~gut** *nt* wine-growing estate; **~karte** *f* wine list.

Weinkrampf *m* crying fit.

Wein- *zW:* **~lese** *f* vintage; **~rebe** *f* vine; **w~selig** *a* merry with wine; **~stein** *m* tartar; **~stock** *m* vine; **~traube** *f* grape.

weise [vī'zə] *a* wise.

Weise *f* **-, -n** manner, way; (*Lied*) tune; **auf diese ~** in this way.

weisen *vt unreg* show; **etw (weit) von sich ~** (*fig*) reject sth (emphatically).

Weise(r) *mf dekl wie a* wise man; wise woman, sage.

Weisheit [vīs'hīt] *f* wisdom.

Weisheitszahn *m* wisdom tooth.

weismachen [vīs'mákhən] *vt:* **er wollte uns ~, daß ...** he would have us believe that ...

weiß [vīs] *1./3. pers sing präs von* **wissen**.

weiß [vīs] *a* white; **W~blech** *nt* tin plate; **W~brot** *nt* white bread; **~en** *vt* whitewash; **W~glut** *f* (*TECH*) incandescence; **jdn bis zur W~glut bringen** (*fig*) make sb see red; **W~kohl** *m* (white) cabbage.

weißt [vīst] *2. pers sing präs von* **wissen**.

weiß- *zW:* **W~waren** *pl* linen *sing*; **W~wein** *m* white wine; **W~wurst** *f* veal sausage.

Weisung [vī'zōong] *f* instruction.

weit [vīt] *a* wide; (*Begriff*) broad; (*Reise, Wurf*) long; **in ~er Ferne** in the far distance ♦ *ad* far; **wie ~ ist es ...?** how far is it ...?; **das geht zu ~** that's going too far; **~ und breit** for miles around; **~ gefehlt!** far from it; **es so ~ bringen, daß ...** bring it about that ...; **~ zurückliegen** be far behind; **vom ~em** from a long way off; **~ab** *ad:* **~ab von** far (away) from; **~aus** *ad* by far; **W~blick** *m* (*fig*) farsightedness; **~blickend** *a* far-seeing.

Weite *f* **-, -n** width; (*Raum*) space; (*von Entfernung*) distance.

weiten *vtr* widen.

weiter [vī'tər] *a* wider; broader; farther (away); (*zusätzlich*) further ♦ *ad* further; **wenn es ~ nichts ist ...** well, if that's all (it is), ...; **das hat ~ nichts zu sagen** that doesn't really matter; **immer ~** on and on; (*Anweisung*) keep on (going); **~ nichts/ niemand** nothing/nobody else; **~arbeiten** *vi* go on working; **~bilden** *vr* continue one's studies; **W~bildung** *f* further education; **~empfehlen** *vt unreg* recommend (to others).

Weitere(s) *nt dekl wie a* further details *pl*;

bis auf w~s for the time being; **ohne w~s** without further ado, just like that.

weiter- *zW:* **W~fahrt** *f* continuation of the journey; **~führend** *a* (*Schule*) high; **~gehen** *vi unreg* go on; **~hin** *ad:* **etw ~hin tun** go on doing sth; **~kommen** *vi unreg:* **nicht ~kommen** (*fig*) be bogged down; **~leiten** *vt* pass on; **~machen** *vti* continue; **~reisen** *vi* continue one's journey; **~sagen** *vt:* **nicht ~sagen!** don't tell anyone!; **~verarbeiten** *vt* process; **~wissen** *vi unreg:* **nicht (mehr) ~wissen** (*verzweifelt sein*) be at one's wits' end.

weit- *zW:* **~gehend** *a* considerable ♦ *ad* largely; **~hergeholt** *a attr* far-fetched; **~hin** *ad* widely; (*~gehend*) to a large extent; **~läufig** *a* (*Gebäude*) spacious; (*Erklärung*) lengthy; (*Verwandter*) distant; **~reichend** *a* (*fig*) far-reaching; **~schweifig** *a* long-winded; **~sichtig** *a* (*lit*) far-sighted (*US*), long-sighted (*Brit*); (*fig*) far-sighted; **W~sprung** *m* long jump; **~verbreitet** *a* widespread; **~verzweigt** *a attr* (*Straßensystem*) extensive; **W~winkelobjektiv** *nt* (*PHOT*) wide-angle lens.

Weizen [vī'tsən] *m* **-s, -** wheat; **~keime** *pl* (*KOCH*) wheatgerm *sing*.

welch [velçh] *pron:* **~ ein(e)** ... what a ...

welche(r, s) *indef pron* (*umg: einige*) some ♦ *rel pron* (*für Personen*) who; (*für Sachen*) which ♦ *interrog pron* (*adjektivisch*) which, what; (*substantivisch*) which one.

welk [velk] *a* withered; **~en** *vi* wither.

Wellblech *nt* corrugated iron.

Welle [ve'lə] *f* **-, -n** wave; (*TECH*) shaft; **(hohe) ~n schlagen** (*fig*) create (quite) a stir.

Wellen- *zW:* **~bereich** *m* waveband; **~brecher** *m* breakwater; **~gang** *m:* **starker ~gang** heavy sea(s) *od* swell; **~länge** *f* (*lit, fig*) wavelength; **mit jdm auf einer ~länge sein** (*fig*) be on the same wavelength as sb; **~linie** *f* wavy line.

Wellensittich *m* parakeet (*US*), budgerigar (*Brit*).

Wellpappe *f* corrugated cardboard.

Welpe [vel'pə] *m* **-n, -n** pup, whelp; (*von Wolf etc*) cub.

Welt [velt] *f* **-, -en** world; **aus der ~ schaffen** eliminate; **in aller ~** all over the world; **vor aller ~** in front of everybody; **auf die ~ kommen** be born; **~all** *nt* universe; **~anschauung** *f* philosophy of life; **w~berühmt** *a* world-famous; **w~bewegend** *a* world-shattering; **~bild** *nt* conception of the world; (*jds Ansichten*) philosophy.

Weltenbummler(in *f)* *m* globetrotter.

Welt- *zW:* **w~fremd** *a* unworldly; **~gesundheitsorganisation** *f* World Health Organization; **~kirchenrat** *m* World Council of Churches; **~krieg** *m* world war; **w~lich** *a* worldly; (*nicht kirchlich*) secular; **~literatur** *f* world literature; **~macht** *f* world power; **w~männisch** *a* sophisticated;

~meister *m* world champion; **~meisterschaft** *f* world's (*US*) *od* world (*Brit*) championship; (*FUSSBALL*) World Cup; **~raum** *m* space; **~raumstation** *f* space station; **~reise** *f* trip round the world; **~ruf** *m* world-wide reputation; **~sicherheitsrat** *m* (*POL*) United Nations Security Council; **~stadt** *f* metropolis; **~untergang** *m* (*lit, fig*) end of the world; **w~weit** *a* world-wide; **~wirtschaftskrise** *f* world economic crisis; **~wunder** *nt* wonder of the world.

wem [vā:m] *pron* (*dat von* **wer**) to whom.

wen [vā:n] *pron* (*akk von* **wer**) whom.

Wende [ven'də] *f* -, -n turn; (*Veränderung*) change; **~kreis** *m* (*GEOG*) tropic; (*AUT*) turning circle.

Wendeltreppe *f* spiral staircase.

wenden *vtir unreg* turn; **bitte ~!** please turn over; **sich an jdn ~** go/come to sb.

Wendepunkt *m* turning point.

wendig *a* (*lit, fig*) agile; (*Auto etc*) maneuverable (*US*), manoeuvrable (*Brit*).

Wendung *f* turn; (*Rede~*) idiom.

wenig [vā:'niç] *a, ad* little; **ein ~** a little; **er hat zu ~ Geld** he doesn't have enough money; **ein Exemplar zu ~** one copy too few.

wenige [vā:'nigə] *pl* few *pl*; **in ~n Tagen** in (just) a few days.

weniger *a, ad* less.

Wenigkeit *f* trifle; **meine ~** (*ung*) yours truly, little me.

wenigstens *ad* at least.

wenigste(r, s) *a* least.

wenn [ven] *kj* if; (*zeitlich*) when; **~ auch ...** even if ...; **~ ich doch ...** if only I ...; **~ wir erst die neue Wohnung haben** once we get the new flat; **W~** *nt*: **ohne W~ und Aber** unequivocally.

wennschon *ad*: **na ~** so what?; **~, dennschon!** if a thing's worth doing, it's worth doing properly.

wer [vā:r] *pron* who.

Werbe- [ver'bə] *zW*: **~agentur** *f* advertising agency; **~aktion** *f* advertising campaign; **~antwort** *f* business reply card; **~fernsehen** *nt* commercial television; **~film** *m* promotional film; **~geschenk** *nt* promotional gift, freebie (*umg*); (*zu Gekauftem*) free gift; **~kampagne** *f* advertising campaign.

werben *unreg vt* win; (*Mitglied*) recruit ♦ *vi* advertise; **um jdn/etw ~** try to win sb/sth; **für jdn/etw ~** promote sb/sth.

Werbe- *zW*: **~spot** *m* commercial; **~texter** *m* copywriter; **~trommel** *f*: **die ~trommel rühren** (*umg*) beat the big drum (*für etw* for sth).

Werbung *f* advertising; (*von Mitgliedern*) recruitment; (*um jdn/etw*) promotion (*um of*).

Werbungskosten *pl* (*von Mensch*) professional outlay *sing od* expenses *pl*; (*von Firma*) business expenses *pl*.

Werdegang [vā:r'dəgáng] *m* development; (*beruflich*) career.

werden [vā:r'dən] *vi unreg* become; **was ist aus ihm/aus der Sache geworden?** what became of him/it?; **daraus ist nichts geworden** it came to nothing; **die Fotos sind gut geworden** the photos turned out well; **mir wird kalt** I'm getting cold; **das muß anders ~** that will have to change; **zu Eis ~** turn to ice; **es wird bald ein Jahr, daß ...** it's almost a year since ...; **er wird am 8. Mai 36** he is 36 on the 8th May ♦ *aux v* (*Futur*) shall, will; (*Passiv*) be; **er wird es tun** he will do it.

werdend *a*: **~e Mutter** expectant mother.

werfen [ver'fən] *unreg vt* throw; **„nicht ~"** "handle with care" ♦ *vi* (*Tier*) have its young.

Werft [verft] *f* -, -en shipyard, dockyard.

Werk [verk] *nt* -(e)s, -e work; (*Tätigkeit*) job; (*Fabrik, Mechanismus*) works *pl*; **ans ~ gehen** set to work; **das ist sein ~** this is his doing; **ab ~** (*COMM*) ex works.

werkeln [ver'kəln] *vi* (*umg*) putter around (*US*), potter about (*Brit*).

Werken *nt* -s (*SCH*) handicrafts *pl*.

Werkschutz *m* works security service.

Werksgelände *nt* factory premises *pl*.

Werk- *zW*: **~statt** *f* -, -stätten workshop; (*AUT*) garage; **~stoff** *m* material; **~stoffbehandlung** *f* materials handling; **~student** *m* self-supporting student; **~tag** *m* working day; **w~tags** *ad* on working days; **w~tätig** *a* working; **~zeug** *nt* tool; **~zeugkasten** *m* toolbox; **~zeugmaschine** *f* machine tool; **~zeugschrank** *m* tool chest.

Wermut [vā:r'mōō:t] *m* -(e)s wormwood; (*Wein*) vermouth.

Wermutstropfen *m* (*fig*) drop of bitterness.

wert [vā:rt] *a* worth; (*geschätzt*) dear; (*würdig*) worthy of; **das ist nichts/viel ~** it's not worth anything/it's worth a lot; **das ist es/er mir ~** it's/he's worth that to me; **ein Auto ist viel ~** (*nützlich*) a car is very useful; **W~** *m* -(e)s, -e worth; (*FIN*) value; **W~ legen auf** (+*akk*) attach importance to; **es hat doch keinen W~** it's useless; **im W~e von** to the value of; **W~angabe** *f* declaration of value; **~beständig** *a* stable in value.

werten *vt* rate; (*beurteilen*) judge (*als* to be); (*SPORT*: *als gültig* ~) allow.

Wert- *zW*: **~gegenstand** *m* article of value; **w~los** *a* worthless; **~losigkeit** *f* worthlessness; **~maßstab** *m* standard; **~papier** *nt* security; **~steigerung** *f* appreciation; **w~voll** *a* valuable; **~vorstellung** *f* moral concept; **~zuwachs** *m* appreciation.

Wesen [vā:'zən] *nt* -s, - (*Geschöpf*) being; (*Natur, Character*) nature.

wesentlich *a* significant; (*beträchtlich*) considerable; **im ~en** essentially; (*im großen*) in the main.

weshalb [veshálp'] *ad* why.

Wespe [ves'pə] *f* -, -n wasp.
wessen [ve'sən] *pron* (*gen von* **wer**) whose.
West- *zW*: ~-**Berlin** *nt*, ~**berlin** *nt* West Berlin; **w**~**berliner** *a attr* West Berlin; ~**berliner(in** *f)* *m* West Berliner; **w**~**deutsch** *a* West German; ~**deutsche(r)** *mf* West German; ~**deutschland** *nt* West Germany.
Weste [ves'tə] *f* -, -n vest (*US*), waistcoat (*Brit*); **eine reine** ~ **haben** (*fig*) have a clean slate.
Westen *m* -s west.
Westentasche *f*: **etw wie seine** ~ **kennen** (*umg*) know sth like the back of one's hand.
Westerwald [ves'tərvált] *m* -s Westerwald (Mountains *pl*).
westeuropäisch [vest'oirópe:'ish] *a* West(ern) European; ~**e Zeit** Central European Time.
Westf. *abk* = **Westfalen.**
Westfale [vestfâ'lə] *m* -n, -n, **Westfälin** [vestfε:'lin] *f* Westphalian.
Westfalen *nt* -s Westphalia.
westfälisch *a* Westphalian.
Westindien [vest'indiən] *nt* -s West Indies *pl*.
west- *zW*: ~**lich** *a* western ♦ *ad* to the west; **W**~**mächte** *pl* (*POL*): **die W**~**mächte** the western powers *pl*; **W**~**mark** *f* (*umg*) West German mark; ~**wärts** *ad* westwards.
weswegen [vesvä:'gən] *ad* why.
wett [vet] *a* even; ~ **sein** be quits.
Wettbewerb *m* competition.
Wettbewerbs- *zW*: ~**beschränkung** *f* restraint of trade; **w**~**fähig** *a* competitive.
Wette *f* -, -n bet, wager; **um die** ~ **laufen** run a race (with each other).
Wett'eifer *m* rivalry.
wett'eifern *vi untr*: **mit jdm um etw** ~ compete with sb for sth.
wetten *vti* bet; **so haben wir nicht gewettet!** that's not part of the bargain!
Wetter [ve'tər] *nt* -s, - weather; (*MIN*) air; ~**aussichten** *pl* weather outlook *sing*; ~**bericht** *m* weather report; ~**dienst** *m* meteorological service; ~**karte** *f* weather chart; ~**lage** *f* (weather) situation.
wettern [ve'tərn] *vi* curse and swear.
Wetter- *zW*: ~**umschlag** *m* sudden change in the weather; ~**vorhersage** *f* weather forecast; ~**warte** *f* weather station; **w**~**wendisch** *a* capricious.
Wett- *zW*: ~**kampf** *m* contest; ~**lauf** *m* race; **ein** ~**lauf mit der Zeit** a race against time; **w**~**laufen** *vi unreg* race.
wettmachen *vt* make good.
Wett- *zW*: ~**rüsten** *nt* arms race; ~**spiel** *nt* match; ~**streit** *m* contest.
wetzen [vet'sən] *vt* sharpen ♦ *vi* (*umg*) scoot.
WEZ *abk* (= *westeuropäische Zeit*) CET.
WG *abk* = **Wohngemeinschaft.**
WHO *f* - *abk* (= *Weltgesundheitsorganisation*) WHO.
wich [viċh] *imperf von* **weichen.**
wichsen [vik'sən] *vti* (*Schuhe*) polish; (*umg!*:

onanieren) jerk *od* toss off (*!*).
Wicht [viċht] *m* -(e)s, -e imp, dwarf; (*pej*) worthless creature.
wichtig *a* important; **sich selbst/etw (zu)** ~ **nehmen** take o.s./sth (too) seriously; **W**~**keit** *f* importance; **W**~**tuer(in** *f)* *m* (*pej*) pompous ass (*!*).
Wicke [vi'kə] *f* -, -n (*BOT*) vetch; (*Garten*~) sweet pea.
Wickelkleid *nt* wrap-around dress.
wickeln [vi'kəln] *vt* wind; (*Haare*) set; (*Kind*) change; **da bist du schief gewickelt!** (*fig umg*) you're very much mistaken; **jdn/etw in etw** (*akk*) ~ wrap sb/sth in sth.
Wickeltisch *m* baby's changing table.
Widder [vi'dər] *m* -s, - ram; (*ASTROL*) Aries.
wider [vē:'dər] *präp* +*akk* against.
widerfah'ren *vi unreg untr* happen (*jdm* to sb).
Widerhaken [vē:'dərhâkən] *m* barb.
Widerhall [vē:'dərhál] *m* echo; **keinen** ~ **finden** (*Interesse*) meet with no response (*bei jdm* from sb).
widerle'gen *vt untr* refute.
widerlich [vē:'dərliċh] *a* disgusting, repulsive; **W**~**keit** *f* repulsiveness.
wider- [vē:'dər] *zW*: ~**rechtlich** *a* unlawful; **W**~**rede** *f* contradiction; **kein W**~**rede!** don't argue!
Widerruf [vē:'dərrōō:f] *m* retraction; countermanding; **bis auf** ~ until revoked.
widerru'fen *vt unreg untr* retract; (*Anordnung*) revoke; (*Befehl*) countermand.
Widersacher(in *f)* [vē:'dərzákhər(in)] *m* -s, - adversary.
widerset'zen *vr untr* oppose (*jdm/etw* sb/sth); **sich jdm** ~ (*der Polizei*) resist sb; **sich einer Sache** ~ (*einem Befehl*) refuse to comply with sth.
widerspenstig [vē:'dərshpenstiċh] *a* willful (*US*), wilful (*Brit*); **W**~**keit** *f* willfulness, wilfulness.
widerspiegeln [vē:'dərshpē:gəln] *vt* reflect.
widerspre'chen *vi unreg untr* contradict (*jdm* sb).
widersprechend *a* contradictory.
Widerspruch [vē:'dərshprōōċh] *m* contradiction; **ein** ~ **in sich** a contradiction in terms.
widersprüchlich [vē:'dərshprüċhliċh] *a* contradictory, inconsistent.
widerspruchslos *ad* without arguing.
Widerstand [vē:'dərshtánt] *m* resistance; **jdm/einer Sache** ~ **leisten** resist sb/sth.
Widerstands- *zW*: ~**bewegung** *f* resistance (movement); **w**~**fähig** *a* resistant, tough; **w**~**los** *a* unresisting.
widerste'hen *vi unreg untr* withstand (*jdm/etw* sb/sth).
widerstre'ben *vi untr* +*dat*: **es widerstrebt mir, so etwas zu tun** I am reluctant to do anything like that.
widerstrebend *a* reluctant; (*gegensätzlich*) conflicting.
Wider- [vē:'dər] *zW*: ~**streit** *m* conflict;

w~wärtig a nasty, horrid; **~wille** m aversion (gegen to); (Abneigung) distaste (gegen for); (~streben) reluctance; **w~willig** a unwilling, reluctant; **~worte** pl answering back sing.

widmen [vit'mən] vt dedicate ♦ vr devote o.s. (dat to).

Widmung f dedication.

widrig [vē:'driᴄⱨ] a (Umstände) adverse; (Mensch) repulsive.

wie [vē:] ad how; ~ **wär's mit einem Whisky?** (umg) how about a whisky?; ~ **nennt man das?** what is that called?; ~ **bitte?** pardon me? (US), pardon? (Brit) ♦ kj: ~ **ich schon sagte** as I said; **(so) schön** ~ ... as beautiful as ...; ~ **du** like you; **singen** ~ **ein** ... sing like a ...; ~ **noch nie** as never before; ~ **(zum Beispiel)** such as (for example).

wieder [vē:'dər] ad again; ~ **da sein** be back (again); **gehst du schon** ~? are you off again?; ~ **ein(e)** ... another ...; **das ist auch** ~ **wahr** that's true; **da sieht man mal** ~ ... it just shows ...

Wieder- präf re; (bei Verben: erneut) again; (zurück) back.

wieder- zW: **W~aufbau** [-ouf'bou] m rebuilding; **~aufbereiten** [-ouf'bərītən] vt recycle; (Atommüll) reprocess; **W~aufbereitungsanlage** f reprocessing plant; **W~aufnahme** [-ouf'nâmə] f resumption; **~aufnehmen** vt unreg resume; (Gedanken, Hobby) take up again; (Thema) revert to; (JUR: Verfahren) reopen; **~bekommen** vt unreg get back; **~beleben** vt revive; **~bringen** vt unreg bring back; **~erkennen** vt unreg recognize; **W~erstattung** f reimbursement; **~finden** vt unreg (fig: Selbstachtung etc) regain.

Wiedergabe f (von Rede, Ereignis) account; (Wiederholung) repetition; (Darbietung) performance; (Reproduktion) reproduction; **~gerät** nt playback unit.

wieder- zW: **~geben** vt unreg (zurückgeben) return; (Erzählung etc) repeat; (Gefühle etc) convey; **W~geburt** f rebirth; **~gutmachen** [-gōō:t'mâᴄⱨən] vt make up for; (Fehler) put right; **W~gut'machung** f reparation; **~her'stellen** vt restore.

wiederho'len vt untr repeat.

wiederholt a: **zum ~en Male** once again.

Wiederholung f repetition.

Wiederholungstäter(in f) m (JUR) second-time offender; (mehrmalig) persistent offender.

wieder- zW: **W~hören** nt: **auf W~hören** (TEL) goodbye; **~käuen** vti ruminate; (fig umg) go over again and again; **W~kehr** f - return; (von Vorfall) repetition, recurrence; **~kehrend** a recurrent; **W~kunft** f -, ⁻e return; **~sehen** vt unreg see again; **auf W~sehen** goodbye; **~um** ad again; (seinerseits etc) in turn; (andererseits) on the other hand; **~vereinigen** vt reunite;

W~vereinigung f reunification; **W~verkäufer** m distributor; **W~wahl** f re-election.

Wiege [vē:'gā] f -, -n cradle.

wiegen vt (schaukeln) rock; (Kopf) shake ♦ vti unreg weigh; **schwer** ~ (fig) carry a lot of weight; (Irrtum) be serious.

wiehern [vē:'ərn] vi neigh, whinny.

Wien [vē:n] nt -s Vienna.

Wiener(in f) m -s, - Viennese ♦ a attr Viennese; ~ **Schnitzel** Wiener schnitzel.

wies [vē:s] imperf von **weisen**.

Wiese [vē:'zə] f -, -n meadow.

Wiesel [vē:'zəl] nt -s, - weasel; **schnell** od **flink wie ein** ~ quick as a flash.

wieso [vē:zō:'] ad why.

wieviel [vē:fē:l'] ad how much; ~ **Menschen** how many people; **~mal** ad how often.

wievielte(r, s) a: **zum ~n Mal?** how many times?; **den W~n haben wir?** what's the date?; **an ~r Stelle?** in what place?; **der ~ Besucher war er?** how many visitors were there before him?

wieweit [vē:vit'] ad to what extent.

Wikinger [vē:'kingər] m -s, - Viking.

wild [vilt] a wild; **~er Streik** unofficial strike; **in ~er Ehe leben** (veraltet, hum) live in sin; ~ **entschlossen** (umg) dead set.

Wild nt -(e)s game; **~bahn** f: **in freier ~bahn** in the wild; **~bret** nt game; (von Rotwild) venison.

wildern [vil'dərn] vi poach.

wild- zW: **W~fang** m little rascal; **~fremd** [vilt'fremt'] a (umg) quite strange and unknown; **W~heit** f wildness; **W~leder** nt suede.

Wildnis f -, -se wilderness.

Wild- zW: **~schwein** nt (wild) boar; **~wechsel** m: „**~wechsel**" "wild animals"; **~westroman** m western.

will [vil] 1./3. pers sing präs von **wollen**.

Wille [vi'lə] m -ns, -n will; **jdm seinen ~n lassen** let sb have his own way; **seinen eigenen ~n haben** be self-willed.

willen präp +gen: **um** ... ~ for the sake of ...

willenlos a weak⁺willed.

willens a (geh): ~ **sein** be willing.

willensstark a strong-willed.

willentlich [vi'ləntlicⱨ] a willful (US), wilful (Brit), deliberate.

willig a willing.

willkommen [vilko'mən] a welcome; **jdn** ~ **heißen** welcome sb; **herzlich** ~ welcome (in +dat to); **W~** nt -s, - welcome.

willkürlich a arbitrary; (Bewegung) voluntary.

willst [vilst] 2. pers sing präs von **wollen**.

wimmeln [vi'məln] vi swarm (von with).

wimmern [vi'mərn] vi whimper.

Wimper [vim'pər] f -, -n eyelash; **ohne mit der** ~ **zu zucken** (fig) without batting an eye(lid).

Wimperntusche f mascara.

Wind [vint] m -(e)s, -e wind; **den Mantel** od **das Fähnchen nach dem** ~ **hängen** trim one's sails to the wind; **etw in den ~ schlagen** turn a deaf ear to sth.

Windbeutel m cream puff; (fig) windbag.

Winde |vin'də| f -, -n (TECH) winch, windlass; (BOT) bindweed.

Windel |vin'dəl| f -, -n diaper (US), nappy (Brit).

windelweich a: **jdn ~ schlagen** (umg) beat the living daylights out of sb.

winden |vin'dən| vi unpers be windy ♦ unreg vt wind; (Kranz) weave; (ent~) twist ♦ vr wind; (Person) writhe; (fig: ausweichen) try to wriggle out.

Wind'energie f wind energy.

Windeseile f: **sich in** od **mit ~ verbreiten** spread like wildfire.

Windhose f whirlwind.

Windhund m greyhound; (Mensch) fly-by-night.

windig |vin'diç| a windy; (fig) dubious.

Wind- zW: **~jacke** f windbreaker (US), windcheater (Brit); **~kraftanlage** f windmill producing electricity; **~mühle** f windmill; **gegen ~mühlen (an)kämpfen** (fig) tilt at windmills.

Windpocken pl chickenpox.

Wind- zW: **~rose** f (NAUT) compass card; (MET) wind rose; **~schatten** m lee; (von Fahrzeugen) slipstream; **~schutzscheibe** f (AUT) windshield (US), windscreen (Brit); **~stärke** f wind force; **~stille** f calm; **~stoß** m gust of wind.

Windung f (von Weg, Fluß etc) meander; (von Schlange, Spule) coil; (von Schraube) thread.

Wink |vingk| m -(e)s, -e (mit Kopf) nod; (mit Hand) wave; (Tip, Hinweis) hint; **ein ~ mit dem Zaunpfahl** a broad hint.

Winkel |ving'kəl| m -s, - (MATH) angle; (Gerät) set square; (in Raum) corner; **~advokat** m (pej) incompetent lawyer; **~messer** m protractor; **~zug** m: **mach keine ~züge** stop evading the issue.

winken |ving'kən| vti wave; **dem Sieger winkt eine Reise nach Italien** the winner will receive (the attractive prize of) a trip to Italy.

winseln |vin'zəln| vi whine.

Winter |vin'tər| m -s, - winter; **w~lich** a wintry; **~reifen** m winter tire (US) od tyre (Brit); **~schlaf** m (ZOOL) hibernation; **~schlußverkauf** m winter sale; **~spiele** pl: **(Olympische) ~spiele** Winter Olympics pl; **~sport** m winter sports pl.

Winzer(in f) |vin'tsər(in)| m -, -s wine grower.

winzig |vin'tsiç| a tiny.

Wipfel |vi'pfəl| m -s, - treetop.

Wippe |vi'pə| f -, -n seesaw.

wir |vēr| pron we; **~ alle** all of us, we all.

Wirbel |vir'bəl| m -s, - whirl, swirl; (Trubel) hurly-burly; (Aufsehen) fuss; (ANAT) vertebra; **~ um jdn/etw machen** make a fuss about sb/sth.

wirbellos a (ZOOL) invertebrate.

wirbeln vi whirl, swirl.

Wirbel- zW: **~säule** f spine; **~tier** nt vertebrate; **~wind** m whirlwind.

wirbst 2. pers sing präs von **werben**.

wirbt |virpt| 3. pers sing präs von **werben**.

wird |virt| 3. pers sing präs von **werden**.

wirfst 2. pers sing präs von **werfen**.

wirft |virft| 3. pers sing präs von **werfen**.

wirken |vir'kən| vi have an effect; (erfolgreich sein) work; (scheinen) seem; **etw auf sich (akk) ~ lassen** take sth in ♦ vt (Wunder) work.

wirklich |virk'liç| a real; **W~keit** f reality; **~keitsgetreu** a realistic.

wirksam |virk'zäm| a effective; **W~keit** f effectiveness.

Wirkstoff m active substance.

Wirkung |vir'kŏong| f effect.

Wirkungs- zW: **~bereich** m field (of activity od interest etc); (Domäne) domain; **w~los** a ineffective; **w~los bleiben** have no effect; **w~voll** a effective.

wirr |vir| a confused; (unrealistisch) wild; (Haare etc) tangled.

Wirren pl disturbances pl.

Wirrwarr |vir'vàr| m -s disorder, chaos; (von Stimmen) hubbub; (von Fäden, Haaren etc) tangle.

Wirsing(kohl) |vir'zing(kō:l)| m -s savoy cabbage.

wirst |virst| 2. pers sing präs von **werden**.

Wirt |virt| m -(e)s, -e landlord; **~in** f landlady.

Wirtschaft |virt'shäft| f (Gaststätte) pub; (Haushalt) housekeeping; (eines Landes) economy; (Geschäftsleben) industry and commerce; (umg: Durcheinander) mess; **w~en** vi (sparsam sein): **gut w~en können** be economical; **~er** m (Verwalter) manager; **~erin** f (im Haushalt, Heim etc) housekeeper; **w~lich** a economical; (POL) economic.

Wirtschafts- zW: **~geld** nt housekeeping (money); **~geographie** f economic geography; **~hilfe** f economic aid; **~krise** f economic crisis; **~minister** m minister of economic affairs; **~ordnung** f economic system; **~prüfer** m certified public accountant (US), chartered accountant (Brit); **~spionage** f industrial espionage; **~wissenschaft** f economics sing; **~wunder** nt economic miracle; **~zweig** m branch of industry.

Wirtshaus nt inn.

Wisch |vish| m -(e)s, -e scrap of paper.

wischen vt wipe.

Wischer m -s, - (AUT) wiper.

Wischiwaschi |vishē:vä'shē:| nt -s (pej umg) drivel.

Wisent |vē:'zent| m -s, -e bison.

WiSo |vi'zō| abk = Wirtschafts- und Sozialwissenschaften.

wispern |vis'pərn| vti whisper.

wiss. *abk* = **wissenschaftlich.**
Wiss. *abk* = **Wissenschaft.**
Wißbegier(de) [vis'bəgē:r(də)] *f* thirst for knowledge.
wißbegierig *a* eager for knowledge.
wissen [vi'sən] *vti unreg* know; **von jdm/etw nichts ~ wollen** not be interested in sb/sth; **sie hält sich für wer weiß wie klug** (*umg*) she doesn't half think she's clever; **gewußt wie** *od* **wo!** *etc* sheer brilliance!; **ich weiß seine Adresse nicht mehr** (*sich erinnern*) I can't remember his address; **W~** *nt* **-s** knowledge; **etw gegen (sein) besseres W~ tun** do sth against one's better judgement; **nach bestem W~ und Gewissen** to the best of one's knowledge and belief.
Wissenschaft [vi'sənshàft] *f* science.
Wissenschaftler(in *f*) *m* **-s,** - scientist; (*Geistes~*) academic.
wissenschaftlich *a* scientific; **W~er Assistent** assistant lecturer.
wissenswert *a* worth knowing.
wissentlich *a* knowing.
wittern [vi'tərn] *vt* scent; (*fig*) suspect.
Witterung *f* weather; (*Geruch*) scent.
Witwe [vit'və] *f* **-, -n** widow.
Witwer *m* **-s,** - widower.
Witz [vits] *m* **-(e)s, -e** joke; **der ~ an der Sache ist, daß** ... the great thing about it is that ...; **~blatt** *nt* comic (paper); **~bold** *m* **-(e)s, -e** joker.
witzeln *vi* joke.
witzig *a* funny.
witzlos *a* (*umg: unsinnig*) pointless, futile.
WiWi [vi'vi] *mf* **-, -s** *abk* (*umg:* = *Wirtschaftswissenschaftler(in)*) economist.
WM *f* - *abk* = **Weltmeisterschaft.**
wo [vō:] *ad* where; (*umg: irgendwo*) somewhere; **im Augenblick, ~** ... the moment (that) ...; **die Zeit, ~** ... the time when ... ♦ *kj* (*wenn*) if.
w.o. *abk* (= *wie oben*) as above.
woanders [vō:án'dərs] *ad* elsewhere.
wob [vō:p] *imperf von* **weben.**
wobei [vō:bi'] *ad* (*rel*) ... in/by/with which; (*interrog*) how; what ... in/by/with; **~ mir gerade einfällt** ... which reminds me ...
Woche [vo'khə] *f* **-, -n** week.
Wochenbett *nt*: **im ~ sterben** die in childbirth.
Wochen- *zW*: **~ende** *nt* weekend; **~karte** *f* weekly ticket; **~lang** *a, ad* for weeks; **~schau** *f* newsreel.
wöchentlich [vœ'çhəntliçh] *a, ad* weekly.
Wochenzeitung *f* weekly (paper).
Wöchnerin [vœçh'nərin] *f woman who has recently given birth.*
wo- *zW*: **~durch** [vōdōōrçh'] *ad* (*rel*) through which; (*interrog*) what ... through; **~für** [vōfü:r'] *ad* (*rel*) for which; (*interrog*) what ... for.
wog [vō:k] *imperf von* **wiegen.**
Woge [vō:'gə] *f* **-, -n** wave.
wogegen [vōgā:'gən] *ad* (*rel*) against which;

(*interrog*) what ... against.
wogen *vi* heave, surge.
wo- *zW*: **~her** [vōhā:r'] *ad* where ... from; **~her kommt es eigentlich, daß ...?** how is it that ...?; **~hin** [vōhin'] *ad* where ... to; **~hin man auch schaut** wherever you look.
wohinge'gen *kj* whereas, while.
wohl [vō:l] *ad* well; (*behaglich*) at ease, comfortable; (*vermutlich*) I suppose, probably; (*gewiß*) certainly; **~ oder übel** whether one likes it or not; **das ist doch ~ nicht dein Ernst!** surely you're not serious!; **er weiß das ~** he knows that perfectly well; **ob das ~ stimmt?** I wonder if that's true; **bei dem Gedanken ist mir nicht ~** I'm not very happy at the thought.
Wohl *nt* **-(e)s** welfare; **zum ~!** cheers!
wohl- *zW*: **~auf** [vō:louf'] *a* well, in good health; **W~befinden** *nt* well-being; **W~behagen** *nt* comfort; **~behalten** *a* safe and sound; **W~ergehen** *nt* welfare; **W~fahrt** *f* welfare; **W~fahrtsstaat** *m* welfare state; **W~gefallen** *nt*: **sich in W~gefallen auflösen** (*hum: Gegenstände, Probleme*) vanish into thin air; (*zerfallen*) fall apart; **~gemeint** *a* well-intentioned; **~gemerkt** *ad* mark you; **~habend** *a* wealthy.
wohlig *a* contented; (*gemütlich*) comfortable.
wohl- *zW*: **W~klang** *m* melodious sound; **~schmeckend** *a* delicious; **W~stand** *m* prosperity; **W~standsgesellschaft** *f* affluent society; **W~tat** *f* (*Gefallen*) favor (*US*), favour (*Brit*); (*gute Tat*) good deed; **W~täter** *m* benefactor; **~tätig** *a* charitable; **~tuend** *a* pleasant; **~tun** *vi unreg* do good (*jdm sb*); **~verdient** *a* (*Ruhe*) well-earned; (*Strafe*) well-deserved; **~weislich** *ad* prudently; **W~wollen** *nt* **-s** good will; **~wollend** *a* benevolent.
Wohnblock *m* **-s, -s** apartment house (*US*), block of flats (*Brit*).
wohnen [vō:'nən] *vi* live.
wohn- *zW*: **W~fläche** *f* living space; **W~geld** *nt* rent allowance; **W~gemeinschaft** *f* apartment *od* flat (*Brit*) sharing; (*von Hippies*) commune; (*Menschen*) people sharing an apartment; **~haft** *a* resident; **W~heim** *nt* (*für Studenten*) dormitory (*US*), hall (of residence); (*für Senioren*) home; (*bes für Arbeiter*) hostel; **W~komfort** *m*: **mit sämtlichem W~komfort** with all mod cons; **~lich** *a* comfortable; **W~mobil** *nt* motor home (*US*), motor caravan (*Brit*); **W~ort** *m* domicile; **W~silo** *nt* concrete block of apartments; **W~sitz** *m* place of residence; **ohne festen W~sitz** of no fixed abode.
Wohnung *f* house; (*Etagen~*) apartment, flat (*Brit*).
Wohnungs- *zW*: **~amt** *nt* housing office; **~markt** *m* housing market; **~not** *f* housing shortage.

wohn- zW: **W~viertel** nt residential area; **W~wagen** m trailer (US), caravan (Brit); **W~zimmer** nt living room.
wölben [væl'bən] vtr curve.
Wölbung f curve.
Wolf [volf] m -(e)s, ⁻e wolf; (TECH) shredder; (Fleisch~) grinder (US), mincer (Brit).
Wölfin [væl'fin] f she-wolf.
Wolke [vol'kə] f -, -n cloud; **aus allen ~n fallen** (fig) be flabbergasted (umg).
Wolken- zW: **w~bruchartig** a torrential; **~kratzer** m skyscraper; **~kuckucksheim** nt cloudland (US), cloud-cuckoo-land (Brit).
wolkig [vol'kiç] a cloudy.
Wolle [vo'lə] f -, -n wool; **sich mit jdm in die ~ kriegen** (fig umg) start squabbling with sb.
wollen [vo'lən] vti unreg want; **und so jemand** od **etwas** (umg) **will Lehrer sein!** and he calls himself a teacher; **das will alles gut überlegt sein** that needs a lot of thought; **oh, das hab ich nicht gewollt** oh, I didn't mean to do that; **ich weiß nicht, was er will** (verstehe ihn nicht) I don't know what he's on about.
Wollsachen pl woolens pl (US), woollens pl (Brit).
wollüstig [vo'lüstiç] a lusty, sensual.
wo- zW: **~mit** [võmit'] ad (rel) with which; (interrog) what ... with; **~mit kann ich dienen?** what can I do for you?; **~möglich** [võmœk'liç] ad probably, I suppose; **~nach** [võnáꭓ'] ad (rel) after/for which; (interrog) what ... for/after.
Wonne [vo'nə] f -, -n joy, bliss.
woran [võrán'] ad (rel) on/at which; (interrog) what ... on/at; **~ liegt das?** what's the reason for it?
worauf [võrouf'] ad (rel) on which; (interrog) what ... on; (zeitlich) whereupon; **~ du dich verlassen kannst** of that you can be sure.
woraus [võrous'] ad (rel) from/out of which; (interrog) what ... from/out of.
worin [võrin'] ad (rel) in which; (interrog) what ... in.
Wort [vort] nt -(e)s, ⁻er od -e word; **jdn beim ~ nehmen** take sb at his word; **ein ernstes ~ mit jdm reden** have a serious talk with sb; **man kann sein eigenes ~ nicht (mehr) verstehen** you can't hear yourself speak; **jdm aufs ~ gehorchen** obey sb's every word; **zu ~ kommen** get a chance to speak; **jdm das ~ erteilen** allow sb to speak; **~art** f (GRAM) part of speech; **w~brüchig** a not true to one's word.
Wörtchen nt: **da habe ich wohl ein ~ mitzureden** (umg) I think I have some say in that.
Wörterbuch [vær'tərbōō:ꭓ] nt dictionary.
Wort- zW: **~fetzen** pl snatches of conversation; **~führer** m spokesman; **w~getreu** a true to one's word; (Übersetzung) literal; **w~gewaltig** a eloquent; **w~karg** a taciturn;

~laut m wording; **im ~laut** verbatim.
wörtlich [vær'tliç] a literal.
Wort- zW: **w~los** a mute; **~meldung** f: **wenn es keine weiteren ~meldungen gibt** ... if nobody else wishes to speak ...; **w~reich** a wordy, verbose; **~schatz** m vocabulary; **~spiel** nt play on words, pun; **~wechsel** m dispute; **w~wörtlich** a word-for-word ♦ ad quite literally.
worüber [võrü:'bər] ad (rel) over/about which; (interrog) what ... over/about.
worum [võrōōm'] ad (rel) about/round which; (interrog) what ... about/round; **~ handelt es sich?** what's it about?
worunter [võrōōn'tər] ad (rel) under which; (interrog) what ... under.
wo- zW: **~von** [võfon'] ad (rel) from which; (interrog) what ... from; **~vor** [võfor'] ad (rel) in front of/before which; (interrog) in front of/before what; of what; **~zu** [võtsōō:'] ad (rel) to/for which; (interrog) what ... for/to; (warum) why; **~zu soll das gut sein?** what's the point of that?
Wrack [vrák] nt -(e)s, -s wreck.
wrang [vráng] imperf von **wringen**.
wringen [vring'gən] vt unreg wring.
WS abk = Wintersemester.
WSV abk = Winterschlußverkauf.
Wttbg. abk = Württemberg.
Wucher [võō:'ꭓər] m -s profiteering; **~er** m -s, -, **Wucherin** f profiteer; **w~isch** a profiteering.
wuchern vi (Pflanzen) grow wild.
Wucherpreis m exorbitant price.
Wucherung f (MED) growth.
wuchs [võō:ks] imperf von **wachsen**.
Wuchs m -es (Wachstum) growth; (Statur) build.
Wucht [võōꭓt] f - force.
wuchtig a massive, solid.
wühlen [vü:'lən] vi scrabble; (Tier) root; (Maulwurf) burrow; (umg: arbeiten) slave away ♦ vt dig.
Wühlmaus f vole.
Wühltisch m (in Kaufhaus) bargain counter.
Wulst [võōlst] m -es, ⁻e bulge; (an Wunde) swelling.
wulstig a bulging; (Rand, Lippen) thick.
wund [võōnt] a sore; **sich** (dat) **die Füße ~ laufen** (lit) get sore feet from walking; (fig) walk one's legs off; **ein ~er Punkt** a sore point; **W~brand** m gangrene.
Wunde [võōn'də] f -, -n wound; **alte ~n wieder aufreißen** (fig) open up old wounds.
wunder [võōn'dər] ad inv: **meine Eltern denken ~ was passiert ist** my parents think goodness knows what has happened; **W~** nt -s, - miracle; **es ist kein W~** it's no wonder; **~bar** a wonderful, marvelous (US), marvellous (Brit); **W~kerze** f sparkler; **W~kind** nt infant prodigy; **~lich** a odd, peculiar.
wundern vr be surprised (über +akk at) ♦ vt surprise.

Wunder- *zW*: **w~schön** *a* beautiful; **~tüte** *f* surprise packet; **w~voll** *a* wonderful.

Wundfieber *nt* **-s** traumatic fever.

Wundstarrkrampf [vo͞ont'shtárkrámpf] *m* tetanus, lockjaw.

Wunsch [vo͞onsh] *m* **-(e)s**, ⁼e wish; **haben Sie (sonst) noch einen ~?** (*beim Einkauf etc*) is there anything else you'd like?; **auf jds (besonderen/ausdrücklichen) ~ hin** at sb's (special/express) request; **~denken** *nt* wishful thinking.

Wünschelrute [vün'shəlro͞o:tə] *f* divining rod.

wünschen [vün'shən] *vt* wish; **sich** (*dat*) **etw ~** want sth, wish for sth; **was ~ Sie?** (*in Geschäft*) what can I do for you?; (*in Restaurant*) what would you like? ♦ *vi*: **zu ~/viel zu ~ übrig lassen** leave something/a great deal to be desired.

wünschenswert *a* desirable.

Wunsch- *zW*: **~kind** *nt* planned child; **~konzert** *nt* (*RAD*) musical request program; **w~los** *a*: **w~los glücklich** perfectly happy; **~zettel** *m* list of things one would like.

wurde [vo͞or'də] *imperf von* **werden**.

Würde [vür'də] *f* **-**, **-n** dignity; (*Stellung*) honor (*US*), honour (*Brit*); **unter aller ~ sein** be beneath contempt.

Würdenträger *m* dignitary.

würdevoll *a* dignified.

würdig [vür'diçh] *a* worthy; (*würdevoll*) dignified.

würdigen [vür'digən] *vt* appreciate; **etw zu ~ wissen** appreciate sth; **jdn keines Blickes ~** not so much as look at sb.

Wurf [vo͞orf] *m* **-s**, ⁼e throw; (*Junge*) litter.

Würfel [vür'fəl] *m* **-s**, **-** dice; (*MATH*) cube; **die ~ sind gefallen** the die is cast; **~becher** *m* (dice) cup.

würfeln *vi* play dice ♦ *vt* dice.

Würfel- *zW*: **~spiel** *nt* game of dice; **~zucker** *m* lump sugar.

Wurf- *zW*: **~geschoß** *nt* projectile; **~sendung** *f* circular.

Würgegriff *m* **-(e)s** (*lit*, *fig*) stranglehold.

würgen [vür'gən] *vti* choke; **mit Hängen und W~** by the skin of one's teeth.

Wurm [vo͞orm] *m* **-(e)s**, ⁼er worm; **da steckt der ~ drin** (*fig umg*) there's something wrong somewhere; (*verdächtig*) there's something fishy about it (*umg*).

wurmen *vt* (*umg*) rile, nettle.

Wurmfortsatz *m* (*MED*) appendix.

wurmig *a* worm-eaten.

wurmstichig *a* worm-ridden.

Wurst [vo͞orst] *f* **-**, ⁼e sausage; **das ist mir ~** (*umg*) I don't care, I don't give a damn; **jetzt geht es um die ~** (*fig umg*) the moment of truth has come.

Würstchenbude *f*, **Würstchenstand** *m* sausage stand, hot dog stand.

Württemberg [vür'təmberk] *nt* Württemberg.

Würze [vür'tsə] *f* **-**, **-n** seasoning.

Wurzel [vo͞or'tsəl] *f* **-**, **-n** root; **~n schlagen** (*lit*) root; (*fig*) put down roots; **(die) ~ aus 4 ist 2** (*MATH*) the square root of 4 is 2.

würzen *vt* season; (*würzig machen*) spice.

würzig *a* spicy.

wusch [vo͞o:sh] *imperf von* **waschen**.

wußte [vo͞os'tə] *imperf von* **wissen**.

Wust [vo͞ost] *m* **-(e)s** (*umg*: *Durcheinander*) jumble; (*Menge*) pile.

wüst [vü:st] *a* untidy, messy; (*ausschweifend*) wild; (*öde*) waste; (*umg*: *heftig*) terrible; **jdn ~ beschimpfen** use vile language to sb.

Wüste *f* **-**, **-n** desert; **die ~ Gobi** the Gobi Desert; **jdn in die ~ schicken** (*fig*) send sb packing.

Wut [vo͞o:t] *f* **-** rage, fury; **eine ~ haben** be furious (*auf jdn/etw* with sb/sth); **~anfall** *m* fit of rage; **w~entbrannt** *a* furious, enraged.

wüten [vü:'tən] *vi* rage.

wütend *a* furious, enraged.

Wz *abk* (= *Warenzeichen*) ®.

X

X, x [iks] *nt* X, x; **jdm ein X für ein U vormachen** put one over on sb (*umg*).

X-Beine [iks'bīnə] *pl* knock-knees *pl*.

x-beliebig [iksbəlē:'bēçh] *a* any (whatever).

Xerographie [ksārōgráfē:'] *f* xerography.

xerokopieren [ksārōkōpē:'rən] *vt untr* xerox, photocopy.

x-fach [iks'fáḵh] *a*: **die ~e Menge** (*MATH*) n times the amount.

x-mal [iks'mál] *ad* any number of times, n times.

x-te [iks'tə] *a* (*MATH*, *umg*) nth; **zum ~n Male** (*umg*) for the nth *od* umpteenth time.

Xylophon [ksylōfō:n'] *nt* **-s**, **-e** xylophone.

Y

Y, y [üp'sēlon] *nt* Y, y.

Yen [yen] *m* **-(s)**, **-(s)** yen.

Yoga [yō:'gà] *m od nt* **-(s)** yoga.

Ypsilon [üp'sēlon] *nt* **-(s)**, **-s** the letter Y.

Z

Z, z [tset] *nt* Z, z.
Zack [tsák] *m*: **auf ~ sein** (*umg*) be on the ball.
Zacke [tsá'kə] *f* -, -n point; (*Berg~*) jagged peak; (*Gabel~*) prong; (*Kamm~*) tooth.
zackig [tsá'kiċh] *a* jagged; (*umg*) smart; (*Tempo*) brisk.
zaghaft [tsák'háft] *a* timid.
Zaghaftigkeit *f* timidity.
zäh [tse:] *a* tough; (*Mensch*) tenacious; (*Flüssigkeit*) thick; (*schleppend*) sluggish; **~flüssig** *a* viscous; (*Verkehr*) slow-moving.
Zähigkeit *f* toughness; tenacity.
Zahl [tsál] *f* -, -en number.
zahlbar *a* payable.
zahlen *vti* pay; **~ bitte!** the check please!
zählen [tse:'lən] *vt* count; **seine Tage sind gezählt** his days are numbered ♦ *vi* (*sich verlassen*): **~ auf** (+*akk*) count on; **~ zu** be numbered among.
Zahlen- *zW*: **~angabe** *f* figure; **~kombination** *f* combination of figures; **z~mäßig** *a* numerical; **~schloß** *nt* combination lock.
Zahler *m* -s, - payer.
Zähler *m* -s, - (*TECH*) meter; (*MATH*) numerator; **~stand** *m* meter reading.
Zahl- *zW*: **~karte** *f* transfer form; **z~los** *a* countless; **~meister** *m* (*NAUT*) purser; **z~reich** *a* numerous; **~tag** *m* payday.
Zahlung *f* payment; **in ~ geben/nehmen** give/take in part exchange.
Zahlungs- *zW*: **~anweisung** *f* draft, transfer order; **~aufforderung** *f* request for payment; **z~fähig** *a* solvent; **~mittel** *nt* means of payment; (*Münzen, Banknoten*) currency; **~rückstände** *pl* arrears *pl*; **z~unfähig** *a* insolvent; **~verzug** *m* default.
Zahlwort *nt* numeral.
zahm [tsám] *a* tame.
zähmen [tse:'mən] *vt* tame; (*fig*) curb.
Zahn [tsán] *m* -(e)s, ⁻e tooth; **die dritten ~e** (*umg*) false teeth *pl*; **einen ~ draufhaben** (*umg*: *Geschwindigkeit*) be going like crazy; **jdm auf den ~ fühlen** (*fig*) sound sb out; **einen ~ zulegen** (*fig*) get a move on; **~arzt** *m* dentist; **~belag** *m* plaque; **~bürste** *f* toothbrush; **~creme** *f* toothpaste; **z~en** *vi* cut teeth; **~fäule** *f* - tooth decay, caries *sing*; **~fleisch** *nt* gums *pl*; **auf dem ~fleisch gehen** (*fig umg*) be all in, be at the end of one's tether; **~medizin** *f* dentistry; **~pasta** *f*, **~paste** *f* toothpaste; **~rad** *nt* cog(wheel); **~radbahn** *f* rack railway; **~schmelz** *m*

(tooth) enamel; **~schmerzen** *pl* toothache *sing*; **~stein** *m* tartar; **~stocher** *m* -s, - toothpick; **~weh** *nt* toothache.
Zaire [zí:r'] *nt* -s Zaire.
Zange [tsá'ngə] *f* -, -n pliers *pl*; (*Zucker~* etc) tongs *pl*; (*Beiß~*, *ZOOL*) pincers *pl*; (*MED*) forceps *pl*; **jdn in die ~ nehmen** (*fig*) put the screws on sb (*umg*).
Zangengeburt *f* forceps delivery.
Zank'apfel *m* bone of contention.
zanken [tsá'ngkən] *vir* quarrel.
zänkisch [tseng'kish] *a* quarrelsome.
Zäpfchen [tsepf'ċhən] *nt* (*ANAT*) uvula; (*MED*) suppository.
zapfen [tsá'pfən] *vt* tap.
Zapfen *m* -s, - plug; (*BOT*) cone; (*Eis~*) icicle.
Zapfenstreich *m* (*MIL*) tattoo.
Zapfsäule *f* gas (*US*) *od* petrol (*Brit*) pump.
zappelig [tsá'pəliċh] *a* wriggly; (*unruhig*) fidgety.
zappeln [tsá'pəln] *vi* wriggle; fidget; **jdn ~ lassen** (*fig umg*) keep sb in suspense.
Zar [tsár] *m* -en, -en Tzar, Czar.
zart [tsárt] *a* (*weich, leise*) soft; (*Braten etc*) tender; (*fein, schwächlich*) delicate; **~besaitet** *a attr* highly sensitive; **~bitter** *a* (*Schokolade*) bittersweet (*US*), plain (*Brit*); **Z~gefühl** *nt* tact; **Z~heit** *f* softness; tenderness; delicacy.
zärtlich [tse:r'tliċh] *a* tender, affectionate; **Z~keit** *f* tenderness; **Z~keiten** *pl* caresses *pl*.
Zäsur [tsezoo:r'] *f* caesura; (*fig*) break.
Zauber [tsou'bər] *m* -s, - magic; (*~bann*) spell; **fauler ~** (*umg*) humbug.
Zauberei [tsoubərí'] *f* magic.
Zauberer *m* -s, -, **Zauberin** *f* magician; (*Zauberkünstler*) conjurer.
Zauber- *zW*: **z~haft** *a* magical, enchanting; **~künstler** *m* conjurer; **~mittel** *nt* magical cure; (*Trank*) magic potion.
zaubern *vi* conjure, do magic.
Zauberspruch *m* (magic) spell.
zaudern [tsou'dərn] *vi* hesitate.
Zaum [tsoum] *m* -(e)s, Zäume bridle; **etw im ~ halten** keep sth in check.
Zaun [tsoun] *m* -(e)s, Zäune fence; **vom ~(e) brechen** (*fig*) start; **~gast** *m* (*Person*) mere onlooker; **~könig** *m* wren; **~pfahl** *m*: **ein Wink mit dem ~pfahl** a big hint.
ZAV *f abk* (= *Zentralstelle für Arbeitsvermittlung*) employment office.
z.B. *abk* (= *zum Beispiel*) e.g.
z.b.V. *abk* (= *zur besonderen Verwendung*) for particular application *od* use.
z.d.A. *abk* (= *zu den Akten*) for our files, to be filed.
ZDF *nt* - *abk* (= *Zweites Deutsches Fernsehen*) West German TV channel.
Zebra [tse:'brá] *nt* -s, -s zebra; **~streifen** *m* crosswalk (*US*), pedestrian crossing (*Brit*).
Zeche [tse'ċhə] *f* -, -n (*Rechnung*) check, bill (*Brit*); (*Bergbau*) mine.

zechen *vi* booze (*umg*).
Zechprellerei |tscçhprɛlərī'| *f* skipping payment in restaurants etc.
Zecke |tsc'kə| *f* -, **-n** tick.
Zedent |tsädɛnt'| *m* assignor.
Zeder |tsä:'dər| *f* -, **-n** cedar.
Zehe |tsä:ə| *f* -, **-n** toe; (*Knoblauch~*) clove.
zehn |tsä:n| *num* ten.
Zehnerpackung *f* packet of ten.
Zehn- *zW:* **~fingersystem** *nt* touch-typing method; **~kampf** *m* (*SPORT*) decathlon.
Zehntel *nt* **-s**, tenth (part).
zehnte(r, s) *a* tenth.
zehren |tsä:'rən| *vi:* **an jdm/etw ~** (*an Mensch, Kraft*) wear sb/sth out.
Zeichen |tsī'çhən| *nt* **-s**, - sign; **jdm ein ~ geben** give sb a signal; **unser/Ihr ~** (*COMM*) our/your reference; **~block** *m* sketch pad; **~code** *m* (*COMPUT*) character code; **~folge** *f* (*COMPUT*) string; **~kette** *f* (*COMPUT*) character string; **~satz** *m* (*COMPUT*) character set; **~setzung** *f* punctuation; **~trickfilm** *m* (animated) cartoon.
zeichnen *vti* draw; (*kenn~*) mark; (*unter~*) sign.
Zeichner(in *f*) *m* **-s**, - artist; **technischer ~** draftsman (*US*), draughtsman (*Brit*).
Zeichnung *f* drawing; (*Markierung*) markings *pl*.
zeichnungsberechtigt *a* authorized to sign.
Zeigefinger *m* index finger.
zeigen |tsī'gən| *vt* show ♦ *vi* point (*auf +akk* to, at) ♦ *vr* show o.s.; **es wird sich ~ time will tell; es zeigte sich, daß** ... it turned out that ...
Zeiger *m* **-s**, - pointer; (*Uhr~*) hand.
Zeile |tsī'lə| *f* -, **-n** line; (*Häuser~*) row.
Zeilen- *zW:* **~abstand** *m* line spacing; **~ausrichtung** *f* justification; **~drucker** *m* line printer; **~umbruch** *m* (*COMPUT*) wraparound; **~vorschub** *m* (*COMPUT*) line feed.
zeit |tsīt| *präp + gen:* **meines Lebens** in my lifetime.
Zeit *f* -, **-en** time; (*GRAM*) tense; **zur ~** at the moment; **sich** (*dat*) **~ lassen** take one's time; **eine Stunde ~ haben** have an hour (to spare); **sich** (*dat*) **für jdn/etw ~ nehmen** devote time to sb/sth; **von ~ zu ~** from time to time; **in letzter ~** recently; **nach ~ bezahlt werden** be paid by the hour; **zu der ~, als** ... (at the time) when ...; **~alter** *nt* age; **~ansage** *f* (*RAD*) time check; (*TEL*) speaking clock; **~aufwand** *m* time (*needed for a task*); **~bombe** *f* time bomb; **~druck** *m:* **unter ~druck stehen** be under pressure; **~geist** *m* spirit of the times; **z~gemäß** *a* in keeping with the times; **~genosse** *m* contemporary.
zeitig *a*, *ad* early.
Zeit- *zW:* **~karte** *f* season ticket; **z~kritisch** *a* (*Aufsatz*) full of comment on contemporary issues; **~lang** *f:* **eine ~lang** a while, a time; **z~le'bens** *ad* all one's life; **z~lich** *a* temporal; **das ~liche segnen** (*euph*) depart

this life ♦ *ad:* **das kann sie z~lich nicht einrichten** she can't find (the) time for that; **~lupe** *f* slow motion; **~lupentempo** *nt:* **im ~lupentempo** (*fig*) at a snail's pace; **~plan** *m* schedule; **~raffer** *m* **-s** time-lapse photography; **z~raubend** *a* time-consuming; **~raum** *m* period; **~rechnung** *f* time, era; **nach/vor unserer ~rechnung** A.D./B.C.; **~schrift** *f* periodical; **~tafel** *f* chronological table.
Zeitung *f* newspaper.
Zeitungs- *zW:* **~anzeige** *f* newspaper advertisement; **~ausschnitt** *m* press cutting; **~händler** *m* newsdealer (*US*), newsagent (*Brit*); **~papier** *nt* newsprint.
Zeit- *zW:* **~verschwendung** *f* waste of time; **~vertreib** *m* pastime, diversion; **z~weilig** *a* temporary; **z~weise** *ad* for a time; **~wort** *nt* verb; **~zeichen** *nt* (*RAD*) time signal; **~zone** *f* time zone; **~zünder** *m* time fuse.
Zelle |tsc'lə| *f* -, **-n** cell; (*Telefon~*) booth.
Zell- *zW:* **~kern** *m* cell, nucleus; **~stoff** *m* cellulose; **~teilung** *f* cell division.
Zelt |tsclt| *nt* **-(e)s**, **-e** tent; **seine ~e aufschlagen/abbrechen** settle down/pack one's bags; **~bahn** *f* groundsheet; **z~en** *vi* camp; **~lager** *nt* camp.
Zement |tsäment'| *m* **-(e)s**, **-e** cement.
zementieren |tsämentē:'rən| *vt* cement.
Zementmaschine *f* cement mixer.
Zenit |tsänē:t'| *m* **-(e)s** (*lit, fig*) zenith.
zensieren |tsenzē:'rən| *vt* censor; (*SCH*) mark.
Zensur |tsenzōō:r'| *f* censorship; (*SCH*) mark.
Zensus |tsen'zōōs| *m* -, census.
Zentimeter |tsentēmā:'tər| *m od nt* centimeter (*US*), centimetre (*Brit*); **~maß** *nt* (metric) tape measure.
Zentner |tsent'nər| *m* **-s**, - hundredweight.
zentral |tsenträl'| *a* central.
Zentrale *f* -, **-n** central office; (*TEL*) exchange.
Zentral- *zW:* **~einheit** *f* (*COMPUT*) central processing unit; **~heizung** *f* central heating.
zentralisieren |tsenträlēzē:'rən| *vt* centralize.
Zentrifugalkraft |tsentrēfōōgäl'kräft| *f* centrifugal force.
Zentrifuge |tsentrēfōō:'gə| *f* -, **-n** centrifuge; (*für Wäsche*) spin-dryer.
Zentrum |tsen'trōōm| *nt* **-s**, **Zentren** center (*US*), centre (*Brit*).
Zepter |tsep'tər| *nt* **-s**, - scepter (*US*), sceptre (*Brit*).
zerbre'chen *vti unreg* break.
zerbrechlich *a* fragile.
zerbröckeln |tserbrœ'kəln| *vti* crumble (to pieces).
zerdeppern |tserde'pərn| *vt* smash.
zerdrü'cken *vt* squash; crush; (*Kartoffeln*) mash.
Zeremonie |tsärämōnē:'| *f* ceremony.
zerfah'ren *a* scatterbrained, distracted.
Zerfall' *m* decay; disintegration; (*von Kultur, Gesundheit*) decline; **z~en** *vi unreg* disinte-

grate, decay; (*sich gliedern*) fall (*in +akk* into).

zerfetzen [tserfet'sən] *vt* tear to pieces.

zerfleischen [tserfli'shən] *vt* = **zerfetzen**.

zerflie'ßen *vi unreg* dissolve, melt away.

zerfres'sen *vt unreg* eat away; (*Motten, Mäuse etc*) eat.

zerge'hen *vi unreg* melt, dissolve.

zerkleinern [tserkli'nərn] *vt* reduce to small pieces.

zerklüftet [tserklüf'tət] *a*: **tief ~es Gestein** deeply fissured rock.

zerknirscht [tserknirsht'] *a* overcome with remorse.

zerknüllen [tserknü'lən] *vt* crumple up.

zerlau'fen *vi unreg* melt.

zerlegbar [tserlā:k'bâr] *a* able to be dismantled.

zerle'gen *vt* take to pieces; (*Fleisch*) carve; (*Satz*) analyse.

zerlumpt [tserlŏompt'] *a* ragged.

zermalmen [tsermál'mən] *vt* crush.

zermürben [tsermür'bən] *vt* wear down.

zerpflü'cken *vt* (*lit, fig*) pick to pieces.

zerplat'zen *vi* burst.

zerquet'schen *vt* squash.

Zerrbild [tser'bilt] *nt* (*fig*) caricature, distorted picture.

zerre'den *vt* (*Problem*) flog to death.

zerrei'ben *vt unreg* grind down.

zerrei'ßen *unreg vt* tear to pieces, dismantle ♦ *vi* tear, rip.

Zerreißprobe *f* (*lit*) pull test; (*fig*) real test.

zerren [tse'rən] *vt* drag ♦ *vi* tuʒ (*an +dat* at).

zerrin'nen *vi unreg* melt away; (*Geld*) disappear.

zerrissen [tserri'sən] *a* torn, tattered ♦ *pp von* **zerreißen**; **Z~heit** *f* tattered state; (*POL*) disunion, discord; (*innere*) disintegration.

Zerrspiegel [tser'shpē:gəl] *m* (*lit*) distorting mirror; (*fig*) travesty.

Zerrung *f*: **eine ~** a pulled ligament *od* muscle.

zerrütten [tserrü'tən] *vt* wreck, destroy.

zerrüttet *a* wrecked, shattered.

Zerrüttungsprinzip *nt* (*Ehescheidung*) principle of irretrievable breakdown.

zerschellen [tsershe'lən] *vi* (*Schiff, Flugzeug*) be smashed to pieces.

zerschie'ßen *vt unreg* shoot to pieces.

zerschla'gen *unreg vt* shatter, smash; (*fig: Opposition*) crush; (: *Vereinigung*) break up ♦ *vr* fall through.

zerschleißen [tsershli'sən] *vti unreg* wear out.

zerschmel'zen *vi unreg* melt.

zerschmet'tern *vti* shatter; (*Feind*) crush.

zerschnei'den *vt unreg* cut up.

zerset'zen *vtr* decompose, dissolve.

zersetzend *a* (*fig*) subversive.

zersplittern [tsershpli'tərn] *vti* split (into pieces); (*Glas*) shatter.

zerspring'en *vi unreg* shatter; (*fig*) burst.

zerstäuben [tsershtoi'bən] *vt* spray.

Zerstäuber *m* **-s, -** atomizer.

zerstö'ren *vt* destroy.

Zerstörer *m* **-s, -** (*NAUT*) destroyer.

Zerstörung *f* destruction.

Zerstörungswut *f* destructive mania.

zersto'ßen *vt unreg* pound, pulverize.

zerstrei'ten *vr unreg* fall out, break up.

zerstreu'en *vt* disperse, scatter; (*Zweifel etc*) dispel ♦ *vr* (*sich verteilen*) scatter; (*fig*) be dispelled; (*sich ablenken*) take one's mind off things.

zerstreut *a* scattered; (*Mensch*) absentminded; **Z~heit** *f* absent-mindedness.

Zerstreuung *f* dispersion; (*Ablenkung*) diversion.

zerstrit'ten *a*: **mit jdm ~ sein** be on very bad terms with sb.

zerstückeln [tsershtü'kəln] *vt* cut into pieces.

zertei'len *vt* divide into parts.

Zertifikat [tsertēfēkât'] *nt* **-(e)s, -e** certificate.

zertre'ten *vt unreg* crush underfoot.

zertrümmern [tsertrü'mərn] *vt* shatter; (*Gebäude etc*) demolish.

zerwüh'len *vt* ruffle up, tousle; (*Bett*) rumple (up).

Zerwürfnis [tservürf'nis] *nt* **-ses, -se** dissension, quarrel.

zerzausen [tsertsou'zən] *vt* (*Haare*) ruffle up, tousle.

Zessionar [tsesēōnâr'] *m* assignee.

zetern [tsā:'tərn] *vi* (*pej*) clamor (*US*), clamour (*Brit*); (*keifen*) scold.

Zettel [tse'təl] *m* **-s, -** piece *od* slip of paper; (*Notiz~*) note; (*Formular*) form; „~ **ankleben verboten"** "post no bills"; **~kasten** *m* card index (box); **~wirtschaft** *f* (*pej*): **eine ~wirtschaft haben** have bits of paper everywhere.

Zeug [tsoik] *nt* **-(e)s, -e** (*umg*) stuff; (*Ausrüstung*) gear; **dummes ~** (stupid) nonsense; **das ~ haben zu** have the makings of; **sich ins ~ legen** put one's shoulder to the wheel; **was das ~ hält** for all one is worth; **jdm am ~ flicken** find fault with sb.

Zeuge [tsoi'gə] *m* **-n, -n, Zeugin** *f* witness.

zeugen *vi* bear witness, testify; **es zeugt von ...** it testifies to ... ♦ *vt* (*Kind*) father.

Zeugen- *zW*: **~aussage** *f* evidence; **~stand** *m* witness stand.

Zeugnis [tsoig'nis] *nt* **-ses, -se** certificate; (*SCH*) report; (*Referenz*) reference; (*Aussage*) evidence, testimony; **~ geben von** be evidence of, testify to; **~konferenz** *f* (*SCH*) staff meeting to decide on grades etc.

Zeugung [tsoi'gŏong] *f* procreation.

zeu'gungs'unfähig *a* sterile.

z.H. *abk* (= *zu Händen*) att., attn.

ZH *abk* = **Zentralheizung**.

z.H(d). *abk* (= *zu Händen*) att., attn.

Zicken [tsi'kən] *pl* (*umg*): **~ machen** make trouble.

zickig *a* (*albern*) silly; (*prüde*) prudish.

Zickzack [tsik'tsák] *m* **-(e)s, -e** zigzag.

Ziege [tsē:'gə] *f* **-, -n** goat; (*pej umg: Frau*)

cow (!).
Ziegel [tsē:'gəl] *m* **-s**, - brick; (*Dach~*) tile.
Ziegelei [tsē:gəlī'] *f* brickworks.
Ziegelstein *m* brick.
Ziegen- *zW*: **~bock** *m* billy goat; **~leder** *nt* kid.
Ziegenpeter *m* mumps *sing*.
zieh [tsē:] *imperf von* **zeihen**.
Ziehbrunnen *m* well.
ziehen [tsē:'ən] *unreg vt* draw; (*zerren*) pull; (*SCHACH etc*) move; (*züchten*) rear; **etw nach sich ~** lead to sth, entail sth; **etw ins Lächerliche ~** ridicule sth; **so was zieht bei mir nicht** I don't like that sort of thing ♦ *vi* draw; (*um~, wandern*) move; (*Rauch, Wolke etc*) drift; (*reißen*) pull; **zu jdm ~** move in with sb ♦ *v unpers*: **es zieht** there is a draft (*US*) *od* draught (*Brit*), it's drafty (*US*) *od* draughty (*Brit*); **mir zieht's im Rücken** my back hurts ♦ *vr* (*Gummi*) stretch; (*Grenze etc*) run; (*Gespräche etc*) be drawn out.
Ziehen *nt* **-s**, - (*Schmerz*) ache; (*im Unterleib*) dragging pain.
Ziehharmonika [tsē:'hármō:nēkà] *f* concertina; accordion.
Ziehung [tsē:'ŏŏng] *f* (*Los~*) drawing.
Ziel [tsē:l] *nt* **-(e)s**, **-e** (*einer Reise*) destination; (*SPORT*) finish; (*MIL*) target; (*Absicht*) goal, aim; **jdm/sich ein ~ stecken** set sb/ o.s. a goal; **am ~ sein** be at one's destination; (*fig*) have reached one's goal; **über das ~ hinausschießen** (*fig*) overshoot the mark; **z~bewußt** *a* purposeful; **z~en** *vi* aim (*auf +akk* at); **~fernrohr** *nt* telescopic sight; **~gruppe** *f* target group; **~linie** *f* (*SPORT*) finishing line; **z~los** *a* aimless; **~ort** *m* destination; **~scheibe** *f* target; **z~strebig** *a* purposeful.
ziemen [tsē:'mən] *vr unpers* (*geh*): **das ziemt sich nicht (für dich)** it is not proper (for you).
ziemlich [tsē:m'liċh] *a attr* (*Anzahl*) fair; **eine ~e Anstrengung** quite an effort ♦ *ad* quite, pretty (*umg*); (*beinahe*) almost, nearly; **~ lange** quite a long time; **~ fertig** almost *od* nearly ready.
Zierde [tsē:r'də] *f* **-**, **-n** ornament, decoration; (*Schmuckstück*) adornment.
zieren [tsē:'rən] *vr* act coy.
Zierleiste *f* border; (*an Wand, Möbeln*) molding (*US*), moulding (*Brit*); (*an Auto*) trim.
zierlich *a* dainty; **Z~keit** *f* daintiness.
Zierstrauch *m* flowering shrub.
Ziff. *abk* = **Ziffer**.
Ziffer [tsi'fər] *f* **-**, **-n** figure, digit; **römische/ arabische ~n** roman/arabic numerals; **~blatt** *nt* dial, clock face.
zig [tsik] *a* (*umg*) umpteen.
Zigarette [tsēgàrɛ'tə] *f* cigarette.
Zigaretten- *zW*: **~automat** *m* cigarette machine; **~pause** *f* break for a cigarette; **~schachtel** *f* cigarette packet *od* pack (*US*); **~spitze** *f* cigarette holder.

Zigarillo [tsēgàri'lō] *nt od m* **-s**, **-s** cigarillo.
Zigarre [tsēgà'rə] *f* **-**, **-n** cigar.
Zigeuner(in *f*) [tsēgoi'nər(in)] *m* **-s**, - gipsy; **~schnitzel** *nt* (*KOCH*) *cutlet served in a spicy sauce with green and red peppers*; **~sprache** *f* Romany, Romany *od* Gypsy language.
Zimbabwe [tsimbá'bŏŏà] *nt* **-s** Zimbabwe.
Zimmer [tsi'mər] *nt* **-s**, - room; **~antenne** *f* indoor antenna (*US*) *od* aerial (*Brit*); **~decke** *f* ceiling; **~lautstärke** *f* reasonable volume; **~mädchen** *nt* chambermaid; **~mann** *m*, *pl* **-leute** carpenter.
zimmern *vt* make from wood.
Zimmer- *zW*: **~pflanze** *f* indoor plant; **~vermittlung** *f* accommodations (*US*) *od* accommodation (*Brit*) service.
zimperlich [tsim'pərliċh] *a* squeamish; (*pingelig*) fussy, finicky.
Zimt [tsimt] *m* **-(e)s**, **-e** cinnamon; **~stange** *f* cinnamon stick.
Zink [tsingk'] *nt* **-(e)s** zinc.
Zinke *f* **-**, **-n** (*Gabel~*) prong; (*Kamm~*) tooth.
zinken *vt* (*Karten*) mark.
Zinken *m* **-s**, - (*umg: Nase*) shnozzle, hooter (*Brit*).
Zinksalbe *f* zinc ointment.
Zinn [tsin] *nt* **-(e)s** (*Element*) tin; (*in ~waren*) pewter; **~becher** *m* pewter tankard.
zinnoberrot [tsinō:'bərrōt] *a* vermilion.
Zinn- *zW*: **~soldat** *m* tin soldier; **~waren** *pl* pewter *sing*.
Zins [tsins] *m* **-es**, **-en** interest.
Zinseszins *m* compound interest.
Zins- *zW*: **~fuß** *m* rate of interest; **z~los** *a* interest-free; **~satz** *m* rate of interest.
Zionismus [tsēōnis'mŏŏs] *m* Zionism.
Zipfel [tsip'fəl] *m* **-s**, - corner; (*von Land*) tip; (*Hemd~*) tail; (*Wurst~*) end; **~mütze** *f* pointed cap.
zirka [tsir'kà] *ad* (round) about.
Zirkel [tsir'kəl] *m* **-s**, - circle; (*MATH*) pair of compasses; **~kasten** *m* geometry set.
zirkulieren [tsirkōōlē:'rən] *vi* circulate.
Zirkus [tsir'kŏŏs] *m* **-**, **-se** circus; (*umg: Getue*) fuss, to-do.
zirpen [tsir'pən] *vi* chirp, cheep.
Zirrhose [tsirō:'zə] *f* **-**, **-n** cirrhosis.
zischeln [tsi'shəln] *vti* whisper.
zischen [tsi'shən] *vi* hiss; (*Limonade*) fizz; (*Fett*) sizzle.
Zitat [tsētát'] *nt* **-(e)s**, **-e** quotation, quote.
zitieren [tsētē:'rən] *vt* quote; (*vorladen, rufen*) summon (*vor +akk* before).
Zitronat [tsētrōnát'] *nt* **-(e)s**, **-e** candied lemon peel.
Zitrone [tsētrō:'nə] *f* **-**, **-n** lemon.
Zitronen- *zW*: **~limonade** *f* lemonade; **~saft** *m* lemon juice; **~säure** *f* citric acid; **~scheibe** *f* lemon slice.
zitt(e)rig [tsit'(ə)riċh] *a* shaky.
zittern [tsi'tərn] *vi* tremble; **vor jdm ~** be

terrified of sb.

Zitze [tsĭtsə] f -, -n teat, dug.

Zivi [tsḗ'vē] m -s, -s abk = **Zivildienstleistender**.

zivil [tsḗvē:l'] a civilian; (anständig) civil; (Preis) moderate; **~er Ungehorsam** civil disobedience; **Z~** nt -s plain clothes pl; (MIL) civilian clothing; **Z~bevölkerung** f civilian population; **Z~courage** f courage of one's convictions; **Z~dienst** m alternative service (for conscientious objectors); **Z~dienstleistender** m conscientious objector doing alternative service in the community.

Zivilisation [tsḗvēlēzátsēō:n'] f civilization.

Zivilisations- zW: **~erscheinung** f phenomenon of civilization; **~krankheit** f disease of civilized man.

zivilisieren [tsḗvēlēzē:'rən] vt civilize.

Zivilist [tsḗvēlist'] m civilian.

Zivilrecht nt civil law.

ZK nt -s, -s abk (= Zentralkomitee) central committee.

ZKB abk (in Zeitungsannonce) = Zimmer, Küche, Bad.

Zobel [tsō:'bəl] m -s, - (auch: **~pelz**) sable (fur).

Zofe [tsō:'fə] f -, -n lady's maid; (von Königin) lady-in-waiting.

zog [tsō:k] imperf von **ziehen**.

zögern [tsœ'gərn] vi hesitate.

Zölibat [tsœlēbát'] nt od m -(e)s celibacy.

Zoll [tsol] m -(e)s, ⁼e customs pl; (Abgabe) duty ♦ m -(e)s, - (Maß) inch; **~abfertigung** f customs clearance; **~amt** nt customs office; **~beamte(r)** m customs official; **~erklärung** f customs declaration; **z~frei** a duty-free; **~gutlager** nt bonded warehouse; **z~pflichtig** a liable to duty, dutiable; **~stock** m inch rule.

Zone [tsō:'nə] f -, -n zone.

Zonen- zW: **~grenze** f: **die ~grenze** (umg) the border (with East Germany); **~randgebiet** nt border area (with East Germany).

Zoo [tsō:] m -s, -s zoo.

Zoologe [tsōōlō:'gə] m -n, -n, **Zoologin** f zoologist.

Zoologie' f zoology.

zoolo'gisch a zoological.

Zoom [zō̄:m] nt -s, -s zoom shot; (Objektiv) zoom lens.

Zopf [tsopf] m -(e)s, ⁼e plait; pigtail; **alter ~** antiquated custom.

Zorn [tsorn] m -(e)s anger.

zornig a angry.

Zote [tsō:'tə] f -, -n dirty joke od remark.

zottig [tso'tiċh] a shaggy.

ZPO abk (= Zivilprozeßordnung) code of civil procedure, ≈ General Practice Act (US).

z.R. abk (= zur Rücksprache) for consultation.

Zs. abk = **Zeitschrift; Zusammensetzung**.

z.T. abk = **zum Teil**.

Ztg. abk = **Zeitung**.

Ztschr. abk = **Zeitschrift**.

zu [tsō̄:] präp +dat (bei Richtung, Vorgang) to; (bei Orts-, Zeit-, Preisangabe) at; (Zweck) for; (Zusatz, Zusammengehörigkeit) with; **bis ~** as far as; **sich ~ jdm setzen** sit down beside od next to sb; **Ausstellung ~m Jahrestag der Revolution** exhibition to mark the anniversary of the revolution; **~ seinem Besten** for his own good; **drei ~ zwei** (SPORT) three two; **~m Fenster herein** through the window; **~ meiner Zeit** in my time ♦ ad too; (in Richtung) towards (sb/sth); man ~ (an Hähnen) on, off ♦ a (umg) shut ♦ kj (mit Infinitiv) to; (mit Partizip): **hoch ~ bezahlende Rechnungen** outstanding bills.

zualler- [tsō̄á'lər] zW: **~erst'** ad first of all; **~letzt'** ad last of all.

zubauen [tsō̄:'bouən] vt (Lücke) fill in; (Platz, Gebäude) build up.

Zubehör [tsō̄:'bəhœr] nt -(e)s, -e accessories pl.

Zuber [tsō̄:'bər] m -s, - tub.

zubereiten [tsō̄:'bərītən] vt prepare.

zubilligen [tsō̄:'biligən] vt grant.

zubinden [tsō̄:'bindən] vt unreg tie up; **jdm die Augen ~** blindfold sb.

zubleiben [tsō̄:'blībən] vi unreg (umg) stay shut.

zubringen [tsō̄:'bringən] vt unreg spend; (herbeibringen) bring to, take to; (umg: Tür) get shut.

Zubringer m -s, - (TECH) feeder, conveyor; (zum Flughafen) airport bus; **~(bus)** m shuttle (bus); **~straße** f entrance ramp (US), slip road (Brit).

Zucht [tsō̄kht] f -, -en (von Tieren) breeding; (von Pflanzen) cultivation; (Rasse) breed; (Erziehung) raising; (Disziplin) discipline; **~bulle** m breeding bull.

züchten [tsüċh'tən] vt (Tiere) breed; (Pflanzen) cultivate, grow.

Züchter(in f) m -s, - breeder; grower.

Zuchthaus nt prison, penitentiary (US).

Zuchthengst m stallion, stud.

züchtig [tsüċh'tiċh] a modest, demure.

züchtigen [tsüċh'tigən] vt chastise.

Züchtigung f chastisement; **körperliche ~** corporal punishment.

Zuchtperle f cultured pearl.

zucken [tsō̄'kən] vi jerk, twitch; (Strahl etc) flicker; **der Schmerz zuckte (mir) durch den ganzen Körper** the pain shot right through my body ♦ vt shrug.

zücken [tsü'kən] vt (Schwert) draw; (Geldbeutel) pull out.

Zucker [tsō̄'kər] m -s, - sugar; (MED) diabetes; **~ haben** be a diabetic; **~dose** f sugar bowl; **~guß** m icing; **~hut** m sugar loaf; **z~krank** a diabetic; **~lecken** nt: **das ist kein ~lecken** (umg) it's no picnic.

zuckern vt sugar.

Zucker- zW: **~rohr** nt sugar cane; **~rübe** f sugar beet; **~spiegel** m (MED) (blood) sugar level; ~**watte** f cotton candy (US), candy-floss (Brit).

Zuckung f convulsion, spasm; (leicht) twitch.

zudecken [tsoo:'dekən] vt cover (up); (im Bett) tuck up od in.

zudem [tsoodā:m'] ad in addition (to this).

zudrehen [tsoo:'drā:ən] vt turn off.

zudringlich [tsoo:'dringliсh] a forward, pushy; (Nachbar etc) intrusive; ~ **werden** make advances (zu to); **Z~keit** f forwardness; intrusiveness.

zudrücken [tsoo:'drükən] vt close; **jdm die Kehle** ~ throttle sb; **ein Auge** ~ turn a blind eye.

zueinander [tsooīnán'dər] ad to one other; (in Verbindung) together.

zuerkennen [tsoo:'erkenən] vt unreg award (jdm etw sth to sb, sb sth).

zuerst [tsooā:rst'] ad first; (zu Anfang) at first; ~ **einmal** first of all.

Zufahrt [tsoo:'fârt] f approach; „**keine** ~ **zum Krankenhaus**" "no access to hospital".

Zufahrtsstraße f approach road; (von Autobahn etc) entrance ramp (US), slip road (Brit).

Zufall [tsoo:'fál] m chance; (Ereignis) coincidence; **durch** ~ by accident; **so ein** ~! what a coincidence!

zufallen vi unreg close, shut; (Anteil, Aufgabe) fall (jdm to sb).

zufällig [tsoo:'feliсh] a chance ♦ ad by chance; (in Frage) by any chance.

Zufallstreffer m **-s, -** lucky shot.

zufassen [tsoo:'fásən] vi (zugreifen) take hold (of it od them); (fig: schnell handeln) seize the opportunity; (helfen) lend a hand.

zufliegen [tsoo:'flē:gən] vi unreg: **ihm fliegt alles nur so zu** (fig) everything comes so easily to him.

Zuflucht [tsoo:'flooсht] f recourse; (Ort) refuge; **zu etw** ~ **nehmen** (fig) resort to sth.

Zufluchtsstätte f place of refuge.

Zufluß [tsoo:'floos] m (Zufließen) inflow, influx; (GEOG) tributary; (COMM) supply.

zufolge [tsoofol'gə] präp +dat od gen judging by; (laut) according to; (aufgrund) as a result of.

zufrieden [tsoofrē:'dən] a satisfied, content(ed); **er ist mit nichts** ~ nothing pleases him; **~geben** vr unreg: **sich mit etw ~geben** be satisfied with sth; **Z~heit** f satisfaction, contentedness; **~lassen** vt unreg: **laß mich damit** ~! (umg) shut up about it!; **~stellen** vt satisfy.

zufrieren [tsoo:'frē:rən] vi unreg freeze up od over.

zufügen [tsoo:'fü:gən] vt add (dat to); (Leid etc) cause (jdm etw sth to sb).

Zufuhr [tsoo:'foo:r] f **-, -en** (Herbeibringen) supplying; (MET) influx; (MIL) supplies pl.

zuführen [tsoo:'fü:rən] vt (bringen) bring; (transportieren) convey; (versorgen) supply ♦ vi: **auf etw** (akk) ~ lead to sth.

Zug [tsoo:k] m **-(e)s, ̈-e** (Eisenbahn~) train; (Luft~) draft (US), draught (Brit); (ziehen) pull(ing); (Gesichts~) feature; (SCHACH etc) move; (Klingel~) pull; (Schrift~, beim Schwimmen) stroke; (Atem~) breath; (Charakter~) trait; (an Zigarette) puff, pull, drag; (Schluck) gulp; (Menschengruppe) procession; (von Vögeln) flight; migration; (MIL) platoon; **etw in vollen ̈-en genießen** enjoy sth to the full; **in den letzten ̈-en liegen** (umg) be at one's last gasp; **im** ~**(e)** (im Verlauf) in the course (gen of); ~ **um** ~ (fig) step by step; **zum** ~**(e) kommen** (umg) get a chance; **etw in groben ̈-en darstellen** od **umreißen** outline sth; **das war kein schöner** ~ **von dir** that wasn't nice of you.

Zugabe [tsoo:'gábə] f extra; (in Konzert etc) encore.

Zug'abteil nt train compartment.

Zugang [tsoo:'gáng] m access, approach.

zugänglich [tsoo:'gengliсh] a accessible; (öffentliche Einrichtungen) open; (Mensch) approachable.

Zug- zW: **~begleiter** m (EISENB) conductor (US), guard (Brit); (: Fahrplan) timetable; **~brücke** f drawbridge.

zugeben [tsoo:'gā:bən] vt unreg (beifügen) add, throw in; (zugestehen) admit; (erlauben) permit; **zugegeben** granted.

zugegebenermaßen [tsoo:'gə:gā:bənərmā'sən] ad admittedly.

zugegen [tsoogā:'gən] ad (geh): ~ **sein** be present.

zugehen [tsoo:'gā:ən] unreg vi (schließen) shut; **auf jdn/etw** ~ walk towards sb/sth; **dem Ende** ~ be finishing; **er geht schon auf die Siebzig zu** he's getting on for seventy; **hier geht es nicht mit rechten Dingen zu** there's something odd going on here ♦ vi unpers (sich ereignen) go on, proceed; **dort geht es ... zu** things are ... there.

Zugehörigkeit [tsoo:'gəhœriсhkīt] f membership (zu of), belonging (zu to).

Zugehörigkeitsgefühl nt feeling of belonging.

zugeknöpft [tsoo:'gəknēpft] a (umg) reserved, stand-offish.

Zügel [tsü:'gəl] m **-s, -** rein(s); (fig auch) curb; **die** ~ **locker lassen** slacken one's hold on the reins; (fig) give free rein (bei to).

zugelassen [tsoo:'gálásən] a authorized; (Heilpraktiker) registered; (Kfz) licensed.

Zügel- zW: **z~los** a unrestrained; (sexuell) licentious; **~losigkeit** f lack of restraint; licentiousness.

zügeln vt curb; (Pferd auch) rein in.

zugesellen vr join (jdm up with).

Zugeständnis [tsoo:'gəshtentnis] nt **-ses, -se** concession; **~se machen** make allowances.

zugestehen vt unreg admit; (Rechte) concede (jdm to sb).

zugetan [tsoo:'gotán] a: **jdm/einer Sache** ~ **sein** be fond of sb/sth.

Zugewinn *m* -(e)s *(JUR) property acquired during marriage.*

Zugezogene(r) [tsōō:'gətsō:gənā(r)] *mf dekl wie a* newcomer.

Zug- *zW:* ~**führer** *m (EISENB)* chief conductor *(US) od* guard *(Brit)*; *(MIL)* platoon commander.

zugig *a* drafty *(US)*, draughty *(Brit)*.

zügig [tsü:'giċḥ] *a* speedy, swift.

zugkräftig *a (fig: Werbeteil, Titel)* eyecatching; *(Schauspieler)* crowd-pulling *attr*, popular.

zugleich [tsōōglīċḥ'] *ad (zur gleichen Zeit)* at the same time; *(ebenso)* both.

Zug- *zW:* ~**luft** *f* draft *(US)*, draught *(Brit)*; ~**maschine** *f* traction engine, tractor.

zugreifen [tsōō:'grīfən] *vi unreg* seize *od* grab; *(helfen)* help; *(beim Essen)* help o.s.

Zugriff [tsōō:'grif] *m (COMPUT)* access; **sich dem ~ der Polizei entziehen** *(fig)* evade justice.

zugrunde [tsōōgrōōn'də] *ad:* ~ **gehen** collapse; *(Mensch)* perish; **er wird daran nicht ~ gehen** he'll survive; *(finanziell)* it won't ruin him; **einer Sache ~ legen** base sth on sth; **einer Sache ~ liegen** be based on sth; ~ **richten** ruin, destroy.

zugunsten [tsōōgoons'tən] *präp +gen od dat* in favor *(US) od* favour *(Brit)* of.

zugute [tsōōgoō:'tə] *ad:* **jdm etw ~ halten** concede sth to sb; **jdm ~ kommen** be of assistance to sb.

Zug- *zW:* ~**verbindung** *f* train connection; ~**vogel** *m* migratory bird; ~**zwang** *m (SCHACH)* zugzwang; **unter ~zwang stehen** *(fig)* be in a tight spot.

zuhalten [tsōō:'hältən] *unreg vt* hold shut; **sich** *(dat)* **die Nase ~** hold one's nose ♦ *vi:* **auf jdn/etw ~** make for sb/sth.

Zuhälter [tsōō:'hcltər] *m* -s, - pimp.

zuhause [tsōōhou'zə] *ad* at home.

Zuhilfenahme [tsōōhil'fənāmə] *f:* **unter ~ von** with the help of.

zuhören [tsōō:'hœrən] *vi* listen *(dat* to).

Zuhörer *m* -s, - listener; ~**schaft** *f* audience.

zujubeln [tsōō:'yōō:bəln] *vi* cheer *(jdm* sb).

zukehren [tsōō:'kā:rən] *vt (zuwenden)* turn.

zuklappen [tsōō:'kläpən] *vt (Buch, Deckel)* close with a bang ♦ *vi aux sein (Tür etc)* click shut.

zukleben [tsōō:'klā:bən] *vt* paste up.

zukneifen [tsōō:'knīfən] *vt (Augen)* screw up; *(Mund)* shut tight(ly).

zuknöpfen [tsōō:'knœpfən] *vt* button up, fasten.

zukommen [tsōō:'komən] *vi unreg* come up *(auf +akk* towards); *(+dat: sich gehören)* be fitting *(jdm* for sb); **diesem Treffen kommt große Bedeutung zu** this meeting is of the utmost importance; **jdm etw ~ lassen** give sb sth; **die Dinge auf sich** *(akk)* ~ **lassen** take things as they come.

Zukunft [tsōō:'kōōnft] *f* -, **Zukünfte** future.

zukünftig [tsōō:'künftiċḥ] *a* future; **mein ~er**

Mann my husband-to-be ♦ *ad* in future.

Zukunfts- *zW:* ~**aussichten** *pl* future prospects *pl*; ~**musik** *f (umg)* wishful thinking; ~**roman** *m* science-fiction novel; **z~trächtig** *a* promising for the future; **z~weisend** *a* trend-setting.

Zulage [tsōō:'lāgə] *f* bonus.

zulande [tsōōlän'də] *ad:* **bei uns ~** in our country.

zulangen [tsōō:'längən] *vi (umg: Dieb, beim Essen)* help o.s.

zulassen [tsōō:'läsən] *vt unreg (hereinlassen)* admit; *(erlauben)* permit; *(Auto)* license; *(umg: nicht öffnen)* keep shut.

zulässig [tsōō:'lcsiċḥ] *a* permissible, permitted; ~**e Höchstgeschwindigkeit** (upper) speed limit.

Zulassung *f (amtlich)* authorization; *(von Kfz)* licensing; *(als praktizierender Arzt)* registration.

Zulauf *m:* **großen ~ haben** *(Geschäft)* be very popular.

zulaufen [tsōō:'loufən] *vi unreg* run *(auf +akk* towards); *(Tier)* adopt *(jdm* sb); **spitz ~** come to a point.

zulegen [tsōō:'lā:gən] *vt* add; *(Geld)* put in; *(Tempo)* accelerate, quicken; *(schließen)* cover over; **sich** *(dat)* **etw ~** *(umg)* get hold of sth.

zuleide [tsōōlī'də] *a:* **jdm etw ~ tun** harm sb.

zuleiten [tsōō:'lītən] *vt (Wasser)* supply; *(schicken)* send.

Zuleitung *f (TECH)* supply.

zuletzt [tsōōlctst'] *ad* finally, at last; **wir blieben bis ~** we stayed to the very end; **nicht ~ wegen** not least because of.

zuliebe [tsōōlī:'bə] *ad:* **jdm ~** to please sb.

Zulieferbetrieb [tsōō:'lc:fərbətrē:p] *m (COMM)* supplier.

zum [tsōōm] = **zu dem**; ~ **dritten Mal** for the third time; ~ **Scherz** as a joke; ~ **Trinken** for drinking; **bis ~ 15. April** until 15th April; *(nicht später als)* by 15th April; ~ **ersten Mal(e)** for the first time; **es ist ~ Weinen** it's enough to make you (want to) weep; ~ **Glück** luckily.

zumachen [tsōō:'mäḥən] *vt* shut; *(Kleidung)* do up, fasten ♦ *vi (umg)* hurry up.

zumal [tsōōmál'] *kj* especially (as).

zumeist [tsōōmīst'] *ad* mostly.

zumessen [tsōō:'mcsən] *vt unreg (Zeit)* allocate *(dat* for); *(Bedeutung)* attach *(dat* to).

zumindest [tsōō:'min'dəst] *ad* at least.

zumutbar [tsōō:'mōō:tbár] *a* reasonable.

zumute [tsōōmōō:'tə] *ad:* **wie ist ihm ~?** how does he feel?

zumuten [tsōō:'mōō:tən] *vt* expect, ask *(jdm* of sb); **sich** *(dat)* **zuviel ~** take on too much.

Zumutung *f* unreasonable expectation *od* demand; *(Unverschämtheit)* impertinence; **das ist eine ~!** that's a bit much!

zunächst [tsōōnc:ċḥst'] *ad* first of all; ~ **ein-**

mal to start with.
zunageln [tsōō:'nágəln] vt (Fenster etc) nail up; (Kiste etc) nail down.
zunähen [tsōō:'nɛːən] vt sew up.
Zunahme [tsōō:'nāmə] f -, -n increase.
Zuname [tsōō:'nāmə] m surname.
zünden [tsün'dən] vi (Feuer) light, ignite; (Motor) fire; (fig) kindle enthusiasm ♦ vt ignite; (Rakete) fire.
zündend a fiery.
Zünder m -s, - fuse; (MIL) detonator.
Zünd- zW: ~**holz** nt match; ~**kabel** nt (AUT) ignition wire; ~**kerze** f (AUT) spark(ing) plug; ~**plättchen** nt cap; ~**schlüssel** m ignition key; ~**schnur** f fuse wire; ~**stoff** m fuel; (fig) dynamite.
Zündung f ignition.
zunehmen [tsōō:'nāːmən] vi unreg increase, grow; (Mensch) put on weight.
zunehmend a: mit ~**em** Alter with advancing age.
zuneigen [tsōō:'nīgən] vi incline, lean; **sich dem Ende** ~ draw to a close; **einer Auffassung** ~ incline towards a view; **jdm zugeneigt sein** be attracted to sb.
Zuneigung f affection.
Zunft [tsōōnft] f -, ⁼e guild.
zünftig [tsünf'tiçh] a (Arbeit) professional; (umg: ordentlich) proper, real.
Zunge [tsōō'ngə] f -, -n tongue; (Fisch) sole; **böse** ~**n behaupten, ...** malicious gossip has it ...
züngeln [tsü'ngəln] vi (Flammen) lick.
Zungen- zW: ~**brecher** m tongue-twister; **z**~**fertig** a glib.
Zünglein [tsüng'līn] nt: **das** ~ **an der Waage sein** (fig) tip the scales.
zunichte [tsōōniçh'tə] ad: ~ **machen** ruin, destroy; ~ **werden** come to nothing.
zunutze [tsōōnōō'tsə] ad: **sich** (dat) **etw** ~ **machen** make use of sth.
zuoberst [tsōō:'oːbərst] ad at the top.
zuordnen [tsōō:'ordnən] vt assign (+dat to).
zupacken [tsōō:'pákən] vi (umg: zugreifen) make a grab for it; (bei der Arbeit) get down to it; **mit** ~ (helfen) give me/them etc a hand.
zupfen [tsōōp'fən] vt pull, pick, pluck; (Gitarre) pluck.
zur [tsōō:r] = **zu der**.
zurechnungsfähig [tsōō:'reçhnōōngsfɛːiçh] a (JUR) responsible, of sound mind; **Z**~**keit** f responsibility, accountability.
zurecht- [tsōō:reçht'] zW: ~**biegen** vt unreg bend into shape; (fig) twist; ~**finden** vr unreg find one's way (about); ~**kommen** vi unreg (rechtzeitig kommen) come in time; (schaffen) cope; (finanziell) manage; ~**legen** vt get ready; (Ausrede etc) have ready; ~**machen** vt prepare; **sich** ~**machen** get ready; (schminken) put on one's make-up; ~**weisen** vt unreg reprimand; **Z**~**weisung** f reprimand, rebuff.
zureden [tsōō:'rāːdən] vi persuade, urge (jdm

sb).
zureiten [tsōō:'rītən] vt unreg (Pferd) break in.
Zürich [tsü:'riçh] nt -s Zurich.
zurichten [tsōō:'riçhtən] vt (Essen) prepare; (beschädigen) batter, bash up.
zürnen [tsür'nən] vi be angry (jdm with sb).
zurück [tsōōrük'] ad back; (mit Zahlungen) behind; (fig: ~**geblieben**: von Kind) backward; ~! get back!
zurück- zW: ~**behalten** vt unreg keep back; **er hat Schäden** ~**behalten** he suffered lasting damage; ~**bekommen** vt unreg get back; ~**bezahlen** vt repay, pay back; ~**bleiben** vi unreg (Mensch) remain behind; (nicht nachkommen) fall behind, lag; (Schaden) remain; ~**bringen** vt unreg bring back; ~**drängen** vt (Gefühle) repress; (Feind) push back; ~**drehen** vt turn back; ~**erobern** vt reconquer; ~**erstatten** vt refund; ~**fahren** unreg vi travel back; (vor Schreck) recoil, start ♦ vt drive back; ~**fallen** vi unreg fall back; (in Laster) relapse; (an Besitzer) revert (an +akk to); (in Leistungen) fall behind; ~**finden** vr unreg find one's way back; ~**fordern** vt demand back; ~**führen** vt lead back; **etw auf etw** (akk) ~**führen** trace sth back to sth; ~**geben** vt unreg give back; (antworten) retort with; ~**geblieben** a retarded; ~**gehen** vi unreg go back; (zeitlich) date back (auf +akk to); (fallen) go down, fall; **Waren** ~**gehen lassen** send back goods; ~**gezogen** a retired, withdrawn; ~**greifen** vi unreg (fig) fall back (auf +akk upon); (zeitlich) go back (auf +akk to); ~**halten** unreg vt hold back; (Mensch) restrain; (hindern) prevent ♦ vr (reserviert sein) be reserved; (im Essen) hold back; (im Hintergrund bleiben) keep in the background; (bei Verhandlung) keep a low profile; ~**haltend** a reserved; **Z**~**haltung** f reserve; ~**holen** vt (COMPUT: Daten) retrieve; ~**kehren** vi return; ~**kommen** vi unreg come back; **auf etw** (akk) ~**kommen** return to sth; ~**lassen** vt unreg leave behind; ~**legen** vt put back; (Geld) put by; (reservieren) keep back; (Strecke) cover ♦ vr lie back; ~**liegen** vi unreg: **der Unfall liegt etwa eine Woche** ~ the accident was about a week ago; ~**nehmen** vt unreg take back; ~**reichen** vi (Tradition etc) go back (in +akk to); ~**rufen** vti unreg call back; **etw ins Gedächtnis** ~**rufen** recall sth; ~**schrauben** vt: **seine Ansprüche** ~**schrauben** lower one's sights; ~**schrecken** vi shrink (vor +dat from); **vor nichts** ~**schrecken** stop at nothing; ~**setzen** vt put back; (im Preis) reduce; (benachteiligen) put at a disadvantage ♦ vi (mit Fahrzeug) reverse, back; ~**stecken** vt put back ♦ vi (fig) moderate (one's wishes); ~**stellen** vt put back, replace; (aufschieben) put off, postpone; (MIL) turn down; (Interessen) defer;

(Ware) keep; **persönliche Interessen hinter etw** *(dat)* ~**stellen** put sth before one's personal interests; ~**stoßen** *vt unreg* repulse; ~**stufen** *vt* downgrade; ~**treten** *vi unreg* step back; *(vom Amt)* retire; *(von einem Vertrag etc)* withdraw *(von* from); **gegenüber** *od* **hinter etw** ~**treten** diminish in importance in view of sth; **bitte** ~**treten!** stand back, please!; ~**verfolgen** *vt (fig)* trace back; ~**versetzen** *vt (in alten Zustand)* restore *(in +akk* to) ♦ *vr* think o.s. back *(in +akk* to); ~**weisen** *vt unreg* turn down; *(Mensch)* reject; ~**werfen** *vt unreg (Ball, Kopf)* throw back; *(Strahlen, Schall)* reflect; *(fig: wirtschaftlich)* set back *(um* by); *(Feind)* repel; **Z~zahlung** *f* repayment; ~**ziehen** *unreg vt* pull back; *(Angebot)* withdraw ♦ *vr* retire.

Zuruf [tsoo:'roo:f] *m* shout, cry.

zus. *abk* = **zusammen; zusätzlich.**

Zusage [tsoo:'zågə] *f* promise; *(Annahme)* consent.

zusagen *vt* promise; **jdm etw auf den Kopf** ~ *(umg)* tell sb sth outright ♦ *vi* accept; **jdm** ~ *(gefallen)* agree with *od* please sb.

zusammen [tsoozä'mən] *ad* together.

zusammen- *zW:* **Z~arbeit** *f* cooperation; ~**arbeiten** *vi* cooperate; **Z~ballung** *f* accumulation; ~**bauen** *vt* assemble; ~**beißen** *vt unreg (Zähne)* clench; ~**bleiben** *vi unreg* stay together; ~**brauen** *vt (umg)* concoct ♦ *vr (Gewitter, Unheil etc)* be brewing; ~**brechen** *vi unreg aux sein* ccollapse; *(Mensch auch)* break down; *(Verkehr etc)* come to a standstill; ~**bringen** *vt unreg* bring *od* get together; *(Geld)* get; *(Sätze)* put together; **Z~bruch** *m* collapse; *(auch* COMPUT*)* crash; ~**fahren** *vi unreg* collide; *(erschrecken)* start; ~**fallen** *vi unreg (einstürzen)* collapse; *(Ereignisse)* coincide; ~**fassen** *vt* summarize; *(vereinigen)* unite; ~**fassend** *a* summarizing ♦ *ad* to summarize; **Z~fassung** *f* summary, résumé; ~**finden** *vir unreg* meet (together); ~**fließen** *vi unreg* flow together, meet; **Z~fluß** *m* confluence; ~**fügen** *vt* join (together), unite; ~**führen** *vt* bring together; *(Familie)* reunite; ~**gehören** *vi* belong together; *(Paar)* match; **Z~gehörigkeitsgefühl** *nt* sense of belonging; ~**gesetzt** *a* compound, composite; ~**gewürfelt** *a* motley; ~**halten** *vt unreg* hold together ♦ *vi* hold together; *(Freunde, fig)* stick together; **Z~hang** *m* connection; **im/aus dem Z~hang** in/out of context; **etw aus dem Z~hang reißen** take sth out of its context; ~**hängen** *vi unreg* be connected *od* linked; ~**hängend** *a (Erzählung)* coherent; ~**hang(s)los** *a* incoherent, disjointed; ~**klappbar** *a* folding, collapsible; ~**knüllen** *vt* crumple up; ~**kommen** *vi unreg* meet, assemble; *(sich ereignen)* occur at once *od* together; ~**kramen** *vt* gather (together); **Z~kunft** *f* -, **-künfte** meeting; ~**laufen** *vi un-*

reg run *od* come together; *(Straßen, Flüsse etc)* converge, meet; *(Farben)* run into one another; ~**legen** *vt* put together; *(stapeln)* pile up; *(falten)* fold; *(verbinden)* combine, unite; *(Termine, Fest)* amalgamate; *(Geld)* collect; ~**nehmen** *unreg vt* summon up; **alles** ~**genommen** all in all ♦ *vr* pull o.s. together; ~**passen** *vi* go well together, match; **Z~prall** *m (lit, fig)* collision; clash; ~**prallen** *vi aux sein* collide; ~**reimen** *vt (umg)*: **das kann ich mir nicht** ~**reimen** I can't make head nor tail of this; ~**reißen** *vr unreg* pull o.s. together; ~**rotten** *vr (pej)* gang up *(gegen* against); ~**schlagen** *vt unreg (Mensch)* beat up; *(Dinge)* smash up; *(falten)* fold; *(Hände)* clap; *(Hacken)* click; ~**schließen** *vtr unreg* join (together); **Z~schluß** *m* amalgamation; ~**schmelzen** *vi unreg (verschmelzen)* fuse; *(zerschmelzen)* melt (away); *(Anzahl)* dwindle; ~**schrecken** *vi unreg* start; ~**schreiben** *vt unreg* write together; *(Bericht)* put together; ~**schrumpfen** *vi aux sein* shrink, shrivel up; **Z~sein** *nt* -s get-together; ~**setzen** *vt* put together ♦ *vr* be composed *(aus* of); **sich** ~**setzen aus** consist of; **Z~setzung** *f* composition; ~**spiel** *nt* teamwork; *(von Kräften etc)* interaction; ~**stellen** *vt* put together; compile; **Z~stellung** *f* list; *(Vorgang)* compilation; **Z~stoß** *m* collision; ~**stoßen** *vi unreg aux sein* collide; ~**strömen** *vi aux sein (Menschen)* flock together; ~**tragen** *vt unreg* collect; ~**treffen** *vi unreg aux sein* coincide; *(Menschen)* meet; **Z~treffen** *nt* meeting; *(Zufall)* coincidence; ~**treten** *vi unreg (Verein etc)* meet; ~**wachsen** *vi unreg* grow together; ~**wirken** *vi* combine; ~**zählen** *vt* add up; ~**ziehen** *unreg vt (verengern)* draw together; *(vereinigen)* bring together; *(addieren)* add up ♦ *vr* shrink; *(sich bilden)* form, develop; ~**zucken** *vi aux sein* start.

Zusatz [tsoo:'zåts] *m* addition; ~**antrag** *m (POL)* amendment; ~**gerät** *nt* attachment.

zusätzlich [tsoo:'zetslich] *a* additional.

Zusatzmittel *nt* additive.

zuschauen [tsoo:'shouən] *vi* watch, look on.

Zuschauer *m* -s, - spectator; *pl (THEAT)* audience.

zuschicken [tsoo:'shikən] *vt* send, forward *(jdm etw* sth to sb).

zuschießen [tsoo:'shē:sən] *unreg vt* fire *(dat* at); *(Geld)* put in ♦ *vi*: ~ **auf** *(+akk)* rush towards.

Zuschlag [tsoo:'shlåk] *m* extra charge; *(Erhöhung)* surcharge; *(EISENB)* supplement.

zuschlagen [tsoo:'shlågən] *unreg vt (Tür)* slam; *(Ball)* hit *(jdm* to sb); *(bei Auktion)* knock down; *(Steine etc)* knock into shape ♦ *vi (Fenster, Tür)* shut; *(Mensch)* hit, punch.

Zuschlags- *zW:* ~**karte** *f (EISENB)* supplementary ticket; **z~pflichtig** *a* subject to surcharge.

zuschließen [tsōō:'shlē:sən] *vt unreg* lock (up).

zuschmeißen [tsōō:sh'mīsən] *vt unreg* (*umg*) slam, bang shut.

zuschmieren [tsōō:sh'mē:rən] *vt* (*umg*) smear over; (*Löcher*) fill in.

zuschneiden [tsōō:sh'nīdən] *vt unreg* cut to size; (*NÄHEN*) cut out; **auf etw** (*akk*) **zugeschnitten sein** (*fig*) be geared to sth.

zuschnüren [tsōō:sh'nü:rən] *vt* tie up; **die Angst schnürte ihm die Kehle zu** (*fig*) he was choked with fear.

zuschrauben [tsōō:'shroubən] *vt* screw down *od* up.

zuschreiben [tsōō:'shrībən] *vt unreg* (*fig*) ascribe, attribute; (*COMM*) credit; **das hast du dir selbst zuzuschreiben** you've only got yourself to blame.

Zuschrift [tsōō:'shrift] *f* letter, reply.

zuschulden [tsōōshōōl'dən] *ad:* **sich** (*dat*) **etw ~ kommen lassen** make o.s. guilty of sth.

Zuschuß [tsōō:'shōōs] *m* subsidy, allowance.

Zuschußbetrieb *m* loss-making concern.

zuschütten [tsōō:'shütən] *vt* fill up.

zusehen [tsōō:'ze:ən] *vi unreg* watch (*jdm/ etw* sb/sth); (*dafür sorgen*) take care; (*etw dulden*) sit back (and watch).

zusehends *ad* visibly.

zusenden [tsōō:'zendən] *vt unreg* forward, send on (*jdm etw* sth to sb).

zusetzen [tsōō:'zetsən] *vt* (*beifügen*) add; (*Geld*) lose ♦ *vi:* **jdm ~ harass** sb; (*Krankheit*) take a lot out of sb; (*unter Druck setzen*) lean on sb (*umg*); (*schwer treffen*) hit sb hard.

zusichern [tsōō:'ziċhərn] *vt* assure (*jdm etw* sb of sth).

Zusicherung *f* assurance.

zusperren [tsōō:'shperən] *vt* bar.

zuspielen [tsōō:'shpē:lən] *vti* pass (*jdm* to sb); **jdm etw ~** (*fig*) pass sth on to sb; **etw der Presse ~** leak sth to the press.

zuspitzen [tsōō:'shpitsən] *vt* sharpen ♦ *vr* (*Lage*) become critical.

zusprechen [tsōō:sh'preċhən] *unreg vt* (*zuerkennen*) award (*jdm etw* sb sth, sth to sb); **jdm Trost ~ comfort** sb ♦ *vi* speak (*jdm* to sb); **dem Essen/Alkohol ~ eat/ drink** a lot.

Zuspruch [tsōō:'shprōōkh] *m* encouragement; (*Anklang*) popularity.

Zustand [tsōō:'shtánt] *m* state, condition; **in gutem/schlechtem ~ in good/poor** condition; (*Haus*) in good/bad repair; **Zustände bekommen** *od* **kriegen** (*umg*) have a fit.

zustande [tsōōshtän'də] *ad:* **~ bringen** *vt unreg* bring about; **~ kommen** *vi unreg* come about.

zuständig [tsōō:'shtendiċh] *a* competent, responsible; **Z~keit** *f* competence, responsibility.

Zuständigkeitsbereich *m* area of responsibility.

zustatten [tsōōshtá'tən] *a:* **jdm ~ kommen** (*geh*) come in useful for sb.

zustehen [tsōō:'shtā:ən] *vi unreg:* **jdm ~ be** sb's right.

zusteigen [tsōō:'shtīgən] *vi unreg:* **noch jemand zugestiegen?** (*in Zug*) any more tickets?

zustellen [tsōō:'shtelən] *vt* (*verstellen*) block; (*Post etc*) send.

Zustellung *f* delivery.

zusteuern [tsōō:'shtoiərn] *vi:* **auf etw** (*akk*) **~ head** for sth; (*beim Gespräch*) steer towards sth ♦ *vt* (*beitragen*) contribute (*zu* to).

zustimmen [tsōō:'shtimən] *vi* agree (*dat* to).

Zustimmung *f* agreement; (*Einwilligung*) consent; **allgemeine ~ finden meet** with general approval.

zustoßen [tsōō:'shtō:sən] *vi unreg* (*fig*) happen (*jdm* to sb).

Zustrom [tsōō:'shtrō:m] *m* (*fig: Menschenmenge*) stream (of visitors *etc*); (*hineinströmend*) influx; (*MET*) inflow.

zustürzen [tsōō:'shtürtsən] *vi:* **auf jdn/etw ~ rush** up to sb/sth.

zutage [tsōōtá'gə] *ad:* **~ bringen** bring to light; **~ treten** come to light.

Zutaten [tsōō:'tátən] *pl* ingredients *pl*; (*fig*) accessories *pl*.

zuteil [tsōōtíl'] *ad* (*geh*): **jdm wird etw ~ sb** is granted sth, sth is granted to sb.

zuteilen [tsōō:'tīlən] *vt* allocate, assign.

zutiefst [tsōōtē:fst'] *ad* deeply.

zutragen [tsōō:'trágən] *unreg vt* bring (*jdm etw* sth to sb); (*Klatsch*) tell ♦ *vr* happen.

zuträglich [tsōō:'tre:kliċh] *a* beneficial.

zutrauen [tsōō:'trouən] *vt* credit (*jdm etw* sb with sth); **sich** (*dat*) **nichts ~ have** no confidence in o.s.; **jdm viel ~ think** a lot of sb; **jdm wenig ~ not** think much of sb; **Z~ nt - s trust** (*zu* in); **zu jdm Z~ fassen begin** to trust sb.

zutraulich *a* trusting; (*Tier*) friendly; **Z~keit** *f* trust.

zutreffen [tsōō:'trefən] *vi unreg* be correct; (*gelten*) apply.

zutreffend *a* (*richtig*) accurate; **Z~es bitte unterstreichen** please underline where applicable.

zutrinken [tsōō:'tringkən] *vi unreg* drink to (*jdm* sb).

Zutritt [tsōō:'trit] *m* access; (*Einlaß*) admittance; **kein ~** *od* **~ verboten** no admittance.

zutun [tsōō:'tōō:n] *vt unreg* add; (*schließen*) shut.

Zutun *nt* -s assistance.

zuunterst [tsōōōōn'tərst] *ad* right at the bottom.

zuverlässig [tsōō:'ferlesiċh] *a* reliable; **Z~keit** *f* reliability.

Zuversicht [tsōō:'ferziċht] *f* - confidence; **z~lich** *a* confident; **~lichkeit** *f* confidence.

zuviel [tsōōfē:l'] *ad* too much; (*umg: zu*

viele) too many; **da krieg' ich** ~ (_umg_) I blow my top.
zuvor [tsoͅofoͅːr'] _ad_ before, previously.
zuvorderst [tsoͅofor'dərst] _ad_ right at the front.
zuvorkommen _vi unreg_ anticipate (_jdm_ sb), beat (sb) to it; (_einer Gefahr_) forestall.
zuvorkommend _a_ courteous; (_gefällig_) obliging.
Zuwachs [tsoͅoː'vàks] _m_ **-es** increase, growth; (_umg_) addition.
zuwachsen _vi unreg_ become overgrown; (_Wunde_) heal (up).
Zuwachsrate _f_ rate of increase.
zuwandern [tsoͅoː'vándərn] _vi_ immigrate.
zuwege [tsoͅoͅovaː'gə] _ad_: **etw** ~ **bringen** accomplish sth; **mit etw** ~ **kommen** manage sth; **gut** ~ **sein** be (doing) well.
zuweilen [tsoͅoͅoviː'lən] _ad_ at times, now and then.
zuweisen [tsoͅoː'vīzən] _vt unreg_ assign, allocate (_jdm_ to sb).
zuwenden [tsoͅoː'vendən] _unreg vt_ turn (_dat_ towards); **jdm seine Aufmerksamkeit** ~ give sb one's attention ♦ _vr_ turn (_dat_ to); (_sich widmen_) devote o.s. (_dat_ to).
zuwenig [tsoͅoͅovaː'niçḥ] _ad_ too little; (_umg: zu wenige_) too few.
zuwerfen [tsoͅoː'verfən] _vt unreg_ throw (_jdm_ to sb).
zuwider [tsoͅoͅovēː'dər] _ad_: **etw ist jdm** ~ sb loathes sth, sb finds sth repugnant ♦ _präp_ +_dat_ contrary to; ~**handeln** _vi_ act contrary (_dat_ to); **einem Gesetz** ~**handeln** contravene a law; **Z**~**handlung** _f_ contravention; ~**laufen** _vi unreg_ run counter (_dat_ to).
zuz. _abk_ = **zuzüglich**.
zuzahlen [tsoͅoː'tsàlən] _vt_: **10 Mark** ~ pay another 10 marks.
zuziehen [tsoͅoː'tsēːən] _unreg vt_ (_schließen: Vorhang_) draw, close; (_herbeirufen: Experten_) call in; **sich** (_dat_) **eine Verletzung** ~ (_form_) sustain an injury; **sich** (_dat_) **etw** ~ (_Krankheit_) catch; (_Zorn_) incur ♦ _vi_ move in, come.
Zuzug [tsoͅoː'tsoͅok] _m_ **-(e)s** (_Zustrom_) influx; (_von Familie etc_) move (_nach_ to).
zuzüglich [tsoͅoː'tsüːkliçḥ] _präp_ +_gen_ plus, with the addition of.
zuzwinkern [tsoͅoː'tsvinkərn] _vi_: **jdm** ~ wink at sb.
zw. _abk_ = **zwischen**.
zwang [tsvàng] _imperf von_ **zwingen**.
Zwang _m_ **-(e)s**, ~**e** compulsion; (_Gewalt_) coercion; **gesellschaftliche** ~̃**e** social constraints; **tu dir keinen** ~ **an** don't feel you have to be polite.
zwängen [tsve'ngən] _vtr_ squeeze.
Zwang- _zW_: **z**~**haft** _a_ compulsive; ~**los** _a_ informal; ~**losigkeit** _f_ informality.
Zwangs- _zW_: ~**abgabe** _f_ (_COMM_) compulsory levy; ~**ernährung** _f_ force feeding; ~**jacke** _f_ straitjacket; ~**lage** _f_ predicament, tight corner; **z**~**läufig** _a_ inevitable;

~**maßnahme** _f_ compulsory measure; (_POL_) sanction; ~**vollstreckung** _f_ execution; ~**vorstellung** _f_ (_PSYCH_) obsession; **z**~**weise** _ad_ compulsorily.
zwanzig [tsvàn'tsiçḥ] _num_ twenty.
zwanzigste(r, s) _a_ twentieth.
zwar [tsvàr] _ad_ to be sure, indeed; **das ist** ~ **...**, **aber ...** that may be ... but ...; **und** ~ in fact, actually; **und** ~ **am Sonntag** on Sunday to be precise; **und** ~ **so schnell, daß ...** in fact so quickly that ...
Zweck [tsvek] _m_ **-(e)s, -e** purpose, aim; **es hat keinen** ~, **darüber zu reden** there is no point (in) talking about it; **z**~**dienlich** _a_ practical; (_nützlich_) useful; **z**~**dienliche Hinweise** (any) relevant information.
Zwecke _f_ **-**, **-n** hobnail; (_Heft~_) thumbtack (_US_), drawing pin (_Brit_).
Zweck- _zW_: **z**~**entfremden** _vt untr_ use for another purpose; ~**entfremdung** _f_ misuse; **z**~**frei** _a_ (_Forschung etc_) pure; **z**~**los** _a_ pointless; **z**~**mäßig** _a_ suitable, appropriate; ~**mäßigkeit** _f_ suitability.
zwecks _präp_ +_gen_ (_form_) for (the purpose of).
zweckwidrig _a_ unsuitable.
zwei [tsvī] _num_ two; ~**deutig** _a_ ambiguous; (_unanständig_) suggestive; **Z**~**drittelmehrheit** _f_ (_PARL_) two-thirds majority; ~**eiig** _a_ (_Zwillinge_) non-identical.
zweierlei [tsvī'ərlī] _a_ two kinds _od_ sorts of; ~ **Stoff** two different kinds of material; ~ **zu tun haben** have two different things to do.
zweifach _a_ double.
Zweifel [tsvī'fəl] _m_ **-s**, **-** doubt; **ich bin mir darüber im** ~ I'm in two minds about it; **z**~**haft** _a_ doubtful, dubious; **z**~**los** _a_ doubtless.
zweifeln _vi_ doubt (_an etw_ (_dat_) sth).
Zweifelsfall _m_: **im** ~ in case of doubt.
Zweifron'tenkrieg _m_ war(fare) on two fronts.
Zweig [tsvīk] _m_ **-(e)s, -e** branch; ~**geschäft** _nt_ (_COMM_) branch.
zweigleisig [tsvī'glīziçḥ] _a_: ~ **argumentieren** argue along two different lines.
Zweigstelle _f_ branch (office).
zwei- _zW_: ~**händig** _a_ two-handed; (_MUS_) for two hands; **Z**~**heit** _f_ duality; ~**hundert** _num_ two hundred; **Z**~**kampf** _m_ duel; ~**mal** _ad_ twice; **das lasse ich mir nicht** ~**mal sagen** I don't have to be told twice; ~**motorig** _a_ twin-engined; ~**reihig** _a_ (_Anzug_) double-breasted; **Z**~**samkeit** _f_ togetherness; ~**schneidig** _a_ (_fig_) two-edged; **Z**~**sitzer** _m_ **-s**, **-** two-seater; ~**sprachig** _a_ bilingual; ~**spurig** _a_ (_AUT_) two-lane; **Z**~**spur-(tonband)gerät** _nt_ twin-track (tape) recorder; ~**stellig** _a_ (_Zahl_) two-digit _attr_, with two digits; ~**stimmig** _a_ for two voices.
zweit _ad_: **zu** ~ (_in Paaren_) in twos.
Zweitaktmotor _m_ two-stroke engine.
zweitens _ad_ secondly.
zweite(r, s) _a_ second; **Bürger** ~**r Klasse**

second-class citizen(s *pl*); ~r Hand (*wissen*) second hand.

zweit- |tsvīt'| *zW*: ~größ'te(r, s) *a* second largest; ~klassig *a* second-class; ~letz'te(r, s) *a* last but one, penultimate; ~rangig *a* second-rate; Z~stimme *f* second vote.

zweitürig |tsvī'türicḥ| *a* two-door.

Zweitwagen *m* second car.

Zwei- *zW*: z~zeilig *a* two-lined; (*TYP: Abstand*) double-spaced; ~zimmerwohnung *f* two-room(ed) apartment.

Zwerchfell |tsvercḥ'fcl| *nt* diaphragm.

Zwerg(in *f)* |tsverk, tsver'gin| *m* -(e)s, -e dwarf; (*fig: Knirps*) midget; ~schule *f* (*umg*) village school.

Zwetschge |tsvetsh'gə| *f* -, -n plum.

Zwickel |tsvi'kəl| *m* -s, - gusset.

zwicken |tsvi'kən| *vt* pinch, nip.

Zwickmühle |tsvik'mü:lə| *f*: in der ~ sitzen (*fig*) be in a dilemma.

Zwieback |tsvē:'bák| *m* -(e)s, -e *od* -bäcke rusk.

Zwiebel |tsvē:'bəl| *f* -, -n onion; (*Blumen~*) bulb; z~artig *a* bulbous; ~turm *m* onion-shaped dome.

Zwie- |tsvē:'| *zW*: ~gespräch *nt* dialogue, dialog (*US*); ~licht *nt* twilight; ins ~licht geraten sein (*fig*) appear in an unfavorable light; z~lichtig *a* shady, dubious; ~spalt *m* conflict; (*zwischen Menschen*) rift, gulf; z~spältig *a* (*Gefühle*) conflicting; (*Charakter*) contradictory; ~tracht *f* discord, dissension.

Zwilling |tsvi'ling| *m* -s, -e twin; ~e *pl* (*ASTROL*) Gemini.

zwingen |tsvi'ngən| *vt unreg* force.

zwingend *a* (*Grund etc*) compelling; (*logisch notwendig*) necessary; (*Schluß, Beweis*) conclusive.

Zwinger *m* -s, - (*Käfig*) cage; (*Hunde~*) run.

zwinkern |tsving'kərn| *vi* blink; (*absichtlich*) wink.

Zwirn |tsvirn| *m* -(e)s, -e thread.

zwischen |tsvi'shən| *präp* +*akk od dat* between; (*bei mehreren*) among.

zwischen- *zW*: Z~aufenthalt *m* stopover; Z~bemerkung *f* (incidental) remark; Z~bilanz *f* (*COMM*) interim balance; ~blenden *vt* (*FILM, RAD, TV*) insert;

Z~ding *nt* cross; Z~dividende *f* interim dividend; ~durch |-dōōrcḥ'| *ad* in between; (*räumlich*) here and there; Z~ergebnis *nt* intermediate result; Z~fall *m* incident; Z~frage *f* question; Z~gas *nt*: Z~gas geben double-declutch; Z~größe *f* in-between size; Z~handel *m* wholesaling; Z~händler *m* middleman, agent; Z~lagerung *f* temporary storage; Z~landung *f* (*AVIAT*) stopover; Z~lösung *f* temporary solution; ~menschlich *a* interpersonal; Z~prüfung *f* intermediate examination; Z~raum *m* gap, space; Z~ruf *m* interjection, interruption; Z~rufe *pl* heckling *sing*; Z~spiel *nt* (*THEAT, fig*) interlude; (*MUS*) intermezzo; ~staatlich *a* interstate; (*international*) international; Z~station *f* intermediate station; Z~stecker *m* (*ELEK*) adapter; Z~stück *nt* connecting piece; Z~summe *f* subtotal; Z~wand *f* partition; Z~zeit *f* interval; in der Z~zeit in the interim, meanwhile; Z~zeugnis *nt* (*SCH*) interim report.

Zwist |tsvist| *m* -es, -e dispute.

zwitschern |tsvit'shərn| *vti* twitter, chirp; einen ~ (*umg*) have a drink.

Zwitter |tsvi'tər| *m* -s, - hermaphrodite.

zwölf |tsvœlf| *num* twelve; fünf Minuten vor ~ (*fig*) at the eleventh hour.

Zwölffingerdarm *m* -(e)s duodenum.

z.w.V. *abk* (= *zur weiteren Veranlassung*) for appropriate action.

Zyankali |tsüänkä'lē| *nt* -s (*CHEM*) potassium cyanide.

Zyklon |tsüklō:n'| *m* -s, -e cyclone.

Zyklus |tsü:'klōōs| *m* -, Zyklen cycle.

Zylinder |tsēlin'dər| *m* -s, - cylinder; (*Hut*) top hat; z~förmig *a* cylindrical.

Zyniker(in *f)* |tsü:'nēkər(in)| *m* -s, - cynic.

zynisch |tsü:'nish| *a* cynical.

Zynismus |tsünis'mōōs| *m* cynicism.

Zypern |tsü:'pərn| *nt* -s Cyprus.

Zypresse |tsüpre'sə| *f* -, -n (*BOT*) cypress.

Zypriot(in *f)* |tsüprēō:t'(in)| *m* -en, -en Cypriot.

zypriotisch, zyprisch |tsü:'prish| *a* Cypriot, Cyprian.

Zyste |tsüs'tə| *f* -, -n cyst.

z.Z(t). *abk* = zur Zeit.

ENGLISH-GERMAN
ENGLISCH-DEUTSCH

A

A, a [ā] *n* (*letter*) A *nt*, a *nt*; **A for Able** ≈ A wie Anton.

a *abbr* = **acre.**

A [ā] *n abbr* (*SCH*: *mark*) ≈ 1.

a, an [ā, ə, an, ən] *indef art* ein/eine/ein; ~ **mirror/lamp** ein Spiegel/eine Lampe; **an apple**, ~ **pear** ein Apfel, eine Birne; **$5** ~ **meter** 5 Dollar pro *or* das Meter; **I haven't got** ~ **car** ich habe kein Auto; **he's** ~ **doctor** er ist Arzt; **3 times** ~ **month** dreimal im Monat.

AA *n abbr* (*US*: = *Associate in/of Arts*) akademischer Grad; (*Brit*: = *Automobile Association*) ≈ ADAC *m*; (= *Alcoholics Anonymous*) ≈ Anonyme Alkoholiker.

AAA [trip'əlā] *n abbr* (= *American Automobile Association*) ≈ ADAC *m*; (*Brit*: = *Amateur Athletics Association*) Amateursportverband.

AAUP *n abbr* (= *American Association of University Professors*) Verband amerikanischer Universitätsprofessoren.

AB *abbr* = **able-bodied seaman**; (*Canada*) = *Alberta*.

ABA *n abbr* = *American Bankers Association*; *American Bar Association*.

aback [əbak'] *ad*: **to be taken** ~ verblüfft sein.

abandon [əban'dən] *vt* (*give up*) aufgeben; (*desert*) verlassen; **to** ~ **ship** das Schiff verlassen ♦ *n* Hingabe *f*.

abandoned [əban'dənd] *a* (*baby*) ausgesetzt; (*unrestrained*: *manner*) selbstvergessen, hemmungslos; (*house*) verlassen.

abase [əbās'] *vt*: **to** ~ **o.s. so far as to do sth** sich dazu erniedrigen, etw zu tun.

abashed [əbasht'] *a* verlegen.

abate [əbāt'] *vi* nachlassen, sich legen.

abatement [əbāt'mənt] *n* (*of pollution, noise*) Bekämpfung *f*; **noise** ~ **society** Gesellschaft *f* zur Bekämpfung von Lärm.

abattoir [abətwâr'] *n* (*Brit*) Schlachthaus *nt*.

abbey [ab'ē] *n* Abtei *f*.

abbot [ab'ət] *n* Abt *m*.

abbreviate [əbrē'vēāt] *vt* abkürzen.

abbreviation [əbrēvēā'shən] *n* Abkürzung *f*.

ABC [ābēsē'] *n* (*lit, fig*) Abc *nt* ♦ *n abbr* (= *American Broadcasting Company*) ABC *f*.

abdicate [ab'dikāt] *vt* aufgeben ♦ *vi* abdanken.

abdication [abdikā'shən] *n* Abdankung *f*; (*Amts*)niederlegung *f*.

abdomen [ab'dəmən] *n* Unterleib *m*.

abdominal [abdâm'ənəl] *a* Unterleibs-.

abduct [abdukt'] *vt* entführen.

abduction [abduk'shən] *n* Entführung *f*.

aberration [abərā'shən] *n* Anomalie *f*; (*mistake*) Irrtum *m*; (*moral*) Verirrung *f*; **in a moment of mental** ~ in einem Augenblick geistiger Verwirrung.

abet [əbet'] *vt see* **aid.**

abeyance [əbā'əns] *n*: **in** ~ in der Schwebe; (*disuse*) außer Kraft.

abhor [abhôr'] *vt* verabscheuen.

abhorrent [abhôr'ənt] *a* verabscheuungswürdig.

abide [əbīd'] *vt* vertragen; leiden.

abide by *vt fus* sich halten an (+*acc*).

ability [əbil'itē] *n* (*power*) Fähigkeit *f*; (*skill*) Geschicklichkeit *f*; **to the best of my** ~ nach (besten) Kräften.

abject [ab'jekt] *a* (*liar*) übel; (*poverty*) bitter; (*apology*) demütig; (*coward*) unterwürfig.

ablaze [əblāz'] *a* in Flammen; ~ **with lights** hell erleuchtet.

able [ā'bəl] *a* geschickt, fähig; **to be** ~ **to do sth** etw tun können.

able-bodied [ā'bəlbâd'ēd] *a* kräftig; (*MIL*) wehrfähig; ~ **seaman** Vollmatrose *m*.

ably [ā'blē] *ad* geschickt.

ABM *n abbr* (= *antiballistic missile*) ABM *f*.

abnormal [abnôr'məl] *a* regelwidrig, abnorm.

abnormality [abnôrmal'ətē] *n* Regelwidrigkeit *f*; (*condition*) Anormale(s) *nt*; (*instance*) Abnormität *f*; (*MED*) krankhafte Erscheinung *f*.

aboard [əbôrd'] *ad*, *prep* an Bord (+*gen*); ~ **the train** im Zug.

abode [əbōd'] *n* (*old*) Behausung *f*, Aufenthalt *m* (*liter*); (*JUR*) Wohnsitz *m*; **of no fixed** ~ ohne festen Wohnsitz.

abolish [əbâl'ish] *vt* abschaffen.

abolition [abəlish'ən] *n* Abschaffung *f*.

abominable [əbâm'inəbəl] *a*, **abominably** [əbâm'inəbəlē] *ad* scheußlich.

aborigine [abərij'ənē] *n* Ureinwohner *m*.

abort [əbôrt'] *vt* abtreiben; (*miscarry*) fehlgebären; (*COMPUT*) abbrechen, aussteigen.

abortion [əbôr'shən] *n* Abtreibung *f*; (*miscarriage*) Fehlgeburt *f*; **to have an** ~ abtreiben lassen.

abortive [əbôr'tiv] *a* mißlungen.

abound [əbound'] *vi* im Überfluß vorhanden sein; **to** ~ **in** Überfluß haben an (+*dat*).

about [əbout'] *ad* (*nearby*) in der Nähe; (*approximately*) ungefähr; (*around*) umher, herum; **they left all their things lying** ~ sie haben alle (ihre) Sachen herumliegen lassen; **it's just ~ finished** es ist fast fertig; **to be ~ to** im Begriff sein zu; **I was ~ to go out** ich wollte gerade weggehen; **I'm not ~ to do all that for nothing** ich habe nicht vor, das alles umsonst zu machen ♦ *prep* (*topic*) über (+*acc*); (*place*) um, um... herum; **he's promised to do something ~ it** er hat versprochen, (in der Sache) etwas zu unternehmen.

about-face [əbout'fās], (*Brit*) **about-turn** [əbout'tûrn] *n* (*MIL*) Kehrtwendung *f*; (*fig*) Wendung *f* um hundertachtzig Grad.

above [əbuv'] *ad* oben ♦ *a* obig ♦ *prep* über; **~ all** vor allem; **he's not ~ a bit of blackmail** er ist sich (*dat*) nicht zu gut für eine kleine Erpressung.

aboveboard [əbuv'bôrd] *a* offen, ehrlich.

above-mentioned [əbuv'men'chənd] *a* obenerwähnt.

abrasion [əbrā'zhən] *n* Abschürfung *f*.

abrasive [əbrā'siv] *n* Schleifmittel *nt* ♦ *a* Abschleif-; (*personality*) zermürbend, aufreibend.

abreast [əbrest'] *ad* nebeneinander; **to keep ~ of** Schritt halten mit.

abridge [əbrij'] *vt* (ab)kürzen.

abroad [əbrôd'] *ad* (*be*) im Ausland; (*go*) ins Ausland; **there is a rumor ~ that ...** ein Gerücht geht um *or* kursiert, daß ...

abrupt [əbrupt'] *a* (*sudden*) abrupt, jäh; (*curt*) schroff.

abscess [ab'ses] *n* Geschwür *nt*.

abscond [abskând'] *vi* flüchten, sich davonmachen.

absence [ab'səns] *n* Abwesenheit *f*; **in the ~ of** (*person*) in Abwesenheit +*gen*; (*thing*) in Ermangelung +*gen*.

absent [ab'sənt] *a* abwesend, nicht da; (*lost in thought*) geistesabwesend.

absentee [absəntē'] *n* Abwesende(r) *mf*.

absentee ballot *n* (*US*) Briefwahl *f*.

absenteeism [absəntē'izəm] *n* Fehlen *nt* (am Arbeitsplatz/in der Schule).

absent-minded [ab'səntmīn'did] *a* zerstreut.

absolute [ab'səlōōt] *a* absolut; (*power*) unumschränkt; (*rubbish*) vollkommen, rein; **~ monopoly** uneingeschränkte marktbeherrschende Stellung *f*.

absolutely [absəlōōt'lē] *ad* absolut, vollkommen; **~!** ganz bestimmt!; **oh yes, ~!** ja, genau!

absolve [abzâlv'] *vt* (*from vow, oath*) entbinden; (*from blame*) freisprechen.

absorb [absôrb'] *vt* aufsaugen, absorbieren; (*fig*) ganz in Anspruch nehmen, fesseln.

absorbent [absôr'bənt] *a* absorbierend.

absorbent cotton *n* (*US*) Verbandwatte *f*.

absorbing [absôr'bing] *a* fesselnd.

absorption [absôrp'shən] *n* Absorption *f*; (*COMM: takeover*) Firmenübernahme *f*.

abstain [abstān'] *vi* (*in vote*) sich enthalten; **to ~ from** (*keep from*) sich enthalten (+*gen*).

abstemious [abstē'mēəs] *a* mäßig, enthaltsam.

abstention [absten'shən] *n* (*in vote*) (Stimm)enthaltung *f*.

abstinence [ab'stənəns] *n* Enthaltsamkeit *f*.

abstract [ab'strakt] *a* abstrakt ♦ *n* Abriß *m* ♦ *vt* [abstrakt'] abstrahieren, aussondern.

abstruse [abstrōōs'] *a* verworren, abstrus.

absurd [absûrd'] *a* absurd.

absurdity [absûr'dətē] *n* Unsinnigkeit *f*, Absurdität *f*.

abundance [əbun'dəns] *n* Überfluß *m* (*of an* +*dat*).

abundant [əbun'dənt] *a* reichlich.

abuse *n* [əbyōōs'] (*rude language*) Beschimpfung *f*; (*ill usage*) Mißbrauch *m*; (*bad practice*) (Amts)mißbrauch *m*; **open to ~** leicht zu mißbrauchen ♦ *vt* [əbyōōz'] (*misuse*) mißbrauchen; (*child*) mißhandeln.

abusive [əbyōō'siv] *a* beleidigend, Schimpf-.

abysmal [əbiz'məl] *a* scheußlich; (*ignorance*) bodenlos.

abyss [əbis'] *n* Abgrund *m*.

AC *abbr* (= *alternating current*) Wechselstrom *m* ♦ *n abbr* (*US*: = *Athletic Club*) SV *m*.

a/c *n abbr* (= *account*) Kto.; (*US*: = *account current*) ≈ Girokonto *nt*.

academic [akədem'ik] *a* akademisch; (*theoretical*) theoretisch; **~ year** akademische(s) Jahr *nt*.

academy [əkad'əmē] *n* (*school*) Hochschule *f*; (*society*) Akademie *f*.

accede [aksēd'] *vi*: **to ~ to** (*office*) antreten; (*throne*) besteigen; (*request*) zustimmen (+*dat*).

accelerate [aksel'ərāt] *vi* schneller werden; (*AUT*) Gas geben ♦ *vt* beschleunigen.

acceleration [akselərā'shən] *n* Beschleunigung *f*.

accelerator [aksel'ərātûr] *n* Gas(pedal) *nt*.

accent [ak'sent] *n* Akzent *m*; (*tones*) Tonfall *m*; (*mark*) Akzent *m*; (*stress*) Betonung *f*.

accentuate [aksen'chōōāt] *vt* (*syllable*) betonen; (*need, difference etc*) hervorheben.

accept [aksept'] *vt* (*take*) annehmen; (*agree to*) akzeptieren.

acceptable [aksep'təbəl] *a* annehmbar.

acceptance [aksep'təns] *n* Annahme *f*; **to meet with general ~** allgemeine Anerkennung finden.

access [ak'ses] *n* Zugang *m*; **the burglars gained ~ through a window** die Einbrecher gelangten durch ein Fenster hinein ♦ *vt* (*COMPUT*) zugreifen auf.

accessible [akses'əbəl] *a* (*easy to approach*) zugänglich; (*within reach*) (leicht) erreichbar.

accession [aksesh'ən] *n* (*to office*) Antritt *m*; (*to library*) (Neu)anschaffung *f*; (*of king*) Thronbesteigung *f*.

accessories [akses'ûrēz] *npl* Zubehör *nt*; **toilet ~** Toilettenartikel *pl*.

accessory [akses'ûrē] *n* Zubehörteil *nt*.

access road n (*Brit*) Zufahrtstraße f; (: *to freeway*) Auffahrt f.

access time n (*COMPUT*) Zugriffszeit f.

accident [ak'sidənt] n Unfall m; (*coincidence*) Zufall m; ~s at work Arbeitsunfälle pl; by ~ zufällig; to meet with *or* have an ~ einen Unfall haben.

accidental [aksiden'təl] a unbeabsichtigt.

accidentally [aksiden'təlē] ad (*by chance*) zufällig; (*unintentionally*) versehentlich.

accident insurance n Unfallversicherung f.

accident-prone [ak'sidəntprōn'] a: to be ~ zu Unfällen neigen.

acclaim [əklām'] vt zujubeln (+*dat*) ♦ n Beifall m.

acclamation [akləmā'shən] n (*approval*) Anerkennung f; (*applause*) Beifall m; by ~ durch Akklamation.

acclimate [əklī'mit] vt (*US*) to become ~d sich akklimatisieren, sich gewöhnen (*to* an +*acc*).

acclimatize [əklī'mətīz] vt (*Brit*) = acclimate.

accolade [akəlād'] n Auszeichnung f.

accommodate [əkâm'ədāt] vt unterbringen; (*hold*) Platz haben für; (*oblige*) (aus)helfen (+*dat*); this car ~s 4 people comfortably in diesem Auto ist gut Platz für 4 Personen.

accommodating [əkâm'ədāting] a entgegenkommend.

accommodations [əkâmədā'shənz], (*Brit*) **accommodation** [əkâmədā'shən] npl Unterkunft f.

accompaniment [əkum'pənimənt] n Begleitung f.

accompanist [əkum'pənist] n (*MUS*) Begleiter(in f) m.

accompany [əkum'pənē] vt begleiten.

accomplice [əkâm'plis] n Helfershelfer m, Komplize m.

accomplish [əkâm'plish] vt (*fulfill*) durchführen; (*finish*) vollenden; (*achieve*) erreichen.

accomplished [əkâm'plisht] a vollendet, ausgezeichnet; (*young lady*) vielseitig.

accomplishment [əkâm'plishmənt] n (*skill*) Fähigkeit f; (*completion*) Vollendung f; (*feat*) Leistung f.

accord [əkôrd'] n Übereinstimmung f; of one's own ~ freiwillig; with one ~ geschlossen, wie aus einem Mund ♦ vt gewähren.

accordance [əkôr'dəns] n: in ~ with in Übereinstimmung mit.

according [əkôr'ding] prep: ~ to nach, laut (+*gen*); it went ~ to plan es verlief nach Plan; it's all ~ (to whether ...) es hängt davon ab(, ob ...).

accordingly [əkôr'dinglē] ad danach, dementsprechend.

accordion [əkôr'dēən] n Ziehharmonika f, Akkordeon m.

accordionist [əkôr'dēənist] n Akkordeonspieler m.

accost [əkôst'] vt ansprechen.

account [əkount'] n (*bill*) Rechnung f; (*narrative*) Bericht m; (*report*) Rechenschaftsbericht m; (*in bank*) Konto nt; (*importance*) Geltung f; ~s payable Verbindlichkeiten pl; ~s receivable ausstehende Forderungen; of no ~ ohne Bedeutung; on no ~ keinesfalls; on ~ of wegen; to take into ~ berücksichtigen; to keep an ~ of ... Buch führen über ...; to bring sb to ~ for sth/for having done sth jdn über etw zur Rechenschaft ziehen; your ~ is still outstanding die Rechnungen stehen noch offen; to buy sth on ~ (*Brit*) etw auf (Kunden)kredit kaufen.

account for vt fus (*expenditure*) Rechenschaft ablegen für; how do you ~ for that? wie erklären Sie (sich) das?; all the children were ~ed for man wußte, wo alle Kinder waren.

accountability [əkountəbil'ətē] n Verantwortlichkeit f.

accountable [əkoun'təbəl] a verantwortlich.

accountancy [əkoun'tənsē] n Buchhaltung f.

accountant [əkoun'tənt] n Wirtschaftsprüfer(in f) m.

accounting [əkoun'ting] n Buchführung f ♦ a: ~ period Abrechnungszeitraum m, Rechnungsabschnitt m.

account number n Kontonummer f.

accouterments [əkōō'tûrmənts] npl Ausrüstung f.

accredited [əkred'itid] a beglaubigt, akkreditiert, zugelassen; ~ agent bevollmächtigte(r) Vertreter m; to be ~ to an embassy bei einer Botschaft akkreditiert sein/werden.

accretion [əkrē'shən] n Zunahme f.

accrue [əkrōō'] vi (*mount up*) sich ansammeln, zusammenkommen; (*interest*) auflaufen; to ~ to sb jdm erwachsen (*from* aus).

accrued [əkrōōd'] a: ~ charges aufgelaufene Kosten pl; ~ interest aufgelaufene Zinsen pl.

acct. abbr = account; accountant.

accumulate [əkyōō'myəlāt] vt ansammeln ♦ vi sich ansammeln.

accumulation [əkyōōmyəlā'shən] n (*act*) Aufhäufung f; (*result*) Ansammlung f.

accuracy [ak'yûrəsē] n Genauigkeit f.

accurate [ak'yûrit] a genau.

accurately [ak'yûritlē] ad genau, richtig.

accursed [əkûr'sid] a verflucht.

accusation [akyōōzā'shən] n Anklage f, Beschuldigung f.

accusative [əkyōō'zətiv] n Akkusativ m, vierte(r) Fall m.

accuse [əkyōōz'] vt (*JUR*) anklagen (*of* wegen + gen); to ~ sb of doing sth jdn beschuldigen, etw getan zu haben.

accused [əkyōōzd'] n Angeklagte(r) mf.

accustom [əkus'təm] vt gewöhnen (*to* an +*acc*); to ~ o.s. to sth sich an etw gewöhnen.

accustomed [əkus'təmd] a gewohnt.

AC/DC abbr (= *alternating current/direct current*) WS/GS, AC/DC.

ace [ās] *n* (*CARDS, TENNIS, col*) As *nt.*

ACE [ās] *n abbr* (= *American Council on Education*) Verband von Universitäten, Colleges *etc.*

Ace bandage *n* ® (*US*) elastische Binde *f.*

acerbic [əsûr'bik] *a* (*lit, fig*) bitter, scharf.

ache [āk] *n* Schmerz *m*; **I've got a stomach** ~ ich habe Bauchschmerzen ♦ *vi* schmerzen, weh tun; **I** ~ **all over** mir tut es überall weh; **to** ~ **to do sth** sich danach sehnen, etw zu tun.

achieve [əchēv'] *vt* zustande bringen; (*aim*) erreichen.

achievement [əchēv'mənt] *n* Leistung *f*; (*act*) Erreichen *nt.*

acid [as'id] *n* Säure *f* ♦ *a* sauer, scharf.

acidity [əsid'itē] *n* Säuregehalt *m.*

acid rain *n* saurer Regen *m.*

acid test *n* (*fig*) Nagelprobe *f.*

acknowledge [aknâl'ij] *vt* (*letter*) bestätigen; (*admit*) zugeben; **to** ~ **receipt of a letter** den Erhalt eines Schreibens bestätigen.

acknowledgement [aknâl'ijmənt] *n* Anerkennung *f*; (*letter*) Empfangsbestätigung *f*; ~**s are due to** ... mein/unser Dank gilt ...

ACLU *n abbr* (= *American Civil Liberties Union*) Vereinigung zum Schutz der bürgerlichen Freiheit.

acme [ak'mē] *n* Höhepunkt *m*, Gipfel *m*; (*of task, elegance*) Inbegriff *m.*

acne [ak'nē] *n* Akne *f.*

acorn [ā'kôrn] *n* Eichel *f.*

acoustic [əkōōs'tik] *a* akustisch.

acoustic coupler [əkōōs'tik kup'lûr] *n* (*COMPUT*) akustische(r) Koppler *m.*

acoustics [əkōōs'tiks] *npl* Akustik *f.*

acoustic screen *n* schalldämpfende Trennwand *f.*

acquaint [əkwānt'] *vt* vertraut machen.

acquaintance [əkwān'təns] *n* (*person*) Bekannte(r) *mf*; (*knowledge*) Kenntnis *f*; **to make sb's** ~ die Bekanntschaft jds machen.

acquiesce [akwēes'] *vi* (*agree*) einwilligen (*in* in +*acc*), sich abfinden (*in* mit).

acquire [əkwī'ûr] *vt* erwerben.

acquired [əkwī'ûrd] *a* (*PSYCH*) erworben; **caviar is an** ~ **taste** Kaviar ist (nur) etwas für Kenner.

acquisition [akwizish'ən] *n* Errungenschaft *f*; (*act*) Erwerb *m.*

acquisitive [əkwiz'ətiv] *a* gewinnsüchtig.

acquit [əkwit'] *vt* (*free*) freisprechen; **to** ~ **o.s.** sich bewähren.

acquittal [əkwit'əl] *n* Freispruch *m.*

acre [ā'kûr] *n* Morgen *m.*

acreage [ā'kûrij] *n* Fläche *f.*

acrid [ak'rid] *a* (*smell*) beißend; (*fig*) bitter.

acrimonious [akrəmō'nēəs] *a* bitter.

acrobat [ak'rəbat] *n* Akrobat *m.*

acrobatics [akrəbat'iks] *npl* akrobatische Kunststücke *pl.*

across [əkrôs'] *prep* über (+*acc*); **he lives** ~ **the river** er wohnt auf der anderen Seite des Flusses ♦ *ad* hinüber, herüber; **ten meters** ~ zehn Meter breit; **he lives** ~ **from us** er wohnt uns gegenüber; **to get sth** ~ **to sb** (*fig*) jdm etw klarmachen; **the lake is 12 km** ~ es sind 12 km quer über den See.

across-the-board [əkrôs'thəbôrd'] *a* pauschal.

acrylic [əkril'ik] *n* Acryl *nt.*

act [akt] *n* (*deed*) Tat *f*; (*JUR*) Gesetz *nt*; (*THEAT*) Akt *m*; (: *turn*) Nummer *f*; ~ **of God** höhere Gewalt *f no pl*; **to catch sb in the** ~ jdn auf frischer Tat ertappen, jdn bei etw erwischen; (*sexually*) jdn in flagranti ertappen; **it's only an** ~ es ist nur Schau/ Theater ♦ *vi* (*take action*) handeln; (*behave*) sich verhalten; (*pretend*) vorgeben; (*THEAT*) spielen; **he's only** ~**ing** er tut (doch) nur so, er spielt (doch) nur; ~**ing in my capacity as chairman** ... in meiner Eigenschaft als Vorsitzender ...; **it** ~**s as a deterrent** das wirkt abschreckend ♦ *vt* (*in play*) spielen.

act out *vt* (*event, fantasies*) durchspielen.

act up *vi* bocken.

ACT *n abbr* (= *American College Test*) standardisierter Eignungstest für Studienbewerber.

acting [ak'ting] *a* stellvertretend; **he is the** ~ **manager** er ist der stellvertretende Manager ♦ *n* Schauspielkunst *f*; (*performance*) Aufführung *f.*

action [ak'shən] *n* (*deed*) Tat *f*; (*of play, novel*) Handlung *f*; (*motion*) Bewegung *f*; (*way of working*) Funktionieren *nt*; (*battle*) Einsatz *m*, Gefecht *nt*; (*lawsuit*) Klage *f*, Prozeß *m*; **to take** ~ etwas unternehmen; **killed in** ~ (*MIL*) gefallen; **to put a plan into** ~ einen Plan in die Tat umsetzen; **to bring an** ~ **against sb** eine Klage gegen jdn anstrengen.

action replay *n* (*Brit TV*) Wiederholung *f.*

activate [ak'təvāt] *vt* in Betrieb setzen, aktivieren.

active [ak'tiv] *a* (*brisk*) rege, tatkräftig; (*working, COMPUT*) aktiv; (*GRAM*) aktiv, Tätigkeits-; **to play an** ~ **part in sth** sich aktiv an etw beteiligen.

active duty *n* (*US*) Einsatz *m.*

actively [ak'tivlē] *ad* aktiv, tätig.

active partner *n* tätige(r) Teilhaber *m.*

activist [ak'tivist] *n* Aktivist(in *f*) *m.*

activity [aktiv'ətē] *n* Aktivität *f*; (*doings*) Unternehmungen *pl*; (*occupation*) Tätigkeit *f.*

actor [ak'tûr] *n* Schauspieler *m.*

actress [ak'tris] *n* Schauspielerin *f.*

actual [ak'chōōəl] *a* wirklich.

actually [ak'chōōəlē] *ad* tatsächlich; ~ **no** eigentlich nicht.

actuary [ak'chōōārē] *n* Aktuar *m.*

actuate [ak'chōōāt] *vt* auslösen; (*fig*) treiben; ~**d by** ausgelöst durch.

acumen [əkyōō'mən] *n* Scharfsinn *m*; **business** ~ Geschäftssinn *m.*

acupuncture [ak'yōopungkchûr] *n* Akupunktur *f*.
acute [əkyōot'] *a* (*severe*) heftig, akut; (*keen, shrewd*) scharfsinnig.
acutely [əkyōot'lē] *ad* akut; scharf.
ad [ad] *n abbr* = **advertisement**.
AD *ad abbr* (= *anno domini*) A.D. ♦ *n abbr* (*US MIL*) = **active duty**.
adage [ad'ij] *n* Sprichwort *nt*.
Adam [ad'əm] *n* Adam *m*; ~'s apple Adamsapfel *m*.
adamant [ad'əmənt] *a* hart; (*refusal*) hartnäckig.
adapt [ədapt'] *vt* anpassen ♦ *vi* sich anpassen (*to* an +*acc*).
adaptability [ədaptəbil'ətē] *n* (*of person, device etc*) Anpassungsfähigkeit *f*.
adaptable [ədap'təbəl] *a* anpassungsfähig.
adaptation [adəptā'shən] *n* (*THEAT etc*) Bearbeitung *f*; (*adjustment*) Anpassung *f*.
adapter [ədap'tûr] *n* (*ELEC*) Zwischenstecker *m*.
ADC *n abbr* (*MIL*) = *aide-de-camp*; (*US*: = *Aid to Dependent Children*) Beihilfe *für* sozialschwache Alleinerziehenden.
add [ad] *vt* (*join*) hinzufügen; (*numbers*) addieren.
add up *vi* (*MATH, fig*) stimmen ♦ *vt* zusammenzählen.
add up to *vt fus* ausmachen; **it doesn't ~ up to much** (*fig*) das ist nicht berühmt.
addendum [əden'dəm] *n* Zusatz *m*.
adder [ad'ûr] *n* Kreuzotter *f*, Natter *f*.
addict [ad'ikt] *n* Süchtige(r) *mf*; **to be a heroin ~** heroinsüchtig sein.
addicted [ədik'tid] *a*: ~ **to heroin** heroinsüchtig.
addiction [ədik'shən] *n* Sucht *f*.
adding machine [ad'ing məshēn'] *n* Addiermaschine *f*.
Addis Ababa [ad'is âb'əbâ] *n* Addis Ababa *nt*.
addition [ədish'ən] *n* Anhang *m*, Addition *f*; (*MATH*) Addition *f*, Zusammenzählen *nt*; **in ~** zusätzlich, außerdem.
additional [ədish'ənəl] *a* zusätzlich, weiter.
additive [ad'ətiv] *n* Zusatz *m*.
addled [ad'əld] *a* (*Brit*) faul, schlecht; (*fig*) verwirrt.
address [ədres'] *n* (*auch COMPUT*) Adresse *f*; (*speech*) Ansprache *f*; **absolute ~** (*COMPUT*) absolute Adresse *f*, Maschinenadresse *f*; **form of ~** (Form *f* der) Anrede *f*; **relative ~** (*COMPUT*) relative Adresse *f* ♦ *vt* (*letter*) adressieren; (*speak to*) ansprechen; (*make speech to*) eine Ansprache halten an (+*acc*); **to ~ o.s. to sb** jdn ansprechen.
addressee [adresē'] *n* Empfänger(in *f*) *m*, Adressat *m*.
Aden [ä'dən] *n* Aden *nt*; **Gulf of ~** Golf *m* von Aden.
adenoids [ad'ənoidz] *npl* Polypen *pl*.
adept [ədept'] *a* geschickt; **to be ~ at** geschickt sein in (+*dat*).

adequacy [ad'əkwəsē] *n* Angemessenheit *f*.
adequate [ad'əkwit] *a* angemessen; **to feel ~ to a task** einer Aufgabe gewachsen sein.
adequately [ad'əkwitlē] *ad* hinreichend.
adhere [adhēr'] *vi*: **to ~ to** (*lit*) haften an (+*dat*); (*fig*) festhalten an (+*dat*).
adhesion [adhē'zhən] *n* (*PHYS*) Adhäsion *f*.
adhesive [adhē'siv] *a* klebend; Kleb(e)- ♦ *n* Klebstoff *m*.
adhesive tape *n* (*US: for wound*) Heftpflaster *nt*.
ad hoc [ad hâk'] *a* (*decision, committee*) ad hoc.
adieu [ədyōō'] *n* (*old*) Adieu *nt*, Lebewohl *nt*.
ad infinitum [ad infənī'təm] *ad* ad infinitum.
adjacent [əjā'sənt] *a* benachbart.
adjective [aj'iktiv] *n* Adjektiv *nt*, Eigenschaftswort *nt*.
adjoin [əjoin'] *vt* grenzen an (+*acc*).
adjoining [əjoi'ning] *a* benachbart, Neben-.
adjourn [əjûrn'] *vt* vertagen; (*US: end*) beenden; **to ~ a meeting till the following week** eine Versammlung auf die nächste Woche vertagen ♦ *vi* abbrechen; **they ~ed to the pub** (*Brit col*) sie begaben sich *or* gingen in die Kneipe.
adjournment [əjûrn'mənt] *n* (*period*) Unterbrechung *f*.
Adjt. *abbr* (= *adjutant*) Adj.
adjudicate [əjōō'dikāt] *vi* entscheiden, ein Urteil fällen ♦ *vt* (*contest*) Preisrichter sein bei; (*claim*) entscheiden.
adjudication [əjōōdikā'shən] *n* Entscheidung *f*.
adjudicator [əjōō'dikātûr] *n* Schiedsrichter *m*, Preisrichter *m*.
adjust [əjust'] *vt* (*alter*) anpassen; (*put right*) regulieren, richtig stellen.
adjustable [əjust'əbəl] *a* verstellbar.
adjuster [əjust'ûr] *n* Schadenssachverständiger *m*.
adjustment [əjust'mənt] *n* (*rearrangement*) Anpassung *f*; (*settlement*) Schlichtung *f*.
adjutant [aj'ətənt] *n* Adjutant *m*.
ad-lib [adlib'] *vti* improvisieren ♦ *n* Improvisation *f* ♦ *a* improvisiert ♦ *ad* aus dem Stegreif.
adman [ad'man] *n* (*col*) Werbefachmann *m*.
admin. [ad'min] *n abbr* (*col*) = **administration**.
administer [admin'istûr] *vt* (*manage*) verwalten; (*dispense*) ausüben; (*justice*) sprechen; (*medicine*) geben.
administration [administrā'shən] *n* Verwaltung *f*; (*POL*) Regierung *f*; **the A~** (*US*) die Regierung.
administrative [admin'istrātiv] *a* Verwaltungs-.
administrator [admin'istrātûr] *n* Verwaltungsbeamte(r) *mf*.
admirable [ad'mûrəbəl] *a* bewundernswert.
admiral [ad'mûrəl] *n* Admiral *m*.
Admiralty [ad'mûrəltē] *n* (*Brit*) Admiralität *f*.
admiration [admərā'shən] *n* Bewunderung *f*.

admire [admī'ûr] *vt* (*respect*) bewundern; (*love*) verehren.

admirer [admī'ərûr] *n* Bewunderer(in *f*) *m*.

admission [admish'ən] *n* (*entrance*) Einlaß *m*; (*fee*) Eintritt(spreis) *m*; (*confession*) Geständnis *nt*; **"free ~"** „Eintritt frei"; **by his own ~** nach eigenem Eingeständnis.

admit [admit'] *vt* (*let in*) einlassen; (*confess*) gestehen; (*accept*) anerkennen; **children not ~ted** kein Zutritt für Kinder; **this ticket ~s two** die Karte ist für zwei (Personen); **I must ~ that** ... ich muß zugeben, daß ...

admittance [admit'əns] *n* (*to club*) Zulassung *f*; **"no ~"** „kein Zutritt".

admittedly [admit'idlē] *ad* zugegebenermaßen.

admonish [admân'ish] *vt* ermahnen.

ad nauseam [ad nô'zēəm] *ad* bis zum Gehtnicht-mehr (*col*), bis zur Vergasung (*col*).

ado [ədōō'] *n*: **without more ~** ohne weitere Umstände.

adolescence [adəles'əns] *n* Jugendalter *nt*.

adolescent [adəles'ənt] *a* heranwachsend, jugendlich ♦ *n* Jugendliche(r) *mf*.

adopt [ədâpt'] *vt* (*child*) adoptieren; (*idea*) übernehmen.

adoption [ədâp'shən] *n* (*of child*) Adoption *f*; (*of idea*) Übernahme *f*.

adorable [ədôr'əbəl] *a* anbetungswürdig; (*lovable*) entzückend.

adoration [ədərā'shən] *n* Liebe *f*; Anbetung *f*.

adore [ədôr'] *vt* über alles lieben; (*God*) anbeten.

adoring [ədôr'ing] *a* bewundernd.

adorn [ədôrn'] *vt* schmücken.

adornment [ədôrn'mənt] *n* Schmuck *m*, Verzierung *f*.

ADP *n abbr* = **automatic data processing**.

adrenalin [ədren'əlin] *n* Adrenalin *nt*.

Adriatic Sea [ādrēat'ik sē] *n* Adriatische(s) Meer *nt*, Adria *f*.

adrift [ədrift'] *ad* Wind und Wellen preisgegeben; **to set ~** (*boat*) losmachen; **to come ~** (*wire, rope etc*) sich lösen.

adroit [ədroit'] *a* gewandt.

adulation [ajōōlā'shən] *n* Verherrlichung *f*.

adult [ədult'] *a* erwachsen ♦ *n* Erwachsene(r) *mf*.

adult education *n* Erwachsenenbildung *f*.

adulterate [ədul'tûrāt] *vt* verfälschen, mischen.

adultery [ədul'tûrē] *n* Ehebruch *m*.

adulthood [ədult'hōōd] *n* Erwachsensein *nt*, Erwachsenenalter *nt*.

advance [advans'] *n* (*progress*) Vorrücken *nt*; (*money*) Vorschuß *m* ♦ *vt* (*move forward*) vorrücken; (*money*) vorschießen; (*argument*) vorbringen ♦ *vi* vorwärtsgehen; **in ~** im voraus; **in ~ of** vor (+*dat*); **to make ~s to sb** (*fig, amorously*) Annäherungsversuche *pl* machen.

advance booking *n* Vorbestellung *f*, Vorverkauf *m*.

advanced [advanst'] *a* (*ahead*) vorgerückt;

(*modern*) fortgeschritten; (*study*) für Fortgeschrittene; **~ in years** in fortgeschrittenem Alter.

advancement [advans'mənt] *n* Förderung *f*; (*promotion*) Beförderung *f*.

advance payment *n* (*part sum*) Vorschuß *m*.

advantage [advan'tij] *n* Vorteil *m*; **to have an ~ over sb** jdm gegenüber im Vorteil sein; **to be of ~** von Nutzen sein; **to take ~ of** (*misuse*) ausnutzen; (*profit from*) Nutzen ziehen aus; **it's to our ~** es ist zu unserem Vorteil.

advantageous [advəntā'jəs] *a* vorteilhaft.

advent [ad'vent] *n* Ankunft *f*.

Advent *n* Advent *m*.

adventure [adven'chûr] *n* Abenteuer *nt*.

adventurous [adven'chûrəs] *a* abenteuerlich, waghalsig.

adverb [ad'vûrb] *n* Adverb *nt*, Umstandswort *nt*.

adversary [ad'vûrsärē] *n* Gegner *m*.

adverse [advûrs'] *a* widrig.

adversity [advûr'sitē] *n* Widrigkeit *f*, Mißgeschick *nt*.

advert [ad'vûrt] *n* (*Brit*) Anzeige *f*.

advertise [ad'vûrtīz] *vt* anzeigen ♦ *vi* annoncieren.

advertisement [advûrtīz'mənt] *n* Anzeige *f*, Annonce *f*, Inserat *nt*.

advertiser [ad'vûrtīzûr] *n* Inserent(in *f*) *m*.

advertising [ad'vûrtīzing] *n* Werbung *f*.

advertising agency *n* Werbeagentur *f*.

advertising campaign *n* Werbekampagne *f*.

advice [advīs'] *n* Rat(schlag) *m*; **legal ~** Rechtsberatung *f*; **to take legal ~** einen Rechtsanwalt zu Rate ziehen; **to ask (sb) for ~** (jdn) um Rat fragen.

advice slip *n* Versandanzeige *f*.

advisable [advī'zəbəl] *a* ratsam.

advise [advīz'] *vt* raten (+*dat*); **you will be well/ill ~d to go** Sie wären gut/schlecht beraten, wenn Sie gehen würden.

adviser [advī'zûr] *n* Berater(in *f*) *m*.

advisory [advī'zûrē] *a* beratend, Beratungs-; **in an ~ capacity** in beratender Funktion.

advocate [ad'vəkāt] *vt* vertreten.

advt. *abbr* = **advertisement**.

AEA *n abbr* (*Brit*: = *Atomic Energy Authority*) Atomenergiekommission *f*.

AEC *n abbr* (*US*: = *Atomic Energy Commission*) Atomenergiekommission *f*.

Aegean Sea [ijē'ən sē] *n* die Ägäis, das Ägäische Meer.

aegis [ē'jis] *n*: **under the ~ of** unter der Schirmherrschaft von.

aeon [ē'ən] *n* (*Brit*) = **eon**.

aerial [är'ēəl] *n* Antenne *f* ♦ *a* Luft-.

aerie [är'ē] *n* (*US*) Horst *m*.

aero- [är'ō] *pref* Luft-.

aerobatics [ärəbat'iks] *npl* Kunstfliegen *nt*; (*stunts*) Stunts *pl*.

aerodynamic [ärōdīnam'ik] *a* aerodynamisch.

aerogramme [är'əgram] *n* Aerogramm *nt*,

Luftpost(leicht)brief *m*.

aeronautics [ärənô'tiks] *n sing* Luftfahrt *f*, Aeronautik *f*.

aeroplane [är'əplān] *n* (*Brit*) Flugzeug *nt*.

aerosol [är'əsôl] *n* Aerosol *nt*; (*can*) Spraydose *f*.

aerospace [är'əspās] *a attr*: ~ **industry** Raumfahrtindustrie *f*.

aesthetic [esthet'ik] *a* (*Brit*) ästhetisch.

aesthetics [esthet'iks] *n sing* (*Brit*) Ästhetik *f*.

a.f. *abbr* (= *audiofrequency*) Tonfrequenz *f*.

afar [əfär'] *ad* weit; **from** ~ aus der Ferne, von weit her.

AFB *n abbr* (*US*: = *Air Force Base*) AFB.

AFDC *n abbr* (*US*: = *Aid to Families with Dependent Children*) Kindergeld.

affable [af'əbəl] *a* umgänglich.

affair [əfär'] *n* (*concern*) Angelegenheit *f*; (*event*) Ereignis *nt*; (*love* ~) (Liebes)verhältnis *nt*; ~**s** (*business*) Geschäfte *pl*; **the Watergate** ~ die Watergate-Affäre.

affect [əfekt'] *vt* (*influence*) (ein)wirken auf (+*acc*); (*move deeply*) bewegen; **this change doesn't** ~ **us** diese Änderung betrifft uns nicht.

affectation [afektā'shən] *n* Affektiertheit *f*, Verstellung *f*.

affected [əfek'tid] *a* affektiert, gekünstelt.

affection [əfek'shən] *n* Zuneigung *f*.

affectionate [əfek'shənit] *a* liebevoll, lieb.

affectionately [əfek'shənitlē] *ad* liebevoll; ~ **yours** herzlichst Dein.

affidavit [afidā'vit] *n* (*JUR*) eidesstattliche Erklärung *f*.

affiliated [əfil'ēātid] *a* angeschlossen (*to dat*).

affiliated company *n* Schwestergesellschaft *f*.

affinity [əfin'ətē] *n* (*attraction*) gegenseitige Anziehung *f*; (*relationship*) Verwandtschaft *f*.

affirm [əfûrm'] *vt* versichern, beteuern.

affirmation [afûrmā'shən] *n* Behauptung *f*.

affirmative [əfûr'mətiv] *a* bestätigend ♦ *n*: **in the** ~ (*GRAM*) nicht verneint; **to answer in the** ~ mit Ja antworten.

affix [əfiks'] *vt* aufkleben, anheften.

afflict [əflikt'] *vt* quälen, heimsuchen.

affliction [əflik'shən] *n* Kummer *m*; (*illness*) Leiden *nt*.

affluence [af'lōoəns] *n* (*wealth*) Wohlstand *m*.

affluent [af'lōoənt] *a* wohlhabend, Wohlstands-; **the** ~ **society** die Wohlstandsgesellschaft.

afford [əfôrd'] *vt* (sich) leisten, erschwingen; (*yield*) bieten, einbringen; **can we** ~ **a car?** können wir uns ein Auto leisten?

affront [əfrunt'] *n* Beleidigung *f*.

affronted [əfrun'tid] *a* beleidigt.

Afghan [af'gan] *a* afghanisch ♦ *n* Afghane *m*, Afghanin *f*.

Afghanistan [afgan'istan] *n* Afghanistan *nt*.

afield [əfēld'] *ad*: **far** ~ weit entfernt.

AFL-CIO *n abbr* (= *American Federation of*

Labor and Congress of Industrial Organizations) Gewerkschaftsverband.

afloat [əflōt'] *a*: **to be** ~ schwimmen.

afoot [əfŏŏt'] *ad* im Gang.

aforementioned [əfôr'menshənd] *a* obengenannt.

aforesaid [əfôr'sed] *a* = **aforementioned**.

afraid [əfrād'] *a* ängstlich; **to be** ~ **of** Angst haben vor (+*dat*); **to be** ~ **to do sth** sich scheuen, etw zu tun; **I am** ~ **I have** ... ich habe leider ...; **I'm** ~ **so!** leider ja!; **I'm** ~ **not!** leider nicht!

afresh [əfresh'] *ad* von neuem.

Africa [af'rikə] *n* Afrika *nt*.

African [af'rikən] *a* afrikanisch ♦ *n* Afrikaner(in *f*) *m*.

Afro-American [af'rōəmär'ikən] *a* afroamerikanisch.

aft [aft] *ad* achtern.

AFT *n abbr* (= *American Federation of Teachers*) Gewerkschaft für Lehrer und verwandte Berufe.

after [af'tûr] *prep* nach; (*following, seeking*) hinter ... (*dat*) ... her; (*in imitation*) nach, im Stil von; ~ **dinner** nach dem Essen; **the day** ~ **tomorrow** übermorgen; **the police are** ~ **him** die Polizei ist hinter ihm her; **quarter** ~ **two** (*US*) viertel nach zwei ♦ *ad*: **soon** ~ bald danach; ~ **all** letzten Endes.

aftercare [af'tûrkär] *n* (*MED*) Nachbehandlung *f*.

after-effects [af'tûrifekts] *npl* Nachwirkungen *pl*.

afterlife [af'tûrlīf] *n* Leben *nt* nach dem Tode.

aftermath [af'tûrmath] *n* Auswirkungen *pl*.

afternoon [aftûrnōōn'] *n* Nachmittag *m*; **good** ~! guten Tag!

after-sales service [af'tûrsālz sûr'vis] *n* (*Brit*) Kundendienst *m*.

after-shave (lotion) [af'tûrshāv (lōshən)] *n* Rasierwasser *nt*.

aftershock [af'tûrshâk] *n* Nachbeben *nt*.

afterthought [af'tûrthôt] *n* nachträgliche(r) Einfall *m*.

afterwards [af'tûrwûrdz] *ad* danach, nachher.

again [əgen'] *ad* wieder, noch einmal; (*besides*) außerdem, ferner; ~ **and** ~ immer wieder; **now and** ~ hin und wieder.

against [əgenst'] *prep* gegen; (*over*) ~ (*as opposed to*) gegenüber (+*dat*); **I was leaning** ~ **the desk** ich stand an den Schreibtisch gelehnt.

age [āj] *n* (*of person*) Alter *nt*; (*in history*) Zeitalter *nt*; **to come of** ~ mündig werden; **what** ~ **is he?** wie alt ist er?; **under** ~ minderjährig ♦ *vi* altern, alt werden ♦ *vt* älter machen.

aged [ājd] *a* ... Jahre alt, -jährig; (*elderly*) [ā'jid] betagt; **the** ~ die Bejahrten *pl*.

age group *n* Altersgruppe *f*, Jahrgang *m*; **the 40 to 50** ~ die Altersgruppe der Vierzig- bis Fünfzigjährigen.

ageless [āj'lis] *a* zeitlos.

age limit *n* Altersgrenze *f*.

agency [ā'jənsē] *n* (*COMM. THEAT*) Agentur *f*; (*CHEM*) Wirkung *f*; **through the ~ of** durch die Vermittlung von.

agenda [əjen'də] *n* Tagesordnung *f*; **on the ~** auf dem Programm.

agent [ā'jənt] *n* (*COMM*) Vertreter *m*; (*spy*) Agent *m*.

aggravate [ag'rəvāt] *vt* (*make worse*) verschlimmern; (*irritate*) reizen.

aggravating [ag'rəvāting] *a* verschlimmernd; ärgerlich.

aggravation [agrəvā'shən] *n* Verschlimmerung *f*; Verärgerung *f*.

aggregate [ag'rəgit] *n* Summe *f*.

aggression [əgresh'ən] *n* Aggression *f*.

aggressive [əgres'iv] *a*, **aggressively** [əgres'ivlē] *ad* aggressiv.

aggressiveness [əgres'ivnis] *n* Aggressivität *f*.

aggrieved [əgrēvd'] *a* bedrückt, verletzt.

aghast [əgast'] *a* entsetzt.

agile [aj'əl] *a* flink, agil; (*mind*) rege.

agitate [aj'ətāt] *vt* rütteln ♦ *vi* agitieren.

agitated [aj'ətātid] *a* aufgeregt.

agitator [aj'itātûr] *n* Agitator *m*; (*pej*) Hetzer *m*.

AGM *n abbr* (*Brit*: = *annual general meeting*) JHV *f*.

agnostic [agnâs'tik] *n* Agnostiker(in *f*) *m*.

ago [əgō'] *ad*: **two days ~** vor zwei Tagen; **not long ~** vor kurzem; **it's so long ~** es ist schon so lange her; **as long ~ as 1960** schon 1960.

agog [əgâg'] *a*, *ad* gespannt; **(all) ~ (for)** gespannt (auf).

agonize [ag'ənīz] *vi* sich (*dat*) den Kopf zermartern (*over* über).

agonized [ag'ənīzd] *a* gequält.

agonizing [ag'ənīzing] *a* quälend.

agony [ag'ənē] *n* Qual *f*.

agony column *n* Schmelzspalte *f*.

agree [əgrē'] *vt* (*date*) vereinbaren ♦ *vi* (*have same opinion, correspond*) übereinstimmen (*with* mit); (*consent*) zustimmen; (*be in harmony*) sich vertragen; **to ~ to do sth** sich bereit erklären, etw zu tun; **garlic doesn't ~ with me** Knoblauch vertrage ich nicht; **I ~** einverstanden, ich stimme zu; **to ~ on sth** sich auf etw (*acc*) einigen; **it was ~d that ...** man kam überein, daß ..., es wurde beschlossen, daß ...

agreeable [əgrē'əbəl] *a* (*pleasing*) angenehm; (*willing to consent*) einverstanden.

agreeably [əgrē'əblē] *ad* angenehm.

agreed [əgrēd'] *a* vereinbart.

agreement [əgrē'mənt] *n* (*agreeing*) Übereinstimmung *f*; (*contract*) Vereinbarung *f*, Vertrag *m*; **by mutual ~** in gegenseitigem Einvernehmen.

agricultural [agrəkul'chûrəl] *a* landwirtschaftlich, Landwirtschafts-.

agriculture [ag'rəkulchûr] *n* Landwirtschaft *f*.

aground [əground'] *a*, *ad* auf Grund.

agt. *abbr* = **agent**.

ahead [əhed'] *ad* vorwärts; **to be ~** voraus sein.

ahoy [əhoi'] *interj* ahoi!

AI *n abbr* (*COMPUT*) = **artificial intelligence**.

aid [ād] *n* (*assistance*) Hilfe *f*, Unterstützung *f*; (*person*) Hilfe *f*; (*thing*) Hilfsmittel *nt*; **with the ~ of** mit Hilfe von ♦ *vt* unterstützen, helfen (+*dat*); **to ~ and abet** Beihilfe leisten (*sb* jdm).

AID *n abbr* (= *artificial insemination by donor*) künstliche Befruchtung durch Spender; (*US*: = *Agency for International Development*) Abteilung zur Koordinierung von Entwicklungshilfe und Außenpolitik.

aide [ād] *n* (*person*) Gehilfe *m*; (*MIL*) Adjutant *m*.

AIDS [ādz] *n abbr* (= *acquired immune deficiency syndrome*) AIDS *nt*.

AIH *n abbr* (= *artificial insemination by husband*) künstliche Befruchtung durch Ehemann.

ailing [ā'ling] *a* kränkelnd.

ailment [āl'mənt] *n* Leiden *nt*.

aim [ām] *vt* (*gun, camera*) richten auf (+*acc*); **that was ~ed at you** das war auf dich gemünzt ♦ *vi* (*with gun*) zielen; (*intend*) beabsichtigen; **to ~ at sth** etw anstreben ♦ *n* (*intention*) Absicht *f*, Ziel *nt*; (*pointing*) Zielen *nt*, Richten *nt*; **to take ~** zielen.

aimless [ām'lis] *a*, **aimlessly** [ām'lislē] *ad* ziellos.

air [är] *n* Luft *f*; (*manner*) Miene *f*, Anschein *m*; (*MUS*) Melodie *f*; **to go by ~** (*travel*) fliegen, mit dem Flugzeug reisen; **to be on the ~** (*RAD, TV: program*) gesendet werden; (: *station*) senden ♦ *vt* (*room, bed, clothes*) lüften; (*fig*) an die Öffentlichkeit bringen; (*grievance*) Luft machen (+*dat*); (*ideas, views*) darlegen.

air base *n* Luftwaffenstützpunkt *m*.

air bed *n* (*Brit*) Luftmatratze *f*.

airborne [är'bôrn] *a*: **as soon as the plane was ~** sobald sich das Flugzeug in der Luft befand.

air cargo *n* Luftfracht *f*.

air-conditioned [är'kəndishənd] *a* mit Klimaanlage.

air-conditioning [är'kəndishəning] *n* Klimaanlage *f*.

aircraft [är'kraft] *n* Flugzeug *nt*, Maschine *f*.

aircraft carrier *n* Flugzeugträger *m*.

airfield [är'fēld] *n* Flugplatz *m*.

air force *n* Luftwaffe *f*.

air freshener *n* Luftverbesserer *m*.

air gun *n* Luftgewehr *nt*.

air hostess *n* (*Brit*) Stewardeß *f*.

airily [är'ilē] *ad* leichthin.

airing [är'ing] *n*: **to give sth an ~** etw gut durch- *or* auslüften; **to give an idea an ~** eine Idee darlegen.

air letter *n* Luftpost(leicht)brief *m*.

airlift [är'lift] *n* Luftbrücke *f*.

airline [är'līn] *n* Luftverkehrsgesellschaft *f*.

airliner [är'līnûr] *n* Verkehrsflugzeug *nt*.

air lock *n* Luftblase *f*.
airmail [är'māl] *n*: **by ~** mit Luftpost.
air mattress *n* Luftmatratze *f*.
airplane [är'plān] *n* Flugzeug *nt*.
airport [är'pôrt] *n* Flughafen *m*, Flugplatz *m*.
air raid *n* Luftangriff *m*.
airsick [är'sik] *a* luftkrank.
airstrip [är'strip] *n* Landestreifen *m*.
air terminal *n* (Air) Terminal *m*.
airtight [är'tīt] *a* luftdicht.
air traffic controller *n* Fluglotse *m*.
air waybill [är' wā'bil] *n* Luftfrachtbrief *m*.
airy [är'ē] *a* luftig; (*manner*) leichtfertig.
aisle [īl] *n* Gang *m*.
ajar [əjär'] *ad* angelehnt, einen Spalt offen.
AK *abbr* (*US MAIL*) = *Alaska*.
aka *abbr* (= *also known as*) alias.
akin to [əkin' tōō] *prep* ähnlich wie.
AL *abbr* (*US MAIL*) = *Alabama*.
ALA *n abbr* (= *American Library Association*) Interessenverband der Bibliothekare.
Ala. *abbr* (*US*) = *Alabama*.
alabaster [al'əbastûr] *n* Alabaster *m*.
à la carte [â lâ kârt'] *a*, *ad* nach der (Speise)karte, à la carte.
alacrity [əlak'ritē] *n* Bereitwilligkeit *f*; **with ~** ohne zu zögern.
alarm [əlärm'] *n* (*warning*) Alarm *m*; (*bell etc*) Alarmanlage *f* ♦ *vt* erschrecken.
alarm clock *n* Wecker *m*.
alarming [əlär'ming] *a* beängstigend; (*worrying*) beunruhigend; (*news*) alarmierend.
alarmist [əlär'mist] *n* Bangemacher *m*.
Alas. *abbr* (*US*) = *Alaska*.
alas [əlas'] *interj* ach, leider.
Albania [albā'nēə] *n* Albanien *nt*.
Albanian [albā'nēən] *a* albanisch ♦ *n* (*person*) Albaner(in *f*) *m*; (*language*) Albanisch *nt*.
albeit [ôlbē'it] *cj* obgleich.
album [al'bəm] *n* Album *nt*.
alcohol [al'kəhôl] *n* Alkohol *m*.
alcoholic [alkəhôl'ik] *a* (*drink*) alkoholisch ♦ *n* Alkoholiker(in *f*) *m*.
alcoholism [al'kəhôlizəm] *n* Alkoholismus *m*.
alcove [al'kōv] *n* Alkoven *m*.
ald. *abbr* = **alderman**.
alderman [ôl'dûrmən] *n*, *pl* **-men** Stadtrat *m*.
ale [āl] *n* Ale *nt*.
alert [əlûrt'] *a* wachsam ♦ *n* Alarm *m* ♦ *vt*: **to ~ sb (to sth)** jdn (vor etw) warnen; **to ~ sb to the dangers** jdn vor den Gefahren warnen.
alertness [əlûrt'nis] *n* Wachsamkeit *f*.
Aleutian Islands [əlōō'shən ī'ləndz] *npl* Aleuten *pl*.
Alexandria [aligzan'drēə] *n* Alexandria *nt*, Alexandrien *nt*.
alfresco [alfres'kō] *a* im Freien.
algebra [al'jəbrə] *n* Algebra *f*.
Algeria [aljē'rēə] *n* Algerien *nt*.
Algerian [aljə'rēən] *a* algerisch ♦ *n* Algerier(in *f*) *m*.
Algiers [aljērz'] *n* Algier *nt*.
algorithm [al'gərit͡həm] *n* Algorithmus *m*.

alias [ā'lēəs] *ad* alias ♦ *n* Deckname *m*.
alibi [al'əbī] *n* Alibi *nt*.
alien [āl'yən] *n* Ausländer(in *f*) *m* ♦ *a* (*foreign*) ausländisch; (*strange*) fremd.
alienate [āl'yənāt] *vt* entfremden.
alienation [ālyənā'shən] *n* Entfremdung *f*.
alight [əlīt'] *a*, *ad* brennend; (*building*) in Flammen ♦ *vi* (*descend*) aussteigen; (*bird*) sich setzen.
align [əlīn'] *vt* ausrichten.
alignment [əlīn'mənt] *n* Ausrichtung *f*; (*of policies etc*) Orientierung *f*.
alike [əlīk'] *a* gleich, ähnlich ♦ *ad* gleich, ebenso.
alimony [al'əmōnē] *n* Unterhalt *m*, Alimente *pl*.
alive [əlīv'] *a* (*living*) lebend; (*lively*) lebendig, aufgeweckt; (*full of*) voll (*with* von), wimmelnd (*with* von).
alkali [al'kəlī] *n* Alkali *nt*.
all [ôl] *a* (*with pl n*) alle; (*with sing n*) ganze(r, s), alle(r, s); **~ day** den ganzen Tag; **for ~ their efforts** trotz all ihrer Bemühungen ♦ *n* (*the whole*) alles, das Ganze; (*everyone*) alle; **~ of the books** alle Bücher; **is that ~?** ist das alles?; (*in shop*) sonst noch etwas? ♦ *ad* (*completely*) vollkommen, ganz; **it's ~ mine** das gehört alles mir; **it's ~ over** es ist alles aus *or* vorbei; **to be** *or* **feel ~ in** (*col*) total erledigt sein; **~ around the edge** rund um den Rand; **~ at once** auf einmal; **~ but** alle(s) außer; (*almost*) fast; **~ in** alles in allem; **~ over town** in der ganzen Stadt; **~ right** okay, in Ordnung; **not at ~** ganz und gar nicht; (*don't mention it*) bitte.
allay [əlā'] *vt* (*fears*) beschwichtigen.
all clear *n* Entwarnung *f*.
allegation [aləgā'shən] *n* Behauptung *f*.
allege [əlej'] *vt* (*declare*) behaupten; (*falsely*) vorgeben; **he is ~d to have said that ...** er soll gesagt haben, daß ...
alleged [əlejd'] *a* angeblich.
allegedly [əlej'idlē] *ad* angeblich.
allegiance [əlē'jəns] *n* Treue *f*, Ergebenheit *f*.
allegory [al'əgôrē] *n* Allegorie *f*.
all-embracing [ôl'embrās'ing] *a* allumfassend.
allergic [əlûr'jik] *a* allergisch (*to* gegen).
allergy [al'ûrjē] *n* Allergie *f*.
alleviate [əlē'vēāt] *vt* erleichtern, lindern.
alleviation [əlēvēā'shən] *n* Erleichterung *f*.
alley [al'ē] *n* Gasse *f*, Durchgang *m*.
alliance [əlī'əns] *n* Bund *m*, Allianz *f*.
allied [əlīd'] *a* vereinigt; (*powers*) alliiert; verwandt (*to* mit).
alligator [al'əgātûr] *n* Alligator *m*.
all-important [ôl'impôr'tənt] *a* äußerst wichtig.
all-inclusive [ôl'inklōō'siv] *a*, *ad* alles inbegriffen, Gesamt-.
all-in wrestling [ô'lin res'ling] *n* (*Brit*) Freistilringen *nt*.
alliteration [əlitərā'shən] *n* Alliteration *f*,

Stabreim *m*.

all-night [ôl'nīt] *a* (*café, cinema*) die ganze Nacht geöffnet, Nacht-.

allocate [al'əkāt] *vt* zuweisen, zuteilen.

allocation [aləkā'shən] *n* Zuteilung *f*.

allot [əlât'] *vt* zuteilen; **in the ~ted time** in(nerhalb) der vorgesehenen Zeit.

allotment [əlât'mənt] *n* (*share*) Anteil *m*; (*Brit: plot*) Schrebergarten *m*.

all-out [ôl'out'] *a, ad* total.

allow [əlou'] *vt* (*permit*) erlauben, gestatten (*sb* jdm); (*grant*) bewilligen; (*deduct*) abziehen; **smoking is not ~ed** Rauchen verboten; **we must ~ 3 days for the journey** wir müssen für die Reise 3 Tage einplanen. **allow for** *vt fus* berücksichtigen, einplanen.

allowance [əlou'əns] *n* Beihilfe *f*; **to make ~s for** berücksichtigen; **you have to make ~(s)** Sie müssen (gewisse) Zugeständnisse machen.

alloy [al'oi] *n* Metallegierung *f*.

all-round [ôl'round'] *a* (*sportsman*) allseitig, Allround-.

all-rounder [ôlroun'dûr] *n* (*SPORT*) vielseitige(r) Sportler *mf*; (*general*) Allerweltskerl *m*; **to be a good ~** (*Brit*) ein (guter) Allroundmann sein.

allspice [ôl'spīs] *n* Piment *m or nt*.

all-time [ôl'tīm] *a* (*record, high*) aller Zeiten, Höchst-.

allude [əlōōd'] *vi* hinweisen, anspielen (*to* auf +*acc*).

alluring [əlōō'ring] *a* verlockend.

allusion [əlōō'zhən] *n* Anspielung *f*, Andeutung *f*.

alluvium [əlōō'vēəm] *n* Schwemmland *nt*.

ally [al'ī] *n* Verbündete(r) *mf*; (*POL*) Alliierte(r) *m*.

almanac [ôl'mənak] *n* Kalender *m*.

almighty [ôlmī'tē] *a* allmächtig ♦ *n*: **the A~** der Allmächtige.

almond [â'mənd] *n* Mandel *f*.

almost [ôl'mōst] *ad* fast, beinahe; **he ~ fell** er wäre beinahe gefallen.

alms [âmz] *npl* Almosen *nt*.

alone [əlōn'] *a, ad* allein.

along [əlông'] *prep* entlang, längs; **~ the river** den Fluß entlang ♦ *ad* (*onward*) vorwärts, weiter; **~ with** zusammen mit; **I knew all ~** ich wußte die ganze Zeit.

alongside [əlông'sīd'] *ad* (*walk*) nebenher; (*come*) nebendran; (*be*) daneben ♦ *prep* (*walk, compared with*) neben (+*dat*); (*come*) neben (+*acc*); (*be*) entlang, neben (+*dat*); (*of ship*) längsseits (+*gen*); **we were moored ~ the pier** (*NAUT*) wir lagen am Pier vor Anker.

aloof [əlōōf'] *a* zurückhaltend ♦ *ad* fern.

aloofness [əlōōf'nis] *n* Zurückhaltung *f*, Sich-Fernhalten *nt*.

aloud [əloud'] *ad* laut.

alphabet [al'fəbet] *n* Alphabet *nt*.

alphabetical [alfəbet'ikəl] *a* alphabetisch; **in**

~ order in alphabetischer Reihenfolge.

alphanumeric [alfənōōmär'ik] *a* alphanumerisch.

alpine [al'pīn] *a* alpin, Alpen-.

Alps [alps] *npl* Alpen *pl*.

already [ôlred'ē] *ad* schon, bereits.

alright [ôlrīt'] *|* = **all right**.

Alsace [alsâs'] *n* Elsaß *nt*.

Alsatian [alsā'shən] *n* (*person*) Elsässer(in *f*) *m*; (*Brit: dog*) Schäferhund *m* ♦ *a* elsässisch.

also [ôl'sō] *ad* auch, außerdem.

Alta. *abbr* (*Canada*) = *Alberta*.

altar [ôl'tûr] *n* Altar *m*.

alter [ôl'tûr] *vt* ändern; (*dress*) umändern ♦ *vi* ändern.

alteration [ôltərā'shən] *n* Änderung *f*; Umänderung *f*; (*to building*) Umbau *m*; ~**s** (*SEWING, ARCHIT*) Änderungen *pl*; **timetable subject to ~** Änderungen (im Fahrplan sind) vorbehalten.

alternate *a* [ôl'tûrnit] abwechselnd ♦ *vi* [ôl'tûrnāt] abwechseln (*with* mit).

alternately [ôl'tûrnitlē] *ad* abwechselnd, wechselweise.

alternating [ôl'tûrnāting] *a*: **~ current** Wechselstrom *m*.

alternative [ôltûr'nətiv] *a* andere(r, s) ♦ *n* (*Aus*)wahl *f*, Alternative *f*; **what's the ~?** welche Alternative gibt es?; **we have no ~** uns bleibt keine andere Wahl.

alternatively [ôltûr'nətivlē] *ad* im anderen Falle.

alternator [ôl'tûrnātûr] *n* (*AUT*) Lichtmaschine *f*.

although [ôlt͡hō'] *cj* obwohl, wenn auch.

altitude [al'tətōōd] *n* Höhe *f*.

alto [al'tō] *n* Alt *m*.

altogether [ôltəget͡h'ûr] *ad* (*on the whole*) im ganzen genommen; (*entirely*) ganz und gar; **how much is that ~?** was kostet das alles zusammen?

altruistic [altrōōis'tik] *a* uneigennützig, altruistisch.

aluminium [alōōmin'ēəm] *n* (*Brit*) = **aluminum**.

aluminum [əlōō'mənəm] *n* (*US*) Aluminium *nt*.

aluminum foil *n* Stanniolpapier *nt*.

alumnus [əlum'nəs] *n* (*US SCH*) Ehemalige(r) *m*.

always [ôl'wāz] *ad* immer; **it was ~ that way** es war schon immer so.

am [am] *1 pers sing pres of* **be**.

a.m. *ad abbr* (= *ante meridiem*) vorm.

AM *n abbr* (= *amplitude modulation*) AM.

AMA *n abbr* (= *American Medical Association*) amerikanischer Medizinerverband.

amalgam [əmal'gəm] *n* Amalgam *nt*; (*fig*) Mischung *f*.

amalgamate [əmal'gəmāt] *vi* (*combine*) sich vereinigen ♦ *vt* (*mix*) amalgamieren.

amalgamation [əmalgəmā'shən] *n* Verschmelzung *f*, Zusammenschluß *m*, Fusion *f*.

amass [əmas'] vt anhäufen.

amateur [am'əchûr] n (pej) Amateur m, Bastler m, Stümper m ♦ a Amateur-, Bastler-.

amateur dramatics npl Laientheater nt.

amateurish [aməchōō'rish] a (pej) dilettantisch, stümperhaft.

amaze [əmāz'] vt erstaunen, in Staunen versetzen; **to be ~d (at)** erstaunt sein (über), verblüfft sein (über).

amazement [əmāz'mənt] n höchste(s) (Er)staunen nt.

amazing [əmā'zing] a höchst erstaunlich; (bargain, offer) erstaunlich.

amazingly [əmā'zinglē] ad erstaunlich.

Amazon [am'əzân] n (river) Amazonas m, Amazonasstrom m; (MYTHOLOGY) Amazone f ♦ a: ~ **basin** Amazonasniederung f.

Amazonian [aməzō'nēən] a amazonisch.

ambassador [ambas'ədûr] n Botschafter m.

amber [am'bûr] n Bernstein m.

ambidextrous [ambidek'strəs] a ambidexter (form), beidhändig.

ambience [am'bēəns] n Ambiente nt.

ambiguity [ambəgyōō'itē] n Zweideutigkeit f; Unklarheit f.

ambiguous [ambig'yōōəs] a zweideutig; (not clear) unklar.

ambition [ambish'ən] n Ehrgeiz m; **to achieve one's** ~ seine Ambitionen erfüllen.

ambitious [ambish'əs] a ehrgeizig.

ambivalent [ambiv'ələnt] n (attitude) zwiespältig.

amble [am'bəl] vi schlendern.

ambulance [am'byələns] n Krankenwagen m.

ambush [am'bōōsh] n Hinterhalt m ♦ vt aus dem Hinterhalt angreifen, überfallen.

AMC n abbr (US) = automatic message counting.

ameba [əmē'bə] n (US) = amoeba.

ameliorate [əmēl'yərāt] vt verbessern.

amelioration [əmēlyərā'shən] n Verbesserung f.

amen [ā'men'] interj amen.

amenable [əmē'nəbəl] a gefügig; (to reason) zugänglich (to dat); (to flattery) empfänglich (to für); (to law) unterworfen (to dat).

amend [əmend'] vt (law etc) abändern, ergänzen ♦ n: **to make ~s for sth** etw wiedergutmachen.

amendment [əmend'mənt] n Abänderung f.

amenities [əmen'itēz] npl Einkaufs-, Unterhaltungs- und Transportmöglichkeiten pl.

amenity [əmen'itē] n (moderne) Einrichtung f.

America [əmär'ikə] n Amerika nt.

American [əmär'ikən] a amerikanisch ♦ n Amerikaner(in f) m.

Americanize [əmär'ikənīz] vt amerikanisieren.

Amerindian [amərin'dēən] a indianisch ♦ n Indianer(in f) m.

amethyst [am'ithist] n Amethyst m.

Amex [am'eks] n abbr (= American Stock Ex-

change) amerikanische Börse f.

amiable [ā'mēəbəl] a liebenswürdig, sympathisch.

amicable [am'ikəbəl] a freundschaftlich; (settlement) gütlich.

amid(st) [əmid(st)'] prep mitten in or unter (+dat).

amiss [əmis'] a verkehrt, nicht richtig ♦ ad: **to take sth** ~ etw übelnehmen.

ammeter [am'mētûr] n Amperemeter m.

ammo [am'ō] n abbr (col) = **ammunition**.

ammonia [əmōn'yə] n Ammoniak nt.

ammunition [amyənish'ən] n (lit, fig) Munition f; (fig) Zündstoff m.

ammunition dump n Munitionslager nt.

amnesia [amnē'zhə] n Gedächtnisverlust m.

amnesty [am'nistē] n Amnestie f; **to grant an** ~ (eine) Amnestie gewähren.

amoeba [əmē'bə] n Amöbe f.

amok [əmuk'] ad = **amuck**.

among(st) [əmung(st)'] prep unter.

amoral [āmôr'əl] a unmoralisch.

amorous [am'ûrəs] a verliebt.

amorphous [əmôr'fəs] a formlos, gestaltlos.

amortization [amûrtəzā'shən] n Amortisation f.

amount [əmount'] n (of money) Betrag m; (of time, energy) Aufwand m (of an +dat); (of water, sand) Menge f; **no** ~ **of** ... **kein(e)** ...; **the total** ~ (of money) die Gesamtsumme ♦ vi: **to** ~ **to** (total) sich belaufen auf (+acc); **this ~s to a refusal** das kommt einer Absage gleich; **this ~s to treachery** das kommt Verrat gleich; **it ~s to the same** es läuft aufs gleiche hinaus; **he won't** ~ **to much** aus ihm wird nie was.

amp [amp] n = **ampère**.

ampère [am'pēr] n Ampere nt.

ampersand [am'pûrsand] n Und-Zeichen nt.

amphibian [amfib'ēən] n Amphibie f.

amphibious [amfib'ēəs] a amphibisch, Amphibien-.

amphitheater, (Brit) **amphitheatre** [am'fəthēətûr] n Amphitheater nt; (lecture hall) Hörsaal m.

ample [am'pəl] a (portion) reichlich; (dress) weit, groß; ~ **time** genügend Zeit.

amplifier [am'pləfiûr] n Verstärker m.

amply [am'plē] ad reichlich.

ampule, (Brit) **ampoule** [am'pyōōl] n (MED) Ampulle f.

amputate [am'pyōōtāt] vt amputieren, abnehmen.

Amsterdam [am'stûrdam] n Amsterdam nt.

amt. abbr (= amount) Betr.

amuck [əmuk'] ad: **to run** ~ Amok laufen.

amuse [əmyōōz'] vt (entertain) unterhalten; (make smile) belustigen; (occupy) unterhalten; **I'm not ~d** das find' ich gar nicht lustig; **if that ~s you** wenn es dir Spaß macht; **to ~ o.s. with sth** sich die Zeit mit etw vertreiben; **to be ~d at sth** sich über etw amüsieren.

amusement [əmyōōz'mənt] n (feeling) Unter-

haltung *f*; *(recreation)* Zeitvertreib *m*; **much to my** ~ zu meiner großen Belustigung.
amusement arcade *n* Spielhalle *f*.
amusement park *n* Vergnügungspark *m*.
amusing [əmyōō'zing] *a* amüsant, unterhaltend.
an [an, ən] *indef art* ein(e).
ANA *n abbr* (= *American Nurses Association*) *amerikanischer Krankenschwesternverband*; = *American Newspaper Association*.
anachronism [ənak'rənizəm] *n* Anachronismus *m*.
anaemia [ənē'mēə] *n* *(Brit)* Anämie *f*.
anaemic [ənē'mik] *a* *(Brit)* blutarm.
anaesthetic [anisthet'ik] *n* *(Brit)* = **anesthetic**.
anaesthetist [ənēs'thətist] *n* *(Brit)* Anästhesist(in *f*) *m*.
anagram [an'əgram] *n* Anagramm *nt*.
analgesic [anəljē'zik] *n* schmerzlindernde(s) Mittel *nt*.
analog, analogue [an'əlôg] *a* analog.
analog computer *n* Analogrechner *m*.
analogous [ənal'əgəs] *a* analog *(with* zu).
analogy [ənal'əjē] *n* Analogie *f*; **to draw an** ~ **(between)** eine Analogie herstellen (zwischen).
analyse [an'əlīz] *vt* *(Brit)* analysieren.
analysis [ənal'isis] *n* Analyse *f*; **in the last** ~ letzten Endes.
analyst [an'əlist] *n* *(also:* **psycho**~) (Psycho)analytiker(in *f*) *m*.
analytic [anəlit'ik] *a* analytisch.
analyze [an'əlīz] *vt* *(US)* analysieren.
anarchist [an'ûrkist] *n* Anarchist(in *f*) *m*.
anarchy [an'ûrkē] *n* Anarchie *f*.
anathema [ənath'əmə] *n* *(fig)* Greuel *nt*.
anatomical [anətâm'ikəl] *a* anatomisch.
anatomy [ənat'əmē] *n* *(structure)* anatomische(r) Aufbau *m*; *(study)* Anatomie *f*.
ANC *n abbr* (= *African National Congress*) ANC *m*.
ancestor [an'sestûr] *n* Vorfahr *m*.
ancestral [anses'trəl] *a* angestammt, Ahnen-.
ancestry [an'sestrē] *n* Abstammung *f*; Vorfahren *pl*.
anchor [ang'kûr] *n* Anker *m* ♦ *vi* ankern, vor Anker liegen ♦ *vt* verankern.
anchorage [ang'kûrij] *n* Ankerplatz *m*.
anchovy [an'chōvē] *n* Sardelle *f*.
ancient [ān'shənt] *a* alt; *(car etc)* uralt; ~ **monument** historische(s) Denkmal *nt*.
ancillary [an'səlārē] *a* Hilfs-.
and [and] *cj* und.
Andes [an'dēz] *npl* Anden *pl*.
anecdote [an'ikdōt] *n* Anekdote *f*.
anemia [ənē'mēə] *n* *(US)* Anämie *f*.
anemic [ənē'mik] *a* *(US)* blutarm.
anemone [ənem'ənē] *n* *(BOT)* Anemone *f*, Buschwindröschen *nt*; *(sea* ~) Seeanemone *f*.
anesthesiologist [an'isthēzēāl'əjist] *n* *(US)* Anästhesist(in *f*) *m*.

anesthetic [anisthet'ik] *n* *(US)* Betäubungsmittel *nt*; **local** ~ örtliche Betäubung *f*; **general** ~ Vollnarkose *f*; **under** ~ unter Narkose.
anew [ənōō'] *ad* von neuem.
angel [ān'jəl] *n* Engel *m*.
angelic [anjel'ik] *a* engelhaft.
anger [ang'gûr] *n* Zorn *m* ♦ *vt* ärgern.
angina [anjī'nə] *n* Angina *f*.
angle [ang'gəl] *n* Winkel *m*; *(point of view)* Standpunkt *m*; **at an** ~ nicht gerade, schräg ♦ *vt* stellen; **to** ~ **for** aussein auf (+*acc*).
angler [ang'glûr] *n* Angler *m*.
Anglican [ang'glikən] *a* anglikanisch ♦ *n* Anglikaner(in *f*) *m*.
anglicize [ang'gləsīz] *vt* anglisieren.
angling [ang'gling] *n* Angeln *nt*.
Anglo- [an'glō] *pref* Anglo-; ~**German** anglodeutsch.
Angola [anggō'lə] *n* Angola *nt*.
Angolan [anggō'lən] *a* angolanisch ♦ *n* *(person)* Angolaner(in *f*) *m*.
angrily [ang'grilē] *ad* ärgerlich, böse.
angry [ang'grē] *a* ärgerlich, ungehalten, böse; *(wound)* entzündet.
anguish [ang'gwish] *n* Qual *f*.
angular [ang'gyəlûr] *a* eckig, winkelförmig; *(face)* kantig.
animal [an'əməl] *n* Tier *nt*; *(living creature)* Lebewesen *nt* ♦ *a* tierisch, animalisch.
animate *vt* [an'əmāt] beleben ♦ *a* [an'əmit] lebhaft.
animated [an'əmātid] *a* lebendig; *(film)* Zeichentrick-.
animation [anəmā'shən] *n* Lebhaftigkeit *f*.
animosity [anəmâs'ətē] *n* Feindseligkeit *f*, Abneigung *f*.
aniseed [an'isēd] *n* Anis *m*.
Ankara [ang'kûrə] *n* Ankara *nt*.
ankle [ang'kəl] *n* (Fuß)knöchel *m*.
ankle socks *npl* Söckchen *pl*.
annex [an'eks] *n* Anbau *m* ♦ *vt* [əneks'] anfügen; *(POL)* annektieren, angliedern.
annihilate [ənī'əlāt] *vt* vernichten.
anniversary [anəvûr'sûrē] *n* Jahrestag *m*.
annotate [an'ōtāt] *vt* kommentieren.
announce [ənouns'] *vt* ankündigen, anzeigen; **he** ~**d that he wasn't going** er gab bekannt, daß er nicht gehen würde.
announcement [ənouns'mənt] *n* Ankündigung *f*; *(official)* Bekanntmachung *f*; **I'd like to make an** ~ *(of impending event, speaker)* ich möchte etwas bekanntgeben; *(over intercom etc)* ich möchte eine Durchsage machen.
announcer [ənoun'sûr] *n* Ansager(in *f*) *m*.
annoy [ənoi'] *vt* ärgern; **to be** ~**ed (at sth/ with sb)** sich ärgern (über etw/jdn).
annoyance [ənoi'əns] *n* Ärgernis *nt*, Störung *f*.
annoying [ənoi'ing] *a* ärgerlich; *(person, habit)* lästig.
annual [an'yōōəl] *a* jährlich; *(salary)* Jahres-; ~ **general meeting** *(Brit)* Jahreshauptver-

sammlung f; ~ **report** Jahresbericht m ♦ n (*plant*) einjährige Pflanze f; (*book*) Jahrbuch nt.
annually [an'yōōəlē] ad jährlich.
annuity [ənōō'itē] n Jahresrente f.
annul [ənul'] vt aufheben, annullieren.
annulment [ənul'mənt] n Aufhebung f, Annullierung f.
Annunciation [ənunsēā'shən] n Mariä Verkündigung f.
anode [an'ōd] n Anode f.
anoint [ənoint'] vt salben.
anomalous [ənâm'ələs] a unregelmäßig, anomal.
anomaly [ənâm'əlē] n Abweichung f von der Regel.
anon [ənân'] abbr = **anonymous.**
anonymity [anənim'itē] n Anonymität f.
anonymous [ənân'əməs] a anonym; **to remain** ~ anonym bleiben.
anorak [ân'ərâk] n Anorak m, Windjacke f.
anorexia [anərek'sēə] n Magersucht f, Anorexie f.
another [ənuth'ûr] a, pron (*different*) ein(e) andere(r, s); (*additional*) noch eine(r, s); ~ **drink?** noch etwas zu trinken?; **in ~ 5 years** nach weiteren 5 Jahren; **some actor or ~** (*US*) irgendein Schauspieler.
ANSI n abbr (= *American National Standards Institute*) ≈ DNA m (= *Deutscher Normenausschuß*).
answer [an'sûr] n Antwort f ♦ vi antworten; (*on phone*) sich melden ♦ vt (*person*) antworten (+*dat*); (*letter, question*) beantworten; (*telephone*) gehen an (+*acc*), abnehmen; (*door*) öffnen; **to ~ to the name of ...** auf den Namen ... hören.
answer back vi frech sein.
answer for vt fus: **to ~ for sth** für etw verantwortlich sein.
answerable [an'sûrəbəl] a beantwortbar; (*responsible*) verantwortlich, haftbar.
answering machine [an'sûring məshēn'] n Anrufbeantworter m.
ant [ant] n Ameise f.
ANTA n abbr (= *American National Theater and Academy*) Vereinigung amerikanischer Theater.
antagonism [antag'ənizəm] n Antagonismus m.
antagonist [antag'ənist] n Gegner m, Antagonist m.
antagonistic [antagənis'tik] a feindselig.
antagonize [antag'ənīz] vt reizen.
Antarctic [antârk'tik] a antarktisch ♦ n die Antarktis.
Antarctica [antârk'tikə] n die Antarktis.
Antarctic Circle n südliche(r) Polarkreis m.
Antarctic Ocean n Südpolarmeer nt.
ante [an'tē] n: **to up the ~** den Einsatz erhöhen.
ante- [an'tē] pref vor-.
anteater [ant'ētûr] n Ameisenbär m.
antecedent [antisē'dənt] n Vorhergehende(s)

nt; ~**s** pl Vorleben nt, Vorgeschichte f.
antechamber [an'tēchâmbûr] n Vorzimmer nt.
antelope [an'təlōp] n Antilope f.
antenatal [antēnā'təl] a (*Brit*) = **prenatal.**
antenatal clinic n Sprechstunde f für werdende Mütter.
antenna [anten'ə] n (*BIOL*) Fühler m; (*RAD*) Antenne f.
anteroom [an'tērōōm] n Vorzimmer nt.
anthem [an'thəm] n Hymne f.
anthill [ant.hil'] n Ameisenhaufen m.
anthology [anthâl'əjē] n Gedichtsammlung f, Anthologie f.
anthropologist [anthrəpâl'əjist] n Anthropologe m, Anthropologin f.
anthropology [anthrəpâl'əjē] n Anthropologie f.
anti- [an'tī] pref Gegen-, Anti-.
antiaircraft [antīâr'kraft] a Flugabwehr-.
antiballistic [antēbəlis'tik] a Anti-Raketen-.
antibiotic [antēbīât'ik] n Antibiotikum nt.
antibody [an'tēbâdē] n Antikörper m.
anticipate [antis'əpāt] vt (*expect: trouble, question*) erwarten, rechnen mit; (*look forward to*) sich freuen auf (+*acc*); (*do first*) vorwegnehmen; (*foresee*) ahnen, vorhersehen; **as ~d** wie erwartet; **this is worse than I ~d** es ist schlimmer, als ich erwartet habe.
anticipation [antisəpā'shən] n Erwartung f; (*foreshadowing*) Vorwegnahme f; **that was good ~** das war gut vorausgesehen.
anticlimax [antēklī'maks] n Ernüchterung f.
anticlockwise [antēklâk'wīz] a (*Brit*) entgegen dem Uhrzeigersinn.
antics [an'tiks] npl Possen pl.
anticyclone [antēsī'klōn] n Hoch nt, Hochdruckgebiet nt.
antidote [an'tidōt] n Gegenmittel nt.
antifreeze [an'tēfrēz] n Frostschutzmittel nt.
antihistamine [antēhis'təmēn] n Antihistamin(ikum) nt.
Antilles [antil'ēz] npl Antillen pl.
antipathy [antip'əthē] n Abneigung f, Antipathie f.
Antipodean [antipədē'ən] a antipodisch.
Antipodes [antip'ədēz] npl Antipodeninseln pl.
antiquarian [antəkwâr'ēən] a altertümlich ♦ n Antiquitätensammler m.
antiquated [an'təkwātid] a antiquiert.
antique [antēk'] n Antiquität f ♦ a antik; (*old-fashioned*) altmodisch.
antique shop n Antiquitätenladen m.
antiquity [antik'witē] n Antike f, Altertum nt.
anti-Semitic [an'tīsəmit'ik] a antisemitisch.
anti-Semitism [antīsem'itizəm] n Antisemitismus m.
antiseptic [antēsep'tik] n Antiseptikum nt ♦ a antiseptisch.
antisocial [antēsō'shəl] a (*person*) ungesellig; (*law*) unsozial.
antitank [antētangk'] a Panzerabwehr-.

antithesis [antith'əsis] *n*, *pl* **antitheses** [antith'əsēz] Gegensatz *m*, Antithese *f*; (*direct opposite*) genaue(s) Gegenteil *nt*.

antitrust [antētrust'] *a* (*US*): ~ **legislation** Kartellgesetzgebung *f*.

antlers [ant'lûrz] *npl* Geweih *nt*.

anus [ā'nəs] *n* After *m*.

anvil [an'vil] *n* Amboß *m*.

anxiety [angzī'ətē] *n* Angst *f*; (*worry*) Sorge *f*.

anxious [angk'shəs] *a* ängstlich; (*worried*) besorgt; **I'm very** ~ **about you** ich mache mir große Sorgen um Sie; **to be** ~ **to do sth** etw unbedingt tun wollen.

anxiously [angk'shəslē] *ad* besorgt; (*keenly*) begierig.

any [en'ē] *a* irgendein(e); (*with pl n*) irgendwelche; (*no matter which*) jede(r,s); **take** ~ **one** nimm irgendein!; **do you want** ~ **apples?** willst du Äpfel (haben)?; **do you want** ~**?** willst du welche?; **not** ~ kein/keine; **have you** ~ **money?** has du Geld (dabei)? ♦ *ad*: ~ **faster** schneller.

anybody [en'ēbâdē] *pron* irgend jemand; (*everybody*) jedermann.

anyhow [en'ēhou] *ad* sowieso, ohnehin; (*carelessly*) einfach so; (*haphazardly*) irgendwie; **I shall go** ~ ich gehe sowieso.

anyone [en'ēwun] *pron* = **anybody**.

anyplace [en'ēplās] *ad col*) = **anywhere**.

anything [en'ēthing] *pron* irgend etwas; ~ **else?** sonst noch etwas?

anytime [en'ētīm] *ad* jederzeit.

anyway [en'ēwā] *ad* sowieso, ohnehin; ~, **let's stop** na ja *or* sei's drum, hören wir auf.

anywhere [en'ēhwär] *ad* irgendwo; (*everywhere*) überall; ~ **in the world** überall auf der Welt.

Anzac [an'zak] *n abbr* = *Australia-New Zealand Army Corps*.

apace [əpās'] *ad* rasch.

apart [əpârt'] *ad* (*parted*) auseinander; (*away*) beiseite, abseits; ~ **from** außer.

apartheid [əpârt'hīt] *n* Apartheid *f*.

apartment [əpârt'mənt] *n* Wohnung *f*; ~**s** *pl* (möblierte Miet)wohnung *f*.

apartment block *or* **building** *or* **house** *n* (*US*) Wohnhaus *nt*.

apathetic [apəthet'ik] *a* teilnahmslos, apathisch.

apathy [ap'əthē] *n* Teilnahmslosigkeit *f*, Apathie *f*.

APB *n abbr* (*US*: = *all points bulletin*) amerikanischer Polizeijargon *für Aufspüren und Verhaftung einer verdächtigen Person*.

ape [āp] *n* (Menschen)affe *m* ♦ *vt* nachahmen.

Apennines [ap'əninz] *npl* Apenninen *pl*, der Apennin.

aperitif [əpārētēf'] *n* Aperitif *m*.

aperture [ap'ûrchûr] *n* Öffnung *f*; (*PHOT*) Blende *f*.

apex [ā'peks] *n* Spitze *f*, Scheitelpunkt *m*.

APEX [ā'peks] *n abbr* (*AVIAT*: = *advance*

purchase excursion) APEX.

aphid [ā'fid] *n* Blattlaus *f*.

aphorism [af'ərizəm] *n* Aphorismus *m*.

aphrodisiac [afrədiz'ēak] *n* Aphrodisiakum *nt*.

API *n abbr* (= *American Press Institute*) API *f*.

apiece [əpēs'] *ad* pro Stück; (*per person*) pro Kopf.

aplomb [əplâm'] *n* selbstbewußte(s) Auftreten *nt*.

APO *n abbr* (*US*: = *Army Post Office*) Feldpostamt *nt*.

Apocalypse [əpâk'əlips] *n* Apokalypse *f*.

apocryphal [əpâk'rəfəl] *a* apokryph, unecht.

apolitical [āpəlit'ikəl] *a* apolitisch.

apologetic [əpâləjet'ik] *a* entschuldigend; **to be** ~ sich sehr entschuldigen.

apologetically [əpâləjet'iklē] *ad* entschuldigend.

apologize [əpâl'əjīz] *vi* sich entschuldigen.

apology [əpâl'əjē] *n* Entschuldigung *f*; **please accept my apologies** ich bitte um Verzeihung.

apoplectic [apəplek'tik] *a* (*MED*) apoplektisch; **he was** ~ **with rage** er platzte fast vor Wut.

apoplexy [ap'əpleksē] *n* Schlaganfall *m*.

apostle [əpâs'əl] *n* Apostel *m*; (*pioneer*) Vorkämpfer *m*.

apostrophe [əpâs'trəfē] *n* Apostroph *m*.

Appalachian Mountains [apəlā'chēən moun'tənz] *npl* Appalachen *pl*.

appall(l) [əpôl'] *vt* erschrecken.

appalling [əpôl'ing] *a* schrecklich; **she's an** ~ **cook** sie kann überhaupt nicht kochen.

apparatus [apərat'əs] *n* Apparat *m*, Gerät *nt*.

apparel [əpar'əl] *n* Kleidung *f*; (*US COMM*) Kleider *pl*.

apparent [əpar'ənt] *a* offenbar; **heir** ~ gesetzliche(r) Erbe *m*; **it is** ~ **that** ... es ist offensichtlich, daß ...

apparently [əpar'əntlē] *ad* anscheinend.

apparition [apərish'ən] *n* (*ghost*) Erscheinung *f*, Geist *m*; (*appearance*) Erscheinen *nt*.

appeal [əpēl'] *vi* dringend ersuchen; dringend bitten (*for* um); sich wenden (*to* an +*acc*); (*to public*) appellieren (*to* an +*acc*); (*JUR*) Berufung einlegen ♦ *n* Aufruf *m*; (*JUR*) Berufung *f*; **right of** ~ Einspruchsrecht *nt*.

appealing [əpē'ling] *a* ansprechend; (*moving*) bittend; (*attractive*) reizvoll.

appear [əpēr'] *vi* (*come into sight*) erscheinen; (*be seen*) auftauchen; (*seem*) scheinen.

appearance [əpē'rəns] *n* (*coming into sight*) Erscheinen *nt*; (*outward show*) Äußere(s) *nt*; **to put in** *or* **make an** ~ sich zeigen; **to all** ~**s** allem Anschein nach; **to keep up** ~**s** den (äußeren) Schein wahren.

appease [əpēz'] *vt* beschwichtigen.

appeasement [əpēz'mənt] *n* (*POL*) Beschwichtigung *f* (durch Zugeständnisse).

appellate court [əpel'it kôrt] *n* (*US*) Berufungsgericht *nt*.

append [əpend'] *vt* (*COMPUT*) anhängen, hinzufügen.

appendage [əpen'dij] *n* Anhang *m*, Anhängsel *nt*.

appendicitis [əpendisī'tis] *n* Blinddarmentzündung *f*.

appendix [əpen'diks] *n* (*in book*) Anhang *m*; (*MED*) Blinddarm *m*; **to have one's ~ out** sich am Blinddarm operieren lassen.

appetite [ap'itīt] *n* Appetit *m*; (*fig*) Lust *f*; **that walk has given me an ~** der Spaziergang hat mich hungrig gemacht.

appetizer [ap'itīzûr] *n* (*food*) Vorspeise *f*, Appetithappen *m*; (*drink*) appetitanregende(s) Getränk *nt*.

appetizing [ap'itīzing] *a* appetitanregend.

applaud [əplôd'] *vti* Beifall klatschen (*+dat*), applaudieren.

applause [əplôz'] *n* Beifall *m*, Applaus *m*.

apple [ap'əl] *n* Apfel *m*.

apple tree *n* Apfelbaum *m*.

appliance [əplī'əns] *n* Gerät *nt*; **electrical ~s** Elektrogeräte *pl*.

applicable [ap'likəbəl] *a* anwendbar; (*in forms*) zutreffend; **the law is ~ from January** das Gesetz gilt ab Januar; **to be ~ to** anwendbar sein auf.

applicant [ap'likənt] *n* (*for job*) Bewerber(in *f*) *m*; (*for benefit etc*) Antragsteller(in *f*) *m*.

application [aplikā'shən] *n* (*request*) Antrag *m*; (*for job*) Bewerbung *f*; (*putting into practice*) Anwendung *f*; (*hard work*) Fleiß *m*.

application form *n* Bewerbungsformular *nt*.

applications [aplikā'shənz] *a* (*COMPUT*) Anwender-.

applied [əplīd'] *a* angewandt.

apply [əplī'] *vi* (*ask*) sich wenden (*to* an *+acc*), sich melden; (*be suitable*) zutreffen ♦ *vt* (*place on*) auflegen; (*cream*) auftragen; (*put into practice*) anwenden; (*devote o.s.*) sich widmen (*to dat*).

appoint [əpoint'] *vt* (*to office*) ernennen, berufen; (*settle*) festsetzen.

appointee [əpointē'] *n* Ernannte(r) *mf*.

appointment [əpoint'mənt] *n* (*meeting*) Verabredung *f*; (*at hairdresser etc*) Bestellung *f*; (*in business*) Termin *m*; (*choice for a position*) Ernennung *f*; (*UNIV*) Berufung *f*; **"~s (vacant)"** (*PRESS*) „Stellenangebote"; **by ~** auf Verabredung; (*to see doctor, lawyer etc*) mit Voranmeldung, nach Vereinbarung; **to make an ~ with sb** einen Termin mit jdm vereinbaren.

appointment book *n* Terminkalender *m*.

apportion [əpôr'shən] *vt* aufteilen, zuteilen.

appraisal [əprā'zəl] *n* Beurteilung *f*.

appraise [əprāz'] *vt* (ab)schätzen.

appreciable [əprē'shēəbəl] *a* (*perceptible*) merklich; (*able to be estimated*) abschätzbar.

appreciate [əprē'shēāt] *vt* (*value*) zu schätzen wissen; (*understand*) einsehen ♦ *vi* (*increase in value*) im Wert steigen; **I ~ your help** ich

weiß Ihre Hilfe zu schätzen.

appreciation [əprēshēā'shən] *n* Wertschätzung *f*; (*COMM*) Wertzuwachs *m*.

appreciative [əprē'shətiv] *a* (*showing thanks*) dankbar; (*showing liking*) anerkennend.

apprehend [aprihend'] *vt* (*arrest*) festnehmen; (*understand*) erfassen.

apprehension [aprihen'shən] *n* Angst *f*.

apprehensive [aprihen'siv] *a* furchtsam.

apprentice [əpren'tis] *n* Lehrling *m* ♦ *vt*: **to be ~d to** bei jdm in der Lehre sein.

apprenticeship [əpren'tisship] *n* Lehrzeit *f*; **to serve one's ~** seine Lehre machen.

approach [əprōch'] *vi* sich nähern ♦ *vt* herantreten an (*+acc*); (*problem*) herangehen an (*+acc*); **to ~ sb about sth** jdn auf etw ansprechen ♦ *n* Annäherung *f*; (*to problem*) Ansatz *m*; (*path*) Zugang *m*, Zufahrt *f*.

approachable [əprō'chəbəl] *a* zugänglich.

approbation [aprəbā'shən] *n* Billigung *f*.

appropriate *vt* [əprōp'rēāt] (*take for o.s.*) sich aneignen; (*set apart*) bereitstellen ♦ *a* [əprōp'rēit] angemessen; (*remark*) angebracht; **~ for *or* to** passend für, geeignet für; **it would not be ~ for me to comment** es wäre nicht angebracht, wenn ich meinen Kommentar dazu geben würde.

appropriately [əprōp'rēitlē] *ad* passend.

appropriation [əprōprēā'shən] *n* Bereitstellung *f* von Geldmitteln.

approval [əprōō'vəl] *n* (*show of satisfaction*) Beifall *m*; (*permission*) Billigung *f*; **to meet with sb's ~** jds Zustimmung *or* Beifall finden; **on ~** (*COMM*) bei Gefallen.

approve [əprōōv'] *vti* billigen (*of acc*); **I don't ~ of it/him** ich halte nichts davon/von ihm.

approx. *abbr* (= *approximately*) ung.

approximate *a* [əprâk'səmit] annähernd, ungefähr ♦ *vt* [əprâk'səmāt] nahekommen (*+dat*).

approximately [əprâk'səmitlē] *ad* rund, ungefähr.

approximation [əprâksəmā'shən] *n* Annäherung *f*.

appt. *abbr* (*US*) = **appointment**.

apr *n abbr* (= *annual percentage rate*) Jahreszins *m*.

Apr. *abbr* (= *April*) Apr.

apricot [ap'rikât] *n* Aprikose *f*.

April [āp'rəl] *n* April *m*; **see September**.

April Fool's Day *n* der erste April.

apron [ā'prən] *n* Schürze *f*; (*AVIAT*) Vorfeld *nt*.

apse [aps] *n* (*ARCHIT*) Apsis *f*.

apt [apt] *a* (*suitable*) passend; (*able*) begabt; (*likely*) geneigt.

Apt. *abbr* (= *apartment*) Apart.

aptitude [ap'tətōōd] *n* Begabung *f*.

aptitude test *n* Eignungsprüfung *f*.

aptly [apt'lē] *ad* passend.

aqualung [ak'wəlung] *n* Unterwasseratmungsgerät *nt*.

aquarium [əkwär'ēəm] *n* Aquarium *nt*.

Aquarius [əkwär'ēəs] *n* Wassermann *m*.
aquatic [əkwat'ik] *a* Wasser-.
aqueduct [ak'widukt] *n* Aquädukt *nt*.
AR *abbr* (*US MAIL*) = *Arkansas*.
Arab [ar'əb] *a* arabisch ♦ *n* (*person*) Araber(in *f*) *m*.
Arabia [ərābēə] *n* Arabien *nt*.
Arabian [ərā'bēən] *a* arabisch; ~ **Desert** Arabische Wüste *f*; ~ **Gulf** Arabische(r) Golf *m*; ~ **Sea** Arabische(s) Meer *nt*.
Arabic [ar'əbik] *a* arabisch ♦ *n* (*language*) Arabisch *nt*.
arable [ar'əbəl] *a* bebaubar, Kultur-.
arbiter [âr'bitûr] *n* (Schieds)richter *m*.
arbitrary [âr'biträrē] *a* willkürlich.
arbitrate [âr'bitrāt] *vti* schlichten.
arbitration [ârbitrā'shən] *n* Schlichtung *f*; **to go to** ~ vor ein Schiedsgericht gehen; **the dispute went to** ~ der Streit wurde vor eine Schlichtungskommission gebracht.
arbitrator [âr'bitrātûr] *n* Schiedsrichter *m*, Schlichter *m*.
arc [ârk] *n* Bogen *m*.
ARC *n abbr* (= *American Red Cross*) ≈ DRK *nt*.
arcade [ârkād'] *n* Säulengang *m*.
arch [ârch] *n* Bogen *m* ♦ *vt* überwölben; (*back*) krumm machen ♦ *vi* sich wölben ♦ *a* durchtrieben.
archaeology [ârkēâl'əjē] *etc* = **archeology** *etc*.
archaic [ârkā'ik] *a* altertümlich.
archangel [ârkān'jəl] *n* Erzengel *m*.
archbishop [ârchbish'əp] *n* Erzbischof *m*.
arched [ârcht] *a* gewölbt.
archenemy [ârch'en'əmē] *n* Erzfeind *m*.
archeological [ârkēəlâj'ikəl] *a* archäologisch.
archeologist [ârkēâl'əjist] *n* Archäologe *m*.
archeology [ârkēâl'əjē] *n* Archäologie *f*.
archer [âr'chûr] *n* Bogenschütze *m*.
archery [âr'chûrē] *n* Bogenschießen *nt*.
archetypal [âr'kitīpəl] *a* archetypisch.
archipelago [ârkəpel'əgō] *n* Archipel *m*; (*sea*) Inselmeer *nt*.
architect [âr'kitekt] *n* Architekt(in *f*) *m*.
architectural [âr'kitekchûrəl] *a* architektonisch.
architecture [âr'kitekchûr] *n* Architektur *f*.
archive file *n* (*COMPUT*) Archivierungsdatei *f*, Archivdatei *f*.
archive [âr'kīv] *n* (*also COMPUT*) Archiv *nt*.
archives [âr'kīvz] *npl* Archiv *nt*.
archivist [âr'kəvist] *n* Archivar *m*.
archway [ârch'wā] *n* Bogen *m*.
Arctic [ârk'tik] *a* arktisch ♦ *n*: **the** ~ die Arktis.
Arctic Circle *n* nördliche(r) Polarkreis *m*.
Arctic Ocean *n* Nordpolarmeer *nt*.
ARD *n abbr* (*US MED*: = *acute respiratory disease*) *akute bakterielle Erkrankung des Respirationstrakts*.
ardent [âr'dənt] *a* glühend.
ardor, (*Brit*) **ardour** [âr'dûr] *n* Begeisterung *f*, Leidenschaft *f*.

arduous [âr'jōōəs] *a* mühsam.
are [âr] *see* **be**.
area [âr'ēə] *n* Fläche *f*; (*of land*) Gebiet *nt*; (*part of sth*) Teil *m*, Abschnitt *m*; **the Washington** ~ die Gegend um Washington.
area code *n* (*TEL*) Vorwahl(nummer) *f*.
arena [ərē'nə] *n* Arena *f*.
aren't [ârnt] = **are not**.
Argentina [ârjəntē'nə] *n* Argentinien *nt*.
Argentinian [ârjəntin'ēən] *a* argentinisch ♦ *n* Argentinier(in *f*) *m*.
arguable [âr'gyōōəbəl] *a* (*doubtful*) diskutabel; (*possible*): **it's** ~ **that** ... man könnte argumentieren, daß ...; **it is** ~ **whether** ... est ist die Frage, ob ...
arguably [âr'gyōōəblē] *ad* wohl.
argue [âr'gyōō] *vt* (*debate*: *case, matter*) diskutieren, erörtern; (*JUR*) vertreten ♦ *vi* diskutieren; (*angrily*) streiten; **don't** ~! keine Widerrede!; **to** ~ **about sth (with sb)** sich (mit jdm) über etw streiten.
argument [âr'gyəmənt] *n* (*theory*) Argument *nt*; (*reasoning*) Argumentation *f*; (*row*) Auseinandersetzung *f*, Streit *m*; ~**s for/against** Gründe *pl*/Gegengründe *pl*; **to have an** ~ sich streiten.
argumentative [ârgyəmen'tətiv] *a* streitlustig.
aria [âr'ēə] *n* Arie *f*.
arid [ar'id] *a* trocken.
aridity [ərid'itē] *n* Dürre *f*.
Aries [âr'ēz] *n* Widder *m*.
arise [ərīz'] *vi irreg* aufsteigen; (*get up*) aufstehen; (*difficulties etc*) entstehen; (*case*) vorkommen; **to** ~ **out of sth** herrühren von etw; **should the need** ~ falls sich die Notwendigkeit ergibt.
arisen [əriz'ən] *pp of* **arise**.
aristocracy [aristâk'rəsē] *n* Adel *m*, Aristokratie *f*.
aristocrat [əris'təkrat] *n* Adlige(r) *mf*, Aristokrat(in *f*) *m*.
aristocratic [əristəkrat'ik] *a* adlig, aristokratisch.
arithmetic [ərith'mətik] *n* Rechnen *nt*, Arithmetik *f*.
arithmetical [arithmet'ikəl] *a* arithmetisch.
Ariz. *abbr* (*US*) = *Arizona*.
Ark. *abbr* (*US*) = *Arkansas*.
ark [ârk] *n*: **Noah's A~** die Arche Noah.
arm [ârm] *n* Arm *m*; (*branch of military service*) Zweig *m*; *see also* **arms** ♦ *vt* bewaffnen.
armaments [âr'məmənts] *npl* (*weapons*) Ausrüstung *f*.
armchair [ârm'chär] *n* Lehnstuhl *m*.
armed [ârmd] *a* (*robbery also*) bewaffnet; **the** ~ **forces** die Streitkräfte *pl*.
Armenia [ârmē'nēə] *n* Armenien *nt*.
Armenian [ârmē'nēən] *a* armenisch ♦ *n* (*person*) Armenier(in *f*) *m*; (*language*) Armenisch *nt*.
armful [ârm'fəl] *n* Armvoll *m*.

armistice [âr'mistis] *n* Waffenstillstand *m*.
armor [âr'mûr] *n* (*US*) (*knight's*) Rüstung *f*; (*MIL*) Panzerplatte *f*.
armored car [ârmûrd kâr'] *n* Panzerwagen *m*.
armory [âr'mûrē] *n* Waffenlager *nt*; (*factory*) Waffenfabrik *f*.
armour [âr'mûr] *etc* (*Brit*) = **armor** *etc*.
armpit [ârm'pit] *n* Achselhöhle *f*.
armrest [ârm'rest] *n* Armlehne *f*.
arms [ârmz] *npl* (*weapons*) Waffen *pl*; **the ~ race** das Wettrüsten.
arms control *n* Abrüstung *f*.
army [âr'mē] *n* Armee *f*, Heer *nt*; (*fig*) Heer *nt*.
aroma [ərō'mə] *n* Duft *m*, Aroma *nt*.
aromatic [arəmat'ik] *a* aromatisch, würzig.
arose [ərōz'] *pt of* **arise**.
around [əround'] *ad* ringsherum; (*about*) ungefähr; **it's the other way ~** es ist genau umgekehrt; **enough to go ~** genug für alle; **I'll be ~ at 6** ich werde um 6 Uhr da sein; **to ask sb ~** jdn zu sich einladen ♦ *prep* um ... herum; **is he ~?** ist er hier?
arouse [ərouz'] *vt* wecken.
arrange [ərānj'] *vt* (*time, meeting*) festsetzen; (*vacation*) festlegen; (*flowers, hair, objects*) anordnen; **I ~d to meet him** ich habe mit ihm ausgemacht, ihn zu treffen; **it's all ~d** es ist alles arrangiert; **it was ~d that ...** es wurde vereinbart, daß ...; **to ~ to do sth** dafür sorgen, daß etw getan wird; **we have ~d for a cab to pick you up** wir haben Ihnen ein Taxi bestellt.
arrangement [ərānj'mənt] *n* (*order*) Reihenfolge *f*; (*agreement*) Übereinkommen *nt*; (*plan*) Vereinbarung *f*; **by ~** nach Vereinbarung; **to come to an ~** (**with sb**) eine Regelung (mit jdm) treffen; **I'll make ~s for you to be met** ich werde dafür sorgen, daß Sie abgeholt werden.
array [ərā'] *n* Aufstellung *f*; (*COMPUT*) Datenfeld *nt*.
arrears [ərērz'] *npl* (*of debts*) Rückstand *m*; (*of work*) Unerledigte(s) *nt*; **in ~** im Rückstand.
arrest [ərest'] *vt* (*person*) verhaften; (*stop*) aufhalten ♦ *n* Verhaftung *f*; **under ~** in Haft; **you're under ~** Sie sind verhaftet.
arresting [əres'ting] *a* (*fig*) atemberaubend.
arrival [ərī'vəl] *n* Ankunft *f*.
arrive [ərīv'] *vi* ankommen (*at* in +*dat*, bei); **to ~ at a decision** zu einer Entscheidung kommen.
arrogance [ar'əgəns] *n* Überheblichkeit *f*, Arroganz *f*.
arrogant [ar'əgənt] *a* anmaßend, arrogant.
arrow [ar'ō] *n* Pfeil *m*.
arse [ârs] *n* (*Brit col!*) Arsch *m*.
arsenal [âr'sənəl] *n* Waffenlager *nt*, Zeughaus *nt*.
arsenic [âr'sənik] *n* Arsen *nt*.
arson [âr'sən] *n* Brandstiftung *f*.
art [ârt] *n* Kunst *f*; **work of ~** Kunstwerk *nt*;

see also **arts**.
artefact [âr'təfakt] *n* (*Brit*) = **artifact**.
arterial [ârtē'rēəl] *a* (*ANAT*) arteriell.
arterial road *n* Fernverkehrsstraße *f*.
artery [âr'tûrē] *n* Schlagader *f*, Arterie *f*.
artful [ârt'fəl] *a* verschlagen, listig.
art gallery *n* Kunstgalerie *f*.
arthritis [ârthrī'tis] *n* Arthritis *f*.
artichoke [âr'tichōk] *n* Artischocke *f*.
article [âr'tikəl] *n* (*PRESS, GRAM*) Artikel *m*; (*thing*) Gegenstand *m*, Artikel *m*; (*clause*) Abschnitt *m*, Paragraph *m*.
articles [âr'tikəlz] *npl*: **~ of association** Gesellschaftsvertrag *m*; **~ of clothing** Kleidungsstücke *pl*.
articulate *a* [ârtik'yəlit] (*able to express o.s.*) redegewandt; (*speaking clearly*) deutlich, verständlich; **to be ~** sich gut ausdrücken können ♦ *vt* [ârtik'yəlāt] (*connect*) zusammenfügen, gliedern.
articulated lorry [ârtik'yəlātid lôr'ē] *n* (*Brit*) Sattelschlepper *m*.
artifact [âr'təfakt] *n* (*US*) Artefakt *nt*.
artifice [âr'təfis] *n* (*skill*) Kunstgriff *m*; (*trick*) Kniff *m*, List *f*.
artificial [ârtəfish'əl] *a* künstlich, Kunst-.
artificial insemination [ârtəfish'əl insemənā'shən] *n* künstliche Befruchtung *f*.
artificial intelligence *n* (*COMPUT*) künstliche Intelligenz *f*.
artificial respiration *n* künstliche Atmung *f*.
artillery [ârtil'ûrē] *n* Artillerie *f*.
artisan [âr'tizən] *n* gelernte(r) Handwerker *m*.
artist [âr'tist] *n* Künstler(in *f*) *m*.
artistic [ârtis'tik] *a* künstlerisch.
artistry [âr'tistrē] *n* künstlerische(s) Können *nt*.
artless [ârt'lis] *a* ungekünstelt; (*character*) arglos.
arts [ârts] *npl* (*UNIV*) Geisteswissenschaften *pl*.
art school *n* Kunsthochschule *f*.
arty [âr'tē] *a* (*col*) **to be ~** auf Kunst machen.
ARV *n abbr* (= *American Revised Version*) amerikanische revidierte Übersetzung der Bibel.
as [az] *ad, cj* (*since*) da, weil; (*while*) als; (*like*) wie; (*in role of*) als; **~ soon ~ he comes** sobald er kommt; **~ big ~ so groß wie**; **~ well auch**; **~ well ~ und auch**; **~ for him** was ihn anbetrifft; **~ if, ~ though** als ob; **~ it were** sozusagen; **old ~ he was** so alt er auch war; **much ~ I admire her ...** so sehr ich sie auch bewundere ...
AS *n abbr* (*US SCH*: = *Associate in*/*of Science*) akademischer Grad ♦ *abbr* (*US MAIL*) = *American Samoa*.
ASAP, a.s.a.p. *abbr* (= *as soon as possible*) so bald wie möglich.
asbestos [asbes'təs] *n* Asbest *m*.
ascend [əsend'] *vi* aufsteigen ♦ *vt* besteigen.
ascendancy [əsen'dənsē] *n* Oberhand *f*.
ascendant [əsen'dənt] *n*: **to be in the ~**

(*ASTROL.*, *fig*) im Aufgang sein.
Ascension [əsen'chən] *n* (*ECCL*) Himmelfahrt *f*.
ascent [əsent'] *n* Aufstieg *m*, Besteigung *f*.
ascertain [asûrtān'] *vt* feststellen.
ascetic [əset'ik] *a* asketisch.
asceticism [əset'isizəm] *n* Askese *f*.
ASCII [as'kē] *n* *abbr* (= *American Standard Code for Information Interchange*) ASCII (- Code *m*).
ascribe [əskrīb'] *vt* zuschreiben (*to dat*).
ASCU *n* *abbr* (*US*: = *Association of State Colleges and Universities*) Verband von Universitäten und staatlichen Einrichtungen.
ASE *n* *abbr* (= *American Stock Exchange*) amerikanische Börse *f*.
ASEAN [á'sēân] *n* *abbr* (= *Association of South-East Asian Nations*) ASEAN *f*.
ash [ash] *n* (*dust*) Asche *f*; (*tree*) Esche *f*.
ashamed [əshāmd'] *a* beschämt.
'A' shares *npl* (*Brit*) stimmrechtslose Aktien *pl*.
ashen [ash'ən] *a* (*pale*) aschfahl.
ashore [əshôr'] *ad* an Land.
ashtray [ash'trā] *n* Aschenbecher *m*.
Ash Wednesday *n* Aschermittwoch *m*.
Asia [ā'zhə] *n* Asien *nt*.
Asian [ā'zhən] *a* asiatisch ♦ *n* Asiat (in *f*) *m*.
Asiatic [āzhēat'ik] *a* asiatisch.
aside [əsīd'] *ad* beiseite; ~ **from** abgesehen von, außer ♦ *n* beiseite gesprochene Worte *pl*.
ask [ask] *vt* fragen; (*permission*) bitten um ♦ *vi* fragen; **to ~ about sth** nach etw fragen, sich nach etw erkundigen; **to ~ sb the time** jdn nach der Zeit fragen; ~ **him his name** frage ihn nach seinem Namen; **he ~ed to see you** er wollte dich sehen; **the ~ing price** der geforderte Preis.
ask after *vt fus* fragen nach.
ask for *vt fus*: **it's just ~ing for trouble** das kann nicht gutgehen; **you ~ed for that!** da bist du selbst schuld.
askance [əskans'] *ad*: **to look ~ at sb** jdn schief ansehen.
askew [əskyōō'] *ad* schief.
asleep [əslēp'] *a*, *ad*: **to be ~** schlafen; **to fall ~** einschlafen.
asp [asp] *n* Espe *f*.
asparagus [əspar'əgəs] *n* Spargel *m*.
ASPCA *n* *abbr* (= *American Society for the Prevention of Cruelty to Animals*) ≈ DTV *m*.
aspect [as'pekt] *n* (*appearance*) Aussehen *nt*; (*of question*) Aspekt *m*.
aspersions [əspûr'zhənz] *npl*: **to cast ~ on sb/sth** sich abfällig über jdn/etw äußern.
asphalt [as'fôlt] *n* Asphalt *m*.
asphyxiate [asfik'sēāt] *vt* ersticken.
asphyxiation [asfiksēā'shən] *n* Erstickung *f*.
aspirate [as'pûrit] *n* Hauchlaut *m*.
aspiration [aspərā'shən] *n* Trachten *nt*; **to have ~s towards sth** etw anstreben.
aspire [əspī'ûr] *vi* streben (*to* nach).
aspirin [as'pûrin] *n* Aspirin *nt*.

ass [as] *n* (*lit*, *fig*) Esel *m*; (*US col!*) Arsch *m*; (: *person*) Armleuchter *m*; **kiss my ~!** (*!*) du kannst mich mal! (*!*).
assailant [əsā'lənt] *n* Angreifer (in *f*) *m*.
assassin [əsas'in] *n* Attentäter (in *f*) *m*.
assassinate [əsas'ənāt] *vt* ermorden.
assassination [əsasinā'shən] *n* Ermordung *f*.
assault [əsôlt'] *n* Angriff *m* ♦ *vt* überfallen; (*woman*) herfallen über (+*acc*).
assemble [əsem'bəl] *vt* versammeln; (*parts*) zusammensetzen ♦ *vi* sich versammeln.
assembly [əsem'blē] *n* (*meeting*) Versammlung *f*; (*construction*) Zusammensetzung *f*, Montage *f*.
assembly language *n* (*COMPUT*) Assemblersprache *f*.
assembly line *n* Fließband *nt*.
assent [əsent'] *n* Zustimmung *f* ♦ *vi* zustimmen (*to dat*).
assert [əsûrt'] *vt* behaupten; **to ~ o.s.** sich behaupten.
assertion [əsûr'shən] *n* Behauptung *f*.
assertive [əsûr'tiv] *a* bestimmt.
assess [əses'] *vt* schätzen.
assessment [əses'mənt] *n* Bewertung *f*, Einschätzung *f*; (*judgement*): ~ (**of**) Beurteilung *f* (+*gen*).
assessor [əses'ûr] *n* Steuerberater *m*; (*tax* ~) Steuerschätzer *m*; (*insurance* ~) Schadensabschätzer *m*.
asset [as'et] *n* Vorteil *m*, Wert *m*; **he is one of our great ~s** er ist einer unserer besten Leute.
assets [as'ets] *npl* Vermögen *nt*; (*estate*) Nachlaß *m*.
asset stripping [as'et striping] *n* (*COMM*) Aufkauf von finanziell gefährdeten Firmen und anschließender Verkauf ihrer Vermögenswerte.
assiduous [əsij'ōōəs] *a* gewissenhaft.
assign [əsīn'] *vt* zuweisen.
assignment [əsīn'mənt] *n* Aufgabe *f*, Auftrag *m*; (*US SCH*) Aufgabe *f*.
assimilate [əsim'əlāt] *vt* sich aneignen, aufnehmen.
assimilation [əsiməlā'shən] *n* Assimilierung *f*, Aufnahme *f*.
assist [əsist'] *vt* beistehen (+*dat*).
assistance [əsis'təns] *n* Unterstützung *f*, Hilfe *f*.
assistant [əsis'tənt] *n* Assistent (in *f*) *m*, Mitarbeiter (in *f*) *m*; (*Brit*: *in shop*) Verkäufer (in *f*) *m*.
assistant manager *n* stellvertretende (r) Geschäftsführer *m*.
assizes [əsī'ziz] *npl* (*Brit*) Landgericht *nt*.
associate *n* [əsō'shēit] (*partner*) Kollege *m*, Teilhaber *m*; (*member*) außerordentliche (s) Mitglied *nt* ♦ *vt* [əsō'shēat] verbinden (*with* mit) ♦ *vi* (*keep company*) verkehren (*with* mit).
associated [əsō'shēātid] *a*: ~ **company** Beteiligungsgesellschaft *f*.
associate director *n* Führungskraft *m* noch

nicht offiziell zum Direktor ernannt.

association [əsōsēā'shən] *n* Verband *m*, Verein *m*; (*PSYCH*) Assoziation *f*; (*link*) Verbindung *f*; **in ~ with** im Zusammenhang mit.

association football *n* (*Brit*) Fußball *nt*.

assorted [əsôr'tid] *a* gemischt, verschieden; **in ~ sizes** in verschiedenen Größen.

assortment [əsôrt'mənt] *n* Sammlung *f*; (*COMM*) Sortiment *nt* (*of* von), Auswahl *f* (*of* an +*dat*).

Asst. *abbr* (= *assistant*) Ass., Assist.

assuage [əswāj'] *vt* (*pain, grief*) lindern; (*thirst, appetite, desire*) stillen, befriedigen.

assume [əsōōm'] *vt* (*take for granted*) annehmen; (*put on*) annehmen, sich geben.

assumed name [əsōōmd' nām] *n* Deckname *m*.

assumption [əsump'shən] *n* Annahme *f*; **on the ~ that ...** vorausgesetzt, daß ...

assurance [əshōōr'əns] *n* (*firm statement*) Versicherung *f*; (*confidence*) Selbstsicherheit *f*; (*Brit: insurance*) (Lebens)versicherung *f*; **I can give you no ~s** ich kann keine Zusicherungen machen.

assure [əshōōr'] *vt* (*make sure*) sicherstellen; (*convince*) versichern (+*dat*); (*life*) versichern.

assuredly [əshōōr'idlē] *ad* sicherlich.

AST *abbr* (*US*) = *Atlantic Standard Time*.

asterisk [as'tûrisk] *n* Sternchen *nt*.

astern [əstûrn'] *ad* achtern.

asteroid [as'təroid] *n* Asteroid *m*.

asthma [az'mə] *n* Asthma *nt*.

asthmatic [azmat'ik] *a* asthmatisch ♦ *n* Asthmatiker(in *f*) *m*.

astigmatism [əstig'mətizəm] *n* Astigmatismus *m*.

astir [əstûr'] *ad* in Bewegung.

ASTM *n abbr* = *American Society for Testing Materials*.

astonish [əstân'ish] *vt* erstaunen.

astonishing [əstân'ishing] *a* erstaunlich; **I find it ~ that ...** es überrascht *or* befremdet mich, daß ...

astonishingly [əstân'ishinglē] *ad*: **~ enough** erstaunlicherweise.

astonishment [əstân'ishmənt] *n* Erstaunen *nt*; **to my ~** zu meinem Erstaunen *or* Befremden.

astound [əstound'] *vt* verblüffen.

astounding [əstound'ing] *a* verblüffend.

astray [əstrā'] *ad* in die Irre; auf Abwege; **to go ~ in one's calculations** sich verrechnen ♦ *a* irregehend.

astride [əstrīd'] *ad* rittlings ♦ *prep* rittlings auf.

astringent [əstrin'jənt] *a* adstringierend; (*MED*) zusammenziehend; (*severe*) streng; (*fig: remark, humor*) ätzend, beißend ♦ *n* Adstringens *nt*.

astrologer [əstrâl'əjûr] *n* Astrologe *m*, Astrologin *f*.

astrology [əstrâl'əjē] *n* Astrologie *f*.

astronaut [as'trənôt] *n* Astronaut(in *f*) *m*.

astronomer [əstrân'əmûr] *n* Astronom *m*.

astronomical [astrənâm'ikəl] *a* (*fig, numbers*) astronomisch; (*success*) riesig.

astronomy [əstrân'əmē] *n* Astronomie *f*.

astrophysics [astrōfiz'iks] *n sing* Astrophysik *f*.

astute [əstōōt'] *a* scharfsinnig; schlau, gerissen.

asunder [əsun'dûr] *ad* entzwei.

ASV *n abbr* (= *American Standard Version*) amerikanische Standardausgabe der Bibel.

asylum [əsī'ləm] *n* (*home*) Heim *nt*; (*refuge*) Asyl *nt*; **to seek political ~** um (politisches) Asyl bitten.

asymmetric(al) [āsəmet'rik(əl)] *a* asymmetrisch.

at [at] *prep*: **~ home** zuhause; **~ John's** bei John; **~ table** bei Tisch; **~ school** in der Schule; **~ Easter** an Ostern; **~ 2 o'clock** um 2 Uhr; **~ night** nachts; **~ (the age of) 16** mit 16; **~ $5** zu 5 Dollar; **~ 20 mph** mit 20 Meilen pro Stunde; **~ full speed** mit voller Geschwindigkeit; **~ that** darauf; (*also*) dazu.

ate [āt] *pt of* **eat**.

atheism [ā'thēizəm] *n* Atheismus *m*.

atheist [ā'thēist] *n* Atheist(in *f*) *m*.

Athenian [əthē'nēən] *a* athenisch ♦ *n* Athener(in *f*) *m*.

Athens [ath'ənz] *n* Athen *nt*.

athlete [ath'lēt] *n* Athlet(in *f*) *m*, Sportler(in *f*) *m*.

athletic [athlet'ik] *a* sportlich, athletisch.

athletics [athlet'iks] *npl* Leichtathletik *f*.

Atlantic [atlan'tik] *a* atlantisch; **the ~ (Ocean)** der Atlantik, der Atlantische Ozean.

atlas [at'ləs] *n* Atlas *m*.

Atlas Mountains *npl* Atlasgebirge *nt*.

A.T.M. *abbr* (= *Automatic Teller Machine*) ≈ Geldautomat *m*.

atmosphere [at'məsfēr] *n* Atmosphäre *f*.

atoll [at'ôl] *n* Atoll *nt*.

atom [at'əm] *n* Atom *nt*; (*fig*) bißchen *nt*.

atomic [ətâm'ik] *a* atomar, Atom-.

atom(ic) bomb *n* Atombombe *f*.

atomic power *n* Atomkraft *f*.

atomizer [at'əmīzûr] *n* Zerstäuber *m*.

atone [ətōn'] *vi* sühnen (*for acc*).

atonement [ətōn'mənt] *n* Sühne *f*, Buße *f*; **the A~** (*REL*) das Sühneopfer (Christi).

atrocious [ətrō'shəs] *a* gräßlich.

atrocity [ətrâs'itē] *n* Scheußlichkeit *f*; (*deed*) Greueltat *f*.

atrophy [at'rəfē] *n* Atrophie *f*, Schwund *m* ♦ *vi* verkümmern, schwinden.

attach [ətach'] *vt* (*fasten*) befestigen; (*importance etc*) legen (*to* auf +*acc*), beimessen (*to dat*); **to be ~ed to sb/sth** an jdm/etw hängen; **the ~ed letter** das beigefügte Schreiben.

attaché [atashā'] *n* Attaché *m*.

attack [ətak'] *vti* angreifen ♦ *n* Angriff *m*; (*MED*) Anfall *m*.

attacker [ətak'ûr] n Angreifer m.
attain [ətān'] vt erreichen.
attainment [ətān'mənt] n Erreichung f.
attainments [ətān'mənts] npl Errungenschaften pl.
attempt [ətempt'] n Versuch m; **he made no ~ to help us** er unternahm keinen Versuch, uns zu helfen ♦ vti versuchen.
attend [ətend'] vt (go to) teilnehmen an (+dat); (lectures) besuchen ♦ vi (pay attention) aufmerksam sein; **to ~ to** (needs) nachkommen (+dat); (person) sich kümmern um.
attendance [əten'dəns] n (presence) Anwesenheit f; (people present) Besucherzahl f; **good ~** gute Teilnahme.
attendant [əten'dənt] n (companion) Begleiter(in f) m; Gesellschafter(in f) m; (in car park etc) Wächter(in f) m; (servant) Bediente(r) mf ♦ a begleitend.
attention [əten'shən] n Aufmerksamkeit f; (care) Fürsorge f; (for machine etc) Pflege f; **it has come to my ~ that ...** man hat mich darauf aufmerksam gemacht, daß ...
attentive [əten'tiv] a, **attentively** [əten'tivlē] ad aufmerksam.
attenuate [əten'yōōāt] vt verdünnen.
attest [ətest'] vt bestätigen; **to ~ to** sich verbürgen für.
attic [at'ik] n Dachstube f, Mansarde f.
attire [ətîûr'] n Gewand nt.
attitude [at'ətōōd] n (position) Haltung f; (mental) Einstellung f.
attorney [ətûr'nē] n (US) Rechtsanwalt m.
Attorney General n (US) ≈ Generalbundesanwalt m; (Brit) Justizminister m.
attract [ətrakt'] vt anziehen; (attention) erregen; (employees) anlocken; **the idea ~s me** ich finde die Idee attraktiv.
attraction [ətrak'shən] n Anziehungskraft f; (thing) Attraktion f.
attractive [ətrak'tiv] a attraktiv; (idea, offer, price) verlockend, reizvoll.
attribute n [at'rəbyōōt] Eigenschaft f, Attribut nt ♦ vt [ətrib'yōōt] zuschreiben (to dat).
attrition [ətrish'ən] n Verschleiß m; **war of ~** Zermürbungskrieg m.
atty. abbr (US) = **attorney.**
Atty. Gen. abbr (US) = **Attorney General.**
ATV n abbr (= all terrain vehicle) Geländewagen nt.
aubergine [ō'bûrzhēn] n Aubergine f.
auburn [ô'bûrn] a kastanienbraun.
auction [ôk'shən] n Versteigerung f, Auktion f ♦ vt versteigern.
auctioneer [ôkshənēr'] n Versteigerer m.
auction room n Auktionshalle f.
aud. abbr = **audit; auditor.**
audacious [ôdā'shəs] a (bold) kühn, verwegen; (impudent) dreist, unverfroren.
audacity [ôdas'itē] n (boldness) Wagemut m; (impudence) Unverfrorenheit f.
audible [ôd'əbəl] a hörbar.
audience [ôd'ēəns] n Zuhörer pl, Zuschauer

pl; (with king etc) Audienz f.
audiovisual [ôd'ēōvizh'ōōəl] a audiovisuell.
audit [ôd'it] n Bücherrevision f ♦ vt prüfen.
audition [ôdish'ən] n Probe f; (THEAT) Vorsprechprobe f; (of musician) Probespiel nt; (of singer) Vorsingen nt ♦ vi vorsprechen; vorspielen; vorsingen.
auditor [ô'ditûr] n (COMM) Rechnungsprüfer m; (US UNIV) Gasthörer m.
auditorium [ôditôr'ēəm] n Zuschauerraum m.
Aug. abbr (= August) Aug.
augment [ôgment'] vt vermehren ♦ vi zunehmen.
augur [ô'gûr] vti bedeuten, voraussagen; **this ~s well** das ist ein gutes Omen.
augury [ô'gyûrē] n Vorbedeutung f, Omen nt.
august [ôgust'] a erhaben.
August [ôg'əst] n August m; see **September.**
aunt [ant] n Tante f.
auntie, aunty [an'tē] n Tantchen nt.
au pair [ō pär'] n (also: **~ girl**) Au-pair-Mädchen nt.
aura [ôr'ə] n Nimbus m.
auspices [ôs'pisiz] npl: **under the ~ of** unter der Schirmherrschaft von.
auspicious [ôspish'əs] a günstig; verheißungsvoll.
austere [ôstēr'] a streng; (room) nüchtern.
austerity [ôstar'itē] n (severity) Strenge f; Nüchternheit f; (POL) wirtschaftliche Einschränkung f.
Australasia [ôstrəlā'zhə] n Australien und Ozeanien nt.
Australasian [ôstrəlā'zhən] n Ozeanier(in f) m.
Australia [ôstrāl'yə] n Australien nt.
Australian [ôstrāl'yən] a australisch ♦ n Australier(in f) m.
Austria [ôs'trēə] n Österreich nt.
Austrian [ôs'trēən] a österreichisch ♦ n Österreicher(in f) m.
authentic [ôthen'tik] a echt, authentisch.
authenticate [ôthen'tikāt] vt beglaubigen.
authenticity [ôthəntis'itē] n Echtheit f.
author [ô'thûr] n Autor(in f) m, Schriftsteller(in f) m; (beginner) Urheber m, Schöpfer m.
authoritarian [əthôritār'ēən] a autoritär.
authoritative [əthôr'itātiv] a (account) maßgeblich; (manner) herrisch.
authority [əthôr'itē] n (power) Autorität f; (expert) Autorität f, Fachmann m; **the authorities** pl die Behörden pl; **to have ~ to do sth** befugt sein, etw zu tun.
authorization [ôthûrəzā'shən] n Genehmigung f; (delegation of authority) Bevollmächtigung f, Autorisation f (form); (right) Recht nt.
authorize [ô'thərīz] vt bevollmächtigen; (permit) genehmigen.
authorized capital [ô'thərīzd kap'itəl] n Grundkapital nt.
autistic [ôtis'tik] a autistisch.
autobiographical [ôtəbīəgraf'ikəl] a autobio-

graphisch.

autobiography [ôtəbīăg'rəfē] n Autobiographie f.

autocracy [ôtăk'rəsē] n Autokratie f.

autocratic [ôtəkrat'ik] a autokratisch.

autograph [ô'təgraf] n (of celebrity) Autogramm nt ♦ vt mit Autogramm versehen.

automat [ô'təmat] n (US) Automatenrestaurant nt.

automate [ô'təmāt] vt automatisieren, auf Automation umstellen.

automatic [ôtəmat'ik] a automatisch ♦ n Selbstladepistole f; (car) Automatik m; (washing machine) Waschautomat m.

automatically [ôtəmat'iklē] ad automatisch.

automatic data processing n automatisierte Datenverarbeitung f.

automation [ôtəmā'shən] n Automation f.

automaton [ôtâm'ətân] n Automat m, Roboter m.

automobile [ôtəməbēl'] n (US) Auto(mobil) nt.

autonomous [ôtân'əməs] a autonom.

autonomy [ôtân'əmē] n Autonomie f, Selbstbestimmung f.

autopsy [ô'tâpsē] n Autopsie f, Obduktion f.

autumn [ô'təm] n Herbst m.

auxiliary [ôgzil'yûrē] a Hilfs- ♦ n Hilfskraft f; (GRAM) Hilfsverb nt.

AV abbr = **audiovisual** ♦ n abbr (= Authorized Version) englische Bibelfassung von 1611.

Av. abbr = **avenue**.

avail [əvāl'] vt: **to ~ o.s. of sth** sich einer Sache bedienen ♦ n: **to no ~** nutzlos.

availability [əvāləbil'ətē] n Erhältlichkeit f, Vorhandensein nt.

available [əvā'ləbəl] a erhältlich; zur Verfügung stehend; (person) erreichbar, abkömmlich; **to make sth ~ to sb** jdm etw zur Verfügung stellen; (accessible: information etc) jdm etw zugänglich machen; **is the manager ~?** ist der Geschäftsführer zu sprechen?

avalanche [av'əlanch] n Lawine f.

avant-garde [avântgârd'] a avantgardistisch ♦ n Avantgarde f.

avarice [av'ûris] n Habsucht f, Geiz m.

avaricious [avərish'əs] a geizig, habgierig, habsüchtig.

avdp. abbr (= avoirdupois) gesetzliches Handelsgewicht.

Ave. abbr = **avenue**.

avenge [əvenj'] vt rächen, sühnen.

avenue [av'ənōō] n Allee f.

average [av'ûrij] n Durchschnitt m; **on ~** durchschnittlich, im Durchschnitt ♦ a durchschnittlich, Durchschnitts- ♦ vt (figures) den Durchschnitt nehmen von; (perform) durchschnittlich leisten; (in car etc) im Schnitt fahren; **to ~ out** at sich belaufen auf or durchschnittlich betragen.

averse [əvûrs'] a: **to be ~ to** eine Abneigung haben gegen.

aversion [əvûr'zhən] n Abneigung f.

avert [əvûrt'] vt (turn away) abkehren; (prevent) abwehren.

aviary [ā'vēärē] n Vogelhaus nt; Aviarium nt (form).

aviation [āvēā'shən] n Luftfahrt f, Flugwesen nt.

aviator [ā'vēātûr] n Flieger m.

avid [av'id] a gierig (for auf +acc).

avidly [av'idlē] ad gierig.

avocado [avəkâd'ō] n Avocado(birne) f.

avoid [əvoid'] vt vermeiden.

avoidable [əvoid'əbəl] a vermeidbar.

avoidance [əvoid'əns] n Vermeidung f.

avow [əvou'] vt: **he ~ed himself to be a royalist** er bekannte (offen), Royalist zu sein.

avowal [əvou'əl] n Erklärung f.

AVP n abbr (US) = assistant vice-president.

AWACS [ā'waks] n abbr (= airborne warning and control system) AWACS.

await [əwāt'] vt erwarten, entgegensehen (+dat); **long ~ed** langersehnt.

awake [əwāk'] a wach ♦ irreg vi aufwachen ♦ vt (auf)wecken.

awaked [əwākt'] pp of **awake**.

awakening [əwā'kəning] n Erwachen nt.

award [əwôrd'] n (judgement) Urteil nt; (prize) Preis m ♦ vt zuerkennen.

aware [əwär'] a bewußt; **to be ~** sich bewußt sein (of gen); **I am fully ~ that** ... es ist mir völlig klar or bewußt, daß ...

awareness [əwär'nis] n Bewußtsein nt.

awash [əwâsh'] a überflutet.

away [əwā'] ad weg, fort; **he's ~ in Milan** er ist in Mailand.

away game n Auswärtsspiel nt.

awe [ô] n Ehrfurcht f.

awe-inspiring [ô'inspīuring] a = **awesome**.

awesome [ô'səm] a ehrfurchtgebietend.

awe-struck [ô'struk] a von Ehrfurcht ergriffen.

awful [ô'fəl] a (very bad) furchtbar; (dreadful) schrecklich; **an ~ lot of** (people, cars, dogs) unheimlich viele.

awfully [ô'fəlē] ad furchtbar, sehr.

awhile [əhwīl'] ad eine kleine Weile, ein bißchen.

awkward [ôk'wûrd] a (clumsy) ungeschickt, linkisch; (embarrassing) peinlich; (difficult: problem, question) schwierig.

awkwardness [ôk'wûrdnis] n Ungeschicklichkeit f.

awl [ôl] n Ahle f, Pfriem m.

awning [ô'ning] n Markise f.

awoke [əwōk'] pt of **awake**.

awoken [əwō'kən] pp of **awake**.

AWOL [ā'wôl] abbr (MIL etc) = absent without leave.

awry [ərī'] ad, a schief; **to go ~** (person) fehlgehen; (plans) schiefgehen.

ax, (Brit) axe [aks] n Axt f, Beil nt; **to have an ~ to grind** (fig) ein persönliches Interesse haben ♦ vt (bring to end suddenly) streichen.

axiom [ak'sēəm] n Grundsatz m, Axiom nt.

axiomatic [aksēəmat'ik] a axiomatisch.

axis [ak'sis] n, pl **axes** [ak'sēz] Achse f.

axle [ak'səl] n Achse f.

ay(e) [ī] interj ja; **the** ~s pl die Jastimmen pl.

AYH n abbr (= American Youth Hostels) ≈ DJH f.

AZ abbr (US MAIL) = Arizona.

azalea [əzāl'yə] n Azalee f.

Azores [əzôrz'] npl Azoren pl.

AZT n abbr (= azidothymidine) AZT nt.

Aztec [az'tek] a aztekisch ♦ n Azteke m, Aztekin f.

azure [azh'ûr] a azurblau, tiefblau.

B

B, b [bē] n (letter) B nt, b nt; **B for Baker** B wie Bertha.

b. abbr (= born) geb.

B [bē] n abbr (SCH: mark) ≈ 2.

BA n abbr (= Bachelor of Arts) B.A. m.

babble [bab'əl] vi schwätzen; (stream) murmeln ♦ n Geschwätz nt.

babe [bāb] n Kindlein nt.

baboon [baboon'] n Pavian m.

baby [bā'bē] n Baby nt.

baby buggy [bā'bē bug'ē] n Sportwagen m.

baby carriage n (US) Kinderwagen m.

babyish [bā'bēish] a kindisch.

baby-minder [bā'bēmīndûr] n (Brit) Tagesmutter f.

baby-sit [bā'bēsit] vi irreg Kinder hüten, babysitten.

baby-sitter [bā'bēsitûr] n Babysitter(in f) m.

bachelor [bach'əlûr] n Junggeselle m; ~ **of Arts** Bakkalaureus m der philosophischen Fakultät; ~ **of Science** Bakkalaureus m der Naturwissenschaften.

bachelor party n (US) Herrenabend m.

back [bak] n (of person, horse) Rücken m; (of house) Rückseite f; (of train) Ende nt; (SOCCER) Verteidiger m; **to have one's** ~ **to the wall** (fig) in die Enge getrieben sein/ werden; **to break the** ~ **of a job** (Brit) mit der Arbeit überm Berg sein; ~ **to front** verkehrt herum; (read) von hinten nach vorne; **at the** ~ **of my mind was the thought that** ... mich beschäftigte der Gedanke, daß ... ♦ vt (support) unterstützen; (wager) wetten auf (+acc); (car) rückwärts fahren ♦ vi (go ~wards) rückwärts gehen or fahren ♦ a (wheel, yard) Hinter-; ~ **garden** Garten m (hinterm Haus); ~ **room** Hinterzimmer nt; **to take a** ~ **seat** (fig) sich zurückhalten or

raushalten ♦ ad zurück; (to the rear) nach hinten; ~ **and forth** hin und her; **as far** ~ **as the 13th century** schon im 13. Jahrhundert; **when will you be** ~? wann kommen Sie wieder?

back down vi zurückstecken.

back on to vt fus: **the house** ~s **on to the golf course** das Haus grenzt hinten an den Golfplatz an.

back out vi sich zurückziehen; (fig: of deal etc) aussteigen (of aus).

back up vt (COMPUT) sicherstellen.

backbencher [bak'benchûr] n (Brit) Parlamentarier(in f) m.

backbiting [bak'bīting] n Verleumdung f.

backbone [bak'bōn] n Rückgrat nt; (support) Rückhalt m; **the** ~ **of the organization** das Rückgrat der Organisation.

back burner n: **to put sth on the** ~ etw verschieben.

backcomb [bak'kōm] vt (Brit) toupieren.

backdrop [bak'drâp] n Hintergrund m.

backer [bak'ûr] n Förderer m.

backfire [bak'fīûr] vi (plan) fehlschlagen; (TECH) fehlzünden.

background [bak'ground] n Hintergrund m; (information) Hintergrund m, Umstände pl; (person's education) Vorbildung f ♦ a: ~ **job** (COMPUT) Hintergrundauftrag m; ~ **noises** Geräuschkulisse f, Geräusch nt im Hintergrund.

backhand [bak'hand] n (SPORT) Rückhand f ♦ a Rückhand-.

backhanded [bak'handid] a (shot) Rückhand-; (compliment) zweifelhaft.

backhander [bak'handûr] n (Brit: bribe) Schmiergeld nt.

backing [bak'ing] n (also COMM: support) Unterstützung f; (MUS) Begleitung f.

backlash [bak'lash] n (TECH) tote(r) Gang m; (fig) Gegenschlag m.

backlog [bak'lôg] n (of work) Rückstand m.

back number n (PRESS) alte Nummer f.

backpack [bak'pak] n Rucksack m.

backpacker [bak'pakûr] n Rucksacktourist(in f) m.

back pay n (Gehalts- or Lohn)nachzahlung f.

backpedal [bak'pedəl] vi (lit) rückwärts treten; (fig) einen Rückzieher machen.

backside [bak'sīd] n (col) Hintern m.

backslash [bak'slash] n Rückwärtsschrägstrich m.

backslide [bak'slīd] vi rückfällig werden.

backspace [bak'spās] vi (in typing) zurücksetzen.

backstage [bak'stāj'] ad hinter den Kulissen; (in dressing-room area) in der Garderobe.

back street n: **he comes from the** ~s **of New York** er kommt aus dem ärmeren Teil von New York.

back-street [bak'strēt] a: ~ **abortionist** Engelmacher(in f) m (col).

backstroke [bak'strōk] n Rückenschwimmen nt.

backtrack [bak'trak] *vi* = **backpedal.**

backup [bak'up] *a* (*train, plane*) Entlastungs-; (*COMPUT*) Reserve-, Sicher(stell)ungs-; ~ **disk** Sicher(stell)ungsdiskette *f*; ~ **file** (*COMPUT*) Sicher(stell)ungsdatei *f* ♦ *n* (*US*: *congestion*) Stau *m*.

backup lights [bak'up lītz] *npl* (*US*) Rückfahrscheinwerfer *pl*.

backward [bak'wûrd] *a* (*less developed*) zurückgeblieben; (*primitive*) rückständig.

backwardness [bak'wûrdnis] *n* (*of child*) Zurückgebliebenheit *f*; (*of country*) Rückständigkeit *f*.

backwards [bak'wûrdz] *ad* (*in reverse*) rückwärts; (*towards the past*) zurück, rückwärts; **to know sth** ~ **and forwards** (*col*) etw in- und auswendig kennen.

backwater [bak'wôtûr] *n* (*fig*) Kaff *nt*; **a cultural** ~ tiefste Provinz *f*.

backyard [bak'yârd] *n* Hinterhof *m*.

bacon [bā'kən] *n* Schinkenspeck *m*.

bacteria [baktē'rēə] *npl* Bakterien *pl*.

bacteriology [baktērēâl'əjē] *n* Bakteriologie *f*.

bad [bad] *a* schlecht, schlimm; ~ **debt** uneinbringliche Forderung *f*; ~ **faith** Unredlichkeit *f*; **to have a** ~ **time of it** es schwer haben; **I feel** ~ **about it** (*guilty*) es tut mir leid.

bad-feeling [badfē'ling] *n* Verstimmung *f*.

badge [baj] *n* Abzeichen *nt*.

badger [baj'ûr] *n* Dachs *m* ♦ *vt* plagen.

badly [bad'lē] *ad* schlecht, schlimm; **things are going** ~ es läuft schlecht *or* nicht gut; **he is** ~ **off** es geht ihm schlecht.

bad-mannered [badman'ûrd] *a* ungezogen, unhöflich.

badminton [bad'mintən] *n* Federballspiel *nt*.

bad-mouth [bad'mouth'] *vt* (*US*) heruntermachen.

bad-tempered [bad'tem'pûrd] *a* schlecht gelaunt.

baffle [baf'əl] *vt* (*puzzle*) verblüffen.

baffling [baf'ling] *a* rätselhaft, verwirrend.

bag [bag] *n* (*sack*) Beutel *m*; (*paper*) Tüte *f*; (*hand*~) Tasche *f*; (*suitcase*) Koffer *m*; (*booty*) Jagdbeute *f*; (*col*: *old woman*) Schachtel *f*; **to pack one's** ~**s** seine Koffer *or* seine Siebensachen packen ♦ *vi* sich bauschen ♦ *vt* (*put in sack*) in einen Sack stecken; (*hunting*) erlegen.

bagful [bag'fəl] *n* Sackvoll *m*.

baggage [bag'ij] *n* Gepäck *nt*.

baggage check *n* Gepäckkontrolle *f*.

baggage claim *n* Gepäckausgabe *f*.

baggy [bag'ē] *a* bauschig, sackartig.

Baghdad [bag'dad] *n* Bagdad *nt*.

bagpipes [bag'pīps] *npl* Dudelsack *m*.

bag-snatcher [bag'snachûr] *n* (*Brit*) Taschendieb *m*.

Bahamas [bəhâm'əz] *npl* Bahamainseln *pl*.

Bahrain [bârān'] *n* Bahrain *nt*.

bail [bāl] *n* (*money*) Kaution *f*; **to be released on** ~ gegen Kaution freigelassen werden ♦ *vt* (*prisoner*) gegen Kaution freilassen;

(*also:* ~ **out:** *boat*) ausschöpfen.

bail out *vt* (*NAUT*: *water*) schöpfen; (: *boat*) leer schöpfen ♦ *vi* (*from a plane*) abspringen.

bailiff [bā'lif] *n* Gerichtsvollzieher(in *f*) *m*.

bait [bāt] *n* Köder *m* ♦ *vt* mit einem Köder versehen; (*fig*) ködern.

bake [bāk] *vti* backen.

baker [bā'kûr] *n* Bäcker *m*.

baker's dozen [bākûrz du'zən] *n*: **a** ~ dreizehn.

bakery [bā'kûrē] *n* Bäckerei *f*.

baking [bā'king] *n* Backen *nt*.

baking pan *n* (*US*) Backform *f*.

baking powder *n* Backpulver *nt*.

baking sheet *n* Backblech *nt*.

baking tin *n* (*Brit*) = **baking pan.**

balance [bal'əns] *n* (*scales*) Waage *f*; (*equilibrium*) Gleichgewicht *nt*; (*FIN*: *state of account*) Saldo *m*; (*difference*) Bilanz *f*; (*amount remaining*) Restbetrag *m*; ~ **carried** *or* **brought forward** Saldovortrag *m* ♦ *vt* (*weigh*) wägen; (*make equal*) ausgleichen; **to** ~ **the books** Bilanz ziehen *or* machen.

balanced [bal'ənst] *a* ausgeglichen.

balance sheet *n* Bilanz *f*, Rechnungsabschluß *m*.

balcony [bal'kənē] *n* Balkon *m*; (*US THEAT*) Rang *m*.

bald [bôld] *a* kahl; (*statement*) knapp.

bale [bāl] *n* Ballen *m*.

bale out (*Brit*) *vt* (*NAUT*: *water*) schöpfen; (: *boat*) leer schöpfen ♦ *vi* (*from a plane*) abspringen.

Balearic Islands [balēâr'ək ī'ləndz] *npl* Balearen *pl*.

baleful [bāl'fəl] *a* (*sad*) unglückselig; (*evil*) böse.

balk [bôk] *vt* (*hinder*) vereiteln ♦ *vi* scheuen (*at vor* +*dat*).

Balkan [bôl'kən] *a* balkanisch, Balkan- ♦ *npl*: **the** ~**s** der Balkan, die Balkanländer *pl*.

ball [bôl] *n* Ball *m*; **to be on the** ~ (*fig*) auf Zack *or* Draht sein (*col*); **to play** ~ (*fig*) mitmachen; **to start the** ~ **rolling** (*fig*) den Stein ins Rollen bringen; **the** ~ **is in your court** (*fig*) Sie sind am Ball.

ballad [bal'əd] *n* Ballade *f*.

ballast [bal'əst] *n* Ballast *m*.

ball bearing *n* Kugellager *nt*.

ballcock [bôl'kâk] *n* Schwimmerhahn *m*.

ballerina [balərē'nə] *n* Ballerina *f*.

ballet [balā'] *n* Ballett *nt*.

ballet dancer *n* Balletttänzer(in *f*) *m*.

ballistic [bəlis'tik] *a* ballistisch; **intercontinental** ~ **missiles** interkontinentale Raketengeschosse *pl*.

ballistics [bəlis'tiks] *n* Ballistik *f*.

balloon [bəlōōn'] *n* (*Luft*)ballon *m*; (*in comic strip*) Sprechblase *f* ♦ *vi* sich (auf)blähen.

ballot [bal'ət] *n* (*geheime*) Abstimmung *f*; (*US*: ~ **paper**) Stimmzettel *m*.

ballot paper *n* Stimmzettel *m*.

ballpark [bôl'pârk] *n* (*US*) Baseballstadion *nt*; **in that** ~ innerhalb dieser Spanne.
ballpark figure *n* Richtzahl *f*.
ballpoint (pen) [bôl'point (pen')] *n* Kugelschreiber *m*.
ballroom [bôl'rōōm] *n* Tanzsaal *m*.
balmy [bâ'mē] *a* lindernd, mild.
balsa [bôl'sə] *n* (*also:* ~ **wood**) Balsaholz *nt*.
Baltic (Sea) [bôl'tik (sē)] *n* Ostsee *f*.
balustrade [bal'əstrād] *n* Brüstung *f*.
bamboo [bambōō'] *n* Bambus *m*.
bamboozle [bambōō'zəl] *vt* (*col*) übers Ohr hauen.
ban [ban] *n* Verbot *nt* ♦ *vt* verbieten.
banal [bənal'] *a* banal.
banana [bənan'ə] *n* Banane *f*.
band [band] *n* Band *nt*; (*group*) Gruppe *f*; (*of criminals*) Bande *f*; (*MUS*) Kapelle *f*, Band *f* ♦ *vi* (+ *together*) sich zusammentun.
bandage [ban'dij] *n* Verband *m*; (*elastic*) Bandage *f*.
Band-Aid [band'ād'] *n* ® (*US*) Heftpflaster *nt*.
B & B [bē and bē] *abbr* = **bed and breakfast.**
bandit [ban'dit] *n* Bandit *m*.
bandstand [band'stand] *n* Musikpavillion *or* -podium *nt*.
bandy [ban'dē] *vt* wechseln.
bandy(-legged) [ban'dē(lеgid)] *a* o-beinig.
bane [bān] *n*: **he is the** ~ **of my life** mit ihm bin ich gestraft.
bang [bang] *n* (*explosion*) Knall *m*; (*blow*) Hieb *m* ♦ *vti* knallen; **I** ~**ed into the table** ich hab(e) mich am Tisch gestoßen ♦ *ad*: **to be** ~ **on time** (*Brit col*) auf die Minute pünktlich sein.
banger [bang'ûr] *n* (*col: firework*) Knallkörper *m*; (*Brit col: sausage*) Würstchen *nt*; (: *old car*) Klapperkiste *f*.
Bangkok [bang'kâk] *n* Bangkok *nt*.
Bangladesh [bangglədesh'] *n* Banglades(c)h *nt*, Bangla Desh *nt*.
bangle [bang'gəl] *n* Armspange *f*.
bangs [bangz] *npl* (*US: hair*) Pony *m*.
banish [ban'ish] *vt* verbannen.
banister(s) [ban'istûr(z)] *n* (*pl*) (Treppen)geländer *nt*.
banjo [ban'jō] *n* Banjo *nt*.
bank [bangk] *n* (*raised ground*) Erdwall *m*; (*of lake etc*) Ufer *nt*; (*FIN*) Bank *f* ♦ *vt* (*AVIAT: tilt*) in die Kurve bringen; (*money*) einzahlen ♦ *vi*: **to** ~ **on sth** mit etw rechnen.
bank account *n* Bankkonto *nt*.
bank card *n* Scheckkarte *f*.
bank charges *npl* Bankgebühren *pl*, Bankspesen *pl*.
bank draft *n* Bankanweisung *f*.
banker [bangk'ûr] *n* (*employee*) Bankier *m*; ~**'s order** Dauerauftrag *m*.
bank holiday *n* (*Brit*) gesetzliche(r) Feiertag *m*.
banking [bangk'ing] *n* Bankwesen *nt*, Bankgeschäft *nt*.

bank loan *n* Bankkredit *m*.
bank manager *n* Bankdirektor *m*.
bank note *n* Banknote *f*.
bank rate *n* Banksatz *m*.
bankrupt [bangk'rupt] *n* Zahlungsunfähige(r) *mf* ♦ *vt* bankrott machen ♦ *a*: **to go** ~ Bankrott machen.
bankruptcy [bangk'ruptsē] *n* Bankrott *m*.
bank statement *n* Kontoauszug *m*.
banner [ban'ûr] *n* Banner *nt*.
banns [banz] *npl* Aufgebot *nt*.
banquet [bang'kwit] *n* Bankett *nt*, Festessen *nt*.
banter [ban'tûr] *n* Neckerei *f*.
BAOR *n abbr* = *British Army of the Rhine.*
baptism [bap'tizəm] *n* Taufe *f*.
baptize [baptīz'] *vt* taufen.
bar [bâr] *n* (*rod*) Stange *f*; (*obstacle*) Hindernis *nt*; (*of chocolate*) Tafel *f*; (*of soap*) Stück *nt*; (*for food, drink*) Buffet *nt*, Bar *f*; (*pub*) Wirtschaft *f*; (*MUS*) Takt(strich) *m*; **behind** ~**s** hinter Gittern, hinter schwedischen Gardinen; **to be admitted to the B**~ als Anwalt zugelassen werden ♦ *vt* (*fasten*) verriegeln; (*hinder*) versperren; (*exclude*) ausschließen ♦ *ad*: ~ **none** ohne Ausnahme.
Barbados [bârbā'dōs] *n* Barbados *nt*.
barbarian [bârbär'ēən] *n* Barbar(in *f*) *m*.
barbaric [bârbar'ik] *a* primitiv, unkultiviert.
barbarity [bârbar'itē] *n* Grausamkeit *f*.
barbarous [bâr'bûrəs] *a* grausam, barbarisch.
barbecue [bâr'bəkyō] *n* Barbecue *nt*.
barbed wire [bârbd wîûr] *n* Stacheldraht *m*.
barber [bâr'bûr] *n* Herrenfriseur *m*.
barbiturate [bârbich'ûrit] *n* Barbiturat *nt*, Schlafmittel *nt*.
Barcelona [bârsəlō'nə] *n* Barcelona *nt*.
bar chart *n* Balkendiagramm *nt*.
bar code *n* Balken-/Strichcode *m*.
bare [bär] *a* nackt; (*trees, country*) kahl; (*mere*) bloß ♦ *vt* entblößen.
bareback [bär'bak] *a* ungesattelt.
barefaced [bär'fāst] *a* unverfroren.
barefoot [bär'fŏŏt] *a* barfuß.
bareheaded [bär'hedid] *a* mit bloßem Kopf.
barely [bär'lē] *ad* kaum, knapp.
bareness [bär'nis] *n* Nacktheit *f*; Kahlheit *f*.
Barents Sea [bär'ənts sē] *n* Barentssee *f*.
bargain [bâr'gin] *n* (*sth cheap*) günstige(r) Kauf *m*; (*agreement: written*) Kaufvertrag *m*; (: *oral*) Geschäft *nt*; **into the** ~ obendrein.
bargain for *vt fus* rechnen mit; **he got more than he** ~**ed for** (*col*) er hat sein blaues Wunder erlebt.
bargaining table [bâr'gining tā'bəl] *n* Verhandlungstisch *m*.
barge [bârj] *n* Lastkahn *m*.
barge in *vi* hereinplatzen.
barge into *vt fus* (*knock against: person*) (hinein)rennen in (+*acc*); (: *thing*) rennen gegen; (*room etc*) hereinplatzen in (+*acc*).
baritone [bar'itōn] *n* Bariton *m*.
barium meal [bar'ēəm mēl'] *n* Bariumbrei

m, Kontrastbrei *m*.

bark [bârk] *n* (*of tree*) Rinde *f*; (*of dog*) Bellen *nt* ♦ *vi* (*dog*) bellen.

barley [bâr'lē] *n* Gerste *f*.

barley sugar *n* Malzzucker *m*.

barmaid [bâr'mād] *n* Bardame *f*.

barman [bâr'mən] *n*, *pl*, **-men** Barkellner *m*.

barn [bârn] *n* Scheune *f*; (*for animals*) Hütte *f*.

barnacle [bâr'nəkəl] *n* Entenmuschel *f*.

barometer [bərâm'itûr] *n* Barometer *nt*.

baron [bar'ən] *n* Baron *m*; (*fig*) Baron *m*, Magnat *m*; **the press ~s** die Pressebarone.

baroness [bar'ənis] *n* Baronin *f*.

baronial [bərō'nēəl] *a* freiherrlich.

baroque [bərōk'] *a* barock.

barracks [bar'əks] *npl* Kaserne *f*.

barrage [bərâzh'] *n* (*gunfire*) Sperrfeuer *nt*; (*dam*) Staudamm *m*, Talsperre *f*; **he was attacked with a ~ of questions** er wurde mit Fragen überschüttet.

barrel [bar'əl] *n* Faß *nt*; (*of gun*) Lauf *m*.

barrel organ *n* Drehorgel *f*.

barren [bar'ən] *a* unfruchtbar.

barrette [bəret'] *n* (*US*) Haarspange *f*.

barricade [bar'əkād] *n* Barrikade *f* ♦ *vt* verbarrikadieren.

barrier [bar'ēûr] *n* (*obstruction*) Hindernis *nt*; (*fence*) Schranke *f*; (*Brit: crash ~*) (Leit)planke *f*.

barrister [bar'istûr] *n* (*Brit*) Rechtsanwalt *m*.

barrow [bar'ō] *n* Schubkarren *m*.

barstool [bâr'stōōl] *n* Barhocker *m*.

bartender [bâr'tendûr] *n* (*US*) Barmann *m*, Barkellner *m*.

barter [bâr'tûr] *n* Tauschhandel *m* ♦ *vi* Tauschhandel treiben.

base [bās] *n* (*bottom*) Boden *m*, Basis *f*; (*MIL*) Stützpunkt *m* ♦ *vt* gründen; (*troops*) stationieren ♦ *a* (*low*) gemein.

baseball [bās'bôl] *n* Baseball *m*.

baseboard [bās'bôrd] *n* (*US*) Fußleiste *f*.

base camp *n* Basislager *nt*, Versorgungslager *nt*.

based [bāst] *a*: **to be ~ on** basieren auf (*+dat*); **I'm ~ in New York** ich arbeite in New York.

Basel [báz'əl] *n* Basel *nt*.

baseless [bās'lis] *a* grundlos.

basement [bās'mənt] *n* Kellergeschoß *nt*.

base pay *n* (*US*) Grundgehalt *nt*.

base rate *n* Eckzins der Londoner Clearing-Banken.

bases [bā'siz] *npl of* **base** ♦ [bā'sēz] *npl of* **basis**.

bash [bash] *vt* (*col*) (heftig) schlagen ♦ *n* Schlag *m*; **I'll have a ~ (at it)** (*Brit*) ich probier's mal (damit) (*col*).

bash up *vt* (*col: car*) demolieren, kaputtfahren; (: *person*) vermöbeln, verkloppen.

bashful [bash'fəl] *a* schüchtern.

bashing [bash'ing] *n*: **Paki-/queer-~** (*col*) Verprügeln *nt* von Pakistanern/Schwulen.

basic [bā'sik] *a* grundlegend; (*elementary: principles*) grundsätzlich.

BASIC [bā'sik] *n abbr* (= *Beginners' All-purpose Symbolic Instruction Code*) BASIC *nt*.

basically [bā'siklē] *ad* im Grunde.

basic rate *n* (*of wage*) Ecklohn *m*; (*of tax*) Eingangssteuersatz *m*.

basil [baz'əl] *n* Basilikum *nt*.

basin [bā'sin] *n* (*for washing, also valley*) Becken *nt*; (*dock*) (Trocken)becken *nt*; (*Brit: for food*) Schüssel *f*.

basis [bā'sis] *n*, *pl* **bases** Basis *f*, Grundlage *f*; **on the ~ of what you've said** aufgrund dessen, was Sie gesagt haben.

bask [bask] *vi* sich sonnen.

basket [bas'kit] *n* Korb *m*.

basketball [bas'kitbôl] *n* Basketball *m*.

basketball player *n* Basketballspieler(in *f*) *m*.

Basle [baz'əl] *n* Basel *nt*.

bass [bās] *n* (*MUS, also instrument*) Baß *m*; (*voice*) Baßstimme *f*.

bass clef [bās klef] *n* Baßschlüssel *m*.

bassoon [basōōn'] *n* Fagott *nt*.

bastard [bas'tûrd] *n* Bastard *m*; (*col!*) Arschloch *nt*.

baste [bāst] *vt* (*meat*) mit Fett begießen; (*seam*) heften.

bastion [bas'chən] *n* Bastion *f*; (*lit, fig*) Bollwerk *nt*.

bat [bat] *n* (*SPORT*) Schlagholz *nt*; (*Brit: for table tennis*) Schläger *m*; (*ZOOL*) Fledermaus *f*; **like a ~ out of hell** (*col*) in einem Affentempo ♦ *vt* (*hit*) schlagen; **he didn't ~ an eyelid** er hat nicht mit der Wimper gezuckt ♦ *vi* (*SPORT*) schlagen.

batch [bach] *n* (*of applicants, letters*) Stoß *m*, Stapel *m*; (*of work*) Schwung *m*; (*of samples*) Satz *m*; (*of goods*) Sendung *f*, Ladung *f*.

batch processing *n* (*COMPUT*) Stapelverarbeitung *f*.

bated [bā'tid] *a*: **with ~ breath** mit verhaltenem Atem.

bath [bath] *n* Bad *nt*; (*tub*) Badewanne *f* ♦ *vt* baden; **to have a ~** baden.

bathe [bāth] *vti* baden.

bather [bāth'ûr] *n* Badende(r) *mf*.

bathing [bā'thing] *n* Baden *nt*.

bathing cap *n* Badekappe *f*.

bathing suit *n* Badeanzug *m*.

bathmat [bath'mat] *n* Badevorleger *m*.

bathrobe [bath'rōb] *n* Morgenrock *m*.

bathroom [bath'rōōm] *n* Bad(ezimmer) *nt*; (*col*) Klo *nt*.

baths [bathz] *npl* (Schwimm)bad *nt*.

bath towel *n* [bath' toul] *n* Badetuch *nt*.

bathtub [bath'tub] *n* Badewanne *f*.

baton [batân'] *n* (*of police*) Gummiknüppel *m*; (*MUS*) Taktstock *m*.

battalion [bətal'yən] *n* Bataillon *nt*.

batten [bat'ən] *n* Leiste *f*, Latte *f*; (*NAUT*) Segellatte *f*, Schalke *f*.

batten down *vt* (*NAUT*) schalken, dicht

machen.
batter [bat'ûr] *vt* verprügeln ♦ *n* Schlagteig *m*; (*for cake*) Biskuitteig *m*.
battered [bat'ûrd] *a* (*hat, pan*) verbeult; (*child*) mißhandelt.
battery [bat'ûrē] *n* (*ELEC*) Batterie *f*; (*MIL*) Geschützbatterie *f*.
battery charger *n* Batterieladegerät *nt*.
battery farming *n* Batteriehaltung *f*.
battery hen *n* Batteriehuhn *nt*.
battle [bat'əl] *n* Schlacht *f*; (*small*) Gefecht *nt*; **that's half the** ~ (*col*) damit ist schon viel gewonnen; **to fight a losing** ~ (*fig*) einen aussichtslosen Kampf führen ♦ *vi* kämpfen.
battlefield [bat'əlfēld] *n* Schlachtfeld *nt*.
battlements [bat'əlmənts] *npl* Zinnen *pl*.
battleship [bat'əlship] *n* Schlachtschiff *nt*.
batty [bat'ē] *a* (*col*) plemplem.
bauble [bô'bəl] *n* Flitter *m*.
baud [bôd] *n* (*COMPUT*) Baud *nt*.
baud rate *n* Baud-Rate *f*, Baud-Zahl *f*.
bauxite [bôk'sīt] *n* Bauxit *m*.
Bavaria [bəvär'ēə] *n* Bayern *nt*.
Bavarian [bəvär'ēən] *a* bay(e)risch ♦ *n* Bayer(in *f*) *m*.
bawdy [bô'dē] *a* unflätig.
bawl [bôl] *vi* brüllen; **to** ~ **sb out** jdn zur Schnecke machen.
bay [bā] *n* (*of sea*) Bucht *f*; (*Brit: for parking*) Parkbucht *f*; (: *for loading*) Ladeplatz *m*; **at** ~ gestellt, in die Enge getrieben; **to keep at** ~ unter Kontrolle halten.
bay leaf *n* Lorbeerblatt *nt*.
bayonet [bā'ənet] *n* Bajonett *nt*.
bay window *n* Erkerfenster *nt*.
bazaar [bəzâr'] *n* Basar *m*.
bazooka [bəzōō'kə] *n* Panzerfaust *f*.
BBA *n abbr* (*US*) = *Bachelor of Business Administration*.
BBB *n abbr* (*US*: = *Better Business Bureau*) ≈ Verbraucherzentrale *f*.
BBC *n abbr* (= *British Broadcasting Corporation*) BBC *f*.
BC *ad abbr* (= *before Christ*) v. Chr. ♦ *abbr* (*Canada*) = *British Columbia* ♦ *n abbr* (*US*) = *Bachelor of Commerce*.
BCG *n abbr* (= *Bacillus Calmette-Guérin*) BCG *m*.
BD *n abbr* (= *Bachelor of Divinity*) akademischer Grad in Theologie.
B/D *abbr* = *bank draft*.
BDS *n abbr* (= *Bachelor of Dental Surgery*) akademischer Grad in Zahnmedizin.
be [bē] *vi irreg* sein; (*become, for passive*) werden; (*be situated*) liegen, sein; **the book is $5** das Buch kostet 5 Dollar; **he wants to** ~ **a teacher** er will Lehrer werden; **how long have you been here?** wie lange sind Sie schon da?; **have you been to Rome?** warst du schon einmal in Rom?, bist du schon einmal in Rom gewesen?; **his name is on the list** sein Name steht auf der Liste; **there is/are** es gibt; **it's only me** ich bin's;

what are you doing? was machen Sie?/was machst du?; **I've been waiting for her for two hours** ich warte schon seit 2 Stunden auf sie; **to** ~ **asked** gefragt werden; **he is nowhere to** ~ **found** er ist nirgendwo zu finden; **the car is to** ~ **sold** das Auto soll verkauft werden; **he was to have come yesterday** er sollte eigentlich gestern kommen; **if I were you** ... an deiner Stelle ...; **it's 8 o'clock** es ist 8 Uhr; **am I to understand that** ...? soll ich etwa verstehen or daraus entnehmen, daß ...?
B/E *abbr* = *bill of exchange*.
beach [bēch] *n* Strand *m* ♦ *vt* (*ship*) auf den Strand setzen.
beach buggy [bēch' bug'ē] *n* Strandbuggy *m*.
beachcomber [bēch'kōmûr] *n* Strandgutsammler *m*.
beachwear [bēch'wär] *n* Strandkleidung *f*.
beacon [bē'kən] *n* (*signal*) Leuchtfeuer *nt*; (*traffic* ~, *radio* ~) Bake *f*.
bead [bēd] *n* Perle *f*; (*of dew, sweat*) Tropfen *m*; ~**s** (*necklace*) Perlenkette *f*.
beady [bē'dē] *a*: ~ **eyes** wache Äuglein *pl*.
beagle [bē'gəl] *n* (*dog*) Beagle *m*.
beak [bēk] *n* Schnabel *m*.
beaker [bē'kûr] *n* Becher *m*.
beam [bēm] *n* (*of wood*) Balken *m*; (*of light*) Strahl *m*; (*smile*) strahlende(s) Lächeln *nt*; (*RAD*) Leitstrahl *m*; **to drive/be on high** ~ (*US*) or **full** (*Brit*) ~ mit Fernlicht fahren/ Fernlicht eingestellt haben ♦ *vi* strahlen; ~ **at sb** (*smile*) jdn anstrahlen.
bean [bēn] *n* Bohne *f*.
bean sprouts *npl* Sojabohnensprossen *pl*.
bear [bär] *vt irreg* (*produce: fruit*) tragen; (*tolerate*) ertragen; (*young*) gebären; (*traces, signs*) aufweisen, zeigen; **I can't** ~ **him** ich kann ihn nicht ertragen; **to** ~ **interest at 10%** (*FIN*) mit 10% verzinslich sein; **to bring pressure to** ~ **on sb** Druck auf jdn ausüben ♦ *vi*: **to** ~ **right/left** sich rechts/ links halten ♦ *n* Bär *m*; (*FIN*) Baissier *m*.
bear on *vt fus* relevant sein für.
bear out *vt* (*theory, suspicion*) bestätigen.
bear up *vi* Haltung (be)wahren; **he bore up well under the strain** er wurde gut mit der Belastung fertig.
bear with *vt fus* (*sb's moods, temper*) tolerieren.
bearable [bär'əbəl] *a* erträglich.
beard [bērd] *n* Bart *m*.
bearded [bērd'id] *a* bärtig.
bearer [bär'ûr] *n* (*carrier*) Träger(in *f*) *m*; (*of passport*) Inhaber(in *f*) *m*.
bearing [bär'ing] *n* (*posture*) Haltung *f*; (*relevance*) Relevanz *f*; (*relation*) Bedeutung *f*; (*TECH*) Kugellager *nt*.
bearings [bär'ingz] *npl* (*direction*) Orientierung *f*; **to get one's** ~ sich zurechtfinden.
bearskin [bär'skin] *n* Bärenfellmütze *f*.
beast [bēst] *n* Tier *nt*, Vieh *nt*; (*person*) Biest *nt*; ~ **of burden** Lasttier *nt*.
beastly [bēst'lē] *a* (*col*) scheußlich; (*person*

also) gemein.

beat [bēt] *n* (*stroke*) Schlag *m*; (*pulsation*) (Herz)schlag *m*; (*police round*) Runde *f*; (*district*) Revier *nt*; (*MUS*) Takt *m*, Beat *m* ♦ *irreg vt pt* **beat** schlagen; **to ~ time** den Takt schlagen; **that ~s everything!** (*col*) das ist doch wirklich der Gipfel *or* die Höhe, das schlägt dem Faß den Boden aus ♦ *vi:* **to ~ on the door** gegen die Tür hämmern *or* schlagen; **to ~ about the bush** wie die Katze um den heißen Brei herumgehen ♦ *a* (*col: tired*) fertig.

beat down *vt* (*door*) einrennen; (*price*) herunterhandeln; (*opposition*) kleinkriegen ♦ *vi* (*rain*) herunterprasseln; (*sun*) herunterbrennen.

beat off *vt* abschlagen.

beat up *vt* zusammenschlagen.

beaten [bē'tən] *pp of* **beat** ♦ *a:* **~ track** gebahnte(r) Weg *m*; (*fig*) herkömmliche Art und Weise; **off the ~ track** abgelegen.

beater [bē'tûr] *n* (*for eggs, cream*) Schneebesen *m*.

beating [bē'ting] *n* (*defeat*) Wiederlage *f*; **to take a ~** eine Schlappe einstecken (*col*).

beat-up [bēt'up] *a* (*col*) zerbeult, ramponiert.

beautiful [byōō'təfəl] *a* (*col*) schön.

beautifully [byōō'təfəlē] *ad* ausgezeichnet.

beautify [byōō'təfī] *vt* verschönern.

beauty [byōō'tē] *n* Schönheit *f*; (*concept*) das Schöne; **the ~ of it is that** ... das Schöne daran ist, daß ... ♦ *in cpds* (*contest, salon etc*) Schönheits-.

beauty queen *n* Schönheitskönigin *f*.

beauty spot *n* Schönheitsfleck *m*; (*Brit TOURISM*) (besonders) schöne(r) Ort *m*.

beaver [bē'vûr] *n* Biber *m*.

becalm [bikâm'] *vt:* **to be ~ed** eine Flaute haben.

became [bikām'] *pt of* **become**.

because [bikôz'] *ad, cj* weil ♦ *prep:* **~ of** wegen (+*gen or* (*col*) *dat*).

beck [bek] *n:* **to be at sb's ~ and call** nach jds Pfeife tanzen.

beckon [bek'ən] *vti* ein Zeichen geben (*sb* jdm).

become [bikum'] *vi irreg* werden; **it became known that** ... es wurde bekannt, daß ... ♦ *vt* (*clothes*) stehen (+*dat*).

becoming [bikum'ing] *a* (*suitable*) schicklich; (*clothes*) kleidsam.

becquerel [bekərel'] *n* Becquerel *nt*.

bed [bed] *n* Bett *nt*; (*of river*) Flußbett *nt*; (*of sea, lake*) Grund *m*, Boden *m*; (*foundation*) Schicht *f*; (*in garden*) Beet *nt*.

bed down *vi* sein Lager aufschlagen.

BEd *n abbr* (= *Bachelor of Education*) *akademischer Grad von Lehrern.*

bed and breakfast *n* Übernachtung *f* mit Frühstück.

bedbug [bed'bug] *n* Wanze *f*.

bedclothes [bed'klōz] *npl* Bettwäsche *f*.

bedding [bed'ing] *n* Bettzeug *nt*.

bedeck [bidek'] *vt* schmücken.

bedevil [bidev'əl] *vt* komplizieren, erschweren, vermasseln (*col*).

bedfellow [bed'felō] *n:* **they are strange ~s** (*fig*) sie sind ein merkwürdiges Gespann.

bedlam [bed'ləm] *n* (*uproar*) tolle(s) Durcheinander *nt*.

bedpan [bed'pan] *n* Bettpfanne *f*, Bettschüssel *f*.

bedraggled [bidrag'əld] *a* ramponiert.

bedridden [bed'ridən] *a* bettlägerig.

bedrock [bed'râk] *n* (*GEOL*) Grundgestein *nt*; **to get down to ~** (*fig*) zum Kern der Sache kommen.

bedroom [bed'rōōm] *n* Schlafzimmer *nt*.

Beds [bedz] *abbr* (*Brit*) = *Bedfordshire.*

bedside [bed'sīd] *n:* **at the ~** am Bett.

bedside lamp *n* Nachttischlampe *f*.

bed-sitter [bed'sitûr] *n* (*Brit*) Einzimmerwohnung *f*, möblierte(s) Zimmer *nt*.

bedspread [bed'spred] *n* Tagesdecke *f*.

bedtime [bed'tīm] *n* Schlafenszeit *f*; **it's ~** es ist Zeit, ins Bett zu gehen.

bee [bē] *n* Biene *f*; **to have a ~ in one's bonnet** einen Fimmel *or* Tick haben (*col*).

beech [bēch] *n* Buche *f*.

beef [bēf] *n* Rindfleisch *nt*.

beef up *vt* (*col*) verstärken.

beefeater [bēf'ētûr] *n* Beefeater *m*; (*US col*) Engländer(in *f*) *m*.

beehive [bē'hīv] *n* Bienenstock *m*.

beeline [bē'līn] *n:* **to make a ~ for** schnurstracks zugehen auf (+*acc*).

been [bin] *pp of* **be**.

beer [bēr] *n* Bier *nt*.

beer can *n* Bierdose *f*.

beet [bēt] *n* (*US*) rote Bete *f*.

beetle [bēt'əl] *n* Käfer *m*.

beetroot [bēt'rōōt] *n* (*Brit*) rote Bete *f*.

befall [bifôl'] *irreg vi* sich ereignen ♦ *vt* zustoßen (+*dat*).

befallen [bifôl'ən] *pp of* **befall**.

befell [bifel'] *pt of* **befall**.

befit [bifit'] *vt* sich schicken für.

before [bifôr'] *prep* vor ♦ *cj* bevor ♦ *ad* (*of time*) zuvor; früher; **I've done it ~** das hab' ich schon mal getan.

beforehand [bifôr'hand] *ad* im voraus.

befriend [bifrend'] *vt* sich annehmen (+ *gen*).

befuddled [bifud'əld] *a* (*confused*) durcheinander, verwirrt.

beg [beg] *vti* (*implore*) dringend bitten; (*alms*) betteln; **I ~ your pardon** (*apologizing*) Entschuldigung; (*not hearing*) wie bitte?, bitte?

began [bigan'] *pt of* **begin**.

beggar [beg'ûr] *n* Bettler(in *f*) *m*.

begin [bigin'] *irreg vt* anfangen, beginnen; (*found*) gründen; **to ~ doing sth, to ~ to do sth** anfangen, etw zu tun; **I can't ~ to thank you** ich kann Ihnen gar nicht genug danken ♦ *vi:* **to ~ with** zunächst (einmal); **to ~ with, I'd like to know ...** zuerst *or* zuallererst möchte ich wissen ...; **~ning (from) Monday** von Montag an.

beginner [bigin'ûr] n Anfänger(in f) m.
beginning [bigin'ing] n Anfang m; **right from the ~** von Anfang an.
begrudge [bigruj'] vt: **to ~ sb sth** jdm etw mißgönnen.
beguile [bigīl'] vt (enchant) betören.
beguiling [bigī'ling] a verführerisch, betörend.
begun [bigun'] pp of **begin**.
behalf [bihaf'] n: **in** (US) or **on** (Brit) **~ of** im Namen (+gen); **on my ~** für mich.
behave [bihāv'] vi sich benehmen.
behavior, (Brit) **behaviour** [bihāv'yûr] n Benehmen nt.
behead [bihed'] vt enthaupten.
beheld [biheld'] pt, pp of **behold**.
behind [bihīnd'] prep hinter ♦ ad (late) im Rückstand; (in the rear) hinten ♦ n (col) Hinterteil nt; **we're ~ them in technology** (fig) auf dem Gebiet der Technologie sind wir hinter ihnen zurück; **to leave sth ~** etw vergessen; **to be ~ with sth** (payments etc) mit etw im Rückstand sein.
behold [bihōld'] vt irreg (old) erblicken.
beige [bāzh] a beige.
being [bē'ing] n (existence) (Da)sein nt; (person) Wesen nt.
Beirut [bārōōt'] n Beirut nt.
belated [bilā'tid] a verspätet.
belch [belch] n Rülpsen nt ♦ vi rülpsen ♦ vt (smoke) ausspeien.
beleaguered [bilē'gûrd] a (city) belagert; (army) umgeben, eingekesselt; (fig) umgeben.
Belfast [bel'fast] n Belfast nt.
belfry [bel'frē] n Glockenturm m.
Belgian [bel'jən] a belgisch ♦ n (person) Belgier(in f) m.
Belgium [bel'jəm] n Belgien nt.
Belgrade [belgrād'] n Belgrad nt.
belie [bilī'] vt Lügen strafen (+acc); (give false impression of) hinwegtäuschen über (+acc).
belief [bilēf'] n Glaube m (in an +acc); (conviction) Überzeugung f; **it's beyond ~** es ist unglaublich or nicht zu glauben; **in the ~ that ...** im Glauben, daß ..., in der Annahme, daß ...
believable [bilēv'əbəl] a glaubhaft.
believe [bilēv'] vt glauben (+dat); (think) glauben, meinen, annehmen ♦ vi (have faith) glauben; **to ~ (that ...)** glauben (‚daß ...), annehmen (‚daß ...); **he is ~d to be abroad** es heißt, daß er im Ausland ist; **to ~ in** (God, ghosts) glauben an (+ acc); (method) Vertrauen haben zu; **I don't ~ in corporal punishment** ich bin nicht für die Prügelstrafe.
believer [bilēv'ûr] n Gläubige(r) mf.
belittle [bilit'əl] vt herabsetzen.
Belize [bəlēz'] n Belize nt.
bell [bel] n Glocke f; **that rings a ~** (fig) das kommt mir bekannt vor.
bellhop [bel'hâp] n Page m, Hoteljunge m.

belligerent [bəlij'ûrənt] a (person) streitsüchtig; (country) kriegsführend.
bellow [bel'ō] vti brüllen, grölen ♦ n Gebrüll nt.
bellows [bel'ōz] npl (TECH) Gebläse nt; (for fire) Blasebalg m.
belly [bel'ē] n Bauch m.
bellyache [bel'ēāk] (col) n Bauchschmerzen pl ♦ vi murren.
belong [bilóng'] vi gehören (to sb jdm); (to club) angehören (+dat); **it does not ~ here** es gehört nicht hierher.
belongings [bilóng'ingz] npl Habe f; **personal ~** persönliche(s) Eigentum nt, persönliche(r) Besitz m.
beloved [biluv'id] a innig geliebt ♦ n Geliebte(r) mf.
below [bilō'] prep unter ♦ ad unten; **temperatures ~ normal** Temperaturen unter dem Durchschnitt.
belt [belt] n (band) Riemen m; (round waist) Gürtel m; **industrial ~** Industriegebiet nt ♦ vt (fasten) mit Riemen befestigen; (col: beat) schlagen ♦ vi (Brit col: go fast) rasen.
belt out vt (song) schmettern.
belt up vi (Brit col) den Mund halten.
beltway [belt'wā] n (US) Umgehungsstraße f.
bemoan [bimōn'] vt beklagen.
bemused [bimyōōzd'] a verwirrt.
bench [bench] n (seat) Bank f; (workshop) Werkbank f; (judge's seat) Richterbank f; (judges) Richterstand m.
bench mark n Maßstab m.
bend [bend] vt irreg (curve) biegen; (stoop) beugen ♦ n Biegung f; (Brit: in road) Kurve f.
bend down vi (person) sich bücken ♦ vt (edges) nach unten biegen.
bend over vi (person) sich bücken ♦ vt umbiegen.
bends [bendz] npl: **the ~** Taucherkrankheit f.
beneath [binēth'] prep unter ♦ ad darunter.
benefactor [ben'əfaktûr] n Wohltäter(in f) m.
beneficial [benəfish'əl] a vorteilhaft; (to health) heilsam; **~ to** gut für; (advice, lesson) nützlich für; (influence also) vorteilhaft für.
beneficiary [benəfish'ēārē] n (JUR) Nutznießer(in f) m.
benefit [ben'əfit] n (advantage) Nutzen m; **unemployment ~** Arbeitslosenunterstützung f ♦ vt fördern ♦ vi Nutzen ziehen (from aus).
Benelux [ben'əluks] n Beneluxstaaten pl.
benevolence [bənev'ələns] n Wohlwollen nt.
benevolent [bənev'ələnt] a wohlwollend.
BEng n abbr (= Bachelor of Engineering) akademische(r) Grad von Ingenieuren.
benign [binīn'] a (person) gütig; (climate) mild; (MED) gutartig.
bent [bent] n (inclination) Neigung f ♦ a (wire, pipe) gebogen; (col: dishonest) unehrlich; **to be ~ on** versessen sein auf (+acc) ♦ pt, pp of **bend**.
bequeath [bikwēth'] vt vermachen.

bequest [bikwest'] n Vermächtnis nt.
bereaved [birēvd'] a leidtragend ♦ npl: **the ~** die Hinterbliebenen.
bereavement [birēv'mənt] n schmerzliche(r) Verlust m.
beret [bərā'] n Baskenmütze f.
Bering Sea [bar'ing sē] n Beringmeer nt.
Berks abbr (Brit) = Berkshire.
Berlin [bûrlin'] n Berlin nt; **East/West ~** Ost-/West-Berlin nt.
Bermuda [bûrmōō'də] n Bermuda nt, Bermudainseln pl.
Bermuda shorts npl Bermudashorts pl.
Bern [bûrn] n Bern nt.
berry [bär'ē] n Beere f.
berserk [bûrsûrk'] a: **to go ~** wild werden.
berth [bûrth] n (for ship) Ankerplatz m; (in ship) Koje f; (in train) Bett nt; **to give sb a wide ~** (fig) einen (weiten) Bogen um jdn machen ♦ vt am Kai festmachen ♦ vi anlegen.
beseech [bisēch'] vt irreg anflehen.
beset [biset'] vt irreg pt, pp **beset** bedrängen; **to be ~ with dangers** voller Gefahren sein.
besetting [biset'ing] a: **his ~ sin** eine ständige Untugend von ihm.
beside [bisīd'] prep neben, bei; (except) außer; (compared with) neben (+dat); **that's ~ the point** das hat damit nichts zu tun; **to be ~ o.s.** außer sich sein (with vor +dat).
besides [bisīdz'] prep außer, neben ♦ ad zudem, überdies.
besiege [bisēj'] vt (MIL) belagern; (surround) umlagern, bedrängen.
besmirch [bismûrch'] vt besudeln.
besotted [bisât'id] a: **~ with** vernarrt in, berauscht von.
bespectacled [bispek'təkəld] a bebrillt.
besought [bisôt'] pt, pp of **beseech**.
best [best] a beste(r, s); **the ~ thing to do is ...** das beste ist/wäre ...; **2,000 dollars or ~ offer** (US) 2,000 Dollar oder das nächstbeste Angebot ♦ ad am besten ♦ n: **at ~** höchstens; **to make the ~ of it** das Beste daraus machen; **for the ~** zum Besten; **he's not exactly patient at the ~ of times** er ist unter normalen Umständen schon ungeduldig.
bestial [bes'tēəl] a bestialisch.
best man n Trauzeuge m.
bestow [bistō'] vt: **to ~ sth on sb** (gift) jdm etw schenken; (honor) jdm etw erweisen; (medal) jdm etw verleihen.
best seller n Bestseller m, meistgekaufte(s) Buch nt.
bet [bet] n Wette f; **it's a safe ~** (fig) das ist ein sicherer Tip ♦ vti irreg pt **bet, betted,** pp **bet, betted** wetten; **to ~ on a horse** auf ein Pferd setzen.
Bethlehem [beth'lēəm] n Bethlehem nt.
betray [bitrā'] vt verraten.
betrayal [bitrā'əl] n Verrat m.
better [bet'ûr] a, ad besser; **that's ~!** so ist

es besser!; **I had ~ go** es ist besser, ich gehe jetzt; **he thought ~ of it** er hat sich eines Besseren besonnen; **~ off** (richer) wohlhabender ♦ vt verbessern ♦ n: **to get the ~ of sb** jdn überwinden; **a change for the ~** eine Wendung zum Guten.
betting [bet'ing] n Wetten nt.
betting shop n (Brit) Wettbüro nt.
between [bitwēn'] prep zwischen; (among) unter; **the road ~ here and Chicago** die Straße zwischen hier und Chicago; **we only had $5 ~ us** wir hatten zusammen nur 5 Dollar ♦ ad dazwischen.
bevel [bev'əl] n Abschrägung f.
bevelled [bev'əld] a: **~ edge** Schrägkante f.
beverage [bev'ûrij] n Getränk nt.
bevy [bev'ē] n Schar f.
bewail [biwāl'] vt beklagen, bejammern; (death) betrauern.
beware [biwär'] vt sich hüten vor (+dat); **"~ of the dog"** „Vorsicht, bissiger Hund!"
bewildered [biwil'dûrd] a verwirrt.
bewildering [biwil'dûring] a verwirrend, verblüffend.
bewitching [biwich'ing] a bestrickend.
beyond [bēând'] prep (place) jenseits (+gen); (time) über ... hinaus; (out of reach) außerhalb (+gen); **it's ~ me** das geht über meinen Horizont ♦ ad darüber hinaus.
b/f abbr (= brought forward) Obertr.
BFPO abbr (= British Forces Post Office) Teil der Anschrift auf Postsendungen an britische Truppenangehörige im Ausland.
bhp n abbr (= brake horsepower) Bremsleistung f.
bi- [bī] pref bi-, Bi-.
biannual [bīan'yōōəl] a zweimal jährlich.
bias [bī'əs] n (slant) Neigung f; (prejudice) Vorurteil nt.
bias(s)ed [bī'əst] a voreingenommen; **to be ~ against** voreingenommen sein gegen.
bib [bib] n Latz m.
Bible [bī'bəl] n Bibel f.
biblical [bib'likəl] a biblisch.
bibliography [biblēâg'rəfē] n Bibliographie f.
bicarbonate of soda [bīkâr'bənit əv sō'də] n (COOK) Natron nt.
bicentenary [bīsen'tənārē] n (Brit) = **bicentennial**.
bicentennial [bīsenten'ēəl] n Zweihundertjahrfeier f.
biceps [bī'seps] npl Bizeps m.
bicker [bik'ûr] vi zanken.
bickering [bik'ûring] n Gezänk nt, Gekeife nt.
bicycle [bī'sikəl] n Fahrrad nt.
bicycle path n (Fahr)radweg m.
bicycle pump n Luftpumpe f, Fahrradpumpe f.
bid [bid] n (offer) Gebot nt; (attempt) Versuch m ♦ vt irreg pt, pp **bid** (offer) bieten; **to ~ farewell** Lebewohl sagen.
bidder [bid'ûr] n (person) Steigerer m.
bidding [bid'ing] n (command) Geheiß nt.

bide [bīd] *vt*: **to ~ one's time** abwarten.
bidet [bēdā'] *n* Bidet *nt*.
bidirectional [bīdirek'shənəl] *a* bidirektional.
biennial [bīen'ēəl] *a* zweijährlich ♦ *n* (*BOT*) zweijährige Pflanze *f*.
bifocals [bīfō'kəlz] *npl* Bifokalbrille *f*.
big [big] *a* groß; **~ business** (*high finance*) Großkapital *nt*, Hochfinanz *f*; **to do things in a ~ way** alles im großen Stil tun.
bigamy [big'əmē] *n* Bigamie *f*.
big dipper [big dip'ûr] *n* (*Brit*) Achterbahn *f*, Berg-und-Tal-Bahn *f*.
big end *n* (*AUT*) Pleuelfuß *m*, Schubstangenkopf *m*.
bigheaded [big'hedid] *a* eingebildet.
bigot [big'ət] *n* Frömmler *m*.
bigoted [big'ətid] *a* bigott.
bigotry [big'ətrē] *n* Bigotterie *f*.
big toe *n* große Zehe *f*.
big top *n* Zirkuszelt *nt*.
big wheel *n* (*at fair*) Riesenrad.
bigwig [big'wig] *n* (*col*) hohe(s) Tier *nt*.
bike [bīk] *n* Rad *nt*.
bikeway [bīk'wā] *n* (*US*) (Fahr)radweg *m*.
bikini [bikē'nē] *n* Bikini *m*.
bilateral [bīlat'ûrəl] *a* bilateral.
bile [bīl] *n* (*BIOL*) Galle(nflüssigkeit) *f*.
bilge [bilj] *n* (*water*) Bilgenwasser *nt*.
bilingual [bīling'gwəl] *a* zweisprachig.
bilious [bil'yəs] *a* (*sick*) gallenkrank; (*peevish*) verstimmt.
bill [bil] *n* (*statement of charges*) Rechnung *f*; (*notice*) Anschlag *m*; (*THEAT*) Programm *nt*; (*POL*) Gesetzentwurf *m*; (*US FIN*) Geldschein *m*; **~ of exchange** Wechsel *m*, Tratte *f*; **~ of lading** Konnossement *nt*; **~ of sale** Verkaufsurkunde *f*; **may I have the ~ please?** die Rechnung bitte!, kann ich bitte bezahlen!; **"post no ~s"** „Plakate ankleben verboten" ♦ *vt* eine Rechnung ausstellen (+*dat*).
billboard [bil'bôrd] *n* Reklametafel *f*.
billet [bil'it] *n* Quartier *nt* ♦ *vt*: **to ~ sb (on sb)** jdn einquartieren (bei jdm).
billfold [bil'fōld] *n* (*US*) Geldscheintasche *f*.
billiards [bil'yûrdz] *n* Billard *nt*.
billion [bil'yən] *n* (*US*) Milliarde *f*; (*Brit*) Billion *f*.
billionaire [bilyənär'] *n* Milliardär(in *f*) *m*.
billow [bil'ō] *n* (*of smoke*) Schwaden *m*; (*of sail*) Blähen *nt* ♦ *vi* (*sail*) sich blähen.
billowy [bil'ōē] *a* (*smoke*) in Schwaden ziehend.
billy (club) [bil'ē (klub')] *n* (*US*) Gummiknüppel *m*.
billy goat [bil'ē gōt] *n* Ziegenbock *m*.
bin [bin] *n* Kasten *m*; (*Brit: dust~*) Mülltonne *f*; **litter ~** (*Brit*) Abfallbehälter *m*.
binary [bī'nûrē] *a* binär; (*MUS*) zweiteilig; **~ code** Binärcode *m*; **~ system** (*COMPUT*) binäre(s) Zahlensystem *nt*.
bind [bīnd] *vt irreg* (*tie*) binden; (*tie together*) zusammenbinden; (*oblige*) verpflichten.
bind over *vt* (*JUR*): **to ~ sb over** jdn ver-

warnen.
bind up *vt* (*wound*) verbinden; **to be bound up in** (*work, research etc*) sehr beschäftigt sein mit; **to be bound up** (*with person*) verbunden *or* verknüpft sein.
binder [bīn'dûr] *n* (*file*) Hefter *m*, Mappe *f*.
binding [bīn'ding] *n* (Buch)einband *m* ♦ *a* verbindlich.
binge [binj] *n* (*col: drinking*) Sauferei *f*; (*: eating*) Freßgelage *nt*; **to go on a ~** eine Sauftour machen.
bingo [bing'gō] *n* Bingo *nt*.
binoculars [bənâk'yəlûrz] *npl* Fernglas *nt*.
biochemistry [bīōkem'istrē] *n* Biochemie *f*.
biodegradable [bīōdigrā'dəbəl] *a* biologisch abbaubar.
biographer [bīâg'rəfûr] *n* Biograph(in *f*) *m*.
biographic(al) [bīəgraf'ik(əl)] *a* biographisch.
biography [bīâg'rəfē] *n* Biographie *f*.
biological [bīəlâj'ikəl] *a* biologisch.
biologist [bīâl'əjist] *n* Biologe *m*, Biologin *f*.
biology [bīâl'əjē] *n* Biologie *f*.
biophysics [bīōfiz'iks] *n sing* Biophysik *f*.
biopsy [bī'âpsē] *n* Biopsie *f*.
biorhythm [bī'ōrith̩əm] *n* Biorhythmus *m*.
biotechnology [bīōteknâl'əjē] *n* Biotechnologie *f*.
biped [bī'ped] *n* Zweifüßler *m*.
birch [bûrch] *n* Birke *f*.
bird [bûrd] *n* Vogel *m*; (*Brit col: girl*) Mädchen *nt*.
bird's-eye view [bûrdz'ī vyōō'] *n* Vogelschau *f*.
bird watcher [bûrd wâch'ûr] *n* Vogelbeobachter(in *f*) *m*.
Biro [bē'rō] *n* ® (*Brit*) Kugelschreiber *m*.
birth [bûrth] *n* Geburt *f*; **of good ~** aus gutem Hause; **to give ~ to** gebären; **to give ~ to sth** (*fig*) etw schaffen *or* gründen.
birth certificate *n* Geburtsurkunde *f*.
birth control *n* Geburtenkontrolle *f*.
birthday [bûrth'dā] *n* Geburtstag *m*.
birthplace [bûrth'plās] *n* Geburtsort *m*.
birth rate [bûrth rāt] *n* Geburtenrate *f*.
biscuit [bis'kit] *n* (*US*) Brötchen *nt*; (*Brit*) Keks *m*.
bisect [bīsekt'] *vt* in zwei Teile *or* Hälften teilen; (*MATH*) halbieren.
bishop [bish'əp] *n* Bischof *m*; (*CHESS*) Läufer *m*.
bison [bī'sən] *n* Bison *m*.
bit [bit] *n* bißchen, Stückchen *nt*; (*horse's*) Gebiß *nt*; (*COMPUT*) Bit *nt*; **a ~ tired** etwas müde; **to do one's ~** das Seine tun, sein(en) Teil tun; **to come to ~s** (*break*) kaputtgehen, aus dem Leim gehen; **bring all your ~s and pieces** bring deine Siebensachen (mit) ♦ *pt of* **bite**.
bitch [bich] *n* (*dog*) Hündin *f*; (*unpleasant woman*) Weibsstück *nt*.
bite [bīt] *vti irreg* beißen ♦ *n* (*wound: of dog, snake etc*) Biß *m*; (*mouthful*) Bissen *m*; (*of food*) Happen *m*.
biting [bī'ting] *a* beißend.

bit part n Nebenrolle f.
bitten [bit'ən] pp of **bite**.
bitter [bit'ûr] a bitter; (*memory etc*) schmerzlich; (*person*) verbittert; (*icy: weather*) bitterkalt, eisig; **to the ~ end** bis zum bitteren Ende ♦ n (*Brit: beer*) dunkle(s) Bier nt.
bitterly [bit'ûrlē] ad (*disappoint, complain, weep*) bitter; (*oppose, criticize*) erbittert, scharf; (*jealous*) wahnsinnig; **it's ~ cold** es ist bitter kalt.
bitterness [bit'ûrnis] n Bitterkeit f.
bittersweet [bit'ûrswēt] a bittersüß.
bitty [bit'ē] a (*col: US*) winzig; (: *Brit*) zusammengestoppelt or -gestückelt.
bitumen [bitōō'mən] n Bitumen nt.
bivouac [biv'ōōak] n Biwak nt.
bizarre [bizâr'] a bizarr.
bk n abbr (= *bank; book*) B.
b/l abbr (= *bill of lading*) FB.
BL n abbr (= *Bachelor of Letters*) akademischer Titel.
blab [blab] vi klatschen ♦ vt ausplaudern.
black [blak] a schwarz; (*night*) finster; **~ and blue** grün und blau; **the ~ country** Industriegebiet in Mittelengland ♦ vt schwärzen; (*shoes*) wichsen; (*eye*) blau schlagen; (*industry*) boykottieren ♦ n: **there it is in ~ and white** (*fig*) da steht es schwarz auf weiß; **in the ~** (*FIN*) in den schwarzen Zahlen.
  black out vi (*faint*) ohnmächtig werden.
black belt n (*SPORT*) Schwarze(r) Gürtel m; (*US: area*) Gebiet, das vorwiegend von Schwarzen bewohnt wird.
blackberry [blak'bärē] n Brombeere f.
blackbird [blak'bûrd] n Amsel f.
blackboard [blak'bôrd] n (Wand)tafel f.
black box n (*AVIAT*) Flugschreiber m.
black coffee n schwarze(r) Kaffee m.
blackcurrant [blakkur'ənt] n schwarze Johannisbeere f.
black economy n (*Brit*) Schattenwirtschaft f.
blacken [blak'ən] vt schwärzen; (*fig*) verunglimpfen.
Black Forest n Schwarzwald m.
blackguard [blag'ârd] n Schuft m.
black ice n Glatteis nt.
blackjack [blak'jak] n 17 und 4 nt.
blackleg [blak'leg] n (*Brit*) Streikbrecher(in f) m.
blacklist [blak'list] n schwarze Liste f ♦ vt auf die schwarze Liste setzen.
blackmail [blak'māl] n Erpressung f ♦ vt erpressen.
blackmailer [blak'mālûr] n Erpresser(in f) m.
black market n Schwarzmarkt m.
blackness [blak'nis] n Schwärze f.
blackout [blak'out] n Verdunklung f; (*TV*) Ausfall m; **to have a ~** (*MED*) bewußtlos werden.
Black Sea n Schwarze(s) Meer nt.
black sheep n schwarze(s) Schaf nt.

blacksmith [blak'smith] n Schmied m.
black spot n (*AUT*) Gefahrenstelle f.
bladder [blad'ûr] n Blase f.
blade [blād] n (*of weapon*) Klinge f; (*of grass*) Halm m; (*of oar*) Ruderblatt nt.
blame [blām] n Tadel m, Schuld f ♦ vt tadeln, Vorwürfe machen (+dat); **and I don't ~ him** und er hat ganz recht; **he is to ~** er ist daran schuld.
blameless [blām'lis] a untadelig.
blanch [blanch] vi (*person*) blaß werden, erbleichen ♦ vt (*COOK*) blanchieren.
blancmange [bləmânzh'] n Pudding m.
bland [bland] a mild.
blank [blangk] a leer, unbeschrieben; (*look*) verdutzt; (*verse*) Blank- ♦ n (*space*) Lücke f, Zwischenraum m; (*cartridge*) Platzpatrone f; **to draw a ~** (*fig*) kein Glück haben.
blank check n Blankoscheck m.
blanket [blang'kit] n (Woll)decke f ♦ cpd (*statement, agreement*) Pauschal-.
blankly [blangk'lē] ad leer; (*look*) verdutzt.
blare [blär] vti (*radio*) plärren; (*horn*) tuten; (*MUS*) schmettern ♦ n Geplärr nt; Getute nt; Schmettern nt.
blasé [blâzā'] a blasiert.
blaspheme [blasfēm'] vi (Gott) lästern.
blasphemous [blas'fəməs] a lästernd, lästerlich.
blasphemy [blas'fəmē] n (Gottes)lästerung f, Blasphemie f.
blast [blast] n Explosion f; (*of wind*) Windstoß m; (*of air, steam*) Schwall m; **(at) full ~** (*also fig*) mit voller Wucht ♦ vt (*blow up*) sprengen ♦ interj (*Brit col*) verdammt! (*col*), so ein Mist! (*col*).
  blast off vi (*spacecraft etc*) abheben, starten.
blast furnace n Hochofen m.
blast-off [blast'ôf] n (*SPACE*) (Raketen)abschuß m.
blatant [blā'tənt] a offenkundig.
blatantly [blā'təntlē] ad: **it's ~ obvious** es ist überdeutlich.
blather [blaᴛʜ'ûr] vi (*col*) quasseln.
blaze [blāz] n (*glow: of fire, sun etc*) Glut f; **in a ~ of glory** mit Glanz und Gloria ♦ vi lodern ♦ vt: **to ~ a trail** Bahn brechen.
blazer [blā'zûr] n Klubjacke f, Blazer m.
bleach [blēch] n Bleichmittel nt ♦ vt bleichen.
bleachers [blē'chûrz] npl (*US*) unüberdachte Zuschauertribüne.
bleak [blēk] a (*landscape, prospect, future*) trostlos; (*weather, fig*) rauh, kalt.
bleary-eyed [blē'rēid] a triefäugig; (*on waking up*) mit verschlafenen Augen.
bleat [blēt] n (*of sheep*) Blöken nt; (*of goat*) Meckern nt ♦ vi blöken; meckern.
bled [bled] pt, pp of **bleed**.
bleed [blēd] irreg vi bluten; **to ~ to death** verbluten ♦ vt (*draw blood*) Blut abnehmen; (*brakes, radiator*) lüften.
bleeding [blē'ding] a blutend.
bleeper [blē'pûr] n (*of doctor etc*) Funk-

rufempfänger *m*.
blemish [blem'ish] *n* Makel *m* ♦ *vt* verunstalten.
blench [blench] *vi* zurückschrecken; *see* **blanch**.
blend [blend] *n* Mischung *f* ♦ *vt* mischen ♦ *vi* sich mischen.
blender [blen'dûr] *n* (*COOK*) Mixer *m*, Mixgerät *nt*.
bless [bles] *vt* segnen; (*give thanks to*) preisen; (*make happy*) glücklich machen; ~ you! Gesundheit!
blessed [bles'id] *a* (*REL*: *holy*) heilig; (*giving joy*) willkommen; **every ~ day** aber auch jeden Tag.
blessing [bles'ing] *n* Segen *m*; (*at table*) Tischgebet *nt*; (*happiness*) Wohltat *f*, Segen *m*; (*good wish*) Glück *nt*; **it was a ~ in disguise** es war schließlich doch ein Segen; **to count one's ~s** von Glück sagen können.
blew [blōō] *pt of* **blow**.
blight [blīt] *n* (*BOT*) Mehltau *m*; (*fig*) schädliche(r) Einfluß *m* ♦ *vt* verderben, zerstören.
blimey [blī'mē] *interj* (*Brit col*) verflucht.
blind [blīnd] *a* blind; (*corner*) unübersichtlich ♦ *n* (*for window*) Rouleau *nt* ♦ *vt* blenden.
blind alley *n* Sackgasse *f*.
blinders [blīn'dûrz] *npl* (*US*) Scheuklappen *pl*.
blindfold [blīnd'fōld] *n* Augenbinde *f* ♦ *a* mit verbundenen Augen ♦ *vt* die Augen verbinden (*sb* jdm).
blindly [blīnd'lē] *ad* blind; (*fig*) blindlings.
blindness [blīnd'nis] *n* Blindheit *f*.
blind spot *n* (*AUT*) tote(r) Winkel *m*; (*fig*) schwache(r) Punkt *m*.
blink [blingk] *vti* blinzeln ♦ *n*: **to be on the ~** (*col*) kaputt sein (*col*).
blinkers [blingk'ûrz] *npl* (*Brit*) Scheuklappen *pl*.
bliss [blis] *n* (Glück)seligkeit *f*.
blissful [blis'fəl] *a* herrlich, paradiesisch, wohltuend; **in ~ ignorance of the fact that** ... in keinster Weise ahnend, daß ...
blissfully [blis'fəlē] *ad* (*sigh, smile*) selig; ~ **happy** überglücklich.
blister [blis'tûr] *n* Blase *f* ♦ *vt* Blasen werfen auf (+*dat*) ♦ *vi* Blasen werfen.
BLit *n abbr* (= *Bachelor of Literature*) akademischer Grad in Literaturwissenschaft.
blithe [blīth] *a*, **blithely** [blīth'lē] *ad* munter.
BLitt *n abbr see* **BLit**.
blitz [blits] *n* Luftkrieg *m* ♦ *vt* bombardieren; **to have a ~ on sth** (*fig*) etw gründlich sauber machen.
blizzard [bliz'ûrd] *n* Schneesturm *m*.
BLM *n abbr* (*US*: = *Bureau of Land Management*) staatliche Organisation zur Verwaltung von Land, Bodenschätzen etc.
bloated [blō'tid] *a* aufgedunsen; (*col: full*) nudelsatt.
blob [bläb] *n* Klümpchen *nt*.
bloc [bläk] *n* (*POL*) Block *m*.
block [bläk] *n* (*of wood*) Block *m*, Klotz *m*; (*of houses*) Häuserblock *m*; (*COMPUT*)

Block *m*; **mental ~** Mattscheibe *f* (*col*); ~ **and tackle** (*TECH*) Flaschenzug *m*; **3 ~s from here** 3 Blocks *or* Straßen weiter ♦ *vt* hemmen; (*COMPUT*) blocken.
block up *vt* blockieren, versperren; (*pipe*) verstopfen.
blockade [bläkād'] *n* Blockade *f* ♦ *vt* blockieren.
blockage [bläk'ij] *n* Verstopfung *f*.
block booking *n* (*travel booking*) Gruppenbuchung *f*; (*THEAT*) Gruppenbestellung *f*.
blockbuster [bläk'bustûr] *n* (*novel*) Knüller *m*; (*film*) Hit *m*, Kassenschlager *m*.
block capitals *npl* Blockschrift *f*.
block letters *npl* Blockbuchstaben *pl*.
block vote *n* geschlossene Stimmabgabe *f*.
bloke [blōk] *n* (*Brit col*) Kerl *m*, Typ *m*.
blond [bländ] *a* blond ♦ *n* (*man*) der Blonde.
blonde [bländ] *a* blond ♦ *n* Blondine *f*.
blood [blud] *n* Blut *nt*; **new ~** (*fig*) frisches Blut.
blood donor *n* Blutspender *m*.
blood group *n* Blutgruppe *f*.
bloodhound [blud'hound] *n* Bluthund *m*; (*fig: detective*) Schnüffler *m* (*col*), Detektiv *m*.
bloodless [blud'lis] *a* blutleer.
bloodletting [blud'leting] *n* (*fig*, *MED*) Aderlaß *m*.
blood poisoning *n* Blutvergiftung *f*.
blood pressure *n* Blutdruck *m*; **to have high/low ~** hohen/niedrigen Blutdruck haben.
blood sausage *n* (*US*) Blutwurst *f*.
bloodshed [blud'shed] *n* Blutvergießen *nt*.
bloodshot [blud'shät] *a* blutunterlaufen.
bloodstained [blud'stānd] *a* blutbefleckt.
bloodstream [blud'strēm] *n* Blut *nt*, Blutkreislauf *m*.
blood test *n* Blutprobe *f*.
bloodthirsty [blud'thûrstē] *a* blutrünstig.
blood transfusion *n* Blutübertragung *f*.
blood vessel *n* Blutgefäß *nt*.
bloody [blud'ē] *a* (*lit*) blutig; (*Brit col*) verdammt, saumäßig.
bloody-minded [blud'ēmīn'did] *a* (*Brit col*) stur.
bloom [blōōm] *n* Blüte *f*; (*freshness*) Glanz *m* ♦ *vi* blühen; **in ~** in Blüte.
blossom [bläs'əm] *n* Blüte *f* ♦ *vi* blühen; **to ~ into** (*fig*) zu etw aufblühen *or* erblühen.
blot [blät] *n* Klecks *m*; **a ~ on the landscape** ein Schandfleck in der Landschaft ♦ *vt* beklecksen; (*ink*) (ab)löschen.
blot out *vt* auslöschen.
blotchy [bläch'ē] *a* fleckig.
blotter [blät'ûr] *n* (Tinten)löscher *m*.
blotting paper [blät'ing pā'pûr] *n* Löschpapier *nt*.
blouse [blous] *n* Bluse *f*.
blow [blō] *n* Schlag *m*; **to come to ~s** handgreiflich werden ♦ *irreg vt* blasen; **to ~ one's top** (vor Wut) explodieren ♦ *vi* (*wind*) wehen.
blow away *vt* wegblasen.

blow down vt umwehen.
blow out vt ausblasen ♦ vi ausgehen.
blow over vi vorübergehen.
blow up vi explodieren ♦ vt sprengen.
blow-dry [blō'drī] n: **to have a** ~ sich fönen lassen ♦ vt fönen.
blowfly [blō'flī] n (US) Schmeißfliege f.
blowlamp [blō'lamp] n (Brit) Lötlampe f.
blown [blōn] pp of **blow**.
blowout [blō'out] n (AUT) geplatzte(r) Reifen m; (col: big meal) Schlemmerei f.
blowtorch [blō'tôrch] n Lötlampe f.
blow-up [blō'up] n Vergrößerung f.
blowy [blō'ē] a windig.
BLS n abbr (US: = Bureau of Labor Statistics) statistisches Bundesamt für den Arbeitsmarkt.
BLT n abbr = bacon, lettuce and tomato (sandwich).
blubber [blub'ûr] n Walfischspeck m.
bludgeon [bluj'ən] vt (fig) zwingen.
blue [blōō] a blau; (col: unhappy) niedergeschlagen; (obscene) pornographisch; (joke) anzüglich; **once in a** ~ **moon** alle Jubeljahre (einmal); **out of the** ~ (fig) aus heiterem Himmel.
blue baby n Baby nt mit angeborenem Herzfehler.
bluebell [blōō'bel] n Glockenblume f.
blueberry [blōō'bärē] n Heidelbeere f.
blue-blooded [blōō'blud'id] a blaublütig.
bluebottle [blōō'bátəl] n Schmeißfliege f.
blue cheese n Blauschimmelkäse m.
blue-chip investment [blōō'chip' invest'mənt] n erstklassige sichere Wertpapieranlage f.
blue-collar [blōō'kâl'ûr] a: ~ **worker** Arbeiter m.
blueprint [blōō'print] n Blaupause f; (fig) Plan m, Entwurf m.
blues [blōōz] npl (MUS) Blues m; **to have the** ~ (col: feeling) den Moralischen haben.
bluff [bluf] vt bluffen, täuschen ♦ n (cliff) Klippe f; (deception) Bluff m ♦ a gutmütig und derb.
bluish [blōō'ish] a bläulich.
blunder [blun'dûr] n grobe(r) Fehler m, Schnitzer m ♦ vi einen groben Fehler machen; **to** ~ **into sb** auf jdn stoßen or (zufällig) treffen; **to** ~ **into sth** in etw hineintappen.
blunt [blunt] a (knife) stumpf; (talk) unverblümt; **this pencil is** ~ der Bleistift ist stumpf; **with a** ~ **instrument** (JUR) mit einem stumpfen Gegenstand ♦ vt abstumpfen.
bluntly [blunt'lē] ad frei heraus.
bluntness [blunt'nis] n Stumpfheit f; (fig) Plumpheit f.
blur [blûr] n Fleck m ♦ vi verschwimmen ♦ vt verschwommen machen.
blurb [blûrb] n Material nt, Informationen pl; (on book cover) Klappentext m, Waschzettel m.
blurred [blûrd] a (TV) verschwommen; (pho-

to) unscharf.
blurt [blûrt] vt: **to** ~ **out** herausplatzen mit.
blush [blush] vi erröten ♦ n (Scham)röte f.
blusher [blush'ûr] n Rouge nt.
blushing [blush'ing] a errötend.
bluster [blus'tûr] vi (wind) brausen; (fig) sich aufblasen ♦ n Gezeter nt, große(s) Geschrei nt.
blustery [blus'tûrē] a sehr windig.
Blvd abbr = boulevard.
BM n abbr (= Bachelor of Medicine) akademischer Grad in Medizin.
BMA n abbr (= British Medical Association) britischer Medizinerverband.
BMus n abbr (= Bachelor of Music) akademischer Grad in Musik.
BO n abbr (col: = body odor) Körpergeruch m; (US) = **box office**.
boa [bō'ə] n Boa f.
boar [bôr] n Keiler m; (male pig) Eber m.
board [bôrd] n (for chess etc) Brett nt; (of card) Pappe f; (committee) Ausschuß m; (of firm) Aufsichtsrat m; (SCH) Direktorium nt; **above** ~ (fig) korrekt; **across the** ~ (fig) allgemein, generell; (criticize, agree, reject) pauschal; **on** ~ (NAUT, AVIAT) an Bord; **to go by the** ~ unter den Tisch fallen ♦ vt (train) einsteigen in (+acc); (ship) an Bord gehen (+gen).
board up vt mit Brettern vernageln.
board and lodging n Unterkunft f und Verpflegung.
boarder [bôr'dûr] n Kostgänger m; (SCH) Internatsschüler(in f) m.
board game n Brettspiel nt.
boarding house [bôr'ding hous] n Pension f.
boarding pass [bôr'ding pas] n (AVIAT) Bordkarte f, Einsteigekarte f.
boarding school [bôr'ding skōōl] n Internat nt.
board meeting n Vorstandssitzung f.
board room n Sitzungszimmer nt.
boardwalk [bôrd'wôk] n (US) Holzsteg m.
boast [bōst] vi prahlen ♦ n Großtuerei f, Prahlerei f.
boastful [bōst'fəl] a prahlerisch.
boastfulness [bōst'fəlnis] n Prahlerei f.
boat [bōt] n Boot nt; (ship) Schiff nt; **to go by** ~ mit dem Schiff reisen or fahren.
boater [bō'tûr] n (hat) Kreissäge f.
boating [bō'ting] n Bootfahren nt.
boatswain [bō'sən] n = **bosun**.
boat train n Zug m mit Schiffsanschluß.
bob [bâb] vi sich auf und nieder bewegen.
bob up vi auftauchen.
bobbin [bâb'in] n Spule f.
bobby pin [bâb'ē pin] n (US) Haarklemme f.
bobsled [bâb'sled] n (US) Bob m.
bobsleigh [bâb'slā] n Bob m.
bode [bōd] vi: **to** ~ **well/ill** ein gutes/ schlechtes Zeichen sein.
bodice [bâd'is] n Mieder nt.
-bodied [bâd'ēd] a -gebaut.
bodily [bâd'əlē] a körperlich; ~ **harm** Kör-

perverletzung *f*; ~ **needs** leibliche Bedürfnisse *pl* ♦ *ad* (*lift*) mit beiden Händen.

body [bâd'ē] *n* Körper *m*; (*dead*) Leiche *f*; (*group*) Mannschaft *f*; (*organization*) Organ *nt*; (*AUT*) Karosserie *f*; (*trunk*) Rumpf *m*; (*of speech, document*) Hauptteil *m*; (*also*: ~ **stocking**) Body *m*; **ruling** ~ amtierende(s) Organ *nt*, amtierende(s) Gremium *nt*; **in a** ~ geschlossen; **the main** ~ **of the work** der Hauptanteil der Arbeit.

bodyguard [bâd'ēgârd] *n* Leibwache *f*.

bodywork [bâd'ēwûrk] *n* Karosserie *f*.

boffin [bâf'in] *n* (*Brit col*) Eierkopf *m*.

bog [bâg] *n* Sumpf *m* ♦ *vi*: **to be** *or* **get** ~**ged down in** (*discussion, essay*) sich verrennen (in +*acc*).

bogey [bō'gē] *n* Schreckgespenst *nt*.

boggle [bâg'əl] *vi*: **the mind** ~**s** das kann man sich (*dat*) kaum ausmalen.

Bogotá [bōgətâ'] *n* Bogota *nt*.

bogus [bō'gəs] *a* unecht, Schein-.

Bohemia [bōhē'mēə] *n* Böhmen *nt*.

Bohemian [bōhē'mēən] *a* böhmisch ♦ *n* Böhme *m*, Böhmin *f*.

boil [boil] *vti* kochen ♦ *n* (*MED*) Geschwür *nt*; **to bring to the** ~ zum Kochen bringen; **to come to the** ~ zu kochen anfangen.

  boil down *vi* (*fig*): **to** ~ **down to** hinauslaufen auf (+*acc*).

  boil over *vi* überkochen.

boiled egg [boild eg] *n* gekochte(s) Ei *nt*.

boiler [boi'lûr] *n* Boiler *m*.

boiling [boi'ling] *a*: **I'm** ~ (**hot**) (*col*) mir ist fürchterlich heiß.

boiling point *n* Siedepunkt *m*.

boisterous [bois'tûrəs] *a* ungestüm.

bold [bōld] *a* (*fearless*) unerschrocken; (*handwriting*) fest und klar.

boldly [bōld'lē] *ad* keck.

boldness [bōld'nis] *n* Kühnheit *f*; (*cheekiness*) Dreistigkeit *f*.

bold type *n* (*TYP*) Fettdruck *m*.

Bolivia [bōliv'ēə] *n* Bolivien *nt*.

Bolivian [bōliv'ēən] *a* bolivianisch, bolivisch ♦ *n* Bolivianer(in *f*) *m*.

bollard [bâl'ûrd] *n* (*NAUT*) Poller *m*; (*Brit: on road*) Pfosten *m*.

bolster [bōl'stûr] *n* Polster *f*.

  bolster up *vt* unterstützen.

bolt [bōlt] *n* Bolzen *m*; (*lock*) Riegel *m* ♦ *vt* verriegeln; (*swallow*) verschlingen ♦ *vi* (*horse*) durchgehen.

bomb [bâm] *n* Bombe *f* ♦ *vt* bombardieren.

bombard [bâmbârd'] *vt* bombardieren.

bombardment [bâmbârd'mənt] *n* Bombardierung *f*, Bombardement *nt*.

bombastic [bâmbas'tik] *a* bombastisch.

bomb disposal expert *n* Bombenräumexperte *m*.

bomber [bâm'ûr] *n* Bomber *m*; (*terrorist*) Bombenattentäter *m*.

bombing [bâm'ing] *n* Bombenangriff *m*.

bombshell [bâm'shel] *n* (*fig*) Bombe *f*.

bomb site *n* Trümmergrundstück *nt*.

bona fide [bō'nə fīd'] *a* echt.

bonanza [bənan'zə] *n* (*fig*) Goldgrube *f*.

bond [bând] *n* (*link*) Band *nt*; (*FIN*) Schuldverschreibung *f*; **in** ~ (*COMM*) unter Zollverschluß.

bondage [bân'dij] *n* Sklaverei *f*.

bonded [bân'did] *a*: ~ **goods** Waren *pl* unter Zollverschluß; ~ **warehouse** Zollgutlager *nt*.

bone [bōn] *n* Knochen *m*; (*of fish*) Gräte *f*; (*piece of* ~) Knochensplitter *m*; ~ **of contention** Zankapfel *m* ♦ *vt* die Knochen herausnehmen (+*dat*); (*fish*) entgräten.

bone up on *vt* büffeln.

bone china *n* Knochen-Porzellan *nt*.

bone-dry [bōn'drī'] *a* knochentrocken.

bone idle *a* stinkfaul.

boner [bō'nûr] *n* (*US col*) Schnitzer *m*.

bonfire [bân'fîûr] *n* Feuer *nt* im Freien.

Bonn [bân] *n* Bonn *nt*.

bonnet [bân'it] *n* Haube *f*; (*for baby*) Häubchen *nt*; (*Brit AUT*) Motorhaube *f*.

bonny [bân'ē] *a* (*esp Scot*) schön, hübsch.

bonus [bō'nəs] *n* Bonus *m*; (*on wages*) Gratifikation *f*.

bony [bō'nē] *a* knochendürr; (*thin: person*) knochig.

boo [bōō] *vt* auspfeifen.

boob [bōōb] *n* (*col: breast*) Busen *m*; (: *Brit: mistake*) Schnitzer *m*.

boo-boo [bōō'bōō] *n* (*US col*) Schnitzer *m*.

booby prize [bōō'bē prīz] *n* Scherzpreis für den schlechtesten Teilnehmer.

booby trap [bōō'bē trap] *n* (*MIL etc*) versteckte Bombe *f*.

book [bōōk] *n* Buch *nt*; **to throw the** ~ **at sb** jdn nach allen Regeln der Kunst fertigmachen; **to keep the** ~**s** die Bücher führen; **by the** ~ buchstabengetreu ♦ *vt* (*ticket etc*) vorbestellen; (*SOCCER*) verwarnen; (*col: driver*) aufschreiben (*col*).

  book in *vt* (*Brit*): **to** ~ **sb in to a hotel** jdm ein Hotelzimmer reservieren lassen.

  book up *vt*: **all seats are** ~**ed up** es ist bis auf den letzten Platz ausverkauft; **the hotel is** ~**ed up** das Hotel ist ausgebucht.

bookable [bōōk'əbəl] *a* im Vorverkauf erhältlich.

bookcase [bōōk'kās] *n* Bücherregal *nt*, Bücherschrank *m*.

booking office [bōōk'ing ôf'is] *n* (*Brit: RAIL*) Fahrkartenschalter *m*; (: *THEAT*) Vorverkaufsstelle *f*.

bookkeeping [bōōkkē'ping] *n* Buchhaltung *f*.

booklet [bōōk'lit] *n* Broschüre *f*.

bookmaker [bōōk'mākûr] *n* Buchmacher *m*.

bookseller [bōōk'selûr] *n* Buchhändler *m*.

bookshop [bōōk'shâp] *n* Buchhandlung *f*.

bookstall [bōōk'stôl] *n* Bücherstand *m*; (*RAIL*) Bahnhofsbuchhandlung *f*.

bookstore [bōōk'stôr] *n* Buchhandlung *f*.

book token *n* Buchgutschein *m*.

book value *n* Buchwert *m*.

bookworm [bōōk'wûrm] *n* Bücherwurm *m*.

boom [bōōm] *n* (*noise*) Dröhnen *nt*; (*busy pe-*

riod) Hochkonjunktur *f* ♦ *vi* dröhnen; (*business*) florieren.
boomerang [bo͞o'mərang] *n* (*lit, fig*) Bumerang *m* ♦ *vi* (*fig*) wie ein Bumerang zurückkommen (*on* zu).
boom town *n* Goldgräberstadt *f*.
boon [bo͞on] *n* Wohltat *f*, Segen *m*.
boorish [bo͞o'rish] *a* grob.
boost [bo͞ost] *n* Auftrieb *m*; (*fig*) Reklame *f*; **to give a ~ to sb** (*morale*) jdm Auftrieb geben; **it gave a ~ to his confidence** das hat sein Selbstvertrauen gestärkt ♦ *vt* Auftrieb geben; (*increase: sales, production*) ankurbeln.
booster [bo͞os'tûr] *n* (*TV*) Zusatzgleichrichter *m*; (*ELEC*) Puffersatz *m*; (*also:* ~ **rocket**) Booster *m*, Startrakete *f*; (*MED*) Wiederholungsimpfung *f*.
boot [bo͞ot] *n* Stiefel *m*; (*ankle* ~) hoh(er) Schuh *m*; (*Brit AUT*) Kofferraum *m*; **to give sb the ~** (*col*) jdn rausschmeißen/an die Luft setzen; **to ~** (*in addition*) obendrein ♦ *vt* (*kick*) einen Fußtritt geben; (*COMPUT*) (durch Ureingabe) laden, urladen.
booth [bo͞oth] *n* (*at fair*) Bude *f*; (*telephone* ~) Zelle *f*; (*also:* **voting** ~) Kabine *f*.
bootleg [bo͞ot'leg] *a* schwarz gebrannt; ~ **record** im Raubdruck hergestellte Schallplatte.
bootlicker [bo͞ot'likûr] *n* (*col*) Arschkriecher *m* (*col*), Radfahrer *m*.
booty [bo͞o'tē] *n* Beute *f*.
booze [bo͞oz] *n* (*col*) Alkohol *m*, Schnaps *m* ♦ *vi* saufen.
boozer [bo͞oz'ûr] *n* (*col: person*) Säufer(in *f*) *m*.
border [bôr'dûr] *n* Grenze *f*; (*edge*) Kante *f*; (*in garden*) (Blumen)rabatte *f*.
border on *vt fus* grenzen an (+*acc*).
borderline [bôr'dûrlīn] *n* Grenze *f*.
bore [bôr] *vt* bohren; (*weary*) langweilen; **he's ~d to tears** *or* ~**d to death** *or* ~**d stiff** er langweilt sich zu Tode ♦ *n* (*person*) Langweiler *m*; (*thing*) langweilige Sache *f*; (*of gun*) Kaliber *nt* ♦ *pt of* **bear**.
boredom [bôr'dəm] *n* Langeweile *f*.
boring [bôr'ing] *a* langweilig.
born [bôrn] *a:* **to be ~** geboren werden.
borne [bôrn] *pp of* **bear**.
Borneo [bôr'nēō] *n* Borneo *nt*.
borough [bûr'ə] *n* Stadt(gemeinde) *f*, Stadtbezirk *m*.
borrow [bâr'ō] *vt* borgen; **may I ~ your car?** kann ich deinen Wagen leihen?
borrower [bâr'ōûr] *n* Ausleiher(in *f*) *m*; (*FIN*) Kreditnehmer(in *f*) *m*.
borrowing [bâr'ōing] *n* Aufnahme *f* von Geldern.
bosom [bo͞oz'əm] *n* Busen *m*.
boss [bôs] *n* Chef *m*, Boß *m*.
boss around *vt* herumkommandieren.
bossy [bôs'ē] *a* herrisch.
bosun [bō'sən] *n* Bootsmann *m*.
botanical [bətan'ikəl] *a* botanisch.

botanist [bât'ənist] *n* Botaniker(in *f*) *m*.
botany [bât'ənē] *n* Botanik *f*.
botch [bâch] *vt* verpfuschen.
both [bōth] *a* beide; ~ **(of) the books** beide Bücher; **I like them** ~ ich mag (sie) beide ♦ *pron* beide; (*two different things*) beides ♦ *ad:* ~ **X and Y** sowohl X wie *or* als auch Y.
bother [bâth̞'ûr] *vt* (*pester*) quälen; **I'm sorry to** ~ **you** es tut mir leid, daß ich Sie stören muß ♦ *vi* (*fuss*) sich aufregen; (*take trouble*) sich Mühe machen; **please don't** ~ machen Sie bitte keine Umstände ♦ *n* Mühe *f*, Umstand *m* ♦ *interj* Mist!; ~ **him!** zum Kuckuck mit ihm!
Botswana [bo͞ochwän'ə] *n* Botswana *nt*.
bottle [bât'əl] *n* (*of perfume, shampoo etc*) Flasche *f*; **a ~ of wine/milk** eine Flasche Wein/Milch; **wine/milk** ~ Wein-/Milchflasche *f* ♦ *vt* (in Flaschen) abfüllen.
bottle up *vt* aufstauen.
bottleneck [bât'əlnek] *n* (*lit, fig*) Engpaß *m*.
bottle opener *n* Flaschenöffner *m*.
bottom [bât'əm] *n* Boden *m*; (*of person*) Hintern *m*; (*riverbed*) Flußbett *nt*; (*of mountain*) Fuß *m*; **at** ~ im Grunde; **to get to the** ~ **of sth** (*fig*) einer Sache auf den Grund gehen ♦ *a* unterste(r, s).
bottomless [bât'əmlis] *a* bodenlos.
bottom line *n* (*fig*): **that's the** ~ das ist das Entscheidende.
bough [bou] *n* Zweig *m*, Ast *m*.
bought [bôt] *pt, pp of* **buy**.
bouillon cube [bo͞ol'yən kyo͞ob] *n* (*US*) Brühwürfel *m*.
boulder [bōl'dûr] *n* Felsbrocken *m*.
bounce [bouns] *vi* (*ball*) hochspringen; (*person*) herumhüpfen; (*check*) platzen ♦ *vt* (auf)springen lassen ♦ *n* (*rebound*) Aufprall *m*; **he's got plenty of** ~ (*fig*) er hat viel Schwung.
bouncer [boun'sûr] *n* Rausschmeißer *m*.
bound [bound] *n* Grenze *f*; (*leap*) Sprung *m*; **out of** ~**s** Zutritt verboten; **to go out of** ~**s** (*ball*) ins Aus gehen ♦ *vi* (*spring, leap*) (auf)springen ♦ *a* gebunden, verpflichtet; **to be** ~ **to do sth** verpflichtet sein, etw zu tun; **it's** ~ **to happen** es muß so kommen; **to be** ~ **for ...** nach ... fahren ♦ *pt, pp of* **bind**.
boundary [boun'dûrē] *n* Grenze *f*, Grenzlinie *f*.
boundless [bound'lis] *a* grenzenlos.
bountiful [boun'təfəl] *a* (*person*) großzügig; (*God*) gütig; (*supply*) (über)reich.
bounty [boun'tē] *n* (*generosity*) Freigebigkeit *f*; (*reward money*) Kopfgeld *nt*.
bounty hunter *n* Kopfgeldjäger *m*.
bouquet [bo͞okā'] *n* Strauß *m*, Bukett *nt*; (*of wine*) Blume *f*.
bourbon [bûr'bən] *n* (*US: also:* ~ **whiskey**) Bourbon *m*.
bourgeois [bo͞or'zhwâ] *a* bürgerlich; (*pej*) spießig ♦ *n* Bürger(in *f*) *m*, Bourgeois *m*.
bout [bout] *n* (*of illness*) Anfall *m*; (*of contest*) Kampf *m*.

boutique [boōtēk'] *n* Boutique *f*.
bow *n* [bō] *(ribbon)* Schleife *f*; *(weapon, MUS)* Bogen *m* ♦ *vi* [bou] sich verbeugen; *(submit)* sich beugen *(+dat)*; **to ~ to the inevitable** sich in das Unvermeidliche fügen ♦ *n* [bou] Verbeugung *f*; *(NAUT: also: ~s)* Bug *m*.
bowels [bou'əlz] *npl* Darm *m*; *(centre)* Innere *nt*.
bowl [bōl] *n (basin)* Schüssel *f*; *(of pipe)* (Pfeifen)kopf *m*; *(wooden ball)* (Holz)kugel *f*; *(US: stadium)* Stadion *nt*; *see also* **bowls** ♦ *vt (ball)* rollen ♦ *vi (CRICKET)* werfen; *(play bowls)* Bowling spielen.
bowlegged [bō'legid] *a* o-beinig.
bowler [bō'lûr] *n* Werfer *m*; *(Brit: hat)* Melone *f*.
bowling [bō'ling] *n* Kegeln *nt*.
bowling alley *n* Kegelbahn *f*.
bowling green *n* Rasen *m* zum Bowling-Spiel.
bowls [bōlz] *npl (Brit: game)* Bowls-Spiel *nt*.
bow tie [bō tī] *n* Fliege *f*.
box [bâks] *n* Schachtel *f*; *(bigger)* Kasten *m*; *(crate: also for money)* Kassette *f*; *(THEAT)* Loge *f* ♦ *vt* einpacken; **to ~ sb's ears** jdm eine Ohrfeige geben ♦ *vi* boxen.
box in *vt* einpferchen.
box car *n (US RAIL)* geschlossene(r) Güterwagen *m*.
boxer [bâk'sûr] *n* Boxer *m*.
boxer shorts *npl (Brit)* Boxer-Shorts *pl*.
box file *n* kastenförmige(r) Aktendeckel *m*.
boxing [bâk'sing] *n (SPORT)* Boxen *nt*.
Boxing Day *n (Brit)* zweite(r) Weihnachtsfeiertag *m*.
boxing ring *n* Boxring *m*.
box lunch *n (US)* Lunchpaket *nt*.
box number *n (for advertisements)* Chiffre *f*.
box office *n* (Theater)kasse *f*.
box room *n (Brit)* Rumpelkammer *f*.
boy [boi] *n* Junge *m*.
boycott [boi'kât] *n* Boykott *m* ♦ *vt* boykottieren.
boyfriend [boi'frend] *n* Freund *m*.
boyish [boi'ish] *a* jungenhaft.
boy scout *n* Pfadfinder *m*.
Bp *abbr* (= *bishop*) Bi., Bisch.
BPOE *n abbr (US: = Benevolent and Protective Order of Elks)* Wohltätigkeitsorganisation.
BR *n abbr* (= *British Rail*) ≈ DB *f*.
bra [brâ] *n* BH *m*.
brace [brās] *n (TECH)* Stütze *f*; *(MED)* Klammer *f*; *see also* **braces** ♦ *vt* stützen.
bracelet [brās'lit] *n* Armband *nt*.
braces [brā'siz] *npl* Hosenträger *pl*; *(US: for teeth)* Klammer *m*.
bracing [brā'sing] *a* kräftigend.
bracken [brak'ən] *n* Farnkraut *nt*.
bracket [brak'it] *n* Halter *m*, Klammer *f*; *(in punctuation)* Klammer *f*; *(group)* Gruppe *f*; **round/square ~s** runde/eckige Klammern

pl; **in ~s** in Klammern ♦ *vt* einklammern; *(fig: also: ~ together)* zusammenfassen.
brackish [brak'ish] *a (water)* brackig.
brag [brag] *vi* sich rühmen.
braid [brād] *n (hair)* Flechte *f*; *(trim)* Borte *f*.
Braille [brāl] *n* Blinden- or Brailleschrift *f*.
brain [brān] *n (ANAT)* Gehirn *nt*; *(intellect: also: ~s)* Intelligenz *f*, Verstand *m*; *(person)* kluge(r) Kopf *m*.
brainchild [brān'chīld] *n* Erfindung *f*; *(idea)* Geistesprodukt *nt*.
brainless [brān'lis] *a* dumm.
brainstorm [brān'stôrm] *n* verrückte(r) Einfall *m*; *(fig US: brain wave)* Geistesblitz *m*.
brainstorming [brān'stôrming] *n* gemeinsame Problembewältigung *f*, Brainstorming *nt*.
brainwash [brān'wâsh] *vt* Gehirnwäsche *f* vornehmen bei.
brain wave *n* gute(r) Einfall *m*, Geistesblitz *m*.
brainy [brā'nē] *a* gescheit.
braise [brāz] *vt* schmoren.
brake [brāk] *n* Bremse *f* ♦ *vti* bremsen.
brake light *n* Bremslicht *nt*.
brake pedal *n* Bremspedal *nt*.
bramble [bram'bəl] *n (fruit)* Brombeere *f*.
bran [bran] *n* Kleie *f*.
branch [branch] *n* Ast *m*; *(division)* Zweig *m* ♦ *vi (road)* sich verzweigen.
branch out *vi*: **to ~ out on one's own** sich selbständig machen.
branch line *n (RAIL)* Zweiglinie *f*, Nebenlinie *f*.
branch manager *n* Zweigstellenleiter *m*.
brand [brand] *n (COMM)* Marke *f*, Sorte *f*; *(on cattle)* Brandmal *nt* ♦ *vt* brandmarken; *(COMM)* eine Schutzmarke geben *(+dat)*.
brandish [bran'dish] *vt* (drohend) schwingen.
brand name *n* Markenname *m*.
brand-new [brand'noō'] *a* funkelnagelneu.
brandy [bran'dē] *n* Weinbrand *m*, Kognak *m*.
brash [brash] *a* unverschämt.
Brasilia [brazil'ēə] *n* Brasilia *nt*.
brass [bras] *n* Messing *nt* ♦ *a* Messing-; **to get down to ~ tacks** *(col)* zur Sache kommen.
brass band *n* Blaskapelle *f*.
brassière [brəzēr'] *n* Büstenhalter *m*.
brat [brat] *n* Gör *nt*.
bravado [brəvâ'dō] *n* Tollkühnheit *f*.
brave [brāv] *a* tapfer ♦ *n* indianische(r) Krieger *m* ♦ *vt* die Stirn bieten *(+dat)*.
bravely [brāv'lē] *ad* tapfer.
bravery [brā'vûrē] *n* Tapferkeit *f*.
bravo [brä'vō] *interj* bravo!
brawl [brôl] *n* Rauferei *f* ♦ *vi* Krawall machen.
brawn [brôn] *n (ANAT)* Muskeln *pl*; *(strength)* Muskelkraft *f*.
brawny [brô'nē] *a* muskulös, stämmig.
bray [brā] *n* Eselsschrei *m* ♦ *vi* schreien.
brazen [brā'zən] *a (shameless)* unverschämt ♦ *vt*: **to ~ it out** sich mit Lügen und Betrügen durchsetzen.

brazier [brā'zhûr] n (of workmen) offene(r) Kohlenofen m.

Brazil [brəzil'] n Brasilien nt.

Brazilian [brəzil'ēən] a brasilianisch ♦ n Brasilianer(in f) m.

breach [brēch] n (gap) Lücke f; (MIL) Durchbruch m; (of discipline) Verstoß m (gegen die Disziplin); (of faith) Vertrauensbruch m; (estrangement) Bruch m; ~ of the peace öffentliche Ruhestörung f; in ~ of unter Verstoß gegen ♦ vt durchbrechen.

bread [bred] n Brot nt; (col: money) Moos nt, Kies m, Flöhe pl; to earn one's daily ~ (sich dat) sein Geld verdienen; he knows which side his ~ is buttered on er weiß, wo was zu holen ist; ~ and butter Butterbrot nt; (fig) Broterwerb m.

breadbin [bred'bin] n (Brit) Brotkasten m.

breadboard [bred'bôrd] n (COMPUT) Leiterplatte f.

breadbox [bred'bâks] n (US) Brotkasten m.

breadcrumbs [bred'krumz] npl Brotkrumen pl; (COOK) Paniermehl nt.

breadline [bred'līn] n: to be on the ~ sich gerade so durchschlagen.

breadth [bredth] n Breite f.

breadwinner [bred'winûr] n Geldverdiener m, Ernährer m.

break [brāk] irreg vt (destroy) (ab- or zer)brechen; (promise) brechen ♦ vi (fall apart) auseinanderbrechen; (collapse) zusammenbrechen; (of dawn) anbrechen; to ~ with sb mit jdm Schluß machen; to ~ free or loose sich losreißen ♦ n (gap) Lücke f; (chance) Chance f, Gelegenheit f; (fracture) Bruch m; (rest) Pause f; (vacation) Kurzurlaub m; to have a lucky ~ (col: chance) Glück or Schwein (col) haben; to have or take a ~ (few minutes) (eine) Pause machen; without a ~ ohne Unterbrechung or Pause, ununterbrochen.

break down vi (car) eine Panne haben; (person) zusammenbrechen ♦ vt (door etc) einrennen; (resistance) brechen.

break in vt (animal) abrichten; (horse) zureiten; (US: car) einfahren ♦ vi (burglar) einbrechen.

break into vt fus (house) einbrechen in (+acc).

break off vt (talks) abbrechen; (engagement) lösen.

break out vi ausbrechen.

break through vt fus (defences, barrier, crowd) durchbrechen ♦ vi: the sun broke through die Sonne kam durch.

break up vi zerbrechen; (fig) sich zerstreuen; (marriage) in die Brüche gehen; (Brit SCH) in die Ferien gehen ♦ vt brechen.

breakable [brā'kəbəl] a zerbrechlich ♦ n: ~s zerbrechliche Ware f.

breakage [brā'kij] n Bruch m, Beschädigung f; to pay for ~s für zerbrochene Ware or Bruch bezahlen.

breakaway [brā'kəwā] a (group etc) abgefallen.

break-dancing [brāk'dansing] n Break-Dancing nt.

breakdown [brāk'doun] n (TECH) Panne f; (of nerves) Zusammenbruch m; (of figures) Aufschlüsselung f.

breakdown van n (Brit) Abschleppwagen m.

breaker [brā'kûr] n Brecher m.

break-even chart [brākē'vən chârt] n Gewinnschwellen-Diagramm nt.

break-even point n Break-Even-Punkt m.

breakfast [brek'fəst] n Frühstück nt.

breakfast cereal n Getreideflocken pl zum Frühstück.

break-in [brāk'in] n Einbruch m.

breaking point [brā'king point] n (TECH) Festigkeitsgrenze f; she has reached ~ sie ist am Ende (ihrer Kräfte).

breakthrough [brāk'throō] n Durchbruch m.

break-up [brāk'up] n (of partnership, marriage) Zerrüttung f.

break-up value n (COMM) Liquidationswert m.

breakwater [brāk'wôtûr] n Wellenbrecher m.

breast [brest] n Brust f.

breast-feed [brest'fēd] vt stillen.

breast stroke n Brustschwimmen nt.

breath [breth] n Atem m; out of ~ außer Atem; under one's ~ flüsternd; to go out for a ~ of air an die frische Luft gehen, frische Luft schnappen gehen.

breathalyze [breth'əliz] vt blasen lassen.

Breathalyzer [breth'əlīzûr] n ® Teströhrchen nt.

breathe [brēth] vti atmen; I won't ~ a word about it ich werde kein Sterbenswörtchen darüber verlauten lassen.

breathe in vti einatmen.

breathe out vti ausatmen.

breather [brē'thûr] n Verschnaufpause f.

breathing [brē'thing] n Atmung f.

breathing space n (fig) Atempause f, Ruhepause f.

breathless [breth'lis] a (with excitement) atemlos.

breathtaking [breth'tāking] a atemberaubend.

bred [bred] pt, pp of breed.

-bred suff: to be well/ill~ gut/schlecht erzogen sein.

breed [brēd] irreg vi sich vermehren ♦ vt züchten; (fig: hate, suspicion) erzeugen ♦ n (race) Rasse f, Zucht f.

breeder [brē'dûr] n (person) Züchter m; (PHYS: also: ~ reactor) Brüter m.

breeding [brē'ding] n Züchtung f; (upbringing) Erziehung f; (education) Bildung f.

breeze [brēz] n Brise f.

breezeblock [brēz'blâk] n (Brit) Ytong m ®.

breezy [brē'zē] a windig; (manner) munter.

Breton [bret'ən] a bretonisch ♦ n (person) Bretone m, Bretonin f; (language) Bretonisch nt.

brevity [brev'itē] n Kürze f.

brew [broo] *vt* brauen; *(plot)* anzetteln ♦ *vi* *(storm)* sich zusammenziehen.

brewer [broo'ûr] *n* Brauer *m*.

brewery [broo'ûrē] *n* Brauerei *f*.

briar [brī'ûr] *n* *(thorny bush)* Dornbusch *m*; *(wild rose)* wilde Rose *f*.

bribe [brīb] *n* Bestechungsgeld/Bestechungsgeschenk *nt* ♦ *vt* bestechen; **to ~ sb to do sth** jdn bestechen, damit er etw tut.

bribery [brī'bûrē] *n* Bestechung *f*.

bric-à-brac [brik'əbrak] *n* Nippes *m*, Nippsachen *pl*.

brick [brik] *n* Backstein *m*.

bricklayer [brik'lāûr] *n* Maurer *m*.

brickwork [brik'wûrk] *n* Mauerwerk *nt*.

brickworks [brik'wûrks] *npl* Ziegelei *f*.

bridal [brīd'əl] *a* Braut-, bräutlich.

bride [brīd] *n* Braut *f*.

bridegroom [brīd'groom] *n* Bräutigam *m*.

bridesmaid [brīdz'mād] *n* Brautjungfer *f*.

bridge [brij] *n* Brücke *f*; *(NAUT)* Kommandobrücke *f*; *(CARDS)* Bridge *nt*; *(ANAT)* Nasenrücken *m* ♦ *vt* eine Brücke schlagen über *(+acc)*; *(fig)* überbrücken.

bridging loan [brij'ing lōn] *n* Überbrückungskredit *m*.

bridle [brīd'əl] *n* Zaum *m* ♦ *vt* *(fig)* zügeln; *(horse)* aufzäumen ♦ *vi* *(in anger etc)* sich entrüstet wehren.

bridle path *n* Saumpfad *m*.

brief [brēf] *a* kurz; **in ~** kurz gesagt ♦ *n* *(JUR)* Akten *pl*; *see also* **briefs** ♦ *vt* instruieren; **to ~ sb (about sth)** jdn instruieren (über etw)/jdn einweisen (in etw).

briefcase [brēf'kās] *n* Aktentasche *f*.

briefing [brē'fing] *n* (genaue) Anweisung *f*.

briefly [brēf'lē] *ad* *(speak, visit)* kurz; **to glimpse sb/sth ~** einen flüchtigen Blick von jdm/etw erhaschen.

briefness [brēf'nis] *n* Kürze *f*.

briefs [brēfs] *npl* Schlüpfer *m*, Slip *m*.

Brig. *abbr* = **brigadier**.

brigade [brigād'] *n* Brigade *f*.

brigadier [brigədi'ûr] *n* Brigadegeneral *m*.

bright [brīt] *a* hell; *(cheerful)* heiter; *(idea)* klug; **to look on the ~ side** zuversichtlich sein, etw von der positiven Seite betrachten.

brighten up [brīt'ən up] *vt* aufhellen; *(person)* aufheitern ♦ *vi* sich aufheitern.

brightly [brīt'lē] *ad* hell; heiter.

brilliance [bril'yəns] *n* Glanz *m*; *(of person)* Scharfsinn *m*; **a man of such ~** ein Mann von so hervorragender Intelligenz.

brilliant [bril'yənt] *a* *(light)* strahlend; *(idea, person, success)* großartig, glänzend.

brilliantly [bril'yəntlē] *ad* glänzend.

brim [brim] *n* Rand *m* ♦ *vi* voll sein.

brimful [brim'fool'] *a* übervoll.

brine [brīn] *n* Salzwasser *nt*.

bring [bring] *vt irreg* bringen; **to ~ sth to an end** etw beenden *or* zu Ende bringen; **I can't ~ myself to fire him** ich bringe es nicht fertig, ihn zu entlassen.

bring about *vt* zustande bringen.

bring back *vt* zurückbringen.

bring down *vt* *(price)* senken.

bring forward *vt* *(in accounts)* übertragen.

bring in *vt* *(person, object)* hereinbringen; *(PARL: bill, legislation)* einbringen; *(JUR: verdict)* fällen; *(produce: income)* (ein)bringen.

bring off *vt* davontragen; *(deal)* zustande bringen.

bring out *vt* *(new product)* herausbringen; *(book)* herausgeben.

bring round *or* **to** *vt* wieder zu sich bringen.

bring up *vt* aufziehen; *(question)* zur Sprache bringen.

brink [bringk] *n*: **to be on the ~ of doing sth** nahe daran sein, etw zu tun; **she was on the ~ of tears** sie war den Tränen nahe.

brisk [brisk] *a* *(abrupt)* forsch; *(walk)* flott; *(wind)* frisch; *(trade etc)* lebhaft, rege; **business is ~** das Geschäft ist rege.

bristle [bris'əl] *n* Borste *f* ♦ *vi* sich sträuben; **bristling with** strotzend vor *(+dat)*.

bristly [bris'lē] *a* *(chin)* Stoppel-, stoppelig; *(beard, hair)* borstig.

Brit [brit] *n abbr* *(col: = British person)* Brite *m*, Britin *f*.

Britain [brit'in] *n* *(also:* **Great ~)** Großbritannien *nt*.

British [brit'ish] *a* britisch; **the ~ Isles** die Britischen Inseln ♦ *npl*: **the ~** die Briten.

British Honduras *n* Britisch-Honduras *nt*.

British Rail *n die Britischen Eisenbahnen pl*, ≈ Deutsche Bundesbahn.

Briton [brit'ən] *n* Brite *m*, Britin *f*.

Brittany [brit'ənē] *n* die Bretagne.

brittle [brit'əl] *a* spröde.

Br(o). *abbr* *(REL)* = **brother**.

broach [brōch] *vt* *(subject)* anschneiden.

broad [brôd] *a* breit; *(hint)* deutlich; *(daylight)* hellicht; *(general)* allgemein; *(accent)* stark ♦ *n* *(US col)* Frau *f*; *(: younger)* Mieze *f*; **the ~ outlines** die groben Umrisse *pl*.

broad bean *n* Bohne *f*, Saubohne *f*.

broadcast [brôd'kast] *n* Rundfunkübertragung *f* ♦ *vt irreg* übertragen, senden ♦ *vi* senden.

broadcasting [brôd'kasting] *n* Rundfunk *m*.

broadcasting station *n* *(RAD)* Rundfunkstation *f*; *(TV)* Fernsehstation *f*.

broaden [brôd'ən] *vt* erweitern ♦ *vi* sich erweitern.

broadly [brôd'lē] *ad* allgemein gesagt.

broad-minded [brôd'mīn'did] *a* tolerant.

brocade [brōkād'] *n* Brokat *m*.

broccoli [brák'əlē] *n* *(BOT)* Brokkoli *pl*, Spargelkohl *m*; *(COOK)* Spargelkohl *m*.

brochure [brōshoor'] *n* Broschüre *f*.

brogue [brōg] *n* *(accent)* Akzent *m*; *(shoe)* feste(r) Schuh *m*.

broil [broil] *vt* *(US)* grillen.

broiler [broi'lûr] *n* Brathähnchen *nt*.

broke [brōk] *a* *(col)* pleite; **to go ~** Pleite *f*

machen ♦ *pt of* **break**.

broken [brō'kən] *a* (*stick*) entzwei; (*fig: marriage*) zerrüttet; (: *promise, vow*) gebrochen ♦ *pp of* **break**.

broken-down [brō'kəndoun'] *a* (*machine, car*) kaputt; (*house*) zerstört.

brokenhearted [brō'kənhâr'tid] *a* untröstlich.

broker [brō'kûr] *n* Makler *m*.

brokerage [brō'kûrij] *n* Maklergebühr *f*, Courtage *f*; (*business*) Maklergeschäft *nt*.

brolly [brál'ē] *n* (*Brit col*) Schirm *m*.

bronchitis [brångkī'tis] *n* Bronchitis *f*.

bronze [brânz] *n* Bronze *f*.

bronzed [brânzd] *a* sonnengebräunt.

brooch [brōch] *n* Brosche *f*.

brood [brōōd] *n* Brut *f* ♦ *vi* brüten.

broody [brōō'dē] *a* brütend.

brook [brōōk] *n* Bach *m*.

broom [brōōm] *n* Besen *m*.

broomstick [brōōm'stik] *n* Besenstiel *m*.

Bros. *abbr* (*COMM*) = *Brothers*) Gebr.

broth [brôth] *n* Suppe *f*, Fleischbrühe *f*.

brothel [bráth'əl] *n* Bordell *nt*.

brother [bruth'ûr] *n* Bruder *m*.

brotherhood [bruth'ûrhōōd] *n* Bruderschaft *f*.

brother-in-law [bruth'ûrinlô] *n* Schwager *m*.

brotherly [bruth'ûrlē] *a* brüderlich.

brought [brôt] *pt, pp of* **bring**.

brow [brou] *n* (*eye*~) (Augen)braue *f*; (*forehead*) Stirn *f*; (*of hill*) Bergkuppe *f*.

browbeat [brou'bēt] *vt irreg* einschüchtern.

brown [broun] *a* (*hair*) braun ♦ *n* Braun *nt* ♦ *vt* bräunen; **to go** ~ (*person*) braun werden, bräunen; (*leaves*) braun werden.

brown bread *n* (*Brit*) Graubrot *nt*.

Brownie [brou'nē] *n* (*Girl Scout*) Wichtel *m*.

brownnose(r) [broun'nōz'(ûr)] *n* (*US col*) Arschkriecher *m* (*col*), Radfahrer *m*.

brown paper *n* Packpapier *nt*.

brown rice *n* geschälte(r) Reis *m*.

browse [brouz] *vi* (*in books*) blättern; (*in shop*) schmökern, herumschauen; (*cattle*) weiden; (*deer*) äsen; **to** ~ **through the books** in den Büchern schmökern ♦ *n*: **to have a** ~ (**around**) sich umsehen.

bruise [brōōz] *n* (*on person*) blaue(r) Fleck *m*, Bluterguß *m* ♦ *vt* (*leg etc*) sich stoßen, sich (*dat*) einen blauen Fleck holen; (*fig: feelings*) verletzen ♦ *vi* einen blauen Fleck bekommen; verletzt werden.

brunette [brōōnet'] *n* Brünette *f*.

brunt [brunt] *n* volle Wucht *f*.

brush [brush] *n* Bürste *f*; (*for sweeping*) Handbesen *m*; (*for painting*) Pinsel *m*; (*fight*) kurze(r) Kampf *m*; (*MIL*) Scharmützel *nt*; (*fig*) Auseinandersetzung *f* ♦ *vt* (*clean*) bürsten; (*sweep*) fegen; (*touch*) streifen; **to have a** ~ **with the police** mit der Polizei zusammenstoßen.

brush aside *vt* abtun.

brush up *vt* (*knowledge*) auffrischen.

brushed [brusht] *a*: ~ **chrome** (*TECH*) gebürstete Mattverchromung *f*; ~ **nylon** Nylon-

Velours *m*; ~ **steel** (*TECH*) gebürstete(r) Mattstahl *m*.

brush-off [brush'ôf] *n*: **to give sb the** ~ (*col*) jdm eine Abfuhr erteilen.

brushwood [brush'wōōd] *n* Gestrüpp *nt*.

brusque [brusk] *a* (*person, manner*) brüsk, schroff; (*tone*) schroff.

Brussels [brus'əlz] *n* Brüssel *nt*.

Brussels sprout *n* Rosenkohl *m*.

brutal [brōōt'əl] *a* brutal.

brutality [brōōtal'itē] *n* Brutalität *f*.

brute [brōōt] *n* (*person*) Scheusal *nt* ♦ *a*: **by** ~ **force** mit brachialer *or* roher Gewalt.

brutish [brōō'tish] *a* tierisch.

bs *abbr* = **bill of sale**.

BS *n abbr* (*US*: = *Bachelor of Science*) akademischer Grad in Naturwissenschaften.

BSA *n abbr* (= *Boy Scouts of America*) amerikanische Pfadfinder.

BSc *n abbr* (= *Bachelor of Science*) akademischer Grad in Naturwissenschaften.

BSI *n abbr* (= *British Standards Institution*) ≈ DNA *m*.

BST *abbr* = *British Summer Time*.

btu *n abbr* (= *British thermal unit*) britische Wärmeeinheit.

bubble [bub'əl] *n* (Luft)blase *f* ♦ *vi* sprudeln; (*with joy*) übersprudeln.

bubble bath *n* Schaumbad *nt*.

Bucharest [bōō'kərest] *n* Bukarest *nt*.

buck [buk] *n* Bock *m*; (*US col*) Dollar *m* ♦ *vi* bocken.

buck up *vi* (*col*) sich zusammenreißen ♦ *vt*: **to** ~ **one's ideas up** sich zusammenreißen (*col*).

bucket [buk'it] *n* Eimer *m* ♦ *vi* (*Brit col*): **the rain is** ~**ing** (**down**) es gießt *or* es schüttet.

buckle [buk'əl] *n* Schnalle *f* ♦ *vt* (an- *or* zusammen)schnallen ♦ *vi* (*bend*) sich verziehen.

buckle down *vi* sich dahinterklemmen (*col*), sich dranmachen (*col*).

Bucks *abbr* (*Brit*) = *Buckinghamshire*.

bud [bud] *n* Knospe *f* ♦ *vi* knospen, keimen.

Budapest [bōō'dəpest] *n* Budapest *nt*.

Buddhism [bōō'dizəm] *n* Buddhismus *m*.

Buddhist [bōō'dist] *n* Buddhist(in *f*) *m* ♦ *a* buddhistisch.

budding [bud'ing] *a* angehend.

buddy [bud'ē] *n* (*US col*) Kumpel *m*.

budge [buj] *vi* sich von der Stelle rühren ♦ *vt* (von der Stelle) bewegen.

budgerigar [buj'ûrēgär] *n* (*Brit*) Wellensittich *m*.

budget [buj'it] *n* Budget *nt*; (*POL*) Haushalt *m*; **I'm on a tight** ~ ich werde kurz gehalten (*col*), ich habe nicht viel Geld zur Verfügung; **she works out her** ~ **every month** sie macht sich jeden Monat einen Haushaltsplan ♦ *vi* haushalten.

budgie [buj'ē] *n* (*Brit*) = **budgerigar**.

Buenos Aires [bwānəs ī'riz] *n* Buenos Aires *nt*.

buff [buf] *a* (*color*) lederfarben ♦ *n* (*col*) Fan *m*, Spezialist(in *f*) *m*.

buffalo [buf'əlō] *n* Büffel *m*.

buffer [buf'ûr] *n* (*COMPUT*) Puffer *m*.

buffering [buf'ûring] *n* (*COMPUT*) Pufferung *f*.

buffet [buf'it] *n* (*blow*) Schlag *m*; [bŏŏfā'] (*Brit*: *bar*) Imbißraum *m*, Erfrischungsraum *m*; (: *food*) (kaltes) Büffet *nt* ♦ *vt* [buf'it] (herum)stoßen.

buffet car [bŏŏfā' kár] *n* (*Brit RAIL*) Speisewagen *m*.

buffet lunch [bŏŏfā' lunch] *n* Stehimbiß *m*.

buffoon [bufŏŏn'] *n* Hanswurst *m*.

bug [bug] *n* (*lit*, *fig*) Wanze *f*; (*COMPUT*) Programmfehler *m*; **I've got the travel ~** (*fig*) die Reiselust hat mich gepackt ♦ *vt* (*room*) verwanzen, Wanzen *pl* installieren in; (*annoy*) nerven (*col*); **that really ~s me** das nervt mich vielleicht *or* unheimlich.

bugbear [bug'bär] *n* Schreckgespenst *nt*.

bugle [byŏŏ'gəl] *n* Jagd- *or* Bügelhorn *nt*.

build [bild] *vt irreg* bauen ♦ *n* Körperbau *m*.

   build on *vt* anbauen; (*fig*) aufbauen.

   build up *vt* (*establish*: *business*) aufbauen; (*increase*: *production*) steigern, erhöhen; **to ~ up a reputation** sich (*dat*) einen Namen machen; **don't ~ your hopes up too soon** mach dir nicht zu früh Hoffnungen.

builder [bil'dûr] *n* Bauunternehmer *m*.

building [bil'ding] *n* Gebäude *nt*.

building contractor *n* Bauunternehmer *m*.

building industry *n* Bauindustrie *f*, Baugewerbe *nt*.

building site *n* Baustelle *f*.

building society *n* (*Brit*) Baugenossenschaft *f*.

building trade *n* = **building industry**.

build-up [bild'up] *n* Aufbau *m*; (*publicity*) Reklame *f*; **to give sb/sth a good ~** (*publicity*) jdn/etw ganz groß herausbringen.

built [bilt] *a*: **well-~** (*person*) gut gebaut ♦ *pt*, *pp of* **build**.

built-in [bilt'in'] *a* (*closet*) eingebaut.

built-in obsolescence *n* geplanter Verschleiß und/oder absichtlich herbeigeführtes Altmodischwerden.

built-up area [bilt'up är'ēə] *n* Wohngebiet *nt*.

bulb [bulb] *n* (*BOT*) (Blumen)zwiebel *f*; (*ELEC*) Glühlampe *f*, Birne *f*.

bulbous [bul'bəs] *a* knollig.

Bulgaria [bulgär'ēə] *n* Bulgarien *nt*.

Bulgarian [bulgär'ēən] *a* bulgarisch ♦ *n* (*person*) Bulgare *m*, Bulgarin *f*; (*language*) Bulgarisch *nt*.

bulge [bulj] *n* (Aus)bauchung *f*; (*in birth rate*, *sales*) Zunahme *f*, Anschwellen *nt* ♦ *vi* sich (aus)bauchen.

bulk [bulk] *n* Größe *f*, Masse *f*; (*greater part*) Großteil *m*; **to buy in ~** in großen Mengen (ein)kaufen.

bulk buying [bulk bī'ing] *n* Mengeneinkauf *m*.

bulkhead [bulk'hed] *n* Schott *nt*.

bulky [bul'kē] *a* (sehr) umfangreich; (*goods*) sperrig.

bull [bŏŏl] *n* (*animal*) Bulle *m*; (*cattle*) Stier *m*; (*REL*) Bulle *f*; (*in stock market*) Haussier *m*.

bulldog [bŏŏl'dôg] *n* Bulldogge *f*.

bulldoze [bŏŏl'dōz] *vt* mit Bulldozern wegräumen, abreißen; (*fig*) durchboxen; **I was ~d into doing it** (*fig col*) ich wurde gezwungen *or* unter Druck gesetzt, es zu tun.

bulldozer [bŏŏl'dōzûr] *n* Planierraupe *f*, Bulldozer *m*.

bullet [bŏŏl'it] *n* Kugel *f*.

bulletin [bŏŏl'itən] *n* Bulletin *nt*, Bekanntmachung *f*.

bulletin board *n* (*for notices*) Anschlagbrett *nt*; (*COMPUT*) Informationstafel *f*.

bulletproof [bŏŏl'itprŏŏf] *a* kugelsicher; **~ vest** kugelsichere Weste *f*.

bullfight [bŏŏl'fit] *n* Stierkampf *m*.

bullhorn [bŏŏl'hôrn] *n* (*US*) Megaphon *nt*.

bullion [bŏŏl'yən] *n* Barren *m*.

bullock [bŏŏl'ək] *n* Ochse *m*.

bullring [bŏŏl'ring] *n* Stierkampfarena *f*.

bull's-eye [bŏŏlz'ī] *n* das Schwarze *nt*.

bully [bŏŏl'ē] *n* Raufbold *m* ♦ *vt* einschüchtern.

bum [bum] *n* (*col*: *backside*) Hintern *m*; (: *tramp*) Landstreicher *m*; (*esp US*: *idler*) Rumtreiber *m*, Schnorrer *m*; (: *nasty person*) fiese(r) Kerl *m*.

   bum around *vi* herumgammeln.

bumble [bum'bəl] *vi* (*walk unsteadily*) stolpern; (*fig*) sich verhaspeln.

bumblebee [bum'bəlbē] *n* Hummel *f*.

bumbling [bum'bling] *n* ungeschickte(s) Verhalten *nt*.

bumf [bumf] *n* (*Brit col*: *forms etc*) Papierkram *m*.

bump [bump] *n* (*blow*) Stoß *m*; (*swelling*) Beule *f*; (*noise*) Bums *m* (*col*) ♦ *vt* stoßen, prallen gegen; **to ~ sb's car** jdm eine Delle ins Auto fahren.

   bump into *vt fus* (*col*: *meet*) über den Weg laufen (+*dat*).

bumper [bum'pûr] *n* (*Brit AUT*) Stoßstange *f* ♦ *a* (*edition*) dick; (*harvest*) Rekord-.

bumper cars *npl* Autoskooter *pl*.

bumptious [bump'shəs] *a* aufgeblasen.

bumpy [bum'pē] *a* (*journey*, *flight*) holprig.

bun [bun] *n* Korinthenbrötchen *nt*; (*hair*) Knoten *m*.

bunch [bunch] *n* (*of flowers*) Strauß *m*; (*of keys*) Bund *m*; (*of people*) Haufen *m*.

bundle [bun'dəl] *n* Bündel *nt* ♦ *vt* bündeln.

   bundle off *vt* fortschicken.

bung [bung] *n* Spund *m* ♦ *vt* (*Brit col*: *throw*) schleudern; (*also*: **~ up**: *pipe*, *hole*) verstopfen.

bungalow [bung'gəlō] *n* einstöckige(s) Haus *nt*, Bungalow *m*.

bungle [bung'gəl] *vt* verpfuschen.

bunion [bun'yən] *n* entzündete(r) Fußballen *m*.

bunk [bungk] *n* Schlafkoje *f*.
bunk bed *n* Etagenbett *nt*.
bunker [bung'kûr] *n* (*coal store*) Kohlenbunker *m*; (*GOLF*) Sandloch *nt*.
bunny [bun'ē] *n* Häschen *nt*.
Bunsen burner [bun'sən bûr'nûr] *n* Bunsenbrenner *m*.
bunting [bun'ting] *n* Fahnentuch *nt*.
buoy [bōō'ē] *n* Boje *f*; (*life*~) Rettungsboje *f*.
  buoy up *vt* Auftrieb geben (+*dat*).
buoyancy [boi'ənsē] *n* Schwimmkraft *f*;
buoyant [boi'ənt] *a* (*floating*) schwimmend; (*fig*) heiter; (*FIN: market, currency*) fest.
burden [bûr'dən] *n* (*weight*) Ladung *f*, Last *f*; (*fig*) Bürde *f*; **to be a ~ to sb** jdm zur Last fallen ♦ *vt* belasten.
bureau [byoor'ō] *n* (*for information etc*) Büro *nt*; (*US: chest of drawers*) Kommode *f*; (*Brit: desk*) Sekretär *m*.
bureaucracy [byoorâk'rəsē] *n* Bürokratie *f*.
bureaucrat [byoor'əkrat] *n* Bürokrat(in *f*) *m*.
bureaucratic [byoorəkrat'ik] *a* bürokratisch.
burgeon [bûr'jən] *vi* schnell wachsen, sprießen; (*trade etc*) blühen.
burglar [bûr'glûr] *n* Einbrecher *m*.
burglar alarm *n* Einbruchssicherung *f*.
burglarize [bûr'glərīz] *vt* (*US*) einbrechen in (+*acc*).
burglary [bûr'glûrē] *n* Einbruch *m*.
burgle [bûr'gəl] *vt* (*Brit*) einbrechen in (+*acc*).
Burgundy [bûr'gəndē] *n* Burgund *nt*.
burial [bär'ēəl] *n* Beerdigung *f*.
burial ground *n* Friedhof *m*.
burlap [bûr'lap] *n* Sackleinen *nt*.
burlesque [bûrlesk'] *n* Burleske *f*.
burly [bûr'lē] *a* stämmig.
Burma [bûr'mə] *n* Birma *nt*, Burma *nt*.
Burmese [bûrmēz'] *a* birmanisch, burmesisch ♦ *n* (*person*) Birmane/Burmese *m*, Birmanin/Burmesin *f*; (*language*) Birmanisch *nt*, Burmesisch *nt*.
burn [bûrn] *irreg vt* verbrennen; **to ~ a hole in sth** ein Loch in etw brennen; **I've ~ed myself** ich habe mich verbrannt; **to ~ one's fingers** sich die Finger verbrennen ♦ *vi* brennen ♦ *n* (*MED*) Brandwunde *f*
  burn down *vti* abbrennen.
  burn out *vr*: **to ~ o.s. out** sich kaputtmachen (*col*), sich völlig verausgaben.
burned [bûrnd] *pt, pp of* **burn**.
burner [bûr'nûr] *n* Brenner *m*.
burning [bûr'ning] *a* (*building, forest, question*) brennend.
burnish [bûr'nish] *vt* polieren.
burnt [bûrnt] *pt, pp of* **burn**.
burrow [bûr'ō] *n* (*of fox*) Bau *m*; (*of rabbit*) Höhle *f* ♦ *vi* sich eingraben ♦ *vt* eingraben.
bursar [bûr'sûr] *n* Kassenverwalter *m*, Quästor *m*.
bursary [bûr'sûrē] *n* (*Brit*) Stipendium *nt*.
burst [bûrst] *irreg vt pt, pp* **burst** zerbrechen; **the river has ~ its banks** der Fluß ist über die Ufer getreten ♦ *vi* platzen; (*into tears*) ausbrechen ♦ *n* Explosion *f*; (*outbreak*) Ausbruch *m*; (*in pipe*) Bruch(stelle *f*) *m*; **a ~ of applause** ein Beifallssturm *m*; **a ~ of speed** ein Spurt *m*.
  burst into *vt fus* (*room etc*) platzen in (+*acc*).
bury [bär'ē] *vt* vergraben; (*in grave*) beerdigen; **to ~ the hatchet** das Kriegsbeil begraben.
bus [bus] *n* (Auto)bus *m*, Omnibus *m*; (*long-distance*) (Überland)bus *m*.
bush [boosh] *n* Busch *m*.
bushel [boosh'əl] *n* Scheffel *m*.
bushy [boosh'ē] *a* buschig.
busily [biz'ilē] *ad* geschäftig.
business [biz'nis] *n* Geschäft *nt*; (*concern*) Angelegenheit *f*; **he's in the insurance ~** er arbeitet in der Versicherungsbranche; **I'm here on ~** ich bin geschäftlich hier; **to do ~ with sb** mit jdm geschäftlich zu tun haben; **it's none of your ~** es geht dich nichts an; **to mean ~** es ernst meinen.
business address *n* Geschäftsadresse *f*.
business card *n* Visitenkarte *f*.
business hours *npl* Geschäftsstunden *pl*.
businesslike [biz'nislīk] *a* geschäftsmäßig.
businessman [biz'nisman] *n, pl* -**men** Geschäftsmann *m*.
business suit *n* Straßenanzug *m*.
businesswoman [biz'niswoomən] *n, pl* -**women** Geschäftsfrau *f*.
busker [bus'kûr] *n* (*Brit*) Straßenmusikant(in *f*) *m*.
bus route *n* Buslinie *f*, (Bus)strecke *f*.
bus station *n* Busbahnhof *m*.
bus-stop [bus'stâp] *n* Bushaltestelle *f*.
bust [bust] *n* Büste *f* ♦ *a* (*broken*) kaputt(gegangen); (*business*) pleite; **to go ~** pleite machen ♦ *vt* (*police: arrest*) verhaften.
bustle [bus'əl] *n* Getriebe *nt* ♦ *vi* hasten.
bustling [bus'ling] *a* geschäftig.
bust-up [bust'up] *n* (*col*) Krach *m*.
busy [biz'ē] *a* beschäftigt; (*road*) belebt; (*telephone, line*) besetzt; **he's a ~ man** (*normally*) er ist ein vielbeschäftigter Mann; (*temporarily*) er hat (zur Zeit) viel zu tun ♦ *vt*: **to ~ o.s.** sich beschäftigen.
busybody [biz'ēbâdē] *n* Übereifrige(r) *mf*.
busy signal *n* (*US TEL*) Besetztzeichen *nt or* -ton *m*.
but [but] *cj* aber; (*only*) nur; (*except*) außer; **not this ~ that** nicht dies, sondern das; **no one ~ him** keiner außer ihm.
butane [byoo'tān] *n* Butan *nt*.
butcher [booch'ûr] *n* Metzger *m*; (*murderer*) Schlächter *m* ♦ *vt* schlachten; (*kill*) abschlachten.
butcher's (shop) [booch'ûrz (shâp')] *n* Metzgerei *f*.
butler [but'lûr] *n* Butler *m*.
butt [but] *n* (*cask*) große(s) Faß *nt*; (*US col: bottom*) Gesäß *nt*; (*Brit: target*) Zielscheibe *f*; (*thick end*) dicke(s) Ende *nt*; (*of gun*) Kolben *m*; (*of cigarette*) Stummel *m* ♦ *vt*

(mit dem Kopf) stoßen.
butt in *vi* (*interrupt*) sich einmischen, dazwischenfunken.
butter [but'ûr] *n* Butter *f* ♦ *vt* buttern.
buttercup [but'ûrkup] *n* Butterblume *f*.
butterfingers [but'ûrfinggûrz] *n* (*col*) Schussel *m*.
butterfly [but'ûrflī] *n* Schmetterling *m*; (*SWIMMING*: also: ~ **stroke**) Delphinstil *m*, Schmetterlingsstil *m*.
buttocks [but'əks] *npl* Gesäß *nt*.
button [but'ən] *n* Knopf *m* ♦ *vt* zuknöpfen ♦ *vi* geknöpft werden.
buttonhole [but'ənhōl] *n* Knopfloch *nt*; (*flower*) Blume *f* im Knopfloch ♦ *vt* rankriegen.
buttress [but'tris] *n* Strebepfeiler *m*, Stützbogen *m*.
buxom [buk'səm] *a* drall.
buy [bī] *vt irreg* kaufen; (*COMM: company*) erwerben, ankaufen ♦ *n*: **a good/bad** ~ ein guter/schlechter Kauf.
buy back *vt* zurückkaufen.
buy in *vt* (*Brit*) einkaufen ♦ *vi* (*FIN*) Deckungskäufe *pl* vornehmen.
buy off *vt* (*col: bribe*) kaufen.
buy out *vt* (*business*) aufkaufen.
buy up *vt* aufkaufen.
buyer [bī'ûr] *n* Käufer(in *f*) *m*; ~'**s market** Käufermarkt *m*.
buzz [buz] *n* Summen *nt* ♦ *vi* summen; **my head is** ~**ing** mir schwirrt der Kopf ♦ *vt* (*call on intercom*) rufen; (*call with buzzer*) (mit dem Summer) rufen; (*AVIAT: plane, building*) dicht vorbeifliegen an (+*dat*).
buzzard [buz'ûrd] *n* Bussard *m*.
buzzer [buz'ûr] *n* Summer *m*.
buzz word *n* (*col*) Modewort *nt*.
by [bī] *prep* (*near*) bei; (*via*) über (+*acc*); (*past*) an (+*dat*) ... vorbei; (*before*) bis; ~ **day/night** tags/nachts; ~ **train/bus** mit dem Zug/Bus; **done** ~ **sb/sth** von jdm/durch etw gemacht; ~ **oneself** allein; ~ **and large** im großen und ganzen; **killed** ~ **lightning** vom Blitz erschlagen; **a painting** ~ **Picasso** ein Bild von Picasso; **surrounded** ~ **enemies** von Feinden umgeben; ~ **saving hard, he managed to** ... durch eisernes Sparen *or* dadurch, daß er eisern sparte, gelang es ihm ...; **it missed me** ~ **inches** es verfehlte mich um Zentimeter; ~ **this time tomorrow** morgen um diese Zeit; ~ **the kilo/meter** kilo-/meterweise; **to pay** ~ **check** mit Scheck bezahlen; **the room is 3 meters** ~ **4** das Zimmer ist 3 mal 4 Meter (groß).
bye(-bye) [bī'(bī')] *interj* (auf) Wiedersehen.
by(e)-law [bī'lô] *n* Verordnung *f*.
by-election [bī'ilekshən] *n* Nachwahl *f*.
bygone [bī'gôn] *a* vergangen ♦ *n*: **let** ~**s be** ~**s** laß(t) das Vergangene vergangen sein.
bypass [bī'pas] *n* Umgehungsstraße *f*.
by-product [bī'prädəkt] *n* Nebenprodukt *nt*.
bystander [bī'standûr] *n* Zuschauer *m*.
byte [bīt] *n* (*COMPUT*) byte *nt*.
byway [bī'wā] *n* Seitenweg *m*.

byword [bī'wûrd] *n* Inbegriff *m*.

C

C, c [sē] *n* (*letter*) C *nt*, c *nt*; **C** ~ **for Charlie** ≈ C wie Cäsar.
c *abbr* (*US etc*) = **cent(s)**; (= *century*) Jhd.; (= *circa*) ca.
C [sē] *n abbr* (*SCH: mark*) ≈ 3 ♦ *abbr* (= *Celsius*; *centigrade*) C.
CA *n abbr* = *Central America*; = **chartered accountant** ♦ *abbr* (*US MAIL*) = *California*.
ca. *abbr* (= *circa*) ca.
c/a *abbr* = **capital account**; **credit account**; **current account**.
CAA *n abbr* (*US*: = *Civil Aeronautics Authority*, *Brit*: *Civil Aviation Authority*) ≈ LBA.
cab [kab] *n* Taxi *nt*; (*of train*) Führerstand *m*; (*of truck*) Führersitz *m*.
cabaret [kabərā'] *n* Kabarett *nt*.
cabbage [kab'ij] *n* Kohl(kopf) *m*.
cabin [kab'in] *n* Hütte *f*; (*NAUT*) Kajüte *f*; (*AVIAT*) Kabine *f*.
cabin cruiser *n* Motorjacht *f*.
cabinet [kab'ənit] *n* Schrank *m*; (*for china*) Vitrine *f*; (*POL*) Kabinett *nt*.
cabinetmaker [kab'ənitmākûr] *n* Kunsttischler *m*.
cabinet minister *n* Mitglied *nt* des Kabinetts, Minister(in *f*) *m*.
cable [kā'bəl] *n* Drahtseil *nt*, Tau *nt*; (*TEL*) (Leitungs)kabel *nt*; (*telegram*) Kabel *nt* ♦ *vti* kabeln, telegraphieren.
cable car [kā'bəl kâr] *n* Seilbahn *f*.
cablegram [kā'bəlgram] *n* (Übersee)telegramm *nt*.
cable railway *n* (*Brit*) (Draht)seilbahn *f*.
cable television *n* Kabelfernsehen *nt*.
cabman [kab'mən] *n* (*US*) Taxifahrer *m*.
cache [kash] *n* Versteck *nt*; (*for ammunition*) geheime(s) Munitionslager *nt*; (*for food*) geheime(s) Proviantlager *nt*.
cackle [kak'əl] *n* Gegacker *nt* ♦ *vi* gacken.
cactus [kak'təs] *n* Kaktus *m*, Kaktee *f*.
CAD *n abbr* (= *computer-aided design*) CAD *nt*.
caddie [kad'ē] *n* Golfjunge *m*.
caddy [kad'ē] *n* Teedose *f*.
cadence [kād'əns] *n* Tonfall *m*; (*MUS*) Kadenz *f*.
cadet [kədet'] *n* Kadett *m*; **police** ~ Polizeianwärter *m*.
cadge [kaj] *vt* (*Brit*) (er)betteln.
cadre [kad'rə] *n* Kader *m*.
Caesarean (section) [sizär'ēən (sek'shən)] *n* (*Brit*) Kaiserschnitt *m*.
CAF *abbr* (= *cost and freight*) c.a.f.

café [kafā'] *n* Café *nt*, Restaurant *nt*.
cafeteria [kafətir'ēə] *n* Selbstbedienungsrestaurant *nt*; (*UNIV*) Mensa *f*.
caffein(e) [ka'fēn] *n* Koffein *nt*.
cage [kāj] *n* Käfig *m* ♦ *vt* einsperren.
cagey [kā'jē] *a* geheimnistuerisch, zurückhaltend.
cagoule [kəgōōl'] *n* Windhemd *nt*.
CAI *n abbr* (= *computer-aided instruction*) CAI *f*.
Cairo [kī'rō] *n* Kairo *nt*.
cajole [kəjōl'] *vt* gut zureden.
cake [kāk] *n* Kuchen *m*; (*of soap*) Stück *nt*;
it's a piece of ~ (*col*) das ist ein Kinderspiel *or* ein Klacks (*col*); **you can't have your** ~ **and eat it too** (*fig*) du kannst nicht alles haben.
caked [kākt] *a* verkrustet.
Cal. *abbr* (*US*) = *California*.
calamine [kal'əmīn] *n* Galmei *m*.
calamity [kəlam'itē] *n* Unglück *nt*, (Schicksals)schlag *m*.
calcium [kal'sēəm] *n* Kalzium *nt*.
calculate [kal'kyəlāt] *vt* berechnen; (*estimate*: *chances*, *effect*) kalkulieren, schätzen.
calculate on *vt*: **I had** ~**d on finishing by this week** ich hatte damit gerechnet, diese Woche fertig zu werden.
calculated [kal'kyəlātid] *a*: **a** ~ **risk** ein kalkuliertes Risiko.
calculating [kal'kyəlāting] *a* berechnend.
calculation [kalkyəlā'shən] *n* Berechnung *f*.
calculator [kal'kyəlātûr] *n* Rechner *m*.
calculus [kal'kyələs] *n* Rechenart *f*.
calendar [kal'əndûr] *n* Kalender *m*.
calendar month *n* Kalendermonat *m*.
calf [kaf] *n*, *pl* **calves** [kavz] Kalb *nt*; (*leather*) Kalbsleder *nt*; (*ANAT*) Wade *f*.
caliber [kal'əbûr] *n* (*US*) Kaliber *nt*.
calibrate [kal'əbrāt] *vt* (*scale of measuring instrument*) eichen; (*gun etc*) kalibrieren.
calibre [kal'əbûr] *n* (*Brit*) Kaliber *nt*.
calico [kal'ikō] *n* (*Brit*) Kattun *m*.
Calif. *abbr* (*US*) = *California*.
calipers, (*Brit*) **callipers** [kal'əpûrz] *npl* (*MED*) Schiene *f*; (*MATH*) Tastzirkel *m*.
call [kôl] *vt* rufen; (*summon*) herbeirufen; (*name*) nennen; (*meeting*) einberufen; (*awaken*) wecken; (*TEL*) anrufen; (*announce*: *flight*) ankündigen; **to be** ~**ed** heißen; **to** ~ **sb names** jdn beschimpfen; **let's** ~ **it a day** (*col*) machen wir Schluß *or* Feierabend für heute; **to** ~ **a strike** zum Streik aufrufen ♦ *vi* (*for help*) rufen, schreien; (*visit*) vorbeikommen; **who is** ~**ing please?** (*TEL*) wer spricht da bitte?;
Chicago ~**ing** (*TEL*) hier ist Chicago ♦ *n* (*shout*) Schrei *m*, Ruf *m*; (*visit*) Besuch *m*; (*TEL*) Anruf *m*; (*summons*: *for flight etc*) Aufruf *m*; (*fig*: *lure*) Ruf *m*, Verlockung *f*; **to pay a** ~ **on sb** jdm einen Besuch abstatten, jdn besuchen; **long-distance** ~ Ferngespräch *nt*; **to make a** ~ ein (Telefon)gespräch führen; **on** ~ in Bereitschaft;

please give me a ~ **at 7** rufen Sie mich bitte um 7 an; **port of** ~ Anlaufhafen *m*; **there's not much** ~ **for these items** es besteht keine große Nachfrage nach diesen Artikeln.
call at *vt fus* (*ship*) anlaufen; (*train*) halten in (+*dat*).
call back *vti* (*TEL*) zurückrufen ♦ *vi* (*return*) wiederkommen.
call for *vt fus* rufen (nach); (*fetch*) abholen; (*fig*: *require*) erfordern, verlangen.
call in *vt* (*doctor*, *expert*, *police*) zu Rate ziehen.
call off *vt* (*meeting*) absagen; (*deal*) rückgängig machen; **the strike was** ~**ed off** der Streik wurde abgesagt.
call on *vt fus* besuchen, aufsuchen; (*request*) fragen.
call out *vt* (*police*, *troops*) alarmieren; (*doctor*) rufen ♦ *vi* rufen.
call up *vt* (*MIL*) einziehen, einberufen.
callbox [kôl'bâks] *n* (*Brit*) Fernsprechzelle *f*.
caller [kôl'ûr] *n* Besucher(in *f*) *m*; (*TEL*) Anrufer *m*; **hold the line,** ~**!** (*TEL*) bitte bleiben Sie am Apparat!
call girl *n* Call-Girl *nt*.
call-in [kôl'in] *n* (*US*) Phone-in *nt*.
calling [kôl'ing] *n* (*vocation*) Berufung *f*.
calling card *n* (*US*) Visitenkarte *f*.
callous [kal'əs] *a*, **callously** [kal'əslē] *ad* herzlos.
callousness [kal'əsnis] *n* Herzlosigkeit *f*.
callow [kal'ō] *a* unerfahren, noch nicht flügge.
calm [kâm] *n* Stille *f*, Ruhe *f*; (*NAUT*) Flaute *f* ♦ *vt* beruhigen ♦ *a* still, ruhig; (*person*) gelassen.
calm down *vi* sich beruhigen ♦ *vt* beruhigen, besänftigen.
calmly [kâm'lē] *ad* ruhig, still.
calmness [kâm'nis] *n* Stille *f*, Ruhe *f*; (*mental*) Gelassenheit *f*.
Calor gas [kā'lûr gas] *n* ® (*Brit*) Propangas *nt*.
calorie [kal'ûrē] *n* Kalorie *f*, Wärmeeinheit *f*; **low-**~ **product** kalorienarme(s) Produkt *nt*.
calve [kav] *vi* kalben.
calves [kavz] *npl of* **calf**.
CAM *n abbr* (= *computer-aided manufacturing*) CAM *f*.
camber [kam'bûr] *n* Wölbung *f*.
Cambodia [kambō'dēə] *n* Kambodscha *nt*.
Cambodian [kambō'dēən] *a* kambodschanisch ♦ *n* Kambodschaner(in *f*) *m*.
Cambs *abbr* (*Brit*) = *Cambridgeshire*.
camcorder [kam'kôrdûr] *n* Camrecorder *m*, Kamera-Recorder *m*.
came [kām] *pt of* **come**.
camel [kam'əl] *n* Kamel *nt*.
cameo [kam'ēō] *n* Kamee *f*.
camera [kam'ûrə] *n* Fotoapparat *m*, Kamera *f*; (*movie* ~) Filmkamera *f*; (*cine* ~) (Schmal)filmkamera *f*; (*TV* ~) Fernsehkamera *f*.
cameraman [kam'ûrəman] *n*, *pl* **-men** Kame-

ramann *m*.

Cameroon, Cameroun [kamərōōn'] *n* Kamerun *nt*.

camomile tea [kam'əmīl tē'] *n* Kamillentee *m*.

camouflage [kam'əflázh] *n* Tarnung *f* ♦ *vt* tarnen; (*fig*) verschleiern, bemänteln.

camp [kamp] *n* Lager *nt*, Camp *nt*; (*MIL*) Feldlager *nt*; (*permanent*) Kaserne *f*; (*camping place*) Zeltplatz *m* ♦ *a* affektiert ♦ *vi* zelten, campen; **to go ~ing** zelten (gehen).

campaign [kampān'] *n* Kampagne *f*; (*MIL*) Feldzug *m*; **electoral ~** Wahlkampf *m* ♦ *vi* (*MIL*) Krieg führen; (*participate*) in den Krieg ziehen; (*fig*) werben, Propaganda machen; (*POL*) den Wahlkampf führen; **to ~ (for/against)** sich einsetzen, sich stark machen (für/gegen) (*col*); (*politician, candidate*) im Wahlkampf stehen (für/gegen), den Wahlkampf führen (für/gegen); (*outdoors also*) auf die Straße gehen (für/gegen).

campaigner [kampān'ûr] *n*: **~ for** Befürworter(in *f*) *m* (+*gen*); **~ against** Gegner(in *f*) *m* (+*gen*).

camp bed *n* Campingbett *nt*.

camper [kam'pûr] *n* Zeltende(r) *mf*, Camper *m*.

camping [kam'ping] *n*: **to go ~** zelten, Camping machen.

campsite [kamp'sīt] *n* Campingplatz *m*.

campus [kam'pəs] *n* (*SCH*) Schulgelände *nt*; (*UNIV*) Universitätsgelände *nt*, Campus *m*.

camshaft [kam'shaft] *n* Nockenwelle *f*.

can [kan] *n* Büchse *f*, Dose *f*; (*for water*) Kanne *f*; **a ~ of beer** eine Dose Bier; **to carry the ~** (*Brit col*) die Sache ausbaden (*col*) ♦ *aux v irreg* (*be able*) können, fähig sein; (*be allowed*) dürfen, können; **they could have forgotten** sie könnten (es) vergessen haben; **he could be in the library** er könnte in der Bücherei sein; **I ~'t see you** ich kann dich nicht sehen; **~ you hear me?** hören Sie mich?; **~ I use your telephone?** kann *or* darf ich bei Ihnen mal telefonieren?; **could I have a word with you?** kann *or* könnte ich Sie mal sprechen? ♦ *vt* konservieren, in Büchsen einmachen.

Canada [kan'ədə] *n* Kanada *nt*.

Canadian [kanā'dēən] *a* kanadisch ♦ *n* Kanadier(in *f*) *m*.

canal [kənal'] *n* Kanal *m*.

Canaries [kənär'ēz] *npl* Kanarische Inseln.

canary [kənär'ē] *n* Kanarienvogel *m* ♦ *a* hellgelb.

Canary Islands *npl* Kanarische Inseln *pl*.

Canberra [kan'bərə] *n* Canberra *nt*.

cancel [kan'səl] *vt* (*delete*) durchstreichen; (*MATH*) kürzen; (*arrangement*) aufheben; (*meeting*) absagen; (*treaty*) annullieren; (*stamp*) entwerten; (*check*) stornieren.

cancel out *vt* (*MATH*) aufheben; (*fig*) zunichte machen.

cancellation [kansəlā'shən] *n* Aufhebung *f*;

Absage *f*; Annullierung *f*; Entwertung *f*.

cancer [kan'sûr] *n* (*also*: *ASTROL*: **C~**) Krebs *m*.

cancerous [kan'sûrəs] *a* krebsartig.

cancer patient *n* Krebskranke(r) *mf*.

cancer research *n* Krebsforschung *f*.

C and F *abbr* (= *cost and freight*) bedingt frachtfrei.

candid [kan'did] *a* offen, ehrlich.

candidacy [kan'didəsē] *n* Kandidatur *f*.

candidate [kan'didāt] *n* Bewerber(in *f*) *m*; (*POL*) Kandidat(in *f*) *m*.

candidly [kan'didlē] *ad* ehrlich.

candle [kan'dəl] *n* Kerze *f*.

candlelight [kan'dəllit] *n* Kerzenlicht *nt*.

candlestick [kan'dəlstik] *n* Kerzenleuchter *m*.

candor, (*Brit*) **candour** [kan'dûr] *n* Offenheit *f*.

candy [kan'dē] *n* (*US*) Bonbons *pl* ♦ *vt* (*fruit*) kandieren.

candy-floss [kan'dēflôs] *n* (*Brit*) Zuckerwatte *f*.

candy store *n* (*US*) Süßwarenladen *m*.

cane [kān] *n* (*for baskets, chairs etc*) Rohr *nt*; (*stick: for walking*) (Spazier)stock *m* ♦ *vt* schlagen.

canister [kan'istûr] *n* Blechdose *f*.

cannabis [kan'əbis] *n* Haschisch *nt*.

canned [kand] *a* Büchsen-, eingemacht; (*Brit col: drunk*) blau, voll; **~ music** (*col*) Musikberieselung *f*.

cannibal [kan'əbəl] *n* Menschenfresser *m*.

cannibalism [kan'əbəlizəm] *n* Kannibalismus *m*.

cannon [kan'ən] *n* Kanone *f*.

cannon fodder *n* Kanonenfutter *nt*.

cannot [kan'ât] = **can not**.

canny [kan'ē] *a* (*shrewd*) schlau, erfahren; (*cautious*) umsichtig, vorsichtig.

canoe [kənōō'] *n* Paddelboot *nt*, Kanu *nt*.

canoeing [kənōō'ing] *n* Kanufahren *nt*.

canoeist [kənōō'ist] *n* Kanufahrer(in *f*) *m*.

canon [kan'ən] *n* Domherr *m*; (*in church law*) Kanon *m*; (*standard*) Grundsatz *m*.

canonize [kan'ənīz] *vt* heiligsprechen.

can opener [kan' ō'pənûr] *n* Büchsenöffner *m*.

canopy [kan'əpē] *n* Baldachin *m*.

can't [kant] = **can not**.

cantankerous [kantang'kûrəs] *a* zänkisch, mürrisch.

canteen [kantēn'] *n* (*in factory*) Kantine *f*; (*Brit: case of cutlery*) Besteckkasten *m*.

canter [kan'tûr] *n* Kanter *m*, kurze(r) leichte(r) Galopp *m* ♦ *vi* in kurzem Galopp reiten.

cantilever [kan'təlevûr] *n* Träger *m*, Ausleger *m*.

canvas [kan'vəs] *n* Segeltuch *nt*, Zeltstoff *m*; (*sail*) Segel *nt*; (*for painting*) Leinwand *f*; (*painting*) Ölgemälde *nt*; **under ~** (*people*) in Zelten; (*boat*) unter Segel.

canvass [kan'vəs] *vt* (*POL: district*) Wahlwerbung machen in (+*dat*); (: *person*) für seine Partei zu gewinnen suchen; (*COMM*: *district*) eine Werbekampagne durchführen in (+*dat*); (*citizens*) werben.

canvasser |kan'vəsûr| *n* (*POL*) Wahlhelfer(in *f*) *m*; (*COMM*) Vertreter(in *f*) *m*, Klinkenputzer *m* (*col*).

canyon |kan'yən| *n* Felsenschlucht *f*.

cap |kap| *n* Kappe *f*, Mütze *f*; (*for swimming*) Bademütze *f* or -kappe *f*; (*lid*) (Verschluß)kappe *f*, Deckel *m*; (*Brit*: *contraceptive*) Pessar *nt* ♦ *vt* verschließen; (*surpass*) übertreffen; **and then to** ~ **it all …** (*Brit*) und, um dem Ganzen die Krone aufzusetzen, …

CAP *n abbr* (= *Common Agricultural Policy*) GAP *f*.

capability |kāpəbil'ətē| *n* Fähigkeit *f*.

capable |kā'pəbəl| *a* fähig; **to be** ~ **of sth** zu etw fähig *or* imstande sein.

capacious |kəpā'shəs| *a* geräumig; (*dress*) weit.

capacity |kəpas'itē| *n* Fassungsvermögen *nt*; (*ability*) Fähigkeit *f*; (*position*) Eigenschaft *f*; **filled to** ~ randvoll; **this work is within/beyond his** ~ er ist zu dieser Arbeit fähig/nicht fähig; **in an advisory** ~ in beratender Funktion.

cape |kāp| *n* (*garment*) Cape *nt*, Umhang *m*; (*GEOG*) Kap *nt*.

Cape of Good Hope *n* Kap *nt* der guten Hoffnung.

caper |kā'pûr| *n* (*COOK*: also: ~**s**) Kaper *f*; (*prank*) Eskapade *f*, Kapriole *f*.

Cape Town *n* Kapstadt *nt*.

capital |kap'itəl| *n* (also: ~ **city**) Hauptstadt *f*; (*FIN*) Kapital *nt*; (also: ~ **letter**) Großbuchstabe *m*; **working** ~ Betriebskapital *nt*.

capital account *n* (*of business*) Kapitalverkehrsbilanz *f*; (*of country*) Kapitalkonto *nt*.

capital allowance *n* Anlagenabschreibung *f*.

capital assets *npl* Kapitalvermögen *nt*.

capital expenditure *n* Kapitalaufwendungen *pl*.

capital gains tax *n* Kapitalertragssteuer *f*.

capital goods *npl* Kapitalgüter *pl*.

capital-intensive |kap'itəlintcn'siv| *a* kapitalintensiv.

capital investment *n* (*in assets*) Kapitalanlage *f*; (*in stocks and shares*) Aktieninvestition *f*; (*through deposit account*) Spareinlage *f*.

capitalism |kap'itəlizəm| *n* Kapitalismus *m*.

capitalist |kap'itəlist| *a* kapitalistisch ♦ *n* Kapitalist(in *f*) *m*.

capitalize |kap'itəlīz| *vt* (*FIN*: *provide with capital*) kapitalisieren.

capitalize on *vt fus* (*fig*) Kapital schlagen aus.

capital letters *npl* Großbuchstaben *pl*.

capital punishment *n* Todesstrafe *f*.

capitulate |kəpich'ōōlāt| *vi* kapitulieren.

capitulation |kəpichōōlā'shən| *n* Kapitulation *f*.

capricious |kəprish'əs| *a* launisch.

Capricorn |kap'rikôrn| *n* Steinbock *m*.

caps |kaps| *abbr* = **capital letters**.

capsize |kap'sīz| *vti* kentern.

capstan |kap'stən| *n* Ankerwinde *f*, Poller *m*.

capsule |kap'səl| *n* Kapsel *f*.

Capt. *abbr* (= *captain*) Kapt.

captain |kap'tin| *n* Führer *m*; (*NAUT*) Kapitän *m*; (*MIL*) Hauptmann *m*; (*SPORT*) (Mannschafts)kapitän *m* ♦ *vt* anführen.

caption |kap'shən| *n* Unterschrift *f*, Text *m*.

captivate |kap'təvāt| *vt* fesseln.

captive |kap'tiv| *n* Gefangene(r) *mf* ♦ *a* gefangen(gehalten).

captivity |kaptiv'ətē| *n* Gefangenschaft *f*.

captor |kap'tûr| *n* Person, *die jdn gefangennimmt*; **his** ~**s treated him kindly** er wurde nach seiner Gefangennahme gut behandelt.

capture |kap'chûr| *vt* fassen, gefangennehmen ♦ *n* Gefangennahme *f*.

car |kâr| *n* Auto *nt*, Wagen *m*; (*RAIL*) Wagen *m*; **by** ~ mit dem Auto.

Caracas |kərak'əs| *n* Caracas *nt*.

carafe |kəraf'| *n* Karaffe *f*.

caramel |kar'əməl| *n* Karamelle *f*.

carat |kar'ət| *n* Karat *nt*; **18** ~ **gold** achtzehnkarätiges Gold.

caravan |kar'əvan| *n* (*in desert*) Karawane *f*; (*Brit*) Wohnwagen *m*.

caravan site *n* (*Brit*) Campingplatz *m* für Wohnwagen.

caraway seed |kar'əwā sēd| *n* Kümmel *m*.

carbohydrate |kârbōhī'drāt| *n* Kohlenhydrat *nt*.

carbolic |kârbâl'ik| *a*: ~ **acid** Karbolsäure *f*.

carbon |kâr'bən| *n* Kohlenstoff *m*; (also: ~ **paper**) Kohlepapier *nt*.

carbonated |kâr'bənātid| *a* (*drink*) mit Kohlensäure (versetzt).

carbon copy *n* Durchschlag *m*.

carbon dioxide *n* Kohlendioxyd *nt*.

carbon monoxide |kâr'bən mənâk'sīd| *n* Kohlenmonoxyd *nt*.

carbon ribbon *n* Kohlefarbband *nt*.

carburetor, (*Brit*) **carburettor** |kâr'bərātûr| *n* Vergaser *m*.

carcass |kâr'kəs| *n* Kadaver *m*.

carcinogenic |kârsinəjcn'ik| *a* karzinogen, krebserregend.

card |kârd| *n* Karte *f*; (*thin cardboard*) Pappe *f*; (*membership* ~) Mitgliedskarte *f*; **to play** ~**s** Karten spielen.

cardamom |kâr'dəməm| *n* Kardamom *m or nt*.

cardboard |kârd'bôrd| *n* Pappe *f*.

cardboard box *n* (Papp)karton *m*, Pappschachtel *f*.

card-carrying |kârd'karēing| *a*: ~ **member** eingetragene(s) Mitglied *nt*.

card game *n* Kartenspiel *nt*.

cardiac |kâr'dēak| *a* Herz-.

cardigan |kâr'digən| *n* Strickjacke *f*.

cardinal number |kâr'dənəl num'bûr| *n* Kardinalzahl *f*.

card index *n* Kartei *f*; (*library*) Katalog *m*.

Cards *abbr* (*Brit*) = *Cardiganshire*.

cardsharp [kârd'shârp] *n* Falschspieler *m*.

care [kär] *n* Sorge *f*, Mühe *f*; (*charge*) Obhut *f*, Fürsorge *f* ♦ *vi*: **I don't ~** es ist mir egal; **to ~ about sb/sth** sich kümmern um jdn/ etw; **~ of** (*abbr* **c/o**: *on letter*) bei; **to take ~** (*watch*) vorsichtig sein; (*take pains*) darauf achten; **to take ~ to do sth** sich bemühen, etw zu tun; **to take ~ of** (*look after*) sorgen für; **to take ~ of sth** (*settle*) etw erledigen; **the child has been taken into ~** das Kind ist in Pflege gegeben worden; "**handle with ~**" „Vorsicht, zerbrechlich!"
care for *vt fus* (*look after*) sorgen für; (*like*) mögen, gern haben.

CARE *n abbr* (*US*) = *Cooperative for American Relief Everywhere*.

career [kərēr'] *n* Karriere *f*, Laufbahn *f*; (*occupation*) Beruf *m* ♦ *vi* rasen.

career girl *n* Karrierefrau *f*.

careers officer *n* Berufsberater(in *f*) *m*.

carefree [kär'frē] *a* sorgenfrei.

careful [kär'fəl] *a* sorgfältig; **he's very ~ with his money** er geht sehr sorgsam mit seinem Geld um.

carefully [kär'fəlē] *ad* sorgfältig.

careless [kär'lis] *a*, **carelessly** [kär'lislē] *ad* unvorsichtig.

carelessness [kär'lisnis] *n* Unachtsamkeit *f*; (*neglect*) Nachlässigkeit *f*.

caress [kəres'] *n* Liebkosung *f* ♦ *vt* liebkosen.

caretaker [kär'tākûr] *n* Hausmeister *m*.

caretaker government *n* geschäftsführende Regierung *f*.

car ferry *n* Autofähre *f*.

cargo [kâr'gō] *n* Kargo *m*, Schiffsladung *f*.

cargo boat *n* Frachter *m*, Frachtschiff *nt*.

cargo plane *n* Transportflugzeug *nt*.

car hire *n* (*Brit*) Autovermietung *f*; (*activity*) Automieten *nt*.

Caribbean [karəbē'ən] *a* karibisch; **the ~ Sea** das Karibische Meer.

caricature [kar'əkəchûr] *n* Karikatur *f* ♦ *vt* karikieren.

caring [kär'ing] *a* (*society, organization*) sozial eingestellt; (*person*) liebevoll.

carnage [kâr'nij] *n* Blutbad *nt*, Gemetzel *nt*.

carnal [kâr'nəl] *a* fleischlich, sinnlich.

carnation [kârnā'shən] *n* Nelke *f*.

carnival [kâr'nəvəl] *n* Karneval *m*, Fasching *m*; (*US: fair*) Kirmes *f*.

carnivore [kâr'nəvôr] *n* Fleischfresser *m*.

carnivorous [kârniv'ûrəs] *a* fleischfressend.

carol [kar'əl] *n* (Weihnachts)lied *nt*.

carouse [kərouz'] *vi* zechen.

carousel [karəsel'] *n* (*US*) Karussell *nt*.

carp [kârp] *n* (*fish*) Karpfen *m*.
carp at *vt fus* herumnörgeln an (+*dat*).

car park *n* (*Brit*) Parkplatz *m*; (: *covered*) Parkhaus *nt*.

carpenter [kâr'pəntûr] *n* Zimmermann *m*.

carpentry [kâr'pəntrē] *n* Zimmerei *f*.

carpet [kâr'pit] *n* Teppich *m* ♦ *vt* mit einem Teppich auslegen.

carpet slippers *npl* Pantoffeln *pl*.

carpet sweeper [kâr'pit swē'pûr] *n* Teppichkehrer *m*.

car phone *n* Autotelefon *nt*.

carping [kâr'ping] *a* (*critical*) krittelnd, Mecker-.

carriage [kar'ij] *n* Wagen *m*; (*of goods*) Beförderung *f*; (*bearing*) Haltung *f*; **~ forward** (*COMM*) Fracht zahlt Empfänger; **~ free** frachtfrei; **~ paid** frei Haus.

carriage return *n* (*typewriter*) Wagenrücklauf *m*; (*COMPUT*) Return *nt*.

carriageway [kar'ijwā] *n* (*Brit: on road*) Fahrbahn *f*.

carrier [kar'ēûr] *n* Träger(in *f*) *m*; (*COMM*) Spediteur *m*.

carrier bag *n* (*Brit*) Tragetasche *m*.

carrier pigeon *n* Brieftaube *f*.

carrion [kar'ēən] *n* Aas *nt*.

carrot [kar'ət] *n* Möhre *f*, Mohrrübe *f*, Karotte *f*.

carry [kar'ē] *vt* tragen; (*COMM: goods*) befördern, transportieren ♦ *vi* weit tragen, reichen; **to be carried away** (*fig*) hingerissen sein; **this loan carries 10% interest** das Darlehen wird mit 10% verzinst; **to ~ interest** (*FIN*) Zinsen tragen *or* abwerfen; ...**and ~ 2** (*MATH: figure*) ...behalte 2, ...und 2 im Sinn.
carry forward *vt* (*MATH, FIN*) vortragen.
carry on *vt* fortführen ♦ *vi* weitermachen.
carry out *vt* (*orders*) ausführen; (*accomplish etc*: *plan*) durchführen; (*perform, implement*: *idea, threat*) wahrmachen.

carryall [kar'ôl] *n* Reisetasche *f*.

carrycot [kar'ēkât] *n* (*Brit*) Babytragetasche *f*.

carry-on [kar'ēân] *n* (*US: hand-luggage*) Handgepäck *nt*.

cart [kârt] *n* Wagen *m*, Karren *m*; (*US: for shopping*) Einkaufswagen *m*; (: *for baggage*) Kofferkuli *m* ♦ *vt* schleppen.

carte blanche [kârt' blânsh'] *n*: **to give sb ~** jdm Carte Blanche *or* (eine) Blankovollmacht geben.

cartel [kârtel'] *n* (*COMM*) Kartell *nt*.

cartilage [kâr'təlij] *n* Knorpel *m*.

cartographer [kârtâg'rəfûr] *n* Kartograph(in *f*) *m*.

carton [kâr'tən] *n* (Papp)karton *m*; (*of cigarettes*) Stange *f*.

cartoon [kârtoon'] *n* (*PRESS*) Karikatur *f*; (*CINE*) (Zeichen)trickfilm *m*.

cartridge [kâr'trij] *n* (*for gun*) Patrone *f*; (*film*) Rollfilm *m*; (*of record player*) Tonabnehmer *m*.

cartwheel [kârt'hwēl] *n*: **to turn a ~** (*SPORT etc*) radschlagen.

carve [kârv] *vti* (*wood*) schnitzen; (*stone*) meißeln; (*meat*) (vor)schneiden.
carve up *vt* (*meat*) aufschneiden.

carving [kâr'ving] *n* (*in wood etc*) Schnitzerei *f*.

carving knife n Tranchiermesser nt.
car wash n Autowäsche f.
Casablanca [kasəblang'kə] n Casablanca nt.
cascade [kaskād'] n Wasserfall m ♦ vi kaskadenartig herabfallen.
case [kās] n (box) Kasten m, Kiste f; (Brit: also: **suit~**) Koffer m; (JUR, matter) Fall m; **in ~** falls, im Falle; **in any ~** jedenfalls, auf jeden Fall; **to have a good ~** gute Chancen haben, durchzukommen; **there's a strong ~ for reform** es spricht viel für Reform; **in lower/upper ~** (TYP) groß/klein geschrieben.
case-hardened [kās'hâr'dənd] a (fig) abgebrüht, abgehärtet.
case history n (MED) Krankengeschichte f.
case study n Fallstudie f.
cash [kash] n (Bar)geld nt; (col: money) Geld nt ♦ vt einlösen; **~ on delivery** per Nachnahme; **to be short of ~** knapp bei Kasse sein (col).
  cash in vt (insurance policy etc) einlösen ♦ vi: **to ~ in on sth** aus etw Kapital schlagen.
cash account n Kassenbuch nt.
cash-and-carry [kash'ənkar'ē] n Cash and Carry m, Abholmarkt m.
cash book n Kassenbuch nt.
cash box n Geldkassette f.
cash card n Geldautomatenkarte f.
cash desk n (Brit) Kasse f.
cash discount n Skonto nt.
cash dispenser n Nachtschalter m (einer Bank), Bankomat m.
cash flow n Cash-flow m.
cashier [kashi'ûr] n Kassierer(in f) m ♦ vt feuern, (unehrenhaft) entlassen.
cashmere [kazh'mēr] n Kaschmirwolle f.
cash payment n Barzahlung f.
cash price n Barzahlungspreis m.
cash register n Registrierkasse f.
cash reserves npl Bargeldreserven pl.
cash sale n Barverkauf m.
casing [kā'sing] n Gehäuse nt.
casino [kəsē'nō] n Kasino nt.
cask [kask] n Faß nt.
casket [kas'kit] n Kästchen nt; (US: coffin) Sarg m.
Caspian Sea [kas'pēən sē'] n Kaspische(s) Meer nt, Kaspisee m.
casserole [kas'ərōl] n Kasserole f; (food) Auflauf m.
cassette [kəset'] n Kassette f.
cassette deck n Kassettendeck nt.
cassette player or **recorder** n Kassettenrecorder m.
cassock [kas'ək] n Soutane f, Talar m.
cast [kast] vt irreg pt, pp cast werfen; (horns etc) verlieren; (metal) gießen; (THEAT) besetzen; (roles) verteilen ♦ n (THEAT) Besetzung f.
  cast aside vt (reject) fallen lassen.
  cast off vi (NAUT) losmachen; (KNITTING) abketten ♦ vt: **to ~ sb off** jdn fallenlassen.
  cast on vi (KNITTING) anschlagen.

castanets [kastənets'] npl Kastagnetten pl.
castaway [kas'təwā] n Schiffbrüchige(r) mf.
caste [kast] n Kaste f.
caster sugar [kas'tûr shōōg'ûr] n (Brit) Streuzucker m.
casting [kas'ting] a: **~ vote** (Brit) entscheidende Stimme f.
cast-iron [kast'ī'ûrn] n Gußeisen nt ♦ a gußeisern; (fig: will) eisern; (: alibi) hieb- und stichfest.
castle [kas'əl] n Schloß nt; (fortress) Burg f; (country mansion) Landschloß nt; (CHESS) Turm m.
cast-offs [kast'ôfs] npl abgelegte Kleider.
castor [kas'tûr] n (wheel) Laufrolle f.
castor oil n Rizinusöl m.
castrate [kas'trāt] vt kastrieren.
casual [kazh'ōōəl] a (arrangement) beiläufig; (attitude) nachlässig; (dress) leger; (meeting) zufällig; (labor) Gelegenheits-.
casually [kazh'ōōəlē] ad (dress) zwanglos, leger; (remark) beiläufig.
casualty [kazh'ōōəltē] n Verletzte(r) mf; (dead) Tote(r) mf.
cat [kat] n Katze f.
catacombs [kat'əkōmz] npl Katakomben pl.
catalog, (Brit) **catalogue** [kat'əlôg] n Katalog m ♦ vt katalogisieren.
catalyst [kat'əlist] n (lit, fig) Katalysator m.
catalytic converter [katelit'ik kânvûrt'ûr] n (AUT) Katalysator m.
catapult [kat'əpult] n Katapult nt; (Brit: slingshot) Schleuder f.
cataract [kat'ərakt] n Wasserfall m; (MED) graue(r) Star m.
catarrh [kətâr'] n Katarrh m.
catastrophe [kətas'trəfē] n Katastrophe f.
catastrophic [katəstráf'ik] a katastrophal.
catcalls [kat'kôlz] npl (at meeting etc) Pfiffe und Buhrufe pl.
catch [kach] vt irreg fangen; (train etc) nehmen, erreichen; (surprise) ertappen; (understand) begreifen; **to ~ a cold** sich erkälten ♦ n (of lock) Sperrhaken m; (of fish) Fang m.
  catch on vi (become popular) ankommen; **to ~ on (to sth)** (understand) (etw) kapieren (col).
  catch out vt (Brit fig: with trick question) hereinlegen.
  catch up vi (fig) aufholen ♦ vt (person) einholen.
catching [kach'ing] a (MED, fig) ansteckend.
catchment area [kach'mənt är'ēə] n (Brit) Einzugsgebiet nt.
catch phrase n Schlagwort nt, Slogan m.
catch-22 [kach'twentētōō'] n: **it's a ~ situation** es ist eine Zwickmühle.
catchy [kach'ē] a (tune) eingängig.
catechism [kat'əkizəm] n Katechismus m.
categorical [katəgôr'ikəl] a, **categorically** [katəgôr'ikəlē] ad kategorisch.
categorize [kat'əgərīz] vt kategorisieren.
category [kat'əgôrē] n Kategorie f.

cater [kā'tûr] vi versorgen.
cater for vt fus (Brit: lit: party) ausrichten; (fig) eingestellt sein auf (+acc); (consider) berücksichtigen.
caterer [kā'tûrûr] n Lieferant(in f) m (von Lebensmitteln, Getränken).
catering [kā'tûring] n (trade) Gastronomie f; (in hotel) Bewirtung f.
caterpillar [kat'ûrpilûr] n Raupe f.
caterpillar track n Gleiskette f.
cathedral [kəthē'drəl] n Kathedrale f, Dom m.
cathode ray tube [kath'ōd rā' tōōb] n Kathodenstrahlröhre f.
Catholic [kath'əlik] a (REL) katholisch ♦ n Katholik(in f) m.
catholic a vielseitig.
cat's eye n (AUT) Katzenauge nt.
catsup [kat'səp] n (US) Ketchup nt or m.
cattle [kat'əl] npl Vieh nt.
catty [kat'ē] a gehässig.
CATV n abbr (US) = community antenna television.
Caucasian [kôkā'zhən] a kaukasisch ♦ n Kaukasier(in f) m.
caucus [kô'kəs] n (US POL) Gremium nt, Ausschuß m; (Brit: POL: group) Gruppierung f.
caught [kôt] pt, pp of catch.
cauliflower [kô'ləflouûr] n Blumenkohl m.
cause [kôz] n Ursache f; (reason) Grund m; (purpose) Sache f ♦ vt verursachen; in a good ~ zu einem guten Zweck; to ~ sth to be done etw veranlassen; to ~ sb to do sth jdn veranlassen, etw zu tun.
causeway [kôz'wā] n Damm m.
caustic [kôs'tik] a ätzend; (fig) bissig.
cauterize [kôt'əriz] vt ätzen, ausbrennen.
caution [kô'shən] n Vorsicht f; (warning) Warnung f; (JUR) Verwarnung f ♦ vt (ver)warnen.
cautious [kô'shəs] a, cautiously [kô'shəslē] ad vorsichtig.
cavalcade [kav'əlkād] n Kavalkade f.
cavalier [kavəliûr'] n (knight) Kavalier m ♦ a (pej: offhand: person, attitude) unbekümmert, keck.
cavalry [kav'əlrē] n Kavallerie f.
cave [kāv] n Höhle f ♦ vi: to go caving auf Höhlenexpedition(en) gehen.
cave in vi einstürzen.
caveman [kāv'mən] n, pl -men Höhlenmensch m.
cavern [kav'ûrn] n Höhle f.
cavernous [kav'ûrnəs] a (cheeks) hohl; (eyes) tiefliegend.
caviar(e) [kav'ēâr] n Kaviar m.
cavil [kav'əl] vi kritteln (at an +dat).
cavity [kav'itē] n Höhlung f; (in tooth) Loch nt.
cavity wall insulation n Schaumisolierung f.
cavort [kəvôrt'] vi umherspringen.
cayenne [kīen'] n (also: ~ pepper) Cayennepfeffer m.
CB n abbr (= Citizens' Band (Radio)) CB; ~ radio (set) CB Radio nt.
CBC n abbr (= Canadian Broadcasting Corporation) CBC f.
CBI n abbr (= Confederation of British Industry) ≈ BDI nt.
CBS n abbr (US: = Columbia Broadcasting System) CBS.
cc abbr (= cubic centimeter(s)) ccm; = carbon copy.
CCA n abbr (US: = Circuit Court of Appeals) Bundesgericht für Berufungen.
CCC n abbr (US: = Commodity Credit Corporation; (US: = Civilian Conservation Corps) von 1933-1943 staatliche Einrichtung zum Schutze von Bodenschätzen etc.
CCU n abbr (US: = coronary care unit) Intensivstation für Herzkranke.
CD n abbr (= Civil Defense (US), Civil Defence (Corps) (Brit)) ≈ ZV; (= compact disc) CD f ♦ abbr (Brit: = Corps Diplomatique) CD.
CDC n abbr (US: = center for disease control) staatliche Einrichtung zur Kontrolle und Prevention von Seuchen etc.
Cdr. abbr (= commander) FKpt.
CDV n abbr (= compact disc video) CD-Video nt.
cease [sēs] vi aufhören ♦ vt beenden.
ceasefire [sēs'fiûr'] n Feuereinstellung f.
ceaseless [sēs'lis] a unaufhörlich.
CED n abbr (US: = Committee for Economic Development) staatliche Einrichtung für wirtschaftliche Entwicklung.
cedar [sē'dûr] n Zeder f.
cede [sēd] vt abtreten.
CEEB n abbr (US: = College Entrance Examination Board) Verband von Universitäten und Schulen.
ceiling [sē'ling] n Decke f; (fig: upper limit) ober(st)e Grenze f, Höchstgrenze f.
celebrate [sel'əbrāt] vt feiern, (anniversary) begehen ♦ vi feiern.
celebrated [sel'əbrātid] a gefeiert.
celebration [seləbrā'shən] n Feier f.
celebrity [səleb'ritē] n gefeierte Persönlichkeit f.
celeriac [səlär'ēak] n (Knollen)sellerie f.
celery [sel'ûrē] n Sellerie f.
celestial [səles'chəl] a himmlisch.
celibacy [sel'əbəsē] n Zölibat nt or m.
cell [sel] n Zelle f; (ELEC) Element nt.
cellar [sel'ûr] n Keller m.
cellist [chel'ist] n Cellist(in f) m.
cello [chel'ō] n Cello nt.
cellophane [sel'əfān] n ® Cellophan nt.
cellular [sel'yəlûr] a zellenförmig, zellular.
celluloid [sel'yəloid] n Zelluloid nt.
cellulose [sel'yəlōs] n Zellulose f.
Celsius [sel'sēəs] a Celsius.
Celt [selt, kelt] n Kelte m, Keltin f.
Celtic [sel'tik, kel'tik] a keltisch ♦ n (language) Keltisch nt.

cement [siment'] *n* Zement *m* ♦ *vt* (*lit*) zementieren; (*fig*) festigen.
cement mixer *n* Betonmischmaschine *f*.
cemetery [sem'itārē] *n* Friedhof *m*.
cenotaph [sen'ətaf] *n* Ehrenmal *nt*, Zenotaph *m*.
censor [sen'sûr] *n* Zensor *m* ♦ *vt* zensieren.
censorship [sen'sûrship] *n* Zensur *f*.
censure [sen'shûr] *vt* rügen.
census [sen'səs] *n* Volkszählung *f*.
cent [sent] *n* (*US*: *coin*) Cent *m*.
centenary [sen'tənārē] *n* (*Brit*) = **centennial**.
centennial [senten'ēəl] *n* (*US*) Jahrhundertfeier *f*.
center [sen'tûr] (*US*) *n* Zentrum *n* ♦ *vt*: **to ~ (on)** (*concentrate*) konzentrieren (auf).
centerfold [sen'tûrfōld] *n* Ausklapper *m*.
centerpiece [sen'tûrpēs] *n* Kernstück *nt*.
centigrade [sen'tigrād] *a*: **10 (degrees)** ~ 10 Grad Celsius.
centiliter, (*Brit*) **centilitre** [sen'təlētûr] *n* Zentiliter *nt or m*.
centimeter, (*Brit*) **centimetre** [sen'təmētûr] *n* Zentimeter *nt*.
centipede [sen'təpēd] *n* Tausendfüßler *m*.
central [sen'trəl] *a* zentral.
Central African Republic *n* Zentralafrikanische Republik *f*.
central heating *n* Zentralheizung *f*.
centralize [sen'trəlīz] *vt* zentralisieren.
central processing unit *n* (*COMPUT*) Zentraleinheit *f*.
central reservation *n* (*Brit AUT*) Mittelstreifen *m*; (*with grass*) Grünstreifen *m*.
centre [sen'tûr] *etc* (*Brit*) = **center** *etc*.
centrifuge [sen'trəfyōōj] *n* Zentrifuge *f*, Schleuder *f*.
century [sen'chûrē] *n* Jahrhundert *nt;* **in the twentieth** ~ im zwanzigsten Jahrhundert.
CEO *n abbr* (*US*) = **chief executive officer**.
ceramic [səram'ik] *a* keramisch.
ceramics [səram'iks] *npl* Keramiken *pl*.
cereal [sēr'ēəl] *n* (*any grain*) Getreide *nt*; (*at breakfast*) Getreideflocken *pl*.
cerebral [sär'əbrəl] *a* zerebral; (*intellectual*) geistig.
ceremonial [särəmō'nēəl] *a* zeremoniell ♦ *n* (*rite*) Zeremoniell *nt*, Ritus *m*.
ceremony [sär'əmōnē] *n* Feierlichkeiten *pl*, Zeremonie *f*.
cert [sûrt] *n*: (*col*) **a dead** ~ eine todsichere Sache.
certain [sûr'tən] *a* sicher; (*particular*) gewiß; **for** ~ ganz bestimmt.
certainly [sûr'tənlē] *ad* sicher, bestimmt.
certainty [sûr'təntē] *n* Gewißheit *f*.
certificate [sûrtif'əkit] *n* Bescheinigung *f*; (*SCH etc*) Zeugnis *nt*.
certified mail [sûr'təfīd māl] *n* (*US*) Einschreiben *nt*.
certified public accountant *n* (*US*) geprüfte(r) Buchhalter *m*.
certify [sûr'təfī] *vt* bescheinigen.
cervical [sûr'vikəl] *a*: ~ **cancer** Gebärmutter-

halskrebs *m*; ~ **smear** Abstrich *m*.
cervix [sûr'viks] *n* Gebärmutterhals *m*.
Cesarean (section) [sizär'ēən (sek'shən)] *n* (*US*) Kaiserschnitt *m*.
cessation [sesā'shən] *n* Einstellung *f*, Ende *nt*.
cesspit [ses'pit] *n* Senkgrube *f*.
CET *abbr* (= *Central European Time*) MEZ *f*.
cf. *abbr* (= *compare*) vgl.
c.f. *abbr* (= *cost and freight*) bedingt frachtfrei.
c/f *abbr* (*COMM*: = *carried forward*) Vortr.
CFC *n abbr* (= *chlorofluorocarbon*) CFC *nt*.
CFI *abbr* (= *cost, freight and insurance*) cif.
cg *abbr* (= *centigram*(*s*)) cg.
CG *n abbr* (*US*: = *coastguard*) Küstenwache *f*.
ch *abbr* (*Brit*: = *central heating*) ZH.
ch. *abbr* (= *chapter*) Kap.
Chad [chad] *n* Tschad *m*, der Tschad.
chafe [chāf] *vti* (*wund*) reiben, scheuern; (*fig*) sich ärgern (*at, against* über +*acc*).
chaffinch [chaf'inch] *n* Buchfink *m*.
chain [chān] *n* Kette *f* ♦ *vt* (*also*: ~ **up**) anketten; mit Ketten fesseln.
chain reaction *n* Kettenreaktion *f*.
chain smoker *n* Kettenraucher(in *f*) *m*.
chain store *n* Kettenladen *m*.
chair [chär] *n* Stuhl *m*; (*arm*~) Sessel *m*; (*UNIV*) Lehrstuhl *m*; **the** ~ (*US: electric* ~) der (elektrische) Stuhl; **please take a** ~ bitte nehmen Sie Platz! ♦ *vt*: **to** ~ **a meeting** in einer Versammlung den Vorsitz führen.
chairlift [chär'lift] *n* Sessellift *m*.
chairman [chär'mən] *n, pl* **-men** Vorsitzende(r) *m*; (*of firm*) Präsident *m*.
chairperson [chär'pûrsən] *n* Vorsitzende(r) *mf*.
chalet [shalā'] *n* Chalet *nt*.
chalice [chal'is] *n* (*Abendmahls*)kelch *m*.
chalk [chôk] *n* Kreide *f*.
chalk up *vt* aufschreiben, notieren; (*fig: success, victory*) verbuchen.
challenge [chal'inj] *n* Herausforderung *f* ♦ *vt* auffordern; (*contest*) bestreiten.
challenger [chal'injûr] *n* Herausforderer *m*.
challenging [chal'injing] *a* (*statement*) herausfordernd; (*work*) anspruchsvoll.
chamber [chām'bûr] *n* Kammer *f*; ~ **of commerce** Handelskammer *f*.
chambermaid [chām'bûrmād] *n* Zimmermädchen *nt*.
chamber music *n* Kammermusik *f*.
chamberpot [chām'bûrpât] *n* Nachttopf *m*.
chameleon [kəmē'lēən] *n* Chamäleon *nt*.
chamois [sham'ē] *n* Gemse *f*.
chamois leather [sham'ē leth'ûr] *n* Sämischleder *nt*.
champagne [shampān'] *n* Champagner *m*, Sekt *m*.
champion [cham'pēən] *n* (*SPORT*) Sieger(in *f*) *m*, Meister *m*; (*of cause*) Verfechter(in *f*) *m* ♦ *vt* eintreten für, sich engagieren für.
championship [cham'pēənship] *n* Meister-

schaft *f*.

chance [chans] *n* (*luck, fate*) Zufall *m*; (*possibility*) Möglichkeit *f*; (*opportunity*) Gelegenheit *f*, Chance *f*; (*risk*) Risiko *nt* ♦ *a* zufällig ♦ *vt*: **to ~ it** es darauf ankommen lassen; **by ~** zufällig; **to take a ~** ein Risiko eingehen; **no ~** keine Chance; **to ~ to do sth** (*form: happen*) zufällig etwas tun; **the ~ of a lifetime** eine einmalige Chance; **the ~s are that ...** aller Wahrscheinlichkeit nach ..., wahrscheinlich ...
chance (up)on *vt fus* (*person*) zufällig begegnen (+*dat*), zufällig treffen; (*thing*) zufällig stoßen auf (+*acc*).

chancellor [chan'sǝlúr] *n* Kanzler *m*.

Chancellor of the Exchequer *n* (*Brit*) Schatzkanzler *m*.

chancy [chan'sē] *a* (*col*) riskant.

chandelier [shandǝliúr'] *n* Kronleuchter *m*.

change [chānj] *vt* ändern; (*money*) wechseln ♦ *vi* sich verändern; (*trains*) umsteigen; (*colour etc*) sich verwandeln; (*clothes*) sich umziehen ♦ *n* Veränderung *f*; (*money*) Wechselgeld *nt*; (*coins*) Kleingeld *nt*; **to ~ gear** (*Brit AUT*) schalten; **she ~d into an old skirt** sie zog sich einen alten Rock an; **can you give me ~ for $10?** können Sie mir 10 Dollar wechseln?; **keep the ~** stimmt so.

changeable [chān'jǝbǝl] *a* (*weather*) wechselhaft; (*person*) unbeständig.

change machine *n* Geldwechselautomat *m*.

changeover [chānj'ōvúr] *n* Umstellung *f*, Wechsel *m*.

changing [chān'jing] *a* veränderlich.

changing room *n* (*Brit*) Umkleideraum *m*.

channel [chan'ǝl] *n* (*stream*) Bachbett *nt*; (*NAUT*) Straße *f*, Meerenge *f*; (*RAD, TV*) Kanal *m*; (*fig*) Weg *m* ♦ *vt* (hindurch)leiten, lenken; **through official ~s** durch die Instanzen; **the (English) C~** der Ärmelkanal; **green ~** (*CUSTOMS*) „Nichts zu verzollen"; **red ~** (*CUSTOMS*) „Waren zu verzollen"; **~s of communications** Informationskanäle *pl*.
channel into *vt* (*fig: interest, energies*) lenken auf (+*acc*).

Channel Islands *npl* Kanalinseln *pl*.

chant [chant] *n* liturgische(r) Gesang *m*; (*monotonous song*) Sprechgesang *m*, (*of crowd*) Sprechchor *m* ♦ *vt* intonieren; **the demonstrators ~ed (their disapproval)** die Demonstranten riefen im (Sprech)chor (ihre Mißbilligung aus).

chaos [kā'ás] *n* Chaos *nt*, Durcheinander *nt*.

chaotic [kāāt'ik] *a* chaotisch.

chap [chap] *n* (*Brit col*) Bursche *m*, Kerl *m*; **old ~** alter Junge (*col*) *or* Knabe (*col*) ♦ *vt* (*skin*) rissig machen ♦ *vi* (*hands etc*) aufspringen.

chapel [chap'ǝl] *n* Kapelle *f*.

chaperon [shap'ǝrōn] *n* Anstandsdame *f* ♦ *vt* begleiten.

chaplain [chap'lin] *n* Geistliche(r) *m*, Pfarrer *m*, Kaplan *m*.

chapter [chap'tûr] *n* Kapitel *nt*.

char [chár] *vt* (*burn*) verkohlen ♦ *vi* (*Brit: clean*) putzen gehen.

character [kar'iktúr] *n* Charakter *m*, Wesen *nt*; (*LITER*) Figur *f*, Gestalt *f*; (*THEAT*) Person *f*, Rolle *f*; (*peculiar person*) Original *nt*; (*in writing*) Schriftzeichen *nt*; (*COMPUT*) Zeichen *nt*; **a person of good ~** ein anständiger *or* guter Mensch.

character code *n* (*COMPUT*) Zeichencode *m*.

characteristic [kariktǝris'tik] *a* charakteristisch ♦ *n* Kennzeichen *nt*, Eigenschaft *f*; **~ of** charakteristisch für, typisch für.

characterize [kar'iktǝrīz] *vt* charakterisieren, kennzeichnen; (*describe*) beschreiben (*as* als).

charade [shǝrād'] *n* Scharade *f*.

charcoal [chár'kōl] *n* Holzkohle *f*.

charge [chárj] *n* (*cost*) Preis *m*; (*JUR*) Anklage *f*; (*of gun*) Ladung *f*; (*attack*) Angriff *m* ♦ *vt* (*gun, battery*) laden; (*price*) verlangen; (*MIL*) angreifen ♦ *vi* (*rush*) angreifen, (an)stürmen; **to reverse the ~s** (*TEL*) ein R-Gespräch führen; **extra ~** Aufpreis *m*; **~ it to my account** das geht auf meine Rechnung; **to be in ~ of** verantwortlich sein für; **to take ~** (die Verantwortung) übernehmen.

charge account *n* Kunden(kredit)konto *nt*.

charge card *n* Kundenkreditkarte *f*.

chargé d'affaires [shárzhā' dâfárz'] *n* Chargé d'affaires *m*.

chargehand [chárj'hand] *n* (*Brit*) Vorarbeiter *m*.

charger [chár'júr] *n* (*also:* **battery ~**) Ladegerät *nt*; (*old: warhorse*) Kavalleriepferd *nt*.

chariot [char'ēǝt] *n* (Streit)wagen *m*.

charitable [char'itǝbǝl] *a* wohltätig; (*lenient*) nachsichtig.

charity [char'itē] *n* (*institution*) Wohlfahrtseinrichtung *f*, Hilfswerk *nt*; (*attitude*) Nächstenliebe *f*, Wohltätigkeit *f*.

charlady [chár'lādē] *n* (*Brit*) Reinemachefrau *f*, Putzfrau *f*.

charlatan [shâr'lǝtǝn] *n* Scharlatan *m*, Schwindler(in *f*) *m*.

charm [chárm] *n* Charme *m*, gewinnende(s) Wesen *nt*; (*in superstition*) Amulett *nt*, Talisman *m* ♦ *vt* bezaubern.

charm bracelet *n* Armband *nt* mit Anhängern.

charming [chár'ming] *a* reizend, liebenswürdig, charmant.

chart [chárt] *n* Tabelle *f*; (*NAUT*) Seekarte *f*; (*MET: weather ~*) Wetterkarte *f* ♦ *vt* (*sales, progress*) auswerten; **to be in the ~s** (*record, pop group*) in der Hitliste sein.

charter [chár'túr] *vt* (*NAUT, AVIAT*) chartern ♦ *n* Schutzbrief *m*; (*cost*) Schiffsmiete *f*; **on ~** gechartert.

chartered accountant [chár'túrd ǝkoun'tǝnt] *n* (*Brit*) Wirtschaftsprüfer(in *f*) *m*.

charter flight *n* Charterflug *m*.

charwoman [chár'woomǝn] *n*, *pl* **-women** (*Brit*) Reinemachefrau *f*, Putzfrau *f*.

chary [chär'ē] *a* zurückhaltend (*of sth* mit etw).

chase [chās] *vt* jagen, verfolgen ♦ *n* Jagd *f*.
  chase up *vt* (*Brit: information*) ranschaffen (*col*); (: *person*) rankriegen (*col*).

chasm [kaz'əm] *n* Kluft *f*.

chassis [shas'ē] *n* Chassis *nt*, Fahrgestell *nt*.

chaste [chāst] *a* keusch.

chastened [chā'sənd] *a* zur Vernunft gebracht.

chastening [chā'səning] *a* ernüchternd.

chastity [chas'titē] *n* Keuschheit *f*.

chat [chat] *vi* plaudern, sich (zwanglos) unterhalten ♦ *n* Plauderei *f*.
  chat up *vt* (*Brit col: girl*) anmachen.

chat show *n* (*Brit*) Talkshow *f*.

chattels [chat'əlz] *npl* bewegliche(s) Vermögen *nt*, bewegliche Habe *f*.

chatter [chat'ûr] *vi* schwatzen; (*teeth*) klappern ♦ *n* Geschwätz *nt*.

chatterbox [chat'ûrbâks] *n* Quasselstrippe *f*.

chatty [chat'ē] *a* geschwätzig.

chauffeur [shō'fûr] *n* Chauffeur *m*, Fahrer *m*.

chauvinist [shō'vənist] *n* (*male ~*) männliche(r) Chauvinist *m*; (*nationalist*) Chauvinist *m*.

chauvinistic [shōvənis'tik] *a* chauvinistisch.

ChE *abbr* (*esp US*) = *Chemical Engineer*.

cheap [chēp] *a* billig; (*joke*) schlecht; (*of poor quality*) minderwertig; (*reduced: ticket, fare*) ermäßigt; ~ **money** billiges Geld.

cheapen [chē'pən] *vt*: **to ~ o.s.** sich herablassen.

cheaply [chēp'lē] *ad* billig.

cheat [chēt] *vt* betrügen ♦ *n* Betrüger(in *f*) *m* ♦ *vi* betrügen; (*in exam*) mogeln (*col*), schummeln (*col*); **he's been ~ing on his wife** er ist seiner Frau untreu gewesen, er hat seine Frau betrogen.

cheating [chēt'ing] *n* Betrug *m*.

check [chek] *vt* prüfen; (*look up, make sure*) nachsehen; (*control*) kontrollieren; (*restrain*) zügeln; (*stop*) anhalten; (*US*) abhaken ♦ *vi* (*official etc*) nachprüfen ♦ *n* (*examination, restraint*) Kontrolle *f*; (*restaurant bill*) Rechnung *f*; (*BANKING*) Scheck *m*; (*pattern*) Karo(muster) *nt* ♦ *a* (*also: ~ed: pattern, cloth*) kariert; **to ~ with sb** bei jdm nachfragen; **to keep a ~ on sb/sth** jdn/etw überwachen *or* kontrollieren; **to pay by ~** mit (einem) Scheck bezahlen.
  check in *vi* einchecken.
  check out *vt* (*investigate: story, person*) überprüfen ♦ *vi* abreisen.

checkbook [chek'bŏŏk] *n* (*US*) Scheckheft *nt*.

checkerboard [chek'ərbôrd] *n* (*US*) Damebrett *nt*.

checkered [chek'ûrd] *a* (*US: lit*) kariert; (: *fig*) bewegt.

checkers [chek'ûrz] *npl* (*US*) Damespiel *nt*.

check-in [chek'in] *n* (*also: ~ desk: at airport*) Abfertigungsschalter *m*.

checking account [chek'ing əkount'] *n* (*US*) Girokonto *nt*.

checklist [chek'list] *n* Prüf- *or* Checkliste *f*.

checkmate [chek'māt] *n* Schachmatt *nt*.

checkout [chek'out] *n* (*in supermarket*) Kasse *f*; (*US: in library: also:* ~ **desk**) Ausleihe *f*.

checkpoint [chek'point] *n* Kontrollpunkt *m*.

checkroom [chek'rŏŏm] *n* (*US*) Gepäckaufbewahrung *f*.

check-up [chek'up] *n* (Nach)prüfung *f*; (*MED*) (ärztliche) Untersuchung *f*.

cheek [chēk] *n* Backe *f*, Wange *f*; (*fig*) Frechheit *f*, Unverschämtheit *f*.

cheekbone [chēk'bōn] *n* Backenknochen *m*.

cheeky [chē'kē] *a* frech, übermütig.

cheep [chēp] *n* (*of bird*) Piep *m*, Piepser *m* ♦ *vi* piepsen.

cheer [chēr] *n* Beifallsruf *m*, Hochruf *m*; ~**s** Prost! ♦ *vt* zujubeln; (*encourage*) ermuntern, aufmuntern ♦ *vi* jauchzen, Hochrufe ausbringen.
  cheer on *vt* (*person etc*) anspornen, anfeuern.
  cheer up *vt* ermuntern ♦ *vi*: ~ **up!** Kopf hoch!

cheerful [chēr'fəl] *a* fröhlich.

cheerfulness [chēr'fəlnis] *n* Fröhlichkeit *f*, Munterkeit *f*.

cheering [chē'ring] *n* Applaus *m* ♦ *a* aufheiternd.

cheerio [chēr'ēō] *interj* (*Brit*) tschüs!

cheerless [chēr'lis] *a* (*prospect*) trostlos; (*person*) verdrießlich.

cheese [chēz] *n* Käse *m*.

cheeseboard [chēz'bôrd] *n* (gemischte) Käseplatte *f*.

cheesecake [chēz'kāk] *n* Käsekuchen *m*.

cheetah [chē'tə] *n* Gepard *m*.

chef [shef] *n* Küchenchef *m*.

chemical [kem'ikəl] *a* chemisch.

chemist [kem'ist] *n* (*CHEM*) Chemiker *m*; (*Brit MED*) Apotheker, Drogist *m*; ~**'s (shop)** (*Brit MED*) Apotheke *f*, Drogerie *f*.

chemistry [kem'istrē] *n* Chemie *f*.

cheque [chek] *n* (*Brit*) Scheck *m*; **to pay by** ~ mit (einem) Scheck bezahlen.

chequebook [chek'bŏŏk] *n* (*Brit*) Scheckbuch *nt*.

cheque card *n* (*Brit*) Scheckkarte *f*.

chequered [chek'ûrd] *a* (*Brit: fig*) bewegt.

cherish [chär'ish] *vt* (*person*) lieben; (*hope*) hegen; (*memory*) bewahren.

cheroot [shərŏŏt'] *n* Zigarillo *nt or m*.

cherry [chär'ē] *n* Kirsche *f*.

chervil [chûr'vil] *n* Kerbel *m*.

Ches *abbr* (*Brit*) = *Cheshire*.

chess [ches] *n* Schach *nt*.

chessboard [ches'bôrd] *n* Schachbrett *nt*.

chessman [ches'man] *n, pl* -**men** Schachfigur *f*.

chessplayer [ches'plâûr] *n* Schachspieler(in *f*) *m*.

chest [chest] *n* Brust *f*, Brustkasten *m*; (*box*) Kiste *f*, Kasten *m*; **to get sth off one's** ~

(col) sich *(dat)* etw von der Seele reden; ~ **of drawers** Kommode *f.*

chest measurement *n* Brustweite *f,* Brustumfang *m.*

chestnut [ches'nut] *n* Kastanie *f;* *(color)* Kastanienbraun *nt* ♦ *a* kastanienbraun, rötlichbraun.

chestnut tree *n* Kastanienbaum *m.*

chew [choo͞] *vti* kauen.

chewing gum [choo͞'ing gum] *n* Kaugummi *m.*

chic [shēk] *a* schick, elegant.

chicanery [shikā'nûrē] *n* Schikane *f.*

chick [chik] *n* Küken *nt; (col)* Biene *f.*

chicken [chik'ən] *n* Huhn *nt; (food: roast)* Hähnchen *nt; (col: coward)* feige(s) Huhn *nt,* Feigling *m.*
    chicken out *vi (col)* kneifen; **to ~ out of sth** vor etw kneifen.

chickenpox [chik'ənpâks] *n* Windpocken *pl.*

chickpea [chik'pē] *n* Kichererbse *f.*

chicory [chik'ûrē] *n* Zichorie *f; (plant)* Chicorée *f.*

chide [chīd] *vt* tadeln, rügen.

chief [chēf] *n* (Ober)haupt *nt;* Anführer *m; (COMM)* Chef *m* ♦ *a* höchst, Haupt-; **C~ of Staff** *(MIL)* Stabschef *m.*

chief executive *n* Geschäftsführer(in *f) m.*

chief executive officer *n* Generaldirektor *m.*

chiefly [chēf'lē] *ad* hauptsächlich.

chieftain [chēf'tin] *n* Häuptling *m.*

chiffon [shifân'] *n* Chiffon *m.*

chilblain [chil'blān] *n* Frostbeule *f.*

child [chīld] *n, pl* **children** [chil'drən] Kind *nt.*

childbirth [chīld'bûrth] *n* Entbindung *f.*

childhood [chīld'hood] *n* Kindheit *f.*

childish [chīl'dish] *a* kindisch.

childless [chīld'lis] *a* kinderlos.

childlike [chīld'līk] *a* kindlich.

child minder *n (Brit)* Tagesmutter *f.*

children [chil'drən] *npl of* **child.**

child's play [chīldz' plā] *n (fig)* Kinderspiel *nt.*

Chile [chil'ē] *n* Chile *nt.*

Chilean [chēl'āən] *a* chilenisch ♦ *n* Chilene *m,* Chilenin *f.*

chill [chil] *n* Kühle *f; (MED)* Erkältung *f.*

chil(l)i [chil'ē] *n* Peperoni *pl; (spice, meal)* Chili *m.*

chilly [chil'ē] *a* kühl, frostig.

chime [chīm] *n* Glockenschlag *m,* Glockenklang *m* ♦ *vi* ertönen, (er)klingen.

chimney [chim'nē] *n* Schornstein *m,* Kamin *m.*

chimney sweep *n* Schornsteinfeger(in *f) m.*

chimpanzee [chimpanzē'] *n* Schimpanse *m.*

chin [chin] *n* Kinn *nt.*

china [chī'nə] *n* Porzellan *nt.*

China *n* China *nt.*

Chinese [chīnēz'] *a* chinesisch ♦ *n (person)* Chinese *m,* Chinesin *f; (language)* Chinesisch *nt.*

chink [chingk] *n (opening)* Ritze *f,* Spalt *m;*

(noise) Klirren *nt.*

chintz [chints] *n* Kattun *m.*

chip [chip] *n (of wood etc)* Splitter *m; (US: snack)* Chip *m; (in gambling)* Chip *m,* Spielmarke *f; (COMPUT)* Chip *m* ♦ *vt* absplittern; **~s** *(Brit: french fries)* Pommes frites *pl;* **when the ~s are down** *(fig)* wenn es drauf ankommt.
    chip in *vi (col: interrupt)* Zwischenbemerkungen machen; **he ~ped in with 3** (: *contribute)* er steuerte 3 bei.

chipboard [chip'bôrd] *n (Brit)* Spanholz *nt.*

chipmunk [chip'mungk] *n* Backenhörnchen *nt.*

chiropodist [kirâp'ədist] *n (Brit)* Fußpfleger(in *f) m.*

chiropody [kirâp'ədē] *n* Fußpflege *f.*

chirp [chûrp] *n* Zwitschern *nt; (of crickets)* Zirpen *nt* ♦ *vi* zwitschern.

chirpy [chûr'pē] *a (col)* munter.

chisel [chiz'əl] *n* Meißel *m.*

chit [chit] *n* Notiz *f.*

chitchat [chit'chat] *n (col)* Geplauder *nt,* Smalltalk *m.*

chivalrous [shiv'əlrəs] *a* ritterlich.

chivalry [shiv'əlrē] *n* Ritterlichkeit *f; (honor)* Ritterschaft *f.*

chives [chīvz] *npl* Schnittlauch *m.*

chloride [klôr'īd] *n* Chlorid *nt.*

chlorinate [klôr'ənāt] *vt* chloren.

chlorine [klôr'ēn] *n* Chlor *nt.*

chock [châk] *n* Keil *m.*

chock-a-block [châk'əblâk'], **chockfull** [châk'fool] *a* vollgepfropft.

chocolate [chôk'əlit] *n* Schokolade *f.*

choice [chois] *n* Wahl *f; (of goods)* Auswahl *f* ♦ *a* auserlesen, Qualitäts-; **I did it by** *or* **from** ~ ich wollte es so; **a wide** ~ eine große Auswahl.

choir [kwī'ûr] *n* Chor *m.*

choirboy [kwīûr'boi] *n* Chorknabe *m.*

choke [chōk] *vi* ersticken ♦ *vt* erdrosseln; *(block)* (ab)drosseln ♦ *n (AUT)* Starterklappe *f.*

cholera [kâl'ərə] *n* Cholera *f.*

cholesterol [kəles'tərôl] *n* Cholesterin *nt.*

choose [choo͞z] *vt irreg* (aus)wählen; *(decide)* beschließen; **to ~ between** wählen zwischen (+*dat*); **to ~ from** wählen *or* eine Wahl treffen (aus *or* unter +*dat*).

choosy [choo͞'zē] *n* wählerisch.

chop [châp] *vt* (zer)hacken; *(wood)* spalten ♦ *vi:* **to ~ and change** schwanken ♦ *n* Hieb *m; (meat)* Kotelett *nt;* **to get the ~** *(Brit col: be axed)* dem Rotstift zum Opfer fallen; (: *be fired)* rausgeschmissen werden; *see also* **chops.**

chopper [châp'ûr] *n (helicopter)* Hubschrauber *m.*

choppy [châp'ē] *a* bewegt.

chops [châps] *npl (jaws)* Lefzen *pl.*

chopsticks [châp'stiks] *npl* (Eß)stäbchen *pl.*

choral [kôr'əl] *a* Chor-.

chord [kôrd] *n* Akkord *m; (string)* Saite *f.*

chore [chôr] *n* Pflicht *f*, harte Arbeit *f*.
choreographer [kôrēăg'rəfûr] *n* Choreo-graph(in *f*) *m*.
chorister [kôr'istûr] *n* Chorknabe *m*; (*US*) Dirigent *m* eines Kirchenchors.
chortle [chôr'təl] *vi* glucksen, tief lachen.
chorus [kôr'əs] *n* Chor *m*; (*in song*) Refrain *m*.
chose [chōz] *pt of* **choose**.
chosen [chō'zən] *pp of* **choose**.
chow [chou] *n* (*dog*) Chow-Chow *m*.
chowder [chou'dûr] *n* (*esp US*) sämige Fisch-suppe *f*.
Christ [krīst] *n* Christus *m*.
christen [kris'ən] *vt* taufen.
christening [kris'əning] *n* Taufe *f*.
Christian [kris'chən] *a* christlich ♦ *n* Christ(in *f*) *m*.
Christianity [krischēan'itē] *n* Christentum *nt*.
Christian name *n* Vorname *m*.
Christmas [kris'məs] *n* Weihnachten *pl*; **Father** ~ der Weihnachtsmann; **happy** *or* **merry** ~! frohe *or* fröhliche Weihnachten!
Christmas card *n* Weihnachtskarte *f*.
Christmas Day *n* der erste Weihnachtstag.
Christmas Eve *n* Heiligabend *m*.
Christmas Island *n* Christmasinsel *f*.
Christmas tree *n* Weihnachtsbaum *m*.
chrome [krōm] *n* = **chromium plating**.
chromium [krō'mēəm] *n* Chrom *nt*.
chromium plating [krō'mēəm plā'ting] *n* Verchromung *f*.
chronic [krân'ik] *a* (*MED, fig: liar, smoker*) chronisch; (*terrible*) scheußlich.
chronicle [krân'ikəl] *n* Chronik *f*.
chronological [krânəlâj'ikəl] *a* chronologisch.
chrysalis [kris'əlis] *n* (*Insekten*)puppe *f*.
chrysanthemum [krisan'thəməm] *n* Chrysantheme *f*.
chubby [chub'ē] *a* (*child*) pausbäckig; (*adult*) rundlich.
chuck [chuk] *vt* werfen; (*also*: ~ **up**, ~ **in**: *job*) hinschmeißen (*col*); (*person*) Schluß machen mit (*col*) ♦ *n* (*TECH*) Spannvorrichtung *f*.
chuckle [chuk'əl] *vi* in sich hineinlachen.
chug [chug] *vi* (*also*: ~ **along**) tuckern, entlangtuckern.
chum [chum] *n* (*child*) Spielkamerad *m*; (*adult*) Kumpel *m*.
chump [chump] *n* (*col*) Einfaltspinsel *m*, Tölpel *m*.
chunk [chungk] *n* Klumpen *m*; (*of food*) Brocken *m*.
chunky [chung'kē] *a* (*furniture etc*) sperrig; (*knitwear*) dick, klobig; (*person*) stämmig, gedrungen.
church [chûrch] *n* Kirche *f*; (*clergy*) Geistlichkeit *f*; **the C~ of England** die Anglikanische Kirche.
churchyard [chûrch'yârd] *n* Kirchhof *m*.
churlish [chûr'lish] *a* ungehobelt.
churn [chûrn] *n* Butterfaß *nt*; (*for transporting*) (große) Milchkanne *f*.

churn out *vt* (*col*) am laufenden Band produzieren.
chute [shoot] *n* Rutsche *f*.
chutney [chut'nē] *n* Chutney *m*.
CIA *n abbr* (*US*: = *Central Intelligence Agency*) CIA *m*.
cicada [sikā'də] *n* Zikade *f*.
CID *n abbr* (*Brit*: = *Criminal Investigation Department*) britische Kriminalpolizei.
cider [sī'dûr] *n* Apfelwein *m*.
cif *abbr* (= *cost, insurance and freight*) cif.
cigar [sigâr'] *n* Zigarre *f*.
cigarette [sigəret'] *n* Zigarette *f*.
cigarette butt *n* Zigarettenstummel *m*.
cigarette case *n* Zigarettenetui *nt*.
cigarette holder *n* Zigarettenspitze *f*.
C in C *abbr* = *Commander in Chief* .
cinch [sinch] *n* (*col*) klare(r) Fall *m*; (*easy*) Kinderspiel *nt*; **it's a** ~ (*col*: *sure thing*) es ist todsicher.
cinder block [sin'dûr blâk] *n* (*US*) Ytong *m* ®.
Cinderella [sindərel'ə] *n* Aschenbrödel *nt*.
cinders [sin'dûrz] *npl* Asche *f*.
cine camera [sin'ē kam'ûrə] *n* (*Brit*) Filmkamera *f*.
cine film [sin'ē film] *n* (*Brit*) Schmalfilm *m*.
cinema [sin'əmə] *n* Kino *nt*.
cinnamon [sin'əmən] *n* Zimt *m*.
cipher [sī'fûr] *n* (*code*) Chiffre *f*; (*numeral*) Ziffer *f*; **in** ~ chiffriert.
circle [sûr'kəl] *n* Kreis *m* ♦ *vi* kreisen ♦ *vt* umkreisen; (*attacking*) umzingeln.
circuit [sûr'kit] *n* Umlauf *m*; (*ELEC*) Stromkreis *m*.
circuit board *n* (*COMPUT*) (Schaltungs)platine *f*.
circuitous [sûrkyoo'itəs] *a* weitschweifig.
circular [sûr'kyəlûr] *a* (kreis)rund, kreisförmig ♦ *n* (*letter*) Rundschreiben *nt*, Rundbrief *m*; (*as advertisement*) Wurfsendung *f*.
circularize [sûr'kyələrīz] *vt* (*inform*) benachrichtigen; (*letter*) herumschicken.
circulate [sûr'kyəlāt] *vi* zirkulieren; (*person*: *socially*) die Runde machen ♦ *vt* in Umlauf setzen.
circulation [sûrkyəlā'shən] *n* (*of blood*) Kreislauf *m*; (*of newspaper etc*) Auflage(nziffer) *f*; (*of money*) Umlauf *m*.
circumcise [sûr'kəmsīz] *vt* beschneiden.
circumference [sûrkum'fûrəns] *n* (Kreis)umfang *m*.
circumscribe [sûrkəmskrīb'] *vt* (*restrict*) eingrenzen; (*MATH*) einen Kreis umbeschreiben (+*dat*).
circumspect [sûr'kəmspekt] *a* umsichtig.
circumstances [sûr'kəmstansiz] *npl* (*facts connected with sth*) Umstände *pl*; (*financial condition*) Verhältnisse *pl*; **in the** ~ unter diesen Umständen; **under no** ~ unter gar keinen Umständen.
circumstantial [sûrkəmstan'shəl] *a* (*report, statement*) ausführlich; ~ **evidence** Indizienbeweis *m*.

circumvent [sûrkəmvent'] vt (rule etc) umgehen.

circus [sûr'kəs] n Zirkus m; (usu C~: in place names) Platz m.

cissy [sis'ē] n Weichling m.

cistern [sis'tûrn] n Zisterne f; (of toilet) Spülkasten m.

citation [sītā'shən] n (quote) Zitat nt; (JUR) Vorladung f (vor Gericht).

cite [sīt] vt zitieren, anführen.

citizen [sit'əzən] n Bürger(in f) m; (of nation) Staatsangehörige(r) mf.

citizenship [sit'əzənship] n Staatsangehörigkeit f.

citric acid [sit'rik as'id] n Zitronensäure f.

citrus fruit [sit'rəs frōōt] n Zitrusfrucht f.

city [sit'ē] n Großstadt f; (center) Zentrum nt, City f.

city center n Stadtzentrum nt.

city hall n (US) Stadtverwaltung f.

civic [siv'ik] a städtisch, Bürger-.

civil [siv'əl] a (of town) Bürger-; (of state) staatsbürgerlich; (not military) zivil; (polite) höflich.

Civil Aviation Authority n (Brit) Zivile Luftfahrtbehörde f.

civil engineer n Bauingenieur m.

civil engineering n Hoch- und Tiefbau m.

civilian [sivil'yən] n Zivilperson f ♦ a zivil, Zivil-.

civilization [sivələzā'shən] n Zivilisation f, Kultur f.

civilized [siv'əlīzd] a zivilisiert; Kultur-.

civil law n bürgerliche(s) Recht nt, Zivilrecht nt.

civil rights npl Bürgerrechte pl; ~ **movement** Bürgerrechtsbewegung f.

civil servant n Staatsbeamte(r) m.

Civil Service n Staatsdienst m.

civil war n Bürgerkrieg m.

cl abbr (= centiliter(s)) cl.

clad [klad] a gekleidet; ~ **in** gehüllt in (+acc).

claim [klām] vt beanspruchen; (have opinion) behaupten ♦ vi (for expenses) sich (dat) etw zurückgeben or -zahlen lassen ♦ n (demand) Forderung f; (right) Anspruch m; Behauptung f; **to put in a ~ for sth** etw beantragen; (for insurance) Ansprüche geltend machen.

claimant [klā'mənt] n Antragsteller(in f) m.

claim form n Antragsformular nt.

clairvoyant [klärvoi'ənt] n Hellseher(in f) m ♦ a hellseherisch.

clam [klam] n Venusmuschel f.

   clam up vi (col) keinen Piep(s) (mehr) sagen.

clamber [klam'bûr] vi kraxeln.

clammy [klam'ē] a feucht(kalt), klamm.

clamor [klam'ûr] (US) n (noise) Lärm m, Lärmen nt; (protest) Aufschrei m ♦ vi: **to ~ for sth** nach etw schreien.

clamorous [klam'ûrəs] a lärmend, laut.

clamour [klam'ûr] n (Brit) = **clamor**.

clamp [klamp] n Schraubzwinge f ♦ vt einspannen.

   clamp down on vt fus (fig) gewaltig bremsen (col).

clan [klan] n Sippe f, Clan m.

clandestine [klandes'tin] a geheim, Geheim-.

clang [klang] n Klang m; (clatter) Scheppern nt ♦ vi klingen; scheppern.

clansman [klanz'mən] n Clanmitglied nt.

clap [klap] vi klatschen ♦ vt Beifall klatschen (+dat) ♦ n: **a ~ of thunder** ein Donnerschlag; **to ~ one's hands** in die Hände klatschen.

clapping [klap'ing] n (Beifall)klatschen nt.

claret [klar'it] n rote(r) Bordeaux(wein) m.

clarification [klarəfəkā'shən] n Erklärung f.

clarify [klar'əfī] vt klären, erklären.

clarinet [klarənet'] n Klarinette f.

clarity [klar'itē] n Klarheit f.

clash [klash] n (fig) Konflikt m, Widerstreit m; (sound) Knall m ♦ vi zusammenprallen; (colors) sich beißen; (argue) sich streiten; (dates, events) sich überschneiden.

clasp [klasp] n Klammer f, Haken m; (on belt) Schnalle f ♦ vt umklammern.

class [klas] n (group, category, SCH) Klasse f ♦ vt einordnen, einstufen.

class-conscious [klas'kân'shəs] a standesbewußt, klassenbewußt.

classic [klas'ik] n Klassiker(in f) m; see also **classics** ♦ a (traditional) klassisch.

classical [klas'ikəl] a klassisch; ~ **music** klassische Musik f.

classics [klas'iks] n (UNIV) Altphilologie f.

classification [klasəfəkā'shən] n Klassifizierung f, Einteilung f.

classified [klas'əfīd] a (col) streng geheim; ~ **advertisement** Kleinanzeige f.

classify [klas'əfī] vt klassifizieren, einteilen.

classmate [klas'māt] n Klassenkamerad(in f) m.

classroom [klas'rōōm] n Klassenzimmer nt.

classy [klas'ē] a (col) todschick.

clatter [klat'ûr] n Klappern nt, Rasseln nt; (of feet) Getrappel nt ♦ vi klappern, rasseln; (feet) trappeln.

clause [klôz] n (JUR) Klausel f; (GRAM) Satz(teil) m, Satzglied nt.

claustrophobia [klôstrəfō'bēə] n Platzangst f, Klaustrophobie f.

claw [klô] n Kralle f ♦ vt (zer)kratzen.

clay [klā] n Lehm m; (for pots) Ton m.

clean [klēn] a sauber; (fig) schuldlos; (shape) ebenmäßig; (cut) glatt ♦ vt saubermachen, reinigen, putzen ♦ ad: **he ~ forgot** (col) das hat er glatt(weg) vergessen; **to come ~** (col: admit guilt) auspacken; **to have a ~ driving record** keine Strafpunkte haben; **to ~ one's teeth** (Brit) sich die Zähne putzen.

   clean off vt abwaschen, abwischen.

   clean out vt gründlich putzen.

   clean up vt aufräumen; (fig: make profit) einstecken (col), absahnen (col).

clean-cut [klēn'kut'] a (person) adrett.

cleaner [klē'nûr] *n* (*person*) Putzfrau *f*; (*for grease etc*) Scheuerpulver *nt*.

cleaners [klē'nûrz] *npl* chemische Reinigung *f*.

cleaning [klē'ning] *n* Reinigen *nt*, Säubern *nt*.

cleaning lady *or* **woman** *n* Reinemachefrau *f*.

cleanliness [klɛn'lēnis] *n* Sauberkeit *f*, Reinlichkeit *f*.

cleanly [klēn'lē] *ad* reinlich.

cleanse [klɛnz] *vt* reinigen, säubern.

cleanser [klɛn'zûr] *n* (*cosmetic*) Reinigungscreme *f or* -milch *f*.

clean-shaven [klēn'shā'vən] *a* glattrasiert.

clean-up [klēn'up] *n* Reinigung *f*.

clear [kli'ûr] *a* (*water*) klar; (*glass*) durchsichtig; (*sound*) deutlich, klar, hell; (*meaning*) genau, klar; (*certain*) klar, sicher; (*road*) frei; **a ~ majority** eine klare Mehrheit; **a ~ profit** ein Reingewinn *m*; **to make o.s. ~** sich klar ausdrücken; **to make it ~ to sb that ...** es jdm (unmißverständlich) klar machen, daß ...; **I have a ~ day tomorrow** (*Brit*) ich habe morgen nichts vor ♦ *n*: **to be in the ~** (*out of debt*) schuldenfrei sein, aus allem heraus sein; (*out of suspicion*) von jedem Verdacht frei sein; (*out of danger*) außer Gefahr sein ♦ *ad*: **to keep ~ of sb/sth** jdm/etw aus dem Weg gehen *or* meiden; **to stand ~ of sth** etw frei halten ♦ *vt* (*road etc*) freimachen; (*site, woodland*) räumen; **to ~ a profit** Profit machen; **to ~ a check** bestätigen, daß ein Scheck gedeckt ist ♦ *vi* (*become ~*) klarwerden.

clear off *vi* (*Brit col*) = **clear out.**

clear out *vi* (*US col*) abhauen, verschwinden.

clear up *vi* (*weather*) sich aufklären ♦ *vt* reinigen, säubern; (*solve*) aufklären.

clearance [klē'rəns] *n* (*removal*) Räumung *f*; (*free space*) Lichtung *f*; (*permission*) Freigabe *f*.

clear-cut [kli'ûrkut'] *a* scharf umrissen; (*case*) eindeutig.

clearing [klē'ring] *n* Lichtung *f*.

clearing bank *n* (*Brit FIN*) Clearingbank *f*.

clearing house *n* (*FIN*) Clearingstelle *f*.

clearly [kli'ûrlē] *ad* klar, deutlich, zweifellos.

clearway [klēr'wā]· *n* (*Brit*) (Straße *f* mit) Halteverbot *nt*.

cleaver [klē'vûr] *n* Hackbeil *f*.

clef [klɛf] *n* Notenschlüssel *m*.

cleft [klɛft] *n* (*in rock*) Spalte *f*.

clement [klɛm'ənt] *a* (*weather*) mild.

clench [klɛnch] *vt* (*teeth*) zusammenbeißen; (*fist*) ballen.

clergy [klûr'jē] *n* Geistliche(n) *pl*.

clergyman [klûr'jēmən] *n*, *pl* **-men** Geistliche(r) *m*.

clerical [klär'ikəl] *a* (*office*) Schreib-, Büro-; (*ECCL*) geistlich, Pfarr(er)-.

clerical error *n* Schreibfehler *m*.

clerk [klûrk] *n* (*in office*) Büroangestellte(r) *mf*; (*US: salesperson*) Verkäufer(in *f*) *m*;

C~ of the Court Protokollführer(in *f*) *m*.

clever [klev'ûr] *a*, **cleverly** [klev'ûrlē] *ad* klug, geschickt, gescheit.

clew [klōō] *n* (*US*) = **clue.**

cliché [klēshā'] *n* Klischee *nt*.

click [klik] *vi* klicken ♦ *n* Klicken *nt*; (*of door*) Zuklinken *nt* ♦ *vt* (*heels*) zusammenklappen; (*tongue*) schalzen mit.

client [klī'ənt] *n* Klient(in *f*) *m*.

clientele [klīəntel'] *n* Kundschaft *f*.

cliff [klif] *n* Klippe *f*.

cliffhanger [klif'hangûr] *n* (*TV*, *fig*) Superthriller *m* (*col*).

climate [klī'mit] *n* Klima *nt*.

climatic [klīmat'ik] *a* klimatisch.

climax [klī'maks] *n* (*of play etc*) Höhepunkt *m*; (*sexual ~*) Orgasmus *m*.

climb [klīm] *vt* besteigen ♦ *vi* steigen, klettern; (*plane*) (auf)steigen ♦ *n* Aufstieg *m*; **to ~ over a wall** über eine Mauer steigen *or* klettern.

climb down *vi* (*Brit fig*) nachgeben, vom hohen Roß heruntersteigen.

climbdown [klīm'doun] *n* (*Brit: from opinion, position*) Abstieg *m*.

climber [klī'mûr] *n* Bergsteiger *m*, Kletterer *m*; (*fig*) Streber *m*.

climbing [klī'ming] *n* Bergsteigen *nt*, Klettern *nt*.

clinch [klinch] *vt* (*decide*) entscheiden; (*deal*) festmachen ♦ *n* (*BOXING*) Clinch *m*.

cling [kling] *vi irreg* (*clothes*) eng anliegen; **to ~ to** sich festklammern an (+*dat*).

clinic [klin'ik] *n* Klinik *f*.

clinical [klin'ikəl] *a* klinisch; (*fig: room, atmosphere*) steril, kalt; (*dispassionate*) klinisch, nüchtern.

clink [klingk] *n* (*of coins*) Klimpern *nt*; (*of glasses*) Klirren *nt*; (*col: prison*) Knast *m* ♦ *vi* klimpern ♦ *vt* klimpern mit; (*glasses*) anstoßen.

clip [klip] *n* Spange *f*; (*also:* **paper ~**) (Büro- *or* Heft)klammer *f* ♦ *vt* (*papers*) heften; (*hair, hedge*) stutzen.

clippers [klip'ûrz] *npl* (*for hedge*) Heckenschere *f*; (*for hair*) Haarschneidemaschine *f*.

clipping [klip'ing] *n* (*from newspaper*) Ausschnitt *m*.

clique [klēk] *n* Clique *f*, Gruppe *f*.

cloak [klōk] *n* lose(r) Mantel *m*, Umhang *m*.

cloakroom [klōk'rōōm] *n* (*for coats*) Garderobe *f*; (*Brit: rest room*) Toilette *f*.

clobber [kláb'ûr] *n* (*col*) Klamotten *pl* ♦ *vt* schlagen.

clock [kläk] *n* (*of cab also*) Uhr *f*; **to work against the ~** gegen die Uhr arbeiten; **(a)round the ~** rund um die Uhr; **30,000 on the ~** (*Brit AUT*) ein Tachostand von 30.000.

clock in, clock on *vi* (den Arbeitsbeginn) stempeln *or* stechen.

clock off, clock out *vi* (das Arbeitsende) stempeln *or* stechen.

clock up *vt* verbuchen.

clockwise [kläk'wīz] *ad* im Uhrzeigersinn.

clockwork [klâk'wûrk] *n* Uhrwerk *nt* ♦ *cpd* (*toy, train*) Aufzieh-; **like** ~ wie am Schnürchen.

clog [klâg] *n* Holzschuh *m* ♦ *vt* verstopfen.

cloister [klois'tûr] *n* Kreuzgang *m.*

clone [klōn] *n* Klon *m.*

close *a* [klōs] nahe; (*march*) geschlossen; (*thorough*) genau, gründlich; (*weather*) schwül; **I/you** *etc* **had a** ~ **shave** das war knapp; **how** ~ **is Houston to Dallas?** wie weit ist Houston von Dallas entfernt?; **at** ~ **quarters** in allernächster Nähe ♦ *ad* knapp; ~ **to** *prep* in der Nähe (+*gen*) ♦ *vt* [klōz] schließen, abschließen; (*bargain, deal*) abschließen, zu einem Abschluß bringen ♦ *vi* [klōz] sich schließen; **to** ~ **with sb** jdn angreifen ♦ *n* [klōz] (*end*) Ende *nt*, Schluß *m*; **to bring sth to a** ~ etw beenden.
close down *vt* schließen ♦ *vi* Geschäft aufgeben, eingehen.
close in *vi* (*evening, winter*) anbrechen; (*night, darkness*) hereinbrechen; (*hunters*) nahen, umzingeln; (*fog*) sich verdichten; **the days are closing in** die Tage werden kürzer.
close in on *vt fus*: **to** ~ **in on sb** jdm auf den Leib rücken.
close off *vt* (*area*) abteilen, abtrennen.

closed [klōzd] *a* (*road*) gesperrt; (*shop etc*) geschlossen.

closed-circuit television [klōzdsûr'kit tel'əvizhən] *n* interne Fernsehanlage *f.*

closed shop *n* Gewerkschaftszwang *m.*

close-knit [klōs'nit'] *a* eng zusammengewachsen.

closely [klōs'lē] *ad* gedrängt, dicht; **we are** ~ **related** wir sind nahverwandt; **a** ~ **guarded secret** ein streng gehütetes Geheimnis.

closet [kläz'it] *n* Abstellraum *m*, Schrank *m.*

close-up [klōs'up] *n* Nahaufnahme *f.*

closing [klō'zing] *a* (*stages, remarks*) abschließend; ~ **price** (*STOCK EXCHANGE*) Schlußkurse *pl*, Schlußnotierungen *pl.*

closure [klō'zhûr] *n* Schließung *f.*

clot [klât] *n* Klumpen *m*; (*of blood*) Blutgerinnsel *nt*; (*Brit: fool*) Blödmann *m* ♦ *vi* gerinnen.

cloth [klôth] *n* (*material*) Stoff *m*, Tuch *nt*; (*for washing etc*) Lappen *m*, Tuch *nt*; (*table* ~) Tischdecke *f*, Tischtuch *nt.*

clothe [klōth] *vt* kleiden, bekleiden.

clothes [klōz] *npl* Kleider *pl*, Kleidung *f*; **to put one's** ~ **on** sich anziehen; **to take one's** ~ **off** sich ausziehen; *see* **bedclothes.**

clothes brush *n* Kleiderbürste *f.*

clothes line *n* Wäscheleine *f.*

clothes pin, (*Brit*) **clothes peg** *n* Wäscheklammer *f.*

clothing [klō'thing] *n* = **clothes.**

clotted cream [klât'id krēm] *n* Sahne aus erhitzter Milch.

cloud [kloud] *n* (*of dust, smoke, gas*) Wolke *f* ♦ *vt* (*liquid*) trüben; **every** ~ **has a silver lining** (*PROVERB*) auf Regen folgt Sonnen-

schein (*PROVERB*); **to** ~ **the issue** es unnötig komplizieren machen; (*hide deliberately*) die Angelegenheit verschleiern.
cloud over *vi* sich bewölken, sich bedecken; (*fig*) sich bewölken.

cloudburst [kloud'bûrst] *n* Wolkenbruch *m.*

cloudland [kloud'land] *n* (*US*) Wolkenkuckucksheim *nt.*

cloudy [klou'dē] *a* wolkig, bewölkt.

clout [klout] (*col*) *n* Schlag *m*; (*fig*) Schlagkraft *f* ♦ *vt* hauen.

clove [klōv] *n* Gewürznelke *f*; ~ **of garlic** Knoblauchzehe *f.*

clover [klō'vûr] *n* Klee *m.*

cloverleaf [klō'vûrlēf] *n* Kleeblatt *nt.*

clown [kloun] *n* Clown *m*, Hanswurst *m* ♦ *vi* kaspern, sich albern benehmen.

cloy [kloi] *vi*: **it** ~**s** es übersättigt einen.

cloying [kloi'ing] *a* (*taste, smell*) übersüß.

CLU *n* *abbr* (*US*) = *Chartered Life Underwriter.*

club [klub] *n* (*weapon*) Knüppel *m*; (*society*) Klub *m*; (*also:* **golf** ~) Golfschläger *m*; *see also* **clubs** ♦ *vt* prügeln.
club together *vi* (*with money etc*) zusammenlegen.

club car *n* (*US RAIL*) Speisewagen *m.*

clubhouse [klub'hous] *n* Klubhaus *nt.*

clubs [klubz] *n* (*CARDS*) Kreuz *nt.*

cluck [kluk] *vi* glucken.

clue [klōō] *n* Anhaltspunkt *m*, Fingerzeig *m*, Spur *f*; **he hasn't a** ~ er hat keine Ahnung.

clued in [klōō d in] *a* (*US col*): **to be** ~ **on sth** über etw (*acc*) im Bilde sein; (*about subject*) mit etw vertraut sein.

clued up [klōō d up] *a* (*Brit col*) = **clued in.**

clueless [klōō'lis] *a* (*col*) ahnungslos, unbedarft.

clump [klump] *n* Gebüsch *nt.*

clumsy [klum'zē] *a* (*person*) ungelenk, unbeholfen; (*object, shape*) unförmig.

clung [klung] *pt, pp of* **cling.**

clunker [klunk'ûr] *n* (*US pej: car*) Kiste *f*, Mühle *f.*

cluster [klus'tûr] *n* Traube *f*; (*of trees etc*) Gruppe *f.*
cluster round *vi* sich scharen um.

clutch [kluch] *n* feste(r) Griff *m*; (*AUT*) Kupplung *f* ♦ *vt* sich festklammern an (+*dat*); (*book*) an sich klammern.

clutter [klut'ûr] *vt* (*also:* ~ **up**) zu voll machen (*col*) or stellen; (*mind*) vollstopfen ♦ *n* (*confusion*) Durcheinander *nt*; (*disorderly articles*) Kram *m* (*col*).

cm *abbr* (= *centimeter(s)*) cm.

CM *abbr* (*US MAIL*) = *North Marianna Islands.*

CND *n abbr* (*Brit*) = *Campaign for Nuclear Disarmament.*

CO *n abbr* (= *commanding officer*) Kdr. ♦ *abbr* (*US MAIL*) = *Colorado.*

Co. *abbr* (= *company*) KG *f*; (= *county*) Land.

c/o *abbr* (*COMM*) = *cash order*; (= *care of*)

c/o.
coach [kōch] *n* (*old*) Kutsche *f*; (*RAIL*) (Personen)wagen *m*; (*trainer*) Trainer *m*; (*Brit*) Omnibus *m*, (Überland)bus *m* ♦ *vt* (*SCH*) Nachhilfeunterricht geben (+*dat*); (*SPORT*) trainieren.
coach trip *n* Busfahrt *f*.
coagulate [kōag'yəlāt] *vi* gerinnen.
coal [kōl] *n* Kohle *f*.
coalesce [kōəles'] *vi* sich verbinden.
coalfield [kōl'fēld] *n* Kohlengebiet *nt*.
coalition [kōəlish'ən] *n* Zusammenschluß *m*; (*POL*) Koalition *f*.
coalman [kōl'mən] *n, pl* **-men** Kohlenhändler *m*.
coal mine *n* Kohlenbergwerk *nt*.
coal miner *n* Bergmann *m*, Kumpel *m* (*col*).
coal mining *n* Kohle(n)bergbau *m*.
coarse [kôrs] *a* (*lit*) grob; (*vulgar: character, laugh, remark*) grob, derb.
coast [kōst] *n* Küste *f*.
coastal [kōs'təl] *a* Küsten-.
coaster [kōs'tûr] *n* (*vessel*) Küstenfahrer *m*; (*for drinks*) Untersetzer *m*.
coastguard [kōst'gârd] *n* Küstenwache *f*.
coastline [kōst'līn] *n* Küste(nlinie) *f*.
coat [kōt] *n* Mantel *m*; (*on animals*) Fell *nt*, Pelz *m*; (*of paint*) Schicht *f* ♦ *vt* überstreichen; (*cover*) bedecken; ~ **of arms** Wappen *nt*.
coated [kō'tid] *a* (*US: tongue*) belegt.
coathanger [kōt'hangûr] *n* Kleiderbügel *m*.
coating [kō'ting] *n* Schicht *f*, Überzug *m*; (*of paint*) Schicht *f*.
co-author [kōōth'ûr] *n* Co-Autor *m*, Mitautor *m*.
coax [kōks] *vt* beschwatzen.
cobbler [kâb'lûr] *n* Schuster *m*.
cobble(stone)s [kâb'əl(stōn)z] *npl* Pflastersteine *pl*.
COBOL [kō'bôl] *n* COBOL *nt*.
cobra [kōb'rə] *n* Kobra *f*.
cobweb [kâb'web] *n* Spinnenwebe *f*.
cocaine [kōkān'] *n* Kokain *nt*.
cock [kâk] *n* Hahn *m* ♦ *vt* (*ears*) spitzen; (*gun*) entsichern.
cock-a-hoop [kâkəhōōp'] *a* ausgelassen, ganz aus dem Häuschen.
cockerel [kâk'ûrəl] *n* junge(r) Hahn *m*.
cockeyed [kâk'īd] *a* (*fig*) verrückt.
cockle [kâk'əl] *n* Herzmuschel *f*.
cockney [kâk'nē] *n* echte(r) Londoner *m*.
cockpit [kâk'pit] *n* (*AVIAT*) Pilotenkanzel *f*.
cockroach [kâk'rōch] *n* Küchenschabe *f*.
cocktail [kâk'tāl] *n* Cocktail *m*; **shrimp** (*US*) or **prawn** (*Brit*) ~ Krabbencocktail *m*.
cocktail cabinet *n* Hausbar *f*.
cocktail party *n* Cocktailparty *f*.
cocktail shaker [kâk'tāl shā'kûr] *n* Mixbecher *m*.
cocoa [kō'kō] *n* Kakao *m*.
coconut [kō'kənut] *n* Kokosnuß *f*.
cocoon [kəkōōn'] *n* Puppe *f*, Kokon *m*.
cod [kâd] *n* Kabeljau *m*.

COD *abbr* (= *cash on delivery*) Nachn.; (*US*) = **collect on delivery**.
code [kōd] *n* Kode *m*; (*JUR*) Kodex *m*; **in** ~ verschlüsselt, in Kode; ~ **of behavior** Sittenkodex *m*; ~ **of practice** Standesordnung *f*.
codeine [kō'dēn] *n* Kodein *nt*.
codicil [kâd'isəl] *n* Kodizill *nt*.
codify [kâd'əfī] *vt* (*message*) verschlüsseln; (*JUR*) kodifizieren.
cod-liver oil [kâd'livûr oil'] *n* Lebertran *m*.
co-driver [kōdrī'vûr] *n* Beifahrer *m*.
co-ed [kōed'] *n abbr* (*US: female student*) Schülerin einer gemischten Schule, Studentin an einer koedukativen Universität ♦ *a abbr* = **coeducational**.
coeducational [kōejōōkā'shənəl] *a* koedukativ, gemischt.
coerce [kōûrs'] *vt* nötigen, zwingen.
coercion [kōûr'shən] *n* Zwang *m*, Nötigung *f*.
coexistence [kōigzis'təns] *n* Koexistenz *f*.
C. of C. *n abbr* (= *Chamber of Commerce*) HK *f*.
C of E *n abbr* = **Church of England**.
coffee [kôf'ē] *n* Kaffee *m*.
coffee bar *n* (*Brit*) Café *nt*.
coffee bean *n* Kaffeebohne *f*.
coffee break *n* Kaffeepause *f*.
coffee cup *n* Kaffeetasse *f*.
coffee pot *n* Kaffeekanne *f*.
coffee table *n* Couchtisch *m*.
coffin [kôf'in] *n* Sarg *m*.
cog [kâg] *n* (Rad)zahn *m*.
cogent [kō'jənt] *a* triftig, überzeugend, zwingend.
cognac [kōn'yak] *n* Kognak *m*.
cohabit [kōhab'it] *vi*: **to** ~ **(with sb)** (*form*) (mit jdm) zusammenleben, (mit jdm) in eheähnlicher Gemeinschaft leben.
coherent [kōhē'rənt] *a* zusammenhängend, einheitlich.
cohesion [kōhē'zhən] *n* Zusammenhang *m*.
cohesive [kōhē'siv] *a* (*fig*) geschlossen.
coil [koil] *n* Rolle *f*; (*of smoke*) Kringel *m*; (*AUT, ELEC*) Spule *f* ♦ *vt* aufrollen, aufwickeln.
coin [koin] *n* Münze *f* ♦ *vt* prägen.
coinage [koi'nij] *n* (*of word*) Prägung *f*.
coincide [kōinsīd'] *vi* (*happen together*) zusammenfallen; (*agree*) übereinstimmen.
coincidence [kōin'sidəns] *n* Zufall *m*; **by a strange** ~ merkwürdigerweise.
coincidental [kōinsiden'təl] *a* zufällig.
coin-operated [koinâp'ərātid] *a* (*machine*) Münz-.
coke [kōk] *n* Koks *m*.
Coke *n* (®): *Coca-Cola*) (Coca-)Cola *f*, Coke *nt*.
Col. *abbr* (= *colonel*) Ob; (*US*) = *Colorado*.
COLA *n abbr* (*US:* = *cost-of-living agreement*) Vertrag, der Lohnerhöhungen bei steigenden Lebenshaltungskosten regelt.
colander [kâl'əndûr] *n* Durchschlag *m*.
cold [kōld] *a* kalt ♦ *n* Kälte *f*; (*illness*) Erkältung *f*; **I'm** ~ mir ist kalt; **the room's**

getting ~ im Zimmer wird's kalt; **to have ~ feet** (fig) kalte Füße haben, Angst haben; **to give sb the ~ shoulder** jdm die kalte Schulter zeigen; **to catch a ~** sich erkälten.

cold-blooded [kōld'blud'id] a kaltblütig.

cold cream n halbfette Feuchtigkeitscreme f.

cold cuts npl (US) Aufschnitt m.

coldly [kōld'lē] ad kalt; (fig) gefühllos.

cold sore n Erkältungsbläschen nt.

coleslaw [kōl'slô] n Krautsalat m.

colic [kâl'ik] n Kolik f.

collaborate [kəlab'ərāt] vi zusammenarbeiten.

collaboration [kəlabərā'shən] n Zusammenarbeit f; (POL) Kollaboration f.

collaborator [kəlab'ərātûr] n Mitarbeiter(in f) m; (POL) Kollaborateur(in f) m.

collage [kəlâzh'] n Collage f.

collagen [kâl'əjən] n Kollagen nt.

collapse [kəlaps'] vi (person) zusammenbrechen; (things) einstürzen; (negotiations) scheitern ♦ n Zusammenbruch m, Einsturz m; (of plans, scheme, business) Scheitern nt, Zusammenbruch m; (of government) Sturz m.

collapsible [kəlaps'əbəl] a zusammenklappbar, Klapp-.

collar [kâl'ûr] n Kragen m; (for dog) Halsband nt; (TECH) Bund m ♦ vt (col: person, object) fassen, schnappen.

collarbone [kâl'ûrbōn] n Schlüsselbein nt.

collate [kəlāt'] vt vergleichen, kollationieren; (TYP) kollationieren, zusammentragen.

collateral [kəlat'ûrəl] n (FIN) (zusätzliche) Sicherheit f.

collation [kəlā'shən] n (TYP) Kollationieren nt; (form: meal) Leerung f.

colleague [kâl'ēg] n Kollege m, Kollegin f.

collect [kəlekt'] vt sammeln; (Brit: fetch) abholen ♦ vi sich sammeln ♦ ad: **to call ~** (US TEL) ein R-Gespräch führen; **to ~ one's thoughts** seine Gedanken ordnen; **~ on delivery** (US) bei Lieferung bezahlen.

collect call n (US) R-Gespräch nt.

collected [kəlek'tid] a gefaßt.

collection [kəlek'shən] n Sammlung f; (ECCL) Kollekte f; (MAIL) Leerung f.

collective [kəlek'tiv] a gemeinsam; (POL) kollektiv ♦ n Kollektiv nt.

collective bargaining n Tarifverhandlungen pl.

collector [kəlek'tûr] n Sammler m; (tax ~) (Steuer)einnehmer m; **~'s item** or **piece** Sammlerstück nt.

college [kâl'ij] n (UNIV) College nt; (of technology, agriculture etc) Fachhochschule f.

collide [kəlīd'] vi zusammenstoßen; (interests, demands) kollidieren, im Widerspruch stehen (with zu).

collie [kâl'ē] n (dog) Collie m.

colliery [kâl'yûrē] n (Brit) (Kohlen)bergwerk nt, Zeche f.

collision [kəlizh'ən] n Zusammenstoß m; (of opinions) Konflikt m; **to be on a ~ course** (also fig) auf Kollisionskurs sein.

colloquial [kəlō'kwēəl] a umgangssprachlich.

collusion [kəlōō'zhən] n (geheime) Absprache f; **to be in ~ with** gemeinsame Sache machen mit, zusammenarbeiten mit.

Colo. abbr (US) = Colorado.

cologne [kəlōn'] n (also: **eau de ~**) n Kölnisch Wasser nt.

Cologne n Köln nt.

Colombia [kəlum'bēə] n Kolumbien nt.

colon [kō'lən] n (GRAM) Doppelpunkt m.

colonel [kûr'nəl] n Oberst m.

colonial [kəlō'nēəl] a Kolonial-.

colonize [kâl'ənīz] vt kolonisieren.

colonnade [kâlənād'] n Säulengang m.

colony [kâl'ənē] n Kolonie f.

color [kul'ûr] (US) n Farbe f; **~s** pl Fahne f; **off ~** nicht wohl ♦ vt (lit, fig) färben ♦ vi (blush) sich verfärben.

Colorado beetle [kâlərâd'ō bē'təl] n Kartoffelkäfer m.

color bar n Rassenschranke f.

color-blind [kul'ûrblīnd] a farbenblind.

colored [kul'ûrd] a farbig.

color film n Farbfilm m.

colorful [kul'ûrfəl] a bunt.

coloring [kul'ûring] n Farbstoff m; (complexion) Gesichtsfarbe f, Teint m.

color scheme n Farbgebung f.

color television n Farbfernsehen nt.

colossal [kəlâs'əl] a kolossall, riesig.

colour [kul'ûr] etc (Brit) = **color** etc.

colt [kōlt] n Fohlen nt.

column [kâl'əm] n Säule f; (MIL) Kolonne f; (of print) Spalte f; (fashion ~, sports ~ etc) Kolumne f; **the editorial ~** der Leitartikel.

columnist [kâl'əmist] n Kolumnist(in f) m.

coma [kō'mə] n Koma nt.

comb [kōm] n Kamm m ♦ vt kämmen; (search) durchkämmen.

combat n [kâm'bat] Kampf m ♦ vt [kəmbat'] bekämpfen.

combination [kâmbənā'shən] n Verbindung f, Kombination f.

combination lock n Kombinationsschloß nt.

combine [kəmbīn'] vt verbinden ♦ vi sich vereinigen ♦ n [kâm'bīn] (COMM) Konzern m, Verband m; **to make a ~d effort** etw mit vereinten Kräften tun.

combine harvester n Mähdrescher m.

combo [kâm'bō] n (esp JAZZ) Combo f.

combustible [kəmbus'təbəl] a brennbar, leicht entzündlich.

combustion [kəmbus'chən] n Verbrennung f.

come [kum] vi irreg pp **come** kommen; (reach) ankommen, gelangen; **~ with me** kommen Sie mit; **we've just ~ from Paris** wir kommen gerade aus Paris; **coming!** ich komme!; **if it ~s to it** wenn es darauf ankommt.

come about vi geschehen.

come across vt fus (find) stoßen auf

(+*acc*) ♦ *vi*: **to ~ across well/badly** gut/
schlecht ankommen.
come around *vi* (*visit*) vorbeikommen;
(*MED*) wieder zu sich kommen.
come away *vi* (*person*) weggehen; (*handle etc*) abgehen.
come back *vi* (*return*) zurückkommen.
come by *vi* vorbeikommen ♦ *vt fus* (*find*):
to ~ by sth zu etw kommen.
come down *vi* (*price*) fallen.
come forward *vi* (*volunteer*) sich melden.
come from *vt fus* (*result*) kommen von;
where do you ~ from? wo kommen Sie
her?; **I ~ from New York** ich komme aus
New York.
come in *vi* (*enter*) hereinkommen.
come in for *vt fus* abkriegen.
come into *vt fus* (*inherit*) erben.
come of *vt fus*: **what came of it?** was ist
daraus geworden?
come off *vi* (*handle*) abgehen; (*happen*)
stattfinden; (*succeed*) klappen ♦ *vt*: **~ off it!**
(*col*) laß den Quatsch!
come on *vi* (*progress*) vorankommen;
how's the book coming on? was macht das
Buch?; **~ on!** komm!; (*hurry*) beeil dich!;
(*encouraging*) los!
come out *vi* herauskommen.
come out with *vt fus* herausrücken mit.
come over *vt fus*: **I don't know what's ~
over him!** ich weiß nicht, was über ihn gekommen ist *or* was mit ihm los ist!
come round *vi* (*Brit*) = **come around.**
come through *vi* (*survive*) überstehen,
überleben; **the call came through** der Anruf
ist durchgekommen.
come to *vi* (*MED*) wieder zu sich kommen
♦ *vt fus* (*bill*) sich belaufen auf (+*acc*);
how much does it ~ to? (*amount*) wieviel
macht das?
come under *vt fus* (*heading*) kommen
unter (+*acc*); **to ~ under sb's influence**
unter jds Einfluß geraten.
come up *vi* hochkommen; (*problem*) auftauchen; **to ~ up against** stoßen auf
(+*acc*).
come upon *vt fus* stoßen auf (+*acc*).
come up to *vt fus* (*approach*) zukommen
auf (+*acc*); (*water*) gehen *or* reichen bis zu
or an (+*acc*); (*expectation*) entsprechen
(+*dat*); **the film didn't ~ up to our
expectations** der Film entsprach nicht unseren Erwartungen.
come up with *vt fus*: **to ~ up with sth**
sich etw einfallen lassen
comeback [kum'bak] *n* (*reaction, response*)
Reaktion *f*; (*THEAT, fig*) Comeback *nt*.
Comecon [kâm'əkân] *n abbr* (= *Council for
Mutual Economic Aid*) Comecon *m*.
comedian [kəmē'dēən] *n* Komiker *m*.
comedienne [kəmēdēen'] *n* Komikerin *f*; (*actress*) Komödiendarstellerin *f*.
comedown [kum'doun] *n* Abstieg *m*.
comedy [kâm'idē] *n* Komödie *f*.

comet [kâm'it] *n* Komet *m*.
comeuppance [kumup'əns] *n*: **to get one's
~** seine Quittung bekommen.
comfort [kum'fûrt] *n* Bequemlichkeit *f*; (*of
body*) Behaglichkeit *f*; (*of mind*) Trost *m*;
see also **comforts** ♦ *vt* trösten.
comfortable [kumf'təbəl] *a* bequem, gemütlich; (*income*) ausreichend; (*majority*) sicher; **I don't feel very ~ about it** mir ist
nicht ganz wohl bei der Sache.
comfortably [kum'fûrtəblē] *ad* (*sit etc*) bequem; (*live*) angenehm.
comforter [kum'fûrtûr] *n* (*US*) Deckbett *nt*.
comforts [kum'fûrts] *npl* Annehmlichkeiten
pl.
comfort station *n* (*US*) öffentliche Toilette
f.
comic [kâm'ik] *n* Comic(heft) *nt*; (*comedian*)
Komiker *m* ♦ *a* komisch, humoristisch.
comical [kâm'ikəl] *a* komisch, ulkig.
comic strip *n* Comic strip *m*.
coming [kum'ing] *n* Kommen *nt*, Ankunft *f* ♦
a (*future*) kommend; **in the ~ weeks** in den
nächsten Wochen.
coming(s) and going(s) *n (pl)* Kommen
und Gehen *nt*.
Comintern [kâm'intûrn] *n* Komintern *f*.
comma [kâm'ə] *n* Komma *nt*.
command [kəmand'] *n* (*auch COMPUT*) Befehl *m*; (*control*) Führung *f*; (*MIL*) Kommando *nt*, (Ober)befehl *m* ♦ *vt* befehlen
(+*dat*); (*MIL*) kommandieren, befehligen;
(*be able to get*) verfügen über (+*acc*) ♦ *vi*
befehlen; **to have at one's ~** (*money, resources etc*) verfügen über; **to have ~ of
sth** das Kommando über etw haben; **to take
~ of** das Kommando übernehmen (+*gen*).
commandeer [kâməndēr'] *vt* (*MIL*) requirieren.
commander [kəman'dûr] *n* Befehlshaber *m*,
Kommandant *m*.
commanding [kəman'ding] *a* (*appearance*)
gebieterisch, hervorstechend; (*voice, tone*)
gebieterisch, Kommando- (*pej*); (*place*) beherrschend; (*lead*) entscheidend; (*position
of authority*) Befehls-.
commanding officer *n* Kommandeur *m*.
commandment [kəmand'mənt] *n* (*REL*) Gebot *nt*.
command module *n* Kommandokapsel *f*.
commando [kəman'dō] *n* (*Mitglied einer*)
Kommandotruppe *f*.
commemorate [kəmem'ərāt] *vt* gedenken
(+*gen*).
commemoration [kəmemərā'shən] *n*: **in ~
of** zum Gedächtnis *or* Andenken an (+*acc*).
commemorative [kəmem'ərātiv] *a*
Gedächtnis-; Gedenk-.
commence [kəmens'] *vti* beginnen.
commencement [kəmens'mənt] *n* Beginn *m*.
commend [kəmend'] *vt* (*recommend*) empfehlen; (*praise*) loben.
commendable [kəmend'əbəl] *a* empfehlenswert, lobenswert.

commendation [kâməndā'shən] n Empfehlung f; (SCH) Lob nt; (for bravery etc) Auszeichnung f.

commensurate [kəmen'sərit] a: ~ **with**, ~ **to** gemessen an, entsprechend (+dat).

comment [kâm'ent] n (remark) Bemerkung f; (note) Anmerkung f; (opinion) Stellungnahme f ♦ vi: **to** ~ **(on)** sich äußern (über +acc, zu), einen Kommentar abgeben (zu); **to** ~ **that** ... bemerken, daß ...; **"no** ~**"** „kein Kommentar!"

commentary [kâm'əntärē] n Kommentar m.

commentator [kâm'əntātûr] n Kommentator m.

commerce [kâm'ûrs] n Handel m.

commercial [kəmûr'shəl] a kommerziell, geschäftlich; (training) kaufmännisch ♦ n (TV) Fernsehwerbung f.

commercial bank n Handelsbank f.

commercialism [kəmûr'shəlizəm] n Kommerzialisierung f; (ART, LITER) Kommerz m.

commercialize [kəmûr'shəlīz] vt kommerzialisieren.

commercial television n Werbefernsehen nt.

commercial vehicle n Lieferwagen m.

commiserate [kəmiz'ərāt] vi Mitleid haben.

commission [kəmish'ən] n (order for work: esp of artist) Auftrag m; (for salesperson) Provision f; (MIL) Offizierspatent nt; (of offense) Begehen nt; (reporting body) Kommission f ♦ vt bevollmächtigen, beauftragen; **I get 10%** ~ ich bekomme 10% Provision; **out of** ~ (machine) außer Betrieb; **to** ~ **sb to do sth** jdn (damit) beauftragen, etw zu tun; **to** ~ **sth from sb** (painting etc) jdm etw in Auftrag geben.

commissionaire [kəmishənär'] n (Brit) Portier m.

commissioner [kəmish'ənûr] n (Regierungs)bevollmächtigte(r) m.

commit [kəmit'] vt (crime) begehen; (entrust) übergeben, anvertrauen; **I don't want to** ~ **myself** ich will mich nicht festlegen; **to** ~ **sb for trial** jdn einem Gericht überstellen; **a** ~**ted writer** (political) ein engagierter Schriftsteller.

commitment [kəmit'mənt] n Verpflichtung f.

committee [kəmit'ē] n Ausschuß m, Komitee nt; **to be on a** ~ in einem Ausschuß or Komitee sein or sitzen.

committee meeting n Ausschußsitzung f.

commodious [kəmō'dēəs] a geräumig.

commodity [kəmâd'itē] n Ware f; (Handelsor Gebrauchs)artikel m.

commodity exchange n Warenbörse f.

commodore [kâm'ədôr] n Flotillenadmiral m.

common [kâm'ən] a (cause) gemeinsam; (public) öffentlich, allgemein; (experience) allgemein, alltäglich; (pej) gewöhnlich; (widespread) üblich, häufig, gewöhnlich ♦ n Gemeindeland nt; **in** ~ **use** allgemein gebräuchlich; see also **Commons**.

commoner [kâm'ənûr] n Bürgerliche(r) mf.

common-law [kâm'ənlô'] a: **she is his** ~ **wife** sie lebt mit ihm in eheähnlicher Gemeinschaft.

commonly [kâm'ənlē] ad im allgemeinen, gewöhnlich.

Common Market n Gemeinsame(r) Markt m.

commonplace [kâm'ənpläs] a alltäglich ♦ n Gemeinplatz m.

common room n (Brit) Gemeinschaftsraum m.

commons [kâm'ənz] n sing (US) Mensa f.

Commons n (Brit): **the** ~ das Unterhaus.

common sense n gesunde(r) Menschenverstand m.

common stock n (US) Stammaktien fpl.

Commonwealth [kâm'ənwelth] n: **the** ~ das Commonwealth.

commotion [kəmō'shən] n Aufsehen nt, Unruhe f.

communal [kəmyōō'nəl] a Gemeinde-; Gemeinschafts-.

commune n [kâm'yōōn] Kommune f ♦ vi [kəmyōōn'] sich mitteilen (with dat), vertraulich verkehren.

communicate [kəmyōō'nikāt] vt (transmit) übertragen ♦ vi (be in touch) in Verbindung stehen; (make o.s. understood) sich verständlich machen.

communication [kəmyōōnikā'shən] n (message) Mitteilung f; (RAD, TV etc) Kommunikationsmittel nt; (making o.s. understood) Kommunikation f; ~**s** pl (transport etc) Verkehrswege pl.

communication cord n (Brit) Notbremse f.

communications satellite n Nachrichtensatellit m.

communications technology n Kommunikationstechnologie f.

communicative [kəmyōō'nikātiv] a mitteilsam, gesprächig.

communion [kəmyōōn'yən] n (group) Gemeinschaft f; (REL) Religionsgemeinschaft f; **(Holy) C**~ Heilige(s) Abendmahl nt, Kommunion f.

communiqué [kəmyōōnikā'] n Kommuniqué nt, amtliche Verlautbarung f.

communism [kâm'yənizəm] n Kommunismus m.

communist [kâm'yənist] n Kommunist(in f) m ♦ a kommunistisch.

community [kəmyōō'nitē] n Gemeinschaft f; (public) Gemeinwesen nt.

community center n Gemeinschaftszentrum nt.

community chest n (US) Wohltätigkeitsfonds m.

community health centre n (Brit) Gemeinde-Ärztezentrum nt.

community spirit n Gemeinschaftssinn m.

commutation ticket [kâmyətā'shən tik'it] n (US) Zeitkarte f.

commute [kəmyōōt'] vi pendeln.

commuter [kəmyōōt'ûr] n Pendler m.
compact [kâm'pakt] a kompakt, fest, dicht ♦ n Pakt m, Vertrag m; (for powder) Puderdose f.
compact disc n Mikrodiskette f.
companion [kəmpan'yən] n Begleiter(in f) m.
companionship [kəmpan'yənship] n Gesellschaft f.
companionway [kəmpan'yənwā] n (NAUT) Niedergang m.
company [kum'pənē] n Gesellschaft f; (also COMM) Firma f; (MIL) Kompanie f; **to keep sb ~** jdm Gesellschaft leisten; **Smith and C~** Smith & Co.
company car n Firmenwagen m.
company director n Direktor(in f) m, Verwaltungsratsmitglied nt.
company secretary n Company Secretary m.
comparable [kâm'pûrəbəl] a vergleichbar.
comparative [kəmpar'ətiv] a (freedom, luxury, cost) relativ; (GRAM) steigernd.
comparatively [kəmpar'ətivlē] ad verhältnismäßig.
compare [kəmpär'] vt vergleichen ♦ vi sich vergleichen lassen; **~d with** or **to** im Vergleich zu, verglichen mit; **how do the prices ~?** wie lassen sich die Preise vergleichen?
comparison [kəmpar'isən] n Vergleich m; (object) Vergleichsgegenstand m; **in ~** im Vergleich (with mit or zu).
compartment [kəmpärt'mənt] n (RAIL) Abteil nt; (in drawer etc) Fach nt.
compass [kum'pəs] n Kompaß m; **within the ~ of** im Rahmen or Bereich (+gen).
compasses [kum'pəsiz] npl Zirkel m.
compassion [kəmpash'ən] n Mitleid nt.
compassionate [kəmpash'ənit] a mitfühlend; **on ~ grounds** aus familiären Gründen.
compatibility [kəmpatəbil'ətē] n Vereinbarkeit f; (COMPUT) Kompatibilität f.
compatible [kəmpat'əbəl] a vereinbar, im Einklang; (COMPUT) kompatibel; **we're not ~** wir vertragen uns nicht.
compel [kəmpel'] vt zwingen.
compelling [kəmpel'ing] a (argument) zwingend.
compendium [kəmpen'dēəm] n Kompendium nt.
compensate [kâm'pənsāt] vt entschädigen; **to ~ for** Ersatz leisten für, kompensieren.
compensation [kâmpənsā'shən] n Entschädigung f; (money) Schadenersatz m; (JUR) Abfindung f; (PSYCH etc) Kompensation f.
compère [kâmpâr'] n (Brit) Conférencier m.
compete [kəmpēt'] vi sich bewerben; konkurrieren, sich messen mit.
competence [kâm'pitəns] n Fähigkeit f; (JUR) Zuständigkeit f.
competent [kâm'pitənt] a kompetent, fähig; (JUR) zuständig.
competition [kâmpitish'ən] n Wettbewerb m;

(COMM) Konkurrenz f; **in ~ with** im Wettbewerb mit.
competitive [kəmpet'ətiv] a Konkurrenz-; (sports) (Wett)kampf-; (COMM: price) wettbewerbs- or konkurrenzfähig.
competitor [kəmpet'itûr] n Mitbewerber(in f) m; (COMM) Konkurrent(in f) m; (SPORT) Teilnehmer(in f) m.
compile [kəmpīl'] vt zusammenstellen.
complacency [kəmplā'sənsē] n Selbstzufriedenheit f, Gleichgültigkeit f.
complacent [kəmplā'sənt] a selbstzufrieden, gleichgültig.
complain [kəmplān'] vi sich beklagen, sich beschweren (about über +acc).
complaint [kəmplānt'] n Beschwerde f; (MED) Leiden nt.
complement n [kâm'pləmənt] Ergänzung f; (ship's crew etc) Bemannung f ♦ vt [kâm'pləment] ergänzen; (make perfect) vervollkommnen, abrunden.
complementary [kâmpləmen'tûrē] a Komplementär-, (sich) ergänzend.
complete [kəmplēt'] a vollständig, vollkommen, ganz ♦ vt vervollständigen; (finish) beenden; **it's a ~ disaster** es ist eine totale Katastrophe.
completely [kəmplēt'lē] ad vollständig, ganz.
completion [kəmplē'shən] n Vervollständigung f; (of building) Fertigstellung f; **to be nearing ~** kurz vor dem Abschluß sein or stehen; **on ~ of contract** bei Vertragsabschluß.
complex [kəmpleks'] a kompliziert, verwickelt ♦ n Komplex m.
complexion [kəmplek'shən] n Gesichtsfarbe f, Teint m; (fig) Anstrich m, Aussehen nt.
complexity [kəmplek'sitē] n Verwicklung f, Kompliziertheit f.
compliance [kəmplī'əns] n Fügsamkeit f, Einwilligung f.
complicate [kâm'pləkāt] vt komplizieren, verwickeln.
complicated [kâm'pləkātid] a kompliziert, verwickelt.
complication [kâmpləkā'shən] n Komplikation f, Erschwerung f.
complicity [kəmplis'ətē] n Mittäterschaft f.
compliment n [kâm'pləmənt] Kompliment nt; see also **compliments** ♦ vt [kâm'pləment]: **to ~ sb** jdm ein Kompliment/Komplimente machen.
complimentary [kâmpləmen'tûrē] a schmeichelhaft; (free) Frei-, Gratis-.
compliments [kâm'pləmənts] npl Grüße pl, Empfehlung f.
compliments slip n Beilegzettel m mit Firmenaufdruck.
comply [kəmplī'] vi: **to ~ with** (conditions, system) erfüllen (+acc), entsprechen (+dat).
component [kəmpō'nənt] a Teil- ♦ n Bestandteil m.
compose [kəmpōz'] vt (arrange) zusammen-

setzen; *(music)* komponieren; *(poetry)* schreiben; *(thoughts)* sammeln; *(features)* beherrschen; *(constitute)* bilden; **to be ~d of** bestehen aus.

composed [kəmpōzd'] *a* ruhig, gefaßt.

composer [kəmpō'zûr] *n* Komponist(in *f*) *m*.

composite [kəmpâz'it] *a* zusammengesetzt; **~ drawing** *(US)* Phantombild *nt*; **~ motion** Sammelantrag *m*.

composition [kâmpəzish'ən] *n* *(MUS)* Komposition *f*; *(SCH)* Aufsatz *m*; *(composing)* Zusammensetzung *f*, Gestaltung *f*; *(structure)* Zusammensetzung *f*, Aufbau *m*.

compositor [kəmpâz'itûr] *n* Schriftsetzer *m*.

compos mentis [kâm'pəs men'tis] *a* klar im Kopf.

compost [kâm'pōst] *n* Kompost *m*.

compost heap *n* Komposthaufen *m*.

composure [kəmpō'zhûr] *n* Gelassenheit *f*, Fassung *f*.

compound [kâm'pound] *n* *(CHEM)* Verbindung *f*; *(mixture)* Gemisch *nt*; *(enclosure)* eingezäunte(s) Gelände *nt*; *(LING)* Kompositum *nt* ♦ *a* zusammengesetzt ♦ *vt* [kəmpound'] *(fig: problem, difficulty)* verschlimmern, vergrößern.

compound fracture *n* komplizierte(r) Bruch *m*.

compound interest *n* Zinseszinsen *pl*.

comprehend [kâmprihend'] *vt* begreifen; *(include)* umfassen, einschließen.

comprehension [kâmprihen'shən] *n* Fassungskraft *f*, Verständnis *nt*.

comprehensive [kâmprihen'siv] *a* umfassend.

comprehensive insurance *n* kombinierte Haftpflicht- und Kaskoversicherung *f*.

comprehensive school *n* *(Brit)* Gesamtschule *f*.

compress *vt* [kəmpres'] zusammendrücken, komprimieren ♦ *n* [kâm'pres] *(MED)* Kompresse *f*, Umschlag *m*.

compression [kəmpresh'ən] *n* Komprimieren *nt*.

comprise [kəmprīz'] *vt* *(also:* **be ~d of**) umfassen, bestehen aus.

compromise [kâm'prəmīz] *n* Kompromiß *m*, Verständigung *f* ♦ *a* *(decision, solution)* Kompromiß- ♦ *vt* *(reputation)* kompromittieren ♦ *vi* einen Kompromiß schließen.

compulsion [kəmpul'shən] *n* Zwang *m*; **under ~** unter Druck *or* Zwang.

compulsive [kəmpul'siv] *a* Gewohnheits-.

compulsory [kəmpul'sûrē] *a* *(obligatory)* obligatorisch, Pflicht-; **~ purchase** Enteignung *f*.

compunction [kəmpungk'shən] *n* Schuldgefühle *pl*, Gewissensbisse *pl*; **to have no ~ about doing sth** etw tun, ohne sich im geringsten schuldig zu fühlen.

computer [kəmpyōō'tûr] *n* Computer *m*, Rechner *m*.

computerize [kəmpyōō'tərīz] *vt* auf Computer umstellen.

computer language *n* Computersprache *f*.

computer peripheral *n* periphere(s) Gerät *nt*.

computer program *n* Programm *nt*.

computer programmer *n* Programmierer(in *f*) *m*.

computer programming *n* Programmieren *nt*.

computer science *n* Computerwissenschaft *f*.

computer virus *n* Computer-Virus *m*.

computing [kəmpyōō'ting] *n* *(science)* Informatik *f*.

comrade [kâm'rad] *n* Kamerad *m*; *(POL)* Genosse *m*.

comradeship [kâm'rədship] *n* Kameradschaft *f*.

comsat [kâm'sat] *n* *abbr* (= *communications satellite*) Nachrichtensatellit *m*.

con [kân] *vt* *(col)*: **to ~ sb into doing sth** jdn durch einen faulen Trick dazu bringen, daß er etw tut ♦ *n* Schwindel *nt*.

concave [kânkāv'] *a* konkav, hohlgeschliffen.

conceal [kənsēl'] *vt* *(secret)* verschweigen; **to ~ o.s.** sich verbergen.

concede [kənsēd'] *vt* *(grant)* gewähren; *(point)* zugeben ♦ *vi* *(admit)* zugeben.

conceit [kənsēt'] *n* Eitelkeit *f*, Einbildung *f*.

conceited [kənsē'tid] *a* eitel, eingebildet.

conceivable [kənsēv'əbəl] *a* vorstellbar; **it is ~ that** ... es ist denkbar, daß ..., man kann sich vorstellen, daß ...

conceivably [kənsēv'əblē] *ad*: **he may ~ be right** es ist durchaus denkbar, daß er recht hat.

conceive [kənsēv'] *vt* *(idea)* ausdenken; *(imagine)* sich vorstellen ♦ *vti* *(baby)* empfangen.

conceive of *vt fus*: **who first ~d of the idea?** wer hatte die Idee zuerst?

concentrate [kân'səntrāt] *vi* sich konzentrieren *(on* auf +*acc)* ♦ *vt* konzentrieren.

concentration [kânsəntrā'shən] *n* Konzentration *f*.

concentration camp *n* Konzentrationslager *nt*, KZ *nt*.

concentric [kənsen'trik] *a* konzentrisch.

concept [kân'sept] *n* Begriff *m*.

conception [kənsep'shən] *n* *(idea)* Vorstellung *f*; *(PHYSIOL)* Empfängnis *f*.

concern [kənsûrn'] *n* *(affair)* Angelegenheit *f*; *(COMM)* Unternehmen *nt*, Konzern *m*; *(worry)* Sorge *f*, Unruhe *f* ♦ *vt* *(interest)* angehen; *(be about)* handeln von; *(have connection with)* betreffen; **"to whom it may ~"** an den betreffenden Sachbearbeiter; **as far as I am ~ed** was mich betrifft; **to be ~ed with** behandeln, handeln von; **the department ~ed** *(involved)* die betreffende Abteilung; *(relevant)* die zuständige Abteilung.

concerned [kənsûrnd'] *a* *(anxious)* besorgt.

concerning [kənsûr'ning] *prep* betreffend, hinsichtlich (+*gen*).

concert [kân'sûrt] *n* Konzert *nt*; **in ~ (with)**

im Einverständnis (mit).

concerted [kənsûr'tid] *a* gemeinsam; *(FIN)* konzertiert.

concert hall *n* Konzerthalle *f.*

concertina [kânsûrtē'nə] *n* Handharmonika *f.*

concertmaster [kân'sûrtmastûr] *n (US)* Konzertmeister *m.*

concerto [kənchär'tō] *n* Konzert *nt.*

concession [kənsesh'ən] *n (yielding)* Zugeständnis *nt; (right to do sth)* Genehmigung *f;* **tax** ~ Steuer-Konzession *f.*

concessionaire [kənseshənär'] *n* Konzessionär *m.*

concessionary [kənsesh'ənārē] *a (ticket, fare)* ermäßigt.

conciliation [kənsilēā'shən] *n* Versöhnung *f; (official)* Schlichtung *f.*

conciliatory [kənsil'ēətôrē] *a* vermittelnd; versöhnlich.

concise [kənsīs'] *a* knapp, gedrängt.

conclave [kän'klāv] *n* Konklave *nt.*

conclude [kənklōōd'] *vt (end)* beenden; *(treaty)* (ab)schließen; *(decide)* schließen, folgern ♦ *vi (finish)* schließen; *(events)* enden.

conclusion [kənklōō'zhən] *n* (Ab)schluß *m;* **in** ~ zum Schluß, schließlich; **to come to the** ~ **that** ... zu dem Schluß *or* Ergebnis kommen, daß ...

conclusive [kənklōō'siv] *a* überzeugend, schlüssig.

conclusively [kənklōō'sivlē] *ad* endgültig.

concoct [kənkâkt'] *vt* zusammenbrauen, aushecken.

concoction [kənkâk'shən] *n (food)* Zusammenstellung *f; (drink)* Gebräu *nt.*

concord [kän'kôrd] *n (harmony)* Eintracht *f; (treaty)* Vertrag *m.*

concourse [kän'kôrs] *n* (Bahnhofs)halle *f,* Vorplatz *m.*

concrete [kän'krēt] *n* Beton *m* ♦ *a* konkret.

concrete mixer *n* Betonmischmaschine *f.*

concur [kənkûr'] *vi* übereinstimmen.

concurrently [kənkûr'əntlē] *ad* gleichzeitig.

concussion [kənkush'ən] *n* (Gehirn)erschütterung *f.*

condemn [kəndem'] *vt* verdammen; *(JUR)* verurteilen; *(building)* abbruchreif erklären.

condemnation [kândemnā'shən] *n* Verurteilung *f; (of object)* Verwerfung *f.*

condensation [kândensā'shən] *n* Kondensation *f.*

condense [kəndens'] *vi (CHEM)* kondensieren ♦ *vt (fig)* zusammendrängen.

condensed milk [kəndenst' milk'] *n* Kondensmilch *f.*

condescend [kândisend'] *vi* sich herablassen; **to** ~ **to do sth** sich herablassen, etw zu tun.

condescending [kândisen'ding] *a* herablassend.

condition [kəndish'ən] *n (state)* Zustand *m; (prerequisite)* Bedingung *f; (disease)* Beschwerden *pl;* **in good/poor** ~ *(person)* in guter/schlechter Verfassung; *(article)* in

gutem/schlechtem Zustand; **on** ~ **that** ... unter der Bedingung, daß ...; *see also* **conditions** ♦ *vt (hair etc)* behandeln; *(regulate)* regeln; ~**ed to** gewöhnt an (+*acc*).

conditional [kəndish'ənəl] *a* bedingt; *(GRAM)* Bedingungs-.

conditioned reflex [kəndish'ənd rē'fleks] *n* bedingte(r) Reflex *m.*

conditioner [kəndish'ənûr] *n (for hair)* Haarspülung *f.*

conditions [kəndish'ənz] *npl (circumstances)* Verhältnisse *pl;* **weather** ~ Wetterlage *f;* ~ **of sale** Verkaufsbedingungen *pl.*

condolences [kəndō'lənsiz] *npl* Beileid *nt.*

condom [kän'dəm] *n* Kondom *nt or m.*

condo(minium) [kândō(min'ēəm)] *n (US)* Eigentumswohnung *f.*

condone [kəndōn'] *vt* gutheißen.

conducive [kəndōō'siv] *a* dienlich *(to dat).*

conduct *n* [kän'dukt] *(behavior)* Verhalten *nt; (management)* Führung *f* ♦ *vt* [kəndukt'] führen, leiten; *(MUS)* dirigieren.

conductor [kənduk'tûr] *n (of orchestra)* Dirigent *m; (in bus)* Schaffner *m; (US RAIL)* Zugführer *m.*

conductress [kənduk'tris] *n (in bus)* Schaffnerin *f.*

conduit [kän'dōōwit] *n (for water)* Rohrleitung *f; (ELEC)* Isolierrohr *nt.*

cone [kōn] *n (MATH)* Kegel *m; (for ice cream)* (Waffel)tüte *f; (fir)* Tannenzapfen *m.*

confectioner [kənfek'shənûr] *n* Konditor *m;* ~'**s (shop)** Süßwarengeschäft *nt.*

confectioner's sugar *n (US)* Puderzucker *m.*

confectionery [kənfek'shənārē] *n (cakes)* Konfekt *nt,* Konditorwaren *pl; (candy)* Süßigkeiten *pl.*

confederate [kənfed'ûrit] *a* konföderiert; *(nations also)* verbündet ♦ *n (pej)* Komplize *m,* Komplizin *f;* **the C**~**s** *(US HIST)* die Konföderierten *pl.*

confederation [kənfedərā'shən] *n* Bund *m.*

confer [kənfûr'] *vt (degree)* verleihen ♦ *vi (discuss)* konferieren, verhandeln; **to** ~ **with sb about sth** sich mit jdm über etw beraten, mit jdm etw besprechen.

conference [kän'fûrəns] *n* Konferenz *f;* **to be in** ~ bei einer Konferenz *or* Besprechung sein.

conference room *n* Sitzungszimmer *nt.*

confess [kənfes'] *vti* gestehen; *(ECCL)* beichten.

confession [kənfesh'ən] *n* Geständnis *nt; (ECCL)* Beichte *f.*

confessional [kənfesh'ənəl] *n* Beichtstuhl *m.*

confessor [kənfes'ûr] *n (ECCL)* Beichtvater *m.*

confetti [kənfet'ē] *n* Konfetti *nt.*

confide [kənfīd'] *vi:* **to** ~ **in** (sich) anvertrauen (+*dat*); *(trust)* vertrauen (+*dat*).

confidence [kän'fidəns] *n* Vertrauen *nt; (assurance)* Selbstvertrauen *nt; (secret)* vertrauliche Mitteilung *f*, Geheimnis *nt*; **in ~** (*speak, write*) vertraulich; **to tell sb sth in strict ~** jdm etw im Vertrauen sagen; **to have (every) ~ that** ... ganz zuversichtlich sein, daß ...; **motion of no ~** Mißtrauensantrag *m*.

confidence game *n* Schwindel *m*.

confident [kân'fidənt] *a* (*sure*) überzeugt; sicher; (*self-assured*) selbstsicher.

confidential [kânfiden'shəl] *a* (*secret*) vertraulich, geheim; (*trusted*) Vertrauens-; (*secretary*) Privat-.

confidentiality [kânfidenshēal'itē] *n* Vertraulichkeit *f*.

configuration [kənfigyərā'shən] *n* (*COMPUT*) Konfiguration *f*.

confine [kənfīn'] *vt* (*limit*) begrenzen, einschränken; (*lock up*) einsperren; **to ~ o.s. to doing sth** sich darauf beschränken, etw zu tun.

confined [kənfīnd'] *a* (*space*) eng, begrenzt.

confinement [kənfīn'mənt] *n* (*of room*) Beengtheit *f*; (*in prison*) Haft *f*; (*MED*) Wochenbett *nt*.

confines [kân'fīnz] *npl* Grenze *f*.

confirm [kənfûrm'] *vt* bestätigen.

confirmation [kânfûrmā'shən] *n* Bestätigung *f*; (*REL*) Konfirmation *f*.

confirmed [kənfûrmd'] *a* unverbesserlich, hartnäckig; (*bachelor*) eingefleischt.

confiscate [kân'fiskāt] *vt* beschlagnahmen, konfiszieren.

confiscation [kânfiskā'shən] *n* Beschlagnahme *f*.

conflagration [kânfləgrā'shən] *n* Feuersbrunst *f*.

conflict *n* [kân'flikt] Kampf *m*; (*of words, opinions*) Konflikt *m*, Streit *m* ♦ *vi* [kənflikt'] im Widerspruch stehen.

conflicting [kənflik'ting] *a* gegensätzlich; (*reports, evidence, opinions*) widersprüchlich.

conform [kənfôrm'] *vi* sich anpassen (*to dat*); (*to rules*) sich fügen (*to dat*); (*to general trends*) sich richten (*to* nach).

conformist [kənfôr'mist] *n* Konformist(in *f*) *m*.

confound [kənfound'] *vt* (*amaze*) verblüffen.

confront [kənfrunt'] *vt* (*enemy*) entgegententen (+*dat*); (*sb with sth*) konfrontieren; (*sb with sb*) gegenüberstellen (*with dat*).

confrontation [kânfrəntā'shən] *n* Gegenüberstellung *f*; (*quarrel*) Konfrontation *f*.

confuse [kənfyōōz'] *vt* verwirren; (*sth with sth*) verwechseln.

confused [kənfyōōzd'] *a* verwirrt, konfus; **to get ~** konfus werden.

confusing [kənfyōō'zing] *a* verwirrend.

confusion [kənfyōō'zhən] *n* (*disorder*) Verwirrung *f*; (*tumult*) Aufruhr *m*; (*embarrassment*) Bestürzung *f*.

congeal [kənjēl'] *vi* (*freeze*) gefrieren; (*clot*) gerinnen.

congenial [kənjēn'yəl] *a* (*agreeable*) angenehm.

congenital [kənjen'itəl] *a* angeboren.

conger eel [kâng'gûr ēl] *n* Meeraal *m*.

congested [kənjes'tid] *a* überfüllt; (*telephone lines*) (dauernd) besetzt.

congestion [kənjes'chən] *n* Stauung *f*, Stau *m*.

conglomerate [kənglâm'ûrit] *n* (*COMM*) Konglomerat *nt*.

conglomeration [kənglâmərā'shən] *n* Anhäufung *f*.

Congo [kân'go] *n* (*state*) Kongo *m*.

congratulate [kəngrach'ōōlāt] *vt* beglückwünschen (*on* zu), gratulieren (+*dat*) (*on* zu).

congratulations [kəngrachōōlā'shənz] *npl* Glückwünsche *pl*; **~!** gratuliere!, herzlichen Glückwunsch!; **~ (on)** Glückwunsch *m*, Glückwünsche *pl* (zu).

congregate [kâng'grəgāt] *vi* sich versammeln.

congregation [kânggrəgā'shən] *n* Gemeinde *f*.

congress [kâng'gris] *n* Kongreß *m*.

congressional [kəngresh'ənəl] *a* Kongreß-.

Congressman [kâng'grismən] *n, pl* **-men** (*US*) Kongreßabgeordnete(r) *m*.

Congresswoman [kâng'griswōōmən] *n, pl* **-women** (*US*) Kongreßabgeordnete *f*.

conical [kân'ikəl] *a* kegelförmig, konisch.

conifer [kō'nifûr] *n* Nadelbaum *m*.

coniferous [kōnif'ûrəs] *a* zapfentragend.

conjecture [kənjek'chûr] *n* Vermutung *f* ♦ *vti* vermuten.

conjugal [kân'jəgəl] *a* ehelich.

conjugate [kân'jəgāt] *vt* konjugieren.

conjunction [kənjungk'shən] *n* Verbindung *f*; (*GRAM*) Konjunktion *f*, Verbindungswort *nt*; **in ~ with** in Verbindung mit.

conjunctivitis [kənjungktəvī'tis] *n* Bindehautentzündung *f*.

conjure [kân'jûr] *vti* zaubern.

   conjure up *vt* heraufbeschwören.

conjurer [kân'jûrûr] *n* Zauberer *m*; (*entertainer*) Zauberkünstler(in *f*) *m*.

conjuring trick [kân'jûring trik] *n* Zauberkunststück *nt*.

conker [kâng'kûr] *n* (*Brit*) (Roß)kastanie *f*.

conk out [kângk out] *vi* (*col*) stehenbleiben, streiken.

Conn. *abbr* (*US*) = *Connecticut*.

connect [kənekt'] *vt* verbinden; (*train*) koppeln; **I am trying to ~ you** (*TEL*) ich versuche, Sie zu verbinden.

connection, connexion [kənek'shən] *n* Verbindung *f*; (*relation*) Zusammenhang *m*; **in ~ with** in Zusammenhang mit; **to miss/ make a ~** Anschluß verpassen/haben; **what is the ~ between them?** welche Verbindung besteht zwischen ihnen?; **she has many business ~s** sie hat viele Geschäftsbeziehungen.

connoisseur [kânisûr'] *n* Kenner *m*.

connotation [kânətā'shən] *n* Konnotation *f*.

conquer [kâng'kûr] *vt* (*overcome*) überwinden, besiegen; (*MIL*) besiegen ♦ *vi* siegen.

conqueror [kâng'kûrûr] *n* Eroberer *m*.

conquest [kân'kwest] n Eroberung f.

conscience [kân'shəns] n Gewissen nt; **in all ~** allen Ernstes.

conscientious [kânshēen'shəs] a gewissenhaft.

conscientious objector n Wehrdienstverweigerer m (aus Gewissensgründen).

conscious [kân'shəs] a bewußt; (deliberate: insult, error) absichtlich; (MED) bei Bewußtsein; **to become ~ of sth** sich (dat) einer Sache bewußt werden.

consciousness [kân'shəsnis] n Bewußtsein nt.

conscript [kân'skript] n (Brit) Wehrpflichtige(r) m.

conscription [kənskrip'shən] n Wehrpflicht f.

consecrate [kân'səkrāt] vt weihen.

consecutive [kənsek'yətiv] a aufeinanderfolgend; **on 3 ~ occasions** bei 3 aufeinanderfolgenden Anlässen.

consensus [kənsen'səs] n: **the ~ of opinion** die allgemeine Meinung.

consent [kənsent'] n Zustimmung f ♦ vi zustimmen (to dat); **by common ~** in allgemeinem Einvernehmen.

consequence [kân'səkwens] n (importance) Bedeutung f, Konsequenz f; (result, effect) Wirkung f; **in ~** folglich.

consequently [kân'səkwentlē] ad folglich.

conservation [kânsûrvā'shən] n Erhaltung f; (nature ~) Umweltschutz m.

conservationist [kânsûrvā'shənist] n Umweltschützer(in f) m; (as regards old buildings etc) Denkmalpfleger(in f) m.

conservative [kənsûr'vətiv] a konservativ; (cautious) mäßig, vorsichtig; **C~** a (Brit: party) konservativ ♦ n Konservative(r) mf.

conservatory [kənsûr'vətôrē] n (greenhouse) Gewächshaus nt; (room) Wintergarten m.

conserve [kənsûrv'] vt erhalten.

consider [kənsid'ûr] vt überlegen; (take into account) in Betracht ziehen; (regard) halten für; **to ~ doing sth** in Erwägung ziehen, etw zu tun; **all things ~ed** alles in allem; **to ~ o.s. lucky** sich glücklich schätzen.

considerable [kənsid'ûrəbəl] a beträchtlich.

considerably [kənsid'ûrəblē] ad (comparison) beträchtlich; (very) höchst.

considerate [kənsid'ûrit] a rücksichtsvoll, aufmerksam.

consideration [kənsidərā'shən] n Rücksicht(nahme) f; (thought) Erwägung f; (reward) Entgelt nt; **to be under ~** im Gespräch sein, geprüft werden; **my first ~ is my family** ich denke zunächst einmal an meine Familie; **on no ~** unter keinen Umständen.

considering [kənsid'ûring] prep in Anbetracht (+gen) ♦ cj da; **~ (that)** wenn man bedenkt (, daß).

consign [kənsīn'] vt übergeben.

consignee [kânsīnē'] n Empfänger(in f) m.

consignment [kənsīn'mənt] n (of goods) Sendung f, Lieferung f.

consignment note n Frachtbrief m.

consignor [kənsī'nûr] n Versender m.

consist [kənsist'] vi bestehen (of aus).

consistency [kənsis'tənsē] n (of material) Festigkeit f; (of argument) Folgerichtigkeit f; (of person) Konsequenz f.

consistent [kənsis'tənt] a gleichbleibend, stetig; (argument) folgerichtig; **she's not ~** sie ist nicht konsequent.

consolation [kânsəlā'shən] n Trost m.

consolation prize n Trostpreis m.

console vt [kənsōl'] trösten ♦ n [kân'sōl] (control panel) (Bedienungs)konsole f.

consolidate [kənsâl'idāt] vt festigen; **~d balance sheet** konsolidierte Bilanz f.

consommé [kânsəmā'] n Fleischbrühe f.

consonant [kân'sənənt] n Konsonant m, Mitlaut m.

consort n [kân'sôrt] Gemahl(in f) m (form), Gatte m (form), Gattin f (form); **prince ~** Prinzgemahl m ♦ vi [kənsôrt']: **to ~ with sb** (often pej) mit jdm verkehren.

consortium [kənsôr'shēəm] n Gruppe f, Konsortium nt.

conspicuous [kənspik'yōōəs] a (prominent) auffallend; (visible) deutlich, sichtbar; **to make o.s. ~** auffallen.

conspiracy [kənspir'əsē] n Verschwörung f, Komplott nt.

conspiratorial [kənspirətôr'ēəl] a verschwörerisch.

conspire [kənspī'ûr] vi sich verschwören.

constable [kân'stəbəl] n (Brit) Polizist(in f) m.

constabulary [kənstab'yəlärē] n Polizei f.

constancy [kân'stənsē] n Beständigkeit f, Treue f.

constant [kân'stənt] a dauernd.

constantly [kân'stəntlē] ad (continually) andauernd; (faithfully) treu, unwandelbar.

constellation [kânstəlā'shən] n (temporary) Konstellation f; (permanent) Sternbild nt.

consternation [kânstûrnā'shən] n (dismay) Bestürzung f.

constipated [kân'stəpātid] a verstopft.

constipation [kânstəpā'shən] n Verstopfung f.

constituency [kənstich'ōōənsē] n (POL) Wahlkreis m; (people) Wähler pl (eines bestimmten Wahlkreises).

constituency party n Parteiorganisation in einem Wahlkreis.

constituent [kənstich'ōōənt] n (POL) Wähler m; (part) Bestandteil m.

constitute [kân'stitōōt] vt ausmachen.

constitution [kânstitōō'shən] n Verfassung f.

constitutional [kânstitōō'shənəl] a Verfassungs-; (monarchy) konstitutionell.

constrain [kənstrān'] vt zwingen.

constraint [kənstrānt'] n (restraint) Beschränkung f, Einschränkung f; (embarrassment) Befangenheit f.

constrict [kənstrikt'] vt zusammenziehen.

constriction [kənstrik'shən] n Zusammenziehung f; (of chest) Zusammenschnürung f, Beklemmung f.

construct [kənstrukt'] *vt* bauen.
construction [kənstruk'shən] *n* (*action*) (Er)bauen *nt*, Konstruktion *f*; (*building*) Bau *m*; (*fig: interpretation*) Deutung *f*; **under** ~ in *or* im Bau.
construction industry *n* Bauindustrie *f*.
constructive [kənstruk'tiv] *a* konstruktiv.
construe [kənstrōō'] *vt* (*interpret*) deuten.
consul [kân'səl] *n* Konsul *m*.
consulate [kân'səlit] *n* Konsulat *nt*.
consult [kənsult'] *vt* um Rat fragen; (*doctor*) konsultieren; (*book*) nachschlagen in (+*dat*); **to** ~ **sb** (**about sth**) jdn (zu etw) konsultieren.
consultancy [kənsul'tənsē] *n* (*act*) Beratung *f*; (*business*) Beratungsbüro *nt*.
consultant [kənsul'tənt] *n* (*MED*) Facharzt *m*; (*other specialist*) Gutachter *m*.
consultation [kânsəltā'shən] *n* Beratung *f*; (*MED*) Konsultation *f*; **in** ~ **with** in gemeinsamer Beratung mit.
consulting room [kənsul'ting rōōm] *n* Sprechzimmer *nt*.
consume [kənsōōm'] *vt* verbrauchen; (*food*) verzehren, konsumieren.
consumer [kənsōō'mûr] *n* Verbraucher(in *f*) *m*.
consumer association *n* Konsumgesellschaft *f*.
consumer credit *n* Verbraucherkredit *m*.
consumer durables *npl* Gebrauchsgüter *pl*, langlebige Konsumgüter *pl*.
consumer goods *npl* Konsumgüter *pl*.
consumerism [kənsōō'mərizəm] *n* Verbraucherschutz *m*.
consummate [kân'səmāt] *vt* vollenden; (*marriage*) vollziehen.
consumption [kənsump'shən] *n* Verbrauch *m*; (*of food*) Konsum *m*; **not fit for human** ~ zum Verzehr ungeeignet.
cont. *abbr* (= *continued*) fortges.
contact [kân'takt] *n* (*touch*) Berührung *f*; (*connection*) Verbindung *f*; (*person*) Kontakt *m*, Beziehung *f* ♦ *vt* sich in Verbindung setzen mit; **business** ~**s** Geschäftsverbindungen *pl*; **to be in** ~ **with sb/sth** (*in communication*) mit jdm/etw in Verbindung *or* Kontakt stehen; (*be touching*) jdn/etw berühren.
contact lenses *npl* Kontaktlinsen *pl*.
contagious [kəntā'jəs] *a* ansteckend.
contain [kəntān'] *vt* enthalten; **to** ~ **o.s.** sich zügeln.
container [kəntā'nûr] *n* Behälter *m*; (*transport*) Container *m*.
containerization [kəntānûrəzā'shən] *n* Containerisierung *f*.
containerize [kəntā'nərīz] *vt* (*freight*) in Container verpacken; (*port*) auf Container umstellen.
contaminate [kəntam'ənāt] *vt* verunreinigen; (*germs*) infizieren.
contamination [kəntamənā'shən] *n* Verunreinigung *f*.
contd. *abbr* (= *continued*) fortges.

contemplate [kân'təmplāt] *vt* (*nachdenklich*) betrachten; (*think about*) überdenken; (*plan*) vorhaben.
contemplation [kântəmplā'shən] *n* Betrachtung *f*; (*REL*) Meditation *f*.
contemporary [kəntem'pərärē] *a* zeitgenössisch ♦ *n* (*of the same age*) Altersgenosse *m*/-genossin *f*.
contempt [kəntempt'] *n* Verachtung *f*; ~ **of court** (*JUR*) Mißachtung *f* (der Würde) des Gerichts, Ungebühr *f* vor Gericht.
contemptible [kəntemp'təbəl] *a* verachtenswert, verächtlich.
contemptuous [kəntemp'chōōəs] *a* voller Verachtung (*of* für).
contend [kəntend'] *vt* (*fight*) kämpfen (um); (*argue*) behaupten; **he has a lot to** ~ **with** er muß mit viel fertigwerden.
contender [kəntend'ûr] *n* (*for post*) Bewerber(in *f*) *m*; (*SPORT*) Wettkämpfer(in *f*) *m*.
content [kəntent'] *a* zufrieden ♦ *vt* befriedigen; **to** ~ **o.s. with sth/with doing sth** sich mit etw zufriedengeben *or* begnügen/sich damit zufriedengeben *or* begnügen, etw zu tun ♦ *n* [kân'tent] (*also:* ~**s**) Inhalt *m*.
contented [kəntent'tid] *a*, **contentedly** [kəntent'tidlē] *ad* zufrieden.
contention [kəntent'shən] *n* (*dispute*) Streit *m*; (*argument*) Behauptung *f*; **bone of** ~ Zankapfel *m*.
contentious [kəntent'shəs] *a* strittig.
contentment [kəntent'mənt] *n* Zufriedenheit *f*.
contest *n* [kân'test] (Wett)kampf *m* ♦ [kəntest'] (*dispute*) bestreiten; (*JUR*) anfechten; (*election, seat*) kämpfen um.
contestant [kəntes'tənt] *n* Bewerber(in *f*) *m*.
context [kân'tekst] *n* Zusammenhang *m*; **in/out of** ~ im Zusammenhang/aus dem Zusammenhang gerissen.
continent [kân'tinənt] *n* Kontinent *m*, Festland *nt*; **the C**~ das europäische Festland, der Kontinent; **on the C**~ in Europa, auf dem Kontinent.
continental [kântənen'təl] *a* kontinental ♦ *n* Bewohner(in *f*) *m* des Kontinents.
continental breakfast *n* kleine(s) Frühstück *nt*.
continental quilt *n* (*Brit*) Steppdecke *f*.
contingency [kəntin'jənsē] *n* Möglichkeit *f*.
contingent [kəntin'jənt] *n* (*MIL*) Kontingent *nt* ♦ *a* abhängig (*upon* von).
continual [kəntin'yōōəl] *a* (*endless*) fortwährend; (*repeated*) immer wiederkehrend.
continually [kəntin'yōōəlē] *ad* immer wieder.
continuation [kəntinyōōā'shən] *n* Fortsetzung *f*.
continue [kəntin'yōō] *vi* (*go on*) anhalten; (*last*) fortbestehen ♦ *vt* fortsetzen; **shall we** ~? wollen wir weitermachen?; **if this** ~**s** wenn das so weitergeht; **the rain** ~**d** es regnete weiter; ~**d on page 10** Fortsetzung auf Seite 10; **to** ~ **doing sth** fortfahren, etw zu tun.

continuing education [kəntin'yōoing ejōōkā'shən] n Weiter- or Fortbildung f.
continuity [kântənōō'itē] n Kontinuität nt; (wholeness) Zusammenhang m; (CINE) Anschluß m.
continuous [kəntin'yōōəs] a ununterbrochen; ~ **performance** (CINE) durchgehende Vorstellung f.
continuously [kəntin'yōōəslē] ad (repeatedly) dauernd, ständig; (uninterruptedly) ununterbrochen.
contort [kəntôrt'] vt verdrehen.
contortion [kəntôr'shən] n Verzerrung f.
contortionist [kəntôr'shənist] n Schlangenmensch m.
contour [kân'tōōr] n Umriß m; (height) Höhenlinie f.
contraband [kân'trəband] n Schmuggelware f ♦ a Schmuggel-.
contraception [kântrəsep'shən] n Empfängnisverhütung f.
contraceptive [kântrəsep'tiv] n empfängnisverhütende(s) Mittel nt ♦ a empfängnisverhütend.
contract [kân'trakt] n (agreement) Vertrag m, Kontrakt m; ~ **of employment** Arbeitsvertrag m; ~ **of service** Dienstvertrag m; **to be under** ~ **to do sth** unter Vertrag stehen, etw zu tun ♦ cpd (work) Kontrakt-; (price, date) vertraglich festgelegt or vereinbart ♦ vi [kən'trakt'] (to do sth) sich vertraglich verpflichten; (muscle) sich zusammenziehen; (become smaller) schrumpfen.
contraction [kəntrak'shən] n (shortening) Verkürzung f.
contractor [kân'traktûr] n Unternehmer m; (supplier) Lieferant m.
contractual [kəntrak'chōōəl] a vertraglich.
contradict [kântrədikt'] vt widersprechen (+dat).
contradiction [kântrədik'shən] n Widerspruch m; **to be in** ~ **with** ... im Widerspruch stehen zu ...
contradictory [kântrədik'tûrē] a widersprüchlich; **to be** ~ **to sth** einer Sache (dat) widersprechen, zu etw im Widerspruch stehen.
contralto [kəntral'tō] n (tiefe) Altstimme f.
contraption [kəntrap'shən] n (col) komische Konstruktion f, komische(s) Ding nt.
contrary [kân'trärē] a entgegengesetzt; (wind) ungünstig, Gegen-; (obstinate) widerspenstig, eigensinnig ♦ n Gegenteil nt; ~ **to what we thought** ganz im Gegenteil zu dem, was wir dachten; **on the** ~ im Gegenteil.
contrast n [kân'trast] Kontrast m ♦ vt [kəntrast'] entgegensetzen; **in** ~ **to** or **with** im Gegensatz/in Kontrast zu.
contrasting [kəntras'ting] a Kontrast-.
contravene [kântrəvēn'] vt verstoßen gegen.
contravention [kântrəven'shən] n Verstoß m (of gegen), Verletzung f (of gen).
contribute [kəntrib'yōōt] vti (in discussion) beitragen; (money) spenden.

contribution [kântrəbyōō'shən] n Beitrag m.
contributor [kəntrib'yətûr] n Beitragende(r) mf.
contributory [kəntrib'yətôrē] a: **a** ~ **cause of a disease** ein Faktor, der zu einer Krankheit beiträgt; ~ **pension** beitragspflichtige Pension f.
contrite [kəntrīt'] a zerknirscht.
contrivance [kəntrī'vəns] n (machine, device) Gerät nt, Apparat m.
contrive [kəntrīv'] vt zustande bringen; **to** ~ **to do sth** es schaffen, etw zu tun.
control [kəntrōl'] vt (direct, test) kontrollieren; (disease, fire) unter Kontrolle bringen ♦ n Kontrolle f; (business) Leitung f; **out of** ~ außer Kontrolle; **under** ~ unter Kontrolle; **to** ~ **o.s.** sich beherrschen, sich zusammennehmen (col); **everything is under** ~ wir haben die Sache im Griff (col); **the car went out of** ~ der Wagen war nicht mehr zu halten; see also **controls**.
control group n (MED, PSYCH etc) Vergleichsgruppe f.
control key n (COMPUT) nichtschreibende Taste f, Funktionstaste f.
controller [kəntrō'lûr] n (RAD, TV) Intendant(in f) m; (AVIAT) (Flug)lotse m.
controlling [kəntrō'ling] a: ~ **interest** Mehrheitsanteil m.
control panel n (on aircraft, ship, TV etc) Bedienungsfeld nt.
control point n Kontrollstelle f.
control room n (NAUT) Kommandoraum m; (RAD, TV) Kontrollraum m; (MIL) (Operations)zentrale f.
controls [kəntrōlz'] npl (of vehicle) Steuerung f; (of engine) Schalttafel f.
control tower n (AVIAT) Kontrollturm m.
control unit n (COMPUT) Steuereinheit f.
controversial [kântrəvûr'shəl] a umstritten, kontrovers.
controversy [kân'trəvûrsē] n Meinungsstreit m, Kontroverse f.
conurbation [kânûrbā'shən] n Ballungsgebiet nt or -raum m or -zentrum nt.
convalesce [kânvəles'] vi gesund werden.
convalescence [kânvəles'əns] n Genesung f.
convalescent [kânvəles'ənt] a auf dem Wege der Besserung ♦ n Genesende(r) mf.
convector [kənvek'tûr] n Heizlüfter m.
convene [kənvēn'] vt (meeting) einberufen ♦ vi sich versammeln.
convenience [kənvēn'yəns] n Annehmlichkeit f; (thing) bequeme Einrichtung f; **at your earliest** ~ (COMM) möglichst bald, baldmöglichst (form); see **public convenience**.
convenience foods npl Fertiggerichte pl.
convenient [kənvēn'yənt] a günstig; **if it is** ~ **for you** wenn es Ihnen (so) paßt, wenn es Ihnen keine Umstände macht.
conveniently [kənvēn'yəntlē] ad (happen) günstigerweise; (situated) günstig, vorteilhaft.
convent [kân'vent] n Kloster nt.

convention [kənven'shən] n Versammlung f; (POL) Übereinkunft f; (custom) Konvention f.
conventional [kənven'shənəl] a herkömmlich, konventionell.
converge [kənvûrj'] vi zusammenlaufen.
conversant [kənvûr'sənt] a vertraut (with mit); (in learning) bewandert (with in +dat).
conversation [kânvûrsā'shən] n Unterhaltung f.
conversational [kânvûrsā'shənəl] a Unterhaltungs-.
conversational mode n (COMPUT) Dialogbetrieb m.
converse vi [kənvûrs'] sich unterhalten; **to ~ with sb about sth** ein Gespräch mit jdm über etw führen ♦ a [kân'vûrs] gegenteilig.
conversely [kənvûrs'lē] ad umgekehrt.
conversion [kənvûr'zhən] n Umwandlung f; (esp REL) Bekehrung f; (Brit: house ~) Umbau m.
conversion table n Umrechnungstabelle f.
convert vt [kənvûrt'] (change) umwandeln; (REL) bekehren ♦ n [kân'vûrt] (lit, fig) Bekehrte(r) mf; (to another denomination) Konvertit(in f) m.
convertible [kənvûr'təbəl] n (AUT) Kabriolett nt ♦ a umwandelbar; (FIN) konvertierbar; ~ **loan stock** konvertierbare(r) Anleihestock m.
convex [kânveks'] a konvex.
convey [kənvā'] vt (carry) befördern; (feelings) vermitteln.
conveyance [kənvā'əns] n (of goods) Beförderung f, Spedition f; (vehicle) Gefährt nt.
conveyancing [kənvā'ənsing] n (JUR) (Eigentums)übertragung f.
conveyor belt [kənvā'ûr belt] n Förderband nt.
convict vt [kənvikt'] verurteilen ♦ n [kân'vikt] Häftling m.
conviction [kənvik'shən] n (verdict) Verurteilung f; (belief) Überzeugung f.
convince [kənvins'] vt überzeugen; **to ~ sb (of sth)** jdn (von etw) überzeugen; **to ~ sb that ...** jdn überzeugen, daß ...
convinced [kənvinst'] a: ~ **that** überzeugt davon, daß ...
convincing [kənvin'sing] a, **convincingly** [kənvin'singlē] ad überzeugend.
convivial [kənviv'ēəl] a festlich, froh.
convoluted [kân'vəlōōtid] a (shape) gewunden, verwickelt; (argument) kompliziert, umständlich.
convoy [kân'voi] n (of vehicles) Kolonne f; (protected) Konvoi m.
convulse [kənvuls'] vt zusammenzucken lassen; **to be ~d with laughter** sich vor Lachen krümmen.
convulsion [kənvul'shən] n (esp MED) Zuckung f, Krampf m.
coo [kōō] vi (dove) gurren.
cook [kōōk] vti (meal) kochen ♦ n Koch m,

Köchin f.
cook up vt (col: excuse, story) sich (dat) einfallen lassen, zurechtbasteln.
cookbook [kōōk'bōōk] n Kochbuch nt.
cooker [kōōk'ûr] n Herd m, Kocher m.
cookery [kōōk'ûrē] n Kochkunst f.
cookery book n (Brit) = **cookbook**.
cookie [kōōk'ē] n (US) Plätzchen nt.
cooking [kōōk'ing] n Kochen nt ♦ cpd (apples, utensils, salt) Koch-.
cooking chocolate n Blockschokolade f.
cooking foil n Backfolie f.
cookout [kōōk'out] n (US) Kochen nt am Lagerfeuer.
cool [kōōl] a kühl ♦ vti (ab)kühlen; **it is ~** (weather) es ist kühl; **to keep sth ~** or **in a ~ place** etw kühl aufbewahren.
cool down vi abkühlen; (fig: person, situation) abkühlen, sich beruhigen; (weather) sich abkühlen.
cool box [kōōl bâks] n (Brit) Kühlbox f.
coolie [kōō'lē] n Kuli m.
cooling tower [kōō'ling tou'ûr] n Kühlturm m.
coolly [kōō'lē] ad (audaciously) kaltblütig, unverfroren, cool; (calmly) ruhig, gefaßt, besonnen; (unenthusiastically) kühl.
coolness [kōōl'nis] n Kühle f; (of temperament) kühle(r) Kopf m.
coop [kōōp] n Hühnerstall m.
coop up vt (fig) einpferchen.
co-op [kō'âp] n abbr (= cooperative) Coop m.
cooperate [kōâp'ərāt] vi zusammenarbeiten; **will he ~?** wird er mitmachen?
cooperation [kōâpərā'shən] n Zusammenarbeit f.
cooperative [kōâp'rətiv] a hilfsbereit; (COMM) genossenschaftlich ♦ n (of farmers) Genossenschaft f; (~ store) Konsumladen m.
co-opt [kōâpt'] vt: **he was ~ed onto the committee** er wurde vom Komitee selbst dazugewählt.
coordinate vt [kōôr'dənāt] koordinieren ♦ n [kōôr'dənit] (MATH) Koordinate f.
coordinates [kōôr'dənits] npl (clothes) Kombinationen pl.
coordination [kōôrdənā'shən] n Koordination f.
coot [kōōt] n Wasserhuhn nt.
co-ownership [kōō'nûrship] n Miteigentum nt.
cop [kâp] n (col) Polyp m, Bulle m.
cope [kōp] vi: **to ~ with** fertig werden mit.
Copenhagen [kōpenhā'gən] n Kopenhagen nt.
copilot [kōpi'lət] n Kopilot m.
copious [kō'pēəs] a reichhaltig.
copper [kâp'ûr] n (metal) Kupfer nt; (coin) Kupfermünze f; (col: policeman) Polyp m, Bulle m.
copse [kâps] n Unterholz nt.
copulate [kâp'yəlāt] vi sich paaren.
copy [kâp'ē] n (imitation) Nachahmung f; (of book etc) Exemplar nt; (of newspaper)

Nummer *f*; *(material: for printing)* Artikel *m*; **this murder story will make good ~** aus diesem Mord kann man etwas machen ♦ *vt (imitate)* nachmachen, nachahmen; *(COMPUT)* kopieren.

copy out *vt* abschreiben.

copycat [kâp'ĕkat] *n* Nachäffer *m*.

copyright [kâp'ĕrīt] *n* Copyright *nt*; **~ reserved** alle Rechte vorbehalten, Nachdruck verboten.

copy typist *n* Schreibkraft *f*.

coral [kôr'əl] *n* Koralle *f*.

coral reef *n* Korallenriff *nt*.

Coral Sea *n* Korallensee *f*.

cord [kôrd] *n* Schnur *f*, Kordel *f*; *(ELEC)* Schnur *f*; *see* **vocal cord.**

cordial [kôr'jəl] *a* herzlich ♦ *n* Fruchtsaft *m*.

cordially [kôr'jəlē] *ad* herzlich.

cordon [kôr'dən] *n* Absperrkette *f*.

cordon off *vt* absperren.

cords [kôrdz] *npl (trousers)* Kordhosen *pl*.

corduroy [kôr'dəroi] *n* Kord(samt) *m*.

core [kôr] *n* Kern *m*; *(nuclear reactor)* Core *nt* ♦ *vt* entkernen; **the ~ of the earth** das Erdinnere.

CORE *n abbr (US: = Congress of Racial Equality)* Kongreß gegen Rassendiskriminierung.

coriander [kôrēan'dûr] *n* Koriander *m*.

cork [kôrk] *n (bark)* Korkrinde *f*; *(stopper)* Korken *m*.

corked [kôrkt] *a (wine)* nach Kork schmeckend.

corkscrew [kôrk'skrōō] *n* Korkenzieher *m*.

corm [kôrm] *n* Knolle *f*.

cormorant [kôr'mûrənt] *n* Kormoran *m*.

corn [kôrn] *n (US: maize)* Mais *m*; *(Brit: wheat)* Getreide *nt*, Korn *nt*; *(on foot)* Hühnerauge *nt*.

cornea [kôr'nēə] *n* Hornhaut *f*.

corned beef [kôrnd bēf] *n* Corned Beef *nt*.

corner [kôr'nûr] *n* Ecke *f*; *(nook)* Winkel *m*; *(on road)* Kurve *f*; *(SOCCER)* Ecke *f*, Eckball *m* ♦ *vt* in die Enge treiben ♦ *vi (AUT)* in die Kurve gehen; **to cut ~s** *(fig)* das Verfahren abkürzen.

corner flag *n* Eckfahne *f*.

corner kick *n* Eckball *m*.

cornerstone [kôr'nûrstōn] *n* Eckstein *m*.

cornet [kôrnet'] *n (MUS)* Kornett *nt*; *(Brit: for ice cream)* Eistüte *f*.

cornflakes [kôrn'flāks] *npl* Corn-flakes *pl*.

cornflour [kôrn'flouûr] *n (Brit)* Maizena ® *nt*, Maisstärke *f*.

cornice [kôr'nis] *n* Gesims *nt*.

Cornish [kôr'nish] *a* kornisch, aus Cornwall.

corn oil *n* (Mais)keimöl *nt*.

cornstarch [kôrn'stârch] *n (US)* Maizena ® *nt*, Maisstärke *f*.

cornucopia [kôrnəkō'pēə] *n* Füllhorn *nt*.

Cornwall [kôr'nwôl] *n* Cornwall *nt*.

corny [kôr'nē] *a (joke)* blöd(e).

corollary [kôr'əlārē] *n* Folgesatz *m*.

coronary [kôr'ənārē] *a (MED)* Koronar- ♦ *n* Herzinfarkt *m*.

coronary thrombosis *n* Koronarthrombose *f*.

coronation [kôrənā'shən] *n* Krönung *f*.

coroner [kôr'ənûr] *n* Untersuchungsrichter *m* und Leichenbeschauer *m*.

coronet [kôr'ənit] *n* Adelskrone *f*.

Corp. *abbr (US: = corporation)* Ges.

corporal [kôr'pûrəl] *n (MIL)* Obergefreite(r) *m*.

corporal punishment *n* Prügelstrafe *f*.

corporate [kôr'pərit] *a* gemeinschaftlich, korporativ; **~ identity** *or* **image** Firmenimage *nt*; **~ planning** Unternehmensplanung *f*.

corporation [kôrpərā'shən] *n* Gemeinde *f*, Stadt *f*; *(esp business)* Körperschaft *f*, Aktiengesellschaft *f*.

corps [kôr] *n* (Armee)korps *nt*; **press ~** Presse *f*.

corpse [kôrps] *n* Leiche *f*.

corpulent [kôr'pyələnt] *a* korpulent.

Corpus Christi [kôr'pəs kris'tē] *n* Fronleichnamsfest *nt*.

corpuscle [kôr'pəsəl] *n* Blutkörperchen *nt*.

corral [kəral'] *n* Pferch *m*, Korral *m*.

correct [kərekt'] *a (accurate)* richtig; *(proper)* korrekt ♦ *vt (mistake)* berichtigen; *(pupil)* tadeln; **you are ~** Sie haben recht.

correction [kərek'shən] *n* Berichtigung *f*.

correctly [kərekt'lē] *ad* richtig; korrekt.

correlate [kôr'əlāt] *vt* aufeinander beziehen ♦ *vi* korrelieren; **to ~ with sth** mit etw in Beziehung stehen.

correlation [kôrəlā'shən] *n* Wechselbeziehung *f*.

correspond [kôrəspând'] *vi* übereinstimmen; *(exchange letters)* korrespondieren.

correspondence [kôrəspân'dəns] *n (similarity)* Entsprechung *f*; *(exchanging letters)* Briefwechsel *m*, Korrespondenz *f*.

correspondence column *n* Leserbriefspalte *f*.

correspondence course *n* Fernkurs *m*.

correspondent [kôrəspân'dənt] *n (PRESS)* Berichterstatter *m*.

corresponding [kôrəspân'ding] *a* entsprechend, gemäß *(to dat)*.

corridor [kôr'idûr] *n* Gang *m*.

corroborate [kərâb'ərāt] *vt* bestätigen, erhärten.

corroboration [kərâbərā'shən] *n* Bekräftigung *f*.

corrode [kərōd'] *vt* zerfressen ♦ *vi* rosten.

corrosion [kərō'zhən] *n* Korrosion *f*.

corrosive [kərō'siv] *a* korrosiv.

corrugated [kôr'əgātid] *a* gewellt.

corrugated cardboard *n* Wellpappe *f*.

corrugated iron *n* Wellblech *nt*.

corrupt [kərupt'] *a* korrupt ♦ *vt* verderben; *(bribe)* bestechen; *(data)* korrumpieren, verstümmeln; **~ practices** *(dishonesty, bribery)* korrupte Praktiken *pl*, dunkle Machenschaften *pl*.

corruption [kərup'shən] *n (of society)* Ver-

dorbenheit *f*; (*bribery*) Bestechung *f*; (*of data*) Korrumpierung *f*.
corset [kôr'sit] *n* Korsett *nt*.
Corsica [kôr'sikə] *n* Korsika *nt*.
Corsican [kôr'sikən] *a* korsisch ♦ *n* Korse *m*, Korsin *f*.
cortège [kôrtezh'] *n* Zug *m*; (*of funeral*) Leichenzug *m*.
cortisone [kôr'tisōn] *n* Kortison *nt*.
cosh [kâsh] (*Brit*) *n* Totschläger *m* ♦ *vt* über den Schädel hauen.
cosignatory [kōsig'nətôrē] *n* Mitunterzeichner(in *f*) *m*.
cosine [kō'sīn] *n* Kosinus *m*.
cosiness [kō'zēnis] *n* (*Brit*) = **coziness**.
cosmetic [kâzmet'ik] *n* Schönheitsmittel *nt*, kosmetische(s) Mittel *nt* ♦ *a* kosmetisch.
cosmic [kâz'mik] *a* kosmisch.
cosmonaut [kâz'mənôt] *n* Kosmonaut(in *f*) *m*.
cosmopolitan [kâzməpâl'itən] *a* international; (*city*) Welt-.
cosmos [kâz'məs] *n* Weltall *nt*, Kosmos *m*.
cosset [kâs'it] *vt* verwöhnen.
cost [kôst] *n* Kosten *pl*, Preis *m* ♦ *vt irreg pt, pp cost* kosten; ~**s** (*JUR*) Kosten *pl*; **at all** ~**s** um jeden Preis; **how much does it** ~? was kostet das?; **what will it** ~ **to have it repaired?** wieviel kostet die Reparatur?; **it** ~ **him his life/job** es kostete ihm sein Leben/seine Stelle.
cost accountant *n* Kalkulator *m*.
co-star [kō'stâr] *n* zweite(r) *or* weitere(r) Hauptdarsteller(in *f*) *m*.
Costa Rica [kâs'tə rē'kə] *n* Costa Rica *nt*.
cost-benefit analysis [kôstben'əfit ənal'isis] *n* Kostennutzenanalyse *f*.
cost center *n* Kostenstelle *f*.
cost control *n* Kostenkontrolle *f*.
cost-effective [kôstifek'tiv] *a* (*gen*) kosteneffektiv, kostengünstig; (*COMM*) rentabel.
cost-effectiveness [kôstifek'tivnis] *n* Kostenrentabilität *f*.
costing [kôs'ting] *n* (*Brit*) Kalkulation *f*.
costly [kôst'lē] *a* kostspielig.
cost of living *n* Lebenshaltungskosten *pl*.
cost-of-living index [kôstəvliv'ing in'deks] *n* Lebenshaltungskostenindex *m*.
cost price *n* Selbstkostenpreis *m*.
costume [kâs'tōōm] *n* Kostüm *nt*; (*fancy dress*) Maskenkostüm *nt*; (*Brit: for bathing*) Badeanzug *m*.
costume jewelry *n* Modeschmuck *m*.
costume party *n* (*US*) Maskenball *m*.
cosy [kō'zē] *a* (*Brit*) = **cozy**.
cot [kât] *n* (*US*) Feldbett *nt*; (*Brit*) Kinderbett(chen) *nt*.
cottage [kât'ij] *n* kleine(s) Haus *nt* (auf dem Land).
cottage cheese *n* Hüttenkäse *m*.
cottage industry *n* Manufaktur *f*, Heimindustrie *f*.
cottage pie *n* Auflauf *m* mit Hackfleisch und Kartoffelbrei.

cotton [kât'ən] *n* (*material*) Baumwollstoff *m*; (*MED*) Watte *f* ♦ *a* (*dress etc*) Baumwoll-.
cotton on to *vt fus*: **to** ~ **on to sth** (*col*) kapieren, schnallen (*col*).
cotton candy *n* (*US*) Zuckerwatte *f*.
cotton wool *n* (*Brit*) Watte *f*.
couch [kouch] *n* (*also PSYCH*) Couch *f* ♦ *vt* (in Worte) fassen, formulieren.
couchette [kōōshet'] *n* (*on train, boat*) Liegewagen(platz) *m*.
cougar [kōō'gûr] *n* Puma *m*.
cough [kôf] *vi* husten ♦ *n* Husten *m*.
cough drop *n* Hustenbonbon *nt*.
cough syrup *n* Hustensaft *m*.
could [kōōd] *pt of* **can**.
couldn't [kōōd'ənt] = **could not**.
council [koun'səl] *n* (*of town*) Stadtrat *m*; **C~ of Europe** Europarat *m*.
council estate *n* (*Brit*) Siedlung *f* des sozialen Wohnungsbaus.
council house *n* (*Brit*) Haus *nt* des sozialen Wohnungsbaus.
councilor, (*Brit*) **councillor** [koun'səlûr] *n* Stadtrat *m*.
counsel [koun'səl] *n* (*barrister*) Anwalt *m*, Rechtsbeistand *m*; (*advice*) Rat(schlag) *m* ♦ *vt*: **to** ~ **sth/sb to do sth** etw empfehlen *or* raten/jdm empfehlen *or* raten, etw zu tun; ~ **for the defense/the prosecution** Verteidiger(in *f*) *m*/Vertreter(in *f*) *m* der Anklage.
counselor, (*Brit*) **counsellor** [koun'səlûr] *n* Berater *m*; (*US: lawyer*) Rechtsanwalt *m*/-anwältin *f*.
count [kount] *vti* (*MATH etc*) zählen ♦ *vi* (*be important*) zählen, gelten ♦ *n* (*reckoning*) Abrechnung *f*; (*nobleman*) Graf *m*; **to** ~ (**up**) **to 10** bis 10 zählen; **to** ~ **the cost of** (*sth*) auf die Kosten für (etw) achten; **not** ~**ing the children** die Kinder nicht mitgerechnet *or* eingerechnet; **10** ~**ing him** 10, ihn mitgerechnet, mit ihm 10; ~ **yourself lucky** Sie können sich glücklich schätzen; **it** ~**s for very little** es spielt keine große Rolle; **to keep** ~ **of sth** etw mitzählen; (*keep track*) die Übersicht über etw behalten.
count on *vt fus* (*depend on*) zählen auf (+*acc*); **to** ~ **on doing sth** (*intend*) die Absicht haben, etw zu tun.
count up *vt* zusammenzählen.
countdown [kount'doun] *n* Countdown *m*.
counter [koun'tûr] *n* (*in shop*) Ladentisch *m*; (*in café*) Tresen *m*, Theke *f*; (*in bank, post office*) Schalter *m*; (*in game*) Spielmarke *f*; (*TECH*) Zähler *m* ♦ *vt* entgegnen ♦ *ad* entgegen; **to buy under the** ~ (*fig*) unter dem Ladentisch bekommen; **to** ~ **sth with sth** auf etw mit etw antworten.
counteract [kountûrakt'] *vt* entgegenwirken (+*dat*).
counter-attack [koun'tûrətak] *n* Gegenangriff *m*.
counterbalance [koun'tûrbaləns] *vt* aufwiegen.

counterclockwise [kountûrklåk'wīz] *ad* entgegen dem Uhrzeigersinn.

counterespionage [kountûres'pēənâzh] *n* Spionageabwehr *f*.

counterfeit [koun'tûrfit] *n* Fälschung *f* ♦ *vt* fälschen ♦ *a* gefälscht, unecht.

counterfoil [koun'tûrfoil] *n* (Kontroll)abschnitt *m*.

counterintelligence [kountûrintel'ijəns] *n* = **counterespionage**.

countermand [kountûrmand'] *vt* aufheben, widerrufen.

countermeasure [koun'tûrmezhûr] *n* Gegenmaßnahme *f*.

counteroffensive [kountûrəfen'siv] *n* Gegenoffensive *f*.

counterpane [koun'tûrpān] *n* Tagesdecke *f*.

counterpart [koun'tûrpârt] *n* (*object*) Gegenstück *nt*; (*person*) Gegenüber *nt*.

counterproductive [kountûrprəduk'tiv] *a* unsinnig, widersinnig.

counterproposal [koun'tûrprəpōzəl] *n* Gegenvorschlag *m*.

countersign [koun'tûrsīn] *vt* gegenzeichnen.

countess [koun'tis] *n* Gräfin *f*.

countless [kount'lis] *a* zahllos, unzählig.

countrified [kun'trəfid] *a* ländlich.

country [kun'trē] *n* Land *nt*; **in the ~** auf dem Land(e); **mountainous ~** gebirgige Landschaft *f*.

country-and-western (music) [kuntrēənwes'tûrn (myōō'zik)] *n* Country- und Westernmusik *f*.

country dancing *n* (*Brit*) Volkstanz *m*.

country house *n* Landhaus *nt*.

countryman [kun'trēmən] *n*, *pl* **-men** (*national*) Landsmann *m*; (*rural*) Bauer *m*.

countryside [kun'trēsīd] *n* Landschaft *f*.

country-wide [kun'trēwīd] *a* landesweit.

county [koun'tē] *n* Landkreis *m*; (*Brit*) Grafschaft *f*.

coup [kōō] *n* Coup *m*.

coup d'état [kōō dātā'] *n* Staatsstreich *m*, Putsch *m*.

coupé [kōōpā'] *n* (*AUT*) Coupé *nt*.

couple [kup'əl] *n* Paar *nt*; **a ~ of** ein paar ♦ *vt* koppeln.

couplet [kup'lit] *n* Reimpaar *nt*.

coupling [kup'ling] *n* Kupplung *f*.

coupon [kōō'pän] *n* Gutschein *m*.

courage [kûr'ij] *n* Mut *m*.

courageous [kərā'jəs] *a* mutig.

courgette [kōōrzhet'] *n* (*Brit*) Zucchino *m*.

courier [kûr'ēûr] *n* (*messenger*) Kurier *m*, Eilbote *m*; (*Brit: for vacation*) Reiseleiter *m*.

course [kôrs] *n* (*race*) Strecke *f*, Bahn *f*; (*of stream*) Lauf *m*; (*of action*) Richtung *f*; (*of lectures*) Vortragsreihe *f*; (*of study*) Studiengang *m*; (*NAUT*) Kurs *m*; (*in meal*) Gang *m*; **of ~** natürlich; **(no,) of ~ not!** natürlich nicht!; **in the ~ of** im Laufe (+*gen*); **in due ~** zu gegebener Zeit; **summer ~** Sommerkurs *m*; **in the ~ of the next few**

days während der nächsten paar Tage; **the best ~ would be** ... das beste wäre ...; **we have no other ~ but to** ... es bleibt uns nichts anderes übrig als zu ...; **there are 2 ~s open to us** wir haben 2 Alternativen *or* Möglichkeiten; **~ of treatment** (*MED*) Kur *f*; *see* **golf course**.

court [kôrt] *n* (*royal*) Hof *m*; (*JUR*) Gericht *nt* ♦ *vt* gehen mit; (*fig: favor, popularity*) werben um, buhlen um (*pej*); (: *death, disaster*) herausfordern; **~ of appeal** Berufungsgericht *nt*; *see* **tennis court**.

courteous [kûr'tēəs] *a* höflich, zuvorkommend.

courtesan [kôr'tizən] *n* Kurtisane *f*.

courtesy [kûr'tisē] *n* Höflichkeit *f*; **by ~ of** freundlicherweise zur Verfügung gestellt von.

courtesy bus *n* gebührenfreie(r) Bus *m*.

courtesy light *n* (*AUT*) Innenleuchte *f*.

courthouse [kôrt'hous] *n* (*US*) Gerichtsgebäude *nt*.

courtier [kôr'tēûr] *n* Höfling *m*.

court-martial [kôrt'mâr'shəl] *n* Kriegsgericht *nt* ♦ *vt* vor ein Kriegsgericht stellen.

courtroom [kôrt'rōōm] *n* Gerichtssaal *m*.

court shoe *n* (*Brit*) Pumps *m*.

courtyard [kôrt'yârd] *n* Hof *m*.

cousin [kuz'in] *n* Cousin *m*, Vetter *m*; (*female*) Kusine *f*.

cove [kōv] *n* kleine Bucht *f*.

covenant [kuv'ənənt] *n* feierliche(s) Abkommen *nt* ♦ *vt*: **to ~ $20 per year to a charity** sich vertraglich verpflichten, 20 Dollar im Jahr für wohltätige Zwecke zu spenden.

Coventry [kuv'intrē] *n*: **to send sb to ~** (*fig*) jdn schneiden (*col*).

cover [kuv'ûr] *vt* (*spread over*) bedecken; (*shield*) abschirmen; (*include*) sich erstrecken über (+*acc*); (*protect*) decken; (*distance*) zurücklegen; (*PRESS: report on*) berichten über (+*acc*) ♦ *n* (*lid*) Deckel *m*; (*for bed*) Decke *f*; (*MIL*) Bedeckung *f*; (*INSURANCE*) Versicherung *f*; **$10 will ~ everything** 10 Dollar reichen für alles; **to take ~** (*from gunfire etc*) in Deckung gehen; (*from rain*) sich unterstellen; **under ~ of** in Schutze (+*gen*); **under separate ~** (*COMM*) mit getrennter Post.

cover up *vt* (*hide: truth, feelings*) vertuschen, verheimlichen; **to ~ up (with)** zudecken (mit).

cover up for *vt fus*: **to ~ up for sb** (*fig*) jdn decken.

coverage [kuv'ûrij] *n* (*PRESS: reports*) Berichterstattung *f*; (*distribution*) Verbreitung *f*; (*INSURANCE*) Versicherung *f*.

coveralls [kuv'ûrôlz] *npl* (*US*) Overall *m*.

cover charge *n* Bedienungsgeld *nt*.

covering [kuv'ûring] *n* Bedeckung *f*.

cover letter, (*Brit*) **covering letter** *n* Begleitbrief *m*.

cover note *n* (*INSURANCE*) Deckungszusage *f*.

cover price n Einzelexemplarpreis m.
covert [kō'vûrt] a geheim.
cover-up [kuv'ûrup] n Vertuschung f, Verschleierung f.
covet [kuv'it] vt begehren.
covetous [kuv'ətəs] a begehrlich.
cow [kou] n Kuh f ♦ vt einschüchtern.
coward [kou'ûrd] n Feigling m.
cowardice [kou'ûrdis] n Feigheit f.
cowardly [kou'ûrdlē] a feige.
cowboy [kou'boi] n Cowboy m.
cower [kou'ûr] vi kauern.
co-worker [kōwûr'kûr] n Mitarbeiter(in f) m.
cowshed [kou'shed] n Kuhstall m.
cowslip [kou'slip] n (BOT) Schlüsselblume f.
coxswain [kâk'sin] n (abbr cox) Steuermann m.
coy [koi] a schüchtern; (girl) spröde.
coyote [kīōt'ē] n Präriewolf m.
coziness [kō'zēnis] n (US) Gemütlichkeit f.
cozy [kō'zē] a (US: room, atmosphere) gemütlich, behaglich.
cp. abbr (= compare) vgl.
c/p abbr (Brit: = carriage paid) frfr.
CP n abbr (= Communist Party) KP f.
CPA n abbr (US) = **certified public accountant**.
CPI n abbr (= Consumer Price Index) Preisindex.
Cpl. n abbr (= corporal) Uffz.
CP/M n abbr (= Central Program for Microprocessors) CP/M.
c.p.s. abbr (= characters per second) Zeichen pro Sekunde.
CPU n abbr (COMPUT: = central processing unit) ZE f.
cr. abbr = **credit; creditor**.
crab [krab] n Krebs m.
crab apple n Holzapfel m.
crab meat n Krabbenfleisch nt.
crack [krak] n Riß m, Sprung m; (noise) Knall m; (drugs) Crack nt; **to have a ~ at sth** (col: attempt) etw mal (aus)probieren ♦ vt (break) springen lassen; (case: solve) lösen; (code) knacken; **to ~ jokes** (col) Witze reißen ♦ vi (break) springen; (noise) krachen, knallen ♦ a erstklassig; (troops) Elite-.
crack down on vt fus hart durchgreifen gegen.
crack up vi (fig) zusammenbrechen.
crackdown [krak'doun] n gewaltsame(s) scharfe(s) Durchgreifen nt.
cracker [krak'ûr] n (firework) Knallkörper m, Kracher m; (biscuit) leichtgewürzte(s) Kleingebäck nt; (Christmas ~) Knallbonbon nt.
crackle [krak'əl] vi knistern; (fire) prasseln.
crackling [krak'ling] n Knistern n; (rind) Kruste f (des Schweinebratens); (on radio, telephone) Störung f.
cradle [krā'dəl] n Wiege f ♦ vt (object) an sich (acc) drücken; (child) fest in den Armen or auf dem Schoß halten.
craft [kraft] n (skill) (Hand- or

Kunst)fertigkeit f; (trade) Handwerk nt; (cunning) Verschlagenheit f; (NAUT) Fahrzeug nt, Schiff nt.
craftsman [krafts'mən] n, pl **-men** gelernte(r) Handwerker m.
craftsmanship [krafts'mənship] n (quality) handwerkliche Ausführung f; (ability) handwerkliche(s) Können nt.
crafty [kraf'tē] a schlau, gerieben.
crag [krag] n Klippe f.
craggy [krag'ē] a schroff, felsig.
cram [kram] vt vollstopfen; (col: teach) einpauken ♦ vi (col: learn) pauken.
cramp [kramp] n Krampf m ♦ vt (hinder) einengen, hemmen.
crampon [kram'pân] n Steigeisen nt.
cranberry [kran'bärē] n Preiselbeere f.
crane [krān] n (machine) Kran m; (bird) Kranich m ♦ vti: **to ~ forward, to ~ one's neck** den Hals or den Kopf recken.
cranium [krā'nēəm] n Schädel m.
crank [krangk] n (lever) Kurbel f; (person) Spinner m ♦ vt ankurbeln.
crankshaft [krangk'shaft] n Kurbelwelle f.
cranny [kran'ē] n Ritze f.
crap [krap] n (col) Mist m, Scheiße f.
craps [kraps] n (US) Würfelspiel nt.
crash [krash] n (noise) Krachen nt; (with cars) Zusammenstoß m; (with plane) Absturz m; (of business, economy) Zusammenbruch m ♦ vi stürzen; (cars) zusammenstoßen; (plane) abstürzen; (economy) zusammenbrechen; (noise) knallen ♦ vt: **he ~ed the car into a wall** er ist mit dem Wagen gegen die Mauer gefahren ♦ a (course) Schnell-.
crash barrier n (AUT) Leitplanke f.
crash course n Schnellkurs m.
crash helmet n Sturzhelm m.
crash landing n Bruchlandung f.
crass [kras] a kraß.
crate [krāt] n (lit, fig) Kiste f.
crater [krā'tûr] n Krater m.
cravat(e) [krəvat'] n Krawatte f.
crave [krāv] vt verlangen (for nach).
craving [krā'ving] n Verlangen nt.
crawfish [krô'fish] n (US) = **crayfish**.
crawl [krôl] vi kriechen; (baby) krabbeln ♦ n Kriechen nt; (swim) Kraul nt; **to ~ to sb** (col: suck up) vor jdm kriechen.
crayfish [krā'fish] n (pl inv) (freshwater) Krebs m; (saltwater) Languste f.
crayon [krā'ân] n Buntstift m.
craze [krāz] n Fimmel m.
crazed [krāzd] a (pottery, glaze) rissig; **he had a ~ look on his face** er hatte den Gesichtsausdruck eines Wahnsinnigen.
crazy [krā'zē] a (foolish) verrückt; (insane) wahnsinnig; **to go ~** verrückt or wahnsinnig werden; **to be ~ about sb/sth** ganz verrückt or wild auf jdn/etw sein.
crazy paving n (Brit) Mosaikpflaster nt.
CRC n abbr (US) = Civil Rights Commission.
creak [krēk] n Knarren nt ♦ vi quietschen,

knarren.

cream [krēm] *n* (*from milk*) Rahm *m*, Sahne *f*; (*polish, cosmetic*) Creme *f*; (*color*) Cremefarbe *f*; (*fig: people*) Elite *f*; **whipped** ~ Schlagsahne *f*.

cream cake *n* (*small*) Sahnetörtchen *nt*; (*large*) Sahnekuchen *m*.

cream cheese *n* Rahmquark *m*.

creamery [krē'mûrē] *n* Molkerei *f*.

creamy [krē'mē] *a* sahnig.

crease [krēs] *n* Falte *f* ♦ *vt* falten; (*crumple*) zerknittern.

crease-resistant [krēsrizis'tənt] *a* knitterfrei.

create [krēāt'] *vt* erschaffen; (*cause*) verursachen; (*impression, fuss*) machen; (*COMPUT: file*) anlegen.

creation [krēā'shən] *n* Schöpfung *f*.

creative [krēā'tiv] *a* schöpferisch, kreativ.

creativity [krēātiv'ətē] *n* schöpferische Begabung *f* or Kraft *f*, Kreativität *f*.

creator [krēā'tûr] *n* Schöpfer *m*.

creature [krē'chûr] *n* Geschöpf *nt*.

crèche, creche [kresh] *n* Krippe *f*.

credence [krēd'əns] *n* Glauben *m*.

credentials [kriden'shəlz] *npl* Beglaubigungsschreiben *nt*; (*letters of reference*) (Ausweis)papiere *pl*.

credibility [kredəbil'ətē] *n* Glaubwürdigkeit *f*.

credible [kred'əbəl] *a* (*witness, source*) glaubwürdig; (*story*) glaubhaft.

credit [kred'it] *n* (*COMM*) Kredit *m*, Guthaben *nt*; (*UNIV: esp US*) ≈ Schein *m* ♦ *vt* Glauben schenken (+*dat*); (*COMM*) gutschreiben; **to sb's** ~ zu jds Ehre; **on** ~ auf Kredit; **he's a** ~ **to his family** er macht seiner Familie Ehre; *see also* **credits**.

creditable [kred'itəbəl] *a* rühmlich.

credit account *n* Kreditkonto *nt*.

credit agency *n* Kreditauskunftei *f*.

credit balance *n* Kreditsaldo *m*.

credit card *n* Kreditkarte *f*.

credit control *n* Kreditüberwachung *f*.

credit facilities *npl* Kreditmöglichkeiten *pl*.

credit limit *n* Kreditgrenze *f*.

credit note *n* (*Brit*) Gutschrift *f*.

creditor [kred'itûr] *n* Gläubiger *m*.

credit rating *n* Kreditwürdigkeit *f*.

credits [kred'its] *npl* (*CINE*) die Mitwirkenden.

credit transfer *n* bargeldlose Überweisung *f*.

creditworthy [kred'itwûrthē] *a* kreditwürdig.

creed [krēd] *n* Glaubensbekenntnis *nt*.

creek [krēk] *n* (*inlet*) kleine Bucht *f*; (*US: river*) kleine(r) Wasserlauf *m*.

creel [krēl] *n* (*also:* **lobster** ~) Hummer(fang)korb *m*.

creep [krēp] *vi irreg* kriechen ♦ *n* (*col*): **he's a** ~ er ist ein fieser Typ; **to** ~ **up on sb** sich an jdn heranschleichen; **old age is** ~**ing up on him** (*fig*) er wird langsam alt; **it gives me the** ~**s** es ist mir nicht geheuer, da bekomme ich eine Gänsehaut.

creeper [krē'pûr] *n* (*plant*) Kletterpflanze *f*; (*US AUT*) Räderschlitten *m*.

creepers [krē'pûrz] *npl* (*US: crampons*) Steig-eisen *pl*.

creepy [krē'pē] *a* (*frightening*) gruselig.

creepy-crawly [krē'pēkrôl'ē] *n* (*col*) Krabbeltier *nt*.

cremate [krē'māt] *vt* einäschern.

cremation [krimā'shən] *n* Einäscherung *f*.

crematorium [krēmətôr'ēəm] *n* Krematorium *nt*.

creosote [krē'əsōt] *n* Kreosot *nt*.

crêpe [krāp] *n* Krepp *m*.

crêpe bandage *n* (*Brit*) elastische Binde *f*.

crêpe paper *n* Kreppapier *nt*.

crêpe sole *n* (*on shoe*) Kreppsohle *f*.

crept [krept] *pt, pp* of **creep**.

crescent [kres'ənt] *n* (*of moon*) Halbmond *m*.

cress [kres] *n* Kresse *f*.

crest [krest] *n* (*of cock*) Kamm *m*; (*of wave*) Wellenkamm *m*; (*coat of arms*) Wappen *nt*.

crestfallen [krest'fôlən] *a* niedergeschlagen.

Crete [krēt] *n* Kreta *f*.

cretin [krē'tən] *n* Idiot(in *f*) *m*.

crevasse [krəvas'] *n* Gletscherspalte *f*.

crevice [krev'is] *n* Riß *m*; (*in rock*) Felsspalte *f*.

crew [krōō] *n* Besatzung *f*, Mannschaft *f*; (*CINE*) Crew *f*; (*gang*) Bande *f*.

crew cut *n* Bürstenschnitt *m*.

crew neck *n* runde(r) Ausschnitt *m*.

crib [krib] *n* (*bed*) Krippe *f*; (*translation*) wortwörtliche Übersetzung *f*, Klatsche *f*.

crick [krik] *n* Muskelkrampf *m*; **a** ~ **in the neck** ein steifes Genick, ein steifer Nacken.

cricket [krik'it] *n* (*insect*) Grille *f*; (*game*) Kricket *nt*.

cricketer [krik'itûr] *n* Kricketspieler *m*.

crime [krīm] *n* Straftat *f*, Verbrechen *nt*.

crime wave *n* Verbrechenswelle *f*.

criminal [krim'ənəl] *n* Verbrecher *m* ♦ *a* kriminell, strafbar.

Criminal Investigation Department *n* (*Brit*) ≈ Kriminalpolizei *f*.

crimp [krimp] *vt* (*hair*) drehen.

crimson [krim'zən] *n* Karmesin *nt* ♦ *a* leuchtend rot.

cringe [krinj] *vi* sich ducken.

crinkle [kring'kəl] *vt* zerknittern ♦ *vi* knittern.

crinkly [kring'klē] *a* (*hair*) kraus.

cripple [krip'əl] *n* Krüppel *m* ♦ *vt* lahmlegen; (*MED*) lähmen, verkrüppeln; (*ship, plane*) aktionsunfähig machen; (*production, exports*) lahmlegen, lähmen; ~**d with arthritis** von Arthritis praktisch gelähmt.

crippling [krip'ling] *a* (*taxes, debts etc*) erdrückend.

crisis [krī'sis] *n* Krise *f*.

crisp [krisp] *a* knusprig.

crisps [krisps] *npl* (*Brit*) Chips *pl*.

crisscross [kris'krôs] *a* gekreuzt; (*pattern*) Kreuz- ♦ *vt* durchkreuzen.

criterion [krītēr'ēən] *n, pl* **criteria** [krītēr'ēə] Kriterium *nt*.

critic [krit'ik] *n* Kritiker(in *f*) *m*.

critical [krit'ikəl] *a* kritisch; **to be** ~ **of sb/ sth** jdn/etw kritisieren.

critically [krit'iklē] *ad* kritisch; **to be ~ ill** schwer krank sein.

criticism [krit'isizəm] *n* Kritik *f*.

criticize [krit'əsīz] *vt* kritisieren; (*comment*) beurteilen.

critique [kritēk'] *n* Kritik *f*.

croak [krōk] *vi* krächzen; (*frog*) quaken ♦ *n* Krächzen *nt*; Quaken *nt*.

crochet [krōshā'] *n* Häkelei *f*.

crock [krâk] *n* (*jar*) Topf *m*; (*pottery chip*) Scherbe *f*; (*col: person: also:* **old ~**) Wrack *nt*; (: *car etc*) Kiste *f*.

crockery [krâk'ûrē] *n* Geschirr *nt*.

crocodile [krâk'ədīl] *n* Krokodil *nt*.

crocus [krō'kəs] *n* Krokus *m*.

croft [krôft] *n* (*Brit*) kleine(s) Pachtgut *nt*.

crone [krōn] *n* Hexe *f*.

crony [krō'nē] *n* (*col*) Kumpel *m*.

crook [krŏŏk] *n* (*criminal*) Gauner *m*, Schwindler *m*; (*stick*) Hirtenstab *m*.

crooked [krŏŏk'id] *a* krumm.

crop [krâp] *n* (*harvest*) Ernte *f*; (*fig: series*) Haufen *m*; (*of bird*) Kropf *m*; (*riding ~*) Reitpeitsche *f* ♦ *vt* (*animals*) stutzen, kupieren; (*cut: grass*) kurz mähen; (: *hair*) stutzen.

crop up *vi* passieren.

crop spraying [krâp sprā'ing] *n* Schädlingsbekämpfung *f* (*durch Besprühen*).

croquet [krōkā'] *n* Krocket *nt*.

croquette [krōket'] *n* Krokette *f*.

cross [krôs] *n* Kreuz *nt*; (*BIOL*) Kreuzung *f*; **it's a ~ between geography and sociology** es ist eine Mischung aus Geographie und Soziologie ♦ *vt* (*road*) überqueren; (*legs*) übereinander legen; (*write*) einen Querstrich ziehen durch; (*BIOL*) kreuzen; (*check*) als Verrechnungsscheck kennzeichnen; (*thwart: person, plan*) durchkreuzen; **the lines are ~ed** (*TEL*) die Leitungen überschneiden sich; **they've got their lines ~ed** (*fig*) sie reden aneinander vorbei ♦ *vi*: **the boat ~es from ... to ...** das Schiff fährt von ... nach ... ♦ *a* (*annoyed*) ärgerlich, böse; **to be ~ about sth** sich über etw ärgern; **to be/get ~ with sb** sich über jdn ärgern.

cross out *vt* streichen.

crossbar [krôs'bâr] *n* Querstange *f*.

crossbreed [krôs'brēd] *n* Kreuzung *f*.

cross-Channel ferry [krôs'chanəl fär'ē] *n* Kanalfähre *f*.

cross-check [krôs'chek] *n* Gegenprobe *f* ♦ *vt* überprüfen.

cross-country (race) [krôs'kun'trē (rās)] *n* Geländelauf *m*.

cross-examination [krôs'igzamənā'shən] *n* Kreuzverhör *nt*.

cross-examine [krôs'igzam'in] *vt* ins Kreuzverhör nehmen.

cross-eyed [krôs'īd] *a*: **to be ~** schielen.

crossfire [krôs'fīûr] *n* Kreuzfeuer *nt*.

crossing [krôs'ing] *n* (*crossroads*) (Straßen)kreuzung *f*; (*of ship*) Überfahrt *f*; (*for pedestrians*) Fußgängerüberweg *m*.

cross-purposes [krôs'pûr'pəsiz] *npl*: **to be at ~ with sb** (*disagree*) mit jdm auf keinen gleichen Nenner kommen; (*misunderstand*) aneinander vorbeireden.

cross-reference [krôs'ref'ûrəns] *n* Querverweis *m* (*to* auf +*acc*).

crossroads [krôs'rōdz] *n* Straßenkreuzung *f*; (*fig*) Scheideweg *m*.

cross section *n* Querschnitt *m*.

crosswalk [krôs'wôk] *n* (*US*) Fußgängerüberweg *m*.

crosswind [krôs'wind] *n* Seitenwind *m*.

crossword (puzzle) [krôs'wûrd (puz'əl)] *n* Kreuzworträtsel *nt*.

crotch [krâch] *n* (*of pants*) Schritt *m*; (*ANAT*) Unterleib *m*.

crotchet [krâch'it] *n* (*Brit*) Viertelnote *f*.

crotchety [krâch'ətē] *a* (*person*) launenhaft.

crouch [krouch] *vi* hocken.

croup [krŏŏp] *n* (*MED*) Krupp *m*.

crouton [krŏŏ'tân] *n* geröstete(r) Brotwürfel *m*.

crow [krō] *n* Krähen *nt* ♦ *vi* krähen.

crowbar [krō'bâr] *n* Stemmeisen *nt*.

crowd [kroud] *n* Menge *f*, Gedränge *nt* ♦ *vt* (*fill*) überfüllen ♦ *vi* drängen; **~s of people** eine Menge Leute.

crowded [krou'did] *a* überfüllt.

crowd scene *n* (*CINE, THEAT*) Massenszene *f*.

crown [kroun] *n* Krone *f*; (*of head, hat*) Kopf *m* ♦ *vt* krönen; (*tooth*) eine Krone machen für; **and to ~ it all, ...** (*fig*) und um dem Ganzen die Krone aufzusetzen, ...

crown court *n* (*JUR*) Bezirksgericht *nt*.

crowning [krou'ning] *a* (*achievement, glory*) krönend.

crown jewels *npl* Kronjuwelen *pl*.

crown prince *n* Kronprinz *m*.

crow's-feet [krōz'fēt] *npl* Krähenfüße *pl*.

crow's-nest [krōz'nest] *n* Krähennest *nt*, Ausguck *m*.

crucial [krŏŏ'shəl] *a* entscheidend; **his approval is ~ to the success of the project** seine Zustimmung ist für den Erfolg des Projekts äußerst wichtig.

crucifix [krŏŏ'səfiks] *n* Kruzifix *nt*.

crucifixion [krŏŏsəfik'shən] *n* Kreuzigung *f*.

crucify [krŏŏ'səfī] *vt* (*also fig*) kreuzigen.

crude [krŏŏd] *a* (*raw*) roh; (*humor, behavior*) grob, unfein.

crudely [krŏŏd'lē] *ad* grob.

crudeness [krŏŏd'nis] *n* Roheit *f*.

crudity [krŏŏ'dətē] *n* Roheit *f*.

cruel [krŏŏ'əl] *a* grausam; (*distressing*) schwer; (*hard-hearted*) hart, gefühllos.

cruelty [krŏŏ'əltē] *n* Grausamkeit *f*.

cruet [krŏŏ'it] *n* Gewürzständer *m*, Menage *f*.

cruise [krŏŏz] *n* Kreuzfahrt *f* ♦ *vi* kreuzen.

cruise missile *n* Cruise Missile *nt*.

cruiser [krŏŏ'zûr] *n* (*MIL*) Kreuzer *m*.

cruising speed [krŏŏ'zing spēd] *n* Reisegeschwindigkeit *f*.

crumb [krum] *n* Krume *f*; (*fig*) Bröckchen *nt*.

crumble [krum'bəl] *vti* zerbröckeln.
crumbly [krum'blē] *a* krümelig.
crummy [krum'ē] *a* (*col*) mies.
crumpet [krum'pit] *n* Tee(pfann)kuchen *m*.
crumple [krum'pəl] *vt* zerknittern.
crunch [krunch] *n* Knirschen *nt*; (*fig*) entscheidende(r) Punkt *m* ♦ *vt* knirschen.
crunchy [krun'chē] *a* knusprig.
crusade [krōōsād'] *n* Kreuzzug *m* ♦ *vi*: **to ~ for/against sb/sth** (*fig*) für/gegen jdn/etw zu Felde ziehen.
crusader [krōōsā'dûr] *n* Kreuzfahrer *m*; (*fig*) Apostel *m*.
crush [krush] *n* Gedränge *nt*; **to have a ~ on sb** für jdn schwärmen ♦ *vt* zerdrücken; (*rebellion*) unterdrücken, niederwerfen; (*grind, break up: garlic, ice*) (zer)stoßen; (*grapes*) (aus)pressen ♦ *vi* (*material*) knittern.
crushing [krush'ing] *a* überwältigend.
crust [krust] *n* (*of bread*) Rinde *f*, Kruste *f*; (*MED*) Schorf *m*.
crustacean [krustā'shən] *n* Schalentier *nt*, Krustazee *f*.
crusty [krus'tē] *a* (*loaf*) knusprig.
crutch [kruch] *n* Krücke *f*; **to use sth/sb as a ~** (*support*) sich an etw/jdn klammern; *see also* **crotch**.
crux [kruks] *n*: **the ~** (*crucial point*) der springende Punkt, der Haken (*col*).
cry [krī] *vi* (*call*) ausrufen; (*shout*) schreien; (*weep*) weinen ♦ *n* (*call*) Schrei *m*; **what are you ~ing about?** warum weinst du?; **to ~ for help** um Hilfe rufen/schreien; **she had a good ~** (*weep*) sie hat sich (mal) richtig ausgeweint; **it's a far ~ from ...** (*fig*) das ist etwas ganz anderes als ...
cry off *vi* (*Brit*) (plötzlich) absagen.
crying [krī'ing] *a* (*fig*) himmelschreiend.
crypt [kript] *n* Krypta *f*.
cryptic [krip'tik] *a* (*secret*) geheim; (*mysterious*) rätselhaft.
crystal [kris'təl] *n* Kristall *m*; (*glass*) Kristallglas *nt*; (*mineral*) Bergkristall *m*.
crystal-clear [kris'təlkli'ûr] *a* (*fig also*) kristallklar, glasklar.
crystallize [kris'təlīz] *vi* kristallisieren ♦ *vt* (*fig*) klären, (feste) Form geben (+*dat*); **~d fruits** (*Brit*) kandierte Früchte *pl*.
CSA *n abbr* = *Confederate States of America*.
CS gas [sē'cs gas'] *n* (*Brit*) Tränengas *nt*.
CST *abbr* (*US*) = *Central Standard Time*.
ct *abbr* (= *carat*) Kt.
CT *abbr* (*US MAIL*) = *Connecticut*.
cub [kub] *n* Junge(s) *nt*; (*young Boy Scout*) Wölfling *m*.
Cuba [kyōō'bə] *n* Kuba *nt*.
Cuban [kyōō'bən] *n* Kubaner(in *f*) *m* ♦ *a* kubanisch.
cubbyhole [kub'ēhōl] *n* Eckchen *nt*.
cube [kyōōb] *n* Würfel *m*; (*MATH*) Kubikzahl *f*.
cube root *n* Kubikwurzel *f*.
cubic [kyōō'bik] *a* würfelförmig; (*centimeter*

etc) Kubik-.
cubic capacity *n* (*AUT*) Hubraum *m*.
cubicle [kyōō'bikəl] *n* Kabine *f*.
cubism [kyōō'bizəm] *n* Kubismus *m*.
cuckoo [kōō'kōō] *n* Kuckuck *m*.
cuckoo clock *n* Kuckucksuhr *f*.
cucumber [kyōō'kumbûr] *n* Gurke *f*.
cuddle [kud'əl] *vt* herzen, drücken (*col*) ♦ *n* enge Umarmung *f*.
cuddly [kud'lē] *a* anschmiegsam; (*teddy*) zum Drücken.
cudgel [kuj'əl] *n* Knüppel *m* ♦ *vt*: **to ~ one's brains** (*fig*) sich das (Ge)hirn zermartern.
cue [kyōō] *n* Wink *m*; (*THEAT*) Stichwort *nt*; (*snooker ~*) Billardstock *m*.
cuff [kuf] *n* (*US: on pants*) Aufschlag *m*; (*Brit: of shirt, coat etc*) Manschette *f*, Aufschlag *m* ♦ *vt* einen Klaps geben (+*dat*).
cuff link *n* Manschettenknopf *m*.
cuisine [kwizēn'] *n* Kochkunst *f*, Küche *f*.
cul-de-sac [kul'dəsak'] *n* Sackgasse *f*.
culinary [kyōō'lənärē] *a* Koch-.
cull [kul] *n* (*selection*) Auswahl *f*, Auslese *f*; **seal ~** Robbenschlag *m* ♦ *vt*: **to ~ seals** Robbenschlag *m* betreiben.
culminate [kul'mənāt] *vi* gipfeln.
culmination [kulmənā'shən] *n* Höhepunkt *m*.
culottes [kyōōläts'] *npl* Hosenrock *m*.
culpable [kul'pəbəl] *a* strafbar, schuldhaft.
culprit [kul'prit] *n* Täter *m*.
cult [kult] *n* Kult *m*; **a ~ figure** eine Kultfigur.
cultivate [kul'təvāt] *vt* (*AGR*) bebauen; (*mind*) bilden.
cultivated [kul'təvātid] *a* (*AGR*) bebaut; (*cultured*) kultiviert.
cultivation [kultəvā'shən] *n* (*AGR*) Bebauung *f*; (*of person*) Bildung *f*.
cultural [kul'chûrəl] *a* kulturell, Kultur-.
culture [kul'chûr] *n* (*refinement*) Kultur *f*, Bildung *f*; (*of community*) Kultur *f*.
cultured [kul'chûrd] *a* gebildet, kultiviert.
cumbersome [kum'bûrsəm] *a* (*task*) beschwerlich; (*object*) schwer zu handhaben.
cumin [kyōōm'in] *n* (*spice*) Kreuzkümmel *m*.
cummerbund [kum'ûrbund] *n* Kummerbund *m*.
cumulative [kyōōm'yələtiv] *a* gehäuft; **to be ~** sich häufen.
cunning [kun'ing] *n* Verschlagenheit *f* ♦ *a* schlau; (*clever: device, idea*) schlau *or* clever (*col*) ausgedacht.
cup [kup] *n* Tasse *f*; (*prize*) Pokal *m*; **a ~ of tea** eine Tasse Tee.
cupboard [kub'ûrd] *n* (*Brit*) Schrank *m*.
cupful [kup'fəl] *n* Tasse(voll) *f*.
cupola [kyōō'pələ] *n* Kuppel *f*.
cup tie *n* (*Brit SOCCER*) Pokalspiel *nt*.
curable [kyōō'rəbəl] *a* heilbar.
curate [kyōō'rit] *n* (*Catholic*) Kurat *m*; (*Protestant*) Vikar *m*.
curator [kyōōrā'tûr] *n* Kustos *m*.
curb [kûrb] *vt* zügeln; (*expenditure*) in Schranken halten, bremsen (*col*) ♦ *n* (*US: of*

sidewalk) Bordstein *m*; (*control*) Zaum *m*; (*on spending etc*) Einschränkung *f*.

curd cheese [kûrd chēz] *n* Quark *m*.

curdle [kûr'dəl] *vi* gerinnen.

cure [kyŏŏr] *n* (*remedy*) Heilmittel *nt*; (*process*) Heilverfahren *nt*; (*health* ~) Kur *f*; **there's no** ~ **for** ... es gibt kein Mittel gegen ...; **to take a** ~ zur *or* in Kur gehen, eine Kur machen ♦ *vt* heilen; **to be** ~**d of sth** von etw geheilt sein.

cure-all [kyŏŏr'ôl] *n* (*also fig*) Allheilmittel *nt*.

curfew [kûr'fyŏŏ] *n* Ausgangssperre *f*, Sperrstunde *f*.

curio [kyŏŏ'rēō] *n* Kuriosität *f*.

curiosity [kyŏŏrēâs'ətē] *n* Neugier *f*; (*for knowledge*) Wißbegierde *f*; (*object*) Merkwürdigkeit *f*.

curious [kyŏŏ'rēəs] *a* neugierig; (*strange*) seltsam; **I'm** ~ **about him** ich bin gespannt auf ihn.

curiously [kyŏŏ'rēəslē] *ad* neugierig; (*oddly*) seltsam, eigenartig; ~ **enough** merkwürdigerweise.

curl [kûrl] *n* Locke *f*; (*of smoke etc*) Kringel *m* ♦ *vt* locken.

curler [kûr'lûr] *n* Lockenwickler *m*.

curlew [kûr'lŏŏ] *n* Brachvogel *m*.

curling irons [kûr'ling i'ûrnz] *npl* (*US: for hair*) Lockenschere *f*, Brennschere *f*.

curling tongs [kûr'ling tôngz] *npl* (*Brit*) = **curling irons.**

curly [kûr'lē] *a* lockig.

currant [kûr'ənt] *n* Korinthe *f*; (*BOT*) Johannisbeere *f*.

currency [kûr'ənsē] *n* Währung *f*; (*of ideas*) Geläufigkeit *f*.

current [kûr'ənt] *n* Strömung *f* ♦ *a* (*expression*) gängig, üblich; (*tendency, price, event*) gegenwärtig, aktuell; **the** ~ **issue of a magazine** die neueste *or* letzte Nummer einer Zeitschrift; **in** ~ **use** allgemein gebräuchlich; **direct/alternating** ~ Gleich-/Wechselstrom *m*.

current account *n* (*Brit*) Girokonto *nt*.

current affairs *npl* Zeitgeschehen *nt*.

current assets *npl* (*FIN*) Umlaufvermögen *nt*.

current liabilities *npl* kurzfristige Verbindlichkeiten *pl*.

currently [kûr'əntlē] *ad* zur Zeit.

curriculum [kərik'yələm] *n* Lehrplan *m*.

curriculum vitae [kərik'yələm vē'tī] *n* Lebenslauf *m*.

curry [kûr'ē] *n* Currygericht *nt*.

curry powder *n* Curry(pulver) *nt*.

curse [kûrs] *vi* (*swear*) fluchen (*at* auf +*acc*) ♦ *vt* (*insult*) verwünschen ♦ *n* Fluch *m*.

cursor [kûr'sûr] *n* (*COMPUT*) Cursor *m*.

cursory [kûr'sûrē] *a* flüchtig.

curt [kûrt] *a* schroff.

curtail [kûrtāl'] *vt* abkürzen; (*rights*) einschränken.

curtain [kûr'tən] *n* Vorhang *m*, Gardine *f*; (*THEAT*) Vorhang *m*; **to draw the** ~**s** (*together*) den Vorhang *or* die Vorhänge zuziehen; (*apart*) den Vorhang *or* die Vorhänge aufziehen.

curtain call *n* (*THEAT*) Vorhang *m*.

curts(e)y [kûrt'sē] *n* Knicks *m* ♦ *vi* knicksen.

curvature [kûr'vəchûr] *n* Krümmung *f*; (*misshapen*) Verkrümmung *f*.

curve [kûrv] *n* Kurve *f*; (*of river*) Biegung *f* ♦ *vt* biegen; (*arch*) wölben ♦ *vi* (*road*) einen Bogen machen.

curved [kûrvd] *a* (*line*) gebogen; (*table legs*) geschwungen; (*surface, arch, side of ship*) gewölbt.

cushion [kŏŏsh'ən] *n* Kissen *nt* ♦ *vt* polstern.

cushy [kŏŏsh'ē] *a*: **to have a** ~ **time** eine ruhige Kugel schieben (*col*).

custard [kus'tûrd] *n* Vanillesoße *f*.

custodian [kustō'dēən] *n* Kustos *m*, Verwalter(in *f*) *m*; (*of museum etc*) Aufseher *m*, Wächter *m*.

custody [kus'tədē] *n* Aufsicht *f*; (*police*) Polizeigewahrsam *m*; **to take sb into** ~ jdn verhaften; **in the** ~ **of** in der Obhut von.

custom [kus'təm] *n* (*tradition*) Brauch *m*; (*business dealing*) Kundschaft *f*.

customary [kus'təmärē] *a* üblich; **it is** ~ **to do sth** etw wird normalerweise *or* gewöhnlich getan.

custom-built [kus'təmbilt'] *a* spezial angefertigt.

customer [kus'təmûr] *n* Kunde *m*, Kundin *f*; **he's a tough** ~ (*col*) er ist ein schwieriger Typ.

customer profile *n* Kundenprofil *nt*.

customer service *n* Kundendienst *m*.

customized [kus'təmīzd] *a* spezial angefertigt.

custom-made [kus'təmmād'] *a* = **customized.**

customs [kus'təmz] *npl* (*duty, organization*) Zoll *m*; **to go through (the)** ~ durch den Zoll gehen.

Customs and Excise *n* (*Brit*) Zollbehörde *f*.

customs officer *n* Zollbeamte(r) *m*.

cut [kut] *irreg vt pt, pp* **cut** schneiden; (*wages*) kürzen; (*prices*) heruntersetzen; (*col: avoid: class, lecture, appointments*) schwänzen ♦ *vi* schneiden; **to get one's hair** ~ sich die Haare schneiden lassen; **I** ~ **my hand** ich habe mir in die Hand geschnitten; **it** ~**s both ways** (*fig*) es trifft auch umgekehrt zu ♦ *n* Schnitt *m*; (*wound*) Schnittwunde *f*; (*in book, income etc*) Kürzung *f*; (*share*) Anteil *m*.

cut back *vt* (*plants*) zurückschneiden, stutzen; (*production*) zurückschrauben; (*expenditure*) einschränken ♦ *vi* (*on expenditure*) sich einschränken.

cut down *vt* (*tree*) fällen; **to** ~ **sb down to size** (*fig*) jdn auf seinen Platz verweisen.

cut down on *vt fus* (*consumption, expenses*) einschränken.

cut in *vi*: **to** ~ **in on sb** (*interrupt: conver-*

sation) jdn unterbrechen; **to** ~ **in** in front of sb (*AUT*) jdn schneiden.
cut off *vt*: **we've been** ~ **off** (*TEL*) wir sind unterbrochen worden.
cut out *vt* ausschneiden; (*delete*) streichen.
cut up *vt* aufschneiden; (*chop: food*) kleinschneiden.
cut-and-dried [kutəndrīd'] *a* (*fig: also*: **cut-and-dry**) abgesprochen, (eine) abgemachte Sache.
cute [kyōōt] *a* reizend, niedlich.
cuticle [kyōō'tikəl] *n* (*on nail*) Nagelhaut *f*.
cutlery [kut'lûrē] *n* Besteck *nt*.
cutlet [kut'lit] *n* (*pork*) Kotelett *nt*; (*veal*) Schnitzel *nt*.
cutoff [kut'ôf] *n* Ausschaltmechanismus *m*; (~ *point*) Trennlinie *f*.
cutout [kut'out] *n* (*ELEC*) Sicherung *f*; (*paper, cardboard figure*) Ausschneidepuppe *f*.
cut-price [kut'prīs] *a* verbilligt.
cut-rate [kut'rāt] *a* verbilligt.
cut-throat [kut'thrōt] *a*: ~ **competition** halsabschneiderische Konkurrenz *f*.
cutting [kut'ing] *a* schneidend ♦ *n* (*Brit: from paper*) Ausschnitt *m*; (*CINE*) Schnitt *m*.
CV *n abbr* = **curriculum vitae**.
C & W *n abbr* = **country-and-western** (music).
cwo *abbr* (*COMM*) = **cash with order.**
cwt. *abbr* (= *hundredweight*) Ztr.
cyanide [sī'ənīd] *n* Zyankali *nt*.
cybernetics [sībûrnet'iks] *n* Kybernetik *f*.
cyclamen [sik'ləmən] *n* Alpenveilchen *nt*.
cycle [sī'kəl] *n* Fahrrad *nt*; (*series*) Reihe *f*; (*of songs*) Zyklus *m* ♦ *vi* radfahren.
cycle race *n* Radrennen *nt*.
cycle rack *n* Fahrradständer *m*.
cycling [sīk'ling] *n* Radfahren *nt*; (*SPORT*) Radsport *m*.
cyclist [sīk'list] *n* Radfahrer(in *f*) *m*.
cyclone [sīk'lōn] *n* Zyklon *m*.
cygnet [sig'nit] *n* junge(r) Schwan *m*.
cylinder [sil'indûr] *n* Zylinder *m*; (*TECH*) Walze *f*.
cylinder block *n* Zylinderblock *m*.
cylinder capacity *n* Zylindervolumen *nt*, Zylinderinhalt *m*.
cylinder head *n* Zylinderkopf *m*.
cylinder head gasket *n* Zylinderkopfdichtung *f*.
cymbals [sim'bəlz] *npl* Becken *nt*.
cynic [sin'ik] *n* Zyniker(in *f*) *m*.
cynical [sin'ikəl] *a* zynisch.
cynicism [sin'əsizəm] *n* Zynismus *m*.
CYO *n abbr* (*US*: = *Catholic Youth Organization*) ≈ KAJ *f*.
cypress [sī'pris] *n* Zypresse *f*.
Cypriot [sip'rēət] *a* zypriotisch, zyprisch ♦ *n* Zypriot(in *f*) *m*.
Cyprus [sīp'rəs] *n* Zypern *nt*.
cyst [sist] *n* Zyste *f*.
cystitis [sistī'tis] *n* Blasenentzündung *f*, Zystitis *f*.

CZ *n abbr* (*US*: = *Canal Zone*) Gebiet um den Panamakanal.
czar [zâr] *n* Zar *m*.
czarina [zârē'nə] *n* Zarin *f*.
Czech [chek] *a* tschechisch ♦ *n* (*person*) Tscheche *m*, Tschechin *f*; (*language*) Tschechisch *nt*.
Czechoslovak [chekəslō'vak] *a*, *n see* **Czechoslovakian.**
Czechoslovakia [chekəsləvâk'ēə] *n* die Tschechoslowakei.
Czechoslovakian [chekəsləvâk'ēən] *a* tschechoslowakisch ♦ *n* (*person*) Tschechoslowake *m*, Tschechoslowakin *f*.

D

D, d [dē] *n* (*letter*) D *nt*, d *nt*; **D for Dog** ≈ D wie Dora.
d. *abbr* (= *died*) gest.
D *abbr* (*US POL*) = **Democrat; Democratic.**
DA *n abbr* (*US*) = **district attorney.**
dab [dab] *vt* (*wound, paint*) betupfen ♦ *n* (*little bit*) bißchen *nt*; (*of paint*) Tupfer *m*; (*smear*) Klecks *m*.
dabble [dab'əl] *vi* (*splash*) plätschern; **to** ~ **in sth** (*fig*) in etw (*dat*) machen.
Dacca [dak'ə] *n* Dacca *nt*.
dachshund [dâks'ōōnd] *n* Dackel *m*.
dad(dy) [dad'(ē)] *n* Papa *m*, Vati *m*.
daddy-long-legs [dadēlông'legz] *n* Weberknecht *m*.
daffodil [daf'ədil] *n* Osterglocke *f*.
daft [daft] *a* (*col*) blöd(e), doof.
dagger [dag'ûr] *n* Dolch *m*.
dahlia [dal'yə] *n* Dahlie *f*.
daily [dā'lē] *a* täglich; **twice** ~ zweimal am Tag/täglich ♦ *n* (*PRESS*) Tageszeitung *f*; (*Brit: cleaning woman*) Haushaltshilfe *f*.
dainty [dān'tē] *a* zierlich; (*attractive*) reizend.
dairy [där'ē] *n* (*on farm*) Molkerei *f*; (*Brit: shop*) Milchgeschäft *nt* ♦ *a* Milch-.
dairy cow *n* Milchkuh *f*.
dairy farm *n* auf Milchviehhaltung spezialisierte(r) Bauernhof.
dairy produce *n* Milch- *or* Molkereiprodukte *pl*.
dais [dā'is] *n* Podium *nt*.
daisy [dā'zē] *n* Gänseblümchen *nt*.
daisy wheel *n* (*on printer*) Typenrad *nt*, Typenscheibe *f*.
daisy wheel printer *n* Typenraddrucker *m*.
Dakar [dâkâr'] *n* Dakar *nt*.
dale [dāl] *n* Tal *nt*.
dally [dal'ē] *vi* tändeln.
dalmation [dalmā'shən] *n* (*dog*) Dalmatiner

m.

dam [dam] *n* (Stau)damm *m*; *(reservoir)* Stausee *m* ♦ *vt* stauen.

damage [dam'ij] *n* Schaden *m* ♦ *vt* beschädigen; ~ **to property** Eigentumsbeschädigung *f.*

damages [dam'ijiz] *npl* *(JUR)* Schaden(s)ersatz *m*; **to pay $5000 in** ~ 5000 Dollar Schaden(s)ersatz bezahlen.

damaging [dam'ijing] *a*: ~ **(to)** schädlich (für).

Damascus [dəmas'kəs] *n* Damaskus *nt.*

dame [dām] *n* Dame *f*; *(US col)* Weib(sbild) *nt*; *(THEAT)* komische Alte *f.*

damn [dam] *vt* verdammen, verwünschen ♦ *a* *(col)* verdammt; ~ **it!** verflucht!

damnable [dam'nəbəl] *a* *(col: behavior, weather)* gräßlich.

damnation [damnā'shən] *n* *(REL)* Verdammung *f* ♦ *interj* *(col)* verdammt.

damning [dam'ing] *a* vernichtend.

damp [damp] *a* feucht ♦ *n* Feuchtigkeit *f* ♦ *vt* *(also:* **dampen**) befeuchten; *(discourage)* dämpfen.

dampcourse [damp'kôrs] *n* Feuchtigkeitsisolierschicht *f.*

damper [dam'pûr] *n* *(MUS)* Dämpfer *m*; *(of fire)* (Luft)klappe *f*; **to put a** ~ **on sth** *(fig: atmosphere, enthusiasm)* einer Sache *(dat)* einen Dämpfer aufsetzen.

dampness [damp'nis] *n* Feuchtigkeit *f.*

damson [dam'zən] *n* Damaszenerpflaume *f.*

dance [dans] *n* Tanz *m*; *(party)* Tanz(abend) *m* ♦ *vi* tanzen; **to** ~ **about** herumtanzen.

dance hall *n* Tanzlokal *nt.*

dancer [dan'sûr] *n* Tänzer *m.*

dancing [dan'sing] *n* Tanzen *nt.*

D and C *n* *abbr* *(MED*: = *dilation and curettage)* Ausschabung *f.*

dandelion [dan'dəliən] *n* Löwenzahn *m.*

dandruff [dan'drəf] *n* (Kopf)schuppen *pl.*

dandy [dan'dē] *n* Dandy *m* ♦ *a* *(US col)* prima.

Dane [dān] *n* Däne *m*, Dänin *f.*

danger [dān'jûr] *n* Gefahr *f*; ~**!** *(sign)* Achtung!; **in** ~ in Gefahr; **out of** ~ außer Gefahr.

danger list *n* *(MED)*: **on the** ~ in Lebensgefahr.

dangerous [dān'jûrəs] *a* gefährlich.

dangerously [dān'jûrəslē] *ad* gefährlich; ~ **ill** schwer krank.

danger zone *n* Gefahrenzone *f.*

dangle [dang'gəl] *vi* baumeln ♦ *vt* herabhängen lassen.

Danish [dā'nish] *a* dänisch ♦ *n* *(language)* Dänisch *nt.*

Danish pastry *n* Plundergebäck *nt.*

dank [dangk] *a* (unangenehm) feucht.

Danube [dan'yōōb] *n* Donau *f.*

dapper [dap'ûr] *a* elegant.

Dardanelles [dârdənelz'] *npl* Dardanellen *pl.*

dare [dār] *vt* herausfordern ♦ *vi*: **to** ~ **(to) do sth** es wagen, etw zu tun; **I** ~ **say** ich würde sagen; ~**n't tell him** *(Brit)* ich wage nicht, es ihm zu sagen; **I** ~ **say he'll turn up** es kann (gut) sein, daß er aufkreuzt.

dare-devil [dār'devəl] *n* Draufgänger(in *f*) *m.*

Dar es Salaam [dâr es səlâm'] *n* Daressalam *nt.*

daring [dār'ing] *a* *(audacious)* verwegen; *(bold)* wagemutig; *(dress)* gewagt ♦ *n* Mut *m.*

dark [dârk] *a* dunkel; *(fig)* düster, trübe; *(deep color)* dunkel- ♦ *n* Dunkelheit *f*; **it is/ is getting** ~ es ist/wird dunkel; **after** ~ nach Anbruch der Dunkelheit; ~ **chocolate** Zartbitterschokolade *f.*

Dark Ages *npl* (finstere(s)) Mittelalter *nt.*

darken [dâr'kən] *vti* (sich) verdunkeln.

dark glasses *npl* Brille *f* mit getönten Gläsern.

darkly [dârk'lē] *ad* *(gloomily)* dunkel; *(sinisterly)* finster.

darkness [dârk'nis] *n* Finsternis *nt.*

darkroom [dârk'rōōm] *n* Dunkelkammer *f.*

darling [dâr'ling] *n* Liebling *m* ♦ *a* lieb.

darn [dârn] *n* Gestopfte(s) *nt* ♦ *vt* stopfen.

dart [dârt] *n* *(leap)* Satz *m*; *(weapon)* Pfeil *m*; *(SPORT)* (Wurf)pfeil *m* ♦ *vi* sausen.

dartboard [dârt'bôrd] *n* Zielscheibe *f.*

darts [dârts] *n* *sing* *(game)* Pfeilwerfen *nt.*

dash [dash] *n* Sprung *m*; *(mark)* (Gedanken)strich *m*; *(small quantity: of liquid)* Schuß *m*, Spritzer *m*; (: *of soda)* ein bißchen ♦ *vt* *(lit)* schmeißen ♦ *vi* stürzen.

dash away *vi* davonstürzen.

dashboard [dash'bôrd] *n* Armaturenbrett *nt.*

dashing [dash'ing] *a* schneidig.

dastardly [das'tûrdlē] *a* heimtückisch, niederträchtig.

data [dā'tə] *npl* Einzelheiten *pl*, Daten *pl.*

database [dā'təbās] *n* *(COMPUT)* Datenbank *f.*

data capture *n* Datenerfassung *f.*

data link *n* Datenübermittlungsabschnitt *m.*

data processing *n* Datenverarbeitung *f.*

data transmission *n* Datenübertragung *f.*

date [dāt] *n* Datum *nt*; *(for meeting etc)* Termin *m*; *(with person)* Verabredung *f*; *(fruit)* Dattel *f* ♦ *vt* *(letter etc)* datieren; *(col: girl)* gehen mit, befreundet sein mit; **what's the** ~ **today?** der wievielte ist heute?; ~ **of birth** Geburtsdatum *nt*; **the closing** ~ *(for application)* der letzte Anmeldetag; **to bring up to** ~ *(information, method)* auf den neuesten Stand bringen; *(correspondence)* aufarbeiten; **to bring sb up to** ~ jdn auf dem laufenden halten; **thank you for your letter** ~**d July 5th** vielen Dank für Ihr Schreiben vom 5. Juli.

dated [dā'tid] *a* altmodisch.

date-line [dāt'lin] *n* Datumsgrenze *f.*

date stamp *n* *(Brit)* Datumsstempel *m*; (: *on fresh food)* Haltbarkeitsdatum *nt.*

dative [dā'tiv] *n* Dativ *m* ♦ *a* Dativ-.

daub [dôb] *vt* beschmieren; *(paint)* schmieren.

daughter [dôt'ûr] n Tochter f.
daughter-in-law [dô'tûrinlô] n Schwiegertochter f.
daunt [dônt] vt entmutigen.
daunting [dôn'ting] a entmutigend.
davenport [dav'ənpôrt] n (US: sofa) Sofa nt.
dawdle [dôd'əl] vi trödeln; **to ~ over one's work** bei der Arbeit bummeln or trödeln.
dawn [dôn] n Morgendämmerung f ♦ vi (also fig) dämmern; **to ~ on sb, that ...** jdm dämmern, daß ...; **at ~** bei Tagesanbruch, im Morgengrauen; **from ~ to dusk** von morgens bis abends.
day [dā] n Tag m; (daylight) Tageslicht nt; **~ by ~** Tag für Tag, täglich; **one ~** eines Tages; **the ~ after, the following ~** am (darauf)folgenden Tag; **the ~ before yesterday** vorgestern; **the ~ after tomorrow** übermorgen; **these ~s** heutzutage; **(on) the ~ that** ... am Tag als ...; **to be paid by the ~** tageweise bezahlt werden; **to work an 8-hour ~** einen Achtstundentag haben; **he works 8 hours a ~** er arbeitet 8 Stunden am or pro Tag.
daybreak [dā'brāk] n Tagesanbruch m.
day-care center [dā'kär sen'tûr] n (Kinder)krippe f.
daydream [dā'drēm] n Wachtraum m, Träumerei f ♦ vi irreg (mit offenen Augen) träumen.
daylight [dā'līt] n Tageslicht nt.
Daylight Saving Time n (US) Sommerzeit f.
day release course n (Brit) Tageskurs m für Berufstätige.
day return (ticket) n (Brit) Tagesrückfahrkarte f.
day shift n Tagschicht f.
daytime [dā'tīm] n Tageszeit f.
day-to-day [dātōōdā'] a (routine) Alltags-, alltäglich; (expenses) täglich; **on a ~ basis** tageweise.
day trip n Tagesausflug m.
daze [dāz] vt benommen machen, betäuben ♦ n Betäubung f.
dazed [dāzd] a benommen.
dazzle [daz'əl] vt blenden ♦ n Blenden nt.
dazzling [daz'ling] a (light, color) blendend; (smile) strahlend.
dB abbr (= decibel) dB nt.
DBS n abbr (= direct broadcasting by satellite) Satellitenübertragung.
DC abbr (= direct current) GS, DC; (US MAIL) = District of Columbia.
DD n abbr (= Doctor of Divinity) Dr. theol. ♦ abbr = **demand draft**; (Brit: = direct debit) Bankeinzug.
D-day [dē'dā] n (HIST, fig) der Tag X.
DDS n abbr (US: = Doctor of Dental Science, Doctor of Dental Surgery) Dr. med. dent.
DDT n abbr DDT nt.
DE abbr (US MAIL) = Delaware.
DEA n abbr (= Drug Enforcement Administration) Amerikanische Drogenbehörde.

deacon [dē'kən] n Diakon m.
dead [ded] a tot, gestorben; (without feeling) gefühllos; (without movement) leer, verlassen; (battery) leer ♦ ad völlig ♦ npl: **the ~** die Toten pl; **~ center** genau in der Mitte; **the line has gone ~** (TEL) die Leitung ist tot.
deaden [ded'ən] vt (pain) abtöten; (sound) ersticken.
dead end n Sackgasse f; **a dead-end job** ein Job ohne Aufstiegsmöglichkeiten.
dead heat n tote(s) Rennen nt.
deadline [ded'līn] n Frist(ablauf) m, Stichtag m; **to work to a ~** auf einen Termin hinarbeiten.
deadlock [ded'lâk] n Stillstand m.
dead loss [ded' lôs] n (col): **a ~** ein böser Reinfall; (person) ein hoffnungsloser Fall.
deadly [ded'lē] a tödlich ♦ ad: **~ dull** tödlich langweilig.
deadly nightshade [ded'lē nīt'shād] n (BOT) Tollkirsche f.
deadpan [ded'pan] a undurchdringlich.
Dead Sea n Tote(s) Meer nt.
dead season n: **in the ~** (for tourists) außerhalb der Saison.
deaf [def] a taub; **to turn a ~ ear to sb/sth** sich jdm/einer Sache (dat) gegenüber taub stellen.
deaf-and-dumb [def'əndum'] a (person) taubstumm; (alphabet) Taubstummen-.
deafen [def'ən] vt taub machen.
deafening [def'əning] a ohrenbetäubend.
deaf-mute [def'myōōt'] n Taubstumme(r) mf.
deafness [def'nis] n Taubheit f.
deal [dēl] n Geschäft nt ♦ vti irreg austeilen; **a great ~ of** sehr viel; **a good ~, a great ~** ziemlich viel; **to strike a ~ with sb** mit jdm ein Geschäft machen; **he got a bad/fair ~ from them** er wurde schlecht/gut von ihnen behandelt; **it's a ~!** (col) abgemacht!
deal in vt fus (COMM) handeln mit.
deal with vt fus (manage, handle) sich kümmern um; (book etc) handeln von.
dealer [dē'lûr] n (COMM) Händler m; (CARDS) Kartengeber m.
dealership [dē'lûrship] n Vertriebsorganisation f.
dealings [dē'lingz] npl (relations) Beziehungen pl, Geschäftsverkehr m; (in goods, FIN) Geschäfte pl.
dealt [delt] pt, pp of **deal**.
dean [dēn] n (Protestant) Superintendent m; (Catholic) Dechant m; (UNIV) Dekan m.
dear [dēr] a lieb; (Brit: expensive) teuer ♦ n Liebling m; **~ me!** du liebe Zeit!; **D~ Sir** Sehr geehrter Herr!; **D~ John** Lieber John!
dearly [dēr'lē] ad (love) herzlich; (pay) teuer.
dearth [dûrth] n Mangel m (of an +dat).
death [deth] n Tod m; (end) Ende nt; (statistic) Sterbefall m.
deathbed [deth'bed] n Sterbebett nt.
death certificate n Totenschein m.

deathly [deth'lē] *a* totenähnlich, Toten-.

death penalty *n* Todesstrafe *f*.

death rate *n* Sterbeziffer *f*.

death sentence *n* Todesurteil *nt*.

deathtrap [deth'trap] *n* Todesfalle *f*.

debacle [dəbâk'əl] *n* Debakel *nt*.

debar [dibár'] *vt* ausschließen.

debase [dibās'] *vt* entwerten.

debatable [dibā'təbəl] *a* anfechtbar; **it is** ~ **whether ...** es ist fraglich, ob ...

debate [dibāt'] *n* Debatte *f*, Diskussion *f* ♦ *vt* debattieren, diskutieren; (*consider*) überlegen.

debauched [dibôcht'] *a* ausschweifend.

debauchery [debô'chûrē] *n* Ausschweifungen *pl*.

debenture [diben'chûr] *n* (*FIN*) Schuldschein *m*.

debenture capital *n* Anleihekapital *nt*.

debilitate [dibil'ətāt] *vt* schwächen.

debilitating [dibil'ətāting] *a* schwächend.

debit [deb'it] *n* Schuldposten *m* ♦ *vt* belasten.

debit balance *n* Debetsaldo *m*.

debit note *n* Lastschriftanzeige *f*.

debonair [debənär'] *a* flott, weltmännisch.

debrief [dēbrēf'] *vt* den Einsatz (anschließend) besprechen mit.

debriefing [dēbrēf'ing] *n* Berichterstattung *f*.

debris [dəbrē'] *n* Trümmer *pl*.

debt [det] *n* Schuld *f*; **to be in** ~ verschuldet sein; ~**s of $5000** 5000 Dollar Schulden; **bad** ~ uneinbringliche Forderung *f*.

debt collector *n* Inkassomandatar *m*, Schuldeneintreiber *m* (*col*).

debtor [det'ûr] *n* Schuldner *m*.

debug [dēbug'] *vt* (*COMPUT*) austesten.

debunk [dibungk'] *vt* (*col: theory, person etc*) den Nimbus nehmen (+*dat*).

debut [dābyōō'] *n* Debüt *nt*.

debutante [debyōōtánt'] *n* Debütantin *f*.

Dec. *abbr* (= *December*) Dez.

decade [dek'ād] *n* Jahrzehnt *nt*.

decadence [dek'ədəns] *n* Verfall *m*, Dekadenz *f*.

decadent [dek'ədənt] *a* dekadent.

decaffeinated [dēkaf'ənātid] *a* kaffeinfrei.

decamp [dikamp'] *vi* (*col*) (bei Nacht und Nebel) verschwinden, sich aus dem Staub machen.

decant [dikant'] *vt* (*wine*) umfüllen.

decanter [dikan'tûr] *n* Karaffe *f*.

decarbonize [dēkâr'bəniz] *vt* entkohlen.

decay [dikā'] *n* Verfall *m* ♦ *vi* verfallen; (*teeth, meat etc*) faulen; (*leaves etc*) verrotten.

decease [disēs'] *n* Hinscheiden *nt*.

deceased [disēst'] *a* verstorben.

deceit [disēt'] *n* Betrug *m*.

deceitful [disēt'fəl] *a* falsch.

deceive [disēv'] *vt* täuschen.

decelerate [dēsel'ərāt] *vi* sich verlangsamen, die Geschwindigkeit verringern.

December [disem'bûr] *n* Dezember *m*; *see* **September**.

decency [dē'sənsē] *n* Anstand *m*.

decent [dē'sənt] *a* (*respectable*) anständig; (*pleasant*) annehmbar.

decently [dē'səntlē] *ad* (*respectably*) anständig; (*kindly*) liebenswürdigerweise, freundlicherweise.

decentralization [dēsentrəlizā'shən] *n* Dezentralisierung *f*.

deception [disep'shən] *n* Betrug *m*.

deceptive [disep'tiv] *a* täuschend, irreführend.

decibel [des'əbəl] *n* Dezibel *nt*.

decide [disīd'] *vt* entscheiden ♦ *vi* sich entscheiden; **to** ~ **on sth** etw beschließen; **to** ~ **against doing sth** sich dagegen entscheiden, etw zu tun.

decided [disī'did] *a* bestimmt, entschieden.

decidedly [disī'didlē] *ad* entschieden.

deciding [disī'ding] *a* entscheidend.

deciduous [disij'ōōəs] *a* jedes Jahr abfallend, Laub-.

decimal [des'əməl] *a* dezimal ♦ *n* Dezimalzahl *f*; **to 3** ~ **places** auf 3 Dezimalstellen.

decimalize [des'əməlīz] *vt* (*Brit*) auf das Dezimalsystem umstellen.

decimal point *n* Komma *nt* (eines Dezimalbruches).

decimal system *n* Dezimalsystem *nt*.

decimate [des'əmāt] *vt* dezimieren.

decipher [disī'fûr] *vt* entziffern.

decision [disizh'ən] *n* Entscheidung *f*, Entschluß *m*; **to make a** ~ eine Entscheidung treffen.

decisive [disī'siv] *a* entscheidend, ausschlaggebend; (*manner, reply*) bestimmt, entschlossen; (*person*) entschlußfreudig.

deck [dek] *n* (*NAUT*) Deck *nt*; (*of cards*) Pack *m*; **cassette** ~ Tape-deck *nt*; **to go up on** ~ an Deck gehen; **below** ~ unter Deck.

deck chair *n* Liegestuhl *m*.

deckhand [dek'hand] *n* Matrose *m*.

declaration [deklərā'shən] *n* Erklärung *f*.

declare [diklär'] *vt* (*state*) behaupten; (*war*) erklären; (*at customs*) verzollen.

declassify [dēklas'əfī] *vt* (*col*) freigeben.

decline [diklīn'] *n* (*decay*) Verfall *m*; (*lessening*) Rückgang *m*, Niedergang *m*; ~ **in living standards** Rückgang *m* or Senkung *f* im Lebensstandard ♦ *vt* (*invitation*) ausschlagen, ablehnen; **to** ~ **to do sth** ablehnen, etw zu tun ♦ *vi* (*strength*) nachlassen; (*say no*) ablehnen.

declutch [dēkluch'] *vi* (*Brit*) auskuppeln.

decode [dēkōd'] *vt* entschlüsseln.

decoder [dēkō'dûr] *n* (*COMPUT*) Decoder *m*.

decompose [dēkəmpōz'] *vi* (sich) zersetzen.

decomposition [dēkâmpəzish'ən] *n* Zersetzung *f*.

decompression [dēkəmpresh'ən] *n* Dekompression *f*, Druckverminderung *f*.

decompression chamber *n* Dekompressionskammer *f*.

decongestant [dēkənjes'tənt] *n* abschwellende(s) Mittel *nt*.

decontaminate [dēkəntam'ənāt] vt entgiften.
decontrol [dēkəntrōl'] vt (Brit: trade, prices) freigeben.
décor [dākôr'] n Ausstattung f.
decorate [dek'ərāt] vt (room) tapezieren; (paint) streichen; (adorn) (aus)schmücken; (cake) verzieren; (honor) auszeichnen.
decoration [dekərā'shən] n (of house) (Wand)dekoration f; (medal) Orden m.
decorative [dek'ûrətiv] a dekorativ, Schmuck-.
decorator [dek'ərātûr] n Maler m, Anstreicher m.
decorum [dikôr'əm] n Anstand m.
decoy [dē'koi] n (lit, fig) Lockvogel m.
decrease n [dē'krēs] Abnahme f ♦ [dikrēs'] vt vermindern ♦ vi abnehmen; **to be on the ~** abnehmen, zurückgehen.
decreasing [dikrēs'ing] a abnehmend, zurückgehend.
decree [dikrē'] n Verfügung f, Erlaß m ♦ vt verordnen, verfügen (that daß); **~ absolute** endgültige(s) Scheidungsurteil nt.
decrepit [dikrep'it] a hinfällig; (person) klapprig (col); (building) baufällig, heruntergekommen.
decry [dikrī'] vt schlechtmachen.
dedicate [ded'ikāt] vt (to God) weihen; (book) widmen.
dedicated [ded'ikātid] a (attitude) hingebungsvoll; (COMPUT) dediziert; **~ computer** Computer m für einen speziellen Zweck; **~ word processor** dedizierte(s) Text(verarbeitungs)system nt.
dedication [dedikā'shən] n (devotion) Ergebenheit f; (in book) Widmung f.
deduce [didōōs'] vt ableiten, schließen (from aus).
deduct [didukt'] vt abziehen.
deduction [diduk'shən] n (of money) Abzug m; (conclusion) Schluß)folgerung f.
deed [dēd] n Tat f; (document) Urkunde f.
deed of covenant n Vertragsurkunde f.
deem [dēm] vt (form) **to ~ sb/sth to be sth** jdn/etw für etw erachten or halten; **to ~ it wise to do sth** etw vorsichtshalber machen.
deep [dēp] a tief.
deepen [dē'pən] vt vertiefen.
deep-freeze [dēp'frēz'] n Tiefkühlung f.
deep-fry [dēp'frī'] vt fritieren.
deep fryer [dēp' frī'ûr] n Friteuse f.
deeply [dēp'lē] ad (dig, cut, breathe) tief; **to regret sth ~** etw zutiefst bereuen.
deep-rooted [dēp'rōō'tid] a (prejudice) tief verwurzelt; (hate) tiefgründig; (habit) fest eingefahren.
deep-sea diver [dēp'sē' dī'vûr] n Tiefseetaucher(in f) m.
deep-seated [dēp'sē'tid] a tiefsitzend.
deep-set [dēp'set] a tiefliegend.
deer [dēr] n Reh nt; (with antlers) Hirsch m.
deerstalker [dēr'stôkûr] n jd, der auf die Pirsch geht; (hat) ≈ Sherlock-Holmes-Mütze f.

deface [difās'] vt entstellen.
defamation [defəmā'shən] n Verleumdung f.
defamatory [difam'ətôrē] a diffamierend, verleumderisch.
default [difôlt'] n Versäumnis nt ♦ a (COMPUT) Vorgabe- ♦ vi versäumen; **by ~** durch Nichterscheinen nt; **to ~ on a debt** einer Zahlungsverpflichtung nicht nachkommen.
defaulter [difôlt'ûr] n Schuldner m, Zahlungsunfähige(r) m.
default option n (COMPUT) Vorbelegung f, Vorgabe f.
defeat [difēt'] n (overthrow) Vernichtung f; (battle) Niederlage f ♦ vt schlagen, zu Fall bringen.
defeatism [difē'tizəm] n Defätismus m.
defeatist [difē'tist] a defätistisch.
defect n [dē'fekt] Defekt m, Fehler m ♦ vi [difekt'] überlaufen; **physical ~** körperliche(r) Schaden m or Defekt m; **mental ~** geistige(r) Schaden m.
defective [difek'tiv] a fehlerhaft, schadhaft.
defector [difek'tûr] n (POL) Überläufer(in f) m.
defence [difens'] etc (Brit) = **defense** etc; **the Ministry of D~** (Brit) das Verteidigungsministerium.
defend [difend'] vt verteidigen.
defendant [difen'dənt] n Angeklagte(r) m.
defender [difen'dûr] n Verteidiger m.
defending [difen'ding] a: **~ champion** (SPORT) Titelverteidiger(in f) m; **~ counsel** (Brit: JUR) Verteidiger(in f) m.
defense [difens'] n (US) Verteidigung f; (excuse) Rechtfertigung f; **~ counsel** (US: JUR) Verteidiger(in f) m.
defenseless [difens'lis] a wehrlos.
defensive [difen'siv] a defensiv, Schutz- ♦ n Defensive f; **on the ~** in der Defensive.
defer [difûr'] vt verschieben ♦ vi: **to ~ to sb/sth** (submit) sich jdm/etw beugen or fügen.
deference [def'ûrəns] n Hochachtung f, Rücksichtnahme f; **out of or in ~ to** aus Achtung (dat) or Respekt (dat) vor.
deferential [defərən'chəl] a ehrerbietig.
deferred [difûrd'] a: **~ creditor** im Range nachstehende(r) Gläubige(r) m.
defiance [difī'əns] n Trotz m, Unnachgiebigkeit f; **in ~ of the order** dem Befehl zum Trotz.
defiant [difī'ənt] a trotzig, unnachgiebig.
defiantly [difī'əntlē] ad herausfordernd, trotzig.
deficiency [difish'ənsē] n Unzulänglichkeit f, Mangel m; (FIN) Defizit nt, Fehlbetrag m.
deficient [difish'ənt] a unzureichend.
deficit [def'isit] n Defizit nt, Fehlbetrag m.
defile [difīl'] vt beschmutzen ♦ n Schlucht f.
define [difīn'] vt bestimmen; (COMPUT, explain) definieren.
definite [def'ənit] a bestimmt; (clear) klar, eindeutig.
definitely [def'ənitlē] ad bestimmt.

definition [defənish'ən] *n* Definition *f*; (*PHOT*) Schärfe *f*.

definitive [difin'ətiv] *a* definitiv, endgültig.

deflate [diflāt'] *vt* die Luft ablassen aus; (*FIN*): **to ~ the currency** eine Deflation herbeiführen; **that was rather deflating for him** das war ein ziemlicher Dämpfer für ihn.

deflation [diflā'shən] *n* (*FIN*) Deflation *f*.

deflationary [diflā'shənärē] *a* (*FIN*) Deflations-, deflationistisch.

deflect [diflekt'] *vt* ablenken.

defog [dēfôg'] *vt* (*US AUT*) freimachen.

defogger [dēfôg'ûr] *n* (*US AUT*) Gebläse *nt*.

deforestation [dēfôristā'shən] *n* Entwaldung *f*.

deform [difôrm'] *vt* deformieren, entstellen.

deformed [difôrmd'] *a* deformiert.

defo∠mity [difôr'mitē] *n* Verunstaltung *f*, Mißbildung *f*.

defraud [difrôd'] *vt* betrügen.

defray [difrā'] *vt* bestreiten.

defrost [difrôst'] *vt* (*fridge*) abtauen; (*food*) auftauen.

defroster [difrôs'tûr] *n* (*US*) Gebläse *nt*.

deft [deft] *a* geschickt.

defunct [difungkt'] *a* verstorben.

defuse [dēfyōōz'] *vt*: **to ~ a situation** (*fig*) eine Situation entschärfen.

defy [difi'] *vt* (*challenge, refuse to obey: person*) sich widersetzen (+*dat*); (*resist*) trotzen (+*dat*), sich stellen gegen.

degenerate *vi* [dijen'ûrāt] degenerieren ♦ *a* [dijen'ûrit] degeneriert.

degradation [degrədā'shən] *n* Erniedrigung *f*.

degrade [digrād'] *vt* erniedrigen.

degrading [digrā'ding] *a* erniedrigend.

degree [digrē'] *n* Grad *m*; (*UNIV*) akademische(r) Grad *m*; **by ~s** allmählich; **to some ~, to a certain ~** einigermaßen, in gewissem Maße; **a considerable ~ of risk** ein ziemliches Risiko; **10 ~s below zero** 10 Grad unter Null; **to take one's ~** sein Examen machen.

dehydrated [dēhī'drātid] *a* getrocknet, Trocken-.

dehydration [dēhīdrā'shən] *n* Austrocknung *f*, Dehydration *f*.

de-ice [dēīs'] *vt* enteisen, auftauen.

de-icer [dēī'sûr] *n* Enteiser *m*.

deign [dān] *vi* sich herablassen.

deity [dē'itē] *n* Gottheit *f*.

dejected [dijek'tid] *a* niedergeschlagen.

dejection [dijek'shən] *n* Niedergeschlagenheit *f*.

Del. *abbr* (*US*) = *Delaware*.

del. *abbr* = **delete**.

delay [dilā'] *vt* (*hold back*) aufschieben; **to ~ payment** mit der Zahlung warten; **the flight was ~ed** die Maschine hatte Verspätung ♦ *vi* (*linger*) sich aufhalten, zögern ♦ *n* Aufschub *m*, Verzögerung *f*; **without ~** unverzüglich.

delayed [dilād'] *a* (*action*) verzögert.

delayed-action [dilād'ak'shən] *a* (*bomb etc*) mit Zeitzünder.

delectable [dilek'təbəl] *a* köstlich; (*fig*) reizend.

delegate *n* [del'əgit] Delegierte(r) *mf*, Abgeordnete(r) *mf* ♦ *vt* [del'əgāt] delegieren; **to ~ sth to sb/sb to do sth** jdm etw übertragen/jdn damit beauftragen, etw zu tun.

delegation [deləgā'shən] *n* Abordnung *f*; (*foreign*) Delegation *f*; (*of work etc*) Delegieren *nt*.

delete [dilēt'] *vt* (aus)streichen; (*COMPUT*) löschen.

Delhi [del'ē] *n* Delhi *nt*.

deliberate *a* [dilib'ûrit] (*intentional*) bewußt, überlegt; (*slow*) bedächtig ♦ *vi* [dilib'ûrāt] (*consider*) überlegen; (*debate*) sich beraten.

deliberately [dilib'ûritlē] *ad* vorsätzlich.

deliberation [dilibərā'shən] *n* Überlegung *f*; (*discussion*) Beratungen *pl*.

delicacy [del'əkəsē] *n* Zartheit *f*; (*weakness*) Anfälligkeit *f*; (*tact*) Zartgefühl *nt*; (*food*) Delikatesse *f*.

delicate [del'əkit] *a* (*fine*) fein; (*fragile*) zart; (*situation*) heikel; (*MED*) empfindlich.

delicately [del'əkitlē] *ad* fein; (*act, express*) gefühlvoll.

delicatessen [deləkətes'ən] *n* Feinkostgeschäft *nt*.

delicious [dilish'əs] *a* köstlich, lecker, delikat.

delight [dilīt'] *n* Wonne *f* ♦ *vt* entzücken.

delighted [dilī'tid] *a*: **~ (at or with sth)** erfreut (über etw); **to be ~ to do sth** etw gerne tun; **I'd be ~** ich würde mich sehr freuen; **I'm ~ that …** ich freue mich, daß …

delightful [dilīt'fəl] *a* entzückend, herrlich.

delimit [dilim'it] *vt* abstecken, abgrenzen.

delineate [dilin'ēāt] *vt* (*draw*) skizzieren; (*describe*) beschreiben, darstellen.

delinquency [diling'kwənsē] *n* Straffälligkeit *f*, Delinquenz *f*.

delinquent [diling'kwint] *n* Straffällige(r) *mf* ♦ *a* straffällig.

delirious [dilēr'ēəs] *a* irre, im Fieberwahn; (*MED*) im Delirium.

delirium [dilēr'ēəm] *n* Fieberwahn *m*, Delirium *nt*.

deliver [diliv'ûr] *vt* (*goods*) (ab)liefern; (*letter*) bringen, zustellen; (*verdict*) aussprechen; (*speech*) halten.

deliverance [diliv'ûrəns] *n* Befreiung *f*, Erlösung *f*.

delivery [diliv'ûrē] *n* (Ab)lieferung *f*; (*of letter*) Zustellung *f*; (*of speech*) Vortragsweise *f*.

delivery slip *n* Lieferschein *m*.

delivery truck, (*Brit*) **delivery van** *n* Lieferwagen *m*.

delouse [dēlous'] *vt* entlausen.

delta [del'ta] *n* Delta *nt*.

delude [dilōōd'] *vt* täuschen.

deluge [del'yōōj] *n* Überschwemmung *f*; (*fig*) Flut *f* ♦ *vt*: **to ~ (with)** (*fig*) überschwem-

men *or* überfluten (mit).
delusion [dilōō'zhən] *n* (Selbst)täuschung *f*.
deluxe [dəluks'] *a* Luxus-.
Dem. *abbr* (*US POL*) = **Democrat; Democratic**.
demand [dimand'] *vt* verlangen; (*need*) erfordern, verlangen; **to ~ sth (from** *or* **of sb)** etw (von jdm) verlangen *or* fordern ♦ *n* (*request*) Verlangen *nt*; (*COMM*) Nachfrage *f*; **in ~** begehrt, gesucht; **on ~** auf Verlangen.
demand draft *n* Zahlungsaufforderung *f*.
demanding [dimand'ing] *a* anspruchsvoll.
demarcation [dēmärkā'shən] *n* Abgrenzung *f*.
demarcation dispute *n* Streit *m* um den Zuständigkeitsbereich.
demean [dimēn'] *vt*: **to ~ o.s.** sich erniedrigen.
demeanor, (*Brit*) **demeanour** [dimē'nûr] *n* Benehmen *nt*.
demented [dimen'tid] *a* wahnsinnig.
demi- [dem'i] *pref* halb-.
demilitarize [dēmil'itərīz] *vt* entmilitarisieren, demilitarisieren.
demise [dimīz'] *n* Ableben *nt*.
demist [dēmist'] *vt* (*Brit AUT*) freimachen.
demister [dimīs'tûr] *n* (*Brit AUT*) Gebläse *nt*.
demo [dem'ō] *n* (*col*) Demo *f*.
demobilization [dēmōbəlizā'shən] *n* Demobilisierung *f*.
democracy [dimâk'rəsē] *n* Demokratie *f*.
Democrat [dem'əkrat] *n* (*US POL*) Demokrat(in *f*) *m*.
democratic [deməkrat'ik] *a*, **democratically** [deməkrat'iklē] *ad* demokratisch.
demography [dimâg'rəfē] *n* Demographie *f*.
demolish [dimâl'ish] *vt* (*lit*) abreißen; (*destroy*) zerstören; (*fig*) vernichten.
demolition [deməlish'ən] *n* Abbruch *m*.
demon [dē'mən] *n* Dämon *m*.
demonstrate [dem'ənstrāt] *vti* demonstrieren (*for/against* für/gegen).
demonstration [demənstrā'shən] *n* Demonstration *f*; (*proof*) Beweisführung *f*; **to hold a ~** (*POL*) eine Demonstration veranstalten *or* durchführen.
demonstrative [dimân'strətiv] *a* demonstrativ.
demonstrator [dem'ənstrātûr] *n* (*POL*) Demonstrant(in *f*) *m*; (*COMM*) Propagandist(in *f*) *m*, Vorführer(in *f*) *m*.
demoralize [dimôr'əlīz] *vt* demoralisieren.
demote [dimōt'] *vt* degradieren, zurückstufen.
demotion [dimō'shən] *n* Degradierung *f*, Zurückstufung *f*.
demur [dimûr'] *vi* (*form*) Einwände *pl* erheben (*at* gegen) ♦ *n*: **without ~** widerspruchslos.
demure [dimyōōr'] *a* sittsam.
demurrage [dimûr'ij] *n* Liegegeld *nt*; (*to shipowner*) Überliegegeld *nt*.
den [den] *n* (*of animal*) Höhle *f*, Bau *m*; (*room*) Bude *f*; **~ of vice** Lasterhöhle *f*.
denationalization [dēnashnəlizā'shən] *n* Re-

privatisierung *f*.
denationalize [dēnash'nəlīz] *vt* reprivatisieren, entstaatlichen.
denial [dinī'əl] *n* Leugnung *f*; **official ~** Dementi *nt*.
denier [den'yûr] *n* Denier *nt*.
denigrate [den'əgrāt] *vt* verunglimpfen.
denim [den'əm] *a* Denim-.
denim jacket *n* Jeansjacke *f*.
denims [den'əmz] *npl* Denim-Jeans *pl*.
denizen [den'izən] *n* (*inhabitant*) Einwohner(in *f*) *m*, Bewohner(in *f*) *m*; (*foreigner*) eingebürgerte(r) Ausländer *m*.
Denmark [den'mârk] *n* Dänemark *nt*.
denomination [dinâmənā'shən] *n* (*ECCL*) Bekenntnis *nt*; (*type*) Klasse *f*; (*FIN*) Wert *m*.
denominator [dinâm'ənātûr] *n* Nenner *m*; **common ~** gemeinsame(r) Nenner.
denote [dinōt'] *vt* bedeuten.
denounce [dinouns'] *vt* brandmarken.
dense [dens] *a* dicht, dick; (*stupid*) schwer von Begriff.
densely [dens'lē] *ad* dicht.
density [den'sitē] *n* Dichte *f*; **single-/double-~ disk** (*COMPUT*) Diskette *f* mit einfacher/ doppelter Bitdichte.
dent [dent] *n* Delle *f* ♦ *vt* einbeulen.
dental [den'təl] *a* Zahn-.
dental surgeon *n* = **dentist**.
dentifrice [den'təfris] *n* Zahnputzmittel *nt*.
dentist [den'tist] *n* Zahnarzt *m*/-ärztin *f*; **~'s office** (*US*) *or* **surgery** (*Brit*) Zahnarztpraxis *f*.
dentistry [den'tistrē] *n* Zahnmedizin *f*.
denture [den'chûr] *n* künstliche(s) Gebiß *nt*.
dentures [den'chûrz] *npl* (*partial ~*) Zahnprothese *f*.
denude [dinōōd'] *vt* entblößen.
deny [dinī'] *vt* leugnen; (*rumor*) widersprechen (+*dat*); (*knowledge*) verleugnen; (*help*) abschlagen; **to ~ o.s. sth** sich etw versagen; **he denies having said it** er leugnet *or* bestreitet, das gesagt zu haben.
deodorant [dēō'dûrənt] *n* Desodorant *nt*.
depart [dipârt'] *vi* abfahren.
departed [dipâr'tid] *a* (*bygone: days, glory*) vergangen; (*dead*) verstorben.
department [dipârt'mənt] *n* (*COMM*) Abteilung *f*, Sparte *f*; (*UNIV. SCH*) Fachbereich *m*; (*POL*) Ministerium *nt*, Ressort *nt*; **that's not my ~** (*also fig*) das ist nicht mein Ressort; **D~ of State** (*US*) Außenministerium *nt*.
departmental [dēpârtmen'təl] *a* Fach-; (*dispute*) Abteilungs-, Fachbereichs-; **~ manager** Abteilungsleiter(in *f*) *m*.
department store *n* Warenhaus *nt*.
departure [dipâr'chûr] *n* (*of person*) Weggang *m*; (*on journey*) Abreise *f*; (*of train*) Abfahrt *f*; (*of plane*) Abflug *m*; **new ~** Neuerung *f*.
departure lounge *n* Abflughalle *f*.
depend [dipend'] *vi* (*person: be dependent on*) abhängig sein von, angewiesen sein auf

(+*acc*); **it ~s** es kommt darauf an.
depend on *vt fus* abhängen von; *(parents etc)* angewiesen sein auf (+*acc*); **~ing on the result** ... abhängend vom Resultat ...
dependable [dipen'dəbəl] *a* zuverlässig.
dependence [dipen'dəns] *n* Abhängigkeit *f*.
dependent [dipen'dənt] *n* *(person)* Familienangehörige(r) *mf* ♦ *a* abhängig *(on* von); **to be ~ (on)** angewiesen sein (auf).
depict [dipikt'] *vt* schildern.
depilatory [dipil'ətôrē] *n* *(also:* **~ cream)** Enthaarungscreme *f*.
deplane [dēplān'] *vi* *(US)* von Bord gehen.
depleted [diplēt'id] *a* aufgebraucht.
deplorable [diplôr'əbəl] *a* bedauerlich.
deplore [diplôr'] *vt* mißbilligen.
deploy [diploi'] *vt* einsetzen.
depopulate [dipâp'yəlāt] *vt* entvölkern.
depopulation [dipâpyəlā'shən] *n* Entvölkerung *f*.
deport [dipôrt'] *vt* deportieren.
deportation [dēpôrtā'shən] *n* Abschiebung *f*.
deportation order *n* Ausweisung *f*.
deportment [dipôrt'mənt] *n* Betragen *nt*.
depose [dipōz'] *vt* absetzen.
deposit [dipâz'it] *n* *(in bank)* Guthaben *nt*; *(down payment)* Anzahlung *f*; *(security)* Kaution *f*; *(CHEM)* Niederschlag *m* ♦ *vt (in bank)* deponieren; *(put down)* niederlegen; **to put down a ~ of $50** eine Anzahlung von 50 Dollar machen.
deposit account *n* *(Brit)* Sparkonto *nt*.
depositor [dipâz'itûr] *n* Deponent(in *f*) *m*, Einzahler(in *f*) *m*.
depository [dipâz'itôrē] *n* Hinterlegungsstelle *f*.
depot [dē'pō] *n* Depot *nt*.
deprave [diprāv'] *vt* *(moralisch)* verderben.
depraved [diprāvd'] *a* verworfen.
depravity [diprav'itē] *n* Verworfenheit *f*.
deprecate [dep'rəkāt] *vt* mißbilligen.
deprecating [dep'rəkāting] *a* *(disapproving)* mißbilligend; **a ~ smile** *(apologetic)* ein abwehrendes Lächeln.
depreciate [diprē'shēāt] *vi* im Wert sinken.
depreciation [diprēshēā'shən] *n* Wertminderung *f*.
depress [dipres'] *vt* *(press down)* niederdrücken; *(in mood)* deprimieren.
depressant [dipres'ənt] *n* *(MED)* Beruhigungsmittel *nt*, Sedativ(um) *nt*.
depressed [diprest'] *a* *(person)* niedergeschlagen, deprimiert; *(FIN: market, trade)* flau; **to get ~** deprimiert werden.
depressed area *n* Notstandsgebiet *nt*.
depressing [dipres'ing] *a* deprimierend.
depression [dipresh'ən] *n* *(mood)* Depression *f*; *(in trade)* Wirtschaftskrise *f*; *(hollow)* Vertiefung *f*; *(MET)* Tief(druckgebiet) *nt*; **the economy is in a state of ~** die Wirtschaft steckt in einer Krise.
deprivation [deprəvā'shən] *n* Entbehrung *f*, Not *f*.
deprive [diprīv'] *vt* berauben *(of +gen)*.

deprived [diprīvd'] *a* *(child)* sozial benachteiligt; *(area)* unterentwickelt.
dept. *abbr* (= *department*) Abt.
depth [depth] *n* Tiefe *f*; **at a ~ of 3 meters** in 3 Meter Tiefe; **don't go out of your ~!**; *(Brit: swimmer)* geh nicht zu tief rein!; **in the ~s of despair** in tiefster Verzweiflung; **to be out of one's ~** *(fig)* keine Ahnung haben, passen; **to study sth in ~** etw gründlich studieren.
depth charge *n* Wasserbombe *f*.
deputation [depyətā'shən] *n* Abordnung *f*.
deputize [dep'yətīz] *vi* vertreten *(for acc)*.
deputy [dep'yətē] *a* stellvertretend ♦ *n* (Stell)vertreter *m*.
deputy leader *n* *(Brit POL)* stellvertretende(r) Vorsitzende(r) *mf*.
derail [dirāl'] *vt* entgleisen lassen; **to be ~ed** entgleisen.
derailment [dirāl'mənt] *n* Entgleisung *f*.
deranged [dirānjd'] *a* irr, verrückt.
derby [dûr'bē] *n* *(US)* Melone *f*.
Derbys *abbr (Brit)* = *Derbyshire*.
deregulate [dēreg'yəlāt] *vi* staatliche Kontrollen aufheben von.
deregulation [dēregyəlā'shən] *n* Aufhebung *f* staatlicher Kontrollen.
derelict [där'əlikt] *a* verlassen; *(building)* baufällig.
deride [dirīd'] *vt* auslachen.
derision [dirizh'ən] *n* Hohn *m*, Spott *m*.
derisory [dirī'sûrē] *a* spöttisch.
derivation [därəvā'shən] *n* Ableitung *f*.
derivative [diriv'ətiv] *n* Abgeleitete(s) *nt* ♦ *a* abgeleitet.
derive [dirīv'] *vt* *(get)* gewinnen; *(deduce)* ableiten ♦ *vi* *(come from)* abstammen.
derived [dirīvd'] *a*: **~ demand** mittelbar entstandene(r) Bedarf *m*.
dermatitis [dûrmətī'tis] *n* Hautentzündung *f*, Dermatitis *f*.
dermatology [dûrmətâl'əjē] *n* Dermatologie *f*.
derogatory [dirâg'ətôrē] *a* geringschätzig.
derrick [där'ik] *n* Drehkran *m*.
derv [dûrv] *n* *(Brit)* Diesel(kraftstoff) *m*, Dieselöl *nt*.
DES *n* *abbr (Brit*: = *Department of Education and Science)* Ministerium für Bildung und Wissenschaft.
desalination [dēsalənā'shən] *n* Entsalzung *f*.
descend [disend'] *vti* hinuntersteigen; **to ~ from** abstammen von; **in ~ing order of importance** nach Wichtigkeit geordnet.
descend on *vt fus* *(enemy, angry person)* überfallen; *(misfortune)* hereinbrechen über; *(fig: gloom, silence)* befallen; **visitors ~ed (up)on us** der Besuch hat uns überfallen.
descendant [disen'dənt] *n* Nachkomme *m*.
descent [disent'] *n* *(coming down)* Abstieg *m*; *(origin)* Abstammung *f*.
describe [diskrīb'] *vt* beschreiben.
description [diskrip'shən] *n* Beschreibung *f*;

(*sort*) Art *f*; **of every** ~ aller Art.
descriptive [diskrip'tiv] *a* beschreibend; (*word*) anschaulich.
desecrate [des'əkrāt] *vt* schänden.
desegregation [dēsegrəgā'shən] *n* Aufhebung *f* der Rassentrennung.
desert *n* [dez'ûrt] Wüste *f*; *see also* **deserts** ♦ [dizûrt'] *vt* verlassen; (*temporarily*) im Stich lassen ♦ *vi* (*MIL*) desertieren.
deserter [dizûr'tûr] *n* Deserteur *m*.
desertion [dizûr'shən] *n* (*of wife*) böswillige(s) Verlassen *nt*; (*MIL*) Fahnenflucht *f*.
desert island [dez'ûrt i'lənd] *n* einsame *or* verlassene Insel *f*.
deserts [dizûrts'] *npl*: **to get one's just** ~ bekommen, was man verdient.
deserve [dizûrv'] *vt* verdienen.
deservedly [dizûr'vidlē] *ad* verdientermaßen.
deserving [dizûr'ving] *a* (*person*) würdig; (*action*) verdienstvoll.
desiccated [des'əkātid] *a* getrocknet.
design [dizīn'] *n* (*plan*) Entwurf *m*; (*drawing*) Zeichnung *f*; (*planning*) Gestaltung *f*, Design *nt*; (*of car*) Konstruktion *f*; (*of dress*) Design *nt* ♦ *vt* entwerfen; (*intend*) bezwecken; **industrial** ~ Konstruktionslehre *f*; **to be** ~**ed for sb/sth** für jdn/etw vorbestimmt *or* bestimmt sein; **to have** ~**s on sb/sth** es auf jdn/etw abgesehen haben.
designate *vt* [dez'ignāt] bestimmen ♦ *a* [dez'ignit] designiert.
designation [dezignā'shən] *n* Bezeichnung *f*.
designer [dizī'nûr] *n* Designer *m*; (*THEAT*) Bühnenbildner(in *f*) *m*.
desirability [dizīûrəbil'ətē] *n* Erwünschtheit *f*.
desirable [dizī'ûrəbəl] *a* wünschenswert; (*woman*) begehrenswert; **it is** ~ **that** ... es ist wünschenswert, daß ...
desire [dizī'ûr] *n* Wunsch *m*, Verlangen *nt* ♦ *vt* (*lust*) begehren, wünschen; (*ask for*) verlangen, wollen; **to** ~ **sth/to do sth/that** ... nach etw verlangen/etw zu tun wünschen/ danach verlangen, daß ...
desirous [dizī'ûrəs] *a* begierig (*of* auf +*acc*).
desist [dizist'] *vi* Abstand nehmen, aufhören.
desk [desk] *n* Schreibtisch *m*; (*Brit: in shop, restaurant*) Kasse *f*.
desktop publishing [desk'tâp pub'lishing] *n* Desktop Publishing *nt*.
desolate [des'əlit] *a* öde; (*sad*) trostlos.
desolation [desəlā'shən] *n* Trostlosigkeit *f*.
despair [dispär'] *n* Verzweiflung *f* ♦ *vi* verzweifeln (*of* an +*dat*); **in** ~ aus *or* in Verzweiflung.
despatch [dispach'] (*Brit*) = **dispatch**.
desperate [des'pûrit] *a* (*measures*) verzweifelt; (*situation*) hoffnungslos; **to be** ~ **for sth** etw unbedingt brauchen; **we are getting** ~ wir verzweifeln allmählich.
desperately [des'pûritlē] *ad* verzweifelt; ~ **ill** schwerkrank *attr*, schwer krank.
desperation [despərā'shən] *n* Verzweiflung *f*.
despicable [des'pikəbəl] *a* abscheulich.
despise [dispīz'] *vt* verachten.

despite [dispīt'] *prep* trotz (+*gen*).
despondent [dispân'dənt] *a* mutlos.
despot [des'pət] *n* Despot *m*.
dessert [dizûrt'] *n* Nachtisch *m*.
dessertspoon [dizûrt'spōōn] *n* Dessertlöffel *m*.
destabilize [dēstā'bəlīz] *vt* (*lit, fig*) destabilisieren, aus dem Gleichgewicht bringen.
destination [destənā'shən] *n* (*of person*) (Reise)ziel *nt*; (*of goods*) Bestimmungsort *m*.
destine [des'tin] *vt* (*set apart*) bestimmen.
destined [des'tind] *a*: ~ **for New York** unterwegs nach New York.
destiny [des'tənē] *n* Schicksal *nt*.
destitute [des'titōōt] *a* notleidend.
destitution [destitōō'shən] *n* Elend *f*.
destroy [distroi'] *vt* zerstören.
destroyer [distroi'ûr] *n* (*NAUT*) Zerstörer *m*.
destruction [distruk'shən] *n* Zerstörung *f*.
destructive [distruk'tiv] *a* zerstörend.
desultory [des'əltôrē] *a* (*reading*) flüchtig; (*conversation*) zwanglos; (*contact*) oberflächlich.
detach [ditach'] *vt* loslösen.
detachable [ditach'əbəl] *a* abtrennbar.
detached [ditacht'] *a* (*attitude*) distanziert, objektiv; (*house*) Einzel-.
detachment [ditach'mənt] *n* (*MIL*) Abteilung *f*, Sonderkommando *nt*; (*fig*) Abstand *m*, Unvoreingenommenheit *f*.
detail [ditāl'] *n* Einzelheit *f*, Detail *nt*; (*minor part*) unwichtige Einzelheit *f*; (*MIL*) Sondertrupp *m* ♦ *vt* (*relate*) ausführlich berichten; (*MIL*) abkommandieren (*for* zu); **in** ~ ausführlichst, bis ins kleinste; **to go into** ~(**s**) auf Einzelheiten eingehen.
detailed [ditāld'] *a* detailliert.
detain [ditān'] *vt* aufhalten; (*imprison*) in Haft halten.
detainee [dētānē'] *n* Häftling *m*.
detect [ditekt'] *vt* entdecken.
detection [ditek'shən] *n* (*of crime*) Aufdeckung *f*, Entdeckung *f*; (*of criminal*) Entlarvung *f*; **to escape** ~ (*criminal*) nicht gefaßt *or* dingfest gemacht werden; (*mistake*) der Aufmerksamkeit (*dat*) entgehen.
detective [ditek'tiv] *n* Detektiv *m*.
detective story *n* Krimi(nalgeschichte *f*) *m*.
detector [ditek'tûr] *n* Detektor *m*.
détente [dātânt'] *n* Entspannung *f*, Detente *f*.
detention [diten'chən] *n* Haft *f*; (*SCH*) Nachsitzen *nt*.
deter [ditûr'] *vt* abschrecken.
detergent [ditûr'jənt] *n* Waschmittel *nt*.
deteriorate [ditē'rēərāt] *vi* sich verschlechtern.
deterioration [ditērēərā'shən] *n* Verschlechterung *f*.
determination [ditûrmənā'shən] *n* Entschlossenheit *f*.
determine [ditûr'min] *vt* bestimmen; **to** ~ **to do sth** sich entschließen, etw zu tun.
determined [ditûr'mind] *a* entschlossen; **to be** ~ **to do sth** entschlossen sein, etw zu

tun; **a ~ effort** ein entschlossener Versuch.

deterrence [ditûr'əns] *n* Abschreckung(smittel *nt*) *f*.

deterrent [ditûr'ənt] *n* Abschreckungsmittel *nt* ♦ *a* abschreckend; **to act as a ~** als Abschreckung(smittel) dienen *(to für)*.

detest [ditest'] *vt* verabscheuen.

detestable [dites'təbəl] *a* abscheulich.

dethrone [dēthrōn'] *vt* entthronen.

detonate [det'ənāt] *vt* detonieren.

detonator [det'ənātûr] *n* Sprengkapsel *f*.

detour [dē'tōōr] *n* Umweg *m*; *(US AUT: diversion)* Umleitung *f* ♦ *vt (US: traffic)* umleiten.

detract [ditrakt'] *vi* schmälern *(from acc)*.

detractor [ditrak'tûr] *n* Gegner(in *f*) *m*.

detriment [det'rəmənt] *n*: **to the ~ of** zum Schaden *(+gen)*; **without ~ to** ohne Schaden für.

detrimental [detrəmen'təl] *a* schädlich.

deuce [dōōs] *n (TENNIS)* Einstand *m*; *(CARDS)* Zwei *f*.

devaluation [dēvalyōōā'shən] *n* Abwertung *f*.

devalue [dēval'yōō] *vt* abwerten.

devastate [dev'əstāt] *vt* verwüsten.

devastating [dev'əstāting] *a* verheerend.

devastation [devəstā'shən] *n* Verwüstung *f*.

develop [divel'əp] *vt* entwickeln; *(resources)* erschließen ♦ *vi* sich entwickeln; **to ~ a taste for sth** Geschmack an etw finden; **this land is to be ~ed** dieses Gebiet soll erschlossen werden; **to ~ into sth** sich zu etw entwickeln, etw werden.

developer [divel'əpûr] *n (PHOT)* Entwickler *m*; *(of land)* Bauunternehmer *m*; *(property ~)* Immobilienmakler *m*.

developing [divel'əping] *a (country)* Entwicklungs-.

development [divel'əpmənt] *n* Entwicklung *f*.

development area *n* Fördergebiet *nt*.

deviant [dē'vēənt] *a* abweichend ♦ *n* Abweichler *m*.

deviate [dē'vēāt] *vi* abweichen.

deviation [dēvēā'shən] *n* Abweichung *f*.

device [divīs'] *n* Vorrichtung *f*, Gerät *nt*; *(explosive ~)* Sprengkörper *m*.

devil [dev'əl] *n* Teufel *m*.

devilish [dev'əlish] *a* teuflisch.

devil-may-care [dev'əlmākār'] *a* unbekümmert, unbesonnen.

devious [dē'vēəs] *a (route)* gewunden; *(means)* krumm; *(person)* verschlagen.

devise [divīz'] *vt* entwickeln.

devoid [divoid'] *a*: **~ of** ohne, bar *(+gen)*.

devolution [devəlōō'shən] *n* Dezentralisierung *f*.

devolve [divālv'] *vi*: **to ~ (up)on** übergehen auf.

devote [divōt'] *vt* widmen *(to dat)*.

devoted [divōt'id] *a* ergeben.

devotee [devōtē'] *n* Anhänger(in *f*) *m*, Verehrer(in *f*) *m*.

devotion [divō'shən] *n (piety)* Andacht *f*; *(loyalty)* Ergebenheit *f*, Hingabe *f*.

devour [divou'ûr] *vt* verschlingen.

devout [divout'] *a* andächtig.

dew [dōō] *n* Tau *m*.

dexterity [dekstär'itē] *n* Geschicklichkeit *f*.

dext(e)rous [dek'strəs] *a (skillful: person, movement)* geschickt.

dg *abbr* *(= decigram(s))* dg.

diabetes [dīəbē'tis] *n* Zuckerkrankheit *f*.

diabetic [dīəbet'ik] *a* zuckerkrank; *(chocolate, jam)* Diabetiker- ♦ *n* Diabetiker(in *f*) *m*.

diabolical [dīəbâl'ikəl] *a* teuflisch; *(col: dreadful)* saumäßig.

diagnose [dīəgnōs'] *vt (MED)* diagnostizieren; feststellen.

diagnosis [dīəgnō'sis] *n* Diagnose *f*.

diagonal [dīag'ənəl] *a* diagonal, schräg ♦ *n* Diagonale *f*.

diagram [dī'əgram] *n* Diagramm *nt*, Schaubild *nt*.

dial. *abbr* *(= dialect)* Dial.

dial [dīl] *n (TEL)* Wählscheibe *f*; *(of clock)* Zifferblatt *nt* ♦ *vt* wählen; **to ~ a wrong number** *(TEL)* sich verwählen; **can I ~ Chicago direct?** kann ich nach Chicago durchwählen?

dial code *n (US)* Vorwahl *f*.

dialect [dī'əlekt] *n* Dialekt *m*.

dialling code [dī'ling kōd] *n (Brit)* Vorwahl *f*.

dialling tone [dī'ling tōn] *n (Brit)* Amtszeichen *nt*.

dialog(ue) [dī'əlôg] *n* Gespräch *nt*; *(LITER)* Dialog *m*.

dial tone *n (US)* Amtszeichen *nt*.

dialysis [dīal'isis] *n* Dialyse *f*.

diameter [dīam'itûr] *n* Durchmesser *m*.

diametrically [dīəmet'riklē] *ad*: **~ opposed to** genau *or* diametral entgegengesetzt *(+dat)*.

diamond [dī'mənd] *n* Diamant *m*; *(CARDS)* Karo *nt*.

diamond ring *n* Diamantring *m*; *(with one diamond)* Solitär *m*.

diaper [dī'pûr] *n (US)* Windel *f*.

diaper pin *n (US)* Sicherheitsnadel *f*.

diaphragm [dī'əfram] *n* Zwerchfell *nt*.

diarrhea, *(Brit)* **diarrhoea** [dīərē'ə] *n* Durchfall *m*.

diary [dī'ûrē] *n* Tagebuch *nt*; **to keep a ~** ein Tagebuch führen.

diatribe [dī'ətrīb] *n* Schmährede *f*.

dice [dīs] *n* Würfel *pl* ♦ *vt (COOK)* in Würfel schneiden.

dicey [dī'sē] *a (col)* riskant.

dichotomy [dīkât'əmē] *n* Kluft, *f* Dichotomie *f*.

Dictaphone [dik'təfōn] *n* ® Diktaphone *nt*.

dictate *vt* [diktāt'] diktieren; *(of circumstances)* gebieten ♦ *n* [dik'tāt] Mahnung *f*, Gebot *nt*.

  dictate to *vt fus (person)* diktieren *(+dat)*; **I won't be ~d to** ich lasse mir keine Vorschriften machen.

dictation [diktā'shən] *n* Diktat *nt*; **at ~ speed** im Diktiertempo.

dictator [dik'tātûr] *n* Diktator *m*.

dictatorship [dik'tātûrship] *n* Diktatur *f*.

diction [dik'shən] *n* Ausdrucksweise *f*.

dictionary [dik'shənārē] *n* Wörterbuch *nt*.

did [did] *pt of* **do**.

didactic [dīdak'tik] *a* didaktisch.

diddle [did'əl] *vt* (*col*) übers Ohr hauen.

didn't [did'ənt] = **did not**; **~ you know?** haben Sie/hast du das nicht gewußt?

die [dī] *vi* sterben; (*end*) aufhören; **to ~** (**of** *or* **from sth**) (an etw *dat*) sterben; **to be dying** im Sterben liegen; **to be dying to do sth** darauf brennen, etw zu tun.

die away *vi* schwächer werden.

die down *vi* nachlassen.

die out *vi* aussterben; (*fig*) nachlassen.

diehard [dī'hârd] *n* zähe(r) Kämpfer *m*.

dieresis [dīär'əsis] *n* Trema *nt*.

diesel [dē'zəl] *n* Diesel *m*.

diesel engine *n* Dieselmotor *m*.

diesel fuel, diesel oil *n* Dieselöl *nt*, Diesel *no art*.

diet [dī'ət] *n* Nahrung *f*, Kost *f*; (*special food*) Diät *f*; (*slimming*) Abmagerungskur *f* ♦ *vi* eine Abmagerungskur machen; **to live on a ~ of** sich ernähren von, leben von.

dietician [dīətish'ən] *n* Ernährungswissenschaftler(in *f*) *m*.

differ [dif'ûr] *vi* sich unterscheiden; (*disagree*) anderer Meinung sein; **we ~ on this** darüber sind wir unterschiedlicher Meinung.

difference [dif'ûrəns] *n* Unterschied *m*; (*disagreement*) (Meinungs)unterschied *m*; **it makes no ~ to me** das ist mir egal *or* einerlei; **to settle one's ~s** die Differenzen *or* Meinungsverschiedenheiten beilegen.

different [dif'ûrənt] *a* verschieden; **that's ~** das ist anders.

differential [difəren'chəl] *n* (*AUT*) Differentialgetriebe *nt*; (*in wages*) Lohnstufe *f*.

differentiate [difəren'chēāt] *vti* unterscheiden.

differently [dif'ûrəntlē] *ad* verschieden, unterschiedlich.

difficult [dif'əkult] *a* schwierig; **~ to understand** schwer zu verstehen.

difficulty [dif'əkultē] *n* Schwierigkeit *f*; **with ~** nur schwer; **to be in ~** in Schwierigkeiten sein; **to have difficulties with** (*police, landlord etc*) in Schwierigkeiten geraten mit.

diffidence [dif'idəns] *n* Bescheidenheit *f*, Zurückhaltung *f*; (*of smile*) Zaghaftigkeit *f*.

diffident [dif'idənt] *a* schüchtern.

diffuse *a* [difyōōs'] langatmig ♦ *vt* [difyōōz'] verbreiten.

dig [dig] *vti irreg* (*hole*) graben; (*garden*) (um)graben; (*claws*) senken ♦ *n* (*prod*) Stoß *m*; (*ARCHEOLOGY*) (Aus)grabung *f*; (*site*) Ausgrabungsstätte *f*; **to ~ into one's pockets for sth** in seinen Taschen nach etw suchen *or* wühlen; *see also* **digs**.

dig in *vi* (*MIL*) sich eingraben; (*col: eat*)

reinhauen, sich hermachen über (+*acc*) ♦ *vt* (*compost*) unter- *or* eingraben; (*knife*) hineinstoßen; (*claw*) festkrallen; **~ in!** hau rein! (*col*); **to ~ in one's heels** (*also fig*) sich auf die Hinterbeine stellen.

dig out *vt* ausgraben.

dig up *vt* ausgraben; (*fig*) aufgabeln.

digest *vt* [dijest'] (*lit, fig*) verdauen ♦ *n* [dī'jest] Auslese *f*.

digestible [dijes'təbəl] *a* verdaulich.

digestion [dijes'chən] *n* Verdauung *f*.

digestive [dijes'tiv] *a* Verdauungs-; **~ system** Verdauungsapparat *m*.

digit [dij'it] *n* einstellige Zahl *f*; (*ANAT*) Finger *m*; (*toe*) Zehe *f*.

digital [dij'itəl] *a* Digital-, digital.

digital computer *n* Digitalrechner *m*.

dignified [dig'nəfīd] *a* würdevoll.

dignify [dig'nəfī] *vt* Würde verleihen (+*dat*).

dignitary [dig'nitārē] *n* Würdenträger *m*.

dignity [dig'nitē] *n* Würde *f*.

digress [digres'] *vi* abschweifen.

digression [digresh'ən] *n* Abschweifung *f*.

digs [digz] *npl* (*Brit col*) Bude *f*.

dike [dīk] *n* (*US*) Deich *m*.

dilapidated [dilap'ədātid] *a* baufällig.

dilate [dīlāt'] *vti* (sich) weiten.

dilatory [dil'ətôrē] *a* hinhaltend.

dilemma [dilem'ə] *n* Dilemma *nt*; **to be in a ~** sich in einem Dilemma befinden, in der Klemme sitzen (*col*).

dilettante [dilitânt'] *n* Dilettant *m*.

diligence [dil'ijəns] *n* Fleiß *m*.

diligent [dil'ijənt] *a* fleißig.

dill [dil] *n* Dill *m*.

dilly-dally [dil'ēdalē] *vi* (*col*) herumtrödeln, bummeln.

dilute [dilōōt'] *vt* verdünnen ♦ *a* verdünnt.

dim [dim] *a* trübe, matt; (*stupid*) schwer von Begriff; **I take a ~ view of this** ich halte nicht viel davon ♦ *vt* verdunkeln; (*US AUT*) abblenden.

dime [dīm] *n* (*US*) Zehncentstück *nt*.

dimension [dimen'chən] *n* Dimension *f*.

-dimensional [dimen'chənəl] *a suff*: **two~** zweidimensional.

dimensions [dimen'chənz] *npl* Maße *pl*.

diminish [dimin'ish] *vti* (sich) verringern.

diminished [dimin'isht] *a*: **~ responsibility** (*JUR*) verminderte Zurechnungsfähigkeit *f*.

diminutive [dimin'yətiv] *a* winzig ♦ *n* Verkleinerungsform *f*.

dimly [dim'lē] *ad* trübe.

dimmer [dim'ûr] *n* (*US AUT*) Abblendschalter *m*.

dimple [dim'pəl] *n* Grübchen *nt*.

dim-witted [dim'witid] *a* (*col*) dämlich.

din [din] *n* Getöse *nt* ♦ *vt*: **to ~ sth into sb** (*col*) jdm etw einbleuen.

dine [dīn] *vi* speisen.

diner [dīn'ûr] *n* (*person: in restaurant*) Speisende(r) *mf*; (*RAIL*) Speisewagen *m*; (*esp US: eating place*) Eßlokal *nt*.

dinghy [ding'ē] *n* kleine(s) Ruderboot *nt*,

Dinghy *nt*.

dingy [din'jē] *a* armselig.

dining car [dīn'ing kár] *n* Speisewagen *m*.

dining room [dīn'ing rōōm] *n* Eßzimmer *nt*; (*in hotel*) Speisezimmer *nt*.

dinner [din'úr] *n* Mittagessen *nt*, Abendessen *nt*; (*public*) Festessen *nt*.

dinner jacket *n* Smoking *m*.

dinner party *n* Tischgesellschaft *f*.

dinner time *n* Tischzeit *f*.

dinosaur [dī'nəsôr] *n* Dinosaurier *m*.

dint [dint] *n*: **we succeeded by ~ of working 24 hours a day** wir schafften es, indem wir 24 Stunden pro Tag arbeiteten.

diocese [dī'əsēs] *n* Diözese *f*, Sprengel *m*.

dioxide [dīǎk'sid] *n* Dioxyd *nt*; **carbon ~** Kohlendioxyd *nt*.

dip [dip] *n* (*hollow*) Senkung *f*; (*bathe*) kurze(s) Bad(en) *nt* ♦ *vt* eintauchen; (*Brit AUT*) abblenden ♦ *vi* (*slope*) sich senken, abfallen.

diphtheria [dipthē'rēə] *n* Diphterie *f*.

diphthong [dif'thông] *n* Diphthong *m*.

diploma [diplō'mə] *n* Urkunde *f*, Diplom *nt*.

diplomacy [diplō'məsē] *n* Diplomatie *f*.

diplomat [dip'ləmət] *n* Diplomat(in *f*) *m*.

diplomatic [dipləmat'ik] *a* diplomatisch; **to break off ~ relations** diplomatische Beziehungen abbrechen.

diplomatic corps *n* diplomatische(s) Korps *nt*.

dipstick [dip'stik] *n* Ölmeßstab *m*.

dipswitch [dip'swich] *n* (*Brit AUT*) Abblendschalter *m*.

dire [dī'úr] *a* schrecklich.

direct [direkt'] *a* direkt; (*manner, person*) direkt, offen ♦ *vt* leiten; (*film*) die Regie führen (+*gen*); (*jury*) anweisen; (*aim*) richten, lenken; (*tell way*) den Weg erklären (+*dat*); (*order*) anweisen; **to ~ sb to do sth** jdn anweisen, etw zu tun.

direct access *n* (*COMPUT*) direkte(r) Zugriff *m*.

direct cost *n* direkte Kosten *pl*.

direct current *n* Gleichstrom *m*.

direct hit *n* Volltreffer *m*.

direction [direk'shən] *n* Führung *f*, Leitung *f*; (*course*) Richtung *f*; (*CINE*) Regie *f*; (*RAD, TV*) Leitung *f*; **~s** *pl* (*for use*) Gebrauchsanleitung *f*; (*orders*) Anweisungen *pl*; (*instructions: to a place*) (Richtungs)angaben *pl*; **to ask for ~s** nach dem Weg fragen; **sense of ~** Orientierungssinn *m*; **in the ~ of Bonn** in Richtung Bonn.

directional [direk'shənəl] *a* Richt-.

directive [direk'tiv] *n* Direktive *f*, Weisung *f*; **a government ~** ein Regierungserlaß *m*.

directly [direkt'lē] *ad* (*in straight line*) gerade, direkt; (*at once*) unmittelbar, sofort.

direct mail *n* Direktwerbung *f* per Post.

direct mailshot *n* (*Brit*) Postwurfsendung *f*.

directness [direkt'nis] *n* (*of person, speech*) Direktheit *f*.

director [direk'tûr] *n* Direktor *m*, Leiter *m*;

(*of film*) Regisseur *m*.

Director of Public Prosecutions *n* (*Brit*) Leiter *m* der Anklagebehörde.

directory [direk'tûrē] *n* Adreßbuch *nt*; (*TEL*) Telefonbuch *nt*; (*COMPUT*) Inhaltsverzeichnis *nt*; **street ~** Straßenverzeichnis *nt*; **trade ~** Branchenverzeichnis *nt*.

directory assistance, (*Brit*) **directory enquiries** *n* (*service*) (Fernsprech)auskunft *f*.

dirt [dûrt] *n* Schmutz *m*, Dreck *m*.

dirt-cheap [dûrt'chēp'] *a* (*col*) spottbillig.

dirt road *n* (*US*) unbefestigte Straße *f*.

dirty [dûr'tē] *a* schmutzig, dreckig; (*despicable*) gemein ♦ *vt* beschmutzen.

disability [disəbil'ətē] *n* Körperbehinderung *f*.

disability allowance *n* Behindertenbeihilfe *f*.

disable [disā'bəl] *vt* (*illness, accident*) behindern; (*tank, gun*) unbrauchbar machen; (*JUR: disqualify*) rechtsunfähig machen.

disabled [disā'bəld] *a* körperbehindert.

disabuse [disəbyōōz'] *vt* befreien.

disadvantage [disədvan'tij] *n* Nachteil *m*.

disadvantaged [disədvan'tijd] *a* benachteiligt.

disadvantageous [disadvəntā'jəs] *a* ungünstig.

disaffected [disəfek'tid] *a* entfremdet; **to be ~ (to** or **towards)** sich entfremden (von).

disaffection [disəfek'shən] *n* Entfremdung *f*.

disagree [disəgrē'] *vi* nicht übereinstimmen; (*quarrel*) (sich) streiten; (*food*) nicht bekommen (*with dat*); **I ~ with you** ich bin anderer Meinung.

disagreeable [disəgrē'əbəl] *a* (*person*) widerlich; (*task*) unangenehm.

disagreement [disəgrē'mənt] *n* (*between persons*) Meinungsverschiedenheit *f*; (*between things*) Widerspruch *m*; **to have a ~ with sb** eine Meinungsverschiedenheit mit jdm haben.

disallow [disəlou'] *vt* nicht zulassen.

disappear [disəpiûr'] *vi* verschwinden.

disappearance [disəpi'ûrəns] *n* Verschwinden *nt*.

disappoint [disəpoint'] *vt* enttäuschen.

disappointed [disəpoin'tid] *a* (*person*) enttäuscht.

disappointing [disəpoin'ting] *a* enttäuschend.

disappointment [disəpoint'mənt] *n* Enttäuschung *f*.

disapproval [disəprōō'vəl] *n* Mißbilligung *f*.

disapprove [disəprōōv'] *vi* mißbilligen (*of acc*); **she ~s of it** sie mißbilligt es.

disapproving [disəprōō'ving] *a* mißbilligend.

disarm [disârm'] *vt* entwaffnen; (*POL*) abrüsten.

disarmament [disâr'məmənt] *n* Abrüstung *f*.

disarmament talks *npl* Abrüstungsgespräche *pl*.

disarming [disârm'ing] *a* (*smile*) entwaffnend.

disarray [disərā'] *n*: **in ~** (*clothes*) unordentlich; (*troops*) in Auflösung; (*thoughts*) durcheinander; **to throw into** ~ durcheinanderbringen.

disaster [dizas'tûr] n Katastrophe f; (AVIAT etc) Unglück nt.

disaster area n Katastrophengebiet nt.

disastrous [dizas'trəs] a verhängnisvoll.

disband [disband'] vt auflösen.

disbelief [disbilēf'] n Ungläubigkeit f; **in** ~ ungläubig.

disbelieve [disbilēv'] vt nicht glauben.

disc [disk] n (Brit) = **disk**.

disc. abbr (COMM) = **discount**.

discard [diskârd'] vt ablegen.

disc brake [disk brāk] n Scheibenbremse f.

discern [disûrn'] vt unterscheiden (können), erkennen.

discernible [disûr'nəbəl] a (with senses) wahrnehmbar; (mentally) erkennbar.

discerning [disûr'ning] a scharfsinnig.

discharge vt [dischârj'] (ship) entladen; (duties) nachkommen (+dat); (dismiss) entlassen; (gun) abschießen; (settle: debt) begleichen ♦ n [dis'chârj] (of ship) Entladung f; (MED) Ausfluß m; (of gas, chemicals) Ausströmen nt.

disciple [disī'pəl] n Jünger m.

disciplinary [dis'əplənārē] a disziplinarisch; **to take** ~ **action against sb** ein Disziplinarverfahren gegen jdn einleiten.

discipline [dis'əplin] n Disziplin f ♦ vt (train) schulen; (punish) bestrafen; **to** ~ **o.s. to do sth** sich dazu anhalten or zwingen, etw zu tun.

disc jockey [disk' jâkē] n Diskjockey m.

disclaim [disklām'] vt nicht anerkennen; (POL) dementieren.

disclaimer [disklām'ûr] n Dementi nt; **to issue a** ~ eine Gegenerklärung abgeben.

disclose [disklōz'] vt enthüllen.

disclosure [disklō'zhûr] n Enthüllung f.

disco [dis'kō] n abbr = **discotheque**.

discoloration, (Brit) **discolouration** [diskulərā'shən] n Verfärben nt; (mark) Verfärbung f.

discolored, (Brit) **discoloured** [diskul'ûrd] a verfärbt, verschossen.

discomfort [diskum'fûrt] n Unbehagen nt; (embarrassment) Verlegenheit f.

disconcert [diskənsûrt'] vt aus der Fassung bringen; (puzzle) verstimmen.

disconnect [diskənekt'] vt abtrennen.

disconsolate [diskân'səlit] a niedergeschlagen.

discontent [diskəntent'] n Unzufriedenheit f.

discontented [diskəntent'id] a unzufrieden.

discontinue [diskəntin'yōō] vt einstellen ♦ vi aufhören.

discord [dis'kôrd] n Zwietracht f; (noise) Dissonanz f.

discordant [diskôr'dənt] a uneinig; (noise) mißtönend.

discotheque [dis'kōtek] n Diskothek f.

discount n [dis'kount] Rabatt m; **at a** ~ mit Rabatt; ~ **for cash** Rabatt or Skonto bei

Barzahlung; **to give sb a** ~ **on sth** jdm auf etw (acc) Rabatt geben ♦ vt [diskount'] außer acht lassen; (report etc) abtun.

discount house n Wechselbank f; (shop) Billigladen m.

discount rate n Diskontsatz m.

discount store n Discountgeschäft nt, Discountladen m.

discourage [diskûr'ij] vt entmutigen; (dissuade, deter) abraten, abbringen (from von).

discouragement [diskûr'ijmənt] n (dissuasion) Abraten nt, Abbringen nt; (depression) Mutlosigkeit f; **to be a** ~ entmutigend sein.

discouraging [diskûr'ijing] a entmutigend.

discourteous [diskûr'tēəs] a unhöflich.

discover [diskuv'ûr] vt entdecken.

discovery [diskuv'ûrē] n Entdeckung f.

discredit [diskred'it] vt in Verruf bringen ♦ n Mißkredit m.

discreet [diskrēt'] a, **discreetly** [diskrēt'lē] ad taktvoll, diskret.

discrepancy [diskrep'ənsē] n Unstimmigkeit f, Diskrepanz f.

discretion [diskresh'ən] n Takt m, Diskretion f; (decision) Gutdünken nt; **to leave sth to sb's** ~ etw jds Gutdünken überlassen; **use your own** ~ Sie müssen nach eigenem Ermessen handeln.

discretionary [diskresh'ənārē] a: ~ **powers** Ermessensspielraum m.

discriminate [diskrim'ənāt] vi unterscheiden; **to** ~ **against** diskriminieren.

discriminating [diskrim'ənāting] a klug; (taste) anspruchsvoll.

discrimination [diskrimənā'shən] n Urteilsvermögen nt; (pej) Diskriminierung f; **sexual** ~ Diskriminierung f aufgrund des Geschlechts; **racial** ~ Rassendiskriminierung f.

discus [dis'kəs] n Diskus m.

discuss [diskus'] vt diskutieren, besprechen.

discussion [diskush'ən] n Diskussion f, Besprechung f; **under** ~ in der Diskussion.

disdain [disdān'] vt verachten, für unter seiner Würde halten ♦ n Verachtung f.

disdainful [disdān'fəl] a geringschätzig.

disease [dizēz'] n Krankheit f.

diseased [dizēzd'] a (lit, fig) krank; (tissue, plant) befallen.

disembark [disembârk'] vt aussteigen lassen ♦ vi von Bord gehen.

disembarkation [disembârkā'shən] n Landung f.

disenchanted [disenchan'tid] a desillusioniert.

disenfranchise [disenfran'chīz] vt Wahlrecht entziehen (+dat); (COMM) Konzession entziehen (+dat).

disengage [disengāj'] vt (AUT) auskuppeln.

disentangle [disentang'gəl] vt entwirren.

disfavor, (Brit) **disfavour** [disfā'vûr] n Ungunst f.

disfigure [disfig'yûr] vt entstellen.

disgorge [disgôrj'] vt (food) ausspucken, ausspeien.

disgrace [disgrās'] *n* Schande *f*; *(thing)* Schandfleck *m* ♦ *vt* Schande bringen über *(+acc)*; *(less strong)* blamieren.

disgraceful [disgrās'fəl] *a* schändlich, unerhört; **it's ~** es ist eine Schande.

disgruntled [disgrun'təld] *a* verärgert.

disguise [disgīz'] *vt* verkleiden; *(feelings)* verhehlen; *(voice)* verstellen ♦ *n* Verkleidung *f*; **in ~** verkleidet, maskiert; **to ~ o.s.** sich verkleiden; **there's no disguising the fact that** ... es kann nicht geleugnet werden, daß ...

disgust [disgust'] *n* Abscheu *f* ♦ *vt* anwidern.

disgusting [disgus'ting] *a* abscheulich; *(terrible)* gemein.

dish [dish] *n* Schüssel *f*; *(food)* Gericht *nt*; **to do the ~es** abwaschen.

dish out *vt (food, money, exam papers)* austeilen; *(advice)* verteilen.

dish up *vt* auftischen.

dish cloth *n* Spüllappen *m*.

dishearten [dis·här'tən] *vt* entmutigen.

disheveled, *(Brit)* **dishevelled** [dishev'əld] *a (hair)* zerzaust; *(clothing)* ungepflegt.

dishonest [disán'ist] *a* unehrlich.

dishonesty [disán'istē] *n* Unehrlichkeit *f*.

dishonor [disán'ûr] *(US) n* Unehre *f* ♦ *vt (check)* nicht einlösen.

dishonorable [disán'ûrəbəl] *a* unehrenhaft.

dishonour [disán'ûr] *etc (Brit)* = **dishonor** *etc*.

dish rag *n (US)* Spüllappen *m*.

dish soap *n (US)* Spülmittel *nt*.

dish towel *n* Küchenhandtuch *nt*.

dishwasher [dish'wâshûr] *n* Geschirrspülmaschine *f*.

dishwashing liquid [dish'wâshing lik'wid] *n* Spülmittel *nt*.

disillusion [disilōō'zhən] *vt* enttäuschen, desillusionieren.

disillusioned [disilōō'zhənd] *a*: **to become ~** Illusionen verlieren *(with sth* über etw).

disillusionment [disilōō'zhənmənt] *n* Desillusionierung *f*, Enttäuschung *f*.

disincentive [disinsen'tiv] *n*: **it acts as a ~** es hält die Leute ab; **to be a ~** keinen Anreiz bieten.

disinclined [disinklīnd'] *a*: **to be ~ to do sth** abgeneigt sein, etw zu tun.

disinfect [disinfekt'] *vt* desinfizieren.

disinfectant [disinfek'tənt] *n* Desinfektionsmittel *nt*.

disinflation [disinflā'shən] *n* Rückgang *m* einer inflationären Entwicklung.

disingenuous [disinjen'yōōəs] *a* unehrlich.

disinherit [disinhär'it] *vt* enterben.

disintegrate [disin'təgrāt] *vi* sich auflösen.

disinterested [disin'tristid] *a* uneigennützig; *(col)* uninteressiert.

disjointed [disjoint'id] *a* unzusammenhängend.

disk [disk] *n* Scheibe *f*; *(record)* (Schall)platte *f*; *(COMPUT)* Diskette *f*; **single-sided/**

double-sided ~ einseitige/beid- *or* doppelseitige Diskette *f*.

disk drive *n* Diskettenlaufwerk *nt*.

diskette [disket'] *n (COMPUT)* Minidiskette *f*.

disk operating system *n* Disketten-Betriebssystem *nt*.

dislike [dislīk'] *n* Abneigung *f* ♦ *vt* nicht leiden können; **I ~ the idea** der Gedanke widerstrebt mir; **to take a ~ to sb/sth** eine Abneigung gegen jdn/etw fassen.

dislocate [dis'lōkāt] *vt* auskugeln; *(upset)* in Verwirrung bringen; **he ~d his shoulder** er hat sich seinen Arm ausgekugelt.

dislodge [dislâj'] *vt* verschieben; *(MIL)* aus der Stellung werfen.

disloyal [disloi'əl] *a* treulos.

dismal [diz'məl] *a* trostlos, trübe.

dismantle [disman'təl] *vt* demontieren.

dismay [dismā'] *n* Bestürzung *f* ♦ *vt* bestürzen; **much to my ~** zu meiner Bestürzung.

dismiss [dismis'] *vt (employee)* entlassen; *(idea)* von sich weisen; *(send away)* wegschicken; *(JUR: complaint)* abweisen.

dismissal [dismis'əl] *n* Entlassung *f*.

dismount [dismount'] *vi* absteigen.

disobedience [disəbē'dēəns] *n* Ungehorsam *m*.

disobedient [disəbē'dēənt] *a* ungehorsam.

disobey [disəbā'] *vt* nicht gehorchen *(+dat)*; *(rule)* übertreten.

disorder [disôr'dûr] *n (confusion)* Verwirrung *f*; *(commotion)* Aufruhr *m*; *(MED)* Erkrankung *f*; **civil ~** öffentliche Unruhen *pl*.

disorderly [disôr'dûrlē] *a (untidy)* unordentlich; *(unruly)* ordnungswidrig; **~ conduct** *(JUR)* ungebührliche(s) Benehmen *nt*.

disorganized [disôr'gənīzd] *a* chaotisch, durcheinander.

disorientated [disô'rēintātid] *a* desorientiert.

disoriented [disôr'ēentid] *a* desorientiert.

disown [disōn'] *vt (son)* verstoßen; **I ~ you** ich will nichts mehr mit dir zu tun haben.

disparaging [dispar'ijing] *a* geringschätzig; **to be ~ about sb/sth** über jdn/etw abschätzig *or* geringschätzig urteilen.

disparity [dispar'itē] *n* Verschiedenheit *f*.

dispassionate [dispash'ənit] *a* gelassen, unparteiisch.

dispatch [dispach'] *vt (goods)* abschicken, abfertigen; *(deal with: business)* erledigen ♦ *n* Absendung *f*; *(esp MIL)* Meldung *f*.

dispatch department *n* Versandabteilung *f*.

dispatcher [dispach'ûr] *n (US)* Fahrbereitschaftsleiter *m*.

dispatch rider *n (MIL)* Meldereiter *m*, Meldefahrer *m*.

dispel [dispel'] *vt* zerstreuen.

dispensable [dispen'səbəl] *a* entbehrlich.

dispensary [dispen'sûrē] *n* Apotheke *f*.

dispensation [dispənsā'shən] *n (ECCL)* Befreiung *f*.

dispense [dispens'] *vt (medicine)* abgeben; *(prescription)* zubereiten.

dispense with *vt fus* verzichten auf

(+*acc*); **that can be ~d with** das ist entbehrlich.

dispenser [dispen'sûr] *n* (*container*) Spender *m*.

dispensing [dispens'ing] *a*: ~ **chemist** (*Brit*) Apotheker *m*.

dispersal [dispûr'səl] *n* Zerstreuung *f*.

disperse [dispûrs'] *vt* zerstreuen ♦ *vi* sich verteilen.

dispirited [dispir'itid] *a* niedergeschlagen.

displace [displās'] *vt* verschieben.

displaced [displāst'] *a*: ~ **person** Verschleppte(r) *mf*.

display [displā'] *n* (*of goods*) Auslage *f*; (*of feeling*) Zurschaustellung *f*; (*military: air* ~) Schau *f*; (*computer* ~) Computerausstellung *or* -vorführung *f* ♦ *vt* zeigen, entfalten; **on** ~ ausgestellt.

display advertising *n* Großwerbung *f*.

displease [displēz'] *vt* mißfallen (+*dat*).

displeasure [displezh'ûr] *n* Mißfallen *nt*.

disposable [dispō'zəbəl] *a* (*container etc*) Wegwerf-; ~ **personal income** verfügbare(s) Einkommen *nt*; ~ **diaper** Papierwindel *f*.

disposal [dispō'zəl] *n* (*of property*) Verkauf *m*; (*by giving away*) Loswerden *nt*; (*throwing away*) Beseitigung *f*; **to be at one's** ~ einem zur Verfügung stehen; **to put sth at sb's** ~ jdm etw zur Verfügung stellen.

disposed [dispōzd'] *a* geneigt.

dispose of [dispōz' uv] *vt fus* loswerden; (*COMM: sell*) veräußern.

disposition [dispəzish'ən] *n* Wesen *nt*, Natur *f*.

dispossess [dispəzes'] *vt*: **to** ~ **sb** jdn enteignen.

disproportion [disprəpôr'shən] *n* Mißverhältnis *nt*.

disproportionate [disprəpôr'shənit] *a* unverhältnismäßig.

disprove [disprōōv'] *vt* widerlegen.

dispute [dispyōōt'] *n* Kontroverse *f*, Streit *m* ♦ *vt* bestreiten; **to be in** *or* **under** ~ (*matter*) verhandelt werden; (*territory*) umstritten sein.

disqualification [diskwâləfəkā'shən] *n* Disqualifizierung *f*.

disqualify [diskwâl'əfī] *vt* disqualifizieren.

disquiet [diskwī'it] *n* Unruhe *f*.

disquieting [diskwī'iting] *a* beunruhigend.

disregard [disrigârd'] *vt* nicht (be)achten ♦ *n* (*indifference*: *for feelings*) Mißachtung *f* (*for gen*); (: *for danger, money*) Geringschätzung *f* (*for gen*).

disrepair [disripär'] *n*: **to fall into** ~ (*building*) verfallen; (*street*) herunterkommen.

disreputable [disrep'yətəbəl] *a* verrufen, anrüchig.

disrepute [disripyōōt'] *n* Verruf *m*, schlechte(r) Ruf *m*; **to bring into** ~ in Verruf bringen.

disrespectful [disrispekt'fəl] *a* respektlos.

disrupt [disrupt'] *vt* stören; (*program*) unter-

brechen; (*plans*) durcheinanderbringen.

disruption [disrup'shən] *n* Störung *f*; Unterbrechung *f*.

disruptive [disrup'tiv] *a* (*col*) störend.

dissatisfaction [dissatisfak'shən] *n* Unzufriedenheit *f*.

dissatisfied [dissat'isfīd] *a* unzufrieden.

dissect [disekt'] *vt* (*lit, fig*) zerlegen, sezieren.

disseminate [disem'ənāt] *vt* verbreiten.

dissent [disent'] *n* abweichende Meinung *f* ♦ *vi* nicht übereinstimmen.

dissenter [disen'tûr] *n* (*REL, POL*) Dissident(in *f*) *m*.

dissertation [disûrtā'shən] *n* (*UNIV*) wissenschaftliche Arbeit *f*.

disservice [dissûr'vis] *n*: **to do sb a** ~ jdm einen schlechten Dienst erweisen.

dissident [dis'idənt] *a* andersdenkend ♦ *n* Dissident(in *f*) *m*, Regimekritiker(in *f*) *m*.

dissimilar [disim'ilûr] *a* unähnlich (*to dat*).

dissipate [dis'əpāt] *vt* (*waste*) verschwenden; (*scatter*) zerstreuen.

dissipated [dis'əpātid] *a* ausschweifend.

dissipation [disəpā'shən] *n* Ausschweifung *f*.

dissociate [disō'shēāt] *vt* trennen; **to** ~ **o.s. from** sich distanzieren von.

dissolute [dis'əlōōt] *a* liederlich.

dissolution [disəlōō'shən] *n* Auflösung *f*.

dissolve [dizâlv'] *vt* auflösen ♦ *vi* sich auflösen.

dissuade [diswād'] *vt* abraten (+*dat*).

distaff [dis'taf] *n*: **on the** ~ **side** mütterlicherseits.

distance [dis'təns] *n* Entfernung *f*; **in the** ~ in der Ferne; **what's the** ~ **to New York?** wie weit ist es nach New York?; **it's within walking** ~ es ist zu Fuß erreichbar.

distant [dis'tənt] *a* entfernt, fern; (*with time*) fern; (*formal*) distanziert.

distaste [distāst'] *n* Abneigung *f*.

distasteful [distāst'fəl] *a* widerlich.

Dist. Atty. *abbr* (*US*) = **district attorney**.

distemper [distem'pûr] *n* (*paint*) Temperafarbe *f*; (*of dogs*) Staupe *f*.

distend [distend'] *vti* (sich) blähen.

distended [distend'id] *a* (*stomach*) aufgebläht.

distill, (*Brit*) **distil** [distil'] *vt* destillieren.

distillery [distil'ûrē] *n* Brennerei *f*.

distinct [distingkt'] *a* (*separate*) getrennt; (*clear*) klar, deutlich; **as** ~ **from** im Unterschied zu.

distinction [distingk'shən] *n* Unterscheidung *f*; (*eminence*) Berühmtheit *f*; (*in exam*) Auszeichnung *f*; **to draw a** ~ **between** einen Unterschied machen zwischen; **a writer of** ~ ein namhafter Schriftsteller.

distinctive [distingk'tiv] *a* bezeichnend.

distinctly [distingkt'lē] *ad* deutlich.

distinguish [disting'gwish] *vt* unterscheiden ♦ *vi*: **to** ~ **between** unterscheiden zwischen (+*dat*).

distinguished [disting'gwisht] *a* (*eminent*) berühmt; (*career*) hervorragend; (*refined*) vornehm.

distinguishing [disting'gwishing] *a* unterscheidend, bezeichnend.

distort [distórt'] *vt* verdrehen; *(account, news)* verzerrt darstellen; *(misrepresent)* entstellen.

distortion [distòr'shən] *n* Verzerrung *f*; *(of truth, facts)* Verdrehung *f*.

distr. *abbr* = **distribution; distributor.**

distract [distrakt'] *vt* ablenken; *(bewilder)* verwirren.

distracting [distrak'ting] *a* verwirrend.

distraction [distrak'shən] *n* Zerstreutheit *f*; *(distress)* Raserei *f*; *(diversion)* Zerstreuung *f*; **to drive sb to** ~ jdn zur Verzweiflung treiben.

distraught [distrôt'] *a* bestürzt.

distress [distres'] *n* Not *f*; *(suffering)* Qual *f* ♦ *vt* quälen; **a ship/plane in** ~ ein Schiff in Seenot/ein Flugzeug in Not.

distressing [distres'ing] *a* erschütternd; *(upsetting)* besorgniserregend; *(regrettable)* bedauerlich, betrüblich.

distress signal *n* Notsignal *nt*.

distribute [distrib'yōōt] *vt* verteilen.

distribution [distrəbyōō'shən] *n* Verteilung *f*.

distribution cost *n* Vertriebskosten *pl*.

distributor [distrib'yətûr] *n* Verteiler *m*; *(COMM)* Großhändler *m*.

district [dis'trikt] *n* *(of country)* Kreis *m*; *(of town)* Bezirk *m*.

district attorney *n* *(US)* Oberstaatsanwalt *m*.

district council *n* *(Brit)* ≈ Bezirksregierung *f*.

district manager *n* Bezirksdirektor *m*.

district nurse *n* *(Brit)* Kreiskrankenschwester *f*.

distrust [distrust'] *n* Mißtrauen *nt* ♦ *vt* mißtrauen (+*dat*).

distrustful [distrust'fəl] *a* mißtrauisch *(of* gegenüber).

disturb [distûrb'] *vt* stören; *(agitate)* erregen; **sorry to** ~ **you** entschuldigen Sie die Störung.

disturbance [distûr'bəns] *n* Störung *f*; ~ **of the peace** Ruhestörung *f*; **to cause a** ~ Unruhe *or* eine Ruhestörung verursachen.

disturbed [distûrbd'] *a* *(socially)* verhaltensgestört; **to be emotionally/mentally** ~ *(PSYCH)* seelisch/geistig gestört sein.

disturbing [distûrb'ing] *a* beunruhigend.

disuse [disyōōs'] *n* Nichtgebrauch *m*; **to fall into** ~ außer Gebrauch kommen.

disused [disyōōzd'] *a* aufgegeben, außer Gebrauch.

ditch [dich] *n* Graben *m* ♦ *vt* im Stich lassen.

dither [dith'ûr] *vi* verdattert sein.

ditto [dit'ō] *n* dito, ebenfalls.

div. *abbr (COMM)* = **dividend.**

divan [divan'] *n* Liegesofa *nt*.

divan bed *n* Liege *f*.

dive [dīv] *n* *(into water)* Kopfsprung *m*; *(AVIAT)* Sturzflug *m*; *(col: club etc)* Spiel-

halle *f* ♦ *vi* tauchen.

diver [dī'vûr] *n* Taucher *m*.

diverge [divûrj'] *vi* auseinandergehen.

divergent [divûr'jənt] *a* auseinandergehend, divergent *(MATH)*.

diverse [divûrs'] *a* verschieden.

diversification [divûrsəfəkā'shən] *n* Verzweigung *f*; *(change, variety)* Abwechslung *f*; *(of business)* Diversifikation *f*, Programmausweitung *f*.

diversify [divûr'səfī] *vt* (ver)ändern ♦ *vi* variieren.

diversion [divûr'zhən] *n* Ablenkung *f*; *(Brit: traffic)* Umleitung *f*.

diversity [divûr'sitē] *n* Verschiedenheit *f*; *(variety)* Mannigfaltigkeit *f*.

divert [divûrt'] *vt* ablenken; *(traffic, plane)* umleiten.

divide [divīd'] *vt* teilen ♦ *vi* sich teilen; **to** ~ **(between, among)** verteilen *or* aufteilen (zwischen, unter); **40** ~**d by 5** 40 geteilt *or* dividiert durch 5.

divide out *or* **up** *vt* *(tasks, candy etc)* aufteilen *(between, among* unter +*acc or dat).*

divided [divīd'id] *a* *(country, opinions)* geteilt; *(couple)* getrennt.

divided highway *n* *(US)* Schnellstraße *f* *(mit Mittelstreifen).*

dividend [div'idend] *n* Dividende *f*; *(fig)* Gewinn *m*.

dividend cover *n* Dividendendeckung *f*.

dividers [divī'dûrz] *npl* Stechzirkel *m*.

divine [divīn'] *a* göttlich ♦ *vt* erraten; *(future, truth)* weissagen, prophezeien; *(water, metal)* aufspüren.

diving [dī'ving] *n* *(SPORT)* Turmspringen *nt*.

diving board [dī'ving bôrd] *n* Sprungbrett *nt*.

divinity [divin'ətē] *n* Gottheit *f*, Gott *m*; *(subject)* Religion *f*; *(as study)* Theologie *f*.

divisible [diviz'əbəl] *a* teilbar.

division [divizh'ən] *n* Teilung *f*; *(MATH)* Division *f*, Teilung *f*; *(MIL)* Division *f*; *(part)* Teil *m*, Abteilung *f*; *(in opinion)* Uneinigkeit *f*; *(SOCCER)* Liga *f*; ~ **of labor** Arbeitsteilung *f*.

divisive [divī'siv] *a*: **to be** ~ Uneinigkeit schaffen.

divorce [divôrs'] *n* (Ehe)scheidung *f* ♦ *vt* scheiden.

divorced [divôrst'] *a* geschieden; **to get** ~ sich scheiden lassen.

divorcee [divôrsē'] *n* Geschiedene(r) *mf*.

divulge [divulj'] *vt* preisgeben.

DIY *n abbr (Brit)* = **do-it-yourself.**

dizziness [diz'ēnis] *n* Schwindelgefühl *nt*.

dizzy [diz'ē] *a* schwindlig; **I feel** ~ mir ist *or* ich bin schwindlig.

DJ *n abbr* (= *disc jockey*) DJ *m*.

Djakarta [jəkâr'tə] *n* Jakarta *nt*.

DJIA *n abbr (US*: = *Dow-Jones Industrial Average)* Dow-Jones Index *m*.

dl *abbr* (= *deciliter(s)*) dl.

DLit(t) *n abbr* (= *Doctor of Literature, Doctor of Letters)* akademischer Grad.

DLO n abbr (= dead-letter office) Dienststelle der Post für unzustellbare Postsachen.

dm abbr (= decimeter(s)) dm.

DMus n abbr (= Doctor of Music) akademischer Grad.

DMZ n abbr (= demilitarized zone) entmilitarisierte Zone.

DNA n abbr (= deoxyribonucleic acid) DNS f.

do [dōō] abbr (= ditto) dto.

do [dōō] aux vb: ~ **you speak English?** sprechen Sie Englisch?; **I don't understand you/that** ich verstehe Sie/das nicht; **DO come!** bitte komm!; **I DO wish I could** ... ich möchte wirklich gerne ...; **but I DO like it!** aber es gefällt mir wirklich; **you speak better than I** ~ du sprichst besser als ich; **so does he** er auch ♦ irreg vt tun, machen; (visit: city, museum) besuchen; **to** ~ **sb out of sth** jdn um etw bringen; **we've done 200 km already** wir sind schon 200 km gefahren; **what can I** ~ **for you?** (in shop) bitte schön?; **what does he** ~ **for a living?** was macht er beruflich?; **I'm going to** ~ **the dishes** ich spüle schon mal; **I'll** ~ **all I can** ich werde alles mir Mögliche tun; **how do you like your steak done?** — **well done** wie möchten Sie Ihr Steak? — durch(gebraten) ♦ vi (proceed) vorangehen; (be suitable) passen; (be enough) genügen; **how** ~ **you** ~? guten Tag! etc; **he's** ~**ing well/badly at school** er ist gut/schlecht in der Schule; **it doesn't** ~ **to upset her** man sollte sie nicht aufregen; **that'll** ~! (in annoyance) jetzt reicht's aber! ♦ n (col: party) Fete f; (formal gathering) Veranstaltung f; **the** ~**s and don'ts** was man tun und nicht tun sollte.

do away with vt fus (abolish) abschaffen; (kill) umbringen.

do for vt fus (col: person) fertigmachen; (: plan) zunichte machen.

do up vt: **to** ~ **o.s. up** sich zurechtmachen.

do with vt fus (with can, could: need) brauchen; **I could** ~ **with some help/a drink** ich könnte Hilfe/etw zu trinken (ge)brauchen; **what has that got to** ~ **with it?** was hat das denn damit zu tun?; **what have you done with my slippers?** was hast du mit meinen Pantoffeln gemacht?

D.O.A. a abbr = dead on arrival.

d.o.b. abbr = date of birth.

docile [dás'əl] a gefügig; (dog) gutmütig.

dock [dák] n Dock nt; (wharf) Kai m; (JUR) Anklagebank f ♦ vi ins Dock gehen ♦ vt (pay etc) kürzen.

dock dues npl Dockgebühren pl.

docker [dák'ûr] n Hafenarbeiter m.

docket [dák'it] n Inhaltsvermerk m; (on parcel etc) Warenbegleitschein m.

dockyard [dák'yârd] n Werft f.

doctor [dák'tûr] n Arzt m, Ärztin f; (UNIV) Doktor m ♦ vt (interfere with: food, drink) beimischen; (text, document) verfälschen;

D~ of Philosophy Doktor der Philosophie.

doctorate [dák'tûrit] n Doktorwürde f.

doctrinaire [dáktrənär'] a doktrinär.

doctrine [dák'trin] n Doktrin f.

document n [dák'yəmənt] Dokument nt ♦ vt [dák'yəment] beurkunden, (urkundlich) belegen.

documentary [dákyəmən'tûrē] n Dokumentarbericht m; (film) Dokumentarfilm m ♦ a dokumentarisch.

documentation [dákyəməntā'shən] n dokumentarische(r) Nachweis m.

DOD n abbr (US: = Department of Defense) Verteidigungsministerium.

doddering [dád'ûring] a zittrig.

doddery [dád'ûrē] a = doddering.

Dodecanese Islands [dōdekənēs' ī'ləndz] npl Dodekanes m.

dodge [dáj] n Kniff m ♦ vt (tax) umgehen; (blow, ball, question) ausweichen (+dat); (work) sich drücken vor ♦ vi: **to** ~ **out of the way** zur Seite springen; **to** ~ **through the traffic** sich durch den Verkehr schlängeln.

dodgems [dáj'əmz] npl Autoskooter m.

dodo [dō'dō] n Dronte f.

doe [dō] n (deer) Reh(geiß f) nt; (rabbit) (Kaninchen)weibchen nt.

DOE n abbr (US: = Department of Energy) Ministerium für Energiewissenschaft; (Brit: = Department of the Environment) ≈ UBA.

does [duz] 3rd pers present of **do**.

doesn't [duz'nt] = **does not**.

dog [dóg] n Hund m; **to go to the** ~**s** (person) auf den Hund kommen ♦ vt (fig: memory etc) verfolgen; **to** ~ **sb** (follow closely) jdm hart auf den Fersen sein or bleiben.

dog biscuit n Hundekuchen m.

dog collar n Hundehalsband nt; (ECCL) Kragen m des Geistlichen.

dog-eared [dóg'ērd] a mit Eselsohren.

dogfish [dóg'fish] n Hundsfisch m.

dog food n Hundefutter nt.

dogged [dóg'id] a hartnäckig.

dogma [dóg'mə] n Dogma nt.

dogmatic [dógmat'ik] a dogmatisch.

do-gooder [dōōgōōd'ûr] n (col): **to be a** ~ ein Weltverbesserer sein.

dogsbody [dógz'bádē] n (Brit) Mädchen nt für alles.

dog tag n (US) Erkennungsmarke f.

doing [dōō'ing] n: **this is your** ~ das ist dein Werk.

doings [dōō'ingz] npl (activities) Treiben nt.

do-it-yourself [dōō'ityōōrself'] n Do-it-yourself nt ♦ a zum Selbermachen.

do-it-yourselfer [dōō'ityōōrself'ûr] n (US) Heimwerker m.

doldrums [dōl'drəmz] npl: **to be in the** ~ (business) in einer Flaute stecken; (person) deprimiert sein.

dole [dōl] n Stempelgeld nt; **to be on the** ~ stempeln gehen.

dole out vt ausgeben, austeilen.
doleful [dōl'fəl] a traurig.
doll [dâl] n Puppe f ♦ vt: **to ~ o.s. up** sich
aufdonnern.
dollar [dâl'ûr] n Dollar m.
dollar area n Dollarblock m.
dollop [dâl'əp] n Brocken m.
dolphin [dâl'fin] n Delphin m, Tümmler m.
domain [dōmān'] n Sphäre f, Bereich m; (fig)
Domäne f.
dome [dōm] n Kuppel f.
domestic [dəmes'tik] a häuslich; (within
country) Innen-, Binnen-; (animal) Haus-;
(news) Inland-, aus dem Inland.
domesticated [dəmes'tikātid] a (person)
häuslich; (animal) zahm.
domesticity [dōmestis'itē] n häusliche(s) Leben nt.
domestic servant n Hausangestellte(r) mf.
domicile [dâm'isil] n (ständiger) Wohnsitz m.
dominant [dâm'ənənt] a vorherrschend.
dominate [dâm'ənāt] vt beherrschen.
domination [dâmənā'shən] n (Vor)herrschaft
f.
domineering [dâmənēr'ing] a herrisch, überheblich.
Dominican Republic [dəmin'əkən ripub'lik]
n Dominikanische Republik f.
dominion [dəmin'yən] n (rule) Regierungsge-
walt f; (land) Staatsgebiet nt mit Selbstverwaltung.
dominoes [dâm'ənōz] n Domino(spiel) nt.
don [dân] n (Brit) akademische(r) Lehrer m.
donate [dō'nāt] vt (blood, little money) spenden; (lot of money) stiften.
donation [dōnā'shən] n Spende f; Stiftung f.
done [dun] pp of **do**.
donkey [dâng'kē] n Esel m.
donkey-work [dâng'kēwûrk] n (Brit col)
Routinearbeit f, Dreckarbeit f (col).
donor [dō'nûr] n Spender m.
don't [dōnt] = **do not**.
donut [dō'nut] n (US) = **doughnut**.
doodle [dōōd'əl] n Gekritzel nt ♦ vi Männchen malen.
doom [dōōm] n böse(s) Geschick nt; (downfall) Verderben nt ♦ vt: **to be ~ed** zum
Untergang verurteilt sein.
doomsday [dōōmz'dā] n der Jüngste Tag.
door [dôr] n Tür f; **from ~ to ~** von Tür zu
Tür.
doorbell [dôr'bel] n Türklingel f.
door-handle [dôr'handəl] n Türklinke f.
doorman [dôr'man] n, pl **-men** Türsteher m.
doormat [dôr'mat] n Fußmatte f.
doorstep [dôr'step] n Türstufe f.
door-to-door [dôr'tədôr'] n Haus-zu-Haus-.
doorway [dôr'wā] n Eingang m, Tür f.
dope [dōp] n (drug) Aufputschmittel nt; (col:
information) Information(en pl) f; (: fool)
Blödmann m.
dopey [dō'pē] a (col) bekloppt.
dormant [dôr'mənt] a schlafend, latent.
dormer [dôr'mûr] n (also: **~ window**) Man-

sardenfenster nt.
dormitory [dôr'mitôrē] n Schlafsaal m; (US:
residence) Wohnheim nt.
dormouse [dôr'mous] n, pl **dormice** [dôr'mīs]
Haselmaus f.
Dors abbr (Brit) = Dorset.
DOS [dōs] n abbr (= disk operating system)
DOS.
dosage [dō'sij] n (on medicine bottle) Dosie-
rung f.
dose [dōs] n (of medicine) Dosis f; **a ~ of flu**
(Brit) eine Grippe ♦ vt dosieren.
doss house [dâs' hous] n (Brit) Bleibe f.
dossier [dâs'ēā] n Dossier nt, Aktenbündel nt;
~ on Dossier or Akte f über.
dot [dât] n Punkt m; **on the ~** pünktlich.
DOT n abbr (US: = Department of Transportation) Verkehrsministerium nt.
dot command n (COMPUT) Punktkomman-
do nt.
dote on [dōt' ân] vt fus vernarrt sein in
(+acc).
dot-matrix printer [dâtmāt'riks prin'tûr] n
Matrixdrucker m.
dotted line [dât'id līn'] n punktierte Linie f;
to sign on the ~ (fig) seine formelle Zustimmung geben.
dotty [dât'ē] a (col: person) verschroben,
übergeschnappt; (: scheme) verrückt.
double [dub'əl] a, ad doppelt ♦ n Doppelgän-
ger m ♦ vt verdoppeln; (fold) zusammenfalten ♦ vi (in amount) sich verdoppeln; **to ~
as** (have two uses etc) eine Doppelrolle haben; **on the ~** im Laufschritt; **spelled with
a ~ "l"** mit Doppel-l or mit zwei „l" geschrieben.
double back vi (person) kehrtmachen,
zurückgehen/-fahren.
double up vi (bend over) sich krümmen;
(share bedroom) ein Zimmer teilen.
double bass n Kontrabaß m.
double bed n Doppelbett nt.
double bend n (Brit) S-Kurve f.
double-breasted [dub'əlbres'tid] a zwei-
reihig.
double-check [dub'əlchek'] vti noch einmal
(über)prüfen.
double cream n (Brit) Schlagsahne f.
double-cross [dub'əlkrôs'] n Betrug m ♦ vt
hintergehen.
double-decker [dub'əldekûr] n Doppeldecker
m.
double glazing [dub'əl glāz'ing] n (Brit)
Doppelfenster pl.
double indemnity [dub'əl indem'nitē] n Ver-
doppelung f der Versicherungssumme bei
Unfalltod.
double-page spread [dub'əlpāj spred] n doppelseitige Anzeige f.
double park vi in zweiter Reihe parken.
double room n Doppelzimmer nt.
doubles [dub'əlz] n sing or pl (TENNIS) Doppel nt.
double time n Lohnverdoppelung f.

doubly [dub'lē] *ad* doppelt.

doubt [dout] *n* Zweifel *m* ♦ *vi* zweifeln ♦ *vt* bezweifeln; **without (a)** ~ ohne (jeglichen) Zweifel; **beyond** ~ außer Zweifel; **I** ~ **it very much** das möchte ich stark bezweifeln.

doubtful [dout'fəl] *a* zweifelhaft, fraglich; **I'm a bit** ~ ich bin nicht ganz sicher; **to be** ~ **about sth** einer Sache gegenüber Zweifel hegen *or* voller Zweifel sein.

doubtless [dout'lis] *ad* ohne Zweifel, sicherlich.

dough [dō] *n* Teig *m*; (*col: money*) Kohle *f*, Knete *f*.

doughnut [dō'nut] *n* Berliner *m*.

douse [dous] *vt* (*with water*) Wasser schütten über (+*acc*); (*flames*) löschen.

dove *n* [duv] Taube *f* ♦ *pp* [dōv] (*US*) *of* dive.

dovetail [duv'tāl] *n* Schwalbenschwanz *m*, Zinke *f* ♦ *vt* verzahnen, verzinken.

dowager [dou'əjûr] *n* (adlige) Witwe *f*.

dowdy [dou'dē] *a* unmodern, schlampig.

Dow-Jones Index [dou'jōnz' in'deks] *n* Dow-Jones Index *m*.

down [doun] *n* (*fluffy*) Flaum *m*; (*hill*) Hügel *m*; (*US FOOTBALL*) Versuch *m* ♦ *ad* unten; (*motion*) herunter; hinunter; ~ **there** da unten; ~ **here** hier unten; **I'll be** ~ **in a minute** ich komme sofort runter; **England is two goals** ~ England liegt mit 2 Toren zurück; **I've been** ~ **with flu** ich habe mit Grippe im Bett gelegen; **the price of meat is** ~ die Fleischpreise sind gefallen; **to pay $20** ~ 20 Dollar anzahlen; **I've got it** ~ **in my diary** ich habe es in meinem (Termin)kalender notiert; ~ **with X!** nieder mit X! ♦ *prep*: **he came** ~ **the street** er kam die Straße herunter; **to go** ~ **the street** die Straße hinuntergehen; **he lives** ~ **the street** er wohnt unten an der Straße; **she went** ~ **the hill** sie ging den Berg hinunter ♦ *vt* niederschlagen; (*drink*) herunterkippen; **to** ~ **tools** (*Brit fig*) die Arbeit niederlegen.

down-and-out [doun'ənout] *a* abgerissen ♦ *n* Tramp *m*, Penner *m* (*col*).

down-at-heel(s) [dounat·hēl(z)'] *a* schäbig.

downbeat [doun'bēt] *n* (*MUS*) Taktstockführung, die den ersten betonten Taktteil anzeigt ♦ *a* (*col*) pessimistisch.

downcast [doun'kast] *a* niedergeschlagen.

downer [dou'nûr] *n* (*col*) Downer *m*, Beruhigungsmittel *nt*, Dämpfer *m*.

downfall [doun'fôl] *n* Sturz *m*.

downgrade [doun'grād] *vt* niedriger einstufen; (*person*) herabstufen; (*job, hotel*) herunterstufen.

down-hearted [doun'hâr'tid] *a* niedergeschlagen, mutlos.

downhill [doun'hil'] *ad* bergab; **to go** ~ (*business*) sich verschlechtern ♦ *n* (*SKI: also:* ~ **race**) Abfahrtslauf *m*.

download [doun'lōd] *vt* fernladen, runterfahren.

downmarket [doun'mâr'kit] *a* (*area*) weniger anspruchsvoll.

down payment *n* Anzahlung *f*.

downplay [doun'plā] *vt* (*US*) herunterspielen.

downpour [doun'pôr] *n* Platzregen *m*.

downright [doun'rīt] *a* völlig, ausgesprochen.

Down's syndrome [dounz' sin'drōm] *n* (*MED*) Down-Syndrom *nt*, Mongolismus *m*.

downstairs [doun'stärz'] *ad* unten; (*motion*) nach unten ♦ *a* untere(r, s); **to come** ~ runterkommen; **to go** ~ runtergehen.

downstream [doun'strēm'] *ad* flußabwärts.

downtime [doun'tīm] *n* (*of machine*) Ausfallzeit *f*; (*of worker*) betrieblich bedingte Verlustzeit *f*.

down-to-earth [dountooûrth'] *a* praktisch.

downtown [doun'toun'] *ad* in die/der Innenstadt ♦ *a* (*US*) im Geschäftsviertel, City-.

downtrodden [doun'trâdən] *a* unterdrückt, geknechtet.

down under *ad* (*Brit col*) in Australien.

downward [doun'wûrd] *a* sinkend, Abwärts-; **a** ~ **trend** ein Abwärtstrend.

downwards [doun'wûrdz] *ad* abwärts, nach unten; **face** ~ (*person*) mit dem Gesicht nach unten; (*object*) umgedreht.

dowry [dou'rē] *n* Mitgift *f*.

doz. *abbr* (= *dozen*) Dtz.

doze [dōz] *vi* dösen ♦ *n* Schläfchen *nt*, Nickerchen *nt*.

doze off *vi* einnicken.

dozen [duz'ən] *n* Dutzend *nt*; **$5 a** ~ 5 Dollar das Dutzend; ~**s of times** x-mal (*col*), tausendmal.

DPH *n abbr* (*US:* = *Department of Health*) Gesundheitsministerium *nt*.

DPh, DPhil *n abbr* (= *Doctor of Philosophy*) Dr. phil.

DPP *n abbr* (*Brit:* = *Director of Public Prosecutions*) ≈ GBA *m*.

DPT *n abbr* (= *diphtheria, pertussis, tetanus*) Diphtherie, Keuchhusten, Tetanus.

DPW *n abbr* (*US:* = *Department of Public Works*) Ministerium für öffentliche Arbeiten.

dr *abbr* (*COMM*) = **debtor.**

Dr. *abbr* (*in street names*) = **Drive.**

Dr, Dr. *abbr* (= *doctor*) Dr.

drab [drab] *a* düster, eintönig.

draft [draft] *n* Skizze *f*, Entwurf *m*; (*FIN*) Wechsel *m*; (*US: of air*) Zug *m*; (: *MIL*) Einberufung *f*; (: *NAUT*) Tiefgang *m*; **on** ~ (*beer*) vom Faß ♦ *vt* skizzieren.

draftee [draftē'] *n* (*US*) Wehrpflichtige(r) *m*.

draftsman [drafts'mən] *n*, *pl* **-men** (*US*) technische(r) Zeichner *m*.

draftsmanship [drafts'mənship] *n* (*US*): **you can tell by the** ~ **that it was done by an expert** an der Qualität der Zeichnung *or* des Entwurfs kann man sehen, daß das ein Fachmann gemacht hat.

drafty [draf'tē] *a* (*US*) zugig.

drag [drag] *vt* schleifen, schleppen; (*river*) mit einem Schleppnetz absuchen ♦ *vi* sich (dahin)schleppen ♦ *n* (*bore*) etwas Blödes; (*hindrance*) Klotz *m* am Bein; (*AVIAT: resistance*) Luft- *or* Strömungswiderstand

m; (*women's clothing*): **in** ~ in Frauenkleidung, im Fummel (*col*).
drag away *vt* wegschleppen *or* -ziehen (*from* von).
drag on *vi* sich in die Länge ziehen.
dragnet [drag'net] *n* (*lit*) Schleppnetz *nt*; (*fig*: *police hunt*) großangelegte Polizeiaktion *f*.
dragon [drag'ən] *n* Drache *m*.
dragonfly [drag'ənflī] *n* Libelle *f*.
dragoon [drəgōōn'] *vt*: **to** ~ **sb into doing sth** (*Brit*) jdn zwingen, etw zu tun ♦ *n* (*cavalryman*) Dragoner *m*.
drain [drān] *n* (*lit*) Abfluß *m*; (*ditch*) Abflußgraben *m*; (*fig*: *burden*) Belastung *f* ♦ *vt* ableiten; (*exhaust*) erschöpfen ♦ *vi* (*water*) abfließen; **to feel** ~**ed (of energy)** (*fig*) sich ausgelaugt fühlen.
drainage [drā'nij] *n* Kanalisation *f*.
drainboard [drān'bôrd] *n* (*US*) Ablaufbrett *nt*.
draining board [drā'ning bôrd] *n* (*Brit*) Ablaufbrett *nt*.
drainpipe [drān'pīp] *n* Abflußrohr *nt*.
drake [drāk] *n* Enterich *m*.
drama [drâm'ə] *n* (*lit, fig*) Drama *nt*.
dramatic [drəmat'ik] *a* dramatisch.
dramatist [dram'ətist] *n* Dramatiker *m*.
dramatize [dram'ətiz] *vt* (*events etc*) dramatisieren; (*adapt: for TV, cinema*) für das Fernsehen/den Film bearbeiten, dramatisieren.
drank [drangk] *pt of* **drink**.
drape [drāp] *vt* drapieren.
drapes [drāps] *npl* (*US*) Vorhänge *pl*.
drastic [dras'tik] *a* drastisch.
draught [draft] *n* (*Brit: of air*) Zug *m*; (: *NAUT*) Tiefgang; **on** ~ (*beer*) vom Faß.
draughtboard [draft'bôrd] *n* (*Brit*) Damebrett *nt*.
draughts [drafts] *n sing* (*Brit*) Damespiel *nt*.
draughtsman [drafts'mən] *etc* (*Brit*) = **draftsman** *etc*.
draughty [draf'tē] *a* (*Brit*) = **drafty**.
draw [drô] *irreg vt* ziehen; (*crowd*) anlocken; (*picture*) zeichnen; (*money*) abheben; (*water*) schöpfen ♦ *vi* (*SPORT*) unentschieden spielen ♦ *n* (*SPORT*) Unentschieden *nt*; (*lottery*) Ziehung *f*; **to** ~ **a conclusion/comparison** eine Schlußfolgerung/einen Vergleich ziehen; **to** ~ **a distinction** eine Unterscheidung treffen; **to** ~ **to a close** (*speech*) zu Ende kommen; (*year*) zu Ende gehen.
draw back *vi*: **to** ~ **back (from)** zurückweichen (von).
draw in *vi* (*Brit: car, train*) anhalten.
draw on *vt fus* (*resources*) sich stützen auf; **you'll have to** ~ **on your powers of imagination** Sie müssen Ihre Phantasie zu Hilfe nehmen.
draw out *vi* (*train*) ausfahren; (*lengthen*) sich hinziehen ♦ *vt* (*money*) abheben.
draw up *vi* (*stop*) halten ♦ *vt* (*document*) aufsetzen; (*plans*) entwerfen.
draw upon *vt fus* = **draw on**.

drawback [drô'bak] *n* (*disadvantage*) Nachteil *m*; (*obstacle*) Haken *m*.
drawbridge [drô'brij] *n* Zugbrücke *f*.
drawee [drôē'] *n* Bezogener *m*.
drawer [drôr] *n* Schublade *f*; [drô'ûr] (*of check*) Aussteller *m*.
drawing [drô'ing] *n* (*picture*) Zeichnung *f*; (*act*) Zeichnen *nt*.
drawing board *n* Reißbrett *nt*.
drawing pin *n* (*Brit*) Reißzwecke *f*.
drawing room *n* Salon *m*.
drawl [drôl] *n* schleppende Sprechweise *f* ♦ *vi* gedehnt sprechen.
drawn [drôn] *a* (*game*) unentschieden; (*face: with worry*) abgehärmt; (: *with tiredness*) abgespannt; (: *with pain*) verzerrt ♦ *pp of* **draw**.
drawstring [drô'string] *n* Vorhangschnur *f*.
dread [dred] *n* Furcht *f*, Grauen *nt* ♦ *vt* fürchten, sich grauen vor (+*dat*).
dreadful [dred'fəl] *a* furchtbar; **I feel** ~! (*ill*) ich fühle mich schrecklich; (*ashamed*) es ist mir schrecklich peinlich.
dream [drēm] *n* Traum *m*; (*fancy*) Wunschtraum *m* ♦ *vti irreg* träumen (*about* von) ♦ *a* (*house etc*) Traum-; **to have a** ~ **about sb/sth** von jdm/etw träumen; **sweet** ~**s!** träum süß!
dream up *vt* (*reason, plan*) sich (*dat*) einfallen lassen *or* ausdenken.
dreamed [drēmd] *pt, pp of* **dream**.
dreamer [drē'mûr] *n* Träumer(in *f*) *m*.
dreamt [dremt] *pt, pp of* **dream**.
dream world *n* Traumwelt *f*.
dreamy [drē'mē] *a* verträumt.
dreary [drēr'ē] *a* trostlos, öde.
dredge [drej] *vt* ausbaggern; (*with flour etc*) mit Mehl bestreuen.
dredge up *vt* ausbaggern; (*fig: unpleasant facts*) ans Licht zerren.
dredger [drej'ûr] *n* Baggerschiff *nt*; (*for flour etc*) (Mehl)streuer *m*.
dregs [dregz] *npl* Bodensatz *m*; (*fig*) Abschaum *m*.
drench [drench] *vt* durchnässen; ~**ed to the skin** naß bis auf die Haut.
dress [dres] *n* Kleidung *f*; (*garment*) Kleid *nt* ♦ *vt* anziehen; (*MED*) verbinden; (*AGR*) düngen; (*food*) anrichten; (*shop window*) dekorieren ♦ *vi* sich anziehen, sich kleiden; **to get** ~**ed** sich anziehen.
dress up *vi* sich fein machen ♦ *vt* verkleiden.
dress circle *n* (*Brit*) erste(r) Rang *m*.
dress designer *n* Modezeichner(in *f*) *m*.
dresser [dres'ûr] *n* (*furniture*) Anrichte *f*, Geschirrschrank *m*; **she's a smart** ~ sie zieht sich elegant an.
dressing [dres'ing] *n* (*MED*) Verband *m*; (*COOK*) Soße *f*.
dressing gown *n* (*Brit*) Morgenrock *m*.
dressing room *n* (*THEAT*) Garderobe *f*; (*SPORT*) Umkleideraum *m*.
dressing table *n* Toilettentisch *m*.

dressmaker [dres'mākûr] *n* Schneiderin *f*.
dressmaking [dres'māking] *n* Schneidern *nt*.
dress rehearsal *n* Generalprobe *f*.
dress shirt *n* Frackhemd *nt*.
dressy [dres'ē] *a* (*col*) schick.
drew [drōō] *pt of* draw.
dribble [drib'əl] *vi* tröpfeln ♦ *vt* sabbern; (*SPORT*) dribbeln.
dried [drīd] *a* getrocknet; (*fruit also*) Dörr-; ~ **milk** Milchpulver *nt*.
drier [drī'ûr] *n* Trockner *m*; *see* dryer.
drift [drift] *n* Trift *f*, Strömung *f*; (*snow*~) Schneewehe *f*; (*fig*) Richtung *f* ♦ *vi* getrieben werden; (*aimlessly*) sich treiben lassen; **to catch sb's** ~ verstehen, worauf jdm hinauswill; **to let things** ~ die Dinge treiben lassen; **to** ~ **apart** (*friends, lovers*) sich auseinanderleben.
drifter [drif'tûr] *n* Gammler *m*.
driftwood [drift'wōōd] *n* Treibholz *nt*.
drill [dril] *n* Bohrer *m*; (*MIL*) Drill *m* ♦ *vt* bohren; (*soldiers*) drillen ♦ *vi* (*MIL*) exerzieren; (*MIN*) bohren (*for* nach); **to** ~ **pupils in grammar** mit den Schülern Grammatik pauken.
drilling [dril'ing] *n* Bohren *nt*; (*hole*) Bohrloch *nt*; (*MIL*) Exerzieren *nt*.
drilling rig *n* (*on land*) Bohrturm *m*; (*at sea*) Bohrinsel *f*.
drily [drī'lē] *ad* (*Brit*) = dryly.
drink [dringk] *n* Getränk *nt*; (*spirits*) Drink *m* ♦ *vti irreg* trinken; **to invite sb for** ~s jdn zum Drink einladen; **would you like something to** ~? möchten Sie etwas zu trinken?; **there's food and** ~ **in the kitchen** Essen und Getränke sind in der Küche.
drink in *vt* (*person: fresh air*) einatmen, einsaugen; (: *story, sight*) (begierig) aufnehmen.
drinkable [dring'kəbəl] *a* (*not poisonous*) trinkbar; (*palatable*) genießbar, trinkbar.
drinker [dring'kûr] *n* Trinker(in *f*) *m*.
drinking [dring'king] *n* (*drunkenness*) Trinken *nt*, Saufen *nt* (*col*).
drinking fountain *n* Trinkwasserbrunnen *m*.
drinking water *n* Trinkwasser *nt*.
drip [drip] *n* Tropfen *m*; (*dripping*) Tröpfeln *nt*; (*col: spineless person*) Flasche *f*; (*Brit MED*) Tropf *m* ♦ *vi* tropfen.
drip-dry [drip'drī] *a* bügelfrei.
dripping [drip'ing] *n* Bratenfett *nt* ♦ *a*: ~ **wet** triefend.
drive [drīv] *n* Fahrt *f*; (*road*) Einfahrt *f*; (*campaign*) Aktion *f*; (*energy*) Schwung *m*, Tatkraft *f*; (*SPORT*) Schlag *m*; (*also: disk* ~) Diskettenlaufwerk *nt*; **sales** ~ Verkaufskampagne *f*; **front-/rear-wheel** ~ Vorderrad-/Hinterradantrieb *m*; **to go for a** ~ ein bißchen (raus)fahren; **it's 3 hours'** ~ **from Boston** es sind 3 Stunden Fahrt von Boston ♦ *irreg vt* (*car*) fahren; (*animals*) treiben; (*nail*) einschlagen; (*ball*) schlagen; (*power*) antreiben; (*force*) treiben; **he** ~**s a cab** er ist Taxifahrer; **he** ~**s a Mercedes** er

fährt einen Mercedes; **to** ~ **sb to desperation** (*fig*) jdn zur Verzweiflung bringen ♦ *vi* fahren; **can you** ~? können Sie (Auto)fahren?; **to** ~ **at 50 km an hour** mit 50 Stundenkilometer fahren.
drive at *vt fus* (*fig: intend, mean*) hinauswollen auf (+*acc*); **what are you driving at?** worauf willst du hinaus?
drive on *vi* weiterfahren ♦ *vt* (*incite, encourage*) antreiben.
drive-in [drīv'in] *a* Drive-in-; ~ **cinema** (*esp US*) Autokino *nt*.
drivel [driv'əl] *n* (*col: nonsense*) Blödsinn *m*, Kokolores *m*.
driven [driv'ən] *pp of* drive.
driver [drī'vûr] *n* Fahrer *m*.
driver's license *n* (*US*) Führerschein *m*.
driveway [drīv'wā] *n* Auffahrt *f*.
driving [drī'ving] *a* (*rain*) stürmisch; **the** ~ **force** die treibende Kraft.
driving instructor *n* Fahrlehrer *m*.
driving lesson *n* Fahrstunde *f*.
driving licence *n* (*Brit*) Führerschein *m*.
driving school *n* Fahrschule *f*.
driving test *n* Fahrprüfung *f*.
drizzle [driz'əl] *n* Nieselregen *m* ♦ *vi* nieseln.
droll [drōl] *a* drollig.
dromedary [drâm'idārē] *n* Dromedar *nt*.
drone [drōn] *n* (*sound*) Brummen *nt*; (*bee*) Drohne *f* ♦ *vi* (*bee*) summen; (*engine, aircraft*) brummen; (*also*: ~ **on**) (*voice, person*) langweilig reden.
drool [drōōl] *vi* sabbern; **to** ~ **over sb/sth** (*fig*) ganz vernarrt in jdm/etw sein.
droop [drōōp] *vi* (*schlaff*) herabhängen.
drop [drâp] *n* (*of liquid*) Tropfen *m*; (*fall: in price*) Rückgang *m*, (Preis)sturz *m*; **a** ~ **in salary** eine Gehaltsverschlechterung ♦ *vt* fallen lassen; (*lower*) senken; (*abandon*) fallenlassen; **to** ~ **sb a line** jdm ein paar Zeilen schreiben; **to** ~ **anchor** ankern, vor Anker gehen ♦ *vi* (*fall*) herunterfallen; (*decrease: wind*) sich legen; (: *numbers, attendance*) geringer werden; (*temperature*) sinken; (*voice*) sich senken; (*price*) fallen.
drop in *vi* (*col: visit*) vorbeikommen, hereinschauen (*on* bei).
drop off *vi* (*sleep*) einschlafen ♦ *vt*: **to** ~ **sb off** jdn absetzen.
drop out *vi* (*withdraw*) ausscheiden.
droplet [drâp'lit] *n* Tröpfchen *nt*.
dropout [drâp'out] *n* (*from society*) Aussteiger(in *f*) *m*; (*from university*) Studienabbrecher(in *f*) *m*.
dropper [drâp'ûr] *n* (*MED*) Pipette *f*.
droppings [drâp'ingz] *npl* Kot *m*.
drops [drâps] *npl* (*MED*) Tropfen *pl*; **cough** ~ Hustentropfen *pl*.
dross [drôs] *n* Unrat *m*.
drought [drout] *n* Dürre *f*.
drove [drōv] *n* (*crowd*) Herde *f* ♦ *pt of* drive.
drown [droun] *vt* ertränken; (*sound*) übertönen ♦ *vi* ertrinken.
drowse [drouz] *vi* (vor sich (*acc*) hin) dösen

or dämmern.
drowsy [drou'zē] *a* schläfrig.
drudge [druj] *n* Kuli *m*.
drudgery [druj'ûrē] *n* Plackerei *f*, Schinderei
f.
drug [drug] *n* (*MED*) Medikament *nt*, Arzneimittel *nt*; (*narcotic*) Rauschgift *nt* ♦ *vt* betäuben; **he's on ~s** (*MED*) er muß Medikamente nehmen; (*addicted*) er ist drogen-
süchtig.
drug addict *n* Rauschgiftsüchtige(r) *mf*.
druggist [drug'ist] *n* (*US*) Drogist *m*.
drug peddler *n* Drogenhändler *m*, Pusher *m*
(*col*).
drugstore [drug'stôr] *n* Drogerie *f*.
drug test *n* Dopingkontrolle *f*.
drum [drum] *n* Trommel *f* ♦ *vt*: **to ~ one's**
fingers on the table mit den Fingern auf
den Tisch trommeln.
  drum up *vt* (*enthusiasm*) erwecken; (*sup-*
  port) auftreiben.
drummer [drum'ûr] *n* Trommler *m*.
drumstick [drum'stik] *n* (*chicken leg*) Keule
f.
drunk [drungk] *a* betrunken ♦ *n* Betrunke-
ne(r) *m*; Trinker(in *f*) *m*; **to get ~** sich betrinken *or* besaufen (*col*) ♦ *pp of* **drink**.
drunkard [drung'kûrd] *n* Trunkenbold *m*.
drunken [drung'kən] *a* betrunken.
drunkenness [drung'kənnis] *n* Betrunkenheit
f.
dry [drī] *a* (*also humor, lecture etc*) trocken ♦
vt (ab)trocknen ♦ *vi* trocknen, trocken werden; **on ~ land** auf festem Boden; **to ~**
one's hands sich die Hände (ab)trocknen;
to ~ one's hair/eyes sich die Haare/Augen
trocknen.
  dry up *vi* austrocknen; (*source of supply*)
  versiegen; (*dishes*) abtrocken; (*fig: imagi-*
  nation etc) keine Ideen mehr haben; (*fall si-*
  lent: speaker) den Faden verlieren ♦ *vt*
  (*dishes*) abtrocknen.
dry-clean [drī'klēn'] *vt* chemisch reinigen; "**~**
only" (*on label*) „chemisch reinigen!‟
dry cleaner *n* Trockner *m*.
dry cleaning *n* chemische Reinigung *f*.
dry dock *n* (*NAUT*) Trockendock *nt*.
dryer [drī'ûr] *n* (*for hair*) Fön *m*, Haartrockner *m*; (*for clothes*) Trockner *m*.
dry goods *npl* (*COMM*) Kurzwaren *pl*.
dry goods store *n* (*US*) Textilgeschäft *nt*.
dry ice *n* Trockeneis *nt*.
dryly [drī'lē] *ad* trocken.
dryness [drī'nis] *n* Trockenheit *f*.
dry rot *n* Hausschwamm *m*.
dry run *n* (*fig*) Probe *f*.
dry ski slope *n* Trockenskipiste *f*.
DSc *n abbr* (= *Doctor of Science*) *akade-*
mischer Grad.
DSS *n abbr* (*Brit*: = *Department of Social Se-*
curity) *Ministerium für soziale Sicherheit*.
DST *n abbr* (*US*: = *Daylight Saving Time*) ≈
SZ *f*.
DT *n abbr* (*COMPUT*: = *data transmission*)

DO *f*.
DTI *n abbr* (*Brit*: = *Department of Trade and*
Industry) *Ministerium für Wirtschaft*.
DT's *n abbr* (*col*: = *delirium tremens*) Delirium tremens, Säuferwahn(sinn) *m*.
dual [dōō'əl] *a* doppelt.
dual carriageway *n* (*Brit*) Schnellstraße *f*
(*mit Mittelstreifen*).
dual-control [dōō'əlkəntrōl'] *a* mit Doppel-
steuerung.
dual nationality *n* doppelte Staatsangehörigkeit *f*.
dual-purpose [dōō'əlpûr'pəs] *a* Mehrzweck-.
dubbed [dubd] *a* (*film*) synchronisiert.
dubious [dōō'bēəs] *a* zweifelhaft; (*character,*
manner) zweifelhaft, fragwürdig; **I'm very**
~ about it ich habe da (doch) starke Zweifel.
Dublin [dub'lin] *n* Dublin *nt*.
duchess [duch'is] *n* Herzogin *f*.
duck [duk] *n* Ente *f* ♦ *vt* (ein)tauchen;
(*plunge in water: person, head*) untertauchen ♦ *vi* sich ducken.
duckling [duk'ling] *n* Entchen *nt*.
duct [dukt] *n* Röhre *f*.
dud [dud] *n* Niete *f* ♦ *a* wertlos, miserabel;
(*Brit: check*) ungedeckt.
dude [dōōd] *n* (*US col*) Kerl *m*.
due [dōō] *a* fällig; (*fitting*) angemessen; **the**
rent's ~ on the 30th die Miete ist am 30.
fällig; **the train is ~ at 8** der Zug kommt
laut Fahrplan um 8 Uhr an; **she is ~ back**
tomorrow sie müßte morgen zurück sein; **I**
am ~ 6 days' leave mir stehen 6 Tage Urlaub zu; **~ to** infolge (+*gen*), wegen (+*gen*)
♦ *n* Gebühr *f*; (*right*) Recht *nt* ♦ *ad* (*south*
etc) genau, gerade.
due date *n* Fälligkeitsdatum *nt*.
duel [dōō'əl] *n* Duell *nt*.
dues [dōōz] *npl* (*for club, union*) Beitrag *m*;
(*in harbor*) Gebühren *pl*.
duet [dōōet'] *n* Duett *nt*.
duff [duf] *a* (*Brit col*) öde, doof.
duffel bag, duffle bag [duf'əl bag] *n* Match-
beutel *m*.
duffel coat, duffle coat [duf'əl kōt] *n* Duffle-
coat *m*.
dug [dug] *pt, pp of* **dig**.
duke [dōōk] *n* Herzog *m*.
dull [dul] *a* (*color, weather*) trübe; (*stupid*)
schwer von Begriff; (*boring*) langweilig ♦ *vt*
(*soften, weaken*) abstumpfen.
duly [dōō'lē] *ad* ordnungsgemäß, richtig; (*on*
time) pünktlich.
dumb [dum] *a* (*lit*) stumm; (*col: stupid*)
doof, blöde; **he was struck ~ with horror**
es hatte ihm vor Schreck die Sprache verschlagen.
dumbbell [dum'bel] *n* (*SPORT*) Hantel *f*;
(*fool*) Blödmann *m*.
dumbfounded [dumfound'id] *a* verblüfft.
dummy [dum'ē] *n* Schneiderpuppe *f*; (*substi-*
tute) Attrappe *f*; (*Brit: pacifier*) Schnuller
m ♦ *a* Schein-; **~ run** Probe *f*.

dump [dump] *n* Abfallhaufen *m*; (*MIL*) Stapelplatz *m*; (*col: place*) Nest *nt*; (*COMPUT*) Dump *m*, Speicherauszug *m* ♦ *vt* abladen, auskippen; (*COMM: goods*) zu Dumpingpreisen verkaufen, verschleudern; (*COMPUT*) ausgeben; **to be (down) in the ~s** (*col*) deprimiert *or* down sein.

dumping [dum'ping] *n* (*COMM*) Schleuderexport *m*; (*of garbage*) Schuttabladen *nt*.

dumpling [dump'ling] *n* Kloß *m*, Knödel *m*.

dumpy [dump'ē] *a* pummelig.

dunce [duns] *n* Dummkopf *m*.

dune [dōōn] *n* Düne *f*.

dung [dung] *n* Mist *m*; (*AGR*) Dünger *m*.

dungarees [dunggərēz'] *npl* (*Brit*) Arbeitsanzug *m*, Arbeitskleidung *f*.

dungeon [dun'jən] *n* Kerker *m*.

dunk [dungk] *vt* einstippen, eintunken.

duo [dōō'ō] *n* (*also MUS*) Duo *nt*.

duodenal ulcer [dōōədē'nəl ul'sûr] *n* Zwölffingerdarmgeschwür *nt*.

duodenum [dōōədē'nəm] *n* Zwölffingerdarm *m*, Duodenum *nt*.

dupe [dōōp] *n* Gefoppte(r) *m* ♦ *vt* hintergehen, übertölpeln.

duplex [dōōp'leks] *n* (*US: also:* **~ apartment**) zweistöckige Wohnung *f*.

duplicate [dōō'plikit] *a* doppelt; (*copy*) zweifach ♦ *n* Duplikat *nt*; (*copy of letter etc*) Kopie *f* ♦ *vt* [dōō'plikāt] verdoppeln; (*make copies*) kopieren; **in ~** in doppelter Ausführung.

duplicate key *n* Zweitschlüssel *m*.

duplicating machine [dōō'plikāting məshēn] *n* Vervielfältigungsapparat *m*.

duplicator [dōōp'likātûr] *n* Vervielfältigungsapparat *m*.

duplicity [dōōplis'ətē] *n* Doppelspiel *nt*.

Dur *abbr* (*Brit*) = Durham.

durability [dōōrəbil'ətē] *n* Dauer *f*, Haltbarkeit *f*, Widerstandsfähigkeit *f*.

durable [dōōr'əbəl] *a* haltbar.

duration [dōōrā'shən] *n* Dauer *f*.

duress [dōōres'] *n*: **under ~** unter Zwang.

Durex [dōō'reks] *n* ® (*Brit*) Kondom *m*, Gummi *m* (*col*).

during [dōōr'ing] *prep* während (*+gen*).

dusk [dusk] *n* Abenddämmerung *f*.

dusky [dus'kē] *a* dunkel; (*maiden*) dunkelhäutig.

dust [dust] *n* Staub *m* ♦ *vt* abstauben; (*sprinkle*) bestäuben.

dust off *vt* hervorkramen.

dustbin [dust'bin] *n* (*Brit*) Mülleimer *m*.

duster [dus'tûr] *n* Staubtuch *nt*.

dust jacket *n* Schutzumschlag *m*.

dustman [dust'man] *n*, *pl* **-men** (*Brit*) Müllmann *m*.

dustpan [dust'pan] *n* Kehrblech *nt*.

dust storm *n* Staubsturm *m*.

dusty [dus'tē] *a* staubig.

Dutch [duch] *a* holländisch, niederländisch ♦ *n* (*language*) Holländisch *nt*, Niederländisch *nt*; **the ~** (*people*) die Holländer *or* Nieder-

länder *pl* ♦ *ad*: **to go ~** *or* **d~** getrennte Kasse machen.

Dutch auction *n* Versteigerung *mit laufend erniedrigtem Ausbietungspreis*.

Dutchman/Dutchwoman [duch'mən/ wōōmən] *n*, *pl* **-men/women** Holländer(in *f*) *m*.

dutiable [dōō'tēəbəl] *a* zollpflichtig.

dutiful [dōō'tifəl] *a* (*child*) gehorsam; (*husband, employee*) pflichtbewußt.

duty [dōō'tē] *n* Pflicht *f*; (*job*) Aufgabe *f*; (*tax*) Einfuhrzoll *m*; (*MED: in hospital*) Dienst *m*; **to make it one's ~ to do sth** es sich (*dat*) zur Pflicht machen, etw zu tun; **to pay ~ on sth** Zoll auf etw (*acc*) bezahlen; **on ~** im Dienst, diensthabend.

duty-free [dōō'tēfrē'] *a* zollfrei.

duty-free shop *n* Duty-free-Shop *m*.

duty officer *n* (*MIL etc*) Offizier *m* vom Dienst.

duvet [dōō'vā] *n* (*Brit*) Steppdecke *f*.

DV *abbr* (= *Deo volente*) so Gott will.

DVM *n abbr* (*US:* = *Doctor of Veterinary Medicine*) Dr. med. vet.

dwarf [dwôrf] *n* Zwerg *m*.

dwell [dwel] *vi irreg* wohnen.

dwell on *vt fus* verweilen bei.

dweller [dwel'ûr] *n* Bewohner(in *f*) *m*; **city ~** Städter(in *f*) *m*.

dwelling [dwel'ing] *n* Wohnung *f*.

dwelt [dwelt] *pt*, *pp of* **dwell**.

dwindle [dwin'dəl] *vi* schwinden.

dwindling [dwin'dling] *a* (*strength, interest*) schwindelnd; (*resources, supplies*) versiegend.

dye [dī] *n* Farbstoff *m* ♦ *vt* färben; **hair ~** Haarfärbemittel *nt*.

dying [dī'ing] *a* (*person*) sterbend; (*moments*) letzt.

dyke [dīk] *n* (*Brit: channel*) (Entwässerungs)graben *m*; (: *embankment*) Deich *m*.

dynamic [dīnam'ik] *a* dynamisch.

dynamics [dīnam'iks] *n sing or pl* Dynamik *f*.

dynamite [dī'nəmīt] *n* Dynamit *nt* ♦ *vt* sprengen.

dynamo [dī'nəmō] *n* Dynamo *m*.

dynasty [dī'nəstē] *n* Dynastie *f*.

dysentery [dis'əntärē] *n* Ruhr *f*.

dyslexic [dislek'sik] *a* legasthenisch ♦ *n* Legastheniker(in *f*) *m*.

dyspepsia [dispep'shə] *n* Verdauungsstörung *f*.

dystrophy [dis'trəfē] *n* Dystrophie *f*, Ernährungsstörung *f*; **muscular ~** Muskelschwund *m*.

E

E, e [ē] n (letter) E nt, e nt; **E for Easy** ≈ E für Emil.

E abbr (= east) O.

E111 n abbr (also: **form** ~) E111 f.

ea. abbr = **each.**

each [ēch] a jeder/jede/jedes; **he comes ~ day** er kommt jeden Tag ♦ pron (ein) jeder/(eine) jede/(ein) jedes; ~ **other** einander, sich; ~ **of us** jeder von uns ♦ ad je; **they cost $5** ~ sie kosten je 5 Dollar.

eager [ē'gûr] a eifrig; (keen: pupil) lerneifrig, lernwillig.

eagerly [ē'gûrlē] ad eifrig.

eagerness [ē'gûrnis] n Eifer m; (impatience) Ungeduld f.

eagle [ē'gəl] n Adler m.

ear [ēr] n Ohr nt; (of corn) Ähre f; **to be up to one's ~s in debt** bis über beide Ohren in Schulden stecken.

earache [ēr'āk] n Ohrenschmerzen pl.

eardrum [ēr'drum] n Trommelfell nt.

earl [ûrl] n Graf m.

early [ûr'lē] a, ad früh; (man) vor- or frühgeschichtlich; ~ **Christians** Urchristen pl; **you're** ~ du bist früh dran; ~ **in the morning/afternoon** früh am Morgen/am frühen Nachmittag; **I can't come any earlier** ich kann nicht früher kommen; **she's in her** ~ **forties** sie ist Anfang Vierzig; **at your earliest convenience** (COMM) möglichst bald.

early retirement n vorzeitige Pensionierung f.

early warning system n Frühwarnungsystem nt.

earmark [ēr'mârk] vt vorsehen.

earn [ûrn] vt verdienen; (interest) bringen; **to** ~ **one's living** seinen Lebensunterhalt verdienen.

earned income [ûrnd' in'kum] n Arbeitseinkommen nt.

earnest [ûr'nist] a ernst; ~ **money** Angeld nt; **in** ~ im Ernst.

earnings [ûr'ningz] npl Verdienst m; (of company etc) Ertrag m.

earphones [ēr'fōnz] npl Kopfhörer pl.

earplugs [ēr'plugz] npl Ohropax ® nt.

earring [ēr'ring] n Ohrring m.

earshot [ēr'shât] n Hörweite f.

earth [ûrth] n Erde f; (Brit ELEC) Erdung f ♦ vt erden.

earthenware [ûr'thənwär] n Steingut nt.

earthly [ûrth'lē] a irdisch; ~ **paradise** Paradies nt auf Erden; **there is no** ~ **reason to think** es besteht nicht der geringste Grund für die Annahme ...

earthquake [ûrth'kwāk] n Erdbeben nt.

earthworm [ûrth'wûrm] n Regenwurm m.

earthworks [ûrth'wûrks] npl (CONSTR) Erdarbeiten pl.

earthy [ûr'thē] a roh; (sensual) sinnlich.

earwig [ēr'wig] n Ohrwurm m.

ease [ēz] n (simplicity) Leichtigkeit f; (social) Ungezwungenheit f; **to feel at** ~/**ill at** ~ sich wohl/unwohl fühlen; **with** ~ mit Leichtigkeit; **at** ~ ungezwungen; (MIL) rührt euch! ♦ vt (pain) lindern; (burden) erleichtern ♦ vi (situation) sich entspannen.

ease off, ease up vi (pressure, tension) sich entspannen.

easel [ē'zəl] n Staffelei f.

easily [ē'zilē] ad leicht.

easiness [ē'zēnis] n Leichtigkeit f; (of manners) Ungezwungenheit f.

east [ēst] n Osten m; **the E~** (POL) der Osten ♦ a östlich ♦ ad nach Osten.

Easter [ēs'tûr] n Ostern nt.

Easter egg n Osterei nt.

Easter Island n Osterinsel f.

easterly [ēs'tûrlē] a östlich, Ost-.

Easter Monday n Ostermontag m.

eastern [ēs'tûrn] a östlich; (attitude) orientalisch; **the E~ bloc** (POL) der Ostblock f.

Easter Sunday n Ostersonntag m.

East Germany n die DDR.

eastward(s) [ēst'wûrd(z)] ad ostwärts.

easy [ē'zē] a (task) einfach; (life) bequem; (carefree) unbekümmert; (manner) ungezwungen, natürlich; **I'm** ~ (col) mir ist alles recht; **easier said than done** leichter gesagt als getan; **payment on** ~ **terms** (COMM) Zahlung zu günstigen Bedingungen ♦ ad: **to take things** ~ (for health) sich schonen; **take it** ~! (don't worry) nimm's nicht so schwer; (don't rush) immer mit der Ruhe!

easy chair n Sessel m.

easy-going [ē'zēgō'ing] a gelassen; (lax) lässig.

eat [ēt] vt irreg essen; (animals) fressen; (destroy) (zer)fressen.

eat away vt (corrode) zerfressen; (sea) auswaschen.

eat out vi zum Essen ausgehen.

eat up vt (meal etc) aufessen; **it ~s up electricity** es verbraucht Strom.

eatable [ē'təbəl] a genießbar.

eaten [ē'tən] pp of **eat.**

Eau de Cologne [ō də kəlōn'] n Kölnisch Wasser nt, Eau de Cologne nt.

eaves [ēvz] npl Dachvorsprung m.

eavesdrop [ēvz'drâp] vi horchen, lauschen; **to** ~ **on sb** jdn belauschen.

ebb [eb] n Ebbe f; ~ **and flow** Ebbe und Flut; (fig) Auf und Ab; **to be at a low** ~ (fig: person, spirits, business also) auf einem Tiefstand sein ♦ vi ebben.

ebb tide n Ebbe f.

ebony [eb'ǝnē] n Ebenholz nt.
ebullient [ibul'yǝnt] a sprudelnd, temperamentvoll.
EC n abbr (= European Community) EG f.
eccentric [iksen'trik] a exzentrisch, überspannt ♦ n exzentrische(r) Mensch m.
ecclesiastical [iklēzēas'tikǝl] a kirchlich, geistlich.
ECG n abbr (= electrocardiogram; electrocardiograph) EKG nt.
echo [ek'ō] n Echo nt; (COMPUT) Echo nt, Rückmeldung f ♦ vt zurückwerfen; (fig) nachbeten ♦ vi widerhallen.
eclair [iklär'] n Eclair nt.
eclipse [iklips'] n Verfinsterung f, Finsternis f ♦ vt verfinstern.
ECM n abbr (US: = European Common Market) EG f.
ecologist [ikál'ǝjist] n Ökologe m, Ökologin f.
ecology [ikál'ǝjē] n Ökologie f.
economic [ēkǝnâm'ik] a (profitable: price) wirtschaftlich; (business) wirtschaftlich, ökonomisch.
economical [ēkǝnâm'ikǝl] a wirtschaftlich; (person) sparsam.
economically [ēkǝnâm'iklē] ad (thriftily) sparsam; (regarding economics) wirtschaftlich.
economics [ēkǝnâm'iks] n sing Volkswirtschaft f; (pl: financial aspects) Wirtschaftlichkeit f, Ökonomie f.
economic warfare n Wirtschaftskrieg m.
economies [ikân'ǝmēz] npl: ~ **of scale** Kostenersparnisse pl durch Erhöhung der Produktion.
economist [ikân'ǝmist] n Volkswirt(schaftler) m.
economize [ikân'ǝmīz] vi sparen (on an +dat).
economy [ikân'ǝmē] n (thrift) Sparsamkeit f; (of country) Wirtschaft f; see also **economies**.
economy class n Touristenklasse f.
economy size n Sparpackung f.
ecosystem [ek'ōsistǝm] n Ökosystem nt.
ECSC n abbr (= European Coal & Steel Community) EGKS f.
ecstasy [ek'stǝsē] n Ekstase f.
ecstatic [ekstat'ik] a hingerissen.
ECT n abbr (= electroconvulsive therapy) EKT f (= Elektrokrampftherapie).
ECU n abbr (= European Currency Unit) EWS f.
Ecuador [ek'wǝdōr] n Ecuador nt, Ekuador nt.
ecumenical [ekyōōmen'ikǝl] a ökumenisch.
eczema [ek'sǝmǝ] n Ekzem nt.
eddy [ed'ē] n Wirbel m.
Eden [ē'dǝn] n (Garten m) Eden nt.
edge [ej] n Rand m; (of knife) Schneide f; on ~ nervös; (nerves) überreizt ♦ vi: to ~ **past** sich vorbeidrücken/-schieben an (+dat); to ~ up to sb sich an jdn heranmachen.

edgeways [ej'wāz] ad mit der Schmalseite voran; I **couldn't get a word in** ~ ich bin überhaupt nicht zu Wort gekommen.
edging [ej'ing] n Einfassung f.
edgy [ej'ē] a nervös.
edible [ed'ǝbǝl] a eßbar.
edict [ē'dikt] n Erlaß m.
edifice [ed'ǝfis] n Gebäude nt.
edifying [ed'ǝfiing] a erbaulich.
Edinburgh [ed'ǝnbûrǝ] n Edinburg nt, Edinburgh nt.
edit [ed'it] vt redigieren; (newspaper, magazine) herausgeben; (COMPUT) aufbereiten, bearbeiten.
edition [idish'ǝn] n Ausgabe f.
editor [ed'itûr] n (of newspaper) Redakteur(in f) m; (of book) Lektor(in f) m; **film** ~ Cutter(in f) m.
editorial [editôr'ēǝl] a Redaktions- ♦ n Leitartikel m.
editorial staff n Redaktion(sangestellte pl) f.
EDP n abbr (= electronic data processing) EDV f.
EDT abbr (US) = Eastern Daylight Time.
educate [ej'ōōkāt] vt erziehen; (mind, tastes etc) (aus)bilden.
education [ejōōkā'shǝn] n (teaching) Unterricht m; (system) Schulwesen nt; (schooling) Erziehung f; Bildung f; (UNIV: subject) Pädagogik f; **elementary/secondary** ~ Primarstufen-/Sekundarstufenerziehung f.
educational [ejōōkā'shǝnǝl] a pädagogisch; ~ **technology** Unterrichtstechnologie f.
Edwardian [edwôr'dēǝn] a aus der Zeit Edwards VII.
EE abbr = **electrical engineer**.
EEC n abbr (= European Economic Community) EG f.
EEG n abbr (= electroencephalogram) EEG nt.
eel [ēl] n Aal m.
EENT n abbr (US MED) = eye, ear, nose and throat.
EEOC n abbr (US: = Equal Employment Opportunity Commission) Kommission zum Schutze der Gleichberechtigung am Arbeitsplatz.
eerie [ē'rē] a unheimlich.
EET abbr (= Eastern European Time) OEZ f.
efface [ifās'] vt auslöschen.
effect [ifekt'] n Wirkung f; **in** ~ in der Tat; **to have an** ~ **on sb/sth** eine Wirkung auf jdn/etw haben; **to put into** ~ (plan) verwirklichen; **his letter is to the** ~ **that** ... sein Brief hat zum Inhalt, daß ...; see also **effects** ♦ vt bewirken.
effective [ifek'tiv] a wirksam, effektiv; (striking: display, outfit) wirkungsvoll, effektvoll; ~ **date** Zeitpunkt m des Inkrafttretens; **to become** ~ (JUR) in Kraft treten.
effectively [ifek'tivlē] ad (efficiently) wirksam, effektiv; (strikingly) wirkungsvoll, effektvoll; (in reality, in effect) effektiv.
effects [ifekts'] npl (sound, visual) Effekte pl;

(*property*) Effekten *pl*.

effeminate [ifem'ənit] *a* weibisch.

effervescent [cfûrves'ənt] *a* (*lit*, *fig*) sprudelnd.

efficacy [ef'ikəsē] *n* Wirksamkeit *f*.

efficiency [ifish'ənsē] *n* Tüchtigkeit *f*; Wirksamkeit *f*; Effizienz *f*; Leistungsfähigkeit *f*.

efficient [ifish'ənt] *a*, **efficiently** [ifish'əntlē] *ad* tüchtig; (*method*) wirksam; (*remedy*, *product*, *system*) effizient; (*machine*, *car*) leistungsfähig.

effigy [ef'ijē] *n* Abbild *nt*.

effluent [ef'lōōənt] *n* (*from a lake*) Ausfluß *m*; (*sewage*) Abwasser *nt*.

effort [ef'ûrt] *n* Anstrengung *f*; **to make an ~** sich anstrengen.

effortless [ef'ûrtlis] *a* mühelos.

effrontery [ifrun'tûrē] *n* Unverfrorenheit *f*.

effusive [ifyōō'siv] *a* (*person*) exaltiert; (*welcome*, *letter*, *thanks*, *apologies*) überschwenglich.

EFL *n abbr* (*SCH*) = *English as a foreign language*.

EFT *n abbr* (*US*) = *electronic funds transfer*.

EFTA [ef'tə] *n abbr* (= *European Free Trade Association*) EFTA *f*.

e.g. *abbr* (= *exempli gratia: for example*) z.B.

egalitarian [igalitär'ēən] *a* Gleichheits-, egalitär.

egg [eg] *n* Ei *nt*.

 egg on *vt* anstacheln.

egg cup *n* Eierbecher *m*.

eggnog [eg'nâg] *n* Ei-Flip *m*.

eggplant [eg'plant] *n* (*esp US*) Aubergine *f*.

eggshell [eg'shel] *n* Eierschale *f*.

egg white *n* Eiweiß *nt*.

egg yolk *n* Eigelb *nt*, Eidotter *m*.

ego [ē'gō] *n* Ich *nt*, Selbst *nt*.

egotism [ē'gətizəm] *n* Ichbezogenheit *f*.

egotist [ē'gətist] *n* Egozentriker(in *f*) *m*.

Egypt [ē'jipt] *n* Ägypten *nt*.

Egyptian [ijip'shən] *a* ägyptisch ♦ *n* (*person*) Ägypter(in *f*) *m*; (*language*) Ägyptisch *nt*.

eiderdown [ī'dûrdoun] *n* Daunendecke *f*.

eight [āt] *num* acht.

eighteen [ā'tēn'] *num* achtzehn.

eighth [ātth] *a* achte(r, s) ♦ *n* Achtel *nt*.

eighth note *n* (*US*) Achtel *m*.

eighty [ā'tē] *num* achtzig.

Eire [är'ə] *n* Irland *nt*.

either [ē'thûr] *a*, *pron* (*one or other*) eine(r,s) (von beiden); (*each*, *both*) jede(r,s), beide *pl*; **I don't want ~** ich will keins von beiden; **on ~ side** auf beiden Seiten ♦ *ad*, *cj* (*after negative statement*) auch nicht; **I don't ~** ich auch nicht; **~ ... or** entweder ... oder; (*after a negative*) weder ... noch.

eject [ijekt'] *vt* ausstoßen, vertreiben ♦ *vi* (*pilot*) den Schleudersitz betätigen.

ejector seat [ijek'tûr sēt] *n* Schleudersitz *m*.

eke out [ēk out] *vt* strecken.

EKG *n abbr* (*US:* = *electrocardiogram*; *electrocardiograph*) EKG *nt*.

el [el] *n abbr* (*US col:* = *elevated railroad*) ≈ S-Bahn *f*.

elaborate *a* [ilab'ûrit] sorgfältig ausgearbeitet, ausführlich ♦ *vt* [ilab'ûrāt] sorgfältig ausarbeiten.

elaborately [ilab'ûritlē] *ad* genau, ausführlich.

elaboration [ilabərā'shən] *n* Ausarbeitung *f*.

elapse [ilaps'] *vi* vergehen.

elastic [ilas'tik] *n* Gummi(band *nt*) *m* ♦ *a* elastisch.

elastic band *n* Gummiband *nt*.

elated [ilā'tid] *a* froh, in gehobener Stimmung.

elation [ilā'shən] *n* gehobene Stimmung *f*.

elbow [el'bō] *n* Ellbogen *m* ♦ *vt*: **to ~ one's way through the crowd** sich durch die Menge boxen; **to ~ sb aside** jdn beiseite stoßen.

elder [el'dûr] *a* älter ♦ *n* Altere(r) *mf*.

elderly [el'dûrlē] *a* ältere(r, s).

elect [ilekt'] *vt* wählen ♦ *a* zukünftig.

election [ilek'shən] *n* Wahl *f*; **to hold an ~** eine Wahl durchführen *or* abhalten.

election campaign *n* Wahlkampagne *f*, Wahlkampf *m*.

electioneering [ilekshənē'ring] *n* Wahlpropaganda *f*.

elective [ilek'tiv] *n* (*US*) Wahlfach *nt*.

elector [ilek'tûr] *n* Wähler(in *f*) *m*.

electoral [ilek'tûrəl] *a* Wahl-.

electoral college *n* Wahlmännerkollegium *nt*.

electoral roll *n* (*Brit*) Wählerverzeichnis *nt*.

electorate [ilek'tûrit] *n* Wähler *pl*, Wählerschaft *f*.

electric [ilek'trik] *a* elektrisch, Elektro-.

electrical [ilek'trikəl] *a* elektrisch.

electrical engineer *n* Elektrotechniker *m*.

electrical failure *n* Stromausfall *m*.

electric blanket *n* Heizdecke *f*.

electric chair *n* elektrische(r) Stuhl *m*.

electric current *n* elektrische(r) Strom *m*.

electrician [ilektrish'ən] *n* Elektriker *m*.

electricity [ilektris'ətē] *n* Elektrizität *f*; **to switch on/off the ~** den Strom an-/abschalten.

electric light *n* elektrische(s) Licht *nt*.

electric shock *n* elektrische(r) Schlag *m*.

electric stove *n* (*for cooking*) Elektroherd *m*.

electrification [ilektrəfəkā'shən] *n* Elektrifizierung *f*.

electrify [ilek'trəfī] *vt* elektrifizieren; (*fig*) elektrisieren.

electro- [ilek'trō] *pref* Elektro-.

electrocardiogram [ilektrōkâr'dēəgram] *n* Elektrokardiogramm *nt*.

electrocardiograph [ilektrōkâr'dēəgraf] *n* Elektrokardiograph *m*.

electro-convulsive therapy [ilek'trōkənvul'siv thär'əpē] *n* Elektrokonvulsivtherapie *f*.

electrocute [ilek'trəkyōōt] *vt* durch elektrischen Strom töten; (*execute*) auf dem elek-

trischen Stuhl hinrichten.
electrode [ilek'trōd] *n* Elektrode *f.*
electroencephalogram [ilektrōensef'ələgram] *n* Elektroenzephalogramm *nt.*
electrolysis [ilektrál'isis] *n* Elektrolyse *f.*
electromagnetic [ilektrōmagnet'ik] *a* elektromagnetisch.
electron [ilek'trân] *n* Elektron *nt.*
electronic [ilektrân'ik] *a* elektronisch, Elektronen-.
electronic data processing *n* elektronische Datenverarbeitung *f.*
electronic mail *n* elektronische Post *f.*
electronics [ilektrân'iks] *n* Elektronik *f.*
electron microscope *n* Elektronenmikroskop *nt.*
electroplated [ilek'trəplätid] *a* (galvanisch) versilbert *or* verchromt.
electrotherapy [ilektrōthär'əpē] *n* Elektrotherapie *f.*
elegance [el'əgəns] *n* Eleganz *f.*
elegant [el'əgənt] *a* elegant.
elegy [el'ijē] *n* Elegie *f.*
element [el'əmənt] *n* Element *nt*; *(fig)* Körnchen *nt.*
elementary [elimen'tûrē] *a* einfach; *(primary)* grundlegend, Anfangs-.
elephant [el'əfənt] *n* Elefant *m.*
elevate [el'əvāt] *vt* emporheben.
elevation [eləvā'shən] *n* *(height)* Erhebung *f*; *(of style)* Niveau *nt*; *(ARCHIT)* (Quer)schnitt *m.*
elevator [el'əvātûr] *n* *(US)* Fahrstuhl *m*, Aufzug *m.*
eleven [ilev'ən] *num* elf ♦ *n* *(team)* Elf *f.*
elevenses [ilev'ənziz] *npl* *(Brit)* zweite(s) Frühstück *nt.*
eleventh [ilev'ənth] *a* elfte(r, s); **at the ~ hour** *(fig)* in letzter Minute, fünf Minuten vor zwölf.
elf [elf] *n*, *pl* **elves** [elvz] Elfe *f.*
elicit [ilis'it] *vt* herausbekommen; **to ~ sth (from sb)** (jdm) etw entlocken.
eligible [el'ijəbəl] *a* wählbar; **he's not ~** er kommt nicht in Frage; **to be ~ for a pension/competition** pensions-/teilnahmeberechtigt sein; **~ bachelor** gute Partie *f.*
eliminate [əlim'ənāt] *vt* *(competitor etc)* ausschalten; *(fault)* beseitigen.
elimination [əlimənā'shən] *n* Ausschaltung *f*; Beseitigung *f*; **by process of ~** durch negative Auslese.
elite [ilēt'] *n* Elite *f.*
elitist [ilē'tist] *a* *(pej)* elitär.
elixir [ilik'sûr] *n* Elixier *nt*, Auszug *m.*
Elizabethan [ilizəbē'thən] *a* elisabethanisch.
elm [elm] *n* Ulme *f.*
elocution [eləkyōō'shən] *n* Sprecherziehung *f*; *(clarity)* Artikulation *f.*
elongated [ilông'gātid] *a* verlängert.
elope [ilōp'] *vi* entlaufen.
elopement [ilōp'mənt] *n* Entlaufen *nt.*
eloquence [el'əkwəns] *n* Beredsamkeit *f.*
eloquent [el'əkwənt] *a*, **eloquently**

[el'əkwəntlē] *ad* redegewandt.
else [els] *ad* sonst; **everyone ~** alle anderen; **nothing ~** nichts weiter; **is there anything ~ I can do?** kann ich sonst noch was tun?; **or ~** *(otherwise)* sonst; **who ~?** wer sonst?; **somebody ~** jd anders.
elsewhere [els'hwär] *ad* anderswo, woanders.
ELT *n abbr* *(SCH)* = *English Language Teaching.*
elucidate [ilōō'sidāt] *vt* erläutern.
elude [ilōōd'] *vt* entgehen (+*dat*).
elusive [ilōō'siv] *a* schwer faßbar.
elves [elvz] *npl of* **elf.**
emaciated [imā'shēātid] *a* abgezehrt.
emanate [em'ənāt] *vi* ausströmen *(from* aus).
emancipate [iman'səpāt] *vt* emanzipieren; *(slave)* freilassen.
emancipation [imansəpā'shən] *n* Emanzipation *f*; Freilassung *f.*
emasculate [imas'kyəlāt] *vt* *(lit)* entmannen; *(fig)* außer Kraft setzen.
embalm [embâm'] *vt* einbalsamieren.
embankment [embangk'mənt] *n* *(of river)* Uferböschung *f*; *(of road)* Straßendamm *m*; *(of railway)* Bahndamm *m.*
embargo [embár'gō] *n* Embargo *nt*; *(fig)* Sperre *f*; **to put an ~ on sth** etw mit einem Embargo belegen.
embark [embârk'] *vi* sich einschiffen.
embark on *vt fus* unternehmen; **to ~ on sth** etw anfangen, etw beginnen.
embarkation [embârkā'shən] *n* Einschiffung *f.*
embarkation card *n* Einsteigekarte *f.*
embarrass [embar'əs] *vt* in Verlegenheit bringen.
embarrassed [embar'əst] *a* verlegen.
embarrassing [embar'əsing] *a* peinlich.
embarrassment [embar'əsmənt] *n* Verlegenheit *f.*
embassy [em'bəsē] *n* Botschaft *f*; **the German E~** die Deutsche Botschaft.
embed [embed'] *vt* einbetten.
embellish [embel'ish] *vt* schmücken; *(fig: story)* ausschmücken; *(: truth)* beschönigen.
embers [em'bûrz] *npl* Glut(asche) *f.*
embezzle [embez'əl] *vt* unterschlagen.
embezzlement [embez'əlmənt] *n* Unterschlagung *f.*
embitter [embit'ûr] *vt* verbittern.
emblem [em'bləm] *n* Emblem *nt*, Abzeichen *nt.*
embodiment [embâd'ēmənt] *n* Verkörperung *f.*
embody [embâd'ē] *vt* *(ideas)* verkörpern; *(new features)* (in sich) vereinigen.
embolden [embōl'dən] *vt* *(TYP)* fett drucken; *(fig)* ermutigen.
embolism [em'bəlizəm] *n* *(MED)* Embolie *f.*
emboss [embôs'] *vt* prägen.
embrace [embrās'] *vt* umarmen; *(include)* einschließen, umfassen ♦ *vi* sich umarmen ♦ *n* Umarmung *f.*
embroider [embroi'dûr] *vt* (be)sticken; *(sto-*

ry) ausschmücken.
embroidery [embroi'dûrē] *n* Stickerei *f*.
embroil [embroil'] *vt*: **to become ~ed (in sth)** (in etw) verwickelt *or* hineingezogen werden.
embryo [em'brēō] *n* (*lit*) Embryo *m*; (*fig*) Keim *m*.
emcee [em'sē'] *n* (*col*) Gastgeber *m*.
emend [imend'] *vt* (*text*) verbessern, korrigieren.
emerald [em'ûrəld] *n* Smaragd *m* ♦ *a* smaragdgrün.
emerge [imûrj'] *vi* auftauchen; (*truth*) herauskommen; **it ~s that ...** (*Brit*) es stellt sich heraus, daß ...
emergence [imûr'jəns] *n* Erscheinen *nt*; (*of nation*) Entstehung *f*.
emergency [imûr'jənsē] *n* Notfall *m*; **to declare a state of ~** den Notstand ausrufen ♦ *a* (*action*) Not-.
emergency exit *n* Notausgang *m*.
emergency flasher [imûr'jənsē flash'ûr] *n* (*US AUT*) Warnblinklicht *nt*.
emergency landing *n* Notlandung *f*.
emergency lane *n* (*US*) Seitenstreifen *m*.
emergency service *n* Not- *or* Hilfsdienst *m*.
emergency stop *n* (*AUT*) Vollbremsung *f*.
emergent [imûr'jənt] *a* (*nation*) aufstrebend.
emery board [em'ûrē bōrd] *n* Papiernagelfeile *f*.
emery paper [em'ûrē pāpûr] *n* Schmirgelpapier *nt*.
emetic [imet'ik] *n* Brechmittel *nt*.
emigrant [em'əgrənt] *n* Auswanderer(in *f*) *m*, Emigrant(in *f*) *m* ♦ *a* Auswanderungs-.
emigrate [em'əgrāt] *vi* auswandern, emigrieren.
emigration [eməgrā'shən] *n* Auswanderung *f*, Emigration *f*.
émigré [em'igrā] *n* Emigrant(in *f*) *m*.
eminence [em'ənəns] *n* hohe(r) Rang *m*; **to gain** *or* **win ~** (hohes) Ansehen gewinnen; **E~** (*title*) Eminenz *f*.
eminent [em'ənənt] *a* bedeutend.
eminently [em'ənəntlē] *ad* ausgesprochen, außerordentlich.
emirate [əmē'rit] *n* Emirat *nt*.
emission [imish'ən] *n* (*of gases*) Ausströmen *nt*.
emit [imit'] *vt* von sich (*dat*) geben.
emolument [imál'yəmənt] *n* (*often pl*: *form*) Vergütung *f*; (*fee*) Honorar *nt*; (*salary*) Bezüge *pl*.
emotion [imō'shən] *n* Emotion *f*, Gefühl *nt*.
emotional [imō'shənəl] *a* (*person*) emotional; (*scene*) ergreifend.
emotionally [imō'shənəlē] *ad* gefühlsmäßig; (*behave*) emotional; (*sing*) ergreifend; (*speak*) gefühlvoll.
emotive [imō'tiv] *a* gefühlsbetont.
empathy [em'pəthē] *n* Einfühlungsvermögen *nt*, Empathie *f*; **to feel ~** Einfühlungsvermögen haben.
emperor [em'pûrûr] *n* Kaiser *m*.

emphasis [em'fəsis] *n* (*LING*) Betonung *f*; (*fig*) Nachdruck *m*; **to lay** *or* **place ~ on sth** (*fig*) etw betonen; **the ~ is on sport** der Schwerpunkt liegt auf Sport, Sport wird betont.
emphasize [em'fəsīz] *vt* betonen.
emphatic [əmfat'ik] *a* nachdrücklich; (*condemnation, denial*) energisch; **to be ~ about sth** etw nachdrücklich betonen.
emphatically [əmfat'iklē] *ad* nachdrücklich.
emphysema [emfisē'mə] *n* (*MED*) Emphysem *nt*, Schwellung *f*.
empire [em'pīûr] *n* Reich *nt*.
empirical [empir'ikəl] *a* empirisch.
employ [emploi'] *vt* (*give job to*) anstellen; (*use*) verwenden; (*make use of*: *thing, method*) anwenden, einsetzen; (: *person*) einsetzen; **he's ~ed in a bank** er ist bei einer Bank angestellt.
employee [emploi'ē] *n* Angestellte(r) *mf*.
employer [emploi'ûr] *n* Arbeitgeber(in *f*) *m*.
employment [emploi'mənt] *n* Beschäftigung *f*; **in ~** beschäftigt; **without ~** ohne Arbeit; **to find ~** eine Arbeit *or* Anstellung finden; **place of ~** Anstellungsort *m*.
employment agency *n* Stellenvermittlung *f*.
empower [empou'ûr] *vt*: **to ~ sb to do sth** jdn ermächtigen, etw zu tun.
empress [em'pris] *n* Kaiserin *f*.
emptiness [emp'tēnis] *n* Leere *f*.
empty [emp'tē] *a* leer ♦ *n* (*bottle*) Leergut *nt* ♦ *vt* (*contents*) leeren; (*container*) ausleeren ♦ *vi*: **to ~ into** (*river*) münden in (+*acc*).
empty-handed [emp'tēhan'did] *a* mit leeren Händen.
empty-headed [emp'tēhed'id] *a* strohdumm.
EMS *n abbr* (= *European Monetary System*) EWS *nt*.
EMT *n abbr* = *emergency medical technician*.
emu [ē'myōō] *n* Emu *m*.
emulate [em'yəlāt] *vt* nacheifern (+*dat*).
emulsion [imul'shən] *n* (*also*: **~ paint**) Emulsionsfarbe *f*.
enable [enā'bəl] *vt* ermöglichen; **it ~s us to ...** das ermöglicht es uns, zu ...
enact [enakt'] *vt* (*law*) erlassen; (*play, scene*) aufführen.
enamel [inam'əl] *n* Email *nt*; (*of teeth*) (Zahn)schmelz *m*.
enamel paint *n* Email(le)lack *m*.
enamored, (*Brit*) **enamoured** [enam'ûrd] *a* verliebt (*of* in +*dat*).
encampment [enkamp'mənt] *n* Lager *nt*.
encase [enkās'] *vt* einschließen; (*TECH*) verschalen; **to ~ in** (*contain*) verkleiden mit.
enchant [enchant'] *vt* bezaubern.
enchanting [enchan'ting] *a* entzückend.
encircle [ensûr'kəl] *vt* umringen.
enc(l). *abbr* (*on letters etc* = *enclosed, enclosure*) Anl.
enclose [enklōz'] *vt* einschließen; (*in letter*) beilegen (*in, with dat*); **~d** (*in letter*) beiliegend, anbei.

enclosure |enklō'zhûr| n Einfriedung f; (in letter) Anlage f.
encoder |enkō'dûr| n (COMPUT) Codierer m.
encompass |enkum'pəs| vt umfassen.
encore |âng'kôr| n Zugabe f; ~! da capo!
encounter |enkoun'tûr| n Begegnung f; (MIL) Zusammenstoß m ♦ vt treffen; (resistance) stoßen auf (+acc).
encourage |enkûr'ij| vt ermutigen; (industry, projects) fördern.
encouragement |enkûr'ijmənt| n Ermutigung f; Förderung f.
encouraging |enkûr'ijing| a ermutigend, vielversprechend.
encroach |enkrōch'| vi eindringen ((up)on in +acc), überschreiten ((up)on acc).
encrust |enkrust'| vt überziehen; ~ed with besetzt mit.
encumber |enkum'bûr| vt: to ~ with (person: with luggage) beladen mit; (: with debts) belasten mit.
encyclopedia, encyclopaedia |ensīkləpē'dēə| n Konversationslexikon nt.
end |end| n Ende nt, Schluß m; (purpose) Zweck m; (of line, rope etc) Ende nt, Rest m; (of pointed object) Spitze f; (of town) Rand m; **from ~ to ~** von einem Ende zum anderen; **to be at an ~** am Ende sein; **at the ~ of the day** (Brit fig) letztlich; **to this ~, with this ~ in view** mit diesem Ziel vor Augen ♦ a End- ♦ vt beenden ♦ vi zu Ende gehen; **to ~ (with)** zum Abschluß.
end up vi landen.
endanger |endān'jûr| vt gefährden; **an ~ed species** (of animal) eine gefährdete Tierart.
endear |endi'ûr| vt: to ~ o.s. to sb sich bei jdm beliebt machen.
endearing |endēr'ing| a gewinnend.
endearment |endēr'mənt| n: **term of ~** Kosename m, Kosewort nt; **to whisper ~s** liebe Worte flüstern.
endeavor, (Brit) **endeavour** |endev'ûr| n Bestrebung f ♦ vi sich bemühen.
endemic |endem'ik| a endemisch.
ending |en'ding| n Ende nt.
endive |en'dīv| n Endiviensalat m.
endless |end'lis| a endlos; (plain) unendlich.
endorse |endôrs'| vt unterzeichnen; (approve) unterstützen.
endorsee |endôrsē'| n Indossat m.
endorsement |endôrs'mənt| n Bestätigung f; (of document) Unterzeichnung f; (approval) Billigung f; (Brit: on driver's license) Strafvermerk m.
endorser |endôrs'ûr| n Indossant m.
endow |endou'| vt: to ~ sb with sth jdm etw verleihen; (with money) jdm etw stiften.
endowment |endou'mənt| n Stiftung f; (amount) Stiftungssumme f; (natural talent etc) Begabung f.
endowment assurance n Lebensversicherung f.
end product n (INDUSTRY) Endprodukt nt;

(fig) Produkt nt.
end result n Endergebnis nt.
endurable |endōō'rəbəl| a erträglich.
endurance |endōōr'əns| n Ausdauer f; (suffering) Ertragen nt.
endurance test n Belastungsprobe f.
endure |endōōr'| vt ertragen ♦ vi (last) (fort)dauern.
enduring |endōōr'ing| a bleibend, dauernd; (illness) langwierig; (hardship) anhaltend.
end user n Endverbraucher m.
enema |en'əmə| n (MED) Klistier nt.
enemy |en'əmē| n Feind m; **to make an ~ of sb** sich (dat) jdn zum Feind machen ♦ a feindlich.
energetic |enûrjet'ik| a tatkräftig.
energy |en'ûrjē| n (of person) Energie f, Tatkraft f; (PHYS) Energie f.
energy crisis n Energiekrise f.
energy-saving |en'ûrjēsāving| a (policy) energiebewußt; (device) energiesparend ♦ n Energiesparen nt.
enervating |en'ûrvāting| a nervenaufreibend.
enforce |enfôrs'| vt durchsetzen; (obedience) erzwingen.
enfranchise |enfran'chīz| vt (give vote to) das Wahlrecht geben or erteilen (+dat); (set free) freilassen.
engage |engāj'| vt (employ) einstellen; (lawyer) sich (dat) nehmen; (MIL) angreifen; (TECH) einrasten lassen, einschalten; **to ~ sb in conversation** jdn in ein Gespräch verwickeln.
engaged |engājd'| a verlobt; (Brit: TEL, toilet) besetzt; (busy) beschäftigt, unabkömmlich; **to get ~** sich verloben.
engaged tone n (Brit TEL) Besetztzeichen nt.
engagement |engāj'mənt| n (appointment) Verabredung f; (to marry) Verlobung f; (MIL) Gefecht nt; **I have a previous ~** ich habe schon eine Verabredung.
engagement ring n Verlobungsring m.
engaging |engā'jing| a gewinnend.
engender |enjen'dûr| vt hervorrufen.
engine |en'jən| n (AUT) Motor m; (RAIL) Lokomotive f.
engine driver n (Brit: of train) Lok(omotiv)führer m.
engineer |enjənēr'| n Ingenieur m; (US RAIL) Lokomotivführer m, Lokführer m; (Brit: for domestic appliances) Techniker m; **mechanical ~** Maschinenbauingenieur m; **civil ~** Bauingenieur m.
engineering |enjənēr'ing| n Technik f; (mechanical ~) Maschinenbau m.
engineering worker n Techniker(in f) m.
engineering works n sing or npl Maschinenfabrik f.
engine failure, engine trouble n Maschinenschaden m; (AUT) Motorschaden m.
England |ing'glənd| n England nt.
English |ing'glish| a englisch; **the ~ Channel** der Ärmelkanal ♦ n (language) Englisch nt;

the ~ (*people*) die Engländer.
English horn n (*US*) Englischhorn nt.
Englishman [ing'glishmən] n, pl **-men** Engländer m.
English-speaker [ing'glishspēkûr] n jd, der *Englisch spricht*.
English-speaking [ing'glishspē'king] a englisch sprechend.
Englishwoman [ing'glishwŏŏmən] n, pl **-women** Engländerin f.
engrave [engrāv'] vt (*carve*) einschneiden; (*fig*) tief einprägen; (*print*) gravieren.
engraving [engrā'ving] n Stich m.
engrossed [engrōst'] a vertieft.
engulf [engulf'] vt verschlingen.
enhance [enhans'] vt (*position, reputation*) verbessern; (*price, chances etc*) erhöhen.
enjoyable [enjoi'əbəl] a erfreulich.
enjoyment [enjoi'mənt] n Genuß m, Freude f.
enlarge [enlârj'] vt erweitern; (*PHOT*) vergrößern; **to ~ on sth** etw weiter ausführen.
enlarged [enlârjd'] a (*MED*: *organ, gland*) übergroß; **~ edition** erweiterte Ausgabe f.
enlargement [enlârj'mənt] n Vergrößerung f.
enlighten [enlīt'ən] vt aufklären.
enlightening [enlīt'əning] a aufschlußreich.
enlightenment [enlīt'ənmənt] n Aufklärung f.
enlist [enlist'] vt gewinnen ♦ vi (*MIL*) sich melden.
enlisted man [enlis'tid man] n (*US MIL*) gemeine(r) Soldat m.
enliven [enlī'vən] vt beleben.
enmity [en'mitē] n Feindschaft f.
ennoble [ennō'bəl] vt erhöhen; (*with title*) adeln.
enormity [inôr'mitē] n Ungeheuerlichkeit f.
enormous [inôr'məs] a, **enormously** [inôr'məslē] ad ungeheuer.
enough [inuf'] a genug; **will $5 be ~?** reichen 5 Dollar?; **that's ~** das ist genug; **that's ~!** das reicht!; **I've had ~!** mir reicht's! ♦ ad genug, genügend; **he was kind ~ to lend me the money** er war so gut und hat mir das Geld geliehen.
enquire [enkwī'ûr] = **inquire**.
enrage [enrāj'] vt wütend machen.
enrich [enrich'] vt bereichern.
enroll, (*Brit*) **enrol** [enrōl'] vt (*MIL*) anwerben; (*UNIV*) immatrikulieren ♦ vi (*register*) sich anmelden.
enrollment, (*Brit*) **enrolment** [enrōl'mənt] n (*for course*) Anmeldung f; (*UNIV*) Einschreibung f.
en route [ôn rōōt'] ad unterwegs; **~ for/ from/to** unterwegs nach/von/zu.
ensconce [enskâns'] vt: **to ~ o.s.** sich (häuslich) niederlassen.
ensemble [ânsâm'bəl] n (*MUS*) Ensemble nt.

enshrine [enshrīn'] vt verwahren, bewahren.
ensign [en'sən] n (*NAUT*) Flagge f.
enslave [enslāv'] vt versklaven.
ensue [ensōō'] vi folgen, sich ergeben.
ensuing [ensōō'ing] a (nach)folgend.
ensure [enshōōr'] vt garantieren.
ENT a abbr (*Brit MED*: = *Ear, Nose & Throat*) HNO.
entail [entāl'] vt mit sich bringen.
entangle [entang'gəl] vt (*thread etc*) verwickeln, verheddern; **to become ~d in sth** (*fig*) sich in etw verstricken or verheddern.
enter [en'tûr] vt eintreten in (+*dat*), betreten; (*club*) beitreten (+*dat*); (*in book*) eintragen; (*COMPUT*) eingeben; **to ~ a profession** einen Beruf ergreifen ♦ vi hereinkommen, hineingehen.
enter for vt fus sich beteiligen an (+*dat*).
enter into vt fus (*agreement*) eingehen; (*argument*) sich einlassen auf (+*acc*); (*negotiations*) aufnehmen.
enter up vt eintragen.
enter upon vt fus beginnen.
enteritis [entərī'tis] n Dünndarmentzündung f.
enterprise [en'tûrprīz] n (*in person*) Initiative f, Unternehmungsgeist m; (*COMM*) Unternehmen nt, Betrieb m.
enterprising [en'tûrprīzing] a unternehmungslustig.
entertain [entûrtān'] vt (*guest*) bewirten; (*amuse*) unterhalten.
entertainer [entûrtān'ûr] n Unterhaltungskünstler(in f) m.
entertaining [entûrtā'ning] a unterhaltend, amüsant ♦ n: **to do a lot of ~** oft Gäste haben.
entertainment [entûrtān'mənt] n (*amusement*) Unterhaltung f; (*show*) Veranstaltung f.
entertainment allowance n Aufwandspauschale f.
enthralled [enthrōld'] a gefesselt.
enthralling [enthrōl'ing] a spannend.
enthuse [enthōōz'] vi: **to ~ (about** or **over)** schwärmen (von).
enthusiasm [enthōō'zēazəm] n Begeisterung f, Enthusiasmus m (*for* für).
enthusiast [enthōō'zēast] n Enthusiast m, Schwärmer(in f) m.
enthusiastic [enthōōzēas'tik] a begeistert; **to be ~ about sth/sb** von etw/jdm begeistert sein.
entice [entīs'] vt verleiten, locken.
enticing [entī'sing] a verlockend.
entire [entī'ûr] a ganz.
entirely [entīûr'lē] ad ganz, völlig.
entirety [entīr'tē] n: **in its ~** in seiner Gesamtheit.
entitle [entīt'əl] vt (*allow*) berechtigen; (*name*) betiteln; **to be ~d to sth/to do sth** das Recht auf etw (*acc*) haben/das Recht haben, etw zu tun.
entity [en'titē] n Ding nt, Wesen nt.
entourage [ântōōrâzh'] n Gefolge nt.

entrails [en'trālz] *npl* Eingeweide *pl.*

entrance *n* [en'trəns] Eingang *m*; *(entering)* Eintritt *m* ♦ *vt* [entrans'] hinreißen.

entrance examination *n* Aufnahmeprüfung *f.*

entrance fee *n* Eintrittsgeld *nt.*

entrance ramp *n* *(US AUT)* Einfahrt *f.*

entrancing [entrans'ing] *a* bezaubernd.

entrant [en'trənt] *n* *(Brit: in exam)* Prüfling *m*; *(for job)* Anfänger(in *f*) *m*; *(MIL)* Rekrut *m*; *(in race)* Teilnehmer(in *f*) *m.*

entreat [entrēt'] *vt* anflehen, beschwören.

entreaty [entrē'tē] *n* flehende Bitte *f*, Beschwörung *f.*

entrée [ântrā'] *n* Zwischengang *m.*

entrenched [entrencht'] *a* *(fig)* verwurzelt.

entrepreneur [ântrəprənûr'] *n* Unternehmer(in *f*) *m*, Entrepeneur *m.*

entrepreneurial [ântrəprənûr'ēəl] *a* unternehmerisch.

entrust [entrust'] *vt* anvertrauen *(sb with sth* jdm etw).

entry [en'trē] *n* Eingang *m*; *(THEAT)* Auftritt *m*; *(in account)* Eintragung *f*; *(in dictionary, diary, log etc)* Eintrag *m*; "no ~" „Eintritt verboten"; *(for cars)* „Einfahrt verboten"; **single/double ~** **book-keeping** einfache/doppelte Buchführung *f.*

entry form *n* Anmeldeformular *nt.*

entry phone *n* *(Brit)* Eingangstelefonanlage *f.*

enumerate [inōō'mərāt] *vt* aufzählen.

enunciate [inun'sēāt] *vt* (deutlich) aussprechen.

envelop [envel'əp] *vt* einhüllen.

envelope [en'vəlōp] *n* Umschlag *m.*

enviable [en'vēəbəl] *a* beneidenswert.

envious [en'vēəs] *a* neidisch.

environment [envī'rənmənt] *n* Umgebung *f*; *(ecology)* Umwelt *f*; **Department of the E~** *(Brit)* Umweltministerium *nt.*

environmental [envīrənmen'təl] *a* Umwelt-; *(social, cultural environment)* Milieu-.

environmentalist [envīrənmen'təlist] *n* Umweltschützer(in *f*) *m.*

environmental studies *npl* *(in school etc)* Umweltkunde *f.*

environment-friendly [envī'rənməntfrend'lē] *a* umweltfreundlich.

envisage [enviz'ij] *vt* sich *(dat)* vorstellen; *(plan)* ins Auge fassen.

envision [envizh'ən] *vt* sich *(dat)* vorstellen, voraussehen.

envoy [en'voi] *n* Gesandte(r) *mf.*

envy [en'vē] *n* Neid *m*; *(object)* Gegenstand *m* des Neides ♦ *vt* beneiden *(sb sth* jdn um etw).

enzyme [en'zīm] *n* Enzym *nt.*

eon [ē'ən] *n* *(US)* Äon *m*, Ewigkeit *f.*

EPA *n abbr* *(US: = Environmental Protection Agency)* ≈ UBA *nt.*

ephemeral [ifem'ûrəl] *a* kurzlebig, vorübergehend.

epic [ep'ik] *n* Epos *nt*; *(film)* Großfilm *m* ♦ *a*

episch; *(fig)* heldenhaft.

epicenter, *(Brit)* **epicentre** [ep'isentûr] *n* Epizentrum *nt.*

epidemic [epidem'ik] *n* Epidemie *f.*

epigram [ep'igram] *n* Epigramm *nt.*

epilepsy [ep'əlepsē] *n* Epilepsie *f.*

epileptic [epəlep'tik] *a* epileptisch ♦ *n* Epileptiker(in *f*) *m.*

epilogue [ep'əlôg] *n* *(of drama)* Epilog *m*; *(of book)* Nachwort *nt.*

episcopal [ipis'kəpəl] *a* bischöflich, Bischofs-.

episode [ep'isōd] *n* *(incident)* Vorfall *m*; *(story)* Episode *f.*

epistle [ipis'əl] *n* Brief *m.*

epitaph [ep'itaf] *n* Grab(in)schrift *f.*

epithet [ep'əthet] *n* Beiname *m.*

epitome [ipit'əmē] *n* Inbegriff *m.*

epitomize [ipit'əmīz] *vt* verkörpern.

epoch [ep'ək] *n* Epoche *f.*

eponymous [epân'əməs] *a* namengebend.

equable [ek'wəbəl] *a* ausgeglichen; **~ climate** gemäßigte(s) Klima *nt.*

equal [ē'kwəl] *a* gleich; **~ to the task** der Aufgabe gewachsen; **the E~ Opportunities Commission** *(Brit)* Ausschuß *m* für Chancengleichheit ♦ *n* Gleichgestellte(r) *mf*; **without ~** ohne seinesgleichen ♦ *vt* gleichkommen *(+dat)*; **two times two ~s four** zwei mal zwei ist (gleich) vier.

equality [ikwâl'itē] *n* Gleichheit *f*; *(equal rights)* Gleichberechtigung *f.*

equalize [ē'kwəlīz] *vt* gleichmachen ♦ *vi* *(SPORT)* ausgleichen.

equalizer [ē'kwəlīzûr] *n* *(SPORT)* Ausgleich(streffer) *m.*

equally [ē'kwəlē] *ad* gleich; **they are ~ clever** sie sind beide gleich klug.

equal(s) sign [e'kwəl(z) sīn] *n* Gleichheitszeichen *nt.*

equanimity [ē'kwənim'itē] *n* Gleichmut *m.*

equate [ikwāt'] *vt* gleichsetzen.

equation [ikwā'zhən] *n* Gleichung *f.*

equator [ikwā'tûr] *n* Äquator *m.*

equatorial [ēkwətôr'ēəl] *a* Äquator-.

Equatorial Guinea *n* Äquatorial-Guinea *nt*, Äquatorialguinea *nt.*

equestrian [ikwes'trēən] *a* Reit-, Reiter- ♦ *n* Reiter(in *f*) *m.*

equilibrium [ēkwəlib'rēəm] *n* Gleichgewicht *nt.*

equinox [ē'kwənâks] *n* Tagundnachtgleiche *f.*

equip [ikwip'] *vt* ausrüsten; **~ped with** *(machinery etc)* ausgestattet mit; **he is well ~ped for the job** er hat die nötigen Kenntnisse *or* das nötige Rüstzeug für die Stelle.

equipment [ikwip'mənt] *n* Ausrüstung *f*; *(TECH)* Gerät *nt.*

equitable [ek'witəbəl] *a* gerecht.

equities [ek'witēz] *npl* *(Brit)* Stammaktien *pl.*

equity [ek'witē] *n* Gerechtigkeit *f.*

equity capital *n* Eigenkapital *nt.*

equivalent [ikwiv'ələnt] *a* gleichwertig *(to* +*dat)*, entsprechend *(to* +*dat)*; **to be ~ to sth** etw *(dat)* entsprechen ♦ *n* *(amount)* gleiche Menge *f*; (*in money*) Gegenwert *m*; Äquivalent *nt*.

equivocal [ikwiv'əkəl] *a* zweideutig; (*suspect*) fragwürdig.

equivocate [ikwiv'əkāt] *vi* ausweichen, ausweichend antworten.

equivocation [ikwivəkā'shən] *n* Ausflucht *f*, ausweichende Antwort *f*.

ER *abbr* (*Brit*) = *Elizabeth Regina*.

era [ē'rə] *n* Epoche *f*, Ära *f*.

ERA *n* *abbr* (*US*: *POL*) = *Equal Rights Amendment*; (: *BASEBALL*: = *earned run average*) *beim Baseball die vom Werfer erlaubten Läufe*.

eradicate [irad'ikāt] *vt* ausrotten.

erase [irās'] *vt* ausradieren; (*tape, also COMPUT*) löschen.

eraser [irā'sûr] *n* Radiergummi *m*.

erect [irekt'] *a* aufrecht ♦ *vt* errichten.

erection [irek'shən] *n* (*ANAT*) Erektion *f*; (*of building*) Errichten *nt*, Bauen *nt*; (*of machinery*) Aufstellen *nt*.

ergonomics [ûrgənâm'iks] *n sing* Ergonomie *f*.

ERISA *n abbr* (*US*: = *Employee Retirement Income Security Act*) *Gesetz zur Rentenversicherung.*

ermine [ûr'min] *n* Hermelin(pelz) *m*.

erode [irōd'] *vt* zerfressen; (*land*) auswaschen.

erosion [irō'zhən] *n* Auswaschen *nt*, Erosion *f*.

erotic [irât'ik] *a* erotisch.

eroticism [irât'isizəm] *n* Erotik *f*.

err [ûr] *vi* sich irren.

errand [är'ənd] *n* (*shopping*) Besorgung *f*; (*message etc*) Botengang *m*; ~ **of mercy** Rettungsaktion *f*; **to run** ~s Besorgungen/Botengänge machen.

errand boy *n* Laufbursche *m*.

erratic [irat'ik] *a* sprunghaft; (*driving*) unausgeglichen.

erroneous [irō'nēəs] *a* irrig, irrtümlich.

error [är'ûr] *n* Fehler *m*; **typing/spelling** ~ Tippfehler *m*/Fehler *m*; **in** ~ aus Versehen; ~**s and omissions excepted** Irrtum vorbehalten.

error message *n* (*COMPUT*) Fehlermeldung *f*.

erstwhile [ûrst'hwīl] *a* einstig, vormalig.

erudite [är'yōōdīt] *a* gelehrt.

erudition [äryōōdish'ən] *n* Gelehrsamkeit *f*.

erupt [irupt'] *vi* ausbrechen.

eruption [irup'shən] *n* Eruption *f*; (*of anger, violence*) Ausbruch *m*.

ESA *n abbr* (= *European Space Agency*) Europäische Weltraumorganisation *f*.

escalate [es'kəlāt] *vt* steigern ♦ *vi* sich steigern; (*costs*) sprunghaft ansteigen, in die Höhe schnellen.

escalation clause [es'kəlāshən klóz] *n* (*COMM*) Gleitklausel *f*.

escalator [es'kəlātûr] *n* Rolltreppe *f*.

escapade [es'kəpād] *n* Eskapade *f*, Streich *m*.

escape [eskāp'] *n* Flucht *f*; (*of gas*) Entweichen *nt* ♦ *vti* entkommen (+*dat*); (*prisoners*) fliehen; (*leak*) entweichen; **to** ~ **notice** unbemerkt bleiben; **it has** ~**d my notice** es ist mir entgangen; **the word** ~**s me** das Wort ist mir entfallen; **to** ~ **to** (*another place*) sich zurückziehen; **to** ~ **to safety** sich in Sicherheit bringen.

escape artist *n* (*US*) Entfesselungskünstler(in *f*) *m*.

escape clause *n* (*fig*: *in agreement*) Befreiungsklausel *f*.

escape hatch *n* (*in submarine, space rocket*) Notluke *f*.

escape key *n* (*COMPUT*) Escape-Taste *f*, schreibende Taste *f* mit Vorschub.

escape route *n* Fluchtweg *m*.

escapism [eskā'pizəm] *n* Flucht *f* (vor der Wirklichkeit).

escapist [eskā'pist] *a* unrealistisch ♦ *n* Eskapist(in *f*) *m*.

escapologist [eskəpál'əjist] *n* (*Brit*) Entfesselungskünstler(in *f*) *m*.

escarpment [eskárp'mənt] *n* Steilhang *m*.

eschew [eschōō'] *vt* meiden.

escort *n* [es'kórt] (*person accompanying*) Begleiter *m*; (*guard*) Eskorte *f* ♦ *vt* [eskórt'] (*lady*) begleiten; (*MIL*) eskortieren.

escort agency *n* Hostessenagentur *f*.

Eskimo [es'kəmō] *a* Eskimo-, eskimoisch ♦ *n* (*person*) Eskimo *m*, Eskimofrau *f*; (*language*) Eskimosprache *f*.

ESL *n abbr* (*SCH*) = *English as a Second Language*.

esophagus [isâf'əgəs] *n* (*US*) Speiseröhre *f*.

esoteric [esətär'ik] *a* esoterisch.

esp. *abbr* (= *especially*) bes.

ESP *n abbr* (= *extrasensory perception*) ASW *f*.

especially [espesh'əlē] *ad* besonders.

espionage [es'pēənâzh] *n* Spionage *f*.

esplanade [esplənād'] *n* Esplanade *f*, Promenade *f*.

espouse [espouz'] *vt* Partei ergreifen für.

Esq. *abbr* (*Brit*) = **Esquire**.

Esquire [es'kwiûr] *n*: **J. Brown, Esq.** (*in address*) Herrn J. Brown.

essay [es'ā] *n* Aufsatz *m*; (*LITER*) Essay *m*.

essence [es'əns] *n* (*quality*) Wesen *nt*; (*extract*) Essenz *f*, Extrakt *m*; **in** ~ im Wesentlichen; **speed is of the** ~ Geschwindigkeit ist von entscheidender Bedeutung.

essential [əsen'chəl] *a* (*necessary*) unentbehrlich; (*basic*) wesentlich; **it is** ~ **that** ... es ist unbedingt erforderlich, daß ... ♦ *n* Hauptbestandteil *m*, Allernötigste(s) *nt*; (*often pl*) wichtige Punkte *pl*, Essentials *pl*.

essentially [əsen'chəlē] *ad* in der Hauptsache, eigentlich.

est. *abbr* (= *established*) gegr.; (= *estimate(d)*) schätzen, geschätzt, Schätzung.

EST *abbr* (*US*) = *Eastern Standard Time*.

establish [əstab'lish] *vt* (*set up*) gründen, einrichten; (*prove: fact, identity, sb's inno-*

cence) beweisen, nachweisen.
establishment [əstab'lishmənt] *n* (*setting up*) Einrichtung *f*; (*business*) Unternehmen *nt*; **the E~** das Establishment; **a teaching ~** eine Lehranstalt.
estate [əstāt'] *n* Gut *nt*; (*housing* ~) Siedlung *f*; (*will*) Nachlaß *m*; (*Brit: car*) Kombiwagen *m*.
estate agent *n* (*Brit*) Grundstücksmakler *m*.
estate car *n* (*Brit*) Kombiwagen *m*.
esteem [əstēm'] *n* Wertschätzung *f*.
esthetic [esthet'ik] *a* (*US*) ästhetisch.
esthetics [esthet'iks] *n sing* (*US*) Ästhetik *f*.
estimate *n* [es'təmit] (*opinion*) Meinung *f*; (*of price*) (Kosten)voranschlag *m*; **to give sb an ~ of sth** jdm einen Kostenvoranschlag für etw geben; **at a rough ~** grob geschätzt, über den Daumen gepeilt (*col*) ♦ *vt* [es'təmāt] schätzen.
estimation [estəmā'shən] *n* Einschätzung *f*; (*esteem*) Achtung *f*; **in my ~** meiner Einschätzung nach.
estimator [es'təmātûr] *n* Schätzer *m*.
Estonia [estō'nēə] *n* Estland *nt*.
estranged [estrānjd'] *a* entfremdet.
estrangement [estrānj'mənt] *n* Entfremdung *f*.
estrogen [es'trəjən] *n* (*US*) Östrogen *nt*.
estuary [es'chōōārē] *n* Mündung *f*.
ETA *n abbr* (= *estimated time of arrival*) voraussichtliche Ankunftzeit *f*.
et al. [et âl] *abbr* (= *et alii: and others*) et al.
etc. *abbr* (= *et cetera*) etc.
etch [ech] *vt* ätzen; (*in copper*) kupferstechen; (*in other metals*) radieren.
etching [ech'ing] *n* Kupferstich *m*.
ETD *n abbr* (= *estimated time of departure*) voraussichtliche Abflugzeit *f*.
eternal [itûr'nəl] *a*, **eternally** [itûr'nəlē] *ad* ewig.
eternity [itûr'nitē] *n* Ewigkeit *f*.
ether [ē'thûr] *n* (*MED*) Äther *m*.
ethereal [ithēr'ēəl] *a* ätherisch, himmlisch.
ethical [eth'ikəl] *a* ethisch.
ethics [eth'iks] *npl* Ethik *f*.
Ethiopia [ēthēō'pēə] *n* Äthiopien *nt*.
Ethiopian [ēthēō'pēən] *a* äthiopisch ♦ *n* Äthiopier(in *f*) *m*.
ethnic [eth'nik] *a* Volks-, ethnisch.
ethos [ē'thâs] *n* Ethos *nt*, Gesinnung *f*.
etiquette [et'əkit] *n* Etikette *f*.
ETV *n abbr* (*US*: = *Educational Television*) Schulfernsehen.
etymology [etəmâl'əjē] *n* Etymologie *f*.
eucalyptus [yōōkəlip'təs] *n* Eukalyptus *m*.
Eucharist [yōō'kûrist] *n* heilige(s) Abendmahl *nt*.
eulogy [yōō'ləjē] *n* Lobrede *f*.
eunuch [yōō'nək] *n* Eunuch *m*.
euphemism [yōō'fəmizəm] *n* Euphemismus *m*.
euphemistic [yōōfəmis'tik] *a* euphemistisch.
euphoria [yōōfôr'ēə] *n* Taumel *m*, Euphorie *f*.

Eurasia [yōōrā'zhə] *n* Eurasien *nt*.
Eurasian [yōōrā'zhən] *a* eurasisch ♦ *n* Eurasier(in *f*) *m*.
Euratom [yōōrat'əm] *n abbr* (= *European Atomic Energy Community*) Euratom *f*.
Euro- [yōō'rō] *pref* Euro-.
Eurocheque [yōō'rōchek] *n* Euroscheck *m*.
Eurocrat [yōō'rəkrat] *n* Eurokrat(in *f*) *m*.
Eurodollar [yōō'rōdálûr] *n* Eurodollar *m*.
Europe [yōō'rəp] *n* Europa *nt*.
European [yōōrəpē'ən] *a* europäisch ♦ *n* Europäer(in *f*) *m*.
European Court of Justice *n* Europäische(r) Gerichtshof *m*.
European Economic Community *n* Europäische Wirtschaftsgemeinschaft *f*.
euthanasia [yōōthənā'zhə] *n* Euthanasie *f*, Sterbehilfe *f*.
evacuate [ivak'yōōāt] *vt* (*place*) räumen; (*people*) evakuieren; (*MED*) entleeren.
evacuation [ivakyōōā'shən] *n* Räumung *f*; Evakuierung *f*; Entleerung *f*.
evade [ivād'] *vt* (*escape*) entkommen (+*dat*); (*avoid*) meiden; (*duty*) sich entziehen (+*dat*).
evaluate [ival'yōōāt] *vt* bewerten; (*information*) auswerten.
evangelical [ēvanjel'ikəl] *a* evangelisch.
evangelist [ivan'jəlist] *n* Evangelist(in *f*) *m*.
evaporate [ivap'ərāt] *vi* verdampfen ♦ *vt* verdampfen lassen.
evaporated milk [ivap'ərātid milk'] *n* Kondensmilch *f*.
evaporation [ivapərā'shən] *n* Verdunstung *f*.
evasion [ivā'zhən] *n* Umgehung *f*; (*excuse*) Ausflucht *f*.
evasive [ivā'siv] *a* ausweichend.
eve [ēv] *n*: **on the ~ of** am Vorabend (+*gen*).
even [ē'vən] *a* (*surface etc*) eben; (*regular*) gleichmäßig; (*quantities, distances etc*) gleich; (*score etc*) unentschieden; (*number*) gerade; **to break ~** plus minus null abschließen; **to get ~** sich revanchieren ♦ *vt* (ein)ebnen, glätten ♦ *ad* sogar, selbst; **~ faster** noch schneller; **not ~** ... nicht einmal ...; **~ you** selbst *or* sogar du; **he ~ said** ... er hat sogar gesagt...; **~ as he spoke** (gerade) da er sprach; **~ if** sogar *or* selbst wenn, wenn auch; **~ so** dennoch.
even out, even up *vi* sich ausgleichen ♦ *vt* ausgleichen.
evening [ēv'ning] *n* Abend *m*; **in the ~** abends, am Abend; **this ~** heute abend; **tomorrow/yesterday ~** morgen/gestern abend.
evening class *n* Abendschule *f*.
evening dress *n* (*man's*) Gesellschaftsanzug *m*; (*woman's*) Abendkleid *nt*.
evenly [ē'vənlē] *ad* gleichmäßig.
evensong [ē'vənsông] *n* (*REL*) Abendandacht *f*.
event [ivent'] *n* (*happening*) Ereignis *nt*; (*SPORT*) Disziplin *f*; (*horses*) Rennen *nt*; **the next ~** der nächste Wettkampf; **in the ~ of**

im Falle (+*gen*); **in the ~ that** ... für den Fall, daß ...; **in any ~** auf jeden Fall; **in the normal course of ~s** normalerweise.

eventful |ivent'fəl| *a* ereignisreich.

eventual |iven'chōōəl| *a* (*final*) schließlich.

eventuality |ivenchōōal'itē| *n* Möglichkeit *f*.

eventually |iven'chōōəlē| *ad* (*at last*) am Ende; (*given time*) schließlich.

ever |ev'ûr| *ad* (*always*) immer; (*at any time*) je(mals); **~ so big** sehr groß; **~ so many** sehr viele; **for ~** für immer; **yours ~** (*Brit*: *in letters*) Alles Liebe; **did you ~ meet him?** haben Sie ihn mal kennengelernt?; **have you ~ been there?** waren Sie schon einmal dort?; **thank you ~ so much** ganz herzlichen Dank.

Everest |ev'ûrist| *n* (*also*: **Mount ~**) Mount Everest *m*.

evergreen |ev'ûrgrēn| *a* immergrün ♦ *n* Immergrün *nt*.

everlasting |evûrlas'ting| *a* immerwährend.

every |ev'rē| *a* jeder/jede/jedes; **~ day** jeden Tag; **~ other day** jeden zweiten Tag; **I have ~ confidence in him** ich habe vollstes Vertrauen zu ihm; **~ so often** hin und wieder.

everybody |ev'rēbádē| *pron* jeder, alle *pl*; **~ knows about it** jeder weiß davon; **~ else** jeder.

everyday |ev'rēdā| *a* (*daily*) täglich; (*commonplace*) alltäglich, Alltags-.

everyone |ev'rēwun| *pron* = **everybody**.

everything |ev'rēthing| *pron* alles; **~ is ready** alles ist fertig; **he did ~ possible** er hat sein Möglichstes getan.

everywhere |ev'rēhwär| *ad* überall; (*wherever*): **~ you look** wo man auch hinsieht ...; **~ you go you meet** ... wo immer man hingeht, trifft man ...

evict |ivikt'| *vt* ausweisen.

eviction |ivik'shən| *n* Ausweisung *f*.

eviction notice *n* Räumungsbescheid *m*.

evidence |ev'idəns| *n* (*sign*) Spur *f*; (*proof*) Beweis *m*; (*testimony*) Aussage *f*; **in ~** (*obvious*) zu sehen.

evident |ev'idənt| *a* augenscheinlich.

evidently |ev'idəntlē| *ad* offensichtlich.

evil |ē'vəl| *a* böse, übel ♦ *n* Böse *nt*; (*thing, circumstance*) Übel *nt*.

evince |ivins'| *vt* an den Tag legen.

evocative |ivák'ətiv| *a*: **to be ~ of sth** an etw (*acc*) erinnern.

evoke |ivōk'| *vt* hervorrufen.

evolution |evəlōō'shən| *n* Entwicklung *f*; (*of life*) Evolution *f*.

evolve |ivâlv'| *vt* entwickeln ♦ *vi* sich entwickeln.

ewe |yōō| *n* Mutterschaf *nt*.

ex- |eks| *pref* Ex-, Alt-, ehemalig; **~directory (phone) number** (*Brit*) Geheimnummer *f*; **~serviceman** ehemalige(r) Soldat *m*.

exacerbate |igzas'ûrbāt| *vt* (*pain*) verschlimmern; (*fig*: *relations, situation*) verschärfen.

exact |igzakt'| *a* genau ♦ *vt* (*demand*) verlangen; (*compel*) erzwingen; (*money, fine*) ein-

ziehen; (*punishment*) vollziehen.

exacting |igzak'ting| *a* anspruchsvoll.

exactitude |igzakt'ətōōd| *n* Genauigkeit *f*.

exactly |igzakt'lē| *ad* genau; **~!** (ganz) genau!

exactness |igzakt'nis| *n* Genauigkeit *f*, Richtigkeit *f*.

exaggerate |igzaj'ərāt| *vti* übertreiben.

exaggerated |igzaj'ərātid| *a* übertrieben.

exaggeration |igzajərā'shən| *n* Übertreibung *f*.

exalt |igzôlt'| *vt* (*praise*) verherrlichen.

exalted |igzôl'tid| *a* (*position, style*) hoch; (*person*) exaltiert.

exam |igzam'| *n* Prüfung *f*.

examination |igzamənā'shən| *n* Untersuchung *f*; (*SCH, UNIV*) Prüfung *f*, Examen *nt*; (*customs*) Kontrolle *f*; **to take an ~** eine Prüfung machen; **the matter is under ~** die Angelegenheit wird überprüft.

examine |igzam'in| *vt* (*MED*) untersuchen; (*SCH*) prüfen; (*consider*) erwägen; (*inspect: machine, premises, luggage*) kontrollieren.

examiner |igzam'inûr| *n* Prüfer *m*.

example |igzam'pəl| *n* Beispiel *nt*; **for ~** zum Beispiel; **to set a good/bad ~** ein gutes/schlechtes Beispiel geben.

exasperate |igzas'pərāt| *vt* zum Verzweifeln bringen; **~d by** *or* **at** *or* **with** verärgert über.

exasperating |igzas'pərāting| *a* ärgerlich, zum Verzweifeln bringend.

exasperation |igzaspərā'shən| *n* Verzweiflung *f*.

excavate |eks'kəvāt| *vt* (*hollow out*) aushöhlen; (*unearth*) ausgraben.

excavation |eks'kəvā'shən| *n* Ausgrabung *f*.

excavator |eks'kəvātûr| *n* Bagger *m*.

exceed |iksēd'| *vt* überschreiten; (*hopes*) übertreffen.

exceedingly |iksē'dinglē| *ad* in höchstem Maße.

excel |iksel'| *vi* sich auszeichnen ♦ *vt* übertreffen.

excellence |ek'sələns| *n* Vortrefflichkeit *f*.

excellency |ek'sələnsē| *n*: **His E~** Seine Exzellenz.

excellent |ek'sələnt| *a* ausgezeichnet.

except |iksept'| *prep* (*also*: **~ for**) außer (+*dat*) ♦ *vt* ausnehmen.

excepting |iksep'ting| *prep* = **except**.

exception |iksep'shən| *n* Ausnahme *f*; **to take ~ to** Anstoß nehmen an (+*dat*); **with the ~ of** mit Ausnahme von; **to make an ~** eine Ausnahme machen.

exceptional |iksep'shənəl| *a*, **exceptionally** |iksep'shənəlē| *ad* außergewöhnlich.

excerpt |ek'sûrpt| *n* Auszug *m*.

excess |ekses'| |ek'ses| Übermaß *nt* (*of* an +*dat*), Exzeß *m*; **in ~ of** mehr als; *see also* **excesses** ♦ *a* |ek'ses| (*money*) Nach-; (*baggage*) Mehr-.

excesses |ekses'iz| *npl* Ausschweifungen *pl*, Exzesse *pl*; (*violent*) Ausschreitungen *pl*.

excess fare n Nachlösegebühr f.
excessive [ikses'iv] a, **excessively** [ikses'ivlē] ad übermäßig.
excess supply n Überangebot nt.
excess weight n (of thing) Mehrgewicht nt; (of person) Übergewicht nt.
exchange [ikschãnj'] n Austausch m; (FIN) Wechselstube f; (TEL) Vermittlung f, Zentrale f; (Post Office) (Fernsprech)amt nt; **foreign ~** (COMM) Devisen pl; **in ~ for money** gegen Geld ♦ vt (goods) tauschen; (greetings) austauschen; (money, blows) wechseln.
exchange control n Devisenkontrolle f.
exchange rate n Wechselkurs m.
exchequer [eks'chekûr] n (Brit) Schatzamt nt.
excisable [iksī'zəbəl] a (verbrauchs)-steuerpflichtig.
excise n [ek'sīz] Verbrauchssteuer f ♦ vt [iksīz'] (MED) herausschneiden.
excitable [iksī'təbəl] a erregbar, nervös.
excite [iksīt'] vt erregen.
excited [iksī'tid] a aufgeregt; **to get ~** sich aufregen.
excitement [iksīt'mənt] n Aufgeregtheit f; (of interest) Erregung f.
exciting [iksī'ting] a aufregend; (book, film) spannend.
excl. abbr (= excluding, exclusive (of)) ausgen.
exclaim [iksklām'] vi ausrufen.
exclamation [eksklәmә'shən] n Ausruf m.
exclamation mark n Ausrufezeichen nt.
exclude [iksklŏŏd'] vt ausschließen.
excluding [iksklŏŏ'ding] prep: **~ VAT** ohne MwSt.
exclusion [iksklŏŏ'zhən] n Ausschluß m; **to the ~ of** mit Ausnahme von.
exclusion clause n Haftungsausschlußklausel f.
exclusive [iksklŏŏ'siv] a (select) exklusiv; (sole) ausschließlich, Allein-; **~ of postage** exklusive Porto; **~ of service** ohne Bedienung; **from 1st to 15th March ~** vom 1. bis ausschließlich 15. März.
exclusively [iksklŏŏ'sivlē] ad nur, ausschließlich.
excommunicate [ekskəmyŏŏ'nəkāt] vt exkommunizieren.
excrement [eks'krəmənt] n Kot m.
excruciating [ikskrŏŏ'shēāting] a qualvoll.
excursion [ikskûr'zhən] n Ausflug m.
excursion ticket n verbilligte(s) Ticket nt.
excusable [ikskyŏŏ'zəbəl] a entschuldbar.
excuse n [ikskyŏŏs'] Entschuldigung f; **to make ~s for sb** jdn entschuldigen ♦ vt [ikskyŏŏz'] entschuldigen; **to ~ o.s. for sth** sich für or wegen etw entschuldigen; **~ me!** entschuldigen Sie!
exec. [igzek'] n abbr = **executive**.
execrable [ek'səkrəbəl] a (manners) scheußlich, abscheulich.
execute [ek'səkyŏŏt] vt (carry out) ausführen; (kill) hinrichten.

execution [eksəkyŏŏ'shən] n Ausführung f; Hinrichtung f.
executioner [eksəkyŏŏ'shənûr] n Scharfrichter m.
executive [igzek'yətiv] n (COMM) leitende(r) Angestellte(r) m, Geschäftsführer m; (POL) Exekutive f ♦ a (powers, committee etc) Exekutiv-; (secretary, car, plane) Privat-; (offices, suite) Vorstands-; (position, job, duties) leitend.
executive director n Vorstandsmitglied nt.
executor [igzek'yətûr] n Testamentsvollstrecker m.
exemplary [igzem'plûrē] a musterhaft.
exemplify [igzem'pləfī] vt veranschaulichen.
exempt [igzempt'] a befreit ♦ vt befreien.
exemption [igzemp'shən] n Befreiung f.
exercise [ek'sûrsīz] n Übung f ♦ vt (power) ausüben; (muscles, patience) üben; (dog) ausführen ♦ vi Sport treiben.
exercise book n (Brit) (Schul)heft nt.
exert [igzûrt'] vt (influence, strength, force) ausüben ♦ vr sich anstrengen.
exertion [igzûr'shən] n Anstrengung f.
ex-gratia payment [eksgra'tēə pā'mənt] n freiwillige Zahlung f.
exhale [eks-hāl'] vt/i ausatmen.
exhaust [igzôst'] n (fumes) Abgase pl; (pipe) Auspuffrohr nt ♦ vt (weary) ermüden; (use up) erschöpfen.
exhausted [igzôs'tid] a erschöpft; **my patience is ~** meine Geduld ist erschöpft or am Ende.
exhausting [igzôs'ting] a anstrengend; **an ~ journey/day** eine strapaziöse Reise/ein anstrengender Tag.
exhaustion [igzôs'chən] n Erschöpfung f.
exhaustive [igzôs'tiv] a erschöpfend.
exhibit [igzib'it] n (ART) Ausstellungsstück nt; (JUR) Beweisstück nt ♦ vt ausstellen.
exhibition [eksəbish'ən] n (ART) Ausstellung f; (of temper etc) Zurschaustellung f.
exhibitionist [eksəbish'ənist] n Exhibitionist(in f) m.
exhibitor [igzib'ətûr] n Aussteller m.
exhilarating [igzil'ərāting] a erhebend.
exhilaration [igzilərā'shən] n erhebende(s) Gefühl nt, Hochgefühl nt.
exhort [igzôrt'] vt ermahnen.
exile [eg'zīl] n Exil nt; (person) im Exil Lebende(r) mf; **in ~** im Exil ♦ vt verbannen.
exist [igzist'] vi existieren; (live) leben.
existence [igzis'məns] n Existenz f; (way of life) Leben nt, Existenz f.
existentialism [egzisten'chəlizəm] n Existentialismus m.
existing [igzis'ting] a vorhanden, bestehend.
exit [eg'zit] n Ausgang m; (THEAT) Abgang m ♦ vi (THEAT) abtreten.
exit poll n bei Wahlen unmittelbar nach Verlassen der Wahllokale durchgeführte Umfrage.
exit ramp n (US AUT) Ausfahrt f.

exit visa n Ausreisegenehmigung f.
ex officio [eks əfish'ēō] ad von Amts wegen.
exonerate [igzân'ərāt] vt entlasten.
exorbitant [igzôr'bətənt] a übermäßig; (price) astronomisch, unverschämt; (demands) maßlos, übertrieben.
exorcize [ek'sôrsīz] vt exorzieren.
exotic [igzât'ik] a exotisch.
exp. abbr = **expenses**; **export**; **express**; **expired**.
expand [ikspand'] vt (spread) ausspannen; (operations) ausdehnen ♦ vi sich ausdehnen; **to ~ on** (notes, story etc) weiter ausführen.
expanse [ikspans'] n weite Fläche f, Weite f.
expansion [ikspan'chən] n Erweiterung f.
expansionism [ikspan'chənizəm] n Expansionspolitik f.
expansionist [ikspan'chənist] a expansionistisch, Expansions-.
expatriate [ekspā'trēit] a Exil- ♦ n im Exil Lebende(r) mf.
expect [ikspekt'] vt erwarten; (suppose) annehmen; **to ~ to do sth** vorhaben, etw zu tun; **as ~ed** wie erwartet; **I ~ so** das nehme ich an ♦ vi: **to be ~ing (a baby)** ein Kind erwarten.
expectancy [ikspek'tənsē] n Erwartung f; **life ~** Lebenserwartung f.
expectant [ikspek'tənt] a (hopeful) erwartungsvoll; (mother) werdend.
expectantly [ikspek'təntlē] ad (look, listen) gespannt.
expectation [ekspektā'shən] n (hope) Hoffnung f; **~s** pl Erwartungen pl; (prospects) Aussicht f; **in ~ of** in Erwartung (+gen); **against** or **contrary to all ~(s)** wider Erwarten; **to come** or **live up to sb's ~s** jds (gen) Erwartungen entsprechen.
expedience [ikspē'dēəns] n Zweckdienlichkeit f.
expediency [ikspē'dēənsē] n = **expedience**.
expedient [ikspē'dēənt] a zweckdienlich ♦ n (Hilfs)mittel nt.
expedite [ek'spidīt] vt beschleunigen.
expedition [ekspədish'ən] n Expedition f.
expeditionary force [ekspədish'ənärē fôrs] n Expeditionskorps nt.
expel [ikspel'] vt ausweisen; (student) (ver)weisen.
expend [ikspend'] vt (money) ausgeben; (effort) aufwenden.
expendable [ikspen'dəbəl] a entbehrlich.
expenditure [ikspen'dichûr] n Kosten pl, Ausgaben pl; (of time, effort) Aufwand m.
expense [ikspens'] n (cost) Auslage f, Ausgabe f; (high cost) Aufwand m; **to meet the ~ of** Kosten begleichen für; **at the ~ of** auf Kosten von; see also **expenses**.
expense account n Spesenkonto nt.
expenses [ikspen'siz] npl Spesen pl.
expensive [ikspen'siv] a teuer.
experience [ikspēr'ēəns] n (incident) Erlebnis nt; (practice) Erfahrung f; **to learn by ~** durch Erfahrung lernen ♦ vt erfahren, erle-

ben; (hardship) durchmachen.
experienced [ikspēr'ēənst] a erfahren.
experiment n [ikspär'əmənt] Versuch m, Experiment nt; **to perform** or **carry out an ~** ein Experiment durchführen; **as an ~** als Experiment ♦ vi [ikspär'əment] experimentieren; **to ~ with a new vaccine** einen neuen Impfstoff versuchsweise einführen.
experimental [ikspärəmen'təl] a versuchsweise, experimentell; **the process is still at the ~ stage** das Verfahren befindet sich noch im Versuchsstadium.
expert [ek'spûrt] n Fachmann m, Experte m, Expertin f; (official) Sachverständige(r) m; **an ~ on the subject** ein Fachmann or Experte auf diesem Gebiet ♦ a erfahren; (practiced) gewandt; **~ witness** (JUR) Sachverständige(r) mf; **to be ~ in** or **at doing sth** Experte für etw sein.
expertise [ekspûrtēz'] n Sachkenntnis f.
expiration [ekspərā'shən] n (breathing) Ausatmen nt; (fig) Ablauf m.
expire [ikspī'ûr] vi (end) ablaufen; (die) sterben; (ticket) verfallen.
expiry [ikspīûr'ē] n (Brit) Ablauf m.
explain [iksplān'] vt (make clear) erklären; (account for) begründen.
explain away vt wegerklären, eine (einleuchtende) Erklärung finden für.
explanation [eksplənā'shən] n Erklärung f; **to find an ~ for sth** eine Erklärung für etw finden.
explanatory [iksplan'ətôrē] a erklärend.
explicable [eksplik'əbəl] a erklärlich.
explicit [iksplis'it] a (clear) ausdrücklich; (outspoken) deutlich.
explicitly [iksplis'itlē] ad deutlich.
explode [iksplōd'] vi explodieren ♦ vt (bomb) zur Explosion bringen; (theory) platzen lassen; **to ~ a fallacy** einen Irrtum aufdecken.
exploit n [eks'ploit] (Helden)tat f ♦ vt [iksploit'] ausbeuten.
exploitation [eksploitā'shən] n Ausbeutung f.
exploration [eksplərā'shən] n Erforschung f.
exploratory [iksplôr'ətôrē] a sondierend, Probe-.
explore [iksplôr'] vt (travel) erforschen; (search) untersuchen.
explorer [iksplôr'ûr] n Forschungsreisende(r) mf, Erforscher(in f) m.
explosion [iksplō'zhən] n (lit) Explosion f; (fig) Ausbruch m.
explosive [iksplō'siv] a explosiv, Spreng- ♦ n Sprengstoff m.
exponent [ikspō'nənt] n Exponent(in f) m.
export vt [ikspôrt'] exportieren ♦ n [eks'pôrt] Export m ♦ a [eks'pôrt] (trade) Export-.
exportation [ekspôrtā'shən] n Ausfuhr f.
export drive n Exportkampagne f.
exporter [ekspôr'tûr] n Exporteur m.
export license n Ausfuhrgenehmigung f.
export manager n Exportmanager m.
export trade n Exporthandel m.
expose [ikspōz'] vt (to danger etc) aussetzen

(*to dat*); (*imposter*) entlarven; (*lie*) aufdecken.

exposé [ekspōzā'] *n* Exposé *nt*.

exposed [ikspōzd'] *a* (*position*) exponiert; (*land, house*) ungeschützt; (*ELEC*: *wire*) bloßliegend; (*pipe, beam*) nicht unter Putz gelegt.

exposition [ekspəzish'ən] *n* Darlegung *f*, Exposition *f*; (*of literature, text*) Kommentar *m*.

exposure [ikspō'zhûr] *n* (*MED*) Unterkühlung *f*; (*PHOT*) Belichtung *f*.

exposure meter *n* Belichtungsmesser *m*.

expound [ikspound'] *vt* (*theory, text, one's views*) darlegen, erläutern, auseinandersetzen.

express [ikspres'] *a* ausdrücklich; (*speedy*) Expreß-, Eil- ♦ *ad*: **to send sth ~ etw** per Expreß schicken ♦ *n* (*RAIL*) D-Zug *m* ♦ *vt* ausdrücken; **to ~ o.s.** sich ausdrücken.

expression [ikspresh'ən] *n* (*phrase*) Ausdruck *m*; (*look*) (Gesichts)ausdruck *m*.

expressionism [ikspresh'ənizəm] *n* Expressionismus *m*.

expressive [ikspres'iv] *a* ausdrucksvoll.

expressly [ikspres'lē] *ad* ausdrücklich, extra.

expressway [ikspres'wā] *n* (*US*) Schnellstraße *f*.

expropriate [eksprōp'rēāt] *vt* enteignen.

expulsion [ikspul'shən] *n* Ausweisung *f*.

expurgate [eks'pûrgāt] *vt* zensieren.

exquisite [ekskwiz'it] *a* erlesen.

exquisitely [ekskwiz'itlē] *ad* ausgezeichnet.

ext. *abbr* (*TEL*: = *extension*) App.

extemporize [ikstem'pərīz] *vi* aus dem Stegreif sprechen *or* spielen, extemporieren.

extend [ikstend'] *vt* (*visit etc*) verlängern; (*building*) vergrößern, ausbauen; (*hand*) ausstrecken; (*welcome*) bieten; (*FIN*: *credit, deadline*) verlängern ♦ *vi*: **the contract ~s to/for ...** der Vertrag gilt bis/für ...

extension [iksten'chən] *n* Erweiterung *f*; (*of building*) Anbau *m*; (*TEL*) Nebenanschluß *m*, Apparat *m*; **~ 3718** Apparat 3718.

extension cord *n* (*ELEC*) Verlängerungsschnur *f*.

extensive [iksten'siv] *a* (*knowledge*) umfassend; (*use*) weitgehend.

extensively [iksten'sivlē] *ad* (*altered, damaged etc*) beträchtlich.

extent [ikstent'] *n* Ausdehnung *f*; (*fig*) Ausmaß *nt*; (*of knowledge, activities, power*) Umfang *m*; **to a certain/large ~** in gewissem/hohen Maße; **debts to the ~ of $5,000** Schulden in Höhe von 5000 Dollar.

extenuating [iksten'yōōāting] *a* mildernd; **~ circumstances** mildernde Umstände *pl*.

exterior [ikstēr'ēûr] *a* äußere(r,s), Außen- ♦ *n* Äußere(s) *nt*.

exterminate [ikstûr'mənāt] *vt* ausrotten.

extermination [ikstûrmənā'shən] *n* Ausrottung *f*.

external [ikstûr'nəl] *a* äußere(r,s), Außen-; **for ~ use only** (*MED*) nur äußerlich (anzu-

wenden) ♦ *n*: **the ~s** die Äußerlichkeiten *pl*.

external affairs *n* Außenpolitik *f*.

externally [ikstûr'nəlē] *ad* äußerlich.

extinct [ikstingkt'] *a* ausgestorben.

extinction [ikstingk'shən] *n* Aussterben *nt*.

extinguish [iksting'gwish] *vt* (aus)löschen.

extinguisher [iksting'gwishûr] *n* Löschgerät *nt*.

extol, extoll, (*Brit*) **extol** [ikstōl'] *vt* (*merits, virtues, person*) preisen, rühmen.

extort [ikstôrt'] *vt* erpressen (*sth from sb* jdn um etw).

extortion [ikstôr'shən] *n* Erpressung *f*.

extortionate [ikstôr'shənit] *a* überhöht, erpresserisch.

extra [eks'trə] *a* zusätzlich ♦ *ad* besonders ♦ *n* (*work*) Sonderarbeit *f*; (*benefit*) Sonderleistung *f*; (*charge*) Zuschlag *m*; (*THEAT*) Statist(in *f*) *m*; **wine will cost ~** der Wein wird extra berechnet; **available in ~ large sizes** vorrätig in Sondergrößen; *see also* **extras.**

extra... [eks'trə] *prefix* außer....

extract *vt* [ikstrakt'] (heraus)ziehen; (*select*) auswählen ♦ *n* [eks'trakt] (*from book etc*) Auszug *m*; (*COOK*) Extrakt *m*.

extraction [ikstrak'shən] *n* (Heraus)ziehen *nt*; (*origin*) Abstammung *f*.

extracurricular [ekstrəkərik'yəlûr] *a* (*SCH*) außerstundenplanmäßig.

extradite [eks'trədīt] *vt* ausliefern.

extradition [ekstrədish'ən] *n* Auslieferung *f*.

extramarital [ekstrəmar'itəl] *a* außerehelich.

extramural [ekstrəmyōōr'əl] *a* (*course*) Volkshochschul-.

extraneous [ikstrā'nēəs] *a* unwesentlich; (*influence*) äußere(r, s).

extraordinary [ikstrôr'dənārē] *a* außerordentlich; (*amazing*) erstaunlich; **the ~ thing is that ...** das Merkwürdige an der Sache ist, daß ...

extraordinary general meeting *n* außerordentliche Hauptversammlung *f*.

extrapolation [ikstrapəlā'shən] *n* Extrapolation *f*.

extras [eks'trəz] *npl* (*additional expense*) zusätzliche Kosten *pl*.

extrasensory perception [ekstrəsen'sûrē pûrsep'shən] *n* außersinnliche Wahrnehmung *f*.

extra time *n* (*Brit SPORT*) Verlängerung *f*.

extravagance [ikstrav'əgəns] *n* Verschwendung *f*; (*lack of restraint*) Zügellosigkeit *f*; (*an ~*) Extravaganz *f*; (*excessive spending*) Verschwendungssucht *f*.

extravagant [ikstrav'əgənt] *a* extravagant.

extreme [ikstrēm'] *a* (*edge*) äußerste(r, s), hinterste(r, s); (*cold*) äußerste(r, s); (*behavior*) ausgefallen, übertrieben; **the ~ left/right** (*POL*) die extreme *or* äußerste Linke/Rechte ♦ *n* Extrem *nt*, das Äußerste; *see also* **extremes.**

extremely [ikstrēm'lē] *ad* äußerst, höchst.

extremes [ikstrēmz'] *npl* (*excesses*) Ausschreitungen *pl*; (*opposites*) Extreme *pl*; ~

of **temperature** extreme Temperaturen *pl.*
extremist [ikstrē'mist] *a* extremistisch ♦ *n*
Extremist (in *f) m.*
extremities [ikstrem'itēz] *npl (hands and feet)* Extremitäten *pl.*
extremity [ikstrem'itē] *n (end)* Spitze *f,* äußerste(s) Ende *nt; (hardship)* bitterste Not *f.*
extricate [ek'strikāt] *vt* losmachen, befreien.
extrovert [ek'strōvûrt] *n* Extravertierte(r) *mf* ♦ *a* extravertiert.
exuberance [igzōō'bûrəns] *n* Überschwang *m; (of person)* Überschwenglichkeit *f.*
exuberant [igzōō'bûrənt] *a* ausgelassen.
exude [igzōōd'] *vt (confidence)* ausstrahlen; *(liquid)* absondern ♦ *vi* sich absondern.
exult [igzult'] *vi* frohlocken.
exultant [igzul'tənt] *a (person)* jubelnd; *(shout)* Jubel-; *(smile)* triumphierend.
exultation [egzultā'shən] *n* Jubel *m;* **sing in ~** *(REL)* jauchzet und frohlocket.
ex works *a (Brit COMM):* **the price ~** der Preis ab Werk.
eye [ī] *n* Auge *nt; (of needle)* Öhr *nt* ♦ *vt* betrachten; *(up and down)* mustern; **to keep an ~ on** aufpassen auf (+*acc);* **in the ~s of** in den Augen (+*gen);* **up to the ~s in** bis zum Hals in; **as far as the ~ can see** so weit das Auge reicht; **to have an ~ for sth** ein Auge für etw haben; **there's more to this than meets the ~** da steckt mehr dahinter.
eyeball [ī'bôl] *n* Augapfel *m.*
eyebath [ī'bath] *n* = **eye cup.**
eyebrow [ī'brou] *n* Augenbraue *f.*
eyebrow pencil *n* Augenbrauenstift *m.*
eye-catching [ī'kaching] *a* auffallend.
eye cup *n* Augenbad *nt.*
eyedrops [ī'dräps] *npl* Augentropfen *pl.*
eyelash [ī'lash] *n* Augenwimper *f.*
eyelet [ī'lit] *n* Öse *f.*
eye-level [ī'levəl] *a (grill)* in Augenhöhe.
eyelid [ī'lid] *n* Augenlid *nt.*
eyeliner [ī'līnûr] *n* Eyeliner *m.*
eye-opener [ī'ōpənûr] *n:* **that was an ~** das hat mir die Augen geöffnet.
eyeshadow [ī'shadō] *n* Lidschatten *m.*
eyesight [ī'sīt] *n* Sehkraft *f.*
eyesore [ī'sôr] *n* Schandfleck *m.*
eyestrain [ī'strān] *n:* **to get ~** die Augen überanstrengen.
eye test *n* Augentest *m.*
eye-tooth [ī'tōōth] *n, pl* **eye-teeth** Eckzahn *m,* Augenzahn *m;* **I'd give my eye-teeth for this** *(col fig)* ich gäbe viel darum.
eyewash [ī'wâsh] *n (lit)* Augenwasser *nt; (fig)* Schwindel *m; (nonsense)* Quatsch *m.*
eye witness *n* Augenzeuge *m.*
eyrie [är'ē] *n* Horst *m.*

F

F, f [ef] *n (letter)* F *nt,* f *nt;* **F for Fox** ≈ F wie Friedrich.
F *abbr (= Fahrenheit)* F; *(US)* = **freeway.**
FA *n abbr (Brit:* = *Football Association)* ≈ DFB *m.*
FAA *n abbr (US:* = *Federal Aviation Administration)* ≈ LBA *nt.*
fable [fā'bəl] *n* Fabel *f.*
fabric [fab'rik] *n* Stoff *m,* Gewebe *nt; (fig)* Gefüge *nt;* **the ~ of the building was quite sound** *(ARCHIT)* das Gebäude als solches war ganz gut.
fabricate [fab'rikāt] *vt* fabrizieren; *(story, lie)* erfinden.
fabrication [fabrikā'shən] *n* Lügengeschichte *f.*
fabric ribbon *n, (for typewriter)* Gewebefarbband *nt.*
fabulous [fab'yələs] *a (imaginary)* legendär, sagenhaft; *(unbelievable)* unglaublich; *(wonderful)* fabelhaft, unglaublich.
façade [fəsâd'] *n (lit, fig)* Fassade *f.*
face [fās] *n* Gesicht *nt; (grimace)* Grimasse *f; (surface)* Oberfläche *f; (of clock)* Zifferblatt *nt; (in mine)* (Abbau)sohle *f,* Streb *m* ♦ *vt (point towards)* liegen nach; *(situation)* sich gegenübersehen (+*dat); (difficulty)* mutig entgegentreten (+*dat);* **to ~** Auge in Auge, direkt; **in the ~ of** angesichts (+*gen);* **rock ~** *(of mountain, cliff)* Steifwand *f;* **to save ~** das Gesicht wahren; **~ down** *(person)* mit dem Gesicht nach unten; *(card)* mit der Vorderseite nach unten; **to ~ up to** sich einer Sache ins Auge sehen; **to ~ the fact that** ... der Tatsache ins Auge sehen, daß ...; **we are ~d with serious problems** wir stehen großen Problemen gegenüber.
facecloth [fās'clôth] *n* Waschlappen *m.*
face cream *n* Gesichtscreme *f.*
faceless [fās'lis] *a (fig)* anonym.
face lift *n* Facelifting *nt.*
face powder *n* (Gesichts)puder *m.*
face-saving [fās'sāving] *a:* **a ~ excuse** eine Entschuldigung, um das Gesicht zu wahren.
facet [fas'it] *n* Seite *f,* Aspekt *m; (of gem)* Kristallfläche *f,* Schliff *m.*
facetious [fəsē'shəs] *a* schalkhaft; *(humorous)* witzig.
facetiously [fəsē'shəslē] *ad* spaßhaft, witzig.
face-to-face [fās'təfās'] *a* persönlich; *(confrontation)* direkt.
face value *n* Nennwert *m;* **to take sth at ~** *(fig)* etw für bare Münze nehmen.

facial [fā'shəl] *a* Gesichts- ♦ *n* (*also:* **beauty** ~) kosmetische Gesichtsbehandlung *f*.

facile [fas'əl] *a* oberflächlich; (*US: easy*) leicht; (*pej: remark, answer*) nichtssagend.

facilitate [fəsil'ətāt] *vt* erleichtern.

facilities [fəsil'ətēz] *npl* Einrichtungen *pl*; **credit** ~ Kreditmöglichkeiten *pl*.

facility [fəsil'ətē] *n* (*ease*) Leichtigkeit *f*; (*skill*) Gewandtheit *f*.

facing [fā'sing] *a* zugekehrt ♦ *prep* gegenüber ♦ *n* (*in construction industry*) Verblendung *f*, Verkleidung *f*; (*SEWING*) Besatz *m*.

facsimile [faksim'əlē] *n* (*document*) Faksimile *nt*; (*also:* ~ **machine**) Telekopierer *m*, Telefax(gerät) *nt*.

fact [fakt] *n* Tatsache *f*; **in** ~ in der Tat; ~**s and figures** genaue Angaben *pl*; **the** ~ (**of the matter**) **is that** ... die Sache ist die, daß ...; **to know for a** ~ **that** ... ganz genau wissen, daß ...; **I told my daughter the** ~**s of life** (*about sex*) ich habe meine Tochter aufgeklärt; **that's just a** ~ **of life** (*fig*) so ist es nun mal im Leben.

fact-finding [fakt'fīnding] *a:* **a** ~ **tour/ mission** eine Erkundungsreise/-mission.

faction [fak'shən] *n* Splittergruppe *f*.

factor [fak'tûr] *n* Faktor *m*; (*COMM*) Kommissionär *m*; **safety** ~ Sicherheitsfaktor *m*; **human** ~ menschliche(r) Faktor *m* ♦ *vi* (*COMM*) Schulden aufkaufen.

factory [fak'tûrē] *n* Fabrik *f*.

factory farming *n* (*Brit*) industriell betriebene Landwirtschaft *f*.

factory ship *n* Fabrikschiff *nt*.

factual [fak'chōōəl] *a* Tatsachen-, sachlich.

faculty [fak'əltē] *n* Fähigkeit *f*; (*UNIV*) Fakultät *f*; (*US: teaching staff*) Lehrpersonal *nt*.

fad [fad] *n* Tick *m*; (*fashion*) Masche *f*.

fade [fād] *vi* (*lose color*) verblassen; (*grow dim*) nachlassen, schwinden; (*sound, memory*) schwächer werden; (*wither*) verwelken ♦ *vt* (*material*) verblassen lassen.

fade away *vi* (*sound*) verklingen.

fade in *vt* (*TV, RAD, CINE*) allmählich einblenden ♦ *vi* allmählich eingeblendet werden.

fade out *vt* (*TV, CINE*) abblenden; (*RAD*) ausblenden ♦ *vi* (*TV, CINE*) abgeblendet werden; (*RAD*) ausgeblendet werden.

faded [fā'did] *a* verwelkt; (*color*) verblichen.

faeces [fē'sēz] *npl* (*Brit*) = **feces**.

fag [fag] *n* Plackerei *f*; (*Brit col: cigarette*) Kippe *f* ♦ *vi* (*Brit: schoolboy slang*) für einen älteren Schüler Dienste leisten.

fag end *n* (*Brit col: cigarette end*) Kippe *f*.

fagged [fagd] *a* (*Brit: exhausted*) erschöpft.

Fahrenheit [far'ənhīt] *n* Fahrenheit *nt*.

fail [fāl] *vt* (*exam*) nicht bestehen; (*student*) durchfallen lassen; (*memory*) im Stich lassen ♦ *vi* (*supplies*) ausbleiben; (*student*) durchfallen; (*eyesight*) nachlassen; (*light*) schwächer werden; (*crop*) fehlschlagen; (*remedy*) nicht wirken; (*brakes*) versagen; **words** ~ **me!** mir fehlen die Worte; **to** ~ **to**

do sth (*neglect*) es unterlassen, etw zu tun; (*be unable*) es nicht schaffen, etw zu tun; **without** ~ ganz bestimmt, unbedingt.

failing [fā'ling] *n* Fehler *m*, Schwäche *f* ♦ *prep* in Ermangelung (+*gen*); ~ **that** (oder) sonst, und wenn das nicht möglich ist.

failsafe [fāl'sāf] *a* (*device etc*) (ab)gesichert.

failure [fāl'yûr] *n* (*person*) Versager *m*; (*act*) Versagen *nt*; (*TECH*) Defekt *m*; (*in exam*) Durchfallen *nt*; (*of crops*) Mißernte *f*; **it was a complete** ~ (*attempt etc*) es war ein totaler Fehlschlag.

faint [fānt] *a* schwach; (*voice*) matt; (*smell, breeze, trace*) leicht ♦ *n* Ohnmacht *f* ♦ *vi* ohnmächtig werden.

fainthearted [fānthārt'id] *a* mutlos, kleinmütig.

faintly [fānt'lē] *ad* schwach.

faintness [fānt'nis] *n* Schwäche *f*; (*MED*) Schwächegefühl *nt*.

fair [fär] *a* schön; (*hair*) blond; (*skin*) hell; (*weather*) schön, trocken; (*just*) gerecht, fair; (*not very good*) leidlich, mittelmäßig; (*conditions*) günstig, gut; ~ **play** faire(s) Verhalten *nt*, Fair play *nt*; **it's not** ~! das ist nicht fair!; **a** ~ **amount of** ziemlich viel; ~ **wear and tear** allgemeine Abnutzung *f* ♦ *ad* (*play*) ehrlich, fair; **to play** ~ (*SPORT*) fair spielen; (*fig*) fair sein ♦ *n* (*carnival*) Jahrmarkt *m*; (*COMM*) Messe *f*.

fair-haired [fär'härd] *a* (*person*) blond.

fairly [fär'lē] *ad* (*honestly*) gerecht, fair; (*rather*) ziemlich; **I'm** ~ **sure** ich bin (mir) ziemlich sicher.

fairness [fär'nis] *n* Schönheit *f*; (*of hair*) Blondheit *f*; (*of game*) Ehrlichkeit *f*, Fairneß *f*; **in all** ~ gerechterweise, fairerweise.

fairway [fär'wā] *n* (*NAUT*) Fahrrinne *f*; (*GOLF*) Fairway *nt*.

fairy [fär'ē] *n* Fee *f*.

fairy godmother *n* gute Fee *f*.

fairyland [fär'ēland] *n* Märchenland *nt*.

fairy lights *npl* (*Brit*) bunte Lichter *pl*.

fairy tale *n* Märchen *nt*.

faith [fāth] *n* (*REL*) Glaube *m*; (*trust*) Vertrauen *nt*; **to have** ~ **in sb/sth** auf jdn/etw vertrauen.

faithful [fāth'fəl] *a* treu.

faithfully [fāth'fəlē] *ad* treu; (*promise*) fest; **yours** ~ (*in letters*) mit freundlichen Grüßen.

faith healer [fāth' hē'lûr] *n* Gesundbeter(in *f*) *m*.

fake [fāk] *n* (*thing*) Fälschung *f*; (*person*) Schwindler *m* ♦ *a* vorgetäuscht ♦ *vt* fälschen.

falcon [fal'kən] *n* Falke *m*.

Falkland Islands [fôlk'land i'ləndz] *npl* Falklandinseln *pl*.

fall [fôl] *n* Fall *m*, Sturz *m*; (*decrease*) Sinken *nt*; (*in population, membership*) Abnahme *f*; (*US: autumn*) Herbst *m*; (*Brit: of snow*) (Schnee)fall *m*; **a** ~ **of earth** ein Grundrutsch; *see also* **falls** ♦ *vi irreg* (*lit, fig*) fallen; (*night*) hereinbrechen; **to ~ flat** (*lit*) platt hinfallen; (*joke*) nicht ankommen; **the plan fell flat** aus dem Plan wurde nichts; **to ~ short of sb's expectations** jds Erwartungen gen nicht entsprechen; **to ~ in love (with sb/sth)** sich (in jdn/etw) verlieben.

fall apart *vi* auseinanderfallen, kaputt gehen.

fall back *vi* zurückweichen.

fall back on *vt fus* zurückgreifen auf.

fall behind *vi* (*fig*: *with payments*) in Rückstand geraten.

fall down *vi* (*person*) hinfallen; (*building*) einstürzen.

fall for *vt fus* (*trick*) hereinfallen auf (+*acc*); (*person*) sich verknallen in (+*acc*).

fall in *vi*: **to ~ in with sb's plans** sich nach jds Plänen richten.

fall off *vi* herunterfallen (von); (*diminish*) sich vermindern.

fall out *vi* sich streiten.

fall over *vi* (*person*) hinfallen; (*vase etc*) umkippen.

fall through *vi* (*plan*) ins Wasser fallen.

fallacy [fal'əsē] *n* Trugschluß *m*.

fallback position [fόl'bak pəzish'ən] *n* Rückzugsbasis *f*.

fallen [fόl'ən] *pp of* **fall**.

fallible [fal'əbəl] *a* fehlbar.

falling-off [fόl'ing·όf'] *n* Rückgang *m*, Abnahme *f*.

Fallopian tube [fəlō'pēən tōōb] *n* (*ANAT*) Eileiter *m*.

fallout [fόl'out] *n* radioaktive(r) Niederschlag *m*.

fallout shelter *n* Atombunker *m*.

fallow [fal'ō] *a* brach(liegend).

falls [fόlz] *npl* (*waterfall*) Fälle *pl*.

false [fόls] *a* falsch; (*artificial*) gefälscht, künstlich; **under ~ pretenses** unter Vorspiegelung falscher Tatsachen.

false alarm *n* Fehlalarm *m*.

falsely [fόls'lē] *ad* fälschlicherweise.

false teeth *npl* Gebiß *nt*.

falsify [fόl'səfī] *vt* (*report, story*) entstellen; (*figures, documents, evidence*) fälschen.

falter [fόl'tûr] *vi* schwanken; (*in speech*) stocken.

fame [fām] *n* Ruhm *m*.

familiar [fəmil'yûr] *a* vertraut, bekannt; (*intimate*) familiär; **to be ~ with** vertraut sein mit, gut kennen; **to make o.s. ~ with sth** sich mit etw vertraut machen; **to be on ~ terms with sb** mit jdm auf vertrautem Fuß stehen.

familiarity [fəmilēar'ətē] *n* Vertrautheit *f*.

familiarize [fəmil'yərīz] *vt* vertraut machen.

family [fam'lē] *n* Familie *f*; (*relations*) Verwandtschaft *f*.

family allowance *n* Kindergeld *nt*.

family business *n* Familienunternehmen *nt*.

family doctor *n* Hausarzt *m*.

family life *n* Familienleben *nt*.

family planning *n* Geburtenkontrolle *f*.

family planning clinic *n* Familienberatungsstelle *f*.

family tree *n* Stammbaum *m*.

famine [fam'in] *n* Hungersnot *f*.

famished [fam'isht] *a* ausgehungert; **I'm ~!** (*col*) ich sterbe vor Hunger!

famous [fā'məs] *a* berühmt.

famously [fā'məslē] *ad* (*get on*) prächtig.

fan [fan] *n* (*folding*) Fächer *m*; (*ELEC*) Ventilator *m*; (*admirer*) begeisterte(r) Anhänger *m*, Fan *m* ♦ *vt* fächeln.

fan out *vi* sich (fächerförmig) ausbreiten.

fanatic [fənat'ik] *n* Fanatiker(in *f*) *m*.

fanatical [fənat'ikəl] *a* fanatisch.

fan belt *n* Keilriemen *m*.

fancied [fan'sēd] *a* beliebt, populär.

fanciful [fan'sifəl] *a* (*odd*) seltsam; (*imaginative*) phantasievoll.

fancy [fan'sē] *n* (*liking*) Neigung *f*; (*imagination*) Phantasie *f*, Einbildung *f*; **when the ~ strikes him** wenn ihm gerade danach ist ♦ *a* schick, ausgefallen ♦ *vt* (*like*) gern haben; (*want*) wollen; (*imagine*) sich (*dat*) einbilden; **(just) ~ (that)!** stellen Sie sich (das nur) vor!

fancy dress *n* (*Brit*) Verkleidung *f*, Maskenkostüm *nt*.

fancy dress ball *n* (*Brit*) Maskenball *m*.

fancy goods *npl* Geschenkartikel *pl*.

fanfare [fan'fär] *n* Fanfare *f*.

fanfold paper [fan'fōld pā'pûr] *n* Endlospapier *nt*.

fang [fang] *n* Fang *m*; (*of snake*) Giftzahn *m*.

fan heater *n* (*Brit*) Heizofen *m*.

fanlight [fan'līt] *n* (*Brit*) Oberlicht *nt*.

fantasize [fan'təsīz] *vi* phantasieren; (*dream*) Fantasievorstellungen haben.

fantastic [fantas'tik] *a* phantastisch.

fantasy [fan'təsē] *n* Phantasie *f*.

FAO *n abbr* (= *Food and Agriculture Organization*) Ernährungs- und Landwirtschaftsorganisation der UNO.

FAQ *abbr* (*US*) = *fair average quality*.

far [fär] *a* weit; **the ~ left/right** (*POL*) die äußerste Linke/Rechte ♦ *ad* weit entfernt; (*very much*) weitaus, (sehr) viel; **~ away, ~ off** weit weg; **by ~** bei weitem; **so ~** (*up to this point*) soweit; (*up to now*) bis jetzt; **is it ~ to Chicago?** ist es weit bis nach Chicago?; **it's not ~ (from here)** es ist nicht weit (von hier); **it's by ~ the best** es ist bei weitem das Beste; **how ~ have you got with your work?** wie weit bist du mit der Arbeit?

faraway [fär'əwā] *a* weit entfernt; (*voice, look*) verträumt.

farce [färs] *n* (*THEAT, fig*) Farce *f*.

farcical [fär'sikəl] *a* (*fig*) lächerlich.

fare [fär] *n* (*charge*) Fahrpreis *m*; (*money*) Fahrgeld *nt*; (*food*) Kost *f* ♦ *vi*: **he is faring well** es ergeht ihm gut.

Far East *n*: **the ~** der Ferne Osten.

farewell [fär'wel'] *n* Abschied(sgruß) *m* ♦ *interj* lebe wohl! ♦ *a* [fär'wel] Abschieds-.

far-fetched [fär'fecht'] *a* weit hergeholt.

farm [färm] *n* Bauernhof *m*, Farm *f* ♦ *vt* bewirtschaften ♦ *vi* Landwirt *m* sein.

farm out *vt*: (*work*) vergeben (*to sb* an jdn).

farmer [fär'mûr] *n* Bauer *m*, Landwirt *m*.

farmhand [färm'hand] *n* Landarbeiter *m*.

farmhouse [färm'hous] *n* Bauernhaus *nt*.

farming [fär'ming] *n* Landwirtschaft *f*; **sheep ~** Schafzucht *f*.

farm laborer *n* Landarbeiter *m*.

farmland [färm'land] *n* Ackerland *nt*.

farm produce *n* landwirtschaftliche Produkte *pl*.

farm worker *n* = **farm laborer**.

farmyard [färm'yärd] *n* (Bauern)hof *m*.

Faroe Islands [fə'rō ī'ləndz] *npl* Färöer *pl*.

far-reaching [fär'rē'ching] *a* weitgehend.

farsighted [fär'sī'tid] *a* weitsichtig.

fart [färt] (*col!*) *n* Furz *m* ♦ *vi* furzen.

farther [fär'thûr] *a*, *ad* weiter.

farthest [fär'thist] *a* weiteste(r, s), fernste(r, s) ♦ *ad* am weitesten.

FAS *abbr* = **free alongside ship**.

fascinate [fas'ənāt] *vt* faszinieren.

fascinating [fas'ənāting] *a* faszinierend.

fascination [fasənā'shən] *n* Faszination *f*.

fascism [fash'izəm] *n* Faschismus *m*.

fascist [fash'ist] *n* Faschist(in *f*) *m* ♦ *a* faschistisch.

fashion [fash'ən] *n* (*of clothes*) Mode *f*; (*manner*) Art *f* (und Weise *f*); **in ~** in Mode; **out of ~** unmodisch; **after a ~** (*finish, manage etc*) recht und schlecht; **in the Greek ~** im griechischen Stil ♦ *vt* machen, gestalten.

fashionable [fash'ənəbəl] *a* (*clothes*) modern, modisch; (*place*) elegant; (*writer*) in Mode; **it is very ~** es ist (große) Mode.

fashion designer *n* Modezeichner(in *f*) *m*.

fashion show *n* Mode(n)schau *f*.

fast [fast] *a* schnell; (*firm*) fest; (*dye*) waschecht; (*PHOT: film*) hochempfindlich; **my watch is 5 minutes ~** meine Uhr geht 5 Minuten vor; **to be in the ~ lane** (*AUT*) auf der Überholspur sein; ♦ *ad* schnell; (*firmly*) fest ♦ *n* Fasten *nt* ♦ *vi* (*not eat*) fasten.

fasten [fas'ən] *vt* (*attach*) befestigen; (*seat belt*) festmachen; (*with rope*) zuschnüren ♦ *vi* sich schließen lassen.

fasten (up)on *vt fus* (*idea*) festhängen an (+*acc*).

fastener [fas'ənûr] *n* Verschluß *m*; (*Brit: zip ~*) Reißverschluß *m*.

fastening [fas'əning] *n* = **fastener**.

fast food *n* Schnellgerichte *pl*.

fastidious [fastid'ēəs] *a* wählerisch.

fat [fat] *a* dick, fett ♦ *n* (*ANAT, COOK*) Fett *nt*; **to live off the ~ of the land** wie Gott in Frankreich *or* wie die Made im Speck leben.

fatal [fāt'əl] *a* tödlich; (*disastrous*) verhängnisvoll.

fatalism [fāt'əlizəm] *n* Fatalismus *m*, Schicksalsglaube *m*.

fatality [fātal'itē] *n* (*road death etc*) Todesopfer *nt*.

fatally [fāt'əlē] *ad* tödlich.

fate [fāt] *n* Schicksal *nt*.

fated [fā'tid] *a* (*governed by fate*) zum Scheitern verurteilt; (*person, project, friendship etc*) unglückselig.

fateful [fāt'fəl] *a* (*prophetic*) schicksalsschwer; (*important*) schicksalhaft.

father [fä'thûr] *n* Vater *m*; (*REL*) Pfarrer *m*.

Father Christmas *n* (*Brit*) der Weihnachtsmann.

fatherhood [fä'thûrhōōd] *n* Vaterschaft *f*.

father-in-law [fä'thûrinlô] *n* Schwiegervater *m*.

fatherland [fä'thûrland] *n* Vaterland *nt*.

fatherly [fä'thûrlē] *a* väterlich.

fathom [fath'əm] *n* Klafter *m* ♦ *vt* (*also: ~ out*) verstehen.

fatigue [fətēg'] *n* Ermüdung *f* ♦ *vt* ermüden.

fatness [fat'nis] *n* Dicke *f*.

fatten [fat'ən] *vt* dick machen; (*animals*) mästen; **chocolate is ~ing** Schokolade macht dick ♦ *vi* dick werden.

fatty [fat'ē] *a* (*food*) fettig ♦ *n* (*person*) Dickerchen *nt*.

fatuous [fach'ōōəs] *a* albern, affig.

faucet [fô'sit] *n* (*US*) Wasserhahn *m*.

fault [fôlt] *n* (*defect*) Defekt *m*; (*ELEC*) Störung *f*; (*blame*) Fehler *m*, Schuld *f*; (*GEOG*) Verwerfung *f*; **it's your ~** du bist daran schuld; **at ~** schuldig, im Unrecht ♦ *vt*: **to ~ sth** etwas an etw (*dat*) auszusetzen haben.

faultless [fôlt'lis] *a* fehlerfrei, tadellos.

faulty [fôl'tē] *a* fehlerhaft, defekt.

fauna [fô'nə] *n* Fauna *f*.

favor [fā'vûr] (*US*) *n* (*approval*) Wohlwollen *nt*; (*kindness*) Gefallen *m*; **to be in ~ of sth/of doing sth** für etw sein/dafür sein, etw zu tun; **to find ~ with sb** bei jdm Anklang finden; **in ~ of** für, zugunsten (+*gen*) ♦ *vt* (*prefer*) vorziehen.

favorable [fā'vûrəbəl] *a*, **favorably** [fā'vûrəblē] *ad* günstig.

favorite [fā'vûrit] *a* Lieblings- ♦ *n* Günstling *m*; (*child*) Liebling *m*; (*SPORT*) Favorit *m*.

favoritism [fā'vûritizəm] *n* (*SCH*) Bevorzugung *f*; (*POL*) Günstlingswirtschaft *f*.

favour [fā'vûr] *etc* (*Brit*) = **favor** *etc*.

fawn [fôn] *a* rehbraun ♦ *n* (*color*) Rehbraun *nt*; (*animal*) (Reh)kitz *nt*.

fawning [fôn'ing] *a* kriecherisch.

fax [faks] *n* (*document*) Telekopie *f*, Fernkopie *f*, Telefax *nt*; (*machine*) Telekopierer *m*, Telefax(gerät) *nt* ♦ *vt* eine Telekopie machen, telekopieren.

fazed [fāzd] *a* (*col*) verdattert, außer Fassung.

FBI *n abbr* (*US*: = *Federal Bureau of Investigation*) FBI *m*, ≈ Kriminalpolizei *f*.

FCA *n abbr* (*US*) = *Farm Credit Administration*.

FCC *n abbr* (*US*) = *Federal Communications Commission*.

FCO *n abbr* (*Brit:* = *Foreign and Commonwealth Office*) ≈ AA *nt.*

FD *n abbr* (*US:* = *Fire Department*) Feuerwehr *f.*

FDA *n abbr* (*US:* = *Food and Drug Administration*) Nahrungs- und Arzneimittelbehörde.

FDIC *n abbr* (*US*) = *Federal Deposit Insurance Corporation.*

FEA *n abbr* (*US*) = *Federal Energy Administration.*

fear [fēr] *n* Angst *f*; ~ **of heights** Höhenangst *f*; **not to** ~!, (*Brit*) **no** ~! keine Angst! ♦ *vt* fürchten; **to** ~ **that** ... (be)fürchten, daß ... ♦ *vi:* **to** ~ **for** fürchten für *or* um.

fearful [fēr'fəl] *a* (*apprehensive*) ängstlich; (*terrible*) furchtbar; **I was** ~ **of waking her** ich befürchtete, daß ich sie aufwecken würde.

fearfully [fēr'fəlē] *ad* (*timidly*) ängstlich, bang; (*col: very*) furchtbar.

fearless [fēr'lis] *a*, **fearlessly** [fēr'lislē] *ad* furchtlos.

fearlessness [fēr'lisnis] *n* Furchtlosigkeit *f.*

fearsome [fēr'səm] *a* (*opponent, sight*) furchterregend.

feasibility [fēzəbil'ətē] *n* Durchführbarkeit *f.*

feasibility study *n* Durchführbarkeitsstudie *f.*

feasible [fē'zəbəl] *a* durchführbar, machbar.

feast [fēst] *n* Festmahl *nt*; (*REL*) Kirchenfest *nt* ♦ *vi* sich gütlich tun (*on* an +*dat*).

feast day *n* kirchliche(r) Feiertag *m.*

feat [fēt] *n* Leistung *f.*

feather [feth'ûr] *n* Feder *f*; (*mattress, bed, pillow*) Feder- *attr* ♦ *vt*: **to** ~ **one's nest** (*fig*) sein Schäfchen ins trockene bringen.

featherweight [feth'ûrwāt] *n* Federgewicht *nt.*

feature [fē'chûr] *n* (*facial*) (Gesichts)zug *m*; (*characteristic*) Merkmal *nt*; (*CINE. PRESS*) Feature *nt*; **a** (**special**) ~ **on sth/sb** ein Sonderbeitrag über etw/jdn ♦ *vt* darstellen; (*advertising etc*) groß herausbringen; **featuring X** mit X ♦ *vi* vorkommen; **it** ~**d prominently in** ... es spielte eine große Rolle in *or* bei ...

feature film *n* Hauptfilm *m.*

featureless [fē'chûrlis] *a* nichtssagend.

Feb. *abbr* (= *February*) Febr.

February [feb'yəwārē] *n* Februar *m*; *see also* **September.**

feces [fē'sēz] *npl* (*US*) Kot *m.*

feckless [fek'lis] *a* nutzlos.

fed [fed] *pt, pp of* **feed.**

Fed *abbr* (*US*) = **federal; federation.**

Fed. [fed] *n abbr* (*US col:* = *Federal Reserve Board*) Aufsichtsrat der Reservebank.

federal [fed'ûrəl] *a* Bundes-.

Federal Republic of Germany *n* die Bundesrepublik Deutschland.

federation [fedərā'shən] *n* (*league*) Föderation *f*, Bund *m*; (*of states*) Staatenbund *m.*

fedora [fədôr'ə] *n* (*US*) weiche(r) Filzhut *m.*

fed-up [fedup'] *a*: **to be** ~ **with sth** etw satt

haben; **I'm** ~ ich habe die Nase voll.

fee [fē] *n* Honorar *nt*; (*entrance* ~, *membership* ~) Gebühr *f*; **for a small** ~ gegen eine geringe Gebühr.

feeble [fē'bəl] *a* (*person*) schwach; (*excuse*) lahm.

feebleminded [fē'bəlmīndid] *a* geistesschwach.

feed [fēd] *n* (*for baby*) Essen *nt*; (*for animals*) Futter *nt* ♦ *irreg vt* füttern; (*support*) ernähren ♦ *vi* (*baby, animal*) füttern.

feed in *vt* (*COMPUT*) füttern.

feed into *vt*: **to** ~ **sth into a machine** etw in eine Maschine eingeben.

feed on *vt fus* leben von.

feedback [fēd'bak] *n* (*TECH*) Rückkopplung *f*; (*information*) Feedback *nt*; (*from person*) Reaktion *f.*

feeder [fē'dûr] *n* (*bottle*) Flasche *f.*

feeding bottle [fē'ding bât'əl] *n* (*Brit*) Flasche *f.*

feel [fēl] *n*: **it has a soft** ~ es fühlt sich weich an; **to get the** ~ **of sth** ein Gefühl für etw bekommen ♦ *irreg vt* (*sense*) fühlen; (*touch*) anfassen; (*think*) meinen; **I** ~ **that you ought to do it** ich glaube, daß Sie es tun sollten; **I'm still** ~**ing my way around** (*fig*) ich versuche noch, mich zu orientieren ♦ *vi* (*person*) sich fühlen; (*thing*) sich anfühlen; **I** ~ **cold** mir ist kalt; **it** ~**s colder out here** hier draußen ist es kälter; **I** ~ **like a cup of tea** ich habe Lust auf eine Tasse Tee.

feeler [fē'lûr] *n* Fühler *m.*

feeling [fē'ling] *n* Gefühl *nt*; (*opinion*) Meinung *f*; (*impression*) Eindruck *m*; **what are your** ~**s on the matter?** wie ist Ihre Meinung dazu?; **to hurt sb's** ~**s** jds Gefühle verletzen; ~**s ran high about it** man ereiferte sich sehr darüber; **I got the** ~ **that** ... ich bekam den Eindruck, daß ...; **there was a general** ~ **that** ... man war allgemein der Ansicht, daß ...

feet [fēt] *npl of* **foot.**

feign [fān] *vt* vortäuschen.

feigned [fānd] *a* vorgetäuscht, Schein-.

feint [fānt] *n* Täuschungsmanöver *nt.*

feline [fē'līn] *a* Katzen-, katzenartig.

fell [fel] *vt* (*tree*) fällen ♦ *n* (*hill*) kahle(r) Berg *m*; ♦ *a*: **at one** ~ **swoop** mit einem Schlag; **with one** ~ **blow** mit einem einzigen gewaltigen Hieb ♦ *pt of* **fall.**

fellow [fel'ō] *n* (*companion*) Gefährte *m*, Kamerad *m*; (*man*) Kerl *m*; (*UNIV*) Stipendiat(in *f*) *m.*

fellow citizen *n* Mitbürger(in *f*) *m.*

fellow countryman *n* Landsmann *m.*

fellow feeling *n* Mitgefühl *nt*; (*togetherness*) Zusammengehörigkeitsgefühl *nt.*

fellow men *npl* Mitmenschen *pl.*

fellowship [fel'ōship] *n* (*group*) Körperschaft *f*; (*friendliness*) Gemeinschaft *f*, Kameradschaft *f*; (*scholarship*) Forschungsstipendium *nt.*

fellow traveler *n* Mitreisende(r) *mf*; (*POL:*

with communists) Mitläufer *m*.

fellow worker *n* Mitarbeiter(in *f*) *m*, Kollege *m*, Kollegin *f*.

felon [fel'ən] *n* (*US JUR*) Schwerverbrecher *m*.

felony [fel'ənē] *n* schwere(s) Verbrechen *nt*.

felt [felt] *n* Filz *m* ♦ *pt, pp of* **feel**.

felt-tip (pen) [felt'tip (pen')] *n* Filzstift *m*.

female [fē'māl] *n* (*of animals*) Weibchen *nt* ♦ *a* weiblich.

feminine [fem'ənin] *a* (*GRAM*) weiblich; (*qualities*) fraulich.

femininity [femənin'ətē] *n* Weiblichkeit *f*; (*quality*) Fraulichkeit *f*.

feminism [fem'ənizəm] *n* Feminismus *m*.

feminist [fem'ənist] *n* Feminist(in *f*) *m*.

fence [fens] *n* Zaun *m*; (*crook*) Hehler *m*; (*SPORT*) Hindernis *nt*; **to sit on the ~** (*fig*) neutral bleiben, nicht Partei ergreifen ♦ *vi* fechten.

fence in *vt* einzäunen.

fence off *vt* absperren.

fencing [fen'sing] *n* Zaun *m*; (*SPORT*) Fechten *nt*.

fend [fend] *vi*: **to ~ for o.s.** sich (allein) durchschlagen.

fend off *vt* (*attacker*) vertreiben; (*blow, awkward question*) abwehren.

fender [fen'dûr] *n* Kaminvorsetzer *m*; (*US AUT*) Kotflügel *m*.

fennel [fen'əl] *n* Fenchel *m*.

Fens [fenz] *npl*: **the ~** die Niederungen *pl* in East Anglia.

FEPC *n abbr* (*US*) = *Fair Employment Practices Committee*.

FERC *n abbr* (*US*) = *Federal Energy Regulatory Commission*.

ferment *vi* [fərment'] (*CHEM*) gären ♦ *n* [fûr'ment] (*excitement*) Unruhe *f*.

fermentation [fûrmentā'shən] *n* Gärung *f*.

fern [fûrn] *n* Farn *m*.

ferocious [fərō'shəs] *a* wild, grausam.

ferociously [fərō'shəslē] *ad* wild.

ferocity [fərâs'itē] *n* Wildheit *f*, Grimmigkeit *f*.

ferret [fär'it] *n* Frettchen *nt*.

ferret around *vi* herumstöbern *or* -schnüffeln.

ferret out *vt* (*person*) aufstöbern, aufspüren; (*secret, truth*) ausgraben.

Ferris wheel [fär'is wēl] *n* Riesenrad *nt*.

ferry [fär'ē] *n* Fähre *f* ♦ *vt* übersetzen; **to ~ sth/sb across** *or* **over a river** etw/jdn über einen Fluß setzen; **to ~ sb to and fro** jdn hin- und herbringen.

ferryman [fär'ēmən] *n, pl* **-men** Fährmann *m*.

fertile [fûr'təl] *a* fruchtbar.

fertility [fûrtil'ətē] *n* Fruchtbarkeit *f*.

fertility drug *n* Fruchtbarkeitspille *f*.

fertilization [fûrtələzā'shən] *n* Befruchtung *f*.

fertilize [fûr'təlīz] *vt* (*AGR*) düngen; (*BIOL*) befruchten.

fertilizer [fûr'təlīzûr] *n* (Kunst)dünger *m*.

fervent [fûr'vənt] *a* (*admirer*) glühend;

(*hope*) innig.

fervor, (*Brit*) **fervour** [fûr'vûr] *n* Inbrunst *m*; (*of public speaker*) Leidenschaft *f*.

fester [fes'tûr] *vi* eitern.

festival [fes'təvəl] *n* (*REL etc*) Fest *nt*; (*ART, MUS*) Festspiele *pl*; (*esp pop* ~) Festival *nt*.

festive [fes'tiv] *a* festlich; **the ~ season** (*Christmas*) die Festzeit *f*.

festivity [festiv'ətē] *n* Festlichkeit *f*.

festoon [festōōn'] *vt*: **to ~ with sth** mit etw behängen *or* schmücken.

FET *n abbr* (*US*) = *Federal Excise Tax*.

fetch [fech] *vt* holen; (*in sale*) einbringen.

fetching [fech'ing] *a* einnehmend, reizend.

fête [fet] *n* Fest *nt*.

fetid [fet'id] *a* übelriechend.

fetish [fet'ish] *n* Fetisch *m*.

fetter [fet'ûr] *vt* (*person*) fesseln; (*goat*) anpflocken; (*fig*) in Fesseln legen.

fetters [fet'ûrz] *npl* (*lit, fig*) Fesseln *pl*.

fettle [fet'əl] *n*: **in fine ~** (*Brit*) in bester Form *or* Verfassung.

fetus [fē'təs] *n* (*US*) Fötus *m*.

feud [fyōōd] *n* Fehde *f*; **a family ~** eine Familienfehde ♦ *vi* sich befehden.

feudal [fyōōd'əl] *a* lehnsherrlich, Feudal-.

feudalism [fyōō'dəlizəm] *n* Lehnswesen *nt*, Feudalismus *m*.

fever [fē'vûr] *n* Fieber *nt*; **he has a ~** er hat Fieber.

feverish [fē'vûrish] *a* (*MED*) fiebrig, Fieber-; (*fig*) fieberhaft.

feverishly [fē'vûrishlē] *ad* (*fig*) fieberhaft.

few [fyōō] *a* wenig ♦ *pron* wenige; **a ~** einige; **a good ~, quite a ~** ziemlich viele; **a ~ more days** noch ein paar Tage; **every ~ weeks** alle paar Wochen; **in** *or* **over the next ~ days** innerhalb der nächsten paar Tage.

fewer [fyōō'ûr] *a* weniger.

fewest [fyōō'ist] *a* wenigste(r, s).

FFA *n abbr* = *Future Farmers of America*.

FHA *n abbr* (*US*) = *Federal Housing Administration*.

fiancé [fēânsā'] *n* Verlobte(r) *m*.

fiancée [fēânsā'] *n* Verlobte *f*.

fiasco [fēas'kō] *n* Fiasko *nt*.

fib [fib] *n* Flunkerei *f* ♦ *vi* flunkern.

fiber, (*Brit*) **fibre** [fī'bûr] *n* Faser *f*; (*material*) Faserstoff *m*.

fiberboard, (*Brit*) **fibreboard** [fī'bûrbôrd] *n* Holzfaserplatte *f*.

fiberglass, (*Brit*) **fibreglass** [fī'bûrglas] *n* Glaswolle *f*.

fibrositis [fibrəsī'tis] *n* Bindegewebsentzündung *f*.

FIC *n abbr* (*US*) = *Federal Information Centers*.

FICA *n abbr* (*US*) = *Federal Insurance Contributions Act*.

fickle [fik'əl] *a* unbeständig, wankelmütig.

fickleness [fik'əlnis] *n* Unbeständigkeit *f*, Wankelmut *m*.

fiction [fik'shən] *n* (*novels*) Romanliteratur *f*;

(*story*) Erdichtung *f*.
fictional [fik'shənəl] *a* erfunden.
fictionalize [fik'shənəlīz] *vt* darstellen, fiktionalisieren.
fictitious [fiktish'əs] *a* erfunden, fingiert.
fiddle [fid'əl] *n* Geige *f*, Fiedel *f*; (*trick*) Schwindelei *f*; **to work a ~** ein krummes Ding drehen (*col*) ♦ *vt* (*Brit: accounts*) frisieren.
fiddle with *vt fus* herumfummeln an (+*dat*).
fiddler [fid'lûr] *n* Geiger *m*.
fiddly [fid'lē] *a* (*task, object*) knifflig.
fidelity [fidel'itē] *n* Treue *f*.
fidget [fij'it] *vi* zappeln ♦ *n* Zappelphilipp *m*.
fidgety [fij'itē] *a* nervös, zappelig.
fiduciary [fidōō'shēārē] *n* Treuhänder *m*.
field [fēld] *n* (*lit, COMPUT*) Feld *nt*; (*range*) Gebiet *nt*; **my particular ~** mein Spezialgebiet; **to lead the ~** (*SPORT, COMM*) anführen; **to give sth a year's trial in the ~** (*fig*) etw ein Jahr lang in der Praxis testen; **~ day** (*gala*) Paradetag *m*; **to have a ~ day** (*fig*) einen inneren Reichsparteitag haben.
field glasses *npl* Feldstecher *m*.
field marshal *n* Feldmarschall *m*.
fieldwork [fēld'wûrk] *n* (*MIL*) Schanze *f*; (*UNIV*) Feldforschung *f*; (*ARCHEOLOGY. GEOG*) Arbeit *f* im Gelände.
fiend [fēnd] *n* Teufel *m*; (*enthusiast*) Fanatiker(in *f*) *m*.
fiendish [fēn'dish] *a* teuflisch.
fierce [fērs] *a*, **fiercely** [fērs'lē] *ad* wild.
fierceness [fērs'nis] *n* Wildheit *f*.
fiery [fī'ûrē] *a* glühend; (*blazing*) brennend; (*hot-tempered*) hitzig, heftig.
FIFA [fē'fa] *n abbr* (= *Fédération Internationale de Football Association*) FIFA *f*.
fifteen [fif'tēn'] *num* fünfzehn.
fifteenth [fif'tēnth] *a* fünfzehnte(r, s).
fifth [fifth] *a* fünfte(r, s) ♦ *n* Fünftel *nt*.
fiftieth [fif'tēith] *a* fünfzigste(r, s).
fifty [fif'tē] *num* fünfzig.
fifty-fifty [fif'tēfif'tē] *a* halbe-halbe, fifty-fifty (*col*); **to go ~ with sb** mit jdm halbe-halbe or fifty-fifty machen; **we have a ~ chance of success** unsere Chancen stehen fifty-fifty.
fig [fig] *n* Feige *f*.
fight [fīt] *n* Kampf *m*; (*brawl*) Schlägerei *f*; (*argument*) Streit *m* ♦ *irreg vt* kämpfen gegen; (*brawl*) sich schlagen mit; (*fig*) bekämpfen; (*JUR: case*) durchkämpfen or -fechten ♦ *vi* kämpfen; sich schlagen; sich streiten.
fight back *vi* zurückschlagen; (*MIL*) sich verteidigen, Widerstand leisten ♦ *vt* (*tears*) unterdrücken.
fight down *vt* (*anger, anxiety, urge*) unterdrücken, bezwingen.
fight off *vt* (*attack, attacker*) abwehren; (*disease, sleep, urge*) ankämpfen gegen.
fight out *vt*: **to ~ it out** es untereinander ausfechten.
fighter [fī'tûr] *n* Kämpfer(in *f*) *m*; (*plane*)

Jagdflugzeug *nt*.
fighter-bomber [fī'tûrbâm'ûr] *n* Jagdbomber *m*.
fighter pilot *n* Jagdflieger *m*.
fighting [fī'ting] *n* Kämpfen *nt*; (*war*) Kampfhandlungen *pl*; (*in streets*) Prügeleien *pl*.
figment [fig'mənt] *n*: **a ~ of one's imagination** reine Einbildung *f*.
figurative [fig'yûrətiv] *a* bildlich; (*ART*) gegenständlich.
figure [fig'yûr] *n* Form *f*; (*of person*) Figur *f*; (*person*) Gestalt *f*; (*illustration*) Zeichnung *f*; (*number*) Ziffer *f*; **public ~** Persönlichkeit *f* des öffentlichen Lebens; **~ of speech** (*GRAM*) Redensart *f*, Redewendung *f* ♦ *vt* (*imagine*) sich (*dat*) vorstellen; (*US: think, reckon*) glauben, schätzen (*col*) ♦ *vi* (*appear*) eine Rolle spielen, erscheinen; (*US: make sense*) hinkommen, hinhauen (*col*).
figure on *vt fus* (*US*) rechnen mit.
figure out *vt* (*understand*) schlau werden aus; (*work out*) ausrechnen; (*how to do sth*) herausbekommen.
figurehead [fig'yûrhed] *n* (*NAUT, fig*) Galionsfigur *f*.
figure skating *n* Eiskunstlaufen *nt*.
Fiji Islands [fē'jē ī'ləndz] *npl* Fidschiinseln *pl*.
FILA *n abbr* (*US* = *Fédération Internationale de Lutte Amateur*) *Internationaler Amateurringerverband.*
filament [fil'əmənt] *n* (*ELEC*) Glühfaden *m*.
filch [filch] *vt* (*col*) filzen.
file [fīl] *n* (*tool*) Feile *f*; (*for nails*) Nagelfeile *f*; (*dossier*) Akte *f*; (*folder*) Aktenordner *m*; (*row*) Reihe *f*; (*COMPUT*) Datei *f*; **to open/ close a ~** (*COMPUT*) eine Datei eröffnen/ (ab)schließen; **in single ~** einer hinter dem anderen ♦ *vt* (*metal, nails*) feilen; (*papers*) abheften; (*claim, protest*) einreichen; (*complaint*) einlegen; **to ~ a suit against sb** eine Klage gegen jdn erheben.
file in *vi* hintereinander hereinkommen.
file out *vi* hintereinander hinausgehen.
file name *n* (*COMPUT*) Dateiname *m*.
filibuster [fil'əbustûr] *n* (*US: speech*) Obstruktion *f*, Dauerrede *f*; (: *person: also*: **~er**) Dauerredner *m* ♦ *vi* filibustern, Obstruktion betreiben.
filing [fī'ling] *n* Feilen *nt*; *see also* **filings**.
filing cabinet *n* Aktenschrank *m*.
filing clerk *n* Angestellte(r) *mf* in der Registratur.
filings [fī'lingz] *npl* Feilspäne *pl*.
fill [fil] *vt* füllen; (*occupy*) ausfüllen; (*satisfy*) sättigen; (*supply: order, requirements, need*) entsprechen; **~ed with admiration (for)** voller Bewunderung (für); **we've already ~ed that vacancy** wir haben diese Stelle schon besetzt; **to ~ the bill** (*fig*) allen Anforderungen genügen ♦ *n*: **to eat one's ~** sich richtig satt essen; **to have had one's ~** genug haben.
fill in *vt* (*hole*) (auf)füllen; (*form*) ausfüllen; (*details, report*) eintragen; **to ~ sb in**

on sth (*col*) jdn über etw aufklären *or* ins Bild setzen ♦ *vi*: **to ~ in for sb** für jdn einspringen.

fill out *vt* (*form, receipt*) ausfüllen.

fill up *vt* (*container*) auffüllen; (*form*) ausfüllen.

fillet [fɪlā'] *n* Filet *nt* ♦ *vt* als Filet herrichten.

fillet steak *n* Filetsteak *nt*.

filling [fɪl'ɪng] *n* (*COOK*) Füllung *f*; (*for tooth*) (Zahn)plombe *f*.

filling station *n* Tankstelle *f*.

fillip [fɪl'əp] *n* (*fig*) Ansporn *m*.

filly [fɪl'ē] *n* Stutfohlen *nt*.

film [fɪlm] *n* Film *m*; (*of dust etc*) Schicht *f*; (*membrane*) Häutchen *nt* ♦ *vt* (*scene*) filmen.

film script *n* Drehbuch *nt*.

film star *n* Filmstar *m*.

filmstrip [fɪlm'strɪp] *n* Filmstreifen *m*.

film studio *n* Filmstudio *nt*.

filter [fɪl'tûr] *n* Filter *m*; (*for traffic*) Abbiegespur *f* ♦ *vt* filtern ♦ *vi* durchscheinen.

filter in, filter through *vi* (*news*) durchsickern.

filter coffee *n* Filterkaffee *m*.

filter lane *n* (*Brit*) Abbiegespur *f*.

filter tip *n* Filter *m*, Filtermundstück *nt*.

filter-tipped cigarette [fɪl'tûrtɪpt sɪgəret'] *n* Filterzigarette *f*.

filth [fɪlth] *n* (*lit*) Dreck *m*; (*fig*) Schweinerei *f*.

filthy [fɪl'thē] *a* dreckig; (*behavior*) gemein; (*weather*) scheußlich.

fin. *abbr* = **finance**.

fin [fɪn] *n* Flosse *f*.

final [fɪ'nəl] *a* letzte(r, s); End-; (*conclusive*) endgültig; ~ **demand** letzte Zahlungsaufforderung *f*; ~ **dividend** Schlußdividende *f* ♦ *n* (*SPORT*) Endspiel *nt*; *see also* **finals**.

finale [fɪnal'ē] *n* (*THEAT*) Schlußszene *f*; (*MUS*) Finale *nt*.

finalist [fɪ'nəlɪst] *n* (*SPORT*) Schlußrundenteilnehmer(in *f*) *m*.

finality [fɪnal'ɪtē] *n* Endgültigkeit *f*; **with an air of** ~ mit Bestimmtheit.

finalize [fɪ'nəlīz] *vt* (*plans etc*) endgültige Form geben (+*dat*); (*deal*) abschließen.

finally [fɪ'nəlē] *ad* (*lastly*) zuletzt; (*eventually*) endlich; (*irrevocably*) endgültig.

finals [fɪ'nəlz] *npl* (*UNIV*) Abschlußexamen *nt*; (*SPORT*) Schlußrunde *f*.

finance [fɪ'nans] *n* Finanzwesen *nt*; (*funds*) (Geld)mittel *pl* ♦ *cpd* (*page, section, company*) Finanz- ♦ *vt* [fɪnans'] finanzieren.

finances [fɪnan'sɪz] *npl* Finanzen *pl*; (*income*) Einkünfte *pl*.

financial [fɪnan'chəl] *a* Finanz-; (*situation, crisis etc*) finanziell.

financially [fɪnan'chəlē] *ad* finanziell.

financial management *n* Finanzverwaltung *f*.

financial statement *n* Bilanz *f*.

financial year *n* Geschäftsjahr *nt*.

financier [fɪnansiûr'] *n* Finanzier *m*.

find [fīnd] *irreg vt* finden; (*realize*) erkennen; **to ~ sb guilty** jdn für schuldig erklären; **to ~ (some) difficulty in doing sth** Schwierigkeiten haben, etw zu tun; **if you still ~ you can't do it** wenn Sie feststellen, daß Sie es immer noch nicht können ♦ *n* Fund *m*.

find out *vt* herausfinden.

findings [fīn'dɪngz] *npl* (*JUR*) Ermittlungsergebnis *nt*; (*of report*) Feststellung *f*, Befund *m*.

fine [fīn] *a* fein; (*thin*) dünn, fein; (*good*) gut; (*clothes*) elegant; (*weather*) schön; **he's ~** es geht ihm gut ♦ *ad* (*well*) gut; (*small*) klein; **you're doing ~** das machen Sie gut; **to cut it ~** (*of time, money*) knapp bemessen ♦ *n* (*JUR*) Geldstrafe *f*; **to get a ~ for sth** eine Geldstrafe für etw bekommen ♦ *vt* (*JUR*) mit einer Geldstrafe belegen.

fine arts *npl* schöne Künste *pl*.

finely [fīn'lē] *ad* (*splendidly*) wunderschön; (*chop*) dünn; (*adjust*) genau.

fineness [fīn'nɪs] *n* Feinheit *f*.

finery [fī'nûrē] *n* Putz *m*.

finesse [fɪnes'] *n* Finesse *f*.

fine-tooth comb [fīn'tōōth kōm] *n*: **to go through sth with a ~** etw gründlich durchkämmen.

finger [fɪng'gûr] *n* Finger *m* ♦ *vt* befühlen.

fingernail [fɪng'gûrnāl] *n* Fingernagel *m*.

fingerprint [fɪng'gûrprɪnt] *n* Fingerabdruck *m* ♦ *vt* (*person*) Fingerabdrücke abnehmen.

fingertip [fɪng'gûrtɪp] *n* Fingerspitze *f*; **to have sth at one's ~s** (*at one's disposal*) etw parat haben; (*know well*) etw aus dem Effeff kennen (*col*).

finicky [fɪn'ikē] *a* pingelig.

finish [fɪn'ɪsh] *n* Ende *nt*; (*SPORT*) Ziel *nt*; (*of products*) Finish *nt* ♦ *vt* beenden; (*course, work*) abschließen; (*book*) zu Ende lesen; **to ~ doing sth** mit etw fertig werden ♦ *vi* aufhören; (*SPORT*) ans Ziel kommen; **to ~ first/second** (*SPORT*) als erster/zweiter durchs Ziel gehen; **I've ~ed with the paper** ich habe die Zeitung zu Ende gelesen, ich bin mit der Zeitung fertig; **she's ~ed with him** er ist für sie untendurch.

finish off *vt* fertigmachen; (*food*) aufessen; (*kill*) den Gnadenstoß geben (+*dat*).

finish up *vi* landen ♦ *vt* = **finish off**.

finished [fɪn'ɪsht] *a* (*product*) fertig; (*performance*) ausgereift, makellos; (*col: tired*) erledigt.

finishing line [fɪn'ɪshɪng līn] *n* Ziellinie *f*.

finishing school [fɪn'ɪshɪng skōōl] *n* Mädchenpensionat *nt*.

finishing touches [fɪn'ɪshɪng tuchəz] *npl*: **the ~** das Tüpfelchen auf dem i.

finite [fɪ'nīt] *a* endlich, begrenzt; (*GRAM*) finit.

Finland [fɪn'lənd] *n* Finnland *nt*.

Finn [fɪn] *n* (*person*) Finne *m*, Finnin *f*.

Finnish [fɪn'ɪsh] *a* finnisch ♦ *n* (*language*) Finnisch *nt*.

fiord, fjord [fyŏrd] *n* Fjord *m*.
fir [fûr] *n* Tanne *f*.
fire [fī'ûr] *n* (*lit, fig*) Feuer *nt*; (*damaging*) Brand *m*; (*Brit: electric* ~ *or gas* ~) Ofen *m*; **to catch** ~ Feuer fangen; **to set** ~ **to sth** etw in Brand stecken; **to be on** ~ brennen; **to be insured against** ~ feuerversichert sein; **to be** *or* **come under** ~ (*lit, fig*) unter Beschuß geraten ♦ *vt* (*rocket*) zünden; (*shot*) abfeuern; (*fig: imagination*) entzünden; (*dismiss*) hinauswerfen ♦ *vi* (*AUT*) zünden; **to** ~ **at sb** auf jdn schießen; ~ **away!** schieß los!
fire alarm *n* Feueralarm *m*.
firearm [fiûr'ârm] *n* Schußwaffe *f*.
fire brigade *n* (*Brit*) Feuerwehr *f*.
fire department *n* (*US*) Feuerwehr *f*.
fire drill *n* (*for passengers, people in building*) Probealarm *m*.
fire engine *n* Feuerwehrauto *nt*.
fire escape *n* Feuerleiter *f*.
fire extinguisher *n* Löschgerät *nt*.
fire hazard *n* Brandgefahr *f*, Feuerrisiko *nt*.
fire hydrant *n* Hydrant *m*.
fire insurance *n* Feuerversicherung *f*.
fireman [fiûr'mən] *n, pl* **-men** Feuerwehrmann *m*.
fireplace [fiûr'plās] *n* offene(r) Kamin *m*.
fire practice *n* = **fire drill**.
fireproof [fiûr'prōōf] *a* feuerfest.
fire regulations *npl* Feuersicherheitsvorschriften *pl*.
fire risk *n* = **fire hazard**.
firescreen [fiûr'skrēn] *n* Ofenschirm *m*.
fireside [fiûr'sīd] *n* Kamin *m*.
fire station *n* Feuerwehrwache *f*.
firewood [fiûr'wōōd] *n* Brennholz *nt*.
fireworks [fiûr'wûrks] *npl* Feuerwerk *nt*.
firing [fiûr'ing] *n* Schießen *nt*.
firing line *n* (*MIL*) Feuer- *or* Schußlinie *f*; **to be in the** ~ (*fig*) in der Schußlinie sein.
firing squad *n* Exekutionskommando *nt*.
firm [fûrm] *a* (*offer, decision*) fest; (*determined*) entschlossen; **to be a** ~ **believer in sth** fest von etw überzeugt sein; **to stand** ~ **on sth** *or* **take a** ~ **stand over sth** (*fig*) fest *or* unerschütterlich bei etw bleiben ♦ *n* Firma *f*.
firmness [fûrm'nis] *n* Festigkeit *f*; Entschlossenheit *f*.
first [fûrst] *a* erste(r, s); **in the** ~ **instance** zuerst *or* zunächst einmal; **I'll do it** ~ **thing tomorrow** ich werde es morgen als Allererstes tun ♦ *ad* zuerst; (*arrive*) als erste(r); (*for the* ~ *time*) zum ersten Mal, das erste Mal; **head** ~ kopfüber; **at** ~ zuerst, anfangs; ~ **of all** zu allererst ♦ *n* (*person: in race*) Erste(r) *mf*; (*AUT: also:* ~ **gear**) erste(r) Gang *m*; **from the (very)** ~ (ganz) von Anfang an.
first aid *n* Erste Hilfe *f*.
first aid kit *n* Verbandskasten *m*.
first aid station, (*Brit*) **first aid post** *n* Sanitätswache *f*.

first-class [fûrst'klas'] *a* erstklassig; (*travel*) erste(r) Klasse; ~ **ticket** (*RAIL etc*) Erster-Klasse-Fahrkarte *f*; ~ **mail** bevorzugt beförderte Post *f*.
firsthand [fûrst'hand'] *a, ad* aus erster Hand.
first lady *n* (*US*) First Lady *f*.
firstly [fûrst'lē] *ad* erstens.
first name *n* Vorname *m*.
first night *n* Premiere *f*.
first-rate [fûrst'rāt'] *a* erstklassig.
fiscal [fis'kəl] *a* fiskalisch, Finanz-; ~ **year** Steuerjahr *nt*.
fish [fish] *n* Fisch *m* ♦ *vt* (*river*) angeln in (+*dat*); (*sea*) fischen in (+*dat*) ♦ *vi* angeln; fischen; **to go** ~**ing** angeln gehen; fischen gehen.
fish out *vt* herausfischen.
fishbone [fish'bōn] *n* (Fisch)gräte *f*.
fisherman [fish'ûrmən] *n, pl* **-men** Fischer *m*.
fishery [fish'ûrē] *n* Fischgrund *m*.
fish factory *n* Fischfabrik *f*.
fish farm *n* Fischzucht *f*.
fish finger *n* (*Brit*) Fischstäbchen *nt*.
fish hook *n* Angelhaken *m*.
fishing boat [fish'ing bōt] *n* Fischerboot *nt*.
fishing industry *n* Fischereiindustrie *f*.
fishing line *n* Angelschnur *f*.
fishing net *n* Fischnetz *nt*.
fishing rod *n* Angel(rute) *f*.
fishing tackle *n* (*for sport*) Angelgeräte *pl*; (*for industry*) Fischereigeräte *pl*.
fish market *n* Fischmarkt *m*.
fishmonger [fish'munggûr] *n* Fischhändler *m*.
fish slice *n* (*Brit*) Fischvorlegemesser *nt*.
fish stick *n* (*US*) Fischstäbchen *nt*.
fishy [fish'ē] *a* (*col: suspicious*) faul.
fission [fish'ən] *n* Spaltung *f*; **atomic** *or* **nuclear** ~ Atomspaltung *f*.
fissure [fish'ûr] *n* Riß *m*.
fist [fist] *n* Faust *f*.
fistfight [fist'fīt] *n* Faustkampf *m*.
fit [fit] *a* (*MED*) gesund; (*SPORT*) in Form, fit; (*suitable*) geeignet; **to keep** ~ sich fit halten; **do as you think** *or* **see** ~ handeln Sie, wie Sie es für richtig halten; **to be** ~ **for work** (*after illness*) wieder arbeiten können ♦ *vt* passen (+*dat*); (*insert, attach*) einsetzen; (*match: facts, description*) entsprechen (+*dat*) ♦ *vi* passen; (*in space, gap*) hineinpassen ♦ *n* (*of clothes*) Sitz *m*; (*MED, outburst*) Anfall *m*; (*of laughter*) Krampf *m*; ~ **of anger** Wutanfall *m*; ~ **of coughing** Hustenanfall *m*; ~ **of enthusiasm** Anwandlung *f* von Enthusiasmus; **to have** *or* **suffer a** ~ einen Anfall haben; **by** ~**s and starts** = fitfully.
fit in *vi* sich einfügen; **to** ~ **in with sb's plans** sich nach jds Plänen richten ♦ *vt* einpassen; (*find space for*) unterbringen; (*fig: appointment, visitor*) einen Termin geben (+*dat*).
fit out, fit up *vt* ausstatten.
fitful [fit'fəl] *a* (*sleep*) unruhig.
fitfully [fit'fəlē] *ad* (*move*) ruckweise; (*work*)

unregelmäßig.

fitment [fit'mənt] n (furniture) Einrichtungsgegenstand m.

fitness [fit'nis] n (suitability) Eignung f;
(MED) Gesundheit f; (SPORT) Fitneß f.

fitness activity n Ausgleichssport m.

fitted [fit'id] a: ~ **carpet** Teppichboden m; ~
kitchen (Brit) Einbauküche f.

fitter [fit'ûr] n (TECH) Monteur m.

fitting [fit'ing] a passend ♦ n (of suit etc) Anprobe f; (part) Zubehörteil nt; see also
fittings.

fitting room n (in shop) Umkleideraum m,
Umkleidekabine f.

fittings [fit'ingz] npl (furniture) Einrichtung f.

five [fīv] num fünf.

five-day week [fīv'dā wēk'] n Fünftagewoche
f.

fix [fiks] vt befestigen; (settle) festsetzen; (repair) richten, reparieren; (make ready:
meal, drink) machen; (castrate) kastrieren;
to ~ **sth in one's mind** sich (dat) etw fest
einprägen ♦ n: **in a** ~ in der Klemme.

fix on vt fus (decide on) sich entscheiden
für.

fix up vt (arrange: date, meeting) arrangieren; **to** ~ **sb up with sth** jdm etw besorgen or verschaffen.

fixation [fiksā'shən] n (PSYCH, fig) Fixierung
f.

fixative [fiks'ətiv] n Fixativ nt.

fixed [fikst] a repariert; (time) abgemacht; **it
was** ~ (dishonest) das war Schiebung; **how
are you** ~ **for money?** wie sieht's bei dir
mit Geld aus?

fixed assets npl (COMM) Anlagevermögen
nt.

fixed charge n feste Belastung f.

fixed-price contract [fikst'prīs' kân'trakt] n
Festpreisvertrag m.

fixture [fiks'chûr] n Installationsteil m;
(SPORT) Spiel nt.

fizz [fiz] n Sprudeln nt ♦ vi sprudeln.

fizzle [fiz'əl] vi zischen.

fizzle out vi (enthusiasm, interest) verpuffen; (plan) im Sande verlaufen.

fizzy [fiz'ē] a Sprudel-, sprudelnd.

fjord [fyôrd] n = **fiord**.

FL abbr (US MAIL) = Florida.

Fla. abbr (US) = Florida.

flabbergasted [flab'ûrgastid] a (col) platt.

flabby [flab'ē] a wabbelig.

flag [flag] n Fahne f; ~ **of convenience** billige
Handelsflagge f ♦ vi (strength) nachlassen;
(spirit) erlahmen.

flag down vt stoppen, abwinken.

flagpole [flag'pōl] n Fahnenstange f.

flagrant [flāg'rənt] a offenkundig; (offense)
schamlos; (violation) flagrant.

flagship [flag'ship] n Flaggschiff nt.

flagstone [flag'stōn] n Steinplatte f.

flag stop n (US) Bedarfshaltestelle f.

flair [flär] n (talent) Talent nt; (stylishness)
Schick m.

flake [flāk] n (of snow) Flocke f; (of rust)
Schuppe f ♦ vi (also: ~ **off**) abblättern.

flaky [flā'kē] a (paintwork) brüchig; (skin)
schuppig.

flaky pastry n (Brit COOK) Blätterteig m.

flamboyant [flamboi'ənt] a extravagant; (colors) prächtig.

flame [flām] n Flamme f; **old** ~ (col) alte
Liebe or Flamme; **to burst into** ~**s** in
Flammen aufgehen.

flaming [flā'ming] a (Brit col) verdammt; (:
row) irre.

flamingo [fləming'gō] n Flamingo m.

flammable [flam'əbəl] a brennbar.

flan [flan] n Obsttorte f.

flank [flangk] n Flanke f ♦ vt flankieren.

flannel [flan'əl] n Flanell m; (Brit: face ~)
Waschlappen m; (col) Geschwafel nt; see
also **flannels**.

flannelette [flanəlet'] n Baumwollflanell m.

flannels [flan'əlz] npl Flanellhose f.

flap [flap] n Klappe f; (AVIAT) (Lande)klappe
f; (col: panic) (helle) Aufregung f ♦ vt
(wings) schlagen mit ♦ vi (wings) schlagen;
(sails) flattern; (col: panic) sich aufregen.

flapjack [flap'jak] n (US: pancake) Pfannkuchen m.

flare [flär] n (signal) Leuchtsignal nt; (in skirt
etc) Weite f.

flare up vi aufflammen; (fig) aufbrausen;
(revolt) (plötzlich) ausbrechen.

flared [flärd] a (skirt, pants) ausgestellt.

flash [flash] n Blitz m; (news ~) Kurzmeldung f; (PHOT) Blitzlicht nt; ~ **of inspiration** Geistesblitz m; **in a** ~ im Nu ♦ vt aufleuchten lassen; (message) durchgeben; **to**
~ **sth about** (fig col: flaunt) mit etw protzen
♦ vi aufleuchten.

flash by, flash past vi vorbeirasen.

flashback [flash'bak] n Rückblende f.

flash bulb n Blitzlichtbirne f.

flash card n (SCH) Leselernkarte f.

flash cube n Blitzwürfel m.

flashlight [flash'līt] n Taschenlampe f.

flash point n Flammpunkt m; (fig) Siedepunkt m.

flashy [flash'ē] a (pej) knallig.

flask [flask] n Flakon m; (CHEM) Glaskolben
m; (vacuum ~) Thermosflasche f ®.

flat [flat] a flach; (dull) matt; (MUS) ernie-
drigt; (beer) schal; (tire) platt; (instrument) zu tief (gestimmt); (Brit: battery)
leer; **A** ~ As nt; ~ **rate of pay** Pauschal-
lohn m ♦ ad (MUS) zu tief; **(to work)** ~ **out**
auf Hochtouren (arbeiten); ~ **broke** (col)
völlig pleite ♦ n (Brit: apartment) Wohnung
f; (MUS) b nt; (AUT) Reifenpanne f, Plat-
te(r) m.

flatfooted [flat'fõotid] a plattfüßig.

flatly [flat'lē] ad glatt.

flatmate [flat'māt] n (Brit): **he's my** ~ er ist
mein Mitbewohner.

flatness [flat'nis] n Flachheit f.

flatten [flat'ən] vt (house, city) dem Erdboden

gleichmachen; (*also:* ~ **out**) platt machen, (ein)ebnen.

flatter [flat'ûr] *vt* schmeicheln (+*dat*); **it** ~**s your figure** das ist sehr vorteilhaft.

flatterer [flat'ûrûr] *n* Schmeichler(in *f*) *m*.

flattering [flat'ûring] *a* schmeichelhaft; (*clothes etc*) vorteilhaft.

flattery [flat'ûrē] *n* Schmeichelei *f*.

flatulence [flach'ələns] *n* Blähungen *pl*.

flaunt [flônt] *vt* prunken mit.

flavor, (*Brit*) **flavour** [flā'vûr] *n* Geschmack *m* ♦ *vt* würzen.

flavoring, (*Brit*) **flavouring** [flā'vûring] *n* Würze *f*.

flaw [flô] *n* Fehler *m*; (*in argument*) schwache(r) Punkt *m*.

flawless [flô'lis] *a* einwandfrei.

flax [flaks] *n* Flachs *m*.

flaxen [flaks'ən] *a* flachsfarben.

flea [flē] *n* Floh *m*.

flea market *n* Flohmarkt *m*.

fleck [flek] *n* (*of mud, paint, color*) Fleck(en) *m*; (*of dust*) Teilchen *nt*, Flöckchen *nt* ♦ *vt* (*with blood, mud etc*) bespritzen; **brown ~ed with white** braun und weiß gesprenkelt, braun mit weißen Punkten.

fled [fled] *pt, pp of* **flee**.

fledg(e)ling [flej'ling] *n* Jungvogel *m*.

flee [flē] *irreg vi* fliehen ♦ *vt* fliehen vor (+*dat*); (*country*) fliehen aus.

fleece [flēs] *n* Schaffell *nt*, Vlies *nt* ♦ *vt* (*col*) schröpfen.

fleecy [flē'sē] *a* (*blanket*) flauschig; ~ **clouds** Schäfchenwolken.

fleet [flēt] *n* Flotte *f*; (*of cars*) Fuhrpark *m*.

fleeting [flē'ting] *a* flüchtig.

Flemish [flem'ish] *a* flämisch.

flesh [flesh] *n* Fleisch *nt*; (*of fruit*) Fruchtfleisch *nt*.

flesh wound *n* Fleischwunde *f*.

flew [flōō] *pt of* **fly**.

flex [fleks] *n* (*Brit*) (Leitungs)kabel *nt* ♦ *vt* beugen, biegen.

flexibility [fleksəbil'ətē] *n* Biegsamkeit *f*; (*fig*) Flexibilität *f*.

flexible [flek'səbəl] *a* biegsam; (*plans*) flexibel; (*working hours*) gleitend; (*disk*) Floppy-.

flick [flik] *n* (*blow*) leichte(r) Schlag *m* ♦ *vt* leicht schlagen.

flick off *vt:* **to** ~ **sth off** etw wegschnippen.

flick through *vt fus* durchblättern.

flicker [flik'ûr] *n* Flackern *nt*; (*of emotion*) Funken *m* ♦ *vi* flackern.

flick knife *n* (*Brit*) Klappmesser *nt*.

flier [flī'ûr] *n* Flieger(in *f*) *m*.

flies [flīz] *npl of* **fly**.

flight [flīt] *n* (*journey*) Flug *m*; (*fleeing*) Flucht *f*; **how long does the ~ take?** wie lange dauert der Flug?; ~ **of stairs** Treppe *f*; **to take** ~ die Flucht ergreifen; **to put to** ~ in die Flucht schlagen.

flight attendant *n* Steward(eß *f*) *m*.

flight deck *n* Flugdeck *nt*.

flight recorder *n* Flugschreiber *m*.

flighty [flī'tē] *a* flatterhaft.

flimsy [flim'zē] *a* nicht stabil; (*thin*) hauchdünn; (*excuse*) fadenscheinig.

flinch [flinch] *vi* zurückschrecken (*away from* vor +*dat*).

fling [fling] *vt irreg* schleudern ♦ *n* kurze(s) Abenteuer *nt*.

flint [flint] *n* (*in lighter*) Feuerstein *m*.

flip [flip] *vt* werfen; **to** ~ **a coin** eine Münze in die Luft werfen; **he** ~**ped the lid off** er klappte den Deckel auf.

flip through *vt fus* (*book*) durchblättern.

flippancy [flip'ənsē] *n* Leichtfertigkeit *f*.

flippant [flip'ənt] *a* schnippisch; **to be** ~ **about sth** etw nicht ernst nehmen.

flipper [flip'ûr] *n* Flosse *f*.

flip side *n* (*of record*) B-Seite *f*.

flirt [flûrt] *vi* flirten ♦ *n:* **he/she is a** ~ er/sie flirtet gern.

flirtation [flûrtā'shən] *n* Flirt *m*.

flit [flit] *vi* flitzen.

float [flōt] *n* (*FISHING*) Schwimmer *m*; (*esp in procession*) Plattformwagen *m*; (*sum of money*) Wechselgeld *nt* ♦ *vi* schwimmen; (*in air*) schweben; (*currency*) floaten ♦ *vt* schwimmen lassen; (*COMM*) gründen; (*currency*) floaten; (*idea*) vorbringen.

floating [flō'ting] *a* (*lit*) schwimmend; (*fig: votes*) unentschieden.

floating voter *n* (*Brit*) Wechselwähler *m*.

flock [flåk] *n* (*of sheep, REL*) Herde *f*; (*of birds*) Schwarm *m*; (*of people*) Schar *f*.

floe [flō] *n* (*ice* ~) Eisscholle *f*.

flog [flåg] *vt* prügeln; (*whip*) peitschen; (*col: sell*) verkaufen.

flood [flud] *n* Überschwemmung *f*; (*fig*) Flut *f*; **the F~** die Sintflut; **to be in** ~ Hochwasser haben ♦ *vt* (*lit, fig*) überschwemmen; (*AUT: carburetor*) absaufen lassen; **to** ~ **the market** (*COMM*) den Markt überschwemmen.

flooding [flud'ing] *n* Überschwemmung *f*.

floodlight [flud'līt] *n* Flutlicht *nt* ♦ *vt* anstrahlen.

floodlighting [flud'līting] *n* Beleuchtung *f*.

floodlit [flud'lit] *pt, pp of* **floodlight** ♦ *a:* ~ **soccer** Fußball bei Flutlicht.

flood tide *n* Flut *f*.

floor [flôr] *n* (Fuß)boden *m*; (*story*) Stock *m*; (*of sea*) Grund *m*; (*of valley*) Boden *m*; **first** ~ (*US*), **ground** ~ (*Brit*) Erdgeschoß *nt*; **second** ~ (*US*), **first** ~ (*Brit*) erste(r) Stock *m*; **top** ~ oberste(s) Stockwerk *nt*; **to have the** ~ (*speaker*) das Wort haben ♦ *vt* (*person*) zu Boden schlagen; (*baffle*) verblüffen; (*silence*) die Sprache verschlagen (+*dat*).

floorboard [flôr'bôrd] *n* Diele *f*.

flooring [flôr'ing] *n* Fußboden(belag) *m*.

floor lamp *n* (*US*) Stehlampe *f*.

floor show *n* Kabarettvorstellung *f*.

floorwalker [flôr'wôkûr] *n* (*US COMM*)

Ladenaufsicht f.

flop [flâp] n Plumps m; (failure) Reinfall m ♦ vi (fail) durchfallen; **the project ~ped** aus dem Plan wurde nichts.

floppy [flâp'ē] a hängend ♦ n = **floppy disk.**

floppy disk n Diskette f, Floppy-disk f.

flora [flôr'ə] n Flora f.

floral [flôr'əl] a Blumen-.

Florence [flâr'əns] n Florenz nt.

Florentine [flôr'əntēn] a florentinisch ♦ n Florentiner(in f) m.

florid [flôr'id] a (style) blumig.

florist [flôr'ist] n Blumenhändler(in f) m; ~'s (shop) Blumengeschäft nt.

flotation [flōtā'shən] n (of ship) Flottmachen nt; (COMM) Gesellschaftsgründung f, Umwandlung f in eine Aktiengesellschaft.

flotsam [flât'səm] n Strandgut nt.

flounce [flouns] n (on dress) Besatz m.

flounce in vi hineinstürmen.

flounce out vi hinausstürmen.

flounder [floun'dûr] vi herumstrampeln; (fig) ins Schleudern kommen ♦ n (fish) Flunder f.

flour [flou'ûr] n Mehl nt.

flourish [flûr'ish] vi (business) blühen; (person, plant) gedeihen ♦ vt (wave) schwingen ♦ n (waving) Schwingen nt; (of trumpets) Tusch m, Fanfare f.

flourishing [flûr'ishing] a blühend.

flout [flout] vt mißachten, sich hinwegsetzen über (+acc).

flow [flō] n Fließen nt; (of sea) Flut f; (of river, ELEC) Fluß m ♦ vi fließen.

flow diagram n Flußdiagramm nt.

flower [flou'ûr] n Blume f; **in ~** in Blüte ♦ vi blühen.

flower bed n Blumenbeet nt.

flowerpot [flou'ûrpât] n Blumentopf m.

flowery [flou'ûrē] a (style) blumenreich.

flowing [flō'ing] a fließend; (hair) wallend; (style) flüssig.

flown [flōn] pt of **fly.**

flu [flōō] n Grippe f.

fluctuate [fluk'chōōāt] vi schwanken.

fluctuation [flukchōōā'shən] n Schwankung f.

flue [flōō] n Rauchfang m, Rauchabzug m.

fluency [flōō'ənsē] n Flüssigkeit f; **his ~ in English** seine Fähigkeit, fließend Englisch zu sprechen.

fluent [flōō'ənt] a (speech) flüssig; **to be ~ in German** fließend Deutsch sprechen.

fluently [flōō'əntlē] ad flüssig.

fluff [fluf] n Fussel f.

fluffy [fluf'ē] a flaumig; (pastry) flockig.

fluid [flōō'id] n Flüssigkeit f ♦ a (lit) flüssig; (fig: plans) veränderbar.

fluke [flōōk] n (col) Dusel m.

flummox [flum'əks] vt verwirren, durcheinanderbringen.

flung [flung] pt, pp of **fling.**

flunky [flung'kē] n Lakai m, Speichellecker m.

fluorescent [flōōəres'ənt] a Leucht-; (lighting, tube) Neon-.

fluoride [flōō'ərīd] n Fluorid nt; ~ **tooth-**

paste Fluorzahnpasta f.

flurry [flûr'ē] n (of activity) Aufregung f; (of snow) Gestöber nt.

flush [flush] n Erröten nt; (fig: of excitement) Glühen nt; (CARDS) Sequenz f ♦ vt (aus)spülen; (also: ~ **out**) (game, birds) aufspüren; (fig: criminal) aufstöbern, aufspüren ♦ vi erröten ♦ a glatt.

flushed [flusht] a rot.

fluster [flus'tûr] n Verwirrung f ♦ vt verwirren; nervös machen.

flustered [flus'tûrd] a verwirrt; nervös.

flute [flōōt] n (Quer)flöte f.

fluted [flōō'tid] a gerillt.

flutter [flut'ûr] n (of wings) Flattern nt; (of excitement) Beben nt ♦ vi flattern ♦ vt: **to ~ one's eyelashes** mit den Wimpern klimpern.

flux [fluks] n: **in a state of ~** im Fluß.

fly [flī] n (insect) Fliege f; (on pants, also: **flies**) (Hosen)schlitz m ♦ irreg vt fliegen ♦ vi fliegen; (flee) fliehen; (flag) wehen; **to ~ open** auffliegen.

fly away vi (person, plane, bird) weg- or fortfliegen; (fig: hopes, cares) schwinden.

fly in vi (plane) einfliegen; **she flew in from New York this morning** sie ist heute morgen mit dem Flugzeug aus New York angekommen.

fly off vi abfliegen, wegfliegen.

fly out vi ausfliegen.

fly-fishing [flī'fishing] n Fliegenfischen nt.

flying [flī'ing] n Fliegen nt ♦ a: **with ~ colors** mit fliegenden Fahnen.

flying buttress n (ARCHIT) Strebebogen m.

flying saucer n fliegende Untertasse f.

flying squad n (MIL etc) Überfallkommando nt.

flying start n gute(r) Start m.

flying visit n Stippvisite f.

flyleaf [flī'lēf] n Vorsatzblatt nt.

flyover [flī'ōvûr] n (US) Luftparade f; (Brit) Überführung f.

flypaper [flī'pāpûr] n Fliegenfänger m.

flypast [flī'past] n (Brit) Luftparade f.

flysheet [flī'shēt] n (for tent) Regendach nt.

flyswatter [flī'swâtûr] n Fliegenwedel m.

flywheel [flī'hwēl] n Schwungrad nt.

FM abbr (RAD) = **frequency modulation;** (Brit MIL: = Field Marshal) FM m.

FMB n abbr (US) = Federal Maritime Board.

FMCS n abbr (US: = Federal Mediation and Conciliation Services) Schlichtungsausschuß f.

foal [fōl] n Fohlen nt.

foam [fōm] n Schaum m; (rubber etc) Schaumgummi m ♦ vi schäumen.

fob [fâb] n (also: **watch ~**) Uhrkette f.

fob off vt (Brit) andrehen (sb with sth jdm etw); (: with promise) abspeisen.

f.o.b. abbr (COMM: = free on board) f.a.B.

foc abbr (Brit COMM: = free of charge) kostenlos.

focal [fō'kəl] a im Brennpunkt (stehend), Brennpunkt-; ~ **point** Brennpunkt m; ~

length Brennweite *f*.

focus [fō'kəs] *n* Brennpunkt *m*; (*fig*) Mittelpunkt *m*; **in** ~ scharf eingestellt; **out of** ~ unscharf (eingestellt) ♦ *vt* (*attention*) konzentrieren; (*camera*) scharf einstellen ♦ *vi* sich konzentrieren (*on* auf +*acc*).

fodder [fâd'ûr] *n* Futter *nt*.

foe [fō] *n* (*liter*) Feind(in *f*) *m*, Gegner(in *f*) *m*.

FOE *n abbr* = *Friends of the Earth*; (*US*: = *Fraternal Order of Eagles*) *Wohltätigkeitsverein*.

foetus [fē'təs] *n* (*Brit*) Fötus *m*.

fog [fôg] *n* Nebel *m* ♦ *vt* (*issue*) verunklären, verwirren.

fog up *vi* sich beschlagen.

fogbound [fôg'bound] *a* (*airport*) wegen Nebel geschlossen.

foggy [fôg'ē] *a* neblig, trüb.

fog light *n* (*AUT*) Nebellampe *f*.

foible [foi'bəl] *n* Schwäche *f*, Faible *nt*.

foil [foil] *vt* vereiteln ♦ *n* (*metal, also fig*) Folie *f*; (*fencing*) Florett *nt*.

foist [foist] *vt*: **to** ~ **sth on sb** *jdm etw andrehen*; (*task*) etw an jdn abschieben.

fold [fōld] *n* (*bend, crease*) Falte *f*; (*AGR*) Pferch *m* ♦ *vt* falten; **to** ~ **one's arms** die Arme verschränken.

fold up *vt* (*map etc*) zusammenfalten ♦ *vi* (*business*) eingehen.

folder [fōl'dûr] *n* (*brochure*) Informationsblatt *nt*; (*binder*) Aktenmappe *f*.

folding [fōl'ding] *a* (*chair etc*) Klapp-.

foliage [fō'lēij] *n* Laubwerk *nt*.

folio [fō'lēō] *n* Foliant *m*.

folk [fōk] *n* Volk *nt*; *see also* **folks** ♦ *a* Volks-.

folklore [fōk'lôr] *n* (*study*) Volkskunde *f*; (*tradition*) Folklore *f*.

folk music *n* Volksmusik *f*, Folk-Musik *f*.

folks [fōks] *npl* Leute *pl*.

folk singer *n* Sänger(in *f*) *m* von Volksliedern *or* Folksongs.

folk song *n* Volkslied *nt*; (*modern*) Folksong *m*.

follow [fâl'ō] *vt* folgen (+*dat*); (*obey*) befolgen; (*fashion*) mitmachen; (*profession*) nachgehen (+*dat*); (*understand*) folgen können (+*dat*); **to** ~ **sb's advice** jds Rat befolgen; **I don't quite** ~ **you** das verstehe ich nicht ganz, da komme ich nicht ganz mit ♦ *vi* folgen; (*result*) sich ergeben; **as** ~**s** wie folgt; **to** ~ **in sb's footsteps** (*fig*) in jds Fußstapfen (*acc*) treten; **it doesn't** ~ **that** ... daraus folgt nicht, daß ...

follow on *vi* (*continue*): **she will** ~ **on from where he left off** sie wird da weitermachen, wo er aufgehört hat.

follow out *vt* (*implement: idea, plan*) zu Ende verfolgen, durchziehen.

follow through *vt* (*plan, idea*) zu Ende verfolgen ♦ *vi* (*SPORT*) durchschwingen.

follow up *vt* (weiter) verfolgen.

follower [fâl'ōûr] *n* Anhänger(in *f*) *m*.

following [fâl'ōing] *a* folgend; **the** ~ **day** der

(darauf) folgende Tag ♦ *n* (*followers*) Anhängerschaft *f*; **she said the** ~ sie sagte folgendes.

follow-up [fâl'ōup] *n* Weiterverfolgen *nt*.

follow-up letter *n* Nachfaßschreiben *nt*.

folly [fâl'ē] *n* Torheit *f*.

fond [fând] *a*: **to be** ~ **of sb** jdn gern mögen; **she's** ~ **of swimming** sie schwimmt sehr gern.

fondle [fân'dəl] *vt* streicheln.

fondly [fând'lē] *ad* (*with love*) liebevoll; (*foolishly*) törichterweise; **he** ~ **believed that ...** er hat fest geglaubt, daß ...

fondness [fând'nis] *n* (*for sb*) Zuneigung *f*; (*for sth*) Vorliebe *f*.

font [fânt] *n* Taufbecken *nt*; (*TYP*) Schriftsatz *m*.

food [fōōd] *n* Essen *nt*, Nahrung *f*; (*for animals*) Futter *nt*.

food mixer *n* Küchenmixer *m*.

food poisoning *n* Lebensmittelvergiftung *f*.

food processor [fōōd' prås'esûr] *n* Küchenmaschine *f*.

foodstuffs [fōōd'stufs] *npl* Lebensmittel *pl*.

fool [fōōl] *n* Narr *m*, Närrin *f*; (*jester*) (Hof)narr *m*; (*Brit COOK*) Mus *nt*; **to make a** ~ **of o.s.** sich blamieren ♦ *vt* (*deceive*) hereinlegen; **you can't** ~ **me** du kannst mich nicht zum Narren halten ♦ *vi* (*behave like a* ~) (herum)albern.

fool about, fool around *vi* (*waste time*) herumtrödeln.

foolhardy [fōōl'hârdē] *a* tollkühn.

foolish [fōō'lish] *a* dumm.

foolishly [fōō'lishlē] *ad* dumm, töricht.

foolishness [fōō'lishnis] *n* Dummheit *f*.

foolproof [fōōl'prōōf] *a* idiotensicher.

foolscap [fōōlz'kap] *n* ≈ Kanzleipapier *nt* (*britisches Papierformat*).

foot [fōōt] *n, pl* **feet** [fēt] Fuß *m*; (*of animal*) Pfote *f*; **on** ~ zu Fuß; **to put one's** ~ **in it** ins Fettnäpfchen treten; **to put one's** ~ **down** (*AUT*) Gas geben; (*say no*) ein Machtwort sprechen; **to find one's feet** sich eingewöhnen ♦ *vt* (*bill*) bezahlen.

footage [fōōt'ij] *n* (*CINE*) Filmmaterial *nt*.

foot-and-mouth (disease) [fōōt'ənmouth' (dizēz')] *n* Maul- und Klauenseuche *f*.

football [fōōt'bôl] *n* Fußball *m*.

footballer [fōōt'bôlûr] *n* (*Brit*) Fußballer *m*.

football game, (*Brit*) **football match** *n* Fußballspiel *nt*.

football player *n* Fußball(spiel)er *m*; (*US*) Footballer *m*.

footbrake [fōōt'brāk] *n* Fußbremse *f*.

footbridge [fōōt'brij] *n* Fußgängerbrücke *f*.

foothills [fōōt'hilz] *npl* Ausläufer *pl*.

foothold [fōōt'hōld] *n* Halt *m*.

footing [fōōt'ing] *n* (*lit*) Halt *m*; (*fig*) Verhältnis *nt*; **to get a** ~ **in society** in der Gesellschaft Fuß fassen; **to be on a good** ~ **with sb** mit jdm auf gutem Fuß stehen.

footlight [fōōt'līt] *n* Rampenlicht *nt*.

footman [fōōt'mən] *n, pl* **-men** Bediente(r)

m.

footnote [fŏŏt'nōt] *n* Fußnote *f.*
footpath [fŏŏt'path] *n* Fußweg *m.*
footprint [fŏŏt'print] *n* Fußabdruck *m;* ~s Fußspuren *pl.*
footrest [fŏŏt'rest] *n* Fußstütze *f.*
footsore [fŏŏt'sôr] *a* fußkrank.
footstep [fŏŏt'step] *n* Schritt *m;* **in his father's** ~s in den Fußstapfen seines Vaters.
footwear [fŏŏt'weûr] *n* Schuhzeug *nt.*
for [fôr] *prep* für; **the train** ~ **Chicago** der Zug nach Chicago; **is this** ~ **me?** ist das für mich?; **it's time** ~ **lunch** es ist Zeit zum Mittagessen; **I'll be away** ~ **3 weeks** ich werde 3 Wochen weg sein; **what** ~? wofür?, wozu?; **what's this button** ~? wofür ist dieser Knopf?; **there's nothing** ~ **it but to jump** (*Brit*) da gibt's nur eins — springen; **the campaign** ~ ... die Kampagne für ...; ~ **all that** (*in spite of*) trotz allem ♦ *cj* denn.
FOR *abbr* = **free on rail.**
forage [fôr'ij] *n* (Vieh)futter *nt* ♦ *vi* nach Nahrung suchen.
foray [fôr'ā] *n* Raubzug *m.*
forbade [fûrbād'] *pt of* **forbid.**
forbearing [fôrbär'ing] *a* geduldig.
forbid [fûrbid'] *vt irreg* verbieten; **to** ~ **sb to do sth** jdm verbieten, etw zu tun.
forbidden [fûrbid'ən] *pp of* **forbid** ♦ *a* verboten.
forbidding [fûrbid'ing] *a* einschüchternd, abschreckend.
force [fôrs] *n* (*physical strength, power*) Kraft *f;* (*of blow, impact*) Wucht *f;* (*compulsion*) Zwang *m;* **a** ~ **5 wind** Windstärke 5; **sales** ~ (*COMM*) Verkäufer- *or* Absatzstab *m;* **to join** ~s sich zusammentun; **in** ~ (*rule*) gültig; (*group*) in großer Stärke; **the F**~**s** (*Brit*) die Armee ♦ *vt* zwingen; (*lock*) aufbrechen; (*plant*) hochzüchten; (*smile, confession*) erzwingen; **to** ~ **sb to do sth** jdn zwingen, etw zu tun.
force back *vt* (*crowd, enemy*) zurückdrängen; (*tears*) unterdrücken.
force down *vt* (*food*) runterwürgen.
forced [fôrst] *a* (*smile*) gezwungen; (*landing*) Not-.
force-feed [fôrs'fēd] *vt* zwangsernähren.
forceful [fôrs'fəl] *a* (*speech*) kraftvoll; (*personality*) resolut.
forceps [fôr'səps] *npl* Zange *f.*
forcible [fôr'səbəl] *a* (*convincing*) wirksam, überzeugend; (*violent*) gewaltsam.
forcibly [fôr'səblē] *ad* unter Zwang, zwangsweise.
ford [fôrd] *n* Furt *f* ♦ *vt* durchwaten.
fore [fôr] *a* vorder, Vorder- ♦ *n:* **to the** ~ in den Vordergrund ♦ *interj* (*GOLF*) Achtung!
forearm [fôr'ârm] *n* Unterarm *m.*
forebear [fôr'beûr] *n* Vorfahr(in *f*) *m,* Ahn(e *f*) *m.*
foreboding [fôrbō'ding] *n* Vorahnung *f.*
forecast [fôr'kast] *n* Vorhersage *f;* (*weather* ~) Wettervorhersage *f,* Wetterbericht *m* ♦ *vt*

irreg voraussagen.
foreclose [fôrklōz'] *vt* (*JUR: also:* ~ **on**) kündigen.
foreclosure [fôrklō'zhûr] *n* Zwangsvollstreckung *f.*
forecourt [fôr'kôrt] *n* (*of gas station*) Vorplatz *m;* (*SPORT*) Vorfeld *nt.*
forefathers [fôr'fàthûrz] *npl* Vorfahren *pl.*
forefinger [fôr'finggûr] *n* Zeigefinger *m.*
forefront [fôr'frunt] *n* Spitze *f.*
forego, forgo [fôrgō'] *vt irreg* verzichten auf (+*acc*).
foregoing [fôrgō'ing] *a* vorangehend.
foregone [fôrgôn'] *pp of* **forego** ♦ *a:* **a** ~ **conclusion** eine ausgemachte Sache.
foreground [fôr'ground] *n* Vordergrund *m* ♦ *cpd* (*COMPUT*) Vordergrund-.
forehand [fôr'hand] *n* (*TENNIS*) Vorhand *f.*
forehead [fôr'hed] *n* Stirn *f.*
foreign [fôr'in] *a* Auslands-; (*country, accent*) ausländisch; (*trade*) Außen-; (*body*) Fremd-.
foreign currency *n* Devisen *pl.*
foreigner [fôr'ənûr] *n* Ausländer(in *f*) *m.*
foreign exchange *n* Devisen *pl;* (*system*) Devisenkurs *m.*
foreign investment *n* Auslandsinvestition *f.*
Foreign Office *n* (*Brit*) Außenministerium *nt.*
foreign secretary *n* (*Brit*) Außenminister *m.*
foreleg [fôr'leg] *n* Vorderbein *nt.*
foreman [fôr'mən] *n, pl* **-men** Vorarbeiter *m;* (*of jury*) Obmann *m.*
foremost [fôr'mōst] *a* erste(r, s) ♦ *ad:* **first and** ~ zunächst, vor allem.
forename [fôr'nām] *n* Vorname *m.*
forensic [fərən'sik] *a* gerichtsmedizinisch; ~ **scientist** Gerichtsmediziner(in *f*) *m.*
forerunner [fôr'runûr] *n* Vorläufer *m.*
foresaw [fôrsô'] *pt of* **foresee.**
foresee [fôrsē'] *vt irreg* vorhersehen.
foreseeable [fôrsē'əbəl] *a* absehbar.
foreseen [fôrsēn'] *pp of* **foresee.**
foreshadow [fôrshad'ō] *vt* andeuten.
foreshore [fôr'shôr] *n* Küste *f,* Küstenland *nt.*
foreshorten [fôrshôr'tən] *vt* (*figure, scene*) verkürzen, perspektivisch darstellen.
foresight [fôr'sīt] *n* Voraussicht *f.*
foreskin [fôr'skin] *n* (*ANAT*) Vorhaut *f.*
forest [fôr'ist] *n* Wald *m.*
forestall [fôrstôl'] *vt* zuvorkommen (+*dat*).
forestry [fôr'istrē] *n* Forstwirtschaft *f.*
foretaste [fôr'tāst] *n* Vorgeschmack *m.*
foretell [fôrtel'] *vt irreg* vorhersagen.
forethought [fôr'thôt] *n* Vorbedacht *m.*
foretold [fôrtōld'] *pt, pp of* **foretell.**
forever [fôrev'ûr] *ad* für immer.
forewarn [fôrwôrn'] *vt* vorher warnen.
forewent [fôrwent'] *pt of* **forego.**
foreword [fôr'wûrd] *n* Vorwort *nt.*
forfeit [fôr'fit] *n* Einbuße *f* ♦ *vt* verwirken.
forgave [fûrgāv'] *pt of* **forgive.**
forge [fôrj] *n* Schmiede *f* ♦ *vt* fälschen; (*iron*)

schmieden.
forge ahead *vi* Fortschritte machen.
forger [fôr'jûr] *n* Fälscher *m*.
forgery [fôr'jûrē] *n* Fälschung *f*.
forget [fûrget'] *vti irreg* vergessen.
forgetful [fûrget'fəl] *a* vergeßlich.
forgetfulness [fûrget'fəlnis] *n* Vergeßlichkeit *f*.
forget-me-not [fûrget'mēnât] *n* Vergißmeinnicht *nt*.
forgive [fûrgiv'] *vt irreg* verzeihen; **to ~ sb for sth/for doing sth** jdm etw verzeihen/jdm verzeihen, daß er etw getan hat.
forgiven [fûrgiv'ən] *pp of* **forgive**.
forgiveness [fûrgiv'nis] *n* Verzeihung *f*.
forgiving [fûrgiv'ing] *a* versöhnlich, nicht nachtragend.
forgo [fôrgō'] = **forego**.
forgone [fôrgôn'] *pp of* **forgo**.
forgot [fûrgât'] *pt of* **forget**.
forgotten [fûrgât'ən] *pp of* **forget**.
fork [fôrk] *n* Gabel *f*; (*in road*) Gabelung *f* ♦ *vi* (*road*) sich gabeln.
  fork out *vti* (*col: pay*) blechen.
forked [fôrkt] *a* gegabelt; (*lightning*) zickzackförmig.
forklift truck [fôrk'lift truk'] *n* Gabelstapler *m*.
forlorn [fôrlôrn'] *a* (*person*) einsam und verlassen; (*hope*) vergeblich; (*deserted: cottage*) verlassen; (*desperate: attempt*) verzweifelt.
form [fôrm] *n* Form *f*; (*type*) Art *f*; (*figure*) Gestalt *f*; (*Brit SCH*) Klasse *f*; (*bench*) (Schul)bank *f*; (*document*) Formular *nt*; **in the ~ of** in Form von; **to be in good ~** (*SPORT, fig*) gut in Form sein ♦ *vt* formen; (*be part of*) bilden; **to ~ a circle/a line** einen Kreis/eine Schlange bilden; **to ~ part of sth** Teil von etw sein.
formal [fôr'məl] *a* förmlich, formell; (*occasion*) offiziell.
formal dress *n* Gesellschaftskleidung *f*; (*evening dress*) Abendkleid *nt*.
formalities [fôrmal'itēz] *npl* Formalitäten *pl*.
formality [fôrmal'itē] *n* Förmlichkeit *f*; (*of occasion*) offizielle(r) Charakter *m*; (*matter of form*) Formalität *f*.
formalize [fôr'məlīz] *vt* (*agreement*) formell machen.
formally [fôr'məlē] *ad* (*ceremoniously*) formell; (*officially*) offiziell.
format [fôr'mat] *n* Format *nt* ♦ *vt* (*COMPUT: text*) formatieren.
formation [fôrmā'shən] *n* (*of government etc*) Bildung *f*; (*AVIAT*) Formation *f*.
formative [fôr'mətiv] *a* (*years*) formend.
format line *n* (*COMPUT*) Formatzeile *f*.
former [fôr'mûr] *a* früher, ehemalig; (*opposite of latter*) erstere(r, s); **the ~ president** der ehemalige Präsident.
formerly [fôr'mûrlē] *ad* früher.
form feed *n* (*on printer*) Papiervorschub *m*.
Formica [fôrmī'kə] *n* ® Resopal *nt* ®.

formidable [fôr'midəbəl] *a* gewaltig.
formula [fôr'myələ] *n* Formel *f*; **F~ One** (*AUT*) Formel Eins.
formulate [fôr'myəlāt] *vt* formulieren.
fornicate [fôr'nikāt] *vi* Unzucht treiben.
forsake [fôrsāk'] *vt irreg* im Stich lassen, verlassen; (*habit*) aufgeben.
forsaken [fôrsā'kən] *pp of* **forsake**.
forsook [fôrsook'] *pt of* **forsake**.
fort [fôrt] *n* Fort *nt*; **to hold the ~** (*fig*) die Stellung halten.
forte [fôr'tā] *n* Stärke *f*, starke Seite *f*.
forth [fôrth] *ad:* **and so ~** und so weiter.
forthcoming [fôrth'kum'ing] *a* kommend; (*character*) entgegenkommend.
forthright [fôrth'rīt] *a* offen, gerade heraus.
forthwith [fôrth'with'] *ad* umgehend.
fortieth [fôr'tēith] *a* vierzigste(r, s).
fortification [fôrtəfəkā'shən] *n* Befestigung *f*.
fortified wine [fôr'təfīd wīn'] *n* weinhaltige(s) Getränk *nt*.
fortify [fôr'təfī] *vt* (ver)stärken; (*protect*) befestigen.
fortitude [fôr'tətood] *n* Seelenstärke *f*, Mut *m*.
fortnight [fôrt'nīt] *n* (*Brit*) zwei Wochen *pl*, vierzehn Tage *pl*; **it's a ~ since ...** es ist vierzehn Tage her, daß ...
fortnightly [fôrt'nītlē] *a* (*Brit*) zweiwöchentlich ♦ *ad* alle vierzehn Tage.
FORTRAN [fôr'tran] *n* FORTRAN *nt*.
fortress [fôr'tris] *n* Festung *f*.
fortuitous [fôrtoo'itəs] *a* zufällig.
fortunate [fôr'chənit] *a* glücklich.
fortunately [fôr'chənitlē] *ad* glücklicherweise, zum Glück.
fortune [fôr'chən] *n* Glück *nt*; (*money*) Vermögen *nt*; **to make a ~** ein Vermögen machen.
fortuneteller [fôr'chəntelûr] *n* Wahrsager(in *f*) *m*.
forty [fôr'tē] *num* vierzig.
forum [fôr'əm] *n* Forum *nt*.
forward [fôr'wûrd] *a* (*in place*) vordere(r, s); (*movement*) Vorwärts- ♦ *ad* vorwärts ♦ *n* (*SPORT*) Stürmer *m* ♦ *vt* (*send*) schicken; (*help*) fördern; **"please ~"** „bitte nachsenden".
forward exchange *n* Devisentermingeschäft *nt*.
forward planning *n* Vorausplanung *f*.
forward rate *n* Terminkurs *m*.
forwards [fôr'wûrdz] *ad* vorwärts.
forward sales *npl* Terminverkauf *m*.
forwent [fôrwent'] *pt of* **forgo**.
fossil [fâs'əl] *n* Fossil *nt*.
fossil fuels *npl* fossile Brennstoffe *pl*.
foster [fôs'tûr] *vt* (*talent*) fördern.
foster child *n* Pflegekind *nt*.
foster mother *n* Pflegemutter *f*.
fought [fôt] *pt, pp of* **fight**.
foul [foul] *a* schmutzig; (*language*) gemein; (*weather*) schlecht ♦ *n* (*SPORT*) Foul *nt* ♦ *vt* (*mechanism*) blockieren; (*SPORT*) foulen;

(*entangle: anchor, propeller*) sich verheddern in (+*dat*).

foul play *n* (*SPORT*) Foulspiel *nt*; (*JUR*) Verbrechen *nt*.

found [found] *vt* (*establish*) gründen ♦ *pt, pp of* **find**.

foundation [foundā'shən] *n* (*act*) Gründung *f*; (*fig*) Grundlage *f*; **to lay the** ~**s** (*fig*) die Grundlagen *or* die Basis schaffen.

foundations [foundā'shənz] *npl* (*of house etc*) Fundament *nt*.

foundation stone *n* Grundstein *m*.

founder [foun'dûr] *n* Gründer(in *f*) *m* ♦ *vi* sinken.

founding [foun'ding] *a*: ~ **fathers** (*esp US*) Väter *pl*; ~ **member** Mitbegründer(in *f*) *m*.

foundry [foun'drē] *n* Gießerei *f*, Eisenhütte *f*.

fount [fount] *n* (*liter*) Quell *m*.

fountain [foun'tin] *n* (Spring)brunnen *m*.

fountain pen *n* Füllfederhalter *m*.

four [fôr] *num* vier; **on all** ~**s** auf allen vieren.

four-footed [fôr'foŏtid] *a* vierfüßig.

four-poster [fôr'pōs'tûr] *n* (*also*: ~ **bed**) Himmelbett *nt*.

foursome [fôr'səm] *n* Quartett *nt*.

fourteen [fôr'tēn'] *num* vierzehn.

fourteenth [fôr'tēnth'] *a* vierzehnte(r, s).

fourth [fôrth] *a* vierte(r, s) ♦ *n* (*AUT: also* ~ **gear**) vierte(r) Gang *m*.

four-wheel drive [fôr'hwēl drīv] *n* Vierradantrieb *m*.

fowl [foul] *n* Huhn *nt*; (*food*) Geflügel *nt*.

fox [fâks] *n* Fuchs *m*.

fox fur *n* Fuchspelz *m*.

foxglove [fâks'gluv] *n* (*BOT*) Fingerhut *m*.

fox hunting *n* Fuchsjagd *f*.

foxtrot [fâks'trât] *n* Foxtrott *m*.

foyer [foi'ûr] *n* Foyer *nt*, Vorhalle *f*.

fr. *abbr* (= *franc*) Fr.

Fr. *abbr* (*REL*: = *Father*) Pf.; (= *friar*) Bruder.

fracas [frâ'kəs] *n* Aufruhr *m*, Tumult *m*.

fraction [frak'shən] *n* (*MATH*) Bruch *m*; (*part*) Bruchteil *m*.

fractionally [frak'shənəlē] *ad* geringfügig.

fractious [frak'shəs] *a* verdrießlich.

fracture [frak'chûr] *n* (*MED*) Bruch *m* ♦ *vt* brechen.

fragile [fraj'əl] *a* zerbrechlich.

fragment [frag'mənt] *n* Bruchstück *nt*; (*MUS, LITER*) Fragment *nt*; (*small part*) Stück *nt*.

fragmentary [frag'məntärē] *a* fragmentarisch.

fragrance [frā'grəns] *n* Duft *m*.

fragrant [frā'grənt] *a* duftend.

frail [frāl] *a* schwach, gebrechlich.

frame [frām] *n* Rahmen *m*; (*body*) Gestalt *f*; (*of spectacles: also* ~**s**) Gestell *nt* ♦ *vt* rahmen; (*answer, excuse*) formulieren; **to** ~ **sb** (*col: incriminate*) jdm (etw) anhängen.

framework [frām'wûrk] *n* Rahmen *m*; (*of society*) Gefüge *nt*.

France [frans] *n* Frankreich *nt*.

franchise [fran'chīz] *n* (*aktive(s)*) Wahlrecht *nt*; (*COMM*) Konzession *f*.

frank [frangk] *a* offen ♦ *vt* (*letter*) frankieren.

Frankfurt [frangk'fûrt] *n* Frankfurt *nt*.

frankfurter [frangk'fûrtûr] *n* Saitenwürstchen *nt*.

frankincense [frang'kinsens] *n* Weihrauch *m*.

frankly [frangk'lē] *ad* offen gesagt.

frankness [frangk'nis] *n* Offenheit *f*.

frantic [fran'tik] *a* (*effort, search*) verzweifelt; (*desperate: need, desire*) übersteigert; (*person*) außer sich, außer Fassung; ~ **with worry** außer sich vor Sorge.

frantically [fran'tiklē] *ad* außer sich; verzweifelt.

fraternal [frətûr'nəl] *a* brüderlich.

fraternity [frətûr'nitē] *n* (*club*) Vereinigung *f*; (*spirit*) Brüderlichkeit *f*; (*US SCH*) Studentenverbindung *f*.

fraternization [fratûrnəzā'shən] *n* Verbrüderung *f*.

fraternize [frat'ûrnīz] *vi* fraternisieren.

fraud [frôd] *n* (*trickery*) Betrug *m*; (*trick*) Schwindel *m*, Trick *m*; (*person*) Schwindler(in *f*) *m*.

fraudulent [frô'jələnt] *a* betrügerisch.

fraught [frôt] *a* voller (*with gen*); ~ **with tension** spannungsgeladen.

fray [frā] *n* Gefecht *nt*, Kampf *m* ♦ *vti* (*cloth*) ausfransen.

FRB *n abbr* (*US*: = *Federal Reserve Board*) ≈ Bundesreserve-Amt *nt*.

freak [frēk] *n* Monstrosität *f*; (*storm etc*) Anomalie *f*; (*weird person*) Irre(r) *mf*; (*col: enthusiast*) Freak *m*; **health** ~ (*col*) Gesundheitsfanatiker(in *f*) *m* ♦ *a* (*storm, conditions*) anormal; (*animal*) monströs.

freak out *vi* (*col*) ausflippen.

freakish [frē'kish] *a* (*result, appearance*) verrückt, irre (*col*); (*weather*) verrückt, launisch.

freckle [frek'əl] *n* Sommersprosse *f*.

freckled [frek'əld] *a* sommersprossig.

free [frē] *a* frei; (*loose*) lose; (*liberal*) freigebig; **to get sth** ~ etw umsonst bekommen; **you're** ~ **to** ... es steht dir frei zu ...; **to give sb a** ~ **hand** jdm freie Hand geben; **is this seat** ~**?** ist der Platz (noch) frei?; **"admission** ~**"** „Eintritt frei"; ~ **and easy** ungezwungen; ~ **of tax** steuerfrei; ~ **on board** frei Schiff; ~ **alongside ship** frei Längsseite Schiff; ~ **on rail** frei Waggon Versandbahnhof, frei Schiene ♦ *vt* (*set* ~) befreien; (*unblock*) freimachen.

-free [frē] *suff* -frei.

freebie [frē'bē] *n* (*col*) Werbegeschenk *nt*.

freedom [frē'dəm] *n* Freiheit *f*; ~ **of association** Vereinsfreiheit *f*.

freedom fighter *n* Freiheitskämpfer *m*.

free enterprise *n* freie(s) Unternehmertum *nt*.

free-for-all [frē'fûrôl'] *n* Gerangel *nt*; (*fight*) allgemeine(s) Handgemenge *nt*.

free gift *n* Werbegeschenk *nt*.

freehold (property) [frē'hōld (prâp'ûrtē)] *n* (freie(r)) Grundbesitz *m*.

free kick *n* Freistoß *m*.

freelance [frē'lans] *a* frei; (*artist*) freischaffend; **to work** ~ freiberuflich arbeiten *or* tätig sein; (*with particular firm*) als freier Mitarbeiter tätig sein.

freely [frē'lē] *ad* frei; lose; (*generously*) reichlich; (*admit*) offen.

freemason [frē'māsən] *n* Freimaurer *m*.

freemasonry [frē'māsənrē] *n* Freimaurerei *f*.

free-range [frē'rānj] *a* (*Brit: eggs*) Land-.

free sample *n* Gratisprobe *f*.

freesia [frē'zhēə] *n* Freesie *f*.

free speech *n* Redefreiheit *f*.

freestyle [frē'stīl] *n*: ~ **wrestling** (*US*) Freistilringen *nt*.

free trade *n* Freihandel *m*.

freeway [frē'wā] *n* (*US*) Autobahn *f*.

freewheel [frē'hwēl'] *vi* im Freilauf fahren.

freewheeling [frē'hwē'ling] *a* ungesteuert, unkontrolliert.

free will *n*: **of one's own** ~ aus freien Stücken.

freeze [frēz] *irreg vi* gefrieren; (*MET*) frieren ♦ *vt* (*lit, fig*) einfrieren; (*water*) gefrieren ♦ *n* (*fig, FIN*) Stopp *m*.

freeze over *vi* (*lake, river*) zufrieren; (*windows, windshield*) vereisen.

freeze up *vi* zufrieren; (*lock, car door etc*) einfrieren.

freeze-dried [frēz'drīd'] *a* gefriergetrocknet.

freezer [frē'zûr] *n* Tiefkühltruhe *f*; (*in fridge*) Gefrierfach *nt*.

freezing [frē'zing] *a* (~ *cold*) eiskalt.

freezing point *n* Gefrierpunkt *m*.

freight [frāt] *n* (*goods*) Fracht *f*; ~ **forward** Fracht gegen Nachnahme; ~ **inward** (*Brit*) Eingangsfracht *f*.

freight car *n* (*US*) Güterwagen *m*.

freighter [frā'tûr] *n* (*NAUT*) Frachtschiff *nt*.

freight forwarder [frāt' fôr'wûrdûr] *n* (*US*) Güterspedition *f*.

freight train *n* (*US*) Güterzug *m*.

French [french] *a* französisch ♦ *n* (*language*) Französisch *nt*; **the** ~ die Franzosen *pl*.

French bean *n* (*Brit*) grüne Bohne *f*.

French Canadian *a* frankokanadisch ♦ *n* Frankokanadier(in *f*) *m*.

French dressing *n* (*COOK*) Salatsoße *f*.

French fries [french frīz] *npl* Pommes frites *pl*.

French Guiana [french gēan'ə] *n* Französisch Guayana *nt*.

Frenchman [french'mən] *n, pl* **-men** Franzose *m*.

French Riviera *n*: **the** ~ die französische Riviera.

French window *n* Verandatür *f*.

Frenchwoman [french'woomən] *n, pl* **-women** Französin *f*.

frenetic [frənet'ik] *a* frenetisch, rasend.

frenzy [fren'zē] *n* Raserei *f*, wilde Aufregung *f*.

frequency [frē'kwənsē] *n* Häufigkeit *f*; (*PHYS*) Frequenz *f*.

frequency modulation *n* Frequenzmodulation *f*.

frequent *a* [frē'kwint] häufig ♦ *vt* [frikwent'] (*regelmäßig*) besuchen.

frequently [frē'kwintlē] *ad* häufig.

fresco [fres'kō] *n* Fresko *nt*.

fresh [fresh] *a* frisch; (*new*) neu; (*cheeky*) frech; **to make a** ~ **start** einen neuen Anfang machen.

freshen [fresh'ən] *vi* (*also*: ~ **up**) (sich) auffrischen; (*person*) sich frisch machen ♦ *vt* auffrischen.

freshener [fresh'ənûr] *n* (*air* ~) Luftverbesserer *m*; **skin** ~ Hauttonikum *nt*.

fresher [fresh'ûr] *n* (*Brit UNIV*) = **freshman**.

freshly [fresh'lē] *ad* gerade.

freshman [fresh'mən] *n, pl* **-men** (*UNIV*) Erstsemester *nt*.

freshness [fresh'nis] *n* Frische *f*.

freshwater [fresh'wôtûr] *a* (*fish*) Süßwasser-.

fret [fret] *vi* sich (*dat*) Sorgen machen (*about* über + *acc*).

fretful [fret'fəl] *a* (*child*) quengelig.

Freudian [froi'dēən] *a* Freudsch *attr*, freudianisch.

Freudian slip *n* Freudsche Fehlleistung *f*.

FRG *n abbr* (= *Federal Republic of Germany*) BRD *f*.

Fri. *abbr* (= *Friday*) Fr.

friar [frī'ûr] *n* (Kloster)bruder *m*.

friction [frik'shən] *n* (*lit, fig*) Reibung *f*.

friction feed *n* (*on printer*) Reibungsvorschub *m*.

Friday [frī'dā] *n* Freitag *m*; *see also* **Tuesday.**

fridge [frij] *n* Kühlschrank *m*.

fried [frīd] *a* gebraten.

fried egg *n* Spiegelei *nt*.

friend [frend] *n* Bekannte(r) *mf*; (*more intimate*) Freund(in *f*) *m*.

friendliness [frend'lēnis] *n* Freundlichkeit *f*.

friendly [frend'lē] *a* freundlich; (*relations*) freundschaftlich.

friendly society *n* Unterstützungsverein *m* auf Gegenseitigkeit.

friendship [frend'ship] *n* Freundschaft *f*.

frieze [frēz] *n* Fries *m*.

frigate [frig'it] *n* Fregatte *f*.

fright [frīt] *n* Schrecken *m*; **you look a** ~! (*col*) du siehst verboten aus!; **to take** ~ mit der Angst zu tun bekommen.

frighten [frīt'ən] *vt* erschrecken; **to be** ~**ed** Angst haben.

frighten away, frighten off *vt* (*birds, children etc*) verscheuchen.

frightening [frīt'ning] *a* furchterregend, schreckenerregend.

frightful [frīt'fəl] *a* furchtbar.

frightfully [frīt'fəlē] *ad* (*col*) schrecklich, furchtbar; **I'm** ~ **sorry** es tut mir sehr leid.

frigid [frij'id] *a* kühl; (*woman*) frigide.

frigidity [frijid'itē] *n* Kälte *f*; Frigidität *f*.

frill [fril] *n* Rüsche *f*; **without** ~**s** (*fig*)

schlicht.

fringe [frinj] n Besatz m; (Brit: hair) Pony m; (fig) äußere(r) Rand m.

fringe benefits npl zusätzliche Leistungen pl.

fringe theater n alternative(s) (Randgruppen)theater nt.

frisk [frisk] vt durchsuchen ♦ vi umhertollen.

frisky [fris'kē] a lebendig, ausgelassen.

fritter [frit'ûr] vt: **to ~ away** vergeuden ♦ n Schmalzgebackene(s) nt mit Füllung.

frivolity [frəvâl'itē] n Leichtfertigkeit f, Frivolität f.

frivolous [friv'ələs] a leichtsinnig, frivol.

frizzy [friz'ē] a kraus.

fro [frō] see **to**.

frock [fråk] n Kleid nt.

frog [fråg] n Frosch m; **to have a ~ in one's throat** einen Frosch im Hals haben.

frogman [fråg'man] n, pl **-men** Froschmann m.

frogmarch [fråg'mârch] vt (Brit): **to ~ sb in/out** jdn herein-/herausschleppen.

frolic [frål'ik] vi ausgelassen sein.

from [frum] prep von; (place) aus; (judging by) nach; (because of) wegen (+gen); **where is he ~?** woher kommt or stammt er?; **where has he come ~?** wo ist er hergekommen?; **(as) ~ Friday** von Freitag (an); **a telephone call ~ Mr. Smith** ein Anruf von Herrn Smith; **prices range ~ $10 to $50** die Preise liegen zwischen 10 und 50 Dollar; **weak ~ hunger** schwach vor Hunger; **~ experience** aus Erfahrung; **~ beneath sth** unter etw (dat) hervor.

frond [frånd] n (of fern) Farnwedel m; (of palm) Palmwedel m.

front [frunt] n Vorderseite f; (of house, fig) Fassade f; (promenade) Strandpromenade f; (MIL, POL, MET) Front f ♦ a (forward) vordere(r, s); (tooth, wheel) Vorder-; (first) vorderste(r, s); (page) erste(r, s); (door) Eingangs-, Haus-; **in ~** vorne; **in ~ of** vor ♦ vi: **the windows ~ onto the street** die Fenster geben auf die Straße hinaus.

frontage [frun'tij] n Front f, Vorderseite f.

frontal [frun'təl] a frontal, Vorder-.

front bench n (Brit POL) vorderste or erste Reihe f (wo die führenden Politiker sitzen).

front desk n (US: in hotel, at doctor's) Rezeption f.

frontier [fruntēûr'] n Grenze f.

frontispiece [frun'tispēs] n Stirnseite f.

front room n (Brit) Vorderzimmer nt, Wohnzimmer nt.

front runner n (fig) Spitzenreiter m, Favorit m.

front-wheel drive [frunt'hwēl drīv] n Vorderradantrieb m.

frost [fróst] n Frost m ♦ vt (cake) mit Zuckerguß überziehen.

frostbite [fróst'bīt] n Erfrierung f.

frosted [fró'stid] a (glass) Milch-; (esp US: cake) glasiert, mit Zuckerguß überzogen.

frosty [fró'stē] a frostig.

froth [fróth] n Schaum m.

frothy [fróth'ē] a schaumig.

frown [froun] n Stirnrunzeln nt ♦ vi die Stirn runzeln.

frown on vt fus mißbilligen, mit Stirnrunzeln betrachten.

froze [frōz] pt of **freeze**.

frozen [frō'zən] pp of **freeze** ♦ a (food) gefroren; (river) zugefroren; (FIN: assets) festgelegt.

FRS n abbr (US: = Federal Reserve System) Bundesreservebank.

frugal [frōō'gəl] a sparsam, bescheiden.

fruit [frōōt] n (particular) Frucht f; (collective) Obst nt.

fruiterer [frōōt'ərûr] n (Brit) Obsthändler m; **~'s shop** Obsthandlung f.

fruitful [frōōt'fəl] a fruchtbar.

fruition [frōōish'ən] n Verwirklichung f; **to come to ~** in Erfüllung gehen.

fruit juice n Fruchtsaft m.

fruitless [frōōt'lis] a (fig) fruchtlos, ergebnislos.

fruit machine n (Brit) Spielautomat m.

fruit salad n Obstsalat m.

frump [frump] n: **to feel a ~** sich wie eine Vogelscheuche vorkommen.

frustrate [frus'trāt] vt vereiteln.

frustrated [frus'trātid] a gehemmt; (PSYCH) frustriert.

frustrating [frus'trāting] a (job, day) frustrierend.

frustration [frusträ'shən] n Frustration f; (of hopes, plans etc) Zerschlagung f.

fry [frī] vt braten.

frying pan [frī'ing pan] n Bratpfanne f.

FSLIC n abbr (US) = Federal Savings and Loan Insurance Corporation.

ft. abbr = **foot, feet.**

FT n abbr (Brit: = Financial Times) Zeitung.

FTC n abbr (US: = Federal Trade Commission) Verband zum Schutze der freien Marktwirtschaft.

fuchsia [fyōō'shə] n Fuchsie f.

fuck [fuk] vti (col!) ficken (!); **~ off!** (!) verpiß dich! (!).

fuddled [fud'əld] a (muddled) verwirrt, verdattert (col); (col: tipsy) beschwipst.

fuddy-duddy [fud'ēdudē] n (pej) Langweiler m.

fudge [fuj] n Karamellen pl ♦ vt aus dem Weg gehen (+dat); **to ~ the issue** einem Problem ausweichen or aus dem Weg gehen.

fuel [fyōō'əl] n Brennstoff m; (for vehicle) Kraftstoff m; (gas) Benzin nt ♦ vt (furnace etc) mit Brennstoff versorgen; (aircraft, ship etc) auftanken, betanken.

fuel oil n (diesel fuel) Heizöl nt.

fuel pump n (AUT) Benzinpumpe f.

fuel tank n Tank m.

fug [fug] n (esp. Brit: col) Mief m.

fugitive [fyōō'jətiv] n Flüchtling m; (from prison) Flüchtige(r) mf; **he is a ~ from the**

law er ist auf der Flucht vor dem Gesetz.
fulfill, (Brit) **fulfil** [fo͝ol'fil'] vt (duty) erfüllen; (promise) einhalten.
fulfilled [fo͝ol'fild'] a (person) ausgefüllt.
fulfillment, (Brit) **fulfilment** [fo͝ol'fil'mənt] n Erfüllung f; Einhaltung f.
full [fo͝ol] a (box, bottle, price) voll; (person: satisfied) satt; (member, power, employment, moon) Voll-; (complete) vollständig, Voll-; (speed) höchste(r, s); (skirt) weit; ~ **name** Vor- und Zuname m; **we are** ~ **up for July** wir sind im Juli völlig ausgebucht ♦ n: **in** ~ vollständig, ungekürzt; **to pay in** ~ den vollen Betrag bezahlen; **to write sth in** ~ etw ausschreiben.
fullback [fo͝ol'bak] n (Brit) Verteidiger m.
full-blooded [fo͝ol'blud'id] a (vigorous: attack) kräftig; (virile: male) Vollblut-.
full-cream milk [fo͝ol'krēm milk'] n (Brit) Vollmilch f.
full-fledged [fo͝ol'flejd'] a (US: lit) flügge; (: fig) vollwertig; **a** ~ **teacher** ein vollqualifizierter Lehrer.
full-grown [fo͝ol'grōn'] a ausgewachsen.
full-length [fo͝ol'lengkth'] a (portrait) lebensgroß; (film) abendfüllend.
fullness [fo͝ol'nis] n Fülle f.
full-scale [fo͝ol'skāl'] a (plan, model, search) groß angelegt; (retreat) auf der ganzen Linie.
full stop n (Brit) Punkt m.
full-time [fo͝ol'tīm] a (job) Ganztags- ♦ ad (work) hauptberuflich.
fully [fo͝ol'ē] a völlig; **it is** ~ **two hours since ...** (at least) es ist volle or gute zwei Stunden her, daß ...
fully-fledged [fo͝ol'ēflejd'] a (Brit) = **full-fledged.**
fully-paid [fo͝ol'ēpād'] a: ~ **share** voll eingezahlte Aktie f.
fulsome [fo͝ol'səm] a übertrieben.
fumble [fum'bəl] vi herumfummeln (with, at an +dat).
fume [fyo͞om] vi rauchen, qualmen; (fig) wütend sein, kochen (col).
fumes [fyo͞omz] npl (from liquids) Dämpfe pl; (of car) Abgase pl.
fumigate [fyo͞o'məgāt] vt ausräuchern.
fun [fun] n Spaß m; **it's** ~ es macht Spaß; **to make** ~ **of** sich lustig machen über (+acc).
function [fungk'shən] n Funktion f; (occasion) Veranstaltung f, Feier f ♦ vi funktionieren; **to** ~ **as** fungieren or dienen als.
functional [fungk'shənəl] a funktionell, praktisch.
function key n (COMPUT) Funktionstaste f.
fund [fund] n (money) Geldmittel pl, Fonds m; (store) Schatz m, Vorrat m.
fundamental [fundəmen'təl] a fundamental, grundlegend.
fundamentalist [fundəmen'təlist] n Fundamentalist m.
fundamentally [fundəmen'təlē] ad im Grunde.

fundamentals [fundəmen'təlz] npl Grundbegriffe pl.
fund-raising [fund'rāzing] n Spendenaktion f.
funeral [fyo͞o'nûrəl] n Beerdigung f ♦ a Beerdigungs-.
funeral director n Beerdigungsunternehmer m.
funeral home, (Brit) **funeral parlour** n Leichenhalle f.
funeral service n Trauergottesdienst m.
funereal [fyo͞onērēəl] a traurig, trübselig; (voice) Trauer-.
funfair [fun'fär] n (Brit) Jahrmarkt m.
fungus [fung'gəs] n, pl **fungi** [fun'jī] Pilz m.
funicular [fyo͞onik'yəlûr] n Seilbahn f.
funnel [fun'əl] n Trichter m; (NAUT) Schornstein m.
funnily [fun'ilē] ad komisch; ~ **enough** komischerweise.
funny [fun'ē] a komisch.
funny bone n Musikantenknochen m.
fur [fûr] n Fell nt, Pelz m.
fur coat n Pelzmantel m.
furious [fyo͞or'ēəs] a wütend; (attempt) heftig; (argument) rasend; **to be** ~ **with sb** auf jdn wütend sein.
furl [fûrl] vt (sail) aufrollen, zusammenrollen.
furlong [fûr'lông] n Achtelmeile f.
furlough [fûr'lō] n (US) Urlaub m.
furnace [fûr'nis] n (Brenn)ofen m.
furnish [fûr'nish] vt einrichten, möblieren; (supply) versehen.
furnished [fûr'nisht] a möbliert.
furnishings [fûr'nishingz] npl Einrichtung f.
furniture [fûr'nichûr] n Möbel pl.
furore [fyo͞or'ôr] n (protests) Protest(e pl) m; (enthusiasm) Furore f.
furrier [fûr'ēûr] n Kürschner(in f) m.
furrow [fûr'ō] n Furche f; (on brow) Runzel f ♦ vt (forehead) runzeln.
furry [fûr'ē] a (animal) Pelz-; (toy) Plüsch-; (Brit: tongue) belegt.
further [fûr'thûr] comp of **far** ♦ a weitere(r, s) ♦ ad weiter; **how much** ~ **is it?** wie weit ist es noch?; ~ **to your letter of ...** (Brit COMM) bezugnehmend auf Ihr Schreiben vom ... ♦ vt fördern.
further education n (Brit) Weiterbildung f, Fortbildung f.
furthermore [fûr'thûrmôr] ad ferner.
furthermost [fûr'thûrmōst] a äußerste(r, s).
furthest [fûr'thist] superl of **far.**
furtive [fûr'tiv] a, **furtively** ad [fûr'tivlē] verstohlen.
fury [fyo͞or'ē] n Wut f, Zorn m.
fuse [fyo͞oz] n (ELEC) Sicherung f; (Brit: of bomb) Zunder m ♦ vt verschmelzen ♦ vi (ELEC) durchbrennen.
fuse box n Sicherungskasten m.
fuselage [fyo͞o'sələzh] n Flugzeugrumpf m.
fuse wire n Schmelzdraht m.
fusillade [fyo͞os'əlād] n (fig also) Salve f.
fusion [fyo͞o'zhən] n Verschmelzung f.
fuss [fus] n Theater nt ♦ vi sich unnötig aufre-

gen ♦ *vt* (*person*) nervös machen.

fuss over *vt fus* (*person*) bemuttern; (*guests*) sich (*dat*) große Umstände machen mit.

fussy [fus'ē] *a* (*difficult*) heikel; (*attentive to detail*) kleinlich; **I'm not** ~ (*col*) es ist mir egal.

futile [fyōō'təl] *a* zwecklos, sinnlos.

futility [fyōōtil'ətē] *n* Zwecklosigkeit *f*.

future [fyōō'chûr] *a* zukünftig ♦ *n* Zukunft *f*; **in (the)** ~ in Zukunft, zukünftig.

futures [fyōō'chûrz] *npl* (*COMM*) Termingeschäfte *pl*.

futuristic [fyōō'chəristik] *a* futuristisch.

fuze [fyōōz] (*US*) *n* (*of bomb*) Zünder *m* ♦ *vt*, *vi* = **fuse.**

fuzzy [fuz'ē] *a* (*indistinct*) verschwommen; (*hair*) kraus.

fwd. *abbr* = **forward.**

fwy *abbr* (*US*) = **freeway.**

FY *abbr* = **fiscal year.**

G

G, g [jē] *n* (*letter*) G *nt*, g *nt*; **G for George** ≈ G wie Gustav.

g *abbr* (= *gram(s)*; *gravity*) g.

G [jē] *n abbr* (*US CINE*: = *general (audience)*) jugendfrei; (*Brit SCH*: = *good*) gut.

GA *abbr* (*US MAIL*) = Georgia.

gab [gab] *n*: **to have the gift of the** ~ (*col*: *talk a lot*) wie ein Wasserfall reden; (: *be persuasive*) nicht auf den Mund gefallen sein.

gabardine [gab'ûrdēn] *n* Gabardine *m*.

gabble [gab'əl] *vi* plappern.

gable [gā'bəl] *n* Giebel *m*.

Gabon [gābán'] *n* Gabun *nt*.

gad about [gad əbout'] *vi* (*col*) herumziehen.

gadget [gaj'it] *n* Gerät *nt*.

gadgetry [gaj'itrē] *n* Vorrichtungen *pl*.

Gaelic [gā'lik] *a* gälisch ♦ *n* (*language*) Gälisch *nt*.

gaffe [gaf] *n* Fauxpas *m*, Entgleisung *f*; (*verbal*) taktlose Bemerkung *f*.

gag [gag] *n* Knebel *m*; (*THEAT*) Gag *m* ♦ *vt* knebeln.

gaga [gâ'gâ] *a*: **to go** ~ (*col*) ausflippen, überschnappen; (*old person*) verkalken.

gage [gāj] (*US*) *n*, *vt* = **gauge.**

gaiety [gā'ətē] *n* Fröhlichkeit *f*.

gaily [gā'lē] *ad* lustig, fröhlich.

gain [gān] *vt* (*obtain*) erhalten; (*reach*: *shore*) erreichen; (*win*) gewinnen; **to** ~ **ground** aufholen; **she has** ~**ed weight** sie hat zugenommen ♦ *vi* (*improve*) gewinnen (*in* an +*dat*); (*make progress*) Vorsprung

gewinnen; (*clock*) vorgehen ♦ *n* Gewinn *m*.

gain (up)on *vt fus* den Vorsprung zu ... vergrößern; (*close gap*) einholen.

gainful [gān'fəl] *a*: ~ **employment** Erwerbstätigkeit *f*.

gala [gā'lə] *n* Fest *nt*; **swimming** ~ große(s) Schwimmfest *nt*.

Galapagos Islands [gəlâ'pəgōs ī'ləndz] *npl* Galapagosinseln *pl*.

galaxy [gal'əksē] *n* Sternsystem *nt*.

gale [gāl] *n* Sturm *m*; ~ **force 10** Windstärke 10.

gal(l). *abbr* = **gallon(s).**

gall [gôl] *n* (*ANAT*) Galle(nsaft *m*) *f*; (*fig*: *impudence*) Frechheit *f* ♦ *vt* (*fig*) maßlos ärgern.

gallant [gal'ənt] *a* tapfer, ritterlich; [gəlânt'] (*polite*) galant.

gallantry [gal'əntrē] *n* (*compliment*) Galanterie *f*; (*bravery*) Tapferkeit *f*; (*chivalry*) Edelmut *m*.

gallbladder [gôl'bladûr] *n* Gallenblase *f*.

galleon [gal'ēən] *n* Galeone *f*.

gallery [gal'ûrē] *n* Galerie *f*; (*for spectators*) Empore *f*; (*in theater*) oberste(r) Rang *m*, Balkon *m*; (*art* ~: *government owned*) staatliche(s) Kunstmuseum *nt*; (: *private*) Privatgalerie *f*.

galley [gal'ē] *n* (*ship's kitchen*) Kombüse *f*; (*ship*) Galeere *f*.

galley proof *n* (*TYP*) Fahne(nabzug *m*) *f*.

Gallic [gal'ik] *a* gallisch.

gallon [gal'ən] *n* Gallone *f*.

gallop [gal'əp] *n* Galopp *m* ♦ *vi* galoppieren.

galloping [gal'əping] *a*: ~ **inflation** galoppierende Inflation *f*.

gallows [gal'ōz] *n* Galgen *m*.

gallstone [gôl'stōn] *n* Gallenstein *m*.

galore [gəlôr'] *ad* in Hülle und Fülle.

galvanize [gal'vənīz] *vt* galvanisieren; **to** ~ **sb into action** (*fig*) jdn plötzlich aktiv werden lassen.

Gambia [gam'bēə] *n* Gambia *nt*.

gamble [gam'bəl] *vi* (*um Geld*) spielen; **to** ~ **on the stock exchange** an der Börse spekulieren ♦ *vt* (*risk*) aufs Spiel setzen ♦ *n* Risiko *nt*.

gambler [gam'blûr] *n* Spieler(in *f*) *m*.

gambling [gam'bling] *n* Glücksspiel *nt*.

gambol [gam'bəl] *vi* herumtollen, herumspringen.

game [gām] *n* Spiel *nt*; (*hunting*) Wild *nt*; ~**s** (*SCH*) Sport *m* ♦ *a* bereit (*for* zu); (*brave*) mutig.

game bird *n* Federwild *nt*.

gamekeeper [gām'kēpûr] *n* Wildhüter *m*.

gamely [gām'lē] *ad* beherzt.

game reserve *n* Wildschutzgebiet *nt*.

gamesmanship [gāmz'mənship] *n* Täuschungsmanöver *nt*.

gammon [gam'ən] *n* Schinken *m*.

gamut [gam'ət] *n*: **to run the (whole)** ~ **of emotions** die ganze Skala der Gefühle durchlaufen.

gander [gan'dûr] *n* Gänserich *m*.
gang [gang] *n* Schar *f*; (*of criminals, youths*) Bande *f*; (*of workmen*) Kolonne *f*.
Ganges [gan'jēz] *n* Ganges *m*.
gangling [gang'gling] *a* schlaksig, hochaufgeschossen.
gangplank [gang'plangk] *n* Laufplanke *f*, Landungssteg *m*.
gangrene [gang'grēn] *n* Brand *m*.
gangster [gang'stûr] *n* Gangster *m*.
gangway [gang'wā] *n* (*NAUT*) Laufplanke *f*.
gantry [gan'trē] *n* (*for crane*) Portal *nt*; (*for rocket*) Abschußrampe *f*; (*for railroad signal*) Signalbrücke *f*.
GAO *n abbr* (*US*: = *General Accounting Office*) Regierungsabteilung.
gaol [jāl] *n* (*Brit*) = **jail.**
gap [gap] *n* (*hole*) Lücke *f*; (*space*) Zwischenraum *m*.
gape [gāp] *vi* glotzen.
gaping [gā'ping] *a* (*wound*) klaffend; (*hole*) gähnend.
garage [gərâzh'] *n* Garage *f*; (*for repair*) (Auto)reparaturwerkstatt *f*; (*Brit: gas station*) Tankstelle *f* ♦ *vt* einstellen.
garb [gârb] *n* Gewand *nt*; (*col*) Kluft *f*.
garbage [gâr'bij] *n* (*esp US*) Abfall *m*; (*fig: film, book*) Schund *m*, Mist *m*; (*nonsense*) Blödsinn *m*, Quatsch *m*.
garbage bag *n* (*US*) Müllbeutel *m*.
garbage can *n* (*US*) Müll- *or* Abfalleimer *m*.
garbage disposal (unit) *n* Müllschlucker *m*.
garbage dump *n* (*US*) Müllablageplatz *m*.
garbage man *n* (*US*) Müllmann *m*.
garbage truck *n* (*US*) Müllwagen *m*.
garbled [gâr'bəld] *a* (*story*) verdreht.
garden [gâr'dən] *n* Garten *m*; ~**s** *pl* (*public*) Park *m*; (*private*) Gartenanlagen *pl* ♦ *vi* gärtnern.
garden center *n* Gartencenter *nt*.
gardener [gârd'nûr] *n* Gärtner(in *f*) *m*.
gardening [gâr'dəning] *n* Gärtnern *nt*.
garden party *n* Gartenfest *nt*.
gargle [gâr'gəl] *vi* gurgeln ♦ *n* Gurgelmittel *nt*.
gargoyle [gâr'goil] *n* Wasserspeier *m*.
garish [gär'ish] *a* grell.
garland [gâr'lənd] *n* Girlande *f*.
garlic [gâr'lik] *n* Knoblauch *m*.
garment [gâr'mənt] *n* Kleidungsstück *nt*.
garner [gâr'nûr] *vt* (an)sammeln.
garnish [gâr'nish] *vt* (*food*) garnieren ♦ *n* Garnierung *f*.
garret [gar'it] *n* Dachkammer *f*, Mansarde *f*.
garrison [gar'isən] *n* Garnison *f* ♦ *vt* besetzen.
garrulous [gar'ələs] *a* geschwätzig.
garter [gâr'tûr] *n* Strumpfband *nt*; (*US: for stocking*) Strumpfhalter *m*.
garter belt *n* (*US*) Strumpfgurtel *m*.
gas [gas] *n* Gas *nt*; (*MED*) Lachgas *nt*; (*esp US*: *gasoline*) Benzin *nt*; **Calor** ~ ® (*Brit*) Butangas *nt*; **to step on the** ~ Gas geben ♦ *vt* vergasen.

gas can *n* (*US*) Benzinkanister *m*.
gas chamber *n* Gaskammer *f*.
Gascony [gas'kənē] *n* Gascogne *f*.
gas cylinder *n* Gasflasche *f*.
gaseous [gas'ēəs] *a* gasförmig.
gash [gash] *n* klaffende Wunde *f* ♦ *vt* tief verwunden.
gasket [gas'kit] *n* Dichtungsring *m*.
gas mask *n* Gasmaske *f*.
gas meter *n* Gaszähler *m*.
gasoline [gasəlēn'] *n* (*US*) Benzin *nt*.
gasp [gasp] *vi* keuchen; (*in astonishment*) nach Luft schnappen (*col*); **to** ~ **for breath** nach Atem ringen ♦ *n* Keuchen *nt*.
gas pedal *n* (*US*) Gas(pedal) *nt*.
gas-permeable [gaspûr'mēəbəl] *a* luftdurchlässig.
gas pump *n* (*US*) Zapfsäule *f*.
gas ring *n* Gasring *m*.
gas station *n* (*US*) Tankstelle *f*.
gas stove *n* Gaskocher *m*.
gassy [gas'ē] *a* (*drink*) sprudelnd.
gas tank *n* (*US AUT*) Benzintank *m*.
gas tap *n* Gashahn *m*.
gastric [gas'trik] *a* Magen-.
gastric ulcer *n* Magengeschwür *nt*.
gastroenteritis [gastrōentərī'tis] *n* Magen- und Darmentzündung *f*.
gastronomy [gastrân'əmē] *n* Kochkunst *f*.
gasworks [gas'wûrks] *n sing or npl* Gaswerk *nt*.
gate [gāt] *n* Tor *nt*; (*barrier, at grade crossing*) Schranke *f*; (*at airport*) Flugsteig *m*.
gâteau [gatō'] *n, pl* **-x** Torte *f*.
gate-crash [gāt'krash] *vt* (*party*) platzen in (+*acc*).
gate-crasher [gāt'krashûr] *n* Eindringling *m*.
gateway [gāt'wā] *n* Toreingang *m*.
gather [gaⁿ'ûr] *vt* (*people*) versammeln; (*collect: things*) sammeln; **to** ~ **(from)** schließen (aus); **as far as I can** ~ (so) wie ich das sehe; **to** ~ **(that ...)** annehmen, (daß ...) ♦ *vi* (*assemble*) sich versammeln; (*dust, objects*) sich (an)sammeln; (*clouds*) sich zusammenziehen.
gathering [gaⁿ'ûring] *n* Versammlung *f*.
GATT [gat] *n abbr* (= *General Agreement on Tariffs and Trade*) Allgemeines Zoll- und Handelsabkommen.
gauche [gōsh] *a* linkisch.
gaudy [gô'dē] *a* knallig (*col*).
gauge [gāj] *n* (*instrument*) Meßgerät *nt*; (*RAIL*) Spurweite *f*; (*dial*) Anzeiger *m*; (*fig*) Maßstab *m*; **gas** ~ Benzinuhr *f* ♦ *vt* (*lit*) (ab)messen; (*fig*) abschatzen; (: *sb's capabilities, character*) beurteilen; **to** ~ **the right moment** den richtigen Moment abwägen.
Gaul [gôl] *n* (*country*) Gallien *nt*; (*person*) Gallier(in *f*) *m*.
gaunt [gônt] *a* hager.
gauntlet [gônt'lit] *n* (*knight's*) Fehdehandschuh *m*; (*glove*) (Stulpen)handschuh *m*; **to throw down the** ~ den Fehdehandschuh

hinwerfen.

gauze [gôz] n Mull m, Gaze f.

gave [gāv] pt of **give**.

gawk [gôk] vi dumm (an)glotzen (at acc).

gawky [gôˈkē] a schlaksig, staksig; (appearance) unbeholfen.

gay [gā] a lustig; (colored) bunt; (homosexual) schwul.

gaze [gāz] n Blick m ♦ vi (an)blicken (at acc).

gazelle [gəzelˈ] n Gazelle f.

gazette [gəzetˈ] n (newspaper) Zeitung f; (official publication) Amtsblatt nt.

gazetteer [gazitērˈ] n geographische(s) Lexikon nt.

GB abbr (= Great Britain) GB.

GCE n abbr (Brit: = General Certificate of Education) Schulabschluß.

GCSE n abbr (Brit: = General Certificate of Secondary Education) Schulabschluß.

Gdns. abbr (Brit: in address) = Gardens.

GDP n abbr = **gross domestic product.**

GDR n abbr (= German Democratic Republic) DDR f.

gear [gēr] n Getriebe nt; (equipment) Ausrüstung f; (AUT) Gang m; **to be out of/in** ~ aus-/eingekuppelt sein ♦ vt (fig: adapt) abstellen (to auf +acc); **our service is ~ed to meet the needs of the disabled** unsere Leistungen sind auf die Bedürfnisse der Behinderten abgestellt.

  gear up vi: **to** ~ **up to** sich einstellen auf.

gearbox [gērˈbâks] n (esp Brit) Getriebe(gehäuse) nt.

gearlever [gērˈlevûr] n (Brit) Schalthebel m.

gearshift [gērˈshift] n Schalthebel m.

GED n abbr (US) = general educational development.

geese [gēs] npl of **goose.**

Geiger counter [gīˈgûr kounˈtûr] n Geigerzähler m.

gel [jel] n Gel nt; (for hair) Haarfestiger m.

gelatin(e) [jelˈətin] n Gelatine f.

gelignite [jelˈignīt] n Plastiksprengstoff m.

gem [jem] n Edelstein m; (fig) Juwel nt.

Gemini [jemˈənī] n Zwillinge pl.

gen [jen] n (Brit col: information) Informationen pl (on über +acc); **to give sb the** ~ **on sth** jdn über etw (acc) informieren.

gen. abbr (= general; generally) allg.

Gen. abbr (MIL: = General) Gen.

gender [jenˈdûr] n (GRAM) Geschlecht nt.

gene [jēn] n (BIOL) Gen nt, Erbfaktor m.

genealogy [jēnēalˈəjē] n Genealogie f, Stammbaumforschung f; (ancestry) Stammbaum m.

general [jenˈûrəl] n General m ♦ a allgemein; **the** ~ **public** die breite Öffentlichkeit; ~ **audit** Jahresabschlußprüfung f.

general anesthetic n Vollnarkose f.

general delivery n (US): **to send sth** ~ etw postlagernd schicken.

general election n allgemeine Wahlen pl.

generalization [jenûrələzāˈshən] n Verallge-

meinerung f.

generalize [jenˈûrəlīz] vi verallgemeinern.

generally [jenˈûrəlē] ad allgemein, im allgemeinen.

general manager n Generaldirektor m.

general practitioner n praktische(r) Arzt m.

general strike n Generalstreik m.

generate [jenˈərāt] vt erzeugen.

generation [jenərāˈshən] n Generation f; (of electricity etc) Erzeugung f; **first/second/third/fourth** ~ **computer** Computer m der ersten/zweiten/dritten/vierten Generation.

generator [jenˈərātûr] n Generator m.

generic [jənärˈik] a artmäßig; (BIOL) Gattungs-.

generosity [jenərâsˈətē] n Großzügigkeit f.

generous [jenˈûrəs] a, **generously** [jenˈûrəslē] ad (noble-minded) hochherzig; (giving freely) großzügig.

genesis [jenˈəsis] n Entstehung f, Genese f; **(the book of) G**~ die Schöpfungsgeschichte f.

genetic [jinetˈik] a genetisch.

genetic engineering n Gentechnologie f.

genetics [jənetˈiks] n sing Genetik f.

Geneva [jənēˈvə] n Genf nt.

genial [jēˈnēəl] a freundlich, jovial.

genitals [jenˈitəlz] npl Geschlechtsteile pl, Genitalien pl.

genitive [jenˈətiv] n Genitiv m, Wesfall m.

genius [jēnˈyəs] n Genie nt.

Genoa [jenˈəwə] n Genua nt.

genocide [jenˈəsīd] n Völkermord m.

Genoese [jenōēzˈ] a genuesich ♦ n Genueser(in f) m.

genteel [jentēlˈ] a vornehm; (affected) geziert.

gentile [jenˈtīl] n Nichtjude m.

gentle [jenˈtəl] a sanft, zart.

gentleman [jenˈtəlmən] n, pl **-men** Herr m; (polite) Gentleman m; ~**'s agreement** Gentleman's Agreement nt.

gentlemanly [jenˈtəlmənlē] a zuvorkommend, gentlemanlike pred.

gentleness [jenˈtəlnis] n Zartheit f, Milde f.

gently [jenˈtlē] ad zart, sanft.

gentrification [jentrifikāˈshən] n Veränderung eines Stadtviertels durch Zuzug von Angehörigen der Mittelklasse.

gentry [jenˈtrē] npl Gentry f (niederer Adel und Stände).

genuine [jenˈyōōin] a echt, wahr.

genuinely [jenˈyōōinlē] ad wirklich, echt.

geographer [jēâgˈrəfûr] n Geograph(in f) m.

geographical [jēəgrafˈikəl] a geographisch.

geography [jēâgˈrəfē] n (SCH) Geographie f, Erdkunde f; (topography) Geographie f.

geological [jēəläjˈikəl] a geologisch.

geologist [jēâlˈəjist] n Geologe m, Geologin f.

geology [jēâlˈəjē] n Geologie f.

geometric(al) [jēəmetˈrik(əl)] a geometrisch.

geometry [jēâmˈətrē] n Geometrie f.

geranium [jərāˈnēəm] n Geranie f.

geriatric [järēat'rik] a geriatrisch, Greisen- ♦ n Greis(in f) m.

germ [jûrm] n Keim m; (MED) Bazillus m.

German [jûr'mən] a deutsch ♦ n (person) Deutsche(r) mf; (language) Deutsch nt.

German Democratic Republic n Deutsche Demokratische Republik f.

German shepherd (dog) n (US) Schäferhund m.

Germany [jûr'mənē] n Deutschland nt; **East/ West** ~ Ost-/West-Deutschland nt.

germination [jûrmənā'shən] n Keimen nt.

germ warfare n biologische Kriegsführung f.

gesticulate [jestik'yəlāt] vi gestikulieren.

gesticulation [jestikyəlā'shən] n Gesten pl, Gestikulieren nt.

gesture [jes'chûr] n Geste f; **as a ~ of friendship** als Zeichen der Freundschaft.

get [get] irreg vi (become, be) werden; (go) (an)kommen, gehen; **to ~ used to sth** sich an etw gewöhnen; **let's ~ going** or **started** laß uns anfangen; **you've got to tell the police** Sie müssen es der Polizei melden ♦ vt (receive, catch) bekommen, kriegen; (obtain: results etc) erhalten; (fetch) holen; (take, move) bringen; (understand) kapieren (col); (col: annoy) ärgern, aufregen; (: thrill) packen; **to ~ sb to do sth** jdn dazu bringen, etw zu tun; **to ~ sth done** (do) etw gemacht kriegen (col); (cause to be done) etw machen lassen; **to ~ sth/sb ready** etw/jdn fertigmachen; **to ~ one's hair cut** sich die Haare schneiden lassen; **the discussion got us nowhere** die Diskussion brachte uns nicht weiter; **can I ~ you a drink?** kann ich Ihnen etwas zu trinken holen?; **~ me Mr. Jones, please** (TEL) verbinden Sie mich bitte mit Mr. Jones.

get about vi herumkommen; (news) sich verbreiten.

get across vi: **to ~ across to** (message, meaning) klarwerden, verständlich werden (+dat); (subj: speaker) ankommen bei.

get along vi (people) (gut) zurechtkommen; (depart) sich (acc) auf den Weg machen; **how are you ~ting along?** wie geht's?, wie kommen Sie zurecht?

get around vt herumkommen; (person) herumkriegen.

get around to vt fus: **to ~ around to doing sth** dazu kommen, etw zu tun.

get at vt fus (facts) herausbekommen; **to ~ at sb** (nag) an jdm herumnörgeln; **what are you ~ting at?** worauf wollen Sie hinaus?

get away vi (leave) sich (acc) davonmachen; (escape) entkommen (from dat).

get away with vt fus: **to ~ away with sth** mit etw davonkommen.

get back vi (return) zurückkommen ♦ vt (possessions) zurückbekommen.

get back at vt fus: **to ~ back at sb for sth** (col) jdm etw heimzahlen.

get by vi (move past) vorbeikommen (an

+dat); **I can ~ by in Dutch** ich kann mich auf Holländisch verständlich machen.

get down vi (her)untergehen ♦ vt (depress) fertigmachen.

get down to vt fus: **to ~ down to business** zur Sache kommen.

get in vi (train) ankommen ♦ vt (arrive home) heimkommen; (bring in: harvest) einbringen; (: coal, shopping) hereinholen; (insert) hineinbringen or -kriegen; **= get into**.

get into vt fus (vehicle) einsteigen in (+acc).

get off vi (from train etc) aussteigen; (from horse) absteigen ♦ vt: **to ~ sth off to a good start** (fig) einer Sache zu einem guten Start verhelfen ♦ vt fus aussteigen aus; absteigen von.

get on vi (progress) vorankommen; (be friends) auskommen; (age) alt werden; **how are you ~ting on?** wie geht's?, wie kommen Sie zurecht? ♦ vt fus (train etc) einsteigen in (+acc); (horse) aufsteigen auf (+acc).

get on to vt fus (deal with) übergehen zu; (Brit col: contact) sich in Verbindung setzen mit.

get out vi (of house) herauskommen; (of vehicle) aussteigen; (news etc) herauskommen ♦ vt (take out) herausholen; (money from bank etc) abheben (of von).

get out of vt fus (vehicle etc) aussteigen aus; (extract: confession, words) herausbekommen or -kriegen; (gain from: pleasure, benefit) haben an (+dat); (duty etc) herumkommen um.

get over vt fus (illness) sich (acc) erholen von; (surprise) verkraften; (news) fassen; (loss) sich abfinden mit; **I couldn't ~ over her** ich konnte sie nicht vergessen ♦ vt (communicate: idea etc) verständlich machen; **let's ~ it over (with)** bringen wir's hinter uns.

get round vt (Brit) = **get around**.

get through vi (also TEL) durchkommen ♦ vt fus (finish: work) fertigmachen, erledigen; (: book) auslesen.

get together vi zusammenkommen ♦ vt zusammenbringen; **to ~ it together** (col) bringen.

get up vi aufstehen ♦ vt: **to ~ up enthusiasm for sth** Begeisterung für etw aufbringen; **to ~ sb up** (out of bed) jdn aus dem Bett holen.

get up to vt fus (reach) erreichen; (prank etc) anstellen.

getaway [get'əwā] n Flucht f.

getaway car n Fluchtauto nt.

get-together [get'təgeᵗhûr] n Treffen nt; (party) Party f.

get-up [get'up] n (col: outfit) Aufzug m, Aufmachung f.

get-well card [getwel' kârd] n Karte f mit Wünschen zur baldigen Genesung.

geyser [gī'zûr] *n* Geiser *m*.

Ghana [gân'ə] *n* Ghana *nt*.

Ghanaian [gənā'ēən] *a* ghanaisch ♦ *n* Ghanaer(in *f*) *m*.

ghastly [gast'lē] *a* (*horrible*) gräßlich; (*pale*) totenbleich.

gherkin [gûr'kin] *n* Gewürzgurke *f*.

ghetto [get'ō] *n* G(h)etto *nt*.

ghetto blaster [get'ō blast'ûr] *n* (*col*) Ghettoblaster *m*.

ghost [gōst] *n* Gespenst *nt*, Geist *m* ♦ *vt*: **to ~ sb's books** für jdn Bücher (als Ghostwriter) schreiben.

ghostly [gōst'lē] *a* gespenstisch.

ghost story *n* Gespenstergeschichte *f*.

ghostwriter [gōst'rītûr] *n* Ghostwriter *m*.

ghoul [gōōl] *n* (*fig*) Mensch *m* mit schaurigen Gelüsten.

GHQ *n abbr* (*MIL*: = *general headquarters*) Hauptquartier *nt*.

GI *n abbr* (*US col*: = *government issue*) GI *m*.

giant [jī'ənt] *n* Riese *m* ♦ *a* riesig, Riesen-; **~(size) packet** Riesenpackung *f*.

gibber [jib'ûr] *vi* (*ape*) schnattern; (*idiot*) brabbeln.

gibberish [jib'ûrish] *n* dumme(s) Geschwätz *nt*.

gibe [jīb] *n* spöttische Bemerkung *f*.

giblets [jib'lits] *npl* Geflügelinnereien *pl*.

Gibraltar [jibrôl'tûr] *n* Gibraltar *nt*.

giddiness [gid'ēnis] *n* Schwindelgefühl *nt*.

giddy [gid'ē] *a* schwindlig; (*frivolous*) leichtsinnig; **I feel ~** mir ist schwindelig.

gift [gift] *n* Geschenk *nt*; (*ability*) Begabung *f*; (*COMM*: *also*: **free ~**) (Werbe)geschenk *nt*; **to have a ~ for sth** (*talent*) Talent für etw haben.

gifted [gif'tid] *a* begabt.

gift certificate, gift voucher, gift token *n* Geschenkgutschein *m*.

gig [gig] *n* (*col*: *concert*) Konzert *nt*.

gigantic [jīgan'tik] *a* riesenhaft, ungeheuer groß.

giggle [gig'əl] *vi* kichern ♦ *n* Gekicher *nt*.

GIGO [gig'ō] *abbr* (*COMPUT col*) = *garbage in, garbage out*.

gild [gild] *vt* vergolden.

gill [gil] *n* (*of fish*) Kieme *f*.

gilt [gilt] *n* Vergoldung *f* ♦ *a* vergoldet.

gilt-edged [gilt'ejd] *a* (*Brit FIN*) erstklassig.

gimlet [gim'lit] *n* Handbohrer *m*.

gimmick [gim'ik] *n* (*for publicity*) Gag *m*; **sales ~** Verkaufstrick *m*, (Verkaufs)masche *f*.

gimmicky [gim'ikē] *a*: **it's so ~** es ist alles nur ein Gag.

gin [jin] *n* Gin *m*.

ginger [jin'jûr] *n* Ingwer *m*.

ginger ale, ginger beer *n* Ingwerbier *nt*.

gingerbread [jin'jûrbred] *n* Pfefferkuchen *m*.

ginger-haired [jin'jûrhärd] *a* rothaarig.

gingerly [jin'jûrlē] *ad* behutsam.

gipsy [jip'sē] *n* (*Brit*) = **gypsy.**

giraffe [jəraf'] *n* Giraffe *f*.

girder [gûr'dûr] *n* (*steel*) Eisenträger *m*; (*wood*) Tragebalken *m*.

girdle [gûr'dəl] *n* (*woman's*) Hüftgürtel *m* ♦ *vt* umgürten.

girl [gûrl] *n* Mädchen *nt*.

girl Friday *n* Allround-Sekretärin *f*.

girlfriend [gûrl'frend] *n* Freundin *f*.

girlish [gûr'lish] *a* mädchenhaft.

Girl Scout, (*Brit*) **Girl Guide** *n* Pfadfinderin *f*.

giro [jī'rō] *n* (*Brit*: *bank* ~) Giro(verkehr *m*) *nt*; (: *post office* ~) Postscheckdienst *m*.

girth [gûrth] *n* (*measure*) Umfang *m*; (*strap*) Sattelgurt *m*.

gist [jist] *n* Wesentliche(s) *nt*, Quintessenz *f*.

give [giv] *irreg vt* geben; **I can ~ you 10 minutes** ich kann Ihnen 10 Minuten Zeit geben; **how much did you ~ for it?** wieviel hast du dafür bezahlt?; **12 o'clock, ~ or take a few minutes** so um 12 (herum); **~ them my regards** grüß sie von mir ♦ *vi* (*break*) nachgeben; **to ~ way** (*to feelings*) nachgeben (*to* +*dat*); (*Brit*: *traffic*) Vorfahrt lassen; **to ~ way to despair** sich der Verzweiflung überlassen.

give away *vt* (*give free*) verschenken; (*betray*) verraten.

give back *vt* zurückgeben.

give in *vi* (*yield*) aufgeben; (*agree*) nachgeben ♦ *vt* (*Brit*: *turn in*) abgeben.

give off *vt* abgeben.

give out *vi* (*be exhausted*: *supplies*) zu Ende gehen; (*fail*: *engine, strength*) versagen ♦ *vt* (*distribute*) austeilen.

give up *vti* aufgeben.

give-and-take [giv'əntāk'] *n* (*col*) Entgegenkommen *nt*, Geben und Nehmen *nt*.

giveaway [giv'əwā] *n* (*col*): **her expression was a ~** ihr Gesicht verriet alles; **the exam was a ~!** die Prüfung war geschenkt.

giveaway prices *npl* Schleuderpreise *pl*.

given [giv'ən] *a* (*fixed*: *time, amount*) vorgegeben, bestimmt ♦ *conj*: **~ the circumstances ...** unter den Umständen ...; **~ (that) ...** vorausgesetzt, (daß) ... ♦ *pp of* **give.**

glacial [glā'shəl] *a* glazial, Gletscher-.

glacier [glā'shûr] *n* Gletscher *m*.

glad [glad] *a* froh; **to be ~ about sth/that ...** froh sein über etw/daß ...; **I was ~ of his help** ich war froh über seine Hilfe; **I was ~ to hear...** ich habe mich gefreut, zu hören....

gladden [glad'ən] *vt* erfreuen.

glade [glād] *n* Lichtung *f*.

gladiator [glad'ēātûr] *n* Gladiator *m*.

gladioli [gladēō'lē] *npl* Gladiolen *pl*.

gladly [glad'lē] *ad* gern(e).

glamor [glam'ûr] *n* (*US*) Glamour *m*; (*of occasion, situation*) Glanz *m*.

glamorous [glam'ûrəs] *a* bezaubernd; (*life*) reizvoll.

glamour [glam'ûr] *n* (*Brit*) = **glamor.**

glance [glans] *n* flüchtige(r) Blick *m* ♦ *vi*

schnell (hin)blicken (at auf +acc).
glance off vt fus (fly off) abprallen von.
glancing [glan'sing] a (blow) abprallend, Streif-.
gland [gland] n Drüse f.
glandular fever [glan'jəlûr fē'vûr] n (Brit) Drüsenfieber nt.
glare [glär] n (light) grelle(s) Licht nt; (stare) wilde(r) Blick m ♦ vi grell scheinen; (angrily) böse ansehen (at acc).
glaring [glär'ing] a (injustice) schreiend; (mistake) kraß.
glass [glas] n Glas nt; (mirror) Spiegel m; see also **glasses**.
glassblowing [glas'blōing] n Glasbläserei f.
glasses [glas'iz] npl Brille f.
glass fiber, (Brit) **glass fibre** n Glasfaser f.
glasshouse [glas'hous] n (Brit) Gewächshaus nt.
glassware [glas'wär] n Glaswaren pl.
glassy [glas'ē] a glasig.
glaze [glāz] vt verglasen; (finish with a ~) glasieren ♦ n (COOK) Glasur f.
glazed [glāzd] a (eyes) glasig; (pottery) glasiert.
glazier [glā'zhûr] n Glaser m.
gleam [glēm] n Schimmer m; **a ~ of hope** ein Hoffnungsschimmer ♦ vi schimmern.
gleaming [glē'ming] a schimmernd.
glean [glēn] vt (gather: facts, news) herausbekommen, ausfindig machen.
glee [glē] n Frohsinn m.
gleeful [glē'fəl] a fröhlich.
glen [glen] n Bergtal nt.
glib [glib] a (rede)gewandt; (superficial) oberflächlich.
glibly [glib'lē] ad glatt.
glide [glīd] vi gleiten ♦ n Gleiten nt; (AVIAT) Segelflug m.
glider [glī'dûr] n (AVIAT) Segelflugzeug nt.
gliding [glī'ding] n Segelfliegen nt.
glimmer [glim'ûr] n Schimmer m; **a ~ of hope** ein Hoffnungsschimmer.
glimpse [glimps] n flüchtige(r) Blick m; **to catch a ~ of sb/sth** einen flüchtigen Blick auf jdn/etw werfen können ♦ vt flüchtig erblicken.
glint [glint] n Glitzern nt ♦ vi glitzern.
glisten [glis'ən] vi glänzen.
glitter [glit'ûr] vi funkeln ♦ n Funkeln nt.
glittering [glit'ûring] a glitzernd.
glitz [glits] n (col) Glimmer m.
gloat [glōt] vi sich großtun; **to ~ over** sich weiden an (+dat).
global [glō'bəl] a (world-wide) global, weltweit.
globe [glōb] n Erdball m; (sphere) Globus m.
globetrotter [glōb'trâtûr] n Weltenbummler(in f) m, Globetrotter(in f) m.
globule [glâb'yōōl] n Klümpchen nt, Kügelchen nt; (of oil, water) Tröpfchen nt.
gloom [glōōm] n (also: **gloominess**) (darkness) Dunkel nt, Dunkelheit f; (depression) düstere Stimmung f.

gloomily [glōō'milē] ad düster.
gloomy [glōō'mē] a düster; **to feel ~** niedergeschlagen sein.
glorification [glôrəfəkā'shən] n Verherrlichung f.
glorify [glôr'əfī] vt verherrlichen; **just a glorified snack bar** nur eine bessere Imbißstube.
glorious [glôr'ēəs] a glorreich; (splendid) prächtig.
glory [glôr'ē] n Herrlichkeit f; (praise) Ruhm m ♦ vi: **to ~ in** sich sonnen in (+dat).
glory hole n (col: cupboard) Rumpel- or Kramecke f; (: box) Rumpelkiste f.
Glos abbr (Brit) = Gloucestershire.
gloss [glôs] n (shine) Glanz m; (also: ~ **paint**) Lackanstrich m.
gloss over vt fus übertünchen.
glossary [glâs'ûrē] n Glossar nt.
glossy [glâs'ē] a (surface) glänzend.
glove [gluv] n Handschuh m.
glove compartment n (AUT) Handschuhfach nt.
glow [glō] vi glühen, leuchten ♦ n (heat) Glühen nt; (color) Röte f; (feeling) Wärme f.
glower [glou'ûr] vi: **to ~ at sb** jdn finster anblicken.
glowing [glō'ing] a (fire) glühend; (complexion) blühend; (fig: report, description etc) begeistert.
glowworm [glō'wûrm] n Glühwürmchen nt.
glucose [glōō'kōs] n Traubenzucker m.
glue [glōō] n Klebstoff m, Leim m ♦ vt kleben, leimen.
glue-sniffing [glōō'snifing] n Patex ® Schnüffeln nt.
glum [glum] a bedrückt.
glut [glut] n Überfluß m ♦ vt überladen.
glutinous [glōōt'ənəs] a klebrig.
glutton [glut'ən] n Vielfraß m; (fig) Unersättliche(r) mf.
gluttonous [glut'ənəs] a gierig.
gluttony [glut'ənē] n Völlerei f; (fig) Unersättlichkeit f.
glycerin(e) [glis'ûrin] n Glyzerin nt.
gm abbr (= gram) g.
GMAT n abbr (US: = Graduate Management Admissions Test) Zugangstest für Handelsschulen.
GMT abbr (= Greenwich Mean Time) WEZ f.
gnarled [nârld] a knorrig.
gnash [nash] vt: **to ~ one's teeth** mit den Zähnen knirschen.
gnat [nat] n Stechmücke f.
gnaw [nô] vt nagen an (+dat).
gnome [nōm] n Gnom m.
GNP n abbr (= gross national product) BSP nt.
go [gō] vi irreg gehen; (travel) reisen, fahren; (depart: train) (ab)fahren; (money) ausgehen; (time) vergehen; (disappear, vanish) verschwinden; (be sold) gehen; (fail, break, wear out) kaputtgehen; (work) gehen, funktionieren; (fit, suit) passen (with zu); (become) werden; **to ~ by car/on foot**

das Auto nehmen/zu Fuß gehen; **to ~ look-ing for sb/sth** nach jdm/etw Ausschau hal-ten; **to make sth ~, to get sth ~ing** etw in Gang bringen; **to ~ to sleep** einschlafen; ... **to ~** (US: food) ... zum Mitnehmen; **to ~ and see sb, to ~ to see sb** jdn besuchen; **my voice has gone** meine Stimme ist weg; **the cake is all gone** der Kuchen ist alle; **the conference went well** die Konferenz verlief gut; **I'll take whatever is ~ing** (Brit) ich nehme, was es gibt; **the money will ~ towards our vacation** das Geld ist für den Urlaub ♦ n (energy) Schwung m; (attempt) Versuch m; **can I have another ~?** darf ich noch mal?

go about vt fus: **to ~ about one's busi-ness** sich um seine eigenen Geschäfte küm-mern ♦ vi (Brit) = **go around.**

go after vt fus (pursue) nachgehen (+dat); (job etc) sich bemühen um, aussein auf (+acc).

go against vt fus (be unfavorable to: re-sults, events) ungünstig verlaufen für; (be contrary to: principles, conscience, sb's wishes) gehen gegen.

go ahead vi (go in front) vorangehen; (proceed) weitergehen.

go along vi dahingehen, dahinfahren.

go along with vt fus (accompany) mitge-hen mit, mitkommen mit; (agree to support) zustimmen (+dat), unterstützen.

go around vi (revolve) sich drehen; (suf-fice) langen, (aus)reichen; (circulate: news, rumor) umgehen; (wander around) herum-gehen, herumlaufen; **to ~ around to sb's** vorbeigehen bei jdm; **to ~ around by X** (make a detour) bei X herumfahren.

go away vi (depart) weggehen.

go back vi (return) zurückgehen.

go back on vt fus (promise) nicht halten.

go by vi (years, time) vergehen; (person) vorbeigehen ♦ vt fus (person) vorbeigehen an (+dat); (judge by) gehen nach; **if that's anything to ~ by** wenn man danach gehen kann.

go down vi hinuntergehen; (sun) unterge-hen; **that should ~ down well with him** das findet er bestimmt gut.

go for vt fus (fetch) holen (gehen); (like) mögen; (attack) sich stürzen auf (+acc).

go in vi hineingehen.

go in for vt fus (competition) teilnehmen an (+dat).

go into vi vt fus (enter) hineingehen in (+acc); (study) sich befassen mit.

go off vi (depart) weggehen; (lights) aus-gehen; (milk etc) sauer werden; (explode) losgehen; **the party went off well** die Party verlief gut ♦ vt fus (dislike) nicht mehr mö-gen.

go on vi (continue) weitergehen; (lights) angehen; (col: complain) meckern; (fit) passen ♦ vt fus (be guided by: evidence etc) sich stützen auf; **what's ~ing on here?** was

ist hier los?; **to ~ on with sth** mit etw wei-termachen.

go on at vt fus (nag) herumnörgeln an (+dat), herumhacken auf (+dat) (col).

go out vi (fire, light) ausgehen; (leave house) hinausgehen; **to ~ out with sb** mit jdm ausgehen; **the tide is ~ing out** es ist Ebbe.

go over vi (cross) hinübergehen ♦ vt fus (examine, check) durchgehen; **to ~ over sth in one's mind** etw überdenken.

go round vi (Brit) = **go around.**

go through vt fus (door, hole etc) gehen durch; (examine: list, book) durchgehen; (search through) durchsuchen; (perform) durchgehen ♦ vi (lit, fig) durchgehen.

go through with vt fus (plan) durchzie-hen (col); (crime) ausführen; **I couldn't ~ through with it** ich brachte es nicht fertig.

go together vi (harmonize: people etc) zusammenpassen.

go under vi (ship, person) untergehen; (fig: business) scheitern; (: firm) eingehen ♦ vt fus (pass under) durchgehen unter (+dat).

go up vi (price) steigen; **to ~ up in flames** in Flammen aufgehen ♦ vt fus (climb: stairs, hill) hinaufgehen (+acc); (: ladder) hinaufsteigen (+acc); (: tree) hin-aufklettern (+acc).

go without vt fus sich behelfen ohne; (food) entbehren.

goad [gōd] vt anstacheln ♦ n Treibstock m.

go-ahead [gō'əhed] a zielstrebig; (progres-sive) fortschrittlich ♦ n grüne(s) Licht nt; **to give sb the ~** jdm grünes Licht geben.

goal [gōl] n Ziel nt; (SPORT) Tor nt.

goalkeeper [gōl'kēpûr] n Torwart m.

goal post n Torpfosten m.

goat [gōt] n Ziege f.

gobble [gâb'əl] vt hinunterschlingen.

go-between [gō'bitwēn] n Mittelsmann m.

Gobi Desert [gō'bē dez'ûrt] n Wüste f Gobi.

goblet [gâb'lit] n Kelch(glas nt) m.

goblin [gâb'lin] n Kobold m.

go-cart [gō'kârt] n = **go-kart.**

god [gâd] n Gott m.

godchild [gâd'chīld] n, pl **-children** Patenkind nt.

goddamn [gâd'dam'] a (US col!) verdammt, saumäßig.

goddaughter [gâd'dôtûr] n Patentochter f.

goddess [gâd'is] n Göttin f.

godfather [gâd'fâthûr] n Pate m.

godforsaken [gâd'fûrsā'kən] a gottverlassen.

godmother [gâd'muthûr] n Patin f.

godparents [gâd'pärənts] npl Paten pl.

godsend [gâd'send] n Geschenk nt des Him-mels.

godson [gâd'sun] n Patensohn m.

goes [gōz] 3rd pers sing pres of **go.**

gofer [gō'fûr] n (US) Mädchen nt für alles.

go-getter [gō'get'ûr] n Tatmensch m.

goggle [gâg'əl] vi (stare) glotzen; **to ~ at** anglotzen.

goggles [gåg'əlz] *npl* Schutzbrille *f*.

going [gō'ing] *n* (*condition of ground*) Stra-ßenzustand *m*; (*horse racing*) Bahn *f*; **it's hard** ~ es ist schwierig; **it was slow** ~ es ging nur langsam (voran) ♦ *a* (*rate*) gängig; (*concern*) gutgehend.

goings-on [gō'ingzân'] *npl* Vorgänge *pl*; (*col*) Dinge *pl*.

go-kart [gō'kârt] *n* Go-kart *m*.

gold [gōld] *n* Gold *nt* ♦ *a* (*reserves*) Gold-.

golden [gōl'dən] *a* (*lit, fig*) golden, Gold-.

golden handshake *n* (*Brit*) Abstandssum-me *f*.

golden rule *n* goldene Regel *f*.

goldfish [gōld'fish] *n* Goldfisch *m*.

gold leaf *n* Blattgold *nt*.

gold medal *n* (*SPORT*) Goldmedaille *f*.

gold mine *n* Goldgrube *f*.

gold-plated [gōldplā'tid] *a* vergoldet.

goldsmith [gōld'smith] *n* Goldschmied *m*.

gold standard *n* Goldstandard *m*.

golf [gâlf] *n* Golf *nt*.

golf ball *n* Golfball *m*; (*Brit: on typewriter*) Kugelkopf *m*.

golf club *n* (*society*) Golfklub *m*; (*stick*) Golfschläger *m*.

golf course *n* Golfplatz *m*.

golfer [gâl'fûr] *n* Golfspieler(in *f*) *m*.

gondola [gân'dələ] *n* Gondel *f*.

gondolier [gândəliûr'] *n* Gondoliere *m*.

gone [gôn] *pp of* **go**.

gong [gông] *n* Gong *m*.

good [gōōd] *n* (*benefit*) Wohl *nt*; (*moral ex-cellence*) Güte *f*; **is this any** ~? (*will it do?*) hilft *or* nützt das?; (*what's it like?*) eignet sich das?; **he's up to no** ~ er führt etwas *or* nichts Gutes im Schilde; **the common** ~ das Gemeinwohl; **for** ~ (*forever*) für im-mer; **it's no** ~ **complaining** Klagen nützt nichts; *see also* **goods** ♦ *a* gut; (*suitable*) passend; **to feel** ~ sich wohlfühlen; **it's** ~ **to see you** es ist schön, Sie zu sehen; **that's very** ~ **of you** das ist wirklich nett von Ihnen; **it's** ~ **for you** das tut dir gut; **it's a** ~ **thing you were there** gut, daß du da warst; **a** ~ **deal of** ziemlich viel; **a** ~ **many** ziemlich viele.

goodbye [gōōdbī'] *interj* auf Wiedersehen! ♦ *n*: **to say** ~ **to** (*person*) auf Wiedersehen sa-gen (+*dat*), sich verabschieden von.

good faith *n*: **in** ~ in gutem Glauben.

good-for-nothing [gōōd'fərnuth'ing] *n* Nichtsnutz *m*, Taugenichts *m*.

Good Friday *n* Karfreitag *m*.

good-humored, (*Brit*) **good-humoured** [gōōd'hyōō'mûrd] *a* (*person*) gut gelaunt; (*remark, joke*) harmlos; (*good-natured*) gut-mütig.

good-looking [gōōd'lōōk'ing] *a* gutaussehend.

good-natured [gōōd'nā'chûrd] *a* (*person*) gutmütig; (*discussion*) freundlich.

goodness [gōōd'nis] *n* Güte *f*; (*virtue*) Tu-gend *f*.

goods [gōōdz] *npl* Güter *pl* (*also COMM*); (*possessions*) Habe *f* (*col*); **all his** ~ **and chattels** sein ganzes Hab und Gut, seine Sie-bensachen *pl*.

goods train *n* (*Brit*) Güterzug *m*.

goodwill [gōōd'wil'] *n* (*favor*) Wohlwollen *nt*; (*COMM*) Firmenansehen *nt*.

goody-goody [gōōd'ēgōōd'ē] *n* (*pej*) Tugend-lamm *nt*, Musterkind *nt*.

goof [gōōf] *vi* (*US col*) patzen.

goose [gōōs] *n*, *pl* **geese** [gēs] Gans *f*.

gooseberry [gōōs'bärē] *n* Stachelbeere *f*.

gooseflesh [gōōs'flesh] *n* Gänsehaut *f*.

goosepimples [gōōs'pimpəlz] *npl* Gänsehaut *f*.

goose step *n* (*MIL*) Stech- *or* Paradeschritt *m*.

GOP *n abbr* (*US POL: col* = *Grand Old Par-ty*) republikanische Partei.

gore [gōr] *vt* durchbohren, aufspießen ♦ *n* Blut *nt*.

gorge [gôrj] *n* Schlucht *f* ♦ *vti* (sich voll)fressen.

gorgeous [gôr'jəs] *a* prächtig; (*person*) bild-hübsch.

gorilla [gəril'ə] *n* Gorilla *m*.

gorse [gôrs] *n* Stechginster *m*.

gory [gôr'ē] *a* blutig.

go-slow [gō'slō'] *n* (*Brit*) Bummelstreik *m*.

gospel [gâs'pəl] *n* Evangelium *nt*.

gossamer [gâs'əmûr] *n* Spinnfäden *pl*.

gossip [gâs'əp] *n* Klatsch *m*; (*person*) Klatschbase *f*; **a piece of** ~ Klatsch *m*, Tratsch *m* (*col*) ♦ *vi* klatschen.

gossip column *n* Klatschspalte *f*.

got [gât] *pt, pp of* **get**.

Gothic [gâth'ik] *a* gotisch.

gotten [gât'ən] *pp* (*US*) *of* **get**.

gouge [gouj] *vt* (*also*: ~ **out:** *hole etc*) boh-ren; (: *initials*) eingravieren; (: *sb's eyes*) ausstechen.

goulash [gōō'lâsh] *n* Gulasch *nt or m*.

gourd [gôrd] *n* Flaschenkürbis *m*.

gourmet [gōōrmā'] *n* Feinschmecker *m*.

gout [gout] *n* Gicht *f*.

govern [guv'ûrn] *vt* regieren; (*school, prov-ince*) verwalten; (*GRAM*) regieren.

governess [guv'ûrnis] *n* Gouvernante *f*.

governing [guv'ûrning] *a* leitend; (*fig*) be-stimmend; (*POL*) regierend.

governing body *n* Vorstand *m*.

government [guv'ûrnmənt] *n* Regierung *f* ♦ *a* Regierungs-.

government stock *n* Staatsanleihe *f*.

governor [guv'ûrnûr] *n* Gouverneur *m*.

Govt. *abbr* (= *Government*) Reg.

gown [goun] *n* Gewand *nt*; (*Brit UNIV*) Robe *f*.

GP *n abbr* (*MED*) = **general practitioner.**

GPO *n abbr* (*US*: = *Government Printing Office*) staatliche Druckanstalt.

gr. *abbr* (*COMM*) = **gross.**

grab [grab] *vt* packen; (*greedily*) an sich rei-ßen ♦ *vi*: **to** ~ **at** greifen *or* grapschen nach

(+acc) ♦ n plötzliche(r) Griff m; (crane) Greifer m.

grace [grās] n (graciousness) Anmut f; (favor) Güte f, Gefälligkeit f; (blessing) Gnade f; (prayer) Tischgebet nt; (COMM) Zahlungsfrist f; **his sense of humor is his saving** ~ was einen mit ihm versöhnt, ist sein Sinn für Humor; **5 days'** ~ 5 Tage Aufschub ♦ vt (adorn) zieren; (honor) auszeichnen.

graceful [grās'fəl] a, **gracefully** [grās'fəlē] ad anmutig, graziös.

gracious [grā'shəs] a gnädig; (kind, courteous) wohlwollend, freundlich ♦ interj: **(good)** ~! du meine Güte!, (ach du) lieber Himmel!

gradation [grādā'shən] n (Ab)stufung f.

grade [grād] n Grad m; (slope) Gefälle nt; (US: gradient) Neigung f; (: SCH: class) Klasse f; (: mark) Note f; **to make the** ~ es schaffen ♦ vt (classify) einstufen.

grade crossing n (US) Bahnübergang m.

grade school n (US) Grundschule f.

gradient [grā'dēənt] n Neigung f; (upward also) Steigung f; (downward also) Gefälle nt.

gradual [graj'ōōəl] a, **gradually** [graj'ōōəlē] ad allmählich.

graduate n [graj'ōōit] (US) Schulabgänger(in f) m; (Brit): **to be a** ~ das Staatsexamen haben ♦ vi [graj'ōōāt] das Staatsexamen machen or bestehen.

graduated pension [graj'ōōātid pen'shən] n gestaffelte Sozialrente f.

graduation [grajōōā'shən] n (UNIV. US SCH) (Ab)schlußfeier f.

graffiti [grəfē'tē] npl Graffiti pl.

graft [graft] n (on plant) Pfropfreis nt; (hard work) Schufterei f; (MED) Transplantat nt; (unfair self-advancement) Schiebung f ♦ vt propfen; (fig) aufpfropfen; (MED) einpflanzen (in in +acc).

grain [grān] n Korn nt, Getreide nt; (particle) Körnchen nt, Korn nt; (in wood) Maserung f.

gram, (Brit) gramme [gram] n Gramm nt.

grammar [gram'ûr] n Grammatik f.

grammatical [grəmat'ikəl] a grammatisch.

gramme [gram] n (Brit) = **gram.**

granary [grā'nûrē] n Kornspeicher m.

grand [grand] a großartig ♦ n (col) ≈ Riese m (1000 Dollar od Pfund).

granddad [gran'dad] n Opa m.

granddaughter [gran'dôtûr] n Enkelin f.

grandeur [gran'jûr] n (of occasion, scenery etc) Erhabenheit f; (of style, house) Vornehmheit f.

grandfather [gran'fâthûr] n Großvater m.

grandiose [gran'dēōs] a (imposing) großartig; (pompous) schwülstig.

grand jury n (US) große(s) Geschworenengericht nt.

grandma [gran'mə] n Oma f.

grandmother [gran'muthûr] n Großmutter f.

grandpa [gran'pə] n = **granddad.**

grandparents [gran'pärənts] npl Großeltern pl.

grand piano n Flügel m.

Grand Prix [grand prē'] n (AUT) Grand Prix m.

grandson [gran'sun] n Enkel m.

grandstand [gran'stand] n Haupttribüne f.

grand total n Gesamt- or Endsumme f.

granite [gran'it] n Granit m.

granny [gran'ē] n Oma f.

grant [grant] vt gewähren; (allow) zugeben; **to** ~ **that** ... (admit) zugeben, daß ...; **to take sb/sth for** ~ed jdn/etw als selbstverständlich (an)nehmen ♦ n Unterstützung f; (UNIV) Stipendium nt.

granulated [gran'yəlātid] a: ~ **sugar** Raffinade f.

granule [gran'yōōl] n Körnchen nt.

grape [grāp] n (Wein)traube f; **a bunch of** ~s eine Weintraube.

grapefruit [grāp'frōōt] n Pampelmuse f, Grapefruit f.

grape juice n Traubensaft m.

grapevine [grāp'vīn] n Weinstock m; (col) Nachrichtendienst m; **I heard it on the** ~ (fig) es ist mir zu Ohren gekommen.

graph [graf] n Schaubild nt.

graphic [graf'ik] a (descriptive) anschaulich, lebendig; (drawing) graphisch.

graphic designer n Grafiker(in f) m.

graphics [graf'iks] n sing (art, process) graphische Darstellung f; (pl: drawings) Zeichnungen pl; (: computer ~) Grafilen pl.

graphite [graf'īt] n Graphit m.

graph paper n Millimeterpapier nt.

grapple [grap'əl] vi sich raufen.

grapple with vt fus (lit, fig) kämpfen mit.

grappling iron [grap'ling i'ûrn] n (NAUT) Enterhaken m.

grasp [grasp] vt ergreifen; (understand) begreifen ♦ n Griff m; (possession) Gewalt f; (of subject) Beherrschung f; **to have a good** ~ **of** (subject) etw gut beherrschen.

grasp at vt fus (rope etc) greifen nach; (fig: opportunity) aufgreifen, beim Schopf(e) packen.

grasping [gras'ping] a habgierig.

grass [gras] n Gras nt; (pasture) Weide(land nt) f; (Brit col: informer) Spitzel m, Singvogel m.

grasshopper [gras'hâpûr] n Heuschrecke f.

grassland [gras'land] n Weideland nt.

grass roots npl (fig) Basis f.

grass snake n Ringelnatter f.

grassy [gras'ē] a grasig, Gras-.

grate [grāt] n Feuerrost m, Kamin m ♦ vi kratzen; (sound) knirschen; (on nerves) zerren (on an +dat) ♦ vt (cheese) reiben.

grateful [grāt'fəl] a, **gratefully** [grāt'fəlē] ad dankbar.

grater [grā'tûr] n Reibe f.

gratification [gratəfəkā'shən] n (of desires) Befriedigung f; (pleasure) Genugtuung f.

gratify [grat'əfī] vt befriedigen.

gratifying [grat'əfiiŋ] *a* erfreulich.

grating [grā'tiŋ] *n* (*iron bars*) Gitter *nt* ♦ *a* (*noise*) knirschend.

gratitude [grat'ətōōd] *n* Dankbarkeit *f*.

gratuitous [grətōō'itəs] *a* (*uncalled-for*) unnötig, überflüssig; (*given free*) unentgeltlich, gratis.

gratuity [grətōō'itē] *n* (Geld)geschenk *nt*; (*COMM*) Gratifikation *f*.

grave [grāv] *n* Grab *nt* ♦ *a* (*serious*) ernst, schwerwiegend; (*solemn*) ernst, feierlich.

gravedigger [grāv'digûr] *n* Totengräber *m*.

gravel [grav'əl] *n* Kies *m*.

gravely [grāv'lē] *ad* schwer, ernst; ~ **ill** schwerkrank.

gravestone [grāv'stōn] *n* Grabstein *m*.

graveyard [grāv'yârd] *n* Friedhof *m*.

gravitate [grav'ətāt] *vi* streben; (*fig*) tendieren.

gravitation [gravitā'shən] *n* Gravitation *f*, Schwerkraft *f*.

gravity [grav'itē] *n* (*PHYS*) Schwerkraft *f*; (*seriousness*) Schwere *f*, Ernst *m*; **center of ~** Schwerpunkt *m*.

gravy [grā'vē] *n* (Braten)soße *f*.

gravy boat *n* Sauciere *f*, Soßenschüssel *f*.

gravy train *n*: **to get on the ~** (*esp US col*) auch ein Stück vom Kuchen abbekommen.

gray [grā] *a* (*US*) grau; **to go ~** grau werden.

grayhound [grā'hound] *n* (*US*) Windhund *m*.

graze [grāz] *vi* grasen ♦ *vt* (*touch*) streifen; (*MED*) abschürfen ♦ *n* (*MED*) Abschürfung *f*.

grazing [grā'ziŋ] *n* Weiden *nt*, Weideland *nt*.

grease [grēs] *n* (*fat*) Fett *nt*; (*lubricant*) Schmiere *f* ♦ *vt* einfetten; (ab)schmieren; **to ~ the skids** (*US fig*) die Maschinerie in Gang halten.

grease gun *n* Schmierspritze *f*.

greasepaint [grēs'pānt] *n* (Fett)schminke *f*.

greaseproof [grēs'prōōf] *a* (*Brit: paper*) Butterbrot-.

greasy [grē'sē] *a* fettig; (*hands, clothes*) schmierig, ölbeschmiert; (*Brit: road, surface*) glitschig, schlüpfrig.

great [grāt] *a* (*pain, heat*) groß; (*important*) groß, bedeutend; (*distinguished*) groß, hochstehend; (*col: good*) prima; **it was ~!** es war toll!; **they're ~ friends** sie sind gute Freunde; **the ~ thing is that ...** das Wichtigste ist, daß ...; **we had a ~ time** wir haben uns prima amüsiert.

Great Barrier Reef *n* Große(s) Barrierriff *nt*.

Great Britain *n* Großbritannien *nt*.

greater [grā'tûr] *a* größer; **G~ London** Groß-London *nt*.

greatest [grā'tist] *a* größte(r, s).

great-grandchild [grāt'gran'chīld] *n*, *pl* **-children** Urenkel(in *f*) *m*.

great-grandfather [grāt'gran'fâthûr] *n* Urgroßvater *m*.

great-grandmother [grāt'gran'muthûr] *n* Urgroßmutter *m*.

Great Lakes *npl*: **the ~** die Großen Seen *pl*.

greatly [grāt'lē] *ad* sehr.

greatness [grāt'nis] *n* Größe *f*.

Greece [grēs] *n* Griechenland *nt*.

greed [grēd] *n* (*also*: **greediness**) Gier *f* (*for* nach); (*meanness*) Geiz *m*.

greedily [grē'dilē] *ad* gierig.

greedy [grē'dē] *a* gefräßig, gierig; ~ **for money** geldgierig.

Greek [grēk] *a* griechisch ♦ *n* (*person*) Grieche *m*, Griechin *f*; (*language*) Griechisch *nt*; **ancient/modern ~** Alt-/Neugriechisch *nt*.

green [grēn] *a* grün; **to have a ~ thumb** (*US*) *or* **fingers** (*Brit*) ein gutes Händchen für Pflanzen haben ♦ *n* (*village ~*) Dorfwiese *f*; (*of golf course*) Grün *nt*; **the G~s** (*POL*) die Grünen *pl*.

greenback [grēn'bak] *n* (*US col*) Dollar-Schein *m*.

green bean *n* Brechbohne *f*.

greenbelt [grēn'belt] *n* Grüngürtel *m*.

green card *n* (*US ADMIN*) ≈ Arbeitserlaubnis *f*; (*for international insurance*) grüne Versicherungskarte *f*.

greenery [grē'nûrē] *n* Grün *nt*; (*foliage*) grüne(s) Laub *nt*, grüne Zweige *f*.

greenfly [grēn'flī] *n* (*Brit*) Blattlaus *f*.

greengage [grēn'gāj] *n* Reneklode *f*, Reineclaude *f*.

greengrocer [grēn'grōsûr] *n* Obst- und Gemüsehändler *m*.

greenhouse [grēn'hous] *n* Gewächshaus *nt*.

greenhouse effect *n* Treibhauseffekt *m*.

greenish [grē'nish] *a* grünlich.

Greenland [grēn'lənd] *n* Grönland *nt*.

Greenlander [grēn'ləndûr] *n* Grönländer(in *f*) *m*.

green light *n* (*lit, fig*) grüne(s) Licht *nt*.

green pepper *n* (grüne) Paprikaschote *f*.

greet [grēt] *vt* grüßen.

greeting [grē'tiŋ] *n* Gruß *m*, Begrüßung *f*; **~s** Grüße *pl*; (*congratulations also*) Glückwünsche *pl*; **Season's ~s** Fröhliche Weihnachten und ein glückliches Neues Jahr; **~ card, ~s card** Glückwunschkarte *f*.

gregarious [grigâr'ēəs] *a* gesellig.

grenade [grinād'] *n* (*also*: **hand ~**) (Hand)granate *f*.

grew [grōō] *pt of* **grow**.

grey [grā] *a* (*Brit*) = **gray**.

greyhound [grā'hound] *n* (*Brit*) = **grayhound**.

grid [grid] *n* Gitter *nt*; (*ELEC*) Leitungsnetz *nt*; (*on map*) Gitternetz *nt*.

griddle [grid'əl] *n* gußeiserne Platte zum Pfannkuchen backen.

gridiron [grid'iûrn] *n* Bratrost *m*.

grief [grēf] *n* Gram *m*, Kummer *m*; **to come to ~** (*plan*) scheitern; (*person*) zu Schaden kommen.

grievance [grē'vəns] *n* Beschwerde *f*; ~ **procedure** Beschwerdeweg *m*.

grieve [grēv] *vi* sich grämen; **to ~ for sb** jds Schmerz teilen; (*dead person*) um jdn trauern ♦ *vt* betrüben.

grievous [grē'vəs] *a* schwer; (*wrong, pain*) groß; ~ **bodily harm** (*JUR*) schwere Körperverletzung *f*.

grill [gril] *n* (*on cooker*) Grill *m* ♦ *vt* grillen; (*question*) in die Mangel nehmen.

grille [gril] *n* (*on car etc*) (Kühler)gitter *nt*.

grilled meat [grild mēt] *n* gegrillte(s) Fleisch *nt*.

grim [grim] *a* grimmig; (*situation*) düster.

grimace [grim'əs] *n* Grimasse *f* ♦ *vi* Grimassen schneiden.

grime [grīm] *n* Schmutz *m*.

grimly [grim'lē] *ad* grimmig, finster.

grimy [grīm'ē] *a* schmutzig.

grin [grin] *n* Grinsen *nt* ♦ *vi* grinsen; **to** ~ **at sb** jdn anlächeln *or* angrinsen (*col*).

grind [grīnd] *irreg vt* mahlen; (*US: meat*) hacken; (*sharpen*) schleifen; (*teeth*) knirschen mit; (*polish: gem, lens*) schleifen ♦ *vi* (*car gears*) knirschen; **to** ~ **to a halt** (*vehicle*) quietschend zum Stehen kommen; (*fig: talks, scheme*) stocken, sich festfahren; (*work, production*) zum Erliegen kommen ♦ *n* (*bore*) Plackerei *f*; **the daily** ~ (*col*) der tägliche Trott.

grinder [grīn'dûr] *n* (*machine: for coffee*) Kaffeemühle *f*; (*: for meat*) Wolf *m*.

grindstone [grīnd'stōn] *n*: **to keep one's nose to the** ~ hart arbeiten.

grip [grip] *n* Griff *m*; (*US: suitcase*) Reisetasche *f*; **to lose one's** ~ (*lit*) den Halt verlieren; (*fig*) nachlassen ♦ *vt* packen.

gripe [grīp] *n* (*col: complaint*) Meckerei *f* ♦ *vi*: **to** ~ (**about sth**) (*complain*) (über etw) meckern, (an etw) herumnörgeln.

gripes [grīps] *npl* (*bowel pains*) Bauchschmerzen *pl*, Bauchweh *nt*.

gripping [grip'ing] *a* (*exciting*) spannend.

grisly [griz'lē] *a* gräßlich.

grist [grist] *n*: **it's (all)** ~ **to his mill** es ist Wasser auf seine Mühle.

gristle [gris'əl] *n* Knorpel *m*.

grit [grit] *n* (*gravel*) Splitt *m*; (*courage*) Mut *m*; **I've got a piece of** ~ **in my eye** ich habe ein Staubkorn im Auge ♦ *vt* (*road*) (mit Splitt be)streuen; **to** ~ **one's teeth** die Zähne zusammenbeißen.

grits [grits] *npl* (*US*) Grütze *f*.

grizzly [griz'lē] *n* (*also*: ~ **bear**) Grisly(bär) *m*.

groan [grōn] *n* Stöhnen *nt* ♦ *vi* stöhnen.

grocer [grō'sûr] *n* Lebensmittelhändler *m*; ~**'s** Lebensmittelgeschäft *nt*.

groceries [grō'sûrēz] *npl* Lebensmittel *pl*.

grocery [grō'sûrē] *n* (*also*: ~ **store**) Lebensmittelgeschäft *nt*.

grog [grág] *n* Grog *m*.

groggy [grág'ē] *a* benommen; (*BOXING*) angeschlagen.

groin [groin] *n* Leistengegend *f*.

groom [grōōm] *n* Bräutigam *m*; (*for horses*) Pferdeknecht *m* ♦ *vt*: **to** ~ **o.s.** (*of man*) sich zurechtmachen, sich pflegen; (**well**)

~**ed** gepflegt; **to** ~ **sb for a career** jdn auf eine Laufbahn vorbereiten.

groove [grōōv] *n* Rille *f*, Furche *f*.

grope [grōp] *vi* tasten.

grosgrain [grō'grān] *n* grob gerippte(s) Seidentuch *nt*.

gross [grōs] *a* (*coarse*) dick, plump; (*bad*) grob, schwer; (*COMM*) brutto ♦ *vt* (*COMM*) brutto verdienen; (*store also*) brutto einnehmen ♦ *n* Gros *nt*.

gross domestic product *n* Bruttoinlandsprodukt *nt*.

gross income *n* Bruttoeinkommen *nt*.

grossly [grōs'lē] *ad* höchst, ungeheuerlich.

gross national product *n* Bruttosozialprodukt *nt*.

gross profit *n* Bruttogewinn *m*.

gross sales *npl* Bruttoumsatz *m sing*.

grotesque [grōtesk'] *a* grotesk.

grotto [grát'ō] *n* Grotte *f*.

grouch [grouch] *vi* (*col*) schimpfen, meckern ♦ *n* (*col: person*) Miesepeter *m*, Muffel *m*.

ground [ground] *n* Boden *m*, Erde *f*; (*land*) Grundbesitz *m*; (*reason*) Grund *m*; (*US ELEC*) Erde *f*; **common** ~ Gemeinsames *nt*; **to gain/lose** ~ Boden gewinnen/verlieren; **below** ~ unter der Erde; **he covered a lot of** ~ **in his lecture** er behandelte eine Menge in seiner Vorlesung; *see also* **grounds** ♦ *vt* (*run ashore*) auf Strand setzen; (*aircraft*) stillegen; (*US ELEC*) erden ♦ *vi* (*run ashore*) stranden, auflaufen ♦ *a* (*a coffee etc*) gemahlen; (*US: meat*) Hack- ♦ *pt, pp of* **grind**.

ground cloth *n* (*US*) Zeltboden *m*.

ground control *n* (*AVIAT, SPACE*) Bodenkontrolle *f*.

ground floor *n* (*Brit*) Erdgeschoß *nt*, Parterre *nt*.

grounding [groun'ding] *n* (*instruction*) Anfangsunterricht *m*.

groundkeeper [ground'kēpûr] *n* (*US*) = **groundskeeper**.

groundless [ground'lis] *a* grundlos, unbegründet.

groundnut [ground'nut] *n* (*Brit*) Erdnuß *f*.

ground rent *n* (*Brit*) Erbbauzins *m*.

grounds [groundz] *npl* (*dregs*) Bodensatz *m*; (*around house*) (Garten)anlagen *pl*.

groundsheet [ground'shēt] *n* (*Brit*) Zeltboden *m*.

groundsman [groundz'mən] *n, pl* **-men** (*Brit SPORT*) Platzwart *m*.

groundskeeper [groundz'kēpûr] *n* (*US SPORT*) Platzwart *m*.

ground swell *n* Dünung *f*; (*fig*) Aufstand *m*.

ground-to-ground missile [ground'tə-ground mis'əl] *n* Boden-Boden-Rakete *f*.

groundwork [ground'wûrk] *n* Grundlage *f*.

group [grōōp] *n* Gruppe *f*; (*MUS: pop* ~) Pop-Musik-Gruppe *f* ♦ *vti* (sich) gruppieren.

grouse [grous] *n* (*bird*) schottische(s) Moorhuhn *nt*; (*complaint*) Nörgelei *f* ♦ *vi* (*complain*) meckern.

grove [grōv] *n* Gehölz *nt*, Hain *m*.

grovel [gruv'əl] *vi* auf dem Bauch kriechen; *(fig)* kriechen.

grow [grō] *irreg vi* wachsen, größer werden; *(grass)* wachsen; *(become)* werden; **to ~ tired of waiting** es leid sein zu warten; **that painting is ~ing on me** allmählich finde ich Gefallen an dem Gemälde; **it ~s on you** man gewöhnt sich daran ♦ *vt (raise)* anbauen, ziehen.

grow apart *vi (fig)* sich auseinanderleben.

grow away from *vt fus (fig)* sich entfremden (+*dat*).

grow out of *vt fus (clothes)* herauswachsen aus; *(habit)* ablegen.

grow up *vi* aufwachsen; *(mature)* erwachsen werden.

grower [grō'ûr] *n (of flowers)* Züchter *m*; *(of tobacco, coffee)* Pflanzer *m*; *(AGR)* Anbauer *m*.

growing [grō'ing] *a* wachsend; *(fig)* zunehmend; **~ pains** *(fig)* Kinderkrankheiten *pl*, Anfangsschwierigkeiten *pl*.

growl [groul] *vi* knurren ♦ *n* Knurren *nt*.

grown [grōn] *pp* of **grow**.

grown-up [grōn'up'] *a* erwachsen ♦ *n* Erwachsene(r) *mf*.

growth [grōth] *n* Wachstum *nt*; *(of person)* Entwicklung *f*; *(increase: in quantity)* Anwachsen *nt*; *(: in size)* Vergrößerung *f*; *(of beard etc)* Wuchs *m*; *(MED)* Wucherung *f*.

growth rate *n* Wachstumsrate *f*.

grub [grub] *n* Made *f*, Larve *f*; *(col: food)* Futter *nt*.

grubby [grub'ē] *a* schmutzig, schmuddelig.

grudge [gruj] *n* Groll *m* ♦ *vt* misgönnen *(sb sth* jdm etw); **to bear sb a ~** einen Groll gegen jdn hegen.

grudging [gruj'ing] *a* neidisch; *(unwilling)* widerwillig.

grueling, *(Brit)* **gruelling** [grōō'əling] *a (climb, race)* mörderisch.

gruesome [grōō'səm] *a* grauenhaft.

gruff [gruf] *a* barsch.

grumble [grum'bəl] *vi* murren, schimpfen ♦ *n* Murren *nt*.

grumpy [grum'pē] *a* verdrießlich.

grunt [grunt] *vi* grunzen ♦ *n* Grunzen *nt*.

GSA *n abbr (US:* = *General Services Administration)* Dienstleistungsorganisation der Regierung.

G-string [jē'string] *n* G-Saite *f*.

GSUSA *n abbr (*= *Girl Scouts of the United States of America)* amerikanische Pfadfinderinnen.

GT *n abbr (AUT:* = *gran turismo)* GT *m*.

GU *abbr (US MAIL)* = **Guam.**

guarantee [garəntē'] *n* Garantie *f (of* für) ♦ *vt* garantieren; **he can't ~ (that) he'll come** er kann nicht dafür garantieren, daß er kommt.

guarantor [gar'əntôr] *n* Gewährsmann *m*, Bürge *m*.

guard [gârd] *n (defense)* Bewachung *f*; *(sentry)* Wache *f*; *(protection)* Schutz *m*; *(safety*

device: on machine) Schutzvorrichtung *f*; *(fire ~)* (Schutz)gitter *nt*; *(Brit RAIL)* Zugbegleiter *m*, Schaffner(in *f*) *m*; **to be on ~ Wache stehen; to be on one's ~** *(fig)* auf der Hut sein, sich vorsehen ♦ *vt* bewachen, beschützen; **to ~ from** abschirmen gegen.

guard against *vt fus* abschirmen gegen; **to ~ against doing sth** sich hüten, etw zu tun.

guard dog *n* Wachhund *m*.

guarded [gâr'did] *a* vorsichtig, zurückhaltend.

guardian [gâr'dēən] *n* Vormund *m*; *(keeper)* Hüter *m*.

guardrail [gârd'rāl] *n* (Leit)planke *f*.

guard's van [gârdz' van] *n (Brit RAIL)* Dienstwagen *m*.

Guatemala [gwâtəmâl'ə] *n* Guatemala *nt*.

Guatemalan [gwâtəmâl'ən] *a* guatemaltekisch, aus Guatemala ♦ *n (person)* Guatemalteke *m*, Guatemaltekin *f*.

Guernsey [gûrn'zē] *n* Guernsey *nt*.

guerrilla [gəril'ə] *n* Guerilla(kämpfer) *m*.

guerrilla warfare *n* Guerillakrieg *m*.

guess [ges] *vt* (er)raten, schätzen; **I ~ you're right** da haben Sie wohl recht ♦ *vi* raten; **to keep sb ~ing** jdn im ungewissen lassen ♦ *n* Vermutung *f*; **good ~!** gut geraten!; **my ~ is that ...** ich tippe darauf *or* vermute, daß ...

guesstimate [ges'təmit] *n* grobe Schätzung *f*.

guesswork [ges'wûrk] *n* Raterei *f*; **I got the answer by ~** ich habe die Antwort (nur) geraten.

guest [gest] *n* Gast *m*; **be my ~** *(col)* nur zu!

guestbook [gest'bŏŏk] *n (US)* Gästebuch *nt*.

guest house *n* Pension *f*.

guest room *n* Gastzimmer *nt*.

guffaw [gufô'] *n* schallende(s) Gelächter *nt* ♦ *vi* schallend lachen.

guidance [gīd'əns] *n (control)* Leitung *f*; *(advice)* Rat *m*, Beratung *f*; **marriage/ vocational ~** Ehe-/Berufsberatung *f*.

guide [gīd] *n* Führer *m* ♦ *vt* führen; **to be ~d by sb/sth** sich von jdm/etw leiten lassen.

guidebook [gīd'bŏŏk] *n* Reiseführer *m*.

guided missile [gī'did mis'əl] *n* Fernlenkgeschoß *nt*.

guidelines [gīd'līnz] *npl* Richtlinien *pl*.

guild [gild] *n (HIST)* Gilde *f*; *(society)* Vereinigung *f*.

guile [gīl] *n* Arglist *f*.

guileless [gīl'lis] *a* arglos.

guillotine [gil'ətēn] *n* Guillotine *f*.

guilt [gilt] *n* Schuld *f*.

guilty [gil'tē] *a* schuldig; **to feel ~** ein schlechtes Gewissen haben; **to plead ~/not ~** sich schuldig/nicht schuldig bekennen.

Guinea [gin'ē] *n*: **Republic of ~** Guinea *nt*.

guinea pig *n* Meerschweinchen *nt*; *(fig)* Versuchskaninchen *nt*.

guise [gīz] *n (appearance)* Verkleidung *f*; **in the ~ of** *(thing)* in der Form (+*gen*); *(person)* gekleidet als.

guitar [gitâr'] *n* Gitarre *f*.

guitarist [gitâr'ist] n Gitarrist(in f) m.
gulch [gulch] n (US) Schlucht f.
gulf [gulf] n Golf m; (fig) Abgrund m.
Gulf States npl: **the** ~ die Golfstaaten pl.
Gulf Stream n: **the** ~ der Golfstrom.
gull [gul] n Möwe f.
gullet [gul'it] n Schlund m.
gullibility [guləbil'ətē] n Leichtgläubigkeit f.
gullible [gul'əbəl] a leichtgläubig.
gully [gul'ē] n (Wasser)rinne f; (gorge)
Schlucht f.
gulp [gulp] vt hinunterschlucken ♦ vi (gasp)
schlucken ♦ n (of liquid) Schluck m; **in** or **at
one** ~ auf einen Schluck.
gum [gum] n (around teeth) Zahnfleisch nt;
(glue) Klebstoff m; (chewing ~) Kaugummi
m ♦ vt gummieren, kleben.
   gum up vt: **to** ~ **up the works** (col) alles
verkleben; (fig) die Arbeit stoppen.
gumboots [gum'bōōts] npl (Brit) Gummistiefel pl.
gum tree n Gummibaum m; **up a** ~ (col) in
der Klemme.
gun [gun] n Schußwaffe f; (rifle) Gewehr nt;
(pistol) Pistole f; **to stick to one's** ~**s** (fig)
nicht nachgeben, festbleiben ♦ vt (also: ~
down) erschießen, zusammenschießen.
gun dog n Jagdhund m.
gunfire [gun'fīûr] n Geschützfeuer nt.
gung-ho [gung'hō'] a (col) übereifrig.
gunk [gungk] n (col) Dreckzeug nt.
gunman [gun'mən] n, pl -**men** bewaffnete(r)
Verbrecher m.
gunner [gun'ûr] n Kanonier m, Artillerist m.
gunpoint [gun'point] n: **at** ~ mit Waffenge-
walt.
gunpowder [gun'poudûr] n Schießpulver nt.
gunrunner [gun'runûr] n Waffenschieber m.
gunrunning [gun'runing] n Waffenschmuggel
m, Waffenschieberei f.
gunshot [gun'shât] n Schuß m.
gunsmith [gun'smith] n Büchsenmacher m.
gurgle [gûr'gəl] n Gluckern nt ♦ vi gluckern.
gush [gush] n Strom m, Erguß m ♦ vi (rush
out) hervorströmen; (fig) schwärmen.
gusset [gus'it] n Keil m, Zwickel m.
gust [gust] n Windstoß m, Bö f.
gusto [gus'tō] n Genuß m, Lust f.
gut [gut] n (ANAT) Gedärme pl; (string)
Darm m; see also **guts** ♦ vt (poultry, fish)
ausnehmen; (house etc) ausräumen, ausschlachten; **the blaze** ~**ted the entire building** das Gebäude war völlig ausgebrannt.
gut reaction n rein gefühlsmäßige Reaktion
f.
guts [guts] npl (col: innards) Eingeweide pl;
(of animals) Darm m; (fig) Schneid m; **to
hate sb's** ~ jdn auf den Tod nicht ausstehen
können (col).
gutter [gut'ûr] n (on roof) Dachrinne f; (in
street) Gosse f.
guttural [gut'ûrəl] a guttural, Kehl-.
guy [gī] n (rope) Halteseil nt; (man) Typ m,
Kerl m.

Guyana [gēân'ə] n Guyana nt, Guayana nt.
guzzle [guz'əl] vti (drink) saufen; (eat) fressen.
gymkhana [jimkâ'nə] n Reiterfest nt.
gym(nasium) [jim(nã'zēəm)] n Turnhalle f.
gymnast [jim'nast] n Turner(in f) m.
gymnastics [jimnas'tiks] n sing Turnen nt,
Gymnastik f.
gym shoes npl Turnschuhe pl.
gym slip n (Brit) Schulträgerrock m.
gynecologist, (Brit) **gynaecologist**
[gīnəkâl'əjist] n Frauenarzt m/-ärztin f, Gynäkologe m, Gynäkologin f.
gynecology, (Brit) **gynaecology** [gīnəkâl'əjē]
n Gynäkologie f, Frauenheilkunde f.
gypsy [jip'sē] n Zigeuner(in f) m.
gyrate [jī'rāt] vi kreisen.
gyroscope [jī'rəskōp] n Gyroskop nt.

H

H, h [āch] n (letter) H nt, h nt; **H for How** ≈
H wie Heinrich.
habeas corpus [hā'bēəs kôr'pəs] n Habeas-
korpusakte f.
haberdashery [hab'ûrdashûrē] n (US) Her-
renmodegeschäft nt; (Brit) Kurzwaren pl.
habit [hab'it] n (An)gewohnheit f; (monk's)
Habit nt or m; **to get out of/into the** ~ **of
doing sth** sich abgewöhnen/angewöhnen, etw
zu tun.
habitable [hab'itəbəl] a bewohnbar.
habitat [hab'itat] n Heimat f; (of animals
also) Lebensraum m; (of plants also) Standort m.
habitation [habitā'shən] n Bewohnen nt;
(place) Wohnung f.
habitual [həbich'ōōəl] a üblich, gewohnheits-
mäßig.
habitually [həbich'ōōəlē] ad gewöhnlich.
hack [hak] vt hacken ♦ n Hieb m; (writer)
Schreiberling m; (old horse) Gaul m.
hacker [hak'ûr] n (COMPUT) Hacker m.
hacking [hak'ing] n (COMPUT) Hacken nt.
hackles [hak'əlz] npl: **to make sb's** ~ **rise**
(fig) jdn auf die Palme bringen.
hackney cab [hak'nē kab] n Taxi nt.
hackneyed [hak'nēd] a abgedroschen.
had [had] pt, pp of **have**.
haddock [had'ək] n Schellfisch m.
hadn't [had'ənt] = **had not**.
haema-, haemo- [hēmə-] (Brit) = **hema-,
hemo-**.
hag [hag] n Hexe f.
haggard [hag'ûrd] a abgekämpft.
haggis [hag'is] n (Scot) Gericht aus ge-
hackten Schafsinnereien und Haferschrot im

Schafsmagen gekocht.

haggle [hag'əl] *vi* feilschen.

haggling [hag'ling] *n* Feilschen *nt*.

Hague [hāg] *n*: **The ~** Den Haag *nt*.

hail [hāl] *n* Hagel *m* ♦ *vt* zujubeln (+*dat*), bejubeln; **to ~ sb as emperor** jdn zum Kaiser ausrufen ♦ *vi* (*MET*) hageln; **he ~s from Scotland** er kommt *or* stammt aus Schottland.

hailstone [hāl'stōn] *n* Hagelkorn *nt*.

hailstorm [hāl'stórm] *n* Hagelschauer *m*.

hair [här] *n* (*collectively*) Haar *nt*, Haare *pl*; (*one ~*) Haar *nt*.

hairbrush [här'brush] *n* Haarbürste *f*.

haircut [här'kut] *n* Haarschnitt *m*; **to get a ~** sich (*dat*) die Haare schneiden lassen.

hairdo [här'dōō] *n* Frisur *f*.

hairdresser [här'dresûr] *n* Friseur *m*, Friseuse *f*.

hairdresser's *n* Friseursalon *m*.

hair dryer *n* Haartrockner *m*; (*handheld*) Fön *m* ®.

-haired [härd] *a suff*: **fair/long~** hell-/langhaarig.

hair gel *n* Haarfestiger *m*.

hair grip *n* (*Brit*) Klemme *f*.

hairline [här'līn] *n* Haaransatz *m*.

hairline fracture *n* Haarriß *m*.

hairnet [här'net] *n* Haarnetz *nt*.

hair oil *n* Haaröl *nt*.

hairpiece [här'pēs] *n* (*lady's*) Haarteil *nt*; (*man's*) Toupet *nt*.

hairpin [här'pin] *n* (*lit*) Haarnadel *f*; (*curve*) Haarnadelkurve *f*.

hair-raising [här'rāzing] *a* haarsträubend.

hair remover *n* Haarentferner *m*.

hair's breadth *n*: **by a ~** um Haaresbreite.

hair spray *n* Haarspray *nt*.

hair style *n* Frisur *f*.

hairy [här'ē] *a* haarig.

Haiti [hā'tē] *n* Haiti *nt*.

hake [hāk] *n* Seehecht *m*.

halcyon [hal'sēən] *a*: **~ days** glückliche Tage *pl*.

hale [hāl] *a*: **~ and hearty** gesund und munter.

half [haf] *n* Hälfte *f*; (*SPORT: of game*) Halbzeit *f*; (: *of ground*) Feldhälfte *f*; **to go halves (with sb)** (mit jdm) halbe-halbe machen ♦ *a* halb ♦ *ad* halb, zur Hälfte; **~ empty/closed** halb leer/geschlossen; **it's ~ after 3** es ist halb vier.

halfback [haf'bak] *n* Läufer *m*.

half-baked [haf'bākt'] *a* (*fig col: idea, scheme*) unausgegoren, blödsinnig.

half-breed [haf'brēd] *n* Mischling *m*.

half brother *n* Halbbruder *m*.

half-caste [haf'kast] *n* Mischling *m*.

halfhearted [haf'hâr'tid] *a* lustlos, unlustig.

half-hour [haf'our'] *n* halbe Stunde *f*.

half note *n* (*US*) halbe Note *f*.

halfpenny [hā'pənē] *n* halbe(r) Penny *m*.

half price *n* halbe(r) Preis *m*.

half term *n* (*Brit SCH*) Ferien in der Mitte

des Trimesters.

half time *n* Halbzeit *f*.

halfway [haf'wā'] *ad* halbwegs, auf halbem Wege; **to meet sb ~** (*fig*) jdm auf halbem Wege entgegenkommen.

half-yearly [haf'yēr'lē] *a* halbjährlich ♦ *ad* halbjährlich, jedes halbe Jahr.

halibut [hal'əbət] *n* Heilbutt *m*.

halitosis [halitō'sis] *n* schlechte(r) Mundgeruch *m*.

hall [hôl] *n* Saal *m*; (*entrance ~ of house*) Hausflur *m*; (*building*) Halle *f*.

hallmark [hôl'márk] *n* (*lit, fig*) Stempel *m*.

hallo [həlō'] = **hello**.

Hallowe'en [haləwēn'] *n* Tag *m* vor Allerheiligen.

hallucination [həlōōsənā'shən] *n* Halluzination *f*.

hallway [hôl'wā] *n* Korridor *m*.

halo [hā'lō] *n* (*of saint*) Heiligenschein *m*; (*of moon*) Hof *m*.

halt [hôlt] *n* Halt *m*; **to call a ~ (to sth)** (*fig*) (einer Sache) ein Ende machen ♦ *vti* anhalten.

halter [hôl'tûr] *n* (*for horse*) Halfter *nt*.

halterneck [hôl'tûrnek] *a* rückenfrei mit Nackenverschluß.

halve [hav] *vt* halbieren.

ham [ham] *n* Schinken *m*; (*col: radio ~*) Funkamateur *m*; (: **~ actor**) Schmierenkomödiant (in *f*) *m*.

hamburger [ham'bûrgûr] *n* Hamburger *m*.

ham-fisted [ham'fis'tid] *a* (*Brit*) = **ham-handed**.

ham-handed [ham'handid] *a* (*US*) ungeschickt.

hamlet [ham'lit] *n* Weiler *m*.

hammer [ham'ûr] *n* Hammer *m* ♦ *vt* hämmern; **to ~ a point home to sb** jdm etw einbleuen.

hammer out *vt* (*metal*) hämmern; (*fig: solution, agreement*) ausarbeiten, aushandeln.

hammock [ham'ək] *n* Hängematte *f*.

hamper [ham'pûr] *vt* (be)hindern ♦ *n* Picknickkorb *m*; Geschenkkorb *m*.

hamster [ham'stûr] *n* Hamster *m*.

hand [hand] *n* Hand *f*; (*of clock*) (Uhr)zeiger *m*; (*worker*) Arbeiter *m*; (*measurement: of horse*) ≈ 10 cm; **to force sb's ~** jdn zwingen; **to have a free ~** freie Hand haben; **we have the matter in ~** wir haben die Sache im Griff; **to have in one's ~** (*knife, victory*) in der Hand haben; **to give sb a ~** jdm helfen; **at first ~** aus erster Hand; **on ~** zur Verfügung; **to ~** zur Hand; **in ~** (*under control*) in fester Hand, unter Kontrolle; (*being done*) im Gange; (*extra*) übrig ♦ *vt* (*give*) reichen, geben.

hand down *vt* (*lit*) herunterreichen; (*tradition*) überliefern, weitergeben; (*US: sentence, verdict*) verhängen; (*heirloom*) vererben.

hand in *vt* abgeben; (*forms*) einreichen.

hand out *vt* (*leaflets*) austeilen, verteilen (*to sb* an jdn); (*advice*) geben, erteilen (*to sb* jdm).

hand over *vt* (*deliver*) übergeben; (*surrender*) abgeben; (: *prisoner*) ausliefern.

hand round *vt* (*Brit*) herumreichen; (: *distribute*) austeilen, verteilen.

handbag [hand'bag] *n* Handtasche *f*.

handball [hand'bôl] *n* Handball *m*.

handbook [hand'book] *n* Handbuch *nt*.

hand brake *n* Handbremse *f*.

h & c *abbr* (*Brit*: = *hot and cold (water)*) k.u.w.

hand cream *n* Handcreme *f*.

handcuffs [hand'kufs] *npl* Handschellen *pl*.

handful [hand'fool] *n* Handvoll *f*; (: *col: person*) Plage *f*.

handicap [han'dēkap] *n* Handikap *nt* ♦ *vt* ein Handikap darstellen für; **to be physically ~ped** körperlich behindert sein; **to be mentally ~ped** geistig behindert sein.

handicraft [han'dēkraft] *n* Kunsthandwerk *nt*.

handiwork [han'dēwûrk] *n* (*SCH*) Werken *nt*; **this looks like Tom's ~** (*pej*) das sieht ganz nach Tom aus.

handkerchief [hang'kûrchif] *n* Taschentuch *nt*.

handle [han'dəl] *n* Griff *m*; (*of door etc*) Klinke *f*; (*of basket, cup etc*) Henkel *m*; (*for winding*) Kurbel *f* ♦ *vt* (*touch*) anfassen, berühren; (*deal with: matter, problem*) sich befassen mit; (: *people*) umgehen mit; (*vehicle*) steuern.

handlebars [han'dəlbârz] *npl* Lenkstange *f*.

handling charge [hand'ling chârj] *n* Umladekosten *pl*; (*in banking*) Kontoführungsgebühr *f*.

hand luggage *n* Handgepäck *nt*.

handmade [hand'mād'] *a* handgefertigt; (*cookies*) selbst gebacken.

handout [hand'out] *n* (*leaflet*) Flugblatt *nt*; (*press ~*) (Presse)mitteilung *f*.

handpicked [hand'pikt] *a* ausgesucht, handverlesen; (*produce*) von Hand geerntet; (*staff etc*) handverlesen.

handrail [hand'rāl] *n* (*on staircase etc*) Geländer *nt*.

handshake [hand'shāk] *n* Händedruck *f*; (*COMPUT*) Quittungsaustausch *m*.

handsome [han'səm] *a* gutaussehend; (*generous*) großzügig.

hands-on experience [handz'án' ikspēr'ēəns] *n* praktische Erfahrung *f*.

handstand [hand'stand] *n* Handstand *m*.

hand-to-mouth [hand'təmouth'] *a* (*existence*) kümmerlich, armselig.

handwriting [hand'rīting] *n* Handschrift *f*.

handwritten [hand'ritən] *a* handgeschrieben.

handy [han'dē] *a* praktisch; (*stores*) leicht erreichbar; **to come in ~** gelegen kommen.

handyman [han'dēman] *n*, *pl* **-men** Mädchen *nt* für alles; (*do-it-yourselfer*) Bastler *m*; (*general ~*) Gelegenheitsarbeiter *m*.

hang [hang] *irreg vt* aufhängen; (*execute*)

hängen; **to ~ sth on sth** etw an etw (*acc*) hängen ♦ *vi* (*droop*) hängen ♦ *n*: **to get the ~ of sth** (*col*) den richtigen Dreh bei etw herauskriegen.

hang about *vi* sich herumtreiben.

hang back *vi* (*hesitate*): **to ~ back (from doing sth)** zögern(, etw zu tun).

hang on *vt fus* (*depend on: decision etc*) abhängen von ♦ *vi* sich festhalten; (*wait*) warten.

hang on to *vt fus* (*keep hold of*) sich festhalten an, sich festklammern an; **to ~ on to sth** (*keep*) etw behalten.

hang out *vt* (*washing*) draußen aufhängen ♦ *vi* (*col: live*) hausen, wohnen; (: *frequent*) herumlungern.

hang together *vi* (*cohere: argument etc*) folgerichtig *or* zusammenhängend sein.

hang up *vi* (*TEL*) auflegen ♦ *vt* (*coat*) aufhängen.

hangar [hang'ûr] *n* Hangar *m*, Flugzeughalle *f*.

hangdog [hang'dôg] *a* (*guilty: look, expression*) niedergeschlagen, trübsinnig.

hanged [hangd] *pt, pp of* **hang**.

hanger [hang'ûr] *n* Kleiderbügel *m*.

hanger-on [hang'ûrân'] *n* Anhänger(in *f*) *m*, Schmarotzer *m*.

hang gliding *n* Drachenfliegen *nt*.

hanging [hang'ing] *n* (*execution*) Hinrichtung *f* (durch den Strang).

hangman [hang'mən] *n*, *pl* **-men** Henker *m*.

hangover [hang'ōvûr] *n* Kater *m*.

hang-up [hang'up] *n* Komplex *m*.

hank [hangk] *n* Strang *m*.

hanker [hang'kûr] *vi* sich sehnen (*for, after* nach).

hankie, hanky [hang'kē] *n* *abbr* (= *handkerchief*) Taschentuch *nt*.

Hants *abbr* (*Brit*) = *Hampshire*.

haphazard [hap'haz'ûrd] *a* wahllos, zufällig.

hapless [hap'lis] *a* unglücklich, unselig.

happen [hap'ən] *vi* sich ereignen, passieren; **what's ~ing?** was ist los?

happen (up)on *vt fus* zufällig stoßen auf (*+acc*); (*person*) zufällig treffen *or* sehen.

happening [hap'əning] *n* Ereignis *nt*.

happily [hap'ilē] *ad* glücklich; (*fortunately*) glücklicherweise.

happiness [hap'ēnis] *n* Glück *nt*.

happy [hap'ē] *a* glücklich; **yes, I'd be ~ to** ja, sehr gern(e); **~ birthday!** herzlichen Glückwunsch zum Geburtstag!; **H~ Christmas/New Year!** frohe Weihnachten/ein frohes neues Jahr!

happy-go-lucky [hap'ēgōluk'ē] *a* sorglos.

harangue [hərang'] *vt* eine Strafpredigt halten (*+dat*).

harass [həras'] *vt* bedrängen, plagen.

harassed [hərast'] *a* abgespannt, mitgenommen.

harassment [həras'mənt] *n* Belästigung *f*.

harbor, (*Brit*) harbour [hâr'bûr] *n* Hafen *m*; **~ dues** Hafengebühren *pl* ♦ *vt* (*retain*:

grudge etc) hegen.
hard [hârd] *a* (*firm*) hart, fest; (*difficult*)
schwer, schwierig; (*physically*) schwer;
(*harsh*) hart(herzig), gefühllos; **to be ~ on
sb** gegenüber jdm hart sein; **I find it ~ to
believe that ...** es fällt mir schwer zu glauben, daß ... ♦ *ad* (*work*) hart; (*try*) sehr;
(*push, hit*) fest; **~ by** (*close*) dicht *or* nahe
an (+*dat*); **he took it ~** er hat es schwer
genommen.
hard-and-fast [hârd'ənfast] *a* fest; (*rules*)
bindend, verbindlich.
hardback [hârd'bak] *n* kartonierte Ausgabe *f*.
hard-boiled [hârd'boild'] *a* hartgekocht.
hard cash *n* Bargeld *nt*.
hard copy *n* Hardcopy *f*, Ausdruck *m*.
hard-core [hârd'kôr'] *a* (*pornography*) knall-
hart ♦ *n* (*fig*) harte(r) Kern *m*.
hard court *n* (*TENNIS*) Hartplatz *m*.
hard disk *n* (*COMPUT*) Festplatte *f*.
harden [hârd'ən] *vt* (*body, muscles*) kräfti-
gen, stählen; (*steel*) härten; (*fig: determination*) verhärten ♦ *vi* (*substance*) hart werden; (*fig*) sich verhärten.
hardened [hârd'ənd] *a* abgehärtet; (*criminal*)
Gewohnheits-; **to be ~ to sth** gegen etw abgehärtet sein.
hardheaded [hârd'hed'id] *a* nüchtern.
hardhearted [hârd'hâr'tid] *a* hartherzig; (*towards sb*) jdm gegenüber).
hardliner [hârdlī'nûr] *n* Vertreter *m* der har-
ten Linie.
hardly [hârd'lē] *ad* kaum; **I can ~ believe it**
das kann ich kaum glauben.
hard sell *n* aggressive Verkaufstaktik *f*.
hardship [hârd'ship] *n* Not *f*; (*injustice*) Unrecht *nt*.
hard shoulder *n* (*Brit AUT*) Seitenstreifen
m.
hard up *a* knapp bei Kasse.
hardware [hârd'wär] *n* Eisenwaren *pl*;
(*household goods*) Haushaltswaren *pl*; (*COM-
PUT*) Hardware *f*.
hardware dealer *n* (*US*) Eisenwarenhändler
m.
hard-wearing [hârd'wär'ing] *a* widerstandsfähig; (*shoes*) strapazierfähig.
hard-working [hârd'wûr'king] *a* (*person*) fleißig; (*engine*) leistungsfähig.
hardy [hâr'dē] *a* (*strong*) widerstandsfähig;
(*brave*) verwegen.
hare [här] *n* Hase *m*.
harelip [här'lip] *n* Hasenscharte *f*.
harem [här'əm] *n* Harem *m*.
hark back [hârk bak] *vi*: **to ~ back to (former days)** zurückkommen auf (vergangene
Zeiten); **this custom ~s back to the days
when ...** dieser Brauch geht auf die Zeit zurück, als ...
harm [hârm] *n* (*bodily*) Verletzung *f*; (*material, PSYCH*) Schaden *m*; **it won't do any ~**
es kann nicht schaden; **there's no ~ in trying** es kann nicht schaden, es zu versuchen
♦ *vt* schaden (+*dat*).

harmful [hârm'fəl] *a* schädlich.
harmless [hârm'lis] *a* harmlos, unschädlich.
harmonica [hârmân'ikə] *n* Mundharmonika *f*.
harmonious [hârmō'nēəs] *a* harmonisch.
harmonize [hâr'mənīz] *vt* abstimmen ♦ *vi*
harmonieren.
harmony [hâr'mənē] *n* Harmonie *f*; (*fig also*)
Einklang *m*.
harness [hâr'nis] *n* Geschirr *nt* ♦ *vt* (*horse*)
anschirren; (*fig*) nutzbar machen.
harp [hârp] *n* Harfe *f*.
harp on *vi* (*col*): **to ~ on about sth** auf
etw (*dat*) herumreiten.
harpist [hâr'pist] *n* Harfenspieler(in *f*) *m*.
harpoon [hârpōōn'] *n* Harpune *f*.
harrow [har'ō] *n* Egge *f* ♦ *vt* eggen.
harrowing [har'ōing] *a* grauenhaft.
harry [har'ē] *vt* (*MIL*) plündern; (*person*) zusetzen (+*dat*).
harsh [hârsh] *a* (*rough*) rauh, grob; (*severe*)
schroff, streng.
harshly [hârsh'lē] *ad* rauh, barsch.
harshness [hârsh'nis] *n* Härte *f*.
harvest [hâr'vist] *n* Ernte *f*; (*time*) Erntezeit
f ♦ *vt* ernten.
harvester [hâr'vistûr] *n* (*person*) Erntearbei-
ter(in *f*) *m*; (*machine*) Mähmaschine *f*;
(*combine ~*) Mähdrescher *m*.
has [haz] *3rd pers sing pres of* **have.**
has-been [haz'bin] *n* (*col: person*) vergangene *or* vergessene Größe *f*; (*: thing*) Ver-
gangene(s) *nt*, Vergessene(s) *nt*.
hash [hash] *vt* kleinhacken ♦ *n* (*mess*) Kuddelmuddel *m*; (*meat: cooked*) Haschee *nt*;
(*: raw*) Gehackte(s) *nt*.
hashish [hash'ēsh] *n* Haschisch *nt*.
hasn't [haz'ənt] = **has not.**
hassle [has'əl] *n* (*col*) Auseinandersetzung *f*;
(*bother, trouble*) Mühe *f*, Theater *nt*.
haste [hāst] *n* (*speed*) Eile *f*; (*hurry*) Hast *f*.
hasten [hā'sən] *vt* beschleunigen ♦ *vi* eilen,
sich beeilen; **I ~ to add that ...** ich muß allerdings hinzufügen, daß ...
hasty [hās'tē] *a*, **hastily** [hās'tēlē] *ad* hastig;
(*hurried*) eilig; (*rash*) vorschnell.
hat [hat] *n* Hut *m*.
hatbox [hat'bâks] *n* Hutschachtel *f*.
hatch [hach] *n* (*NAUT*) Luke *f*; (*in house*)
Durchreiche *f* ♦ *vi* brüten; (*young*) ausschlüpfen ♦ *vt* (*brood*) ausbrüten; (*plot*) aushecken.
hatchback [hach'bak] *n* (Auto *m* mit) Heck-
klappe *f*.
hatchet [hach'it] *n* Beil *nt*.
hate [hāt] *n* Haß *m* ♦ *vt* hassen; **I ~ standing
in line** ich stehe nicht gern Schlange; **I ~ to
trouble you, but ...** es ist mir sehr unangenehm, daß ich Sie belästigen muß, aber ....
hateful [hāt'fəl] *a* verhaßt.
hatred [hā'trid] *n* Haß *m*; (*dislike*) Abneigung
f.
hat trick *n* (*SPORT*): **to get a ~** einen Hat-
trick *or* einen dreifachen Erfolg erzielen.
haughty [hô'tē] *a*, **haughtily** [hô'tēlē] *ad*

hochnäsig, überheblich.

haul [hôl] *vt* ziehen, schleppen ♦ *n* (*pull*) Zug *m*; (*catch*) Fang *m*.

haulage [hô'lij] *n* Transport *m*; (*COMM*) Spedition *f*.

haulage contractor *n* (*Brit*: *firm*) Transportunternehmen *nt*, Spedition(sfirma) *f*; (: *person*) Transportunternehmer *m*, Spediteur *m*.

haulier [hôl'ēûr] *n* (*Brit*) Transportunternehmer *m*, Spediteur *m*.

haunch [hônch] *n* Lende *f*; **to sit on one's ~es** hocken.

haunt [hônt] *vt* (*ghost*) spuken in (+*dat*), umgehen in (+*dat*); (*memory*) verfolgen; (*frequent*) häufig besuchen; **the castle is ~ed** in dem Schloß spukt es ♦ *n* Lieblingsplatz *m*.

haunted [hôn'tid] *a* (*look*) gehetzt, gequält.

haunting [hôn'ting] *a* (*sight, music*) unheimlich.

Havana [həvan'ə] *n* Havanna *nt*.

have [hav] *irreg vt* haben; (*at meal*) essen; (*drink*) trinken; (*baby*) bekommen; (*col: trick*) hereinlegen; **to ~ breakfast** frühstücken; **to ~ lunch** zu Mittag essen; **to ~ dinner** zu Abend essen; **I'll ~ a coffee** ich nehme einen Kaffee; **to ~ an operation** operiert werden; **let me ~ a try** laß mich mal versuchen; **to ~ a party** eine Party geben; **rumor has it (that)** ... Gerüchten zufolge heißt es, (daß) ... ♦ *aux v*: **to ~ eaten** gegessen haben; **to ~ arrived** angekommen sein; **to ~ sth done** etw machen lassen; **to ~ to do sth** (*be obliged*) etw tun müssen; *see also* **haves.**

have in *vt*: **to ~ it in for sb** (*col*) jdn auf dem Kieker haben.

have on *vt* (*wear*) anhaben; **to ~ sb on** (*Brit col: tease*) jdn auf den Arm nehmen; **~ you anything on tomorrow?** (*Brit*) haben Sie morgen etwas vor?; **I don't ~ any money on me** ich habe kein Geld bei mir.

have out *vt*: **I'll ~ it out with him** ich werde mit ihm reden.

haven [hā'vən] *n* Hafen *m*; (*fig*) Zufluchtsort *m*.

haversack [hav'ûrsak] *n* Rucksack *m*.

haves [havz] *npl* (*col*): **the ~ and the have-nots** die Betuchten und die Habenichtse.

havoc [hav'ək] *n* Verwüstung *f*.

Hawaii [həwī'yē] *n* Hawaii *nt*.

Hawaiian [həwī'ən] *a* hawaiisch ♦ *n* Hawaiianer(in *f*) *m*.

hawk [hôk] *n* Habicht *m* ♦ *vt* (*goods for sale*) verkaufen, feilhalten.

hawthorn [hô'thôrn] *n* Weiß- *or* Rotdorn *m*.

hay [hā] *n* Heu *nt*.

hay fever *n* Heuschnupfen *m*.

haystack [hā'stak] *n* Heuschober *m*.

haywire [hā'wīûr] *a* (*col*) durcheinander.

hazard [haz'ûrd] *n* (*chance*) Zufall *m*; (*risk*) Risiko *nt*; **to be a health/fire ~** gesundheitsschädigend/feuergefährlich sein ♦ *vt* aufs Spiel setzen, riskieren; **to ~ a re-**

mark sich eine Bemerkung erlauben; **to ~ a guess** (es) wagen, eine Vermutung anzustellen.

hazardous [haz'ûrdəs] *a* gefährlich, risikoreich.

hazardous pay *n* (*US*) Gefahrenzulage *f*.

hazard warning lights *npl* (*Brit AUT*) Warnblinklicht *nt*.

haze [hāz] *n* Dunst *m*; (*fig*) Unklarheit *f*.

hazel [hā'zəl] *n* (*tree*) Haselnußbaum *m* ♦ *a* (*eyes*) haselnußbraun.

hazelnut [hā'zəlnut] *n* Haselnuß *f*.

hazy [hā'zē] *a* (*misty*) dunstig, diesig; (*vague*) verschwommen.

H-bomb [āch'bâm] *n* H-bombe *f*.

he [hē] *pron* er.

HE *abbr* (*REL. DIPLOMACY*: = *His* (*or Her*) *Excellency*) S.E., I.E.; = **high explosive.**

head [hed] *n* (*also COMPUT*) Kopf *m*; (*top*) Spitze *f*; (*leader*) Leiter *m*; **to have a ~ for business** einen Sinn fürs Geschäft haben; **to have no ~ for heights** nicht schwindelfrei sein; **to lose/keep one's ~** den Kopf verlieren/nicht verlieren; **~s** (*on coin*) Kopf *m*; **~ first** mit dem Kopf nach unten; **to sit at the ~ of the table** am (Kopf)ende des Tisches sitzen; **to come to a ~** (*fig: situation etc*) sich zuspitzen; **$10 a** *or* **per ~** 10 Dollar pro Kopf; **on your ~ be it** auf Ihre eigene Verantwortung *or* Kappe (*col*); **they went over my ~ to the manager** sie sind über meinen Kopf hinweg zum Manager gegangen; **it was above** *or* **over their ~s** es ging über ihren Horizont ♦ *a* Kopf-; (*leading*) Ober- ♦ *vt* (an)führen, leiten; (*ball*) köpfen.

head for *vt fus* Richtung nehmen auf (+*acc*), zugehen auf (+*acc*).

head off *vt* (*threat, danger*) abwehren.

headache [hed'āk] *n* Kopfschmerzen *pl*, Kopfweh *nt*; **to have a ~** Kopfschmerzen haben.

headcheese [hed'chēz] *n* (*US*) Sülze *f*.

headdress [hed'dres] *n* (*of Indian etc*) Kopfschmuck *m*; (*of bride*) Brautkranz *m*.

header [hed'ûr] *n* (*dive*) Kopfsprung *m*, Köpfer *m*; (*Brit col: SOCCER*) Kopfball *m*.

headhunter [hed'huntûr] *n* Personal(ab)werber *m*.

heading [hed'ing] *n* Überschrift *f*.

headlamp [hed'lamp] *n* (*Brit*) Scheinwerfer *m*.

headland [hed'land] *n* Landspitze *f*.

headlights [hed'līts] *npl* Beleuchtung *f*.

headline [hed'līn] *n* Schlagzeile *f*; **to make the ~s** Schlagzeilen machen.

headlong [hed'lông] *ad* kopfüber.

headmaster [hed'mas'tûr] *n* (*Brit*: *of grade school*) Rektor *m*; (: *of high school*) Direktor *m*.

headmistress [hed'mis'tris] *n* (*Brit*) Rektorin *f*; Direktorin *f*.

head-on [hed'ân'] *a* Frontal-.

headphones [hed'fōnz] *npl* Kopfhörer *pl*.

headquarters [hed'kwôrtûrz] *npl* Zentrale *f*; (*MIL*) Hauptquartier *nt*.

headrest |hed'rest| n Kopfstütze f.
headroom |hed'rōōm| n (of bridges etc) lichte Höhe f; (in car) Kopfraum nt.
headscarf |hed'skárf| n Kopftuch nt.
headset |hed'set| n Kopfhörer pl.
headstone |hed'stōn| n (on grave) Grabstein m.
headstrong |hed'stróng| a eigenwillig.
head waiter n Oberkellner m.
headway |hed'wā| n: **to make** ~ (lit, fig) vorankommen.
headwind |hed'wind| n Gegenwind m.
heady |hed'ē| a (rash) hitzig; (intoxicating) stark, berauschend.
heal |hēl| vt heilen ♦ vi verheilen.
health |helth| n Gesundheit f; **your** ~! prost!
health centre n (Brit) Ärztezentrum nt.
health food(s) n(pl) Reformhauskost f.
health food store n Reformhaus nt.
health hazard n Gesundheitsrisiko nt.
Health Service n: **the** ~ (Brit) das Gesundheitswesen.
healthy |hel'thē| a (lit, fig) gesund.
heap |hēp| n Haufen m; ~**s (of)** (col: lots) ein(en) Haufen ♦ vt häufen; **to** ~ **praise on sb** über jdn voll des Lobes sein; **to** ~ **favors/gifts on sb** jdm mit Gefälligkeiten/ Geschenken überhäufen.
hear |hēr| irreg vt hören; (listen to) anhören; **to** ~ **a case** (JUR) einen Fall verhandeln ♦ vi hören; **I've never heard of that book** von dem Buch habe ich noch nie (was) gehört.
hear out vt (person) ausreden lassen; (story) zu Ende hören.
heard |hûrd| pt, pp of **hear**.
hearing |hē'ring| n Gehör nt; (Brit JUR) Verhandlung f; **to give sb a** ~ jdn anhören.
hearing aid n Hörapparat m.
hearsay |hēr'sā| n Gerüchte pl.
hearse |hûrs| n Leichenwagen m.
heart |härt| n Herz nt; (center also) Zentrum nt; (courage) Mut m; **to have a weak** ~ ein schwaches Herz haben; **by** ~ auswendig; **the** ~ **of the matter** der Kern der Sache; **to take** ~ Mut fassen; **to set one's** ~ **on sth/on doing sth** sein Herz an etw (acc) hängen/alles daransetzen, etw zu tun; **I did not have the** ~ **to tell her** ich brachte es nicht übers Herz, es ihr zu erzählen.
heart attack n Herzanfall m.
heartbeat |härt'bēt| n Herzschlag m.
heartbreak |härt'brāk| n große(r) Kummer m, Leid f.
heartbreaking |härt'brāking| a herzzerbrechend.
heartbroken |härt'brōkən| a todunglücklich.
heartburn |härt'bûrn| n Sodbrennen nt.
-hearted |härt'id| a suff: **a kind**~ **person** eine gutherzige or gütige Person.
heartening |här'təning| a ermutigend.
heart failure n (MED) Herzversagen nt.
heartfelt |härt'felt| a aufrichtig.
hearth |härth| n Herd m.
heartily |här'təlē| ad herzlich; (eat) herzhaft;

to be ~ **sick of sth** (Brit) etw wahnsinnig satt haben.
heartland |härt'land| n Kernland nt.
heartless |härt'lis| a herzlos.
heart-to-heart |härt'təhärt'| a, ad ganz offen.
heart transplant n Herztransplantation f, Herzverpflanzung f.
hearty |här'tē| a kräftig; (friendly) freundlich.
heat |hēt| n Hitze f; (of food, water etc) Wärme f; (SPORT) Ausscheidungsrunde f; (excitement) Feuer nt; **in the** ~ **of the moment** in der Hitze des Gefechts; **in** or (Brit) **on** ~ (ZOOL) brünstig, läufig ♦ vt (house) heizen; (substance) heiß machen, erhitzen.
heat up vi warm werden ♦ vt aufwärmen.
heated |hē'tid| a erhitzt; (fig) hitzig.
heater |hē'tûr| n (Heiz)ofen m.
heath |hēth| n (Brit) Heide f.
heathen |hē'thən| n Heide m ♦ a heidnisch, Heiden-.
heather |heth'ûr| n Heidekraut nt, Erika f.
heating |hē'ting| n Heizung f.
heat-resistant |hēt'rizistənt| a hitzebeständig.
heatstroke |hēt'strōk| n Hitzschlag m.
heat wave n Hitzewelle f.
heave |hēv| vt hochheben; (sigh) ausstoßen ♦ vi (pull) ziehen; (breast) sich heben ♦ n Heben nt.
heave to vi (NAUT) beidrehen.
heaven |hev'ən| n Himmel m; (bliss) (der siebte) Himmel; **for** ~**'s sake!** (pleading, protesting) um Himmels willen!; **thank** ~! Gott sei Dank!
heavenly |hev'ənlē| a himmlisch.
heavenly body n Himmelskörper m.
heavily |hev'ilē| ad schwer.
heavy |hev'ē| a schwer.
heavy cream n (US) Schlagsahne f.
heavy-duty |hev'ēdōō'tē| a strapazierfähig.
heavy goods vehicle n (Brit) Lastkraftwagen m.
heavy-handed |hev'ēhan'did| a (clumsy, tactless) schwerfällig, ungeschickt.
heavy industry n Schwerindustrie f.
heavy-set |hev'ēset| a untersetzt.
heavy user n Großverbraucher m.
heavyweight |hev'ēwāt| n (SPORT) Schwergewicht nt.
Hebrew |hē'brōō| a hebräisch ♦ n (LING) Hebräisch nt.
Hebrides |heb'ridēz| npl Hebriden pl.
heckle |hek'əl| vt unterbrechen ♦ vi dazwischenrufen, störende Fragen stellen.
heckler |hek'lûr| n Zwischenrufer m, Störer m.
hectic |hek'tik| a hektisch.
hector |hek'tûr| vt tyrannisieren.
he'd |hēd| = **he had; he would.**
hedge |hej| n Hecke f; **as a** ~ **against inflation** (fig) als Absicherung or Schutz gegen die Inflation ♦ vt einzäunen; **to** ~ **one's bets** sich absichern ♦ vi (fig) ausweichen.
hedgehog |hej'hâg| n Igel m.

hedgerow [hej'rō] *n* Hecke *f*, Knick *m*.
hedonism [hēd'ənizəm] *n* Hedonismus *m*.
heed [hēd] *vt* beachten ♦ *n* Beachtung *f*; **to pay (no)** ~ **to, to take (no)** ~ **of** (nicht) beachten.
heedful [hēd'fəl] *a* achtsam.
heedless [hēd'lis] *a* achtlos.
heel [hēl] *n* Ferse *f*; (*of shoe*) Absatz *m*; **to take to one's** ~**s** (*col*) sich aus dem Staub machen; **to bring to** ~ (*person*) jdn an die Kandare nehmen; (*dog*) bei Fuß gehen lassen ♦ *vt* (*shoes*) mit Absätzen versehen.
hefty [hef'tē] *a* (*person*) stämmig; (*portion*) reichlich; (*bite*) kräftig; (*weight*) schwer.
heifer [hef'ûr] *n* Färse *f*.
height [hīt] *n* (*of person*) Größe *f*; (*of object*) Höhe *f*; (*high place*) Gipfel *m*; **what** ~ **are you?** wie groß sind Sie?; ~ **average** ~ Durchschnittsgröße *f*; **to be afraid of** ~**s** nicht schwindelfrei sein; **it's the** ~ **of fashion** das ist die neueste Mode.
heighten [hīt'ən] *vt* erhöhen.
heinous [hā'nəs] *a* abscheulich, verabscheuungswürdig.
heir [är] *n* Erbe *m*.
heiress [är'is] *n* Erbin *f*.
heirloom [är'lōōm] *n* Erbstück *nt*.
heist [hīst] *n* (*col: hold-up*) Raubüberfall *m*.
held [held] *pt, pp of* **hold**.
helicopter [hel'əkâptûr] *n* Hubschrauber *m*.
heliport [hel'əpôrt] *n* (*AVIAT*) Hubschrauberlandeplatz *m*.
helium [hē'lēəm] *n* Helium *nt*.
hell [hel] *n* Hölle *f* ♦ *interj* verdammt!
he'll [hēl] = **he will, he shall.**
hellish [hel'ish] *a* höllisch, verteufelt.
hello [helō'] *interj* (*greeting*) hallo; (*surprise*) hallo, he.
hell's angels *npl* Hell's Angels *pl*.
helm [helm] *n* Ruder *nt*, Steuer *nt*.
helmet [hel'mit] *n* Helm *m*.
helmsman [helmz'mən] *n, pl* **-men** Steuermann *m*.
help [help] *n* Hilfe *f*; **with the** ~ **of** mit Hilfe (+*gen*); **to be of** ~ **to sb** jdm behilflich sein ♦ *vt* helfen (+*dat*); **to** ~ **sb (to) do sth** jdm (dabei) helfen, etw zu tun; **I can't** ~ **it** ich kann nichts dafür; **I couldn't** ~ **laughing** ich mußte einfach lachen; **can I** ~ **you?** (*in shop*) bitte schön?, was darf es sein?; ~ **yourself** bedienen Sie sich.
helper [hel'pûr] *n* Helfer(in *f*) *m*.
helpful [help'fəl] *a* hilfreich.
helping [hel'ping] *n* Portion *f*.
helpless [help'lis] *a* hilflos.
Helsinki [hel'singkē] *n* Helsinki *nt*.
helter-skelter [hel'tûrskel'tûr] *n* (*Brit: at amusement park*) (hohe Spiral-)Rutschbahn *f*.
hem [hem] *n* Saum *m*.
hem in *vt* einschließen; (*fig*) einengen; **to feel** ~**med in** (*fig*) sich eingeengt fühlen.
he-man [hē'man] *n, pl* **-men** (*col*) He-man *m*, richtige(r) Mann *m*.

hematology [hēmətâl'əjē] *n* (*US*) Hämatologie *f*.
hemisphere [hem'isfēr] *n* Hemisphäre *f*.
hemline [hem'līn] *n* Rocklänge *f*.
hemlock [hem'lâk] *n* Schierling *m*.
hemoglobin [hē'məglōbin] *n* (*US*) Hämoglobin *nt*.
hemophilia [hēməfil'ēə] *n* (*US*) Bluterkrankheit *f*.
hemorrhage [hem'ûrij] *n* (*US*) Blutung *f*.
hemorrhoids [hem'əroidz] *npl* (*US*) Hämorrhoiden *pl*.
hemp [hemp] *n* Hanf *m*.
hen [hen] *n* Henne *f*; (*female bird*) Weibchen *nt*.
hence [hens] *ad* von jetzt an; (*therefore*) daher.
henceforth [hens'fôrth] *ad* von nun an; (*from then on*) von da an.
henchman [hench'mən] *n, pl* **-men** Anhänger *m*, Gefolgsmann *m*.
henna [hen'ə] *n* Henna *f*.
hen party *n* (*col*) Damenkränzchen *nt*, ≈ Kaffeeklatsch *m*.
henpecked [hen'pekt] *a*: **to be** ~ unter dem Pantoffel stehen.
hepatitis [hepətī'tis] *n* Hepatitis *f*.
her [hûr] *pron* (*acc*) sie; (*dat*) ihr ♦ *poss a* ihre(r, s).
herald [här'əld] *n* Herold *m*; (*fig*) (Vor)bote *m* ♦ *vt* verkünden, anzeigen.
heraldic [hiral'dik] *a* heraldisch, Wappen-.
heraldry [här'əldrē] *n* Wappenkunde *f*, Heraldik *f*; (*signs*) Wappen *pl*.
herb [ûrb] *n* Kraut *nt*.
herbaceous [hûrbā'shəs] *a* krautig; ~ **border** Staudenrabatte *f*.
herbal [hûr'bəl] *a* Kräuter-.
herbicide [hûr'bisīd] *n* Unkrautvertilgungsmittel *nt*.
herd [hûrd] *n* Herde *f* ♦ *vt* (*drive, gather: animals, people*) treiben.
herd together *vi* sich zusammendrängen ♦ *vt* zusammentreiben.
here [hēr] *ad* hier; (*to this place*) hierher; **come** ~! kommen Sie her!, komm her!; ~ **and there** hier und da.
hereabouts [hē'rəbouts] *ad* hier herum, in dieser Gegend.
hereafter [hēraf'tûr] *ad* hernach, künftig ♦ *n* Jenseits *nt*.
hereby [hērbī'] *ad* hiermit.
hereditary [həred'itärē] *a* erblich.
heredity [həred'itē] *n* Vererbung *f*.
heresy [här'isē] *n* Ketzerei *f*.
heretic [här'itik] *n* Ketzer(in *f*) *m*.
heretical [həret'ikəl] *a* ketzerisch.
herewith [hērwith'] *ad* hiermit; (*COMM*) anbei.
heritage [här'itij] *n* Erbe *nt*; **our national** ~ unser nationales Erbe.
hermetically [hûrmet'iklē] *ad* luftdicht, hermetisch; ~ **sealed** hermetisch verschlossen.
hermit [hûr'mit] *n* Einsiedler *m*.

hernia [hûr'nēə] n Bruch m.
hero [hē'rō] n, pl **-es** Held m.
heroic [hirō'ik] a heroisch.
heroin [här'ōin] n Heroin nt.
heroin addict n Heroinsüchtige(r) mf.
heroine [här'ōin] n Heldin f.
heroism [här'ōizəm] n Heldentum nt.
heron [här'ən] n Reiher m.
hero worship n Heldenverehrung f.
herring [här'ing] n Hering m.
hers [hûrz] pron ihre(r, s); **a friend of** ~ ein Freund von ihr; **this is** ~ das gehört ihr.
herself [hûrself'] pron sich (selbst); (emphatic) selbst; **she's not** ~ mit ihr ist etwas los or nicht in Ordnung.
Herts abbr (Brit) = Hertfordshire.
he's [hēz] = **he is, he has.**
hesitant [hez'ətənt] a zögernd; (speech) stockend; **to be** ~ **about doing sth** zögern, etw zu tun.
hesitate [hez'ətāt] vi zögern; (feel doubtful) unschlüssig sein; **don't** ~ **to ask (me)** fragen Sie (mich) ruhig.
hesitation [hezətā'shən] n Zögern nt, Schwanken nt; **I have no** ~ **in saying (that ...)** ich kann ohne weiteres sagen(, daß ...).
hessian [hesh'ən] n Sackleinwand f, Rupfen m.
heterogeneous [hetûrəjē'nēəs] a heterogen.
heterosexual [hetûrəsek'shōōəl] a heterosexuell ♦ n Heterosexuelle(r) mf.
het up [het up] a (col) aufgeregt.
hew [hyōō] vt irreg hauen, hacken.
hex [heks] (US) n Fluch m ♦ vt verhexen.
hexagon [hek'səgän] n Sechseck nt.
hexagonal [heksag'ənəl] a sechseckig.
hey [hā] interj he (du or Sie).
heyday [hā'dā] n Blüte f, Höhepunkt m.
HF n abbr = high frequency.
HGV n abbr (Brit: = heavy goods vehicle) LKW m.
HHFA n abbr (US) = Housing and Home Finance Agency.
hi [hī] interj he, hallo.
HI abbr (US MAIL) = Hawaii.
hiatus [hīā'təs] n (gap) Lücke f; (GRAM) Hiatus m.
hibernate [hī'bûrnāt] vi Winterschlaf halten.
hibernation [hībûrnā'shən] n Winterschlaf m.
hiccough, hiccup [hik'up] n Schluckauf m; **to have the** ~**s** den Schluckauf haben.
hick [hik] n (US) Hinterwäldler m (col); (female) Landpomeranze f (col).
hid [hid] pt of **hide.**
hidden [hid'ən] a: **there are no** ~ **extras** es gibt keine versteckten Extrakosten ♦ pp of **hide.**
hide [hīd] n (skin) Haut f, Fell nt ♦ irreg vt verstecken; (keep secret) verbergen ♦ vi sich verstecken.
hide-and-seek [hīd'ənsēk'] n Versteckspiel nt.
hideaway [hīd'əwā] n Versteck nt.
hideous [hid'ēəs] a abscheulich.

hideously [hid'ēəslē] ad scheußlich.
hide-out [hīd'out] n Versteck nt.
hiding [hī'ding] n (beating) Tracht f Prügel; **to be in** ~ sich versteckt halten.
hiding place n Versteck nt.
hierarchy [hī'ərärkē] n Hierarchie f.
hieroglyphic [hīûrəglif'ik] a hieroglyphisch ♦ n: ~**s** pl Hieroglyphen(schrift f) pl.
hi-fi [hī'fī'] n abbr (= high fidelity) Hi-Fi nt.
higgledy-piggledy [hig'əldēpig'əldē] ad durcheinander, wie Kraut und Rüben (col).
high [hī] a hoch; (importance) groß; (spirits) Hoch-; (wind) stark; (living) extravagant, üppig; (col: on drugs) high; (: on drink) blau; (: game) anbrüchig; **to pay a** ~ **price for sth** etw teuer bezahlen ♦ ad hoch ♦ n: **exports have reached a new** ~ der Export hat einen neuen Höchststand erreicht.
highball [hī'bôl] n (drink) Highball m.
highbrow [hī'brou] n Intellektuelle(r) mf ♦ a (betont) intellektuell; (pej) hochgestochen.
highchair [hī'chär] n Hochstuhl m, Sitzer m.
high-class [hī'klas'] a (neighborhood) vornehm; (hotel) erstklassig; (person) aus der Oberschicht; (food) hochwertig.
high court n (Brit JUR) oberste(s) or höchste(s) Gericht nt.
higher [hī'ûr] a (form of life, study etc) höher (entwickelt) ♦ ad höher.
higher education n Hochschulbildung f.
high explosive n hochexplosive(r) Sprengstoff m.
high finance n Hochfinanz f.
highflier [hī'flī'ûr] n Senkrechtstarter m.
highhanded [hī'han'did] a eigenmächtig.
high-heeled [hī'hēld] a hochhackig.
highjack [hī'jak] = **hijack.**
high jump n (SPORT) Hochsprung m.
highlands [hī'ləndz] npl Hochland nt.
high-level [hī'levəl] a (meeting) wichtig, Spitzen-; (talks etc) auf höchster Ebene.
high-level language n (COMPUT) höhere Programmiersprache f.
highlight [hī'līt] n (fig) Höhepunkt m.
highly [hī'lē] ad in hohem Maße, höchst; (praise) in hohen Tönen; ~ **paid** hoch bezahlt; **to speak** ~ **of sb/sth** sich über jdn/etw sehr positiv äußern.
highly-strung [hī'lēstrung'] a (Brit) = **highstrung.**
High Mass n Hochamt nt.
highness [hī'nis] n Höhe f; **H**~ Hoheit f.
high-pitched [hī'picht'] a (voice) hoch, schrill, hell.
high-powered [hī'pou'ûrd] a (engine) Hochleistungs-; (fig: person) Spitzen-.
high-pressure [hī'presh'ûr] a Hochdruck-; (fig) aufdringlich.
high school n Oberschule f.
high season n Hochsaison f.
high-speed [hī'spēd] a Schnell-.
high-spirited [hī'spir'itid] a temperamentvoll, lebhaft.
high street n (Brit) Hauptstraße f.

high-strung [hī'strung'] a (US) überempfind-
lich, reizbar.
high tide n Flut f.
highway [hī'wā] n Landstraße f.
Highway Code n (Brit) Straßenverkehrsordnung f.
highwayman [hī'wāmən] n, pl -men Räuber
m, Wegelagerer m.
highway robbery n (US fig) offene(r) Diebstahl m.
hijack [hī'jak] vt hijacken, entführen ♦ n
(also: ~ing) Entführung f.
hijacker [hī'jakûr] n Entführer m, Luftpirat
m.
hike [hīk] vi wandern ♦ vt (also: ~ up) hochziehen ♦ n Wanderung f; (col: in prices etc)
Erhöhung f.
hiker [hī'kûr] n Wanderer(in f) m.
hiking [hī'king] n Wandern nt.
hilarious [hilär'ēəs] a zum Schreien komisch.
hilarity [hilar'itē] n Lustigkeit f.
hill [hil] n Berg m.
hillbilly [hil'bilē] n (US pej) Hinterwäldler(in
f) m; (: female) Landpomeranze f.
hillock [hil'ək] n Hügel m, Anhöhe f.
hillside [hil'sïd] n (Berg)hang m.
hilltop [hil'tâp] n Bergspitze f.
hilly [hil'ē] a hügelig.
hilt [hilt] n Heft nt; **up to the** ~ (fig: support) voll und ganz; (involved, in debt also)
bis über beide Ohren.
him [him] pron (acc) ihn; (dat) ihm.
Himalayas [himəlā'əz] npl Himalaja m.
himself [himself'] pron sich (selbst);
(emphatic) selbst; **he's not** ~ mit ihm ist
etwas los or nicht in Ordnung.
hind [hīnd] a hinter, Hinter- ♦ n Hirschkuh f.
hinder [hin'dûr] vt (stop) hindern; (delay) behindern.
hindquarters [hīnd'kwôrtûrz] npl (ZOOL)
Hinterteil nt.
hindrance [hin'drəns] n (delay) Behinderung
f; (obstacle) Hindernis nt.
hindsight [hīnd'sīt] n: **with the benefit of** ~
im nachhinein.
Hindu [hin'dōō] n Hindu m.
hinge [hinj] n Scharnier nt; (on door) Türan-
gel f ♦ vt mit Scharnieren versehen ♦ vi
(fig) abhängen (on von).
hint [hint] n Tip m, Andeutung f; (trace) Anflug m; **to drop a** ~ eine Andeutung machen; **give me a** ~ geben Sie mir einen Hinweis ♦ vt andeuten (to gegenüber); **what
are you ~ing (at)?** was wollen Sie damit andeuten?
hip [hip] n Hüfte f; (BOT) Hagebutte f.
hip flask n Flachmann m.
hippie [hip'ē] n Hippie m.
hip pocket n Gesäßtasche f.
hippopotamus [hipəpāt'əməs] n Nilpferd nt.
hippy [hip'ē] n = **hippie**.
hire [hiûr] vt (worker) anstellen; (Brit: car)
mieten ♦ n Miete f; **for** ~ (taxi) frei; **to
have for** ~ verleihen; **on** ~ geliehen, gemie-

tet.
hire out vt vermieten, verleihen.
hire(d) car n (Brit) Mietwagen m.
hire purchase n (Brit) Ratenkauf m; **to buy
sth on** ~ etw auf Raten kaufen.
his [hiz] poss pron sein(e) ♦ poss seine(r, s);
this is ~ das gehört ihm.
hiss [his] vi zischen ♦ n Zischen nt.
histogram [his'təgram] n Säulendiagramm nt.
historian [histôr'ēən] n Historiker(in f) m.
historic [histôr'ik] a historisch.
historical [histôr'ikəl] a historisch, geschichtlich.
history [his'tûrē] n Geschichte f; (personal)
Entwicklung f; **there's a long** ~ **of that illness in his family** die Krankheit liegt in der
Familie.
histrionics [histrēân'iks] npl Theater nt, Getue nt.
hit [hit] vt irreg pt, pp **hit** schlagen; (injure)
treffen, verletzen ♦ n (blow) Schlag m, Stoß
m; (success) Erfolg m; (on target) Treffer
m; (MUS) Hit m.
hit back vi: **to** ~ **back at** zurückschlagen.
hit out at vt fus: **to** ~ **out at sb** auf jdn
einschlagen or losschlagen; (fig) jdn scharf
angreifen or attackieren.
hit (up)on vt fus (answer, solution) stoßen
auf (+acc), finden.
hitch [hich] vt festbinden; (pull up) hochziehen ♦ n (loop) Knoten m; (difficulty)
Schwierigkeit f, Haken m; **technical** ~ tech-
nische(r) Haken m.
hitch up vt (horse, cart) anschirren, anspannen.
hitchhike [hich'hīk] vi trampen, per Anhalter
fahren.
hitchhiker [hich'hīkûr] n Tramper(in f) m,
Anhalter(in f) m.
hi-tech [hī'tek'] a Hi-Tech-.
hitherto [hith'ûrtōō] ad bis jetzt, bisher.
hit man n Killer m.
hit-or-miss [hit'ərmis'] a: **it was a** ~ **affair**
es ging alles aufs Geratewohl.
hit parade n Hitparade f.
hive [hīv] n Bienenkorb m; **the shop was a** ~
of activity (fig) der Laden glich einem Bie-
nenhaus.
hive off vt (col) ausgliedern, abspalten.
hl abbr (= hectoliter(s)) hl.
HM abbr (= His (or Her) Majesty) S.M., I.M.
HMG abbr (Brit) = His (or Her) Majesty's
Government.
HMO n abbr (US: = health maintenance organization) (freiwillige) Krankenversicherung.
HMS abbr (Brit) = His (or Her) Majesty's
Ship.
hoard [hôrd] n Schatz m ♦ vt horten, hamstern.
hoarding [hôr'ding] n (Brit) Bretterzaun m;
(for advertising) Reklamewand f.
hoarfrost [hôr'frâst] n (Rauh)reif m.
hoarse [hôrs] a heiser, rauh.

hoax [hōks] *n* Streich *m.*
hob [hâb] *n* Kochmulde *f.*
hobble [hâb'əl] *vi* humpeln.
hobby [hâb'ē] *n* Steckenpferd *nt*, Hobby *nt.*
hobbyhorse [hâb'ēhôrs] *n* (*fig*) Steckenpferd *nt.*
hobnob [hâb'nâb] *vi*: **to ~ (with sb)** (mit jdm) auf Du und Du stehen.
hobo [hō'bō] *n* (*US*) Tippelbruder *m.*
hock [hâk] *vt* (*col*) versetzen, verpfänden ♦ *n* (*of animal*) Sprunggelenk *nt*; (*Brit: wine*) weiße(r) Rheinwein *m*; (*col*): **in ~** (*pawned*) verpfändet, versetzt, im Leihhaus.
hockey [hâk'ē] *n* Hockey *nt.*
hocus-pocus [hō'kəspō'kəs] *n* (*trickery*) faule Tricks *pl*, Hokuspokus *m*; (*words: of magician*) Hokuspokus *m.*
hodgepodge [hâj'pâj] *n* (*US*) Durcheinander *nt*, Mischmasch *m.*
hoe [hō] *n* Hacke *f* ♦ *vt* hacken.
hog [hôg] *n* Schlachtschwein *nt* ♦ *vt* in Beschlag nehmen.
hoist [hoist] *n* Winde *f* ♦ *vt* hochziehen.
hold [hōld] *irreg vt* halten; (*keep*) behalten; (*contain*) enthalten; (*be able to contain*) fassen; (*keep back*) zurück(be)halten; (*breath*) anhalten; (*meeting*) abhalten; **to ~ office** (*POL*) (ein) Amt innehaben; **he ~s the view that ...** er vertritt die Meinung, daß ...; **to ~ sb responsible for sth** jdn für etw verantwortlich machen ♦ *vi* (*withstand pressure*) standhalten, aushalten; (*be valid*) gelten; **to ~ firm** *or* **fast** (fest)halten ♦ *n* Griff *m*; (*grasp*) Halt *m*; (*NAUT. AVIAT*) Laderaum *m*; **to get ~ of sb/sth** jdn/etw finden *or* auftreiben (*col*).
hold back *vt* zurückhalten; **to ~ sb back from doing sth** jdn daran hindern, etw zu tun.
hold down *vt* niederhalten; (*job*) behalten.
hold forth *vi* sich ergehen, sich auslassen (*on* über +*acc*).
hold off *vi*: **if the rain ~s off** wenn es nicht regnet.
hold on *vi* sich festhalten; (*resist*) durchhalten; (*wait*) warten.
hold on to *vt fus* festhalten an (+*dat*); (*keep*) behalten.
hold out *vt* hinhalten, bieten ♦ *vi* aushalten; **to ~ out (against)** sich behaupten (gegen).
hold over *vt* (*meeting etc: postpone*) verschieben (*until* auf +*acc*).
hold up *vt* (*delay*) aufhalten; (*traffic*) ins Stocken bringen; (*rob*) überfallen.
holdall [hōld'ôl] *n* (*Brit*) Reisetasche *f.*
holder [hōl'dûr] *n* (*container*) Behälter *m*; (*of passport, post*) Inhaber(in *f*) *m.*
holding [hōl'ding] *n* (*share*) (Aktien)anteil *m.*
holding company *n* Dachgesellschaft *f.*
hold-up [hōld'up] *n* (*in traffic*) Stockung *f*; (*robbery*) Überfall *m.*
hole [hōl] *n* Loch *nt*; **to pick ~s in sth** (*fig*)

etw auseinandernehmen; **a ~ in the heart** (*MED*) ein Loch im Herz ♦ *vt* durchlöchern; **to be ~d** (*ship*) leck schlagen.
hole up *vi* sich verkriechen.
holiday [hâl'idā] *n* (*day*) Feiertag *m*; (*from work*) freie(r) Tag *m*; (*Brit: vacation*) Urlaub *m*; (: *SCH*) Ferien *pl*; **to be on ~** im Urlaub *or* in den Ferien sein.
holiday camp *n* (*Brit*) Feriendorf *nt.*
holiday-maker [hâl'idāmākûr] *n* (*Brit*) Feriengast *m*, Urlauber(in *f*) *m.*
holiday pay *n* (*Brit*) Urlaubsgeld *nt.*
holiday season *n* (*US: Christmas etc*) Festzeit *f*; (*Brit*) Ferienzeit *f.*
holiness [hō'lēnis] *n* Heiligkeit *f.*
Holland [hâl'ənd] *n* Holland *nt.*
hollow [hâl'ō] *a* hohl; (*fig*) leer ♦ *n* Vertiefung *f*; (*in rock*) Höhle *f.*
hollow out *vt* aushöhlen.
holly [hâl'ē] *n* Stechpalme *f.*
hollyhock [hâl'ēhâk] *n* Malve *f.*
holocaust [hâl'əkôst] *n* Inferno *nt*, Holocaust *m.*
holster [hōl'stûr] *n* Pistolenhalfter *m.*
holy [hō'lē] *a* heilig; (*religious*) fromm; **the H~ Father** der Heilige Vater.
Holy Communion *n* Heilige Kommunion *f.*
Holy Ghost, Holy Spirit *n* Heilige(r) Geist *m.*
homage [hâm'ij] *n* Huldigung *f*; **to pay ~ to** huldigen (+*dat*).
home [hōm] *n* Heim *nt*, Zuhause *nt*; (*institution*) Heim *nt*, Anstalt *f*; **it's near my ~** es ist bei mir in der Nähe; **at ~** zu Hause ♦ *a* einheimisch; (*POL*) inner; (*SPORT: team, game, win*) Heim- ♦ *ad* heim, nach Hause; **to go ~** nach Hause gehen *or* fahren.
home address *n* Heimatadresse *f.*
home-brew [hōm'brōō'] *n* selbstgebraute(s) Bier *nt.*
homecoming [hōm'kuming] *n* Heimkehr *f.*
Home Counties *npl* (*Brit*) Grafschaften, die an London angrenzen.
home economics *n sing* Hauswirtschaft(slehre) *f.*
home-grown [hōm'grōn'] *a* selbstgezogen, einheimisch.
home key *n* (*COMPUT*) Home-Taste *f.*
homeland [hōm'land] *n* Heimat(land *nt*) *f.*
homeless [hōm'lis] *a* obdachlos ♦ *npl*: **the ~** die Obdachlosen *pl.*
home loan *n* Wohnungsbaudarlehen *nt.*
homely [hōm'lē] *a* häuslich; (*US: ugly*) unscheinbar.
homemade [hōm'mād'] *a* selbstgemacht.
Home Office *n* (*Brit*) Innenministerium *nt.*
homeopath [hō'mēəpath] *n* (*US*) Homöopath(in *f*) *m.*
homeopathic [hōmēəpath'ik] *a* (*US*) homöopathisch.
homeopathy [hōmēâp'əthē] *n* (*US*) Homöopathie *f.*
home rule *n* Selbstverwaltung *f.*
Home Secretary *n* (*Brit*) Innenminister(in

f) *m.*

homesick [hōm'sik] *a*: **to be** ~ Heimweh haben.

homestead [hōm'sted] *n* Heimstätte *f*, Gehöft *nt*; (*US*) Siedlerstätte *f*.

homeward(s) [hōm'wûrd(z)] *a* nach Haus(e), heim.

homework [hōm'wûrk] *n* Hausaufgaben *pl*.

homicidal [hâmisīd'əl] *a* gemeingefährlich; (*mood also*) Morde-.

homicide [hâm'isīd] *n* (*US*) Totschlag *m*, Mord *m.*

homily [hâm'ilē] *n* Predigt *f.*

homing [hō'ming] *a* (*device, missile*) mit Zielsucheinrichtung.

homing pigeon *n* Brieftaube *f.*

homoeopath [hō'mēəpath] *etc* (*Brit*) = **homeopath** *etc.*

homogeneous [hōməjē'nēəs] *a* homogen, gleichartig.

homogenize [həmâj'əniz] *vt* homogenisieren.

homosexual [hōməsek'shōoəl] *a* homosexuell ♦ *n* Homosexuelle(r) *mf.*

Hon. *abbr* (= *honorable; honorary*) *Titel.*

Honduras [hundōo'rəs] *n* Honduras *nt.*

hone [hōn] *n* Schleifstein *m* ♦ *vt* feinschleifen; (*sharpen: also fig*) schärfen.

honest [ân'ist] *a* ehrlich; (*upright*) aufrichtig; **to be quite** ~ **with you** ... um ehrlich mit Ihnen zu sein, ...

honestly [ân'istlē] *ad* ehrlich.

honesty [ân'istē] *n* Ehrlichkeit *f.*

honey [hun'ē] *n* Honig *m*; (*col*) Schätzchen *nt.*

honeycomb [hun'ēkōm] *n* Honigwabe *f* ♦ *vt* (*fig*) durchlöchern.

honeymoon [hun'ēmōon] *n* Flitterwochen *pl*, Hochzeitsreise *f.*

honeysuckle [hun'ēsukəl] *n* Geißblatt *nt.*

Hong Kong [hâng' kông'] *n* Hongkong *nt.*

honk [hângk] *n* (*AUT*) Hupensignal *nt* ♦ *vi* hupen.

Honolulu [hânəlōo'lōo] *n* Honolulu *nt.*

honor [ân'ûr] (*US*) *vt* ehren; (*check*) annehmen; (*debts*) begleichen; (*contract*) einhalten ♦ *n* (*respect*) Ehre *f*; (*reputation*) Ansehen *nt*, gute(r) Ruf *m*; ~**s** (*titles*) Auszeichnungen *pl*; **in** ~ **of** zu Ehren von; **it's a great** ~ es ist eine große Ehre.

honorable [ân'ûrəbəl] *a* ehrenwert, rechtschaffen; (*intention*) ehrenhaft.

honorary [ân'ərärē] *a* Ehren-.

honor-bound [ân'ûrbound'] *a*: **if you've promised, then you're** ~ **to** ... wenn du es versprochen hast, bist du auch (moralisch) verpflichtet, zu ...

honors [ân'ûrz] *n* (*US*) akademischer Grad *mit Prüfung in Spezialfach.*

honour [ân'ûr] *etc* (*Brit*) = **honor** *etc.*

honours degree *n* (*Brit*) = **honors.**

Hons. *abbr* (*UNIV*) = **honors.**

hood [hōod] *n* Kapuze *f*; (*US AUT*) Kühlerhaube *f*; (*Brit AUT*: *roof*) Verdeck *nt*; (*US col*) Gangster(in *f*) *m*, Ganove *m*, Ganovin *f.*

hooded [hōod'id] *a* (*robber*) maskiert.

hoodlum [hōod'ləm] *n* Rowdy *m*; (*member of gang*) Gangster *m.*

hoodwink [hōod'wingk] *vt* reinlegen.

hoof [hōof] *n, pl* **-s** *or* **hooves** [hōovz] Huf *m.*

hook [hōok] *n* Haken *m*; ~**s and eyes** Haken und Ösen; **by** ~ **or by crook** auf Biegen und Brechen ♦ *vt* einhaken; **to be** ~**ed on** (**sth**) (*col*) auf (etw) stehen.

hook up *vt* (*RAD, TV etc*) anschließen (*with* an +*acc*).

hooker [hōok'ûr] *n* (*col*) Nutte *f.*

hook-up [hōok'up] *n* Gemeinschaftssendung *f.*

hooky [hōok'ē] *n* (*US col*): **to play** ~ (die Schule) schwänzen.

hooligan [hōo'ligən] *n* Rowdy *m.*

hooliganism [hōo'ligənizəm] *n* Rowdytum *nt.*

hoop [hōop] *n* Reifen *m.*

hoot [hōot] *vi* (*owl*) schreien, rufen; (*Brit AUT*) hupen; **to** ~ **with laughter** schallend lachen ♦ *n* (*shout*) Johlen *nt*; (*AUT*) Hupen *nt.*

hooter [hōo'tûr] *n* (*NAUT*) Dampfpfeife *f*; (*AUT*) (Auto)hupe *f*; (*Brit: factory* ~) Sirene *f.*

hoover [hōo'vûr] (*Brit*) *n* ® Staubsauger *m* ♦ *vt* staubsaugen.

hooves [hōovz] *npl of* **hoof.**

hop [hâp] *vi* hüpfen, hopsen ♦ *n* (*jump*) Hopser *m*; (*BOT*) Hopfen *m.*

hope [hōp] *vi* hoffen; **I** ~ **that...** hoffentlich... ♦ *n* Hoffnung *f.*

hopeful [hōp'fəl] *a* hoffnungsvoll; (*promising*) vielversprechend; **I'm** ~ **that she'll manage to come** ich hoffe, daß sie kommen kann.

hopefully [hōp'fəlē] *ad* hoffnungsvoll; (*I etc hope*) hoffentlich.

hopeless [hōp'lis] *a* hoffnungslos; (*useless*) unmöglich.

hopelessly [hōp'lislē] *ad* (*live etc*) hoffnungslos; (*involved, complicated*) aussichtslos; **I'm** ~ **confused/lost** ich bin total verwirrt/ ich habe mich total verirrt.

hopper [hâp'ûr] *n* (*chute*) Einfülltrichter *m.*

horde [hôrd] *n* Horde *f.*

horizon [hərī'zən] *n* Horizont *m.*

horizontal [hôrizân'təl] *a* horizontal.

hormone [hôr'mōn] *n* Hormon *nt.*

horn [hôrn] *n* Horn *nt*; (*AUT*) Hupe *f.*

horned [hôrnd] *a* gehörnt, Horn-.

hornet [hôr'nit] *n* Hornisse *f.*

horny [hôr'nē] *a* schwielig; (*col*) scharf.

horoscope [hôr'əskōp] *n* Horoskop *nt.*

horrible [hôr'əbəl] *a*, **horribly** [hôr'əblē] *ad* fürchterlich.

horrid [hôr'id] *a*, **horridly** [hôr'idlē] *ad* abscheulich, scheußlich.

horrific [hôrif'ik] *a* (*accident*) entsetzlich; (*film*) schrecklich.

horrify [hôr'əfi] *vt* entsetzen.

horrifying [hôr'əfiing] *a* schrecklich, fürchterlich.

horror [hôr'ûr] *n* Schrecken *m*; (*great dislike*)

Abscheu *m* (*of* vor +*dat*).

horror film *n* Horrorfilm *m*.

horror-stricken [hôr'ûrstrikən] *a* = **horror-struck**.

horror-struck [hôr'ûrstruk] *a* von Entsetzen *or* Grauen gepackt.

hors d'œuvre [ôr dûrv'] *n* Vorspeise *f*.

horse [hôrs] *n* Pferd *nt*.

horseback [hôrs'bak] *n*: **on** ~ zu Pferd.

horseback riding *n* (*US*) Reiten *nt*.

horsebox [hôrs'bâks] *n* (*Brit*) = **horsetrailer**.

horse chestnut *n* Roßkastanie *f*.

horse-drawn [hôrs'drôn] *a* von Pferden gezogen, Pferde-.

horsefly [hôrs'flī] *n* (Pferde)bremse *f*.

horseman [hôrs'mən] *n*, *pl* **-men** Reiter *m*.

horsemanship [hôrs'mənship] *n* Reitkunst *f*.

horseplay [hôrs'plā] *n* Alberei *f*, Balgerei *f*.

horsepower [hôrs'pouûr] *n* Pferdestärke *f*.

horse racing *n* Pferderennen *nt*.

horseradish [hôrs'radish] *n* Meerrettich *m*.

horse riding *n* (*Brit*) = **horseback riding**.

horseshoe [hôrs'shōō] *n* Hufeisen *nt*.

horse show *n* Pferdeschau *f*, Querfeldeinrennen *nt*.

horse-trader [hôrs'trādûr] *n* Pferdehändler *m*.

horsetrailer [hôrs'trāl'ûr] *n* (*US*) Pferdetransporter *m*.

horse trials *npl* = **horse show**.

horsewhip [hôrs'hwip] *vt* auspeitschen.

horsewoman [hôrs'wōōmən] *n*, *pl* **-women** Reiterin *f*.

hors(e)y [hôr'sē] *a* (*col*: *person*) pferdenärrisch.

horticulture [hôr'təkulchûr] *n* Gartenbau *m*.

hose [hōz] *n* (*also*: ~**pipe**) Schlauch *m*.

   hose down *vt* abspritzen.

hosiery [hō'zhûrē] *n* Strumpfwaren *pl*.

hospice [hâs'pis] *n* Hospiz *nt*.

hospitable [hâspit'əbəl] *a* gastfreundlich.

hospital [hâs'pitəl] *n* Krankenhaus *nt*.

hospitality [hâspətal'itē] *n* Gastfreundschaft *f*.

hospitalize [hâs'pitəlīz] *vt* ins Krankenhaus einweisen.

host [hōst] *n* Gastgeber *m*; (*innkeeper*) (Gast)wirt *m*; (*large number*) Heerschar *f*; (*ECCL*) Hostie *f*; (*TV, RAD*) Gastgeber *m* ♦ *vt* (*program, games*) Gastgeber sein bei.

hostage [hâs'tij] *n* Geisel *f*.

hostel [hâs'təl] *n* (*for students, nurses etc*) (Wohn)heim *nt*; (*for homeless people*) Herberge *f*.

hostelling [hâs'təling] *n*: **to go (youth)** ~ in Jugendherbergen übernachten.

hostess [hōs'tis] *n* Gastgeberin *f*; (*in nightclub*) Hosteß *f*; (*Brit AVIAT*) Stewardeß *f*.

hostile [hâs'təl] *a* feindlich.

hostility [hâstil'ətē] *n* Feindschaft *f*.

hostilities [hâstil'ətēz] *npl* Feindseligkeiten *pl*.

hot [hât] *a* heiß; (*drink, food, water*) warm; (*spiced*) scharf; (*angry*) hitzig; **to be** ~ (*col*: *person*) fähig sein; (: *thing*) zugkräftig

sein; ~ **news** das Neueste vom Neuen.

   hot up *vi* (*Brit col*: *situation*) sich verschärfen *or* zuspitzen; (: *party*) in Schwung kommen; (: *pace*) steigern; (: *engine*) frisieren.

hot air *n* (*col*) Gewäsch *nt*.

hot-air balloon [hâtär' bəlōōn'] *n* (*AVIAT*) Heißluftballon *m*.

hotbed [hât'bed] *n* (*fig*) Nährboden *m*.

hot-blooded [hât'blud'id] *a* heißblütig.

hotchpotch [hâch'pâch] *n* (*Brit*) = **hodgepodge**.

hot dog *n* heiße(s) Würstchen *nt*.

hotel [hōtel'] *n* Hotel *nt*.

hotelier [ôtelyā'] *n* Hotelier *m*.

hotel industry *n* Hotelgewerbe *nt*.

hotel room *n* Hotelzimmer *nt*.

hotfoot [hât'fōōt] *ad* eilends.

hotheaded [hât'hedid] *a* hitzig, aufbrausend.

hothouse [hât'hous] *n* (*lit, fig*) Treibhaus *nt*.

hot line [hât līn] *n* (*POL*) heiße(r) Draht *m*.

hotly [hât'lē] *ad* (*argue*) hitzig; (*pursue*) dicht.

hotplate [hât'plāt] *n* Kochplatte *f*.

hotpot [hât'pât] *n* (*Brit COOK*) Fleischeintopf *f* mit Kartoffeleinlage.

hot seat *n* Schleudersitz *m*.

hot spot *n* Krisenherd *m*.

hot spring *n* heiße Quelle *f*, Thermalquelle *f*.

hot-tempered [hât'tem'pûrd] *a* leicht aufbrausend, jähzornig.

hot-water bottle [hâtwôt'ûr bâtəl] *n* Wärmflasche *f*.

hound [hound] *n* Jagdhund *m* ♦ *vt* jagen, hetzen.

hour [ou'ûr] *n* Stunde *f*; (*time of day*) (Tages)zeit *f*; **lunch** ~ Mittagspause *f*; **at 30 miles an** ~ mit 30 Meilen in der Stunde; **to pay sb by the** ~ jdn stundenweise bezahlen.

hourly [ouûr'lē] *a*, *ad* stündlich.

hourly rate *n* Stundenlohn *m*.

house *n* [hous] Haus *nt*; **at my** ~ bei mir zu Hause; **to my** ~ zu mir nach Hause ♦ *vt* [houz] (*accommodate*) unterbringen; (*shelter*) aufnehmen.

houseboat [hous'bōt] *n* Hausboot *nt*.

housebound [hous'bound] *a* ans Haus gefesselt.

housebreaking [hous'brāking] *n* Einbruch *m*.

housebroken [hous'brōkən] *a* (*US: animal*) stubenrein.

housecoat [hous'kōt] *n* Morgenrock *m*.

household [hous'hōld] *n* Haushalt *m*.

householder [hous'hōldûr] *n* Haus-/Wohnungsinhaber(in *f*) *m*; (*head of house*) Hausherr(in *f*) *m*.

house hunting *n*: **to go** ~ auf Haussuche gehen.

housekeeper [hous'kēpûr] *n* Haushälterin *f*.

housekeeping [hous'kēping] *n* Haushaltung *f*; (*COMPUT*) Organisation *f*; (*also*: ~ **money**) Haushalts- *or* Wirtschaftsgeld *nt*.

houseman [hous'mən] *n*, *pl* **-men** (*Brit MED*) Medizinalassistent *m*.

house plant n Zimmerpflanze f.
house-proud [hous'proud] a: **she is very ~** sie ist eine penible Hausfrau.
house-to-house [houstəhous'] a (collection, search) Haus-.
house-trained [hous'trānd] a (Brit) = **housebroken**.
housewarming [hous'wôrming] n (also: ~ party) Einweihungsparty f.
housewife [hous'wīf] n Hausfrau f.
housework [hous'wûrk] n Hausarbeit f.
housing [hou'zing] n (act) Unterbringung f; (houses) Wohnungen pl; (building of houses) Wohnungsbau m; (covering) Gehäuse nt ♦ cpd (problem, shortage) Wohnungs-.
housing association n Wohnungsbaugesellschaft f.
housing conditions npl Wohnungsbedingungen pl or -verhältnisse pl.
housing development, (Brit) **housing estate** n (Wohn)siedlung f.
housing project n (Wohn)siedlung f.
hovel [huv'əl] n elende Hütte f; (fig) Loch nt.
hover [huv'ûr] vi (bird) schweben; (person) wartend herumstehen; (helicopter) stehen; **to ~ on the brink of disaster** (fig) am Rande des Ruins stehen.
hovercraft [huv'ûrkraft] n Luftkissenboot nt, Hovercraft nt.
hoverport [huv'ûrpôrt] n Anlegestelle f für Hovercrafts.
how [hou] ad wie; **~ many** wie viele; **~ much** wieviel; **~ about a drink?** wie wär's mit etwas zu trinken?; **~ is school?** was macht die Schule?; **~ do you do?** (Brit) wie geht es Ihnen?
however [houev'ûr] ad (but) (je)doch, aber; **~ you phrase it** wie Sie es auch ausdrücken.
howitzer [hou'itsûr] n (MIL) Haubitze f.
howl [houl] n Heulen nt ♦ vi heulen.
howler [hou'lûr] n grobe(r) Schnitzer m.
hp n abbr (AUT: = horsepower) PS.
HP n abbr (Brit) = **hire purchase**.
HQ n abbr (= headquarters) HQ.
HR n abbr (US: = House of Representatives) Unterhaus des US-Kongresses.
HRH abbr (Brit: = His (or Her) Royal Highness) S.Kgl.H., I.Kgl.H.
hr(s). abbr (= hour; hours) Std.
HS abbr (US) = **high school**.
HST n abbr (US) = Hawaiian Standard Time.
hub [hub] n Radnabe f; (of the world) Mittelpunkt m; (of commerce) Zentrum nt.
hubbub [hub'ub] n Tumult m.
hub cap n (AUT) Radkappe f.
HUD n abbr (US: = Department of Housing and Urban Development) Behörde für Städteplanung.
huddle [hud'əl] vi sich zusammendrängen ♦ n Grüppchen nt.
hue [hyōō] n Färbung f, Farbton m; **~ and cry** Zetergeschrei nt.
huff [huf] n Eingeschnapptsein nt; **to go into**

a ~ einschnappen.
hug [hug] vt umarmen; (fig) sich dicht halten an (+acc) ♦ n Umarmung f.
huge [hyōōj] a groß, riesig.
hulk [hulk] n (ship) abgetakelte(s) Schiff nt; (person) Koloß m.
hulking [hul'king] a ungeschlacht.
hull [hul] n Schiffsrumpf m.
hullabaloo [huləbəlōō'] n (col: noise) Radau m.
hullo [həlō'] = **hello**.
hum [hum] vi summen; (engine, tool) brummen; (traffic) brausen ♦ vt summen ♦ n (also ELEC) Summen nt, Surren nt; (of traffic, machines) Brausen nt, Summen nt; (of voices etc) Gemurmel nt.
human [hyōō'mən] a menschlich ♦ n (also: ~ being) Mensch m.
humane [hyōōmān'] a human.
humanism [hyōō'mənizəm] n Humanismus m.
humanitarian [hyōōmanitär'ēən] a humanitär.
humanity [hyōōman'itē] n Menschheit f; (kindliness) Menschlichkeit f.
humanly [hyōō'mənlē] ad menschlich.
humanoid [hyōō'mənoid] a wie ein Mensch, in Menschengestalt.
human relations npl Human Relations pl.
humble [hum'bəl] a demütig; (modest) bescheiden ♦ vt demütigen.
humbly [hum'blē] ad demütig.
humbug [hum'bug] n (col: talk) Humbug m, Mumpitz m; (Brit: candy) Pfefferminzbonbon nt.
humdrum [hum'drum] a eintönig, langweilig.
humid [hyōō'mid] a feucht.
humidifier [hyōōmid'əfiûr] n Verdunster m.
humidity [hyōōmid'ətē] n Feuchtigkeit f.
humiliate [hyōōmil'ēāt] vt demütigen.
humiliation [hyōōmilēā'shən] n Demütigung f.
humility [hyōōmil'ətē] n Demut f.
humor [hyōō'mûr] (US) n (fun) Humor m; (mood) Stimmung f; **sense of ~** (Sinn m für) Humor m; **to be in a good/bad ~** gute/schlechte Laune haben ♦ vt nachgeben (+dat).
humorist [hyōō'mûrist] n Humorist m.
humorless [hyōō'mûrlis] a humorlos.
humorous [hyōō'mûrəs] a humorvoll, komisch.
humour [hyōō'mûr] etc (Brit) = **humor** etc.
hump [hump] n Buckel m.
humus [hyōō'məs] n (BIOL) Humus m.
hunch [hunch] n (feeling) Ahnung f; **I have a ~ that ...** ich habe den (leisen) Verdacht, daß ... ♦ vt (shoulders) hochziehen.
hunchback [hunch'bak] n Bucklige(r) m.
hunched [huncht] a gekrümmt.
hundred [hun'drid] num hundert; **around a ~ people** ungefähr hundert Personen; **I'm a ~ per cent sure** ich bin absolut sicher; **~s of people** Hunderte von Leuten.

hundredweight [hun'dridwāt] n Zentner m.
hung [hung] pt, pp of **hang**.
Hungarian [hunggär'ēən] a ungarisch ♦ n (person) Ungar(in f) m; (language) Ungarisch nt.
Hungary [hung'gûrē] n Ungarn nt.
hunger [hung'gûr] n Hunger m; (fig) Verlangen nt (for nach) ♦ vi hungern.
hunger strike n Hungerstreik m.
hungrily [hung'grilē] ad hungrig.
hungry [hung'grē] a hungrig; **to be ~** Hunger haben; **to be ~ for** (fig) sich sehnen nach.
hunk [hungk] n Stück nt.
hunt [hunt] vt jagen; (search): **to ~ for** suchen ♦ vi jagen ♦ n Jagd f.
hunt down vt Jagd machen auf (+acc); (capture) zur Strecke bringen.
hunter [hun'tûr] n Jäger m; (Brit: horse) Jagdpferd nt.
hunting [hun'ting] n Jagen nt, Jagd f.
hurdle [hûr'dəl] n (lit, fig) Hürde f.
hurl [hûrl] vt schleudern.
hurrah [hərä'] n Hurra nt.
hurray [hərä'] n = **hurrah**.
hurricane [hûr'əkən] n Orkan m.
hurried [hûr'ēd] a eilig; (hasty) übereilt.
hurriedly [hûr'ēdlē] ad übereilt, hastig.
hurry [hûr'ē] n Eile f; **to be in a ~** es eilig haben ♦ vi sich beeilen; **~!** mach schnell!; **I must ~ back/home** ich muß schnell zurück/nach Hause ♦ vt (an)treiben; (job) übereilen.
hurry along vi sich beeilen.
hurry away, hurry off vi schnell weggehen, forteilen.
hurry on vi: **to ~ on to sth** mit etw weitermachen.
hurry up vi sich beeilen ♦ vt (person) zur Eile antreiben; (work) vorantreiben.
hurt [hûrt] irreg vt pt, pp **hurt** weh tun (+dat); (injure, fig) verletzen; (business, interests etc) schaden; **I ~ my arm** ich habe mir am Arm weh getan; (injure also) ich habe mir den Arm verletzt ♦ vi weh tun; **where does it ~?** wo tut es weh?
hurtful [hûrt'fəl] a schädlich; (remark) verletzend.
hurtle [hûr'təl] vt schleudern ♦ vi sausen.
husband [huz'bənd] n (Ehe)mann m, Gatte m.
hush [hush] n Stille f ♦ vt zur Ruhe bringen ♦ vi still sein ♦ interj pst, still.
hush up vt (fact) vertuschen.
hushed [husht] a gedämpft, leise.
hush-hush [hush'hush] a (col) streng geheim.
husk [husk] n Spelze f.
husky [hus'kē] a (voice) rauh; (burly) stämmig ♦ n Eskimohund m.
hustings [hus'tingz] npl (Brit POL) Wahlkampf m; (: meeting) Wahlveranstaltung f.
hustle [hus'əl] vt (push) stoßen; (hurry) antreiben, drängen ♦ n (Hoch)betrieb m; **~ and bustle** Geschäftigkeit f.
hut [hut] n Hütte f.

hutch [huch] n (Kaninchen)stall m.
hyacinth [hī'əsinth] n Hyazinthe f.
hybrid [hī'brid] n Kreuzung f ♦ a Misch-.
hydrant [hī'drənt] n Hydrant m.
hydraulic [hīdrô'lik] a hydraulisch.
hydraulics [hīdrô'liks] n sing Hydraulik f.
hydrochloric acid [hīdrəklôr'ik as'id] n Salzsäure f.
hydroelectric [hīdrōilek'trik] a hydroelektrisch.
hydrofoil [hī'drəfoil] n Tragflächen- or Tragflügelboot nt.
hydrogen [hī'drəjən] n Wasserstoff m.
hydrogen bomb n Wasserstoffbombe f.
hydrophobia [hīdrəfō'bēə] n Hydrophobie f, Wasserscheu f.
hydroplane [hī'drəplān] n Wasserflugzeug nt, Flugboot nt.
hyena [hīē'nə] n Hyäne f.
hygiene [hī'jēn] n Hygiene f.
hygienic [hījēen'ik] a hygienisch.
hymn [him] n Kirchenlied nt.
hype [hīp] n (col) Gag m.
hyperactive [hīpûrak'tiv] a äußerst aktiv.
hypermarket [hī'pûrmârkit] n (Brit) Hypermarket m.
hypertension [hīpûrten'chən] n (MED) Hypertonie f, erhöhte(r) Blutdruck m.
hyphen [hī'fən] n Bindestrich m; (at end of line) Trennungszeichen nt.
hypnosis [hipnō'sis] n Hypnose f.
hypnotic [hipnât'ik] a hypnotisierend.
hypnotism [hip'nətizəm] n Hypnotismus m.
hypnotist [hip'nətist] n Hypnotiseur m.
hypnotize [hip'nətīz] vt hypnotisieren.
hypoallergenic [hīpōalûrjen'ik] a für äußerst empfindliche Haut.
hypochondriac [hīpəkân'drēak] n eingebildete(r) Kranke(r) mf, Hypochonder m.
hypocrisy [hipâk'rəsē] n Heuchelei f, Scheinheiligkeit f.
hypocrite [hip'əkrit] n Heuchler(in f) m, Scheinheilige(r) mf.
hypocritical [hipəkrit'ikəl] a heuchlerisch, scheinheilig.
hypodermic [hīpədûr'mik] n Subkutanspritze f.
hypothermia [hīpōthûr'mēə] n Unterkühlung f, Kältetod m.
hypothesis [hīpâth'əsis] n, pl **hypotheses** [hīpâth'əsēz] Hypothese f.
hypothetic(al) [hīpəthet'ik(əl)] a hypothetisch.
hysterectomy [histərek'təmē] n Hysterektomie f, Totaloperation f.
hysteria [histē'rēə] n Hysterie f.
hysterical [histär'ikəl] a hysterisch.
hysterics [histär'iks] npl hysterische(r) Anfall m; **to have ~** einen hysterischen Anfall haben.
Hz abbr (= hertz) Hz.

I, i [ī] *n* (*letter*) I *nt*, i *nt*; **I for Item** ≈ I wie Ida.

I [ī] *pron* ich ♦ *abbr* (= *island, isle*) I; (*US*) = *Interstate* (*Highway*).

IA *abbr* (*US MAIL*) = *Iowa*.

IAEA *n abbr* (= *International Atomic Energy Agency*) IAEA *f*.

IBA *n abbr* (*Brit*: = *Independent Broadcasting Authority*) Aufsichtsgremium der Fernseh- und Rundfunkanstalten.

Iberian [ibēr'ēən] *a* iberisch.

Iberian Peninsula *n* Iberische Halbinsel *f*.

IBEW *n abbr* (*US*: = *International Brotherhood of Electrical Workers*) Gewerkschaft.

ib(id). *abbr* (= *ibidem: from the same source*) ibd.

i/c *abbr* (*Brit*: = *in charge*) verantw.

ICBM *n abbr* (= *intercontinental ballistic missile*) Interkontinentalrakete *f*.

ICC *n abbr* (*US*: = *Interstate Commerce Commission*) Kommission *f* zur Regelung des Güterverkehrs zwischen den einzelnen Staaten; = **International Chamber of Commerce.**

ice [īs] *n* Eis *nt*; **to keep sth on** ~ (*fig*: *plan, project*) etw auf Eis legen ♦ *vt* (*COOK*) mit Zuckerguß überziehen ♦ *vi* (*also*: ~ **up**) vereisen.

Ice Age *n* Eiszeit *f*.

ic ax, (*Brit*) **ice axe** *n* Eispickel *m*.

iceberg [īs'bûrg] *n* Eisberg *m*; **the tip of the** ~ (*also fig*) die Spitze des Eisbergs.

icebox [īs'bâks] *n* (*US*: *old*) Kühlschrank *m*.

icebreaker [īs'brākûr] *n* Eisbrecher *m*.

ice bucket *n* Eiskühler *m*.

ice-cold [īs'kōld'] *a* eiskalt.

ice cream *n* Eis *nt*.

ice-cream soda [īs'krēm sō'də] *n* Eisbecher mit Milch, Sodawasser und Aromastoff.

ice cube *n* Eiswürfel *m*.

iced [īst] *a* (*drink*) eisgekühlt; (*coffee, tea*) Eis-; (*cake*) glasiert.

ice hockey *n* Eishockey *nt*.

Iceland [īs'lənd] *n* Island *nt*.

Icelander [īs'landûr] *n* Isländer(in *f*) *m*.

Icelandic [īslan'dik] *a* isländisch ♦ *n* (*language*) Isländisch *nt*.

ice lolly [īs lâl'ē] *n* (*Brit*) Eis *nt* am Stiel.

ice pick *n* Eispickel *m*.

ice rink *n* (Kunst)eisbahn *f*.

ice skate *n* Schlittschuh *m*.

ice-skate [īs'skāt] *vi* Schlittschuh laufen.

ice-skating [īs'skāting] *n* Eislauf *m*, Schlittschuhlaufen *nt*.

icicle [ī'sikəl] *n* Eiszapfen *m*.

icing [ī'sing] *n* (*on cake*) Zuckerguß *m*; (*on window*) Vereisung *f*.

icing sugar *n* (*Brit*) Puderzucker *m*.

ICJ *n abbr* = **International Court of Justice.**

icon [ī'kân] *n* Ikone *f*; (*COMPUT*) ikonische(s) Zeichen *nt*.

ICR *n abbr* (*US*: = *Institute for Cancer Research*) Krebsforschungsinstitut *nt*.

ICU *n abbr* (= *intensive care unit*) Intensivstation *f*.

icy [ī'sē] *a* (*slippery*) vereist; (*cold*) eisig.

ID *abbr* (*US MAIL*) = *Idaho*.

I'd [īd] = **I would; I had.**

Ida. *abbr* (*US*) = *Idah.*

ID card *n* (= *identification card*) ≈ Personalausweis *m*.

idea [īdē'ə] *n* Idee *f*; **no** ~ keine Ahnung; **good** ~! gute Idee!; **my** ~ **of a vacation** wie ich mir einen Urlaub vorstelle; **to have an** ~ **that** ... (so) ein Gefühl haben, daß ...; **I haven't the least** ~ ich habe nicht die leiseste Ahnung.

ideal [īdē'əl] *n* Ideal *nt* ♦ *a* ideal.

idealism [īdē'əlizəm] *n* Idealismus *m*.

idealist [īdē'əlist] *n* Idealist(in *f*) *m*.

ideally [īdē'əlē] *ad* ideal(erweise); ~ **the house should have four rooms** es wäre ideal, wenn das Haus vier Zimmer hätte.

identical [īden'tikəl] *a* identisch; (*twins*) eineiig.

identification [īdentəfəkā'shən] *n* Identifizierung *f*.

identify [īden'təfī] *vt* identifizieren; (*regard as the same*) gleichsetzen ♦ *vi*: **to** ~ **with** gleichsetzen mit.

Identikit (picture) [īden'təkit (pik'chûr)] *n* (*Brit*) Phantombild *nt*.

identity [īden'titē] *n* Identität *f*.

identity card *n* (*Brit*) Personalausweis *m*.

identity papers *npl* (Ausweis)papiere *pl*.

identity parade *n* (*Brit*) Gegenüberstellung *f*.

ideological [īdēəlâj'ikəl] *a* ideologisch, weltanschaulich.

ideology [īdēâl'əjē] *n* Ideologie *f*.

idiocy [id'ēəsē] *n* Idiotie *f*.

idiom [id'ēəm] *n* (*expression*) Redewendung *f*; (*dialect*) Idiom *nt*.

idiomatic [idēəmat'ik] *a* idiomatisch.

idiosyncrasy [idēəsing'krəsē] *n* Eigenart *f*.

idiot [id'ēət] *n* Idiot(in *f*) *m*.

idiotic [idēât'ik] *a* idiotisch.

idle [ī'dəl] *a* (*doing nothing*) untätig, müßig; (*lazy*) faul; (*useless*) vergeblich, nutzlos; (*machine*) außer Betrieb; (*engine*) im Leerlauf; (*threat, talk*) leer ♦ *vi* (*engine*) im Leerlauf sein.

idle away *vt* (*time*) vertrödeln, verbummeln.

idle capacity *n* Leerlaufkapazität *f*.

idle money *n* (*COMM*) brachliegende(s) Kapital *nt*.

idleness [ī'dəlnis] *n* Untätigkeit *f*; Faulheit *f*.

idler [īd'lûr] *n* Faulenzer(in *f*) *m*.

idle time n Leerlaufzeit f.
idol [ī'dəl] n Idol nt.
idolize [ī'dəlīz] vt vergöttern.
idyllic [īdil'ik] a idyllisch.
i.e. abbr (= id est: that is) d.h.
if [if] cj wenn, falls; (whether) ob; ~ only ...
wenn ... doch nur; ~ **not** falls nicht; ~ **necessary** falls nötig; **as** ~ als ob; **even** ~
auch wenn; **I'd be pleased** ~ **you could do
it** ich würde mich freuen, wenn Sie das machen könnten ♦ n: ~**s and buts** Wenn und
Aber nt.
igloo [ig'lōō] n Iglu m or nt.
ignite [ignīt'] vt (an)zünden.
ignition [ignish'ən] n Zündung f.
ignition key n (AUT) Zündschlüssel m.
ignoble [ignō'bəl] a schändlich, unwürdig.
ignominious [ignəmin'ēəs] a schmachvoll,
entwürdigend.
ignoramus [ignərā'məs] n Ignorant m.
ignorance [ig'nûrəns] n Unwissenheit f, Igno-
ranz f; **to keep sb in** ~ **of sth** jdn in Unkenntnis über etw (acc) lassen.
ignorant [ig'nûrənt] a unwissend; **to be** ~ **of**
(subject) sich nicht auskennen in, nicht bewandert sein in; (events) nicht informiert
sein über.
ignore [ignôr'] vt ignorieren.
ikon [ī'kán] n = **icon**.
IL abbr (US MAIL) = Illinois.
ILA n abbr (US: = International Longshore-
men's Association) Gewerkschaft.
ILGWU n abbr (US: = International Ladies'
Garment Workers Union) Gewerkschaft.
ill [il] a krank; (evil) schlecht, böse; **to feel** ~
sich unwohl fühlen ♦ n Übel nt; see also **ills**.
Ill. abbr (US) = Illinois.
I'll [īl] = **I will, I shall**.
ill-advised [il'advīzd'] a schlecht beraten, unklug.
ill-at-ease [il'ətēz'] a unbehaglich.
ill-considered [il'kənsid'ûrd] a (plan) übereilt, unüberlegt.
ill-disposed [il'dispōzd'] a: **to be** ~ **towards
sb/sth** jdm/etw nicht wohlgesinnt sein.
illegal [ilē'gəl] a, **illegally** [ilē'gəlē] ad illegal.
illegible [ilej'əbəl] a unleserlich.
illegitimate [ilijit'əmit] a unzulässig; (child)
unehelich.
ill-fated [il'fā'tid] a unselig.
ill-favored, (Brit) **ill-favoured** [il'fā'vûrd] a
(liter) ungestalt, häßlich.
ill-feeling [il'fē'ling] n (Brit) Verstimmung f.
ill-gotten gains [il'gát'ən gānz] npl unrechtmäßig erworbene(s) Gut nt.
illicit [ilis'it] a verboten.
ill-informed [il'infôrmd'] a (judgement,
speech) wenig sachkundig; (person) schlecht
informiert or unterrichtet.
illiterate [ilit'ûrit] a ungebildet.
ill-mannered [il'man'ûrd] a ungehobelt.
illness [il'nis] n Krankheit f.
illogical [ilâj'ikəl] a unlogisch.
ills [ilz] npl Übel nt; (fig) Mißstände pl.

ill-suited [il'sōō'tid] a (couple) nicht zusammenpassend; **he is** ~ **to the job** er ist für
die Stelle nicht geeignet.
ill-timed [il'tīmd] a ungelegen, unpassend.
ill-treat [il'trēt] vt mißhandeln.
ill-treatment [il'trēt'mənt] n Mißhandlung f.
illuminate [ilōō'mənāt] vt beleuchten.
illuminated sign [ilōō'mənātid sīn] n Leucht-
zeichen nt.
illuminating [ilōō'mənāting] a aufschlußreich.
illumination [ilōōmənā'shən] n Beleuchtung f.
illusion [ilōō'zhən] n Illusion f; **to be under
the** ~ **that** ... sich einbilden, daß ...
illusive [ilōō'siv] a illusorisch, trügerisch.
illusory [ilōō'sərē] a illusorisch, trügerisch.
illustrate [il'əstrāt] vt (book) illustrieren; (explain) veranschaulichen.
illustration [iləstrā'shən] n Illustration f; (explanation) Veranschaulichung f.
illustrator [il'əstrātûr] n Illustrator m.
illustrious [ilus'trēəs] a berühmt.
ill will n Groll m.
ILO n abbr = **International Labour Organization**.
ILWU n abbr (US: = International Longshore-
men's and Warehousemen's Union) Gewerkschaft.
I'm [īm] = **I am**.
image [im'ij] n Bild nt; (likeness) Abbild nt;
(public ~) Image nt.
imagery [im'ijrē] n Symbolik f.
imaginable [imaj'ənəbəl] a vorstellbar, denkbar.
imaginary [imaj'ənärē] a eingebildet; (world)
Phantasie-.
imagination [imajənā'shən] n Einbildung f;
(creative) Phantasie f.
imaginative [imaj'ənətiv] a phantasiereich,
einfallsreich.
imagine [imaj'in] vt sich vorstellen; (wrongly) sich einbilden.
imbalance [imbal'əns] n Unausgeglichenheit
f.
imbecile [im'bəsil] n Schwachsinnige(r) mf.
imbue [imbyōō'] vt durchdringen.
IMF n abbr (= International Monetary Fund)
IWF m.
imitate [im'ətāt] vt nachahmen, imitieren.
imitation [imətā'shən] n Nachahmung f, Imitation f.
imitator [im'ətātûr] n Nachahmer m.
immaculate [imak'yəlit] a makellos; (dress)
tadellos; (ECCL) unbefleckt.
immaterial [imətē'rēəl] a unwesentlich; **it is**
~ **whether** ... es ist unwichtig, ob ...
immature [imətōōr'] a unreif.
immaturity [imətōō'ritē] n Unreife f.
immeasurable [imezh'ûrəbəl] a (amount, distance) unmeßbar.
immediacy [imē'dēəsē] n Unmittelbarkeit f,
Direktheit f.
immediate [imē'dēit] a (instant) sofortig;
(near) unmittelbar; (relatives) nächste(r,
s); (needs) dringlich; **in the** ~ **future** in un-

mittelbarer Zukunft.

immediately [imē'dēitlē] ad sofort; (in position) unmittelbar.

immense [imens'] a unermeßlich.

immensely [imens'lē] ad ungeheuerlich; (grateful) unheimlich.

immensity [imen'sitē] n (of size, difference) ungeheure Größe f, Unermeßlichkeit f; the ~ of the problem das (gewaltige) Ausmaß des Problems.

immerse [imûrs'] vt eintauchen; to be ~d in (fig) vertieft sein in (+acc).

immersion heater [imûr'zhən hē'tûr] n (Brit) Heißwassergerät nt.

immigrant [im'əgrənt] n Einwanderer m, Einwanderin f.

immigrate [im'əgrāt] vi einwandern.

immigration [iməgrā'shən] n Einwanderung f.

immigration authorities npl Einwanderungsbehörden pl.

immigration laws npl Einwanderungsgesetze or -bestimmungen pl.

imminent [im'ənənt] a bevorstehend; (danger) drohend.

immobile [imō'bəl] a unbeweglich.

immobilize [imō'bəlīz] vt lähmen.

immoderate [imâd'ûrit] a (person) zügellos; (opinion, reaction, demand) übertrieben, extrem.

immodest [imâd'ist] a (indecent) unanständig; (boasting) unbescheiden.

immoral [imôr'əl] a unmoralisch; (sexually) unsittlich.

immorality [iməral'itē] n Verderbtheit f.

immortal [imôr'təl] a unsterblich ♦ n Unsterbliche(r) mf.

immortality [imôrtal'itē] n Unsterblichkeit f; (of book etc) Unvergänglichkeit f.

immortalize [imôr'təlīz] vt unsterblich machen.

immovable [imōō'vəbəl] a (object) unbeweglich; (person) fest; (fig) unüberwindlich.

immune [imyōōn'] a (secure) geschützt (from gegen), sicher (from vor +dat); (MED) immun (to gegen).

immunity [imyōō'nitē] n (MED, JUR, diplomatic) Immunität f; (fig) Freiheit f.

immunization [imyōōnəzā'shən] n Immunisierung f.

immunize [im'yənīz] vt immunisieren.

imp [imp] n (small devil) Kobold m; (col: child) Racker m.

impact [im'pakt] n (lit) Aufprall m; (force) Wucht f; (fig) Wirkung f.

impair [impär'] vt beeinträchtigen.

impale [impāl'] vt aufspießen.

impart [impârt'] vt (make known) mitteilen; (bestow) verleihen, geben (to dat).

impartial [impâr'shəl] a unparteiisch.

impartiality [impârshēal'itē] n Unparteilichkeit f.

impassable [impas'əbəl] a unpassierbar.

impasse [im'pas] n Sackgasse f.

impassioned [impash'ənd] a leidenschaftlich.

impassive [impas'iv] a gelassen.

impatience [impā'shəns] n Ungeduld f.

impatient [impā'shənt] a ungeduldig; to be ~ to do sth es nicht erwarten können, etw zu tun.

impatiently [impā'shəntlē] ad ungeduldig.

impeachment [impēch'mənt] n (öffentliche) Anklage f.

impeccable [impek'əbəl] a tadellos.

impecunious [impəkyōō'nēəs] a mittellos.

impede [impēd'] vt (be)hindern.

impediment [imped'əmənt] n Hindernis nt; (in speech) Sprachfehler m.

impel [impel'] vt (force): to ~ sb (to do sth) jdn nötigen(, etw zu tun).

impending [impen'ding] a bevorstehend.

impenetrable [impen'itrəbəl] a (lit, fig) undurchdringlich; (fortress) uneinnehmbar; (theory) undurchschaubar; (mystery) unergründlich.

imperative [impär'ətiv] a (necessary) unbedingt erforderlich ♦ n (GRAM) Imperativ m, Befehlsform f.

imperceptible [impûrsep'təbəl] a nicht wahrnehmbar.

imperfect [impûr'fikt] a (faulty) fehlerhaft; (incomplete) unvollständig ♦ n (GRAM) Imperfekt nt.

imperfection [impûrfek'shən] n Unvollkommenheit f; (fault) Fehler m; (faultiness) Fehlerhaftigkeit f.

imperial [impēr'ēəl] a kaiserlich.

imperialism [impēr'ēəlizəm] n Imperialismus m.

imperil [impär'əl] vt gefährden.

imperious [impēr'ēəs] a herrisch, gebieterisch.

impersonal [impûr'sənəl] a unpersönlich.

impersonate [impûr'sənāt] vt sich ausgeben als; (for amusement) imitieren.

impersonation [impûrsənā'shən] n Verkörperung f; (THEAT) Imitation f.

impersonator [impûr'sənātûr] n (THEAT) Imitator(in f) m.

impertinence [impûr'tənəns] n Unverschämtheit f.

impertinent [impûr'tənənt] a unverschämt, frech.

imperturbable [impûrtûr'bəbəl] a unerschütterlich.

impervious [impûr'vēəs] a undurchlässig; (fig) unempfänglich (to für).

impetuous [impech'ōōəs] a heftig, ungestüm.

impetus [im'pitəs] n Triebkraft f; (fig) Auftrieb m.

impinge on [impinj' ân] vt beeinträchtigen.

impish [imp'ish] a schelmisch.

implacable [implak'əbəl] a erbittert, unversöhnlich.

implant [implant'] vt (MED) implantieren; (fig: idea, principle) einpflanzen.

implausible [implô'zəbəl] a unglaubwürdig, nicht überzeugend.

implement n [im'pləmənt] Werkzeug nt, Gerät nt ♦ vt [im'pləment] ausführen.
implicate [im'plikāt] vt verwickeln, hineinziehen; **to ~ sb in sth** jdn in etw verwickeln.
implication [implikā'shən] n (meaning) Bedeutung f; (effect) Auswirkung f; (hint) Andeutung f; (in crime) Verwicklung f; **by ~** implizit.
implicit [implis'it] a (suggested) unausgesprochen; (utter) vorbehaltlos.
implicitly [implis'itlē] ad implizit; (agree) stillschweigend.
implore [implôr'] vt anflehen.
imploring [implôr'ing] a flehentlich, flehend.
imply [implī'] vt (hint) andeuten; (be evidence for) schließen lassen auf (+acc); **what does that ~?** was bedeutet das?
impolite [impəlīt'] a unhöflich.
impolitic [impâl'itik] a undiplomatisch.
imponderable [impân'dûrəbəl] a unwägbar.
import vt [impôrt'] einführen, importieren ♦ n [im'pôrt] Einfuhr f, Import m; (meaning) Bedeutung f, Tragweite f.
importance [impôr'təns] n Bedeutung f; (influence) Einfluß m; **to be of great/little ~** von großer/geringer Bedeutung sein.
important [impôr'tənt] a wichtig; (influential) bedeutend, einflußreich; **it's not ~** es ist unwichtig; **it is ~ that** ... es ist wichtig, daß ...
importantly [impôr'təntlē] ad (pej) wichtigtuerisch; **but, more ~** ... aber wichtiger noch ...
import duty [im'pôrt dōō'tē] n Einfuhrzoll m.
imported [impôr'tid] a eingeführt, importiert.
importer [impôr'tûr] n Importeur m.
import license n Einfuhrgenehmigung f.
import quota n Einfuhrkontingent nt.
impose [impōz'] vti auferlegen (on dat); (penalty, sanctions) verhängen (on gegen); **to ~ (o.s.) on sb** sich jdm aufdrängen; **to ~ on sb's kindness** jds Liebenswürdigkeit ausnützen.
imposing [impō'zing] a eindrucksvoll.
imposition [impəzish'ən] n Aufzwingen nt, Zumutung f; (of burden, fine) Auferlegung f; (SCH) Strafarbeit f.
impossibility [impâsəbil'itē] n Unmöglichkeit f.
impossible [impâs'əbəl] a unmöglich; **it is ~ for me to leave now** ich kann jetzt unmöglich gehen.
impossibly [impâs'əblē] ad unmöglich.
impostor [impâs'tûr] n Hochstapler(in f) m.
impotence [im'pətəns] n Impotenz f.
impotent [im'pətənt] a machtlos; (sexually) impotent.
impound [impound'] vt beschlagnahmen.
impoverished [impâv'ûrisht] a verarmt.
impracticable [imprak'tikəbəl] a undurchführbar.
impractical [imprak'tikəl] a unpraktisch.
imprecise [imprisīs'] a ungenau.
impregnable [impreg'nəbəl] a (castle) uneinnehmbar.

impregnate [impreg'nāt] vt (saturate) sättigen; (fertilize) befruchten; (fig) durchdringen.
impresario [imprəsâ'rēō] n Impresario m.
impress [impres'] vt (influence) beeindrucken; (imprint) (auf)drücken; **to ~ sth on sb** jdm etw einschärfen.
impression [impresh'ən] n Eindruck m; (on wax, footprint) Abdruck m; (of stamp) Aufdruck m; (of book) Auflage f; (takeoff) Nachahmung f; **I was under the ~ that** ... ich hatte den Eindruck, daß ...; **to make a good/bad ~ on sb** einen guten/schlechten Eindruck auf jdn machen.
impressionable [impresh'ənəbəl] a für Eindrücke empfänglich.
impressionist [impresh'ənist] n Impressionist(in f) m.
impressive [impres'iv] a eindrucksvoll.
imprint n [im'print] (on wax etc) Abdruck m; (TYP) Impressum nt ♦ vt [imprint'] aufdrucken.
imprison [impriz'ən] vt ins Gefängnis schicken.
imprisonment [impriz'ənmənt] n (action) Inhaftierung f; (state) Gefangenschaft f; **3 years' ~** eine Gefängnisstrafe von 3 Jahren.
improbable [impräb'əbəl] a unwahrscheinlich.
impromptu [imprâmp'tōō] a, ad aus dem Stegreif, improvisiert.
improper [imprâp'ûr] a (indecent) unanständig; (wrong) unrichtig, falsch; (unsuitable) unpassend.
impropriety [imprəprī'ətē] n Ungehörigkeit f.
improve [improōv'] vt verbessern ♦ vi besser werden.
improve (up)on vt fus (offer) überbieten.
improvement [improōv'mənt] n (Ver)besserung f; (of appearance) Verschönerung f; **to make ~s to** Verbesserungen vornehmen an.
improvisation [imprəvəzā'shən] n Improvisation f.
improvise [im'prəvīz] vti improvisieren.
imprudence [improōd'əns] n Unklugheit f.
imprudent [improōd'ənt] a unklug.
impudent [im'pyədənt] a unverschämt.
impugn [impyōōn'] vt (evidence etc) bekämpfen, bezweifeln; (person) angreifen; (motives) in Zweifel ziehen.
impulse [im'puls] n Impuls m; (desire) Drang m; **my first ~ was to...** ich wollte zuerst...; **to act on ~** aus einem Impuls heraus handeln.
impulse buying n Kauf m aus einem Impuls heraus.
impulsive [impul'siv] a impulsiv.
impunity [impyōō'nitē] n Straflosigkeit f.
impure [impyōōr'] a (dirty: water etc) unrein; (thoughts, motives) unsauber.
impurity [impyōōr'itē] n Unreinheit f; (TECH) Verunreinigung f.

in [in] *prep* in; *(made of)* aus; ~ **here/there** hierin/darin, hier/da drin *(col)*; ~ **the United States** in den Vereinigten Staaten; ~ **1986** (im Jahre) 1986; ~ **May/spring** im Mai/Frühling; ~ **the morning** am Morgen, morgens; ~ **writing** schriftlich; ~ **person** persönlich; ~ **all** insgesamt; **to be dressed** ~ **green** grüne Sachen anhaben; **to be** ~ **teaching** Lehrer(in *f*) *m* sein; **to be** ~ **publishing** im Verlagswesen (beschäftigt) sein; ~ **Dickens/a child** bei Dickens/einem Kind; ~ **him you'll have** ... an ihm hast du...; ~ **doing this he has** ... dadurch, daß er das tat, hat er ...; ~ **saying that I mean** ... wenn ich das sage, meine ich ...; **I haven't seen him** ~ **years** ich habe ihn seit Jahren nicht mehr gesehen; **once** ~ **a hundred years** alle hundert Jahre einmal; **a rise** ~ **prices** eine Preissteigerung; **to pay** ~ **dollars** mit *or* in Dollar bezahlen; **blind** ~ **the left eye** auf dem linken Auge *or* links blind; ~ **itself** an sich; ~ **that,** ~ **so** *or* **as far as** insofern als ♦ *ad* hinein; **to be** ~ zuhause sein; *(train)* da sein; *(fashionable)* in (Mode) sein; **to have it** ~ **for sb** *(col)* es auf jdn abgesehen haben ♦ *n*: ~**s and outs** Einzelheiten *pl*; **to know the** ~**s and outs** sich auskennen.
IN *abbr (US MAIL)* = *Indiana.*
in., ins. *abbr* = **inch; inches.**
inability [inəbil'ətē] *n* Unfähigkeit *f*; ~ **to pay** Zahlungsunfähigkeit *f*.
inaccessible [inakses'əbəl] *a* unzugänglich.
inaccuracy [inak'yûrəsē] *n* Ungenauigkeit *f*.
inaccurate [inak'yûrit] *a* ungenau; *(wrong)* unrichtig.
inaction [inak'shən] *n* Untätigkeit *f*.
inactive [inak'tiv] *a* untätig.
inactivity [inaktiv'itē] *n* Untätigkeit *f*.
inadequacy [inad'əkwəsē] *n* Unzulänglichkeit *f*; *(of punishment)* Unangemessenheit *f*.
inadequate [inad'əkwit] *a* unzulänglich; *(punishment)* unangemessen.
inadmissible [inədmis'əbəl] *a* unzulässig.
inadvertent [inədvûr'tənt] *a,* **inadvertently** [inədvûr'təntlē] *ad* unbeabsichtigt, ungewollt.
inadvisable [inədvī'zəbəl] *a* nicht ratsam.
inane [inān'] *a* dumm, albern.
inanimate [inan'əmit] *a* leblos.
inapplicable [inap'likəbəl] *a* unzutreffend.
inappropriate [inəprō'prēit] *a* unpassend, unangebracht.
inaptitude [inap'tətōōd] *n (for work etc)* Untauglichkeit *f*; *(of remark)* Ungeschicktheit *f*.
inarticulate [inârtik'yəlit] *a* unklar; **to be** ~ sich nicht ausdrücken können.
inartistic [inârtis'tik] *a* unkünstlerisch.
inasmuch as [inəzmuch' az] *ad* da, weil; *(in so far as)* soweit.
inattention [inəten'chən] *n* Unaufmerksamkeit *f*.
inattentive [inəten'tiv] *a* unaufmerksam.
inaudible [inô'dəbəl] *a* unhörbar.

inaugural [inô'gyûrəl] *a* Eröffnungs-; *(UNIV)* Antritts-.
inaugurate [inô'gyərāt] *vt (open)* einweihen; *(admit to office)* (feierlich) einführen.
inauguration [inôgyərā'shən] *n* Eröffnung *f*; (feierliche) Amtseinführung *f*.
inauspicious [inôspish'əs] *a* unheilverheißend, unheilträchtig.
in-between [in'bitwēn'] *a* Zwischen-.
inborn [in'bôrn] *a* angeboren.
inbred [in'bred] *a (quality)* angeboren.
inbreeding [in'brēding] *n* Inzucht *f*.
Inc. *abbr* = **incorporated.**
Inca [ing'kə] *a (also:* ~**n)** Inka-, inkaisch ♦ *n (person)* Inka *mf*.
incalculable [inkal'kyələbəl] *a (person)* unberechenbar; *(consequences, damage)* unabsehbar; *(amount)* unschätzbar, unermeßlich.
incapability [inkāpəbil'ətē] *n* Unfähigkeit *f*.
incapable [inkā'pəbəl] *a* unfähig; *(not able)* nicht einsatzfähig; **to be** ~ **(of doing sth)** unfähig sein(, etw zu tun).
incapacitate [inkəpas'ətāt] *vt* untauglich machen.
incapacitated [inkəpas'ətātid] *a* behindert; *(machine)* nicht gebrauchsfähig.
incapacity [inkəpas'itē] *n* Unfähigkeit *f*.
incarcerate [inkâr'sûrit] *vt* einkerkern.
incarnate [inkâr'nit] *a* menschgeworden; *(fig)* leibhaftig.
incarnation [inkârnā'shən] *n (ECCL)* Menschwerdung *f*; *(fig)* Inbegriff *m*.
incendiary [insen'dēârē] *a* Brand-; *(fig)* aufrührerisch ♦ *n* Brandstifter *m*; *(bomb)* Brandbombe *f*.
incense *n* [in'sens] Weihrauch *m* ♦ *vt* [insens'] erzürnen.
incentive [insen'tiv] *n* Anreiz *m*.
incentive bonus *n* Leistungszulage *f*.
incentive scheme *n* Prämiensystem *nt*.
inception [insep'shən] *n* Beginn *m*, Anfang *m*.
incessant [inses'ənt] *a,* **incessantly** [inses'əntlē] *ad* unaufhörlich.
incest [in'sest] *n* Inzest *m*.
inch [inch] *n* Zoll *m*; **a few** ~**es** ein paar Zentimeter; **he didn't give an** ~ er gab kein Zentimeter nach.
inch forward *vi* sich millimeterweise *or* stückchenweise vorwärts schieben.
incidence [in'sidəns] *n* Auftreten *nt*; *(of crime)* Quote *f*.
incident [in'sidənt] *n* Vorfall *m*; *(diplomatic etc)* Zwischenfall *m*.
incidental [insiden'təl] *a (music)* Begleit-; *(expenses)* Neben-; *(unplanned)* zufällig; *(unimportant)* nebensächlich; *(remark)* beiläufig; ~ **to sth** mit etw verbunden.
incidentally [insiden'təlē] *ad (by chance)* nebenbei; *(by the way)* nebenbei bemerkt, übrigens.
incinerate [insin'ərāt] *vt* verbrennen.
incinerator [insin'ərātûr] *n* Verbrennungsofen *m*.
incipient [insip'ēənt] *a* beginnend.

incision [insizh'ən] *n* Einschnitt *m*.
incisive [insī'siv] *a* (*style*) treffend; (*person*) scharfsinnig.
incisor [insī'zûr] *n* Schneidezahn *m*.
incite [insīt'] *vt* anstacheln.
incl. *abbr* (= *including, inclusive (of)*) inkl.
inclement [inklem'ənt] *a* (*weather*) rauh, unfreundlich.
inclination [inklənā'shən] *n* Neigung *f*.
incline *n* [in'klīn] Abhang *m* ♦ *vt* [inklīn'] neigen; (*fig*) veranlassen; **to be** ~**d to do sth** Lust haben, etw zu tun; (*have tendency*) dazu neigen, etw zu tun ♦ *vi* sich neigen.
include [inklood'] *vt* einschließen; (*on list, in group*) aufnehmen; **the tip is/is not** ~**d** das Trinkgeld ist/ist nicht inbegriffen.
including [inklood'ing] *prep:* ~ **tip** *etc* Trinkgeld *etc* inbegriffen.
inclusion [inkloo'zhən] *n* Aufnahme *f*, Einbeziehung *f*.
inclusive [inkloo'siv] *a* einschließlich; (*Brit COMM*) inklusive; **$50,** ~ **of all surcharges** 50 Dollar alles inklusive.
incognito [inkâgnē'tō] *ad* inkognito.
incoherent [inkōhē'rənt] *a* zusammenhanglos.
income [in'kum] *n* Einkommen *nt*; (*from business*) Einkünfte *pl*; ~ **and expenditure account** (*US*) Gewinn- und Verlustrechnung *f*.
income bracket *n* Einkommensgruppe *f*.
income tax *n* Lohnsteuer *f*; (*of self-employed*) Einkommenssteuer *f*.
income tax return *n* Steuererklärung *f*.
incoming [in'kuming] *a* (*passengers*) ankommend; (*succeeding*) folgend; (*government, tenant*) nachfolgend; (*mail*) eingehend; (*tide*) steigend.
incommunicado [inkəmyoonəkâ'dō] *a:* **to hold sb** ~ jdm jeden Kontakt mit der Außenwelt verweigern.
incomparable [inkâm'pûrəbəl] *a* nicht vergleichbar; (*skill, beauty*) unvergleichlich.
incompatible [inkəmpat'əbəl] *a* unvereinbar; (*people*) unverträglich.
incompetence [inkâm'pitəns] *n* Unfähigkeit *f*.
incompetent [inkâm'pitənt] *a* unfähig; (*not qualified*) nicht berechtigt.
incomplete [inkəmplēt'] *a* unvollständig.
incomprehensible [inkâmprihen'səbəl] *a* unverständlich.
inconceivable [inkənsē'vəbəl] *a* unvorstellbar, undenkbar.
inconclusive [inkənkloo'siv] *a* nicht schlüssig.
incongruity [inkânggroo'itē] *n* Seltsamkeit *f*; (*of remark etc*) Unangebrachtsein *nt*.
incongruous [inkâng'grooəs] *a* seltsam; (*remark*) unangebracht.
inconsequential [inkânsəkwen'chəl] *a* belanglos.
inconsiderable [inkənsid'ûrəbəl] *a* unerheblich.
inconsiderate [inkənsid'ûrit] *a* rücksichtslos; (*hasty*) unüberlegt.
inconsistency [inkənsis'tənsē] *n* (*of work*)

Unbeständigkeit *f*; (*of actions etc*) Widersprüchlichkeit *f*; (*of statement etc*) Widersprüchlichkeit *f*, Ungereimtheit *f*.
inconsistent [inkənsis'tənt] *a* unvereinbar; (*behavior*) inkonsequent; (*action, speech*) widersprüchlich; (*person, work*) unbeständig.
inconsolable [inkənsō'ləbəl] *a* untröstlich.
inconspicuous [inkənspik'yooəs] *a* unauffällig.
inconstancy [inkân'stənsē] *n* Unbeständigkeit *f*.
inconstant [inkân'stənt] *a* unbeständig.
incontinence [inkân'tənəns] *n* (*MED*) Unfähigkeit *f*, Stuhl und Harn zurückzuhalten; (*fig*) Zügellosigkeit *f*.
incontinent [inkân'tənənt] *a* (*MED*) nicht fähig, Stuhl und Harn zurückzuhalten; (*fig*) zügellos.
incontrovertible [inkântrəvûr'təbəl] *a* unbestreitbar, unwiderlegbar.
inconvenience [inkənvēn'yəns] *n* Unbequemlichkeit *f*; (*trouble to others*) Unannehmlichkeiten *pl*; **to put sb to great** ~ jdm große Umstände bereiten ♦ *vt:* **don't** ~ **yourself** machen Sie (sich) keine Umstände.
inconvenient [inkənvēn'yənt] *a* (*time*) ungelegen; (*house, design*) unbequem, unpraktisch; **that time is very** ~ **for me** der Zeitpunkt ist sehr ungünstig für mich.
incorporate [inkôr'pûrāt] *vt* (*include*) aufnehmen; (*unite*) vereinigen; (*US COMM*) (amtlich) als Aktiengesellschaft eintragen.
incorporated [inkôr'pərātid] *a* (*US COMM: in titles*) GmbH.
incorporated company *n* (*US*) Gesellschaft *f* mit beschränkter Haftung, GmbH *f*.
incorrect [inkərekt'] *a* unrichtig; (*behavior*) inkorrekt.
incorrigible [inkôr'ijəbəl] *a* unverbesserlich.
incorruptible [inkərup'təbəl] *a* unzerstörbar; (*person*) unbestechlich.
increase *n* [in'krēs] Zunahme *f*, Erhöhung *f*; (*pay* ~) Gehaltserhöhung *f*; (*in size*) Vergrößerung *f*; **an** ~ **of 5%** 5% mehr, eine Erhöhung von 5%; **to be on the** ~ ständig zunehmen ♦ [inkrēs'] *vt* erhöhen; (*wealth, rage*) vermehren; (*business*) erweitern ♦ *vi* zunehmen; (*prices*) steigen; (*in size*) größer werden; (*in number*) sich vermehren.
increasingly [inkrēs'inglē] *ad* zunehmend.
incredible [inkred'əbəl] *a*, **incredibly** [inkred'əblē] *ad* unglaublich.
incredulity [inkridoo'litē] *n* Ungläubigkeit *f*.
incredulous [inkrej'ələs] *a* ungläubig.
increment [in'krəmənt] *n* Zulage *f*.
incriminate [inkrim'ənāt] *vt* belasten.
incriminating [inkrim'ənāting] *a* belastend.
incrust [inkrust'] *vt* = **encrust.**
incubate [in'kyəbāt] *vt* (*eggs*) ausbrüten; (*disease*) ausbrüten (*col*) ♦ *vi* (*egg*) ausgebrütet werden.
incubation [inkyəbā'shən] *n* Ausbrüten *nt*.
incubation period *n* Inkubationszeit *f*.

incubator [in'kyəbātûr] *n* (*MED*) Brutkasten *m*.

inculcate [in'kulkāt] *vt*: **to** ~ **sth in sb** jdm etw einprägen.

incumbent [inkum'bənt] *n* Amtsinhaber(in *f*) *m* ♦ *a*: **it is** ~ **on him to do it** es obliegt ihm, es zu tun.

incur [inkûr'] *vt* sich zuziehen; (*debts*) machen.

incurable [inkyōōr'əbəl] *a* unheilbar; (*fig*) unverbesserlich.

incursion [inkûr'zhən] *n* (feindliche(r)) Einfall *m*.

Ind. *abbr* (*US*) = *Indiana*.

indebted [indet'id] *a* (*obliged*) verpflichtet (*to sb* jdm); (*owing*) verschuldet.

indecency [indē'sənsē] *n* Unanständigkeit *f*, Anstößigkeit *f*.

indecent [indē'sənt] *a* unanständig.

indecent assault *n* (*JUR*) Notzucht *f*.

indecent exposure *n* (*JUR*) Erregung *f* öffentlichen Ärgernisses.

indecipherable [indisī'fûrəbəl] *a* nicht zu entziffern; (*handwriting*) unleserlich.

indecision [indisizh'ən] *n* Unschlüssigkeit *f*.

indecisive [indisī'siv] *a* (*battle*) nicht entscheidend; (*result*) unentschieden; (*person*) unentschlossen.

indeed [indēd'] *ad* tatsächlich, in der Tat.

indefatigable [indifat'əgəbəl] *a* unermüdlich.

indefensible [indifen'səbəl] *a* (*conduct*) unentschuldbar.

indefinable [indifī'nəbəl] *a* undefinierbar; (*vague*) unbestimmt.

indefinite [indef'ənit] *a* unbestimmt.

indefinitely [indef'ənitlē] *ad* auf unbestimmte Zeit; (*wait*) unbegrenzt lange.

indelible [indel'əbəl] *a* unauslöschlich; ~ **pencil** Tintenstift *m*.

indelicate [indel'əkit] *a* (*tactless*) taktlos; (*not polite*) ungehörig, geschmacklos.

indemnify [indem'nafī] *vt* entschädigen; (*safeguard*) versichern.

indemnity [indem'nitē] *n* Schadensersatz *m*, Wiedergutmachung *f*.

indent [indent'] *vt* (*text*) einrücken.

indentation [indentā'shən] *n* Einbuchtung *f*; (*TYP*) Einrückung *f*.

indented [inden'tid] *a* (*TYP*) eingerückt.

independence [indipen'dəns] *n* Unabhängigkeit *f*.

independent [indipen'dənt] *a* unabhängig (*of* von); (*person: in attitude*) selbständig.

indescribable [indiskrī'bəbəl] *a* unbeschreiblich.

indestructible [indistruk'təbəl] *a* unzerstörbar.

indeterminate [inditûr'mənit] *a* unbestimmt.

index [in'deks] *n*, *pl* **-es** (*in book*) Register *nt*; *pl* **indices** [in'disēz] (*on scale*) (An)zeiger *m*.

index card *n* Karteikarte *f*.

indexed [in'dekst] *a* (*US*) (*salaries*) der Inflationsrate (*dat*) angeglichen; (*pensions*) dynamisch.

index finger *n* Zeigefinger *m*.

index-linked [in'dekslingkt'] *a* (*Brit*) = **indexed**.

India [in'dēə] *n* Indien *nt*.

Indian [in'dēən] *a* (*from India*) indisch; (*from America*) indianisch ♦ *n* Inder(in *f*) *m*; Indianer(in *f*) *m*.

Indian Ocean *n* Indische(r) Ozean *m*.

Indian summer *n* Altweiber- *or* Nachsommer *m*.

indicate [in'dikāt] *vt* anzeigen; (*hint*) andeuten ♦ *vi*: **to** ~ **left/right** (*Brit AUT*) links/rechts blinken.

indication [indikā'shən] *n* Anzeichen *nt*; (*information*) Angabe *f*.

indicative [indik'ətiv] *n* (*GRAM*) Indikativ *m* ♦ *a*: **to be** ~ **of sth** auf etw (*acc*) schließen lassen.

indicator [in'dikātûr] *n* (*sign*) (An)zeichen *nt*; (*Brit AUT*) Richtungsanzeiger *m*.

indices [in'disēz] *npl of* **index**.

indict [indīt'] *vt* anklagen.

indictable [indīt'əbəl] *a* (*person*) strafrechtlich verfolgbar; (*offense*) strafbar.

indictment [indīt'mənt] *n* Anklage *f*.

indifference [indif'ûrəns] *n* (*lack of interest*) Gleichgültigkeit *f* (*to, towards* gegenüber); (*mediocrity*) Mittelmäßigkeit *f*.

indifferent [indif'ûrənt] *a* (*not caring*) gleichgültig; (*unimportant*) unwichtig; (*mediocre*) mäßig.

indigenous [indij'ənəs] *a* einheimisch; **a plant** ~ **to X** eine in X vorkommende Pflanze.

indigestible [indijes'təbəl] *a* unverdaulich.

indigestion [indijes'chən] *n* Magenverstimmung *f*.

indignant [indig'nənt] *a* ungehalten, entrüstet.

indignation [indignā'shən] *n* Entrüstung *f*.

indignity [indig'nitē] *n* Demütigung *f*.

indigo [in'dəgō] *n* Indigo *m or nt* ♦ *a* indigofarben.

indirect [indirekt'] *a* indirekt; (*answer*) nicht direkt; **by** ~ **means** auf Umwegen.

indirectly [indirekt'lē] *ad* indirekt.

indiscernible [indisûr'nəbəl] *a* nicht wahrnehmbar.

indiscreet [indiskrēt'] *a* (*insensitive*) unbedacht; (*improper*) taktlos; (*telling secrets*) indiskret.

indiscretion [indiskresh'ən] *n* Taktlosigkeit *f*; Indiskretion *f*.

indiscriminate [indiskrim'ənit] *a* wahllos; (*reader, shopper*) unkritisch.

indispensable [indispen'səbəl] *a* unentbehrlich.

indisposed [indispōzd'] *a* unpäßlich.

indisposition [indispəzish'ən] *n* Unpäßlichkeit *f*.

indisputable [indispyōō'təbəl] *a* unbestreitbar; (*evidence*) unanfechtbar.

indistinct [indistingkt'] *a* undeutlich.

indistinguishable [indisting'gwishəbəl] *a*

nicht unterscheidbar (*from* von); (*differ-ence*) unmerklich.

individual [indəvij'ōōəl] *n* Einzelne(r) *mf*, Individuum *nt* ♦ *a* individuell; (*case*) Einzel-; (*of, for one person*) eigen, individuell; (*characteristic*) eigentümlich.

individualist [indəvij'ōōəlist] *n* Individualist(in *f*) *m*.

individuality [indəvijōōal'itē] *n* Individualität *f*.

individually [indəvij'ōōəlē] *ad* einzeln, individuell.

indivisible [indəviz'əbəl] *a* unteilbar.

Indochina [in'dōchī'nə] *n* Indochina *nt*.

indoctrinate [indǎk'trənāt] *vt* indoktrinieren.

indoctrination [indǎktrənā'shən] *n* Indoktrination *f*.

indolence [in'dələns] *n* Trägheit *f*.

indolent [in'dələnt] *a* träge.

Indonesia [indənē'zhə] *n* Indonesien *nt*.

Indonesian [indənē'zhən] *a* indonesisch ♦ *n* Indonesier(in *f*) *m*.

indoor [in'dôr] *a* Haus-; (*plant*) Zimmer-; (*photography*) Innen-; (*SPORT*) Hallen-.

indoors [indôrz'] *ad* drinnen, im Haus; **to go** ~ hinein *or* ins Haus gehen.

indubitable [indōō'bitəbəl] *a* unzweifelhaft.

indubitably [indōō'bitəblē] *ad* zweifellos.

induce [indōōs'] *vt* dazu bewegen, veranlassen; (*reaction*) hervorrufen; **to ~ sb to do sth** jdn dazu bewegen, etw zu tun.

inducement [indōōs'mənt] *n* Veranlassung *f*; (*incentive*) Anreiz *m*.

induct [indukt'] *vt* in sein Amt einführen.

indulge [indulj'] *vt* (*give way*) nachgeben (+*dat*); (*gratify*) frönen (+*dat*); **to ~ o.s. in sth** sich (*dat*) etw gönnen ♦ *vi* frönen (*in dat*), sich gönnen (*in acc*).

indulgence [indul'jəns] *n* Nachsicht *f*; (*enjoyment*) Genuß *m*.

indulgent [indul'jənt] *a* nachsichtig; (*pej*) nachgiebig.

industrial [indus'trēəl] *a* Industrie-, industriell; (*dispute, injury*) Arbeits-.

industrial action *n* Arbeitskampfmaßnahmen *pl*.

industrial estate *n* (*Brit*) = **industrial park**.

industrial goods *npl* Investitionsgüter *pl*.

industrialist [indus'trēəlist] *n* Industrielle(r) *mf*.

industrialize [indus'trēəlīz] *vt* industrialisieren.

industrial park *n* (*US*) Industriegelände *nt*.

industrial relations *npl* Verhältnis *nt* zwischen Arbeitgebern und Arbeitnehmern.

industrial tribunal *n* (*Brit*) ≈ Arbeitsgericht *nt*.

industrial unrest *n* (*Brit*) Arbeitsunruhen *pl*.

industrious [indus'trēəs] *a* fleißig.

industry [in'dəstrē] *n* Industrie *f*; (*diligence*) Fleiß *m*.

inebriated [inēb'rēātid] *a* betrunken, berauscht.

inedible [ined'əbəl] *a* ungenießbar.

ineffective [inifek'tiv] *a* unwirksam, wirkungslos; (*person*) untauglich.

ineffectual [inifek'chōōəl] *a* = **ineffective**.

inefficiency [inifish'ənsē] *n* Ineffizienz *f*.

inefficient [inifish'ənt] *a* ineffizient; (*ineffective*) unwirksam.

inelegant [inel'əgənt] *a* unelegant; (*clothes also*) ohne Schick *or* Eleganz.

ineligible [inel'ijəbəl] *a* nicht berechtigt; (*candidate*) nicht wählbar.

inept [inept'] *a* (*behavior*) ungeschickt; (*remark*) unpassend; (*comparison*) ungeeignet.

ineptitude [inep'tətōōd] *n* Ungeschicktheit *f*, Unbeholfenheit *f*.

inequality [inikwâl'itē] *n* Ungleichheit *f*.

inequitable [inek'witəbəl] *a* ungerecht.

ineradicable [inirad'ikəbəl] *a* unausrottbar; (*mistake*) unabänderlich; (*guilt*) tiefsitzend.

inert [inûrt'] *a* träge; (*CHEM*) inaktiv; (*motionless*) unbeweglich.

inertia [inûr'shə] *n* Trägheit *f*.

inertia-reel seat belt [inûr'shərēl sēt belt] *n* Automatikgurt *m*.

inescapable [inəskā'pəbəl] *a* unvermeidbar.

inessential [inisen'chəl] *a* unwesentlich.

inestimable [ines'təməbəl] *a* unschätzbar.

inevitability [inevitəbil'ətē] *n* Unvermeidlichkeit *f*.

inevitable [inev'itəbəl] *a* unvermeidlich.

inevitably [inev'itəblē] *ad*: **if it's ~ the case that ...** wenn es zwangsläufig so sein muß, daß ...; **as ~ happens ...** wie es immer so ist *or* vorkommt ...

inexact [in'igzakt'] *a* ungenau.

inexcusable [inikskyōō'zəbəl] *a* unverzeihlich, unentschuldbar.

inexhaustible [inigzôs'təbəl] *a* (*wealth, patience*) unerschöpflich; (*talker*) unermüdlich; (*curiosity*) unstillbar.

inexorable [inek'sûrəbəl] *a* unerbittlich.

inexpensive [inikspen'siv] *a* preiswert.

inexperience [inikspēr'ēəns] *n* Unerfahrenheit *f*.

inexperienced [inikspēr'ēənst] *a* unerfahren; **to be ~ in sth** in etw (*dat*) wenig Übung haben.

inexplicable [ineks'plikəbəl] *a* unerklärlich.

inexpressible [inikspres'əbəl] *a* (*pain, joy*) unbeschreiblich; (*thoughts*) nicht ausdrückbar.

inextricable [ineks'trikəbəl] *a* (*tangle*) unentwirrbar; (*difficulties*) verwickelt, unlösbar.

inextricably [ineks'trikəblē] *ad* untrennbar.

infallibility [infaləbil'ətē] *n* Unfehlbarkeit *f*.

infallible [infal'əbəl] *a* unfehlbar.

infamous [in'fəməs] *a* (*place*) verrufen; (*person*) niederträchtig; (*deed*) schändlich.

infamy [in'fəmē] *n* Verrufenheit *f*; Niedertracht *f*; (*disgrace*) Schande *f*.

infancy [in'fənsē] *n* frühe Kindheit *f*; (*fig*) Anfangsstadium *nt*.

infant [in'fənt] *n* kleine(s) Kind *nt*; (*baby*) Säugling *m*.

infantile [in'fəntīl] *a* kindisch, infantil.
infant mortality *n* Säuglingssterblichkeit *f*.
infantry [in'fəntrē] *n* Infanterie *f*.
infantryman [in'fəntrēmən] *n*, *pl* -men Infanterist *m*.
infant school *n* (*Brit*) Grundschule *f* (*für die ersten beiden Jahrgänge*).
infatuated [infach'ōōātid] *a* vernarrt; **to become ~ with** sich vernarren *or* verknallen (*col*) in (*+acc*).
infatuation [infachōōā'shən] *n* Vernarrtheit *f* (*with* in *+acc*).
infect [infekt'] *vt* anstecken (*also fig*), infizieren; **to become ~ed** (*wound*) sich entzünden.
infection [infek'shən] *n* Ansteckung *f*, Infektion *f*.
infectious [infek'shəs] *a* ansteckend.
infer [infûr'] *vt* schließen (*from* aus).
inference [in'fûrəns] *n* Schlußfolgerung *f*.
inferior [infē'rēûr] *a* (*rank*) untergeordnet, niedriger; (*quality*) minderwertig; **to feel ~** sich unterlegen vorkommen ♦ *n* Untergebene(r) *m*.
inferiority [infērēôr'itē] *n* Minderwertigkeit *f*; (*of person*) Unterlegenheit *f*.
inferiority complex *n* Minderwertigkeitskomplex *m*.
infernal [infûr'nəl] *a* höllisch.
inferno [infûr'nō] *n* Hölle *f*, Inferno *nt*.
infertile [infûr'təl] *a* unfruchtbar.
infertility [infûrtil'ətē] *n* Unfruchtbarkeit *f*.
infest [infest'] *vt* plagen, heimsuchen; **to be ~ed with** wimmeln von.
infidel [in'fidəl] *n* Ungläubige(r) *mf*.
infidelity [infidel'itē] *n* Untreue *f*.
infighting [in'fīting] *n* Nahkampf *m*.
infiltrate [infil'trāt] *vt* infiltrieren; (*spies*) einschleusen; (*liquid*) durchdringen ♦ *vi* (*MIL, liquid*) einsickern; (*POL*) unterwandern (*into acc*).
infinite [in'fənit] *a* unendlich; **an ~ amount of time/money** unendlich viel Zeit/Geld.
infinitely [in'fənitlē] *ad* unendlich; (*fig also*) grenzenlos.
infinitesimal [infinites'əməl] *a* unendlich klein, winzig; (*MATH*) infinitesimal.
infinitive [infin'ətiv] *n* Infinitiv *m*, Nennform *f*.
infinity [infin'ətē] *n* Unendlichkeit *f*.
infirm [infûrm'] *a* schwach, gebrechlich.
infirmary [infûr'mûrē] *n* Krankenhaus *nt*.
infirmity [infûr'mitē] *n* Schwäche *f*, Gebrechlichkeit *f*.
inflame [inflām'] *vt* (*MED*) entzünden; (*person*) reizen; (*anger*) erregen.
inflamed [inflāmd'] *a* entzündet.
inflammable [inflam'əbəl] *a* feuergefährlich.
inflammation [infləmā'shən] *n* Entzündung *f*.
inflammatory [inflam'ətôrē] *a* (*speech*) aufrührerisch, Hetz-.
inflatable [inflā'təbəl] *a* aufblasbar.
inflate [inflāt'] *vt* aufblasen; (*tire*) aufpumpen; (*prices*) hochtreiben.

inflated [inflā'tid] *a* (*prices*) überhöht, inflationär; (*pride*) übersteigert; (*style*) geschwollen.
inflation [inflā'shən] *n* Inflation *f*.
inflationary [inflā'shənärē] *a* (*increase*) inflationistisch; (*situation*) inflationär.
inflationary spiral *n* Inflationsspirale *f*.
inflexible [inflek'səbəl] *a* (*person*) nicht flexibel; (*opinion*) starr; (*thing*) unbiegsam.
inflict [inflikt'] *vt* zufügen (*sth on sb* jdm etw); (*punishment*) auferlegen (*on dat*); (*wound*) beibringen (*on dat*).
infliction [inflik'shən] *n* Zufügung *f*; Auferlegung *f*; (*suffering*) Heimsuchung *f*.
in-flight [in'flīt] *a* (*entertainment*) während des Fluges.
inflow [in'flō] *n* Einfließen *nt*, Zustrom *m*.
influence [in'flōōəns] *n* Einfluß *m* ♦ *vt* beeinflussen.
influential [inflōōen'chəl] *a* einflußreich.
influenza [inflōōen'zə] *n* Grippe *f*.
influx [in'fluks] *n* (*of money*) Zufuhr *f*; (*of people*) Zustrom *m*; (*of ideas*) Zufluß *m*.
inform [infôrm'] *vt* informieren; **to keep sb ~ed** jdn auf dem laufenden halten (*of* über *+acc*) ♦ *vi*: **to ~ on sb** jdn denunzieren.
informal [infôr'məl] *a* zwanglos; (*language*) ungezwungen.
informality [infôrmal'itē] *n* Ungezwungenheit *f*.
informally [infôr'məlē] *ad* inoffiziell; (*invite*) zwanglos.
informant [infôr'mənt] *n* Informant *m*, Gewährsmann *m*.
informatics [infôrmat'iks] *n sing* Informatik *f*.
information [infûrmā'shən] *n* Auskunft *f*, Information *f*; **for your ~** zu Ihrer Kenntnisnahme.
information bureau *n* Auskunft(sbüro *nt*) *f*.
information desk *n* Auskunftsschalter *m*.
information line *n* (*COMPUT*) Informationszeile *f*.
information processing *n* Informationsverarbeitung *f*.
information retrieval *n* Informationsabruf *m*.
information science *n* Informatik *f*.
information technology *n* Informationstechnik *f*.
informative [infôr'mətiv] *a* informativ; (*person*) mitteilsam.
informed [infôrmd'] *a* (*observer*) informiert, (*gut*) unterrichtet; **it was an ~ guess** es war gut geschätzt.
informer [infôr'mûr] *n* Denunziant(in *f*) *m*; **police ~** Polizeispitzel *m*.
infra dig [in'frə dig] *abbr* (*col*: = *infra dignitatem: beneath one's dignity*) unter meiner (*or seiner etc*) Würde.
infrared [in'frəred'] *a* infrarot.
infrastructure [in'frəstruk'chûr] *n* Infrastruktur *f*.
infrequent [infrē'kwint] *a* selten.
infringe [infrinj'] *vt* (*law*) verstoßen gegen.

infringe upon *vt fus* verletzen.
infringement [infrinj'mənt] *n* Verstoß *m*, Verletzung *f*.
infuriate [infyŏŏr'ēāt] *vt* wütend machen; **to be ~d** wütend sein.
infuriating [infyŏŏr'ēāting] *a* ärgerlich.
infuse [infyŏŏz'] *vt*: **to ~ sb with sth** (*courage, enthusiasm*) jdm etw einflößen ♦ *vi* (*tea etc*) ziehen.
infusion [infyŏŏ'zhən] *n* (*tea etc*) Aufguß *m*.
ingenious [injēn'yəs] *a* genial; (*thing*) raffiniert.
ingenuity [injənŏŏ'itē] *n* Genialität *f*; Raffiniertheit *f*.
ingenuous [injen'yŏŏəs] *a* offen, unbefangen; (*naive*) naiv, unverdorben.
ingot [ing'gət] *n* Barren *m*.
ingratiate [ingrā'shēāt] *vt* einschmeicheln (*o.s. with sb* sich bei jdm).
ingratiating [ingrā'shēāting] *a* schmeichlerisch.
ingratitude [ingrat'ətŏŏd] *n* Undankbarkeit *f*.
ingredient [ingrē'dēənt] *n* Bestandteil *m*; (*COOK*) Zutat *f*.
ingrowing [in'grōing] *a*: **~ (toe)nail** eingewachsene(r) Zehennagel *m*.
ingrown [in'grōn] *a* = **ingrowing**.
inhabit [inhab'it] *vt* bewohnen.
inhabitable [inhab'itəbəl] *a* bewohnbar.
inhabitant [inhab'ətənt] *n* Bewohner(in *f*) *m*; (*of island, town*) Einwohner(in *f*) *m*.
inhale [inhāl'] *vt* einatmen; (*MED, cigarettes*) inhalieren.
inherent [inhär'ent] *a* innewohnend (*in dat*).
inherently [inhär'entlē] *ad* (*easy, difficult*) von Natur aus, an sich; **~ lazy** von Natur aus faul.
inherit [inhär'it] *vt* erben.
inheritance [inhär'itəns] *n* Erbe *nt*, Erbschaft *f*.
inhibit [inhib'it] *vt* hemmen; (*restrain*) hindern.
inhibited [inhib'itid] *a* (*person*) gehemmt.
inhibition [inibish'ən] *n* Hemmung *f*.
inhospitable [inhâspit'əbəl] *a* (*person*) ungastlich; (*country*) unwirtlich.
inhuman [inhyŏŏ'mən] *a* unmenschlich.
inhumane [inhyŏŏmān'] *a* inhuman.
inimitable [inim'itəbəl] *a* unnachahmlich.
iniquity [inik'witē] *n* Ungerechtigkeit *f*.
initial [inish'əl] *a* anfänglich, Anfangs- ♦ *n* Initiale *f* ♦ *vt* abzeichnen; (*POL*) paraphieren.
initialize [inish'əliz] *vt* (*COMPUT*) initialisieren.
initially [inish'əlē] *ad* anfangs.
initiate [inish'ēāt] *vt* einführen; (*negotiations*) einleiten; (*set in motion*) den Anstoß geben zu; (*instruct*) einweihen; **to ~ proceedings against sb** (*JUR*) gegen jdn einen Prozeß anstrengen.
initiation [inishēā'shən] *n* Einführung *f*; Einleitung *f*; Einweihung *f*.
initiative [inish'ēətiv] *n* Initiative *f*; **to take the ~** die Initiative ergreifen.

inject [injekt'] *vt* einspritzen; (*fig*) einflößen; (*money*) hineinpumpen (*into* in); **to ~ enthusiasm into sb** jdn mit Begeisterung erfüllen.
injection [injek'shən] *n* (*Brit*) Spritze *f*, Injektion *f*; **to have an ~** eine Spritze bekommen.
injudicious [injŏŏdish'əs] *a* unklug.
injunction [injungk'shən] *n* (*JUR*) gerichtliche Verfügung *f*.
injure [in'jûr] *vt* verletzen; (*fig*) schaden (*+dat*); **to ~ o.s.** sich verletzen.
injured [in'jûrd] *a* (*person, leg etc*) verletzt; (*tone, feelings*) gekränkt; **the ~ party** (*JUR*) der *or* die Geschädigte.
injurious [injŏŏr'ēəs] *a*: **to be ~ to sb** jdm schaden.
injury [in'jûrē] *n* Verletzung *f*; **to escape without ~** unverletzt davonkommen; **to play ~ time** (*SPORT*) nachspielen.
injustice [injus'tis] *n* Ungerechtigkeit *f*; **you do me an ~** Sie tun mir Unrecht.
ink [ingk] *n* Tinte *f*.
ink-jet printer [ingk'jet prin'tûr] *n* Tintenstrahldrucker *m*.
inkling [ingk'ling] *n* dunkle Ahnung *f*.
inkpad [ingk'pad] *n* Stempelkissen *nt*.
inlaid [in'lād] *a* eingelegt, Einlege-.
inland [in'land] *a* Binnen-; (*domestic*) Inlands- ♦ *ad* landeinwärts.
Inland Revenue *n* (*Brit*) ≈ Finanzamt *nt*.
in-law [in'lô] *n* angeheiratete(r) Verwandte(r) *mf*.
inlet [in'let] *n* (*of sea*) Meeresarm *m*; (*of river*) Flußarm *m*; (*TECH*) Zuleitung *f*.
inmate [in'māt] *n* Insasse *m*, Insassin *f*.
inmost [in'mōst] *a* innerst.
inn [in] *n* Gasthaus *nt*, Wirtshaus *nt*.
innards [in'ûrdz] *npl* (*col*) Innereien *pl*.
innate [ināt'] *a* angeboren, eigen (*+dat*).
inner [in'ûr] *a* innere(r, s), Innen-; (*fig*) verborgen.
inner city *n* Innenstadt *f*.
innermost [in'ûrmōst] *a* innerst.
inner tube *n* (*in tire*) Schlauch *m*.
innings [in'ingz] *n sing* (*SPORT*) Innenrunde *f*.
innocence [in'əsəns] *n* Unschuld *f*; (*ignorance*) Unkenntnis *f*.
innocent [in'əsənt] *a* unschuldig.
innocuous [inâk'yŏŏəs] *a* harmlos.
innovation [inəvā'shən] *n* Neuerung *f*.
innuendo [inyŏŏen'dō] *n* versteckte Anspielung *f*.
innumerable [inŏŏ'mûrəbəl] *a* unzählig.
inoculate [inâk'yəlāt] *vt*: **to ~ sb with sth/against sth** jdm etw einimpfen/jdn gegen etw impfen.
inoculation [inâkyəlā'shən] *n* Impfung *f*.
inoffensive [inəfen'siv] *a* harmlos.
inopportune [inâpûrtŏŏn'] *a* (*remark*) unangebracht; (*visit*) ungelegen.
inordinate [inôr'dənit] *a*, **inordinately** [inôr'dənitlē] *ad* unmäßig, ungeheuer.
inorganic [inôrgan'ik] *a* unorganisch; (*CHEM*)

anorganisch.

inpatient [in'pāshənt] *n* stationäre(r) Patient(in *f*) *m*.

input [in'pŏot] *n* (*COMPUT*) Eingabe *f*, Input *m or nt*; (*of capital*) Investition *f*; (*power* ~) Energiezufuhr *f* ♦ *vt* (*data*) eingeben.

inquest [in'kwest] *n* gerichtliche Untersuchung *f*.

inquire [inkwīûr'] *vi* sich erkundigen; **to** ~ **into sth** etw untersuchen ♦ *vt* (*price*) sich erkundigen nach; **to** ~ **when/where/whether** sich erkundigen, wann/wo/ob.

inquire into *vt fus* untersuchen.

inquiring [inkwīûr'ing] *a* (*mind*) wissensdurstig.

inquiry [inkwīûr'ē] *n* (*question*) Erkundigung *f*, Nachfrage *f*; (*investigation*) Untersuchung *f*; **to hold an** ~ **into** eine Untersuchung (+*gen*) durchführen.

inquiry desk *n* (*Brit*) Auskunftsschalter *m*.

inquiry office *n* (*Brit*) Auskunft(sbüro *nt*) *f*.

inquisition [inkwizish'ən] *n* (*JUR*) Untersuchung *f*.

inquisitive [inkwiz'ətiv] *a* neugierig; (*look*) forschend.

inroad [in'rōd] *n* (*MIL*) Einfall *m*; (*fig*) Eingriff *m*; **extra work has made** ~**s into my spare time** zusätzliche Arbeit hat meine Freizeit sehr eingeschränkt; **that makes** ~**s into my savings** das greift meine Ersparnisse stark an.

insane [insān'] *a* wahnsinnig; (*MED*) geisteskrank.

insanitary [insan'itärē] *a* unhygienisch, gesundheitsschädlich.

insanity [insan'itē] *n* Wahnsinn *m*.

insatiable [insā'shəbəl] *a* unersättlich.

inscription [inskrip'shən] *n* (*on stone*) Inschrift *f*; (*in book*) Widmung *f*.

inscrutable [inskrŏō'təbəl] *a* unergründlich.

inseam measurement [insēm' mezh'ûrmənt] *n* (*US*) innere Beinlänge *f*.

insect [in'sekt] *n* Insekt *nt*.

insect bite *n* Insektenstich *m*.

insecticide [insek'tisīd] *n* Insektenvertilgungsmittel *nt*.

insect repellent *n* Insektenbekämpfungsmittel *nt*.

insecure [insikyŏor'] *a* (*person*) unsicher; (*thing*) nicht fest *or* sicher.

insecurity [insikyŏor'itē] *n* Unsicherheit *f*.

insensible [insen'səbəl] *a* gefühllos; (*unconscious*) bewußtlos; (*imperceptible*) unmerklich; ~ **of** *or* **to sth** unempfänglich für etw.

insensitive [insen'sətiv] *a* (*to pain*) unempfindlich; (*without feelings*) gefühllos.

insensitivity [insensətiv'itē] *n* (*emotional*) Gefühllosigkeit *f*; (*unappreciativeness*) Unempfänglichkeit *f*; (*physical*) Unempfindlichkeit *f*.

inseparable [insep'ûrəbəl] *a* (*people*) unzertrennlich; (*word*) untrennbar.

insert *vt* [insûrt'] (*also COMPUT*) einfügen; (*coin*) einwerfen; (*stick into*) hineinstecken;

(*advert*) aufgeben ♦ *n* [in'sûrt] Beifügung *f*; (*in book*) Einlage *f*; (*in magazine*) Beilage *f*.

insertion [insûr'shən] *n* Einfügung *f*; Einwerfen *nt*; Hineinstecken *nt*.

in-service [in'sûr'vis] *a*: ~ **training** Fortbildung *f*, berufsbegleitende Weiterbildung *f*.

inshore [in'shôr] *a* Küsten- ♦ *ad* an der Küste.

inside [in'sīd'] *n* Innenseite *f*, Innere(s) *nt*; (*of road*) Innenspur *f*; ~ **out** links *or* verkehrt herum; **to know sth** ~ **out** etw in- und auswendig kennen ♦ *a* innere(r, s), Innen- ♦ *ad* (*place*) innen; (*direction*) nach innen, hinein ♦ *prep* (*place*) in (+*dat*); (*direction*) in (+*acc*) ... hinein; (*time*) innerhalb (+*gen*).

inside forward *n* (*SPORT*) Halbstürmer *m*.

inside information *n* Insider-Informationen *pl*.

inside leg (measurement) *n* (*Brit*) = **inseam measurement**.

insider [insī'dûr] *n* Insider *m*, Eingeweihte(r) *mf*; (*member*) Mitglied *nt*.

insider dealing *n* (*FIN*) Insider-Handel *m*.

inside story *n* Inside-Story *f*.

insidious [insid'ēəs] *a* heimtückisch.

insight [in'sīt] *n* Verständnis *nt*; Einblick *m* (*into* in +*acc*); **to gain** *or* **get an** ~ **into sth** in etw (einen) Einblick gewinnen *or* bekommen.

insignia [insig'nēə] *npl* Insignien *pl*.

insignificant [insignif'ikənt] *a* unbedeutend.

insincere [insinsēr'] *a* unaufrichtig, falsch.

insincerity [insinsār'itē] *n* Unaufrichtigkeit *f*, Falschheit *f*.

insinuate [insin'yŏōāt] *vt* (*hint*) andeuten; **to** ~ **o.s. into sth** sich in etw (*acc*) einschleichen.

insinuation [insinyŏōā'shən] *n* Anspielung *f* (*about* auf +*acc*).

insipid [insip'id] *a* fad(e).

insist [insist'] *vi* bestehen (*on* auf +*acc*).

insistence [insis'təns] *n* Bestehen *nt*.

insistent [insis'tənt] *a* hartnäckig; (*urgent*) dringend.

insole [in'sōl] *n* Einlegesohle *f*.

insolence [in'sələns] *n* Frechheit *f*.

insolent [in'sələnt] *a* frech.

insoluble [insâl'yəbəl] *a* unlösbar; (*CHEM*) unlöslich.

insolvency [insâl'vənsē] *n* Zahlungsunfähigkeit *f*.

insolvent [insâl'vənt] *a* zahlungsunfähig.

insomnia [insâm'nēə] *n* Schlaflosigkeit *f*.

insomniac [insâm'nēak] *n*: **to be an** ~ an Schlaflosigkeit leiden.

inspect [inspekt'] *vt* (*examine*) kontrollieren, prüfen; (*officially*) inspizieren.

inspection [inspek'shən] *n* Besichtigung *f*, Inspektion *f*.

inspector [inspek'tûr] *n* (*official*) Aufsichtsbeamte(r) *m*, Inspektor *m*; (*police*) Polizeikommissar *m*; (*RAIL*) Kontrolleur *m*.

inspiration [inspərā'shən] *n* Inspiration *f*.

inspire [inspīûr'] *vt* (*respect*) einflößen (*in dat*); (*hope*) wecken (*in* in +*dat*); (*person*) inspirieren; **to ~ sb to do sth** jdn inspirieren, etw zu tun.

inspired [inspīûrd'] *a* begabt, einfallsreich; (*writer, book etc*) inspiriert; **in an ~ moment** in einem Augenblick der Inspiration.

inspiring [inspī'ûring] *a* begeisternd.

inst. *abbr* (*Brit COMM*: = *instant*) d.M.

instability [instəbil'ətē] *n* Instabilität *f*; (*of character*) Labilität *f*.

install [instôl'] *vt* (*put in*) einbauen, installieren; (*telephone*) anschließen; (*establish*) einsetzen.

installation [instəlā'shən] *n* (*of person*) (Amts)einsetzung *f*; (*of machinery*) Einbau *m*, Installierung *f*; (*machines etc*) Anlage *f*.

installment [instôl'mənt] *n* (*US*) Rate *f*; (*of story*) Fortsetzung *f*; **to pay in ~s** in Raten abzahlen.

installment plan *n* (*US*) Ratenkauf *m*.

instalment [instôl'mənt] *n* (*Brit*) = **installment.**

instance [in'stəns] *n* Fall *m*; (*example*) Beispiel *nt*; **for ~** zum Beispiel; **in that ~** in diesem Fall; **in the first ~** zuerst *or* zunächst (einmal).

instant [in'stənt] *n* Augenblick *m* ♦ *a* augenblicklich, sofortig.

instantaneous [instəntā'nēəs] *a* unmittelbar.

instant coffee *n* Pulverkaffee *m*.

instantly [in'stəntlē] *ad* sofort.

instant replay *n* (*US TV*) Wiederholung *f*.

instead [insted'] *ad* statt dessen; **~ of** (an)statt (+*gen*).

instigate [in'stəgāt] *vt* (*rebellion, strike, crime*) anstiften, anzetteln; (*new ideas etc*) initiieren.

instigation [instəgā'shən] *n* Veranlassung *f*; (*of crime etc*) Anstiftung *f*; **at sb's ~** auf jds Betreiben *or* Veranlassung.

instill, (*Brit*) **instil** [instil'] *vt* (*fig*) beibringen (*in sb* jdm).

instinct [in'stingkt] *n* Instinkt *m*.

instinctive [insting'tiv] *a*, **instinctively** [insting'tivlē] *ad* instinktiv.

institute [in'stit<del>oo</del>t] *n* Institut *nt*; (*society*) Gesellschaft *f* ♦ *vt* einführen; (*search*) einleiten.

institution [instit<del>oo</del>'shən] *n* (*custom*) Einrichtung *f*, Brauch *m*; (*society*) Institution *f*; (*home*) Anstalt *f*; (*beginning*) Einführung *f*, Einleitung *f*.

institutional [instit<del>oo</del>'shənəl] *a* (*life etc*) Anstalts-.

instruct [instrukt'] *vt* anweisen; (*officially*) instruieren.

instruction [instruk'shən] *n* Unterricht *m*; *see also* **instructions.**

instruction book *n* Bedienungsanleitung *f*.

instructions [instruk'shənz] *npl* Anweisungen *pl*; (*for use*) Gebrauchsanweisung *f*.

instructive [instruk'tiv] *a* lehrreich.

instructor [instruk'tûr] *n* Lehrer *m*; (*US*

UNIV) ≈ Assistent *m*; (*MIL*) Ausbilder *m*.

instrument [in'strəmənt] *n* (*tool*) Instrument *nt*, Werkzeug *nt*; (*MUS*) (Musik)instrument *nt*.

instrumental [instrəmen'təl] *a* (*MUS*) Instrumental-; (*helpful*) behilflich (*in* bei); **to be ~ in sth** eine bedeutende Rolle bei etw spielen.

instrumentalist [instrəmen'təlist] *n* Instrumentalist *m*.

instrument panel *n* Armaturenbrett *nt*.

insubordinate [insəbôr'dənit] *a* aufsässig, widersetzlich.

insubordination [insəbôrdənā'shən] *n* Gehorsamsverweigerung *f*.

insufferable [insuf'ûrəbəl] *a* unerträglich.

insufficient [insəfish'ənt] *a*, **insufficiently** [insəfish'əntlē] *ad* ungenügend.

insular [in'sələr] *a* (*fig*) engstirnig.

insularity [insəlar'itē] *n* (*fig*) Engstirnigkeit *f*.

insulate [in'səlāt] *vt* (*ELEC*) isolieren; (*fig*) abschirmen (*from* vor +*dat*).

insulating tape [in'səlāting tāp] *n* Isolierband *nt*.

insulation [insəlā'shən] *n* Isolierung *f*.

insulator [in'səlātûr] *n* Isolator *m*.

insulin [in'səlin] *n* Insulin *nt*.

insult *n* [in'sult] Beleidigung *f* ♦ *vt* [insult'] beleidigen.

insulting [insul'ting] *a* beleidigend.

insuperable [ins<del>oo</del>'pûrəbəl] *a* unüberwindlich.

insurance [inshûr'əns] *n* Versicherung *f*; **to take out ~ (against)** eine Versicherung abschließen (gegen).

insurance agent *n* Versicherungsvertreter *m*.

insurance broker *n* Versicherungsmakler *m*.

insurance policy *n* Versicherungspolice *f*.

insurance premium *n* Versicherungsprämie *f*.

insure [insh<del>oo</del>r'] *vt* versichern; **to ~ (against sth)** sich (gegen etw) versichern; **to ~ sb** *or* **sb's life** jdn versichern; **to be ~d for $5000** für 5000 Dollar versichert sein.

insured [insh<del>oo</del>rd'] *n*: **the ~** der/die Versicherte.

insurer [insh<del>oo</del>'rûr] *n* Versicherungsgeber *m*.

insurgent [insûr'jənt] *a* aufständisch ♦ *n* Aufständische(r) *mf*.

insurmountable [insûrmoun'təbəl] *a* unüberwindlich.

insurrection [insərek'shən] *n* Aufstand *m*.

intact [intakt'] *a* intakt, unangetastet, ganz.

intake [in'tāk] *n* (*place*) Einlaßöffnung *f*; (*act*) Aufnahme *f*; (*amount*) aufgenommene Menge *f*; (*Brit SCH*) Neuaufnahme *f*.

intangible [intan'jəbəl] *a* unfaßbar; (*thing*) nicht greifbar.

integer [in'tijûr] *n* ganze Zahl *f*.

integral [in'təgrəl] *a* (*essential*) wesentlich; (*complete*) vollständig; (*MATH*) Integral-.

integrate [in'təgrāt] *vt* vereinigen; (*people*) eingliedern, integrieren.

integrated circuit [in'təgrātid sûr'kit] *n* (*COMPUT*) integrierte(r) Schaltkreis *m*.
integration [intəgrā'shən] *n* Eingliederung *f*, Integration *f*.
integrity [integ'ritē] *n* (*honesty*) Redlichkeit *f*, Integrität *f*; (*COMPUT*) (System)integrität *f*.
intellect [in'təlekt] *n* Intellekt *m*.
intellectual [intəlek'chōōəl] *a* geistig, intellektuell ♦ *n* Intellektuelle(r) *mf*.
intelligence [intel'ijəns] *n* (*understanding*) Intelligenz *f*; (*news*) Information *f*; (*MIL*) Geheimdienst *m*.
intelligence quotient *n* Intelligenzquotient *m*.
intelligence test *n* Intelligenztest *m*.
intelligent [intel'ijənt] *a* intelligent.
intelligently [intel'ijəntlē] *ad* klug; (*write, speak*) verständlich.
intelligible [intel'ijəbəl] *a* verständlich.
intemperate [intem'pûrit] *a* unmäßig.
intend [intend'] *vt* beabsichtigen; **that was ~ed for you** das war für dich gedacht.
intense [intens'] *a* stark, intensiv; (*person*) ernsthaft.
intensely [intens'lē] *ad* äußerst; (*study*) intensiv.
intensify [inten'səfī] *vt* verstärken, intensivieren ♦ *vi* zunehmen.
intensity [inten'sitē] *n* Intensität *f*, Stärke *f*.
intensive [inten'siv] *a* intensiv; **to be in ~ care** auf der Intensivstation sein.
intensively [inten'sivlē] *ad* intensiv.
intent [intent'] *n* Absicht *f*; **to all ~s and purposes** im Grunde ♦ *a*: **to be ~ on doing sth** (*determined*) entschlossen sein, etw zu tun.
intention [inten'chən] *n* Absicht *f*; **with good ~s** mit guten Vorsätzen.
intentional [inten'chənəl] *a*, **intentionally** [inten'chənəlē] *ad* absichtlich.
intently [intent'lē] *ad* aufmerksam; (*look*) forschend.
inter [intûr'] *vt* beerdigen.
inter- [in'tûr] *pref* zwischen-, Zwischen-.
interact [intûrakt'] *vi* aufeinander einwirken.
interaction [intûrak'shən] *n* Wechselwirkung *f*.
interactive computing [intûrak'tiv kəmpyōōt'ing] *n* Dialogbetrieb *m*.
intercede [intûrsēd'] *vi* sich verwenden; (*in argument*) vermitteln; **to ~ with sb/on behalf of sb** sich bei jdm/für jdn einsetzen.
intercept [intûrsept'] *vt* abfangen.
interception [intûrsep'shən] *n* Abfangen *nt*.
interchange *n* [in'tûrchānj] (*exchange*) Austausch *m*; (*on roads*) Verkehrskreuz *nt* ♦ *vt* [intûrchānj'] austauschen.
interchangeable [intûrchān'jəbəl] *a* austauschbar.
intercity [in'tûrsitē] *n*: **~ (train)** Intercity(zug) *m*.
intercom [in'tûrkâm] *n* (Gegen)sprechanlage *f*.
interconnect [intûrkənekt'] *vt* miteinander

verbinden ♦ *vi* miteinander verbunden sein; (*roads*) zusammenführen.
intercontinental [intûrkântənen'təl] *a* interkontinental.
intercourse [in'tûrkôrs] *n* (*exchange*) Verkehr *m*; (*sexual*) Geschlechtsverkehr *m*.
interdependence [intûrdipen'dəns] *n* gegenseitige Abhängigkeit *f*.
interdependent [intûrdipen'dənt] *a* voneinander abhängig.
interest [in'trist] *n* Interesse *nt*; (*FIN*) Zinsen *pl*; (*COMM: share*) Anteil *m*; (*: group*) Interessentengruppe *f*; **to be of ~** von Interesse sein; **simple ~** einfache Zinsen *pl*; **business ~s** Geschäftsinteressen *pl*; **American ~s in the Middle East** amerikanische Interessen im Nahen Osten ♦ *vt* interessieren.
interested [in'tristid] *a* (*having claims*) beteiligt; (*attentive*) interessiert; **to be ~ in** sich interessieren für.
interest-free [in'tristfrē] *a* zinsfrei.
interesting [in'tristing] *a* interessant.
interest rate *n* Zinssatz *m*.
interface [in'tûrfās] *n* (*COMPUT*) Schnittstelle *f*.
interfere [intûrfēr'] *vi* (*meddle*) sich einmischen (*with* in +*acc*); (*disrupt, obstruct*) stören (*with acc*); (*with an object*) sich zu schaffen machen (*with* an +*dat*).
interference [intûrfēr'əns] *n* Einmischung *f*; (*TV*) Störung *f*.
interfering [intûrfēr'ing] *a* sich ständig einmischend.
interim [in'tûrim] *a* vorläufig ♦ *n*: **in the ~** inzwischen.
interim dividend *n* Abschlagsdividende *f*.
interior [intē'rēûr] *n* Innere(s) *nt* ♦ *a* innere(r, s), Innen-.
interior decorator *n* Dekorateur(in *f*) *m*.
interjection [intûrjek'shən] *n* Ausruf *m*; (*GRAM*) Interjektion *f*.
interlock [intûrlâk'] *vi* ineinandergreifen ♦ *vt* zusammenschließen, verzahnen.
interloper [intûrlō'pûr] *n* Eindringling *m*.
interlude [in'tûrlōōd] *n* Pause *f*; (*in entertainment*) Zwischenspiel *nt*.
intermarriage [intûrmar'ij] *n* Mischehe *f*.
intermarry [intûrmar'ē] *vi* untereinander heiraten.
intermediary [intûrmē'dēârē] *n* Vermittler *m*.
intermediate [intûrmē'dēit] *a* Zwischen-, Mittel-.
interminable [intûr'mənəbəl] *a* endlos.
intermission [intûrmish'ən] *n* Pause *f*.
intermittent [intûrmit'ənt] *a* periodisch, stoßweise.
intermittently [intûrmit'əntlē] *ad* mit Unterbrechungen.
intern *vt* [intûrn'] internieren ♦ *n* [in'tûrn] (*US*) Assistenzarzt *m*.
internal [intûr'nəl] *a* (*inside*) innere(r, s); (*domestic*) Inlands-; **~ injuries** innere Verletzungen *pl*.
internally [intûr'nəlē] *ad* innen; (*MED*) inner-

lich; (*in organization*) intern; "not to be taken ~" „nicht zum Einnehmen".

Internal Revenue Service *n* (*US*) ≈ Steueramt *nt*, Finanzamt *nt*.

international [intûrnash'ənəl] *a* international ♦ *n* (*Brit* SPORT) Nationalspieler(in *f*) *m*; (*match*) internationale(s) Spiel *nt*.

International Atomic Energy Agency *n* Internationale Atomenergiekommission *f*.

International Chamber of Commerce *n* Internationale Handelskammer *f*.

International Court of Justice *n* Internationale(r) Gerichtshof *m*.

International Labour Organization *n* Internationale(s) Arbeitsamt *nt*.

internationally [intûrnash'ənəlē] *ad* international, weltweit.

International Monetary Fund *n* Internationale(r) Währungsfond *m*.

International Olympic Committee *n* Internationale(s) Olympische(s) Komitee *nt*.

internecine [intûrnē'sīn] *a* mörderisch.

internee [intûrnē'] *n* Internierte(r) *mf*.

internment [intûrn'mənt] *n* Internierung *f*.

interplanetary [intûrplan'itārē] *a* interplanetar.

interplay [in'tûrplā] *n* Wechselspiel *nt*.

Interpol [in'tûrpōl] *n* Interpol *f*.

interpret [intûr'prit] *vt* (*explain*) auslegen, interpretieren; (*translate*) dolmetschen; (*represent*) darstellen.

interpretation [intûrpritā'shən] *n* Deutung *f*, Interpretation *f*; (*translation*) Dolmetschen *nt*.

interpreter [intûr'pritûr] *n* Dolmetscher(in *f*) *m*.

interrelated [intərilā'tid] *a* untereinander zusammenhängend.

interrogate [intär'əgāt] *vt* befragen; (*JUR*) verhören.

interrogation [intärəgā'shən] *n* Verhör *nt*.

interrogative [intərâg'ətiv] *a* fragend, Frage-.

interrogator [intär'əgātûr] *n* Vernehmungsbeamte(r) *m*.

interrupt [intərupt'] *vt* unterbrechen.

interruption [intərup'shən] *n* Unterbrechung *f*.

intersect [intûrsekt'] *vt* durchschneiden ♦ *vi* sich schneiden.

intersection [intûrsek'shən] *n* (*of roads*) Kreuzung *f*; (*of lines*) Schnittpunkt *m*.

intersperse [intûrspûrs'] *vt* (*scatter*) verstreuen; **to ~ sth with sth** etw mit etw durchsetzen.

interstate highway [in'tûrstāt hī'wā] *n* (*US*) ≈ Autobahn *f*.

intertwine [intûrtwīn'] *vti* (sich) verflechten.

interval [in'tûrvəl] *n* Abstand *m*; (*Brit: break*) Pause *f*; (*MUS*) Intervall *nt*; **at ~s** hier und da; (*time*) dann und wann; **sunny ~s** (*MET*) Aufheiterungen *pl*.

intervene [intûrvēn'] *vi* dazwischenliegen; (*act*) einschreiten (*in* gegen), eingreifen (*in* in +*acc*).

intervening [intûrvēn'ing] *a* dazwischenliegend.

intervention [intûrven'chən] *n* Eingreifen *nt*, Intervention *f*.

interview [in'tûrvyōō] *n* (*in media*) Interview *nt*; (*for job*) Vorstellungsgespräch *nt* ♦ *vt* interviewen; (*job applicant*) das Vorstellungsgespräch führen mit.

interviewer [in'tûrvyōōûr] *n* Interviewer *m*.

intestate [intes'tāt] *a* ohne Hinterlassung eines Testaments.

intestinal [intes'tənəl] *a* Darm-.

intestine [intes'tin] *n* Darm *m*; **~s** *pl* Eingeweide *nt*.

intimacy [in'təməsē] *n* Vertrautheit *f*; (*sexual*) Intimität *f*.

intimate *a* [in'təmit] (*inmost*) innerste(r, s); (*knowledge*) eingehend; (*familiar*) vertraut; (*friends*) eng ♦ *vt* [in'təmāt] andeuten.

intimately [in'təmitlē] *ad* vertraut; eng.

intimidate [intim'idāt] *vt* einschüchtern.

intimidation [intimidā'shən] *n* Einschüchterung *f*.

into [in'tōō] *prep* (*motion*) in (+*acc*) ... hinein; **5 ~ 25** 25 durch 5; **to change pounds ~ dollars** Pfunde in Dollars wechseln.

intolerable [intâl'ûrəbəl] *a* unerträglich.

intolerance [intâl'ûrəns] *n* Intoleranz *f*.

intolerant [intâl'ûrənt] *a* intolerant; **~ of** unduldsam gegen(über).

intonation [intōnā'shən] *n* Intonation *f*.

intoxicate [intâk'sikāt] *vt* betrunken machen; (*fig*) berauschen.

intoxicated [intâk'sikātid] *a* betrunken; (*fig*) trunken.

intoxication [intâksikā'shən] *n* Rausch *m*.

intractable [intrak'təbəl] *a* (*problem*) schwer lösbar; (*illness*) hartnäckig.

intransigence [intran'sijəns] *n* Unnachgiebigkeit *f*.

intransigent [intran'sijənt] *a* unnachgiebig.

intransitive [intran'sətiv] *a* intransitiv.

intravenous [intrəvē'nəs] *a* intravenös.

in-tray [in'trā] *n* Ablage *f* für Eingänge.

intrepid [intrep'id] *a* unerschrocken.

intricacy [in'trəkəsē] *n* Kompliziertheit *f*.

intricate [in'trəkit] *a* kompliziert.

intrigue [intrēg'] *n* Intrige *f* ♦ *vt* faszinieren ♦ *vi* intrigieren.

intriguing [intrē'ging] *a* faszinierend.

intrinsic [intrin'sik] *a* innere(r, s); (*difference*) wesentlich; **~ value** intrinsische(r) Wert *m*.

introduce [intrədōōs'] *vt* (*person*) vorstellen (*to sb* jdm); (*something new*) einführen; (*subject*) anschneiden; **to ~ sb to sth** jdn in etw (*acc*) einführen; **may I ~ ...?** darf ich ... vorstellen?

introduction [intrəduk'shən] *n* Einführung *f*; (*to book*) Einleitung *f*; **letter of ~** Einführungsbrief *m* *or* -schreiben *nt*.

introductory [intrəduk'tûrē] *a* Einführungs-, Vor-; **an ~ offer** ein Einführungsangebot; **his ~ remarks** seine einleitenden Bemerkun-

gen.
introspection [intrəspek'shən] n Selbstbeobachtung f, Introspektion f.
introspective [intrəspek'tiv] a nach innen gekehrt.
introvert [in'trəvûrt] n Introvertierte(r) mf ♦ a introvertiert.
intrude [introod'] vi stören (on acc).
intruder [introo'dûr] n Eindringling m.
intrusion [introo'zhən] n Störung f; (coming into) Eindringen nt.
intrusive [introo'siv] a aufdringlich.
intuition [intooish'ən] n Intuition f.
intuitive [intoo'ətiv] a, **intuitively** [intoo'ətivlē] ad intuitiv.
inundate [in'undāt] vt (lit, fig) überschwemmen.
inure [inyoor'] vt gewöhnen (to an +acc).
invade [invād'] vt einfallen in (+acc).
invader [invā'dûr] n Eindringling m.
invalid [in'vəlid] n Kranke(r) mf; (disabled) Invalide m ♦ a (ill) krank; (disabled) invalide; (not valid) [inval'id] ungültig.
invalidate [inval'idāt] vt (passport) (für) ungültig erklären; (fig) entkräften.
invalid chair n (Brit) Rollstuhl m.
invaluable [inval'yōoəbəl] a unschätzbar.
invariable [invär'ēəbəl] a unveränderlich.
invariably [invär'ēəblē] ad ausnahmslos, ständig, unweigerlich; **she is ~ late** sie kommt immer zu spät.
invasion [invā'zhən] n Invasion f, Einfall m.
invective [invek'tiv] n Beschimpfung f.
inveigle [invē'gəl] vt: **to ~ sb into doing sth** jdn dazu verleiten or verlocken, etw zu tun.
invent [invent'] vt erfinden.
invention [inven'chən] n Erfindung f.
inventive [inven'tiv] a erfinderisch.
inventiveness [inven'tivnis] n Erfindungsgabe f.
inventor [inven'tûr] n Erfinder(in f) m.
inventory [in'vəntôrē] n (Bestands)verzeichnis nt, Inventar nt.
inventory control n Bestandsüberwachung f.
inverse [invûrs'] n Umkehrung f ♦ a umgekehrt, entgegengesetzt; **in ~ proportion (to)** im umgekehrten Verhältnis (zu).
invert [invûrt'] vt umdrehen.
invertebrate [invûr'təbrit] n wirbellose(s) Tier nt.
inverted commas [invûr'tid kâm'əz] npl (Brit) Anführungsstriche pl.
invest [invest'] vt (FIN) anlegen, investieren; (endow) ausstatten; (fig: time, effort) investieren; **to ~ sb with sth** jdm etw verleihen.
investigate [inves'təgāt] vt untersuchen.
investigation [inves'təgāshən] n Untersuchung f.
investigative [inves'təgātiv] a: **~ journalism** Enthüllungsjournalismus m.
investigator [inves'təgātûr] n Ermittler m; **a private ~** ein Privatdetektiv m.

investiture [inves'tichûr] n Amtseinsetzung f.
investment [invest'mənt] n Investition f.
investment grant n Investitionszuschuß m.
investment income n Erträge pl aus Anlagen.
investment portfolio n Wertpapierportefeuille nt.
investment trust n Investmenttrust m.
investor [inves'tûr] n (Geld)anleger m.
inveterate [invet'ûrit] a unverbesserlich.
invigilator [invij'əlātûr] n (Brit) Aufsicht f, Aufsichtführende(r) mf.
invigorating [invig'ərāting] a stärkend.
invincible [invin'səbəl] a unbesiegbar, unschlagbar.
inviolate [invī'əlit] a unverletzt.
invisible [inviz'əbəl] a unsichtbar; (ink) Geheim-.
invisible exports npl unsichtbare Ausfuhren pl.
invisible imports npl unsichtbare Einfuhren pl.
invisible mending n Kunststopfen nt.
invitation [invitā'shən] n Einladung f; **by ~ only** nur auf Einladung; **at sb's ~** auf jds Aufforderung (hin).
invite [invīt'] vt einladen; (criticism, discussion) herausfordern; **to ~ sb (to do sth)** jdn auffordern(, etw zu tun); **to ~ sb to dinner** jdn zum Abendessen einladen.
invite out vt einladen.
invite over vt (zu sich) einladen.
inviting [invī'ting] a einladend; (prospect, meal) verlockend.
invoice [in'vois] n Rechnung f ♦ vt (goods) in Rechnung stellen; **to ~ sb for goods** jdm für Waren eine Rechnung ausstellen.
invoke [invōk'] vt anrufen.
involuntary [invâl'əntārē] a (unwilling) unfreiwillig; (unintentional) unabsichtlich.
involve [invâlv'] vt (entangle) verwickeln; (entail) mit sich bringen; **to ~ o.s. in sth** in etw (acc) verwickelt werden.
involved [invâlvd'] a verwickelt; **the person ~** die betreffende Person.
involvement [invâlv'mənt] n Verwicklung f.
invulnerable [invul'nûrəbəl] a unverwundbar; (fig) unangreifbar.
inward [in'wûrd] a innere(r, s); (curve) Innen-.
inwardly [in'wûrdlē] ad im Innern.
inward(s) [in'wûrd(z)] ad nach innen.
I/O abbr (COMPUT: = input/output) E/A; **~ error** Ein-/Ausgabefehler m.
IOC n abbr = **International Olympic Committee.**
iodine [ī'ədīn] n Jod nt.
ion [ī'ən] n Ion nt.
Ionian Sea [īō'nēən sē] n Ionische(s) Meer nt.
iota [īō'tə] n (fig) bißchen nt.
IOU n abbr (= I owe you) Schuldschein m.
IOW abbr (Brit) = Isle of Wight.
IPA n abbr (= International Phonetic Alpha-

bet) IPA *nt.*

IQ *n abbr* (= *intelligence quotient*) IQ *m.*

IRA *n abbr* (= *Irish Republican Army*) IRA *f*; (*US*) = *individual retirement account.*

Iran [iran'] *n* (der) Iran.

Iranian [irā'nēən] *a* iranisch ♦ *n* (*person*) Iraner(in *f*) *m*; (*language*) Iranisch *nt.*

Iraq [irak'] *n* der Irak.

Iraqi [irák'ē] *a* irakisch ♦ *n* (*person*) Iraker(in *f*) *m*; (*language*) Irakisch *nt.*

irascible [iras'əbəl] *a* reizbar.

irate [īrāt'] *a* zornig.

Ireland [īūr'lənd] *n* Irland *nt*; **Republic of ~** Republik *f* Irland.

iris [ī'ris] *n* Iris *f.*

Irish [ī'rish] *a* irisch; **~ Sea** Irische See *f* ♦ *n* (*language*) Irisch *nt*, Irische(s) Gälisch *nt*; **the ~** die Iren *pl*, die Irländer *pl.*

Irishman [ī'rishmən] *n, pl* -men Ire *m*, Irländer *m.*

Irishwoman [ī'rishwo͞omən] *n, pl* -women Irin *f*, Irländerin *f.*

irk [ûrk] *vt* verdrießen.

irksome [ûrk'səm] *a* lästig.

IRN *n abbr* = *Independent Radio News.*

IRO *n abbr* (*US*: = *International Refugee Organization*) Internationale Flüchtlingsorganisation *f.*

iron [ī'ûrn] *n* Eisen *nt*; (*for clothes*) Bügeleisen *nt*; **~s** *pl* (*chains*) Hand-/Fußschellen *pl* ♦ *a* eisern ♦ *vt* bügeln.

iron out *vt* (*lit, fig*) ausbügeln; (*differences*) ausgleichen.

Iron Curtain *n* Eiserne(r) Vorhang *m*; **the ~ countries** die Länder hinter dem Eisernen Vorhang.

iron foundry *n* (Eisen)gießerei *f.*

ironic(al) [īrân'ik(əl)] *a* ironisch; (*coincidence etc*) witzig.

ironically [īrân'iklē] *ad* ironisch; witzigerweise.

ironing [ī'ûrning] *n* Bügeln *nt*; (*laundry*) Bügelwäsche *f.*

ironing board *n* Bügelbrett *nt.*

iron lung *n* (*MED*) eiserne Lunge *f.*

ironmonger [ī'ûrnmunggûr] *n* (*Brit*) Eisenwarenhändler *m*; **~'s (shop)** Eisenwarenhandlung *f.*

iron ore [ī'ûrn ôr] *n* Eisenerz *nt.*

ironworks [ī'ûrnwûrks] *n sing or pl* Eisenhütte *f.*

irony [ī'rənē] *n* Ironie *f*; **the ~ of it was …** das Witzige daran war …

irrational [irash'ənəl] *a* unvernünftig, irrational.

irreconcilable [irek'ənsīləbəl] *a* unvereinbar.

irredeemable [iridē'məbəl] *a* (*COMM: money*) nicht einlösbar; (*loan*) unkündbar; (*fig*) rettungslos.

irrefutable [irifyo͞o'təbəl] *a* unwiderlegbar.

irregular [ireg'yəlûr] *a* unregelmäßig; (*shape*) ungleich(mäßig); (*fig*) unüblich; (*behavior*) ungehörig.

irregularity [iregyəlar'itē] *n* Unregelmäßigkeit

f; Ungleichmäßigkeit *f*; (*fig*) Vergehen *nt.*

irrelevance [irel'əvəns] *n* Irrelevanz *f.*

irrelevant [irel'əvənt] *a* belanglos, irrelevant.

irreligious [irilij'əs] *a* unreligiös, irreligiös.

irreparable [irep'ûrəbəl] *a* nicht gutzumachen.

irreplaceable [iriplā'səbəl] *a* unersetzlich.

irrepressible [iripres'əbəl] *a* nicht zu unterdrücken; (*joy*) unbändig.

irreproachable [iriprō'chəbəl] *a* untadelig.

irresistible [irizis'təbəl] *a* unwiderstehlich.

irresolute [irez'əlo͞ot] *a* unentschlossen.

irrespective of [irispek'tiv uv] *prep* ungeachtet (+*gen*).

irresponsibility [irispânsəbil'ətē] *n* Verantwortungslosigkeit *f.*

irresponsible [irispân'səbəl] *a* verantwortungslos.

irretrievable [iritrē'vəbəl] *a* (*object*) nicht mehr wiederzubekommen; (*loss*) unersetzlich; (*damage*) nicht wieder gutzumachen.

irretrievably [iritrē'vəblē] *ad* unwiederbringlich.

irreverence [irev'ûrəns] *n* Mißachtung *f.*

irreverent [irev'ûrənt] *a* respektlos.

irrevocable [irev'əkəbəl] *a* unwiderrufbar.

irrigate [ir'igāt] *vt* bewässern.

irrigation [irigā'shən] *n* Bewässerung *f.*

irritability [iritəbil'ətē] *n* Reizbarkeit *f.*

irritable [ir'itəbəl] *a* reizbar.

irritant [ir'ətənt] *n* Reizmittel *nt.*

irritate [ir'ətāt] *vt* irritieren, reizen (*also MED*).

irritating [ir'ətāting] *a* irritierend, aufreizend.

irritation [iritā'shən] *n* (*anger*) Ärger *m*; (*MED*) Reizung *f.*

IRS *n abbr* (*US*) = **Internal Revenue Service.**

is [iz] *3rd pers sing pres of* **be.**

ISBN *n abbr* (= *International Standard Book Number*) ISBN *f.*

Islam [iz'lâm] *n* Islam *m.*

island [ī'lənd] *n* Insel *f.*

islander [ī'ləndûr] *n* Inselbewohner(in *f*) *m.*

isle [īl] *n* (kleine) Insel *f.*

isn't [iz'ənt] = **is not.**

isobar [ī'sōbâr] *n* Isobare *f.*

isolate [ī'səlāt] *vt* isolieren.

isolated [ī'səlātid] *a* isoliert; (*case*) Einzel-.

isolation [īsəlā'shən] *n* Isolierung *f*; **to treat sth in ~** etw vereinzelt *or* isoliert behandeln.

isolationism [īsəlā'shənizəm] *n* Isolationismus *m.*

isolation ward *n* Isolierstation *f.*

isotope [ī'sətōp] *n* Isotop *nt.*

Israel [iz'rāəl] *n* Israel *nt.*

Israeli [izrā'lē] *a* israelisch ♦ *n* Israeli *mf*, Israelit(in *f*) *m.*

issue [ish'o͞o] *n* (*matter*) Problem *nt*, Frage *f*; (*outcome*) Resultat *nt*, Ergebnis *nt*; (*of newspaper, shares*) Ausgabe *f*; (*offspring*) Nachkommenschaft *f*; (*of river*) Mündung *f*; **that's not at ~** das steht nicht zur Debatte; **to make an ~ out of sth** ein Theater machen wegen etw; **to avoid the** ~ das Thema vermeiden; **to take** ~ **with sb over sth** jdm in etw (*dat*) widersprechen; **to confuse** *or* **obscure the** ~ die Frage verworren *or* unklar machen ♦ *vt* ausgeben; (*warrant*) erlassen; (*documents*) ausstellen; (*orders*) erteilen; (*books*) herausgeben; (*verdict*) aussprechen; **to** ~ **sb with sth** etw (*acc*) an jdn ausgeben; **to** ~ **sb with a visa** jdm ein Visum ausstellen ♦ *vi* (*people*) (heraus)strömen; (*liquid, gas*) austreten.

issued capital [ish'ōōd kap'itəl] *n* ausgegebene(s) Kapital *nt*.

Istanbul [istambōōl'] *n* Istanbul *nt*.

isthmus [is'məs] *n* Landenge *f*.

it [it] *pron* (*nom, acc*) es; (*dat*) ihm; **of** ~/ **about** ~/**out of** ~ *etc* davon/darüber/daraus *etc*; **who is** ~? wer ist da?; **what is** ~? was ist das?; (*what's the matter?*) was ist los?; ~'**s Friday tomorrow** morgen ist Freitag; ~'**s me** ich bin's; ~'**s 6 o'clock** es ist 6 Uhr; ~'**s 2 hours on the train** es dauert 2 Stunden mit dem Zug.

IT *n abbr* (= *information technology*) IT *f*.

Italian [ital'yən] *a* italienisch ♦ *n* (*person*) Italiener(in *f*) *m*; (*language*) Italienisch *nt*.

italic [ital'ik] *a* kursiv ♦ *npl*: ~**s** Kursivschrift *f*; **in** ~**s** kursiv gedruckt.

Italy [it'əlē] *n* Italien *nt*.

itch [ich] *n* Juckreiz *m* ♦ *vi* jucken; **to be** ~**ing to do sth** darauf brennen, etw zu tun.

itching [ich'ing] *n* Jucken *nt*.

itchy [ich'ē] *a* juckend.

it'd [it'əd] = **it would**; **it had**.

item [i'təm] *n* Gegenstand *m*; (*on list*) Posten *m*; (*in program*) Nummer *f*; (*on agenda*) (Programm)punkt *m*; (*in newspaper*) (Zeitungs)notiz *f*; ~**s of clothing** Kleidungsstücke *pl*.

itemize [i'təmīz] *vt* verzeichnen.

itinerant [ītin'ûrənt] *a* (*person*) umherreisend.

itinerary [ītin'ərärē] *n* Reiseroute *f*; (*records*) Reisebericht *m*.

it'll [it'əl] = **it will, it shall**.

its [its] *poss a* (*masculine, neuter*) sein(e); (*feminine*) ihr(e) ♦ *poss pron* seine(r, s); ihre(r, s).

it's [its] = **it is, it has**.

itself [itself'] *pron* sich (selbst); (*emphatic*) selbst.

ITV *n abbr* (*US*) = *instructional television*; (*Brit*: = *Independent Television*) unabhängige Fernsehgesellschaft.

IUD *n abbr* (= *intra-uterine device*) IUP *nt*.

IV *n abbr* (*US*: = *intravenous*) Tropf *m*.

I've [īv] = **I have**.

ivory [i'vûrē] *n* Elfenbein *nt*.

Ivory Coast *n* Elfenbeinküste *f*.

ivory tower *n* (*fig*) Elfenbeinturm *m*.

ivy [i'vē] *n* Efeu *m*.

Ivy League *n* (*US*) Eliteuniversitäten im Nordosten der USA.

J

J, j [jā] *n* (*letter*) J *nt*, **J for Jig** ≈ J wie Julius.

JA *n abbr* (*US*: = *judge advocate*) Militäranwalt *m*.

J/A *abbr* = **joint account**.

jab [jab] *vti* (hinein)stechen; **to** ~ **at sb with sth** mit etw auf jdn zustoßen ♦ *n* Stich *m*, Stoß *m*; (*col: injection*) Spritze *f*.

jabber [jab'ûr] *vi* plappern.

jack [jak] *n* Wagenheber *m*; (*CARDS*) Bube *m*.

jack in *vt* (*Brit col*) stecken, aufgeben.

jack up *vt* aufbocken.

jackal [jak'əl] *n* Schakal *m*.

jackass [jak'as] *n* Eselhengst *m*.

jackdaw [jak'dô] *n* Dohle *f*.

jacket [jak'it] *n* Jacke *f*, Jackett *nt*; (*of book*) Schutzumschlag *m*; (*TECH*) Ummantelung *f*.

jack-in-the-box [jak'intḫəbáks] *n* Schachtel- *or* Kastenteufel *m*.

jackknife [jak'nīf] *n* Klappmesser *nt* ♦ *vi* (*Brit: truck*) sich zusammenschieben.

jack-of-all-trades [jak'əvôltrádz'] *n* Alleskönner *m*.

jack plug *n* (*Brit*) Stecker *m*.

jackpot [jak'pât] *n* Haupttreffer *m*.

jacuzzi [jəkōō'zē] *n* ® Jacuzzi *nt* ®.

jade [jād] *n* (*stone*) Jade *m*.

jaded [jā'did] *a* ermattet.

JAG *n abbr* (*US*: = *Judge Advocate General*) Chef der Militärjustiz.

jagged [jag'id] *a* zackig; (*blade*) schartig.

jaguar [jag'wâr] *n* Jaguar *m*.

jail [jāl] *n* Gefängnis *nt* ♦ *vt* einsperren.

jailbird [jāl'bûrd] *n* (*col*) Knastbruder *m*.

jailbreak [jāl'brāk] *n* Gefängnisausbruch *m*.

jailer [jā'lûr] *n* Gefängniswärter *m*.

jalopy [jəlâp'ē] *n* (*col*) alte (Klapper)kiste *or* Mühle *f*.

jam [jam] *n* Marmelade *f*; (*crowd*) Gedränge *nt*; (*col: trouble*) Klemme *f*; (*traffic* ~) Verkehrsstauung *f*; **to get sb out of a** ~ (*fig*) jdm aus der Klemme helfen ♦ *vt* (*people*) zusammendrängen; (*wedge*) einklemmen; (*cram*) hineinzwängen; (*obstruct*) blockieren; **to** ~ **on the brakes** auf die Bremse treten; **the telephone lines are** ~**med** die (Telefon)leitungen sind belegt.

Jamaica [jəmā'kə] *n* Jamaika *nt*.

Jamaican [jəmā'kən] *a* jamaikanisch, jamaikisch ♦ *n* Jamaikaner(in *f*) *m*, Jamaiker(in *f*) *m*.

jamb [jam] *n* (Tür-/Fenster)pfosten *m*.

jamboree [jambərē'] *n* (Pfadfinder)treffen *nt*.

jam-packed [jam'pakt'] *a*: ~ **(with)** überfüllt

(mit).

jam session n Jam Session f.

Jan. abbr (= January) Jan.

jangle [jang'gəl] vi klimpern; (bells) bimmeln ♦ vt klimpern mit; bimmeln lassen.

janitor [jan'itûr] n Hausmeister m.

January [jan'yōōwārē] n Januar m; see **September**.

Japan [jəpan'] n Japan nt.

Japanese [japənēz'] a japanisch ♦ n (person) Japaner(in f) m; (language) Japanisch nt.

jar [jâr] n Glas nt ♦ vi kreischen; (colors etc) nicht harmonieren.

jargon [jâr'gən] n Fachsprache f, Jargon m.

jarring [jâr'ing] a (sound) kreischend; (color) unharmonisch.

Jas. abbr = James.

jasmin(e) [jaz'min] n Jasmin m.

jaundice [jôn'dis] n Gelbsucht f.

jaundiced [jôn'dist] a (fig) mißgünstig.

jaunt [jônt] n Spritztour f.

jaunty [jôn'tē] a (lively) munter; (brisk) flott; (attitude) unbekümmert.

javelin [jav'lin] n Speer m.

jaw [jô] n Kiefer m; ~s pl (fig) Rachen m; (TECH: of vice etc) (Klemm)backen pl.

jawbone [jô'bōn] n Kieferknochen m.

jay [jā] n Eichelhäher m.

jaywalker [jā'wôkûr] n unvorsichtige(r) Fußgänger m, Verkehrssünder m.

jazz [jaz] n Jazz m.

jazz up vt (MUS) verjazzen; (enliven) aufpolieren.

jazz band n Jazzband f.

jazzy [jaz'ē] a (color) schreiend, auffallend.

JCC n abbr (US) = Junior Chamber of Commerce.

JCS n abbr (US: = Joint Chiefs of Staff) Chefs des Stabs.

JD n abbr (US: = Doctor of Laws) Dr. jur.; (: = Justice Department) Justizministerium nt.

jealous [jel'əs] a eifersüchtig; (envious) neidisch; (watchful) bedacht (of auf +acc).

jealously [jel'əslē] ad eifersüchtig; (enviously) neidisch; (watchfully) sorgsam, sorgfältig.

jealousy [jel'əsē] n Eifersucht f; Neid f.

jeans [jēnz] npl Jeans pl.

jeep [jēp] n Jeep m.

jeer [jēr] vi höhnisch lachen (at über +acc), verspotten (at sb jdn) ♦ n Hohn m; (remark) höhnische Bemerkung f.

jeering [jē'ring] a höhnisch; (crowd) johlend ♦ n Johlen nt, Gejohle nt.

jelly [jel'ē] n Gelee nt; (on meat) Gallert nt; (dessert) Grütze f.

jellyfish [jel'ēfish] n Qualle f.

jemmy [jem'ē] n (Brit) Brecheisen nt.

jeopardize [jep'ûrdīz] vt gefährden.

jeopardy [jep'ûrdē] n Gefahr f.

jerk [jûrk] n Ruck m; (col: idiot) Trottel m, Dämlack m ♦ vt ruckartig bewegen ♦ vi sich ruckartig bewegen; (muscles) zucken.

jerkin [jûr'kin] n Wams nt.

jerky [jûr'kē] a (movement) ruckartig; (writing) zitterig; (ride) rüttelnd.

jerry-built [jär'ēbilt] a schlampig gebaut.

jerry can [jär'ē kan] n große(r) (Blech)kanister m.

jersey [jûr'zē] n Pullover m; (fabric) Jersey m.

Jersey [jûr'zē] n Jersey nt.

Jerusalem [jərōō'sələm] n Jerusalem nt.

jest [jest] n Scherz m; **in ~** im Spaß ♦ vi spaßen.

jester [jes'tûr] n Narr m, Spaßvogel m.

Jesus [jē'səs] n Jesus m; **~ Christ** Jesus Christus m.

jet [jet] n (stream: of water etc) Strahl m; (spout) Düse f; (AVIAT) Düsenflugzeug nt.

jet-black [jet'blak'] a rabenschwarz.

jet engine n Düsenmotor m.

jet lag n Schwierigkeiten durch die Zeitumstellung beim Fliegen.

jetsam [jet'səm] n Strandgut nt.

jettison [jet'əsən] vt über Bord werfen.

jetty [jet'ē] n Landesteg m, Mole f.

Jew [jōō] n Jude m, Jüdin f.

jewel [jōō'əl] n (lit, fig) Juwel nt; (stone) Edelstein m.

jeweler, (Brit) **jeweller** [jōō'əlûr] n Juwelier m; **~'s (shop)** Schmuckwarengeschäft nt, Juwelier m.

jewelry, (Brit) **jewellery** [jōō'əlrē] n Schmuck m, Juwelen pl.

Jewess [jōō'is] n Jüdin f.

Jewish [jōō'ish] a jüdisch.

JFK n abbr (US) = John Fitzgerald Kennedy International Airport.

jib [jib] n (NAUT) Klüver m ♦ vi sich scheuen (at vor +dat); (horse) scheuen, bocken (vor +dat); **to ~ at doing sth** sich dagegen sträuben, etw zu tun.

jibe [jīb] n spöttische Bemerkung f.

jiffy [jif'ē] n (col): **in a ~** sofort.

jig [jig] n (dance, tune) lebhafte(r) Volkstanz m.

jigsaw [jig'sô] n (also: **~ puzzle**) Puzzle(spiel) nt; (tool) Tischler-Bandsäge f.

jilt [jilt] vt den Laufpaß geben (+dat).

jimmy [jim'ē] n (US) Brecheisen nt.

jingle [jing'gəl] n (advertisement) Werbesong m; (verse) Reim m ♦ vi klimpern; (bells) bimmeln ♦ vt klimpern mit; bimmeln lassen.

jingoism [jing'gōizəm] n Hurrapatriotismus m.

jinx [jingks] n Fluch m; **to put a ~ on sth** etw verhexen.

jitters [jit'ûrz] npl (col): **to get the ~** einen Bammel kriegen.

jittery [jit'ûrē] a (col) nervös, rappelig.

jiujitsu [jōōjit'sōō] n Jiu-Jitsu nt.

job [jâb] n (piece of work) Arbeit f; (occupation) Stellung f, Arbeit f; (duty) Aufgabe f; (difficulty) Mühe f; (COMPUT) Auftrag m, Job m; **what's your ~?** was machen Sie von

Beruf?; **it's a good ~ he...** es ist ein Glück, daß er...; **just the ~** genau das Richtige; **a part-time/full-time ~** eine Halbtags-/ Ganztagsstelle; **that's not my ~** dafür bin ich nicht zuständig; **he's only doing his ~** er tut nur seine Pflicht.

jobber [jáb'ûr] n (*pieceworker*) Akkordarbeiter m; (*Brit FIN*) Börsenhändler m.

jobbing [jáb'ing] a (*Brit: in factory*) Akkord-; (: *gardener, carpenter etc*) Gelegenheits-.

Jobcentre [jáb'sentûr] n (*Brit*) Arbeitsvermittlung(samt nt) f.

job creation scheme n Arbeitsplatzbeschaffungsmaßnahmen pl.

job description n Arbeitsplatzbeschreibung f.

jobless [jáb'lis] a arbeitslos.

job lot n (Waren)posten m.

job satisfaction n Zufriedenheit f am Arbeitsplatz.

job security n Sicherheit f des Arbeitsplatzes.

job specification n Arbeitsplatzbeschreibung f.

jockey [ják'ē] n Jockei m ♦ vi: **to ~ for position** sich in einer gute Position drängeln.

jocular [ják'yəlûr] a scherzhaft, witzig.

jodhpurs [jád'pûrz] npl Reithose f.

jog [jág] vt (an)stoßen ♦ vi (*run*) einen Dauerlauf machen, joggen.

jogging [jág'ing] n Jogging nt.

john [ján] n (US col) Klo nt.

join [join] vt (*put together*) verbinden (*to* mit); (*club*) beitreten (+*dat*); (*person*) sich anschließen (+*dat*); **will you ~ us for dinner?** wollen Sie mit uns zu Abend essen?; **I'll ~ you later** ich komme nach ♦ vi (*unite*) sich vereinigen; (*bones*) zusammenwachsen ♦ n Verbindungsstelle f, Naht f.

join in vt *fus* mitmachen (*sth* bei etw) ♦ vi mitmachen.

join up vi (*MIL*) zur Armee gehen; (*meet: road etc*) sich treffen ♦ vt (miteinander) verbinden.

joiner [joi'nûr] n Schreiner m.

joinery [joi'nûrē] n Schreinerei f.

joint [joint] n (*TECH*) Fuge f; (*of bones*) Gelenk nt; (*of meat*) Braten m; (*col: place*) Lokal nt; (*DRUGS*) Marihuana- or Haschischzigarette f ♦ a gemeinsam.

joint account n gemeinsame(s) Konto nt.

jointly [joint'lē] ad gemeinsam.

joint owners npl Miteigentümer pl.

joint stock company n Aktiengesellschaft f.

joint venture n Joint-venture nt.

joist [joist] n Träger m.

joke [jōk] n Witz m; **it's no ~** es ist nicht zum Lachen ♦ vi spaßen, Witze machen; **you must be joking** das ist doch wohl nicht dein Ernst.

joker [jō'kûr] n Witzbold m; (*CARDS*) Joker m.

joking [jō'king] a scherzhaft.

jokingly [jō'kinglē] ad zum Spaß; (*talk*) im Spaß, scherzhaft.

jollity [jál'itē] n Fröhlichkeit f.

jolly [jál'ē] a lustig, vergnügt ♦ ad (*col*) ganz schön; **~ good!** (*Brit*) prima!

jolt [jōlt] n (*shock*) Schock m; (*jerk*) Stoß m, Rütteln nt ♦ vt (*push*) stoßen; (*shake*) durchschütteln; (*fig*) aufrütteln ♦ vi holpern.

Jordan [jór'dun] n (*river*) Jordan m; (*country*) Jordanien m.

jostle [jás'əl] vt anrempeln.

jot [ját] n (*of sense etc*) Funken m; **not one ~** kein Jota nt.

jot down vt schnell aufschreiben, notieren.

jotter [ját'ûr] n (*Brit*) Notizbuch nt; (*SCH*) Schulheft nt.

journal [jûr'nəl] n (*diary*) Tagebuch nt; (*magazine*) Zeitschrift f.

journalese [jûrnəlēz'] n Zeitungsstil m.

journalism [jûr'nəlizəm] n Journalismus m.

journalist [jûr'nəlist] n Journalist(in f) m.

journey [jûr'nē] n Reise f; (*by train, car also*) Fahrt f; **a 5 hour ~** eine Fahrt von 5 Stunden.

jovial [jō'vēəl] a jovial.

jowl [joul] n (*jaw*) (Unter)kiefer m; (*often pl: cheek*) Backe f.

joy [joi] n Freude f.

joyful [joi'fəl] a freudig; (*gladdening*) erfreulich.

joyfully [joi'fəlē] ad freudig.

joyous [joi'əs] a freudig.

joy ride n Schwarzfahrt f.

joystick [joi'stik] n (*AVIAT*) Steuerknüppel m; (*COMPUT*) Joystick m.

JP n abbr = **Justice of the Peace.**

Jr. abbr (= *junior*) Jun., jun.

JTPA n abbr (US: = *Job Training Partnership Act*) staatliches Programm zur beruflichen Aus- und Weiterbildung.

jubilant [jōō'bələnt] a triumphierend.

jubilation [jōōbəlā'shən] n Jubel m.

jubilee [jōō'bəlē] n Jubiläum nt; **silver ~** 25 jähriges Jubiläum.

judge [juj] n Richter m; (*fig*) Kenner m ♦ vt (*JUR: person*) die Verhandlung führen über (+*acc*); (*case*) verhandeln; (*assess*) beurteilen; (*criticize*) verurteilen; **I ~d it necessary to inform him** ich hielt es für notwendig, ihn zu informieren ♦ vi ein Urteil abgeben; **as far as I can ~** soweit ich das beurteilen kann; **judging by sth** nach etw zu urteilen.

judgement, judgment [juj'mənt] n (*JUR*) Urteil nt; (*ECCL*) Gericht nt; (*opinion*) Ansicht f; (*estimation*) Einschätzung f; (*discernment*) Urteilsvermögen nt; **in my ~** meines Erachtens.

judicial [jōōdish'əl] a gerichtlich, Justiz-.

judicious [jōōdish'əs] a weis(e).

judo [jōō'dō] n Judo nt.

jug [jug] n Krug m.

juggernaut [jug'ûrnôt] n (*Brit: truck*) Fernlastwagen m.

juggle [jug'əl] *vi* jonglieren ♦ *vt* (*facts*) verdrehen; (*figures*) frisieren.

juggler [jug'lûr] *n* Jongleur *m*.

jugular [jug'yəlûr] *a* (*vein*) Hals-.

juice [jo͞os] *n* Saft *m*.

juiciness [jo͞o'sēnis] *n* Saftigkeit *f*.

juicy [jo͞o'sē] *a* (*lit*, *fig*) saftig; (*story*) schlüpfrig.

jujitsu [jo͞ojit'so͞o] = **jiujitsu**.

jukebox [jo͞ok'báks] *n* Musikautomat *m*.

Jul. *abbr* = **July**.

July [julī'] *n* Juli *m*; *see* **September**.

jumble [jum'bəl] *n* Durcheinander *nt* ♦ *vt* (*also:* ~ **up**) durcheinanderwerfen; (*facts*) durcheinanderbringen.

jumble sale *n* (*Brit*) Basar *m*, Flohmarkt *m*.

jumbo (jet) [jum'bō (jet)] *n* Jumbo(-Jet) *m*.

jump [jump] *vi* springen; (*nervously*) zusammenzucken; **to** ~ **to conclusions** voreilige Schlüsse ziehen ♦ *vt* überspringen; **to** ~ **the gun** (*fig*) voreilig handeln ♦ *n* Sprung *m*; **to give sb a** ~ jdn erschrecken.

jump about, jump around *vi* herumspringen.

jump at *vt fus* (*fig*) sofort zugreifen bei; (*suggestion also*) sofort aufgreifen; **he** ~**ed at the offer** er griff bei dem Angebot sofort zu.

jumped-up [jumpt'up] *a* (*col*) eingebildet.

jumper [jum'pûr] *n* (*US*) Trägerkleid *nt*; (*Brit*) Pullover *m*.

jumper cables *npl* Starthilfekabel *pl*.

jump leads *npl* (*Brit*) = **jumper cables**.

jump rope *n* (*US*) Hüpfseil *nt*.

jump suit *n* Overall *m*.

jumpy [jum'pē] *a* nervös.

Jun. *abbr* = **June**.

junction [jungk'shən] *n* (*of roads*) (Straßen)kreuzung *f*; (*RAIL*) Knotenpunkt *m*.

juncture [jungk'chûr] *n*: **at this** ~ in diesem Augenblick.

June [jo͞on] *n* Juni *m*; *see* **September**.

jungle [jung'gəl] *n* Dschungel *m*, Urwald *m*.

junior [jo͞on'yûr] *a* (*younger*) jünger; (*after name*) junior; (*SPORT*) Junioren-; (*lower position*) untergeordnet; (*for young people*) Junioren- ♦ *n* Jüngere(r) *m*.

junior executive *n* zweite(r) Geschäftsführer *m*.

junior high school *n* (*US*) Mittelschule *f*.

junior school *n* (*Brit*) Grundschule *f*.

juniper [jo͞o'nəpûr] *n* Wacholder *m*.

junk [jungk] *n* (*rubbish*) Plunder *m*; (*ship*) Dschunke *f* ♦ *vt* ausrangieren.

junk bond *n* niedrig eingestuftes Wertpapier mit hohen Ertragschancen bei erhöhtem Risiko.

junk foods *npl* ungesunde Kost *f*.

junkie [jung'kē] *n* (*col*) Fixer(in *f*) *m*.

junk room *n* Rumpelkammer *f*.

junkshop [jungk'sháp] *n* Ramschladen *m*.

junkyard [jungk'yârd] *n* Schrottplatz *m*.

Jun(r)., Jun. *abbr* (= *junior*) Jun., jun.

junta [ho͞on'tə] *n* Junta *f*.

jurisdiction [jo͞orisdik'shən] *n* Gerichtsbarkeit *f*; (*range of authority*) Zuständigkeit(sbereich *m*) *f*.

jurisprudence [jo͞orispro͞od'əns] *n* Rechtswissenschaft *f*, Jura *no art*.

juror [jo͞o'rûr] *n* Schöffe *m*, Schöffin *f*; (*for capital crimes*) Geschworene(r) *mf*; (*in competition*) Preisrichter *m*.

jury [jo͞o'rē] *n* (*court*) Geschworene *pl*; (*in competition*) Jury *f*, Preisgericht *nt*.

jury box *n* Schöffen-/Geschworenenbank *f*.

juryman [jo͞or'ēmən] *n*, *pl* **-men** = **juror**.

just [just] *a* gerecht ♦ *ad* (*recently, now*) gerade, eben; (*barely*) gerade noch; (*exactly*) genau, gerade; (*only*) nur, bloß; (*a small distance*) gleich; (*absolutely*) einfach; ~ **as I arrived** gerade als ich ankam; ~ **as nice** genauso nett; ~ **as well** um so besser; ~ **about** so etwa; ~ **now** soeben, gerade; **not** ~ **now** nicht im Moment; ~ **try** versuch es bloß *or* mal; **I've** ~ **seen him** ich habe ihn gerade gesehen; ~ **a minute!**, ~ **one moment!** einen Moment, bitte!

justice [jus'tis] *n* (*fairness*) Gerechtigkeit *f*; (*magistrate*) Richter *m*.

Justice of the Peace *n* Friedensrichter *m*.

justifiable [jus'tifiəbəl] *a* berechtigt.

justifiably [jus'təfiəblē] *ad* berechtigterweise, zu Recht.

justification [justəfəkā'shən] *n* Rechtfertigung *f*.

justify [jus'təfī] *vt* rechtfertigen; (*TYP etc*) ausrichten, ausschließen; **to be justified in doing sth** gerechtfertigt sein, etw zu tun.

justly [just'lē] *ad* (*say*) mit Recht; (*condemn*) gerecht.

justness [just'nis] *n* Gerechtigkeit *f*.

jut [jut] *vi* (*also:* ~ **out**) herausragen, vorstehen.

juvenile [jo͞o'vənəl] *a* (*young*) jugendlich; (*for the young*) Jugend- ♦ *n* Jugendliche(r) *mf*.

juvenile delinquency *n* Jugendkriminalität *f*.

juvenile delinquent *n* jugendliche(r) Straftäter(in *f*) *m*.

juxtapose [jukstəpōz'] *vt* nebeneinanderstellen.

juxtaposition [jukstəpəzish'ən] *n* Nebeneinanderstellung *f*.

K

K, k [kā] *n* (*letter*) K *nt*, k *nt*; **K for King** ≈ K wie Kaufmann.

K [kā] *n abbr* (= *one thousand*) K, Tsd. ♦ *abbr* (*COMPUT*: = *kilobyte*) K.

Kalahari Desert [kâləhâr'ē dez'ûrt] *n* Kalahari(steppe) *f.*

kaleidoscope [kəlī'dəskōp] *n* Kaleidoskop *nt.*

Kampuchea [kampōōchē'ə] *n* Kampuchea *nt,* Kambodscha *nt.*

kangaroo [kanggəroo'] *n* Känguruh *nt.*

Kans. *abbr (US)* = *Kansas.*

Kashmir [kazh'mēr] *n* Kaschmir *nt.*

kayak [kī'ak] *n* Kajak *m or nt.*

kd *abbr (US:* = *knocked down)* (in Einzelteile) zerlegt.

keel [kēl] *n* Kiel *m;* **on an even ~** *(fig)* im Lot.

keen [kēn] *a* eifrig, begeistert; *(intelligence, wind, blade)* scharf; *(sight, hearing)* gut; *(price)* günstig; **I'm not ~ on going** ich bin nicht erpicht darauf, zu gehen.

keenly [kēn'lē] *ad (feel)* leidenschaftlich; *(sharply)* scharf; *(enthusiastically)* begeistert; *(acutely)* sehr, scharf.

keenness [kēn'nis] *n* Schärfe *f; (eagerness)* Begeisterung *f.*

keep [kēp] *irreg vt (retain)* behalten; *(have)* haben; *(animals, one's word)* halten; *(support)* versorgen; *(maintain in state)* halten; *(preserve)* aufbewahren; *(restrain)* abhalten; **~ the change** stimmt so!; **to ~ sb waiting** jdn warten lassen; **to ~ an appointment** eine Verabredung einhalten; **to ~ a note of sth** sich etw notieren; **to ~ a record of sth** über etw Buch führen ♦ *vi (continue in direction)* sich halten; *(remain: quiet etc)* sein, bleiben; **to ~ doing sth** *(not stop)* etw weiter tun; *(repeatedly)* etw immer wieder tun; *(constantly)* etw dauernd tun; **it ~s happening** es passiert immer wieder ♦ *n* Unterhalt *m; (tower)* Burgfried *m;* **for ~s** *(col)* für immer.

keep back *vt* fernhalten; *(secret)* verschweigen ♦ *vi* zurückbleiben.

keep down *vt (prices)* niedrig halten; *(spending)* einschränken; *(food)* bei sich behalten ♦ *vi* unten bleiben.

keep off *vi* wegbleiben ♦ *vt fus:* "**~ off the grass**" „Betreten des Rasens verboten".

keep on *vi:* **to ~ on doing sth** etw immer weiter tun ♦ *vt* anbehalten; *(hat)* aufbehalten.

keep out *vt* draußen lassen, nicht hereinlassen ♦ *vi:* "**~ out!**" „Eintritt verboten!"

keep up *vi* Schritt halten ♦ *vt* aufrechterhalten; *(continue)* weitermachen.

keep-fit [kēp'fit'] *n (Brit)* Keep-Fit-Training *nt.*

keeping [kē'ping] *n (care)* Obhut *f;* **in ~ (with)** in Übereinstimmung (mit).

keepsake [kēp'sāk] *n* Andenken *nt.*

keg [keg] *n* Faß *nt.*

Ken. *abbr (US)* = *Kentucky.*

kennel [ken'əl] *n* Hundehütte *f.*

Kenya [ken'yə] *n* Kenia *nt.*

Kenyan [ken'yən] *a* kenianisch ♦ *n* Kenianer(in *f*) *m.*

kept [kept] *pt, pp of* **keep.**

kerb(stone) [kûrb'(stōn)] *n (Brit)* Bordstein *m.*

kernel [kûr'nəl] *n* Kern *m.*

kerosene [kär'əsēn] *n (US)* Paraffin *nt.*

kestrel [kes'trəl] *n* Turmfalke *m.*

ketchup [kech'əp] *n* Ketchup *nt or m.*

kettle [ket'əl] *n* Kessel *m.*

kettledrum [ket'əldrum] *n* Pauke *f.*

key [kē] *n (lit, fig)* Schlüssel *m; (of piano, typewriter etc)* Taste *f; (MUS)* Tonart *f; (explanatory note)* Zeichenerklärung *f* ♦ *a (position etc)* Schlüssel-.

key in *vt (text)* eintasten.

keyboard [kē'bôrd] *n (of piano, typewriter etc)* Tastatur *f* ♦ *vt (text)* eintasten.

keyed up [kēd up] *a:* **to be (all) ~** (ganz) aufgedreht sein.

keyhole [kē'hōl] *n* Schlüsselloch *nt.*

key man *n* Schlüsselfigur *f.*

keynote [kē'nōt] *n* Grundton *m; (of a speech)* Leitgedanke *m.*

keynote speech *n (POL etc)* programmatische Rede *f.*

keypad [kē'pad] *n (keyboard)* Tastatur *f.*

key ring *n* Schlüsselring *m.*

keystroke [kē'strōk] *n* Tastenanschlag *m.*

kg *abbr (= kilogram(s))* kg.

KGB *n abbr* KGB *m.*

khaki [kak'ē] *n* K(h)aki *nt* ♦ *a* k(h)aki(farben).

kick [kik] *vt* einen (Fuß)tritt geben (*+dat*), treten ♦ *vi* treten; *(baby)* strampeln; *(horse)* ausschlagen ♦ *n* (Fuß)tritt *m; (thrill)* Spaß *m.*

kick around *vt* herumkicken; *(person)* herumstoßen.

kick off *vi (SPORT)* anstoßen.

kick up *vt (col)* schlagen.

kickoff [kik'ôf] *n (SPORT)* Anstoß *m.*

kid [kid] *n (child)* Kind *nt; (goat)* Zicklein *nt; (leather)* Glacéleder *nt* ♦ *vt* auf den Arm nehmen ♦ *vi* Witze machen.

kidnap [kid'nap] *vt* entführen, kidnappen.

kidna(p)per [kid'napûr] *n* Kidnapper(in *f*) *m,* Entführer(in *f*) *m.*

kidna(p)ping [kid'naping] *n* Entführung *f,* Kidnapping *nt.*

kidney [kid'nē] *n* Niere *f.*

kidney machine *n* künstliche Niere *f.*

Kilimanjaro [kiləmənjär'ō] *n* Kilimandscharo *m.*

kill [kil] *vt* töten, umbringen; *(chances)* ruinieren; **to ~ time** Zeit totschlagen ♦ *vi* töten ♦ *n* Tötung *f; (hunting)* (Jagd)beute *f.*

killer [kil'ûr] *n* Mörder(in *f*) *m.*

killing [kil'ing] *n (of person)* Töten *nt;* **to make a ~** *(FIN)* einen Riesengewinn machen.

killjoy [kil'joi] *n* Spaßverderber(in *f*) *m.*

kiln [kiln] *n* Brennofen *m.*

kilo [kē'lō] *n abbr (= kilogram(me))* Kilo *nt.*

kilobyte [kil'əbit] *n (COMPUT)* Kilobyte *nt.*

kilogram, *(Brit)* **kilogramme** [kil'əgram] *n* Kilogramm *nt.*

kilometer, (*Brit*) **kilometre** [kil'əmētûr] *n* Kilometer *m*.

kilowatt [kil'əwât] *n* Kilowatt *nt*.

kilt [kilt] *n* Schottenrock *m*.

kilter [kil'tûr] *n*: **out of** ~ durcheinander.

kimono [kimō'nō] *n* Kimono *m*.

kin [kin] *n* Verwandtschaft *f*, Verwandte(n) *pl*.

kind [kīnd] *a* freundlich, gütig; **would you be** ~ **enough to ...?, would you be so** ~ **as to ...?** wären Sie (vielleicht) so nett und ...?; **it's very** ~ **of you** es ist wirklich nett von Ihnen ♦ *n* Art *f*; **a** ~ **of** eine Art von; **(two) of a** ~ (zwei) von der gleichen Art; **in** ~ auf dieselbe Art; (*in goods*) in Naturalien.

kindergarten [kin'dûrgârtən] *n* (*Brit*) Kindergarten *m*.

kindhearted [kīnd'hârtid] *a* gutherzig.

kindle [kin'dəl] *vt* (*set on fire*) anzünden; (*rouse*) reizen, (er)wecken.

kindliness [kīnd'lēnis] *n* Freundlichkeit *f*, Güte *f*.

kindly [kīnd'lē] *a* freundlich ♦ *ad* liebenswürdig(erweise); **would you** ~ **...?** wären Sie so freundlich und ...?

kindness [kīnd'nis] *n* Freundlichkeit *f*.

kindred [kin'drid] *a* verwandt.

kindred spirit *n* Gleichgesinnte(r) *mf*.

kinetic [kinet'ik] *a* kinetisch.

king [king] *n* König *m*.

kingdom [king'dəm] *n* Königreich *nt*.

kingfisher [king'fishûr] *n* Eisvogel *m*.

kingpin [king'pin] *n* (*TECH*) Bolzen *m*; (*AUT*) Achsschenkelbolzen *m*; (*fig*) Stütze *f*.

king-size(d) [king'sīz(d)] *a* (*cigarette*) Kingsize.

kink [kingk] *n* Knick *m*.

kinky [king'kē] *a* (*fig*) exzentrisch.

kiosk [kēâsk'] *n* (*TEL*) Telefonhäuschen *nt*; (*newspaper* ~) Zeitungskiosk *m*.

kipper [kip'ûr] *n* Räucherhering *m*.

kiss [kis] *n* Kuß *m* ♦ *vt* küssen; **to** ~ **sb goodbye** jdm einen Abschiedskuß geben ♦ *vi*: **they** ~**ed** sie küßten sich.

kit [kit] *n* Ausrüstung *f*; (*tools*) Werkzeug *nt*.

kit bag *n* Seesack *m*.

kitchen [kich'ən] *n* Küche *f*.

kitchen garden *n* Gemüsegarten *m*.

kitchen sink *n* Spülbecken *nt*.

kitchen unit *n* Küchenschrank *m*.

kitchenware [kich'ənwär] *n* Küchengeschirr *nt*.

kite [kīt] *n* Drachen *m*.

kith [kith] *n*: ~ **and kin** Blutsverwandte *pl*; **with** ~ **and kin** mit Kind und Kegel.

kitten [kit'ən] *n* Kätzchen *nt*.

kitty [kit'ē] *n* (*money*) (gemeinsame) Kasse *f*.

KKK *n abbr* (*US*) = Ku Klux Klan.

kleptomaniac [kleptəmā'nēak] *n* Kleptomane *m*, Kleptomanin *f*.

km *abbr* (= *kilometer(s)*) km.

km/h *abbr* (= *kilometers per hour*) km/h.

knack [nak] *n* Dreh *m*, Trick *m*.

knapsack [nap'sak] *n* Rucksack *m*; (*MIL*) Tornister *m*.

knave [nāv] *n* (*old*) Schurke *m*.

knead [nēd] *vt* kneten.

knee [nē] *n* Knie *nt*.

kneecap [nē'kap] *n* Kniescheibe *f*.

knee-deep [nē'dēp] *a* knietief.

kneel [nēl] *vi irreg* knien.

knell [nel] *n* Grabgeläute *nt*.

knelt [nelt] *pt, pp of* **kneel**.

knew [nōō] *pt of* **know**.

knickers [nik'ûrz] *npl* (*US*) Knickerbockenhosen *pl*; (*Brit*) Schlüpfer *m*.

knife [nīf] *n, pl* **knives** [nīvz] Messer *nt* ♦ *vt* erstechen.

knight [nīt] *n* Ritter *m*; (*CHESS*) Springer *m*, Pferd *nt*.

knighthood [nīt'hōōd] *n* Ritterwürde *f*.

knit [nit] *vt* stricken ♦ *vi* stricken; (*bones*) zusammenwachsen; (*people*) harmonieren.

knitting [nit'ing] *n* (*occupation*) Stricken *nt*; (*work*) Strickzeug *nt*.

knitting machine *n* Strickmaschine *f*.

knitting needle *n* Stricknadel *f*.

knitwear [nit'wär] *n* Strickwaren *pl*.

knives [nīvz] *npl of* **knife**.

knob [nâb] *n* Knauf *m*; (*on door also*) Griff *m*; (*on instrument*) Knopf *m*; (*of butter etc*) kleine(s) Stück *nt*.

knock [nâk] *vt* schlagen; (*criticize*) heruntermachen ♦ *vi* klopfen; (*knees*) zittern; **he** ~**ed at the door** er klopfte an die Tür ♦ *n* Schlag *m*; (*on door*) Klopfen *nt*.

knock down *vt* (*pedestrian*) anfahren; (: *fatally*) überfahren; (*boxer*) zu Boden schlagen; (*price*) herunterhandeln.

knock off *vt* (*do quickly*) hinhauen; (*col: steal*) klauen ♦ *vi* (*finish*) Feierabend machen.

knock out *vt* lahmlegen; (*tooth*) ausschlagen; (*BOXING*) k.o. schlagen.

knock over *vt* (*person, object*) umwerfen; (*with car*) anfahren; (: *fatally*) überfahren.

knockdown [nâk'doun] *a* (*Brit: price*) heruntergehandelt.

knocker [nâk'ûr] *n* (*on door*) Türklopfer *m*.

knock-for-knock [nâk'fûrnâk'] *a*: ~ **agreement** (*Brit INSURANCE*) Schadensteilungsvereinbarung *f*.

knock-kneed [nâk'nēd] *a* x-beinig.

knock-on effect [nâk'ân ifekt'] *n* Folgewirkung *f*.

knockout [nâk'out] *n* (*lit*) K.o.-Schlag *m*; (*fig*) Sensation *f*.

knot [nât] *n* Knoten *m*; (*in wood*) Astloch *nt*; (*group*) Knäuel *nt or m*; **to tie a** ~ einen Knoten machen ♦ *vt* (ver)knoten.

knotted [nât'id] *a* verknotet.

knotty [nât'ē] *a* knorrig; (*problem*) kompliziert.

know [nō] *vti irreg* wissen; (*be able to*) können; (*be acquainted with*) kennen; (*recognize*) erkennen; **to** ~ **how to do sth** (*in theory*) wissen, wie man etw macht; (*in practice*) etw tun können; **to** ~ **about** *or* **of sth/sb** etw/jdn kennen; **you** ~ nicht (wahr).

to be well ~n bekannt sein; **to get to ~ sth** etw kennenlernen; **I ~ nothing about it** davon weiß ich nichts; **I don't ~ him** ich kenne ihn nicht; **to ~ right from wrong** Gut und Böse unterscheiden können; **as far as I ~** ... soviel ich weiß ...; **yes, I ~** ja, ich weiß; **I don't ~** ich weiß (es) nicht.

know-all [nō'ôl] n (Brit) = **know-it-all.**

know-how [nō'hou] n Kenntnis f, Know-how nt.

knowing [nō'ing] a schlau; (look, smile) wissend.

knowingly [nō'inglē] ad wissend; (intentionally) wissentlich.

know-it-all [nō'itôl] n (US) Alleswisser m.

knowledge [nâl'ij] n Wissen nt, Kenntnis f; **to have no ~ of** nichts wissen von, keine Kenntnisse haben von; **not to my ~** nicht, daß ich wüßte; **to have a working ~ of German** Grundkenntnisse in Deutsch haben.

knowledgeable [nâl'ijəbəl] a informiert.

known [nōn] pp of **know.**

knuckle [nuk'əl] n Fingerknöchel m.

KO abbr (= knock out) n K.o.(-Schlag) m ♦ vt k.o. schlagen.

kook [kōōk] n (US col) Spinner m.

Korea [kôrē'ə] n Korea nt.

Korean [kôrē'ən] a koreanisch ♦ n (person) Koreaner(in f) m; (language) Koreanisch nt.

kosher [kō'shûr] a koscher.

KS abbr (US MAIL) = Kansas.

kudos [kyōō'dōs] n Ansehen nt, Ehre f.

Kuwait [kōōwāt'] n Kuwait nt.

kW abbr (= kilowatt(s)) kW.

KY abbr (US MAIL) = Kentucky.

L

L, l [el] n (letter) L nt, l nt; **L for Love** ≈ L wie Ludwig.

l abbr (= liter(s)) l.

L abbr (= lake, large) L; (= left) l.; (Brit AUT: = learner) L.

LA n abbr (US) = Los Angeles ♦ abbr (US MAIL) = Louisiana.

lab [lab] n abbr (= laboratory) Labor nt.

Lab. abbr (Canada) = Labrador.

label [lā'bəl] n Etikett nt, Schild nt ♦ vt mit einer Aufschrift versehen, etikettieren.

labor [lā'bûr] n (US) Arbeit f; (workmen) Arbeitskräfte pl; (MED) Wehen pl; **to be in ~** in den Wehen liegen; **hard ~** Zwangsarbeit f.

laboratory [lab'rətôrē] n Laboratorium nt.

labor cost n Arbeitslöhne pl.

Labor Day n Tag m der Arbeit.

labor dispute n arbeitsrechtliche Auseinandersetzung f.

labored [lā'bûrd] a (style) schwerfällig; **his breathing became ~** er begann, schwer zu atmen.

laborer [lā'bûrûr] n Arbeiter m.

labor force n Arbeiterschaft f.

labor-intensive [lā'bûrintensiv] a arbeitsintensiv.

laborious [ləbôr'ēəs] a, **laboriously** [ləbôr'ēəslē] ad mühsam.

labor market n Arbeitsmarkt m.

labor relations npl Verhältnis nt zwischen Arbeitgebern und Arbeitnehmern.

labor-saving [lā'bûrsā'ving] a arbeitssparend.

labor union n (US) Gewerkschaft f.

labor unrest n Arbeitsunruhen pl.

labour [lā'bûr] n (Brit) = **labor** ♦ a (Brit POL) Labour-.

laburnum [ləbûr'nəm] n Goldregen m.

labyrinth [lab'ûrinth] n (lit, fig) Labyrinth nt.

lace [lās] n (fabric) Spitze f; (of shoe) Schnürsenkel m; (braid) Litze f ♦ vt (also: ~ up) (zu)schnüren; **to ~ a drink** (with spirits) einen Schuß Alkohol in ein Getränk geben.

lacemaking [lās'māking] n Klöppelei f.

lacerate [las'ərāt] vt zerschneiden, tief verwunden.

laceration [lasərā'shən] n Verletzung f, Fleischwunde f; (tear) Rißwunde f.

lace-up [lās'up] a (shoes etc) Schnür-.

lack [lak] vt nicht haben; **we ~ time** uns fehlt die nötige Zeit ♦ vi: **to be ~ing** fehlen; **sb is ~ing in sth** es fehlt jdm an etw (dat) ♦ n Mangel m; **for ~ of** aus Mangel an (+dat).

lackadaisical [lakədā'zikəl] a lasch.

lackey [lak'ē] n (also fig) Lakei m.

lackluster, (Brit) **lacklustre** [lak'lustûr] a (surface) stumpf, glanzlos; (style) farblos, langweilig; (eyes) trübe.

laconic [ləkân'ik] a lakonisch.

lacquer [lak'ûr] n Lack m; (hair ~) Haarspray nt.

lacrosse [ləkrôs'] n Lacrosse nt.

lacy [lā'sē] a spitzenartig, Spitzen-.

lad [lad] n (boy) Junge m; (Brit: in stable etc) Bursche m.

ladder [lad'ûr] n Leiter f; (Brit: in stocking) Laufmasche f ♦ vt (Brit) Laufmaschen bekommen in (+dat).

laden [lā'dən] a beladen, voll; **fully ~** (truck, ship) voll beladen.

ladle [lā'dəl] n Schöpfkelle f.

lady [lā'dē] n Dame f; (title) Lady f; **young ~** junge Dame; (toilets) "Ladies", "Damen".

ladybird [lā'dēbûrd] n (Brit) Marienkäfer m.

ladybug [lā'debug] n (US) Marienkäfer m.

lady doctor n Ärztin f.

lady-in-waiting [lā'dēinwā'ting] n Hofdame f.

ladykiller [lā'dēkilûr] n Frauenheld m, Herzensbrecher m.

ladylike [lā'dēlīk] a damenhaft, vornehm.

lag [lag] n (delay) Verzug m; (time ~) Zeitabstand m ♦ vi (also: ~ behind) zurückblei-

ben ♦ *vt* (*pipes*) verkleiden.
lager [lâ'gûr] *n* helle(s) Bier *nt*.
lagging [lag'ing] *n* Isolierung *f*.
lagoon [ləgōōn'] *n* Lagune *f*.
laid [lād] *pt, pp of* **lay**.
laid-back [lād'bak'] *a* (*col*) locker.
laid up *a*: **to be** ~ ans Bett gefesselt sein.
lain [lān] *pp of* **lie**.
lair [lär] *n* Lager *nt*.
laissez-faire [lesâfär'] *n* Laisser-faire *nt*.
laity [lā'itē] *n* Laien *pl*.
lake [lāk] *n* See *m*.
Lake District *n* Lake District *m*.
lamb [lam] *n* Lamm *nt*; (*meat*) Lammfleisch *nt*.
lamb chop *n* Lammkotelett *nt*.
lambswool [lamz'wōōl] *n* Lammwolle *f*.
lame [lām] *a* lahm; (*person also*) gelähmt; (*excuse*) faul; (*firm*) wackelig; ~ **duck** (*fig: person*) Niete *f* (*col*).
lamely [lām'lē] *ad* (*fig*) lahm.
lament [ləment'] *n* Klage *f* ♦ *vt* beklagen.
lamentable [ləmen'təbəl] *a* bedauerlich; (*bad*) erbärmlich.
lamentation [laməntā'shən] *n* Wehklage *f*.
laminated [lam'ənātid] *a* beschichtet.
lamp [lamp] *n* Lampe *f*; (*in street*) Straßenlaterne *f*.
lamplight [lamp'līt] *n*: **by** ~ bei Lampenlicht.
lampoon [lampōōn'] *vt* verspotten.
lamppost [lamp'pōst] *n* Laternenpfahl *m*.
lampshade [lamp'shād] *n* Lampenschirm *m*.
lance [lans] *n* Lanze *f* ♦ *vt* (*MED*) aufschneiden.
lance corporal *n* (*Brit*) ≈ Obergefreite(r) *m*.
lancet [lan'sit] *n* (*MED*) Lanzette *f*.
Lancs [langks] *abbr* (*Brit*) = *Lancashire*.
land [land] *n* Land *nt*; **to go/travel by** ~ auf dem Landweg reisen; **to own** ~ Land besitzen ♦ *vi* (*from ship*) an Land gehen; (*AVIAT, end up*) landen; **to** ~ **on one's feet** (*lit*) auf den Füßen landen; (*fig*) auf die Füße fallen ♦ *vt* (*obtain*) gewinnen, kriegen; (*passengers*) absetzen; (*goods*) abladen; (*troops, space probe*) landen.
landed [lan'did] *a* Land-.
landing [lan'ding] *n* (*of troops, people, plane*) Landung *f*; (*on stairs*) (Treppen)absatz *m*.
landing card *n* Einreisekarte *f*.
landing craft *n* Landungsboot *nt*.
landing gear *n* (*AVIAT*) Fahrwerk *nt*.
landing strip *n* Landebahn *f*.
landlady [land'lādē] *n* (Haus)wirtin *f*.
landlocked [land'lâkt] *a* landumschlossen, Binnen-.
landlord [land'lôrd] *n* (*of house*) Hauswirt *m*, Besitzer *m*; (*of pub*) Gastwirt *m*; (*of land*) Grundbesitzer *m*.
landlubber [land'lubûr] *n* Landratte *f*.
landmark [land'mârk] *n* Wahrzeichen *nt*; (*fig*) Meilenstein *m*.
landowner [land'ōnûr] *n* Grundbesitzer *m*.
landscape [land'skāp] *n* Landschaft *f*.

landscape architecture, landscape gardening *n* Landschaftsgärtnerei *or* -gestaltung *f*, Gartengestaltung *f*.
landscape painting *n* (*ART*) Landschaftsmalerei *f*.
landslide [land'slīd] *n* (*GEOG*) Erdrutsch *m*; **a** ~ **victory** (*POL*) ein überwältigender Sieg.
lane [lān] *n* (*in town*) Gasse *f*; (*in country*) Weg *m*; (*of freeway*) Fahrbahn *f*, Spur *f*; (*SPORT*) Bahn *f*.
language [lang'gwij] *n* Sprache *f*; (*style*) Ausdrucksweise *f*.
language laboratory *n* Sprachlabor *nt*.
language studies *npl* Sprachenstudium *nt*.
languid [lang'gwid] *a* schlaff, matt.
languish [lang'gwish] *vi* schmachten; (*pine*) sich sehnen (*for* nach).
languor [lang'gûr] *n* Mattigkeit *f*.
languorous [lang'gûrəs] *a* schlaff, träge.
lank [langk] *a* dürr.
lanky [lang'kē] *a* schlacksig.
lanolin(e) [lan'əlin] *n* Lanolin *nt*.
lantern [lan'tûrn] *n* Laterne *f*.
lap [lap] *n* Schoß *m*; (*SPORT*) Runde *f* ♦ *vt* auflecken ♦ *vi* (*water*) plätschern.
lap up *vt* auflecken, aufschlecken; (*fig: compliments, attention*) genießen.
lapdog [lap'dôg] *n* Schoßhund *m*.
lapel [ləpel'] *n* Rockaufschlag *m*, Revers *m or nt*.
Lapland [lap'lənd] *n* Lappland *nt*.
Laplander [lap'landûr] *n* Lappländer(in *f*) *m*, Lappe *m*, Lappin *f*.
lapse [laps] *n* (*mistake*) Irrtum *m*; (*fault*) Fehler *m*; (*in behavior*) Rückfall *m*; (*moral*) Fehltritt *m*; (*time*) Zeitspanne *f*; **he had a** ~ **of memory** es ist ihm entfallen.
laptop [lap'tâp] *n* (*also:* ~ **computer**) Laptop *m*.
larceny [lâr'sənē] *n* Diebstahl *m*.
lard [lârd] *n* Schweineschmalz *nt*.
larder [lâr'dûr] *n* Speisekammer *f*.
large [lârj] *a* groß; **to make** ~**r** vergrößern; **a** ~ **number of people** eine große Anzahl Leute; **on a** ~ **scale** weitreichend ♦ *n*: **at** ~ auf freiem Fuß ♦ *ad*: **by and** ~ im großen und ganzen.
largely [lârj'lē] *ad* zum größten Teil.
large-scale [lârj'skāl] *a* groß angelegt, Groß-; (*map, drawing etc*) in großem Maßstab; ~ **changes** (*reforms, business activities*) Veränderungen *pl* in großem Umfang *or* Rahmen.
largesse [lârjes'] *n* Freigebigkeit *f*.
lark [lârk] *n* (*bird*) Lerche *f*; (*joke*) Jux *m*.
lark about *vi* (*col*) herumalbern.
larva [lâr'və] *n*, *pl* **larvae** [lâr'vā] Larve *f*.
laryngitis [larənjī'tis] *n* Kehlkopfentzündung *f*.
larynx [lar'ingks] *n* Kehlkopf *m*.
lascivious [ləsiv'ēəs] *a*, **lasciviously** [ləsiv'ēəslē] *ad* wollüstig.
laser beam [lā'zûr bēm] *n* Laserstrahl *m*.
laser printer *n* Laserdrucker *m*.
lash [lash] *n* Peitschenhieb *m* ♦ *vt* (*beat*

against) schlagen an (+_acc_); (_rain_) schlagen gegen; (_whip_) peitschen; (_bind_) festbinden.
lash down _vt_ festbinden ♦ _vi_ (_rain_) niederprasseln.
lash out _vi_ (_with fists_) um sich schlagen; (_spend money_) sich in Unkosten stürzen ♦ _vt_ (_money etc_) springen lassen.
lass [las] _n_ Mädchen _nt_.
lassitude [las'ətōōd] _n_ Abgespanntheit _f_.
lasso [las'ō] _n_ Lasso _nt_ ♦ _vt_ mit einem Lasso fangen.
last [last] _a_ letzte(r, s); ~ **night** gestern abend ♦ _ad_ zuletzt; (~ _time_) das letztemal ♦ _n_ (_person_) Letzte(r) _mf_; (_thing_) Letzte(s) _nt_; (_for shoe_) (Schuh)leisten _m_; **at ~** endlich ♦ _vi_ (_continue_) dauern; (_remain good_) sich halten; (_money_) ausreichen; **it ~s (for) 2 hours** es dauert 2 Stunden.
last-ditch [last'dich'] _a_ allerletzte(r, s); (_attempt etc_) in letzter Minute.
lasting [las'ting] _a_ dauerhaft, haltbar; (_shame etc_) andauernd.
lastly [last'lē] _ad_ schließlich, zum Schluß.
last-minute [last'min'it] _a_ in letzter Minute.
latch [lach] _n_ Riegel _m_.
latch on to _vt fus_: **she ~ed on to me at the party** sie hängte sich auf der Party an mich (_col_); **he ~ed on to the idea of coming (with us)** er hat es sich (_dat_) in den Kopf gesetzt mitzukommen.
latchkey [lach'kē] _n_ Hausschlüssel _m_.
latchkey child _n_ Schlüsselkind _nt_.
late [lāt] _a_ spät, spät; (_recent_) jüngste(r, s); (_former_) frühere(r, s); (_dead_) verstorben; **to be (10 minutes) ~** (10 Minuten) zu spät kommen; **to be ~ with sth** sich mit etw verspäten; **~ delivery** zweite (Post)zustellung _f_ ♦ _ad_ spät; (_after proper time_) zu spät; **of ~** in letzter Zeit; **~ in the day** (_lit_) spät; (_fig_) reichlich spät; **to work ~** länger arbeiten; **he took up the piano rather ~ in life** er begann ziemlich spät mit dem Klavierspielen.
latecomer [lāt'kumûr] _n_ Nachzügler _m_.
lately [lāt'lē] _ad_ in letzter Zeit, neulich.
lateness [lāt'nis] _n_ (_of person_) Zuspätkommen _nt_; (_of train_) Verspätung _f_; **the ~ of the hour** die vorgerückte Stunde.
latent [lā'tənt] _a_ latent.
latent defect _n_ verborgene(r) Mangel _m_.
later [lā'tûr] _a_, _ad_ später; **~ on today** im Laufe des Tages.
lateral [lat'ûrəl] _a_ seitlich.
latest [lā'tist] _n_ (_news_) Neu(e)ste(s) _nt_; **at the ~** spätestens ♦ _a_: **the ~ news** die neuesten Nachrichten.
latex [lā'teks] _n_ Milchsaft _m_, Latex _m_.
lath [lath] _n_ Latte _f_, Leiste _f_.
lathe [lāth] _n_ Drehbank _f_.
lather [lath'ûr] _n_ (Seifen)schaum _m_ ♦ _vt_ einschäumen ♦ _vi_ schäumen.
Latin [lat'in] _n_ Latein _nt_ ♦ _a_ lateinisch; (_Roman_) römisch.

Latin America _n_ Lateinamerika _nt_.
Latin-American [lat'inəmär'ikən] _a_ lateinamerikanisch ♦ _n_ Lateinamerikaner(in _f_) _m_.
latitude [lat'ətōōd] _n_ (_GEOG_) Breite _f_; (_freedom_) Spielraum _m_.
latrine [lətrēn'] _n_ Latrine _f_.
latter [lat'ûr] _a_ (_second of two_) letztere(r, s); (_coming at end_) letzte(r, s), später ♦ _n_: **the ~** der/die/das letztere; die letzteren.
latter-day [lat'ûrdā] _a_ modern.
latterly [lat'ûrlē] _ad_ in letzter Zeit.
lattice window [lat'is win'dō] _n_ Gitterfenster _nt_.
lattice work _n_ Lattenwerk _nt_, Gitterwerk _nt_.
Latvia [lat'vēə] _n_ Lettland _nt_.
laudable [lô'dəbəl] _a_ löblich.
laugh [laf] _n_ Lachen _nt_ ♦ _vi_ lachen.
laugh at _vt fus_ lachen über (+_acc_).
laugh off _vt_ lachend abtun.
laughable [laf'əbəl] _a_ lachhaft, lächerlich.
laughing [laf'ing] _a_ lachend ♦ _n_ Lachen _nt_.
laughing gas _n_ Lachgas _nt_.
laughing matter _n_: **this is no ~** das ist nicht zum Lachen, das ist gar nicht komisch.
laughing stock _n_ Zielscheibe _f_ des Spottes.
laughter [laf'tûr] _n_ Lachen _nt_, Gelächter _nt_.
launch [lônch] _n_ (_of ship_) Stapellauf _m_; (_of rocket_) Raketenabschuß _m_; (_of company_) Gründung _f_; (_boat_) Barkasse _f_; (_pleasure boat_) Vergnügungsboot _nt_ ♦ _vt_ (_set afloat_) vom Stapel laufen lassen; (_rocket_) (ab)schießen; (_set going_) in Gang setzen, starten.
launch forth, launch out _vi_: **to ~ forth into a violent speech** (_fig_) eine wütende Rede vom Stapel lassen.
launching [lôn'ching] _n_ Stapellauf _m_.
launch(ing) pad _n_ Abschußrampe _f_.
launder [lôn'dûr] _vt_ waschen und bügeln.
launderette [lôndəret'] _n_ (_Brit_) Waschsalon _m_.
laundromat [lôn'drəmat] _n_ (_US_) Waschsalon _m_.
laundry [lôn'drē] _n_ (_place_) Wäscherei _f_; (_clothes_) Wäsche _f_.
laureate [lô'rēit] _a_ _see_ **poet laureate**.
laurel [lôr'əl] _n_ Lorbeer _m_; **to rest on one's ~s** sich auf seinen Lorbeeren ausruhen.
lava [lâv'ə] _n_ Lava _f_.
lavatory [lav'ətôrē] _n_ Toilette _f_.
lavender [lav'əndûr] _n_ Lavendel _m_.
lavish [lav'ish] _a_ (_extravagant_) verschwenderisch; (_generous_) großzügig ♦ _vt_ (_money_) verschwenden (_on_ auf +_acc_); (_attentions, gifts_) überschütten mit (_on sb_ jdn).
lavishly [lav'ishlē] _ad_ verschwenderisch; (_give, spend_) großzügig; (_furnished_) luxuriös.
law [lô] _n_ Gesetz _nt_; (_system_) Recht _nt_; (_of game etc_) Regel _f_; (_as studies_) Jura _no art_, Rechtswissenschaft _f_.
law-abiding [lô'əbīding] _a_ gesetzestreu, friedlich.
lawbreaker [lô'brākûr] _n_ Gesetzesübertreter

m.

law court *n* Gerichtshof *m.*

lawful [lô'fəl] *a* gesetzlich, rechtmäßig.

lawfully [lô'fəlē] *ad* rechtmäßig.

lawless [lô'lis] *a* gesetzlos.

lawmaker [lô'mākûr] *n* Gesetzgeber *m.*

lawn [lôn] *n* (*grass*) Rasen *m.*

lawnmower [lôn'mōûr] *n* Rasenmäher *m.*

lawn tennis *n* Rasentennis *m.*

law school [lô' skōōl] *n* Rechtsakademie *f*; (*US*) juristische Fakultät *f.*

law student [lô' stōōd'ənt] *n* Jurastudent(in *f*) *m.*

lawsuit [lô'sōōt] *n* Prozeß *m*; **to bring a ~ against** eine Klage *or* einen Prozeß anstrengen gegen.

lawyer [lô'yûr] *n* Rechtsanwalt *m*, Rechtsanwältin *f.*

lax [laks] *a* (*person: careless*) lax, nachlässig; (*on discipline*) lasch.

laxative [lak'sətiv] *n* Abführmittel *nt.*

laxity [lak'sitē] *n* Laxheit *f.*

lay [lā] *a* Laien- ♦ *pt of* **lie** ♦ *vt irreg* (*place*) legen; (*Brit: table*) decken; (*fire*) anrichten; (*egg*) legen; (*trap*) stellen; (*money*) wetten; **to ~ the facts/one's proposals before sb** jdm die Tatsachen/seine Vorschläge vortragen.

lay aside *vt* zurücklegen.

lay by *vt* (*set aside*) beiseite legen.

lay down *vt* hinlegen; (*rules*) vorschreiben; (*arms*) strecken.

lay in *vt* einlagern, anlegen.

lay into *vt fus*: **to ~ into sb** (*col: attack, scold*) jdn fertigmachen *or* runterputzen.

lay off *vt* (*workers*) (vorübergehend) entlassen.

lay on *vt* auftragen; (*concert etc*) veranstalten.

lay out *vt* (her)auslegen; (*money*) ausgeben; (*corpse*) aufbahren.

lay up *vt* (*store*) aufspeichern; (*supplies*) anlegen; (*save*) zurücklegen.

layabout [lā'əbout] *n* (*Brit*) Faulenzer *m.*

lay-by [lā'bī] *n* (*Brit*) Parkbucht *f*; (*bigger*) Rastplatz *m.*

lay days *npl* (*NAUT*) Liegezeit *f.*

layer [lā'ûr] *n* Schicht *f.*

layette [lā'et'] *n* Babyausstattung *f.*

layman [lā'mən] *n, pl* **-men** Laie *m.*

layoff [lā'ôf] *n* Feierschicht *f.*

layout [lā'out] *n* Anlage *f*; (*ART*) Layout *nt.*

layover [lā'ōvûr] *n* (*US*) Zwischenaufenthalt *m.*

laze [lāz] *vi* faulenzen.

lazily [lā'zilē] *ad* faul; träge.

laziness [lā'zēnis] *n* Faulheit *f.*

lazy [lā'zē] *a* faul; (*slow-moving*) träge.

lb. *abbr* (= *libra: pound*) ≈ Pfd.

LB *abbr* (*Canada*) = *Labrador.*

lc *abbr* (*TYP: = lower case*) Kleinbuchstaben *pl.*

LC *n abbr* (*US*) = *Library of Congress.*

LCD *abbr* = **liquid crystal display.**

LDS *n abbr* = *Latter-day Saints.*

lead [led] *n see also following entry* Blei *nt*; (*of pencil*) (Bleistift)mine *f* ♦ *a* bleiern, Blei-.

lead [lēd] *n see also previous entry* (*front position*) Führung *f*; (*distance, time ahead*) Vorsprung *f*; (*example*) Vorbild *nt*; (*clue*) Tip *m*; (*of police*) Spur *f*; (*THEAT*) Hauptrolle *f*; (*dog's*) Leine *f*; **to take the ~** (*SPORT*) in Führung gehen; (*fig*) mit gutem Beispiel vorangehen ♦ *irreg vt* (*guide*) führen; (*group*) leiten; (*orchestra: US*) leiten; (: *Brit*) führen; **to ~ sb to do sth** jdn dazu bringen, etw zu tun; **to ~ sb to believe that** ... jdm den Eindruck vermitteln, daß ... ♦ *vi* (*be first*) führen; **to ~ astray** irreführen.

lead away *vt* wegführen; (*prisoner*) abführen.

lead back *vti* zurückführen.

lead off *vt* abführen ♦ *vi* abgehen.

lead on *vt* anführen.

lead to *vt fus* (*street*) (hin)führen nach; (*result in*) führen zu.

lead up *vt* hinaufführen (*to* auf +*acc*); (*lead across*) führen (*to* zu).

lead up to *vt fus* (*speaker etc*) hinführen auf (+*acc*) ♦ *vi*: **the years that led up to the war** die Jahre, die dem Krieg vorausgingen.

leaded [led'id] *a* (*gas*) verbleit.

leaded windows [led'id win'dōz] *npl* Bleiglasfenster *pl.*

leader [lē'dûr] *n* Führer *m*, Leiter *m*; (*of orchestra: US*) Dirigent *m*; (: *Brit*) Konzertmeister *m*; (*of party*) Vorsitzende(r) *m*; (*Brit: in newspaper*) Leitartikel *m*; **they are ~s in their field** (*fig*) sie sind auf diesem Gebiet führend.

leadership [lē'dûrship] *n* (*office*) Leitung *f*; (*quality*) Führerschaft *f*; **under the ~ of** ... unter (der) Führung von ...; **qualities of ~** Führungsqualitäten *pl.*

lead-free [ledfrē'] *a* bleifrei.

leading [lē'ding] *a* führend; **a ~ question** eine Suggestivfrage.

leading lady *n* (*THEAT*) Hauptdarstellerin *f.*

leading light *n* (*person*) Nummer eins *f*, große(s) Licht *nt.*

leading man *n* (*THEAT*) Hauptdarsteller *m.*

leading role *n* führende Rolle *f.*

lead pencil [led pen'səl] *n* Bleistift *m.*

lead poisoning [led' poi'zəning] *n* Bleivergiftung *f.*

lead weight [led wāt] *n* Bleigewicht *nt.*

leaf [lēf] *n, pl* **leaves** [lēvz] Blatt *nt*; (*of table*) Ausziehplatte *f*; **to turn over a new ~** (*fig*) einen neuen Anfang machen; **to take a ~ out of sb's book** (*fig*) sich (*dat*) von jdm eine Scheibe abschneiden.

leaf through *vt fus* (*book*) durchblättern.

leaflet [lēf'lit] *n* Blättchen *nt*; (*advertisement*) Prospekt *m*; (*pamphlet*) Flugblatt *nt*; (*for information*) Merkblatt *nt.*

leafy [lē'fē] *a* belaubt.

league [lēg] *n* (*union*) Bund *m*, Liga *f*; (*SPORT*) Liga *f*, Tabelle *f*; (*measure*) 3 englische Meilen.

leak [lēk] *n* (*fig also*) undichte Stelle *f*; (*in ship*) Leck *nt* ♦ *vt* (*liquid etc*) durchlassen; (*information*) zuspielen ♦ *vi* (*pipe etc*) undicht sein; (*liquid etc*) auslaufen.

leak out *vi* (*liquid etc*) auslaufen; (*information*) durchsickern.

leakage [lē'kij] *n*: **there is still a ~ in the pipe** das Rohr ist immer noch undicht.

leaky [lē'kē] *a* (*pipe, bucket, roof, shoe*) undicht; (*boat*) undicht, leck.

lean [lēn] *a* mager ♦ *irreg vi* sich neigen (*to* nach); (*rest*) sich lehnen (*against* gegen +*acc*); **she ~ed across the table** sie beugte sich über den Tisch ♦ *vt* (an)lehnen; (*rest*) aufstützen (*on* auf +*dat or acc*); **to ~ one's elbow on sth** sich mit dem Ellbogen auf etw (*acc*) stützen.

lean back *vi* sich zurücklehnen.

lean forward *vi* sich vorbeugen.

lean on *vt fus* sich stützen auf (+*acc*).

lean out *vi*: **to ~ out (of)** sich hinauslehnen (aus).

lean over *vi* sich hinüberbeugen.

lean towards *vt fus* neigen zu.

leaning [lē'ning] *n* Neigung *f* ♦ *a*: **the L~ Tower of Pisa** der schiefe Turm von Pisa.

leant [lent] *pt, pp of* **lean.**

lean-to [lēn'tōō] *n* (*roof*) Anbau *m*; (*building*) Wetterschutz *m*, Wetterschirm *m*.

leap [lēp] *n* Sprung *m*; **by ~s and bounds** sprunghaft ♦ *vi irreg* springen; **to ~ at an offer** sich auf ein Angebot stürzen.

leap up *vi* (*person*) aufspringen.

leapfrog [lēp'frâg] *n* Bockspringen *nt* ♦ *vi*: **the children ~ged over one another** die Kinder spielten *or* machten Bockspringen.

leapt [lept] *pt, pp of* **leap.**

leap year *n* Schaltjahr *nt*.

learn [lûrn] *vti irreg* lernen; (*find out*) erfahren, hören; **to ~ that ...** erfahren, daß ...; **we were sorry to ~ that ...** es hat uns sehr leid getan, daß ...; **to ~ about *or* of sth** (*SCH*) etw lernen; (*hear*) von etw hören *or* erfahren.

learned [lûr'nid] *a* gelehrt.

learner [lûr'nûr] *n* Anfänger(in *f*) *m*; (*Brit AUT*) Fahrschüler(in *f*) *m*.

learning [lûr'ning] *n* Gelehrsamkeit *f*.

learnt [lûrnt] *pt, pp of* **learn.**

lease [lēs] *n* (*of property*) Mietvertrag *m*; (*of land*) Pachtvertrag *m*; **on ~** zur Pacht ♦ *vt* mieten; pachten.

lease back *vt* (*Brit*) verkaufen und gleichzeitig rückmieten.

leaseback [lēs'bak] *n* (*Brit*) Verkauf *m* mit gleichzeitiger Rückmiete.

leasehold [lēs'hōld] *a* gepachtet, in Pacht ♦ *n* (*contract*) Pachtvertrag *m*; (*property*) Pachtbesitz *m*.

leash [lēsh] *n* Leine *f*.

least [lēst] *a* kleinste(r, s); (*slightest*) geringste(r, s) ♦ *n* Mindeste(s) *nt*; **at ~** zumindest; **not in the ~!** durchaus nicht!

leather [leth'ûr] *n* Leder *nt* ♦ *a* ledern, Leder-.

leather goods *npl* Lederwaren *pl*.

leathery [leth'ûrē] *a* zäh, ledern.

leave [lēv] *irreg vt* verlassen; (~ *behind*) zurücklassen; (*forget*) vergessen; (*allow to remain*) lassen; (*after death*) hinterlassen; (*entrust*) überlassen (*to sb* jdm); **to be left** (*remain*) übrigbleiben; **to ~ school** die Schule verlassen; **~ it to me!** laß mich nur machen ♦ *vi* weggehen, wegfahren; (*for journey*) abreisen; (*bus, train*) abfahren; **he's already left for the airport** er ist schon zum Flughafen gefahren ♦ *n* Erlaubnis *f*; (*MIL*) Urlaub *m*; **on ~** auf Urlaub; **to take one's ~ of** Abschied nehmen von; **to be on ~ of absence** beurlaubt sein.

leave behind *vt* (*also fig*) zurücklassen; (*forget*) liegen- *or* stehenlassen; (*outstrip*) hinter sich (*dat*) lassen.

leave off *vi* aufhören ♦ *vt* (*clothes*) nicht anziehen; (*radio, lights*) auslassen.

leave on *vt* (*clothes*) anbehalten, anlassen; (*light, fire, stove*) anlassen.

leave out *vt* auslassen.

leave over *vt* (*leave surplus*) übriglassen; (*postpone*) verschieben, vertagen.

leaves [lēvz] *npl of* **leaf.**

leavetaking [lēv'tāking] *n* Abschied *m*.

Lebanon [leb'ənən] *n* der Libanon.

lecherous [lech'ûrəs] *a* lüstern.

lectern [lek'tûrn] *n* Lesepult *nt*.

lecture [lek'chûr] *n* Vortrag *m*; (*UNIV*) Vorlesung *f* ♦ *vi* einen Vortrag halten; (*UNIV*) lesen ♦ *vt* (*reprove*) tadeln, abkanzeln.

lecture hall *n* Hörsaal *m*.

lecturer [lek'chûrûr] *n* Vortragende(r) *mf*; (*Brit UNIV*) Dozent(in *f*) *m*.

led [led] *pt, pp of* **lead.**

LED *n abbr* (*ELEC*: = *light-emitting diode*) Leuchtdiode *f*.

ledge [lej] *n* Leiste *f*; (*window ~*) Sims *m or* *nt*; (*of mountain*) (Fels)vorsprung *m*.

ledger [lej'ûr] *n* Hauptbuch *nt*.

lee [lē] *n* Windschatten *m*; (*NAUT*) Lee *f*; **in the ~** im Schutz *or* Windschatten.

leech [lēch] *n* Blutegel *m*.

leek [lēk] *n* Lauch *m*.

leer [lēr] *n* schiefe(r) Blick *m* ♦ *vi* schielen (*at* nach).

leeward [lē'wûrd] *a* (*NAUT*) Lee- ♦ *n* (*NAUT*) Lee(seite) *f*; **to ~** an der Leeseite.

leeway [lē'wā] *n* (*fig*) Rückstand *m*; (*freedom*) Spielraum *m*.

left [left] *a* linke(r, s) ♦ *ad* links, nach links ♦ *n* (*side*) linke Seite *f*; **on the ~, to the ~** links, auf der linken Seite; **the L~** (*POL*) die Linke *f* ♦ *pt, pp of* **leave.**

left-hand drive [left'hand' drīv] *n* Linkssteuerung *f*.

left-handed [left'han'did] *a* linkshändig; **~ scissors** Schere *f* für Linkshänder.

left-hand side [left'hand' sīd] *n* linke Seite *f*.
leftist [left'tist] *a* (*POL*) linke(r, s).
left-luggage (office) [leftlug'ij   (ôf'is)] *n* (*Brit*) Gepäckaufbewahrung *f*.
leftovers [left'ōvŭrz] *npl* Reste *pl*, Überbleibsel *pl*.
left wing *n* linke(r) Flügel *m*.
left-wing [left'wing] *a* linke(r, s).
left-winger [left'wingŭr] *n* (*POL*) Linke(r) *mf*.
leg [leg] *n* Bein *nt*; (*of meat*) Keule *f*; (*stage*) Etappe *f*; **to stretch one's ~s** sich die Beine vertreten.
legacy [leg'əsē] *n* (*lit, fig*) Erbe *nt*, Erbschaft *f*.
legal [lē'gəl] *a* gesetzlich, rechtlich; (*allowed*) legal, rechtsgültig; **to take ~ action** *or* **proceedings against sb** gerichtlich gegen jdn vorgehen.
legal adviser *n* juristische(r) Berater *m*.
legal holiday *n* (*US*) gesetzliche(r) Feiertag *m*.
legality [lēgal'itē] *n* Legalität *f*.
legalize [lē'gəlīz] *vt* legalisieren.
legally [lē'gəlē] *ad* legal; (*guaranteed*) gesetzlich; **~ binding** rechtsverbindlich.
legal tender *n* gesetzliche(s) Zahlungsmittel *nt*.
legatee [legətē'] *n* Vermächtnisnehmer *m*.
legation [ligā'shən] *n* Gesandtschaft *f*.
legend [lej'ənd] *n* Legende *f*.
legendary [lej'əndārē] *a* legendär.
-legged [leg'id] *a* -beinig.
leggings [leg'ingz] *npl* (hohe) Gamaschen *pl*; (*for baby*) Gamaschenhose *f*.
legibility [lejəbil'ətē] *n* Leserlichkeit *f*.
legible [lej'əbəl] *a*, **legibly** [lej'əblē] *ad* leserlich.
legion [lē'jən] *n* Legion *f*.
legionnaire [lējənär'] *n* Legionär *m*.
legionnaire's disease *n* Legionärskrankheit *f*.
legislate [lej'islāt] *vi* Gesetze geben.
legislation [lejislā'shən] *n* Gesetzgebung *f*; **to enact ~** Gesetze erlassen.
legislative [lej'islātiv] *a* gesetzgebend.
legislator [lej'islātŭr] *n* Gesetzgeber *m*.
legislature [lej'islāchŭr] *n* Legislative *f*.
legitimacy [lijit'əməsē] *n* Rechtmäßigkeit *f*; (*of birth*) Ehelichkeit *f*.
legitimate [lijit'əmit] *a* rechtmäßig, legitim; (*child*) ehelich.
legitimize [lijit'əmīz] *vt* legitimieren; (*child*) für ehelich erklären.
legroom [leg'rōōm] *n* Platz *m* für die Beine.
Leics *abbr* (*Brit*) = Leicestershire.
leisure [lē'zhŭr] *n* Freizeit *f*; **to be at ~** Zeit haben ♦ *a* Freizeit-.
leisurely [lē'zhŭrlē] *a* gemächlich.
leisure suit *n* Hausanzug *m*.
lemming [lem'ing] *n* Lemming *m*.
lemon [lem'ən] *n* Zitrone *f*; (*color*) Zitronengelb *nt*; (*US col: person*) Niete *f*.
lemonade [lemənād'] *n* Limonade *f*.

lemon cheese *n*, **lemon curd** *n* zähflüssiger Brotaufstrich mit Zitronengeschmack.
lemon juice *n* Zitronensaft *m*.
lemon juicer [lem'ən jōō'sŭr] *n* Zitronenpresse *f*.
lend [lend] *vt irreg* leihen; **to ~ sb sth** jdm etw leihen; **it ~s itself to** es eignet sich zu; **to ~ a hand** mit anfassen.
lender [len'dŭr] *n* Verleiher *m*.
lending library [len'ding li'brärē] *n* Leihbibliothek *f*.
length [lengkth] *n* Länge *f*; (*section of road, pipe etc*) Strecke *f*; (*of material*) Stück *nt*; **it is 2 meters in ~** es ist 2 Meter lang; **what ~ is it?** wie lang ist es?; **to fall full ~** der Länge nach hinfallen; **to go to any ~s to do sth** vor nichts zurückschrecken, um etw zu tun; **~ of time** Zeitdauer *f*; **at ~** (*lengthily*) ausführlich; (*at last*) schließlich.
lengthen [lengk'thən] *vt* verlängern ♦ *vi* länger werden.
lengthwise [length'wīz] *ad* längs.
lengthy [lengk'thē] *a* sehr lang; (*speech also*) langatmig.
leniency [lē'nēənsē] *n* Nachsicht *f*.
lenient [lē'nēənt] *a* nachsichtig (*towards* gegenüber); (*judge, attitude*) milde.
leniently [lē'nēəntlē] *ad* nachsicht; milde.
lens [lenz] *n* Linse *f*; (*PHOT*) Objektiv *nt*.
lent [lent] *pt, pp* of **lend**.
Lent [lent] *n* Fastenzeit *f*.
lentil [len'təl] *n* Linse *f*.
Leo [lē'ō] *n* Löwe *m*.
leopard [lep'ŭrd] *n* Leopard *m*.
leotard [lē'ətârd] *n* Trikot *nt*, Gymnastikanzug *m*.
leper [lep'ŭr] *n* Leprakranke(r) *mf*.
leper colony *n* Leprasiedlung *f*.
leprosy [lep'rəsē] *n* Lepra *f*.
lesbian [lez'bēən] *a* lesbisch ♦ *n* Lesbierin *f*.
lesion [lē'zhən] *n* (*MED*) Verletzung *f*.
Lesotho [lisōō'tōō] *n* Lesotho *nt*.
less [les] *a, ad, n* weniger ♦ *prep*: **~ 5%** abzüglich 5%; **~ than $1/a kilo/3 meters** weniger als 1 Dollar/ein Kilo/3 Meter.
lessee [lesē'] *n* Pächter *m*; (*of house, apartment*) Mieter *m*.
lessen [les'ən] *vi* abnehmen ♦ *vt* verringern, verkleinern.
lesser [les'ŭr] *a* kleiner, geringer; **to a ~ extent** *or* **degree** in geringerem Maße.
lesson [les'ən] *n* (*SCH*) Stunde *f*; (*unit of study*) Lektion *f*; (*fig*) Lehre *f*; (*ECCL*) Lesung *f*; **to give ~s in** Stunden geben in; **~s start at 9** der Unterricht beginnt um 9; **it taught him a ~** (*fig*) es war ihm eine Lehre.
lessor [les'ôr] *n* Verpächter *m*; (*of apartment etc*) Vermieter *m*.
lest [lest] *cj* damit ... nicht.
let [let] *n*: **without ~ or hindrance** völlig unbehindert ♦ *vt irreg pt, pp* **let** lassen; (*Brit: lease*) vermieten; **to ~ fly** (*shoot*) losschießen; (*verbally*) loswettern; (*insults*) loslas-

sen; ~'s go! gehen wir!; to ~ sb do sth
jdn etw tun lassen; she ~ me borrow the
car sie hat mir das Auto geliehen.

let down vt hinunterlassen; (disappoint)
enttäuschen; to ~ down a tire die Luft aus
einem Reifen lassen.

let go vi loslassen ♦ vt (things) loslassen;
(person) gehen lassen.

let in vt (water) durchlassen; (visitor) hereinlassen; what have you ~ yourself in
for? worauf hast du dich (da) eingelassen?

let off vt (gun) abfeuern; (emit: gases) absondern; (forgive) laufen lassen; (subject:
cab driver, bus driver) aussteigen lassen; to
~ off steam (fig col) sich abreagieren, sich
austoben.

let on vi (col): don't ~ on you know laß
dir bloß nicht anmerken, daß du das weißt.

let out vt herauslassen; (scream) fahren
lassen; (rent out) vermieten.

let up vi nachlassen; (stop) aufhören.

letdown [let'doun] n Enttäuschung f.

lethal [lē'thəl] a tödlich.

lethargic [ləthâr'jik] a lethargisch, träge.

lethargy [leth'ûrjē] n Lethargie f, Teilnahmslosigkeit f.

letter [let'ûr] n (of alphabet) Buchstabe m;
(message) Brief m; small/capital ~ Klein-/
Großbuchstabe m; covering ~ Begleitschrei-
ben m; ~ of credit Kreditbrief m; documentary ~ of credit Dokumentarakkreditiv
nt; see also letters.

letter bomb n Briefbombe f.

letterbox [let'ûrbâks] n (Brit) Briefkasten m.

letterhead [let'ûrhed] n Briefkopf m.

lettering [let'ûring] n Beschriftung f.

letter-opener [let'ûrōpənûr] n Brieföffner m.

letterpress [let'ûrpres] n Hochdruck m.

letter quality n Briefqualität f, Korrespon-
denzqualität f.

letters [let'ûrz] npl (literature) (schöne) Literatur f.

letters patent npl Patenturkunde f.

lettuce [let'is] n (Kopf)salat m.

letup [let'up] n (col) Nachlassen nt; there
was no ~ es hörte nicht auf, es ließ nicht
nach.

leukemia, (Brit) leukaemia [lōōkē'mēə] n
Leukämie f.

level [lev'əl] a (ground) eben; (at same
height) auf gleicher Höhe; (equal) gleich
gut; (head) kühl; a ~ spoonful (COOK) ein
gestrichener Löffel; to draw ~ with gleich-
ziehen mit; to do one's ~ best sein möglichstes tun ♦ ad auf gleicher Höhe ♦ n (instrument) Wasserwaage f; (altitude) Höhe
f; (flat place) ebene Fläche f; (position on
scale) Niveau nt; (amount, degree) Grad m;
O ~ (Brit) Abschluß m der Sekundarstufe 1,
≈ mittlere Reife f; A ~ (Brit) ≈ Abitur nt;
talks at ministerial ~ Gespräche auf mini-
sterieller Ebene; profits keep on the same
~ Gewinne halten sich auf dem gleichen
Stand; on the moral ~ aus moralischer

Sicht; on the ~ (lit) auf gleicher Höhe;
(fig: honest) ehrlich ♦ vt (ground) einebnen;
(building) abreißen; (town) dem Erdboden
gleichmachen; (blow) versetzen (at sb
jdm); (remark) richten (at gegen); (gun)
richten (at auf); (accusation) erheben
(against gegen); to ~ with sb offen und
ehrlich mit jdm sein.

level off, level out vi flach or eben werden; (fig) sich ausgleichen; (plane) horizontal fliegen, sich fangen ♦ vt (ground) planieren; (differences) ausgleichen.

level crossing n (Brit) Bahnübergang m.

levelheaded [lev'əlhed'id] a vernünftig.

leveling, (Brit) levelling [lev'əling] a
(process, effect) gleichmachend, ausglei-
chend.

lever [lev'ûr] n Hebel m; (fig) Druckmittel nt
♦ vt (hoch)stemmen.

leverage [lev'ûrij] n Hebelkraft f; (fig) Einfluß m.

levity [lev'itē] n Leichtfertigkeit f.

levy [lev'ē] n (of taxes) Erhebung f; (tax) Abgaben pl; (MIL) Aushebung f ♦ vt erheben;
(MIL) ausheben.

lewd [lōōd] a unzüchtig, unanständig.

LF abbr = low frequency.

LI abbr (US) = Long Island.

liability [līəbil'ətē] n (burden) Belastung f;
(duty) Pflicht f; (debt) Verpflichtung f;
(proneness) Anfälligkeit f; (responsibility)
Haftung f.

liability insurance n (US) Haftpflichtversicherung f.

liable [lī'əbəl] a (responsible) haftbar; (prone)
anfällig; to be ~ for sth etw (dat) unterliegen; to be ~ to a fine strafbar sein; it's ~ to
happen es kann leicht vorkommen.

liaise [lēāz'] vi: to ~ (with) als Verbindungsmann (zwischen) fungieren.

liaison [lēā'zán] n Verbindung f.

liar [lī'ûr] n Lügner(in f) m.

libel [lī'bəl] n Verleumdung f ♦ vt verleumden.

libelous, (Brit) libellous [lī'bələs] a verleumderisch.

liberal [lib'ûrəl] a (generous) großzügig;
(open-minded) aufgeschlossen; (POL) liberal
♦ n liberal denkende(r) Mensch m; L~
(POL) Liberale(r) mf.

liberality [libəral'itē] n (generosity) Großzügigkeit f.

liberalize [lib'ûrəlīz] vt liberalisieren.

liberally [lib'ûrəlē] ad (abundantly) reichlich.

liberal-minded [lib'ûrəlmīn'did] a liberal
(eingestellt).

liberate [lib'ərāt] vt befreien.

liberation [libərā'shən] n Befreiung f.

Liberia [lībē'rēə] n Liberia nt.

Liberian [lībē'rēən] a liberianisch, liberisch ♦
n Liberianer(in f) m, Liberier(in f) m.

liberty [lib'ûrtē] n Freiheit f; (permission) Erlaubnis f; to be at ~ to do sth etw tun dürfen; to take liberties with sich (dat) Freiheiten herausnehmen gegenüber.

libido [libē'dō] *n* Libido *f*.
Libra [lēb'rə] *n* Waage *f*.
librarian [lībrär'ēən] *n* Bibliothekar(in *f*) *m*.
library [lī'brärē] *n* Bibliothek *f*; (*lending* ~) Bücherei *f*.
library book *n* Buch *nt* aus der Bücherei.
libretto [libret'ō] *n* Libretto *nt*.
Libya [lib'ēə] *n* Libyen *nt*.
Libyan [lib'ēən] *a* libysch ♦ *n* Libyer(in *f*) *m*.
lice [līs] *npl of* **louse**.
licence [lī'səns] *n* (*Brit*) = **license**.
license [lī'səns] (*US*) *n* (*permit*) Erlaubnis *f*, amtliche Zulassung *f*; (*driver's* ~) Führerschein *m*; (*excess*) Zügellosigkeit *f*; **produced under** ~ unter Lizenz hergestellt ♦ *vt* genehmigen, konzessionieren; **a car must be** ~**d every year** die Kfz-Steuer muß jedes Jahr bezahlt werden.
license plate *n* (*US AUT*) Nummernschild *nt*.
licentious [līsen'chəs] *a* ausschweifend.
lichen [lī'kən] *n* Flechte *f*.
lick [lik] *vt* lecken; (*col: defeat*) in die Pfanne hauen, einseifen ♦ *vi* (*flames*) züngeln ♦ *n* Lecken *nt*; (*small amount*) Spur *f*.
licorice [lik'ûris] *n* (*US*) Lakritze *f*.
lid [lid] *n* Deckel *m*; (*eye*~) Lid *nt*; **to take the** ~ **off sth** (*fig*) etw enthüllen *or* aufdecken.
lido [lē'dō] *n* Freibad *nt*.
lie [lī] *n* Lüge *f*; **to tell** ~**s** lügen ♦ *vi* lügen ♦ *vi irreg* (*rest, be situated*) liegen; (*put o.s. in position*) sich legen; **to** ~ **idle** stillstehen.
lie around *vi* (*things*) herumliegen; (*person*) faulenzen, herumlümmeln.
lie back *vi* sich zurücklehnen.
lie down *vi* sich hinlegen.
lie up *vi* (*hide*) untertauchen.
Liechtenstein [lēch'tenstīn] *n* Liechtenstein *nt*.
lie detector *n* Lügendetektor *m*.
lie detector test *n* Lügendetektortest *m*.
lieu [loo] *n*: **in** ~ **of** anstatt (+*gen*).
Lieut. *abbr* (= *lieutenant*) Lt., Ltn.
lieutenant [looten'ənt] *n* Leutnant *m*.
lieutenant colonel *n* Oberstleutnant *m*.
life [līf] *n, pl* **lives** [livz] Leben *nt*; (*energy*) Lebendigkeit *f*; **to be sent to prison for** ~ zu einer lebenslänglichen Freiheitsstrafe verurteilt werden; **country/city** ~ Land-/Stadtleben *nt*; **true to** ~ lebensecht; **painted from** ~ aus dem Leben gegriffen.
life annuity *n* Leibrente *f*.
life belt *n* Rettungsring *m*.
lifeblood [līf'blud] *n* (*fig*) Lebensnerv *m*.
lifeboat [līf'bōt] *n* Rettungsboot *nt*.
life buoy *n* Rettungsring *m*.
life expectancy *n* Lebenserwartung *f*.
lifeguard [līf'gârd] *n* Badewärter *m*; (*on beach*) Rettungsschwimmer *m*.
life imprisonment *n* lebenslängliche Freiheitsstrafe *f*.
life insurance *n* Lebensversicherung *f*.
life jacket *n* Schwimmweste *f*.

lifeless [līf'lis] *a* (*dead*) leblos, tot; (*dull*) langweilig.
lifelike [līf'līk] *a* lebenswahr, naturgetreu.
lifeline [līf'līn] *n* (*lit*) Rettungsleine *f*; (*fig*) Rettungsanker *m*.
lifelong [līf'lông] *a* lebenslang.
life preserver [līf prēzûrv'ûr] *n* (*US*) Rettungsring *m*; Schwimmweste *f*.
life raft *n* Rettungsfloß *nt*.
lifesaver [līf'sāvûr] *n* Lebensretter(in *f*) *m*.
life-sentence [līfsen'təns] *n* lebenslängliche Freiheitsstrafe *f*.
life-sized [līf'sīzd] *a* in Lebensgröße.
life span *n* Lebensspanne *f*.
lifestyle [līf'stīl] *n* Lebensstil *m*.
life support system *n* (*MED*) Lebenserhaltungssystem *nt*.
lifetime [līf'tīm] *n* Lebenszeit *f*; (*of animal, battery etc*) Lebensdauer *f*; **once in a** ~ einmal im Leben; **the chance of a** ~ eine einmalige Chance.
lift [lift] *vt* hochheben ♦ *vi* sich heben ♦ *n* (*raising*) (Hoch)heben *nt*; (*Brit: elevator*) Aufzug *m*, Lift *m*; **to give sb a** ~ (*Brit*) jdn mitnehmen.
lift off *vti* abheben.
lift out *vt* herausheben (*of* aus); (*troops, evacuees etc*) evakuieren.
lift up *vt* hochheben; (*window*) hochschieben.
lift-off [lift'ôf] *n* (*AVIAT*) Start *m*.
ligament [lig'əmənt] *n* Sehne *f*, Band *nt*.
light [līt] *n* Licht *nt*; (*lamp*) Lampe *f*; (*flame*) Feuer *nt*; **to turn the** ~ **on/off** das Licht an-/ausmachen; **to cast** *or* **shed** *or* **throw** ~ **on sth** etw beleuchten; **in the** ~ **of** angesichts (+*gen*) ♦ *vt irreg* beleuchten; (*lamp*) anmachen; (*fire, cigarette*) anzünden; (*brighten*) erleuchten, erhellen ♦ *a* (*bright*) hell, licht; (*pale*) hell-; (*not heavy, easy*) leicht; (*punishment*) milde; (*taxes*) niedrig; (*touch*) leicht; **to make** ~ **of sth** (*fig*) etw herunterspielen ♦ *ad*: **to travel** ~ mit wenig *or* leichtem Gepäck reisen.
light up *vi* (*lamp*) angehen; (*face*) aufleuchten ♦ *vt* (*illuminate*) beleuchten; (*cigarette*) anzünden.
light bulb *n* Glühbirne *f*.
lighten [lī'tən] *vi* hell werden ♦ *vt* (*give light to*) erhellen; (*hair*) aufhellen; (*gloom*) aufheitern; (*make less heavy*) leichter machen; (*fig*) erleichtern.
lighter [lī'tûr] *n* (*cigarette* ~) Feuerzeug *nt*.
light-fingered [līt'fing'gûrd] *a* langfingerig.
lightheaded [līt'hed'id] *a* (*thoughtless*) leichtsinnig; (*giddy*) schwindlig.
lighthearted [līt'hâr'tid] *a* leichtherzig, fröhlich.
lighthouse [līt'hous] *n* Leuchtturm *m*.
lighting [lī'ting] *n* Beleuchtung *f*.
lightly [līt'lē] *ad* leicht; (*irresponsibly*) leichtfertig; **to get off** ~ glimpflich davonkommen.
light meter *n* (*PHOT*) Belichtungsmesser *m*.

lightness [līt'nis] *n* (*of weight*) Leichtigkeit *f*; (*of color*) Helle *f*; (*light*) Helligkeit *f*.

lightning [līt'ning] *n* Blitz *m*.

lightning rod, (*Brit*) **lightning conductor** *n* Blitzableiter *m*.

lightning strike *n* (*Brit*) spontane(r) Streik *m*, spontane Arbeitsniederlegung *f*.

light pen *n* Lichtstift *m*.

lightweight [līt'wāt] *a* (*suit*) leicht; (*boxer*) Leichtgewichts-.

light-year [līt'yēr] *n* Lichtjahr *nt*.

lignite [lig'nīt] *n* Lignit *m*.

like [līk] *vt* mögen, gernhaben; **would you ~ ...?** hätten Sie gern ...?; **would you ~ to ...?** möchten Sie gern ...?; **if you ~** wenn Sie wollen ♦ *prep* wie; **what's it/he ~?** wie ist es/er denn?; **that's just ~ him** das sieht ihm ähnlich; **~ that/this** so; **what's the weather ~?** wie ist das Wetter?; **something ~ that** so ähnlich; **I feel ~ a drink** ich würde gern(e) etwas trinken ♦ *a* (*similar*) ähnlich; (*equal*) gleich ♦ *n* Gleiche(s) *nt*.

likeable [lī'kəbəl] *a* sympathisch.

likelihood [līk'lēhŏŏd] *n* Wahrscheinlichkeit *f*; **in all ~** aller Wahrscheinlichkeit nach.

likely [līk'lē] *a* (*probable*) wahrscheinlich; (*suitable*) geeignet ♦ *ad* wahrscheinlich; **not ~!** wohl kaum!

like-minded [līk'mīn'did] *a* gleichgesinnt.

liken [lī'kən] *vt* vergleichen (*to* mit).

likeness [līk'nis] *n* (*similarity*) Ähnlichkeit *f*.

likewise [līk'wīz] *ad* ebenfalls.

liking [lī'king] *n* Zuneigung *f*; (*taste for*) Vorliebe *f*; **to be to sb's ~** nach jds Geschmack sein; **to take a ~ to sb** Zuneigung für jdn empfinden.

lilac [lī'lək] *n* Flieder *m*.

lilt [lilt] *n* (*song*) muntere(r) Rhythmus *m*; (*voice*) singende(r) Tonfall *m*.

lilting [lil'ting] *a* (*accent*) singend; (*tune*) munter.

lily [lil'ē] *n* Lilie *f*; **~ of the valley** Maiglöckchen *nt*.

limb [lim] *n* Glied *nt*; **to be out on a ~** (*fig*) (ganz) allein (da)stehen.

limber up [lim'bûr up] *vi* sich auflockern; (*fig*) sich vorbereiten.

limbo [lim'bō] *n*: **to be in ~** (*fig*) in der Schwebe sein.

lime [līm] *n* (*tree*) Linde *f*; (*fruit*) Limone *f*; (*substance*) Kalk *m*.

lime juice *n* Limonensaft *m*.

limelight [līm'līt] *n* (*fig*) Rampenlicht *nt*.

limerick [lim'ûrik] *n* Limerick *m*.

limestone [līm'stōn] *n* Kalkstein *m*.

limit [lim'it] *n* Grenze *f*; (*limitation*) Beschränkung *f*; (*col*) Höhe *f*; **within ~s** bis zu einem gewissen Grad(e) ♦ *vt* begrenzen, einschränken; **to be ~ed to** sich beschränken auf (+*acc*).

limitation [limitā'shən] *n* Grenzen *pl*, Einschränkung *f*.

limited [lim'itid] *a* beschränkt; **~ edition** beschränkte Ausgabe *f*.

limited (liability) company *n* (*Brit*) Gesellschaft *f* mit beschränkter Haftung, GmbH *f*.

limitless [lim'itlis] *a* grenzenlos.

limousine [lim'əzēn] *n* Limousine *f*.

limp [limp] *n* Hinken *nt* ♦ *vi* hinken ♦ *a* schlaff.

limpet [lim'pit] *n* (*lit*) Napfschnecke *f*; (*fig*) Klette *f*.

limpid [lim'pid] *a* klar.

limply [limp'lē] *ad* schlaff.

linchpin [linch'pin] *n* Achs(en)nagel *m*; (*fig*) Stütze *f*.

Lincs [lingks] *abbr* (*Brit*) = Lincolnshire.

line [līn] *n* Linie *f*; (*rope*) Leine *f*; (*on face*) Falte *f*; (*row*) Reihe *f*; (*of hills*) Kette *f*; (*US: people waiting*) Schlange *f*; (*shipping ~ etc*) Linie *f*; (*RAIL*) Strecke *f*; (*TEL*) Leitung *f*; (*written*) Zeile *f*; (*direction*) Richtung *f*; (*fig: business*) Branche *f*, Beruf *m*; (*range of items*) Kollektion *f*; **it's a bad ~** (*TEL*) die Verbindung ist schlecht; **hold the ~** (*Brit TEL*) bleiben Sie am Apparat; **in ~ with** in Einklang mit, in Übereinstimmung mit; **to come on ~** (*power plant etc*) in Betrieb genommen werden; **to bring sth into ~ with sth** etw auf die gleiche Linie wie etw (*acc*) bringen; **~ of research** Forschungsgebiet *nt*; **a new ~ in cosmetics** eine neue Kollektion Kosmetikartikel; **to be in ~ for sth** (*fig*) als nächster an der Reihe sein mit etw; **on the right ~s** auf dem richtigen Weg; **to draw the ~ at (doing) sth** (*fig*) bei etw nicht mehr mitmachen; **he took the ~ that** ... er vertrat den Standpunkt, daß ...; *see also* **lines** ♦ *vt* (*coat*) füttern; (*streets*) säumen.

line up *vi* sich aufstellen ♦ *vt* aufstellen; (*prepare*) sorgen für; (*support*) mobilisieren; (*surprise*) planen; **to have sth ~d up** etw geplant haben.

linear [lin'ēûr] *a* gerade; (*measure*) Längen-.

lined [līnd] *a* (*paper*) liniert, liniiert; (*face*) faltig; (*clothes*) gefüttert.

line editing *n* (*COMPUT*) zeilenweise Aufbereitung *f*.

line feed *n* (*COMPUT*) Zeilenvorschub *m*.

linen [lin'ən] *n* Leinen *nt*; (*sheets etc*) Wäsche *f*.

line printer *n* Zeilendrucker *m*.

liner [lī'nûr] *n* (*ship*) Überseedampfer *m*; (*for garbage can*) Müllsack *m*.

lines [līnz] *npl* (*RAIL*) Gleise *pl*.

linesman [līnz'mən] *n*, *pl* **-men** (*SPORT*) Linienrichter *m*.

lineup [līn'up] *n* Aufstellung *f*; (*also:* **police ~**) Gegenüberstellung *f*.

linger [ling'gûr] *vi* (*remain long*) verweilen; (*taste*) (zurück)bleiben; (*delay*) zögern, verharren.

lingerie [lán'jərā] *n* Damenunterwäsche *f*.

lingering [ling'gûring] *a* lang; (*doubt*) zurückbleibend; (*disease*) langwierig; (*taste*) nachhaltend.

lingo [ling'gō] *n* (*col*) Sprache *f*.
linguist [ling'gwist] *n* Sprachkundige(r) *mf*; (*UNIV*) Sprachwissenschaftler(in *f*) *m*.
linguistic [linggwis'tik] *a* (*concerning language*) sprachlich; (*of linguistics*) sprachwissenschaftlich.
linguistics [linggwis'tiks] *n sing* Sprachwissenschaft *f*, Linguistik *f*.
liniment [lin'əmənt] *n* Einreibemittel *nt*.
lining [lī'ning] *n* (*of clothes*) Futter *nt*; (*TECH*) Auskleidung *f*; (*of brake*) (Brems)belag *m*.
link [lingk] *n* Glied *nt*; (*connection*) Verbindung *f*; **rail** ~ Zug- *or* Bahnverbindung *f* ♦ *vt* verbinden.
  link up *vt* verbinden ♦ *vi* zusammenkommen; (*companies*) sich zusammenschließen.
links [lingks] *npl* Golfplatz *m*.
linkup [lingk'up] *n* (*TEL. RAD. TV*) Verbindung *f*; (*of spaceships*) Kopplung (smanöver *nt*) *f*.
linoleum [linō'lēəm] *n* Linoleum *nt*.
linseed oil [lin'sēd oil] *n* Leinöl *nt*.
lint [lint] *n* Verbandstoff *m*.
lintel [lin'təl] *n* (*ARCHIT*) Sturz *m*.
lion [lī'ən] *n* Löwe *m*.
lioness [lī'ənis] *n* Löwin *f*.
lip [lip] *n* Lippe *f*; (*of jug*) Tülle *f*, Schnabel *m*.
lip-read [lip'rēd] *vi irreg* von den Lippen ablesen.
lip salve [lip sav] *n* Lippenbalsam *m*.
lip service *n*: **to pay** ~ ein Lippenbekenntnis ablegen (*to* zu).
lipstick [lip'stik] *n* Lippenstift *m*.
liquefy [lik'wəfī] *vt* verflüssigen ♦ *vi* sich verflüssigen.
liqueur [lik'ûr] *n* Likör *m*.
liquid [lik'wid] *n* Flüssigkeit *f* ♦ *a* flüssig.
liquidate [lik'widāt] *vt* liquidieren.
liquidation [likwidā'shən] *n* Liquidation *f*; **to go into** ~ in Liquidation gehen.
liquid crystal display *n* Flüssigkristallanzeige *f*.
liquidity [likwid'itē] *n* (*FIN*) Liquidität *f*.
liquidize [lik'widīz] *vt* (*COOK*) (im Mixer) purieren.
liquidizer [lik'widīzûr] *n* (*Brit COOK*) Mixer *m*.
Liquid Paper *n* ® (*US*) ≈ Tippex *nt* ®.
liquor [lik'ûr] *n* Alkohol *m*, Spirituosen *pl*.
liquorice [lik'ûris] *n* (*Brit*) Lakritze *f*.
liquor store *n* (*US*) ≈ Wein- und Spirituosengeschäft *nt*.
Lisbon [liz'bən] *n* Lissabon *nt*.
lisp [lisp] *n* Lispeln *nt* ♦ *vti* lispeln.
lissom [lis'əm] *a* geschmeidig, gelenkig.
list [list] *n* Liste *f*, Verzeichnis *nt*; (*of ship*) Schlagseite *f*; *see also* **lists** ♦ *vt* (*write down*) eine Liste machen von; (*verbally*) aufzählen; (*COMPUT*) (auf)listen ♦ *vi* (*ship*) Schlagseite haben.
listed company [lis'tid kum'pənē] *n* börsennotierte Firma *f*.
listen [lis'ən] *vi* hören, horchen.

listen to *vt fus* zuhören (+*dat*).
listener [lis'ənûr] *n* (Zu)hörer(in *f*) *m*.
listing [lis'ting] *n* (*COMPUT*) Auflisten *nt*, Auflistung *f*.
listless [list'lis] *a*, **listlessly** [list'lislē] *ad* lustlos, teilnahmslos.
listlessness [list'lisnis] *n* Lustlosigkeit *f*, Teilnahmslosigkeit *f*.
lists [lists] *npl* (*HIST*) Schranken *pl*.
lit [lit] *pt, pp of* **light**.
litany [lit'ənē] *n* Litanei *f*.
liter [lē'tûr] *n* (*US*) Liter *m*.
literacy [lit'ûrəsē] *n* Fähigkeit *f* zu lesen und zu schreiben; ~ **campaign** Kampagne *f* gegen das Analphabetentum.
literal [lit'ûrəl] *a* eigentlich, buchstäblich; (*translation*) wortwörtlich.
literally [lit'ûrəlē] *ad* buchstäblich; wörtlich.
literary [lit'ərärē] *a* literarisch.
literate [lit'ûrit] *a* des Lesens und Schreibens kundig.
literature [lit'ûrəchûr] *n* Literatur *f*.
litho(graph) [lith'ō(graf)] *n* Lithographie *f*.
lithography [lithág'rəfē] *n* Lithographie *f*, Steindruck *m*.
Lithuania [lithōōā'nēə] *n* Litauen *nt*.
litigate [lit'əgāt] *vi* prozessieren.
litigation [litəgā'shən] *n* Prozeß *m*.
litmus paper [lit'məs pā'pûr] *n* Lackmuspapier *nt*.
litre [lē'tûr] *n* (*Brit*) Liter *m*.
litter [lit'ûr] *n* (*garbage*) Abfall *m*; (*of animals*) Wurf *m* ♦ *vt*: **to be** ~**ed with** übersät sein mit.
litter bin *n* (*Brit*) Abfalleimer *m*.
litterbug [lit'ûrbug] *n* Dreckspatz *m* (*col*).
little [lit'əl] *a* klein; (*unimportant*) unbedeutend; ~ **finger** kleine(r) Finger *m*; **for a** ~ **while** für ein Weilchen; **with** ~ **difficulty** mit geringen Schwierigkeiten ♦ *ad* wenig; **a** ~ ein bißchen; **the** ~ das wenige; **as** ~ **as possible** so wenig wie möglich.
liturgy [lit'ûrjē] *n* Liturgie *f*.
live [liv] *a see also following entry* lebendig; (*burning*) glühend; (*ELEC*) geladen; (*broadcast*) live; (*issue*) aktuell; (*unexploded*) scharf ♦ *ad* (*broadcast*) live.
live [liv] *vi see also previous entry* leben; (*last*) fortleben; (*dwell*) wohnen; **to** ~ **in Munich** in München wohnen; **to** ~ **together** zusammenleben ♦ *vt* (*life*) führen.
  live down *vt* Gras wachsen lassen über (+*acc*); **I'll never** ~ **it down** das wird man mir nie vergessen.
  live off *vt fus* (*land, fish etc*) leben von, sich ernähren von; **to** ~ **off one's relatives** (*pej*) auf Kosten seiner Verwandten leben.
  live on *vi* weiterleben ♦ *vt fus*: **to** ~ **on sth** von etw leben; **to** ~ **on $100 a week** von 100 Dollar in der Woche leben.
  live out *vi* (*Brit: students*) außerhalb (des Heims/des Universitätsgeländes) wohnen ♦ *vt*: **to** ~ **out one's days/life** seine Tage/sein Leben verbringen.

live up vt: **to ~ it up** (col) die Puppen tanzen lassen.
live up to vt fus (standards) gerecht werden (+dat); (principles) anstreben; (hopes) entsprechen (+dat).
livelihood [līv'lēhōod] n Lebensunterhalt m.
liveliness [līv'lēnis] n Lebendigkeit f.
lively [līv'lē] a lebhaft, lebendig.
liven up [līv'ən up] vt (room, discussion, evening etc) beleben, Leben bringen in (+acc).
liver [liv'ûr] n (ANAT) Leber f.
liverish [liv'ûrish] a (bad-tempered) gallig.
livery [liv'ûrē] n Livree f.
lives [līvz] npl of **life**.
livestock [līv'stâk] n Vieh nt.
livid [liv'id] a (lit) bläulich; (furious) fuchsteufelswild.
living [liv'ing] n (Lebens)unterhalt m ♦ a lebendig; (language etc) lebend; (wage) ausreichend; **within ~ memory** seit Menschengedenken.
living conditions npl Wohnverhältnisse pl.
living expenses npl Lebenshaltungskosten pl.
living room n Wohnzimmer nt.
living wage n ausreichende(r) Lohn m.
lizard [liz'ûrd] n Eidechse f.
llama [lâm'ə] n Lama nt.
LLB n abbr (= Bachelor of Laws) akademischer Grad.
LLD n abbr (= Doctor of Laws) ≈ Dr. jur.
load [lōd] n (burden) Last f; (amount) Ladung f, Fuhre f; **~s of** (col) massenhaft ♦ vt (be)laden; (fig) überhäufen; (camera) Film einlegen in (+acc); (COMPUT, gun) laden.
loaded [lō'did] a: **to be ~** (col: rich) steinreich sein, im Geld schwimmen; **a ~ question** eine Fangfrage.
loading [lō'ding] n (COMM) Prämienzuschlag m.
loading dock n (US) Ladeplatz m.
loaf [lōf] n, pl **loaves** [lōvz] Brot nt, Laib m ♦ vi herumlungern, faulenzen.
loafer [lō'fûr] n Faulenzer m.
loam [lōm] n Lehmboden m.
loan [lōn] n Leihgabe f; (FIN) Darlehen nt; **on ~** geliehen; (book, painting: to another museum etc) verliehen; **to raise a ~** (money) ein Darlehen aufnehmen ♦ vt leihen.
loan account n Darlehenskonto nt.
loan capital n Fremdkapital nt.
loath [lōth] a: **to be ~ to do sth** etw ungern tun.
loathe [lōth] vt verabscheuen.
loathing [lō'thing] n Abscheu f.
loathsome [lōth'səm] a abstoßend, abscheulich; (person) abscheulich, widerlich.
loaves [lōvz] npl of **loaf**.
lob [lâb] vt (ball) lobben.
lobby [lâb'ē] n Vorhalle f; (POL) Lobby f ♦ vt politisch beeinflussen (wollen).
lobbyist [lâb'ēist] n Lobbyist m.
lobe [lōb] n Ohrläppchen nt.

lobster [lâb'stûr] n Hummer m.
lobster pot n Hummer(fang)korb m.
local [lō'kəl] a ortsansässig, hiesig, Orts-; (anesthetic) örtlich ♦ n (pub) Stammwirtschaft f ♦ npl: **the ~s** die Ortsansässigen pl.
local anesthetic n örtliche Betäubung f.
local authority n (Brit) städtische Behörden pl, Gemeinde-/Stadtverwaltung f.
local call n (TEL) Ortsgespräch nt.
local government n Stadtverwaltung f.
locality [lōkal'itē] n Ort m.
localize [lō'kəlīz] vt lokalisieren.
locally [lō'kəlē] ad örtlich, am Ort.
locate [lō'kāt] vt ausfindig machen; (establish) errichten.
location [lōkā'shən] n Platz m, Lage f; **on ~** (CINE) auf Außenaufnahme.
loch [lâk] n (Scot) See m.
lock [lâk] n (of door, box) Schloß nt; (NAUT) Schleuse f; (of hair) Locke f; **he offered me the house ~, stock and barrel** er bat mir das Haus mit allem Drum und Dran an ♦ vt (fasten) (ver)schließen ♦ vi (door etc) sich schließen (lassen); (wheels) blockieren.
lock away vt (valuables) einschließen; (criminal) einsperren.
lock out vt aussperren.
lock up vi abschließen ♦ vt (house, object) abschließen; (person) einsperren.
locker [lâk'ûr] n Spind m.
locker room n (US) Umkleideraum m.
locket [lâk'it] n Medaillon nt.
lockout [lâk'out] n (in industry) Aussperrung f.
locksmith [lâk'smith] n Schlossermeister m.
lockup [lâk'up] n (prison) Gefängnis nt.
locomotive [lōkəmō'tiv] n Lokomotive f.
locum tenens [lō'kəm tē'nenz] n (MED) Vertreter (in f) m.
locust [lō'kəst] n Heuschrecke f.
lodge [lâj] n (gatehouse) Pförtnerhaus nt; (freemasons') Loge f ♦ vi (in Untermiete) wohnen (with bei); (get stuck) stecken(-bleiben) ♦ vt (protest) einreichen; (complaint) einlegen.
lodger [lâj'ûr] n (Unter)mieter (in f) m.
lodgings [lâj'ingz] npl (Miet)wohnung f, Zimmer nt.
loft [lôft] n (Dach)boden m.
lofty [lôf'tē] a hoch(ragend); (proud) hochmütig; (sentiments) erhaben; (aims, ideas) hoch(fliegend).
log [lôg] n Baumstamm m; (for fire) Scheit nt; (NAUT) Log nt; **to sleep like a ~** wie ein Stein schlafen ♦ n abbr (= logarithm) lg ♦ vt verzeichnen.
log off vi (COMPUT) abmelden.
log on vi (COMPUT) anmelden.
logarithm [lôg'ərithəm] n Logarithmus m.
logbook [lôg'bŏōk] n (NAUT) Bordbuch nt, Logbuch nt; (for truck) Fahrtenschreiber m; (AUT) Kraftfahrzeugbrief m.
log cabin n Blockhaus nt or -hütte f.
log fire n Holzfeuer nt.

loggerheads [lôg'ûrhedz] *npl*: **to be at ~** sich in den Haaren liegen.
logic [lâj'ik] *n* Logik *f*.
logical [lâj'ikəl] *a* logisch.
logically [lâj'iklē] *ad* logisch(erweise).
logistics [lōjis'tiks] *npl* Logistik *f*.
logo [lō'gō] *n* Firmenzeichen *nt*.
loin [loin] *n* Lende *f*.
loincloth [loin'klôth] *n* Lendenschurz *m*.
loiter [loi'tûr] *vi* herumstehen, sich herumtreiben.
loll [lâl] *vi* sich rekeln.
lollipop [lâl'ēpâp] *n* (Dauer)lutscher *m*.
London [lun'dən] *n* London *nt*.
Londoner [lun'dənûr] *n* Londoner(in *f*) *m*.
lone [lōn] *a* einsam.
loneliness [lōn'lēnis] *n* Einsamkeit *f*.
lonely [lōn'lē] *a* einsam.
loner [lō'nûr] *n* Einzelgänger(in *f*) *m*.
lonesome [lōn'səm] *a* einsam.
long [lông] *a* lang; (*distance*) weit; **how ~ is the lesson?** wie lange dauert die Stunde?; **two-day-~** zwei Tage lang; **in the ~ run** auf die Dauer; **I won't be ~** ich bin gleich fertig; **don't be ~!** bleib nicht so lang!, beeil dich! ♦ *ad* lange; **~ ago** vor langer Zeit; **before ~** bald; **as ~ as** solange; **he no ~er comes** er kommt nicht mehr ♦ *n*: **the ~ and the short of it is that ...** (*fig*) kurz gesagt ... ♦ *vi* sich sehnen (*for* nach).
long-distance [lông'dis'təns] *a* Fern-.
longevity [lânjev'itē] *n* Langlebigkeit *f*.
long-haired [lông'hârd] *a* langhaarig.
longhand [lông'hand] *n* Langschrift *f*.
longing [lông'ing] *n* Verlangen *nt*, Sehnsucht *f* ♦ *a* sehnsüchtig.
longingly [lông'inglē] *ad* sehnsüchtig.
longish [lông'ish] *a* ziemlich lang.
longitude [lân'jətōōd] *n* Längengrad *m*.
long jump *n* Weitsprung *m*.
long-lost [lông'lôst] *a* längst verloren geglaubt.
long-playing record [lông'plā'ing rek'ûrd] *n* Langspielplatte *f*.
long-range [lông'rānj] *a* Langstrecken-, Fern-; (*weather forecast*) langfristig.
longshoreman [lông'shôrmən] *n*, *pl* **-men** (*US*) Hafenarbeiter *m*.
long-sighted [lông'sītid] *a* weitsichtig.
long-standing [lông'stan'ding] *a* alt, seit langer Zeit bestehend.
long-suffering [lông'suf'ûring] *a* schwer geprüft.
long-term [lông'tûrm'] *a* langfristig.
long wave *n* (*RAD*) Langwelle *f*.
long-winded [lông'win'did] *a* langatmig.
loo [lōō] *n* (*Brit col*) Klo *nt*.
loofah [lōō'fə] *n* (*Brit: sponge*) Luffa(-schwamm) *m*.
look [lōōk] *vi* schauen, blicken; (*seem*) aussehen; (*face*): **to ~ north** nach Norden gehen; **it ~s about 4 meters long** es scheint ungefähr 4 Meter lang zu sein; **it ~s all right to me** es scheint mir in Ordnung zu

sein; **to ~ ahead** nach vorne sehen; (*fig*) vorausschauen ♦ *n* Blick *m*; **to have a ~ at sth** sich (*dat*) etw ansehen; **to have a ~ for sth** sich nach etw umsehen; *see also* **looks**.
look after *vt fus* (*care for*) sorgen für; (*watch*) aufpassen auf (+*acc*).
look around *vi* (*turn*) sich umsehen; **to ~ around for sth** sich nach etw umsehen.
look at *vt fus* (*also examine*) ansehen; (*consider*) sich (*dat*) überlegen.
look back *vi* sich umsehen; **to ~ back at sth/sb** auf etw/jdn zurückblicken; **to ~ back on sth** (*event, period*) einen Rückblick auf etw (*acc*) werfen.
look down on *vt fus* (*lit, fig*) herabsehen auf (+*acc*).
look for *vt fus* (*seek*) suchen (nach); (*expect*) erwarten.
look forward to *vt fus* sich freuen auf (+*acc*); **I'm not ~ing forward to it** ich freue mich nicht darauf; **~ing forward to hearing from you** (*in letter*) ich hoffe, bald von Ihnen zu hören.
look in *vi* hinein-/hereinsehen; **to ~ in on sb** (*visit*) bei jdm vorbeikommen.
look into *vt fus* (*matter, possibility*) untersuchen.
look on *vi* (*watch*) zusehen ♦ *vt fus* (*consider as*) betrachten; **to ~ on sb as a friend** jdn als Freund betrachten.
look out *vi* hinaussehen; (*take care*) aufpassen.
look out for *vt fus* Ausschau halten nach; (*be careful*) achtgeben auf (+*acc*).
look over *vt* (*essay*) durchsehen; (*town, building*) sich (*dat*) ansehen; (*person*) mustern.
look round *vi* (*Brit*) = **look around**.
look through *vt fus* (*papers, book, telescope*) durchsehen; (*briefly*) durchblättern.
look to *vt fus* (*take care of*) achtgeben auf (+*acc*); (*rely on*) sich verlassen auf (+*acc*).
look up *vi* aufblicken; (*improve*) sich bessern ♦ *vt* (*word*) nachschlagen; (*person*) besuchen.
look up to *vt fus* aufsehen zu.
lookout [lōōk'out] *n* (*watch*) Ausschau *f*; (*person*) Wachposten *m*; (*place*) Ausguck *m*; (*prospect*) Aussichten *pl*.
looks [lōōks] *npl* Aussehen *nt*.
look-up table [lōōk'up tā'bəl] *n* Nachschlagetabelle *f*.
loom [lōōm] *n* Webstuhl *m* ♦ *vi* sich abzeichnen.
LOOM *n abbr* (*US*: = *Loyal Order of Moose*) Wohltätigkeitsverein.
loony [lōō'nē] *a* (*col*) Verrückte(r) *mf*.
loop [lōōp] *n* Schlaufe *f*; (*also COMPUT*) Schleife *f* ♦ *vt* schlingen.
loophole [lōōp'hōl] *n* (*fig*) Hintertürchen *nt*, Lücke *f*.
loose [lōōs] *a* lose, locker; (*free*) frei; (*inexact*) unpräzise; **~ connection** (*ELEC*) Wackelkontakt *m*; **~ change** Kleingeld *nt*;

to be at ~ ends *or* (*Brit*) **a ~ end** nicht wissen, was man tun soll; **to tie up ~ ends** (*fig*) ein paar offene *or* offenstehende Probleme lösen ♦ *vt* lösen, losbinden; (*free*) befreien; (*slacken*) lockern.
loose-fitting [lōōs'fit'ing] *a* weit.
loose-leaf [lōōs'lēf] *a:* ~ **binder** *or* **folder** Ringbuch *nt*.
loosely [lōōs'lē] *ad* locker, lose; ~ **speaking** grob gesagt.
loosen [lōō'sən] *vt* lockern, losmachen.
loosen up *vi* (*before game*) Lockerungsübungen machen; (*col: relax*) auftauen.
looseness [lōōs'nis] *n* Lockerheit *f*.
loot [lōōt] *n* Beute *f* ♦ *vt* plündern.
looter [lōō'tûr] *n* Plünderer *m*.
looting [lōō'ting] *n* Plünderung *f*.
lop off [lâp' ôf] *vt* abhacken.
lopsided [lâp'sīdid] *a* schief; (*fig*) einseitig.
lord [lôrd] *n* (*ruler*) Herr *m*, Gebieter *m*; (*title*) Lord *m*; **the L~** (Gott) der Herr *m*.
lordly [lôrd'lē] *a* vornehm; (*proud*) stolz.
lore [lôr] *n* Überlieferung *f*.
lorry [lôr'ē] *n* (*Brit*) Lastwagen *m*.
lose [lōōz] *irreg vt* verlieren; (*chance*) verpassen; **to get lost** (*object*) verlorengehen, verschwinden; (*person*) sich verlaufen; **to ~ no time** keine Zeit verlieren ♦ *vi* verlieren.
lose out *vi* zu kurz kommen (*on* bei).
loser [lōō'zûr] *n* Verlierer(in *f*) *m*; **to be a bad ~** ein schlechter Verlierer sein.
losing [lōō'zing] *a* Verlierer-; (*COMM*) verlustbringend.
loss [lôs] *n* Verlust *m*; **to cut one's ~es** seine Verluste abschreiben; **at a ~** (*COMM*) mit Verlust; (*unable*) außerstande; **I am at a ~ for words** mir fehlen die Worte.
loss leader *n* (*COMM*) Lockvogelangebot *nt*.
lost [lôst] *a* verloren; **to be ~ in thought** in Gedanken *or* gedankenverloren sein ♦ *pt, pp* *of* **lose**.
lost and found *n* (*US*) Fundbüro *nt*.
lost cause *n* aussichtslose Sache *f*.
lost property *n* (*Brit*) Fundsachen *pl*.
lost property office *or* **department** *n* (*Brit*) Fundbüro *nt*.
lot [lât] *n* (*quantity*) Menge *f*; (*of land*) (Grund)stück *nt*; (*fate, at auction*) Los *nt*; (*col: people, things*) Haufen *m*; **the ~** alles; (*people*) alle; **a ~ of** viel; *pl* viele; **~s of** massenhaft, viel(e).
lotion [lō'shən] *n* Lotion *f*.
lottery [lât'ûrē] *n* Lotterie *f*.
loud [loud] *a* laut; (*showy*) schreiend ♦ *ad* laut; **to say sth out** ~ etw laut sagen.
loudly [loud'lē] *ad* laut.
loudness [loud'nis] *n* Lautheit *f*.
loudspeaker [loud'spēkûr] *n* Lautsprecher *m*.
lounge [lounj] *n* (*in hotel*) Gesellschaftsraum *m*; (*in house*) Wohnzimmer *nt*; (*in airport*) Warteraum *m*; (*on ship*) Salon *m* ♦ *vi* sich herumlümmeln.
lounge bar *n* Salon *m*.
lounge suit *n* (*Brit*) Straßenanzug *m*.

louse [lous] *n, pl* **lice** [līs] Laus *f*.
louse up *vt* (*col*) vermasseln.
lousy [lou'zē] *a* (*lit*) verlaust; (*fig*) lausig, miserabel.
lout [lout] *n* (*Brit*) Lümmel *m*.
louver, (*Brit*) **louvre** [lōō'vûr] *n* Jalousie *f*.
lovable [luv'əbəl] *a* liebenswert.
love [luv] *n* Liebe *f*; (*person*) Liebling *m*, Schatz *m*; (*SPORT*) null; **for the ~ of** aus Liebe zu; **to send one's ~ to sb** jdn grüßen lassen; ~, **Anne** (*in letter*) liebe Grüße von Anne, Anne läßt herzlich grüßen; **to make ~** sich lieben; **to make ~ to** *or* **with sb** jdn lieben ♦ *vt* (*person*) lieben; (*activity*) gerne mögen; **to ~ to do sth** etw (sehr) gerne tun; **I'd ~ to come** ich würde gern(e) kommen.
love affair *n* (Liebes)verhältnis *nt*.
love letter *n* Liebesbrief *m*.
love life *n* Liebesleben *nt*.
lovely [luv'lē] *a* schön; (*person, object also*) entzückend, reizend; **we had a ~ time** es war sehr schön.
love-making [luv'māking] *n* Liebe *f*.
lover [luv'ûr] *n* Liebhaber *m*, Geliebte(r) *mf*; (*of books etc*) Liebhaber *m*; **the ~s** die Liebenden, das Liebespaar.
lovesick [luv'sik] *a* liebeskrank.
lovesong [luv'sông] *n* Liebeslied *nt*.
loving [luv'ing] *a* liebend, liebevoll.
lovingly [luv'inglē] *ad* liebevoll.
low [lō] *a* niedrig; (*rank*) niedere(r, s); (*level, note, neckline*) tief; (*intelligence, density*) gering; (*vulgar*) ordinär; (*not loud*) leise; (*depressed*) gedrückt ♦ *ad* (*aim*) nach unten; (*not loudly*) leise ♦ *n* (*low point*) Tiefstand *m*; (*MET*) Tief *nt*; **to reach a new ~/an all-time ~** einen neuen Tiefpunkt/einen Tiefststand erreichen.
lowbrow [lō'brou] *a* (*person*) anspruchslos, ungebildet.
low-calorie [lō'kal'ûrē] *a* kalorienarm.
low-cut [lō'kut'] *a* (*dress*) tiefausgeschnitten.
lowdown [lō'doun] *n* (*col*): **he gave me the ~ on it** er hat mich darüber aufgeklärt ♦ *a* (*mean*) gemein, fies.
lower [lō'ûr] *vt* see also following entry herunterlassen; (*eyes, gun*) senken; (*US AUT*) abblenden; (*reduce: price*) herabsetzen, senken; (*resistance*) herabsetzen; **to ~ o.s. to** (*fig*) sich herablassen zu ♦ *a* niedriger, tiefer ♦ *ad* tiefer, leiser.
lower [lou'ûr] *vi* see also previous entry (*sky*) bedrohlich dunkel *or* überzogen sein; **to ~ at sb** jdn finster *or* drohend ansehen.
lower case *n* (*TYP*) Kleinbuchstaben *pl*.
low-fat [lō'fat'] *a* fettarm, Mager-.
low-key [lō'kē'] *a* zurückhaltend; (*operation*) einfach.
lowland [lō'lənd] *n* Flachland *nt*.
low-level [lō'levəl] *a* zwanglos; (*flying*) tief.
lowly [lō'lē] *a* bescheiden.
low-lying [lō'lī'ing] *a* tiefgelegen.
loyal [loi'əl] *a* (*true*) treu; (*to king*) loyal,

treu.

loyalist [loi'əlist] *n* Loyalist *m*.

loyally [loi'əlē] *ad* treu; loyal.

loyalty [loi'əltē] *n* Treue *f*; Loyalität *f*.

lozenge [lȧz'inj] *n* Pastille *f*.

LP *n abbr* (= *long-playing record*) LP *f*.

L-plates [el plāts] *npl* (*Brit*) *Schild mit der Aufschrift "L" (für Fahrschüler)*.

LPN *n abbr* (*US*: = *Licensed Practical Nurse*) *staatlich zugelassene(r) Krankenschwester oder Krankenpfleger*.

LSAT *n abbr* (*US*) = *Law School Admissions Test*.

LSD *n abbr* (= *lysergic acid diethylamide*) LSD *nt*.

LSE *n abbr* = *London School of Economics*.

LST *abbr* (*US*) = *local standard time*.

Lt. *abbr* (= *lieutenant*) Lt., Ltn.

LT *abbr* (*ELEC*) = *low tension*.

Ltd *abbr* (*COMM*: = *limited* (*liability*) *company*) ≈ GmbH *f*.

lubricant [lōōb'rikənt] *n* Schmiermittel *nt*.

lubricate [lōōb'rikāt] *vt* (ab)schmieren, ölen.

lubrication [lōōbrikā'shən] *n* (Ein- *or* Ab)schmierung *f*.

lucid [lōō'sid] *a* klar; (*sane*) bei klarem Verstand; (*moment*) licht.

lucidity [lōōsid'itē] *n* Klarheit *f*.

lucidly [lōō'sidlē] *ad* klar.

luck [luk] *n* Glück *nt*; **good** ~ viel Glück; **bad** ~ Pech *nt*; **to be in** ~ Glück haben; **to be out of** ~ kein Glück haben.

luckily [luk'ilē] *ad* glücklicherweise, zum Glück.

lucky [luk'ē] *a* glücklich, Glücks-; **to be** ~ Glück haben.

lucrative [lōō'krətiv] *a* einträglich.

ludicrous [lōō'dəkrəs] *a* grotesk.

luffa [luf'ə] *n* (*US*: *sponge*) Luffa(schwamm) *m*.

lug [lug] *vt* schleppen.

luggage [lug'ij] *n* Gepäck *nt*.

luggage car *n* (*US RAIL*) Gepäckwagen *m*.

luggage checkroom *n* (*US*) Gepäckaufbewahrung *f*.

luggage rack *n* (*RAIL*) Gepäckablage *f*; (*AUT*) Gepäckträger *m*.

lugubrious [lōōgōō'brēəs] *a* schwermütig, wehmütig; (*expression*) kummervoll.

lukewarm [lōōk'wôrm'] *a* lauwarm; (*indifferent*) lau.

lull [lul] *n* Flaute *f* ♦ *vt* einlullen; (*calm*) beruhigen.

lullaby [lul'əbī] *n* Schlaflied *nt*.

lumbago [lumbā'gō] *n* Hexenschuß *m*.

lumber [lum'bûr] *n* Plunder *m*; (*wood*) Holz *nt* ♦ *vt* (*Brit col*): **to** ~ **sb with sth/sb** jdm etw/jdn aufhängen ♦ *vi* (*also*: ~ **about**, ~ **along**) trampeln, walzen.

lumberjack [lum'bûrjak] *n* Holzfäller *m*.

lumberyard [lum'bûryârd] *n* Holzlager *nt*.

luminous [lōō'minəs] *a* leuchtend, Leucht-.

lump [lump] *n* Klumpen *m*; (*MED*) Schwellung *f*; (*in breast*) Knoten *m*; (*of sugar*)

Stück *nt* ♦ *vt* zusammentun.

lump together *vt* (*fig*) in einen Topf werfen.

lump sum *n* Pauschalsumme *f*.

lumpy [lum'pē] *a* klumpig; **to go** ~ klumpen.

lunacy [lōō'nəsē] *n* Irrsinn *m*.

lunar [lōō'nûr] *a* Mond-.

lunatic [lōō'nətik] *n* Wahnsinnige(r) *mf* ♦ *a* wahnsinnig, irr.

lunatic asylum *n* Irrenanstalt *f*.

lunatic fringe *n* Chaotenfraktion *f*.

lunch [lunch] *n* Mittagessen *nt*; **to invite sb to** *or* **for** ~ jdn zum Mittagessen einladen ♦ *vi* (zu) Mittag essen.

lunch break, lunch hour *n* Mittagspause *f*.

luncheon [lun'chən] *n* = **lunch**.

luncheon meat *n* Frühstücksfleisch *nt*.

lunchtime [lunch'tīm] *n* Mittagszeit *f*, Mittagspause *f*.

lung [lung] *n* Lunge *f*.

lung cancer *n* Lungenkrebs *m*.

lunge [lunj] *vi* (los)stürzen; **to** ~ **at** sich stürzen auf (+*acc*).

lupin [lōō'pin] *n* Lupine *f*.

lurch [lûrch] *vi* taumeln; (*NAUT*) schlingern ♦ *n* Taumeln *nt*; (*NAUT*) plötzliche(s) Schlingern *nt*; **to leave sb in the** ~ jdn im Stich lassen.

lure [lōōr] *n* Köder *m*; (*fig*) Lockung *f* ♦ *vt* (ver)locken.

lurid [lōō'rid] *a* (*shocking*) grausig, widerlich; (*color*) grell.

lurk [lûrk] *vi* lauern.

luscious [lush'əs] *a* köstlich; (*color*) satt.

lush [lush] *a* satt; (*vegetation*) üppig.

lust [lust] *n* sinnliche Begierde *f* (*for* nach); (*sensation*) Wollust *f*; (*greed*) Gier *f* ♦ *vi* gieren (*after, for* nach).

luster [lus'tûr] *n* (*US*) Glanz *m*.

lustful [lust'fəl] *a* wollüstig, lüstern.

lustre [lus'tûr] *n* (*Brit*) = **luster**.

lusty [lus'tē] *a* gesund und munter; (*old person*) rüstig.

lute [lōōt] *n* Laute *f*.

Luxembourg [luk'səmbûrg] *n* (*state, city*) Luxemburg *nt*.

luxuriant [lōōgzhōōr'ēənt] *a* üppig.

luxurious [lōōgzhōōr'ēəs] *a* luxuriös, Luxus-.

luxury [luk'shûrē] *n* Luxus *m*; **the little luxuries** die kleinen Genüsse.

LW *abbr* (*RAD*: = *long wave*) LW.

lying [lī'ing] *n* Lügen *nt* ♦ *a* (*person*) verlogen; (*statement, story*) verlogen, lügnerisch.

lynch [linch] *vt* lynchen.

lynx [lingks] *n* Luchs *m*.

lyre [lī'ûr] *n* Leier *f*.

lyric [lir'ik] *n* Lyrik *f*; (*often pl*: *words for song*) (Lied)text *m* ♦ *a* lyrisch.

lyrical [lir'ikəl] *a* lyrisch, gefühlvoll.

M

M, m [em] n (letter) M nt, m nt; **M for Mike**
≈ M wie Martha.
m abbr (= meter(s)) m; (= mile(s)) M.
M abbr (= million(s)) Mio., Mill.; (= medium) M; (Brit) = **motorway**.
MA n abbr (US: = military academy)
Militärakademie f; (= Master of Arts) M. A.
m ♦ abbr (US MAIL) = Massachusetts.
mac [mak] n (Brit col) Regenmantel m.
macabre [məkâ'brə] a makaber.
macaroni [makərō'nē] n Makkaroni pl.
macaroon [makərōōn'] n Makrone f.
mace [mās] n (of mayor) Amtsstab m;
(spice) Muskat m.
machinations [makənə'shənz] npl Machenschaften pl.
machine [məshēn'] n Maschine f ♦ vt (dress
etc) mit der Maschine nähen; (TECH) maschinell herstellen or bearbeiten.
machine code n (COMPUT) Maschinencode
m.
machine gun n Maschinengewehr nt.
machine language n Maschinensprache f.
machine readable a (COMPUT) maschinen-
lesbar, maschinell lesbar.
machinery [məshē'nûrē] n Maschinerie f, Maschinen pl.
machine shop n Maschinensaal m.
machine tool n Werkzeugmaschine f.
machine washable a waschmaschinenfest.
machinist [məshē'nist] n Machinist m.
macho [mâch'ō] a macho.
mackerel [mak'ûrəl] n Makrele f.
mackintosh [mak'intâsh] n (Brit) Regenmantel m.
macro- [mak'rō] pref Makro-, makro-.
macroeconomics [makrōēkənâm'iks] npl
Makroökonomie f.
mad [mad] a wahnsinnig, verrückt; (dog) toll-
wütig; (angry) wütend; **~ at** or **with sb**
böse or sauer auf jdn; **to go ~** wahnsinnig
werden; **~ about** (fond of) verrückt nach,
versessen auf (+acc); **to be ~ (keen) on**
sth auf etw (acc) verrückt sein.
madam [mad'əm] n gnädige Frau f; **M~**
Chairman Frau Vorsitzende.
madden [mad'ən] vt verrückt machen;
(make angry) ärgern.
maddening [mad'əning] a unerträglich, zum
Verrücktwerden.
made [mād] pt, pp of **make**.
Madeira [mədē'rə] n (GEOG) Madeira nt;
(wine) Madeira m.
made-to-measure [mād'təmezh'ûr] a (Brit)

Maß-.
made-to-order [mād'tōōór'dûr] a (US) Maß-.
made-up [mād'up'] a (story) erfunden.
madly [mad'lē] ad wahnsinnig.
madman [mad'man] n, pl **-men** Verrückte(r)
m, Irre(r) m.
madness [mad'nis] n Wahnsinn m.
Madonna [mədân'ə] n Madonna f.
Madrid [mədrid'] n Madrid nt.
madrigal [mad'rəgəl] n Madrigal nt.
Mafia [mâf'ēə] n Mafia f.
magazine [magəzēn'] n Zeitschrift f; (in gun)
Magazin nt.
maggot [mag'ət] n Made f.
magic [maj'ik] n Zauberei f, Magie f; (fig)
Zauber m ♦ a magisch, Zauber-.
magical [maj'ikəl] a magisch.
magician [məjish'ən] n Zauberer m.
magistrate [maj'istrāt] n (Friedens)richter
m.
magnanimity [magnənim'itē] n Großmut f.
magnanimous [magnan'əməs] a großmütig.
magnate [mag'nāt] n Magnat m.
magnesium [magnē'zēəm] n Magnesium nt.
magnet [mag'nit] n Magnet m.
magnetic [magnet'ik] a magnetisch; (fig) anziehend, unwiderstehlich.
magnetic disk n (COMPUT) Magnetplatte f.
magnetic tape n Magnetband nt.
magnetism [mag'nitizəm] n Magnetismus m;
(fig) Ausstrahlungskraft f.
magnification [magnəfəkā'shən] n Vergrößerung f.
magnificence [magnif'isəns] n Pracht f,
Großartigkeit f.
magnificent [magnif'əsənt] a, **magnificently**
[magnif'əsəntlē] ad großartig.
magnify [mag'nəfī] vt vergrößern.
magnifying glass [mag'nəfīing glas] n Vergrößerungsglas nt, Lupe f.
magnitude [mag'nətōōd] n (size) Größe f;
(importance) Ausmaß nt.
magnolia [magnōl'yə] n Magnolie f.
magpie [mag'pī] n Elster f.
maharajah [mâhərâ'jə] n Maharadscha m.
mahogany [məhâg'ənē] n Mahagoni nt ♦ a
Mahagoni-.
maid [mād] n Dienstmädchen nt; **old ~** alte
Jungfer f.
maiden [mād'ən] n (liter) Maid f ♦ a (flight,
speech) Jungfern-.
maiden name n Mädchenname m.
mail [māl] n Post f; **by ~** mit der Post ♦ vt
aufgeben.
mailbox [māl'bâks] n (US) Briefkasten m;
(ELEC) (elektronische(s)) Postfach nt.
mailing [mā'ling] n Postwurfsendung f.
mailing list [mā'ling list] n Anschriftenliste
f.
mailman [māl'man] n, pl **-men** (US) Brief-trä-
ger m.
mail order n Bestellung f durch die Post.
mail-order firm [māl'ôrdûr fûrm] n Versand-
haus nt.

mailshot [māl'shât] *n* (*Brit*) Postwurfsendung *f*.

mail train *n* Postzug *m*.

mail truck, (*Brit*) **mail van** *n* Postauto *nt*.

maim [mām] *vt* verstümmeln.

main [mān] *a* hauptsächlich, Haupt- ♦ *n* (*pipe*) Hauptleitung *f*; **the ~s** (*Brit ELEC*) das Stromnetz; **in the ~** im großen und ganzen.

main course *n* (*COOK*) Hauptgericht *nt*.

mainframe [mān'frām] *n* (*also*: ~ **computer**) Großrechner *m*, Mainframe *m*.

mainland [mān'lənd] *n* Festland *nt*.

main line *n* Hauptstrecke *f*.

mainly [mān'lē] *ad* hauptsächlich.

main road *n* Hauptstraße *f*.

mainstay [mān'stā] *n* (*fig*) Hauptstütze *f*.

mainstream [mān'strēm] *n* (*fig*) Hauptrichtung *f*.

maintain [māntān'] *vt* (*building, roads*) instand halten; (*TECH*) warten; (*support*) unterhalten; (*keep up*) aufrechterhalten; (*claim*) behaupten; (*innocence*) beteuern; **to ~ that ...** behaupten, daß ...

maintenance [mān'tənəns] *n* (*TECH*) Wartung *f*; (*of family*) Unterhalt *m*.

maintenance contract *n* Wartungsabkommen *nt*.

maintenance order *n* (*JUR*) Unterhaltsurteil *nt*.

maisonette [māzənet'] *n* (*Brit*) Wohnung *f*.

maize [māz] *n* Mais *m*.

Maj. *abbr* (*MIL*: = *major*) Maj., Mjr.

majestic [məjes'tik] *a* majestätisch.

majesty [maj'istē] *n* Majestät *f*.

major [mā'jûr] *n* Major *m*; (*US UNIV*) Hauptfach *nt* ♦ *a* (*MUS*) Dur; (*more important*) Haupt-; (*bigger*) größer; **a ~ operation** eine größere Operation ♦ *vi*: **to ~ in French** (*US UNIV*) Französisch als Hauptfach studieren.

Majorca [məyôr'kə] *n* Mallorca *nt*.

major general *n* (*MIL*) Generalmajor *m*.

majority [məjôr'itē] *n* Mehrheit *f*; (*JUR*) Volljährigkeit *f*.

majority holding *n* (*FIN*): **to have a ~** Mehrheitsanteile *pl* besitzen.

make [māk] *vt irreg* machen; (*appoint*) ernennen (zu); (*cause to do sth*) veranlassen; (*reach*) erreichen; (*connection*) schaffen; (*earn*) verdienen; **to ~ a profit of $10,000** 10000 Dollar Gewinn machen; **to ~ sth happen** etw geschehen lassen ♦ *n* Marke *f*, Fabrikat *nt*.

make for *vt fus* gehen *or* fahren nach.

make off *vi* sich davonmachen.

make out *vi* zurechtkommen ♦ *vt* (*write out*) ausstellen; (*understand*) verstehen; (*pretend*) (so) tun (als ob); **to ~ out a case for sth** für etw argumentieren; **to ~ out that ...** (*claim, imply*) behaupten, daß ...

make over *vt* (*assign*): **to ~ over (to)** überschreiben (+*dat*).

make up *vt* (*make*) machen, herstellen; (*face*) schminken; (*quarrel*) beilegen; (*story*

etc) erfinden; **to be made up of** bestehen aus ♦ *vi* sich versöhnen.

make up for *vt fus* wiedergutmachen; (*COMM*) vergüten.

make-believe [māk'bilēv] *n*: **it's ~** es ist nicht wirklich ♦ *a* Phantasie-, ersonnen.

maker [mā'kûr] *n* (*COMM*) Hersteller *m*.

makeshift [māk'shift] *a* behelfsmäßig, Not-.

make-up [māk'up] *n* Schminke *f*, Make-up *nt*.

make-up bag *n* Schminktäschchen *nt*.

make-up remover *n* Make-up-Entferner *m*.

making [mā'king] *n*: **in the ~** im Entstehen; **to have the ~s of** das Zeug haben zu.

maladjusted [maləjus'tid] *a* fehlangepaßt, umweltgestört.

maladroit [malədroit'] *a* ungeschickt.

malaise [malāz'] *n* Unbehagen *nt*.

malaria [məlär'ēə] *n* Malaria *f*.

Malawi [mâ'lâwē] *n* Malawi *nt*.

Malay [məlā'] *a* malaiisch ♦ *n* (*person*) Malaie *m*, Malaiin *f*; (*language*) Malaiisch *nt*.

Malaya [məlā'yə] *n* (*old*) Malaya *nt*.

Malayan [məlā'yən] = **Malay**.

Malaysia [məlā'zhə] *n* Malaysia *nt*.

Malaysian [məlā'zhən] *a* malayisch ♦ *n* (*person*) Malaysier (in *f*) *m*.

Maldive Islands [maldīv' ī'ləndz] *npl* Malediven *pl*.

male [māl] *n* Mann *m*; (*animal*) Männchen *nt* ♦ *a* männlich.

male chauvinist pig [māl' shō'vənist pig'] *n* (*col pej*) Chauvi *m*.

male nurse *n* Krankenpfleger *m*.

malevolence [məlev'ələns] *n* Böswilligkeit *f*.

malevolent [məlev'ələnt] *a* übelwollend.

malfunction [malfungk'shən] *vi* versagen, nicht funktionieren.

malice [mal'is] *n* Bosheit *f*.

malicious [məlish'əs] *a*, **maliciously** [məlish'əslē] *ad* böswillig, gehässig.

malign [məlīn'] *vt* verleumden.

malignant [məlig'nənt] *a* bösartig.

malinger [məling'gûr] *vi* simulieren.

malingerer [məling'gûrûr] *n* Simulant *m*.

mall [môl] *n* (*US*) Einkaufszentrum *nt*.

malleable [mal'ēəbəl] *a* formbar.

mallet [mal'it] *n* Holzhammer *m*.

malnutrition [malnōōtrish'ən] *n* Unterernährung *f*.

malpractice [malprak'tis] *n* Amtsvergehen *nt*.

malt [môlt] *n* Malz *nt*.

Malta [môl'tə] *n* Malta *nt*.

Maltese [môltēz'] *a* maltesisch ♦ *n* (*person*) Malteser (in *f*) *m*; (*language*) Maltesisch *nt*.

maltreat [maltrēt'] *vt* mißhandeln.

mammal [mam'əl] *n* Säugetier *nt*.

mammoth [mam'əth] *n* Mammut-, Riesen-.

Man. *abbr* (*Canada*) = *Manitoba*.

man [man] *n, pl* **men** Mann *m*; (*human race*) der Mensch, die Menschen *pl* ♦ *vt* bemannen.

manacles [man'əkəlz] *npl* Handfesseln *pl*, Ketten *pl*.

manage [man'ij] *vi* zurechtkommen; **to ~**

without sth/sb ohne etw/jdn auskommen ♦ *vt (company, organization)* leiten; *(task, person, animal)* zurechtkommen mit; *(cope with)* fertigwerden mit; **to ~ to do sth** es schaffen, etw zu tun.

manageable [man'ijəbəl] *a (person, animal)* lenksam, fügsam; *(object)* handlich.

management [man'ijmənt] *n (control)* Führung *f*, Leitung *f*, Management *nt*; *(persons: of business, firm)* Unternehmensleitung *f*; (: *of hotel, shop)* Leitung *f*; *(THEAT)* Intendanz *f*; **"under new ~"** „neuer Inhaber"; *(shop)* „neu eröffnet"; *(pub)* „unter neuer Bewirtschaftung".

management accounting *n* Rechnungswesen *nt* im Dienste der Unternehmensführung.

management consultant *n* Unternehmensberater *m*.

manager [man'ijûr] *n* Geschäftsführer *m*, (Betriebs)leiter *m*; **sales ~** Verkaufsleiter *m*, Sales manager *m*.

manageress [man'ijûris] *n (Brit)* Geschäftsführerin *f*.

managerial [manijē'rēəl] *a* leitend; *(problem etc)* Management-.

managing director [man'ijing direk'tûr] *n* Betriebsleiter *m*.

Mancunian [mangkyōō'nēən] *n* Bewohner(in *f*) *m* Manchesters ♦ *a* aus Manchester.

mandarin [man'dûrin] *n (fruit)* Mandarine *f*; *(official: Chinese)* Mandarin *m*; (: *gen)* Funktionär *m*, Bonze *m (pej)*.

mandate [man'dāt] *n* Mandat *nt*.

mandatory [man'dətôrē] *a* obligatorisch.

mandolin(e) [man'dəlin] *n* Mandoline *f*.

mane [mān] *n* Mähne *f*.

maneuver [mənōō'vûr] *(US) vti* manövrieren; **to ~ sb into doing sth** jdn dazu bringen, etw zu tun ♦ *n (MIL)* Feldzug *m*; *(clever plan)* Manöver *nt*, Schachzug *m*; **~s** *pl* Truppenübungen *pl*, Manöver *nt*.

maneuverable [mənōō'vrəbəl] *a (US)* manövrierfähig; *(car)* wendig.

manful [man'fəl] *a*, **manfully** [man'fəlē] *ad* beherzt, mannhaft.

manganese [mang'gənēz] *n* Mangan *nt*.

mangle [mang'gəl] *vt* verstümmeln.

mango [mang'gō] *n* Mango(pflaume) *f*.

mangrove [mang'grōv] *n* Mangrove *f*.

mangy [mān'jē] *a (dog)* räudig.

manhandle [man'handəl] *vt* grob behandeln; *(move by hand: goods)* abfertigen.

manhole [man'hōl] *n* Kanalschacht *m*.

manhood [man'hŏŏd] *n* Mannesalter *nt*; *(manliness)* Männlichkeit *f*.

man-hour [man'ouûr] *n* Arbeitsstunde *f*.

manhunt [man'hunt] *n* Fahndung *f*.

mania [mā'nēə] *n (craze)* Sucht *f*, Manie *f*; *(madness)* Wahn(sinn) *m*.

maniac [mā'nēak] *n* Wahnsinnige(r) *mf*, Verrückte(r) *mf*.

manic-depressive [man'ikdipres'iv] *n (PSYCH)* Manisch-Depressive(r) *mf* ♦ *a* manisch-depressiv.

manicure [man'əkyōōr] *n* Maniküre *f* ♦ *vt* maniküren.

manicure set *n* Necessaire *nt*.

manifest [man'əfest] *n* Manifest *nt* ♦ *vt* offenbaren ♦ *a* offenkundig.

manifestation [manəfestā'shən] *n (showing)* Ausdruck *m*, Bekundung *f*; *(sign)* Anzeichen *nt*.

manifestly [man'əfestlē] *ad* offenkundig.

manifesto [manəfes'tō] *n* Manifest *nt*.

manifold [man'əfōld] *a* vielfältig, mannigfaltig ♦ *n (AUT etc)*: **exhaust ~** Auspuffrohr *nt*.

Manila [mənil'ə] *n* Manila *nt*.

manil(l)a envelope *n* braune(r) Umschlag *m*.

manipulate [mənip'yəlāt] *vt* handhaben; *(fig)* manipulieren.

manipulation [mənipyəlā'shən] *n* Manipulation *f*.

mankind [man'kīnd'] *n* Menschheit *f*.

manliness [man'lēnis] *n* Männlichkeit *f*.

manly [man'lē] *a* männlich, mannhaft.

man-made [man'mād] *a (fiber)* künstlich.

manna [man'ə] *n* Manna *nt*.

mannequin [man'əkin] *n (dummy)* Gliederpuppe *f*; *(Brit: fashion model)* Mannequin *nt*.

manner [man'ûr] *n* Art *f*, Weise *f*; *(style)* Stil *m*; **all ~ of** allerlei, die verschiedensten; **in such a ~ so**; **in a ~ of speaking** sozusagen; *see also* **manners**.

mannerism [man'ərizəm] *n (of person)* Angewohnheit *f*; *(of style)* Maniertheit *f*.

mannerly [man'ûrlē] *a* wohlerzogen.

manners [man'ûrz] *npl* Manieren *pl*; **good/bad ~** gutes/schlechtes Benehmen.

manoeuvre [mənōō'vûr] *etc (Brit)* = **maneuver** *etc*.

manor [man'ûr] *n* Landgut *nt*.

manor house *n* Herrenhaus *nt*.

manpower [man'pouûr] *n* Arbeitskräfte *pl*.

Manpower Services Commission *n (Brit) Behörde für Arbeitsbeschaffung, Arbeitsvermittlung und Berufsausbildung.*

manservant [man'sûrvənt] *n* Diener *m*.

mansion [man'chən] *n* Herrenhaus *nt*, Landhaus *nt*.

manslaughter [man'slôtûr] *n* Totschlag *m*.

mantelpiece [man'təlpēs] *n* Kaminsims *m*.

mantle [man'təl] *n (cloak)* Umhang *m*.

man-to-man [man'təman'] *a* von Mann zu Mann.

manual [man'yōōəl] *a* manuell, Hand- ♦ *n* Handbuch *nt*.

manual worker *n* (Hand)arbeiter *m*.

manufacture [manyəfak'chûr] *vt* herstellen ♦ *n* Herstellung *f*.

manufactured goods [manyəfak'chûrd gŏŏdz] *npl* Fertigwaren *pl*.

manufacturer [manyəfak'chûrûr] *n* Hersteller *m*.

manufacturing industries [manyəfak'chûring in'dəstrēz] *npl* verarbeitende Indu-

strie *f sing.*
manure [mənōōr'] *n* Dünger *m.*
manuscript [man'yəskript] *n* Manuskript *nt.*
many [men'ē] *a, pron* viele; **too ~ difficulties**
zu viele Schwierigkeiten; **twice as ~** zweimal so viel(e); **how ~?** wie viele?; **as ~ as
20** sage und schreibe 20; **~ a good soldier**
so mancher gute Soldat; **~'s the time** ... oft
...
map [map] *n* (Land)karte *f*; (*of town*) Stadtplan *m* ♦ *vt* eine Karte machen von.
  map out *vt* (*fig: essay*) anlegen; (: *career, vacation*) planen, festlegen.
maple [mā'pəl] *n* Ahorn *m.*
mar [mâr] *vt* verderben, beeinträchtigen.
Mar. *abbr* (= *March*) Mrz.
marathon [mar'əthân] *n* (*SPORT*) Marathonlauf *m*; (*fig*) Marathon *m* ♦ *a*: **a ~ session**
eine Marathonsitzung.
marathon runner *n* Marathonläufer(in *f*)
m.
marauder [mərôd'ûr] *n* Plünderer *m.*
marble [mâr'bəl] *n* Marmor *m*; (*for game*)
Murmel *f.*
march [mârch] *vi* marschieren ♦ *n* Marsch *m.*
March [mârch] *n* März *m; see* **September.**
marcher [mâr'chûr] *n* Demonstrant(in *f*) *m.*
marching [mâr'ching] *a*: **to give sb his ~
orders** (*fig*) jdm den Laufpaß geben.
march-past [mârch'past] *n* Vorbeimarsch *m.*
mare [mâr] *n* Stute *f.*
margarine [mâr'jûrin] *n* Margarine *f.*
marg(e) [mârj] *n abbr* (*col*) = **margarine.**
margin [mâr'jin] *n* Rand *m*; (*extra amount*)
Spielraum *m*; (*COMM*) Spanne *f.*
marginal [mâr'jinəl] *a* (*note*) Rand-; (*difference etc*) geringfügig; **a ~ seat** (*POL*) *ein
Wahlkreis, der mit einer knappen Mehrheit
erworben wurde.*
marginally [mâr'jinəlē] *ad* nur wenig;
(*bigger, better*) etwas, ein wenig; (*different*)
unwesentlich.
marigold [mar'əgōld] *n* Ringelblume *f.*
marijuana [marəwâ'nə] *n* Marihuana *nt.*
marina [mərē'nə] *n* Yachthafen *m.*
marinade [mar'ənād] *n* Marinade *f.*
marinate [mar'ənāt] *vt* marinieren.
marine [mərēn'] *a* Meeres-, See- ♦ *n* (*MIL*)
Marineinfanterist *m*; (*fleet*) Marine *f.*
marine insurance *n* Seeversicherung *f.*
mariner [mar'inûr] *n* Seemann *m.*
marionette [marēənet'] *n* Marionette *f.*
marital [mar'itəl] *a* ehelich, Ehe-.
marital status *n* Familienstand *m.*
maritime [mar'itīm] *a* See-.
maritime law *n* Seerecht *nt.*
marjoram [mâr'jûrəm] *n* Majoran *m.*
mark [mârk] *n* (*FIN*) Mark *f*; (*spot*) Fleck *m*;
(*scar*) Kratzer *m*; (*sign*) Zeichen *nt*; (*target*) Ziel *nt*; (*Brit SCH*) Note *f*; **quick off the
~** blitzschnell; **on your ~s** auf die Plätze;
to be up to the ~ (*in efficiency*) den Anforderungen entsprechen; (*Brit TECH*): **Cortina
M~ 3** Cortina 3 ♦ *vt* (*make ~*) Flecken *or*

Kratzer machen auf (+*acc*); (*indicate*) markieren, bezeichnen; (*note*) sich (*dat*) merken; (*exam*) korrigieren; (*SPORT: player*)
decken; **to ~ time** (*lit, fig*) auf der Stelle
treten.
  mark down *vt* (*reduce: prices, goods*)
  herab- *or* heruntersetzen.
  mark off *vt* (*tick off*) abhaken.
  mark out *vt* bestimmen; (*area*) abstecken.
  mark up *vt* (*write up*) notieren (*on* auf
  +*dat*); (*price*) heraufsetzen, erhöhen.
marked [mârkt] *a* deutlich.
markedly [mâr'kidlē] *ad* merklich.
marker [mâr'kûr] *n* (*in book*) (Lese)zeichen
nt; (*on road*) Schild *nt.*
market [mâr'kit] *n* Markt *m*; (*stock ~*) Börse
f; **to be on the ~** auf dem Markt sein; **to
play the ~** (an der Börse) spekulieren; **falling ~** (*COMM*) Baissemarkt *m*; **open ~** of-
fene(r) *or* freie(r) Markt *m* ♦ *vt* (*COMM*:
new product) auf den Markt bringen; (:
sell) vertreiben; (: *promote*) vermarkten,
verkaufen.
marketable [mâr'kitəbəl] *a* marktfähig.
market analysis *n* Marktanalyse *f.*
market day *n* Markttag *m.*
market demand *n* Marktbedarf *m.*
market forces *npl* Marktkräfte *pl.*
market garden *n* (*Brit*) Handelsgärtnerei *f.*
marketing [mâr'kiting] *n* Marketing *nt.*
marketing manager *n* Marketing-Manager
m.
market leader *n* Marktführer *m*, Spitzenreiter *m.*
market place *n* Marktplatz *m.*
market price *n* Marktpreis *m.*
market research *n* Marktforschung *f.*
market value *n* Marktwert *m.*
marking [mâr'king] *n* (*on animal*) Zeichnung
f; (*on road*) Markierung *f*; (*SCH*) Korrektur
f.
marking ink *n* Wäschetinte *f.*
marksman [mârks'mən] *n, pl* **-men**
(Scharf)schütze *m.*
marksmanship [mârks'mənship] *n* Schieß-
kunst *f*, Treffsicherheit *f.*
markup [mârk'up] *n* (*COMM: margin*) Han-
delsspanne *f*; (: *increase*) Preiserhöhung *f*
or -aufschlag *m.*
marmalade [mâr'məlād] *n* Orangenmarmela-
de *f.*
maroon [mərōōn'] *vt* aussetzen ♦ *a* (*color*)
kastanienbraun.
marquee [mârkē'] *n* große(s) Zelt *nt*; (*US:
canopy*) Schutzdach *nt.*
marquess, marquis [mâr'kwis] *n* Marquis *m.*
marriage [mar'ij] *n* Ehe *f*; (*wedding*) Heirat
f; (*fig*) Verbindung *f.*
marriage bureau *n* Heiratsinstitut *nt.*
marriage certificate *n* Heiratsurkunde *f.*
marriage counseling, (*Brit*) **marriage
guidance** *n* Eheberatung *f.*
married [mar'ēd] *a* (*person*) verheiratet;
(*couple, life*) Ehe-.

marrow [mar'ō] *n* (Knochen)mark *nt*; (*Brit: vegetable*) Kürbis *m*.

marry [mar'ē] *vt* (*join*) trauen; (*take as husband, wife*) heiraten ♦ *vi* (*also:* **get married**) heiraten.

Mars [mârz] *n* Mars *m*.

Marseilles [mârsā'] *n* Marseilles *nt*.

marsh [mârsh] *n* Marsch *f*, Sumpfland *nt*.

marshal [mâr'shəl] *n* (*US*) Bezirkspolizeichef *m*; (*for demonstration, meeting*) Ordner *m* ♦ *vt* (an)ordnen, arrangieren.

marshal(l)ing yard [mârshəling yârd] *n* (*Brit RAIL*) Rangierbahnhof *m*.

marshmallow [mârsh'melō] *n* (*BOT*) Eibisch *m*; (*sweet*) Marshmallow *nt*.

marshy [mâr'shē] *a* sumpfig.

marsupial [mârsōō'pēəl] *n* Beuteltier *nt*.

martial [mâr'shəl] *a* kriegerisch.

martial law *n* Kriegsrecht *nt*.

martin [mâr'tən] *n* (*house* ~) (Mehl)schwalbe *f*.

martyr [mâr'tûr] *n* (*lit, fig*) Märtyrer(in *f*) *m* ♦ *vt* zum Märtyrer machen.

martyrdom [mâr'tûrdəm] *n* Martyrium *nt*.

marvel [mâr'vəl] *n* Wunder *nt* ♦ *vi* staunen, sich wundern (*at* über +*acc*).

marvelous, (*Brit*) **marvellous** [mâr'vələs] *a* wunderbar.

marvelously, (*Brit*) **marvellously** [mâr'vələslē] *ad* wunderbar.

Marxism [mârk'sizəm] *n* Marxismus *m*.

Marxist [mâr'ksist] *n* Marxist(in *f*) *m*.

marzipan [mâr'zəpan] *n* Marzipan *nt*.

mascara [maskar'ə] *n* Wimperntusche *f*.

mascot [mas'kət] *n* Maskottchen *nt*.

masculine [mas'kyəlin] *a* männlich ♦ *n* Maskulinum *nt*.

masculinity [maskyəlin'itē] *n* Männlichkeit *f*.

mash [mash] *vt* (*COOK*) zerstampfen ♦ *n* Brei *m*.

MASH [mash] *n* *abbr* (*US MIL*: = *mobile army surgical hospital*) mobiles Lazarett.

mashed potatoes [masht pətā'tōz] *npl* Kartoffelbrei *m* or -püree *nt*.

mask [mask] *n* (*lit, fig, ELEC*) Maske *f* ♦ *vt* maskieren, verdecken.

masochism [mas'əkizəm] *n* Masochismus *m*.

masochist [mas'əkist] *n* Masochist(in *f*) *m*.

mason [mā'sən] *n* (*stone*~) Steinmetz *m*; (*free*~) Freimaurer *m*.

masonic [məsân'ik] *a* Freimaurer-.

masonry [mā'sənrē] *n* Mauerwerk *nt*.

masquerade [maskərâd'] *n* Maskerade *f* ♦ *vi* sich maskieren, sich verkleiden; **to** ~ **as** sich ausgeben als.

mass [mas] *n* Masse *f*; (*greater part*) Mehrheit *f*; (*REL*) Messe *f*; **to go to** ~ zur Messe gehen; ~**es of** massenhaft ♦ *vt* sammeln, anhäufen ♦ *vi* sich sammeln.

Mass. *abbr.* (*US*) = *Massachusetts*.

massacre [mas'əkûr] *n* Massaker *nt* ♦ *vt* massakrieren.

massage [məsâzh'] *n* Massage *f* ♦ *vt* massieren.

masseur [masûr'] *n* Masseur *m*.

masseuse [məsōōs'] *n* Masseuse *f*.

massive [mas'iv] *a* gewaltig, massiv.

mass media [mas mē'dēə] *npl* Massenmedien *pl.*

mass meeting *n* (*huge*) Massenveranstaltung *f*; (*of everyone concerned*) Vollversammlung *f*; (*in company*) Betriebsversammlung *f*.

mass-produce [mas'prədōōs'] *vt* in Massenproduktion herstellen.

mass production *n* Serienproduktion *f*, Massenproduktion *f*.

mast [mast] *n* Mast *m*; (*RAD. TV*) Sendeturm *m*.

master [mas'tûr] *n* Herr *m*; (*NAUT*) Kapitän *m*; (*teacher*) Lehrer *m*; (*artist*) Meister *m* ♦ *vt* meistern; (*language etc*) beherrschen.

master disk *n* (*COMPUT*) Hauptplatte *f* or -diskette *f*.

masterful [mas'tûrfəl] *a* meisterhaft.

master key *n* Hauptschlüssel *m*.

masterly [mas'tûrlē] *a* meisterhaft.

mastermind [mas'tûrmīnd] *n* (führende(r)) Kopf *m* ♦ *vt* geschickt lenken; **who** ~**ed the robbery?** wer steckt hinter dem Raubüberfall?

Master of Arts *n* Magister Artium *m*.

master of ceremonies *n* (*at function*) Zeremonienmeister *m*; (*on stage*) Conférencier *m*.

masterpiece [mas'tûrpēs] *n* Meisterstück *nt*; (*ART*) Meisterwerk *nt*.

master plan *n* kluge(r) Plan *m*.

masterstroke [mas'tûrstrōk] *n* Glanzstück *nt*.

mastery [mas'tûrē] *n* Können *nt*; **to gain** ~ **over sb** die Oberhand über jdn gewinnen .

mastiff [mas'tif] *n* Dogge *f*.

masturbate [mas'tûrbāt] *vi* masturbieren, onanieren.

masturbation [mastûrbā'shən] *n* Masturbation *f*, Onanie *f*.

mat [mat] *n* Matte *f*; (*for table*) Untersetzer *m* ♦ *vi* (*hair, wool*) sich verfilzen ♦ *vt* verfilzen ♦ *a* = **matt**.

match [mach] *n* Streichholz *nt*; (*sth corresponding*) Pendant *nt*; (*SPORT*) Wettkampf *m*; (*ball games*) Spiel *nt*; **it's a good** ~ es paßt gut (*for* zu); **to be a** ~ **for sb** sich mit jdm messen können; (*be able to handle*) jdm gewachsen sein; **he's a good** ~ er ist eine gute Partie ♦ *vt* (*be like, suit*) passen zu; (*equal*) gleichkommen (+*dat*); (*SPORT*) antreten lassen ♦ *vi* zusammenpassen.

matchbox [mach'bâks] *n* Streichholzschachtel *f.*

matching [mach'ing] *a* passend.

matchless [mach'lis] *a* unvergleichlich.

matchmaker [mach'mākûr] *n* Kuppler(in *f*) *m.*

mate [māt] *n* (*spouse*) Lebensgefährte *m*; (*of animal*) Weibchen *nt* or Männchen *nt*; (*NAUT*) Schiffsoffizier *m*; (*Brit: companion*) Kamerad *m* ♦ *vi* (*animals*) sich paaren ♦ *vt*

(*CHESS*) matt setzen.

material [mətē'rēəl] *n* Material *nt*; (*for book, cloth*) Material *nt*, Stoff *m* ♦ *a* (*important*) wesentlich; (*damage*) Sach-; (*comforts etc*) materiell; *see also* **materials**.

materialistic [mətērēəlis'tik] *a* materialistisch.

materialize [mətēr'ēəlīz] *vi* sich verwirklichen, zustande kommen.

materially [mətēr'ēəlē] *ad* grundlegend, wesentlich.

materials [mətē'rēəlz] *npl* Material *nt*.

maternal [mətûr'nəl] *a* mütterlich, Mutter-.

maternal grandmother *n* Großmutter *f* mütterlicherseits.

maternity [mətûr'nitē] *n* Mutterschaft *f*.

maternity benefit *n* Mutterschaftsgeld *nt*.

maternity dress *n* Umstandskleid *nt*.

maternity leave *n* Schwangerschaftsurlaub *m*.

math [math] *n abbr* (*US*: = *mathematics*) Mathe *f*.

mathematical [mathəmat'ikəl] *a*, **mathematically** [mathəmat'ikəlē] *ad* mathematisch.

mathematician [mathəmətish'ən] *n* Mathematiker(in *f*) *m*.

mathematics [mathəmat'iks] *n* Mathematik *f*.

maths [maths] *n abbr* (*Brit*: = *mathematics*) Mathe *f*.

matinée [matənā'] *n* Matinee *f*.

mating [mā'ting] *n* Paarung *f*.

mating call *n* Lockruf *m*.

matins [mat'ənz] *n* (Früh)mette *f*.

matriarchal [mātrēâr'kəl] *a* matriarchalisch.

matrices [māt'risēz] *npl of* **matrix**.

matrimonial [matrəmō'nēəl] *a* ehelich, Ehe-.

matrimony [mat'rəmōnē] *n* Ehestand *m*.

matrix [mā'triks] *n*, *pl* **~es** *or* **matrices** (*BIOL*) Gebärmutter *f*; (*GEOL. MATH, COMPUT*) Matrix *f*.

matron [mā'trən] *n* (*MED*) Oberin *f*; (*SCH*) Hausmutter *f*.

matronly [mā'trənlē] *a* matronenhaft.

matt [mat] *a* (*paint*) matt.

matter [mat'ûr] *n* (*substance*) Materie *f*; (*affair*) Sache *f*, Angelegenheit *f*; (*content*) Inhalt *m*; (*MED*) Eiter *m*; **no ~ how/what** egal wie/was; **what is the ~?** was ist los?; **as a ~ of fact** eigentlich ♦ *vi* darauf ankommen; **it doesn't ~** es macht nichts.

matter-of-fact [mat'ûrəvfakt'] *a* sachlich, nüchtern.

mattress [mat'ris] *n* Matratze *f*.

mature [mətōōr'] *a* reif ♦ *vi* reif werden.

maturity [mətōō'ritē] *n* Reife *f*.

maudlin [môd'lin] *a* (*story*) rührselig; (*person*) gefühlsselig.

maul [môl] *vt* übel zurichten.

Mauritania [môritā'nēə] *n* Mauritanien *nt*.

Mauritius [môrish'ēəs] *n* Mauritius *nt*.

mausoleum [môsəlē'əm] *n* Mausoleum *nt*.

mauve [mōv] *a* mauve.

maverick [mav'ûrik] *n* (*fig*) Einzelgänger(in *f*) *m*; (*dissenter*) Abtrünnige(r) *mf*.

mawkish [môk'ish] *a* kitschig; (*taste*) süßlich.

max. *abbr* = **maximum**.

maxi [maks'ē] *pref* Maxi-.

maxim [mak'sim] *n* Maxime *f*.

maximize [mak'səmīz] *vt* (*profits etc*) maximieren; (*chances*) vergrößern.

maximum [mak'səməm] *a* höchste(r, s), Höchst-, Maximal- ♦ *n* Höchstgrenze *f*, Maximum *nt*.

may [mā] *aux v* (*be possible*) können; (*have permission*) dürfen; **I ~** *or* **might come** ich komme vielleicht, es kann sein, daß ich komme; **we ~ as well go** wir können ruhig gehen; **~ you be very happy** ich hoffe, ihr seid glücklich; **~ I sit here?** kann ich mich hier hinsetzen?

May [mā] *n* Mai *m*; *see* **September**.

maybe [mā'bē] *ad* vielleicht; **~ not** vielleicht nicht.

May Day *n* der 1. Mai.

mayday [mā'dā] *n* (*message*) SOS *nt*.

mayhem [mā'hem] *n* Chaos *nt*; (*US JUR*) Körperverletzung *f*.

mayonnaise [māənāz'] *n* Mayonnaise *f*.

mayor [mā'ûr] *n* Bürgermeister *m*.

mayoress [mā'ûris] *n* (*Brit*: *wife*) Frau *f* Bürgermeister; (: *lady* **~**) Bürgermeisterin *f*.

maypole [mā'pōl] *n* Maibaum *m*.

maze [māz] *n* (*lit*) Irrgarten *m*; (*fig*) Wirrwarr *nt*; **to be in a ~** (*fig*) durcheinander sein.

MB *abbr* (*Canada*) = *Manitoba*.

MBA *n abbr* (= *Master of Business Administration*) MBA *m*.

MBBS, MBChB *n abbr* (*Brit*: = *Bachelor of Medicine and Surgery*) akademischer Grad in Medizin.

MC *n abbr* = **master of ceremonies**.

MCAT *n abbr* (*US*) = *Medical College Admissions Test*.

MCP *n abbr* (*Brit col*) = **male chauvinist pig**.

MD *n abbr* (= *Doctor of Medicine*) Dr. med.; = **managing director** ♦ *abbr* (*US MAIL*) = *Maryland*.

me [mē] *pron* (*acc*) mich; (*dat*) mir; **it's ~** ich bin's; **it's for ~** das ist für mich.

ME *n abbr* (*US*: = *medical examiner*) Arzt, der Obduktionen durchführt ♦ *abbr* (*US MAIL*) = *Maine*.

meadow [med'ō] *n* Wiese *f*.

meager, (*Brit*) **meagre** [mē'gûr] *a* dürftig, spärlich.

meal [mēl] *n* Essen *nt*, Mahlzeit *f*; (*grain*) Schrotmehl *nt*; **to have a ~** essen (gehen); **to go out for a ~** essen gehen *or* zum Essen gehen.

meal ticket *n* (*US*) Essensmarke *f*.

mealtime [mēl'tīm] *n* Essenszeit *f*.

mealy-mouthed [mē'lēmouthd] *a:* **to be ~** d(a)rum herumreden.

mean [mēn] *a* (*stingy*) geizig; (*spiteful*) gemein; (*shabby*) armselig, schäbig; (*aver-*

age) durchschnittlich, Durchschnitts-; (*US*: *vicious*: *animal*) bösartig; (: *person*) böse, bösartig ♦ *irreg vt* (*signify*) bedeuten ♦ *vi* (*intend*) vorhaben, beabsichtigen; (*be resolved*) entschlossen sein; **he ~s well** er meint es gut; **I ~ it!** ich meine das ernst!; **do you ~ me?** meinen Sie mich?; **it ~s nothing to me** es sagt mir nichts ♦ *n* (*average*) Durchschnitt *m*; *see also* **means**.

meander [mēan'dûr] *vi* sich schlängeln.

meaning [mē'ning] *n* Bedeutung *f*; (*of life*) Sinn *m*.

meaningful [mē'ningfəl] *a* bedeutungsvoll; (*life*) sinnvoll; **a ~ relationship** eine feste Beziehung.

meaningless [mē'ninglis] *a* sinnlos.

meanness [mēn'nis] *n* (*stinginess*) Geiz *m*; (*spitefulness*) Gemeinheit *f*; (*shabbiness*) Schäbigkeit *f*.

means [mēnz] *npl* Mittel *pl*; (*wealth*) Vermögen *nt*; **by ~ of** durch; **by all ~** selbstverständlich; **by no ~** keineswegs.

means test *n* Vermögensprüfung *f*.

meant [ment] *pt, pp of* **mean**.

meantime [mēn'tīm] *ad* inzwischen, mittlerweile.

meanwhile [mēn'wīl] *ad* inzwischen, mittlerweile.

measles [mē'zəlz] *n* Masern *pl*; **German ~** Röteln *pl*.

measly [mēz'lē] *a* (*col*) poplig.

measurable [mezh'ûrəbəl] *a* meßbar.

measure [mezh'ûr] *vti* messen ♦ *n* Maß *nt*; (*step*) Maßnahme *f*; **a liter ~** ein Litermaß; **some ~ of success** ein gewisses Maß an Erfolg; **to take ~s to do sth** Maßnahmen ergreifen, um etw zu tun; **to be a ~ of sth** etw erkennen lassen.

measure up *vi*: **to ~ up to sth** an etw (*acc*) herankommen, etw (*dat*) gewachsen sein.

measured [mezh'ûrd] *a* (*slow*) gemessen.

measurement [mezh'ûrmənt] *n* (*way of measuring*) Messung *f*; (*amount measured*) Maß *nt*; **to take sb's ~s** an *or* bei jdm Maß nehmen.

meat [mēt] *n* Fleisch *nt*; **cold ~s** (*Brit*) Aufschnitt *m*.

meatball [mēt'bôl] *n* Fleischkloß *m*.

meaty [mē'tē] *a* (*lit*) fleischig; (*fig*) gehaltvoll.

Mecca [mek'ə] *n* Mekka *nt* (*also fig*).

mechanic [məkan'ik] *n* Mechaniker *m*; *see also* **mechanics**.

mechanical [məkan'ikəl] *a* mechanisch.

mechanical engineering *n* (*science*) Maschinenbauwesen *nt*; (*industry*) Maschinenbau *m*.

mechanics [məkan'iks] *n sing* Mechanik *f*.

mechanism [mek'ənizəm] *n* Mechanismus *m*.

mechanization [mekənizā'shən] *n* Mechanisierung *f*.

mechanize [mek'ənīz] *vt* mechanisieren.

MEd *n abbr* (= *Master of Education*) akade-

mischer Grad für Lehrer.

medal [med'əl] *n* Medaille *f*; (*decoration*) Orden *m*.

medalist [med'əlist] *n* (*US*) Medaillengewinner(in *f*) *m*.

medallion [mədal'yən] *n* Medaillon *nt*.

medallist [med'əlist] *n* (*Brit*) Medaillengewinner(in *f*) *m*.

meddle [med'əl] *vi* sich einmischen (*in* in +*acc*); (*tamper*) hantieren (*with* an +*dat*); **to ~ with sb** sich mit jdm einlassen.

meddlesome [med'əlsəm] *a* (*interfering*): **she's a ~ old busybody** sie mischt sich dauernd in alles ein.

meddling [med'ling] *a* = **meddlesome**.

media [mē'dēə] *npl* Medien *pl*.

mediaeval [mēdēē'vəl] = **medieval**.

median [mē'dēən] *n* Median *m*.

median strip [mē'dēən strip] *n* (*US*) Mittelstreifen *m*; (*with grass*) Grünstreifen *m*.

media research *n* Medienforschung *f*.

mediate [mē'dēāt] *vi* vermitteln.

mediation [mēdēā'shən] *n* Vermittlung *f*.

mediator [mē'dēātûr] *n* Vermittler *m*.

medical [med'ikəl] *a* medizinisch; (*student*) Medizin-; (*treatment, examination*) ärztlich ♦ *n* (ärztliche) Untersuchung *f*.

medical certificate *n* (*report on health*) Gesundheitszeugnis *nt*.

Medicare [med'əkär] *n* (*US*) *staatliche Krankenversicherung und Gesundheitsfürsorge.*

medicated [med'ikātid] *a* medizinisch.

medication [medikā'shən] *n* (*drugs etc*) Medikamente *pl*.

medicinal [mədis'ənəl] *a* medizinisch, Heil-.

medicine [med'isin] *n* Medizin *f*; (*drugs*) Arznei *f*.

medicine chest *n* (*Brit*) Hausapotheke *f*.

medicine man *n* Medizinmann *m*.

medieval, mediaeval [mēdēē'vəl] *a* mittelalterlich.

mediocre [mē'dēōkûr] *a* mittelmäßig.

mediocrity [mēdēâk'ritē] *n* Mittelmäßigkeit *f*.

meditate [med'ətāt] *vi* nachdenken (*on* über +*acc*); (*REL*)meditieren (*on* über +*acc*).

meditation [medətā'shən] *n* Nachsinnen *nt*; (*REL*) Meditation *f*.

Mediterranean [meditərā'nēən] *a* Mittelmeer-; **~ Sea** Mittelmeer *nt*.

medium [mē'dēəm] *a* mittlere(r, s), Mittel-, mittel- ♦ *n* Mitte *f*; (*means*) Mittel *nt*; (*person*) Medium *nt*.

medium-sized [mē'dēəmsīzd] *a* (*tin etc*) mittelgroß; (*clothes*) mittel, mittlere Größe *f*.

medium wave *n* (*RAD*) Mittelwelle *f*.

medley [med'lē] *n* Gemisch *nt*.

meek [mēk], **meekly** [mēk'lē] *ad* sanft(mütig); (*pej*) duckmäuserisch.

meet [mēt] *irreg vt* (*encounter*) treffen, begegnen (+*dat*); (*by arrangement*) sich treffen mit; (*difficulties*) stoßen auf (+*acc*); (*become acquainted with*) kennenlernen; (*fetch*) abholen; (*join*) zusammentreffen

mit; (*river*) fließen in (+*acc*); (*satisfy*) entsprechen (+*dat*); (*debt*) bezahlen; (*bill, expenses*) begleichen; **pleased to** ~ **you!** guten Tag *or* Abend, (sehr) angenehm! (*form*)
♦ *vi* sich treffen; (*become acquainted*) sich kennenlernen; (*join*) sich treffen; (*rivers*) ineinanderfließen; (*roads*) zusammenlaufen
♦ *n* (*US SPORT*) Sportfest *nt*; (*Brit HUNTING*) Jagd(veranstaltung) *f*.
meet up *vi*: **to** ~ **up with sb** sich mit jdm treffen.
meet with *vt fus* (*problems*) stoßen auf (+*acc*); (*US: people*) zusammentreffen mit.
meeting [mē'ting] *n* Treffen *nt*; (*business* ~) Besprechung *f*, Konferenz *f*; (*discussion*) Sitzung *f*; (*assembly*) Versammlung *f*; (*SPORT: rally*) Veranstaltung *f*, Begegnung *f*; **to call a** ~ eine Sitzung *or* Versammlung einberufen.
meeting place *n* Treffpunkt *m*.
megabyte [meg'əbīt] *n* (*COMPUT*) Megabyte *nt*.
megalomaniac [megəlōmā'nēak] *n* Größenwahnsinnige(r) *mf*.
megaphone [meg'əfōn] *n* Megaphon *nt*.
melancholy [mel'ənkâlē] *n* Melancholie *f* ♦ *a* (*person*) melancholisch, schwermütig; (*sight, event*) traurig.
mellow [mel'ō] *a* mild, weich; (*fruit*) reif, weich; (*fig*) gesetzt ♦ *vi* reif werden.
melodious [məlō'dēəs] *a* wohlklingend.
melodrama [mel'ədrâmə] *n* Melodrama *nt*.
melodramatic [melədrəmat'ik] *a* melodramatisch.
melody [mel'ədē] *n* Melodie *f*.
melon [mel'ən] *n* Melone *f*.
melt [melt] *vi* schmelzen; (*anger*) verfliegen; (*butter*) zerlassen ♦ *vt* schmelzen.
melt away *vi* dahinschmelzen.
melt down *vt* einschmelzen.
meltdown [melt'doun] *n* Kernschmelze *f*.
melting point [melt'ing point] *n* Schmelzpunkt *m*.
melting pot [melt'ing pât] *n* (*fig*) Schmelztiegel *m*; **to be in the** ~ in der Schwebe sein.
member [mem'bûr] *n* (*of club, political party*) Mitglied *nt*; (*of tribe, species*) Angehörige(r) *mf*; (*ANAT*) Glied *nt*.
membership [mem'bûrship] *n* Mitgliedschaft *f*; **to seek** ~ einen Antrag auf Mitgliedschaft stellen.
membership card *n* Mitgliedsausweis *m*.
membrane [mem'brān] *n* Membrane *f*.
memento [məmen'tō] *n* Andenken *nt*.
memo [mem'ō] *n* *abbr* (= *memorandum*) Memo *nt*.
memoirs [mem'wârz] *npl* Memoiren *pl*.
memo pad *n* Notizblock *m*.
memorable [mem'ûrəbəl] *a* denkwürdig.
memorandum [meməran'dəm] *n* Notiz *f*; (*in business*) Mitteilung *f*; (*POL*) Memorandum *nt*.
memorial [məmô'rēəl] *n* Denkmal *nt* ♦ *a* Gedenk-.

memorize [mem'ərīz] *vt* sich einprägen.
memory [mem'ûrē] *n* Gedächtnis *nt*; (*of computer*) Speicher *m*; (*sth recalled*) Erinnerung *f*; **in** ~ **of** zur Erinnerung an (+*acc*); **from** ~ aus dem Kopf; **to have a good/bad** ~ ein gutes/schlechtes Gedächtnis haben; **loss of** ~ Gedächtnisschwund *m*.
men [men] *npl of* **man.**
menace [men'is] *n* Drohung *f*; (*danger*) Gefahr *f*; (*col: nuisance*) (Land)plage *f*; **a public** ~ eine Gefahr für die Öffentlichkeit ♦ *vt* bedrohen.
menacing [men'ising] *a*, **menacingly** [men'isinglē] *ad* drohend.
ménage [mānâzh'] *n* Haushalt *m*.
menagerie [mənaj'ûrē] *n* Tierschau *f*.
mend [mend] *vt* reparieren, flicken ♦ *vi* (ver)heilen ♦ *n* ausgebesserte Stelle *f*; **on the** ~ auf dem Wege der Besserung.
mending [mend'ing] *n* (*articles*) Flickarbeit *f*.
menial [mē'nēəl] *a* niedrig, untergeordnet.
meningitis [meninji'tis] *n* Hirnhautentzündung *f*, Meningitis *f*.
menopause [men'əpôz] *n* Wechseljahre *pl*, Menopause *f*.
menstrual [men'strōōəl] *a* Monats-, Menstruations-.
menstruate [men'strōōāt] *vi* menstruieren.
menstruation [menstrōōā'shən] *n* Menstruation *f*.
mental [men'təl] *a* geistig, Geistes-; (*arithmetic*) Kopf-; (*hospital*) Nerven-; (*cruelty*) seelisch; (*col: mad*) verrückt.
mental illness *n* Geisteskrankheit *f*.
mentality [mental'itē] *n* Mentalität *f*.
mentally [men'təlē] *ad* geistig; ~ **ill** geisteskrank; **to be** ~ **handicapped** geistig behindert sein.
menthol [men'thôl] *n* Menthol *nt*.
mention [men'chən] *n* Erwähnung *f* ♦ *vt* erwähnen; (*names*) nennen; **don't** ~ **it!** (sehr), gern geschehen; **I need hardly** ~ **that ...** es versteht sich wohl von selbst, daß ...; **not to** ~, **without** ~**ing** nicht zu vergessen, geschweige denn.
mentor [men'tûr] *n* Mentor *m*.
menu [men'yōō] *n* Speisekarte *f*; (*food*) Speisen *pl*; (*COMPUT*) Menü *nt*.
menu-driven [men'yōōdriv'ən] *a* (*COMPUT*) menügesteuert.
meow [mēou'] *vi* (*US*) miauen.
MEP *n abbr* (*Brit*: = *Member of the European Parliament*) Mitglied *nt* des Europäischen Parlaments.
mercantile [mûr'kəntil] *a* Handels-.
mercenary [mûr'sənerē] *a* (*person*) geldgierig; (*MIL*) Söldner- ♦ *n* Söldner *m*.
merchandise [mûr'chəndīs] *n* (Handels)ware *f*.
merchandiser [mûr'chəndīzûr] *n* Fachmann *m* für Warengestaltung.
merchant [mûr'chənt] *n* Kaufmann *m* ♦ *a* Handels-.

merchant bank n (Brit) Handelsbank f.
merchantman [mûr'chəntmən] n, pl -men Handelsschiff f.
merchant marine, (Brit) **merchant navy** n Handelsmarine f.
merciful [mûr'sifəl] a gnädig, barmherzig.
mercifully [mûr'sifəlē] ad barmherzig, gnädig; (fortunately) glücklicherweise, zum Glück.
merciless [mûr'silis] a, **mercilessly** [mûr'silislē] ad erbarmunglos.
mercurial [mûrkyōō'rēəl] a quecksilbrig, Quecksilber-.
mercury [mûrk'yûrē] n Quecksilber nt.
mercy [mûr'sē] n Erbarmen nt; (in judgement) Gnade f; (blessing) Segen m; **at the ~ of** ausgeliefert (+dat).
mercy killing n Euthanasie f.
mere [mēr] a, **merely** [mēr'lē] ad bloß.
merge [mûrj] vt verbinden; (COMM) fusionieren; (COMPUT: files, text) mischen ♦ vi verschmelzen; (roads) zusammenlaufen; (COMM) fusionieren; **to ~ into** übergehen in (+acc).
merger [mûr'jûr] n (COMM) Fusion f.
meridian [mərid'ēən] n Meridian m.
meringue [mərang'] n Baiser nt, Meringue f.
merit [mär'it] n Verdienst nt; (advantage) Vorzug m; **to judge on ~** nach Leistung beurteilen ♦ vt verdienen.
meritocracy [märiták'rəsē] n Leistungsgesellschaft f.
mermaid [mûr'mād] n Wassernixe f, Meerjungfrau f.
merrily [mär'ilē] ad lustig.
merriment [mär'imənt] n Fröhlichkeit f; (laughter) Gelächter nt.
merry [mär'ē] a fröhlich; (col) angeheitert; **M~ Christmas!** Frohe Weihnachten!
merry-go-round [mär'ēgōround] n Karussell nt.
mesh [mesh] n Masche f ♦ vi (gears) ineinandergreifen.
mesmerize [mez'mərīz] vt hypnotisieren; (fig) faszinieren.
mess [mes] n Unordnung f; (dirt) Schmutz m; (trouble) Schwierigkeiten pl; (MIL) Messe f; **to look a ~** fürchterlich aussehen; **to make a ~ of sth** etw verpfuschen; **to be (in) a ~** unordentlich sein; (fig) verkorkst sein (col).
mess around vi (tinker with) herummurksen (with an +dat); (play the fool) herumalbern; (do nothing in particular) herumgammeln.
mess up vt verpfuschen; (make untidy) in Unordnung bringen.
message [mes'ij] n Mitteilung f, Nachricht f; **to get the ~** kapieren.
message switching n Speichervermittlung f.
messenger [mes'injûr] n Bote m.
Messiah [misī'ə] n Messias m.
Messrs, Messrs. [mes'ûrz] abbr (on letters: =

messieurs) An die Herren.
messy [mes'ē] a schmutzig; (untidy) unordentlich; (confused: situation etc) durcheinander.
met [met] pt, pp of **meet** ♦ a abbr (Brit) = **meteorological.**
Met [met] n abbr (US: = Metropolitan Opera) Met f.
metabolism [mətab'əlizəm] n Stoffwechsel m.
metal [met'əl] n Metall nt.
metallic [mital'ik] a metallisch.
metallurgy [met'əlûrjē] n Metallurgie f.
metalwork [met'əlwûrk] n (craft) Schmiedehandwerk nt.
metamorphosis [metəmôr'fəsis] n Metamorphose f.
metaphor [met'əfôr] n Metapher f.
metaphorical [metəfôr'ikəl] a bildlich, metaphorisch.
metaphysics [metəfiz'iks] n sing Metaphysik f.
meteor [mē'tēôr] n Meteor m.
meteoric [mētēôr'ik] a meteorisch, Meteor-; (fig) kometenhaft.
meteorite [mē'tēərīt] n Meteorit m.
meteorological [mētēûrəlâj'ikəl] a meteorologisch.
meteorology [mētēərál'əjē] n Meteorologie f.
meter [mē'tûr] n (machine) Zähler m; (US: measurement) Meter m or nt; (verse) Metrum nt.
methane [meth'ān] n Methan nt.
method [meth'əd] n Methode f; **~ of payment** Zahlungsweise f.
methodical [məthâd'ikəl] a methodisch.
Methodist [meth'ədist] a methodistisch ♦ n Methodist(in f) m.
methodology [methədâl'əjē] n Methodik f.
meths [meths] n abbr (Brit) = **methylated spirits.**
methylated spirits [meth'əlātid spir'its] n (Brit) (Brenn)spiritus m.
meticulous [mətik'yələs] a (über)genau.
metre [mē'tûr] n (Brit) Meter m or nt; (verse) Metrum nt.
metric [met'rik] a (also: **metrical**) metrisch; **to go ~** auf das metrische Maßsystem umstellen.
metrication [metrikā'shən] n Umstellung f auf das Dezimalsystem.
metric system n metrische(s) System nt.
metric ton n Metertonne f.
metronome [met'rənōm] n Metronom nt.
metropolis [mitrâp'əlis] n Metropole f.
metropolitan [metrəpâl'itən] a städtisch; **the M~ Police** (Brit) die Londoner Polizei.
mettle [met'əl] n Mut m.
mew [myōō] vi (cat) miauen.
mews flat [myōōz flat] n (Brit) Wohnung in einem umgebauten Kutscherhaus.
Mexican [mek'səkən] a mexikanisch ♦ n Mexikaner(in f) m.
Mexico [mek'səkō] n Mexiko nt; **~ City** Mexiko nt.

mezzanine [mez'ənēn] *n* Hochparterre *nt*.
MFA *n abbr* (*US:* = *Master of Fine Arts*) akademischer Grad in Kunst.
mfr *abbr* (= *manufacture, manufacturer*) Herst.
mg *abbr* (= *milligram*) mg.
mgr *abbr* (= *manager*) Manager *m*.
Mgr *abbr* (= *Monseigneur, Monsignor*) Mgr.
MHR *n abbr* (*US:* = *Member of the House of Representatives*) Mitglied des Unterhauses des amerikanischen Kongresses.
MHz *abbr* (= *megahertz*) MHz.
MI *abbr* (*US MAIL*) = *Michigan*.
MI5 *n abbr* (*Brit:* = *Military Intelligence 5*) ≈ SD.
MI6 *n abbr* (*Brit:* = *Military Intelligence 6*) ≈ BND.
MIA *abbr* (= *missing in action*) verm.
mice [mīs] *npl of* **mouse**.
Mich. *abbr* (*US*) = *Michigan*.
microbe [mī'krōb] *n* Mikrobe *f*.
microbiology [mīkrōbīâl'əjē] *n* Mikrobiologie *f*.
microchip [mī'krəchip] *n* (*ELEC*) Mikrochip *nt*.
microcomputer [mīkrōkəmpyōō'tûr] *n* Mikro- or Kleincomputer *m*.
microcosm [mī'krəkázəm] *n* Mikrokosmos *m*.
microeconomics [mīkrōēkənâm'iks] *npl* Mikroökonomie *f*.
microfiche [mī'krōfēsh] *n* Mikrofiche *m*.
microfilm [mī'krəfilm] *n* Mikrofilm *m*.
micrometer [mīkrâm'itûr] *n* Mikrometer *m*.
microphone [mī'krəfōn] *n* Mikrophon *nt*.
microprocessor [mīkrōprâs'esûr] *n* Mikroprozessor *m*.
microscope [mī'krəskōp] *n* Mikroskop *nt*; **under the** ~ unter dem Mikroskop.
microscopic [mī'krəskâp'ik] *a* mikroskopisch.
microwave [mī'krōwāv] *n* (*also:* ~ **oven**) Mikrowelle(nherd) *nt*.
mid [mid] *a* mitten in (+*dat*); **in the** ~ **eighties** Mitte der achtziger Jahre; **he's in his** ~ **thirties** er ist Mitte dreißig; **in** ~ **course** mittendrin.
midday [mid'dā] *n* Mittag *m*.
middle [mid'əl] *n* Mitte *f*; (*waist*) Taille *f*; **in the** ~ **of** mitten in (+*dat*); **I'm in the** ~ **of reading it** ich lese es gerade, ich bin mittendrin ♦ *a* mittlere(r, s), Mittel-; **the** ~ **Ages** *pl* das Mittelalter; **the M**~ **East** der Nahe Osten.
middle-aged [mid'əlājd'] *a* mittleren Alters.
middle-class [mid'əlklas] *n* Mittelstand *m* or -klasse *f* ♦ *a* Mittelstands-, Mittelklassen-.
middleman [mid'əlman] *n, pl* **-men** (*COMM*) Zwischenhändler *m*.
middle management *n* mittlere(s) Management *nt*.
middle name *n* zweite(r) Vorname *m*.
middle-of-the-road [mid'ələvthərōd'] *a* gemäßigt.
middleweight [mid'əlwāt] *n* (*BOXING*) Mittelgewicht *nt*.

middling [mid'ling] *a* mittelmäßig.
Middx *abbr* (*Brit*) = *Middlesex*.
midge [mij] *n* Mücke *f*.
midget [mij'it] *n* Liliputaner(in *f*) *m* ♦ *a* Kleinst-.
Midlands [mid'ləndz] *npl* die Midlands *pl*.
midnight [mid'nīt] *n* Mitternacht *f*; **at** ~ um Mitternacht.
midriff [mid'rif] *n* Taille *f*.
midst [midst] *n*: **in the** ~ **of** (*persons*) mitten unter (+*dat*); (*things*) mitten in (+*dat*); **in our** ~ unter uns.
midsummer [mid'sum'ûr] *n* Hochsommer *m*.
Midsummer's Day *n* Sommersonnenwende *f*.
midway [mid'wā] *ad* auf halbem Wege ♦ *a* Mittel-.
midweek [mid'wēk] *ad* mitten in der Woche.
midwife [mid'wīf] *n, pl* **midwives** [mid'wīvz] Hebamme *f*.
midwifery [mid'wīfûrē] *n* Geburtshilfe *f*.
midwinter [mid'win'tûr] *n* tiefste(r) Winter *m*.
might [mīt] *n* Macht *f*, Kraft *f* ♦ *pt of* **may; I** ~ **come** ich komme vielleicht.
mightily [mī'təlē] *ad* mächtig.
mightn't = **might not**.
mighty [mī'tē] *a, ad* mächtig.
migraine [mī'grān] *n* Migräne *f*.
migrant [mī'grənt] *n* (*bird*) Zugvogel *m*; (*worker*) Saison- *or* Wanderarbeiter *m* ♦ *a* Wander-; (*bird*) Zug-.
migrate [mī'grāt] *vi* (ab)wandern; (*birds*) (fort)ziehen.
migration [mīgrā'shən] *n* Wanderung *f*, Zug *m*.
mike [mīk] *n* = **microphone**.
Milan [milan'] *n* Mailand *nt*.
mild [mīld] *a* mild; (*medicine, interest*) leicht; (*person*) sanft.
mildew [mil'dōō] *n* (*on plants*) Mehltau *m*; (*on food*) Schimmel *m*.
mildly [mīld'lē] *ad* leicht; **to put it** ~ gelinde gesagt.
mildness [mīld'nis] *n* Milde *f*.
mile [mīl] *n* Meile *f*; **how many** ~**s per gallon does your car do?** ≈ wieviel verbraucht Ihr Auto?
mileage [mī'lij] *n* Meilenzahl *f*.
mileage allowance *n* Kilometergeld *nt*.
mileometer [mīlâm'itûr] *n* (*Brit*) = **milometer**.
milestone [mīl'stōn] *n* (*lit, fig*) Meilenstein *m*.
milieu [mēlyōō'] *n* Milieu *nt*.
militant [mil'ətənt] *n* Militante(r) *mf* ♦ *a* militant.
militarism [mil'itərizəm] *n* Militarismus *m*.
militaristic [militəris'tik] *a* militaristisch.
military [mil'itärē] *a* militärisch, Militär-, Wehr- ♦ *n* Militär *nt*.
militate [mil'ətāt] *vi* sprechen (*against* gegen).
militia [milish'ə] *n* Miliz *f*, Bürgerwehr *f*.

milk [milk] *n* Milch *f* ♦ *vt* (*lit*, *fig*) melken.
milk chocolate *n* Milchschokolade *f*.
milk float *n* (*Brit*) Milchwagen *m*.
milking [mil'king] *n* Melken *nt*.
milkman [milk'man] *n*, *pl* **-men** Milchmann *m*.
milk shake *n* Milchmixgetränk *nt*.
milk tooth *n* Milchzahn *m*.
milk truck *n* (*US*) Milchwagen *m*.
milky [mil'kē] *a* milchig.
Milky Way *n* Milchstraße *f*.
mill [mil] *n* Mühle *f*; (*factory*) Fabrik *f* ♦ *vt* mahlen ♦ *vi* (*move around*) umherlaufen.
milled [mild] *a* gemahlen.
millennium [milen'ēəm] *n* Jahrtausend *nt*.
miller [mil'ûr] *n* Müller *m*.
millet [mil'it] *n* Hirse *f*.
milligram(me) [mil'əgram] *n* Milligramm *nt*.
milliliter, (Brit) millilitre [mil'əlētûr] *n* Milliliter *m*.
millimeter, (Brit) millimetre [mil'əmētûr] *n* Millimeter *m*.
milliner [mil'inûr] *n* Hutmacher(in *f*) *m*.
millinery [mil'ənärē] *n* (*hats*) Hüte *pl*, Modewaren *pl*; (*business*) Hutgeschäft *nt*.
million [mil'yən] *n* Million *f*.
millionaire [milyənär'] *n* Millionär(in *f*) *m*.
millipede [mil'əpēd] *n* Tausendfüßler *m*.
millstone [mil'stōn] *n* Mühlstein *m*.
mill wheel *n* Mühlrad *nt*.
milometer [mī'lōmētûr] *n* (*Brit*) ≈ Kilometerzähler *m*.
mime [mīm] *n* Pantomime *f*; (*actor*) Mime *m*, Mimin *f* ♦ *vti* mimen.
mimic [mim'ik] *n* Mimiker *m* ♦ *vt* nachahmen.
mimicry [mim'ikrē] *n* Nachahmung *f*; (*BIOL*) Mimikry *f*.
min. *abbr* (= *minute*) Min.; (= *minimum*) min.
Min. *abbr* (*Brit POL*: = *Ministry*) Min.
minaret [minəret'] *n* Minarett *nt*.
mince [mins] *vt* (zer)hacken ♦ *vi* (*walk*) trippeln ♦ *n* (*Brit*: *meat*) Hackfleisch *nt*.
mincemeat [mins'mēt] *n* süße Pastetenfüllung *f*.
mince pie *n* gefüllte (süße) Pastete .
mincing [min'sing] *a* (*manner*) affektiert.
mind [mīnd] *n* Verstand *m*, Geist *m*; (*opinion*) Meinung *f*; **on my ~** auf dem Herzen; **to my ~** meiner Meinung nach; **to be out of one's ~** wahnsinnig sein; **to bear** *or* **keep in ~** bedenken, nicht vergessen; **to change one's ~** es sich (*dat*) anders überlegen; **to make up one's ~** sich entschließen; **to have sb in ~** an jdn denken; **to have sth in ~** an etw (*acc*) denken; (*intend*) etw beabsichtigen; **to have a good ~ to do sth** große Lust haben, etw zu tun; **it went right out of my ~** das habe ich total vergessen; **to bring** *or* **call sth to ~** etw in Erinnerung rufen; **to be in** *or* **of two ~s about sth** sich (*dat*) über etw (*acc*) nicht im Klaren sein ♦ *vt* aufpassen auf (+*acc*); (*object to*) etwas

haben gegen; **I don't ~ the rain** der Regen macht mir nichts aus; **~ your own business** kümmern Sie sich um Ihre eigenen Angelegenheiten ♦ *vi* etwas dagegen haben; **do you ~ if I ...?** macht es Ihnen etwas aus, wenn ich ...?; **do you ~!** na hören Sie mal!; **never ~!** macht nichts!
-minded [mīnd'id] *suff*: **fair~** gerecht; **an industrially~ nation** ein auf Industrie ausgerichtetes Land.
minder [mīnd'ûr] *n* Aufpasser(in *f*) *m*.
mindful [mīnd'fəl] *a* achtsam (*of* auf +*acc*).
mindless [mīnd'lis] *a* achtlos, dumm; (*violence, crime*) sinnlos.
mine [mīn] *poss pron* meine(r, s) ♦ *n* (*coal~*) Bergwerk *nt*; (*MIL*) Mine *f*; (*source*) Fundgrube *f* ♦ *vt* abbauen; (*MIL*) verminen ♦ *vi* Bergbau betreiben; **to ~ for sth** etw gewinnen.
mine detector *n* Minensuchgerät *nt*.
minefield [mīn'fēld] *n* Minenfeld *nt*.
miner [mīn'ûr] *n* Bergarbeiter *m*.
mineral [min'ûrəl] *a* mineralisch, Mineral- ♦ *n* Mineral *nt*.
mineral water *n* Mineralwasser *nt*.
minesweeper [mīn'swēpûr] *n* Minensuchboot *nt*.
mingle [ming'gəl] *vt* vermischen ♦ *vi* sich mischen (*with* unter +*acc*).
mingy [min'jē] *a* (*col*) knickerig.
mini [min'ē] *pref* Mini-, Klein-.
miniature [min'ēəchûr] *a* Miniatur-, Klein- ♦ *n* Miniatur *f*; **in ~** en miniature.
miniature golf *n* Minigolf *nt*.
minibus [min'ēbus] *n* Kleinbus *m*, Minibus *m*.
minicab [min'ēkab] *n* Kleintaxi *nt*.
minicomputer [min'ēkəmpyōōtûr] *n* Minicomputer *m*, Minirechner *m*.
minim [min'əm] *n* (*Brit*) halbe Note *f*.
minimal [min'əməl] *a* kleinste(r, s), minimal, Mindest-.
minimize [min'əmīz] *vt* auf das Mindestmaß beschränken; (*belittle*) herabsetzen.
minimum [min'əməm] *n* Minimum *nt*; **to reduce to a ~** auf ein Minimum reduzieren ♦ *a* Mindest-.
minimum wage *n* Mindestlohn *m*.
mining [mī'ning] *n* Bergbau *m* ♦ *a* Bergbau-, Berg-.
minion [min'yən] *n* (*pej*) Trabant *m*.
miniskirt [min'ēskûrt] *n* Minirock *m*.
minister [min'istûr] *n* (*POL*) Minister *m*; (*ECCL*) Geistliche(r) *m*, Pfarrer *m* ♦ *vi*: **to ~ to sb** sich um jdn kümmern.
ministerial [ministēr'ēəl] *a* ministeriell, Minister-.
ministry [min'istrē] *n* (*ECCL*: *office*) geistliche(s) Amt *nt*; (*Brit*: *government body*) Ministerium *nt*.
Ministry of Defence *n* (*Brit*) Verteidigungsministerium *nt*.
mink [mingk] *n* Nerz *m*.
Minn. *abbr* (*US*) = *Minnesota*.
minnow [min'ō] *n* Elritze *f*.

minor [mī'nûr] *a* kleiner; *(operation)* leicht; *(problem, poet)* unbedeutend; *(MUS)* Moll ♦ *n* *(US UNIV)* Nebenfach *nt*; *(Brit: under 18)* Minderjährige(r) *mf*.

Minorca [minôr'kə] *n* Menorca *nt*.

minority [minôr'itē] *n* Minderheit *f*; **to be in a ~ in** der Minderheit sein.

minority interest *n* Minderheitsbeteiligung *f*.

minster [min'stûr] *n* Münster *nt*, Kathedrale *f*.

minstrel [min'strəl] *n* *(HIST)* Spielmann *m*, Minnesänger *m*.

mint [mint] *n* Minze *f*; *(sweet)* Pfefferminzbonbon *nt*; *(place)* Münzstätte *f* ♦ *a* *(condition)* (wie) neu; *(stamp)* ungestempelt.

mint sauce *n* Minzsoße *f*.

minuet [minyōōet'] *n* Menuett *nt*.

minus [mī'nəs] *n* Minuszeichen *nt*; *(amount)* Minusbetrag *m* ♦ *prep* minus, weniger.

minuscule [min'əskyōōl] *a* winzig.

minute *a* [mīnōōt'] winzig, sehr klein; **in ~ detail** minuziös ♦ *n* [min'it] Minute *f*; *(moment)* Augenblick *m*; **it is 5 ~s past 3** es ist 5 Minuten nach 3; **wait a ~!** einen Augenblick!; **up to the ~** auf dem neuesten Stand; *see also* **minutes.**

minute book *n* Protokollbuch *nt*.

minute hand *n* Minutenzeiger *m*.

minutely [mīnōōt'lē] *ad* *(in detail)* genau; *(by a small amount)* ganz geringfügig.

minutes [min'its] *npl* *(official record)* Protokoll *nt*.

miracle [mir'əkəl] *n* Wunder *nt*.

miracle play *n* geistliche(s) Drama *nt*.

miraculous [mirak'yələs] *a* wunderbar.

miraculously [mirak'yələslē] *ad* auf wunderbare Weise.

mirage [mirázh'] *n* Luftspiegelung *f*, Fata Morgana *f*.

mire [mī'ûr] *n* Morast *m*.

mirror [mir'ûr] *n* Spiegel *m* ♦ *vt* (wider)spiegeln.

mirror image *n* Spiegelbild *nt*.

mirth [mûrth] *n* Freude *f*; *(laughter)* Heiterkeit *f*.

misadventure [misədven'chûr] *n* Mißgeschick *nt*, Unfall *m*.

misanthropist [misan'thrəpist] *n* Menschenfeind *m*.

misapply [misəplī'] *vt* falsch anwenden.

misapprehension [misaprihen'chən] *n* Mißverständnis *nt*; **to be under the ~ that ...** irrtümlicherweise annehmen, daß...

misappropriate [misəprō'prēāt] *vt* *(funds)* veruntreuen.

misappropriation [misəprōprēā'shən] *n* Veruntreuung *f*.

misbehave [misbihāv'] *vi* sich schlecht benehmen.

misc. *abbr* = **miscellaneous.**

miscalculate [miskal'kyəlāt] *vt* falsch berechnen ♦ *vi* sich verrechnen.

miscalculation [miskalkyəlā'shən] *n* Rechenfehler *m*.

miscarriage [miskar'ij] *n* *(MED)* Fehlgeburt *f*; **~ of justice** Fehlurteil *nt*.

miscarry [miskar'ē] *vi* *(MED)* eine Fehlgeburt haben; *(fail: plans)* fehllaufen *or* -schlagen.

miscellaneous [misəlā'nēəs] *a* verschieden; **~ expenses** sonstige Unkosten *pl*.

miscellany [mis'əlānē] *n* (bunte) Sammlung *f*.

mischance [mischans'] *n* Mißgeschick *nt*; **by (some) ~** durch einen unglücklichen Zufall.

mischief [mis'chif] *n* Unfug *m*; *(harm)* Schaden *m*.

mischievous [mis'chəvəs] *a*, **mischievously** [mis'chəvəslē] *ad* *(person)* durchtrieben; *(glance)* verschmitzt; *(rumor)* bösartig.

misconception [miskənsep'shən] *n* fälschliche Annahme *f*.

misconduct [miskân'dukt] *n* Vergehen *nt*.

misconstrue [miskənstrōō'] *vt* mißverstehen.

miscount [miskount'] *vt* falsch (be)rechnen ♦ *vi* sich verzählen.

misdeed [misdēd'] *n* *(old)* Missetat *f*.

misdemeanor, *(Brit)* **misdemeanour** [misdimē'nûr] *n* Vergehen *nt*.

misdirect [misdirekt'] *vt* *(person)* irreleiten; *(letter)* fehlleiten.

miser [mī'zûr] *n* Geizhals *m*.

miserable [miz'ûrəbəl] *a* *(unhappy)* unglücklich; *(headache, weather)* fürchterlich; *(poor)* elend; *(contemptible)* erbärmlich; **to feel ~** sich elend fühlen.

miserably [miz'ûrəblē] *ad* unglücklich; *(fail)* kläglich; *(wretchedly: live)* elend, jämmerlich; *(pay)* miserabel.

miserly [mī'zûrlē] *a* geizig.

misery [miz'ûrē] *n* Elend *nt*, Qual *f*.

misfire [misfīr'] *vi* *(gun)* versagen; *(engine)* fehlzünden; *(plan)* fehlgehen.

misfit [mis'fit] *n* Außenseiter *m*.

misfortune [misfôr'chən] *n* Unglück *nt*.

misgiving [misgiv'ing] *n* *(often pl)* Befürchtung *f*, Bedenken *pl*; **to have ~s about sth** sich bei etw *(dat)* nicht wohl fühlen.

misguided [misgī'did] *a* irregeleitet; *(opinions)* irrig.

mishandle [mis·han'dəl] *vt* falsch handhaben.

mishap [mis'hap] *n* Unglück *nt*; *(slight)* Panne *f*.

mishear [mis·hiûr'] *vt irreg* falsch hören, sich verhören.

mishmash [mish'mash] *n* *(col)* Mischmasch *m*.

misinform [misinfôrm'] *vt* falsch unterrichten.

misinterpret [misintûr'prit] *vt* falsch auffassen.

misinterpretation [misintûrpritā'shən] *n* falsche Auslegung *f*.

misjudge [misjuj'] *vt* falsch beurteilen.

mislay [mislā'] *vt irreg* verlegen.

mislead [mislēd'] *vt irreg* *(deceive)* irreführen.

misleading [mislē'ding] *a* irreführend.

misled [misled'] *pt, pp of* **mislead.**

mismanage [misman'ij] *vt* schlecht verwalten.

mismanagement [misman'ijmənt] *n* Mißwirtschaft *f*.

misnomer [misnō'mûr] *n* falsche Bezeichnung *f*.

misogynist [misâj'ənist] *n* Frauenfeind *m*.

misplace [misplās'] *vt* verlegen; **to be ~d** (*trust etc*) fehl am Platz *or* unangebracht sein.

misprint [mis'print] *n* Druckfehler *m*.

mispronounce [misprənouns'] *vt* falsch aussprechen.

misquote [miskwōt'] *vt* falsch zitieren.

misread [misrēd'] *vt irreg* falsch lesen.

misrepresent [misreprizent'] *vt* falsch darstellen.

misrepresentation [misreprizentā'shən] *n* (*JUR*) falsche Angaben *pl*.

miss [mis] *vt* (*fail to hit or catch*) verfehlen; (*not notice*) verpassen; (*be too late for*) versäumen, verpassen; (*omit*) auslassen; (*regret the absence of*) vermissen; (*escape*) entgehen (*+gen*); (*avoid: obstacle*) (noch) ausweichen können (*+dat*); **you're ~ing the point** das geht an der Sache vorbei; **the bus just ~ed the wall** der Bus wäre um ein Haar gegen die Mauer gefahren; **I ~ you** du fehlst mir ♦ *vi* nicht treffen; (*not attend*) fehlen ♦ *n* (*shot*) Fehlschuß *m*; (*failure*) Fehlschlag *m*; (*title*) Fräulein *nt*.

miss out *vt* (*Brit*) auslassen.

miss out on *vt fus* verpassen.

Miss. [mis] *abbr* (*US*) = *Mississippi*.

missal [mis'əl] *n* Meßbuch *nt*.

misshapen [mis·shā'pən] *a* mißgestaltet.

missile [mis'əl] *n* Geschoß *nt*, Rakete *f*.

missile base *n* Raketenbasis *f*.

missile launcher *n* Abschuß- *or* Startrampe *f*.

missing [mis'ing] *a* (*person*) vermißt; (*thing*) fehlend; **to be ~** fehlen.

missing person *n* Vermißte(r) *mf*.

mission [mish'ən] *n* (*work*) Auftrag *m*, Mission *f*; (*people*) Delegation *f*; (*REL*) Mission *f*; **he's on a secret ~** er ist in geheimer Mission unterwegs.

missionary [mish'ənärē] *n* Missionar(in *f*) *m*.

misspell [misspel'] *vt* falsch schreiben.

misspent [misspent'] *a* (*youth*) vergeudet.

mist [mist] *n* Dunst *m*, Nebel *m* ♦ *vi* (*also: ~ over, ~ up*) sich beschlagen.

mistake [mistāk'] *n* Fehler *m*; **to make a ~** sich irren (*about sb/sth* in jdm/etw); (*in writing, calculating etc*) einen Fehler machen; **by ~** aus Versehen ♦ *vt irreg* (*misunderstand*) mißverstehen; (*mix up*) verwechseln (*for* mit).

mistaken [mistā'kən] *a* (*idea*) falsch; **to be ~** sich irren ♦ *pp of* **mistake**.

mistaken identity *n* Verwechslung *f*.

mistakenly [mistā'kənlē] *ad* versehentlich.

mister [mis'tûr] *n* Herr *m*.

mistletoe [mis'əltō] *n* Mistel *f*.

mistook [mistōōk'] *pt of* **mistake**.

mistranslation [mistranzlā'shən] *n* falsche Übersetzung *f*.

mistreat [mistrēt'] *vt* schlecht behandeln.

mistress [mis'tris] *n* (*in house*) Herrin *f*; (*lover*) Geliebte *f*; (*title*) Frau *f*; (*Brit: teacher*) Lehrerin *f*.

mistrust [mistrust'] *vt* mißtrauen (*+dat*) ♦ *n* Mißtrauen *nt* (*of* gegenüber).

mistrustful [mistrust'fəl] *a* mißtrauisch (*of* gegenüber).

misty [mis'tē] *a* neblig.

misty-eyed [mis'tēīd'] *a* verträumt, mit verschleiertem Blick.

misunderstand [misundûrstand'] *vti irreg* mißverstehen, falsch verstehen.

misunderstanding [misundûrstan'ding] *n* Mißverständnis *nt*; (*disagreement*) Meinungsverschiedenheit *f*.

misunderstood [misundûrstōōd'] *a* (*person*) unverstanden.

misuse *n* [misyōōs'] falsche(r) Gebrauch *m* ♦ *vt* [misyōōz'] falsch gebrauchen.

MIT *n abbr* (*US*) = *Massachusetts Institute of Technology*.

miter [mī'tûr] *n* (*US ECCL*) Mitra *f*.

mitigate [mit'əgāt] *vt* (*pain*) lindern; (*punishment*) mildern; **mitigating circumstances** mildernde Umstände *pl*.

mitigation [mitəgā'shən] *n* Linderung *f*, Milderung *f*.

mitre [mī'tûr] *n* (*Brit ECCL*) = **miter**.

mitt(en) [mit'(ən)] *n* Fausthandschuh *m*.

mix [miks] *vt* (*blend*) (ver)mischen; **to ~ business with pleasure** das Angenehme mit dem Nützlichen verbinden ♦ *vi* (*liquids*) sich (ver)mischen lassen; (*people: get on*) sich vertragen; (: *associate*) Kontakt haben; **he ~es well** er ist kontaktfreudig ♦ *n* (*mixture*) Mischung *f*; **cake ~** Backmischung *f*.

mix in *vt* (*eggs etc*) unterrühren.

mix up *vt* (*mix*) zusammenmischen; (*confuse*) verwechseln; **to be ~ed up in sth** in etw (*acc*) verwickelt sein.

mixed [mikst] *a* gemischt.

mixed doubles *npl* (*SPORT*) gemischte(s) Doppel *nt*.

mixed economy *n* gemischte Wirtschaftsform *f*.

mixed grill *n* (*Brit*) Grillteller *m*.

mixed-up [mikst'up] *a* (*papers, person*) durcheinander.

mixer [mik'sûr] *n* (*for food*) Mixer *m*.

mixture [miks'chûr] *n* (*assortment*) Mischung *f*; (*MED*) Saft *m*.

mix-up [miks'up] *n* Durcheinander *nt*, Verwechslung *f*.

mk *abbr* (*FIN*) = **mark**.

Mk *abbr* (*Brit TECH*) = **mark**.

mkt *abbr* (= *market*) Markt *m*.

MLitt *n abbr* (= *Master of Literature, Master of Letters*) *akademischer Grad*.

MLR *n abbr* (*Brit*: = *minimum lending rate*) *Mindestzins*.

mm *abbr* (= *millimeter(s)*) mm.
MN *abbr* (*US MAIL*) = *Minnesota*; (*Brit*: = *Merchant Navy*) HM *f*.
mo *abbr* = *month*.
m.o. *abbr* = **money order**.
MO *n abbr* = *medical officer*; (*col*: *esp US*) = **modus operandi** ♦ *abbr* (*US MAIL*) = *Missouri*.
moan [mōn] *n* Stöhnen *nt*; (*complaint*) Klage *f* ♦ *vi* stöhnen; (*complain*) maulen.
moaning [mō'ning] *n* Stöhnen *nt*; Gemaule *nt*.
moat [mōt] *n* (Burg)graben *m*.
mob [mâb] *n* Mob *m*; (*the masses*) Pöbel *m* ♦ *vt* (*star*) herfallen über (+*acc*).
mobile [mō'bəl] *a* beweglich; (*library etc*) fahrbar ♦ *n* (*decoration*) Mobile *nt*.
mobile home *n* Wohnwagen *m*.
mobility [mōbil'ətē] *n* Beweglichkeit *f*; **~ of labor** Mobilität *f* der Arbeitskräfte.
mobilize [mō'bəlīz] *vt* mobilisieren.
moccasin [mâk'əsin] *n* Mokassin *m*.
mock [mâk] *vt* verspotten; (*defy*) trotzen (+*dat*) ♦ *a* Schein-.
mockery [mâk'ûrē] *n* Spott *m*; (*person*) Gespött *nt*; **to make a ~ of sth** etw lächerlich machen.
mocking [mâk'ing] *a* (*tone*) spöttisch.
mockingbird [mâk'ingbûrd] *n* Spottdrossel *f*.
mock-up [mâk'up] *n* Modell *nt*.
MOD *n abbr* (*Brit*: = *Ministry of Defence*) Verteidigungsministerium *nt*.
mod cons [mâd kânz] *npl abbr* (*Brit*: = *modern conveniences*) Komfort *m*.
mode [mōd] *n* (Art *f* und) Weise *f*; (*COMPUT*) Modus *m*; **~ of transport** Transportmittel *nt*.
model [mâd'əl] *n* Modell *nt*; (*example*) Vorbild *nt*; (*in fashion*) Mannequin *nt* ♦ *vt* (*make*) formen, modellieren, bilden; (*clothes*) vorführen; **to ~ o.s.** *or* **one's life on sb** sich (*dat*) jdn zum Vorbild nehmen ♦ *a* (*railway*) Modell-; (*perfect*) Muster-, vorbildlich.
modeling, (*Brit*) **modelling** [mâd'əling] *n* (*modelmaking*) Basteln *nt*.
modem [mō'dem] *n* Modem *nt*.
moderate [mâd'ûrit] *a* gemäßigt; (*fairly good*) mittelmäßig ♦ *n* (*POL*) Gemäßigte(r) *mf* ♦ [mâd'ərāt] *vi* sich mäßigen ♦ *vt* mäßigen.
moderately [mâd'ûritlē] *ad* mäßig; (*expensive, difficult*) nicht allzu; (*pleased, happy*) ziemlich.
moderation [mâdərā'shən] *n* Mäßigung *f*; **in ~** mit Maßen.
modern [mâd'ûrn] *a* modern; (*history*) neuere(r, s); (*Greek etc*) Neu-.
modernity [mâdûr'nitē] *n* Modernität *f*.
modernization [mâdûrnəzā'shən] *n* Modernisierung *f*.
modernize [mâd'ûrnīz] *vt* modernisieren.
modern languages *npl* neuere Sprachen *pl*, moderne Fremdsprachen *pl*.

modest [mâd'ist] *a* (*attitude*) bescheiden; (*meal, home*) einfach; (*chaste*) schamhaft.
modestly [mâd'istlē] *ad* bescheiden.
modesty [mâd'istē] *n* Bescheidenheit *f*; (*chastity*) Schamgefühl *nt*.
modicum [mâd'əkəm] *n* bißchen *nt*.
modification [mâdəfəkā'shən] *n* (Ab)änderung *f*; **to make ~s to sth** (Ver)änderungen an etw (*dat*) vornehmen, etw modifizieren.
modify [mâd'əfī] *vt* abändern; (*GRAM*) modifizieren.
modular [mâj'əlûr] *a* (*filing, unit*) Baustein-.
modulate [mâj'əlāt] *vt* modulieren.
modulation [mâjəlā'shən] *n* Modulation *f*.
module [mâj'ōōl] *n* (Raum)kapsel *f*.
modus operandi [mō'dəs âpəran'dī] *n* Modus operandi *m*.
Mogadishu [mâgədish'ōō] *n* Mogadischu *nt*.
mogul [mō'gəl] *n* (*fig*) Mogul *m*.
mohair [mō'här] *n* Mohair *m* ♦ *a* Mohair-.
Mohammed [mōham'id] *n* Mohammed *m*.
moist [moist] *a* feucht.
moisten [mois'ən] *vt* befeuchten.
moisture [mois'chûr] *n* Feuchtigkeit *f*.
moisturize [mois'chərīz] *vt* (*skin*) mit einer Feuchtigkeitscreme behandeln.
moisturizer [mois'chərīzûr] *n* Feuchtigkeitscreme *f*.
molar [mō'lûr] *n* Backenzahn *m*.
molasses [məlas'iz] *npl* Melasse *f*.
mold [mōld] (*US*) *n* Form *f*; (*mildew*) Schimmel *m* ♦ *vt* (*lit, fig*) formen.
molder [mōl'dûr] *vi* vermodern.
molding [mōl'ding] *n* Formen *nt*; (*ARCHIT*) Deckenfries *m or* -stück *m*.
moldy [mōl'dē] *a* schimmelig.
mole [mōl] *n* (*spot*) Leberfleck *m*; (*animal*) Maulwurf *m*; (*pier*) Mole *f*.
molecular [məlek'yəlûr] *a* molekular, Molekular-.
molecule [mâl'əkyōōl] *n* Molekül *nt*.
molest [məlest'] *vt* belästigen.
moll [mâl] *n* (*slang*) Gangsterbraut *f*.
mollusk, (*Brit*) **mollusc** [mâl'əsk] *n* Molluske *f*, Weichtier *nt*.
mollycoddle [mâl'ēkâdəl] *vt* verhätscheln.
molt [mōlt] *vi* (*US*) sich mausern.
molten [mōl'tən] *a* geschmolzen.
mom [mâm] *n* (*US col*) Mutti *m*.
moment [mō'mənt] *n* Moment *m*, Augenblick *m*; (*importance*) Tragweite *f*; **~ of truth** Stunde *f* der Wahrheit; **any ~** jeden Augenblick; **for the ~** vorläufig; **in a ~** gleich; **at the ~** im Augenblick; **one ~ please** (*TEL*) bleiben Sie am Apparat.
momentarily [mōməntar'ilē] *ad* (für) einen Augenblick *or* Moment; (*US*: *very soon*) jeden Augenblick *or* Moment.
momentary [mō'məntärē] *a* kurz.
momentous [mōmen'təs] *a* folgenschwer.
momentum [mōmen'təm] *n* (*lit, fig*) Schwung *m*.
Mon. *abbr* (= *Monday*) Mo.

Monaco [mân'əkō] *n* Monaco *nt*.
monarch [mân'ûrk] *n* Herrscher(in *f*) *m*.
monarchist [mân'ûrkist] *n* Monarchist(in *f*) *m*.
monarchy [mân'ûrkē] *n* Monarchie *f*.
monastery [mân'əstärē] *n* Kloster *nt*.
monastic [mənas'tik] *a* klösterlich, Kloster-.
Monday [mun'dā] *n* Montag *m*; *see* **Tuesday**.
Monegasque [mânāgask'] *a* monegassisch ♦ *n* Monegasse *m*, Monegassin *f*.
monetarist [mân'itärist] *n* Monetarist *m*.
monetary [mân'itärē] *a* geldlich, Geld-; (*of currency*) Währungs-, monetär.
monetary policy *n* Währungspolitik *f*.
money [mun'ē] *n* Geld *nt*; **I've got no ~ left** ich habe kein Geld mehr.
moneyed [mun'ēd] *a* vermögend.
moneylender [mun'ēlendûr] *n* Geldverleiher *m*.
moneymaker [mun'ēmākûr] *n* Verkaufsschlager *m*.
moneymaking [mun'ēmāking] *a* einträglich, gewinnbringend ♦ *n* Gelderwerb *m*.
money market *n* Geldmarkt *m*.
money order *n* Postanweisung *f*.
money-spinner [mun'ēspinûr] *n* (*col*) Verkaufsschlager *m*.
money supply *n* Geldvolumen *nt*.
mongol [mâng'gəl] *n* (*MED*) mongoloide(s) Kind *nt*; **M~** (*language*) Mongolisch *nt* ♦ *a* mongolisch; (*MED*) mongoloid.
Mongolia [mânggō'lēə] *n* Mongolei *f*.
Mongolian [mânggō'lēən] *a* mongolisch ♦ *n* (*person*) Mongole *m*, Mongolin *f*; (*language*) Mongolisch *nt*.
mongoose [mâng'gōōs] *n* Mungo *m*.
mongrel [mung'grəl] *n* Promenadenmischung *f* ♦ *a* Misch-.
monitor [mân'itûr] *n* (*SCH*) Klassenordner *m*; (*US*) Aufsicht *f*, Aufsichtführende(r) *mf*; (*TV, TECH: screen*) Monitor *m*, Überwachungsgerät *nt* ♦ *vt* (*broadcasts*) abhören; (*control*) überwachen.
monk [mungk] *n* Mönch *m*.
monkey [mung'kē] *n* Affe *m*; **no ~ business!, none of your ~ tricks!** (*col*) mach(t) mir keinen Unfug!
monkey nut *n* (*Brit*) Erdnuß *f*.
monkey wrench *n* (*TECH*) verstellbare(r) Schraubenschlüssel *m*, Engländer *m*, Franzose *m*.
mono- [mân'ō] *pref* Mono-, mono-.
monochrome [mân'əkrōm] *a* schwarz-weiß.
monocle [mân'əkəl] *n* Monokel *nt*.
monogram [mân'əgram] *n* Monogramm *nt*.
monolith [mân'əlith] *n* Monolith *m*.
monolithic [mânəlith'ik] *a* monolithisch.
monolog(ue) [mân'əlôg] *n* Monolog *m*.
mononucleosis [mânōnōōklēō'sis] *n* (*US*) Drüsenfieber *nt*.
monoplane [mân'əplān] *n* Eindecker *m*.
Monopolies [mənâp'əlēz] *npl*: **~ and Mergers Commission** (*Brit*) Kartellamt *nt*.
monopolist [mənâp'əlist] *n* Monopolist *m*.

monopolize [mənâp'əlīz] *vt* beherrschen.
monopoly [mənâp'əlē] *n* Monopol *nt*.
monorail [mân'ərāl] *n* Einschienenbahn *f*.
monosyllabic [mânəsilab'ik] *a* einsilbig.
monosyllable [mân'əsiləbəl] *n* einsilbige(s) Wort *nt*.
monotone [mân'ətōn] *n* gleichbleibende(r) Ton(fall) *m*.
monotonous [mənât'ənəs] *a* eintönig, monoton.
monotony [mənât'ənē] *n* Eintönigkeit *f*, Monotonie *f*.
monoxide [mənâk'sīd] *n* Monoxyd *nt*.
monseigneur, monsignor [mânsēn'yûr] *n* Monsignore *m*.
monsoon [mânsōōn'] *n* Monsun *m*.
monster [mân'stûr] *n* Ungeheuer *nt*; (*person*) Scheusal *nt* ♦ *a* (*col*) Riesen-.
monstrosity [mânstrâs'ətē] *n* Ungeheuerlichkeit *f*; (*thing*) Monstrosität *f*.
monstrous [mân'strəs] *a* (*shocking*) gräßlich, ungeheuerlich; (*huge*) riesig.
Mont. *abbr* (*US*) = Montana.
montage [mântâzh'] *n* Montage *f*.
Mont Blanc [mânt blangk'] *n* Montblanc *m*.
month [munth] *n* Monat *m*; **300 dollars a ~** 300 Dollar im Monat; **every other ~** jeden zweiten Monat.
monthly [munth'lē] *a* monatlich, Monats-; (*installment*) Monats- ♦ *ad* einmal im Monat; **twice ~** zweimal monatlich ♦ *n* (*magazine*) Monatsschrift *f*.
monument [mân'yəmənt] *n* Denkmal *nt*.
monumental [mânyəmen'təl] *a* (*huge*) gewaltig; (*ignorance*) ungeheuer.
moo [mōō] *vi* muhen.
mood [mōōd] *n* Stimmung *f*, Laune *f*; **to be in the ~ for** aufgelegt sein zu; **I am not in the ~ for laughing** mir ist nicht zum Lachen zumute.
moodily [mōō'dilē] *ad* launisch.
moodiness [mōō'dēnis] *n* Launenhaftigkeit *f*.
moody [mōō'dē] *a* launisch.
moon [mōōn] *n* Mond *m*.
moonbeam [mōōn'bēm] *n* Mondstrahl *m*.
moon landing *n* Mondlandung *f*.
moonless [mōōn'lis] *a* mondlos.
moonlight [mōōn'lit] *n* Mondlicht *nt* ♦ *vi* schwarzarbeiten.
moonlighting [mōōn'līting] *n* Schwarzarbeit *f*.
moonlit [mōōn'lit] *a* mondhell.
moonshot [mōōn'shât] *n* Mondflug *m*.
moonstruck [mōōn'struk] *a* mondsüchtig.
moor [mōōr] *n* Heide *f*, Hochmoor *nt* ♦ *vt* (*ship*) festmachen, verankern ♦ *vi* anlegen.
moorings [mōōr'ingz] *npl* Liegeplatz *m*.
moorland [mōōr'land] *n* Heidemoor *nt*.
moose [mōōs] *n* Elch *m*.
moot [mōōt] *vt* aufwerfen ♦ *a*: **~ point** strittige(r) Punkt *m*.
mop [mâp] *n* Mop *m*; (*of hair*) Mähne *f* ♦ *vt* (auf)wischen.
mop up *vt* aufwischen.

mope [mōp] *vi* Trübsal blasen.
 mope about, **mope around** *vi* mit einer Jammermiene herumlaufen.
moped [mō'ped] *n* Moped *nt*.
moping [mō'ping] *a* trübselig.
moquette [mōket'] *n* Plüschgewebe *nt*.
moral [môr'əl] *a* moralisch; (*values*) sittlich; (*virtuous*) tugendhaft ♦ *n* Moral *f*; *see also* **morals**.
morale [məral'] *n* Moral *f*, Stimmung *f*.
morality [məral'itē] *n* Sittlichkeit *f*.
moralize [môr'əlīz] *vi*: **to ~ about sth** sich über etw moralisch entrüsten.
morally [môr'əlē] *ad* moralisch.
morals [môr'əlz] *npl* Moral *f*.
morass [məras'] *n* Sumpf *m*.
moratorium [môrətôr'ēəm] *n*, *pl* **-ria** *or* **-riums** Stopp *m*.
morbid [môr'bid] *a* morbid, krankhaft; (*jokes*) makaber.
more [môr] *a*, *n*, *ad* mehr; **~ or less** mehr oder weniger; **~ than ever** mehr denn je; **a few ~** noch ein paar; **~ beautiful** schöner; **many** *or* **much ~** viel mehr; **is there any ~?** gibt es noch mehr?; **~ and ~** mehr und mehr; **and what's ~ ...** und außerdem ...; **once ~** noch einmal, noch mal; **no ~,** **not any ~** nicht mehr.
moreover [môrō'vûr] *ad* überdies.
morgue [môrg] *n* Leichenschauhaus *nt*.
MORI [mō'rē] *n abbr* (*Brit*) = *Market & Opinion Research Institute.*
moribund [môr'əbund] *a* todgeweiht, moribund; (*policy*) zum Scheitern verurteilt.
Mormon [môr'mən] *n* Mormone *m*, Mormonin *f*.
morning [môr'ning] *n* Morgen *m*; **in the ~** am Morgen; (*tomorrow*) morgen früh; **this ~** heute morgen ♦ *a* morgendlich, Morgen-, Früh-.
morning sickness *n* (*MED*) (Schwangerschafts)übelkeit *f*.
Moroccan [mərâk'ən] *a* marokkanisch ♦ *n* Marokkaner(in *f*) *m*.
Morocco [mərâk'ō] *n* Marokko *nt*.
moron [môr'ân] *n* Schwachsinnige(r) *mf*.
moronic [mərân'ik] *a* schwachsinnig.
morose [mərōs'] *a* mürrisch.
morphine [môr'fēn] *n* Morphium *nt*.
Morse [môrs] *n* (*also:* **~ code**) Morsealphabet *nt*.
morsel [môr'səl] *n* Stückchen *nt*, bißchen *nt*.
mortal [môr'təl] *a* sterblich; (*deadly*) tödlich; (*very great*) Todes- ♦ *n* (*human being*) Sterbliche(r) *mf*.
mortality [môrtal'itē] *n* Sterblichkeit *f*; (*death rate*) Sterblichkeitsziffer *f*.
mortally [môr'təlē] *ad* tödlich.
mortar [môr'tûr] *n* (*for building*) Mörtel *m*; (*bowl*) Mörser *m*; (*MIL*) Granatwerfer *m*.
mortgage [môr'gij] *n* Hypothek *f* (*on* auf +*acc*); **to take out a ~** eine Hypothek aufnehmen ♦ *vt* mit einer Hypothek belasten.
mortgage company *n* (*US*) ≈ Bausparkas-

se *f*, ≈ Hypothekenbank *f*.
mortgagee [môrgəjē'] *n* Hypothekengläubiger *m*.
mortgagor [môr'gəjûr] *n* Hypothekenschuldner *m*.
mortice [môr'tis] = **mortise**.
mortician [môrtish'ən] *n* (*US*) Bestattungsunternehmer *m*.
mortification [môrtəfəkā'shən] *n* Beschämung *f*.
mortified [môr'təfīd] *a*: **I was ~** es war mir schrecklich peinlich.
mortise (lock) [môr'tis lâk] *n* (*Brit*) (Ein)steckschloß *nt*.
mortuary [môr'chōōārē] *n* Leichenhalle *f*.
mosaic [mōzā'ik] *n* Mosaik *nt*.
Moscow [mâs'kou] *n* Moskau *nt*.
Moslem [mâz'ləm] = **Muslim**.
mosque [mâsk] *n* Moschee *f*.
mosquito [məskē'tō] *n* Moskito *m*.
moss [môs] *n* Moos *nt*.
mossy [môs'ē] *a* bemoost.
most [mōst] *a* meiste(r, s); **~ men** die meisten Männer ♦ *ad* am meisten; (*very*) höchst; **the ~ beautiful** der/die/das Schönste ♦ *n* das meiste, der größte Teil; (*people*) die meisten, meisten Männer; **~ of the time** die meiste Zeit; (*usually*) meistens; **~ of the winter** fast den ganzen Winter über; **at the (very) ~** allerhöchstens; **to make the ~ of** das Beste machen aus.
mostly [mōst'lē] *ad* größtenteils.
MOT *n abbr* (*Brit*: = *Ministry of Transport*) Verkehrsministerium *nt*; **the ~ (test)** ≈ TÜV *m*.
motel [mōtel'] *n* Motel *nt*.
moth [môth] *n* Nachtfalter *m*; (*wool-eating*) Motte *f*.
mothball [môth'bôl] *n* Mottenkugel *f*.
moth-eaten [môth'ētən] *a* mottenzerfressen.
mother [muth'ûr] *n* Mutter *f* ♦ *vt* bemuttern ♦ *a* (*tongue*) Mutter-; (*country*) Heimat-.
mother board *n* (*COMPUT*) Grundplatine *f*.
motherhood [muth'ûrhōōd] *n* Mutterschaft *f*.
mother-in-law [muth'ûrinlô] *n* Schwiegermutter *f*.
motherly [muth'ûrlē] *a* mütterlich.
mother-of-pearl [muth'ûrəvpûrl'] *n* Perlmutt *nt*.
mother-to-be [muth'ûrtəbē'] *n* werdende Mutter *f*.
mothproof [môth'prōōf] *a* mottenfest.
motif [mōtēf'] *n* Motiv *nt*.
motion [mō'shən] *n* Bewegung *f*; (*in meeting*) Antrag *m*; (*Brit*: *bowel ~*) Stuhlgang *m*; **to be in ~** (*vehicle*) fahren; **to set sth in ~** etw in Gang bringen *or* setzen; **to go through the ~s of doing sth** (*fig*) etw der Form halber tun; (*pretend*) so tun, als ob (+*subjunctive*) ♦ *vti* winken (+*dat*), zu verstehen geben (+*dat*).
motionless [mō'shənlis] *a* regungslos.
motion picture *n* Film *m*.
motivate [mō'təvāt] *vt* (*act, decision, person*)

motivieren.
motivated [mō'təvātid] a motiviert.
motivation [mōtəvā'shən] n Motivierung f.
motive [mō'tiv] n Motiv nt, Beweggrund m;
from the best ~**s** mit den besten Absichten ♦ a treibend.
motley [mât'lē] a bunt.
motor [mō'tûr] n Motor m; (car) Auto nt ♦ vi (im Auto) fahren ♦ a Motor-.
motorbike [mō'tûrbīk] n Motorrad nt.
motorboat [mō'tûrbōt] n Motorboot nt.
motorcar [mō'tûrkâr] n (Brit) Auto nt.
motorcoach [mō'tûrkōch] n (Brit) Autobus m.
motorcycle [mō'tûrsī'kəl] n Motorrad nt.
motorcycle racing n Motorradrennen nt.
motorcyclist [mō'tûrsīklist] n Motorradfahrer(in f) m.
motor home n (US) Wohnmobil nt.
motoring [mō'tûring] n (Brit) Autofahren nt ♦ a Auto-; (offense) Verkehrs-.
motorist [mō'tûrist] n Autofahrer(in f) m.
motorize [mō'tərīz] vt motorisieren.
motor oil n Motorenöl m.
motor racing n Autorennen nt.
motor scooter n Motorroller m.
motor vehicle n Kraftfahrzeug nt.
motorway [mō'tûrwā] n (Brit) Autobahn f.
mottled [mât'əld] a gesprenkelt.
motto [mât'ō] n Motto nt, Wahlspruch m.
mould [mōld] etc (Brit) = **mold** etc.
moult [mōlt] vi (Brit) = **molt**.
mound [mound] n (Erd)hügel m.
mount [mount] n (liter: hill) Berg m; (old: horse) Roß nt; (for jewel etc) Fassung f ♦ vt (horse) steigen auf (+acc); (put in setting) fassen; (stairs) hochgehen or -steigen; (exhibition, attack) organisieren; (picture) mit einem Passepartout versehen; (stamp) aufkleben ♦ vi (increase: also: ~ **up**) sich häufen; (on horse) aufsitzen.
mountain [moun'tən] n Berg m; **to make a** ~ **out of a molehill** aus einer Mücke einen Elefanten machen (col).
mountaineer [mountənēr'] n Bergsteiger(in f) m.
mountaineering [mountənē'ring] n Bergsteigen nt; **to go** ~ klettern gehen.
mountainous [moun'tənəs] a bergig.
mountain rescue team n Bergwacht f.
mountainside [moun'tənsīd] n Berg(ab)hang m.
mounted [moun'tid] a (on horseback) beritten; (MIL: with motor vehicle) motorisiert.
Mount Everest [mount ev'ûrist] n Mount Everest m.
mourn [môrn] vt betrauern, beklagen ♦ vi trauern (for um).
mourner [môr'nûr] n Trauernde(r) mf.
mournful [môrn'fəl] a traurig.
mourning [môr'ning] n (grief) Trauer f; **in** ~ (period etc) in Trauer; (dress) in Trauerkleidung f.
mouse [mous] n, pl **mice** [mīs] (also COMPUT)

Maus f.
mousetrap [mous'trap] n Mausefalle f.
mousse [mōōs] n (COOK) Creme(speise) f; (for hair) Schaumfestiger m.
moustache [məstash'] n (Brit) Schnurrbart m.
mousy [mou'sē] a (color) mausgrau; (person) schüchtern.
mouth n [mouth] Mund m; (opening) Öffnung f; (of river) Mündung f; (of harbor) Einfahrt f; **down in the** ~ niedergeschlagen ♦ vt [mouth] (words) affektiert sprechen.
mouthful [mouth'fōōl] n Mundvoll m.
mouth organ n Mundharmonika f.
mouthpiece [mouth'pēs] n (lit) Mundstück nt; (fig) Sprachrohr nt.
mouth-to-mouth resuscitation [mouthtəmouth' risusətā'shən] n Mund-zu-Mund Beatmung f.
mouthwash [mouth'wôsh] n Mundwasser nt.
mouthwatering [mouth'wôtûring] a lecker, appetitlich.
movable [mōō'vəbəl] a beweglich.
move [mōōv] n (movement) Bewegung f; (in game) Zug m; (turn) Schritt m; (of house) Umzug m; **on the** ~ in Bewegung; **to get a** ~ **on** sich beeilen ♦ vt bewegen; (object) rücken; (people) transportieren; (in job) versetzen; (emotionally) bewegen, ergreifen; **to** ~ **sb to do sth** jdn veranlassen, etw zu tun; **to be** ~**d** gerührt sein; **to** ~ **house** umziehen ♦ vi sich bewegen; (change place) gehen; (vehicle, ship) fahren; (take action) etwas unternehmen; (go to another house) umziehen; **to** ~ **closer to** or **towards sth** sich etw (dat) nähern.
move around vi sich hin- und herbewegen; (travel) unterwegs sein.
move along vi weiterfahren; (cars) weiterfahren.
move away vi weggehen.
move back vi zurückgehen; (to the rear) zurückweichen.
move down vt (downwards) (weiter) nach unten stellen; (demote) zurückstufen; (SPORT) absteigen lassen ♦ vi nach unten rücken.
move forward vi vorwärtsgehen, sich vorwärtsbewegen ♦ vt vorschieben; (in time) vorverlegen.
move in vi (to house) einziehen; (troops) einrücken.
move off vt (people) wegschicken ♦ vi weggehen; (set off) sich in Bewegung setzen; (train, car) abfahren.
move on vi weitergehen ♦ vt weitergehen lassen.
move out vi (of house) ausziehen; (troops) abziehen.
move over vi zur Seite rücken or rutschen.
move up vi aufsteigen; (in job) befördert werden ♦ vt nach oben bewegen; (in job) befördern; (SCH) versetzen.

movement [mōōv'mənt] *n* Bewegung *f*; (*MUS*) Satz *m*; (*of clock*) Uhrwerk *nt*; **bowel** ~ (*MED*) Stuhlgang *m*.

mover [mōō'vûr] *n* (*of proposition*) Antragsteller(in *f*) *m*; (*furniture* ~) Möbelpacker *m*; (*firm*) Spediteur *m*.

movie [mōō'vē] *n* Film *m*; **the** ~**s** (*the cinema*) das Kino.

movie camera *n* Filmkamera *f*.

moviegoer [mōō'vēgōūr] *n* Kinogänger(in *f*) *m*.

movie projector *n* (*US*) Filmvorführgerät *nt*.

movie theater *n* (*US*) Kino *nt*.

moving [mōō'ving] *a* beweglich; (*force*) treibend; (*touching*) ergreifend.

moving van *n* (*US*) Möbelwagen *m*.

mow [mō] *vt irreg* mähen.

    mow down *vt* (*fig*) niedermähen.

mowed [mōd] *pt, pp of* **mow**.

mower [mō'ûr] *n* (*machine*) Mähmaschine *f*; (*lawn*~) Rasenmäher *m*.

mown [mōn] *pt of* **mow**.

Mozambique [mōzambēk'] *n* Mozambique *nt*.

MP *n abbr* (= *Military Police*) MP *f*; (*Canada*: = *Mounted Police*) berittene Polizei; (*Brit*: = *Member of Parliament*) Abgeordnete(r) *mf*.

mpg *n abbr* (= *miles per gallon*) Meilen pro Gallone.

mph *abbr* (= *miles per hour*) Meilen pro Stunde.

MPhil *n abbr* (*US*: = *Master of Philosophy*) *akademischer Grad*.

Mr, Mr. [mis'tûr] *n*: ~ **X** Herr X.

Mrs, Mrs. [mis'iz] *n*: ~ **X** Frau X.

MS *n abbr* (= *manuscript*) Ms; (*US*: = *Master of Science*) *akademischer Grad*; (= *multiple sclerosis*) MS *f* ♦ *abbr* (*US MAIL*) = *Mississippi*.

Ms, Ms. [miz] *n* (= *Miss or Mrs*): ~ **X** Frau X.

MSA *n abbr* (*US*: = *Master of Science in Agriculture*) *akademischer Grad*.

MSc *n abbr* (= *Master of Science*) *akademischer Grad*.

MSG *n abbr* = *monosodium glutamate*.

MST *abbr* (*US*) = *Mountain Standard Time*.

MSW *n abbr* (*US*: = *Master of Social Work*) *akademischer Grad*.

Mt *abbr* (*GEOG*) = **Mount**.

MT *n abbr* (= *machine translation*) MÜ *f* ♦ *abbr* (*US MAIL*) = *Montana*.

much [much] *a* viel; **how** ~? wieviel?; **too** ~ zuviel, zu sehr ♦ *ad* (*with v*) sehr; (*with a, ad*) viel; **so** ~ soviel; **I like it very/so** ~ es gefällt mir sehr/so gut; **thank you very** ~ vielen Dank; ~ **better** viel besser; ~ **the same size** so ziemlich gleich groß; ~ **to my surprise** zu meiner großen Überraschung; ~ **as I should like to** so gern ich möchte ♦ *n* viel, eine Menge *f*.

muck [muk] *n* (*lit*) Mist *m*; (*fig*) Schmutz *m*.

    muck about *or* **around** (*Brit col*) *vi* herumlungern; (*meddle*) herumalbern; (*tinker*) herumfummeln (*with* an +*dat*) ♦ *vt*: **to** ~ **sb about** mit jdm treiben, was man will.

    muck in *vi* (*Brit col*) mit anpacken.

    muck out *vt* (*stable*) (aus)misten.

    muck up *vt* (*col: ruin*) vermasseln; (: *dirty*) dreckig machen.

muckraking [muk'rāk'ing] *n* (*fig col*) Sensationsmache(rei) *f*.

mucky [muk'ē] *a* (*dirty*) dreckig.

mucus [myōō'kəs] *n* Schleim *m*.

mud [mud] *n* Schlamm *m*; (*fig*) Schmutz *m*.

muddle [mud'əl] *n* Durcheinander *nt* ♦ *vt* (*also*: ~ **up**) durcheinanderbringen.

    muddle along, muddle on *vi* vor sich (*acc*) hinwursteln.

    muddle through *vi* sich durchwursteln.

muddle-headed [mud'əlhedid] *a* (*person*) zerstreut.

muddy [mud'ē] *a* schlammig.

mudguard [mud'gârd] *n* Schutzblech *nt*.

mudpack [mud'pak] *n* Moorpackung *f*, Schlammpackung *f*.

mudslinging [mud'slinging] *n* (*col*) Verleumdung *f*.

muff [muf] *n* Muff *m* ♦ *vt* (*shot*) danebensetzen; (*catch etc*) danebengreifen; **to** ~ **it** es vermasseln *or* verpatzen.

muffin [muf'in] *n* süße(s) Teilchen *nt*.

muffle [muf'əl] *vt* (*sound*) dämpfen; (*wrap up*) einhüllen.

muffler [muf'lûr] *n* (*scarf*) (dicke(r)) Schal *m*; (*US AUT*) Auspuff(topf) *m*; (: *on motorbike*) Schalldämpfer *m*.

mufti [muf'tē] *n*: **in** ~ in Zivil.

mug [mug] *n* (*cup*) Becher *m*; (*col: face*) Visage *f*; (: *fool*) Trottel *m* ♦ *vt* überfallen und ausrauben.

    mug up *vt* (*Brit col: also*: ~ **up on**) pauken.

mugger [mug'ûr] *n* Straßenräuber *m*.

mugging [mug'ing] *n* Straßenraub *m*.

muggy [mug'ē] *a* (*weather*) schwül.

mulatto [məlat'ō] *n* Mulatte *m*, Mulattin *f*.

mulberry [mul'bärē] *n* (*fruit*) Maulbeere *f*; (*tree*) Maulbeerbaum *m*.

mule [myōōl] *n* Maulesel *m*.

mull over [mul ō'vûr] *vt* nachdenken über (+*acc*).

mulled [muld] *a* (*wine*) Glüh-.

mullioned [mul'yənd] *a* (*windows*) längs unterteilt.

multi- [mul'tē] *pref* Multi-, multi-.

multi-access [multēak'ses] *a* (*COMPUT*) Mehrbenutzer-.

multicolored, (*Brit*) **multicoloured** [mul'tikulûrd] *a* mehrfarbig.

multifarious [multəfär'ēəs] *a* mannigfaltig, vielfältig.

multilateral [multilat'ûrəl] *a* multilateral.

multimillionaire [multēmilyənär'] *n* Multimillionär(in *f*) *m*.

multinational [multənash'ənəl] *a* multinational ♦ *n* multinationale(r) Konzern *m*, Multi

m (col).
multiple [mul'təpəl] *n* Vielfache(s) *nt* ♦ *a* mehrfach; (*many*) mehrere.
multiple choice *n* Multiple Choice *f*.
multiple crash *n* Massenkarambolage *f*.
multiple sclerosis [mul'təpəl sklirō'sis] *n* multiple Sklerose *f*.
multiple store *n* (*Brit*) Kettenladen *m*.
multiplication [multəpləkā'shən] *n* Multiplikation *f*.
multiplication table *n* Multiplikationstabelle *f*.
multiplicity [multəplis'ətē] *n* Vielzahl *f*, Fülle *f*.
multiply [mul'təplī] *vt* multiplizieren (*by* mit) ♦ *vi* (*BIOL*) sich vermehren.
multiracial [multērā'shəl] *a* gemischtrassig.
multiracial policy *n* Rassenintegration *f*.
multiracial school *n* Schule *f* ohne Rassentrennung.
multistory, (*Brit*) **multistorey** [multēstôr'ē] *a* (*building*) mehrstöckig.
multi-tasking [multētas'king] *n* (*COMPUT*) Multitasking *nt*.
multitude [mul'tətood] *n* Menge *f*.
mum [mum] (*Brit*) *a*: **to keep ~** den Mund halten (*about* über +*acc*) ♦ *n* (col) Mutti *f*.
mumble [mum'bəl] *vti* murmeln ♦ *n* Gemurmel *nt*.
mummify [mum'əfī] *vt* einbalsamieren, mumifizieren.
mummy [mum'ē] *n* (*dead body*) Mumie *f*; (*Brit col*) Mami *f*.
mumps [mumps] *n sing* Mumps *m*.
munch [munch] *vti* mampfen.
mundane [mundān'] *a* weltlich; (*fig*) profan.
Munich [myoo'nik] *n* München *nt*.
municipal [myoonis'əpəl] *a* städtisch, Stadt-.
municipality [myoonisəpəl'itē] *n* Stadt *f* mit Selbstverwaltung.
munificence [myoonif'əsəns] *n* Freigebigkeit *f*.
munitions [myoonish'ənz] *npl* Munition *f*.
mural [myoor'əl] *n* Wandgemälde *nt*.
murder [mûr'dûr] *n* Mord *m*; **to commit ~** einen Mord begehen; **it was ~** (*fig*) es war mörderisch; **to get away with ~** (*fig*) sich alles erlauben können ♦ *vt* ermorden.
murderer [mûr'dûrûr] *n* Mörder *m*.
murderess [mûr'dûris] *n* Mörderin *f*.
murderous [mûr'dûrəs] *a* Mord-; (*fig*) mörderisch.
murk [mûrk] *n* Dunkelheit *f*.
murky [mûr'kē] *a* finster.
murmur [mûr'mûr] *n* Murmeln *nt*; (*of water, wind*) Rauschen *nt*; **without a ~** ohne zu murren; **heart ~** Herzgeräusche *pl* ♦ *vti* murmeln.
MusB(ac) *n abbr* (= *Bachelor of Music*) akademischer Grad.
muscle [mus'əl] *n* Muskel *m*.
muscle in *vi* mitmischen (*on* bei).
muscular [mus'kyəlûr] *a* Muskel-; (*strong*) muskulös.

MusD(oc) *n abbr* (= *Doctor of Music*) akademischer Grad.
muse [myooz] *vi* (nach)sinnen.
museum [myoozē'əm] *n* Museum *nt*.
mush [mush] *n* Brei *m*.
mushroom [mush'room] *n* Pilz *m*; (*button ~*) Champignon *m* ♦ *vi* (*fig*) emporschießen.
mushy [mush'ē] *a* breiig; (*sentimental*) gefühlsduselig.
music [myoo'zik] *n* Musik *f*; (*printed*) Noten *pl*.
musical [myoo'zikəl] *a* (*sound*) melodisch; (*person*) musikalisch ♦ *n* (*show*) Musical *nt*.
musical box *n* (*Brit*) = **music box**.
musical instrument *n* Musikinstrument *nt*.
musically [myoo'ziklē] *ad* musikalisch; (*sing*) melodisch.
music box *n* (*US*) Spieldose *f*.
music hall *n* (*Brit*) Varieté *nt*.
musician [myoozish'ən] *n* Musiker(in *f*) *m*.
music stand *n* Notenständer *m*.
musk [musk] *n* Moschus *m*.
musket [mus'kit] *n* Muskete *f*.
muskrat [musk'rat] *n* Bisamratte *f*.
musk rose *n* (*BOT*) Moschusrose *f*.
Muslim [muz'lim] *a* moslemisch ♦ *n* Moslem.
muslin [muz'lin] *n* Musselin *m*.
musquash [mus'kwäsh] *n* Bisamratte *f*.
muss [mus] *vt* (*US*: *also*: **~ up**) durcheinanderbringen; (*hair*) zersausen.
mussel [mus'əl] *n* Miesmuschel *f*.
must [must] *aux v* müssen; (*in negation*) dürfen; **I ~ go** ich muß gehen; **I ~n't say that** ich darf das nicht sagen ♦ *n* Muß *nt*; **the film is a ~** den Film muß man einfach gesehen haben.
mustache [məstash'] *n* (*US*) Schnurrbart *m*.
mustard [mus'tûrd] *n* Senf *m*.
mustard gas *n* (*CHEM*) Senfgas *nt*.
muster [mus'tûr] *vt* (*MIL*) antreten lassen; (*courage*) zusammennehmen; (*also*: **~ up**: *strength*) aufbringen ♦ *n*: **to pass ~** die Anforderungen genügen.
mustiness [mus'tēnis] *n* Muffigkeit *f*.
mustn't [mus'ənt] = **must not**.
musty [mus'tē] *a* muffig.
mutant [myoo'tənt] *a* Mutations- ♦ *n* Mutation *f*.
mutate [myoo'tāt] *vi* sich verändern; (*BIOL*) mutieren.
mutation [myootā'shən] *n* (*process*) Veränderung *f*; (*BIOL*) Mutation *f*.
mute [myoot] *a* stumm ♦ *n* (*person*) Stumme(r) *mf*; (*MUS*) Dämpfer *m*.
muted [myoo'tid] *a* (*noise*) gedämpft; (*criticism*) leise, leicht.
mutilate [myoo'təlāt] *vt* verstümmeln.
mutilation [myootəlā'shən] *n* Verstümmelung *f*.
mutinous [myoo'tənəs] *a* meuterisch.
mutiny [myoo'tənē] *n* Meuterei *f* ♦ *vi* meutern.
mutter [mut'ûr] *vti* murmeln.
mutton [mut'ən] *n* Hammelfleisch *nt*.

mutual [myōō'chōōəl] a (respect etc) gegenseitig; (satisfaction) beiderseitig.
mutual fund n (US) Investmentgesellschaft f.
mutually [myōō'chōōəlē] ad beide; (distrust) gegenseitig; (agreed, rejected) von beiden Seiten.
muzzle [muz'əl] n (of animal) Schnauze f; (for animal) Maulkorb m; (of gun) Mündung f ♦ vt einen Maulkorb anlegen (+dat).
MVP n abbr (US SPORT: = most valuable player) bester Spieler (der Saison).
MW abbr (= medium wave) MW.
my [mī] poss a mein(e).
myopic [mīáp'ik] a kurzsichtig.
myrrh [mûr] n Myrrhe f.
myself [mīself'] pron mich (acc); mir (dat); (emphatic) selbst; **I'm not** ~ mit mir ist etwas nicht in Ordnung.
mysterious [mistēr'ēəs] a geheimnisvoll, mysteriös.
mysteriously [mistēr'ēəslē] ad auf unerklärliche Weise.
mystery [mis'tûrē] n (secret) Geheimnis nt; (sth difficult) Rätsel nt.
mystery play n Mysterienspiel nt.
mystic [mis'tik] n Mystiker m ♦ a mystisch.
mystical [mis'tikəl] a mystisch.
mysticism [mis'tisizəm] n Mystizismus m.
mystification [mistəfəkā'shən] n Verblüffung f.
mystify [mis'təfī] vt ein Rätsel sein (+dat).
mystique [mistēk'] n geheimnisvolle Natur f.
myth [mith] n Mythos m; (fig) Erfindung f.
mythical [mith'ikəl] a mythisch, Sagen-.
mythological [mithəlâj'ikəl] a mythologisch.
mythology [mithâl'əjē] n Mythologie f.

N

N, n [en] n (letter) N nt, n nt; **N for Nan** ≈ N wie Nordpol.
N. abbr (= north) N.
n/a abbr (COMM etc) = no account; (= not applicable) nicht zutreffend.
NA n abbr (US: = Narcotics Anonymous) Anonyme Drogenabhangige pl; (: = National Academy) Nationalakademie f.
NAACP n abbr (US: = National Association for the Advancement of Colored People) Vereinigung zur Förderung Farbiger.
nab [nab] vt (col) schnappen.
NACU n abbr (US: = National Association of Colleges and Universities) Verband von Colleges und Universitäten.
nadir [nā'dûr] n (ASTRON) Nadir m, Fußpunkt m; (fig) Tiefstpunkt m.

nag [nag] n (horse) Gaul m; (person) Nörgler(in f) m ♦ vti herumnörgeln (sb an jdm).
nagging [nag'ing] a (doubt) nagend ♦ n Nörgelei f.
nail [nāl] n Nagel m; **to pay cash on the** ~ (Brit) auf der Stelle or sofort (bar) bezahlen ♦ vt nageln.
nail down vt (lit, fig) festnageln.
nailbrush [nāl'brush] n Nagelbürste f.
nailfile [nāl'fīl] n Nagelfeile f.
nail polish n Nagellack m.
nail polish remover n Nagellackentferner m.
nail scissors npl Nagelschere f.
nail varnish n (Brit) Nagellack m.
naïve [nīēv'] a, **naïvely** [nīēv'lē] ad naiv.
naïveté, naivety [nīēvtā'] n Naivität f.
naked [nā'kid] a nackt; **with the** ~ **eye** mit bloßem Auge.
nakedness [nā'kidnis] n Nacktheit f.
NAM n abbr (US: = National Association of Manufacturers) Herstellerverband.
name [nām] n Name m; (reputation) Ruf m; **what's your** ~? wie heißen Sie?; **my** ~ **is Peter** ich heiße Peter; **to take sb's** ~ **and address** Name und Adresse von jdm aufschreiben; **to make a** ~ **for o.s.** sich (dat) einen Namen machen; **to get (o.s.) a bad** ~ in Verruf kommen, (sich) in Verruf bringen; **by** ~ mit Namen; **in the** ~ **of** im Namen (+gen); (for the sake of) um (+gen) willen ♦ vt nennen; (sth new) benennen; (appoint) ernennen.
name-drop [nām'drâp] vi (col): **he's always name-dropping** er wirft immer mit großen Namen um sich.
nameless [nām'lis] a namenlos.
namely [nām'lē] ad nämlich.
nameplate [nām'plāt] n (on door etc) Türschild nt.
namesake [nām'sāk] n Namensvetter m.
nanny [nan'ē] n Kindermädchen nt.
nap [nap] n (sleep) Nickerchen nt; (on cloth) Strich m; **to have a** ~ ein Nickerchen machen.
NAPA n abbr (US: = National Association of Performing Artists) Gewerkschaft der vortragenden Künstler.
napalm [nā'pâm] n Napalm nt.
nape [nāp] n Nacken m.
napkin [nap'kin] n (at table) Serviette f; (sanitary ~) (Damen)binde f; (Brit: for baby) Windel f.
Naples [nā'pəlz] n Neapel nt.
nappy [nap'ē] n (Brit: for baby) Windel f.
narcissism [nâr'sisizəm] n Narzißmus m.
narcissus [nârsis'əs] n, pl **narcissi** [nârsis'ī] Narzisse f.
narcotic [nârkât'ik] n Betäubungsmittel nt.
narrate [nar'āt] vt erzählen.
narration [narā'shən] n Erzählung f; (of events, journey) Schilderung f.
narrative [nar'ətiv] n Erzählung f ♦ a erzählend.

narrator [nar'ātûr] *n* Erzähler(in *f*) *m*.
narrow [nar'ō] *a* eng, schmal; *(limited)* beschränkt ♦ *vi* sich verengen.
narrow down *vt:* **to ~ sth down to sth** etw auf etw *(acc)* einschränken.
narrowly [nar'ōlē] *ad (miss)* knapp; *(escape)* mit knapper Not.
narrow-minded [nar'ōmīn'did] *a* engstirnig.
narrow-mindedness [nar'ōmīn'didnis] *n* Engstirnigkeit *f*.
NAS *n abbr (US:* = *National Academy of Sciences) Akademie der Wissenschaften.*
NASA [nas'ə] *n abbr (US:* = *National Aeronautics and Space Administration)* NASA *f*.
nasal [nā'zəl] *a* Nasal-; *(voice)* näselnd.
nastily [nas'tilē] *ad* böse, schlimm.
nastiness [nas'tēnis] *n* Scheußlichkeit *f*; *(of person)* Gemeinheit *f*, Bosheit *f*; *(spitefulness)* Gehässigkeit *f*; *(of remarks)* Bosheit *f*, Gehässigkeit *f*.
nasturtium [nəstûr'shəm] *n* (Kapuziner)kresse *f*, Kapuziner *m*.
nasty [nas'tē] *a* scheußlich; *(person, behavior)* ekelhaft, fies; *(business, wound)* schlimm; **to turn ~** gemein werden; *(situation, person)* unangenehm werden; *(weather)* schlecht werden.
nation [nā'shən] *n* Nation *f*, Volk *nt*.
national [nash'ənəl] *a* national, National-, Landes- ♦ *n* Staatsangehörige(r) *mf*.
national anthem *n* Nationalhymne *f*.
national debt *n* Staatsverschuldung *f*.
national dress *n* Nationaltracht *f*.
National Forest Service *n (US)* Forstverwaltung *f*.
National Guard *n (US)* Nationalgarde *f*.
National Health Service *n (Brit)* Staatliche(r) Gesundheitsdienst *m*.
National Insurance *n (Brit)* ≈ Sozialversicherung *f*.
nationalism [nash'ənəlizəm] *n* Nationalismus *m*.
nationalist [nash'nəlist] *n* Nationalist(in *f*) *m* ♦ *a* nationalistisch.
nationality [nashənal'ətē] *n* Staatsangehörigkeit *f*, Nationalität *f*.
nationalization [nashnələzā'shən] *n* Verstaatlichung *f*.
nationalize [nash'nəliz] *vt* verstaatlichen; **~d industry** verstaatlichte(r) Industriezweig *m*.
nationally [nash'nəlē] *ad* national; *(nationwide)* landesweit.
national park *n (US)* Naturschutzgebiet *nt*.
national press *n* überregionale Presse *f*.
national service *n (MIL)* Wehrdienst *m*.
National Weather Service *n (US)* das Wetteramt.
nationwide [nā'shənwīd'] *a, ad* allgemein, landesweit.
native [nā'tiv] *n (born in)* Einheimische(r) *mf*; *(original inhabitant)* Eingeborene(r) *mf*; **a ~ of Germany** ein gebürtiger Deutscher ♦ *a (coming from a certain place)* einheimisch; *(of the original inhabitants)*

Eingeborenen-; *(belonging by birth)* heimatlich, Heimat-; *(inborn)* angeboren, natürlich.
native language *n* Muttersprache *f*.
Nativity [nətiv'ətē] *n:* **the ~** Christi Geburt.
NATO [nā'tō] *n abbr* (= *North Atlantic Treaty Organization)* NATO *f*.
natter [nat'ûr] *vi (Brit col: chat)* quatschen ♦ *n* Gequatsche *nt*; **to have a ~** einen Schwatz halten.
natural [nach'ûrəl] *a* natürlich; *(laws, silk, phenomena)* Natur-; *(inborn)* (an)geboren; **death from ~ causes** *(JUR)* Tod durch natürliche Ursachen.
natural childbirth *n* natürliche Geburt *f*.
natural gas *n* Erdgas *nt*.
naturalist [nach'ûrəlist] *n* Naturkundler(in *f*) *m*.
naturalization [nachûrələzā'shən] *n* Naturalisierung *f*, Einbürgerung *f*.
naturalize [nach'ûrəliz] *vt (foreigner)* einbürgern, naturalisieren; *(plant etc)* einführen.
naturally [nach'ûrəlē] *ad* natürlich.
naturalness [nach'ûrəlnis] *n* Natürlichkeit *f*.
natural resources *npl* Naturschätze *pl*.
natural wastage *n (COMM)* natürliche Personalreduzierung *f*.
nature [nā'chûr] *n* Natur *f*; **by ~** von Natur (aus); **documents of a confidential ~** Dokumente vertraulichen Inhalts.
nature reserve *n (Brit)* Naturschutzgebiet *nt*.
nature trail *n* Naturlehrpfad *m*.
naturist [nā'chûrist] *n* FKK-Anhänger(in *f*) *m*.
naught [nôt] *n* Null *f*.
naughtily [nôt'ilē] *ad* unartig.
naughtiness [nôt'ēnis] *n* Frechheit *f*; Unartigkeit *f*.
naughty [nôt'ē] *a* frech; *(child)* unartig, ungezogen; *(action)* ungehörig; *(joke, word)* unanständig.
nausea [nô'zēə] *n (sickness)* Übelkeit *f*; *(disgust)* Ekel *m*.
nauseate [nô'zēāt] *vt* anekeln.
nauseating [nô'zēāting] *a* ekelerregend; *(job)* widerlich; *(fig: person)* ekelhaft, widerlich; *(: film, book, style)* gräßlich.
nauseous [nô'shəs] *a (fig)* widerlich; **that made me feel ~** *(MED)* dabei wurde mir übel.
nautical [nô'tikəl] *a* nautisch, See-; *(expression)* seemännisch.
nautical mile *n* Seemeile *f* (= *1853 m)*.
naval [nā'vəl] *a* Marine-, Flotten-.
naval officer *n* Marineoffizier *m*.
nave [nāv] *n* Kirchen(haupt)schiff *nt*.
navel [nā'vəl] *n* Nabel *m*.
navigable [nav'əgəbəl] *a* schiffbar.
navigate [nav'əgāt] *vt (ship etc)* steuern ♦ *vi (sail)* (zu Schiff) fahren; *(AUT)* den Fahrer dirigieren; *(in rally)* Beifahrer sein.
navigation [navəgā'shən] *n* Navigation *f*.
navigator [nav'əgātûr] *n* Steuermann *m*; *(explorer)* Seefahrer *m*; *(AVIAT)* Navigator *m*; *(AUT)* Beifahrer(in *f*) *m*.

navvy [nav'ē] n (Brit) Straßenarbeiter m; (: on railway) Streckenarbeiter m.

navy [nā'vē] n Marine f, Flotte f; (warships etc) (Kriegs)flotte f.

navy-blue [nā'vēbloō] n Marineblau nt ♦ a marineblau.

nay [nā] ad (old: no) nein; (: even) ja sogar.

Nazareth [naz'ûrith] n Nazareth nt.

Nazi [nât'sē] a Nazi- ♦ n Nazi m.

NB abbr (= nota bene) NB; (Canada) = New Brunswick.

NBA n abbr (US: = National Basketball Association) ≈ DBB m; = National Boxing Association.

NBC n abbr (US: = National Broadcasting Company) NBC f.

NBS n abbr (US: = National Bureau of Standards) Verband zur Förderung von Industrie und Wirtschaft.

NC abbr (COMM etc) = no charge; (US MAIL) = North Carolina.

NCC n abbr (US: = National Council of Churches) Zusammenschluß protestantischer und östlich-orthodoxer Kirchen.

NCO n abbr (= non-commissioned officer) Uffz m.

ND abbr (US MAIL) = North Dakota.

N. Dak. abbr (US) = North Dakota.

NE abbr (US MAIL) = Nebraska, New England; = northeast.

NEA n abbr (US: = National Education Association) Lehrergewerkschaft.

Neapolitan [nēəpál'ətən] a neapolitanisch ♦ n Neapolitaner(in f) m.

neap tide [nēp tīd] n Nippflut f.

near [nēr] a nah; the vacation is ~ es sind bald Ferien; a ~ miss knapp daneben; (AVIAT) ein Beinahzusammenstoß m; a ~ thing knapp; in the ~ future in naher Zukunft, bald ♦ ad in der Nähe; to come ~er näher kommen; (time) näher rücken; ~ at hand nicht weit weg ♦ prep (also: ~ to) (space) in der Nähe (+gen); (time) um (+acc) ... herum; ~ here/there hier/dort in der Nähe ♦ vt sich nähern (+dat); the building is ~ing completion der Bau steht kurz vor dem Abschluß.

nearby [nēr'bī'] a nahe (gelegen) ♦ ad in der Nähe.

nearly [nēr'lē] ad fast; not ~ bei weitem nicht, nicht annähernd.

nearness [nēr'nis] n Nähe f.

nearside [nēr'sīd] (Brit AUT) n Beifahrerseite f ♦ a auf der Beifahrerseite.

nearsighted [nēr'sītid] a kurzsichtig.

neat [nēt] a (tidy) ordentlich; (clever) treffend; (solution) sauber; (skillful) gewandt; (col: great) prima; (pure) unverdünnt, rein.

neatly [nēt'lē] ad (tidily) ordentlich; (cleverly) treffend; (work, solve) sauber.

neatness [nēt'nis] n Ordentlichkeit f; Sauberkeit f; Gewandtheit f.

Nebr. abbr (US) = Nebraska.

nebulous [neb'yələs] a nebelhaft, verschwommen.

necessarily [nesəsär'ilē] ad unbedingt, notwendigerweise; not ~ nicht unbedingt.

necessary [nes'isärē] a notwendig, nötig; if ~ falls nötig.

necessitate [nəses'ətāt] vt erforderlich machen.

necessity [nəses'itē] n (need) Not f; (compulsion) Notwendigkeit f; in case of ~ im Notfall; **necessities of life** Bedürfnisse pl des Lebens.

neck [nek] n Hals m; ~ **and** ~ Kopf an Kopf; **to stick one's** ~ **out** (col) seinen Kopf riskieren ♦ vi (col) knutschen.

necklace [nek'lis] n Halskette f.

neckline [nek'līn] n Ausschnitt m.

necktie [nek'tī] n (US) Krawatte f.

nectar [nek'tûr] n Nektar m.

nectarine [nektərēn'] n Nektarine f.

née [nā] a geborene.

need [nēd] n (requirement) Bedürfnis nt (for für); (want) Mangel m; (necessity) Notwendigkeit f; (poverty) Not f; if ~ **be** wenn nötig; **there is no** ~ **for you to come** du brauchst nicht zu kommen; **in case of** ~ notfalls; **there's no** ~ **for it** das ist nicht nötig; **to be in** ~ **of (sth), to have** ~ **of (sth)** (etw) brauchen; **10 will meet my immediate** ~s mit 10 komme ich erst einmal aus; **consumer** ~s Verbraucherbedürfnisse pl ♦ vt brauchen; **I** ~ **it** ich brauche das; **a signature is** ~**ed** das bedarf einer Unterschrift (gen) ♦ aux v: **I** ~ **to do it** ich muß das tun.

needle [nē'dəl] n Nadel f.

needless [nēd'lis] a, **needlessly** [nēd'lislē] ad unnötig.

needlework [nēd'əlwûrk] n Handarbeit f.

needy [nē'dē] a bedürftig.

negation [nigā'shən] n Verneinung f.

negative [neg'ətiv] n (PHOT) Negativ nt ♦ a negativ; (answer) abschlägig.

negative cash flow n Überhang m der Zahlungsausgänge.

neglect [niglekt'] vt (leave undone) versäumen; (not take care of) vernachlässigen; **to** ~ **to do sth** es versäumen or unterlassen, etw zu tun ♦ n Vernachlässigung f.

neglected [niglek'tid] a vernachlässigt; (garden etc) verwahrlost.

neglectful [niglekt'fəl] a nachlässig; (father, government, etc) pflichtvergessen; **to be** ~ **of sb/sth** sich nicht um jdn/etw kümmern, jdn/etw vernachlässigen.

negligée [neg'ləzhā] n Negligé nt.

negligence [neg'lijəns] n Nachlässigkeit f.

negligent [neg'lijənt] a, **negligently** [neg'lijəntlē] ad nachlässig, unachtsam.

negligible [neg'lijəbəl] a unbedeutend, geringfügig.

negotiable [nigō'shəbəl] a (check) übertragbar, einlösbar; (road) befahrbar.

negotiate [nigō'shēāt] vi verhandeln; **to** ~ **with sb for sth** mit jdm über etw verhandeln ♦ *vt* (*treaty*) abschließen, aushandeln; (*difficulty*) überwinden; (*curve in road*) nehmen.

negotiation [nigōshēā'shən] *n* Verhandlung *f*; **to enter into ~s with sb** Verhandlungen mit jdm aufnehmen.

negotiator [nigō'shēātûr] *n* Unterhändler(in *f*) *m*.

Negress [nēg'ris] *n* Negerin *f*.

Negro [nēg'rō] *n* Neger *m* ♦ *a* Neger-.

neigh [nā] *vi* wiehen.

neighbor [nā'bûr] *n* (*US*) Nachbar(in *f*) *m*.

neighborhood [nā'bûrhōōd] *n* Nachbarschaft *f*; (*district*) Gegend *f*.

neighboring [nā'bûring] *a* benachbart, angrenzend.

neighborly [nā'bûrlē] *a* freundlich.

neighbour [nā'bûr] *etc* (*Brit*) = **neighbor** *etc*.

neither [nē'thûr] *a*, *pron* keine(r, s) (von beiden) ♦ *ad*: ~ ... **nor** weder ... noch ♦ *cj* auch nicht; **he can't do it, and ~ can I** er kann es nicht und ich auch nicht.

neo- [nē'ō] *pref* neo-.

neolithic [nēəlith'ik] *a* jungsteinzeitlich, neolithisch.

neologism [nēal'əjizəm] *n* (Wort)neubildung *f*, Neologismus *m*.

neon [nē'ân] *n* Neon *nt*.

neon light *n* Neonlicht *nt*.

Nepal [nəpôl'] *n* Nepal *nt*.

nephew [nef'yōō] *n* Neffe *m*.

nepotism [nep'ətizəm] *n* Vetternwirtschaft *f*.

nerve [nûrv] *n* Nerv *m*; (*courage*) Mut *m*; (*impudence*) Frechheit *f*; **to lose one's ~** (*self-confidence*) den Mut verlieren.

nerve center *n* (*ANAT*) Nervenknoten *m*; (*fig*) Schaltzentrale *f*.

nerve gas *n* Nervengas *nt*.

nerve-racking [nûrv'raking] *a* nervenaufreibend.

nervous [nûr'vəs] *a* (*of the nerves*) Nerven-; (*timid*) nervös, ängstlich.

nervous breakdown *n* Nervenzusammenbruch *m*.

nervously [nûr'vəslē] *ad* nervös.

nervousness [nûr'vəsnis] *n* Nervosität *f*.

nest [nest] *n* Nest *nt* ♦ *vi* nisten.

nest egg *n* (*fig*) Notgroschen *m*.

nestle [nes'əl] *vi* sich kuscheln; (*village*) sich schmiegen.

nestling [nest'ling] *n* Nestling *m*.

net [net] *n* Netz *nt*; (*fabric*) Tüll *m* ♦ *a* (*also*: **nett**) netto, Netto-, Rein-; **~ of tax** steuerfrei; **he earns $10,000 ~ per year** er verdient 10.000 Dollar netto im Jahr ♦ *vt* verdienen; (*in deal, sale*) einbringen.

NET *n abbr* (*US*) = *National Educational Television*.

net assets *npl* Reinvermögen *nt*.

netball [net'bôl] *n* Netzball *m*.

net curtains *npl* (*Brit*) Store *m*.

Netherlands [neth'ûrləndz] *npl* die Niederlande *pl*.

net income *n* Nettoeinkommen *nt*.

net loss *n* Nettoverlust *m*.

net profit *n* Nettogewinn *m*.

nett [net] *a* = **net**.

netting [net'ing] *n* Netz(werk) *nt*, Drahtgeflecht *nt*; (*fabric*) Netzgewebe *nt*.

network [net'wûrk] *n* Netz *nt*; (*RAD, TV*) Sendenetz *nt*; (*COMPUT*) Network *nt*.

neuralgia [nōōral'jə] *n* Neuralgie *f*, Nervenschmerzen *pl*.

neurosis [nōōrō'sis] *n* Neurose *f*.

neurotic [nōōrât'ik] *a* neurotisch ♦ *n* Neurotiker(in *f*) *m*.

neuter [nōō'tûr] *a* (*BIOL*) geschlechtslos; (*GRAM*) sächlich ♦ *n* (*GRAM*) Neutrum *nt* ♦ *vt* kastrieren.

neutral [nōō'trəl] *a* neutral.

neutrality [nōōtral'itē] *n* Neutralität *f*.

neutralize [nōō'trəlīz] *vt* neutralisieren.

neutron bomb [nōō'trân bâm] *n* Neutronenbombe *f*.

Nev. *abbr* (*US*) = *Nevada*.

never [nev'ûr] *ad* nie(mals); **well I ~!** na so was!

never-ending [nev'ûren'ding] *a* endlos.

nevertheless [nevûrthəles'] *ad* trotzdem, dennoch.

new [nōō] *a* neu; **they are still ~ to the work** die Arbeit ist ihnen noch neu; **~ from** frisch aus *or* von; **as good as ~** so gut wie neu.

newborn [nōō'bôrn] *a* neugeboren.

newcomer [nōō'kumûr] *n* Neuankömmling *m*.

newfangled [nōō'fang'gəld] *a* (*pej*) neumodisch.

newfound [nōō'found] *a* neuentdeckt.

New Guinea [nōō gin'ē] *n* Neuguinea *nt*.

newly [nōō'lē] *ad* frisch, neu.

newlyweds [nōō'lēwedz] *npl* Neu- *or* Jungvermählte *pl*.

new moon *n* Neumond *m*.

newness [nōō'nis] *n* Neuheit *f*; (*of bread, cheese, etc*) Frische *f*.

news [nōōz] *n* Nachricht *f*; (*RAD, TV*) Nachrichten *pl*; **good/bad ~** gute/schlechte Nachricht; **financial ~** (*in newspaper*) Wirtschaftsteil *m*; (*RAD, TV*) Wirtschaftsbericht *m*.

news agency *n* Nachrichtenagentur *f*.

newsagent [nōōz'ājənt] *n* (*Brit*) Zeitungshändler *m*.

news bulletin *n* (*RAD, TV*) Bulletin *nt*.

newscaster [nōōz'kastûr] *n* (*RAD, TV*) Nachrichtensprecher(in *f*) *m*.

newsdealer [nōōz'dēlûr] *n* (*US*) Zeitungshändler *m*.

news flash *n* Kurzmeldung *f*.

news item *n* Nachricht *f*.

newsletter [nōōz'letûr] *n* Rundschreiben *nt*, Mitteilungsblatt *nt*.

newspaper [nōōz'pāpûr] *n* Zeitung *f*; **daily ~** Tageszeitung *f*; **weekly ~** Wochenzeitung *f*.

newspaper kiosk *n* Zeitungskiosk *m*.

newsprint [nōōz'print] n Zeitungspapier nt.
newsreader [nōōz'rēdûr] n (Brit) Nachrichtensprecher(in f) m.
newsreel [nōōz'rēl] n Wochenschau f.
newsroom [nōōz'rōōm] n (of newspaper) Nachrichtenredaktion f; (RAD, TV) Nachrichtenstudio nt or -zentrale f.
newsstand [nōōz'stand] n Zeitungsstand m.
newt [nōōt] n Wassermolch m.
New Year n Neujahr nt; **Happy** ~ Frohes Neues Jahr!; **to wish sb a happy** ~ jdm ein frohes Neues Jahr wünschen.
New Year's Day n Neujahrstag m.
New Year's Eve n Silvester(abend m) nt.
New York [nōō yôrk] n New York nt.
New Zealand [nōō zē'lənd] n Neuseeland nt ♦ a neuseeländisch.
New Zealander [nōō zē'ləndûr] n Neuseeländer(in f) m.
next [nekst] a nächste(r, s); **the** ~ **day** am nächsten or folgenden Tag; ~ **door** nebenan; ~ **year** nächstes Jahr; ~ **month** nächsten Monat; **the week after** ~ übernächste Woche; **"turn to the** ~ **page"** „blättern Sie um"; **you're** ~ Sie sind an der Reihe ♦ ad (after) dann, darauf; (~ time) das nächste Mal; ~ **to** (gleich) neben (+dat); ~ **to nothing** so gut wie nichts; **to do sth** ~ etw als nächstes tun; **what** ~? was denn noch (alles)?
next-of-kin [nekst'əvkin'] n nächste(r) Verwandte(r) mf.
n/f abbr (FIN: = no funds) keine Deckung.
NF n abbr (Brit POL: = National Front) rechtsradikale Partei ♦ abbr (Canada) = Newfoundland.
NFL n abbr (US: = National Football League) ≈ Fußballbundesliga f.
Nfld. abbr (Canada) = Newfoundland.
NG n abbr (US: = National Guard) Nationalgarde f.
NGO n abbr (US: = non-governmental organization) nichtstaatliche Organisation f.
NH abbr (US MAIL) = New Hampshire.
NHL n abbr (US: = National Hockey League) ≈ Eishockeybundesliga f.
NHS n abbr (Brit) = **National Health Service**.
NI abbr = **Northern Ireland**; (Brit) **National Insurance**.
nib [nib] n Spitze f.
nibble [nib'əl] vt knabbern an (+dat).
Nicaragua [nikərâg'wə] n Nicaragua nt.
Nicaraguan [nikərâg'wən] a nicaraguanisch ♦ n Nicaraguaner(in f) m.
nice [nīs] a nett; (girl, dress etc) hübsch; (intensifier) schön; (subtle) fein; (taste, smell, meal) gut.
Nice [nēs] n Nizza nt.
nice-looking [nīs'lōōk'ing] a hübsch, gutaussehend.
nicely [nīs'lē] ad gut, fein, nett; **that will do** ~ das reicht (vollauf).
niceties [nī'sətēz] npl Feinheiten pl.

niche [nich] n (ARCHIT) Nische f.
nick [nik] n Einkerbung f; **in the** ~ **of time** gerade zur rechten Zeit ♦ vt (wood) einkerben; (Brit col: arrest) einsperren, einlochen; **to** ~ **o.s.** (cut o.s.) sich schneiden.
nickel [nik'əl] n Nickel nt.
nickname [nik'nām] n Spitzname m.
nicotine [nik'ətēn] n Nikotin nt.
niece [nēs] n Nichte f.
nifty [nif'tē] a (col: car, jacket) flott; (: gadget, tool) schlau.
Niger [nī'jûr] n (country) Niger nt.
Nigeria [nījē'rēə] n Nigeria nt.
Nigerian [nījē'rēən] a nigerianisch ♦ n Nigerianer(in f) m.
niggardly [nig'ûrdlē] a schäbig; (person) geizig, knauserig; (allowance, amount) armselig.
niggle [nig'əl] vt plagen, quälen ♦ vi (person) herumkritisieren (about an +dat).
niggling [nig'ling] a pedantisch; (detail) kleinlich, pingelig (col); (doubt, pain) bohrend, quälend.
night [nīt] n Nacht f; (evening) Abend m; **good** ~! gute Nacht!; **at** or **by** ~ nachts; abends; **in the** ~ in der Nacht; **during the** ~ während der Nacht; **the** ~ **before last** vorletzte Nacht; vorgestern abend.
nightcap [nīt'kap] n Schlafmütze f; (drink) Schlummertrunk m.
nightclub [nīt'klub] n Nachtlokal nt.
nightdress [nīt'dres] n = **nightgown**.
nightfall [nīt'fôl] n Einbruch m der Nacht.
nightgown [nīt'goun] n Nachthemd nt.
nightie [nī'tē] n (Brit col) = **nightgown**.
nightingale [nī'təngāl] n Nachtigall f.
night life n Nachtleben nt.
nightly [nīt'lē] a (every night) (all)nächtlich, Nacht-; (every evening) (all)abendlich, Abend- ♦ ad jede Nacht; jeden Abend.
nightmare [nīt'mär] n Alptraum m.
night owl n (fig) Nachteule f.
night porter n Nachtportier m.
night safe n Nachtsafe m.
night school n Abendschule f.
night shift n Nachtschicht f.
nightstick [nīt'stik] n (US) Gummiknüppel m.
nighttime [nīt'tīm] n Nacht f; **at** ~ nachts.
night watchman n Nachtwächter m.
NIH n abbr (US) = National Institutes of Health.
nihilism [nē'əlizəm] n Nihilismus m.
nil [nil] n Nichts nt, Null f.
Nile [nīl] n Nil m.
nimble [nim'bəl] a behend(e), flink; (mind) beweglich.
nimbly [nim'blē] ad flink.
nine [nīn] n Neun f ♦ a neun.
nineteen [nīn'tēn'] n Neunzehn f ♦ a neunzehn.
nineteenth [nīn'tēnth'] a neunzehnte(r, s).
ninety [nīn'tē] n Neunzig f ♦ a neunzig.
ninth [nīnth] a neunte(r, s) ♦ n Neuntel nt.
nip [nip] vt kneifen ♦ vi (Brit col): **to** ~ **out**

hinaussausen; **to ~ up/down(stairs)** hoch-/runtersausen ♦ *n* Kneifen *nt*; *(drink)* Schlückchen *nt*.

nipple [nip'əl] *n* (ANAT) Brustwarze *f*; *(on nursing bottle)* Sauger *m*.

nippy [nip'ē] *a* *(Brit col: person)* flink; *(: car)* flott; *(: cold)* frisch.

nit [nit] *n* *(of louse)* Nisse *f*; *(col: idiot)* Dummkopf *m*.

nit-pick [nit'pik] *vi* *(col)* kleinlich *or* pingelich sein.

nitrogen [nī'trəjən] *n* Stickstoff *m*.

nitroglycerin(e) [nītrəglis'ûrin] *n* Nitroglyzerin *nt*.

nitty-gritty [nit'ēgrit'ē] *n* *(col)*: **to get down to the ~** zur Sache kommen.

nitwit [nit'wit] *n* *(col)* Dummkopf *m*.

NJ *abbr* (US MAIL) = New Jersey.

NLF *n abbr* (= National Liberation Front) NLF *f*.

NLQ *n abbr* (= near letter quality) korrespondenzfähiges Schriftbild.

NLRB *n abbr* (US: = National Labor Relations Board) Bundesausschuß zur Regelung von Beziehungen zwischen Arbeitgebern und -nehmern.

NM *abbr* (US MAIL) = New Mexico.

N. Mex. *abbr* (US) = New Mexico.

no [nō] *a* kein ♦ *ad* nein; **~ further** nicht weiter; **~ more time** keine Zeit mehr; **in ~ time** schnell ♦ *n* Nein *nt*; **I won't take ~ for an answer** ich bestehe darauf.

no., nos. *abbr* (= number(s)) Nr.

nobble [nâb'əl] *vt* *(Brit col: horse, dog)* lahmlegen; *(: catch)* schnappen.

Nobel prize [nō'bel prīz'] *n* Nobelpreis *m*.

nobility [nōbil'ətē] *n* Adel *m*; **the ~ of this deed** diese edle Tat.

noble [nō'bəl] *a* *(rank)* adlig; *(splendid)* nobel, edel ♦ *n* Adlige(r) *mf*.

nobleman [nō'bəlmən] *n, pl* **-men** Edelmann *m*, Adlige(r) *m*.

nobly [nō'blē] *ad* edel, großmütig; *(selflessly)* nobel, edel(mütig).

nobody [nō'bâdē] *pron* niemand, keiner ♦ *n* Niemand *m*.

no-claims bonus [nō'klāmz' bō'nəs] *n* (Brit) = **no-claims discount**.

no-claims discount [nō'klāmz' dis'kount] *n* (US) Schadensfreiheitsrabatt *m*.

nocturnal [nâktûr'nəl] *a* nächtlich; *(animal, bird)* Nacht-.

nod [nâd] *vi* nicken ♦ *vt*: **to ~ one's head** mit dem Kopf nicken; **they ~ded their agreement** sie nickten zustimmend ♦ *n* Nicken *nt*.

nod off *vi* einnicken.

no fault agreement *n* (US) Schadensteilungsvereinbarung *f*.

noise [noiz] *n* *(sound)* Geräusch *nt*; *(unpleasant, loud)* Lärm *m*.

noisily [noi'zilē] *ad* lärmend, laut.

noisy [noi'zē] *a* laut; *(crowd)* lärmend.

nomad [nō'mad] *n* Nomade *m*.

nomadic [nōmad'ik] *a* nomadisch.

no man's land *n* *(lit, fig)* Niemandsland *nt*.

nominal [nâm'ənəl] *a* nominell; (GRAM) Nominal-.

nominate [nâm'ənāt] *vt* *(suggest)* vorschlagen; *(in election)* aufstellen; *(appoint)* ernennen.

nomination [nâmənā'shən] *n* *(election)* Nominierung *f*; *(appointment)* Ernennung *f*.

nominee [nâmənē'] *n* Kandidat(in *f*) *m*.

non- [nân] *pref* Nicht-, un-.

nonalcoholic [nânalkəhôl'ik] *a* alkoholfrei.

nonarrival [nânərī'vəl] *n* Ausbleiben *nt*.

nonce word [nâns' wûrd] *n* Neuschöpfung *f*.

nonchalant [nânshəlânt'] *a* lässig.

noncommissioned officer [nânkəmish'ənd ôf'isûr] *n* Unteroffizier *m*.

noncommittal [nânkəmit'əl] *a* *(reserved)* zurückhaltend; *(uncommitted)* unverbindlich.

nonconformist [nânkənfôr'mist] *n* (REL also) Nonkonformist(in *f*) *m*.

noncontributory [nânkəntrib'yətôrē] *a*: **~ pension plan** beitragsfreie(s) Betriebsrentensystem *nt*.

noncooperation [nânkōâpərā'shən] *n* unkooperative Haltung *f*.

nondescript [nân'diskript] *a* mittelmäßig.

none [nun] *a, pron* kein(e, er, es); **I have ~ left** ich habe keine(n) mehr; **~ of you** keiner von euch; **do you have any milk/bread? — I have ~** haben Sie Milch/Brot? — ich habe (gar) keine/keins; **there is ~ left** es ist nichts übrig; **~ of your cheek!** sei nicht so frech! ♦ *ad*: **~ the wiser** keineswegs klüger.

nonentity [nânen'titē] *n* Nichts *nt*, Null *f* *(col)*.

nonessential [nânəsen'chəl] *a* unnötig ♦ *npl*: **~s** nicht (lebens)notwendige Dinge *pl*.

nonetheless [nun'thəles'] *ad* nichtsdestoweniger, trotzdem.

nonexecutive director [nânigzek'yətiv direk'tûr] *n* Führungskraft ohne Entscheidungsgewalt bei der Geschäftsführung.

nonexistent [nânigzis'tənt] *a* nicht vorhanden.

nonfiction [nânfik'shən] *n* Sachbücher *pl*.

nonintervention [nânintûrven'chən] *n* Nichteinmischung *f*, Nichteingreifen *nt* *(in +acc)*.

non obst. *ad abbr* (= non obstante) trotzdem.

nonpayment [nânpā'mənt] *n* Nichtzahlung *f*, Zahlungsverweigerung *f*.

nonplused, *(Brit)* **nonplussed** [nânplust'] *a* verdutzt.

nonprofit-making [nânprâf'itmāking] *a* keinen Gewinn anstrebend *attr*; *(charity etc)* gemeinnützig.

nonsense [nân'sens] *n* Unsinn *m*; **it is ~ to say that ...** es ist dummes Gerede, zu sagen, daß ...

nonskid [nânskid'] *a* rutschsicher.

nonsmoker [nânsmō'kûr] *n* Nichtraucher(in *f*) *m*.

nonstick [nânstik'] *a* *(pan etc)* Teflon- ®.

nonstop [nân'stâp'] *a* pausenlos, Nonstop-.
nontaxable income [nântak'səbəl in'kum] *n* nicht zu versteuernde(s) Einkommen *nt*.
nonvolatile memory [nânvâl'ətəl mem'ûrē] *n* (*COMPUT*) nichtflüchtige(r) Speicher *m*, Festwertspeicher *m*.
nonvoting shares [nânvō'ting shärz] *npl* stimmrechtslose Aktien *pl*.
nonwhite [nânwīt'] *a* farbig ♦ *n* Farbige(r) *mf*.
noodles [nōō'dəlz] *npl* Nudeln *pl*.
nook [nook] *n* Winkel *m*, Eckchen *nt*.
noon [nōōn] *n* (12 Uhr) Mittag *m*.
no one *pron* = **nobody**.
noose [nōōs] *n* Schlinge *f*.
nor [nôr] *cj* = **neither** ♦ *ad see* **neither**.
Norf *abbr* (*Brit*) = **Norfolk**.
norm [nôrm] *n* Norm *f*, Regel *f*.
normal [nôr'məl] *a* normal ♦ *n*: **to return to** ~ sich wieder normalisieren.
normality [nôrmal'itē] *n* Normalität *f*.
normally [nôr'məlē] *ad* normal; (*usually*) normalerweise.
Normandy [nôr'məndē] *n* Normandie *f*.
north [nôrth] *n* Norden *m* ♦ *a* nördlich, Nord- ♦ *ad* nördlich, nach *or* im Norden.
North Africa *n* Nordafrika *nt*.
North African *a* nordafrikanisch ♦ *n* Nordafrikaner(in *f*) *m*.
North America *n* Nordamerika *nt*.
North American *a* nordamerikanisch ♦ *n* Nordamerikaner(in *f*) *m*.
Northants [nôrthants'] *abbr* (*Brit*) = Northamptonshire.
northbound [nôrth'bound'] *a* (*traffic*) in Richtung Norden; (*freeway*) nach Norden (führend).
Northd *abbr* (*Brit*) = Northumberland.
northeast [nôrthēst'] *n* Nordosten *m*.
northerly [nôr'thûrlē] *a* (*wind, direction*) nördlich.
northern [nôr'thûrn] *a* nördlich, Nord-.
Northern Ireland *n* Nordirland *nt*.
North Korea *n* Nordkorea *nt*.
North Pole *n* Nordpol *m*.
North Sea *n* Nordsee *f*; ~ **oil** Nordseeöl *nt*.
North star *n* Polarstern *m*.
northward(s) [nôrth'wûrd(z)] *ad* nach Norden.
northwest [nôrthwest'] *n* Nordwesten *m*.
Norway [nôr'wā] *n* Norwegen *nt*.
Norwegian [nôrwē'jən] *a* norwegisch ♦ *n* (*person*) Norweger(in *f*) *m*; (*language*) Norwegisch *nt*.
nose [nōz] *n* Nase *f*; **to pay through the** ~ (*col*) viel blechen, sich dumm und dämlich zahlen ♦ *vi*: **the car/ship** ~**d (its way) through the fog** das Auto/Schiff tastete sich durch den Nebel.
nose around *vi* herumschnüffeln.
nosebleed [nōz'blēd] *n* Nasenbluten *nt*.
nose dive *n* Sturzflug *m*.
nose drops *npl* Nasentropfen *pl*.
nosey [nō'zē] *a* neugierig.

nostalgia [nəstal'jə] *n* Sehnsucht *f*, Nostalgie *f*.
nostalgic [nəstal'jik] *a* wehmütig, nostalgisch.
nostril [nâs'trəl] *n* Nasenloch *nt*; (*of animal*) Nüster *f*.
nosy [nō'zē] *a* = **nosey**.
not [nât] *ad* nicht; **he is** ~ **an expert** er ist kein Experte; ~ **at all** überhaupt nicht, keineswegs; (*don't mention it*) nichts zu danken, gern geschehen; **I hope** ~ hoffentlich nicht.
notable [nō'təbəl] *a* bemerkenswert.
notably [nō'təblē] *ad* (*especially*) besonders; (*noticeably*) bemerkenswert; (*in particular*) hauptsächlich.
notary [nō'tûrē] *n* (*also*: ~ **public**) Notar(in *f*) *m*.
notation [nōtā'shən] *n* Zeichensystem *nt*, Notation *f*; (*MUS*) Notenschrift *f*.
notch [nâch] *n* Kerbe *f*, Einschnitt *m*.
note [nōt] *n* (*MUS*) Note *f*, Ton *m*; (*short letter*) Nachricht *f*; (*comment, attention*) Notiz *f*; (*of lecture etc*) Aufzeichnung *f*; (*bank*~) Schein *m*; (*fame*) Ruf *m*, Ansehen *nt*; **just a quick** ~ **to let you know that** ... nur ein paar Zeilen, um Ihnen zu sagen, daß ...; **to compare** ~**s** (*fig*) Eindrücke *or* Erfahrungen austauschen; **a man of** ~/**nothing of** ~ ein bedeutender Mann/nichts Beachtens- *or* Erwähnenswertes; **to take** ~ zur Kenntnis nehmen; **to take a** ~ **of sth** sich (*dat*) etw notieren ♦ *vt* (*observe*) bemerken; (*write down*) notieren.
notebook [nōt'book] *n* Notizbuch *nt*; (*for shorthand*) Notizheft *nt*.
notecase [nōt'kās] *n* (*Brit*) Brieftasche *f*.
noted [nō'tid] *a* bekannt.
notepad [nōt'pad] *n* Notizblock *m*.
notepaper [nōt'pāpûr] *n* Briefpapier *nt*.
noteworthy [nōt'wûrthē] *a* beachtenswert, erwähnenswert.
nothing [nuth'ing] *n* nichts; **for** ~ umsonst; **it is** ~ **to me** es bedeutet mir nichts; ~ **at all** überhaupt nichts.
notice [nō'tis] *vt* bemerken ♦ *n* (*announcement*) Anzeige *f*, Bekanntmachung *f*; (*attention*) Beachtung *f*; (*warning*) Ankündigung *f*; (*dismissal*) Kündigung *f*; (*Brit: review: of play etc*) Kritik *f*, Rezension *f*; **without** ~ ohne Ankündigung, unangemeldet; **advance** ~ Vorankündigung *f*; **at short** ~ kurzfristig; **until further** ~ bis auf weiteres; **to give sb** ~ **of sth** jdn von etw benachrichtigen; **to give** ~, **to hand in one's** ~ kündigen; **it has come to my** ~ **that** ... es ist mir zu Ohren gekommen, daß ...; **it might not have escaped your** ~ **that** ... es ist Ihnen sicherlich nicht entgangen, daß ...; **to take** ~ **of** beachten; **to bring sth to sb's** ~ jdn auf etw (*acc*) aufmerksam machen; **take no** ~! kümmere dich nicht darum!
noticeable [nō'tisəbəl] *a* merklich.
notice board *n* (*Brit*) Anschlagbrett *nt*.
notification [nōtəfəkā'shən] *n* Benachrichti-

gung *f*; (*announcement*) Meldung *f*.
notify [nō'təfī] *vt* benachrichtigen.
notion [nō'shən] *n* (*idea*) Vorstellung *f*, Idee *f*; (*fancy*) Lust *f*.
notions [nō'shənz] *npl* (*US*) Kurzwaren *pl*.
notoriety [nōtərī'ətē] *n* traurige Berühmtheit *f*.
notorious [nōtôr'ēəs] *a* berüchtigt.
notoriously [nōtôr'ēəslē] *a* notorisch.
Notts [nāts] *abbr* (*Brit*) = *Nottinghamshire*.
notwithstanding [nātwithstan'ding] *ad* trotzdem ♦ *prep* trotz.
nougat [nōō'gət] *n* weiße(r) Nougat *m*.
nought [nôt] *n* Null *f*.
noun [noun] *n* Hauptwort *nt*, Substantiv *nt*.
nourish [nûr'ish] *vt* nähren.
nourishing [nûr'ishing] *a* nahrhaft.
nourishment [nûr'ishmənt] *n* Nahrung *f*.
Nov. *abbr* (= *November*) Nov.
novel [nâv'əl] *n* Roman *m* ♦ *a* neu(artig).
novelist [nâv'əlist] *n* Schriftsteller(in *f*) *m*.
novelty [nâv'əltē] *n* Neuheit *f*.
November [nōvem'bûr] *n* November *m*; *see* **September**.
novice [nâv'is] *n* Neuling *m*; (*ECCL*) Novize *m*.
now [nou] *ad* jetzt; **just** ~ gerade; **right** ~ sofort; ~ **and then**, ~ **and again** ab und zu, manchmal; ~, ~ na, na; ~ ... ~ *or* **then** bald ... bald, mal ... mal; **that's all for** ~ das ist erstmal alles; **between** ~ **and Monday** bis (zum) Montag; **by** ~ inzwischen, mittlerweile; **in 3 days from** ~ in drei Tagen.
NOW [nou] *n abbr* (*US*: = *National Organization for Women*) Frauenvereinigung.
nowadays [nou'ədāz] *ad* heutzutage.
nowhere [nō'wär] *ad* nirgends; ~ **else** nirgendwo anders.
noxious [nâk'shəs] *a* schädlich.
nozzle [nâz'əl] *n* Düse *f*.
NP *n abbr* = **notary public**.
NS *abbr* (*Canada*) = *Nova Scotia*.
NSC *n abbr* (*US*: = *National Security Council*) Sicherheitsausschuß.
NSF *n abbr* (*US*: = *National Science Foundation*) (*unabhängige*) Organisation zur Förderung der Wissenschaft.
NSW *abbr* (*Australia*) = *New South Wales*.
NT *n abbr* (= *New Testament*) N.T. *nt*.
nth [enth] *a* (*col*): **for the** ~ **time** zum x-ten Mal.
nuance [nōō'ânts] *n* Nuance *f*.
nubile [nōō'bīl] *a* (*attractive*) gut entwickelt; (*girl*) heiratsfähig.
nuclear [nōō'klēûr] *a* (*energy etc*) Atom-, Kern-; (*warfare*) Atom-.
nuclear disarmament *n* atomare Abrüstung *f*.
nucleus [nōō'klēəs] *n* Kern *m*.
nude [nōōd] *a* nackt ♦ *n* (*person*) Nackte(r) *mf*; (*ART*) Akt *m*; **in the** ~ nackt.
nudge [nuj] *vt* leicht anstoßen.
nudist [nōō'dist] *n* Nudist(in *f*) *m*.

nudist colony *n* FKK-Kolonie *f*.
nudity [nōō'ditē] *n* Nacktheit *f*.
nugget [nug'it] *n* Klumpen *m*; (*fig: of information, knowledge*) Brocken *m*, Bröckchen *nt*.
nuisance [nōō'səns] *n* Ärgernis *nt*; **that's a** ~ das ist ärgerlich; **he's a** ~ er geht einem auf die Nerven.
nuke [nōōk] *n* (*col*) Atombombe *f* ♦ *vt* atomar vernichten.
null [nul] *a*: ~ **and void** null und nichtig.
nullify [nul'əfī] *vt* für null und nichtig erklären.
numb [num] *a* taub, gefühllos; ~ **with cold** vor Kälte taub *or* gefühllos; ~ **with fear/ grief** (*fig*) starr vor Furcht/Schmerz ♦ *vt* (*with injection*) betäuben; (*with cold*) taub *or* gefühllos machen.
number [num'bûr] *n* Nummer *f*; (*numeral also*) Zahl *f*; (*quantity*) (An)zahl *f*; (*of magazine also*) Ausgabe *f*; **they were 20 in** ~ Sie waren 20 an der Zahl; **wrong** ~ (*TEL*) falsch verbunden; **N~ Ten** (*Brit POL*) Nummer Zehn (Downing Street) ♦ *vt* (*give a* ~ *to*) numerieren; (*amount to*) sein; **his days are** ~**ed** seine Tage sind gezählt.
numbered account [num'bûrd əkount'] *n* Nummernkonto *nt*.
number plate *n* (*Brit AUT*) Nummernschild *nt*.
numbness [num'nis] *n* Benommenheit *f*, Betäubung *f*; (*due to cold*) Taubheit *f*, Starre *f*.
numbskull [num'skul] *n* Idiot *m*.
numeral [nōō'mûrəl] *n* Ziffer *f*.
numerical [nōōmär'ikəl] *a* (*order*) zahlenmäßig.
numerous [nōō'mûrəs] *a* zahlreich.
nun [nun] *n* Nonne *f*.
nuptial [nup'shəl] *a* ehelich, Ehe-; (*celebration*) Hochzeits-; (*vow*) Ehe-.
nurse [nûrs] *n* Krankenschwester *f*; (*for children*) Kindermädchen *nt*; (*male* ~) Krankenpfleger *m* ♦ *vt* (*patient*) pflegen; (*doubt etc*) hegen; (*US: baby*) stillen; futtern.
nursery [nûr'sûrē] *n* (*for children*) Kinderzimmer *nt*; (*for plants*) Gärtnerei *f*; (*for trees*) Baumschule *f*.
nursery rhyme *n* Kinderreim *m*.
nursery school *n* Kindergarten *m*.
nursery slope *n* (*Brit SKI*) Anfängerhügel *m*.
nursing [nûrs'ing] *n* (*profession*) Krankenpflege *f*.
nursing bottle *n* (*US*) Flasche *f*.
nursing home *n* Privatklinik *f*; (*for convalescents*) Pflegeheim *nt*.
nut [nut] *n* Nuß *f*; (*for screw*) Schraubenmutter *f*; (*col*) Verrückte(r) *nf* ♦ *a* (*chocolate etc*) Nuß-.
nutcase [nut'kās] *n* (*Brit col*) Verrückte(r) *mf*.
nutcracker(s) [nut'krakûr(z)] *n(pl)* Nußknacker *m*.
nutmeg [nut'meg] *n* Muskat(nuß *f*) *m*.

nutrient [nōō'trēənt] *n* Nährstoff *m* ♦ *a* (*substance*) nahrhaft; (*properties*) Nähr-.

nutrition [nōōtrish'ən] *n* Nahrung *f*.

nutritionist [nōōtrish'ənist] *n* Ernährungswissenschaftler(in *f*) *m*.

nutritious [nōōtrish'əs] *a* nahrhaft.

nuts [nuts] *a* (*col: crazy*) verrückt; **to be ~** *or* **to go ~** spinnen, durchdrehen ♦ *excl* Mist!

nutshell [nut'shel] *n*: **in a ~** in aller Kürze.

nuzzle [nuz'əl] *vi*: **to ~ up to sb** sich an jdn schmiegen *or* drücken.

NV *abbr* (*US MAIL*) = *Nevada*.

NWT *abbr* (*Canada*) = *Northwest Territories*.

NY *abbr* (*US MAIL*) = *New York*.

NYC *abbr* (*US MAIL*) = *New York City*.

nylon [nī'lân] *n* Nylon *nt* ♦ *a* Nylon-.

nymph [nimf] *n* Nymphe *f*.

nymphomaniac [nimfəmā'nēak] *a* nymphoman ♦ *n* Nymphomanin *f*.

NYSE *n abbr* (*US*) = *New York Stock Exchange*.

NZ *abbr* = **New Zealand**.

O

O, o [ō] *n* (*letter*) O *nt*, o *nt*; (*TEL*) Null *f*; **O for Oboe** ≈ O wie Otto.

O [ō] *n abbr* (*US SCH: mark = outstanding*) ≈ 1.

oaf [ōf] *n* Trottel *m*.

oak [ōk] *n* Eiche *f* ♦ *a* Eichen(holz)-.

O&M *n abbr* = *organization and method*.

OAP *n abbr* (*Brit*) = **old-age pensioner**.

oar [ōr] *n* Ruder *nt*; **to put one's ~ in** (*fig col*) mitmischen, sich einmischen.

oarlock [ōr'lâk] *n* (*US*) Rudergabel *f*.

OAS *n abbr* (= *Organization of American States*) Vereinigung von amerikanischen Staaten.

oasis [ōā'sis] *n*, *pl* **oases** [ōā'sēz] Oase *f*.

oath [ōth] *n* (*statement*) Eid *m*, Schwur *m*; (*swearword*) Fluch *m*.

oatmeal [ōt'mēl] *n* (*US*) Haferbrei *m*; (*Brit*) Haferschrot *m*.

oats [ōts] *npl* Hafer *m*; (*COOK*) Haferflocken *pl*.

OAU *n abbr* (= *Organization of African Unity*) OAU *f*.

obdurate [âb'dyərit] *a* (*stubborn*) hartnäckig; (*sinner*) verstockt; (*unyielding*) unnachgiebig.

obedience [ōbē'dēəns] *n* Gehorsam *m*.

obedient [ōbē'dēənt] *a* gehorsam, folgsam; **to be ~ to sb** jdm gehorchen; **to be ~ to sth** auf etw (*acc*) reagieren.

obelisk [âb'əlisk] *n* Obelisk *m*.

obesity [ōbē'sitē] *n* Korpulenz *f*, Fettleibigkeit *f*.

obey [ōbā'] *vti* gehorchen (+*dat*), folgen (+*dat*).

obituary [ōbich'ōōärē] *n* Nachruf *m*.

object *n* [âb'jikt] (*thing*) Gegenstand *m*, Objekt *nt*; (*abstract etc*) Objekt *nt*, Ding *nt*; (*purpose*) Ziel *nt*; (*GRAM*) Objekt *nt*; **what's the ~ of the exercise?** was ist der Zweck *or* Sinn der Übung?; **money is no ~** Geld spielt keine Rolle ♦ *vi* [əbjekt'] dagegen sein, Einwände haben (*to* gegen); (*morally*) Anstoß nehmen (*to* an +*acc*); **do you ~ to my smoking?** haben Sie etwas dagegen, wenn ich rauche?

objection [əbjek'shən] *n* (*reason against*) Einwand *m*, Einspruch *m*; (*dislike*) Abneigung *f*; **to make** *or* **raise an ~** einen Einwand machen *or* erheben.

objectionable [əbjek'shənəbəl] *a* nicht einwandfrei; (*language*) anstößig.

objective [əbjek'tiv] *n* Ziel *nt* ♦ *a* objektiv.

objectively [əbjek'tivlē] *ad* objektiv.

objectivity [âbjektiv'ətē] *n* Objektivität *f*.

object lesson *n* (*fig*) Paradebeispiel *nt*, Musterbeispiel *nt*.

objector [əbjek'tûr] *n* Gegner(in *f*) *m*.

obligation [âbləgā'shən] *n* (*duty*) Pflicht *f*; (*promise*) Verpflichtung *f*; **no ~** unverbindlich; **"without ~"** „unverbindlich"; **to be under an ~ to sb/to do sth** jdm verpflichtet sein/verpflichtet sein, etw zu tun.

obligatory [əblig'ətôrē] *a* bindend, obligatorisch; **it is ~ to ...** es ist Pflicht, zu ...

oblige [əblij'] *vt* (*compel*) zwingen; (*do a favor*) einen Gefallen tun (+*dat*); **you are not ~d to do it** Sie sind nicht verpflichtet, es zu tun; **much ~d!** herzlichen Dank!; **anything to ~ a friend!** (*col*) was tut man nicht alles für einen Freund!

obliging [əblī'jing] *a* entgegenkommend.

oblique [əblēk'] *a* schräg, schief ♦ *n* (*Brit: also:* **~ stroke**) Schrägstrich *m*.

obliterate [əblit'ərāt] *vt* auslöschen.

oblivion [əbliv'ēən] *n* Vergessenheit *f*.

oblivious [əbliv'ēəs] *a* nicht bewußt (*of gen*); **he was ~ of it** er hatte es nicht bemerkt.

oblong [âb'lông] *n* Rechteck *nt* ♦ *a* länglich.

obnoxious [əbnâk'shəs] *a* abscheulich, widerlich.

o.b.o. *abbr* (*US*) = **or best offer**.

oboe [ō'bō] *n* Oboe *f*.

obscene [əbsēn'] *a* obszön, unanständig.

obscenities [əbsen'itēz] *npl* Zoten *pl*.

obscenity [əbsen'itē] *n* Obszönität *f*.

obscure [əbskyōōr'] *a* unklar; (*indistinct*) undeutlich; (*unknown*) unbekannt, obskur; (*dark*) düster ♦ *vt* verdunkeln; (*view*) verbergen; (*confuse*) verwirren.

obscurity [əbskyōōr'itē] *n* Unklarheit *f*; (*darkness*) Dunkelheit *f*; (*lack of fame*) Vergessenheit *f*.

obsequious [əbsē'kwēəs] *a* servil.

observable [əbzûr'vəbəl] *a* wahrnehmbar, sichtlich.

observance [əbzûr'vəns] *n* Befolgung *f*; **religious ~s** religiöse *or* kirchliche Feste *pl*.

observant [əbzûr'vənt] *a* aufmerksam.

observation [âbzûrvā'shən] *n* (*noticing*) Beobachtung *f*; (*surveillance*) Überwachung *f*; (*remark*) Bemerkung *f*.

observation post *n* (*MIL*) Beobachtungsposten *m*.

observatory [əbzûr'vətôrē] *n* Sternwarte *f*, Observatorium *nt*.

observe [əbzûrv'] *vt* (*notice*) bemerken; (*watch*) beobachten; (*customs*) einhalten.

observer [əbzûr'vûr] *n* Beobachter(in *f*) *m*.

obsess [əbses'] *vt* verfolgen, quälen; **to be ~ed by** *or* **with sb/sth** von jdm/etw besessen sein.

obsession [əbsesh'ən] *n* Besessenheit *f*, Wahn *m*.

obsessive [əbses'iv] *a* krankhaft.

obsolescence [âbsəles'əns] *n* Veralten *nt*.

obsolescent [âbsəles'ənt] *a* allmählich außer Gebrauch kommend.

obsolete [âbsəlēt'] *a* überholt, veraltet.

obstacle [âb'stəkəl] *n* Hindernis *nt*.

obstacle race *n* Hindernisrennen *nt*.

obstetrics [əbstet'riks] *n sing* Geburtshilfe *f*.

obstinacy [âb'stənəsē] *n* Hartnäckigheit *f*, Sturheit *f*.

obstinate [âb'stənit] *a*, **obstinately** [âb'stənitlē] *ad* hartnäckig, stur.

obstreperous [əbstrep'ûrəs] *a* aufmüpfig.

obstruct [əbstrukt'] *vt* versperren; (*block*) verstopfen; (*hinder*) hemmen.

obstruction [əbstruk'shən] *n* Versperrung *f*; Verstopfung *f*; (*obstacle*) Hindernis *nt*.

obstructive [əbstruk'tiv] *a* hemmend; obstruktiv (*esp POL*), behindernd; **stop being ~!** mach doch keine Schwierigkeiten!

obtain [əbtān'] *vt* erhalten, bekommen; (*result*) erzielen; **to ~ sth (for o.s.)** (sich) etw beschaffen *or* verschaffen.

obtainable [əbtān'əbəl] *a* erhältlich.

obtrusive [əbtrōō'siv] *a* aufdringlich.

obtuse [əbtōōs'] *a* begriffsstutzig; (*angle*) stumpf.

obverse [âb'vûrs] *n* (*of medal, coin*) Vorderseite *f*; (*fig*) Kehrseite *f*.

obviate [âb'vēāt] *vt* vermeiden; (*need*) vorbeugen (+*dat*).

obvious [âb'vēəs] *a* offenbar, offensichtlich; **it's ~ that ...** es ist klar *or* offensichtlich, daß ...

obviously [âb'vēəslē] *ad* offensichtlich; **is he there? — well, ~ not** ist er da? — offensichtlich nicht.

OCAS *n abbr* (= *Organization of Central American States*) Vereinigung zentralamerikanischer Staaten.

occasion [əkā'zhən] *n* Gelegenheit *f*; (*special event*) große(s) Ereignis *nt*; (*reason*) Grund *m*, Anlaß *m*; **on ~** gelegentlich; **on that ~** bei der Gelegenheit; **to rise to the ~** (*fig*)

sich der Lage gewachsen zeigen ♦ *vt* veranlassen.

occasional [əkā'zhənəl] *a* gelegentlich; (*worker*) Gelegenheits-.

occasionally [əkā'zhənəlē] *ad* gelegentlich; **very ~** sehr selten, nicht sehr oft.

occasional table *n* kleine(r) Wohnzimmertisch *m*, Beistelltisch *m*.

occult [əkult'] *n*: **the ~** der Okkultismus ♦ *a* okkult.

occupancy [âk'yəpənsē] *n* Bewohnen *nt*.

occupant [âk'yəpənt] *n* Inhaber(in *f*) *m*; (*of house etc*) Bewohner(in *f*) *m*; (*of boat, car etc*) Insasse *m*, Insassin *f*.

occupation [âkyəpā'shən] *n* (*employment*) Tätigkeit *f*, Beruf *m*; (*pastime*) Beschäftigung *f*; (*of country*) Besetzung *f*, Okkupation *f*.

occupational [âkyəpā'shənəl] *a* (*hazard*) Berufs-; (*therapy*) Beschäftigungs-.

occupational accident *n* Berufsunfall *m*.

occupational pension plan *n* betriebliche Altersversorgung *f*.

occupational therapy *n* Beschäftigungstherapie *f*.

occupied [âk'yəpīd] *a* besetzt.

occupier [âk'yəpīûr] *n* Bewohner(in *f*) *m*.

occupy [âk'yəpī] *vt* (*take possession of*) besetzen; (*seat*) belegen; (*live in*) bewohnen; (*position, office*) bekleiden; (*position in sb's life*) einnehmen; (*time*) beanspruchen; (*mind*) beschäftigen; **to be occupied with sth/in doing sth** mit etw beschäftigt sein/ damit beschäftigt sein, etw zu tun.

occur [əkûr'] *vi* (*happen*) vorkommen, geschehen; (*appear*) vorkommen; (*come to mind*) einfallen (*to dat*).

occurrence [əkûr'əns] *n* (*event*) Ereignis *nt*; (*appearing*) Auftreten *nt*.

ocean [ō'shən] *n* Ozean *m*, Meer *nt*; **~s of** (*col*) jede Menge.

ocean bed *n* Meeresboden *m*.

oceangoing [ō'shəngōing] *a* Hochsee-.

Oceania [ōshēan'ēə] *n* Ozeanien *nt*.

ocean liner *n* Ozeandampfer *m*.

ocher, (*Brit*) **ochre** [ō'kûr] *n* Ocker *m or nt*.

o'clock [əklâk'] *ad*: **it is 5 ~** es ist 5 Uhr.

OCR *n abbr* = *optical character recognition*; = *optical character reader.*

Oct. *abbr* (= *October*) Okt.

octagonal [âktag'ənəl] *a* achteckig.

octane [âk'tān] *n* Oktan *nt*; **high-~ gas** Benzin *nt* mit hoher Oktanzahl.

octave [âk'tiv] *n* Oktave *f*.

October [âktō'bûr] *n* Oktober *m*; *see* **September.**

octogenarian [âktəjənär'ēən] *n* Achtzigjährige(r) *mf*.

octopus [âk'təpəs] *n* Krake *f*; (*small*) Tintenfisch *m*.

oculist [âk'yəlist] *n* Augenarzt *m*.

odd [âd] *a* (*strange*) sonderbar; (*not even*) ungerade; (*the other part missing*) einzeln; (*about*) ungefähr; (*surplus*) übrig; (*casual*)

Gelegenheits-, zeitweilig.
oddball [âd'bôl] *n* (*col*) komische(r) Kauz *m*.
oddity [âd'itē] *n* (*strangeness*) Merkwürdigkeit *f*; (*queer person*) komische(r) Kauz *m*; (*thing*) Kuriosität *f*.
odd-job man [âdjâb' man] *n* Mädchen *nt* für alles.
odd jobs *npl* gelegentlich anfallende Arbeiten *pl*.
oddly [âd'lē] *ad* seltsam; ~ **enough** merkwürdigerweise.
odds [âdz] *npl* Chancen *pl*; (*in betting*) Gewinnchancen *pl*; **it makes no** ~ es spielt keine Rolle; **at** ~ uneinig; **to succeed against all the** ~ wider Erwarten *or* entgegen allen Erwartungen erfolgreich sein; ~ **and ends** Krimskrams *m*, Kram *m*.
ode [ōd] *n* Ode *f*.
odious [ō'dēəs] *a* verhaßt; (*action*) abscheulich.
odometer [ōdâm'itûr] *n* (*US*) ≈ Kilometerzähler *m*.
odor [ō'dûr] *n* (*US*) Geruch *m*.
odorless [ō'dûrlis] *a* geruchlos.
odour [ō'dûr] *etc* (*Brit*) = **odor** *etc*.
OECD *n abbr* (= *Organization for Economic Cooperation and Development*) OECD *f*.
oesophagus [isâf'əgəs] *n* (*Brit*) Speiseröhre *f*.
oestrogen [es'trəjən] *n* (*Brit*) Östrogen *nt*.
of [uv] *prep* von; (*indicating material*) aus; **the first** ~ **May** der erste Mai; **within a month** ~ **his death** einen Monat nach seinem Tod; **a girl** ~ **ten** ein zehnjähriges Mädchen; **fear** ~ **God** Gottesfurcht *f*; **love** ~ **money** Liebe zum Geld; **the six** ~ **us** wir sechs; **that was very kind** ~ **you** das war sehr nett von Ihnen; **a kilo** ~ **flour** ein Kilo Mehl; **a quarter** ~ **4** (*US*) Viertel vor vier.
off [ôf] *ad* (*absent*) weg, fort; **it's a long way** ~ das ist weit weg; **the lid was** ~ der Deckel war nicht drauf; ~ **and on** ab und zu; **3%** ~ 3% Nachlaß; **I'm** ~ ich gehe jetzt; **the button's (come)** ~ der Knopf ist ab ♦ *a* (*switch*) aus(geschaltet); (*food: bad*) verdorben, schlecht; **to be well-/badly** ~ sich gut/schlecht stehen; **he was** ~ **in his calculations** seine Berechnungen waren nicht richtig; **that's a bit** ~! (*fig col*) das ist ein dicker Hund! ♦ *prep* von; (*distant from*) ab(gelegen) von; **just** ~ **Broadway** gleich bei Broadway; **I'm** ~ **sausages** ich kann keine Wurst mehr sehen; **I'm** ~ **smoking** ich rauche nicht mehr.
offal [ôf'əl] *n* Innereien *pl*.
off-center, (*Brit*) **off-centre** [ôf'sen'tûr] *a* nicht in der Mitte; (*construction*) asymmetrisch.
off-color, (*Brit*) **off-colour** [ôf'kul'ûr] *a* (*joke*) zweideutig; **to feel** ~ sich nicht wohl fühlen.
offence [əfens'] *n* (*Brit*) = **offense.**
offend [əfend'] *vt* beleidigen ♦ *vi:* **to** ~ **against** (*law, rule*) verstoßen gegen.
offender [əfen'dûr] *n* Gesetzesübertreter *m*.

offending [əfen'ding] *a* verletzend.
offense [əfens'] *n* (*US: crime*) Vergehen *nt*, Straftat *f*; (: *insult*) Beleidigung *f*; **to commit an** ~ sich strafbar machen.
offensive [əfen'siv] *a* (*unpleasant*) übel, abstoßend; (*weapon*) Kampf-; (*remark*) verletzend ♦ *n* Angriff *m*, Offensive *f*.
offer [ôf'ûr] *n* Angebot *f*; **on** ~ zum Verkauf angeboten; **to make an** ~ **for sth** ein Angebot für etw machen ♦ *vt* anbieten; (*reward*) aussetzen; (*opinion*) äußern; (*resistance*) leisten; **to** ~ **sth to sb, to** ~ **sb sth** jdm etw anbieten; **to** ~ **to do sth** anbieten, etw zu tun.
offering [ôf'ûring] *n* Gabe *f*; (*collection*) Kollekte *f*.
offer price *n* Briefkurs *m*.
offhand [ôf'hand'] *a* lässig ♦ *ad* ohne weiteres; **I can't tell you** ~ das kann ich Ihnen auf Anhieb nicht sagen.
office [ôf'is] *n* Büro *nt*; (*position*) Amt *nt*; (*duty*) Aufgabe *f*; (*ECCL*) Gottesdienst *m*; **through his good** ~s durch seine guten Dienste; **doctor's** ~ (*US*) Praxis *f*.
office automation *n* Büroautomatisierung *f*.
office bearer *n* (*of club etc*) Amtsträger(in *f*) *m*.
office block *n* (*Brit*) = **office building.**
office boy *n* Laufjunge *m*.
office building *n* Büro(hoch)haus *nt*.
office hours *npl* Dienstzeit *f*; (*on sign*) Geschäfts- *or* Öffnungszeiten *pl*; (*US MED*) Sprechstunde *f*.
office manager *n* Geschäftsstellenleiter *m*.
officer [ôf'isûr] *n* (*MIL*) Offizier *m*; (*public* ~) Beamte(r) *m* im öffentlichen Dienst; (*of club etc*) Amtsträger(in *f*) *m*.
office work *n* Büroarbeit *f*.
office worker *n* Büroangestellte(r) *mf*.
official [əfish'əl] *a* offiziell, amtlich ♦ *n* Beamte(r) *m*; (*POL*) amtliche(r) Sprecher *m*; (*of club etc*) Funktionär *m*, Offizielle(r) *mf*.
officialdom [əfish'əldəm] *n* Bürokratie *f*.
officially [əfish'əlē] *ad* offiziell.
official strike *n* gewerkschaftlich genehmigte(r) Streik *m*.
officiate [əfish'ēāt] *vi* (*REL*) Messe lesen; **to** ~ **as mayor** das Amt des Bürgermeisters ausüben; **to** ~ **at a marriage** eine Trauung vornehmen.
officious [əfish'əs] *a* aufdringlich.
offing [ôf'ing] *n:* **in the** ~ in (Aus)sicht.
off-key [ôfkē'] *a, ad* (*MUS*) falsch.
off-licence [ôf'līsəns] *n* (*Brit*) Wein- und Spirituosenhandlung *f*.
off-limits [ôf'lim'its] *a* verboten; "~" (*US MIL*) „kein Zutritt für Soldaten".
off line *a* (*COMPUT*) rechnerunabhängig; (: *switched off*) abgetrennt.
off-load [ôf'lōd'] *vt* (*goods*) ausladen; (*passengers*) aussteigen lassen.
off-peak [ôf'pēk'] *a* (*heating*) Speicher-; (*charges*) verbilligt.
off-putting [ôf'pŏŏt'ing] *a* abstoßend.

off-ramp |ôf'ramp| *n* (*US*) Ausfahrt *f*.
off-season |ôf'sēzən| *ad* außer Saison.
offset |ôfsct'| *vt irreg* ausgleichen.
offshoot |ôf'shōōt| *n* (*BOT*) Ausläufer *m*, Ableger *m*; (*fig: family*) Nebenlinie *f*; (: *organization*) Nebenzweig *m*.
offshore *ad* |ôf'shôr'| in einiger Entfernung von der Küste ♦ *a* |ôf'shôr| küstennah, Küsten-.
offside *a* |ôf'sīd'| (*SPORT*) im Abseits (stehend); (*AUT*) auf der Fahrerseite ♦ *n* |ôf'sīd| (*AUT*) Fahrerseite *f*.
offspring |ôf'spring| *n* Nachkommenschaft *f*; (*one*) Sprößling *m*.
offstage |ôf'stāj'| *ad* hinter den Kulissen.
off-the-job training |ôf'thəjäb trā'ning| *n* außerbetriebliche Weiterbildung *f*.
off-the-peg |ôf'thəpcg'| *ad* (*Brit*) = **off-the-rack.**
off-the-rack |ôf'thərak'| *ad* (*US*) von der Stange.
off-the-wall |ôf'thəwôl'| *a* radikal neu.
off-white |ôf'wīt| *a* naturweiß.
off-year election |ôf'yēr ilck'shən| *n* (*US*) Nachwahl *f*.
often |ôf'ən| *ad* oft.
ogle |ō'gəl| *vt* liebäugeln mit.
ogre |ō'gür| *n* Menschenfresser *m*; (*fig*) Unmensch *m*.
oh |ō| *interj* oh, ach.
OH *abbr* (*US MAIL*) = *Ohio*.
OHMS *abbr* (*Brit*: = *On His or Her Majesty's Service*) *Poststempel auf portofreien Dienstsachen*.
oil |oil| *n* Öl *nt* ♦ *vt* ölen.
oilcan |oil'kan| *n* Ölkännchen *nt*.
oil field *n* Ölfeld *nt*.
oil filter *n* (*AUT*) Ölfilter *m*.
oil-fired |oil'fīūrd| *a* Öl-.
oil gauge *n* Ölstandsmesser *m*.
oil industry *n* Erdölindustrie *f*.
oil level *n* Ölstand *m*.
oil painting *n* Ölgemälde *nt*.
oil pan *n* (*US*) Ölwanne *f*.
oil refinery *n* Ölraffinerie *f*.
oil rig *n* Ölplattform *f*.
oilskins |oil'skinz| *npl* Ölzeug *nt*.
oil tanker *n* (Öl)tanker *m*.
oil well *n* Ölquelle *f*.
oily |oi'lē| *a* ölig; (*dirty*) ölbeschmiert; (*manners*) schleimig.
ointment |oint'mənt| *n* Salbe *f*.
OJT *n abbr* (*US*) = **on-the-job training.**
OK *abbr* (*US MAIL*) = *Oklahoma*.
O.K., okay |ōkā'| *interj* in Ordnung, O.K. ♦ *a* in Ordnung; **that's ~ with** *or* **by me** das ist mir recht; **are you ~ for money?** (*col*) hast du (noch) genug Geld? ♦ *n* Zustimmung *f*; **to give sth one's ~** seine Zustimmung zu etw geben ♦ *vt* genehmigen.
Okla. *abbr* (*US*) = *Oklahoma*.
old |ōld| *a* alt; (*former*) alt, ehemalig; **in the ~ days** früher; **any ~ thing** irgend etwas; **any ~ thing will do** alles ist recht; **she's a**

funny ~ thing sie ist eine komische alte Tante.
old age *n* Alter *nt*.
old-age pension |ōld'āj pcn'chən| *n* (*Brit*) Rente *f*.
old-age pensioner |ōld'āj pcn'chənūr| *n* (*Brit*) Rentner(in *f*) *m*.
olden |ōl'dən| *a* (*liter*) alt, vergangen.
old-fashioned |ōld'fash'ənd'| *a* altmodisch.
old maid *n* alte Jungfer *f*.
old-time |ōld'tīm'| *a* alt.
old-timer |ōld'tī'mûr| *n* Alteingediente(r) *mf*.
old wives' tale *n* Ammenmärchen *nt*.
olive |âl'iv| *n* (*fruit*) Olive *f*; (*color*) Olive *nt* ♦ *a* Oliven-; (*colored*) olivenfarbig.
olive branch *n* Ölzweig *m*.
olive oil *n* Olivenöl *nt*.
Olympic |ōlim'pik| *a* olympisch.
Olympic Games *npl* Olympische Spiele *pl*.
Oman |ō'mán| *n* Oman *nt*.
OMB *n abbr* (*US*: = *Office of Management and Budget*) *Regierungsabteilung*.
omelet, (*Brit*) **omelette** |âm'lit| *n* Omelett *nt*.
omen |ō'mən| *n* Zeichen *nt*, Omen *nt*.
ominous |âm'ənəs| *a* bedrohlich.
omission |ōmish'ən| *n* Auslassung *f*; (*neglect*) Versäumnis *nt*.
omit |ōmit'| *vt* auslassen; **to ~ to do sth** versäumen, etw zu tun.
omnivorous |âmniv'ûrəs| *a* allesfressend.
on |ân| *prep* auf; **~ TV** im Fernsehen; **a ring ~ his finger** ein Ring am Finger; **~ the main road/the bank of the river** an der Hauptstraße/dem Flußufer; **to be ~ to sth** einer Sache auf der Spur sein; **~ foot** zu Fuß; **a lecture ~ Dante** eine Vorlesung über Dante; **~ the left** links; **~ the right** rechts; **~ Sunday** am Sonntag; **~ Sundays** sonntags; **to be ~ vacation** in Ferien *or* im Urlaub sein; **~ the Continent** in Europa, auf dem Kontinent; **I haven't any money ~ me** ich habe kein Geld bei mir; **we're ~ irregular verbs** wir behandeln unregelmäßige Verben; **he's ~ $60,000 a year** er verdient *or* kriegt 60.000 Dollar im Jahr; **this round's ~ me** diese Runde geht auf meine Kosten; **~ hearing this, he left** als er das hörte, ging er ♦ *ad* (dar)auf; **he had nothing ~** sie hatte nichts an; (*no plans*) sie hatte nichts vor; **to move ~** weitergehen; **go ~** mach weiter; **from that day ~** von diesem Tag an; **~ and off** hin und wieder; **it was well ~ in the evening** es war ziemlich spät am Abend; **my father's always ~ at me to get a job** (*Brit col*) mein Vater liegt mir dauernd in den Ohren, eine Stelle zu suchen ♦ *a*: **the light is ~** das Licht ist an; **what's ~ at the movies?** was läuft im Kino?; **you're ~** (*col: agreed*) akzeptiert; **it's not ~** (*col*) das ist nicht drin.
ON *abbr* (*Canada*) = *Ontario*.
once |wuns| *ad* einmal ♦ *cj* wenn ... einmal; **~ you've seen him** wenn du ihn erst einmal gesehen hast; **~ she had seen him** sobald

sie ihn gesehen hatte; ~ **he had left** nachdem er gegangen war; **at** ~ sofort; (*at the same time*) gleichzeitig; **all at** ~ plötzlich; ~ **more** noch einmal; **more than** ~ mehr als einmal; ~ **in a while** ab und zu; ~ **and for all** ein für allemal; ~ **upon a time** es war einmal; **I knew him** ~ ich kannte ihn früher (mal).

oncoming [ân'kuming] a (*traffic*) Gegen-, entgegenkommend.

one [wun] a (*number*) ein/eine/ein; (*only*) einzig; ~ **day** eines Tages; **it's** ~ (o'clock) es ist eins, es ist ein Uhr ♦ n Eins *f*; **to be** ~ **up on sb** jdm um etw voraussein; **to be at** ~ **(with sb)** (mit jdm) einig sein ♦ *pron* eine(r, s); (*impersonal*) man; **this** ~ diese(r, s); **that** ~ der/die/das; **the blue** ~ der/die/das blaue; **which** ~ welche(r, s); **which** ~ **do you want?** welche möchten Sie?; **he is** ~ **of us** er ist einer von uns; ~ **by** ~ einzeln; ~ **another** einander.

one-armed bandit [wun'ârmd ban'dit] *n* einarmige(r) Bandit *m*, Spielautomat *m*.

one-man [wun'man] a Einmann-.

one-off [wun'ôf] (*Brit col*) a einmalig ♦ n: **a** ~ etwas Einmaliges.

one-piece [wun'pēs] a (*bathing suit*) einteilig.

onerous [ân'ûrəs] a (*task, duty*) schwer, beschwerlich; (*responsibility*) schwer(wiegend).

oneself [wunself'] *pron* (*reflexive*; *after prep*) sich; (~ *personally*) sich selber; **to do sth by** ~ etw allein tun.

one-shot [wun'shât] a (*US col*) einmalig.

one-sided [wun'sīdid] a (*decision, view, game, contest*) einseitig; (*judgement, account*) parteiisch.

one-time [wun'tīm] a ehemalig.

one-to-one [wun'təwun'] a (*relationship*) eins-zu-eins.

one-upmanship [wunup'mənship] *n*: **that's just a form of** ~ damit will er den anderen nur um eine Nasenlänge voraussein.

one-way [wun'wā'] a (*street*) Einbahn-.

one-way ticket *n* einfache Fahrkarte *f*.

ongoing [ân'gōing] a stattfindend, momentan; (*progressing*) sich entwickelnd.

onion [un'yən] *n* Zwiebel *f*.

on line a (*COMPUT*) rechnerabhängig; (: *switched on*) gekoppelt.

onlooker [ân'lŏŏkûr] *n* Zuschauer(in *f*) *m*.

only [ōn'lē] *ad* nur, bloß ♦ a einzige(r, s); ~ **just arrived** gerade erst angekommen; **I saw her** ~ **yesterday** ich habe sie erst gestern gesehen; **I'd be** ~ **too pleased to help** ich würde nur zu gerne helfen ♦ *cj* bloß, nur; **I would come,** ~ **I'm very busy** ich würde (schon) kommen, ich bin nur sehr beschäftigt; **not** ~ ... **but also** nicht nur ... sondern auch.

ono *abbr* (*Brit*) = **or nearest offer**.

on-ramp [ân'ramp] *n* (*US AUT*) Einfahrt *f*.

onset [ân'set] *n* (*beginning*) Beginn *m*.

onshore [ân'shôr'] *ad* an Land ♦ a Küsten-.

onslaught [ân'slôt] *n* Angriff *m*.

Ont. *abbr* (*Canada*) = **Ontario**.

on-the-job training [ânth̩əjâb' trā'ning] *n* Ausbildung *f* am Arbeitsplatz.

onto [ân'tŏŏ] *prep* = **on to**.

onus [ō'nəs] *n* Last *f*, Pflicht *f*; **the** ~ **is upon him to prove it** es liegt an ihm, das zu beweisen.

onwards [ân'wûrdz] *ad* (*place*) voran, vorwärts; **from that day** ~ von dem Tag an; **from today** ~ ab heute.

onyx [ân'iks] *n* Onyx *m*.

ooze [ŏŏz] *vi* sickern ♦ *vt* (aus)schwitzen; (*fig*) verströmen.

opacity [ōpas'itē] *n* Undurchsichtigkeit *f*.

opal [ō'pəl] *n* Opal *m*.

opaque [ōpāk'] a undurchsichtig.

OPEC [ō'pek] *n abbr* (= *Organization of Petroleum-Exporting Countries*) OPEC *f*.

open [ō'pən] a offen; (*public*) öffentlich; ~ **sandwich** belegte(s) Brot *nt*; **in the** ~ (air) im Freien; **to keep a day** ~ einen Tag freihalten; **to have an** ~ **mind on sth** einer Sache aufgeschlossen gegenüberstehen ♦ *vt* öffnen, aufmachen; (*trial, freeway, account*) eröffnen ♦ *vi* (*begin*) anfangen; (*shop*) aufmachen; (*door, flower*) aufgehen; (*play*) Premiere haben.

open on to *vt fus* sich öffnen auf (+*acc*).

open out *vt* ausbreiten; (*hole, business*) erweitern ♦ *vi* (*person*) aus sich herausgehen.

open up *vt* (*route*) erschließen; (*shop, prospects*) eröffnen.

open-air [ō'pənär'] a Frei(luft)-.

open-and-shut [ō'pənənshut'] a: ~ **case** klare(r) Fall *m*.

open day *n* (*Brit*) Tag *m* der offenen Tür.

open-ended [ō'pənen'did] a (*fig*) offen, unbegrenzt.

opener [ō'pənûr] *n* Öffner *m*; **can** ~ Dosenöffner *m*.

open ground *n* (*among trees*) Lichtung *f*; (*waste ground*) unbebaute(s) Gelände *nt*.

open-heart surgery [ō'pənhârt sûr'jûrē] *n* Herzeingriff *m* am offenen Herzen.

open house *n* Tag *m* der offenen Tür.

opening [ō'pəning] *n* (*hole*) Öffnung *f*, Loch *nt*; (*beginning*) Eröffnung *f*, Anfang *m*; (*good chance*) Gelegenheit *f*.

opening night *n* Eröffnungsvorstellung *f*.

openly [ō'pənlē] *ad* offen; (*publicly*) öffentlich.

open-minded [ō'pənmīn'did] a aufgeschlossen.

open-necked [ō'pənnekt'] a mit offenem Kragen.

openness [ō'pənnis] *n* (*frankness*) Offenheit *f*, Aufrichtigkeit *f*.

open-plan [ō'pənplan'] a frei angelegt, Großraum-.

open return *n* offene(s) Rückflugticket *nt*.

open shop *n* *Unternehmen, das die Beschäftigten nicht verpflichtet, einer Ge-*

werkschaft beizutreten.

Open University *n* (*Brit*) Fernuniversität *f*.

open verdict *n* Todesfeststellung *f* ohne Angabe des Grundes.

opera [ập'rə] *n* Oper *f*.

opera glasses *npl* Opernglas *nt*.

opera house *n* Opernhaus *nt*.

opera singer *n* Opernsänger(in *f*) *m*.

operate [ập'ərāt] *vt* (*machine*) bedienen; (*brakes, light*) betätigen ♦ *vi* (*machine*) laufen, in Betrieb sein; (*person*) arbeiten; **to ~ on** (*MED*) operieren.

operatic [ậpərat'ik] *a* Opern-.

operating costs [ập'ərāting kôsts] *npl* Betriebskosten *pl*.

operating profit *n* Betriebsgewinn *m*.

operating room *n* (*US*) Operationssaal *m*.

operation [ậpərā'shən] *n* (*working*) Betrieb *m*, Tätigkeit *f*; (*MED*) Operation *f*; (*undertaking*) Unternehmen *nt*; (*MIL*) Einsatz *m*; **in full ~** in vollem Gang; **to be in ~** (*JUR*) in Kraft sein; (*machine*) in Betrieb sein; **to have a serious ~** sich einer schweren Operation unterziehen; **the company's ~s during the year** die Geschäfte der Firma während des Jahres.

operational [ậpərā'shənəl] *a* einsatzbereit; (*COMM*) Betriebs-; (*ready for use or action*) betriebsbereit *or* -fähig; **when the machine is fully ~** wenn die Maschine voll einsatzfähig ist.

operative [ập'ûrətiv] *a* wirksam; (*law*) rechtsgültig; (*MED*) operativ; **"if" being the ~ word** wobei ich „wenn" betone ♦ *n* Mechaniker *m*; (*spy*) Agent *m*.

operator [ập'ərātûr] *n* (*of machine*) Arbeiter *m*; (*TEL*) Telefonist(in *f*) *m*; **phone the ~** rufen Sie die Vermittlung *or* das Fernamt an.

operetta [ậpəret'ə] *n* Operette *f*.

ophthalmic [âfthal'mik] *a* Augen-.

ophthalmologist [âfthalmâl'əjist] *n* Augenoptiker(in *f*) *m*.

opinion [əpin'yən] *n* Meinung *f*; **in my ~** meiner Meinung nach; **a matter of ~** Ansichtssache *f*; **to seek a second ~** ein zweites Gutachten *or* einen zweiten Befund einholen.

opinionated [əpin'yənātid] *a* starrsinnig.

opinion poll *n* Meinungsumfrage *f*.

opium [ō'pēəm] *n* Opium *nt*.

opponent [əpō'nənt] *n* Gegner(in *f*) *m*.

opportune [âpûrtōōn'] *a* günstig; (*remark*) passend.

opportunist [âpûrtōō'nist] *n* Opportunist *m*.

opportunity [âpûrtyōō'nitē] *n* Gelegenheit *f*, Möglichkeit *f*; **to take the ~ to do** *or* **of doing sth** die Gelegenheit nutzen *or* ergreifen, etw zu tun.

oppose [əpōz'] *vt* entgegentreten (+*dat*); (*argument, idea*) ablehnen; (*plan*) bekämpfen.

opposed [əpōzd'] *a*: **to be ~ to sth** gegen etw sein; **as ~ to** im Gegensatz zu.

opposing [əpōz'ing] *a* gegnerisch; (*points of view*) entgegengesetzt.

opposite [ập'əzit] *a* (*house*) gegenüberliegend; (*direction*) entgegengesetzt; **the ~ sex** das andere Geschlecht ♦ *ad* gegenüber ♦ *prep* gegenüber; **~ me** mir gegenüber ♦ *n* Gegenteil *nt*.

opposite number *n* (*person*) Pendant *nt*; (*SPORT*) Gegenspieler *m*.

opposition [âpəzish'ən] *n* (*resistance*) Widerstand *m*; (*POL*) Opposition *f*; (*contrast*) Gegensatz *m*.

oppress [əpres'] *vt* unterdrücken; (*heat etc*) bedrücken.

oppression [əpresh'ən] *n* Unterdrückung *f*.

oppressive [əpres'iv] *a* (*authority, law*) ungerecht; (*burden, thought*) bedrückend; (*heat*) drückend.

opprobrium [əprō'brēəm] *n* (*form*) Schande *f*, Schmach *f*.

opt [ậpt] *vi*: **to ~ for sth** sich für etw entscheiden; **to ~ to do sth** sich entscheiden, etw zu tun.

opt out of *vt fus* sich drücken vor (+*dat*); (*of society*) ausflippen aus (+*dat*).

optical [ập'tikəl] *a* optisch.

optical character reader *n* optische(r) Klarschriftleser *m*.

optical fiber network *n* Glasfasernetz *nt*.

optician [âptish'ən] *n* Optiker(in *f*) *m*.

optics [ập'tiks] *n sing* Optik *f*.

optimism [ập'təmizəm] *n* Optimismus *m*.

optimist [ập'təmist] *n* Optimist(in *f*) *m*.

optimistic [âptəmis'tik] *a* optimistisch.

optimum [ập'təməm] *a* optimal.

option [ập'shən] *n* Wahl *f*; (*COMM*) Vorkaufsrecht *m*, Option *f*; (*extra*) Extra *nt*; **I have no ~** mir bleibt keine andere Wahl.

optional [ập'shənəl] *a* freiwillig; (*subject*) wahlfrei; **~ extras** (*Brit*) Extras *pl*.

opulence [ập'yələns] *n* Reichtum *m*.

opulent [ập'yələnt] *a* sehr reich.

opus [ō'pəs] *n* Werk *nt*, Opus *nt*.

or [ôr] *cj* oder; **he could not read ~ write** er konnte weder lesen noch schreiben; **let me go ~ I'll scream!** laß mich los, oder ich schreie!

OR *abbr* (*US MAIL*) = *Oregon*.

oracle [ôr'əkəl] *n* Orakel *nt*.

oral [ôr'əl] *a* mündlich ♦ *n* (*exam*) mündliche Prüfung *f*, Mündliche(s) *nt*.

orange [ôr'inj] *n* (*fruit*) Apfelsine *f*, Orange *f*; (*color*) Orange *nt* ♦ *a* orange.

orangeade [ôrinjād'] *n* Orangenlimonade *f*.

orange juice *n* Orangensaft *m*.

orange squash *n* (*Brit*) ≈ Orangensaft *m*.

orang-outang, orang-utan [ôrang'ōōtang] *n* Orang-Utan *m*.

oration [ôrā'shən] *n* feierliche Rede *f*.

orator [ôr'ətûr] *n* Redner(in *f*) *m*.

oratorio [ôrətôr'ēō] *n* Oratorium *nt*.

orbit [ôr'bit] *n* Umlaufbahn *f*; **2 ~s** 2 Umkreisungen; **to be in/go into ~** in der Erdumlaufbahn sein/in die Erdumlaufbahn eintreten ♦ *vt* umkreisen ♦ *vi* kreisen.

orchard [ôr'chŭrd] *n* Obstgarten *m*; **apple** ~ Obstgarten mit Apfelbäumen.

orchestra [ôr'kistrə] *n* Orchester *nt*; (*US THEAT*) Parterre *nt*.

orchestral [ôrkes'trəl] *a* Orchester-, orchestral.

orchestrate [ôr'kistrāt] *vt* (*MUS. fig*) orchestrieren.

orchid [ôr'kid] *n* Orchidee *f*.

ordain [ôrdān'] *vt* (*ECCL*) weihen; (*decide*) verfügen.

ordeal [ôrdēl'] *n* schwere Prüfung *f*, Qual *f*.

order [ôr'dûr] *n* (*sequence*) Reihenfolge *f*; (*good arrangement*) Ordnung *f*; (*command*) Befehl *m*; (*JUR*) Anordnung *f*; (*peace*) Ordnung *f*, Ruhe *f*; (*condition*) Zustand *m*; (*rank*) Klasse *f*; (*COMM. in restaurant*) Bestellung *f*; (*ECCL, honor*) Orden *m*; **to be out of** ~ (*machine, toilets*) außer Betrieb sein; (*telephone*) nicht funktionieren; **to be under** ~**s to do sth** Instruktionen haben, etw zu tun; **to place an** ~ **for sth with sb** eine Bestellung für etw bei jdm aufgeben; **payable to the** ~ **of** (*FIN*) zahlbar an (+*acc*); **a machine in working** ~ eine Maschine in betriebsfähigem Zustand; **a point of** ~ eine Verfahrensfrage; **to be on** ~ bestellt sein; **made to** ~ auf Bestellung (gemacht *or* hergestellt); **his income is on** (*US*) *or* **of** (*Brit*) **the** ~ **of $70000 per year** sein Einkommen beträgt etwa 70000 Dollar im Jahr; **holy** ~**s** Priesterweihe *f*; **in** ~ **to do sth** um etw zu tun; **in** ~ **that** damit ♦ *vt* (*arrange*) ordnen; (*command*) befehlen (*sth* etw *acc*, *sb* jdm); (*COMM*) bestellen.

order book *n* Auftragsbuch *nt*.

order form *n* Bestellschein *m*, Bestellformular *nt*.

orderly [ôr'dûrlē] *n* (*MIL*) Offiziersbursche *m*; (*MIL MED*) Sanitäter *m*; (*MED*) Pfleger *m* ♦ *a* (*tidy*) ordentlich; (*well-behaved*) ruhig.

order number *n* Bestellnummer *f*.

ordinal [ôr'dənəl] *a* Ordnungs-, Ordinal-.

ordinarily [ôrdənär'ilē] *ad* gewöhnlich.

ordinary [ôr'dənärē] *a* (*usual*) gewöhnlich, normal; (*commonplace*) gewöhnlich, alltäglich ♦ *n*: **out of the** ~ außergewöhnlich.

ordinary seaman *n* Leichtmatrose *m*.

ordinary share *n* (*Brit*) Stammaktie *f*.

ordination [ôrdənā'shən] *n* Priesterweihe *f*; (*Protestant*) Ordination *f*.

ordnance [ôrd'nəns] *n* (*MIL*: *artillery*) Geschütze *pl*; (: *supply*) Material *nt*.

ordnance factory *n* Munitionsfabrik *f*.

ore [ôr] *n* Erz *nt*.

Ore., Oreg. (*US*) *abbr* = *Oregon*.

organ [ôr'gən] *n* (*MUS*) Orgel *f*; (*BIOL, fig*) Organ *nt*.

organic [ôrgan'ik] *a* organisch.

organism [ôr'gənizəm] *n* Organismus *m*.

organist [ôr'gənist] *n* Organist(in *f*) *m*.

organization [ôrgənəzā'shən] *n* Organisation *f*; (*make-up*) Struktur *f*.

organization chart *n* Organisationsplan *m*.

organize [ôr'gəniz] *vt* organisieren; **to get (o.s.)** ~**d** sich fertigmachen.

organizer [ôr'gənizûr] *n* Organisator *m*, Veranstalter *m*.

orgasm [ôr'gazəm] *n* Orgasmus *m*.

orgy [ôr'jē] *n* Orgie *f*.

Orient [ôr'ēənt] *n* Orient *m*.

oriental [ôrēen'təl] *a* orientalisch ♦ *n* Orientale *m*, Orientalin *f*.

orientate [ôr'ēəntāt] *vt* orientieren.

orifice [ôr'əfis] *n* Öffnung *f*.

origin [ôr'ijin] *n* Ursprung *m*; (*of the world*) Anfang *m*, Entstehung *f*; **country of** ~ Herkunftsland *nt*.

original [ərij'ənəl] *a* (*first*) ursprünglich; (*painting*) original; (*idea*) originell ♦ *n* Original *nt*.

originality [ərijənal'itē] *n* Originalität *f*.

originally [ərij'ənəlē] *ad* ursprünglich; (*in an original way*) originell.

originate [ərij'ənāt] *vi* entstehen; **to** ~ **from** stammen aus ♦ *vt* ins Leben rufen.

originator [ərij'inātûr] *n* (*of movement*) Begründer *m*; (*of invention*) Erfinder *m*.

Orkney Islands [ôrk'nē i'ləndz] *npl* Orkneyinseln *pl*.

Orkneys [ôrk'nēz] *npl* Orkneyinseln *pl*.

ornament [ôr'nəmənt] *n* Schmuck *m*; (*on mantelpiece*) Nippesfigur *f*; (*fig*) Zierde *f*.

ornamental [ôrnəmen'təl] *a* schmückend, Zier-.

ornamentation [ôrnəməntā'shən] *n* Verzierung *f*.

ornate [ôrnāt'] *a* reich verziert; (*style*) überladen.

ornithologist [ôrnəthâl'əjist] *n* Ornithologe *m*, Ornithologin *f*.

ornithology [ôrnəthâl'əjē] *n* Vogelkunde *f*, Ornithologie *f*.

orphan [ôr'fən] *n* Waise *f*, Waisenkind *nt* ♦ *vt* zur Waise machen.

orphanage [ôr'fənij] *n* Waisenhaus *nt*.

orthodox [ôr'thədâks] *a* orthodox.

orthopedic, (*Brit*) **orthopaedic** [ôrthəpē'dik] *a* orthopädisch.

O/S *abbr* (= *out of stock*) nicht auf Lager.

oscillation [âsəlā'shən] *n* Schwingung *f*, Oszillation *f*.

OSHA *n abbr* (*US*: = *Occupational Safety and Health Administration*) Abteilung des Arbeitsministerium.

Oslo [âz'lō] *n* Oslo *nt*.

ostensible [âsten'səbəl] *a*, **ostensibly** [âsten'səbəlē] *ad* vorgeblich, angeblich.

ostentation [âstentā'shən] *n* Zurschaustellen *nt*.

ostentatious [âstentā'shəs] *a* großtuerisch, protzig.

ostracize [âs'trəsiz] *vt* ausstoßen.

ostrich [ôs'trich] *n* Strauß *m*.

OT *n abbr* (= *Old Testament*) A.T. *nt*.

OTB *n abbr* (*US*) = *off-track betting*.

other [uth'ûr] *a* andere(r, s); **the** ~ **one** der/

die/das andere; **the ~ day** neulich; **every ~ day** jeden zweiten Tag; **any person ~ than him** alle außer ihm; **some ~ people have still to arrive** ein paar Leute kommen noch; **some actor or ~** (*Brit*) irgendein Schauspieler ♦ *pron* andere(r, s); **somebody or ~ ir**gendjemand; **there are 6 ~s** da sind noch 6 ♦ *ad*: **~ than** anders als; **it was none ~ than Jane** es war niemand anders als Jane.

otherwise [uth'ûrwīz] *ad* (*in a different way*) anders; (*in other ways*) sonst, im übrigen; (*or else*) sonst; **an ~ good piece of work** eine sonst gute Arbeit.

OTT *a abbr* (*col*: = *over the top*) übertrieben.

otter [ât'ûr] *n* Otter *m*.

ouch [ouch] *interj* autsch.

ought [ôt] *aux v* sollen; **he behaves as he ~** er benimmt sich, wie es sich gehört; **you ~ to do that** Sie sollten das tun; **he ~ to win** er müßte gewinnen; **that ~ to do** das müßte *or* dürfte reichen; **you ~ to go and see it** das sollten Sie sich wirklich ansehen.

ounce [ouns] *n* Unze *f*.

our [ou'ûr] *poss a* unser.

ours [ou'ûrz] *poss pron* unsere(r, s).

ourselves [ouûrselvz'] *pron* uns (selbst); (*emphatic*) (wir) selbst; **we did it (all) by ~** wir haben das alles selbst gemacht.

oust [oust] *vt* verdrängen.

out [out] *ad* hinaus, heraus; (*not indoors*) draußen ♦ *a* (*not alight*) aus; (*unconscious*) bewußtlos; (*results*) bekanntgegeben; **to eat/go ~** auswärts essen/ausgehen; **that fashion's ~** das ist nicht mehr Mode; **the ball was ~** der Ball war aus; **the flowers are ~** die Blumen blühen; **he was ~ in his calculations** (*Brit*) seine Berechnungen waren nicht richtig; **to be ~ for sth** auf etw (*acc*) aus sein; **he likes to be ~ and around** (*US*) *or* **about** (*Brit*) er ist gern unterwegs; **the journey ~** die Hinreise; **the boat was 10 km ~** das Boot war 10 km weit draußen; **~ loud** laut; **the workers are ~** (*on strike*) die Arbeiter streiken; **before the week was ~** vor Ende der Woche; **he's ~ for all he can get** er will haben, was er nur bekommen kann; *see also* **out of**.

out-and-out [out'əndout'] *a* (*liar*) Erz-, ausgemacht; (*fool*) vollkommen, ausgemacht.

outback [out'bak] *n* Hinterland *nt*.

outbid [outbid'] *vt* überbieten.

outboard (motor) [out'bôrd (mō'tûr)] *n* Außenbordmotor *m*.

outbreak [out'brāk] *n* Ausbruch *m*.

outbuilding [out'bilding] *n* Nebengebäude *nt*.

outburst [out'bûrst] *n* Ausbruch *m*.

outcast [out'kast] *n* Ausgestoßene(r) *mf*.

outclass [outklas'] *vt* übertreffen.

outcome [out'kum] *n* Ergebnis *nt*.

outcrop [out'kräp] *n*: **an ~ (of rocks)** eine Felsnase.

outcry [out'krī] *n* Protest *m*.

outdated [outdā'tid] *a* veraltet, überholt.

outdistance [outdis'təns] *vt* hinter sich (*dat*) lassen.

outdo [outdōo'] *vt irreg* übertrumpfen.

outdoor [out'dôr] *a* Außen-; (*SPORT*) im Freien.

outdoors [outdôrz'] *ad* draußen, im Freien; **to go ~** ins Freie *or* nach draußen gehen.

outer [out'ûr] *a* äußere(r, s).

outer space *n* Weltraum *m*.

outfit [out'fit] *n* Ausrüstung *f*; (*set of clothes*) Kleidung *f*; (*col: organization*) Laden *m*, Verein *m*.

outfitters [out'fitûrz] *npl* (*for men's clothes*) Herrenausstatter *m*.

outgoing [out'gōing] *a* (*means of transport*) hinausfahrend; (*character*) aus sich herausgehend; (*tenant*) ausziehend; (*president*) (aus)scheidend.

outgoings [out'gōingz] *npl* Ausgaben *pl*.

outgrow [outgrō'] *vt irreg* (*clothes*) herauswachsen aus; (*habit*) ablegen.

outhouse [out'hous] *n* (*US: toilet*) Außenabort *m*, Außenklosett *nt*; (*Brit*) Nebengebäude *nt*.

outing [ou'ting] *n* Ausflug *m*.

outlandish [outlan'dish] *a* eigenartig.

outlast [outlast'] *vt* (*outlive*) überleben; (*endure*) länger aus- *or* durchhalten als.

outlaw [out'lô] *n* Geächtete(r) *mf* ♦ *vt* ächten; (*thing*) verbieten.

outlay [out'lā] *n* Auslage *f*.

outlet [out'let] *n* Auslaß *m*, Abfluß *m*; (*COMM*) Absatzmarkt *m*; (*store*) Verkaufsstelle *f*; (*for emotions*) Ventil *nt*; (*US ELEC*) Steckdose *f*.

outline [out'līn] *n* Umriß *m*.

outlive [outliv'] *vt* überleben.

outlook [out'lŏŏk] *n* (*lit, fig*) Aussicht *f*; (*attitude*) Einstellung *f*.

outlying [out'līing] *a* entlegen; (*district*) Außen-.

outmaneuver, (*Brit*) **outmanoeuvre** [outmənōō'vûr] *vt* (*MIL, fig*) ausmanövrieren.

outmoded [outmō'did] *a* veraltet.

outnumber [outnum'bûr] *vt* zahlenmäßig überlegen sein (+*dat*).

out of *prep* aus; (*away from*) außerhalb (+*gen*); **to be ~ milk** *etc* keine Milch *etc* mehr haben; **it's ~ stock** (*COMM*) es ist nicht vorrätig *or* auf Lager; **made ~ wood** aus Holz gemacht; **~ danger** außer Gefahr; **~ place** fehl am Platz; **~ curiosity** aus Neugier; **nine ~ ten** neun von zehn.

out-of-bounds [outəvboundz'] *a* verboten.

out-of-date [outəvdāt'] *a* (*passport, ticket*) abgelaufen; (*theory, idea*) überholt, veraltet; (*custom, clothes*) altmodisch, veraltet.

out-of-doors [outəvdôrz'] *ad* im Freien.

out-of-the-way [outəvthəwā'] *a* (*remote*) abgelegen; (*unusual*) ungewöhnlich.

outpatient [out'pāshənt] *n* ambulante(r) Patient(in *f*) *m*.

outpost [out'pōst] *n* (*MIL, fig*) Vorposten *m*.

output [out'pŏŏt] *n* Leistung *f*, Produktion *f*; (*COMPUT*) Ausgabe *f* ♦ *vt* (*COMPUT*) ausgeben.

outrage |out'rāj| *n* (*cruel deed*) Ausschreitung *f*, Verbrechen *nt*; (*indecency*) Skandal *m* ♦ *vt* (*morals*) verstoßen gegen; (*person*) empören.

outrageous |outrā'jəs| *a* unerhört, empörend; (*clothes*) ausgefallen, unmöglich.

outright *ad* |outrīt'| (*at once*) sofort; (*openly*) ohne Umschweife; **to refuse ~** rundweg ablehnen ♦ *a* |out'rīt| (*denial*) völlig; (*sale*) Total-; (*winner*) unbestritten.

outrun |outrun'| *vt irreg* schneller laufen als.

outset |out'set| *n* Beginn *m*.

outshine |outshīn'| *vt irreg* (*fig*) in den Schatten stellen.

outside |out'sīd'| *n* Außenseite *f*; **on the ~** außen; **at the very ~** höchstens ♦ *a* äußere(r, s), Außen-; (*price*) Höchst-; (*chance*) gering; **an ~ broadcast** (*RAD, TV*) eine nicht im Studio produzierte Sendung; **that is done by ~ contractors** damit ist ein Elektriker *or* Monteur *or* Spediteur *etc* (einer anderen Firma) beauftragt; **an ~ chance** (*remote*) eine kleine Chance ♦ *ad* außen; **to go ~** nach draußen *or* hinaus gehen ♦ *prep* außerhalb (+*gen*).

outside line *n* (*TEL*) Amtsanschluß *m*.

outsider |outsī'dûr| *n* Außenseiter(in *f*) *m*.

outsize |out'sīz| *a* (*Brit*) übergroß.

outskirts |out'skûrts| *npl* Stadtrand *m*.

outsmart |outsmärt'| *vt* austricksen (*col*).

outspoken |out'spō'kən| *a* offen, freimütig.

outspread |out'spred| *a* ausgebreitet; (*wings*) ausgespannt.

outstanding |outstan'ding| *a* hervorragend; (*debts etc*) ausstehend.

outstretched |outstrecht'| *a* ausgestreckt.

outstrip |outstrip'| *vt* (*also fig*) übertreffen (*in an* +*dat*).

out-tray |out'trā| *n* (*COMM*) Ausgangsablage *f*.

outvote |outvōt'| *vt*: **I was ~d** ich wurde überstimmt.

outward |out'wûrd| *a* äußere(r, s); (*journey*) Hin-; (*freight*) ausgehend ♦ *ad* nach außen.

outwardly |out'wûrdlē| *ad* äußerlich.

outweigh |outwā'| *vt* (*fig*) überwiegen.

outwit |outwit'| *vt* überlisten.

outworn |outwôrn'| *a* (*expression*) abgedroschen.

oval |ō'vəl| *a* oval ♦ *n* Oval *nt*.

ovary |ō'vûrē| *n* Eierstock *m*.

ovation |ōvā'shən| *n* Beifallssturm *m*.

oven |uv'ən| *n* Backofen *m*.

ovenproof |uv'ənprōōf| *a* feuerfest.

oven-ready |uv'ənred'ē| *a* bratfertig.

ovenware |uv'ənwär| *n* feuerfeste Formen *pl*.

over |ō'vûr| *ad* (*across*) hinüber, herüber; (*finished*) vorbei; (*left*) übrig; (*again*) wieder, noch einmal; (*excessively*) allzu, übermäßig; **all ~** (*everywhere*) überall; (*finished*) vorbei; **~ and ~** immer wieder; **~ and above** darüber hinaus ♦ *prep* über; (*in every part of*) in; **famous the world ~** in

der ganzen Welt berühmt; **five times ~** fünfmal; **~ the weekend** übers Wochenende; **~ coffee** bei einer Tasse Kaffee; **~ the phone** am Telephon.

over- |ō'vûr| *pref* über-.

overact |ōvûrakt'| *vi* übertreiben.

overall |ō'vûrôl| *n* (*Brit: for woman*) Kittelschürze *f* ♦ *a* (*situation*) allgemein; (*length*) Gesamt- ♦ *ad* |ōvûrôl'| insgesamt.

overalls |ō'vûrôlz| *npl* (*for man*) Overall *m*.

overanxious |ōvûrangk'shəs| *a* überängstlich.

overawe |ōvûrô'| *vt* (*frighten*) einschüchtern; (*make impression*) überwältigen.

overbalance |ōvûrbal'əns| *vi* Übergewicht bekommen.

overbearing |ōvûrbär'ing| *a* aufdringlich.

overboard |ō'vûrbôrd| *ad* über Bord; **to go ~ for sth** (*fig*) von etw ganz hingerissen sein.

overbook |ō'vûrbook'| *vt* überbuchen.

overcapitalize |ōvûrkap'itəlīz| *vt* überkapitalisieren.

overcast |ō'vûrkast| *a* bedeckt.

overcharge |ōvûrchärj'| *vt* zuviel verlangen von.

overcoat |ō'vûrkōt| *n* Mantel *m*.

overcome |ōvûrkum'| *vt irreg* überwinden; (*sleep, emotion*) übermannen; **she was quite ~ by the occasion** sie war von dem Ereignis ganz ergriffen.

overconfident |ōvûrkän'fidənt| *a* übertrieben selbstsicher.

overcrowded |ōvûrkrou'did| *a* überfüllt.

overcrowding |ōvûrkrou'ding| *n* Überfüllung *f*.

overdo |ōvûrdoo'| *vt irreg* (*cook too much*) verkochen; (*exaggerate*) übertreiben; **to ~ it, to ~ things** (*work too hard*) es übertreiben.

overdose |ō'vûrdōs| *n* Überdosis *f*.

overdraft |ō'vûrdraft| *n* (Konto)überziehung *f*; **to have an ~** sein Konto überzogen haben.

overdrawn |ōvûrdrôn'| *a* (*account*) überzogen.

overdrive |ō'vûrdrīv| *n* (*AUT*) Schnellgang *m*.

overdue |ōvûrdoo'| *a* überfällig; **that change was long ~** diese Veränderung war schon längst fällig.

overenthusiastic |ōvûrenthoozēas'tik| *a* zu begeistert.

overestimate |ōvûres'təmāt| *vt* überschätzen.

overexcited |ōvûriksī'tid| *a* überreizt, aufgedreht (*col*); (*children*) aufgeregt.

overexertion |ōvûrigzûr'shən| *n* Überanstrengung *f*.

overexpose |ōvûrikspōz'| *vt* (*PHOT*) überbelichten.

overflow |ō'vûrflō| *vi* überfließen ♦ *n* (*excess*) Überschuß *m*; (*outlet*) Überlauf *m*.

overfly |ōvûrflī'| *vt irreg* überfliegen.

overgenerous |ōvûrjen'ûrəs| *a* übertrieben großzügig.

overgrown |ōvûrgrōn'| *a* (*garden*) verwil-

dert; **he's just an ~ schoolboy** (*fig*) er ist
ein großes Kind.

overhang [ōvúrhang'] *irreg vt* hängen über
(*+acc*), hinausragen über (*+acc*) ♦ *vi* über-
hängen.

overhaul *vt* [ōvúrhôl'] (*car*) überholen;
(*plans*) überprüfen ♦ *n* [ō'vúrhôl] Überholung
f.

overhead [ō'vúrhed] *a* Hoch-; (*wire*) oberir-
disch; (*lighting*) Decken- ♦ *n* (*US*) allgemeine Unkosten *pl* ♦ *ad* [ō'vúrhed'] oben.

overheads [ō'vúrhedz] *npl* (*Brit*) = **overhead**.

overhear [ōvúrhiûr'] *vt irreg* (mit an)hören.

overheat [ōvúrhēt'] *vi* (*engine*) heiß laufen.

overjoyed [ōvúrjoid'] *a* überglücklich.

overkill [ō'vúrkil] *n* (*MIL*) Overkill *m*; (*fig*)
Rundumschlag *m*, Kahlschlag *m*.

overland [ō'vúrland] *a* Überland- ♦ *ad* (*travel*) über Land.

overlap *vi* [ōvúrlap'] sich überschneiden; (*objects*) sich teilweise decken ♦ *n* [ō'vúrlap]
Überschneidung *f*.

overleaf [ō'vúrlēf] *ad* umseitig, umstehend.

overload [ōvúrlōd'] *vt* überladen.

overlook [ōvúrlook'] *vt* (*view from above*)
überblicken; (*not notice*) übersehen; (*pardon*) hinwegsehen über (*+acc*).

overlord [ō'vúrlôrd] *n* Lehnsherr *m*.

overmanning [ōvúrman'ing] *n* Überbesetzung
f mit Arbeitskräften.

overnight *a* [ōvúrnīt'] (*journey*) Nacht- ♦ *ad*
[ō'vúrnīt] über Nacht.

overnight bag *n* Reisetasche *f*.

overnight stay *n* Übernachtung *f*.

overpass [ō'vúrpas] *n* Überführung *f*.

overpay [ōvúrpā'] *vt irreg*: **to ~ sb by $50**
jdm 50 Dollar zuviel bezahlen.

overpower [ōvúrpou'ûr] *vt* überwältigen.

overpowering [ōvúrpou'ûring] *a* überwältigend.

overproduction [ōvúrprøduk'shøn] *n* Über-
produktion *f*.

overrate [ōvørrāt'] *vt* überschätzen.

overreach [ōvørēch'] *vt*: **to ~ o.s.** sich übernehmen.

override [ōvørīd'] *vt irreg* (*order, decision*)
aufheben; (*objection*) übergehen.

overriding [ōvørīd'ing] *a* Haupt-, vorherrschend.

overrule [ōvørool'] *vt* verwerfen; **we were
~d** unser Vorschlag/unsere Entscheidung *etc*
wurde verworfen.

overrun [ō'vørun] *irreg vt* (*MIL: country etc*)
einfallen in (*+dat*); (*time limit etc*) überziehen, überschreiten; **the town is ~ with
tourists** die Stadt ist von Touristen überlaufen ♦ *vi* überziehen.

overseas *ad* [ō'vúrsēz'] nach *or* in Übersee ♦
a [ō'vúrsēz] überseeisch, Übersee-.

overseer [ō'vúrsēûr] *n* Aufseher *m*.

overshadow [ōvúrshad'ō] *vt* überschatten.

overshoot [ōvúrshoot'] *vt irreg* (*runway*) hinausschießen über (*+acc*).

oversight [ō'vúrsīt] *n* (*mistake*) Versehen *nt*;
(*supervision*) Aufsicht *f*; **due to an ~** aufgrund eines Versehens.

oversimplify [ōvúrsim'pløfī] *vt* zu sehr vereinfachen.

oversize [ō'vúrsīz] *a* (*US*) übergroß.

oversleep [ōvúrslēp'] *vi irreg* verschlafen.

overspend [ōvúrspend'] *vi irreg* zuviel ausgeben; **we have overspent by 50 dollars** wir
haben 50 Dollar zuviel ausgegeben.

overspill [ō'vúrspil] *n* (Bevölke-
rungs)überschuß *m*.

overstaffed [ō'vúrstaft] *a*: **to be ~** überbe-
setzt sein, zu viel Personal haben.

overstate [ōvúrstāt'] *vt* übertreiben.

overstatement [ōvúrstāt'mønt] *n* Übertreibung *f*.

overstay [ōvúrstā'] *vt*: **to ~ one's welcome**
länger bleiben als erwünscht.

overstep [ōvúrstep'] *vt*: **to ~ the mark** zu
weit gehen; **to ~ the limits** die Grenzen
überschreiten.

overstock [ōvúrstâk'] *n* Überbevorratung *f*.

overstrike *n* [ō'vúrstrīk] (*on printer*) Mehr-
fachdruck *m* ♦ *vt* [ōvúrstrīk'] mehrfach-
drucken.

oversubscribed [ōvúrsøbskrībd'] *a* (*FIN*)
überzeichnet.

overt [ōvúrt'] *a* offen(kundig).

overtake [ōvúrtāk'] *vti irreg* (*Brit*) überholen.

overtax [ōvúrtaks'] *vt* (*FIN*) übermäßig besteuern; (*fig: strength, patience*) überfor-
dern; **to ~ o.s.** sich übernehmen.

overthrow *vt irreg* [ōvúrthrō'] (*POL*) stürzen.

overtime [ō'vúrtīm] *n* Überstunden *pl*; (*US
SPORT*) Verlängerung *f*; **to do** *or* **work ~**
Überstunden *pl* machen.

overtime ban *n* Überstundenverbot *nt*.

overtone [ō'vúrtōn] *n* (*fig*) Note *f*.

overture [ō'vúrchûr] *n* (*MUS*) Ouvertüre *f*.

overtures [ō'vúrchûrz] *npl* (*fig*) Annäherungsversuche *pl*.

overturn *vti* [ōvúrtúrn'] umkippen.

overweight [ōvúrwāt'] *a* zu dick, zu schwer.

overwhelm [ōvúrwelm'] *vt* überwältigen.

overwhelming [ōvúrwel'ming] *a* überwältigend.

overwhelmingly [ōvúrwel'minglē] *ad*: **they
voted ~ for it** sie haben mit überwältigender Mehrheit dafür gestimmt.

overwork [ōvúrwûrk'] *n* Überarbeitung *f* ♦ *vt*
überlasten ♦ *vi* sich überarbeiten.

overwrite [ōvúrīt'] *vt irreg* (*COMPUT*) überschreiben.

overwrought [ō'vøröt'] *a* überreizt.

ovulation [âvyølā'shøn] *n* Eisprung *m*.

owe [ō] *vt* schulden; **to ~ sth to sb** *or* **sb
sth** (*money*) jdm etw schulden; (*favor etc*)
jdm etw verdanken.

owing to [ō'ing too] *prep* wegen (*+gen*).

owl [oul] *n* Eule *f*.

own [ōn] *vt* besitzen; (*admit*) zugeben; **who
~s that?** wem gehört das? ♦ *a* eigen ♦ *pron*:
can I have it for my (very) ~? darf ich das

(ganz) für mich allein behalten?; **to come into one's ~** in seinem Element sein; **I have money of my ~** ich habe mein eigenes Geld; **on one's ~** (ganz) allein.

own up *vi* es zugeben (*to sth* etw *acc*); **to ~ up to having done sth** zugeben, etw getan zu haben.

own brand *n* (*COMM*) Hausmarke *f*.

owner [ō'nûr] *n* Besitzer(in *f*) *m*, Eigentümer(in *f*) *m*.

owner-occupier [ō'nûrák'yəpīûr] *n* Bewohner *m* im eigenen Haus.

ownership [ō'nûrship] *n* Besitz *m*; **under new ~** unter neuer Leitung.

ox [âks] *n* Ochse *m*.

Oxfam [âks'fam] *n abbr* (*Brit*: = *Oxford Committee for Famine Relief*) Wohlfahrtsverband.

oxide [âk'sīd] *n* Oxyd *nt*.

oxtail soup [âks'tāl sōōp] *n* Ochsenschwanzsuppe *f*.

oxyacetylene [âksēəset'əlin] *a* Azetylensauerstoff-; **~ burner** *or* **torch** Schneidbrenner *m*.

oxygen [âk'sijən] *n* Sauerstoff *m*.

oxygen mask *n* Sauerstoffmaske *f*.

oxygen tent *n* Sauerstoffzelt *nt*.

oyster [ois'tûr] *n* Auster *f*.

oz. *abbr* = **ounce**.

ozone [ō'zōn] *n* Ozon *nt*.

ozone-friendly [ō'zōnfrend'lē] *a* (*spray*) FCKW-frei.

ozone layer *n* Ozonschicht *f*.

P

P, p [pē] *n* (*letter*) P *nt*, p *nt*; **P for Peter** ≈ P wie Peter.

p *abbr* (= *page*) S; (*Brit*) = **penny, pence**.

P *abbr* (= *president*; *prince*) Pr.

PA *n abbr* = **personal assistant**; **public address system**; (= *Press Association*) ≈ Deutsche(r) Presserat *m* ♦ *abbr* (*US MAIL*) = *Pennsylvania*.

p.a. *abbr* (= *per annum*) p.a.

pa [pâ] *n* (*col*) Papa *m*.

PAC *n abbr* (*US*: = *political action committee*) politisches Aktionskomitee.

pace [pās] *n* Schritt *m*; (*speed*) Geschwindigkeit *f*, Tempo *nt*; **to keep ~ with** Schritt halten mit; **to put sb through his ~s** (*fig*) jdn auf Herz und Nieren prüfen; **to set the ~** (*running*, *fig*) das Tempo angeben ♦ *vi* schreiten.

pacemaker [pās'mākûr] *n* Schrittmacher *m*.

Pacific [pəsif'ik] *a*: **the ~ islands** die Pazifi-

schen Inseln; **the ~ (Ocean)** der Pazifische Ozean, der Pazifik.

pacification [pasəfəkā'shən] *n* Befriedung *f*.

pacifier [pas'əfīûr] *n* (*US*) Schnuller *m*.

pacifism [pas'əfizəm] *n* Pazifismus *m*.

pacifist [pas'əfist] *n* Pazifist(in *f*) *m*.

pacify [pas'əfī] *vt* befrieden; (*calm*) beruhigen.

pack [pak] *n* Packen *m*; (*of wolves*) Rudel *nt*; (*of hounds*) Meute *f*; (*of cards*) Spiel *nt*; (*gang*) Bande *f*; (*packet*) Paket *nt*; (*COMM*) Packung *f*; (*of cigarettes*) Packung *f*, Schachtel *f* ♦ *vt* (*case*) packen; (*clothes*) einpacken; (*COMPUT*) packen, verdichten; **the place was ~ed** es war gerammelt voll *or* proppenvoll (*col*) ♦ *vt* (*person*) packen; **the crowd ~ed into the stadium** die Menge drängte sich in das Stadion; **to send sb ~ing** (*col*) jdn kurz abfertigen.

pack in *vt* (*Brit col*) hinschmeißen ♦ *vi* (*Brit*: *break down*: *watch*, *car*) seinen Geist aufgeben.

pack up *vt* (*belongings*, *clothes*) zusammenpacken; (*goods*) verpacken ♦ *vi* (*Brit col*: *machine*) seinen Geist aufgeben; (: *person*) Feierabend machen.

package [pak'ij] *n* Paket *nt* ♦ *vt* (*COMM*: *goods*) verpacken.

package bomb *n* (*US*) Paketbombe *f*.

package holiday *n* (*Brit*) Pauschalreise *f*.

package tour *n* Pauschalreise *f*.

packaging [pak'ijing] *n* Verpackung *f*.

packed lunch [pakt lunch] *n* (*Brit*) Lunchpaket *nt*.

packer [pak'ûr] *n* (*person*) Packer(in *f*) *m*.

packet [pak'it] *n* Päckchen *nt*.

packet switching *n* (*COMPUT*) Paketvermittlung *f*.

packhorse [pak'hôrs] *n* Packpferd *nt*.

pack ice [pak īs] *n* Packeis *nt*.

packing [pak'ing] *n* (*action*) Packen *nt*; (*material*) Verpackung *f*.

packing case *n* (Pack)kiste *f*.

pact [pakt] *n* Pakt *m*, Vertrag *m*.

pad [pad] *n* (*of paper*) (Schreib)block *m*; (*for inking*) Stempelkissen *nt*; (*padding*) Polster *nt* ♦ *vt* polstern ♦ *vi*: **to ~ in/about** *etc* herein-/herumtappen.

padding [pad'ing] *n* Polsterung *f*.

paddle [pad'əl] *n* Paddel *nt*; (*US*: *racket*) Schläger *m* ♦ *vt* (*boat*) paddeln ♦ *vi* (*in sea*) planschen.

paddle steamer *n* Raddampfer *m*.

paddling pool [pad'ling pōōl] *n* (*Brit*) Planschbecken *nt*.

paddock [pad'ək] *n* Koppel *f*.

paddy [pad'ē] *n* Reisfeld *nt*.

padlock [pad'läk] *n* Vorhängeschloß *nt*.

Padua [paj'ōōə] *n* Padua *nt*.

paediatrics [pēdēat'riks] *n sing* (*Brit*) = **pediatrics**.

pagan [pā'gən] *a* heidnisch.

page [pāj] *n* Seite *f*; (*person*) Page *m* ♦ *vt* (*in hotel etc*) ausrufen lassen.

pageant [paj'ənt] *n* Festzug *m*.
pageantry [paj'əntrē] *n* Gepränge *nt*.
page break *n* Seitenlänge *f*.
paginate [paj'ənāt] *vt* paginieren.
pagination [pajənā'shən] *n* Seitennumerierung *f*, Paginierung *f*.
pagoda [pəgō'də] *n* Pagode *f*.
paid [pād] *pt, pp of* **pay**.
paid-up [pād'up] *a* (*share*) eingezahlt; **fully ~ member** Mitglied *nt* ohne Beitragsrückstände.
paid-up capital *n* voll eingezahlte(s) Kapital *nt*.
pail [pāl] *n* Eimer *m*.
pain [pān] *n* Schmerz *m*, Schmerzen *pl*; **on ~ of death** bei Todesstrafe, unter Androhung der Todesstrafe; *see also* **pains**.
pained [pānd] *a* (*expression*) gequält.
painful [pān'fəl] *a* (*physically*) schmerzhaft; (*embarrassing*) peinlich; (*difficult*) mühsam.
pain-killer [pān'kilûr] *n* schmerzstillende(s) Mittel *nt*.
painless [pān'lis] *a* schmerzlos.
pains [pānz] *npl* (*efforts*) große Mühe *f*, große Anstrengungen *pl*; **to be at ~ to do sth** sich (*dat*) Mühe geben, etw zu tun.
painstaking [pānz'tāking] *a* gewissenhaft.
paint [pānt] *n* Farbe *f* ♦ *vt* anstreichen; (*picture*) malen.
paintbox [pānt'bâks] *n* (*Brit*) Farb- *or* Malkasten *m*.
paintbrush [pānt'brush] *n* Pinsel *m*.
painter [pān'tûr] *n* Maler(in *f*) *m*; (*decorator*) Maler(in *f*) *m*, Anstreicher(in *f*) *m*.
painting [pān'ting] *n* (*act*) Malen *nt*; (*ART*) Malerei *f*; (*picture*) Bild *nt*, Gemälde *nt*.
paintwork [pānt'wûrk] *n* (*Brit*) Anstrich *m*; (: *of car*) Lack *m*.
pair [pär] *n* Paar *nt*; **~ of scissors** Schere *f*; **~ of pants** Hose *f*.
pair off *vi* in Zweiergruppen einteilen.
pajamas [pəjâm'əz] *npl* (*US*) Schlafanzug *m*, Pyjama *m*; **a pair of ~** ein Schlafanzug.
Pakistan [pak'istan] *n* Pakistan *nt*.
Pakistani [pak'əstan'ē] *a* pakistanisch ♦ *n* Pakistaner(in *f*) *m*, Pakistani *mf*.
pal [pal] *n* (*col: man*) Kumpel *m*; (: *woman*) (gute) Freundin *f*.
palace [pal'is] *n* Palast *m*, Schloß *nt*.
palatable [pal'ətəbəl] *a* schmackhaft.
palate [pal'it] *n* Gaumen *m*; (*taste*) Geschmack *m*.
palaver [pəlav'ûr] *n* (*col*) Theater *nt*.
pale [pāl] *a* (*face*) blaß, bleich; (*color*) blaß; **to turn ~** bleich *or* blaß werden ♦ *n*: **he is now regarded as beyond the ~** man betrachtet ihn jetzt als indiskutabel ♦ *vi* erbleichen, blaß *or* bleich werden; **to ~ into insignificance** zur Bedeutungslosigkeit herabsinken.
paleness [pāl'nis] *n* Blässe *f*.
Palestine [pal'istīn] *n* Palästina *nt*.
Palestinian [palistin'ēən] *a* palästinensisch,

palästinisch ♦ *n* Palästinenser(in *f*) *m*.
palette [pal'it] *n* Palette *f*.
paling [pā'ling] *n* (*stake*) Zaunpfahl *m*.
palisade [palisād'] *n* Palisade *f*.
pall [pôl] *n* Bahr- *or* Leichentuch *nt*; (*of smoke*) (Rauch)wolke *f* ♦ *vi* an Reiz verlieren.
pallbearer [pôl'bärûr] *n* Sargträger *m*.
pallet [pal'it] *n* (*for goods*) Palette *f*.
palletization [palitəzā'shən] *n* Palettisierung *f*.
palliative [pal'ēātiv] *n* Linderungsmittel *nt*, Palliativ(um) *nt*.
pallid [pal'id] *a* blaß, bleich.
pally [pal'ē] *a* (*col*) befreundet.
palm [pâm] *n* (*of hand*) Handfläche *f*; (*also*: **~ tree**) Palme *f*.
palmist [pâm'ist] *n* Handleserin *f*.
Palm Sunday *n* Palmsonntag *m*.
palpable [pal'pəbəl] *a* (*lit, fig*) greifbar.
palpably [pal'pəblē] *ad* offensichtlich.
palpitation [palpitā'shən] *n* Herzklopfen *nt*; **to have ~s** Herzklopfen haben.
paltry [pôl'trē] *a* armselig.
pamper [pam'pûr] *vt* verhätscheln.
pamphlet [pam'flit] *n* Broschüre *f*; (*political*) Flugblatt *nt*.
pan [pan] *n* Pfanne *f*; (*sauce~*) Topf *m*; (*of lavatory*) Becken *nt* ♦ *vt* (*criticize*) verreißen ♦ *vi* (*CINE*) schwenken; **to ~ for gold** (*prospectors*) Gold waschen.
pan- [pan] *pref* Pan-, All-.
panacea [panəsē'ə] *n* (*fig*) Allheilmittel *nt*.
panache [pənash'] *n* Schwung *m*, Elan *m*.
Panama [pan'əmâ] *n* Panama *nt*.
Panama Canal *n* Panamakanal *m*.
pancake [pan'kāk] *n* Pfannkuchen *m*.
Pancake Day *n* (*Brit*) Fastnachtsdienstag *m*.
pancreas [pan'krēəs] *n* Bauchspeicheldrüse *f*, Pankreas *nt*.
panda [pan'də] *n* Panda *m*.
pandemonium [pandəmō'nēəm] *n* Hölle *f*; (*noise*) Höllenlärm *m*.
pander [pan'dûr] *vi* sich richten (*to* nach).
p&h *abbr* (*US:* = *postage and handling*) Porto und Umschlagspesen.
P&L *abbr* (= *profit and loss*) GuV.
p&p *abbr* (*Brit:* = *postage and packing*) Porto und Umschlagspesen.
pane [pān] *n* (Fenster)scheibe *f*.
panel [pan'əl] *n* (*of wood*) Tafel *f*; (*TV*) Diskussionsteilnehmer *pl*.
panel game *n* Ratespiel *nt*.
paneling, (*Brit*) **panelling** [pan'əling] *n* Täfelung *f*.
panelist, (*Brit*) **panellist** [pan'əlist] *n* Diskussionsteilnehmer(in *f*) *m*.
pang [pang] *n* Stich *m*, Qual *f*; **~s of conscience** Gewissensbisse *pl*.
panic [pan'ik] *n* Panik *f* ♦ *vi* in Panik geraten; **don't ~** (nur) keine Panik.
panicky [pan'ikē] *a* (*person*) überängstlich.
panic-stricken [pan'ikstrikən] *a* von pani-

schem Schrecken erfaßt; (*look*) panisch.
pannier [pan'yûr] *n* (Trage)korb *m*; (*on bike*) Satteltasche *f*.
panorama [panəram'ə] *n* Rundblick *m*, Panorama *nt*.
panoramic [panəram'ik] *a* Panorama-.
pansy [pan'zē] *n* (*flower*) Stiefmütterchen *nt*; (*col: homosexual*) Schwule(r) *m*.
pant [pant] *vi* keuchen; (*dog*) hecheln.
panther [pan'thûr] *n* Panther *m*.
panties [pan'tēz] *npl* (Damen)slip *m*.
pantihose [pan'tēhōz] *n* (*US*) Strumpfhose *f*.
pantomime [pan'təmīm] *n* (*Brit: at Christmas*) Märchenkomödie *f* um Weihnachten.
pantry [pan'trē] *n* Vorratskammer *f*.
pants [pants] *npl* (*US*) Hose *f*; (*Brit*) Unterhose *f*.
pants press *n* (*US*) Hosenpresse *f*.
pantsuit [pant'sōōt] *n* (*US*) Hosenanzug *m*.
papal [pā'pəl] *a* päpstlich.
paper [pā'pûr] *n* Papier *nt*; (*also:* **news~**) Zeitung *f*; (*essay*) Vortrag *m*; (*academic*) Referat *nt*; **a piece of** ~ (*odd bit*) ein Zettel, ein Stück Papier; (*sheet*) ein Blatt Papier; **to put sth down on** ~ etw schriftlich festhalten; *see also* **papers** ♦ *a* Papier-, aus Papier ♦ *vt* (*wall*) tapezieren.
paper advance *n* (*on printer*) Papiervorschub *m*.
paperback [pā'pûrbak] *n* Taschenbuch *nt*.
paper bag *n* Tüte *f*.
paperboy [pā'pûrboi] *n* (*selling, delivering*) Zeitungsjunge *m*.
paper clip *n* Büroklammer *f*.
paper hankie *n* (*Brit*) Tempotaschentuch ® *nt*.
paper money *n* Papiergeld *nt*.
paper profit *n* rechnerische(r) Gewinn *m*.
papers [pā'pûrz] *npl* (*identity* ~) Ausweis(papiere *pl*) *m*.
paperweight [pā'pûrwāt] *n* Briefbeschwerer *m*.
paperwork [pā'pûrwûrk] *n* Schreibarbeit *f*.
papier-mâché [pā'pûrməshā'] *n* Papiermaché *nt*.
paprika [paprē'kə] *n* Paprika *m*.
Pap test [pap test] *n* (*US MED*) Abstrich *m*.
papyrus [pəpī'rəs] *n* Papyrus *m*.
par [pâr] *n* (*FIN*) Pariwert *m*, Nennwert *m*; (*of currency*) Parität *f*; (*GOLF*) Par *nt*; **below** *or* **under** ~ (*fig*) in schlechter Verfassung, nicht auf der Höhe; **at** ~ (*shares*) zum Nennwert; **on a** ~ **with** ebenbürtig (+*dat*); **to be on a** ~ **with sb** sich mit jdm messen können.
parable [par'əbəl] *n* Parabel *f*; (*REL*) Gleichnis *nt*.
parachute [par'əshōōt] *n* Fallschirm *m* ♦ *vi* (mit dem Fallschirm) abspringen.
parachutist [par'əshōōtist] *n* Fallschirmspringer(in *f*) *m*.
parade [pərād'] *n* Parade *f* ♦ *vt* aufmarschieren lassen ♦ *vi* paradieren, vorbeimarschieren.

parade ground *n* Truppenübungsplatz *m*, Exerzierplatz *m*.
paradise [par'ədīs] *n* Paradies *nt*.
paradox [par'ədâks] *n* Paradox *nt*.
paradoxical [parədâk'sikəl] *a* paradox, widersinnig.
paradoxically [parədâk'siklē] *ad* paradoxerweise.
paraffin [par'əfin] *n* (*Brit*) Paraffin *nt*.
paragon [par'əgân] *n* Muster *nt*.
paragraph [par'əgraf] *n* Absatz *m*, Paragraph *m*; **to begin a new** ~ mit einem neuen Absatz anfangen.
Paraguay [par'əgwā] *n* Paraguay *nt*.
Paraguayan [parəgwā'an] *a* paraguayisch ♦ *n* Paraguayer(in *f*) *m*.
parakeet [par'əkēt] *n* (*US*) Wellensittich *m*.
parallel [par'əlel] *a* parallel; ~ **with** *or* **to** parallel zu ♦ *n* Parallele *f*.
paralysis [pəral'isis] *n*, *pl* **paralyses** [pəral'isēz] Lähmung *f*.
paralytic [parəlit'ik] *a* paralytisch, Lähmungs-; (*Brit col: very drunk*) total blau.
paralyze [par'əlīz] *vt* lähmen.
paramedic [parəmed'ik] *n* (*US*) Sanitär *m*.
parameter [pəram'itûr] *n* Parameter *m*; ~**s** *pl* Rahmen *m*.
paramilitary [parəmil'itärē] *a* (*organization, operation*) paramilitärisch.
paramount [par'əmount] *a* höchste(r, s), oberste(r, s).
paranoia [parənoi'ə] *n* Paranoia *f*.
paranormal [parənôr'məl] *a* übersinnlich, paranormal.
parapet [par'əpit] *n* Brüstung *f*.
paraphernalia [parəfûrnāl'yə] *n* Zubehör *nt*, Utensilien *pl*.
paraphrase [par'əfrāz] *vt* umschreiben.
paraplegic [parəplē'jik] *n* Paraplegiker(in *f*) *m*.
parapsychology [parəsīkâl'əjē] *n* Parapsychologie *f*.
parasite [par'əsīt] *n* (*lit, fig*) Parasit *m*.
parasol [par'əsôl] *n* Sonnenschirm *m*.
paratrooper [par'ətrōōpûr] *n* Fallschirmjäger *m*.
parcel [pâr'səl] *n* Paket *nt*; **to be part and** ~ **of sth** (*fig*) fester Bestandteil von etw sein ♦ *vt* (*also:* ~ **up**) einpacken.
parcel out *vt* aufteilen.
parcel bomb *n* (*Brit*) Paketbombe *f*.
parcel post *n* Paketpost *f*.
parch [pârch] *vt* (aus)dörren; **I'm** ~**ed** ich bin am Verdursten.
parchment [pârch'mənt] *n* Pergament *nt*.
pardon [pâr'dən] *n* Verzeihung *f* ♦ *vt* (*JUR*) begnadigen; ~ **me!**, **I beg your** ~**!** verzeihen Sie bitte!; (*objection*) aber ich bitte Sie!; ~ **me?**, (*Brit*) ~**?** wie bitte?
pare [pär] *vt* (*Brit: nails*) schneiden; (*fruit etc*) schälen.
parent [pär'ənt] *n* Elternteil *m*; ~**s** *pl* Eltern *pl*.

parentage [pär'əntij] n Herkunft f.
parental [pəren'təl] a elterlich, Eltern-.
parent company n Muttergesellschaft f.
parenthesis [pəren'thəsis] n, pl **parentheses** [pəren'thəsēz] Klammer f; (sentence) Parenthese f; **in ~** in Klammern.
parenthood [pär'ənthŏŏd] n Elternschaft f.
parent ship n Mutterschiff nt.
Paris [par'is] n Paris nt.
parish [par'ish] n Gemeinde f.
parish council n (Brit) Gemeinderat m.
parishioner [pərish'ənûr] n Gemeindemitglied nt.
Parisian [pərizh'ən] a pariserisch, parisisch, Pariser inv ♦ n Pariser(in f) m.
parity [par'itē] n (FIN) Umrechnungskurs m, Parität f.
park [pârk] n Park m ♦ vti parken.
parka [pâr'kə] n Parka m.
parking [pâr'king] n Parken nt; "no ~" „Parken verboten".
parking lights npl Parklicht nt, Parkleuchte f.
parking lot n (US) Parkplatz m.
parking meter n Parkuhr f.
parking offence n (Brit) = **parking violation**.
parking place n Parkplatz m.
parking ticket n Strafzettel m.
parking violation n (US) Falschparken nt.
parkway [pârk'wā] n (US) Allee f.
parlance [pâr'ləns] n: **in common ~** im allgemeinen Sprachgebrauch.
parley [pâr'lē] vi verhandeln.
parliament [pâr'ləmənt] n Parlament nt.
parliamentary [pârləmen'tûrē] a parlamentarisch, Parlaments-.
parlor, (Brit) **parlour** [pâr'lûr] n Salon m, Wohnzimmer nt.
parlous [pâr'ləs] a (form) gefährlich, prekär; (state) schlimm.
Parmesan [pâr'məzân] n (also: ~ **cheese**) Parmesankäse m.
parochial [pərō'kēəl] a Gemeinde-, gemeindlich; (narrow-minded) engstirnig, Provinz-.
parody [par'ədē] n Parodie f ♦ vt parodieren.
parole [pərōl'] n: **on ~** (prisoner) auf Bewährung.
paroxysm [par'əksizəm] n (MED) Anfall m; (of anger) Wutanfall m; (of grief) Verzweiflungsanfall m; (of laughter) Lachkrampf m; (of coughing) Hustenanfall m.
parquet [pârkā'] n Parkett nt.
parrot [par'ət] n Papagei m.
parrot fashion ad wie ein Papagei.
parry [par'ē] vt parieren, abwehren.
parsimonious [pârsəmō'nēəs] a knauserig.
parsley [pârz'lē] n Petersilie f.
parsnip [pârs'nip] n Pastinake f, Petersilienwurzel f.
parson [pâr'sən] n Pfarrer m.
part [pârt] n (piece) Teil m, Stück nt; (THEAT) Rolle f; (of machine) Teil nt; (US: in hair) Scheitel m; **~ of speech** (GRAM)

Wortart f; **for the better ~ of the day** fast den ganzen Tag; **to take sb's ~** sich auf jds Seite stellen; **for my ~** ich für meinen Teil; **for the most ~** meistens, größtenteils ♦ ad = partly ♦ vt trennen; (hair) scheiteln ♦ vi (people) sich trennen, Abschied nehmen.
part with vt fus hergeben; (renounce) aufgeben.
partake [pârtāk'] vi (form): **to ~ of sth** etw zu sich (dat) nehmen.
part exchange n (Brit): **in ~** in Zahlung.
partial [pâr'shəl] a (incomplete) teilweise, Teil-; (biased) eingenommen, parteiisch; (eclipse) partiell; **to be ~ to** eine (besondere) Vorliebe haben für.
partially [pâr'shəlē] ad teilweise, zum Teil.
participant [pârtis'əpənt] n Teilnehmer(in f) m.
participate [pârtis'əpāt] vi teilnehmen (in an +dat).
participation [pârtisəpā'shən] n Teilnahme f; (sharing) Beteiligung f.
participle [pâr'tisipəl] n Partizip nt, Mittelwort nt.
particleboard [pâr'tikəlbôrd] n (US) Spanholz nt.
particular [pûrtik'yəlûr] a bestimmt, speziell; (exact) genau; (fussy) eigen; **to be very ~** (fussy, fastidious) eigen or pingelig (col) sein; (choosy) wählerisch sein; **I'm not ~** es kommt mir nicht so d(a)rauf an, es ist mir gleich ♦ n Einzelheit f; **in ~** besonders, vor allem; see also **particulars**.
particularly [pûrtik'yəlûrlē] ad besonders.
particulars [pûrtik'yəlûrz] npl (details) Einzelheiten pl; (Brit: about person) Personalien pl.
parting [pâr'ting] n (separation) Abschied m, Trennung f; (Brit: in hair) Scheitel m ♦ a Abschieds-; **he made a ~ threat** zum Abschied stieß er eine Drohung aus.
partisan [pâr'tizən] n Parteigänger m; (guerrilla) Partisan m ♦ a Partei-; Partisanen-.
partition [pârtish'ən] n (wall) Trennwand f; (division) Teilung f ♦ vt aufteilen.
partly [pârt'lē] ad zum Teil, teilweise.
partner [pârt'nûr] n Partner(in f) m; (COMM also) Gesellschafter(in f) m, Teilhaber(in f) m ♦ vt der Partner sein von.
partnership [pârt'nûrship] n Partnerschaft f, Gemeinschaft f; (COMM) Teilhaberschaft f; **to go into ~ with sb, to form a ~ with sb** sich mit jdm assoziieren.
part payment n Anzahlung f, Teilzahlung f.
partridge [pâr'trij] n Rebhuhn n.
part-time [pârt'tīm] a (half-day only) halbtägig, Halbtags-; (part of the week only) nebenberuflich ♦ ad halbtags; nebenberuflich.
part-timer [pârtī'mûr] n Teilzeitarbeiter(in f) m.
party [pâr'tē] n (POL. JUR) Partei f; (group) Gesellschaft f; (celebration) Party f; **dinner ~** Abendgesellschaft f (mit Essen); **to have** or **give** or **throw a ~** eine Party geben or

schmeißen (*col*); **to be a ~ to a crime** an einem Verbrechen beteiligt sein ♦ *a* (*politics*) Partei-; (*dress*) Party-.

party line *n* (*POL*) Parteilinie *f*; (*TEL*) Gemeinschaftsanschluß *m*.

pass [pas] *vt* vorbeikommen an (*+dat*); (*on foot*) vorbeigehen an (*+dat*); (*in car etc*) vorbeifahren an (*+dat*); (*surpass*) übersteigen; (*hand on*) weitergeben; (*approve*) gelten lassen, genehmigen; (*time*) verbringen; (*exam*) bestehen; **to ~ the time of day with sb** mit jdm die Zeit verplaudern ♦ *vi* (*go by*) vorbeigehen; vorbeifahren; (*years*) vergehen; (*be successful*) bestehen; (*be accepted: behavior*) gehen; **to bring sth to ~** (*plan*) etw bewirken ♦ *n* (*in mountains*) Paß *m*; (*MIL etc*) Passierschein *m*; (*travel ~*) Zeitkarte *f*; (*SPORT*) Paß *m*, Abgabe *f*; (*in exam*) Bestehen *nt*; **to get a ~** bestehen; **to make a ~ at sb** (*col*) sich an jdn heranmachen.

pass away *vi* (*euph*) verscheiden.

pass by *vi* vorbeigehen; (*car etc*) vorbeifahren; (*years*) vergehen.

pass down *vt* (*customs, inheritance*) weitergeben (*to* an *+acc*), überliefern (*to dat*).

pass for *vt fus* angesehen werden als; **she could ~ for 25** sie könnte für 25 durchgehen.

pass on *vt*: **to ~ on (to)** (*news, information, object*) weitergeben (an *+acc*); (*cold, illness*) übertragen (auf *+acc*); (*benefits, price, rises*) weitergeben (an *+acc*) ♦ *vi* (*die*) entschlafen, verscheiden.

pass out *vi* (*faint*) ohnmächtig werden.

pass over *vt* übergehen.

pass up *vt* (*opportunity*) vorübergehen lassen.

passable [pas'əbəl] *a* (*road*) passierbar, befahrbar; (*fairly good*) passabel, leidlich.

passably [pas'əblē] *ad* leidlich, ziemlich.

passage [pas'ij] *n* (*corridor*) Gang *m*, Korridor *m*; (*in book*) (Text)stelle *f*; (*voyage*) Überfahrt *f*.

passageway [pas'ijwā] *n* Passage *f*, Durchgang *m*.

passbook [pas'bŏŏk] *n* Sparbuch *nt*.

passenger [pas'injûr] *n* Passagier *m*; (*on bus*) Fahrgast *m*.

passer-by [pasûrbī'] *n* Passant(in *f*) *m*.

passing [pas'ing] *n* (*death*) Ableben *nt*; **in ~** beiläufig ♦ *a* (*car*) vorbeifahrend; (*thought, affair*) momentan.

passing place *n* (*AUT*) Ausweichstelle *f*.

passion [pash'ən] *n* Leidenschaft *f*.

passionate [pash'ənit] *a*, **passionately** [pash'ənitlē] *ad* leidenschaftlich.

passive [pas'iv] *n* Passiv *nt* ♦ *a* Passiv-, passiv.

passkey [pas'kē] *n* Hauptschlüssel *m*.

Passover [pas'ōvûr] *n* Passahfest *nt*.

passport [pas'pôrt] *n* (Reise)paß *m*.

passport control *n* Paßkontrolle *f*.

password [pas'wûrd] *n* Parole *f*, Kennwort

nt; (*COMPUT*) Kennwort *nt*, Paßwort *nt*.

past [past] *n* (*also GRAM*) Vergangenheit *f*; **in the ~** in der Vergangenheit, früher ♦ *ad* vorbei ♦ *prep*: **to go ~ sth** an etw (*dat*) vorbeigehen; **to be ~ 10** (*aged*) über 10 sein; (*time*) nach 10 sein; **quarter/half ~ four** Viertel nach vier/halb fünf; **I'm ~ caring** es kümmert mich nicht mehr; **he's ~ his prime** er ist über sein bestes Alter ♦ *a* (*years*) vergangen; (*president etc*) ehemalig.

pasta [pâs'tə] *n* Teigwaren *pl*.

paste [pāst] *n* (*for pastry*) Teig *m*; (*fish ~ etc*) Paste *f*; (*glue*) Kleister *m* ♦ *vt* kleben; (*put ~ on*) mit Kleister bestreichen.

pastel [pastel'] *a* (*color*) Pastell-.

pasteurized [pas'chərīzd] *a* pasteurisiert.

pastille [pastēl'] *n* Pastille *f*.

pastime [pas'tīm] *n* Hobby *nt*, Zeitvertreib *m*.

pastor [pas'tûr] *n* Pastor *m*, Pfarrer *m*.

pastoral [pas'tûrəl] *a* (*literature*) Schäfer-, Pastoral-.

pastries [pās'trēz] *npl* Gebäck *nt*.

pastry [pās'trē] *n* Blätterteig *m*; (*tarts etc*) Tortengebäck *nt*.

pasture [pas'chûr] *n* Weide *f*.

pasty *n* [pas'tē] (Fleisch)pastete *f* ♦ *a* [pās'tē] bläßlich, käsig.

pat [pat] *n* leichte(r) Schlag *m*, Klaps *m*; **to give sb/o.s. a ~ on the back** (*fig*) jdm/sich selbst auf die Schulter klopfen ♦ *ad*: **he has the rules down ~** (*US*), **he knows the rules off ~** (*Brit*) er kennt die Regeln aus dem Effeff (*col*) ♦ *vt* tätscheln.

patch [pach] *n* Fleck *m*; (*COMPUT*) Direktkorrektur *f*, Korrekturroutine *f*; **a ~ of fog** ein Nebelfeld ♦ *vt* flicken.

patch up *vt* flicken; (*quarrel*) beilegen.

patchwork [pach'wûrk] *n* Patchwork *nt*.

patchy [pach'ē] *a* (*irregular*) ungleichmäßig.

pate [pāt] *n* Schädel *m*.

pâté [pátā'] *n* Pastete *f*.

patent [pat'ənt] *n* Patent *nt* ♦ *vt* patentieren lassen; (*by authorities*) patentieren ♦ *a* offenkundig.

patent leather *n* Lackleder *nt*.

patently [pat'əntlē] *ad* offensichtlich.

patent medicine *n* patentrechtlich geschützte(s) Arzneimittel *nt*.

patent office *n* Patentamt *nt*.

patent rights *npl* Patentrechte *pl*.

paternal [pətûr'nəl] *a* väterlich; **his ~ grandmother** seine Großmutter väterlicherseits.

paternalistic [pətûrnəlis'tik] *a* väterlich, onkelhaft.

paternity [pətûr'nitē] *n* Vaterschaft *f*.

paternity suit *n* (*JUR*) Vaterschaftsprozeß *m*.

path [path] *n* (*lit, fig*) Weg *m*; (*small*) Pfad *m*; (*of the sun*) Bahn *f*.

pathetic [pəthet'ik] *a* mitleiderregend; (*very bad*) erbärmlich; **it's ~** es ist zum Weinen.

pathetically [pəthet'iklē] *ad* mitleiderregend; erbärmlich.

pathological [pathǝlâj'ikǝl] a krankhaft, pathologisch.
pathologist [pǝthâl'ǝjist] n Pathologe m.
pathology [pǝthâl'ǝjē] n Pathologie f.
pathos [pā'thâs] n Rührseligkeit f.
pathway [path'wā] n Pfad m, Weg m.
patience [pā'shǝns] n Geduld f; (Brit CARDS) Patience f; **to lose one's** ~ die Geduld verlieren.
patient [pā'shǝnt] n Patient(in f) m, Kranke(r) mf ♦ a geduldig.
patiently [pā'shǝntlē] ad geduldig.
patio [pat'ēō] n Innenhof m; (outside) Terrasse f.
patriot [pā'trēǝt] n Patriot(in f) m.
patriotic [pātrēât'ik] a patriotisch.
patriotism [pā'trēǝtizǝm] n Patriotismus m.
patrol [pǝtrōl'] n Patrouille f; (police) Streife f; **to be on** ~ patrouillieren; (police car) Streife fahren ♦ vt patrouillieren in (+dat) ♦ vi (police) die Runde machen; (MIL) patrouillieren.
patrol boat n Patrouillenboot nt.
patrol car n Streifenwagen m.
patrolman [pǝtrōl'mǝn] n, pl -men (US) (Streifen)polizist m.
patron [pā'trǝn] n (in shop) Kunde m, Kundin f; (in hotel) Gast m; (supporter) Förderer m.
patronage [pā'trǝnij] n Schirmherrschaft f; (COMM) Kundschaft f.
patronize [pā'trǝnīz] vt (support) unterstützen; (shop) besuchen; (treat condescendingly) von oben herab behandeln.
patronizing [pā'trǝnīzing] a (attitude) herablassend.
patron saint n Schutzheilige(r) mf, Schutzpatron(in f) m.
patter [pat'ûr] n (sound: of feet) Trappeln nt; (: of rain) Prasseln nt; (sales talk) Gerede nt ♦ vi (feet) trappeln; (rain) prasseln.
pattern [pat'ûrn] n Muster nt; (SEWING) Schnittmuster nt; (KNITTING) Strickanleitung f; **the** ~ **of events** der Ablauf der Ereignisse; **behavior** ~s Verhaltensmuster pl ♦ vt: **to be** ~ed **on sth** einer Sache (dat) nachgebildet sein.
patterned [pat'ûrnd] a (material) gemustert, bedruckt.
paucity [pô'sitē] n Mangel m (of an +dat).
paunch [pônch] n dicke(r) Bauch m, Wanst m.
pauper [pô'pûr] n Arme(r) mf.
pause [pôz] n Pause f ♦ vi innehalten; **to** ~ **for breath** eine Verschnaufpause machen.
pave [pāv] vt pflastern; **to** ~ **the way for** den Weg bahnen für.
pavement [pāv'mǝnt] n (US) Straße f; (Brit) Bürgersteig m.
pavilion [pǝvil'yǝn] n Pavillon m; (SPORT) Klubhaus nt; (changing ~) Umkleideräume pl.
paving [pā'ving] n Straßenpflaster nt.
paving stone n Pflasterstein m.

paw [pô] n Pfote f; (of big cats) Tatze f, Pranke f ♦ vt (scrape) scharren; (handle) betatschen.
pawn [pôn] n Pfand nt; (CHESS) Bauer m ♦ vt versetzen, verpfänden.
pawnbroker [pôn'brōkûr] n Pfandleiher m.
pawnshop [pôn'shâp] n Pfandhaus nt.
pay [pā] n Bezahlung f, Lohn m; **to be in sb's** ~ für jdn arbeiten ♦ irreg vt zahlen; (person, debt) bezahlen; (be profitable to, also fig) sich lohnen für; **it would** ~ **you to** ... es würde sich für dich lohnen, zu ...; **to** ~ **attention** achtgeben (to auf +acc); **that's put paid to my vacation** damit ist mein Urlaub geplatzt or gestorben (col); **that's put paid to him** damit ist für ihn der Ofen aus (col), das war's dann wohl für ihn (col); **to** ~ **one's way** (contribute one's share) seinen Teil beitragen; (remain solvent: company) seinen Verbindlichkeiten nachkommen; **to** ~ **dividends** (FIN) Dividenden zahlen; (fig) sich lohnen, sich bezahlt machen; ♦ vi zahlen; (be profitable) sich bezahlt machen; (fig): **it doesn't** ~ es lohnt sich nicht; **it doesn't** ~ **to be kind nowadays** es lohnt sich heutzutage nicht mehr, freundlich zu sein.
pay back vt zurückzahlen.
pay for vt bezahlen für.
pay in vt einzahlen.
pay off vt (debts) abbezahlen, tilgen; (creditor) befriedigen; (mortgage) ablösen; (workers) auszahlen; **to** ~ **sth off in installments** etw ab(be)zahlen ♦ vi (scheme, patience) sich bezahlt machen.
pay out vt (money) ausgeben; (rope) ablaufen lassen.
pay up vt bezahlen, seine Schulden begleichen.
payable [pā'ǝbǝl] a zahlbar, fällig; **to make a check** ~ **to sb** einen Scheck auf jdn ausstellen.
payday [pā'dā] n Zahltag m.
PAYE n abbr (Brit: = pay as you earn) Steuersystem, bei dem die Lohnsteuer direkt einbehalten wird.
payee [pāē'] n Zahlungsempfänger m.
pay envelope n (US) Lohntüte f.
paying [pā'ing] a einträglich, rentabel; ~ **guest** zahlende(r) Gast m.
payload [pā'lōd] n Nutzlast f.
payment [pā'mǝnt] n Bezahlung f; (total sum) Vorauszahlung f; **deferred** ~ Ratenzahlung f; **monthly** ~ monatliche Rate f; **in** ~ **for** (goods, sum owed) als Bezahlung für; **on** ~ **of** bei Bezahlung von.
pay packet n (Brit) Lohntüte f.
pay phone n Münzfernsprecher m.
payroll [pā'rōl] n Lohnliste f; **to be on a firm's** ~ bei einer Firma beschäftigt sein.
pay slip n (Brit) Lohn-/Gehaltsstreifen m.
pay station n (US) öffentliche(r) Fernsprecher m.
PBS n abbr (US: = Public Broadcasting Ser-

vice) öffentliche *Rundfunkanstalt.*

PBX *n abbr* = *private branch (telephone) exchange.*

pc *abbr* (= *postcard*) Pk.; (= *per cent*) Pr.

p/c *abbr* = **petty cash.**

PC *n abbr* (= *personal computer*) PC *m;* (*Brit*) = **police constable.**

PCB *n abbr* = **printed circuit board.**

pd. *abbr* (= *paid*) bez.

PD *n abbr* (*US*) = **police department.**

PDQ *ad abbr* (*col:* = *pretty damn quick*) verdammt schnell.

PDT *n abbr* (*US*) = *Pacific Daylight Time.*

PE *n abbr* (= *physical education*) Turnen *nt.*

pea [pē] *n* Erbse *f.*

peace [pēs] *n* Friede(n) *m;* **to be at ~ with sb/sth** mit jdm/etw in Frieden leben; **to keep the ~** (*police*) die öffentliche Ordnung aufrechterhalten; (*citizen*) die öffentliche Ordnung wahren.

peaceable [pē'səbəl] *a,* **peaceably** [pē'səblē] *ad* friedlich.

Peace Corps *n* (*US*) ≈ Deutsche(r) Entwicklungsdienst *m.*

peaceful [pēs'fəl] *a* friedlich, ruhig.

peacekeeping [pēs'kēping] *a* Friedens-.

peacekeeping role *n* Vermittlerrolle *f.*

peace offering *n* Friedensangebot *nt;* (*fig*) Versöhnungsgeschenk *nt.*

peacetime [pēs'tim] *n* Friede(n) *m.*

peach [pēch] *n* Pfirsich *m.*

peacock [pē'kâk] *n* Pfau *m.*

peak [pēk] *n* Spitze *f;* (*of mountain*) Gipfel *m;* (*fig*) Höhepunkt *m;* (*of cap*) (Mützen)schirm *m.*

peaked [pēkt] *a* (*US col*) blaß, verhärmt; **I'm feeling a bit ~** es geht mir nicht so gut.

peak hour *n* (*ELEC*) Hauptbelastungszeit *f.*

peak hour traffic *n* Hauptverkehrszeit *f,* Stoßzeit *f.*

peak period *n* Stoßzeit *f,* Hauptzeit *f.*

peaky [pē'kē] *a* (*Brit col*) = **peaked.**

peal [pēl] *n* (Glocken)läuten *nt.*

peanut [pē'nut] *n* Erdnuß *f.*

peanut butter *n* Erdnußbutter *f.*

peanut oil *n* Erdnußöl *nt.*

pear [pär] *n* Birne *f.*

pearl [pûrl] *n* Perle *f.*

peasant [pez'ənt] *n* Bauer *m.*

peat [pēt] *n* Torf *m.*

pebble [peb'əl] *n* Kiesel *m.*

peck [pek] *vti* picken ♦ *n* (*with beak*) Schnabelhieb *m;* (*kiss*) flüchtige(r) Kuß *m.*

pecking order [pek'ing ôrdûr] *n* (*fig*) Hackordnung *f.*

peckish [pek'ish] *a* (*Brit col*) ein bißchen hungrig.

peculiar [pikyōōl'yûr] *a* (*odd*) seltsam; (*particular: importance, qualities*) eigentümlich; (*characteristic*) wesenseigen; **~ to** charakteristisch für; **an animal ~ to Africa** ein Tier, das nur in Afrika vorkommt.

peculiarity [pikyōōlēar'itē] *n* (*singular quality*) Besonderheit *f;* (*strangeness*) Eigenar-

tigkeit *f.*

peculiarly [pikyōōl'yûrlē] *ad* seltsam; (*especially*) besonders.

pedal [ped'əl] *n* Pedal *nt* ♦ *vti* (*cycle*) fahren, radfahren.

pedal bin *n* (*Brit*) Treteimer *m.*

pedant [ped'ənt] *n* Pedant *m.*

pedantic [pədan'tik] *a* pedantisch.

pedantry [ped'əntrē] *n* Pedanterie *f.*

peddle [ped'əl] *vt* hausieren gehen mit; (*goods*) feilbieten, verkaufen; (*gossip*) verbreiten; **to ~ drugs** mit Drogen handeln.

peddler [ped'lûr] *n* (*US*) Hausierer(in *f*) *m;* (*of drugs*) Pusher(in *f*) *m.*

pedestal [ped'istəl] *n* Sockel *m.*

pedestrian [pədes'trēən] *n* Fußgänger *m* ♦ *a* Fußgänger-; (*humdrum*) langweilig.

pedestrian crossing *n* (*Brit*) Fußgängerüberweg *m.*

pedestrian precinct *n* (*Brit*) Fußgängerzone *f.*

pediatrician [pēdēətrish'ən] *n* (*US*) Kinderarzt *m*/Kinderärztin *f.*

pediatrics [pēdēat'riks] *n sing* (*US*) Kinderheilkunde *f.*

pedigree [ped'əgrē] *n* Stammbaum *m* ♦ *a* (*animal*) reinrassig, Zucht-.

pedlar [ped'lûr] *n* (*Brit*) Hausierer(in *f*) *m.*

pee [pē] *vi* (*col*) pissen, pinkeln.

peek [pēk] *n* flüchtige(r) Blick *m* ♦ *vi* gucken.

peel [pēl] *n* Schale *f* ♦ *vt* schälen ♦ *vi* (*paint etc*) abblättern; (*skin*) sich schälen.

peel back *vt* abziehen.

peelings [pē'lingz] *npl* Schalen *pl.*

peep [pēp] *n* (*sound*) Piepsen *nt;* (*look*) neugierige(r) Blick *m* ♦ *vi* (*bird*) piepen; (*horn, car*) tuten; (*whistle*) pfeifen; (*Brit: look*) neugierig gucken.

peep out *vi* herausgucken.

peephole [pēp'hōl] *n* Guckloch *nt.*

peer [pēr] *vi* starren ♦ *n* (*nobleman*) Peer *m;* (*equal*) Ebenbürtige(r) *m;* **his ~s** seinesgleichen.

peerage [pē'rij] *n* Peerswürde *f.*

peerless [pēr'lis] *a* einzigartig, unvergleichlich.

peeve [pēv] *vt* (*col*) verärgern.

peeved [pēvd] *a* ärgerlich; (*person*) sauer.

peevish [pē'vish] *a* verdrießlich, brummig.

peevishness [pē'vishnis] *n* Verdrießlichkeit *f.*

peg [peg] *n* Stift *m;* (*hook*) Haken *m;* (*stake*) Pflock *m* ♦ *vt* (*clothes*) anklammern; (*fig: prices, wages*) festsetzen.

PEI *abbr* (*Canada*) = *Prince Edward Island.*

pejorative [pijôr'ətiv] *a* pejorativ, herabsetzend.

pekinese [pēkənēz'] *n* (*dog*) Pekinese *m.*

Peking [pēking'] *n* Peking *nt.*

pelican [pel'ikən] *n* Pelikan *m.*

pelican crossing *n* (*Brit AUT*) Ampelüberweg *m.*

pellet [pel'it] *n* Kügelchen *nt.*

pell-mell [pel'mel'] *ad* durcheinander.

pelmet [pel'mit] *n* Blende *f.*

pelt [pelt] *vt* bewerfen ♦ *n* Pelz *m*, Fell *nt*.
pelt down *vi* niederprasseln.
pelvis [pel'vis] *n* Becken *nt*.
pen [pen] *n* (*fountain* ~) Federhalter *m*; (*ballpoint*) Kuli *m*; (*felt-tip* ~) Filzstift *m*; (*for sheep*) Pferch *m*; **to put** ~ **to paper** zur Feder greifen.
penal [pē'nəl] *a* Straf-; ~ **servitude** Zwangsarbeit *f*.
penalize [pē'nəlīz] *vt* (*make punishable*) unter Strafe stellen; (*punish*) bestrafen; (*disadvantage*) benachteiligen.
penalty [pen'əltē] *n* Strafe *f*; (*SOCCER*) Elfmeter *m*.
penalty clause *n* Vertragsstrafe *f*.
penalty kick *n* Elfmeter *m*.
penance [pen'əns] *n* Buße *f*.
pence [pens] *npl* (*Brit*) Pence *pl*; *see* **penny**.
penchant [pen'chənt] *n* Vorliebe *f*, Schwäche *f*.
pencil [pen'səl] *n* Bleistift *m* ♦ *vt* (*also*: ~ **in**) vormerken.
pencil case *n* Federmäppchen *nt*.
pencil sharpener *n* Bleistiftspitzer *m*.
pendant [pen'dənt] *n* Anhänger *m*.
pending [pen'ding] *prep* bis (zu); ~ **the arrival of** bis zur Ankunft von ♦ *a* unentschieden, noch offen.
pendulum [pen'jələm] *n* Pendel *nt*.
penetrate [pen'itrāt] *vt* durchdringen; (*enter into*) eindringen in (+*acc*).
penetrating [pen'itrāting] *a* durchdringend; (*analysis*) scharfsinnig.
penetration [penitrā'shən] *n* Durchdringen *nt*; Eindringen *nt*.
pen friend *n* Brieffreund(in *f*) *m*.
penguin [pen'gwin] *n* Pinguin *m*.
penicillin [penisil'in] *n* Penizillin *nt*.
peninsula [pənin'sələ] *n* Halbinsel *f*.
penis [pē'nis] *n* Penis *m*.
penitence [pen'itəns] *n* Reue *f*.
penitent [pen'itənt] *a* reuig.
penitentiary [peniten'chûrē] *n* (*US*) Zuchthaus *nt*.
penknife [pen'nīf] *n*, *pl* **-knives** Taschenmesser *nt*.
pen name [pen' nām] *n* Pseudonym *nt*.
Penn., Penna. *abbr* (*US*) = *Pennsylvania*.
pennant [pen'ənt] *n* Wimpel *m*; (*official* ~) Stander *m*; (*US SPORT*) Siegeszeichen *nt*.
penniless [pen'ēlis] *a* mittellos, ohne einen Pfennig.
Pennines [pen'īnz] *npl* Pennines *pl*.
penny *n*, *pl* **pennies** *or* **pence** [pen'ē, pen'ēz, pens] (*US*) Centstück *nt*; (*Brit*) Penny *m*.
pen pal *n* Brieffreund(in *f*) *m*.
pension [pen'chən] *n* Rente *f*; (*for civil servants, executives etc*) Ruhegehalt *nt*, Pension *f*.
pension off *vt* vorzeitig pensionieren.
pensionable [pen'chənəbəl] *a* (*person*) pensionsberechtigt; (*job*) mit Renten- *or* Pensionsanspruch.

pensioner [pen'chənûr] *n* (*civil servant, executive*) Pensionär *m*; (*Brit*) Rentner(in *f*) *m*.
pension fund *n* Rentenfonds *m*.
pensive [pen'siv] *a* nachdenklich.
pentagon [pen'təgân] *n* Fünfeck *nt*; **the P**~ (*US POL*) das Pentagon.
Pentecost [pen'təkôst] *n* Pfingsten *nt*.
penthouse [pent'hous] *n* Dachterrassenwohnung *f*.
pent-up [pent'up'] *a* (*emotions*) angestaut.
penultimate [pinul'təmit] *a* vorletzte(r, s).
penury [pen'yûrē] *n* Armut *f*, Not *f*.
people [pē'pəl] *n* (*nation*) Volk *nt*; (*inhabitants*) Bevölkerung *f*; (*persons*) Leute *pl*; **old** ~ alte Leute *pl*; **young** ~ junge Leute *pl*; ~ **at large** die Allgemeinheit; **a man of the** ~ ein Mann des Volkes ♦ *vt* besiedeln.
pep [pep] *n* (*col*) Schwung *m*, Schmiß *m*.
pep up *vt* aufmöbeln.
pepper [pep'ûr] *n* Pfeffer *m*; (*vegetable*) Paprika *m* ♦ *vt* (*pelt*) bombardieren.
pepper mill *n* Pfeffermühle *f*.
peppermint [pep'ûrmint] *n* (*plant*) Pfefferminze *f*; (*sweet*) Pfefferminz *nt*.
pepperpot [pep'ûrpât] *n* (*US*) gepfefferte Suppe *f*; (*esp Brit*) Pfefferstreuer *m*.
pepper shaker [pep'ûr shā'kûr] *n* (*US*) Pfefferstreuer *m*.
pep talk *n* (*col*) Anstachelung *f*.
per [pûr] *prep* pro; ~ **annum** pro Jahr; ~ **capita** pro Kopf, pro Person; **as** ~ **your instructions** gemäß Ihren Anweisungen.
perceive [pûrsēv'] *vt* (*realize*) wahrnehmen, spüren; (*understand*) verstehen.
per cent, percent [pûr sent'] *n* Prozent *nt*; **a 20** ~ **discount** 20 Prozent Rabatt.
percentage [pûrsen'tij] *n* Prozentsatz *m*; **on a** ~ **basis** prozentual, auf Prozentbasis; **to get a** ~ **on all sales** prozentual am Umsatz beteiligt sein.
perceptible [pûrsep'təbəl] *a* merklich, wahrnehmbar.
perception [pûrsep'shən] *n* Wahrnehmung *f*; (*insight*) Einsicht *f*.
perceptive [pûrsep'tiv] *a* (*person*) aufmerksam; (*analysis*) tiefgehend.
perch [pûrch] *n* Stange *f*; (*fish*) Flußbarsch *m* ♦ *vi* sitzen, hocken.
percolate [pûr'kəlāt] *vt* (*coffee*) (in einer Kaffeemaschine) zubereiten ♦ *vi* durchsickern.
percolator [pûr'kəlātûr] *n* Kaffeemaschine *f*.
percussion [pûrkush'ən] *n* (*MUS*) Schlagzeug *nt*.
percussionist [pûrkush'ənist] *n* Schlagzeuger(in *f*) *m*.
peremptory [pəremp'tûrē] *a* schroff.
perennial [pəren'ēəl] *a* wiederkehrend ♦ *n* mehrjährige Pflanze *f*.
perfect [pûr'fikt] *a* vollkommen; (*crime, solution*) perfekt; (*GRAM*) vollendet; **he's a** ~ **stranger to me** er ist mir völlig fremd ♦ *n* (*GRAM*) Perfekt *nt* ♦ *vt* [pərfekt'] vervoll-

kommnen.

perfection [pûrfek'shən] *n* Vollkommenheit *f*, Perfektion *f*.

perfectionist [pûrfek'shənist] *n* Perfektionist *m*.

perfectly [pûr'fiktlē] *ad* vollkommen, perfekt; *(quite)* ganz, einfach; **I'm ~ happy about it** ich bin damit völlig zufrieden; **you know ~ well, that** ... du weißt ganz genau, daß ...

perforate [pûr'fûrāt] *vt* durchlöchern.

perforated [pûr'fərātid] *a* durchlöchert, perforiert; **~ ulcer** *(MED)* durchgebrochene(s) Geschwür *nt*.

perforation [pûrfərā'shən] *n* Perforation *f*.

perform [pûrfôrm'] *vt* *(carry out)* durch- or ausführen; *(task)* verrichten; *(THEAT)* spielen, geben; *(duty)* erfüllen ♦ *vi* *(THEAT)* auftreten.

performance [pûrfôr'məns] *n* Durchführung *f*; *(efficiency)* Leistung *f*; *(show)* Vorstellung *f*.

performer [pûrfôr'mûr] *n* Künstler(in *f*) *m*.

performing [pûrfôr'ming] *a* *(animal)* dressiert.

perfume [pûr'fyōōm] *n* Duft *m*; *(lady's)* Parfüm *nt*.

perfunctory [pûrfungk'tûrē] *a* oberflächlich, mechanisch.

perhaps [pûrhaps'] *ad* vielleicht; **~ so** das kann *or* mag sein; **~ not** vielleicht nicht.

peril [pär'əl] *n* Gefahr *f*.

perilous [pär'ələs] *a* gefährlich.

perilously [pär'ələslē] *ad* gefährlich; **she came ~ close to falling** sie wäre um ein Haar (herunter)gefallen.

perimeter [pərim'itûr] *n* Peripherie *f*; *(of circle etc)* Umfang *m*.

period [pēr'ēəd] *n* Periode *f*, Zeit *f*; *(GRAM)* Punkt *m*; *(MED)* Periode *f*; *(Brit SCH)* Stunde *f*; **the holiday ~** die Urlaubszeit; **for a ~ of three weeks** für eine Dauer *or* einen Zeitraum von drei Wochen ♦ *a* *(costume)* historisch.

periodic [pērēād'ik] *a* periodisch.

periodical [pērēād'ikəl] *n* Zeitschrift *f* ♦ *a* = periodic.

periodically [pērēād'iklē] *ad* periodisch.

peripatetic [päripətet'ik] *a* *(salesman)* reisend; *(teacher)* an mehreren Schulen unterrichtend.

peripheral [pərif'ûrəl] *a* Rand-; *(COMPUT also)* peripher ♦ *n* *(COMPUT)* periphere(s) Gerät *nt*, Peripheriegerät *nt*.

periphery [pərif'ûrē] *n* Peripherie *f*, Rand *m*.

periscope [pär'iskōp] *n* Periskop *nt*, Sehrohr *nt*.

perish [pär'ish] *vi* umkommen; *(material)* unbrauchbar werden; *(fruit)* verderben; **~ the thought!** daran wollen wir nicht denken.

perishable [pär'ishəbəl] *a* *(fruit)* leicht verderblich.

perishables [pär'ishəbəlz] *npl* leicht verderbliche Ware(n).

peritonitis [pär'itənī'tis] *n* Bauchfellentzün-

dung *f*.

perjure [pûr'jûr] *vr*: **to ~ o.s.** einen Meineid leisten.

perjury [pûr'jûrē] *n* Meineid *m*.

perk [pûrk] *n* *(col: fringe benefit)* Vorteil *m*, Vergünstigung *f*.

perk up *vi* munter werden ♦ *vt* *(ears)* spitzen.

perky [pûr'kē] *a* *(cheerful)* keck.

perm [pûrm] *n* Dauerwelle *f* ♦ *vt*: **to have one's hair ~ed** sich eine Dauerwelle machen lassen.

permanence [pûr'mənəns] *n* Dauer(haftigkeit) *f*, Beständigkeit *f*.

permanent [pûr'mənənt] *a* dauernd, ständig; *(job, position)* fest, Dauer-; *(dye, ink)* wasserfest; **my ~ address** mein ständiger *or* fester Wohnsitz; **I'm not ~ here** ich bin hier nicht fest angestellt ♦ *n* *(US)* = **perm**.

permanently [pûr'mənəntlē] *ad* dauernd, ständig.

permeate [pûr'mēāt] *vti* durchdringen.

permissible [pûrmis'əbəl] *a* zulässig.

permission [pûrmish'ən] *n* Erlaubnis *f*, Genehmigung *f*; **to give sb ~ to do sth** jdm die Erlaubnis geben *or* jdm erlauben, etw zu tun; **with your ~** mit Ihrer Erlaubnis.

permissive [pûrmis'iv] *a* nachgiebig; *(society etc)* permissiv.

permit *n* [pûr'mit] Zulassung *f*, Erlaubnis(schein *m*) *f*; *(entrance pass)* Genehmigung *f*, Ausweis *m*; **export ~** Exportgenehmigung *f*; **fishing ~** Angelschein *m* ♦ [pərmit'] *vt* erlauben, zulassen ♦ *vi*: **weather ~ting** wenn es das Wetter erlaubt.

permutation [pûrmyətā'shən] *n* Veränderung *f*; *(MATH)* Permutation *f*.

pernicious [pûrnish'əs] *a* schädlich.

pernickety [pûrnik'ətē] *n* *(Brit)* = **persnickety**.

perpendicular [pûrpəndik'yəlûr] *a* senkrecht.

perpetrate [pûr'pitrāt] *vt* begehen; *(crime)* begehen, verüben.

perpetual [pûrpech'ōōəl] *a*, **perpetually** [pûrpech'ōōəlē] *ad* dauernd, ständig.

perpetuate [pûrpech'ōōāt] *vt* verewigen, bewahren.

perpetuity [pûrpətōō'itē] *n* Ewigkeit *f*.

perplex [pûrpleks'] *vt* verblüffen.

perplexed [pûrplekst'] *a* verblüfft, perplex.

perplexing [pûrplek'sing] *a* verblüffend.

perplexity [pûrplek'sitē] *n* Verblüffung *f*.

perquisites [pûr'kwizits] *npl* *(also:* **perks)** Sondervergünstigungen *pl*.

persecute [pûr'səkyōōt] *vt* verfolgen.

persecution [pûrsəkyōō'shən] *n* Verfolgung *f*.

perseverance [pûrsəvēr'əns] *n* Ausdauer *f*.

persevere [pûrsəvēr'] *vi* beharren, durchhalten.

Persia [pûr'zhə] *n* Persien *nt*.

Persian [pûr'zhən] *a* persisch ♦ *n* *(person)* Perser(in *f*) *m*; *(language)* Persisch *nt*.

Persian Gulf *n* Persische(r) Golf *m*.

persist [pûrsist'] *vi* *(in belief etc)* bleiben *(in*

bei); (*rain, smell*) andauern; (*continue*) nicht aufhören.

persistence [pûrsis'təns] *n* Beharrlichkeit *f*.

persistent [pûrsis'tənt] *a* beharrlich; (*unending*) ständig; (*rain*) Dauer-, andauernd.

persistently [pûrsis'təntlē] *ad* beharrlich; (*unending*) ständig.

persnickety [pûrsnik'ətē] *a* (*US col: task*) heikel; (: *person*) pingelig.

person [pûr'sən] *n* Person *f*, Mensch *m*; (*GRAM*) Person *f*; **a ~ to ~ call** (*TEL*) ein Gespräch mit Voranmeldung; **on** *or* **about one's ~** (*weapon, money*) bei sich; **in ~** persönlich.

personable [pûr'sənəbəl] *a* gut aussehend.

personal [pûr'sənəl] *a* persönlich; (*private*) privat; (*of body*) körperlich, Körper-.

personal allowance *n* persönliche(r) Steuerfreibetrag *m*.

personal assistant *n* Stellvertreter(in *f*) *m*.

personal belongings *npl* persönliche(s) Eigentum *nt*, persönliche(r) Besitz *m*.

personal column *n* Familienanzeigen *pl*.

personal computer *n* Personal-Computer *m*.

personal effects *npl* bewegliche Habe *pl*.

personal interview *n* Vorstellungsgespräch *nt*.

personality [pûrsənal'itē] *n* Persönlichkeit *f*.

personal loan *n* Personaldarlehen *nt*.

personally [pûr'sənəlē] *ad* persönlich.

personal property *n* Privateigentum *nt*, persönliche(s) Eigentum *nt*.

personification [pûrsânəfəkā'shən] *n* Verkörperung *f*.

personify [pûrsân'əfī] *vt* verkörpern, personifizieren.

personnel [pûrsənel'] *n* Personal *nt*; (*in factory*) Belegschaft *f*.

personnel department *n* Personalabteilung *f*.

personnel management *n* Personalführung *f*.

personnel manager *n* Personalchef *m*.

perspective [pûrspek'tiv] *n* Perspektive *f*; **try to keep things in ~** versuchen Sie, nüchtern und sachlich zu bleiben; **to get sth into ~** etw nüchtern und sachlich sehen.

Perspex [pûr'speks] *n* ® (*Brit*) Acrylglas ® *nt*.

perspicacity [pûrspəkə'sitē] *n* Scharfsinn *m*.

perspiration [pûrspərā'shən] *n* Transpiration *f*.

perspire [pûrspīr'] *vi* transpirieren.

persuade [pûrswād'] *vt* überreden; (*convince*) überzeugen; **to ~ sb of sth/that ...** jdn von etw überzeugen/jdn davon überzeugen, daß ...; **I am ~d that ...** ich bin überzeugt, daß ...

persuasion [pûrswā'zhən] *n* Überredung *f*; (*belief*) Überzeugung *f*.

persuasive [pûrswā'siv] *a*, **persuasively** [pûrswā'sivlē] *ad* überzeugend.

pert [pûrt] *a* keck; (*hat*) keß.

pertain [pûrtān'] *vt* gehören (*to* zu); **~ing to** betreffend (+*acc*).

pertinent [pûr'tənənt] *a* relevant.

perturb [pûrtûrb'] *vt* beunruhigen.

perturbing [pûrtûrb'ing] *a* beunruhigend.

Peru [pərōō'] *n* Peru *nt*.

perusal [pərōō'zəl] *n* Durchsicht *f*.

peruse [pərōōz'] *vt* lesen.

Peruvian [pərōō'vēən] *a* peruanisch ♦ *n* Peruaner(in *f*) *m*.

pervade [pûrvād'] *vt* erfüllen, durchziehen.

pervasive [pûrvā'siv] *a* (*smell*) durchdringend; (*influence etc*) allgegenwärtig; (*gloom, feelings*) um sich greifend.

perverse [pûrvûrs'] *a*, **perversely** [pûrvûrs'lē] *ad* pervers; (*obstinate*) eigensinnig.

perverseness [pûrvûrs'nis] *n* Perversität *f*; Eigensinn *m*.

perversion [pûrvûr'zhən] *n* Perversion *f*; (*of justice*) Verdrehung *f*.

perversity [pûrvûr'sitē] *n* Perversität *f*.

pervert *n* [pûr'vûrt] perverse(r) Mensch *m* ♦ *vt* [pûrvûrt'] verdrehen; (*morally*) verderben.

pessimism [pes'əmizəm] *n* Pessimismus *m*.

pessimist [pes'əmist] *n* Pessimist(in *f*) *m*.

pessimistic [pesəmis'tik] *a* pessimistisch.

pest [pest] *n* Plage *f*; (*insect*) Schädling *m*; (*fig: person*) Nervensäge *f*.

pest control *n* Schädlingsbekämpfung *f*.

pester [pes'tûr] *vt* plagen.

pesticide [pes'tisīd] *n* Insektenvertilgungsmittel *nt*.

pestle [pes'əl] *n* Stößel *m*.

pet [pet] *n* (*animal*) Haustier *nt*; (*person*) Liebling *m* ♦ *vt* liebkosen, streicheln ♦ *a attr* (*favorite: pupil etc*) Lieblings-; **smoking is my ~ hate** Rauchen ist mir ein besonderer Greuel.

petal [pet'əl] *n* Blütenblatt *nt*.

peter out [pē'tûr out'] *vi* allmählich zu Ende gehen.

petite [pətēt'] *a* zierlich.

petition [pətish'ən] *n* Bittschrift *f* ♦ *vi* eine Unterschriftenliste einreichen; **to ~ for divorce** die Scheidung einreichen.

pet name *n* (*Brit*) Kosename *m*.

petrel [pet'rəl] *n* Sturmvogel *m*.

petrified [pet'rəfīd] *a* (*person*) starr (vor Schreck).

petrify [pet'rəfī] *vt* (*lit*) versteinern; (*person*) erstarren lassen.

petrochemical [petrōkem'ikəl] *a* petrochemisch.

petrodollar [petrōdâl'ûr] *n* Petrodollar *m*.

petrol [pet'rəl] *n* (*Brit*) Benzin *nt*, Kraftstoff *m*; **two-/four-star ~** Normal-/Superbenzin *nt*.

petrol can *n* (*Brit*) Benzinkanister *m*.

petrol engine *n* (*Brit*) Benzinmotor *m*.

petroleum [petrō'lēəm] *n* Petroleum *nt*.

petroleum jelly *n* Vaseline *f*.

petrol pump *n* (*Brit: in car*) Benzinpumpe *f*; (: *at garage*) Zapfsäule *f*, Tanksäule *f*.

petrol station n (*Brit*) Tankstelle f.
petrol tank n (*Brit*) Benzintank m.
petticoat [pet'ēkōt] n Petticoat m.
pettifogging [pet'ēfäging] a kleinlich.
pettiness [pet'ēnis] n Geringfügigkeit f; (*meanness*) Kleinlichkeit f.
petty [pet'ē] a (*unimportant*) geringfügig, unbedeutend; (*mean*) kleinlich.
petty cash n Portokasse f.
petty cash book n Bargeldkassenbuch nt.
petty officer n Maat m.
petulant [pech'ələnt] a leicht reizbar.
pew [pyōō] n Kirchenbank f.
pewter [pyōō'tûr] n Zinn nt.
Pfc abbr (*US MIL*: = *private first class*) OGefr.
PG n abbr (*CINE*) = *parental guidance*; ~-13 (*US*) ≈ frei ab 14.
PGA n abbr (= *Professional Golfers' Association*) Golfsportverband.
pH n abbr (= *pH value*) pH.
PH n abbr (*US MIL*: = *Purple Heart*) Verwundetenabzeichen.
PHA n abbr (*US*: = *Public Housing Administration*) Verwaltung von öffentlichen Wohnungen.
phallic [fal'ik] a phallisch, Phallus-.
phantom [fan'təm] n Phantom nt, Geist m.
pharmaceutical [fârməsōō'tikəl] a pharmazeutisch.
pharmacist [fâr'məsist] n Pharmazeut m; (*druggist*) Apotheker m.
pharmacy [fâr'məsē] n Pharmazie f; (*shop*) Apotheke f.
phase [fāz] n Phase f ♦ vt: ~d withdrawal schrittweise(r) Abzug m.
phase out vt langsam abbauen; (*model*) auslaufen lassen; (*person*) absetzen.
PhD n abbr (= *Doctor of Philosophy*) ≈ Dr. phil.
pheasant [fez'ənt] n Fasan m.
phenomenal [finâm'ənəl] a, **phenomenally** [finâm'ənəlē] ad phänomenal.
phenomenon [finâm'ənân] n, pl **phenomena** [finâm'ənə] Phänomen nt; **common** ~ häufige Erscheinung f.
phial [fī'əl] n Fläschchen nt, Ampulle f.
philanderer [filan'dûrûr] n Schwerenöter m.
philanthropic [filənthráp'ik] a philanthropisch.
philanthropist [filan'thrəpist] n Philanthrop m, Menschenfreund m.
philatelist [filat'əlist] n Briefmarkensammler m, Philatelist m.
philately [filat'əlē] n Briefmarkensammeln nt, Philatelie f.
Philippines [fil'ipēnz] npl Philippinen pl.
philosopher [filás'əfûr] n Philosoph(in f) m.
philosophical [filəsâf'ikəl] a philosophisch.
philosophize [filás'əfīz] vi philosophieren.
philosophy [filás'əfē] n Philosophie f; (*of life*) Weltanschauung f.
phlegm [flem] n (*MED*) Schleim m; (*calmness*) Gelassenheit f.

phlegmatic [flegmat'ik] a gelassen.
phobia [fō'bēə] n krankhafte Furcht f, Phobie f.
phoenix [fē'niks] n Phönix m.
phone [fōn] n Telefon nt ♦ vti telefonieren, anrufen.
phone back vti zurückrufen.
phone book n Telefonbuch nt.
phone booth, (*Brit*) **phone box** n Telefonzelle f.
phone call n Telefonanruf m.
phone-in [fōn'in] n (*Brit*) Phone-in nt.
phonetics [fənet'iks] n sing Phonetik f, Laut(bildungs)lehre f; pl Lautschrift f.
phon(e)y [fō'nē] a (*col*) unecht; (*excuse*) faul; (*money*) gefälscht ♦ n (*person*) Schwindler m; (*thing*) Fälschung f; (*dollar bill*) Blüte f.
phonograph [fō'nəgraf] n (*US*) Grammophon nt.
phonology [fənâl'əjē] n Phonologie f, Lautlehre f.
phosphate [fás'fāt] n Phosphat nt.
phosphorus [fás'fûrəs] n Phosphor m.
photo [fō'tō] n Foto nt.
photocopier [fō'təkâpēûr] n Kopiergerät nt.
photocopy [fō'təkâpē] n Fotokopie f ♦ vt fotokopieren.
photoelectric [fōtōilek'trik] a fotoelektrisch; ~ **cell** Photozelle f.
photo finish n Zielfotografie f.
photogenic [fōtəjen'ik] a fotogen.
photograph [fō'təgraf] n Fotografie f, Aufnahme f; **to take a** ~ **of sb** jdn fotografieren, eine Aufnahme or ein Bild von jdm machen ♦ vt fotografieren, aufnehmen.
photographer [fətâg'rəfûr] n Fotograf(in f) m.
photographic [fōtəgraf'ik] a fotografisch.
photography [fətâg'rəfē] n Fotografie f, Fotografieren nt; (*of film, book*) Aufnahmen pl.
Photostat [fō'təstat] n ® Fotokopie f.
photosynthesis [fōtəsin'thəsis] n Photosynthese f.
phrase [frāz] n (kurze(r)) Satz m; (*GRAM*) Phrase f; (*expression*) Redewendung f, Ausdruck m ♦ vt ausdrücken; (*letter*) formulieren.
phrase book n Sprachführer m.
physical [fiz'ikəl] a (*of physics*) physikalisch; (*bodily*) körperlich, physisch ♦ n = **physical examination**.
physical examination n ärztliche Untersuchung f.
physical exercises npl Gymnastik f, Leibesübungen pl.
physically [fiz'iklē] ad körperlich, physisch.
physical training n Turnen nt.
physician [fizish'ən] n Arzt m, Ärztin f.
physicist [fiz'əsist] n Physiker(in f) m.
physics [fiz'iks] n sing Physik f.
physiological [fizēəlâj'ikəl] a physiologisch.
physiology [fizēâl'əjē] n Physiologie f.
physiotherapist [fizēōthär'əpist] n Heilgym-

nast (in *f*) *m*.

physiotherapy [fizēōthär'əpē] *n* Heilgymnastik *f*, Physiotherapie *f*.

physique [fizēk'] *n* Körperbau *m*.

pianist [pēan'ist] *n* Pianist (in *f*) *m*.

piano [pēan'ō] *n* Klavier *nt*, Piano *nt*.

piano accordion *n* (*Brit*) Akkordeon *nt*.

piccolo [pik'əlō] *n* kleine Flöte *f*, Pikkoloflöte *f*.

pick [pik] *n* (*tool*) Pickel *m*; (*choice*) Auswahl *f*; **the ~ of** das Beste von ♦ *vt* (*gather*) (auf)lesen, sammeln; (*fruit*) pflücken; (*choose*) aussuchen; (*scab, spot*) kratzen an (+*dat*); **to ~ sb's brains** sich von jdm inspirieren lassen; **to ~ one's nose** in der Nase bohren; **to ~ sb's pocket** jdm bestehlen; **to ~ a fight with sb** einen Streit mit jdm anfangen; **to ~ one's way through sth** seinen Weg durch etw finden ♦ *vi*: **to ~ and choose** wählerisch sein.

pick at *vt fus*: **to ~ at one's food** im Essen herumstochern.

pick off *vt* (*kill*) abschießen.

pick on *vt fus* (*person*) herumhacken auf (+*dat*); **why ~ on me?** warum ich?

pick out *vt* auswählen.

pick up *vt* (*lift up*) aufheben; (*learn*) (schnell) mitbekommen; (*word*) aufschnappen; (*collect*) abholen; (*AUT: passenger*) mitnehmen; (*girl*) (sich *dat*) anlachen; (*speed*) gewinnen an (+*dat*); (*RAD. TV. TEL*) empfangen ♦ *vi* (*improve*) sich erholen; **to ~ up where one left off** da weitermachen, wo man aufgehört hat.

pickax, (*Brit*) **pickaxe** [pik'aks] *n* Spitzhacke *f*, Picke *f*, Pickel *m*.

picket [pik'it] *n* (*stake*) Pfahl *m*, Pflock *m*; (*guard*) Posten *m*; (*striker*) Streikposten *m*; **to be on ~ duty** Streikposten sein ♦ *vt* (*factory*) Streikposten aufstellen vor (+*dat*) ♦ *vi* Streikposten stehen.

picketing [pik'iting] *n* Streikwache *f*.

picket line *n* Streikpostenlinie *f*.

pickings [pik'ingz] *npl*: **the ~ are good** (*pilfering*) es lohnt sich, die Ausbeute ist gut.

pickle [pik'əl] *n* (*salty mixture*) Pökel *m*; (*US: cucumber*) Essiggurke *f*; (*col*) Klemme *f*; **to be in a ~** in der Klemme sitzen ♦ *vt* (in Essig) einlegen.

pick-me-up [pik'mēup] *n* Schnäpschen *nt*.

pickpocket [pik'påkit] *n* Taschendieb *m*.

pickup [pik'up] *n* (*small truck*) offene(r) Lieferwagen *m*, Kleintransporter *m*; (*Brit: on record player*) Tonabnehmer *m*.

picnic [pik'nik] *n* Picknick *nt* ♦ *vi* picknicken.

pictorial [piktôr'ēəl] *a* in Bildern ♦ *n* Illustrierte *f*.

picture [pik'chūr] *n* (*also TV*) Bild *nt*; (*likeness*) Abbild *nt*; (*drawing*) Zeichnung *f*; (*film*) Film *m*; (*painting*) Gemälde *nt*; **in the ~** (*fig*) im Bild; **to put sb in the ~** jdn ins Bild setzen; **the overall ~** der Überblick; **to take a ~ of sb/sth** ein Bild *or* eine Aufnahme von jdm/etw machen; **the garden**

is a ~ in June der Garten ist im Juni eine Pracht; **we get a good ~ here** (*TV*) wir haben hier einen guten Empfang ♦ *vt* darstellen; (*fig: paint*) malen; (*imagine*) sich (*dat*) vorstellen.

picture book *n* Bilderbuch *nt*.

picturesque [pikchəresk'] *a* malerisch.

piddling [pid'ling] *a* (*col*) lumpig; (: *task*) pingelig.

pidgin (English) [pij'in (in'glish)] *n* Pidgin-Englisch *nt*.

pie [pī] *n* (*meat*) Pastete *f*; (*fruit*) Torte *f*.

piebald [pī'bôld] *a* gescheckt.

piece [pēs] *n* Stück *nt*; (*in chess*) Figur *f*; (*in draughts*) Stein *m*; **a 10 cent ~** ein 10-Cent-Stück; **~ by ~** Stück für Stück; **a six-~ band** eine sechsköpfige Band; **in one ~** (*object*) heil, unversehrt; **to say one's ~** seine Meinung sagen; **a ~ of news** eine Nachricht, eine Neuigkeit; **to go to ~s** (*work, standard*) wertlos werden; **he's gone to ~s** er ist vollkommen fertig; **in ~s** entzwei, kaputt; (*taken apart*) auseinandergenommen; **a ~ of cake** (*col*) ein Kinderspiel *nt*.

piece together *vt* zusammensetzen.

piecemeal [pēs'mēl] *ad* stückweise, Stück für Stück.

piece rate *n* Akkordlohnsatz *m*.

piecework [pēs'wûrk] *n* Akkordarbeit *f*.

pie chart *n* Kreisdiagramm *nt*.

pie crust pastry *n* (*US*) Mürbeteig *m*.

Piedmont [pēd'mânt] *n* Piemont *nt*.

pier [pēr] *n* Pier *m*, Mole *f*.

pierce [pērs] *vt* durchstechen; (*look, knife, bullet*) durchbohren; (*fig, sound, cold*) durchdringen; **to have one's ears ~d** sich (*dat*) die Ohrläppchen durchstechen lassen.

piercing [pērs'ing] *a* durchdringend; (*cry*) gellend; (*look*) durchbohrend; (*cold, sarcasm*) beißend.

piety [pī'ətē] *n* Frömmigkeit *f*.

pig [pig] *n* Schwein *nt*.

pigeon [pij'ən] *n* Taube *f*.

pigeonhole [pij'ənhōl] *n* (*compartment*) Ablegefach *nt* ♦ *vt* (*lit*) (in Fächer) einordnen, ablegen; (*idea*) zu den Akten legen; (*fig: categorize*) einordnen, ein- *or* aufteilen.

piggy bank [pig'ē bangk] *n* Sparschwein *nt*.

pig-headed [pig'hedid] *a* dickköpfig.

piglet [pig'lit] *n* Ferkel *nt*, Schweinchen *nt*.

pigment [pig'mənt] *n* Farbstoff *m*, Pigment *nt* (*also BIOL*).

pigmentation [pigməntā'shən] *n* Färbung *f*, Pigmentation *f*.

pigmy [pig'mē] *n* = **pygmy**.

pigskin [pig'skin] *n* Schweinsleder *nt*; (*US col: football*) Pille *f*, Leder *nt* ♦ *a* schweinsledern.

pigsty [pig'stī] *n* (*lit, fig*) Schweinestall *m*.

pigtail [pig'tāl] *n* Zopf *m*.

pike [pīk] *n* Pike *f*; (*fish*) Hecht *m*.

pilchard [pil'chûrd] *n* Sardine *f*.

pile [pīl] *n* Haufen *m*; (*of books, wood*) Stapel *m*, Stoß *m*; (*in ground*) Pfahl *m*; (*of bridge*)

Pfeiler *m*; (*on carpet*) Flausch *m*; **to put things in a ~** etw (auf)stapeln; *see also* **piles ♦** *vti* (*also:* **~ up**) sich anhäufen.

pile on *vt*: **to ~ on the pressure** (*col*) unter Druck setzen; **to ~ it on** (*col*) dick auftragen.

piles [pīlz] *npl* (*MED*) Hämorrhoiden *pl*.

pile-up [pīl'up] *n* (*AUT*) Massenzusammenstoß *m*.

pilfer [pil'fûr] *vt* stehlen, klauen (*col*).

pilfering [pil'fûring] *n* Diebstahl *m*.

pilgrim [pil'grim] *n* Wallfahrer(in *f*) *m*, Pilger(in *f*) *m*.

pilgrimage [pil'grəmij] *n* Wallfahrt *f*, Pilgerfahrt *f*.

pill [pil] *n* Tablette *f*, Pille *f*; **the ~** die (Antibaby)pille; **to be on the ~** die Pille nehmen.

pillage [pil'ij] *vt* plündern.

pillar [pil'ûr] *n* Pfeiler *m*, Säule *f* (*also fig*).

pillar box *n* (*Brit*) Briefkasten *m*.

pillion [pil'yən] *n* Sozius(sitz) *m*; **to ride ~** auf dem Sozius(sitz) mitfahren.

pillion passenger *n* Soziusfahrer(in *f*) *m*.

pillory [pil'ûrē] *n* Pranger *m* ♦ *vt* an den Pranger stellen; (*fig*) anprangern.

pillow [pil'ō] *n* Kissen *nt*.

pillowcase [pil'ōkās] *n* (Kopf)kissenbezug *m*.

pillowslip [pil'ōslip] *n* = **pillowcase**.

pilot [pī'lət] *n* Pilot *m*; (*NAUT*) Lotse *m* ♦ *a* (*scheme etc*) Versuchs- ♦ *vt* führen; (*ship*) lotsen.

pilot light *n* Zündflamme *f*.

pimento [pimen'tō] *n* Paprikaschote *f*.

pimp [pimp] *n* Zuhälter *m*.

pimple [pim'pəl] *n* Pickel *m*.

pimply [pim'plē] *a* pick(e)lig.

pin [pin] *n* Nadel *f*; (*SEWING*) Stecknadel *f*; (*TECH*) Stift *m*, Bolzen *m*; (*in grenade*) Sicherungsstift *m*; (*Brit: drawing ~*) Reißzwecke *f*; (*Brit ELEC: of plug*) Pol *m*; **~s and needles** Kribbeln *nt*; **I have ~s and needles in my leg** mein Bein ist (mir) eingeschlafen ♦ *vt* stecken, heften (*to* an *+acc*); (*keep in one position*) pressen, drücken; **to ~ sth on sb** (*fig*) jdm etw anhängen.

pin down *vt* (*fig: person*) festnageln (*to* auf *+acc*); **there's something strange here but I can't quite ~ it down** hier stimmt was nicht, aber was, weiß ich nicht genau.

pinafore [pin'əfôr] *n* Schürze *f*.

pinafore dress *n* (*Brit*) Trägerkleid *nt*.

pinball [pin'bôl] *n* (*also:* **~ machine**) Flipper(automat) *m*.

pincers [pin'sûrz] *npl* Kneif- *or* Beißzange *f*; (*MED*) Pinzette *f*.

pinch [pinch] *n* Zwicken *nt*, Kneifen *nt*; (*of salt*) Prise *f*; **at a ~** notfalls, zur Not; **to feel the ~** (*fig*) die schlechte Lage zu spüren bekommen ♦ *vti* zwicken, kneifen; (*shoe*) drücken ♦ *vt* (*col: steal*) klauen; (*arrest*) schnappen.

pinched [pincht] *a* (*drawn*) verhärmt; **~**

with cold verfroren; **to be ~ for money** (*short*) knapp bei Kasse sein (*col*); **to be ~ for space** ein wenig beengt sein.

pincushion [pin'kōōshən] *n* Nadelkissen *nt*.

pine [pīn] *n* (*also:* **~ tree**) Kiefer *f*, Föhre *f*, Pinie *f* ♦ *vi*: **to ~ for** sich sehnen *or* verzehren nach; **to ~ away** sich zu Tode sehnen.

pineapple [pīn'apəl] *n* Ananas *f*.

pine nut *n* Fichtenkern *m*.

ping [ping] *n* (*of bullet*) Peng *nt*; (*of bell*) Klingeln *nt*.

ping-pong [ping'pông] *n* Pingpong *nt*.

pink [pingk] *n* (*plant*) Nelke *f*; (*color*) Rosa *nt* ♦ *a* rosa *inv* ♦ *vt* (*SEWING*) mit der Zickzackschere schneiden.

pin money *n* Nadelgeld *nt*.

pinnacle [pin'əkəl] *n* Spitze *f*.

pinpoint [pin'point] *vt* festlegen.

pinstripe [pin'strīp] *n* Nadelstreifen *m*.

pint [pīnt] *n* Pint *nt*.

pin-up [pin'up] *n* Pin-up-girl *nt*.

pinwheel [pin'wēl] *n* Feuerrad *nt*.

pioneer [pīənēr'] *n* Pionier *m*; (*fig also*) Bahnbrecher *m* ♦ *vt*: **to ~ sth** den Weg bahnen für etw.

pious [pī'əs] *a* fromm; (*literature*) geistlich.

pip [pip] *n* Kern *m*; (*on uniform*) Stern *m*.

pipe [pīp] *n* (*smoking*) Pfeife *f*; (*MUS*) Flöte *f*; (*tube*) Rohr *nt*; (*in house*) (Rohr)leitung *f* ♦ *vti* (durch Rohre) leiten; (*MUS*) blasen.

pipe down *vi* (*be quiet*) die Luft anhalten.

pipe cleaner *n* Pfeifenreiniger *m*.

piped music [pīpt myōō'zik] *n* Berieselungsmusik *f*.

pipe dream *n* Luftschloß *nt*.

pipeline [pīp'līn] *n* (*for oil, natural gas*) Pipeline *f*; **to be in the ~** (*fig*) in Vorbereitung sein.

piper [pī'pûr] *n* (*on bagpipes*) Dudelsackbläser *m*.

pipe tobacco *n* Pfeifentabak *m*.

piping [pī'ping] *n* Leitungsnetz *nt*; (*on cake*) Dekoration *f*; (*on uniform*) Tresse *f* ♦ *ad*: **~ hot** siedend heiß.

piquant [pē'kənt] *a* (*lit, fig*) pikant.

pique [pēk] *n* gekränkte(r) Stolz *m*.

piqued [pēkt] *a* pikiert.

piracy [pī'rəsē] *n* Piraterie *f*, Seeräuberei *f*; (*plagiarism*) Plagiat *nt*.

pirate [pī'rit] *n* Pirat *m*, Seeräuber *m*; (*plagiarist*) Plagiator *m* ♦ *vt* (*record*) eine Raubpressung machen *or* herstellen; (*video*) eine Raubkopie machen *or* herstellen; (*book*) einen Raubdruck herstellen.

pirated [pī'ritid] *a* (*book, record etc*) Raub-.

pirate radio (station) *n* Piratensender *m*.

pirouette [pirōōet'] *n* Pirouette *f* ♦ *vi* pirouettieren, eine Pirouette drehen.

Pisces [pī'sēz] *n* Fische *pl*.

piss [pis] *vi* (*col*) pissen (*!*).

pissed [pist] *a* (*Brit col: drunk*) sturz- *or* stockbesoffen.

pistol [pis'təl] *n* Pistole *f*.

piston [pis'tən] *n* Kolben *m*.

pit |pit| *n* Grube *f*; (*THEAT*) Parterre *nt*; (*orchestra* ~) Orchestergraben *m*; (*US: of fruit*) Stein *m*; Kern *m*; **the ~s** (*SPORT*) die Boxen ♦ *vt* (*mark with scars*) zerfressen; (*compare: o.s.*) messen (*against* mit); (: *sb/sth*) messen (*against* an +*dat*); (*US: fruit*) entkernen; **his face was ~ted with smallpox scars** sein Gesicht war voller Pockennarben; **the underside of the car was ~ted with rustholes** die Unterseite des Wagens war voll von Rostlöchern; **the road was ~ted with potholes** die Straße war voller Schlaglöcher.

pitapat |pit'əpat| *ad*: **to go ~** (*heart*) pochen, klopfen; **the rain went ~** der Regen platschte *or* klatschte.

pitch |pich| *n* Wurf *m*; (*of trader*) Stand *m*; (*Brit SPORT*) (Spiel)feld *nt*; (*slope*) Neigung *f*; (*MUS*) Tonlage *f*; (*substance*) Pech *nt*; (*fig: degree*) Grad *m*; (*sales* ~) Verkaufsmasche *f*, Taktik *f*; **perfect ~** absolute(s) Gehör *nt*; **to queer sb's ~** (*col*) jdm alles verderben; **I can't keep working at this ~** ich kann dieses Arbeitstempo nicht mehr lange durchhalten; **at its (highest) ~** auf dem Höhepunkt *or* Gipfel; **his anger reached such a ~ that** ... sein Ärger hat einen derartigen Grad erreicht, daß ... ♦ *vt* werfen, schleudern; (*set up*) aufschlagen; (*song*) anstimmen ♦ *vi* (*fall*) (längelang) hinschlagen; (*NAUT*) rollen.

pitch-black |pich'blak'| *a* pechschwarz.

pitched battle |picht bat'əl| *n* offene Schlacht *f*.

pitcher |pich'ûr| *n* Krug *m*.

pitchfork |pich'fôrk| *n* Heugabel *f*.

piteous |pit'ēəs| *a* kläglich, erbärmlich.

pitfall |pit'fôl| *n* (*fig*) Falle *f*.

pith |pith| *n* Mark *nt*; (*of speech*) Kern *m*.

pithy |pith'ē| *a* prägnant.

pitiable |pit'ēəbəl| *a* bedauernswert; (*contemptible*) jämmerlich.

pitiful |pit'ifəl| *a* mitleidig; (*deserving pity*) bedauernswert; (*contemptible*) jämmerlich.

pitifully |pit'ifəlē| *ad see* **pitiful**; **it's ~ obvious** es ist schon allzu offensichtlich.

pitiless |pit'ilis| *a*, **pitilessly** |pit'ilislē| *ad* erbarmungslos.

pittance |pit'əns| *n* Hungerlohn *m*.

pity |pit'ē| *n* (*sympathy*) Mitleid *nt*; (*shame*) Jammer *m*; **for ~'s sake** um Himmels willen; **what a ~!** wie schade!; **it's a ~** es ist schade; **it is a ~ that you can't come** schade, daß du nicht kommen kannst; **to have** *or* **take ~ on sb** mit jdm Mitleid haben ♦ *vt* bemitleiden, bedauern; **I ~ you** du tust mir leid.

pitying |pit'ēing| *a* mitleidig.

pivot |piv'ət| *n* Drehpunkt *m*; (*pin*) (Dreh)zapfen *m*; (*fig*) Angelpunkt *m* ♦ *vi* sich drehen (*on* um).

pixel |pik'səl| *n* (*COMPUT*) Bildelement *nt*, Pixel *nt*.

pixie |pik'sē| *n* Elf *m*, Elfe *f*.

pizza |pēt'sə| *n* Pizza *f*.

placard |plak'ârd| *n* Plakat *nt*, Anschlag *m* ♦ *vt* anschlagen.

placate |plā'kāt| *vt* beschwichtigen, besänftigen.

place |plās| *n* Platz *m*; (*spot*) Stelle *f*; (*town etc*) Ort *m*; (*in street names*) Platz *m*; **in ~** am rechten Platz; **out of ~** nicht am rechten Platz; (*fig: remark*) unangebracht; **in ~ of** anstelle von; **in the first/second** *etc* **~** erstens/zweitens *etc*; **~ of worship** Stätte *f* des Gebets; **to give ~ to** Platz machen (+*dat*); **market ~** (*COMM*) Marktplatz *m*; (*fig*) Markt *m*; **to change ~s with sb** mit jdm den Platz tauschen; **from ~ to ~** von einem Ort zum anderen; **all over the ~** überall; **he's going ~s** (*fig col*) er bringt's noch (mal) zu was; **I feel rather out of ~ here** ich fühle mich hier fehl am Platz; **it is not my ~ to do it** es steht mir nicht zu, das zu tun; **to invite sb to one's ~** jdn zu sich (nach Hause) einladen; **to keep sb in his ~** jdn in seinen Schranken halten; **to put sb in his ~** jdn in seine Schranken weisen ♦ *vt* setzen, stellen, legen; (*order*) aufgeben; (*SPORT*) plazieren; (*identify*) unterbringen; **we are better ~d than a month ago** es geht uns besser als vor einem Monat; **goods that are difficult to ~** kaum absatzfähige Waren; **to ~ an order with sb (for)** eine Bestellung bei jdm aufgeben *or* machen (für).

placebo |pləsē'bō| *n* Placebo *nt*.

place mat *n* Platzdeckchen *nt*, Set *nt*.

placement |plās'mənt| *n* Einstellung *f*.

place name *n* Ortsname *m*.

placenta |pləsen'tə| *n* Plazenta *f*.

placid |plas'id| *a* gelassen, ruhig.

placidity |pləsid'itē| *n* Gelassenheit *f*, Ruhe *f*.

plagiarism |plā'jərizəm| *n* Plagiat *nt*.

plagiarist |plā'jûrist| *n* Plagiator *m*.

plagiarize |plā'jərīz| *vt* abschreiben, plagiieren.

plague |plāg| *n* Pest *f*; (*fig*) Plage *f* ♦ *vt* (*fig*) plagen, quälen; **to ~ sb with questions** jdn mit Fragen belästigen.

plaice |plās| *n* Scholle *f*.

plaid |plad| *n* Plaid *nt*.

plain |plān| *a* (*clear*) klar, deutlich; (*simple*) einfach, schlicht; (*not beautiful*) einfach, nicht attraktiv; (*honest*) offen; **to make sth ~ to sb** jdm etw klarmachen *or* klar zu verstehen geben; **in ~ clothes** (*police*) in Zivil(kleidung); **it is ~ sailing** das ist ganz einfach ♦ *n* Ebene *f*.

plain chocolate *n* (*Brit*) Bitterschokolade *f*.

plainly |plān'lē| *ad* (*clearly*) deutlich; (*simply*) einfach; (*frankly*) offen, direkt.

plainness |plān'nis| *n* Einfachheit *f*.

plaintiff |plān'tif| *n* Kläger(in *f*) *m*.

plaintive |plān'tiv| *a* (*voice*) klagend; (*look*) leidend; (*song*) schwermütig.

plait |plat| *n* Zopf *m* ♦ *vt* flechten.

plan |plan| *n* Plan *m*; **according to ~** planmäßig; **have you got any ~s for today?**

hast du heute etwas vor? ♦ *vt* planen; *(intend)* beabsichtigen, vorhaben; **to ~ to do sth** vorhaben, etw zu tun; **how long do you ~ to stay?** wie lange hast du vor, zu bleiben? ♦ *vi* planen; **to ~ for** sich einstellen auf (+*acc*).

plan out *vt* vorbereiten.

plane [plän] *n* Ebene *f*; *(AVIAT)* Flugzeug *nt*; *(tool)* Hobel *m*; *(tree)* Platane *f* ♦ *a* eben, flach ♦ *vt* hobeln.

planet [plan'it] *n* Planet *m*.

planetarium [planitär'ēəm] *n* Planetarium *nt*.

planetary [plan'itärē] *a* planetarisch.

plank [plangk] *n* Planke *f*, Brett *nt*; *(POL)* Programmpunkt *m*.

plankton [plangk'tən] *n* Plankton *nt*.

planner [plan'ûr] *n* Planer *m*; *(chart)* Jahresplaner *m*; **city** *(US)* **or town** *(Brit)* **~** Stadt- or Städteplaner (in *f*) *m*.

planning [plan'ing] *n* Planen *nt*; *(POL, FIN)* Planung *f*.

plant [plant] *n* Pflanze *f*; *(TECH)* (Maschinen)anlage *f*; *(factory)* Fabrik *f*, Werk *nt* ♦ *vt* pflanzen; *(set firmly)* stellen.

plantain [plan'tin] *n* Mehlbanane *f*.

plantation [plantā'shən] *n* Plantage *f*.

planter [plan'tûr] *n* Pflanzer *nt*.

plant pot *n* *(Brit)* Blumentopf *m*.

plaque [plak] *n* Gedenktafel *f*.

plasma [plaz'mə] *n* Plasma *nt*.

plaster [plas'tûr] *n* Gips *m*; *(for fracture: also:* **~ of Paris)** Gipsverband *m*; *(Brit: for wound)* Pflaster *nt*; **in ~** *(leg etc)* in Gips ♦ *vt* gipsen; *(hole)* zugipsen; *(ceiling)* verputzen; *(fig: with pictures etc)* bekleben, verkleben; *(col: cover)* vollkleistern; **to be ~ed with mud** schlammbedeckt sein.

plaster cast *n* *(MED)* Gipsverband *m*; *(model, statue)* Gipsform *f*.

plastered [plas'tûrd] *a* *(col)* besoffen.

plasterer [plas'tərûr] *n* Gipser *m*.

plastic [plas'tik] *n* Kunststoff *m* ♦ *a* *(made of* **~)** Kunststoff-, Plastik-; *(soft)* formbar, plastisch; *(ART)* plastisch, bildend.

plastic bag *n* Plastiktüte *f*.

plastic surgery *n* plastische Chirurgie *f*; *(for cosmetic reasons)* Schönheitsoperation *f*.

plate [plät] *n* Teller *m*; *(gold or silver)* vergoldete(s) *or* versilberte(s) Tafelgeschirr *nt*; *(flat sheet)* Platte *f*; *(in book)* (Bild)tafel *f*; *(on door)* Schild *nt*; *(AUT: license ~)* Kennzeichen *nt* ♦ *vt* überziehen, plattieren; **to silver-/gold-~** versilbern/vergolden.

plateau [platō'] *n*, *pl* **~s** *or* **plateaux** Hochebene *f*, Plateau *nt*.

plateful [plāt'fəl] *n* Teller(voll) *m*.

plate glass *n* Tafelglas *nt*.

platen [plat'ən] *n* *(on typewriter, printer)* Schreibwalze *f*.

platform [plat'fôrm] *n* *(at meeting)* Plattform *f*, Podium *nt*; *(stage)* Bühne *f*; *(RAIL)* Bahnsteig *m*; *(POL)* Parteiprogramm *nt*; **the train leaves from ~ 7** der Zug fährt von

Gleis 7 ab.

platinum [plat'ənəm] *n* Platin *nt*.

platitude [plat'ətōōd] *n* Gemeinplatz *m*, Platitüde *f*.

platoon [plətōōn'] *n* *(MIL)* Zug *m*.

platter [plat'ûr] *n* Platte *f*.

plaudits [plô'dits] *npl* Beifall *m*, Ovation *f*.

plausibility [plôzəbil'ətē] *n* Plausibilität *f*.

plausible [plô'zəbəl] *a* plausibel, einleuchtend; *(liar)* überzeugend.

play [plā] *n* *(also TECH)* Spiel *nt*; *(THEAT)* (Theater)stück *nt*, Schauspiel *nt*; **to bring or call into ~** ins Spiel bringen; *(plan)* aufbieten, einsetzen ♦ *vt* spielen; *(another team)* spielen gegen; *(put in a team)* einsetzen, spielen lassen; **to ~ a joke on sb** jdm einen Streich spielen; **to ~ a trick on sb** jdn an der Nase herumführen, jdn reinlegen *(col)*; **to ~ sb off against somebody else** jdn gegen jdn anders ausspielen; **to ~ a part in** *(fig)* eine Rolle spielen bei ♦ *vi* spielen; **they're ~ing (at) soldiers** sie spielen Soldaten; **to ~ for time** *(fig)* Zeit gewinnen wollen; **to ~ into sb's hands** *(fig)* jdm in die Hände spielen; **a smile ~ed on his lips** ein Lächeln spielte um seine Lippen.

play around *vi* spielen.

play along *vi*: **to ~ along with** *(fig: person)* auf jdn eingehen; **to ~ along with a suggestion** auf einen Vorschlag eingehen.

play back *vt* abspielen.

play down *vt* bagatellisieren, herunterspielen.

play on *vt fus* *(sb's feelings, credulity)* geschickt ausnutzen; **to ~ on sb's nerves** jdn zermürben.

play up *(Brit)* *vi* *(cause trouble)* frech werden; *(bad leg etc)* weh tun; **to ~ up to sb** jdm schmeicheln ♦ *vt* *(person)* plagen.

playact [plā'akt] *vi* *(fig)* Theater spielen.

playacting [plā'akting] *n* Schauspielerei *f*.

playboy [plā'boi] *n* Playboy *m*.

player [plā'ûr] *n* Spieler(in *f*) *m*.

playful [plā'fəl] *a* spielerisch, verspielt.

playground [plā'ground] *n* Spielplatz *m*.

playgroup [plā'grōōp] *n* Spielgruppe *f*.

playing card [plā'ing kârd] *n* Spielkarte *f*.

playing field *n* Sportplatz *m*.

playmate [plā'māt] *n* Spielkamerad(in *f*) *m*.

play-off [plā'ôf] *n* *(SPORT)* Entscheidungsspiel *nt*.

playpen [plā'pen] *n* Laufstall *m*.

playroom [plā'rōōm] *n* Spielzimmer *nt*.

plaything [plā'thing] *n* Spielzeug *nt*.

playtime [plā'tīm] *n* *(SCH)* große Pause *f*.

playwright [plā'rīt] *n* Theaterschriftsteller *m*.

plc *n abbr* *(Brit:* = *public limited company)* ≈ GmbH *f*.

plea [plē] *n* (dringende) Bitte *f*, Gesuch *nt*; *(JUR)* Antwort *f* des Angeklagten; *(excuse)* Ausrede *f*, Vorwand *m*; **to enter a ~ of guilty** ein Geständnis ablegen.

plead [plēd] *vt* *(poverty)* zur Entschuldigung anführen; *(JUR: sb's case)* vertreten ♦ *vi* *(beg)* dringend bitten *(with sb* jdn); *(JUR)* plädieren; **to ~ for sth** *(beg for)* um etw bitten; **to ~ guilty/not guilty** *(defendant)* sich schuldig/nicht schuldig bekennen.

pleasant [plez'ənt] *a,* **pleasantly** [plez'əntlē] *ad* angenehm, freundlich.

pleasantness [plez'əntnis] *n* Angenehme(s) *nt; (of person)* angenehme(s) Wesen *nt,* Freundlichkeit *f.*

pleasantry [plez'əntrē] *n* Scherz *m;* **to exchange pleasantries** *(polite remarks)* Höflichkeiten austauschen.

please [plēz] *interj* bitte; **~ don't cry!** ach, wein doch nicht! ♦ *vr:* **to ~ o.s.** tun, was einem gefällt; **~ yourself!** wie du willst! ♦ *vt (be agreeable to)* gefallen (+dat); *(give pleasure to)* eine Freude machen (+dat); *(satisfy)* zufriedenstellen; *(do as sb wants)* gefällig sein (+dat) ♦ *vi:* **do as you ~** mach' was du willst.

pleased [plēzd] *a (satisfied)* zufrieden; *(glad)* erfreut *(with* über +acc); **to be ~** sich freuen *(about sth* über etw *acc);* **~ to meet you!** angenehm! freut mich!; **we are ~ to inform you that ...** es freut uns, Ihnen mitteilen zu können, daß ...

pleasing [plē'zing] *a* erfreulich.

pleasurable [plezh'ûrəbəl] *a,* **pleasurably** [plezh'ûrəblē] *ad* angenehm, erfreulich.

pleasure [plezh'ûr] *n* Vergnügen *nt,* Freude *f;* *(old: will)* Wünsche *pl;* **it's a ~** gern geschehen; **with ~** sehr gern(e), mit Vergnügen; **they take (no/great) ~ in going** es macht ihnen (keinen/großen) Spaß zu gehen; **is this trip for business or ~?** ist es eine Geschäftsreise oder eine Vergnügungsreise?; **I have much ~ in informing you that ...** ich freue mich (sehr), Ihnen mitteilen zu können, daß ...

pleasure ground *n (Brit)* Vergnügungspark *m.*

pleasure-seeking [plezh'ûrsēking] *a* vergnügungshungrig.

pleasure steamer *n* Vergnügungsdampfer *m.*

pleat [plēt] *n* Falte *f.*

pleb [pleb] *n* Plebejer(in *f)* m; **the ~s** der Plebs.

plebeian [pləbē'ən] *n* Plebejer(in *f)* m ♦ *a* plebejisch.

plebiscite [pleb'isit] *n* Volksentscheid *m,* Plebiszit *nt.*

plectrum [plek'trəm] *n* Plektron *nt.*

pledge [plej] *n* Pfand *nt; (promise)* Versprechen *nt* ♦ *vt* verpfänden; *(promise)* geloben, versprechen; **to take the ~** dem Alkohol abschwören; **to ~ support for sb** jdm seine Unterstützung zusichern; **to ~ sb to secrecy** jdn zum Schweigen verpflichten.

plenary session [plē'nûrē sesh'ən] *n* Plenarsitzung *f,* Vollversammlung *f.*

plenipotentiary [plenēpəten'chēärē] *n* Bevollmächtiger *m* ♦ *a* bevollmächtigt.

plentiful [plen'tifəl] *a* reichlich.

plenty [plen'tē] *n* Fülle *f,* Überfluß *m* ♦ *ad (col)* ganz schön; **~ of** eine Menge, viel; **in ~** reichlich, massenhaft; **we've got ~ of time to get there** wir haben noch genug Zeit, um (dort) hinzukommen; **to be ~** genug sein, reichen.

plethora [pleth'ərə] *n* Übermaß *nt,* Fülle *f.*

pleurisy [plōōr'isē] *n* Rippenfellentzündung *f.*

Plexiglas [plek'səglas] *n* ® *(US)* Plexiglas ® *nt.*

pliability [plīəbil'ətē] *n* Biegsamkeit *f; (of person)* Beeinflußbarkeit *f.*

pliable [plī'əbəl] *a* biegsam; *(person)* beeinflußbar.

pliers [plī'ûrz] *npl* (Kneif)zange *f.*

plight [plīt] *n* Not *f,* Notlage *f.*

plimsolls [plim'səlz] *npl (Brit)* Turnschuhe *pl.*

plinth [plinth] *n* Säulenplatte *f,* Plinthe *f.*

PLO *n abbr (= Palestine Liberation Organization)* PLO *f.*

plod [pläd] *vi (work)* sich abplagen; *(walk)* stapfen, trotten.

plodder [pläd'ûr] *n* Arbeitstier *nt.*

plodding [pläd'ing] *a* schwerfällig.

plonk [plängk] *n (Brit col: wine)* billige(r) Wein *m.*

plot [plät] *n* Komplott *nt,* Verschwörung *f; (story)* Handlung *f; (of land)* Stück *nt* Land, Grundstück *nt* ♦ *vt* markieren; *(curve)* zeichnen; *(movements)* nachzeichnen ♦ *vi (plan secretly)* sich verschwören, ein Komplott schmieden.

plotter [plät'ûr] *n* Verschwörer *m; (COMPUT)* Plotter *m.*

plotting [plät'ing] *n* Intrigen *pl.*

plough [plou] *etc (Brit)* = **plow** *etc.*

plow [plou] *(US)* *n* Pflug *m* ♦ *vt* pflügen.

plow back *vt (COMM)* wieder in das Geschäft stecken.

plow through *vt fus (water)* durchpflügen; *(book)* sich kämpfen durch.

plowing [plou'ing] *n (US)* Pflügen *nt.*

ploy [ploi] *n* Masche *f.*

pluck [pluk] *vt (fruit)* pflücken; *(guitar)* zupfen; *(goose)* rupfen; **to ~ one's eyebrows** sich die Augenbrauen zupfen; **to ~ up courage** all seinen Mut zusammennehmen ♦ *n* Mut *m.*

plucky [pluk'ē] *a* beherzt.

plug [plug] *n* Stöpsel *m; (ELEC)* Stecker *m; (of tobacco)* Pfriem *m; (col: publicity)* Schleichwerbung *f; (AUT)* Zündkerze *f* ♦ *vt* (zu)stopfen; *(col: advertise)* Reklame machen für; **to give sb/sth a ~** für jdn/etw Schleichwerbung machen; **to ~ a cord into a socket** ein Kabel anschließen.

plug in *vt (ELEC)* hineinstecken, einstöpseln, anschließen ♦ *vi:* **where does the TV ~ in?** wo wird der Fernseher angeschlossen?

plughole [plug'hōl] *n (Brit)* Abfluß(loch *nt) m.*

plum [plum] *n* Pflaume *f,* Zwetschge *f* ♦ *a (job etc)* Bomben-.

plumage [ploo'mij] n Gefieder nt.
plumb [plum] n Lot nt; **out of** ~ nicht im Lot
♦ a senkrecht ♦ ad (exactly) genau ♦ vt ausloten; (fig) sondieren; (mystery) ergründen.
  plumb in vt (washing machine) installieren.
plumber [plum'ûr] n Klempner m, Installateur m.
plumbing [plum'ing] n (craft) Installieren nt;
(fittings) Leitungen pl, Installationen pl.
plumbline [plum'līn] n Senkblei nt.
plume [ploom] n Feder f; (of smoke etc)
Fahne f.
plummet [plum'it] n Senkblei nt ♦ vi
(ab)stürzen.
plump [plump] a rundlich, füllig ♦ vi plumpsen, sich fallen lassen ♦ vt plumpsen lassen.
  plump up vt aufschütteln.
plumpness [plump'nis] n Rundlichkeit f.
plunder [plun'dûr] n Plünderung f; (loot)
Beute f ♦ vt plündern; (things) rauben.
plunge [plunj] n Sprung m, Stürzen nt ♦ vt
stoßen ♦ vi (sich) stürzen; (ship) rollen; **the
room was ~d into darkness** das Zimmer
war in Dunkelheit getaucht.
plunging [plun'jing] a (neckline) offenherzig.
pluperfect [ploopûr'fikt] n Plusquamperfekt
nt, Vorvergangenheit f.
plural [ploor'əl] a Plural-, Mehrzahl- ♦ n Plural m, Mehrzahl f.
plus [plus] prep plus, und ♦ a Plus-; **a** ~
factor (fig) ein Pluspunkt.
plush [plush] a (col: luxurious) feudal ♦ n
Plüsch m.
plutonium [plootō'nēəm] n Plutonium nt.
ply [plī] n: **three-**~ (wood) dreischichtig;
(wool) Dreifach- ♦ vt (trade) (be)treiben;
(with questions) zusetzen (+dat); (ship,
cab) befahren ♦ vi (ship, cab) verkehren.
plywood [plī'wood] n Sperrholz nt.
PM n abbr = prime minister.
p.m. ad abbr (= post meridiem) nachm.
pneumatic [noomat'ik] a pneumatisch;
(TECH) Luft-.
pneumatic drill n Preßlufthammer m.
pneumonia [nyoomōn'yə] n Lungenentzündung f.
po abbr (Brit: = postal order) PA, PAnw.
PO n abbr (= Post Office) PA nt; (MIL) =
petty officer.
poach [pōch] vt (COOK) pochieren; (game)
stehlen ♦ vi (steal) wildern (for nach).
poached [pōcht] a (egg) pochiert, verloren.
poacher [pō'chûr] n Wilddieb m.
poaching [pō'ching] n Wildern nt.
PO Box n abbr (= Post Office Box) Postfach
nt.
pocket [pâk'it] n Tasche f; (of ore) Ader f;
air ~ Luftloch nt; **breast** ~ Brusttasche f;
~ **of resistance** (fig) Widerstandsnest nt ♦
vt einstecken, in die Tasche stecken.
pocketbook [pâk'itbook] n (notebook) Notizbuch nt; (US: handbag) Handtasche f.
pocketful [pâk'itfool] n Tasche(voll) f.

pocket knife n Taschenmesser nt.
pocket money n Taschengeld nt.
pockmarked [pâk'mârkt] a (face) pockennar-
big.
pod [pâd] n Hülse f; (of peas) Schote f.
podgy [pâj'ē] a pummelig.
podiatrist [pədī'ətrist] n (US) Fußspezialist(in
f) m.
podium [pō'dēəm] n Podest nt.
POE n abbr (= port of embarkation) Einschif-
fungshafen m; (= port of entry) Eingangs-
hafen m.
poem [pō'əm] n Gedicht nt.
poet [pō'it] n Dichter m, Poet m.
poetic [pōet'ik] a poetisch, dichterisch; (beauty) malerisch, stimmungsvoll.
poet laureate [pō'it lô'rēit] n Hofdichter m.
poetry [pō'itrē] n Poesie f; (poems) Gedichte
pl.
poignant [poin'yənt] a, **poignantly**
[poin'yəntlē] ad scharf, stechend; (touching)
ergreifend, quälend.
point [point] n Punkt m (also in discussion,
scoring); (spot) Punkt m, Stelle f;
(sharpened tip) Spitze f; (moment)
(Zeit)punkt m, Moment m; (purpose) Zweck
m; (idea) Argument nt; (decimal): **three** ~
two drei Komma zwei; (personal characteristic) Seite f; (Brit ELEC: also: **power** ~)
Steckdose f; see also **points** ♦ vt zeigen
mit; (gun) richten ♦ vi zeigen; ~ **of departure** (also fig) Ausgangspunkt m; **a** ~ **of
order** ein Geschäftsordnungspunkt; ~ **of
sale** (COMM) Verkaufsort m; **to be on the**
~ **of doing sth** im Begriff sein, etw zu tun;
in ~ **of fact** eigentlich; (in reality) tatsächlich, in Wirklichkeit; (after all) (dann)
doch; (to make previous statement more
precise) nämlich; **the train stops at Boston
and all** ~**s south** der Zug hält in Boston und
allen Orten weiter südlich; **when it comes
to the** ~ wenn es darauf ankommt; **that's
the whole** ~ **of doing it this way** gerade
deshalb machen wir das so; **to be beside
the** ~ unerheblich or irrelevant sein; **to
make a** ~ **of doing sth** Wert darauf legen,
etw zu tun; **you've got a** ~ **there!** da könnten Sie recht haben, da ist was dran (col);
my ~ **of view** mein Stand- or Gesichts-
punkt; **what's the** ~? was soll das?
point out vt hinweisen auf (+acc).
point to vt fus zeigen auf (+acc).
point-blank [point'blangk'] ad (at close
range) aus nächster Entfernung; (bluntly)
unverblümt.
pointed [poin'tid] a, **pointedly** [poin'tidlē] ad
spitz, scharf; (fig) gezielt.
pointer [poin'tûr] n Zeigestock m; (on dial)
Zeiger m; (clue) Anzeichen nt, Hinweis m;
(advice) Hinweis m, Tip m.
pointless [point'lis] a, **pointlessly** [point'lislē]
ad zwecklos, sinnlos.
pointlessness [point'lisnis] n Zwecklosigkeit
f, Sinnlosigkeit f.

point-of-sale advertising [point'əvsäl ad'vûrtīzing] *n* Werbung *f* am Verkaufsort.

points [points] *npl* (*Brit RAIL*) Weichen *pl*.

poise [poiz] *n* Haltung *f*; (*fig also*) Gelassenheit *f* ♦ *vti* balancieren; (*knife, pen*) bereithalten; (*o.s.*) sich bereitmachen.

poised [poizd] *a* beherrscht.

poison [poi'zən] *n* (*lit, fig*) Gift *nt* ♦ *vt* vergiften.

poisoning [poi'zəning] *n* Vergiftung *f*.

poisonous [poi'zənəs] *a* giftig, Gift-; (*fumes, rumors*) giftig; (*ideas, literature*) zersetzend; **he's a ~ individual** er ist ein richtiger Giftzwerg.

poke [pōk] *vt* stoßen; (*put*) stecken; (*fire*) schüren; (*hole*) bohren; **to ~ one's nose into** seine Nase stecken in (+*acc*); **to ~ fun at sb** sich über jdn lustig machen; **to ~ one's head out of the window** seinen Kopf aus dem Fenster strecken ♦ *n* Stoß *m*; (*with elbow*) Schubs *m* (*col*); **to give the fire a ~** das Feuer schüren.

poke about *vi* herumstochern.

poker [pō'kûr] *n* Schürhaken *m*; (*CARDS*) Poker *nt*.

poker-faced [pō'kûrfāst'] *a* undurchdringlich.

poky [pō'kē] *a* eng.

Poland [pō'lənd] *n* Polen *nt*.

polar [pō'lûr] *a* Polar-, polar.

polar bear *n* Eisbär *m*.

polarization [pōlûrəzā'shən] *n* Polarisation *f*.

polarize [pō'lərīz] *vt* polarisieren ♦ *vi* sich polarisieren.

pole [pōl] *n* Stange *f*, Pfosten *m*; (*flag~, telegraph ~ also*) Mast *m*; (*ELEC. GEOG*) Pol *m*; (*SPORT: vaulting ~*) Stab *m*; (*ski ~*) Stock *m*; **~s apart** durch Welten getrennt.

Pole [pōl] *n* (*person*) Pole *m*, Polin *f*.

pole bean *n* (*US*) Stangenbohne *f*.

polecat [pōl'kat] *n* Iltis *m*; (*US: skunk*) Skunk *m*, Stinktier *nt*.

Pol. Econ. [pâl'ēkân] *n abbr* (= *political economy*) VW *f*.

polemic [pəlem'ik] *n* Polemik *f*.

polestar [pōl'stár] *n* Polarstern *m*.

pole vault *n* Stabhochsprung *m*.

police [pəlēs'] *n* Polizei *f* ♦ *vt* (*road, frontier*) kontrollieren.

police captain *n* (*US*) ≈ Komissar(in *f*) *m*.

police car *n* Polizeiwagen *m*.

police constable *n* (*Brit*) Polizist *m*, Polizeibeamter *m*.

police department *n* Dezernat *nt*.

police force *n* Polizei *f*.

policeman [pəlēs'mən] *n, pl* **-men** Polizist *m*; **traffic ~** ≈ Verkehrspolizist *m*.

police officer *n* Polizeibeamter *m*.

police record *n*: **to have a ~** vorbestraft sein.

police state *n* Polizeistaat *m*.

police station *n* (Polizei)revier *nt*, Wache *f*.

policewoman [pəlēs'wōōmən] *n, pl* **-women** Polizistin *f*.

policy [pâl'isē] *n* Politik *f*; (*of business*) Usus *m*; (*insurance*) (Versicherungs)police *f*; (*prudence*) Klugheit *f*; (*principle*) Grundsatz *m*; (*of newspaper*) Linie *f*; (*company ~*) Geschäfts- *or* Firmenpolitik *f*; **it is our ~ to do that** das ist bei uns so üblich; **to take out an insurance ~** eine Versicherung abschließen.

policy decision *n* Grundsatzentscheidung *f*.

policy holder *n* Versicherungsnehmer(in *f*) *m*.

polio [pō'lēō] *n* Kinderlähmung *f*, Polio *f*.

polish [pâl'ish] *n* (*for floor*) Wachs *nt*; (*for shoes*) Creme *f*; (*nail ~*) Lack *m*; (*shine*) Glanz *m*; (*of furniture*) Politur *f*; (*fig*) Schliff *m* ♦ *vt* polieren; (*shoes*) putzen; (*fig*) den letzten Schliff geben (+*dat*), aufpolieren.

polish off *vt* (*col: work*) erledigen; (*: food*) wegputzen; (*: drink*) hinunterschütten.

polish up *vt* (*silver, shoes etc*) polieren; (*essay*) aufpolieren; (*knowledge*) auffrischen.

Polish [pō'lish] *a* polnisch ♦ *n* (*language*) Polnisch *nt*.

polished [pâl'isht] *a* glänzend (*also fig*); (*manners*) verfeinert.

polite [pəlit'] *a* höflich; (*society*) fein; **it's not ~ to do that** das ist nicht höflich.

politely [pəlit'lē] *ad* höflich.

politeness [pəlit'nis] *n* Höflichkeit *f*; Feinheit *f*.

politic [pâl'itik] *a* (*prudent*) diplomatisch.

political [pəlit'ikəl] *a* politisch; **~ asylum** politische(s) Asyl *nt*; **~ levy** Anteil des Gewerkschaftsbeitrages eines Arbeitnehmers, der zur Öffentlichkeitsarbeit der Gewerkschaft verwendet wird.

politically [pəlit'iklē] *ad* politisch.

politician [pâlitish'ən] *n* Politiker(in *f*) *m*, Staatsmann *m*.

politics [pâl'itiks] *npl* Politik *f*.

polka [pōl'kə] *n* Polka *f*.

polka dot *n* Tupfen *m*.

poll [pōl] *n* Abstimmung *f*; (*in election*) Wahl *f*; (*votes cast*) Wahlbeteiligung *f*; (*opinion ~*) Umfrage *f* ♦ *vt* (*votes*) erhalten, auf sich vereinigen; **to go to the ~s** (*voters*) wählen *or* zur Wahl gehen; (*government*) sich der Wählerschaft stellen.

pollen [pâl'ən] *n* Blütenstaub *m*, Pollen *m*.

pollen count *n* Pollenkonzentration *f*.

pollination [pâlənā'shən] *n* Befruchtung *f*.

polling [pō'ling] *n* Stimmabgabe *f*, Wahl *f*; (*TEL*) Abrufen *nt*, Sendeaufruf *m*.

pollute [pəlōōt'] *vt* verschmutzen, verunreinigen.

pollution [pəlōō'shən] *n* Verschmutzung *f*.

polo [pō'lō] *n* Polo *nt*.

polo neck *n* Rollkragen *m*.

poly [pâl'ē] *n abbr* (*Brit*) = **polytechnic**.

poly- [pâl'ē] *pref* Poly-.

polygamy [pəlig'əmē] *n* Polygamie *f*.

polymath [pâl'ēmath] *n* Universalgelehrter *m*.

Polynesia [pâlənē'zhə] *n* Polynesien *nt*.

Polynesian |pálənē'zhən| *a* polynesisch ♦ *n* Polynesier(in *f*) *m*.

polyp |pál'ip| *n* (*MED*) Polyp *m*.

polystyrene |pálēstī'rēn| *n* Polysterol *nt*; (*extended also*) Styropor *nt*.

polytechnic |pálētek'nik| *n* (*Brit*) technische Hochschule *f*.

polythene |pál'əthēn| *n* Plastik *nt*.

polythene bag *n* Plastiktüte *f*.

polyurethane |pálēyōōr'əthān| *n* Polyurethan *pl*.

pomegranate |pám'əgranit| *n* Granatapfel *m*.

pommel |pum'əl| *vt* mit den Fäusten bearbeiten ♦ *n* Sattelknopf *m*.

pomp |pámp| *n* Pomp *m*, Prunk *m*.

pompom |pám'pám| *n* Troddel *f*, Pompon *m*.

pompon |pám'pán| *n* = **pompom**.

pompous |pám'pəs| *a* (*person*) wichtigtuerisch, aufgeblasen; (*language*) geschwollen.

pond |pánd| *n* Teich *m*, Weiher *m*.

ponder |pán'dûr| *vt* nachdenken *or* nachgrübeln über (+*acc*).

ponderous |pán'dûrəs| *a* schwerfällig.

pong |pông| (*Brit col*) *n* Gestank *m*, Mief *m* ♦ *vi* stinken, miefen.

pontiff |pán'tif| *n* Pontifex *m*.

pontificate |pántif'ikāt| *vi* (*fig*) geschwollen reden.

pontoon |pántōōn'| *n* Ponton *m*; (*Brit CARDS*) 17 und 4 *nt*.

pony |pō'nē| *n* Pony *nt*.

ponytail |pō'nētāl| *n* Pferdeschwanz *m*.

pony trekking |pō'nē trek'ing| *n* (*Brit*) Ponyreiten *nt*.

poodle |pōō'dəl| *n* Pudel *m*.

pooh-pooh |pōōpōō'| *vt* die Nase rümpfen über (+*acc*).

pool |pōōl| *n* (*swimming* ~) Schwimmbad *nt*; (*private*) Swimming-pool *m*; (*of spilt liquid, blood*) Lache *f*; (*fund*) (gemeinsame) Kasse *f*; (*COMM: consortium*) Interessengemeinschaft *f*; (*US: monopoly trust*) Pool *m*, Kartell *nt*; (*billiards*) Poolspiel *nt*; **to do the (football)** ~**s** (*Brit*) Toto spielen ♦ *vt* (*money etc*) zusammenlegen; *see* **secretary pool, typing pool**.

pooped |pōōpd| *a* (*US col*) fertig.

poor |pōōr| *a* arm; (*not good*) schlecht, schwach ♦ *npl*: **the** ~ die Armen *pl*.

poorly |pōōr'lē| *ad* schlecht, schwach; (*dressed*) ärmlich ♦ *a* schlecht, elend.

pop |páp| *n* Knall *m*; (*music*) Popmusik *f*; (*drink*) Limo(nade) *f*; (*US col: dad*) Pa *m* ♦ *vt* (*put*) stecken; (*balloon*) platzen lassen; **she** ~**ped her head out of the window** sie streckte den Kopf aus dem Fenster ♦ *vi* knallen; **to** ~ **in/out** (*person*) vorbeikommen/hinausgehen; (*jump*) hinein-/hinausspringen.

    pop up *vi* auftauchen.

pop concert *n* Popkonzert *nt*.

popcorn |páp'kórn| *n* Puffmais *m*.

pope |pōp| *n* Papst *m*.

poplar |páp'lûr| *n* Pappel *f*.

poplin |páp'lin| *n* Popelin *m*.

poppy |páp'ē| *n* Mohn *m*.

poppycock |páp'ēkâk| *n* (*col*) Unsinn *m*, Blödsinn *m*.

Popsicle |páp'sikəl| *n* ® (*US*) Eis *nt* am Stiel.

populace |páp'yələs| *n* Volk *nt*.

popular |páp'yəlûr| *a* beliebt, populär; (*of the people*) volkstümlich, Populär-; (*widespread*) allgemein; **to be** ~ (*person*) beliebt sein (*with* bei); (*decision*) populär sein (*with* bei).

popularity |pápyəlar'itē| *n* Beliebtheit *f*, Popularität *f*.

popularize |páp'yələrīz| *vt* popularisieren.

popularly |páp'yəlûrlē| *ad* allgemein, überall.

populate |páp'yəlāt| *vt* bevölkern; (*town*) bewohnen.

population |pápyəlā'shən| *n* Bevölkerung *f*; (*of town*) Einwohner *pl*.

population explosion *n* Bevölkerungsexplosion *f*.

populous |páp'yələs| *a* dicht besiedelt.

porcelain |pôr'səlin| *n* Porzellan *nt*.

porch |pôrch| *n* Vorbau *m*; (*US*) Veranda *f*; (*in church*) Portal *nt*.

porcupine |pôr'kyəpīn| *n* Stachelschwein *nt*.

pore |pôr| *n* Pore *f*.

    pore over *vt* brüten *or* hocken über (+*dat*).

pork |pôrk| *n* Schweinefleisch *nt*.

pork chop *n* Schweine- *or* Schweinskotelett *nt*.

pornographic |pôrnəgraf'ik| *a* pornographisch.

pornography |pôrná'grəfē| *n* Pornographie *f*.

porous |pôr'əs| *a* porös; (*skin*) porig.

porpoise |pôr'pəs| *n* Tümmler *m*.

porridge |pôr'ij| *n* Porridge *m*, Haferbrei *m*.

port |pôrt| *n* Hafen *m*; (*town*) Hafenstadt *f*; (*NAUT: left side*) Backbord *nt*; (*opening for loads*) Luke *f*; (*wine*) Portwein *m*; (*COMPUT*) Anschluß *m*; ~ **of call** Anlaufhafen *m*; (*fig*) Station *f*.

portable |pôr'təbəl| *a* tragbar; (*radio*) Koffer-; (*typewriter*) Reise-.

portal |pôr'təl| *n* Portal *nt*.

port authorities *npl* Hafenbehörde *f*.

portcullis |pôrtkul'is| *n* Fallgitter *nt*.

portend |pôrtend'| *vt* anzeigen, hindeuten auf (+*acc*).

portent |pôr'tent| *n* schlimme(s) Vorzeichen *nt*.

porter |pôr'tûr| *n* Pförtner(in *f*) *m*; (*for luggage*) (Gepäck)träger *m*; (*US RAIL*) Schlafwagenschaffner *m*.

portfolio |pôrtfō'lēō| *n* (*POL: office*) Portefeuille *nt* (*form*), Geschäftsbereich *m*; (*FIN*) Portefeuille *nt*; (*of artist*) Kollektion *f*.

porthole |pôr'hōl| *n* Bullauge *nt*.

portico |pôr'tikō| *n* Säulengang *m*.

portion |pôr'shən| *n* Teil *m*, Stück *nt*; (*of food*) Portion *f*.

portly |pôrt'lē| *a* korpulent, beleibt.

portrait |pôr'trit| *n* Porträt *nt*, Bild(nis) *nt*.

portray [pôrträ'] *vt* darstellen; *(describe)* schildern.

portrayal [pôrträ'əl] *n* Darstellung *f*; Schilderung *f*.

Portugal [pôr'chəgəl] *n* Portugal *nt*.

Portuguese [pôrchəgēz'] *a* portugiesisch ♦ *n* *(person)* Portugiese *m*, Portugiesin *f*; *(language)* Portugiesisch *nt*; ~ **man-of-war** *(jellyfish)* Staats- *or* Röhrenqualle *f*, Portugiesische Galeere *f*.

pose [pōz] *n* Stellung *f*, Pose *f* *(also affectation)* ♦ *vi* posieren, sich in Positur setzen ♦ *vt* stellen; **to** ~ **as** sich ausgeben als; **to strike a** ~ sich in Positur werfen.

poser [pō'zûr] *n* knifflige Frage *f*.

poseur [pōzir'] *n* Wichtigtuer *m*, Aufschneider *m*.

posh [päsh] *a* *(col)* (piek)fein ♦ *ad*: **to talk** ~ mit vornehmen Akzent sprechen.

position [pəzish'ən] *n* Stellung *f*; *(place)* Position *f*, Lage *f*; *(job)* Stelle *f*; *(attitude)* Standpunkt *m*, Haltung *f*; **to be in a** ~ **to do sth** in der Lage sein, etw zu tun ♦ *vt* aufstellen.

positive [päz'ətiv] *a* positiv; *(convinced)* sicher; *(definite)* eindeutig; ~ **cash flow** Überhang *m* der Zahlungseingänge; **we look forward to a** ~ **reply** *(COMM)* wir hoffen auf einen positiven Bescheid; **he's a** ~ **nuisance** er ist wirklich eine Plage.

positively [päz'ətivlē] *ad* positiv; *(really, absolutely)* wirklich.

posse [päs'ē] *n* *(US)* Aufgebot *nt*.

possess [pəzes'] *vt* besitzen; **what** ~**ed you to** ...? was ist bloß in dich gefahren, daß...?

possessed [pəzest'] *a* besessen; **like one** ~ wie ein Besessener.

possession [pəzesh'ən] *n* Besitz *m*; **to take** ~ **of sth** etw in Besitz nehmen.

possessive [pəzes'iv] *a* besitzergreifend, eigensüchtig; *(GRAM)* Possessiv-, besitzanzeigend.

possessively [pəzes'ivlē] *ad* besitzergreifend, eigensüchtig.

possessor [pəzes'ûr] *n* Besitzer(in *f*) *m*.

possibility [päsəbil'ətē] *n* Möglichkeit *f*; **he's a** ~ **for the part** er kommt für die Rolle in Frage *or* Betracht.

possible [päs'əbəl] *a* möglich; **if** ~ wenn möglich, möglichst; **as big as** ~ so groß wie möglich, möglichst groß; **as far as** ~ so weit wie möglich; **it is** ~ **to do it** das läßt sich machen; **a** ~ **candidate** ein möglicher Kandidat.

possibly [päs'əblē] *ad* möglicherweise, vielleicht; **as soon as I** ~ **can** sobald ich irgendwie kann; **could you** ~ ...? könntest du vielleicht ...?

post [pōst] *n* Post *f*; *(pole)* Pfosten *m*, Pfahl *m*; *(place of duty)* Posten *m*; *(job)* Stelle *f*; *(trading* ~*)* Handelsniederlassung *f*; ~**-free** *(Brit)* portofrei; **by** ~ *(Brit)* mit der Post; **by return of** ~ *(Brit)* postwendend ♦ *vt* *(notice)* anschlagen; *(letters)* aufgeben; *(sol-*

diers) aufstellen; **to keep sb** ~**ed** jdn auf dem laufenden halten.

post- *pref* nach-; *(esp with foreign words)* post-; ~**1950** nach 1950.

postage [pōs'tij] *n* Postgebühr *f*, Porto *nt*; ~ **prepaid** *(US)* portofrei.

postage stamp *n* Briefmarke *f*.

postal [pōs'təl] *a* Post-.

postal order *n* *(Brit)* Postanweisung *f*.

postbag [pōst'bag] *n* *(Brit)* Postsack *m*.

postbox [pōst'bäks] *n* *(Brit)* Briefkasten *m*.

postcard [pōst'kärd] *n* Postkarte *f*.

postcode [pōst'kōd] *n* *(Brit)* Postleitzahl *f*.

postdate [pōst'dāt] *vt* *(check)* nachdatieren.

poster [pōs'tûr] *n* Plakat *nt*, Poster *m*.

posterior [pâstēr'ēûr] *n* *(col)* Hintern *m*.

posterity [pâstär'itē] *n* Nachwelt *f*; *(descendants)* Nachkommenschaft *f*.

poster paint *n* Plakatfarbe *f*.

post-free [pōst'frē'] *a* *(Brit)* portofrei, gebührenfrei.

postgraduate [pōstgraj'ōōit] *n* Weiterstudierender(in *f*) *m*.

posthumous [päs'chəməs] *a*, **posthumously** [päs'chəməslē] *ad* post(h)um.

postman [pōst'mən] *n, pl* **-men** Briefträger *m*, Postbote *m*.

postmark [pōst'märk] *n* Poststempel *m*.

postmaster [pōst'mastûr] *n* Postmeister *m*.

Postmaster General *n* Postminister *m*.

postmistress [pōst'mistris] *n* Postmeisterin *f*.

post-mortem [pōstmôr'təm] *n* Obduktion *f*, Autopsie *f*; *(fig)* nachträgliche Erörterung *f*.

postnatal [pōstnāt'əl] *a* nach der Geburt, postnatal.

post office *n* Postamt *nt*, Post *f* *(also organization)*.

postpone [pōstpōn'] *vt* verschieben, aufschieben.

postponement [pōstpōn'mənt] *n* Verschiebung *f*, Aufschub *m*.

postscript [pōst'skript] *n* Nachschrift *f*, Postskript *nt*; *(in book)* Nachwort *nt*.

postulate [päs'chəlāt] *vt* voraussetzen; *(maintain)* behaupten.

postulation [päschəlā'shən] *n* Voraussetzung *f*; Behauptung *f*.

posture [päs'chûr] *n* Haltung *f* ♦ *vi* posieren.

postwar [pōst'wôr'] *a* Nachkriegs-.

posy [pō'zē] *n* Blumenstrauß *m*.

pot [pât] *n* Topf *m*; *(tea*~, *coffee*~*)* Kanne *f*; *(col: marijuana)* Hasch *m*; ~**s of** *(Brit col)* jede Menge, massenhaft ♦ *vt* *(plant)* eintopfen.

potash [pât'ash] *n* Pottasche *f*.

potassium [pətas'ēəm] *n* Kalium *nt*.

potato [pətā'tō] *n, pl* **potatoes** Kartoffel *f*.

potato chips, *(Brit)* **potato crisps** *npl* Kartoffelchips *pl*.

potato peeler [pətā'tō pē'lûr] *n* Schälmesser *m*, Kartoffelschäler *m*.

potbellied [pât'belēd] *a* *(from overeating)* spitzbäuchig; *(from malnutrition)* blähbäuchig.

potency [pōt'ənsē] *n* Stärke *f*, Potenz *f*.

potent [pōt'ənt] *a* stark; (*argument*) zwingend.

potentate [pāt'əntāt] *n* Machthaber *m*.

potential [pəten'chəl] *a* potentiell; **he is a ~ virtuoso** er hat das Zeug zum Virtuosen ♦ *n* Potential *nt*; **to have ~** ausbaufähig sein (*col*).

potentially [pəten'chəlē] *ad* potentiell.

pothole [pāt'hōl] *n* (*underground*) Höhle *f*; (*in road*) Schlagloch *nt*.

potholer [pāt'hōlûr] *n* (*Brit*) Höhlenforscher *m*.

potion [pō'shən] *n* Trank *m*.

potluck [pāt'luk] *n*: **to take ~ with sth** etw auf gut Glück nehmen.

potpourri [pōpərē'] *n* Potpourri *nt*.

pot roast *n* Schmorbraten *m*.

potshot [pāt'shāt] *n*: **to take a ~ at sth** auf etw (*acc*) ballern.

potted [pāt'id] *a* (*food*) eingelegt, eingemacht; (*plant*) Topf-; (*fig: book, version*) konzentriert; (: *shortened*) gekürzt, zusammengefaßt.

potter [pāt'ûr] *n* Töpfer *m* ♦ *vi* (*Brit*) = **putter** *vi*.

potter's wheel *n* Töpferscheibe *f*.

pottery [pāt'ûrē] *n* Töpferwaren *pl*, Steingut *nt*; (*place*) Töpferei *f*; **a piece of ~** etwas Getöpfertes.

potty [pāt'ē] *n* Töpfchen *nt*.

potty-trained [pāt'ētrānd] *a* (*child*) sauber.

pouch [pouch] *n* Beutel *m*; (*under eyes*) Tränensack *m*; (*for tobacco*) Tabaksbeutel *m*.

pouffe [pōōf] *n* Sitzkissen *nt*.

poultice [pōl'tis] *n* Packung *f*.

poultry [pōl'trē] *n* Geflügel *nt*.

poultry farm *n* Geflügelfarm *f*.

poultry farmer *n* Geflügelzüchter *m*.

pounce [pouns] *vi* sich stürzen (*on* auf +*acc*) ♦ *n* Sprung *m*, Satz *m*.

pound [pound] *n* Pfund *nt* (*weight* = 453*g, 16 ounces*; *money* = 100 *pence*); (*for cars, animals*) Auslösestelle *f*; (*for stray animals*) (Tier)asyl *nt* ♦ *vi* klopfen, hämmern ♦ *vt* (*zer*)stampfen; **half a ~** ein halbes Pfund; **a one-~ note** eine Einpfundnote; **one ~ sterling** ein Pfund Sterling.

pounding [poun'ding] *n* starke(s) Klopfen *nt*, Hämmern *nt*; (*of feet, hooves etc*) (Zer)stampfen *nt*; (*of heart*) Pochen *nt*; **our team took quite a ~** unsere Mannschaft mußte eine ziemliche Schlappe einstecken.

pour [pôr] *vt* gießen, schütten ♦ *vi* gießen; (*crowds etc*) strömen; **to come ~ing in** (*water, cars, people*) hereinströmen.

pour away, pour off *vt* abgießen.

pour in *vi* (*people*) hereinströmen.

pour out *vi* (*people*) herausströmen.

pouring [pôr'ing] *a*: **~ rain** strömende(r) Regen *m*.

pout [pout] *n* Schnute *f*, Schmollmund *m* ♦ *vi* eine Schnute ziehen, schmollen.

poverty [pāv'ûrtē] *n* Armut *f*.

poverty-stricken [pāv'ûrtēstrikən] *a* verarmt, notleidend.

POW *n abbr* (= *prisoner of war*) Kgf, Kriegsgefangene(r) *mf*.

powder [pou'dûr] *n* Pulver *nt*; (*cosmetic*) Puder *m* ♦ *vt* pulverisieren; (*sprinkle*) bestreuen; **to ~ one's nose** sich (*dat*) die Nase pudern; (*euph*) kurz verschwinden.

powder compact *n* Puderdose *f*.

powdered milk [pou'dûrd milk] *n* Milchpulver *nt*.

powdered sugar [pou'dûrd shōōg'ûr] *n* (*US*) Streuzucker *m*.

powder puff *n* Puderquaste *f*.

powder room *n* Damentoilette *f*.

powdery [pou'dûrē] *a* pulverig, Pulver-.

power [pou'ûr] *n* Macht *f* (*also POL*); (*ability*) Fähigkeit *f*; (*strength*) Stärke *f*; (*authority*) Macht *f*, Befugnis *f*; (*MATH*) Potenz *f*; (*ELEC*) Strom *m*; **to be in ~** an der Macht sein; **to do all in one's ~ to help sb** alles tun, was in seiner Macht *or* in seinen Kräften steht, um jdm zu helfen; **the world ~s** die Weltmächte *pl* ♦ *vt* (*fuel*) betreiben; (*engine*) antreiben.

power cut *n* (*Brit*) Stromausfall *m*.

power-driven [pou'ûrdrivən] *a* (*ELEC also*) Motor-.

powered [pou'ûrd] *a*: **~ by** betrieben mit; **nuclear-~ submarine** atomgetriebene(s) U-boot *nt*.

power failure *n* Stromausfall *m*.

powerful [pou'ûrfəl] *a* (*person*) mächtig; (*engine, government*) stark.

powerhouse [pou'ûrhous] *n* (*fig: person*) treibende Kraft *f*; **he's a ~ of new ideas** er hat einen unerschöpflichen Vorrat an neuen Ideen.

powerless [pou'ûrlis] *a* machtlos.

power line *n* (Haupt)stromleitung *f*.

power station *n* Elektrizitätswerk *nt*.

power steering *n* (*AUT*) Servolenkung *f*.

powwow [pou'wou] *n* Besprechung *f* ♦ *vi* eine Besprechung abhalten.

pp *abbr* (= *per procurationem*: *by proxy*) ppa., pp; = *pages*.

PPS *n abbr* (= *post postscriptum*) PPS *nt*.

PQ *abbr* (*Canada*) = *Province of Quebec*.

Pr. *abbr* (= *prince*) Pr.

PR *n abbr* (= *public relations*) PR; (= *proportional representation*) ♦ *abbr* (*US MAIL*) = *Puerto Rico*.

practicability [praktikəbil'ətē] *n* Durchführbarkeit *f*.

practicable [prak'tikəbəl] *a* durchführbar.

practical [prak'tikəl] *a* praktisch.

practicality [praktikal'itē] *n* (*of person*) praktische Veranlagung *f*; (*of situation*) Durchführbarkeit *f*.

practical joke *n* Streich *m*.

practically [prak'tiklē] *ad* praktisch.

practice [prak'tis] *n* Übung *f*; (*custom*) Brauch *m*; (*in business*) Verfahrensweise *f*; (*doctor's, lawyer's*) Praxis *f*; **out of ~**

außer Übung; **it's common** ~ es ist allgemein üblich; **to put sth into** ~ etw in die Praxis umsetzen; **to set up a** ~ **as a doctor/lawyer** eine Arzt-/Rechtsanwaltspraxis aufmachen, sich als Arzt/ Rechtsanwalt niederlassen; *see* **target practice** ♦ *vt* (*US*) üben; (*profession*) ausüben; **to** ~ **law/medicine** als Rechtsanwalt/ Arzt arbeiten ♦ *vi* (*US*) (sich) üben; (*doctor, lawyer*) praktizieren.

practiced [prak'tist] *a* (*person*) geübt; (*performance*) gekonnt; (*liar*) erfahren; **with a** ~ **eye** mit geübtem Auge.

practice test *n* Übungsarbeit *f*.

practicing [prak'tising] *a* praktizierend; (*Christian etc*) aktiv.

practise [prak'tis] *etc* (*Brit*) = **practice** *etc*.

practitioner [praktish'ənûr] *n* praktische(r) Arzt *m*, praktische Ärztin *f*.

pragmatic [pragmat'ik] *a* pragmatisch.

pragmatism [prag'mətizəm] *n* Pragmatismus *m*.

pragmatist [prag'mətist] *n* Pragmatiker *m*.

Prague [prâg] *n* Prag *nt*.

prairie [prär'ē] *n* Prärie *f*, Steppe *f*.

praise [prāz] *n* Lob *nt*, Preis *m* ♦ *vt* (*worship also*) loben.

praiseworthy [prāz'wûrthē] *a* lobenswert.

pram [pram] *n* (*Brit*) Kinderwagen *m*.

prance [prans] *vi* (*horse*) tänzeln; (*person*) stolzieren; (*gaily*) herumhüpfen.

prank [prangk] *n* Streich *m*.

prattle [prat'əl] *vi* schwatzen, plappern.

prawn [prôn] *n* Garnele *f*, Krabbe *f*.

pray [prā] *vi* beten; **to** ~ **for forgiveness** um Vergebung bitten.

prayer [prär] *n* Gebet *nt*.

prayer book *n* Gebetbuch *nt*.

pre- [prē] *pref* prä-, vor-; ~**1970** vor 1970.

preach [prēch] *vi* predigen.

preacher [prē'chûr] *n* (*minister*) Prediger *m*.

preamble [prē'ambəl] *n* Einleitung *f*.

prearrange [prēərānj'] *vt* vereinbaren, absprechen.

prearranged [prēərānjd'] *a* vereinbart.

prearrangement [prēərānj'mənt] *n* Vereinbarung *f*, vorherige Absprache *f*.

precarious [prikär'ēəs] *a*, **precariously** [prikär'ēəslē] *ad* prekär, unsicher.

precaution [prikô'shən] *n* (Vorsichts)maßnahme *f*, Vorbeugung *f*.

precautionary [prikô'shənārē] *a* (*measure*) vorbeugend, Vorsichts-.

precede [prisēd'] *vt* vorausgehen (+*dat*); (*be more important*) an Bedeutung übertreffen.

precedence [pres'idəns] *n* Priorität *f*, Vorrang *m*; **to take** ~ **over** den Vorrang haben vor (+*dat*).

precedent [pres'idənt] *n* Präzedenzfall *m*; **to establish** *or* **set a** ~ einen Präzedenzfall schaffen.

preceding [prisē'ding] *a* vorhergehend.

precept [prē'sept] *n* Gebot *nt*, Regel *f*.

precinct [prē'singkt] *n* Gelände *f*; (*US: PO-*

LICE) (Polizei)revier *nt*; (: *POL*) (Wahl)bezirk *m*; (*Brit: shopping* ~) Einkaufszone *f*; *see* **pedestrian precinct**.

precious [presh'əs] *a* kostbar, wertvoll; (*affected*) preziös, geziert ♦ *ad*: ~ **little/few** (*col*) herzlich wenig/wenige.

precipice [pres'əpis] *n* Abgrund *m*.

precipitate *a* [prisip'itit] überstürzt, übereilt ♦ *vt* [prisip'itāt] hinunterstürzen; (*events*) heraufbeschwören.

precipitation [prisipitā'shən] *n* Niederschlag *m*.

precipitous [prisip'itəs] *a* abschüssig; (*action*) überstürzt.

précis [prā'sē] *n* (kurze) Übersicht *f*, Zusammenfassung *f*; (*SCH*) Inhaltsangabe *f*.

precise [prisīs'] *a*, **precisely** [prisīs'lē] *ad* genau, präzis.

precision [prisizh'ən] *n* Präzision *f*.

preclude [priklōōd'] *vt* ausschließen; (*person*) abhalten.

precocious [prikō'shəs] *a* frühreif.

preconceived [prēkənsēvd'] *a* (*idea*) vorgefaßt.

preconception [prēkənsep'shən] *n* vorgefaßte Meinung *f*.

precondition [prēkəndish'ən] *n* Vorbedingung *f*, Voraussetzung *f*.

precursor [prikûr'sûr] *n* Vorläufer *m*.

predate [prēdāt'] *vt* (*precede*) zeitlich vorangehen (+*dat*).

predator [pred'ətûr] *n* Raubtier *nt*.

predatory [pred'ətôrē] *a* (*animal*) Raub-; (*attack*) räuberisch.

predecessor [pred'isesûr] *n* Vorgänger(in *f*) *m*.

predestination [prēdestinā'shən] *n* Vorherbestimmung *f*, Prädestination *f*.

predestine [prēdes'tin] *vt* vorherbestimmen.

predetermine [prēditûr'min] *vt* vorherentscheiden, vorherbestimmen.

predicament [pridik'əmənt] *n* mißliche Lage *f*; **to be in a** ~ in der Klemme sitzen.

predicate [pred'əkit] *n* Prädikat *nt*, Satzaussage *f*.

predict [pridikt'] *vt* voraussagen.

predictable [pridikt'əbəl] *a* vorher- *or* voraussagbar.

predictably [pridikt'əblē] *ad*: ~ **he was late** wie vorauszusehen kam er zu spät.

prediction [pridik'shən] *n* Voraussage *f*.

predispose [prēdispōz'] *vt*: **I'm not** ~**d to help him** ich bin nicht geneigt, ihm zu helfen.

predominance [pridâm'ənəns] *n* (*in power*) Vorherrschaft *f*; (*fig*) Vorherrschen *nt*, Überwiegen *nt*.

predominant [pridâm'ənənt] *a* vorherrschend; (*fig*) vorherrschend, überwiegend.

predominantly [pridâm'ənəntlē] *ad* überwiegend, hauptsächlich.

predominate [pridâm'ənāt] *vi* vorherrschen; überwiegen.

preeminent [prēem'ənənt] *a* hervorragend,

herausragend.

preempt [prēempt'] *vt* (*action, decision*) vorwegnehmen.

preemptive strike [prēemp'tiv strīk] *n* Präventivschlag *m*.

preen [prēn] *vt* putzen; **to ~ o.s. on sth** sich (*dat*) etwas auf etw (*acc*) einbilden.

prefab [prē'fab'] *n* Fertighaus *nt*.

prefabricated [prēfab'rikātid] *a* vorgefertigt, Fertig-.

preface [pref'is] *n* Vorwort *nt*, Einleitung *f*.

prefect [prē'fekt] *n* Präfekt *m*; (*Brit SCH*) Aufsichtsschüler(in *f*) *m*.

prefer [prifûr'] *vt* vorziehen, lieber mögen; (*action*) bevorzugen; **to ~ to do sth** etw lieber tun; **to ~ coffee to tea** lieber Kaffee als Tee trinken; **to ~ charges (against sb)** (*JUR*) (gegen jdn) klagen, Klage (gegen jdn) erheben.

preferable [pref'ûrəbəl] *a* vorzuziehen(d) (*to dat*).

preferably [prifûr'əblē] *ad* vorzugsweise, am liebsten.

preference [pref'ûrəns] *n* Präferenz *f*, Vorzug *m*; **he chose to stay at home in ~ to going abroad** er zog es vor, in der Heimat zu bleiben, statt ins Ausland zu gehen.

preference shares *npl* (*Brit*) Vorzugsaktien *pl*.

preferential [prefəren'chəl] *a* bevorzugt, Vorzugs-.

preferred stock [prifûrd' stâk] *n* (*US*) Prioritäten *pl*.

prefix [prē'fiks] *n* Vorsilbe *f*, Präfix *nt*.

pregnancy [preg'nənsē] *n* Schwangerschaft *f*.

pregnant [preg'nənt] *a* schwanger; **to be 3 months ~** im dritten Monat sein; **~ with meaning** (*fig*) bedeutungsschwer *or* -voll.

prehistoric [prēhistôr'ik] *a* prähistorisch, vorgeschichtlich.

prehistory [prēhis'tûrē] *n* Urgeschichte *f*.

prejudge [prējuj'] *vt* vorschnell beurteilen.

prejudice [prej'ədis] *n* Vorurteil *nt*, Voreingenommenheit *f*; (*harm*) Schaden *m* ♦ *vt* beeinträchtigen; **to ~ sb in favor of/against** jdn positiv/negativ beeinflussen.

prejudiced [prej'ədist] *a* (*person*) voreingenommen; **to be ~ against sb/sth** gegen jdn/etw voreingenommen sein.

prelate [prel'it] *n* Prälat *m*.

preliminaries [prilim'ənārēz] *npl* die vorbereitenden Maßnahmen *pl*.

preliminary [prilim'ənārē] *a* einleitend, Vor-.

prelude [prā'lōōd] *n* Vorspiel *nt*; (*MUS*) Präludium *nt*; (*fig also*) Auftakt *m*.

premarital [prēmar'itəl] *a* vorehelich.

premature [prēməchōōr'] *a* (*birth, arrival*) vorzeitig, Früh-; (*decision, action*) verfrüht; **you are being a little ~** da sind Sie ein wenig voreilig.

prematurely [prēmətōōr'lē] *ad* vorzeitig; verfrüht; voreilig.

premeditate [primed'ətāt] *vt* im voraus planen.

premeditated [primed'ətātid] *a* geplant; (*murder*) vorsätzlich.

premeditation [primeditā'shən] *n* Planung *f*.

premenstrual [prēmen'strōōəl] *a* prämenstruell.

premenstrual tension *n* prämenstruelle(s) Syndrom *nt*, Beschwerden *pl* vor der Periode.

premier [primyēr'] *a* erste(r, s), oberste(r, s), höchste(r, s) ♦ *n* Premier *m*.

première [primyēr'] *n* Premiere *f*, Uraufführung *f*.

premise [prem'is] *n* Voraussetzung *f*, Prämisse *f*.

premises [prem'isiz] *npl* Räumlichkeiten *pl*; (*grounds*) Grundstück *nt*; **business ~** Geschäftsräume *pl*.

premium [prē'mēəm] *n* Prämie *f*; (*gasoline*) Super *nt*; **to sell at a ~** mit Gewinn verkaufen; (*shares*) über pari verkaufen.

premium bond *n* (*Brit*) Prämienanleihe *f*.

premium gasoline *n* (*US*) Super *nt*.

premonition [premənish'ən] *n* Vorahnung *f*.

prenatal [prēnāt'l] *a* vor der Geburt.

preoccupation [prēâkyəpā'shən] *n* Sorge *f*.

preoccupied [prēâk'yəpīd] *a* (*look*) geistesabwesend; **to be ~ with sth** mit dem Gedanken an etw (*acc*) beschäftigt sein.

prep [prep] *a* *abbr*: **~ school** = **preparatory school**.

prepaid [prēpād'] *a* vorausbezahlt; (*letter*) frankiert; **~ envelope** Freiumschlag *m*.

preparation [prepərā'shən] *n* Vorbereitung *f*; (*SCH: study*) Hausaufgabe *f*; **in ~ for sth** als Vorbereitung für etw.

preparatory [pripar'ətôrē] *a* Vor(bereitungs)-; **~ school** (*US*) *private Vorbereitungsschule für die Hochschule*; (*Brit*) *private Vorbereitungsschule für die Public School*; **the ~ arrangements** die Vorbereitungen *pl*.

prepare [pripär'] *vt* vorbereiten (*for* auf +*acc*) ♦ *vi* sich vorbereiten; **to be ~d to ...** bereit sein zu ...

preponderance [pripân'dûrəns] *n* Übergewicht *nt*.

preposition [prepəzish'ən] *n* Präposition *f*, Verhältniswort *nt*.

prepossessing [prēpəzes'ing] *a* einnehmend, anziehend.

preposterous [pripâs'tûrəs] *a* absurd, widersinnig.

prerecorded [prērikôr'did] *a*: **~ broadcast** aufgezeichnete Sendung *f*; **~ cassette** bespielte Kassette *f*.

prerequisite [prirek'wizit] *n* (unerläßliche) Voraussetzung *f*.

prerogative [prərâg'ətiv] *n* Vorrecht *nt*, Privileg *nt*.

presbytery [prez'bitärē] *n* (*house*) Presbyterium *nt*; (*Catholic*) Pfarrhaus *nt*.

Presbyterian [prezbitēr'ēən] *a* presbyterianisch ♦ *n* Presbyterier(in *f*) *m*.

preschool [prē'skōōl'] *a*: **~ child** Vorschulkind *nt*; ~ **age** Vorschulalter *nt*.

prescribe [priskrīb'] *vt* vorschreiben, anordnen; (*MED*) verschreiben.

prescription [priskrip'shən] *n* Vorschrift *f*; (*MED*) Rezept *nt*; **to fill a** ~ eine Medizin zubereiten.

prescriptive [priskrip'tiv] *a* normativ.

presence [prez'əns] *n* Gegenwart *f*, Anwesenheit *f*; ~ **of mind** Geistesgegenwart *f*.

present [prez'ənt] *a* anwesend; (*existing*) gegenwärtig, augenblicklich; **to be** ~ **at** bei etw anwesend sein; **those** ~ die Anwesenden ♦ *n* Gegenwart *f*; (*GRAM*) Präsens *nt*; (*gift*) Geschenk *nt*; **at** ~ im Augenblick; **to make sb a** ~ **of sth** jdm etw schenken ♦ *vt* [prizent'] vorlegen; (*introduce*) vorstellen; (*show*) zeigen; (*give*) überreichen; **to** ~ **sb with sth** jdm etw überreichen; **to** ~ **o.s. for an interview** zu einem Vorstellungsgespräch erscheinen; **may I** ~ **Miss Clark?** darf ich Ihnen Fräulein Clark vorstellen?

presentable [prizen'təbəl] *a* präsentabel.

presentation [prezəntā'shən] *n* Überreichung *f*; **on** ~ **of the voucher** bei Vorlage des Gutscheins.

present-day [prez'əntdā'] *a* heutig, gegenwärtig, modern.

presenter [prizen'tûr] *n* (*RAD, TV*) Moderator(in *f*) *m*.

presently [prez'əntlē] *ad* bald; (*at present*) im Augenblick; (*now*) zur Zeit, im Augenblick.

present participle *n* Partizip *nt* des Präsens, Mittelwort *nt* der Gegenwart.

present tense *n* Präsens *nt*, Gegenwart *f*.

preservation [prezûrvā'shən] *n* Erhaltung *f*.

preservative [prizûr'vətiv] *n* Konservierungsmittel *nt*.

preserve [prizûrv'] *vt* erhalten, schützen; (*food*) einmachen, konservieren ♦ *n* (*jam*) Eingemachte(s) *nt*; (*HUNTING*) Schutzgebiet *nt*.

preserving jar [prizûrv'ing jâr] *n* Einmachglas *nt*.

preshrunk [prē'shrungk'] *a* vorgewaschen.

preside [prizīd'] *vi* den Vorsitz haben.

presidency [prez'idənsē] *n* (*POL*) Präsidentschaft *f*; (*US: of company*) Aufsichtsratsvorsitz *m*.

president [prez'idənt] *n* Präsident *m*; (*US: of company*) Aufsichtsratsvorsitzende(r) *mf*.

presidential [prezidən'chəl] *a* Präsidenten-; (*election*) Präsidentschafts-; (*system*) Präsidial-.

press [pres] *n* Presse *f*; (*printing house*) Druckerei *f*; **to go to** ~ (*newspaper*) in Druck gehen; **to be in the** ~ (*being printed*) im Druck sein; (*in the newspapers*) in der Zeitung sein; (*ironing*): **to give the clothes a** ~ die Kleider bügeln ♦ *vt* drücken, pressen; (*iron*) bügeln; (*urge*) (be)drängen; (*doorbell, button, brake*) drücken auf (+*acc*); **to** ~ **sb to do** *or* **into doing sth** (*urge*) jdn drängen, etw zu tun;

to ~ **for sth** drängen auf etw (*acc*); **to** ~ **charges against sb** (*JUR*) Klage gegen jdn erheben; **to be** ~**ed for time** unter Zeitdruck stehen; **to be** ~**ed for money/space** wenig Geld/Platz haben ♦ *vi* (*push*) drücken, pressen.

press on *vi* vorwärtsdrängen.

press agency *n* Presseagentur *f*.

press clipping *n* Zeitungsausschnitt *m*.

press conference *n* Pressekonferenz *f*.

press cutting *n* (*Brit*) Zeitungsausschnitt *m*.

pressing [pres'ing] *a* dringend.

press release *n* Presseverlautbarung *f*.

press stud *n* (*Brit*) Druckknopf *m*.

press-up [pres'up] *n* (*Brit*) Liegestütz *m*.

pressure [presh'ûr] *n* Druck *m*; **high/low** ~ Hoch-/Tiefdruck *m*; **to put** ~ **on sb** jdn unter Druck setzen ♦ *vt*: **to** ~ **sb into doing sth** (*US*) jdn so unter Druck setzen, daß er schließlich etw tut.

pressure cooker *n* Schnellkochtopf *m*.

pressure gauge *n* Druckmesser *m*.

pressure group *n* Interessenverband *m*, Pressure Group *f*.

pressurize [presh'ərīz] *vt* unter Druck setzen; **to** ~ **sb into doing sth** (*Brit fig*) jdn so unter Druck setzen, daß er schließlich etw tut.

pressurized [presh'ərīzd] *a* Druck-.

prestige [prestēzh'] *n* Ansehen *nt*, Prestige *nt*.

prestigious [prestij'əs] *a* Prestige-.

presumably [prizoo'məblē] *ad* vermutlich.

presume [prizoom'] *vti* annehmen; (*dare*) sich erlauben.

presumption [prizump'shən] *n* Annahme *f*; (*impudent behavior*) Anmaßung *f*.

presumptuous [prizump'chooəs] *a* anmaßend.

presuppose [prēsəpōz'] *vt* voraussetzen.

presupposition [prēsupəzish'ən] *n* Voraussetzung *f*.

pretax [prē'taks'] *a* vor Steuern.

pretence [pritens'] *n* (*Brit*) = **pretense**.

pretend [pritend'] *vt* vorgeben, so tun als ob ... ♦ *vi* so tun.

pretense [pritens'] *n* (*US*) Vorgabe *f*, Vortäuschung *f*; (*pretext*) Vorwand *m*; **she is devoid of all** ~ sie ist völlig natürlich; **on** *or* **under the** ~ **of doing sth** unter dem Vorwand, etw zu tun.

pretension [priten'chən] *n* (*claim*) Anspruch *m*; (*impudent claim*) Anmaßung *f*; **he makes no** ~**s to originality** er beansprucht keineswegs, originell zu sein.

pretentious [priten'chəs] *a* angeberisch.

pretext [prē'tekst] *n* Vorwand *m*; **on** *or* **under the** ~ **of doing sth** unter dem Vorwand, etw zu tun.

prettily [prit'ilē] *ad* hübsch, nett.

pretty [prit'ē] *a* hübsch, nett ♦ *ad* (*col*) ganz schön.

prevail [privāl'] *vi* siegen (*against, over* über +*acc*); (*custom*) vorherrschen; **to** ~ **upon sb to do sth** jdn dazu bewegen, etw zu tun.

prevailing [privā'ling] a vorherrschend.
prevalent [prev'ələnt] a vorherrschend.
prevarication [privarikā'shən] n Ausflucht f.
prevent [privent'] vt (stop) verhindern, verhüten; **to ~ sb from doing sth** jdn (daran) hindern, etw zu tun.
preventable [privent'əbəl] a verhütbar.
preventative [priven'tətiv] n Vorbeugungsmittel nt.
prevention [priven'chən] n Verhütung f, Schutz m (of gegen).
preventive [priven'tiv] a vorbeugend, Schutz-♦ n Vorbeugungsmittel nt.
preview [prē'vyōō] n private Voraufführung f; (trailer) Vorschau f ♦ vt (film) privat vorführen.
previous [prē'vēəs] a früher, vorherig; **he has no ~ experience in that field** er hat keine Vorkenntnisse auf diesem Gebiet; **I have a ~ engagement** ich habe schon einen Termin.
previously [prē'vēəslē] ad früher.
prewar [prē'wôr'] a Vorkriegs-.
prey [prā] n Beute f; **bird/beast of ~** Raubvogel m/Raubtier nt.
prey on vt fus Jagd machen auf (+acc); (mind) nagen an (+dat).
price [prīs] n Preis m; (value) Wert m; (betting: odds) Quote f; **to go up** or **rise in ~** teurer werden, im Preis steigen; **what is the ~ of ...?** was kostet ...?; **to put a ~ on sth** einen Preis für etw nennen; **he regained his freedom, but at what a ~!** er hat seine Freiheit wiedererlangt, aber zu welchem Preis! ♦ vt schätzen; (label) auszeichnen; **to be ~d out of the market** (article) durch zu hohe Preise konkurrenzunfähig sein; (producer, nation) durch niedrigere Preise vom Markt verdrängt werden.
price control n Preiskontrolle f.
price-cutting [prīs'kuting] n Preissenkung f.
priceless [prīs'lis] a (lit, fig) unbezahlbar; (col: amusing) köstlich.
price list n Preisliste f.
price range n Preisklasse f; **it's within my ~** es entspricht meinen Preisvorstellungen.
price tag n Preisschild nt.
price war n Preiskrieg m.
pricey [prī'sē] a (col) teuer, kostspielig.
prick [prik] n Stich m ♦ vti stechen; **to ~ up one's ears** die Ohren spitzen.
prickle [prik'əl] n Stachel m, Dorn m ♦ vi brennen.
prickly [prik'lē] a stachelig; (fig: person) reizbar.
prickly heat n Hitzebläschen pl.
prickly pear n Feigenkaktus m; (fruit) Kaktusfeige f.
pride [prīd] n Stolz m; (arrogance) Hochmut m; **to take (a) ~ in sth** auf etw stolz sein; **her ~ and joy** ihr ganzer Stolz ♦ vt: **to ~ o.s. on sth** auf etw (acc) stolz sein.
priest [prēst] n Priester m.
priestess [prēs'tis] n Priesterin f.

priesthood [prēst'hŏŏd] n Priesteramt nt.
prig [prig] n Selbstgefällige(r) mf.
prim [prim] a prüde.
prima donna [prē'mə dân'ə] n Primadonna f.
prima facie [prē'mə fā'sē] a: **to have a ~ case** (JUR) genügend Beweise haben.
primarily [prīmär'ilē] ad vorwiegend, hauptsächlich.
primary [prī'märē] a Haupt-, Grund-, primär.
primary color n Grundfarbe f.
primary education n Grundschul(-aus)bildung f.
primary election n (US) (innerparteiliche) Vorwahl f.
primary products npl Grundstoffe pl.
primary school n (Brit) Grundschule f, Volksschule f.
primate n [prī'mit] (ECCL) Primas m; [prī'māt] (BIOL) Primat m.
prime [prīm] a oberste(r, s), erste(r, s), wichtigste(r, s); (excellent) erstklassig, prima inv ♦ vt vorbereiten; (gun) laden ♦ n (of life) beste(s) Alter nt.
prime minister n Premierminister(in f) m, Ministerpräsident(in f) m.
primer [prī'mûr] n Elementarlehrbuch nt, Fibel f; (paint) Grundierfarbe f.
prime time n (TV) Hauptsendezeit f.
primeval [primē'vəl] a vorzeitlich; (forests) Ur-.
primitive [prim'ətiv] a primitiv.
primly [prim'lē] ad prüde.
primrose [prim'rōz] n (gelbe) Primel f.
primula [prim'yələ] n Primel f.
primus (stove) [prī'məs (stōv)] n ® (Brit) Primuskocher m.
prince [prins] n Prinz m; (ruler) Fürst m.
princess [prin'sis] n Prinzessin f; (wife of ruler) Fürstin f.
principal [prin'səpəl] a Haupt-, wichtigste(r, s) ♦ n (SCH) (Schul)direktor m, Rektor m; (FIN) (Grund)kapital nt; (of debt) Kreditsumme f; (in play) Hauptperson f.
principality [prinsəpal'itē] n Fürstentum nt.
principally [prin'səpəlē] ad hauptsächlich.
principle [prin'səpəl] n Grundsatz m, Prinzip nt; **in ~** im Prinzip, prinzipiell; **on ~** aus Prinzip.
print [print] n Druck m; (made by feet, fingers) Abdruck m; (PHOT) Abzug m; (cotton) Kattun m ♦ vt drucken; (name) in Druckbuchstaben schreiben; (PHOT) abziehen; **is the book still in ~?** wird das Buch noch gedruckt?; **out of ~** vergriffen.
print out vt (text) ausdrucken.
printed circuit [prin'tid sûr'kit] n gedruckte Schaltung f.
printed circuit board n Leiterplatte f.
printed matter n Drucksache f.
printer [prin'tûr] n Drucker m; **at the ~'s** (book) im Druck.
printhead [print'hed] n Druckkopf m.
printing [prin'ting] n Drucken nt; (of photos) Abziehen nt.

printing press n Druckerpresse f.
printout [print'out] n Ausdruck m.
print run n Auflage f.
print wheel n Typenrad nt, Typenscheibe f.
prior [prī'ûr] a früher; ~ **to sth** vor etw (dat); ~ **to going abroad, she had ... bevor sie ins Ausland ging, hatte sie ...; without ~ notice** ohne vorherige Ankündigung; **to have a ~ claim to sth** schon Anspruch auf etw haben ♦ n Prior m.
prioress [prī'ûris] n Priorin f.
priority [prīôr'itē] n Vorrang m, Priorität f; **to have** or **take ~ over sth** Vorrang vor etw haben.
priory [prī'ərē] n Kloster nt.
prise [prīz] vt (Brit) = **prize.**
prism [priz'əm] n Prisma nt.
prison [priz'ən] n Gefängnis nt.
prison camp n Gefangenenlager nt.
prisoner [priz'ənûr] n Gefangene(r) mf; **the ~ at the bar** der Angeklagte(r) mf; **to take sb ~** jdn gefangennehmen; **to be taken ~ in** Gefangenschaft geraten; ~ **of war** Kriegsgefangene(r) mf.
prissy [pris'ē] a zimperlich.
pristine [pris'tēn] a makellos.
privacy [prī'vəsē] n Privatleben nt; **in the strictest ~** unter strengster Geheimhaltung.
private [prī'vit] a privat, Privat-; (secret) vertraulich, geheim; **in his ~ life** in seinem Privatleben; **he is a very ~ person** er führt ein sehr privates Leben ♦ n (Brit MIL) einfache(r) Soldat m; **in ~** privat.
private enterprise n Privatunternehmen nt; (free enterprise) freie(s) Unternehmen nt.
private eye n Privatdetektiv m.
private hearing n (JUR) Verhandlung f unter Ausschluß der Öffentlichkeit.
private limited company n (Brit) Gesellschaft f mit beschränkter Haftung.
privately [prī'vitlē] ad privat; (in confidence) vertraulich, geheim.
private parts npl (ANAT) Geschlechtsteile pl.
private practice n: **to be in ~** Privatpatienten haben.
private property n Privatbesitz m.
private school n Privatschule f.
privation [prīvā'shən] n (state) Armut f, Not f.
privatize [prī'vətīz] vt privatisieren.
privet [priv'it] n Liguster m.
privilege [priv'əlij] n Vorrecht nt, Privileg nt; (honor) Ehre f.
privileged [priv'əlijd] a bevorzugt, privilegiert; **to be ~ to do sth** die Ehre or das Privileg haben, etw zu tun.
privy [priv'ē] a geheim, privat.
privy council n Geheime(r) Staatsrat m.
prize [prīz] n Preis m ♦ a (example) erstklassig; (idiot) Voll- ♦ vt (US) (hoch)schätzen; **to ~ open** aufbrechen.
prize fighter n Berufsboxer m.
prize fighting n Berufsboxkampf m.

prize-giving [prīz'giving] n Preisverteilung f.
prize money n Geldpreis m, Barpreis m.
prizewinner [prīz'winûr] n Preisträger(in f) m; (of money) Gewinner(in f) m.
prizewinning [prīz'wining] a (novel, essay etc) preisgekrönt; (ticket) Gewinn-.
pro [prō] n (professional) Profi m; (advantage): **the ~s and cons** pl das Für und Wider.
pro- [prō] pref (in favor of) pro-; ~**Soviet** prosowjetisch.
PRO n abbr = **public relations officer.**
probability [prâbəbil'ətē] n Wahrscheinlichkeit f; **in all ~** aller Wahrscheinlichkeit nach, höchstwahrscheinlich.
probable [prâb'əbəl] a wahrscheinlich; **it is ~/hardly ~ that ...** es ist wahrscheinlich/ziemlich unwahrscheinlich, daß ...
probably [prâb'əblē] ad wahrscheinlich.
probate [prō'bāt] n (JUR) gerichtliche Testamentsbestätigung f; (will) beglaubigte Testamentsabschrift f.
probation [prəbā'shən] n Probe(zeit) f; (JUR) Bewährung f; **on ~** auf Probe; auf Bewährung.
probationary [prəbā'shənârē] a Probe-; ~ **period** Probezeit f.
probationer [prəbā'shənûr] n (nurse: female) Lernschwester f; (: male) Pfleger m in der Ausbildung; (JUR) auf Bewährung freigelassene(r) Gefangene(r) mf.
probation officer n Bewährungshelfer m.
probe [prōb] n Sonde f; (enquiry) Untersuchung f ♦ vti untersuchen, erforschen, sondieren.
probity [prō'bitē] n Rechtschaffenheit f.
problem [prâb'ləm] n Problem nt; **what's the ~?** was ist los?; **no ~!** kein Problem!; **to have ~s with the car** Schwierigkeiten mit dem Wagen haben; **I had no ~ in finding her** ich habe sie ohne Schwierigkeiten gefunden.
problematic [prâbləmat'ik] a problematisch.
procedural [prəsē'jûrəl] a verfahrensmäßig, Verfahrens-.
procedure [prəsē'jûr] n Verfahren nt, Vorgehen nt; **cashing a check is a simple ~** es ist sehr einfach, einen Scheck einzulösen.
proceed [prəsēd'] vi (advance) vorrücken; (start) anfangen; (carry on) fortfahren; (set about) vorgehen; (come from) entstehen (from aus); (JUR) gerichtlich vorgehen; **I am not sure how to ~** ich weiß nicht genau, wie ich vorgehen soll; **to ~ against sb** (JUR) gegen jdn gerichtlich vorgehen.
proceedings [prəsē'dingz] npl Verfahren nt; (record of things) Sitzungsbericht m.
proceeds [prō'sēds] npl Erlös m, Gewinn m.
process [prâs'es] n Vorgang m, Prozeß m; (method also) Verfahren nt; **we are in the ~ of moving** wir sind im Umzug begriffen (to nach), wir sind gerade dabei, umzuziehen (to nach) ♦ vt bearbeiten; (food) verarbeiten; (film) entwickeln.

process(ed) cheese [prås'es(t) chēz] *n* Schmelzkäse *m*.

processing [prås'esing] *n* (*PHOT*) Entwickeln *nt*.

procession [prəsesh'ən] *n* Prozession *f*, Umzug *m*.

proclaim [prəklām'] *vt* verkünden, proklamieren; (*state of emergency*) ausrufen; **to ~ sb king** jdn zum König ausrufen.

proclamation [prákləmā'shən] *n* Verkündung *f*, Proklamation *f*; Ausrufung *f*.

proclivity [prōkliv'ətē] *n* Schwäche *f*, Vorliebe *f*.

procrastination [prōkrastənā'shən] *n* Hinausschieben *nt*.

procreation [prōkrēā'shən] *n* (Er)zeugung *f*.

procure [prəkyŏŏr'] *vt* beschaffen.

procurement [prəkyŏŏr'mənt] *n* Beschaffung *f*.

prod [prád] *vt* stoßen; **to ~ sb** (*fig*) jdn anspornen (*to do sth, into sth* zu etw) ♦ *n* Stoß *m*.

prodigal [prád'əgəl] *a* verschwenderisch (*of* mit); **the ~ son** der verlorene Sohn.

prodigious [prədij'əs] *a* gewaltig, erstaunlich; (*wonderful*) wunderbar.

prodigy [prád'əjē] *n* Wunder *nt*; **a child ~** ein Wunderkind.

produce *n* [prō'dōōs] (*AGR*) (Boden)produkte *pl*, (Natur)erzeugnis *nt* ♦ *vt* [prədōōs'] herstellen, produzieren; (*cause*) hervorrufen; (*farmer*) erzeugen; (*yield*) liefern, bringen; (*THEAT: play*) inszenieren; (*bring, show*) hervorholen; (*: proof of identity*) vorlegen.

producer [prədōō'sûr] *n* Erzeuger *m*, Hersteller *m*, Produzent *m* (*also CINE*).

product [prád'əkt] *n* Produkt *nt*, Erzeugnis *nt*.

production [prəduk'shən] *n* Produktion *f*, Herstellung *f*; (*thing*) Erzeugnis *nt*, Produkt *nt*; (*THEAT*) Inszenierung *f*; **to put into ~** die Herstellung *or* Produktion aufnehmen.

production agreement *n* (*US*) Produktivitätsvereinbarung *f*.

production control *n* Überwachung *f* des Produktionsablaufs.

production line *n* Fließband *nt*.

production manager *n* Produktionsmanager *m*.

productive [prəduk'tiv] *a* produktiv; (*fertile*) ertragreich, fruchtbar; **to be ~ of** führen zu, erzeugen.

productivity [prádəktiv'ətē] *n* Produktivität *f*; (*COMM*) Leistungsfähigkeit *f*; (*fig*) Fruchtbarkeit *f*.

productivity agreement *n* (*Brit*) = **production agreement**.

productivity bonus *n* Leistungszulage *f*.

Prof. [práf] *n abbr* (= *professor*) Prof.

profane [prəfān'] *a* weltlich, profan, Profan-.

profess [prəfes'] *vt* bekennen; (*show*) zeigen; (*claim to be*) vorgeben; **I do not ~ to be an expert** ich behaupte nicht, ein Fachmann zu sein.

profession [prəfesh'ən] *n* Beruf *m*; (*declaration*) Bekenntnis *nt*; **the ~s** die gehobenen Berufe.

professional [prəfesh'ənəl] *n* Fachmann *m*; (*SPORT*) Berufsspieler(in *f*) *m* ♦ *a* Berufs-; (*expert*) fachlich; (*player*) professionell; **to seek ~ advice** fachmännischen Rat einholen.

professionalism [prəfesh'ənəlizəm] *n* (fachliche(s)) Können *nt*; (*SPORT*) Berufssportlertum *nt*.

professionally [prəfesh'ənəlē] *ad*: **I only know him ~** ich kenne ihn nur geschäftlich.

professor [prəfes'ûr] *n* Professor *m*; (*US: teacher*) Dozent(in *f*) *m*.

professorship [prəfes'ûrship] *n* Professur *f*.

proffer [práf'ûr] *vt* (*remark*) machen; (*apologies*) aussprechen; (*arm*) anbieten.

proficiency [prəfish'ənsē] *n* Fertigkeit *f*, Können *nt*.

proficiency test *n* Leistungstest *m*.

proficient [prəfish'ənt] *a* fähig.

profile [prō'fil] *n* Profil *nt*; (*fig: report*) Kurzbiographie *f*; **to keep a low ~** (*fig*) sich zurückhalten; **to maintain a high ~** sich in den Vordergrund spielen.

profit [práf'it] *n* Gewinn *m*, Profit *m*; **~ and loss statement** Gewinn- und Verlustrechnung *f*; **to sell sth at a ~** etw mit Gewinn verkaufen ♦ *vi* profitieren (*by, from* von), Nutzen *or* Gewinn ziehen (*by, from* aus).

profitability [práfitəbil'ətē] *n* Rentabilität *f*.

profitable [práf'itəbəl] *a* einträglich, rentabel; (*fig: beneficial: scheme*) nützlich, vorteilhaft; (*: meeting, visit*) nützlich.

profitably [práf'itəblē] *ad* rentabel; nützlich.

profit center *n* Bilanzeinheit *f*.

profiteering [práfitēr'ing] *n* Profitmacherei *f*.

profit-making [práf'itmāking] *a* rentabel.

profit margin *n* Gewinnspanne *f*.

profit sharing [práf'it shä'ring] *n* Gewinnbeteiligung *f*.

profligate [práf'ləgit] *a* (*dissolute: behavior, act*) lasterhaft, verworfen; **he's very ~ with his money** (*extravagant*) er geht sehr verschwenderisch mit seinem Geld um ♦ *n* (*person*) Windhund *m*, Leichtfuß *m*.

pro forma invoice [prō fôr'mə in'vois] *n* Pro-forma-Rechnung *f*.

profound [prəfound'] *a* tief; (*knowledge*) profund; (*book, thinker*) tiefschürfend.

profoundly [prəfound'lē] *ad* zutiefst.

profuse [prəfyōōs'] *a* überreich; **to be ~ in** überschwenglich sein bei.

profusely [prəfyōōs'lē] *ad* überschwenglich; (*sweat*) reichlich.

profusion [prəfyōō'zhən] *n* Überfülle *f*, Überfluß *m* (*of* an +*dat*).

progeny [práj'ənē] *n* Nachkommenschaft *f*.

program *n* [prō'grəm] Programm *nt* ♦ *vt* [prō'gram] planen; (*COMPUT*) programmieren.

programer [prō'gramûr] *n* Programmierer(in *f*) *m*.

programing [prō'graming] *n* Programmieren *nt*, Programmierung *f*.

programing language *n* Programmiersprache *f*.

programme [prō'gram] *etc* (*Brit*) = **program** *etc*.

progress *n* [prâg'res] Fortschritt *m*; **to be in** ~ (*meeting, work etc*) im Gange sein; **to make** ~ Fortschritte machen ♦ *vi* [prəgres'] fortschreiten, weitergehen; **as the match** ~**ed** im Laufe des Spiels.

progression [prəgresh'ən] *n* Fortschritt *m*, Progression *f*; (*walking etc*) Fortbewegung *f*.

progressive [prəgres'iv] *a* fortschrittlich, progressiv.

progressively [prəgres'ivlē] *ad* zunehmend.

progress report *n* (*MED*) Fortschrittsbericht *m*; (*of work*) Tätigkeitsbericht *m*.

prohibit [prōhib'it] *vt* verbieten; **to** ~ **sb from doing sth** jdm etw verbieten *or* untersagen; "**smoking** ~**ed**" „Rauchen verboten".

prohibition [prōəbish'ən] *n* Verbot *nt*; (*US HIST*) Alkoholverbot *nt*, Prohibition *f*.

prohibitive [prōhib'ətiv] *a* (*price etc*) unerschwinglich.

project *n* [prâj'ekt] Projekt *nt*; (*SCH, UNIV*) Referat *nt* ♦ [prəjekt'] *vt* vorausplanen; (*PSYCH*) hineinprojizieren; (*film etc*) projizieren; (*personality, voice*) zum Tragen bringen ♦ *vi* (*stick out*) hervorragen, (her)vorstehen.

projectile [prəjek'təl] *n* Geschoß *nt*, Projektil *nt*.

projection [prəjek'shən] *n* Projektion *f*; (*sth prominent*) Vorsprung *m*.

projectionist [prəjek'shənist] *n* (*CINE*) Filmvorführer *m*.

projection room *n* (*CINE*) Vorführraum *m*.

projector [prəjek'tûr] *n* Projektor *m*, Vorführgerät *nt*.

proletarian [prōlitär'ēən] *a* proletarisch, Proletarier- ♦ *n* Proletarier(in *f*) *m*.

proletariat [prōlitär'ēət] *n* Proletariat *nt*.

proliferate [prōlif'ərāt] *vi* sich vermehren.

proliferation [prōlifərā'shən] *n* Vermehrung *f*.

prolific [prōlif'ik] *a* fruchtbar; (*author etc*) produktiv.

prolog(ue) [prō'lôg] *n* Prolog *m*; (*event*) Vorspiel *nt*.

prolong [prəlông'] *vt* verlängern.

prom [prâm] *n abbr* = **promenade, promenade concert** ♦ *n* (*US: college ball*) Studentenball *m*.

promenade [prâmənâd'] *n* Promenade *f*.

promenade concert *n* Promenadenkonzert *nt*, Stehkonzert *nt*.

promenade deck *n* Promenadendeck *nt*.

prominence [prâm'ənəns] *n* (große) Bedeutung *f*, Wichtigkeit *f*; (*sth standing out*) vorspringende(r) Teil *m*.

prominent [prâm'ənənt] *a* bedeutend; (*politician*) prominent; (*easily seen*) herausragend, auffallend; **he is** ~ **in the field of** ... er ist eine führende Persönlichkeit im Bereich ... (+*gen*).

prominently [prâm'ənəntlē] *ad* (*display, set*) deutlich sichtbar; **he figured** ~ **in the case** er spielte in dem Fall eine bedeutende Rolle.

promiscuity [prâmiskyōō'itē] *n* Promiskuität *f*.

promiscuous [prəmis'kyōōəs] *a* lose.

promise [prâm'is] *n* Versprechen *nt*; (*hope*) Aussicht *f* (*of* auf + *acc*); **to show** ~ vielversprechend sein; **to make sb a** ~ jdm ein Versprechen geben; **a writer of** ~ ein vielversprechender Schriftsteller ♦ *vt* versprechen; **to** ~ (**sb**) **to do sth** (jdm) versprechen, etw zu tun; **the** ~**d land** das Gelobte Land ♦ *vi*: **to** ~ **well** vielversprechend sein.

promising [prâm'ising] *a* vielversprechend.

promissory note [prâm'isôrē nōt] *n* Schuldschein *m*.

promontory [prâm'əntôrē] *n* Vorsprung *m*.

promote [prəmōt'] *vt* befördern; (*help on*) fördern, unterstützen; (*product*) werben für; (*put on the market*) auf den Markt bringen; **the team was** ~**d to the second division** (*Brit SOCCER*) die Mannschaft stieg in die zweite Liga auf.

promoter [prəmō'tûr] *n* (*in sport, entertainment*) Veranstalter *m*; (*for charity etc*) Organisator *m*; (*of company, business*) Mitbegründer *m*.

promotion [prəmō'shən] *n* (*in rank*) Beförderung *f*; (*furtherance*) Förderung *f*; (*COMM*) Werbung *f* (*of* für).

prompt [prâmpt] *n* (*COMPUT*) Aufforderungsmeldung *f*, Prompt *m* ♦ *a* prompt, schnell; **to be** ~ **to do sth** etw sofort *or* prompt erledigen; **they're very** ~ (*punctual*) sie sind sehr pünktlich ♦ *ad* (*punctually*) genau; **at two o'clock** ~ punkt zwei Uhr ♦ *vt* veranlassen; (*THEAT*) einsagen (+*dat*), soufflieren (+*dat*).

prompter [prâmp'tûr] *n* (*THEAT*) Souffleur *m*, Souffleuse *f*.

promptly [prâmpt'lē] *ad* sofort.

promptness [prâmpt'nis] *n* Schnelligkeit *f*, Promptheit *f*.

promulgate [prâm'əlgāt] *vt* (öffentlich) bekanntmachen, verkünden; (*beliefs*) verbreiten.

prone [prōn] *a* (*lying*) hingestreckt; **to be** ~ **to sth** zu etw neigen; **she is** ~ **to burst into tears** sie neigt dazu, in Tränen auszubrechen.

prong [prông] *n* Zinke *f*.

pronoun [prō'noun] *n* Pronomen *nt*, Fürwort *nt*.

pronounce [prənouns'] *vt* aussprechen; (*JUR*) verkünden; **they** ~**d him unfit to drive** er wurde für fahruntüchtig erklärt ♦ *vi* (*give an opinion*) sich äußern (*on* zu).

pronounced [prənounst'] *a* ausgesprochen.

pronouncement [prənouns'mənt] *n* Erklärung *f*.

pronto [prän'tō] *ad* (*col*) fix, pronto.

pronunciation [prən unsēā'shən] *n* Aussprache *f*.

proof [proof] *n* Beweis *m*; (*of book*) Korrekturfahne *f*; (*of alcohol*) Alkoholgehalt *m*; (*PHOT*) Probeabzug *m*; **35 per cent** ~ ≈ 40° Vol.; **to put to the** ~ unter Beweis stellen ♦ *a* (*resistant*) sicher; (*alcohol*) prozentig.

proofreader [proof'rēdûr] *n* Korrektor(in *f*) *m*.

prop [präp] *n* Stütze *f* (*also fig*); (*MIN*) Stempel *m*; (*THEAT*) Requisit *nt* ♦ *vt* (*also*: ~ **up**) (ab)stützen.

Prop. *abbr* (*COMM*: = *proprietor*) Inh.

propaganda [präpəgan'də] *n* Propaganda *f*.

propagate [präp'əgāt] *vt* fortpflanzen; (*news*) propagieren, verbreiten.

propagation [präpəgā'shən] *n* Fortpflanzung *f*; (*of knowledge also*) Verbreitung *f*.

propel [prəpel'] *vt* (an)treiben.

propeller [prəpel'ûr] *n* Propeller *m*.

propensity [prəpen'sitē] *n* Tendenz *f*.

proper [präp'ûr] *a* richtig; (*seemly*) schicklich; **to go through the** ~ **channels** (*officially*) den Dienstweg einhalten.

properly [präp'ûrlē] *ad* richtig; ~ **speaking** genau genommen.

proper noun *n* Eigenname *m*.

properties [präp'ûrtēz] *npl* (*THEAT*) Requisiten *pl*.

property [präp'ûrtē] *n* Eigentum *nt*, Besitz *m*, Gut *nt*; (*quality*) Eigenschaft *f*; (*land*) Grundbesitz *m*.

property developer *n* (*Brit*) Häusermakler *m*.

property owner *n* Grundbesitzer *m*.

property tax *n* Vermögenssteuer *f*.

prophecy [präf'isē] *n* Prophezeiung *f*.

prophesy [präf'isī] *vt* prophezeien, vorhersagen.

prophet [präf'it] *n* Prophet *m*.

prophetic [prəfet'ik] *a* prophetisch.

prophylactic [prōfəlak'tik] *n* (*US*) Kondom *m*.

proportion [prəpôr'shən] *n* Verhältnis *nt*, Proportion *f*; (*share*) Teil *m*; **to be in/out of** ~ **to** *or* **with sth** im Verhältnis/in keinem Verhältnis zu etw stehen; **to see sth in** ~ (*fig*) etw objektiv betrachten ♦ *vt* abstimmen (*to* auf +*acc*).

proportional [prəpôr'shənəl] *a* proportional, verhältnismäßig; **to be** ~ **to** entsprechen (+*dat*).

proportionally [prəpôr'shənəlē] *ad* proportional, verhältnismäßig.

proportional representation *n* (*POL*) Verhältnis- *or* Proportionalwahl *f*.

proportional spacing *n* (*on printer*) Proportionaldruck *m*, Proportionalschrift *f*.

proportionate [prəpôr'shənit] *a*, **proportionately** [prəpôr'shənitlē] *ad* verhältnismäßig.

proportioned [prəpôr'shənd] *a* proportioniert.

proposal [prəpō'zəl] *n* Vorschlag *m*, Antrag *m*; (*of marriage*) Heiratsantrag *m*.

propose [prəpōz'] *vt* vorschlagen; (*toast*) ausbringen; **to** ~ **sth/to do** *or* **doing sth** (*have in mind*) etw vorschlagen/vorschlagen, etw zu tun ♦ *vi* (*offer marriage*) einen Heiratsantrag machen.

proposer [prəpō'zûr] *n* (*of motion*) Antragsteller(in *f*) *m*.

proposition [präpəzish'ən] *n* Angebot *nt*; (*MATH*) Lehrsatz *m*; (*statement*) Satz *m*; **to make sb a** ~ jdm ein Angebot machen.

propound [prəpound'] *vt* (*theory*) vorlegen.

proprietary [prəprī'itärē] *a* Eigentums-; (*medicine*) gesetzlich geschützt.

proprietary article *n* (*COMM*) Markenartikel *m*.

proprietary brand *n* Markenname *m*, Markenware *f*.

proprietary goods *npl* Markenartikel *pl*.

proprietor [prəprī'ətûr] *n* Besitzer *m*; (*COMM*) Inhaber *m*.

propulsion [prəpul'shən] *n* Antrieb *m*.

pro rata [prō ra'tə] *a*, *ad* anteilmäßig.

prosaic [prōzā'ik] *a* prosaisch, alltäglich.

Pros. Atty. *abbr* (*US*: = *prosecuting attorney*) St.-Anw.

proscribe [prōskrīb'] *vt* (*forbid*) verbieten.

prose [prōz] *n* Prosa *f*.

prosecute [präs'əkyoot] *vt* (strafrechtlich) verfolgen; **"trespassers will be** ~**d"** „widerrechtliches Betreten wird strafrechtlich verfolgt".

prosecution [präsəkyoo'shən] *n* (*form: carrying out*) Durchführung *f*; (*JUR*) strafrechtliche Verfolgung *f*; (: *party*) Anklage *f* (*for* wegen).

prosecutor [präs'əkyootûr] *n* Vertreter *m* der Anklage.

prospect *n* [präs'pekt] Aussicht *f*; **we are faced with the** ~ **of nuclear war** wir müssen mit der Möglichkeit eines Atomkrieges rechnen; **there is every** ~ **of an early victory** es besteht die Möglichkeit eines baldigen Sieges ♦ *vi* [präspekt'] suchen (*for* nach).

prospecting [präs'pekting] *n* (*for minerals*) Suche *f*.

prospective [prəspek'tiv] *a* möglich; (*legislation, son-in-law*) zukünftig; ~ **buyer** interessierte(r) Kunde *m*.

prospector [präs'pektûr] *n* Goldsucher *m*.

prospectus [prəspek'təs] *n* (Werbe)prospekt *m*.

prosper [präs'pûr] *vi* blühen, gedeihen; (*person*) erfolgreich sein.

prosperity [präspär'itē] *n* Wohlstand *m*.

prosperous [präs'pûrəs] *a* wohlhabend, reich; (*business*) gutgehend, blühend.

prostate [präs'tāt] *n* (*also*: ~ **gland**) Prostata *f*, Vorsteherdrüse *f*.

prostitute [präs'titoot] *n* Prostituierte *f*; **male** ~ männliche(r) Prostituierte(r) *m*, Strichjunge *m* (*col*).

prostitution [prästitoo'shən] *n* (*lit, fig*) Prostitution *f*; (*of one's talents, honor etc*) Verkaufen *nt.*

prostrate [prås'trāt] *a* ausgestreckt (liegend); ~ **with grief/exhaustion** von Schmerz/ Erschöpfung übermannt ♦ *vt*: **to ~ o.s. before sb** sich vor jdm niederwerfen; **to ~ o.s. on the floor** sich zu Boden werfen.

protagonist [prōtag'ənist] *n* Hauptperson *f*, Held *m*.

protect [prətekt'] *vt* (be)schützen.

protection [prətek'shən] *n* Schutz *m*; **to be under sb's ~** unter jds Schutz (*dat*) stehen.

protectionism [prətek'shənizəm] *n* Protektionismus *m*.

protection racket *n* organisierte(s) Erpresserunwesen *nt.*

protective [prətek'tiv] *a* Schutz-, (be)schützend.

protective custody *n* (*JUR*) Schutzhaft *f*.

protector [prətek'tûr] *n* Beschützer *m*.

protégé [prō'təzhā] *n* Schützling *m*.

protein [prō'tēn] *n* Protein *nt*, Eiweiß *nt.*

pro tem [prō tem] *abbr* (= *pro tempore*: *for the time being*) vorl.

protest *n* [prō'test] Protest *m* ♦ [prōtest'] *vi* protestieren (*against, about* gegen) ♦ *vt* (*innocence, loyalty*) beteuern.

Protestant [prât'istənt] *a* protestantisch ♦ *n* Protestant(in *f*) *m.*

protester [prōtes'tûr] *n* Protestierende(r) *mf*; (*in demonstration*) Demonstrant(in *f*) *m.*

protest march *n* Protestmarsch *m.*

protocol [prō'təkól] *n* Protokoll *nt.*

prototype [prō'tətīp] *n* Prototyp *m.*

protracted [prōtrak'tid] *a* sich hinziehend.

protractor [prōtrak'tûr] *n* Winkelmesser *m.*

protrude [prōtrōod'] *vi* (her)vorstehen.

protuberance [prōtōo'bûrəns] *n* Auswuchs *m.*

protuberant [prōtōo'bûrənt] *a* (her)vorstehend.

proud [proud] *a* stolz (*of* auf +*acc*); **to be ~ to do sth** stolz darauf sein, etw zu tun ♦ *ad*: **to do sb/o.s. ~** jdn/sich verwöhnen.

proudly [proud'lē] *ad* stolz.

prove [prōov] *vt* beweisen ♦ *vi* sich herausstellen, sich zeigen; **he was ~d right in the end** er hat schließlich doch recht behalten.

proverb [prâv'ûrb] *n* Sprichwort *nt.*

proverbial [prəvûr'bēəl] *a*, **proverbially** [prəvûr'bēəlē] *ad* sprichwörtlich.

provide [prəvīd'] *vt* versehen; (*supply*) besorgen; (*person*) versorgen; **to be ~d with sth** (*food, clothing etc*) mit etw versorgt sein; (*equipped*) mit etw versehen *or* ausgestattet sein; **blankets will be ~d** Decken werden gestellt.

provide for *vt fus* sorgen für, sich kümmern um; (*emergency*) Vorkehrungen treffen für.

provided [prəvī'did] *cj*: ~ **(that)** vorausgesetzt (daß).

Providence [prâv'idəns] *n* die Vorsehung.

providing [prəvī'ding] *cj* = **provided.**

province [prâv'ins] *n* Provinz *f*; (*division of work*) Bereich *m*; **the ~s** die Provinz *sing.*

provincial [prəvin'chəl] *a* provinziell, Provinz- ♦ *n* Provinzler(in *f*) *m.*

provision [prəvizh'ən] *n* Vorkehrung *f*, Maßnahme *f*; (*condition*) Bestimmung *f*; **to make ~ for one's family/future** für seine Familie/für die Zukunft Vorsorge *or* Vorkehrungen treffen; *see also* **provisions.**

provisional [prəvizh'ənəl] *a* vorläufig, provisorisch ♦ *n*: **P~** (*col: Irish POL*) Mitglied *m* der Provisional IRA.

provisional licence *n* (*Brit AUT*) vorläufige Fahrerlaubnis *f* für Fahrschüler.

provisions [prəvizh'ənz] *npl* (*food*) Vorräte *pl*, Proviant *m.*

proviso [prəvī'zō] *n* Vorbehalt *m*, Bedingung *f*; **with the ~ that ...** unter (dem) Vorbehalt *or* vorausgesetzt, daß ...

Provo [prō'vō] *n* *abbr* (*Irish POL*) = **Provisional.**

provocation [prâvəkā'shən] *n* Provokation *f*, Herausforderung *f.*

provocative [prəvâk'ətiv] *a* provokativ, herausfordernd.

provoke [prəvōk'] *vt* provozieren; (*cause*) hervorrufen; **to ~ sb to do** *or* **into doing sth** jdn dazu bringen, daß er etw tut; (*taunt*) jdn dazu treiben *or* so provozieren, daß er etw tut.

provoking [prəvōk'ing] *a* provozierend, ärgerlich.

provost [prâv'əst] *n* (*UNIV*) Dekan *m*; (*Scot*) Bürgermeister *m.*

prow [prou] *n* Bug *m.*

prowess [prou'is] *n* überragende(s) Können *nt*; (*valor*) Tapferkeit *f*; **his ~ as a football player** (*skill*) sein (spielerisches) Können als Fußballspieler.

prowl [proul] *vt* (*streets*) durchstreifen ♦ *vi* herumstreichen; (*animal*) schleichen ♦ *n*: **on the ~** umherstreifend.

prowler [prou'lûr] *n* Eindringling *m.*

proximity [prâksim'itē] *n* Nähe *f.*

proxy [prâk'sē] *n* (Stell)vertreter *m*, Bevollmächtigte(r) *m*; (*document*) Vollmacht *f*; **by ~** durch einen Stellvertreter.

prude [prōod] *n*: **to be a ~** prüde sein.

prudence [prōo'dəns] *n* Klugheit *f*, Umsicht *f.*

prudent [prōo'dənt] *a*, **prudently** [prōo'dəntlē] *ad* klug, umsichtig.

prudish [prōo'dish] *a* prüde.

prudishness [prōo'dishnis] *n* Prüderie *f.*

prune [prōon] *n* Backpflaume *f* ♦ *vt* ausputzen; (*fig*) zurechtstutzen.

pruning shears [prōon'ing shirz] *npl* Gartenschere *f.*

pry [prī] *vi* seine Nase stecken (*into* in +*acc*).

PS *n abbr* (= *postscript*) PS *nt.*

psalm [sâm] *n* Psalm *m.*

PSAT *n abbr* (*US:* = *Preliminary Scholastic Aptitude Test*) Eignungstest.

pseudo [sōo'dō] *a* Pseudo-; (*false*) falsch, unecht.

pseudonym [sōo'dənim] *n* Pseudonym *nt*, Deckname *m.*

PST *n abbr* (*US*) = *Pacific Standard Time*.
psyche [sī'kē] *n* Psyche *f*.
psychiatric [sīkēat'rik] *a* psychiatrisch.
psychiatrist [sikī'ətrist] *n* Psychiater(in *f*) *m*.
psychiatry [sikī'ətrē] *n* Psychiatrie *f*.
psychic [sī'kik] *a* übersinnlich; (*person*) paranormal begabt; **you must be** ~ du kannst wohl hellsehen.
psychoanalyse, psychoanalyze [sīkōan'əlīz] *vt* psychoanalytisch behandeln.
psychoanalysis [sīkōənal'isis] *n, pl* **psychoanalyses** [sīkōənal'isēz] Psychoanalyse *f*.
psychoanalyst [sīkōan'əlist] *n* Psychoanalytiker(in *f*) *m*.
psychological [sīkəlåj'ikəl] *a*, **psychologically** [sīkəlåj'ikəlē] *ad* psychologisch.
psychologist [sīkâl'əjist] *n* Psychologe *m*, Psychologin *f*.
psychology [sīkâl'əjē] *n* Psychologie *f*.
psychopath [sī'kəpath] *n* Psychopath(in *f*) *m*.
psychosis [sīkō'sis] *n, pl* **psychoses** [sīkō'sēz] Psychose *f*.
psychosomatic [sīkōsōmat'ik] *a* psychosomatisch.
psychotherapy [sīkōthär'əpē] *n* Psychotherapie *f*.
psychotic [sīkât'ik] *a* psychotisch ♦ *n* Psychotiker(in *f*) *m*.
pt *abbr* = **point; pint.**
PT *n abbr* (= *physical training*) Turnen *nt*.
PTA *n abbr* (= *Parent-Teacher Association*) *Eltern-Lehrer-Verband*.
Pte. *abbr* (*Brit MIL*) = *private*.
PTO *abbr* (= *please turn over*) b.w.
PTV *n abbr* (*US*) = *pay television*; *public television*.
pub [pub] *n* (*Brit*: = *public house*) Wirtschaft *f*, Kneipe *f*.
puberty [pyōō'bûrtē] *n* Pubertät *f*.
pubic [pyōō'bik] *a* Scham-.
public [pub'lik] *a* öffentlich; **to make sth** ~ etw bekanntgeben, etw publik machen; (*officially*) etw öffentlich bekanntmachen; **to be** ~ **knowledge** ein öffentliches Geheimnis sein; **to go** ~ (*COMM*) in eine Aktiengesellschaft umgewandelt werden; (*FIN*) an der Börse notiert werden ♦ *n* (*also:* **general** ~) Öffentlichkeit *f*; **in** ~ in der Öffentlichkeit.
public address system *n* öffentliche Lautsprecheranlage *f*.
publican [pub'likən] *n* (*Brit*) Gastwirt(in *f*) *m*.
publication [publikā'shən] *n* Publikation *f*, Veröffentlichung *f*.
public company *n* (*Brit*) Aktiengesellschaft *f*.
public convenience *n* öffentliche Toiletten *pl*.
public holiday *n* (*Brit*) gesetzliche(r) Feiertag *m*.
public house *n* (*Brit*) Lokal *nt*, Kneipe *f*.
public housing unit *n* (*US*) Haus *nt* des sozialen Wohnungsbaus.

publicity [publis'ətē] *n* Publicity *f*, Werbung *f*.
publicize [pub'ləsīz] *vt* bekanntmachen, an die Öffentlichkeit bringen.
public limited company *n* (*Brit*) Aktiengesellschaft *f*.
publicly [pub'liklē] *ad* in aller Öffentlichkeit.
public opinion *n* öffentliche Meinung *f*.
public ownership *n* Staatseigentum *nt*; **to be taken into** ~ in öffentlichen Besitz genommen werden.
Public Prosecutor *n* Staatsanwalt *m*.
public relations *npl* Public Relations *pl*.
public relations officer *n* Pressesprecher(in *f*) *m*.
public school *n* (*US*) staatliche Schule *f*; (*Brit*) Privatschule *f*, Internatsschule *f*.
public sector *n* öffentliche(r) Sektor *m*.
public service vehicle *n* öffentliche(s) Verkehrsmittel *nt*.
public-spirited [pub'likspir'itid] *a* mit Gemeinschaftssinn; **to be** ~ Gemeinschaftssinn haben.
public transportation, (*Brit*) **public transport** *n* öffentliche Verkehrsmittel *pl*.
public utility *n* öffentliche(r) Versorgungsbetrieb *m*.
public works *npl* öffentliche Arbeiten *pl*.
publish [pub'lish] *vt* veröffentlichen, publizieren; (*event*) bekanntgeben.
publisher [pub'lishûr] *n* Verleger *m*; (*firm*) Verlag *m*.
publishing [pub'lishing] *n* Herausgabe *f*, Verlegen *nt*; (*business*) Verlagswesen *nt*.
publishing company *n* Verlagshaus *nt*.
puce [pyōōs] *a* violettbraun.
puck [puk] *n* Puck *m*, Scheibe *f*.
pucker [puk'ûr] *vt* (*face*) verziehen; (*lips*) kräuseln.
pudding [pŏōd'ing] *n* Pudding *m*.
puddle [pud'əl] *n* Pfütze *f*.
pudgy [puj'ē] *a* (*US*) pummelig.
puerile [pyōō'ûrəl] *a* kindisch.
Puerto Rico [pwär'tō rē'kō] *n* Puerto Rico *nt*.
puff [puf] *n* (*of wind etc*) Stoß *m*; (*cosmetic*) Puderquaste *f* ♦ *vt* blasen, pusten; (*pipe*) paffen; (*also:* ~ **out:** *sails*) blähen ♦ *vi* keuchen, schnaufen; (*smoke a cigarette*) paffen.
puffed [puft] *a* (*col: out of breath*) außer Puste.
puffin [puf'in] *n* Papageitaucher *m*.
puff paste, (*Brit*) **puff pastry** *n* Blätterteig *m*.
puffy [puf'ē] *a* aufgedunsen.
pull [pŏōl] *n* Ruck *m*; (*at pipe*) Zug *m*; (*tug*) Ziehen *nt*; (*influence*) Beziehung *f* ♦ *vt* ziehen; (*trigger*) abdrücken; (*strain: muscle, tendon*) zerren; **to** ~ **a face** ein Gesicht schneiden; **to** ~ **sb's leg** jdn auf den Arm nehmen; **to** ~ **strings** Beziehungen spielen lassen; **to** ~ **to pieces** (*lit*) in Stücke reißen; (*fig*) verreißen; **to** ~ **one's weight** sich in die Riemen legen; **to** ~ **o.s. together** sich zusammenreißen ♦ *vi* ziehen.
pull apart *vt* (*break*) zerreißen; (*disman-*

tle) auseinandernehmen; (*fighters*) trennen.

pull around *vt* (*handle roughly: object*) herumzerren; (: *person*) herumzerren an (+*dat*).

pull down *vt* (*house*) abreißen.

pull in *vi* hineinfahren; (*Brit: stop*) anhalten; (*RAIL*) einfahren.

pull off *vt* (*violently*) abreißen; (*clothes, shoes*) abziehen; (*cover*) abnehmen; (*col: succeed in*) schaffen; (: *deal*) zuwege bringen.

pull out *vi* (*car*) herausfahren; (*fig: of deal etc*) aussteigen ♦ *vt* herausziehen.

pull over *vt* hinüber-/herüberziehen (*über* +*acc*); (*topple*) umreißen ♦ *vi* (*AUT*) an die Seite fahren.

pull round, pull through *vi* durchkommen.

pull up *vi* (*stop*) anhalten ♦ *vt* hochziehen; (*uproot*) herausreißen.

pulley [pŏŏl'ē] *n* Rolle *f*, Flaschenzug *m*.

Pullman [pŏŏl'mən] *n* (*US*) Schlafwagen *m*.

pullout [pŏŏl'out] *n* (*supplement*) heraustrennbare(r) Teil *m*; (*withdrawal*) Abzug *m* ♦ *a* (*table, seat*) Auszieh-.

pullover [pŏŏl'ōvûr] *n* Pullover *m*.

pulp [pulp] *n* Brei *m*; (*of fruit*) Fruchtfleisch *nt*; (*also:* ~ **magazine**) Schundmagazin *nt*; **to reduce sth to** ~ etw in Brei auflösen.

pulpit [pŏŏl'pit] *n* Kanzel *f*.

pulsate [pul'sāt] *vi* pulsieren.

pulse [puls] *n* Puls *m*; (*COOK*) Hülsenfrucht *f*; **to feel** *or* **take sb's** ~ jdm den Puls fühlen.

pulverize [pul'vərīz] *vt* pulverisieren, in kleine Stücke zerlegen (*also fig*).

puma [pyŏŏ'mə] *n* Puma *m*.

pumice stone [pum'is stōn] *n* Bimsstein *m*.

pummel [pum'əl] *vt* mit den Fäusten bearbeiten.

pump [pump] *n* Pumpe *f*; (*shoe*) leichte(r) (Tanz)schuh *m* ♦ *vt* pumpen; **to** ~ **sb for information** jdn aushorchen.

pump up *vt* (*inflate*) aufpumpen.

pumpkin [pump'kin] *n* Kürbis *m*.

pun [pun] *n* Wortspiel *nt*.

punch [punch] *n* (*tool*) Locher *m*; (*blow*) (Faust)schlag *m*; (*drink*) Punsch *m*, Bowle *f* ♦ *vt* (*hole*) lochen; (*strike*) schlagen, boxen.

punch in *vi* (*US*) (den Arbeitsbeginn) stempeln *or* stechen.

punch out *vi* (*US*) (das Arbeitsende) stempeln *or* stechen.

punch-drunk [punch'drungk] *a* (*Brit*) benommen.

punch(ed) card [punch(t) kârd] *n* Lochkarte *f*.

punch line *n* Pointe *f*.

punch-up [punch'up] *n* (*Brit col*) Keilerei *f*, Schlägerei *f*.

punctual [pungk'chŏŏəl] *a* pünktlich.

punctuality [pungkchŏŏal'itē] *n* Pünktlichkeit *f*.

punctually [pungk'chŏŏəlē] *ad*: **it will start** ~ **at 6** es fängt pünktlich um 6 an.

punctuate [pungk'chŏŏāt] *vt* mit Satzzeichen versehen, interpunktieren; (*fig*) unterbrechen.

punctuation [pungkchŏŏā'shən] *n* Zeichensetzung *f*, Interpunktion *f*.

punctuation mark *n* Satzzeichen *nt*.

puncture [pungk'chûr] *n* Loch *nt*; (*Brit AUT*) Reifenpanne *f* ♦ *vt* durchbohren.

pundit [pun'dit] *n* Gelehrte(r) *m*.

pungent [pun'jənt] *a* scharf.

punish [pun'ish] *vt* bestrafen; (*in boxing etc*) übel zurichten.

punishable [pun'ishəbəl] *a* strafbar.

punishing [pun'ishing] *n*: **to take a** ~ (*team etc*) vorgeführt werden (*col*) ♦ *a* (*fig: exhausting*) hart, strapazierend.

punishment [pun'ishmənt] *n* Strafe *f*; (*action*) Bestrafung *f*; **to take a lot of** ~ (*fig col: boxer*) vorgeführt werden; (: *car*) stark strapaziert werden.

punitive [pyŏŏ'nətiv] *a* strafend.

punk [pungk] *n* (*person*) Punker *m*; (*music*) Punk *m*; (*US col: hoodlum*) Ganove *m*.

punt [punt] *n* Stechkahn *m*.

puny [pyŏŏ'nē] *a* kümmerlich.

pup [pup] *n* = **puppy**.

pupil [pyŏŏ'pəl] *n* Schüler(in *f*) *m*; (*in eye*) Pupille *f*.

puppet [pup'it] *n* Puppe *f*, Marionette *f*.

puppet government *n* Marionettenregierung *f*.

puppy [pup'ē] *n* junge(r) Hund *m*.

purchase [pûr'chis] *n* Kauf *m*, Anschaffung *f*; (*grip*) Halt *m* ♦ *vt* kaufen, erwerben.

purchase order *n* Kunden- *or* Kaufauftrag *m*, Bestellung *f*.

purchase price *n* Kaufpreis *m*.

purchaser [pûr'chisûr] *n* Käufer(in *f*) *m*.

purchasing power [pûr'chising pouûr] *n* Kaufkraft *f*.

pure [pyŏŏr] *a* pur, rein (*also fig*); **a** ~ **wool jumper** ein Pullover *or* Pulli aus reiner Wolle; **it's laziness** ~ **and simple** es ist reine Faulheit.

purebred [pyŏŏr'bred'] *a* reinrassig.

purée [pyŏŏrā'] *n* Püree *nt*.

purely [pyŏŏr'lē] *ad* rein; (*only*) nur.

purgatory [pûr'gətôrē] *n* Fegefeuer *nt*.

purge [pûrj] *n* Säuberung *f* (*also POL*); (*medicine*) Abführmittel *nt* ♦ *vt* reinigen; (*body*) entschlacken.

purification [pyŏŏrəfəkā'shən] *n* Reinigung *f*.

purify [pyŏŏr'əfī] *vt* reinigen.

purist [pyŏŏr'ist] *n* Purist(in *f*) *m*.

puritan [pyŏŏr'itən] *n* Puritaner(in *f*) *m*.

puritanical [pyŏŏritan'ikəl] *a* puritanisch.

purity [pyŏŏr'itē] *n* Reinheit *f*.

purl [pûrl] *n* linke Masche *f* ♦ *vt* links stricken.

purloin [pûrloin'] *vt* (*form*) stehlen, entwenden.

purple [pûr'pəl] *a* violett; (*face*) dunkelrot ♦

n Violett *nt*.

purpose [pûr'pəs] *n* (*goal*) Zweck *m*; (*intention*) Absicht *f*; **on ~** absichtlich; **to no ~** ohne Erfolg; **for teaching** ~s zu Unterrichtszwecken *pl*; **for the** ~s **of this meeting** zum Zweck dieser Konferenz.

purpose-built [pûr'pəsbilt'] *a* (*Brit*) spezial angefertigt, Spezial-.

purposeful [pûr'pəsfəl] *a* zielbewußt, entschlossen.

purposely [pûr'pəslē] *ad* absichtlich.

purr [pûr] *n* Schnurren *nt* ♦ *vi* schnurren.

purse [pûrs] *n* (*US*) Handtasche *f*; (*Brit*) Portemonnaie *nt*, Geldbeutel *m* ♦ *vt* (*lips*) zusammenpressen, schürzen.

purser [pûr'sûr] *n* Zahlmeister *m*.

purse snatcher [pûrs' snach'ûr] *n* (*US*) Taschendieb *m*.

pursue [pûrsōō'] *vt* verfolgen; (*pleasures*) nachjagen (+*dat*); (*inquiry, matter*) durchführen; (*study*) nachgehen (+*dat*).

pursuer [pûrsōō'ûr] *n* Verfolger *m*.

pursuit [pûrsōōt'] *n* Jagd *f* (*of* nach), Verfolgung *f*; (*occupation*) Beschäftigung *f*; **to go in (the) ~ of sth** sich auf die Jagd nach etw machen.

purveyor [pûrvā'ûr] *n* Lieferant *m*.

pus [pus] *n* Eiter *m*.

push [pōosh] *n* Stoß *m*, Schub *m*; (*energy*) Schwung *m*; (*MIL*) Vorstoß *m*; **at a ~** (*Brit col*) notfalls, im Notfall ♦ *vt* stoßen, schieben; (*button*) drücken; (*advance: idea*) durchsetzen; **to ~ a door open/shut** eine Tür auf-/zustoßen; **she is** ~ing **50** (*col*) sie geht auf die 50 zu; **to be** ~ed **for time/ money** mit der Zeit/mit Geld knapp dran sein ♦ *vi* stoßen, schieben; "*~*" (*on door*) „drücken"; (*on bell*) „klingeln".

push aside *vt* beiseiteschieben.

push for *vt fus* (*better pay, conditions*) drängen auf.

push in *vt* hineinschieben ♦ *vi* sich hineindrängen *or* -drängeln (*col*).

push off *vt* hinunterschieben; (*lid, cap*) wegdrücken ♦ *vi* (*col*) abschieben.

push on *vt* (*top, lid*) festdrücken ♦ *vi* weitermachen.

push through *vt* durchdrücken; (*policy*) durchsetzen.

push up *vt* (*lit*) hinaufschieben; (*window*) hochschieben; (*total*) erhöhen; (*prices*) hochtreiben.

push button *n* Drucktaste *f* ♦ *a* mit Drucktaste.

pushchair [pōosh'chär] *n* (*Brit*) (Kinder)sportwagen *m*.

pusher [pōosh'ûr] *n* (*also:* **drug ~**) Pusher(in *f*) *m*.

pushover [pōosh'ōvûr] *n* (*col*) Kinderspiel *nt*.

push-up [pōosh'up] *n* Liegestütz *m*.

pushy [pōosh'ē] *a* (*col*) aufdringlich.

pussycat [pōos'ēkat] *n* Mieze(katze) *f*.

put [pōot] *vt irreg, pt, pp* **put** setzen, stellen, legen; (*express*) ausdrücken, sagen; (*write*)

schreiben; **to ~ money into a company** Geld in einer Firma anlegen *or* in eine Firma stecken (*col*); **to ~ money on a horse** auf ein Pferd setzen; **to ~ sb to a lot of trouble** jdm viel Arbeit *or* Umstände machen; **to ~ a lot of time into sth** viel Zeit in etw (*acc*) stecken; **how shall I ~ it?** wie soll ich (es) sagen?; **to ~ sb in a good/bad mood** jdn fröhlich/mißmutig stimmen; **we ~ the children to bed** wir haben die Kinder ins Bett gebracht; **to stay ~** liegen- *or* stehen- *or* hängen- *etc* bleiben.

put about *vi* (*NAUT: turn back*) wenden ♦ *vt* (*spread*) verbreiten.

put across *vt* (*explain*) erklären.

put aside *vt* (*lay down: book etc*) beiseite legen; (*save*) beiseite *or* auf die Seite legen, zurücklegen; (*in shop*) zurücklegen.

put away *vt* weglegen; (*store*) beiseitelegen.

put back *vt* zurückstellen *or* -legen; (*set back: watch, clock*) zurückstellen; **this will ~ us back 10 years** das wirft uns 10 Jahre zurück.

put by *vt* zurücklegen, sparen.

put down *vt* hinstellen *or* -legen; (*stop*) niederschlagen; (*animal*) einschläfern; (*in writing*) niederschreiben; **~ me down for 15** für mich kannst du 15 eintragen.

put forward *vt* (*idea*) vorbringen; (*clock*) vorstellen.

put in *vt* hineinsetzen, hineinstellen, hineinlegen; (*insert*) einfügen; (*enter: application*) einreichen; (*install*) einbauen.

put in for *vt fus* (*job*) sich bewerben um; (*promotion*) beantragen.

put off *vt* verlegen, verschieben; (*discourage*) abbringen von; **it ~ me off smoking** das hat mir die Lust am Rauchen verdorben.

put on *vt* (*clothes etc*) anziehen; (*light etc*) anschalten, anmachen; (*brake*) anziehen; (*assume: accent, manner*) annehmen; (*: airs*) aufsetzen; (*col: kid: esp US*) verkohlen; (*play etc*) aufführen; (*concert, exhibition etc*) veranstalten; (*extra bus, train etc*) einsetzen; **to ~ sb on to a plumber/ dentist** *etc* (*inform about*) jdm einen Installateur/Zahnarzt *etc* empfehlen.

put out *vt* (*hand etc*) (her)ausstrecken; (*news, rumor*) verbreiten; (*light etc*) ausschalten, ausmachen; (*Brit: dislocate: shoulder, knee*) ausrenken; (*: back*) verrenken ♦ *vi* (*NAUT*): **to ~ out to sea** in See stechen; **to ~ out from Boston** von Boston auslaufen.

put through *vt* (*call*) durchstellen (*to* zu); **~ me through to Ms Blair** verbinden Sie mich bitte mit Frau Blair.

put together *vt* (*put in same room, case etc*) zusammentun; (*assemble: furniture*) zusammensetzen, zusammenbauen; (*meal*) auf die Beine stellen; (*seat together*) zusammensetzen.

put up *vt* (*tent*) aufstellen; (*building*) errichten; (*price*) erhöhen; (*person*) unterbringen; **to ~ sth up for sale** etw zum Verkauf anbieten; **to ~ sb up to doing sth** jdn zu etw anstiften.

put upon *vt fus*: **to be ~ upon** (*imposed on*) ausgenutzt werden.

put up with sich abfinden mit; **I won't ~ up with it** das laß ich mir nicht gefallen.

putrid [pyōō'trid] *a* faul.

putsch [pōōch] *n* Putsch *m*.

putt [put] *vt* (*GOLF*) putten, einlochen ♦ *n* (*GOLF*) Putten *nt*, leichte(r) Schlag *m*.

putter [put'ûr] *n* Putter *m* ♦ *vi* herumhantieren, herumwursteln; **to ~ around the house** im Haus herumwerkeln.

putting green [put'ing grēn] *n* Rasenfläche *f* zum Putten.

putty [put'ē] *n* Kitt *m*; (*fig*) Wachs *nt*.

put-up [pōōt'up] *a*: **~ job** abgekartete(s) Spiel *nt*.

puzzle [puz'əl] *n* Rätsel *nt*; (*toy*) Geduldspiel *nt* ♦ *vt* verwirren; **to be ~d about sth** sich über etw im unklaren sein ♦ *vi*: **to ~ over sth** sich (*dat*) über etw den Kopf zerbrechen.

puzzling [puz'ling] *a* rätselhaft; (*question, attitude, set of instructions*) verwirrend.

PVC *n abbr* (= *polyvinyl chloride*) PVC *nt*.

Pvt. *abbr* (*US MIL*: = *private*) Gefr.

pw *abbr* (= *per week*) wö.

PW *n abbr* (*US*) = **prisoner of war**.

PX *n abbr* (*US MIL*: = *post exchange*) Laden oder Kantine für Armeeangehörige.

pygmy [pig'mē] *n* Pygmäe *m*; (*fig*) Zwerg *m*.

pyjamas [pəjâm'əz] *npl* (*Brit*) = **pajamas**.

pylon [pī'lân] *n* Mast *m*.

pyramid [pir'əmid] *n* Pyramide *f*.

Pyrenean [pirənē'ən] *a* pyrenäisch.

Pyrenees [pir'ənēz] *npl*: **the ~** die Pyrenäen *pl*.

python [pī'thân] *n* Pythonschlange *f*.

Q

Q, q [kyōō] *n* (*letter*) Q *nt*, q *nt*; **Q for Queen** ≈ Q wie Quelle.

Qatar [kə'târ] *n* Katar *nt*.

QC *n abbr* (= *Queen's Counsel*) Staatsanwalt, der die Krone vertritt.

QED *n abbr* (*MATH*: = *quod erat demonstrandum*) q.e.d.

QM *n abbr* = **quartermaster**.

q.t. *n abbr* (*col*: = *quiet*): **on the ~** heimlich.

qty *abbr* (= *quantity*) M.

quack [kwak] *n* Quacken *nt*; (*hum: doctor*)

Medizinmann *m*; (*pej*) Kurpfuscher *m* ♦ *vi* quaken.

quad [kwâd] *n abbr* = **quadrangle**, **quadruple**, **quadruplet**.

quadrangle [kwâd'ranggəl] *n* (*court*) Hof *m*; (*MATH*) Viereck *nt*.

quadruped [kwâd'rōōped] *n* Vierfüßler *m*.

quadruple [kwâdrōō'pəl] *a* vierfach ♦ *vi* sich vervierfachen ♦ *vt* vervierfachen.

quadruplet [kwâdru'plit] *n* Vierling *m*.

quagmire [kwag'mīûr] *n* Morast *m*.

quail [kwāl] *vi* vor Angst zittern.

quaint [kwānt] *a* (*col*) kurios; (*picturesque*) malerisch.

quaintly [kwānt'lē] *ad* kurios.

quaintness [kwānt'nis] *n* Kuriosität *f*.

quake [kwāk] *vi* beben, zittern.

Quaker [kwā'kûr] *n* Quäker(in *f*) *m*.

qualification [kwâləfəkā'shən] *n* Qualifikation *f*; (*sth which limits*) Einschränkung *f*; **what are your ~s?** was für Qualifikationen haben Sie?

qualified [kwâl'əfid] *a* (*competent*) qualifiziert; (*limited*) bedingt; **to be ~ for sth/to do sth** qualifiziert sein für etw/qualifiziert sein, etw zu tun; **he's not ~ for the job** ihm fehlt die Qualifikation für die Stelle; **it was a ~ success** es war kein voller Erfolg.

qualify [kwâl'əfi] *vt* (*prepare, equip*) befähigen; (*limit*) einschränken ♦ *vi* sich qualifizieren; **to ~ as an engineer** die Ingenieurausbildung abschließen.

qualifying exam [kwâl'əfīing igzam'] *n* Auswahlprüfung *f*.

qualitative [kwâl'itātiv] *a* qualitativ.

quality [kwâl'itē] *n* Qualität *f*; (*characteristic*) Eigenschaft *f* ♦ *a* Qualitäts-; **of good/ poor ~** von guter/schlechter Qualität, qualitativ gut/schlecht.

quality control *n* Qualitätskontrolle *f*.

qualm [kwâm] *n* Bedenken *nt*, Zweifel *m*; **without the slightest ~** ohne die geringsten Skrupel *or* Bedenken.

quandary [kwân'drē] *n* Verlegenheit *f*; **to be in a ~** in Verlegenheit sein.

quantitative [kwân'titātiv] *a* quantitativ.

quantity [kwân'titē] *n* Menge *f*, Quantität *f*; **in ~** in großen Mengen.

quarantine [kwôr'əntēn] *n* Quarantäne *f*.

quarrel [kwôr'əl] *n* Streit *m*; **to have a ~ with sb** (einen) Streit mit jdm haben, sich mit jdm streiten ♦ *vi* sich streiten; **I can't ~ with that** ich habe nichts dagegen einzuwenden.

quarrelsome [kwôr'əlsəm] *a* streitsüchtig.

quarry [kwôr'ē] *n* Steinbruch *m*; (*animal*) Wild *nt*; (*fig*) Opfer *nt*.

quart [kwôrt] *n* Quart *nt*.

quarter [kwôr'tûr] *n* Viertel *nt*; (*of year*) Quartal *nt*, Vierteljahr *nt*; (*US, Canada: 25 cents*) 25-Centstück *nt* ♦ *vt* (*divide*) vierteln, in Viertel teilen; (*MIL*) einquartieren; **to pay by the ~** vierteljährlich bezahlen; **from all ~s** aus allen Himmelsrichtungen; **at**

close ~**s** aus unmittelbarer Nähe; ~ **of an hour** Viertelstunde *f*; **it's a** ~ **of 3** (*US*), **it's a** ~ **to 3** (*Brit*) es ist Viertel vor drei; **it's a** ~ **after 3**, **it's a** ~ **past 3** (*Brit*) es ist Viertel nach drei; *see also* **quarters**.

quarter-deck [kwôr'tûrdek] *n* Achterdeck *nt*.

quarter final *n* Viertelfinale *nt*.

quarterly [kwôr'tûrlē] *a* vierteljährlich ♦ *n* (*magazine*) Vierteljahresschrift *f*.

quartermaster [kwôr'tûrmastûr] *n* Quartiermeister *m*.

quarter note *n* (*US*) Viertelnote *f*.

quarters [kwôr'tûrz] *npl* (*esp MIL*) Quartier *nt*.

quartet(te) [kwôrtet'] *n* Quartett *nt*.

quarto [kwôr'tō] *n* (*TYP*) Quart(format) *nt* ♦ *a attr* (*paper, volume*) in Quart.

quartz [kwôrts] *n* Quarz *m*.

quash [kwâsh] *vt* (*verdict*) aufheben.

quasi [kwā'zī] *ad* quasi.

quaver [kwā'vûr] *n* (*Brit MUS*) Achtelnote *f* ♦ *vi* (*tremble*) zittern.

quay [kē] *n* Kai *m*.

Que. *abbr* (*Canada*) = *Quebec*.

queasiness [kwē'zēnis] *n* Übelkeit *f*.

queasy [kwē'zē] *a* übel; **he feels** ~ ihm ist übel.

Quebec [kwibek'] *n* Quebec *nt*.

queen [kwēn] *n* Königin *f*.

queen mother *n* Königinmutter *f*.

queer [kwēr] *a* seltsam, sonderbar, kurios; ~ **fellow** komische(r) Kauz *m* ♦ *n* (*pej: homosexual*) Schwule(r) *m*.

quell [kwel] *vt* unterdrücken.

quench [kwench] *vt* (*thirst*) löschen, stillen; (*extinguish*) löschen.

querulous [kwär'ələs] *a* nörglerisch.

query [kwiûr'ē] *n* (*question*) (An)frage *f*; (*question mark*) Fragezeichen *nt* ♦ *vt* in Zweifel ziehen, in Frage stellen; (*disagree with, dispute*) bezweifeln.

quest [kwest] *n* Suche *f*.

question [kwes'chən] *n* Frage *f* ♦ *vt* (*ask*) (be)fragen; (*suspect*) verhören; (*doubt*) in Frage stellen, bezweifeln; **beyond** ~ ohne Frage; **out of the** ~ ausgeschlossen; **to ask sb a** ~, **to put a** ~ **to sb** jdm eine Frage stellen; **the** ~ **is** ... es geht darum, ...; **to bring** *or* **call sth into** ~ etw in Frage stellen.

questionable [kwes'chənəbəl] *a* zweifelhaft.

questioner [kwes'chənûr] *n* Fragesteller(in *f*) *m*.

questioning [kwes'chəning] *a* fragend.

question mark *n* Fragezeichen *nt*.

questionnaire [kweschənâr'] *n* Fragebogen *m*; (*enquiry*) Umfrage *f*.

queue [kyōō] (*Brit*) *n* Schlange *f*; **to jump the** ~ sich in der Schlange vordrängen ♦ *vi* (*also*: ~ **up**) Schlange stehen.

quibble [kwib'əl] *n* Spitzfindigkeit *f* ♦ *vi* kleinlich sein.

quick [kwik] *a* schnell; **she was** ~ **to see that** ... sie hat schnell begriffen, daß ...; **to**

be ~ **to act** schnell handeln, schnell dabei sein, etw zu tun ♦ *n* (*of nail*) Nagelhaut *f*; (*old: the living*) die Lebenden; **to the** ~ (*fig*) bis ins Innerste.

quicken [kwik'ən] *vt* (*hasten*) beschleunigen; (*stir*) anregen ♦ *vi* sich beschleunigen.

quick-fire [kwik'fiûr] *a* (*questions etc*) Schnellfeuer-.

quickly [kwik'lē] *ad* schnell; **we must act** ~ wir müssen schnell was unternehmen, wir müssen schnell handeln.

quickness [kwik'nis] *n* Schnelligkeit *f*; (*of mind*) Scharfsinn *m*.

quicksand [kwik'sand] *n* Treibsand *m*.

quickstep [kwik'step] *n* Quickstep *m*.

quick-tempered [kwik'tempûrd] *a* hitzig, leicht erregbar.

quick-witted [kwik'wit'id] *a* schlagfertig, hell.

quid [kwid] *n* (*pl inv*) (*Brit col: pound*) Pfund *nt*.

quid pro quo [kwid' prō' kwō] *n* Gegenleistung *f*.

quiet [kwī'it] *a* (*silent*) still; (*music, car, voice*) leise; (*peaceful, calm*) still, ruhig; (*not noisy: engine*) ruhig; (*not busy: day*) ruhig; **business is** ~ **at this time of year** um diese Jahreszeit ist nicht viel los ♦ *n* Stille *f*, Ruhe *f* ♦ *vb* (*US: also* ~ **down**) *vi* ruhig werden ♦ *vt* beruhigen.

quieten [kwī'itən] (*Brit: also:* ~ **down**) *vi, vt* = **quiet**.

quietly [kwī'itlē] *ad* leise, ruhig.

quietness [kwī'itnis] *n* Ruhe *f*, Stille *f*.

quill [kwil] *n* (*of porcupine*) Stachel *m*; (*pen*) Feder *f*.

quilt [kwilt] *n* Steppdecke *f*.

quilting [kwil'ting] *n* Füllung *f*, Wattierung *f*.

quin [kwin] *n* (*Brit*) = **quintuplet**.

quince [kwins] *n* Quitte *f*.

quinine [kwī'nīn] *n* Chinin *nt*.

quintet(te) [kwintet'] *n* Quintett *nt*.

quintuplet [kwintu'plit] *n* Fünfling *m*.

quip [kwip] *n* witzige *or* geistreiche Bemerkung *f* ♦ *vi* witzeln.

quire [kwiûr] *n* 25 Bogen Papier.

quirk [kwûrk] *n* (*oddity*) Eigenart *f*; **by some** ~ **of fate** durch eine Laune des Schicksals.

quit [kwit] *irreg vt, pt, pp* **quit** *or* **quitted** verlassen ♦ *vi* (*leave job*) kündigen; (*go away*) wegfahren; (*stop*) aufhören; ~ **stalling!** hören Sie auf, um die Sache herumzureden!

quite [kwīt] *ad* (*completely*) ganz, völlig; (*fairly*) ziemlich; ~ (**so!**) richtig!; **not** ~ **as many as last time** nicht ganz so viel wie das letzte Mal; **she's** ~ **pretty** sie ist ganz hübsch; ~ **new** (*entirely*) ganz neu; (*fairly*) ziemlich neu; **that's not** ~ **right** das ist nicht ganz richtig, das stimmt nicht ganz.

Quito [kē'tō] *n* Quito *nt*.

quits [kwits] *a* quitt.

quitted [kwit'id] *pt, pp of* **quit**.

quiver [kwiv'ûr] *vi* zittern ♦ *n* (*for arrows*) Köcher *m*.

quiz [kwiz] *n* (*competition*) Quiz *nt*; (*series of questions*) Befragung *f* ♦ *vt* prüfen.
quizzical [kwiz'ikəl] *a* fragend, verdutzt.
quoit [kwoit] *n* Wurfring *m*.
quorum [kwôr'əm] *n* beschlußfähige Anzahl *f*.
quota [kwō'tə] *n* Anteil *m*; (*COMM*) Quote *f*.
quotation [kwōtā'shən] *n* Zitat *nt*; (*Brit COMM*) Kostenvoranschlag *m*.
quotation marks *npl* Anführungszeichen *pl*.
quote [kwōt] *n* Zitat *nt*; (*COMM*) Kostenvoranschlag *m* ♦ *vi* (*from book*) zitieren; ~ ... **unquote** (*in dictation*) Anfang des Zitats ... Ende des Zitats ♦ *vt* (*from book*) zitieren; (*COMM: price, figure*) Preis angeben; **the figure ~d for the repairs** der für die Reparatur genannte Preis.
quotes [kwōts] *npl* (*inverted commas*) Anführungszeichen *pl*.
quotient [kwō'shənt] *n* Quotient *m*.
qv *abbr* (= *quod vide: which see*) qv.
qwerty keyboard [kwûr'tē kē'bôrd] *n* englische *or* amerikanische Tastatur *f*.

R

R, r [âr] *n* (*letter*) R *nt*, r *nt*; **R for Roger** ≈ R wie Richard.
R *abbr* (*Brit*) = *Rex*; *Regina*; (= *Réaumur (scale)*) R; (= *river*) Fl.; (*US POL*) = **Republican**; (= *right*) r.; (*US CINE*: = *restricted*) frei ab 16.
RA *abbr* (= *rear admiral*) Flottillenadmiral *m*.
RAAF *n abbr* = *Royal Australian Air Force*.
Rabat [räbât'] *n* Rabat *nt*.
rabbi [rab'ī] *n* Rabbiner *m*; (*title*) Rabbi *m*.
rabbit [rab'it] *n* Kaninchen *nt*.
rabbit hutch *n* Kaninchenstall *m*.
rabble [rab'əl] *n* Pöbel *m*.
rabies [rā'bēz] *n* Tollwut *f*.
RAC *n abbr* (*Brit*: = *Royal Automobile Club*) ≈ ADAC *m*.
raccoon [rakōōn'] *n* Waschbär *m*.
race [rās] *n* (*species*) Rasse *f*; (*competition*) Rennen *nt*; (*on foot also*) Wettlauf *m*; (*rush*) Hetze *f*; (*the arms* ~ das Wettrüsten, der Rüstungswettlauf; **the human** ~ die Menschheit, das Menschengeschlecht (*liter*) ♦ *vt* um die Wette laufen mit; (*horses*) laufen lassen ♦ *vi* (*run*) rennen; (*in contest*) am Rennen teilnehmen; **to** ~ **in/out** hinein-/hinausstürzen; **he** ~**d across the road** er raste über die Straße.
race car *n* (*US*) Rennwagen *m*.
race car driver *n* (*US*) Rennfahrer *m*.
racecourse [rās'kôrs] *n* Rennbahn *f*.

racehorse [rās'hôrs] *n* Rennpferd *nt*.
race meeting *n* (Pferde)rennen *nt*.
race relations *npl* Beziehungen *pl* zwischen den Rassen.
racetrack [rās'trak] *n* Rennbahn *f*.
raceway [rās'wā] *n* (*US*) Rennbahn *f*.
racial [rā'shəl] *a* Rassen-.
racial discrimination *n* Rassendiskriminierung *f*.
racial integration *n* Rassenintegration *f*.
racialism [rā'shəlizəm] *n* Rassismus *m*.
racialist [rā'shəlist] *a* rassistisch ♦ *n* Rassist *m*.
racing [rā'sing] *n* Rennen *nt*.
racing car *n* (*Brit*) Rennwagen *m*.
racing driver *n* (*Brit*) Rennfahrer *m*.
racism [rā'sizəm] *n* Rassismus *m*.
racist [rā'sist] *a* rassistisch ♦ *n* Rassist *m*.
rack [rak] *n* Ständer *m*, Gestell *nt*; **off the** ~ (*US*) von der Stange; **to go to** ~ **and ruin** (*building*) verfallen; (*business*) dem Ruin entgegengehen ♦ *vt* (zer)martern; **to** ~ **one's brains** sich (*dat*) den Kopf zerbrechen.
rack up *vt* zusammenraffen.
rack-and-pinion [rak'əndpin'yən] *n* (*TECH*) Zahnstangenersatz *m*.
racket [rak'it] *n* (*din*) Krach *m*; (*scheme*) Schwindelgeschäft *nt*; (*TENNIS*) (Tennis)-schläger *m*.
racketeer [rakitēr'] *n* (*esp US*) Gauner *m* (*col*); (*making excessive profit*) Halsabschneider *m* (*col*).
racquet [rak'it] *n* (*SPORT*) = **racket**.
racy [rā'sē] *a* gewagt; (*style*) spritzig.
radar [rā'dâr] *n* Radar *nt or m*.
radar trap *n* Radarfalle *f*.
radial tire, (*Brit*) **radial tyre** [rā'dēəl tīûr] *n* Gürtelreifen *m*.
radiance [rā'dēəns] *n* strahlende(r) Glanz *m*.
radiant [rā'dēənt] *a* (*bright*) strahlend.
radiate [rā'dēāt] *vti* ausstrahlen; (*roads, lines*) strahlenförmig wegführen.
radiation [rādēā'shən] *n* (Aus)strahlung *f*.
radiation sickness *n* Strahlenkrankheit *f*.
radiator [rā'dēātûr] *n* (*for heating*) Heizkörper *m*; (*AUT*) Kühler *m*.
radiator cap *n* (*AUT*) Kühlerdeckel *m*.
radiator grill *n* (*AUT*) Kühlergitter *nt*.
radical [rad'ikəl] *a*, **radically** [rad'ikəlē] *ad* radikal.
radii [rā'dēī] *npl of* **radius**.
radio [rā'dēō] *n* Rundfunk *m*, Radio *nt*; (*set*) Radio(apparat) *nt* ♦ *vt* (*information, one's position*) funken, durchgeben; (*person*) per *or* über Funk verständigen ♦ *vi*: **to** ~ **to sb** mit jdm per Funk sprechen.
radioactive [rādēōak'tiv] *a* radioaktiv.
radioactivity [rādēōaktiv'ətē] *n* Radioaktivität *f*.
radio announcer *n* Rundfunkansager(in *f*) *m*, Rundfunksprecher(in *f*) *m*.
radio-controlled [rā'dēōkəntrōld'] *a* ferngesteuert, ferngelenkt.

radiographer [rādēăg'rəfûr] *n* Röntgenassistent(in *f*) *m*.
radiography [rādēăg'rəfē] *n* Radiographie *f*, Röntgenphotographie *f*.
radiology [rādēăl'əjē] *n* Strahlenkunde *f*.
radio station *n* Rundfunkstation *f*.
radio taxi *n* Funktaxi *nt*.
radio telephone *n* Funksprechgerät *nt*.
radio telescope *n* Radioteleskop *nt*.
radiotherapist [rādēōthär'əpist] *n* Radiologieassistent(in *f*) *m*.
radiotherapy [rādēōthär'əpē] *n* Röntgentherapie *f*.
radish [rad'ish] *n* (*big*) Rettich *m*; (*small*) Radieschen *nt*.
radium [rā'dēəm] *n* Radium *nt*.
radius [rā'dēəs] *n*, *pl* **radii** [rā'dēī] Radius *m*, Halbkreis *m*; (*area*) Umkreis *m*; **within a ~ of 50 miles** in einem Umkreis von 50 Meilen.
RAF *n abbr* (*Brit*) = **Royal Air Force**.
raffia [raf'ēə] *n* Bast *m*.
raffle [raf'əl] *n* Verlosung *f*, Tombola *f* ♦ *vt* (*object*) verlosen.
raft [raft] *n* Floß *nt*.
rafter [raf'tûr] *n* Dachsparren *m*.
rag [rag] *n* (*cloth*) Lumpen *m*, Lappen *m*; (*col: newspaper*) Käseblatt *nt*; (*Brit UNIV: for charity*) studentische Sammelaktion *f*; **in ~s** zerlumpt, abgerissen.
rag-and-bone man [ragənbōn' man] *n* (*Brit*) Lumpensammler *m*.
ragbag [rag'bag] *n* (*fig*) Sammelsurium *nt*.
rag doll *n* Flickenpuppe *f*.
rage [rāj] *n* Wut *f*; (*desire*) Sucht *f*; (*fashion*) große Mode *f*; **to be in a ~** wütend sein; **to fly into a ~** einen Wutanfall bekommen ♦ *vi* wüten, toben.
ragged [rag'id] *a* (*edge*) gezackt; (*clothes*) zerlumpt; **~ left/right** (*text*) Flattersatz linksseitig/rechtsseitig.
raging [rā'jing] *a* (*storm, sea*) tobend; (*thirst*) Heiden-, brennend; (*person*) wütend; (*fever*) heftig; (*pain*) rasend; **to be in a ~ temper** eine fürchterliche Laune haben.
ragman [rag'man] *n* Lumpensammler *m*.
rag trade *n*: **the ~** (*col*) die Kleiderbranche.
raid [rād] *n* Überfall *m*; (*MIL*) Angriff *m*; (*by police*) Razzia *f* ♦ *vt* überfallen.
raider [rā'dûr] *n* (*person*) (Bank)räuber *m*; (*NAUT*) Kaperschiff *nt*.
rail [rāl] *n* Schiene *f*, Querstange *f*; (*on stairs*) Geländer *nt*; (*of ship*) Reling *f*; (*RAIL*) Schiene *f*; **by ~** per Bahn, mit der Bahn.
railing(s) [rāl'ing(z)] *n(pl)* Geländer *nt*.
rail link *n* Zug- od Bahnverbindung *f*.
railroad [rāl'rōd] *n* (*US*) Eisenbahn *f*.
railroader [rāl'rōdûr] *n* (*US*) Eisenbahner *m*.
railroad line *n* (Eisen)bahnlinie *f*; (*track*) Gleis *nt*; (*rails*) Schienen *pl*.
railroad station *n* Bahnhof *m*.
railway [rāl'wā] *etc* (*Brit*) = **railroad** *etc*.
railway engine *n* (*Brit*) Lokomotive *f*.
railwayman [rāl'wāmən] *n*, *pl* **-men** (*Brit*) =

railroader.
rain [rān] *n* Regen *m*; **the ~s** die Regenzeit ♦ *vi*: **it's ~ing** es regnet ♦ *vt* regnen; **it's ~ing cats and dogs** es gießt *or* es regnet in Strömen.
rainbow [rān'bō] *n* Regenbogen *m*.
raincoat [rān'kōt] *n* Regenmantel *m*.
raindrop [rān'dráp] *n* Regentropfen *m*.
rainfall [rān'fôl] *n* Niederschlag *m*.
rainforest [rān'fôr'ist] *n* Regenwald *m*.
rainproof [rān'prōōf] *a* regendicht.
rainstorm [rān'stôrm] *n* heftige(r) Regenguß *m*.
rainwater [rān'wôtûr] *n* Regenwasser *nt*.
rainy [rā'nē] *a* (*region, season*) Regen-; (*day*) regnerisch, verregnet.
raise [rāz] *n* (*esp US: increase*) (Lohn- *or* Gehalts- *or* Preis)erhöhung *f* ♦ *vt* (*lift*) (hoch)heben; (*increase*) erhöhen; (*question*) aufwerfen; (*doubts*) äußern; (*funds*) beschaffen; (*family*) großziehen; (*livestock*) züchten; (*build*) errichten; (*end: siege, embargo*) aufheben, beenden; **to ~ sb's hopes** jdm Hoffnung machen; **to ~ one's glass to sb/sth** jdm zutrinken/auf etw trinken; **to ~ a laugh/a smile** Gelächter ernten/ein Lächeln hervorrufen.
raisin [rā'zin] *n* Rosine *f*.
rajah [rá'jə] *n* Radscha *m*.
rake [rāk] *n* Harke *f*; (*person*) Wüstling *m* ♦ *vt* harken; (*gun, searchlight*) bestreichen; (*search*) (durch)suchen.
  rake in, rake together *vt* zusammenscharren.
rake-off [rāk'ôf] *n* (betrügerische(r)) Gewinnanteil *m*.
rakish [rā'kish] *a* verwegen; **at a ~ angle** (*hat*) verwegen aufgesetzt.
rally [ral'ē] *n* (*POL etc*) Kundgebung *f*; (*AUT*) Sternfahrt *f*, Rallye *f*; (*improvement*) Erholung *f* ♦ *vt* (*MIL*) sammeln ♦ *vi* Kräfte sammeln.
  rally around *vti* (sich) scharen um; (*help*) zu Hilfe kommen (+*dat*).
rallying point [ral'ēing point] *n* (*POL. MIL*) Sammelplatz *m*.
ram [ram] *n* Widder *m*; (*instrument*) Ramme *f* ♦ *vt* (*strike*) rammen; (*stuff*) (hinein)stopfen.
RAM [ram] *n abbr* (*COMPUT*: = *random access memory*) Direktzugriffsspeicher *m*.
ramble [ram'bəl] *n* Wanderung *f*, Ausflug *m* ♦ *vi* (*wander*) umherstreifen; (*talk*) schwafeln.
rambler [ram'blûr] *n* Wanderer *m*; (*plant*) Kletterrose *f*.
rambling [ram'bling] *a* (*plant*) Kletter-; (*speech*) weitschweifig; (*town*) ausgedehnt; (*house*) weitläufig.
rambunctious [rambungk'shəs] *a* (*US*) derb.
ramification [raməfəkā'shən] *n* (*of arteries etc*) Verästelung *f*; (*fig*) Tragweite *f*.
ramp [ramp] *n* Rampe *f*.
rampage [ram'pāj] *n*: **to be on the ~** randa-

lieren ♦ *vi* randalieren.
rampant [ram'pənt] *a (heraldry)* aufgerichtet; **to be ~** (wild) wuchern.
rampart [ram'pârt] *n* (Schutz)wall *m*.
ramshackle [ram'shakəl] *a* baufällig.
ran [ran] *pt of* **run**.
ranch [ranch] *n* Ranch *f*.
rancher [ran'chûr] *n* Rancher *m*.
rancid [ran'sid] *a* ranzig.
rancor, *(Brit)* **rancour** [rang'kûr] *n* Verbitterung *f*, Groll *m*.
R & B *n abbr* = *rhythm and blues.*
R & D *n abbr* (= *research and development*) FuE *f*.
random [ran'dəm] *a* ziellos, wahllos ♦ *n*: **at ~** aufs Geratewohl.
random access *n (COMPUT)* wahlfreie(r) Zugriff *m*.
R and R *n abbr (US MIL)* = *rest and recuperation.*
randy [ran'dē] *a (Brit)* geil, scharf.
rang [rang] *pt of* **ring**.
range [rānj] *n* Reihe *f*; *(of mountains)* Kette *f*; *(COMM)* Sortiment *nt*; *(selection)* (große) Auswahl *f* *(of* an *+dat)*; *(reach)* (Reich)weite *f*; *(of gun)* Schußweite *f*; *(for shooting practice)* Schießplatz *m*; *(stove)* (großer) Herd *m*; **within (firing) ~** in Schußweite; **do you have anything else in this price ~?** haben Sie sonst noch was in dieser Preisklasse?; **intermediate-/short-~ missile** Mittel-/Kurzstreckenrakete *f* ♦ *vt* *(set in row)* anordnen, aufstellen; *(roam)* durchstreifen; **~d left/right** *(Brit: text)* links-/rechtsbündig (angeordnet) ♦ *vi (extend)* sich erstrecken; **prices ranging from 5 to 10 dollars** Preise, die sich zwischen 5 und 10 Dollar bewegen.
ranger [rān'jûr] *n* Förster *m*.
Rangoon [ranggōōn'] *n* Rangun *nt*.
rangy [rān'jē] *a* langglied(e)rig.
rank [rangk] *n (row)* Reihe *f*; *(Brit: for cabs)* Stand *m*; *(MIL)* Dienstgrad *m*, Rang *m*; *(social position)* Stand *m*; **the ~s** *(MIL)* die Mannschaften *pl*; **the ~ and file** *(fig)* die breite Masse; **to close ~s** *(MIL)* die Reihen schließen; *(fig)* zusammenhalten ♦ *vt* einschätzen; **he is ~ed 6th** er steht an sechster Stelle ♦ *vi*: **to ~ among** gehören zu ♦ *a (strong-smelling)* stinkend; *(extreme)* krass; *(smell)* übel; *(hypocrisy, injustice etc)* wahr.
rankle [rang'kəl] *vi* nagen; **it still ~s with me** es wurmt mich immer noch.
ransack [ran'sak] *vt (plunder)* plündern; *(search)* durchwühlen.
ransom [ran'səm] *n* Lösegeld *nt*; **to hold sb to ~** jdn gegen Lösegeld festhalten.
rant [rant] *vi* hochtrabend reden, toben.
ranting [ran'ting] *n* Wortschwall *m*.
rap [rap] *n* Schlag *m* ♦ *vt* klopfen.
rape [rāp] *n* Vergewaltigung *f*; *(plant)* Raps *m* ♦ *vt* vergewaltigen.
rape(seed) oil [rāp'(sēd) oil] *n* Rapsöl *nt*.

rapid [rap'id] *a* rasch, schnell.
rapidity [rəpid'itē] *n* Schnelligkeit *f*.
rapidly [rap'idlē] *ad* schnell.
rapids [rap'idz] *npl* Stromschnellen *pl*.
rapier [rā'pēûr] *n* Florett *nt*.
rapist [rā'pist] *n* Vergewaltiger *m*.
rapport [rapôr'] *n* gute(s) Verhältnis *nt*.
rapprochement [raprōchmônt'] *n* (Wieder)annäherung *f*.
rapt [rapt] *a* hingerissen; *(attention)* atemlos; **to be ~ in contemplation** in Betrachtungen versunken sein.
rapture [rap'chûr] *n* Entzücken *nt*.
rapturous [rap'chûrəs] *a (applause)* stürmisch; *(expression)* verzückt.
rare [rär] *a* selten, rar; *(especially good)* vortrefflich; *(underdone)* nicht durchgebraten; **it is ~ to find that ...** es kommt selten vor, daß ...
rarefied [rär'əfīd] *a (air, atmosphere)* dünn.
rarely [reûr'lē] *ad* selten.
raring [rär'ing] *a*: **to be ~ to go** *(col)* es kaum erwarten können, bis es losgeht.
rarity [rär'itē] *n* Seltenheit *f*.
rascal [ras'kəl] *n* Schuft *m*; *(child)* Strick *m*.
rash [rash] *a* übereilt; *(reckless)* unbesonnen ♦ *n* Ausschlag *m*; **to come out in a ~** einen Ausschlag bekommen.
rasher [rash'ûr] *n* Speckscheibe *f*.
rashly [rash'lē] *ad* vorschnell, unbesonnen.
rashness [rash'nis] *n* Voreiligkeit *f*; *(recklessness)* Unbesonnenheit *f*.
rasp [rasp] *n* Raspel *f* ♦ *vt (speak: also: ~ out)* krächzen.
raspberry [raz'bärē] *n* Himbeere *f*.
rasping [ras'ping] *a (noise)* kratzend.
rat [rat] *n (animal)* Ratte *f*; *(person)* Halunke *m*.
ratchet [rach'it] *n* Sperrad *nt*.
rate [rāt] *n (proportion)* Ziffer *f*, Rate *f*; *(price)* Tarif *m*, Gebühr *f*; *(speed)* Geschwindigkeit *f* ♦ *vt* (ein)schätzen; **at a ~ of 60 kph** mit 60 (Stundenkilometern); **at any ~** auf jeden Fall; **at this ~** wenn es so weitergeht; **bank ~** Diskontsatz *m*; **failure ~** Durchfallrate *f or* -quote *f*; **pulse ~** Puls(zahl *f*) *m*; **~ of growth** Wachstumsrate *f*; **~ of exchange** (Wechsel)kurs *m*; **~ of pay** Lohntarif *m*; **~ of return** Rendite *f*; **to ~ sb/sth highly** jdn/etw hoch schätzen; *see also* **rates.**
rates [rāts] *npl (Brit)* Grundsteuer *f*, Gemeindeabgaben *pl*.
rather [rath'ûr] *ad (in preference)* lieber, eher; *(to some extent)* ziemlich; *(somewhat)* etwas; **or ~** *(more accurately)* vielmehr; **I'd ~ not** lieber nicht; **~!** und ob!
ratification [ratəfəkā'shən] *n* Ratifikation *f*.
ratify [rat'əfī] *vt* bestätigen; *(POL)* ratifizieren.
rating [rā'ting] *n* Klasse *f*; *(Brit: sailor)* Matrose *m*.
ratings [rā'tingz] *npl (TV)* Einschaltquote *f*.
ratio [rā'shō] *n* Verhältnis *nt*; **in the ~ of 2**

to 1 im Verhältnis 2 zu 1.
ration [rash'ən] n (usually pl) Ration f ♦ vt rationieren.
rational [rash'ənəl] a rational, vernünftig.
rationale [rashənal'] n Grundprinzip nt.
rationalization [rashənələzā'shən] n Rationalisierung f.
rationalize [rash'ənəlīz] vt rationalisieren.
rationally [rash'ənəlē] ad rational, vernünftig.
rationing [rash'əning] n Rationierung f, Rationieren nt.
rat race n Konkurrenzkampf m.
rattan [ratan'] n Rattan nt, Peddigrohr nt.
rattle [rat'əl] n (sound) Rattern nt, Rasseln nt; (toy) Rassel f ♦ vi ratteln, klappern ♦ vt (keys etc) schütteln; (col: disconcert) nervös machen.
rattlesnake [rat'əlsnāk] n Klapperschlange f.
ratty [rat'ē] a (col: US) schäbig; (: Brit) gereizt.
raucous [rô'kəs] a, **raucously** [rô'kəslē] ad heiser, rauh.
ravage [rav'ij] vt verheeren.
ravages [rav'ijiz] npl verheerende Wirkungen pl; **the ~ of time** der Zahn der Zeit.
rave [rāv] vi (talk wildly) phantasieren; (rage) toben ♦ cpd: **~ review** (col) glänzende or begeisterte Kritik f.
raven [rā'vən] n Rabe m.
ravenous [rav'ənəs] a heißhungrig; (appetite) unersättlich.
ravine [rəvēn'] n Schlucht f, Klamm f.
raving [rā'ving] a tobend ♦ ad: **~ mad** total verrückt.
ravings [rā'vingz] npl Phantasien pl, Delirien pl.
ravioli [ravēō'lē] n Ravioli pl.
ravish [rav'ish] vt (delight) entzücken; (JUR: woman) vergewaltigen.
ravishing [rav'ishing] a hinreißend.
raw [rô] a roh; (tender) wund(gerieben); (wound) offen; (inexperienced) unerfahren; **to give sb a ~ deal** (col: bad bargain) jdn unfair behandeln; **to get a ~ deal** (harsh treatment) schlecht wegkommen; **~ data** (COMPUT) Ursprungsdaten pl.
Rawalpindi [râwəlpin'dē] n Rawalpindi nt.
raw material n Rohmaterial nt.
ray [rā] n (of light) (Licht)strahl m; (gleam) Schimmer m.
rayon [rā'ân] n Kunstseide f, Reyon nt or m.
raze [rāz] vt zerstören; **to ~ to the ground** dem Erdboden gleichmachen.
razor [rā'zûr] n Rasierapparat m.
razor blade n Rasierklinge f.
razzmatazz [raz'mətaz] n (col) Tamtam nt, Rummel m.
RC a, n abbr = **Roman Catholic.**
RCAF n abbr = Royal Canadian Air Force.
RCMP n abbr (= Royal Canadian Mounted Police) kanadische berittene Polizei.
RCN n abbr = Royal Canadian Navy.
Rd abbr (= road) Str.
RD abbr (US MAIL: = rural delivery) Land-

postzustellung f.
re [rā] prep (COMM) betreffs (+ gen).
re- [rē] pref wieder-.
reach [rēch] n Reichweite f; (of river) Flußstrecke f; **within ~** (shops etc) in erreichbarer Weite or Entfernung ♦ vt erreichen; (pass on) reichen, geben; **can I ~ you at your hotel?** sind Sie in Ihrem Hotel zu erreichen?; **to ~ sb by phone** jdn telefonisch erreichen ♦ vi (try to get) langen (for nach); (territory etc) sich erstrecken; (stretch out hand) greifen.
reach out vi die Hand ausstrecken.
react [rēakt'] vi reagieren.
reaction [rēak'shən] n Reaktion f.
reactionary [rēak'shənärē] a reaktionär.
reactor [rēak'tûr] n Reaktor m.
read [rēd] vti irreg, pt, pp **read** [red] lesen; (aloud) vorlesen; (COMPUT) (ein)lesen; **it ~s as follows** es lautet folgendermaßen; **to take sth as read** (fig) etw als selbstverständlich voraussetzen; **do you ~ me?** (TEL) können Sie mich verstehen?; **to ~ between the lines** zwischen den Zeilen lesen.
read out vt vorlesen.
read over vt durchlesen.
read through vt (quickly) flüchtig durchlesen; (thoroughly) genau durchlesen.
read up (on) vt nachlesen über (+acc).
readable [rē'dəbəl] a lesbar; (worth reading) lesenswert.
reader [rē'dûr] n (person) Leser(in f) m; (book) Lesebuch nt.
readership [rē'dûrship] n Leserschaft f.
readily [red'əlē] ad (willingly) bereitwillig; (easily) prompt.
readiness [red'ēnis] n (willingness) Bereitwilligkeit f; (being ready) Bereitschaft f.
reading [rēd'ing] n Lesen nt; (interpretation) Interpretation f; (from instruments) Anzeige f.
reading lamp n Leselampe f.
reading room n Lesezimmer nt, Lesesaal m.
readjust [rēəjust'] vt wieder in Ordnung bringen; neu einstellen; **to ~ (o.s.) to sth** sich wieder anpassen an etw (acc).
readjustment [rēəjust'mənt] n Wiederanpassung f.
ready [red'ē] a (prepared) bereit, fertig; (willing) bereit, willens; (in condition to) reif; (quick) schlagfertig; (money) verfügbar, bar ♦ ad bereit ♦ n: **at the ~** bereit; **~ for use** gebrauchsfertig; **to be ~ to do sth** (willing) bereit sein, etw zu tun; (quick) schnell dabei sein, etw zu tun; **to get sth ~** etw fertigmachen, etw bereitmachen.
ready cash n Bargeld nt.
ready-made [red'ēmād'] a gebrauchsfertig, Fertig-; (clothes) Konfektions-.
ready money n Bargeld nt.
ready-to-wear [red'ētəwär'] a von der Stange.

reagent [rēā'jənt] n Reagenz nt.
real [rēl] a wirklich; (actual) eigentlich; (true) wahr; (not fake) echt; **in ~ life** im wirklichen Leben; **~ time** (COMPUT) Echtzeit f.
real estate n Immobilien pl.
real estate agency n Maklerbüro nt.
real estate agent n Grundstücksmakler m.
realism [rē'əlizəm] n Realismus m.
realist [rē'əlist] n Realist(in f) m.
realistic [rēəlis'tik] a, **realistically** [rēəlis'tiklē] ad realistisch.
reality [rēal'itē] n (real existence) Wirklichkeit f, Realität f; (facts) Tatsachen pl.
realization [rēələzā'shən] n (understanding) Erkenntnis f; (fulfillment) Verwirklichung f.
realize [rē'əlīz] vt (understand) begreifen; (make real) verwirklichen; (money) einbringen; **I didn't ~** ... ich wußte nicht, ...; **I ~ that** ... es ist mir klar, daß ...
really [rē'əlē] ad wirklich.
realm [relm] n Reich nt.
realtor [rē'əltûr] n (US) Grundstücksmakler(in f) m.
ream [rēm] n Ries nt; **he always writes ~s** (fig col) er schreibt immer ganze Bände.
reap [rēp] vt ernten.
reaper [rē'pûr] n Mähmaschine f.
reappear [rēəpi'ûr] vi wieder erscheinen.
reappearance [rēəpēr'əns] n Wiedererscheinen nt.
reapply [rēəplī'] vi wiederholt beantragen (for acc); (for job) sich erneut bewerben (for um).
reappoint [rēəpoint'] vt wiederernennen.
reappraisal [rēəprā'zəl] n Neubeurteilung f, Neubewertung f.
rear [rēr] a hintere(r, s), Rück- ♦ n Rückseite f; (last part) Schluß m ♦ vt (children, animals) aufziehen ♦ vi (horse) sich aufbäumen.
rear-engined [rēr'en'jənd] a mit Heckmotor.
rear guard n Nachhut f.
rearm [rēârm'] vt wiederbewaffnen ♦ vi wiederaufrüsten.
rearmament [rēârm'əmənt] n Wiederaufrüstung f.
rearrange [rēərānj'] vt umordnen; (plans) ändern.
rearview mirror [rēr'vyōō' mir'ûr] n Rückspiegel m.
reason [rē'zən] n (cause) Grund m; (ability to think) Verstand m; (sensible thoughts) Vernunft f; **the ~ for/why** der Grund für/weshalb; **she claims with good ~ that she's underpaid** sie behauptet mit gutem Grund, unterbezahlt zu sein; **all the more ~ why you should not sell it** um so mehr Grund, warum du's nicht verkaufen solltest ♦ vi (think) denken; (use arguments) argumentieren; **to ~ with sb** mit jdm diskutieren.
reasonable [rē'zənəbəl] a vernünftig.
reasonably [rē'zənəblē] ad vernünftig; (fair-

ly) ziemlich; **one could ~ suppose** man könnte doch (mit gutem Grund) annehmen.
reasoned [rē'zənd] a (argument) durchdacht.
reasoning [rē'zəning] n Urteilen nt; (arguing) Beweisführung f.
reassemble [rēəsem'bəl] vt wieder versammeln; (TECH) wieder zusammensetzen, wieder zusammenbauen ♦ vi sich wieder versammeln.
reassert [rēəsûrt'] vt wieder geltend machen.
reassurance [rēəshōōr'əns] n Beruhigung f; (confirmation) Bestätigung f.
reassure [rēəshōōr'] vt beruhigen; (confirm) versichern (sb jdm).
reassuring [rēəshōōr'ing] a beruhigend.
reawakening [rēəwā'kəning] n Wiedererwachen nt.
rebate [rē'bāt] n Rabatt m; (money back) Rückzahlung f.
rebel [reb'əl] n Rebell m ♦ a Rebellen- ♦ vi [ribel'] rebellieren.
rebellion [ribel'yən] n Rebellion f, Aufstand m.
rebellious [ribel'yəs] a rebellisch; (fig) widerspenstig.
rebirth [rēbûrth'] n Wiedergeburt f.
rebound vi [ribound'] zurückprallen ♦ n [rē'bound] Rückprall m; **on the ~** (fig) als Reaktion.
rebuff [ribuf'] n Abfuhr f ♦ vt abblitzen lassen.
rebuild [rēbild'] vt irreg wiederaufbauen; (fig) wiederherstellen.
rebuilding [rēbil'ding] n Wiederaufbau m.
rebuke [ribyōōk'] n Tadel m ♦ vt tadeln, rügen.
rebut [ribut'] vt widerlegen.
recalcitrant [rikal'sitrənt] a widerspenstig, aufsässig.
recall [rikôl'] vt (call back) zurückrufen; (remember) sich erinnern an (+acc); (COMPUT) abrufen.
recant [rikant'] vi (öffentlich) widerrufen.
recap [rē'kap] n kurze Zusammenfassung f ♦ vti (information) wiederholen.
recapture [rēkap'chûr] vt wieder (ein)fangen.
recd. abbr (= received) erh.
recede [risēd'] vi zurückweichen.
receding [risē'ding] a: **~ hair** Stirnglatze f.
receipt [risēt'] n (document) Quittung f; (receiving) Empfang m; **to acknowledge ~ of sth** den Empfang einer Sache (gen) bestätigen; **we are in ~ of your letter of** ... wir haben Ihr Schreiben vom ... erhalten.
receipts [risēts'] npl Einnahmen pl.
receivable [risē'vəbəl] a zulässig; **accounts ~** ausstehende Forderungen pl.
receive [risēv'] vt erhalten; (visitors etc) empfangen; **"~d with thanks"** (COMM) „dankend erhalten".
receiver [risē'vûr] n (TEL) Hörer m; (RAD) Empfänger m; (official) ~ Konkursverwalter m.
recent [rē'sənt] a vor kurzem (geschehen),

neuerlich; (*modern*) neu; **in ~ years** in den letzten Jahren.

recently [rē'səntlē] *ad* kürzlich, neulich; **until ~** bis vor kurzem.

receptacle [risep'təkəl] *n* Behälter *m*.

reception [risep'shən] *n* Empfang *m*; (*welcome*) Aufnahme *f*; (*in hotel, hospital, offices*) Rezeption *f*.

reception center *n* Durchgangslager *nt*.

reception desk *n* Empfang *m*; (*in hotel*) Rezeption *f*.

receptionist [risep'shənist] *n* (*in hotel*) Empfangschef *m*/-dame *f*; (*MED*) Sprechstundenhilfe *f*.

receptive [risep'tiv] *a* aufnahmebereit.

recess [rē'ses] *n* (*alcove*) Nische *f*; (*secret place*) Winkel *m*; (*short break*) Ferien *pl*; (*US SCH*) Pause *f*.

recession [risesh'ən] *n* (*FIN*) Rezession *f*.

recharge [rēchârj'] *vt* (*battery*) aufladen.

rechargeable battery [rēchâr'jəbəl bat'ûrē] *n* aufladbare Batterie *f*.

recipe [res'əpē] *n* Rezept *nt*.

recipient [risip'ēənt] *n* Empfänger(in *f*) *m*.

reciprocal [risip'rəkəl] *a* gegenseitig; (*mutual*) wechselseitig.

reciprocate [risip'rəkāt] *vt* erwidern.

recital [risīt'əl] *n* (*MUS*) Konzert *nt*, Vortrag *m*; **song ~** Liederabend *m*.

recitation [resitā'shən] *n* Rezitation *f*.

recite [risīt'] *vt* (*poetry*) vortragen; (*facts*) aufzählen.

reckless [rek'lis] *a*, **recklessly** [rek'lislē] *ad* leichtsinnig; (*driving*) rücksichtslos.

recklessness [rek'lisnis] *n* Leichtsinn *m*; Rücksichtslosigkeit *f*.

reckon [rek'ən] *vt* (*count*) berechnen; (*consider*) halten für; **I ~ (that)** (*think, suppose*) ich glaube(, daß); (*estimate*) ich schätze(, daß) ♦ *vi* (*suppose*) annehmen; **he is somebody to be ~ed with** er ist nicht zu unterschätzen; **to ~ without sb/sth** mit jdm/etw nicht rechnen.

reckon on *vt fus* rechnen mit.

reckoning [rek'əning] *n* (*calculation*) Rechnen *nt*.

reclaim [riklām'] *vt* (*land*) abgewinnen (*from dat*); (*expenses*) zurückverlangen.

reclamation [rekləmā'shən] *n* (*of land*) Gewinnung *f*.

recline [riklīn'] *vi* sich zurücklehnen.

reclining [riklīn'ing] *a* verstellbar, Liege-.

recluse [rek'lōōs] *n* Einsiedler *m*.

recognition [rekəgnish'ən] *n* (*recognizing*) Erkennen *nt*; (*acknowledgement*) Anerkennung *f*; **in ~ of** in Anerkennung (*+gen*).

recognizable [rekəgnī'zəbəl] *a* erkennbar.

recognize [rek'əgnīz] *vt* erkennen; (*POL, approve*) anerkennen.

recoil [rikoil'] *n* Rückstoß *m* ♦ *vi* (*in horror*) zurückschrecken; (*rebound*) zurückprallen; **to ~ from doing sth** davor zurückschrecken, etw zu tun.

recollect [rekəlekt'] *vt* sich erinnern an

(*+acc*).

recollection [rekəlek'shən] *n* Erinnerung *f*; **to the best of my ~** soweit ich mich erinnern kann.

recommend [rekəmend'] *vt* empfehlen; **she has a lot to ~ her** es spricht sehr viel für sie.

recommendation [rekəmendā'shən] *n* Empfehlung *f*.

recommended retail price [rekəmen'did rē'tāl prīs] *n* (*Brit*) empfohlene(r) Einzelhandelspreis *m*.

recompense [rek'əmpens] *n* (*compensation*) Entschädigung *f*; (*reward*) Belohnung *f* ♦ *vt* entschädigen; belohnen.

reconcilable [rek'ənsīləbəl] *a* vereinbar.

reconcile [rek'ənsīl] *vt* (*facts*) vereinbaren, in Einklang bringen; (*people*) versöhnen.

reconciliation [rekənsilēā'shən] *n* Versöhnung *f*.

recondite [rek'əndīt] *a* abstrus.

reconditioned [rēkəndi'shənd] *a* überholt, erneuert.

reconnaissance [rikân'isəns] *n* Aufklärung *f*.

reconnoiter, (*Brit*) **reconnoitre** [rēkənoi'tûr] *vt* erkunden ♦ *vi* aufklären.

reconsider [rēkənsid'ûr] *vti* von neuem erwägen, (es) überdenken.

reconstitute [rēkân'stitōōt] *vt* neu bilden.

reconstruct [rēkənstrukt'] *vt* wiederaufbauen; (*crime*) rekonstruieren.

reconstruction [rēkənstruk'shən] *n* Rekonstruktion *f*.

record [rek'ûrd] *n* Aufzeichnung *f*; (*in card file*) Karteikarte *f*; (*MUS*) Schallplatte *f*; (*best performance*) Rekord *m*; (*COMPUT*) Datensatz *m*; (*also:* **criminal ~**) Vorstrafen *pl*; **public ~s** Nationalarchiv *nt*; **he is on ~ as saying that ...** es ist belegt, daß er gesagt hat ...; **Germany's excellent ~** (*achievements*) Deutschlands ausgezeichnete Leistungen; **off the ~** vertraulich ♦ *a* (*time*) Rekord- ♦ *vt* [rikôrd'] aufzeichnen (*also COMPUT*); (*MUS etc*) aufnehmen.

record card *n* (*in file*) Karteikarte *f*.

recorded delivery [rikôr'did diliv'ûrē] *n* (*Brit MAIL*): **~ letter** Einschreiben *nt*.

recorded music *n* Musikaufnahmen *pl*.

recorder [rikôr'dûr] *n* (*MUS*) Blockflöte *f*.

record holder *n* (*SPORT*) Rekordinhaber(in *f*) *m*.

recording [rikôr'ding] *n* (*MUS*) Aufnahme *f*.

recording studio *n* Aufnahmestudio *nt*.

record library *n* Schallplattenarchiv *nt*.

record player *n* Plattenspieler *m*.

recount *n* [rē'kount] (*POL: of votes*) Nachzählung *f* ♦ *vt* [rēkount'] (*count again*) nachzählen; [rikount'] (*tell*) berichten.

recoup [rikōōp'] *vt* (*money*) wieder einbringen; (*loss*) wettmachen.

recourse [rē'kôrs] *n* Zuflucht *f*.

recover [rikuv'ûr] *vt* (*get back*) zurückerhalten; [rēkuv'ûr] (*quilt etc*) neu überziehen sich erholen.

recovery [rikuv'ûrē] *n* Wiedererlangung *f*; (*of health*) Genesung *f*.
re-create [rēkrēāt'] *vt* wiederherstellen.
recreation [rekrēā'shən] *n* Erholung *f*; (*pastime*) Hobby *nt*.
recreational [rekrēā'shənəl] *a* Erholungs-.
recreation center *n* Freizeitzentrum *nt*.
recrimination [rikrimənā'shən] *n* Gegenbeschuldigung *f*.
recruit [rikrōōt'] *n* Rekrut *m* ♦ *vt* rekrutieren.
recruiting office [rikrōōt'ing óf'is] *n* Wehrmeldeamt *nt*.
recruitment [rikrōōt'mənt] *n* Rekrutierung *f*.
rectangle [rek'tanggəl] *n* Rechteck *nt*.
rectangular [rektang'gyəlûr] *a* rechteckig, rechtwinklig.
rectify [rek'təfī] *vt* berichtigen.
rector [rek'tûr] *n* (*Brit UNIV*) Rektor(in *f*) *m*.
rectory [rek'tûrē] *n* Pfarrhaus *nt*.
rectum [rek'təm] *n* (*ANAT*) Rektum *nt*, Mastdarm *m*.
recuperate [rikōō'pərāt] *vi* sich erholen.
recur [rikûr'] *vi* sich wiederholen.
recurrence [rikûr'əns] *n* Wiederholung *f*.
recurrent [rikûr'ənt] *a* wiederkehrend.
recycle [rēsī'kəl] *vt* (*waste, paper etc*) wiederverwerten.
red [red] *n* Rot *nt*; (*POL*) Rote(r) *m* ♦ *a* rot; **in the ~** in den roten Zahlen.
red carpet treatment *n* Sonderbehandlung *f*, große(r) Bahnhof *m*.
Red Cross *n* Rote(s) Kreuz *nt*.
red currant *n* rote Johannisbeere *f*.
redden [red'ən] *vti* (sich) röten; (*blush*) erröten.
reddish [red'ish] *a* rötlich.
redecorate [rēdek'ərāt] *vt* renovieren.
redecoration [rēdekərā'shən] *n* Renovierung *f*.
redeem [ridēm'] *vt* (*COMM*) einlösen; (*set free*) freikaufen; (*compensate*) retten; **to ~ sb from sin** jdn von seinen Sünden erlösen.
redeemable [ridē'məbəl] *a* rückkaufbar, einlösbar.
redeeming [ridē'ming] *a* (*virtue, feature*) rettend.
redeploy [rēdiploi'] *vt* (*resources*) umverteilen.
redeployment [rēdiploi'mənt] *n* Einsatz *m* an einem anderen Arbeitsplatz.
redevelop [rēdivel'əp] *vt* sanieren.
redevelopment [rēdivel'əpmənt] *n* Sanierung *f*.
red-haired [red'härd] *a* rothaarig.
red-handed [red'han'did] *ad* auf frischer Tat.
redhead [red'hed] *n* Rothaarige(r) *mf*.
red herring *n* Ablenkungsmanöver *nt*.
red-hot [red'hät'] *a* rotglühend; (*excited*) hitzig; (*tip*) heiß.
redirect [rēdərekt'] *vt* umleiten.
rediscover [rēdiskuv'ûr] *vt* wiederentdecken.
rediscovery [rēdiskuv'ûrē] *n* Wiederentdeckung *f*.
redistribute [rēdistrib'yōōt] *vt* neu verteilen.

red-letter day [red'let'ûr dā] *n* (*lit, fig*) Festtag *m*.
red light *n*: **to go through a ~** bei Rot über die Ampel fahren.
red-light district [red'līt dis'trikt] *n* Strichviertel *nt*.
redness [red'nis] *n* Röte *f*.
redo [rēdōō'] *vt irreg* nochmals tun *or* machen.
redolent [red'ələnt] *a*: **~ of** riechend nach; (*fig*) erinnernd an (+*acc*).
redouble [rēdub'əl] *vt* verdoppeln.
redraft [rēdraft'] *vt* umformulieren.
redress [ridres'] *vt* wiedergutmachen; **to ~ the balance** das Gleichgewicht wiederherstellen.
Red Sea *n*: **the ~** das Rote Meer.
red tape *n* Papierkrieg *m*, Behördenkram *m* (*col*).
reduce [ridōōs'] *vt* (*price*) herabsetzen (*to* auf +*acc*); (*speed, temperature*) vermindern; (*photo*) verkleinern; **to ~ sth by $10/to $10** etw um 10 Dollar reduzieren/etw auf 10 Dollar reduzieren; **to ~ sb to silence/despair/tears** jdn zum Schweigen/zur Verzweiflung/zum Weinen bringen.
reduced [ridōōst'] *a* (*decreased*) verringert, reduziert; **at a ~ price** zu ermäßigtem Preis, ermäßigt; "**greatly ~ prices**" „stark reduzierte Preise".
reduction [riduk'shən] *n* Herabsetzung *f*; Verminderung *f*; Verkleinerung *f*; (*amount of money*) Nachlaß *m*.
redundancy [ridun'dənsē] *n* Überflüssigkeit *f*; (*Brit: of workers*) Entlassung *f*; **compulsory ~** Entlassung *f*; **voluntary ~** freiwillige Arbeitsplatzaufgabe *f*.
redundancy payment *n* (*Brit*) Abfindung *f*.
redundant [ridun'dənt] *a* überflüssig; (*Brit: workers*) ohne Arbeitsplatz; **to be made ~** arbeitslos werden.
reed [rēd] *n* Schilf *nt*; (*MUS*) Rohrblatt *nt*.
reedy [rē'dē] *a* (*voice, instrument*) durchdringend.
reef [rēf] *n* Riff *nt*.
reek [rēk] *vi* stinken (*of* nach).
reel [rēl] *n* Spule *f*, Rolle *f* ♦ *vt* (*wind*) wickeln, spulen; (*stagger*) taumeln ♦ *vi*: **my head is ~ing** mir dreht sich der Kopf.
reel off *vt* herunterrasseln.
reelection [rēilek'shən] *n* Wiederwahl *f*.
reenter [rēen'tûr] *vti* wieder eintreten (in +*acc*).
reentry [rēen'trē] *n* (*also SPACE*) Wiedereintritt *m*; (*for exam*) Wiederantritt *m* (*for* zu).
reexamine [rēigzam'in] *vt* neu überprüfen.
reexport *n* [rēeks'pôrt] wieder ausgeführte Ware *pl*, Wiederausfuhr *f* ♦ *vt* [rēekspôrt'] wieder ausführen.
ref [ref] *n* (*col*: = *referee*) Schiri *m*.
ref. *abbr* (*COMM*: = *with reference to*) betr.
refectory [rifek'tûrē] *n* (*UNIV*) Mensa *f*; (*SCH*) Speisesaal *m*; (*ECCL*) Refektorium *nt*.

refer [rifûr'] *vt*: **to ~ sb to sb/sth** jdn an jdn/etw verweisen; **he ~red me to the manager** er verwies mich an den Geschäftsleiter ♦ *vi*: **to ~ to** hinweisen auf (+*acc*); (*to book*) nachschlagen in (+*dat*); (*mention*) sich beziehen auf (+*acc*).

referee [refǝrē'] *n* Schiedsrichter *m*; (*Brit: for job*) Referenz *f* ♦ *vt* schiedsrichtern.

reference [ref'ûrǝns] *n* (*mentioning*) Hinweis *m*; (*allusion*) Anspielung *f*; (*for job*) Referenz *f*; (*in book*) Verweis *m*; (*number, code*) Katalognummer *f*; **with ~ to** in bezug auf (+*acc*); **with ~ to your letter of** (*COMM*) bezugnehmend auf Ihr Schreiben vom ....

reference book *n* Nachschlagewerk *nt*.

reference number *n* Aktenzeichen *nt*.

referendum [refǝren'dǝm] *n*, *pl* **-s** *or* **referenda** [refǝren'dǝ] Volksabstimmung *f*, Referendum *nt*.

refill *vt* [rēfil'] nachfüllen ♦ *n* [rē'fil] Nachfüllung *f*; (*for pen*) Ersatzmine *f*.

refine [rifīn'] *vt* (*purify*) raffinieren; (*fig*) bilden, kultivieren.

refined [rifīnd'] *a* fein.

refinement [rifīn'mǝnt] *n* (*of oil, sugar*) Raffination *f*; (*of person etc*) Vornehmheit *f*.

refinery [rifī'nûrē] *n* Raffinerie *f*.

refit *n* [rē'fit] (*NAUT*) Neuausrüstung *f* ♦ *vt* [rēfit'] (*ship*) neu ausrüsten.

reflate [riflāt'] *vt* (*economy*) bewußt inflationieren, ankurbeln.

reflation [riflā'shǝn] *n* Reflation *f*, Ankurbelung *f* der Konjunktur.

reflationary [riflā'shǝnärē] *a* bewußt *or* gewollt inflationär.

reflect [riflekt'] *vt* (*light*) reflektieren; (*fig*) (wider)spiegeln, zeigen ♦ *vi* (*meditate*) nachdenken (*on über* +*acc*).
reflect on *vt fus*: **it ~s badly/well on him** das stellt ihn in ein schlechtes/gutes Licht.

reflection [riflek'shǝn] *n* Reflexion *f*; (*image*) Spiegelbild *nt*; (*thought*) Überlegung *f*, Gedanke *m*.

reflector [riflek'tûr] *n* Reflektor *m*.

reflex [rē'fleks] *n* Reflex *m*.

reflexive [riflek'siv] *a* (*GRAM*) Reflexiv-, rückbezüglich, reflexiv.

reforest [rēfôr'ist] *vt* wiederaufforsten.

reform [rifôrm'] *n* Reform *f* ♦ *vt* (*person*) bessern.

reformat [rēfôr'mat] *vt* (*COMPUT*) umformatieren.

Reformation [refûrmā'shǝn] *n*: **the ~** die Reformation *f*.

reformatory [rifôr'mǝtôrē] *n* Besserungsanstalt *f*.

reformer [rifôr'mûr] *n* Reformer *m*; (*ECCL*) Reformator *m*.

refrain [rifrān'] *vi* unterlassen (*from acc*) ♦ *n* (*MUS etc*) Refrain *m*.

refresh [rifresh'] *vt* erfrischen.

refresher course [rifresh'ûr kôrs] *n* Wiederholungskurs *m*.

refreshing [rifresh'ing] *a* (*drink, sleep, idea*) erfrischend; (*change etc*) angenehm.

refreshments [rifresh'mǝnts] *npl* Erfrischungen *pl*.

refreshment stand *n* Trinkhalle *f*.

refrigeration [rifrijǝrā'shǝn] *n* Kühlung *f*.

refrigerator [rifrij'ǝrātûr] *n* Kühlschrank *m*.

refuel [rēfyōō'ǝl] *vti* auftanken.

refueling, (*Brit*) **refuelling** [rēfyōō'ǝling] *n* Auftanken *nt*.

refuge [ref'yōōj] *n* Zuflucht *f*.

refugee [refyōōjē'] *n* Flüchtling *m*.

refugee camp *n* Flüchtlingslager *nt*.

refund *n* [rē'fund] Rückvergütung *f* ♦ *vt* [rifund'] zurückerstatten, rückvergüten.

refurbish [rēfûr'bish] *vt* aufpolieren.

refurnish [rēfûr'nish] *vt* neu möblieren.

refusal [rifyōō'zǝl] *n* (Ver)weigerung *f*; (*official*) abschlägige Antwort *f*; **to have first ~ on sth** etw als erster angeboten bekommen.

refuse *n* [ref'yōōs] Abfall *m*, Müll *m* ♦ [rifyōōz'] *vt* abschlagen; **to ~ to do sth** sich weigern, etw zu tun ♦ *vi* sich weigern.

refuse collection *n* (*Brit*) Müllabfuhr *f*.

refuse disposal *n* (*Brit*) Müllbeseitigung *f*.

refute [rifyōōt'] *vt* widerlegen.

regain [rigān'] *vt* wiedergewinnen; (*consciousness*) wiedererlangen.

regal [rē'gǝl] *a* königlich.

regale [rigāl'] *vt* verwöhnen.

regalia [rigā'lēǝ] *npl* Insignien *pl*; (*of mayor etc*) Amtsornat *m*.

regard [rigârd'] *n* Achtung *f*; *see also* **regards** ♦ *vt* ansehen; **as ~s, with ~ to** bezüglich (+*gen*), in bezug auf (+*acc*).

regarding [rigâr'ding] *prep* bezüglich (+*gen*), in bezug auf (+*acc*).

regardless [rigârd'lis] *a* ohne Rücksicht (*of auf* +*acc*) ♦ *ad* trotzdem.

regards [rigârdz'] *npl* Grüße *pl*; **with kind ~** mit freundlichen Grüßen; **(please give my) ~ to Maria** schöne Grüße an Maria, grüß mir bitte Maria.

regatta [rigât'ǝ] *n* Regatta *f*.

regency [rē'jǝnsē] *n* Regentschaft *f*.

regenerate [rējen'ûrāt] *vt* erneuern.

regent [rē'jǝnt] *n* Regent *m*.

régime [rāzhēm'] *n* Regime *nt*.

regiment *n* [rej'ǝmǝnt] Regiment *nt* ♦ *vt* [rej'ǝment] (*fig*) reglementieren.

regimental [rejǝmen'tǝl] *a* Regiments-.

regimentation [rejǝmǝntā'shǝn] *n* Reglementierung *f*.

region [rē'jǝn] *n* Gegend *f*, Bereich *m*.

regional [rē'jǝnǝl] *a* örtlich, regional.

regional development grant *n* Staatszuschuß *m* zur regionalen Förderung der Wirtschaft.

register [rej'istûr] *n* Register *nt*, Verzeichnis *nt*, Liste *f* ♦ *vt* (*list*) registrieren, eintragen; (*emotion*) zeigen; (*write down*) eintragen; **to ~ a protest** Protest anmelden ♦ *vi* (*at hotel*) sich eintragen; (*with police*) sich melden (*with bei*); (*make impression*) wirken, ankommen; **to ~ for a course** einen Kurs belegen.

registered [rej'istûrd] a (design) eingetragen; (Brit: letter) Einschreibe-, eingeschrieben; (student) eingeschrieben; (voter) eingetragen.

registered company n eingetragene Gesellschaft f.

registered nurse n (US) staatlich geprüfte Krankenschwester f.

registered office n eingetragene(r) Gesellschaftssitz m.

registered trademark n eingetragene(s) Warenzeichen nt.

registrar [rej'istrár] n Standesbeamte(r) m; (MED) Krankenhausarzt m/-ärztin f.

registration [rejistrā'shən] n (act) Erfassung f, Registrierung f; (number) Autonummer f, polizeiliche(s) Kennzeichen nt.

registry office [rej'istrē ôfis] n (Brit) Standesamt nt.

regret [rigret'] n Bedauern nt; **to have no ~s** nichts bedauern ♦ vt bedauern; **we ~ to inform you that ...** wir müssen Ihnen leider mitteilen, daß ...

regretful [rigret'fəl] a traurig; **to be ~ about sth** etw bedauern.

regretfully [rigret'fəlē] ad mit Bedauern, ungern.

regrettable [rigret'əbəl] a bedauerlich.

regrettably [rigret'əblē] ad bedauerlicherweise, leider.

regroup [rēgrōōp'] vt umgruppieren ♦ vi sich umgruppieren.

regt. abbr (= regiment) Reg.

regular [reg'yəlûr] a regelmäßig; (usual) üblich; (fixed by rule) geregelt; (col: disaster) regelrecht ♦ n (client etc) Stammkunde m; (MIL) Berufssoldat m; (US: gas) Normalbenzin nt.

regularity [regyəlar'itē] n Regelmäßigkeit f.

regularly [reg'yəlûrlē] ad regelmäßig.

regulate [reg'yəlāt] vt regeln, regulieren.

regulation [regyəlā'shən] n (rule) Vorschrift f; (control) Regulierung f.

rehabilitation [rēhəbilətā'shən] n (of criminal) Resozialisierung f.

rehash [rēhash'] vt (col) aufwärmen.

rehearsal [rihûr'səl] n Probe f.

rehearse [rihûrs'] vt proben.

rehouse [rēhouz'] vt neu unterbringen.

reign [rān] n Herrschaft f ♦ vi herrschen.

reigning [rā'ning] a (monarch) herrschend; (champion) gegenwärtig.

reimburse [rēimbûrs'] vt entschädigen, zurückzahlen (sb for sth jdm etw).

rein [rān] n Zügel m; **to give sb free ~** (fig) jdm freien Lauf lassen.

reincarnation [rēinkârnā'shən] n Wiedergeburt f.

reindeer [rān'dēr] n (pl inv) Ren nt.

reinforce [rēinfôrs'] vt verstärken.

reinforced concrete [rēinfôrst' kân'krēt] n Stahlbeton m.

reinforcement [rēinfôrs'mənt] n Verstärkung f.

reinforcements [rēinfôrs'mənts] npl (MIL, fig) Verstärkungstruppen pl.

reinstate [rēinstāt'] vt wiedereinsetzen.

reinstatement [rēinstāt'mənt] n Wiedereinstellung f.

reissue [rēish'ōō] vt neu herausgeben.

reiterate [rēit'ərāt] vt wiederholen.

reject n [rē'jekt] (COMM) Ausschuß(artikel) m ♦ vt [rijekt'] ablehnen; (throw away) ausrangieren.

rejection [rijek'shən] n Zurückweisung f.

rejoice [rijois'] vi sich freuen.

rejoinder [rijoin'dûr] n Erwiderung f.

rejuvenate [rijōō'vənāt] vt verjüngen.

rekindle [rēkin'dəl] vt wieder anfachen.

relapse [rilaps'] n Rückfall m.

relate [rilāt'] vt (tell) berichten, erzählen; (connect) verbinden ♦ vi: **to ~ to** (connect) zusammenhängen mit.

related [rilā'tid] a verwandt (to mit).

relating to [rilā'ting tōō] prep bezüglich (+gen).

relation [rilā'shən] n Verwandte(r) mf; (connection) Beziehung f; **in ~ to** (as regards) in bezug auf (+acc); (compared with) im Verhältnis zu; **diplomatic/international ~s** diplomatische/internationale Beziehungen pl; **to bear a ~ to** in Beziehung stehen zu.

relationship [rilā'shənship] n Verhältnis nt, Beziehung f.

relative [rel'ətiv] n Verwandte(r) mf ♦ a relativ, bedingt.

relatively [rel'ətivlē] ad (fairly, rather) relativ, verhältnismäßig.

relative pronoun n Verhältniswort nt, Relativpronomen nt.

relax [rilaks'] vi (slacken) sich lockern; (muscles, person) sich entspannen; (be less strict) freundlicher werden ♦ vt (ease) lockern, entspannen; **~!** reg' dich ab!

relaxation [rēlaksā'shən] n Entspannung f.

relaxed [rilakst'] a entspannt, locker.

relaxing [rilaks'ing] a entspannend.

relay n [rē'lā] (SPORT) Staffel f ♦ vt [rēlā'] (message) weiterleiten; (RAD, TV) übertragen.

release [rilēs'] n (freedom) Entlassung f; (TECH) Auslöser m ♦ vt befreien; (prisoner) entlassen; (report, news) verlautbaren, bekanntgeben.

relegated [rel'əgātid] a: **to be ~** (SPORT) absteigen.

relent [rilent'] vi nachgeben.

relentless [rilent'lis] a, **relentlessly** [rilent'lislē] ad unnachgiebig.

relevance [rel'əvəns] n Relevanz f.

relevant [rel'əvənt] a wichtig, relevant.

reliability [rilīəbil'ətē] n Zuverlässigkeit f.

reliable [rilī'əbəl] a, **reliably** [rilī'əblē] ad zuverlässig.

reliance [rilī'əns] n Abhängigkeit f (on von).

reliant [rilī'ənt] a: **to be ~ on sth/sb** auf

etw/jdn angewiesen sein.

relic [rel'ik] n *(from past)* Überbleibsel nt; *(REL)* Reliquie f.

relief [rilēf'] n Erleichterung f; *(help)* Hilfe f, Unterstützung f; *(person)* Ablösung f; *(ART)* Relief nt; **by way of light** ~ um eine kleine Abwechslung zu schaffen.

relief road n *(Brit)* Entlastungsstraße f.

relieve [rilēv'] vt *(ease)* erleichtern; *(bring help)* entlasten; *(person)* ablösen; **to ~ sb of sth** jdm etw abnehmen; **to ~ sb of his command** *(MIL)* jdn des Kommandos entheben; **I am ~d to hear you are better** ich bin erleichtert, zu erfahren, daß es dir besser geht.

religion [rilij'ən] n Religion f.

religious [rilij'əs] a religiös.

religiously [rilij'əslē] ad religiös; *(conscientiously)* gewissenhaft.

reline [rēlīn'] vt *(brakes)* neu beschuhen.

relinquish [riling'kwish] vt aufgeben.

relish [rel'ish] n Würze f, pikante Beigabe f ♦ vt genießen.

relive [rēliv'] vt noch einmal durchleben.

relocate [rēlō'kāt] vt verlegen ♦ vi umziehen.

reluctance [riluk'təns] n Widerstreben nt, Abneigung f.

reluctant [riluk'tənt] a widerwillig; **I am ~ to do it** es widerstrebt mir, es zu tun.

reluctantly [riluk'təntlē] ad ungern.

rely on [rilī' ân] vt fus sich verlassen auf *(+acc)*; **you can ~ on my discretion** Sie können sich auf meine Verschwiegenheit verlassen.

remain [rimān'] vi *(be left)* übrigbleiben; *(stay)* bleiben; **to ~ silent** weiterhin schweigen.

remainder [rimān'dûr] n Rest m.

remaining [rimā'ning] a übrig(geblieben).

remains [rimānz'] npl Überreste pl; *(dead body)*: **(human) ~** sterbliche Überreste pl.

remand [rimand'] *(Brit)* n: **on ~** in Untersuchungshaft ♦ vt: **to ~ in custody** in Untersuchungshaft schicken.

remark [rimârk'] n Bemerkung f ♦ vt bemerken ♦ vi: **to ~ on sth** über etw *(acc)* eine Bemerkung machen, sich zu etw äußern.

remarkable [rimâr'kəbəl] a, **remarkably** [rimâr'kəblē] ad bemerkenswert.

remarry [rēmar'ē] vi wieder heiraten.

remedial [rimē'dēəl] a Heil-; *(teaching)* Hilfsschul-.

remedy [rem'idē] n Mittel nt ♦ vt *(pain)* abhelfen *(+dat)*; *(trouble)* in Ordnung bringen.

remember [rimem'bûr] vt sich erinnern an *(+acc)*; **I ~ seeing it, I ~ having seen it** ich erinnere mich daran, daß ich es gesehen habe; **she ~ed to do it** sie hat daran gedacht, es zu tun; **~ me to them** grüße sie von mir.

remembrance [rimem'brəns] n Erinnerung f; *(official)* Gedenken nt.

remind [rimīnd'] vt erinnern *(of* an *+acc)*; **that ~s me ...** dabei fällt mir (gerade) ein

...

reminder [rimīnd'ûr] n Mahnung f.

reminisce [remənis'] vi in Erinnerungen schwelgen.

reminiscences [remənis'ənsiz] npl Erinnerungen pl.

reminiscent [remənis'ənt] a erinnernd *(of* an *+acc)*, Erinnerungen nachrufend *(of* an *+acc)*.

remiss [rimis'] a nachlässig.

remission [rimish'ən] n *(REL)* Nachlaß m; *(of debt, sentence)* Erlaß m.

remit [rimit'] vt *(money)* überweisen *(to* an *+acc)*.

remittance [rimit'əns] n Geldanweisung f.

remnant [rem'nənt] n Rest m.

remonstrate [rimän'strāt] vi protestieren.

remorse [rimôrs'] n Gewissensbisse pl.

remorseful [rimôrs'fəl] a reumütig.

remorseless [rimôrs'lis] a, **remorselessly** [rimôrs'lislē] ad unbarmherzig.

remote [rimōt'] a abgelegen, entfernt; *(slight)* gering; *(COMPUT)* rechnerfern; **I haven't the ~st idea** ich habe nicht die leiseste Ahnung.

remote control n Fernsteuerung f.

remote-controlled [rimōt'kəntrōld'] a ferngesteuert, ferngelenkt.

remotely [rimōt'lē] ad entfernt.

remoteness [rimōt'nis] n Entlegenheit f.

remould [rē'mōld] n *(Brit)* runderneuerte(r) Reifen m.

removable [rimōō'vəbəl] a entfernbar.

removal [rimōō'vəl] n Beseitigung f; *(Brit: of furniture)* Umzug m; *(from office)* Entlassung f.

removal van n *(Brit)* Möbelwagen m.

remove [rimōōv'] vt beseitigen, entfernen; *(dismiss)* entlassen; **a cousin once ~d** ein Cousin ersten Grades.

remover [rimōō'vûr] n *(for paint etc)* Fleckenentferner m; **make-up ~** Reinigungscreme f.

removers [rimōō'vûrz] npl *(Brit: company)* Möbelspedition f.

remunerate [rimyōō'nərāt] vt bezahlen.

remuneration [rimyōōnərā'shən] n Vergütung f, Honorar nt.

Renaissance [ren'isâns] n: **the ~** die Renaissance.

rename [rēnām'] vt umbenennen.

rend [rend] vt irreg zerreißen.

render [ren'dûr] vt machen; *(translate)* übersetzen.

rendering [ren'dûring] n *(MUS)* Wiedergabe f.

rendezvous [rân'dāvōō] n Verabredung f, Rendezvous nt; *(of spaceships)* Begegnung von Raumfahrzeugen im Weltraum ♦ vi sich treffen.

renegade [ren'əgād] n Überläufer m.

renew [rinōō'] vt erneuern; *(contract, license)* verlängern; *(replace)* ersetzen.

renewable [rinōō'əbəl] a *(lease, contract)* verlängerbar; *(energy, resources)* erneuerbar.

renewal [rinōō'əl] *n* Erneuerung *f*; Verlängerung *f*.

renounce [rinouns'] *vt* (*give up*) verzichten auf (+*acc*); (*disown*) verstoßen.

renovate [ren'əvāt] *vt* renovieren; (*building*) restaurieren.

renovation [renəvā'shən] *n* Renovierung *f*; Restauration *f*.

renown [rinoun'] *n* Ruf *m*.

renowned [rinound'] *a* namhaft.

rent [rent] *n* (*for room, house*) Miete *f*; (*for land, factory*) Pacht *f* ♦ *vt* (*hire: house, apartment, car*) mieten; (: *farm, factory*) pachten; (*let*) vermieten; verpachten; (*also:* ~ **out**: *car, TV*) verleihen ♦ *pt, pp of* **rend**.

rental [ren'təl] *n* Miete *f*; Pacht *f*, Pachtgeld *nt*; (*on car: also:* ~ **fee**) Leihgebühr *f*.

rental car *n* (*US*) Mietwagen *m*.

renunciation [rinunsēā'shən] *n* Verzicht *m* (*of* auf +*acc*).

reopen [rēō'pən] *vt* wiedereröffnen.

reorder [rēôr'dûr] *vt* wieder bestellen.

reorganization [rēôrgənəzā'shən] *n* Neugestaltung *f*; (*COMM etc*) Umbildung *f*.

reorganize [rēôr'gənīz] *vt* umgestalten, reorganisieren.

rep [rep] *n abbr* (*COMM*: = *representative*) Vertreter *m*; (*THEAT*: = *repertory*) Repertoire *nt*.

rep. *abbr* (= *republic*) Rep.

Rep. *n abbr* (*US POL*: = *Representative*) Abg.; (: = *Republican*) Rep.

repair [ripär'] *n* Reparatur *f*; **in good** ~ in gutem Zustand; **under** ~ in Reparatur ♦ *vt* reparieren; (*damage*) wiedergutmachen.

repair kit *n* Werkzeugkasten *m*.

repair man *n* Mechaniker *m*.

repair shop *n* Reparaturwerkstatt *f*.

repartee [repûrtē'] *n* Witzeleien *pl*.

repast [ripast'] *n* (*form*) Mahl *nt*.

repatriate [rēpā'trēāt] *vt* in das Heimatland zurücksenden, repatriieren.

repay [ripā'] *vt irreg* zurückzahlen; (*reward*) vergelten.

repayment [ripā'mənt] *n* Rückzahlung *f*; (*fig*) Vergelten *nt*.

repeal [ripēl'] *n* Aufhebung *f* ♦ *vt* aufheben.

repeat [ripēt'] *n* (*RAD, TV*) Wiederholung(ssendung) *f* ♦ *vt* wiederholen; **to place a** ~ **order for** (*COMM*) nachbestellen.

repeatedly [ripēt'idlē] *ad* wiederholt.

repel [ripel'] *vt* (*drive back*) zurückschlagen; (*disgust*) abstoßen.

repellent [ripel'ənt] *a* abstoßend ♦ *n*: **insect** ~ Insektenmittel *nt*.

repent [ripent'] *vti* bereuen.

repentance [ripen'təns] *n* Reue *f*.

repercussion [rēpûrkush'ən] *n* Auswirkung *f*; **to have** ~**s** ein Nachspiel haben.

repertoire [rep'ûrtwâr] *n* Repertoire *nt*.

repertory [rep'ûrtōrē] *n* Repertoire *nt*.

repertory company *n* Repertoire-Ensemble *nt*.

repetition [repitish'ən] *n* Wiederholung *f*.

repetitious [repitish'əs] *a* (*work*) eintönig; (*speech*) sich wiederholend.

repetitive [ripet'ətiv] *a* = **repetitious**.

rephrase [rēfrāz'] *vt* anders formulieren.

replace [riplās'] *vt* ersetzen; (*put back*) zurückstellen.

replacement [riplās'mənt] *n* Ersatz *m*.

replacement cost *n* Wiederbeschaffungskosten *pl*.

replacement part *n* Ersatzteil *nt*.

replacement value *n* Wiederbeschaffungswert *m*.

replay [rēplā'] *n* (*TV: playback*) Wiederholung *f*, Replay *f*; (*of match*) Wiederholungsspiel *nt*.

replenish [riplen'ish] *vt* (wieder) auffüllen.

replete [riplēt'] *a* reichlich versehen *or* ausgestattet (*with* mit).

replica [rep'ləkə] *n* Kopie *f*.

reply [riplī'] *n* Antwort *f*, Erwiderung *f* ♦ *vi* antworten, erwidern; **in** ~ (als Antwort) darauf.

report [ripôrt'] *n* Bericht *m*; (*Brit SCH*) Zeugnis *nt*; (*of gun*) Knall *m* ♦ *vt* (*tell*) berichten; (*give information against*) melden; (*to police*) anzeigen; **it is** ~**ed from Berlin that** ... aus Berlin wird berichtet *or* gemeldet, daß ... ♦ *vi* (*make* ~) Bericht erstatten; (*present o.s.*) sich melden.

report card *n* (*US, Scot*) Zeugnis *nt*.

reportedly [ripôr'tidlē] *ad* angeblich.

reporter [ripôr'tûr] *n* (*PRESS, RAD, TV*) Reporter(in *f*) *m*, Berichterstatter(in *f*) *m*.

repose [ripōz'] *n*: **in** ~ (*face, mouth*) gelassen.

repossess [rēpəzes'] *vt* wieder in Besitz nehmen.

reprehensible [reprihen'səbəl] *a* tadelnswert.

represent [reprizent'] *vt* darstellen, zeigen; (*act*) darstellen; (*speak for*) vertreten.

representation [reprizentā'shən] *n* Darstellung *f*; (*being represented*) Vertretung *f*.

representative [reprizen'tətiv] *n* (*COMM*) Vertreter(in *f*) *m*; **R**~ (*US POL*) Abgeordnete(r) *mf* des Repräsentantenhauses ♦ *a* repräsentativ; ~ **of** typisch für.

repress [ripres'] *vt* unterdrücken.

repression [ripresh'ən] *n* Unterdrückung *f*.

repressive [ripres'iv] *a* Unterdrückungs-; (*PSYCH*) Hemmungs-.

reprieve [riprēv'] *n* Aufschub *m*; (*JUR*) Begnadigung *f*; (*fig*) Gnadenfrist *f* ♦ *vt* (*JUR*) begnadigen; Gnadenfrist gewähren (+*dat*).

reprimand [rep'rəmand] *n* Verweis *m* ♦ *vt* einen Verweis erteilen (+*dat*).

reprint *n* [rē'print] Neudruck *m*, Neuauflage *f* ♦ *vt* [rēprint'] wieder abdrucken, neu auflegen.

reprisal [riprī'zəl] *n* Vergeltung *f*; **to take** ~**s** zu Repressalien greifen.

reproach [riprōch'] *n* (*blame*) Vorwurf *m*, Tadel *m*; (*disgrace*) Schande *f*; **beyond** ~ über jeden Vorwurf erhaben ♦ *vt* Vorwürfe

machen (+*dat*), tadeln.
reproachful [riprōch'fəl] *a* vorwurfsvoll.
reproduce [rēprədōōs'] *vt* reproduzieren ♦ *vi* (*have offspring*) sich vermehren.
reproduction [rēprəduk'shən] *n* Wiedergabe *f*; (*ART, PHOT*) Reproduktion *f*; (*breeding*) Fortpflanzung *f*.
reproductive [rēprəduk'tiv] *a* reproduktiv; (*breeding*) Fortpflanzungs-.
reprove [riprōōv'] *vt* tadeln.
reptile [rep'tīl] *n* Reptil *nt*.
Repub. *abbr* (*US POL*: = *Republican*) Rep.
republic [ripub'lik] *n* Republik *f*.
Republican [ripub'likən] (*US POL*) *a* republikanisch ♦ *n* Republikaner(in *f*) *m*.
repudiate [ripyōō'dēāt] *vt* zurückweisen, nicht anerkennen.
repudiation [ripyōōdēā'shən] *n* Nichtanerkennung *f*.
repugnance [ripug'nəns] *n* Widerwille *m*.
repugnant [ripug'nənt] *a* widerlich.
repulse [ripuls'] *vt* (*drive back*) zurückschlagen; (*reject*) abweisen.
repulsion [ripul'shən] *n* Abscheu *m*.
repulsive [ripul'siv] *a* abstoßend.
repurchase [rēpûr'chis] *vt* zurückkaufen.
reputable [rep'yətəbəl] *a* angesehen.
reputation [repyətā'shən] *n* Ruf *m*; **he has a ~ for being awkward** er hat den Ruf, schwierig zu sein.
repute [ripyōōt'] *n* hohe(s) Ansehen *nt*.
reputed [ripyōō'tid] *a* angeblich; **to be ~ to be rich/intelligent** *etc* als reich/intelligent *etc* gelten.
reputedly [ripyōō'tidlē] *ad* angeblich.
request [rikwest'] *n* (*asking*) Ansuchen *nt*; (*demand*) Wunsch *m*; **at sb's ~** auf jds Bitte ♦ *vt* (*thing*) erbitten; (*person*) ersuchen; **"you are ~ed not to smoke"** „bitte nicht rauchen".
request stop *n* (*Brit*) Bedarfshaltestelle *f*.
requiem [rek'wēəm] *n* Requiem *nt*.
require [rikwīûr'] *vt* (*need*) brauchen; (*wish*) wünschen; **to ~ sth of sb** etw von jdm verlangen; **to be ~d to do sth** etw tun müssen; **what qualifications are ~d?** welche Qualifikationen sind erforderlich?; **to ~ sb to do sth** von jdm verlangen, daß er etw tut; **as ~d by law** gemäß den gesetzlichen Bestimmungen.
requirement [rikwīûr'mənt] *n* (*condition*) Anforderung *f*; (*need*) Bedarf *m*.
requisite [rek'wizit] *n* Erfordernis *nt* ♦ *a* erforderlich.
requisition [rekwizish'ən] *n* Anforderung *f* ♦ *vt* (*order*) anfordern.
reroute [rērout'] *vt* umleiten.
resale price maintenance [rē'sāl prīs mān'tənəns] *n* Einhaltung *f* von Wiederverkaufspreisen.
rescind [risind'] *vt* aufheben.
rescue [res'kyōō] *n* Rettung *f* ♦ *vt* retten; **to come to sb's ~** jdm zu Hilfe kommen.
rescue party *n* Rettungsmannschaft *f*.

rescuer [res'kyōōûr] *n* Retter(in *f*) *m*.
research [risûrch'] *n* Forschung *f*; **a piece of ~** eine Forschungsarbeit; **~ and development** Forschung und Entwicklung ♦ *vi* Forschungen anstellen (*into* über +*acc*) ♦ *vt* erforschen.
researcher [risûr'chûr] *n* Forscher(in *f*) *m*.
research work *n* Forschungsarbeit *f*.
research worker *n* wissenschaftliche(r) Mitarbeiter(in *f*) *m*.
resemblance [rizem'bləns] *n* Ähnlichkeit *f*; **to bear a strong ~ to sb/sth** starke Ähnlichkeit mit jdm/etw haben.
resemble [rizem'bəl] *vt* ähneln (+*dat*).
resent [rizent'] *vt* übelnehmen.
resentful [rizent'fəl] *a* nachtragend, empfindlich.
resentment [rizent'mənt] *n* Verstimmung *f*, Unwille *m*.
reservation [rezûrvā'shən] *n* (*booking*) Reservierung *f*; (*THEAT*) Vorbestellung *f*; (*doubt*) Vorbehalt *m*; (*land*) Reservat *nt*; **with ~s** unter Vorbehalt.
reservation desk *n* (*US: in hotel*) Rezeption *f*.
reserve [rizûrv'] *n* (*store*) Vorrat *m*, Reserve *f*; (*manner*) Zurückhaltung *f*; (*game ~*) Naturschutzgebiet *nt*; (*native ~*) Reservat *nt*; (*SPORT*) Ersatzspieler(in *f*) *m*; **in ~** in Reserve; *see also* **reserves** ♦ *vt* reservieren; (*judgement*) sich (*dat*) vorbehalten.
reserve currency *n* Reservewährung *f*.
reserved [rizûrvd'] *a* reserviert; **all rights ~** alle Rechte vorbehalten.
reserve price *n* Mindestpreis *m*.
reserves [rizûrvz'] *npl* (*MIL*) Reserve *f*.
reservist [rizûr'vist] *n* Reservist *m*.
reservoir [rez'ûrvwâr] *n* (*artificial lake*) Reservoir *nt*.
reset [rēset'] *vt irreg* (*COMPUT*) rücksetzen.
reshape [rēshāp'] *vt* umformen.
reshuffle [rēshuf'əl] *vt* (*POL*) umbilden.
reside [rizīd'] *vi* wohnen, ansässig sein.
residence [rez'idəns] *n* (*house*) Wohnung *f*, Wohnsitz *m*; (*living*) Wohnen *nt*, Aufenthalt *m*; **to take up ~** sich niederlassen; **in ~** (*queen etc*) anwesend sein; (*doctor*) am Ort.
resident [rez'idənt] *n* (*in house*) Bewohner(in *f*) *m*; (*in area*) Einwohner(in *f*) *m*; (*in hotel*) Gast *m* ♦ *a* wohnhaft, ansässig; (*COMPUT*) resident.
residential [reziden'chəl] *a* Wohn-.
residue [rez'idōō] *n* Rest *m*; (*CHEM*) Rückstand *m*; (*fig*) Bodensatz *m*.
resign [rizīn'] *vt* (*office*) aufgeben, zurücktreten von; **to be ~ed to sth, to ~ o.s. to sth** sich mit etw abfinden ♦ *vi* (*from office*) zurücktreten.
resignation [rezignā'shən] *n* (*resigning*) Aufgabe *f*; (*POL*) Rücktritt *m*; (*submission*) Resignation *f*; **to tender one's ~** seinen Rücktritt *or* seine Kündigung einreichen.
resigned [rizīnd'] *a* resigniert.
resilience [rizil'yəns] *n* Spannkraft *f*; (*of per-*

son) Unverwüstlichkeit f.
resilient [rizil'yənt] a unverwüstlich.
resin [rez'in] n Harz nt.
resist [rizist'] vt widerstehen (+dat).
resistance [rizis'təns] n Widerstand m.
resistant [rizis'tənt] a (material, surface) strapazierfähig; (MED) immun (to gegen).
resolute [rez'əloot] a, **resolutely** [rez'əlootlē] ad entschlossen, resolut.
resolution [rezəloo'shən] n (determination) Entschlossenheit f; (intention) Vorsatz m; (decision) Beschluß m; (COMPUT: on screen) (Bild)auflösung f; **to make a ~** einen Vorsatz fassen.
resolve [rizâlv'] n Entschlossenheit f ♦ vt (decide) beschließen ♦ vr sich lösen.
resolved [rizâlvd'] a (fest) entschlossen.
resonance [rez'ənəns] n Resonanz f.
resonant [rez'ənənt] a widerhallend; (voice) volltönend.
resort [rizôrt'] n (vacation spot) Erholungsort m, Urlaubsort m; (help) Zuflucht f ♦ vi Zuflucht nehmen (to zu); **as a last ~** als letzter Ausweg; **seaside/winter sports ~** Badeort m/Wintersportort m.
resound [rizound'] vi widerhallen.
resounding [rizoun'ding] a nachhallend; (success) groß.
resource [rē'sôrs] n (expedient) Ausweg m; see also **resources**.
resourceful [risôrs'fəl] a findig.
resourcefulness [risôrs'fəlnis] n Findigkeit f.
resources [rē'sôrsiz] npl (of energy) Energiequellen pl; (of money) Quellen pl; (of a country etc) Bodenschätze pl; **to leave sb to his (or her) own ~** (fig) jdn sich (dat) selbst überlassen.
respect [rispekt'] n Respekt m; (esteem) (Hoch)achtung f; **to have or show ~ for** Respekt or Achtung haben/zeigen vor (+dat); **out of ~ for** aus Rücksicht auf (+acc); **with due ~ ...** bei allem Respekt ...; **in some ~s** in gewisser Hinsicht; **in this ~** in dieser Hinsicht; **with ~ to** in bezug auf (+acc), hinsichtlich (+gen); **in ~ of** in bezug auf (+acc) ♦ vt achten, respektieren; see also **respects**.
respectability [rispektəbil'ətē] n Anständigkeit f, Achtbarkeit f.
respectable [rispek'təbəl] a (decent) anständig, achtbar; (quite big: amount etc) ansehnlich, beachtlich; (quite good: player) ordentlich; (: result etc) beachtlich.
respected [rispek'tid] a angesehen.
respectful [rispek'fəl] a respektvoll (towards, of gegenüber).
respectfully [rispekt'fəlē] ad respektvoll, ehrerbietig; (in letter) mit vorzüglicher Hochachtung.
respecting [rispek'ting] prep bezüglich (+gen).
respective [rispek'tiv] a jeweilig.
respectively [rispek'tivlē] ad beziehungsweise.

respects [rispekts'] npl Grüße pl; **to pay one's last ~** die letzte Ehre erwiesen.
respiration [respərā'shən] n Atmung f, Atmen nt.
respiratory [res'pûrətôrē] a Atem-; (organs, problem) Atmungs-.
respite [res'pit] n Ruhepause f; **without ~** ohne Unterlaß.
resplendent [risplen'dənt] a strahlend.
respond [rispând'] vi antworten; (react) reagieren (to auf +acc).
respondent [rispân'dənt] n (JUR) Scheidungsbeklagte(r) mf.
response [rispâns'] n Antwort f; (reaction) Reaktion f; (to advert etc) Resonanz f; **in ~ to** als Antwort auf (+acc).
responsibility [rispânsəbil'ətē] n Verantwortung f; **to take ~ for sth/sb** die Verantwortung für etw/jdn übernehmen.
responsible [rispân'səbəl] a verantwortlich; (reliable) verantwortungsvoll; **to be ~ to sb (for sth)** jdm gegenüber (für etw) verantwortlich sein.
responsibly [rispân'səblē] ad verantwortungsvoll.
responsive [rispân'siv] a empfänglich.
rest [rest] n Ruhe f; (break) Pause f; (remainder) Rest m; **the ~ of them** die übrigen; **to set sb's mind at ~** jdn beruhigen ♦ vi sich ausruhen; (be supported) (auf)liegen; (remain) liegen (with bei); **~ assured that ...** Sie können versichert sein, daß ... ♦ vt: **to ~ one's eyes or gaze on sb/sth** den Blick auf jdn/etw heften.
rest area n (US AUT) Raststätte f.
restaurant [res'tûrənt] n Restaurant nt, Gaststätte f.
restaurant car n (Brit) Speisewagen m.
restaurant owner n Inhaber(in f) m eines Restaurants.
rest cure n Erholung f.
restful [rest'fəl] a erholsam, ruhig.
rest home n Erholungsheim nt.
restitution [restitoo'shən] n Rückgabe f, Entschädigung f; **to make ~ to sb for sth** jdn für etw entschädigen.
restive [res'tiv] a unruhig; (disobedient) störrisch.
restless [rest'lis] a unruhig; **to get ~** unruhig werden.
restlessly [rest'lislē] ad ruhelos.
restlessness [rest'lisnis] n Ruhelosigkeit f.
restock [rēstâk'] vt auffüllen.
restoration [restərā'shən] n Wiederherstellung f; Neueinführung f; Wiedereinsetzung f; Rückgabe f; Restauration f; **the R~** die Restauration.
restorative [ristôr'ətiv] n Stärkungsmittel nt ♦ a stärkend.
restore [ristôr'] vt (order) wiederherstellen; (customs) wieder einführen; (person to position) wiedereinsetzen; (give back) zurückgeben; (paintings) restaurieren.
restorer [ristôr'ûr] n (ART etc) Restaurator(in

f) m.

restrain [ristrān'] *vt* zurückhalten; *(curiosity etc)* beherrschen.

restrained [ristrānd'] *a (style etc)* gedämpft, verhalten.

restraint [ristrānt'] *n (restraining)* Einschränkung *f*; *(being restrained)* Beschränkung *f*; *(self-control)* Zurückhaltung *f*; **wage ~** Lohnstopp *m*.

restrict [ristrikt'] *vt* einschränken.

restricted [ristrik'tid] *a* beschränkt.

restriction [ristrik'shən] *n* Einschränkung *f*.

restrictive [ristrik'tiv] *a* einschränkend; **~ practices** *(INDUSTRY)* wettbewerbsbeschränkende Geschäftspraktiken *pl.*

rest room *n (US)* Toilette *f.*

restructure [rēstruk'chûr] *vt* umstrukturieren.

rest stop *n (US)* Rastplatz *m.*

result [rizult'] *n* Resultat *nt*, Folge *f*; *(of exam, game)* Ergebnis *nt*; **as a ~ of this** und folglich, als Folge davon ♦ *vi* zur Folge haben *(in acc)*; **to ~ (from)** sich ergeben (aus).

resultant [rizul'tənt] *a* resultierend, sich daraus ergebend.

resume [rēzōōm'] *vt* fortsetzen; *(occupy again)* wieder einnehmen; *(sum up)* zusammenfassen.

résumé [rez'ōōmā'] *n* Zusammenfassung *f.*

resumption [rizump'shən] *n* Wiederaufnahme *f.*

resurgence [risûr'jəns] *n* Wiedererwachen *nt.*

resurrection [rezərek'shən] *n* Auferstehung *f.*

resuscitate [risus'ətāt] *vt* wiederbeleben.

resuscitation [risusətā'shən] *n* Wiederbelebung *f.*

retail [rē'tāl] *n* Einzelhandel *m* ♦ *a* Einzelhandels-, Laden- ♦ *vt* im kleinen verkaufen ♦ *vi*: **to ~ at ...** *(COMM)* im Einzelhandel ... kosten.

retailer [rē'tālûr] *n* Einzelhändler *m*, Kleinhändler *m.*

retail outlet *n* Einzelhandelsverkaufsstelle *f.*

retail price *n* Einzelhandelspreis *m.*

retail price index *n* Einzelhandelspreisindex *m.*

retain [ritān'] *vt (keep)* behalten; *(money, object)* zurück(be)halten.

retainer [ritā'nûr] *n (servant)* Gefolgsmann *m; (fee)* Vorschuß *m.*

retaliate [rital'ēāt] *vi* zum Vergeltungsschlag ausholen.

retaliation [ritalēā'shən] *n* Vergeltung *f*; **in ~** als Revanche, zur Vergeltung.

retarded [ritär'did] *a* zurückgeblieben.

retch [rech] *vi* würgen.

retention [riten'chən] *n* Behalten *nt.*

retentive [riten'tiv] *a (memory)* gut.

rethink [rēthingk'] *vt irreg* nochmals durchdenken.

reticence [ret'isəns] *n* Schweigsamkeit *f.*

reticent [ret'isənt] *a* schweigsam.

retina [ret'ənə] *n* Netzhaut *f.*

retinue [ret'ənōō] *n* Gefolge *nt.*

retire [ritīûr'] *vi (from work)* in den Ruhestand treten; *(withdraw)* sich zurückziehen; *(go to bed)* schlafen gehen.

retired [ritīûrd'] *a (person)* pensioniert, im Ruhestand.

retirement [ritīûr'mənt] *n (period, state)* Ruhestand *m*; **early ~** frühzeitige *or* vorzeitige Pensionierung *f*; **on his ~ he hopes to travel** nach seiner Pensionierung hofft er zu reisen.

retiring [ritīûr'ing] *a (shy)* zurückhaltend, schüchtern; *(departing: chairman)* ausscheidend.

retort [ritôrt'] *n (reply)* Erwiderung *f*; *(CHEM)* Retorte *f* ♦ *vi (scharf)* erwidern.

retrace [rētrās'] *vt* zurückverfolgen.

retract [ritrakt'] *vt (statement)* zurücknehmen; *(undercarriage, claws)* einziehen.

retractable [ritrakt'əbəl] *a (aerial)* ausziehbar.

retrain [rētrān'] *vt* umschulen.

retraining [rētrā'ning] *n* Umschulung *f.*

retread [rē'tred] *n* runderneuerte(r) Reifen *m.*

retreat [ritrēt'] *n* Rückzug *m*; *(place)* Zufluchtsort *m* ♦ *vi* sich zurückziehen; **to beat a hasty ~** *(fig)* (schleunigst) das Feld räumen.

retrial [rētrīl'] *n* Wiederaufnahmeverfahren *nt.*

retribution [retrəbyōō'shən] *n* Strafe *f.*

retrieval [ritrē'vəl] *n* Wiedergewinnung *f.*

retrieve [ritrēv'] *vt* wiederbekommen; *(rescue)* retten.

retriever [ritrē'vûr] *n* Apportierhund *m.*

retroactive [retrōak'tiv] *a* rückwirkend.

retrograde [ret'rəgrād] *a* rückläufig; *(step)* Rück-; *(policy)* rückschrittlich; *(order)* umgekehrt.

retrospect [ret'rəspekt] *n*: **in ~** im Rückblick, rückblickend.

retrospective [retrəspek'tiv] *n* Retrospektive *f*, Rückschau *f* ♦ *a* rückwirkend; rückblickend.

return [ritûrn'] *n* Rückkehr *f*; *(profits)* Ertrag *m*, Gewinn *m*; *(report)* amtliche(r) Bericht *m*; *(Brit: rail ticket)* Rückfahrkarte *f*; *(: plane ticket)* Rückflugkarte *f*; *(: bus ticket)* Rückfahrschein *m*; *(COMM: merchandise)* zurückgesandte Ware *pl*, Retouren *pl*; **by ~ (of post)** *(Brit)* postwendend; **in ~ for** für; **tax ~** Steuererklärung *f* ♦ *a (journey, match)* Rück-; **by ~ mail** *(US)* postwendend ♦ *vi* zurückkehren *or* -kommen ♦ *vt* zurückgeben, zurücksenden; *(pay back)* zurückzahlen; *(elect)* wählen; *(verdict)* aussprechen.

returnable [ritûr'nəbəl] *a (bottle etc)* Mehrweg-; *(with deposit)* Pfand-.

return key *n (COMPUT)* Return-Taste *f.*

reunion [rēyōōn'yən] *n* Wiedervereinigung *f*; *(SCH etc)* Treffen *nt.*

reunite [rēyōōnīt'] *vt* wiedervereinigen.

rev [rev] *n abbr (AUT: = revolution)* Drehzahl *f* ♦ *vi (also: ~ up)* den Motor auf Touren bringen.

revaluation [rēval'yōōāshən] *n* Aufwertung *f.*
revamp [rēvamp'] *vt* aufpolieren.
Rev(d). *abbr* = **reverend.**
reveal [rivēl'] *vt* enthüllen.
revealing [rivē'ling] *a* aufschlußreich.
reveille [rev'əlē] *n* Wecken *nt.*
revel [rev'əl] *vi* genießen (*in acc*).
revelation [revəlā'shən] *n* Offenbarung *f.*
reveler, (*Brit*) **reveller** [rev'əlûr] *n* Schwelger *m.*
revelry [rev'əlrē] *n* Rummel *m.*
revenge [rivenj'] *n* Rache *f* ♦ *vt* rächen; **to get one's ~ (for sth)** sich (für etw) rächen, seine Rache (für etw) bekommen; (*SPORT*) sich (für etw) revanchieren, seine Revanche (für etw) bekommen.
revengeful [rivenj'fəl] *a* rachsüchtig.
revenue [rev'ənōō] *n* Einnahmen *pl*, Staatseinkünfte *pl.*
reverberate [rivûr'bərāt] *vi* widerhallen.
reverberation [rivûrbərā'shən] *n* Widerhall *m.*
revere [rivēr'] *vt* verehren.
reverence [rev'ûrəns] *n* Ehrfurcht *f.*
reverend [rev'ûrənd] *n*: **R~ Jones** ≈ Pfarrer Jones.
reverent [rev'ûrənt] *a* ehrfurchtsvoll.
reverie [rev'ûrē] *n* Träumerei *f.*
reversal [rivûr'səl] *n* Umkehrung *f.*
reverse [rivûrs'] *n* Rückseite *f*; (*AUT*: *gear*) Rückwärtsgang *m*; **the ~** das Gegenteil; **to go into ~** den Rückwärtsgang einlegen ♦ *a* (*order, direction*) entgegengesetzt; **in ~ order** in umgekehrter Reihenfolge ♦ *vt* umkehren ♦ *vi* (*AUT*) rückwärts fahren.
reverse-charge call [rivûrs'chärj kôl] *n* (*Brit*) R-Gespräch *nt.*
reverse video *n* invertierte Darstellung *f.*
reversible [rivûr'səbəl] *a* (*garment*) Wende-; (*procedure*) umkehrbar.
reversing lights [rivûr'sing līts] *npl* (*Brit AUT*) Rückfahrscheinwerfer *pl.*
reversion [rivûr'zhən] *n* Umkehrung *f.*
revert [rivûrt'] *vi* zurückkehren (*to* zu), zurückfallen (*to* in).
review [rivyōō'] *n* (*MIL*) Inspektion *f*; (*of book*) Rezension *f*; (*magazine*) Zeitschrift *f*; **to come under ~** (nochmals) geprüft werden; **to be under ~** untersucht werden ♦ *vt* Rückschau halten auf (+*acc*); (*US SCOL*) durchsehen, verbessern; (*MIL*) mustern; (*book*) rezensieren; (*reexamine*) von neuem untersuchen.
reviewer [rivyōō'ûr] *n* Rezensent(in *f*) *m.*
revile [rivīl'] *vt* schmähen, verunglimpfen.
revise [rivīz'] *vt* durchsehen, verbessern; (*book*) überarbeiten; (*reconsider*) ändern, revidieren.
revised edition [rivīzd' idish'ən] *n* überarbeitete Ausgabe *f.*
revision [rivizh'ən] *n* Durchsicht *f*, Prüfung *f*; (*of book*) überarbeitete Ausgabe *f*; (*SCH*) Wiederholung *f.*
revisit [rēviz'it] *vt* wieder besuchen.

revitalize [rēvī'təlīz] *vt* neu beleben.
revival [rivī'vəl] *n* Wiederbelebung *f*; (*REL*) Erweckung *f*; (*THEAT*) Wiederaufnahme *f.*
revive [rivīv'] *vt* wiederbeleben; (*fig*) wieder auffrischen ♦ *vi* wiedererwachen; (*fig*) wieder aufleben.
revoke [rivōk'] *vt* aufheben.
revolt [rivōlt'] *n* Aufstand *m*, Revolte *f* ♦ *vi* (*rebel*) rebellieren (*against* gegen +*acc*) ♦ *vt* (*disgust*) entsetzen.
revolting [rivōl'ting] *a* widerlich.
revolution [revəlōō'shən] *n* (*turn*) Umdrehung *f*; (*change*) Umwälzung *f*; (*POL*) Revolution *f.*
revolutionary [revəlōō'shənärē] *a* revolutionär ♦ *n* Revolutionär *m.*
revolutionize [revəlōō'shənīz] *vt* revolutionieren.
revolve [rivâlv'] *vi* kreisen; (*on own axis*) sich drehen.
revolver [rivâl'vûr] *n* Revolver *m.*
revolving credit [rivâl'ving kred'it] *n* Revolvingkredit *m.*
revue [rivyōō'] *n* Revue *f.*
revulsion [rivul'shən] *n* (*disgust*) Ekel *m.*
reward [riwôrd'] *n* Belohnung *f* ♦ *vt* belohnen.
rewarding [riwôrd'ing] *a* lohnend; **financially ~** einträglich, lohnend.
rewind [rēwīnd'] *vt irreg* (*watch*) wieder aufziehen; (*film, tape*) zurückspulen.
rewire [rēwīûr'] *vt* (*house*) neu verkabeln.
reword [rēwûrd'] *vt* anders formulieren.
rewrite [rērīt'] *vt irreg* umarbeiten, neu schreiben.
Reykjavik [rā'kyəvik] *n* Reykjavik *nt.*
RFD *abbr* (*US MAIL*: = *rural free delivery*) freie Landpostzustellung *f.*
Rh *abbr* (= *rhesus*) Rh.
rhapsody [rap'sədē] *n* Rhapsodie *f*; (*fig*) Schwärmerei *f.*
rhetoric [ret'ûrik] *n* Rhetorik *f*, Redekunst *f.*
rhetorical [ritôr'ikəl] *a* rhetorisch.
rheumatic [rōōmat'ik] *a* rheumatisch.
rheumatism [rōō'mətizəm] *n* Rheumatismus *m*, Rheuma *nt.*
rheumatoid arthritis [rōō'mətoid ärthrī'tis] *n* Gelenkrheumatismus *m.*
Rh factor *n* (*MED*) Rhesusfaktor *m.*
Rhine [rīn] *n* Rhein *m.*
rhinoceros [rīnâs'ûrəs] *n* Nashorn *nt*, Rhinozeros *nt.*
Rhodes [rōdz] *n* Rhodos *nt.*
rhododendron [rōdəden'drən] *n* Rhododendron *m.*
Rhone [rōn] *n* Rhone *f.*
rhubarb [rōō'bärb] *n* Rhabarber *m.*
rhyme [rīm] *n* Reim *m*; **without ~ or reason** ohne Sinn und Verstand ♦ *vi*: **to ~ (with)** sich reimen (auf +*acc*).
rhythm [rith'əm] *n* Rhythmus *m.*
rhythmic(al) [rith'mik(əl)] *a*, **rhythmically** [rith'miklē] *ad* rhythmisch.
RI *abbr* (*US MAIL*) = *Rhode Island.*
rib [rib] *n* Rippe *f* ♦ *vt* (*mock*) hänseln, aufzie-

hen.
ribald [rib'əld] *a* saftig, derb.
ribbon [rib'ən] *n* Band *nt*.
rice [rīs] *n* Reis *m*.
rice paddy *n* Reisfeld *nt*.
rich [rich] *a* reich, wohlhabend; *(fertile)*
fruchtbar; *(splendid)* kostbar; *(food)* reichhaltig; **to be ~ in sth** reich an etw *(dat)*
sein.
riches [rich'iz] *npl* Reichtum *m*, Reichtümer
pl.
richly [rich'lē] *ad* reich; *(deserve)* völlig.
richness [rich'nis] *n* Reichtum *m*; *(of food)*
Reichhaltigkeit *f*; *(of colors)* Sattheit *f*.
rickets [rik'its] *n* Rachitis *f*.
rickety [rik'ətē] *a* wack(e)lig.
rickshaw [rik'shô] *n* Rikscha *f*.
ricochet [rikəshā'] *n* Abprallen *nt*; *(shot)*
Querschläger *m* ♦ *vi* abprallen.
rid [rid] *vt irreg, pt, pp* **rid** befreien *(of* von*)*;
to get ~ of loswerden.
riddance [rid'əns] *n:* **good ~!** den/die/das
wären wir los!
ridden [rid'ən] *pp of* ride.
-ridden *suff:* **disease~** von Krankheiten geplagt.
riddle [rid'əl] *n* Rätsel *nt* ♦ *vt (esp passive)*
durchlöchern.
ride [rīd] *n (in vehicle)* Fahrt *f*; *(on horse)*
Ritt *m*; **to go for a ~** *(in car, on bike etc)*
spazierenfahren; **to give sb a ~** *(to work
etc)* jdn mitnehmen ♦ *irreg vt (horse)* reiten; *(bicycle)* fahren ♦ *vi* reiten; fahren;
(ship) vor Anker liegen.
ride out *vt:* **to ~ out the storm** *(fig)* den
Sturm überstehen.
rider [rī'dûr] *n (on horse)* Reiter(in *f*) *m*; *(on
bicycle, motorbike)* Fahrer(in *f*) *m*; *(addition)* Zusatz *m*.
ridge [rij] *n (of hills)* Bergkette *f*; *(top)* Grat
m, Kamm *m*; *(of roof)* Dachfirst *m*.
ridicule [rid'əkyōōl] *n* Spott *m* ♦ *vt* lächerlich
machen; **to hold sb/sth up to ~** sich über
jdn/etw lustig machen.
ridiculous [ridik'yələs] *a*, **ridiculously** [ri-
dik'yələslē] *ad* lächerlich.
riding [rī'ding] *n* Reiten *nt*; **to go ~** reiten gehen.
riding habit *n* Reitkleid *nt*.
riding school *n* Reitschule *f*.
rife [rīf] *a* weit verbreitet.
riffraff [rif'raf] *n* Gesindel *nt*, Pöbel *m*.
rifle [rī'fəl] *n* Gewehr *nt* ♦ *vt* berauben.
rifle through *vt fus* durchwühlen.
rifle range *n* Schießstand *m*.
rift [rift] *n* Ritze *f*, Spalte *f*; *(fig)* Bruch *m*.
rig [rig] *n (outfit)* Takelung *f*; *(fig)* Aufmachung *f*; *(oil-~)* Bohrinsel *f* ♦ *vt (election
etc)* manipulieren.
rig up *vt* zusammenbasteln, konstruieren.
rigging [rig'ing] *n* Takelage *f*.
right [rīt] *a (correct, just)* richtig, recht; *(~
side)* rechte(r, s) ♦ *n* Recht *nt*; *(not left,
POL)* Rechte *f* ♦ *ad (on the ~)* rechts; *(to

the ~) nach rechts; *(look, work)* richtig,
recht; *(directly)* gerade; *(exactly)* genau ♦
vt in Ordnung bringen, korrigieren ♦ *interj*
gut; **to be ~** recht haben; **to get sth ~** etw
richtig machen, etw richtig verstehen; **die
richtige Antwort geben; the ~ time** die genaue (Uhr)zeit; **you did the ~ thing** das
hast du richtig gemacht; **let's get it ~ this
time!** mach es diesmal richtig; **~ and
wrong** Recht und Unrecht; **~ of way** Vorfahrt *f*; **film ~s** Filmrechte *pl*; **by ~s** von
Rechts wegen; **on the ~** rechts; **~ before/
after** gleich davor/danach; **~ away** sofort;
~ now in diesem Augenblick, eben; **I'm/I
feel all ~ now** es geht mir wieder gut; **to
go ~ to the end of** ganz bis zum Ende gehen; **~, who's next?** (also dann) wer ist
jetzt dran?; **all ~!** gut!, in Ordnung!, schön!
right angle *n* Rechteck *nt*.
righteous [rī'chəs] *a* rechtschaffen.
righteousness [rī'chəsnis] *n* Rechtschaffenheit *f*.
rightful [rīt'fəl] *a* rechtmäßig.
rightfully [rīt'fəlē] *ad* rechtmäßig; *(justifiably)* zu Recht.
right-hand drive [rīt'hand' drīv] *n:* **to have
~** das Steuer rechts haben.
right-handed [rīt'handid] *a* rechtshändig.
right-hand man [rīt'hand' man] *n* rechte
Hand *f*.
right-hand side [rīt'hand' sīd] *n* rechte Seite
f.
rightly [rīt'lē] *ad* mit Recht; **if I remember ~**
(Brit) wenn ich mich recht erinnere *or* ent-
sinne.
right-minded [rīt'mīndid] *a* vernünftig.
rights issue *n* Bezugsrechtsemission *f*.
right wing *n* rechte(r) Flügel *m*.
right-winger [rīt'wing'ûr] *n (POL)* Rechte(r)
mf; *(SPORT)* Rechtsaußen *m*.
rigid [rij'id] *a (stiff)* starr, steif; *(strict)*
streng.
rigidity [rijid'itē] *n* Starrheit *f*, Steifheit *f*;
Strenge *f*.
rigidly [rij'idlē] *ad* starr, steif; streng.
rigmarole [rig'mərōl] *n* Gewäsch *nt*, Getue *nt*.
rigor [rig'ûr] *n (US)* Strenge *f*, Härte *f*, Strikt-
heit *f*.
rigor mortis [rig'ûr môr'tis] *n* Totenstarre *f*.
rigorous [rig'ûrəs] *a*, **rigorously** [rig'ûrəslē] *ad*
streng.
rigour [rig'ûr] *n (Brit)* = **rigor**.
rig-out [rig'out] *n (Brit col)* Aufzug *m*.
rile [rīl] *vt* ärgern.
rim [rim] *n (edge)* Rand *m*; *(of wheel)* Felge
f.
rimless [rim'lis] *a* randlos.
rimmed [rimd] *a* gerändert.
rind [rīnd] *n* Rinde *f*.
ring [ring] *n* Ring *m*; *(of people)* Kreis *m*;
(arena) Ring *m*, Manege *f*; *(of telephone)*
Klingeln *nt*, Läuten *nt*; **that has the ~ of
truth about it** das klingt sehr wahrscheinlich; **to give sb a ~** *(Brit TEL)* jdn anrufen;

it has a familiar ~ es klingt bekannt ♦ *vti irreg* (*bell*) läuten; (*in ears*) klingen; (*also:* ~ **up**) anrufen; **that ~s a bell** das kommt mir bekannt vor; **the name doesn't ~ a bell (with me)** der Namen sagt mir nichts.
ring back *vti* (*Brit*) zurückrufen.
ring off *vi* (*esp Brit TEL*) aufhängen.
ring binder *n* Ringbuch *nt*.
ring finger *n* Ringfinger *m*.
ringing [ring'ing] *n* (*of bell, telephone*) Klingeln *nt*; (*of church bells*) Läuten *nt*.
ringing tone *n* (*TEL*) Rufzeichen *nt*.
ringleader [ring'lēdûr] *n* Anführer *m*, Rädelsführer *m*.
ringlets [ring'lits] *npl* Ringellocken *pl*.
ring road *n* (*Brit*) Umgehungsstraße *f*.
rink [ringk] *n* (*ice* ~) Eisbahn *f*; (*rollerskating* ~) Rollschuhbahn *f*.
rinse [rins] *n* Spülen *nt*; (*colorant*) Tönung *f* ♦ *vt* spülen.
Rio (de Janeiro) [rē'ō (dē zhənɛr'ō)] *n* Rio de Janeiro *nt*.
riot [rī'ət] *n* Aufruhr *m* ♦ *vi* randalieren.
rioter [rī'ətûr] *n* Randalierer *m*; (*rebel*) Aufrührer *m*.
riotous [rī'ətəs] *a*, **riotously** [rī'ətəslē] *ad* aufrührerisch; (*noisy*) lärmend.
riot police *n* Bereitschaftspolizei *f*.
rip [rip] *n* Schlitz *m*, Riß *m* ♦ *vti* (zer)reißen.
rip up *vt* zerreißen.
RIP *abbr* (= *rest in peace*) R.I.P.
rip cord *n* Reißleine *f*.
ripe [rīp] *a* (*fruit*) reif; (*cheese*) ausgereift.
ripen [rī'pən] *vt* reifen lassen ♦ *vi* reifen, reif werden.
ripeness [rīp'nis] *n* Reife *f*.
rip-off [rip'ôf] *n* (*col*): **it's a ~!** das ist Wucher!
riposte [ripōst'] *n* Nachstoß *m*; (*fig*) schlagfertige Antwort *f*.
ripple [rip'əl] *n* kleine Welle *f* ♦ *vt* kräuseln ♦ *vi* sich kräuseln.
rise [rīz] *n* (*slope*) Steigung *f*; (*Brit*: *esp in wages*) Erhöhung *f*; (*growth, fig*: *ascendancy*) Aufstieg *m*; **to give** ~ **to** Anlaß geben zu ♦ *vi irreg* aufstehen; (*sun*) aufgehen; (*smoke*) aufsteigen; (*mountain*) sich erheben; (*ground*) ansteigen; (*prices*) steigen; (*in revolt*) sich erheben; **to** ~ **to the occasion** sich der Lage gewachsen zeigen.
risen [riz'ən] *pp of* **rise**.
rising [rī'zing] *a* (*increasing*: *tide, numbers, prices*) steigend; (*sun, moon*) aufgehend ♦ *n* (*uprising*) Aufstand *m*.
rising damp *n* Bodenfeuchtigkeit *f*.
risk [risk] *n* Gefahr *f*, Risiko *nt*; **fire/security** ~ Feuer-/Sicherheitsrisiko *nt*; **health** ~ Gefahr für die Gesundheit ♦ *vt* (*venture*) wagen; (*chance loss of*) riskieren, aufs Spiel setzen; **I'll** ~ **it** das riskiere ich.
risk capital *n* Eigenkapital *nt*, Risikokapital *nt*.
risky [ris'kē] *a* gewagt, gefährlich, riskant.
risqué [riskā'] *a* gewagt.

rissole [ris'âl] *n* Fleischklößchen *nt*.
rite [rīt] *n* Ritus *m*; **last ~s** Letzte Ölung *f*.
ritual [rich'ōōəl] *n* Ritual *nt* ♦ *a* Ritual-; (*fig*) rituell.
rival [rī'vəl] *n* Rivale *m*, Rivalin *f*, Konkurrent(in *f*) *m* ♦ *a* rivalisierend ♦ *vt* rivalisieren mit; (*COMM*) konkurrieren mit.
rivalry [rī'vəlrē] *n* Rivalität *f*, Konkurrenz *f*.
river [riv'ûr] *n* Fluß *m*, Strom *m*; **up/down** ~ flußaufwärts/-abwärts.
riverbank [riv'ûrbangk] *n* Flußufer *nt*.
riverbed [riv'ûrbed] *n* Flußbett *nt*.
riverside [riv'ûrsīd] *n* Flußufer *nt* ♦ *a* am Ufer gelegen, Ufer-.
rivet [riv'it] *n* Niete *f* ♦ *vt* (*fasten*) (ver)nieten.
riveting [riv'iting] *a* (*fig*) fesselnd.
Riviera [rivēâr'ə] *n*: **the Italian** ~ die Riviera, die italienische Riviera; **the French** ~ die französische Riviera.
Riyadh [rēyâd'] *n* Riad *nt*, Er-Riad *nt*.
RN *n abbr* (*Brit*) = **Royal Navy**; (*US*: = *registered nurse*) staatlich geprüfte Krankenschwester.
RNA *n abbr* (= *ribonucleic acid*) RNS *f*.
road [rōd] *n* Straße *f*; **it takes four hours by** ~ man braucht vier Stunden mit dem Auto *or* dem Bus; **on the** ~ **to success** auf dem Weg zum Erfolg.
roadblock [rōd'blâk] *n* Straßensperre *f*.
road haulage *n* Spedition *f*, Straßengüterverkehr *m*.
road hog *n* Verkehrsrowdy *m*.
road map *n* Straßenkarte *f*.
road safety *n* Verkehrssicherheit *f*.
roadside [rōd'sīd] *n* Straßenrand *m*; **by the** ~ am Straßenrand ♦ *a* an der Straße (gelegen).
road sign *n* Straßenschild *nt*.
roadsweeper [rōd'swēpûr] *n* (*Brit*: *person*) Straßenkehrer(in *f*) *m*.
road transport *n* = **road haulage**.
road user *n* Verkehrsteilnehmer *m*.
roadway [rōd'wā] *n* Fahrbahn *f*.
roadworthy [rōd'wûrthē] *a* verkehrssicher.
roam [rōm] *vi* (umher)streifen ♦ *vt* durchstreifen.
roar [rôr] *n* Brüllen *nt*, Gebrüll *m* ♦ *vi* brüllen.
roaring [rôr'ing] *a* (*fire*) Bomben-, prasselnd; (*trade*) schwunghaft, Bomben-; **a** ~ **success** ein Bombenerfolg *m* (*col*).
roast [rōst] *n* Braten *m* ♦ *vt* (*meat*) braten; (*coffee*) rösten.
roast beef *n* Roastbeef *nt*.
rob [râb] *vt* bestehlen, berauben; (*bank*) ausrauben.
robber [râb'ûr] *n* Räuber(in *f*) *m*.
robbery [râb'ûrē] *n* Raub *m*.
robe [rōb] *n* (*dress*) Gewand *nt*; (*US*: *for house wear*) Hauskleid *nt*; (*judge's*) Robe *f* ♦ *vt* feierlich ankleiden.
robin [râb'in] *n* Rotkehlchen *nt*.
robot [rō'bət] *n* Roboter *m*.

robotics [rōbât'iks] *n sing* Robotik *f*.
robust [rōbust'] *a* stark, robust.
rock [râk] *n* Felsen *m*; (*piece*) Stein *m*; (*bigger*) Fels(brocken) *m*; (*Brit*: *candy*) Zuckerstange *f*; (*MUS*) Rock *m* ♦ *vti* wiegen, schaukeln; **on the ~s** (*drink*) mit Eis(würfeln); (*marriage*) gescheitert; (*ship*) aufgelaufen.
rock and roll *n* Rock and Roll *m*.
rock-bottom [râk'bât'əm] *n* (*fig*) Tiefpunkt *m*; **to reach** *or* **touch ~** den Tiefpunkt erreichen *or* auf dem Tiefpunkt sein.
rock climber *n* (Felsen)kletterer(in *f*) *m*.
rock climbing *n* (*SPORT*) Klettern *nt* (im Fels); **to go ~** (steil)klettern gehen.
rocket [râk'it] *n* Rakete *f* ♦ *vi* (*prices*) hochschießen, hochschnellen.
rocket launcher [râk'it lônch'ûr] *n* Raketenabschußgerät *nt*; (*on plane*) Raketenwerfer *m*.
rock face *n* Felswand *f*.
rock garden *n* Steingarten *m*.
rocking chair [râk'ing chär] *n* Schaukelstuhl *m*.
rocking horse [râk'ing hôrs] *n* Schaukelpferd *nt*.
rocky [râk'ē] *a* felsig.
rococo [rəkō'kō] *a* Rokoko- ♦ *n* Rokoko *nt*.
rod [râd] *n* (*bar*) Stange *f*; (*stick*) Rute *f*.
rode [rōd] *pt of* ride.
rodent [rō'dənt] *n* Nagetier *nt*.
rodeo [rō'dēō] *n* Rodeo *m or nt*.
roe [rō] *n* (*deer*) Reh *nt*; (*of fish*) Rogen *m*; **soft ~** Milch *f*.
rogue [rōg] *n* Schurke *m*; (*hum*) Spitzbube *m*.
roguish [rō'gish] *a* schurkisch; (*hum*) schelmisch.
ROI *n abbr* (*US*) = *return on investment*.
role [rōl] *n* Rolle *f*.
roll [rōl] *n* Rolle *f*; (*bread*) Brötchen *nt*; (*movement, of sea*) Rollen *nt*; (*list*) Liste *f*; (*of drum*) Wirbel *m*; **cheese ~** Käsebrötchen *nt* ♦ *vt* (*turn*) rollen, (herum)wälzen; (*grass etc*) walzen ♦ *vi* rollen; (*swing*) schlingern; (*sound*) grollen; **tears ~ed down her cheeks** Tränen kullerten über ihre Wangen; **he's ~ing in money** er schwimmt im Geld.
roll around *vi* herumkugeln; (*ship*) schlingern; (*dog*) sich wälzen.
roll by *vi* (*time*) verfließen.
roll in *vt* herein-/hineinrollen ♦ *vi* (*mail*) hereinkommen.
roll out *vt* (*pastry*) ausrollen; (*barrel*) heraus-/hinausrollen.
roll over *vi* sich (herum)drehen.
roll up *vi* (*arrive*) kommen, auftauchen ♦ *vt* (*carpet*) aufrollen; (*cloth, map*) auf- *or* zusammenrollen; (*sleeves*) hochkrempeln; **to ~ o.s. up into a ball** sich zusammenrollen.
roll call *n* Namensaufruf *m*.
roller [rō'lûr] *n* Rolle *f*, Walze *f*; (*road ~*)

Straßenwalze *f*.
roller coaster *n* Achterbahn *f*.
roller skates *npl* Rollschuhe *pl*.
rollicking [râl'iking] *a* ausgelassen.
rolling [rō'ling] *a* (*landscape*) wellig.
rolling mill *n* (*factory*) Walzwerk *nt*; (*machine*) Walze *f*.
rolling pin *n* Nudel- *or* Wellholz *nt*.
rolling stock *n* Wagenmaterial *nt*.
ROM [râm] *n abbr* (*COMPUT*: = *read-only memory*) Festwertspeicher *m*.
romaine [rōmān'] *n* (*US*) Romagna-Salat *m*, römische(r) Salat *m*.
Roman [rō'mən] *a* römisch ♦ *n* Römer(in *f*) *m*.
Roman Catholic *a* römisch-katholisch ♦ *n* Katholik(in *f*) *m*.
romance [rōmans'] *n* Romanze *f*; (*story*) (Liebes)roman *m*.
Romanesque [rōmənesk'] *a* romanisch.
Romania [rəmā'nēə] *etc* = **Rumania** *etc*.
Roman numeral *n* römische Ziffer *f*.
romantic [rōman'tik] *a* romantisch.
Romanticism [rōman'tisizəm] *n* Romantik *f*.
Romany [rōm'ənē] *n* (*person*) Zigeuner(in *f*) *m*; (*language*) Zigeunersprache *f*, Romani *nt* ♦ *a* Zigeuner-.
Rome [rōm] *n* Rom *nt*.
romp [râmp] *n* Tollen *nt* ♦ *vi* (*also*: **~ around**) herumtollen; **to ~ home** (*horse*) spielend gewinnen.
rompers [râm'pûrz] *npl* Spielanzug *m*.
roof [rōōf] *n* Dach *nt*; (*of mouth*) Gaumen *m* ♦ *vt* überdachen, überdecken.
roofing [rōō'fing] *n* Deckmaterial *nt*.
roof rack *n* (*AUT*) Dachgepäckträger *m*.
rook [rōōk] *n* (*bird*) Saatkrähe *f*; (*CHESS*) Turm *m* ♦ *vt* (*cheat*) betrügen.
room [rōōm] *n* Zimmer *nt*, Raum *m*; (*public hall, ball~ etc*) Saal *m*; (*space*) Platz *m*; (*fig*) Spielraum *m*; **~s** *pl* (*lodging*) Wohnung *f*; **~ and board** Unterkunft und Verpflegung; **is there ~ for this?** ist genügend Platz dafür da?; **to make ~ for sb** für jdn Platz machen *or* schaffen; **there is ~ for improvement in your work** Ihre Arbeit könnte um einiges besser sein.
roominess [rōō'mēnis] *n* Geräumigkeit *f*.
rooming house [rōō'ming hous] *n* Pension *f*.
room-mate [rōōm'māt] *n* Mitbewohner(in *f*) *m*.
room service *n* Zimmerbedienung *f*.
room temperature *n* Zimmertemperatur *f*.
roomy [rōō'mē] *a* geräumig.
roost [rōōst] *n* Hühnerstange *f* ♦ *vi* auf der Stange hocken.
rooster [rōōs'tûr] *n* Hahn *m*.
root [rōōt] *n* (*lit, fig*) Wurzel *f*; **to take ~** (*plant, idea*) Wurzeln schlagen; **the ~ of the problem** der Kern des Problems ♦ *vt* einwurzeln.
root about *vi* (*Brit*) = **root around**.
root around *vi* (*fig*) herumwühlen.
root for *vt fus* Stimmung machen für.

root out vt ausjäten; (fig) ausrotten.
rooted [rōō'tid] a (fig) verwurzelt.
rope [rōp] n Seil nt, Strick m; **to know the ~s** sich auskennen; **to jump** or **skip ~** (US) Seil springen; **to be at the end of one's ~** völlig am Ende sein ♦ vt (tie) festschnüren; **to ~ sb in** jdn rankriegen.
rope off vt absperren.
rope ladder n Strickleiter f.
rosary [rō'zûrē] n Rosenkranz m.
rose [rōz] pt of **rise** ♦ n Rose f ♦ a Rosen-, rosenrot.
rosé [rōzā'] n Rosé m.
rosebed [rōz'bed] n Rosenbeet nt.
rosebud [rōz'bud] n Rosenknospe f.
rosebush [rōz'bōōsh] n Rosenstock m, Rosenstrauch m.
rosemary [rōz'märē] n Rosmarin m.
rosette [rōzet'] n Rosette f.
roster [râs'tûr] n Dienstplan m.
rostrum [râs'trəm] n Rednerbühne f.
rosy [rō'zē] a rosig.
rot [rât] n Fäulnis f; (nonsense) Quatsch m, Blödsinn m ♦ vti verfaulen (lassen); **to stop the ~** (Brit fig) den Fäulnisprozeß aufhalten; **dry/wet ~** Haus- or Holzschwamm m/ Naßfäule f.
rota [rō'tə] n Dienstliste f.
rotary [rō'tûrē] a rotierend, sich drehend.
rotate [rō'tāt] vt rotieren lassen; (two or more things in order) turnusmäßig wechseln ♦ vi rotieren.
rotating [rō'tāting] a rotierend.
rotation [rōtā'shən] n Umdrehung f, Rotation f; **in ~** der Reihe nach, abwechselnd, im Turnus.
rote [rōt] n: **to learn by ~** auswendig lernen.
rotor [rō'tûr] n Rotor m.
rotten [rât'ən] a faul, verfault; (fig) schlecht, gemein; **~ to the core** durch und durch verdorben.
rotund [rōtund'] a rund; (person) rundlich.
rouge [rōōzh] n Rouge nt.
rough [ruf] a (not smooth, also weather) rauh; (path) uneben; (violent) roh, grob; (crossing, sea) stürmisch; (without comforts) hart, unbequem; (unfinished, makeshift) grob; (approximate) ungefähr; **~ estimate** grobe Schätzung f; **to have a ~ time (of it)** eine harte Zeit haben ♦ n (GOLF) Rauh nt; (Brit: person) Rowdy m, Rohling m ♦ vt: **to ~ it** primitiv leben ♦ ad: **to play ~** (SPORT) wild spielen.
rough out vt entwerfen, flüchtig skizzieren.
roughage [ruf'ij] n Ballaststoffe pl.
rough-and-ready [ruf'ənred'ē] a provisorisch, zusammengepfuscht (col).
rough-and-tumble [ruf'əntum'bəl] n Balgerei f; (fighting) Keilerei f.
roughcast [ruf'kast] n Rauhputz nt.
rough copy, rough draft n Entwurf m.
roughen [ruf'ən] vt aufrauhen.
roughly [ruf'lē] ad grob; (about) ungefähr; ~

speaking grob gesagt.
roughness [ruf'nis] n Rauheit f; (of manner) Ungeschliffenheit f.
roughshod [ruf'shâd'] ad: **to ride ~ over sb/sth** rücksichtslos über jdn/etw hinweggehen.
rough work n Konzept nt.
roulette [rōōlet'] n Roulette nt.
round [round] a rund; (figures) aufgerundet; **in ~ figures** in runden Zahlen ♦ ad (in a circle) rundherum; ♦ prep um ... herum; (approximately) ungefähr; **she arrived ~ (about) noon** (Brit) sie kam gegen mittag an ♦ n Runde f; (of ammunition) Magazin nt; (song) Kanon m; **the daily ~** (fig) die tägliche Arbeit, der tägliche Trott (pej); **~ of applause** Beifall m ♦ vt (corner) biegen um; (make ~) runden.
round off vt abrunden.
round up vt (animals) zusammentreiben; (figures) aufrunden.
roundabout [round'əbout] n (Brit: traffic) Kreisverkehr m; (: merry-go-round) Karussell nt ♦ a: **by a ~ way** (lit, fig) auf Umwegen.
rounded [roun'did] a gerundet.
rounders [roun'dûrz] npl (game) ≈ Schlagball m.
roundly [round'lē] ad (fig) gründlich.
round-shouldered [round'shōldûrd] a mit abfallenden Schultern.
round trip n Rundreise f.
round trip ticket n (US) Rückfahrkarte f.
roundup [round'up] n Zusammentreiben nt, Sammeln nt; **a ~ of the latest news** eine Zusammenfassung der Nachrichten vom Tage.
rouse [rouz] vt (waken) (auf)wecken; (stir up) erregen.
rousing [rou'zing] a (welcome) stürmisch; (speech) zündend.
rout [rout] n (defeat) Sieg m ♦ vt in die Flucht schlagen.
route [rōōt] n Weg m, Route f.
routine [rōōtēn'] n Routine f (also COMPUT) ♦ a Routine-; **~ procedure** Routinesache f.
rover [rō'vûr] n Wanderer m.
roving [rō'ving] a (reporter) im Außendienst.
row [rō] n (line) Reihe f ♦ vti (boat) rudern ♦ [rou] n (noise) Lärm m, Krach m; (dispute) Streit m; (scolding) Krach m; **to make a ~** (col) Krach schlagen; **to have a ~ with sb** mit jdm Streit or Krach haben ♦ vi sich streiten.
rowboat [rō'bōt] n (US) Ruderboot m.
rowdy [rou'dē] a rüpelhaft ♦ n (person) Rowdy m.
rowdyism [rou'dēizəm] n Rowdytum nt.
row house n (US) Reihenhaus nt.
rowing [rō'ing] n Rudern nt; (SPORT) Rudersport m.
rowing boat n (Brit) = **rowboat**.
rowlock [rō'lâk] n (Brit) Rudergabel f.
royal [roi'əl] a königlich, Königs-.

Royal Air Force n (Brit) Königliche Luftwaffe f.

royal blue a königsblau.

royalist [roi'əlist] n Royalist m ♦ a königstreu.

Royal Navy n (Brit) Königliche Marine f.

royalty [roi'əltē] n (family) königliche Familie f; (for invention) Patentgebühr f; (for book) Tantieme f.

RP n abbr (Brit) = received pronunciation.

rpm abbr (= revolutions per minute) UpM.

RR n abbr (= Right Reverend) Anrede für einen Bischof; (US) = **railroad**; (: = rural route) Landstraße f.

RSVP abbr (= répondez s'il vous plaît) u.A.w.g.

Rt Hon. abbr (Brit: = Right Honourable) Anrede für Abgeordnete.

Rt Rev. abbr (= Right Reverend) Anrede für einen Bischof.

rub [rub] n (problem) Haken m; **to give sth a ~** etw (ab)reiben ♦ vt reiben.

  rub down vt (body) abrubbeln (col), abfrottieren; (horse) abreiben.

  rub in vt (ointment) einreiben; **to ~ it in** (fig) darauf herumreiten.

  rub off vi (lit, fig) abfärben (on auf +acc).

  rub out vt (stain) herausreiben; (with eraser) ausradieren ♦ vi herausgehen; sich ausradieren lassen.

rubber [rub'ûr] n Gummi m; (US col) Kondom nt; (Brit: eraser) Radiergummi m.

rubber band n Gummiband nt.

rubber plant n Gummibaum m.

rubber stamp n Stempel m.

rubber-stamp [rubûrstamp'] vt (fig) genehmigen.

rubbery [rub'ûrē] a gummiartig; (meat) wie Gummi.

rubbing alcohol [rub'ing al'kəhôl] n (US) Wundbenzin nt.

rubbish [rub'ish] n (waste) Abfall m; (nonsense) Blödsinn m, Quatsch m ♦ vt (Brit col) in den Dreck ziehen.

rubbish bin n (Brit) Mülleimer m.

rubbish dump n (Brit) Müllablageplatz m.

rubbishy [rub'ishē] a (Brit: worthless) wertlos; (ideas) blödsinnig.

rubble [rub'əl] n (Stein)schutt m.

ruble [rōō'bəl] n Rubel m.

ruby [rōō'bē] n Rubin m ♦ a rubinrot.

RUC n abbr (Brit: = Royal Ulster Constabulary) Polizeitruppe in Nordirland.

rucksack [ruk'sak] n Rucksack m.

rudder [rud'ûr] n Steuerruder nt.

ruddy [rud'ē] a (col) rötlich.

rude [rōōd] a unhöflich, unverschämt; (shock) hart; (awakening) unsanft; (unrefined, rough) grob; **to be ~ to sb** jdn grob anfahren, gegen jdn unhöflich sein.

rudely [rōōd'lē] ad unhöflich, unverschämt; unsanft; grobe.

rudeness [rōōd'nis] n Unhöflichkeit f, Unverschämtheit f; Grobheit f.

rudiment [rōō'dəmənt] n Grundlage f.

rudimentary [rōōdəmen'tûrē] a rudimentär.

rueful [rōō'fəl] a, **ruefully** [rōō'fəlē] ad reuevoll.

ruff [ruf] n Halskrause f.

ruffian [ruf'ēən] n Rohling m.

ruffle [ruf'əl] vt (surface, water) kräuseln; (hair, feathers) zerzausen.

rug [rug] n Teppich m, Brücke f; (in bedroom) Bettvorleger m.

rugby [rug'bē] n (also: ~ **football**) Rugby nt.

rugged [rug'id] a (coastline) zerklüftet; (features) markig.

ruin [rōō'in] n Ruine f; (downfall) Ruin m; **~s** pl Trümmer pl; **it will be the ~ of him** das wird ihn ruinieren ♦ vt ruinieren.

ruination [rōōinā'shən] n Zerstörung f, Ruinierung f.

ruinous [rōō'inəs] a ruinierend.

rule [rōōl] n Regel f; (government) Herrschaft f, Regierung f; (for measuring) Maßstab m; **as a ~** in der Regel; **it's against the ~s** es ist nicht erlaubt; **the ~s of the road** ≈ die Straßenverkehrsordnung; **by ~ of thumb** über den Daumen gepeilt; **majority ~** (POL) Mehrheitsregierung f; **under British ~** unter britischer Herrschaft ♦ vti (govern) herrschen (über +acc), regieren; (decide) anordnen, entscheiden; (make lines) linieren; **to ~ that ...** entscheiden, daß ...; **to ~ against/in favor of/on** (JUR) entscheiden gegen/für/in +dat.

  rule out vt (exclude) ausschließen.

ruled [rōōld] a (paper) liniert.

ruler [rōō'lûr] n (for measuring) Lineal nt; (person) Herrscher m.

ruling [rōō'ling] a (party) Regierungs-; (class) herrschend.

rum [rum] n Rum m.

Rumania [rōōmā'nēə] n Rumänien nt.

Rumanian [rōōmā'nēən] n (person) Rumäne m, Rumänin f; (language) Rumänisch nt ♦ a rumänisch.

rumble [rum'bəl] n Rumpeln nt; (of thunder) Rollen nt ♦ vi rumpeln; grollen.

rumbustious [rumbus'chəs] a (Brit) derb.

ruminate [rōō'mənāt] vi grübeln; (cows) wiederkäuen.

rummage [rum'ij] vi durchstöbern.

rummage sale n Basar m, Flohmarkt m.

rumor, (Brit) **rumour** [rōō'mûr] n Gerücht nt ♦ vt: **it is ~ed that** man sagt or man munkelt, daß.

rump [rump] n Hinterteil nt.

rumple [rum'pəl] vt (hair) zerzausen; (clothes) zerknittern.

rump steak n Rumpsteak nt.

rumpus [rum'pəs] n Spektakel m, Krach m; **to kick up a ~** einen Spektakel or Heidenlärm machen (col); (complain) Krach schlagen (col).

run [run] n Lauf m; (in car) (Spazier)fahrt f; (series) Serie f, Reihe f; (of play) Spielzeit f; (sudden demand) Ansturm m; (for ani-

mals) Auslauf *m*; (*ski* ~) (Ski)abfahrt *f*; (*in stocking*) Laufmasche *f* ♦ *irreg vt, pp* **run** (*cause to* ~) laufen lassen; (*car, train, bus*) fahren; (*pay for: car etc*) unterhalten; (*race, distance*) laufen, rennen; (*manage*) leiten, verwalten, führen; (*sword*) stoßen; (*pass: hand, eye*) gleiten lassen; (*COMPUT: program*) fahren ♦ *vi* laufen; (*move quickly also*) rennen; (*bus, train*) fahren; (*flow*) fließen, laufen; (*colors*) (ab)färben; **on the** ~ auf der Flucht; **in the long** ~ auf die Dauer; **to go for a** ~ **in the car** eine Fahrt *or* einen Ausflug im Auto machen; **a** ~ **of luck/bad luck** eine Glücks-/Pechsträhne; **to make a** ~ **for it** weglaufen, wegrennen; **to have the** ~ **of sb's house** das Haus von jdn übernehmen; **to** ~ **riot** Amok laufen; **to** ~ **a risk** ein Risiko eingehen; **it's very cheap to** ~ (*car*) es ist sehr billig im Unterhalt; **to** ~ **errands** Besorgungen machen; **to** ~ **a stoplight** bei Rot drüberfahren; **to** ~ **on diesel** mit Diesel fahren; **to** ~ **off batteries/the mains** auf Batterie/Netz laufen; **to** ~ **for the bus** zum Bus rennen; **to** ~ **for president** für die Präsidentschaft kandidieren; **we shall have to** ~ **for it** wir müssen rennen, was das Zeug hält; **the car ran into a lamppost** das Auto fuhr gegen einen Laternenpfahl.

run across *vt fus* (*find*) stoßen auf (+*acc*).

run around *vi* (*children*) umherspringen.

run away *vi* weglaufen; (*horse*) durchgehen.

run down *vi* (*clock*) ablaufen ♦ *vt* (*with car*) überfahren; (*talk against*) heruntermachen; (*Brit: reduce: production*) herunterschrauben; (: *factory, shop*) allmählich auflösen; **to be** ~ **down** (*person*) nicht auf der Höhe sein.

run in *vt* (*Brit: car*) einfahren.

run into *vt fus* (*meet: person*) zufällig treffen; (: *trouble*) bekommen; (*collide*) rennen *or* fahren (*with* gegen); **to** ~ **into debt** in Schulden geraten.

run off *vi* fortlaufen.

run out *vi* (*person*) hinausrennen; (*liquid*) auslaufen; (*lease*) ablaufen; (*money*) ausgehen.

run out of *vt fus*: **I've** ~ **out of gas** ich habe kein Benzin mehr.

run over *vt* (*in accident*) überfahren ♦ *vt fus* (*read quickly*) überfliegen.

run through *vt fus* (*read quickly: instructions*) durchgehen.

run up *vt* (*debt, bill*) machen; **to** ~ **up against** (*difficulties*) stoßen auf (+*acc*).

runabout [run'əbout] *n* (*small car*) kleine(r) Flitzer *m*.

runaway [run'əwā] *a* (*horse*) ausgebrochen; (*person*) flüchtig ♦ *n* (*person*) Ausreißer(in *f*) *m*.

rundown [run'doun] *n* (*Brit: of industry etc*) allmähliche Auflösung *f*.

rung [rung] *pp of* **ring** ♦ *n* Sprosse *f*.

run-in [run'in] *n* (*col*) Krach *m*, Streit *m*.

runner [run'ûr] *n* Läufer(in *f*) *m*; (*messenger*) Bote *m*; (*for sleigh*) Kufe *f*.

runner bean *n* (*Brit*) Stangenbohne *f*.

runner-up [runûrup'] *n* Zweite(r) *mf*.

running [run'ing] *n* (*of business*) Leitung *f*; (*of machine*) Laufen *nt*, Betrieb *m* ♦ *a* (*water*) fließend; (*commentary*) laufend; **3 days** ~ 3 Tage lang *or* hintereinander; **to be in/out of the** ~ im Rennen liegen/aus dem Rennen sein.

running costs *npl* (*of business*) Betriebs(un)kosten *pl*; (*of car*) Unterhaltskosten *pl*.

running head *n* (*TYP*) lebende(r) Kolumnentitel *m*.

running mate *n* (*US POL*) Kandidat *für die Vizepräsidentschaft*.

runny [run'ē] *a* dünn.

run-off [run'ôf] *n* (*in contest, election*) Entscheidung *f*; (*extra race*) Entscheidungslauf *m*.

run-of-the-mill [runəvtḥəmil'] *a* gewöhnlich, alltäglich.

run-up [run'up] *n* (*SPORT*) Anlauf *m*; (*Brit: to election*) Vorwahlzeit *f*.

runway [run'wā] *n* (*AVIAT*) Runway *m*, Start- und Landebahn *f*.

rupee [rōō'pē] *n* Rupie *f*.

rupture [rup'chûr] *n* (*MED*) Bruch *m* ♦ *vt*: **to** ~ **o.s.** sich (*dat*) einen Bruch zuziehen.

rural [rōōr'əl] *a* ländlich, Land-.

ruse [rōōz] *n* Kniff *m*, List *f*.

rush [rush] *n* Eile *f*, Hetze *f*; (*of crowd*) Andrang *m*, Gedränge *nt*; (*FIN*) starke Nachfrage *f*; (*BOT*) Schilf(rohr) *nt*; **gold** ~ Goldrausch *m*; **we've had a** ~ **of orders** wir hatten sehr viele Bestellungen; **I'm in a** ~ ich bin in Eile, ich habe es eilig; **is there any** ~ **for this?** eilt das? ♦ *vt* (*carry along*) auf dem schnellsten Wege schaffen *or* transportieren; (*attack*) losstürmen auf (+*acc*); **to** ~ **sth off** etw schnell erledigen; **don't** ~ **me** dräng mich nicht ♦ *vi* (*hurry*) eilen, stürzen; **to** ~ **into sth** etw überstürzen.

rush through *vt* (*book, work*) durchjagen; (*town*) durchrasen; **I had to** ~ **through my meal** ich mußte ganz schnell essen ♦ *vt* (*COMM: order*) schnell erledigen.

rush hour *n* Hauptverkehrszeit *f*.

rush job *n* (*urgent*) eilige(r) Auftrag *m*.

rush matting [rush mat'ing] *n* Binsenmatte *f*.

rusk [rusk] *n* Zwieback *m*.

Russia [rush'ə] *n* Rußland *nt*.

Russian [rush'ən] *n* (*person*) Russe *m*, Russin *f*; (*language*) Russisch *nt* ♦ *a* russisch.

rust [rust] *n* Rost *m* ♦ *vi* rosten.

rustic [rus'tik] *a* bäuerlich, ländlich, Bauern-.

rustle [rus'əl] *n* Rauschen *nt*, Rascheln *nt* ♦ *vi* rauschen, rascheln ♦ *vt* rascheln lassen; (*cattle*) stehlen.

rustproof [rust'prōōf] *a* nichtrostend, rostfrei.

rusty [rus'tē] *a* rostig.

rut [rut] *n* (*in track*) Radspur *f*; (*of deer*) Brunst *f*; (*fig*) Trott *m*; **to be in a** ~ **im**

Trott stecken.
rutabaga [rōōtəbā'gə] *n* (*US*) Steck- *or* Kohl-
rube *f*.
ruthless [rōōth'lis] *a*, **ruthlessly** [rōōth'lislē]
ad unbarmherzig, rücksichtslos.
ruthlessness [rōōth'lisnis] *n* Unbarmherzig-
heit *f*, Rücksichtslosigkeit *f*.
RV *n abbr* (*Bible*: = *revised version*) britische Bibelausgabe; *abbr* (*US*) = *recreational vehicle*.
rye [rī] *n* Roggen *m*.
rye bread *n* Roggenbrot *nt*.

S

S, s [es] *n* (*letter*) S *nt*, s *nt*; **S for Sugar** ≈ S
wie Samuel.
S *abbr* (= *Saint*) Skt., St.; (*US SCH*:
grade: = *satisfactory*) ≈ 3; (= *small*) S.
S. *abbr* (= *south*) S.
SA *n abbr* = **South Africa; South America.**
sabbath [sab'əth] *n* Sabbat *m*.
sabbatical year [səbatikəl yēr] *n*
Beurlaubungs- *or* Forschungsjahr *nt*.
saber [sā'bûr] *n* (*US*) Säbel *m*.
sabotage [sab'ətâzh] *n* Sabotage *f* ♦ *vt* sabotieren.
sabre [sā'bûr] *n* (*Brit*) = **saber.**
saccharin(e) [sak'ûrin] *n* Saccharin *nt*.
sachet [sashā'] *n* Beutel *m*; (*of shampoo*)
Briefchen *nt*; (*of lavender*) Kissen *nt*.
sack [sak] *n* Sack *m* ♦ *vt* (*col*) hinauswerfen;
(*pillage*) plündern.
sackful [sak'fəl] *n* Sack(voll) *m*.
sacking [sak'ing] *n* (*material*) Sackleinen *nt*;
(*col*) Rausschmiß *m*.
sacrament [sak'rəmənt] *n* Sakrament *nt*.
sacred [sā'krid] *a* (*building, music etc*) geistlich, Kirchen-; (*altar, oath*) heilig.
sacrifice [sak'rəfīs] *n* Opfer *nt*; **to make ~s
(for sb)** (*lit, fig*) (für jdn) Opfer bringen ♦ *vt*
(*lit, fig*) opfern.
sacrilege [sak'rəlij] *n* Schändung *f*.
sacrosanct [sak'rōsangkt] *a* sakrosankt.
sad [sad] *a* traurig; (*deplorable*) bedauerlich.
sadden [sad'ən] *vt* traurig machen, betrüben.
saddle [sad'əl] *n* Sattel *m* ♦ *vt* (*horse*) satteln; **to be/have been ~d with sb/sth** (*col*:
task, bill, name) jdn/etw auf dem *or* am
Hals haben (*col*); **to ~ sb with sth** jdm etw
aufhalsen.
saddlebag [sad'əlbag] *n* Satteltasche *f*.
sadism [sā'dizəm] *n* Sadismus *m*.
sadist [sā'dist] *n* Sadist(in *f*) *m*.
sadistic [sədis'tik] *a* sadistisch.
sadly [sad'lē] *ad* betrübt, beklagenswert;
(*very*) arg; (*regrettably*) bedauerlich; **he is**

~ **lacking in humor** ihm fehlt jeglicher Humor.
sadness [sad'nis] *n* Traurigkeit *f*.
sae *abbr* (*Brit* = **stamped addressed envelope**).
safari [səfâ'rē] *n* Safari *f*.
safari park *n* Safaripark *m*.
safe [sāf] *a* (*free from danger*) sicher; (*careful*) vorsichtig; ~ **journey!** gute Fahrt *or*
Reise!; **it's ~ to say** ... man kann ruhig behaupten ...; ~ **and sound** gesund und munter; **(just) to be on the ~ side** um ganz sicher zu gehen ♦ *n* Safe *m*, Tresor *m*,
Geldschrank *m*.
safe-breaker [sāf'brākûr] *n* (*Brit*) = **safecracker.**
safe-conduct [sāf'kân'dukt] *n* freie(s) *or* si-
chere(s) Geleit *nt*.
safecracker [sāf'krakûr] *n* (*US*) Safeknacker
m (*col*).
safe-deposit [sāf'dipâzit] *n* (*vault*) Tresorraum *m*; (*box*) Banksafe *m or nt*.
safeguard [sāf'gârd] *n* Sicherung *f* ♦ *vt* sichern, schützen.
safekeeping [sāfkē'ping] *n* sichere Verwahrung *f*.
safely [sāf'lē] *ad* sicher; (*arrive*) wohlbehalten; **I can ~ say** ... ich kann wohl sagen ....
safeness [sāf'nis] *n* Zuverlässigkeit *f*.
safe(r) sex [sāf('ûr) seks] *n* sicherer sex.
safety [sāf'tē] *n* Sicherheit *f*; **road ~** Verkehrssicherheit *f*.
safety belt *n* Sicherheitsgurt *m*.
safety curtain *n* eiserne(r) Vorhang *m*.
safety net *n* Sprung- *or* Sicherheitsnetz *nt*.
safety pin *n* Sicherheitsnadel *f*.
safety valve *n* Sicherheitsventil *nt*.
saffron [saf'rən] *n* Safran *m*.
sag [sag] *vi* (durch)sacken, sich senken.
saga [sâg'ə] *n* Saga *f*; (*fig*) Geschichte *f*, Story *f* (*col*).
sage [sāj] *n* (*herb*) Salbei *m*; (*man*) Weise(r)
m.
Sagittarius [sajitär'ēəs] *n* Schütze *m*.
sago [sā'gō] *n* Sago *m*.
Sahara Desert [səhär'ə dez'ûrt] *n* Sahara *f*,
die (Wüste) Sahara.
said [sed] *a* besagt ♦ *pt, pp of* **say.**
Saigon [sīgân'] *n* Saigon *nt*.
sail [sāl] *n* Segel *nt*; (*trip*) Fahrt *f* ♦ *vt* segeln
♦ *vi* (*yacht*) segeln; (*NAUT*) fahren; (*begin
voyage*: *person*) abfahren; (: *ship*) auslaufen; (*fig*: *cloud etc*) dahinsegeln; **to set ~**
losfahren.
sail through *vi, vt fus* (*fig*) spielend schaffen.
sailboat [sāl'bōt] *n* (*US*) Segelboot *nt*.
sailing [sā'ling] *n* Segeln *nt*; **to go ~** segeln
gehen.
sailing ship *n* Segelschiff *nt*.
sailor [sā'lûr] *n* Matrose *m*, Seemann *m*.
saint [sānt] *n* Heilige(r) *mf*.
saintliness [sānt'lēnis] *n* Heiligkeit *f*.
saintly [sānt'lē] *a* heilig, fromm.

sake [sāk] *n*: **for the ~ of** um (+*gen*) willen; **for your ~** um deinetwillen, deinetwegen, wegen dir; **to talk for talking's ~** reden, nur damit etwas gesagt wird; **for the ~ of argument** rein theoretisch; **art for art's ~** Kunst um der Kunst willen; **for heaven's ~!** um Gottes willen!

salad [sal'əd] *n* Salat *m*; **tomato ~** Tomatensalat *m*.

salad bowl *n* Salatschüssel *f*.

salad cream *n* (*Brit*) ≈ Mayonnaise *f*.

salad dressing *n* Salatsoße *f*.

salad oil *n* Speiseöl *nt*, Salatöl *nt*.

salami [sələ'mē] *n* Salami *f*.

salaried [sal'ûrēd] *a* Gehalts-; **~ staff** Gehaltsempfänger *pl*.

salary [sal'ûrē] *n* Gehalt *nt*.

salary scale *n* Tariflohn *m*.

sale [sāl] *n* Verkauf *m*; (*reduced prices*) Schlußverkauf *m*; **liquidation ~** Räumungsverkauf *m*, Totalausverkauf *m*; **~ and lease back** Rückvermietung *f* durch die Leasinggesellschaft an den Verkäufer; **"for ~"** „zu verkaufen"; **on ~** zu verkaufen.

saleroom [sāl'rōōm] *n* (*Brit*) = **salesroom**.

sales assistant *n* (*Brit*) = **sales clerk**.

sales campaign *n* Verkaufskampagne *f*.

sales clerk *n* (*US*) Verkäufer(in *f*) *m*.

sales conference *n* Versammlung *f* des Verkaufsstabs.

sales drive *n* Verkaufskampagne *f*.

sales figures *npl* Absatzziffern *pl*.

sales force *n* Verkäufer- *or* Absatzstab *m*.

salesman [sālz'mən] *n*, *pl* **-men** Verkäufer *m*; (*representative*) Vertreter *m*.

sales manager *n* Verkaufsleiter *m*, Salesmanager *m*.

salesmanship [sālz'mənship] *n* Verkaufstechnik *f*.

sales meeting *n* Handelsvertreterversammlung *f*.

salesroom [sālz'rōōm] *n* (*US*) Verkaufsraum *m*.

sales slip *n* (*US*) Quittung *f*.

sales tax *n* (*US*) nach dem Großhandelspreis *berechnete Steuer.*

saleswoman [sālz'wōōmən] *n*, *pl* **-women** Verkäuferin *f*.

salient [sā'lēənt] *a* hervorspringend, bemerkenswert.

saline [sā'lēn] *a* salzig.

saliva [səli'və] *n* Speichel *m*.

sallow [sal'ō] *a* fahl; (*face*) bleich.

salmon [sam'ən] *n* Lachs *m*.

salon [səlân'] *n* Salon *m*.

saloon [səlōōn'] *n* (*ship's lounge*) Salon *m*; (*US*) Kneipe *f*; (*Brit AUT*) Limousine *f*.

Salop [sal'əp] *abbr* (*Brit*) = Shropshire.

salt [sôlt] *n* Salz *nt*; **an old ~** ein (alter) Seebär ♦ *vt* (*cure*) einsalzen; (*flavour*) salzen.

salt away *vt* auf die hohe Kante legen.

SALT [sôlt] *n abbr* (= *Strategic Arms Limitation Talks/Treaty*) SALT.

saltcellar [sôlt'selûr] *n* (*Brit*) Salzfaß *nt*.

salt mine *n* Salzbergwerk *nt*.

salt shaker [sôlt shā'kûr] *n* (*US*) Salzfaß *nt*.

saltwater [sôlt'wôtûr] *a* *attr* (*fish etc*) Meeres-.

salty [sôl'tē] *a* salzig.

salubrious [səlōō'brēəs] *a* gesund; (*district etc*) ersprießlich.

salutary [sal'yətārē] *a* gesund, heilsam.

salute [səlōōt'] *n* (*MIL*) Gruß *m*, Salut *m*; (*with guns*) Salutschüsse *pl* ♦ *vt* (*MIL*) salutieren.

salvage [sal'vij] *n* (*from ship*) Bergung *f*; (*property*) Rettung *f*; (*scrap*) Altmaterial *nt* ♦ *vt* bergen; retten.

salvage vessel *n* Bergungsschiff *nt*.

salvation [salvā'shən] *n* Rettung *f*.

Salvation Army *n* Heilsarmee *f*.

salver [sal'vûr] *n* Tablett *nt*.

salvo [sal'vō] *n* Salve *f*.

same [sām] *a* (*similar*) gleiche(r, s); (*identical*) derselbe/dieselbe/dasselbe; **on the ~ day** am gleichen *or* am selben Tag; **at the ~ time** zur gleichen Zeit, gleichzeitig; (*however*) zugleich, andererseits ♦ *pron*: **the ~ again** (*in bar etc*) das gleiche noch mal; **all or just the ~** trotzdem; **it's all the ~ to me** das ist mir egal; **they all look the ~ to me** für mich sehen sie alle gleich aus; **the ~ to you** gleichfalls; **they're one and the ~** (*person*) das ist doch ein- und derselbe/dieselbe; (*thing*) das ist doch der/die/das gleiche, das ist doch derselbe/dieselbe/dasselbe; **~ here!** ich *etc* auch!

sampan [sam'pan] *n* Sampan *m*.

sample [sam'pəl] *n* (*specimen*) Probe *f*; (*example of sth*) Muster *nt*, Probe *f* ♦ *vt* probieren; **to take a ~** eine (Stich)probe machen; **free ~** kostenlose Probe.

sanatorium [sanətôr'ēəm] *n*, *pl* **sanatoria** [sanətôr'ēə] Sanatorium *nt*.

sanctify [sangk'təfī] *vt* weihen.

sanctimonious [sangktəmō'nēəs] *a* scheinheilig.

sanction [sangk'shən] *n* Sanktion *f*; **to impose economic ~s** wirtschaftliche Sanktionen verhängen (*on, against* gegen).

sanctity [sangk'titē] *n* Heiligkeit *f*; (*fig*) Unverletzlichkeit *f*.

sanctuary [sangk'chōōärē] *n* Heiligtum *nt*; (*for fugitive*) Asyl *nt*; (*refuge*) Zufluchtsort *m*; (*for animals*) Naturpark *m*, Schutzgebiet *nt*.

sand [sand] *n* Sand *m* ♦ *vt* mit Sand bestreuen; (*also*: **~ down**: *wood etc*) (ab)schmirgeln; *see also* **sands**.

sandal [san'dəl] *n* Sandale *f*.

sandbag [sand'bag] *n* Sandsack *m*.

sandblast [sand'blast] *vt* sandstrahlen.

sandbox [sand'bâks] *n* (*US*) Sandkasten *m*.

sand castle *n* Sandburg *f*.

sand dune *n* Sanddüne *f*.

sandpaper [sand'pāpûr] *n* Sandpapier *nt*.

sand pie *n* Sandburg *f*.

sandpit [sand'pit] *n* (*Brit*) = **sandbox**.

sands [sandz] *npl* Sand *m*.
sandstone [sand'stōn] *n* Sandstein *m*.
sandstorm [sand'stôrm] *n* Sandsturm *m*.
sandwich [sand'wich] *n* Sandwich *m or nt* ♦ *vt* einklemmen; **to be ~ed between two things/people** zwischen zwei Dingen/ Menschen eingekeilt sein.
sandwich board *n* Reklameschild *m*.
sandy [san'dē] *a* sandig, Sand-; *(color)* sand- farben; *(hair)* rotblond.
sane [sān] *a* geistig gesund *or* normal; *(sen- sible)* vernünftig, gescheit.
sang [sang] *pt of* **sing**.
sanguine [sang'gwin] *a* *(hopeful)* zuversicht- lich.
sanitarium [sanitär'ēəm] *n* Sanatorium *nt*.
sanitary [san'itärē] *a* hygienisch (einwand- frei); *(against dirt)* hygienisch, Gesundheits-.
sanitary napkin *n* (Monats)binde *f*.
sanitation [sanitā'shən] *n* Hygiene *f*; *(toilets)* sanitäre Anlagen *pl*.
sanity [san'itē] *n* geistige Gesundheit *f*; *(good sense)* gesunde(r) Verstand *m*, Vernunft *f*.
sank [sangk] *pt of* **sink**.
San Marino [san marē'nō] *n* San Marino *nt*.
Santa Claus [san'tə klôz] *n* Nikolaus *m*, der Weihnachtsmann.
Santiago [santēä'gō] *n* Santiago *nt*, Santiago de Chile *nt*.
sap [sap] *n* *(of plants)* Saft *m* ♦ *vt* *(strength)* schwächen; *(health)* untergraben.
sapling [sap'ling] *n* junge(r) Baum *m*.
sapphire [saf'īûr] *n* Saphir *m*.
sarcasm [sâr'kazəm] *n* Sarkasmus *m*.
sarcastic [sârkas'tik] *a* sarkastisch.
sarcophagus [sârkâf'əgəs] *n*, *pl* **sarcophagi** [sârkâf'əgī] Sarkophag *m*.
sardine [sârdēn'] *n* Sardine *f*.
Sardinia [sârdin'ēə] *n* Sardinien *nt*.
Sardinian [sârdin'ēən] *n* *(person)* Sardinier(in *f*) *m* ♦ *a* sardinisch, sardisch.
sardonic [sârdân'ik] *a* zynisch.
sari [sâ'rē] *n* Sari *m*.
SAS *n abbr (Brit MIL*: = *Special Air Service)* Spezialeinheit, besonders bei Terroranschlä- gen eingesetzt.
SASE *n abbr (US)* = **self-addressed stamped envelope.**
sash [sash] *n* Schärpe *f*.
Sask. *abbr (Canada)* = Saskatchewan.
sassy [sas'ē] *a* *(US)* frech, übermütig.
sat [sat] *pt*, *pp of* **sit**.
Sat. *abbr* (= *Saturday)* Sa.
SAT *n abbr (US*: = *Scholastic Aptitude Test)* Eignungstest.
Satan [sā'tən] *n* Satan *m*, der Teufel.
satanic [sətan'ik] *a* satanisch, teuflisch.
satchel [sach'əl] *n* Handtasche *f*; *(SCH)* Schul- ranzen *m*, Schulmappe *f*.
sated [sā'tid] *a* *(appetite, person)* gesättigt.
satellite [sat'əlīt] *n* Satellit *m*; *(fig)* Trabant *m* ♦ *a* Satelliten-.
satellite dish *n* Parabolantenne *f*.

satiate [sā'shēāt] *vt* stillen, sättigen.
satin [sat'ən] *n* Satin *m* ♦ *a* Satin-; **with a ~ finish** mit Seidenglanz.
satire [sat'īûr] *n* Satire *f*.
satirical [sətir'ikəl] *a* satirisch.
satirist [sat'ûrist] *n* *(writer etc)* Satiriker(in *f*) *m*; *(cartoonist)* Karikaturist(in *f*) *m*.
satirize [sat'ərīz] *vt* (durch Satire) verspotten.
satisfaction [satisfak'shən] *n* Befriedigung *f*, Genugtuung *f*; **it gives me great ~** es ist mir eine große Genugtuung; **has it been done to your ~?** sind Sie damit zufrieden?
satisfactorily [satisfak'tərəlē] *ad* zufrieden- stellend.
satisfactory [satisfak'tûrē] *a* zufriedenstel- lend, befriedigend.
satisfy [sat'isfī] *vt* befriedigen, zufriedenstel- len; *(convince)* überzeugen; *(conditions)* er- füllen; **to ~ the requirements** die Bedürf- nisse erfüllen, den Bedingungen entspre- chen; **to ~ sb** jdn zufriedenstellen; **to ~ o.s. of sth** sich von etw überzeugen.
satisfying [sat'isfīing] *a* befriedigend; *(meal)* sättigend.
saturate [sach'ûrāt] *vt* (durch)tränken.
saturation [sachərā'shən] *n* Durchtränkung *f*; *(CHEM, fig)* Sättigung *f*.
Saturday [sat'ûrdā] *n* Samstag *m*, Sonnabend *m*; *see* **Tuesday.**
sauce [sôs] *n* Soße *f*, Sauce *f*.
saucepan [sôs'pan] *n* Kochtopf *m*, Kasserolle *f*.
saucer [sô'sûr] *n* Untertasse *f*.
saucily [sô'silē] *ad* frech.
sauciness [sô'sēnis] *n* Frechheit *f*.
saucy [sôs'ē] *a* frech, keck.
Saudi Arabia [sou'dē ərā'bēə] *n* Saudi- Arabien *nt*.
Saudi Arabian [sou'dē ərā'bēən] *n* *(person)* Saudiarabier(in *f*) *m* ♦ *a* saudiarabisch, sau- disch.
sauna [sô'nə] *n* Sauna *f*.
saunter [sôn'tûr] *vi* schlendern ♦ *n* Schlen- dern *nt*.
sausage [sô'sij] *n* *(salami etc)* Wurst *f*.
sausage roll *n* Wurst *f* im Schlafrock, Wurst- pastete *f*.
sauté [sōtā'] *vt* dünsten, leicht *or* kurz anbra- ten ♦ *a*: **~ potatoes** Brat- *or* Röstkartoffeln *pl*; **~ onions** gedünstete Zwiebeln *pl*.
savage [sav'ij] *a* *(fierce)* wild, brutal, grau- sam; *(uncivilized)* wild, primitiv ♦ *n* Wil- de(r) *mf* ♦ *vt* *(animals)* zerfleischen.
savagely [sav'ijlē] *ad* grausam.
savagery [sav'ijrē] *n* Roheit *f*, Grausamkeit *f*.
save [sāv] *vt* retten; *(money, electricity etc)* sparen; *(strength etc)* aufsparen; *(COMPUT)* sicherstellen; **God ~ the Queen!** Gott schüt- ze die Königin!; **I ~d you a piece of cake** ich habe dir ein Stück Kuchen aufgehoben; **to ~ face** das Gesicht wahren; **it will ~ me an hour** dadurch gewinne ich eine Stunde; **to ~ you the trouble** um dir Mühe zu er- sparen ♦ *vi* *(also:* **~ up)** sparen ♦ *n* *(SPORT)*

(Ball)abwehr *f* ♦ *prep, cj* außer, ausgenommen.

saving [sā'ving] *a* rettend ♦ *n* Sparen *nt*, Ersparnis *f*; *(rescue)* Rettung *f*; **the ~ grace of** das Versöhnende an (+*dat*); **to make ~s** sparen.

savings [sā'vingz] *npl (amount saved)* Ersparnisse *pl.*

savings account *n* Sparkonto *nt.*

savings and loan association *n* (*US*) Baugenossenschaft *f.*

savings bank *n* Sparkasse *f.*

savior, *(Brit)* **saviour** [sāv'yûr] *n* Retter *m*; *(ECCL)* Heiland *m*, Erlöser *m.*

savoir-faire [savwârfār'] *n* Gewandtheit *f.*

savor, *(Brit)* **savour** [sā'vûr] *n* Wohlgeschmack *m* ♦ *vt (taste)* schmecken; *(fig)* genießen ♦ *vi* schmecken *(of* nach), riechen *(of* nach).

savory, *(Brit)* **savoury** [sā'vûrē] *a* schmackhaft; *(food)* pikant, würzig.

saw [sô] *n (tool)* Säge *f* ♦ *vti irreg* sägen; **to ~ sth up** etw zersägen ♦ *pt of* **see.**

sawdust [sô'dust] *n* Sägemehl *nt.*

sawed [sôd] *pt of* **saw.**

sawed-off shotgun [sôd'ôf shât'gun] *n* (*US*) Gewehr *nt* mit abgesägtem Lauf.

sawmill [sô'mil] *n* Sägewerk *nt.*

sawn [sôn] *pp of* **saw.**

sawn-off shotgun [sôn'ôf shât'gun] *n (Brit)* = **sawed-off shotgun.**

saxophone [sak'səfōn] *n* Saxophon *nt.*

say [sā] *n* Meinung *f*; *(right)* Mitspracherecht *nt*; **to have a ~ in sth** Mitspracherecht bei etw haben; **let him have his ~** laß ihn doch reden ♦ *vti irreg* sagen; **to ~ yes/no** ja/nein sagen; **when all is said and done** letzten Endes; **I couldn't ~** schwer zu sagen; **how old would you ~ he is?** wie alt schätzt du ihn?; **you don't ~!** was du nicht sagst!; **~ after me ...** sprechen Sie mir nach ...; **I should ~ it's worth about $100** ich schätze, es ist etwa 100$ wert; **there is something/a lot to be said for it** es spricht dafür/es spricht vieles dafür; **don't ~ you forgot** sag bloß nicht, daß du es vergessen hast; **there are, ~, 50 ...** es sind, sagen wir mal, 50 ...; **that is to ~** das heißt; *(more precisely)* beziehungsweise, mit anderen Worten; **to ~ nothing of ...** ganz zu schweigen von ...; **my watch ~s 3 o'clock** nach meiner or auf meiner Uhr ist es 3 Uhr; **shall we ~ Tuesday?** sagen wir Dienstag?; **she said (that) I was to give you this** sie sagte, ich soll dir das geben; **that doesn't ~ much for him** das spricht nicht für ihn.

saying [sā'ing] *n* Sprichwort *nt.*

say-so [sā'sō] *n (col)* Ja *nt*, Zustimmung *f.*

SBA *n abbr* (*US*) = *Small Business Administration.*

s/c *a abbr* (= *self-contained*) abg.

SC *abbr* (*US MAIL*) = *South Carolina.*

S.C. *n abbr* (*US*: = *Supreme Court*) ≈ BG *nt.*

scab [skab] *n* Schorf *m*; *(pej)* Streikbrecher

m.

scabby [skab'ē] *a (skin)* schorfig.

scaffold [skaf'əld] *n (for execution)* Schafott *nt.*

scaffolding [skaf'əlding] *n* (Bau)gerüst *nt.*

scald [skôld] *n* Verbrühung *f* ♦ *vt (burn)* verbrühen; *(clean)* (ab)brühen.

scalding [skôl'ding] *a (also: ~* **hot**) siedend heiß.

scale [skāl] *n (of fish)* Schuppe *f*; *(MUS)* Tonleiter *f*; *(dish for measuring)* Waagschale *f*; *(on map, size)* Maßstab *m*; *(gradation)* Skala *f*; **pay ~** Tariflohn *m*; **to draw sth to ~** etw im Maßstab or maßstabgerecht zeichnen; **on a large ~** *(fig)* im großen, in großem Umfang; *see also* **scales** ♦ *vt (climb)* erklimmen.

scale down *vt* verkleinern; *(FIN)* herunterschrauben; *(fig)* verringern.

scale drawing *n* maßstabgerechte Zeichnung *f.*

scale model *n* maßstabgetreue(s) Modell *nt.*

scales [skālz] *npl:* **pair of ~** Waage *f.*

scallion [skal'yən] *n* (*US*) Schalotte *f.*

scallop [skâl'əp] *n* Kammuschel *f.*

scalp [skalp] *n* Kopfhaut *f* ♦ *vt* skalpieren.

scalpel [skal'pəl] *n* Skalpell *nt.*

scamper [skam'pûr] *vi:* **to ~ away, to ~ off** verschwinden.

scampi [skam'pē] *npl* Scampi *pl.*

scan [skan] *n (MED)* Scan *m* ♦ *vt (examine)* genau prüfen; *(quickly)* überfliegen; *(horizon)* absuchen; *(poetry)* skandieren.

scandal [skan'dəl] *n (disgrace)* Skandal *m*; *(gossip)* Skandalgeschichte *f.*

scandalize [skan'dəlīz] *vt* schockieren.

scandalous [skan'dələs] *a* skandalös, schockierend.

Scandinavia [skandənā'vēə] *n* Skandinavien *nt.*

Scandinavian [skandənā'vēən] *a* skandinavisch ♦ *n* Skandinavier(in *f*) *m.*

scanner [skan'ûr] *n (RADAR)* Richtantenne *f.*

scant [skant] *a* knapp.

scantily [skan'tilē] *ad* knapp, dürftig; **~ clad** *or* **dressed** leicht bekleidet.

scantiness [skan'tēnis] *n* Knappheit *f.*

scanty [skan'tē] *a* knapp, unzureichend.

scapegoat [skāp'gōt] *n* Sündenbock *m.*

scar [skâr] *n* Narbe *f* ♦ *vt* durch Narben entstellen.

scarce [skârs] *a* selten, rar; *(goods)* knapp.

scarcely [skârs'lē] *ad* kaum; **~ anybody** kaum einer *or* jemand; **I can ~ believe it** ich kann es kaum glauben.

scarceness [skârs'nis], **scarcity** [skâr'sitē] *n (rarity)* Seltenheit *f*; *(shortage)* Mangel *m*, Knappheit *f.*

scarcity value *n* Seltenheitswert *m.*

scare [skâr] *n* Schrecken *m*, Panik *f*; **there was a bomb ~ at Bloomingdales** bei Bloomingdales war ein Bombenalarm ♦ *vt (startle)* erschrecken; *(worry)* ängstigen; **to be ~d** Angst haben.

scare away, scare off vt (dog) verscheuchen.

scarecrow [skär'krō] n Vogelscheuche f.

scaremonger [skär'munggûr] n Bangemacher m.

scarf [skârf] n, pl **scarves** [skârvz] Schal m; (head~) Kopftuch nt.

scarlet [skâr'lit] a scharlachrot ♦ n Scharlachrot nt.

scarlet fever n Scharlach m.

scarred [skârd] a narbig.

scarves [skârvz] pl of **scarf**.

scary [skär'ē] a (col) schaurig.

scathing [skā'thing] a scharf, vernichtend; **to be ~ about sth** bissige or schneidende Bemerkungen pl über etw machen.

scatter [skat'ûr] n Streuung f ♦ vt (sprinkle) (ver)streuen; (disperse) zerstreuen ♦ vi sich zerstreuen.

scatterbrained [skat'ûrbrānd] a flatterhaft, schusselig.

scavenge [skav'inj] vi (person) durchstöbern (for nach); (hyenas etc) Nahrung suchen.

scavenger [skav'injûr] n (animal) Aasfresser m.

scenario [sinär'ēō] n (THEAT, CINE, TV) Szenar(ium) nt; (fig) Szenario nt.

scene [sēn] n (of happening) Ort m; (of play, incident) Szene f; (canvas etc) Bühnenbild nt; (view) Anblick m; (argument) Szene f, Auftritt m; **on the ~** am Ort, dabei; **behind the ~s** (also fig) hinter den Kulissen; **to make a ~** (fam: fuss) eine Szene machen; **to appear** or **come on the ~** (also fig) auftauchen, auf der Bildfläche erscheinen; **the political ~ in Germany** Deutschlands politische Landschaft.

scenery [sē'nûrē] n (THEAT) Bühnenbild nt; (landscape) Landschaft f.

scenic [sē'nik] a landschaftlich, Landschafts-.

scent [sent] n Parfüm nt; (smell) Duft m; (of animal) Fährte f; **to put** or **throw sb off the ~** (fig) jdm von der Spur or Fährte abbringen or ablenken ♦ vt parfümieren

scepter, (Brit) **sceptre** [sep'tûr] n (US) Szepter m.

sceptic etc [skep'tik] (Brit) = **skeptic** etc.

schedule [skej'ool] n (list) Liste f, Tabelle f; (plan) Programm nt, Zeitplan m; (of lessons) Stundenplan m; **we are working on** or **to a very tight ~** wir arbeiten nach einem knapp bemessenen Zeitplan; **everything went according to ~** alles ist planmäßig verlaufen; **on ~** pünktlich, fahrplanmäßig; **behind ~** mit Verspätung ♦ vt: **it is ~d for 2** es soll um 2 abfahren/stattfinden etc.

scheduled [skej'oold] a (date, time) geplant, planmäßig; ~ **flight** Linienflug m.

scheme [skēm] n Schema nt; (dishonest) Intrige f; (plan of action) Plan m, Programm nt ♦ vi sich verschwören, intrigieren ♦ vt planen; **color ~** Farbzusammenstellung f.

scheming [skēm'ing] a intrigierend, ränkevoll.

schism [skiz'əm] n Spaltung f; (ECCL) Schisma nt, Kirchenspaltung f.

schizophrenia [skitsəfrē'nēə] n Schizophrenie f.

schizophrenic [skitsəfren'ik] a schizophren.

scholar [skâl'ûr] n Gelehrte(r) mf; (holding scholarship) Stipendiat m; (student) Student(in f) m; Schüler(in f) m.

scholarly [skâl'ûrlē] a gelehrt.

scholarship [skâl'ûrship] n Gelehrsamkeit f, Belesenheit f; (grant) Stipendium nt.

school [skool] n Schule f; (UNIV) Fakultät f; (of fish) (Fisch)schwarm m ♦ vt schulen; (dog) trainieren.

school age n schulpflichtige(s) Alter nt, Schulalter nt.

schoolbag [skool'bag] n Schulmappe f.

schoolbook [skool'book] n Schulbuch nt.

schoolboy [skool'boi] n Schüler m, Schuljunge m.

schoolchild [skool'chīld] n, pl **-children** Schulkinder pl, Schüler pl.

school days npl (alte) Schulzeit f.

schoolgirl [skool'gûrl] n Schülerin f, Schulmädchen nt.

schooling [skoo'ling] n Schulung f, Ausbildung f.

schoolmaster [skool'mastûr] n Lehrer m.

schoolmistress [skool'mistris] n Lehrerin f.

schoolroom [skool'room] n Klassenzimmer nt.

schoolteacher [skool'tēchûr] n Lehrer(in f) m.

schoolyard [skool'yârd] n Schulhof m.

schooner [skoo'nûr] n Schoner m; (glass) große(s) Sherryglas nt.

sciatica [sīat'ikə] n Ischias m or nt.

science [sī'əns] n Wissenschaft f; (natural ~) Naturwissenschaft f.

science fiction n Science-fiction f.

scientific [sīəntif'ik] a (equipment etc) wissenschaftlich; (of natural sciences) naturwissenschaftlich.

scientist [sī'əntist] n Wissenschaftler(in f) m.

sci-fi [sī'fī'] n abbr (col: = science fiction) Sci-Fi f.

Scilly Islands [sil'ē ī'ləndz] npl Scillyinseln pl.

scintillating [sin'təlāting] a sprühend.

scissors [siz'ûrz] npl Schere f; **a pair of ~** eine Schere.

scoff [skâf] vi (mock) spotten (at über +acc).

scold [skōld] vt schimpfen.

scone [skōn] n weiche(s) Teegebäck nt.

scoop [skoop] n (instrument) Schaufel f; (news) Knüller m (col).

scoop out vt (take out) herausschaufeln; (liquid) herausschöpfen.

scoop up vt aufschaufeln; (liquid) aufschöpfen.

scooter [skoo'tûr] n Motorroller m; (child's) Roller m.

scope [skōp] n Ausmaß nt; (opportunity) (Spiel)raum m, Bewegungsfreiheit f; **there**

is plenty of ~ **for improvement** (*Brit*) es könnte noch viel verbessert werden.

scorch [skôrch] *n* Brandstelle *f* ♦ *vt* versengen, verbrennen.

scorcher [skôr'chûr] *n* (*col*) heiße(r) Tag *m*.

scorching [skôrch'ing] *a* brennend, glühend.

score [skôr] *n* (*in game*) Punktzahl *f*, (*Spiel*)ergebnis *nt*; (*MUS*) Partitur *f*; (*line*) Kratzer *m*; (*twenty*) 20, 20 Stück; **on that** ~ in dieser Hinsicht; **what's the** ~? wie steht's? ♦ *vt* (*goal*) schießen; (*points*) machen; (*mark*) einkerben; (*scratch*) zerkratzen, einritzen ♦ *vi* (*keep record*) Punkte zählen.

score out *vt* ausstreichen.

scoreboard [skôr'bôrd] *n* Anschreibetafel *f*.

scorecard [skôr'kârd] *n* (*SPORT*) Punktliste *f*.

scorer [skôr'ûr] *n* (*FOOTBALL*) Torschütze *m*; (*recorder*) (Auf)schreiber *m*.

scorn [skôrn] *n* Verachtung *f* ♦ *vt* verhöhnen.

scornful [skôrn'fəl] *a*, **scornfully** [skôrn'fəlē] *ad* höhnisch, verächtlich.

Scorpio [skôr'pēō] *n* Skorpion *m*.

scorpion [skôr'pēən] *n* Skorpion *m*.

Scot [skât] *n* Schotte *m*, Schottin *f*.

scotch [skâch] *vt* (*end*) unterbinden ♦ *n*: **S**~ Scotch *m*.

Scotch tape *n* ® (*US*) Tesafilm *m* ®.

scot-free [skât'frē'] *ad*: **to get off** ~ (*unpunished*) ungeschoren davonkommen.

Scotland [skât'lənd] *n* Schottland *nt*.

Scots [skâts] *a* schottisch.

Scotsman [skâts'mən] *n*, *pl* **-men** Schotte *m*.

Scotswoman [skâts'wo͞omən] *n*, *pl* **-women** Schottin *f*.

Scottish [skât'ish] *a* schottisch.

scoundrel [skoun'drəl] *n* Schurke *m*, Schuft *m*.

scour [skour] *vt* (*search*) absuchen; (*clean*) schrubben.

scourer [skour'ûr] *n* (*pad*) Topfkratzer *m*; (*powder*) Scheuersand *m*.

scourge [skûrj] *n* (*whip*) Geißel *f*; (*plague*) Qual *f*.

scouring pad [skour'ing pad] *n* Topfkratzer *m*.

scout [skout] *n* (*MIL*) Späher *m*, Aufklärer *m* ♦ *vi* (*reconnoitre*) auskundschaften; *see* **boy scout**.

scout around *vi* sich umsehen (*for* nach).

scowl [skoul] *n* finstere(r) Blick *m* ♦ *vi* finster blicken.

scrabble [skrab'əl] *vi* (*claw*) kratzen (*at* an +*dat*); (*also*: ~ **around**: *search*) (herum)tasten ♦ *n*: **S**~ ® Scrabble *nt* ®.

scraggy [skrag'ē] *a* dürr, hager.

scram [skram] *vi* (*col*) verschwinden, abhauen.

scramble [skram'bəl] *n* (*climb*) Kletterei *f*; (*struggle*) Kampf *m* ♦ *vi* klettern; (*fight*) sich schlagen; **to** ~ **out/through** krabbeln aus/durch; **to** ~ **for sth** sich um etw raufen.

scrambled eggs [skram'bəld egz] *npl* Rührei *nt*.

scrambling [skram'bling] *n* (*SPORT*): **to go** ~ Querfeldeinrennen gehen.

scrap [skrap] *n* (*bit*) Stückchen *nt*; (*fight*) Keilerei *f*; (*also*: ~ **iron**) Schrott *m*; **to sell sth for** ~ etw als Schrott *or* zum Verschrotten verkaufen; *see also* **scraps** ♦ *a* Abfall- ♦ *vt* verwerfen ♦ *vi* (*fight*) streiten, sich prügeln.

scrapbook [skrap'bo͝ok] *n* Einklebealbum *nt*.

scrap dealer *n* Schrotthändler(in *f*) *m*.

scrape [skrāp] *n* Kratzen *nt*; (*trouble*) Klemme *f* ♦ *vt* kratzen; (*car*) zerkratzen; (*clean*) abkratzen ♦ *vi* (*make harsh noise*) kratzen.

scrape through *vi* (*in exam*) durchrutschen (*col*).

scraper [skrā'pûr] *n* Kratzer *m*.

scrap heap *n* Abfallhaufen *m*; (*for metal*) Schrotthaufen *m*; **to throw sth on the** ~ (*fig*) etw vergessen.

scrap iron *n* Alteisen *nt*.

scrap metal *n* Schrott *m*.

scrappy [skrap'ē] *a* zusammengestoppelt.

scraps [skraps] *npl* Reste *pl*; (*waste*) Abfall *m*.

scrap yard *n* (*Brit*: *for cars also*) Schrottplatz *m*.

scratch [skrach] *n* (*wound*) Kratzer *m*, Schramme *f*; **to start from** ~ ganz von vorne anfangen; **to be up to** ~ den Anforderungen entsprechen ♦ *a* (*improvised*) zusammengewürfelt ♦ *vt* kratzen; (*car*) zerkratzen ♦ *vi* (sich) kratzen.

scratchpad [skrach'pad] *n* (*US*) Notizblock *m*.

scrawl [skrôl] *n* Gekritzel *nt* ♦ *vti* kritzeln.

scrawny [skrô'nē] *a* (*person, neck*) dürr.

scream [skrēm] *n* Schrei *m* ♦ *vti* schreien; **it/he was a** ~ (*fig col*) es/er war zum Schreien; **to** ~ **at sb** jdn anschreien (*to do sth* etw zu tun).

scree [skrē] *n* Geröll(halde *f*) *nt*.

screech [skrēch] *n* Schrei *m* ♦ *vi* kreischen.

screen [skrēn] *n* (*protective*) Schutzschirm *m*; (*film*) Leinwand *f*; (*TV*) Bildschirm *m*; (*against insects*) Fliegengitter *nt*; (*ECCL*) Lettner *m* ♦ *vt* (*shelter*) (be)schirmen; (*film*) zeigen, vorführen; (*fig*: *person*: *for security*) überprüfen; (: *for illness*) eine Reihenuntersuchung machen (+*dat*).

screen editing *n* (*COMPUT*) Bildschirmaufbereitung *f*.

screening [skrē'ning] *n* (*of film*) Vorführung *f*; (*medical* ~) Untersuchung *f*; (*for security*) Überprüfung *f*.

screen memory *n* (*COMPUT*) Bildschirmspeicher *m*.

screenplay [skrēn'plā] *n* Drehbuch *nt*.

screen test *n* Probeaufnahmen *pl*.

screw [skro͞o] *n* Schraube *f*; (*NAUT*) Schiffsschraube *f* ♦ *vt* (*fasten*) schrauben; (*col*: *cheat*) hereinlegen; (*vulgar*) bumsen; **to** ~ **sth to the wall** etw an die Wand schrauben; **to** ~ **money out of sb** (*col*) jdm das Geld aus der Tasche ziehen.

screw up *vt* (*paper, material*) zusammenknüllen; (*col: ruin*) vermasseln; **to ~ up one's face** das Gesicht verziehen.

screwball [skrōō'ból] *n* Spinner *m*.

screwdriver [skrōō'drĭvûr] *n* Schraubenzieher *m*.

screwy [skrōō'ē] *a* (*col*) verrückt.

scribble [skrĭb'əl] *n* Gekritzel *nt* ♦ *vt* kritzeln; **to ~ sth down** etw hinkritzeln.

scribe [skrīb] *n* Schreiber *m*; (*Jewish*) Schriftgelehrte(r) *m*.

script [skrĭpt] *n* (*handwriting*) Handschrift *f*; (*writing*) Schrift *f*; (*for film*) Drehbuch *nt*; (*THEAT*) Manuskript *nt*, Text *m*.

scripted [skrĭp'tĭd] *a*: **a ~ discussion** (*RAD, TV*) eine vorbereitete Diskussion.

Scripture [skrĭp'chûr] *n* Heilige Schrift *f*.

scriptwriter [skrĭpt'rĭtûr] *n* Textverfasser(in *f*) *m*.

scroll [skrōl] *n* Schriftrolle *f* ♦ *vi* (*COMPUT*) den Bildschirminhalt verschieben.

scrotum [skrō'təm] *n* Hodensack *m*, Skrotum *nt*.

scrounge [skrounj] *vt* schnorren ♦ *n*: **on the ~** beim Schnorren.

scrub [skrub] *n* (*clean*) Schrubben *nt*; (*in countryside*) Gestrüpp *nt* ♦ *vt* (*clean*) schrubben; (*reject*) fallenlassen.

scrubbing brush [skrub'ĭng brush] *n* (*Brit*) = **scrub brush**.

scrub brush *n* (*US*) Schrubbürste *f*, Wurzelbürste *f*.

scruff [skruf] *n* (*of neck*) Genick *nt*, Kragen *m*.

scruffy [skruf'ē] *a* unordentlich, vergammelt.

scrum(mage) [skrum('ĭj)] *n* (*RUGBY*) Gedränge *nt*.

scruple [skrōō'pəl] *n* Skrupel *m*, Bedenken *nt*; **to have no ~s about doing sth** keine Skrupel haben, etw zu tun.

scrupulous [skrōō'pyələs] *a* peinlich genau, gewissenhaft.

scrupulously [skrōō'pyələslē] *ad* gewissenhaft; **he tries to be ~ fair/honest** er bemüht sich, äußerst fair/ehrlich zu sein.

scrutinize [skrōō'tənīz] *vt* genau prüfen *or* untersuchen.

scrutiny [skrōō'tənē] *n* genaue Untersuchung *f*; **everybody was subject to police ~** jeder wurde einer Überprüfung durch die Polizei unterzogen.

scuba [skōō'bə] *n* (Schwimm)tauchgerät *nt*.

scuba diving *n* (Sport)tauchen *nt*.

scuff [skuf] *vt* (*shoes*) abstoßen.

scuffle [skuf'əl] *n* Handgemenge *nt*.

scullery [skul'ûrē] *n* Spülküche *f*.

sculptor [skulp'tûr] *n* Bildhauer *m*.

sculpture [skulp'chûr] *n* (*ART*) Bildhauerei *f*; (*statue*) Skulptur *f*.

scum [skum] *n* (*lit, fig*) Abschaum *m*.

scurrilous [skûr'ələs] *a* unflätig.

scurry [skûr'ē] *vi* huschen.

scurvy [skûr'vē] *n* Skorbut *m*.

scuttle [skut'əl] *n* (*also:* **coal ~**) Kohleneimer *m* ♦ *vt* (*ship*) versenken ♦ *vi* (*scamper*): **to**

~ away *or* **off** sich davonmachen.

scythe [sīth] *n* Sense *f*.

SD *abbr* (*US MAIL*) = *South Dakota*.

S. Dak. *abbr* (*US*) = *South Dakota*.

SDI *n abbr* (= *Strategic Defense Initiative*) SDI *f*.

SDLP *n abbr* (*Brit POL*) = *Social Democratic and Labour Party*.

SDP *n abbr* (*Brit POL*) = *Social Democratic Party*.

sea [sē] *n* Meer *nt* (*also fig*), See *f* ♦ *a* Meeres-, See-; **out to** *or* **at ~** aufs Meer (hinaus); **to go by ~** mit dem Schiff fahren; **heavy/rough ~(s)** schwere/rauhe See; **by** *or* **beside the ~** (*vacation*) am Meer; (*village*) am Meer, an der See; **a ~ of flames** ein Flammenmeer *nt*.

sea bed *n* Meeresboden *m*, Meeresgrund *m*.

sea bird *n* Meervogel *m*.

seaboard [sē'bôrd] *n* Küste *f*.

sea breeze *n* Seewind *m*.

seadog [sē'dôg'] *n* Seebär *m*.

seafarer [sē'fârûr] *n* Seefahrer *m*.

seafaring [sē'fâring] *a* (*community*) seefahrend; **~ man** Seefahrer *m*.

seafood [sē'fōōd] *n* Meeresfrüchte *pl*.

sea front *n* Strandpromenade *f*.

seagoing [sē'gōing] *a* seetüchtig, Hochsee-.

seagull [sē'gul] *n* Möwe *f*.

seal [sēl] *n* (*animal*) Seehund *m*; (*stamp, impression*) Siegel *nt*; **~ of approval** offizielle Zustimmung *f* ♦ *vt* versiegeln; (*bargain, sb's fate*) besiegeln.

seal cull *n* Robbenschlag *m*.

sea level *n* Meeresspiegel *m*.

sealing wax [sē'lĭng waks] *n* Siegellack *m*.

sea lion *n* Seelöwe *m*.

sealskin [sēl'skĭn] *n* Seehundfell *nt*, Seal *m*.

seam [sēm] *n* Saum *m*; (*edges joining*) Naht *f*; (*layer*) Schicht *f*; (*of coal*) Flöz *nt*; **the hall was bursting at the ~s** der Saal war proppenvoll.

seaman [sē'mən] *n, pl* **-men** Seemann *m*.

seamanship [sē'mənshĭp] *n* Seemannschaft *f*.

seamless [sēm'lĭs] *a* nahtlos.

seamy [sē'mē] *a* (*people, café*) zwielichtig; (*life*) anrüchig; **the ~ side of life** die dunkle Seite des Lebens.

seaplane [sē'plān] *n* Wasserflugzeug *nt*.

seaport [sē'pôrt] *n* Seehafen *m*, Hafenstadt *f*.

search [sûrch] *n* Suche *f* (*for* nach) ♦ *vi* suchen ♦ *vt* (*examine*) durchsuchen; (*COMPUT*) suchen; **in ~ of** auf der Suche nach; **to ~ for** suchen nach; **"~ and replace"** (*COMPUT*) ,,suchen und ersetzen''.

search through *vt fus* durchsuchen.

searcher [sûr'chûr] *n* Durchsuchungsbeamte *m*, Durchsuchungsbeamtin *f*.

searching [sûr'chĭng] *a* (*look*) forschend; (*question*) durchdringend.

searchlight [sûrch'līt] *n* Scheinwerfer *m*.

search party *n* Suchmannschaft *f*.

search warrant *n* Durchsuchungsbefehl *m*.

searing [sē'rĭng] *a* (*heat*) glühend; (*pain*)

brennend, stechend.

seashore [sē'shôr] *n* Meeresküste *f*; **on the ~** am Strand.

seasick [sē'sik] *a* seekrank.

seasickness [sē'siknis] *n* Seekrankheit *f*.

seaside [sē'sīd] *n* Küste *f*; **at the ~** an der See; **to go to the ~** an die See fahren.

seaside resort *n* Badeort *m*.

season [sē'zən] *n* Jahreszeit *f*; (*Christmas etc*) Zeit *f*, Saison *f*; **busy ~** (*for shops*) Hochbetrieb *m*; (*for hotels etc*) Hochsaison *f*; **the open ~** (*HUNTING*) die Jagdzeit *f*; **strawberries are in/out of ~** für Erdbeeren ist jetzt die richtige Zeit/nicht die richtige Zeit ♦ *vt* (*flavor*) würzen.

seasonal [sē'zənəl] *a* Saison-.

seasoned [sē'zənd] *a* (*wood*) abgelagert; (*fig: worker, actor*) erfahren; (*fig: troops also*) kampfgestählt; **a ~ campaigner** ein erfahrener *or* erprobter Befürworter *or* Gegner.

seasoning [sē'zəning] *n* Gewürz *nt*, Würze *f*.

season ticket *n* (*THEAT*) Abonnement *nt*; (*Brit RAIL*) Zeitkarte *f*.

seat [sēt] *n* Sitz *m*, Platz *m*; (*POL, center of government*) Sitz *m*; (*part of body*) Gesäß *nt*; (*part of garment*) Sitzfläche *f*; (*of pants*) Hosenboden *m*; **to take one's ~** sich setzen; **are there any ~s left?** sind noch Plätze frei? ♦ *vt* (*place*) setzen; (*have space for*) Sitzplätze bieten für; **to be ~ed** sitzen.

seat belt *n* Sicherheitsgurt *m*.

seating [sē'ting] *n* Sitzplätze *pl*.

seating arrangements *npl* Sitzordnung *f*.

seating capacity [sē'ting kəpas'itē] *n* Platz *m* zum Sitzen.

SEATO [sē'tō] *n abbr* (= *Southeast Asia Treaty Organization*) SEATO *f*.

sea water *n* Meerwasser *nt*, Seewasser *nt*.

seaweed [sē'wēd] *n* (See)tang *m*, Alge *f*.

seaworthy [sē'wûrṭhē] *a* seetüchtig.

sec. *abbr* (= *second*) Sek., sek.

SEC *n abbr* (*US: = Securities and Exchange Commission*) Einrichtung zum Schutze von privaten Anlegern auf dem Aktienmarkt.

secateurs [sek'ətûrz] *npl* (*Brit*) Gartenschere *f*.

secede [sisēd'] *vi* sich lossagen *or* abspalten (*from* von).

secluded [siklōō'did] *a* abgelegen, ruhig.

seclusion [siklōō'zhən] *n* Zurückgezogenheit *f*.

second [sek'ənd] *a* zweite(r, s); **it is ~ nature to him** es ist ihm zur zweiten Natur geworden; **~ floor** (*US*) erste(r) Stock *m*; (*Brit*) zweite(r) Stock *m*; **to ask for a ~ opinion** (*MED*) ein zweites Gutachten *or* einen zweiten Befund einholen; **~ cousin** Cousin *m* *or* Cousine *f* zweiten Grades; **Charles the S~** Karl der Zweite; **to have ~ thoughts about sth** sich (*dat*) etw anders überlegen; **~ mortgage** zweite Hypothek *f* ♦ *ad* (*in ~ position*) an zweiter Stelle; (*RAIL*) zweite(r) Klasse ♦ *n* (*time*) Sekunde *f*; (*person*) Zweite(r) *mf*; (*COMM: imperfect*) zwei-

te Wahl *f*; (*SPORT*) Sekundant *m*; **just a ~!** (einen) Augenblick! ♦ *vt* (*support*) unterstützen; [sikând'] (*employee*) abordnen.

secondary [sek'əndārē] *a* zweitrangig.

secondary education *n* Sekundarstufe *f*.

secondary picket *n* Streikposten *bei einem nur mittelbar beteiligten Betrieb*.

secondary school *n* höhere Schule *f*, Mittelschule *f*.

second-best [sek'əndbest'] *a* zweitbeste(r, s).

second-class [sek'əndklas'] *a*: **~ citizen** Bürger *m* zweiter Klasse ♦ *ad*: **to send sth ~** etw zweiter Klasse (mit der Post) schicken; **to travel ~** zweiter Klasse reisen.

seconder [sek'əndûr] *n* Unterstützer *m*.

secondhand [sek'əndhand'] *a* (*information, knowledge*) aus zweiter Hand; (*buy: car etc*) gebraucht ♦ *ad*: **to hear sth ~** etw aus zweiter Hand haben.

second hand *n* (*on clock*) Sekundenzeiger *m*.

second-in-command [sek'əndinkəmand'] *n* (*ADMIN*) Stellvertreter *m*; (*MIL*) stellvertretende(r) Kommandeur *m*.

secondly [sek'əndlē] *ad* zweitens.

second-rate [sek'əndrāt'] *a* mittelmäßig.

secrecy [sē'krisē] *n* Geheimhaltung *f*.

secret [sē'krit] *n* Geheimnis *nt*; **in ~** geheim, heimlich; **to make no ~ of sth** kein Geheimnis *or* keinen Hehl aus etw machen; **to keep sth ~ (from sb)** etw (vor jdm) geheimhalten ♦ *a* geheim, heimlich, Geheim-; **~ agent** Geheimagent(in *f*) *m*.

secretarial [sekritär'ēəl] *a* Sekretärs-; **~ work** Büroarbeit *f*.

secretariat [sekritär'ēət] *n* Sekretariat *nt*.

secretary [sek'ritārē] *n* Sekretär(in *f*) *m*; (*government*) Staatssekretär(in *f*) *m*, Minister(in *f*) *m*.

secretary pool *n* (*US*) = **typing pool**.

secrete [sikrēt'] *vt* (*MED, BIOL*) absondern; (*hide*) verbergen.

secretion [sikrē'shən] *n* (*MED: act*) Absonderung *f*.

secretive [sē'kritiv] *a* geheimtuerisch.

secretly [sē'kritlē] *ad* heimlich.

sect [sekt] *n* Sekte *f*.

sectarian [sektär'ēən] *a* (*belonging to a sect*) Sekten-.

section [sek'shən] *n* Teil *m*, Ausschnitt *m*; (*department*) Abteilung *f*; (*of document*) Abschnitt *m*, Paragraph *m*; **the business ~** (*PRESS*) der Wirtschaftsteil.

sectional [sek'shənəl] *a* (*US: furniture*) Anbau-; (*regional*) partikularistisch.

sector [sek'tûr] *n* Sektor *m*; (*COMPUT*) (Platten)sektor *m*.

secular [sek'yəlûr] *a* weltlich, profan.

secure [sikyōōr'] *a* (*safe*) sicher; (*firmly fixed*) fest; **to make sth ~** etw festmachen *or* sichern ♦ *vt* (*make firm*) befestigen, sichern; (*obtain*) sichern; (*FIN: loan*) (ab)sichern; **to ~ sth for sb** jdm etw sichern.

secured creditor [sikyōōrd' kred'itûr] *n* abgesicherte(r) Gläubiger *m*.

securely [sikyōōr'lē] *ad* sicher, fest.

security [sikyōōr'itē] *n* Sicherheit *f*; (*pledge*) Pfand *nt*; (*document*) Sicherheiten *pl*; (*national* ~) Staatssicherheit *f*; **job** ~ gesicherte(r) Arbeitsplatz *m*; **securities** (*FIN*) Effekten, (Wert)papiere *pl*; ~ **of tenure** Kündigungsschutz *m*; **to increase** *or* **tighten** ~ Sicherheitsvorkehrungen verschärfen; *see* **social security.**

security forces *npl* Friedensstreitmacht *f*.

security guard *n* Sicherheitsbeamte(r) *m*, Wache *f*.

security risk *n* Sicherheitsrisiko *nt*.

secy. *abbr* (= *secretary*) Sekr.

sedan [sidan'] *n* (*US AUT*) Limousine *f*.

sedate [sidāt'] *a* (*calm*) gelassen; (*serious*) gesetzt ♦ *vt* (*MED*) ein Beruhigungsmittel geben (+*dat*).

sedation [sidā'shən] *n* (*MED*) Einfluß *m* von Beruhigungsmitteln; **to put sb under** ~ jdm Beruhigungsmittel geben.

sedative [sed'ətiv] *n* Beruhigungsmittel *nt* ♦ *a* beruhigend, einschläfernd.

sedentary [sed'əntärē] *a* (*job*) sitzend.

sediment [sed'əmənt] *n* (Boden)satz *m*.

sedimentary [sedəmen'tûrē] *a* (*GEOG*) Sediment-.

sedition [sidish'ən] *n* Aufwiegelung *f*.

seduce [sidōōs'] *vt* verführen.

seduction [siduk'shən] *n* Verführung *f*.

seductive [siduk'tiv] *a* verführerisch.

see [sē] *irreg vt* sehen; (*understand*) (ein)sehen, erkennen; **it** ~**s that** ... es (*find out*) sehen, herausfinden; (*make sure*) dafür sorgen (daß); (*accompany*) begleiten, bringen; (*visit*) besuchen ♦ *vi* (*be aware*) sehen; (*find out*) nachsehen ♦ *n* (*ECCL*: *R.C.*) Bistum *nt*; (: *Protestant*) Kirchenkreis *m*; **to** ~ **a doctor** zum Arzt gehen; **to go and** ~ **sb** jdn besuchen (gehen); ~ **you soon/later/tomorrow!** bis bald/später/morgen!; **there was nobody to be seen** es war niemand zu sehen; **to** ~ **sb off** jdn zum Zug *etc* begleiten; **as far as I can** ~ soweit ich das beurteilen kann; **I don't know what she** ~**s in him** ich weiß nicht, was sie an ihm findet; **I** ~ ach so, ich verstehe; **let me** ~ (*wait*) warte mal; (*show me*) laß mich (mal) sehen; (*let me think*) laß mich mal überlegen; ~ **for yourself** überzeug dich (doch) selbst; **we'll** ~ werden (mal) sehen.

see about *vt fus* (*deal with*) sich kümmern um, erledigen.

see through *vt*: **to** ~ **sth through** etw durchfechten ♦ *vt fus*: **to** ~ **through sb/sth** jdn/etw durchschauen.

see to *vt fus*: **to** ~ **to it** dafür sorgen.

seed [sēd] *n* Samen *m*, (Samen)korn *nt* ♦ *vt* (*TENNIS*) plazieren.

seedless [sēd'lis] *a* kernlos.

seedling [sēd'ling] *n* Setzling *m*.

seedy [sē'dē] *a* (*ill*) flau, angeschlagen;

(*clothes*) schäbig; (*person*) zweifelhaft.

seeing [sē'ing] *cj* da.

seek [sēk] *vt irreg* suchen; **to** ~ **advice/help from sb** jdn um Rat fragen/um Hilfe bitten.

seek out *vt* (*person*) ausfindig machen.

seem [sēm] *vi* scheinen; **it** ~**s that** ... es scheint, daß ...; **what** ~**s to be the trouble?** worum geht es denn?; (*doctor*) was kann ich für Sie tun?

seemingly [sē'minglē] *ad* anscheinend.

seemly [sēm'lē] *a* geziemend.

seen [sēn] *pp of* **see.**

seep [sēp] *vi* sickern.

seer [sēr] *n* Seher *m*.

seersucker [sēr'sukûr] *n* Krepp *m*, Seersucker *m*.

seesaw [sē'sô] *n* Wippe *f*.

seethe [sēth] *vi* kochen; (*with crowds*) wimmeln von.

see-through [sē'thrōō] *a* (*dress*) durchsichtig.

segment [seg'mənt] *n* Teil *m*; (*of circle*) Ausschnitt *m*.

segregate [seg'rəgāt] *vt* trennen, absondern.

segregation [segrəgā'shən] *n* Rassentrennung *f*.

Seine [sān] *n* Seine *f*.

seismic [sīz'mik] *a* seismisch, Erdbeben-.

seize [sēz] *vt* (*grasp*) ergreifen, packen; (*power*) ergreifen; (*take legally*) beschlagnahmen; (*point*) erfassen, begreifen.

seize up *vi* (*TECH*) sich festfressen.

seize (up)on *vt fus* sich stürzen auf (+*acc*).

seizure [sē'zhûr] *n* (*illness*) Anfall *m*; (*confiscation*) Beschlagnahme *f*.

seldom [sel'dəm] *ad* selten.

select [silekt'] *a* ausgewählt; (*hotel, restaurant, club*) exklusiv; **a** ~ **few** wenige Auserwählte ♦ *vt* auswählen.

selection [silek'shən] *n* Auswahl *f*.

selection committee *n* Auswahlkomitee *nt*.

selective [silek'tiv] *a* (*person*) wählerisch.

self [self] *n*, *pl* **selves** [selvz] Selbst *nt*, Ich *nt*.

self-addressed (stamped) envelope [self'ədrest' (stampt) ân'vəlōp] *n* frankierte(r) Rückumschlag *m*.

self-adhesive [self'adhē'siv] *a* selbstklebend.

self-appointed [self'əpoin'tid] *a* selbsternannt.

self-assertive [self'əsûr'tiv] *a* selbstbewußt.

self-assurance [self'əshōōr'əns] *n* Selbstsicherheit *f*.

self-assured [self'əshōōrd'] *a* selbstbewußt.

self-catering [self'kā'tûring] *a*: ~ **apartment** Wohnung *f* für Selbstversorger.

self-centered [self'sen'tûrd] *a* egozentrisch, ichbezogen.

self-cleaning [self'klē'ning] *a* selbstreinigend.

self-colored [self'kul'ûrd] *a* einfarbig.

self-confessed [self'kənfest'] *a*: **he is a** ~ **alcoholic** er ist Alkoholiker und gibt es offen zu.

self-confidence [self'kân'fidəns] *n* Selbstver-

trauen *nt*, Selbstbewußtsein *nt*.
self-confident [self'kân'fidənt] *a* selbstsicher.
self-conscious [self'kân'chəs] *a* gehemmt, befangen.
self-contained [self'kəntând'] *a* (*complete*) (in sich) geschlossen; (*person*) verschlossen.
self-control [self'kəntrōl'] *n* Selbstbeherrschung *f*.
self-defeating [self'difē'ting] *a* sinnlos, unsinnig; **to be ~** ein Widerspruch in sich sein.
self-defense [self'difens'] *n* Selbstverteidigung *f*; (*JUR*) Notwehr *f*; **to act in ~** in Notwehr handeln.
self-discipline [self'dis'əplin] *n* Selbstdisziplin *f*.
self-employed [self'imploid'] *a* frei(-schaffend).
self-esteem [self'əstēm'] *n* Selbstachtung *f*.
self-evident [self'ev'idənt] *a* offensichtlich.
self-explanatory [self'iksplan'ətôrē] *a* für sich (selbst) sprechend.
self-financing [self'finan'sing] *n* Eigenfinanzierung *f*.
self-governing [self'guv'ûrning] *a* selbstverwaltet, sich selbst verwaltend.
self-help [self'help'] *n* Selbsthilfe *f*.
self-importance [self'impôr'təns] *n* Eigendünkel *m*.
self-indulgent [self'indul'jənt] *a* zügellos.
self-inflicted [self'inflik'tid] *a* selbst zugefügt.
self-interest [self'in'trist] *n* Eigennutz *m*.
selfish [sel'fish] *a*, **selfishly** [sel'fishlē] *ad* egoistisch, selbstsüchtig.
selfishness [sel'fishnis] *n* Egoismus *m*, Selbstsucht *f*.
selfless [self'lis] *a*, **selflessly** [self'lislē] *ad* selbstlos.
self-made [self'mād'] *a* selbstgemacht; **~ man** Selfmademan *m*.
self-pity [self'pit'ē] *n* Selbstmitleid *nt*.
self-portrait [self'pôr'trit] *n* Selbstbildnis *nt*.
self-possessed [self'pəzest'] *a* selbstbeherrscht.
self-preservation [self'prezûrvā'shən] *n* Selbsterhaltung *f*.
self-propelled [self'prəpeld'] *a* mit Eigenantrieb.
self-raising flour [self'rā'zing flour] *n* (*Brit*) = **self-rising flour**.
self-reliant [self'rili'ənt] *a* unabhängig.
self-respect [self'rispekt'] *n* Selbstachtung *f*.
self-respecting [self'rispekt'ing] *a* mit Selbstachtung.
self-righteous [self'rī'chəs] *a* selbstgerecht.
self-rising flour [self'rī'zing flour] *n* (*US*) selbsttreibende(s) Mehl *nt*, Mehl mit bereits *beigemischtem Backpulver*.
self-sacrifice [self'sak'rəfīs] *n* Selbstaufopferung *f*.
self-same [self'sām] *a* genau der/die/das gleiche, der-/die-/dasselbe.
self-satisfied [self'sat'isfīd] *a* selbstzufrieden.
self-service [self'sûr'vis] *a* Selbstbedienungs-.
self-styled [self'stīld'] *a* selbsternannt.

self-sufficient [self'səfish'ənt] *a* selbstgenügsam.
self-supporting [self'səpôrt'ing] *a* (*FIN*) Eigenfinanzierungs-; (*person*) eigenständig.
self-taught [self'tôt'] *a* selbsterlernt.
self-test [self'test'] *n* (*COMPUT*) Eigendiagnose *f*.
sell [sel] *irreg vt* verkaufen ♦ *vi* verkaufen, (*goods*) sich verkaufen (lassen); **to ~ sb an idea** (*fig*) jdm eine Idee verkaufen *or* schmackhaft machen.
sell off *vt* verkaufen.
sell out *vi* (*COMM*) sein Geschäft/seine Firma/seinen Anteil verkaufen *or* abstoßen ♦ *vt* ausverkaufen; **the tickets are all sold out** die Karten sind alle ausverkauft.
sell-by date [sel'bī dāt] *n* Haltbarkeitsdatum *nt*.
seller [sel'ûr] *n* Verkäufer(in *f*) *m*.
seller's market *n* Verkäufermarkt *m*.
selling price [sel'ing prīs] *n* Verkaufspreis *m*.
Sellotape [sel'ōtāp] *n* ® (*Brit*) Tesafilm *m* ®.
sellout [sel'out] *n* (*of tickets*): **it was a ~** es war ausverkauft.
selves [selvz] *npl of* **self**.
semantic [siman'tik] *a* semantisch.
semaphore [sem'əfôr] *n* Winkzeichen *pl*.
semblance [sem'bləns] *n* Anschein *m*, Anflug *m*.
semester [simes'tûr] *n* Semester *nt*.
semi [sem'ē] *n* (*Brit*) = **semidetached house**.
semi ... *pref* halb ..., Halb ...
semiannually [semēan'yōōəlē] *a* halbjährlich ♦ *ad* halbjährlich, jedes halb Jahr.
semibreve [sem'ēbrēv] *n* (*Brit*) = **whole note**.
semicircle [sem'ēsûrkəl] *n* Halbkreis *m*.
semicircular [semēsûr'kyəlûr] *a* halbkreisförmig.
semicolon [sem'ēkōlən] *n* Semikolon *nt*.
semiconductor [semēkənduk'tûr] *n* Halbleiter *m*.
semiconscious [semēkân'chəs] *a* halbbewußt.
semidetached house [semēditacht' hous'] *n* (*Brit*) Zweifamilienhaus *nt*, Doppelhaus *nt*.
semifinal [semēfī'nəl] *n* Halbfinale *nt*.
seminar [sem'ənâr] *n* Seminar *nt*.
semiprecious stone [semēpresh'əs stōn'] *n* Halbedelstein *m*.
semiquaver [sem'ēkwāvûr] *n* (*Brit*) = **sixteenth note**.
semiskilled [semēskild'] *a* angelernt.
semi(trailer) [sem'ē(trā'lûr)] *n* (*US*) Sattelschlepper *m*.
semitone [sem'ētōn] *n* Halbton *m*.
semolina [seməlē'nə] *n* Grieß *m*.
Sen., sen. *abbr* (*US*) = **senator**; (= *senior*) Sen.
senate [sen'it] *n* Senat *m*.
senator [sen'ətûr] *n* Senator *m*.
send [send] *vt irreg* senden, schicken; **to ~ by mail** mit der Post schicken; **to ~ sb for**

sth jdn etw holen lassen; **to ~ word that** ...
Nachricht geben, daß ...; **she ~s (you) her
love** sie läßt (dich) grüßen; **to ~ sb to
sleep** jdn einschläfern; **to ~ sb/sth flying**
jdn/etw umschmeißen *or* umwerfen.
send (a)round *vt* (*letter, document etc*)
verschicken.
send away *vt* wegschicken.
send away for *vt fus* anfordern.
send back *vt* zurückschicken.
send for *vt fus* holen lassen; (*by mail*) anfordern, sich (*dat*) kommen lassen.
send in *vt* (*report, application, resignation*) einsenden, einschicken.
send off *vt* (*goods*) abschicken.
send on *vt* (*letter*) nachschicken; (*luggage
etc: in advance*) vorausschicken.
send out *vt* (*invitation*) aussenden; (*emit:
light, heat*) ausstrahlen; (: *signals*) aussenden.
send up *vt* hinaufsenden.
sender [send'ûr] *n* Absender(in *f*) *m*.
send-off [send'ôf] *n* Verabschiedung *f*.
send-up [send'up] *n* (*Brit col*) Verulkung *f*.
Senegal [sen'əgâl] *n* Senegal *nt*.
Senegalese [senəgəlēz'] *n* Senegalese *m*, Se-
negalesin *f*, Senegaler(in *f*) *m* ♦ *a* senegale-
sisch, senegalisch.
senile [sē'nîl] *a* senil, Alters-.
senility [sinil'ətē] *n* Altersschwachheit *f*.
senior [sēn'yûr] *a* (*older*) älter; (*higher rank*)
Ober-; **P. Jones S~** P. Jones Senior ♦ *n*
(*older person*) Ältere(r) *mf*; (*higher-
ranking*) Rangälteste(r) *mf*.
senior citizens *npl* ältere Bürger *pl*, Rent-
ner *pl*.
senior high school *n* (*US*) Oberstufe *f*.
seniority [sēnyôr'itē] *n* (*of age*) höhere(s) Alter *nt*; (*in rank*) höhere Position *f*; (*MIL*)
höhere(r) Rang *m*; (*in civil service*) höhe-
re(r) Dienstgrad *m*.
sensation [sensā'shən] *n* (*feeling*) Gefühl *nt*;
(*of heat, cold etc*) Empfindung *f*; (*great success*) Sensation *f*, Aufsehen *nt*.
sensational [sensā'shənəl] *a* sensationell,
Sensations-.
sense [sens] *n* Sinn *m*; (*understanding*) Verstand *m*, Vernunft *f*; (*meaning*) Sinn *m*, Bedeutung *f*; (*feeling*) Gefühl *nt*; **~ of humor**
Sinn *m* für Humor; **there is no ~ in doing
that** es ist zwecklos *or* sinnlos, das zu tun;
to make ~ Sinn ergeben; **to come to one's
~s** (*regain consciousness*) zur Besinnung
kommen; **to take leave of one's ~s** den
Verstand verlieren ♦ *vt* fühlen, spüren.
senseless [sens'lis] *a* sinnlos; (*unconscious*)
besinnungslos.
senselessly [sens'lislē] *ad* (*stupidly*) sinnlos.
sensibility [sensəbil'ətē] *n* Empfindsamkeit *f*;
(*feeling hurt*) Empfindlichkeit *f*.
sensible [sen'səbəl] *a*, **sensibly** [sen'səblē] *ad*
vernünftig.
sensitive [sen'sətiv] *a* empfindlich (*to* gegen);
(*easily hurt*) sensibel, feinfühlig; (*film*)

lichtempfindlich; **he is very ~ about it** er
reagiert sehr empfindlich darauf.
sensitivity [sensətiv'ətē] *n* Empfindlichkeit *f*;
(*artistic*) Feingefühl *nt*; (*tact*) Feinfühlig-
keit *f*.
sensual [sen'shōōəl] *a* sinnlich.
sensuous [sen'shōōəs] *a* sinnlich, sinnenfreu-
dig.
sent [sent] *pt, pp of* **send**.
sentence [sen'təns] *n* Satz *m*; (*JUR*) Strafe *f*,
Urteil *nt* ♦ *vt* verurteilen; **to pass ~ on sb**
über jdn das Urteil verkünden; (*fig*) jdn verurteilen.
sentiment [sen'təmənt] *n* Gefühl *nt*;
(*thought*) Gedanke *m*, Gesinnung *f*.
sentimental [sentəmen'təl] *a* sentimental; (*of
feelings rather than reason*) gefühlsmäßig.
sentimentality [sentəmental'itē] *n* Sentimentalität *f*.
sentinel [sen'tənəl] *n* Wachtposten *m*.
sentry [sen'trē] *n* (Schild)wache *f*.
sentry duty *n*: **to be on ~** auf Wache sein.
Seoul [sōl] *n* Seoul *nt*.
separable [sep'ûrəbəl] *a* (ab)trennbar.
separate *a* [sep'rit] getrennt, separat; **~
from** gesondert von; **under ~ cover**
(*COMM*) mit getrennter Post ♦ [sep'ərāt] *vt*
trennen; **to ~ into** aufteilen in (+*acc*); **he
is ~d from his wife, but not divorced** er
lebt von seiner Frau getrennt, aber sie sind
nicht geschieden ♦ *vi* sich trennen.
separately [sep'ritlē] *ad* getrennt.
separates [sep'rits] *npl* (*clothes*) Röcke, Pullover *etc*.
separation [sepərā'shən] *n* Trennung *f*.
sepia [sē'pēə] *a* Sepia-.
Sept. *abbr* (= *September*) Sept.
September [septem'bûr] *n* September *m*; **the
first of ~** der erste September; **at the end/
beginning of ~** Anfang/Ende September; **in
~** im September.
septic [sep'tik] *a* vereitert, septisch; **to go ~**
eitern, septisch werden.
septicemia, (*Brit*) **septicaemia** [septisē'mēə]
n Vergiftung *f* des Blutes, Septikämie *f*.
septic tank *n* Faulbehälter *m*, Klärbehälter
m.
sequel [sē'kwəl] *n* Folge *f*.
sequence [sē'kwins] *n* (Reihen)folge *f*; **in ~**
der Reihe nach.
sequential access [sikwen'chəl ak'ses] *n*
(*COMPUT*) sequentielle(r) Zugriff *m*.
sequin [sē'kwin] *n* Paillette *f*.
Serbo-Croat [sûr'bəkrōat] *n* (*language*) Ser-
bokroatisch *nt*.
serenade [särənād'] *n* Ständchen *nt*, Serenade
f ♦ *vt* ein Ständchen bringen (+*dat*).
serene [sərēn'] *a*, **serenely** [sərēn'lē] *ad* heiter, gelassen, ruhig.
serenity [sərcn'itē] *n* Heiterkeit *f*, Gelassenheit *f*, Ruhe *f*.
serf [sûrf] *n* Leibeigene(r) *mf*.
serge [sûrj] *n* Serge *f*.
sergeant [sâr'jənt] *n* Feldwebel *m*; (*police*)

(Polizei)wachtmeister *m*.
sergeant major *n* Oberfeldwebel *m*.
serial [sēr'ēəl] *n* Fortsetzungsroman *m*; (*TV*) Fernsehserie *f* ♦ *a* (*number*) (fort)laufend.
serial access *n* (*COMPUT*) serielle(r) Zugriff *m*.
serial interface *n* serielle Schnittstelle *f*.
serialize [sēr'ēəlīz] *vt* in Fortsetzungen veröffentlichen.
serial number *n* Seriennummer *f*.
serial printer *n* serielle(r) Drucker *m*.
series [sēr'ēz] *n* Serie *f*, Reihe *f*.
serious [sēr'ēəs] *a* ernst; (*injury*) schwer; (*development*) ernstzunehmend; **I'm ~ das meine ich ernst; are you ~ (about it)?** meinst du das ernst?
seriously [sē'rēəslē] *ad* ernst(haft); (*hurt*) schwer; **to take sth/sb ~** etw/jdn ernst nehmen.
seriousness [sē'rēəsnis] *n* Ernst *m*, Ernsthaftigkeit *f*.
sermon [sûr'mən] *n* Predigt *f*.
serpent [sûr'pənt] *n* Schlange *f*.
serrated [särā'tid] *a* gezackt; **~ knife** Sägemesser *nt*.
serum [sēr'əm] *n* Serum *nt*.
servant [sûr'vənt] *n* Bedienstete(r) *mf*, Diener(in *f*) *m*; *see* **civil servant**.
serve [sûrv] *vt* dienen (+dat); (*guest, customer*) bedienen; (*food*) servieren; (*writ*) zustellen (*on sb* jdm) ♦ *vi* dienen, nützen; (*at table*) servieren; (*TENNIS*) geben, aufschlagen; (*servant, soldier etc*) dienen; **it ~s my purpose** das ist das, was ich brauche; **to ~ a summons on sb** jdn vor Gericht laden; **are you being ~d?** (*Brit*) werden Sie (schon) bedient?; **the power station ~s the entire region** das Kraftwerk versorgt das ganze Gebiet; **it ~s him right** das geschieht ihm recht; **that'll ~ the purpose** das reicht; **to ~ on a committee** in einem Ausschuß sitzen; **to ~ on a jury** Geschworene(r) sein; **that'll ~ as a table** das geht als Tisch.
serve out, serve up *vt* (*food*) auftragen, servieren.
service [sûr'vis] *n* (*help*) Dienst *m*; (*trains etc*) Verkehrsverbindungen *pl*; (*hotel*) Service *m*, Bedienung *f*; (*set of dishes*) Service *nt*; (*MIL*) Militärdienst *f*; (*car*) Inspektion *f*; (*for TVs etc*) Kundendienst *m*; (*TENNIS*) Aufschlag *m*; (*REL*) Gottesdienst *m*; **to be of ~ to sb** jdm einen großen Dienst erweisen; **can I be of ~?** kann ich Ihnen behilflich sein?; **the essential ~s** das Versorgungsnetz; **medical/social ~s** ärztliche Versorgung *f*/Sozialversorgung *f*; **the train ~ to Boston** die Zugverbindung nach Boston; **to hold a ~** einen Gottesdienst halten ♦ *vt* (*AUT, TECH*) warten, überholen; *see also* **Services**.
serviceable [sûr'visəbəl] *a* brauchbar.
service area *n* (*Brit AUT*) Raststätte *f*.
service charge *n* Bedienung(sgeld *nt*) *f*; (*of bank*) Bearbeitungsgebühr *f*.

service industries *npl* Dienstleistungsbranche *f*.
serviceman [sûr'visman] *n, pl* **-men** (*soldier etc*) Militärangehörige(r) *m*.
Services [sûr'visiz] *npl*: **the Armed ~** die Streitkräfte *pl*.
service station *n* (Groß)tankstelle *f*.
servicing [sûr'vising] *n* Wartung *f*.
serviette [sûrvēet'] *n* (*Brit*) Serviette *f*.
servile [sûr'vīl] *a* sklavisch, unterwürfig.
serving cart [sûr'ving kârt] *n* (*US*) Servierwagen *m*.
session [sesh'ən] *n* Sitzung *f*; (*POL*) Sitzungsperiode *f*.
set [set] *n* (*collection of things*) Satz *m*, Set *nt*; (*RAD, TV*) Apparat *m*; (*TENNIS*) Satz *m*; (*group of people*) Kreis *m*; (*CINE*) Szene *f*; (*THEAT*) Bühnenbild *nt*; **a ~ of false teeth** ein Gebiß *nt*, künstliche Zähne *pl*; **a ~ of dining-room furniture** eine Eßzimmer-Garnitur ♦ *a* festgelegt; (*ready*) bereit; **to be all ~ to do sth** (*have made all arrangements*) sich darauf eingerichtet haben, etw zu tun; (*be mentally prepared*) fest entschlossen *or* drauf und dran sein, etw zu tun; **to be ~ in one's ways** in seinen Gewohnheiten festgefahren sein ♦ *irreg vt, pt, pp* **set** (*place*) setzen, stellen, legen; (*arrange*) (an)ordnen; (*table*) decken; (*time, price*) festsetzen; (*alarm, watch, task*) stellen; (*jewels*) (ein)fassen; (*exam*) ausarbeiten; (*assign: task, homework*) aufgeben; **to ~ on fire** anstecken; **to ~ free** freilassen; **to ~ sth going** etw in Gang bringen; **to ~ sail** losfahren; **the novel is ~ in Hamburg** der Roman spielt in Hamburg; **to ~ one's hair** die Haare eindrehen ♦ *vi* (*sun*) untergehen; (*become hard*) fest werden; (*bone*) zusammenwachsen.
set about *vt fus* (*task*) anpacken; **to ~ about doing sth** sich daranmachen, etw zu tun.
set aside *vt* beiseitelegen.
set back *vt* (*by a certain length of time*) zurückwerfen; (*watch, clock*) zurückstellen; (*progress*) verzögern, behindern; **the house is ~ back from the road** das Haus liegt etwas von der Straße ab.
set down *vt* absetzen.
set in *vi* (*infection, complications*) sich einstellen; **the rain has ~ in** es hat sich eingeregnet.
set off *vi* (*depart*) ausbrechen ♦ *vt* (*explode*) zur Explosion bringen; (*alarm*) losgehen lassen; (*show up well*) hervorheben.
set out *vi* aufbrechen, sich auf den Weg machen ♦ *vt* (*arrange*) anlegen, arrangieren; (*state*) darlegen.
set up *vt* (*organization*) aufziehen; (*machine*) installieren; (*record*) aufstellen; (*monument*) erstellen.
setback [set'bak] *n* Rückschlag *m*; (*in health*) gesundheitliche(r) Rückschlag *m*.
set menu *n* Tageskarte *f*.

set phrase *n* (*idiom*) feststehende(r) Ausdruck *m*.

set square *n* (*Brit*) Zeichendreieck *nt*.

settee [set'ē'] *n* Sofa *nt*.

setting [set'ing] *n* (*MUS*) Vertonung *f*; (*scenery*) Hintergrund *m*, Umgebung *f*.

settle [set'əl] *vt* (*nerves*, *stomach*) beruhigen; (*pay*: *bill*, *account*) begleichen, bezahlen; (*colonize*: *land*) besiedeln; (*agree*) regeln; **that's ~d then** das ist also klar *or* abgemacht ♦ *vi* (*also*: ~ **down**) sich einleben; (*come to rest*) sich niederlassen; (*sink*) sich setzen; (*calm down*) sich beruhigen.

settle in *vi* sich eingewöhnen.

settle up *vi*: **to ~ up with sb** mit jdm abrechnen.

settlement [set'əlmənt] *n* Regelung *f*; (*payment*) Begleichung *f*; (*colony*) Siedlung *f*, Niederlassung *f*; **in ~ of our account** (*COMM*) zur Begleichung unserer Rechnung.

settler [set'lûr] *n* Siedler(in *f*) *m*.

setup [set'up] *n* (*arrangement*) Aufbau *m*, Gliederung *f*; (*situation*) Situation *f*, Lage *f*.

seven [sev'ən] *num* sieben.

seventeen [sev'əntēn'] *num* siebzehn.

seventh [sev'ənth] *a* siebte(r, s) ♦ *n* Siebtel *nt*; **to be in ~ heaven** im siebten Himmel sein.

seventy [sev'əntē] *num* siebzig.

sever [sev'ûr] *vt* abtrennen.

several [sev'ûrəl] *a* mehrere, verschiedene ♦ *pron* mehrere; ~ **times** einige Male, mehrmals.

severance [sev'ûrəns] *n* Abtrennung *f*; (*fig*) Abbruch *m*.

severance pay *n* (*INDUSTRY*) Abfindung *f*.

severe [sivēr'] *a* (*strict*) streng; (*serious*) schwer; (*climate*) rauh; (*plain*) streng, schmucklos.

severely [sivēr'lē] *ad* (*strictly*) streng, strikt; (*seriously*) schwer, ernstlich; (*wounded*, *ill*) schwer.

severity [sivär'itē] *n* Strenge *f*; Schwere *f*, Ernst *m*.

sew [sō] *vti irreg* nähen.

sew up *vt* zunähen.

sewage [soo'ij] *n* Abwässer *pl*.

sewer [soo'ûr] *n* (Abwasser)kanal *m*.

sewing [sō'ing] *n* Näharbeit *f*.

sewing machine *n* Nähmaschine *f*.

sex [seks] *n* Sex *m*; (*gender*) Geschlecht *nt*; **the opposite ~** das andere Geschlecht.

sex act *n* Geschlechtsakt *m*.

sexism [sek'sizəm] *n* Sexismus *m*.

sexist [seks'ist] *a* sexistisch.

sextant [seks'tənt] *n* Sextant *m*.

sextet [sekstet'] *n* Sextett *nt*.

sexual [sek'shōōəl] *a* sexuell, geschlechtlich, Geschlechts-.

sexual assault *n* Notzucht *f*.

sexual intercourse *n* (Geschlechts)verkehr *m*.

sexually [sek'shōōəlē] *ad* geschlechtlich, sexuell.

sexy [sek'sē] *a* sexy.

Seychelles [sāshel'] *npl* Seychellen *pl*.

SF *n abbr* (= *science fiction*) Science-fiction *f*.

SG *n abbr* (*US*: = *Surgeon General*) Genstarzt *m*.

Sgt. *abbr* (= *sergeant*) ≈ Fw.

shabbily [shab'ilē] *ad* schäbig.

shabbiness [shab'ēnis] *n* (*of dress*, *person*, *building*) Schäbigkeit *f*.

shabby [shab'ē] *a* (*lit*, *fig*) schäbig.

shack [shak] *n* Hütte *f*.

shackle [shak'əl] *vt* fesseln.

shackles [shak'əlz] *npl* (*lit*, *fig*) Fesseln *pl*, Ketten *pl*.

shade [shād] *n* Schatten *m*; (*for lamp*) Lampenschirm *m*; (*color*) Farbton *m*; (*small quantity*) Spur *f*, Idee *f*; (*US*: *window* ~) Jalousie *f*; ~**s** *pl* (*sunglasses*) Sonnenbrille *f* ♦ *vt* abschirmen.

shadow [shad'ō] *n* Schatten *m* ♦ *vt* (*follow*) beschatten; **without** *or* **beyond a ~ of a doubt** ohne den geringsten Zweifel.

shadow cabinet *n* (*Brit POL*) Schattenkabinett *nt*.

shadowy [shad'ōē] *a* schattig.

shady [shā'dē] *a* schattig; (*fig*) zwielichtig.

shaft [shaft] *n* (*of spear etc*) Schaft *m*; (*in mine*) Schacht *m*; (*TECH*) Welle *f*; (*of light*) Strahl *m*; **ventilator ~** Luftschacht *m*.

shaggy [shag'ē] *a* struppig.

shake [shāk] *irreg vt* schütteln, rütteln; (*shock*) erschüttern; **to ~ hands** die Hand geben (*with dat*); **they shook hands** sie gaben sich die Hand; **to ~ one's head** den Kopf schütteln ♦ *vi* (*move*) schwanken; (*tremble*) zittern, beben; **to ~ in one's shoes** (*fig*) das Flattern kriegen (*col*) ♦ *n* (*jerk*) Schütteln *nt*, Rütteln *nt*.

shake off *vt* abschütteln.

shake up *vt* (*lit*) aufschütteln; (*fig*) aufrütteln.

shaken [shā'kən] *pp of* shake.

shake-up [shāk'up] *n* Aufrüttelung *f*; (*POL*) Umgruppierung *f*.

shakily [shā'kilē] *ad* zitternd, unsicher; (*reply*) zitt(e)rig; (*walk*, *write*) wack(e)lig.

shakiness [shā'kēnis] *n* Wackeligkeit *f*.

shaky [shā'kē] *a* zitt(e)rig; (*weak*: *memory*) unsicher; (*knowledge*) unsicher, wack(e)lig.

shale [shāl] *n* Schiefer(ton) *m*.

shall [shal] *v aux irreg* werden; (*must*) sollen.

shallot [shəlät'] *n* Schalotte *f*.

shallow [shal'ō] *a* flach, seicht; (*fig*) oberflächlich.

shallows [shal'ōz] *npl* flache Stellen *pl*.

sham [sham] *n* Täuschung *f*, Trug *m*, Schein *m* ♦ *a* unecht, falsch.

shambles [sham'bəlz] *n* Durcheinander *nt*; **the economy is (in) a complete ~** die Wirtschaft befindet sich in einem totalen Chaos.

shame [shām] *n* Scham *f*; (*disgrace*, *pity*) Schande *f* ♦ *vt* beschämen; **what a ~!** wie schade!; **to put sb/sth to ~** (*fig*) jdn/etw in den Schatten stellen; ~ **on you!** schäm dich!

shamefaced [shām'fāst] a beschämt.

shameful [shām'fəl] a, **shamefully** [shām'fəlē] ad schändlich.

shameless [shām'lis] a schamlos; (immodest) unverschämt.

shampoo [shampōō'] n Schampoon nt ♦ vt schampunieren; ~ **and set** Waschen nt und Legen; **to have a** ~ **and set** sich (dat) die Haare waschen und legen lassen.

shamrock [sham'râk] n Kleeblatt nt.

shandy [shan'dē] n (Brit) Radlermaß nt.

shan't [shant] = **shall not**.

shanty [shan'tē] n (cabin) Hütte f, Baracke f.

shanty town n Elendsviertel nt.

shape [shāp] n Form f, Gestalt f ♦ vt formen, gestalten; (clay) formen; (fig: ideas, character) formen, prägen; (course of events) bestimmen; (stone) bearbeiten; **to take** ~ (fig) Gestalt annehmen; **to get o.s. into** ~ sich auf Vordermann bringen; **in the** ~ **of a heart** in Herzform; **I don't accept gifts in any** ~ **or form** ich nehme überhaupt keine Geschenke an.

SHAPE [shāp] n abbr (= Supreme Headquarters Allied Powers, Europe) SHAPE.

-shaped [shāpt] suff: **heart**~ herzförmig.

shapeless [shāp'lis] a formlos.

shapely [shāp'lē] a wohlgeformt, wohlproportioniert.

share [shär] n (An)teil m; (FIN) Aktie f; **to have a** ~ **in the profits** am Gewinn beteiligt sein; **he has a 50%** ~ **in a new business venture** er ist bei einem neuen Unternehmen mit 50% beteiligt ♦ vt teilen; (fig: have in common) gemeinsam haben ♦ vi: **to** ~ **in** (gen) sich an etw (dat) beteiligen.

share capital n Kapitalanteil m.

share certificate n Aktienzertifikat nt.

shareholder [shär'hōldûr] n Aktionär(in f) m.

share index n Aktienindex m.

share issue n Aktienemission f.

share price n Aktienkurs m.

shark [shârk] n Hai(fisch) m; (swindler) Gauner m.

sharp [shârp] a scharf; (pin) spitz; (person) clever; (child) aufgeweckt; (unscrupulous) gerissen, raffiniert; (MUS) erhöht; ~ **practices** pl Machenschaften pl; **to be** ~ **with sb** schroff mit jdm sein ♦ n (MUS) Kreuz nt ♦ ad (MUS) zu hoch; **nine o'clock** ~ Punkt neun; **look** ~! mach schnell!; **to turn** ~ **left** scharf nach links abbiegen.

sharpen [shâr'pən] vt schärfen; (pencil) spitzen.

sharpener [shâr'pənûr] n Spitzer m.

sharp-eyed [shârp'īd] a scharfsichtig.

sharply [shârp'lē] ad (abruptly) abrupt; (clearly) deutlich; (harshly) schroff.

sharpness [shârp'nis] n Schärfe f.

sharp-tempered [shârp'tempûrd] a jähzornig.

sharp-witted [shârp'wit'id] a scharfsinnig, aufgeweckt.

shatter [shat'ûr] vt zerschmettern; (fig) zerstören ♦ vi zerspringen.

shattered [shat'ûrd] a (lit, fig) kaputt; (grief-stricken) zerschmettert; (exhausted) erledigt, zerschlagen.

shattering [shat'ûring] a (experience) furchtbar.

shatterproof [shat'ûrprōōf] a splitterfest or -frei.

shave [shāv] n Rasur f, Rasieren nt; **to have a** ~ sich rasieren (lassen) ♦ vt rasieren ♦ vi sich rasieren.

shaven [shā'vən] a (head) geschoren.

shaver [shā'vûr] n (ELEC) Rasierapparat m, Rasierer m.

shaving [shā'ving] n (action) Rasieren nt; see also **shavings**.

shaving brush n Rasierpinsel m.

shaving cream n Rasierkrem f.

shavings [shā'vingz] npl (of wood etc) Späne pl.

shaving soap n Rasierseife f.

shawl [shôl] n Schal m, Umhang m.

she [shē] pron sie; **there** ~ **is** da ist sie ♦ a weiblich; ~**-bear** Bärenweibchen nt.

sheaf [shēf] n, pl **sheaves** [shēvz] Garbe f.

shear [shē'ûr] vt irreg scheren.

shear off vt abscheren ♦ vi (break off) abbrechen.

sheared [shē'ûrd] pt of **shear**.

shears [shē'ûrz] npl Heckenschere f.

sheath [shēth] n Scheide f.

sheathe [shēth] vt einstecken; (TECH) verkleiden.

sheath knife n Fahrtenmesser nt.

sheaves [shēvz] npl of **sheaf**.

shed [shed] n Schuppen m; (for animals) Stall m; (INDUSTRY, RAIL) Schuppen m, Halle f ♦ vt irreg, pt, pp **shed** (leaves etc) abwerfen, verlieren; (tears) vergießen; **to** ~ **light on sth** etw erhellen, Licht auf etw (acc) werfen.

she'd [shēd] = **she had**; **she would**.

sheen [shēn] n Glanz m.

sheep [shēp] n (pl inv) Schaf nt.

sheepdog [shēp'dôg] n Schäferhund m.

sheep farmer n Schaffarmer m, Schafzüchter m.

sheepish [shē'pish] a verschämt, betreten.

sheepskin [shēp'skin] n Schaffell nt.

sheepskin jacket n Schaffelljacke f.

sheer [shēr] a bloß, rein; (steep) steil, jäh; (transparent) (hauch)dünn, durchsichtig ♦ ad (directly) direkt; **by** ~ **chance** rein zufällig.

sheet [shēt] n Bettuch nt, Bettlaken nt; (of paper) Blatt nt; (of metal etc) Platte f; (of ice) Fläche f.

sheet feed n (on printer) automatische(r) Papiereinzug m.

sheet lightning n Wetterleuchten nt.

sheet metal n Walzblech nt.

sheet music n Notenblätter f.

sheik(h) [shēk] n Scheich m.

shelf [shelf] *n, pl* **shelves** [shelvz] Bord *nt*, Regal *nt*.

shelf life *n* (COMM) Haltbarkeit *f*.

shell [shel] *n* Schale *f*; (*sea*~) Muschel *f*; (*explosive*) Granate *f*; (*of building*) Mauerwerk *nt* ♦ *vt* (*peas*) schälen; (*fire on*) beschießen. **shell out** *vi* (col) blechen (*for sth* für etw).

she'll [shēl] = **she will**; **she shall**.

shellfish [shel'fish] *n* Schalentier *nt*; (*as food*) Meeresfrüchte *pl*.

shelter [shel'tûr] *n* Schutz *m*; (*air-raid* ~) Bunker *m*; **bus** ~ Wartehäuschen *nt*; **to take** ~ sich in Sicherheit bringen, sich schützen (*from* vor +*dat*) ♦ *vt* schützen, bedecken; (*refugees*) aufnehmen ♦ *vi* sich unterstellen.

sheltered [shel'tûrd] *a* (*life*) behütet; (*spot*) geschützt.

shelve [shelv] *vt* aufschieben ♦ *vi* abfallen.

shelves [shelvz] *npl of* **shelf**.

shelving [shel'ving] *n* Regale *pl*.

shepherd [shep'ûrd] *n* Schäfer *m* ♦ *vt* treiben, führen.

shepherdess [shep'ûrdis] *n* Schäferin *f*.

sherbet [shûr'bit] *n* (*US*) Fruchteis *nt*; (*Brit*: *powder*) Brausepulver *nt*.

sheriff [shär'if] *n* Sheriff *m*.

sherry [shär'ē] *n* Sherry *m*.

she's [shēz] = **she is**; **she has**.

Shetland [shet'lənd] *n* Shetlandinseln *pl*.

shield [shēld] *n* Schild *m*; (*fig*) Schirm *m*, Schutz *m* ♦ *vt* (be)schirmen; (TECH) abschirmen.

shift [shift] *n* Veränderung *f*, Verschiebung *f*; (*work*) Schicht *f*; ~ **in demand** Nachfrageverschiebung *f* ♦ *vt* (ver)rücken, verschieben; (*office*) verlegen; (*arm*) wegnehmen ♦ *vi* sich verschieben; (*col*) schnell fahren; **to** ~ **gear** (*US AUT*) schalten; **the wind has** ~**ed to the south** der Wind ist nach Süden umgesprungen.

shift key *n* (*on typewriter etc*) Umschalttaste *f*.

shiftless [shift'lis] *a* faul, träge.

shift work *n* Schichtarbeit *f*; **to do** ~ Schicht arbeiten.

shifty [shif'tē] *a* verschlagen.

shilling [shil'ing] *n* (*Brit old*) Shilling *m*.

shilly-shally [shil'ēshalē] *vi* zögern.

shimmer [shim'ûr] *n* Schimmer *m* ♦ *vi* schimmern.

shimmering [shim'ûring] *a* schillernd; (*haze*, *satin etc*) schimmernd.

shin [shin] *n* Schienbein *nt* ♦ *vi*: **to** ~ **up/down a tree** einen Baum hinauf-/hinunterklettern.

shindig [shin'dig] *n* (col) Remmidemmi *nt*.

shine [shīn] *n* Glanz *m*, Schein *m* ♦ *irreg vt* polieren; **to** ~ **a torch on sb** jdn (mit einer Lampe) anleuchten ♦ *vi* scheinen; (*fig*) glänzen.

shingle [shing'gəl] *n* Schindel *f*; (*on beach*) Strandkies *m*.

shingles [shing'gəlz] *npl* (MED) Gürtelrose *f*.

shining [shī'ning] *a* (*light*) strahlend; (*surface*, *hair*) glänzend.

shiny [shī'nē] *a* glänzend.

ship [ship] *n* Schiff *nt*; **on board** ~ an Bord ♦ *vt* an Bord bringen, verladen; (*transport as cargo*) verschiffen.

shipbuilder [ship'bildûr] *n* Schiff(s)bauer *m*.

shipbuilding [ship'bilding] *n* Schiffbau *m*.

ship canal *n* Seekanal *m*.

ship chandler [ship chan'dlûr] *n* Lieferant *m* von Schiffsbedarf.

shipment [ship'mənt] *n* Verladung *f*; (*goods shipped*) Schiffsladung *f*.

shipowner [ship'ōnûr] *n* Schiffseigner *m*; (*of many ships*) Reeder *m*.

shipper [ship'ûr] *n* Verschiffer *m*; (*sender*) Absender *m*; (*company*) Speditionsfirma *f*, Spediteure *pl*.

shipping [ship'ing] *n* (*act*) Verschiffung *f*; (*ships*) Schiffahrt *f*.

shipping agent *n* Reedereivertreter *m*.

shipping company *n* Schiffahrtsgesellschaft *f* or -linie *f*, Reederei *f*.

shipping lane *n* Schiffahrtsstraße *f*.

shipping line *n* = **shipping company**.

shipshape [ship'shāp] *a* in Ordnung.

shipwreck [ship'rek] *n* Schiffbruch *m*; (*destroyed ship*) Wrack *nt* ♦ *vt*: **to be** ~**ed** (*lit*) schiffbrüchig sein; (*fig*) Schiffbruch erleiden.

shipyard [ship'yârd] *n* Werft *f*.

shirk [shûrk] *vt* ausweichen (+*dat*).

shirt [shûrt] *n* (Ober)hemd *nt*.

shirt-sleeves [shûrt'slēvz] *npl*: **in** ~ in Hemdsärmeln.

shit [shit] *n, interj* (!) Scheiße *f* (!).

shiver [shiv'ûr] *n* Schauer *m* ♦ *vi* frösteln, zittern.

shoal [shōl] *n* (Fisch)schwarm *m*.

shock [shâk] *n* Stoß *m*, Erschütterung *f*; (*mental*) Schock *m*; (ELEC) Schlag *m*; **to be suffering from** ~ unter Schock stehen, sich in einem Schockzustand befinden; **it gave us a** ~ es hat uns erschreckt; **it came as a** ~ **to her that** ... mit Bestürzung hörte sie, daß ... ♦ *vt* erschüttern; (*offend*) schockieren.

shock absorber [shâk absôrb'ûr] *n* Stoßdämpfer *m*.

shocking [shâk'ing] *a* unerhört, schockierend; (*very bad*: *weather*, *handwriting*) schrecklich, furchtbar; (: *results*) schrecklich.

shockproof [shâk'prōōf] *a* (*watch*) stoßsicher.

shock treatment *n* (MED) Schockbehandlung *f*.

shod [shâd] *pt, pp of* **shoe** ♦ *a* beschuht.

shoddiness [shâd'ēnis] *n* Schäbigkeit *f*.

shoddy [shâd'ē] *a* schäbig.

shoe [shōō] *n* Schuh *m*; (*of horse*) Hufeisen *nt*; (*brake* ~) Bremsbacke *f* ♦ *vt irreg* (*horse*) beschlagen.

shoe brush *n* Schuhbürste *f*.

shoehorn [shōō'hôrn] *n* Schuhlöffel *m*.

shoelace [shoo'lās] n Schnürsenkel m.
shoemaker [shoo'mākûr] n Schumacher m, Schuster m.
shoe polish n Schuhcreme f.
shoe shop n Schuhgeschäft nt.
shoestring [shoo'string] n (shoelace) Schnürsenkel m; **to do sth on a ~** (fig) etw mit ein paar Pfennigen or Mark tun.
shone [shōn] pt, pp of **shine**.
shoo [shoo] vt (also: **~ away, ~ off**) ver- or wegscheuchen ♦ interj (to child) husch!; (to dog) pfui!
shook [shook] pt of **shake**.
shoot [shoot] n (branch) Schößling m; (preserve) (Jagd)revier nt; (competition) (Wett)schießen nt; (~ing party) Jagdgesellschaft f ♦ irreg vt (gun) abfeuern; (goal, arrow) schießen; (kill) erschießen; (film) drehen, filmen; **shot in the leg** ins Bein getroffen ♦ vi (gun: move quickly) schießen; **don't ~!** nicht schießen!; **to ~ past sb** an jdm vorbeischießen.
shoot down vt abschießen.
shoot up vi (fig) aus dem Boden schießen.
shooting [shoo'ting] n Schießerei f; (act: murder) Erschießung f; (CINE) Drehen nt.
shooting star n Sternschnuppe f.
shop [shâp] n Geschäft nt, Laden m; (work~) Werkstatt f; **repair ~** Reparaturwerkstatt f; **to talk ~** (fig) über die or von der Arbeit reden; (of professional people also) fachsimpeln ♦ vi (also: **go ~ping**) einkaufen gehen.
shop around vi (lit, fig) sich umsehen (for nach).
shop assistant n (Brit) Verkäufer(in f) m.
shopkeeper [shâp'kēpûr] n Geschäftsinhaber(in f) m.
shoplift [shâp'lift] vi Ladendiebstahl begehen.
shoplifter [shâp'liftûr] n Ladendieb(in f) m.
shoplifting [shâp'lifting] n Ladendiebstahl m.
shopper [shâp'ûr] n Käufer(in f) m.
shopping [shâp'ing] n Einkaufen nt, Einkauf m.
shopping bag n Einkaufstasche f.
shopping cart n (US) Einkaufswagen m.
shopping center n Einkaufszentrum nt.
shopping list n Einkaufszettel m.
shopping mall n (US) Einkaufszentrum nt.
shop-soiled [shâp'soild] a (Brit) = **shopworn**.
shop steward n (Brit) Betriebsrat m.
shop window n Schaufenster nt.
shopworn [shâp'wôrn] a (US) angeschmutzt.
shore [shôr] n Ufer nt; (of sea) Strand m, Küste f; **on ~** an Land.
shore up vt abstützen.
shore leave n (NAUT) Landurlaub m.
shorn [shôrn] pp of **shear**.
short [shôrt] a kurz; (person) klein; (curt) kurz angebunden; (measure) zu knapp; **a ~ time ago** vor kurzer Zeit; **to be in ~ supply** knapp sein; **to be ~ of ...** zu wenig ... haben; **I'm ~ of time** ich habe wenig Zeit; **for ~** kurz; **two ~** zwei zu wenig ♦ n (ELEC:

~-circuit) Kurzschluß m; see also **shorts** ♦ ad (suddenly) plötzlich; **to run ~ of supplies** nicht mehr viel Vorräte haben; **to cut ~** abkürzen; **to fall ~** nicht erreichen ♦ vi (ELEC) einen Kurzschluß haben.
shortage [shôr'tij] n Knappheit f, Mangel m.
shortbread [shôrt'bred] n Mürbegebäck nt, Heidesand m.
shortchange [shôrt'chānj'] vt: **to ~ sb** jdm zuwenig Wechselgeld geben, jdm zuwenig herausgeben.
short circuit n Kurzschluß m ♦ vi einen Kurzschluß haben.
shortcoming [shôrt'kuming] n Fehler m, Mangel m.
short(crust) pastry [shôrt('krust) pās'trē] n (Brit) Mürbeteig m.
short cut n Abkürzung f.
shorten [shôr'tən] vt (ab)kürzen; (clothes) kürzer machen.
shortfall [shôrt'fôl] n Defizit nt.
shorthand [shôrt'hand] n Stenographie f, Kurzschrift f; **to take sth down in ~** etw stenographieren.
shorthand notebook n Steno(graphie)block m.
shorthand typist n (Brit) Stenotypist(in f) m.
short list n engere Wahl f.
short-lived [shôrt'livd'] a kurzlebig.
shortly [shôrt'lē] ad bald.
shortness [shôrt'nis] n Kürze f.
shorts [shôrts] npl (also: **a pair of ~**) Shorts pl.
short-sighted [shôrt'sī'tid] a (lit, fig) kurzsichtig.
short-sightedness [shôrt'sī'tidnis] n Kurzsichtigkeit f.
short-staffed [shôrt'staft'] a (Brit): **to be ~** zuwenig Personal haben.
short story n Kurzgeschichte f.
short-tempered [shôrt'tempûrd] a leicht aufbrausend.
short-term [shôrt'tûrm'] a (effect) kurzfristig.
short time n: **to work ~, to be on ~** (INDUSTRY) kurzarbeiten, Kurzarbeit haben.
short-time working [shôrt'tīm wûr'king] n Kurzarbeit f.
shortwave [shôrt'wāv'] n (RAD) Kurzwelle f.
shot [shât] n (from gun) Schuß m; (~gun pellets) Schrot m; (person) Schütze m; (try) Versuch m; (MED) Spritze f; (PHOT) Aufnahme f, Schnappschuß m; **like a ~** wie der Blitz; **a big ~** (col) ein hohes Tier; **to fire a ~ at sb/sth** einen Schuß auf jdn/etw abfeuern or abgeben; **to have a ~** (MED) eine Spritze bekommen; **to have a ~ at sth** or **doing sth** es (mal) versuchen; **to get ~ of sb/sth** (col) jdn/etw loswerden ♦ pt, pp of **shoot**.
shotgun [shât'gun] n Schrotflinte f.
should [shood] aux v: **I ~ go now** ich sollte jetzt gehen; **I ~ say** ich würde sagen; **~ he**

phone falls er anruft ... ♦ *pt of* **shall**.
shoulder [shōl'dúr] *n* Schulter *f* ♦ *vt* (*rifle*) schultern; (*fig*) auf sich nehmen; **to look over one's** ~ über die Schulter blicken; **to rub** ~**s with sb** (*fig*) mit jdm in Berührung kommen; **to give sb the cold** ~ (*fig*) jdm die kalte Schulter zeigen.
shoulder bag *n* Umhängetasche *f*.
shoulder blade *n* Schulterblatt *nt*.
shoulder strap *n* (*MIL*) Schulterklappe *f*; (*of dress etc*) Träger *m*.
shouldn't [shōōd'ənt] = **should not**.
shout [shout] *n* Schrei *m*; (*call*) Ruf *m* ♦ *vt* rufen ♦ *vi* schreien, laut rufen; **to** ~ **at** anbrüllen.
shouting [shout'ing] *n* Geschrei *nt*.
shove [shuv] *n* Schubs *m*, Stoß *m* ♦ *vt* schieben, stoßen, schubsen; **he** ~**d me out of the way** er stieß mich zur Seite.
shove off *vi* (*NAUT*) abstoßen; (*fig col*) abhauen.
shovel [shuv'əl] *n* Schaufel *f* ♦ *vt* schaufeln.
show [shō] *n* (*display*) Schau *f*; (*COMM. TECH*) Ausstellung *f*; (*CINE. THEAT*) Vorstellung *f*, Show *f*; (*organization*) Laden *m* (*col*); **who's running the** ~ **here?** wer ist hier verantwortlich?, wer hat hier das Sagen?; **to be on** ~ ausgestellt sein; **it's just for** ~ das ist nur zur Schau; **to ask for a** ~ **of hands** um Handzeichen bitten ♦ *irreg vt* zeigen; (*kindness*) erweisen; **to** ~ **a profit/ loss** (*COMM*) Gewinn/Verlust aufweisen; **as** ~**n in the illustration** wie in der Abbildung dargestellt; **it just goes to** ~ **that** ... da sieht man mal wieder, daß ...; **I have nothing to** ~ **for it** ich habe am Ende nichts vorzuweisen; **to** ~ **sb to his seat/to the door** jdn an seinen Platz/an die *or* zur Tür bringen; **to** ~ **sb in** jdn hereinführen; **to** ~ **sb out** jdn hinausbegleiten ♦ *vi* zu sehen sein; **it doesn't** ~ man sieht es nicht.
show off *vi* (*pej*) angeben, protzen ♦ *vt* (*display*) ausstellen.
show up *vi* (*stand out*) sich abheben; (*arrive*) erscheinen ♦ *vt* aufzeigen; (*unmask*) bloßstellen.
show business *n* Showbusineß *nt*.
showcase [shō'kās] *n* Schaukasten *m*; (*COMM*) Ausstellungsvitrine *f*; (*advertising*) gute Werbung *f*.
showdown [shō'doun] *n* Kraftprobe *f*, endgültige Auseinandersetzung *f*.
showed [shōd] *pt of* **show**.
shower [shou'ûr] *n* (*of rain etc*) Schauer *m*; (*of stones*) (Stein)hagel *m*; (*of sparks*) (Funken)regen *m*; (*also:* ~ **bath**) Dusche *f*; (*US: party*) Party, *auf der jeder ein Geschenk für den Ehrengast mitbringt*; **to have** *or* **take a** ~ duschen ♦ *vt* (*fig*) überschütten ♦ *vi* duschen.
shower cap *n* Duschhaube *f*.
showerproof [shou'ûrprōōf] *a* wasserabstoßend, regenfest.
showery [shou'ûrē] *a* (*weather*) regnerisch.

showground [shō'ground] *n* (*Brit*) Ausstellungsgelände *nt*.
showing [shō'ing] *n* (*of film*) Vorführung *f*.
show jumping [shō' jump'ing] *n* Turnierreiten *nt*.
showman [shō'mən] *n*, *pl* **-men** (*at fair, circus*) Showman *m*; (*fig*) Schauspieler *m*.
showmanship [shō'mənship] *n* Talent *nt* als Showman.
shown [shōn] *pp of* **show**.
show-off [shō'óf] *n* Angeber(in *f*) *m*.
showpiece [shō'pēs] *n* Paradestück *nt*; (*of exhibition*) Schaustück *nt*.
showroom [shō'rōōm] *n* (*COMM*) Ausstellungsraum *m*.
showy [shō'ē] *a* protzig; (*person*) auffallend.
shrank [shrangk] *pt of* **shrink**.
shrapnel [shrap'nəl] *n* Schrapnell *nt*.
shred [shred] *n* Fetzen *m* ♦ *vt* zerfetzen; (*COOK*) raspeln; (*documents*) durch den Reißwolf geben; **in** ~**s** in Fetzen; **not a** ~ **of truth** (*fig*) kein Fünkchen Wahrheit.
shredder [shred'ûr] *n* (*for documents, papers*) Papierwolf *m*, Reißwolf *m*.
shrewd [shrōōd] *a*, **shrewdly** [shrōōd'lē] *ad* scharfsinnig, clever.
shrewdness [shrōōd'nis] *n* Scharfsinn *m*.
shriek [shrēk] *n* Schrei *m* ♦ *vti* kreischen, schreien.
shrill [shril] *a* schrill, gellend.
shrimp [shrimp] *n* Garnele *f*.
shrine [shrīn] *n* Schrein *m*.
shrink [shringk] *irreg vi* schrumpfen, eingehen; **to** ~ **from doing sth** davor zurückschrecken, etw zu tun *or* sich davor scheuen, etw zu tun ♦ *vt* einschrumpfen lassen.
shrink away *vi* zurückschrecken (*from* vor +*dat*).
shrinkage [shringk'ij] *n* (*of clothes*) Einlaufen *nt*; (*COMM: in shops*) Schwund *m*, Einbußen *pl*.
shrink-wrap [shringk'rap] *vt* einschweißen, in Schrumpffolie verpacken und einschweißen.
shrivel [shriv'əl] *vi* (*also:* ~ **up**) schrumpfen.
shroud [shroud] *n* Leichentuch *nt* ♦ *vt* umhüllen, (ein)hüllen.
Shrove Tuesday [shrōv tōōz'dā] *n* Fastnachtsdienstag *m*.
shrub [shrub] *n* Busch *m*, Strauch *m*.
shrubbery [shrub'ûrē] *n* Gebüsch *nt*.
shrug [shrug] *n* Achselzucken *nt* ♦ *vi* die Achseln zucken.
shrug off *vt* auf die leichte Schulter nehmen; (*cold, illness*) abschütteln.
shrunk [shrungk] *pp of* **shrink**.
shrunken [shrungk'ən] *a* eingelaufen.
shudder [shud'ûr] *n* Schauder *m* ♦ *vi* schaudern.
shuffle [shuf'əl] *n* (*CARDS*) (Karten)mischen *nt* ♦ *vt* (*cards*) mischen ♦ *vi* (*walk*) schlurfen.
shun [shun] *vt* scheuen, (ver)meiden.
shunt [shunt] *vt* rangieren.
shut [shut] *pt*, *pp* **shut**, *irreg vt* schließen, zu-

machen ♦ *vi* sich schließen (lassen).
shut down *vti* schließen; (*machine*) außer
Betrieb setzen, stillegen.
shut off *vt* (*supply*) abdrehen; (*stop*:
power, water) abstellen; (: *engine*) ab- *or*
ausschalten.
shut out *vt* (*person*) aussperren; (*block*:
view) versperren; (*memory*) unterdrücken;
(*noise, cold*) nicht hereinlassen.
shut up *vi* (*keep quiet*) den Mund halten;
~ **up!** halt den Mund! ♦ *vt* (*close*) zuschließen; (*silence*) zum Schweigen bringen.
shutdown [shut'doun] *n* Stillegung *f*.
shutter [shut'ûr] *n* Fensterladen *m*, Rolladen
m; (*PHOT*) Verschluß *m*.
shuttle [shut'əl] *vi* pendeln; (*vehicle*) hin- und
herfahren ♦ *vt* (*to and fro*: *passengers*) hin-
und hertransportieren ♦ *n* (*plane*) Pendel-
flugzeug *nt*; ~ **service** Pendelverkehr *m*.
shuttlecock [shut'əlkâk] *n* Federball *m*.
shy [shī] *a* schüchtern, scheu; **to be** ~ **of**
doing sth Hemmungen haben, etw zu tun.
shy away *vi*: **to** ~ **away from sth** vor etw
zurückschrecken; **to** ~ **away from doing**
sth (*fig*) vor etw zurückscheuen.
shyly [shī'lē] *ad* schüchtern, scheu.
shyness [shī'nis] *n* Schüchternheit *f*, Zurückhaltung *f*.
Siam [sīam'] *n* Siam *nt*.
Siamese [sīəmēz'] *a* siamesisch ♦ *n* (*person*)
Siamese *m*, Siamesin *f*; (*language*) Siamesisch *nt*.
Siamese cat *n* Siamkatze *f*.
Siamese twins *npl* siamesische Zwillinge *pl*.
Siberia [sībē'rēə] *n* Sibirien *nt*.
sibling [sib'ling] *n* (*form*) Geschwister *nt*.
Sicilian [sisil'yən] *a* sizilianisch ♦ *n* (*person*)
Sizilianer(in *f*) *m*.
Sicily [sis'ilē] *n* Sizilien *nt*.
sick [sik] *a* krank; (*humor*) schwarz; (*joke*)
makaber; **a** ~ **person** ein Kranker, eine
Kranke; **to fall** *or* **take** ~ krank werden; **to**
be off ~ (wegen Krankheit) fehlen; **I feel** ~
to my stomach mir ist schlecht; **I was** ~
(*Brit*) ich habe gebrochen; **to be** ~ **of sb/**
sth jdn/etw satt haben.
sick bay *n* (Schiffs)lazarett *nt*.
sickbed [sik'bed] *n* Krankenbett *nt*.
sick benefit *n* (*US*) Krankengeld *nt*.
sicken [sik'ən] *vt* (*disgust*) krankmachen ♦ *vi*
krank werden.
sickening [sik'əning] *a* (*sight*) widerlich; (*an-*
noying) zum Weinen.
sickle [sik'əl] *n* Sichel *f*.
sick leave *n*: **to be on** ~ krank geschrieben
sein.
sick list *n* Krankenliste *f*.
sickly [sik'lē] *a* kränklich, blaß; (*causing nau-*
sea) widerlich.
sickness [sik'nis] *n* Krankheit *f*; (*Brit*: *vom-*
iting) Übelkeit *f*, Erbrechen *nt*.
sickness benefit *n* (*Brit*) Krankengeld *nt*.
sick pay *n* Krankengeld *nt*.
sickroom [sik'rōōm] *n* Krankenzimmer *nt*.

side [sīd] *a* (*door, entrance*) Seiten-, Neben- ♦
n Seite *f*; (*team*: *SPORT*) Mannschaft *f*;
(*POL etc*) Partei *f*; **the right/wrong** ~ (*of*
cloth) die rechte/linke Seite *f*; ~ **of beef** Flanke *f* von Rindfleisch; **by the** ~ **of** neben; **on**
all ~**s** von allen Seiten; **they are on our** ~
sie stehen auf unserer Seite; **to take** ~**s**
(with) Partei nehmen (für) ♦ *vi*: **to** ~ **with**
sb es halten mit jdm.
sideboard [sīd'bôrd] *n* Anrichte *f*, Sideboard
nt.
sideburns [sīd'bûrnz] *npl* Koteletten *pl*.
sidecar [sīd'kâr] *n* Beiwagen *m*.
side dish *n* Beilage *f*.
side drum *n* (*MUS*) kleine Trommel *f*.
side effect *n* Nebenwirkung *f*.
sidekick [sīd'kik] *n* (*col*) Handlanger *m*.
sidelight [sīd'līt] *n* (*Brit AUT*) Parkleuchte *f*,
Standlicht *nt*.
sideline [sīd'līn] *n* (*SPORT*) Seitenlinie *f*; (*fig*:
hobby) Nebenbeschäftigung *f*.
sidelong [sīd'lông] *a*: **to give sb a** ~ **glance**
etw kurz aus den Augenwinkeln *or* verstoh-
len anblicken.
side plate *n* kleine(r) Teller *m*.
side road *n* Nebenstraße *f*.
sidesaddle [sīd'sadəl] *ad* im Damensattel.
sideshow [sīd'shō] *n* Nebenausstellung *f*.
sidestep [sīd'step] *vt* (*question*) ausweichen;
(*problem*) ausweichen, umgehen ♦ *vi* (*BOX-*
ING etc) zur Seite ausweichen.
side street *n* Seitenstraße *f*.
sidetrack [sīd'trak] *vt* (*fig*) ablenken.
sidewalk [sīd'wôk] *n* (*US*) Bürgersteig *m*.
sideways [sīd'wāz] *ad* seitwärts.
siding [sī'ding] *n* Nebengleis *nt*.
sidle [sī'dəl] *vi*: **to** ~ **up** sich heranmachen
(*to an* +*acc*).
SIDS *n abbr* (= *sudden infant death syndro-*
me) Krippentod *m*.
siege [sēj] *n* Belagerung *f*; **to lay** ~ **to** belagern.
Sierra Leone [sēär'ə lēōn'] *n* Sierra Leone *f*.
siesta [sēes'tə] *n* Siesta *f*.
sieve [siv] *n* Sieb *nt* ♦ *vt* sieben.
sift [sift] *vt* sieben; (*fig*) sichten; **to** ~
through sichten, durchgehen.
sigh [sī] *n* Seufzer *m* ♦ *vi* seufzen.
sight [sīt] *n* (*power of seeing*) Sehvermögen
nt, Augenlicht *nt*; (*view*) (An)blick *m*;
(*scene*) Aussicht *f*, Blick *m*; (*of gun*) Ziel-
vorrichtung *f*, Korn *nt*; **on** ~ bei Sicht; **at**
first ~ auf den ersten Blick; **to lose** ~ **of**
sb/sth jdn/etw nicht mehr sehen können,
jdn/etw aus dem Blickfeld verlieren; **I know**
her by ~ ich kenne sie vom Sehen; **to catch**
~ **of sth/sb** etw/jdn erblicken; **to set one's**
~**s on sth/on doing sth** etw im Auge auf etw
werfen, etw anstreben/danach streben, etw
zu tun; ~**s** *pl* (*of city etc*) Sehenswürdigkeiten *pl*; **in** ~ in Sicht; **out of** ~ außer Sicht ♦
vt sichten.
sighted [sī'tid] *a* sehend; **to be partially-~**
keine volle Sehkraft haben, sehbehindert

sein.

sightseeing [sīt'sēing] *n* Besuch *m* von Sehenswürdigkeiten; **to go ~** Sehenswürdigkeiten besichtigen.

sightseer [sīt'sēr] *n* Tourist (in *f*) *m*.

sign [sīn] *n* Zeichen *nt*; (*notice*, *road ~ etc*) Schild *nt*; **as a ~ of** zum Zeichen (+*gen*); **it's a good/bad ~** das ist ein gutes/schlechtes Zeichen; **plus/minus ~** Plus-/Minuszeichen *nt*; **to show ~s of sth** Anzeichen von etw erkennen lassen; **he shows ~s/no ~s of doing it** es sieht/sieht nicht so aus, als ob er es tun würde; **there is no ~ of their agreeing** nichts deutet darauf hin, daß sie zustimmen werden ♦ *vt* unterschreiben; **to ~ one's name** unterschreiben.

sign away *vt* (*rights etc*) verzichten (auf).

sign off *vi* (*RAD. TV*) sich verabschieden.

sign on *vi* (*Brit*: *as unemployed*: *apply*) beantragen; (: *regularly*) sich melden; **to ~ on for a course** (*enrol*) sich zu einem Kurs anmelden.

sign out *vi* sich austragen.

sign over *vt*: **to ~ sth over to sb** jdm etw überschreiben.

sign up (*MIL*) *vi* sich verpflichten ♦ *vt* verpflichten.

signal [sig'nəl] *n* Signal *nt*; **the busy** (*US*) *or* **engaged** (*Brit*: ~ (*TEL*) der Besetztton; **the ~ is very weak** (*TV*) der Empfang ist sehr schwach ♦ *vt* ein Zeichen geben (+*dat*); **to ~ a left/right turn** (*AUT*) nach links/rechts anzeigen ♦ *vi*: **to ~ to sb to do sth** jdm das Zeichen geben, etw zu tun.

signal box *n* (*Brit RAIL*) Stellwerk *nt*.

signalman [sig'nəlmən] *n, pl* **-men** (*RAIL*) Stellwerkswärter *m*.

signatory [sig'nətôrē] *n* Signatar *m*, Unterzeichnete(r) *mf*.

signature [sig'nəchûr] *n* Unterschrift *f*.

signature tune *n* Erkennungsmelodie *f*.

signet ring [sig'nit ring] *n* Siegelring *m*.

significance [signif'əkəns] *n* Bedeutung *f*; **that is of no ~** das ist belanglos *or* bedeutungslos.

significant [signif'ikənt] *a* (*meaning sth*) bedeutsam; (*important*) bedeutend, wichtig; **it is ~ that** ... es ist bezeichnend, daß ...

significantly [signif'ikəntlē] *ad* bezeichnenderweise; (*smile*) vielsagend; (*improve, increase*) erheblich.

signify [sig'nəfī] *vt* bedeuten; (*show*) andeuten, zu verstehen geben.

sign language *n* Zeichensprache *f*, Fingersprache *f*.

signpost [sīn'pōst] *n* Wegweiser *m*, Schild *nt*.

silage [sī'lij] *n* Silage *f*, Silofutter *nt*.

silence [sī'ləns] *n* Stille *f*, Ruhe *f*; (*of person*) Schweigen *nt* ♦ *vt* zum Schweigen bringen.

silencer [sī'lənsûr] *n* Schalldämpfer *m*.

silent [sī'lənt] *a* still; (*person*) schweigsam; **to keep** *or* **remain ~** still sein *or* bleiben, sich still verhalten; **~ partner** (*US*) stille(r) Teilhaber *m*.

silently [sī'ləntlē] *ad* schweigend, still.

silhouette [silōōet'] *n* Silhouette *f*, Umriß *m*; (*picture*) Schattenbild *nt* ♦ *vt*: **to be ~d against sth** sich als Silhouette gegen etw abheben.

silicon [sil'ikən] *n* Silizium *nt*.

silicone [sil'əkōn] *n* Silikon *nt*.

silk [silk] *n* Seide *f* ♦ *a* seiden, Seiden-.

silky [sil'kē] *a* seidig.

sill [sil] *n* (*AUT*) Türleiste *f*; (*also:* **window~**) (Fenster)sims *m or nt*, Fensterbank *f*; (*esp of wood*) Fensterbrett *nt*.

silliness [sil'ēnis] *n* Albernheit *f*, Dummheit *f*.

silly [sil'ē] *a* dumm, albern; **to do something ~** etwas Dummes tun.

silo [sī'lō] *n* Silo *nt*; (*for missile*) unterirdische Startrampe *f*.

silt [silt] *n* Schlamm *m*, Schlick *m*.

silver [sil'vûr] *n* Silber *nt* ♦ *a* silbern, Silber-.

silver foil *n* Alufolie *f*.

silver plate *n* Silber (geschirr) *nt*.

silver-plated [sil'vûrplā'tid] *a* versilbert.

silversmith [sil'vûrsmith] *n* Silberschmied *m*.

silverware [sil'vûrwär] *n* Silber *nt*.

silver wedding (anniversary) *n* Silberhochzeit *f*.

silvery [sil'vûrē] *a* silbern.

similar [sim'əlûr] *a* ähnlich (*to dat*).

similarity [siməlar'itē] *n* Ähnlichkeit *f*.

similarly [sim'əlûrlē] *ad* ähnlich, in ähnlicher Weise; (*in a similar way*) genauso, ebenso.

simile [sim'əlē] *n* Vergleich *m*.

simmer [sim'ûr] *vti* sieden (lassen).

simmer down *vi* (*fig*) sich beruhigen, sich abregen.

simpering [sim'pûring] *a* geziert, albern.

simple [sim'pəl] *a* einfach; (*dress also*) schlicht; **~ interest** (*FIN*) Zinsen *pl*; **the ~ truth is** ... es ist nun mal so, daß ...

simple-minded [sim'pəlmīn'did] *a* naiv, einfältig.

simpleton [sim'pəltən] *n* Einfaltspinsel *m*.

simplicity [simplis'ətē] *n* Einfachheit *f*; (*of person*) Einfältigkeit *f*.

simplification [simpləfəkā'shən] *n* Vereinfachung *f*.

simplify [sim'pləfī] *vt* vereinfachen.

simply [sim'plē] *ad* einfach; (*only*) bloß, nur.

simulate [sim'yəlāt] *vt* simulieren.

simulation [simyəlā'shən] *n* Vortäuschung *f*; (*simulated appearance*) Imitation *f*; (*of animals*) Tarnung *f*; (*reproduction*) Simulation *f*.

simultaneous [sīməltā'nēəs] *a* gleichzeitig.

simultaneously [sīməltā'nēəslē] *ad* gleichzeitig, simultan.

sin [sin] *n* Sünde *f* ♦ *vi* sündigen.

since [sins] *ad* seither ♦ *prep* seit, seitdem ♦ *cj* (*time*) seit; (*because*) da, weil; **~ Monday** seit Montag; **(ever) ~ I arrived** (schon) seitdem ich hier bin.

sincere [sinsēr'] *a* aufrichtig, ehrlich, offen.

sincerely [sinsēr'lē] *ad* aufrichtig, offen; **~ yours**, (*Brit*) **yours ~** (*at end of letter*) Mit freundlichen Grüßen, Hochachtungsvoll (*form*).

sincerity [sinsär'itē] *n* Aufrichtigkeit *f*.

sinecure [sī'nəkyŏŏr] *n* einträgliche(r) Ruheposten *m*.

sinew [sin'yŏŏ] *n* Sehne *f*; (*of animal*) Flechse *f*.

sinful [sin'fəl] *a* sündig, sündhaft.

sing [sing] *irreg vt* singen ♦ *vi* singen; (*kettle*) summen; (*ears*) dröhnen.

Singapore [sing'gəpôr] *n* Singapur *nt*.

singe [sinj] *vt* versengen.

singer [sing'ûr] *n* Sänger(in *f*) *m*.

Singhalese [singəlēz'] *a* = **Sinhalese**.

singing [sing'ing] *n* (*of person, bird*) Singen *nt*, Gesang *m*; (*of kettle*) Summen *nt*; (*of bullet*) Zischen *nt*; (*in ears*) Dröhnen *nt*.

single [sing'gəl] *a* (*one only*) einzig; (*bed, room*) Einzel-, einzeln; (*unmarried*) ledig; (*ticket*) einfach; (*having one part only*) einzeln ♦ *n* (*Brit*: *ticket*) einfache Fahrkarte *f*; **not a ~ piece was left** es war kein einziges Stück übrig; **every ~ day** jeden Tag; **in ~ file** hintereinander; *see also* **singles**.

single out *vt* aussuchen, auswählen.

single bed *n* Einzelbett *nt*.

single-breasted [sing'gəlbres'tid] *a* einreihig.

single-density disk [sing'gəldensitē disk] *n* Diskette *f* mit einfacher Bitdichte.

single-entry book-keeping [sing'gəlen'trē bŏŏk'kēping] *n* einfache Buchführung *f*.

single-handed [sing'gəlhan'did] *a* allein.

single-minded [sing'gəlmīn'did] *a* zielstrebig.

single parent *n* unverheiratete Mutter *f*, unverheiratete(r) Vater *m*.

single room *n* Einzelzimmer *nt*.

singles [sing'gəlz] *npl* (*TENNIS*) Einzel *nt*.

single-sided [sing'gəlsī'did] *a* (*disk*) einseitig.

single spacing *n* einzeilige(r) Abstand *m*.

singly [sing'glē] *ad* einzeln, allein.

singsong [sing'sông] *a*: **in his ~ voice** mit *or* in seinem Singsang.

singular [sing'gyəlûr] *a* (*GRAM*) Singular-; (*odd*) merkwürdig, seltsam ♦ *n* (*GRAM*) Einzahl *f*, Singular *m*; **in the feminine ~** im Singular weiblich.

singularly [sing'gyəlûrlē] *ad* besonders, höchst, außerordentlich.

Sinhalese [sinhəlēz'] *a* singhalesisch.

sinister [sin'istûr] *a* (*evil*) böse; (*ghostly*) unheimlich.

sink [singk] *n* Spülbecken *nt*, Ausguß *m* ♦ *irreg vt* (*ship*) versenken; (*dig*) einsenken ♦ *vi* sinken; **he sank into a chair** er sank in einen Sessel; **he sank into the mud** er sank im Schlamm ein; **the shares** *or* **share prices have sunk to 3 dollars** die Aktien sind auf 3 Dollar gefallen.

sink in *vi* (*news etc*) eingehen (+*dat*); **it took a long time to ~ in** es dauerte lange, bis er *or* sie *etc* es kapiert hatte.

sinking [sing'king] *a* (*feeling*) flau; **~ fund** Tilgungsfonds *m*.

sink unit *n* Spültisch *m*.

sinner [sin'ûr] *n* Sünder(in *f*) *m*.

sinuous [sin'yŏŏəs] *a* gewunden, sich schlängelnd.

sinus [sī'nəs] *n* (*ANAT*) Nasenhöhle *f*, Sinus *m*.

sip [sip] *n* Schlückchen *nt* ♦ *vt* nippen an (+*dat*).

siphon [sī'fən] *n* Siphon(flasche *f*) *m* ♦ *vt* (*funds*) abschöpfen.

siphon off *vt* absaugen; (*fig*) abschöpfen.

sir [sûr] *n* (*respect*) Herr *m*; (*knight*) Sir *m*; **yes S~** ja(wohl, mein Herr); **Dear S~** (*in letter*) Sehr geehrte Damen und Herren!; **Dear S~s** Sehr geehrte Herren!

siren [sī'rən] *n* Sirene *f*.

sirloin steak [sûr'loin stāk'] *n* Filetsteak *nt*.

sirocco [sərak'ō] *n* Schirokko *m*.

sisal [sī'səl] *n* Sisal *m*.

sissy [sis'ē] *n* = **cissy**.

sister [sis'tûr] *n* Schwester *f*; (*Brit*: *nurse*) Oberschwester *f*; (*nun*) Ordensschwester *f*.

sister city *n* (*US*) Partnerstadt *f*.

sister-in-law [sis'tûrinlô] *n* Schwägerin *f*.

sister organization *n* Schwestergesellschaft *f*.

sister ship *n* Schwesterschiff *nt*.

sit [sit] *irreg vi* sitzen; (*hold session*) tagen, Sitzung halten; (*dress etc*) sitzen; **to ~ tight** abwarten; **that jacket ~s well** die Jacke sitzt *or* paßt gut; **to be ~ting down** sitzen; **to ~ on a committee** in einem Ausschuß sitzen ♦ *vt* (*exam*) machen.

sit about *vi* (*Brit*) = **sit around**.

sit around *vi* herumsitzen.

sit back *vi* (*in seat*) sich zurücklehnen.

sit down *vi* sich hinsetzen.

sit in on *vt fus*: **to ~ in on a discussion** bei einer Diskussion dabeisein.

sit up *vi* (*after lying*) sich aufsetzen; (*straight*) sich gerade setzen; (*at night*) aufbleiben.

sitcom [sit'käm] *n abbr* (= *situation comedy*) Situationskomödie *f*.

sit-down [sit'doun] *a*: **a ~ strike** ein Sitzstreik; **a ~ meal** ein Essen am gedeckten Tisch.

site [sīt] *n* Platz *m* ♦ *vt* plazieren, legen.

sit-in [sit'in] *n* Sit-in *nt*.

siting [sī'ting] *n* (*location*) Platz *m*, Lage *f*.

sitter [sit'ûr] *n* (*also*: **baby~**) Babysitter *m*.

sitting [sit'ing] *n* (*meeting*) Sitzung *f*, Tagung *f*.

sitting member *n* (*POL*) (derzeitiger) Abgeordnete *m*, (derzeitige) Abgeordnete *f*.

sitting room *n* Wohnzimmer *nt*.

situate [sich'ŏŏāt] *vt* legen.

situated [sich'ŏŏātid] *a*: **to be ~** liegen.

situation [sichŏŏā'shən] *n* Situation *f*, Lage *f*; (*place*) Lage *f*; (*employment*) Stelle *f*.

situation comedy *n* (*TV, RAD*) Situationskomödie *f*.

six [siks] *num* sechs.

sixteen [siks'tēn'] *num* sechzehn.

sixteenth [siks'tēnth'] *a* sechzehnte(r, s).

sixteenth note n (US) Sechzehntel nt.

sixth [siksth] a sechste(r, s) ♦ n Sechstel nt; **upper/lower** ~ (Brit SCH) ≈ Unter-/Oberprima f.

sixty [siks'tē] num sechzig; **the sixties** die 60er Jahre; **to be in one's sixties** in den 60ern sein.

size [sīz] n Größe f; (of project) Umfang m; (glue) Kleister m; **I take** ~ **5 shoes** ich habe Schuhgröße 5; **I take** ~ **14 in a dress** ich habe Kleidergröße 14; **I'd like the small/large** ~ (of soap powder etc) ich möchte die kleine/große Packung; **it's the** ~ **of ...** es ist so groß wie ...; **cut to** ~ auf die richtige Größe zurechtgeschnitten.

size up vt (assess) abschätzen, einschätzen.

sizeable [sī'zəbəl] a ziemlich groß, ansehnlich.

sizzle [siz'əl] n Zischen nt ♦ vi zischen; (COOK) brutzeln.

SK abbr (Canada) = Saskatchewan.

skate [skāt] n Schlittschuh m; (fish) Rochen m ♦ vi Schlittschuh laufen.

skate over, skate round vt fus (problem, issue) einfach übergehen.

skateboard [skāt'bôrd] n Skateboard nt.

skater [skā'tûr] n Schlittschuhläufer(in f) m.

skating [skā'ting] n Eislauf m; **to go** ~ Eislaufen gehen; **figure** ~ Eiskunstlauf m.

skating rink n Eisbahn f.

skeleton [skel'itən] n Skelett nt; (fig) Gerüst nt.

skeleton key n Dietrich m, Nachschlüssel m.

skeleton staff n Notbesetzung f.

skeptic [skep'tik] n (US) Skeptiker(in f) m.

skeptical [skep'tikəl] a (US) skeptisch.

skepticism [skep'tisizəm] n (US) Skepsis f.

sketch [skech] n Skizze f; (THEAT) Sketch m ♦ vt skizzieren, eine Skizze machen von.

sketchbook [skech'bŏŏk] n Skizzenbuch nt.

sketching [skech'ing] n Skizzieren nt.

sketch pad n Skizzenblock m.

sketchy [skech'ē] a skizzenhaft.

skewer [skyŏŏ'ûr] n Fleischspieß m.

ski [skē] n Ski m, Schi m ♦ vi Ski or Schi laufen.

ski boot n Skistiefel m.

skid [skid] n (AUT) Schleudern nt; **to go into a** ~ ins Schleudern geraten or kommen ♦ vi rutschen; (AUT) schleudern.

skid mark n Reifenspur f; (from braking) Bremsspur f.

skier [skē'ûr] n Skiläufer(in f) m.

skiing [skē'ing] n Skilaufen nt; **to go** ~ Skilaufen gehen.

ski instructor n Skilehrer m.

ski jump n Sprungschanze f ♦ vi Ski springen.

skilful [skil'fəl] a, **skilfully** [skil'fəlē] ad (Brit) = **skillful(ly)**.

ski lift n Skilift m.

skill [skil] n Können nt, Geschicklichkeit f;

(technique) Fertigkeit f; **there's a certain** ~ **to doing it** dazu gehört ein gewisses Geschick.

skilled [skild] a geschickt; (worker) Fach-, gelernt.

skillet [skil'it] n Bratpfanne f.

skillful [skil'fəl] a (US) geschickt.

skillfully [skil'fəlē] ad (US) geschickt.

skim [skim] vt (liquid) abschöpfen; (milk) entrahmen; (read) überfliegen; (glide over) gleiten über (+acc).

skimmed milk [skimd milk] n Magermilch f.

skimp [skimp] vt (do carelessly) oberflächlich tun ♦ vi: **to** ~ **on** (work) hudeln, nachlässig erledigen; **to** ~ **on sth** (material etc) an etw sparen.

skimpy [skim'pē] a (work) schlecht gemacht; (dress) knapp.

skin [skin] n Haut f; (of fruit, vegetable) Schale f; **to have a thick/thin** ~ (fig) ein dickes Fell (col)/eine dünne Haut haben; **to be wet** or **soaked to the** ~ bis auf die Haut naß sein ♦ vt abhäuten; schälen.

skin-deep [skin'dēp'] a oberflächlich.

skin diver n Sporttaucher(in f) m.

skin diving n Schwimmtauchen nt.

skinflint [skin'flint] n Geizkragen m.

skinny [skin'ē] a dünn.

skintight [skin'tīt] a (dress etc) hauteng.

skip [skip] n Sprung m, Hopser m ♦ vi hüpfen, springen; (with rope) Seil springen ♦ vt (pass over) übergehen.

ski pants npl Skihose(n pl) f.

ski pole n Skistock m.

skipper [skip'ûr] n (NAUT) Schiffer m, Kapitän m; (SPORT) Mannschaftskapitän m ♦ vt führen.

skipping rope [skip'ing rōp] n (Brit) Hüpfseil nt.

ski resort n Wintersportort m.

skirmish [skûr'mish] n Scharmützel nt.

skirt [skûrt] n Rock m ♦ vt herumgehen um; (fig) umgehen.

skirting board [skûr'ting bôrd] n (Brit) Fußleiste f.

ski run n Skiabfahrt f.

ski suit n Skianzug m.

skit [skit] n Parodie f.

ski tow n Schlepplift m.

skittle [skit'əl] n Kegel m; ~**s** pl (Brit: game) Kegeln nt.

skive [skīv] vi (Brit col) schwänzen.

skulk [skulk] vi sich herumdrücken.

skull [skul] n Schädel m.

skullcap [skul'kap] n (worn by Jews or Pope) Scheitelkäppchen nt.

skunk [skungk] n Stinktier nt.

sky [skī] n Himmel m; **to praise sb to the skies** jdn über den grünen Klee loben (col).

sky-blue [skī'blōō'] a himmelblau ♦ n Himmelblau nt.

sky-high [skī'hī'] ad (throw) zum Himmel; **prices have gone** ~ die Preise sind enorm gestiegen.

skylark [skī'lârk] n (bird) Feldlerche f.
skylight [skī'līt] n Dachfenster nt, Oberlicht nt.
skyline [skī'līn] n (horizon) Horizont m; (of city) Skyline f, Silhouette f.
skyscraper [skī'skrāpûr] n Wolkenkratzer m.
slab [slab] n (of stone) Platte f; (of chocolate, wood) Tafel f; (of meat, cheese) dicke Scheibe f, dicke(s) Stück nt.
slack [slak] a (loose) lose, schlaff, locker; (COMM: market, business) flau; (careless) nachlässig, lasch; (demand) schwach; (period) ruhig; **business is** ~ es ist nicht viel los ♦ vi nachlässig sein ♦ n (in rope etc) durchhängende(s) Teil nt; **to take up the** ~ straffziehen; see also **slacks**.
slacken [slak'ən] (also: ~ **off**) vi schlaff/locker werden; (become slower) nachlassen, stocken ♦ vt (loosen) lockern.
slackness [slak'nis] n Schlaffheit f.
slacks [slaks] npl Hose(n pl) f.
slag [slag] n Schlacke f.
slag heap n Halde f.
slain [slān] pp of **slay**.
slake [slāk] vt (one's thirst) löschen, stillen.
slalom [slä'ləm] n Slalom m.
slam [slam] n Knall m ♦ vt (door) zuschlagen, zuknallen; (throw down) knallen ♦ vi zuschlagen.
slander [slan'dûr] n Verleumdung f ♦ vt verleumden.
slanderous [slan'dûrəs] a verleumderisch.
slang [slang] n Slang m; (army ~, schoolboy ~) Jargon m.
slant [slant] n (lit) Schräge f; (fig) Tendenz f, Einstellung f; **to give a new** ~ **on sth** etw aus einer anderen Perspektive betrachten ♦ vt schräg legen ♦ vi schräg liegen.
slanting [slan'ting] a schräg.
slap [slap] n Schlag m, Klaps m ♦ vt schlagen, einen Klaps geben (+dat) ♦ ad (directly) geradewegs.
slapdash [slap'dash] a salopp.
slapstick [slap'stik] n (comedy) Klamauk m.
slash [slash] n Hieb m, Schnittwunde f; (US) Schrägstrich m ♦ vt (auf)schlitzen; (expenditure) radikal kürzen.
slat [slat] n (of wood) Leiste f, Latte f.
slate [slāt] n (stone) Schiefer m; (roofing) Dachziegel m ♦ vt (criticize) verreißen.
slaughter [slô'tûr] n (of animals) Schlachten nt; (of people) Gemetzel nt ♦ vt schlachten; (people) niedermetzeln.
slaughterhouse [slô'tûrhous] n Schlachthof m.
Slav [släv] a slawisch.
slave [släv] n Sklave m, Sklavin f ♦ vi schuften, sich schinden; **to** ~ (**away**) **at sth** or **at doing sth** sich mit etw herumschlagen.
slave labor n Sklavenarbeit f.
slaver [slä'vûr] n (dribble) speicheln, geifern.
slavery [slä'vûrē] n Sklaverei f; (work) Schinderei f.
slavish [slä'vish] a sklavisch; (devotion) skla-

visch, unterwürfig.
slay [slā] vt irreg (old) erschlagen; (with gun etc) ermorden.
SLD n abbr (Brit POL) = Social and Liberal Democratic Party.
sleazy [slē'zē] a (place) schmierig.
sled [sled] n Schlitten m.
sledge [slej] n (Brit) = **sled**.
sledgehammer [slej'hamûr] n Schmiedehammer m.
sleek [slēk] a glatt, glänzend; (shape) rassig.
sleep [slēp] n Schlaf m; **to have a good night's** ~ sich richtig ausschlafen; **to go to** ~ einschlafen; **to put to** ~ (patient) einschläfern; (euph: kill: animal) einschläfern ♦ irreg vi schlafen; **to** ~ **lightly** einen leichten Schlaf haben; **to** ~ **with sb** (euph: have sex) mit jdm schlafen ♦ vt: **we can** ~ **4** wir können 4 Leute unterbringen.
sleep in vi ausschlafen; (oversleep) verschlafen.
sleeper [slē'pûr] n (person) Schläfer(in f) m; (Brit RAIL: carriage) Schlafwagen m; (: tie) Schwelle f.
sleepily [slē'pilē] ad schläfrig.
sleepiness [slē'pēnis] n Schläfrigkeit f.
sleeping bag [slē'ping bag] n Schlafsack m.
sleeping car n Schlafwagen m.
sleeping partner n (Brit COMM) = **silent partner**.
sleeping pill n Schlaftablette f.
sleepless [slēp'lis] a (night) schlaflos.
sleeplessness [slēp'lisnis] n Schlaflosigkeit f.
sleepwalker [slēp'wôkûr] n Schlafwandler(in f) m.
sleepy [slē'pē] a schläfrig; **to be** or **feel** ~ müde sein.
sleet [slēt] n Schneeregen m.
sleeve [slēv] n Ärmel m; (of record) Umschlag m, Hülle f.
sleeveless [slēv'lis] a (garment) ärmellos.
sleigh [slā] n Pferdeschlitten m.
sleight [slīt] n: ~ **of hand** Fingerfertigkeit f.
slender [slen'dûr] a schlank; (fig) gering.
slept [slept] pt, pp of **sleep**.
sleuth [slooth] n (col) Spürhund m.
slew [sloo] pt of **slay** ♦ vi (Brit: veer) (herum)schwenken.
slice [slīs] n Scheibe f ♦ vt in Scheiben schneiden; ~**d bread** (auf)geschnittene(s) Brot nt, Scheibenbrot nt.
slick [slik] a (clever) raffiniert, aalglatt ♦ n Ölteppich m.
slid [slid] pt, pp of **slide**.
slide [slīd] n Rutschbahn f; (PHOT) Dia(positiv) nt; (Brit: for hair) (Haar)spange f; (fall in prices) (Preis)rutsch m; **microscope** ~ Objektträger m ♦ irreg vt schieben ♦ vi (slip) gleiten, rutschen; **to let things** ~ (fig) die Dinge laufen or schleifen lassen (col).
slide projector n (PHOT) Diaprojektor m.
slide rule n Rechenschieber m.
sliding [slī'ding] a (door) Schiebe-; ~ **roof**

(AUT) Schiebedach *nt.*

slight [slīt] *a* zierlich; *(trivial)* geringfügig; *(small)* leicht, gering; **a ~ improvement** eine leichte Verbesserung; **there's not the ~est possibility** es besteht nicht die geringste Möglichkeit ♦ *n* Kränkung *f* ♦ *vt (offend)* kränken.

slightly [slīt'lē] *ad* etwas, ein bißchen; **~ built** zierlich.

slim [slim] *a* schlank; *(book)* dünn; *(chance)* gering ♦ *vi* eine Schlankheitskur machen.

slime [slīm] *n* Schleim *m.*

slimming [slim'ing] *n* Abnehmen *nt* ♦ *a (diet, pills)* schlankmachend.

slimness [slim'nis] *n* Schlankheit *f.*

slimy [slī'mē] *a* schleimig; *(stone, wall)* glitschig; *(hands)* schmierig; *(person)* schleimig, schmierig.

sling [sling] *n* Schlinge *f*; *(weapon)* Schleuder *f*; **to have one's arm in a ~** den Arm in der Schlinge tragen ♦ *vt irreg* werfen; *(hurl)* schleudern.

slingshot [sling'shát] *n (US)* Schleuder *f.*

slink [slingk] *vi irreg*: **to ~ away, to ~ off** sich davonschleichen.

slip [slip] *n (slipping)* Ausgleiten *nt*, Rutschen *nt*; *(mistake)* Flüchtigkeitsfehler *m*; *(petticoat)* Unterrock *m*; *(of paper)* Zettel *m*; **a Freudian ~** ein Freudscher Versprecher; **to give sb the ~** jdn entwischen; **a ~ of the tongue** ein Versprecher *m* ♦ *vt (put)* stecken, schieben; **to ~ on a sweater** einen Pullover überziehen; **it ~ped my mind** das ist mir entfallen, ich habe es vergessen ♦ *vi (lose balance)* ausrutschen; *(move)* gleiten, rutschen; *(make mistake)* einen Fehler machen; *(decline)* nachlassen; **to let things ~** die Dinge schleifen lassen; **to let a chance ~ by** eine Gelegenheit ungenutzt lassen; **it ~ped from her hand** es rutschte ihr aus der Hand.

slip away *vi* sich wegstehlen.

slip by *vi (time)* verstreichen.

slip in *vt* hineingleiten lassen ♦ *vi (errors)* sich einschleichen.

slip off *vt*: **to ~ sth off** etw abstreifen ♦ *vi* sich wegstehlen.

slip out *vi* hinausschlüpfen.

slip-on [slip'án] *a* zum Überziehen.

slip-ons [slip'ónz] *npl (shoes)* Slipper *pl.*

slipped disc [slipt disk] *n* Bandscheibenschaden *m.*

slipper [slip'ûr] *n* Hausschuh *m.*

slippery [slip'ûrē] *a* glatt; *(tricky)* aalglatt, gerissen.

slip road *n (Brit: to freeway)* Auffahrt *f*; *(: leaving freeway)* Ausfahrt *f.*

slipshod [slip'shád] *a* schlampig.

slipstream [slip'strēm] *n* Windschatten *m.*

slip-up [slip'up] *n* Panne *f.*

slipway [slip'wā] *n* Auslaufbahn *f.*

slit [slit] *n* Schlitz *m* ♦ *vt irreg, pt, pp* **slit** aufschlitzen; **to ~ sb's throat** jdm die Kehle aufschlitzen.

slither [sliTH'ûr] *vi* schlittern; *(snake)* sich schlängeln.

sliver [sliv'ûr] *n (of glass, wood)* Splitter *m*; *(of cheese, sausage)* Scheibchen *nt.*

slob [sláb] *n (col: man)* Dreckschwein *nt (!)*; *(: woman)* Schlampe *f.*

slog [slág] *n (Brit: great effort)* Plackerei *f* ♦ *vi (work hard)* schuften.

slogan [slō'gən] *n* Schlagwort *nt*; *(COMM)* Werbespruch *m.*

slop [sláp] *vi* überschwappen ♦ *vt* verschütten.

slope [slōp] *n* Neigung *f*, Schräge *f*; *(of mountains)* (Ab)hang *m* ♦ *vi*: **to ~ down** sich senken; **to ~ up** ansteigen.

sloping [slō'ping] *a* schräg; *(shoulders)* abfallend; *(ground)* abschüssig.

sloppily [sláp'ilē] *ad* schlampig.

sloppiness [sláp'ēnis] *n* Matschigkeit *f*; *(of work)* Nachlässigkeit *f.*

sloppy [sláp'ē] *a (wet)* matschig; *(careless)* schlampig; *(silly)* rührselig.

slosh [slásh] *vt (col: liquid)* platschen ♦ *vi (col)*: **to ~ around** *(children)* (herum)planschen; *(liquid)* (herum)schwappen.

slot [slát] *n* Schlitz *m*; *(fig: RAD, TV)* gewohnte Sendezeit *f* ♦ *vt*: **to ~ sth in** etw einlegen.

sloth [slōth] *n (vice)* Trägheit *f*, Faulheit *f*; *(ZOOL)* Faultier *nt.*

slot machine *n (for gambling)* Spielautomat *m*; *(Brit: vending machine)* Automat *m.*

slouch [slouch] *vi* krumm dasitzen *or* dastehen.

slovenly [sluv'ənlē] *a* schlampig; *(speech)* salopp.

slow [slō] *a* langsam; **to be ~** *(clock)* nachgehen; *(stupid)* begriffsstutzig sein; **my watch is 20 minutes ~** meine Uhr geht 20 Minuten nach; **to be ~ to act** *or* **decide** sich Zeit lassen/lange brauchen, um sich zu entscheiden; **at a ~ speed** langsam; **the ~ lane** die Kriechspur *f*; **in ~ motion** in Zeitlupe; **business is ~** *(COMM)* es ist nicht viel los; **bake for two hours in a ~ oven** bei schwacher Hitze 2 Stunden backen ♦ *ad*: **to go ~** *(driver)* langsam fahren; *(in industrial dispute)* einen Bummelstreik machen.

slow down *vi* langsamer werden; **~ down!** mach langsam! ♦ *vt* aufhalten, langsamer machen, verlangsamen.

slow up *vi* sich verlangsamen, sich verzögern ♦ *vt* aufhalten, langsamer machen.

slowdown [slō'doun] *n (US)* Bummelstreik *m.*

slowly [slō'lē] *ad* langsam; *(gradually)* allmählich; **to drive ~** langsam fahren; **~ but surely** langsam aber sicher.

slow-moving [slō'mŌō'ving] *a* sich (nur) langsam bewegend.

slowpoke [slō'pōk] *n (US)* Bummeler(in *f*) *m.*

sludge [sluj] *n* Schlamm *m*, Matsch *m.*

slue [slŌō] *vi (US: veer)* (herum)schwenken.

slug [slug] *n* Nacktschnecke *f*; (*col: bullet*) Kugel *f*.

sluggish [slug'ish] *a* träge; (*COMM*) schleppend; (*business, market, sales*) flau.

sluggishly [slug'ishlē] *ad* träge.

sluggishness [slug'ishnis] *n* Trägheit *f*.

sluice [sloōs] *n* Schleuse *f* ♦ *vt*: **to ~ down** abspritzen ♦ *vi*: **to ~ out** herausschießen.

slum [slum] *n* Elendsviertel *nt*, Slum *m*.

slumber [slum'bûr] *n* Schlummer *m*.

slump [slump] *n* Rückgang *m*; **the ~ in the price of copper** der Preissturz bei Kupfer ♦ *vi* fallen, stürzen; **he was ~ed over the wheel** er war über dem Steuer zusammengesackt (*col*).

slung [slung] *pt, pp of* **sling**.

slunk [slungk] *pt, pp of* **slink**.

slur [slûr] *n* Undeutlichkeit *f*; (*insult*) Verleumdung *f*; **to cast a ~ on sb** jdn verunglimpfen ♦ *vt* (*also*: **~ over**) hinweggehen über (+*acc*).

slurred [slûrd] *a* (*pronunciation*) undeutlich.

slush [slush] *n* (*snow*) Schneematsch *m*; (*mud*) Schlamm *m*.

slush fund *n* Schmiergelder *pl*, Schmiergeldfonds *m*.

slushy [slush'ē] *a* (*lit*) matschig; (*fig: sentimental*) schmalzig; (*Brit col: poetry etc*) kitschig.

slut [slut] *n* Schlampe *f*.

sly [slī] *a*, **slyly** [slī'lē] *ad* schlau, verschlagen.

slyness [slī'nis] *n* Schlauheit *f*.

smack [smak] *n* Klaps *m* ♦ *vt* einen Klaps geben (+*dat*); **to ~ one's lips** schmatzen, sich (*dat*) die Lippen lecken ♦ *vi*: **to ~ of** riechen nach ♦ *ad*: **it fell ~ in the middle** (*col*) es fiel direkt in die Mitte (hinein).

smacker [smak'ûr] *n* (*col: kiss*) Schmatz *m*; (: *dollar bill or pound note*) Dollar *m*, Pfund *nt*.

small [smôl] *a* (*in height*) klein; **to get** *or* **grow ~er** (*stain, town*) kleiner werden; (*debt, organization, numbers*) reduzieren; **to make ~er** (*amount, income*) kürzen; (*garden, object*) kleiner machen; (*garment*) enger machen; **~ capitals** Kapitälchen *pl*; **a ~ storekeeper** ein Inhaber *m* eines kleinen Ladens ♦ *n*: **the ~ of the back** das Kreuz.

small ads *npl* (*Brit*) Kleinanzeigen *pl*.

small change *n* Kleingeld *nt*.

smallholding [smôl'hōlding] *n* (*Brit*) kleine(r) Landbesitz *m*.

small hours *npl* frühe Morgenstunden *pl*.

smallish [smô'lish] *a* ziemlich klein.

small-minded [smôl'mīn'did] *a* engstirnig, kleinkariert.

smallness [smôl'nis] *n* Kleinheit *f*.

smallpox [smôl'pâks] *n* Pocken *pl*.

small print *n*: **the ~** das Kleingedruckte.

small-scale [smôl'skāl] *a* klein; (*map, model*) in verkleinertem Maßstab; (*business, farming*) kleinangelegt.

small talk *n* Konversation *f*, Geplauder *nt*.

small-time [smôl'tīm'] *a* mickerig, armselig;

---

a ~ thief ein kleiner Ganove.

smart [smârt] *a* (*fashionable*) elegant, schick; (*neat*) adrett; (*clever*) clever; (*quick*) scharf; **the ~ set** die Schickeria *f*; **to look ~** flott *or* schick aussehen ♦ *vi* brennen, schmerzen; **my eyes are ~ing** mir brennen die Augen.

smart-ass [smârt'as] *n* (*US col*) Klugschießer *m*.

smarten up [smârt'ən up] *vi* sich in Schale werfen ♦ *vt* herausputzen.

smartness [smârt'nis] *n* (*cleverness*) Schlauheit *f*; (*elegance*) Eleganz *f*.

smash [smash] *n* Zusammenstoß *m*; (*TENNIS*) Schmetterball *m*; (*sound*) Scheppern *nt* ♦ *vt* (*break*) zerschmettern; (*destroy*) vernichten ♦ *vi* (*break*) zersplittern, zerspringen.

smash up *vt* (*car*) kaputtfahren; (*room*) zertrümmern.

smash hit *n* Superhit *m*.

smattering [smat'ûring] *n* oberflächliche Kenntnis *f*.

smear [smēûr] *n* Fleck *m*; (*insult*) Verleumdung *f*; (*MED*) Abstrich *m* ♦ *vt* beschmieren; **his hands were ~ed with oil/ink** seine Hände waren mit Öl/Tinte beschmiert.

smear campaign *n* Verleumdungskampagne *f*.

smell [smel] *n* Geruch *m*; (*sense*) Geruchssinn *m* ♦ *irreg vt* riechen ♦ *vi* riechen (*of* nach); (*unpleasantly also*) stinken; (*fragrantly*) duften; **it ~s good** es riecht gut.

smelled [smeld] *pt, pp of* **smell**.

smelly [smel'ē] *a* übelriechend.

smelt [smelt] *vt* (*ore*) schmelzen ♦ *pt, pp of* **smell**.

smile [smīl] *n* Lächeln *nt* ♦ *vi* lächeln.

smiling [smī'ling] *a* lächelnd.

smirk [smûrk] *n* blöde(s) Grinsen *nt* ♦ *vi* blöde grinsen.

smith [smith] *n* Schmied *m*.

smithy [smith'ē] *n* Schmiede *f*.

smitten [smit'ən] *a*: **he's really ~ with her** er ist wirklich vernarrt in sie.

smock [smák] *n* Kittel *m*.

smog [smâg] *n* Smog *m*.

smoke [smōk] *n* Rauch *m*; **to go up in ~** (*house etc*) in Rauch (und Flammen) aufgehen; (*fig*) sich in Wohlgefallen auflösen ♦ *vt* rauchen; (*food*) räuchern ♦ *vi* rauchen; **do you ~?** rauchen Sie?

smoked [smōkt] *a* (*bacon*) geräuchert; (*glass*) Rauch-.

smokeless fuel [smōk'lis fyoō'əl] *n* rauchlose Kohle *f*.

smoker [smō'kûr] *n* Raucher(in *f*) *m*; (*RAIL*) Raucherabteil *nt*.

smoke screen *n* Rauchwand *f*.

smoking [smō'king] *n* Rauchen *nt*; **he's given up ~** er hat aufgehört zu rauchen; "**no ~**" „Rauchen verboten".

smoking car *n* Raucherabteil *nt*.

smoky [smō'kē] *a* rauchig; (*room*) verraucht; (*taste*) geräuchert.

smolder [smōl'dûr] *vi* (*US*) glimmen, schwelen.

smooth [smo͞oͭh] *a* (*texture, landing, takeoff, flight*) glatt; (*cigarette*) mild; (*movement*) geschmeidig; (*person*) glatt, gewandt ♦ *vt* (*also*: ~ **out**) glätten, glattstreichen.
smooth over *vt*: **to** ~ **things over** (*fig*) eine Sache geradebiegen.

smoothly [smo͞oͭh'lē] *ad* glatt, eben; (*fig*) reibungslos; (*easily*) glatt; **everything went** ~ alles ist glatt über die Bühne gegangen.

smoothness [smo͞oͭh'nis] *n* Glätte *f*.

smother [smuͭh'ûr] *vt* ersticken.

smoulder [smōl'dûr] *vi* (*Brit*) = **smolder**.

smudge [smuj] *n* Schmutzfleck *m* ♦ *vt* beschmieren.

smug [smug] *a* selbstgefällig.

smuggle [smug'əl] *vt* schmuggeln; **to** ~ **in/ out** (*goods etc*) einschmuggeln/herausschmuggeln.

smuggler [smug'lûr] *n* Schmuggler(in *f*) *m*.

smuggling [smug'ling] *n* Schmuggel *m*.

smugly [smug'lē] *ad* selbstgefällig.

smugness [smug'nis] *n* Selbstgefälligkeit *f*.

smut [smut] *n* (*grain of soot*) Rußflocke *f*; (*mark*) Fleck *m*; (*in conversation etc*) Schmutz *m*.

smutty [smut'ē] *a* (*fig: obscene*) obszön, schmutzig.

snack [snak] *n* Imbiß *m*; **to have a** ~ eine Kleinigkeit essen, einen Imbiß zu sich (*dat*) nehmen.

snack bar *n* Imbißstube *f*.

snag [snag] *n* Haken *m*; (*in stocking*) gezogene(r) Faden *m*; **to run into** *or* **hit a** ~ auf Schwierigkeiten stoßen.

snail [snāl] *n* Schnecke *f*.

snake [snāk] *n* Schlange *f*.

snap [snap] *n* Schnappen *nt*; (*photograph*) Schnappschuß *m*; **a cold** ~ (*col*) ein Kälteeinbruch *m* ♦ *a* (*decision*) schnell ♦ *vt* (*break*) zerbrechen; **to** ~ **one's fingers** mit den Fingern schnipsen *or* schnalzen; **to** ~ **one's fingers at sb/sth** (*fig*) auf jdn/etw pfeifen ♦ *vi* (*break*) brechen; (*dog*) schnappen; (*speak*) anfauchen; **to** ~ (**at sb**) (jdn) anschnauzen (*col*); ~ **out of it!** raff dich auf!
snap off *vt* (*break*) abbrechen.
snap up *vt* aufschnappen.

snap fastener *n* Druckknopf *m*.

snappy [snap'ē] *a* flott.

snapshot [snap'shät] *n* Schnappschuß *m*.

snare [snär] *n* Schlinge *f* ♦ *vt* mit einer Schlinge fangen.

snarl [snärl] *n* Zähnefletschen *nt* ♦ *vi* (*dog*) knurren; (*engine*) brummen, dröhnen ♦ *vt* (*wool*) verheddern; **I got** ~**ed up in a traffic jam** ich bin im Verkehr steckengeblieben; **to get** ~**ed up** (*plans*) durcheinander kommen.

snatch [snach] *n* (*grab*) Schnappen *nt*; (*of conversation*) Fetzen *pl*; (*small amount*) Bruchteil *m* ♦ *vt* schnappen, packen.
snatch up *vt* schnappen.

sneak [snēk] *vi* schleichen ♦ *vt*: **to** ~ **a look at sth** verstohlen auf etw schielen.

sneakers [snē'kûrz] *npl* Freizeitschuhe *pl*, Leisetreter *pl*, Turnschuhe *pl*.

sneaking [snē'king] *a*: **to have a** ~ **feeling/ suspicion that** ... ein ungewisses Gefühl/ein leisen Verdacht haben, daß ...

sneaky [snē'kē] *a* raffiniert.

sneer [snēr] *n* Hohnlächeln *nt* ♦ *vi* höhnisch grinsen; spötteln; **to** ~ **at sb/sth** jdn/etw verhöhnen, jdn/etw auslachen.

sneeze [snēz] *n* Niesen *nt* ♦ *vi* niesen.

snicker [snik'ûr] *n* Kichern *nt* ♦ *vi* hämisch kichern.

snide [snīd] *a* (*col: sarcastic*) schneidend.

sniff [snif] *n* Schnüffeln *nt* ♦ *vi* schnieben; (*smell*) schnüffeln ♦ *vt* schnuppern; (*glue, drug*) schnüffeln.
sniff at *vt fus*: **it's not to be** ~**ed at** es ist nicht zu verachten.

snigger [snig'ûr] *n* Kichern *nt* ♦ *vi* hämisch kichern.

snip [snip] *n* Schnippel *m*, Schnipsel *m* ♦ *vt* schnippeln.

sniper [snī'pûr] *n* Heckenschütze *m*.

snippet [snip'it] *n* Schnipsel *m*; (*of conversation*) Fetzen *m*.

sniveling, (*Brit*) **snivelling** [sniv'əling] *a* weinerlich.

snob [snäb] *n* Snob *m*.

snobbery [snäb'ûrē] *n* Snobismus *m*.

snobbish [snäb'ish] *a* versnobt.

snobbishness [snäb'ishnis] *n* Versnobtheit *f*, Snobismus *m*.

snooker [sno͞ok'ûr] *n* Snooker *nt*.

snoop [sno͞op] *vi*: **to** ~ **around** herumschnüffeln.

snooper [sno͞o'pûr] *n* Schnüffler(in *f*) *m*.

snooty [sno͞o'tē] *a* (*col*) hochnäsig.

snooze [sno͞oz] *n* Nickerchen *nt* ♦ *vi* ein Nickerchen machen, dösen.

snore [snôr] *vi* schnarchen ♦ *n* Schnarchen *nt*.

snoring [snôr'ing] *n* Schnarchen *nt*.

snorkel [snôr'kəl] *n* Schnorchel *m*.

snort [snôrt] *n* Schnauben *nt* ♦ *vi* schnauben ♦ *vt* (*drugs col*) schnupfen.

snotty [snät'ē] *a* (*col*) rotzig.

snout [snout] *n* Schnauze *f*; (*of pig*) Rüssel *m*.

snow [snō] *n* Schnee *m* ♦ *vi* schneien.
snow under *vt*: **to be** ~**ed under with work** mit Arbeit reichlich eingedeckt sein.

snowball [snō'bôl] *n* Schneeball *m*.

snow-blind [snō'blīnd] *a* schneeblind.

snowbound [snō'bound] *a* eingeschneit.

snowcapped [snō'kapt] *a* (*mountain, peak*) schneebedeckt.

snowdrift [snō'drift] *n* Schneewehe *f*.

snowdrop [snō'dräp] *n* Schneeglöckchen *nt*.

snowfall [snō'fôl] *n* Schneefall *m*.

snowflake [snō'flāk] *n* Schneeflocke *f*.

snowline [snō'līn] *n* Schneegrenze *f*.

snowman [snō'man] *n*, *pl* -**men** Schneemann *m*.

snowplow, (*Brit*) **snowplough** [snō'plou] *n* Schneepflug *m*.
snowshoe [snō'shōō] *n* Schneeschuh *m*.
snowstorm [snō'stôrm] *n* Schneesturm *m*.
snowy [snō'ē] *a* schneereich.
SNP *n abbr* = *Scottish National Party*.
snub [snub] *vt* schroff abfertigen ♦ *n* Verweis *m*, schroffe Abfertigung *f*.
snub-nosed [snub'nōzd] *a* stupsnasig.
snuff [snuf] *n* Schnupftabak *m* ♦ *vt* (*also*: ~ **out**: *candle*) auslöschen.
snuffbox [snuf'bâks] *n* Schnupftabakdose *f*.
snug [snug] *a* gemütlich, behaglich.
snuggle [snug'əl] *vi*: **to** ~ **down in bed** sich ins Bett kuscheln; **to** ~ **up to sb** sich an jdn kuscheln.
snugly [snug'lē] *ad* gemütlich, behaglich; **it fits** ~ (*object in holder*) es paßt genau (rein); (*garment*) es paßt wie angegossen.
so [sō] *ad* so ♦ *cj* daher, folglich, also; ~ **quickly** (*early*) so früh, schon; (*fast*) so schnell; **quite** ~**!** genau!; **even** ~ (aber) trotzdem; ~ **it is!**, ~ **it does!** (ja) tatsächlich; ~ **to speak** sozusagen; **she didn't** ~ **much as send me a birthday card** sie hat mir nicht mal eine Geburtstagskarte geschickt; ~ **as to** um zu; **or** ~ so etwa; ~ **long!** (*goodbye*) tschüß!; ~ **many** so viele; ~ **much** soviel; ~ **that** damit; ~ (**what**)? (*col*) (na) und?; ~ **that's the reason!** das ist also der Grund!
SO *abbr* (*FIN*: = *standing order*) DA.
soak [sōk] *vt* durchnässen; (*leave in liquid*) einweichen.
soak in *vi* einsickern in (+*acc*).
soak up *vt* aufsaugen.
soaking [sō'king] *n* Einweichen *nt* ♦ *a*: ~ **wet** klatschnaß, triefend (naß).
so-and-so [sō'ənsō] *n* (*somebody*) Soundso *m*.
soap [sōp] *n* Seife *f*.
soapflakes [sōp'flâks] *npl* Seifenflocken *pl*.
soap opera *n* Seifenoper *f* (*col*).
soap powder *n* Waschpulver *nt*.
soapsuds [sōp'sudz] *npl* Seifenschaum *m*.
soapy [sō'pē] *a* seifig, Seifen-.
soar [sôr] *vi* aufsteigen; (*price*) hochschnellen; (*morale, spirits*) einen Aufschwung bekommen.
soaring [sôr'ing] *a* (*flight*) aufsteigend, in die Luft steigend; (*prices*) in die Höhe schnellend; (*inflation*) unaufhaltsam.
sob [sâb] *n* Schluchzen *nt* ♦ *vi* schluchzen.
s.o.b. *n abbr* (*US col!*: = *son of a bitch*) Mistkerl *m* (*!*).
sober [sō'bûr] *a* (*lit, fig*) nüchtern.
sober up *vi* nüchtern werden.
soberly [sō'bûrlē] *ad* nüchtern.
sobriety [səbrī'ətē] *n* (*not being drunk*) Nüchternheit *f*; (*seriousness, sedateness*) Solidität *f*.
Soc. *abbr* (= *society*) Ges.
so-called [sō'kôld'] *a* sogenannt.
soccer [sâk'ûr] *n* Fußball *m*.

soccer player *n* Fußballspieler *m*.
sociability [sōshəbil'ətē] *n* Umgänglichkeit *f*.
sociable [sō'shəbəl] *a* umgänglich, gesellig.
social [sō'shəl] *a* sozial; (*friendly, living with others*) gesellig.
social class *n* Gesellschaftsklasse *f*.
social climber *n* Emporkömmling *m* (*pej*), soziale(r) Aufsteiger *m*.
social club *n* Verein *m* (*für Freizeitgestaltung*).
Social Democrat *n* Sozialdemokrat(in *f*) *m*.
socialism [sō'shəlizəm] *n* Sozialismus *m*.
socialist [sō'shəlist] *n* Sozialist(in *f*) *m* ♦ *a* sozialistisch.
socialite [sō'shəlīt] *n* Angehörige(r) *mf* der Schickeria *or* der feinen Gesellschaft.
socialize [sō'shəlīz] *vi*: **to** ~ **with sb** (*meet socially*) mit jdm gesellschaftlich verkehren; (*chat to*) sich mit jdm unterhalten.
socially [sō'shəlē] *ad* gesellschaftlich, privat.
social science *n* Sozialwissenschaft *f*.
social security *n* Sozialversicherung *f*.
social welfare *n* Fürsorge *f*, soziale(s) Wohl *nt*.
social work *n* Sozialarbeit *f*.
social worker *n* Sozialarbeiter(in *f*) *m*.
society [səsī'ətē] *n* Gesellschaft *f*; (*fashionable world*) die große Welt ♦ *cpd* (*party, column*) Gesellschafts-.
socioeconomic grouping [sō'sēōēkənâm'ik grōō'ping] *n* sozialwirtschaftliche Gruppierung *f*.
sociological [sōsēəlâj'ikəl] *a* soziologisch.
sociologist [sōsēâl'əjist] *n* Soziologe *m*, Soziologin *f*.
sociology [sōsēâl'əjē] *n* Soziologie *f*.
sock [sâk] *n* Socke *f*; **to pull one's** ~**s up** (*fig*) sich am Riemen reißen ♦ *vt* (*col*) schlagen.
socket [sâk'it] *n* (*Brit ELEC*) Steckdose *f*; (*of eye*) Augenhöhle *f*; (*TECH*) Rohransatz *m*.
sod [sâd] *n* (*of earth*) Rasenstück *nt*; (*Brit col!*) Saukerl *m* (*!*).
soda [sō'də] *n* Soda *f*; (*US*: *also*: ~ **pop**) Brause *f*, Limo *f*.
soda water *n* Mineralwasser *nt*, Soda(wasser) *nt*.
sodden [sâd'ən] *a* durchweicht.
sodium [sō'dēəm] *n* Natrium *nt*.
sodium chloride *n* Natriumchlorid *nt*, Kochsalz *nt*.
sofa [sō'fə] *n* Sofa *nt*.
Sofia [sōfē'ə] *n* Sofia *nt*.
soft [sôft] *a* weich; (*not loud*) leise, gedämpft; (*kind*) weichherzig, gutmütig; (*weak*) weich, nachgiebig; (*teacher, parent*) nachsichtig, gutmütig.
soft-boiled [sôft'boild'] *a* (*egg*) weich(gekocht).
soft drink *n* alkoholfreie(s) Getränk *nt*.
soft drugs *npl* weiche Drogen *pl*.
soften [sôf'ən] *vt* weich machen; (*blow*) abschwächen, mildern ♦ *vi* weich werden.
softener [sôf'ənûr] *n* Weichmacher *m*.

soft furnishings *npl* Vorhänge, Teppiche, Kissen etc.

softhearted [sôft'hâr'tid] *a* weichherzig.

softly [sôft'lē] *ad* (*gently*) sanft; (*not loud*) leise.

softness [sôft'nis] *n* Weichheit *f*; (*fig*) Sanftheit *f*.

soft sell *n* Softsell *m*, weiche Verkaufstaktik *f*.

soft toy *n* Stofftier *nt*.

software [sôft'wär] *n* (*COMPUT*) Software *f*.

soft water *n* weiche(s) Wasser *nt*.

soggy [säg'ē] *a* (*ground*) sumpfig; (*bread*) aufgeweicht.

soil [soil] *n* Erde *f*, Boden *m* ♦ *vt* beschmutzen.

soiled [soild] *a* beschmutzt, schmutzig.

sojourn [sō'jûrn] *n* Aufenthalt *m*.

solace [sâl'is] *n* Trost *m*.

solar [sō'lûr] *a* Sonnen-, Solar-.

solarium [sōlär'ēəm] *n*, *pl* **solaria** [sōlär'ēə] Solarium *nt*.

solar plexus [sō'lûr plek'səs] *n* (*ANAT*) Solarplexus *m*, Magengrube *f*.

solar system *n* Sonnensystem *nt*.

sold [sōld] *pt*, *pp* of **sell**.

solder [sâd'ûr] *vt* löten ♦ *n* Lötmetall *nt*.

soldier [sōl'jûr] *n* Soldat *m*; **toy ~** Spielzeugsoldat *m*.

sold out *a* (*COMM*) ausverkauft.

sole [sōl] *n* Sohle *f*; (*fish*) Seezunge *f* ♦ *vt* besohlen ♦ *a* alleinig, Allein-; **the ~ reason** der einzige Grund; **~ trader** Einzelkaufmann *m*.

solely [sōl'lē] *ad* ausschließlich, nur, (einzig und) allein; **I will hold you ~ responsible** ich mache Sie allein (dafür) verantwortlich.

solemn [sâl'əm] *a* feierlich; (*serious*) feierlich, ernst.

solicit [səlis'it] *vt* (*request*) erbitten, bitten um ♦ *vi* (*prostitute*) Kunden anwerben.

solicitor [səlis'itûr] *n* (*Brit*) Rechtsanwalt *m*.

solid [sâl'id] *a* (*hard*) fest; (*of same material*) rein, massiv; (*not hollow*) massiv, stabil; (*without break*) voll, ganz; (*reliable*) solide, zuverlässig; (*sensible*) solide, gut; (*united*) eins, einig; (*vote*) einstimmig; (*meal*) kräftig; (*line*) ununterbrochen; **we waited 2 ~ hours** wir haben zwei volle Stunden gewartet ♦ *n* Feste(s) *nt*.

solidarity [sâlidar'itē] *n* Solidarität *f*, Zusammenhalt *m*.

solid figure *n* (*MATH*) Körper *m*.

solid ground *n*: **to be on ~** (*lit*, *fig*) auf festem Boden sein.

solidify [səlid'əfī] *vi* fest werden, sich verdichten, erstarren ♦ *vt* fest machen, verdichten.

solidity [səlid'itē] *n* Festigkeit *f*.

solidly [sâl'idlē] *ad* (*fig*: *support*) einmütig; (: *work*) ununterbrochen.

solid-state [sâl'idstāt'] *a* (*ELEC*) Halbleiter-.

soliloquy [səlil'əkwē] *n* Monolog *m*.

solitaire [sâl'itär] *n* (*CARDS*) Patience *f*; (*gem*) Solitär *m*.

solitary [sâl'itärē] *a* einsam, einzeln; **to be in ~ confinement** (*JUR*) in Einzelhaft sein.

solitude [sâl'ətōōd] *n* Einsamkeit *f*.

solo [sō'lō] *n* Solo *nt*.

soloist [sō'lōist] *n* Solist(in *f*) *m*.

Solomon Islands [sâl'əmən ī'ləndz] *npl* Salomonen *pl*, Salomoninseln *pl*.

solstice [sâl'stis] *n* Sonnenwende *f*.

soluble [sâl'yəbəl] *a* (*substance*) löslich; (*problem*) (auf)lösbar.

solution [səlōō'shən] *n* (*lit*, *fig*) Lösung *f*; (*of mystery*) Erklärung *f*.

solve [sâlv] *vt* (auf)lösen.

solvency [sâl'vənsē] *n* Solvenz *f*; (*FIN*) Zahlungsfähigkeit *f*.

solvent [sâl'vənt] *a* (*FIN*) zahlungsfähig.

solvent abuse *n* Lösungsmittelmißbrauch *m*.

Som. *abbr* (*Brit*) = Somerset.

Somali [sōmâ'lē] *a* somalisch, somali ♦ *n* Somalier(in *f*) *m*, Somali *mf*.

Somalia [sōmâ'lēə] *n* Somalia *nt*.

somber, (*Brit*) **sombre** [sâm'bûr] *a* düster.

some [sum] *a* (*people etc*) einige; (*water etc*) etwas; (*unspecified*) (irgend)ein; (*remarkable*) toll, enorm; **that's ~ house** das ist vielleicht ein Haus; **in ~ form or other** irgendwie; **after ~ time** nach einiger Zeit; **~ day** eines Tages; **at ~ length** ziemlich lang(e); **~ people say that ...** manche Leute sagen, daß ...; **would you like ~ more biscuits?** möchten Sie noch (ein paar) Kekse? ♦ *pron* (*amount*) etwas; (*number*) einige; **could I have ~ of that cheese?** könnte ich etwas von dem Käse haben?

somebody [sum'bâdē] *pron* (irgend) jemand; **~ or other** irgend jemand ♦ *n*: **he is ~** er ist jemand or wer.

someday [sum'dā] *ad* irgendwann.

somehow [sum'hou] *ad* (*in a certain way*) irgendwie; (*for a certain reason*) aus irgendeinem Grunde.

someone [sum'wun] *pron* = **somebody**.

someplace [sum'plās] *ad* (*US*) = **somewhere**.

somersault [sum'ûrsôlt] *n* Purzelbaum *m*; (*fig*, *SPORT*) Salto *m* ♦ *vi* Purzelbäume schlagen; einen Salto machen.

something [sum'thing] *pron* (irgend) etwas; **~ to do** etwas zu tun; **it's ~ of a problem** das ist schon ein Problem ♦ *ad*: **you look ~ like him** du siehst ihm irgendwie ähnlich.

sometime [sum'tīm] *ad* (irgend) einmal; **I'll finish it ~** ich werde es irgendwann fertig haben.

sometimes [sum'tīmz] *ad* manchmal, gelegentlich.

somewhat [sum'wut] *ad* etwas, ein wenig, ein bißchen.

somewhere [sum'wär] *ad* irgendwo; (*to a place*) irgendwohin; **~ else** irgendwo anders, anderswo; (*to a place*) irgendwo andershin, anderswohin.

son [sun] *n* Sohn *m*.

sonar [sō'när] n Sonar(gerät) nt, Echolot nt.
sonata [sənät'ə] n Sonate f.
song [sông] n Lied nt.
songwriter [sông'rī'tûr] n Texter(in f) m und Komponist(in f) m.
sonic [sân'ik] a Schall-.
sonic boom n Überschallknall m.
son-in-law [sun'inlô] n Schwiegersohn m.
sonnet [sân'it] n Sonett nt.
sonny [sun'ē] n (col) Kleine(r) m.
soon [sōōn] ad bald; **too ~** zu früh; **it's too ~ to tell** das kann man jetzt noch nicht sagen; **very/quite ~** sehr/ziemlich bald; **as ~ as possible** so bald wie möglich; **how ~ can you be ready?** wann kannst du fertig sein?; **how ~ can you come back?** wann können Sie zurückkommen?; **see you ~!** bis bald!
sooner [sōō'nûr] ad (time) eher, früher; (for preference) lieber; **no ~** kaum; **no ~ had we left than ...** wir waren gerade gegangen, da ...; **the ~ the better** je früher or eher, desto besser; **no ~ said than done** gesagt, getan.
soot [sōōt] n Ruß m.
soothe [sōōth] vt (person) beruhigen; (pain) lindern.
soothing [sōō'thing] a beruhigend; (for pain) (schmerz)lindernd.
sop [sâp] n (bribe) Schmiergeld nt.
SOP n abbr (= standard operating procedure) normale(s) Betriebsverfahren nt.
sophisticated [səfis'tikātid] a (person) kultiviert, weltgewandt; (machinery) differenziert, hochentwickelt; (plan) ausgeklügelt.
sophistication [səfis'tikā'shən] n Weltgewandtheit f, Kultiviertheit f; (TECH) technische Verfeinerung f.
sophomore [sâf'əmôr] n (US) College-Student(in f) m im 2. Jahr.
soporific [sâpərif'ik] a einschläfernd, Schlaf-.
sopping [sâp'ing] a (very wet) patschnaß, triefend.
soprano [səpran'ō] n Sopran m.
sorbet [sôrbā'] n Fruchteis nt.
sorcerer [sôr'sərûr] n Hexenmeister m.
sordid [sôr'did] a (dirty) schmutzig; (mean) niederträchtig.
sore [sôr] a schmerzend; (point) wund; **~ throat** Halsschmerzen pl; **my eyes are ~, I have ~ eyes** meine Augen tun mir weh; **it's a ~ point** das ist ein wunder Punkt; **to be ~** weh tun; (angry) böse sein ♦ n Wunde f.
sorely [sôr'lē] ad (tempted) stark, sehr.
soreness [sôr'nis] n Schmerzhaftigkeit f, Empfindlichkeit f.
sorrel [sôr'əl] n (BOT) große(r) Sauerampfer m.
sorrow [sâr'ō] n Kummer m, Leid nt.
sorrowful [sâr'ōfəl] a traurig, sorgenvoll.
sorrowfully [sâr'ōfəlē] ad traurig.
sorry [sâr'ē] a traurig, erbärmlich; (condition, tale) traurig; (sight, failure) jämmerlich; **(I'm) ~** es tut mir leid; **I'm ~ to hear that ...** es tut mir leid, daß ...; **I feel ~ for him** er tut mir leid.

sort [sôrt] n Art f, Sorte f; (make: of coffee etc) Sorte f; **what ~ do you want?** welche Sorte möchten Sie?; **what ~ of car?** was für ein Auto?; **I'll do nothing of the ~!** ich werde nichts dergleichen tun!, von wegen! (col); **it's ~ of awkward** (col) es ist ein bißchen peinlich or schwierig ♦ vt (also: **~ out:** papers) sortieren, sichten; (: problems) in Ordnung bringen; (COMPUT) sortieren.
sortie [sôr'tē] n (MIL) Ausfall m; (AVIAT) (Einzel)einsatz m, Feindflug m.
sorting office [sôr'ting ô'fis] n Sortierstelle f.
SOS [es'ō'es'] n SOS nt.
so-so [sō'sō'] ad so(-so) la-la, mäßig.
soufflé [sōōflā'] n Auflauf m, Soufflé nt.
sought [sôt] pt, pp of **seek.**
sought-after [sôt'af'tûr] a begehrt.
soul [sōl] n Seele f; (music) Soul m; **I didn't see a ~** ich habe keine Menschenseele gesehen; **the poor ~ had nowhere to sleep** der Arme hatte keine Bleibe or Unterkunft; **God rest his ~** Gott hab ihn selig.
soul-destroying [sōl'distroiing] a trostlos.
soulful [sōl'fəl] a seelenvoll.
soulless [sōl'lis] a seelenlos, gefühllos.
soul mate n Seelenfreund m.
soul-searching [sōl'sûrching] n: **after much ~** nach reiflicher or ernsthafter Überlegung.
sound [sound] a (healthy) gesund; (safe) sicher, solide; (theory) stichhaltig; (thorough) tüchtig, gehörig; (dependable: person) zuverlässig; (valid: argument, policy, claim, move) vernünftig; **to be of ~ mind** bei klarem Verstand sein; (JUR) im Vollbesitz seiner geistigen Kräfte sein ♦ n (noise) Geräusch nt, Laut m; (GEOG) Meerenge f, Sund m; **I don't like the ~ of it** das klingt gar nicht gut ♦ vt erschallen lassen; (alarm) schlagen; (MED) abhorchen; **to ~ one's horn** hupen ♦ vi (make a ~) schallen, tönen; (seem) klingen; **it ~s as if ...** es hört sich so an or klingt, als ob ...
sound off vi (col: give one's opinions) sich verbreiten or auslassen (about über +acc).
sound out vt (opinion) erforschen; (person) auf den Zahn fühlen (+dat).
sound barrier n Schallmauer f.
sound effect n Toneffekt m.
sound engineer n Toningenieur m.
sounding [soun'ding] n (NAUT etc) Lotung f.
sounding board n (MUS) Resonanzboden m.
soundly [sound'lē] ad (sleep) fest, tief; (beat) tüchtig.
soundproof [sound'prōōf] a (room) schalldicht ♦ vt schalldicht machen.
sound track n Filmmusik f.
sound wave n (PHYS) Schallwelle f.
soup [sōōp] n Suppe f; **in the ~** (col) in der Tinte.
soup kitchen n Volksküche f.
soup plate n Suppenteller m.

soup spoon n Suppenlöffel m.
sour [sou'ûr] a (lit, fig) sauer; **to go** or **turn** ~ (milk, wine) sauer werden; **to go** or **turn** ~ **on sb** (fig) jdn anöden.
source [sôrs] n (lit, fig) Quelle f; **I have it from a reliable** ~ **that** ... ich habe es aus sicherer Quelle, daß ...
source language n (COMPUT) Quellsprache f.
sourness [souûr'nis] n Säure f; (fig) Bitterkeit f.
south [south] n Süden m; (**to the**) ~ **of** im Süden or südlich von; **the S~ of France** Südfrankreich nt ♦ a Süd-, südlich ♦ ad nach Süden, südwärts; **to travel** ~ in südliche Richtung or nach Süden fahren.
South Africa n Südafrika nt.
South African a südafrikanisch ♦ n Südafrikaner(in f) m.
South America n Südamerika nt.
South American a südamerikanisch ♦ n Südamerikaner(in f) m.
southbound [south'bound'] a (in) Richtung Süden; (carriageway) Richtung Süden.
southeast [southêst'] n Südosten m.
Southeast Asia n Südostasien nt.
southerly [suth'ûrlē] a südlich.
southern [suth'ûrn] a südlich, Süd-; **the** ~ **hemisphere** die südliche Halbkugel or Hemisphäre; **to have a** ~ **aspect** Südlage haben.
South Korea n Südkorea nt.
South Pole n Südpol m.
South Sea Islands npl Südseeinseln pl.
South Seas npl Südsee pl.
southward(s) [south'wûrd(z)] ad südwärts, nach Süden.
southwest [southwest'] n Südwesten m.
souvenir [sōōvənēr'] n Andenken nt, Souvenir nt.
sovereign [sáv'rin] n (ruler) Herrscher(in f) m ♦ a (independent) souverän.
sovereignty [sáv'rəntē] n Oberhoheit f, Souveränität f.
soviet [sō'vēit] a sowjetisch.
Soviet Union n Sowjetunion f.
sow n [sou] Sau f ♦ vti irreg [sō] (lit, fig) säen.
sowed [sōd] pt, pp of **sow**.
sown [sōn] pp of **sow**.
soy [soi] n Soja f; ~ **bean** Sojabohne f; ~ **sauce** Sojasoße f.
soya [soi'ə] n (Brit) = **soy**.
spa [spâ] n (spring) Mineralquelle f; (place) Kurort m, Bad nt.
space [spās] n Platz m, Raum m; (outer ~ also) Weltraum m; (length of time) Abstand m; (between words) Zwischenraum m; (COMPUT) Leerzeichen nt; **in a confined** ~ auf engem Raum; **to clear a** ~ **for sth** für etw Platz schaffen; **in a short** ~ **of time** in kurzer Zeit; **(with)in the** ~ **of an hour/ three generations** innerhalb einer Stunde/in drei Generationen.
space out vt Platz lassen zwischen; (typ-

ing) gesperrt schreiben.
space bar n (on typewriter) Leertaste f.
spacecraft [spās'kraft] n Raumschiff nt.
spaceman [spās'man] n, pl **-men** Raumfahrer m.
spaceship [spās'ship] n Raumschiff nt.
space shuttle n Raumfähre f.
spacesuit [spās'sōōt] n Raumanzug m.
spacing [spā'sing] n Abstand m; (also: ~ out) Verteilung f.
spacious [spā'shəs] a geräumig, weit.
spade [spād] n Spaten m.
spades [spādz] npl (CARDS) Pik nt, Schippe f.
spadework [spād'wûrk] n (fig) Vorarbeit f.
spaghetti [spəget'ē] n Spaghetti pl.
Spain [spān] n Spanien nt.
span [span] n (of hand) Spanne f; (of bridge etc) Spannweite f ♦ vt überspannen.
Spaniard [span'yûrd] n Spanier(in f) m.
spaniel [span'yəl] n Spaniel m.
Spanish [span'ish] a spanisch; ~ **omelette** Omelett mit Piment, Paprika und Tomaten ♦ n (language) Spanisch nt; **the** ~ (people) die Spanier pl.
spank [spangk] vt verhauen, versohlen.
spanner [span'ûr] n (Brit) Schraubenschlüssel m.
spar [spâr] n (NAUT) Sparren m ♦ vi (BOXING) einen Sparring machen.
spare [spär] a Ersatz- ♦ n see **spare part** ♦ vt (lives, feelings) verschonen; (trouble) ersparen; **4 to** ~ 4 übrig; **to** ~ **no expense** an nichts sparen, keine Kosten scheuen; **we have no time to** ~ wir haben keine Zeit (mehr); **I've a few minutes to** ~ ich habe ein paar Minuten Zeit; **can you** ~ **the time?** haben Sie Zeit?; **can you** ~ **(me) $10?** kannst du mir 10$ leihen or geben?
spare part n Ersatzteil nt.
spare room n Gästezimmer nt.
spare time n Freizeit f.
spare tire, (Brit) **spare tyre** n (AUT) Ersatzreifen m.
spare wheel n (AUT) Ersatzrad nt.
sparing [spär'ing] a sparsam; **to be** ~ **with** geizen mit.
sparingly [spär'inglē] ad sparsam; (eat, spend etc) in Maßen.
spark [spârk] n Funken m.
spark plug n Zündkerze f.
sparkle [spâr'kəl] n Funkeln nt, Glitzern nt; (gaiety) Lebhaftigkeit f, Schwung m ♦ vi funkeln, glitzern.
sparkling [spâr'kling] a funkelnd, sprühend; (wine) Schaum-; (conversation) spritzig, geistreich.
sparrow [spar'ō] n Spatz m.
sparse [spârs] a, **sparsely** [spârs'lē] ad spärlich, dünn.
spasm [spaz'əm] n (MED) Krampf m; (fig) Anfall m.
spasmodic [spazmâd'ik] a krampfartig, spasmodisch; (fig) sprunghaft.
spastic [spas'tik] a spastisch.

spat [spat] *n* (*US col*) Knatsch *m*, Stunk *m* ♦ *pt, pp of* **spit**.
spate [spāt] *n* (*fig*) Flut *f*, Schwall *m*; **in** ~ (*river*) angeschwollen.
spatial [spā'shəl] *a* räumlich.
spatter [spat'ûr] *n* Spritzer *m* ♦ *vt* bespritzen, verspritzen ♦ *vi* spritzen.
spatula [spach'ələ] *n* Spachtel *m*; (*MED*) Spatel *m*.
spawn [spôn] *vt* laichen; (*pej*) erzeugen.
SPCA *n abbr* (*US*: = *Society for the Prevention of Cruelty to Animals*) Tierschutzverein *m*.
SPCC *n abbr* (*US*: = *Society for the Prevention of Cruelty to Children*) Kinderschutzverein *m*.
speak [spēk] *irreg vt* sprechen, reden; (*truth*) sagen; (*language*) sprechen ♦ *vi* sprechen (*to* mit *or* zu); **to** ~ **one's mind** seine Meinung sagen; ~**ing!** (*on telephone*) am Apparat!; **to** ~ **at a conference/in a debate** bei einer Tagung/Debatte das Wort ergreifen; **he has no money to** ~ **of** er hat so gut wie kein Geld.
speak for *vt fus* sprechen *or* eintreten für; **to** ~ **for sb** (*on behalf of*) in jds Namen (*dat*) sprechen; (*in favour of*) sich für jdn verwenden; **that picture is already spoken for** (*in shop*) das Bild ist schon verkauft *or* schon vergeben.
speak up *vi* lauter sprechen.
speaker [spē'kûr] *n* Sprecher(in *f*) *m*, Redner(in *f*) *m*; **are you a Welsh-**~**?** ist Walisisch Ihre Muttersprache?
speaking [spē'king] *a* sprechend.
-speaking *suff* -sprechend; **German**~ **people** deutsch-sprachige Bevölkerung *f*.
spear [spi'ûr] *n* Speer *m*, Lanze *f*, Spieß *m* ♦ *vt* aufspießen, durchbohren.
spearhead [spēr'hed] *n* Speerspitze *f*; (*MIL*) Angriffsspitze *f*; (*fig*) Bahnbrecher *m* ♦ *vt* (*attack etc*) anführen.
spearmint [spēr'mint] *n* (*BOT etc*) grüne Minze *f*.
special [spesh'əl] *a* besondere(r, s); (*specific, exceptional*) speziell; **nothing** ~ nichts Besonderes ♦ *n* (*RAIL*) Sonderzug *m*.
special agent *n* Agent(in *f*) *m*.
special correspondent *n* Sonderberichterstatter(in *f*) *m*.
special delivery *n* (*MAIL*): **by** ~ per Eilboten.
specialist [spesh'əlist] *n* Fachmann *m*; (*MED*) Spezialist(in *f*) *m*; Facharzt *m*/-ärztin *f*; **a heart** ~ (*MED*) ein Facharzt *or* Spezialist für Herzkrankheiten.
speciality [speshēal'ətē] *n* (*Brit*) = **specialty**.
specialize [spesh'əlīz] *vi* sich spezialisieren (*in* auf +*acc*).
specially [spesh'əlē] *ad* besonders; (*explicitly*) extra, ausdrücklich.
special offer *n* (*COMM*) Sonderangebot *nt*.
special train *n* Sonderzug *m*.
specialty [spesh'əltē] *n* Spezialität *f*; (: *study*)

Spezialgebiet *nt*.
species [spē'shēz] *n* (*pl inv*) Art *f*.
specific [spisif'ik] *a* spezifisch, besondere(r, s); **to be** ~ **to sth** für etw eigentümlich sein.
specifically [spisif'iklē] *ad* genau, spezifisch; (*explicitly*: *state, warn*) ausdrücklich; (*especially*: *design, intend*) speziell.
specifications [spesəfəkā'shənz] *npl* genaue Angaben *pl*; (*TECH*) technische Daten *pl*; (*for building*) Raum- und Materialangaben *pl*, Baubeschreibung *f*.
specify [spes'əfī] *vt* genau angeben ♦ *vi*: **unless otherwise specified** wenn nicht anders angegeben.
specimen [spes'əmən] *n* Probe *f*, Muster *nt*.
specimen copy *n* (*of signature*) Belegexemplar *nt*; (*of publication*) Probeexemplar *nt*.
specimen signature *n* Unterschriftsprobe *f*.
speck [spek] *n* Fleckchen *nt*.
speckled [spek'əld] *a* gesprenkelt.
specs [speks] *npl* (*col*) Brille *f sing*; (*TECH*) technische Daten *pl*.
spectacle [spek'təkəl] *n* (*show*) Schauspiel *nt*; (*sight*) Anblick *m*; *see also* **spectacles**.
spectacles [spek'təkəlz] *npl* Brille *f sing*.
spectacular [spektak'yəlûr] *a* aufsehenerregend, spektakulär.
spectator [spek'tātûr] *n* Zuschauer(in *f*) *m*.
specter [spek'tûr] *n* (*US*) Geist *m*, Gespenst *nt*.
spectra [spek'trə] *npl of* **spectrum**.
spectre [spek'tûr] *n* (*Brit*) = **specter**.
spectrum [spek'trəm] *n, pl* **spectra** Spektrum *nt*.
speculate [spek'yəlāt] *vi* vermuten, spekulieren (*also FIN*).
speculation [spekyəlā'shən] *n* Vermutung *f*, Spekulation *f* (*also FIN*).
speculative [spek'yəlātiv] *a* spekulativ.
speculator [spek'yəlātûr] *n* (*FIN*) Spekulant(in *f*) *m*.
sped [sped] *pt, pp of* **speed**.
speech [spēch] *n* (*language*) Sprache *f*; (*address*) Rede *f*, Ansprache *f*; (*manner of speaking*) Sprechweise *f*.
speech day *n* (*SCH*) (Jahres)schlußfeier *f*.
speech impediment *n* Sprachfehler *m*, Sprachstörung *f*.
speechless [spēch'lis] *a* sprachlos.
speech therapy *n* Sprachheilpflege *f*.
speed [spēd] *n* Geschwindigkeit *f*; (*gear*) Gang *m* ♦ *vi irreg* rasen; (*JUR*) (zu) schnell fahren; (*MOT*) **transmission** Fünfganggetriebe *nt*; **at a** ~ **of 70 km/h** mit 70 Stundenkilometern; **shorthand/typing** ~**s** Silben/Anschläge pro Minute; **the years sped by** die Jahre verlogen *or* vergingen wie im Fluge.
speed up *vt* beschleunigen ♦ *vi* schneller werden *or* fahren.
speedboat [spēd'bōt] *n* Schnellboot *nt*.
speeded [spē'did] *pt, pp of* **speed**.
speedily [spē'dilē] *ad* schnell, schleunigst.

speeding [spē'ding] n Geschwindigkeits-überschreitung f.

speed limit n Geschwindigkeitsbegrenzung f.

speedometer [spēdâm'itûr] n Geschwindig-keitsmesser m.

speed trap n (AUT) Radarfalle f.

speedway [spēd'wā] n (bike racing) Motorradrennstrecke f.

speedy [spē'dē] a schnell, zügig.

spell [spel] n (magic) Bann m, Zauber m; (period of time) Zeit f, Zeitlang f, Weile f; **sunny** ~s Aufheiterungen pl; **rainy** ~s ver-einzelte Schauer pl ♦ vt irreg buchstabieren; (imply) bedeuten; **how do you** ~ ...? wie schreibt man ...?; **how do you** ~ **your name?** wie schreiben Sie sich?; **can you** ~ **it for me?** könn(t)en Sie das bitte buchsta-bieren?

spellbound [spel'bound] a (wie) gebannt.

spelled [speld] pt, pp of **spell**.

spelling [spel'ing] n Buchstabieren nt; **Eng-lish** ~ die englische Rechtschreibung.

spelling mistake n (Recht)schreibfehler m.

spelunker [spēlung'kûr] n (US) Höhlenfor-scher m.

spelt [spelt] pt, pp of **spell**.

spend [spend] vt irreg (money) ausgeben; (time) verbringen; **to** ~ **time/money/effort on sth** (devote to) Zeit/Geld/Mühe für etw aufbringen.

spending [spen'ding] n Ausgaben pl; **govern-ment** ~ Etat m.

spending money n Taschengeld nt.

spending power n Kaufkraft f.

spendthrift [spend'thrift] n Verschwender(in f) m.

spent [spent] a (patience) erschöpft; (car-tridge, bullets) verbraucht ♦ pt, pp of **spend**.

sperm [spûrm] n (BIOL) Samenflüssigkeit f.

sperm whale n Pottwal m.

spew [spyōō] vt erbrechen.

sphere [sfēr] n (globe) Kugel f; (fig) Sphäre f, Gebiet nt.

spherical [sfär'ikəl] a kugelförmig.

sphinx [sfingks] n Sphinx f.

spice [spīs] n Gewürz nt ♦ vt würzen.

spiciness [spī'sēnis] n Würze f.

spick-and-span [spik'ənspan'] a blitzblank.

spicy [spī'sē] a würzig, pikant (also fig).

spider [spī'dûr] n Spinne f; ~'s web Spinnen-gewebe f, Spinnennetz nt.

spidery [spī'dûrē] a (writing) krakelig.

spiel [spēl] n (col) Blabla nt.

spike [spīk] n Dorn m, Spitze f; (ELEC) Über-schwingspitze f ♦ vt: **to** ~ **a story** (in news-paper) eine Story in der Schublade ver-schwinden lassen.

spikes [spīks] npl (SPORT) Spikes pl.

spiky [spī'kē] a (bush, animal) stach(e)lig; (branch) dornig.

spill [spil] irreg vt verschütten; (blood) ver-gießen ♦ vi sich ergießen; **to** ~ **the beans** (col) alles ausplaudern.

spill out vi sich ergießen.

spill over vi überlaufen; (fig) sich ausbrei-ten.

spilled [spild] pt, pp of **spill**.

spilt [spilt] pt, pp of **spill**.

spin [spin] n Umdrehung f; (trip in car) Spa-zierfahrt f; (AVIAT) (Ab)trudeln nt; (on ball) Drall m ♦ irreg vt (thread) spinnen; (like top) schnell drehen, (herum)wirbeln; (clothes) schleudern; (ball, coin) (hoch)werfen ♦ vi sich drehen.

spin out vt in die Länge ziehen; (story) ausmalen.

spinach [spin'ich] n Spinat m.

spinal [spī'nəl] a spinal, Rückgrat-, Rückenmark-.

spinal column n Wirbelsäule f.

spinal cord n Rückenmark nt.

spindly [spind'lē] a spindeldürr.

spin-dry [spindrī'] vt schleudern.

spin-dryer [spindrī'ûr] n Wäscheschleuder f.

spine [spīn] n Rückgrat nt; (thorn) Stachel m.

spine-chilling [spīn'chiling] a schaurig, gruse-lig.

spineless [spīn'lis] a (lit, fig) rückgratlos.

spinet [spin'it] n Spinett nt.

spinner [spin'ûr] n (of thread) Spinner(in f) m.

spinning [spin'ing] n (of thread) (Fa-den)spinnen nt.

spinning wheel n Spinnrad nt.

spin-off [spin'ôf] n Nebenprodukt nt.

spinster [spin'stûr] n unverheiratete Frau f; (pej) alte Jungfer f.

spiral [spī'rəl] n Spirale f ♦ a gewunden, spi-ralförmig, Spiral- ♦ vi sich ringeln; **the in-flationary** ~ die Inflationsspirale f; **price** ~ Preisspirale f.

spiral staircase n Wendeltreppe f.

spire [spī'ûr] n Turm m.

spirit [spir'it] n Geist m; (humor, mood) Stimmung f; (courage) Mut m; (verve) Elan m; (alcohol) Alkohol m; **Holy S**~ Hei-lige(r) Geist m; **community** or **public** ~ Ge-meinschaftssinn m; ~s pl (alcohol) Spirituo-sen pl; (state of mind) Stimmung f, Laune f; **in good** ~s gut aufgelegt.

spirit duplicator n Hektograph m.

spirited [spir'itid] a beherzt.

spirit level n Wasserwaage f.

spiritual [spir'ichōōəl] a geistig, seelisch; (REL) geistlich ♦ n Spiritual nt.

spiritualism [spir'ichōōəlizəm] n Spiritismus m.

spit [spit] n (for roasting) (Brat)spieß m; (spittle) Speichel m; (saliva) Spucke f ♦ vi irreg spucken; (rain) sprühen; (make a sound) zischen; (cat) fauchen.

spite [spīt] n Gehässigkeit f ♦ vt ärgern, krän-ken; **in** ~ **of** trotz (+gen or dat).

spiteful [spīt'fəl] a gehässig; (tongue, re-mark) boshaft, gemein.

spitting [spit'ing] n: "~ **prohibited**"

„spucken verboten" ♦ *a*: **to be the** ~ **image of sb** jdm wie aus dem Gesicht geschnitten sein, jdm zum Verwechseln ähnlich sehen.

splash [splash] *n* Spritzer *m*; (*of color*) (Farb)fleck *m* ♦ *vt* bespritzen ♦ *vi* spritzen; **to** ~ **paint on the floor** den (Fuß)boden mit Farbe bespritzen.

splashdown [splash'doun] *n* (*SPACE*) Wasserung *f*.

spleen [splēn] *n* (*ANAT*) Milz *f*.

splendid [splen'did] *a*, **splendidly** [splen'didlē] *ad* glänzend, großartig.

splendor, (*Brit*) **splendour** [splen'dûr] *n* Pracht *f*.

splice [splīs] *vt* spleißen.

splint [splint] *n* Schiene *f*.

splinter [splin'tûr] *n* Splitter *m* ♦ *vi* (zer)splittern.

splinter group *n* Splittergruppe *f*.

split [split] *n* Spalte *f*; (*fig*) Spaltung *f*; (*division*) Trennung *f* ♦ *irreg vt, pt, pp* **split** spalten ♦ *vi* (*divide*) reißen; sich spalten; (*col: depart*) abhauen; **to do the** ~**s** (einen) Spagat machen; **he** ~ **his head open** er hat sich den Kopf aufgeschlagen; **to** ~ **the difference** (*fig*) sich auf halbem Wege einigen.

split up *vi* sich trennen ♦ *vt* aufteilen, teilen.

split-level [split'lev'əl] *a*: ~ **house** Haus *nt* mit Zwischenstock.

split peas *npl* getrocknete (halbe) Erbsen *pl*.

split personality *n* gespaltene Persönlichkeit *f*.

split second *n* Bruchteil *m* einer Sekunde.

splitting [split'ing] *a* (*headache*) rasend, wahnsinnig.

splutter [splut'ûr] *vi* (*Brit*) spritzen; (: *person, engine*) stottern.

spoil [spoil] *irreg vt* (*ruin*) verderben; (*child*) verwöhnen, verziehen; (*ballot paper*) ungültig machen ♦ *vi* (*food*) verderben; **to be** ~**ing for a fight** Streit suchen.

spoiled [spoild] *pt, pp of* **spoil**.

spoiler [spoi'lûr] *n* (*AUT*) Spoiler *m*.

spoils [spoilz] *npl* Beute *f*.

spoilsport [spoil'spôrt] *n* Spielverderber *m*.

spoilt [spoilt] *pt, pp of* **spoil**.

spoke [spōk] *n* Speiche *f* ♦ *pt of* **speak**.

spoken [spō'kən] *pp of* **speak**.

spokesman [spōks'mən] *n, pl* -**men** Sprecher *m*, Vertreter *m*.

spokeswoman [spōks'wōōmən] *n, pl* -**women** Sprecherin *f*.

sponge [spunj] *n* Schwamm *m*; (*COOK: also:* ~ **cake**) Rührkuchen *m* ♦ *vt* mit dem Schwamm abwaschen ♦ *vi* auf Kosten leben (*on gen*).

sponge bag *n* (*Brit*) Kulturbeutel *m*, Waschbeutel *m*.

sponge cake *n* Rührkuchen *m*.

sponger [spun'jûr] *n* (*col*) Schmarotzer *m*.

spongy [spun'jē] *a* schwammig.

sponsor [spân'sûr] *n* (*for membership*) Bürge

m, Bürgin *f*; (*in advertising*) Sponsor(in *f*) *m*; (*of enterprise, bill*) Förderer *m*, Förderin *f* ♦ *vt* bürgen für; fördern; **I** ~**ed him at 25¢ a mile** (*for fund-raising*) ich habe ihn mit 25 Cents pro Meile gesponsert.

sponsorship [spân'sûrship] *n* Bürgschaft *f*; (*public*) Schirmherrschaft *f*.

spontaneity [spântənē'itē] *n* Spontanität *f*.

spontaneous [spântā'nēəs] *a*, **spontaneously** [spântā'nēəslē] *ad* spontan.

spooky [spōō'kē] *a* (*col*) gespenstisch.

spool [spōōl] *n* Spule *f*, Rolle *f*.

spoon [spōōn] *n* Löffel *m*.

spoon-feed [spōōn'fēd] *vt irreg* (*lit*) mit dem Löffel füttern; (*fig*) hochpäppeln.

spoonful [spōōn'fōōl] *n* Löffel(voll) *m*.

sporadic [spôrad'ik] *a* vereinzelt, sporadisch.

sport [spôrt] *n* Sport *m*; (*fun, amusement*) Spaß *m*; (*person*) feine(r) Kerl *m*; **indoor/outdoor** ~**s** Hallensport *m*/Freiluftsport *m*; **to say sth in** ~ etw im *or* zum Spaß sagen.

sporting [spôr'ting] *a* (*fair*) sportlich, fair.

sports car [spôrts kâr] *n* Sportwagen *m*.

sport(s) coat *n* (*US*) Sportjackett *nt*.

sports field, (*Brit*) **sports ground** *n* Sportplatz *m*.

sports jacket *n* (*Brit*) Sportjackett *nt*.

sportsman [spôrts'mən] *n, pl* -**men** Sportler *m*; (*fig*) anständige(r) Kerl *m*.

sportsmanship [spôrts'mənship] *n* Sportlichkeit *f*; (*fig*) Anständigkeit *f*.

sports page *n* Sportseite *f*.

sportswear [spôrts'weûr] *n* Sportkleidung *f*.

sportswoman [spôrts'wōōmən] *n, pl* -**women** Sportlerin *f*.

sporty [spôr'tē] *a* sportlich.

spot [spât] *n* Punkt *m*; (*dirty*) Fleck(en) *m*; (*place*) Stelle *f*, Platz *m*; (*MED*) Pickel *m*, Pustel *f*; (*small amount*) Schluck *m*, Tropfen *m*; (*for advert: on TV*) Werbespot *m*; **to pay cash on the** ~ (*US*) auf der Stelle *or* sofort (bar) bezahlen ♦ *vt* erspähen; (*mistake*) bemerken; **to do sth on the** ~ etw auf der Stelle tun; **to put sb on the** ~ jdn in Verlegenheit bringen.

spot check *n* Stichprobe *f*.

spotless [spât'lis] *a*, **spotlessly** [spât'lislē] *ad* fleckenlos.

spotlight [spât'līt] *n* Scheinwerferlicht *nt*; (*lamp*) Scheinwerfer *m*.

spot price *n* Kassapreis *m*.

spotted [spât'id] *a* gefleckt; (*dress*) gepunktet.

spotty [spât'ē] *a* (*face*) pickelig.

spouse [spous] *n* Gatte *m*; Gattin *f*.

spout [spout] *n* (*of pot*) Tülle *f*; (*jet*) Wasserstrahl *m* ♦ *vi* speien, spritzen.

sprain [sprān] *n* Verrenkung *f* ♦ *vt* verrenken.

sprang [sprang] *pt of* **spring**.

sprawl [sprôl] *n* (*of city*) Ausbreitung *f*; **urban** ~ wildwuchernde Ausbreitung des Stadtgebietes ♦ *vi* sich strecken; **to send sb** ~**ing** jdn zu Boden werfen.

sprawling [sprôl'ing] *a* sich ausdehnend.

spray [sprā] *n* Spray *nt*; (*off sea*) Gischt *f*; (*perfume* ~) Zerstäuber *m*; (*implement*) Sprühdose *f*; (*of flowers*) Zweig *m* ♦ *cpd* (*deodorant*) Sprüh- ♦ *vt* besprühen, sprayen.

spread [spred] *n* (*extent*) Verbreitung *f*; (*of wings*) Spannweite *f*; (*col: meal*) Schmaus *m*; (*for bread*) Aufstrich *m*; (*in newspaper etc: two pages*) Doppelseite *f* ♦ *vt irreg, pt, pp* **spread** ausbreiten; (*scatter*) verbreiten; (*butter*) streichen; (*payments*) verteilen; **a full-page/double** ~ ein ganz-/zweiseitiger Bericht; **middle-age** ~ Fülligkeit *f*.

spread-eagled [spred'ēgəld] *a*: **to be** *or* **lie** ~ mit ausgestreckten Armen und Beinen daliegen.

spreadsheet [spred'shēt] *n* (*COMPUT*) Kalkulationsprogramm *nt*.

spree [sprē] *n* lustige(r) Abend *m*; (*shopping*) Einkaufsbummel *m*; **to go out on a** ~ einen draufmachen.

sprig [sprig] *n* kleine(r) Zweig *m*.

sprightly [sprīt'lē] *a* munter, lebhaft.

spring [spring] *n* (*leap*) Sprung *m*; (*metal*) Feder *f*; (*season*) Frühling *m*; (*water*) Quelle *f*; (*bounciness*) Federung *f*; **to walk with a** ~ **in one's step** mit federnden Schritten gehen; **in** ~, **in the** ~ im Frühling ♦ *irreg vi* (*leap*) springen; **to** ~ **into action** aktiv werden ♦ *vt*: **to** ~ **a leak** (*pipe etc*) undicht werden; **he sprang the news on me** er hat mich mit der Nachricht überrascht.

spring up *vi* (*problem*) entstehen, auftauchen.

springboard [spring'bôrd] *n* Sprungbrett *nt*.

spring-clean [spring'klēn'] *vt* Frühjahrsputz machen in (+*dat*).

spring-cleaning [spring'klē'ning] *n* Frühjahrsputz *m*.

springiness [spring'ēnis] *n* Elastizität *f*.

spring onion *n* Frühlingszwiebel *f*.

springtime [spring'tīm] *n* Frühling *m*.

springy [spring'ē] *a* federnd, elastisch.

sprinkle [spring'kəl] *n* Prise *f* ♦ *vt* (*salt*) streuen; (*liquid*) sprenkeln.

sprinkler [spring'klûr] *n* (*for lawn etc*) (Rasen)sprenger *m*; (*for fire-fighting*) Sprinkler *m*.

sprinkling [spring'kling] *n* Spur *f*, ein bißchen; (*of water*) ein paar Tropfen; (*of salt, sugar*) Prise *f*.

sprint [sprint] *n* (*race*) Sprint *m*; **the 200-meter** ~ der 200-m-Lauf ♦ *vi* sprinten.

sprinter [sprin'tûr] *n* Sprinter(in *f*) *m*.

sprite [sprīt] *n* Elfe *f*, Kobold *m*.

sprocket [språk'it] *n* (*on printer etc*) Stachelband *nt*.

sprocket feed *n* Stachelbandführung *f*.

sprout [sprout] *vi* sprießen ♦ *n see* **Brussels sprout**.

spruce [sproos] *n* Fichte *f* ♦ *a* schmuck, adrett.

spruce up *vt* (*tidy*) auf Vordermann bringen (*col*); **to** ~ **o.s. up** sein Äußeres pflegen; (*dress up*) sich in Schale werfen.

sprung [sprung] *pp of* **spring**.

spry [sprī] *a* flink, rege.

SPUC *n abbr* (= *Society for the Protection of Unborn Children*) Gesellschaft *f* zum Schutze ungeborener Kinder.

spud [spud] *n* (*col*) Kartoffel *f*.

spun [spun] *pt, pp of* **spin**.

spur [spûr] *n* Sporn *m*; (*fig*) Ansporn *m* ♦ *vt* (*also*: ~ **on**) (*fig*) anspornen; **on the** ~ **of the moment** spontan.

spurious [spyōor'ēəs] *a* falsch, unecht, Pseudo-.

spurn [spûrn] *vt* verschmähen.

spurt [spûrt] *n* (*jet*) Strahl *m*; (*acceleration*) Spurt *m* ♦ *vt* spritzen ♦ *vi* (*jet*) steigen; (*liquid*) schießen; (*run*) spurten; **to put in** *or* **on a** ~ (*lit, fig*) einen Spurt vorlegen.

sputter [sput'ûr] *vi* (*US*) spritzen; (: *person, engine*) stottern.

spy [spī] *n* Spion(in *f*) *m* ♦ *cpd* (*film, story*) Spionage- ♦ *vi* spionieren ♦ *vt* erspähen; **to** ~ **on sb** jdm nachspionieren.

spying [spī'ing] *n* Spionage *f*.

sq. *abbr* (*MATH etc*: = *square*) q.

Sq. *abbr* (*in address*: = *Square*) Pl.

squabble [skwâb'əl] *n* Zank *m* ♦ *vi* sich zanken.

squabbling [skwâb'ling] *n* Zankerei *f*.

squad [skwâd] *n* (*MIL*) Abteilung *f*.

squad car *n* (*for police*) Streifenwagen *m*.

squadron [skwâd'rən] *n* (*cavalry*) Schwadron *f*; (*NAUT*) Geschwader *nt*; (*air force*) Staffel *f*.

squalid [skwâl'id] *a* schmutzig, verkommen.

squall [skwôl] *n* Bö *f*, Windstoß *m*.

squally [skwô'lē] *a* (*weather*) stürmisch; (*wind*) böig.

squalor [skwâl'ûr] *n* Verwahrlosung *f*, Schmutz *m*.

squander [skwân'dûr] *vt* verschwenden.

square [skwär] *n* (*MATH*) Quadrat *nt*; (*open space*) Platz *m*; (*TECH*) Winkel *m*; (*col: person*) Spießer *m*; (*US: block of houses*) Block *m* ♦ *a* viereckig, quadratisch; (*fair*) ehrlich, reell; (*meal*) reichlich; (*col: ideas, tastes*) spießig ♦ *ad* (*exactly*) direkt, gerade ♦ *vt* (*arrange*) ausmachen, aushandeln; (*MATH*) ins Quadrat erheben; (*bribe*) schmieren; (*reconcile*) in Einklang bringen ♦ *vi* (*agree*) übereinstimmen; **we're back to** ~ **one** (*fig*) jetzt sind wir wieder da, wo wir angefangen haben; **all** ~ quitt; **2 meters** ~ 2 Meter im Quadrat; **2** ~ **meters** 2 Quadratmeter; ~ **bracket** eckige Klammer *f*; **to get one's accounts** ~ abrechnen; **I'll** ~ **it with him** (*col*) ich werde es mit ihm abrechnen.

squarely [skwär'lē] *ad* fest, gerade; (*honestly, fairly*) ehrlich, gerade.

square root *n* Quadratwurzel *f*, zweite Wurzel *f*.

squash [skwâsh] *n* (*vegetable*) (Pâtisson-)Kürbis *m*; (*Brit: drink*) Saft *m* ♦ *vt* zerquetschen.

squat [skwât] *a* untersetzt, gedrungen ♦ *vi*

hocken; (*on property*) besetzen.

squatter [skwât'ûr] *n* (*on land*) Squatter *m*, Siedler *m* ohne Rechtstitel; (*in house*) Squatter *m*, Hausbesetzer *m*.

squaw [skwô] *n* Squaw *f*.

squawk [skwók] *n* Kreischen *nt* ♦ *vi* kreischen.

squeak [skwēk] *n* Gequiek(s)e *nt*; (*of hinge, wheel, shoes etc*) Quietschen *nt*; (*of mouse etc*) Piepsen *nt* ♦ *vi* quiek(s)en; quietschen; piepsen.

squeaky [skwē'kē] *a* quiek(s)end; quietschend.

squeal [skwēl] *n* schrille(r) Schrei *m*; (*of brakes etc*) Quietschen *nt* ♦ *vi* schrill schreien.

squeamish [skwē'mish] *a* empfindlich; **that made me ~** davon wurde mir übel.

squeamishness [skwē'mishnis] *n* Überempfindlichkeit *f*.

squeeze [skwēz] *n* Drücken *nt*; (*hug*) Umarmung *f*; (*credit ~*) Kreditbeschränkung *f*; **a ~ of lemon** ein Schuß Zitronensaft ♦ *vt* pressen, drücken; (*orange*) auspressen ♦ *vi*: **to ~ past sth** sich an etw vorbeidrücken; **to ~ under sth** sich unter etw durchzwängen.

squeeze out *vt* ausquetschen.

squelch [skwelch] *vi* platschen.

squid [skwid] *n* Tintenfisch *m*.

squiggle [skwig'əl] *n* Schnörkel *m*.

squint [skwint] *n* Schielen *nt* ♦ *vi* schielen; (*in strong light*) blinzeln; **to ~ at sth** auf etw schielen.

squirm [skwûrm] *vi* sich winden.

squirrel [skwûr'əl] *n* Eichhörnchen *nt*.

squirt [skwûrt] *n* Spritzer *m*, Strahl *m* ♦ *vti* spritzen.

Sr *abbr* (= *senior*) Sen., sen.; (*REL* = *sister*) Schw.

Sri Lanka [srē lângk'ə] *n* Sri Lanka *nt*.

SRO *abbr* (*US:* = *standing room only*) nur Stehplätze.

SS *abbr* = *steamship*.

SSA *n abbr* (*US:* = *Social Security Administration*) Sozialversicherungsträger *m*.

SST *n abbr* (*US:* = *supersonic transport*) Überschallverkehr *m*.

St *abbr* (= *Street*) Str.; (= *Saint*) Skt., St.

stab [stab] *n* (*blow*) Stoß *m*, Stich *m*; (*col: try*) Versuch *m* ♦ *vt* erstechen; **to ~ sb to death** jdn erstechen.

stabbing [stab'ing] *n* Messerstecherei *f*; **there's been a ~** es hat eine Messerstecherei gegeben ♦ *a* (*pain*) stechend.

stability [stəbil'ətē] *n* Festigkeit *f*, Stabilität *f*.

stabilization [stābiləzā'shən] *n* Festigung *f*, Stabilisierung *f*.

stabilize [stā'bəlīz] *vt* festigen, stabilisieren ♦ *vi* sich stabilisieren.

stabilizer [stā'bəlīzûr] *n* (*NAUT. CHEM*) Stabilisator *m*; (*AVIAT*) Stabilisierungsfläche *f*.

stable [stā'bəl] *n* Stall *m*; **riding ~s** Reitstall *m* ♦ *vt* im Stall unterbringen ♦ *a* fest, stabil; (*person*) gefestigt.

stableboy [stā'bəlboi] *n* Stallbursche *m*.

staccato [stəkâ'tō] *a* stakkato.

stack [stak] *n* Stoß *m*, Stapel *m*; (*col*) Haufen *m* ♦ *vt* (auf)stapeln.

stadium [stā'dēəm] *n* Stadion *nt*.

staff [staf] *n* (*stick, MIL*) Stab *m*; (*personnel*) Personal *nt*; (*Brit SCH*) Lehrkräfte *pl*; **the teaching ~** das Lehrpersonal, der Lehrkörper (*form*) ♦ *vt* (*with people*) besetzen.

Staffs *abbr* (*Brit*) = Staffordshire.

stag [stag] *n* Hirsch *m*; (*Brit FIN*) Spekulant *m*.

stage [stāj] *n* Bühne *f*; (*of journey*) Etappe *f*; (*degree*) Stufe *f*; (*point*) Stadium *nt* ♦ *vt* (*put on*) aufführen; (*play*) inszenieren; (*demonstration*) veranstalten; **in ~s** etappenweise; **in the early/final ~s** im Anfangs-/Endstadium; **to go through a difficult ~** eine schwierige Phase durchmachen.

stagecoach [stāj'kōch] *n* Postkutsche *f*.

stage door *n* Bühneneingang *m*.

stagehand [stāj'hand] *n* Bühnenarbeiter(in *f*) *m*.

stage-manage [stāj'man'ij] *vt* (*lit*) Inspizient sein bei; (*fig: demonstration, argument*) inszenieren.

stage manager *n* Spielleiter *m*, Intendant *m*.

stagger [stag'ûr] *vi* wanken, taumeln ♦ *vt* (*amaze*) verblüffen; (*hours*) staffeln.

staggering [stag'ûring] *a* unglaublich.

stagnant [stag'nənt] *a* stagnierend; (*water*) stehend.

stagnate [stag'nāt] *vi* (*economy, pool*) stagnieren; (*mind*) einrosten.

stagnation [stagnā'shən] *n* Stillstand *m*, Stagnation *f*.

stag party *n* Herrenabend *m*.

staid [stād] *a* gesetzt.

stain [stān] *n* Fleck *m*; (*coloring for wood*) Beize *f* ♦ *vt* beflecken, Flecken machen auf (+*acc*); beizen.

stained-glass window [stānd'glas win'dō] *n* bunte(s) Glasfenster *nt*.

stainless [stān'lis] *a* (*steel*) rostfrei, nichtrostend.

stain remover *n* Fleckentferner *m*.

stair [stär] *n* (Treppen)stufe *f*; *see also* **stairs**.

staircase [stär'kās] *n* Treppenhaus *nt*, Treppe *f*.

stairs [stärz] *npl* Treppe *f*.

stairway [stär'wā] *n* Treppenaufgang *m*.

stairwell [stär'wel] *n* Treppenauge *nt*.

stake [stāk] *n* (*post*) Pfahl *m*, Pfosten *m*; (*money*) Einsatz *m* ♦ *vt* (*bet: money*) setzen; (*also:* **~ out**) abstecken; **to be at ~** auf dem Spiel stehen; **to have a ~ in sth** einen Anteil an etw (*dat*) haben; **to ~ a claim to sth** sich (*dat*) ein Anrecht auf etw (*acc*) sichern.

stalactite [stəlak'tīt] *n* Stalaktit *m*.

stalagmite [stəlag'mīt] *n* Stalagmit *m*.

stale [stāl] *a* alt; (*beer*) schal; (*bread*) altbacken.

stalemate [stāl'māt] *n* (*CHESS*) Patt *nt*; (*fig*) Stillstand *m*.

stalk [stók] *n* Stengel *m*, Stiel *m* ♦ *vt* (*game*) sich anpirschen an (+*acc*), jagen ♦ *vi* (*walk*) stolzieren.

stall [stól] *n* (*in stable*) Stand *m*, Box *f*; (*in market*) (Verkaufs)stand *m*; **a newspaper/ flower** ~ (*Brit*) ein Zeitungs-/Blumenstand *m*; *see also* **stalls** ♦ *vt* (*AUT*) (den Motor) abwürgen ♦ *vi* (*AUT*) stehenbleiben; (*avoid*) Ausflüchte machen, ausweichen.

stallholder [stól'hōldûr] *n* (*Brit*) Standbesitzer(in *f*) *m*.

stallion [stal'yən] *n* Hengst *m*.

stalls [stólz] *npl* (*THEAT*) Parkett *nt*.

stalwart [stól'wûrt] *a* standhaft ♦ *n* treue(r) Anhänger *m*.

stamen [stā'mən] *n* Staubgefäß *nt*, Staubfaden *m*.

stamina [stam'inə] *n* Durchhaltevermögen *nt*, Zähigkeit *f*.

stammer [stam'ûr] *n* Stottern *nt* ♦ *vti* stottern, stammeln.

stamp [stamp] *n* Briefmarke *f*; (*with foot*) Stampfen *nt*; (*for document*) Stempel *m* ♦ *vi* stampfen ♦ *vt* (*mark*) stempeln; (*mail*) frankieren; (*foot*) stampfen mit; **a self-addressed ~ed envelope**, (*Brit*) **a ~ed addressed envelope** ein frankierter Rückumschlag.

stamp out *vt* (*fire*) austreten; (*crime*) ausrotten; (*opposition*) unterdrücken, zunichte machen.

stamp album *n* Briefmarkenalbum *nt*.

stamp collecting *n* Briefmarkensammeln *nt*.

stampede [stampēd'] *n* (*of cattle*) wilde Flucht *f*; (*of people*) Massensturm *m* (*on* auf +*acc*) ♦ *vi* durchgehen; (*crowd*) losstürmen (*for* auf +*acc*) ♦ *vt* in Panik versetzen.

stamp machine *n* Briefmarkenautomat *m*.

stance [stans] *n* (*posture*) Haltung *f*, Stellung *f*; (*opinion*) Einstellung *f*.

stand [stand] *n* Standort *m*, Platz *m*; (*for objects*) Gestell *nt*; (*seats*) Tribüne *f*; **to make a ~** Widerstand leisten; **to take a ~ on an issue** zu einem Thema einen Standpunkt vertreten *or* haben; **a music ~** ein Notenständer *m* ♦ *irreg vi* stehen; (*rise*) aufstehen; (*decision*) feststehen; **to ~ still** still stehen; **to let sth ~ as it is** etw bestehenlassen; **as things ~** nach Lage der Dinge; **nothing ~s in our way** es steht uns nichts im Weg; **it ~s to reason** es ist einleuchtend ♦ *vt* setzen, stellen; (*endure*) aushalten; (*person*) ausstehen, leiden können; (*nonsense*) dulden; **to ~ sb a drink/meal** jdm einen Drink/ein Essen spendieren; **the company will have to ~ the loss** die Firma wird den Verlust hinnehmen müssen; **I can't ~ him** ich kann ihn nicht ausstehen; **to ~ guard** *or* **watch** (*MIL*) Wache halten *or* stehen.

stand aside *vi* (*lit*) zur Seite treten; (*fig*) zurücktreten.

stand by *vi* (*be ready*) bereitstehen ♦ *vt fus* (*opinion*) treu bleiben (+*dat*).

stand down *vi* (*withdraw*) verzichten, zurücktreten; (*MIL*) aufgelöst werden; (*JUR*) den Zeugenstand verlassen.

stand for *vt fus* (*represent*) stehen für; (*permit, tolerate*) hinnehmen; (*Brit: be candidate for*) kandidieren für.

stand in for *vt fus* einspringen für.

stand out *vi* (*be prominent*) hervorstechen.

stand up *vi* (*rise*) aufstehen.

stand up for *vt fus* sich einsetzen für.

stand up to *vt fus*: **to ~ up to sth/sb** einer Sache gewachsen sein/sich jdm gegenüber behaupten.

stand-alone [stand'əlōn'] *a* (*COMPUT*) betriebssystemunabhängig.

standard [stan'dûrd] *n* (*average, the norm*) Norm *f*; (*degree, level*) Niveau *nt*; (*flag*) Standarte *f*, Fahne *f*; **the gold ~** (*FIN*) der Goldstandard; **~ of living** Lebensstandard *m*; **high/low ~** hohes/niedriges Niveau; **below** *or* **not up to ~** (*work*) unter der Norm; **to apply a double ~** verschiedene Maßstäbe anlegen; **to be** *or* **come up to ~** den Anforderungen genügen *or* entsprechen ♦ *a* (*size etc*) Normal-, Durchschnitts-; (*usual, customary*) üblich.

standardization [standûrdəzā'shən] *n* Vereinheitlichung *f*.

standardize [stan'dûrdīz] *vt* vereinheitlichen, normen.

standard lamp *n* (*Brit*) Stehlampe *f*.

standard model *n* Standardmodell *nt*.

standard practice *n* übliche(s) Verfahren *nt*.

standard rate *n* (Steuer)normalsatz *m*.

standard time *n* Normalzeit *f*.

standby [stand'bī] *n* Reserve *f*; **to be on ~** in Bereitschaft sein; (*doctor*) Bereitschaftsdienst haben.

standby flight *n* Standby-Flug *m*.

standby generator *n* Reserve- *or* Ersatzgenerator *m*.

standby passenger *n* (*AVIAT*) Passagier, der mit einem Standby-Ticket reist.

stand-in [stand'in] *n* Ersatz(mann) *m*, Hilfskraft *f*; (*FILM*) Double *nt*.

standing [stan'ding] *a* (*erect*) stehend; (*permanent*) ständig, dauernd; (*invitation*) offen; (*rule*) bestehend; (*army*) stehend; (*grievance*) alt, langjährig; **to receive a ~ ovation** stürmischen Beifall ernten; **a ~ joke** ein Standardwitz *m* ♦ *n* (*duration*) Dauer *f*; (*reputation*) Ansehen *nt*; **a man of some ~** ein angesehener Mann; **of 6 months' ~** seit 6 Monaten.

standing jump *n* Sprung *m* aus dem Stand.

standing order *n* (*at bank*) Dauerauftrag *m*.

standing orders *npl* (*MIL*) Vorschrift *f*.

standing room *n* Stehplatz *m*.

standoffish [standôf'ish] *a* zurückhaltend,

sehr reserviert.

standpat [stand'pat] *a* (*US*) konservativ.

standpipe [stand'pīp] *n* Steigrohr *nt*.

standpoint [stand'point] *n* Standpunkt *m*.

standstill [stand'stil] *n*: **to be at a** ~ stillstehen; **to come to a** ~ zum Stillstand kommen.

stank [stangk] *pt of* **stink**.

stanza [stan'zə] *n* (*verse*) Strophe *f*; (*poem*) Stanze *f*.

staple [stā'pəl] *n* (*clip*) Krampe *f*; (*in paper*) Heftklamme *f*; (*article*) Haupterzeugnis *nt* ♦ *a* (*crop, industry, chief product*) Grund-, Haupt- ♦ *vt* (*fest*)klammern.

stapler [stā'plûr] *n* Heftmaschine *f*.

star [stâr] *n* Stern *m*; (*person*) Star *m*; **four-~ hotel** Vier-Sterne-Hotel *nt*; **4-~ petrol** (*Brit*) Super *nt* ♦ *vi* die Hauptrolle spielen.

star attraction *n* Hauptattraktion *f*.

starboard [stâr'bûrd] *n* Steuerbord *nt* ♦ *a* Steuerbord-.

starch [stârch] *n* Stärke *f* ♦ *vt* stärken.

starchy [stâr'chē] *a* (*food*) stärkehaltig; (*formal*) steif.

stardom [stâr'dəm] *n* Berühmtheit *f*.

stare [stär] *n* starre(r) Blick *m* ♦ *vi* starren (*at* auf +*acc*).

stare at *vt* anstarren.

starfish [stâr'fish] *n* Seestern *m*.

staring [stär'ing] *a* (*eyes*) starrend.

stark [stârk] *a* öde; (*simplicity*) schlicht; (*reality, poverty, truth*) nackt; (*color*) eintönig ♦ *ad*: ~ **naked** splitternackt.

starless [stâr'lis] *a* sternlos.

starlet [stâr'lit] *n* (*CINE*) (Film)sternchen *nt*, Starlet *nt*.

starlight [stâr'līt] *n* Sternenlicht *nt*.

starling [stâr'ling] *n* Star *m*.

starlit [stâr'lit] *a* sternklar.

starring [stâr'ing] *a* mit ... in der Hauptrolle.

starry [stâr'ē] *a* Sternen-.

starry-eyed [stâr'ēid] *a* (*innocent, idealistic*) blauäugig; (*gullible*) arglos; **to be** ~ (*from wonder*) große Augen machen; (*from love*) verzückt sein.

star-studded [stâr'studid] *a* mit Spitzenstars; **a** ~ **cast** eine Starbesetzung.

start [stârt] *n* Beginn *m*, Anfang *m*, Start *m*; (*SPORT*) Start *m*; (*lead, advantage*) Vorsprung *m*; **at the** ~ am Anfang, zu Beginn; **for a** ~ (*to begin with*) fürs erste; **to make an early** ~ frühzeitig aufbrechen; **the thieves had 3 hours'** ~ die Diebe hatten 3 Stunden Vorsprung; **to give a** ~ zusammenfahren; **to give sb a** ~ jdm zu einem guten Start verhelfen, jdm eine Starthilfe geben ♦ *vt* in Gang setzen, anfangen; (*car*) anlassen; (*found: business, newspaper*) gründen; **to** ~ **a fire** ein Feuer anzünden; (*arson*) ein Feuer legen ♦ *vi* anfangen; (*car*) anspringen; (*on journey*) aufbrechen; (*SPORT*) starten; **to** ~ (**off**) **with** ... (*firstly*) zunächst einmal ...; (*at the beginning*) fürs erste ...

start off *vi* anfangen; (*begin moving*)

losgehen/-fahren.

start over *vi* (*US*) wieder anfangen, noch (ein)mal von vorn anfangen.

start up *vi* anfangen; (*startled*) auffahren ♦ *vt* beginnen; (*car*) anlassen; (*engine*) starten.

starter [stâr'tûr] *n* (*AUT*) Anlasser *m*; (*for race*) Starter *m*; **for ~s** (*to begin with*) fürs erste.

starting point [stâr'ting point] *n* Ausgangspunkt *m*.

starting price [stâr'ting prīs] *n* (*horse-racing*) letzte(r) Kurs *m* vor dem Start.

startle [stâr'təl] *vt* erschrecken.

startling [stâr'ling] *a* erschreckend.

starvation [stârvā'shən] *n* Verhungern *nt*; **to die of** ~ verhungern; ~ **wages** Hungerlöhne *pl*.

starve [stârv] *vi* verhungern ♦ *vt* verhungern lassen; **to be ~d of** *or* (*US*) **for affection** unter Mangel an Liebe leiden.

starve out *vt* aushungern.

starving [stâr'ving] *a* hungernd.

state [stāt] *n* (*condition*) Zustand *m*; (*POL*) Staat *m*; (*col: anxiety*) (schreckliche) Verfassung *f*; (*pomp*) Aufwand *m*, Pomp *m*; **to lie in** ~ (feierlich) aufgebahrt sein; ~ **of emergency** Notstand *m*; ~ **of mind** Verfassung *f*, Geisteszustand *m*; **the** ~ **of the nation** die Lage der Nation ♦ *vt* erklären; (*facts*) angeben.

state control *n* staatliche Kontrolle *f*.

stated [stā'tid] *a* festgesetzt.

State Department *n* (*US*) Außenministerium *nt*.

state highway *n* (*US*) ≈ Landstraße *f*.

stateless [stāt'lis] *a* staatenlos.

stateliness [stāt'lēnis] *n* Pracht *f*, Würde *f*.

stately [stāt'lē] *a* würdevoll, erhaben.

statement [stāt'mənt] *n* Aussage *f*; (*POL*) Erklärung *f*; **official** ~ (amtliche) Erklärung *f*; ~ **of account, bank** ~ (*FIN*) (Konto)auszug *m*.

state-owned [stāt'ōnd'] *a* verstaatlicht, staatseigen.

States [stāts] *npl*: **the** ~ die Staaten.

state secret *n* Staatsgeheimnis *nt*.

statesman [stāts'mən] *n, pl* **-men** Staatsmann *m*.

statesmanship [stāts'mənship] *n* Staatskunst *f*.

static [stat'ik] *n* Statik *f* ♦ *a* statisch.

station [stā'shən] *n* (*RAIL etc*) Bahnhof *m*; (*police* ~, *fire* ~ *etc*) Wache *f*; (*US: gas* ~) Tankstelle *f*; (*in society, MIL*) Stellung *f*; (*RAD, TV*) Sender *m*; **battle** (*US*) *or* **action** (*Brit*) ~**s!** Stellung!; (*fig*) auf die Plätze! ♦ *vt* aufstellen; **to be ~ed in X** (*MIL*) in X stationiert sein.

stationary [stā'shənārē] *a* stillstehend; (*car*) parkend.

stationer [stā'shənûr] *n* Schreibwarenhändler *m*.

stationery [stā'shənārē] *n* (*writing paper*)

Briefpapier *nt*; (*writing materials*) Schreibwaren *pl*.

station master *n* Bahnhofsvorsteher *m*.

station wagon *n* (*US*) Kombiwagen *m*.

statistic [stətis'tik] *n* Statistik *f*.

statistical [stətis'tikəl] *a* statistisch.

statistics [stətis'tiks] *n* (*science*) Statistik *f*.

statue [stach'ōō] *n* Statue *f*.

statuesque [stachōōesk'] *a* statuenhaft.

statuette [stachōōet'] *n* Statuette *f*.

stature [stach'ûr] *n* Wuchs *m*, Statur *f*; (*fig*) Größe *f*.

status [stā'təs] *n* Stellung *f*; (*legal ~, social ~*) Status *m*; **the ~ quo** der Status quo.

status line *n* (*COMPUT*) Statuszeile *f*, Auskunftszeile *f*.

status symbol *n* Statussymbol *nt*.

statute [stach'ōōt] *n* Gesetz *nt*.

statute book *n* Gesetzbuch *nt*.

statutory [stach'ōōtôrē] *a* gesetzlich; **~ meeting** Gründungsversammlung *f*.

staunch [stônch] *a* treu, zuverlässig; (*Catholic*) standhaft, erz- ♦ *vt* (*flow*) stauen; (*blood*) stillen.

stave off [stāv ôf] *vt* (*attack*) abwehren; (*threat*) abwenden.

stay [stā] *n* Aufenthalt *m*; (*support*) Stütze *f*; (*for tent*) Schnur *f*; **~ of execution** (*JUR*) Aussetzung *f*; (*fig*) Galgenfrist *f* ♦ *vi* bleiben; (*reside*) wohnen; **to ~ put** an Ort und Stelle bleiben; **to ~ with friends** bei Freunden untergebracht sein; **to ~ the night** übernachten.

stay behind *vi* zurückbleiben.

stay in *vi* (*at home*) zu Hause bleiben.

stay on *vi* (*continue*) länger bleiben.

stay out *vi* (*strikers*) weiterstreiken.

stay up *vi* (*at night*) aufbleiben.

staying power [stā'ing pou'ûr] *n* Stehvermögen *nt*, Durchhaltevermögen *nt*, Ausdauer *f*.

STD *n abbr* (= *sexually transmitted disease*) *Krankheit, die durch sexuelle Kontakte verbreitet wird*; (*Brit*: = *subscriber trunk dialling*) Selbstwählfernverkehr *m*.

stead [sted] *n*: **in sb's ~** an jds Stelle.

steadfast [sted'fast] *a* standhaft, treu.

steadily [sted'ilē] *ad* stetig, regelmäßig.

steadiness [sted'ēnis] *n* Festigkeit *f*; (*fig*) Beständigkeit *f*.

steady [sted'ē] *a* (*firm*) fest, stabil; (*regular*) gleichmäßig; (*reliable*) zuverlässig, beständig; (*hand*) ruhig; (*job, boyfriend*) fest ♦ *vt* festigen; **to ~ o.s.** sich stützen (*on or against* auf *or* gegen +*acc*).

steak [stāk] *n* Steak *nt*; (*fish*) Filet *nt*.

steal [stēl] *irreg vti* stehlen ♦ *vi* (*move quietly*) sich stehlen; **to ~ away** *or* **off** sich weg- *or* davonschleichen.

stealth [stelth] *n* Heimlichkeit *f*.

stealthy [stel'thē] *a* verstohlen, heimlich.

steam [stēm] *n* Dampf *m* ♦ *vt* (*COOK*) im Dampfbad erhitzen ♦ *vi* dampfen; (*ship*) dampfen, fahren; **to let off ~** (*lit, fig*) Dampf ablassen; (*fig also*) sich (*dat*) Luft machen; **under one's own ~** (*fig*) allein, ohne Hilfe; **to run out of ~** (*fig: person*) den Schwung verlieren.

steam up *vi* (*window*) beschlagen ♦ *vt*: **to get ~ed up about sth** (*fig*) sich über etw aufregen.

steam engine *n* Dampfmaschine *f*.

steamer [stē'mûr] *n* Dampfer *m*; (*COOK*) Dampfkochtopf *m*.

steam iron *n* Dampfbügeleisen *nt*.

steamroller [stēm'rōlûr] *n* Dampfwalze *f*.

steamy [stē'mē] *a* dampfig.

steel [stēl] *n* Stahl *m* ♦ *a* Stahl-; (*fig*) stählern.

steel band *n* *Band aus der Karibik, die Schlaginstrumente aus Metall benutzt.*

steel industry *n* Stahlindustrie *f*.

steel mill *n* Stahlwalzwerk *nt*.

steelworks [stēl'wûrks] *n sing or pl* Stahlwerke *pl*.

steely [stē'lē] *a* (*determination*) eisern, ehern; (*gaze*) hart, stählern; **~-eyed** mit hartem *or* stählernem Blick.

steep [stēp] *a* steil; (*price*) gepfeffert ♦ *vt* einweichen.

steeple [stē'pəl] *n* Kirchturm *m*.

steeplechase [stē'pəlchās] *n* Hindernisrennen *nt*.

steeplejack [stē'pəljak] *n* Turmarbeiter *m*, Klettermaxe *m* (*col*).

steeply [stēp'lē] *ad* steil.

steepness [stēp'nis] *n* Steilheit *f*.

steer [stēr] *n* Mastochse *m* ♦ *vti* steuern; (*car etc*) lenken; **to ~ clear of sb/sth** (*fig*) jdm aus dem Wege gehen/etw meiden.

steering [stēr'ing] *n* (*AUT*) Steuerung *f*.

steering column *n* Lenksäule *f*.

steering committee *n* vorbereitende(r) Ausschuß *m*.

steering wheel *n* Steuer- *or* Lenkrad *nt*.

stellar [stel'ûr] *a* Stern(en)-.

stem [stem] *n* (*BIOL*) Stengel *m*, Stiel *m*; (*of glass*) Stiel *m* ♦ *vt* aufhalten.

stem from *vt fus* abstammen von.

stench [stench] *n* Gestank *m*.

stencil [sten'səl] *n* Schablone *f*; (*paper*) Matrize *f* ♦ *vt* (auf)drucken.

stenographer [stənåg'rəfûr] *n* (*US*) Stenotypist(in *f*) *m*, Stenograph(in *f*) *m*.

step [step] *n* Schritt *m*; (*stair*) Stufe *f*; **out of ~ (with)** nicht im Gleichklang (mit); **to keep in ~ (with)** (*lit*) Tritt halten (mit); (*fig*) Schritt halten (mit); **to take ~s** Schritte unternehmen; **to take ~s to solve a problem** Maßnahmen ergreifen, um ein Problem zu lösen; **~ by ~** (*also fig*) Schritt für Schritt; *see also* **steps** ♦ *vi* treten, schreiten.

step down *vi* (*fig*) abtreten.

step in *vi* eintreten; (*fig*) eingreifen.

step over *vt fus*: **to ~ over sth** über etw treten.

step up *vt* steigern.

stepbrother [step'bruthûr] *n* Stiefbruder *m*.

stepchild [step'chīld] *n, pl* **-children** Stiefkind

nt.

stepdaughter [step'dôtûr] *n* Stieftochter *f.*
stepfather [step'fâthûr] *n* Stiefvater *m.*
stepladder [step'ladûr] *n* Trittleiter *f.*
stepmother [step'muthûr] *n* Stiefmutter *f.*
steppe [step] *n* Steppe *f.*
stepping stone [step'ing stōn] *n* Stein *m;* *(fig)* Sprungbrett *nt.*
stepsister [step'sistûr] *n* Stiefschwester *f.*
stepson [step'sun] *n* Stiefsohn *m.*
stereo [stär'ēō] *n* Stereoanlage *f;* **in ~** in Stereo.
stereophonic [stärēəfân'ik] *a* stereophonisch.
stereotype [stär'ēətīp] *n* Prototyp *m ♦ vt* stereotypieren; *(fig)* stereotyp machen.
sterile [stär'əl] *a* steril, keimfrei; *(person)* unfruchtbar; *(after operation)* steril.
sterility [stəril'ətē] *n* Unfruchtbarkeit *f,* Sterilität *f.*
sterilization [stärələzā'shən] *n* Sterilisation *f,* Sterilisierung *f.*
sterilize [stär'əlīz] *vt* sterilisieren.
sterling [stûr'ling] *a* (*FIN*) Sterling-; *(silver)* von Standardwert; *(character)* bewährt, gediegen; **in pounds ~** in Pfund Sterling.
sterling area *n* Sterlingblock *m.*
stern [stûrn] *a* streng ♦ *n* Heck *nt.*
sternly [stûrn'lē] *ad* streng.
sternness [stûrn'nis] *n* Strenge *f.*
sternum [stûr'nəm] *n* Brustbein *nt,* Sternum *nt.*
steroid [stär'oid] *n* Steroid *nt.*
stethoscope [steth'əskōp] *n* Stethoskop *nt,* Hörrohr *nt.*
stew [stōō] *n* Eintopf *m ♦ vti* schmoren.
steward [stōō'ûrd] *n* Steward *m;* *(in club)* Kellner *m;* *(organizer)* Verwalter *m;* *(shop ~)* Gewerkschaftsvertreter *m.*
stewardess [stōō'ûrdis] *n* Stewardeß *f.*
stewed fruit [stōōd frōōt] *n* Obstkompott *nt,* Kompott *nt.*
stewing meat [stōō'ing mēt] *n* (*Brit*) = **stew meat.**
stew meat *n* (*US*) Rindfleisch *nt* für Eintopf.
stewpan [stōō'pan] *n* (*US*) (große(r)) Kochtopf *m.*
St. Ex. *abbr* (= *Stock Exchange*) Börse *f.*
stg *abbr* = **sterling.**
stick [stik] *n* Stock *m,* Stecken *m;* *(of chalk etc)* Stück *nt ♦ irreg vt* (*stab*) stechen; *(fix)* stecken; *(put)* stellen; *(gum)* (an)kleben; *(col: tolerate)* vertragen ♦ *vi* (*stop*) steckenbleiben; *(get stuck)* klemmen; *(hold fast)* kleben, haften; **to ~ to** (*one's word, promise*) halten, treubleiben (+*dat*); *(principles*) treubleiben (+*dat*); **it stuck in my mind** es ist mir im Gedächtnis haftengeblieben.
stick around *vi* (*col*) (da/hier) bleiben.
stick out *vi* (*project*) hervorstehen aus ♦ *vt:* **to ~ it out** (*col*) es durchstehen *or* aushalten.
stick up *vi* (*project*) in die Höhe stehen.
stick up for *vt fus* (*defend*) eintreten für.
sticker [stik'ûr] *n* Klebezettel *m,* Aufkleber *m.*

sticking plaster [stik'ing plas'tûr] *n* (*Brit*) Heftpflaster *nt.*
stickleback [stik'əlbak] *n* Stichling *m.*
stickler [stik'lûr] *n* Pedant *m* (*for* in +*acc*).
stick-up [stik'up] *n* (*col*) (Raub)überfall *m.*
sticky [stik'ē] *a* klebrig; *(atmosphere)* stickig.
stiff [stif] *a* steif; *(difficult)* schwierig, hart; *(paste)* dick, zäh; *(drink)* stark; **to have a ~ neck/back** einen steifen Hals/Rücken haben; **the door's ~** die Tür klemmt.
stiffen [stif'ən] *vt* versteifen, (ver)stärken ♦ *vi* sich versteifen.
stiffness [stif'nis] *n* Steifheit *f.*
stifle [stī'fəl] *vt* (*yawn etc*) unterdrücken.
stifling [stīf'ling] *a* (*atmosphere*) drückend.
stigma [stig'mə] *n* (*disgrace*) Stigma *nt.*
stile [stīl] *n* Steige *f.*
stiletto [stilet'ō] *n* (*Brit: also:* **~ heel**) Pfennigabsatz *m.*
still [stil] *a* still; *(Brit: orange juice etc)* ohne Kohlensäure; **keep ~!** halt(e) still! ♦ *n* (*CINE*) Standfoto *nt ♦ ad* (*immer*) noch; *(anyhow)* immerhin; **he ~ hasn't arrived** er ist immer noch nicht angekommen.
stillborn [stil'bôrn] *a* totgeboren.
still life *n* Stilleben *nt.*
stillness [stil'nis] *n* Stille *f.*
stilt [stilt] *n* Stelze *f.*
stilted [stil'tid] *a* gestelzt.
stimulant [stim'yələnt] *n* Anregungsmittel *nt,* Stimulanz *nt;* *(fig)* Ansporn *m.*
stimulate [stim'yəlāt] *vt* anregen, stimulieren.
stimulating [stim'yəlāting] *a* anregend, stimulierend.
stimulation [stimyəlā'shən] *n* Anregung *f,* Stimulation *f.*
stimulus [stim'yələs] *n, pl* **stimuli** [stim'yəlī] Anregung *f,* Reiz *m.*
sting [sting] *n* Stich *m;* (*col*) Trick *m ♦ irreg vi* stechen; *(on skin)* brennen; **my eyes are ~ing** meine Augen brennen ♦ *vt* stechen; *(jellyfish etc)* verbrennen.
stingily [stin'jilē] *ad* knickerig, geizig.
stinginess [stin'jēnis] *n* Geiz *m.*
stinging nettle [sting'ing net'əl] *n* Brennessel *f.*
stingy [stin'jē] *a* geizig, knauserig; **to be ~ with** (**one's praise/money**) mit (Lob/Geld) knausern.
stink [stingk] *n* Gestank *m ♦ vi irreg* stinken.
stinker [stingk'ûr] *n* (*col: person*) gemeine(r) Hund *m;* (: *problem*) böse Sache *f.*
stinking [sting'king] *a* (*fig*) widerlich ♦ *ad:* **~ rich** steinreich.
stint [stint] *n* Pensum *nt;* *(period)* Betätigung *f ♦ vt* einschränken, knapphalten; **to do one's ~** seine Arbeit leisten *or* tun.
stipend [stī'pend] *n* Gehalt *nt.*
stipulate [stip'yəlāt] *vt* festsetzen.
stipulation [stipyəlā'shən] *n* Bedingung *f;* *(act)* Festsetzung *f.*
stir [stûr] *n* Bewegung *f;* (*COOK*) Rühren *nt;* *(sensation)* Aufsehen *nt ♦ vt* (um)rühren ♦ *vi* sich rühren; **to give sth a ~** etw rühren;

to cause a ~ Aufsehen erregen.
stir up vt (mob) aufhetzen; (fire) entfachen; (mixture) umrühren; (dust) aufwirbeln; **to ~ things up** Ärger machen.
stirring [stûr'ing] a ergreifend.
stirrup [stûr'əp] n Steigbügel m.
stitch [stich] n (with needle) Stich m; (MED) Faden m; (of knitting) Masche f; (pain) Stich m, Stechen nt ♦ vt nähen.
stoat [stōt] n Wiesel nt.
stock [stâk] n Vorrat m; (COMM) (Waren)lager nt; (live~) Vieh nt; (COOK) Brühe f; (FIN) Grundkapital nt; (RAIL: also: **rolling ~**) rollende(s) Material nt; (descent, origin) Abstammung f ♦ a stets vorrätig; (standard) Normal-; (fig: response, arguments, excuse, greeting) Standard- ♦ cpd (COMM: goods, size) Standard- ♦ vt versehen, versorgen; (in shop) führen; **in ~** auf Vorrat; **out of ~** nicht vorrätig; **to have sth in ~** etw auf Vorrat haben; **~s and shares** (Aktien und) Wertpapiere pl; **government ~** Staatsanleihe f; **to take ~** Inventur machen; (fig) Bilanz ziehen.
stock up vi Reserven anlegen (with von).
stockade [stâkād'] n Palisade f; (US MIL) Gefängnis nt.
stockbroker [stâk'brōkûr] n Börsenmakler m.
stock control n Bestandsüberwachung f.
stock cube n (Brit COOK) Brühwürfel m.
stock exchange n Börse f.
stockholder [stâk'hōldûr] n Aktionär(in f) m.
Stockholm [stâk'hōm] n Stockholm nt.
stocking [stâk'ing] n Strumpf m.
stock-in-trade [stâk'intrād'] n (lit, fig) Handwerkszeug nt; (stock) Warenbestand m.
stockist [stâk'ist] n (Brit) Händler m.
stock market n Börse f, Effektenmarkt m.
stock phrase n Standardsatz m.
stockpile [stâk'pīl] n Vorrat m; **nuclear ~** Kernwaffenvorräte pl ♦ vt aufstapeln.
stockroom [stâk'rōōm] n Lager(raum m) nt.
stocktaking [stâk'tāking] n (Brit) Inventur f, Bestandsaufnahme f.
stocky [stâk'ē] a untersetzt.
stodgy [stâj'ē] a füllend, stopfend; (fig) langweilig, trocken.
stoic [stō'ik] n Stoiker m.
stoical [stō'ikəl] a stoisch.
stoicism [stō'əsizəm] n Stoizismus m; (fig) Gelassenheit f.
stoke [stōk] vt schüren.
stoker [stō'kûr] n Heizer m.
stole [stōl] n Stola f ♦ pt of **steal**.
stolen [stō'lən] a gestohlen ♦ pp of **steal**.
stolid [stâl'id] a schwerfällig; (silence) stur.
stomach [stum'ək] n Bauch m, Magen m; **I have no ~ for it** das ist nichts für mich ♦ vt vertragen.
stomachache [stum'əkāk] n Magen- or Bauchschmerzen pl.
stomach pump n Magenpumpe f.
stomach ulcer n Magengeschwür nt.
stomp [stâmp] vi: **to ~ in/out** etc herein-/

hineinsta(m)pfen, heraus-/hinaussta(m)pfen.
stone [stōn] n Stein m; (seed) Stein m, Kern m; (Brit: weight) = 6.35 kg; **within a ~'s throw of the station** nur einen (Katzen)sprung vom Bahnhof entfernt ♦ a steinern, Stein-; **the S~ Age** die Steinzeit ♦ vt entkernen; (kill) steinigen.
stone-cold [stōn'kōld'] a eiskalt.
stone-deaf [stōn'def'] a stocktaub.
stonemason [stōn'māsən] n Steinmetz m.
stonework [stōn'wûrk] n Mauerwerk nt.
stony [stō'nē] a steinig.
stood [stood] pt, pp of **stand**.
stool [stōōl] n Hocker m.
stoop [stōōp] vi sich bücken; **to ~ to sth/doing sth** (fig) sich zu etw herablassen or hergeben/sich dazu herablassen or hergeben, etw zu tun.
stop [stâp] n Halt m; (bus-~) Haltestelle f; (punctuation) Punkt m ♦ vt stoppen, anhalten; (engine, machine) abstellen; (bring to end) aufhören (mit), sein lassen; (prevent) verhindern; (tooth) füllen, plombieren ♦ vi aufhören; (clock) stehenbleiben; (remain) bleiben; **to ~ doing sth** aufhören, etw zu tun; **to ~ sb (from) doing sth** jdn davon abhalten or daran hindern, etw zu tun; **~ it!** laß das!, hör auf!; **to ~ dead** plötzlich aufhören, innehalten.
stop by vi kurz vorbeikommen or vorbeischauen.
stop in vi (at home) zu Hause bleiben.
stop off vi kurz haltmachen.
stop out vi (of house) ausbleiben.
stop over vi übernachten, über Nacht bleiben; (AVIAT) zwischenlanden.
stop up vt (hole) zustopfen, verstopfen.
stopcock [stâp'kâk] n Absperrhahn m.
stopgap [stâp'gap] n (person) Lückenbüßer m; (scheme) Notlösung f; (measures, solution) Überbrückungsmaßnahme f.
stop lights npl (AUT) Bremslichter pl.
stopover [stâp'ōvûr] n (on journey) Zwischenaufenthalt m.
stoppage [stâp'ij] n (An)halten nt; (traffic) Verkehrsstockung f; (strike) Arbeitseinstellung f.
stopper [stâp'ûr] n Propfen m, Stöpsel m.
stopping [stâp'ing] n: **"no ~"** (US AUT) „Halteverbot".
stop-press [stâp'pres'] n letzte Meldung f.
stopwatch [stâp'wâch] n Stoppuhr f.
storage [stôr'ij] n Lagerung f.
storage capacity n (of computer) Speicherkapazität f.
storage heater n (Brit) (Nachtstrom)-speicherheizung f.
store [stôr] n Vorrat m; (place) Lager nt, Warenhaus nt; (large shop) Kaufhaus nt ♦ vt lagern; (in filing system) lagern, aufbewahren, speichern; (COMPUT) (ab)speichern; **~s** pl (supplies) Vorräte pl; **who knows what is in ~ for us?** wer weiß, was uns bevorsteht?; **to set great/little ~ by sth**

viel/wenig von etw halten, einer Sache *(dat)* viel/wenig Bedeutung beimessen.

store up *vt* sich eindecken mit.

storehouse [stôr'hous] *n* Lager(haus) *nt*.

storekeeper [stôr'kēpûr] *n (shopkeeper)* Ladenbesitzer(in *f)* *m*, Geschäftsinhaber(in *f)* *m*.

storeroom [stôr'rōōm] *n* Lagerraum *m*, Vorratsraum *m*; *(junk room)* Rumpelkammer *f*.

storey [stôr'ē] *n (Brit)* Stock *m*, Stockwerk *nt*.

stork [stôrk] *n* Storch *m*.

storm [stôrm] *n (lit, fig)* Sturm *m* ♦ *vti* stürmen; **to take by** ~ *(MIL, fig)* im Sturm erobern.

storm cloud *n* Gewitterwolke *f*.

storm door *n* äußere Windfangtür *f*.

stormy [stôr'mē] *a* stürmisch.

story [stôr'ē] *n* Geschichte *f*, Erzählung *f*; *(lie)* Märchen *nt*; *(US: floor)* Stock *m*, Stockwerk *nt*; **newspaper** ~ Artikel *m*.

storybook [stôr'ēbōōk] *n* Geschichtenbuch *nt*.

storyteller [stôr'ētelûr] *n* Geschichtenerzähler(in *f)* *m*.

stout [stout] *a (bold)* mannhaft, tapfer; *(too fat)* beleibt, korpulent.

stoutness [stout'nis] *n* Festigkeit *f*; *(of body)* Korpulenz *f*.

stove [stōv] *n* (Koch)herd *m*; *(for heating)* Ofen *m*; **gas/electric** ~ *(cooker)* Gas-/Elektroherd *m*; *(heater)* Gasofen *m/* elektrische(r) Heizkörper *m*.

stow [stō] *vt* verstauen.

stowaway [stō'əwā] *n* blinde(r) Passagier *m*.

straddle [strad'əl] *vt (horse, fence)* rittlings sitzen auf *(+dat)*; *(fig)* überbrücken.

strafe [strāf] *vt* beschießen, bombardieren.

straggle [strag'əl] *vi (branches etc)* wuchern; *(people)* nachhinken.

straggler [strag'lûr] *n* Nachzügler *m*.

straggling [strag'ling], **straggly** [strag'lē] *a (hair)* zottig.

straight [strāt] *a* gerade; *(honest)* offen, ehrlich; *(in order)* in Ordnung; *(drink)* pur, unverdünnt; *(continuous, direct)* ununterbrochen; *(plain, uncomplicated)* einfach; *(THEAT: part, play)* ernsthaft; *(person: conventional)* etabliert, spießig *(pej)*; *(: heterosexual)* normal ♦ *ad (direct)* direkt, geradewegs ♦ *n (SPORT)* Gerade *f*; **to be (all)** ~ *(tidy)* in Ordnung sein; *(clarified)* (völlig) geklärt sein; **our team had ten** ~ **wins** unsere Mannschaft gewann zehnmal hintereinander; **I went** ~ **home** ich bin direkt nach Haus(e) gegangen; ~ **away** sofort, direkt nacheinander; ~ **on** geradeaus.

straighten [strā'tən] *vt (also:* ~ **out)** *(lit)* gerade machen; *(fig)* in Ordnung bringen, klarstellen; **to** ~ **things out** *(clarify)* Klarheit in die Sache bringen.

straight-faced [strāt'fāst] *a, ad* ohne eine Miene zu verziehen.

straightforward [strātfôr'wûrd] *a* einfach, unkompliziert.

strain [strān] *n* Belastung *f*; *(streak, trace)* Zug *m*; *(of music)* Fetzen *m*; *(breed: of animals)* Rasse *f*; *(lineage)* Abstammung *f*, Geschlecht *nt*; *(of virus)* Art *f*; *(of plants)* Sorte *f*; **she's under a lot of** ~ sie ist stark beansprucht ♦ *vt* überanstrengen; *(stretch)* anspannen; *(muscle)* zerren; *(filter)* (durch)seihen; *(meaning)* dehnen; **don't** ~ **yourself** überanstrenge dich nicht ♦ *vi (make effort)* sich anstrengen.

strained [strānd] *a (laugh)* gezwungen; *(relations)* gespannt.

strainer [strā'nûr] *n* Sieb *nt*.

strait [strāt] *n* Straße *f*, Meerenge *f*; **to be in dire** ~**s** *(fig)* in großen Nöten sein, in einer ernsten Notlage sein.

straitened [strāt'ənd] *a (circumstances)* beschränkt.

strait-jacket [strāt'jakit] *n* Zwangsjacke *f*.

strait-laced [strāt'lāst] *a* engherzig, streng.

strand [strand] *n (lit, fig)* Faden *m*; *(of hair)* Strähne *f* ♦ *vt:* **to be** ~**ed** *(lit, fig)* gestrandet sein.

strange [strānj] *a* fremd; *(unusual)* merkwürdig, seltsam.

strangely [strānj'lē] *ad* fremd; merkwürdig; ~ **enough** merkwürdigerweise.

strangeness [strānj'nis] *n* Fremdheit *f*.

stranger [strān'jûr] *n* Fremde(r) *mf*; **I'm a** ~ **here** ich bin hier fremd.

strangle [strang'gəl] *vt* erdrosseln, erwürgen.

stranglehold [strang'gəlhōld] *n (fig)* Umklammerung *f*.

strangulation [stranggyəlā'shən] *n (act)* Erwürgen *nt*, Erdrosseln *nt*; *(being strangled)* Ersticken *nt*.

strap [strap] *n* Riemen *m*; *(on clothes)* Träger *m* ♦ *vt (fasten)* festschnallen.

strap-hanging [strap'hanging] *n* Pendeln *nt*.

strapless [strap'lis] *a (bra, dress)* trägerlos, schulterfrei.

strapping [strap'ing] *a* stramm.

Strasbourg [stras'bûrg] *n* Straßburg *nt*.

stratagem [strat'əjəm] *n (MIL)* Kriegslist *f*; *(artifice)* List *f*.

strategic [strətē'jik] *a*, **strategically** [strətē'jikəlē] *ad* strategisch.

strategist [strat'ijist] *n* Stratege *m*.

strategy [strat'ijē] *n* Kriegskunst *f*; *(fig)* Strategie *f*.

stratosphere [strat'əsfēr] *n* Stratosphäre *f*.

stratum [strat'əm] *n* Schicht *f*.

straw [strô] *n* Stroh *nt*; *(single stalk, drinking* ~) Strohhalm *m* ♦ *a* Stroh-; **that's the last** ~! das ist der Gipfel!

strawberry [strô'bärē] *n* Erdbeere *f*.

stray [strā] *n* verirrte(s) Tier *nt* ♦ *vi* herumstreunen; *(wander: person)* sich verirren; *(speaker)* abschweifen ♦ *a (animal)* verirrt; *(thought)* zufällig.

streak [strēk] *n* Streifen *m*; *(in character)* Einschlag *m*; *(in hair)* Strähne *f*; **a winning/losing** ~ eine Glücks-/Pechsträhne; ~ **of bad luck** Pechsträhne *f* ♦ *vt* streifen.

streaky [strē'kē] *a* gestreift; (*Brit*: *bacon*) durchwachsen.

stream [strēm] *n* (*brook*) Bach *m*; (*fig*) Strom *m*; (*flow of liquid*) Strom *m*, Flut *f* ♦ *vi* strömen, fluten; **against the ~** gegen den Strom.

streamer [strē'mûr] *n* (*pennon*) Wimpel *m*; (*of paper*) Luftschlange *f*.

streamline [strēm'līn] *vt* windschlüpfrig machen, Stromlinienform geben (+*dat*); (*fig*) rationalisieren.

streamlined [strēm'līnd] *a* stromlinienförmig; (*effective*) rationell.

street [strēt] *n* Straße *f*; **the back ~s** die Seitensträßchen *pl*; **to walk the ~s** (*homeless*) obdachlos sein; (*as prostitute*) auf den Strich gehen (*col*).

streetcar [strēt'kâr] *n* (*US*) Straßenbahn *f*.

street light *n* Straßenlaterne *f*.

street lighting *n* Straßenbeleuchtung *f*.

street market *n* Straßenmarkt *m*.

street plan *n* Stadtplan *m*.

streetsweeper [strēt'swēp'ûr] *n* (*US*) Straßenkehrer(in *f*) *m*.

streetwise [strēt'wīz] *a* (*col*): **to be ~** wissen, wo es lang geht.

strength [strengkth] *n* Stärke *f* (*also fig*); (*of person, feelings*) Kraft *f*; (*of chemical solution*) Konzentration *f*; (*of wine*) Schwere *f*; **on the ~ of sth** aufgrund einer Sache (*gen*); **to be up to/below ~** (die) volle Stärke/nicht die volle Stärke haben.

strengthen [strengk'thən] *vt* (ver)stärken.

strenuous [stren'yōōəs] *a* anstrengend; (*opposition*) heftig; (*efforts, resistance*) unermüdlich.

strenuously [stren'yōōəslē] *ad* angestrengt.

stress [stres] *n* Druck *m*; (*mental*) Streß *m*; (*GRAM*) Betonung *f*; (*emphasis*) Betonung *f*, Akzent *m* ♦ *vt* betonen; **to be under ~** großen Belastungen ausgesetzt sein; (*as regards work*) unter Streß stehen, im Streß sein; **to lay great ~ on sth** großen Wert auf etw (*acc*) legen.

stressful [stres'fəl] *a* (*job*) anstrengend, stark beanspruchend.

stretch [strech] *n* (*of river, countryside*) Stück *nt*; (*of road*) Strecke *f*; (*of time*) Zeit *f*, Zeitraum *m*, Zeitspanne *f* ♦ *vt* ausdehnen, strecken ♦ *vi* sich erstrecken; (*person*) sich strecken; **at a ~** (*continuously*) ununterbrochen; **to ~ one's legs** (*walk*) sich (*dat*) die Beine or Füße vertreten (*col*); **to ~ (to)** (*money, food*) reichen (für).

stretch out *vi* sich ausstrecken ♦ *vt* ausstrecken.

stretcher [strech'ûr] *n* Tragbahre *f*.

stretcher-bearer [strech'ûrbârûr] *n* Krankenträger *m*.

stretch marks *npl* Dehnungsstreifen *pl*; (*through pregnancy*) Schwangerschaftsstreifen *pl*.

strewn [strōōn] *a*: **~ with** übersät mit.

stricken [strik'ən] *a* (*person*) befallen, ergrif-

fen; (*city, country*) heimgesucht; **~ with grief** untröstlich, tieftraurig.

strict [strikt] *a* (*exact*) genau; (*severe*) streng; (*order, rule, discipline, ban*) strikt; **in ~ confidence** streng vertraulich.

strictly [strikt'lē] *ad* streng, genau; **~ speaking** streng or genau genommen; **~ confidential** privat or streng vertraulich; **~ between ourselves** ... ganz unter uns ...

strictness [strikt'nis] *n* Strenge *f*.

stridden [strid'ən] *pp* of **stride**.

stride [strīd] *n* lange(r) Schritt *m* ♦ *vi* irreg schreiten; **to take sth in one's ~** (*fig*: *changes etc*) mit etw spielend fertigwerden.

strident [strīd'ənt] *a* schneidend, durchdringend.

strife [strīf] *n* Streit *m*.

strike [strīk] *n* Streik *m*, Ausstand *m*; (*discovery*) Fund *m*; (*attack*) Schlag *m*; **to go on** or **come out on ~** in den Streik or Ausstand treten; **to call a ~** zum Streik aufrufen ♦ *irreg vt* (*hit*) schlagen; (*stone, bullet etc*) treffen; (*collide*) stoßen gegen; (*come to mind*) einfallen (+*dat*); (*stand out*) auffallen; (*find*) stoßen auf (+*acc*), finden; (*produce, make*: *coin, medal*) prägen; (*agreement, deal*) treffen, machen; **to ~ a balance** (*fig*) einen Mittelweg finden; **to ~ a bargain** ein Geschäft abschließen ♦ *vi* (*stop work*) streiken; (*clock*) schlagen; (*attack*: *MIL etc*) angreifen, zuschlagen.

strike back *vi* (*MIL*) zurückschlagen; (*fig*) sich gegen jdn wehren.

strike down *vt* (*lay low*) niederschlagen.

strike off *vt* (*from list*) (aus)streichen; (*doctor etc*) die Zulassung entziehen (+*dat*).

strike out *vt* (*cross out*) ausstreichen.

strike up *vt fus* (*friendship*) schließen.

strikebreaker [strīk'brākûr] *n* Streikbrecher *m*.

strike pay *n* Streikgeld *nt*.

striker [strī'kûr] *n* Streikende(r) *mf*.

striking [strī'king] *a*, **strikingly** [strī'kinglē] *ad* auffallend, bemerkenswert.

string [string] *n* (*cord*) Schnur *f*, Bindfaden *m*; (*row*) Reihe *f*; (*of people, vehicles*) Schlange *f*; (*MUS*) Saite *f*; (*COMPUT*) Zeichenfolge *f*; **to get a job by pulling ~s** eine Stelle durch Beziehungen bekommen; **with no ~s attached** (*fig*) ohne Bedingungen ♦ *vt irreg* (*put on ~*) aufreihen; **to ~ together** aneinanderreihen.

string along *vt*: **to ~ sb along** (*fig*) jdn hinters Licht führen.

string bean *n* grüne Bohne *f*.

string(ed) instrument [string(d)' in'strəmənt] *n* (*MUS*) Saiteninstrument *nt*.

stringency [strin'jənsē] *n* Schärfe *f*.

stringent [strin'jənt] *a* streng, scharf.

string quartet *n* Streichquartett *nt*.

strip [strip] *n* Streifen *m*; (*Brit SPORT*) Trikot *nt*, Dreß *m* ♦ *vt* (*uncover*) abstreifen, abziehen; (*clothes*) ausziehen; (*TECH*) auseinandernehmen ♦ *vi* (*undress*) sich ausziehen.

strip club *n* Striptease-Club *m*.
stripe [strīp] *n* Streifen *m*.
striped [strīpt] *a* gestreift.
stripper [strip'ûr] *n* Stripteasetänzer(in *f*) *m*.
striptease [strip'tēz] *n* Striptease *nt*.
strive [strīv] *vi irreg* streben (*for* nach).
striven [striv'ən] *pp of* **strive**.
strode [strōd] *pt of* **stride**.
stroke [strōk] *n* (*blow*) Schlag *m*, Hieb *m*; (*swim, row*) Zug *m*; (*TECH*) Hub *m*; (*MED*) Schlaganfall *m*; (*caress*) Streicheln *nt*; (*type of* ~) Stil *m* ♦ *vt* streicheln; **at a** ~ mit einem Schlag; **on the** ~ **of 5** Schlag 5; **a** ~ **of luck** ein Glücksfall *m*; **two-~ engine** Zweitaktmotor *m*.
stroll [strōl] *n* Spaziergang *m* ♦ *vi* spazierengehen, schlendern; **to go for a** ~, **to have** *or* **take a** ~ einen Spaziergang *or* Bummel machen.
stroller [strō'lûr] *n* (*US*) (Klapp- *or* Kinder)sportwagen *m*.
strong [strông] *a* stark; (*firm*) fest; ~ **language** (*swearing*) Kraftausdrücke *pl*, Schimpfwörter *pl* ♦ *ad*: **to be going** ~ (*company*) sehr erfolgreich sein; (*person*) gut in Schuß sein (*col*); **they are 50** ~ sie sind 50 Mann stark.
strong-arm [strông'ârm] *a* (*tactics, methods*) brutal, Gewalt-.
strongbox [strông'bâks] *n* (Geld)kassette *f*.
strong drink *n* steife(r) Drink *m*.
stronghold [strông'hōld] *n* Hochburg *f*.
strongly [strông'lē] *ad* stark; **to feel** ~ **about sth** in bezug auf etw (*acc*) stark engagiert sein; **I feel** ~ **about it** es bedeutet mir viel *or* es liegt mir sehr am Herzen; (*negative*) ich bin sehr dagegen.
strongman [strông'man] *n, pl* **-men** (*lit, fig*) starke(r) Mann *m*.
strongroom [strông'rōōm] *n* Tresor *m*.
strove [strōv] *pt of* **strive**.
struck [struk] *pt, pp of* **strike**.
structural [struk'chûrəl] *a* strukturell.
structure [struk'chûr] *n* Struktur *f*, Aufbau *m*; (*building*) Gebäude *nt*, Bau *m*.
struggle [strug'əl] *n* Kampf *m*, Anstrengung *f* ♦ *vi* (*fight*) kämpfen; **to** ~ **to do sth** sich (ab)mühen, etw zu tun.
strum [strum] *vt* (*guitar*) klimpern auf (+*dat*).
strung [strung] *pt, pp of* **string**; *see* **highly strung**.
strut [strut] *n* Strebe *f*, Stütze *f* ♦ *vi* stolzieren.
strychnine [strik'nīn] *n* Strychnin *nt*.
stub [stub] *n* Stummel *m*; (*of cigarette*) Kippe *f*; (*US: of check*) Abschnitt *m* ♦ *vt*: **to** ~ **out a cigarette** eine Zigarette ausdrücken; **to** ~ **one's toe (on sth)** sich (*dat*) den Zeh (an etw *dat*) stoßen.
stubble [stub'əl] *n* Stoppel *f*.
stubbly [stub'lē] *a* stoppelig, Stoppel-.
stubborn [stub'ûrn] *a*, **stubbornly** [stub'ûrnlē] *ad* stur, hartnäckig.
stubbornness [stub'ûrnis] *n* Sturheit *f*, Hart-

näckigkeit *f*.
stubby [stub'ē] *a* untersetzt.
stucco [stuk'ō] *n* Stuck *m*.
stuck [stuk] *pt, pp of* **stick** ♦ *a* (*caught*) steckengeblieben; (*drawer etc*) geklemmt; **to get** ~ (*fig*) nicht weiterkommen, nicht zurechtkommen.
stuck-up [stuk'up'] *a* hochnäsig.
stud [stud] *n* (*nail*) Beschlagnagel *m*; (*button*) Kragenknopf *m*; (*number of horses*) Stall *m*; (*place*) Gestüt *nt*.
studded [stud'id] *a*: ~ **with** übersät mit.
student [stōō'dənt] *n* Student(in *f*) *m*; (*US also*) Schüler(in *f*) *m*; **law/medical** ~ Jura-/Medizinstudent(in *f*) *m*; **fellow** ~ Kommilitone *m*; Kommilitonin *f*; **he's a** ~ **teacher** er ist Referendar.
student driver *n* (*US*) Fahrschüler(in *f*) *m*.
studied [stud'ēd] *a* absichtlich.
studio [stōō'dēō] *n* Studio *nt*; (*for artist*) Atelier *nt*.
studio apartment *n* Einzimmerwohnung *f*.
studious [stōō'dēəs] *a*, **studiously** [stōō'dēəslē] *ad* lernbegierig.
study [stud'ē] *n* Studium *nt*; (*investigation also*) Untersuchung *f*; (*room*) Arbeitszimmer *nt*; (*essay etc*) Studie *f* ♦ *vt* studieren; (*face*) erforschen; (*evidence*) prüfen ♦ *vi* studieren; **to make a** ~ **of sth** etw untersuchen; (*academic*) etw studieren; **to** ~ **for an exam** sich auf eine Prüfung vorbereiten, für eine Prüfung lernen.
study group *n* Arbeitsgruppe *f*.
stuff [stuf] *n* Stoff *m*; (*col*) Zeug *nt*; **that's hot** ~! das ist Klasse! ♦ *vt* stopfen, füllen; (*animal*) ausstopfen; **my nose is** ~**ed up** meine Nase ist verstopft; **to** ~ **o.s.** sich vollstopfen; ~**ed full** vollgepfropft; **get** ~**ed!** (*Brit col!*) du kannst mich mal! (*!*).
stuffed toy [stuft toi'] *n* Stofftier *nt*.
stuffiness [stuf'ēnis] *n* Schwüle *f*; Spießigkeit *f*.
stuffing [stuf'ing] *n* Füllung *f*.
stuffy [stuf'ē] *a* (*room*) schwül; (*person*) spießig.
stumble [stum'bəl] *vi* stolpern; **to** ~ **on** *or* **across** zufällig stoßen auf (+*acc*).
stumbling block [stum'bling blâk] *n* Hindernis *nt*.
stump [stump] *n* Stumpf *m* ♦ *vt* umwerfen; **to be** ~**ed for an answer** um eine Antwort verlegen sein.
stun [stun] *vt* betäuben; (*shock*) niederschmettern.
stung [stung] *pt, pp of* **sting**.
stunk [stungk] *pp of* **stink**.
stunning [stun'ing] *a* betäubend; (*news*) überwältigend, umwerfend.
stunt [stunt] *n* Kunststück *nt*, Trick *m* ♦ *vt* verkümmern lassen.
stunted [stun'tid] *a* verkümmert.
stuntman [stunt'mən] *n, pl* **-men** Stuntman *m*.
stupefaction [stōōpəfak'shən] *n* Verblüffung

f.

stupefy [stōō'pəfī] *vt* betäuben; (*by news*) bestürzen.

stupefying [stōō'pəfīing] *a* betäubend; bestürzend.

stupendous [stōōpen'dəs] *a* erstaunlich, enorm.

stupid [stōō'pid] *a* dumm.

stupidity [stōōpid'itē] *n* Dummheit *f.*

stupidly [stōō'pidlē] *ad* dumm.

stupor [stōō'pûr] *n* Betäubung *f.*

sturdily [stûr'dilē] *ad* kräftig, stabil.

sturdiness [stûr'dēnis] *n* Robustheit *f.*

sturdy [stûr'dē] *a* kräftig, robust.

sturgeon [stûr'jən] *n* Stör *m.*

stutter [stut'ûr] *n* Stottern *nt* ♦ *vi* stottern.

Stuttgart [stōōt'gârt] *n* Stuttgart *nt.*

sty [stī] *n* Schweinestall *m.*

stye [stī] *n* Gerstenkorn *nt.*

style [stīl] *n* Stil *m*; (*of dress etc*) Stil *m*, Schnitt *m*; (*fashion*) Mode *f*; **hair** ~ Frisur *f*; **in** ~ mit Stil; **in the latest** ~ im neue(ste)n Stil, nach der neue(ste)n Mode ♦ *vt* (*hair*) frisieren.

styling [stī'ling] *n* (*of car etc*) Formgebung *f.*

stylish [stī'lish] *a*, **stylishly** [stī'ishlē] *ad* modisch, schick, flott.

stylist [stī'list] *n*: **hair** ~ Friseur *m*, Friseuse *f.*

stylized [stī'līzd] *a* stilisiert.

stylus [stī'ləs] *n*, *pl* **styli** [stī'lē] or **styluses** [stī'ləsiz] (Grammophon)nadel *f.*

suave [swâv] *a* zuvorkommend.

sub [sub] *n abbr* = **submarine; subscription.**

sub- [sub] *pref* Unter-.

subcommittee [sub'kəmitē] *n* Unterausschuß *m.*

subconscious [subkân'chəs] *a* unterbewußt ♦ *n*: **the** ~ das Unterbewußte.

subcontinent [subkân'tənənt] *n*: **the (Indian)** ~ der (indische) Subkontinent.

subcontract *n* [subkân'trakt] Nebenvertrag *m*, Untervertrag *m*; (*COMM*) Subunternehmervertrag *m* ♦ *vt* [subkəntrakt'] (vertraglich) weitervergeben; an einen Subunternehmer vergeben.

subcontractor [subkân'traktûr] *n* Subunternehmer *m.*

subdivide [subdivīd'] *vt* unterteilen.

subdivision [subdivizh'ən] *n* Unterteilung *f*; (*department*) Unterabteilung *f.*

subdue [səbdōō'] *vt* unterwerfen.

subdued [səbdōōd'] *a* (*lighting*) gedämpft; (*person*) still.

subject *n* [sub'jikt] (*of kingdom*) Untertan *m*; (*citizen*) Staatsangehörige(r) *mf*; (*topic*) Thema *nt*; (*SCH*) Fach *nt*; (*GRAM*) Subjekt *nt*, Satzgegenstand *m*; **to change the** ~ das Thema wechseln ♦ *vt* [səbjekt'] (*subdue*) unterwerfen, abhängig machen; (*expose*) aussetzen [sub'jikt]: ♦ *a* ~ **to confirmation in writing** vorausgesetzt, es wird schriftlich bestätigt; **to be** ~ **to** (*under control of*) unterworfen sein (+*dat*); (*disease*) anfällig

sein für.

subjection [səbjek'shən] *n* (*conquering*) Unterwerfung *f*; (*being controlled*) Abhängigkeit *f.*

subjective [səbjek'tiv] *a*, **subjectively** [səbjek'tivlē] *ad* subjektiv.

subject matter *n* Thema *nt.*

sub judice [sub jōō'disē] *a* (*JUR*): **to be** ~ verhandelt werden.

subjugate [sub'jəgāt] *vt* unterwerfen, unterjochen.

subjunctive [səbjungk'tiv] *n* Konjunktiv *m* ♦ *a* Konjunktiv-, konjunktivisch.

sublease [sublēs'] (*US*) *vt* verkaufen und gleichzeitig rückmieten ♦ *n* Verkauf *m* mit gleichzeitiger Rückmiete.

sublet [sublet'] *irreg vt* untervermieten, weitervermieten ♦ *vi* untervermieten.

sublime [səblīm'] *a* erhaben.

subliminal [sublim'ənəl] *a* unterschwellig.

submachine gun [subməshēn' gun] *n* Maschinenpistole *f.*

submarine [sub'mərēn] *n* Unterseeboot *nt*, U-Boot *nt.*

submerge [səbmûrj'] *vt* untertauchen; (*flood*) überschwemmen ♦ *vi* untertauchen.

submersion [səbmûr'zhən] *n* Untertauchen *nt*; (*flood*) Überschwemmung *f.*

submission [səbmish'ən] *n* (*obedience*) Ergebenheit *f*, Gehorsam *m*; (*claim*) Behauptung *f*; (*to committee etc*) Vorlage *f.*

submit [səbmit'] *vt* behaupten; (*plan*) unterbreiten; (*proposal, claim*) einreichen; **I** ~ **that** ... ich behaupte, daß ... ♦ *vi* (*give in*) sich ergeben.

subnormal [subnôr'məl] *a* unterdurchschnittlich; (*person*) minderbegabt.

subordinate [səbôr'dənit] *a* untergeordnet ♦ *n* Untergebene(r) *mf.*

subpoena [səpē'nə] *n* (*JUR*) Vorladung *f* ♦ *vt* (*JUR*) vorladen.

subroutine [subrōōtēn'] *n* (*COMPUT*) Unterprogramm *nt.*

subscribe [səbskrīb'] *vi* spenden, Geld geben; (*to view etc*) unterstützen (+*acc*), beipflichten (+*dat*); (*to newspaper*) abonnieren (*to acc*).

subscribed capital [səbskrībd' kap'itəl] *n* gezeichnete(s) Kapital *nt.*

subscriber [səbskrīb'ûr] *n* (*to periodical*) Abonnent(in *f*) *m*; (*TEL*) Telefonteilnehmer(in *f*) *m.*

subscript [sub'skript] *n* (*TYP*) Index *m.*

subscription [səbskrip'shən] *n* (*to newspaper etc*) Abonnement *nt*; (*money paid*) (Mitglieds)beitrag *m*; **to take out a** ~ **to sth** etw abonnieren.

subsequent [sub'səkwənt] *a* folgend, später; ~ **to** im Anschluß an (+*acc*).

subsequently [sub'səkwəntlē] *ad* später.

subservient [səbsûr'vēənt] *a*: ~ **(to)** unterwürfig (gegenüber).

subside [səbsīd'] *vi* sich senken.

subsidence [səbsīd'əns] *n* Senkung *f.*

subsidiary [səbsid'ēärē] a (UNIV also) Neben-
♦ n (company) Zweig m, Tochtergesellschaft
f.
subsidize [sub'sidīz] vt subventionieren.
subsidy [sub'sidē] n Subvention f.
subsist [səbsist'] vi: **to ~ on sth** sich von etw
ernähren or leben.
subsistence [səbsis'təns] n Unterhalt m.
subsistence allowance n Unterhaltszu-
schuß m.
subsistence level n Existenzminimum nt.
subsistence wage n Mindestlohn m.
substance [sub'stəns] n Substanz f, Stoff m;
(most important part) Hauptbestandteil m;
to lack ~ (argument) keine Durchschlagskraft haben; (accusation) grundlos sein;
(film, book) keine Substanz haben.
substandard [substan'dûrd] a unterdurchschnittlich; (goods) minderwertig; (housing)
unzulänglich.
substantial [səbstan'chəl] a (strong) fest,
kräftig; (important) wesentlich.
substantially [səbstan'chəlē] ad erheblich; ~
bigger erheblich größer.
substantiate [səbstan'chēāt] vt begründen,
belegen.
substation [sub'stāshən] n (ELEC) Nebenwerk
nt.
substitute [sub'stitōōt] n Ersatz m; (SPORT)
Reservespieler m ♦ vt ersetzen.
substitute teacher (US) Aushilfslehrer(in
f) m.
substitution [substitōō'shən] n Ersetzung f.
subterfuge [sub'tûrfyōōj] n (trick) Tricks pl;
(trickery) Täuschung f, List f.
subterranean [subtərā'nēən] a unterirdisch.
subtitle [sub'tītəl] n Untertitel m.
subtle [sut'əl] a fein; (sly) raffiniert.
subtlety [sut'əltē] n Feinheit f, Raffinesse f.
subtly [sut'lē] ad fein, raffiniert; (flavored
also) delikat; (argue, reply) scharfsinnig,
subtil.
subtotal [subtō'təl] n Zwischen- or Teilsumme
f, Zwischen- or Teilergebnis nt.
subtract [səbtrakt'] vt abziehen, subtrahieren.
subtraction [səbtrak'shən] n Abziehen nt,
Subtraktion f.
subtropical [subtráp'ikəl] a subtropisch.
suburb [sub'ûrb] n Vorort m.
suburban [səbûr'bən] a Vorort(s)-,
Stadtrand-.
suburbia [səbûr'bēə] n die Vororte pl.
subvention [səbven'chən] n (US) Unterstützung f, Subvention f.
subversion [səbvûr'zhən] n Subversion f, Um-
sturz m.
subversive [səbvûr'siv] a subversiv.
subway [sub'wā] n (US) U-Bahn f, Untergrundbahn f; (Brit) Unterführung f.
subway station n (US) U-Bahnstation f.
sub-zero [sub'zē'rō] a unter Null, unter dem
Gefrierpunkt; ~ **temperatures** Temperaturen unter Null.
succeed [səksēd'] vi gelingen (+dat), Erfolg

haben; **he ~ed** es gelang ihm ♦ vt
(nach)folgen (+dat).
succeeding [səksē'ding] a (nach)folgend; ~
generations spätere or nachfolgende Generationen pl.
success [səkses'] n Erfolg m.
successful [səkses'fəl] a, **successfully**
[səkses'fəlē] ad erfolgreich.
succession [səksesh'ən] n (Aufeinander)folge
f; (to throne) Nachfolge f; **in ~** nacheinander, hintereinander.
successive [səkses'iv] a aufeinanderfolgend;
on 3 ~ days 3 Tage nacheinander or hintereinander.
successor [səkses'ûr] n Nachfolger(in f) m.
succinct [səksingkt'] a kurz und bündig,
knapp.
succulent [suk'yələnt] a saftig.
succulents [suk'yələnts] npl (BOT) Fettpflan-
zen pl, Sukkulente pl.
succumb [səkum'] vi zusammenbrechen (to
unter +dat); (yield) nachgeben (to dat);
(die) erliegen.
such [such] a solche(r, s); ~ **a** so ein; ~ **a**
lot so viel; ~ **books as I have** die Bücher,
die ich habe; **I said no ~ thing** das habe ich
nie gesagt ♦ ad: **it's** ~ **a long time since**
we saw each other wir haben uns schon so
lange nicht mehr gesehen; ~ **a long time**
ago vor so langer Zeit ♦ pron solch; ~ **is**
life so ist das Leben; ~ **is my wish** das ist
mein Wunsch; ~ **as** wie; ~ **as I have** die,
die ich habe.
such-and-such [such'ənsuch] a: ~ **a time/**
town die und die Zeit/Stadt.
suchlike [such'līk] a derartig ♦ pron dergleichen; **and** ~ (col) und dergleichen.
suck [suk] vt saugen; (ice-cream etc) lecken;
(toffee etc) lutschen ♦ vi saugen.
sucker [suk'ûr] n (col) Idiot m, Dummkopf m.
suckle [suk'əl] vt säugen; (child) stillen ♦ vi
saugen.
sucrose [sōō'krōs] n Saccharose f, pflanzli-
che(r) Zucker m.
suction [suk'shən] n Saugen nt, Saugkraft f.
suction pump n Saugpumpe f.
Sudan [sōōdan'] n der Sudan.
Sudanese [sōōdənēz'] a sudanesisch, suda-
nisch ♦ n Sudanese m, Sudanesin f, Suda-
ner(in f) m.
sudden [sud'ən] a plötzlich ♦ n: **all of a** ~
ganz plötzlich, auf einmal.
suddenly [sud'ənlē] ad plötzlich.
suddenness [sud'ənis] n Plötzlichkeit f.
suds [sudz] npl Seifenlauge f; (lather) Seifenschaum m.
sue [sōō] vt verklagen; **to ~ sb for sth** jdn
auf etw (acc) or wegen etw verklagen ♦ vi:
to ~ for damages auf Schadenersatz klagen; **to ~ for divorce** die Scheidung einreichen.
suede [swād] n Wildleder nt ♦ a Wildleder-.
suet [sōō'it] n Nierenfett nt.
Suez [sōōez'] n Sues nt, Suez nt; ~ **Canal**

Sueskanal *m*, Suezkanal *m*.

Suff *abbr* (*Brit*) = *Suffolk*.

suffer [suf'ûr] *vt* (*undergo*: *loss*, *setback*) (er)leiden; (*old*: *allow*) zulassen, dulden ♦ *vi* leiden; **to ~ from** leiden an *or* unter; **he is still ~ing from the effects** er leidet noch immer an *or* unter den Folgen.

sufferance [suf'ûrəns] *n*: **he was only there on ~** er wurde nur geduldet.

sufferer [suf'ûrûr] *n* (*MED*) Leidende(r) *mf* (*from* an +*dat*).

suffering [suf'ûring] *n* Leiden *nt*; (*hardship*, *deprivation*) Leid *nt*.

suffice [səfīs'] *vi* genügen.

sufficient [səfish'ənt] *a*, **sufficiently** [səfish'əntlē] *ad* ausreichend.

suffix [suf'iks] *n* Nachsilbe *f*.

suffocate [suf'əkāt] *vti* ersticken.

suffocation [sufəkā'shən] *n* Ersticken *nt*.

suffrage [suf'rij] *n* Wahlrecht *nt*.

suffragette [sufrəjet'] *n* Suffragette *f*.

suffuse [səfyōōz'] *vt*: **to ~ (with)** übergießen (mit), durchfluten (mit); **a blush ~d her face** (eine) Röte überzog ihr Gesicht; **her face was ~d with joy** sie strahlte vor Freude.

sugar [shōōg'ûr] *n* Zucker *m* ♦ *vt* zuckern.

sugar beet *n* Zuckerrübe *f*.

sugar bowl *n* Zuckerdose *f*.

sugar cane *n* Zuckerrohr *nt*.

sugar-coated [shōōg'ûrkō'tid] *a* mit Zucker überzogen.

sugar lump *n* Zuckerwürfel *m*.

sugar refinery *n* Zuckerraffinerie *f*.

sugary [shōōg'ûrē] *a* süß.

suggest [səgjest'] *vt* vorschlagen; (*show*) schließen lassen auf (+*acc*); **what does this painting ~ to you?** was drückt das Bild für dich aus?; **what do you ~ I do?** was soll ich tun? was meinen Sie?

suggestion [səgjes'chən] *n* Vorschlag *m*; **there's no ~ that he was involved** niemand deutet an *or* unterstellt, daß er beteiligt war.

suggestive [səgjes'tiv] *a* anregend; (*indecent*) zweideutig, anzüglich; **to be ~ of sth** an etw (*acc*) erinnern.

suicidal [sōōisīd'əl] *a* selbstmörderisch; **that's ~** das ist glatter Selbstmord.

suicide [sōō'isīd] *n* Selbstmord *m*; **to commit ~** Selbstmord begehen.

suicide attempt, suicide bid *n* Selbstmord- *or* Suizidversuch *m*.

suit [sōōt] *n* Anzug *m*; (*CARDS*) Farbe *f*; (*law~*) Prozeß *m*, Verfahren *nt*; **to bring a ~ against sb** gegen jdn Klage erheben *or* einen Prozeß anstrengen; **to follow ~** (*fig*) jds Beispiel (*dat*) folgen; (*CARDS*) bedienen ♦ *vt* passen (+*dat*); (*clothes*) stehen (+*dat*); (*adapt*) anpassen; **to be ~ed to sth** (*suitable for*) geeignet sein für etw; **that ~s me** das ist mir recht (*col*); (*clothes*, *hair style*) das paßt mir, das steht mir; **~ yourself** mach doch, was du willst.

suitability [sōōtəbil'ətē] *n* Eignung *f*.

suitable [sōō'təbəl] *a* geeignet, passend; **would tomorrow be ~?** würde Ihnen *etc* morgen passen?

suitably [sōō'təblē] *ad* passend, angemessen.

suitcase [sōōt'kās] *n* Koffer *m*.

suite [swēt] *n* (*of rooms*) Zimmerflucht *f*; (*of furniture*) Einrichtung *f*; (*MUS*) Suite *f*; **a three-piece ~** eine Polstergarnitur.

suited [sōō'tid] *a*: **well ~** (*couple*) gut zusammenpassend.

suitor [sōō'tûr] *n* (*JUR*) Kläger(in *f*) *m*.

sulfate [sul'fāt] *n* (*US*) Sulfat *nt*, schwefelsauere(s) Salz *nt*; **copper ~** Kupfersulfat *nt* *or* -vitriol *nt*.

sulfur [sul'fûr] *n* Schwefel *m*.

sulfuric acid [sulfyōōr'ik as'id] *n* (*US*) Schwefelsäure *f*.

sulk [sulk] *vi* schmollen.

sulky [sul'kē] *a* schmollend.

sullen [sul'ən] *a* (*gloomy*) düster; (*bad-tempered*) mürrisch, verdrossen.

sulphur [sul'fûr] *etc* (*Brit*) = **sulfur** *etc*.

sultan [sul'tən] *n* Sultan *m*.

sultana [sultan'ə] *n* (*woman*) Sultanin *f*; (*raisin*) Sultanine *f*.

sultry [sul'trē] *a* schwül.

sum [sum] *n* Summe *f*; (*money also*) Betrag *m*; (*arithmetic*) Rechenaufgabe *f*; *see also* **sums**.

sum up *vt* zusammenfassen; (*evaluate rapidly*) ab- *or* einschätzen ♦ *vi* zusammenfassen.

Sumatra [sōōmât'rə] *n* Sumatra *nt*.

summarize [sum'əriz] *vt* kurz zusammenfassen.

summary [sum'ûrē] *n* Zusammenfassung *f*; (*of book etc*) Inhaltsangabe *f*.

summer [sum'ûr] *n* Sommer *m*; **in (the) ~** im Sommer ♦ *a* Sommer-.

summer camp *n* (*US*) Feriendorf *nt*.

summerhouse [sum'ûrhous] *n* (*in garden*) Gartenhaus *nt*.

summertime [sum'ûrtīm] *n* Sommerzeit *f*.

summery [sum'ûrē] *a* sommerlich.

summing-up [sum'ingup'] *n* Zusammenfassung *f*; (*JUR*) Resümee *nt*.

summit [sum'it] *n* Gipfel *m*.

summit conference *n* Gipfelkonferenz *f*.

summon [sum'ən] *vt* bestellen, kommen lassen; (*JUR*) vorladen; (*gather up*) aufbieten, aufbringen; **to ~ a witness** einen Zeugen vorladen.

summons [sum'ənz] *n sing* (*JUR*) Vorladung *f*; **to serve a ~ on sb** jdn vorladen lassen, jdn vor Gericht laden.

sump [sump] *n* (*Brit*) Ölwanne *f*.

sumptuous [sump'chōōəs] *a* prächtig.

sumptuousness [sump'chōōəsnis] *n* Pracht *f*.

sun [sun] *n* Sonne *f*; **they have everything under the ~** sie haben alles Mögliche; **you've caught the ~** dich hat die Sonne erwischt.

Sun. *abbr* (= *Sunday*) So.

sunbathe [sun'bāth] *vi* sich sonnen.

sunbathing [sun'bāθ̱ing] n Sonnenbaden nt.
sunbeam [sun'bēm] n Sonnenstrahl m.
sunbed [sun'bed] n Sonnenbett nt.
sunburn [sun'bûrn] n (painful) Sonnenbrand m; (tan) Bräune f.
sunburnt [sun'bûrnt], **sunburned** [sun'bûrnd] a: **to be** ~ (Brit) einen Sonnenbrand haben; sonnengebräunt sein.
sundae [sun'dē] n Eisbecher m.
Sunday [sun'dā] n Sonntag m; see **Tuesday**.
Sunday school n Sonntagsschule f.
sundial [sun'dīl] n Sonnenuhr f.
sundown [sun'doun] n Sonnenuntergang m.
sundries [sun'drēz] npl Verschiedene(s) nt.
sundry [sun'drē] a verschieden ♦ pron: **all and** ~ alle.
sunflower [sun'flouûr] n Sonnenblume f.
sung [sung] pp of **sing**.
sunglasses [sun'glasiz] npl Sonnenbrille f.
sunk [sungk] pp of **sink**.
sunken [sung'kən] a versunken; (eyes) eingesunken; (bath) eingelassen.
sunlamp [sun'lamp] n Höhensonne f.
sunlight [sun'līt] n Sonnenlicht nt.
sunlit [sun'lit] a sonnenbeschienen.
sunny [sun'ē] a sonnig; **it is** ~ es ist sonnig.
sunrise [sun'rīz] n Sonnenaufgang m.
sunroof [sun'rōof] n (on building) Sonnenterrasse f; (AUT) Schiebedach nt.
sunset [sun'set] n Sonnenuntergang m.
sunshade [sun'shād] n Sonnenschirm m.
sunshine [sun'shīn] n Sonnenschein m.
sunspot [sun'spät] n Sonnenfleck m.
sunstroke [sun'strōk] n Hitzschlag m.
suntan [sun'tan] n (Sonnen)bräune f; **to get a** ~ braun werden.
suntanned [sun'tand] a braungebrannt.
suntan oil n Sonnenöl nt.
suntrap [sun'trap] n (Brit) sonnige(r) Platz m.
sun-up [sun'up] n (col) Sonnenaufgang m.
super [sōō'pûr] a (col) prima, klasse.
superannuation [sōōpûranyōōā'shən] n Pension f.
superb [sōōpûrb'] a, **superbly** [sōōpûrb'lē] ad ausgezeichnet, hervorragend.
supercilious [sōōpûrsil'ēəs] a herablassend.
superficial [sōōpûrfish'əl] a, **superficially** [sōōpûrfish'əlē] ad oberflächlich.
superfluous [sōōpûr'flōōəs] a überflüssig.
superhuman [sōōpûrhyōō'mən] a (effort) übermenschlich.
superimpose [sōōpûrimpōz'] vt übereinanderlegen.
superintend [sōōpûrintend'] vt beaufsichtigen.
superintendent [sōōpûrinten'dənt] n (POLICE) Polizeichef m.
superior [səpēr'ēûr] a (higher) höher(stehend); (better) besser; (COMM: goods, quality) bester Qualität; (smug: person) eingebildet; (smile, air) überlegen; (remark) überheblich ♦ n Vorgesetzte(r) mf; **Mother S**~ (REL) Ehrwürdige Mutter f,

Oberin f.
superiority [səpērēôr'itē] n Überlegenheit f.
superlative [səpûr'lətiv] a höchste(r, s) ♦ n (GRAM) Superlativ m.
superman [sōō'pûrman] n, pl **-men** Übermensch m.
supermarket [sōō'pûrmârkit] n Supermarkt m.
supernatural [sōōpûrnach'ûrəl] a übernatürlich.
superpower [sōō'pûrpou'ûr] n Weltmacht f.
supersede [sōōpûrsēd'] vt ersetzen.
supersonic [sōōpûrsän'ik] n Überschall-.
superstition [sōōpûrstish'ən] n Aberglaube m.
superstitious [sōōpûrstish'əs] a abergläubisch.
superstore [sōō'pûrstôr] n große(s) Warenhaus nt.
supertanker [sōō'pûrtangkûr] n Super- or Riesentanker m.
supervise [sōō'pûrvīz] vt beaufsichtigen, kontrollieren.
supervision [sōōpûrvizh'ən] n Aufsicht f; **under medical** ~ unter ärztlicher Aufsicht.
supervisor [sōō'pûrvīzûr] n Aufsichtsperson f; (UNIV) Tutor(in f) m.
supervisory [sōōpûrvī'zûrē] a beaufsichtigend, überwachend.
supine [sōō'pīn] a auf dem Rücken liegend.
supper [sup'ûr] n Abendessen nt; **to have** ~ zu Abend essen, Abendbrot essen.
supplant [səplant'] vt ablösen, ersetzen; (forcibly) verdrängen.
supple [sup'əl] a gelenkig, geschmeidig; (wire) biegsam.
supplement [sup'ləmənt] n Ergänzung f; (in book) Nachtrag m ♦ vt [sup'ləment] ergänzen.
supplementary [supləmən'tûrē] a ergänzend, Ergänzungs-, Zusatz-; ~ **benefit** (Brit) Fürsorgeunterstützung f, Sozialhilfe f.
supplier [səplī'ûr] n Lieferant m.
supplies [səplīz'] npl (food) Vorräte pl; (MIL) Nachschub m.
supply [səplī'] vt (material, food etc) sorgen für; (deliver: goods) liefern; (fill: need) befriedigen; (: want) abhelfen (+dat) ♦ n Vorrat m; (supplying) Lieferung f; **to be in short** ~ knapp sein; **office supplies** Bürobedarf m, Büroartikel m; **the electricity/water/gas** ~ die Strom-/Wasser-/Gasversorgung; ~ **and demand** Angebot nt und Nachfrage.
supply teacher n (Brit) Aushilfslehrer(in f) m.
support [səpôrt'] n Unterstützung f; (TECH) Stütze f; **they stopped work in** ~ (of) ... sie sind in den Streik getreten, um für ... einzutreten ♦ vt (hold up) stützen, tragen; (provide for) ernähren; (speak in favor of) befürworten, unterstützen; **he** ~**s the LA Rams** er ist (ein) LA-Rams-Anhänger; **to** ~ **o.s.** (financially) finanziell unabhängig sein.
supporter [səpôr'tûr] n Anhänger(in f) m.

supporting [səpôr'ting] *a* (*program*) Bei-; (*role*) Neben-; ~ **actor** Schauspieler, der eine Nebenrolle spielt.

suppose [səpōz'] *vti* annehmen, denken, glauben; **I** ~ **so** ich glaube schon; ~ **he comes** ... angenommen, er kommt ...; **I don't** ~ **she'll come** vermutlich *or* wahrscheinlich kommt sie nicht; **he's** ~**d to be an expert** er soll (angeblich) (ein) Experte sein.

supposedly [səpō'zidlē] *ad* angeblich.

supposing [səpō'zing] *cj* angenommen.

supposition [supəzish'ən] *n* Voraussetzung *f*.

suppository [səpâz'itôrē] *n* Zäpfchen *nt*.

suppress [səpres'] *vt* unterdrücken.

suppression [səpresh'ən] *n* Unterdrückung *f*.

suppressor [səpres'ûr] *n* (*ELEC*) Entstörungselement *nt*.

supra- [sōō'prə] *pref* Über-.

supremacy [səprem'əsē] *n* Vorherrschaft *f*, Oberhoheit *f*.

supreme [səprēm'] *a*, **supremely** [səprēm'lē] *ad* oberste(r, s), höchste(r, s).

Supreme Court (*US*) *n* oberste(r) Gerichtshof *m*.

Supt. *abbr* (*POLICE*) = **superintendent**.

surcharge [sûr'chârj] *n* Zuschlag *m*.

sure [shōōr] *a* sicher, gewiß; **to be** ~ sicher sein; **I'm not** ~ **how/why/when** ich bin (mir) nicht sicher *or* ich weiß nicht genau, wie/warum/wann; **to be** ~ **of o.s.** (*generally self-confident*) selbstsicher sein; **to be** ~ **about sth** sich (*dat*) einer Sache sicher sein; **we are** ~ **to win** wir werden ganz sicher gewinnen; **to make** ~ **of** sich vergewissern (+*gen*) ♦ *ad* sicher; ~**!** (*of course*) ganz bestimmt!, natürlich!, klar!; **that** ~ **is pretty** (*col*) das ist aber schön.

sure-footed [shōōr'fōōt'id] *a* sicher (auf den Füßen).

surely [shōōr'lē] *ad* (*certainly*) sicherlich, gewiß; ~ **it's wrong** das ist doch wohl falsch; ~ **not!** das ist doch wohl nicht wahr!; ~ **you don't mean that!** das meinen Sie doch bestimmt *or* sicher nicht (so)!

surety [shōōr'ətē] *n* Sicherheit *f*; (*person*) Bürge *m*; **to go** *or* **stand** ~ **for sb** für jdn bürgen.

surf [sûrf] *n* Brandung *f*.

surface [sûr'fis] *n* Oberfläche *f*; **on the** ~ **it seems that** ... (*fig*) oberflächlich betrachtet sieht es so aus, als ... ♦ *cpd* (*MIL, NAUT*) Boden- ♦ *vt* (*roadway*) teeren ♦ *vi* auftauchen.

surface area *n* Fläche *f*.

surface mail *n* gewöhnliche Post *f*, Post *f* per Bahn.

surface-to-air missile [sûr'fistōōâr' mis'əl] *n* Boden-Luft-Rakete *f*.

surfboard [sûrf'bôrd] *n* Wellenreiterbrett *nt*.

surfeit [sûr'fit] *n* Übermaß *nt*.

surfer [sûrf'ûr] *n* Wellenreiter(in *f*) *m*, Surfer(in *f*) *m*.

surfing [sûrf'ing] *n* Wellenreiten *nt*, Surfing *nt*.

surge [sûrj] *n* Woge *f*; (*ELEC*) Überspannung

f ♦ *vi* wogen; **to** ~ **forward** nach vorn drängen.

surgeon [sûr'jən] *n* Chirurg(in *f*) *m*.

surgery [sûr'jûrē] *n* Praxis *f*; (*treatment*) Operation *f*; (*Brit: room*) Sprechzimmer *nt*; (: *time*) Sprechstunde *f*; **he needs** ~ er muß operiert werden.

surgical [sûr'jikəl] *a* chirurgisch.

surgical spirit *n* (*Brit*) Wundbenzin *nt*.

surly [sûr'lē] *a* verdrießlich, grob.

surmise [sûrmīz'] *vt* vermuten.

surmount [sûrmount'] *vt* überwinden.

surname [sûr'nām] *n* Zuname *m*.

surpass [sûrpas'] *vt* übertreffen.

surplus [sûr'pləs] *n* Überschuß *m* ♦ *a* überschüssig, Über(schuß)-; **to have a** ~ **of sth** einen Überschuß an etw (*dat*) haben; ~ **(stock)** (*FIN, COMM*) Überschuß *m*; **it is** ~ **to our requirements** das benötigen wir nicht.

surprise [sûrprīz'] *n* Überraschung *f* ♦ *vt* überraschen; **to take sb by** ~ jdn überraschen; **to take by** ~ (*MIL: town, fort*) mit einem Überraschungsangriff einnehmen *or* erobern.

surprising [sûrprī'zing] *a* überraschend.

surprisingly [sûrprī'zinglē] *ad* überraschend(erweise); **(somewhat)** ~, **he agreed** erstaunlicherweise war er damit einverstanden.

surrealism [sərē'əlizəm] *n* Surrealismus *m*.

surrealist [sərē'əlist] *a* surrealistisch ♦ *n* Surrealist(in *f*) *m*.

surrender [sərən'dûr] *n* Übergabe *f*, Kapitulation *f* ♦ *vi* sich ergeben, kapitulieren ♦ *vt* übergeben; (*claim, right*) aufgeben.

surrender value *n* Rückkaufswert *m*.

surreptitious [sûrəptish'əs] *a*, **surreptitiously** [sûrəptish'əslē] *ad* verstohlen.

surrogate [sûr'əgit] *n* (*substitute*) Ersatz *m* ♦ *a* Ersatz-.

surrogate mother *n* Leihmutter *f*.

surround [səround'] *vt* umgeben; (*crowd round*) umringen; ~**ed by** umgeben von.

surrounding [səroun'ding] *a* (*countryside*) umliegend.

surroundings [səroun'dingz] *npl* Umgebung *f*; (*environment*) Umwelt *f*.

surtax [sûr'taks] *n* Steuerzuschlag *m*.

surveillance [sûrvā'ləns] *n* Überwachung *f*.

survey *n* [sûr'vā] Übersicht *f*; (*comprehensive view*) Überblick *m*; (*poll*) Umfrage *f* ♦ *vt* [sərvā'] überblicken; (*land*) vermessen; (*of building*) inspizieren; **to carry out a** ~ Vermessungsarbeiten durchführen; (*report*) ein Gutachten erstellen.

surveying [sûrvā'ing] *n* (*of land*) Landvermessung *f*.

surveyor [sûrvā'ûr] *n* Landvermesser(in *f*) *m*.

survival [sûrvī'vəl] *n* Überleben *nt*; (*relic*) Überbleibsel *nt*.

survival course *n* Überlebenstraining *nt*.

survival kit *n* Überlebensausrüstung *f*.

survive [sûrvīv'] *vti* überleben.

survivor [sûrvī'vûr] *n* Überlebende(r) *mf*.

susceptibility [səseptəbil'ətē] *n* Anfälligkeit *f* (*to* für).

susceptible [səsep'təbəl] *a*: ~ **(to)** empfindlich (gegen); (*charms etc*) empfänglich (für).

suspect [sus'pekt] *n* Verdächtige(r) *mf* ♦ *a* verdächtig ♦ *vt* [səspekt'] verdächtigen; (*think*) vermuten.

suspend [səspend'] *vt* verschieben; (*from work*) suspendieren; (*hang up*) aufhängen; (*SPORT*) sperren.

suspended sentence [səspen'did sen'təns] *n* (*JUR*) zur Bewährung ausgesetzte Strafe *f*.

suspender belt [səspen'dûr belt] *n* (*Brit*) Strumpf(halter)gürtel *m*.

suspenders [səspen'dûrz] *npl* Strumpfhalter *m*; (*US*) Hosenträger *m*.

suspense [səspens'] *n* Spannung *f*.

suspense account *n* Interimskonto *nt*.

suspension [səspen'chən] *n* (*hanging*) (Auf)hängen *nt*, Aufhängung *f*; (*postponing*) Aufschub *m*; (*from work*) Suspendierung *f*; (*SPORT*) Sperrung *f*; (*AUT*) Federung *f*.

suspension bridge *n* Hängebrücke *f*.

suspicion [səspish'ən] *n* Verdacht *m*; (*distrust*) Mißtrauen *nt*; **to be under** ~ unter Verdacht stehen; **arrested on** ~ **of murder** wegen Mordverdacht(s) festgenommen.

suspicious [səspish'əs] *a* (*feeling suspicion*) mißtrauisch; (*causing suspicion*) verdächtig; **to be** ~ **of** *or* **about sb/sth** jdm/etw gegenüber mißtrauisch sein.

suspiciousness [səspish'əsnis] *n* Mißtrauen *nt*.

suss out [sus out] *vt* (*Brit col*) rausfinden, dahinterkommen.

sustain [səstān'] *vt* (*hold up*) stützen, tragen; (*maintain*) aufrechterhalten; (*confirm*) bestätigen; (*JUR*) anerkennen; (*injury*) davontragen.

sustained [səstānd'] *a* (*effort*) anhaltend.

sustenance [sus'tənəns] *n* Nahrung *f*.

suture [sōō'chûr] *n* Naht *f*.

SW *abbr* (= *short wave*) KW.

swab [swâb] *n* (*MED*) Tupfer *m* ♦ *vt* (*wound*) abtupfen; (*NAUT*: *also*: ~ **down**) wischen.

swagger [swag'ûr] *vi* stolzieren; (*behave*) prahlen, angeben.

swallow [swâl'ō] *n* (*bird*) Schwalbe *f*; (*of food, drink etc*) Schluck *m* ♦ *vt* (ver)schlucken.

swallow up *vt* verschlingen.

swam [swam] *pt of* **swim**.

swamp [swâmp] *n* Sumpf *m* ♦ *vt* überschwemmen.

swampy [swâmp'ē] *a* sumpfig.

swan [swân] *n* Schwan *m*.

swank [swangk] *n* (*col*: *vanity, boastfulness*) Angabe *f*, Protzerei *f* ♦ *vi* (*col*) angeben, sich wichtig machen.

swan song *n* (*fig*) Schwanengesang *m*.

swap [swâp] *n* Tausch *m* ♦ *vt* (ein)tauschen (*for* gegen) ♦ *vi* tauschen.

SWAPO [swâ'pō] *n abbr* (= *South-West Africa People's Organization*) SWAPO *f*.

swarm [swôrm] *n* Schwarm *m* ♦ *vi* (*place*) wimmeln (*with* von); (*crawling insects, people*) schwärmen.

swarthy [swôr'thē] *a* dunkel, braun.

swashbuckling [swâsh'bukling] *a* verwegen, draufgängerisch.

swastika [swâs'tikə] *n* Hakenkreuz *nt*.

swat [swât] *vt* totschlagen.

swatter [swât'ûr] *n* (*also*: **fly** ~) Fliegenklatsche *f*.

sway [swā] *vi* schwanken; (*branches*) schaukeln, sich wiegen ♦ *vt* schwenken; (*influence*) beeinflussen, umstimmen ♦ *n* (*rule, power*) Macht *f*; **to hold** ~ **over sb** jdn beherrschen *or* in seiner Macht haben.

Swaziland [swâ'zēland] *n* Swasiland *nt*.

swear [swär] *irreg vi* (*promise*) schwören; (*curse*) fluchen; **to** ~ **to sth** schwören auf etw (*acc*) ♦ *vt*: **to** ~ **an oath** einen Eid leisten *or* ablegen.

swear in *vt* vereidigen.

swearword [swär'wûrd] *n* Fluch *m*.

sweat [swet] *n* Schweiß *m* ♦ *vi* schwitzen.

sweatband [swet'band] *n* (*SPORT*) Schweißband *nt*.

sweater [swet'ûr] *n* Pullover *m*.

sweatshirt [swet'shûrt] *n* Sweatshirt *nt*.

sweatshop [swet'shâp] *n* Ausbeuterbetrieb *m* (*pej*).

sweat suit *n* (*US*) Trainingsanzug *m*.

sweaty [swet'ē] *a* verschwitzt.

swede [swēd] *n* (*Brit*) Steck- *or* Kohlrübe *f*.

Swede [swēd] *n* Schwede *m*, Schwedin *f*.

Sweden [swēd'ən] *n* Schweden *nt*.

Swedish [swē'dish] *a* schwedisch ♦ *n* (*language*) Schwedisch *nt*.

sweep [swēp] *n* (*cleaning*) Kehren *nt*; (*wide curve*) Bogen *m*; (*with arm*) schwungvolle Bewegung *f*; (*also*: **chimney** ~) Schornsteinfeger *m* ♦ *irreg vt* fegen, kehren; (*disease*) um sich greifen in (+*dat*); (*fashion, craze*) überrollen ♦ *vi* (*road*) sich dahinziehen; (*go quickly*) rauschen.

sweep away *vt* wegfegen; (*river*) wegspülen.

sweep past *vi* vorbeisausen.

sweep up *vti* zusammenkehren.

sweeping [swē'ping] *a* weitreichend; (*gesture*) schwungvoll; (*statement*) verallgemeinernd.

sweepstake [swēp'stāk] *n* Sweepstake *nt*; (*race*) Rennen *nt, in dem die Pferdebesitzer alle Einsätze machen*.

sweet [swēt] *n* (*Brit*: *course*) Nachtisch *m*; (: *candy*) Bonbon *nt* ♦ *a* süß; (*charming*: *person*) lieb, süß; (: *smile, character*) lieb ♦ *ad*: **to smell/taste** ~ süß riechen/ schmecken.

sweet and sour *a* süßsauer.

sweetbread [swēt'bred] *n* Bries *nt*.

sweetcorn [swēt'kôrn] *n* Zuckermais *m*.

sweeten [swēt'ən] *vt* süßen; (*fig*) versüßen.

sweetener [swēt'ənûr] *n* (*COOK*) Süßstoff *m*.
sweetheart [swēt'hârt] *n* Liebste(r) *mf*.
sweetly [swēt'lē] *ad* süß.
sweetness [swēt'nis] *n* Süße *f*.
sweet pea *n* Gartenwicke *f*.
sweet potato *n* Süßkartoffel *f*, Batate *f*.
sweetshop [swēt'shâp] *n* (*Brit*) Süßwarenladen *m or* -geschäft *nt*.
sweet-talk [swēt'tôk] *vt* (*US col*) anmachen.
sweet tooth *n*: **to have a ~** gern Süßes essen.
swell [swel] *n* Seegang *m* ♦ *a* (*col*) todschick ♦ *irreg vt* (*numbers*) vermehren ♦ *vi* (*also*: **~ up**) (an)schwellen.
swelled [sweld] *pt*, *pp of* **swell**.
swelling [swel'ing] *n* Schwellung *f*.
sweltering [swel'tûring] *a* drückend.
swept [swept] *pt*, *pp of* **sweep**.
swerve [swûrv] *n* Bogen *m*; (*in car*) Schlenker *m*; (*of road, coastline*) Schwenkung *f*, Biegung *f* ♦ *vi* einen Bogen machen (*around* um); (*car, driver*) ausschwenken.
swift [swift] *n* (*bird*) Mauersegler *m* ♦ *a* geschwind, schnell, rasch.
swiftly [swift'lē] *ad* geschwind, schnell, rasch.
swiftness [swift'nis] *n* Schnelligkeit *f*.
swig [swig] *n* Zug *m*.
swill [swil] *n* (*for pigs*) Schweinefutter *nt* ♦ *vt* spülen.
swim [swim] *n*: **to go for a ~** schwimmen gehen ♦ *irreg vi* schwimmen; **my head is ~ming** mir dreht sich der Kopf; **to go ~ming** schwimmen gehen ♦ *vt* (*river etc*) (durch)schwimmen; **to ~ a length** eine Bahn *or* Länge schwimmen.
swimmer [swim'ûr] *n* Schwimmer(in *f*) *m*.
swimming [swim'ing] *n* Schwimmen *nt*.
swimming baths *npl* (*Brit*) Schwimmbad *nt*.
swimming cap *n* Badehaube *f*, Badekappe *f*.
swimming costume *n* (*Brit*) Badeanzug *m*.
swimming pool *n* Schwimmbecken *nt*; (*private*) Swimming-Pool *m*.
swimming trunks *npl* Badehose *f*.
swimsuit [swim'sōōt] *n* Badeanzug *m*.
swindle [swin'dəl] *n* Schwindel *m*, Betrug *m* ♦ *vt* betrügen.
swindler [swind'lûr] *n* Schwindler(in *f*) *m*.
swine [swīn] *n* (*pl inv*) (*lit*, *fig*) Schwein *nt*.
swing [swing] *n* (*child's*) Schaukel *f*; (*~ing*) Schwingen *m*, Schwung *m*; (*MUS*) Swing *m* ♦ *irreg vt* schwingen, (herum)schwenken ♦ *vi* schwingen, pendeln, schaukeln; (*turn quickly*) schwenken; **to get into the ~ of things** in eine Sache reinkommen; **in full ~** in vollem Gange; **to be in full ~** voll im Gang sein; **a ~ to the left** ein Ruck nach links; **there has been a ~ towards/away from the Democrats** (*in election*) die Demokraten haben Stimmen gewonnen/verloren; **the road ~s south** die Straße biegt nach Süden.

swing bridge *n* Drehbrücke *f*.
swing door *n* (*Brit*) Schwingtür *f*.
swinging [swing'ing] *a* (*col*) locker.
swinging door *n* (*US*) Schwingtür *f*.
swingeing [swin'jing] *a* (*Brit*) hart; (*taxation, cuts*) extrem.
swipe [swīp] *n* Hieb *m* ♦ *vt* (*col*: *hit*) hart schlagen; (: *steal*) klauen.
swirl [swûrl] *n* Wirbel *m* ♦ *vi* wirbeln.
swish [swish] *n* (*sound*: *of whip*) Zischen *nt*; (*of skirts, grass*) Rauschen *nt*.
Swiss [swis] *a* Schweizer, schweizerisch ♦ *n* Schweizer(in *f*) *m*.
Swiss French *n* (*person*) Französischschweizer(in *f*) *m*.
Swiss German *n* (*person*) Deutschschweizer(in *f*) *m*.
Swiss roll *n* Biskuitrolle *f*.
switch [swich] *n* (*ELEC*) Schalter *m*; (*change*) Wechsel *m*; *see also* **switches** ♦ *vti* (*ELEC*) schalten; (*change*) wechseln; (*also*: **~ around**, **~ over**) vertauschen.
switch off *vt* ab- *or* ausschalten.
switch on *vt* an- *or* einschalten.
switchback [swich'bak] *n* (*Brit*) Achterbahn *f*.
switchblade [swich'blād] *n* (*US*) Schnappmesser *nt*.
switchboard [swich'bôrd] *n* Vermittlung *f*, Zentrale *f*; (*board*) Schaltbrett *nt*.
switches [swich'əz] *npl* (*US RAIL*) Weichen *pl*.
switchtower [swich'touûr] *n* (*US*) Stellwerk *nt*.
switchyard [swich'yârd] *n* (*US*) Rangierbahnhof *m*.
Switzerland [swit'sûrlənd] *n* die Schweiz *f*.
swivel [swiv'əl] *vti* (*also*: **~ around**) (sich) drehen.
swollen [swō'lən] *a* geschwollen ♦ *pp of* **swell**.
swoon [swōōn] *vi* (*old*) in Ohnmacht fallen.
swoop [swōōp] *n* (*of bird etc*) Sturzflug *m*; (*esp by police*) Razzia *f* ♦ *vi* (*also*: **~ down**) stürzen.
swop [swâp] = **swap**.
sword [sôrd] *n* Schwert *nt*.
swordfish [sôrd'fish] *n* Schwertfisch *m*.
swordsman [sôrdz'mən] *n*, *pl* **-men** Fechter *m*.
swore [swôr] *pt of* **swear**.
sworn [swôrn] *pp of* **swear**.
swot [swât] *vti* (*Brit*) pauken.
swum [swum] *pp of* **swim**.
swung [swung] *pt*, *pp of* **swing**.
sycamore [sik'əmôr] *n* (*US*) Platane *f*; (*Brit*) Bergahorn *m*.
sycophant [sik'əfənt] *n* Speichellecker *m*.
sycophantic [sikəfan'tik] *a* schmeichlerisch, kriecherisch.
Sydney [sid'nē] *n* Sydney *nt*.
syllable [sil'əbəl] *n* Silbe *f*.
syllabus [sil'əbəs] *n* Lehrplan *m*; **on the ~** im Lehrplan.

symbol [sim'bəl] *n* Symbol *nt*.
symbolic(al) [simbâl'ik(əl)] *a* symbolisch; **to be ~ of sth** etw symbolisieren, symbolisch sein für etw.
symbolism [sim'bəlizəm] *n* symbolische Bedeutung *f*; (*ART*) Symbolismus *m*.
symbolize [sim'bəlīz] *vt* versinnbildlichen, symbolisieren.
symmetrical [simet'rikəl] *a*, **symmetrically** [simet'rikəlē] *ad* symmetrisch, gleichmäßig.
symmetry [sim'itrē] *n* Symmetrie *f*.
sympathetic [simpəthet'ik] *a* mitfühlend; **to be ~ to sth** (*well-disposed*) einer Sache wohlwollend gegenüberstehen; **to be ~ towards sb** mit jdm mitfühlen.
sympathize [sim'pəthīz] *vi* (*feel compassion*) sympathisieren; (*agree*) mitfühlen; (*understand*) Verständnis haben (*with* für).
sympathizer [sim'pəthīzûr] *n* Mitfühlende(r) *mf*; (*POL*) Sympathisant(in *f*) *m*.
sympathy [sim'pəthē] *n* Mitleid *nt*, Mitgefühl *nt*; (*condolence*) Beileid *nt*; **letter of ~** Beileidsbrief *m*.
symphonic [simfân'ik] *a* sinfonisch.
symphony [sim'fənē] *n* Sinfonie *f*.
symphony orchestra *n* Sinfonieorchester *nt*.
symposium [simpō'zēəm] *n* Tagung *f*.
symptom [simp'təm] *n* Symptom *nt*, Anzeichen *nt*.
symptomatic [simptəmat'ik] *a* symptomatisch (*of* für).
synagogue [sin'əgâg] *n* Synagoge *f*.
synchromesh [sing'krəmesh] *n* Synchronschaltung *f*, Synchrongetriebe *nt*.
synchronize [sing'krəniz] *vt* synchronisieren ♦ *vi* gleichzeitig sein *or* ablaufen.
syncopated [sing'kəpâtid] *a* synkopiert.
syndicate [sin'dəkit] *n* Konsortium *nt*, Verband *m*, Ring *m*; (*PRESS*) (Presse)zentrale *f*.
syndrome [sin'drōm] *n* Syndrom *nt*.
synonym [sin'ənim] *n* Synonym *nt*.
synonymous [sinân'əməs] *a* gleichbedeutend.
synopsis [sinâp'sis] *n*, *pl* **synopses** [sinâp'sēz] Abriß *m*, Zusammenfassung *f*.
syntactic [sintak'tik] *a* syntaktisch.
syntax [sin'taks] *n* Syntax *f*.
syntax error *n* (*COMPUT*) Syntaxfehler *m*.
synthesis [sin'thəsis] *n*, *pl* **syntheses** [sin'thəsēz] Synthese *f*.
synthesizer [sin'thisīzûr] *n* (*MUS*) Synthesizer *m*.
synthetic [sinthet'ik] *a* synthetisch, künstlich ♦ *n* Kunststoff *m*; (*textile*) synthetische(r) Stoff *m*.
syphilis [sif'əlis] *n* Syphilis *f*.
syphon [sī'fən] = **siphon**.
Syria [sēr'ēə] *n* Syrien *nt*.
Syrian [sēr'ēən] *a* syrisch ♦ *n* Syrier(in *f*) *m*, Syrer(in *f*) *m*.
syringe [sərinj'] *n* Spritze *f*.
syrup [sir'əp] *n* Sirup *m*; (*of sugar*) Melasse *f*.

system [sis'təm] *n* System *nt*; **it was quite a shock to his ~** es machte ihm schwer zu schaffen.
systematic [sistəmat'ik] *a*, **systematically** [sistəmat'ikəlē] *ad* systematisch, planmäßig.
system disk *n* (*COMPUT*) Systemplatte *f*.
systems analyst [sis'təmz an'əlist] *n* Systemanalytiker(in *f*) *m*.

T

T, t [tē] *n* (*letter*) T *nt*, t *nt*; **to a T** genau; **T for Tommy** ≈ T wie Theodor.
ta *interj* (*Brit col*) danke.
TA *n abbr* (*US*: = *teaching assistant*) ≈ Wiss. Ass.
tab [tab] *n abbr* = **tabulator** ♦ *n* Schlaufe *f*, Aufhänger *m*; (*name ~*) Schild *nt*; **to keep ~s on** (*fig*) genau im Auge behalten.
tabby [tab'ē] *n* (*female cat*) (weibliche) Katze *f* ♦ *a* (*striped*) getigert.
tabernacle [tab'ûrnakəl] *n* Tabernakel *nt or m*.
table [tā'bəl] *n* Tisch *m*; (*list, chart*) Tabelle *f*, Tafel *f*; **to clear the ~** den Tisch abräumen; **to lay sth on the ~** (*fig*) etw zur Diskussion stellen.
tableau [tablō'] *n*, *pl* **-s** *or* **-x** lebende(s) Bild *nt*.
tablecloth [tā'bəlklôth] *n* Tischtuch *nt*, Tischdecke *f*.
table d'hôte [tâb'əl dōt'] *n* Tagesmenü *nt*.
tableland [tā'bəlland] *n* Tafelland *nt*, Plateau *nt*, Hochebene *f*.
tablemat [tā'bəlmat] *n* Untersatz *m*.
tablespoon [tā'bəlspōōn] *n* Eßlöffel *m*.
tablespoonful [tā'bəlspōōnfəl] *n* Eßlöffel(voll) *m*.
tablet [tab'lit] *n* (*MED*) Tablette *f*; (*for writing*) Täfelchen *nt*; (*of paper*) Schreibblock *m*.
table talk *n* Tischgespräch *nt*.
table tennis *n* Tischtennis *nt*.
table wine *n* Tafelwein *m*.
tabloid [tab'loid] *n* (*newspaper*) Boulevardzeitung *f*, Revolverblatt *nt* (*pej*).
taboo [tabōō'] *n* Tabu *nt* ♦ *a* tabu.
tabulate [tab'yəlāt] *vt* tabellarisch ordnen.
tabulator [tab'yəlātûr] *n* Tabulator *m*.
tachograph [tak'əgraf] *n* Fahrtenschreiber *m*.
tachometer [təkâm'ətûr] *n* Drehzahlmesser *m*.
tacit [tas'it] *a*,. **tacitly** [tas'itlē] *ad* stillschweigend.
taciturn [tas'itûrn] *a* schweigsam, wortkarg.
tack [tak] *n* (*small nail*) Stift *m*; (*US*:

thumb~) Reißzwecke *f*; (*stitch*) Heftstich *m*; (NAUT) Lavieren *nt*; (*course*) Kurs *m* ♦ *vt*: **to ~ sth on to sth** (*letter, book*) etw an etw feststecken.

tackle [tak'əl] *n* (*for lifting*) Flaschenzug *m*; (NAUT) Takelage *f*; (SPORT) Angriff *m*, Tackling *nt* ♦ *vt* (*deal with*) anpacken, in Angriff nehmen; (*person*) festhalten; (*player*) angreifen, angehen; **he couldn't ~ it** er hat es nicht bewältigt.

tacky [tak'ē] *a* (*sticky*) klebrig; (*US: shabby*) verlottert.

tact [takt] *n* Takt *m*.

tactful [takt'fəl] *a* taktvoll.

tactfully [takt'fəlē] *ad* taktvoll.

tactical [tak'tikəl] *a* taktisch.

tactics [tak'tiks] *n, npl* Taktik *f*.

tactless [takt'lis] *a*, **tactlessly** [takt'lislē] *ad* taktlos.

tadpole [tad'pōl] *n* Kaulquappe *f*.

taffeta [taf'itə] *n* Taft *m*.

taffy [taf'ē] *n* (*US*) Sahnebonbon *nt*.

tag [tag] *n* (*label*) Schild *nt*, Anhänger *m*; (*maker's name*) Etikett *nt*; (*phrase*) Floskel *f*, Spruch *m*; **price/name ~** Preis-/Namensschild(chen) *nt*.

    tag along *vi* mitkommen.

tag question *n* Bestätigungsfrage *f*.

Tahiti [təhē'tē] *n* Tahiti *nt*.

tail [tāl] *n* Schwanz *m*; (*of list*) Schluß *m*; (*of comet*) Schweif *m* ♦ *vt* folgen (+*dat*); **to turn ~** ausreißen, die Flucht ergreifen; *see also* **tails**.

    tail away, tail off *vi* abfallen, schwinden.

tailback [tāl'bak] *n* (*Brit* AUT) (Rück)stau *m*.

tail coat *n* Frack *m*.

tail end *n* Schluß *m*, Ende *nt*.

tailgate [tāl'gāt] *n* (AUT) Hecktür *f*.

taillight [tāl'līt] *n* (AUT) Rücklicht *nt*.

tailor [tā'lûr] *n* Schneider *m*; **~'s (shop)** Schneiderei *f* ♦ *vt*: **~ed to meet her needs** auf ihre Bedürfnisse abgestimmt.

tailoring [tā'lûring] *n* Schneidern *nt*, Schneiderarbeit *f*.

tailor-made [tā'lûrmād] *a* (*lit*) maßgeschneidert; (*fig*) wie auf den Leib geschnitten (*for sb* jdm).

tails [tālz] *n* (*of coin*) Zahlseite *f*; **heads or ~?** Wappen oder Zahl?

tailwind [tāl'wind] *n* Rückenwind *m*.

taint [tānt] *vt* (*meat, food*) verderben; (*reputation*) beflecken, beschmutzen.

tainted [tānt'id] *a* verdorben.

Taiwan [tī'wân'] *n* Taiwan *nt*.

take [tāk] *irreg vt* nehmen; (*prize*) entgegennehmen; (*trip, exam*) machen; (*capture: person*) fassen; (: *town*) einnehmen; (*carry to a place*) bringen; (MATH: *subtract*) abziehen (*from* von); (*extract, quotation*) entnehmen (*from dat*); (*get for o.s.*) sich (*dat*) nehmen; (*gain, obtain*) bekommen; (FIN, COMM) einnehmen; (*record*) aufnehmen; (*consume*) zu sich nehmen; (PHOT) aufnehmen, machen; (*put up with*) hinnehmen;

(*respond to*) aufnehmen; (*understand, interpret*) auffassen; (*assume*) annehmen; (*contain*) fassen, Platz haben für; (GRAM) stehen mit; (*conduct: meeting*) abhalten ♦ *vi* (*dye*) angenommen werden; (*fire*) angehen ♦ *n* (CINE) Aufnahme *f*; **it won't ~ long** es dauert nicht lang(e); **it ~s 4 hours** man braucht 4 Stunden; **it ~s him 4 hours** er braucht 4 Stunden; **to ~ sth from sb** jdm etw wegnehmen; **to ~ part in** teilnehmen an (+*dat*); **to ~ place** stattfinden; **to ~ sb's hand** jds Hand nehmen; **to ~ notes** sich (*dat*) Notizen machen; **to be ~n ill** krank werden; **it will ~ at least 5 people to complete the job** es werden mindestens 5 Leute benötigt, um diese Arbeit zu erledigen; **to be ~n with sb/sth** (*attracted*) jdn/etw sympathisch finden; **~ the first (street) on the left** fahren *or* gehen Sie die erste (Straße) rechts; **I only took Russian for one year** ich habe nur ein Jahr lang Russisch gemacht; **I took him for a doctor** ich habe ihn für einen Arzt gehalten.

take after *vt fus* ähnlich sein (+*dat*).

take apart *vt* auseinandernehmen.

take away *vt* wegnehmen; (*subtract*) abziehen ♦ *vi*: **to ~ away from sth** etw schmälern; (*merit, reputation*) etw mindern; (*pleasure, fun*) etw beeinträchtigen.

take back *vt* (*return*) zurückbringen; (*retract*) zurücknehmen; (*remind*) zurückversetzen (*to in* +*acc*).

take down *vt* (*pull down*) abreißen; (*dismantle: scaffolding*) abbauen; (*write down*) aufschreiben.

take in *vt* (*deceive*) hereinlegen; (*understand*) begreifen; (*include*) einschließen; (*child, stray dog*) zu sich nehmen, ins Haus nehmen; (*dress, suit etc*) enger machen.

take off *vi* (*plane*) starten; (*col*) stiftengehen ♦ *vt* (*remove*) wegnehmen, abmachen; (*clothing*) ausziehen; (*imitate*) nachmachen.

take on *vt* (*undertake*) übernehmen; (*engage*) einstellen; (*opponent*) antreten gegen.

take out *vt* (*girl, dog*) ausführen; (*extract*) herausnehmen; (*insurance*) abschließen; (*license*) sich (*dat*) geben lassen; (*book*) ausleihen; (*remove*) entfernen; **to ~ sth out on sb** etw an jdm auslassen; **don't ~ it out on me!** laß es nicht an mir aus!

take over *vt* übernehmen ♦ *vi* ablösen (*from acc*).

take to *vt fus* (*like*) mögen; (*adopt as practice*) sich (*dat*) angewöhnen; **to ~ to doing sth** anfangen, etw zu tun.

take up *vt* (*raise*) aufnehmen; (*dress etc*) kürzer machen; (*occupy*) in Anspruch nehmen; (*absorb*) aufsaugen; (*engage in*) sich befassen mit; (*accept: offer, challenge*) annehmen; **to ~ sb up on sth** jdn beim Wort nehmen.

take up with *vt fus*: **to be ~n up with sb/sth** (*involved with*) mit jdm/etw sehr beschäftigt sein.

take upon vt: **he took it ~ himself to answer for me** er meinte, er müsse für mich antworten.

takeaway [tā'kəwā] a (Brit) = **takeout**.

taken [tā'kən] pp of **take**.

takeoff [tāk'ôf] n (AVIAT) Abflug m, Start m; (imitation) Nachahmung f.

takeout [tāk'out] a (US) zum Mitnehmen.

takeover [tāk'ōvûr] n (COMM) Übernahme f.

takeover bid n Übernahmeangebot nt.

takings [tā'kingz] npl (COMM) Einnahmen pl.

talc [talk] n (also: **talcum powder**) Talkumpuder m.

tale [tāl] n Geschichte f, Erzählung f; **to tell ~s** (fig) Geschichten erfinden.

talent [tal'ənt] n Talent nt, Begabung f.

talented [tal'əntid] a talentiert, begabt.

talent scout n Talentsucher m.

talk [tôk] n (conversation) Gespräch nt; (rumor) Gerede nt; (speech) Vortrag m; **to give a ~** einen Vortrag halten (on über +acc) ♦ vi sprechen, reden; (gossip) klatschen, reden; **~ing of films, have you seen ...?** wo wir gerade von Filmen sprechen, hast du ... gesehen?; **~ about impertinence!** so eine Frechheit! ♦ vt: **to ~ sb into doing sth** jdn überreden, etw zu tun; **to ~ shop** fachsimpeln; see also **talks**.

talk over vt besprechen.

talkative [tô'kətiv] a redselig, gesprächig.

talker [tô'kûr] n Schwätzer(in f) m.

talking point [tô'king point] n Gesprächsthema nt.

talking-to [tô'kingtōō] n: **to give sb a good ~** jdm eine Standpauke halten (col).

talks [tôks] npl (POL etc) Gespräche pl.

talk show n Talkshow f.

tall [tôl] a groß; (building) hoch; **how ~ are you?** wie groß sind Sie?

tallboy [tôl'boi] n (Brit) Kommode f.

tallness [tôl'nis] n Größe f; Höhe f.

tall story n übertriebene Geschichte f.

tally [tal'ē] n Abrechnung f ♦ vi übereinstimmen; **to keep a ~ of sth** über etw Buch führen.

talon [tal'ən] n Kralle f, Klaue f.

tambourine [tam'bərēn] n Tamburin nt.

tame [tām] a zahm; (fig) fade, langweilig ♦ vt zähmen.

tameness [tām'nis] n Zahmheit f; (fig) Langweiligkeit f.

tamper with [tam'pûr with] vt herumpfuschen an (+dat); (documents) fälschen.

tampon [tam'pân] n Tampon m.

tan [tan] n (on skin) (Sonnen)bräune f; (color) Gelbbraun nt; **to get a ~** braun werden ♦ a (color) gelbbraun.

tandem [tan'dəm] n Tandem nt.

tang [tang] n Schärfe f, scharfe(r) Geschmack m or Geruch m.

tangent [tan'jənt] n Tangente f; **to go off at a ~** (fig) (plötzlich) vom Thema abkommen or abschweifen.

tangerine [tanjərēn'] n Mandarine f.

tangible [tan'jəbəl] a (lit) greifbar; (real) handgreiflich; **~ assets** Sachanlagen pl.

Tangier [tanjiûr'] n Tanger nt.

tangle [tang'gəl] n Durcheinander nt; (trouble) Schwierigkeiten pl ♦ vt verwirren.

tango [tang'gō] n Tango m.

tank [tangk] n (container) Tank m, Behälter m; (MIL) Panzer m.

tankard [tangk'ûrd] n Seidel nt, Deckelkrug m.

tanker [tangk'ûr] n (for oil) Tanker m, Tankschiff nt; (vehicle) Tankwagen m.

tankful [tangk'fəl] n volle(r) Tank m.

tanned [tand] a (person) braun (gebrannt); (skins) gegerbt.

tannin [tan'in] n Tannin nt.

tanning [tan'ing] n (of leather) Gerben nt.

tantalizing [tan'təlīzing] a verlockend.

tantamount [tan'təmount] a gleichbedeutend (to mit).

tantrum [tan'trəm] n Wutanfall m; **to throw a ~** einen Koller or Wutanfall haben or bekommen.

Tanzania [tanzənē'ə] n Tansania nt.

Tanzanian [tanzənē'ən] a tansanisch ♦ n Tansanier(in f) m.

tap [tap] n (gentle blow) leichte(r) Schlag m, Klopfen nt; (for water) Hahn m; **on ~** (fig: resources) zur Hand; **beer on ~** Bier vom Faß ♦ vt (strike) klopfen; (supply) anzapfen; (telephone) anzapfen, abhören; **to ~ a telephone conversation** ein Telefongespräch abhören.

tap-dance [tap'dans] vi steppen.

tape [tāp] n Band nt; (magnetic) (Ton)band nt; (adhesive) Klebstreifen m; **on ~** auf Band ♦ vt (record) (auf Band) aufnehmen.

tape deck n Tapedeck nt.

tape measure n Maßband nt.

taper [tā'pûr] n (dünne) Wachskerze f ♦ vi (also: **~ off**) sich zuspitzen; (pants) nach unten enger werden.

tape-record [tāp'rikôrd'] vt auf Band aufnehmen.

tape recorder n Tonbandgerät nt.

tape recording n Tonbandaufnahme f.

tapered [tā'pûrd] a spitz zulaufend.

tapering [tā'pûring] a spitz zulaufend.

tapestry [tap'istrē] n Wandteppich m, Gobelin m.

tapeworm [tāp'wûrm'] n Bandwurm m.

tapioca [tap'ēōka] n Tapioka f.

tappet [tap'it] n Stößel m; (AUT) Nocke f.

tar [târ] n Teer m; **low-/middle-~ cigarettes** Zigaretten mit niedrigem/mittlerem Teergehalt.

tarantula [təran'chōōlə] n Tarantel f.

tardy [târ'dē] a langsam, spät.

tare [tär] n (COMM) Tara f; (of vehicle) Leergewicht nt.

target [târ'git] n Ziel nt; (board) Zielscheibe f; **to be on ~** (project) das Ziel erreichen.

target audience n Zielgruppe f.

target market n Zielmarkt m.

target practice n Zielschießen nt.

tariff [tar'if] n (duty paid) Zoll m; (list) Tarif m.

tariff barrier n Zollschranke f.

tarmac [târ'mak] n (AVIAT) Rollfeld nt.

tarn [târn] n Gebirgssee m.

tarnish [târ'nish] vt (lit) matt machen; (fig) beflecken.

tarpaulin [târpô'lin] n Plane f, Persenning f.

tarragon [tar'əgən] n Estragon m.

tarry [tar'ē] vi (old: stay) bleiben; (: delay) säumen.

tart [târt] n (Obst)torte f; (Brit col) Nutte f ♦ a scharf, sauer; (remark) scharf, spitz.

tart up vt (col) aufmachen; (person) auftakeln (col).

tartan [târ'tən] n (material) schottischkarierte(r) Stoff m; (pattern) Schottenkaro nt.

tartar [târ'tûr] n Zahnstein m.

tartare sauce [târ'tûr sôs] n Remouladensoße f.

tartly [târt'lē] ad spitz.

task [task] n Aufgabe f; (duty) Pflicht f; **to take sb to** ~ sich (dat) jdn vornehmen.

task force n Sondertrupp m.

taskmaster [task'mastûr] n: **he's a hard** ~ er ist ein strenger (Lehr)meister.

Tasmania [tazmā'nēə] n Tasmanien nt.

tassel [tas'əl] n Quaste f.

taste [tāst] n Geschmack m; (sense) Geschmackssinn m; (small quantity) Kostprobe f; (liking) Vorliebe f; **to be in bad** or **poor** ~ geschmacklos sein ♦ vt schmecken; (try) versuchen ♦ vi schmecken (of nach).

taste bud n Geschmacksknospe f.

tasteful [tāst'fəl] a, **tastefully** [tāst'fəlē] ad geschmackvoll.

tasteless [tāst'lis] a (insipid) ohne Geschmack, fade; (in bad taste) geschmacklos.

tastelessly [tāst'lislē] ad geschmacklos.

tastily [tās'tilē] ad schmackhaft.

tastiness [tās'tēnis] n Schmackhaftigkeit f.

tasty [tās'tē] a schmackhaft.

ta-ta [tâtâ'] interj (Brit col) tschüß.

tattered [tat'ûrd] a zerrissen, zerlumpt.

tatters [tat'ûrz] npl: **in** ~ in Fetzen.

tattoo [tatōō'] n (MIL) Zapfenstreich m; (on skin) Tätowierung f ♦ vt tätowieren.

tatty [tat'ē] a (Brit col) schäbig.

taught [tôt] pt, pp of **teach**.

taunt [tônt] n höhnische Bemerkung f ♦ vt verhöhnen.

Taurus [tôr'əs] n Stier m.

taut [tôt] a straff.

tavern [tav'ûrn] n Taverne f.

tawdry [tô'drē] a (bunt und) billig.

tawny [tô'nē] a gelbbraun.

tax [taks] n Steuer f ♦ vt besteuern; (strain) strapazieren; (strength) angreifen; **free of** ~ steuerfrei; **before/after** ~ brutto/netto, vor/nach Abzug der Steuern.

taxable [tak'səbəl] a (person) steuerpflichtig; (income) (be)steuerbar; (goods) besteuert, abgabenpflichtig.

tax allowance n Steuerfreibetrag m.

taxation [taksā'shən] n Besteuerung f; **system of** ~ Steuerwesen nt.

tax avoidance n Steuerumgehung f.

tax collector n Steuereinnehmer m.

tax disc n (Brit AUT) Kraftfahrzeugsteuerplakette f (die an der Windschutzscheibe angebracht wird).

tax evasion n Steuerhinterziehung f.

tax exemption n Steuerbefreiung f.

tax-free [taks'frē'] a steuerfrei.

tax haven n Steuerparadies nt.

taxi [tak'sē] n Taxi nt ♦ vi (plane) rollen.

taxidermist [tak'sidûrmist] n Tierausstopfer m.

taxi driver n Taxifahrer m.

taximeter [tak'simētûr] n Fahrpreisanzeiger m, Taxameter m.

tax inspector n (Brit) Steuerinspektor(in f) m.

taxi stand, (Brit) **taxi rank** n Taxistand m.

taxpayer [taks'pāûr] n Steuerzahler m.

tax rebate n Steuerrückvergütung f.

tax relief n Steuervergünstigung f.

tax return n Steuererklärung f.

tax shelter n Möglichkeit, durch Investitionen Steuerzahlungen auszuweichen.

tax year n Steuerjahr nt.

TB n abbr (= tuberculosis) Tb f, Tbc f.

TD n abbr (FOOTBALL) = **touchdown**; (US: = Treasury Department) Finanzministerium nt.

tea [tē] n Tee m; (Brit: meal) (frühes) Abendessen nt.

tea bag n Tee(aufguß)beutel m.

tea break n (Brit) Teepause f.

teach [tēch] vti irreg lehren; (SCH also) unterrichten; (show) zeigen, beibringen (sb sth jdm etw); **that'll** ~ **him!** das hat er nun davon!; **it taught me a lesson** (fig) dadurch habe ich gelernt.

teacher [tē'chûr] n Lehrer(in f) m; **French** ~ Französischlehrer(in f) m.

teacher training college n (for elementary schools) pädagogische Hochschule f; (for high schools) Studienseminar nt.

teach-in [tēch'in] n Teach-in nt.

teaching [tē'ching] n (teacher's work) Unterricht m, Lehren nt; (doctrine) Lehre f.

teaching aids npl Lehr- or Unterrichtsmittel pl.

teaching hospital n Ausbildungskrankenhaus nt.

tea cosy n Teewärmer m.

teacup [tē'kup] n Teetasse f.

teak [tēk] n Teakbaum m ♦ a Teak(holz)-.

tea leaves npl Teeblätter pl.

team [tēm] n (workers) Team nt; (SPORT) Mannschaft f; (animals) Gespann nt.

team up vi sich zusammentun.

team spirit n Gemeinschaftsgeist m; (SPORT) Mannschaftsgeist m.

teamwork [tēm'wûrk] n Zusammenarbeit f,

Teamwork *nt*.

tea party *n* Kaffeeklatsch *m*.

teapot [tē'påt] *n* Teekanne *f*.

tear [tär] *n* Riß *m*; [tēr] Träne *f*; **in ~s** in Tränen (aufgelöst) ♦ [tär] *irreg vt* zerreißen; *(muscle)* zerren; **to ~ to pieces** *or* **to bits** *or* **to shreds** *(also fig)* in Stücke reißen; **the critics tore the play to pieces** die Kritiker haben das Stück total verrissen; **I am torn between ...** ich schwanke zwischen ... ♦ *vi* (zer)reißen; *(rush)* rasen, sausen.

tear apart *vt (also fig)* völlig durcheinanderbringen.

tear away *vt*: **to ~ o.s. away (from sth)** *(fig)* sich (von etw) losreißen.

tear out *vt (sheet of paper, check)* herausreißen.

tear up *vt (paper etc)* zerreißen.

tearaway [tär'əwā] *n (Brit col)* Feger *m*, Rabauke *m*.

teardrop [tēr'dråp] *n* Träne *f*.

tearful [tēr'fəl] *a* weinend; *(voice)* weinerlich.

tear gas *n* Tränengas *nt*.

tearing [tär'ing] *a*: **to be in a ~ hurry** es schrecklich eilig haben.

tearoom [tē'rōōm] *n* Teestube *f*.

tease [tēz] *n* Hänsler *m* ♦ *vt* necken, aufziehen; *(animal)* quälen; *(hair)* toupieren; **I was only teasing** ich habe nur Spaß gemacht.

tea set *n* Teeservice *nt*.

teashop [tē'shåp] *n* Café *nt*.

teaspoon [tē'spōōn] *n* Teelöffel *m*.

teaspoonful [tē'spōōnfəl] *n* Teelöffel(voll) *m*.

tea strainer *n* Teesieb *nt*.

teat [tēt] *n (of woman)* Brustwarze *f*; *(of animal)* Zitze *f*; *(Brit: of bottle)* Sauger *m*, Schnuller *m*.

tea time *n (in the afternoon)* Teestunde *f*; *(mealtime)* Abendessen *nt*.

tea towel *n (Brit)* Geschirrtuch *nt*, Küchenhandtuch *nt*.

tea urn *n* Teemaschine *f*.

tech. [tek] *n abbr (col)* = **technology; technical college.**

technical [tek'nikəl] *a* technisch; *(knowledge, terms)* Fach-.

technical college *n (Brit)* Technische Fachschule *f*.

technicality [teknikal'itē] *n* technische Einzelheit *f*; *(JUR)* Formsache *f*; **because of a legal ~** aufgrund einer juristischen Formsache.

technically [tek'niklē] *ad* technisch; *(speak)* spezialisiert; *(fig)* genau genommen.

technician [teknish'ən] *n* Techniker *m*.

technique [teknēk'] *n* Technik *f*.

technocrat [tek'nəkrat] *n* Technokrat(in *f*) *m*.

technological [teknəlåj'ikəl] *a* technologisch.

technologist [teknål'əjist] *n* Technologe *m*.

technology [teknål'əjē] *n* Technologie *f*.

teddy (bear) [ted'ē (bär)] *n* Teddybär *m*.

tedious [tē'dēəs] *a*, **tediously** [tē'dēəslē] *ad* langweilig, ermüdend.

tedium [tē'dēəm] *n* Langweiligkeit *f*.

tee [tē] *n (GOLF)* Abschlagstelle *f*; *(object)* Tee *nt*.

teem [tēm] *vi (swarm)* wimmeln *(with* von); *(pour)* gießen.

teenage [tēn'āj] *a (fashions etc)* Teenager-, jugendlich.

teenager [tēn'ājûr] *n* Teenager *m*, Jugendliche(r) *mf*.

teens [tēnz] *npl* Jugendjahre *pl*.

tee shirt *n* T-shirt *nt*.

teeter [tē'tûr] *vi* schwanken.

teeth [tēth] *npl of* **tooth**.

teethe [tēth] *vi* zahnen.

teething ring [tē'thing ring] *n* Beißring *m*.

teething troubles [tē'thing trub'əlz] *npl (fig)* Kinderkrankheiten *pl*.

teetotal [tētōt'əl] *a* abstinent.

teetotaler, *(Brit)* **teetotaller** [tētōt'əlûr] *n* Antialkoholiker(in *f*) *m*, Abstinenzler(in *f*) *m*.

TEFL [tef'əl] *n abbr* = *Teaching of English as a Foreign Language.*

tel. *abbr* (= *telephone*) Tel.

Tel Aviv [tel'əvēv'] *n* Tel Aviv *nt*.

telecast [tel'əkast] *vti* über Fernsehsender ausstrahlen.

telecommunications [teləkəmyōōnikā'shənz] *npl* Fernmeldewesen *nt*.

telegram [tel'əgram] *n* Telegramm *nt*.

telegraph [tel'əgraf] *n* Telegraph *m*.

telegraph pole *n* Telegraphenmast *m*.

telegraph wire *n* Telegraphendraht *m or* -leitung *f*.

telepathic [teləpath'ik] *a* telepathisch.

telepathy [təlep'əthē] *n* Telepathie *f*, Gedankenübertragung *f*.

telephone [tel'əfōn] *n* Telefon *nt*, Fernsprecher *m*; **cordless ~** schnurlose(s) Telefon *nt* ♦ *vi* telefonieren ♦ *vt* anrufen; *(message)* telefonisch mitteilen; **to be on the ~** *(be speaking)* gerade telefonieren.

telephone booth, *(Brit)* **telephone box** *n* Telefonzelle *f*, Fernsprechzelle *f*.

telephone call *n* Telefongespräch *nt*, Anruf *m*.

telephone directory *n* Telefonbuch *nt*.

telephone exchange *n* Telefonvermittlung *f*, Telefonzentrale *f*.

telephone kiosk *n (Brit)* Telefonzelle *f*, Fernsprechzelle *f*.

telephone number *n* Telefonnummer *f*.

telephone operator *n* Telefonist(in *f*) *m*.

telephonist [tel'əfōnist] *n (Brit)* = **telephone operator.**

telephoto lens [teləfō'tō lenz] *n* Teleobjektiv *nt*.

teleprinter [tel'əprintûr] *n* Fernschreiber *m*.

telescope [tel'əskōp] *n* Teleskop *nt*, Fernrohr *nt* ♦ *vti* ineinanderschieben.

telescopic [teliskåp'ik] *a (view)* teleskopisch; *(aerial, umbrella etc)* ausziehbar, zusammenschiebbar.

teletext [tel'ətekst] *n* Bildschirmtext *m*, Btx *m*.

telethon [tel'əthân] *n sehr lange Fernseh-sendung, in deren Verlauf Spenden für wohltätige Zwecke gesammelt werden*.

televise [tel'əvīz] *vt* durch das Fernsehen übertragen.

television [tel'əvizhən] *n* Fernsehen *nt*; *(set)* Fernsehapparat *m*, Fernseher *m*; **to watch** ~ fernsehen; **on** ~ im Fernsehen.

television licence *n (Brit)* Fernsehgeneh-migung *f*.

television set *n* Fernsehapparat *m*, Fernse-her *m*.

telex [tel'eks] *n (message, document)* Fernschreiben *nt*, Telex *nt*; *(machine)* Fernschreiber *m*; *(service)* Telexdienst *m* ♦ *vti (message)* über Fernschreiber *or* fernschriftlich mitteilen; *(person)* ein Fernschreiben *or* Telex schicken (+*dat*).

tell [tel] *irreg vt (story)* erzählen; *(secret)* ausplaudern; *(say, make known)* sagen *(sth to sb* jdm etw); *(talk)* sprechen *(of* von); *(distinguish)* erkennen *(sb by sth* jdn an etw *dat)*; *(be sure)* wissen; *(order)* sagen, be-fehlen *(sb* jdm); **to** ~ **a lie** lügen; **can you** ~ **me the time?** können Sie mir sagen, wie spät es ist?; **to be able to** ~ **the time** die Uhr kennen; **(I)** ~ **you what** ... weißt du was ...; **I couldn't** ~ **them apart** ich konnte sie nicht auseinanderhalten; **to** ~ **sb about sth** jdm von etw erzählen; **to** ~ **sth from** etw unterscheiden von ♦ *vi (be sure)* wissen; *(di-vulge)* es verraten; *(have effect)* sich aus-wirken.

tell off *vt* schimpfen.

tell on *vt fus* verraten, verpetzen.

teller [tel'ûr] *n* Kassenbeamte(r) *mf*.

telling [tel'ing] *a* verräterisch; *(blow)* hart; *(moment)* der Wahrheit. ˙

telltale [tel'tāl] *a* verräterisch.

telly [tel'ē] *n (Brit col)* Fernseher *m*.

temerity [təmär'itē] *n* (Toll)kühnheit *f*.

temp [temp] *(Brit col) n abbr (= temporary office worker)* Aushilfskraft im Büro ♦ *vi* jobben.

temper [tem'pûr] *n (disposition)* Wesen *nt*; *(anger)* Wut *f*, Zorn *m*; **to lose one's** ~ die Beherrschung verlieren *(with sb* bei jdm); **to keep one's** ~ sich beherrschen; **to be in a (bad)** ~ wütend *or* gereizt sein; **quick** ~**ed** jähzornig, aufbrausend ♦ *vt (tone down)* mil-dern; *(metal)* härten.

temperament [tem'pûrəmənt] *n* Tempera-ment *nt*, Veranlagung *f*.

temperamental [tempûrəmen'təl] *a (moody)* launisch.

temperance [tem'pûrəns] *n* Mäßigung *f*; *(ab-stinence)* Enthaltsamkeit *f*.

temperate [tem'pûrit] *a* gemäßigt.

temperature [tem'pûrəchûr] *n* Temperatur *f*; *(MED: high* ~) Fieber *nt*.

tempered [tem'pûrd] *a (steel)* gehärtet.

tempest [tem'pist] *n* (wilder) Sturm *m*.

tempestuous [tempes'chōōəs] *a* stürmisch; *(fig)* ungestüm; *(relationship)* leidenschaft-

lich.

tempi [tem'pē] *npl of* **tempo**.

template [tem'plit] *n* Schablone *f*.

temple [tem'pəl] *n* Tempel *m*; *(ANAT)* Schlä-fe *f*.

tempo [tem'pō] *n, pl* **-s** *or* **tempi** [tem'pē] Tempo *nt*.

temporal [tem'pûrəl] *a (of time)* zeitlich; *(worldly)* irdisch, weltlich.

temporarily [tempərär'ilē] *ad* zeitweilig, vor-übergehend.

temporary [tem'pərärē] *a* vorläufig; *(road, building)* provisorisch; ~ **teacher** Aushilfs-lehrer(in *f*) *m*.

tempt [tempt] *vt (persuade)* verleiten, in Ver-suchung führen; *(attract)* reizen, (ver)-locken; **to be** ~**ed to do sth** versucht sein, etw zu tun.

temptation [temptā'shən] *n* Versuchung *f*.

tempting [temp'ting] *a (person)* verführe-risch; *(object, situation)* verlockend.

ten [ten] *num* zehn; ~**s of thousands** Zehn-tausende *pl*.

tenable [ten'əbəl] *a (fig: opinion, theory)* ver-tretbar; *(MIL: position)* haltbar.

tenacious [tənā'shəs] *a*, **tenaciously** [tənā'shəslē] *ad* zäh, hartnäckig.

tenacity [tənas'itē] *n* Zähigkeit *f*, Hartnäckig-keit *f*.

tenancy [ten'ənsē] *n* Mietverhältnis *nt*; Pachtverhältnis *nt*.

tenant [ten'ənt] *n* Mieter(in *f*) *m*; *(of larger property)* Pächter(in *f*) *m*.

tend [tend] *vt (look after)* sich kümmern um; *(sick etc)* pflegen; *(cattle)* hüten; *(machine)* bedienen ♦ *vi* neigen, tendieren *(to* zu); **to** ~ **to do sth** etw gewöhnlich tun.

tendency [ten'dənsē] *n* Tendenz *f*; *(of person also)* Neigung *f*.

tender [ten'dûr] *a (soft)* weich, zart; *(delic-ate)* zart; *(loving)* liebevoll, zärtlich ♦ *n (COMM: offer)* Kostenanschlag *m*; **to put in a** ~ **for sth** ein Angebot *or* eine Submissionsofferte *(form)* für etw machen *or* einreichen ♦ *vt*: **to** ~ **one's resignation** seinen Rücktritt *or* seine Kündigung einrei-chen.

tenderize [ten'dərīz] *vt* weich machen.

tenderly [ten'dûrlē] *ad* liebevoll; *(touch also)* zart.

tenderness [ten'dûrnis] *n* Zartheit *f*; *(affec-tion)* Zärtlichkeit *f*.

tendon [ten'dən] *n* Sehne *f*.

tendril [ten'dril] *n* Ranke *f*.

tenement [ten'əmənt] *n* Mietshaus *nt*.

Tenerife [tenərēf'] *n* Teneriffa *nt*.

tenet [ten'it] *n* Lehre *f*.

Tenn. *abbr (US)* = *Tennessee*.

tenner [ten'ûr] *n (col)* Zehner *m*.

tennis [ten'is] *n* Tennis *nt*.

tennis ball *n* Tennisball *m*.

tennis club *n* Tennisclub *or* -verein *m*.

tennis court *n* Tennisplatz *m*.

tennis elbow *n (MED)* Tennisarm *m*.

tennis match n Tennismatch nt.
tennis player n Tennisspieler(in f) m.
tennis racket n Tennisschläger m.
tennis shoes npl Tennisschuhe pl.
tenor [ten'ûr] n (voice) Tenor(stimme f) m; (singer) Tenor m; (meaning) Sinn m, wesentliche(r) Inhalt m.
tenpin bowling [ten'pin bō'ling] n (Brit) Bowling nt.
tenpins [ten'pinz] n (US) Bowling nt.
tense [tens] a angespannt; (stretched tight) gespannt, straff ♦ n Zeitform f ♦ vt (tighten: muscles) anspannen.
tensely [tens'lē] ad (an)gespannt.
tenseness [tens'nis] n Spannung f; (strain) (An)gespanntheit f.
tension [ten'chən] n Spannung f; (strain) (An)gespanntheit f.
tent [tent] n Zelt nt.
tentacle [ten'təkəl] n Fühler m; (of sea creatures) Fangarm m.
tentative [ten'tətiv] a (movement) unsicher; (offer) Probe-; (arrangement) vorläufig; (suggestion) unverbindlich.
tentatively [ten'tətivlē] ad versuchsweise; (try, move) vorsichtig.
tenterhooks [ten'tûrhŏŏks] npl: **to be on ~** auf die Folter gespannt sein.
tenth [tenth] a zehnte(r, s) ♦ n (fraction) Zehntel nt; (in series) Zehnte(r, s).
tent peg n Hering m.
tent pole n Zeltstange f.
tenuous [ten'yŏŏəs] a fein; (air) dünn; (connection, argument) schwach.
tenure [ten'yûr] n (of land) Besitz m; (of office) Amtszeit f; **to have ~** (of property) innehaben.
tepid [tep'id] a lauwarm.
term [tûrm] n (period of time) Zeitraum m; (limit) Frist f; (Brit SCH) Quartal nt; (UNIV) Semester nt, Trimester nt; (expression) Ausdruck m; **during his ~ of office** während seiner Amtszeit; **in the short/long ~** auf kurze/lange Sicht; **to come to ~s with** (person) sich einigen mit; (problem) sich abfinden mit; see also **terms** ♦ vt nennen.
terminal [tûr'mənəl] n (COMPUT) Datenendgerät nt, Terminal nt; (AVIAT) Terminal m; (Brit rail, bus ~) Endstation f ♦ a Schluß-; (MED) unheilbar.
terminate [tûr'mənāt] vt beenden ♦ vi enden, aufhören (in auf +dat).
termination [tûrmənā'shən] n Ende nt; (act) Beendigung f; (of contract) Ablauf m, Erlöschen nt; **~ of pregnancy** Schwangerschaftsabbruch m.
termini [tûr'mənē] npl of **terminus**.
terminology [tûrmənâl'əjē] n Terminologie f.
terminus [tûr'mənəs] n, pl **termini** [tûr'mənē] Endstation f.
termite [tûr'mīt] n Termite f.
terms [tûrmz] npl (conditions) Bedingungen pl; (relationship) Beziehungen pl; **to be on**

good ~ with sb mit jdm gut auskommen; **in ~ of money/time** geldlich/zeitlich.
Ter(r). abbr = **Terrace**.
terrace [tär'əs] n (in garden etc) Terrasse f; (Brit: of houses) Häuserreihe f; **the ~s** (Brit SPORT) die Ränge pl.
terraced [tär'əst] a (garden) terrassenförmig angelegt; **~ house** (Brit) Reihenhaus nt.
terracotta [tärəkât'ə] n Terrakotta f.
terrain [tərān'] n Gelände nt, Terrain nt.
terrible [tär'əbəl] a schrecklich, entsetzlich, fürchterlich.
terribly [tär'əblē] ad fürchterlich.
terrier [tär'ēûr] n Terrier m.
terrific [tərif'ik] a unwahrscheinlich; **~!** klasse!
terrify [tär'əfī] vt erschrecken; **to be terrified** schreckliche Angst haben.
terrifying [tär'əfīing] a erschreckend, grauenvoll.
territorial [täritôr'ēəl] a Gebiets-, territorial.
territorial waters npl Hoheitsgewässer pl, Territorialgewässer pl.
territory [tär'itôrē] n Gebiet nt.
terror [tär'ûr] n Schrecken m; (POL) Terror m.
terrorism [tär'ərizəm] n Terrorismus m.
terrorist [tär'ûrist] n Terrorist(in f) m.
terrorize [tär'ərīz] vt terrorisieren.
terse [tûrs] a knapp, kurz, bündig.
tertiary [tûr'shēärē] a tertiär.
Terylene [tär'əlēn] n ® Terylen(e) nt, ≈ Trevira ® nt, Diolen ® nt.
TESL [tes'əl] n abbr = Teaching of English as a Second Language.
test [test] n Probe f; (examination) Prüfung f; (PSYCH, TECH) Test m ♦ vt prüfen; (PSYCH) testen; **to put sth to the ~** etw auf die Probe stellen; **to ~ sth for accuracy** etw auf Genauigkeit prüfen.
testament [tes'təmənt] n Testament nt.
test ban n: **(nuclear) ~** Atomteststopp m.
test case n (JUR) Präzedenzfall m; (fig) Musterbeispiel nt.
test flight n Probeflug m.
testicle [tes'tikəl] n Hoden m.
testify [tes'təfī] vi bezeugen (to acc).
testimonial [testimō'nēəl] n (of character) Referenz f.
testimony [tes'təmōnē] n (JUR) Zeugenaussage f; (fig) Zeugnis nt.
testing [tes'ting] a (difficult: time) hart.
testing ground n Test- or Versuchsgebiet nt; (fig) Versuchsfeld nt.
test match n (Brit SPORT) Länderkampf m.
test paper n schriftliche (Klassen)arbeit f.
test pattern n (US TV) Testbild nt.
test pilot n Testpilot m.
test tube n Reagenzglas nt ♦ a: **~ baby** Kind nt aus der Retorte, Retortenbaby nt.
testy [tes'tē] a gereizt, reizbar.
tetanus [tet'ənəs] n Wundstarrkrampf m, Tetanus m.
tetchy [tech'ē] a gereizt.

tether [teth'ûr] *vt* anbinden; **to be at the end of one's** ~ (*Brit*) völlig am Ende sein.

Tex. *abbr* (*US*) = *Texas.*

text [tekst] *n* Text *m*; (*of document*) Wortlaut *m.*

textbook [tekst'boōk] *n* Lehrbuch *nt.*

textile [teks'təl] *n* Gewebe *nt*; ~s Textilien *pl,* Textilwaren *pl.*

texture [teks'chûr] *n* Beschaffenheit *f*, Struktur *f*; (*of food*) Substanz *f*; (*of minerals*) Gestalt *f.*

TGIF *abbr* = *thank God it's Friday.*

Thai [tī] *a* thailändisch ♦ *n* Thailänder(in *f*) *m*, Thai *mf*; (*language*) Thai *nt.*

Thailand [tī'lənd] *n* Thailand *nt.*

thalidomide [thəlid'əmīd] *n* ® Contergan ® *nt*, Thalidomid *nt.*

Thames [temz] *n* Themse *f.*

than [than] *prep, cj* als; **it is better to phone** ~ **to write** es ist besser zu telefonieren als zu schreiben; **no sooner did he leave** ~ **the phone rang** kaum war er gegangen, da klingelte das Telefon.

thank [thangk] *vt* danken (+*dat*); ~ **heavens** *or* **God!** Gott sei Dank!; **you've him to** ~ **for your success** Sie haben Ihren Erfolg ihm zu verdanken; *see also* **thanks.**

thankful [thangk'fəl] *a* dankbar (*for* für); ~ **that** (*relieved*) froh, daß.

thankfully [thangk'fəlē] *ad* (*luckily*) zum Glück; (*gratefully*) dankbar; ~ **there were few victims** zum Glück gab es nur wenige Opfer.

thankless [thangk'lis] *a* undankbar.

thanks [thangks] *npl* Dank *m*; ~ **to** dank (+*gen*) ♦ *interj* danke.

Thanksgiving Day [thangksgiv'ing dā] *n* (*US*) Thanksgiving Day *m.*

thank you *interj* danke (schön).

that [that] *demonstrative a, pl* **those** der/die/das, jene(r, s) ♦ *demonstrative pron, pl* **those** das ♦ *rel pron* der/die/das; *pl* die ♦ *cj* daß; **so** ~, **in order** ~ damit, um; **not** ~ **I know of** nicht daß ich wüßte; **and** ~'**s** ~ und damit Schluß; ~ **is** das heißt; ~ **one over there** das da; **what is** ~? was ist das?; **at** *or* **with** ~, **she got up and left** damit stand sie auf und ging; **do it like** ~ mach es (doch) so; **after** ~ danach; **at** ~ dazu noch; ~ **big** so groß.

thatched [thacht] *a* strohgedeckt.

thaw [thô] *n* Tauwetter *nt* ♦ *vi* tauen; (*frozen foods, fig: people*) auftauen ♦ *vt* (auf)tauen lassen.

the [thə] *def art* der/die/das; *pl* die; **to play** ~ **piano** Klavier spielen; **I haven't** ~ **time/money** ich hab die Zeit/das Geld nicht; **do you know** ~ **Smiths?** kennen Sie die Smiths?; **twenty pence** ~ **pound** zwanzig Pence das *or* pro Pfund; **paid by** ~ **hour** pro Stunde bezahlt; **Richard** ~ **Second** Richard der Zweite ♦ *ad*: ~ **sooner** ~ **better** je eher desto besser; ~ **more he works** ~ **more he earns** je mehr er arbeitet, desto

mehr verdient er.

theater, (*Brit*) **theatre** [thē'ətûr] *n* Theater *nt*; (*for lectures etc*) Saal *m*; (*MED*) Operationssaal *m.*

theatergoer, (*Brit*) **theatregoer** [thē'ətûrgōūr] *n* Theaterbesucher(in *f*) *m.*

theatrical [thēat'rikəl] *a* Theater-; (*career*) Schauspieler-; (*showy*) theatralisch.

theft [theft] *n* Diebstahl *m.*

their [thär] *poss a* ihr.

theirs [thärz] *poss pron* ihre(r, s).

them [them] *pron* (*acc*) sie; (*dat*) ihnen; **both of** ~ beide; **give me a few of** ~ geben Sie mir ein paar davon.

theme [thēm] *n* Thema *nt*; (*MUS*) Motiv *nt.*

theme song *n* Titelmusik *f.*

themselves [themselvz'] *pl pron* (*reflexive*) sich (selbst); (*emphatic*) selbst.

then [then] *ad* (*at that time*) damals; (*next*) dann ♦ *cj* also, folglich; (*furthermore*) ferner ♦ *a* damalig; **until** ~ bis dann; **and** ~ **what?** und was dann?; **what do you want me to do** ~? was soll ich denn machen?; **from** ~ **on** von da an; **before** ~ davor; **by** ~ bis dahin; **not till** ~ erst dann.

theologian [thēəlō'jən] *n* Theologe *m*, Theologin *f.*

theological [thēəlâj'ikəl] *a* theologisch.

theology [thēâl'əjē] *n* Theologie *f.*

theorem [thēr'əm] *n* Grundsatz *m*, Theorem *nt.*

theoretical [thēəret'ikəl] *a*, **theoretically** [thēəret'ikəlē] *ad* theoretisch.

theorize [thē'ərīz] *vi* theoretisieren.

theory [thēûr'ē] *n* Theorie *f.*

therapeutic(al) [thärəpyōōtik(əl)] *a* (*MED*) therapeutisch; (*fig*) erholsam.

therapist [thär'əpist] *a* Therapeut(in *f*) *m.*

therapy [thär'əpē] *n* Therapie *f*, Behandlung *f.*

there [thär] *ad* dort; (*to a place*) dorthin ♦ *interj* (*see*) na also; (*to child*) (sei) ruhig, na na; ~ **is** es gibt; ~ **are** es sind, es gibt; ~ **he is!** da ist er!; ~'**s the bus** da kommt der Bus; **back** ~ da drüben/dahinten; **down** ~ da unten; **over** ~ da drüben; **in** ~ da drin; **through** ~ da durch.

thereabouts [thär'əbouts] *ad* so ungefähr.

thereafter [thäraf'tûr] *ad* danach, später.

thereby [thärbī'] *ad* dadurch, damit.

therefore [thär'fôr] *ad* daher, deshalb.

there's [thärz] = **there is; there has.**

thereupon [thärəpân'] *ad* (*at that point*) darauf(hin); (*form: on that subject*) darüber.

thermal [thûr'məl] *a* Thermal-; (*PHYS*) thermisch; ~ **paper** Thermopapier *nt*; ~ **printer** Thermodrucker *m.*

thermodynamics [thûrmōdīnam'iks] *npl* Thermodynamik *f.*

thermometer [thûrmâm'itûr] *n* Thermometer *nt.*

thermonuclear [thûrmōnōō'klēûr] *a* thermonuklear.

Thermos [thûr'məs] *n* ® Thermosflasche *f.*

thermostat [thûr'məstat] *n* Thermostat *m*.
thesaurus [thisôr'əs] *n* Synonymwörterbuch *nt*.
these [ŧhēz] *pl pron, a* diese.
thesis [thē'sis] *n, pl* **theses** [thē'sēz] (*for discussion*) These *f*; (*UNIV*) Dissertation *f*, Doktorarbeit *f*.
they [ŧhā] *pl pron* sie; (*people in general*) man.
they'd [ŧhād] = **they had, they would.**
they'll [ŧhāl] = **they shall, they will.**
they're [ŧhār] = **they are.**
they've [ŧhāv] = **they have.**
thick [thik] *a* dick; (*forest*) dicht; (*liquid*) dickflüssig; (*slow, stupid*) dumm, schwer von Begriff ♦ *n*: **in the ~ of** mitten in (+*dat*).
thicken [thik'ən] *vi* (*fog*) dichter werden ♦ *vt* (*sauce etc*) verdicken.
thicket [thik'it] *n* Dickicht *nt*.
thickly [thik'lē] *ad* (*spread, cut*) dick; (*populated*) dicht.
thickness [thik'nis] *n* (*of object*) Dicke *f*; Dichte *f*; Dickflüssigkeit *f*; (*of person*) Dummheit *f*.
thickset [thik'set'] *a* untersetzt.
thickskinned [thik'skind'] *a* dickhäutig.
thief [thēf] *n, pl* **thieves** [thēvz] Dieb(in *f*) *m*.
thieving [thē'ving] *n* Stehlen *nt* ♦ *a* diebisch.
thigh [thī] *n* Oberschenkel *m*.
thighbone [thī'bōn] *n* Oberschenkelknochen *m*.
thimble [thim'bəl] *n* Fingerhut *m*.
thin [thin] *a* dünn; (*person also*) mager; (*not abundant*) spärlich; (*fog, rain*) leicht; (*excuse*) schwach ♦ *vi* (*fog, hair*) sich lichten; (*also:* ~ **out:** *crowd*) kleiner werden ♦ *vt* (*also:* ~ **down:** *sauce, paint*) verdünnen.
thing [thing] *n* Ding *nt*; (*affair*) Sache *f*; **the main ~ is** ... die Hauptsache ist ...; **I'll do it first ~ in the morning** ich mache es morgen früh gleich als erstes; **last ~ (at night)** vor dem Schlafengehen; **the ~ is** ... die Sache ist die, ...; **she's got a ~ about mice** (*col*) sie kann Mäuse (einfach) nicht ausstehen; **poor ~!** das arme Ding!; **my ~s** (*belongings*) meine Sachen *pl*.
think [thingk] *vti irreg* denken; (*believe*) meinen, denken; (*be of opinion*) glauben; **to ~ of sb/sth** an jdn/etw (*acc*) denken; **what do you ~ of it?** was halten Sie davon?; **to ~ of doing sth** vorhaben *or* beabsichtigen, etw zu tun; ~ **again!** denk noch mal nach!; **to ~ aloud** laut denken; **I ~ so** ich denke *or* glaube (schon); **I'll ~ about it** ich überlege es mir.
think out *vt* (*plan*) durchdenken; (*solution*) ausdenken.
think over *vt* überdenken; **I'd like to ~ things over** (*offer, suggestion*) ich möchte darüber nachdenken, ich möchte es mir nochmal überlegen.
think through *vt* (gründlich) durchdenken.

think up *vt* sich (*dat*) ausdenken.
thinking [thingk'ing] *a* denkend ♦ *n*: **to my (way of)** ~ meiner Meinung nach.
think tank *n* Planungsstab *m*.
thinly [thin'lē] *ad* dünn; (*disguised*) kaum.
thinness [thin'is] *n* Dünnheit *f*; Magerkeit *f*; Spärlichkeit *f*.
third [thûrd] *a* dritte(r, s) ♦ *n* (*person*) Dritte(r) *mf*; (*part*) Drittel *nt*.
third-degree burns [thûrd'digrē bûrnz] *npl* Verbrennungen *pl* dritten Grades.
thirdly [thûrd'lē] *ad* drittens.
third party insurance *n* (*Brit*) Haftpflichtversicherung *f*.
third-rate [thûrd'rāt'] *a* minderwertig.
Third World *n* Dritte Welt *f* ♦ *a* Dritte-Welt-.
thirst [thûrst] *n* (*lit, fig*) Durst *m*; (*fig*) Verlangen *nt*.
thirsty [thûrs'tē] *a* (*person*) durstig; (*work*) durstig machend; **to be ~** Durst haben.
thirteen [thûr'tēn'] *num* dreizehn.
thirteenth [thûr'tēnth'] *a* dreizehnte(r, s) ♦ *n* (*in series*) Dreizehnte(r, s); (*fraction*) Dreizehntel *nt*.
thirtieth [thûr'tēith] *a* dreißigste(r, s) ♦ *n* (*in series*) Dreißigste(r, s); (*fraction*) Dreißigstel *nt*.
thirty [thûr'tē] *num* dreißig.
this [ŧhis] *demonstrative a, pl* **these** diese(r, s) ♦ *demonstrative pron, pl* **these** dies, das; ~ **time** diesmal, dieses Mal; ~ **way** auf diese Weise; ~ **time last year** letztes Jahr um diese Zeit; **who/what is ~?** wer/was ist das?; ~ **is Mr Brown** (*in introductions, in photo*) das (hier) ist Mr. Brown; (*on telephone*) Brown (hier); **they were talking of ~ and that** sie sprachen über alles mögliche; **it was ~ long** es war so lang.
thistle [this'əl] *n* Distel *f*.
thong [thông] *n* (Leder)riemen *m*.
thorn [thôrn] *n* Dorn *m*, Stachel *m*; (*plant*) Dornbusch *m*.
thorny [thôr'nē] *a* dornig; (*problem*) schwierig.
thorough [thûr'ō] *a* gründlich; (*contempt*) tief.
thoroughbred [thûr'ōbred] *n* Vollblut *nt* ♦ *a* reinrassig, Vollblut-.
thoroughfare [thûr'ōfär] *n* Durchgangsstraße.
thoroughly [thûr'ōlē] *ad* gründlich; (*extremely*) vollkommen, äußerst.
thoroughness [thûr'ōnis] *n* Gründlichkeit *f*, Sorgfältigkeit *f*.
those [ŧhōz] *pl pron* die (da), jene ♦ *a* die, jene; ~ **who** diejenigen, die.
though [ŧhō] *cj* obwohl ♦ *ad* trotzdem, doch; **it's not so easy,** ~ ... es ist nicht so einfach, doch ...; **even** ~ obwohl, obgleich; **as** ~ als ob.
thought [thôt] *n* (*idea*) Gedanke *m*; (*opinion*) Auffassung *f*; (*thinking*) Denken *nt*, Denkvermögen *nt*; **after much** ~ nach langer Überlegung *or* langem Überlegen; **I've**

just had a ~ mir ist gerade ein Gedanke gekommen, mir ist gerade etw eingefallen; **to give sth some** ~ sich (dat) Gedanken über etw (acc) machen, etw bedenken or überlegen ♦ pt, pp of **think.**

thoughtful [thôt'fəl] a (thinking) gedankenvoll, nachdenklich; (kind) rücksichtsvoll, aufmerksam.

thoughtfully [thôt'fəlē] ad nachdenklich; rücksichtsvoll.

thoughtless [thôt'lis] a gedankenlos, unbesonnen; (unkind) rücksichtslos.

thoughtlessly [thôt'lislē] ad gedankenlos; rücksichtslos.

thousand [thou'zənd] num tausend; **two** ~ zweitausend; ~**s of** Tausende (von).

thousandth [thou'zəndth] a tausendste(r, s).

thrash [thrash] vt (lit) verdreschen; (fig) (vernichtend) schlagen.

thrash about vi um sich schlagen.

thrash out vt ausdiskutieren.

thrashing [thrash'ing] n: **to give sb a** ~ (beat) jdm eine Tracht Prügel verpassen; (SPORT: defeat) jdn vernichtend schlagen.

thread [thred] n Faden m, Garn nt; (on screw) Gewinde nt; (in story) Faden m, Zusammenhang m ♦ vt (needle) einfädeln; **to** ~ **one's way** sich hindurchschlängeln.

threadbare [thred'bär] a (lit, fig) fadenscheinig.

threat [thret] n Drohung f; (danger) Bedrohung f, Gefahr f; **under** ~ **of sth** unter Androhung (+gen); **to be under** ~ **of exposure** Gefahr laufen, bloßgestellt or entlarvt zu werden.

threaten [thret'ən] vt bedrohen; **to** ~ **sb with sth** jdm etw androhen ♦ vi drohen.

threatening [thret'əning] a drohend; (letter) Droh-.

three [thrē] num drei.

three-dimensional [thrē'dimen'chənəl] a dreidimensional.

threefold [thrē'fōld] a dreifach.

three-piece suit [thrē'pēs sōōt] n dreiteilige(r) Anzug m.

three-piece suite [thrē'pēs swēt] n dreiteilige Polstergarnitur f.

three-ply [thrē'plī] a (wool) dreifach; (wood) dreischichtig.

three-quarter [thrē'kwôr'tûr] a dreiviertel.

three-quarters [thrē'kwôr'tûrz] npl Dreiviertel nt ♦ ad: ~ **full** dreiviertel voll.

thresh [thresh] vti dreschen.

threshing machine [thresh'ing məshēn'] n Dreschmaschine f.

threshold [thresh'ōld] n Schwelle f; **to be on the** ~ **of sth** (also fig) vor or an der Schwelle zu etw sein.

threshold agreement n Lohnschwellenvereinbarung f.

threw [thrōō] pt of **throw.**

thrift [thrift] n Sparsamkeit f.

thrifty [thrif'tē] a sparsam.

thrill [thril] n Reiz m, Erregung f; **it gave me**

quite a ~ **to** ... es war ein Erlebnis für mich, zu ... ♦ vt begeistern, packen; **to be** ~**ed with** (gift etc) sich unheimlich freuen über (+acc) ♦ vi beben, zittern.

thriller [thril'ûr] n Krimi m.

thrilling [thril'ing] a (book, play etc) spannend, packend; (news) aufregend; (discovery) überwältigend.

thrive [thrīv] vi gedeihen (on bei).

thriving [thrī'ving] a blühend, gut gedeihend; (industry etc) florierend, blühend.

throat [thrōt] n Hals m, Kehle f; **to have a sore** ~ Halsschmerzen haben.

throb [thrâb] n vi (engine, heart, pulse) klopfen; (wound) pochen; **my head is** ~**bing** ich habe wahnsinnige Kopfschmerzen.

throes [thrōz] npl: **in the** ~ **of** mitten in (+dat).

thrombosis [thrâmbō'sis] n Thrombose f.

throne [thrōn] n Thron m; (ECCL) Stuhl m.

throng [thrông] n Scharen pl von Menschen, Menschenmenge f ♦ vt belagern ♦ vi sich drängen.

throttle [thrât'əl] n (of motorcycle) Gashebel m; **to open the** ~ Gas geben ♦ vt erdrosseln.

through [thrōō] prep durch; (time) während (+gen); (because of) aus, durch; **to go** ~ **sb's papers** jds Akten durchlesen; **I am halfway** ~ **the book** ich habe das Buch halb durch; **(from) Monday** ~ **Friday** (US) von Montag bis (einschließlich) Freitag ♦ ad durch; **the soldiers didn't let us** ~ die Soldaten ließen uns nicht durch; **to put sb** ~ (TEL) jdn verbinden (to mit); **we're** ~ (with relationship) es ist aus zwischen uns; (with job) wir sind fertig ♦ a (ticket, train) durchgehend; (finished) fertig; **no** ~ **road** Durchfahrt verboten!

throughout [thrōōout'] prep (place) überall in (+dat); (time) während (+gen) ♦ ad überall; die ganze Zeit.

throughput [thrōō'pŏŏt] n (of goods, materials) Durchsatz m; (COMPUT) Leistung f.

throw [thrō] n Wurf m ♦ vt irreg werfen; **to** ~ **a party** ein Party geben.

throw about vt (Brit) = **throw around.**

throw around vt (remarks, money etc) herumwerfen.

throw away vt wegwerfen; (waste) verschenken; (money) verschwenden.

throw off vt abwerfen; (pursuer) abschütteln.

throw open vt (doors, windows) aufreißen; (house, gardens etc) (öffentlich) zugänglich machen (to für); (competition, race) Teilnahme ermöglichen.

throw out vt hinauswerfen; (garbage) wegwerfen; (plan) verwerfen.

throw together vt (clothes) zusammenpacken; (essay) hinhauen; (ingredients) zusammenwerfen.

throw up vi (vomit) speien.

throwaway [thrō'əwā] a (disposable)

Wegwerf-; (: *bottle*) Einweg-.

throwback [thrō'bak] *n*: **he's a ~ to his Irish ancestors** bei ihm kommen seine irischen Vorfahren wieder durch.

throw-in [thrō'in] *n* Einwurf *m*.

thrown [thrōn] *pp of* **throw**.

thru [thrōō] *prep, a, ad* (*US*) = **through**.

thrush [thrush] *n* Drossel *f*; (*MED*: *esp in children*) Soor *m*, Schwämmchen *nt*; (*Brit MED*: *in women*) Pilzkrankheit *f*.

thrust [thrust] *n* (*TECH*) Schubkraft *f* ♦ *vti irreg, pt, pp* **thrust** (*push*) stoßen; (*fig*) (sich) drängen; **to ~ o.s. on sb** sich jdm aufdrängen.

thrusting [thrust'ing] *a* (*person*) aufdringlich, unverfroren.

thud [thud] *n* dumpfe(r) (Auf)schlag *m*.

thug [thug] *n* Schlägertyp *m*.

thumb [thum] *n* Daumen *m*; **to give sb the ~s up** jdm zu verstehen geben, daß alles in Ordnung ist; **to give sth the ~s up** grünes Licht für etw geben ♦ *vt* (*book*) durchblättern; **a well-~ed book** ein abgegriffenes Buch; **to ~ a lift** per Anhalter fahren (wollen).

thumb index *n* Daumenregister *nt*.

thumbnail [thum'nāl] *n* Daumennagel *m*.

thumbnail sketch *n* kleine Skizze *f*.

thumbtack [thum'tak] *n* (*US*) Reißzwecke *f*.

thump [thump] *n* (*blow*) Schlag *m*; (*noise*) Bums *m* ♦ *vi* hämmern, pochen ♦ *vt* schlagen auf (+*acc*).

thunder [thun'dûr] *n* Donner *m* ♦ *vi* donnern; **to ~ past** (*train etc*) vorbeidonnern ♦ *vt* brüllen.

thunderbolt [thun'dûrbōlt] *n* Blitz *m*.

thunderclap [thun'dûrklap] *n* Donnerschlag *m*.

thunderous [thun'dûrəs] *a* stürmisch.

thunderstorm [thun'dûrstôrm] *n* Gewitter *nt*, Unwetter *nt*.

thunderstruck [thun'dûrstruk] *a* wie vom Donner gerührt.

thundery [thun'dûrē] *a* gewitterschwül.

Thur(s). *abbr* (= *Thursday*) Do.

Thursday [thûrz'dā] *n* Donnerstag *m*; *see* **Tuesday**.

thus [thus] *ad* (*in this way*) so; (*therefore*) somit, also, folglich.

thwart [thwôrt] *vt* vereiteln, durchkreuzen; (*person*) hindern.

thyme [tīm] *n* Thymian *m*.

thyroid [thī'roid] *n* Schilddrüse *f*.

tiara [tēar'ə] *n* Diadem *nt*.

Tiber [tī'bûr] *n* Tiber *m*.

Tibet [tibet'] *n* Tibet *nt*.

Tibetan [tibet'ən] *a* tibetanisch, tibetisch ♦ *n* (*person*) Tibetaner(in *f*) *m*, Tibeter(in *f*) *m*; (*language*) Tibetisch *nt*.

tibia [tib'ēə] *n* Schienbein *nt*.

tic [tik] *n* Tick *m*.

tick [tik] *n* (*sound*) Ticken *nt*; (*mark*) Häkchen *nt*; **to put a ~ against sth** etw abhaken ♦ *vi* ticken ♦ *vt* abhaken.

tick off *vt* abhaken; (*person*) ausschimpfen.

tick over *vi* (*Brit*: *engine*) im Leerlauf sein.

ticker tape [tik'ûr tāp] *n* Lochstreifen *m*.

ticket [tik'it] *n* (*for travel*) Fahrkarte *f*; (*for entrance*) (Eintritts)karte *f*; (*price ~*) Preisschild *nt*; (*luggage ~*) (Gepäck)schein *m*; (*raffle ~*) Los *nt*; (*parking ~*) Strafzettel *m*; (*in car park*) Parkschein *m*; (*US POL*) Wahlliste *f*; **to get a parking ~** (*AUT*) einen Strafzettel bekommen.

ticket agency *n* (*THEAT*) Vorverkaufsstelle *f*.

ticket collector *n* (*Brit*) Fahrkartenkontrolleur *m*.

ticket holder *n* Karteninhaber *m*.

ticket inspector *n* (Fahrkarten)kontrolleur *m*.

ticket office *n* (*RAIL etc*) Fahrkartenschalter *m*; (*THEAT etc*) Kasse *f*.

tickle [tik'əl] *n* Kitzeln *nt* ♦ *vt* kitzeln; (*amuse*) amüsieren; **that ~d her fancy** das gefiel ihr.

ticklish [tik'lish] *a* (*lit, fig*) kitzlig; (*which tickles*: *blanket*) rauh; (: *cough*) kratzend.

tidal [tīd'əl] *a* Flut-, Tide-.

tidal wave *n* Flutwelle *f*.

tidbit [tid'bit] *n* (*US*) Leckerbissen *m*.

tiddlywinks [tid'lēwingks] *n* Floh(hüpf)spiel *nt*.

tide [tīd] *n* Gezeiten *pl*, Ebbe *f* und Flut; **high/low ~** Flut *f*/Ebbe *f*; **the ~ is in/out** es ist Flut/Ebbe; **the ~ of public opinion** (*fig*) der Trend der öffentlichen Meinung ♦ *vt*: **is that enough to ~ you over?** (*fig*) reicht Ihnen das vorläufig?

tidily [tī'dilē] *ad* sauber, ordentlich; **to arrange ~** Ordnung machen; **to dress ~** sich ordentlich kleiden *or* anziehen.

tidiness [tī'dēnis] *n* Ordnung *f*.

tidy [tī'dē] *a* ordentlich; (*in character*) korrekt; (*in mind*) klar ♦ *vt* aufräumen, in Ordnung bringen.

tie [tī] *n* (*Brit*: *also*: **neck~**) Krawatte *f*, Schlips *m*; (*sth connecting*) Band *nt*; (*US RAIL*) Schwelle *f*; (*SPORT*) Unentschieden *nt*; **cup ~** (*Brit SPORT*: *·match*) Pokalspiel *nt*; **family ~s** familiäre Bindungen *pl* ♦ *vt* (*fasten, restrict*) binden; (*knot*) schnüren, festbinden ♦ *vi* (*SPORT*) unentschieden spielen; (*in competition*) punktgleich sein.

tie down *vt* (*lit*) festbinden; (*fig*) binden.

tie in *vi*: **to ~ in with sth** (*correspond*) zu etw passen.

tie on *vt* (*Brit*: *label etc*) anbinden, festbinden.

tie up *vt* (*dog*) anbinden; (*parcel*) verschnüren; (*boat*) festmachen; (*person*) fesseln; **I am ~d up right now** ich bin im Moment beschäftigt.

tie-break(er) [tī'brāk(ûr)] *n* (*TENNIS*) Tiebreak *m*; (*in quiz*) Stechen *nt*.

tie-on label [tī'ânlā'bəl] *n* Anhängeschildchen

nt.
tie pin n (Brit) Krawattennadel f.
tier [tēr] n Reihe f, Rang m; (of cake) Etage f.
tie tack n (US) Krawattennadel f.
tiff [tif] n (col) Krach m.
tiger [tī'gûr] n Tiger m.
tight [tīt] a (close) eng, knapp; (schedule) gedrängt; (firm) fest, dicht; (screw) festsitzend; (control) streng; (stretched) stramm, (an)gespannt; (col) blau, stramm ♦ ad: **to be packed** ~ (suitcase) voll gestopft sein; (with people) gerammelt voll sein; **hold** ~! festhalten!
tighten [tīt'ən] vt anziehen, anspannen; (restrictions) verschärfen ♦ vi sich spannen.
tightfisted [tīt'fis'tid] a knauserig.
tightly [tīt'lē] ad eng; fest, dicht; (stretched) straff.
tightness [tīt'nis] n Enge f; Festigkeit f; Straffheit f; (of money) Knappheit f.
tightrope [tīt'rōp] n Seil nt.
tightrope walker n Seiltänzer(in f) m.
tights [tīts] npl (Brit) Strumpfhose f.
tigress [tī'gris] n Tigerin f.
tilde [til'də] n Tilde f.
tile [tīl] n (on roof) Dachziegel m; (on wall or floor) Fliese f, Kachel f ♦ vt (floor, bathroom etc) fliesen, kacheln.
tiled [tīld] a (roof) gedeckt, Ziegel-; (floor) mit Fliesen or Platten ausgelegt; (wall, bathroom) gefliest, gekachelt.
till [til] n Kasse f ♦ vt (land) bestellen ♦ prep, cj bis; **not** ~ (in future) nicht vor; (in past) erst.
tiller [til'ûr] n Ruderpinne f.
tilt [tilt] vt kippen, neigen ♦ vi sich neigen ♦ n (slope) Neigung f; **to wear one's hat at a** ~ den Hut schief aufhaben; **(at) full** ~ mit Volldampf, volle Pulle (col).
timber [tim'bûr] n Holz nt; (trees) Baumbestand m.
time [tīm] n Zeit f; (occasion) Mal nt; (rhythm) Takt m; **I have no** ~ **for people like him** für Leute wie ihn habe ich nichts übrig; **in 2 weeks'** ~ in 2 Wochen; **for the** ~ **being** vorläufig; **from** ~ **to** ~ von Zeit zu Zeit, dann und wann; ~ **after** ~, ~ **and again** immer wieder; **at all** ~s immer; **at one** ~ früher; **at no** ~ nie; **in no** ~ im Handumdrehen; **at** ~s manchmal; **any** ~ jederzeit; **by the** ~ bis; **this** ~ diesmal, dieses Mal; **to have a good** ~ viel Spaß haben, sich amüsieren; **to have a hard** ~ es schwer haben; **in** ~ (soon enough) rechtzeitig; (after some time) mit der Zeit; (MUS) im Takt; **on** ~ pünktlich, rechtzeitig; **five** ~s fünfmal; **local** ~ Ortszeit f; **what** ~ **is it?** wieviel Uhr ist es?, wie spät ist es?; **to be 30 minutes behind/ahead of** ~ eine halbe Stunde zu spät/zu früh dran sein; **to take one's** ~ sich Zeit lassen; **he does everything in his own (good)** ~ (without being hurried) er läßt sich nicht hetzen; **he'll do it**

in or (US) **on his own** ~ (out of working hours) er macht es in seiner Freizeit; **by the** ~ **he arrived** als er ankam; **to carry 3 boxes at a** ~ 3 Schachteln auf einmal tragen; **to keep** ~ (beat) den Takt angeben or schlagen; **to be behind the** ~s rückständig sein, hinter dem Mond leben (col) ♦ vt zur rechten Zeit tun, zeitlich einrichten; (SPORT) stoppen; **to** ~ **sth well/badly** den richtigen/falschen Zeitpunkt für etw wählen; **the bomb was** ~d **to explode 5 minutes later** die Bombe war so eingestellt, daß sie 5 Minuten später explodieren sollte.
time-and-motion expert [tīm'ənmō'shən ek'spûrt] n Fachmann m für Zeitstudien, ≈ REFA-Fachmann m.
time-and-motion study [tīm'ənmō'shən stu'dē] n Zeit- und Bewegungsstudie f.
time bomb n Zeitbombe f.
time card n Stechkarte f, Arbeitszeitkontrolliste f.
time clock n Stechuhr f.
time-consuming [tīm'kənsōōming] a zeitraubend.
time-honored [tīm'ânûrd] a althergebracht, altehrwürdig.
timekeeper [tīm'kēpûr] n Zeitnehmer m.
time-lag [tīm'lag] n (Brit: in travel) Verzögerung f; (: difference) Zeitunterschied m.
timeless [tīm'lis] a (beauty) zeitlos.
time limit n Frist f.
timely [tīm'lē] a rechtzeitig.
timer [tī'mûr] n (TECH) Zeitmesser m; (switch) Schaltuhr f.
time off n freie Zeit f.
time-out [tīm'out'] n (US SPORT) Auszeit f.
timesaving [tīm'sāving] a zeitsparend.
time scale n Zeitvorgabe f, Zeitspanne f.
time sharing [tīm' shä'ring] n (COMPUT) zeitlich verzahnte Verarbeitung f, Time-Sharing nt.
time sheet n = **time card**.
time signal n Zeitzeichen nt.
time switch n (Brit) Zeitschalter m.
timetable [tīm'tābəl] n Fahrplan m; (SCH) Stundenplan m; (program of events etc) Programm nt.
time zone n Zeitzone f.
timid [tim'id] a ängstlich, schüchtern.
timidity [timid'itē] n Ängstlichkeit f, Schüchternheit f.
timidly [tim'idlē] ad ängstlich.
timing [tī'ming] n Wahl f des richtigen Zeitpunkts, Timing nt; (AUT) Einstellung f.
timpani [tim'pənē] npl Kesselpauken pl.
tin [tin] n (metal) Blech nt; (Brit: container) Büchse f, Dose f.
tinfoil [tin'foil] n Stanniolpapier nt.
tinge [tinj] n (color) Färbung f; (fig) Anflug m ♦ vt färben, einen Anstrich geben (+dat).
tingle [ting'gəl] n Prickeln nt ♦ vi (from cold) prickeln; (from bad circulation) stechen.
tinker [tingk'ûr] n Kesselflicker m.
tinker with vt fus herumfuschen an

(+*dat*).
tinkle [ting'kəl] *n* Klingeln *nt* ♦ *vi* klingeln.
tin mine *n* Zinnmine *f*.
tinned [tind] *a* (*Brit*: *food*) Dosen-, Büchsen-.
tinny [tin'ē] *a* Blech-, blechern.
tin opener [tin' ōp'ənûr] *n* (*Brit*) Dosen- *or* Büchsenöffner *m*.
tinsel [tin'səl] *n* Girlanden *pl* aus Rauschgold *nt*, Lametta *nt*.
tint [tint] *n* Farbton *m*; (*slight color*) Anflug *m*; (*hair*) Tönung(smittel *nt*) *f* ♦ *vt* (*hair*) tönen.
tinted [tin'tid] *a* getönt.
T-intersection [tē'intərsek'shən] *n* (*US*) T-Kreuzung *f*.
tiny [tī'nē] *a* winzig.
tip [tip] *n* (*pointed end*) Spitze *f*; (*money*) Trinkgeld *nt*; (*hint*) Wink *m*, Tip *m*; **it's on the ~ of my tongue** es liegt mir auf der Zunge ♦ *vt* (*slant*) kippen; (*hat*) antippen; (*~ over*) umkippen; (*waiter*) ein Trinkgeld geben (+*dat*); (*predict: winner*) tippen auf (+*acc*); (: *horse*) setzen auf (+*acc*).
tip off *vt* jdm einen Tip geben.
tip-off [tip'ôf] *n* Hinweis *m*, Tip *m*.
tipped [tipt] *a* (*Brit*: *cigarette*) Filter-.
Tipp-Ex [tip'eks] *n* ® (*Brit*) Tippex ® *nt* ♦ *vt* auslacken.
tipple [tip'əl] *n* (*Brit*: *drink*) Schnäpschen *nt*.
tippy-toe [tip'ētō] *n* (*US*): **on ~** auf Zehenspitzen.
tipsy [tip'sē] *a* beschwipst.
tiptoe [tip'tō] *n*: **on ~** auf Zehenspitzen ♦ *vi* auf Zehenspitzen gehen.
tiptop [tip'tâp] *a*: **in ~ condition** tipptopp, erstklassig.
tire [tīûr'] *n* (*US*) Reifen *m* ♦ *vti* ermüden, müde machen *or* werden.
tire out *vt* (*völlig*) erschöpfen.
tired [tīûrd'] *a* müde; **to be ~ of sth** etw satt haben; **~ out** erschöpft.
tiredness [tīûrd'nis] *n* Müdigkeit *f*.
tireless [tīûr'lis] *a*, **tirelessly** [tīûr'lislē] *ad* unermüdlich.
tiresome [tīûr'səm] *a* lästig.
tiring [tīûr'ing] *a* ermüdend.
tissue [tish'ōō] *n* Gewebe *nt*; (*paper handkerchief*) Papiertaschentuch *nt*.
tissue paper *n* Seidenpapier *nt*.
tit [tit] *n* (*bird*) Meise *f*; (*col!*: *breast*) Titte *f*; **~ for tat** wie du mir, so ich dir.
titbit [tit'bit] *n* (*esp Brit*) Leckerbissen *m*.
titillate [tit'əlāt] *vt* kitzeln.
titillation [titəlā'shən] *n* Kitzeln *nt*.
titivate [tit'əvāt] *vt* schniegeln.
title [tīt'əl] *n* Titel *m*; (*in law*): **~ (to)** (Rechts)anspruch *m* (auf +*acc*).
title deed *n* Eigentumsurkunde *f*.
title page *n* Titelseite *f*.
title role *n* Hauptrolle *f*.
titter [tit'ûr] *vi* kichern.
tittle-tattle [tit'əltatəl] *n* Klatsch *m*.
titular [tich'əlûr] *a* Titular-, nominell; (*possessions*) Titel-.

T-junction [tē'jung'kshən] *n* (*Brit*) T-Kreuzung *f*.
TM *n abbr* (= *transcendental meditation*) TM *f*; (= *trademark*) Wz.
TN *abbr* (*US MAIL*) = *Tennessee*.
TNT *n abbr* (= *trinitrotoluene*) TNT *nt*.
to [tōō] *prep* (*towards*) zu; (*with countries, towns*) nach; (*indir obj*) *dat*; (*as far as*) bis; (*next to, attached to*) an (+*dat*); (*per*) pro; (*with expressions of time*) vor; **~ the left/the right** nach links/rechts; **the road ~ Boston** die Straße nach Boston; **to count ~ 10** bis 10 zählen; **to count ~** bis 10 zählen; **a ~ a kilo** 8 Äpfel auf ein Kilo; **it belongs ~ him** es gehört ihm; **to go ~ school/the theater/bed** in die Schule/ins Theater/ins Bett gehen; **I have never been ~ Germany** ich war noch nie in Deutschland; **to give sth ~ sb** jdm etw geben; **~ this day** bis auf den heutigen Tag; **20 (minutes) ~ 4** 20 (Minuten) vor 4; **it's 25 ~ 3** es ist fünf nach halb 2; **superior ~ sth** besser als etw; **superior ~ the others** den anderen überlegen; **they tied him ~ a tree** sie banden ihn an einen Baum ♦ *with v* (*simple infinitive*): **~ go/eat** gehen/essen; (*in order to*) um... zu; **I don't want ~ do** ich will nicht; **I have things ~ do** ich habe noch einiges zu erledigen; **to be ready ~ go** fertig sein; **to want ~ do** tun wollen; **to try ~ do** zu tun versuchen; **in order ~** (*purpose, result*) um zu; **he did it ~ help you** er tat es, um Ihnen zu helfen ♦ *ad*: **~ and fro** hin und her.
toad [tōd] *n* Kröte *f*.
toadstool [tōd'stōōl] *n* Giftpilz *m*.
toady [tō'dē] *n* Speichellecker *m*, Kriecher *m* ♦ *vi* kriechen (*to* vor +*dat*).
toast [tōst] *n* (*bread*) Toast *m*; (*drinking*) Trinkspruch *m* ♦ *vt* trinken auf (+*acc*); (*bread*) toasten; (*warm*) wärmen.
toaster [tōs'tûr] *n* Toaster *m*.
toastmaster [tōst'mastûr] *n* Zeremonienmeister *m*.
toast rack *n* Toastständer *m*.
tobacco [təbak'ō] *n* Tabak *m*.
tobacconist [təbak'ənist] *n* Tabakhändler *m*; **~'s (shop)** *n* Tabakladen *m*.
tobacco plantation *n* Tabakplantage *f*.
Tobago [tōbā'gō] *n see* **Trinidad and Tobago**.
toboggan [təbâg'ən] *n* (Rodel)schlitten *m*.
today [tədā'] *ad* heute; (*at the present time*) heutzutage ♦ *n* (*day*) heutige(r) Tag *m*; (*time*) Heute *nt*, heutige Zeit *f*; **what day is it ~?** was (für ein Tag) ist heute?; **what date is it ~?** der wievielte ist heute?; **~ is the 4th of March** heute ist der vierte März; **~'s paper** die Zeitung von heute; **a week ~** heute in einer Woche.
toddle [tâd'əl] *vi* watscheln.
toddler [tâd'lûr] *n* Kleinkind *nt*.
toddy [tâd'ē] *n* (Whisky)grog *m*.
to-do [tədōō'] *n* Aufheben *nt*, Theater *nt*.
toe [tō] *n* Zehe *f*; (*of sock, shoe*) Spitze *f*; **the big ~** der große Zeh; **the little ~** der kleine

Zeh ♦ *vt:* **to ~ the line** (*fig*) sich einfügen.
toehold [tō'hōld] *n* Halt *m* für die Fußspitzen.
toenail [tō'nāl] *n* Zehennagel *m*.
toffee [tôf'ē] *n* Sahnebonbon *nt*.
toffee apple *n* (*Brit*) kandierte(r) Apfel *m*.
tofu [tō'fōō] *n* Tofu *m*.
toga [tō'gə] *n* Toga *f*.
together [tōōgeth'ûr] *ad* zusammen; (*at the same time*) gleichzeitig.
togetherness [tōōgeth'ûrnis] *n* (*company*) Beisammensein *nt*; (*feeling*) Zusammengehörigkeitsgefühl *nt*.
toggle (switch) [tág'əl (swich)] *n* (*COMPUT etc*) Kippschalter *m*.
Togo [tō'gō] *n* Togo *nt*.
togs [tágz] *npl* (*Brit: clothes*) Sachen *pl*, Klamotten *pl*.
toil [toil] *n* Mühe *f*, Plage *f* ♦ *vi* sich abmühen, sich plagen.
toilet [toi'lit] *n* Toilette *f*; **to go to the ~** auf die Toilette gehen; *see also* **toilets** ♦ *a* Toiletten-.
toilet bag *n* (*Brit*) Waschbeutel *m*, Kulturbeutel *m*.
toilet paper *n* Toilettenpapier *nt*.
toiletries [toi'litrēz] *npl* Toilettenartikel *pl*.
toilet roll *n* Rolle *f* Toilettenpapier.
toilets [toi'lits] *npl* (*Brit*) Toiletten *pl*.
toilet soap *n* Toilettenseife *f*.
toilet water *n* Toilettenwasser *nt*.
token [tō'kən] *n* Zeichen *nt*; (*gift* ~) Gutschein *m*; **by the same** ~ (*fig*) ebenso; (*with negative*) aber auch; ~ **action** Scheinhandlung *f*, symbolische Handlung *f*; ~ **strike** Warnstreik *m*.
Tokyo [tō'kēyō] *n* Tokio *nt*.
told [tōld] *pt, pp of* **tell**.
tolerable [tâl'ûrəbəl] *a* (*bearable*) erträglich; (*fairly good*) leidlich.
tolerably [tâl'ûrəblē] *ad* leidlich.
tolerance [tâl'ûrəns] *n* Toleranz *f*.
tolerant [tâl'ûrənt] *a*, **tolerantly** [tâl'ûrəntlē] *ad* tolerant; (*patient*) geduldig.
tolerate [tâl'ərāt] *vt* dulden; (*noise*) ertragen.
toleration [tâlərā'shən] *n* Toleranz *f*.
toll [tōl] *n* Gebühr *f*; **it took a heavy ~ of human life** es forderte *or* kostete viele Menschenleben ♦ *vi* (*bell*) läuten.
toll bridge *n* gebührenpflichtige Brücke *f*.
toll free *a* (*US*) gebührenfrei.
toll road *n* gebührenpflichtige Autostraße *f*.
tomato [təmā'tō] *n, pl* **tomatoes** Tomate *f*.
tomato paste *n* Tomatenmark *nt*.
tomb [tōōm] *n* Grab(mal) *nt*.
tomboy [tâm'boi] *n* Wildfang *m*.
tombstone [tōōm'stōn] *n* Grabstein *m*.
tomcat [tâm'kat] *n* Kater *m*.
tome [tōm] *n* (*volume*) Band *m*; (*big book*) Wälzer *m*.
tomorrow [təmôr'ō] *n* Morgen *nt* ♦ *ad* morgen; ~ **morning** morgen früh; **a week ~** morgen in einer Woche; **the day after ~** übermorgen.

ton [tun] *n* (*metric* ~) Tonne *f* (*US: also:* **short ~** = *907,18 kg; Brit: = 1016 kg*).
tonal [tō'nəl] *a* tonal, Klang-.
tone [tōn] *n* Ton *m*; **dial** (*US*) *or* **dialling** (*Brit*) ~ (*TEL*) Amtszeichen *nt* ♦ *vi* (*harmonize*) passen (*with* zu), harmonisieren (*with* mit) ♦ *vt* eine Färbung geben (+*dat*).
tone down *vt* (*criticism, demands*) mäßigen; (*colors*) abtönen.
tone up *vt* in Form bringen.
tone-deaf [tōn'def] *a* ohne musikalisches Gehör.
toner [tō'nûr] *n* (*for photocopier, printer*) Toner *m*.
Tonga Islands [táng'gə ī'ləndz] *npl* Tongainseln *pl*.
tongs [tôngz] *npl* Zange *f*; (*curling* ~) Lockenstab *m*.
tongue [tung] *n* Zunge *f*; (*language*) Sprache *f*; **with ~ in cheek** ironisch, scherzhaft.
tongue-tied [tung'tīd] *a* stumm, sprachlos.
tongue twister [tung' twis'tûr] *n* Zungenbrecher *m*.
tonic [tân'ik] *n* (*MED*) Stärkungsmittel *nt*; (*MUS*) Grundton *m*, Tonika *f*; **this will be a ~ to her** das wird ihr guttun; ~ **(water)** (*Brit*) Tonic(water) *m*.
tonight [tənīt'] *n* heutige(r) Abend *m*; diese Nacht *f* ♦ *ad* heute abend; heute nacht; **I'll see you ~** bis heute abend!
tonnage [tun'ij] *n* Tonnage *f*.
tonsil [tân'səl] *n* Mandel *f*.
tonsillitis [tânsəli'tis] *n* Mandelentzündung *f*; **to have ~** eine Mandelentzündung haben.
too [tōō] *ad* zu; (*also*) auch; **it's ~ sweet** es ist zu süß; **I went ~** ich ging auch (mit); **I'm not ~ sure about that** da bin ich mir nicht ganz *or* keineswegs sicher; ~ **bad!** Pech!
took [tōōk] *pt of* **take**.
tool [tōōl] *n* (*lit, fig*) Werkzeug *nt*.
toolbox [tōōl'báks] *n* Werkzeugkasten *m*.
toolkit [tōōl'kit] *n* Werkzeug *nt*.
toolshed [tōōl'shed] *n* Geräteschuppen *m*.
toot [tōōt] *n* Hupen *nt* ♦ *vi* tuten; (*AUT*) hupen.
tooth [tōōth] *n, pl* **teeth** [tēth] Zahn *m*; **to brush one's teeth** sich die Zähne putzen; **to have a ~ pulled** (*US*) *or* **out** (*Brit*) sich (*dat*) einen Zahn ziehen lassen; **by the skin of one's teeth** mit knapper Not, mit Ach und Krach (*col*).
toothache [tōōth'āk] *n* Zahnschmerzen *pl*, Zahnweh *nt*.
toothbrush [tōōth'brush] *n* Zahnbürste *f*.
toothpaste [tōōth'pāst] *n* Zahnpasta *f*.
toothpick [tōōth'pik] *n* Zahnstocher *m*.
tooth powder *n* Zahnpulver *nt*.
top [táp] *n* Spitze *f*; (*of mountain*) Gipfel *m*; (*of tree*) Wipfel *m*; (*toy*) Kreisel *m*; (~ *gear*) vierte(r) Gang *m*; (*clothes*) Oberteil *nt*, Top *nt*; (*of pajamas*) Schlafanzugjacke *f*, Oberteil *nt*; (*of table, bed, sheet*) Kopfende *nt*, obere(s) Ende *nt*; (*US AUT*) Verdeck *m*

◆ *a* oberste(r, s) ◆ *vt* (*list*) an erster Stelle stehen auf (+*dat*); **at the ~ of the stairs/ page/list** oben auf der Treppe/Seite/Liste; **at the ~ of one's voice** (*fig*) in voller Lautstärke; **to go over the ~** es übertreiben; **to ~ it all, he said …** und er setzte dem noch die Krone auf, indem er sagte …; **from ~ to toe** (*Brit*) von Kopf bis Fuß; **at ~ speed** mit Höchstgeschwindigkeit; **a ~ surgeon** ein Spitzenchirurg, einer der besten Chirurgen.

top off, (*Brit*) **top up** *vt* auffüllen, nachfüllen.

topaz [tō'paz] *n* Topas *m*.

topcoat [tâp'kōt] *n* Mantel *m*.

top-flight [tâp'flīt'] *a* erstklassig, prima.

top hat *n* Zylinder *m*.

top-heavy [tâp'hevē] *a* oben schwerer als unten, kopflastig.

topic [tâp'ik] *n* Thema *nt*, Gesprächsgegenstand *m*.

topical [tâp'ikəl] *a* aktuell.

topless [tâp'lis] *a* (*dress*) oben ohne.

top-level [tâp'lev'əl] *a* auf höchster Ebene.

topmost [tâp'mōst] *a* oberste(r, s), höchste(r, s).

topography [təpâg'rəfē] *n* Topographie *f*.

topping [tâp'ing] *n* (*COOK*): **with a chocolate ~** mit Schokolade überzogen.

topple [tâp'əl] *vti* stürzen, kippen.

top-ranking [tâp'rang'king] *a* von hohem Rang.

top-secret [tâp'sē'krit] *a* streng geheim.

topsy-turvy [tâp'sētûr'vē] *ad* durcheinander ◆ *a* auf den Kopf gestellt.

top-up [tâp'up] *n* (*Brit*): **would you like a ~?** (*coffee etc*) soll ich Ihnen nachschenken?

torch [tôrch] *n* (*with flame*) Fackel *f*; (*Brit ELEC*) Taschenlampe *f*.

tore [tôr] *pt of* **tear**.

torment *n* [tôr'ment] Qual *f* ◆ *vt* [tôrment'] (*annoy*) plagen; (*distress*) quälen.

torn [tôrn] *a* hin- und hergerissen ◆ *pp of* **tear**.

tornado [tôrnā'dō] *n* Tornado *m*, Wirbelsturm *m*.

torpedo [tôrpē'dō] *n* Torpedo *m*.

torpedo boat *n* Torpedoboot *nt*.

torpor [tôr'pûr] *n* Erstarrung *f*.

torrent [tôr'ənt] *n* Sturzbach *m*.

torrential [tôren'chəl] *a* wolkenbruchartig.

torrid [tôr'id] *a* (*lit, fig*) heiß; (*heat, air, sun*) sengend.

torso [tôr'sō] *n* Torso *m*.

tortoise [tôr'təs] *n* Schildkröte *f*.

tortoiseshell [tôr'təs-shel] *n* Schildpatt *m*.

tortuous [tôr'chōōəs] *a* (*winding*) gewunden; (*deceitful*) krumm, unehrlich.

torture [tôr'chûr] *n* Folter *f* ◆ *vt* foltern.

torturer [tôr'chûrûr] *n* (*lit*) Folterknecht *m*; (*fig: tormentor*) Peiniger(in *f*) *m*.

Tory [tôr'ē] (*Brit POL*) *n* Tory *m* ◆ *a* Tory-, konservativ.

toss [tôs] *vt* werfen, schleudern; **to ~ a coin for sth** etw mit einer Münze entscheiden ◆

vi: **to ~ and turn** (*in bed*) sich hin und her werfen ◆ *n* (*of coin*) Münzwurf *m*; **with a proud ~ of her head** mit einer stolzen Kopfbewegung; **to win/lose the ~** (*esp SPORT*) die Seitenwahl gewinnen/verlieren.

tot [tât] *n* (*small child*) Knirps *m*; (*Brit: of alcohol*) Schluckchen *nt*.

total [tōt'əl] *n* Gesamtheit *f*, Ganze(s) *nt*; (*money, figures*) Endsumme *f*; **grand ~** Gesamtmenge *f*; **in ~** insgesamt ◆ *a* ganz, gesamt, total; **~ loss** Totalschaden *m* ◆ *vt* (*add up*) zusammenzählen; (*amount to*) sich belaufen auf.

totalitarian [tōtalitär'ēən] *a* totalitär.

totality [tōtal'itē] *n* Gesamtheit *f*.

totally [tō'təlē] *ad* gänzlich, total, völlig.

tote [tōt] *vt* (*col: carry*) schleppen.

tote bag *n* Reisetasche *f*.

totem pole [tō'təm pōl] *n* Totempfahl *m*.

totter [tât'ûr] *vi* wanken, schwanken, wackeln.

touch [tuch] *n* Berührung *f*; (*sense of feeling*) Tastsinn *m*; (*small amount*) Spur *f*; (*style*) Stil *m*; **in ~ with** in Verbindung mit; **I'll be in ~** ich lasse von mir hören, ich melde mich; **to be out of ~ with events** nicht mehr auf dem laufenden sein; **the personal ~** die persönliche Note; **to put the finishing ~es to sth** einer Sache (*dat*) den letzten Schliff geben ◆ *vt* (*feel*) berühren; (*come against*) leicht anstoßen; (*emotionally*) bewegen, rühren; **no artist in the country can ~ him** (*fig*) kein Künstler im ganzen Land kommt an ihn heran.

touch on *vt fus* (*topic*) berühren, erwähnen.

touch up *vt* (*paint*) auffrischen.

touch-and-go [tuch'əngō'] *a* riskant, knapp.

touchdown [tuch'doun] *n* Landen *nt*, Niedergehen *nt*; (*US FOOTBALL*) Versuch *m*.

touchiness [tuch'ēnis] *n* Empfindlichkeit *f*.

touching [tuch'ing] *a* rührend, ergreifend.

touchline [tuch'līn] *n* Seitenlinie *f*.

touch-type [tuch'tīp] *vi* blindschreiben.

touchy [tuch'ē] *a* empfindlich, reizbar.

tough [tuf] *a* (*strong*) zäh, widerstandsfähig; (*difficult*) schwierig, hart; (*meat*) zäh; (*journey*) strapaziös, anstrengend; (*task, problem, situation*) schwierig; (*rough*) rauh; **they got ~ with the workers** sie griffen gegen die Arbeiter hart durch; **~ luck** Pech *nt* ◆ *n* Schläger(typ) *m*.

toughen [tuf'ən] *vt* zäh machen; (*make strong*) abhärten ◆ *vi* zäh werden.

toughness [tuf'nis] *n* Zähigkeit *f*; Härte *f*; Widerstandsfähigkeit *f*.

toupée [tōōpā'] *n* Toupet *nt*.

tour [tōōr] *n* Reise *f*, Tour *f*, Fahrt *f*; **to go on a ~ of Scotland** eine Schottlandreise machen; **to go on a ~ of a castle** an einer Schloßführung teilnehmen; **to go/be on ~** (*THEAT*) auf Gastspielreise *or* Tournee gehen/sein ◆ *vi* umherreisen; (*THEAT*) auf Tour sein *or* gehen.

touring [tōō'ring] n Umherreisen nt; (THEAT) Tournee f.

tourism [tōōr'izəm] n Fremdenverkehr m, Tourismus m.

tourist [tōōr'ist] n Tourist(in f) m ♦ a (class) Touristen- ♦ ad in der Touristenklasse.

tourist office n Verkehrsamt nt.

tourist trade n: **the** ~ das Fremdenverkehrsgewerbe.

tournament [tōōr'nəmənt] n Tournier nt.

tourniquet [tûr'nikit] n (MED) Aderpresse f, Tourniquet nt.

tour operator n Reiseveranstalter m.

tousled [tou'zəld] a zerzaust.

tout [tout] n (Brit: ticket ~) (Karten)schwarzhändler m ♦ vi: **to** ~ **for** auf Kundenfang gehen für.

tow [tō] n Schleppen nt ♦ vt (ab)schleppen; **to give sb a** ~ (AUT) jdm das Auto abschleppen.

toward(s) [tôrd(z)] prep (with time) gegen; (in direction of) nach; ~ **noon/the end of the year** gegen mittag/Ende des Jahres; **he walked** ~ **me/the town** er kam auf mich zu/er ging auf die Stadt zu; **to feel friendly** ~ **sb** jdm gegenüber freundlich sein; **my feelings** ~ **him** meine Gefühle ihm gegenüber.

towel [tou'əl] n Handtuch nt; **to throw in the** ~ (fig) das Handtuch werfen.

towelling [tou'əling] n (fabric) Frottee nt or m.

towel rack, (Brit) **towel rail** n Handtuchstange f.

tower [tou'ûr] n Turm m ♦ vi (building, mountain: also: ~ **up**) ragen.

tower above, tower over vt fus (buildings etc) emporragen über (+acc); (person) überragen.

tower block n (Brit) Hochhaus nt.

towering [tou'ûring] a hochragend; (rage) rasend.

town [toun] n Stadt f; **in (the)** ~ in der Stadt; **to be out of** ~ nicht in der Stadt sein.

town center n Stadtzentrum nt.

town clerk n Stadtdirektor m.

town council n Stadtrat m.

town hall n Rathaus nt.

town house n Stadthaus nt; (US: in a complex) Reihenhaus nt.

town planner n (Brit) Stadtplaner m.

townspeople [tounz'pēpəl] npl Stadtbewohner pl.

towpath [tō'path] n Leinpfad m.

towrope [tō'rōp] n Abschlepptau nt.

tow truck n (US) Abschleppwagen m.

toxic [tâk'sik] a giftig, Gift-.

toxin [tâk'sin] n Gift(stoff m) nt, Toxin nt.

toy [toi] n Spielzeug nt.

toy with vt fus spielen mit.

toyshop [toi'shâp] n Spielwarengeschäft nt.

toy train n Spielzeugeisenbahn f.

trace [trās] n Spur f; **there was no** ~ **of the**

book das Buch war spurlos verschwunden ♦ vt (follow a course) nachspüren (+dat); (find) aufspüren; (copy) zeichnen, durchpausen.

trace element n Spurenelement nt.

trachea [trā'kēə] n (ANAT) Luftröhre f.

tracing paper [trā'sing pā'pûr] n Pauspapier nt.

track [trak] n (mark) Spur f; (path) Weg m, Pfad m; (SPORT) Rennbahn f; (RAIL) Gleis nt; (COMPUT) Speicherspur f, Spur f; (of tape, record) Spur f; **a 4-~ tape** ein vierspuriges Tonband; **to be on the right** ~ (fig) auf der richtigen Spur sein, auf dem richtigen Weg sein; **to keep** ~ **of sb** jdn im Auge behalten; **to keep** ~ **of an argument** einer Argumentation folgen können; **to keep** ~ **of the situation** die Lage verfolgen; **to make** ~**s (for)** gehen (nach) ♦ vt verfolgen.

track down vt aufspüren.

track events npl (SPORT) Laufwettbewerb m.

tracking station [trak'ing stā'shən] n (in space) Bodenstation f.

trackless [trak'lis] a pfadlos.

track record n: **to have a good** ~ (fig) gute Leistungen or Voraussetzungen vorweisen.

tracksuit [trak'sōōt] n (Brit) Trainingsanzug m.

tract [trakt] n (of land) Gebiet nt; (booklet) Abhandlung f, Traktat nt.

traction [trak'shən] n (power) Zugkraft f; (AUT: grip) Bodenhaftung f; (MED): **in** ~ im Steckverband.

tractor [trak'tûr] n Traktor m.

tractor feed n (on printer) Papiertransport m, Traktor m.

trade [trād] n (commerce, industry) Handel m; (business) Geschäft nt, Gewerbe nt; (people) Geschäftsleute pl; (skilled manual work) Handwerk nt; **foreign** ~ Außenhandel m ♦ vi handeln (in mit) ♦ vt tauschen.

trade in vt in Zahlung geben.

trade barrier n Handelsschranke f.

trade deficit n Handelsdefizit nt.

trade discount n Händlerrabatt m.

trade fair n Messe f.

trade-in price [trād'in prīs] n Preis m, zu dem etw in Zahlung genommen wird.

trademark [trād'mârk] n Warenzeichen nt.

trade mission n Handelsdelegation f.

trade name n Handelsbezeichnung f.

trade price n Großhandelspreis m.

trader [trā'dûr] n Händler m.

trade reference n Kreditauskunft f.

trade secret n Betriebsgeheimnis nt.

tradesman [trādz'mən] n, pl **-men** (shopkeeper) Geschäftsmann m; (workman) Handwerker m; (delivery man) Lieferant m.

trade union n Gewerkschaft f.

trade unionist [trād yōōn'yənist] n Gewerkschaftler(in f) m.

trade wind n Passat m.

trading [trā'ding] n Handel m.

trading account n Betriebskonto nt.
trading estate n (Brit) Industriegelände nt.
trading stamp n Rabattmarke f.
tradition [trədish'ən] n Tradition f.
traditional [trədish'ənəl] a traditionell, herkömmlich.
traditionally [trədish'ənəlē] ad traditionell; (customarily) üblicherweise, schon immer.
traffic [traf'ik] n Verkehr m; (esp in drugs) Handel m (in mit) ♦ vt (esp drugs) handeln.
traffic circle n (US) Kreisverkehr m.
traffic island n Verkehrsinsel f.
traffic jam n Verkehrsstauung f.
trafficker [traf'ikûr] n Händler m, Schieber m (pej).
traffic lights npl Verkehrsampeln pl.
traffic offence n (Brit) = **traffic violation**.
traffic violation n (US) Verkehrsdelikt nt.
traffic warden n (Brit) ≈ Verkehrspolizist m, Politesse f (ohne amtliche Befugnisse).
tragedy [traj'idē] n (lit, fig) Tragödie f.
tragic [traj'ik] a tragisch.
tragically [traj'iklē] ad tragisch, auf tragische Weise.
trail [trāl] n (track) Spur f, Fährte f; (of meteor) Schweif m; (of smoke) Rauchfahne f; (of dust) Staubwolke f; (road) Pfad m, Weg m ♦ vt (animal) verfolgen; (person) folgen (+dat); (drag) schleppen ♦ vi (hang loosely) schleifen; (plants) sich ranken; (be behind) hinterherhinken; (SPORT) weit zurückliegen; (walk) zuckeln; **on the ~** auf der Spur; **to be on sb's ~** jdm auf der Spur sein.
trail away, trail off vi (sound) verhallen; (interest, voice) sich verlieren.
trail behind vi zurückbleiben.
trailer [trā'lûr] n Anhänger m; (US: for sleeping in etc) Wohnwagen m; (for film) Vorschau f.
trailer park n (US) Campingplatz m für Wohnwagen.
trail truck n (US) Sattelschlepper m.
train [trān] n Zug m; (of dress) Schleppe f; (Brit: of events) Folge f, Kette f; **to go by ~** mit dem Zug oder der Bahn fahren oder reisen ♦ vt (teach: person) ausbilden; (: animal) abrichten; (: mind) schulen; (SPORT) trainieren; (aim) richten (on auf +acc); (plant) wachsen lassen, ziehen; **to ~ sb to do sth** jdn dazu erziehen, etw zu tun ♦ vi (exercise) trainieren; (study, learn a skill) ausgebildet werden.
train attendant n (US RAIL) Schlafwagenschaffner m.
trained [trānd] a (eye) geschult; (person, voice) ausgebildet.
trainee [trānē'] n (technical, academic) Praktikant(in f) m; (management) Trainee m.
trainer [trā'nûr] n (SPORT) Trainer m; (shoe) Trainingsschuh m.
training [trā'ning] n (for occupation) Ausbildung f; (SPORT) Training nt; **in ~** im Training.
training college n Pädagogische Hochschule

f, Lehrerseminar nt; (for priests) Priesterseminar nt.
training course n Ausbildungskurs m.
training shoe n Trainingsschuh m.
train station n (US) Bahnhof m.
traipse [trāps] vi latschen.
trait [trāt] n Zug m, Merkmal nt.
traitor [trā'tûr] n Verräter m.
trajectory [trəjek'tûrē] n Flugbahn f.
tram [tram] n (Brit) Straßenbahn f.
tramline [tram'līn] n Straßenbahnschiene f; (route) Straßenbahnlinie f.
tramp [tramp] n Landstreicher m ♦ vi (walk heavily) stampfen, stapfen; (travel on foot) wandern.
trample [tram'pəl] vt (nieder)trampeln ♦ vi (herum)trampeln.
trampoline [trampəlēn'] n Trampolin nt.
trance [trans] n Trance f; **to go into a ~** in Trance verfallen.
tranquil [trang'kwil] a ruhig, friedlich.
tranquility, (Brit) **tranquillity** [trangkwil'itē] n Ruhe f.
tranquilizer, (Brit) **tranquillizer** [trang'kwəlīzûr] n Beruhigungsmittel nt.
trans- [trans] pref Trans-.
transact [transakt'] vt (durch)führen, abwickeln.
transaction [transak'shən] n Durchführung f, Abwicklung f; (piece of business) Geschäft nt, Transaktion f; **cash ~s** Bargeldtransaktionen pl.
transatlantic [transətlan'tik] a transatlantisch.
transcend [transend'] vt übersteigen.
transcendent [transen'dənt] a transzendent.
transcendental meditation [transenden'təl meditā'shən] n transzendentale Meditation f.
transcribe [transkrīb'] vt abschreiben, transkribieren.
transcript [tran'skript] n Abschrift f, Kopie f; (JUR) Protokoll nt.
transcription [transkrip'shən] n Transkription f; (product) Abschrift f.
transept [tran'sept] n Querschiff nt.
transfer n [trans'fûr] (transferring) Übertragung f; (of business) Umzug m; (being transferred) Versetzung f; (design) Abziehbild nt; (SPORT) Transfer m; (player) Transferspieler m; **by bank ~** per Banküberweisung ♦ vt [transfûr'] (business) verlegen; (person) versetzen; (prisoner) überführen; (drawing) übertragen; (money) überweisen; **to ~ money from one account to another** Geld von einem Konto auf ein anderes überweisen; **to ~ sth to sb's name** etw auf jds Namen übertragen.
transferable [transfûr'əbəl] a übertragbar; **not ~** nicht übertragbar.
transfix [transfiks'] vt annageln, feststecken (to an +acc); (butterflies) aufspießen; **~ed with fear** (fig) starr vor Angst.
transform [transfôrm'] vt umwandeln, verändern.

transformation [transfûrmā'shən] n Umwandlung f, Veränderung f, Verwandlung f.

transformer [transfôr'mûr] n (ELEC) Transformator m.

transfusion [transfyōō'zhən] n Blutübertragung f, Transfusion f.

transgress [transgres'] vt (go beyond) überschreiten; (violate) verstoßen gegen, verletzen.

tranship [tranship'] vt umschlagen.

transient [tran'shənt] a kurz(lebig).

transistor [tranzis'tûr] n (ELEC) Transistor m; (radio) Transistorradio nt.

transistorized [tranzis'tərīzd] a (circuit) transistorisiert.

transit [tran'sit] n: **in** ~ unterwegs, auf dem Transport.

transit camp n Durchgangslager nt.

transition [tranzish'ən] n Übergang m.

transitional [tranzish'ənəl] a Übergangs-.

transition period n Übergangsperiode or -zeit f.

transitive [tran'sətiv] a, **transitively** [tran'sətivlē] ad transitiv.

transitory [tran'sitōrē] a vorübergehend.

transit visa n Transitvisum nt, Durchreisevisum nt.

translate [tranz'lāt] vti übersetzen; **to** ~ **sth from German into English** etw vom Deutschen ins Englische übersetzen.

translation [tranzlā'shən] n Übersetzung f.

translator [tranzlā'tûr] n Übersetzer(in f) m.

translucent [translōō'sənt] a durchscheinend, lichtdurchlässig.

transmission [transmish'ən] n (of information) Übermittlung f; (ELEC, MED, TV) Übertragung f; (AUT) Getriebe nt.

transmit [transmit'] vt (message) übermitteln; (ELEC, MED, TV) übertragen.

transmitter [transmit'ûr] n Sender m.

transom [tran'səm] n (US) Oberlicht nt.

transparency [transpär'ənsē] n Durchsichtigkeit f, Transparenz f; (PHOT) Dia(positiv) nt.

transparent [transpär'ənt] a (lit) durchsichtig; (fig) offenkundig.

transpire [transpīûr'] vi (happen) passieren; (become known): **it finally** ~**d that ...** es sickerte schließlich durch, daß ...

transplant vt [transplant'] umpflanzen; (MED, also fig: person) verpflanzen ♦ n [trans'plant] (MED) Transplantation f; (organ) Transplantat nt; **to have a heart** ~ sich einer Herztransplantation unterziehen.

transport n [trans'pôrt] Transport m, Beförderung f; (vehicle) fahrbare(r) Untersatz m; **public** ~ öffentliche Verkehrsmittel pl; **means of** ~ Transportmittel nt ♦ vt [transpôrt'] befördern, transportieren.

transportable [transpôr'təbəl] a transportabel.

transportation [transpûrtā'shən] n Transport m, Beförderung f; (means) Beförderungsmittel nt; (cost) Transportkosten pl.

transport café n (Brit) Fernfahrerlokal nt.

transpose [tranzpōz'] vt vertauschen, umstellen.

transship [transship'] vt umladen, umschlagen.

transverse [transvûrs'] a Quer-; (position) horizontal; (engine) querliegend.

transvestite [transves'tīt] n Transvestit m.

trap [trap] n Falle f; (carriage) zweirädrige(r) Einspänner m; (col: mouth) Klappe f; **to set** or **lay a** ~ **(for sb)** (jdm) eine Falle stellen ♦ vt fangen; (person) in eine Falle locken; **the miners were** ~**ped** die Bergleute waren eingeschlossen; **to** ~ **one's finger in the door** sich den Finger in der Tür einklemmen.

trapdoor [trap'dôr] n Falltür f.

trapeze [trapēz'] n Trapez nt.

trapper [trap'ûr] n Fallensteller m, Trapper m.

trappings [trap'ingz] npl Aufmachung f.

trash [trash] n (nonsense) Mist m, Blech nt; (US: garbage) Abfall m; (book, play etc) Schund m ♦ vt (US col) in den Dreck ziehen.

trash can n (US) Mülleimer m.

trash can liner n (US) Müllsack m.

trashy [trash'ē] a wertlos; (novel etc) Schund-.

trauma [trou'mə] n Trauma nt.

traumatic [trômat'ik] a (PSYCH, fig) traumatisch.

travel [trav'əl] n Reisen nt ♦ vi reisen, eine Reise machen; **this wine doesn't** ~ **well** dieser Wein verträgt den Transport nicht ♦ vt (distance) zurücklegen; (country) bereisen.

travel agency n Reisebüro nt.

travel agent n Reisebürokaufmann m.

travel brochure n Reiseprospekt m.

traveler, (Brit) **traveller** [trav'əlûr] n Reisende(r) mf; (sales representative) Vertreter m, Handlungsreisende(r) m.

traveler's check, (Brit) **traveller's cheque** n Reisescheck m.

traveling, (Brit) **travelling** [trav'əling] n (US) Reisen nt.

traveling bag n Reisetasche f.

traveling circus n Wanderzirkus m.

traveling exhibition n Wanderausstellung f.

traveling salesman n Vertreter m, Handelsreisende(r) m.

travelling [trav'əling] etc Brit = **traveling** etc.

travelog(ue) [trav'əlôg] n (book, film, talk) Reisebericht m.

travel sickness n Reisekrankheit f.

traverse [trav'ûrs] vt (cross) durchqueren; (bridge, water) überqueren; (lie across) überspannen.

travesty [trav'istē] n Zerrbild nt, Travestie f; **a** ~ **of justice** ein Hohn auf die Gerechtigkeit.

trawler [trô'lûr] n Fischdampfer m, Trawler m.

tray [trā] n (tea ~) Tablett nt; (receptacle) Schale f; (for mail) Ablage f.

treacherous [trech'ûrəs] *a* verräterisch; *(memory)* unzuverlässig; *(road)* tückisch; **road conditions today are** ~ heute ist der Straßenzustand äußerst gefährlich.

treachery [trech'ûrē] *n* Verrat *m*; *(of road)* tückische(r) Zustand *m*.

treacle [trē'kəl] *n (Brit)* Sirup *m*, Melasse *f*.

tread [tred] *n* Schritt *m*, Tritt *m*; *(of stair)* Stufe *f*; *(on tire)* Profil *nt* ♦ *vi irreg* treten; *(walk)* gehen.
tread on *vt fus (Brit)* treten auf (+*acc*).

treadle [tred'əl] *n (of sewing machine)* Tretkurbel *f*, Pedal *nt*; *(of lathe also)* Fußhebel *m*.

treas. *abbr* = **treasurer.**

treason [trē'zən] *n* Verrat *m (to an* +*dat)*.

treasure [trezh'ûr] *n* Schatz *m* ♦ *vt* schätzen.

treasure hunt *n* Schatzsuche *f*.

treasurer [trezh'ûrûr] *n* Kassenverwalter *m*, Schatzmeister *m*; *(US)* Kassenverwalter *m*, Quästor *m*.

treasury [trezh'ûrē] *n (US: treasurer's office)* Quästur *f*.

treasury bill *n* kurzfristige(r) Schatzwechsel *m*.

Treasury Department, *(Brit)* **Treasury** *n* Finanzministerium *nt*.

treat [trēt] *n* besondere Freude *f*; *(school* ~ *etc)* Fest *nt*; *(outing)* Ausflug *m* ♦ *vt (deal with)* behandeln; *(entertain)* bewirten; *(consider)* betrachten *(as* als); **to** ~ **sth as a joke** etw als Witz *or* Spaß betrachten *or* ansehen; **to** ~ **sb to sth** jdn zu etw einladen, jdm etw spendieren.

treatise [trē'tis] *n* Abhandlung *f*.

treatment [trēt'mənt] *n (of person, object, MED)* Behandlung *f*; **to have** ~ **for sth** wegen etw in Behandlung sein.

treaty [trē'tē] *n* Vertrag *m*.

treble [treb'əl] *a* dreifach ♦ *vt* verdreifachen ♦ *n (voice)* Sopran *m*; *(music)* Diskant *m*.

treble clef *n* Violinschlüssel *m*.

tree [trē] *n* Baum *m*.

tree-lined [trē'līnd] *a* baumbestanden.

tree trunk *n* Baumstamm *m*.

trek [trek] *n* Treck *m*, Zug *m* ♦ *vi* trecken.

trellis [trel'is] *n* Gitter *nt*; *(for gardening)* Spalier *nt*.

tremble [trem'bəl] *vi* zittern; *(ground)* beben.

trembling [trem'bling] *n* Zittern *nt* ♦ *a* zitternd.

tremendous [trimen'dəs] *a* gewaltig, kolossal; *(col: very good)* prima.

tremendously [trimen'dəslē] *ad* ungeheuer, enorm; *(col)* unheimlich; **he enjoyed it** ~ es hat ihm ausgezeichnet gefallen.

tremor [trem'ûr] *n* Zittern *nt*; *(of earth)* Beben *nt*.

trench [trench] *n* Graben *m*; *(MIL)* Schützengraben *m*.

trench coat *n* Trenchcoat *m*, Regenmantel *m*.

trench warfare *n* Grabenkrieg *m*.

trend [trend] *n* Richtung *f*, Tendenz *f*; **the** ~

towards der Trend *or* die Tendenz zu (+*dat)*; **the** ~ **away from** die zunehmende Abkehr von; **to set the** ~ richtungweisend sein ♦ *vi* verlaufen *(towards* nach).

trendy [tren'dē] *a (col)* modisch.

trepidation [trepidā'shən] *n* Beklommenheit *f*.

trespass [tres'pas] *vi* widerrechtlich betreten *(on acc)*.

trespasser [tres'pasûr] *n* Unbefugte(r) *mf*; **"~s will be prosecuted"** „widerrechtliches Betreten wird strafrechtlich verfolgt".

tress [tres] *n* Locke *f*.

trestle [tres'əl] *n* Bock *m*.

trestle table *n (Brit)* Klapptisch *m*.

tri- [trī] *pref* Drei-, drei-.

trial [trīl] *n (JUR)* Prozeß *m*, Verfahren *nt*; *(test)* Versuch *m*, Probe *f*; *(hardship)* Prüfung *f*; **~s** *pl (SPORT)* Qualifikationsspiel *nt*; **by** ~ **and error** durch Ausprobieren; ~ **by jury** Schwurgericht *f*; **to bring sb to** ~ *(for a crime)* jdn vor Gericht stellen, jdm den Prozeß machen.

trial balance *n* Probebilanz *f*.

trial basis *n*: **on a** ~ versuchsweise, probeweise.

trial offer *n* Probeangebot *nt*.

trial run *n* Probelauf *m*.

triangle [trī'anggəl] *n* Dreieck *nt*; *(MUS)* Triangel *f*; *(US)* Zeichendreieck *nt*.

triangular [trīang'gyəlûr] *a* dreieckig.

tribal [trī'bəl] *a* Stammes-.

tribe [trīb] *n* Stamm *m*.

tribesman [trībz'mən] *n, pl* **-men** Stammesangehörige(r) *m*.

tribulation [tribyəlā'shən] *n* Not *f*, Mühsal *f*.

tribunal [trībyōō'nəl] *n* Gericht *nt*; *(inquiry)* Untersuchungsausschuß *m*.

tributary [trib'yətârē] *n* Nebenfluß *m*.

tribute [trib'yōōt] *n (admiration)* Zeichen *nt* der Hochachtung.

trice [trīs] *n*: **in a** ~ im Nu.

trick [trik] *n* Trick *m*; *(mischief)* Streich *m*; *(habit)* Angewohnheit *f*; *(CARDS)* Stich *m*; **it's a** ~ **of the light** da täuscht das Licht ♦ *vt* überlisten, beschwindeln; **to** ~ **sb out of sth** jdn um etw prellen; **to** ~ **sb into doing sth** jdn (mit List) dazu bringen, etw zu tun.

trickery [trik'ûrē] *n* Betrügerei *f*, Tricks *pl*.

trickle [trik'əl] *n* Tröpfeln *nt*; *(small river)* Rinnsal *nt* ♦ *vi* tröpfeln; *(seep)* sickern.

trick question *n* Falle *f*, Fangfrage *f*.

trickster [trik'stûr] *n* Gauner(in *f*) *m*.

tricky [trik'ē] *a (problem)* schwierig; *(situation)* kitzlig.

tricycle [trī'sikəl] *n* Dreirad *nt*.

tried [trīd] *a* erprobt, bewährt.

trifle [trī'fəl] *n* Kleinigkeit *f*; *(COOK)* Trifle *m* ♦ *ad*: **a** ~ ein bißchen.
trifle with *vi* zu leicht nehmen.

trifling [trī'fling] *a* geringfügig.

trigger [trig'ûr] *n* Drücker *m*.
trigger off *vt* auslösen.

trigonometry [trigənám'ətrē] *n* Trigonometrie *f*.

trilby [tril'bē] n (Brit) weiche(r) Filzhut m.

trill [tril] n (MUS) Triller m; (of bird) Trillern nt.

trillion [tril'yən] n (US) Billion f.

trilogy [tril'əjē] n Trilogie f.

trim [trim] a ordentlich, gepflegt; (figure) schlank ♦ n (gute) Verfassung f; (embellishment, on car) Verzierung f; **to give sb's hair a ~** jdm die Haare etwas schneiden; **to keep in (good) ~** in Form bleiben ♦ vt (clip) schneiden; (trees) stutzen; (decorate) besetzen; (sails) trimmen.

trimmings [trim'ingz] npl (decorations) Verzierung(en pl) f; (extras) Zubehör nt.

Trinidad and Tobago [trin'idad ən tōbā'gō] n Trinidad und Tobago nt.

Trinity [trin'itē] n: **the ~** die Dreieinigkeit.

trinket [tring'kit] n kleine(s) Schmuckstück nt.

trio [trē'ō] n Trio nt.

trip [trip] n (kurze) Reise f; (outing) Ausflug m; (stumble) Stolpern nt ♦ vi (walk quickly) trippeln; (stumble) stolpern.
trip over vt fus stolpern über (+acc).
trip up vi stolpern; (fig also) einen Fehler machen ♦ vt zu Fall bringen; (fig) hereinlegen.

tripartite [trīpâr'tīt] a (agreement, talks) dreiseitig.

tripe [trīp] n (food) Kutteln pl.

triple [trip'əl] a dreifach; **~ the distance** dreimal so weit; **at ~ the speed** mit dreifacher Geschwindigkeit.

triplets [trip'lits] npl Drillinge pl.

triplicate [trip'ləkit] n: **in ~** in dreifacher Ausfertigung.

tripod [trī'pâd] n Dreifuß m; (PHOT) Stativ nt.

Tripoli [trip'əlē] n Tripolis nt.

tripwire [trip'wiûr] n Stolperdraht m.

trite [trīt] a banal.

triumph [trī'əmf] n Triumph m ♦ vi triumphieren.

triumphal [trīum'fəl] a triumphal, Sieges-.

triumphant [trīum'fənt] a triumphierend; (victorious) siegreich.

triumphantly [trīum'fəntlē] ad triumphierend; siegreich.

trivia [triv'ēə] npl Trivialitäten pl.

trivial [triv'ēəl] a gering(fügig), trivial.

triviality [trivēal'ətē] n Trivialität f, Nebensächlichkeit f.

trivialize [triv'ēəlīz] vt trivialisieren.

trod [trâd] pt of tread.

trodden [trâd'ən] pp of tread.

trolley [trâl'ē] n Handwagen m; (in shop) Einkaufswagen m; (for luggage) Kofferkuli m; (Brit: table) Teewagen m.

trolley bus n Oberleitungsbus m, Obus m.

trollop [trâl'əp] n Hure f; (slut) Schlampe f.

trombone [trâmbōn'] n Posaune f.

troop [trōōp] n Schar f; (MIL) Trupp m ♦ vi; see also **troops**.
troop in vi hineinströmen.

troop out vi hinausströmen.

troop carrier n (plane) Truppentransportflugzeug nt.

trooper [trōō'pûr] n Kavallerist m; (US: policeman) Polizist m.

troops [trōōps] npl Truppen pl.

troopship [trōōp'ship] n Truppentransporter m.

trophy [trō'fē] n Trophäe f.

tropic [trâp'ik] n Wendekreis m; **the ~s** pl die Tropen pl.

tropical [trâp'ikəl] a tropisch.

trot [trât] n Trott m ♦ vi trotten.
trot out vt (excuse, reason, names, facts) aufwarten mit.

trouble [trub'əl] n (worry) Sorge f, Kummer m; (in country, industry) Unruhen pl; (effort) Umstand m, Mühe f; (in system) Störung f; (with sth mechanical) Schwierigkeiten pl, Ärger m (col) ♦ vt (worry) beunruhigen; (bother, inconvenience) stören, belästigen; **to ~ to do sth** sich bemühen, etw zu tun; **please don't ~ yourself** bemühen Sie sich nicht; **to make ~** Schwierigkeiten or Unannehmlichkeiten machen; **to have ~ with** Ärger haben mit; **to have ~ doing sth** Schwierigkeiten haben, etw zu tun; **the ~ is that ...** das Problem ist, daß ...; **to be in/get into ~** Ärger haben/bekommen.

troubled [trub'əld] a (person) beunruhigt; (country) geplagt.

trouble-free [trub'əlfrē] a sorglos.

troublemaker [trub'əlmākûr] n Unruhestifter m.

troubleshooter [trub'əlshōōtûr] n Vermittler m.

troublesome [trub'əlsəm] a lästig, unangenehm; (child) schwierig.

trouble spot n Unruheherd m.

trough [trôf] n (vessel) Trog m; (channel) Rinne f, Kanal m; (MET) Tief nt.

troupe [trōōp] n Truppe f.

trouser press [trou'zûr pres] n Hosenpresse f.

trousers [trou'zûrz] npl (esp Brit) (lange) Hose f, Hosen pl.

trouser suit [trou'zûr sōōt] n (Brit) Hosenanzug m.

trousseau [trōō'sō] n, pl **-x** or **-s** [trōō'sōz] Aussteuer f.

trout [trout] n Forelle f.

trowel [trou'əl] n Kelle f.

truant [trōō'ənt] n: **to be** or (Brit) **play ~** (die Schule) schwänzen.

truce [trōōs] n Waffenstillstand m.

truck [truk] n Lastwagen m, Lastauto nt; (RAIL) offene(r) Güterwagen m; (barrow) Gepäckkarren m; **to have no ~ with sb** nichts zu tun haben mit jdm.

truck driver n Lastwagenfahrer(in f) m.

trucker [truk'ûr] n (truck driver) Lastwagenfahrer(in f) m; (contractor) Spediteur m.

truck farm n (US) Gemüsegärtnerei f.

trucking [truk'ing] n Spedition f, Transport

m.

trucking company *n* (*US*) Speditionsfirma *f*, Transportunternehmen *nt*.

truckload [truk'lōd] *n* Wagenladung *f*.

truck stop *n* (*US*) Fernfahrerlokal *nt*.

truculent [truk'yələnt] *a* trotzig.

trudge [truj] *vi* sich (mühselig) dahinschleppen.

true [trōō] *a* (*exact*) wahr; (*genuine*) echt; (*friend*) treu; (*wall, beam*) gerade; **to come ~** Wirklichkeit werden, wahr werden; (*fears*) sich bewahrheiten; **~ to life** lebensnah.

truffle [truf'əl] *n* Trüffel *f*.

truly [trōō'lē] *ad* (*really*) wirklich; (*exactly*) genau; (*faithfully*) treu; **yours ~** (*in letter-writing*) mit freundlichen Grüßen.

trump [trump] *n* (*CARDS*) Trumpf *m*; **to turn up ~s** (*fig col*) alles rausreißen.

trump card *n* Trumpf(karte *f*) *m*; (*fig*) Trumpf *m*.

trumped-up [trumpt'up'] *a* erfunden.

trumpet [trum'pit] *n* Trompete *f* ♦ *vt* ausposaunen ♦ *vi* trompeten.

truncated [trung'kātid] *a* verstümmelt.

truncheon [trun'chən] *n* (*Brit*) Gummiknüppel *m*.

trundle [trun'dəl] *vt* schieben ♦ *vi*: **to ~ along** (*person*) dahinschlendern; (*vehicle*) entlangrollen.

trunk [trungk] *n* (*of tree*) (Baum)stamm *m*; (*ANAT*) Rumpf *m*; (*box*) Truhe *f*, Überseekoffer *m*; (*of elephant*) Rüssel *m*; (*US AUT*) Kofferraum *m*; *see also* **trunks**.

trunk road *n* Fernstraße *f*.

trunks [trungks] *npl* Badehose *f*.

truss [trus] *n* (*MED*) Bruchband *nt*.

truss up *vt* fesseln.

trust [trust] *n* (*confidence*) Vertrauen *nt*; (*for property etc*) Treuhandvermögen *nt*; **in ~** in treuhänderischer Verwaltung; **you'll have to take it on ~** Sie müssen sich einfach glauben ♦ *vt* (*rely on*) vertrauen (+*dat*), sich verlassen auf (+*acc*); (*hope*) hoffen; **to ~ (that)** hoffen, (daß); **~ him to break it!** er muß es natürlich kaputt machen, typisch!; **to ~ sth to sb** jdm etw anvertrauen.

trust company *n* Trust *m*.

trusted [trus'tid] *a* treu.

trustee [trustē'] *n* Vermögensverwalter *m*.

trustful [trust'fəl] *a* vertrauensvoll.

trust fund *n* Treuhandvermögen *nt*.

trusting [trus'ting] *a* vertrauensvoll.

trustworthy [trust'wûrthē] *a* vertrauenswürdig; (*account*) glaubwürdig.

trusty [trus'tē] *a* treu, zuverlässig.

truth [trōōth] *n* Wahrheit *f*.

truthful [trōōth'fəl] *a* (*person*) ehrlich; (*statement*) wahrheitsgemäß.

truthfully [trōōth'fəlē] *ad* ehrlich; wahrheitsgemäß.

truthfulness [trōōth'fəlnis] *n* Ehrlichkeit *f*; Wahrheit *f*.

try [trī] *n* Versuch *m*; **to have a ~** es versu-

chen; **to give sth a ~** etw versuchen, etw ausprobieren ♦ *vt* (*attempt*) versuchen; (*test*) (aus)probieren; (*JUR*: *person*) unter Anklage stellen; (: *case*) verhandeln; (*strain*) anstrengen; (*courage, patience*) auf die Probe stellen; **to ~ one's (very) best** *or* **hardest** sein Bestes tun *or* versuchen ♦ *vi* versuchen; (*make effort*) sich bemühen.

try on *vt* (*dress*) anprobieren; (*hat*) aufprobieren.

try out *vt* ausprobieren.

trying [trī'ing] *a* schwierig; (*physically*) anstrengend.

tsar [zär] *n* Zar *m*.

T-shirt [tē'shûrt] *n* T-shirt *nt*.

T-square [tē'skwär] *n* Reißschiene *f*.

TT *abbr* (*US MAIL*) = *Trust Territory* ♦ *a abbr* (*Brit col* = *teetotal*) abstinent.

tub [tub] *n* Wanne *f*, Kübel *m*; (*for margarine etc*) Becher *m*.

tuba [tōō'bə] *n* Tuba *f*.

tubby [tub'ē] *a* rundlich, klein und dick.

tube [tōōb] *n* (*pipe*) Röhre *f*, Rohr *nt*; (*for toothpaste etc*) Tube *f*; (*AUT*: *for tire*) Schlauch *m*; (*col*: *television*) Glotze *f*, Röhre *f*; (*Brit*: *subway*) U-Bahn *f*; **down the ~s** (*US col*) in Eimer.

tubeless [tōōb'lis] *a* (*tire*) schlauchlos.

tuber [tōō'bûr] *n* (*BOT*) Knolle *f*.

tuberculosis [tōōbûrkyəlō'sis] *n* Tuberkulose *f*.

tube station [tōōb' stā'shən] *n* (*Brit*) U-Bahnstation *f*.

tubular [tōō'byəlûr] *a* röhrenförmig.

TUC *n abbr* (*Brit*: = *Trades Union Congress*) ≈ DGB *m*.

tuck [tuk] *n* (*fold*) Falte *f*, Einschlag *m* ♦ *vt* (*put*) stecken; (*gather*) fälteln, einschlagen.

tuck away *vt* wegstecken.

tuck in *vt* hineinstecken; (*blanket etc*) feststecken; (*person*) zudecken ♦ *vi* (*eat*) hineinhauen, zulangen.

tuck up *vt* (*child*) zudecken.

Tue(s). *abbr* (= *Tuesday*) Di.

Tuesday [tōōz'dā] *n* Dienstag *m*; **on ~** am Dienstag; **on ~s** dienstags; **every ~** jeden Dienstag; **every other ~** jeden zweiten Dienstag; **last/next ~** letzten/nächsten Dienstag; **a week on ~, ~ week** am Dienstag in einer Woche.

tuft [tuft] *n* Büschel *m*.

tug [tug] *n* (*jerk*) Zerren *nt*, Ruck *m*; (*NAUT*) Schleppdampfer *m* ♦ *vti* zerren, ziehen; (*boat*) schleppen.

tug-of-war [tug'əvwôr'] *n* Tauziehen *nt*.

tuition [tōōish'ən] *n* (*US*) Schulgeld *nt*; (*Brit*) Unterricht *m*.

tulip [tōō'lip] *n* Tulpe *f*.

tumble [tum'bəl] *n* (*fall*) Sturz *m* ♦ *vi* (*fall*) fallen, stürzen.

tumble to *vt fus* kapieren.

tumbledown [tum'bəldoun] *a* baufällig.

tumble dryer *n* (*Brit*) Trockner *m*.

tumbler [tum'blûr] *n* (*glass*) Trinkglas *nt*,

Wasserglas *nt*; (*US*) Trockner *m*.
tummy [tum'ē] *n* (*col*) Bauch *m*.
tumor, (*Brit*) **tumour** [tōō'múr] *n* Tumor *m*, Geschwulst *f*.
tumult [tōō'məlt] *n* Tumult *m*.
tumultuous [tōōmul'chōōəs] *a* lärmend, turbulent.
tuna [tōō'nə] *n* Thunfisch *m*.
tundra [tun'drə] *n* Tundra *f*.
tune [tōōn] *n* Melodie *f* ♦ *vt* (*put in tune*) stimmen; (*AUT*) richtig einstellen; **to sing in ~/out of** ~ richtig/falsch singen; **to be in/out of** ~ **with** ~ (*fig*) harmonieren/nicht harmonieren mit; **to the** ~ **of** (*fig: amount*) in Höhe von.
tune in *vi* einstellen (*to acc*).
tune up *vi* (*MUS*) stimmen.
tuneful [tōōn'fəl] *a* melodisch.
tuner [tōō'núr] *n* (*person*) (Instrumenten)stimmer *m*; (*radio set*) Empfangsgerät *nt*, Steuergerät *nt*; (*part*) Tuner *m*, Kanalwähler *m*.
tungsten [tung'stən] *n* Wolfram *nt*.
tunic [tōō'nik] *n* Kasack *m*, Hemdbluse *f*; (*of uniform*) Uniformrock *m*.
tuning [tōō'ning] *n* (*RAD. AUT*) Einstellen *nt*; (*MUS*) Stimmen *nt*.
tuning fork *n* Stimmgabel *f*.
Tunis [tōō'nis] *n* Tunis *nt*.
Tunisia [tōōnē'zhə] *n* Tunesien *nt*.
Tunisian [tōōnē'zhən] *a* tunesisch ♦ *n* Tunesier(in *f*) *m*.
tunnel [tun'əl] *n* Tunnel *m*, Unterführung *f* ♦ *vi* einen Tunnel anlegen.
tunny [tun'ē] *n* Thunfisch *m*.
turban [tûr'bən] *n* Turban *m*.
turbid [tûr'bid] *a* trübe; (*fig*) verworren.
turbine [tûr'bīn] *n* Turbine *f*.
turboprop [tûr'bōpráp] *n* (*engine*) Propellerturbine *f*, Turboprop *f*; (*aircraft*) Turbo-Prop-Flugzeug *nt*.
turbot [tûr'bət] *n* Steinbutt *m*.
turbulence [tûr'byələns] *n* (*AVIAT*) Turbulenz *f*.
turbulent [tûr'byələnt] *a* stürmisch.
tureen [tərēn'] *n* Terrine *f*.
turf [tûrf] *n* Rasen *m*; (*piece*) Sode *f* ♦ *vt* mit Grassoden belegen.
turf out *vt* (*Brit col: person*) rauswerfen; (*: throw away*) wegschmeißen.
turgid [tûr'jid] *a* geschwollen.
Turin [tōō'rin] *n* Turin *nt*.
Turk [tûrk] *n* Türke *m*, Türkin *f*.
turkey [tûr'kē] *n* Puter *m*, Truthahn *m*.
Turkey [tûr'kē] *n* die Türkei.
Turkish [tûr'kish] *a* türkisch ♦ *n* (*language*) Türkisch *nt*.
turmeric [tûr'múrik] *n* Kurkuma *f*, Gelbwurz *f*.
turmoil [tûr'moil] *n* Aufruhr *m*, Tumult *m*.
turn [tûrn] *n* (*rotation*) (Um)drehung *f*; (*performance*) (Programm)nummer *f*; (*shock*) Schock *m*; **to make a** ~ **to the left** nach links abbiegen; **the** ~ **of the tide** der Gezei-

tenwechsel; **(at) the** ~ **of the century** (um) die Jahrhundertwende; **at the** ~ **of the year** am Jahresende; **to take a** ~ **for the worse** sich zum Schlechteren wenden; **it's your** ~ du bist dran *or* an der Reihe; **in** ~, **by** ~**s** abwechselnd; **to take** ~**s** sich abwechseln; **to do sb a good/bad** ~ jdm einen guten/ schlechten Dienst erweisen; **it gave me quite a** ~ das hat mich schön erschreckt ♦ *vt* (*rotate*) drehen; (*change position of*) umdrehen, wenden; (*page*) umblättern; (*transform*) verwandeln; (*direct*) zuwenden; (*shape: wood*) drechseln; (*: metal*) drehen; **they** ~**ed him against us** sie haben ihn gegen uns aufgehetzt; **the car** ~**ed the corner** das Auto fuhr um die Ecke; **to** ~ **sb loose** jdn los- *or* freilassen ♦ *vi* (*rotate*) sich drehen; (*change direction: in car*) abbiegen; (*: wind*) drehen; (~ *round*) umdrehen, wenden; (*become*) werden; (*leaves*) sich verfärben; (*milk*) sauer werden; (*weather*) umschlagen; **to** ~ **left** (*AUT*) links abbiegen; **to** ~ **to stone** zu Stein werden.
turn around *vi* (*person, vehicle*) sich herumdrehen; (*rotate*) sich drehen.
turn away *vi* sich abwenden ♦ *vt* (*reject: person*) wegschicken, abweisen; (*: business*) zurückweisen, ablehnen.
turn back *vt* umdrehen; (*person*) zurückschicken; (*clock*) zurückstellen ♦ *vi* umkehren.
turn down *vt* (*refuse*) ablehnen; (*fold down*) umschlagen.
turn in *vi* (*go to bed*) ins Bett gehen ♦ *vt* (*fold inwards*) einwärts biegen; (*hand in*) abgeben.
turn into *vt fus* sich verwandeln in (+*acc*).
turn off *vi* abbiegen ♦ *vt* (*light*) ausschalten; (*tap*) zudrehen; (*machine, gas*) abstellen.
turn on *vt* (*light*) anschalten, einschalten; (*tap*) aufdrehen; (*machine*) anstellen.
turn out *vi* (*prove to be*) sich herausstellen, sich erweisen; (*people*) sich entwickeln; (*appear, attend: troops*) ausrücken; (*doctor*) einen Krankenbesuch machen; **how did the cake** ~ **out?** wie ist der Kuchen geworden? ♦ *vt* (*light*) ausschalten; (*gas*) abstellen; (*produce*) produzieren.
turn over *vt* (*mattress, card*) umdrehen, wenden; (*page*) umblättern.
turn round *vi* (*Brit*) = **turn around**.
turn to *vt fus* sich zuwenden (+*dat*); **she has no-one to** ~ **to** sie hat niemanden, an den sie sich wenden kann.
turn up *vi* auftauchen; (*happen*) passieren, sich ereignen ♦ *vt* (*collar*) hochklappen, hochstellen; (*nose*) rümpfen; (*radio*) lauter stellen; (*heat*) höher stellen, aufdrehen.
turnabout [tûr'nəbout] *n* Kehrtwendung *f*.
turnaround [tûrn'əround] *n* (*of ship, aircraft*) Abfernigung *f*; (*of situation, company*) Umschwung *m*.
turncoat [tûrn'kōt] *n* Abtrünnige(r) *mf*, Über-

läufer *m*.
turned-up [tûrnd'up] *a* (*nose*) Stups-.
turning [tûr'ning] *n* (*Brit*: *in road*) Abzweigung *f*; **the first ~ on the right** die erste Abfahrt *or* Straße rechts.
turning point *n* Wendepunkt *m*.
turnip [tûr'nip] *n* Steckrübe *f*.
turnkey system [tûrn'kē sis'təm] *n* (*COM-
PUT*) schlüsselfertige(s) System *nt*.
turnout [tûrn'out] *n* (Besucher)zahl *f*;
(*COMM*) Produktion *f*.
turnover [tûrn'ōvûr] *n* Umsatz *m*; (*of staff*)
Wechsel *m*; (*COOK*) Tasche *f*.
turnpike [tûrn'pīk] *n* (*US*) gebührenpflichtige
Straße *f*.
turnround [tûrn'round] *n* (*Brit*) = **turnaround**.
turn signal *n* (*US AUT*) Anzeiger *m*.
turnstile [tûrn'stīl] *n* Drehkreuz *nt*.
turntable [tûrn'tābəl] *n* (*of record player*)
Plattenteller *m*; (*RAIL*) Drehscheibe *f*.
turn-up [tûrn'up] *n* (*Brit*: *on pants*) Aufschlag *m*.
turpentine [tûr'pəntīn] *n* Terpentin *nt*.
turquoise [tûr'koiz] *n* (*gem*) Türkis *m*;
(*color*) Türkis *nt* ♦ *a* türkisfarben.
turret [tûr'it] *n* Turm *m*.
turtle [tûr'təl] *n* Schildkröte *f*.
turtle neck *n* Schildkrötkragen *m*.
Tuscany [tus'kənē] *n* die Toskana.
tusk [tusk] *n* Stoßzahn *m*.
tussle [tus'əl] *n* Balgerei *f*.
tutor [tōō'tûr] *n* (*teacher*) Privatlehrer *m*;
(*college instructor*) Tutor *m*.
tutorial [tōōtôr'ēəl] *n* (*UNIV*) Kolloquium *nt*,
Seminarübung *f*.
tuxedo [tuksē'dō] *n* Smoking *m*.
TV [tēvē] *n abbr* (= *television*) Fernseher *m* ♦
a Fernseh-.
TV dinner *n* (*US*) Fertigmahlzeit *f*.
twaddle [twâd'əl] *n* (*col*) Gewäsch *nt*.
twang [twang] *n* scharfe(r) Ton *m*; (*of voice*)
Näseln *nt* ♦ *vt* zupfen ♦ *vi* klingen.
tweak [twēk] *vt* (*nose, ear, hair*) ziehen.
tweed [twēd] *n* Tweed *m*.
tweezers [twē'zûrz] *npl* Pinzette *f*.
twelfth [twelfth] *a* zwölfte(r, s).
Twelfth Night *n* Dreikönigsabend *m*.
twelve [twelv] *num a* zwölf.
twentieth [twen'tēith] *a* zwanzigste(r, s).
twenty [twen'tē] *num a* zwanzig.
twerp [twûrp] *n* (*col*) Knülch *m*.
twice [twīs] *ad* zweimal; **~ as much** doppelt
soviel; **~ my age** doppelt so alt wie ich; **~
a week** zweimal wöchentlich, zweimal in
der *or* pro Woche.
twiddle [twid'əl] *vti*: **to ~ (with) sth** an etw
(*dat*) herumdrehen; **to ~ one's thumbs**
(*fig*) Däumchen drehen.
twig [twig] *n* dünne(r) Zweig *m* ♦ *vt* (*Brit
col*) kapieren, merken.
twilight [twī'līt] *n* Dämmerung *f*, Zwielicht
nt; **in the ~** in der Dämmerung.
twill [twil] *n* Köper *m*.

twin [twin] *n* Zwilling *m* ♦ *a* Zwillings-; (*very
similar*) Doppel-; **~ beds** zwei (gleiche)
Einzelbetten ♦ *vt* (*town*) zu Partnerstädten
machen.
twin carburetors *npl* Doppelvergaser *m*.
twine [twin] *n* Bindfaden *m* ♦ *vi* binden.
twin-engined [twin'enjənd] *a* zweimotorig; **~
aircraft** zweimotorige(s) Flugzeug *nt*.
twinge [twinj] *n* stechende(r) Schmerz *m*,
Stechen *nt*.
twinkle [twing'kəl] *n* Funkeln *nt*, Blitzen *nt* ♦
vi funkeln.
twin town *n* (*Brit*) Partnerstadt *f*.
twirl [twûrl] *n* Wirbel *m* ♦ *vti* (herum)wirbeln.
twist [twist] *n* (*twisting*) Biegen *nt*, Drehung
f; (*curve*) Kurve *f*, Biegung *f* ♦ *vt* (*turn*)
drehen; (*make crooked*) verbiegen; (*distort*)
verdrehen; **to ~ one's ankle/neck** sich den
Fuß vertreten/den Hals verrenken ♦ *vi* sich
drehen; (*curve*) sich winden.
twisted [twis'tid] *a* (*wire, rope*) (zusammen)gedreht; (*ankle, wrist*) verrenkt; (*fig*:
logic, mind) verdreht.
twit [twit] *n* (*Brit col*) Idiot *m*.
twitch [twich] *n* Zucken *nt* ♦ *vi* zucken.
two [tōō] *num a* zwei; **to break in ~** in zwei
Teile brechen; **~ by ~**, **in ~s** immer zwei
auf einmal, zu zweit; **to be in ~ minds**
nicht genau wissen; **to put ~ and ~ together** seine Schlüsse ziehen.
two-door [tōō'dôr] *a* zweitürig.
two-faced [tōō'fāst] *a* falsch.
twofold [tōō'fōld] *a, ad* zweifach; (*increase*)
doppelt; **to increase ~** um das Doppelte ansteigen.
two-piece [tōō'pēs] *a* zweiteilig.
two-seater [tōō'sē'tûr] *n* (*plane, car*) Zweisit-
zer *m*.
twosome [tōō'səm] *n* Paar *nt*.
two-stroke [tōō'strōk] *n* (*engine*) Zweitakter
m ♦ *a* Zweitakt-.
two-tone [tōō'tōn] *a* (*color*) zweifarbig.
two-way [tōō'wā] *a* (*traffic*) Gegen-; **~
radio** Funksprechgerät *nt*.
TX *abbr* (*US MAIL*) = *Texas*.
tycoon [tīkōōn'] *n* (Industrie)magnat *m*.
type [tīp] *n* Typ *m*, Art *f*, Sorte *f*; (*TYP*) Type
f; **what ~ do you want?** welche Sorte
möchten Sie?; **in bold/italic ~** fett/kursiv
gedruckt ♦ *vi* maschineschreiben, tippen ♦ *vt*
tippen, mit der Maschine) schreiben.
type-cast [tīp'kast] *a* (*THEAT, TV*) auf eine
Rolle festgelegt.
typeface [tīp'fās] *n* Schrift *f*, Schriftbild *nt*.
typescript [tīp'skript] *n* maschinegeschriebe-
ne(r) Text *m*.
typeset [tīp'set] *vt* Schrift setzen.
typesetter [tīp'setûr] *n* (*person*) Schriftset-
zer(in *f*) *m*; (*machine*) Setzmaschine *f*.
typewriter [tīp'rītûr] *n* Schreibmaschine *f*.
typewritten [tīp'ritən] *a* maschinegeschrie-
ben, getippt.
typhoid [tī'foid] *n* Typhus *m*.
typhoon [tīfōōn'] *n* Taifun *m*.

typhus |tī'fəs| n Flecktyphus m.
typical |tip'ikəl| a, **typically** |tip'ikəlē| ad typisch (of für).
typify |tip'əfī| vt typisch sein für.
typing |tī'ping| n Maschineschreiben nt.
typing pool n Schreibzentrale f.
typist |tī'pist| n Maschinenschreiber(in f) m, Tippse f (col).
typo |tī'pō| n abbr (col: = typographical error) Tippfehler m.
typography |tīpág'rəfē| n Typographie f.
tyranny |tĕr'ənē| n Tyrannei f, Gewaltherrschaft f.
tyrant |tī'rənt| n Tyrann m.
tyre |tīūr'| n (Brit) Reifen m.
Tyrol |tirōl'| n Tirol nt.
Tyrolean |tirō'lēən|, **Tyrolese** |tirəlēz'| n Tiroler(in f) m ♦ a Tiroler-.
Tyrrhenian Sea |tīrē'nēən sē'| n Tyrrhenische(s) Meer nt.

U

U, u |yōō| n (letter) U nt, u nt; **U for Uncle** ≈ U wie Ulrich.
U |yōō| n abbr (Brit CINE: = universal) jugendfrei.
U-bend |yōō'bend| n (in pipe) U-Bogen m.
ubiquitous |yōōbik'witəs| adj allgegenwärtig.
UDA n abbr (Brit: = Ulster Defence Association) protestantische paramilitärische Organisation in Nordirland.
udder |ud'ûr| n Euter nt.
UDI n abbr (Brit POL) = unilateral declaration of independence.
UDR n abbr (Brit: = Ulster Defence Regiment) Regiment aus Teilzeitsoldaten zur Unterstützung von Armee und Polizei in Nordirland.
UEFA |yōōā'fa| n abbr (= Union of European Football Associations) UEFA f.
UFO |yōōefō'| n abbr (= unidentified flying object) UFO nt.
Uganda |yōōgan'də| n Uganda nt.
Ugandan |yōōgan'dən| n Ugander(in f) m ♦ a ugandisch.
ugh |u| interj hu.
ugliness |ug'lēnis| n Häßlichkeit f.
ugly |ug'lē| a häßlich; (bad) böse, schlimm.
UHF n abbr (= ultrahigh frequency) UHF.
UHT a abbr = ultra-heat treated.
UK n abbr (= United Kingdom) Vereinigte(s) Königreich nt.
ukulele |yōōkəlā'lē| n Ukulele f.
ulcer |ul'sûr| n Geschwür nt; **mouth ~** Abszeß m im Mund.
Ulster |ul'stûr| n Ulster nt.

ulterior |ultēr'cûr| a: **~ motive** Hintergedanke m.
ultimate |ul'təmit| a äußerste(r, s), allerletzte(r, s) ♦ n: **the ~ in luxury** das Höchste an Luxus.
ultimately |ul'təmitlē| ad schließlich, letzten Endes.
ultimatum |ultimā'təm| n, pl **-s** or **ultimata** |ultimā'tə| Ultimatum nt.
ultra- |ul'trə| pref ultra-.
ultrasonic |ultrəsən'ik| a Ultraschall-, Überschall-.
ultrasound |ul'trəsound| n (MED) Ultraschall m.
ultraviolet |ultrəvī'əlit| a ultraviolett.
umbilical cord |umbil'ikəl kôrd| n Nabelschnur f.
umbrage |um'brij| n: **to take ~** Anstoß nehmen (at an +dat).
umbrella |umbrel'ə| n Schirm m; **under the ~ of** (fig) unter der Kontrolle von.
umpire |um'pīûr| n Schiedsrichter(in f) m ♦ vti schiedsrichtern.
umpteen |ump'tēn'| num (col) zig.
umpteenth |ump'tēnth'| a (col) x-te(r, s).
UMW n abbr (= United Mineworkers of America) Gewerkschaft der Berg- und Metallarbeiter.
UN n abbr = **United Nations**.
un- |un| pref un-.
unabashed |unəbasht'| a unerschrocken.
unabated |unəbā'tid| a unvermindert.
unable |unā'bəl| a außerstande; **to be ~ to do sth** etw nicht tun können, außerstande sein, etw zu tun.
unabridged |unəbrijd'| a ungekürzt.
unacceptable |unaksep'təbəl| a (proposal, behavior) nicht akzeptabel; (price) unannehmbar; **it's ~ that we should be expected to** ... es kann doch nicht von uns verlangt werden, daß ...
unaccompanied |unəkum'pənēd| a ohne Begleitung.
unaccountably |unəkount'əblē| ad unerklärlich.
unaccounted |unəkoun'tid| a: **two passengers are ~ for** zwei Passagiere fehlen noch.
unaccustomed |unəkus'təmd| a nicht gewöhnt (to an +acc); (unusual) ungewohnt.
unacquainted |unəkwān'tid| a: **to be ~ with the facts** mit den Tatsachen nicht vertraut sein.
unadulterated |unədul'tərātid| a rein, unverfälscht; (wine) ungepanscht.
unaffected |unəfek'tid| a (person, behavior) natürlich, unaffektiert; **our plans were ~ by the strike** unsere Pläne wurden durch den Streik nicht betroffen.
unafraid |unəfrād'| a: **to be ~** keine Angst haben.
unaided |unā'did| a selbständig, ohne Hilfe.
unanimity |yōōnənim'itē| n Einstimmigkeit f.
unanimous |yōōnan'əməs| a, **unanimously**

[yōōnan'əməslē] *ad* einmütig; (*vote*) einstimmig.

unanswered [unan'sûrd] *a* (*question, letter*) unbeantwortet; (*criticism*) zwingend, unwiderlegbar.

unappetizing [unap'itīzing] *a* unappetitlich.

unappreciative [unəprē'shēətiv] *a* undankbar.

unarmed [unârmd'] *a* (*person*) unbewaffnet; (*combat*) ohne Waffen.

unashamed [unəshāmd'] *a* schamlos.

unassisted [unəsis'tid] *a, ad* ohne fremde Hilfe.

unattached [unətacht'] *a* ungebunden.

unattended [unəten'did] *a* (*person*) unbeaufsichtigt; (*thing*) unbewacht.

unattractive [unətrak'tiv] *a* unattraktiv.

unauthorized [unôth'ərīzd] *a* unbefugt.

unavailable [unəvā'ləbəl] *a* (*article, room, book*) nicht verfügbar; (*person*) nicht zu erreichen.

unavoidable [unəvoi'dəbəl] *a* unvermeidlich.

unavoidably [unəvoi'dəblē] *ad* unvermeidlich; **to be ~ detained** verhindert sein.

unaware [unəwär'] *a*: **to be ~ of sth** sich (*dat*) einer Sache nicht bewußt sein.

unawares [unəwärz'] *ad* unversehens.

unbalanced [unbal'ənst] *a* unausgeglichen; (*mentally*) gestört.

unbearable [unbär'əbəl] *a* unerträglich.

unbeatable [unbē'təbəl] *a* unschlagbar.

unbeaten [unbēt'ən] *a* (*team*) ungeschlagen; (*record*) ungebrochen, nicht überboten; (*army*) unbesiegt.

unbecoming [unbikum'ing] *a* (*unflattering*: *garment*) unvorteilhaft; (*unseemly*: *language, behavior*) unpassend, unschicklich.

unbeknown(st) [unbinōn(st)'] *ad*: **~ to him** ohne sein Wissen.

unbelief [unbilēf'] *n* Unglaube *m*.

unbelievable [unbilē'vəbəl] *a* unglaublich.

unbelievingly [unbilē'vinglē] *ad* ungläubig.

unbend [unbend'] *irreg vt* geradebiegen, gerademachen ♦ *vi* aus sich herausgehen.

unbending [unben'ding] *a* (*fig*) unnachgiebig.

unbias(s)ed [unbī'əst] *a* unvoreingenommen; (*opinion, report also*) unparteiisch.

unblemished [unblem'isht] *a* (*lit, fig*) makellos.

unblock [unblâk'] *vt* (*pipe*) reinigen.

unborn [unbôrn'] *a* ungeboren.

unbounded [unboun'did] *a* unbegrenzt.

unbreakable [unbrā'kəbəl] *a* unzerbrechlich.

unbridled [unbrī'dəld] *a* ungezügelt.

unbroken [unbrō'kən] *a* (*period*) ununterbrochen; (*spirit*) ungebrochen; (*record*) unübertroffen, ungebrochen.

unbuckle [unbuk'əl] *vt* aufmachen, aufschnallen.

unburden [unbûr'dən] *vt*: **to ~ o.s. (to sb)** (jdm) sein Herz ausschütten.

unbusinesslike [unbiz'nislīk] *a* (*trader*) nicht geschäftsmännisch; (*transaction*) ungeschäftsmäßig; (*fig*: *person*) nicht geschäfts-

tüchtig.

unbutton [unbut'ən] *vt* aufknöpfen.

uncalled-for [unkôld'fôr] *a* unnötig.

uncanny [unkan'ē] *a* unheimlich.

unceasing [unsē'sing] *a* unaufhörlich.

unceremonious [unsärəmō'nēəs] *a* (*abrupt, rude*) brüsk; (*exit, departure*) überstürzt.

uncertain [unsûr'tən] *a* unsicher; (*doubtful*) ungewiß; (*unreliable*) unbeständig; (*vague*) undeutlich, vage; **it's ~ whether ...** es ist nicht sicher, ob ...; **we were ~ whether ...** wir waren uns nicht sicher, ob ...; **in no ~ terms** klar und deutlich, unzweideutig.

uncertainty [unsûr'təntē] *n* Ungewißheit *f*.

unchallenged [unchal'injd] *a* unbestritten, unangefochten; (*JUR*) nicht abgelehnt; **to go ~** nicht überboten werden.

unchanged [unchānjd'] *a* unverändert.

uncharitable [unchar'itəbəl] *a* hartherzig; (*remark*) unfreundlich.

uncharted [unchâr'tid] *a* nicht verzeichnet.

unchecked [unchekt'] *a* ungeprüft; (*not stopped*: *advance*) ungehindert.

uncivil [unsiv'əl] *a* unhöflich, grob.

uncivilized [unsiv'ilīzd] *a* unzivilisiert.

uncle [ung'kəl] *n* Onkel *m*.

unclear [unkliûr'] *a* unklar; **I'm still ~ about what I'm supposed to do** ich bin mir immer noch nicht im klaren darüber, was ich tun soll.

uncoil [unkoil'] *vt* abwickeln ♦ *vi* (*wire etc*) sich abwickeln, sich abspulen.

uncomfortable [unkumf'təbəl] *a* unbequem, ungemütlich.

uncomfortably [unkumf'təblē] *ad* unbequem; (*uneasily*: *say*) unangenehm, ungut.

uncommitted [unkəmit'id] *a* (*attitude, country*) neutral; **to remain ~ to sth** (*policy, party*) sich auf etw nicht festlegen.

uncommon [unkâm'ən] *a* (*unusual*) ungewöhnlich; (*outstanding*) außergewöhnlich.

uncommunicative [unkəmyōō'nikətiv] *a* verschlossen, wortkarg.

uncomplicated [unkâm'plikātid] *a* unkompliziert.

uncompromising [unkâm'prəmīzing] *a* kompromißlos, unnachgiebig.

unconcerned [unkənsûrnd'] *a* (*unworried*) unbekümmert; **to be ~ about sth** sich nicht um etw kümmern.

unconditional [unkəndish'ənəl] *a* bedingungslos.

uncongenial [unkənjēn'yəl] *a* unangenehm.

unconnected [unkənek'tid] *a* (*unrelated*) nicht miteinander in Beziehung stehend; **his illness is ~ with that accident** es besteht keine Beziehung zwischen seiner Krankheit und dem Unfall.

unconscious [unkân'chəs] *a* (*MED*) bewußtlos; (*not aware*) nicht bewußt; (*not meant*) unbeabsichtigt; **the blow knocked him ~** er wurde bewußtlos durch den Schlag ♦ *n*: **the ~** das Unbewußte.

unconsciously [unkân'chəslē] *ad* unwissentlich, unbewußt.

unconsciousness [unkân'chəsnis] *n* Bewußtlosigkeit *f*.

unconstitutional [unkânstitoo'shənəl] *a* nicht verfassungsgemäß, verfassungswidrig.

uncontested [unkəntes'tid] *a* (*champion*) unangefochten; (*Brit POL: seat*) ohne Gegenkandidat.

uncontrollable [unkəntrō'ləbəl] *a* unkontrollierbar, unbändig.

uncontrolled [unkəntrōld'] *a* (*child, dog*) unbeaufsichtigt; (*inflation, price rises*) nicht unter Kontrolle; (*laughter*) unkontrolliert; (*weeping*) hemmungslos, haltlos.

unconventional [unkənven'chənəl] *a* unkonventionell.

unconvinced [unkənvinst'] *a*: **to be/remain ~** nicht überzeugt *or* unüberzeugt sein/bleiben.

unconvincing [unkənvin'sing] *a* nicht überzeugend.

uncork [unkôrk'] *vt* entkorken.

uncorroborated [unkərâb'ərātid] *a* unbestätigt.

uncouth [unkooth'] *a* grob, ungehobelt.

uncover [unkuv'ûr] *vt* aufdecken.

uncovered [unkuv'ûrd] *a* (*US: check*) ungedeckt.

undamaged [undam'ijd] *a* (*goods*) unbeschädigt; (*fig: reputation*) makellos.

undaunted [undôn'tid] *a* unerschrocken.

undecided [undisī'did] *a* unschlüssig.

undelivered [undiliv'ûrd] *a* nicht geliefert; **if ~ return to sender** falls unzustellbar bitte zurück an Absender.

undeniable [undinī'əbəl] *a* unleugbar.

undeniably [undinī'əblē] *ad* unbestreitbar.

under [un'dûr] *prep* unter ♦ *ad* darunter; **~ repair** in Reparatur; **in ~ 2 hours** in weniger als 2 Stunden; **~ anesthetic** in der Narkose; **to be ~ discussion** zur Diskussion stehen, in der Diskussion sein; **~ the circumstances** unter diesen Umständen.

underage [undərāj'] *a* minderjährig.

underarm [un'dûrârm] *a, ad* (*SPORT*) von unten ♦ *n* Unterarm *m*.

undercapitalized [undûrkap'itəlīzd] *a* unterkapitalisiert.

undercarriage [un'dûrkarij] *n* (*Brit AVIAT*) Fahrgestell *nt*.

undercharge [undûrchârj'] *vt* zuwenig berechnen.

underclothes [un'dûrklōz] *npl* Unterwäsche *f*.

undercoat [un'dûrkōt] *n* (*paint*) Grundierung *f* ♦ *vt* (*US AUT*) mit Unterbodenschutz versehen.

undercover [undûrkuv'ûr] *a* Geheim-.

undercurrent [un'dûrkûrənt] *n* Unterströmung *f*.

undercut [undûrkut'] *vt irreg* unterbieten.

underdeveloped [un'dûrdivel'əpt] *a* unterentwickelt.

underdog [un'dûrdôg] *n* Unterlegene(r) *mf*.

underdone [un'dûrdun'] *a* (*COOK*) nicht gar, nicht durchgebraten.

underemployment [undûremploi'mənt] *n* Unterbeschäftigung *f*.

underestimate [undûres'təmāt] *vt* unterschätzen.

underexposed [undûrikspōzd'] *a* unterbelichtet.

underfed [undûrfed'] *a* unterernährt.

underfoot [undûrfoot'] *ad* am Boden.

undergo [undûrgō'] *vt irreg* (*experience*) durchmachen; (*operation, test*) sich unterziehen (+*dat*); **the car is ~ing repairs** der Wagen ist in Reparatur.

undergraduate [undûrgraj'ooit] *n* Student(in *f*) *m*; **~ courses** Kurse *pl* für nichtgraduierte Studenten.

underground [un'dûrground] *n* (*Brit*) Untergrundbahn *f*, U-Bahn *f* ♦ *a* (*press etc*) Untergrund-.

undergrowth [un'dûrgrōth] *n* Gestrüpp *nt*, Unterholz *nt*.

underhand(ed) [un'dûrhan'd(id)] *a* hinterhältig.

underinsured [undûrinshoord'] *a* unterversichert.

underlie [undûrlī'] *vt irreg* (*form the basis of*) zugrundeliegen (+*dat*); **the underlying cause** die (zugrundeliegende) Ursache.

underline [un'dûrlīn] *vt* unterstreichen; (*emphasize*) betonen.

underling [un'dûrling] *n* (*pej*) Befehlsempfänger(in *f*) *m*.

undermanning [un'dûrman'ing] *n* Personalmangel *m*.

undermentioned [un'dûrmenchənd] *a* untengenannt, untenerwähnt.

undermine [un'dûrmīn] *vt* unterhöhlen; (*fig*) unterminieren, untergraben.

underneath [undûrnēth'] *ad* darunter ♦ *prep* unter.

undernourished [undûrnûr'isht] *a* unterernährt.

underpaid [undûrpād'] *a* unterbezahlt.

underpants [un'dûrpants] *npl* (*Brit*) Unterhose *f*.

underpass [un'dûrpas] *n* Unterführung *f*.

underpin [undûrpin'] *vt* (*argument, case*) untermauern.

underplay [undûrplā'] *vt* (*Brit*) herunterspielen.

underpopulated [undûrpâp'yəlātid] *a* unterbevölkert.

underprice [undûrprīs'] *vt* zu niedrig ansetzen.

underpriced [undûrprīst'] *a*: **to be ~** zu billig gehandelt werden.

underprivileged [undûrpriv'əlijd] *a* benachteiligt, unterprivilegiert.

underrate [undərāt'] *vt* unterschätzen.

underscore [undûrskôr'] *vt* unterstreichen.

underseal [un'dûrsēl] *vt* (*Brit AUT*) mit Unterbodenschutz versehen.

undersecretary [un'dûrsek'ritärē] *n* Staatsse-

kretär(in *f*) *m*.
undersell [undûrsel'] *vt irreg* (*competitors*) unterbieten.
undershirt [un'dûrshûrt] *n* (*US*) Unterhemd *nt*.
undershorts [un'dûrshôrts] *npl* (*US*) Unterhose *f*.
underside [un'dûrsīd] *n* Unterseite *f*.
undersigned [un'dûrsīnd'] *n* Unterzeichnete(r) *mf* ♦ *a* unterzeichnet.
underskirt [un'dûrskûrt] *n* (*Brit*) Unterrock *m*.
understaffed [undûrstaft'] *a*: **to be ~** zu wenig Personal haben.
understand [undûrstand'] *vti irreg* verstehen; **I ~ that ...** ich habe gehört, daß ...; **am I to ~ that ...?** soll das (etwa) heißen, daß ...?; **what do you ~ by that?** was verstehen Sie darunter?; **it is understood that ...** es wurde vereinbart, daß ...; **to make o.s. understood** sich verständlich machen; **is that understood?** ist das klar?; **I ~ you are going to Australia** ich höre, Sie gehen nach Australien.
understandable [undûrstan'dəbəl] *a* verständlich.
understanding [undûrstan'ding] *n* Verständnis *nt*; **on the ~ that ...** unter der Voraussetzung, daß ...; **to come to an ~ with sb** eine Abmachung mit jdm treffen ♦ *a* verständnisvoll.
understate [undûrstāt'] *vt* untertreiben.
understatement [un'dûrstāt'mənt] *n* Untertreibung *f*, Understatement *nt*.
understood [undûrsto͞od'] *a* (*agreed*) klar; (*believed*) angenommen, geglaubt ♦ *pt*, *pp* of **understand**.
understudy [un'dûrstudē] *n* Ersatz(schau)spieler(in *f*) *m*.
undertake [undûrtāk'] *vt irreg* unternehmen; (*promise*) sich verpflichten; **to ~ to do sth** etw übernehmen.
undertaker [un'dûrtākûr] *n* Leichenbestatter *m*; **~'s** Beerdigungsinstitut *nt*.
undertaking [un'dûrtāking] *n* (*enterprise*) Unternehmen *nt*; (*promise*) Verpflichtung *f*.
undertone [un'dûrtōn] *n* (*of criticism etc*) Unterton *m*; **in an ~** (*in a low voice*) mit gedämpfter Stimme.
undervalue [undûrval'yo͞o] *vt* (*fig*) unterschätzen; (*COMM etc*) zu niedrig schätzen *or* veranschlagen.
underwater [un'dûrwôt'ûr] *ad* unter Wasser ♦ *a* Unterwasser-.
underwear [un'dûrwär] *n* Unterwäsche *f*.
underweight [un'dûrwāt] *a*: **to be ~** Untergewicht haben.
underworld [un'dûrwûrld] *n* (*of crime*) Unterwelt *f*.
underwrite [un'dərīt] *vt irreg* (*FIN*) tragen, garantieren, bürgen für; (*INSURANCE*) versichern.
underwriter [un'dərītûr] *n* Assekurant *m*.
undeserving [undēzûr'ving] *a*: **to be ~ of sth**

einer Sache (*gen*) unwürdig sein.
undesirable [undizīûr'əbəl] *a* unerwünscht.
undeveloped [undivel'əpt] *a* (*land, resources*) ungenutzt, unerschlossen.
undies [un'dēz] *npl* (*col*) (Damen)-unterwäsche *f*.
undiluted [undilo͞o'tid] *a* (*concentrate*) unverdünnt.
undiplomatic [undipləmat'ik] *a* undiplomatisch.
undischarged [undischârjd'] *a*: **~ bankrupt** nicht entlastete(r) Gemeinschuldne(r) *mf*.
undisciplined [undis'əplind] *a* undiszipliniert.
undiscovered [undiskuv'ûrd] *a* unentdeckt.
undisguised [undisgīzd'] *a* (*dislike, amusement etc*) unverhohlen.
undisputed [undispyo͞o'tid] *a* unbestritten.
undistinguished [undisting'gwisht] *a* unbekannt, nicht ausgezeichnet.
undisturbed [undistûrbd'] *a* (*sleep*) ungestört; **to leave sth ~** etw unberührt lassen.
undivided [undivī'did] *a*: **I want your ~ attention** ich möchte Ihre ungeteilte *or* volle Aufmerksamkeit.
undo [undo͞o'] *vt irreg* (*unfasten*) öffnen, aufmachen; (*work*) zunichte machen.
undoing [undo͞o'ing] *n* Verderben *nt*.
undone [undun'] *a*: **to come ~** aufgehen ♦ *pp* of **undo**.
undoubted [undou'tid] *a* unbezweifelt.
undoubtedly [undou'tidlē] *ad* zweifellos, ohne Zweifel.
undress [undres'] *vti* (sich) ausziehen.
undrinkable [undringk'əbəl] *a* (*unpalatable*) ungenießbar; (*poisonous*) nicht trinkbar.
undue [undo͞o'] *a* übermäßig.
undulating [un'jəlāting] *a* wellenförmig; (*country*) wellig.
unduly [undo͞o'lē] *ad* übermäßig.
undying [undī'ing] *a* unsterblich, ewig.
unearned [unûrnd'] *a* (*praise, respect*) unverdient; **~ income** Kapitaleinkommen *nt*.
unearth [unûrth'] *vt* (*dig up*) ausgraben; (*discover*) ans Licht bringen.
unearthly [unûrth'lē] *a* schauerlich; **at the ~ hour of 5 o'clock** (*col*) zu nachtschlafender Zeit um 5 Uhr.
unease [unēz'] *n* Unbehagen *nt*; (*public*) Unruhe *f*.
uneasy [unē'zē] *a* (*worried*) unruhig; (*feeling*) ungut; (*embarrassed*) unbequem; **I feel ~ about it** mir ist nicht wohl dabei.
uneconomic(al) [unēkənâm'ik(əl)] *a* unwirtschaftlich.
uneducated [unej'o͞okātid] *a* (*person*) ungebildet.
unemployed [unemploid'] *a* arbeitslos ♦ *npl*: **the ~** die Arbeitslosen *pl*.
unemployment [unemploi'mənt] *n* Arbeitslosigkeit *f*.
unemployment benefit *n* Arbeitslosenunterstützung *f*.
unending [unen'ding] *a* endlos.
unenviable [unen'vēəbəl] *a* wenig beneidens-

wert.
unequal [unēk'wəl] a (length, objects) unterschiedlich; (amounts, division of labor) ungleich.
unequaled, (Brit) **unequalled** [unēk'wəld] a unübertroffen; (beauty, stupidity) beispiellos.
unequivocal [unikwiv'əkəl] a (answer) unzweideutig; (person) aufrichtig.
unerring [unûr'ing] a unfehlbar.
UNESCO [yo͞ones'kō] n abbr (= United Nations Educational, Scientific and Cultural Organization) UNESCO f.
unethical [uneth'ikəl] a unethisch; (methods) unmoralisch; **it's ~ for a doctor to do that** es verstößt gegen das Berufsethos, wenn ein Arzt das macht.
uneven [unē'vən] a (surface) uneben; (quality) ungleichmäßig.
uneventful [univent'fəl] a (day, meeting) ereignislos; (career) wenig bewegt.
unexceptional [uniksep'shənəl] a durchschnittlich.
unexciting [uniksī'ting] a (news) nicht besonders aufregend; (film, evening) langweilig.
unexpectedly [unikspek'tidlē] ad unerwartet.
unexplained [unikspländ'] a nicht geklärt, ungeklärt.
unexploded [uniksplō'did] a nicht explodiert.
unfailing [unfā'ling] a nie versagend.
unfair [unfär'] a ungerecht, unfair.
unfair dismissal n ungerechtfertigte Entlassung f.
unfairly [unfär'lē] ad unfair; (treat) ungerecht.
unfaithful [unfāth'fəl] a untreu.
unfamiliar [unfəmil'yûr] a: **to be ~ with sth** etw nicht kennen, mit etw nicht vertraut sein.
unfashionable [unfash'ənəbəl] a (clothes) unmodern; (district) wenig gefragt.
unfasten [unfas'ən] vt öffnen, aufmachen.
unfathomable [unfaṯẖ'əməbəl] a unergründlich.
unfavorable, (Brit) **unfavourable** [unfā'vûrəbəl] a ungünstig.
unfavorably, (Brit) **unfavourably** [unfā'vûrəblē] ad: **to look ~ upon sth** einer Sache (dat) ablehnend gegenüberstehen.
unfeeling [unfē'ling] a gefühllos, kalt.
unfinished [unfin'isht] a unvollendet.
unfit [unfit'] a ungeeignet (for zu, für); (in bad health) schlecht in Form, unfit.
unflagging [unflag'ing] a unermüdlich.
unflappable [unflap'əbəl] a unerschütterlich.
unflattering [unflat'ûring] a (dress, hairstyle) unvorteilhaft.
unflinching [unflin'ching] a unerschrocken.
unfold [unfōld'] vt entfalten; (paper) auseinanderfalten ♦ vi (develop) sich entfalten.
unforeseeable [unfôrsē'əbəl] a unvorhersehbar.
unforeseen [unfôrsēn'] a unvorhergesehen.
unforgettable [unfûrget'əbəl] a unvergeßlich.

unforgivable [unfûrgiv'əbəl] a unverzeihlich.
unformatted [unfôr'matid] a (disk, text) nicht formatiert.
unfortunate [unfôr'chənit] a unglücklich, bedauerlich.
unfortunately [unfôr'chənitlē] ad leider; (chosen) unglücklich; (worded) ungeschickt.
unfounded [unfoun'did] a unbegründet.
unfriendly [unfrend'lē] a unfreundlich.
unfulfilled [unfo͞olfild'] a (person) unausgefüllt; (ambition, promise) unerfüllt; (prophecy, terms of contract) nicht erfüllt; **to have an ~ desire** schon immer den Wunsch gehabt haben.
unfurl [unfûrl'] vt (flag) aufrollen; (sail) losmachen; (peacock: tail) entfalten.
unfurnished [unfûr'nisht] a unmöbliert.
ungainly [ungān'lē] a linkisch.
ungodly [ungåd'lē] a (hour) nachtschlafend; (row) heillos.
ungrateful [ungrāt'fəl] a undankbar (to gegenüber)
unguarded [ungär'did] a (moment) unbewacht.
unhappily [unhap'ilē] ad (unfortunately) leider, unglücklicherweise.
unhappiness [unhap'ēnis] n Unglück nt, Unglückseligkeit f.
unhappy [unhap'ē] a unglücklich.
unharmed [unhârmd'] a wohlbehalten, unversehrt.
unhealthy [unhel'thē] a ungesund; (interest) krankhaft.
unheard-of [unhûrd'əv] a unerhört.
unhelpful [unhelp'fəl] a (person) nicht hilfsbereit, unbehilflich; (advice, book) nutzlos, wenig hilfreich.
unhesitating [unhez'itāting] a (loyalty) bereitwillig; (reply, offer) prompt, unverzüglich.
unhook [unho͞ok'] vt (from wall) vom Haken nehmen; (dress) loshaken.
unhurt [unhûrt'] a unverletzt.
unhygienic [unhijēen'ik] a unhygienisch.
UNICEF [yo͞o'nisef] n abbr (= United Nations International Children's Emergency Fund) UNICEF f.
unicolor [yo͞onəkul'ûr] a (US) einfarbig.
unicorn [yo͞o'nəkôrn] n Einhorn nt.
unidentified [unīden'təfid] a unbekannt, nicht identifiziert; **~ flying object** unbekannte(s) Flugobjekt nt.
unification [yo͞onifikā'shən] n Vereinigung f.
uniform [yo͞o'nəfôrm] n Uniform f ♦ a einheitlich.
uniformity [yo͞onəfôr'mitē] n Einheitlichkeit f.
unify [yo͞o'nəfi] vt vereinigen.
unilateral [yo͞onəlat'ûrəl] a einseitig.
unimaginable [unimaj'ənəbəl] a unvorstellbar.
unimaginative [unimaj'ənətiv] a phantasielos, einfallslos.
unimpaired [unimpärd'] a (quality, prestige) unbeeinträchtigt; (health) unvermindert.

unimportant [unimpôr'tənt] *a* unwichtig, unbedeutend.

unimpressed [unimprest'] *a* nicht beeindruckt.

uninhabited [uninhab'itid] *a* unbewohnt.

uninhibited [uninhib'itid] *a* (*person*) ohne Hemmungen; (*greed etc*) hemmungslos, ungezügelt.

uninjured [unin'jûrd] *a* (*person*) unverletzt.

unintelligent [unintel'ijənt] *a* unintelligent, (*etwas*) dumm.

unintentional [uninten'chənəl] *a* unabsichtlich.

unintentionally [uninten'chənəlē] *ad* unabsichtlich, ohne Absicht.

uninvited [uninvī'tid] *a* (*guest*) ungeladen, ungebeten.

uninviting [uninvī'ting] *a* (*place*) nicht einladend; (*offer*) nicht (gerade) verlockend; (*food*) unappetitlich.

union [yōōn'yən] *n* (*uniting*) Vereinigung *f*; (*alliance*) Bund *m*, Union *f*; (*trade ~*) Gewerkschaft *f*; **the U~** (*US*) die Vereinigten Staaten.

union card *n* Gewerkschaftsausweis *m*.

unionize [yōōn'yənīz] *vt* gewerkschaftlich organisieren.

Union Jack *n* Union Jack *m*.

Union of Soviet Socialist Republics *n* Union *f* der Sozialistischen Sowjetrepubliken.

union shop *n* gewerkschaftliche(r) Betrieb *m*.

unique [yōōnēk'] *a* einzig(artig).

unisex [yōō'niseks] *n* Unisex-, unisex.

unison [yōō'nisən] *n* Einstimmigkeit *f*; **in ~** einstimmig.

unissued capital [unish'ōōd kap'itəl] *n* noch nicht ausgegebene(s) Aktienkapital *nt*.

unit [yōō'nit] *n* Einheit *f*; **production ~** Produktion *f*.

unit cost *n* Stückkosten *pl.*

unite [yōōnīt'] *vt* vereinigen ♦ *vi* sich vereinigen.

united [yōōnī'tid] *a* vereinigt; (*together*) vereint.

United Arab Emirates *npl* Vereinigte Arabische Emirate *pl.*

United Kingdom *n* Vereinigte(s) Königreich *nt.*

United Nations (Organization) *n* Vereinte Nationen *pl.*

United States (of America) *npl* Vereinigte Staaten *pl* (von Amerika).

unit price *n* Preis *m* pro Maßeinheit.

unit trust *n* (*Brit FIN: company*) Unit Trust *m*, Investmentgesellschaft *f*; (: *share*) Unit-Trust-Papiere *pl*, Investmentpapiere *pl.*

unity [yōō'nitē] *n* Einheit *f*; (*agreement*) Einigkeit *f.*

Univ. *abbr* = **University.**

universal [yōōnəvûr'səl] *a*, **universally** [yōōnəvûr'səlē] *ad* allgemein.

universe [yōō'nəvûrs] *n* (*Welt*)all *nt*, Universum *nt.*

university [yōōnəvûr'sitē] *n* Universität *f*; **to be at** *or* **go to ~** studieren ♦ *cpd* (*student, professor, education*) Universitäts-; **~ degree** akademische(r) Grad *m*; **~ year** Universitätsjahr *nt.*

unjust [unjust'] *a* ungerecht.

unjustifiable [unjus'tifīəbəl] *a* ungerechtfertigt, nicht zu rechtfertigen.

unjustified [unjus'təfīd] *a* (*text*) nicht ausgerichtet.

unkempt [unkempt'] *a* ungepflegt, verwahrlost.

unkind [unkīnd'] *a*, **unkindly** [unkīnd'lē] *ad* unfreundlich.

unknown [unnōn'] *a* unbekannt (to *dat*); **~ quantity** (*fig*) unbekannte Größe *f* ♦ *ad*: **~ to me** ohne daß ich es wußte ♦ *n* (*MATH*) Unbekannte *f.*

unladen [unlā'dən] *a* (*weight*) Leer-, unbeladen.

unleaded [unled'id] *a* bleifrei, unverbleit.

unleash [unlēsh'] *vt* entfesseln.

unleavened [unlev'ənd] *a* ungesäuert.

unless [unles'] *cj* wenn nicht, es sei denn; **~ I am mistaken ...** wenn *or* falls ich mich nicht irre ...

unlicensed [unlī'sənst] *a* (*Brit: to sell alcohol*) unkonzessioniert.

unlike [unlīk'] *a* unähnlich ♦ *prep* im Gegensatz zu.

unlikelihood [unlīk'lēhōōd] *n* Unwahrscheinlichkeit *f.*

unlimited [unlim'itid] *a* unbegrenzt; **~ liability** unbeschränkte Haftung *f.*

unlisted [unlis'tid] *a*: **~ company** amtlich nicht notierte Gesellschaft *f*; **~ number** (*US*) Nummer *f*, die nicht im Telefonbuch steht.

unlit [unlit'] *a* (*room*) unbeleuchtet.

unload [unlōd'] *vt* entladen.

unlock [unläk'] *vt* aufschließen.

unlucky [unluk'ē] *a*: **to be ~** (*person*) Pech haben; (*not succeed*) keinen Erfolg haben.

unmanageable [unman'ijəbəl] *a* (*unwieldy: tool, vehicle*) schwer zu handhaben; (*situation*) unkontrollierbar.

unmanned [unmand'] *a* (*spacecraft*) unbemannt.

unmannerly [unman'ûrlē] *a* unmanierlich.

unmarked [unmârkt'] *a* (*unstained*) ohne Flecken, fleckenlos; **~ police car** nicht gekennzeichnete(s) Polizeiauto *nt.*

unmarried [unmar'ēd] *a* unverheiratet, ledig.

unmask [unmask'] *vt* demaskieren; (*fig*) entlarven.

unmatched [unmacht'] *a* unübertroffen.

unmentionable [unmen'chənəbəl] *a* (*topic, vice*) tabu; (*word*) unaussprechlich.

unmerciful [unmûr'sifəl] *a* unbarmherzig, erbarmungslos.

unmistakable [unmistā'kəbəl] *a* unverkennbar.

unmistakably [unmistā'kəblē] *ad* unverwechselbar, unverkennbar.

unmitigated [unmit'əgātid] *a* ungemildert, ganz.

unnamed [unnāmd'] *a* (*nameless*) namenlos; (*anonymous*) ungenannt.

unnecessary [unnes'isärē] *a* unnötig.

unnerve [unnûrv'] *vt* entnerven; (*gradually*) zermürben; (*discourage: speaker*) entmutigen.

unnoticed [unnō'tist] *a*: **to go** *or* **pass** ~ unbemerkt bleiben.

UNO [ōō'nō] *n abbr* (= *United Nations Organization*) UNO *f*.

unobservant [unəbzûr'vənt] *a*: **to be** ~ ein schlechter Beobachter sein.

unobtainable [unəbtā'nəbəl] *a*: **this number is** ~ kein Anschluß unter dieser Nummer.

unobtrusive [unəbtrōō'siv] *a* unauffällig.

unoccupied [unâk'yəpīd] *a* (*seat*, US: *toilet*) frei; (*house*) leerstehend, unbewohnt; (*also* *MIL*: *zone*) unbesetzt.

unopened [unō'pənd] *a* (*letter*) ungeöffnet; (*present*) noch nicht aufgemacht.

unopposed [unəpōzd'] *a* (*enter*) ohne Widerstand; (*be elected*) ohne Gegenstimmen.

unorthodox [unôr'thədâks] *a* unorthodox.

unpack [unpak'] *vti* auspacken.

unpaid [unpād'] *a* (*bill, vacation, work*) unbezahlt.

unpalatable [unpal'ətəbəl] *a* (*food etc*) ungenießbar; (*truth*) bitter.

unparalleled [unpar'əleld] *a* beispiellos.

unpatriotic [unpātrēât'ik] *a* (*person, speech, attitude*) unpatriotisch.

unplanned [unpland'] *a* (*visit, baby*) nicht geplant.

unpleasant [unplez'ənt] *a* unangenehm; (*person, remark*) unliebenswürdig, unfreundlich; (*day, experience*) unerfreulich.

unplug [unplug'] *vt* den Stecker herausziehen von.

unpolluted [unpəlōō'tid] *a* unverschmutzt.

unpopular [unpâp'yəlûr] *a* unbeliebt, unpopulär; **to be** ~ **with sb** (*person*) bei jdm unbeliebt sein; **to make o.s.** ~ **(with)** sich unbeliebt machen (bei).

unprecedented [unpres'identid] *a* noch nie dagewesen; (*step*) unerhört.

unpredictable [unpridik'təbəl] *a* unvorhersehbar; (*weather, person*) unberechenbar.

unprejudiced [unprej'ədist] *a* (*not biased*) objektiv, unparteiisch; (*having no prejudices*) vorurteilslos.

unprepared [unpripärd'] *a* (*person, speech*) unvorbereitet.

unprepossessing [unprēpəzes'ing] *a* wenig gewinnend, wenig einnehmend.

unprincipled [unprin'səpəld] *a* skrupellos.

unproductive [unprəduk'tiv] *a* nicht gewinnbringend, keinen Gewinn bringend; (*discussion*) unproduktiv, unergiebig.

unprofessional [unprəfesh'ənəl] *a*: ~ **conduct** berufswidrige(s) Verhalten *nt*.

unprofitable [unprâf'itəbəl] *a* (*financially*) keinen Profit bringend, wenig einträglich;

(*job, deal*) unrentabel.

unprovoked [unprəvōkt'] *a* ohne Anlaß, grundlos.

unpunished [unpun'isht] *a*: **if this goes** ~ ... wenn das nicht bestraft wird ...

unqualified [unkwâl'əfid] *a* (*success*) uneingeschränkt, voll; (*person*) unqualifiziert.

unquestionably [unkwes'chənəblē] *ad* fraglos, zweifellos.

unquestioning [unkwes'chəning] *a* (*obedience, acceptance*) bedingungslos.

unravel [unrav'əl] *vt* (*disentangle*) auffasern, entwirren; (*solve*) lösen.

unreal [unrēl'] *a* unwirklich.

unrealistic [unrēəlis'tik] *a* (*idea, estimate*) unrealistisch.

unreasonable [unrē'zənəbəl] *a* unvernünftig; (*demand*) übertrieben; **that's** ~ das ist zuviel verlangt; **he makes** ~ **demands on me** er verlangt zuviel von mir.

unrecognizable [unrek'əgnīzəbəl] *a* nicht wiederzuerkennen.

unrecognized [unrek'əgnīzd] *a* (*talent, genius*) ungewürdigt, unerkannt; (*POL*: *régime*) nicht anerkannt.

unrecorded [unrikôr'did] *a* nicht aufgenommen; (*in documents*) nicht schriftlich festgehalten.

unrefined [unrifīnd'] *a* (*sugar, petroleum*) nicht raffiniert.

unrehearsed [unrihûrst'] *a* (*THEAT etc*) nicht geprobt; (*spontaneous*) spontan.

unrelated [unrilā'tid] *a* ohne Beziehung; (*by family*) nicht verwandt.

unrelenting [unrilen'ting] *a* unerbittlich.

unreliable [unrilī'əbəl] *a* unzuverlässig.

unrelieved [unrilēvd'] *a* (*monotony*) tödlich.

unremitting [unrimit'ing] *a* (*efforts, attempts*) unermüdlich.

unrepeatable [unripē'təbəl] *a* nicht wiederholbar.

unrepentant [unripen'tənt] *a* nicht reuig, nicht reumütig; **he is** ~ **about it** er bereut es nicht.

unrepresentative [unreprizen'tətiv] *a* nicht repräsentativ.

unreserved [unrizûrvd'] *a* (*seat*) nicht reserviert; (*approval, admiration*) uneingeschränkt.

unresponsive [unrispân'siv] *a* nicht reagierend, gleichgültig.

unrest [unrest'] *n* (*discontent*) Unruhe *f*; (*fighting*) Unruhen *pl*.

unrestricted [unristrik'tid] *a* (*power, time*) unbeschränkt, uneingeschränkt; (*access*) ungehindert.

unrewarded [unriwôr'did] *a* unbelohnt.

unripe [unrīp'] *a* unreif.

unrivaled, (*Brit*) **unrivalled** [unrī'vəld] *a* unübertroffen.

unroll [unrōl'] *vt* aufrollen.

unruffled [unruf'əld] *a* (*person*) unbewegt, unberührt; (*hair*) ordentlich.

unruly [unrōō'lē] *a* wild; (*child*) undiszipliniert.

unsafe [unsāf'] *a (machine, car)* nicht sicher; *(method)* unsicher; *(wiring)* gefährlich; ~ **to drink** nicht trinkbar; ~ **to eat** ungenießbar.

unsaid [unsed'] *a*: **to leave sth** ~ etw ungesagt sein lassen.

unsalable, *(Brit)* **unsaleable** [unsā'ləbəl] *a* unverkäuflich.

unsatisfactory [unsatisfak'tûrē] *a* unbefriedigend; *(service, hotel)* unzulänglich.

unsatisfied [unsat'isfīd] *a (desire, need etc)* unbefriedigt.

unsavory, *(Brit)* **unsavoury** [unsā'vûrē] *a (fig)* widerwärtig.

unscathed [unskāṯhd'] *a* unversehrt.

unscientific [unsīəntif'ik] *a* unwissenschaftlich.

unscrew [unskrōō'] *vt* aufschrauben.

unscrupulous [unskrōō'pyələs] *a* skrupellos.

unsecured [unsikyōōrd'] *a (FIN)* nicht abgesichert.

unseen [unsēn'] *a (person)* unbemerkt; *(danger)* versteckt.

unselfish [unsel'fish] *a (act)* selbstlos; *(person)* uneigennützig.

unsettled [unset'əld] *a* unstet; *(person)* rastlos; *(weather)* wechselhaft; *(dispute)* nicht beigelegt.

unsettling [unset'ling] *a* aufreibend; *(time also)* aufregend; *(news)* beunruhigend.

unshak(e)able [unshā'kəbəl] *a* unerschütterlich.

unshaven [unshā'vən] *a* unrasiert.

unsightly [unsīt'lē] *a* unansehnlich.

unskilled [unskild'] *a* ungelernt.

unsociable [unsō'shəbəl] *a (person, behavior)* ungesellig.

unsocial [unsō'shəl] *a*: **to work** ~ **hours** außerhalb der normalen Arbeitszeiten arbeiten.

unsold [unsōld'] *a* unverkauft.

unsolicited [unsəlis'itid] *a* unerbeten.

unsophisticated [unsəfis'tikātid] *a* einfach, natürlich.

unsound [unsound'] *a (ideas)* anfechtbar; *(health)* angegriffen; *(policy)* unklug; *(judgement, investment)* unzuverlässig; *(advice)* unvernünftig; *(in construction: floor, foundations)* unsicher, schwach.

unspeakable [unspē'kəbəl] *a (joy)* unsagbar; *(crime)* scheußlich.

unspoken [unspō'kən] *a (words)* unausgesprochen; *(agreement, approval)* stillschweigend.

unstinting [unstin'ting] *a (kindness, support)* uneingeschränkt.

unstuck [unstuk'] *a*: **to come** ~ *(lit)* sich lösen; *(fig)* ins Wasser fallen.

unsubstantiated [unsəbstan'chēātid] *a* unbegründet.

unsuccessful [unsəkses'fəl] *a* erfolglos.

unsuitable [unsōō'təbəl] *a* unpassend.

unsuited [unsōō'tid] *a*: **to be** ~ **for** *or* **to sth**

für etw ungeeignet *or* untauglich sein.

unsupported [unsəpôr'tid] *a (claim, theory)* ohne Beweise, nicht auf Fakten gestützt.

unsure [unshōōr'] *a*: **to be** ~ **(of** *or* **about sth)** (sich *(dat)* einer Sache *gen*) nicht sicher sein; **to be** ~ **of o.s.** unsicher sein.

unsuspecting [unsəspek'ting] *a* nichtsahnend.

unsweetened [unswēt'ənd] *a* ungesüßt.

unswerving [unswûr'ving] *a (loyalty)* unerschütterlich.

unsympathetic [unsimpəthet'ik] *a (attitude)* ablehnend, abweisend; *(person)* unsympathisch; **to be** ~ **to sb/sth** jdm/etw ablehnend gegenüberstehen.

untangle [untang'gəl] *vt* entwirren.

untapped [untapt'] *a (resources)* ungenützt.

untaxed [untakst'] *a (goods)* unbesteuert; *(income)* steuerfrei.

unthinkable [unthingk'əbəl] *a* unvorstellbar.

untidy [untī'dē] *a* unordentlich.

untie [untī'] *vt* aufmachen, aufschnüren.

until [until'] *prep, cj* bis; ~ **now** bis jetzt; ~ **then** bis dahin; **from morning** ~ **night** von morgens bis abends, vom Morgen bis zum Abend; ~ **he comes** bis er kommt.

untimely [untīm'lē] *a (death)* vorzeitig.

untold [untōld'] *a* unermeßlich.

untouched [untucht'] *a (not used etc)* unberührt, unangetastet; *(safe: person)* heil, unversehrt; ~ **by** *(unaffected)* unberührt von.

untoward [untôrd'] *a* widrig, ungünstig.

untrammeled, *(Brit)* **untrammelled** [untram'əld] *a* unbeschränkt.

untranslatable [untranz'lātəbəl] *a* unübersetzbar.

untried [untrīd'] *a (plan)* noch nicht ausprobiert.

untrue [untrōō'] *a (statement)* falsch.

untrustworthy [untrust'wûrṯhē] *a (person)* unzuverlässig.

unusable [unyōō'zəbəl] *a* unbrauchbar.

unused [unyōōzd'] *a* unbenutzt; [unyōōst']: **to be** ~ **to sth** nicht an etw *(acc)* gewöhnt sein; **to be** ~ **to doing sth** nicht daran gewöhnt sein, etw zu tun.

unusual [unyōō'zhōōəl] *a*, **unusually** [unyōō'zhōōəlē] *ad* ungewöhnlich.

unveil [unvāl'] *vt* enthüllen.

unwanted [unwôn'tid] *a (person, effect)* unerwünscht.

unwarranted [unwôr'əntid] *a* ungerechtfertigt.

unwary [unwär'ē] *a* unvorsichtig, unbesonnen.

unwavering [unwā'vûring] *a* standhaft, unerschütterlich.

unwelcome [unwel'kəm] *a* unwillkommen; **to feel** ~ sich nicht willkommen fühlen.

unwell [unwel'] *a* unpäßlich; **to feel** ~ sich nicht wohlfühlen.

unwieldy [unwēl'dē] *a* unhandlich, sperrig.

unwilling [unwil'ing] *a*, **unwillingly** [unwil'inglē] *ad* widerwillig.

unwind [unwīnd'] *irreg vt (lit)* abwickeln ♦ *vi (relax)* sich entspannen.

unwise [unwīz'] *a* (*decision, act*) unklug.

unwitting [unwit'ing] *a* unwissentlich.

unworkable [unwûr'kəbəl] *a* (*plan etc*) undurchführbar.

unworthy [unwûr'thē] *a* (*person*) nicht wert (*of gen*); (*conduct also*) unwürdig (*of gen*).

unwrap [unrap'] *vt* auswickeln, auspacken.

unwritten [unrit'ən] *a* ungeschrieben.

unzip [unzip'] *vt* (den Reißverschluß) aufmachen (an +*dat*).

up [up] *prep* auf ♦ *ad* nach oben, hinauf; (*out of bed*) auf; **to be** ~ (*building*) stehen; (*tent*) aufgeschlagen sein; (*curtains, shutters, wallpaper*) hängen; **to be** ~ **by** (*in price, value*) gestiegen sein um; **when the year was** ~ (*finished*) als das Jahr vorüber war; **prices are** ~ **on last year** die Preise sind gegenüber letztem Jahr gestiegen; ~ **to** (*temporally*) bis; **it is** ~ **to you** es liegt bei Ihnen; **what is he** ~ **to?** was hat er vor?; **he is not** ~ **to it** er kann es nicht (tun); **what's** ~**?** (*col: wrong*) was ist los?; **"this side** ~**"** „oben!"; **time's** ~ die Zeit ist um; **to stop halfway** ~ auf halber Höhe anhalten ♦ *vi* (*col*): **she** ~**ped and left** sie rannte davon ♦ *vt* (*col: price*) raufsetzen ♦ *n*: **the** ~**s and downs** das Auf und Ab.

up-and-coming [upənkum'ing] *a* im Aufstieg.

upbeat [up'bēt] *n* (*MUS*) Auftakt *m*; (*in economy, prosperity*) Aufschwung *m* ♦ *a* (*col*) optimistisch.

upbraid [upbrād'] *vt* tadeln, rügen.

upbringing [up'bringing] *n* Erziehung *f*.

update [updāt'] *vt* auf den neuesten Stand bringen.

upend [upend'] *vt* auf Kante stellen.

upgrade [upgrād'] *vt* höher einstufen; (*COMPUT*) ausbauen.

upheaval [uphē'vəl] *n* Umbruch *m*.

uphill *a* [up'hil'] ansteigend; (*fig*) mühsam ♦ *ad* [uphil'] bergauf.

uphold [uphōld'] *vt irreg* unterstützen.

upholstery [uphōl'stûrē] *n* Polsterung *f*.

UPI *n abbr* = *United Press International*.

upkeep [up'kēp] *n* Instandhaltung *f*.

up-market [up'mâr'kit] *a* anspruchsvoll.

upon [əpân'] *prep* auf.

upper [up'ûr] *n* (*on shoe*) Oberleder *nt* ♦ *a* obere(r, s), höhere(r, s); **the** ~ **class** die Oberschicht; **to have the** ~ **hand** die Oberhand haben.

upper-class [up'ûrklas'] *a* (*district, people, accent*) vornehm, fein; ~ **attitude** Haltung *f* der Oberschicht.

uppermost [up'ûrmōst] *a* oberste(r, s), höchste(r, s); **what was** ~ **in my mind** was mich in erster Linie beschäftigte.

Upper Volta [up'ûr vōl'tə] *n* Obervolta *nt*.

upright [up'rīt] *a* (*erect*) aufrecht; (*honest*) aufrecht, rechtschaffen ♦ *n* Pfosten *m*.

uprising [up'rīzing] *n* Aufstand *m*.

uproar [up'rôr] *n* Aufruhr *m*.

uproot [uprōōt'] *vt* ausreißen; (*tree*) entwurzeln.

upset *n* [up'set] Aufregung *f*; **to have a stomach** ~ (*Brit*) sich (*dat*) den Magen verdorben haben, eine Magenverstimmung haben ♦ [upset'] *vt irreg* (*overturn*) umwerfen; (*disturb*) aufregen, bestürzen; (*plans*) durcheinanderbringen ♦ *a* (*person*) aufgeregt; (*stomach*) verdorben; **to get** ~ sich aufregen (*about* über +*acc*).

upset price *n* Mindestgebot *nt*.

upsetting [upset'ing] *a* bestürzend, traurig; (*offending*) beleidigend, verletzend; (*annoying*) ärgerlich.

upshot [up'shât] *n* (*result*) (End)ergebnis *nt*, Ausgang *m*; **the** ~ **of it all was that** ... es lief darauf hinaus, daß ...

upside down [up'sīd doun'] *ad* verkehrt herum; (*fig*) drunter und drüber.

upstairs [up'stärz'] *ad* oben, im oberen Stockwerk; (*go*) nach oben ♦ *a* (*room*) obere(r, s), Ober- ♦ *n* obere(s) Stockwerk *nt*.

upstart [up'stârt] *n* Emporkömmling *m*.

upstream [up'strēm] *ad* stromaufwärts.

upsurge [up'sûrj] *n*: **she felt an** ~ **of revulsion** sie fühlte Ekel in sich (*dat*) aufwallen.

uptake [up'tāk] *n*: **to be quick on the** ~ schnell begreifen; **to be slow on the** ~ schwer von Begriff sein.

uptight [up'tīt'] *a* (*col: nervous*) nervös; (: *inhibited*) verklemmt.

up-to-date [up'tədāt'] *a* (*clothes*) modisch, modern; (*information*) neueste(r, s); **to bring sb** ~ (**on sth**) jdn über den neuesten Stand (der Dinge) informieren.

upturn [up'tûrn] *n* (*in luck*) Aufschwung *m*; (*in value of currency*) Kursanstieg *m*.

upturned [uptûrnd'] *a*: ~ **nose** Stupsnase *f*.

upward [up'wûrd] *a* nach oben gerichtet ♦ *ad* aufwärts.

upwards [up'wûrdz] *ad* aufwärts.

URA *n abbr* (*US*: = *Urban Renewal Administration*) städtische Sanierungsbehörde.

Urals [yōōr'əlz] *npl*: **the** ~ der Ural, das Uralgebirge.

uranium [yōōrā'nēəm] *n* Uran *nt*.

Uranus [yōōr'ənəs] *n* (*ASTRON*) Uranus *m*.

urban [ûr'bən] *a* städtisch, Stadt-.

urbane [ûrbān'] *a* höflich, weltgewandt.

urbanization [ûrbənəzā'shən] *n* Urbanisierung *f*.

urchin [ûr'chin] *n* (*boy*) Schlingel *m*; (*sea* ~) Seeigel *m*.

urge [ûrj] *n* Drang *m* ♦ *vt* drängen, dringen in (+*acc*); **to** ~ **sb to do sth** (*plead with*) jdn eindringlich bitten, etw zu tun; (*earnestly recommend*) darauf dringen, daß jd etw tut.

urge on *vt* antreiben.

urgency [ûr'jənsē] *n* Dringlichkeit *f*.

urgent [ûr'jənt] *a*, **urgently** [ûrjəntlē] *ad* dringend.

urinal [yōōr'ənəl] *n* (*MED*) Urinflasche *f*; (*public*) Pissoir *nt*.

urinate [yōōr'ənāt] *vi* urinieren, Wasser lassen.

urine [yōōr'in] *n* Urin *m*, Harn *m*.

urn [ûrn] *n* Urne *f*; *(tea ~)* Teemaschine *f*.
Uruguay [yōō'rəgwā] *n* Uruguay *nt*.
Uruguayan [yōōrəgwā'ən] *a* uruguayisch ♦ *n* Uruguayer(in *f*) *m*.
us [us] *pron* uns; **give ~ a kiss** *(col: me)* gib mir einen Kuß.
US *n abbr* = **United States**.
USA *n abbr* (= *United States of America*) USA *pl*; *(MIL)* = *United States Army*.
usable [yōō'zəbəl] *a* verwendbar.
USAF *n abbr* = *United States Air Force*.
usage [yōō'sij] *n* Gebrauch *m*; *(esp LING)* Sprachgebrauch *m*.
USCG *n abbr* (= *United States Coast Guard*) Küstenwachdienst.
USDA *n abbr* (= *United States Department of Agriculture*) Landwirtschaftsministerium.
USDI *n abbr* (= *United States Department of the Interior*) Innenministerium.
use *n* [yōōs] Verwendung *f*; *(custom)* Brauch *m*, Gewohnheit *f*; *(employment)* Gebrauch *m*; *(point)* Zweck *m*; **in ~** in Gebrauch; **out of ~** außer Gebrauch; **ready for ~** gebrauchsfertig; **to be of ~** von Nutzen sein, nützlich sein; **to make ~ of sth** etw (aus)nutzen *or* (aus)nützen; **it's no ~** es hat keinen Zweck; **what's the ~?** was soll's? ♦ *vt* [yōōz] gebrauchen; **what's this ~d for?** wofür wird das benutzt *or* gebraucht?
use up [yōōz up] *vt* aufbrauchen, verbrauchen.
used [yōōzd] *a (car)* Gebraucht-; **~ to** [yōōst] gewöhnt an (+*acc*); **to get ~ to sth** sich an etw gewöhnen; **she ~ to live here** sie hat früher mal hier gewohnt.
useful [yōōs'fəl] *a* nützlich; **to come in ~** sich als nützlich erweisen.
usefulness [yōōs'fəlnis] *n* Nützlichkeit *f*.
useless [yōōs'lis] *a* nutzlos, unnütz; *(unusable: object)* unbrauchbar.
uselessly [yōōs'lislē] *ad* nutzlos.
uselessness [yōōs'lisnis] *n* Nutzlosigkeit *f*.
user [yōō'zûr] *n* Benutzer(in *f*) *m*; *(of gasoline, gas etc)* Verbraucher(in *f*) *m*.
user-friendly [yōō'zûrfrend'lē] *a* benutzerfreundlich.
USES *n abbr* (= *United States Employment Service*) Abteilung des Arbeitsministeriums.
usher [ush'ûr] *n* Platzanweiser *m* ♦ *vt*: **to ~ sb in** jdn hinein-/hereinführen *or* -bringen; **it ~ed in a new era** *(fig)* es leitete ein neues Zeitalter ein.
usherette [ushəret'] *n* Platzanweiserin *f*.
USIA *n abbr* (= *United States Information Agency*) Informations- und Kulturamt.
USM *n abbr* (= *United States Mint*) Münzanstalt; (= *United States Mail*) ≈ DBP *f*.
USN *n abbr* = *United States Navy*.
USPHS *n abbr* = *United States Public Health Service*.
USPS *n abbr* (= *United States Postal Service*) ≈ DBP *f*.
USS *abbr* = *United States Ship*.
USSR *n abbr* (= *Union of Soviet Socialist Republics*) UdSSR *f*.
usu. *abbr* (= *usually*) gew.
usual [yōō'zhōōəl] *a* gewöhnlich, üblich; **as ~** wie gewöhnlich.
usually [yōō'zhōōəlē] *ad* gewöhnlich.
usurer [yōō'zhûrûr] *n* Wucherer *m*.
usurp [yōōsûrp'] *vt* an sich reißen.
usurper [yōōsûr'pûr] *n* Usurpator *m*.
usury [yōō'zhûrē] *n* Wucher *m*.
UT *abbr* (*US MAIL*) = *Utah*.
utensil [yōōten'səl] *n* Gerät *nt*, Utensil *nt*; **kitchen ~s** Küchengeräte *pl*.
uterus [yōō'tûrəs] *n* Gebärmutter *f*, Uterus *m*.
utilitarian [yōōtilitär'ēən] *a* Nützlichkeits-.
utility [yōōtil'itē] *n* *(usefulness)* Nützlichkeit *f*; *(also: public ~)* öffentliche(r) Versorgungsbetrieb *m*.
utility room *n* Geräteraum *m*.
utilization [yōōtəlizā'shən] *n* Nutzbarmachung *f*, Benutzung *f*.
utilize [yōō'təlīz] *vt* verwenden; *(talent)* nutzen.
utmost [ut'mōst] *a* äußerste(r, s); **it is of the ~ importance that ...** es ist äußerst wichtig, daß ... ♦ *n*: **to do one's ~** sein möglichstes tun.
utter [ut'ûr] *a* äußerste(r, s), höchste(r, s), völlig ♦ *vt* äußern, aussprechen.
utterance [ut'ûrəns] *n* Äußerung *f*.
utterly [ut'ûrlē] *ad* äußerst, absolut, völlig.
U-turn [yōō' tûrn] *n* *(AUT)* Kehrtwendung *f*; *(fig)* Wende *f*.

V

V, v [vē] *n (letter)* V *nt*, v *nt*; **V for Victor** ≈ V wie Viktor.
v *abbr* (= *versus*) v.; (= *verse*) Vers; (= *volt*) V; (= *vide: see*) s.
VA *abbr* (*US MAIL*) = *Virginia*.
vac [vak] *n abbr* (*Brit col*) = **vacation**.
vacancy [vā'kənsē] *n (room)* freie(s) Zimmer *nt*; *(Brit: job)* offene Stelle *f*; **have you any vacancies?** *(in boarding house)* haben Sie noch Zimmer frei?; *(job)* haben Sie noch Stellen frei?
vacant [vā'kənt] *a* leer; *(unoccupied)* frei; *(house)* leerstehend, unbewohnt; *(stupid)* (gedanken)leer.
vacant lot *n* *(US)* unbebaute(s) Grundstück *nt*.
vacate [vā'kāt] *vt* *(seat)* frei machen; *(room)* räumen.
vacation [vākā'shən] *n* Ferien *pl*, Urlaub *m*; **to take a ~** Urlaub machen; **on ~** im *or* auf Urlaub.
vacation course *n* Ferienkurs *m*.

vacationer [vākā'shənûr] n (US) Ferienrei-
sende(r) mf.
vacation pay n (US) Urlaubsgeld nt.
vacation season n (US) Ferienzeit f.
vaccinate [vak'sənāt] vt impfen.
vaccination [vak'sənā'shən] n Impfung f.
vaccine [vaksēn'] n Impfstoff m.
vacuum [vak'yōōm] n luftleere(r) Raum m,
Vakuum nt ♦ staubsaugen.
vacuum bottle n (US) Thermosflasche f.
vacuum cleaner n Staubsauger m.
vacuum flask n (Brit) Thermosflasche f.
vacuum-packed [vak'yōōmpakt'] a vakuum-
verpackt.
vagabond [vag'əbând] n Vagabund m.
vagary [vā'gûrē] n Laune f.
vagina [vəji'nə] n Scheide f, Vagina f.
vagrancy [vā'grənsē] n Landstreichertum nt,
Landstreicherei f/Stadtstreicherei f.
vagrant [vā'grənt] n Landstreicher(in f) m/
Stadtstreicher(in f) m.
vague [vāg] a unbestimmt, vage; (outline)
verschwommen; (absent-minded) geistesabwesend; **I haven't the ~st idea** ich habe
nicht die leiseste Ahnung.
vaguely [vāg'lē] ad unbestimmt, vage;
(understand, correct) ungefähr.
vagueness [vāg'nis] n Unbestimmtheit f;
Verschwommenheit f.
vain [vān] a (worthless) eitel, nichtig; (attempt) vergeblich; (conceited) eitel, eingebildet ♦ n: **in ~** vergebens, umsonst.
vainly [vān'lē] ad vergebens, vergeblich; eitel,
eingebildet.
valance [val'əns] n (of bed) Volant m.
valedictory [validik'tûrē] a Abschieds-.
valentine [val'əntīn] n Valentinsgruß m.
valet [valā'] n Kammerdiener m.
valet service n Reinigungsdienst m.
valiant [val'yənt] a, **valiantly** [val'yəntlē] ad
tapfer.
valid [val'id] a gültig; (argument) stichhaltig;
(objection) berechtigt.
validate [val'idāt] vt (contract, document) für
gültig erklären; (argument, claim) bestätigen.
validity [vəlid'itē] n (of ticket) Gültigkeit f;
(of argument) Stichhaltigkeit f.
valise [vəlēs'] n Reisetasche f.
valley [val'ē] n Tal nt.
valor, (Brit) **valour** [val'ûr] n Tapferkeit f.
valuable [val'yōōəbəl] a wertvoll; (time) kostbar.
valuables [val'yōōəbəlz] npl Wertsachen pl.
valuation [valyōōā'shən] n (FIN) Schätzung f;
(judgement) Beurteilung f.
value [val'yōō] n Wert m; (usefulness) Nutzen
m ♦ vt (prize) (hoch)schätzen; (estimate)
schätzen; ~**s** pl (moral stan-
dards) (sittliche) Werte pl; **to lose (in) ~**
(currency, property) im Wert fallen; **to gain
(in) ~** (currency, property) im Wert steigen;
to be of great ~ to sb jdm sehr wertvoll or
nützlich sein; **you get good ~ (for money)**

in that shop in dem Geschäft bekommen Sie
etwas für Ihr Geld; **it is ~d at $80** es wird
auf 80 $ geschätzt.
value added tax n Mehrwertsteuer f.
valued [val'yōōd] a (hoch)geschätzt.
valueless [val'yōōlis] a wertlos.
valuer [val'yōōûr] n Schätzer m.
valve [valv] n Ventil nt; (BIOL) Klappe f;
(RAD) Röhre f.
vampire [vam'pîûr] n Vampir m.
van [van] n Lieferwagen m; (Brit RAIL) Waggon m.
vandal [van'dəl] n Vandale m.
vandalism [van'dəlizəm] n mutwillige Beschädigung f, Vandalismus m.
vandalize [van'dəlīz] vt mutwillig zerstören
or beschädigen.
vanguard [van'gârd] n (fig) Spitze f.
vanilla [vənil'ə] n Vanille f.
vanish [van'ish] vi verschwinden.
vanity [van'itē] n Eitelkeit f, Einbildung f.
vanity case n Schminkkoffer m.
vantage point [van'tij point] n gute(r) Aus-
sichtspunkt m.
vapor [vā'pûr] n (US: mist) Dunst m; (: gas)
Dampf m.
vaporize [vā'pərīz] vt verdampfen ♦ vi verdampfen, verdunsten.
vapor trail n (AVIAT) Kondensstreifen m.
vapour [vā'pûr] etc (Brit) = **vapor** etc.
variable [vär'ēəbəl] n Variable f; (fig) verän-
derliche Größe f ♦ a wechselhaft, veränderlich; (speed, height) regulierbar.
variance [vär'ēəns] n: **to be at ~** uneinig
sein.
variant [vär'ēənt] n Variante f.
variation [värēā'shən] n Variation f, Veränderung f; (of temperature, prices) Schwankung f.
varicose veins [var'əkōs vānz'] npl Krampf-
adern pl.
varied [vär'ēd] a verschieden, unterschiedlich; (life) abwechslungsreich.
variety [vərī'ətē] n (difference) Abwechslung
f; (varied collection) Vielfalt f; (COMM)
Auswahl f; (sort) Sorte f, Art f; **for a ~ of
reasons** aus verschiedenen Gründen; **a wide
~ of ...** die verschiedensten ...
variety show n Varieté nt.
various [vär'ēəs] a verschieden; (several)
mehrere; **at ~ times** (different) zu verschiedenen Zeiten; (several) mehrmals,
mehrere Male.
varnish [vâr'nish] n Lack m; (on pottery)
Glasur f ♦ vt lackieren; (truth) beschönigen.
vary [vär'ē] vt (alter) verändern; (give variety to) abwechslungsreicher gestalten ♦ vi
sich (ver)ändern; (prices) schwanken;
(weather) unterschiedlich sein; **to ~ from
sth** sich von etw unterscheiden; **it varies
with the weather** es richtet sich nach dem
Wetter.
varying [vär'ēing] a unterschiedlich; (changing) veränderlich.

vase [vās] *n* Vase *f.*

vasectomy [vasek'təmē] *n* Vasektomie *f,* Sterilisation *f (des Mannes).*

Vaseline [vas'əlēn] *n* ® Vaseline *f.*

vast [vast] *a* weit, groß, riesig.

vastly [vast'lē] *ad* wesentlich; *(grateful, amused)* äußerst.

vastness [vast'nis] *n* Unermeßlichkeit *f,* Weite *f.*

vat [vat] *n* große(s) Faß *nt.*

VAT [vat] *n abbr* (= *value added tax*) MwSt *f.*

Vatican [vat'ikən] *n:* **the** ~ der Vatikan.

vaudeville [vôd'vil] *n (US)* Varieté *nt.*

vault [vôlt] *n (of roof)* Gewölbe *nt; (tomb)* Gruft *f; (in bank)* Tresorraum *m; (leap)* Sprung *m* ♦ *vt* überspringen.

vaunted [vôn'tid] *a* gerühmt, gepriesen.

VCR *n abbr* (= *video cassette recorder*) VCR *m.*

VD *n abbr* (= *venereal disease*) Geschlechtskrankheit *f.*

VDT *n abbr (COMPUT: = visual display terminal)* Bildschirm *nt.*

VDU *n abbr* = **visual display unit.**

veal [vēl] *n* Kalbfleisch *nt.*

veer [vēr] *vi* sich drehen; *(car)* ausscheren.

vegetable [vej'təbəl] *n* Gemüse *nt; (plant)* Pflanze *f.*

vegetable garden *n* Gemüsegarten *m.*

vegetarian [vejitär'ēən] *n* Vegetarier(in *f) m* ♦ *a* vegetarisch.

vegetate [vej'itāt] *vi* (dahin)vegetieren.

vegetation [vejitā'shən] *n* Vegetation *f.*

vehemence [vē'əməns] *n* Heftigkeit *f.*

vehement [vē'əmənt] *a* vehement, heftig; *(feelings)* leidenschaftlich; *(dislike, hatred)* heftig, stark.

vehicle [vē'ikəl] *n* Fahrzeug *nt; (fig)* Mittel *nt.*

vehicular [vēhik'yəlûr] *a* Fahrzeug-; *(traffic)* Kraft-.

veil [vāl] *n (lit, fig)* Schleier *m;* **under a** ~ **of secrecy** *(fig)* unter dem Mantel der Verschwiegenheit ♦ *vt* verschleiern.

veiled [vāld] *a (lit, fig)* versteckt.

vein [vān] *n* Ader *f; (ANAT)* Vene *f; (mood)* Stimmung *f.*

vellum [vel'əm] *n (writing paper)* Pergament *nt.*

velocity [vəlâs'itē] *n* Geschwindigkeit *f.*

velvet [vel'vit] *n* Samt *m.*

vendetta [vendet'ə] *n* Fehde *f; (in family)* Blutrache *f.*

vending machine [ven'ding məshēn'] *n* Automat *m.*

vendor [ven'dûr] *n* Verkäufer *m;* **street** ~ Straßenhändler *m.*

veneer [vənēr'] *n (lit)* Furnier(holz) *nt; (fig)* äußere(r) Anstrich *m.*

venerable [ven'ûrəbəl] *a* ehrwürdig.

venereal [vənēr'ēəl] *a:* ~ **disease** Geschlechtskrankheit *f.*

Venetian blind [vənē'shən blīnd] *n* Jalousie *f.*

Venezuela [venizwā'lə] *n* Venezuela *nt.*

Venezuelan [venizwā'lən] *a* venezolanisch ♦ *n* Venezolaner(in *f) m.*

vengeance [ven'jəns] *n* Rache *f;* **with a** ~ gewaltig.

vengeful [venj'fəl] *a* rachsüchtig.

Venice [ven'is] *n* Venedig *nt.*

venison [ven'isən] *n* Reh(fleisch) *nt.*

venom [ven'əm] *n* Gift *nt.*

venomous [ven'əməs] *a,* **venomously** [ven'əməslē] *ad* giftig, gehässig.

vent [vent] *n* Öffnung *f; (in coat)* Schlitz *m; (fig)* Ventil *nt* ♦ *vt (emotion)* abreagieren.

ventilate [ven'təlāt] *vt* belüften.

ventilation [ventəlā'shən] *n* Belüftung *f,* Ventilation *f.*

ventilation shaft *n* Luftschacht *m.*

ventilator [ven'təlātûr] *n* Ventilator *m.*

ventriloquist [ventril'əkwist] *n* Bauchredner(in *f) m.*

venture [ven'chûr] *n* Unternehmung *f,* Projekt *nt;* **a business** ~ ein geschäftliches Unternehmen ♦ *vt* wagen; *(life)* aufs Spiel setzen; **to** ~ **to do sth** sich wagen, etw zu tun ♦ *vi* sich wagen.

venture capital *n* Eigenkapital *nt,* Risikokapital *nt.*

venue [ven'yōō] *n (scene)* Schauplatz *m; (meeting place)* Treffpunkt *m.*

Venus [vē'nəs] *n (ASTRON)* Venus *f.*

veracity [vəras'itē] *n (of person)* Ehrlichkeit *f,* Aufrichtigkeit *f; (of report, evidence)* Wahrheit *f,* Richtigkeit *f.*

veranda(h) [vəran'də] *n* Veranda *f.*

verb [vûrb] *n* Zeitwort *nt,* Verb *nt.*

verbal [vûr'bəl] *a (spoken)* mündlich; *(translation)* wörtlich; *(of a verb)* verbal, Verbal-.

verbally [vûr'bəlē] *ad* mündlich; *(as a verb)* verbal.

verbatim [vûrbā'tim] *ad* Wort für Wort ♦ *a* wortwörtlich.

verbose [vûrbōs'] *a* wortreich.

verdict [vûr'dikt] *n* Urteil *nt;* ~ **of guilty/not guilty** Schuldspruch *m*/Freispruch *m.*

verge [vûrj] *n* Rand *m;* **on the** ~ **of doing sth** im Begriff, etw zu tun.

verge on *vt fus* grenzen an (+ *acc).*

verger [vûr'jûr] *n* Kirchendiener *m,* Küster *m.*

verification [värəfəkā'shən] *n* Bestätigung *f; (checking)* Überprüfung *f; (proof)* Beleg *m.*

verify [vär'əfī] *vt* (über)prüfen; *(confirm)* bestätigen; *(theory)* beweisen; *(COMPUT)* prüfen.

veritable [vär'itəbəl] *a* wahr.

vermin [vûr'min] *n* Ungeziefer *nt.*

vermouth [vûrmōōth'] *n* Wermut *m.*

vernacular [vûrnak'yəlûr] *n* Landessprache *f; (dialect)* Dialekt *m,* Mundart *f; (jargon)* Fachsprache *f.*

versatile [vûr'sətəl] *a* vielseitig.

versatility [vûrsətil'itē] *n* Vielseitigkeit *f.*

verse [vûrs] *n (poetry)* Poesie *f; (stanza)* Strophe *f; (of Bible)* Vers *m;* **in** ~ in Versform.

versed [vûrst] *a*: ~ **in** bewandert in (+*dat*), beschlagen in (+*dat*).

version [vûr'zhən] *n* Version *f*; (*of car*) Modell *nt*.

versus [vûr'səs] *prep* gegen.

vertebra [vûr'təbrə] *n*, *pl* **vertebrae** [vûr'təbrē] Rückenwirbel *m*.

vertebrate [vûr'təbrāt] *a* (*animal*) Wirbel-.

vertical [vûr'tikəl] *a*, **vertically** [vûr'tikəlē] *ad* senkrecht, vertikal.

vertigo [vûr'təgō] *n* Schwindel *m*, Schwindelgefühl *nt*; **to suffer from** ~ leicht schwindlig werden, an Gleichgewichtsstörungen leiden (*MED*).

verve [vûrv] *n* Schwung *m*.

very [vär'ē] *ad* sehr; ~ **well** sehr gut; ~ **little** sehr wenig; **it's** ~ **cold** es ist sehr kalt; ~ **high frequency** (*RAD*) Ultrakurzwelle *f*; **at the** ~ **latest** allerspätestens; **the** ~ **same day** noch am selben Tag ♦ *a* (*extreme*) äußerste(r, s); **the** ~ **book** genau das Buch; **at that** ~ **moment** gerade *or* genau in dem Augenblick; **the** ~ **thought (of it) alarms me** allein der Gedanke (daran) beunruhigt mich.

vespers [ves'pûrz] *npl* Vesper *f*.

vessel [ves'əl] *n* (*ship*) Schiff *nt*; (*container*) Gefäß *nt*.

vest [vest] *n* (*US*: *waistcoat*) Weste *f*; (*Brit*: *undershirt*) Unterhemd *nt* ♦ *vt*: **to** ~ **sb with sth** *or* **sth in sb** jdm etw verleihen.

vested interest [ves'tid in'trist] *n* finanzielle Beteiligung *f*; (*people*) finanziell Beteiligte *pl*; (*fig*) persönliche(s) Interesse *nt*.

vestibule [ves'təbyōōl] *n* Vorhalle *f*.

vestige [ves'tij] *n* Spur *f*.

vestry [ves'trē] *n* Sakristei *f*.

Vesuvius [vəsōō'vēəs] *n* Vesuv *m*.

vet [vet] *n* Tierarzt *m*/-ärztin *f* ♦ *vt* genau prüfen; (*candidate*) überprüfen.

veteran [vet'ûrən] *n* Veteran(in *f*) *m* ♦ *a* altgedient; **she's a** ~ **campaigner for women's rights** sie ist eine Veteranin der Frauenbewegung.

veteran car *n* Oldtimer *m*.

veterinarian [vetûrənär'ēən] *n* (*US*) Tierarzt *m*/-ärztin *f*.

veterinary [vet'ûrənärē] *a* Veterinär-.

veterinary surgeon *n* (*Brit*) = **veterinarian**.

veto [vē'tō] *n* Veto *nt*; **power of** ~ Vetorecht *nt*; **to put a** ~ **on** ein Veto einlegen gegen ♦ *vt* sein Veto einlegen gegen.

vex [veks] *vt* ärgern.

vexed [vekst] *a* verärgert; ~ **question** umstrittene Frage *f*.

vexing [vek'sing] *a* ärgerlich.

VFD *n abbr* (*US*: = *voluntary fire department*) freiwillige Feuerwehr.

VHF *n abbr* (= *very high frequency*) UKW *f*.

VI *abbr* (*US MAIL*) = *Virgin Islands*.

via [vī'ə] *prep* über (+*acc*).

viability [vīəbil'ətē] *n* (*of plan, scheme*) Durchführbarkeit *f*, Realisierbarkeit *f*; (*of company*) Rentabilität *f*; (*of life forms, economy*) Lebensfähigkeit *f*.

viable [vī'əbəl] *a* (*plan*) durchführbar; (*company*) rentabel; (*life form, economy*) lebensfähig.

viaduct [vī'ədukt] *n* Viadukt *m*.

vibrant [vī'brənt] *a* (*sound*) volltönend; (*color*) voll.

vibrate [vī'brāt] *vi* zittern, beben; (*machine, string*) vibrieren; (*notes*) schwingen.

vibration [vībrā'shən] *n* Schwingung *f*; (*of machine*) Vibrieren *nt*; (*of voice, ground*) Beben *nt*.

vicar [vik'ûr] *n* Pfarrer *m*.

vicarage [vik'ûrij] *n* Pfarrhaus *nt*.

vicarious [vīkär'ēəs] *a* indirekt, mittelbar, nachempfunden; (*authority*) stellvertretend.

vice [vīs] *n* (*evil*) Laster *nt*; (*TECH*) Schraubstock *m*.

vice-chairman [vīs'chär'mən] *n*, *pl* **-men** stellvertretende(r) Vorsitzende(r) *m*.

vice-chancellor [vīs'chan'səlûr] *n* (*Brit UNIV*) ≈ Rektor *m*.

vice-president [vīs'prez'idənt] *n* Vizepräsident *m*.

vice versa [vīs'vûr'sə] *ad* umgekehrt.

vicinity [visin'ətē] *n* Umgebung *f*; (*closeness*) Nähe *f*.

vicious [vish'əs] *a* gemein, böse; ~ **circle** Teufelskreis *m*, Circulus vitiosus *m*.

viciousness [vish'əsnis] *n* Bösartigkeit *f*, Gemeinheit *f*.

vicissitudes [visis'ətōōdz] *npl* Wechselfälle *pl*.

victim [vik'tim] *n* Opfer *nt*; **to be the** ~ **of sth** einer Sache (*dat*) zum Opfer fallen.

victimization [viktiməzā'shən] *n* Benachteiligung *f*.

victimize [vik'təmīz] *vt* benachteiligen.

victor [vik'tûr] *n* Sieger(in *f*) *m*.

Victorian [viktōr'ēən] *a* viktorianisch; (*fig*) (sitten)streng.

victorious [viktôr'ēəs] *a* siegreich.

victory [vik'tûrē] *n* Sieg *m*; **to win a** ~ **over sb** einen Sieg über jdn erringen, jdn besiegen.

video [vid'ēō] *a* Fernseh-, Bild- ♦ *n* (~ *film*) Video *nt*; (*also*: ~ **cassette**) Videokassette *f*; (*also*: ~ **cassette recorder**) Videogerät *nt*.

video cassette *n* Videokassette *f*.

video cassette recorder *n* Videogerät *nt*.

video recording *n* Fernsehaufnahme *f*, Videoaufnahme *f*.

video tape *n* Videoband *nt*.

videotex [vid'ēōteks] *n* Bildschirmtext *m*.

vie [vī] *vi* wetteifern.

Vienna [vēen'ə] *n* Wien *nt*.

Viennese [vēənēz'] *a* wienerisch ♦ *n* Wiener(in *f*) *m*.

Vietnam, Viet Nam [vēetnâm'] *n* Vietnam *nt*.

Vietnamese [vēetnâmēz'] *a* vietnamesisch ♦ *n* (*person*) Vietnamese *m*, Vietnamesin *f*; (*language*) Vietnamesisch *nt*.

view [vyōō] *n* (*sight*) Sicht *f*, Blick *m*; (*scene*) Aussicht *f*; (*opinion*) Ansicht *f*,

Meinung *f*; (*intention*) Absicht *f*; **to be within** ~ zu sehen sein; **in full** ~ **of thousands of people** vor den Augen von Tausenden von Menschen; **to have sth in** ~ etw beabsichtigen; **in** ~ **of** wegen (+*gen*), angesichts (+*gen*); **to take** *or* **hold the** ~ **that ...** die Ansicht vertreten, daß ...; **with a** ~ **to doing sth** mit der Absicht, etw zu tun; **an overall** ~ **of the situation** ein allgemeiner *or* umfassender Überblick über die Lage ♦ *vt* (*situation*) betrachten; (*house*) besichtigen.

viewdata [vyōō'dātə] *n* (*Brit*) Bildschirmtext *m*.

viewer [vyōō'úr] *n* (*viewfinder*) Sucher *m*; (*PHOT*: *small projector*) Gucki *m*; (*TV*) Fernsehteilnehmer(in *f*) *m*.

viewfinder [vyōō'fīndûr] *n* Sucher *m*.

viewpoint [vyōō'point] *n* Standpunkt *m*.

vigil [vij'əl] *n* (Nacht)wache *f*; **to keep** ~ Wache halten, wachen.

vigilance [vij'ələns] *n* Wachsamkeit *f*.

vigilance committee *n* Bürgerwacht *f*.

vigilant [vij'ələnt] *a* wachsam.

vigilantly [vij'ələntlē] *ad* aufmerksam.

vigor [vig'úr] *n* (*US*) Kraft *f*, Vitalität *f*; (*of protest*) Heftigkeit *f*.

vigorous [vig'úrəs] *a*, **vigorously** [vig'úrəslē] *ad* kräftig; (*protest*) energisch, heftig.

vigour [vig'úr] *n* (*Brit*) = **vigor**.

vile [vīl] *a* (*mean*) gemein; (*foul*) abscheulich.

vilify [vil'əfī] *vt* diffamieren, verleumden.

villa [vil'ə] *n* Villa *f*.

village [vil'ij] *n* Dorf *nt*.

villager [vil'ijûr] *n* Dorfbewohner(in *f*) *m*.

villain [vil'in] *n* Schurke *m*, Bösewicht *m*.

vindicate [vin'dikāt] *vt* rechtfertigen; (*clear*) rehabilitieren.

vindication [vindikā'shən] *n* Rechtfertigung *f*; Rehabilitation *f*; **in** ~ **of** zur Rechtfertigung (+*gen*).

vindictive [vindik'tiv] *a* nachtragend, rachsüchtig.

vine [vīn] *n* Rebstock *m*, Rebe *f*.

vinegar [vin'əgûr] *n* Essig *m*.

vine-growing [vīn'grōing] *a* Wein-.

vineyard [vin'yûrd] *n* Weinberg *m*.

vintage [vin'tij] *n* (*of wine*) Jahrgang *m*; **the 1970** ~ der Jahrgang 1970, der 70er.

vintage car *n* Vorkriegsmodell *nt*, Vintage-Car *nt*.

vintage wine *n* edle(r) Wein *m*.

vintage year *n* besondere(s) Jahr *nt*.

viola [vēō'lə] *n* Bratsche *f*.

violate [vī'əlāt] *vt* (*promise*) brechen; (*law*) übertreten; (*rights, rule, neutrality*) verletzen; (*sanctity, woman*) schänden.

violation [vīəlā'shən] *n* Verletzung *f*; Übertretung *f*; ~ **of a treaty** Vertragsbruch *m*.

violence [vī'ələns] *n* (*force*) Heftigkeit *f*; (*brutality*) Gewalttätigkeit *f*; **acts of** ~ Gewalttaten *pl*.

violent [vī'ələnt] *a* (*strong*) heftig; (*brutal*) gewalttätig, brutal; (*contrast*) kraß; (*death*) gewaltsam; **a** ~ **dislike of sb/sth** eine heftige Abneigung gegen jdn/etw.

violently [vī'ələntlē] *ad* (*severely*: *ill*) schwer; (*brutally*) brutal.

violet [vī'əlit] *n* Veilchen *nt* ♦ *a* veilchenblau, violett.

violin [vīəlin'] *n* Geige *f*, Violine *f*.

violinist [vīəlin'ist] *n* Geiger(in *f*) *m*.

VIP *n abbr* (= *very important person*) VIP *mf*.

viper [vī'pûr] *n* Viper *f*; (*fig*) Schlange *f*.

virgin [vûr'jin] *n* Jungfrau *f* ♦ *a* jungfräulich, unberührt; (*wool*) neu.

virginity [vûrjin'ətē] *n* Unschuld *f*.

Virgo [vûr'gō] *n* Jungfrau *f*.

virile [vir'əl] *a* männlich; (*fig*) kraftvoll.

virility [vəril'ətē] *n* Männlichkeit *f*.

virtual [vûr'chōōəl] *a* eigentlich; **it was a** ~ **disaster** es war geradezu eine Katastrophe; **it was a** ~ **failure** es war praktisch ein Mißerfolg.

virtually [vûr'chōōəlē] *ad* praktisch, fast; **it is** ~ **impossible** es ist (fast) unmöglich.

virtue [vûr'chōō] *n* (*moral goodness*) Tugend *f*; (*good quality*) Vorteil *m*, Vorzug *m*; **by** ~ **of** aufgrund (+*gen*).

virtuoso [vûrchōōō'sō] *n* Virtuose *m*.

virtuous [vûr'chōōəs] *a* tugendhaft.

virulence [vir'yələns] *n* Bösartigkeit *f*; Stärke *f*; Schärfe *f*.

virulent [vir'yələnt] *a* (*MED*) bösartig; (*poison*) stark, tödlich; (*fig*) scharf, virulent.

virus [vī'rəs] *n* (*also COMPUT*) Virus *m*.

visa [vē'zə] *n* Visum *nt*, Sichtvermerk *m*.

vis-à-vis [vēzávē'] *prep* gegenüber.

viscount [vī'kount] *n* Viscount *m*.

viscous [vis'kəs] *a* zähflüssig.

vise [vīs] *n* (*US TECH*) Schraubstock *m*.

visibility [vizəbil'ətē] *n* Sichtbarkeit *f*; (*MET*) Sicht(weite) *f*.

visible [viz'əbəl] *a* sichtbar; ~ **exports/imports** sichtbare Ausfuhr/Einfuhr.

visibly [viz'əblē] *ad* sichtlich.

vision [vizh'ən] *n* (*ability*) Sehvermögen *nt*; (*foresight*) Weitblick *m*; (*in dream, image*) Vision *f*.

visionary [vizh'ənârē] *n* Hellseher *m*; (*dreamer*) Phantast *m* ♦ *a* phantastisch.

visit [viz'it] *n* Besuch *m* ♦ *vt* besuchen; **to pay a** ~ **to sb** jdm einen Besuch abstatten (*form*), jdn besuchen; **to be on a private/official** ~ inoffiziell/offiziell da sein.

visiting [viz'iting] *a* (*speaker, professor, team*) Gast-.

visiting card *n* Visitenkarte *f*.

visiting hours *npl* Besuchszeiten *pl*.

visitor [viz'itûr] *n* (*in house*) Besucher(in *f*) *m*; (*in hotel*) Gast *m*.

visitors' book *n* Gästebuch *nt*.

visor [vī'zûr] *n* Visier *nt*; (*on cap*) Schirm *m*; (*AUT*) Blende *f*.

vista [vis'tə] *n* Aussicht *f*.

VISTA [vis'tə] *n abbr* (= *Volunteers in Service to America*) staatliches Förderpro-

gramm für entwicklungsschwache Gebiete Amerikas, durchgeführt von Freiwilligen.

visual [vizh'ōōəl] *a* Seh-, visuell.

visual aid *n* Anschauungsmaterial *nt.*

visual display unit *n* Bildsichtgerät *nt,* Datensichtgerät *nt.*

visualize [vizh'ōōəlīz] *vt (imagine)* sich *(dat)* vorstellen; *(expect)* erwarten.

visually [vizh'ōōəlē] *ad* visuell; ~ **handicapped** sehbehindert.

vital [vīt'əl] *a (important)* unerläßlich; *(necessary for life)* Lebens-, lebenswichtig; *(lively)* vital; **to be of** ~ **importance (to sb/sth)** von äußerster Wichtigkeit sein (für jdn/etw); ~ **statistics** *(of population)* Bevölkerungsstatistik *f;* *(col: woman's)* Maße *pl.*

vitality [vītal'itē] *n* Vitalität *f,* Lebendigkeit *f.*

vitally [vī'təlē] *ad* äußerst, ungeheuer.

vitamin [vī'təmin] *n* Vitamin *nt.*

vitamin pill *n* Vitamintablette *f.*

vitreous [vit'rēəs] *a (china, enamel)* Glas-.

vitriolic [vitrēâl'ik] *a (fig)* beißend, haßerfüllt.

viva [vē'və] *n (also:* ~ **voce)** mündliche Prüfung *f.*

vivacious [vivā'shəs] *a* lebhaft.

vivacity [vivas'itē] *n* Lebhaftigkeit *f,* Lebendigkeit *f.*

vivid [viv'id] *a (graphic)* lebendig, deutlich; *(memory)* lebhaft; *(bright)* leuchtend.

vivisection [vivisek'shən] *n* Vivisektion *f.*

vixen [vik'sən] *n* Füchsin *f;* *(pej: woman)* Drachen *m.*

viz. [viz] *abbr (= videlicet: namely)* nämlich.

VLF *abbr = very low frequency.*

V-neck [vē'nek] *n* V-Ausschnitt *m.*

VOA *n abbr (= Voice of America)* Stimme Amerikas *f.*

vocabulary [vōkab'yəlärē] *n* Wortschatz *m,* Vokabular *nt.*

vocal [vō'kəl] *a* Vokal-, Gesang-; *(fig)* lautstark.

vocal cord *n* Stimmband *nt.*

vocalist [vō'kəlist] *n* Sänger(in *f) m.*

vocation [vōkā'shən] *n (calling)* Berufung *f.*

vocational [vōkā'shənəl] *a* Berufs-.

vocational guidance *n* Berufsberatung *f.*

vocational training *n* Berufsausbildung *f.*

vociferous [vōsif'ûrəs] *a,* **vociferously** [vōsif'ûrəslē] *ad* lautstark.

vodka [vâd'kə] *n* Wodka *m.*

vogue [vōg] *n* Mode *f;* **to be in** ~ *or* **be the** ~ **in** Mode sein.

voice [vois] *n (lit)* Stimme *f;* *(fig)* Mitspracherecht *nt;* *(GRAM)* Aktionsart *f;* **in a loud/soft** ~ mit lauter/leiser Stimme; **to give** ~ **to sth** etw aussprechen, einer Sache *(dat)* Ausdruck verleihen; **active/passive** ~ Aktiv *nt/*Passiv *nt;* **with one** ~ einstimmig ♦ *vt* äußern.

void [void] *n* Leere *f* ♦ *a (empty)* leer; *(JUR)* ungültig; ~ **of** *(lacking)* ohne, bar; *see* **null.**

voile [voil] *n* Voile *m.*

vol. *abbr (= volume)* Bd.

volatile [vâl'ətəl] *a (gas)* flüchtig; *(person)*

impulsiv; *(situation)* brisant.

volatile memory *n (COMPUT)* flüchtige(r) Speicher *m.*

volcanic [vâlkan'ik] *a* vulkanisch, Vulkan-.

volcano [vâlkā'nō] *n* Vulkan *m.*

volition [vōlish'ən] *n* Wille *m;* **of one's own** ~ aus freiem Willen.

volley [vâl'ē] *n (of guns)* Salve *f;* *(of stones)* Hagel *m;* *(of words)* Schwall *m;* *(TENNIS)* Flugball *m.*

volleyball [vâl'ēbôl] *n* Volleyball *m.*

volt [vōlt] *n* Volt *nt.*

voltage [vōl'tij] *n* (Volt)spannung *f;* **high/low** ~ Hoch-/Niederspannung *f.*

volte-face [vōltfâs'] *n* Kehrtwendung *f.*

voluble [vâl'yəbəl] *a* redselig.

volume [vâl'yōōm] *n (book)* Band *m;* *(size)* Umfang *m;* *(of tank)* Rauminhalt *m,* Volumen *nt;* *(of sound)* Lautstärke *f;* ~ **one/two** Band eins/zwei; **his expression spoke** ~**s** sein Gesichtsausdruck sprach Bände.

volume control *n (RAD, TV)* Lautstärkeregler *m.*

volume discount *n* Mengenrabatt *m.*

voluminous [vəlōō'minəs] *a* üppig; *(clothes)* wallend; *(correspondence, notes)* umfangreich.

voluntarily [vâləntär'ilē] *ad* freiwillig.

voluntary [vâl'əntärē] *a* freiwillig.

voluntary liquidation *n (COMM)* freiwillige Liquidation *f.*

volunteer [vâləntēr'] *n* Freiwillige(r) *mf* ♦ *vi* sich freiwillig melden ♦ *vt* anbieten.

voluptuous [vəlup'chōōəs] *a* sinnlich, wollüstig.

vomit [vâm'it] *n* Erbrochene(s) *nt;* *(act)* Erbrechen *nt* ♦ *vt* speien ♦ *vi* sich übergeben.

vote [vōt] *n* Stimme *f;* *(ballot)* Wahl *f,* Abstimmung *f;* *(result)* Wahl- or Abstimmungsergebnis *nt;* *(right to vote)* Wahlrecht *nt;* ~ **for/against** Stimme für/gegen; **to give a** ~ **of confidence** das Vertrauen aussprechen; ~ **of no confidence** Mißtrauensvotum *nt;* **to take a** ~ **on sth, to put sth to the** ~ über etw *(acc)* abstimmen (lassen) ♦ *vt* wählen; **he was** ~**d secretary** er wurde zum Sekretär *or* Schriftführer gewählt; **to** ~ **to do sth** wählen, etw zu tun ♦ *vi* wählen; **to** ~ **against/in favor of sth** gegen/für etw stimmen.

voter [vō'tûr] *n* Wähler(in *f) m.*

voting [vō'ting] *n* Wahl *f;* **low** ~ geringe Wahlbeteiligung *f.*

voting right *n* Wahlrecht *nt.*

voucher [vou'chûr] *n* Gutschein *m;* **luncheon** ~ Essensmarke *f,* Essensbon *m.*

vouch for [vouch fôr] *vt fus* bürgen für.

vow [vou] *n* Versprechen *nt;* *(REL)* Gelübde *nt* ♦ *vt* geloben; *(vengeance)* schwören; **to take** *or* **make a** ~ **to do sth** geloben, etw zu tun.

vowel [vou'əl] *n* Vokal *m,* Selbstlaut *m.*

voyage [voi'ij] *n* Reise *f.*

VP *n abbr (= vice-president)* VP *m.*

vs *abbr* (= *versus*) vs.

VSO *n abbr* (*Brit*: = *Voluntary Service Overseas*) ≈ Deutsche(r) Entwicklungsdienst *m*.

VT *abbr* (*US MAIL*) = *Vermont*.

VTR *n abbr* = *video tape recorder*.

vulgar [vul'gûr] *a* (*rude*) vulgär; (*of common people*) allgemein, Volks-.

vulgarity [vulgar'itē] *n* Gewöhnlichkeit *f*, Vulgarität *f*.

vulnerability [vulnûrəbil'ətē] *n* Verwundbarkeit *f*; Verletzlichkeit *f*.

vulnerable [vul'nûrəbəl] *a* (*easily injured*) verwundbar; (*sensitive*) verletzlich.

vulture [vul'chûr] *n* Geier *m*.

W

W, w [dub'əlyōō] *n* (*letter*) W *nt*, w *nt*; **W for William** ≈ W wie Wilhelm.

W *abbr* (*ELEC*: = *watt*) W; (= *west*) W.

WA *abbr* (*US MAIL*) = *Washington*.

wad [wâd] *n* (*bundle*) Bündel *nt*; (*of paper*) Stoß *m*; (*of money*) Packen *m*.

wadding [wâd'ing] *n* Material *nt* zum Ausstopfen; (*in jacket etc*) Wattierung *f*.

waddle [wâd'əl] *vi* watscheln.

wade [wâd] *vi* waten.

wading pool [wâd'ing pōōl] *n* (*US*) Planschbecken *nt*.

wafer [wā'fûr] *n* Waffel *f*; (*ECCL*) Hostie *f*; (*COMPUT*) Scheibe *f*, Wafer *nt*.

wafer-thin [wā'fûrthin'] *a* hauchdünn.

waffle [wâf'əl] *n* Waffel *f*; (*col: empty talk*) Geschwafel *nt* ♦ *vi* (*col*) schwafeln.

waffle iron *n* Waffeleisen *nt*.

waft [waft] *vti* wehen.

wag [wag] *vt* (*tail*) wedeln mit; **the dog ~ged its tail** der Hund wedelte mit dem Schwanz ♦ *vi* (*tail*) wedeln; **her tongue never stops ~ging** ihr Mund steht nie still.

wage [wāj] *n* (*Arbeits*)lohn *m* ♦ *vt* führen; **a day's ~s** ein Tageslohn.

wage claim *n* Lohnforderung *f*.

wage differential *n* Lohngefälle *nt*.

wage earner *n* Lohnempfänger(in *f*) *m*.

wage freeze *n* Lohnstopp *m*.

wage packet *n* (*Brit*) Lohntüte *f*.

wager [wā'jûr] *n* Wette *f* ♦ *vti* wetten.

waggle [wag'əl] *vt* (*tail*) wedeln mit ♦ *vi* wedeln.

wagon, (*Brit*) **waggon** [wag'ən] *n* (*horse-drawn*) Fuhrwerk *nt*; (*US AUT*) Wagen *m*; (*Brit RAIL*) Waggon *m*.

wail [wāl] *n* Wehgeschrei *nt* ♦ *vi* wehklagen, jammern.

waist [wāst] *n* Taille *f*.

waistcoat [wāst'kōt] *n* (*Brit*) Weste *f*.

waistline [wāst'līn] *n* Taille *f*.

wait [wāt] *n* Wartezeit *f* ♦ *vi* warten (*for* auf +*acc*); **to ~ for sb to do sth** darauf warten, daß jd etw tut; **~ a minute** einen Augenblick *or* Moment (mal)!; **~ and see!** abwarten!; **to ~ on tables** *or* (*Brit*) **at table** servieren; **to keep sb ~ing** jdn warten lassen; **"repairs while you ~"** „Sofortreparaturen", „Reparaturschnelldienst".

wait behind *vi* zurückbleiben.

wait on *vt fus* bedienen.

wait up *vi* aufbleiben (*for* wegen, für); **don't ~ up for me** warte nicht auf mich.

waiter [wā'tûr] *n* Kellner *m*; **~!** Herr Ober!

waiting list [wāt'ing list] *n* Warteliste *f*.

waiting room *n* (*MED*) Wartezimmer *nt*; (*RAIL*) Wartesaal *m*.

waitress [wā'tris] *n* Kellnerin *f*; **~!** Fräulein!

waive [wāv] *vt* verzichten auf (+*acc*).

waiver [wā'vûr] *n* Verzicht *m*.

wake [wāk] *irreg vt* wecken ♦ *vi* aufwachen; **to ~ up to** (*fig*) sich bewußt werden (+*gen*) ♦ *n* (*NAUT*) Kielwasser *nt*; (*for dead*) Totenwache *f*; **in the ~ of** unmittelbar nach, im Gefolge (+*gen*); **to follow in sb's ~** (*fig*) in jds Kielwasser segeln.

waked [wākt] *pt, pp of* **wake**.

waken [wā'kən] *vt* aufwecken.

Wales [wālz] *n* Wales *nt*.

walk [wôk] *n* Spaziergang *m*; (*way of walking*) Gang *m*; (*route*) Weg *m*; **~s of life** Sphären *pl*; **to go for a ~** einen Spaziergang machen, spazierengehen; **to take sb for a ~** mit jdm einen Spaziergang machen; **a 10-minute ~** 10 Minuten zu Fuß ♦ *vi* gehen; (*stroll*) spazierengehen; (*longer*) wandern; **to ~ in one's sleep** schlafwandeln ♦ *vt*: **I'll ~ you home** ich bringe dich nach Hause.

walk out *vi* (*strike*) streiken, in Streik treten; **to ~ out of a meeting** (*as protest*) eine Versammlung verlassen.

walk out on *vt fus*: **to ~ out on sb** jdn verlassen.

walker [wôk'ûr] *n* Spaziergänger(in *f*) *m*; (*hiker*) Wanderer(in *f*) *m*.

walkie-talkie [wô'kētô'kē] *n* Walkie-talkie *nt*.

walking [wô'king] *n* Gehen *nt*; (*as pastime*) Spazieren(gehen) *nt*; (*hiking*) Wandern *nt* ♦ *a* Wander-; **it's within ~ distance** es ist zu Fuß zu erreichen.

walking shoes *npl* Wanderschuhe *pl*.

walking stick *n* Spazierstock *m*.

walk-on [wôk'ân] *a* (*THEAT: part*) Statisten-.

walkout [wôk'out] *n* Streik *m*.

walkover [wôk'ōvûr] *n* (*col*) leichter Sieg *m*.

walkway [wôk'wā] *n* Fuß(gänger)weg *m*.

wall [wôl] *n* (*inside*) Wand *f*; (*outside*) Mauer *f*; **to go to the ~** (*fig*: *firm etc*) kaputtgehen.

wall in *vt* (*garden etc*) mit einer Mauer *or* von Mauern umgeben.

walled [wôld] *a* von Mauern umgeben.

wallet [wâl'it] *n* Brieftasche *f*.

wallflower [wôl'flouûr] *n* Goldlack *m*; **to be a ~** (*fig*) ein Mauerblümchen sein.
wall hanging *n* Wandbehang *m*, Wandteppich *m*.
wallop [wâl'əp] *vt* (*col*) schlagen, verprügeln.
wallow [wâl'ō] *vi* sich wälzen *or* suhlen; **to ~ in one's grief** in Kummer schwelgen.
wallpaper [wôl'pāpûr] *n* Tapete *f*.
wall-to-wall carpeting [wôl'təwôl kâr'piting] *n* Teppichboden *m*.
wally [wā'lē] *n* (*Brit col*) Trottel *m*.
walnut [wôl'nut] *n* Walnuß *f*; (*tree*) Walnußbaum *m*; (*wood*) Nußbaumholz *nt*.
walrus [wôl'rəs] *n* Walroß *nt*.
waltz [wôlts] *n* Walzer *m* ♦ *vi* Walzer tanzen.
wan [wân] *a* bleich.
wand [wând] *n* Stab *m*.
wander [wân'dûr] *vi* (*roam*) (herum)wandern; (*fig*) abschweifen.
wanderer [wân'dûrûr] *n* Wanderer(in *f*) *m*.
wandering [wân'dûring] *a* (*tribe*) umherziehend; (*minstrel, actor*) fahrend; (*path, river*) gewunden; (*glance, mind, thoughts*) (ab)schweifend.
wane [wān] *vi* abnehmen; (*fig*) schwinden.
wangle [wang'gəl] (*col*) *vt* organisieren, verschaffen ♦ *n* Mauschelei *f*.
want [wônt] *n* (*lack*) Mangel *m* (*of* an +*dat*); (*need*) Bedürfnis *nt*; (*poverty*) Not *f*; **to be in ~** Not leiden; **for ~ of** aus Mangel an (+*dat*); mangels (+*gen*) ♦ *vt* (*need*) brauchen; (*desire*) wollen; (*lack*) nicht haben; **I ~ to go** ich will gehen; **I ~ you to come here** ich will, daß du herkommst; **you're ~ed on the phone** Sie werden am Telefon verlangt *or* gewünscht; **"cook ~ed"** „Koch/Köchin gesucht"; **he ~s confidence** ihm fehlt das Selbstvertrauen.
want ads *npl* (*US*) Kaufgesuche *pl*.
wanting [wôn'ting] *a*: **he is ~ in confidence** es fehlt ihm an Selbstvertrauen.
wanton [wân'tən] *a* mutwillig, zügellos.
war [wôr] *n* Krieg *m*; **to make ~** Krieg führen.
warble [wôr'bəl] *n* (*of bird*) Trällern *nt* ♦ *vi* trällern.
war cry *n* Kriegsruf *m*; (*fig*) Schlachtruf *m*.
ward [wôrd] *n* (*in hospital*) Station *f*; (*child*) Mündel *nt*; (*of city*) Bezirk *m*.
ward off *vt* abwenden, abwehren.
warden [wôr'dən] *n* (*guard*) Wächter *m*, Aufseher *m*; (*US: prison ~*) Gefängniswärter *m*; (*Brit: in youth hostel*) Herbergsvater *m*; (*Brit UNIV*) Heimleiter(in *f*) *m*.
warder [wôr'dûr] *n* (*Brit*) Gefängniswärter *m*.
wardrobe [wôrd'rōb] *n* Kleiderschrank *m*; (*clothes*) Garderobe *f*.
warehouse [wär'hous] *n* Lagerhaus *nt*.
wares [wärz] *npl* Waren *pl*.
warfare [wôr'fär] *n* Krieg *m*.
war game *n* Kriegsspiel *nt*.
warhead [wôr'hed] *n* Sprengkopf *m*.
warily [wär'ilē] *ad* vorsichtig.

warlike [wôr'līk] *a* kriegerisch.
warm [wôrm] *a* warm; (*welcome*) herzlich ♦ *vti* wärmen; (*supporter*) eifrig, heftig; **to keep sth ~** etw warmhalten.
warm up *vt* aufwärmen ♦ *vi* warm werden.
warm-blooded [wôrm'blud'id] *a* warmblütig; (*fig*) heißblütig.
war memorial *n* Kriegerdenkmal *nt*.
warmhearted [wôrm'hâr'tid] *a* warmherzig.
warmly [wôrm'lē] *ad* warm; herzlich.
warmonger [wôr'munggûr] *n* Kriegshetzer *m*.
warmongering [wôr'munggûring] *n* Kriegshetze *f*.
warmth [wôrmth] *n* (*lit, fig*) Wärme *f*; (*of welcome*) Herzlichkeit *f*.
warm-up [wôrm'up] *n* (*SPORT*) Aufwärmen *nt*.
warn [wôrn] *vt* warnen (*of, against* vor +*dat*); **to ~ sb not to do sth** *or* **against doing sth** jdn davor warnen, etw zu tun.
warning [wôr'ning] *n* Warnung *f*; **gale ~** (*MET*) Sturmwarnung *f*; **without (any) ~** unerwartet, ohne Vorwarnung.
warning light *n* Warnlicht *nt*.
warning triangle *n* (*AUT*) Warndreieck *nt*.
warp [wôrp] *n* (*TEXTILES*) Kette *f* ♦ *vt* verziehen; (*fig*) verzerren ♦ *vi* sich verziehen.
warpath [wôr'path] *n*: **on the ~** (*fig*) auf dem Kriegspfad.
warped [wôrpt] *a* (*lit*) wellig, verzogen; (*fig: character, sense of humor*) abartig; (: *judgement*) verzerrt.
warrant [wôr'ənt] *n* Haftbefehl *m* ♦ *vt* (*justify, merit*) rechtfertigen.
warranty [wôr'əntē] *n* Garantie *f*; **it's still under ~** darauf ist noch Garantie.
warren [wôr'ən] *n* Labyrinth *nt*.
warring [wô'ring] *a* (*nations*) sich bekriegend; (*interests etc*) gegensätzlich.
warrior [wôr'êûr] *n* Krieger *m*.
Warsaw [wôr'sô] *n* Warschau *nt*.
warship [wôr'ship] *n* Kriegsschiff *nt*.
wart [wôrt] *n* Warze *f*.
wartime [wôr'tīm] *n* Kriegszeit *f*, Krieg *m*.
wary [wär'ē] *a* vorsichtig; (*look*) mißtrauisch; **to be ~ about doing sth** seine Zweifel *or* Bedenken haben, ob man etw tun soll.
was [wuz] *sing pt of* **be**.
Wash. *abbr* (*US*) = *Washington*.
wash [wâsh] *n* Wäsche *f*; **to give sth a ~** etw waschen; **to have a ~** sich waschen ♦ *vt* waschen; (*dishes*) abwaschen; (*sweep, carry: sea etc*) spülen; **he was ~ed overboard** er wurde über Bord gerissen ♦ *vi* sich waschen; (*do washing*) waschen.
wash away *vt* abwaschen, wegspülen.
wash down *vt* (*clean*) abwaschen; (*meal*) hinunterspülen.
wash off *vt* abwaschen.
wash up *vi* (*US: have a wash*) sich waschen; (*Brit: dishes*) abwaschen.
washable [wâsh'əbəl] *a* waschbar.
washbag [wâsh'bag] *n* Kulturbeutel *m*.

washbasin [wâsh'bāsin] *n* Waschbecken *nt*.
washcloth [wâsh'klôth] *n* (*US*) Waschlappen *m*.
washer [wâsh'ûr] *n* (*TECH*) Dichtungsring *m*; (*machine*) Wasch- *or* Spülmaschine *f*.
washing [wâsh'ing] *n* Wäsche *f*.
washing line *n* (*Brit*) Wäscheleine *f*.
washing machine *n* Waschmaschine *f*.
washing powder *n* (*Brit*) Waschpulver *nt*.
Washington [wâsh'ingtən] *n* Washington *nt*.
washing-up [wâsh'ingup'] *n* (*Brit*) Abwasch *m*.
washing-up liquid *n* (*Brit*) Spülmittel *nt*.
wash leather *n* Waschleder *nt*.
wash-out [wâsh'out] *n* (*col: event*) Reinfall *m*; (: *person*) Niete *f*.
washroom [wâsh'rōōm] *n* Waschraum *m*.
wasn't [wuz'ənt] = **was not**.
wasp [wâsp] *n* Wespe *f*.
Wasp, WASP [wâsp] *n abbr* (*US col*: = *White Anglo-Saxon Protestant*) *weißer angelsächsischer Protestant, Angehöriger der privilegierten Mittelklasse*.
waspish [wâs'pish] *a* giftig.
wastage [wās'tij] *n* Verlust *m*; **natural ~** Verschleiß *m*.
waste [wāst] *n* (*wasting*) Verschwendung *f*; (*what is wasted*) Abfall *m*; **~s** *pl* Einöde *f*; **it's a ~ of money** das ist Geldverschwendung; **to go to ~** (*food*) umkommen ♦ *a* (*useless*) überschüssig; (*energy, heat*) Abfall-; (*land, ground: in city*) unbebaut; (: *in country*) brachliegend, ungenutzt; **to lay ~** verwüsten ♦ *vt* (*object*) verschwenden; (*time, life*) vergeuden; (*talent etc*) verkümmern.
waste away *vi* verfallen.
waste bin *n* (*Brit*) Abfalleimer *m*.
wasteful [wāst'fəl] *a* verschwenderisch; (*process*) aufwendig.
wastefully [wāst'fəlē] *ad* verschwenderisch.
waste ground *n* (*Brit*) unbebaute(s) Grundstück *nt*.
wasteland [wāst'land] *n* (*US*) Ödland *nt*; (*fig*) Einöde *f*.
wastepaper basket [wāst'pāpûr bas'kit] *n* Papierkorb *m*.
waste products *npl* (*INDUSTRY*) Abfallprodukte *pl*.
watch [wâch] *n* (*act of watching*) Wache *f*; (*for time*) Uhr *f*; **to be on the ~ (for sth)** (auf etw *acc*) aufpassen; **to keep a close ~ on sb/sth** jdn/etw scharf bewachen ♦ *vt* ansehen; (*observe*) beobachten; (*be careful of*) aufpassen auf (+*acc*); (*guard*) bewachen; **to ~ TV** fernsehen; **to ~ sb doing sth** jdm bei etw zuschauen; **~ how you drive** fahr vorsichtig *or* sei beim Fahren auf; **~ what you are doing** paß auf ♦ *vi* zusehen; (*guard*) Wache halten; **to ~ for sb/sth** nach jdm/etw Ausschau halten; **~ out!** paß auf!
watchband [wâch'band] *n* (*US*) Uhrarmband *nt*.
watchdog [wâch'dôg] *n* (*lit*) Wachthund *m*;

(*fig*) Aufpasser(in *f*) *m*, Überwachungsbeauftragte(r) *mf*.
watchful [wâch'fəl] *a*, **watchfully** [wâch'fəlē] *ad* wachsam.
watchmaker [wâch'mākûr] *n* Uhrmacher *m*.
watchman [wâch'mən] *n*, *pl* **-men** (Nacht)wächter *m*.
watch stem *n* (*US*) Krone *f*, (Aufzieh)rädchen *nt*.
watchstrap [wâch'strap] *n* (*Brit*) Uhrarmband *nt*.
watchword [wâch'wûrd] *n* Parole *f*, Losung *f*.
water [wô'tûr] *n* Wasser *nt*; **~s** *pl* Gewässer *nt*; **to pass ~** Wasser lassen ♦ *vt* (be)gießen; (*river*) bewässern; (*horses*) tränken ♦ *vi* (*eye*) tränen; **my mouth is ~ing** mir läuft das Wasser im Mund zusammen; **to make sb's mouth ~** jdm den Mund wäßrig machen.
water down *vt* verwässern.
water closet *n* (*Brit*) (Wasser)klosett *nt*.
watercolor, (*Brit*) **watercolour** [wô'tûrkulûr] *n* (*painting*) Aquarell *nt*; (*paint*) Wasserfarbe *f*.
water-cooled [wô'tûrkōōld] *a* wassergekühlt.
watercress [wô'tûrkres] *n* (Brunnen)kresse *f*.
waterfall [wô'tûrfôl] *n* Wasserfall *m*.
waterfront [wô'tûrfrunt] *a* (*seafront*) am Wasser ♦ *n* (*at docks*) Hafenviertel *nt*.
water heater *n* Heißwassergerät *nt*.
water hole *n* Wasserloch *nt*.
watering can [wô'tûring kan] *n* Gießkanne *f*.
water level *n* Wasserstand *m*.
water lily *n* Seerose *f*.
waterline [wô'tûrlīn] *n* Wasserlinie *f*.
waterlogged [wô'tûrlôgd] *a* (*ground*) voll Wasser; (*wood*) mit Wasser vollgesogen.
water main *n* Haupt(wasser)leitung *f*.
watermark [wô'tûrmârk] *n* (*on paper*) Wasserzeichen *nt*.
watermelon [wô'tûrmelən] *n* Wassermelone *f*.
water polo *n* Wasserball(spiel) *nt*.
waterproof [wô'tûrprōōf] *a* wasserdicht.
water-repellent [wô'tûripel'ənt] *a* wasserabstoßend.
watershed [wô'tûrshed] *n* (*GEOG*) Wasserscheide *f*; (*fig*) Wendepunkt *m*.
water-skiing [wô'tûrskēing] *n* Wasserschilaufen *nt*; **to go ~** wasserschilaufen gehen.
water softener *n* Wasserenthärter *m*.
water tank *n* Wassertank *m*.
watertight [wô'tûrtīt] *a* wasserdicht.
water vapor *n* Wasserdampf *m*.
waterway [wô'tûrwā] *n* Wasserstraße *f*.
waterworks [wô'tûrwûrks] *n sing* (*place*) Wasserwerk *nt*.
watery [wô'tûrē] *a* wäss(e)rig.
WATS *n abbr* (*US*) = *Wide Area Telecommunications Service*.
watt [wât] *n* Watt *nt*.
wattage [wât'ij] *n* Wattleistung *f*.
wattle [wât'əl] *n* (*material*) Flechtwerk *nt*.
wave [wāv] *n* (*lit, fig*) ·Welle *f*; (*with hand*)

Winken *nt*; **the new ~** (*CINE, MUS*) die neue Welle *f*; **short/medium/long ~** (*RAD*) Kurz-/Mittel-/Langwelle *f* ♦ *vt* (*move to and fro*) schwenken; (*hand, flag*) winken mit; (*hair*) wellen; **to ~ sb goodbye** jdm zum Abschied winken; **he ~d us over to his table** er winkte uns zu sich an den Tisch ♦ *vi* (*person*) winken; (*flag*) wehen; (*hair*) sich wellen; **to ~ to sb** jdm zuwinken.

wave aside, wave away *vt* (*fig: suggestion, objection*) ab- *or* zurückweisen; (: *doubts*) zurückweisen; **to ~ sb aside** jdn auf die Seite *or* zur Seite winken.

wave band *n* Wellenband *nt*.

wavelength [wāv'lengkth] *n* (*lit, fig*) Wellenlänge *f*.

waver [wā'vûr] *vi* (*hesitate*) schwanken; (*flicker*) flackern.

wavy [wā'vē] *a* wellig.

wax [waks] *n* Wachs *nt*; (*sealing ~*) Siegellack *m*; (*in ear*) Ohrenschmalz *nt* ♦ *vt* (*floor*) (ein)wachsen ♦ *vi* (*moon*) zunehmen.

waxen [wak'sən] *a* (*fig: pale*) wachsbleich, wächsern.

wax paper *n* Butterbrotpapier *nt*.

waxworks [waks'wûrks] *npl* Wachsfigurenkabinett *nt*.

way [wā] *n* Weg *m*; (*road also*) Straße *f*; (*method*) Art und Weise *f*, Methode *f*; (*direction*) Richtung *f*; (*habit*) Eigenart *f*, Gewohnheit *f*; (*distance*) Entfernung *f*; (*state*) Zustand *m*; **on the ~** (*en route*) auf dem Weg; (*expected*) unterwegs; **it's a long ~ away** es ist weit entfernt; **you pass it on your ~ home** Sie kommen auf dem Nachhauseweg dran vorbei; **the village is that way out of the ~** das Dorf ist (ziemlich) abseits gelegen; **to keep out of sb's ~** jdm nicht in den Weg kommen; **to lose one's ~** sich verlaufen, sich verirren; **to fight one's ~ through the crowd** sich durch die Menge (durch)kämpfen; **to lie one's ~ out of sth** sich aus einer Verlegenheit herauslügen; **to make ~ for sb/sth** (*lit, fig*) jdm/etw Platz machen; **put it the right ~ up** stell es richtig (herum) hin; **to be the wrong ~ around** verkehrt herum sein; **he's in a bad ~** er ist in schlechter Verfassung; **do it this ~** machen Sie es so; **"give ~"** (*Brit AUT*) „Vorfahrt achten!"; **~ of thinking** Meinung *f*; **to get one's own ~** seinen Willen bekommen; **one ~ or another** irgendwie; **in a ~** in gewisser Weise; **in the ~** im Wege; **by the ~** übrigens; **by ~ of** (*via*) über (+*acc*); (*in order to*) um ... zu; (*instead of*) als; **to be under ~** (*work, project*) im Gang sein; **~ in** Eingang *m*; **~ out** Ausgang *m*.

waybill [wā'bil] *n* (*COMM*) Frachtbrief *m*.

waylaid [wā'lād] *pt, pp of* **waylay**.

waylay [wālā'] *vt irreg* auflauern (+*dat*).

wayside [wā'sīd] *n* Wegrand *m*; **to fall by the ~** (*fig*) auf der Strecke bleiben.

way station *n* (*US RAIL*) Zwischenstation *f*.

wayward [wā'wûrd] *a* eigensinnig.

WC *n abbr* (*Brit: = water closet*) WC *nt*.

WCC *n abbr* (= *World Council of Churches*) Weltkirchenrat *m*.

we [wē] *pl pron* wir.

weak [wēk] *a* schwach; **to grow ~(er)** schwächer werden.

weaken [wē'kən] *vt* schwächen, entkräften ♦ *vi* schwächer werden, nachlassen.

weak-kneed [wēk'nēd] *a* (*fig*) schwach, feige.

weakling [wēk'ling] *n* Schwächling *m*.

weakly [wēk'lē] *ad* schwach.

weakness [wēk'nis] *n* Schwäche *f*.

wealth [welth] *n* Reichtum *m*; (*abundance*) Fülle *f*.

wealth tax *n* Vermögenssteuer *f*.

wealthy [wel'thē] *a* reich.

wean [wēn] *vt* entwöhnen.

weapon [wep'ən] *n* Waffe *f*.

wear [wär] *n* (*clothing*) Kleidung *f*; (*use*) Verschleiß *m* ♦ *irreg vt* (*clothing, jewelry, beard*) tragen; (*smile etc*) haben; (*use*) abnutzen ♦ *vi* (*last*) halten; (*become old*) (sich) verschleißen; (*clothes*) sich abtragen; **to ~ a hole in sth** etw durchwetzen *or* durchlaufen.

wear away *vt* verbrauchen ♦ *vi* schwinden.

wear down *vt* (*people*) zermürben.

wear off *vi* sich verlieren; (*pain, excitement etc*) nachlassen.

wear out *vt* verschleißen; (*person*) erschöpfen.

wearable [wär'əbəl] *a* tragbar.

wear and tear *n* Abnutzung *f*, Verschleiß *m*.

wearer [wär'ûr] *n* Träger(in *f*) *m*.

wearily [wē'rilē] *ad* müde, lustlos.

weariness [wē'rēnis] *n* Müdigkeit *f*.

wearisome [wē'rēsəm] *a* (*tiring*) ermüdend; (*boring*) langweilig.

weary [wēr'ē] *a* (*tired*) müde; (*tiring*) ermüdend ♦ *vt* ermüden ♦ *vi* überdrüssig werden (*of gen*).

weasel [wē'zəl] *n* Wiesel *nt*.

weather [weth'ûr] *n* Wetter *nt* ♦ *vt* verwittern lassen; (*resist*) überstehen; **under the ~** (*fig: ill*) angeschlagen; **what's the ~ like?** wie ist das Wetter?

weather-beaten [weth'ûrbētən] *a* verwittert; (*skin*) wettergegerbt.

weathercock [weth'ûrkâk] *n* (*Brit*) = **weather vane**.

weather forecast *n* Wettervorhersage *f*.

weatherman [weth'ûrman] *n, pl* **-men** Mann *m* vom Wetteramt.

weatherproof [weth'ûrprōōf] *a* (*garment*) wetterfest.

weather report *n* Wetterbericht *m*.

weather strip *n* Dichtungsmaterial *nt*.

weather vane *n* Wetterhahn *m*.

weave [wēv] *vt irreg* weben; **to ~ one's way through sth** sich durch etw durchschlängeln ♦ *vi* (*fig: move in and out*) sich schlängeln.

weaved [wēvd] (*old*) *pt, pp of* **weave**.

weaver [wē'vûr] n Weber(in f) m.
weaving [wē'ving] n Weben nt, Weberei f.
web [web] n Netz nt; (of duck etc) Schwimmhaut f.
webbed [webd] a Schwimm-, schwimmhäutig.
webbing [web'ing] n Gewebe nt.
wed [wed] vt irreg, pt, pp **wed** (old) heiraten.
Wed. abbr (= Wednesday) Mi.
we'd [wēd] = **we had; we would.**
wedded [wed'id] pt, pp of **wed.**
wedding [wed'ing] n Hochzeit f.
wedding anniversary n Hochzeitstag m.
wedding day n Hochzeitstag m.
wedding present n Hochzeitsgeschenk nt.
wedding ring n Trau- or Ehering m.
wedge [wej] n Keil m; (of cheese etc) Stück nt ♦ vt (fasten) festklemmen; (pack tightly) einkeilen.
wedge-heeled [wej'hēld] a mit Keilabsätze.
wedlock [wed'läk] n Ehe f.
Wednesday [wenz'dā] n Mittwoch m; see **Tuesday.**
wee [wē] a (esp Scot) klein, winzig.
weed [wēd] n Unkraut nt ♦ vti jäten.
weed killer n Unkrautvertilgungsmittel nt.
weedy [wē'dē] a (person) schmächtig.
week [wēk] n Woche f; a ~ **today** heute in einer Woche; **once/twice a** ~ einmal/zweimal die Woche; **this** ~ diese Woche; **in 2 ~s' time** in 2 Wochen; **Tuesday** ~, a ~ **from Tuesday** am Dienstag in acht Tagen or einer Woche; **every other** ~ jede zweite Woche.
weekday [wēk'dā] n Wochentag m; **on** ~s an Wochentagen.
weekend [wēk'end] n Wochenende nt.
weekend case n (Brit) Reisetasche f.
weekly [wēk'lē] a wöchentlich; (wages, magazine) Wochen- ♦ ad wöchentlich.
weekly newspaper n Wochenzeitung f.
weep [wēp] vi irreg weinen; (MED: wound etc) tränen, nässen.
weft [weft] n (of textiles) Einschlagfaden m, Schlußfaden m.
weigh [wā] vti wiegen.
weigh down vt niederdrücken.
weigh out vt (goods) auswiegen.
weigh up vt prüfen, abschätzen; **to** ~ **up the pros and cons** das Für und Wider or Pro und Kontra abwägen.
weighing machine [wā'ing məshēn'] n (for people) Personenwaage f; (for goods) Waage f.
weight [wāt] n Gewicht nt; **to lose/put on** ~ abnehmen/zunehmen; ~s **and measures** Maße und Gewichte pl.
weighting [wā'ting] n Zulage f.
weightlessness [wāt'lisnis] n Schwerelosigkeit f.
weight-lifter [wāt'liftûr] n Gewichtheber m.
weight limit n Gewichtsbeschränkung f.
weighty [wā'tē] a (heavy) gewichtig; (important) schwerwiegend.

weir [wēr] n (Stau)wehr nt.
weird [wērd] a seltsam.
welcome [wel'kəm] n Willkommen nt, Empfang m ♦ vt begrüßen; **we** ~ **this step** wir begrüßen diesen Schritt ♦ a: **you're** ~ (after thanks) nichts zu danken!, keine Ursache!, bitte sehr!; **you're** ~ **to try** Sie können es gerne versuchen; **to make sb** ~ jdm das Gefühl geben, ein willkommener or gerngesehener Gast zu sein.
welcoming [wel'kəming] a zur Begrüßung.
weld [weld] n Schweißnaht f ♦ vt schweißen.
welder [weld'ûr] n Schweißer(in f) m.
welding [weld'ing] n Schweißen nt.
welfare [wel'fär] n Wohl nt; (social) Fürsorge f; **to look after sb's** ~ für jds Wohl sorgen; **to be on** ~ (US) Sozialhilfeempfänger sein.
welfare state n Wohlfahrtsstaat m.
welfare work n Fürsorge f.
well [wel] n Brunnen m; (oil ~) Quelle f ♦ a (in good health) gesund; **are you** ~? geht es Ihnen gut?; **I don't feel** ~ ich fühle mich nicht gut or wohl ♦ interj nun, na schön; (starting conversation) nun, tja; ~, ~! na, na!; ~, **as I was saying** ... also, wie (bereits) gesagt ... ♦ ad gut; ~ **over 40** weit über 40; **it may** ~ **be** es kann wohl sein; **as** ~ (in addition) auch; **as** ~ **as** sowohl als auch; **it would be (as)** ~ **to** ... es wäre wohl gut, zu ...; **it would be as** ~ **to ask** es wäre besser, sich erst mal zu erkundigen; **you did** ~ **(not) to** ... Sie haben gut daran getan, (nicht) zu ...; **very** ~ (O.K.) nun gut; **to be doing** ~ gut vorankommen; **to think** ~ **of sb** über or von jdm positiv denken; **you might as** ~ **go** du könntest eigentlich auch gehen.
well up vi emporsteigen; (fig) aufsteigen.
we'll [wēl] = **we will, we shall.**
well-behaved [welbihāvd'] a wohlerzogen.
well-being [wel'bē'ing] n Wohl nt, Wohlergehen nt.
well-bred [wel'bred'] a (polite: person) wohlerzogen, gut erzogen; (manners) vornehm, gepflegt; (accent) distinguiert; (of good stock: animal) aus guter Zucht.
well-built [wel'bilt'] a kräftig gebaut.
well-chosen [wel'chō'zən] a (remarks, words) gut gewählt.
well-deserved [wel'dizûrvd'] a wohlverdient.
well-developed [wel'divel'əpt] a (girl) gut entwickelt; (economy) hochentwickelt.
well-disposed [wel'dispōzd'] a: **to be** ~ **to(wards) sb/sth** jdm/einer Sache gewogen sein or freundlich gesonnen sein.
well-dressed [wel'drest'] a gut gekleidet.
well-earned [wel'ûrnd'] a (rest) wohlverdient.
well-groomed [wel'grōōmd] a gepflegt.
well-heeled [wel'hēld'] a (col: wealthy) gut gepolstert.
well-informed [wel'infôrmd'] a (having knowledge) gut informiert.
Wellington [wel'ingtən] n Wellington nt.

wellingtons [wel'ingtənz] *npl* Gummistiefel *pl.*

well-kept [wel'kept'] *a* (*house, grounds, hair, hands*) gepflegt; (*secret*) gehütet.

well-known [wel'nōn'] *a* (*person*) weithin bekannt.

well-mannered [wel'man'ûrd] *a* wohlerzogen.

well-meaning [wel'mē'ning] *a* (*person*) wohlmeinend; (*action*) gutgemeint.

well-nigh [wel'nī'] *ad*: ~ **impossible** beinahe *or* nahezu unmöglich.

well-off [wel'ôf'] *a* gut situiert.

well-read [wel'red'] *a* (sehr) belesen.

well-spoken [wel'spō'kən] *a*: **to be** ~ gutes Deutsch *or* Englisch *etc* sprechen.

well-stocked [wel'stäkt'] *a* (*shop, larder*) gut gefüllt.

well-timed [wel'tīmd'] *a*: **that was a** ~ **interruption** die Unterbrechung kam im richtigen Augenblick.

well-to-do [wel'tədōō'] *a* wohlhabend.

well-wisher [wel'wishûr] *n* wohlwollende(r) Freund *m*, Gratulant(in *f*) *m*; **"from a** ~**"** „jemand, der es gut mit Ihnen meint".

Welsh [welsh] *a* walisisch ♦ *n* (*language*) Walisisch *nt*; **the** ~ (*people*) die Waliser *pl.*

Welshman [wel'shmən] *n, pl* **-men** Waliser *m.*

Welsh rarebit [welsh rär'bit] *n* überbackene Käseschnitte *pl.*

Welshwoman [welsh'wōōmən] *n, pl* **-women** Waliserin *f.*

welter [wel'tûr] *n* (*jumble*) Chaos *nt*, Durcheinander *nt.*

went [went] *pt of* **go.**

wept [wept] *pt, pp of* **weep.**

were [wûr] *pl pt of* **be.**

we're [wēr] = **we are.**

weren't [wûr'ənt] = **were not.**

werewolf [wär'wōōlf] *n, pl* **-wolves** Werwolf *m.*

west [west] *n* Westen *m* ♦ *a* West-, westlich ♦ *ad* westwärts, nach Westen.

westbound [west'bound] *a* (*traffic, lane*) in Richtung Westen.

westerly [wes'tûrlē] *a* westlich.

western [wes'tûrn] *a* westlich, West- ♦ *n* (*CINE*) Western *m.*

westernized [wes'tûrnīzd] *a* vom Westen beeinflußt.

West German *a* westdeutsch ♦ *n* Westdeutsche(r) *mf.*

West Germany *n* Westdeutschland *nt*, Bundesrepublik *f* (Deutschland).

West Indian *a* westindisch ♦ *n* Westinder(in *f*) *m.*

West Indies [west in'dēz] *npl* Westindien *nt*, Westindische Inseln *pl.*

westward(s) [west'wûrd(z)] *ad* westwärts.

wet [wet] *a* naß; ~ **blanket** (*fig*) Triefel *m*; **"**~ **paint"** „frisch gestrichen" ♦ *vt* naß machen; **to** ~ **one's pants** *or* **o.s.** in die Hose(n) machen.

wetness [wet'nis] *n* Nässe *f*, Feuchtigkeit *f.*

wet suit *n* Taucheranzug *m.*

we've [wēv] = **we have.**

whack [wak] *n* Schlag *m* ♦ *vt* schlagen.

whale [wāl] *n* Wal *m.*

whaler [wā'lûr] *n* (*person, ship*) Walfänger *m.*

wharf [wôrf] *n* Kai *m.*

what [wut] *pron, interj* was; ~ **money I had** das Geld, das ich hatte; ~ **about ...?** (*suggestion*) wie wär's mit ...?; ~ **about it?, so** ~**?** na und?; **well,** ~ **about him?** was ist mit ihm?; **and** ~ **about me?** und ich?; ~ **for?** wozu?; ~**'s happening?** was läuft? (*col*), was ist los?; ~ **is his address?** wie ist seine Adresse?; ~ **will it cost?** was kostet es?; **I don't know** ~ **to do** ich weiß nicht, was ich machen soll; ~ **I want is a cup of tea** was ich jetzt gerne hätte, (das) ist ein Tee ♦ *a* welche(r, s); **for** ~ **reason?** aus welchem Grund?; ~ **a hat!** was für ein Hut!

whatever [wutev'ûr] *pron*: ~ **he says** egal, was er sagt ♦ *a*: **no reason** ~ überhaupt kein Grund.

wheat [wēt] *n* Weizen *m.*

wheat germ *n* Weizenkeim *m.*

wheat meal *n* Weizenmehl *nt.*

wheedle [wēd'əl] *vt*: **to** ~ **sb into doing sth** jdn bequatschen (*col*) *or* herumkriegen, etw zu tun; **to** ~ **sth out of sb** jdm etw abluchsen.

wheel [wēl] *n* Rad *nt*; (*steering* ~) Lenkrad *nt*; (*disc*) Scheibe *f* ♦ *vt* schieben ♦ *vi* (*revolve*) sich drehen; **four-**~ **drive** (*AUT*) Allradantrieb *m*; **front-/rear-**~ **drive** (*AUT*) Vorder-/Hinterradantrieb *m.*

wheelbarrow [wēl'barō] *n* Schubkarren *m.*

wheelbase [wēl'bās] *n* Rad(ab)stand *m.*

wheelchair [wēl'chär] *n* Rollstuhl *m.*

wheeler-dealer [wē'lûrdē'lûr] *n* gerissene(r) Kerl *m.*

wheeling [wē'ling] *n*: ~ **and dealing** (*col*) Geschäftemacherei *f.*

wheeze [wēz] *n* Keuchen *nt* ♦ *vi* keuchen.

when [wen] *ad interrog* wann ♦ *ad, cj* (*with present tense*) wenn; (*with past tense*) als; (*with indirect question*) wann; **on the day** ~ an dem Tag, an dem *or* als *or* wo (*col*).

whenever [wenev'ûr] *ad* (*each time*) jedesmal; (*at whatever time*) wann immer; **I go** ~ **I can** ich gehe, wann immer ich kann.

where [wär] *ad* (*place*) wo; (*direction*) wohin; ~ **from** woher; ~ **are you from?** woher kommen Sie?; ~ **possible** soweit möglich.

whereabouts [wär'əbouts] *ad* wo ♦ *n* Aufenthalt *m*, Verbleib *m.*

whereas [wäraz'] *cj* während, wo ... doch.

whereby [wärbī'] *ad* (*form*) wodurch.

whereupon [wärəpân'] *ad* worauf.

wherever [wärev'ûr] *ad* wo (immer); **sit** ~ **you like** nehmen Sie Platz, wo immer Sie wollen.

wherewithal [wär'withôl] *n*: **the** ~ **(to do sth)** (*money*) das nötige Kleingeld(, etw zu tun).

whet [wet] *vt* (*appetite*) anregen.

whether [weth'ûr] *cj* ob.

whey [wā] *n* Molke *f*.

which [wich] *a* (*from selection*) welche(r, s) ♦ *rel pron* der/die/das; (*rel: which fact*) was; (*interrog*) welche(r, s); **by ~ time I was asleep** und zu dieser Zeit schlief ich (bereits); **~ do you want?** welche(r, s) möchtest du?; **after ~** nachdem.

whichever [wichev'ûr] *a*, *pron* welche(r, s) auch immer.

whiff [wif] *n* Hauch *m*; **to catch a ~ of sth** den Geruch von etw wahrnehmen.

while [wīl] *n* Weile *f* ♦ *cj* während; **for a ~** eine Zeitlang; **in a ~** bald; **all the ~** die ganze Zeit (über); **we'll etc make it worth your ~** es soll Ihr Schaden nicht sein.

while away *vt* (*time*) sich (*dat*) vertreiben.

whilst [wīlst] *cj* während.

whim [wim] *n* Laune *f*.

whimper [wim'pûr] *n* Wimmern *nt* ♦ *vi* wimmern.

whimsical [wim'zikəl] *a* launisch.

whine [wīn] *n* Gewinsel *nt*, Gejammer *nt* ♦ *vi* heulen, winseln.

whip [wip] *n* Peitsche *f*; (*Brit PARL*) Einpeitscher *m* ♦ *vt* (*beat*) peitschen; (*snatch*) reißen; (*COOK: cream etc*) schlagen.

whip up *vt* (*cream*) schlagen; (*col: meal*) hinzaubern; (*stir up: support, feeling*) anheizen, entfachen.

whiplash [wip'lash] *n* (*MED: also: ~ injury*) Peitschenhiebverletzung *f*.

whipped cream [wipt krēm] *n* Schlagsahne *f*.

whipping boy [wip'ing boi] *n* (*fig*) Prügelknabe *m*.

whip-round [wip'round] *n* (*Brit col*) Geldsammlung *f*.

whirl [wûrl] *n* Wirbel *m* ♦ *vti* (herum)wirbeln.

whirlpool [wûrl'pōōl] *n* Wirbel *m*.

whirlwind [wûrl'wind] *n* Wirbelwind *m*.

whirr [wär] *vi* schwirren, surren.

whisk [wisk] *n* Schneebesen *m* ♦ *vt* (*cream etc*) schlagen.

whisker [wis'kûr] *n* (*of animal*) Barthaare *pl*; **~s** *pl* (*of man*) Backenbart *m*.

whiskey (*US, Ireland*), **whisky** (*Brit*) [wis'kē] *n* Whisky *m*.

whisper [wis'pûr] *n* Flüstern *nt* ♦ *vi* flüstern; (*leaves*) rascheln *f*, flüstern, munkeln; **to ~ sth to sb** jdm etw zuflüstern.

whispering [wis'pûring] *n* Flüstern *nt*, Geflüster *nt*.

whist [wist] *n* (*CARDS*) Whist *nt*.

whistle [wis'əl] *n* Pfiff *m*; (*instrument*) Pfeife *f* ♦ *vti* pfeifen.

whistle-stop tour [wis'əlstâp tōōr] *n* (*US POL*) Wahlreise *f*; (*fig*) Reise *f* mit Kurzaufenthalten an allen Orten.

Whit [wit] *n* Pfingsten *nt*.

white [wīt] *n* Weiß *nt*; (*of egg*) Eiweiß *nt*; (*of eye*) Weiße(s) *nt*; **the ~s** (*washing*) die Weißwäsche; **the tennis players were wearing ~s** die Tennisspieler trugen Weiß ♦ *a* weiß; (*with fear*) blaß; **to turn** *or* **go ~** (*person*) bleich *or* blaß werden.

whitebait [wīt'bāt] *n* Breitling *m*.

white coffee *n* (*Brit*) Kaffee *m* mit Milch, Milchkaffee *m*.

white-collar worker [wīt'kâl'ûr wûr'kûr] *n* Angestellte(r) *m*.

white elephant *n* (*fig*) Fehlinvestition *f*.

white goods *npl* große Haushaltsgeräte *pl*; (*household linen*) Weißwaren *pl*.

white-hot [wīt'hât'] *a* (*metal*) weißglühend.

white lie *n* Notlüge *f*.

whiteness [wīt'nis] *n* Weiß *nt*.

white noise *n* weiße(s) Rauschen *nt*.

whiteout [wīt'out] *n* (*MET*) starke(s) Schneegestöber *nt*.

white paper *n* Weißbuch *nt*.

whitewash [wīt'wâsh] *n* (*paint*) Tünche *f*; (*fig*) Ehrenrettung *f* ♦ *vt* weißen, tünchen; (*fig*) reinwaschen.

white-water rafting [wīt'wôtûr raf'ting] *n* Wildwasserflößen *nt*.

whiting [wī'ting] *n* Weißfisch *m*.

Whit Monday *n* Pfingstmontag *m*.

Whitsun [wit'sən] *n* Pfingsten *nt*.

whittle [wit'əl] *vt*: **to ~ away, to ~ down** stutzen, verringern.

whizz [wiz] *vi* sausen, zischen, schwirren.

whizz kid *n* (*col*) Kanone *f*.

who [hōō] *pron* (*interrog*) wer; (*rel*) der/die/das; **"Who's Who"** „Wer ist Wer".

WHO *n abbr* (= *World Health Organization*) WGO *f*.

whodunit [hōōdun'it] *n* (*col*) Krimi *m*.

whoever [hōōev'ûr] *pron* wer *etc* (auch immer); (*no matter who*) ganz gleich wer *etc*.

whole [hōl] *a* ganz; (*uninjured*) heil; **~ villages were destroyed** ganze Dörfer wurden zerstört ♦ *n* Ganze(s) *nt*; **the ~ of the year** das ganze Jahr; **on the ~** im großen und ganzen.

wholefood [hōl'fōōd] *n* Reformkost *f*.

wholehearted [hōl'hâr'tid] *a* rückhaltlos.

wholeheartedly [hōl'hâr'tidlē] *ad* von ganzem Herzen.

wholemeal [hōl'mēl] *a* (*Brit: flour, bread*) Vollkorn-.

whole milk *n* (*US*) Vollmilch *f*.

whole note *n* (*US*) ganze Note *f*.

wholesale [hōl'sāl] *n* Großhandel *m* ♦ *a* (*trade*) Großhandels-; (*destruction*) vollkommen, Massen-.

wholesaler [hōl'sälûr] *n* Großhändler *m*.

wholesome [hōl'səm] *a* bekömmlich, gesund.

whole-wheat [hōl'wēt'] *a* (*US: flour, bread*) Vollkorn-.

wholly [hōl'lē] *ad* ganz, völlig.

whom [hōōm] *pron* (*interrog*) wen; (*rel: sing*) den/die/das; (*: pl*) die; **those to ~ I spoke** die, mit denen ich sprach.

whooping cough [hōō'ping kôf] *n* Keuchhusten *m*.

whoosh [wŏŏsh] *n, vi*: **a train ~ed past, a train came by with a ~** ein Zug brauste vorbei.

whopper [wǎp'ûr] *n* (*col: large thing*) Mordsding *nt*; (*: lie*) faustdicke Lüge *f*.

whopping [wǎp'ing] *a* (*col*) kolossal, Riesen-.

whore [hôr] *n* Hure *f*.

whose [hŏŏz] *pron* (*interrog*) wessen; (*rel*) dessen; (*after f and pl*) deren.

why [wī] *ad* warum ♦ *interj* nanu; **that's ~** deshalb; **that's not ~ I'm here** ich bin nicht deswegen hier.

WI *abbr* (= *West Indies*) Westindische Inseln; (*US MAIL*) = *Wisconsin*.

wick [wik] *n* Docht *m*.

wicked [wik'id] *a* böse.

wickedness [wik'idnis] *n* Bosheit *f*, Schlechtigkeit *f*.

wicker [wik'ûr] *n* Weidengeflecht *nt*, Korbgeflecht *nt*.

wicket [wik'it] *n* Tor *nt*, Dreistab *m*; (*playing pitch*) Spielfeld *nt*.

wide [wīd] *a* breit; (*plain*) weit; (*in firing*) daneben; **~ of** weitab von; **it is 3 meters ~** es ist 3 Meter breit ♦ *ad* weit; (*far from target*) daneben.

wide-angle [wīd'ang'gəl] *a* (*lens*) Weitwinkel-.

wide-awake [wīd'əwāk'] *a* hellwach.

wide-eyed [wīd'īd] *a* mit großen Augen.

widely [wīd'lē] *ad* weit; (*known*) allgemein; **to be ~ read** (*author*) überall gelesen werden; (*reader*) sehr belesen sein.

widen [wī'dən] *vt* erweitern.

wideness [wīd'nis] *n* Breite *f*.

wide-open [wīd'ō'pən] *a* weit geöffnet.

wide-ranging [wīd'rān'jing] *a* (*survey, report*) weitreichend; (*interests*) vielfältig.

widespread [wīdspred'] *a* weitverbreitet.

widow [wid'ō] *n* Witwe *f*.

widowed [wid'ōd] *a* verwitwet.

widower [wid'ōûr] *n* Witwer *m*.

width [width] *n* Breite *f*, Weite *f*; **7 meters in ~** (*fabric*) 7 Meter breit.

widthwise [width'wīz] *ad* der Breite nach.

wield [wēld] *vt* schwingen, handhaben.

wife [wīf] *n, pl* **wives** [wīvz] (Ehe)frau *f*, Gattin *f*.

wig [wig] *n* Perücke *f*.

wiggle [wig'əl] *n* Wackeln *nt* ♦ *vt* wackeln mit ♦ *vi* wackeln.

wiggly [wig'lē] *a* (*line*) Schlangen-.

wigwam [wig'wâm] *n* Wigwam *m*, Indianerzelt *nt*.

wild [wīld] *a* wild; (*violent*) heftig; (*plan, idea*) verrückt; (*col: angry*) wütend, rasend; **to be ~ about sth** (*col: enthusiastic*) scharf *or* versessen auf etw sein; **in its ~ state** im Naturzustand ♦ *n*: **the ~s** *pl* die Wildnis *f*.

wild card *n* (*COMPUT*) Stellvertretersymbol *nt*, Ersatzzeichen *nt*.

wildcat [wīld'kat] *n* Wildkatze *f*.

wildcat strike *n* wilde(r) Streik *m*.

wilderness [wil'dûrnis] *n* Wildnis *f*, Wüste *f*.

wildfire [wīld'fiûr] *n*: **to spread like ~** sich wie ein Lauffeuer ausbreiten.

wild-goose chase [wīld'gŏŏs' chās] *n* fruchtlose(s) Unternehmen *nt*.

wildlife [wīld'līf] *n* Tierwelt *f*.

wildly [wīld'lē] *ad* wild, ungestüm; (*exaggerated*) irrsinnig.

wiles [wīlz] *npl* List *f*, Schliche *pl*.

wilful [wil'fəl] *a* (*Brit*) = **willful.**

will [wil] *v aux*: **he ~ come** er wird kommen; **I ~ do it!** ich werde es tun; **you won't lose it, ~ you?** du wirst es doch nicht verlieren, oder?; **that ~ be the mailman** (*in conjectures*) das ist bestimmt der Briefträger; **~ you sit down** (*politely*) bitte, nehmen Sie Platz; (*angrily*) nun setz dich doch; **the car won't start** das Auto springt nicht an ♦ *n* (*power to choose*) Wille *m*; (*wish*) Wunsch *m*, Bestreben *nt*; (*JUR*) Testament *nt*; **against sb's ~** gegen jds Willen; **to do sth of one's own free ~** etw aus freien Stücken tun ♦ *vt* (*urge by ~power*) (durch Willenskraft) erzwingen.

willful [wil'fəl] *a* (*US: intended*) vorsätzlich; (*: obstinate*) eigensinnig.

willing [wil'ing] *a* gewillt, bereit; **to show o.s. ~** sich willig zeigen.

willingly [wil'inglē] *ad* bereitwillig, gern.

willingness [wil'ingnis] *n* (Bereit)willigkeit *f*.

will-o'-the-wisp [wil'ŏthəwisp'] *n* Irrlicht *nt*; (*fig*) Trugbild *nt*.

willow [wil'ō] *n* Weide *f*.

willpower [wil'pouûr] *n* Willenskraft *f*.

willy-nilly [wil'ēnil'ē] *ad* wohl oder übel.

wilt [wilt] *vi* (ver)welken.

Wilts [wilts] *abbr* (*Brit*) = *Wiltshire.*

wily [wī'lē] *a* gerissen.

wimp [wimp] *n* (*col*) Memme *f*.

win [win] *n* Sieg *m* ♦ *irreg vt* gewinnen; (*contract*) bekommen ♦ *vi* (*be successful*) siegen; **to ~ sb over** jdn gewinnen, jdn dazu bringen.

wince [wins] *n* Zusammenzucken *nt* ♦ *vi* zusammenzucken, zurückfahren.

winch [winch] *n* Winde *f*.

Winchester disk [win'chestûr disk] *n* (*COMPUT*) Winchester-Festplatte *f*.

wind [wīnd] *irreg vt* (*rope*) winden; (*bandage*) wickeln; **to ~ one's way** sich schlängeln ♦ *vi* (*turn*) sich winden; (*change direction*) wenden ♦ *n* [wind] Wind *m*; (*MED*) Blähungen *pl*; **into** *or* **against the ~** gegen den Wind, in den Wind; **to get ~ of sth** (*lit, fig*) von etw Wind bekommen; **to break ~** einen Wind streichen lassen.

wind down [wīnd' doun] *vt* (*fig: production, business*) zurückschrauben; (*car window*) herunterdrehen *or* -kurbeln.

wind up [wīnd' up] *vt* (*clock*) aufziehen; (*debate*) (ab)schließen.

windbreak [wind'brāk] *n* Windschutz *m*.

windbreaker [wind'brākûr] *n* ® (*US*) Windjacke *f or* -bluse *f*.

windfall [wind'fôl] n unverhoffte(r) Glücksfall m.

winding [wīn'ding] a (road) gewunden, sich schlängelnd.

wind instrument [wind in'strəmənt] n Blasinstrument nt.

windmill [wind'mil] n Windmühle f.

window [win'dō] n Fenster nt; (COMPUT) Fenster nt, Bildfenster nt.

window box n Blumenkasten m.

window cleaner n Fensterputzer m.

window dressing n Auslagen pl, Schaufensterdekoration f.

window envelope n Fensterumschlag m.

window frame n Fensterrahmen m.

window ledge n Fenstersims m.

window pane n Fensterscheibe f.

window-shopping [win'dōshåping] n Schaufensterbummel m; **to go** ~ einen Schaufensterbummel machen.

windowsill [win'dōsil] n Fensterbank f.

windpipe [wind'pīp] n Luftröhre f.

windscreen [wind'skrēn] etc (Brit) = **windshield** etc.

windshield [wind'shēld] n Windschutzscheibe f.

windshield washer n Scheibenwaschanlage f.

windshield wiper n Scheibenwischer m.

windswept [wind'swept] a vom Wind gepeitscht; (person) zerzaust.

wind tunnel n Windkanal m.

windy [win'dē] a windig.

wine [wīn] n Wein m ♦ vt: **to** ~ **and dine sb** jdn zu einem guten Abendessen einladen.

wineglass [wīn'glas] n Weinglas nt.

wine list n Weinkarte f.

wine merchant n Weinhändler m.

wine tasting n Weinprobe f.

wine waiter n Weinkellner m.

wing [wing] n Flügel m; (MIL) Gruppe f; (SPORT) Flügelstürmer m; see also **wings**.

winger [wing'ûr] n (Brit SPORT) Flügelstürmer m.

wing mirror n (Brit) Seitenspiegel m.

wing nut n Flügelmutter f.

wings [wingz] npl (THEAT) Seitenkulisse f.

wingspan [wing'span] n Flügelspannweite f.

wingspread [wing'spred] n Flügelspannweite f.

wink [wingk] n Zwinkern nt ♦ vi zwinkern, blinzeln; **to** ~ **at sb** jdm zublinzeln; **to have forty** ~s ein Nickerchen machen.

winkle [win'kəl] n Strandschnecke f.

winner [win'ûr] n Gewinner(in f) m; (SPORT) Sieger(in f) m.

winning [win'ing] a (team) siegreich, Sieger-; (goal) entscheidend; (charming) gewinnend, einnehmend.

winning post n (Brit) Ziel nt.

winnings [win'ingz] npl Gewinn m.

winsome [win'səm] a gewinnend.

winter [win'tûr] n Winter m ♦ a (clothes) Winter- ♦ vi überwintern.

winter sports npl Wintersport m.

wintry [win'trē] a Winter-, winterlich.

wipe [wīp] n Wischen nt ♦ vt wischen, abwischen; **to give sth a** ~ etw abwischen; **to** ~ **one's nose** sich die Nase putzen.

wipe off vt weg- or abwischen.

wipe out vt (debt) löschen; (destroy) auslöschen.

wipe up vt aufwischen.

wire [wī'ûr] n Draht m; (telegram) Telegramm nt ♦ vt telegrafieren (sb jdm, sth etw); (ELEC: house) die (elektrischen) Leitungen verlegen in (+dat).

wire cutters npl Drahtschere f.

wire mesh, **wire netting** n Maschendraht m.

wiretapping [wī'ûrtaping] n Abhören nt, Abzapfen nt von Leitungen.

wiring [wīûr'ing] n (ELEC) elektrische Leitungen pl, Stromkabel pl.

wiry [wīûr'ē] a drahtig.

Wis., **Wisc.** abbr (US) = Wisconsin.

wisdom [wiz'dəm] n Weisheit f; (of decision) Klugheit f.

wisdom tooth n Weisheitszahn m.

wise [wīz] a klug, weise; **I'm none the** ~r ich bin nicht klüger als zuvor.

wise up vi (col: esp US): **he is never going to** ~ **up** der lernt's nie!

...wise ad suff ...mäßig.

wisecrack [wīz'krak] n Witzelei f.

wisely [wīz'lē] ad klug, weise.

wish [wish] n Wunsch m; **with best** ~es herzliche Grüße; **I had no** ~ **to upset you** ich wollte dich nicht verletzen ♦ vt wünschen; **he** ~es **us to do it** er möchte, daß wir es tun; **to** ~ **sb goodbye** jdn verabschieden; **to** ~ **to do sth** etw tun wollen; **to** ~ **sth on sb** jdm etw aufhängen.

wishful thinking [wish'fəl thingk'ing] n Wunschdenken nt.

wishy-washy [wish'ēwåshē] a wischiwaschi; (color) verwaschen.

wisp [wisp] n (Haar)strähne f; (of smoke) Wölkchen nt.

wistful [wist'fəl] a sehnsüchtig; (nostalgic) wehmütig.

wit [wit] n (usu pl: intelligence) Verstand m no pl; (amusing ideas) Witz m; (person) Witzbold m; **at one's** ~s' **end** mit seinem Latein am Ende; **to have** or **keep one's** ~s **about one** seine (fünf) Sinne zusammenhalten, einen klaren Kopf behalten.

witch [wich] n Hexe f.

witchcraft [wich'kraft] n Hexerei f.

witch doctor n Medizinmann m.

witch-hunt [wich'hunt] n (POL) Hexenjagd f.

with [with, with] prep mit; (in spite of) trotz (+gen or dat); ~ **him** it's ... es ist es ...; **to stay** ~ **sb** bei jdm wohnen; **she stayed** ~ **friends** sie blieb bei Freunden; **I have no money** ~ **me** ich habe kein Geld bei mir; **shaking** ~ **fright** vor Angst zitternd; **she's down** ~ **the flu** sie ist an Grippe erkrankt.

withdraw [wiᵗʰdrô'] *irreg vt* zurückziehen; (*money*) abheben; (*remark*) zurücknehmen ♦ *vi* sich zurückziehen; **to** ~ **into o.s.** sich in sich (*acc*) (selber) zurückziehen.

withdrawal [wiᵗʰdrô'əl] *n* Zurückziehung *f*; Abheben *nt*; Zurücknahme *f*.

withdrawal symptoms *npl* Entzugserscheinungen *pl*.

withdrawn [wiᵗʰdrôn'] *a* (*person*) verschlossen; (*manner also*) reserviert, zurückhaltend ♦ *pp of* **withdraw.**

wither [wiᵗʰ'ûr] *vi* (ver)welken.

withered [wiᵗʰ'ûrd] *a* verwelkt, welk.

withhold [withhōld'] *vt irreg* vorenthalten (*from sb* jdm).

within [wiᵗʰin'] *prep* innerhalb (+*gen*); **to be** ~ **the law** im Rahmen des Gesetzes sein; ~ **an hour from now** innerhalb einer Stunde; ~ **reach** in Reichweite ♦ *ad* innen.

without [wiᵗʰout'] *prep* ohne; **it goes** ~ **saying** es ist selbstverständlich; **to have to do** ~ **sth** ohne etw auskommen müssen; ~ **anybody knowing** ohne daß jemand es wußte.

with-profits [with'prâf'its] *a*: ~ **endowment insurance** Versicherung *f* auf den Erlebensfall mit Gewinnbeteiligung.

withstand [withstand'] *vt irreg* widerstehen (+*dat*).

witness [wit'nis] *n* Zeuge *m*; Zeugin *f* ♦ *vt* (*see*) sehen, miterleben; (*sign: document*) beglaubigen ♦ *vi* aussagen; ~ **for the prosecution/defense** Zeuge/Zeugin der Anklage/Verteidigung; **to** ~ **to sth** etw bestätigen *or* bezeugen.

witness box *n* (*Brit*) = **witness stand.**

witness stand *n* Zeugenstand *m*.

witticism [wit'əsizəm] *n* witzige Bemerkung *f*.

witty [wit'ē] *a*, **wittily** [wit'əlē] *ad* witzig, geistreich.

wives [wīvz] *npl of* **wife.**

wizard [wiz'ûrd] *n* Zauberer *m*.

wizened [wiz'ənd] *a* verhutzelt, verschrumpelt.

wk. *abbr* (= *week*) Wo.

Wm. *abbr* = *William*.

WO *n abbr* (= *warrant officer*) *Rang zwischen Unteroffizier und Offizier*.

wobble [wâb'əl] *vi* wackeln.

wobbly [wâb'lē] *a* (*hand, voice*) zitt(e)rig, zitternd; (*table, chair*) wack(e)lig.

woe [wō] *n* Weh *nt*, Leid *nt*, Kummer *m*.

woke [wōk] *pt of* **wake.**

woken [wō'kən] *pp of* **wake.**

wolf [wōōlf] *n*, *pl* **wolves** [wōōlvz] Wolf *m*.

woman [wōōm'ən] *n*, *pl* **women** [wim'ən] Frau *f*.

woman doctor *n* Ärztin *f*.

woman friend *n* Freundin *f*.

womanize [wōōm'əniz] *vi* Weibergeschichten haben.

womanly [wōōm'ənlē] *a* weiblich.

womb [wōōm] *n* Gebärmutter *f*.

women [wim'ən] *npl of* **woman.**

Women's (Liberation) Movement *n* Frauenbewegung *f*.

won [wun] *pt, pp of* **win.**

wonder [wun'dûr] *n* (*marvel*) Wunder *nt*; (*surprise*) Staunen *nt*, Verwunderung *f* ♦ *vi* sich wundern; **I** ~ **whether** ... ich frage mich, ob ...

wonderful [wun'dûrfəl] *a* wunderbar, herrlich.

wonderfully [wun'dûrfəlē] *ad* wunderbar.

wonky [wâng'kē] *a* (*Brit col*) wackelig; (: *machine*) nicht (ganz) in Ordnung.

won't [wōnt] = **will not.**

wood [wōōd] *n* Holz *nt*; (*forest*) Wald *m* ♦ *cpd* Holz-.

wood alcohol *n* (*US*) (Brenn)spiritus *m*.

wood carving *n* Holzschnitzerei *f*.

wooded [wōōd'id] *a* bewaldet, waldig, Wald-.

wooden [wōōd'ən] *a* (*lit, fig*) hölzern.

woodland [wōōd'land] *n* Waldland *nt*, Waldung *f*.

woodpecker [wōōd'pekûr] *n* Specht *m*.

wood pigeon *n* Ringeltaube *f*.

woodwind [wōōd'wind] *n* Blasinstrumente *pl*.

woodwork [wōōd'wûrk] *n* Holzwerk *nt*; (*craft*) Holzarbeiten *pl*.

woodworm [wōōd'wûrm] *n* Holzwurm *m*.

woof [wōōf] *n* (*of dog*) Wuff *nt* ♦ *vi* kläffen.

wool [wōōl] *n* Wolle *f*; **knitting** ~ (Strick)wolle *f*.

woolen, (*Brit*) **woollen** [wōōl'ən] *a* Woll- ♦ *n*: ~**s** *pl* Wollsachen *pl*.

wooly, (*Brit*) **woolly** [wōōl'ē] *a* wollig; (*fig*) schwammig.

word [wûrd] *n* Wort *nt*; (*news*) Bescheid *m*; **by** ~ **of mouth** mündlich; ~ **for** ~ Wort für Wort, wörtlich; **to put sth into** ~**s** etw in Worte fassen *or* kleiden; **to leave** ~ **(with sb/for sb) that** ... (bei jdm/für jdn) den Nachricht hinterlassen, daß ...; **what's the** ~ **for "pen" in German?** was heißt ,,pen'' auf Deutsch?; **to have a** ~ **with sb** mit jdm sprechen; **to have** ~**s with sb** (*quarrel with*) mit jdm eine Auseinandersetzung haben ♦ *vt* formulieren.

wording [wûr'ding] *n* Wortlaut *m*, Formulierung *f*.

word-perfect [wûrd'pûrfikt] *a* (*speech etc*) sicher im Text.

word processing *n* Textverarbeitung *f*.

word processor *n* Text(verarbeitungs)system *nt*, Textverarbeitungsanlage *f*.

wordwrap [wûrd'rap] *n* (*COMPUT*) Zeilenumbruch *m*.

wordy [wûr'dē] *a* wortreich, langatmig (*pej*).

wore [wôr] *pt of* **wear.**

work [wûrk] *n* Arbeit *f*; (*ART, LITER*) Werk *nt* ♦ *vi* arbeiten; (*machine*) funktionieren; (*medicine*) wirken; (*succeed*) klappen ♦ *vt* (*make* ~) arbeiten lassen; **to be at** ~ **(on sth)** (an etw *dat*) arbeiten; **to set to** ~, **to start** ~ sich an die Arbeit machen; **to go to** ~ arbeiten gehen; **his life's** ~ sein Lebenswerk; **to** ~ **hard** schwer arbeiten; **to** ~ **to rule** (*INDUSTRY*) streng nach Vorschrift (planmäßig langsam) arbeiten; *see also* **works**.

work off *vt* (*debt*) abarbeiten; (*anger*) abreagieren.

work on *vi* weiterarbeiten ♦ *vt fus* (*be engaged in*) arbeiten an (+*dat*); (*influence*) bearbeiten; he's ~ing on his car er arbeitet an seinem Auto.

work out *vi* (*sum*) aufgehen; (*plan*) klappen; (*SPORT*) trainieren ♦ *vt* (*problem*) lösen; (*plan*) ausarbeiten.

work up *vt*: to ~ one's way up to the top of a company sich in einer Firma zur Spitze hocharbeiten.

work up to *vt fus* hinarbeiten auf (+*acc*).

workable [wûr'kəbəl] *a* (*soil*) bearbeitbar; (*plan*) ausführbar.

workaholic [wûrkəhâl'ik] *n* Arbeitstier *nt*.

workbench [wûrk'bench] *n* Werkbank *f*.

workbook [wûrk'boŏk] *n* (Schul)heft *nt*.

work conditions *npl* Arbeitsbedingungen *pl*.

work council *n* Betriebsrat *m*.

worked up [wûrkt up] *a*: to get ~ sich aufregen.

worker [wûr'kûr] *n* Arbeiter(in *f*) *m*.

work force *n* Arbeiterschaft *f*.

working [wûr'king] *a* (*woman*) berufstätig; (*partner*) aktiv; (*Brit*: *day*, *week*, *clothes*, *conditions*) Arbeits-; in order in betriebsfähigem Zustand; ~ knowledge Grundkenntnisse *pl*.

working capital *n* (*COMM*) Betriebskapital *nt*.

working class *n* Arbeiterklasse *f* ♦ *a*: **working-class** Arbeiter-.

working man *n* Arbeiter *m*.

working model *n* Arbeitsmodell *nt*.

work-in-progress [wûrkinprâg'res] *n* (*products*) halbfertige Erzeugnisse *pl*.

workload [wûrk'lōd] *n* Arbeit(slast) *f*.

workman [wûrk'mən] *n*, *pl* **-men** Arbeiter *m*.

workmanship [wûrk'mənship] *n* Arbeit *f*, Ausführung *f*.

workmate [wûrk'māt] *n* Arbeitskollege *m*, Arbeitskollegin *f*.

workout [wûrk'out] *n* (*SPORT*) Training *nt*.

work party *n* (Arbeits)ausschuß *m*.

work permit *n* Arbeitserlaubnis *f*.

works [wûrks] *n* (*Brit*: *factory*) Fabrik *f*, Werk *nt* ♦ *npl* (*of watch*) Werk *nt*; road ~ Baustelle *f*.

worksheet [wûrk'shēt] *n* Arbeitsblatt *nt*.

workshop [wûrk'shâp] *n* Werkstatt *f*.

work station *n* Arbeitsplatz *m*.

work study *n* Zeitstudie *f*.

work week *n* Arbeitswoche *f*.

world [wûrld] *n* Welt *f*; (*animal* ~ *etc*) Reich *nt*; the business ~ die Geschäftswelt, das Geschäftsleben; all over the ~ auf der ganzen Welt; out of this ~ himmlisch; to come into the ~ auf die Welt kommen; to do sb/sth the ~ of good jdm/etw sehr gut tun; to be the ~ to sb jds ein und alles sein; to think the ~ of sb große Stücke auf

jdn halten; what in the ~ ... was in aller Welt ...

world champion *n* Weltmeister(in *f*) *m*.

World Cup *n* (*SOCCER*) Fußballweltmeisterschaft *f*.

world-famous [wûrldfā'məs] *a* weltberühmt.

worldly [wûrld'lē] *a* weltlich, irdisch.

worldwide [wûrld'wīd'] *a* weltweit.

WORM *n abbr* (*COMPUT*: *write once read many times*) WORM *m*.

worm [wûrm] *n* Wurm *m* ♦ *vt*: to ~ one's way into sth sich in etw hineinzwängen.

worm drive *n* (*COMPUT*) Worm-Laufwerk *nt*.

worn [wôrn] *a* (*clothes*) abgetragen ♦ *pp of* **wear**.

worn-out [wôrn'out'] *a* (*object*) abgenutzt; (*person*) völlig erschöpft.

worried [wûr'ēd] *a* besorgt, beunruhigt; to be ~ about sth wegen etw besorgt sein.

worrier [wûr'ēûr] *n*: he is a ~ er macht sich (*dat*) ewig Sorgen.

worrisome [wûr'ēsəm] *a* erschreckend.

worry [wûr'ē] *n* Sorge *f*, Kummer *m* ♦ *vt* quälen, beunruhigen ♦ *vi* (*feel uneasy*) sich sorgen, sich (*dat*) Gedanken machen; to ~ about *or* over sth/sb sich Sorgen um etw/jdn machen.

worrying [wûr'ēing] *a* beunruhigend.

worse [wûrs] *a comp of* **bad** schlechter, schlimmer; to get ~, to grow ~ sich verschlechtern, schlechter werden; he is none the ~ for it er hat sich nichts dabei getan; so much the ~! um so schlimmer! ♦ *ad comp of* **badly** schlimmer, ärger ♦ *n* Schlimmere(s) *nt*, Schlechtere(s) *nt*.

worsen [wûr'sən] *vt* verschlimmern ♦ *vi* sich verschlechtern.

worse off *a* (*fig*) schlechter dran; he is now ~ than before er ist jetzt schlechter dran als vorher.

worship [wûr'ship] *n* Anbetung *f*, Verehrung *f*; (*religious service*) Gottesdienst *m*; (*Brit*: *title*) Hochwürden *m* ♦ *vt* anbeten.

worshiper, (*Brit*) **worshipper** [wûr'shipûr] *n* Gottesdienstbesucher(in *f*) *m*.

worst [wûrst] *a superl of* **bad** schlimmste(r, s), schlechteste(r, s) ♦ *ad superl of* **badly** am schlimmsten, am ärgsten; to come off ~ den kürzeren ziehen ♦ *n* Schlimmste(s) *nt*, Ärgste(s) *nt*; if ~ comes to ~ wenn alle Stricke reißen (*col*).

worsted [woõs'tid] *n* Kammgarn *nt*.

worth [wûrth] *n* Wert *m*; $10 ~ of food Essen für 10 $ ♦ *a* wert; ~ seeing sehenswert; it's not ~ the trouble es ist nicht der Mühe wert; how much is it ~? was *or* wieviel ist das wert?; it's ~ $10 es ist 10 $ wert; to be ~ one's while (to do sth) die Mühe wert sein(, etw zu tun).

worthless [wûrth'lis] *a* wertlos; (*person*) nichtsnutzig.

worthwhile [wûrth'wīl'] *a* lohnend, der Mühe wert; it's not ~ going es lohnt sich nicht, dahin zu gehen.

worthy [wûr'ᵺē] *a* (*having worth*) wertvoll; wert (*of gen*), würdig (*of gen*).

would [wōōd] *pt of* **will** ♦ *aux v*: **she ~ come** sie würde kommen; **if you asked he ~ come** wenn Sie ihn fragten, würde er kommen; **~ you like a drink?** möchten Sie etwas trinken?; **it ~ seem so** es sieht so aus; **you WOULD say that, ~n't you!** von dir kann man ja nichts anderes erwarten.

would-be [wōōd'bē'] *a* angeblich.

wouldn't [wōōd'ənt] = **would not.**

wound [wōōnd] *n* (*lit, fig*) Wunde *f* ♦ *vt* verwunden, verletzen (*also fig*) ♦ [wound] *pt, pp of* **wind.**

wove [wōv] *pt of* **weave.**

woven [wō'vən] *pp of* **weave.**

WP *n abbr* = **word processing; word processor.**

WPC *n abbr* (*Brit*) = *woman police constable.*

wpm *abbr* (= *words per minute*) ≈ ApM.

wrangle [rang'gəl] *n* Streit *m* ♦ *vi* sich zanken.

wrap [rap] *n* (*stole*) Umhang *m*, Schal *m*; **under ~s** (*fig: plan, scheme*) geheim ♦ *vt* (*also: ~ up*) einwickeln; (*deal*) abschließen.

wrapper [rap'ûr] *n* (*on chocolate*) Papier(chen) *nt.*

wrapping paper [rap'ing pā'pûr] *n* Einwickel- *or* Packpapier *nt.*

wrath [rath] *n* Zorn *m.*

wreak [rēk] *vt* (*destruction*) anrichten; **to ~ havoc** Chaos anrichten *or* verbreiten; **to ~ vengeance on** Rache üben an (+*dat*).

wreath [rēth] *n* Kranz *m.*

wreck [rek] *n* Schiffbruch *m*; (*ship*) Wrack *nt*; (*sth ruined*) Ruine *f*, Trümmerhaufen *m*; **a nervous ~** ein Nervenbündel *nt* ♦ *vt* zerstören.

wreckage [rek'ij] *n* Wrack *nt*, Trümmer *pl.*

wrecker [rek'ûr] *n* (*US: breakdown van*) Abschleppwagen *m.*

wrecking yard [rek'ing yârd] *n* (*US*) Autofriedhof *m.*

wren [ren] *n* Zaunkönig *m.*

WREN [ren] *n* weibliches Mitglied der britischen Marine.

wrench [rench] *n* (*TECH*) Schraubenschlüssel *m*; (*twist*) Ruck *m*, heftige Drehung *f* ♦ *vt* reißen, zerren.

wrest [rest] *vt*: **to ~ sth from sb** jdm etw abringen.

wrestle [res'əl] *vi* ringen.

wrestling [res'ling] *n* Ringen *nt.*

wrestling match *n* Ringkampf *m.*

wretch [rech] *n* arme(r) Teufel *m or* Schlucker *m* (*col*); **little ~!** (*often hum*) kleiner Schlingel!

wretched [rech'id] *a* (*hovel*) elend; (*col*) verflixt; **I feel ~** mir ist elend.

wriggle [rig'əl] *n* Schlängeln *nt* ♦ *vi* sich winden.

wring [ring] *vt irreg* wringen.

wringer [ring'ûr] *n* (Wäsche)mangel *f.*

wringing [ring'ing] *a* (*also: ~ wet*) tropfnaß.

wrinkle [ring'kəl] *n* Falte *f*, Runzel *f* ♦ *vt* runzeln ♦ *vi* sich runzeln; (*material*) knittern.

wrinkled [ring'kəld] *a* (*fabric, paper*) zerknittert; (*nose*) gerümpft; (*surface*) gekräuselt; (*skin*) schrumpelig.

wrinkly [ring'klē] *a* = **wrinkled.**

wrist [rist] *n* Handgelenk *nt.*

wristwatch [rist'wâch] *n* Armbanduhr *f.*

writ [rit] *n* gerichtliche(r) Befehl *m*; **to serve a ~ on sb** (*JUR*) jdn vorladen.

write [rīt] *vti irreg* schreiben; **to ~ sb a letter** jdm einen Brief schreiben.

write away *vi*: **to ~ away for sth** (*information, goods*) etw anfordern.

write down *vt* niederschreiben, aufschreiben.

write off *vt* (*debt, loss etc*) abschreiben; (*smash up: car*) zu Schrott fahren.

write out *vt* (*essay*) abschreiben; (*check*) ausstellen.

write up *vt* schreiben.

write-off [rīt'ôf] *n*: **it is a ~** (*failure*) das kann man abschreiben; **the car was a complete ~** (*Brit*) das Auto war total im Eimer (*col*).

write protect *n* (*COMPUT*) Schreibschutz *m.*

writer [rī'tûr] *n* Verfasser(in *f*) *m*; (*author*) Schriftsteller(in *f*) *m.*

write-up [rīt'up] *n* Besprechung *f*; (*review*) Kritik *f.*

writing [rī'ting] *n* (*act*) Schreiben *nt*; (*hand~*) (Hand)schrift *f*; **to put sth in ~** etw schriftlich machen *or* festlegen; **in sb's own ~** handgeschrieben; *see also* **writings.**

writing case *n* Schreibmappe *f.*

writing desk *n* Schreibtisch *m.*

writing paper *n* Schreibpapier *nt.*

writings [rī'tingz] *npl* Schriften *pl*, Werke *pl.*

written [rit'ən] *pp of* **write.**

wrong [rông] *a* (*incorrect*) falsch; (*morally*) unrecht; (*out of order*) nicht in Ordnung; **to be ~** (*answer*) falsch *or* verkehrt sein; (*in doing, saying*) unrecht haben; **you have the ~ number** (*TEL*) Sie haben die falsche Nummer; **there's nothing ~** (*amiss*) (es ist) alles in Ordnung; **what's ~ with the car?** was ist mit dem Auto los?; **something went ~ with the brakes** die Bremsen haben nicht funktioniert; **he was ~ in doing that** es war nicht recht von ihm, das zu tun; **what's ~ with your leg?** was ist mit deinem Bein los?; **to go ~** (*plan*) schiefgehen; (*person: be mistaken*) einen Fehler machen; (: *morally*) auf Abwege geraten ♦ *n* Unrecht *nt* ♦ *vt* Unrecht tun (+*dat*).

wrongful [rông'fəl] *a* unrechtmäßig; **~ dismissal** ungerechtfertigte Entlassung *f.*

wrongly [rông'lē] *ad* (*answer, do, count*) falsch, verkehrt; (*accuse*) zu Unrecht.

wrote [rōt] *pt of* **write.**

wrought iron [rôt ī'ûrn] *n* Schmiedeeisen *nt.*

wrung [rung] *pt, pp of* **wring.**

wry [rī] *a* schief, krumm; (*ironical*) trocken; **to make a ~ face** das Gesicht verziehen.

wt. *abbr* (= *weight*) Gew.
WV *abbr* (*US MAIL*) = *West Virginia.*
W. Va. *abbr* (*US*) = *West Virginia.*
WY *abbr* (*US MAIL*) = *Wyoming.*
Wyo. *abbr* (*US*) = *Wyoming.*

X

X, x [eks] *n* (*letter*) X *nt*, x *nt*; **X for Xmas** ≈ X wie Xanthippe; **if you have X dollars a year** wenn man X Dollar pro Jahr hat.
Xerox [zē'råks] *n* ® (*copy*) Xerokopie *f* ♦ *vt* xerokopieren, xeroxen (*col*).
XL *abbr* (= *extra large*) XL.
Xmas [eks'mis] *n abbr* (= *Christmas*) Weihnachten *nt.*
X-rated [eks'rātid] *a* (*US: film*) für Jugendliche nicht geeignet.
X-ray [eks'rā] *n* Röntgenaufnahme *f* ♦ *vt* röntgen.
xylophone [zī'ləfōn] *n* Xylophon *nt.*

Y

Y, y [wī] *n* (*letter*) Y *nt*, y *nt*; **Y for Yoke** ≈ Y wie Ypsilon.
yacht [yât] *n* Jacht *f.*
yachting [yât'ing] *n* (*Sport*) segeln *nt.*
yachtsman [yâts'mən] *n, pl* **-men** Sportsegler *m.*
yam [yam] *n* Yamswurzel *f.*
yank [yangk] *n* Ruck *m* ♦ *vt:* **he ~ed the rope free** er riß das Seil los.
Yank [yangk] *n* (*pej*) Ami *m* (*col*), Yankee *m* (*col*).
Yankee [yang'kē] *n* (*pej*) Ami *m* (*col*), Yankee *m* (*col*).
yap [yap] *vi* (*dog*) kläffen; (*people*) quasseln.
yard [yârd] *n* Hof *m*; (*US: garden*) Garten *m*; (*measure*) (englische) Elle *f*, Yard *nt* (= *0,91 m; 3 feet*); **builder's ~** Bauhof *m.*
yardstick [yârd'stik] *n* (*fig*) Maßstab *m.*
yarn [yârn] *n* (*thread*) Garn *nt*; (*story*) (Seemanns)garn *nt.*
yawn [yôn] *n* Gähnen *nt* ♦ *vi* gähnen.
yawning [yôn'ing] *a* gähnend.
yd. *abbr* = **yard.**
yeah [ye] *ad* (*col*) ja.
year [yēr] *n* Jahr *nt*; (*Brit SCH, UNIV*) Jahrgang *m*; **this ~** dieses Jahr; **~ in, ~ out**

jahrein, jahraus; **she's three ~s old** sie ist drei Jahre alt; **an eight-~-old child** ein achtjähriges Kind; **a** *or* **per ~** pro Jahr.
yearbook [yēr'bōok] *n* Jahrbuch *nt.*
yearling [yēr'ling] *n* (*racehorse*) Einjährige(r) *mf.*
yearly [yēr'lē] *a* jährlich ♦ *ad* jährlich; **twice ~** zweimal im Jahr.
yearn [yûrn] *vi* sich sehnen (*for* nach).
yearning [yûr'ning] *n* Verlangen *nt*, Sehnsucht *f.*
yeast [yēst] *n* Hefe *f.*
yell [yel] *n* gellende(r) Schrei *m* ♦ *vi* laut schreien.
yellow [yel'ō] *a* gelb ♦ *n* Gelb *nt.*
yellow fever *n* Gelbfieber *nt.*
yellowish [yel'ōish] *a* gelblich.
Yellow Sea *n* Gelbe(s) Meer *nt.*
yelp [yelp] *n* Gekläff *nt* ♦ *vi* kläffen.
Yemen [yem'ən] *n* (der) Jemen.
Yemeni [yem'ənē] *a* jemenitisch ♦ *n* Jemenit(in *f*) *m.*
yen [yen] *n* (*currency*) Yen *m*; (*longing*): **~ for/to do** Lust *f* auf (+*acc*)/zu machen.
yeoman [yō'mən] *n, pl* **-men:** **Y~ of the Guard** Leibgardist *m.*
yes [yes] *ad* ja; **to say ~** ja sagen; **to say ~ to sth** etw bejahen *or* mit Ja beantworten ♦ *n* Ja *nt*, Jawort *nt.*
yes-man [yes'man] *n, pl* **-men** Jasager *m.*
yesterday [yes'tûrdā] *ad* gestern ♦ *n* Gestern *nt*; **~ morning/evening** gestern morgen/ abend; **the day before ~** vorgestern; **all day ~** gestern den ganzen Tag.
yet [yet] *ad* noch; (*in question*) schon; (*up to now*) bis jetzt; **and ~ again** und wieder *or* noch einmal; **as ~** bis jetzt; (*in past*) bis dahin ♦ *cj* doch, dennoch.
yew [yōō] *n* Eibe *f.*
YHA *n abbr* (*Brit:* = *Youth Hostels Association*) ≈ DJH *nt.*
Yiddish [yid'ish] *n* Jiddisch *nt.*
yield [yēld] *n* Ertrag *m*; (*FIN*): **a ~ of 5%** ein Ertrag *or* Gewinn *m* von 5% ♦ *vt* (*result, crop*) hervorbringen; (*interest, profit*) abwerfen; (*concede*) abtreten ♦ *vi* nachgeben; (*MIL*) sich ergeben; **"~"** (*US AUT*) „Vorfahrt achten".
YMCA *n abbr* (= *Young Men's Christian Association*) CVJM *m.*
yodel [yōd'əl] *vi* jodeln.
yoga [yō'gə] *n* Joga *m.*
yog(h)ourt, yog(h)urt [yō'gûrt] *n* Joghurt *m.*
yoke [yōk] *n* (*lit, fig*) Joch *nt* ♦ *vt* (*also:* **~ together:** *oxen*) einspannen.
yolk [yōk] *n* Eidotter *m*, Eigelb *nt.*
yonder [yân'dûr] *ad* dort drüben, da drüben ♦ *a* jene(r, s) dort.
Yorks. *abbr* (*Brit*) = Yorkshire.
you [yōō] *pron* (*familiar*) (*sing: nom*) du; (: *acc*) dich; (: *dat*) dir; (*pl: nom*) ihr; (: *acc, dat*) euch; (*polite: nom, acc*) Sie; (: *dat*) Ihnen; (*impers: one*) man; (: *acc*) einen; (: *dat*) einem; **I'll see ~ tomorrow** bis mor-

gen; **if I was** or **were** ~ wenn ich an deiner/Ihrer Stelle wäre; **fresh air does** ~ **good** frische Luft tut gut.

you'd [yōōd] = **you had; you would.**

you'll [yōōl] = **you will; you shall.**

young [yung] a jung; **a** ~ **lady** eine junge Dame od Frau; **a** ~ **man** ein junger Mann; **the** ~**er generation** die jungen Leute, die jüngere Generation ♦ npl (people): **the** ~ die Jungen.

youngish [yung'ish] a ziemlich jung.

youngster [yung'stûr] n Junge m, junge(r) Bursche m; junge(s) Mädchen nt.

your [yōōr] poss a (familiar: sing) dein/deine/dein; (: pl) euer/eure/euer; (polite: sing, pl) Ihr/Ihre/Ihr; ~ **house** (sing) dein/Ihr Haus; (pl) euer/Ihr Haus.

you're [yōōr] = **you are.**

yours [yōōrz] poss pron (familiar: sing) deiner/deine/deins; (: pl) eurer/eure/euers; (polite: sing, pl) Ihrer/Ihre/Ihr(e)s; **a friend of** ~ dein or Ihr Freund.

yourself [yōōrself'] pron pl, **yourselves** [yōōrselvz'] (emphatic) selbst; (reflexive: familiar: sing: acc) dich (selbst); (: dat) dir (selbst); (: pl) euch (selbst); (polite) sich (selbst); **you** ~ **told me** du hast es mir selbst erzählt; **did you do it (all) by** ~? hast du das ganz allein(e) gemacht?; **you're not** ~ mit dir ist etwas nicht in Ordnung.

youth [yōōth] n Jugend f; (young man) junge(r) Mann m; (young people) Jugend f; **in my** ~ in meiner Jugend(zeit).

youth club n Jugendzentrum nt.

youthful [yōōth'fəl] a jugendlich.

youthfulness [yōōth'fəlnis] n Jugendlichkeit f.

youth hostel n Jugendherberge f.

youth movement n Jugendbewegung f.

you've [yōōv] = **you have.**

yowl [youl] n (of dog) Jaulen nt; (of cat) klägliche(s) Miauen nt; (of person) Heulen nt ♦ vi jaulen; kläglich miauen; heulen.

yr. abbr (= year) J.

YT abbr (Canada) = Yukon Territory.

yuck [yuk] interj (col) igitt!

Yugoslav [yōō'gōslâv] a jugoslawisch ♦ n Jugoslawe m, Jugoslawin f.

Yugoslavia [yōō'gōslâ'vēə] n Jugoslawien nt.

Yugoslavian [yōō'gōslâ'vēən] a jugoslawisch ♦ n (person) Jugoslawe m, Jugoslawin f.

YWCA n abbr (= Young Women's Christian Association) CVJF m.

wie Zacharias.

Zaïre [zâēr'] n Zaire nt.

Zambia [zam'bēə] n Sambia nt.

Zambian [zam'bēən] a sambisch ♦ n Sambier(in f) m.

zany [zā'nē] a komisch.

zap [zap] vt (COMPUT) löschen und addieren.

zeal [zēl] n Eifer m.

zealot [zel'ət] n Fanatiker(in f) m.

zealous [zel'əs] a eifrig.

zebra [zēb'rə] n Zebra nt.

zebra crossing n (Brit) Zebrastreifen m.

zenith [zē'nith] n (ASTRON. fig) Zenit m.

zero [zē'rō] n Null f; (on scale) Nullpunkt m; **5 degrees below** ~ 5 Grad unter Null ♦ vi: **to** ~ **in on** (target) sich einschießen auf (+acc).

zero hour n die Stunde X.

zero-rated [zē'rōrā'tid] a (Brit) befreit von Mehrwertsteuer.

zest [zest] n Begeisterung f; ~ **for living** Lebensfreude f.

zigzag [zig'zag] n Zickzack m ♦ vi im Zickzack laufen/fahren.

Zimbabwe [zimbâ'bwä] n Zimbabwe nt, Simbabwe nt.

Zimbabwean [zimbâ'bwäən] a zimbabwisch, simbabwisch ♦ n Zimbabwer(in f) m, Simbabwer(in f) m.

zinc [zingk] n Zink nt.

Zionism [zī'ənizəm] n Zionismus m.

Zionist [zī'ənist] a zionistisch ♦ n Zionist(in f) m.

zip [zip] n Reißverschluß m; (energy) Schwung m ♦ vt (also: ~ **up**) den Reißverschluß zumachen (+gen) ♦ vi: **to** ~ **along to the shops** schnell (ein paar) Einkäufe machen.

ZIP [zip] n abbr (US: = Zoning Improvement Plan) ≈ PLZ f.

zip code n (US MAIL) Postleitzahl f.

zipper [zip'ûr] n Reißverschluß m.

zither [ziTH'ûr] n Zither f.

zodiac [zō'dēak] n Tierkreis m.

zombie [zâm'bē] n Trantüte f.

zone [zōn] n Zone f; (area) Gebiet nt.

zoo [zōō] n Zoo m.

zoological [zōəlâj'ikəl] a zoologisch.

zoologist [zōâl'əjist] n Zoologe m, Zoologin f.

zoology [zōâl'əjē] n Zoologie f.

zoom [zōōm] vi (engine, plane etc) sausen; **to** ~ **in (on sb/sth)** (PHOT, CINE) (jdn/etw) heranholen.

zoom lens n Zoomobjektiv nt.

zucchini [zōōkē'nē] npl (US) Zucchini pl.

Zulu [zōō'lōō] a Zulu- ♦ n Zulu m, Zulufrau f.

Zürich [zûr'ik] n Zürich nt.

Z

Z, z [zē] n (letter) Z nt, z nt; **Z for Zebra** ≈ Z